BIOGRAPHICAL
DICTIONARY AND
SYNOPSIS *of* BOOKS
ANCIENT AND MODERN

CHARLES DUDLEY WARNER

EDITOR

HAMILTON WRIGHT MABIE
LUCIA GILBERT RUNKLE
GEORGE HENRY WARNER

ASSOCIATE EDITORS

The Werner Company
AKRON, OHIO

Republished, 1965

Gale Research Company — Book Tower — Detroit, Michigan 48226

THE ADVISORY COUNCIL

CRAWFORD H. TOY, A. M., LL. D.,
>Professor of Hebrew, HARVARD UNIVERSITY, Cambridge, Mass.

THOMAS R. LOUNSBURY, LL. D., L. H. D.,
>Professor of English in the Sheffield Scientific School of
>>YALE UNIVERSITY, New Haven, Conn.

WILLIAM M. SLOANE, PH. D., L. II. D.,
>Professor of History and Political Science,
>>PRINCETON UNIVERSITY, Princeton, N. J.

BRANDER MATTHEWS, A. M., LL. B.,
>Professor of Literature, COLUMBIA UNIVERSITY, New York City.

JAMES B. ANGELL, LL. D.,
>President of the UNIVERSITY OF MICHIGAN, Ann Arbor, Mich.

WILLARD FISKE, A. M., PH. D.,
>Late Professor of the Germanic and Scandinavian Languages
>and Literatures, CORNELL UNIVERSITY, Ithaca, N. Y.

EDWARD S. HOLDEN, A. M., LL. D.,
>Director of the Lick Observatory, and Astronomer,
>>UNIVERSITY OF CALIFORNIA, Berkeley, Cal.

ALCÉE FORTIER, LIT. D.,
>Professor of the Romance Languages,
>>TULANE UNIVERSITY, New Orleans, La.

WILLIAM P. TRENT, M. A.,
>Dean of the Department of Arts and Sciences, and Professor of
>English and History,
>>UNIVERSITY OF THE SOUTH, Sewanee, Tenn.

PAUL SHOREY, PH. D.,
>Professor of Greek and Latin Literature,
>>UNIVERSITY OF CHICAGO, Chicago, Ill.

WILLIAM T. HARRIS, LL. D.,
>United States Commissioner of Education,
>>BUREAU OF EDUCATION, Washington, D. C.

MAURICE FRANCIS EGAN, A. M., LL. D.,
>Professor of Literature in the
>>CATHOLIC UNIVERSITY OF AMERICA, Washington, D. C.

PREFACE TO THE DICTIONARY.

THE first object of the Dictionary is to afford a handy, condensed reference to the names of the authors written of and quoted in Noted Books or Current Literature, and to enable the reader to get at a glance the main facts of the lives of such authors and the titles of their principal works. But besides these, some thousands of additional names have been selected, which will be of service to the reader in many departments of intellectual activity. It has not been any part of the plan to attempt a comprehensive list of those who have written books ; but, following the idea of similar works to present names, in many departments, fairly representative of literary history. While this general and cosmopolitan plan has been adhered to, considerable prominence has been given to American names, and to writers who have won distinction in works on law, art, travel, and exploration, and indeed in all liberal pursuits.

A literary dictionary, within the space at the editor's command, can only give a clue to the great maze of literature ; but in doing this is promoted the object of the whole work, which is to encourage, stimulate, and assist the general reader, not only in the acquisition of knowledge and the widening of his mental horizon, but in the rational enjoyment of life. The "promotion and diffusion of knowledge among mankind" has been held to be an object worthy of the highest human effort. To have contributed to this effort has been the purpose of those engaged in this work.

In preparing it the best authorities in many languages have been consulted ; but those familiar with dictionaries and cyclopædias know how liable they are to err. If we have erred as to dates or names in this, it has probably been from having to make a choice between several authorities disagreeing and of good standing.

BIOGRAPHICAL DICTIONARY
OF AUTHORS

ANCIENT AND MODERN

Aar, Alexis (är), pseudonym of Anselm Rumpelt. A German poet; born at Chemnitz, Saxony, Feb. 10, 1853. His collection entitled 'Will o' the Wisps' (1878) manifests a noteworthy talent in the field of historical lyrics.

Aarestrup, Emil (â're-ströp). A Danish poet (1800–56). He was not duly appreciated until after his death, but is now acknowledged as one of the foremost lyric poets of Denmark, being ranked by critics next to Christian Winther. 'Collected Poems,' with critical sketch by G. Brandes (Copenhagen, 1877).

Aasen, Ivar Andreas (â'sen). A Norwegian philologist and poet; born in 1813; died in 1896. His great aim was to construct from the older elements of the various Norwegian dialects a new national language ("Landsmaal"), as a substitute for Danish, in pursuance of which end he published several valuable philological works. As a poet he produced 'Symra,' a collection of lyrics (3d ed., 1875); 'Ervingen,' a drama (4th ed., 1887).

Abba, Giuseppe Cesare (äb'bä). An Italian poet; born in 1838 at Cairo Montenotte. He took part in the expedition of Garibaldi into Sicily in 1860, which he celebrated in his poem 'Arrigo.' Among his other works are a tragedy, 'Bpartaco,' a historical novel, and lyric poems.

Abbe, Cleveland. A distinguished American meteorologist; born in New York city, Dec. 3, 1838. He studied astronomy in Germany, and was director of the Cincinnati Observatory from 1868 to 1870. Since 1871 he has been professor of meteorology in the National Weather Bureau. Among his chief publications are: 'Treatise on Meteorological Apparatus'; 'Preparatory Studies for Deductive Methods in Meteorology'; 'Solar Spots and Terrestrial Temperature'; 'Atmospheric Radiation'; 'Physical Basis of Long Range Forecasting.'

Abbot, Ezra. An American Greek scholar; born at Jackson, Me., April 28, 1819; died at Cambridge, Mass., March 21, 1884. Besides his valuable work as one of the editors of the American edition of Smith's 'Bible Dictionary,' he wrote 'The Authorship of the Fourth Gospel' (1880), in which was announced the important discovery of Tatian's "Diatessaron," and which took high rank; compiled 'Literature of the Doctrine of a Future Life' (1864), etc. He was one of the American committee of New Testament revisers.

Abbot, Francis Ellingwood. An American philosophical writer and journalist; born at Boston, 1836. Besides notable magazine articles, he wrote: 'Scientific Theism' (1886); 'The Way Out of Agnosticism' (1890); etc. He was for a number of years editor of the liberal journal, The Index. Died Oct. 23, 1903.

Abbot, Willis John. An American journalist and author; born in Connecticut in 1863. He is connected with the New York press. With the exception of a 'Life of Carter Harrison,' his works consist principally of popular histories for young people, among which are: 'Blue Jackets of 1776'; 'Blue Jackets of 1812'; 'Blue Jackets of '61'; 'Battle Fields and Camp Fires '; 'American Ships and Sailors.'

Abbott, Charles Conrad. An American writer on archæology and natural history; born at Trenton, N. J., 1843. He has discovered palæolithic human remains in the Delaware valley, and shown the likelihood of the early existence of the Eskimo race as far south as New Jersey. His principal works are: 'Primitive Industry' (1881); 'A Naturalist's Rambles about Home' (1884); 'Cyclopædia of Natural History' (1886); 'Upland and Meadow' (1886); 'Wasteland Wanderings' (1887) ; 'Rambles of an Idler.'

Abbott, Edward. An American clergyman, editor, and author, son of Jacob Abbott; born in Farmington, Me., July 15, 1841. He was the editor of the Congregationalist from 1869 to 1878, and of the Literary World from 1878. Among his works are: 'Dialogues of Christ'; 'Paragraph History of the American Revolution' (1875); 'Revolutionary Times' (1876); 'Long Look Series of Juvenile Tales.' D. 1908.

Abbott, Jacob. An American writer; born in Hallowell, Me., Nov. 14, 1803; died at Farmington, Me., Oct. 31, 1879. His works, comprising over 200 titles, chiefly of stories for the young, were widely read in his own day. Among the best known are: 'The Rollo

Books' (28 vols.); 'The Franconia Stories' (10 vols.); 'The Marco Paul Series' (6 vols.).

Abbott, John Stevens Cabot. An American biographer and historical writer; born at Brunswick, Me., Sept. 18, 1805; died at Fair Haven, Conn., June 17, 1877. Brother of the preceding; author of 'The Mother at Home' (1833); 'History of Napoleon'; 'History of the Civil War' (1863-66); 'History of Frederick the Great' (1871); 'The French Revolution of 1789'; 'Napoleon at St. Helena'; 'History of Napoleon III.' (1868); and numerous other works on kindred themes.

Abbott, Lyman. An American author; born at Roxbury, Mass., Dec. 18, 1835. At first a lawyer, he was ordained minister of the Congregational Church in 1860. After a pastorate of five years in Indiana he came to New York, and rose rapidly to distinction through his contributions to periodical literature. He is pastor of Plymouth Church, Brooklyn, being the immediate successor of Henry Ward Beecher. He was associated with Mr. Beecher in the editorship of the Christian Union, and is now editor of The Outlook, formerly the Christian Union. His writings include 'Jesus of Nazareth' (1869); a 'Life of Henry Ward Beecher' (1883); 'In Aid of Faith' (1886); 'Christianity and Social Problems' (1896); 'The Evolution of Christianity'; 'Signs of Promise'; 'An Evolutionist's Theology'; 'New Streams in Old Channels'; 'Personality of God'; 'Industrial Problems.'

Abbt, Thomas (äpt). A German essayist; born at Ulm, 1738; died 1766. Fired with admiration for Frederick the Great and his generals, he wrote his best-known work, 'On Death for One's Fatherland' (1761). In 1762 he became associated in Berlin with Nicolai and Moses Mendelssohn in the publication of the 'Literary Letters,' from which Lessing had just retired. After a tour through Southern Germany, Switzerland, and France, he wrote the work which securely established his fame, 'Of Merit' (1765).

A Beckett, Arthur William. An English dramatist; born at Hammersmith, Oct. 25, 1844. Son of the following, and since 1891 editor of the London Sunday Times; he has written several comedies, including 'About Town' and 'Long Ago.' His 'Papers from Pump-handle Court' were a feature in Punch, whose staff he joined in 1874.

A Beckett, Gilbert Abbott. An English humorist (1811-56). An original founder of Punch (1841), and author of the 'Comic Black-stone,' one of the cleverest burlesques in the language (London, 1845); he also published a 'Comic History of England' (1848); 'Quizziology of the British Drama' (1846), and more than 50 plays, some of which still keep the stage.

À Becket, Thomas. See **Thomas.**

Abélard, Pierre (ä-bā-lär'). A noted French scholastic philosopher and theologian; born near Nantes, 1079; died April 21, 1142. Lect-

uring on theology, he attracted students from all parts of Europe. Several of his disciples afterward became famous; for example, Pope Celestin II., Peter Lombard, Berengarius, and Arnold of Brescia. The story of his romantic and tragic love for Héloïse is told in his 'Story of My Misfortunes'; in her first 'Letter' to him on receipt of the 'Story'; and in the two 'Letters' from her that followed. The poets have taken the loves of this unfortunate pair as the theme of their elegies in every age since the death of the lovers.

Abonyi, Lajos (ob'on-yē). A Hungarian novelist; born Jan. 9, 1833. His subjects are taken from popular life and national history: 'Tales by the Fireside'; 'The Poor Lad's Cloth'; 'The Widow's Cow'; 'Lena's Inheritance.'

About, Edmond (ä-bö'). A distinguished French novelist; born in Dieuze, Lorraine, Feb. 14, 1828; died in Paris, Jan. 17, 1885. One of the few younger authors of note who adhered to the second empire, he enjoyed the special favor of Napoleon III., and in 1870 accompanied the army of Marshal MacMahon as reporter for Le Soir. In that paper, after the war, and from 1875 as editor-in-chief of the XIX. Siècle, he was the champion of the moderate republicans. He was elected a member of the Academy in 1884. Among his best works are: 'Contemporaneous Greece' (1854); 'Tolla Féraldi' (1855); 'The King of the Mountains' (1856); 'The Marriages of Paris' (6 tales, 1856); 'The Man with the Broken Ear' (1861); 'A Notary's Nose' (1862); 'Madelon' (1863); 'The Infamous One' (1866-69); 'Romance of a Good Man' (1880), directed against Zola and his school; 'The Roman Question' (1859), a political treatise; 'The Money Question' (1865).

Abraham a Sancta-Clara (ä'brä-häm ä sänk'tä-klä'rä). A celebrated German pulpit orator and satirist; born at Krähenheinstetten, Baden, July 4, 1644; died in Vienna, Dec. 1, 1709. His family name was Megerle. He was appointed preacher to the imperial court, 1669, and thereafter was one of the celebrities of Vienna. His sermons were characterized by force, broad humor, and impartial denunciation of the follies of all classes, but especially of the courtiers. A good specimen of his manner, both in its elevation of thought and in its grotesqueness, is seen in his 'Judas the Arch-Knave' (1686-95).

Abraham ben Meir ibn Ezra (ä'bra-ham ben mā-ēr' 'b'n ez'rä). A noted Jewish-Arabic poet and scholar; born at Toledo, Spain, 1092; died, 1167. He wrote 150 liturgical poems which are still used in the Jewish worship, besides works on Hebrew grammar and philosophy, a treatise on chess, 'Sefer Moznaïm,' a 'Book of Weights,' etc. He was one of the earliest Biblical critics.

Abrányi, Emil (o'brän-yē). A Hungarian poet; born in Buda-Pesth, 1851. Brother of the following. He is a representative of the cosmopolitan tendency in poetry, his verse being published under the collective title 'Home of Freedom' (1888). He translated into Hungarian, Byron's 'Manfred' and 'Don Juan.'

Abrányi, Kornel (o'brän-yē). A Hungarian poet, novelist, and publicist; born in Buda-Pesth, Dec. 31, 1849. As a member of the Hungarian Diet and as editor of the Pesti Naplo, he is an important political figure in Hungary. His poems are mainly of a political tendency, and his novels deal with the problem of matrimony. 'The Infallible,' a comedy, and the fictions 'The Husband's Philosophy'; 'Who Is the Stronger?'; 'The Only Remedy against Deceit,' and 'Memoirs' are best known.

Abulfaraj (ä'böl-fä-räj') or **Abulfaragius** (ab'ul-ṭa-rä'ji-us). A Syriac and Arabic writer; born at Malatia, Armenia, 1226; died at Maragha, Persia, 1286. His full name was Gregory Abulfaraj ibn al Harun; his father was a Jew. Of numerous writings, the best now known are a universal history in Syriac from the time of Adam down to his own date, and an autobiography.

Abulfeda, Ismail ibn Ali (ä-böl-fä'dä). A celebrated Arabian historian and scholar (1273–1331). Prince of Hamah, and patron of men of letters. He compiled an abridged 'History of the Human Race,' portions of which have been translated into Latin and published under the titles of 'Moslem Annals,' etc.

Abu-Nuvas (ä'bö-nö'vas). An Arabic poet; died 815. He flourished at the court of the caliphs of Bagdad, writing, in the style of Anacreon, some of the most notable songs of love and wine in all Arabic literature.

Accius or **Attius, Lucius** (ak'shi-us). A Latin tragic poet; born about 170 B. C. He took most of his themes from Grecian history and mythology; but in some instances he dramatized scenes from the history of Rome, for example, in his tragedy of 'Brutus': but only fragments of his works remain.

Accolti, Bernardo (äk-kōl'tē). An Italian poet (1465–1535). Greatly admired by his contemporaries, especially for his brilliant gift as an improviser, he was styled "The Only (one) of Arezzo" (L'Unico Aretino). Leo X. esteemed him highly, and made him apostolic secretary, cardinal, and papal legate at Ancona. He drew up the Papal Bull against Luther (1520).

Achard, Louis Amédée (äsh-är'). A French novelist and publicist (1814–75). Originally a merchant, he became a contributor to several papers in Paris in 1838. After the revolution of 1848 he was for a time active as a political writer in support of the royalist cause. From 1848 to 1872 the Revue des Deux Mondes brought out a new story from his pen almost every year. He depicts pre-eminently conflicts in family life and society. 'Parisian Letters' (1838, under the pseudonym "Grimm") made his reputation; his other works are: 'Belle Rose' (1847); 'The Royal Chase' (1849–50); 'Castles in Spain' (1854), a collection of stories; 'The Shirt of Nessus' (1855); etc.

Achilles Tatius (a-kil'ēz tä'shi-us). A Greek writer of romances; born at Alexandria; flourished in the 5th century of our era. He wrote 'The Loves of Clitophon and Leucippe,' an erotic story in florid style, and without much regard to unity or consistency of plot. That the story was very popular in its day is proved by the number of copies of it that are still in MS. An English translation by Anthony Hodges was published in 1638.

Achsharúmov, Nikoléi Dmitriyevich (äch-shä-rö'mof). A Russian novelist and critic; born in St. Petersburg, Dec. 15, 1819. Among his successful novels are: 'The Double' (1850); 'The Gambler'; 'The False Name'; 'An Unusual Case'; and 'The Model.' As a critic he attracted attention by his comments on the writings of Herbert Spencer, Tolstoy, Turgeniev, Dostoievski, etc.

Ackermann, Louise Victorine (äk'er-män). A French poet; born in Paris, Nov. 30, 1813; died near Nice, Aug. 3, 1890. Maiden name Choquet. Her philological studies took her to Berlin, where she married the theologian Paul Ackermann. After his death in 1846 she lived in retirement in an old convent near Nice. Her poems are for the most part pessimistic but passionate. Principal works: 'Tales in Verse' (1855), chiefly Oriental and Ancient Greek subjects; 'Tales and Poems' (1863); 'Philosophical Poems' (1872); 'Thoughts of a Lonely Woman' (1883).

Aclocque, Charles Paul Jacques (äk-lok'). A French novelist and journalist; born in 1832. He was a frequent contributor to the Parisian journals and the author of several romances. His best-known works are: 'Breton Legends' (1862); 'Contraband Love' (1866); 'Love by Double Entry' (1868). In collaboration with his brother he has written 'The Eccentric Huntsmen' (1876) and other works.

Acosta, José d' (ä-kos'ta). A Spanish Jesuit historian; born at Medina del Campo, Old Castile, 1540; died at Salamanca, Feb. 15, 1600. Besides various theological works, he wrote 'Natural and Moral History of the Indies' (1590), which was translated into several European languages. He visited Peru and Rome, resided for some time in Mexico, and was head of the Jesuits' College at Valladolid and of the college at Salamanca.

Acuña, Manuel (ä-kön'yä). A Mexican poet (1849–73), the principal theme of whose poems was disappointed love, which is said to have induced him to die by his own hand.

Acuña de Figueroa, Francisco (ä-kön'yä dè fē-gä-rö'ä). A Uruguayan poet; born at Montevideo, in 1791; died there, Oct. 6, 1862. His works are, in the best sense, a classic in Spanish-American literature, owing to the perfection of his verse in the collection styled 'Poetic Mosaic,' which comprises odes, satires, epigrams, heroic poems, and even Biblical hymns and psalms. In most respects flawless as metrical compositions, these pieces have been criticized as wanting in the ardor usually associated with the southern temperament. A diary in verse, called 'The Siege of Montevideo,' contains many fine passages.

Adam, Juliette. See Lamber.

Adam de la Hale (ä-doṅ' de lä äl). A French poet and composer; born at Arras, about 1235; died at Naples, about 1287. Nicknamed the Hunchback of Arras, although he was not deformed. His satirical extravaganza, 'The Play of Adam, or The Play in the Arbor' (1262), constitutes the earliest comedy in the vulgar tongue; while the pastoral drama 'The Play of Robin and of Marion' may be looked upon as the earliest specimen of comic opera.

Adami, Friedrich (ä-dä'mē). A German author; born at Suhl, Oct. 18, 1816; died in Berlin, Aug. 5, 1893. Besides numerous dramatic pieces, prologues, stories, and short novels, he wrote a very popular biography of 'Louise, Queen of Prussia' (13th ed., 1890) and 'The Book of Emperor William' (1887–90).

Adams, Abigail. Wife of John Adams, second President of the United States; born at Weymouth, Mass., Nov. 23, 1744; died at Quincy, Mass., Oct. 28, 1818. Her letters, contained in 'Familiar Letters of John Adams and his Wife Abigail Adams, during the Revolution,' evince keen political sagacity, and throw valuable light upon the men and the public affairs of the time.

Adams, Bertha Leith (Mrs. Laffan). An English novelist; her first work, 'Mabel Meredith's Love Story,' was published in All the Year Round. This was followed in 1877 by 'Winstowe,' 'Madelon Lemoine,' and 'Aunt Hepsy's Foundling,' the last being her best-known work.

Adams, Brooks. An American essayist and politician; born at Quincy, Mass., 1848. He is the son of Charles Francis Adams, and a lawyer by profession. Besides contributions to magazines, he has written 'The Emancipation of Massachusetts' (1887) and 'The Law of Civilization and Decay.'

Adams, Charles. An American historical and religious writer; born in New Hampshire in 1808; died in 1890. He was a Methodist clergyman. Among his numerous works are: 'Evangelism in the Middle of the 19th Century' (1851); 'Women of the Bible' (1851); 'Life of Cromwell' (1867); 'The Earth and its Wonders' (1869); 'Life Sketches of Macaulay' (1880).

Adams, Charles Follen. An American dialect poet; born at Dorchester, Mass., April 21, 1842. Published 'Leedle Yawcob Strauss and Other Poems' (1878); 'Dialect Ballads' (1887).

Adams, Charles Francis. An eminent American statesman, publicist, and miscellaneous writer; born at Boston, Aug. 18, 1807; died at Boston, Nov. 21, 1886. He was a candidate for Vice-President in 1848, twice elected to Congress, was minister to England from 1861 to 1868, and member of the Geneva Arbitration Commission of 1871. His chief literary work was 'Life and Works of John Adams' (10 vols., 1850–56), his grandfather. He also edited the writings of his father, John Quincy Adams.

Adams, Charles Francis (Jr.). A prominent American publicist, lawyer, and politician; born at Boston, May 27, 1835. He served in the Union army during the Civil War. Besides notable articles in the North American Review on railroad management, he has published: 'Chapters of Erie' (1871); 'Three Episodes of Massachusetts History' (1892); 'Essays on Educational Topics' (1879). He was for several years president of the Union Pacific Railway, but resigned in 1890.

Adams, Charles Kendall. An American historian and educator; born at Derby, Vt., Jan. 24, 1835. He became president of Cornell University (1885), of the American Historical Association (1890), of the University of Wisconsin (1892). He wrote: 'Democracy and Monarchy in France' (1872); 'Christopher Columbus, His Life and Work' (1892); besides many valuable papers on historical and educational topics in reviews. He died in 1902.

Adams, Francis Colburn. An American writer; prominent in the South about the time of the Civil War. He was a resident of Charleston, S. C., and wrote extensively under several pseudonyms. Among his works are: 'Manuel Pereira, or the Sovereign Rule of South Carolina' (1853); 'Uncle Tom at Home' (1853); 'Life and Adventures of Major Potter' (1858); 'An Outcast, a Novel' (1861); 'The Story of a Trooper' (1865); 'The Von Toodleburgs' (1868).

Adams, George Burton. An American historical writer; born in Vermont in 1851. He is a professor of history at Yale University. He is the author of 'Civilization during the Middle Ages' (1883) and 'The Growth of the French Nation'; 'European History.'

Adams, Hannah. An American literary pioneer; born at Medfield, Mass., 1755; died at Brookline, Mass., Nov. 15, 1832. Her principal works were: an 'Autobiography'; 'History of New England' (1799); 'History of the Jews' (1812); besides several writings on topics connected with religion.

Adams, Henry. An American historian; born in Boston, Mass., Feb. 16, 1838; grandson of J. Q. Adams. He was for some time editor of the North American Review, and professor of history in Harvard College. He wrote biographies of eminent public men: 'The Life of Albert Gallatin' (1879); 'John Randolph' (1882);—and studies of particular episodes of American history: 'Documents Relating to New England Federalism' (1877). His principal work is the 'History of the United States from 1801 to 1817,' which constitutes an authoritative history of that period.

Adams, Henry Carter. An American writer on political economy; born at Davenport, Iowa, Dec. 31, 1852. He has been instructor at Iowa and Cornell Universities, and is now professor in the University of Michigan. At one time he was statistician to the Interstate Commerce Commission. His chief works are: 'Taxation in the United States, 1789–1816' (1884); 'Public Debts' (1887); 'Economics and Jurisprudence.'

Adams, Herbert Baxter. An American historian; born near Amherst, Mass., April 16, 1850. After a course of study at Amherst, Heidelberg, and Berlin, he was appointed instructor in history at Johns Hopkins University, and is now professor there. He is the editor of 'Johns Hopkins University Studies in Historical and Political Science,' and author of 'The Study of History in American Colleges and Universities' and 'Jefferson and Higher Education in Virginia.' Died in 1901.

Adams, John. An eminent American statesman and publicist; second President of the United States; born at Braintree (now Quincy), Mass., Oct. 19, 1735; died there, July 4, 1826. In the days preceding the outbreak of the Revolution, he frequently defended in the public prints the right of the colonies to throw off the English yoke. His most important contribution to the literature of the science of government is his 'Defence of the Constitution and Government of the United States' (1787). The 'Familiar Letters' of John Adams and his wife are of great value for the history of the American Revolution.

Adams, John Quincy. An American statesman and publicist; sixth President of the United States; born at Braintree, Mass., July 11, 1767; died in Washington, D. C., Feb. 21, 1848. Before he reached the Presidency he had served as his country's representative in England, France, Prussia, and Holland; in his youth, too, he had accompanied his father, John Adams, when he was American minister at London. He was a frequent contributor to the press, of articles on political topics. He translated Wieland's 'Oberon' into English (1797); published 'Letters on Silesia' (1803). The 'Diary of J. Q. Adams,' with his 'Memoirs,' in 12 vols., was published in 1874–77, edited by his son.

Adams, Myron. An American clergyman and writer, a native of New York State; born in 1841; died in December 1895. He was pastor of a Congregational church in Rochester, N. Y. His chief works are: 'The Creation of the Bible'; 'The Continuous Creation, an Application of the Evolutionary Philosophy to the Christian Religion.'

Adams, Nehemiah. An American clergyman and author; born in Salem, Mass., Feb. 19, 1806; died in Boston, Mass., Oct. 6, 1878. He will be chiefly remembered as the author of a work entitled 'A South Side View of Slavery' (1854), which was severely criticized by the antislavery party. Among his other publications are: 'Under the Mizzenmast' (1871); 'Walks to Emmaüs' (1879); 'Remarks on Unitarian Belief'; 'Life of John Eliot.'

Adams, Oscar Fay. An American compiler and miscellaneous writer of the present day. Besides various compilations, including a 'Dictionary of American Authors' (1897), he has written: 'Dear Old Story-Tellers' (1889); 'The Story of Jane Austen's Life' (1891); 'The Presumption of Sex, and Other Papers' (1892).

Adams, Sarah Flower. An English hymn-writer; born at Great Harlow, Essex, Feb. 22, 1805; died August 1848. In 1834 she was married to William Bridges Adams, a noted inventor. She was the author of 'Vivia Perpetua,' a dramatic poem (London, 1841); and of many lyrics and hymns, the most popular of which is 'Nearer, My God, to Thee' (1860).

Adams, William. A prominent American clergyman and religious writer; born at Colchester, Conn., Jan. 25, 1807; died at Orange Mountain, N. J., Aug. 31, 1880. He was long pastor of the Madison Square Presbyterian Church, New York, and was president of the Union Theological Seminary in New York city from 1873 to 1880. Among his publications are: 'In the World, not of the World' (1866); 'The Three Gardens' (1867); 'Conversations of Jesus Christ with Representative Men' (1868).

Adams, William Davenport. An English journalist and critic; born in 1851. He has published: 'A Dictionary of English Literature' (1878); 'The Witty and Humorous Side of the English Poets' (1880); 'By-Ways in Bookland' (1888); 'A Book of Burlesque'; 'With Poet and Player.' Died July 27, 1904.

Adams, William Taylor. See **Optic, Oliver.**

Addison, Joseph. A celebrated English essayist and poet; born at Milston, Wiltshire, May 1, 1672; died in London, June 17, 1719. He was educated at Oxford. He was Under-Secretary of State in 1706, and in 1709 secretary to Wharton, Lord Lieutenant of Ireland, where he formed a friendship with Swift. In 1716 he married the Countess of Warwick; in 1717 was appointed Secretary of State, but resigned in 1718. He wrote 41 original papers in the Tatler, and 34 with Steele; 274 in the Spectator, embodying his famous creation, the character of Sir Roger de Coverley; 51 essays in the Guardian, which succeeded the Spectator; 24 to a revived Spectator, and 2 to Steele's 'Lover.' His tragedy 'Cato' was acted at Drury Lane in 1713; although it is weak and incongruous, it was greatly admired and variously translated. Besides Latin poems, occasional addresses, and political essays, the following works deserve mention: 'Letter from Italy,' a poem (1703); 'The Campaign' (1704).

Ade, George. An American journalist and author; born in Illinois in 1866. He has published: 'Artic, a Story of the Streets and Town'; 'Pink Marsh' (1897), a dialect story; and the plays, 'The Sultan of Sulu' (1902); 'The Sho-Gun'; 'The College Widow' (1904); 'Marse Covington' (1906).

Adelung, Johann Christoph (ä'de-löng). An eminent German philologist and lexicographer; born at Spantekow, Aug. 8, 1732; died in Dresden, Sept. 10, 1806. His life was devoted to an exhaustive investigation of his native language, which he traced to its remotest origins with a patience and a thoroughness that have remained unsurpassed, the principal result being 'A Grammatical and Critical Dictionary of the High German Tongue.' Science is further indebted to him for 'Mithridates, or Universal Language Lore,' in which all living tongues are directly or indirectly represented; and for a series of text-books that are still authoritative, and to all appearances will long continue so.

Adenet Le Roi (äd-nā' lĕ-rwä'). A French troubadour of the 13th century, whose surname is interpreted as meaning king (leader) of the minstrels, which function he performed at the court of Henri III., Duke of Brabant. His work consists of remodelings of three famous Chansons de Gestes and of the romance of adventure, 'Cleomades,' his last and most important effort.

Adler, Felix (ä'dler). An American lecturer and scholar; born at Alzey, Germany, 1851. The son of an eminent Jewish rabbi, he emigrated when young to the United States, where and at Berlin and Heidelberg he was educated. After being for some time professor at Cornell University, he founded in New York (1876) the Society of Ethical Culture, of which he is lecturer. Similar societies have been established elsewhere in the United States and in other countries. He is also an effective writer and speaker. He has published: 'Creed and Deed' (1878); 'The Moral Instruction of Children' (1892); 'Religion of Duty'; and 'Essentials of Spirituality' (1905).

Adler, Hermann (ä'dler). A German writer; born in Hanover, May 29, 1839. He has lived most of his life in England, where he has held many positions of high trust connected with his race, having been since 1891 chief rabbi of the British empire, and has been active in general benevolence. Besides sermons, lectures, etc., he has written: 'The Jews in England'; 'The Chief Rabbis of England'; 'Ibn Gabirol, the Poet Philosopher,' etc.

Adlersfeld, Eufemia von. See **Ballestrem.**

Adolphus, John. An English historical and miscellaneous writer; born Aug. 7, 1768; died July 16, 1845. He was admitted an attorney in 1790, but after a few years abandoned his profession and devoted himself to literature. His principal work is a 'History of England from the Accession of George III. to the Conclusion of Peace in 1783' (1802).

Ælianus, Claudius (ē-li-ā'nus). A Roman sophist who flourished in the first half of the second century. Of his works, written in Greek, three are extant: 'Peasants' Letters,' purporting to be written by peasants in Attica; 'Various Histories,' or narratives, in 14 books; 'Of the Nature of Animals,' anecdotes of animals.

Æschines (es'ki-nēz). A great Athenian orator (389–314 B. C.), rival of Demosthenes. Only three of his 'Orations' have come down to our time. He was specially brilliant in his extemporaneous efforts. In his more studied orations his great merit was the clearness and fullness of the narrative part.

Æschylus (es'ki-lus). The greatest of the Greek dramatists; born at Eleusis, Attica, 525 B. C.; died at Gela, Sicily, 456 B. C. Of his very numerous works (72 or even 90 dramas), seven tragedies only remain: 'The Suppliants,' one of his earliest productions; 'The Persians,' founded on the contemporary triumph of Greece over the invading Persian hosts; 'The Seven against Thebes,' the only extant member of a tetralogy, the other members of which were 'Laius,' 'Œdipus,' and 'The Sphinx.' The grand tragedy, 'Prometheus Bound,' is the sole survivor of a trilogy, the other two members of which were 'Prometheus the Fire-Bearer' and 'Prometheus Loosed.' In portrayal of grandeur of action and sublimity of heroic character, the 'Prometheus' is almost without an equal in the history of dramatic literature. The remaining three tragedies, 'Agamemnon,' 'Choephori,' and 'Eumenides,' are specially precious, constituting the only complete trilogy that is extant from any ancient Greek tragic poet.

Æsop (ē'sop). A Greek fabulist who lived in the 7th century B. C. According to tradition, he was a captive of war and for part of his life a slave. Many of his fables have been traced to Egyptian and Indian sources. Socrates, during his imprisonment, put into verse a portion of the Æsopian fables. A more complete collection of them was by Babrius, a Greek fabulist. In the lapse of time what might be called the Æsopian canon was much obscured, and spurious fables were incorporated into it.

Afzelius, Arvid August (äf-tsā'li-ös). A Swedish writer and poet (1785–1871), esteemed particularly for his researches in old Norse history and literature; translated the poetical Edda, and with Geijer edited a famous collection of old Swedish folksongs (Stockholm, 1814–17, 3 vols.). As a poet he is best known by his 'Romances.'

Ágai, Adolf (ä'goy). A Hungarian humorist; born 1836. Editor of Borzsem Jankó (John Peppercorn), the best Hungarian comic paper. His sketches from society, character drawings of national types, and personal reminiscences, constitute a rare mine of witty ideas and sound humor, clothed in brilliant language.

Agassiz, Alexander (ä-gä-sē'). An American zoölogist and geologist, son of J. L. R. Agassiz; born in Neuchâtel, Switzerland, Dec. 17, 1835. He came to this country with his father in 1849; graduated from Harvard in 1855; and received the degree of B. S. from the Lawrence Scientific School in 1857. In 1859 he went to California as assistant on the

United States Coast Survey. From 1860 to 1865 he was assistant curator of the Museum of Comparative Zoölogy at Harvard University; and from 1866 to 1869, superintendent of the Calumet and Hecla mines, Lake Superior. On the death of his father in 1873, he was appointed curator of the Museum of Comparative Zoölogy, holding that position until he resigned in 1885. His chief works are: 'List of Echinoderms' (1863); 'Exploration of Lake Titicaca' (1875-76); 'Three Cruises of the Blake, a Contribution to American Thalassography' (1880).

Agassiz, Mrs. Elizabeth (Cary). An American scientific writer, wife of J. L. R. Agassiz; born in Massachusetts in 1822. She is part author, with Alexander Agassiz, of 'Seaside Studies in Natural History' (1865), 'Marine Animals of Massachusetts Bay' (1871). She also wrote a life of her husband.

Agassiz, Jean Louis Rodolphe. An eminent Swiss naturalist; born at Motier, Switzerland, May 28, 1807; died at Cambridge, Mass., Dec. 14, 1873. He studied medicine and comparative anatomy in the universities of Zürich, Heidelberg, and Munich. He gave many years to study of fossil fishes, and his first great work bore that title (1834). His next special researches were directed toward the explanation of glaciers, and he published 'Studies of Glaciers' (1844). In 1846 he made a lecturing tour of the United States, and in 1848 became professor of geology at Harvard, and in 1859 curator of the Museum of Comparative Zoölogy. His contributions to the development of the facts and principles of natural science in his special departments are very numerous and of highest authority. Chief among his works written in English are: 'Principles of Zoölogy'; 'The Structure of Animal Life'; 'Scientific Results of a Journey in Brazil.'

Agathias (a-gā'thi-as). A Greek poet and historian; about 536-581. He collected a 'Cycle' of contemporary poems, in which were a few of his own composition. We have still 101 of his 'Epigrams,' and the whole of his 'History' of the years 553-558.

Agathon (ag'a-thon). A Greek tragic poet (448-402 B. C.). He was a close friend of Euripides and of Plato; and the famous 'Symposium' of Plato immortalizes the banquet given on the occasion of Agathon's dramatic triumph, 416 B. C.

Agoult, Countess d'. See Stern, Daniel.

Agrippa, Heinrich Cornelius (a-grip'ä). A German philosopher (1486-1535); born at Cologne. He was of all professions in turn,— university professor, soldier, magistrate, physician, court historiographer to Charles V. His most notable writings are: 'Of the Nobleness and Pre-eminence of the Female Sex'; 'Occult Philosophy'; 'Uncertainty and Vanity of the Sciences and Arts.'

Aguilar, Grace (ä-gē-lär'). An English novelist; born at Hackney, June 2, 1816; died in Frankfort-on-the-Main, Sept. 16, 1847. She was the daughter of Jewish parents of Spanish origin. Her first books were in defense of the Jewish religion : 'The Spirit of Judaism' (1842); 'The Jewish Faith' (1846); and 'Women of Israel' (1846). She is now best known by her domestic and sentimental novels, only one of which, 'Home Influence' (1847), appeared in her lifetime. Among others are: 'The Vale of Cedars' (1850) and 'The Days of Bruce' (1852).

Aguilera, Ventura Ruiz (ä-gē-lā'rä). A Spanish poet; born in Salamanca, Nov. 2, 1820; died in Madrid, July 1, 1881. Studied but did not practice medicine; afterwards went to Madrid, where he pursued journalism, and later on became director of the archæological museum. Among his works are: 'National Echoes', 'Elegies' (considered masterpieces and translated into nearly all European languages); 'The Book of the Fatherland' (1869); 'Christmas Legend' (1872); Complete Works (Madrid, 1873).

Ahlgren, Ernst (äl'gren), pseudonym of Victoria Benedictsson. A Swedish novelist (1850-88): author of 'From Schonen' (1884), a collection of tales descriptive of native types; 'Money' (1885) and 'Dame Marianne' (1887), novels; 'Folk-Life' (1887), a collection of stories; and others. She ranks very high among the recent female writers of Sweden.

Ahlquist, August Engelbert (äl'qvist). A Finnish poet and philologist; born at Kuopio, Aug. 7, 1826; died at Helsingfors, Nov. 20, 1889. He was appointed professor of Finnish language and literature at the University of Helsingfors in 1862. His poems appeared under the title 'Sparks' (4th ed., 1881); besides which he wrote several grammatical and philological works, and translated Schiller and others into Finnish.

Ahlwardt, Theodor Wilhelm (äl'värt). A German Orientalist; born at Greifswald, July 4, 1828. He is the first living authority on old Arabic poetry. His chief works are: 'On the Poetry and Poetics of the Arabians' (1856); 'The Divans of the Six Ancient Arabic Poets' (1870).

Aicard, Jean (ā-kär'). A French poet; born in Toulon, Feb. 4, 1848. His 'Poems of Provence' (1874) and 'The Child's Song' (1876), were both crowned by the Academy. Noteworthy among his other works are: 'Miette and Noré' (1880), an idyl in Provençal, which caused him to be ranked with Mistral, the modern troubadour; 'On the Border of the Desert' (1888), poems, enthusiastic traveling impressions from Algiers; 'Father Lebonnard' (1890), a drama; 'The King of Camargue' a novel of Provence; 'The Black Diamond' (1895).

Aïdé, Hamilton (ä-ē-dä'). An English novelist and poet; born in Paris, France, in 1830. He was educated at Bonn, and became an officer in the British army. His poems include: 'Eleanore and Other Poems' (1856); 'The Romance of the Scarlet Leaf and Other

Poems' (1865), and 'Songs without Music'
(1882). Among a long list of novels are:
'Rita,' an autobiography (1859); 'Carr of Car-
lyon'; 'The Marstons' (1868); 'Poet and
Peer' (1880); 'The Cliff Mystery' (1888);
'Voyage of Discovery,' depicting American
society (1892); 'Elizabeth's Pretenders' (1895).

Aikin, Lucy. An English poet and historical writer (1781–1864); daughter of John Aikin
(1747–1822), a physician and author, from whom
she received a thorough classical education;
subsequently devoted herself to the study of
English history and literature. Her works include: 'Epistles on Women' (1810); 'Lorimer' (1814), a tale; 'Memoirs of the Court of
Elizabeth' (1818); 'Memoirs of the Court of
James I.' (1822); 'Memoirs of the Court and
Reign of Charles I.' (1833); 'Life of Addison'
(1843).

Aikman, William. An American religious
writer; born in Ireland in 1824. He was a
Presbyterian clergyman. Among his works
are: 'The Moral Power of the Sea' (1864); 'Life
at Home' (1870); 'A Bachelor's Talks about
Married Life' (1884); 'Heavenly Recognitions.'

Aimard, Gustave (ā-mär'). A French novelist (1818–83). He came to America as a boy
and spent a number of years among the Indians; and afterwards traveled through Spain,
Turkey, and the Caucasus, and returned to Paris
in 1848. His stories, in imitation of Cooper's
Indian tales, although abounding in improba-
bilities, hold the attention of the reader:
'The Trappers of Arkansas' (1858); 'The
Great Chief of the Aucas' (1858); 'The Pirates of the Prairie' (1859); 'The White
Scalpers' (1873); 'The Rat Hunters' (1876).

Aimwell, Walter. See **Simonds, William.**

Ainslie, Hew. A Scottish poet; born in the
parish of Dailly, Ayrshire, April 5, 1792; died
at Louisville, Kentucky, March 11, 1878. He
emigrated to America when thirty, and is
remembered for the good verse in his 'A Pilgrimage to the Land of Burns' (1820), and for
various songs and ballads, the most popular
being 'The Rover of Loch Ryan.'

Ainsworth, William Francis. An English
naturalist and writer of travels; born at Exeter, Nov. 9, 1807; died Nov. 27, 1896. He
accompanied Chesney's Euphrates expedition
as physician and naturalist, and was sent in
1838 by the Geographical Society and the
Society for the Diffusion of Christian Knowledge, to make investigations in Asia Minor
and Kurdistan. His chief works are: 'Researches in Assyria, Babylonia, etc.' (1838);
'Travels and Researches in Asia Minor, Mesopotamia, etc.' (1842); 'Travels in the Track
of the 10,000 Greeks' (1844); 'Wanderings in
Every Clime' (1870); 'A Personal Narrative
of the Euphrates Expedition' (2 vols., 1888).
He was for a time proprietor and editor of the
New Monthly Magazine.

Ainsworth, William Harrison. An English novelist; born in Manchester, Feb. 4, 1805;

died in Reigate, Jan. 3, 1882. Educated in
Manchester, he went to London, edited Bentley's Magazine in 1840, Ainsworth's Magazine 1842–53, and the New Monthly Magazine.
He wrote 250 novels and enjoyed enormous
popularity. His books are still read for their
vivacious narrative and powerful descriptions.
The most widely known among them is probably 'Jack Sheppard' (1839).

Aird, Thomas. A Scottish poet (1802–76);
studied in the University of Edinburgh, where
he formed an intimacy with Carlyle which was
maintained to his death. As a contributor to
Blackwood's Magazine he earned the good-
will and praise of Professor Wilson, became
editor of the Weekly Journal in 1832, and of
the Dumfriesshire and Galloway Herald
(Dumfries) in 1835, retiring from it in 1863
His principal works are: 'Religious Characteristics,' a series of prose essays (1827);
'The Captive of Fez,' a narrative poem
(1830); 'The Old Bachelor in the Scottish Village' (1846), a prose delineation of Scottish
character, which became very popular.

Airy, Sir George Biddell. A celebrated
English astronomer; born at Alnwick, Northumberland, July 27, 1801; died Jan. 4, 1892.
Soon after graduation from Trinity College,
Cambridge, he was appointed professor of astronomy and director of the observatory. Here
he introduced improvements and inventions
that led to his selection as director of the
Greenwich Observatory. It was due to his
efforts that the observations taken at Greenwich from 1750 to 1830 were compiled. Among
his works are: 'Reduction of Observations of
the Moon' (1837); 'Sound and Atmospheric
Vibrations' (1871); 'Treatise on Magnetism'
(1871).

Akenside, Mark. An English poet; born
at Newcastle-on-Tyne, Nov. 9, 1721; died in
London, June 23, 1770. Studied at first theology, then medicine in Edinburgh and in Leyden, where he took his degree, 1744. Having
practiced, not very successfully, at Northampton and later (1745–47) at Hampstead, he soon
after, through the aid of a friend, became
prosperous and eminent in London, and in
1761 was appointed physician to the queen.
His literary fame rests on the 'Pleasures of the
Imagination,' a didactic poem (1744, remodeled
and enlarged 1757 and 1765).

Aksákof, Konstantin Sergeyévich (äk-sä'-
kof). A Russian poet and prose writer (1817–
60), son of the following. From 1846 he
was the leader of the Slavophile party, and
one of the most active contributors to all
periodicals of that tendency. Works: 'The
Life of the Old Slavs in General and of the
Russians in Particular' (1852); 'Prince Lupo-
vickij,' a comedy (1857); 'Oleg before Constantinople,' a dramatic parody (1858); 'Lyrics.'

Aksákof, Sergey Timoféyévich. A Russian
author (1791–1859), distinguished for a rare
charm of diction and warmth of feeling, especially apparent in his principal work, 'Family

Chronicle and Reminiscences' (1856), a masterly description of Russian family life; 'The Childhood of Bragoff, the Grandson' (1858), a sequel to the former.

Alaman, Lúcas (ä-lä-män'). A Mexican historian and statesman; born at Guanajuato, Oct. 18, 1792; died in Mexico, June 2, 1853. He is best known by his 'History of the Mexican Republic' (1844-49) and 'History of Mexico' (1849-52). He performed important political services for Mexico, among others as Secretary of the Interior, 1823-25; and established many important public works, including the Mexican Museum.

Alamanni, Luigi (ä-lä-män'nē) An Italian poet; born in Florence, Oct. 28, 1495; died at Amboise, France, April 18, 1556. At first in great favor with Cardinal Giuliano de' Medici, he became implicated in a conspiracy against the life of his patron, 1522, and had to flee to Venice and thence to France. On the expulsion of the Medici in 1527 he returned to Florence; but on their restoration in 1532 again took refuge in France, where Francis I. and Henry II. intrusted him with embassies to Charles V. and the republic of Genoa. His fame rests chiefly on the didactic poem on agriculture, 'Cultivation' (1533), one of the best imitations of Virgil's 'Georgics.'

Alanus ab Insulis (a-lā'nus ab in'sū-lis) or **Alain de Lille** (ä-lan' dé lēl). A noted French scholastic philosopher (1114-1203). Of his voluminous theological writings the best known is the treatise on 'The Articles of the Faith.' His poem 'Anti-Claudianus, or On the Duties of a Good and Perfect Man' is one of the most celebrated poetic compositions of the Middle Ages.

Alarcon (y Ariza), Pedro Antonio de (ä-lär-kōn'). A distinguished Spanish novelist, poet, and politician; born in Guadix, March 10, 1833; died at Valdemoro, near Madrid, July 19, 1891. His critical contributions to papers, political and literary, his description of the Moroccan campaign, but especially his novels and short stories, are among the best of their kind, and present a picture of modern Spanish society as true to life as it is variegated. His clever essay 'The Poet's Christmas' went through over 100 editions. An imposing number of his stories appeared under the collective titles 'Love and Friendship'; 'National Tales'; 'Improbable Stories.' Among them 'The Three-Cornered Hat' and 'The Scandal' deserve special mention.

Alarcón y Mendóza, Don Juan Ruiz de (ä-lär-kōn ē män-dō'thä). A noted Spanish dramatist; born at Tasco, Mexico, about 1580 or 1590; died in Madrid, Aug. 4, 1639. Little is known about his early life, but he came to Spain in 1600 and became royal attorney in Seville. From 1608 to 1611 he was in Mexico; then he took up his residence in Madrid, where he was appointed reporter of the royal council of the Indies, about 1628. The last great dramatist of the old Spanish school, he may be considered also as the creator of the so-called character comedy. Elevated sentiment, harmony of verse, and correctness of language distinguish his works, the principal of which are: 'The Weaver of Segovia'; 'Suspicious Truth,' the model for Corneille's 'Liar'; 'Walls Have Ears'; 'The Proof of Promises'; 'The Anti-Christ.' Complete edition of his works by Hartzenbusch (Madrid, 1866).

Albee, John. An American miscellaneous writer; born at Bellingham, Mass., 1833. His best known works are: 'Prose Idyls'; 'St. Aspenquid of Agamenticus' (1879), an Indian idyl; 'Literary Art' (1881), a conversation; 'Poems' (1883); 'New Castle, Historic and Picturesque' (1884), descriptive of New Castle or Great Island, on the coast of New Hampshire, his place of residence.

Alberdingk-Thijm, Josephus Albertus (äl-ber-dink-tīm). A Dutch poet and art critic (1820-89), brought up to be a merchant, and for a time head of a publishing firm; soon devoted himself entirely to art and literature, and was appointed professor of art history at the Royal Academy of Fine Arts in Amsterdam in 1876. As a prose writer he excels in the historical tale and literary sketch in narrative style, of which his 'Portraits of Joost van den Vondel' (1876) is a masterly specimen. Besides this the 'Collected Tales in Prose' (1879-83, 3 vols.) are noteworthy.

Albergati Capacelli, Francesco (äl-ber-gä'-tē kä'pä-chel'lē). An Italian dramatist (1728-1804). Of an old patrician family, he devoted his time and fortune to the promotion of dramatic art. Having killed his wife in a fit of jealousy in 1785, he had to take refuge in various cities, and only returned to his estate at Zola after a number of years. He excelled as a comedy writer. Voltaire was his ideal; next to whom he esteemed Goldoni. His comedies 'The Wise Friend' and 'The Slanderous Gossip' hold the Italian stage to this day.

Albert, Paul (äl-bär'). A French literary historian (1827-80); succeeded Loménie as professor of French Literature at the College of France. His works include: 'French Literature' (1872-82); 'Poets and Poetry' (1881); 'Moral and Literary Varieties' (1881).

Alberti, Konrad (äl-ber'tē), pseudonym of Konrad Sittenfeld. A German novelist and critic; born at Breslau, July 9, 1862. He is an uncompromising exponent of the naturalist school, and his occupation is that of dramatic critic. His novels are: 'Who Is the Stronger' (1888); 'The Old and the Young' (1889); 'Rosa of Hildesheim' (1895), an historical romance; and 'The Beautiful Theotaki' (1899).

Alberti, Leone Battista. An eminent Italian architect, philosopher, writer on art, and poet; born in Venice, Feb. 18, 1404; died in Rome, April 1472. He excelled simultaneously in Latin comedy with his 'Philodoxios,' long accepted as an ancient classic, in criticism with his 'On Painting,' in architectural theory with his 'Building Art,' and in theology and law with his interesting and sensible essays; moreover, he painted well, designed and built many noble structures, and penned some of the most delightful Latin and Italian poetry in the fifteenth-century anthology.

Alberti, Luigi (äl-ber'te). An Italian dramatist and poet; born in Florence, 1822. Of his numerous comedies (collected, Florence, 1875), 'Peter the Workman' is considered the best. A fantastic drama, 'Asmodeo' (1885), gave rise to lively literary discussions on its first performance in 1887.

Alberti, Sophie. See **Verena**.

Albertus Magnus (al-ber'tus mag'nus). ("Albert the Great," Count von Bollstädt.) A famous German scholastic philosopher; born at Lauingen, Suabia, 1193; died at Cologne, Nov. 15, 1280. He became Bishop of Ratisbon in 1260. One of the greatest scholars of his age, he taught philosophy and theology at Cologne and Paris, the celebrated Thomas Aquinas being among his pupils. So great was his knowledge that he was accounted a magician by his contemporaries. He introduced Aristotle's philosophy to the comprehension of his age. His works, which constitute an encyclopædia of the learning of the times, though treating chiefly of physical science, fill twenty-one volumes. They appeared in 1651.

Alberus, Erasmus (äl'ber-ös). A German poet and scholar (1500–53). He studied theology in Wittenberg; was active as a teacher and preacher in many places; a friend of Luther, and one of the stanchest champions of the Reformation. His most noteworthy works are: 'The Book of Virtue and Wisdom' (1550), containing 49 rhymed fables with a strong satirical element; 'The Barefooted Friars' Owlglass and Alkoran' (1542), a satire in prose, with a preface by Luther.

Albery, James. An English dramatist; born in 1832; died Aug. 16, 1889. He studied architecture, but entered upon a commercial career. He early devoted himself to playwriting, but it was not until 1870 that he achieved success with 'The Two Roses.' Among his other comedies are: 'Pink Dominoes'; 'The Denhams'; and 'Featherbrain.'

Alcæus (al-sē'us). One of the foremost Greek lyric poets; native of Mitylene; flourished in the sixth century B.C. Of his poems we have only fragments; some were hymns to the gods, others battle songs, still others were in praise of liberty; very many were love songs of pronounced erotic character. He is said to have been the literary model of Horace.

Alcantara-Chaves, Pedro Carlos de (äl-kan'tä-rä chä'ves). A Portuguese dramatist; born in Lisbon in 1829. Among his best known works are: 'Garibaldi' and 'Sin and Forgive-

ness.' He has also published a volume of lyric poetry.

Alcázar, Baltasar de (äl-kä'thär). A Spanish poet; born at Seville in 1530; died at Ronda, Jan. 15, 1606. His light poems, not very numerous, received flattering notice from Cervantes and others. He had, in his time, many imitators, but few equals. His best known poem is 'The Jovial Supper.'

Alciphron (al'si-fron). A Greek rhetorician who flourished in the second century of the Christian era, and attained celebrity through his series of more than a hundred imaginary letters purporting to be written by the very dregs of the Athenian population, including courtesans and petty rogues. Their importance in literature is due almost wholly to the insight they afford into the social conditions and manners and morals of the day. The letters from the courtesans (hetairai) are based upon incidents in Menander's lost plays, and the new Attic comedy was likewise drawn upon for material.

Alcman (alk'man). One of the earliest and greatest of Greek lyric poets, belonging to the 7th century B.C. He is supposed to have been a native of Lydia, and to have been taken as a slave to Sparta. Only small fragments of his odes remain. He used the broad, homely Doric dialect. His poems were love ditties, hymns, pæans, processional chants, etc.

Alcott, Amos Bronson (âl'kot). An American philosophical writer and educator, one of the founders of the transcendental school of philosophy in New England; born at Wolcott, Conn., Nov. 29, 1799; died at Boston, March 4, 1888. From 1834–37 his private school in Boston, conducted on the plan of adapting instruction to the individuality of each pupil, attracted attention. He was on terms of friendship with Emerson, Hawthorne, Channing, Thoreau, Margaret Fuller, and many other noted persons. After 1840 he lived in Concord, Mass., and was the projector and dean of the Concord school of philosophy. Lectures on speculative and practical subjects occupied his later years. His chief works are: 'Orphic Sayings,' contributed to the Dial (1840); 'Tablets' (1868); 'Concord Days' (1872); 'Table-Talk' (1877); 'Sonnets and Canzonets' (1882); 'Ralph Waldo Emerson, his Character and Genius' (1882); 'New Connecticut' (1886).

Alcott, Louisa May. An American author, daughter of the preceding; born in Germantown, Pa., Nov. 29, 1832; died in Boston, Mass., March 6, 1888. She wrote at an early age; her 'Flower Fables' (1855) and 'Moods' (1865, revised ed., 1881) made little impression; but 'Hospital Sketches' (1869), 'Little Women' (1868), 'Little Men' (1871), and many others of like character and popularity, made her famous.

Alcuin (al'kwin). An eminent English scholar; born at or near York, about 735; died at Tours, France, May 19, 804. One of the most learned men of his time, teacher and intimate adviser of Charlemagne. 'Lives of the Saints'; 'Poems on the Saints of the Church at York,' and a treatise 'On Grammar,' are among his celebrated works. In Prof. West's 'Alcuin' (1893) a full account of his life and work is given.

Aldana, Ramón (äl-dä'nä). A Mexican poet (1832–82). Besides four dramas, among which are 'Honor and Happiness' and 'Nobility of Heart,' he produced lyric poems and sonnets, and contributed many literary articles to journals.

Alden, Henry Mills. An American editor, poet, and prose writer; born at Mt. Tabor, Vt., Nov. 11, 1836. He was graduated at Williams College and Andover Theological Seminary; settled in New York in 1861, became managing editor of Harper's Weekly in 1864, and editor of Harper's Monthly Magazine in 1868, which post he now holds. He has published: 'The Ancient Lady of Sorrow,' a poem (1872); 'God in His World' (1890); 'A Study of Death' (1895); 'Pictorial History of the Rebellion.'

Alden, Isabella. An American writer of juvenile books; born in New York in 1841. She has written extensively under the name of « Pansy,» the series called the 'Pansy Books' numbering about sixty titles.

Alden, Joseph. An American educator, editor, and writer of juvenile literature; born at Cairo, N. Y., Jan. 4, 1807; died in New York city, Aug. 30, 1885. During his career he was professor of Latin, rhetoric, and political economy at Williams College, and of mental and moral philosophy at Lafayette College. He was president of Jefferson College, Cannonsburg, Pa., from 1857 to 1862, and principal of the Normal School at Albany, N. Y., from 1867 to 1881. He was also editor of the New York Observer. Besides books for young people he wrote: 'Citizens' Manual'); 'Christian Ethics' (1866); 'Science of Government' (1866); 'Elements of Intellectual Philosophy' (1866).

Alden, William Livingston. An American humorous writer and journalist; born at Williamstown, Mass., Oct. 9, 1837. He introduced the sport of canoeing into the United States. He was for a time United States consul-general at Rome. Among his principal writings may be named: 'Domestic Explosives' (1877); 'Shooting Stars' (1878); 'The Canoe and the Flying Proa' (1878); 'Moral Pirates' (1880); 'The Comic Liar' (1882); 'Cruise of the Ghost' (1882); 'Life of Christopher Columbus' (1882); 'A New Robinson Crusoe' (1888). Died 1908.

Aldrich, Anne Reeve. An American poet and novelist; born in New York, April 25, 1866; died there, June 29, 1892. She was the author of: 'The Rose of Flame' (1889); 'The Feet of Love,' a novel (1890); and 'Songs about Life, Love, and Death' (1892).

Aldrich, James. An American poet; born at Mattituck, L. I., July 14, 1810; died in New York, Sept. 9, 1856. Of his poems the best known is 'A Death-Bed,' to which Poe's comment called particular attention.

Aldrich, Thomas Bailey. A distinguished American poet, essayist, and writer of fiction; born in Portsmouth, N. H., Nov. 11, 1836. He spent his early youth in Louisiana, but at the age of seventeen entered a mercantile house in New York. Removing to Boston in 1866, he became editor of Every Saturday, and in 1881 editor of the Atlantic Monthly. He has become almost equally eminent as a prose writer and poet. Among his prose works the best known are: 'The Story of a Bad Boy' (1870); 'Marjorie Daw and Other People' (1873); 'Prudence Palfrey' (1874); 'The Queen of Sheba,' a romance of travel (1877); 'The Stillwater Tragedy' (1880). Of his poems, formerly published in separate collections, most are included in 'Complete Poems' (1882) and 'Household Edition' (1895). Died Mar. 19, 1907.

Aleandro, Girolamo, the Younger, (äl-ä-än'drō). An Italian poet and antiquary; born in Friuli, 1574; died in Rome, 1629. He was distinguished for the accuracy of his taste in literature. The 'Tears of Penitence,' a series of tenderly conceived odes, was completed when he was sixteen years old. A later work is the 'Penitential Psalms'; but the most solid memorial of his talent is a volume on 'Ancient Marble Tablets.'

Aleardi, Aleardo, Count (ä-lä-är'dē). An Italian poet and patriot; born near Verona, Nov. 4, 1812; died there, July 17, 1878. He studied first philosophy and natural science, and then jurisprudence. His political principles, as revealed in his poem 'Arnaldo' (1842), brought him under suspicion, and public office under the (Austrian) government was denied him. Others of his works are: 'Primal Histories' (1857), a poem on the intellectual, ethical, and social evolution of man; 'An Hour in My Youth,' a piece inspired at once with tenderest love of nature and intense devotion to Italian independence; 'Letters to Mary'; 'Raffaele and the Fornarina'; 'The Maritime Cities of Italy'; and 'A Political Ode,' directed against Pope Pius IX. (1862).

Alecsandrescu, Grigoie (ä-lek-sän-dres'kö). A Rumanian poet and statesman (1812–86). After serving three years as an officer in the army he became a writer and a politician. His 'Satires' and 'Fables' enjoyed wide popularity. His poem 'The Year 1840' was like a bugle call, and aroused the enthusiasm of the Wallachians and Servians to the highest pitch. His collected works, 'Meditations, Elegies, Epistles, Satires, and Fables,' were published at Bucharest, 1863.

Alecsandri, Basile (ä-lek-sän'drē). A Rumanian poet (1821–90). He pursued literary studies in Paris, 1834–39; edited a patriotic journal, Literary Dacia, at Bucharest; was afterward director of the French Theatre at Jassy, for which he composed a series of comedies. He excels in the description of natural scenery.

His war poems (1877–78) had a powerful influence on public opinion in the Danubian principalities. Other works are a poem, 'In Praise of the Latin Race' (1874) ; 'Rumanian Folk-Songs,' and the drama 'Prince Despot' (1880).

Alemán, Matteo (ä-lä-män'). A Spanish novelist; born in Seville about 1550; died in Mexico after 1609. For some time an official in the royal treasury, he either resigned or was dismissed in consequence of an annoying lawsuit, and about 1608 went to Mexico. His fame rests on the satirical romance, 'The Life and Deeds of the Picaroon Guzman de Alfarache,' which, like its forerunner and model, the 'Lazarillo de Tormes' by Mendoza, is one of the most famous representatives of the "picaresque" novel. Its first part, under the title of 'Watch-Tower of Human Life,' appeared in 1599 in three editions, and up to 1605 attained to 26 more editions of over 50,000 copies. This immense success induced a literary freebooter to publish a spurious second part in 1603, which was followed by the genuine in 1605. The work was translated into every European language, and in 1623 even into Latin. The best edition of the original is in vol. iii. of Aribau's 'Library of Spanish Authors' (Madrid, 1846).

Alembert, Jean Baptiste le Rond d' (ä-lon̄-bär'). An eminent French philosopher, mathematician, and man of letters ; born in Paris, Nov. 16, 1717; died there, Oct. 9, 1783. His treatises on mathematical and physical problems brought him celebrity while yet under middle age. For the great French 'Encyclopedia' he wrote the admirable 'Preliminary Discourse' or introduction. Among his works of more or less popular or literary character may be named 'Literary and Philosophical Miscellanies' and 'Elements of Philosophy.'

Alencar, José Martinião de (ä-len-kär'). A noted Brazilian novelist; born at Fortaleza, May 1, 1829; died in Rio de Janeiro, Dec. 12, 1877. A lawyer by profession, he was also active as a conservative politician, and in 1868–69 was minister of justice. His novels, in the style of Cooper, treat subjects from Brazilian history, and city and country life, chiefly based on Indian traditions, and contain masterly descriptions of tropical nature.

Alexander, Archibald. An American theological and philosophical writer; born near Lexington, Rockbridge county, Va., April 17, 1772; died at Princeton, N. J., Oct. 22, 1851. He was a Presbyterian minister, president of Hampden Sidney College, Virginia, and professor at Princeton Theological Seminary. His principal works were : 'Evidences of Christianity' (1823) ; 'Treatise on the Canon of the Old and New Testaments' (1826); 'Outlines of Moral Science' (1852). He was a distinguished preacher.

Alexander, Sir James Edward. A British general and explorer; born in Scotland, 1803; died April 2, 1885. He served in the East, in Africa, and the Crimean war, and explored Central Africa. He wrote : 'Travels through Russia and the Crimea' (1830) ; 'Expedition of Discovery into the Interior of Africa' (1838); etc.

Alexander, Mrs., pseudonym of Annie Hector. An Irish novelist; born in Dublin in 1825. She began to write at an early age, and is a prolific and popular novelist. Her books include : 'The Wooing O't' (1873) ; 'Ralph Wilton's Weird' (1875); 'Her Dearest Foe' (1876) ; 'The Freres' (1882) ; 'A Golden Autumn' (1897); and 'A Winning Hazard' (1897).

Alexander, Mrs. Cecil Frances (Humphrey). An Irish poet; born in County Wicklow in 1818; died in Londonderry, Oct. 12, 1895. She was very active in religious and charitable works. She is best known as a writer of hymns and religious poems. Among the most noted are the hymns 'Roseate Hue of Early Dawn' and 'All Things Bright and Beautiful.' Her most famous poem is 'The Burial of Moses.'

Alexander of Hales. A noted English philosopher and theologian; born at Hales, Gloucestershire; died in Paris, 1245. One of the greatest of the schoolmen, he was among the first to study Aristotle from the point of view of the Arabic commentators. His chief work was 'The Sum of Theology' (1475). He was called "The Irrefutable Doctor," "The Doctor of Doctors," "The Fountain of Life."

Alexis, Wilibald (ä-lek'sis), pseudonym of Wilhelm Häring. A notable German novelist; born at Breslau, June 29, 1798; died at Arnstadt, Dec. 16, 1871. The writings of Sir Walter Scott made so profound an impression upon his imagination that almost all his work plainly shows the influence of the author of 'Waverley.' His first important work, indeed, —a romance, 'Walladmor,'—purported to be a translation from Scott, as did his second, 'Avalon Castle.' The finest products of his genius are historical tales of Prussia, with Frederick the Great as hero, and among them 'Cabanis' stands prominently forth. 'The False Waldemar' and 'Peace is the First Civic Duty' are also excellent novels. As a poet he is pleasing and not infrequently impressive, but his stanzas are wanting in true originality. His popularity as a writer of fiction was due to a capacity for presenting the interesting phase of historical themes, and to his fecundity of plot and incident; but his best stories are marred by over-elaboration, and by tricks of style.

Alfieri, Vittorio, Count (äl-fē-ā'rē). A celebrated Italian dramatist; born at Asti in Piedmont, Jan. 17, 1749; died at Florence, Oct. 8, 1803. He came into his vast paternal inheritance at the age of 14; and two or three years afterward began a series of travels which extended over nearly all the European countries, returning to Turin, 1772. He was the hero of many romantic adventures, and his first bent toward literature was given him by his desire to lessen the tedium of illness for a lady of whom he was enamored. His success determined his after career. He elaborated the slender sketch of a dramatic dialogue into a tragedy in five acts, 'Cleopatra,' which was put on the stage in Turin, 1775. Conscious of his imperfect acquaintance with literature and the niceties of his native language, he now began the study of Latin and of the Tuscan dialect. At Florence he formed an attachment for the Countess of Albany, which ended only with his life. His tragedies, 'Cleopatra,' 'Polinice,' 'Antigone,' 'Agide,' 'Bruto,' and several others, are founded on classic themes, and formed on the Hellenic model. 'Saul,' founded on Hebrew sacred history, but elaborated according to the canons of Grecian dramaturgy, was by far the most popular of Alfieri's dramas. The 'Filippo' presents, in lineaments that could be drawn only by the hand of a master, the sombre character of Philip II. of Spain. He wrote in all twenty-one tragedies and six comedies, and composed many sonnets; among his odes are five on 'American Independence.' His prose works comprise an essay on 'Tyranny,' a volume of 'Essays on Literature and Government,' and 'Memoirs of his Life.'

Alfonso X., the Wise. King of Leon and Castile. A Spanish poet, historian, and scholar (1252-84). Of his poetical compositions many are still extant; among them a poem on 'The Chase,' one on chemistry, some love songs, and 'Canticles of Saint Mary.' He was a student of astronomy, and reformed the Ptolemaic planetary tables, called after him 'Alfonsine Tables.' From his hand we have also a history of the Crusades, 'The Great Conquest Over Sea,' and a 'General Chronicle' of Spain; and he had commenced a 'Great and General History' of the world before his death. He was the first to codify the laws of the kingdoms of Spain. He had all accessible classic and Arabic works on philosophy and the sciences translated into Castilian.

Alford, Henry. An English poet and miscellaneous writer, philologist, critic, artist, and preacher; born in London, Oct. 7, 1810; died at Canterbury, Jan. 12, 1871. He became dean of Canterbury in 1856. An accomplished man, his literary work attracted attention in several departments. Besides sermons and university lectures, he wrote: 'The School of the Heart, and Other Poems' (1835), his most popular volume of verse; 'The Queen's English' (1866). He was best known by his celebrated edition of the Greek New Testament (1844-52), which, incorporating the results of German Biblical scholarship, formed a landmark in New Testament study in England and America. He was the first editor of the Contemporary Review.

Alfred the Great. King of England, translator of several works of antiquity into the English tongue of his day (849-901). One of his biographers credits him with having translated into Saxon nearly the whole extant Latin literature: it is certain that he did, himself, translate many of the monuments of the Christian religion, as Gregory the Great's 'Pastoral Care,' selections from the writings of St. Augustine, and Boethius's 'Consolations of Philosophy'; he also translated Bede's 'Church History of the English Nation.'

Algarotti Francesco, Count (äl-gä-rot-tē). An Italian littérateur (1712-64). Frederick the Great held him in high regard and made him a count of Prussia. He was an accomplished critic of the arts of painting, sculpture, and architecture. Among his works is 'The Plurality of Worlds' (1733), an exposition, for ladies' use, of Newton's philosophy. He is at his best in his letters, especially his 'Poetical Epistles' (1759).

Alger, Horatio. An American writer of juvenile fiction; born at Revere, Mass., Jan. 13, 1834. Graduated from Harvard in 1852, settled in New York in 1866, and became interested in the condition of self-supporting boys, described in his series of more than fifty books, including 'Ragged Dick,' 'Tattered Tom,' 'Luck and Pluck,' which became very popular. Other works: 'Nothing to Do: A Tilt at our Best Society,' a poem (1857); 'Helen Ford,' a novel (1860); a series of juvenile biographies of Webster, Lincoln, Garfield, etc.; and 'The Young Salesman' (1896). He died in 1899.

Alger, William Rounseville. An American Unitarian clergyman and miscellaneous writer; born at Freetown, Mass., Dec. 30, 1822. His chief works are: 'History of the Doctrine of a Future Life' (1863); 'Genius of Solitude' (1865); and 'Friendships of Women' (1867). He occupied pulpits in New York, Denver, Boston, and San Francisco. D. in 1905.

Alighieri. See **Dante.**

Alis, Hippolyte Percher (ä-lē'). A French novelist and journalist, born at Couleuvre, Oct. 7, 1857. He has contributed to various Paris journals, and is the author of several naturalistic novels, among which are: 'Hara-Kiri' (1882); 'A Daughter of the Soil' (1885); 'Some Foolish People' (1889).

Alishan, Leon M. An Armenian poet and historian; born in Constantinople, July 30, 1820. He studied in Venice, where he took orders in 1840, and was appointed professor in the College Raphael, of which he became director in 1848. Having taken charge of the Armenian college in Paris in 1858, he returned to Venice in 1865 as director of Saint Lazare. He is regarded by his countrymen as their leading poet. Among his numerous writings are: 'Poems Complete' (1857-67); 'Popular Songs of the Armenians' (1867); 'Historical Monographs' (1870); 'History and Geography of Armenia' (1885), which was seized and suppressed by the Turkish authorities.

Alison, Archibald. A Scottish writer; born in Edinburgh, Nov. 13, 1757; died there, May

17, 1839. The charm of his pulpit oratory drew general attention to his published sermons; and by his 'Essay on the Nature and Principles of Taste' and kindred themes, he won an acknowledged but inconspicuous position in literature.

Alison, Sir Archibald. A Scottish historian, son of the above; born at Kenley, Shropshire, Dec. 29, 1792; died at Glasgow, May 23, 1867. He studied at the University of Edinburgh, and was admitted to the bar in 1814. His principal work is a 'History of Europe,' covering the period from 1789 to 1815, which was received with remarkable favor, and translated into the leading languages of Europe, and even into Arabic. The work contains a vast amount of information and many interesting descriptions; but is prolix in style, often inaccurate, and so strongly partisan that it has been said to have been designed "to prove that Providence was on the side of the Tories."

Allan, William. An American military writer; born in Virginia in 1837; died in 1889. During the Civil War he served as lieutenant-colonel in the Confederate army. His works are: 'Jackson's Valley Campaign' (1862); 'Battle Fields of Virginia' (1867); 'Army of Northern Virginia.'

Allen, Alexander Viets Griswold. An American ecclesiastical historian; born at Otis, Mass., May 4, 1841. Professor of ecclesiastical history at the Episcopal Theological School, Cambridge, Mass. He has written: 'The Continuity of Christian Thought' (1883); 'The Greek Theology and the Renaissance of the 19th Century' (1884, the Bohlen lectures for that year), and a 'Life of Jonathan Edwards' (1889); 'Freedom in the Church' (1906), etc.

Allen, Elizabeth Akers. An American poet; born (Elizabeth Chase) at Strong, Me., Oct. 9, 1832. She was married in 1860 to Paul Akers, the sculptor, who died in 1861, and in 1865 to E. M. Allen of New York. Her first volume, 'Forest Buds,' appeared under the pen-name of "Florence Percy" (1855). Other works: 'The Silver Bridge and Other Poems' (1866); a volume of 'Poems' (1866), which contains 'Rock Me to Sleep, Mother'; (her authorship of this popular ballad, once disputed, is proved in the New York Times, May 27, 1867;) 'The High-Top Sweeting and Other Poems' (1891).

Allen, Ethan. An American Revolutionary hero; born at Litchfield, Conn., Jan. 10, 1737; died near Burlington, Vt., Feb. 12, 1789. His services in the war of independence, as colonel of the "Green Mountain Boys," capturing Fort Ticonderoga "in the name of the great Jehovah and the Continental Congress," his attack on Montreal, sufferings as a prisoner in England, skillful diplomacy in behalf of Vermont, etc., are well known. He wrote an account of his captivity (1799), 'A Vindication of Vermont' (1784), and 'Allen's Theology, or

the Oracles of Reason' (1784), in which he declared reason to be the only oracle of man.

Allen, Fred Hovey. An American clergyman and writer; born in New Hampshire in 1845. He has written the text of several popular art works, among which are included: 'Great Cathedrals of the World'; 'Modern German Masters' (1886); 'The Doré Album'; 'Discovery and Conquest of Peru'; 'Discovery and Conquest of Mexico'; 'Heart of Europe.'

Allen, Grant (Charles Grant Blairfindie Allen). An English naturalist, essayist, and novelist; born in Alwington, Canada, Feb. 24, 1848; died in London, Eng., Oct. 28, 1899. He graduated from Oxford, and was professor at Queen's College, Jamaica, until he settled in England. He early became a follower of Charles Darwin and Herbert Spencer, and wrote scientific essays in a picturesque and attractive style. From 1883 he produced a large number of novels, many of which are based on a psychological theme. Among the best of them are: 'Babylon' (1885), 'The Devil's Die' (1888), and 'Under Sealed Orders' (1896).

Allen, James Lane. An American novelist; born at Lexington, Ky., in 1848. He graduated at Transylvania University, taught there for a time, and became subsequently professor of Latin and English in Bethany College. His fame rests mainly upon his powerful and popular novels of manners and people in the blue-grass region and elsewhere, the best known being 'Summer in Arcady' (1896); 'The Choir Invisible'; 'A Kentucky Cardinal'; 'Aftermath'; 'The Bride of the Mistletoe' (1909).

Allen, Joel Asaph. An American naturalist; born at Springfield, Mass., July 19, 1838. From 1865 to 1869 he was a member of various scientific expeditions to Brazil, the Rocky Mountains, and Florida. In 1870 he was appointed assistant in ornithology at the Museum of Comparative Zoölogy at Cambridge, Mass., and in 1885 curator of ornithology and mammalogy in the American Museum of Natural History in New York city. He is part author with E. Coues of 'Monographs of North American Rodentia' (1877); and has also published among other works, 'History of North American Pinnipeds'; 'Mammals of Patagonia.'

Allen, Joseph Henry. An American Unitarian minister, educator and writer; born at Northboro, Mass., Aug. 21, 1821; died at Cambridge, March 20, 1898. His chief works were: 'Ten Discourses on Orthodoxy' (2d ed.) 1889); 'Hebrew Men and Times' (2d ed., 1879); 'Outline of Christian History' (1884); 'Our Liberal Movement in Theology' (1889); 'Positive Religion, Essays, Fragments, and Hints' (1891). He was editor of the well-known Allen and Greenough series of Latin classics, and of the Unitarian Review; senior editor of the 'History of Unitarianism.' He had parishes at Jamaica Plain, Mass., Washington, D. C., and Bangor, Me.; and lectured for several years on ecclesiastical history in Harvard University.

Allen, Karl Ferdinand. A Danish historian; born at Copenhagen, April 23, 1811; died there, Dec. 27, 1871. He became professor of history and northern archæology at the University of Copenhagen in 1862. His principal works, 'Handbook of the History of the Fatherland' (1840), very democratic in tone, and 'History of the Three Northern Kingdoms' (1864-72), produced a marked impression, as did also minor writings relating to Schleswig.

Allen, Paul. An American miscellaneous writer and journalist; born at Providence, R. I., Feb. 15, 1775; died at Baltimore, Aug. 18, 1826. He studied law originally, but became a journalist, and edited newspapers in Philadelphia and Baltimore. He wrote: 'Poems' (1801); 'Lewis and Clark's Travels' (1814); 'Life of Alexander I.' (1818), etc.

Allen, William. An American preacher and miscellaneous writer; born at Pittsfield, Mass., Jan. 2, 1784; died at Northampton, Mass., July 16, 1868. He became president of Dartmouth University in 1817; was president of Bowdoin College, 1820-39. Of numerous works, both in prose and verse, the best known is 'American Biographical and Historical Dictionary' (3d ed., 1857).

Allen, Willis Boyd. An American writer; born in Maine in 1855. Besides a collection of verse, entitled 'In the Morning,' he has written a large number of works for young people, among which are: 'The Red Mountain of Alaska'; 'Pine Cones' (1885); 'Silver Rags' (1886); 'Kelp' (1888); 'The Mammoth Hunters.'

Allibone, Samuel Austin (al'i-bōn). An American bibliographer; born at Philadelphia, April 17, 1816; died at Lucerne, Switzerland, Sept. 2, 1889. He was at one time librarian of the Lenox Library, New York. He was the author of a 'Dictionary of English Literature, and British and American Authors' (3 vols., 1854-71; Supplement by Dr. John Foster Kirk, 2 vols., 1891), 'Poetical Quotations'; 'Prose Quotations,' etc. It took twenty years to write the Dictionary, which is familiar in libraries the world over wherever English is spoken.

Allies, Jabez. An English antiquary and one of the earliest writers on folklore; born at Lulsley, Worcestershire, Oct. 22, 1787; died at Cheltenham, Jan. 29, 1856. He devoted nearly his entire life to the study of Roman and Saxon antiquities in Worcestershire, the results being embodied in his monumental work, 'The Ancient British, Roman, and Saxon Antiquities and Folklore of Worcestershire' (1852).

Allingham, William. An Irish poet; born at Ballyshannon, March 19, 1828; died at Hampstead, near London, Nov. 18, 1889. Having for some years been an officer in the Customs, he became assistant editor of Fraser's Magazine in 1871 and succeeded Froude as editor in 1874, when he also married Helen Paterson, the illustrator and water-color artist. His graceful poems excel in descriptions of Irish scenery and life; some of them were illustrated by Rossetti, Kate Greenaway, and other distinguished artists. Prominent among his works is 'Lawrence Bloomfield in Ireland' (1864), a narrative poem on contemporary Irish life.

Allmers, Hermann (äl'mers). A German poet; born at Rechtenfleth, near Bremen, Feb. 11, 1821. He wrote: 'Book of the Marshes' (1857), a faithful portrayal of nature and men in his native country; 'Poems' (1860); 'Roman Sauntering Days' (1869), subtle 'delineations of Italian life'; 'Electra' (1872), a drama, continuing and concluding the plot of Goethe's 'Iphigenia.'

Allston, Washington. An eminent American painter, poet, and romancer; born at Waccamaw, S. C., Nov. 5, 1779; died in Cambridge, Mass., July 9, 1843. He graduated at Harvard in 1800; studied at the Royal Academy, London, and in Rome, and returned to Boston in 1809. He is the author of: 'The Sylph of the Seasons and Other Poems' (1813); 'Monaldi,' a romance (1841), and 'Lectures on Art and Poems' (1850). See his 'Life' by Flagg.

Almeida, Nicolao Tolentino de (äl-mä'ē-dä). A Portuguese poet (1741-1811), noted for his satires, ridiculing the manners of his day. One of them, on the ex-Minister Pombal, procured for him a position as secretary in the Ministry of the Interior. 'Poetical Works' (Lisbon, 1802; new ed., 1861).

Almeida-Garrett, João Baptista de Silva Leitão de (äl-mä'ē-dä gär-ret'). A distinguished Portuguese poet, dramatist, and politician; born in Oporto, Feb. 4, 1799; died in Lisbon, Dec. 10, 1854. He studied law at Coimbra, and joining the democratic movement in 1820, became minister of public instruction when scarcely twenty-one, but on the restoration in 1823 was banished and went to England. He subsequently returned, and experienced many vicissitudes owing to his political activity. As a man of letters he endeavored to free Portuguese poetry from the shackles of pseudo-classicism and to inspire it with new life by basing it on national forms and traditions. His efforts were also directed towards the creation of a purely national drama. His principal works are: 'Catão,' a tragedy (1820), among the best in Portuguese literature; 'Camões,' a romantic epic (1825), glorifying the life and death of Portugal's greatest poet; 'Dona Branca,' a satirical epic (1826), scourging monasticism; 'Adozinda,' a lyrical epic (1828); 'Bernal Francez,' a cycle of romances (1829); 'Auto de Gil Vicente' (1838), pronounced the first purely Portuguese drama; 'O Arco de Sant' Anna,' a historical novel (1846); 'Romancerio,' a collection of Portuguese ballads (3 vols., 1851-53).

Almquist, Karl Jonas Ludvig (älm'kvist). A notable Swedish poet, novelist, and miscellaneous writer; born in Stockholm, Nov. 28, 1793; died in Bremen, Sept. 26, 1866. A writer of great versatility, author of a series of educational works, treatises on the mental, moral, and political sciences, on philology, religion, mathematics, philosophy, and national economy, etc., of novels and tales, dramas, poems, lyric and epical. ‹The Book of the Rose,› a collection of dramatic and lyric pieces, is his best known work. ‹It's All Right› and ‹The Palace,› novels, ‹Araminta May› and ‹Skällnora's Will,› tales, are also popular.

Alpuche, Wenceslao (äl-pö'che). A Mexican poet (1804–41). His first poems, published when he was little more than a youth, brought him great popularity. The best among his works are: ‹Hidalgo› and the odes: ‹Independence› and ‹The Return from Exile.›

Alsop, Richard (âl'sǫp). An American poet and scholar; born at Middletown, Conn., Jan. 23, 1761; died at Flatbush, L. I., Aug. 20, 1815. In conjunction with Theodore Dwight he edited from 1791 to 1795 the Echo, a satirical journal. Among his works are: ‹The Charms of Fancy›; ‹A Monody on the Death of Washington› (1800); and the translations entitled ‹The Enchanted Lake of the Fairy Morgana› (1808), and Molina's ‹Geographical, Natural, and Civil History of Chili.›

Altamirano, Ignacio Manuel (äl-tä-mē-rä-'nō). A Mexican poet, orator, and journalist; born in Guerrero, about 1835; died in Italy, Feb. 1893. He wrote ‹Clemencia›; ‹Julia›, etc. He held political office, rose to the rank of colonel in the army during the French invasion, and was of pure Indian blood, said to have been descended from the ancient Aztec monarchs.

Altaroche, Marie Michel (äl-tä-rosh'). A French poet and journalist (1811–84), studied law in Paris, then turned to journalism and in 1834–48 was editor-in-chief of the Charivari, which owed to his witty articles a good deal of its brilliant success. In 1850–52 he managed several theatrical enterprises. His works include: ‹Political Songs and Verses› (1835); ‹Democratic Tales› (1837); ‹Adventures of Victor Augerol› (1838), an imitation of Louvet's famous ‹Faublas› romance.

Alvarez do Oriente, Fernan (äl'vä-reth dō ō-rē-en-te). A Portuguese poet (1540–99) of the school of Camoens. His life-work, ‹Lusitania Transformed,› is a pastoral romance in the manner of Sannazaro's ‹Arcadia,› composed of prose and poetry and containing elegies, sonnets, and idyls of such beauty as to have caused some of them to be ascribed to Camoens.

Alvin, Louis Joseph (äl-van'). A Belgian poet and art critic (1806–87); became secretary (1830), then chief, of a department in the ministry of public instruction, member of the Belgian Academy in 1845, and chief librarian of the royal library in Brussels in 1850. Among his works are: ‹Sardanapalus,› a tragedy (1834); ‹The Anonymous Pamphleteer,› a comedy (1835); ‹Re-Contemplations› (1856), a satirical imitation of the romantic style.

Alxinger, Johann Baptist von (älk'sing-er). An Austrian poet (1755–97), especially esteemed for his chivalrous epics in the manner of Wieland: ‹Doolin von Mainz› (1787) and ‹Bliomberis› (1791).

Amalie, Marie Friederike Auguste (ä-mä'lē-e). A German dramatist (1794–1870), who wrote under the pseudonym "Amalie Heiter." She was Duchess of Saxony, sister of King John of Saxony. Comedies and dramas of simple conception, but careful delineation of character, and well adapted for the stage, have given her eminence, among them: ‹The Uncle›; ‹The Prince's Fiancée›; ‹Primogeniture›; ‹The Young Lady from the Country›; and ‹The Agriculturist.›

Ambros, August Wilhelm (äm'brōs). A notable Austrian writer on music; born at Mauth, Bohemia, Nov. 17, 1816; died in Vienna, June 28, 1876. He was trained for the civil service and served in it with distinction; but his aptitude for music, and particularly for the criticism and literature of music, led him in another direction, and he rose to eminence as the author of ‹The Limits of Music and Poetry,› besides numerous essays and studies connected with art. His masterpiece, however, he left unfinished: ‹The History of Music,› a work which cost him many years of labor and which he carried only to the fourth volume. He attempted musical composition, but in it won no popularity.

Ambrose, Saint (am'brōz). One of the fathers of the Latin Church; born at Trèves, Gaul, probably 340; died at Milan, April 4, 397. He became bishop of Milan in 374. His writings include: ‹Of the Duties of the Clergy› (in imitation of Cicero's ‹Of Duties›); ‹Hexaëmeron›; hymns, etc. He is supposed to have been the author of the style of singing known as the ‹Ambrosian Chant.› Works, Milan, 6 vols., 1875–86.

Ambrosius, Johanna (äm-brō'zi-ös). A German poet and story writer; born at Lengwethen, East Prussia, Aug. 3, 1854. Daughter of an artisan, and married in 1874 to a peasant's son by the name of Voigt, she led the hard life of a peasant woman till in middle age she wrote verses, which were published in a weekly newspaper; their success led to the publication of other poems and stories of hers, which have had extremely wide circulation.

Ames, Charles Gordon. An American Unitarian clergyman and writer; born at Dorchester, Mass., Oct. 3, 1828. He has published ‹George Eliot's Two Marriages› (1886); ‹As Natural as Life›; ‹Studies of the Inner Kingdom›; and is distinguished as a preacher.

Ames, Mrs. Eleanor Maria (Easterbrook). An American writer; born in 1830. She is a resident of Brooklyn, N. Y. Under the pseudonym of "Eleanor Kirk" she wrote: ‹Up Broadway and Its Sequel› (1870); ‹Information for Authors› (1888); ‹Perpetual Youth.›

Ames, Fisher. A famous American orator and statesman; born at Dedham, Mass., April

9, 1758; died there, July 4, 1808. Admitted to the bar in 1781, he became a Member of Congress in 1789, where he gained a national reputation by his oratory. Two of his finest efforts were in support of John Jay's treaty with Great Britain, and a eulogy on Washington before the Massachusetts Legislature. He was elected president of Harvard College in 1804, but declined. A brilliant talker, he was distinguished in conversation for wit and imagination, while his character was spotless. His works consist of orations, essays, and letters, 2 vols., 1854.

Ames, Mary Clemmer. An American writer; born in Utica, N. Y., in 1839; died in Washington, D. C., Aug. 18, 1884. She was a frequent contributor to the Springfield Republican, and afterwards to the New York Independent. Married to and divorced from the Rev. Daniel Ames, she became in 1883 the wife of Edward Hudson at Washington. Among her works are the novels 'Victoria' (1864); 'Eirene' (1870), and 'His Two Wives' (1874); a volume of 'Poems' (1882); and biographies of Alice and Phœbe Cary.

Ames, Nathaniel. An American physician and humorist; born in Bridgewater, Mass., in 1708; died at Dedham, Mass., July 11, 1764. He was a resident of Dedham, Mass. From 1725 to 1764 he published an Astronomical Diary and Almanac, which enjoyed great popularity on account of its wit.

Amicis, Edmondo de (ä-mē′chēs). A distinguished Italian writer; born at Oneglia in Liguria, Oct. 21, 1846. From 1865 till the occupation of Rome by the Italian army he was in the military service of King Victor Emanuel's government; then he returned to civil life at Turin, devoting himself wholly to literature, in which he had already won distinction by several graphic sketches of camp life. Among his writings of this kind the most noteworthy are: 'Army Life' (1869) and 'Recollections of 1870-71.' Of novels we have from his pen: 'The College Friends'; 'A Great Day'; 'The Paternal Home' (1872), and 'Cuore' (Hearts), published in English as 'The Heart of a Schoolboy.' His works of travel—including 'Spain'; 'Recollections of London'; 'Holland'; 'Constantinople'; 'Recollections of Paris'; 'Morocco'—have had a very wide circulation, and have been translated into several languages. He has published also a volume of 'Verses.' Died March 11, 1908.

Amiel, Henri Frédéric (ä-mē-el′). A distinguished Swiss essayist, philosophical critic, and poet; born at Geneva, Sept. 27, 1821; died there, March 11, 1881. He was for five years a student in German universities, and on his return home became professor of philosophy in the Geneva Academy. He is author of several works on the history of literature, as 'The Literary Movement in Romanish Switzerland' (1849); 'Study on Mme. de Staël' (1878); and of several poems, among them 'Millet Grains' (1854). But his fame rests principally on the 'Journal,' which appeared after the author's death.

Ammen, Daniel. A distinguished American admiral and author; born May 15, 1820, in Ohio. He entered the United States Navy July 7, 1836. He was executive officer of the North Atlantic blockading squadron at the outbreak of the Civil War. From 1861 to 1865 he rendered signal service in the attacks on Port Royal, Fort Macallister, Fort Fisher, and both the ironclad attacks on Fort Sumter. On June 4, 1878, he was retired with the rank of rear-admiral. He was the designer of the Ammen life-raft and harbor defense ram. Among his works are: 'The Atlantic Coast' (1883); 'The Old Navy and the New'; 'Navy in the Civil War' (1883). Died in 1898.

Amory, Thomas (am′o-ri). An English memoir writer; born 1691 (?); died Nov. 25, 1788. He has been called the "English Rabelais." He wrote: 'Memoirs Containing the Lives of Several Ladies of Great Britain, etc.' (1755); 'Life of John Buncle, Esq.' (1756-66); etc.

Amory, Thomas Coffin. An American lawyer, politician, biographer, and poet; born in Boston, 1812; died 1889. He held municipal office in Boston for many years. He wrote: 'Life of James Sullivan, with Selections from his Writings' (2 vols., 1859); 'Military Services and Public Life of Major-General John Sullivan' (1868); 'General Sullivan Not a Pensioner of Luzerne' (2d ed. 1875); 'The Transfer of Erin' (1877); 'Life of Sir Isaac Coffin' (1886); and two poems: 'The Siege of Newport' (1888) and 'Charles River' (1888).

Ampère, Jean Jacques Antoine (oñ-pär′). A French literary historian (1800-64), son of the physicist André M. Ampère. He became professor in Marseilles, then at the Sorbonne, and in 1833 at the College of France in Paris, being elected member of the Academy in 1847. His best work is 'Literary History of France before the XII. Century' (1840).

Amyntor, Gerhard von (ä-min′tōr), pseudonym of Dagobert von Gerhardt. A German novelist and poet; born at Liegnitz, Silesia, July 12, 1831. He entered the army in 1849, took part in the campaigns of 1864 and 1870-71 as a major, was severely wounded in the former and resigned in 1872; settled in Potsdam in 1874. His principal works are: 'Peter Quidam's Rhine-Journey' (1877), an epic; 'Songs of a German Night Watchman' (1878); 'The New Romancero' (1880), poems; 'The Priest' (1881), an epic; novels: 'It Is You' (1882); 'A Problem' (1884); 'Praise of Woman' (1885); and 'Gerke Suteminne' (1887), a historical romance.

Amyot, Jacques (ä-mē-ō′). A French author (1513-93), famous for his translations from the Greek, which, owing to their elegant style, are considered classical literature. They are: the 'Theagenes and Chariclea' of Heliodorus; 'Seven Books of Diodorus Siculus'; the 'Daphnis and Chloe' of Longus; the 'Parallel

2

Lives' and the 'Morals' of Plutarch. The most noteworthy among these is the translation of 'Plutarch's Lives,' which was used by Corneille as a source for his antique tragedies, and by Shakespeare (in its English version by Sir Thomas North) for some of his plays.

Anacreon (a-nak're-on). A renowned lyric poet of Greece; born at Teos in Ionia, 562 (?) B. C.; died 477 B. C. He enjoyed the patronage of Polycrates, autocrat of Samos; and while at his court, composed most of the odes In praise of wine and women which won for him pre-eminence among singers. A few of his authentic compositions have come down to us: under his name as many as 68 extant poems circulate, but the authorship of many of these is extremely doubtful.

Anagnos, Mrs. Julia Rowana (**Howe**) (a-näg'nos). An American poet and littérateur, daughter of Julia Ward Howe; born in 1844; died in 1886. In 1870 she married M. Anagnos, superintendent of the Perkins Institute for the Blind, Boston, Mass. She wrote 'Stray Chords' (1883) and 'Philosophiæ Quæstor' (1885).

Anaxagoras (an-aks-ag'ō-ras). A famous Greek philosopher of the Ionic school; born at Clazomenæ, 500 (?) B. C.; died 428 B. C. He explained eclipses and advanced physical science. In philosophy, he taught that the universe is regulated by an eternal self-existent and infinitely powerful principle, called by him mind; matter he seems to have asserted to be eternal, what is called generation and destruction being merely the temporary union and separation of ever existing elements; he disproved the doctrine that things may have arisen by chance. Fragments of his 'Treatise on Nature' are still in existence.

Anaximander (an-aks-i-man'der). A Greek philosopher of the Ionian school; born at Miletus, about 611 B. C.; died about 547 B. C. He was a friend and pupil of Thales of Miletus, and is said to have written the first philosophical work in Greek prose. His system of philosophy declared that the principle, or substance, out of which all things arise and to which they return, is "immortal and imperishable," being in nature intermediate between air and water. He is reputed to have invented the sun-dial.

Anaximenes (an-aks-im'e-nēz). A Greek philosopher of the Ionian school; born at Miletus, and lived in the 6th century B. C. He was probably a pupil of Anaximander. He held that air is the original substance, from which, by thickening and thinning, all other elements, as fire, water, earth, are produced. But little is known of him, there being extant but a single fragment of his lost work 'On Nature.'

Ancelot, Jacques Arsène Polycarpe (oṅs-lō'). A French dramatist (1794–1854), whose first success was the tragedy 'Louis IX.' (1819). In 1841 he was elected a member of the Academy. His works include: 'Fiesco'

(1824), a successful imitation of Schiller's play; 'Maria Padilla' (1838); 'Marie of Brabant,' an epic (1825); 'Six Months in Russia,' a medley of prose and verse (1827); 'The Man of the World,' a novel (1827); 'Familiar Epistles' (1842), satires of great elegance of style. His wife Marguerite Louise Virginie, née Chardon (1792–1875), was frequently his co-laborer and also the author of plays and novels. Of the former, 'Marie, or the Three Epochs' (1836) is the best; of the latter, 'Renée de Varville' (1853) and 'The Banker's Niece' (1853) found most favor.

Anczyc, Vladislav Ludvig (än'tsich). A Polish dramatist (1823–83), who lived mostly at Cracow, and wrote national plays which became very popular. The best among them are: 'The Peasant-Aristocrats' (1851); 'The Inhabitants of Lobsov' (1854); The Raftsmen' (1875); 'The Peasants' Emigration' (1876); besides which he wrote 'Tyrtæus,' a poetical tale (1883), and many juvenile works, partly under the pseudonym "Kasimir Góralczyk."

Andersen, Hans Christian (än'der-sen). An eminent Danish poet and story writer; born at Odense, April 2, 1805; died Aug. 4, 1875. Having received his father early in childhood, the boy received his elementary education in a charity school. He traveled in Germany, 1828, making the acquaintance of Chamisso and Tieck; then he made tours in France, Italy, and the East. His impressions of Italy are embodied in 'The Improvvisatore' (1835), the work which first gave him fame at home and abroad. In the same year appeared 'O. T.,' a novel of life and nature in the North. 'Only a Fiddler' (1837) is founded on the experiences of the author's early life. 'The Poet's Bazar' (1842) is inspired by the impressions of Oriental travel. He is seen at his very best in 'The Picture Book without Pictures.' Among his dramatic compositions are: 'The Mulatto,' a romantic play which was received with high popular favor; 'The Flowers of Happiness,' a comedy; 'Raphaella,' a romantic drama; 'Ahasuerus,' designed to emphasize certain problems of philosophy; 'The Two Baronesses,' a comedy of Danish life. In the English-speaking world Andersen's great fame will ever rest upon his stories for children, the celebrated 'Wonder Tales.'

Andersen, Karl. A Danish poet; born in Copenhagen, Oct. 26, 1828; died there, Sept. 1, 1883. Among his epic and lyrical productions are: 'Strife and Peace' (1858); 'Pictures of Travel' (1864); 'On the Arno and the Ganges' (1865); 'Light and Shade' (1868); 'Romances and Songs' (1880). In the prose tale, 'Over Cliff and Surf' (1883), he described admirably nature and life in Iceland, where he spent his youth; but his most popular work is 'Genre Pictures' (1876–81), seven collections of scenes from daily life.

Anderson, Mary. See **Navarro, Mary (Anderson) de.**

Anderson, Rasmus Björn. An American author; born in Albion, Wis., Jan. 12, 1846, of Norwegian parents. He was educated at Norwegian Lutheran College, Decorah, Iowa; becoming professor of Scandinavian languages in the University of Wisconsin in 1875-84, and United States minister to Denmark in 1885. His books include: 'America not Discovered by Christopher Columbus' (1874); 'Norse Mythology' (1875); 'Viking Tales of the North' (1877), 'Translation of the Younger Edda' (1880); 'First Chapter of Norwegian Immigration, 1821-40.'

Anderson, Robert. An English dialect poet; born in Carlisle, Feb. 1, 1770; died there, Sept. 26, 1833. He was a mill hand who produced delightfully humorous and gracefully pathetic verse in his native Cumbrian dialect; typical examples being 'The Impatient Lass,' 'Lucy Gray,' and 'The Lass abuin Thirty.'

Andreä, Johann Valentin (än-dra'e). A German theologian and satirist (1586-1654). He traveled as the tutor of young noblemen through France, Switzerland, and Italy in 1607-14; became court preacher at Stuttgart in 1639, and abbot of Adelberg in 1650. The chief among his writings, partly in Latin, partly in German, full of ingenious thought, are: 'Turbo' (1616), a dramatic satire on the scholarship of his day; 'Menippus' (1617), 100 satirical dialogues; 'Spiritual Pastime' (1619).

Andreini, Giovanni Battista (än-dra-ē'nē). An Italian comedian and poet; born in Florence, 1578; died in Paris about 1650. From his sacred drama 'Adam' (1613), Milton is by some supposed to have derived the idea of 'Paradise Lost.'

Andrews, Charles McLean. An American historical and descriptive writer; born in Connecticut, 1863. He is professor at Bryn Mawr College. He has written: 'Historical Development of Modern Europe'; 'River Towns of Connecticut'; 'The Old English Manor.'

Andrews, Christopher Columbus. An American diplomat and writer; born at Hillsborough, N. H., Oct. 27, 1829. He was brevetted major-general in the Civil War, was minister to Sweden from 1869 to 1877, and consul-general to Brazil from 1882 to 1885. Among his numerous works are: 'Minnesota and Dakota' (1857); 'Practical Treatise on the Revenue Laws of the United States' (1858); 'History of the Campaign of Mobile' (1867); 'Brazil, its Condition and Prospects' (1887); 'Administrative Reforms.'

Andrews, Elisha Benjamin. An American historical and economical writer; born at Hinsdale, N. H., Jan. 10, 1844. After serving in the Civil War, finishing his college and theological education, preaching about a year at Beverly, Mass., being president of a university in Ohio, professor in Newton Theological Institute and Brown and Cornell Universities, he became president of Brown University (1889). He went as one of the United States commissioners to the monetary conference at Brussels in 1892.

He has written: 'Institutes of our Constitutional History, English and American' (1887); 'Institutes of General History' (1889); 'Institutes of Economics' (1889); 'History of the United States'; 'History of the Last Quarter-Century in the U.S.'; 'History of U.S. in Our Own Times.'

Andrews, Ethan Allen. An American educator and lexicographer; born at New Britain, Conn., April 7, 1787; died there, March 24, 1858. He was professor of ancient languages at the University of North Carolina, 1822-28; edited the Religious Magazine with Jacob Abbott, whom he succeeded as principal of the Young Ladies' School in Boston; but his chief work was compiling classical text-books. He edited the well-known 'Latin-English Lexicon' (1850), based on Freund; and 'Andrews and Stoddard's Latin Grammar' (with Solomon Stoddard; 65th ed. 1857) was for many years the leading one in America.

Andrews, James Pettit. An English historian and antiquary; born near Newbury, Berkshire, about 1737; died in London, Aug. 6, 1797. His principal works were: 'A Collection of Anecdotes, etc., Ancient and Modern' (1789); 'History of Great Britain, etc.' (1794-95); 'Henry's History of Britain, Continued' (1796); etc.

Andrews, Jane. An American juvenile-story writer; born in Massachusetts in 1833; died in 1887. Among her stories for children, which have enjoyed great popularity, are: 'Seven Little Sisters who Live on the Round Ball that Floats in the Air' (1876); 'The Stories Mother Nature Told'; 'The Seven Little Sisters Prove their Sisterhood' (1878); 'Ten Boys on the Road from Long Ago to Now' (1885); 'Only a Year and What it Brought' (1887).

Andrews, Stephen Pearl. An American miscellaneous writer; born at Templeton, Mass., March 22, 1812; died at New York, May 21, 1886. He was a prominent abolitionist, practiced law in the South, and settled in New York in 1847. He paid much attention to phonographic reporting, and also to the development of a universal philosophy which he called "Integralism," and of a universal language, "Alwato." Besides numerous works relating to these subjects, he wrote: 'Comparison of the Common Law with the Roman, French, or Spanish Civil Law on Entails, etc.'; 'Love, Marriage, and Divorce'; 'French, with or without a Master'; 'The Labor Dollar' (1881); 'Transactions of the Colloquium' (a society founded by himself and his friends for philosophical discussion, 1882-83). He contributed to the London Times and other papers, and was a member of the American Academy of Arts and Sciences and the American Ethnological Society.

Andrieux, François Jean Stanislas (oñ-drē-è). A French poet and dramatist; born in Strasbourg, May 6, 1759; died in Paris, May 9, 1833. Practicing law in Paris at the outbreak of the Revolution, he became a zealous adherent of the latter, and in 1798 was elected to the Council of the Five Hundred. In 1795 he was elected a member, and in 1823 secretary for life, of the Academy. His forte is the poetical tale, in which he aims at classical purity of language and prosody. The most noted are: 'The Miller of Sanssouci' (1797); 'Fenelon's Walk'; and 'The Trial of the Senate of Capua.' Of his dramatic work may be mentioned the comedies 'The Heedless' (1787); 'Molière with his Friends' (1804); 'The Comedian' (1816); and the tragedy 'Junius Brutus' (1794).

Andronicus, Livius (an-drō-nī'cus). An early Roman dramatic poet and actor; born at Tarentum, about 284 B.C.; died about 204. A Greek by birth, captured in war and sold as a slave in Rome, he was afterward freed, and became a teacher of Latin and Greek. His plays, mostly tragedies, with a few comedies, were translated from the Greek. They were first played in Rome, 240 B. C.

Aneurin. A famous Welsh bard of the 6th century. Of his epic and songs we possess the 'Godolin,' which is believed to be a description of one of the last great battles of the native Britons with the Saxon invaders. The poem as it has come down to us contains nearly 1,000 lines, but it is not complete and lacks unity. The sense is obscure, and several passages are capable of various interpretations.

Angell, James Burrill. An American educator, diplomatist, and writer; born at Scituate, R. I., Jan. 7, 1829. He was graduated from Brown University in 1849, and professor of modern languages there from 1853 to 1860. From 1860 to 1866 he was editor of the Providence Journal. He was president of the University of Vermont from 1866 to 1871. In 1871 he became president of the University of Michigan. He was minister to China from 1880 to 1881, and from 1897-1898 to Turkey. Among his works are: 'Manual of French Literature' (1857); 'Progress of International Law' (1875).

Angelo, Michel. See **Michel Angelo.**

Angelus Silesius (än'je-lus si-lē'shi-us), pseudonym of Johannes Scheffler. A German mystic and sacred poet (1624–77), brought up in the Lutheran faith, but in 1653 embraced Catholicism, in 1661 was ordained priest, and in 1664 became councilor of the Prince-Bishop of Breslau. His poems, some of which are exquisite sacred lyrics, appeared collected as 'Spiritual Joys' (1657) and 'Cherubic Wanderer' (1675).

Angely, Louis (än'je-li). A German dramatist (1787–1835). He was for several years a favorite comic actor in Berlin, and skillfully adapted to local conditions a number of French comedies, among which the most popular were: 'Schoolboy Pranks'; 'The Journey at Common Expense'; 'Of Seven the Ugliest'; 'The Artisans' Festival'; 'Seven Girls in Uniform.'

Anicet-Bourgeois, Auguste (ä-nē-sā' börzhwä'). A French dramatist; born in Paris, Dec. 25, 1806; died there, Jan. 12, 1871. He wrote about 200 comedies, vaudevilles, melodramas, often in collaboration with Barbier, Ducange, Féval, Labiche, and others; while on the other hand he is the real and sole author of some of the best plays ascribed to the elder Dumas (for instance 'Térésa,' 'Angèle,' 'Catherine Howard'). Among his own productions the following deserve mention: 'The Venetian' (1834); 'The Poor Girl' (1838); 'Stella' (1843).

Annunzio, Gabriele d' (än-nön'tsē-ō). An Italian novelist and poet; born on the yacht Irene in the Adriatic, near Pescara, in 1864. Educated at Prato; went to Rome in 1880; and is one of the most conspicuous Italian writers of the day. He abandoned Italian traditions for the modern French realism. His poems and novels are brilliant but sensual, the later works pessimistic. They include: 'Pleasure' (1889); 'The Triumph of Death' (1894); and 'Maidens of the Crag' (1895). Among his poems are: 'The New Song' (Rome, 1882); 'Interludes of Verse' (1883); and 'Marine Odes' (1893); 'The Fire' (1900).

Ansbach, Elizabeth, Margravine of. See **Craven, Lady.**

Anslo, Reimér (äns'lō). A Dutch poet; born at Amsterdam, 1622 or 1626; died at Perugia, May 16, 1669. He is an imitator of Vondel, and one of the foremost Dutch poets of his time. He went to Italy and lived for many years in Rome, where he wrote his finest poems. His most famous work is 'The Plague at Naples,' and the next in importance 'The Eve of St. Bartholomew,' both epics.

Anspach, Frederick Rinehart. An American clergyman and religious writer; born in central Pennsylvania, Jan. 1815; died in Baltimore, Md., Sept. 16, 1867. He was educated at Pennsylvania College and the Lutheran Theological Seminary. His works include: 'Sons of the Sires' (1854); 'Sepulchres of the Departed' (1854); 'The Two Pilgrims' (1857).

Anstey, Christopher. An English poet (1724–1805). He was a gentleman of fortune, and wrote 'The New Bath Guide' (1766), humorous letters in rhyme describing life at that fashionable watering-place. These became famous, and Smollett borrowed largely from the work for 'Humphrey Clinker.' He also wrote 'An Election Ball and Other Verses' (1776).

Anstey, F., pseudonym of Thomas Anstey Guthrie. An English humorist; born in Kensington in 1856. He graduated from Cambridge in 1875, was called to the bar in 1880, and joined Punch staff in 1887. He is the author of: 'Vice Versâ' (1882); 'The Giant's Robe' (1883); 'The Black Poodle' (1884); 'The Tinted Venus' (1885); 'The Pariah' (1889); 'Voces Populi' (1890); 'Mr. Punch's Pocket Ibsen' (1893); and 'Puppets at Large' (1897).

Antar (än'tär) or **Antarah, ben Shedad el Absi.** A famous Arab poet; born about the middle of the sixth century A. D., died about 615 A. D. He is the author of one of the seven celebrated «suspended poems.» He lauds the beauty of his mistress, and rehearses the story of his adventures in Arabia. Portions were translated into English verse by Terrick Hamilton (1820.)

Antheunis, Gentil Theodoor (än'tĕ-nes). A Flemish poet; born at Oudenaarde, Sept. 9, 1840. At first a teacher in his native place and at Dendermonde, he afterwards became a justice of the peace in Brussels. His lyrics, excelling in euphony and tender sentiment, have frequently been set to music. They appeared in collections: 'From the Heart' (1875); 'Songs and Poems' (1874); 'Life, Love, and Song' (1879).

Anthon, Charles. A celebrated American classical scholar; born in New York city, Nov. 19, 1797; died July 29, 1867. He was for many years professor of ancient languages at Columbia College. A beautiful edition of Horace first made him famous among scholars. His best known work was an edition of Lemprière's 'Classical Dictionary' (1841). He was also the editor of over fifty classical text-books.

Antimachus (an-tim'ạ-kus). A Greek epic and elegiac poet; flourished about 400 B. C. He was called «The Colophonian,» from Colophon, his native place. His chief works were the epic 'Thebaïs,' and an elegy on his dead love Lyde. The Alexandrine critics greatly admired him, esteeming him next to Homer.

Antipater of Sidon (an-tip'ạ-tėr). A Greek poet; lived about 100 B. C. Famous during his life as an improvisator, he is best known by a collection of witty epigrams, which may be found in the 'Greek Anthology.'

Antona-Traversi, Camillo (än-tō'nä trä-ver'si). An Italian literary historian and dramatist; born in Milan, Nov. 27, 1857. Besides numerous essays and studies on Boccaccio, Ugo Foscolo, and Leopardi, he produced several comedies, including 'George's Sacrifice'; 'Albert's Marriage'; 'Stop and Recommence.'

Antonides van der Goes, Joannes (än-tō-nĕ'dän der gös). A Dutch poet; born at Goes, May 3, 1647; died at Rotterdam, Sept. 18, 1684. The most distinguished disciple of Vondel, and a violent opponent of the one-sided French classicism, he exercised a wholesome influence upon his native literature. When only nineteen, his tragedy, 'Trazil, or the Conquest of China' (1664), attracted universal attention and won him the lifelong friendship of Vondel. His most famous work is 'De Y-Stroom' (1671), an epic on the river Y, glorifying the great international commerce of Amsterdam, and is a masterly delineation of the life in that city.

Antoninus, Marcus Aurelius. See **Aurelius.**

Anton Ulrich, Duke of Brunswick-Wolfenbüttel (än'tōn öl'rich). A German novelist and poet (1633–1714), a zealous patron of art and science, author of two voluminous novels, highly famed in their time. They were 'The Serene Syrian Aramena' (1669–73) and 'The Roman Octavia' (1677). He also composed numerous sacred poems.

Anzengruber, Ludwig (än'tsen-grö-ber). An Austrian dramatist and novelist; born in Vienna, Nov. 29, 1839; died there, Dec. 10, 1889. His great merit lies in the creation of a genuine Austrian national drama, by which he sprang at once into fame in his native country; afterwards he wrote stories of village life with equal success. Of his dramatic works the most noteworthy are: 'The Parson of Kirchfeld (1870); 'The Perjured Peasant' (1871). Of his narrative productions, 'The Stigma,' a novel (1876); 'The Sternstein Farm,' a village story (1885), deserve particular mention.

Apel, Johann August (ä'ple). A German novelist and poet (1771–1816) chiefly known by his tales, collected as 'Ghost-Book' (4 vols., 1810–14) and 'Wonder-Book' (4 vols., 1815–17). He also wrote several dramas. His son Guido Theodor (1811–67) attempted dramatic and epic poetry.

Apollonius of Rhodes (ap-o-lō'ni-us). A Greek grammarian and poet; born 280 B. C. His one poetic composition, 'Argonautics,' gives but scant proof of its author's poetic inspiration, though it has a few passages of high artistic beauty. It was widely read by the Romans; both Virgil and Ovid borrowed a little from Apollonius.

Appleton, Thomas Gold. An American writer; born in Boston, March 31, 1812; died in New York, April 17, 1884. He was a patron of art, and an amateur painter of merit; he aided libraries and museums of Boston. Author of 'Nile Journal' (Boston, 1876); 'Syrian Sunshine' (1877); and a volume of poems, 'Faded Leaves.'

Apthorp, William Foster. An American musical and dramatic critic; born in Massachusetts in 1848. He is on the staff of the Boston Evening Transcript. His chief work is 'Musicians and Music Lovers, and Other Essays.' He is also the translator of Zola's 'Jacques Damour,' and of 'Hector Berlioz' (1879); 'The Opera Past and Present.'

Apuleius, Lucius (ap-ū-lē'us). A famous Latin satirist and writer of fiction; lived in the 2d century, and was a native of northern Africa. Having inherited an ample fortune, he devoted himself to study and travel; attending first the schools of Carthage, then the Athenian schools of philosophy. His principal work is 'Metamorphosis' or 'The Golden Ass,' which includes the charming epilogue of 'Cupid and Psyche'; well known also is his witty 'Apology,' a defense against a charge of sorcery brought by the sons of a widow twice his age whom he had married.

Aquinas, Thomas, St. See **Thomas.**

Arago, Dominique François (är-ä-gō'). An eminent French astronomer and physicist; born near Perpignan, Feb. 26, 1786; died in Paris, Oct. 2, 1853. His biographical notices of distinguished men of science hold a high place in literature for clearness of thought and beauty of style. Elected to the Chamber of Deputies after the revolution of 1830, he eloquently took part with the advanced republicans. After the fall of Louis Philippe in 1848, he effected as Minister of War and of Marine many salutary reforms, such as the abolition of flogging in the navy and of negro slavery in the colonies. His scientific observations and discoveries were numerous and important. English translations of separate portions of his works have been published, notably his 'Autobiography'; 'Popular Lectures on Astronomy'; 'Meteorological Essays'; and 'Biographies of Scientific Men.'

Arago, Étienne Vincent. A French poet, journalist, and playwright; born at Perpignan, Feb. 9, 1802; died in Paris, March 6, 1892. Brother of the preceding. He wrote, mostly in collaboration with others, a number of comedies, vaudevilles, and melodramas; and under the pseudonym of Jules Ferney, made himself known through his feuilletons in the Siècle. By far his best production, however, is 'Spa, its Origin, History, Waters, etc.' (1851), an epic in seven cantos. Besides this, 'A Voice from Exile' (1860) and 'The Blue and the White' (1862), a historical romance of the wars in the Vendée, deserve mention.

Arago, Jacques Étienne. A French writer of travels; born at Estagel, March 10, 1790; died in Brazil, January 1855. Brother of the preceding. Till 1837 his literary work consisted in the production of light theatrical pieces. He then lost his sight and made a voyage around the globe, which afforded material for two charming books: 'Promenade around the World' (1838) and 'A Blind Man's Voyage round the World.' He had some painful experiences on this side of the globe, which are detailed in the 'Travels of a Blind Man in California (1851).

Arany, János (or'ony). An eminent Hungarian poet; born at Nagy-Szalonta, March 1, 1817; died in Buda-Pesth, Oct. 22, 1882. Educated in the college at Debreczin, 1832–36, he was employed as a teacher in his native place; in 1840 was appointed notary there; and won immediate success with his first epical production in 1845. During the Hungarian revolution he held a government position; then lived in needy circumstances in his native town until 1854, when he obtained a professorship at Nagy-Körös. Thence he was called to Buda-Pesth in 1860 as director of the Kisfaludy Society; founded the literary weekly Koszorú (The Wreath); and in 1865 was appointed secretary of the Hungarian Academy, of which he had been a member since 1859. Owing to his feeble health he resigned in 1878. As a national poet he ranks immediately after Petöfi and Vörösmarty, his epical creations deserving to be acknowledged as ornaments not only of Hungarian but of modern poetry in general. He is a master of the ballad and a translator of highest merit, as proven by his versions of Tasso, Goethe, Shakespeare, and above all, his translation of Aristophanes (3 vols., 1880). Works: 'The Lost Constitution,' a humorous epic (1845, prize of Kisfaludy Society), depicting the doings at the county elections; 'The Taking of Murány' (1848, prize); 'Katalin' (1850); 'Toldi,' an epical trilogy (1851–54–80), exalting the deeds of the Hungarian Samson; 'The Gipsies of Nagy-Ida' (1852); 'Buda's Death' (1864, prize), 'Prose Writings' (1879).

Arany, László. A Hungarian poet; born at Nagy-Szalonta, March 24, 1844. Son of the preceding; member of the Academy since 1872; author of 'Elfrida,' a poetical tale (1868, prize); 'The Battle of the Huns' (1874); 'The Hero of Disenchantment,' a humorous epic (1873), which won a prize and ranks among the best productions of Hungarian literature.

Aratus (a-rā'tus). A Greek poet and astronomer; born at Soli, Cilicia, flourishing about 290–260 B. C. His chief work was an astronomical poem entitled 'Phænomena' (Aspects of the Heavens), in 1,154 verses; the plan being in imitation of Hesiod, while the style is borrowed from Homer. Greatly admired in antiquity, it was translated into Latin by Cicero and others. He was a friend of the poets Theocritus and Callimachus.

Araujo Porto-Alegre, Manoel de (ä-rou'zhö pōr'tö ä-lā'gre). A Brazilian poet; born at Rio Pardo, Nov. 29, 1806; died in Lisbon, Portugal, Dec. 30, 1879. He frequented the Academy of Arts in Rio de Janeiro, 1826–28; studied painting in Paris and architecture there and in Italy until 1837, when he returned to Rio and was made professor at the Academy of Arts, later at the Military Academy. He was Brazilian consul-general at Stettin in 1859–65, but lived mostly in Berlin, afterwards at Lisbon. His principal works are: 'Colombo,' an epic, celebrating the discovery of America; and 'Brasilianas,' a lyric cycle, abounding in splendid descriptions of nature.

Arblay, Madame d'. See **Burney.**

Arbois de Jubainville, Henri d' (är-bwä' dè zhübań'vēl). A distinguished French archæologist; born at Nancy, Dec. 5, 1827. He is the most eminent authority in France on Gallic antiquity and the Celtic languages. Of his works the most noteworthy are: 'History of the Dukes and Counts of Champagne' (1859–69); 'The First Inhabitants of Europe' (1877); 'A Course of Celtic Literature' (5 vols., 1883).

Arboleda, Julio (är-bō-lā'THä). A South American poet, orator, journalist, and revolutionist; born in Colombia, June 9, 1817; died about 1872. Having assumed the supreme power in New Granada, he was assassinated. He was one of the best-known poets of

Spanish America. Of his principal work, 'Gonzalo de Oyón,' only such parts as happened to exist in duplicate were published, the manuscript having been destroyed by a bitter personal enemy.

Arbuthnot, John. A Scottish humorist; born near Arbuthnot Castle, Kincardineshire, Scotland, April 29, 1667; died in London, Feb. 27, 1735. He was physician to Queen Anne. His literary fame rests mainly on 'The History of John Bull' (1712), at first attributed to Swift, but proved to have been the work of Arbuthnot. Primarily designed to satirize the Duke of Marlborough, and to oppose the continuance of the War of the Spanish Succession, this work was the means of fastening the sobriquet and the typical character of John Bull upon the English nation; but owing to its ardent and extreme Toryism it is now little read, and known chiefly by brilliant extracts. It is said to have suggested to Swift the composition of 'Gulliver's Travels.' He also wrote a number of serious works which have been highly valued.

Archenholz, Johann Wilhelm von (är′chen-hölts). A German historian (1743-1812). He took part in the closing campaigns of the Seven Years' War and retired as captain, 1763; traveled extensively in Europe, lived in England the greater part of 1769-79, and settled in Hamburg in 1792. His book on 'England and Italy' (1785), extensively translated, obtained a phenomenal success. A sequel to it was 'Annals of British History' (1789-98, 20 vols.). His 'History of the Seven Years' War' (1789, augmented 1793, 13th ed. 1892) is still the most popular account of that war.

Archer, Thomas. An English novelist and essayist. His works deal with the conditions of the working classes and with social evils. Among the best known are: 'A Fool's Paradise' (1870); 'Profitable Plants' (1874).

Archer, William. A Scottish critic; born at Perth, Sept. 23, 1856. He graduated at Edinburgh University, 1876, and was called to the bar, 1883. He has long been dramatic critic for various London papers, and has published books on the drama, including: 'English Dramatists of To-day' (1882); 'Masks or Faces: a Study in the Psychology of Acting' (1888); 'Henry Irving,' a critical study (1883); 'William Ch. Macready, a Biography' (1890). He is the English translator of Ibsen's dramas (1890-91).

Archilochus (är-kil′ō-kus). An eminent Greek poet; flourished in the 7th century B. C. Of his life nothing is definitely known. He was classed by the ancients with the greatest poets, Homer, Pindar, Sophocles; but of his works only a few fragments have come down to us. His lyrics, in iambic verse, were often pointed with the bitterest satire; besides satires he wrote hymns, elegies, and epodes.

Arène, Paul Auguste (ä-rän′). A French writer of stories and travels; born at Sisteron, June 26, 1843; died at Antibes, Dec. 16, 1896. At first engaged in teaching at Marseilles and in Paris; but from 1865 on he devoted himself to literature, and became favorably known through his brilliant descriptions of his Provençal home. Notable among various collections of stories are: 'The Perfumed Beggar Woman' (1876); 'In the Kindly Sun' (1879); 'The True Temptation of St. Anthony'; 'Christmas Stories.' He also wrote two novels,—'John of the Figs' (1868) and 'The Golden Goat' (1889); several comedies, partly in conjunction with others, especially Alphonse Daudet, whose collaborator he was in the 'Letters from my Mill.' Equally charming as his stories are the pictures of travel: 'Twenty Days in Tunis' (1884); 'From the Alps to the Pyrenees' (1891); 'Select Tales' (1896).

Aretino, Pietro (ä-rā-tē′nō). An Italian satirical poet and dramatist; born at Arezzo, April 20, 1492; died in Venice, Oct. 21, 1556. He had already won some fame as a writer of satires, when he settled in Rome in 1517, where his bent for witty effusions led to his banishment in 1524. Turning to Florence, he won the favor of John de' Medici, and at Milan ingratiated himself with Francis I. of France, through whose intercession he was allowed to return to Rome. Of his works only his five comedies in prose, and 'Orazia,' a tragedy in verse, numbering among the best in Italian literature, are of lasting merit. His 'Letters' are a valuable contribution to the history of the times.

Argensola, Bartolomeo Leonardo de (är-Hen-sō′lä). A Spanish poet and historian (1565-1631). His verse lacks native force, but shows considerable depth of sentiment, while in form it displays exquisite finish. His history of 'The Conquest of the Moluccas' is a model of correct and idiomatic Spanish prose.

Argensola, Lupercio Leonardo de. A notable Spanish poet; born at Barbastro, Aragon, Dec. 14, 1559; died at Naples in March 1613. Brother of the preceding. His three tragedies, 'Isabella,' 'Alexandra,' and 'Phyllis,' brought him fame while still a young man; but his forte was lyric poetry, in which he won distinction. His ballads and songs are notable for vigor of thought and richness of pictorial fancy. Some of his 'Sonnets' are masterpieces; and his 'Epistles,' both in substance and form, are models of that species of composition.

Argyle or **Argyll, George Douglas Campbell** (är-gīl′), eighth Duke of. An English philosophical, scientific, and political writer, and statesman; born in Ardencaple Castle, Dumbartonshire, April 30, 1823; died at London, April 24, 1900. He was Lord Privy Seal (1860) and Postmaster-General (1855), being reappointed to both offices in 1860, to the former again in 1880; was Secretary for India (1868-74). He wrote: 'The Reign of Law' (1866), a striking work upholding theism; 'Primeval Man' (1869); 'Iona' (1870); 'The Eastern Question' (2 vols., 1879); 'The Unity of Nature (2d ed., 1884); 'Geology and the Deluge' (1885); 'Scotland as It Was and as It Is' (2 vols., 1887); and 'The Unseen Foundations of Society.'

Arici, Cesare (ä-rē'chē). An Italian poet; born in Brescia, July 2, 1782; died there, July 2, 1836. He laid the foundation of his success with a poem on 'The Cultivation of the Olive' (1808), which won for him a professorship of history and literature; it still ranks among the best specimens of Italian didactic poetry. He wrote many lyric pieces, but his chief distinction is as a poet of bucolic and pastoral themes. He left in an incomplete state an epic on 'The Destruction of Jerusalem.'

Ariosto, Ludovico (ä-rē-ōs'tō). A celebrated Italian poet; born at Reggio, Sept. 8, 1474; died at Ferrara, June 6, 1533. He was one of the three great epic poets of Italy, and styled «The Divine» by his countrymen. He early abandoned the study of law for that of the classics. Having attracted attention through two comedies, he entered the service of Cardinal Ippolito d'Este, who intrusted him with several diplomatic missions; after whose death in 1520 he was employed by the reigning duke of Ferrara, Alfonso, the cardinal's brother. His imperishable fame rests mainly on his great romantic-heroic poem 'Orlando Furioso'; of which Orlando's love for the fair Angelica, and his madness induced by her treachery, form the theme. It is really a continuation of Bojardo's 'Orlando Innamorato,' a knowledge of which is most helpful to a thorough appreciation of the Furioso. Of his other poetical efforts the most noteworthy are his seven epistolary satires, conceived in the spirit of Horace, which contain sundry bits of autobiographical information and rank among the treasures of Italian literature.

Aristides or **Aristeides** (ar-is-tī'dēz). A Greek writer who lived in the 2d century B.C. He was the father of Greek prose romance. He wrote a series of love stories in six or more books, entitled 'Milesiaca' (Milesian Tales), from the place in which their scene was laid.

Aristocles. See Plato.

Aristophanes (ar-is-tof'a-nēz). The greatest of the Greek writers of comedy (B.C. 448?–380?); born at Athens. His comedy 'The Knights' is said to have been put on the stage when the author was but 20 years old. Of his 44 plays only eleven have come down to us. These are: 'The Knights'; 'The Clouds,'—prized by him above all the rest,—wherein he ridicules the Sophists and with them Socrates; 'The Wasps,' in which the Athenians are lashed for their litigiousness; 'The Acharnians'; 'The Peace' and 'The Lyristrate,' arguments for concord among Grecian States; 'The Birds,' a satire against the «Greater Athens» idea; in 'The Thesmophoriazusæ' the Athenian women carry off to court the poet Euripides in punishment of his misogyny; 'The Frogs,'

directed against Euripides, as the cause of the degeneration of dramatic art; in 'The Ecclesiazusæ' or 'Ladies in Parliament,' he reduces to absurdity the overweening expectation of the righting of all wrongs through political reforms; in the 'Plutus' the blind god of wealth is made to see and the good old times come back again.

Aristotle (ar'is-totl). The most renowned of Greek philosophers; born at Stagira, Macedonia, 384 B.C.; died at Chalcis, Eubœa, 322 B.C. He was for twenty years a student of philosophy in the school of Plato at Athens, but at the same time a teacher, in the mean time mastering and digesting all the accessible results of philosophical and scientific research and speculation in his time. After Plato's death, he opened a school of philosophy at the court of Hermias, king of Atarneus in Mysia, who had been his fellow student in Plato's Academy, and whose adopted daughter he afterwards married. At the invitation of Philip of Macedon he undertook the education of his son, Alexander. When Alexander succeeded to the throne, the philosopher returned to Athens and opened a school in the Lyceum, so called from the neighboring temple of the Lycian Apollo. From being held in the covered walk (*peripatos*) of the Lyceum the school obtained the name of the Peripatetic. He taught in the Lyceum for 13 years, and to that period we owe the composition of most of his numerous writings. The number of his separate treatises is given by Diogenes Laertius as 146: only 46 separate works bearing the name of the philosopher have come down to our time.

Ari Thorgilsson (ä'rē tōr'gils-son). The father of Icelandic literature (1067–1148). He was the first Icelander to use his mother tongue as a literary medium, in writing his 'Islendingabók,' a concise history of Iceland from its settlement (about 870) until 1120. This work was finished between 1134 and 1138.

Arlincourt, Victor Vicomte d' (är-laṅ-kör'). A French poet and novelist (1789–1856). His chief poetical work is 'Charlemagne, or the Caroleid' (1818), an epic; and of his novels the most successful was 'Le Solitaire' (1821), which was translated into all European languages. Among several pamphlets, written in support of the Legitimist cause in 1848, one entitled 'God Wills It' went through 64 editions.

Armitage, Thomas. An American clergyman; born at Pontefract, England, Aug. 2, 1819; died Jan. 21, 1896. He was an important influence in the Baptist Church in New York city, and the prime mover in the establishment of the American Bible Union in 1850. He was president of that body from 1856 to 1875. Among his works are: 'Jesus, His Self-Introspection'; and 'History of the Baptists' (1887).

Armstrong, Edmund John. An Irish poet; born in Dublin, July 23, 1841; died at Kingstown, Feb. 24, 1865. His most elaborate poem is 'The Prisoner of Mount Saint Michael' (1863), a romantic tale of passion and crime, the scene being suggested by the author's rambles in France in 1862. Next in importance is 'Ovoca,' an idyllic poem, partly dramatic, partly narrative in form.

Armstrong, George Francis. An Irish poet; born in the county of Dublin, May 5, 1845. Brother of the preceding. Professor of history and English literature at Queen's College, Cork, since 1871. His works include: 'Poems, Lyrical and Dramatic' (1869); 'Ugone,' a tragedy (1870); 'Tragedy of Israel,' a trilogy comprising 'King Saul' (1872), 'King David' (1874), and 'King Solomon' (1876); 'Essays' (1877); and 'Mephistopheles in Broadcloth' (1888), a satire in verse.

Armstrong, John. An American author and soldier; born at Carlisle, Pa., Nov. 25, 1758; died at Red Hook, N. Y., April 1, 1843. Served in the war of the Revolution on the staff of General Gates; was United States minister to France, 1804-10, afterwards to Spain; and Secretary of War, 1813-14. Author of 'Newburg Letters,' begun in camp 1783, anonymously, and intended to arouse Congress to redress army grievances. They gave General Washington displeasure. He also wrote 'Notices of the War of 1812' (1836).

Arnaboldi, Alessandro (är-nä-bol'di). An Italian poet; born in Milan, Dec. 19, 1827; studied law in Pavia and entered the government service, but resigned in 1873 owing to an optic infirmity, and has since lived in retirement near Milan. On the publication of a volume of 'Verses' (1872), he was hailed by his countrymen as the peer of Manzoni and Leopardi, while Dall' Ongaro even styled him the greatest living poet of Italy. A second collection of his poems appeared as 'New Verses' (1888).

Arnason, Jón (är-nà-son). An Icelandic writer; born at Hof, Akàgaströnd, Nov. 13, 1819; died at Reykjavik, Aug. 17, 1888. He was for many years librarian of the National Library, and devoted himself assiduously to the collection of Icelandic folk tales. He has hence been called the "Grimm of Iceland." His principal literary work is 'Popular Legends and Tales of Iceland' (1862-64).

Arnault, Antoine Vincent (är-nō'). A French poet and dramatist (1766-1834). He came into public notice through his tragedy 'Marius à Minturnæ' (1791); but more especially deserves remembrance for his satirical fables, in which he guarded successfully against imitation of Lafontaine, and for his graceful poems, of which 'The Leaf' has become most widely known. His 'Souvenirs of a Sexagenarian' (1833) contain excellent delineations of character, and many interesting disclosures about the history of the time up to 1804.

Arndt, Ernst Moritz (ärnt). A German poet, miscellaneous writer, and patriot; born at Schoritz, Isle of Rügen, Dec. 29, 1769; died in Bonn, Jan. 29, 1860. On the publication, in 1806, of the first series of his 'Spirit of the Times,' which kindled patriotic enthusiasm throughout the German lands, he was compelled to take refuge in Sweden. Some years later he was the editor at Cologne of a political journal, The Watchman. In 1848 a member of the National Assembly, he belonged to the so-called imperial party, advocating the union of Germany under the leadership of Prussia. On his ninetieth birthday (1859) the whole nation united in paying him homage. His influence was due to his devotion to the national cause. Many of his poems have become national lyrics, intimately linked with the stirring events to which they owe their origin. Among them are: 'What is the German's Fatherland?' and 'The Song of the Field Marshal.'

Arneth, Alfred von (är'net). An Austrian historian; born in Vienna, July 10, 1819; died there, July 31, 1897. He was member of the House of Lords after 1869, and president of the Academy of Sciences after 1879. His life of 'Prince Eugene of Savoy' (1858-59) is noteworthy as the first authoritative work on that great leader. Next in importance is the 'History of Maria Theresa' (1863-79).

Arnim, Achim von (är'nim). A noted German poet and novelist; born in Berlin, Jan. 26, 1781; died at Wiepersdorf, Jan. 31, 1831. He is the main representative of the younger generation of the Romantic school. Settling at Heidelberg in 1806 after extensive travels, he formed a close friendship with Clemens Brentano, and edited with him 'The Boy's Wonder-Horn,' a collection of old German legends and songs, which was received with much favor. In 1811 he married Brentano's sister Bettina, and thereafter lived alternately in Berlin, and on his estate Wiepersdorf in the province of Brandenburg. He was at his best as a story-teller. His principal works are: 'Poverty, Riches, Guilt, and Penitence of Countess Dolores,' a novel (1810); and 'The Crown-Guardians,' a fantastic historical romance (1817), a glowing picture of life towards the wane of the 15th century. Among his short stories, published mostly in collections, the following deserve mention: 'The Mad Invalid at Fort Ratonneau'; 'The Three Loving Sisters and the Happy Dyer'; 'Prince All-god and Singer Demi-god.' His complete works, with an introduction by W. Grimm, were edited by his wife (1839-46).

Arnim, Bettina von. See **Brentano.**

Arnold, Arthur. An English traveler, journalist, and statesman; born in Sussex, May 28, 1833. From 1863 to 1866 he was a member of a commission to examine into the causes of the "Cotton Famine," and published a treatise on that subject. In 1885 he became president of the Free Land League. Among his works are: 'From the Levant'; 'Through Persia by Caravan' (1877); 'Social Politics'; and 'Free Land,'

Arnold, Edwin, Sir. A distinguished English poet and journalist; born in Rochester, June 10, 1832. He graduated from Oxford in 1854; taught for a while in Birmingham; and became principal of the Sanskrit College at Poona in the Bombay Presidency, where he rendered important service to the government during the great rebellion in India. Returning to London in 1861, he joined the editorial staff of the Daily Telegraph. He has twice visited the United States on lecture tours. Of his original poetry, inspired by Oriental themes and legends, the most famous work is 'The Light of Asia, a Poetic Presentation of the Life and Teaching of Gautama' (1876). 'Indian Idylls' (1883); 'Pearls of the Faith'; 'Sa'di in the Garden'; 'The Light of the World'; 'Potiphar's Wife and Other Poems'; 'India Revisited' and 'Japonica' are among his many works. He died at London, Mar. 24, 1904.

Arnold, Edwin Lester. An English novelist and writer of travels; son of Sir Edwin Arnold. He has written: 'A Summer Holiday in Scandinavia' (1877); 'On the Indian Hills, or Coffee-Planting in Southern India' (1881); 'Bird Life in England' (1887); 'England as She Seems' (1888);—the novels 'Phra, the Phœnician' (1890); 'The Story of Ulla' (1895).

Arnold, George. An American poet; born in New York, June 24, 1834; died at Strawberry Farms, N. J., Nov. 3, 1865. Author of 'McArone Papers,' contributed to Vanity Fair (1860–65). His poetry is of merit: 'Drift and Other Poems' (1866); 'Poems Grave and Gay' (1867). Collected edition, with memoir, by William Winter (new ed. 1889).

Arnold, Hans, pseudonym of Bertha von Bülow. A German story-writer; born at Warmbrunn, Silesia, Sept. 30, 1850. Among her stories which enjoy great popularity are: 'Merry Tales' (1891); 'Once in May and Other Stories' (1892). She also wrote some good comedies, viz.: 'Theory and Practice' (1890); 'Two Peaceful Ones' (1892).

Arnold, Isaac Newton. An American lawyer, politician, and author; born at Hartwick, N. Y., Nov. 30, 1815; died at Chicago, Ill., April 24, 1884. He was a member of Congress from 1861 to 1865. His works are: 'Life of Abraham Lincoln' (1866); 'Life of Benedict Arnold' (1880); 'Recollections of the Early Chicago and Illinois Bar' (1880).

Arnold, Johann Georg Daniel. An Alsatian dialect poet; born in Strassburg, Feb. 18, 1780; died there, Feb. 18, 1829. His lyrics (in High German) are meritorious, but he is at his best in 'Pentecost Monday' (1816), a comedy in Strassburg dialect and rhymed Alexandrine verse, pronounced by Goethe «an incomparable monument of ancient Strassburg custom and language, a work which in clearness and completeness of intuition and ingenious delineation of detail can scarcely be equaled.»

Arnold, Matthew. An eminent English poet, critic, and essayist; born at Laleham, Dec. 24, 1822; died in Liverpool, April 15, 1888. He graduated at Oxford in 1844, and was professor of poetry there from 1857 to 1867. The degree of Doctor of Laws was conferred by the University of Edinburgh in 1869, and by Oxford in 1870. He was government inspector of schools from 1851, and repeatedly visited the Continent to inquire into and report upon systems of education. In 1883–84 he made a lecturing tour through the United States. His works include: 'The Strayed Reveler and Other Poems' (1848); 'Empedocles on Etna' (1853); 'Merope,' a tragedy (1857); 'New Poems' (1868). His prose writings comprise: 'Essays in Criticism' (1865, 2d series 1888); 'Lectures on the Study of Celtic Literature' (1867); 'Culture and Anarchy' (1869); 'Friendship's Garland' (1871), a humorous work; 'Literature and Dogma' (1873); 'Last Essays on Church and Religion' (1877); 'Mixed Essays' (1879); 'Irish Essays' (1882); and 'Discourses on America' (1885); 'Civilization in the U. S.'

Arnold, Thomas. A notable English educator and historical writer; born at Cowes, Isle of Wight, June 13, 1795; died at Oxford, June 12, 1842. Studied at Winchester school; was student and fellow of Oxford 1811–19. He was head-master of the school at Rugby 1828–41. As an educator, he was remarkable for the training of the character of his pupils to a lofty and noble standard. In 1841 he became professor of modern history at Oxford. His writings include: an annotated edition of Thucydides (1830); 'Sermons' (1829–34); 'History of Rome' (1838); 'Lectures on Modern History' (1842).

Arnold, Thomas. An English writer on literature and editor of old texts, son of Dr. Arnold of Rugby and brother of Matthew Arnold; born at Laleham, Nov. 30, 1823; died at Dublin, Nov. 12, 1900. He became a Roman Catholic, and spent a number of years in New Zealand and Tasmania. Among his works are: 'A manual of English Literature'; 'Select English Works of Wyclif' (3 vols., 1869); 'Selections from the Spectator'; 'Beowulf' (text, translation, and notes); 'Henry of Huntingdon'; 'Symeon of Durham'; 'Chronicles of the Abbey of Bury St. Edmunds.'

Arnould, Arthur (är-nö'). A French novelist, dramatist, and journalist; born in Paris in 1833; died there, Nov. 25, 1895. At an early age he devoted himself to journalism, and soon attracted attention by his hostility to the Empire. In 1870 he founded La Marseillaise and the famous Journal du Peuple. After the fall of the Empire he became a member of the Commune, and with its downfall barely escaped with his life. Besides essays and dramas, he is the author of a history of the Commune and over 30 novels, the best known being 'Zoé' and 'Princess Belladonna.'

Arnulfi, Alberto (är-nöl'fi). A Piedmontese dialect poet; born in Turin, July 13, 1849; died in Rome, March 27, 1888. He is the author of 'Turin Blots' (1879), a collection of satirical sonnets, under the pseudonym of "Fulberto Alarni"; and of 'Drolleries,' a comedy. In conjunction with Eraldo Baretti he wrote 'The Dukes of Nemi' (1887), a drama depicting Roman society at the downfall of the temporal power.

Arolas, Juan de (ä-rō'läs). A Spanish poet (1805–49). His first poems were amatory, but the works on which his fame rests are poems of chivalry and romance. A specimen of his best work is to be found in 'The Sylph of the Aqueduct,' a traditional Spanish legend told in various metres.

Arouet. See **Voltaire.**

Arrebo, Anders Christensen (är-e-bō'). A Danish poet (1587–1637). Bishop of Drontheim, Norway, when only thirty-one, but deposed in 1622 owing to his objectionable life; he was afterwards rehabilitated as preacher in Vordingborg. As the pioneer of the renaissance movement, he is considered the father of modern poetry in Denmark. His rhymed translation of the 'Psalms of David' (1623), but especially his 'Hexæmeron' (1641), an imitation of a once famous poem of the French poet Du Bartas on the Creation, are highly esteemed.

Arrianus, Flavius (ar-i-ā'nus). A Greek philosopher and historian (95–180); born at Nicomedia. He aimed to imitate Xenophon in the direction of his studies; and as Xenophon recorded the sayings of Socrates, so Arrianus became the reporter of the 'Discoveries of Epictetus.' These were comprised in eight books, but only the first four remain. He next wrote 'Epictetus's Handbook,' a compendium of that teacher's moral doctrine. He wrote also an 'Anabasis,' a history of Alexander's conquests in Asia; this is still extant complete.

Arrington, Alfred W. An American lawyer, author, and poet; born in Iredell County, N. C., Sept. 18, 1810; died in Chicago, Ill., Dec. 31, 1867. He was admitted to the Missouri bar in 1834. He practiced throughout the Southwest and later in Chicago. Among his works are: 'The Rangers and Regulators of the Tanaha' (1856); 'Sketches of the Southwest'; 'Poems, with Memoir' (1869).

Arrivabene, Ferdinando (är-rē-vä-bä'ne). An Italian poet and littérateur (1770–1834). While confined as a political prisoner at Sebenico, he wrote and published a poem, 'The Tomb of Sebenico,' which made a stir throughout Italy. Of works on the history of literature, he wrote 'The Age of Dante' (1827) and others. The Academy of Brescia crowned his work 'On the Humanity of the Judge' (1817).

Arrom, Cecilia de. See **Caballero.**

Arthur, Timothy Shay. An American author; born at Newburg, N. Y., in 1809; died at Philadelphia, Pa., March 6, 1885. In 1852 he founded Arthur's Home Magazine. He was a voluminous writer of tales of domestic life. His works are over 100 in number, and have had a large sale in England as well as in this country. His most popular work was the famous 'Ten Nights in a Bar-Room.' Among his other publications were: 'Tales for Rich and Poor'; 'Tales of Married Life'; 'Lights and Shadows.'

Arwidson, Adolf Ivar (är'vēds-son). A Swedish poet (1791–1858), chiefly known through his collection of 'Old Swedish Folksongs' (1834–42), which forms a supplement to that of Geijer and Afzelius. His own poems were published under the title of 'Youth's Hoarfrost' (1832).

Asbjörnsen, Peter Kristen (äs-byèrn'sen). A Norwegian folklorist; born in Christiania, Jan. 15, 1812; died there, Jan. 6, 1885. While pursuing botanical and zoölogical studies, and subsequently during various travels at government expense, he eagerly collected folk tales and legends, aided by his lifelong friend Jörgen Moe, with whom he published 'Norwegian Folk Tales' (1842–44, 5th ed. 1874) and 'Norwegian Gnome Stories and Folk Legends' (1845–48, 3d ed. 1870), pronounced by Jacob Grimm the best fairy tales in existence.

Ascham, Roger. An English scholar and prose writer; born at Kirby Wiske, near Northallerton, in 1515; died in London, Dec. 30, 1568. Graduated at Cambridge, and struggled with poverty until patrons came to his relief. He was famous for his general knowledge and acquirements in Greek and Latin, and is classed with Spenser, Sir Thomas More, and Sir Philip Sidney. Though he wrote Latin with ease and elegance at a time when custom favored the use of that language for important works, he urged and practiced the writing of English, and his beautiful style in his own language has given him the name of the "Father of English Prose." In 1548–50 he was tutor of the Princess (afterward Queen) Elizabeth, by whom he was much beloved. His most noted works are: 'Toxophilus,' a treatise on archery (his favorite exercise), in the form of a dialogue (1545); and 'The Scholemaster,' a treatise on education (1570).

Asmus, Georg (äs'mös). A German poet; born at Giessen, Nov. 27, 1830; died in Bonn, May 31, 1892. Employed as an engineer in 1854–62, he came to America to conduct some mining operations in the copper region of Lake Superior; then lived in New York until 1884, when he returned to Europe. Among the German population of America he had an enormous success with his 'American Sketch-Booklet' (1875), an epistle in verse, written in Upper-Hessian dialect and overflowing with delicious humor. It was followed by 'New American Sketch-Booklet' (1876). Besides these he wrote 'Camp Paradise' (1877), a story, and a collection of miscellaneous poems (1891).

Asnyk, Adam (äs'nik). A Polish poet; born at Kalisz, Sept. 11, 1838; died at Cracow, Aug. 2, 1897. Studied in Warsaw, Breslau, and Heidelberg, where he took his degree of Ph. D. in lived in Cracow. Besides numerous lyrics, counted among the most finished of their kind, he wrote the historical tragedy 'Kiejstut' (1878), based on an incident in Lithuanian history; and the comedies 'Job's Friends' (1879), 'Lerche Brothers,' and 'Prize-Comedy' (1888). His 'Poems' appeared collected in 1888, 3 vols.

Assollant, Alfred (ä-sō-lon'). A French novelist and political writer; born at Aubusson, March 20, 1827; died in Paris, March 4, 1886. He taught for a number of years in Paris and other cities, then set out for America; and having traveled extensively over the United States, published on his return 'Scenes from Life in the United States' (1858), a series of tales which attracted a good deal of attention. Among his numerous novels are: 'Two Friends in 1792' (1859), a story of the Reign of Terror; 'Brancas' (1859), a picture of the corruption under Louis Philippe; 'Gabrielle de Chênevert' (1865), portraying the provincial nobility before the Revolution; 'Pendragon' (1881); 'Plantagenet' (1885).

Astor, John Jacob. An American writer; born 1864 in New York City. He published in 1894 an imaginative work, entitled 'A Journey in Other Worlds.'

Astor, William Waldorf. An American romancer; born in New York, March 31, 1848. He is the great-grandson of John Jacob Astor, and graduated at Columbia Law School. He was United States minister to Italy, 1882–85, and now resides in London, and is the proprietor of the Pall Mall Gazette. He is the author of 'Valentino,' a historical romance (1886), and 'Sforza,' a story of Milan (1889).

Athanasius, Saint (ath-a-nā'shi-us). One of the fathers of the Christian Church; born at Alexandria about 296 A.D.; died there, May 2, 373. He distinguished himself by his eloquence at the Synod of Nice (325), where his efforts were instrumental in securing the acceptance of the Nicene Creed. The creed which bears his name was supposed to have been formulated by him, but the term Athanasian was not applied to it until some centuries after his death. He became Patriarch of Alexandria in 328, being afterward deposed and reinstated five times. His chief works, including 'Orations against the Arians' and 'Festal Letters,' appeared in an English translation by Archibald Robertson (New York, 1892).

Athenæus (ath-e-nē'us). A Greek writer of the third century, reputed to have been born at Naucratis in the Nile Delta, and to have lived at Alexandria and afterwards at Rome. He is famous for one work, his 'Feast of the Learned,' a series of books giving with little connection or literary art a vast assemblage of quotations from nearly 800 writers and 2,400 distinct writings, covering practically every department of ancient learning. It has been valued by scholars of all succeeding times as a treasure-house of quotation and anecdote. *

Atherstone, Edwin. An English poet; born at Nottingham, England, about 1788; died Jan. 29, 1872. He was the author of 'The Last Days of Herculaneum' and 'The Fall of Nineveh.' In addition to these poems he wrote 'Israel in Egypt' and 'The Handwriting on the Wall.'

Atkinson, Edward. An American political economist and statistician; born at Brookline, Mass., Feb. 10, 1827. Besides numerous pamphlets and articles in periodicals, he has written: 'Our National Domain' (1879); 'The Distribution of Products' (1885); 'The Margin of Profits' (1887); 'Bi-Metallism in Europe' (1888); 'The Industrial Progress of the Nation (1889); 'Science of Nutrition' (1892). Died Dec. 11, 1905.

Attâr, Ferîd eddin (ät-tär'). A celebrated Persian poet; born near Nishapur in 1119; died about 1229. (?) Son of a spicer, he followed his father's trade (whence his surname of Attâr), but afterward became a dervish and one of the greatest mystics of Persia. He is said to have been killed by a Mongol soldier during the invasion by Jenghiz Khan. Of his extant political works the most famous are: 'The Book of Council,' a series of didactic poems on ethics; 'The Parliament of Birds' (1184–87). His principal work in prose is 'Biographies of the Saints.'

Atterbom, Per Daniel Amadeus (ät'tėr-bom). An eminent Swedish poet; born in the parish of Asbo, East-Gothland, Jan. 19, 1790; died in Upsala, July 21, 1855. He was early influenced by German literature, and having visited Germany and Italy in 1817–19, he formed ties of friendship with Schelling and Thorwaldsen; he became instructor to Crown Prince Oscar in 1820, and professor at the university in Upsala in 1828. Although unquestionably the foremost among the lyric poets of the romantic school in Sweden, it must be acknowledged that his rare talent was much impaired by his groping in Schelling's and Hegel's philosophy. His most celebrated work is 'The Isle of Blessedness' (1823), a romantic drama in the manner of Tieck; but he also wrote: 'The Flowers,' a cycle of lyrics; 'The Blue Bird,' a play; and 'Swedish Seers and Poets,' a volume of criticism.

Atwood, Isaac Morgan. An American clergyman; born in New York State in 1838. He is an important leader of the Universalist Church, and president of the Theological Seminary at St. Lawrence University. His chief works are: 'Have We Outgrown Christianity' (1870); 'Latest Word of Universalism' (1878); 'Manual of Revelation' (1888); 'Walks about Zion' (1881); 'Balance Sheet of Bible Criticism.'

Aubanel, Théodore (ō-bä-nel'). A Provençal poet and dramatist; born in Avignon, March 26, 1829; died there, Oct. 31, 1886. His lyrics are collected under the title 'The Pomegranate Opening' (1860); but he is especially noteworthy as a dramatist, as seen in his strikingly realistic dramas: 'The Shepherd'; 'The Bread of Sin' (1878); 'The Elopement.'

Aubert, Joachim Marie Jean Jacques Alexandre Jules (ō-bār'). A distinguished French general and military writer; born in 1804; died in 1890. Was prominent in several campaigns, and was made commander of the Legion of Honor in 1860. He is best known to the public as a journalist and historical writer. Among his works are: 'Gauls and Germans'; 'The Invasion' (1870); 'History of the War of 1870-71' (1873).

Aubignac, François Hédelin, Abbé d' (ō-bēn-yäk'). A French essayist and miscellaneous prose-writer; born in Paris, Aug. 4, 1604; died at Nemours, July 20, 1676. 'The Practical Side of the Theatre' is his best-known work,—an attempt to handle the theory and technique of the drama after the theory of Scaliger. It is in harmony with the Corneille school.

Aubigné, Théodore Agrippa d' (ō-bē-nyä). A French poet, historian, and statesman (1551-1630). After the death of Henri IV., his friend and patron, he fled from religious persecution in France to Geneva. His greatest work is 'The Tragics' (1616), in which are portrayed the horrors of wars of religion. His satires, too, have reference to the religious strifes of the time; famous among them is 'The Catholic Confession of the Sieur de Sancy.' His 'Universal History' is one of the most authoritative sources for the history of the latter half of the 16th century.

Audouard, Olympe (ō-dö-är'). A French writer (1830-90); married to a notary in Marseilles, but soon after divorced, she traveled in Egypt, Turkey, and Russia; and having conducted various journals in Paris since 1860, made a successful lecture tour through America in 1868-69. After her return she became interested in spiritism. She was an ardent advocate of woman's rights. Among her novels and books of travel may be mentioned: 'How Men Love' (1861); 'The Mysteries of the Seraglio and of the Turkish Harems' (1863); 'The Mysteries of Egypt Unveiled' (1865); 'War to Man' (1866); 'Across America' (1869-71); 'Parisian Silhouettes' (1882).

Audsley, George Ashdown (âds'li). A Scottish architect and writer on art; born at Elgin, Scotland, 1838. His present home is at Plainfield, N. J. He has published, with his brother William James Audsley, 'Color in Dress' (1863); 'Dictionary of Architecture and the Allied Arts' (1880, 10 vols.), etc.; alone, 'Handbook of Christian Symbolism' (1865); 'The Ornamental Arts of Japan' (2 vols., 1882-86); etc.

Audubon, John James. An eminent American naturalist; born in New Orleans, May 4, 1780; died in New York, Jan. 27, 1851. An artist, but above all a lover of animated nature, the best years and efforts of his life were devoted to 'Birds of America' and to 'American Ornithological Biography,' in which his skill with the brush, the effective simplicity of his literary style, and his mastery of his subject, have equal claims to admiration. Another series of studies, 'The Quadrupeds of America,' 'Synopsis of the Birds of North America,' and 'Biography of American Quadrupeds,' have added to a fame which no subsequent labor in the same field has tended to discredit.

Aue. See **Hartmann von Aue.**

Auer, Adelheid von (ou'er), pseudonym of Charlotte von Cosel. A German novelist; born in Berlin, Jan. 6, 1818. She is author of a great many stories of real life, among them: 'Footprints in Sand' (1868); 'A Sister of Charity' (1870); 'In the World's Labyrinth' (1878); 'Castles in the Air' (1882); all written in the tone and spirit of a moderate conservative.

Auerbach, Berthold (ou'er-bäch). An eminent German novelist; born at Nordstetten, Würtemberg, Feb. 28, 1812; died at Cannes, France, Feb. 8, 1882. He began to write while a student in Heidelberg, and under the pseudonym "Theobald Chauber" produced a 'Biography of Frederick the Great' (1834-36). A series of novels from the history of Judaism, under the collective title 'The Ghetto,' of which 'Spinoza' (1837), and 'Poet and Merchant' (1839) were printed in separate editions, was followed by a translation of the works of Spinoza, with a critical biography (1841); and by 'The Educated Citizen, a Book for the Thinking Human Mind' (1842), intended to bring philosophical problems within the comprehension of the uninitiated. His next work, 'Black Forest Village Stories' (1843), was received with universal favor, translated into nearly all European languages, and established his fame. To this class of tales belong also 'The Professor's Lady' (1847); 'Little Barefoot' (1856); 'Joseph in the Snow' (1860); 'Edelweiss' (1861); 'After Thirty Years,' new village stories (1876). His first effort in the field of the novel, 'New Life' (1851), met with little favor; but 'On the Heights' (1865) constituted the crowning success of his literary career. It was followed by 'The Villa on the Rhine' (1868); 'Waldfried, a Family History' (1874); and 'The Head Forester' (1879); 'Brigitta' (1880).

Auersperg, Count Anton Alexander von. See **Grün, Anastasius.**

Auffenberg, Joseph von, Baron (ouf'fenberg). A German dramatist (1798-1857), whose historical tragedies had a temporary success. Among them are: 'Pizarro' (1823); 'The Spartans'; 'The Lion of Kurdistan' (after Scott's 'Talisman'). Of a trip to Spain in 1832 he published a sprightly description under the title 'Humorous Pilgrimage to Granada and Cordova' (1833).

Augier, Émile (ō-zhē-ā'). A distinguished French dramatist; born at Valence, Sept. 17, 1820; died at Croissy, Oct. 25, 1889. With his first play, 'The Hemlock' (1844), he won popular favor, as it commenced a needed reaction against the overstrained romanticism of the time. He lashed the dominant vices of modern society in a series of plays: 'The Marriage of Olympia' (1855); 'The Poor Lionesses' (1858); 'The Brazen-Fronted' (1861); and 'Giboyer's Boy' (1862). 'The Fourchambaults' (1878) is esteemed his best work.

Augustine, Saint (Aurelius Augustinus). The most illustrious of the Latin fathers of the Church, and of patristic writers; born in Tagasta, Numidia, Nov. 13, 354; died at Hippo, Aug. 28, 430. His most celebrated works are his 'Confessions'; 'Grace of Christ'; 'City of God'; and 'Original Sin.' We owe to him also reflections on music, mankind, and other themes.

Aulnoy, Marie Catherine, Comtesse d' (ōl-nwä'). A French writer; born about 1650; died in Paris, 1705. She is now remembered chiefly by her 'Fairy Tales,' in which she successfully imitated Perrault. Of her novels only 'Hippolyte, Count of Douglas' (1690) deserves mention. She also wrote 'Memoirs of the Court of Spain' (1690).

Aumale, Duc d', Henri Eugène Philippe, Louis d'Orléans (dük dō-mäl'). A French biographical and military writer and prince of the blood; born in Paris, Jan. 16, 1822; died at Zucco, Sicily, May 7, 1897. He served with distinction in Algiers, and was a member of the Assembly and the Academy. He was expelled from France in 1886, the sentence being revoked in 1889. He has written: 'Histories of the Princes of Condé' (1869); 'Military Institutions of France' (1897); etc.

Aurbacher, Ludwig (our'bä-ċher). A German author (1784–1847), well remembered by his 'Volksbüchlein' (1827–29); a collection of popular tales, ranking among the best productions of this kind in German literature.

Aureli, Mariano (ō-rāl'-ē). An Italian dramatist and miscellaneous writer; born at Bologna, Dec. 24, 1820. In his youth he studied law, music, and design, but the love of letters finally triumphed. After the war of 1848–49, in which he took part, he became a lecturer and instructor in the government schools. His works include: 'Ernestina' (1845), a novel; 'Charles I. and Oliver Cromwell' (1875), a historical drama; 'Justice and Rigor' (1876), a comedy; and others.

Aurelius, Marcus (mär'kus ä-rē'li-us). The Roman emperor; born in Rome, April 20, 121 A. D.; died in Pannonia, March 17, 180. On account of his devotion to literature and philosophy he is often styled « The Philosopher,» but he is known in history as Marcus Aurelius Antoninus. During his reign, his empire was visited by earthquake, famine, plague, and frequent wars; yet, amid the turmoil, he cherished always his love of peace, truth, and humanity. He founded in Athens chairs of philosophy for the Platonic, Stoic, Peripatetic, and Epicurean sects. His 'Meditations,' containing the inmost thoughts and purest aspirations of one of the noblest souls that ever lived, has always been highly prized.

Auriac, Jules Berlioz d' (dō-rē-äk'). A French novelist; born at Grenoble in 1820. Educated for the law, he was for some years a magistrate in his native city, but finally abandoned this profession to devote himself entirely to letters, and became a regular contributor to the Journal Pour Tous. From a long list of his works may be cited: 'The White Spirit' (1866); 'The Foresters of Michigan' (1866); 'A Duel in the Desert' (1884).

Auringer, Obadiah Cyrus. An American poet; born at Glens Falls, N. Y., June 4, 1849. He served for some years in the United States navy. Since 1875 he has been a farmer in his native place. Among his works are: 'Voices of a Shell'; 'Scythe and Sword' (1887); 'Episode of Jane McCrea'; 'The Book of the Hills,' and 'The Christ' (1900).

Ausonius, Decimus Magnus (â-sō'ni-us). A Roman poet of the 4th century (310–94); born at Bordeaux. He stood in high favor with the emperors Valentinian and Gratian. One of his most ambitious poems is a fulsome eulogy of Gratian. He wrote a number of 'Idyls,' 'Elegies,' and 'Epistles.' He is at his best in 'The Moselle,' one of his idyls, in which he describes a voyage on that river and the Rhine.

Austen, Jane. An English novelist; born in Steventon, Hampshire, Dec. 16, 1775; died in Winchester, July 18, 1817. Her books received little attention during her life, but are accorded high place to-day. They describe with great fidelity ordinary English middle-class life, rural scenes, and characters familiar to her. Long after her death Walter Scott, and still later Macaulay, paid just tribute to her genius. Her best-known works are: 'Sense and Sensibility' (1811); 'Pride and Prejudice.'

Austin, Alfred. An English poet, critic, and journalist; born at Headingly, near Leeds, May 30, 1835. He graduated from the University of London in 1853, was called to the bar in 1857, and became editor of the National Review 1883–93. He was appointed poet laureate of England in 1896. He is the author of political books, novels, and many volumes of verse. The latter include: 'The Season: a Satire' (1862); 'The Human Tragedy' (1862); 'The Golden Age: a Satire' (1871); 'The Tower of Babel,' a drama (1874); 'Savonarola,' a tragedy (1881); and 'Veronica's Garden,' in prose and verse (1895). Some of his happiest effects are attained in 'Prince Lucifer' and 'The Garden that I Love,' although opinion is very much divided on the subject of his merits as a poet, particularly in such works as 'Fortunatus the Pessimist' (1891).

Austin, George Lowell. An American physician and miscellaneous writer; born in Lawrence, Mass., Sept. 11, 1849; died in Melrose, June 5, 1893. Among his works are 'Perils of American Women,' 'Water-Analysis' (1882); 'Under the Tide'; 'Life of Franz Schubert'; 'Popular History of Massachusetts'; 'Life of Wendell Phillips' (1888).

Austin, Henry. An American lawyer and legal writer; born in Mass., Dec. 21, 1858. He has written several valuable books on: 'American Farm and Game Laws'; 'American Fish and Game Laws'; 'Liquor Law in New England.'

Austin, Henry Willard. An American journalist and poet; born in Massachusetts in 1858. He is the author of 'Vagabond Verses.'

Austin, James Trecothic. An American lawyer and biographer; born in Boston, Mass., Jan. 7, 1784; died there, May 8, 1870. He graduated from Harvard in 1802, and was attorney-general of Massachusetts from 1832 to 1843. He was a pronounced opponent of the abolition movement. He is the author of a 'Life of Elbridge Gerry' (1828).

Austin, Jane Goodwin. An American novelist; born in Worcester, Mass., Feb. 25, 1831; died in Boston, March 30, 1894. She was educated and thenceforward lived in Boston. Her reputation rests on excellent stories describing the Pilgrim Fathers and the early colonists of Massachusetts, and including 'Fairy Dreams' (1860); 'Moonfolk' (1874); 'Mrs. Beauchamp Brown' (1880); 'A Nameless Nobleman' (1881); 'The Desmond Hundred' (1882); 'Nantucket Scraps' (1882); 'Standish of Standish' (1889); 'Betty Alden' (1891); and 'David Alden's Daughter and Other Stories' (1892).

Austin, William. An American descriptive and story writer; born in Charlestown, Mass., March 2, 1778; died there, June 27, 1841. Graduated from Harvard in 1798, and afterwards became prominent as a lawyer. A two-years' residence in England (1802-4) resulted in 'Letters from London,' containing descriptions of many distinguished residents of that city. He is the author of 'Peter Rugg, the Missing Man' (1824-26), a legendary tale published in the New England Galaxy, which attracted much attention.

Autran, Joseph (ō-troń'). A French poet; born in Marseilles in June 1813; died there, March 6, 1877. His verse is admired for its purity of form and refined sentiment. He attracted attention in 1832 with an ode to Lamartine, 'The Departure for the East.' His works include: 'The Sea,' poems (1835); 'Milianah,' an epic (1842); 'Rural Life' (1856); and 'The Daughter of Æschylus,' drama (1848), which won a prize from the French Academy.

Avdyeyev, Michael Vassilyevich (äv-dyä'-yef). A Russian novelist (1821-76), whose first effort was 'Tamarin' (1852), a trilogy; and whose second novel, 'The Cliff' (1862), created a great sensation, its theme being free love.

Avellaneda y Arteaga, Gertrudis Gomez de (ä-vä-lyä-na'thä ē är-tā-ä'gä). A distinguished Spanish poet, dramatist, and novelist; born at Puerto Principe, Cuba, March 23, 1814; died in Madrid, Feb. 2, 1873. Under the pseudonym « Peregrina » she contributed to Andalusian journals many 'Lyric Poems' (1851-54), and afterward wrote a series of spirited novels:

'Two Women'; 'The Baroness de Joux'; 'Dolores'; and others. She gained still higher distinction with the tragedies 'Alfonso Munio,' the hero of which was her own ancestor, and 'The Prince of Viana.' Her later compositions have a tone of melancholy, but are not inferior to those that went before them either in grace of style or in forcefulness of thought; among these are: Biblical dramas, as 'Saul' and 'Balthasar'; the spiritual song, 'At the Cross'; and 'The Last Accent of my Harp' (1850). But she did not abandon dramatic composition; in the later years of her life she composed 16 plays which have a place on the Spanish stage.

Avenel, Paul (äv-nel'). A French poet and novelist; born at Chaumont, Oct. 9, 1823. Educated for commerce, he turned to literature and was active in connection with several periodicals. Besides a number of vaudevilles, he wrote: 'The Peasant Woman from the Abruzzi' (1861), a drama; 'The King of Paris' (1860), a historical romance; 'The Calicoes' (1866), scenes of real life. Among several collections of poems may be mentioned 'Alcove and Boudoir,' interdicted 1855 and republished 1885. He died April 19, 1902.

Averkiyev, Dmitry Vassilyévich (ä-ver-kē'-yef). A Russian dramatist and critic; born Oct. 12, 1836. He wrote over twenty dramas and comedies, besides numerous literary criticisms. Among the former, mostly taken from old Russian life, the best are: 'In Old Kashira' (1872), a historical tragedy; and 'Frol Skobejeff' (1868), a comedy.

Averroës or **Averrhoës** (a-ver'o-ez), properly **Ibn Rushd.** An eminent Spanish-Arabian philosopher and physician; born at Cordova, Spain, in 1126; died in Morocco, Dec. 10, 1198. Through translations of his works into Latin and Hebrew, he exerted a profound influence for centuries upon both Christian and Jewish thought.

Avery, Benjamin Parke. An American journalist and diplomatist; born in New York city in 1829; died in Pekin, China, Nov. 8, 1875. He went to California in 1849 and became connected with several papers on the Pacific coast, among them being the San Francisco Bulletin. In 1872 he was appointed editor of the Overland Monthly. From 1874 to 1875 he was minister to China. His chief work is 'Californian Pictures in Prose and Verse' (1877).

Avianus, Flavius (ā-vi-ā'nus). A Roman fabulist of the latter end of the 4th century. He wrote 42 Æsopic fables in elegiac metre, which were used as a text-book in mediæval schools.

Avicebron or **Avencebrol** (ä-vē-thä-brōn'), properly Solomon ben Jehuda ibn Gabirol. A celebrated Hebrew poet and philosopher; born at Cordova, about 1028; died about 1058. Of his poetical works, 'The Royal Crown' is the most famous; of the philosophical, 'The Fountain of Life,' written in Arabic, but known only through a Latin translation (re-edited, Münster, 1895).

Avicenna. See **Ibn Sina.**

Ayala, Adelardo Lopez de (ä-yä'lä). A Spanish dramatist; born at Guadalcanal, Badajoz, March 1829; died Dec. 30, 1879. After studying law in Seville, he went to Madrid, where he devoted himself entirely to poetry and speedily won national fame. His first drama, 'A Statesman' (1851), met with immediate success, and was followed in the same year by 'The Two Noblemen' and 'Penalty and Pardon.' To the modern comedy of manners, his specific domain, he first contributed 'The Glass Roof,' and in 1861 attained to wide reputation with 'Percentage.' Of his other works the most noteworthy are: 'The Modern Don Juan' (1863); and 'Consuelo' (1878), a drama. He has also written beautiful sonnets.

Ayala, Pedro Lopez de. A Spanish historian, poet, and statesman (1332–1407). In great favor with the Castilian kings Peter the Cruel, Henry II., John I., and Henry III., he was invested with the highest dignities of State. His 'Chronicles of the Kings of Castile' contains the history of that kingdom from 1350 to 1396. Of his poetical works, the 'Rhyme-Work of the Palace,' a didactic poem on social and political questions, stands foremost.

Aylmer-Gowing, Mrs. Emilia. An English poet and reciter; born in Bath, October 1846. She was educated partly in Brighton, partly in Paris, where she received the attention of Lamartine. After a short career on the stage she successfully produced two dramas: 'A Life Race' and 'A Crown for Love.' Her 'Ballads and Poems' and 'The Cithern' have become popular, as well as two novels: 'The Jewel Reputation' and 'An Unruly Spirit.' In 1891 she published 'Ballads of the Tower and Other Poems.'

Ayrer, Jacob (ī'rer). A German dramatist; died in Nuremberg, March 26, 1605. Next to Hans Sachs the most prolific dramatist of Germany in the 16th century; in 1595–1605 he wrote more than 100 plays, of which the 'Opus Theatricum' (Nuremberg, 1618) contains 30 tragedies and comedies, and 36 Shrovetide plays and vaudevilles. In his dramas the influence of the English stage is apparent.

Ayres, Anne. An American author; born in England in 1816; died in February 1896. She was the first member of an American sisterhood in the Protestant Episcopal Church. She wrote: 'Evangelical Sisterhood' (1867); 'Life of Augustus Muhlenberg.'

Ayton or **Aytoun, Sir Robert** (ā'tǫn). A Scottish poet; born in his father's castle of Kinaldie in 1570; died in London in February 1638. His Latin and English verses made him famous at the courts of James I. and Charles I., where he held posts of honor and was knighted in 1612. He also wrote in Greek and French. Ayton is supposed to have been the author of 'Auld Lang Syne,' which was remodeled by Burns.

Aytoun, William Edmonstoune. A Scottish humorist; born in Edinburgh, June 21, 1813; died at Blackhills, near Elgin, Aug. 4, 1865. He joined the editorial staff of Blackwood's Magazine in 1844, and to his death continued an unwearying and fertile contributor to its pages. Professor of literature in the University of Edinburgh, 1845-64. After John Wilson's death (1854), he was considered the most important man of letters in Scotland during his life, famous for his humor, satire, and criticism. His most celebrated work is 'Lays of the Scottish Cavaliers' (1848, 29th ed. 1883), a series of ballads replete with genuine poetry, glorifying the champions of the Stuart cause. Noteworthy is his critical and annotated collection of the 'Ballads of Scotland' (1858, 4th ed. 1870). With Theodore Martin he wrote the famous 'Bon Gaultier Ballads' (1844, 13th ed. 1877), and translated 'Poems and Ballads of Goethe' (1858).

Azarias, Brother. See **Mullany, Patrick Francis.**

Azeglio, Massimo Taparelli, Marchese d' (äd-zäl'yō). A distinguished Italian writer, statesman, and artist; born in Turin, Oct. 15, 1798; died in Milan, Jan. 15, 1866. Of his literary productions the most noteworthy are the two historical romances 'Ettore Fieramosca' (1833) and 'Nicolò de' Lapi' (1841); but first in importance is his autobiography 'My Recollections' (1867), translated into English by Count Maffei. Supplements to these are: 'Letters to his Wife, Luisa Blondel' (1870); 'to Giuseppe Torelli' (1870); 'to Carlo di Persano' (1878); and 'to Emanuele d'Azeglio' (1883); but especially 'Italy from 1847 to 1865, Political Correspondence of M. d'Azeglio' (Paris, 1866).

Azevedo, Manoel Antonio Alvares de (ä-zā-vä'dö). A Brazilian poet; born in São Paulo, 1831; died 1852. While studying law in 1848–51, he produced an abundance of romantic poetry in the vein of Byron, Heine, and Musset, which made him the most widely read poet of Brazil after Gonçalves Dias. His 'Complete Works' (1863) contain also prose writings and three dramatic pieces.

Azulai, Hayim David (hä'gēm dä'vēd ä-zö-lī'). A Jewish bibliographer; born in Jerusalem; died at Leghorn, Italy. He lived in the 18th century. Most of his life was spent at Leghorn. Of his numerous works, the best known is 'Shem-ha-Gedôlîm' (The Names of the Great), a bibliography containing the names of over 1,300 Jewish authors, and more than 2,200 of their works.

B

Babbage, Charles (bab'aj). A celebrated English mathematician; born near Teignmouth, Devonshire, Dec. 26, 1792; died in London, Oct. 18, 1871. He was professor of mathematics at Cambridge (1828-39) and one of the founders, secretaries, and vice-presidents of the Astronomical Society. He is best known as the inventor of the only partially successful calculating machine. His principal work was 'On the Economy of Machinery' (1832), which was translated into several languages. Among his other writings were: 'Passages from the Life of a Philosopher' (1864) and 'Chapter on Street Nuisances' (1864).

Baber or **Babar, Zehir-Eddin Mohammed,** surnamed (bä'bèr). Conqueror of India and founder of the Mogul dynasty; born 1483; died at Agra, Dec. 28, 1530. He was a lineal descendant of Jenghiz Khan and Timur, and at the age of 12 years succeeded his father as king of Ferghana, a district to the east of Samarcand. In 1521, gathering an army of 12,-000 followers, he invaded India, then preparing to revolt against the intolerable exactions of Ibrahim, emperor at Delhi; and in six years made himself absolute master of the whole country. He wrote a volume of 'Memoirs' which shows him to have been a man of well-cultivated intellect, a sagacious observer, and a wise statesman.

Babeuf or **Babœuf, François Noel** (bä-bèf). A French communist, who called himself Caius Gracchus; born at Saint-Quentin, 1760; died in Paris, May 27, 1797. He founded in Paris a journal called the Tribune of the People (1794), in which he advocated his system of communism, known as "Babœuvism" and contemplating absolute equality and community of property. His followers were called "Babœuvists." Betrayed in a conspiracy against the Directory, aiming to put his theories into practice, he was guillotined. His principal works were: 'Perpetual Register of the Survey of Lands' (1780); 'Of the System of Population' (1794).

Babo, Joseph Marius von (bä'bō). A German dramatist (1756-1822); author of a series of plays of chivalry in imitation of Goethe's 'Götz,' among which 'Otto von Wittelsbach' (1781) had the greatest success. Two comedies, 'Homely Happiness' (1792) and 'The Pulse' (1804), also found much favor.

Babrius (bä'bri-us). A Greek writer of fables in verse; variously referred to the time immediately preceding the Augustan age, and to the third century of our era; his name also shows variants, as Babrias, Gabrius. Till 1842 only a few fragments of Babrius were known to be extant; but in that year, in the Laura of Mt. Athos was discovered a MS. containing 123 of his fables. In 1846 Sir George Cornewall Lewis

published them together with the pre-existing fragments, and in 1859 or 1860 appeared a good English version by James Davies. The fables have also been edited by W. G. Rutherford (1883), and by F. G. Schneidewin (1880).

Baccalar y Saña, Vicente, Marquis of St. Philip (bäk'ä lär ē sän'yä). A Spanish historian and statesman; born in Sardinia; died in Madrid, 1726. He served the King of Spain with less disinterestedness than distinction during the revolt of his native isle, and was ennobled after writing a very rhetorical 'History of the Kingdom of the Jews,' as well as 'Memoirs for a History of Philip V.,' the latter work covering the period between 1699 and 1725.

Bache, Alexander Dallas (bäch). A distinguished American scientist and educator, great-grandson of Benjamin Franklin; born at Philadelphia, July 19, 1806; died at Newport, Feb. 17, 1867. Graduating from West Point at the head of his class (1825), he became professor of natural philosophy and chemistry at the University of Pennsylvania (1828); organizer and first president of Girard College (1836); superintendent of the United States Coast Survey (1843), his services in that position being invaluable; active member of the sanitary commission during the Civil War; a regent of the Smithsonian Institution (1846-67); president of the National Academy of Sciences (1863). He wrote 'Observations at the Magnetic and Meteorological Observatory at the Girard College,' a scientifically valuable work; a helpful report on education in Europe (1839); and a long series of notable annual reports of the United States Coast Survey.

Bache, Franklin (bäch). A distinguished American physician and chemist; born at Philadelphia, Oct. 25, 1792; died there, March 19, 1864. He was professor of chemistry at the Philadelphia College of Pharmacy (1831) and the Jefferson Medical College (1841). Besides writing 'A System of Chemistry for Students of Medicine' (1819), he was one of the authors of Wood and Bache's 'Dispensatory of the United States' (1833), an acknowledged authority.

Bacher, Julius (bäch'er). A German story-writer and dramatist; born in Ragnit, East Prussia, Aug. 8, 1810. He was a practicing physician, who turned man of letters and attained reputation with 'The First Love of Charles XII.' (1850), a tragedy; 'Princess Sidonie' (1870), a novel; and various other pieces.

Bacheracht, Therese von (bä'chèr-ächt). A German novelist (1804-52), who chose her subjects mostly from the life of the upper classes, and was distinguished for her careful delineation of character. The best among her novels are: 'Falkenberg' (1843); 'Lydia' (1844);

'Heinrich Burkart' (1846). Much credit is due her for the publication of W. von Humboldt's 'Letters to a Friend' (1847).

Bachman, John (bak'man). An American clergyman and naturalist; born in Dutchess county, N. Y., Feb. 4, 1790; died at Charleston, S. C., Feb. 25, 1874. He was associated with Audubon in the 'Quadrupeds of North America,' writing the principal part of the work, which Audubon and his sons illustrated.

Back, Sir George. An English admiral and Arctic explorer; born in Stockport, Cheshire, Nov. 6, 1796; died in London, June 23, 1878. Having accompanied Franklin in several expeditions, he discovered the' Great Fish or Back River (1833–35), commanded the Terror in an Arctic expedition (1836–37), and became admiral (1857). He wrote: 'Narrative of the Arctic Land Expedition to the Mouth of the Great Fish River'; 'Narrative of an Expedition in H. M. S. Terror'; etc.

Bäckström, Per Johan Edvard (bāk'strĕm). A Swedish dramatist and lyric poet; born in Stockholm, Oct. 27, 1841; died there, Feb. 13, 1886. His principal work is 'Dagvard Frey' (1876), a tragedy; besides this the dramas 'A Crown' (1869), 'Eva's Sisters' (1869), 'The Prisoner of Kallö' (1870), met with success. His lyrics were published in three collections (1860, 1870, 1876).

Bacon, Delia. An American writer (1811–59), daughter of Leonard Bacon. She is best remembered for her 'Philosophy of the Plays of Shakespeare' (1857); to which Nathaniel Hawthorne (without concurring) wrote a preface, and which brought into prominence the Bacon-Shakespeare controversy.

Bacon, Francis. The English philosopher; born in London, Jan. 22, 1561; died April 9, 1626. His immortal 'Essays' were published in 1597, and in the same year appeared 'On the Colors of Good and Evil.' The two books of 'The Advancement of Learning' appeared in 1605; and in 1620 the 'Novum Organum,' written, like very many of Bacon's works, in Latin. The 'Novum Organum' is «an essay toward the science of a better use of reason in the investigation of things.» His histories of 'Henry VII.,' of 'Henry VIII.,' and of 'Elizabeth,' are of unequal value and authority: the first is eminently faithful and trustworthy; the other two are probably biased by the author's desire to stand well at court. His 'New Atlantis' is one of the world's great Utopian speculations.

Bacon, Leonard. An American clergyman; born at Detroit, Mich., Feb. 19, 1802; died in New Haven, Conn., Dec. 24, 1881. He graduated at Yale in 1820, after which he studied theology at Andover, Mass. In 1825 he became pastor of the First Congregational Church in New Haven, a position which he held officially, though not always actively, until his death. He was professor of didactic theology in Yale (1866–71). He was throughout his life an active opponent of slavery. In 1847 he joined with Drs. Storrs and Thompson to found the New York Independent, in the joint editorship of which he continued for 16 years. Besides a vast number of reviews and pamphlets, he published many theological and historical works.

Bacon, Leonard Woolsey. An American Congregational minister and religious writer, son of Leonard Bacon; born at New Haven, 1830. Among his writings are : ' The Vatican Council ' (1872); 'Church Music Papers' (1876) ; 'Sunday Evening Essays' (1877). Died May 12, 1907.

Bacon, Roger. An English philosopher, one of the greatest mediæval scholars. He was born of good family in Somersetshire, about 1214; died about 1294. He studied at Oxford, taking orders there 1233; proceeded to Paris, returned, and entered the Franciscan Order 1250. His discoveries in chemistry and physics brought upon him accusations of magic, and he was imprisoned at Paris, 1257. At the request of Pope Clement IV. in 1265 he drew up his 'Opus Majus.' He gained his liberty a little later, but suffered a further imprisonment of ten years under Nicholas II., and was not finally liberated till 1292, two years before his death. He was learned in several languages and wrote elegant Latin. His wide knowledge gained for him the name of Doctor Admirabilis. His chief work, the 'Opus Majus,' shows great learning and remarkably advanced thinking, considering the age in which he lived. He treats of the unity of the sciences, of the necessity of a true linguistic science for the understanding either of philosophy, science, or the Scriptures; he treats also of mathematics, as «the alphabet of philosophy,» and of geography and astronomy as related thereto, of perspective, and of experimental science, foreshadowing the inductive method. The portion relating to geography was read by Columbus, who was strongly influenced by it.

Bacon, Thomas Scott. An American theological writer; born at Saratoga, N. Y., Feb. 1, 1825. Originally a lawyer, he became an Episcopalian clergyman (1854). Besides sermons, addresses, reviews, etc., he has written: 'Both Sides of the Controversy between the Roman and the Reformed Church' (1858); 'The Reign of God, not the' Reign of Law' (1879); 'The Beginnings of Religion' (1887) ; 'Primitive and Catholic Doctrine as to Holy Scripture'; etc.

Bacsányi, János (bo'chän-yē). A Hungarian poet, prose-writer, and journalist; born at Tapolcza, May 11, 1763; died at Linz, May 12, 1845. With Baróti and Kazinczy, he founded a journal, the Magyar Museum (1788), and was editor of the Magyar Minerva. Having translated Napoleon's proclamation to the Hungarians (1809), he was obliged to flee to Paris, whence he was extradited after Napoleon's fall, but was compelled to live at Linz.

Baculard d'Arnaud, François (bä-kü-lär' där-nō'). A French novelist and dramatist (1718–1805), protégé of Voltaire, for two year» literary correspondent, in Paris, of Frederick the Great, who afterwards called him to Berlin. Thence he went to Dresden, and on his return to France wrote a considerable number of sentimental novels in the taste of the times. Of his dramas, in which the sombre and horrible element prevails, only 'The Count of Comminges' (1765) was performed.

Badeau, Adam. An American soldier and author; born in New York city, Dec. 29, 1831; died in Ridgewood, N. J., March 19, 1895. He served in the United States army during the Civil War, was military secretary to General Grant in 1864-69, then secretary of legation in London, and from 1870 till 1881 consul-general there, and in 1882-84 in Havana. He accompanied General Grant on his tour around the world in 1877-78. Author of: 'The Vagabond' (New York, 1858); 'Military History of U. S. Grant' (3 vols., 1867-81); 'Conspiracy: a Cuban Romance' (1885); 'Aristocracy in England' (1886); and 'Grant in Peace' (1886).

Baden-Powell, Sir George Smyth (bā'den-pou'l). An English politician and political writer; born at Oxford, Dec. 24, 1847. He has been member of various important commissions, among others that on United States and Canadian fisheries (1886-87), the Bering Sea inquiry (1891); of the Joint Commission (Washington, 1892). He has written: 'New Homes for the Old Country' (1872), a storehouse of information about Australia; 'Protection and Bad Times' (1879); 'State Aid and State Interference' (1882); 'The Truth about Home Rule' (1888); 'The Land Systems of India' (1892); etc. He died Nov. 20, 1898.

Baena, Antonio (bä-yä'nä). A Portuguese-Brazilian historian and geographer; born in Portugal about 1795; died in Pará, March 28, 1850. He was an officer in the Portuguese, afterward in the Brazilian, army. He studied the geography and history of the Amazon valley. His principal works were: 'The Ages of Pará' (1838), a historic compend stopping at 1823, and 'Chorographic Essay on the Province of Pará' (1839), a geographical and statistical work giving the details of explorations made by himself.

Baer, Karl Ernst von (bär). A noted Russian naturalist, famous especially as an embryologist; born at Piep, Esthonia, Feb. 28, 1792; died at Dorpat, Nov. 28, 1876. He was professor of zoölogy at Königsberg (1819), and librarian of the Academy of Sciences at St. Petersburg (1834). His principal works were: 'History of the Development of Animals' (2 vols., 1828-37); 'Researches into the Development of Fishes' (1835).

Baffin, William. A noted English navigator and explorer; born probably in London, 1584; died at the siege of Ormuz, Jan. 23, 1622. In the second of two arctic expeditions, he discovered Baffin's Bay. Of these voyages he wrote two accounts, in the first giving a new method of computing longitude at sea. These accounts have been recently edited by Clements R. Markham for the Hakluyt Society, 'Voyages of William Baffin' (1881).

Bagby, George William. An American physician, journalist, and humorist; born in Buckingham County, Va., Aug. 13, 1828; died at Richmond, Va., Nov. 29, 1883. He wrote under the pseudonym "Mozis Addums." He was editor of the Lynchburg Express (1853) and Southern Literary Messenger (1859), State Librarian of Virginia (1870-78), and contributor to various magazines: 'John M. Daniel's Latch-Key' (1868); 'What I Did with My Fifty Millions' (1875); 'Meckins's Twinses' (1877).

Bage, Robert (bāj). An English novelist; born at Darley, Derbyshire, Feb. 29, 1728; died at Tamworth, Sept. 1, 1801. He only began to write at the age of fifty-three. Among his works were: 'Mount Henneth' (1781); 'Barham Downs' (1784); 'Hermsprong, or Man as He is Not' (1796); etc.

Bagehot, Walter (baj'ot). An English writer on political economy and government; born in Langport, Somersetshire, Feb. 3, 1826; died there, March 24, 1877. After graduating from University College, London, he studied law and was admitted to the bar; but never entered practice, being drawn rather to the study of economics and political science. His principal works are: 'The English Constitution' (1867); 'Physics and Politics,' in which the life and growth of nations are studied in the light of Darwin's theory (1863); and 'Lombard Street: a Description of the Money Market.' His complete works, edited by Forrest Morgan, were published at Hartford, Conn., 1889.

Baggesen, Jens (bäg'e-sen). A noted Danish poet; born at Korsör, Zealand, Feb. 15, 1764; died in Hamburg, Oct. 3, 1826. He became involved in a great literary feud with Oehlenschläger. His first poetic effort, 'Comic Tales' (1785), at once attracted attention; but 'The Labyrinth' (1792), afterwards entitled 'Wanderings of a Poet,' a description of his traveling impressions, equally distinguished for its overflowing humor and finished style, is his most important work, a landmark in Danish prose literature.

Bahr, Hermann (bär). An Austrian dramatist, novelist, and critic; born in Linz, July 19, 1863. He took a firm stand in opposition to the "naturalism," "modernism," and "symbolism" of the dominant school of French novelists, and published two collections of his strictures on these phases of literature, under the titles 'A Critique of Modernism' (1890) and 'The Overthrow of Naturalism' (1891). He is author of several dramas, among them 'The New Men' (1888); 'The Mother' (1891); of 'The Domestic Woman' (1893), a comedy; and of some novels and romances, among them 'Dora, Stories of Vienna' (1893); 'The Apostle' (1901).

Bähr, Johann Christian (bär). A distinguished German philologist; born at Darmstadt,

June 13, 1798; died at Heidelberg, Nov. 29, 1872. He was professor of classical literature at the University of Heidelberg. Besides editing several of Plutarch's 'Lives,' making a Latin translation of Herodotus, with notes, etc., his principal work was 'History of Roman Literature' (2 vols., 1828; 4th ed. 1868–73).

Bahrdt, Karl Friedrich (bärt). A German theologian; born at Bischofswerda, Saxony, Aug. 25, 1741; died near Halle, April 23, 1792. He was condemned to imprisonment in 1789 for publishing 'The Religious Edict: a Comedy.' As a theologian, he was noted for extreme rationalism. He wrote: 'Letters on Systematic Theology' (2 vols., 1770–72); 'Newest Revelations of God' (1773); while in prison, 'History of his Life' (4 vols., 1790), etc.

Bahya ben Joseph ben Pakoda (bä'hē-yä ben yō'sef ben pä-kō'dä). A noted Jewish poet and religious writer; lived at Saragossa, Spain, in the 11th century. He is best known by his celebrated religious work, 'Duties of the Heart,' written by him in Arabic and translated into Hebrew. It abounds in spiritual meditations and exhortations, and occupies among the Jews a position similar to that held among Christians by the 'Imitation of Christ.' It was translated into Spanish (1610) and English (1894).

Baïf, Jean Antoine de (bä-ēf'). A French poet (1532–89), one of the literary league known as the "Pléiade," and the chief advocate of its plan of reducing French poetry to the metres of the classic tongues; also a spelling reformer, in favor of the phonetic system. His most meritorious works were translations of Greek and Roman dramas. Among his original productions, 'The Mimes, Precepts, and Proverbs' (6 editions, 1576–1619) are the most noteworthy.

Bailey, Gamaliel. An American journalist; born at Mt. Holly, N. J., Dec. 3, 1807; died at sea, on his way to Europe, June 5, 1859. With J. G. Birney, he founded the anti-slavery journal, the Cincinnati Philanthropist (1836), the office of which was destroyed by a mob, though it continued to be published till 1847. He established the well-known newspaper, the Washington National Era (1847), in which the famous novel 'Uncle Tom's Cabin' appeared first.

Bailey, James Montgomery. An American author; born in Albany, N. Y., Sept. 25, 1841; died in Danbury, Conn., March 4, 1894. He served in the 17th Connecticut regiment during the war; returned to Danbury, founded the Danbury News in 1870. His articles in this paper were widely quoted. He wrote: 'Life in Danbury' (Boston, 1873); 'They All Do It' (1877); and 'The Danbury Boom' (1880).

Bailey, Nathan. An English lexicographer and classical scholar; died at Stepney, June 27, 1742. He was a school-teacher at Stepney, and a Seventh-day Baptist. Besides educational books, he was the author of a 'Universal Etymological English Dictionary' (1721), the first English dictionary with any pretensions to

being complete, and the basis of Dr. Johnson's better known work. He wrote also a 'Domestic Dictionary' (1736).

Bailey, Philip James. An English poet; born in Basford, Nottinghamshire, April 22, 1816. He was educated in Glasgow, and studied law at Lincoln's Inn, being admitted to the bar in 1840. In his twentieth year he began 'Festus,' a lyrico-dramatic poem on the Faust legend. The poem was published in 1839, and attracted unusual attention. The eleventh edition was published in 1889. His other works—'The Angel World' (1850); 'The Mystic' (1855); 'The Age' a colloquial satire (1858); and 'The Universal Hymn' (1867)— did not increase his reputation. Died at Nottingham, Sept. 6, 1902.

Bailey, Samuel. An English writer on philosophy and political economy; born at Sheffield, 1791; died there, Jan. 18, 1870. He was chairman of the Sheffield Banking Company and several times president of the Sheffield Literary and Philosophical Society. Besides works on political economy, he wrote: 'On the Formation and Publication of Opinions' (3d ed. 1831); 'The Pursuit of Truth and the Progress of Knowledge' (2d ed. 1844); 'Letters from an Egyptian Kafir in Search of Religion' (1837, anonymously); 'Maro, or Poetic Sensibility' (1846, anonymously); 'Theory of Reasoning' (2d ed., 1852); 'Philosophy of the Human Mind' (three series, 1855, 1858, 1863); 'The Received Text of Shakespeare's Dramatic Writings' (2 vols., 1861–62); etc.

Baillie, Joanna. A Scottish poet; born in Bothwell, Lanarkshire, Sept. 11, 1762; died at Hampstead, England, Feb. 23, 1851. At an early age she removed to London and settled at Hampstead, where, with her sister Agnes, she passed the remainder of her life. The first volume of her 'Plays on the Passions' was published in 1798; one of them, 'The Family Legend,' was successfully presented at Edinburgh under the patronage of Sir Walter Scott. Miss Baillie published many short poems and songs of great beauty. She enjoyed the close friendship of Scott, Jeffrey (who at first had severely criticized her work), Lucy Aikin, Mrs. Siddons, and other eminent persons. For her benevolent deeds at Hampstead, the poor gave her the name of "Lady Bountiful."

Bailly, Jean Sylvain (bä-yē'). A distinguished French astronomer and statesman; born in Paris, Sept. 15, 1736; died there, Nov. 12, 1793. The first president of the States-General or National Assembly (1789), and mayor of Paris (1789). He was the advocate of order and moderation, and having offended the Jacobins, he died on the guillotine. He wrote 'History of Astronomy' (4 vols., 1775–83), which became very popular; 'Memoirs of the Revolution' (3 vols., 1804); etc.

Baily, Francis (bā'lē). An English astronomer; born at Newbury, Berkshire, April 28, 1774; died in London, Aug. 30, 1844. He reformed the 'Nautical Almanac,' and was the author of the 'Astronomical Society's Catalogue of Stars.' He wrote also a 'Life of Flamsteed' (1835); 'Journal of a Tour in Unsettled Parts of North America' (1856, edited by De Morgan); etc.

Bain, Alexander (bān). A distinguished Scotch philosophical writer; born at Aberdeen, 1818. He became professor of natural philosophy in the Andersonian University, Glasgow, (1845); examiner in logic and moral philosophy for the University of London (1857-62, 1864-69); professor of logic (1860-80) at, and lord rector (1881) of, the University of Aberdeen. He belongs to the Spencerian or experiential school of philosophy, and teaches physiological psychology. His chief works are: 'The Senses and the Intellect' (1855); 'The Emotions and the Will' (1859), the two forming a complete course of mental philosophy; 'English Composition and Rhetoric' (1866); 'Mental and Moral Science' (1868); 'Logic' (2 vols., 1870); 'Mind and Body' (1873); 'Education as a Science' (1879); 'James Mill and John Stuart Mill' (1882); 'Practical Essays' (1884); etc. He died Sept. 6, 1902.

Baird, Charles Washington. An American historian and religious writer, son of Robert Baird; born at Princeton, N. J., Aug. 28, 1828; died in Rye, N. Y., Feb. 10, 1881. Besides works on the Presbyterian liturgies (which he was the first to collect and investigate) and local histories, he wrote: 'History of the Huguenot Emigration to America' (2 vols., 1885). It is interesting especially to the genealogist.

Baird, Henry Carey. An American writer on political economy, nephew of Henry C. Carey; born at Bridesburg, Pa., 1825. He was a publisher at Philadelphia; died there — 1901. A protectionist, his economical views generally are similar to those of his distinguished uncle. He wrote numerous economic pamphlets.

Baird, Henry Martyn. An American author; born in Philadelphia, Pa., Jan. 17, 1832. He graduated from the University of the City of New York in 1850, and after spending some years in Europe, took a course in theology at Union and Princeton. In 1859 he was appointed professor of the Greek language and literature in the University of the City of New York. His principal works are the 'History of the Rise of the Huguenots' (1879); 'The Huguenots and Henry of Navarre' (1886); and 'The Huguenots and the Revocation of the Edict of Nantes' 1895). Died Nov. 11, 1906.

Baird, Robert. An American historian and divine; born in Fayette County, Pa., Oct. 6, 1798; died at Yonkers, N. Y., March 15, 1863. Among his works were: 'History of the Waldenses, Albigenses, and Vaudois'; 'History of the Temperance Societies' (1836); 'Religion in America' (1844); etc. He was corresponding secretary of the American and Foreign Christian Union (1849-55, 1861-63).

Baird, Spencer Fullerton. A distinguished American naturalist; born at Reading, Pa.,

Feb. 3, 1823; died at Wood's Holl, Mass., Aug. 19, 1887. He became professor of natural sciences at Dickinson College, Carlisle, Pa., 1845; United States commissioner of fish and fisheries, 1871; secretary of the Smithsonian Institution, 1878. A very prolific writer, among his more important works may be named: a 'Catalogue of North American Reptiles' (1853); 'Birds of North America' (with Cassin and Lawrence, 1860); 'Mammals of North America' (1858); 'History of North American Birds' (with Brewer and Ridgeway, 1874-84); etc. His writings cover nearly every branch of natural history.

Bajza, Joseph (boy'zä). A Hungarian poet and critic (1804-58). He devoted himself to the field of history, and edited a 'Historical Library' (1843-45) and the 'New Plutarch' (1845-47). Since 1831 he was a member of the Hungarian Academy, and since 1836 of the Kisfaludy Society. He ranks among the best lyric poets of Hungary. His 'Poems' were published in 1835, and his 'Collected Works' (2d ed., in 6 vols., by Toldy) in 1861.

Baker, George Augustus. An American writer of verse and stories; born in New York, N. Y., in August 1849. He graduated from Columbia College Law School, and has written: 'Point Lace and Diamonds,' light society verse (New York, 1875); 'Bad Habits of Good Society' (1876); 'Mrs. Hephæstus and Other Stories' (1887); and comedies.

Baker, Mrs. Harriette Newell (Woods) (pseudonyms "Madeline Leslie" and "Aunt Hatty"). An American writer of juvenile stories; born at Andover, 1815; died at Brooklyn, April 23, 1893. Several of her works have been translated into French and German. She has written: 'Tim the Scissors-Grinder' (1861, sequel in 1862), her most popular work; 'Up the Ladder' (1862); 'The Two Homes' (1862); 'The Organ-Grinder' (1863); 'White and Black Lies' (1864); 'Worth and Wealth' (1864); 'Tim's Sister' (1864); 'Wheel of Fortune' (1865); 'Courtesies of Wedded Life' (1869); 'Paul Barton' (1869); 'Fashion and Folly' (1869); 'Lost but Found' (1869); 'Ingleside' (1886); 'This and That' (1887); etc. She is daughter of Rev. Leonard Woods and wife of Rev. S. R. Baker.

Baker, Samuel White, Sir. An English traveler and author; born in London, Eng., June 8, 1821; died at Sandford Orleigh, Dec. 30, 1893. At an early age he went to Ceylon, and established a sanitarium at Newera Ellia 6,200 feet above sea level; in 1861 undertook to explore the sources of the Nile, discovered and named Lake Albert Nyanza, and reached Gondokoro in 1865. In 1866 he was knighted. He afterwards traveled in India, Syria, Japan, and America. His books include: 'The Rifle and Hound in Ceylon' (1856); 'Eight Years' Wanderings in Ceylon' (1855); 'The Albert Nyanza' (1866); 'The Nile Tributaries of Abyssinia' (1867); 'Ismailia' (1874); 'Cyprus' (1879); 'Wild Beasts and their Ways' (1890);

and 'Cast up by the Sea,' a popular tale of adventure (1869).

Baker, William Mumford. An American descriptive and miscellaneous writer; born in Washington, D. C., June 27, 1825; died in South Boston, Mass., Aug. 20, 1883. He graduated from Princeton in 1846, and became pastor of churches in Texas and in South Boston, Mass. His most important book was 'Inside: A Chronicle of Secession' (New York, 1866). He also wrote many stories, including 'His Majesty Myself' (Boston, 1879).

Baki (bä'kē). The greatest lyric poet of Turkey; died about 1600. His 'Divan' contains almost exclusively odes in praise of the Sultan.

Balaguer, Victor (bä-lä-gär'). A noted Spanish-Catalan poet, novelist, and historian; born in Barcelona, Dec. 11, 1824. As a poet he first attracted notice by his dramas, taken partly from antiquity, partly from Catalan history; among them are: 'Sappho'; 'Don Enrique the Magnificent'; 'Juan de Padilla'; 'Coriolanus.' Of his lyrics the best are embodied in the collection 'The Troubadour of Montserrat' (1850). He also wrote widely read historical romances and tales, among which 'Don Juan de Serravalle' deserves especial mention. Other works are: 'Historical and Political Studies' (1876); 'History of Catalonia' (1886–89), and 'Political and Literary History of the Troubadours' (1878–80). A complete edition of his works appears in the 'Collection of Castilian Writers.' Died in 1901.

Balbi, Gasparo (bäl'bē). A Venetian merchant and writer of travels; lived in the 16th century. He visited Aleppo, spent the years 1579–88 in India, and published 'Journey in the East Indies' (1590). It contained the first European description of India beyond the Ganges.

Balbo, Count Cesare (bäl'bō). An Italian statesman, historian, and publicist; born at Turin, Nov. 21, 1789; died there, June 3, 1853. A moderate and liberal patriot, he became prominent in the revolutionary disturbances of 1848, being premier of Sardinia in that year. He wrote: 'Life of Dante' (1839); 'Hopes of Italy' (1843), advocating Italian independence; 'History of Italy' (1849), which takes high rank.

Balboa or **Balvoa, Miguel Cabello de** (bäl-bō'ä). A Spanish historian; born in Archidona, about 1525; died, probably in Peru, after 1586. At first a soldier, he became afterward a priest and went to America (about 1566), residing at Bogota, later in Lima and Cuzco. He left in manuscript a history; which was published 1840, when it appeared in a French translation entitled 'History of Peru.' It treats of the origin of the Incas.

Balbuena, Don Bernardo de (bäl-bwä'nä). A Spanish poet; born at Val de Peñas in 1568; died in Porto Rico in 1627. At an early age he went to Mexico, where he completed his theological studies and acquired reputation as a poet. Of his works only the following are extant: 'The Greatness of Mexico' (1604), a poetic description of that city; 'The Age of Gold in the Forests of Eryphile' (1608), a pastoral romance in prose, interspersed with lyrics; 'Bernardo, or the Victory of Roncesvalles' (1624), an epic treating of the national hero Bernardo del Carpio.

Baldovini, Francesco (bäl-dō-vē'nē). An Italian poet; born at Florence, Feb. 27, 1635; died Nov. 18, 1716. He wrote 'Lament of Cecco of Varlungo, etc.' (1694), etc.

Balducci, Francesco (bäl-dö'chē). A leading Italian Anacreontic poet; born at Palermo; died at Rome, 1642. He wrote 'Sicilian Songs' in the Sicilian dialect, etc.

Baldwin, John Denison. An American journalist, politician, poet, and writer on archæology; born at North Stonington, Conn., Sept. 28, 1809; died at Worcester, Mass., July 8, 1883. After studying law and theology, he entered journalism, was long editor and proprietor of the Worcester Spy, and became member of Congress (1863–69). He wrote: 'Raymond Hill and Other Poems' (1847); 'Prehistoric Nations' (1869); 'Ancient America' (1872).

Bale, John. An English theologian and dramatist; born at Cove, Suffolk, Nov. 21, 1495; died at Canterbury, probably 1563. Originally a Catholic, he became Protestant bishop of Ossory, Ireland (1552). Besides numerous controversial works, he wrote in Latin a 'Catalogue of the Illustrious Writers of Great Britain' (1548–59), the first history of English literature, and a number of interludes and moralities (i. e., religious plays) in the interest of Protestantism, the most important of these being the historical drama 'King John.' On account of his bad temper he was known as "Bilious Bale." Select works, Cambridge, 1849.

Balestier, Charles Wolcott (bal-es-tēr'). An American journalist and novelist; born in Rochester, N. Y., Dec. 13, 1861; died in Dresden, Germany, Dec. 6, 1891. He engaged in publishing and in journalism, and was a writer of much promise. His novels include: 'A Fair Device' (New York, 1884); (and posthumously) 'An Average Woman' (1892); 'Benefits Forgot' (1894); and 'Naulahka: a Story of East and West,' in collaboration with Rudyard Kipling (1892).

Balfour, Alexander (bal'för). A Scotch poet and novelist; born at Monikie, Forfarshire, March 1, 1767; died Sept. 12, 1829. He wrote: 'Campbell, or the Scottish Probationer' (1819); 'Contemplation and Other Poems' (1820); 'Farmer's Three Daughters' (1822); 'The Foundling of Glenthorn, or the Smuggler's Cave' (1823); 'Highland Mary' (1827).

Balfour, Arthur James. An English author and statesman; born July 25, 1848. He was educated at Eton, and at Trinity College, Cambridge, from which he graduated in 1873. He has been lord rector of Glasgow University, and is Chancellor of the University of Edinburgh. He is a leader of the Conservative party, was Chief Secretary for Ireland in 1887, and First Lord of the Treasury, 1891-92, and again in 1895. He is the author of 'A Defence of Philosophic Doubt' (1879); 'Essays and Addresses' (1893). His 'Foundations of Belief' (1895) attracted wide-spread attention and interest both in Europe and America.

Ball, Robert Stawell, Sir. A British astronomer; born in Dublin, July 1, 1840. He was educated at Trinity College, Dublin; Royal astronomer of Ireland in 1874, and since 1892 has been Lowndean professor of astronomy at Cambridge, England. He was knighted in 1886. Author of scientific works and popular books on astronomy, including : 'Story of the Heavens' (1885); 'Time and Tide : a Romance of the Moon' (1888); 'Starland' (1889); and 'In Starry Realms' (1892); 'The Earth's Beginning' 1901.

Ballantine, James. A Scotch poet; born in Edinburgh, June 11, 1808; died Dec. 18, 1877. In addition to achieving distinction as an artist, he wrote various noted poems, including 'The Gaberlunzie's Wallet' (1843); 'One Hundred Songs' (1865); and two or three collections of verse.

Ballantyne, Robert Michael. A Scotch writer of juvenile literature; born in Edinburgh, 1825; died in Rome, Italy, Feb. 8, 1894. He spent his youth in Canada in the service of the Hudson Bay Company. In 1856 he adopted literature as a profession. He has been very popular in England as a writer of stories for boys. Among the best known are: 'Deep Down'; 'Coral Island'; 'The World of Ice'; 'Ungava'; 'The Dog Crusoe'; and others.

Ballestrem, Countess Eufemia von (bäl'lesträm). A German novelist and poet, born at Ratibor, Aug. 18, 1859. Married to Major von Adlersfeld in 1884, she has lived at Karlsruhe since 1889. Of her novels may be mentioned: 'Lady Melusine' (1878); 'The Falconers of Falcon Court' (1890). A collection of lyrics, 'Drops in the Ocean' (1878), a romantic poem, 'Raoul the Page' (1881), and the drama 'A Meteor' (1880), bear witness to her poetic talent.

Ballou, Hosea (ba-lö'). An American Universalist divine, journalist, and historian; born at Halifax, Vt., Oct. 18, 1796; died at Somerville, Mass., May 27, 1861. He was the first president of Tufts College (1854-61), and was very successful as editor of the Universalist Magazine. He wrote: 'Ancient History of Universalism' (1829) and a hymn-book (1837).

Ballou, Maturin Murray. An American journalist and miscellaneous writer, son of Hosea Ballou; born at Boston, April 14, 1820; died 1895. Besides editing Ballou's Pictorial, The Flag of Our Union, Ballou's Monthly, etc., and making a valuable compilation of quotations, he wrote: 'History of Cuba' (1854); 'Biography of Hosea Ballou'; 'Life Work of Hosea Ballou.' Becoming in later life an extensive traveler, he wrote a number of books

of travel, including: 'Due West'; 'Due South' (1885); 'Due North'; 'Under the Southern Cross'; 'Footprints of Travel'; etc. In 1872 he became one of the founders and the editor-in-chief of the Boston Globe.

Balucki, Michael (bä-löts'kē). A Polish dramatist and novelist; born in Cracow, Sept. 29, 1837. He wrote at first under the pseudonym "Elpidon," and is most popular as a story-teller of satirical tendency, ridiculing the shortcomings and prejudices of Polish society. Of his novels may be mentioned: 'The Awakened' (1864); 'The Old and the Young' (1866); 'Life among Ruins' (1870); 'The Jewess' (1871); 'For Sins not Committed' (1879); '250,000' (1883). The best among his comedies are: 'The Chase after a Man' (1869); 'The Emancipated' (1873); 'Amateur Theatre' (1879); 'The Open House' (1883). He also wrote good lyric poetry, and essays on Polish literature. He died Oct. 17, 1901.

Balzac, Honoré de (bäl-zäk'). The greatest of French novelists; born in Tours, May 16, 1799; died in Paris, Aug. 18, 1850. He gave to his works the general title 'The Human Comedy,' in which are embraced the sub-series: 'Scenes of Private Life,' 27 stories and sketches (among them: 'The Woman of Thirty Years,' 'The Grenadier Woman'); 'Scenes of Paris Life' (among them: 'Père Goriot,' 'César Birotteau,' 'Cousin Betty'); 'Scenes of Political Life'; 'Scenes of Military Life'; and so on. According to Larousse's Dictionary, Balzac's novels amount in all to 97 titles; but this does not include all miscellaneous studies and short stories contributed to periodicals.

Balzac, Jean Louis Guez de. A noted French essayist and letter-writer; born at Angoulême in 1597; died on his estate (Balzac) near there, Feb. 18, 1654. His influence upon French prose is usually compared to that of Malherbes upon poetry; the euphony and symmetry of his phraseology, the elegance of his metaphors, served for a long time as models. Under Richelieu he became royal councilor, and historiographer of France, and was one of the most influential members of the Academy from its foundation, likewise a sort of oracle of the Hôtel Rambouillet. Besides his 'Letters' (1624), which are elaborate epistles with a definite attempt at style, he wrote: 'The Prince' (1631), a glorification of absolute monarchy; 'The Dotard' (1648); 'The Christian Socrates' (1652); and 'Aristippus' (1658), the latter intended to portray the ideal statesman.

Ban, Mathias (bän). A Servian dramatist; born in Ragusa, Dec. 18, 1818. He has been a tutor, journalist, and critic; but his best work was done for the theatre, 'Dobrila and Milenko' being a masterpiece in tragedy, as is in a less degree 'The Muscovite.' His poems, notably 'Odes to the Sultan,' are virile and correct. He died in 1903.

Bancroft, George. An eminent American historian and statesman; born in Worcester, Mass., Oct. 3, 1800; died in Washington, D. C.,

Jan. 17, 1891. After graduation from Harvard in 1817, he studied at Göttingen and Heidelberg. He taught Greek at Harvard; founded the Round Hill School at Northampton, Mass.; was collector of the port of Boston in 1838; and in 1845 was appointed Secretary of the Navy in Polk's Cabinet. His principal literary work is the 'History of the United States,' the first volume of which appeared in 1834. The last revised edition is in 6 volumes (New York, 1884-85). His minor publications include: 'Poems' (Cambridge, 1823); a translation of Heeren's 'Politics of Ancient Greece' (Boston, 1824); 'Literary and Historical Miscellanies' (New York, 1855); and 'Abraham Lincoln,' an address (Washington, 1866).

Bancroft, Hubert Howe. An American historian; born in Granville, Ohio, May 5, 1832. In 1852 he went to California to establish a book business, and began to collect documents, maps, books, and MSS. for a complete 'History of the Pacific States' from Mexico to Alaska. In 1893 this library numbered 60,000 vols. to which many additions have been made. His histories are still in preparation. 'Literary Industries' (vol. 40, San Francisco, 1890) describes his work. He also wrote 'Resources of Mexico'; 'The New Pacific.'

Bandelier, Adolph Francis Alphonse (ban-de-lēr'). A Swiss-American archæologist; born at Bern, Switzerland, Aug. 6, 1840. In the employ of the Archæological Institute of America, he has been engaged in explorations in New Mexico, Arizona, Mexico, and Central and South America. He has written: 'The Art of War and Mode of Warfare' (1877); 'Archæological Tour in Mexico' (1885); etc.; and 'The Delight Makers,' a novel of Pueblo Indian life.

Bandello, Matteo (bän-del'lō). An Italian novelist; born at Castelnuovo, Piedmont, about 1480; died after 1561. In Rome he became a Dominican friar, then entered a monastery in Milan, but led on the whole a roving life, sojourning in various cities and at several of the petty courts of Italy until 1525, when he went to France. Made bishop of Agen by Henry II. in 1550, he resigned that dignity in 1555. His tales, 214 in number, present vivid delineations of the loose manners of those times, and have frequently served as a source to many succeeding story-writers and dramatists; 'Mr. Münchhausen' (1901) 'Uncle Sam, Trustee' (1902); 'Proposal under Difficulties' (1905); 'Alice in Municipaland' (1907).

Bangs, John Kendrick. An American humorist and novelist; born in 1862. He was one of the founders of Life, and he has long been famed for his light verse and humorous stories, among which may be mentioned: 'New Waggings of Old Tales with F. D. Sherman' (Boston, 1887); 'Coffee and Repartee' (New York, 1886); 'Mr. Bonaparte of Corsica' (1895); 'Water Ghost and Other Stories' (1896); 'The Mantel-Piece Minstrels' (1896); 'The Bicyclers and Other Farces' (1896); 'A Houseboat on the Styx' (1896), 'A Rebellious Heroine' (1896), and 'The Pursuit of the Houseboat' (1897).

Banim, John. An Irish novelist, dramatist, and poet; born in Kilkenny, April 3, 1798; died there, Aug. 13, 1842. Removed to Dublin in 1820 to devote himself to literature. His best work is contained in the 'O'Hara Tales' (2 series, London, 1825-27). His chief novels are 'The Nowlans,' 'Boyne Water,' and 'The Croppy.' His brother Michael was associated in his work, and 'The Bit o' Writin' and Other Tales' (1838) is ostensibly a joint composition. A tragedy, 'Damon and Pythias,' was represented in London in 1821.

Banim, Michael. An Irish novelist; born in Kilkenny, Aug. 5, 1796; died in Booterstown, Aug. 30, 1874. He claimed to have written 13 out of the 24 books of fiction confusedly associated with the names of John and Michael Banim, and called himself the author of 'Crohoore of the Bill Hook,' one of the most popular of the 'O'Hara Tales'; 'The Ghost Hunter' (1833); 'Father Connell' (1842); and 'The Town of the Cascades' (2 vols., 1864).

Banks, Louis Albert. An American Methodist minister and religious writer; born in Oregon, 1855. Among his works are: 'The Saloon-Keeper's Ledger,' a series of temperance addresses; 'White Slaves'; 'Honeycombs of Life'; 'The Healing of Souls.'

Banvard, John. An American artist, poet, and dramatist; born in New York about 1820; died 1891. He was best known by his panorama of the Mississippi River, covering three miles of canvas, which was exhibited in the chief cities of Europe and America. He wrote a great number of poems; several plays; 'Banvard, or the Adventures of an Artist' (1849); 'Pilgrimage to the Holy Land' (1852); etc.

Banvard, Joseph. An American Baptist divine and historical writer, brother of the preceding; born in New York, 1810; died 1887. Among his writings were: 'Plymouth and the Pilgrims' (1851); 'Romance of American History' (1852); 'Memoir of Webster' (1853); a historical novel, 'Priscilla' (1854); 'Soldiers and Patriots of the Revolution' (1876); etc.

Banville, Théodore Faullain de (boṅ-vēl'). A French poet and novelist; born at Moulins, March 14, 1823; died in Paris, March 13, 1891. He was the son of a naval officer, and came early in life to Paris, where he devoted himself exclusively to literature, contributed to many journals and reviews, and lived in close friendship with some of the foremost artists and men of letters of the day. First known as a poet through two volumes entitled 'The Caryatides' (1842) and 'The Stalactites' (1846), he established his reputation with the 'Odes Funambulesques' (1857), a sort of great lyrical parody, published under the pseudonym "Bracquemond"; which immediately found great favor, and were followed by 'New Odes Funambulesques' (1868, afterwards reprinted as 'Occidentales')); 'Russian Idyls' (1872); 'Thirty-six Merry Ballads' (1873); etc. His dramatic efforts did not meet with equal success, only 'Gringoire' (1866) holding the stage for some time. As a prose writer he is favorably known by a number of humorous and highly finished tales and sketches, like 'The Poor Mountebanks' (1853); 'The Parisians of Paris' (1866); 'Tales for Women' (1881); 'The Soul of Paris' (1890); etc. Of considerable literary interest are 'My Recollections' (1882); 'Marcelle Rabe' (1891).

Baour-Lormian, Louis Pierre Marie François (bä-ör'lōr-myoṅ'). A French poet and dramatist (1772–1854), who first attracted wide notice through his 'Poems of Ossian' (1801), an extremely clever imitation of Caledonian verse; and afterwards won success with a tragedy, 'Omasis, or Joseph in Egypt' (1807). Of his other works may be mentioned: 'Political and Moral Vigils' (1811), in the manner of Young; 'Duranti, or The League in the Province' (1828), a historical novel; and 'Legends, Ballads, and Fabliaux' (1829). But his best work is probably a poetical translation of the Book of Job, completed after he had lost his eyesight.

Baralt, Rafael Maria (bä-rält'). A Venezuelan poet and historian; born in Maracaibo, Venezuela, July 2, 1814; died in Madrid, Jan. 2, 1860. He was educated in Bogotá and at Caracas; served in the Venezuelan army, and went to Spain in 1843, where he held posts of honor and attained literary fame. He wrote: 'Ancient and Modern History of Venezuela' (1841); and 'Odes to Columbus and to Spain.'

Barante, Aimable Guillaume Prosper Brugière, Baron de (bär-änt'). A French historian and statesman; born in Riom, Auvergne, June 10, 1782; died at his estate near Thiers, Nov. 22, 1866. In politics he was usually Legitimist, but his public career on the whole was a failure. In letters his achievements are: 'View of French Literature in the Eighteenth Century' (8th ed. 1857); 'History of the Valois Dukes of Burgundy, 1364 1477' (8th ed. 1858), this being his masterpiece; 'Story of Joan of Arc' (4th ed. 1880); and various works on periods of the great French Revolution.

Barattani, Felipe (bär-ät-ä'nē). An Italian poet and dramatist; born at Filottrano, Ancône, March 1, 1825. He has won most applause for 'Lyric Tragedies' (1858), in which his poetical capacities are most happily exploited; 'Stella' (1866), a drama in verse; and 'The Sons of Alexander VI.,' a powerful metrical play.

Baratynsky, Jevgén; Abrámovich (bä-rä-tin'skē). A Russian poet (1800–44); served in the army, and afterwards lived on an estate near Moscow until 1843, when he set out to travel; the year following he suddenly died in Naples. His best-known works are: 'Eda' (1826), a delineation of Finland character and nature; and 'The Gipsy,' a picture from Russian high life.

Barbauld, Anna Lætitia. An English poet and essayist; born in Kibworth-Harcourt, Leicestershire, in 1743; died in Stoke Newington, March 9, 1825. She was the daughter of the Rev. John Aikin, and in 1774 married the Rev. Rochemont Barbauld. She was well educated, and numbered among her friends many famous authors, including Sir Walter Scott and Wordsworth. Her first poems (1773) went through four editions in one year. She wrote: 'Early Lessons for Children' (about 1774); 'Devotional Pieces,' (1775); 'Hymns in Prose for Children' (1776), translated in many languages; 'Eighteen Hundred and Eleven,' her longest effort (1811); and prepared an edition of the best English novels in fifty volumes.

Barbey d'Aurévilly, Jules (bär-bā' dō re vē-yē). A French critic and novelist; born at Saint-Sauveur-le-Vicomte, Manche, Nov. 2, 1808; died in Paris, April 24, 1889. As a contributor to the Pays in Paris, where he settled in 1851, he created a sensation by the unreserved tone and peculiar style of his literary criticisms; in 1858 he founded the Réveil with Granier de Cassagnac and Escudier. Works: 'On Dandyism and G. Brummel' (1845); 'The Prophets of the Past' (1851); 'Goethe and Diderot' (1880); 'Polemics of Yesterday' (1889); 'Nineteenth Century: The Works and the Men' (1861–92). Of his novels the best are: 'The Bewitched' (1854); and 'The Chevalier des Touches' (1864).

Barbier, Henri Auguste (bär-bē-ā). A French poet; born in Paris, April 29, 1805; died at Nice, Feb. 13, 1882. He studied law, but followed his inclination for literature: and having first written a historical novel (1830, with Royer), depicting French mediæval society, was led, through the July revolution, to enter his proper sphere, that of the poetical satire; in which he obtained a brilliant success with 'The Iambes' (1831, 31st ed. 1882), a series of poignant satires, political and social, lashing the moral depravity of the higher classes,—notably the ignoble scramble for office under the new government, the subject of 'The Quarry' the most famous among these satires. His next works, 'Lamentation' (1833), bewailing the misfortunes of Italy, and 'Lazarus' (1837), in which he describes the misery of the English and Irish laborer, show a considerable falling off; and in those that followed, the poet of 'The Iambes' is scarcely to be recognized. He was elected to the Academy in 1869.

Barbier, Jules. A French dramatist; born in Paris, March 8, 1822. Having won success with his first effort, 'A Poet' (1847), a drama in verse, he produced 'The Shades of Molière' (1847); 'André Chenier' (1849); 'Willy Nilly,' a comedy (1849); and thereafter in collaboration, mostly with Michel Carré, a number of dramas and vaudevilles, also many librettos for comic operas. After the war of 1870–71 he published 'The Sharpshooter, War Songs' (1871), a collection of patriotic poems; and later two other volumes of lyrics, 'The Sheaf' (1882) and 'Faded Flowers' (1890); besides 'Plays in Verse' (1879). Died Jan., 1901.

Barbiera, Raphaël (bärb-yä´rä). An Italian poet and journalist; born in Venice, 1851. His contributions to periodical literature are particularly valuable, and a volume of ' Poems' has been received with pleasure, while works on Italian literature and numerous anthologies indicate good taste, ' The Calendar of the Muses' (1888) being an instance.

Barbieri, Giuseppe (bär-bē-ā´rē). An Italian poet and pulpit orator; born in Bassano, 1783; died at Padua in 1852. He was distinguished for the tasteful eloquence of his sermons. In ' Little Poems,' ' Sermons on Feast Days,' and ' The Euganean Hills,' he displays the resources of his well-stored mind with the utmost elegance.

Barbour, John. A Scottish poet; born about 1316; died in Aberdeen, March 13, 1395. He was educated, it is thought, at Oxford and Paris; and was a clerk in the King's household. Barbour is one of the most ancient poets of Scotland; and his great epic, ' The Bruce,' tells the story of Robert Bruce and the battle of Bannockburn. It was written in 1375 and brought him favor from the King. First printed in Edinburgh in 1571; best modern edition by Skeat (Early Eng. Text Soc'y). He also wrote ' Legends of the Saints,' of 33,533 verses; and a fragment on the Trojan war.

Barclay, Alexander. A British author; born about 1475; died in Croydon, June 1552. The best authorities call him a Scotchman, and suppose him to have been educated at either Cambridge or Oxford, or possibly at both those universities. He traveled extensively, spoke many languages, and was long a priest in the College of Ottery St. Mary in Devonshire. Afterward he was a priest and monk of Ely, and joined the Franciscans at Canterbury. His ' Eclogues,' undated but written at Ely, are the first in the English language. Of more value is his translation (1509) of Sebastian Brandt's ' Ship of Fools,' which had appeared in Basel in 1494. It had great influence on English literature.

Barclay, John. A Scottish poet; born in Pont-à-Mousson, France, Jan 28, 1582; died in Rome, Aug. 12, 1621. Educated in the Jesuit college of his native town; went to England in 1603, and attained the favor of James I. He wrote important books in Latin. ' Argenis,' a romance (Paris, 1621), unites classical with modern fiction. Fénélon was indebted to it for ' Telemachus.' It has always won the admiration of literary men, especially Richelieu and Coleridge. Another romance, ' Satyricon' (London, 1603), partly autobiographical, attacks the Jesuits and Puritans. Other works include: ' Sylvæ,' Latin poems (1606); ' Apologia' (1611), and ' Icon Animorum' (1614).

Baretti, Giuseppe Marcantonio (bä-ret´tē). An Italian critic and poet (1719–89), who, after a roaming life in Italy, settled in London in 1751, whither he returned again about 1766, having left England in 1760 and founded

in Venice the critical periodical Frusta· Letteraria (Literary Scourge), which contained his most important work and is considered as epoch-making in Italian literature. Of his writings in English, the ' Account of the Manners and Customs of Italy' (1768–69) attracted much attention. His ' Dictionary of the English and Italian Languages' (1760, lately 1873) is still highly esteemed.

Barham, Richard Harris. An English poet; born in Canterbury, Dec. 6, 1788; died in London, June 17, 1845. He was educated at St. Paul's and Oxford; took orders in 1813; was rector of two country churches, and later of one in London. Under the name of " Thomas Ingoldsby " he wrote the ' Ingoldsby Legends,' prose and verse (London, 1840–47), which were accorded a high place in humorous literature, and are now classics. He also wrote: ' My Cousin Nicholas,' a novel (1841); and ' Life of Theodore Hook' (1849).

Baring-Gould, Sabine. An English antiquary and novelist; born in Exeter in 1834. He graduated from Cambridge in 1856, and has been since 1881 rector of Lew-Trenchard in Devon. He is author of ' Iceland: Its Scenes and Sagas' (1864); ' The Book of Werewolves' (1865); ' Curious Myths of the Middle Ages' (series 1 and 2, 1866–67); ' Lives of the Saints' (1872–79); ' Yorkshire Oddities' (2 vols., 1874); and ' Germany Past and Present' (2 vols., 1879). He has written religious books, and of late years novels which have become popular. They include: ' Mehalah: a Story of the Salt Marshes' (2 vols., London, 1880); ' John Herring' (2 vols., 1883); ' Red Spider' (1887); ' Grettis the Outlaw' (1890); and ' The Broom Squire' (1896).

Barker, Matthew Henry. An English novelist; born at Deptford in 1790; died in London, June 29, 1846. He followed the sea, and under the name of " The Old Sailor " wrote spirited sea tales, very popular in their day. They include: ' Land and Sea Tales' (London, 1836); ' Life of Nelson' (1836); ' Topsailsheet Blocks' (3 vols., 1838; new ed. 1881); and ' The Victory, or the Wardroom Mess' (1844).

Barlæus or **Baerle, Kaspar van** (bär-lī´üs). A Dutch poet, historian, and learned writer; born in Antwerp, Feb. 12, 1584; died in Amsterdam, Jan. 14, 1648. His ' Poems,' mostly Latin, are not fiery, but his ' History of Brazil under Maurice of Nassau' is decidedly so; and he composed also numerous fine orations, the influence he exercised upon thought being very considerable.

Barlow, Jane. An Irish poet and storywriter; born in county Dublin about 1857. She is the daughter of Prof. Barlow of Dublin University, a writer of historical and philosophical works. Her popular books include: ' Irish Idylls' (1892); ' Bogland Studies'; ' Kerrigan's Quality'; ' Walled Out, or Eschatology in a Bog'; ' The Mockers of the Shallow Waters' (1893); ' Strangers at Lisconnel' (1895).

Barlow, Joel. An American poet and statesman; born in Reading, Conn., March 24, 1754; died near Cracow, Poland, Dec. 24, 1812. He published political works and poems, which contain many philosophical and political dissertations. 'The Vision of Columbus' (Hartford, 1787) was extended into 'The Columbiad,' a long epic (Phila., 1807). He also wrote 'The Conspiracy of Kings' (London, 1792); and the celebrated poem 'Hasty Pudding.'

Barnard, Lady Ann. A Scotch poet; born at Lindsay in Fifeshire, 1750; died 1825. She is famous for 'Auld Robin Gray,' a ballad which has attained great popularity throughout Scotland. She also wrote other poems.

Barnard, Charles. An American dramatist; born in Boston, Mass., Feb. 13, 1838. He is a journalist and dramatist. His most popular play is 'The County Fair' (1888). Author of 'The Tone-Masters' (New York, 1871); 'Knights of To-day' (1881); 'The Whistling Buoy' (1887); dramas, and books on gardening and electricity.

Barnard, Henry. A prominent American educator; born at Hartford, Conn., Jan. 24, 1811. He was president of the University of Wisconsin (1856–59) and St. John's College, Annapolis, Md. (1865–66); founded the American Journal of Education (1855); was United States Commissioner of Education (1867–70). Among his numerous writings may be named: 'Hints and Methods for Teachers' (1857); 'Pestalozzi and Pestalozzianism' (1861); 'German Educational Reformers' (1862). D. 1900.

Barnard, John. A noted American Congregational divine; born at Boston, Nov. 6, 1681; died at Marblehead, Mass., Jan. 24, 1770. He was one of the earliest New England dissenters from Calvinism. Ordained colleague minister of Marblehead (1716); he took great interest in the local fisheries and commerce. He wrote 'History of the Strange Adventures of Philip Ashton' (1725), etc.

Barnes, Albert. An American Presbyterian minister and religious writer; born at Rome, N. Y., Dec. 1, 1798; died at Philadelphia, Dec. 24, 1870. For thirty-seven years pastor of the First Presbyterian Church in Philadelphia; he was best known by his 'Notes' on the New Testament (of which over a million volumes are said to have circulated), Isaiah, Job, Psalms, etc. He wrote also 'The Church and Slavery' (1857); 'Life at Threescore and Ten' (1869); etc. His heterodox views caused the formation of the New School of Presbyterian theology (1837).

Barnes, Barnabe. An English poet; born in Yorkshire about 1569; died in St. Mary-le-Bow, Durham, in December 1609. He was the son of the Bishop of Durham; was educated at Oxford; and went to Normandy in 1591 with the Earl of Essex. His fame rests on a collection of sonnets, madrigals, and odes, called 'Parthenophil and Parthenope' (London, about 1593). Other books: 'A Divine Century of Spiritual Sonnets' (1595); and 'The Devil's Charter,' a tragedy (1607).

Barnes, William. An English poet and philologist; born in Dorsetshire, Feb. 22, 1800; died in Winterbourne Came, in October 1886. He wrote many books on philology; and three series of 'Poems of Rural Life in the Dorsetshire Dialect' (London, 1844, 1846, and 1863), and 'Poems of Rural Life' (1866). His "fad" was the disuse of all but the Anglo-Saxon elements of the English language.

Barni, Jules Romain (bär-nē). A French scholar and philosophical writer and critic; born in Lille, June 1, 1818; died in Mers, dept. Somme, July 4, 1878. His efforts to propagate the Kantian philosophy through the medium of 'Observations on the Sense of the Sublime and Beautiful' (1836), 'Foundations of Ethical Metaphysic' (1848), and 'Kantian Philosophy' (1850), earned him distinction; as did also, in another but contiguous field, a 'History of Moral and Political Ideas in France in the Eighteenth Century' (1866).

Barnum, Mrs. Frances Courtenay (Baylor). An American novelist; born in Arkansas, 1848. Her home is in Savannah. She has written: 'On Both Sides,' an international novel; 'Behind the Blue Ridge'); 'Juan and Juanita,' a story for boys and girls; 'Claudia Hyde.' She has also been a frequent contributor to magazines, and a writer of short stories.

Barnum, Phineas Taylor. A famous American showman; born at Bethel, Conn., July 5, 1810; died at Bridgeport, Conn., April 7, 1891. After various unsuccessful business ventures, he finally established Barnum's Museum in New York (1841), which was twice burned. He introduced Tom Thumb, Jenny Lind, Commodore Nutt, Admiral Dot, the Woolly Horse, Jumbo, etc., to the American public. In 1871 he established his great circus. He was mayor of Bridgeport, and four times member of the Connecticut Legislature. His benefactions were large and frequent. He wrote: 'Humbugs of the World' (1865); 'Struggles and Triumphs' (1869); 'Lion Jack, a Story' (1876); 'Autobiography' (1855, new editions 1869 and later). He was a lecturer on temperance and other popular subjects.

Barr, Amelia Edith. An Anglo-American novelist; born in Ulverton, Lancashire, England, March 29, 1831. She was the daughter of the Rev. William Huddleston, and in 1850 married Robert Barr. She came to America in 1854, and lived for some years in Texas; but after her husband's death removed to New York, where her first book, 'Romance and Reality,' was published in 1872. She is a prolific writer, and her novels are very popular. They include: 'Jan Vedder's Wife' (New York, 1885); 'A Daughter of Fife' (1885); 'A Bow of Orange Ribbon' (1886); 'A Border Shepherdess' (1887); 'Friend Olivia' (1890).

Barr, Robert. A Scottish author; born in Glasgow about 1855. He spent his childhood in Canada, drifted into journalism, joined the staff of Detroit Free Press, and wrote under the name of «Luke Sharp.» He went to London in 1881 and founded The Idler with Jerome K. Jerome, but retired to devote himself to fiction. He is author of a number of novels : ‹In the Midst of Alarms› (1894) ; ‹The Face and the Mask› (1895) ; ‹One Day's Court- ship› (1896) ; ‹A Woman Intervenes› (1896); and others.

Barracand, Léon Henri (bär-ä-kän). A French poet and novelist; born at Romans, Drôme, May 2, 1844. He gave up the law when a very young man in order to write verses; but he was not much known as a poet until ‹Dananiel› (1886) appeared, under the pseudonym of «Léon Grandet,» followed by a sequel, ‹Doctor Gal› (1870). He had already, however, attracted attention by some fictions, and has steadily risen in importance as a nov- elist; — ‹Yolande› (1867) ; ‹Hilaire Gervais› (1885) ; ‹The Second Lieutenant's Manuscript› (1887); and ‹The Cousin› (1888), being per- haps best known. His ‹Lamartine and the Muse› (1883) was crowned by the French Academy.

Barrantes, Vicente (bär-rän′tes). A Span- ish miscellaneous writer, novelist, and poet; born at Badajoz, March 24, 1829. He first stud- ied theology, but in 1848 settled in Madrid to pursue literature ; held responsible government offices ; became member of the Academy in 1872. Among his works are the stories ‹Al- ways Late› (1851) ; ‹Juan de Padilla›; ‹The Widow of Padilla›; and a series of historical studies, dealing with strictly local Philippine Island and Estremaduran topics. His ‹Tales and Legends› are well chosen and well writ- ten; but a work on ‹The Defects and Dangers of Universal Suffrage,› partly fiction and partly satire, is weak.

Barrès, Maurice (bär-äs′). A French nov- elist and publicist; born at Charmes-sur-Mo- selle, Aug. 17, 1862. His political career has been successful, but less important than his work in literature, being conspicuous in the «decadent» school owing to his fictions: ‹Under the Eye of the Barbarians,› a study in egoism; ‹The Sensation of Paris›; and ‹The Latin Quarter› (all in 1888), in all of which the artificialities of an over-refined culture are apparent.

Barrett, Benjamin Fisk. An American Swe- denborgian theologian; born at Dresden, Me., June 24, 1808; died at Germantown, Pa., Aug. 6, 1892. Settled in Philadelphia, he edited the New Church Monthly and founded the Swe- denborgian Publication Society in 1885. He wrote a number of works on Swedenborgian- ism, including a ‹Life of Swedenborg›; ‹Swe- denborg and Channing›; etc.

Barrie, James Matthew. A Scottish author; born in Kirriemuir, Forfarshire, May 9, 1860. He graduated from Edinburgh University in 1882, and went to London in 1885 to engage in journalism. His peculiar talent for depicting

Scottish village life and rustic characters with fidelity, pathos, humor, and poetic charm, has brought him fame. ‹Better Dead› (1887) and ‹When a Man's Single› (1888) were followed by ‹Auld Licht Idylls› (1888) and ‹A Win- dow in Thrums› (1889), which first made him widely known; ‹An Edinburgh Eleven› (1890); ‹My Lady Nicotine,› humorous essays on smoking (1890) ; ‹The Little Minister› (1891) ; ‹Sentimental Tommy› (1896) ; ‹Margaret Ogilvy› (1896), a biography of his mother. He has also written numerous short sketches and three comedies: ‹Walker, London› (1892); ‹Jane Annie› (1893); and ‹The Professor's Love Story.›

Barrière, Jean François (bä-rē-är′). A French historical writer; born in Paris, May 12, 1786; died there, Aug. 22, 1868. His ener- gies were first directed to periodical literature ; but he subsequently produced ‹The Court and the City under Louis XIV., Louis XV., and Louis XVI.,› besides editing a numerous series of memoirs of personages connected with the Grand Monarch.

Barrière, Théodore (bä-rē-är′). A French dramatist, born in Paris, 1823; died there, Oct. 16, 1877. In collaboration with others he sup- plied the French stage with a great number of dramas and comedies, some of which met with much favor, especially ‹Bohemian Life› (1848, with Murger) ; ‹The Maids of Marble› (1853, with Thiboust), a counterpart to Dumas's ‹La Dame aux Camélias› ; and ‹The Spurious Men of Honor› (1856, with Capendu), a scath- ing satire and his masterpiece.

Barrili, Antonio Giulio (bär-rē′lē). An Ital- ian novelist; born in Savona, 1836. Engaging in journalism when only eighteen, he assumed the management of Il Movimento in 1860, and became proprietor and editor of Il Caffaro in Genoa in 1872. He had taken part in the cam- paigns of 1859 and 1866 (with Garibaldi in Ty- rol) and in the Roman expedition of 1867, and sat in the Chamber of Deputies in 1876–79. One of the most prolific writers of modern Italy. Among his numerous stories are : ‹Elm- tree and Ivy› (1868) ; ‹The Vale of Olives› (1871) ; ‹As in a Dream› ; ‹The Devil's Portrait› (1882) ; ‹The Eleventh Commandment›; ‹A Whimsical Wooing› (the last three translated into English and published by Geo. Gotts- berger Peck, New York).

Barros, João de (bär′rös). The foremost Portuguese historian; born at Vizeu, 1496; died near Lisbon, Oct. 20, 1570. His principal work, ‹Asia,› a history of Portuguese discover- ies and conquests in East India, 1415–1539, was afterwards continued by Diogo de Couto. He also wrote the ‹Chronicle of Emperor Clari- mundo,› a historical romance, distinguished for great beauty of style.

Barrow, Frances Elizabeth (Mease). An American author ; born in Charleston, S. C., Feb. 22, 1822 ; died in New York, May 7, 1894. She was educated in New York, where she was married to James Barrow. She wrote under the name of «Aunt Fanny» numerous books for children; among them 'Six Nightcaps,' which has been translated into French, German, and Swedish. Another, 'The Letter G' (1864), was widely known and very popular. She also wrote a novel, 'The Wife's Stratagem.'

Barrow, Sir John. A notable English writer on travels; born at Dragley Beck, Lancashire, June 19, 1764; died in London, Nov. 23, 1848. His numerous and extended journeys are recounted in 'Travels to China,' 'Voyage to Cochin-China,' 'Travels in the Interior of Southern Africa,' and various diaries, with an accuracy beyond question, and a conscientious devotion to science equaled only by the modesty of his own disparagement of the results of his investigations.

Barrows, John Henry. An American Presbyterian minister, president of Oberlin College; born at Medina, Mich., July 11, 1847; died at Oberlin, Mich., June 2, 1902. He wrote: 'The Gospels are True Histories' (1891); 'Henry Ward Beecher, the Pulpit Jupiter' (1893); 'Life of Henry Ward Beecher'; etc.

Barry, John Daniel. An American novelist; born 1866. He has written: 'A Daughter of Thespis'; 'The Intriguers'; 'Mademoiselle Blanche'; 'The Princess Margarethe, a Fairy Tale'; 'The Leading Woman; Our Best Society.'

Barthélemy, Auguste Marseille (bär-tāl-mē'). A French satirist; born in Marseilles, 1796; died there, Aug. 23, 1867. In collaboration with his friend, Joseph Méry, he wrote several satirical epics, directed against the Bourbon dynasty, which appealed to a large circle of readers. The great historical epic 'Napoleon in Egypt' (1828) describes the poetical side of that wonderful campaign with great skill.

Barthélemy, Jean Jacques. A French antiquarian; born at Cassis, Provence, Jan. 20, 1716; died in Paris, April 30, 1795. He won European fame with his 'Travels of Young Anacharsis in Greece' (1788), a fascinating picture of domestic and social life in ancient Greece, which was translated into many languages, into English by Beaumont (1791). As a romancer he tried his hand with 'The Loves of Carites and Polydorus' (1760), purporting to be translated from the Greek.

Barthélemy-Saint-Hilaire, Jules (bär-tāl-mē' sañ-te-lär'). A French scholar and man of letters; born in Paris, Aug. 19, 1805; died there Nov. 25, 1895. He wrote for leading periodicals, and his best-known work is probably the 'Commentary on Aristotle' (1837-70). He also published: 'The Vedas' (1854); 'Mahomet and the Koran' (1865); and 'Philosophy in Relation to Science and Religion' (1889).

Barthet, Armand (bär-tā'). A French poet and novelist (1820-74), best remembered as the author of 'The Sparrow of Lesbia' (1849), a comedy in verse, written for the famous Rachel.

Bartlett, John. An American publisher and compiler of books of reference; born at Plymouth, Mass., June 14, 1820. Since 1878 a member of the publishing-house of Little, Brown & Co., Boston. He has compiled: 'Familiar Quotations' (1855), a ninth edition of which appeared in 1891; 'The Shakspere Phrase Book' (1881); 'A Shakspere Concordance' (1894), etc. Died Dec. 3, 1905.

Bartlett, John Russell. An American author; born in Providence, R. I., Oct. 23, 1805; died there, May 28, 1886. He was Secretary of State of Rhode Island from 1855 to 1872. Besides many books of local interest, he prepared a 'Dictionary of Americanisms,' which is widely known as a work of reference.

Bartlett, Samuel Colcord. American educator and Congregational divine; born at Salisbury, N. H., Nov. 25, 1817; died at Hanover, N.H., Dec. 16, 1898. Was president of Dartmouth College (1877-92). He wrote 'From Egypt to Palestine' (1879), and several religious works.

Bartók, Ludwig von (bär-tōk'). A Hungarian poet and dramatist; born in 1851. He is widely known as a versifier of taste, 'Carpathian Songs' being his happiest verse. As a playwright he is even more distinguished; the comedy of 'The Most Beautiful' (1880), and the historical tragedy 'Margareta Kendi,' as well as 'Anna Thuran,' a historical drama, having been frequently acted.

Bartol, Cyrus Augustus (bär-tol'). An American Unitarian divine and essayist; born at Freeport, Me., April 30, 1813; died in Boston, Dec. 16, 1900. He was prominent as a radical in religious thought, and pastor of the West Church, Boston, after 1861. He has written: 'Pictures of Europe' (1855); 'Radical Problems' (1872); and several ethical and religious works.

Bartoli, Adolfo (bär-tō'lē). An Italian historian of literature; born in Fivizzano, Nov. 19, 1833. He has long been a recognized arbiter of taste and the elegancies in connection with his country's literature; his 'First Two Centuries of Italian Literature' (1870-80) and 'History of Italian Literature' (1878-89) being masterpieces. He died May 16, 1894.

Barton, Bernard. An English poet; born in Carlisle, Jan. 31, 1784; died in Woodbridge, Feb. 19, 1849. Educated at a Quaker school in Ipswich. He is called the «Quaker Poet,» and is best known because of his friendship with Charles Lamb. His life was spent in Woodbridge. He published many volumes of verse, now neglected. They include: 'Metrical Effusions' (London, 1812); 'Devotional Verses' (1826); and 'Household Verses' (1845).

Bartram, John (bär'tram). A celebrated American botanist; born in Chester county, Pa., March 23, 1699; died at Kingsessing, near Philadelphia, Pa., Sept. 22, 1777. He was called the «father of American botany,» and founded at Kingsessing the first botanical garden in America. Linnæus termed him «the greatest natural botanist in the world.» He published

'Observations on the Inhabitants, Climate, Soil, Diverse Productions, Animals, etc., made in his travels from Pennsylvania to Lake Ontario,' and a similar volume on eastern Florida (1766).

Bascom, John. An American educator and philosophical writer; born at Geneva, N. Y., 1827. He was president of the University of Wisconsin (1874-87). He has written a number of philosophical works, among them: 'Philosophy of English Literature' (1874), lectures before the Lowell Institute; 'Comparative Psychology' (1878); 'Sociology' (1887), etc.

Basedow or **Bassedau** (bäs'ĕ-dou). A celebrated German pedagogue; born in Hamburg, Sept. 11, 1723; died in Magdeburg, July 25, 1790. He became one of the most acute thinkers of his day, the problem of education enlisting his intellectual powers particularly; and in the famous 'Elementary Treatise' (1774), he inaugurated a pedagogical revolution, the work being analogous to that of Comenius in the 'Pictured (or Painted) World.' The German, however, was strictly scientific and modern, the numerous works he subsequently prepared being elaborations of the original treatise, and all of vital importance in the history of education.

Bashkirtseff, Marie (bäsh-kērts'ef). A Russian author; born in Russia in 1860; died in Paris in 1884. She came of a noble and wealthy family, went to Italy to study singing, and to Paris to study art. Her fame rests on her private 'Journal,' which seems to have been written with ultimate publication in view.

Basile, Giovan Batista (bä-sēl'ĕ), Count of Torone. An Italian poet and writer of fairy tales; died before 1634. His most prominent works are written in Neopolitan dialect, of which they are the most valuable literary monument. 'The Pentameron' (1637) is a collection of 50 folk-tales, distributed over five days, which became a great favorite and was widely translated.

Basselin or **Bachelin, Olivier** (bäs-laṅ'). A French poet, born in the Val-de-Vire, Normandy, about 1350; died there (?) about 1419. His career has been investigated with some pains because of the assertion that the vocabulary of theatrical and poetical literature is indebted to him for the word "vaudeville"; it would appear he was a cloth fuller or presser, with a mill in his native vale, which brought him in quite a revenue. He was much given to versified narration and iteration of convivial themes, in rhymed fragments dubbed vaux-de-vire in honor of the poet's purlieus. In the 'Book of New Songs and Vaux-de-Vire' (1610) appears a collection of these Bacchanalian stanzas, the most touching of which is addressed by the singer 'To My Nose,' the rubescence thereof being tastefully and exquisitely celebrated.

Bassett, James (bas'et). A Presbyterian missionary in Persia; born at Glenford, near Hamilton, Canada, Jan. 31, 1834. He served in the Civil War, 1862-63. A missionary in Persia since 1871, he wrote a volume of hymns in Persian (Teheran, 1875 and 1884). Among his other works are: 'Among the Turcomans' (1880); 'Persia, the Land of the Imam' (1886). The establishment of a U. S. legation in Persia was largely owing to his efforts and writings.

Bastiat, Frederic (bäst-yä'). A French political economist; born at Bayonne, 1801; died at Rome, 1850. He is most celebrated for the 'Economic Harmonies' (1849). For a long time he edited the great economic journal Libre Échange, and strove to spread free-trade doctrines. 'On the Influence of French and English tariffs on the Future of the Two Nations' is one of his free-trade studies, and he also wrote various manuals of political economy.

Bates, Arlo. An American author; born in East Machias, Me., Dec. 16, 1850. He graduated from Bowdoin in 1876, when he engaged in literary work in Boston. He is now professor of English literature at the Institute of Technology. He is author of poems and novels, including: 'The Pagans' (New York, 1884); 'A Lad's Love'; 'The Wheel of Fire' (1885); 'The Philistines' (1888); 'Berries of the Brier' (1886), poems; 'Talks on Writing English'; and 'Talks on the Study of Literature' (1897); 'Love in a Cloud' (1900); 'The Diary of a Saint' (1901).

Bates, Charlotte Fiske. An American poet and miscellaneous prose-writer; born in New York city, Nov. 30, 1838. She was educated in Cambridge, Mass., where she still resides. She assisted Longfellow in compiling 'Poems of Places'; edited the 'Cambridge Book of Poetry and Song' (Boston, 1882); has contributed to magazines and has published 'Risk and Other Poems' (1879); 'The Art and Literature of Business.'

Bates, Clara Doty. An American author; born in Ann Arbor, Mich., 1838; died 1895. She lived in Chicago and published many juvenile books. Also 'From Heart's Content' (Chicago, 1892).

Bates, Mrs. Harriet Leonora (Vose), better known as "Eleanor Putnam." An American story and sketch writer, wife of Arlo Bates; born 1856; died 1886. She wrote: 'A Woodland Wooing'; 'Old Salem' (1886); with her husband, 'Prince Vance'; etc.

Bates, Katharine Lee. An American story-writer, poet, and educator; born in Falmouth, Mass., Aug. 12, 1859. She fills the chair of English literature in Wellesley College; has edited collections of ballads, etc.; has written juvenile stories, including 'Rose and Thorn' (Boston, 1889); also 'The English Religious Drama' (New York, 1893); and 'The College Beautiful and Other Poems' (1887); 'Tennyson's Princess'.

Baudelaire, Charles (bōd-lâr'). A French poet and critic; born in Paris, April 9, 1821; died there, Aug. 31, 1867. His works include a translation of Poe (1856); the collection of poems 'Flowers of Evil' (1857); 'Théophile Gautier' (1859); 'Artificial Paradises, Opium and Hashish' (1860); 'Little Prose Poems'; besides essays and sketches.

Baudissin, Wolf Heinrich, Count von (bou'-dis-sēn). A German littérateur (1789–1878), one of the chief contributors to the famous German translation of Shakespeare edited by Schlegel and Tieck, of which he rendered: 'Comedy of Errors'; 'Love's Labour's Lost'; 'All's Well that Ends Well'; 'Taming of the Shrew'; 'Much Ado about Nothing'; 'Merry Wives of Windsor'; 'Measure for Measure'; 'Titus Andronicus'; 'King Lear'; 'Antony and Cleopatra'; 'Troilus and Cressida', 'Othello'; and 'Henry VIII.' Under the title 'Ben Jonson and his School' (1836) he published translations of old English dramas.

Bauer, Bruno (bour). A German biblical critic and scholar; born in Eisenberg, Sept. 9, 1809; died in Rixdorf, April 13, 1882. He has carried the "new movement" in rational theology very far, his 'Critical Exposition of the Religion of the Old Testament' (1838) and 'Critique of the Gospels' (1850) being extreme in their various expositions.

Bauer, Klara. See **Detlef.**

Bäuerle, Adolf (boi'er-le). An Austrian dramatist and novelist (1784–1859), who cultivated with much success the field of popular comedy and local farce in Vienna, where in 1804 he founded the Vienna Theatre-Gazette, until 1847 the most widely read paper in the Austrian monarchy and now a valuable source for the history of the stage in Vienna. Of his numerous plays the following became known also outside of Austria: 'Leopold's Day' (1814); 'The Enchanted Prince' (1818); 'The Counterfeit Prima Donna' (1818); 'A Deuce of a Fellow' (1820); 'The Friend in Need.' Under the pseudonym "Otto Horn" he wrote the novels 'Therese Krones' (1855) and 'Ferdinand Raimund' (1855), full of the personal element and local anecdote.

Bauernfeld, Eduard von (bou'ern fold). An Austrian dramatist; born in Vienna, Jan. 13, 1802; died there, Aug. 9, 1890. He studied law and entered the government service in 1826, but resigned after the revolutionary events of 1848, to devote himself exclusively to his literary pursuits. A brilliant conversationalist, he soon became a universal favorite in Vienna society. Intimate from childhood with the genial painter Moritz von Schwind and the composer Franz Schubert, he also kept up a lifelong intercourse with Grillparzer. Among his comedies, distinguished for their subtle dialogue and sprightly humor, particularly the descriptions of fashionable society have made his great reputation. The best-known and most successful were: 'Reckless from Love' (1831); 'Love's Protocol' (1831); 'Confessions' (1834); 'Domestic and Romantic' (1835); 'Of Age' (1846); 'The Categorical Imperative' (1851); 'From Society' (1866); 'Modern Youth' (1868).

Baumbach, Rudolf (boum'bäch). A German poet; born at Kranichfeld, Saxe-Meiningen,

Sept. 28, 1840. After studying natural science in Würzburg, Leipsic, Freiburg, and Heidelberg, he lived as a tutor in Austria, last at Trieste (since 1870), where he devoted himself afterwards exclusively to writing. In 1885 he returned to Meiningen. He has most successfully cultivated the poetical tale, based upon ancient popular legends. Epics: 'Zlatorog,' a Slovenic Alpine legend (1875, 37th ed. 1892); 'Horand and Hilda' (1879); 'Lady Fair' (1881); 'The Godfather of Death' (1884); 'Emperor Max and his Huntsmen' (1888). Lyrics: 'Songs of a Traveling Journeyman' (1878); 'Minstrel's Songs' (1882); 'From the Highway' (1882); 'Traveling Songs from the Alps' (1883); 'Adventures and Pranks Imitated from Old Masters' (1883); 'Jug and Inkstand' (1887); 'Thuringian Songs' (1891). He is also an excellent prose-writer, author of 'False Gold' (1878), a historical romance of the 17th century; 'Summer Legends' (1881); 'Once upon a Time' (1889); 'New Fairy Tales' (1894).

Baur, Ferdinand Christian (bour). A German theologian of eminence; born in Schmiden, near Stuttgart, June 21, 1792; died at Tübingen, Dec. 2, 1860. The profundity not only of his learning but of his intellectual insight made him the founder of a new school of theology, the classics of which are his 'History of the Doctrine of the Atonement' (1838) and 'The Christian Dogma of the Trinity and Incarnation' (1843), although every one of his numerous works is of great authority.

Baxter, Richard. A celebrated English divine and author; born at Rowton, Shropshire, Nov. 12, 1615; died in London, Dec. 8, 1691. His early education was neglected, and he was never a student at any university, but by private study became eminent for learning. Among his numerous works, the most celebrated is 'The Saints' Everlasting Rest,' published in 1650.

Baxter, Sylvester. An American journalist and magazinist; born in Massachusetts, 1850. Attached to the Boston Herald, he has been prominent in pushing the metropolitan park system and advocating a "Greater Boston." He has written 'The Cruise of a Land Yacht, a Boy's Book of Mexican Travel'; 'Old Marblehead.'

Baxter, William. An American clergyman, educator, poet, and novelist; born at Leeds, England, 1820. President of Arkansas College, Fayetteville; when it was burned in the Civil War, he removed to Cincinnati. He has written: 'The Loyal West in the Time of the Rebellion'; 'Pea Ridge and Prairie Grove, or Scenes and Incidents of the War in Arkansas' (1864). His 'War Lyrics,' originally published in Harper's Weekly, were very popular at the time of their publication.

Bayard, Jean François Alfred (bā'ard or bä-yär'). A French dramatist (1796–1853), one of the principal collaborators of Scribe, and a most prolific and skillful writer for the stage; who, jointly with others, produced 225 plays for the theatres of Paris. The favorites among them were: 'The Queen of Sixteen' (1828); 'My Place and my Wife' (1830); 'The Gamin of Paris' (1836); 'The First Arms of Richelieu' (1839); 'A Parisian Household' (1844); 'The Husband in the Country' (1844); 'A Son of Good Family' (1853). He is also the author of the comic opera 'The Daughter of the Regiment' (1840), well known through Donizetti's music.

Bayer, Karl Robert Emerich von. See **Byr.**

Bayle, Pierre (bāl). A distinguished French philosopher and critic; born at Carlat, Languedoc, Nov. 18, 1647; died in Rotterdam, Dec. 28, 1706. Son of a Reformed Church minister, he was converted to Catholicism while studying theology at the Jesuit College in Toulouse, but within two years his family prevailed upon him to resume the Protestant faith. Withdrawing to Geneva, he studied the philosophy of Descartes, acted for some years as tutor at Coppet, Rouen, and in Paris, and in 1675 was appointed to the chair of philosophy at the Protestant University of Sedan. The latter being suppressed in 1681, he accepted a call to Rotterdam as professor of philosophy and history, but was removed in 1693 on account of his liberal opinions, after a bitter controversy with his colleague and former friend Jurieu, whose envy had been aroused by the great success of Bayle's critical writings. He then devoted all his time and strength to the completion of the great work, identified with his name, the 'Historical and Critical Dictionary' (1697), which brought him into conflict with the consistory; while some of his subsequent writings awakened new enmities and theological controversies which embittered the remaining years of his life.

Baylor, Frances Courtenay. See **Barnum.**

Bayly, Ada Ellen. See **Lyall, Edna.**

Bayly, Thomas Haynes. An English poet and novelist; born in Bath, Oct. 13, 1797; died in Cheltenham, April 22, 1839. He wrote '36 dramas, including: 'Perfection'; 'The Aylmers'; 'The Legend of Killarney'; and other novels and many fanciful poems, after the style of Moore.

Bazán, Emilia Pardo (bä-thän'). A Spanish novelist; born in Coruña in 1852. She has published works on history and philosophy, and is the author of 'Studies in Darwinism'; 'Saint Francis of Assisi'; and many novels. These, translated into English by Mary J. Serrano, have become very popular, and include: 'A Christian Woman' (New York and London, 1891); 'Homesickness' (1891); 'The Swan of Vilamorta' (1891); and 'The Wedding Trip' (1891).

Bazancourt, César Lécat, Baron de (bäzäṅ-kör'). A French writer of fiction and works on military science; born in Paris, 1810; died there, Jan. 25, 1865. The novelty of his theories of warfare and the merits of his style imparted

very general interest to 'The Crimean Expedition' and 'The Campaign in Italy in 1859.' He has also written 'Georges de Montagnard' and 'The Princess Pallianci,' novels; as well as 'The Secrets of the Sword,' a manual of fencing.

Beaconsfield, Benjamin Disraeli, Lord. An eminent English statesman and novelist; born in London, Dec. 21, 1804; died April 19, 1881. The first volume of his novel 'Vivian Grey' appeared in 1826, the second volume in 1827. This was followed by 'The Young Duke' (1831); 'Contarini Fleming' (1832); 'The Wondrous Tale of Alroy' (1833); 'The Rise of Iskander'; 'The Revolutionary Epic' (1834); 'Henrietta Temple' (1837); 'Venetia' (1837); 'Alarcos' (1839); 'Coningsby' (1844); 'Sibyl' (1845); 'Tancred' (1847); 'Lothair' (1870); 'Endymion' (1880); etc.

Beard, George Miller. An American physician and medical and hygienic writer; born at Montville, Conn., May 8, 1839; died in New York, Jan. 23, 1883. He made a specialty of the study of stimulants and narcotics, hypnotism, spiritualism, etc. Among his works were: 'Our Home Physician' (1869); 'Eating and Drinking' (1871); 'Stimulants and Narcotics' (1871); 'American Nervousness' (1881); 'Sea-Sickness' (1882); etc.

Beardsley, Eben Edwards. An American Episcopal clergyman, historian, and biographer; born at Stepney, Conn., 1808; died at New Haven, Dec. 22, 1891. He became a pastor in New Haven in 1848. He wrote: 'History of the Episcopal Church in Connecticut' (4th ed. 1883); and lives of 'Samuel Johnson, First President of King's College, New York' (1874); 'William Samuel Johnson, President of Columbia College' (1876); and 'Samuel Seabury, First Bishop of Connecticut' (1881).

Beattie, James (bē'ti *or* Sc. bā'ti). A Scottish poet; born in Laurencekirk, Kincardineshire, Oct. 25, 1735; died in Aberdeen, Aug. 18, 1803. He studied in Aberdeen, and was professor of moral philosophy in Marischal College from 1760 till his death. He wrote metaphysical essays and poems. 'The Minstrel' is his chief work. The first book (1771) passed through four editions before the second part appeared (1774).

Beaumarchais, Pierre Augustin Caron de (bō-mär-shā'). A French dramatist; born in Paris, Jan. 24, 1732; died there, May 18, 1799. He was the son of a Parisian watchmaker named Caron, learned his father's trade, and by his vehement attack on a rival who pirated his patent attracted attention at court. His handsome appearance and manners procured advancement. He taught the daughters of Louis XV. to play the harp; married a rich widow. His first plays, 'Eugénie' (1767) and 'The Two Friends' (1770), had only moderate success. His great plays are: 'The Barber of Seville' (1775) and 'The Marriage of Figaro' (1784), which had unprecedented success. The 'Memoirs of Sieur Beaumarchais' by himself (1774-78; new ed. by Sainte-Beuve, 1873), have never been surpassed for their satire and logic. Beaumarchais is a figure in Goethe's drama 'Clavigo.' His 'Theatre' has been edited by Saint-Marc Girardin (Paris, 1861); his 'Complete Works,' by Moland (1774) and by Fournier (1875); the 'Barber of Seville,' by Austin Dobson (Oxford, 1884).

Beaumont, Francis. An English dramatist; born in 1584, at Grace-Dieu, Leicestershire, the family seat; died in London, March 6, 1615-16. He wrote first 'Salmacis and Hermaphroditus,' a poem on Ovid's legend (1602), and a 'Masque of the Inner Temple,' represented at court in 1612-13. From early youth he was associated with John Fletcher. Their differences are best appreciated by comparing Beaumont's 'Triumph of Love' with Fletcher's 'Triumph of Death,' included in 'Four Plays or Moral Representations in One' (1647). Their plays written together include: 'Philaster'; 'The Maid's Tragedy'; 'King and No King'; 'The Scornful Lady'; 'The Knight of the Burning Pestle'; Cupid's Revenge'; and 'The Coxcomb.' Their first collected edition, 'Comedies and Tragedies,' appeared in 1647; more complete in 1679.

Beaunoir, Alexandre Louis Bertrand (bōn-wär') [true name Robinoir]. A French dramatist (1746-1823). His more than 200 comedies were very popular. Among the best of them are: 'Love Goes A-Begging'; 'Jennie, or The Losers Don't Pay.'

Bebel, Ferdinand August (bä'bel). A German socialist; born in Cologne in 1840. In his youth he was an apprentice, and while learning and practicing the turner's trade, he acquired a practical knowledge of the difficulties and disabilities of the workingmen. He settled in Leipzig in 1860, joined various labor organizations, and became one of the editors of the Volkstaat and of the better-known Vorwärts. Membership in the North German Reichstag was followed by his election to the German Reichstag, of which he was a member from 1871 to 1881, and which he entered again in 1883. He is the leader of his party in the Reichstag. Bebel's earnestness, large sympathy, and wide range of knowledge impress his hearers, although his appearance and manner in the Reichstag do not at first win them. These qualities are also characteristic of his numerous published books, among which are: 'Our Aims' (1874); 'The German Peasant War' (1876); 'The Life and Theories of Charles Fourier' (1888); 'Women in Socialism, the Christian Point of View in the Woman Question' (1893); 'Social Democracy and Universal Suffrage' (1895).

Bebel, Heinrich (bä'bel). A notable German humanist (1472-1518). He was an alumnus of Cracow and Basel Universities, and from 1497 professor of poetry and rhetoric at Tübingen. His fame rests principally on his 'Facetiæ' (1506), a curious collection of bits of homely and rather coarse-grained humor and anecdote, directed mainly against the clergy;

and on his 'Triumph of Venus,' a keen satire on the depravity of his time.

Beccadelli, Antonio degli (bek'ä-del'ē). An Italian humanist and poet (1394-1471); born at Palermo. His book of epigrams, 'Hermaphroditus' (1432), shows abundant wit and fancy, but oversteps the bounds of decency.

Beccari, Agostini (bek-är'ē). An Italian pastoral poet; born in Ferrara, 1540 (?); died there (?) 1590. He wrote 'The Sacrifice' (1554) before his fifteenth birthday, this piece being a pastoral in rather stilted metro and quite sophomoric in flavor; but as the maiden essay of the kind in literature, and as the model upon which Tasso constructed his 'Aminta,' it is not to be overlooked.

Bechstein, Ludwig (bech'stīn). A German poet and novelist (1801-60), chiefly remembered for 'The Legend Treasure and the Legendary Cycles of Thuringia' (1835-38); 'German Fairy-Tale Book' (1845, 41st ed. 1893); and others. Among his epical poems are: 'The Children of Haymon' (1830); 'The Dance of Death' (1831); 'New Natural History of Pet Birds' (1846), a humorous didactic poem; and 'Thuringia's Royal House' (1865). Of his numerous novels, chiefly historical, the best-known is 'Journeys of a Musician' (1836-37).

Beck, Karl (bek). An Austrian poet; born at Baja, Hungary, May 1, 1817; died in Vienna, April 10, 1879. His poems reflect the passionate temperament of his Hungarian countrymen in sonorous verses of consummate finish. Among his works are: 'Nights' (1838); 'The Poet Errant' (1838); 'Jankó' (1842), a romance in verse; 'Songs of the Poor Man' (1847); 'Jadwiga' (1863), a tale in verse; 'Mater Dolorosa' (1854), a novel.

Becke, Louis. An Australian author; born in Port Macquarrie, Australia, about 1850. He went to sea at the age of fourteen, and has spent his life trading in the South Pacific. His publications are: 'By Reef and Palm' (1895); 'South Sea Stories' (1896); 'The Ebbing of the Tide' (1896); and with W. Jeffrey, 'A First-Fleet Family' (1896).

Becker, August (bek'er). A German poet and novelist (1828-91); author of 'Young Friedel, the Minstrel' (1854), a lyrical epic, and the novels: 'The Rabbi's Bequest' (1866); 'Proscribed' (1868); 'The Carbuncle' (1870); 'My Sister' (1876), descriptive of the doings of Lola Montez and the events of 1848 in Bavaria; 'Painter Fairbeard' (1878); 'The Sexton of Horst' (1889); 'Gray Jane' (1890).

Becker, Karl Friedrich. A German historical writer; born in Berlin, 1777; died there, March 15, 1806. He wrote various popular works on historical topics, the best-known being 'The World's History for Children and their Teachers' (1801-5), a truly successful undertaking.

Becker, Nikolaus. A German poet (1809-45), known as the author of the Rhine-song

'They never shall obtain it, the free, the German Rhine,' which became immensely popular throughout Germany, and provoked Alfred de Musset's 'We have had it, your German Rhine,' and Lamartine's more conciliatory 'Peace-Marseillaise' (1841).

Beckford, William. A noted English man of letters; born at Fonthill, Wiltshire, Sept. 29, 1759; died at Bath, May 2, 1844. Heir to a large fortune, he traveled extensively, and after his return home built a costly residence at Fonthill, where he amassed many art treasures. He is famous as the author of 'Vathek,' an Oriental romance of great power and luxurious imagination, written originally in French (1781 or 1782), and translated into English by himself, although another translation (by Henley) had been published anonymously and surreptitiously in 1784(?). Among his other writings are: 'Biographical Memoirs of Extraordinary Painters' (1780), a satirical burlesque; 'Dreams, Waking Thoughts, and Incidents' (1783), a series of letters from various parts of Europe; 'Italy, with Sketches of Spain and Portugal' (1834).

Becque, Henri François (bek). A French dramatist; born in Paris, April 9, 1837, the pioneer realism on the Parisian stage, where he produced 'The Prodigal Son' (1868); The Abduction' (1871); 'The Ravens' (1882); 'The Parisian' (1885); 'Literary Quarrels' (1891). D. 1899.

Becquer, Gustavo Adolfo (bek'ker). A Spanish poet and novelist; born in Seville, Feb. 17, 1836; died in Madrid, Dec. 22, 1870. His lyrics, chiefly elegiac, show much feeling, and his tales and legends are among the best creations of modern Spanish prose.

Beddoes, Thomas Lovell. An English poet; born in Rodney Place, Clifton, July 20, 1803; died in Basle, Jan. 26, 1849. He was educated at Oxford and Göttingen, and lived a strange wandering life as a doctor and politician in Germany and Switzerland, with occasional visits to England. 'The Bride's Tragedy' (1822) was quite remarkable and attracted attention; but his best is 'Death's Jest-Book,' on which he was at work from 1825 until his death. It was published posthumously by T. F. Kelsau (1850), who also edited his other poems with memoir (1851).

Bede or Bæda. The greatest figure in ancient English literature; was born near Monkwearmouth, Durham, about 673; died in the monastery of Jarrow, May 26, 735. Left an orphan at the age of six, he was educated in the Benedictine Abbey at Monkwearmouth and entered the monastery of Jarrow, where he was ordained priest in his thirtieth year. His industry was enormous. "First," says Green, "among English scholars, first among English theologians, first among English historians, it is in the monk of Jarrow that English literature strikes its roots. In the six hundred scholars who gathered around him for instruction he is the father of our national education." Bede wrote homilies, lives of saints, hymns,

epigrams, works on grammar and chronology, and the great 'Ecclesiastical History of England' in five books, gleaned from native chronicles and oral tradition. This was translated from Latin into Anglo-Saxon by King Alfred. The first editions were issued from Strassburg in the 15th century.

Bede, Cuthbert, pseudonym of Edward Bradley. An English author; born in Kidderminster in 1827; died in Lenton, Dec. 12, 1889. He graduated at Durham University, and was rector of Denton, Stretton, and finally Lenton from 1883 until his death. He contributed to Punch and other London periodicals, and published the 'Adventures of Mr. Verdant Green, an Oxford Freshman' (London, 1855), a humorous picture of college life. His other works include: 'Mr. Verdant Green Married and Done For' (1856); 'The White Wife,' a collection of Scottish legends (1864); 'Little Mr. Bouncer and his Friend Verdant Green' (1873-74); and many books of travels.

Beecher, Catherine Esther. An American author and educator, daughter of Lyman, and sister of Henry Ward Beecher; born in Easthampton, L. I., Sept. 6, 1800; died in Elmira, N. Y., May 12, 1878. From 1822 to 1832 she conducted a school in Hartford, Conn.; and afterwards taught for two years in Cincinnati, Ohio. The remainder of her life was devoted to training teachers and supplying them to needy fields, especially in the Western and Southern States. She wrote numerous works on education and on the woman question, among which are: 'The Religious Training of Children in the School, the Family, and the Church' (1864); 'Woman's Profession as Mother and Educator, with Views in Opposition to Woman Suffrage' (1871).

Beecher, Charles. An American clergyman and author, brother of Henry Ward Beecher; born in Litchfield, Conn., Oct. 7, 1815. He graduated from Bowdoin College in 1834, and has had charge of Congregational and Presbyterian churches; especially in Fort Wayne, Ind., Newark, N. J., and Georgetown, Mass. Among his published works are: 'David and his Throne' (1855); 'Spiritual Manifestations' (1879); and 'The Autobiography and Correspondence of Lyman Beecher' (1863).

Beecher, Edward. An American clergyman and author, brother of Henry Ward Beecher; born in Easthampton, N. Y., Aug. 27, 1803; died in Brooklyn, N. Y., July 28, 1895. He graduated at Yale, studied theology at Andover and New Haven; was pastor of various Congregational churches, especially at Park Street, Boston (1826-30), and Salem Street, Boston (1844-55). He was president of Illinois College, Jacksonville (1830-44), and for some years professor of Exegesis in the Chicago Theological Seminary. He wrote many religious books, including 'The Conflict of Ages' (1853) and 'The Concord of Ages' (1860); in which he explained the existence of sin and misery in the world as the results of a pre-existent state, to be harmonized at last in an eternal concord of good.

Beecher, Henry Ward. An American clergyman; born in Litchfield, Conn., June 24, 1813; died in Brooklyn, N. Y., March 8, 1887. He was the son of Lyman Beecher; graduated from Amherst in 1834; studied in Lane Theological Seminary, near Cincinnati, Ohio; and began clerical duty as pastor of a church in Lawrenceburg, Ind., removing to Indianapolis in 1839. From 1847 until his death he was pastor of Plymouth Congregational Church in Brooklyn. He was one of the founders of the Independent and of the Christian Union (now the Outlook). He was also a prominent anti-slavery orator, as well as a famous lecturer. Among his numerous publications are: 'Star Papers; or Experiences of Art and Nature' (1855); 'Freedom and War' (1863); 'Eyes and Ears' (1864); and a novel, 'Norwood, or Village Life in New England' (1867). His 'Sermons' were edited by Dr. Lyman Abbott (2 vols., 1868).

Beecher, Lyman. An American clergyman; born in New Haven, Conn., Oct. 2, 1775; died in Brooklyn, N. Y., June 10, 1863. His ancestors were Puritans. He graduated from Yale in 1796, and became pastor of the Presbyterian Church in East Hampton, L. I.; then of a Congregational church in Litchfield, Conn., in 1810; and then of the Hanover Street Congregational Church in Boston, Mass. In 1832 he became president of Lane Theological Seminary, near Cincinnati, Ohio. His influence throughout the country was very great, especially on the questions of temperance and of slavery. His 'Six Sermons on Intemperance' had a great effect, and have been frequently republished and translated into many languages. His sermon on the death of Alexander Hamilton in 1804, with his 'Remedy for Dueling' (1809), did much toward breaking up the practice of dueling in the United States. His collected 'Sermons and Addresses' were published in 1852.

Beecher, Thomas Kinnicutt. An American clergyman, son of Lyman, and brother of Henry Ward Beecher; born in Litchfield, Conn., Feb. 10, 1824. He became pastor in Brooklyn in 1852, and in Elmira, N. Y., in 1854. He has been a very successful lecturer and an effective writer on current topics. He had published in book form 'Our Seven Churches'(1870). D. 1900.

Beers, Ethel Lynn. An American poet; born in Goshen, N. Y., Jan. 13, 1827; died in Orange, N. J., Oct. 10, 1879. She was a descendant of John Eliot, the apostle to the Indians. She has published 'All Quiet along the Potomac, and Other Poems' (1879).

Beers, Henry Augustin. An American author; born in Buffalo, N. Y., July 2, 1847. He graduated from Yale in 1859, became tutor there in 1871, and professor of English literature in 1880. He has published among other works: 'A Century of American Literature' (1878); 'The Thankless Muse,' poems (1886);

'From Chaucer to Tennyson' (1890); 'Initial Studies in American Letters' (1892); 'A Suburban Pastoral, and Other Tales' (1894); 'The Ways of Yale' (1895); 'Points at Issue' (1904).

Beers, Jan van (bārz). A Flemish poet (1821–88); from 1860 professor at the Athenæum in Antwerp. His principal works, full of sentiment and melodious quality, are: 'Youth's Dreams' (1853); 'Pictures of Life' (1858); 'Sentiment and Life' (1869).

Beethoven, Ludwig van (bā'tō-ven). A German composer of Dutch extraction; born at Bonn, 1770; died at Vienna, 1827. His music is world-famous. In his 'Correspondence' and in the noted 'Brentano Letters' he is a writer of personal impressions of great interest and charm.

Beets, Nicolaas (bāts). A Dutch poet, novelist, and critic; born in Haarlem, Sept. 13, 1814. His early lyrics, and the poetical tales 'José' (1834); 'Kuser' (1835); 'Guy the Fleming' (1837), are in the vein of Byron. He showed a maturer talent in 'Ada of Holland' (1840), and the lyric cycles 'Cornflowers' (1853), 'The Children of the Sea' (1861), and others; but is chiefly esteemed as a prose-writer of rare excellence, author of 'Camera Obscura' (1839, 18th ed. 1888), a series of tales and sketches of Dutch types. His pseudonym was "Hildebrand." Died at Utrecht, Mar., 1903.

Behn, Aphra. An English novelist and dramatist; born in Wye, Kent, in July 1640; died in London, April 16, 1689. She is buried in the Poet's Corner of Westminster Abbey. Her life was adventurous and interesting. She early went to the West Indies, returned to London about 1658, and gaining entrance to court, pleased Charles II. by her wit. He sent her to Antwerp as a spy. She was the first woman in England to live by her pen. Her plays and poems are superior to her novels; but they are all stamped with indelicacy, and do not deserve the praise bestowed on them by Dryden, Otway, and others. Her dramas long held the stage. They include: 'Abdelazar, or the Moor's Revenge'; 'The Forced Marriage'; and many others. Among her novels, 'Oroonoko, or the Royal Slave' (founded on the adventures of a West-Indian native prince of that name) alone has any merit.

Behrens, Bertha. See **Heimburg.**

Bekker, Elisabeth (bek'er). A Dutch novelist; born at Vlissingen, July 24, 1738; died in The Hague, Nov. 5, 1804. Married to Adrian Wolff, a Reformed Church minister at Beemster, who died in 1777, she lived afterwards in closest friendship with Agathe Deken, who also collaborated in her most important works, to wit: 'History of Sara Burgerhart' (1782); 'History of William Leevend' (1784–85); 'Letters of Abraham Blankaart' (1787–89); 'Cornelia Wildschut' (1793–96).

Belcikovski, Adam (bel-chē-kov-skē). A Polish dramatist; born in Cracow, 1839. Among his numerous historical dramas and comedies are: 'King Don Juan' (1869); 'Hunyadi' (1870); 'Francesca da Rimini' (1873); 'The Oath' (1878); 'King Boleslav the Bold' (1882). He also wrote valuable essays on Polish literature.

Belinsky, Vissárion Grigóryevich (bel-in'-skē). A Russian literary critic (1811–48). He wrote an excellent 'View of Russian Literature since the 18th Century.'

Bell, Acton. See **Brontë, Anne.**

Bell, Currer. See **Brontë, Charlotte.**

Bell, Ellis. See **Brontë, Emily.**

Bell, Lilian. An American novelist; born in Chicago, 1867. She has written 'The Love Affairs of an Old Maid' and 'A Little Sister to the Wilderness'; 'Caroline Lee.'

Bell, Robert. An Irish author and editor; born in Cork, Jan. 16, 1800; died in London, April 12, 1867. Educated at Trinity College, Dublin, he went to London in 1828. He became editor of magazines and useful editions of books. He is best known for his annotated edition of English poets from Chaucer to Cowper (24 vols., 1854–57). He wrote: 'History of Russia' (3 vols., London, 1836); 'Life of Canning' (1846); 'Wayside Pictures through France, Belgium, and Holland' (1849); two novels; three comedies; and a collection of 'Early Ballads' (1864).

Bellamy, Edward. An American writer; born in Chicopee Falls, Mass., March 29, 1850; died there May 22, 1898. He was educated in Germany; admitted to the bar; was on the staff of the Evening Post of New York in 1871–72; and on his return from the Sandwich Islands in 1877, he founded the Springfield News. He is best known by his novel 'Looking Backward' (1888), a socialistic work, of which an immense number of copies were sold in two years. His other books are: 'Six to One: a Nantucket Idyl' (1878); 'Dr. Heidenhoff's Process' (1880); 'Miss Ludington's Sister' (1884); 'Equality' (1897); and 'The Wonder Children' (1906).

Bellamy, Mrs. Elizabeth Whitfield (Croom). An American novelist, writing under the pseudonym "Kamba Thorpe"; born at Quincy, Fla., 1839. She has written: 'Four Oaks' (1867); 'Little Joanna' (1876); 'Old Man Gilbert'; 'The Luck of the Pendennings.' D. 1900.

Bellamy, Jacobus (bel'ä-mi). A Dutch poet; born at Vlissingen, Nov. 12, 1757; died in Utrecht, March 11, 1786. First known through his Anacreontic 'Songs of my Youth' (1782), which were followed by the inspired 'Patriotic Songs' (1783), he is now chiefly remembered for his poetical romance 'Roosje' (1784), which in touching simplicity and ardent feeling is unequaled in Dutch literature.

Bellamy, Joseph. An American clergyman and educator; born in Cheshire, Conn., in 1719; died in Bethlehem, Conn., March 6, 1790. He graduated at Yale in 1735; in 1740 became pastor of the church in Bethlehem, where he remained until his death. About 1742 he established a divinity school, in which many celebrated clergymen were trained. Among his published works, besides his 'Sermons' are: 'True Religion Delineated' (1750); 'The Nature and Glory of the Gospel' (1762); and 'The Half-Way Covenant' (1769).

Bellay, Joachim du (bc-lā'). A distinguished French poet and prose-writer; born at the Château de Liré, near Angers, about 1524; died in Paris, Jan. 1, 1560. Next to Ronsard the most prominent member of the famous "Pléiade." He had few of the advantages of a school education, but by his own industry became acquainted with the poets of antiquity and of France. His first volume of poems was a collection of his 'Sonnets to Olive.' His 'Antiquities of Rome' was done into English verse by Edmund Spenser, 'The Ruins of Rome' (1591). His principal work is a 'Defense and Illustration of the French Language' (1549), in which he depreciates the old forms of French poetry and sets up the classic poets of antiquity as models. After his death were published more of his sonnets, also odes, and some translations.

Belleau, Rémy (bel-lo'). A noted French poet; born at Nogent-le-Rotrou, 1528; died in Paris, March 16, 1577. One of the "Pléiade," and ranked by some as its best poet, in preference to Bellay. His poems are graceful and melodious, and show less affectation of sentiment than those of many of his contemporaries. He made an elegant and spirited translation of 'The Odes of Anacreon' (1576). His 'Bergerie' (1572), a compound of prose and verse, is of unequal merit; but it contains some passages — e. g., the 'April' — which are of consummate beauty. A curious work is his fanciful 'Loves and New Exchanges of Precious Stones' (1566): it is perhaps his best performance.

Belli, Giuseppe Gioachino (bel'lē). A noted Roman humorist and satirical poet (1791–1863). He wrote in the popular dialect of the Trastevere; and in early life scourged with stinging, irreverent, and often vulgar satire, the tyranny of the popes and the scandalous lives of the clergy. Becoming afterward a zealous convert to the faith of the Roman Church, he endeavored to call in and destroy the wicked indiscretions of his youth. In his last years he published a beautiful translation of the Roman Breviary. His published sonnets amount to more than 2,000; his other published Italian verses fill four considerable volumes; while two thirds of his vast remains have never been gathered and edited. Of this last, much is clothed in language too coarse to bear the light of modern culture.

Bellman, Carl Michael (bel'män). A noted Swedish poet; born in Stockholm, Feb. 4, 1740; died there, Feb. 11, 1795. His poems were often improvisations, and the airs of his songs were largely of his own composition. As singer of the rollicking life of a capital city he is unsurpassed. A colossal bronze bust of Bellman by Byström was erected in the Zoölogical Garden at Stockholm in 1829, and there a popular festival is held yearly in his honor.

Bellows, Henry Whitney. A prominent Unitarian divine and miscellaneous writer; born at Walpole, N. H., June 11, 1814; died in New York, Jan. 30, 1882. He became pastor of All Souls Church, New York, 1839; was chief founder and long editor of the Christian Inquirer (1846); president and chief originator of the United States Sanitary Commission during the Civil War (1861-65). He wrote: 'Public Life of Washington' (1866); 'Relation of Public Amusements to Public Morality'; 'The Old World in its New Face' (2 vols., 1868-69), a record of travel in Europe. He was an effective preacher and public speaker.

Belloy, Pierre Laurent de (bel-wä'), properly Buirette. A French dramatist; born 1727; died 1775. He won success with the tragedies 'The Siege of Calais' (1765) and 'Gaston and Bayard' (1771), and was elected to the Academy in 1771.

Belmontet, Louis (bel-môn-tā'). A French poet and publicist (1799-1879); studied and practiced law in Toulouse, until involved in difficulties with the magistracy on account of some satirical poems, when he went to Paris and there produced his principal works: 'The Sad Ones' (1824), a cycle of elegies; 'The Supper of Augustus' (1828); and with Soumet, 'A Festival of Nero' (1829), a tragedy which exceeded 100 performances. Subsequently he became an ardent partisan of Bonapartism, pleading its cause as a journalist and poetically extolling the Napoleonic dynasty in many enthusiastic odes.

Belot, Adolphe (be-lō'). A French novelist and dramatist (1829-90); traveled extensively and settled at Nancy as a lawyer. He won reputation with a witty comedy, 'The Testament of César Girodot' (1859, with Villetard); and being less successful with his following dramatic efforts, devoted himself to fiction. Of his novels may be mentioned: 'The Venus of Gordes' (1867, with Ernest Daudet); 'The Drama of the Rue de la Paix' (1868); 'Article 47' (1870): all of which were dramatized.

Bembo, Pietro (bem'bō). A celebrated Italian humanist; born in Venice, May 20, 1470; died in Rome, Jan. 18, 1547. In 1513 he became secretary of Latin letters to Pope Leo X.; the Venetian republic appointed him in 1530 State historiographer. His poetical works, Latin and Italian, are marked rather by elegance of style, purity of idiom, and correctness of taste, than by force or originality of thought or liveliness of fancy. His works include a 'History of Venice 1487-1513,' and a number of poems, dialogues, and essays. There are 16 books of his 'Latin Letters' written in the name of Leo X.

Bender, Prosper (bend'er). An American descriptive writer; born at Quebec, 1844. Originally a Canadian physician, he removed to Boston, Mass. (1883), and practices medicine there. He has written: 'Old and New Canada'; 'Literary Sheaves' (1881).

Benedict, David. A Baptist divine and historian; born at Norwalk, Conn., 1779; died 1874. He was pastor at Pawtucket, R. I., for twenty-five years, and preached till over ninety years of age. Among his chief works were: 'History of All Religions'; 'Fifty Years among the Baptists'; 'History of the Donatists'; etc.

Benedict, Frank Lee. A popular American novelist and poet; born in New York, 1834. Among his numerous novels may be named: 'John Worthington's Name'; 'Miss Van Kortland' (1870); 'Her Friend Lawrence' (1879); 'The Price She Paid' (1883); 'A Late Remorse.'

Benedictoff, Vladimir Grigórjevich (be-ne-dik'tof). A Russian poet (1810-73), whose lyrics excel in deep sentiment and ideal enthusiasm; some, like 'Two Apparitions,' 'The Lake,' 'The Mountain Peaks,' may be ranked with the finest of any literature.

Benedictsson, Victoria. See **Ahlgren.**

Benedix, Roderich Julius (be'ne-diks). A German dramatist; born in Leipsic, Jan. 21, 1811; died there, Sept. 26, 1873. His first comedy, 'The Moss-Covered Pate' (1841), was received throughout Germany with extraordinary popular favor. Its successor, 'Doctor Wasp,' was no less successful. Of the long catalogue of his comedies, nearly every one was received with marked favor in Germany and in foreign countries wherever they were presented. The secret of this success is found in the ever lively action, and in the author's intimate knowledge of the stage with its immemorial yet ever fresh and telling effects. His 'Collected Dramatic Works' were published in 27 volumes.

Beniczky-Bajza, Illona (ben-is'skē bī'tsä). A Hungarian novelist; born in Buda-Pesth, in June 1840. Daughter of the critic Joseph Bajza, and one of the most prolific writers of Hungary. Her most noteworthy works are: 'Prejudice and Enlightenment' (1872); 'It is She' (1888); 'Martha' (1890); 'The Mountain Fairy' (1890).

Benjamin, Park. An American journalist, poet, and lecturer; born at Demerara, British Guiana, Aug. 14, 1809; died in New York, Sept. 12, 1864. He studied law originally. His poems, of a high order of merit, have never been collected. 'The Contemplation of Nature,' read on taking his degree at Washington College, Hartford, 1829; the satires 'Poetry' (1843); 'Infatuation' (1845); 'The Nautilus'; 'To One Beloved'; and 'The Old Sexton,' are among his works. He was associated editorially with Epes Sargent and Rufus W. Griswold.

Benjamin, Park. An American lawyer, editor, and miscellaneous writer, son of the preceding; born in New York, May 11, 1849. A graduate of the United States Naval Academy (1867), he served on Admiral Farragut's flagship, but resigned in 1869. As a lawyer he has been a patent expert. He edited the Scientific American (1872-78). He has written: 'Shakings; Etchings from the Naval Academy' (1867); 'The Age of Electricity' (1886); 'The Intellectual Rise in Electricity, a History'; etc.

Benjamin, Samuel Green Wheeler. An American traveler, artist, and miscellaneous writer; born at Argos, Greece, Feb. 13, 1837. He was United States minister to Persia (1883-85). Among his numerous works, both in prose and verse, are: 'Art in America'; 'Contemporary Art in Europe' (1877); 'Constantinople' (1860); 'Persia and the Persians' (1886); 'The Choice of Paris' (1870), a romance; 'Sea-Spray' (1887), a book for yachtsmen; etc.

Bennett, Charles Wesley. An American Methodist divine and educator; born at East Bethany, N. Y., July 18, 1828; died at Evanston, Ill., April 17, 1891. He was principal of Genesee Wesleyan Seminary (1869-71), professor of history and logic at Syracuse University (1871-85), professor of historical theology at Garrett Biblical Institute, Evanston (1885-91). He wrote 'National Education in Italy, France, Germany, England, and Wales' (1878); and 'Christian Art and Archæology of the First Six Centuries' (1888).

Bennett, William Cox. An English songwriter; born in Greenwich, Oct. 14, 1820; died in Blackheath, March 4, 1895. He was the son of a watchmaker, had comparatively little education, and is known for his songs and ballads: 'Queen Eleanor's Vengeance and Other Poems' (1856); 'War Songs' (1857); 'Our Glory Roll and Other National Poems' (1867); 'Songs for Sailors' (1872); 'Sea Songs' (1878).

Benoît de Sainte-Maure (be-nwä' dĕ sant-mōr). A French trouvère and chronicler of the 12th century; born in Touraine. He wrote in about 42,000 octosyllabic verses a 'Chronicle of the Dukes of Normandy' to the year 1135. To him is usually ascribed the 'Romance of Troy,' founded on the story of the siege of Troy as written by Dictys Cretensis and Dares; it was translated into the languages of western Europe. Boccaccio, Chaucer, and Shakespeare would seem to be indebted to Benoît for the story of the loves of Troilus and Briseis (Cryseyde or Cressida being originally called Briseida).

Bensel, James Berry. A well-known American poet and novelist; born in New York, 1856; died 1886. He lived the most of his life at Lynn, Mass., and was a contributor to magazines. He wrote: 'King Kophetua's Wife' (1884), a novel; 'In the King's Garden and Other Poems' (1886).

Benson, Carl. See **Bristed, Charles Astor.**

Benson, E. F. An English novelist, born 18—. His greatest success was 'Dodo' (1893), a novel of London society; he has also written

'Limitations'; 'The Babe, B. A.'; 'The Rubicon'; and 'The Vintage' (1897).

Benson, Eugene. An American artist and miscellaneous writer; born at Hyde Park, N. Y., 1840. Residing in Rome, Italy, he has contributed to American magazines. He has written: 'Gaspara Stampa' (1881), a biography with selections from her sonnets; 'Art and Nature in Italy' (1882).

Bensserade, Isaac de (bans-räd). A French poet (1613-91), chiefly remembered as author of the ballets, much in vogue then, in which the king and his courtiers tòok part; also by his dainty lyrics,—especially the sonnet on 'Job,' which, in rivalry with Voiture's sonnet to 'Urania,' incited a literary feud in 1651.

Bentham, Jeremy. An English writer on ethics and jurisprudence (1748-1832). He was educated for the bar and studied the theory of law. Treatises on Government (1776), Usury (1787), Civil and Penal Legislation (1813), Fallacies (1824), and others; formed his collected works (11 vols., 1843). His guiding principle was the doctrine of utility.

Bentivoglio, Guido (ben-tē-vōl'yō). An Italian historian, memoirist, and cardinal; born in Ferrara, 1579; died near Rome (?), 1644. His ecclesiastical career was exceedingly brilliant; but almost at the hour when his election to the papacy as successor to Urban VIII. seemed inevitable, he suddenly died. In his 'History of the War in Flanders' and 'Memoirs' he evinces decided literary abilities.

Bentley, Richard. An English critic and essayist; born in Oulton, Yorkshire, Jan. 27, 1662; died July 1742. He is pronounced by some authorities the best classical scholar England has produced. His writings are: 'Latin Epistle to John Mill, Containing Critical Observations on the Chronicle of Joannes Malala' (1691); the very celebrated 'Dissertation on the Epistles of Phalaris' (1697); and editions of Horace and Terence, besides commentaries on the classics, all of great value.

Benton, Joel. A well-known American poet and critic; born at Amenia, Dutchess County, N. Y., 1832. He has written: 'Under the Apple Boughs,' a collection of verse; 'Emerson as a Poet' (1883), and a large number of poems.

Benton, Thomas Hart. An American statesman and author; born near Hillsborough, Orange county, N. C., March 14, 1782; died in Washington, D. C., April 10, 1858. Before he was eight years old, his father died, and his early opportunities for study were few. He took a partial course at the University of North Carolina. The family removed to the yet unsettled territory south of Nashville, Ky., and in 1811 he was admitted to the bar in Nashville. He became a member of the State Legislature. He served in the United States army (1810-11 and 1812-13) and attained the rank of lieutenant-colonel. He settled in St. Louis, Mo., in 1815, and established a newspaper, the Missouri Inquirer, which he edited for many years. He was elected United States Senator from Missouri in 1820, and continued to hold that office for the next thirty years. He was a champion of the rights of settlers on the public lands; and of a gold and silver currency rather than paper money as a medium of exchange (hence called "Old Bullion"). He was a steadfast opponent of the Nullification doctrine, of the repeal of the Missouri Compromise, and of the Kansas-Nebraska bill. He was one of the earliest and most strenuous advocates of the building of a Pacific Railroad. His chief publications are his 'Thirty Years' View' of the workings of the national government (1854–56), and his 'Abridgment of the Debates of Congress,' covering the period from the foundation of the government to the year 1850.

Bentzel-Sternau, Count Karl Christian Ernst von (bents'el stär'nou). A German novelist and miscellaneous writer; born in Mentz, April 9, 1767; died at Mariahalden, Switzerland, Aug. 13, 1843. He is esteemed as a humorist in the manner of Jean Paul; and his satirical romances, 'The Golden Calf' (1802–3), 'The Stone-Guest' (1808), 'Old Adam' (1819–20), 'The Master of the Chair,' together form a series.

Bentzon, Thérèse (bants-ôn'), pseudonym of Marie Thérèse Blanc. A French novelist and littérateur; born at Seine-Port, Sept. 21, 1840. She has been for many years on the editorial staff of the Revue des Deux Mondes, to which she has contributed notable translations and reviews of many American, English, and German authors. Her literary essays on these contemporaneous writers were collected in 'Foreign Literature and Customs' (1882) and 'Recent American Novelists' (1885). Her first work to attract attention was 'A Divorce' (1871), published in the Journal des Débats. Two other novels, 'A Remorse' (1879) and 'Tony' (1889), were crowned by the French Academy. Other stories are: 'Georgette' and 'Jacqueline' (1893). The fruit of her first visit to the United States was 'Condition of Woman in the United States' (1895); 'Tales from All Countries.'

Beöthy, Zoltán (bè'tē). A Hungarian poet and critic; born at Komorn, Sept. 4, 1848. Since 1882 he has been professor of æsthetics at the University of Buda-Pesth. His numerous tales show unusual talent for psychological delineation; among them are: 'Judge Martin' (1872); 'The Nameless Ones' (1875); 'Kálozdi Béla' (1875), a novel. His dramaturgic studies and criticisms appeared under the title 'Playwrights and Actors' (1881). He has also written an excellent history of Hungarian literature (6th ed. 1891).

Béranger, Pierre Jean de (bā-roñ-zhä'). A French poet; born in Paris, Aug. 19, 1780; died there, July 16, 1857. His father took him to Paris in 1802; but they soon quarreled, and he began life in that garret which became famous. In 1804 Lucien Bonaparte helped him out of his distress, by giving him a clerkship in the Imperial University. Meanwhile he had composed many convivial and political songs, but it did not occur to him to write them down until 1812. They were so universally sung that he could have dispensed with the printing-press. When his poems were published in 1815, he was recognized as the champion of the faction opposed to the Bourbons. His popularity with the working-classes was immense, and he made the song a powerful political weapon. His republicanism and enthusiasm for Napoleon suited the multitude. Two volumes published in 1821 led to his imprisonment; and another in 1825 caused a second incarceration. 'New Songs' appeared in 1830, and his 'Autobiography' in 1840. In 1848 he was elected to Parliament, but begged to be released. His songs are full of wit, light-heartedness, and musical grace, ranging in theme from epicurean trivialities to passionate and burning social and political satire. Among the best are the 'King of Yvetot'; 'The Old Flag'; 'The Old Corporal'; 'Roger Bontemps'; 'My Grandmother'; 'Little Red Man'; 'Little Gray Man'; and 'The Marquis of Carabas.'

Berchet, Giovanni (bär-shä or berk'et). An Italian poet; born in Milan, Dec. 23, 1783; died in Turin, March 23, 1851. He was a leader in the school of poets and thinkers who sought to restore Italian literature to its ancient eminence by a purely national development. Coming under suspicion of Carbonarism, he had to quit his country, and lived several years abroad. His songs and romantic ballads — 'Italian Poems' (1848) — made him the favorite popular singer of Italy. His best performance is 'The Fugitives of Parga.'

Berczik, Árpád (bär-sêk'). A Hungarian dramatist; born at Temesvar, 1842 or 1852. He studied at the University of Pesth, and almost immediately upon his graduation became distinguished for his writings. Dramatic criticism and comedy are his congenialities; 'Public Affairs,' 'The Veterans,' and 'In the Czechs' Country,' three very diverting plays, bringing him his greatest fame.

Bergerat, Auguste Émile (berzh-rä'). A French journalist, playwright, and novelist: born in Paris, April 29, 1845. Son-in-law of Théophile Gautier, and since 1884 particularly known as the amusing chronicler of the Figaro under the pseudonym of "Caliban." His feuilletons for that paper were published collectively as 'Life and Adventures of Sieur Caliban' (1886); 'The Book of Caliban' (1887); 'Caliban's Laughter' (1890); etc. He also wrote two novels: 'Faublas in Spite of Himself' (1884); 'The Rape' (1886); besides two volumes to the memory of his father-in-law, 'Théophile Gautier, Painter' (1877), and 'Th. Gautier, Conversations, Souvenirs, and Correspondence' (1879).

Bergh, Henry. A noted American philanthropist and miscellaneous writer; born in New York, 1823; died there, March 12, 1888. He was founder and president of the American Society for the Prevention of Cruelty to Animals

(1866), founder of the American Society for the Prevention of Cruelty to Children (1881), secretary of legation and acting vice-consul at St. Petersburg (1862–64). He wrote: 'Love's Alternatives' (1881), a play; 'Married Off' (1859), a poem; 'The Streets of New York'; 'The Ocean Paragon'; etc.

Bergh, Pieter Theodoor Helvetius van den (bèrg). A Dutch dramatist and poet (1799–1873); attracted attention with his comedy 'The Nephew' (1837), considered one of the best in modern Dutch literature, but did not justify expectations by his subsequent dramatic efforts. He also published a collection, 'Prose and Poetry' (3d ed. 1863).

Bergk, Theodor (berk). A German classical philologist; born in Leipsic, May 22, 1812; died at Ragaz, Switzerland, July 20, 1881. He became an indisputable authority on Hellenic poetry, producing two works of surpassing importance in that department of scholarship: 'Greek Lyric Poets' (4th ed. 1878–82), and 'History of Greek Literature' (1872); the latter not quite completed at his death, but brought to perfection with the aid of his posthumous papers. He contributed much of value, likewise, to our knowledge of special departments of classical learning.

Bergsöe, Jörgen Vilhelm (berg'se). A Danish novelist, poet, and naturalist; born in Copenhagen, Feb. 8, 1835. While suffering partial blindness caused by excessive use of the microscope in his memorable biological researches at Messina, he turned to literary composition; and soon appeared the first of a cycle of novels, 'From the Piazza del Popolo' (1866), which had an extraordinary success. The following year he published his first volume of poems, 'Now and Then.' Of his many novels, the one which excels for fineness of touch is 'Who Was He?' All his stories are characterized by rich imagination, fine observation, and great originality; his poetry is inferior in these respects to his prose.

Berkeley, George, Bishop. A celebrated Irish clergyman and author; born near Kilkenny, March 12, 1685; died at Oxford, England, Jan. 14, 1753. He resided in America, at Newport, R. I., for about three years, beginning 1728. His estate of Whitehall at Newport he conveyed to Yale College for the maintenance of scholarships. Among his published works are the celebrated 'Commonplace Book, 1703–6'; 'Essay towards a New Theory of Vision' (1709); 'The Principles of Human Knowledge' (1710); 'Dialogues between Hylas and Philonous' (1713); 'Alciphron, or the Minute Philosopher' (1732); 'The Analyst' (1735); 'Siris' (1744: on Tar-Water); and others.

Berlichingen, Götz (Gottfried) von, of the Iron Hand (ber'lich-ing''en). A famous German knight and autobiographer; born in Jagsthausen in the present kingdom of Würtemberg, 1480; died July 23, 1562. He became very popular with the masses; this and other facts concerning him being apparent in his 'Auto-biography' (late ed. 1886), a work drawn upon by Goethe for the play bearing his name.

Berlioz, Hector (bär-lē-ōz'). A great French musical composer and critic; born near Grenoble, Dec. 11, 1803; died in Paris, March 8, 1869. In 1830 his cantata 'Sardanapalus' won for him the "prize of Rome," which afforded him the means of spending 18 months in Italy. He had already made his mark in Paris with the overtures 'Waverley' and 'The Vehm Judges'; and among the fruits of his studies in Italy were the overture to 'King Lear' and the symphony 'The Return to Life.' Then followed the long series of his musical works. Among his literary works are 'A Musical Tour in Italy and Germany'; 'Orchestra Soirées'; and 'Treatise on Instrumentation' (1844).

Bernard, Charles de (ber-när'). [Properly Bernard du Grail de La Villette.] A French novelist; born in Besançon, Feb. 25, 1804; died at Neuilly, March 6, 1850. He was a disciple of Balzac, whom he resembles in his power of realistic description and psychological analysis; but he possesses a purer and more nervous style, and above all is content with a less minute elaboration of story and characters. His first piece, 'The Gerfalcon,' made a hit with its clever description of the literary cliques. Everywhere he evinces clear insight into the foibles of society. Of his novels, the following may be named as only second in rank to his masterpiece 'The Gerfalcon': 'A Magistrate's Adventure'; 'The Gordian Knot'; 'Wings of Icarus'; 'The Lion's Skin'; 'The Country Gentleman.'

Bernard of Clairvaux or **St. Bernard** (bernärd'—klär-vo'). A French theologian, church father, and saint; born at Fontaines, near Dijon, 1091; died at Clairvaux, Jan. 12, 1153. His five books on 'Reflection' are written in a clear and cheerful style; and the hymn, 'Jesu! the Very Thought of Thee,' is in use in all the churches of our day.

Bernard of Cluny (klü-nē'). A French monk and poet who flourished in the twelfth century, and is noted for his work 'On Contempt of the World' (1597); but very little is known of the author's life.

Bernard de Ventadour (ber-när' dė ven-tädör'). A French troubadour poet; born in Ventadour (?) about 1125 (?); died in the monastery at Dalon about 1197 (?). Love songs 'To Eleonore,' and various amatory lays to courtly dames, form the riches of his delicate verse.

Bernardakis, Demetrios (ber-när'däk-is''). A Greek poet, dramatist, and scholar; born at Santa Marina, Lesbos, Dec. 2, 1834. After a course of study at Athens and in German universities, he was (with one considerable intermission) professor of history and philology in the University of Athens from 1861 to 1882, when he went back to Lesbos. He is author of a spirited Pindaric ode for a jubilee occasion, of several dramas, and of a satire, 'The Battle of Cranes and Mice'; he has also written

a 'Universal History'; a 'Church History'; and a spirited tractate, 'Confutation of a False Atticism,' directed against the would-be Attic purists. He died in 1907.

Bernardes, Diogo (ber-när'des). A Portuguese poet; born in Ponte de Lima, about 1530; died in 1605. He was called in his day "the Sweet Singer of the Lima," a streamlet immortalized in his verse. He left his native valley in 1550 and attached himself to the mastersinger Sá de Miranda, who then retired on his estate Quinta da Tapada, a devotee of the Muses. Here Bernardes composed verses in all kinds, elegies, sonnets, odes, songs, full of tender sympathies and perfect melody. Here he wrote: 'The Lima'; 'Various Rimes — Flowers from Lima's Banks'; 'Various Rimes to the Good Jesu.'

Berneck, Gustave von. See **Guseck.**

Berners, Juliana. An English prioress and writer; said to have been born in Essex, and flourished in the fifteenth century. She was at the head of a convent in Sopewell, and is celebrated for her work on fishing, hunting, and like pastimes, entitled 'Book of St. Albans' (1486).

Bernhard, Karl (bärn'här), pseudonym of Nicolai de Saint Aubain. A celebrated Danish novelist; born in Copenhagen, Nov. 18, 1798; died there, Nov. 25, 1865. His induction into the republic of letters was under the auspices of his noted kinswoman, Madame Gyllembourg. The poet Heiberg was his uncle; the nephew has almost overshadowed the older writer through the brilliance of 'The Favorite of Fortune,' 'Two Friends,' 'For and Against,' and many other novels, all founded either on historical occurrences or the author's observations of contemporary life.

Bernhardi, Theodor von (bern-här'dē). A German historian and diplomat; born in Berlin, Nov. 6, 1802; died at Kunersdorf, Silesia, Feb. 12, 1887. His diplomatic career was important, and afforded him special facilities for compiling a 'History of Russia and of European Politics during the Years 1814–31' (1863–77); 'Frederick the Great as a Military Commander' (1881); and similar works, all of value.

Bernhardy, Gottfried. A German classical philologist; born in Landsberg-on-the-Warthe, March 20, 1800; died in Halle, May 14, 1875. He lectured very brilliantly at the leading universities, his principal works being 'Greek Syntax Scientifically Considered' (1829), a historical study of the subject; 'Outlines of Roman Literature' (5th ed. 1872); 'Outlines of Greek Literature' (part i., 5th ed. 1892; part ii., 2d–3d ed. 1876–80; part iii. wanting), and a supplement to the first-named treatise, entitled 'Paralipomena [Omissions] in [the Work on] Greek Syntax' (1854–62); although he has written many other important books.

Bernstein, Aaron (bern'stīn). A German publicist and novelist (1812–84); born at Dantzic. He was in politics a radical and in religion a reformer, and his life was a continued battle against obscurantism and conservatism. Yet he wrote some charming stories of life among the Jews, among them 'Mendel Gibbor' (1860). He wrote also some notable historical sketches, as 'The People's Years' and 'The Years of Reaction.'

Berrian, William (ber'i-an). An American Episcopal divine and religious writer; born 1787; died 1862. He was rector of Trinity Church, New York (1830–62). Besides various religious works, he wrote 'Travels in France and Italy' and a 'Historical Sketch of Trinity Church.'

Bersezio, Vittorio (ber-sets'yō). An Italian novelist and playwright; born at Peveragno, Piedmont, in 1830. Both as a writer of tales and of comedies he is conspicuous for vivid and faithful delineation of Piedmontese life; especially in his dialect comedies, among which 'The Misfortunes of Monssù Travett' is considered to be his masterpiece. He also wrote excellent historical works. 'The Reign of Victor Emanuel II.'; 'Rome, the Capital of Italy.'

Bertaut, Jean (bär-tō). A French poet and prelate; born in Caen, 1570; died 1611. He seems to have entered holy orders as a result of the favor he acquired at court through his love poems, which comprise stanzas, odes, and couplets, published as 'Songs' (?) (1602). He also composed "canticles" on 'The Conversion of Henry IV.,' as well as a funeral oration in eulogy of the same monarch.

Berthet, Elie (ber-tā). A French novelist (1815–91), of whose numerous works the best known are: 'The Storks' Nest' (1848); 'The Catacombs of Paris' (1854); 'The Good Old Times' (1867); 'Prehistoric Novels' (1876).

Berthold, Franz (ber-tōld'), pseudonym of Adelheid Reinbold. A German novelist (1802–39), warmly appreciated and furthered by Ludwig Tieck. Her story 'Fred of the Will o' the Wisp' (1830) met with great favor, after her death appeared 'King Sebastian' (1839), a historical romance, and 'Collected Tales' (1842).

Bertin, Antoine (ber-tan'). A French poet (1752–90), much admired by his contemporaries, who, somewhat extravagantly, styled him the French Propertius. He was a friend of Parny, and like him excelled in elegiac and epistolary verse. His principal works are: 'Voyage in Burgundy' (1777) and 'The Loves' (1780).

Besant, Walter, Sir (bes'ant). An English novelist; born in Portsmouth, Aug. 14, 1836; died at Hampstead, June 9, 1901. After graduation, he went to Mauritius as professor in the Royal College, but returned to London, where he became secretary of the Palestine Exploration Fund. In 1871 he formed a literary partnership with James Rice, which continued until the death of the latter. They wrote many novels, some of which were dramatized. Among them are: 'Ready Money Mortiboy' (London, 1871); 'The Golden Butterfly' (1876); 'The Seamy Side'

'The Chaplain of the Fleet' (1881). Alone he has written: 'Studies in Early French Poetry' (1868); 'When George the Third was King' (1872); 'The French Humorists' (1873); 'All Sorts and Conditions of Men' (1882), which led to the establishment of the People's Palace in the East End of London; 'All in a Garden Fair' (1883); 'Dorothy Forster' (1884); 'The World Went Very Well Then' (1887); 'Armorel of Lyonnesse' (1890); 'St. Katharine's By the Tower' (1891); 'The Ivory Gate' (1892); 'Beyond the Dreams of Avarice'; 'The Master Craftsman'; and others. He was knighted in 1896.

Bestúsheff, Alexander Alexandrovich (bestö'zhef *or* bes-tö'shef). A Russian novelist and soldier; born in St. Petersburg, Nov. 3, 1797 (not 1795); killed in battle in the Caucasus, July 19, 1837. Of his numerous novels the most celebrated are: 'Ammalat-Beg'; 'The Nadeshda Frigate'; 'The Terrible Prophecy.' His 'Private Correspondence' is highly prized.

Bethune, George Washington (be-thön'). A distinguished American Dutch Reformed clergyman and poet; born in New York, March 18, 1805; died at Florence, Italy, April 27, 1862. He was a most lovable man, noted as an orator and a wit. He had charges at Rhinebeck and Utica, N.Y., Philadelphia, Brooklyn, and New York city. Besides religious works he wrote: 'British Female Poets'; 'Lays of Love and Faith' (1847), several of the hymns in which are widely used. He also published an edition of Izaak Walton's 'Complete Angler' (1846); etc.

Betteloni, Vittorio (bet-el-ō'ne). An Italian poet; born in Verona, 1840. He was educated in Pisa, and is now professor of Italian literature and history in the Female College in Verona. His verse proves him an adherent of that Italian classical school which dates from 1869, and includes: 'In the Springtime' (1869); 'New Stanzas' (1880); and a translation of Goethe's 'Hermann and Dorothea.'

Betts, Craven Langstroth. An American poet and story-writer; born in New Brunswick, 1853. Besides translating 'Songs from Béranger' in the original metres, he wrote: 'The Perfume Holder, a Persian Love Poem'; and with A. W. H. Eaton, 'Tales of a Garrison Town' and 'A Garland of Sonnets.'

Beyle, Marie-Henri (bāl), better known under the pseudonym of "Stendhal." A notable French novelist and critic; born in Grenoble, Jan. 23, 1783; died in Paris, March 23, 1842. In spite of interruptions due to the political upheavals in which he became involved, he found time to display his critical and imaginative genius in 'Rome, Naples, and Florence in 1817,' 'History of Painting in Italy,' and 'About Love': but his celebrity now rests principally upon 'The Chartreuse [Carthusian Nun] of Parma,' a magnificent fiction, brilliantly original, witty, and absorbing; and to a less extent upon 'The Red and the Black' [*i. e.*, Priests and Soldiers], a romance possible only to a writer with the widest knowledge of men and things.

Bhatti (bhat-tē *or* bě-hat'tē). An Indian epic poet of the 6th or the 7th century. His poem named after him 'Bhattikâvyam' is in 22 cantos. Its theme is the deeds of Râma; but the author designed the work to be also an exemplification of the rules of grammatical and rhetorical composition. It was published with a twofold commentary at Calcutta (1828).

Bhavabhuti (bha-va-bhō'ti *or* bě-ha-va-běhō'ti). An Indian dramatic poet next in celebrity to Kâlidâsa; he lived in the 8th century. His 'Mâlatîmâdhava,' which might be entitled 'The Secret Marriage,' portrays Indian society in effective traits. The 'Mahâvîratsharita' ('Fortunes of the Great Hero') deals with the deeds of Râma and his victory over the giant Râvana, ravisher of Sîta, Râma's consort. The 'Uttararâmatsharita' ('Other Fortunes of Râma') portrays the long-suffering of Sîta and her reconcilement with Râma, all in a sympathetic vein and sometimes with great force.

Biart, Lucien (bē-är'). A French novelist, poet, and writer of travels; born at Versailles, June 21, 1829. He published a number of novels, containing masterly descriptions of Mexican and South-American nature and customs. Among his works are: 'The Mexican Women' (1853), poems; 'Adventures of a Young Naturalist' (1869); 'The Clients of Dr. Bernagius' (1873); 'Across America' (1876), crowned by the Academy. He died March 26, 1897.

Bibbiena (bēb-bē-ä'nä). [Bernardo Dovizio, who was styled Bibbiena.] An Italian poet; born at Bibbiena, Aug. 4, 1470; died Nov. 9, 1520. For many years secretary to Cardinal Giovanni de' Medici, in whose election as Pope Leo X. he is said to have had a considerable share, he was appointed treasurer, and soon after raised to the dignity of cardinal. In this dignity he became an ardent promoter of art and science. His comedy 'Calandria' is probably the earliest in Italian literature.

Bicci, Ersilio (bē'chē). An Italian poet; born in Pisa, 1845. He studied in Florence, and is now professor of Italian literature in the Licei Dante and Toscanelli of that city. His best is in the collection styled 'New Verses.'

Bickersteth, Edward Henry. An English poet; born at Islington, Jan. 25, 1825. He is a graduate of Trinity College, Cambridge, and is noted for his scholarly devotional works; but is most famous as a poet,—'Yesterday, To-day, and Forever' being particularly admired.

Bickmore, Albert Smith. An American naturalist and writer of travels; born at St. George's, Me., March 1, 1839. An extensive traveler in the East, he founded and is curator of the museum of natural history at Central Park, New York. Besides scientific publications, he has written: 'Travels in the East Indian Archipelago' (1869); 'A Journey from Canton to Hankow' (1868); etc.

Biddle, Anthony Joseph Drexel (bid'l). An American publisher, journalist, and miscellaneous writer; born in Pennsylvania, 1874. He has written: 'A Dual Rôle, and Other Stories'; 'An Allegory and Three Essays'; 'The Madeira Islands'; 'The Froggy Fairy Book '; 'The Land of the Wine.'

Biddle, Nicholas. A noted American financier and writer; born in Philadelphia, Jan. 8, 1786; died there, Feb. 27, 1844. He was president of the United States Bank 1823–39, during Jackson's war against its being the depository of the government moneys, and the later speculations which ruined it. Besides miscellaneous writings, he published a 'Commercial Digest,' and 'History of the Expedition under Lewis and Clarke to the Pacific Ocean.'

Biedermann, Karl (bē'der-män). A German historian and publicist; born in Leipsic, Sept. 25, 1812. His influence in public affairs, although indirect, has long been considerable: and as a writer of literary and philosophical history he has struck out a path of his own with 'Germany in the Eighteenth Century' (2d ed. in part, 1880); 'German Philosophy from Kant's Day to Our Own' (1842–43); 'Thirty Years of German History, 1840–70' (2d ed. 1883); and many other allied studies. D. 1901.

Bielovski, August (bē-löv'skē). A Polish poet (1806–76); born at Krechowice, Galicia. Among his poetical compositions is to be mentioned the historical rhapsody 'Lay of Henry the Pious.' He wrote a 'Critical Introduction to the History of Poland.'

Bierbaum, Otto Julius (bēr'boum). A German poet; born in Grünieberg, Silesia, June 28, 1865. He is a rising man of letters; his 'Songs of Experience' (or 'Poems That Were Lived') (1892) is as yet his most noteworthy volume.

Biernatzki, Johann Christoph (bēr-näts'kē). A German pietist, poet, and story-writer; born at Elmshorn, Holstein, Oct. 17, 1795; died at Friedrichstadt, May 11, 1840. A country pastor, he devoted himself to the versification of his own precepts and beliefs, the volume 'Faith' being the result. In 'The Brown Boy,' and 'Hallig, or the Adventures of Castaways on an Island in the North Sea,' he displays a not unpleasing capacity for prose narrative.

Biester, João Ernesto (bēs'ter). A Portuguese dramatist (1829–80); born at Lisbon. He wrote some 90 plays, the most noteworthy among them 'The Nineteenth-Century Gentleman'; 'Luck and Labor'; 'The Scandal-Mongers'; and 'Eternal Spring.'

Bigelow, John. An American author and diplomat; born in Malden, N. Y., Nov. 25, 1817. After graduation from Union College in 1835, he studied law, and in 1849 became associated with William Cullen Bryant in the New York Evening Post, of which he was managing editor until 1861. He was consul in Paris, 1861–65; U. S. minister to France, 1865–67; and held important offices on his return to New York. His specialty is American biography

and history, and his books include: 'Life of John C. Fremont' (1856); 'Lafayette' (1882); 'Molinos, the Quietist' (1882); 'Life of William Cullen Bryant' (1889); 'The United States of America,' in French (1863); and 'France and the Confederate Navy' (1888). He edited the Autobiography of Benjamin Franklin from the original manuscript, which he found in France, and later the complete works of Franklin (10 vols., 1887–88).

Bigelow, Poultney. An American biographical and historical writer; born in New York, N. Y., Sept. 10, 1855. He is the son of John Bigelow; was educated at Yale College and in Germany; and is the author of: 'The German Emperor' (1892); 'Paddles and Politics down the Danube' (1892); 'Borderland of Czar and Kaiser' (1894); and 'History of the German Struggle for Liberty'; 'White Man's Africa.'

Bijns, Anna (bīnz). A noted Flemish poet; born in Antwerp, 1494; died there, April 10, 1575. Much admired for her melodious verses, full of metaphors and showing great technical skill, she was styled the "Brabantine Sappho" by her contemporaries. The first of her volumes of collected verse bore the title 'This is a Beautiful and Truthful [or 'Sincere'] Little Book'; while a second is known as 'Spiritual Refrains.'

Bikelas, Dimitrios (bē-kā'las). An eminent Greek poet and essayist; born at Hermopolis, in the island of Syra, in 1835. After completing his studies, he went to London, where his parents had settled, and since 1874 he has lived in Paris. After having published a collection of his poems in London in 1862, he devoted himself to the task of making Shakespeare's dramas known in Greece through excellent metrical translations. As a prose-writer he has won wide reputation with his tale 'Lukis Laras' (1879), which was translated into thirteen languages. He died July 21, 1908.

Bilderdijk, Willem (bil'der-dīk). A celebrated Dutch poet; born at Amsterdam, Sept. 7, 1756; died Dec. 18, 1831. He reached the highest point of his lyric genius in the 'Miscellaneous Poems' and patriotic pieces, notably the hymn 'Willem Frederik' and 'The True Love of Fatherland.' Of his great didactic poems most are imitations; e. g., the 'Country Life,' after a French original; 'Man,' after Pope's 'Essay on Man.' His epic, 'Destruction of the First World,' a work not unworthy of his genius, was left uncompleted.

Billaut, Adam (bē-yō'), better known as "Maître Adam" (Father Adam). A French poet; born at the beginning of the 17th century; died 1662. A carpenter by trade, he wrote rude but original poems, the gayety of which, together with the contrast they afforded with his occupation, made them very popular at the time. Voltaire called him "Virgil with the Plane." The three collections of his poems were entitled 'The Pegs,' 'The Centre-Bit,' and 'The Plane.'

Billings, John Shaw. An American surgeon and medical and hygienic writer; born in Indiana, 1839. He was librarian of the surgeon-general's office, Washington; president of the American Public Health Association (1880); he is now chief librarian of the New York Library (the combined Astor, Lenox, and Tilden libraries). His chief work is a voluminous ‘Index-Catalogue’ (1880) of the library of the surgeon-general's office. He has written also: ‘Hygienics of the United States Army Barracks’; ‘Mortality and Vital Statistics of the United States Army’ (1880); ‘Ventilation and Heating’ (1884), revised and enlarged 1893,—a very comprehensive and authoritative work.

Billings, Josh. See **Shaw, Henry W.**

Bion (bī'on). A Greek pastoral poet; born near Smyrna in the 3d century B. C. He appears to have passed the latter part of his life in Sicily. His pastorals betray a degree of refinement and sentimentality not found in the earlier and more spontaneous bucolic poets. Still extant is his ‘Lament for Adonis,’ often imitated by subsequent poets. Besides this there remain of his works only short pieces, many of them fragmentary.

Birch-Pfeiffer, Charlotte (bĕrċh-pfī'fĕr). A German actress and dramatist (1800–68). She joined the Court Theatre Company at Munich at the age of 13 years; at 18 she had won distinction in tragic rôles. She married Christian Birch in 1825; thereafter till her death she was in active relations with the stage, whether as actress or conductress. Her numerous dramatic compositions were produced on nearly every stage in Germany. They evince remarkable skill in the employment of stage effects. Her plays are in many instances grounded on novels; among them are: ‘Graffenstein Castle’; ‘The Favorites’; ‘The Bell-Ringers of Notre Dame’ (Victor Hugo); ‘The Woman in White’ (Wilkie Collins); ‘The Orphan of Lowood’ (Charlotte Brontë).

Bird, Robert Montgomery. An American dramatist and novelist; born in Newcastle, Del., Feb. 5, 1805 (?); died in Philadelphia, Pa., Jan. 22, 1854. He was the author of three tragedies: ‘Oraloosa’; ‘The Broker of Bogota’; and ‘The Gladiator,’ frequently played by Forrest. His novels include: ‘Calavar’ (1834); ‘The Infidel’ (1835); ‘Nick of the Woods’ (1837); ‘Peter Pilgrim’ (1838); and ‘Robin Day’ (1839).

Birney, James Gillespie. A noted American statesman and publicist; born at Danville, Ky., Feb. 4, 1792; died at Perth Amboy, N. J., Nov. 25, 1857. Though a Southern planter, he emancipated his slaves and became a prominent anti-slavery leader in the South, proprietor and editor of the anti-slavery journal The Philanthropist, etc. He was candidate of the « Liberty » party for President (1840 and 1844). He wrote: ‘Ten Letters on Slavery and Colonization’; ‘Addresses and Speeches’; ‘American Churches the Bulwark of American Slavery.’

Birrell, Augustine. An English essayist; born in Wavertree, near Liverpool, Jan. 19, 1850. He graduated from Cambridge and was called to the bar. He is author of charming critical and biographical essays on literary subjects, collected in the two series of ‘Obiter Dicta’ (1884, 2d series 1887), and ‘Res Judicatæ’ (1892, really the third of the same series). ‘Men, Women, and Books’ (1895) is a collection of short newspaper pieces. In 1887 he published a ‘Life of Charlotte Brontë.’

Bischoff. J. E. K. See **Bolanden.**

Bishop, Nathaniel Holmes. An American traveler; born at Medway, Mass., 1837. He has written: ‘A Thousand Miles’ Walk Across South America’ (1869); ‘Voyage of the Paper Canoe from Quebec to the Gulf of Mexico’; ‘Four Months in a Sneak-Box.’ Died 1902.

Bishop, William Henry. An American novelist; born in Hartford, Conn., Jan. 7, 1847. He is the author of several novels, including: ‘Detmold’ (1879); ‘The House of a Merchant Prince’ (1882); ‘A Pound of Cure: A Story of Monte Carlo’ (1894); ‘Old Mexico and her Lost Provinces’ (1884); ‘Fish and Men in the Maine Islands’; ‘A House-Hunter in Europe’; ‘Writing to Russia,’ a story; ‘The Golden Justice’; ‘Choy Susan, and Other Stories’; ‘The Brown-Stone Boy and Other Queer People’; and ‘The Yellow Snake.’

Bisland, Elizabeth. An American descriptive and story writer; by marriage Mrs. Wetmore; born 1862. She is author of ‘A Flying Trip around the World’ (1891), the account of a trip performed in 76 days in the year 1876; and of ‘A Widower Indeed,’ with Rhoda Broughton’ (1892); ‘The Secret Life’ (1907).

Bismarck, Otto Edward Leopold von (biz'märk). A German statesman; born at Schönhausen, April 1, 1815. He was a member of the United Diet, 1847; ambassador at St. Petersburg, 1859; ambassador at Paris, 1862; premier of Prussia, 1862 to 1866; and chancellor of the Germam Empire from its inception in 1870 to 1890. He holds a place in literature through the volume of ‘Bismarck's Letters,’ and through his State papers, a series of which appears in Hahn's ‘Fürst Bismarck’; while as a thinker and economist he is seen to advantage in ‘Bismarck als Volkswirth,’ by Poschinger, containing many of the Prince's papers on sociological and fiscal subjects. Died July 30, 1898.

Bissell, Edwin Cone (bis'l). A prominent American Congregational divine and religious writer; born at Schoharie, N. Y., March 2, 1832; died in Chicago, April 9, 1894. Having served in the Civil War (1862–63), he became pastor in Massachusetts and California, missionary in Austria (1873–78), professor in the Hartford Congregational Theological Seminary (1881–92), and the McCormick Presbyterian Theological Seminary, Chicago (1892–94). He published ‘Historic Origin of the Bible’ (1873) and various other religious works, including a curious edition of ‘Genesis Printed in Colors,

Showing the Original Sources from which it is Supposed to have been Compiled ' (1892).

Bisson, Alexandre (bis-sôn'). A French dramatist and musical composer; born in 1848. His vaudeville ' Four Cuts with a Penknife ' (1873) won for him instant celebrity. ' The Deputy from Bombignac ' is his masterpiece. Other comedies or operettas were: ' The Late Toupinel ' (1890); ' The Joys of Paternity ' (1891); ' The Pont-Biquet Family ' (1892) ; ' Madame X.' With Théodore de Lajarte he was joint author of a ' Grammar of Music ' (1879) and of a ' Little Encyclopædia of Music ' (1881).

Bitter, Arthur (bĭt'er), pseudonym of Samuel Haberstich. A Swiss poet and story-writer; born in Ried near Schlosswyl, Oct. 21, 1821; died at Berne, Feb. 20, 1872. Novelettes, stories, and poems proceeded from his pen for many years, all characterized by sympathy of tone and inoffensive realism; ' Tales, Romances, and Poems ' (1865–66), being most pleasing.

Bitzius, Albert. See Gotthelf.

Bjerregaard, Henrik Anker (byer'e̞-gär). A Norwegian dramatic poet; born at Ringsaker, 1792; died 1842. His position in his country's literature is very influential, the plays ' Magnus Barefoot's Sons ' and ' A Mountain Adventure ' being national models. A volume of ' Poems ' (1829) also displays genius.

Björnson, Björnstjerne (byêrn'sọn). An eminent Norwegian novelist, poet, and dramatist; born at Kvikne, Norway, Dec. 8, 1832. He published his first story, ' Synnöve Solbakken,' in 1857; and that, with ' Arne ' (1858) and ' A Lively Fellow ' (1860), established his reputation as a novelist. ' Halte Hulda '; ' Between Battles ' (1858); and ' Sigurd Slembe ' (1862), are among his plays. Of his novels and romances since 1866 the most notable are : ' The Bridal March '; ' Magnhild '; ' The Fisher Maiden '; and ' Captain Mansana ' His principal dramatic works are : ' Mary Stuart ' (1864) ; ' The Editors '; ' A Bankruptcy '; ' Leonarda ' (1879) ; ' A Glove ' (1889). He published a volume of ' Poems and Songs ' in 1870.

Black, William. A Scottish novelist; born in Glasgow November 9, 1841 ; died at London, December 10, 1898. He was educated at private schools. In 1874 he abandoned the career of journalism, visited America in 1876, and returning to London, devoted himself anew to literature. In addition to an interesting story, his novels contain fine descriptions of scenery. They are very popular, and include : ' Love or Marriage ' (1867); ' In Silk Attire ' (1869); ' A Daughter of Heth ' (1871); ' The Strange Adventures of a Phaeton ' (1872) ; ' A Princess of Thule ' (1873); ' Three Feathers ' (1875) ; ' Madcap Violet ' (1876) ; ' Macleod of Dare ' (1878) ; ' White Wings: a Yachting Romance ' (1880); ' Yolande ' (1883) ; ' Judith Shakespeare ' (1884) ; ' White Heather ' (1885); ' The Strange Adventures of a House-Boat ' (1888); ' Wolfenberg ' (1892); ' Highland Cousins.'

He has also written a ' Life of Goldsmith ' (1879), translated into German by Katscher.

Blackburn, William Maxwell. An American Presbyterian divine and educator, historian and biographer; born at Carlisle, Ind., Dec. 30, 1828 ; died —— 1900. He became president of the University of North Dakota (1884–85) and Pierre University, South Dakota (1885). He wrote: ' St. Patrick and the Early Irish Church ' (1869); ' Admiral Coligny and the Rise of the Huguenots ' (2 vols., 1869); ' History of the Christian Church ' (1879); etc. ; and the ' Uncle Alick' juvenile stories.

Blackie, John Stuart. A Scottish author; born in Glasgow in July 1809; died in Edinburgh, March 2, 1895. He received his education in Edinburgh, Göttingen, Berlin, and Rome; was professor of Greek in Edinburgh University from 1852 till 1882, and continued to write and lecture till his death. He was one of the most important men of his day; promoted educational reform, and championed Scottish nationality. He advocated preserving the Gaelic language, and by his own efforts founded a Celtic chair in Edinburgh University. His books include translations from the Greek and German; moral and religious and other philosophy; ' Lays of the Highlands and Islands ' (1872); ' Self-Culture ' (1874) ; ' Language and Literature of the Scottish Highlands ' (1875); ' Altavona: Fact and Fiction from my Life in the Highlands ' (1882) ; Wisdom of Goethe ' (1883) ; ' Life of Burns ' (1888); ' Essays on Subjects of Moral and Social Interest ' ; and ' A Song of Heroes ' (1890).

Blackmore, Sir Richard. An English physician and poet; born in Wiltshire about 1650; died 1729. Besides medical works, Scripture paraphrases, and satirical verse, he wrote in Popian couplets ' Prince Arthur, a Heroic Poem ' (1695), and a voluminous religious epic, ' The Creation ' (1712), very successful and much praised then, but not now read.

Blackmore, Richard Doddridge. An English novelist; born in Longworth, Berkshire, June 7, 1825 ; died in London, Jan. 20, 1900. He graduated from Oxford in 1847, was called to the bar in 1852, and later devoted himself to literature. Among his novels are : ' Lorna Doone ' (London, 1869 ; far the most celebrated, having reached dozens of editions, some of them magnificent extra-illustrated ones); ' Clara Vaughan ' (1864) ; ' The Maid of Sker ' (1872); ' Alice Lorraine ' (1875); ' Cripps the Carrier ' (1876) ; ' Erema ' (1877); ' Mary Anerley ' (1880) ; ' Christowell ' (1882) ; ' Sir Thomas Upmore' (1884) ; ' Springhaven' (1887) ; ' Kit and Kitty' (1889); ' Perlycross' (1894); ' Dariel' (1897); and other novels. He also published a version of Virgil's ' Georgics.'

Blackstone, Sir William. An English jurist and writer on law; born in London, 1723; died in 1780. His ' Commentaries on the Laws of England ' have conferred great celebrity on his name, not only by reason of the profound learning of the work but because it possesses

literary merits of a high order. The first
volume appeared in 1765, the last in 1769.

Blackwell, Mrs. Antoinette Louisa (Brown).
A prominent American woman-suffragist and
Unitarian minister; born at Henrietta, N. Y.,
May 20, 1825. A graduate of Oberlin (1847),
she "preached on her own orders," at first in
Congregational churches, becoming at length a
champion of women's rights. She married
Samuel C., a brother of Dr. Elizabeth Blackwell (1856). She has written: 'Shadows of
our Social System' (1855); 'The Island Neighbors' (1871), a novel of American life; 'Sexes
throughout Nature' (1875); 'Sea Drift' (1903).

Blackwell, Elizabeth. A noted American
physician and medical and ethical writer;
born at Bristol, England, 1821. She is the
first woman that ever obtained the degree of
M. D. in the United States (1849), beginning
practice in New York (1851). With her sister
Emily, she opened the New York infirmary
for women and children (1854), organizing in
connection with it the Women's Medical College (1867). In 1868 she became professor in
a woman's medical college that she had assisted in organizing in London. She has written:
'Laws of Life' (1852); 'Counsel to Parents on
the Moral Education of their Children' (1879);
'Pioneer Work in Opening the Medical Profession to Women'; 'The Human Element in Sex.'

Blaikie, William (blā'ki). A noted American athlete and writer on physical training;
born at York, N. Y., 1843. He became a
lawyer in New York. He has written: 'How
to Get Strong' (2d ed. 1880); 'Sound Bodies
for our Boys and Girls.' Died Dec. 6, 1904.

Blaine, James Gillespie. An eminent
American statesman; born in West Browns-
ville, Pa., Jan. 31, 1830; died in Washington,
D. C., Jan. 27, 1893. He graduated at Washington College, Pa., in 1847. In 1854 he removed
to Augusta, Me., and engaged in journalism.
He was one of the founders of the Republican
party, and in 1856 was a delegate to the first
Republican national convention, which nomi-
nated Frémont for the Presidency. In 1858
he was elected to the Legislature of Maine,
and in 1862 to the House of Representatives
of the national Congress. He became Speaker
of the House in 1869, and held that position
for six years; was a member of the Senate
from 1876 to 1881; was twice Secretary of
State (1881-82 and 1889-92). He was nom-
inated for the Presidency in 1884. Besides
his numerous speeches and writings on the
public questions of his day, his best known
work is his 'Twenty Years in Congress' (2
vols., 1884-86), a historical production of great
and permanent value.

Blair. Hugh. A Scotch divine, sermonist,
and educational writer; born in Edinburgh,
1718; died 1800. He was noted for the eloquence of his sermons, and also for 'Lectures
on Rhetoric' (1783), which attained great popularity, 'Blair's Rhetoric' being familiar to all
students.

Blake, James Vila. An American poet,
essayist, and Unitarian divine; born in New
York, 1842. He is now settled in Chicago.
He has written: 'Essays' (1886); 'Poems and
Essays' (2 vols., 1887); 'Legends from Story
Land'; 'Sonnets' (1902); 'Discoveries' (1904).

Blake, Mrs. Lillie (Devereux) Umstead.
A prominent American advocate of woman's
rights, a novelist; born at Raleigh, N. C., 1835.
Her first husband, Frank G. Quay Umstead,
died in 1859; she married Grenfill Blake in
1866. She has written and spoken much on
woman suffrage and the like, and her novels
bear on this theme. She has written: 'Southwold' (1859); 'Rockford' (1863); 'Fettered for
Life' (new ed. 1885); 'Woman's Place To-
Day' (1883), a reply to Dr. Morgan Dix's
'Lenten Lectures on Women,' which attracted
attention; etc.

Blake, Mrs. Mary Elizabeth (McGrath).
An American poet and writer of travels;
1840-1907. In verse, she has written: 'Poems'
(1882); 'Youth in Twelve Centuries' (1886);
etc. Of her travels, may be named: 'On the
Wing' (1883); 'A Summer Holiday.'

Blake, William. An English poet and artist; born in London, Nov. 28, 1757; died there,
Aug. 12, 1827. He learned to draw; became
a noted illustrator and engraver; had a print-
shop in London; and exhibited at the Royal
Academy. His imagination was strange, powerful, grotesque, and poetic; and his belief was
that his poems and drawings were communications from the spirit world. His 'Poetical
Sketches' (London, 1783); 'Songs of Innocence' (1789); and 'Songs of Experience'
(1794), contain pastoral and lyrical poems of
great beauty. His 'Prophetic Books,' including 'Book of Thel' (1789); 'Marriage of
Heaven and Hell' (1790); 'Book of Urizen'
(1794); 'Book of Los' (1795); 'Book of Ahania'
(1795); 'Jerusalem' (1804); and 'Milton' (1804),
are famous. His greatest artistic work is in
'Illustrations to the Book of Job' (1826).

Blanc, Charles (blŏn). A French art critic
(1813-82). He was director of the government
department of fine art, 1848-52. His contributions to the history and philosophy of art comprise: 'A History of Painters of all Schools'
(14 vols., 1849-69); 'The Treasure of Curiosity' (1858); 'Grammar of the Arts of Design,'
his greatest work (1867); 'Art in Personal
Adornment and Attire'; (posthumously) 'History of the Artistic Renaissance in Italy' (2
vols., 1889).

Blanchard, Edward Laman. An English
dramatist and novelist (1820-89); born in London. His novels, 'Temple Bar' and 'A Man
Without a Destiny,' evinced no special talent
for story-telling; on the other hand, he composed for Drury Lane Theatre about 100
'Christmas Pantomimes' in the vein of gro-
tesque-burlesque, among them 'Sindbad the
Sailor,' which were received with unbounded
popular favor.

Blanche, August Theodor (blänsh). A Swedish dramatist and novelist; born in Stockholm, Sept. 17, 1811; died there, Nov 30, 1868. His comedies and farces—more particularly 'Jenny, or the Steamboat Trip,' 'The Doctor' 'The Rich Uncle,' and 'The Foundling'—have made all Sweden laugh; while his realistic fictions—among them 'The Spectre,' 'Tales of a Cabman,' and 'Sons of North and South'—are eagerly read.

Blavatsky, Helena Petrovna (blä-vät'ski). A noted Theosophist; born at Yekaterinoslav, Russia, 1831; died in London, May 8, 1891. She founded the "Theosophical Society" in New York (1875). She wrote: 'Isis Unveiled' (1876); 'The Secret Doctrine' (1888); 'Key to Theosophy' (1889); etc.

Blaze de Bury, Ange Henri (bläz dĕ bü-rē'). A French literary critic and historian (1813-88); born at Paris. He was profoundly conversant with German literature, and published many admirable studies on that subject. His historical sketches,—'The Königsmarcks' (1855), 'The Legend of Versailles' (1870), 'Women of the Renaissance' (1886), etc.,—and his numerous brief memoirs of great musicians, are worthy of mention.

Bledsoe, Albert Taylor (bled'sō). A prominent American clergyman, educator, lawyer, editor, soldier, and miscellaneous writer; born at Frankfort, Ky., Nov. 9, 1809; died at Alexandria, Va., Dec. 1, 1877. He was Assistant Secretary of War of the Southern Confederacy, and both an Episcopal and a Methodist minister. Besides editing the Southern Review and contributing frequently to leading literary, scientific, and theological periodicals, he wrote: 'Examination of Edwards on the Will' (1845); 'Theodicy' (new ed. 1853); 'Philosophy of Mathematics' (1868); etc.

Bleibtreu, Karl August (blīb'troi). A German poet and novelist; born at Berlin, Jan. 13, 1859. He is one of the foremost representatives of the "Youngest German" school in literature, and a pronounced realist. All his views are radical, as shown by the very titles of his works: e. g., 'Revolution in Literature' (1885); 'Literature's Struggle for Life.' He also wrote: 'Dies Iræ'; 'Napoleon at Leipsic'; 'Cromwell at Marston Moor.' His dramas are: 'Lord Byron' (1888); 'The Day of Judgment'; 'The Queen's Necklace'; 'From Robespierre to Buddha.'

Blessington, Marguerite, Countess of. An Irish descriptive writer and novelist; born in Knockbrit, Tipperary, Sept. 1, 1789; died in Paris, June 4, 1849. In 1818 she was married to the Earl of Blessington, and became a favorite in distinguished society in London and on the Continent. Her connection with the Count d'Orsay dated from 1822. She wrote a number of novels: 'The Idler in Italy' (London, 1839-40); 'The Idler in France' (1841); and 'Conversations with Lord Byron' (1834).

Blicher, Steen Steensen (blich'ẽr). A Danish poet and novelist (1782-1848); born at Viborg His first work was a translation of 'Ossian' (2 vols., 1807-9); and his first original poems appeared in 1814, but attracted little notice. He quickly won a national reputation with his novels, and in 1842 appeared his masterpiece of novel-writing, 'The Knitting-Room,' a collection of short stories in the Jutland dialect.

Blind, Mathilde. A German-English poet; born in Mannheim, March 21, 1847; died in London, Nov. 26, 1896. She went to England in 1849, and won fame by her writings: 'The Prophecy of St. Oran, and Other Poems' (London, 1881); 'Life of George Eliot' (1883); 'Madame Roland' (1886); 'The Heather on Fire,' a tale (1886); 'Ascent of Man' (1889); 'Dramas in Miniature' (1892); 'Songs and Sonnets' (1893); and 'Birds of Passage' (1895).

Bliss, William Dwight Porter. A prominent American Episcopal clergyman and writer on Christian Socialism; born in Italy, 1856. He has written a 'Handbook of Socialism'; 'What is Christian Socialism?' etc., and compiled the 'Encyclopædia of Socialism' (1897), besides editing a Christian Socialist weekly, The Dawn, now The Fabian.

Bloede, Gertrude (blē'dĕ). An American poet and novelist, better known as "Stuart Sterne"; born in Saxony, Germany, 1845. She has written in verse: 'Angelo' (new ed. 1879), 'Giorgio and Other Poems' (1881), etc.; and 'The Story of the Two Lives,' a novel. D. 1905.

Blommaert, Philipp (blom'märt). A Flemish poet, historian, and dramatist; born in Ghent, Aug. 27, 1809; died there, Aug. 14, 1871. His great ambition was to make his native Flemish tongue a literary language, and to unify the people who wrote and spoke it. His works include: 'History of the Belgian Lowlanders,' a specimen of stately prose; 'Theophilus,' a poem; and 'Old Flemish Ballads.'

Bloomfield, Robert. An English poet; born at Honington, Dec. 3, 1766; died in Shefford, 1823. Apprenticed to a shoemaker in London, he chanced upon odd volumes of the poets, and thus was awakened his native poetic genius. He first came into public notice with 'The Milk-Maid,' and good fortune attended his 'The Sailor's Return.' He essayed a longer flight in 'The Farmer's Boy' (1800), by which he established his title to rank among the minor poets.

Bloomfield-Moore, Mrs. Clara Sophia (Jessup). An American poet and novelist; born in Pennsylvania, 1824. Her home is in Philadelphia, though she has lived much abroad, particularly in England. She has written: 'Miscellaneous Poems,' 'The Warden's Tale, and Other Poems,' etc., and the romance 'On Dangerous Ground,' besides essays on science and in promotion of inventions.

Blouet, Paul (blö-ā'). ["Max O'Rell."] A French lecturer and author; born in Brittany, France, March 2, 1848. During his early life he was an officer of cavalry in the French army, but in 1873 went to England and became a teacher. After the publication of his first book, 'John Bull and his Island' (1883), he abandoned teaching and devoted himself to literature. He has made several lecturing-tours of the United States. His works include: 'John Bull and his Daughters' (1884); 'Jonathan and his Continent' (1888, with Jack Allyn); 'A Frenchman in America' (1891). Died at Paris, May 24, 1903.

Blum, Ernest (blüm). A French dramatist; born in Paris, Aug. 15, 1836. Either alone or in collaboration with other dramatists he is author of many highly successful plays. The drama of 'Rose Michel' (1877), of his own composition, insured his place among the most successful French dramatists of the time. Among his later compositions are: 'Adam and Eve' (1886); 'The Nervous Women' (1888); 'End of the Century' (1890); 'A Winter Soiree' (1900).

Blumenreich, Franziska (blö'men-rich). A German novelist; born in Bohemia, April 2, 1849. Among her very numerous novels these are the more notable: 'At the Abyss of Marriage' (1888); 'Freighted with Bliss' (1890); 'Storms in Port' (1892); 'Beyond the Good and Bad.' She is a zealous advocate of woman's rights.

Blumenthal, Oskar (blö'men-täl). A German dramatist and critic; born in Berlin, March 13, 1852. Sprightliness of dialogue is the most distinguishing character of his plays; the most successful of them are: 'The Big Bell'; 'A Drop of Poison'; 'The Black Veil'; 'Severe Masters.' He has published several volumes of critical and miscellaneous essays.

Blunt, Wilfrid Scawen. An Irish poet; born at Crabbet Park, Sussex, in 1840. He was attaché of legation at The Hague, Athens, Madrid, Buenos Ayres, and elsewhere. He supported Arabi Pasha in a revolt in 1881, in Egypt; and was imprisoned in 1888 for his insurrectionary actions in Ireland. He is author of: 'Sonnets and Songs by Proteus' (London, (1875); 'The Love Sonnets of Proteus' (1881; new ed. 1885); 'The Future of Islam' (1882); 'The Wind and the Whirlwind,' political poems (1884); 'Ideas about India' (1885); 'Esther: a Young Man's Tragedy'; 'Odes of Pagan Arabia.'

Blüthgen, August Edward Viktor (blüt'gen). A German novelist; born at Zörbig, near Halle, Jan. 4, 1844. He has won high distinction as a writer for the young. Among his stories for boys and girls are: 'The Rogues' Looking-Glass' (1876); 'The Battle of Frogs and Mice' (1878); and with these is to be classed the letterpress (verses) of O. Pletsch's 'Picture Books.' Of novels and romances he is author of a great many: e. g., 'The Peace-Breaker' (1883); 'The Step-Sister' (1887); 'Madame the Countess' (1892).

Blyden, Edward Wilmot. A negro author; born at St. Thomas, W. I., Aug. 3, 1832. After vainly seeking, in 1845, admission to some college in the United States, he went to Liberia, and graduated at the Alexander High School,

of which he afterwards became principal. In 1880 he became president of Liberia College, has held important governmental positions, and has twice been commissioner to the Presbyterian General Assembly of the United States (in 1861 and 1880). He is proficient in many languages, including Latin, Greek, Spanish, Hebrew, and Arabic. He has published: 'Liberia's Offering' (1873); 'From West Africa to Palestine' (1873); 'The Negro in Ancient History'; etc.

Boardman, George Dana. A distinguished American clergyman and author; born at Tavoy, British Burma, Aug. 18, 1828. He was the son of the eminent American Baptist missionary of the same name. He was educated in the United States, graduating at Brown University in 1852 and at Newton Theological Institution in 1855. He became pastor at Barnwell, S. C.; afterwards at Rochester, N. Y., till 1864, when he became pastor of the First Baptist Church in Philadelphia. Besides sermons and essays, his chief works are: 'Studies in the Creative Week' (1878); 'Studies in the Model Prayer' (1879); 'Epiphanies of the Risen Lord' (1879); 'Studies in the Mountain Instruction' (1880). Died April 28, 1903.

Boccaccio, Giovanni (bok-kä'chō). A celebrated Italian novelist, poet, and humanist; born at Paris, 1313; died Dec. 21, 1375. His first romance was 'Filocopo,' dedicated to his mistress Fiammetta. The romantic epic the 'Theseid' followed; it is the first Italian work of the kind. Both for itself and for its associations, the 'Theseid' is of interest to students of English literature, having been a source of inspiration to Chaucer in his 'Knightes Tale.' 'Fiammetta in Love' is a work of the finest psychological analysis, clothed in every grace of poesy. 'Love's Labyrinth' is a vigorous satire on woman. But Boccaccio's enduring fame rests on the 'Decameron'; a collection of stories original and borrowed, set in a narrative framework, all of the highest charm.

Bodenstedt, Friedrich Martin von (bō'denstet). ["Mirza Schaffy."] A German poet and journalist; born at Peine, April 22, 1819; died in Berlin, April 19, 1892. His works include: 'Poetical Ukraine'; 'The People of the Caucasus and their Struggle for Freedom against the Russians'; 'Thousand and One Days in the East'; 'Songs of Mirza Schaffy'; 'From the Atlantic to the Pacific.'

Bodmer, Johann Jakob (bod'mer). A Swiss scholar and literary critic; born near Zürich, July 19, 1698; died Jan. 2, 1783. He was the first to make English literature known in Germany; and wrote dramas, and the epics 'The Deluge' (1751) and 'Noah' (1752). He published two volumes of 'Critical Letters,' and prepared editions of ancient German poetry: 'Specimens of Thirteenth-Century Suabian Poetry'; 'Fables from the Time of the Minnesingers'; 'Kriemhilde's Revenge'; etc.

Bödtcher, Ludwig (bet'che). A Danish lyrist (1793–1874); born at Copenhagen. He spent many years in Italy, and nature and man in Italy equally with nature and man in Denmark are the themes of his finest poems, — notably 'Bacchus,' and the collection called 'Poems Old and New.'

Boëtius or **Boëthius, Anicius Manlius Torquatus Severinus** (bō-ē'thi-us). A Roman didactic poet and statesman; born between 470 and 475; died about 525. While in prison, rightly anticipating execution, he composed his celebrated 'Consolation of Philosophy.' It purports to be a dialogue between Philosophy and her votary, and is in both prose and verse.

Bogaers, Adriaan (bō'gärs). A Dutch poet (1795-1870); born at The Hague. He holds eminent place among the many disciples of Tollens, and surpasses his master in correctness of taste. He long withheld his compositions from publication, and not till 1832 did he become known to his countrymen; he then published his first lyric poem, 'Volharding,' — an appeal to his countrymen to stand fast in the struggle with Belgium, — together with other patriotic pieces. His first poem of any considerable compass, the epic 'Jochebed,' and his masterpiece, 'The Voyage of Heemskerk to Gibraltar,' were first formally published in 1860-61, though they had had for many years a private circulation among friends. He afterward published three volumes: 'Ballads and Romances'; 'Flowers of Poesy from Abroad'; and 'Poems.'

Bogart, William Henry (bō'gärt). An American biographer; born at Albany, N. Y., 1810; died 1888. He wrote: 'Life of Daniel Boone' (7th thousand, 1856); 'Who Goes There?' etc.

Bogdanóvich, Ippolit Feodorovich (bog-dä-nō'vich). A Russian poet (1744-1803); born in Little Russia. His early poems, written when he was a boy, won for him admission to the university. His most celebrated work is a charming free elaboration of Lafontaine's 'Loves of Psyche and Cupid.' He also wrote dramas and comedies, and published a collection of 'Proverbs.'

Bogdanóvich, Modést Ivanovich. A Russian military historian and commander; born 1805; died in Oranienbaum, Aug. 6, 1882. He was a very able soldier, and even abler with the pen; his 'Bonaparte's Campaign in Italy, 1796' (2d ed. 1860) and 'History of the Art of War,' and particularly his 'History of the Campaign of 1812' (2d ed. 1861), having attracted wide notice.

Bögh, Erik (bég). A Danish poet and dramatist; born in Copenhagen, Jan. 17, 1822; died there Aug. 17, 1899. He is best known for his witty stanzas and epigrams in periodicals for 'This and That,' a collection of humorous essays, and for many plays and farces. A novel, 'Jonas Tvärmose's Vexations,' has merit.

Bogovic, Mirko (bō'-gō-vich). A Croatian poet (1816-93); born at Agram. His first literary work was in translating Serb poetry into German. His original lyric poems appeared under the title 'Violets' (1844); being followed by two successful volumes of his collected verse. He wrote also dramas, among them the tragedy 'Stephen, Last King of Bosnia'; and several novels.

Boguslavski, Adalbert (bō-gō-slav'ske). A Polish dramatist (1759-1829); born near Posen. He composed the first opera ever written in the Polish language. For several years he was director of theatres in various towns, and in 1790 became director of the National Theatre at Warsaw. As an actor he excelled alike in tragedy and in comedy, and he formed many pupils who gained high distinction on the stage. The best of his dramatic compositions is the popular melodrama 'The Wonder, or the Men of Krakau and the Mountaineers.'

Böhlau, Helene (bē'lou). A German novelist; born at Weimar, Nov. 22, 1859. She shows now and then a leaning toward the romantic school, but on the whole her high power of description is realistic and her writings are imbued with passion. Among her novels are : 'Under Death's Ban' (1882); 'Guilty of a Pure Heart' (1888); 'In Freshwater'; 'A Half-Animal.'

Böhme, Jakob (bē'mé). A German mystic theologian; born in Altseidenburg, in the Oberlausitz, 1575; died in Görlitz, Nov. 17, 1624. He was a peasant's son and learned the shoemaker's trade; but his lack of early advantages was recompensed by the heavenly illuminations with which he was favored, and which are set forth in about twenty books, — among them 'Aurora, or the Sunrise' (1612). He was very widely read at one time, and still has devoted adherents. But he himself acknowledges the obscurity of his writings.

Boileau-Despréaux, Nicolas (bwä-lō'dä-prā-ō'). A noted French poet and critic; born in Paris, Nov. 1, 1636; died March 13, 1711. His first effort was 'The Farewell of a Poet to the City of Paris' (1660), and six years later published collectedly seven satires (afterward increased to twelve), in which he castigates even the magnates of the literary world. Following the vein worked by Horace, he published 'The Art of Poetry' (1674). In reply to the critics Boileau composed 'The Reading-Desk,' a comic epic which is esteemed a masterpiece.

Boisard, François Marie (bwä-zär). A French fabulist (1744-1833). Of all the French fabulists he is least an imitator of the great Lafontaine. His 'Fables' were at first published in the newspaper Mercure de France, and afterwards gathered in two collections. His 'Ode on the Deluge' was crowned by the Rouen Academy, 1790.

Boisgobey, Fortuné-Abraham du (bwä-gō-bä'). A French novelist; born in Granville, Sept. 11, 1821; died in February 1891. In 1844-48 he was paymaster in the army at Algiers, and began to write in 1868, somewhat on the lines of Émile Gaboriau. His novels

5

were popular, and include: 'The Scoundrels' (Paris, 1873); 'Chevalier Casse-Con' (1873); 'The Mysteries of Modern Paris' (1876); 'The Demi-Monde under the Terror' (1877); 'The Old Age of M. Lecoq' (1878); 'The Cat's Eye' (1888); and 'The Cold Hand' (1879).

Boissier, Gaston (bwä-syā'). A French biographical and critical writer; born at Nîmes, 1823. He is a member of the Academy, and has won celebrity with 'Cicero and his Friends'; 'Life of Madame de Sévigné'; 'Archæological Walks in Rome and Naples'; and others. He was a frequent contributor to French periodical literature. Died June 10, 1908.

Boito, Arrigo (bō-ē'tō). An Italian poet and musician; born at Padua, 1842. His father was an Italian painter and his mother was a Polish lady, and the son inherits the gifts of both nations. His librettos written for Verdi, Bottesíni, and Ponchielli, and his own operas, 'Mefistofele' and 'Nerone,' are of a high order of poetry. In 1877 he published a separate volume of verse.

Bojardo, Matteo Maria (bō-yär'dō). A celebrated Italian poet; born at Scandiano, about 1434; died at Reggio, Dec. 21, 1494. He was of noble origin in Lombardy, and all his life held high and responsible posts in the civil government at Modena and at Reggio. His great fame rests on the romantic epic 'Orlando in Love,' which tells of the loves of Charlemagne's knight Roland and the fair Angelica and the adventures connected therewith. The epic was planned to be completed in three books, but at the author's death only two books, of 29 and 31 cantos respectively, were finished; the composition of the third book had reached only the ninth canto. Niccolò degli Agostini wrote a continuation in 33 cantos. In point of imagination and invention Bojardo ranks among the greatest poets. But his versification is far from perfect, and his language lacks grace and purity; because of these and other blemishes the 'Orlando' was recast and polished by Francesco Berni, and with eminent success.

Bok, Edward William. An American editor and essayist; born in Holland, 1863. He has edited the Ladies' Home Journal, and written 'The Young Man in Business' and 'Successward.'

Boker, George Henry. An American poet and dramatist; born in Philadelphia, Pa., Oct. 6, 1823; died there, Jan. 2, 1890. He graduated from Princeton in 1842; studied law; and was United States minister to Turkey in 1871–75, and to Russia in 1875–79. His plays include: 'Calaynos' (1848); 'Anne Boleyn' (1850); 'Francesca di Rimini'; 'The Betrothed'; and 'All the World's a Mask.' Collected plays and poems (Boston, 1856). Also 'Poems of the War' (1864); 'Königsmark and other Poems' (1869); 'The Book of the Dead' (1882); and 'Sonnets' (1886).

Bolanden, Konrad von (bō'län-den), pseudonym of Joseph Eduard Konrad Bischoff. A German novelist; born at Niedergailbach, Aug. 9, 1828. A Catholic theologian, and high in favor at the papal court, his fictions, all brilliant in style and conception, attack the Protestant standpoint from all directions;—'A Wedding Trip'; 'Queen Bertha'; 'Barbarossa'; 'The Free-Thinkers'; and 'Historical Tales of Frederick II. and his Times,' being noteworthy examples.

Boldrewood, Rolf, pseudonym of Thomas Alexander Browne. An Australian author; born in England in 1827. He is a son of Capt. Sylvester J. Browne, a founder of Melbourne, Australia. He was educated in Sidney College, and has written: 'Ups and Downs: a Story of Australian Life' (London, 1879); 'Robbery under Arms: Life and Adventures in the Bush' (1888); 'A Squatter's Dream Story' (1890); 'A Modern Buccaneer'; 'In Bad Company.'

Bolingbroke, Henry St. John, Viscount. A celebrated English statesman, orator, and author; born at Battersea, Oct. 1, 1678; died there, Dec. 12, 1751. He entered Parliament in 1701; became Secretary of War 1704-8, and Secretary of State in 1710. In 1712 he entered the House of Lords, and in 1713 negotiated the Peace of Utrecht. On the accession of George I. he fled to the Continent, and in 1715 was attainted of treason; but in 1723 he was permitted to return. His chief works are: 'A Dissertation on Parties'; 'Letters on the Study of History'; 'Letters on the Spirit of Patriotism'; and 'The Idea of a Patriot King.' He was a Deist, but taught that a statesman should profess the doctrines of the Church of England. He was an effective orator; but the style of his philosophical and political works, though polished, is heavy and declamatory.

Bolintineanu, Dimitrie (bō-lēn-tē-na-än'). A Roumanian poet; born at Bolintina in Wallachia, 1826; died Sept. 1, 1872. He is widely known for the beauty of the stanzas comprising his earliest collected verse, 'Songs and Plaints.' He wrote also a successful novel, 'Helena,' and an epic poem, 'The Trajanid,' besides Roumanian ballads and the philosophical epic of 'Manoïl.'

Bolles, Frank (bōlz). American essayist and poet; born in Winchester, Mass., Oct. 31, 1856; died Cambridge, Jan. 10, 1894. He wrote: 'From Blomidon to Smoky,' 'Land of the Lingering Snow,' etc.; in verse, Chocorua's Tenants.'

Bolton, Charles Knowles (bōl'tọn). An American poet and miscellaneous writer, son of Mrs. Sarah Knowles Bolton; born in Ohio, 1867. He is librarian of Brookline, Mass. He has written in prose: 'Gossiping Guide to Harvard,' 'Saskia, the Wife of Rembrandt,' etc.; in verse: 'The Wooing of Martha Pitkin'; 'Love Story of Ursula Wolcott'; 'The Private Soldier under Washington.'

Bolton, Henry Carrington. An American scientific writer; born in New York, 1843. He was professor of chemistry and natural science at Trinity College, Hartford, Conn. Besides works on chemistry he has written: 'The

Counting-Out Rhymes of Children, a Study in Folk-Lore'; 'Literature of Manganese'; and other works. Died Washington, D. C., Nov., 1903.

Bolton, Sarah Knowles. An American author; born in Farmington, Conn., Sept. 15, 1841. She married Charles E. Bolton, a merchant and philanthropist, and resides in Cleveland, O. She is author of a number of books, including: 'Girls who Became Famous' (1886); 'Famous American Authors' (1887); 'Famous American Statesmen' (1888); 'Famous Types of Womanhood' (1892); 'Famous American Authors' (1905).

Bolton, Sarah Tittle. An American poet; born in Newport, Ky., Dec. 18, 1815; died in Indianapolis, Ind., Aug. 4, 1893. She is known for her patriotic and war poems, including: 'Paddle Your Own Canoe'; 'Left on the Battlefield'; etc. 'Poems' (New York, 1865; Indianapolis, 1886).

Bonacci-Brunamonti, Maria Alinda (bō-nä'chē-brö-nä-mon'tē). An Italian poet; born in Perugia, 1842. She was only fourteen years old when her first 'Collection of Poems' appeared and attracted much attention. Her 'National Songs' (1859-78) were inspired by Italy's struggle for freedom.

Bonar, Horatius (bon'är). A celebrated Scotch hymnist; born in Edinburgh, Dec. 19, 1808; died July 31, 1889. He wrote 'Hymns of Faith and Hope,' many of which have been taken into the hymnals of most of the Protestant churches. He also wrote more than 20 volumes on theological and religious subjects.

Bonaventura, Saint (bō''nä-ven-tö'rä). An Italian theologian and scholar; born at Bagnarea, 1221; died 1274. His real name was Giovanni di Fidenza. His writings include: 'Life of Saint Francis'; 'Progress of the Mind towards God'; 'Breviloquium'; and many sermons and treatises on theological subjects.

Bonavino, Cristoforo. See Franchi.

Bondi, Clemente (bon'dē). An Italian poet; born near Parma, June 27, 1742; died at Vienna, June 20, 1821. At the suppression of the Company of Jesus, he, though a Jesuit, lauded that act in a poem and had to flee his country. While yet a member of the Jesuit order he wrote a spirited humorous poem, 'Rural Days' (1773), in three cantos, descriptive of the pranks and sports of a band of students.

Boner, John Henry. An American poet and literary worker; born at Salem, N. C., Jan. 31, 1845. A contributor to the magazines, he was on the editorial staff of the 'Century Dictionary' and the 'Standard Dictionary,' and was once literary editor of the New York World. He has written 'Whispering Pines' (1883), a volume of verse. Died in 1905.

Bonghi, Ruggero (bon'gē). An Italian scholar and controversial writer; born in Naples, March 20, 1826; died at Torre del Greco, Oct. 22, 1895. His early career indicated scholarly activities only, for he made fine studies and versions of Aristotle and Plato; but later he

took up such subjects as 'The Financial History of Italy, 1864-88' (1868); 'The Life and Times of Valentino Pasini' (1867); and 'The Life of Jesus' (1890); the popularity and value of these and other works giving him great prominence.

Boniface. See Saintine.

Bonnechose, Émile Boisnormand de (bôn-shōz'). A French poet and historian (1801-75); born at Leyerdorp in Holland. His one notable poetical composition is 'The Death of Dailly' (1833). Besides a 'History of France' he is author of: 'Reformers before the 16th-Century Reformation' (1844); 'The Four Conquests of England' (2 vols., 1851); 'History of England' (4 vols., 1859).

Bonnières, Robert de (bôn-yär'). A French journalist and novelist; born at Paris, April 7, 1850. He commenced his literary career as contributor to Paris journals of spirited but waspish biographs of contemporary men: these were collected and published in three successive volumes of 'Memoirs of To-day.' His novels are full of transparent allusions to noted persons, and have had a very great vogue. In one of them, 'The Monarch,' he portrays high Jewish society in Paris.

Booth, Mary Louise. An American writer; born in Yaphank, L. I., April 19, 1831; died in New York city, March 5, 1889. She was editor of Harper's Bazar from 1867 until her death; translated many novels and histories, including Gasparin's 'Uprising of a Great People,' and H. Martin's 'History of France' (6 vols., 1880).

Borel, Pétrus (bo-rel'). [Properly Pierre Borel d'Hauterive.] A French journalist and author; born in Lyons, June 28, 1809; died in Algeria, July 14, 1859. His character was eccentric: he surnamed himself the "Werewolf," and his writings both prose and verse were romantic and bizarre. They include: 'Rhapsodies,' poems (Paris, 1831); 'Champavert,' stories (1833); and 'Madam Potiphar,' a novel (2 vols., 1839).

Börne, Ludwig (bèr'ne). An eminent German political writer; born at Frankfort-on-the-Main, of Jewish parents, May 6, 1786; died at Paris, Feb. 12, 1837. He founded and for three years conducted Die Wage, a journal devoted to civics, science, and art. Of his numerous satirical sketches, all full of humor and wit, these are perhaps the most brilliant: 'Monograph on the German Postal Snail'; 'The Art of Becoming an Original Author in Three Days'; 'Memorial Address to Jean Paul.' Fierce animosity toward the dynastic policies of Germany permeated whatever he wrote: even his literary and dramatic criticism was biased by this passion. His last completed work, 'Menzel the French-devourer' (Franzosenfresser), is proof that to the last his voice was still for war. His 'Complete Works,' in 12 vols., were published in 1863.

Borneil, Giraut de (bor-näy'). A Provençal troubadour of the 12th century; a native of

Exideuil, Dordogne. His contemporaries bestowed on him the sobriquet "Master of Troubadours." Some 80 of his songs are extant; among them the charming song of the morning, 'Alba.'

Bornemann, Wilhelm (bōr'ne-män). A Low-German dialect poet (1766-1851); born at Gardelegen. He is one of the foremost representatives of modern Low-German poetry. His works are: 'Low-German Poems' (1810), republished in a 10th edition in 1891; 'Pictures of Nature and the Chase' (1829); 'Humorous Hunting Songs.'

Bornier, Henri Vicomte de (bōr-nē-ā'). A French dramatist, member of the Academy; born at Lunel, Dec. 25, 1825; died in Paris, Jan. 27, 1901. His plays are notable for splendor of diction. Among them are: 'Luther's Wedding' (1845); 'Dante and Beatrice'; 'The Daughter of Roland.' He twice won the prize of the Academy, with the lyrics 'The Isthmus of Suez' (1861) and 'France in the Extreme East' (1863). He was the author of several successful novels and romances.

Borrow, George. An English philologist and traveler; born in East Dereham, Norfolk, February 1803; died in Oulton, Suffolk, July 30, 1881. His linguistic talents are shown in 'Targum; or, Metrical Translations from Thirty Languages' (St. Petersburg, 1835), and 'Romano Lavo-Lil, or Word-Book of the Romany' (1874). The other chief of his fourteen works are: 'The Zincali, or Gipsies of Spain' (London, 1841); 'The Bible in Spain' (1843); 'Lavengro' (1851); 'The Romany Rye,' its sequel (1857); and 'Wild Wales' (1862).

Bosboom, Anna Louisa Geertruida (bos'-bōm). A Dutch novelist (1812-86); born (Toussaint) at Alkmaar. Her first work, 'Almagro,' was published in 1837. It was followed by a long series of others; but she won no high distinction till 1860, when she published 'The House of Lauernesse,' by far her most successful novel, which was translated into several languages. Nearly all her works are historical novels; and in the two very essential particulars of knowledge of the historical epochs and of the human heart, she has a just claim to rank among the notable writers in that department of literature.

Boscan Almogavr, Juan (bos-kän' äl-mō-gä-vär'). A distinguished Spanish poet (1493-1540); born in Barcelona. While attached to the court of Charles V. at Granada he was led to a study of Italian poetry, and was the first to employ the Italian measures in Castilian song. Again, in a poem imitative of Musæus's 'Hero and Leander,' he was the first to introduce in Spain rhymeless verse. His poems, collected and published in 1543, had 21 editions in the 16th century.

Bosio, Ferdinando (bōs'yō or bō'zē-ō). An Italian man of letters; born at Alba, Piedmont, 1829; died there, Oct. 16, 1881. He was for several years teacher of rhetoric and literature, and afterward chief clerk of the ministry of public education. In 1853 he published a volume of lyrics: 'Democracy, with a Collection of Ballads.' He wrote many novels, all possessing the charm of an exquisite style,— 'Home Scenes and Stories' (1874). Among his historical writings is a 'Popular History of the Popes.' His miscellaneous writings, political and literary, 'A Little of Everything,' were published in 1878.

Bossuet, Jacques Bénigne (bo-sü-ā'). A French theologian and pulpit orator; born at Dijon, Sept. 27, 1627; died April 12, 1704. He became in 1681 Bishop of Meaux. The 'History of the Variations of the Protestant Churches' (1688) is still a standard work. One of his most elaborate works is the 'Defense of the Famous Declaration which the Gallican Clergy Approved regarding the Power of the Church' (1730). Hardly less celebrated is his 'Discourse upon Universal History down to the Empire of Charlemagne' (1681). His 'Complete Works,' in 46 vols., were published by the Benedictines (1815-19).

Boswell, Sir Alexander. A Scottish antiquary and poet; born at Auchinleck, Ayrshire, Oct. 9, 1775; died in Balmuto, March 27, 1822. He was the son of James Boswell the biographer of Johnson; was educated at Oxford; and at his father's death in 1795, succeeded to Auchinleck. He studied the literature of Scotland, imitated the ballad style, and published original poems and reprints from his private printing-press. His 'Songs Chiefly in the Scottish Dialect' (1803) were very popular.

Boswell, James. A Scottish biographer; born in Edinburgh, Oct. 29, 1740; died in London, May 19, 1795. He was educated at Edinburgh and Glasgow, admitted to the bar in 1766, and early showed a love for letters. His 'Life of Dr. Samuel Johnson' (1791) is considered the most entertaining biography in the English language. The best modern editions are by Napier (4 vols., 1884), and G. Birkbeck Hill (6 vols., 1887). He also wrote 'Journal of a Tour to the Hebrides with Samuel Johnson' (1746), and many other books, the most successful of which was 'An Account of Corsica and Memoirs of Pascal Paoli' (1768).

Botero, Giuseppe (bō'tä-rō). An Italian romancist; born at Novara, 1815; died 1885. He was all his life an educator, serving as director of high schools or lyceums in various cities of northern Italy. He wrote many stories, among them: 'Ricciarda' (1854); 'Raffaele' (1858); 'Nella of Cortemiglia'; and several apologues, among them: 'My Lady'; 'To Live Well is to Do Good'; 'Love and Nature.'

Botta, Anna Charlotte Lynch. An American poet and essayist; born in Bennington, Vt., Nov. 11, 1815; died in New York city, March 23, 1891. She came to New York in 1842, and in 1855 was married to Vincenzo Botta. Mrs Botta's home in New York was a centre for literary and artistic people from the days of Poe,

Willis, and Bryant, until her death. She was the author of stories, essays, 'Poems' (1848; new ed. 1884), and 'A Handbook of Universal Literature' (1845).

Botta, Carlo Giuseppe Guglielmo (bot-tä). An eminent Italian historian; born near Canavese in the Piedmontese, Nov. 6, 1766; died Aug. 10, 1837. For his sympathy with the French Revolution he suffered imprisonment two years, and then went to France, where he entered the military service as surgeon. He afterward held several offices of responsibility under the empire and the restored monarchy. Besides numerous minor works in French, he published in Italian (1809) a 'History of the War of Independence of the United States of America'; and (1824) a 'History of Italy from 1789 to 1814,' in four volumes. He also continued Guicciardini from 1535 to 1789 (10 vols.).

Böttger, Adolf (bĕt'cher). A German poet (1815-70); born at Leipsic. He made admirable translations into German verse of 'Byron's Complete Works' (1840; 7th ed. 1891), of Pope, Goldsmith, 'Songs of Ossian,' and Longfellow's 'Hiawatha'; he was less successful with some pieces of Shakespeare. Of his original poetry the best specimens are the poetical fairy tales 'Pilgrimage of the Flower Sprites'; and especially the fantasy of 'The Little Man of the Gallows,' a little 'Faustiad.'

Böttiger, Carl Vilhelm (bĕt'tē-ger). A Swedish poet; born in Westerås, May 15, 1807; died at Upsala, Dec. 22, 1878. Although noted for the pleasing prose of his essays on literary topics, his fame must depend upon versions of Dante, Tasso, and Uhland, the 'Lyric Poems,' the 'New Songs,' 'Poetic Memories of My Youth,' and one or two plays, including 'A May Day at Voerend.'

Bouchardy, Joseph (bö-shär-dē'). A French dramatic poet; born at Paris in 1810; died May 28, 1870. He was at first associated with Eugène Deligny in dramatic composition, and afterward composed a series of comedies alone. Notable among his productions are: 'Gaspardo the Fisherman'; 'The Foundlings'; 'The Orphans of Antwerp'; 'The Cavalier's Secret'; 'The Armorer of Santiago.'

Bouchor, Maurice (bö-shôr'). A French poet; born at Paris, 1855. At the age of 19 years he published a volume of 'Merry Lays,' which was followed by 'Poems of Love and the Sea' (1875); 'The Modern Faust' (1878); 'Stories of Paris in Rhyme'; and 'The Dawn,' esteemed his best work. He attempted to revive, but in no reverential spirit, the mediæval "mystery play" in 1889, with 'Tobit' and 'Nativity'; the "actors" being lay figures of life size, while the author and his cronies spoke "the lines" from behind the wings.

Boucicault, Dion (bö'sē-kō). A British dramatist and actor; born in Dublin, Dec. 26, 1822; died in New York, Sept. 18, 1890. His first drama, 'London Assurance,' was written before he was 19 years of age, and made him famous. He also attained celebrity as an actor and manager in England and the United States; established a school for acting, and produced about 300 dramas, many of which were original and many adaptations from the French. He dramatized Washington Irving's 'Rip Van Winkle,' which Joseph Jefferson enlarged; and produced a series of Irish dramas which were extraordinarily popular, such as: 'The Colleen Bawn' (1860); 'Arrah-na-Pogue' (1864); and 'The Shaughraun' (1875), in which he played the principal parts. 'Old Heads on Young Shoulders', 'The Corsican Brothers'; 'The Streets of London'; 'Flying Scud'; and 'After Dark,' were among his later productions.

Boudinot, Elias (bö'di-not). A distinguished American patriot and philanthropist; born at Philadelphia, May 2, 1740; died at Burlington, N. J., Oct. 24, 1821. He was president of the Continental Congress (1782), and first president of the American Bible Society (1816-21). He wrote: 'The Second Advent of the Messiah'; 'The Age of Revelation,' a reply to Thomas Paine; 'The Star in the West,' an attempt to identify the American Indians with the Ten Lost Tribes of Israel.

Boufflers, Stanislas, Marquis de (bö-flär'). A French poet; born at Nancy, May 31, 1738; died at Paris, Jan. 18, 1815. He was reputed to be son of Stanislas II. of Poland. While an ecclesiastical student he wrote in prose the story of 'Aline, Queen of Golconda,' for which Stanislas awarded him a pension of 40,000 livres. Quitting the ecclesiastical career, he entered the military service and rose to the rank of major-general. Meanwhile he was earning the plaudits of the gay world by his erotic verses. He was one of the émigrés of 1792, but returned to France in 1800. His 'Complete Works' were published in 2 vols., 1813.

Bouilhet, Louis (bö-lyä'). A French poet (1821-69). He first achieved fame with 'Melænis, a Story of Rome' in the time of the Cæsars, and 'The Fossils,' a series of delineations of antediluvians. His versified dramas, 'Mme. de Montarcy' (1856); 'Dolorès' (1862); and especially 'The Conspiracy of Amboise,' are elegant in style, rich in imagery, perfect in melody, but lack compactness of structure and are open to moral censure. The same faults are found in his comedies 'Uncle Million' (1861); 'Faustine' (1864); and specially in his posthumous 'Mdlle. Aïssé.'

Bouilly, Jean Nicholas (bö-yē'). A French poet (1763-1842). He made his début with the comic opera 'Peter the Great' (1790). For a few years he was judge and prosecuting attorney at Tours, and then was called to Paris to assist in organizing the primary-school system. He was a man of ancient Roman virtue, and his character is reflected in all his works. His comedies and comic operas (music by the first masters) were eminently successful as well in Germany as in France, particularly these: 'The Abbé de l'Epée'; 'The Two Days'; 'Mme.

de Sévigné.' He also wrote 'Stories for French Children' and 'Counsels to my Daughter.'

Bourdillon, Francis W. Born in 1852. He was educated at Oxford, and became tutor to the children of the Princess Christian of England. He is famous for a short poem, 'The Night Has a Thousand Eyes,' and has published a novel, 'Nephelé' (New York and London, 1896), besides 'Among the Flowers and Other Poéms' (1872), and 'Young Maids and Old China' (1888) ; 'Minussula' (1896).

Bourget, Paul (bör-zhā'). A French novelist and critic; born at Amiens, Sept. 2, 1852. His first book was 'Restless Life,' followed by other poems; but he turned to prose and has become widely known as essayist, critic, and descriptive writer, and famous for his novels. The latter include: 'A Cruel Enigma'; 'A Crime of Love'; 'Lies'; 'The Disciple'; 'André Cornelis'; 'Cosmopolis'; and volumes of stories like 'The Irreparable.' His essays are contained in the volumes: 'Essays in Contemporary Psychology'; 'New Essays in Contemporary Psychology'; 'Studies and Portraits'; and others. 'Outre-Mer.' is a book on America.

Bouton, John Bell (bö-ton'). An American journalist and writer; born at Concord, N. H., 1830; died in New York, Nov. 18, 1892. He wrote: 'Loved and Lost' (1857, essays); 'Round the Block' (1864, a novel); 'Roundabout to Moscow' (1887); 'Uncle Sam's Church' (1895), etc.

Boutwell, George Sewall (bout'wel). An American statesman and publicist; born at Brookline, Mass., Jan. 28, 1818. He was governor of Massachusetts (1852-53), United States Commissioner of Internal Revenue (1862-63), Member of Congress (1863-69), Secretary of the Treasury (1869-73), United States Senator (1873-77). He has written: 'Thoughts on Educational Topics' (1860) ; 'A History of the Republican Party' (1884) ; 'The Lawyer, the Statesman, and the Soldier.' Died 1905.

Bouvet, Marguerite (bö-vā'). An American writer for children ; born in Louisiana, 1865. She has written : 'Sweet William' ; 'Prince Tip-Top' ; 'Little Majorie's Love Story'; 'Pierrette'; 'Bernardo and Laurette'; 'The Fortunes of Clothilde.'

Bowen, Mrs. Sue (Petigru) (King). An American novelist; born in South Carolina, 1824; died 1875. Her home was in Charleston, S. C. She wrote: 'Sylvia's World'; 'Gerald Gray's Wife'; 'Busy Moments of an Idle Woman,' a collection of stories; etc.

Bowker, Richard Rogers (bou'ker). An American editor, bibliographer, and writer on political economy; born in Massachusetts, 1848. He edited for a number of years the Publishers' Weekly; and compiled the 'American Catalogue' (2 vols., 1885), of inestimable value to book-dealers, librarians, and literary workers. Among his writings on political economy are: 'Work and Wealth'; 'Economics for the People'; 'Copyright — Its Law and Its Literature.'

Bowles, Samuel (bōlz). A noted American journalist; born at Springfield, Mass., Feb. 9, 1826; died there, Jan. 16, 1878. He was editor and proprietor of the Springfield Republican (1844-78). He wrote: 'Across the Continent' (1865) ; 'The Switzerland of America' (1869) ; 'Our New West' (1869); etc. As one of the most able journalists in a land of journalism, his fame is both great and enduring.

Bowles, William Lisle. An English poet; born in King's Sutton, Northamptonshire, Sept. 24, 1762; died in Salisbury, April 7, 1850. He was educated at Oxford, and from 1804 until a few years before his death was vicar of Bremhill, Wiltshire. His 'Fourteen Sonnets Written Chiefly on Picturesque Spots during a Journey' (1789) was received with extraordinary favor. Coleridge, Wordsworth, and Southey greatly admired the poems, which reflected the author's thoughts and the moods of nature to such an extent that Bowles is considered to have created by his influence the Lake School of poetry. In 1806 he issued a critical edition of Pope, which led to a memorable controversy (1809-25), in which Byron and Campbell were his opponents. His other works include: 'The Grave of Howard' (1790); 'Coombe Ellen' (1798) ; 'The Battle of the Nile' (1799) ; 'The Spirit of Discovery' (1804), his longest poem; and 'St. John in Patmos' (1832).

Bowne, Borden Parker (boun). An American philosophical writer; born at Leonardville, N. J., Jan. 14, 1847. He was religious editor of the New York Independent 1875-76, becoming professor of philosophy at Boston University 1876. He has written: 'Philosophy of Herbert Spencer' (1874) ; 'Metaphysics' (1882); 'The Immanence of God'; 'Personalism.'

Bowring, Sir John. An English linguist, author, and noted diplomat; born in Exeter, Oct. 17, 1792; died there, Nov. 23, 1872. He was a great traveler and a close student; and boasted that he knew 200 languages and could speak 100. In 1825 he became editor of the Westminster Review, in which he advocated Free Trade by repeal of the Corn Laws in advance of Bright and Cobden. He was a Member of Parliament in 1835-37 and 1841-47; was appointed on various commissions, to France, Switzerland, Italy, Syria, etc. In 1849 he was British consul at Hong-Kong, where he became governor in 1853. In 1855 he concluded a treaty with Siam; he was knighted in 1854. He rendered great service to English literature by translating the popular poems and folk-songs of various nations. Among his works are: 'Specimens of the Russian Poets' (London, 1821-23) ; 'Ancient Poetry and Romances of Spain' (1824) ; 'Specimens of the Polish Poets' (1827) ; 'Servian Popular Poetry' (1827) ; 'Poetry of the Magyars' (1830) ; 'Cheskian Anthology' (1832) ; 'The Flowery Scroll: a Chinese Novel' (1868) ; 'The Oak: Original Tales and Sketches' (1869); and two important volumes of travel: 'The Kingdom and People of Siam' (1857), and 'A Visit to the

Philippine Islands' (1859). He edited with a biography (22 vols., London, 1838) the works of Jeremy Bentham, of whom he was a disciple and admirer; and wrote a number of books on political and social topics, and also hymns and poems.

Boye, Kaspar Johan (bō'yĕ). A Danish poet and dramatist; born in Kongsberg, Norway, Dec. 27, 1791; died in Copenhagen, July 6, 1853. He was a clergyman who wrote anonymously for the stage, becoming "Denmark's great unknown" upon the appearance of 'Juta, Queen of Denmark,' 'King Sigurd,' and other plays, of which only 'William Shakespeare' continues on the boards. His 'There Is a Beautiful Country in the Far North' has become a national favorite hymn.

Boyesen, Hjalmar Hjorth (boi'e-sen). An American novelist; born at Frederiksvärn, Norway, Sept. 23, 1848; died in New York, Oct. 4, 1895. After completing his university studies at Christiania, he came to the United States in 1869 and was editor of a Norwegian journal in Chicago. He returned to Europe in 1872 and studied Germanic philology at Leipsic two years; then returning to this country he was professor of German in Cornell University for six years, and then of Germanic languages and literature in Columbia College till his death. His story of Norwegian life, 'Gunnar,' published in the Atlantic Monthly (1873), and his 'Idyls of Norway and Other Poems' (1883), give proof of his rare imaginative faculty and his deep human sympathies. Besides these, he wrote: 'Tales from Two Hemispheres' (1875); 'A Norseman's Pilgrimage'; 'Ilka on the Hilltop and Other Stories'; 'A Daughter of the Philistines.'

Bozděch, Emanuel (bōz'dyeĕh). A Bohemian dramatist; born at Prague, July 21, 1841. His first notable success in 1867, with the comedy 'From the Days of Cotillons,' was surpassed the following year when he brought out his tragedy 'Baron Görtz.' Other noteworthy productions are: 'The World's Master in his Night-Shirt,' the private life of Napoleon I.; 'The Test of a Statesman' (Prince Kaunitz). He wrote also some novels. Died 1889.

Brabourne, Edward Huggessen Knatchbull-Huggessen, Lord. An English juvenile-story writer; born in Kent, April 29, 1829; died Feb. 6, 1893. Has been Member of Parliament. His literary fame is due mostly to his stories for children, including: 'Moonshine' (1871); 'Tales at Tea-Time' (1872); 'Queer Folk' (1873); 'River Legends' (1874); and many others.

Brace, Charles Loring. An American author and philanthropist; born in Litchfield, Connecticut, June 19, 1826; died in the Tyrol, Austria, Aug. 11, 1890. After graduation at Yale in 1846, he studied theology, but held no pastorate. He devoted himself to philanthropy in New York, and lectured, wrote, and worked to enlist aid for the children of the poor. His

books include: 'Hungary in 1851' (New York, 1852); 'Home Life in Germany' (1853); 'The Norse Folk' (1857); 'Short Sermons to Newsboys' (1861); 'The Dangerous Classes of New York and Twenty Years' Work among Them' (1872; 3d ed. 1880); 'Free Trade as Promoting Peace and Good-Will among Men' (1879); 'Gesta Christi' (1883), a review of the achievements of Christianity from the earliest days in bettering the moral and social condition of the world; and 'To the Unknown God' (1889).

Brachmann, Karoline Luise (bräch'män). A German poet (1777–1822); born at Rochlitz. Her 'Lyric Poems' are full of life and melody. She wrote also a poem of chivalry, 'The Judgment of God,' in five cantos, and several romances.

Brachvogel, Albert Emil (bräch'fō''gel). A German dramatist and novelist (1824–78); born at Breslau. His first dramatic compositions had but little success; but in 1856 he produced 'Narcissus,' which established his fame. A long series of dramas then followed; among them: 'Adalbert von Babanberge' (1858), most poetical of his dramas; 'Mons de Caus' (1860), the tragedy of a genius who is in advance of his time; 'The Usurer's Son' (1863). He wrote a great many historical novels; among them: 'Schubart and his Contemporaries' (1864); 'Beaumarchais' (1865); 'William Hogarth': but his novels are now forgotten.

Brachvogel, Udo. A German poet; born near Dantzic in 1835. He published a volume of 'Juvenile Poems' at Vienna in 1860, and 'The Land of the Theiss and its Poets' (1882). He came to the United States in 1867 and edited journals in the German language. He made an excellent translation of 'Bret Harte's Poems' (1882).

Brackel, Ferdinande, Baroness von (bräck'el). A German novelist; born in the Circle of Warburg, Westphalia, Nov. 25, 1835. She published a volume of 'Poems' in 1873, and thereafter devoted herself to prose fiction, containing opinions regarding the social and labor questions from the Catholic point of view. Many of her tales have been translated into foreign languages. Among her stories are: 'The Spinning-Master of Carrara'; 'Princess Ada'; 'Of the Ancient Stock'; 'In the Battle of the Time.'

Brackenridge, Henry Marie (brak'en-rij). A distinguished American lawyer, historian, and writer of travels, son of Hugh Henry; born at Pittsburg, Pa., May 11, 1786; died at Pensacola, Fla., Jan. 18, 1871. He was a judge in Louisiana and Florida; and was United States commissioner to the South American republics in 1817–18. He wrote: 'History of the Late War between the United States and Great Britain' (after 1820); 'Voyage to South America' (1820); 'Persons and Places in the West' (1834); etc.

Brackenridge, Hugh Henry. A distinguished American lawyer and humorist; born near Campbelton, Scotland, 1748; died at Carlisle, Pa., June 25, 1816. He was judge of the

Supreme Court of Pennsylvania (1799). He wrote: 'Modern Chivalry, or the Adventures of Captain Farrago and Teague O'Regan, his Servant' (1796-1806), a satire very popular early in the present century.

Braddon, Mary Elizabeth, maiden name of Mrs. M. E. Maxwell; born in London, 1837. At an early age she began to write verses and stories. Her novels are old-fashioned, based on sensational plots, but with much narrative power and descriptions of scenery, and have long been popular. Among them are: 'Lady Audley's Secret' (1862; 11th ed. 1863); 'Aurora Floyd' (1863; 8th ed. 1864); 'The Story of Barbara' (1880); 'Asphodel' (1881); 'Ishmael' (1884); 'Wyllard's Weird' (1886); 'The Venetians' (1892); 'London Pride'(1896); 'In High Places' (1898); 'His Darling Sin' (1899). She has also written several comedies.

Bradford, Alden. An American historian and journalist; born at Duxbury, Mass., Nov. 19, 1765; died at Boston, Oct. 26, 1843. Originally a Congregational divine, he became Secretary of State of Massachusetts (1812-24), and edited the Boston Gazette (1826). He wrote: 'History of Massachusetts, 1764-1820'; 'History of the Federal Government'; etc.

Bradford, Joseph. An American journalist and dramatic author; born near Nashville, Tenn., Oct. 24, 1843; died in Boston, Mass., April 13, 1886. His real name was William Randolph Hunter. Besides satirical verses he wrote a number of poems which were highly esteemed, especially those on the death of Victor Hugo and of General Grant. His plays, 'Our Bachelors' and 'One of the Finest,' were very successful and are still popular.

Bradford, William. An American colonial governor and author; born in Austerfield, Yorkshire, England, March 1588; died in Plymouth, Mass., May 9, 1657. He was one of the signers of the celebrated compact on the Mayflower; and in 1621, on the death of the first governor, John Carver, was elected to the same office, which he continued to fill (with the exception of a brief period when he declined re-election) until his death. His administration was remarkably efficient and successful, especially in dealing with the Indians. His 'Diary of Occurrences,' covering the first year of the colony, was published in 1622. He left a number of religious compositions in verse; and historical prose compositions of great value, the most important being his 'History of the Plymouth Plantation' from the formation of the society in England in 1602 down to 1647.

Bradley, Edward. See **Bede, Cuthbert.**

Braga, Theophilo (brä'gä). A Portuguese poet and scholar; born at St. Michael, Azores, Feb. 24, 1843. On quitting the university of Coimbra, he took up the study of Portuguese literature, and made a great collection of popular romances, songs, and fairy tales, publishing the results in a series of volumes. Also in 20 volumes he published a pretty complete history of the national literature (1870-76). Besides these works on the history of Portuguese letters, he issued in 1877 a 'General Outline of the Positive Philosophy'; in 1878 'Positive Solutions of Portuguese Politics'; and in 1884 a 'System of Sociology.' His poetical writings comprise: 'Green Leaves,' written in boyhood; 'The Vision of Time' (1864), a series of pictures of the process of world-evolution, in the manner of Victor Hugo; and 'Undine of the Lake'; 'Torrents' and 'World Pictures.'

Brainard, John Gardiner Calkins. An American poet; born in New London, Conn., Oct. 21, 1796; died there, Sept. 26, 1828. After graduation at Yale in 1815, he went to Hartford in 1822 and took charge of the Connecticut Mirror. His poems were published in 1825; the third edition, called 'Literary Remains,' was edited with a biography by John G. Whittier (1832).

Brandes, Edvard (brän'des). A Danish dramatist, story-writer, and essayist; born in Copenhagen, Oct. 21, 1847. Of his plays, 'A Visit,' 'Love,' and 'Under the Rule' are best known; while studies on art subjects denote his critical taste, and 'The Politician' shows him capable of well-planned and well-told fiction.

Brandes, Georg Morris Cohen. A Danish man of letters; born at Copenhagen, Feb. 4, 1842. At the university he won a gold medal for an essay on 'The Idea of Fate among the Ancients' (1862). He then made extended travels in England, France, and Germany, making acquaintance of men of note in letters and in science. He afterward wrote works which attained a European reputation, on the history of contemporary literature in the countries named; 'Main Currents of 19th-Century Literature,' a work of profound research and the author's masterpiece. He made a special study of 'French Æsthetics in our Day' (1870), and published volumes of miscellaneous 'Æsthetic Studies' and 'Modern Ghosts, Portraits of the 19th Century.' He settled in Berlin in 1877; in 1883 returned to Copenhagen, where he now resides.

Brandes, Johann Christian. A German dramatist (1735-99); born at Stettin. He was an indifferent actor, but his dramatic compositions were received with great favor in his day. Some of his comedies possess very high merit; especially 'Appearances are Deceitful,' and 'The Ennobled Shopkeeper.' Shortly before his death he wrote a very instructive 'History of his Life.'

Brandt or **Brant, Sebastian** (bränt). A celebrated German satirical poet and humanist (1458-1521); born at Strasburg. He was named an imperial councillor by the Emperor Maximilian in 1503, and made count palatine. He was not in sympathy with the Reformers. Though he wrote Latin poems, and treatises on jurisprudence, he is remembered as author of

'The Ship of Fools,' a satire on the follies and vices of the time (1494). Its distinguishing note is its abounding humor; but it owed its great popular success very largely to the clever woodcuts with which it was illustrated. It was translated into Latin and several European vernacular languages; into English by Henry Watson, 'The Grete Shyppe of Fooles of the Worlde' (1517). Barclay's 'Shyp of the Folys of the Worlde' (1508) is in part a translation, in part an adaptation. A more recent imitation is W. H. Ireland's 'Modern Ship of Fools' (1807).

Brantôme, Pierre de Bourdeille, Seigneur de (bron-tom'). A French chronicler (about 1527–1614); born at Périgord. He was for many years traveler or soldier; retired to his estate twenty years before his death, and used his leisure in writing his 'Memoirs,' in sections devoted to 'Lives of Illustrious Men and Great Captains of Foreign Countries'; of 'Illustrious Men, etc., of France'; of 'Illustrious Women'; of 'Courteous Dames'; 'Anecdotes of Duels'; 'Spanish Rhodomontades and Oaths'; etc. The author is vain and egotistical, but thoroughly naïve and honest. The style is charmingly piquant, with frequent sallies of wit and flashes of eloquence. He is indeed a fascinating chronicler. His 'Complete Works,' 10 vols., were published at the Hague (1740).

Brassey, Annie, Lady. An English descriptive writer; born in London, about 1840; died at sea on the Sunbeam, Sept. 14, 1887. After her marriage she spent half of her life at sea, on Lord Brassey's yacht the Sunbeam. She was buried at sea. Her travels are interesting, popular, and have passed through many editions. They are: 'Natural History of a Voyage on the Sunbeam' (1878); 'Sunshine and Storm in the East' (1879); 'Tahiti' (1882); 'In the Trades, the Tropics, and the Roaring Forties' (1884); and 'Three Voyages in the Sunbeam' (1886).

Braun, Karl (broun). A German political writer (1822–93); born at Hadamar in Nassau. Of his very numerous writings it suffices to name: 'For Free Trade and Free Traffic throughout all Germany' (1858); 'Frankfort's Cry of Distress'; 'Pictures from Germany's Littlestatedom.'

Braun, Wilhelm von. A Swedish poet; born Nov. 8, 1813; died Sept. 12, 1860. He abandoned the military career for literature, and speedily became one of the most popular poets. His 'Collected Works' contain every conceivable form of poetical composition, but his writings are characterized by licentiousness.

Braun von Braunthal (broun fōn broun'täl). An Austrian dramatist and novelist (1802–66); born at Eger. He essayed all kinds of poetry, and in all displayed no ordinary talent, but he was deficient in correct taste and judgment. Among his lyric compositions we have: 'Songs of a Hermit'; 'Morning, Noon, and Night in a Poet's Life'; the dramas 'Count Julian' and

'Knight Shakspere'; and several novels, as 'Donna Quixote, or the Life and Opinions of a Sagacious Noble Lady of Young Germany.'

Bray, Anna Eliza. An English woman of letters; born in London, Dec. 25, 1790; died there, Jan. 21, 1883. Her maiden name was Kempe; she studied for the stage, but in 1818 was married to Charles A. Stothard, son of the famous artist, and after his death became the wife of the Rev. Edward A. Bray, vicar of Tavistock. From 1826 to 1874 she wrote at least a dozen novels, one of which, 'The Talba, or the Moor of Portugal,' brought her the acquaintance of Southey. She wrote the 'Life of Thomas Stothard' (1856), and many books of travels. Her letters addressed to Southey on the superstitions and scenery of Tavistock, entitled 'The Borders of the Tamar and the Tavy' (3 vols., 1836; new ed. 1879), and 'A Peep at the Pixies, or Legends of the West' (1854), are esteemed. Mrs. Bray's 'Autobiography' appeared in 1884.

Breckinridge, Robert Jefferson (brek'in-rij). A noted Presbyterian divine and theological writer; born at Cabell's Dale, Ky., March 8, 1800; died at Danville, Ky., Dec. 27, 1871. He was originally a lawyer. He became president of Jefferson College, 1845–47; from 1847 he was pastor at Lexington, Ky. He was a leader in the division of the Presbyterian Church in 1837 into Old and New Schools. His chief work was 'Knowledge of God, Objectively Considered' (1857); 'Knowledge of God, Subjectively Considered' (1859).

Breden, Christiane. See **Christen.**

Brederoo, Gerbrant Adriaenszoon (brä'de-rō). A distinguished Dutch dramatist and poet; born at Amsterdam, March 16, 1585; died there, July 8, 1618. His best poesy is in 'The Meditative Song-Book' and 'The Great Fountain of Love'; collections of grave and gay pieces, all of which have been very popular, and since his time often reprinted. His lyrics are admired for their musical verse and their tender sensibility; but his masterpiece is unquestionably the 'Jerolimo' (Spaansche Brabander Jerolimo), a comedy based upon a French version of one of Mendoza's plays. Another comedy, 'Moortje,' is an adaptation from Terence.

Brehm, Alfred Edmund (bräm). A German naturalist and zoölogist; born in Renthendorf, Feb. 2, 1829; died there, Nov. 11, 1884. He traveled widely and studied long, partly taught by his father, likewise a distinguished scientist; producing finally, among a variety of works, his monumental 'Animal Life, Illustrated' (3d ed. 1890–93), a series of volumes translated and quoted extensively.

Bremer, Fredrika (bräm'er). A Swedish novelist (1801–65); born in Åbo, Finland. She was brought up in the neighborhood of Stockholm. She was a voluminous writer, and the income from her publications enabled her to make extensive travels over Europe and in America. Till 1839 her fame was restricted to Sweden; then it began to extend to Germany; in 1842 was published in London, in English, 'The Neighbors,' and forthwith in rapid succession translations appeared of 'The Diary'; 'The H. Family'; 'The President's Family'; and several others of her charming delineations of domestic life in Sweden. She visited the United States in 1849; and in 1851 her 'Homes of the New World' was published simultaneously in England, Sweden, and this country.

Brentano, Clemens (bren-tä'nō). A German poet and novelist (1778–1842); born at Ehrenbreitstein. He wrote a 'Life of the Virgin Mary,' based on alleged revelations. Among the works of his early days are found some gems of lyric poetry; and his dramatic productions — 'The Merry Musicians' (1803); 'Ponce de Leon' (1804); 'The Founding of Prague' (1815) — manifest great power. Some of his minor novels were very successful; among them 'The Good Caspar and the Fair Annie' (1817), called by German critics "a masterpiece in miniature." His 'Fairy Tales' did not appear till after his death.

Brentano, Elizabeth, commonly known as Bettina von Arnim. A German writer (1785–1859), sister of Clemens Brentano, and famed for 'Goethe's Correspondence with a Child'; which, to a great extent fictitious, is, from a purely poetic point of view, one of the fairest specimens of romanticism. It was translated by her into English, and in that garb constitutes a literary curiosity. Of a similar nature is her correspondence with Caroline von Günderode, the friend of her youth, published under the title 'Die Günderode' (1840). She also wrote 'This Book Belongs to the King' (1843), an attempt to solve the question of pauperism.

Breton, Nicholas. An English poet of whose life little is known (1545–1626). He was very versatile, and wrote moral and religious poems, satires, romances, books of character, a complete letter-writer, pastorals, and lyrics. At his best his verse compares favorably with the sweetest of the Elizabethan singers. Some of his works have only lately been recovered. Grosart, 'Breton's Poems.'

Breton de los Herreros, Manuel (brä tōn' dä lōs är-rā'rōs). A Spanish poet (1800–73); born in the province of Logroño. He is the most notable Spanish poet of the first half of the 19th century. He gave to the Spanish stage 150 plays, some of them original, others derived from ancient Spanish sources or translated from French or Italian. In him the old French comedy finds not so much an imitator as its last true representative. Among his best original comedies are: 'I'm Going Back to Madrid'; 'Here I am in Madrid'; 'This World is All a Farce'; 'Die Once and You'll See.' He was less successful in the historic drama than in comedy. His satiric poems,

'Hypocrisy'; 'Moral Epistle on the Manners of the Age'; and 'Shamelessness,' are not unworthy of their author's great fame.

Bretschneider, Heinrich Gottfried von (bret'shnī-der). An Austrian satirist (1739–1810.) Being in government office, he published nearly all his writings anonymously. Most notable perhaps of all his compositions is the fine street ballad, 'Frightful Story of the Murder of Young Werther.' Worthy of mention too is the 'Saints' Kalendar for 1788,' admired by Joseph II for its witty sallies; also 'George Waller's Life and Morals,' a lively satire on the intrigues of the court counselors and their agents.

Bretzner, Christian Friedrich (brets'ner). A German dramatist (1748–1807); born at Leipsic. He wrote several successful comedies, foremost among them 'The Marriage Broker' and 'The Go-Between'; also two musical dramas, one of which, 'Belmont and Constantia, or the Elopement from the Seraglio,' was used by Mozart as a libretto. He wrote, on the basis of designs by Chodoviecki and Hogarth, a story, 'Life of a Rake,' in three volumes (1787–88), which for a while was very popular.

Brewer, Antony. An English dramatist who lived in the 17th century. He is the author of 'The Love-Sick King' (1655), reprinted as 'The Perjured Nun' (1680). The famous play 'Lingua, or the Combat of the Five Senses for Supremacy' (1607), half masque, half morality, was long ascribed to him and bestowed fame on his name. 'The Merry Devil of Edmonton' (1608) and 'The Country Girl' (1647) were long taken for his.

Brewer, E. Cobham. An English clergyman and lexicographer; born in London May 2, 1810; died at Newark, Eng., March 6, 1897. He was educated at Cambridge, and entered the ministry. He edited many valuable reference books, among which are: 'Guide to Science' (1850; Dictionary of Phrase and Fable' (1885); 'Reader's Handbook' (1884); 'Dictionary of Miracles'; etc.

Bridges, Robert. An American essayist and critic, writing under the pseudonym "Droch"; born in Pennsylvania, 1858. He has been assistant editor of Scribner's Magazine since 1877, literary critic of Life since 1883. He has written: 'Overheard in Arcady,' dialogues about contemporary writers; 'Suppressed Chapters and Other Bookishness'; 'Bramble Brae.'

Brierley, Benjamin. An English sketch-writer; born in Failsworth, Lancashire, in 1825. His reputation rests on numerous stories and sketches written in the Lancashire dialect. His pseudonym is "Ab-o'-th' Yate." Among his best books are: 'Tales and Sketches of Lancashire Life' (London, 1862) and 'Chronicles of Waverlow' (1863). 'Ab-o'-th'-Yate in Yankeeland,' two visits to America (1887). Died at Manchester, Jan. 18, 1896.

Briggs, Charles Augustus. An American clergyman and religious writer; born in New York city. Jan. 15, 1841. For a number of years he was pastor of the Presbyterian Church at Roselle, N. J. In 1874 he was appointed professor of Hebrew in Union Theological Seminary in New York city. He was tried for heresy in 1892, but was acquitted. Among his works are: 'American Presbyterianism' (1885); 'The Messiah of the Apostles' (1886) ; 'The Messiah of the Gospels' ; 'The Higher Criticism of the Hexateuch'; and 'The Bible, the Church, and the Reason' ; 'Ethical Teachings of Jesus.'

Briggs, Charles Frederick. An American journalist and author; born at Nantucket, Mass., in 1804; died in Brooklyn, N. Y., June 20, 1877. He was prominently connected with several newspapers, among others the New York Times and New York Independent. Besides several poems, he wrote: 'The Adventures of Harry Franco' (1839) ; 'The Haunted Merchant' (1843) ; 'History of the Atlantic Telegraph Cable' (1860), in collaboration with Augustus Maverick.

Bright, John. An English statesman; born near Rochdale in Lancashire, Nov. 16, 1811; died March 27, 1889. The son of a wealthy Quaker cotton manufacturer, after his father's death his brother's generously sharing the profits of the business with him enabled him to remain in public life. In early life he began to take an active part in social and political reform. He entered Parliament in 1843, and voted for repeal of the Corn Laws and for factory regulation. He sympathized with the North in the Civil War. He first entered the government in 1868, as president of the Board of Trade. Thereafter he held office under every Liberal administration till 1882. He was an eloquent and impressive orator. His speeches and addresses were published n successive volumes, 1867-69-79, and his 'Public Letters' in 1885.

Brillat-Savarin, Anthelme (bre-yä'-sä-vä-ran'). A French author (1755–1826). He was a deputy to the national convention in 1789; emigrated in 1793 and passed some time in the United States; returned to France in 1796. His writings were mostly anonymous; his title to fame is the work 'Physiology of Taste,' an essay on the social implications of gastronomy, written in elegant style with profound knowledge of the subject-matter.

Brink, Jan ten (brink). A Dutch novelist and critic ; born at Appingedam, June 15, 1834. Besides essays on the literature of his own country, of France, and of England, he has written several novels; among them : 'Mrs. de Roggeveen's Son-in-Law' ; 'Holland Dames and Cavaliers' ; 'Jan Starter and his Wife'; and a 'Historic Essay on the French Revolution.'

Brinton, Daniel Garrison. An American surgeon, archæologist and ethnologist; born at Thornbury, Pa., May 13, 1837 ; died at Atlantic City, N. J., July 31, 1899. During the Civil War he was a surgeon in the Union army. From 1867 to 1887 he was editor of the Medical and Surgical Reporter. In 1884 he was appointed professor of ethnology at the Academy of Natural Sciences in Philadelphia ; and in 1886 professor of American linguistics and archæology in the University of Pennsylvania. Among his many works are : Notes on the 'Floridian Peninsula' (1859); 'American Hero Myths' (1882); 'Aboriginal American Anthology'; etc. He edited the Maya chronicles, and is a high authority on all American archæological topics.

Brisebarre, Edouard Louis (brēz-bär'). A French dramatist (1818–71); born at Paris. He made a brilliant theatrical success with his first piece, 'Cagliostro's Vial' (1835). Thereafter he produced more than 100 dramas and low comedies, mostly in collaboration with other writers. His most notable productions are : 'A Bengal Tiger'; 'Leonard,' which had an almost unexampled "run"; 'The Mad Cow.'

Bristed, Charles Astor. ("Carl Benson.") An American scholar and author; born in New York city, Oct. 6, 1820; died in Washington, D. C., Jan. 15, 1874. He graduated from Yale University in 1839, and from Trinity College, Cambridge, England, in 1845. He traveled extensively in Europe, and was a frequent contributor to the magazines. Among his works are : 'Five Years in an English University' (1851); 'The Upper Ten Thousand' (1852) ; 'Interference Theory of Government' (1868).

Britton, Nathaniel Lord. An American scientific writer; born on Staten Island, N. Y., January 15, 1859. He is director of the New York Botanical Garden. Among his works are: 'Geology of Staten Island' (1880) ; 'Catalogue of the Flora of New Jersey' (1882); and 'An Illustrated Flora of the Northern United States, Canada, and the British Possessions, from Newfoundland to the Parallel of the Southern Boundary of Virginia and from the Atlantic Ocean to the 102d Meridian,' in collaboration with A. Brown,—a very authoritative work, and published by Charles Scribner's Sons.

Brizeux, Julien Auguste Pélage (brē-zē'). A French poet (1803–58) ; born at Lorient. He made his début with the charming idyl 'Marie' (1831), in which are seen all the graces of perfect poetic form conjoined with tenderest sentiment. His reputation as a true poet was well sustained by the works which followed : 'The Bretons' and 'Stories in Verse,' both crowned by the Academy. He composed some verses also in his native Breton speech. His 'Complete Works' are in four volumes.

Broadhurst, George H., an American dramatist. He wrote : 'What Happened to Jones' ; 'Why Smith Left Home'; 'The Wrong Mr. Wright' ; 'A Fooland His Money' ; 'The Man of the Hour' ; 'The Dollar Mark' ; 'The Law of Love.'

Brockes, Barthold Heinrich (brok'es). A German poet (1680–1747); He became a magistrate at Ritzebüttel. There he composed his 'Country Life at Ritzebüttel,' and afterward published 'Earthly Employment in God : Poems of Nature and Morality,'

Brockett, Linus Pierpont. An American historical and miscellaneous writer; born in Canton, Conn., Oct. 16, 1820; died Jan. 13, 1893. He graduated from Yale Medical College in 1843. Since 1847 he has devoted himself to literature; he has contributed largely to encyclopædias, and has published over 40 works, among which are: 'History of Education' (1849); 'History of the Civil War' (1866); 'The Silk Industry of America' (1876).

Brodhead, Mrs. Eva Wilder (McGlasson). An American novelist. Among her most popular works are: 'One of the Visconti'; 'Diana's Livery'; 'An Earthly Paragon'; 'Bound in Shallows.'

Brodzinski, Kazimierz (brod-zins'kē). A Polish poet; born at Krolovka, Galicia, March 8, 1791; died at Dresden, Oct. 10, 1835. In 1818 he lectured in Warsaw on Polish literature, and was afterward professor in the university. In his idyl 'Wieslav' (1820) the life of the Polish peasantry is beautifully idealized. His works were published in 1842 (10 vols.).

Brofferio, Angelo (brof-fā'rē-ō). An Italian poet and journalist; born near Asti, Piedmont, in 1802; died May 26, 1866. He wrote several dramas and comedies: 'Salvator Rosa'; 'Return of the Proscript'; 'My Cousin'; 'All for the Best': they met with much popular favor. By a volume of patriotic 'Songs,' he obtained from his countrymen the title "Piedmontese Béranger." His journal, Voce della Libertà, was a powerful instrument in bringing about the unification of Italy. He published two volumes of 'Memoirs.'

Brome, Alexander. An English poet; born, 1620; died 1666. He was of pronounced royalist sympathies, and is remembered for various stanzas, published under the title 'Songs and Poems' (1661), and a comedy called 'The Cunning Lovers' (1654).

Brome, Richard. An English dramatist; supposed to have died in 1652. Nothing is known of his birth or early history, save that he was of humble origin. He was the servant of Ben Jonson, and wrote himself into high repute. He is mentioned in the induction to Jonson's 'Bartholomew Fair.' Jonson praised his work, and Brome always refers to Jonson with pride. Jonson was of course his model, men and manners his study. His most successful play appears to have been 'The Northern Lass' (1632), frequently acted at the Globe and Blackfriars; 'The Sparagus Garden' (1635) was also popular. The best known dramas besides these are: 'The Antipodes' (1640); 'The Jovial Crew' (1652); 'The City Wit' (1653); and 'The Court Beggar' (1653). With Thomas Heywood he wrote 'The Late Lancashire Witches' (1634). Brome also wrote minor poems. Two volumes of 'Works' were published in London, 1653–59; and Brome's 'Dramatic Works' in London, 1873.

Brontë, Anne. ("Acton Bell.") An English novelist, sister of Charlotte; born in Thornton, Yorkshire, 1820; died in Scarborough, May 28, 1849. She spent her life in her father's parsonage at Haworth; had a short experience as a governess; and published poems with her sisters. Her novels are: 'Agnes Grey' (1847); 'The Tenant of Wildfell Hall' (1848). (See 'Charlotte Brontë and her Sisters.')

Brontë, Charlotte. An English novelist; born in Thornton, April 21, 1816; died in Haworth, March 31, 1855. Her 'Jane Eyre' (London, 1847) was published under her pseudonym "Currer Bell"; and many personal experiences are embodied in her novels, which are: 'Jane Eyre' (1847); 'Shirley' (1849); 'Villette' (1853); 'The Professor' (1855); and 'Emma,' unfinished. Collective edition, 7 vols., 1872.

Brontë, Emily. ["Ellis Bell."] An English novelist, sister of Charlotte; born in Thornton, 1818; died in Haworth, Dec. 19, 1848. Her novel 'Wuthering Heights' (1847) shows a powerful and fantastic imagination. (See 'Charlotte Brontë and her Sisters.')

Brooke, Henry. An Irish novelist and dramatist; born in Rantavan, County Cavan, Ireland, about 1703; died in Dublin, Oct. 10, 1783. He was educated at Trinity College, Dublin, and studied law in London, where he became a friend of Pope. His play 'Gustavus Vasa' (1739) was performed in Dublin as 'The Patriot.' 'The Fool of Quality, or the History of Henry, Earl of Moreland' (5 vols., London, 1760) is his best novel. It was republished under the supervision of Charles Kingsley in 1859. Brooke's works were collected in 4 vols., London, 1778.

Brooke, Stopford Augustus. An Irish critic; born in Letterkenny, Ireland, in 1832. He graduated at Trinity College, Dublin; seceded from the Church of England, and now has charge of a Unitarian chapel in Bloomsbury. He has published religious books; but is noted for his scholarly and interesting works on English literature, including 'History of Early English Literature' (1892); Tennyson: his Art and Relation to Modern Life'; 'The Gospel of Joy.'

Brooks, Charles Timothy. An American clergyman, translator, and author; born in Salem, Mass., June 20, 1813; died in Newport, R. I., June 14, 1883. He became a minister in the Unitarian Church in 1835. He is best known as a translator from the German of Schiller, Richter, Goethe, and Schefer. Among his original works are: 'Controversy Touching the Old Stone Mill' (1851); 'Songs of Field and Flood' (1854); 'Poems, Original and Translated' (1885).

Brooks, Charles William Shirley. An English humorist; born in London, April 29, 1816; died there, Feb. 23, 1874. He was the son of an architect, and forsook law for journalism. In 1853 he was sent on a mission to report on the condition of labor and the poor in Russia, Syria, and Egypt; the result of which appeared in 'The Russians of the South' (1856). He wrote political articles, attracted attention by several dramas and burlesques, and in 1854 joined the staff of the London Punch. In 1870 he succeeded Mark Lemon as its editor. His novels — which include: 'Aspen Court' (1855); 'The Gordian Knot' (1860); 'The Silver Cord' (1861); 'Sooner or Later,' with illustrations by Du Maurier (3 vols., 1866–68); 'The Naggletons' (1875) show keen observation. He also wrote 'Amusing Poetry' (1857). His son, Reginald Shirley, collected Brooks's 'Wit and Humor from Punch' (1875).

Brooks, Elbridge Streeter. Born in Lowell, Mass., April 14, 1846; died at Somerville, Mass., Jan. 7, 1902. He wrote many juvenile books: 'Historic Boys' (New York, 1885); 'Chivalric Days' (1886); 'The Story of the American Indian' (1887); 'The Story of New York' (1888).

Brooks, Maria Gowan. An American poet, pseudonym "Maria del Occidente"; born in Medford, Mass., about 1795; died in Matanzas, Cuba, Nov. 11, 1845. She spent her youth in Charlestown, Mass., and the rest of her life in London, New York, and Cuba. Her chief poem is 'Zophiel, or the Bride of Seven'; the first canto of which appeared in Boston in 1825, and the rest was finished under Southey's influence in 1833. 'Idomen, or the Vale of Yumuri,' is an autobiography (1843).

Brooks, Noah. An American journalist and author; born in Castine, Me., Oct. 24, 1830. Since 1850 he has been connected with newspapers in Massachusetts, California, Washington, and New York. He has written many popular books for boys, among which are: 'The Fairport Nine' (1880); 'Our Baseball Club' (1884); 'How the Republic is Governed.' He has recently edited and enlarged Bryant and Gay's 'History of the U. S.' Died Aug. 6, 1903.

Brooks, Phillips. An American clergyman of the Episcopal Church; born in Boston, Dec. 13, 1835; died there, Jan. 23, 1893. He was rector of Protestant Episcopal churches successively in Philadelphia and in Boston, and was made Bishop of Massachusetts in 1891. He was an impressive pulpit orator and great spiritual force, and published many volumes of sermons and lectures; notably: 'Letters of Travel'; 'Lectures on Preaching' (1877); and 'Essays and Addresses' (1894).

Brossböll, Johan Carl Christian. See Etlar.

Bross, William. A noted American journalist; born in Montague, Sussex County, N. J., Nov. 4, 1813; died in 1890. He graduated from Williams College in 1838 and taught school for ten years. Later he settled in Chicago and entered the publishing business. He was a member of the city council from 1855 to 1856, and lieutenant-governor of Illinois from 1865 to 1869. Among his works are: 'History of Chicago' (1876); 'Tom Quick, a Romance of Indian Warfare.' He is best remembered as the proprietor of the Chicago Tribune.

Brotherton, Mrs. Alice (Williams). An American poet and magazine writer; born in Cambridge, Ind. She is a resident of Cincinnati, O. Her chief works are: 'Beyond the Veil' (1886); 'What the Wind Told the Tree-Tops,' prose and verse for children; 'The Sailing of King Olaf, and Other Poems' (1887).

Brougham, Henry Peter, Lord Brougham and Vaux (brö'am or bröm). An eminent British statesman, orator, and author; born in Edinburgh, Sept. 19, 1778; died at Cannes, France, May 7, 1868. He entered the University of Edinburgh in 1792. In 1802 he helped to found the Edinburgh Review, contributing to the first four numbers twenty-one articles, and to the first twenty numbers eighty articles. The article on Byron's 'Hours of Idleness' provoked the poet to write his 'English Bards and Scotch Reviewers.' In 1810 Brougham entered Parliament; where his remarkable eloquence gave him at once a commanding place. He was counsel for Queen Caroline in George IV.'s suit against her (1820), winning a decisive victory which raised him to the height of fame and popularity. He became Lord Chancellor in 1830, and was at the same time created a baron; he resigned on the defeat of the Whigs in 1834, and never again held public office, though still taking effective part in the business and debates of the House of Lords. His later years were passed partly in England, and partly in the beautiful retreat he had fitted up at Cannes. He was the steadfast and powerful champion of revision and reform of the laws, popular education, the abolition of slavery, and the maintenance of peace. The famous Reform Bill of 1832 was carried during his chancellorship, and largely by his agency. His miscellaneous writings in their collected edition (11 vols., 1855–61) cover a vast number and variety of subjects. His best works are his 'Sketches of the Statesmen of the Time of George III.' and 'Lives of Men of Letters and Science.' An edition of his 'Speeches,' corrected by himself, was published in four volumes in 1838. His 'Autobiography' was written in extreme old age, and is unreliable.

Brougham, John. An American actor and playwright; born in Dublin, Ireland, May 9, 1814; died in New York, June 7, 1880. He made his début as an actor in England in 1830. He came to America in 1842, and with the exception of a short return trip to England in 1860, remained here until his death. He was the author of over 100 comedies, farces, and burlesques. Among his most successful plays were: 'Vanity Fair'; 'The Irish Emigrant'; 'The Game of Love'; and 'London Assurance,' written in collaboration with Dion Boucicault. He is also author of sketches entitled 'Basket of Chips' (1855) and 'Bunsby Papers.'

Broughton, Rhoda. An English novelist; born in Segrwyd Hall, Denbighshire, Wales,

Nov. 29, 1840. She is the daughter of a clergyman, and now resides at Broughton Hall,
Cheshire. Her novels are very popular, and
include: 'Cometh Up as a Flower' (1867);
'Not Wisely but Too Well' (1867); 'Red as
a Rose is She' (1870); 'Good-by, Sweetheart'
(1872); 'Nancy' (1873); 'Belinda' (1883);
'Doctor Cupid' (1886); 'Alas' (1890); 'Mrs.
Bligh' (1892); and 'A Beginner' (1894).

Brown, Alice. An American essayist and
miscellaneous writer; born in New Hampshire
in 1857. She is on the staff of the Youth's
Companion. Among her works are: 'Fools of Nature,' a novel (1887); 'Meadow Grass'; 'Robert
Louis Stephenson'); 'Life of Mercy Otis Warren'; 'The Country Road'); 'The Court of Love.'

Brown, Charles Brockden. An American
novelist; born in Philadelphia, Pa., Jan. 17, 1771;
died Feb. 22, 1810. His most famous novels
are: 'Wieland, or the Transformation,' a tale
of ventriloquism (1798); 'Ormund, or the Secret
Witness' (1799); 'Arthur Mervyn,' containing
a description of the yellow-fever plague of
1793 in Philadelphia (1799–80); 'Jane Talbot'
(1801); 'Edgar Huntly, or the Sleep-Walker'
(1801); and 'Clara Howard,' reprinted as 'Philip
Stanley' (1806). His novels have attained a
considerable vogue in foreign countries, translations of them into French and German proving popular. They also sold largely at one
time in England.

Brown, David Paul. An American lawyer,
playwright, and author; born in Philadelphia,
Pa., Sept. 28, 1795; died there, July 11, 1872.
He was admitted to the bar in 1816. Among
his works are: 'Sertorius,' a tragedy (1830);
'Love and Honor,' a farce. He also wrote
'The Forum, or Forty Years' Full Practice at
the Philadelphia Bar' (1856).

Brown, Emma Elizabeth. An American
biographical writer; born in New Hampshire
in 1847. She is a resident of Newton, Mass.
Her works include popular lives of Washington, Garfield, Holmes, and Lowell; and among
other volumes: 'The Child Toilers of Boston
Streets' (1878); 'True Manliness' (1880).

Brown, Frances. An Irish poet; born in
Stranorlar, County Donegal, Ireland, in 1816.
She is called « The Blind Poetess of Ulster,»
and is known by 'The Star of Attéghéi and
Other Poems' (London, 1844), and 'Lyrics and
Miscellaneous Poems' (1847).

Brown, John. A Scotch essayist; born at
Biggar, 1810; died 1882. He practiced medicine in Edinburgh. Whatever his pen touched
it adorned. The objects of his affection were
homely landscapes, old-fashioned people, the
departed, children, and dogs. Humor and pathos tinged all he wrote. The story of Rab,
the dog, and that of Marjorie Fleming, the
child, will live long in English literature.
Three volumes contain all his writings: 'Horæ
Subsecivæ' (2 vols.), and 'John Leech and
other Papers.'

Brown, Oliver Madox. An English author
and artist; born in Finchley, Jan. 20, 1855; died
in London, Nov. 5, 1874. He inherited great
talent for painting from his father, Ford Madox
Brown (1821–93), and at an early age exhibited
remarkable water-colors. Although he died
young, his literary work, including stories and
poems, is valued for its imaginative power.
His 'Literary Remains' (London, 1876) contain his story 'The Black Swan,' originally
published as 'Gabriel Denver' (1873), and a
sonnet to his memory by Dante Gabriel Rossetti. See J. H. Ingram, 'O. M. Brown' (London, 1883).

Brown, T. E. An English poet; born at Douglas, Isle of Man, in 1830; died at Clifton, Oct. 30,
1897. He was a clergyman of the Church of England, and had made a special study of manners
and people in the Isle of Man, where he was
stationed. His poems comprised narratives in the
Manx dialect, and personal lyrics and elegiacs.
The most notable are: 'Betsy Lee'; 'Fo'c's'le
Yarns'; 'The Manx Witch' and 'The Doctor.'

Browne, Charles Farrar. ("Artemus Ward.»)
An American humorist; born at Waterford,
Me., April 26, 1834; died at Southampton, England, March 6, 1867. He is most celebrated for
the collections of humor called 'Artemus Ward,
his Book' (1862); 'Artemus Ward, his Travels' (1863?). His productions were widely
quoted, and his popularity as a lecturer was
very great. In 1866 he visited England on a
lecture tour, and contributed to Punch.

Browne, Irving. An American lawyer, editor, and author; born in Marshall, Oneida
County, N. Y., Sept. 14, 1835. In 1857 he graduated from the Albany Law School and practiced in Troy. In 1879 he became editor of
the Albany Law Journal. His works include:
'Humorous Phases of the Law' (1876); 'Law
and Lawyers in Literature' (1883); 'The Elements of Criminal Law.' Died Feb. 6, 1899.

Browne, John Ross. An Irish-American
traveler and author; born in Ireland in 1817;
died in Oakland, Cal., Dec. 9, 1875. He came
when a child to the United States. His chief
works are: 'Etchings of a Whaling Cruise,
with Notes of a Sojourn on the Island of Zan-
zibar' (1846); 'Yusef, or the Journey of the
Fragi: a Crusade in the East' (1853); 'The
Land of Thor' (1866); and 'Adventures in the
Apache Country' (1869).

Browne, Junius Henri. An American jour-
nalist; born at Seneca Falls, N. Y., in 1833.
He died in New York city, April 2, 1902.
Among his works are: 'Four Years in Secessia'
(1865); 'The Great Metropolis, a Mirror of
New York' (1869); 'Sights and Sensations in
Europe' (1872).

Browne, Sir Thomas. An English antiquary and physician (1605–82); born in London. After receiving an academic and a
professional (medical) education in England,
he visited the Continent and took the degree
M. D. at Leyden. He was knighted by **Charles**

II. His principal work is 'Religio Medici' (1642), a liberal confession of faith for that day. Four years later he published a treatise on 'Vulgar Errors,' directed against the current superstitions of his contemporaries. 'Urn Burial' appeared in 1658. After his death a collection of his fugitive pieces was published; and this was followed by 'Christian Morals,' a collection of aphorisms.

Browne, Thomas Alexander. See **Boldrewood.**

Browne, William. An English poet; born in Tavistock, Devonshire, in 1591; died in Ottery St. Mary, about 1643. He was educated at Oxford, and spent a quiet, tranquil life. His poetry is graceful and fanciful, and abounds in beautiful pictures of English scenery. Browne has always been much admired by the poets. His chief work is 'Britannia's Pastorals' (1613-16). 'The Shepherd's Pipe' (1614) is a collection of eclogues, and 'The Inner Temple Masque' (1614-15) tells the story of Ulysses and Circe. His minor poems are very fine. The best modern editions are by Hazlitt for the Roxburghe Club, and by Gordon Goodwin, 'The Muse's Library.'

Brownell, Henry Howard. An American poet and writer of historical sketches; born at Providence, R. I., Feb. 6, 1820; died at East Hartford, Conn., Oct. 31, 1872. His first poetic venture was a spirited versification of Farragut's 'General Orders' to the fleet below New Orleans. Afterward he was appointed to an honorary place on the Hartford flagship, and had opportunity to observe actual naval warfare. In 'The Bay Fight' he describes with truth and force the battle of Mobile Bay. He collected and published his many occasional verses in 'Lyrics of a Day, or Newspaper Poetry by a Volunteer in the U. S. Service' (1864).

Brownell, William Crary. An American essayist and critic; born in New York city, Aug. 30, 1851. He graduated from Amherst, and has devoted himself to critical and editorial work in New York. He is editor of Scribner's Magazine, and has written: 'French Traits: an Essay on Comparative Criticism' (1889); 'French Art' (1892); and 'Newport' (1896).

Browning, Elizabeth Barrett. An English poet; born in Durham, March 6, 1809; died in Florence, June 30, 1861. She was the daughter of an English country gentleman, Edward Moulton, who took the name of Barrett. In September 1846 she married Robert Browning. Her chief poems are: 'The Seraphim' (1838); 'Romaunt of the Page' (1839); 'The Drama of Exile' (1844); 'A Vision of Poets' (1844); 'The Cry of the Children' (1844); 'Casa Guidi Windows' (1851); 'Aurora Leigh' (1856), in a measure autobiographical. Her poem 'Lady Geraldine's Courtship' contains a striking characterization of the poetry of Browning. Her 'Sonnets from the Portuguese' are among the noblest of love-poems. The 'Romance of the Swan's Nest'; the 'Rhyme of the

Duchess May'; the 'Romaunt of Margret'; 'Bertha in the Lane'; and 'Isobel's Child,' are romantic and original ballads. ''Prometheus Bound,' a metrical translation of Æschylus, was published in 1850.

Browning, Robert. An English poet; born in Camberwell, May 7, 1812; died in Venice, Dec. 12, 1889. His first dramatic poem, 'Pauline,' which appeared anonymously in 1833, was followed two years later by 'Paracelsus'; 'Strafford' (1837); 'Sordello' (1840); and a series of plays and dramatic lyrics under the title of 'Bells and Pomegranates' (1841-46). This collection included: 'Pippa Passes'; 'King Victor and King Charles', 'Colombe's Birthday'; 'The Return of the Druses'; 'A Blot on the 'Scutcheon'; 'Luria'; and 'A Soul's Tragedy.' In 1846 he married Elizabeth Barrett, and resided in Florence until her death in 1861, when he returned to London; but much of the latter part of his life was spent in Italy. 'The Ring and the Book' was published in 1869. His other works include: 'Christmas Eve and Easter Day' (1850); 'Men and Women' (1855); 'Dramatis Personæ' (1864); 'Balaustion's Adventure' (1871); 'Fifine at the Fair' (1872); 'Red-Cotton Nightcap Country' (1873); 'Dramatic Idylls' (1879-80); 'Jocoseria' (1883); 'Ferishtah's Fancies' (1884); and 'Parleyings with Certain People of Importance in their Day' (1887). The 'Complete Poetic and Dramatic Works: Cambridge Edition' are published in 1 vol. by Houghton, Mifflin & Co.; the 'Complete Works' (1897), edited by Augustine Birrell, in 2 vols., are published by the Macmillan Company.

Brownlow, William Gannaway. ("Parson Brownlow.") An American politician, journalist, and author; born in Wythe County, Va., Aug. 29, 1805; died in Knoxville, Tenn., April 29, 1877. During his early career he was an itinerant preacher, editor, and lecturer. He was a Union champion during the Civil War, and banished from the Confederate lines on that ground. In 1865 he was elected governor of Tennessee, and was re-elected in 1867. He was U. S. Senator from 1869 to 1875. Among his works are: 'The Great Iron Wheel Examined' (1858); 'Sketches of the Rise, Progress, and Decline of Secession' (1862).

Brownson, Orestes Augustus. An American author; born in Stockbridge, Vt., Sept. 16, 1803; died in Detroit, Mich., April 17, 1876. His early education was slight. Originally a Presbyterian, he became a Universalist minister, afterward a Unitarian, and finally a Roman Catholic. He was an ardent champion of popular rights, and advocated a mild form of socialism. His greatest work was the establishment and editorship of the Boston Quarterly Review (1838-43) and Brownson's Review (1844-64 and 1873-75). Of his extensive works, the best known are: 'The Convert, or Leaves from my Experience' (1857); and 'The American Republic, its Constitution, Tendencies, and Destiny' (1865).

Bruce, Wallace. An American lecturer and poet; born in Hillsdale, Columbia County, N. Y., Nov. 10, 1844. He is a prominent lecturer on literary subjects. Among his works are: 'The Land of Burns' (1879); 'From the Hudson to the Yosemite' (1884); 'Wayside Poems'; 'Here's a Hand'; 'Leaves of Gold'; 'Wanderers.'

Brun, Friederike Sophie Christiane (brön). A German poet and writer of travels (1765–1835); born (Münter) at Gräfentonna in the district of Gotha. She traveled extensively through Switzerland, southern France, Italy, and other countries, and came into personal acquaintance with many of the foremost personages of her day; Johann von Müller, Matthisson, Necker, Angelica Kauffmann, Mme. de Staël, etc. Her books of travel were held in very high esteem. She published three small volumes of 'Poems'; and 'Truth from Morning Dreams and Ida's Æsthetic Development,' containing reminiscences of her early years.

Brunetière, Ferdinand (brün-tyär'). A distinguished French critic; born in Toulon, July 19, 1849. He is the editor of the 'Revue des Deux Mondes' and became a member of the French Academy, 1893. In criticism he inclines to the idealist as opposed to the naturalist school. His principal works are: 'History and Literature' (1884, 3 vols.); 'The Naturalist Romance' (1883); 'Essays on Contemporary Literature' (1892); 'Epochs of the French Theatre' (1892). Died Dec. 9, 1906.

Bruni, Leonardo (brö'nē), surnamed Aretino. A noted Italian humanist; born at Arezzo, 1369; died in Florence, March 9, 1444. He forsook the study of jurisprudence to devote himself wholly to the ancient classics; was secretary to four popes from 1404 to 1415, but then resigned, to write the history of Florence (in 10 books). In reward he was made chancellor of Florence. His principal service to the cause of letters was in translations of Aristotle, Plato, Plutarch, Demosthenes, into Latin. He wrote a Latin comedy. His 'Epistles' are of value for the history of his time.

Bruno, Giordano (brö'nō). A renowned Italian philosopher; born at Nola, near Naples, Italy, 1548; burned at the stake in Rome, Feb. 17, 1600, charged with heresy. His best-known works are: 'Ash-Wednesday Conversations'; 'The Work of the Great Key'; 'The Exploration of the Thirty Seals'; 'The Taper'; 'Expulsion of the Triumphant Beast'; 'The Heroic Enthusiasts'; and a great number of other writings in prose and verse.

Brush, Mrs. Christine (Chaplin). An American artist and novelist; born in Bangor, Me., in 1842; died at Brooklyn, Feb. 3, 1892. She was a resident of Brooklyn. Her chief work, 'The Colonel's Opera Cloak,' a novel, was published anonymously in 1879. She also wrote two stories: 'Inside our Gates'; 'One Summer's Lessons in Perspective.'

Bryant, William Cullen. An American poet; born in Cummington, Mass., Nov. 3, 1794; died in New York, June 12, 1878. After two years in Williams College he left it, and turned his attention to law. But in early youth he produced 'Thanatopsis,' and some of his best lyrics,—'To a Waterfowl,' 'The Yellow Violet,' etc.,—which were the opening of a high literary career. His longest poem, 'The Ages,' was recited at Harvard in 1821. In 1829 he became editor-in-chief of the New York Evening Post. His books include: 'Letters of a Traveler' (1855); 'Letters from Spain' (1859); 'Letters from the East' (1869); and a 'Popular History of the United States,' with S. H. Gay (4 vols., 1878–82). His 'Poems' appeared in New York in 1832, and Washington Irving reprinted them in London, where they went through several editions. This book was followed by 'The Fountain and Other Poems' (1842) and 'The White-Footed Deer and Other Poems' (1844). His first complete edition was issued in Philadelphia in 1846. In his old age Bryant began a translation of the 'Iliad' and 'Odyssey' in blank verse; and his last great poem was 'The Flood of Years,' a noble pendant to 'Thanatopsis.' Among his poems that have become popular favorites are: the 'Forest Hymn'; 'The West Wind'; 'June'; 'Death of the Flowers'; and 'Hymn to Death.'

Bryce, James. An Irish historian; born in Belfast, May 10, 1838. After graduating at Oxford in 1862, he studied at Heidelberg, and subsequently practiced law in London. From 1870 till 1893 he was regius professor of civil law in Oxford, has had a distinguished political career. He has supported Home Rule, city reforms, and international copyright. His chief works are: 'The Holy Roman Empire' (1864); 'Transcaucasia and Ararat' (1877); 'The American Commonwealth' (1888). Since 1906 Ambassador to U. S.

Bryce, Lloyd. An American editor and novelist; born in Long Island, N.Y., 1851. He was editor of the North American Review from 1889 to 1896. His works are: 'Paradise'; 'A Dream of Conquest'; 'The Romance of an Alter Ego'; 'Friends in Exile'; 'After Christianity, What'?

Bube, Adolf (bö'bạ). A German poet (1802–73); born at Gotha. He published two volumes of miscellaneous 'Poems,' characterized by sincere feeling for nature. He compiled several volumes of 'Popular Legends,' especially of Thuringia, which he rendered in verse.

Buchanan, Robert Williams. An English author; born at Caverswall, Staffordshire, Aug. 18, 1841; died in London, June 10, 1901. He was educated at Glasgow, and went to London to engage in literature. His attack upon Dante Gabriel Rossetti drew a famous letter from that poet and a scathing pamphlet from Swinburne. His poems include: 'Undertones' (1863); 'Idylls and Legends of Inverburn' (1865); 'London Poems,' his best effort (1866); 'North Coast Poems' (1867); 'Napoleon Fallen: a Lyrical Drama' (1871); 'The Drama of Kings' (1871); 'Ballads of Love, Life, and Humor' (1882); and 'The City of Dreams' (1888). His best novels are: 'The Shadow of the Sword' (1876); 'A Child of Nature' (1879); 'God and the Man' (1881); 'The Martyrdom of Madeline' (1882); and 'Foxglove Manor' (1884). Buchanan also wrote successful plays. His poems have been collected (3 vols., London, 1874).

Buchez, Philippe Benjamin Joseph (bü-shā'). A French annalist and physician; born in Mortagne, Ardennes, March 31, 1796; died at Rhodez, Aveyron, Aug. 12, 1865. With Roux Lavergne he projected the 'Parliamentary History of the French Revolution' (40 vols., 1833-38), a work of inestimable utility.

Buchner, Ludwig, a German scientist and author; born at Darmstadt, March 28, 1824; died there May 1, 1899. His first publication, 'Force and Matter' (1885), aroused vehement opposition. His other writings include 'Nature and Spirit'; 'From Nature and Science'; 'Man and his Position in Nature'; 'The Darwinian Theory of the Origin and Change of Living Matter'; 'God and Science'; 'The Power of Heriditary Transmission'; 'Future Life and Modern Science; 'Darwinism and Socialism.'

Büchner, Georg (büch'ner). A German poet; born near Darmstadt, Oct. 17, 1813; died Feb. 19, 1837. He studied natural science and medicine in the universities of Strasburg and Giessen. In 1834 he entered the political arena with a manifesto entitled 'The Rural Messenger,' and bearing the motto "Peace to the cabin, war to the palace." To escape arrest he fled to Strasburg, where he studied the philosophies of Descartes and Spinoza. He was preparing to open a course of lectures in Zürich when he died. He wrote a drama in 1834 on 'The Death of Danton,' the work of a genuine but undisciplined poet. His 'Complete Works,' with biography, were published in 1879.

Büchner, Luise. A German poet and novelist (1821-77), sister of Georg. Her first publication, 'Women and their Calling' (1855), was followed by many others on the "woman's-rights question"; it commanded much attention, and reached a fifth edition (1883). She wrote a volume of tales, 'From Life' (1861); 'Poet-Voices of Home and Foreign Lands'; several original poems, 'Woman's Heart'; some 'Christmas Stories'; etc.

Buck, Dudley. An American organist, composer, and author; born in Hartford, Conn., March 10, 1839. He is organist of the Church of the Holy Trinity, Brooklyn, N. Y. Aside from several cantatas, he has written two books: 'A Dictionary of Musical Terms' and a work on the 'Influence of the Organ in History' (1882).

Buckland, Francis Trevelyan. An English naturalist; born at Oxford, Dec. 17, 1826; died Dec. 19, 1880. His preferences were for practical science; and after retiring from his place as surgeon to the Second Life Guards he founded the journal Land and Water, of which he was editor. He was an authority on fish-culture, and as such was consulted by foreign

governments. He was a resolute opponent of Darwinism. Besides his works on fish-culture, he wrote: 'Log-Book of a Fisherman and Zoölogist' (1876); 'Notes and Jottings on Animal Life' (1882); 'Curiosities of Natural History.'

Buckle, Henry Thomas. An English historian; born in Lee, Kent, Nov. 24, 1821; died in Damascus, May 29, 1862. A self-educated man, he is known for his great work 'The History of Civilization in England' (2 vols., 1857-61). His 'Miscellaneous and Posthumous Works' were edited by Helen Taylor (London, 1872), new ed. by Grant Allen, 1880.

Buckley, James Monroe. An American clergyman; born in Rahway, N. J., Dec. 16, 1836. In 1858 he entered the ministry in the Methodist Church. Since 1881 he has been the editor of the Christian Advocate. Among his works are: 'Two Weeks in the Yosemite Valley' (1872); 'Oats or Wild Oats' (1885); 'The Land of the Czar and the Nihilist' (1886); 'Travels in Three Continents.'

Buckstone, John Baldwin. An English dramatist; born in Hoxton, London, Sept. 14, 1802; died in Sydenham, near London, Oct. 31, 1879. From 1823 to 1853 he was a well-known London actor; he became manager of the Haymarket Theatre, and produced nearly 200 plays, which were all successful, largely owing to his knowledge of stage effect and humor. Among the best are: 'The Wreck Ashore'; 'Victorine'; 'Green Bushes'; 'The Flowers of the Forest'; 'Married Life'; 'Leap Year'; 'Second Thoughts'; and 'Nicholas Flam.'

Büdinger, Max (bü-ding-er). A German historian; born in Cassel, April 1, 1828. He exerted great influence among the universities; the most admired of his books being on 'Austrian History' (1858; the work coming down to the mediæval period only), and 'King Richard III. of England.' Died Feb. 22, 1902.

Buel, Clarence Clough. An American editor and author; born at Laona, Chautauqua County, N. Y., July 29, 1850. He was connected with the New York Tribune from 1875 to 1881, when he joined the staff of the Century Magazine; and in 1883, in conjunction with Robert Underwood Johnson, he began the editing of the celebrated 'Century War Articles,' which were afterwards expanded into the notable 'Battles and Leaders of the Civil War' (1887).

Buffon, George Louis le Clerc, Comte de (bü-fön'). A famous French naturalist; born at Montbard, Sept. 7, 1707; died April 16, 1788. His 'Natural History' widely popularized the study of zoölogy and of nature in general, owing to the author's luminous and attractive style and his very plausible generalizations; it was translated into nearly all the languages of Europe. The definitive edition of this 'General and Particular Natural History' is in 36 volumes (1749-88).

Bulfinch, Thomas. An American author; born in Boston, Mass., July 15, 1796; died there,

6

May 27, 1867. He graduated from Harvard University in 1814. Although engaged in business, he managed to devote considerable time to literature. Among his best-known works are: 'The Age of Fable' (1855); 'Age of Chivalry' (1858); 'Legends of Charlemagne' (1864); 'Oregon and Eldorado' (1866).

Bülow, Bertha von. See Arnold, Hans.

Bülow, Karl Eduard von (bü'lō). A German story-teller (1803-53); born at Berg vor Eilenburg in Saxony. His literary fame rests mainly on his 'Book of Tales,' after ancient Italian, Spanish, French, English, Latin, and German originals (4 vols., 1834-36), which was followed by a supplementary volume. Of his own original compositions, the 'Springtide Wandering among the Harz Mountains' is one of the best. He wrote also the very interesting story of 'The Youth of a Poor Man of Toggenburg,' founded on the autobiography of Ulrich Brüker, a Swiss weaver. He published the original later.

Bülow, Margarete von. A German novelist (1860-85); born in Berlin. She wrote four volumes of stories, viz.: 'Stories' (1885); 'Jonas Briccius' (1886); 'Chronicle of the Riffelshausen Folks'; and 'New Stories.' She delineated character with great precision, and showed true insight into the human heart. She lost her life in an attempt to rescue a boy from drowning.

Buloz, François (bü-lō). A French publicist (1803-77); born at Bulbens in Haute-Savoie. He founded the great French review, Revue des Deux Mondes (1831), and was its editor for 40 years. He wrote little, but his 'Letters and Memoirs' are of great value for the history of French letters in his time.

Bulthaupt, Heinrich Alfred (bölt'houpt). A German poet and dramatist; born at Bremen, Oct. 26, 1849. On quitting the university he was for a while a private tutor; then he traveled in the East, in Greece, and in Italy. He was a lawyer in his native town for some years, and in 1879 became custodian of the city library. Of his dramatic compositions the list is very long, comprising tragedies: 'Saul,' 'A Corsican Tragedy'; plays dealing with the questions of the time: 'The Workmen'; comedies; comic operas; etc. He has also written a work, already of high authority, on 'Dramaturgy of the Theatre' (3 vols.); also 'Dramaturgy of the Opera' (2 vols.).

Bulwer, Henry Lytton Earle (Lord Dalling). An English author and diplomatist, brother of Sir Edward Bulwer-Lytton; born Feb. 13, 1801; died in Naples, May 23, 1872. He was minister to Madrid in 1843; in 1849 had a diplomatic mission to Washington, and was one of the negotiators of the Clayton-Bulwer treaty; was ambassador to Turkey 1858-65. Among his works are: 'An Autumn in Greece' (1826); 'France, Social, Literary, and Political' (1834-36); and 'Life of Byron' (1835).

Bulwer-Lytton, Edward, Lord Lytton. An English novelist, playwright, and poet; born in London, May 25, 1803; died in Torquay, Jan. 18, 1873. He was the son of Gen. Earle Bulwer and Elizabeth B. Lytton, heiress of Knebworth, to whose estates he succeeded in 1844 and assumed the surname of Lytton. In 1847 and again in 1852, he sat in Parliament; and in 1858-59 was colonial secretary, during which he called into existence the colonies of British Columbia and Queensland. In 1866 he was raised to the peerage as Baron Lytton. Altogether his works exceed sixty in number, and fill 110 volumes. His novels display great versatility, range of power, power of handling psychological and social problems, variety of incident and portraiture; and many are based on romantic and occult themes. Among the most famous are: 'Falkland' (1827); 'Pelham' (1828); 'Devereux' (1829); 'Paul Clifford' (1830); 'Eugene Aram' (1832); 'Godolphin' (1833); 'Pilgrims of the Rhine' (1834); 'Last Days of Pompeii' (1834); 'Rienzi' (1837); 'Ernest Maltravers' (1837); 'Alice, or the Mysteries' (1838); 'Last of the Barons' (1843); 'Harold' (1843); 'The Caxtons' (1850); 'My Novel' (1853); 'What Will He Do with It?' (1859); 'A Strange Story' (1862); 'The Coming Race' (1871); 'Kenelm Chillingly' (1873); and 'The Parisians' (1873). Three of his dramas—'The Lady of Lyons' (1838); 'Richelieu' (1838); and 'Money' (1848)—still hold the stage.

Bunce, Oliver Bell. An American publisher and writer; born in New York city, in 1828; died there, May 15, 1890. At an early age he became connected with the publishing business in New York. Among his books are: 'Romance of the Revolution' (1852); 'A Bachelor's Story' (1859); 'Don't: a Manual of Mistakes and Improprieties' (1883); 'My House' (1884); and 'Adventures of Timias Terrystone,' a novel (1885).

Bundy, Jonas Mills. An American journalist and author; born in Columbia, N. H., in 1835; died in Paris, France, Sept. 8, 1891. He gained experience in journalism in the West, and served in the Civil War. He was editor of the New York Mail and Express, and wrote 'Life of Garfield' (1880).

Bungay, George Washington. An American journalist and poet; born in Walsingham, England, July 22, 1818; died July 10, 1892. He came to this country in 1827. For some time he was connected with the New York Tribune. He was employed in the Custom House from 1873 to 1877. Among his numerous poems the best known is 'The Creed of the Bells.' His other works include: 'Abraham Lincoln Songster'; 'Pen Portraits of Illustrious Abstainers' (1881).

Bunge, Rudolf (böng'ạ). A German poet; born at Köthen, March 27, 1836. Among his works are a volume of his collected short poems, 'Flowers' (1854); a tragedy, 'The Duke of Courland' (1871); a cycle of five tragedies showing forth the action of Christianity upon the political life of nations, the members of the cycle being: 'Nero'; 'Alaric'; 'Desiderata'; 'The Bayonne Festival'; and 'The Cloister.' He wrote the libretti of several operas, among them that of 'The Trumpeter of Säckingen.'

Bunner, Henry Cuyler. An American poet and story-writer; born in Oswego, N. Y., Aug. 3, 1855; died in Nutley, N. J., May 11, 1896. He became a journalist in 1873, and was editor of Puck from shortly after its start till his death. Author of: 'A Woman of Honor' (New York, 1883); 'Airs from Arcady and Elsewhere' (1884); 'The Midge' (1886); 'The Story of a New York House' (1887); 'Zadoc Pine and Other Stories' (1891); 'Short Sixes' (1891); 'The Runaway Browns' (1892); 'Jersey Street and Jersey Lane' (1896); and 'In Partnership,' with Brander Matthews (1883). Also a play, 'The Tower of Babel' (1883); and uncollected magazine articles.

Bunyan, John. An English author; born in Elstow, Bedford, in November 1628; died in London, Aug. 31, 1688. He was the son of a tinker, went to the village school, and at seventeen enlisted in the Parliamentary army and served during the decisive year of 1645. In 1653 he joined a little community sometimes described as a Baptist church, and preached in the villages near Bedford until imprisoned in the Bedford jail. Here he remained for twelve years, being only released after the Declaration of Indulgence in 1672. The 'Pilgrim's Progress' was begun while the author was in prison, and was issued in 1678, a second part appearing in 1684. His other important works are 'Grace Abounding,' written in prison, and the 'Holy War' (1682). Altogether he wrote nearly sixty books.

Burdett, Charles. An American journalist and novelist; born in New York State in 1815; died 18—. His works were at one time very popular. Among the best known are: 'Life of Kit Carson'; 'The Beautiful Spy' (1865); 'The Gambler'; 'Trials and Triumphs.'

Burdette, Robert Jones. An American journalist and humorist; born in Greensborough, Pa., July 30, 1844. He served in the Union army during the Civil War. He is famous for humorous newspaper skits, of rare variety, charm, and unrepetitious freshness; begun in the Burlington (Iowa) Hawkeye, of which he became associate editor in 1874. Among his works are: 'The Rise and Fall of the Mustache,' a lecture (1877); 'Hawkeyes,' collected articles (1880); 'Life of William Penn' (1882).

Bürger, Gottfried August. An eminent German poet; born at Molmerswende, near Ballenstedt, Anhalt, Dec. 31, 1747, or Jan. 1, 1748; died in Göttingen, June 8, 1794. Shakespeare and Percy's 'Reliques of English Ballad Poetry' had a decisive influence in giving direction to his efforts at poetic expression. 'Lenore' (1773) established his reputation as a poet, which was sustained by the ballads that

followed it: 'The Parson's Daughter'; 'The Wild Huntsman'; 'The Song of the Brave Man'; 'Kaiser and Abbot.' Specimens of his burlesque ballads are: 'The Robber Count'; 'The Wives of Weinsberg.'

Burgos, Francisco Javier de (bör'gōs). A Spanish statesman and poet (1778-1845); born at Motril in Granada. In his dramatic compositions he sought to restore the classical Spanish comedy. Among them are: 'The Three (Women) Equals'; 'The Masked Ball'; 'The Optimist and the Pessimist.' He wrote a celebrated 'Ode to Reason.'

Burke, Edmund. An eminent British statesman and orator; born in Dublin, Jan. 12 (?), 1729; died in Beaconsfield, England, July 9, 1797. He graduated from Trinity College, Dublin, 1748; studied law, and in 1750 began literary work. Elected to Parliament, he made his first speech in 1766; and from that date until 1790 was one of the chief guides and inspirers of the revived Whig party. His speeches and pamphlets are still considered the most striking and suggestive manuals of political philosophy in modern times. They, with his miscellaneous writings, are all included in his 'Works and Correspondence' (8 vols., 1852). Among his most important works aside from his speeches are: 'A Philosophical Inquiry into the Origin of our Ideas of the Sublime and Beautiful' (1756); 'Reflections on the French Revolution' (1790); and 'Letters on a Regicide Peace.'

Burleigh, George Shepard. An American poet and miscellaneous writer; born at Plainfield, Conn., in 1821. He is the author of 'Anti-Slavery Hymns' (1842); 'The Maniac, and Other Poems' (1849); 'Signal Fires, or the Trail of the Pathfinder' (1856). Died 1903.

Burleigh, William Henry. An American journalist, lecturer, and poet; born in Woodstock, Conn., Feb. 2, 1812; died in Brooklyn, N. Y., March 18, 1871. He lectured extensively in behalf of the anti-slavery movement. In 1843 he became editor of the Charter Oak, of Hartford, Conn. A collection of his poems was published in 1840.

Burmeister, Hermann (bür-mīs'ter). A German scientific writer; born in Stralsund, Jan. 15, 1807; died in Buenos Ayres, Argentine Republic, May 2, 1892. He distinguished himself as a geologist and zoölogist in his native country, and settled permanently in the Argentine, where he continued his investigations. 'Manual of Entomology' (1832-44); 'History of Creation' (1843); and 'The Fossils of Horses Found among the South American Pampas' (1875), are among his books.

Burnaby, Frederick Gustavus. An English descriptive writer; born in Bedford, March 3, 1842; died at Abu Klea in the Soudan, Jan. 17, 1885. He served in the Royal Horse Guards, in which he became lieutenant-colonel in 1881. Distinguished in military service and with a love of adventure and literary skill, his

life and books are equally interesting. His
'Ride to Khiva' (London, 1875) ran through
eleven editions in a year. 'On Horseback
through Asia Minor' (1877) was nearly as
popular. See R. K. Mann, 'Life and Adventures of Burnaby' (London, 1882).

Burnand, Sir Francis Cowley. An English
humorist; born in London, Nov. 29, 1837. After
graduation from Cambridge, he devoted his
attention to play-writing, and has written about
100 burlesques, extravaganzas, and successful
comedies. Since 1880 he has been the editor of
Punch. Among his books, 'Happy Thoughts'
(1868) and its sequels are the most popular.
The 'New History of Sandford and Merton'
(1872) 'Quite at Home' (1890), and 'The Colonel' are also favorites.

Burnett, Frances (Hodgson). An Anglo-
American novelist; born in Manchester, England, Nov. 24, 1849; her family emigrated to
America and settled in Tennessee in 1865.
She early wrote stories. In 1873 Miss Hodgson
married Dr. Burnett, and in 1875 settled in
Washington, where she has since resided. After
various short stories, she published as a serial
in Scribner's Magazine 'That Lass o' Low-
rie's,' which became very popular, was promptly
issued in book form (1877), and was dramatized.
It was followed by a number of novels, among
which are: 'Haworth's' (1879); 'Louisiana'
(1881); 'Esmeralda'; 'A Fair Barbarian' (1882);
'Through One Administration' (1883); 'Little
Lord Fauntleroy,' a juvenile story, also dramatized (1887); 'The Pretty Sister of José' (1889);
'The One I Knew Best of All,' an autobiography (1893); 'A Lady of Quality' (1895); 'His
Grace of Osmonde,' a sequel to the preced-
ing; and a drama, 'The First Gentleman of
Europe,' with George Fleming; 'Nixie'; 'A
Lady of Quality'; 'The Shuttle.'

Burney, Charles. An English author; born
in Shrewsbury, April 7, 1726; died in Chelsea,
April 12, 1814. He became a famous and influential musician in London; was given the
degree of doctor of music by Oxford in 1769;
and sacrificed time, money, and personal comfort to travel and collect material for his 'History of Music' (4 vols., London, 1776–89). He
also wrote 'Memoirs and Letters of Metastasio'
(3 vols., 1796). Madame D'Arblay was his
daughter.

Burney, Frances—Madame D'Arblay. An
English novelist, daughter of Charles Burney;
born in King's Lynn, Norfolk, June 13, 1752;
died in Bath, Jan. 6, 1840. After she had published 'Evelina, or a Young Lady's Entrance
into the World' (1778), she became the favorite
of the literary men of the day, especially Dr.
Johnson. Her second novel, 'Cecilia' (1782),
was no less admired. In 1786 she was made
Second Keeper of the Robes to Queen Charlotte; and in 1793 she was married to M. D'Arblay, a French army officer. Her other books
are: 'Camilla' (1795); and 'The Wanderer, or
Female Difficulties' (1814). Her 'Diary and
Letters,' edited by her niece (7 vols., 1842–46),

are affected, but entertaining. She also wrote
memoirs of her father (1832). 'Evelina' and
'Cecilia' were published with introductions by
Annie R. Ellis (London, 1881–82).

Burnham, Clara Louise. An American
story-writer; born in Newton, Mass., May 25,
1854. She is the daughter of George F. Root,
the composer, and has lived in Chicago since
childhood. She has written several novels, including: 'Dearly Bought' (1884); 'Next Door'
(1886); 'Young Maids and Old' (1888); 'Miss
Bagg's Secretary' (1892); and 'Sweet Clover,
a Romance of the White City' (1894). She
has also written libretti for her father's cantatas.

Burns, Robert. A Scotch poet; born in Al-
loway, Jan. 25, 1759; died in Dumfries, July
21, 1796. Among the poems to which he owes
his fame are: 'The Cotter's Saturday Night';
'Hallowe'en'; 'Tam O'Shanter' (1790); 'To
a Mountain Daisy'; 'To a Mouse'; 'Twa
Dogs'; 'Highland Mary.' His principal collected editions are, in the order of publication: 'Poems, Chiefly in the Scottish Dialect'
(1786); 'The Scots' Musical Museum' (6 vols.,
1787–1803); 'A Select Collection of Original
Scottish Airs . . . with Select and Characteristic Verses,' which contains 100 songs by
the poet. But such editions have been issued
almost annually since 1805.

Burr, Enoch Fitch. An American mathe-
matical and religious writer; born at Green's
Farms, Fairfield County, Conn., Oct. 21, 1818.
He graduated from Yale in 1839, and became
pastor of the Congregational Church in Lyme,
Conn., in 1850. Since 1868 he has been a lect-
urer at Amherst College. Among his works
are: 'A Treatise on the Application of the
Calculus to the Theory of Neptune' (1848);
'A Song of the Sea' (1873); 'Aleph, the
Chaldean' (1891). He died in 1907.

Burr, George Lincoln. An American writer
and professor of history; born at Oramel,
N. Y., Jan. 30, 1857. From 1881 to 1884 he was
instructor at Cornell University. In 1892 he
was appointed professor of ancient and mediæval history in that institution. His published
works include: 'The Literature of Witchcraft'
(1890); 'Charlemagne' ('Heroes of History'
series); 'The Fate of Dietrich Slade.'

Burritt, Elihu. An American author, called
"The Learned Blacksmith"; born in New
Britain, Conn., Dec. 8, 1811; died there, March
7, 1879. He was a blacksmith, linguist, lecturer,
reformer, and a noted advocate of peace. His
books include: 'Sparks from the Anvil' (1848);
'Olive Leaves' (1853); and 'Chips from Many
Blocks' (1878). See Charles Northend, 'Life
of Elihu Burritt' (New York, 1879).

Burroughs, John. An American essayist;
born in Roxbury, N. Y., April 3, 1837. He is
the son of a farmer, became a journalist in
New York, and engaged in other pursuits until
1874, when he settled on a farm at Esopus,
N. Y., to devote himself to literature and to
fruit-culture. His essays are remarkable for

their descriptions of nature and their style. His books on rural themes include: 'Wake-Robin' (1871); 'Winter Sunshine' (1875); 'Birds and Poets' (1877); 'Locusts and Wild Honey' (1879); 'Pepacton: Notes of a Walker' (1881); 'Fresh Fields' (1884); 'Signs and Seasons' (1886); and 'Sharp Eyes' (1888). He has also written 'Notes on Walt Whitman' (1867); and 'Ways of Nature' (1905).

Burton, Nathaniel J. An American Congregational clergyman and writer; born at Trumbull, Conn., Dec. 17, 1824; died at Hartford, Conn., Oct. 13, 1887. He graduated in 1857 from Wesleyan College, Middletown, Conn., and from the Yale Divinity School in 1854. Translated 'Sacred History from the French of J. N. Loriquet' (1872); and wrote 'Yale Lectures on Preaching and Other Writings,' edited by Richard E. Burton, his son.

Burton, Richard. An American poet and journalist, son of Nathaniel J.; born in Hartford, Conn., March 14, 1859. He graduated from Trinity College, Hartford, and took a degree at Johns Hopkins University. His published poems are: 'Dumb in June' (1895); 'Memorial Day' (1897); 'Rahab' (1906), a drama.

Burton, Sir Richard Francis. An English Orientalist and explorer; born at Trieste, March 19, 1821; died Oct. 20, 1890. He was an officer of the Indian army, for several years engaged in surveys for public works; in this pursuit he learned the languages, habits, beliefs of many races. Obtaining leave of absence, he went to Mecca and Medina in the guise of a Mohammedan devotee; afterward he made extensive explorations in Africa, Brazil, Syria, Iceland; visited the United States twice and traversed the country from Atlantic to Pacific. Of his books of travel, the following may be particularized: 'Pilgrimage to El Medinah'; 'Highlands of Brazil'; 'Gold Coast'; 'City of the Saints'; 'Unexplored Palestine.' He translated into English from the Arabic: 'The Thousand Nights and a Night'; and 'The Scented Garden,' a collection of stories left in MS. and never published. He wrote a 'Life of Camoens,' with translation of the 'Lusiads.'

Burton, Robert. An English writer of peculiar characteristics; born at Lindley, Leicestershire, Feb. 8, 1576–7; died at Oxford, Jan. 25, 1639–40. Obtaining two church livings, he resided at Christ Church, Oxford. Here he wrote the 'Anatomy of Melancholy' (published about 1621); a vast storehouse of shrewd comment, apt and learned quotation, humor, and erudition, from which Milton, Sterne, and others did not scruple to borrow. The work mirrors his own mind and temperament.

Busch, Wilhelm (bösh). A German poet and delineator; born at Wiedensahl in Hanover, April 15, 1832. He was employed on the Fliegende Blätter, the great German comic journal, in 1859. The text for his comic designs is often supplied by himself. Among his most celebrated productions, whether with pencil or pen, are to be named: 'St. Antony of Padua'; 'The Pious Helen'; 'Max and Moritz'; 'Father Filucius.' Died 1908.

Bush, George. An American Swedenborgian clergyman and Bible commentator; born in Norwich, Vt., June 12, 1796; died in Rochester, N. Y., Sept. 19, 1859. He graduated from Dartmouth in 1818, and studied theology at Princeton, N. J., from 1820 to 1822. In 1831 he became professor of Hebrew and Oriental literature in the University of New York. Among his works are: 'Life of Mohammed' (1832); 'Hebrew Grammar' (1835); 'Bible Commentaries' (1840).

Bushnell, Horace. An eminent American clergyman; born near Litchfield, Conn., 1802; died at Hartford, Conn., in 1876. He was settled over a Congregational Church in Hartford until 1853. His numerous works on religion, theology, and morals, and other topics, comprise: 'Christian Nurture'; 'God in Christ'; 'Christ in Theology'; 'The Vicarious Sacrifice'; 'Nature and the Supernatural'; 'Moral Uses of Dark Things'; 'Forgiveness and Law'; 'The Age of Homespun'; 'Moral Tendencies and Results of Human History'; 'The Character of Jesus'; 'Work and Play'; 'Christ and His Salvation'; 'Politics the Law of God'; 'Woman Suffrage.' See 'Life and Letters,' edited by his daughter, Mrs. Mary Cheney.

Busse, Karl (büs'ě). A German story-writer and poet; born in Lindenstadt-Birnbaum, Posen, Nov. 12, 1872. He appeared early in literature with 'Poems' (1892), and 'Quiet Histories' (1894), the latter a volume of fiction.

Butler, Joseph. An English divine and theological writer; born at Wantage, 1692; died in 1752. He had a distinguished career in the Church, but his fame rests upon the 'Analogy of Religion, Natural and Revealed, to the Constitution and Course of Nature' (1736), which is an argumentative and philosophical treatise on Christianity.

Butler, Samuel. An English satirist; born in Strensham, Worcestershire, in February 1612; died in London, Sept. 25, 1680. Little is known of his life except what Anthony-a-Wood relates. He was educated at Oxford or Cambridge, occupied his leisure in studying music and painting, became a man of wide and curious learning, and gained his living as secretary and clerk to aristocratic personages. His famous poem, 'Hudibras,' a witty and sharp satire on the Puritans, secured instant favor with the king and the public; yet after the appearance of the first part in 1663, he spent seventeen years in poverty and obscurity. The second and third divisions of 'Hudibras' appeared in 1664 and 1678. The general design of the great poem was derived from 'Don Quixote.' The situations of the mock epic are few but ludicrous, and the whole canvas is embellished with imagination, raillery, subtle casuistry, brilliant epigrams, and sparkling wit. 'Hudibras' consists of 10,000 verses, and is one of the most frequently quoted books in the language. The standard edition by Dr. Z. Grey (1744) has frequently been reprinted. Butler's next important works are: 'The Elephant in the Moon,' a satire on the Royal Society; a series of prose 'Characters'; and an 'Ode to Duval,' the famous highwayman. 'The Posthumous Works of Mr. S. Butler' were published with great success (1715).

Butler, William Allen. An American poet; born in Albany, N. Y., Feb. 20, 1825. He graduated from the University of the City of New York in 1843, and later practiced law in New York. He wrote: 'Nothing to Wear' (1857), a satirical poem which attracted wide attention; 'Two Millions,' a satire (1858); and 'Mrs. Limber's Raffle.' Died Sept. 9, 1902.

Butterworth, Hezekiah. An American story-writer; born in Warren, R. I., Dec. 22, 1839. Since 1871 he has been on the staff of the Youth's Companion. Author of popular juvenile stories and travels, including: 'Zig-Zag Journeys' (1876–80); 'Songs of History: Poems and Ballads upon Important Episodes in American History' (1887); 'The Wampum Belt, or the Fairest Page of History' (1896). D. 1905.

Butz, Kaspar (büts). A German-American versifier; born in Hagen, Westphalia, Oct. 23, 1825; died at Des Moines, Iowa, Oct. 17, 1885. He was a prominent political journalist in his native land in the stirring days of 1848, but was forced to flee to this country. Here he became a noted (Chicago) newspaper man, and produced pleasing verse, collected in 'A German-American's Poems' (1879) and 'Grandfather Songs' (1887).

Byers, Samuel Hawkins Marshall. An American historical and descriptive writer; born in 1838. During the Civil War he served in the Union army. He was taken prisoner; and while in prison in Columbia, S. C., wrote the famous song 'Sherman's March to the Sea.' He was consul at Zürich, Switzerland, from 1869 to 1884, and consul-general to Italy in 1885. Among his works are: 'Switzerland' (1875); 'History of Switzerland' (1886); 'Military History of Iowa' (1888).

Bynner, Edwin Lassetter. An American novelist; born in Brooklyn, N. Y., in 1842; died Sept. 4, 1893, in Boston, Mass., where he was librarian of the Boston Law Library. He was the author of short stories, and of several novels,

including: 'Tritons' (Boston, 1878); 'Agnes Surriage' (1886); 'Penelope's Suitors' (London, 1887).

Byr, Robert (bir), pseudonym of Karl Robert Emerich von Bayer. A German novelist; born at Bregenz, April 15, 1835. He is a very popular and exceedingly prolific story-teller, and his volume-a-year since 1862 has had a wide circulation. Among his best-known novels are: 'The Struggle for Life'; 'Masks'; 'A Secret Dispatch'; 'The Road to Fortune'; 'Meadow Maidenhair'; 'The Ironworm.'

Byrne, Julia Clara (Busk). An English novelist, born in 1819, and married to William Pitt Byrne in 1842. She died in London Mar. 29, 1894. Her best-known books are: 'Flemish Interiors' (1856): 'Red, White and Blue: Sketches of Military Life (1863); and 'Pictures of Hungarian Life' (1869).

Byron, George Noel Gordon, Lord. A celebrated English poet; born in London, Jan. 22, 1788; died at Missolonghi, Greece, April 19, 1824. His poems appear in an immense number of editions, but a complete bibliography is impossible here, and any attempt at characterization or criticism is wholly superfluous. The collected 'Life and Works,' published by Murray (1832–35), includes all the recognized poems. The dates of issue of a few of the most celebrated single works are as follows: 'Hours of Idleness' (1807); 'English Bards and Scotch Reviewers' (1809); 'Childe Harold's Pilgrimage' (1812–22); 'The Giaour' (1813); 'The Bride of Abydos' (1813); 'The Corsair' (1814); 'Lara' (1814); 'Hebrew Melodies' (1815); 'The Prisoner of Chillon' (1816); 'Manfred' (1817); 'The Lament of Tasso' (1817); 'Don Juan' (1819–24); 'Marino Faliero' (1820); 'The Two Foscari' (1821); and 'Cain' (1821).

Byron, Henry James. An English dramatist; born in Manchester, in January 1834; died in London, April 11, 1884. Forsaking law and medicine for the stage, he acted with success in London, and was for many years a popular author of burlesques, plays, extravaganzas, farces, and light comedies. Among the best are: 'Cyril's Success' (1868); and 'Our Boys' (1875), which ran for four years. With Dion Boucicault he wrote 'Lost at Sea' (1869); and with F. C. Burnand, W. S. Gilbert, and R. Reece, 'Forty Thieves' (1878). Byron was the first editor of Fun, and wrote a novel, 'Paid in Full' (3 vols., London, 1865).

C

Caballero, Fernan (kä-bäl-yā'rō), pseudonym of Cecilia Böhl de Faber. A Spanish novelist; born at Morges, Switzerland, Dec. 25, 1796; died in Seville, Spain, April 7, 1877. Not until 1849 did her first bo_k, 'The Sea-Gull,' appear, forthwith establishing her fame as the creator of the modern Spanish realistic novel. A strictly Roman Catholic and extremely conservative tendency prevails in all her work. Her novels include : 'The Family of Alvareda'; 'A Summer Season at Bornos'; 'Clemencia'; 'Elia'; 'Tears'; 'Poor Dolores'; 'Lucas Garcia'; and others. Besides several collections of short stories, she also published the first collection of Spanish fairy tales, under the title 'Andalusian Popular Tales and Poems' (1859).

Cabanis, Jean Louis (kä-bä-nës'). A German ornithological writer; born in Berlin, March 8, 1816. His studies in two continents are ably elaborated in 'Ornithological Observations,' a work of authority in the science, and succeeded by many invaluable notices and investigations.

Cabanis, Pierre Jean Georges. A French physician and philosophical writer; born in Cosnac, 1757; died near Meulan, May 5, 1808. He attended Mirabeau in that great Frenchman's final illness, and wrote 'Journal of the Illness and Death of Mirabeau' (1791); besides being the author of an interesting work on 'Connections [*rapports*] between Man's Physical and Moral Constitutions [or Natures]' (new ed. 1866), which has proved an incentive to thought.

Cabell, Isa Carrington. An American miscellaneous writer; born in Virginia, 18 . She has written for various periodicals, and has published 'Seen from a Saddle.'

Cable, George Washington. An American novelist; born in New Orleans, La., Oct. 12, 1844. After the Civil War he began to contribute sketches to newspapers, and afterward published stories in magazines. Among his published works are : 'Old Creole Days' (1879); 'The Grandissimes' (1880); 'Madame Delphine' (1881); 'Dr. Sevier' (1883); 'The Creoles of Louisiana' (1884) ; 'The Silent South' (1885); 'John March, Southerner'; 'Bonaventure', 'Strange, True Stories of Louisiana'; 'The Busy Man's Bible'; 'The Negro Question'; 'Strong Hearts' ; 'The Cavalier'; 'Bylow Hill.'

Caccianiga, Antonio (kä''chä-nē'gä). An Italian novelist; born in Treviso, June 30, 1823. Exiled after the revolution of 1848, he lived as reporter in Paris until 1854, and there wrote his novel 'The Proscript' (1853); esteemed as an excellent portrayal of French life. Among his other works are : 'Sweet Idleness' (1869),

a picture of Venetian life in the 18th century; 'Countess Savina's Kiss' (1875); 'The Family of Bonifazio' (1886) : all notable for facility and legitimate popularity of style. Died 1903.

Cadahalso or **Cadalso, Don José de** (kä-dä äl'ōō *or* kä däl'ōō). A Spanish poet, dramatist, and story-writer; born in Cadiz, Oct. 8, 1741; killed at Gibraltar, Feb. 27, 1782. Military and literary capacity were equally characteristic of this well-born and well-educated man, who, after writing elegant verses, dainty satires, and especially 'The Sages of the Violet' (or 'Learned Men who are Fashionable'), a specimen of original and unforced humor, was killed during a siege by the explosion of a shell.

Caderas, Gian Frederic (kä-dā'räs). A distinguished Swiss dialect poet and story-writer; born at Modena, Italy, July 13, 1830; died at Samaden, Switzerland, Nov. 25, 1891. He cultivated the old Rhætian tongue, which still survives among some of the Tyrolese and elsewhere; producing much sprightly verse, the collections 'Alpine Flowers' (1883) and 'Smiles and Tears' (1887) containing fine specimens. His comedy of 'The Apothecary' (1864) has been successful.

Cadol, Victor Edouard (kä-dōl). A French dramatist and novelist; born in Paris, Feb. 11, 1831, died there June 2, 1898. He began as a writer of theatrical criticism for various periodicals; but after the brilliant success of his comedy, 'The Good-for-Nothings' (1868), which ran for 200 consecutive nights, he became known as a dramatist, and numerous plays came from his pen. Among his novels may be mentioned : 'Rose : Splendor and Miseries of Theatrical Life' (1874); and 'Hortense Maillot' (1885).

Cadoudal, Louis Georges de (kä-dö-däl'). A French essayist and critic; born at Auzon, Haute-Loire, Feb. 10, 1823. Journalism, the cause of Bourbon restoration, and love of the Church have occasioned his 'Signs of the Times' (1861); 'Memories of Fifteen Years' (1862); and 'Madame Acarie' (1863), a study of the religious life in the sixteenth and seventeenth centuries.

Caedmon (kad'mon). An English poet; born —; died 680. He is styled "the father of English song" on account of his epics of sacred history, written in old Northumberland dialect, mostly without titles, although one is called 'Genesis.'

Cæsar, Caius Julius (sē'zär). The great Roman general and writer of memoirs; was born probably about 100 B. C.; killed March 15, 44 B. C. He wrote 'Commentaries' or notes on all his wars, but those on the wars in Gaul and those on the Civil War alone remain. Besides the 'Commentaries,' he wrote a grammatical treatise 'On Analogy,' but it has not come down to us; of his orations, too, no example is extant.

Cahan, Abraham (kä'hạn). An American journalist and novelist; born in Russia, 1860. He is editor of the New York Zukunft (Future). He has written: 'Yekl, a Tale of the New York Ghetto'; 'Raphael Narizokh' in Yiddish; and 'The Chasm.'

Cahen, Isidore (kä-an'). A French Hebraist historian and critic, son of Samuel; born in Paris, Sept. 16, 1826. 'The Philosophy of the Poem of Job' (1851) and 'The Immortality of the Soul among the Jews' (1857) are his masterpieces.

Cahen, Samuel. An eminent French Hebraist; born in Metz, Aug. 4, 1796; died in Paris, Jan. 8, 1862. His version of the Old Testament (1841–53) must remain a permanent monument to his memory.

Caine, Thomas Henry Hall. An English novelist; born at Runcorn, Cheshire, May 14, 1853. His works are: 'Recollections of Rossetti' (1882); 'The Shadow of a Crime' (1885); 'A Son of Hagar' (1887); 'The Deemster,' a romance of the Isle of Man (1887); 'The Little Manx Nation' (1891); 'The Scapegoat' (1891); 'The Manxman' (1893); 'The Christian' (1897); 'The Eternal City' (1901); 'The Prodigal Son' (1904).

Caldas Pereira de Souza, Antonio (käl'däs pe-rä'rä de sö'zä). A Brazilian poet; born in Rio Janeiro, Nov. 23, 1762; died there, March 2, 1814. He spent the greater part of his life in Portugal, France, and Rome, where he took orders, and returned to Brazil in 1808. His 'Poems, Sacred and Profane' (1821; new ed. 1836), in Spanish, contain many splendid passages; the best examples being, probably, the ode on 'Man as a Barbarian' and 'The Birds.'

Calderon, Don Serafin Estébanez (käl-dä-rōn'). A Spanish writer (1801–67). He was professor of poetry and rhetoric at Granada, 1822–30; but resigned and went to Madrid. There he collected a vast library of old Spanish literature, especially of ballads, whether MS. or in print: the collection is in the national library at Madrid. He wrote a volume of 'Poems' (1833); a novel, 'Christians and Moriscos' (1838); and a very valuable study of 'The Literature of the Moriscos.' He also wrote 'The Conquest and the Loss of Portugal,' and a charming volume of 'Andalusian Scenes.'

Calderon de la Barca, Pedro (käl-dä-rōn' dä lä bär'kä). A great Spanish dramatist; born at Madrid, Jan. 17, 1600; died May 25, 1681. Of 'Sacramental Acts'—out-door plays for Corpus Christi day—he wrote 72 on themes Scriptural, classical, or moral: of these, 'The Divine Orpheus' is reputed the best. Of religious dramas he wrote 16, among them 'The Wonder-Working Magician,' the action of which centres on a human soul's surrender to Satan;

it was translated by Shelley and beautifully paraphrased by Fitzgerald. Another drama of this series is 'The Schism of England.' Of his dramas of secular history may be cited the powerful domestic tragedy, 'The Alcalde of Zalamea.' His dramas include: 'No Magic Like Love,' founded on the myth of Circe, and 'Echo and Narcissus'; while his best known comedies of intrigue, or "of the cloak and sword," are: 'The Fairy Lady' and ''Tis Ill Keeping a House with Two Doors.'

Calderón y Beltrán, Fernando (käl-dä-rōn ē bel"trän'). A Mexican dramatist and poet; born in Guadalajara, July 20, 1809; died at Ojocaliente, Jan. 18, 1845. His plays, especially 'The Tourney,' 'Anne Boleyn,' and 'The Return of the Crusader,' are very popular throughout Spanish America, while as a lyric poet he is also highly esteemed among his countrymen.

Calderwood, Henry. A Scotch philosophical writer; born at Peebles, May 10, 1830; died at Edinburgh, Nov. 19, 1897. An opponent of the doctrines of Sir William Hamilton, he brought out 'The Philosophy of the Infinite' (1854); 'The Handbook of Moral Philosophy' (1872); and similar works, which ran through many editions.

Caldwell, Joseph (käld'wel). An American divine and educator; born at Lamington, N. J., April 21, 1773; died at Chapel Hill, N. C., Jan. 27, 1835. He was president of the University of North Carolina (1804). He wrote: 'Letters of Carleton'; etc.

Caldwell, William Warren. An American writer of verse; born in Massachusetts, 1823. His home is in Newburyport. Besides translating numerous lyrics from the German, he has published 'Poems, Original and Translated.'

Calef, Robert (kä'lef). An American satirist; born in Massachusetts, about 1648; died 1719. He was a Boston merchant. He wrote: 'More Wonders of the Invisible World' (1700), a reply to Cotton Mather's 'Wonders of the Invisible World,' and opposing persecution for witchcraft. The book was publicly burned by Increase Mather.

Calemard de la Fayette, Charles (käl-mär' dẹ lä fï-yet or fä-yet). A French poet, critic, and essayist; born in Puy, April 9, 1815. He has enriched polite literature with studies of 'Dante, Michael Angelo, Machiavelli' (1852), with an artistic version of 'The Inferno of Dante Alighieri' (1855), and with 'The Adieu' (1885), a collection of well-polished verse.

Calentius or **Calenzio** (kä-len'shus). A noted late Latin poet; died 1503. He wrote elegies, satires, and epigrams that were greatly admired for their pure Latinity; also a poem founded upon the Homeric legends.

Calenzóli, Giuseppe (kä-len'tsō-lē). An Italian dramatist; born in Florence, 1815; author of some thirty comedies, mostly in one act, showing an excellent sense of stage effect, and a ready and always refined wit. The best among them are: 'A Search for a Husband' (1852); 'Father Zappata' (1876). His 'Dialogues and Comedies for Young Girls' (1874) are also highly esteemed. Died 1882.

Calfa, Ambroise (käl-fä'). A French-Armenian historian and miscellaneous writer; born in Constantinople, March 2, 1830. A 'Universal History' (1851), and Armenian versions of French masterpieces, are typical of his talent and industry.

Calfa, Coròno. An Armenian poet and prose-writer, brother of Ambroise; born in Constantinople in 1835. His poems and songs are immensely popular with his countrymen; his translation of Lamartine's 'Poetic Harmonies' is adequate and spirited; besides which should be mentioned a 'History of Armenia,' well written and authoritative.

Calhoun, John Caldwell. An American statesman; born Abbeville dist., S. C., March 18, 1782; died in Washington, March 31, 1850. He was elected Representative in Congress in 1811, and there soon attained note; was Secretary of War in Monroe's administration (1817); was Vice-President of the United States under J. Q. Adams (1825–29), and under Jackson (1829–32). He first distinctly promulgated his doctrine of Nullification in 1829. He became United States Senator in 1832 and so remained till 1843, when he was made Secretary of State by President Tyler; he was again elected to the Senate in 1845, and in that office died. As a speculative thinker, according to John Stuart Mill, he "displayed powers superior to [those of] any one who has appeared in American politics since the authors of 'The Federalist.'" His most memorable treatise is 'On the Constitution and Government of the United States.' A 'Discourse on Government' is also notable.

Callender, James Thomas. An American politician and publicist; born in England, 17—; died 1803. He was exiled from England for his pamphlet 'The Political Progress of Great Britain.' He wrote: 'Sketches of the History of America'; 'The Prospect before Us.'

Callender, John. An American historian; born in Boston, Mass., 1706; died in Newport, R. I., Jan. 26, 1748. He collected many valuable papers relating to the Baptists in America; and published 'A Centennial Discourse on the Civil and Religious Affairs of the Colony of Rhode Island' (1739), which was the only history of that State for more than a century. The State Historical Society reprinted it, with notes by Rev. Romeo Elton, D. D. (1838) and a memoir of the author.

Callimachus (kal-im'ä-kus). A Greek poet; born in Cyrene; flourished third century B. C. He wrote epics called 'Hecale' and 'Galatea,' besides tragedies, comedies, elegies, and hymns; but only some epigrams, sacred songs, and verses have come down to us, among which are a 'Hymn to Jupiter,' an 'Epitaph on Heracleitus,' and one on himself.

Calonne, Ernest de (kä-lon'). A French poet and dramatist; born in Paris, Jan. 11, 1822. His maiden effort, 'Cupid and Psyche' (1842), was a revelation of true poetic gifts; and in comedy he has succeeded, with 'The Amorous Doctor' and 'Bertha and Suzanne,' in attaining felicitous literary if not theatrical effects.

Calpurnius Siculus, Titus (kal-pèr'ni-us sik'ū-lus). A Roman poet; born about 30 A. D.; died about 80 A. D. He appears toward the commencement of Nero's reign with various eclogues and bucolics, palpable imitations of Virgil and of Theocritus, and conceived in a spirit of servile adulation of his imperial master.

Calthrop, Samuel Robert. An American Unitarian divine and essayist; born in England, 1829. He is settled in Syracuse, N. Y. He has written: 'Essay on Religion and Science'; 'The Rights of the Body'; 'God in his Word.'

Calverley, Charles Stuart. An English poet and humorist; born at Martley, Worcestershire, Dec. 22, 1831; died Feb. 17, 1884. He won a prize at Oxford with a Latin poem; afterward becoming a member of Cambridge, he was there made Fellow. He possessed an exquisite wit. His 'Verses and Translations' (1862) have been often reprinted. His 'Society Verses' are marked by great elegance and geniality.

Calvert, George Henry. An American writer of prose and verse; born in Baltimore, Md., Jan. 2, 1803; died in Newport, R. I., May 24, 1889. He was a great-grandson of Lord Baltimore. After graduating at Harvard (1823), he studied in Germany; then returning to Baltimore, became editor of the American, and a contributor to various periodicals. His published books include: 'Poems' (1847); 'Joan of Arc' (1860); 'Goethe, his Life and Works' (1872), 'Brief Essays and Brevities' (1874), and 'Wordsworth: a Biographic Æsthetic Study' (1875).

Calvi, Felice, Count (käl'vē). An Italian historian and novelist; born in Milan, Dec. 16, 1822. His earliest work was 'A Castle in the Roman Campagna,' a novel, followed by several valuable historical works, among them: 'Diplomatic and Historical Curiosities of the Seventeenth Century' (1878); 'A Family of Noted Milanese' (1875-87).

Calvin, John (kal'vin). A celebrated reformer and theologian; born at Noyon, in Picardy, July 10, 1509; died in Geneva, May 27, 1564. Soon after taking a degree, he went to Paris for the study of the humanities. In Paris he came under the influence of the teachers of the new theology; and before long (1534) had to flee from France, seeking refuge at Basel. There he published his greatest work: 'Institutes of the Christian Religion' (1536), first in Latin, then in a French version; he afterward revised and enlarged the work, and the author's definitive edition was published in 1559. Next after the 'Institutes,' Calvin's most important work is his 'Commentaries on the New Testament.' His complete works were published in 12 folio volumes (1617). In the libraries of Geneva and Zürich are about 3,000 of his unpublished sermons and other writings.

Calvo, Carlo, author of international law (1824-93); born at Buenos Ayres. He wrote 'Historical Review of Treaties, Conventions, etc., of all Latin-American States' (1862-69), and 'The International Law in Theory and Practice' (1887-90).

Cambridge, Richard Owen. An English miscellaneous writer; born in London, 1717; died 1802. He wrote: 'The Scribleriad,' a heroic poem; 'History of the War in India between the French and the English from 1755 to 1761'; and other works.

Camden, William. An English antiquarian; born in London, 1551; died, 1623. He was renowned for his Anglo-Saxon learning, and wrote : 'Description of Great Britain in Ancient Times'; 'Annals of the Reign of Elizabeth'; and other works.

Cameron, H. Lovett. An English novelist, widow of Verney L. Her novels deal mostly with personal complications, and include : 'The Cost of a Lie' (1886); 'The Dead Past' (1886); and 'Pure Gold' (1887),—all involving the sombre side of sentiment.

Cameron, Verney Lovett. An English explorer and writer of adventure; born in Radipole, Dorsetshire, July 1, 1844; died at Leighton-Buzzard, March 27, 1894. Famed for his feats of travel, he turned them to account in 'Harry Raymond' (1886), a tale of adventure among pirates; 'The Cruise of the Black Prince Privateer' (1886); and 'Across Africa' (1877).

Camoens, Luiz de (kam'ō-ens). Portugal's greatest poet; born at Lisbon in 1524 or 1525; died June 10, 1580. He passed some time in India as a soldier; later he held a lucrative office at Macao; there he composed a part of 'The Lusiads.' He returned to Portugal beggared, and died at Lisbon in a public hospital. The 'Lusiads' served to determine the ultimate literary forms of Portuguese: it is regarded as the national epic of Portugal.

Camp, Walter. A well-known American writer on athletics; born in Connecticut, 1859. He has written: 'Book of College Sports'; 'American Football'); 'Football Facts and Figures'; 'Drives and Puts'; etc.

Campan, Jeanne Louise Henriette (koṅ-poṅ'). A French writer of memoirs, recollections, and essays on education; born (Genest) in Paris, Oct. 6, 1752; died at Mantes, May 16, 1822. Her 'Memoirs of the Private Life of Marie Antoinette' were based upon personal knowledge obtained in the capacity of lady-in-waiting; the 'Correspondence with Queen Hortense' is a revelation of character of no small value; but the 'Treatise on Education' is unimportant.

Campanella, Tomaso (käm-pän-el'ä). A famous Italian philosopher; born at Stilo, Calabria, Sept. 5, 1568; died at Paris, May 21, 1639. At an unusually early age he had embraced the monastic life, astonishing his religious superiors with the precocious ripeness of his Thomistic scholarship, and writing poems and treatises that are still not beneath respect. For twenty-seven years, however, he lay in a Spanish prison, because of his political indiscretions with the pen. During this period many of his treatises were compiled : but the ordeal broke his spirit and induced the impotence so characteristic of his thought in the very hour of its realization; the consequence being that even such great works as the 'Treatise on Material Philosophy' (1623) and 'Rational Philosophy' (1637) are painfully inadequate. Only his 'Kingdom [or City] of the Sun' (1623), a work not unlike More's 'Utopia,' is very widely known.

Campardon, Émile (käm-pär-dôn'). A French biographer and historian; born in Paris, July 18, 1834. He has made exhaustive studies of 'The Revolutionary Tribunal of Paris' (1866); 'Marie Antoinette and the Necklace Case' (1863); and 'Madame de Pompadour and the Court of Louis XV.' (1867); 'Memoirs of Frederick II.'

Campbell, Alexander (kam'bel *or* kam'el). A celebrated American Presbyterian divine and theological writer; born near Ballymena, Ireland, Sept. 12, 1788; died at Bethany, W. Va., March 4, 1866. With his father, he founded the sect of «Campbellites» or «Disciples of Christ» (about 1827), numbering at the time of his death over 400,000 communicants; he founded also, and was the first president of, Bethany College (1841). He published the monthly magazine the Christian Baptist (1823-30), called afterward the Millennial Harbinger (1830-63). Among his works were: 'Christian System'; 'Popular Lectures and Addresses' (1862); 'Letters to a Sceptic' (1869); etc.

Campbell, Bartley. An American dramatist; born in Allegheny City, Pa., Aug. 12, 1843; died in Middletown, N. Y., July 30, 1888. He established the Evening Mail in Pittsburg (1868); the Southern Magazine in New Orleans (1869). His first drama that met with success in New York city was 'My Partner,' appearing in 1879. 'Fairfax, or Life in the Sunny South,' and 'The Galley Slave,' were on the metropolitan boards during the same season. Included in his plays are: 'Matrimony'; 'The White Slave'; 'Siberia'; and 'Paquita.' Several of his plays were brought out in England.

Campbell, Charles. An American historian; born in Petersburg, Va., May 1, 1807; died in Staunton, Va., July 11, 1876. Among his publications are: 'The Bland Papers' (1840-43); 'An Introduction to the History of the Colony and Ancient Dominion of Virginia' (1849); 'Genealogy of the Spotswood Family' (1868). He belonged to the Historical Society of Virginia; was a contributor of the Historical

Register and the Southern Literary Messenger; and editor of the 'Orderly Book' of Gen. Andrew Lewis in 1776 (Richmond, 1860).

Campbell, Douglas. An American lawyer and historical writer, son of W. W. Campbell; born at Cooperstown, N. Y., July 13, 1839; died at Schenectady, N. Y., March 7, 1893. He practiced law in New York (1865–90). He wrote 'The Puritan in Holland, England, and America' (1892), considered an authoritative work.

Campbell, George. A Scottish divine and philosophical writer; born in Aberdeen, Dec. 25, 1719; died there (?), April 6, 1796. In his 'Dissertation on Miracles' (1762) and 'Philosophy of Rhetoric' (1776), he shows learning, ingenuity, and grace.

Campbell, Sir George. An English descriptive writer; born in 1824; died at Cairo, Feb. 18, 1892. He is best represented by his 'Modern India' (1852); 'White and Black in the United States'; and 'The British Empire' (1889).

Campbell, Helen Stuart. An American sociological writer; born in Lockport, N. Y., July 4, 1839. Her early writings were published in newspapers and magazines. She has given close attention to the study of social problems in such works as 'Prisoners of Poverty.' From 1881 till 1884 she was literary editor of Our Continent, Philadelphia. Her style is serious, witty, and emotional. Among her published books are: 'The Problem of the Poor' (1882); 'The What-to-do Club' (1884); 'Miss Melinda's Opportunity' (1886); 'Household Economics' (1896); 'Ballantyne' (1901).

Campbell, John. A British historical writer; born in Edinburgh, March 8, 1708; died Dec. 28, 1775. His writings before 1742 were published anonymously. From 1755 to the close of his life, he was agent of the British government for the province of Georgia. His works are in part: 'Concise History of Spanish America' (1741); 'Lives of the English Admirals' (1744); 'A Survey of the Present State of Europe' (1750); and 'Trade of Great Britain to America' (1772).

Campbell, John, Baron. A British legal biographer; born in Springfield, near Cupar, Fifeshire, Scotland, Sept. 15, 1779; died in London, June 22, 1861. He was Lord Chancellor of England (1859–61); and wrote: 'Lives of the Lord Chancellors' (1845–48) and 'Lives of the Chief Justices' (1849–57), both well known and authoritative works.

Campbell, Sir John Douglas Sutherland. See **Lorne.**

Campbell, John Francis. A Scotch folklorist and descriptive writer; born about 1822; died at Cannes, France, Feb. 7, 1885. His first success was 'Popular Tales of the West Highlands' (1860–62), an accurate and discriminating compilation; to which succeeded 'Frost and Fire' (1865), a volume of semi-scientific and semi-descriptive miscellany.

Campbell, Loomis J. An American philologist and writer; born in Oneonta, N. Y., 1831; died there, Nov. 6, 1896. He was author of a 'United States History,' also of the popular 'Franklin Series' of school-books; and edited a 'Young Folks' Book of Poetry' and a 'Hand-Book of Synonyms.' The degree of LL.D. was conferred upon him by Hamilton College.

Campbell, Thomas. A celebrated Scottish poet; born at Glasgow, July 27, 1777; died at Boulogne, France, June 15, 1844. In 1799 was published his 'Pleasures of Hope,' which in a year reached a fourth edition. 'Gertrude of Wyoming' (1809); 'The Exile of Erin'; 'Hohenlinden'; 'Lochiel's Warning'; 'Ye Mariners of England'; and 'Battle of the Baltic,' are among his best known poems.

Campbell, William W. A prominent American lawyer and historical writer; born in New York State, 1806; died 1881. Settled in N. Y. city, he was a judge of the State Supreme Court. He wrote: 'Annals of Tryon County' (reissued as 'Border Warfare'); 'Life and Writings of De Witt Clinton'; 'Sketches of Robin Hood and Captain Kidd'; etc.

Campbell, William Wilfred. A Canadian poet; born in Western Ontario, Canada, 1861. He has published 'Lake Lyrics' (1889); 'The Dread Voyage' (1893); 'Mordred, a Tragedy,' and 'Hildebrand' (1895), the two latter being dramas in blank verse; and numerous separate poems, among them 'England' (1897). He is cited, in the Victorian Anthology, among the notable poets of Canada. He is at present an official of the Privy Council of the government at Ottawa.

Campe, Joachim Heinrich (käm'pe). A German lexicographer and writer of juvenile tales (1746–1818). His educational works were long widely read and highly esteemed; especially 'Robinson the Younger' (1779; 115th ed. 1890), an adaptation of Defoe's 'Robinson Crusoe,' which was translated into every European language. Next in popularity came a 'History of the Discovery of America' (1781; 26th ed. 1881).

Campion, Thomas. An English poet; born between 1570 and 1580; died at London, March 1, 1619. He was by profession a medical man. He wrote a volume of 'Poems' (1595), being Latin elegies and epigrams. He published (1610–12) four 'Books of Airs,' containing songs written by himself to airs of his own composition: the first book contains 'Divine and Moral Songs'; the second 'Light Conceits of Lovers'; the third and fourth are not distinguished by any separate sub-title. In his songs the verse and the music are most happily wedded.

Campistron, Jean Galbert de (koñ-pēs-troñ'). A French dramatist (1656–1713), a disciple and faithful imitator of Racine, and often called "Racine's ape." His finest tragedies were 'Andronicus' (1685), the dramatized story of Don Carlos, son of Philip II. of Spain; and

'Tiridates' (1691). A comedy, 'Jealousy Undeceived' (1709), ranks among his best productions.

Campoamor y Campoosorio, Don Ramon de (käm″pō-mōr″ ē käm-pō-sō′rē-ō). A Spanish poet and miscellaneous writer; born at Navia in 1817. He is at once one of the most popular and most prolific of the peninsula's versifiers; in 'Moral and Political Fables' and 'Colon' his talent is most at home, although 'Doloras' (Sorrows), a collection of poems in which he gives expression to the best in contemporary Spanish ideals, has attracted most attention. His stories in verse, 'The Good and the Wise' and 'Juana's Loves' more particularly, are deemed by many his masterpieces; but his plays—among them 'Dies Iræ,' a drama—are not without a claim to that distinction. He has written, as well, on political and social subject's in sonorous prose. Died 1901.

Camprodon, Francisco (käm-prō-don′). A Spanish dramatist; born at Vich, Catalonia, 1816; died at Havana, 1870. His masterpiece is 'The Flower of a Day,' written in euphonious and well-scanned metre, and a drama of no ordinary merit; a sequel to it, entitled 'Thorns of a Flower,' being published afterwards.

Cañete, Manuel (kän-yā′te). A Spanish poet and dramatist; born at Seville, Aug. 6, 1822; died in Madrid, Nov. 4, 1891. A volume of 'Poems' first drew popular attention to his genius, which is strong in lyric compositions and in odes, but strongest in the drama, as 'A Dispute in Granada' and 'The Flower of Bresalú' denote. His studies in dramatic criticism, especially those of the infancy of the Spanish theatre, possess a permanent value as contributions to history, in addition to their merits as specimens of a correct taste and an almost faultless style.

Canini, Marco Antonio (kä-nē′nē). An Italian poet and political agitator (1822-91); born at Venice. He fled from Italy in 1849 and took refuge in Greece. He published, at Athens, a volume of poems: 'Mind, Fancy, and Heart' (1852). Returning to Italy in 1859, he edited journals in various cities. He wrote a novel in verse, 'George the Monk and Leila.' Another collection of his poems, 'Love and Sorrow,' was published in 1880; he has also issued 'The Book of Love,' a volume of translations of love songs from nearly 150 languages.

Canis, Jean (kä-nē′ or kä-nis′). A French historian; born in Paris, Nov. 20, 1840. His realistic style, vivid narration, and scholarly impartiality have attracted special attention to two of his productions: 'The Massacres in Ireland,' and 'History of the French Republic from 1870 to 1883.'

Canivet, Charles Alfred (kä-nē-vä′). A French journalist, novelist, and poet; born in Valognes, Manche, Feb. 10, 1839. His reputation was made by a series of articles in the Soleil, under the pseudonym of «Jean de Nivelle»; but in fiction he is well known as the author of word-pictures of Normandy life, among them 'Poor Devils' and 'The Organist's Niece.' His 'Lost Colonies' is an account of the French forfeiture of India and of Canada through an impotent foreign policy; and his best poetry is probably in the collection 'Along the Coast.'

Cañizares, José (kän-yē-thär′es). A Spanish dramatist; born in Madrid, July 4, 1676; died there, Sept. 4, 1750. His precocity, of which much is made, took the form of dramatic composition, in which he excelled at fourteen; nor was he much older when his 'Balance Sheets (or Accounts) of the Great Captain' was completed,—a historical play made noteworthy by one scene of infinite effectiveness. The Spanish stage owes to him, moreover, 'What Passes from Sceptre to Sceptre'; 'England's Cruelty'; and other productions of merit.

Canning, George. An English statesman, orator, and writer; born in London, April 11, 1770; died at Chiswick, Aug. 8, 1827. A Liberal in extreme youth, he early joined the Tory party, distinguished himself as wit and Parliamentary manager, held repeated Cabinet office, and became Premier in the last year of his life. He had grown more Liberal in his later years, sickened at the stagnant and cruel reactionism that followed the panic over the French Revolution, and assisted the South-American republics to obtain independence. His contributions to pure literature were mostly contained in the short-lived Anti-Jacobin, a Tory periodical after the fashion of the previous Whig Rolliad, and full of wit; among them are 'The Needy Knife-Grinder,' and 'The Rovers,' which contains 'The University of Gottingen.' His speeches, however, are often genuine literary productions; they were published after his death, greatly altered (largely for the worse) from their form as delivered.

Cannizzaro, Tommaso (kän-its-är′ō). An Italian poet; born in Messina, Aug. 17, 1838. The volume of poems styled 'In Solitude' shows him an idealist, and perhaps symbolist. He uses the French language with dexterity and grace in 'Thorns and Roses,' another volume of verse. He also wrote 'India' (1899).

Cannon, Charles James. An American novelist, poet, and dramatist; born in New York city, Nov. 4, 1800; died there, Nov. 9, 1860. His publications include: 'Ravellings from the Web of Life' (1856); 'Dramas' (1857); 'The Poet's Quest'; 'Father Felix, a Catholic Story'; 'Dolores, a Tragedy'; and 'Better Late than Never,' a drama (1852). He compiled a 'Practical English Spelling Book,' and series of Readers.

Canonge, Jules (kä-nônzh). A French poet; born in Nîmes, March 20, 1812; died March 14, 1870. His delicate poesy is preserved in 'Preludes' (1835); 'Tasso at Sorrento'; and 'Olim' (1859); besides other volumes, in addition to which he turned his attention to legend and story and produced worthy prose.

Cánovas del Castillo, Antonio (kä'nō-väs del käs-tēl'yō). A distinguished Spanish statesman and man of letters; born in Malaga, Feb. 8, 1826; assassinated at the baths of Santa Aqueda, Aug. 8, 1897. In his 25th year he was editor of the Conservative journal Patria, and in 1854 entered the public service as member of the Cortes; thereafter he held various posts in the government. At his death he had been for some years prime minister. He is author of 'Literary Studies' (2 vols., 1868); 'History of the Austrian Dominion in Spain' (1869), 'Problems of the Time' (2 vols., 1884); 'Studies on the Reign of Philip IV.' (3 vols., 1888–90). He was editor-in-chief of a 'General History of Spain,' consisting of monographs by sundry writers, of which the first volume appeared in 1890.

Cano y Masas, Leopoldo (kä'nō ē mäs'äs). A distinguished Spanish poet and dramatist; born at Valladolid, Nov. 13, 1844. He graduated from the Spanish Military Academy at Madrid (1865), and was appointed professor of analytical and descriptive geometry there in 1867, retiring in 1885. His first comedy was 'Laurels of a Poet' (1852). His many other plays include: 'The Code of Honor'; 'Modern Idolatry'; and 'The Death of Lucretia.' He is the author of a volume of poems, 'Arrows.'

Cantacuzenus, John (kan''tȧ-kū-zē'nus). Emperor of Constantinople; born in the twelfth century (?); died after 1355. His 'Byzantine History' is a noted work.

Cantemir or **Kantemir, Prince Antiochus** (kän'te-mēr). See **Kantemir.**

Cantoni, Carlo (kän-tō'nē). An Italian philosopher; born in Grapello, Pavia, Nov., 1840. For years he has expounded the Kantian philosophy, attaining an international fame with his 'Lectures on the Human Understanding'; 'Immanuel Kant'; 'The Philosophical-Literary Faculty in its Relation to Scientific and National Education'; and 'Elementary Course Philosophy.'

Cantù, Cesare (kän-tö'). An Italian historian; born at Brivio, Lombardy, Dec. 2, 1805; died near Milan, March 11, 1895. Imprisoned for political causes in 1833, he employed his leisure in writing a historical romance, 'Margherita Pusterla' (1838), one of the most successful of modern Italian romances; it gives a graphic picture of prison life. He wrote numerous historical and biographical works; his 'Universal History' (35 vols.) has passed through several editions, and has been translated into other languages.

Capecelatro, Alphonse, Cardinal (kä''pe-chel-ät'rō). An Italian Pietist biographer and controversialist; born in Marseilles, Feb. 5, 1824. He has won distinction as Italy's leading contemporary Church writer, with a 'History of St. Catherine of Siena and of the Papacy of her Day' (1856); 'The Errors of Renan'; a 'Life of Jesus'; and a 'Life of St. Philip of Neri' (1882).

Capefigue, Baptiste Honoré Raymond (käp-fēg'). A French historian and journalist; born in Marseilles,1802; died in Paris, Dec. 23, 1872. His contributions to historical science are the 'History of Philip Augustus' (1829); and 'History of the Restoration and of the Causes that Led to the Fall of the Elder Branch of the House of Bourbon' (1831).

Capen, Nahum (kā'pen). An American historical writer; born at Canton, Mass., 1804; died 1886. Postmaster of Boston, Mass. (1857–61), he introduced street letter-box collections. He wrote: 'The Republic of the United States'; 'History of Democracy' (1874); etc. He also wrote and edited works on phrenology.

Capern, Edward. An English poet; born at Tiverton, Devonshire, Jan. 29, 1811. He attracted the notice of Walter Savage Landor in consequence of the beauty and feeling of his poems, descriptive of life and character in his native county, where he was long in the mail service, and known in consequence as «The Rural Postman of Bideford.» His best work is in 'Wayside Warbles'; 'Sungleams and Shadow'; and 'Ballads and Songs.' Died at Braunton, June 4, 1894.

Capponi, Gino, Marchese (käp-ō'nē). An Italian historian and scholar; born in Florence, Sept. 14, 1792; died there, Feb. 3, 1876. A 'History of the Florentine Republic' (1875) is his chief work.

Capuana, Luigi (kä-pū-ä'nä). An Italian poet, novelist, and critic; born at Mineo, Sicily, May 27, 1839. Having devoted himself to journalism, he settled (1864) in Florence, where he wrote dramatic criticisms; from 1868 until 1877 he lived in his native town, then in Milan, again as a journalist. His best-known work is 'Giacinta' (1879), a naturalistic novel. Besides this he published several volumes of short stories, among them: 'Profiles of Women' (1881); 'Homo' (1883); and two collections of charming fairy tales: 'Once upon a Time' (1882) and 'Fairy Land' (1883). A curious specimen of rhythmical prose is his 'Semi-Rhythms' (1888), in praise of worldly joy and beauty.

Carayon, Auguste (kä-rī-yôṅ or kä-rä-yôṅ). A French historian; born at Saumur, March 31, 1813; died at Poitiers, May 15, 1874. A distinguished Jesuit, he wrote: 'First Canadian Missions of the Jesuits' (1864); 'Banishment of the Jesuits from Louisiana' (1865); and similar studies.

Carcano, Giulio (kär-kä'nō). An Italian poet (1812–84); born in Milan. He wrote a narrative poem, 'Ida Della Torre,' while a student at Pavia (1834). His next work, 'Angiola Maria' (1839), had extraordinary success; it is a deeply sympathetic story of Italian family life, and is regarded as the highest type of that class in Italian. In the same vein is the volume 'Simple Narratives' (1843). He wrote also 'Damiano, the Story of a Poor Family'

(1851), and 'Twelve Tales' (1856). He published translations of several of Shakespeare's plays. His latest volume of poetry was 'Various Poems' (1875). Among his later novels are 'Gabrio and Camilla, a Milanese Story' (1874); and 'Carlo Barbiano' (1882).

Cárdenas y Rodriguez, José M. de (kär'dä-näs ē rō-drē'ges). A Cuban poet and prose-writer; born at Matanzas in 1812; died in 1882. Many of his humorous sketches of Cuban life have been translated into French and published in the Revue des Deux Mondes. Besides a good comedy, 'A Deaf Uncle,' he has written a collection of fables, some of which have been translated into English; and numerous poems.

Cárdenas y Rodriguez, Nicolás de. A Cuban poet and novelist; born in Havana, 1814; died in 1868. His works comprise: 'Poetical Essays' (1836); 'Scenes from Life in Cuba' (1841); 'The Two Weddings,' a novel (1844); 'Diego de Velazquez,' a drama. He was also a regular contributor to periodicals.

Carducci, Giosuè (kär-dö'chi). A distinguished Italian poet and philologist; born at Valdicastello, Tuscany, July 27, 1835. He was made professor of Italian literature in the University of Bologna in 1860. He had previously written essays on the history of literature; and a small volume of lyrics, 'Rimes,' (1857). But his poetical genius is better shown in the collections of his fugitive pieces published a little later: 'Serious Trifles' and 'The Decennials.' His 'Hymn to Satan' (1863), published under the pseudonym 'Enotrio Romano,' made an extraordinary impression, and was formally defended in 'Satan and Satanic Polemics' (1879). The breadth and range of his genius, as well as his mastery of poetic form, are seen in the 'Poems of Enotrio Romano' (1871); 'New Poems' (1873); 'Iambics and Epodes'; 'New Rimes.' Died Feb. 15, 1907.

Carew, Thomas. An English poet (about 1598-1639). He stood high in favor with Charles I., and was an intimate friend of the greatest poets and scholars of his time in England, including Ben Jonson, Sir John Suckling, and Sir Kenelm Digby. His poems are light and airy, sometimes licentious, always graceful and elegant in form. They are mostly songs or odes; he also wrote 'Cœlum Britannicum,' a masque performed at Whitehall (1633), with Charles I. and his courtiers in the cast.

Carey, Henry. An English poet and playwright; born about 1696; died in London (?), 1743. As the author of 'Sally in our Alley' his claim to the notice of posterity is a strong one, and 'Namby Pamby' is another of his good songs. His farces, among them 'Hanging and Marriage,' are not so lively.

Carey, Henry Charles. A leading American economist; born in Philadelphia, Dec. 15, 1793; died there, Oct. 13, 1879. Trained in his father's publishing-house, he accumulated a competence from the business and retired to devote himself to study. The 'Essay on the Rate of Wages' (1836) and 'The Principles of Political Economy' (1837-40) won him an authoritative international position, in spite of what was then an extravagantly unorthodox opposition to Adam Smith and his followers. He next produced: 'The Credit System in France, Great Britain, and the United States' (1838); 'The Past, The Present, and The Future' (1848); and 'The Principles of Social Science' (1858-59).

Carey, Mathew. An American publisher and prose-writer; born in Ireland, Jan. 28, 1760; died in Philadelphia, Pa., Sept. 16, 1839. The best known of his political writings was his 'Olive Branch' (1814). It was an effort to promote harmony among political parties during the War of 1812. It passed through ten editions. In 1819 he published his 'Vindiciæ Hibernicæ'; and in 1822, 'Essays on Political Economy.'

Carlén, Emilia Flygare- (fle-gär'ë-kär-län'). A Swedish novelist; born at Strömstad, Aug. 8, 1807; died at Stockholm, Feb. 5, 1892. Her first story was 'Waldemar Klein' (1838). A long series of novels followed, most notable among them being: 'Gustav Lindorm' (1839); 'The Professor' (1840); 'Chamberlain Lassmann' (1842); 'A Warehouse on the Cliffs' (1860), her best story. Her latest work was 'Reminiscences of Swedish Literary Life' (1878). She had clear insight into the conditions of human life, especially of life in the middle class, and she describes it with admirable fidelity.

Carlén, Rosa (kär-län'). A Swedish novelist (1836-83). Her first story, 'Agnes Tell' (1861), had a very favorable reception. Then followed: 'Tuva' (1862); 'Helena, a Woman's History' (1863); 'Three Years and Three Days' (1864); 'The Gypsy's Son' (1866), which is regarded as her most perfect work.

Carleton, Henry Guy. An American journalist and dramatist; born in Fort Union, N. Mex., June 21, 1855. He pursued journalism in New Orleans and New York city, and has written several plays including: 'Memnon, a Tragedy'; 'Victor Durand'; 'The Pembertons'; 'A Gilded Fool'; 'The Butterflies'; 'Jack's Honeymoon.'

Carleton, Will. An American poet; born in Hudson, Mich., Oct. 21, 1845. He is best known in literature by his ballads of home life, many of them having gained great popularity. His books include: 'Poems' (1871); 'Farm Legends' (1875); 'City Ballads' (1888); and 'City Legends' (1889); 'In Old School Days' (1907).

Carleton, William. An Irish novelist; born in Prillisk, County Tyrone, 1794; died in Dublin, Jan. 30, 1869. His intimate acquaintance with the traits and tendencies of Irish peasant character, and his harmless, graceful, and unwearying humor, were conspicuous in his first success, 'Traits and Stories of the Irish Peasantry.' Then came: 'Willy Reilly'; 'The Fair of Emyvale'; 'Fardorougha the

Miser'; and several other novels of great power, in which much that seems anomalous in the manners and methods of the author's countrymen is made clear through the medium of a happy style and a realistic humor.

Carlson, Fredrik Ferdinand (kärl'son). A Swedish historian; born in Upland, June 13, 1811; died in Stockholm, March 18, 1887. He was prominent in public affairs for many years, and wrote, among other works, a 'History of Sweden' (1855–87), which ranks high because of its exhaustive accuracy and literary merit.

Carlyle, Jane Welsh. Wife of Thomas Carlyle; born at Haddington, Scotland, July 14, 1801; died in London, April 21, 1866. Her 'Letters,' edited by her husband, were published in 1883, the work being given to the world by J. A. Froude.

Carlyle, Thomas. A Scotch biographer, historian, and miscellaneous writer; born at Ecclefechan, Dec. 4, 1795; died in London, Feb. 4, 1881. His works, as published, are: 'Wilhelm Meister's Apprenticeship,' a translation (1824); 'Legendre's Elements of Geometry and Trigonometry,' a translation (1824); 'Life of Schiller' (1825); 'German Romance,' translations from Tieck, Musäus, Richter, etc. (1827); 'Sartor Resartus' (first edition in book form, Boston, 1835; second, London, 1838); 'The French Revolution' (1837); 'Chartism' (1839); 'Heroes, Hero Worship, and the Heroic in History' (1841); 'Past and Present' (1843); 'Life and Letters of Oliver Cromwell' (1845); 'Latter-Day Pamphlets' (1850); 'Life of Sterling' (1851); 'Friedrich II.' (1858–65); 'Inaugural Address at Edinburgh' (1866); 'Reminiscences of my Irish Journey in 1849' (1882); 'Last Words of Thomas Carlyle' (1882). He wrote also innumerable magazine articles, still uncollected.

Carman, Bliss. A Canadian poet; born at Fredericton, N. B., April 15, 1861. His first publication, 'Low Tide on Grand Pré: A Book of Lyrics' (1893), had a very favorable reception. Other volumes of his collected poems are: 'Songs from Vagabondia' (1894); 'Behind the Arras: a Book of the Unseen' (1895). His poems usually appear first in American magazines and other periodicals.

Carmen Sylva. See **Sylva**.

Carmontel, Louis Carrogis, called (kär-môn-tel'). A French poet and proverb-writer: born in Paris, Aug. 15, 1717; died there, Dec. 26, 1806. His fame rests upon 'Dramatic Proverbs,' or epigrammatic plays upon words.

Carnegie, Andrew (kär-nā'gi). A noted Scotch-American manufacturer, and writer of travels and essays on affairs; born at Dunfermline, Scotland, Nov. 25, 1837. He is proprietor of the largest iron and steel works in the world, at Pittsburg, Pa. His benefactions have been large and numerous, among them gifts of public libraries to Allegheny City and to Pittsburg. Besides many articles in periodicals, he has written : 'An American Four-in-Hand in Britain' (1883); 'Round the World' (1884); 'Triumphant Democracy' (1886); 'The Life of Business' (1902); 'The Life of James Watt' (1906).

Carneri, Bartholomäus von (kär-nā'rē). An Austrian poet; born at Trent, 1821. His volume of poems 'Plough and Sword' was greatly admired. He has published 'Foundation of Ethic' (1881), and 'Modern Man' (1901).

Caro, Miguel Antonio (kä'rō). A Colombian prose-writer and poet; born in Bogotá, Colombia, Nov. 10, 1843. He has been an editor and contributor to periodicals. His principal works are: 'Poems' (1866); 'Hours of Love,' a prose work; and a translation into Spanish verse of Virgil's complete works (3 vols., 1873–75). He is a correspondent of the Royal Spanish Academy, and in 1886 was national librarian in the Colombian congress.

Carpenter, Esther Bernon. An American prose-writer; born in Wakefield, R. I., March 4, 1848; died there Oct. 22, 1893. She wrote for magazines; published 'The Huguenot Influence in Rhode Island,' and 'South Country Neighbors' (1887).

Carpenter, Stephen Cutter. An American journalist and prose-writer; born in England; died about 1820. He came to the United States (1803) and settled in Charleston, S. C., where he soon founded and published with John Bristed the Monthly Register Magazine and Review of the United States. Later he was editor of the Mirror of Taste and Dramatic Censor, in which appeared some clever sketches of American actors. His works include: 'Memoirs of Jefferson, Containing a Concise History of the United States from the Acknowledgment of their Independence, with a View of the Rise and Progress of French Influence and French Principles in that Country' (2 vols., 1809); 'Select American Speeches, Forensic and Parliamentary, with Prefatory Remarks: a Sequel to Dr. Chapman's Select Speeches' (1815); and under the pen-name of "Donald Campbell," 'Overland Journey to India' (2d ed. 1809–10), and 'Letter on the Present Times.'

Carr, Lucien. An American archæologist; born in Missouri, 1829. He has written: 'Mounds of the Mississippi Valley' (1883); 'Missouri, a Bone of Contention' (1888); and 'Prehistoric Remains of Kentucky' (with Shaler).

Carrér, Luigi (kä-rär'). An Italian poet (1801–50); born at Venice. His first volume of 'Poems' contained sonnets, odes, and ballads (1832). He wrote a poetical account of the history of Venice, and published four volumes of 'Prose and Poetry' (1837). He is ranked among the best of the later Italian poets.

Carrera, Valentino (kär-rā'rä). An Italian dramatic poet; born at Turin, Dec. 19, 1834. He is one of the most original dramatists of Italy, especially in comedy. Among his many comedies, vaudevilles, etc., the play which won for him a wide reputation was 'La Quaderna di Nanni' (1870), a perfect picture of Florentine life. He wrote some historical sketches and narratives of travel.

Carrington, Henry Beebe. A distinguished American soldier and military writer; born at Wallingford, Conn., March 2, 1824. Originally a lawyer, he became brigadier-general of volunteers in the Civil War, served in the West till 1868, and was appointed professor of military science at Wabash College, Crawfordsville, Ind. His present home is in Boston. He wrote: 'Battles of the American Revolution' (3d ed. 1878); 'Apsaraka, or Indian Operations on the Plains'; 'Battles of the Bible'; 'The Americans and their Future.'

Carroll, Anna Ella. An American Political writer; born in Maryland, 1815; died in 1894. She wrote: 'The Great American Battle' (1856); 'The Star of the West' (1856); 'The War Powers of the General Government' (1861); etc.

Carroll, Lewis, pseudonym of Charles Lutwidge Dodgson. A notable English humorist; born near Warrington, Jan. 27, 1832; died at Guildford, England, Jan. 14, 1898. His fame is based on the stories—nominally for the nursery, but only appreciable in their full merit by adults—'Alice's Adventures in Wonderland' (1865), and its sequel 'Through the Looking-Glass' (1872). They are fantasy-fables, full of what seems pure nonsense, but is really based largely on « reductions to absurdity » of illogical popular usages in language or reasoning. They have been translated into most of the languages of Europe. Some excellent nonsense verse is also found in the collections 'Phantasmagoria' (1869), the poem 'The Hunting of the Snark' (1876), and the inferior prose fairy-tale 'Sylvie and Bruno.' The author has published several works on mathematics and logic, in both serious and humorous form.

Carruthers, William A. An American novelist; born in Virginia about 1800; died in Savannah, Ga., about 1850. He was professionally a physician, but wrote a number of spirited romances founded on incidents in American history. His best work is 'The Cavaliers of Virginia, or the Recluse of Jamestown, an Historical Romance of the Old Dominion' (1832). He is the author also of 'The Knights of the Horse-Shoe, a Traditionary Tale of the Cocked Hat Gentry in the Old Dominion' (1845).

Carryl, Charles Edward. An American story-writer; born in New York city, Dec. 30, 1841. In 1885 he published 'Davy and the Goblin,' followed by 'The Admiral's Caravan,' both juveniles in the manner of Lewis Carroll. He is a broker in New York city.

Carter, Elizabeth. An English writer; born in Kent, 1717; died in London, 1806. She is remembered for her version of Epictetus, although her 'Ode to Wisdom' (1746) is admired.

Carter, Robert. An American littérateur; born in Albany, N. Y., Feb. 5, 1819; died in Cambridge, Mass., Feb. 15, 1879. At first associated with Lowell in a monthly magazine, later the private secretary of Prescott, then coeditor of a newspaper with Hildreth, he passed his life in miscellaneous journalistic and literary work; the most important being a large share in editing (1859–63) the first two editions of the 'American Cyclopædia.' His one book, 'A Summer Cruise on the Coast of New England' (1864), was long popular as an entertaining travel sketch, and among naturalists for its account of New England fishes.

Carteret, Antoine Alfred Désiré (kär-trä'). A Swiss statesman and fabulist; born in Geneva, April 2, 1813; died there, Jan 31, 1889. His political career was long and brilliant; and in literature he has made a name with pleasing 'Fables' (1873), frequently treating political subjects, and a novel, 'Two Friends' (1872), descriptive of Genevese customs.

Cartwright, Peter. An American controversialist and sermonist; born in Virginia, Sept. 1, 1785; died Sept. 25, 1872. He was a Methodist clergyman, of great power and eccentricity, and preached, it is said, fully 15,000 sermons. He published 'A Controversy with the Devil'; 'Autobiography of a Backwoods Preacher'; 'Fifty Years a Presiding Elder.'

Cartwright, William. An English dramatist and poet; born in Northway, September 1611, or Aug. 16, 1615; died at Oxford, Nov. 29, 1643. His plays were immensely successful at the time; 'The Ordinary' is probably the best, but 'The Royal Slave' is meritorious, and both contain much lively wit and satire at the expense of the Puritans. The poems are not so good.

Carutti di Cantogno, Domenico, Baron (kä-röt'ē dē kän-tōn'yō). An Italian historian and publicist; born in Cumiana, near Turin, Nov. 26, 1821. As a young man he took to romance-writing, but was speedily absorbed in politics and rose to great distinction. When he resumed the pen, it was to compile such solid works as 'History of the Reign of Victor Amadeus II.' (1856), and 'History of the Reign of Charles Emanuel III.' (1859), which are interesting and scholarly.

Cary, Alice. An American poet; born near Cincinnati, O., April 26, 1820; died in New York city, Feb. 12, 1871. When quite young she commenced writing sketches and poems for the press. In 1852 she, with her sister Phœbe, removed to New York city, where they lived during the rest of their lives. In 1850 the sisters published a volume entitled 'Poems by Alice and Phœbe Cary.' Alice soon after published 'Clovernook, or Recollections of our Neighborhood in the West' (1851–53); 'Hagar, a Story of To-Day' (1852); 'Married not Mated' (1856); 'The Lover's Diary' (1867); and Snow-Berries: A Book for Young Folks' (1869).

Cary, Edward. An American journalist; born in New York State, 1840. He has long been connected with the New York Times. His principal published work is a 'Life of George William Curtis.'

Cary, Henry Francis. An English poet and translator of Dante; born at Gibraltar, Spain, Dec. 6, 1772; died in London, Aug. 14, 1844. Although his fame rests upon his version of Dante's 'Divine Comedy,' he possessed an intimate knowledge of Latin, Greek, and French, and translated masterpieces from those languages adequately and with grace.

Cary, Phœbe. An American poet and prose-writer, sister of Alice; born in Cincinnati, O., Sept. 4, 1824; died in Newport, R. I., July 31, 1871. She contributed numerous sketches to various periodicals; and with her sister published many books, among which are 'Poems and Parodies' (1854), and 'Poems of Faith, Hope, and Love.'

Casanova de Seingalt, Giovanni Jacopo (kä''sa-nō'vä de sĭn'gält). An Italian adventurer; born at Venice, 1725; died in Bohemia, June 4, 1803. Expelled from Venice for his scandalous irregularities, he returned there and was imprisoned; after some months he made his escape, and for twenty years traveled over Europe, imposing upon all classes of society with his pretensions to occult science and knowledge of all the secrets of alchemy, including rejuvenation of the old. Among his dupes were Mme. de Pompadour, Frederick the Great, and even that other prince of charlatans, Cagliostro. He wrote his 'Memoirs,' which were published (1828) in 12 volumes.

Casas, Bartolomeo de las (kä'säs). A Spanish missionary to the aborigines of New Spain; born at Seville, 1474; died at Madrid, July 1566. Moved to compassion by the inhuman treatment of the natives by their Spanish taskmasters, he labored to have them put under protection of the law, and to have slaves imported from Africa for labor in the mines and on the plantations. He wrote memoirs in the interest of the aborigines, as 'A Very Brief Account of the Ruin of the Indies' (1542); 'Twenty Reasons'; etc. He wrote a 'History of the Indies,' but it has not been printed.

Casgrain, Abbe Henry Raymond (kä-gran'). A Canadian historical writer; born in Rivière Quelle, Quebec, Dec. 16, 1831. Oct. 5, 1856, he was ordained a priest. He was professor at Ste. Anne's College until 1859, and afterward vicar at Quebec Cathedral from 1860 till 1873. Among his most important works are: 'History of the Hôtel Dieu de Quebec'; 'My Canadian Parish in the Seventeenth Century.' A collection of his entire works was published in 1886.

Cass, Lewis. A famous American statesman, diplomatist, and soldier; born at Exeter, N. H., Oct. 9, 1872; died at Detroit, Mich., June 17, 1866. He served in the War of 1812; was governor of Michigan Territory (1813-31); Secretary of War (1831-36); minister to France (1836-42); United States Senator (1845-48); Presidential candidate (1848); United States Senator (1849-57); Secretary of State (1857-60). He wrote: 'History, Traditions, and Languages of the Indians' (1823); 'France, its King, Court, and Government'; etc.

Cassin, John. An American ornithologist; born near Chester, Pa., Sept. 6, 1813; died in Philadelphia, Jan. 10, 1869. Among his more important works may be named: 'Mammalogy and Ornithology of the Wilkes Exploring Expedition'; 'Ornithology of Perry's Expedition to Japan'; etc.

Castanheda, Fernão Lopez de (käs-tän-ä'dä). A Portuguese historian; born 1500 (?); died 1559. His father having been appointed to an important post in India, he was taken thither in youth, and was thus led to make the careful and unremitting researches embodied in the 'History of the Discovery and Conquest of India by the Portuguese' (1551-61), a work upon which Camoens drew largely in the course of his epic activity.

Castelar, Emilio (käs-tä-lär'). A Spanish orator, statesman, and writer; born at Cadiz, Sept. 8, 1832; died at Murcia, May 25, 1899. In early life he was a journalist. In 1864 he became professor of history in the University of Madrid. He was always a "Progressist" and became a leader in all the struggles of the Liberal party of Spain. His eloquence is poetic and rhetorical, of marvelous fluency and enthusiasm. He wrote many historical and political works; among them: 'Civilization in the First Five Centuries of Christianity'; 'Questions Political and Social'; 'History of the Republican Movement in Europe'; 'Historical Gallery of Celebrated Women'; 'History's Tragedies.'

Castelein, Matthijs de (käs-tel-in'). A Dutch poet (1485-1550); born at Pamele (Oudenarde). He was the acknowledged lawgiver and pattern of all the Dutch rhetoricians of his time, in his 'Art of Rhetoric.' He composed many plays, but only two of them were published: one of these is the 'Story of Pyramus and Thisbe.' He wrote also 'Ballads' and a volume of 'Various Lays,' in melodious verse.

Castelli, Ignaz Franz (käs-tel'lē). An Austrian poet (1781-1862). He wrote many war songs; one of which, 'War-Song of the Austrian Army' (1809), was deemed not unworthy of notice by the official organ of the French government. His opera 'The Swiss Family' (1811) was produced on every German stage. His theatrical pieces numbered over 200.

Castello-Branco, Camillo (käs-tel'lo bränk'ō). A notable Portuguese novelist and poet; born in Lisbon, March 16, 1826; died at San Miguel de Seïde, June 6, 1890. He is the most popular of the modern romancists of Portugal, and at the same time the most national in tone, spirit, and form. Realism characterizes his numerous novels (over 100); the best known being: 'Love of Perdition' (1862); 'The Marquis of Torres Novas'; 'Brilliant from Brazil.' All of them are genuine pictures of Portuguese life. Among his poetic compositions, the collection published under the title 'A Book' (1854) holds the first place.

Castelnovo, Leo di (käs-tel-nō'vō), pseudonym of Count Leopoldo Pullè. An Italian dramatist and poet; born in Verona, April 17, 1835. He is conspicuous politically, and has written a number of plays, mostly comedies; the best being probably 'Drink or Choke' ['O bere o affogare,' meaning a case of Hobson's choice] and 'A Dead Heart.' 'Harp and Guitar' is a verse collection. Notable too is his novel, 'Do the Dead Return?'

Castelnuovo, Enrico (käs''tel-nö-ō'vō). An Italian novelist; born at Florence, 1839. His stories have attained great popularity; among them : 'Prof. Romualdo' (1878); 'Smiles and Tears' (1882) ; 'Reminiscences and Fancies' (1886) ; 'The Return of Aretusa' (1901). He is one of the acknowledged Italian masters of the « novel of the inner life » (romano intimo).

Castelvecchio, Riccardo (käs''tel-vek'ē-ō), pseudonym of Count Giulio Pullè. An Italian dramatist, father of Count Leopoldo Pullè; born in Verona. His greatest success was 'The Romantic Lady and the Homœopathic Doctor' (new ed. 1869), a comedy; another, 'The Discreet [Lady's] Maid,' is also very popular.

Casti, Giambattista (käs'tē). An Italian poet (1721–1803). He entered the service of the Emperor Joseph II.; accompanied embassies to St. Petersburg, etc. He won fame by his 'Gay Stories in Ottava Rima,' and added to it by his witty satiric 'Talking Animals' (1802). The latter work was immediately translated into most of the languages of Europe. The English translation, with numerous additions, was made by W. S. Rose, and published as 'The Court and Parliament of Beasts' (1819). Casti wrote also two very successful comic operas, and a poetic satire on court life in the reign of Catharine II. of Russia.

Castiglione, Baldassare, Count (käs-tēl-yō'nē). An Italian poet and statesman (1478–1529); born in the district of Mantua. He wrote a volume of 'Poems Vernacular and Latin.' But the work to which he owes his literary fame is 'The Book of the Courtier,' a masterpiece of elegant and ornate prose. It lays down the laws of courtesy and of courtly manners, and incidentally gives a view of life in the highest society in the author's time.

Castilho, Antonio Feliciano (käs-tēl'ō). A Portuguese poet (1800–75). Though almost blind, he studied jurisprudence at Coimbra. His first poetical composition, 'Letters of Echo and Narcissus,' published while he was a student, won him great celebrity. He excelled in pastorals; and to this class belong his 'Spring,' and 'Love and Melancholy, or the Latest Heloïse.' He had a deep sympathy with nature, and was a master of elegiac verse.

Castillejo, Christóval de (käs-tēl-yä'hō). The last representative of the ancient Spanish poetry (1490–1556); born at Ciudad Rodrigo. He opposed the introduction of Italian styles into the poetry of Spain, and justified his opposition by demonstrating in his own work the competence of the traditional styles of Spain for the expression of all moods and all sentiments. His satiric vein, especially in the 'Dialogue on the Condition of Women' and the 'Sermon on Loves,' offended both clergy and laity.

Castillo-Solorzano, Alonso del (käs-tēl'yō-sō-lōr'thä'nō). A Spanish romancer and poet of the 17th century. His stories, 'The Garrulous Humbug,' 'The Allurement of Money,' and others, are still popular and are still reprinted. Of his comedies the most notable is 'The Marquis of Cigarral.' His fables after the manner of Ovid would not be deemed unworthy of the Roman poet.

Castlemon, Harry. See **Fosdick, Charles Austin.**

Castro, Agustin (käs'trō). A Mexican poet; born in Cordova, Vera Cruz, Jan. 24, 1728; died in Bologna, Italy, 1790. A Jesuit priest, an unpedantic scholar, he taught philosophy, and also translated masterpieces with almost unfailing sureness of touch. His original verse, always warm and pure, includes 'Hernán Cortés,' and 'Charts' to guide the budding poetic genius; while the versions he made of Seneca, Horace, Sappho, Milton, Fénelon, and Euripides, receive merited praise.

Catherine, St., of Sienna. An Italian saint and religious writer; born in Sienna, Italy, 1347; died 1380. Her letters and treatises are greatly admired. She is styled « the seraphic virgin » on account of her insight into spiritual things. A new edition of her 'Writings,' dictated to her secretary by the saint in moments of ecstasy, appeared in 1896.

Catherwood, Mary Hartwell. An American writer of historical romances; born in Luray, O., Dec. 16, 1847. Died at Chicago, Dec. 26, 1902. She wrote: 'Craque-o'-Doom'; 'The Romance of Dollard'; 'The Story of Tonty'; 'A Woman in Armor'; 'The Lady of Fort St. John'; 'The Chase of St. Castin, and Other Tales'; 'The Spirit of an Illinois Town'; 'The White Islander'; and other novels. Died 1902.

Catlin, George. An American prose-writer and painter; born in Wilkesbarre, Pa., 1796; died in Jersey City, N. J., Dec. 23, 1872. From 1832 till 1839 he traveled and lived among the Indians of America, of whom he painted hundreds of portraits; in 1841 he published 'Illustrations of the Manners, etc., of the North American Indians;' and subsequently, 'Life among the Indians' and 'The Breath of Life.' His little book 'Shut Your Mouth' was widely read; it was founded on his theory that the Indians owed their vigor of health to their habit of breathing through the nose.

Cato, Marcus Porcius (kā'tō), the Censor. A Roman statesman and pamphleteer (234-

149 B. C.). He exercised the broad powers of the censor's office with inflexible, almost fanatical rigor, and absolute impartiality. In his eyes nothing was good that was not ancient. He wrote many tractates on different subjects; but one only of them is extant, 'On Farming,' a collection of the rules of good husbandry. Of his summary of the early annals of Rome, 'Beginnings,' we have only a few fragments.

Caton, John Dean. An American lawyer and miscellaneous writer; born at Monroe, N. Y., 1812; died in Ohio, 1895. He was Chief Justice of Illinois (1855–64). He wrote: 'A Summer in Norway' (1875); 'The Last of the Illinois, and a Sketch of the Pottawatomies' (1876); 'The Antelope and Deer of America' (1877); etc.

Cats, Jacob (käts). A Dutch poet; born in Brouwershaven, Zeeland, Nov. 10, 1577; died at his estate of Zorgvliet, near the Hague, Sept. 12, 1660. He had a distinguished public career as a diplomat, jurist, and educator; but his enduring renown depends upon his various poems, 'Emblems,' 'Maiden Duty,' 'Inward Strife,' and others, in all of which the ethics of domestic life are expounded with much cheerful dullness. The collected edition, under the title of 'Father Cats's Book,' has attained a practically universal circulation throughout Holland.

Catullus, Caius Valerius (ka̤-tul'us). The greatest of Roman lyric poets (84–54 B. C.); born at Verona. Of his compositions 116 have come down to our time. The finest are those 'To Lesbia'; 'The Boat'; and 'Address to Himself.'

Cavalcanti, Guido (kä-väl-kän'tē). One of the earliest Italian poets (about 1235–1300). His poems consist of sonnets, ballads, and songs, to a young woman whose acquaintance he made at Toulouse on a pilgrimage to Santiago.

Cavalcaselle, Giovanni Battista (kä-väl-kä'sel). An Italian historian of art; born at Legnano, Jan. 22, 1820; died November 1897. He became the literary associate of J. A. Crowe, with whom he produced the epoch-making 'History of Painting in Italy' (1864–71), the most complete work on the subject; 'Early Flemish Painters' (1857–72); 'Life of Titian' (1877); and others.

Cavallotti, Felice Carlo Emanuele (kä-väl-ōt'tē). An Italian poet; born at Milan, Nov. 6, 1842; died in Rome, March 6, 1898. His 'Political Poems' brought upon him censure from the public authorities. With his tragedies, 'Agnes de Gonzaga' and 'Alcibiades' (1874), he established his dramatic reputation. He was the author of other dramas and of two volumes of lyric poetry. His best work is 'The Canticle of Canticles.'

Cavendish, Margaret (Duchess of Newcastle). An English writer; born in Essex, 1624; died 1673–4. She wrote 'Philosophical Fancies'; and a collection of poems, 'The Pastime and Recreation of the Queen of Fairies.'

Cavour, Count Camillo Benso di (kä-vör'). A celebrated Italian statesman; was born at Turin, Aug. 10, 1810; died June 6, 1861. His great services to Italy are apparent in his 'Letters' (1821–61); 'Unprinted Letters' (1862); 'Parliamentary Speeches' (1863); and 'Correspondence and Writings' (1892).

Cawein, Madison Julius. An American poet; born in Louisville, Ky., March 23, 1865. Among his works are: 'Blooms of the Berry' (1887); 'The Triumph of Music' (1888); 'Lyrics and Idyls' (1890); 'Days and Dreams'; 'Moods and Memories'; 'Intimations of the Beautiful'; 'Accolon of Gaul'; 'Poems of Nature and Love'; 'Red Leaves and Roses'; 'Undertones'; 'The Vale of Tampa'; 'Nature—Notes and Impressions.'

Caxton, William. An English printer and scholar; born in the Weald of Kent, 1422 (?); died 1491. His 'Recuyell [collection] of the Histories of Troy,' translated by him from the French, appears to have been printed in 1474, most probably at Bruges in Belgium. It was the first book in English reproduced by typography. He set up a printing-office in Westminster, 1477; and on Nov. 18 of that year issued 'The Dictes and Sayings of the Philosophers,' folio, a work ever memorable as the first book printed in England—only 420 years ago! He printed in all 71 separate works, very many of them translated by him from the French; his translations even of Latin classic authors were made, not directly from the original language, but from French versions.

Caylus, Marthe Marguerite de Villette, Marquise de (kä'lüs). A French writer of memoirs; born in Poitou, 1673; died at Paris (?), April 15, 1729. Long an ornament of the brilliant court of Louis XIV., she passed her declining years in dictating 'My Recollections,' in which a valuable insight into the life of Louis XIV. is afforded, through the medium of a singularly happy style.

Cazotte, Jacques (kä-zot'). A French poet and humorist (1719–92). His masterpieces are: 'Oliver' (1762), a poem of chivalry after the manner of Ariosto; and 'The Devil in Love' (1772), a tale of wonder which is still a popular favorite. He had extraordinary skill in versifying, as shown by his adding a seventh canto to Voltaire's 'Civil War of Geneva' with such perfect imitation of Voltaire's style and manner as to deceive all Paris.

Cecchi, Giammaria (chek'ē). An Italian dramatist; born in Florence, April 14, 1518; died there, Oct. 28, 1587. He was the rival of Bibbiena, Machiavelli, and Ariosto in portraiture of character and in liveliness of dialogue. Of his plays, 95 in number, but few have been printed. These are mainly imitations of Plautus and Terence; the best of them are: 'The Hammer,' 'The Slave,' and (the most famous of all) 'The Owl.' He wrote also religious dramas; among them 'The Exaltation of the Holy Cross' (1589).

Cecco d'Ascoli (chek'ō däs-kō'lē), properly Francesco Stabili. An Italian poet; born at

Ascoli, about 1257; died in Florence, Sept. 16, 1327. He was a devoted student of astrology and of demonology. For the expression and defense of certain erroneous opinions he was burned at the stake. His heretical or impious doctrines are contained in a poem, unfinished but of encyclopædic compass, 'Bitternesses,' of which he lived to complete four books. The subject of the first book was astronomy with meteorology; of the second, stellar influence with physiognomy; of the third, minerals; of the fourth, sundry problems, moral and physical.

Cech, Svatopluk (chech). A notable Czech poet and prose writer; born at Ostredek, Feb. 21, 1846. He was editor in succession of several journals, and at the same time practiced law. After winning some celebrity as a writer of stories and short poems, he made a bolder flight in 1872 with 'Dreams,' in which he shows great epic power. Besides 'Dreams,' he has written several other poems, as 'The Adamites'; 'The Storm'; 'Songs of Morning.' He is the most popular of Czech poets. As a novelist he excels in lively wit and rich humor. Among his works of prose fiction may be named: 'Stories, Arabesques, and Humoresques,' and the most amusing 'Candidate for Immortality.' He wrote also (1885) 'Memories from the Orient,' fruit of his travels.

Celakovsky, Frantisek Ladislav (chel'äkŏv"skē). A Czech poet and philologist; born in Strakonitz, March 7, 1799; died in Prague, Aug. 5, 1852. His earlier work was journalistic and pedagogical, his reputation in poesy dating from the appearance of 'Slav Folk-Songs' (1822), to which succeeded various brilliant performances of a like nature: 'Echo of Russian Folk Songs' (1829); 'Echo of Bohemian Folk Songs' (1840); etc. He translated Herder and Scott into his own vernacular with felicitous results.

Cellini, Benvenuto (chel-lē'nē). An Italian sculptor, metal-worker, and writer of memoirs; born in Florence, Nov. 3, 1500; died there, Feb. 13, 1571. His tremendous adventures and his miraculous genius (as set forth by himself in his 'Autobiography') gives the fascinating story of his life an important place in letters, particularly as he is a master of style.

Celsus (sel'sus). A Roman controversial writer; flourished in the second century. His 'True Discourse,' an attack on Christianity, is lost; but it figures conspicuously in the history of the early Church.

Celtes, Konrad (tsel'tes). [The Greek equivalent of his real name, Pickel.] A celebrated German humanist; born 1459; died 1508. His most celebrated work is a volume of 'Odes' (1513). He did much to promote the study of the classics, and wrote his own poems in Latin.

Centlivre, Susannah. An English dramatist; born (Freeman?) in Ireland (?), 1667 (?);

died in London, Dec. 1, 1723. Her third husband, from whom she derives the name by which she is known in literature, was cook to Queen Anne. 'The Gamester' and 'The Busy Body' are her best comedies, but 'The Perjured Husband' is widely known. These plays are very witty in dialogue, but unoriginal in plot.

Ceo, Violante do (sā'ō) A famed Portuguese poet; born in Lisbon, 1601; died, 1693. She was styled "the tenth Muse." Her 'Portuguese Parnassus' and miscellaneous poems are greatly admired.

Cerretti, Luigi (cher-et'tē). An Italian poet and rhetorician; born in Modena, Nov. 1, 1738; died in Pavia, March 5, 1808. The purity and elegance of his diction made him, at an early age, the most distinguished professor of rhetoric and oratory in Italy. His 'Poems and Select Prose,' collected into a posthumous volume, were instantly successful, and have retained their rank ever since.

Cervantes Saavedra, Miguel de (sẽr-van'tēz or ther-vän'tes sä-ä-vä'drä). A celebrated Spanish romancist; born at Alcalá de Henares in 1547; died at Madrid, April 23, 1616. He wrote many romances and stories, but he lives in fame through 'Don Quixote.' He served some years in the army; was captured by corsairs and held five years in servitude. His fellow captives testified to his self-denying services to them while in the hands of the Algerines. His first attempt in literature was the composition of a pastoral romance, 'Galatea,' in the traditional style and spirit. Of twenty or thirty plays written by him, two only survive, and they have no celebrity. The first part of 'Don Quixote' was published in 1605, and it had a hearty reception from the beginning among the populace, though not among the cultured classes. Before the year was out. five editions, some authorized, others pirated, were published, and the Don and his grotesque retainer appeared like immemorial traditional characters in every pageant. The continuation of the immortal story, however, did not appear till 1615 — and then because spurious continuations published under his name fairly forced Cervantes's hand. Meanwhile he busied himself with writing poems and novels now forgotten. On all these dead works he bestowed great care before he gave them to the public: he wrote 'Don Quixote' with "running pen."

Cesarotti, Melchiore (chā-sär-ōt'tē). A distinguished Italian poet and scholar; born in Padua, May 15, 1730; died at Solvaggiano, Nov. 3, 1808. He held a professorship at Padua. His translation of 'Ossian' (1763) was hailed as a work of genius. 'A Course in Greek Literature' remains incomplete; but an 'Essay on the Philosophy of Language Applied to the Italian Tongue' (1785), and on analogous theses, are perfect specimens of criticism; and his poetry, though now falling into secondary rank, is tasteful and ornate.

Cesnola, Luigi Palma di, Count (ches-nō'lä). A noted Italian-American archæologist; born at Rivarola, near Turin, July 29, 1832. Appointed United States consul at Cyprus, he discovered a large number of antiquities there; the collection is now in the Metropolitan Museum, New York, of which he is a director. He has written: 'Cyprus, its Ancient Cities, Tombs, and Temples' (1877); 'The Metropolitan Museum of Art' (1882). Died Nov., 1904.

Cetina, Gutierre de (chet-ē-nä *or* thä-tē'nä). A Spanish poet; born at Seville, early in the 16th century; died there (?), about 1560. He was a soldier, and served the Prince of Ascoli till the death of that patron, when he departed for Mexico. He spent some years in New Spain, returning to Seville shortly before he died. He chose to write in Italian measures and forms, though in the Spanish tongue. His sonnets, ballads, and epistles in terza rima, are consummately graceful in expression, simple in form, and inspired by tender feeling.

Ceva, Tommaso (chā'vä). An Italian poet and mathematician; born in Milan, Dec. 20, 1648; died there, Feb. 3, 1736. He was a Jesuit who attained peculiar proficiency in geometry, and who also aided in spreading a knowledge of Newton's discovery of the law of gravitation. His poetry comprises a rhymed history of Christ's youth, 'The Boy Jesus' (1699); and a 'New-Ancient Philosophy' (1729).

Chadbourne, Paul Ansel (chad'bern). A distinguished American educator and miscellaneous writer; born at North Berwick, Me., Oct. 21, 1823; died in New York, Feb. 23, 1883. He was president of the Massachusetts Agricultural College at Amherst (1867 and 1882); of the University of Wisconsin (1867-70); of Williams College (1872-81). He wrote: 'Natural Theology' (1867); 'Instinct in Animals and Men' (1872); etc.

Chadwick, John White. An American poet, prose writer, and Unitarian divine; born in Marblehead, Mass., Oct. 19, 1840. His radical sermons have attracted attention, and he has been a liberal contributor to current literature. Among his works are: 'A Book of Poems' (1875); 'The Bible of To-Day' (1878); 'Origin and Destiny' (1883); 'A Daring Faith' (1885); 'The Man Jesus'; 'The Faith of Reason'; 'Old and New Unitarian Belief'); 'The Power of an Endless Life.' Died Brooklyn, Dec. 12, 1904.

Chaillé-Long, Charles (shä-yä'lôn). An American explorer; born of French parentage, at Baltimore, Md. 1843. After serving in the Confederate army he went to Egypt, where he was appointed lieutenant-colonel by the Khedive (1870). Gordon made him chief-of-staff and sent him on a mission to King Mtesa of Uganda. He wrote: 'The Three Prophets' (1886); 'Central Africa' (1887); 'The Sources of the Nile.'

Chalkley, Thomas (châk'li). A noted American Quaker itinerant preacher; born in London, March 3, 1675; died in Tortola, West Indies, Sept. 4, 1741. He spent his life preaching in New England and the Southern colonies; toward its end he made his home near Philadelphia. His chief work was his 'Life, Labors, and Travels,' whose quaintness made it popular even outside the Society of Friends, and has caused it to be several times reprinted.

Challemel-Lacour, Paul Armand (shäl-mel' lä-kör'). A French statesman; born at Avranches, May 19, 1827; died in Paris, Oct. 26, 1896. He figured conspicuously in journalism, and published 'Individualist Philosophy' (1864) and numerous essays

Chalmers, George. A Scottish historian; born at Fochabers, 1742; died in London, May 31, 1825. In 1763 he came to America and settled in Baltimore, where he practiced law for several years. At the beginning of the Revolutionary War, he opposed the action of the colonists; not meeting with success, he returned to England. His writings are political, historical, and biographical. Among his works are: 'Churchyard Chips Concerning Scotland'; 'Life of Daniel Defoe'; and 'Caledonia,' an account of Scotland from the earliest period (1807-24).

Chalmers, Thomas. A Scotch theologian and social reformer; born at Anstruther, Fifeshire, March 17, 1780; died in Edinburgh, May 1847. He was one of the greatest pulpit orators of Great Britain. His most important works are: 'Political Economy' (1832); 'On the Adaptation of External Nature to the Moral and Intellectual Constitution of Man' (1833); and many widely read volumes of sermons.

Chamberlain, Nathan Henry. An American Episcopal divine, biographer, and essayist; born in Massachusetts, 1830; died there, April 2, 1901. He wrote: 'Autobiography of a New England Farmhouse' (1864); 'Samuel Sewall and the World He Lived in' (1895); 'The Sphinx in Aubrey Parish.'

Chamberlin, Joseph Edgar. An American journalist; born in Vermont, 1851. He is known as the "Listener" of the Boston Transcript, and is also attached to the Youth's Companion. He has written 'The Listener in the Town' and 'The Listener in the Country.'

Chambers, Charles Julius. An American novelist; born in Bellefontaine, O., Nov 21, 1850. In 1870 he traveled through the West Indies, Europe, the United States, and Canada, as special correspondent of the New York Herald. In 1876 he published an account of his few weeks of experience (incognito) in an insane institution, entitled 'A Mad World,' which excited great interest. He is a contributor to various periodicals; also author of the two novels: 'On a Margin' (1884); and 'Lovers Four and Maidens Five' (1886).

Chambers, Robert. An eminent Scotch prose-writer and publisher; born at Peebles, July 10, 1802; died at St. Andrews, March 17, 1871. He and his brother began in poverty as small booksellers; issued penny leaflets of useful information for the people, written in a clear and simple though not infantile style, which became very popular, and at last took regular periodical form in Chambers' Journal; and the great publishing-house which bears the name of both developed gradually. The excellent 'Chambers' Encyclopædia for the People' was an outgrowth of the Journal, and edited by the brothers. Robert wrote also 'Traditions of Edinburgh' and works on Scotch history; but his most noted book was the anonymous 'Vestiges of Creation,' for years an unequaled theologic-scientific sensation.

Chambers, Robert William. An American artist and novelist; born in Long Island, N. Y., 1865. His home is in New York. He has written: 'The King in Yellow'; 'The Red Republic'; 'A King and a Few Dukes'; etc.; and 'With the Band,' a volume of ballads; 'Cardigan'; 'The Maids of Paradise'; 'Jole'; 'Mountain Land'; 'The Tree of Heaven.'

Chambers, William. A Scotch prose-writer and editor ; born 1800; died in 1883. He wrote: 'Things as They Are in America' (1854); 'American Slavery and Color' (1857); 'France, its History and Revolutions' (1871); 'Stories of Old Families and Remarkable Persons' (1878). He also compiled a 'Hand-book of American Literature' (1857).

Chambray, Georges, Marquis de (shäm-brā'). A French soldier and military writer; born in Paris, 1783; died 1848. He served in the Napoleonic wars, was in the fatal Russian campaign, and during his active service saw much fighting. 'The History of the Expedition to Russia in 1812' (3d ed. 1839) is widely known.

Chamfort, Sébastien Roch Nicolas, called (shon-for'). A French moralist and critic (1741–1794). Among his works are comedies, literary criticisms, political articles, and poems; but none compare with his 'Maxims and Thoughts,' which are worthy to rank next after La Rochefoucauld's 'Maxims.' Sainte-Beuve says of them that they are like "well-minted coins that retain their value." Chamfort's tragedy 'Mustapha and Zeangir' has some scenes of genuine passion, but as a whole it is artificial. He wrote some tales in verse, but their licentiousness is not redeemed even by grace of style.

Chamier, Frederick. An English novelist; born in London in 1796; died at Liverpool (?), October 1870. He was a naval officer. He wrote 'Ben Brace'; 'Tom Bowline'; 'Jack Adams'; 'The Arethusa'; and other once popular sea tales, now neglected. He employs the methods of Marryat.

Chamisso, Adelbert von (shä-mēs'sō). A German lyrist; born at the castle of Boncourt, Champagne, Jan. 30, 1781; died at Berlin, Aug. 21, 1838. His love of poetry brought him into intimate association with many kindred spirits, as Varnhagen von Ense, Theremin, Hitzig, and La Motte Fouqué. He made a voyage of circumnavigation as a naturalist on a Russian

ship, 1815–18. The first of his poetical compositions were published (1804) in 'The Muses' Almanac.' By far his most celebrated work is 'Peter Schlemihl,' a tale of a man who lost his shadow. In association with Gaudy he translated some of Béranger's 'Songs.' He was the first to naturalize fully in German poesy the terzine verse; in that measure is written 'Salaz y Gomez,' one of his finest poems.

Champfleury (shon-flê-rē'), pseudonym of Jules Fleury-Husson. A French novelist and miscellaneous writer; born at Laon, Sept. 10, 1821; died at Sèvres, Dec. 5, 1889. His story of 'Les Chien-Caillous' was in Victor Hugo's opinion a masterpiece of realistic description. He wrote an autobiographical novel of his youthful years in 'The Confessions of Sylvius' (1849), continuing the story in 'The Adventures of Mariette' (1856). But his 'Burghers of Molinchart' (1855), a satiric delineation of the provincial bourgeoisie, made him famous. He is a pronounced "realist." Among his later novels, 'The Tourangeau Girls' (1864) and 'The Little Rose,' are most worthy of mention. He compiled a 'General History of Caricature' (5 vols., 1865-85), with a supplementary volume, 'Secret Museum of Caricature' (1888); and several other works on the arts of design and ceramics.

Champier, Symphorien (shon-pyā'). A French historian, poet, and physician; born, 1471 or 1472, in St. Symphorien-le-Loise, Lyonnais; died at Lyons, about 1540. Famed as a physician, with powerful friends at court and an ample fortune, he took delight in literature and the society of literary men, himself writing a series of poems for 'Virtuous Ladies' (1503), in four divisions, entitled 'The Flower of Dames,' 'The Rule of Love,' 'The Prophecies of the Sibyls,' and 'The Book of True Love,' respectively. His best history is an account of 'Princes and Battles' (1502).

Champlin, James Tift. An American prose-writer; born in Colchester, Conn., June 9, 1811; died in Portland, Me., March 15, 1882. He was a Baptist minister in Portland, Me., 1838-41; then professor of ancient languages at Colby University (Waterville, Me.), and its president 1857-73. A portion of his extensive writings are: 'Text-Book of Intellectual Philosophy' (1860); 'First Principles of Ethics' (1861); 'Constitution of the United States, with Brief Comments' (1880).

Champlin, John Denison. An American prose-writer; born in Stonington, Conn., Jan. 29, 1834. He began his literary career in New York in 1869, with contributions to periodicals. In 1873 he edited 'Fox's Mission to Russia,' and became a reviser, and in 1875 assistant editor, of the 'American Cyclopædia.' He has written: 'Young Folks' Catechisms of Common Things' (1880); 'Young Folks' Cyclopædia of Persons and Places' (1880); 'Young Folks' Astronomy'; and 'Chronicle of the Coach' (1886). In 1894 he was editor of Scribner's Art Cyclopædias, of which two

103

volumes of the first part were published (1886) as 'Cyclopædia of Painters and Paintings.'

Champney, Mrs. Elizabeth (Williams). An American novelist and writer of juveniles; born at Springfield, O., 1850. Many of her books are illustrated by her husband, the artist J. W. Champney. Among them are the Vassar Girls series,—'Three Vassar Girls Abroad,' 'In England,' 'In South America,' etc.; 'In the Sky-Parlor'; 'All Around a Palette'; 'Rosemary and Rue'; 'The Bubbling Teapot'; 'Bourbon Lilies'; 'Sebia's Tangled Web'; 'Romance of the French Abbeys'; 'Romance of the French Villas.'

Chandler, Elizabeth Margaret. An American poet; born near Wilmington, Del., Dec. 24, 1807; died Nov. 22, 1834. Her most popular poem was 'The Slave Ship.' Many of her subsequent verses were written in the same strain, and published in the Genius of Universal Emancipation, a Philadelphia abolitionist periodical. Her poems were published with a memoir by Benjamin Lundy (1836).

Chaney, George Leonard. A Unitarian clergyman and miscellaneous writer; born in Massachusetts, 1836. He was pastor of the Hollis Street Church in Boston (1862–79); afterward at Atlanta, Ga., where he edited the Southern Unitarian (1893–96). Among his works are: 'F. Grant & Co.' (1874), a book for boys; 'Alóha' (1880), travels in the Sandwich Islands; 'Every-Day Life and Every-Day Morals' (1884), a volume of essays; etc.

Chanler, Mrs. Amélie Rives. See Troubetskoi.

Channing, William Ellery. An eminent American theologian, one of the founders of American Unitarianism; born at Newport, R. I., April 7, 1780; died at Bennington, Vt., April 1842. His works were published in 1848.

Channing, William Ellery. An American poet, nephew of the above; born in Boston, Mass., June 10, 1818; died at Concord, Dec. 23, 1901. He was author of 'Poems' (1843-47); 'The Woodman' (1849); 'Near Home' (1858); 'The Wanderer' (1872); 'Conversations in Rome' (1847); and 'Thoreau, the Poet-Naturalist' (1873).

Channing, William Henry. An American Unitarian divine and biographer, nephew of W. E. Channing the elder; born at Boston, May 25, 1810; died in London, Dec. 23, 1884. Settling in England, he succeeded James Martineau as pastor at Liverpool. His daughter married Sir Edwin Arnold. His principal work was 'Memoir of William Ellery Channing' (3 vols., 1848).

Chapelain, Jean (shäp-lan'). A French poet and critic; born in Paris, Dec. 5, 1595; died there, Feb. 24, 1674. By his own unaided efforts he acquired a knowledge of Greek and Latin, Italian and Spanish. He won the favor of Cardinal Richelieu by his preface to Marini's notorious poem 'Adone,' and was a leading founder of the French Academy, whose first meetings were held at his house. Through

court influence he rose to be a recognized lawgiver of literature. He published in 1756 the first installment, 12 cantos, of a great epic, 'The Maid of Orleans,' on which he had been at work 20 years. But the critics, headed by Boileau, were so unfavorable that though of the first installment six editions were sold in 18 months, no publisher could be found for the sequel.

Chapelle, Claude Emmanuel Luillier, called (shä-pel'). A French poet (1626–86). He was illegitimate son of a man of wealth, who gave him an excellent education and left him a large fortune. He owes his place in literary records to his good fortune in having been associated with the foremost literary men of his time,—Racine, Molière, Boileau. He wrote some verses of indifferent merit; with Bachaumont he was joint author of 'Travels in Provence and Languedoc' (1663), written in mixed prose and verse, a fashion which prevailed for a while in France.

Chapin, Edwin Hubbell. A noted American Universalist divine and essayist; born at Union Village, N. Y., Dec. 29, 1814; died in New York, his long-time residence, Dec. 27, 1880. An effective preacher and lecturer, he was one of the powers for good in his day. He wrote: 'Moral Aspects of City Life' (1853); 'True Manliness' (1854); 'Crown of Thorns'; etc.

Chaplin, Heman White. An American lawyer and short-story writer; born in Rhode Island, 1847. His 'Five Hundred Dollars and Other Stories of New England Life' ranks with the best works of its kind.

Chaplin, Jeremiah. An American historical writer; born in Danvers, Mass., 1813; died in New Utrecht, N. Y., March 5, 1886. He was author of: 'Life of Charles Sumner'; 'Life of Franklin'; 'Riches of Bunyan'; 'Life of Galen'; and 'Life of Henry Dunster, First President of Harvard College' (1872), which is a work of much historical value.

Chapman, George. An English dramatist and translator of Homer; born in Hitchin, Hertford, 1559; died at London, May 12, 1634. What distinguishes his plays is the intuitive appreciation they reveal of the material and mechanical limitations of the theatre. The comedies 'All Fools but the Fool' and 'May Day' are well known; as are the tragedies 'Bussy d'Amboise' and 'The Tragedy of Charles, Duke of Byron.' The version of Homer (new ed. 1897) is celebrated.

Chapone, Hesther (shä-pōn'). An English story-writer and poet; born in Northamptonshire, Oct. 27, 1727; died 1801. She wrote: 'Ode to Peace'; 'Fidelia,' a story; 'Miscellanies in Prose and Verse'; and other works.

Charisi, Jehuda ben Salomo (chä-rē'zē), known also as Alcharisi. A Spanish Jewish poet; born in Xeres, about 1190 (?); died 1235. A devoted student of Arabian poetry, he rendered the 'Sittings' or 'Assemblies' of the great poet Hariri into Hebrew; but his masterpiece is the exquisite 'Tach-Kemoni,' or picture of every-day Jewish life and character in his own time,— a poem in which an Arabian influence predominates.

Charras, Jean Baptiste Adolphe (shär-ä'). A French military historian and expert; born in Pfalzburg, Lorraine, Jan. 7, 1810; died in Basel, Switzerland, Jan. 23, 1865. His vicissitudes in the army, the result of his own republicanism and the revolutionary precipitateness of French politics, did not prevent his rise to distinction, although his promotion was interfered with. He wrote : 'History of the Campaign of 1815 : Waterloo' (6th ed. 1869), and 'History of the War of 1813 in Germany' (2d ed. 1870).

Charrière, Isabelle Agnète de Saint Hyacinthe de (shä-ryär'). A French novelist, dramatist, and miscellaneous writer; born (Van Tuyll) in Utrecht, 1740 or 1746(?); died at Colombier, Switzerland, Dec. 25, 1805. She was one of the most accomplished women of her day. Her fictions and studies, 'Caliste' (1788) and 'Neuchatel Letters' (1784), and the drama 'The Thou and the You,' contain much that is admirable.

Chartier, Alain (shär-tyä'). A French poet; born in Bayeux, Normandy, about 1386; died in 1449. Early taken into royal favor for his brilliance in rhetoric and rhyme, he won fame with the 'Book of the Four Ladies' (1415), inspired by the battle of Agincourt, and the 'Ballad of Fougières' (1449), a patriotic piece.

Chase, Salmon Portland. An American statesman; born in Cornish, N. H., Jan. 13, 1808; died in New York city, May 7, 1873. He became eminent as lawyer, United States Senator from and governor of Ohio, Secretary of the Treasury, and Chief Justice of the United States Supreme Court. He was one of the able and strong-willed men whom Mr. Lincoln called about him during the war era, and did signal service to the government and the Union. He compiled a summary of the laws of Ohio, with a historical sketch of the State (3 vols., 1832).

Chase, Thomas. An American educator and prose-writer; born in Worcester, Mass., June 16, 1827; died in Providence, R. I., Oct. 5, 1892. In 1855 became professor of philology and classical literature at Haverford College, near Philadelphia; in 1875 its president. In 1878 Harvard gave him the degree of LL. D. Among his publications are : 'Hellas: her Monuments and Scenery' (1861); an address on 'Liberal Education: Its Aims and Methods.'

Chasles, Philarète (shäl). A French historical and literary critic; born in Mainvilliers, near Chartres, Oct. 8, 1798; died in Venice, July 18, 1873. The son of a Jacobin, and educated according to Rousseau, he acquired the point of view which, enlarged by life abroad, makes his essays so unique and instructive. He has written in every imaginable prose form, from a romance to a riddle: but his enduring work is contained in 'French Language and Literature from the Beginning of the Sixteenth Century to 1610' (1828); 'Studies of Antiquity' (1847); 'Studies of the Sixteenth Century in France' (1848); 'Journeys of a Critic through Life and Books' (2d series, 2d ed. 1866–68); and 'Memoirs' (1876–78).

Châteaubriand, François René Auguste, Vicomte de (shä-tō-brē-oṅ'). A great French statesman, traveler, novelist, and historical writer; born at St. Malo, September 1768; died at Paris, July 4, 1848. He made a voyage in search of the Northwest Passage in 1791; but on touching the American continent abandoned that quest, and proposed to himself a study of the life of the American Indians. He lived for some time among the aborigines, and the fruits of his observations were the three novels 'Atala,' 'René,' and 'The Natchez,' which by the charms of the literary style and the interesting poetical descriptions of life remote from civilization, won instant and great popularity. Perhaps his greatest and certainly his most ambitious work is 'The Genius of Christianity' (5 vols., 1856–57), in which the dogmas, practices, etc., of Catholic Christianity are defended against infidel attack. Other writings of his in the direction of Christian apologetic are : 'The Martyrs, or Triumph of the Christian Religion' (2 vols., 1809); 'A Journey from Paris to Jerusalem' (3 vols., 1811). Of works connected with literature and its history, he wrote 'An Essay on English Literature' and translated Milton's 'Paradise Lost.'

Châteaubrun, Jean Baptiste Vivien (shä-tō-brün'). A French dramatist; born at Angoulême, 1686; died 1775. He was elected to the French Academy, 1753. His tragedy of 'The Trojan Woman' was once very popular.

Chatfield-Taylor, Hobart Chatfield. An American novelist; born in Illinois, 1865; resident in Chicago. He has written : 'With Edge Tools'; 'An American Peeress'; 'Two Women and a Fool'; 'The Land of the Castanet; 'The Vice of Fools'; 'Idle Born'; 'The Crimson Wing'; 'Molière, a Biography.'

Chatterton, Thomas. An English poet, reputed the "marvelous youth" of literature; born in Bristol, Nov. 20, 1752; committed suicide at London, Aug. 25, 1770. He had precocious taste and considerable poetic talent, perhaps overrated from the interest of his pathetic fate and youth, and the literary sensation of his spurious "Rowley" poems,— supposed to have been found in the chest of a mediæval "clerk," but written by Chatterton in a palpably impossible dialect. 'An Excelente Balade of Charitie' is much the best. His poems and plays in common English are mere boy's-work, but show fertility and facility, which with his manly taste might have matured into greatness.

Chaucer, Geoffrey. The father of English poetry; born in London (?), 1328 or 1340; died there, Oct. 25, 1400. His 'Canterbury Tales' is his most celebrated work. Among the others are: 'Troilus and Cressida'; 'The Parliament of Fowles'; 'Boke of the Duchesse'; 'The House of Fame'; 'The Legend of Good Women'; and minor poems and translations.

Chaulieu, Guillaume Amfrye de (shō-lyĕ'). A French poet (1639-1720). He was preceptor of the young princes de Vendôme, Henri IV.'s sons by Gabrielle d'Estrées, and through their good offices obtained some valuable sinecures. His erotic poems won him the title of "the Anacreon of the Temple" (residence of the young princes). But apart from licentiousness he proved himself a true poet in several lyrics, as in 'Fontenoy' and 'The Retreat.' His best poem is perhaps that on 'Country Life,' which in fact the poet could not endure.

Chaussard, Pierre Jean Baptiste (shō-sär'). A French historian, poet, and miscellaneous writer; born in Paris, Oct. 8, 1766; died there, Jan. 9, 1823. He plunged ardently into literary warfare in behalf of the French Revolution, and was distinguished in the diplomacy of the first republic, writing 'The Revolution in Belgium' (1793) and many patriotic odes. He also produced: 'Germany and the House of Austria' (1792); 'The Spirit of Mirabeau' (1797); and other works in harmony with the French sentiment of his day.

Chauveau, Pierre Joseph Olivier (shō-vō'). A Canadian statesman and writer of prose and verse; born in Quebec, May 30, 1820; died there, April 4, 1890. Among his contributions to literature were many popular poems, including 'Simple Joys'; 'Donnaconna'; 'Letters to M. de Puibusque'; also many valuable prose works: 'Tour of H. R. H. Prince of Wales in America' (1861); 'Souvenirs and Legends' (in prose and verse) (1877); and 'François Xavier Garneau, His Life and Works' (1883).

Cheever, George Barrell. An American journalist, poet, and divine; born in Hallowell, Me., April 17, 1807; died in Englewood, N. J., Oct. 1, 1890. He was editor of the New York Evangelist from 1845 to 1846, and at different times connected with the New York Observer and Independent. He was an able and vigorous writer and speaker, and the author of a large number of works in prose and verse. Among his publications are: 'Studies in Poetry' (1830); 'God's Hand in America' (1841); 'Poets of America' (1847); 'Windings of the River of the Water of Life' (1849); 'The Voice of Nature to her Foster-Child, the Soul of Man' (1852); 'Lectures on the Life, Genius, and Insanity of Cowper' (1856), arguing that Cowper's religious terrors proved him sane instead of insane; and 'God against Slavery, and the Freedom and Duty of the Pulpit to Rebuke It' (1857). One of his most effective works was 'Deacon Giles's Distillery.'

Cheever, Henry Theodore. An American prose-writer and divine, brother of G. B.; born in Hallowell, Me., Feb. 6, 1814; died 1897. His writings were popular, and include: 'The Island World of the Pacific' (1852); 'Short Yarns for Long Voyages' (1855); and 'Correspondences of Faith and Views of Madame Guyon' (1886).

Chemnitz, Matthäus Friedrich (chem'nits). A German song-writer; born in Barmstedt, Holstein, June 10, 1815; died at Altona, Holstein, April 14, 1870. He was a legal functionary, whose patriotic song of 'Sea-Girt Schleswig-Holstein' came universally into favor and obtained a place for his name in literature.

Chemnitzer, Ivan Ivanovich (chem'nit-sėr), A Russian fabulist (1745-84); born at Jenotajevsk, government of Astrakhan. At first he wrote in German, his masters and models in literature were Russian, though he was powerfully influenced by Gellert and La Fontaine. His 'Fables and Tales' appeared in two parts anonymously (1779 and 1782) during his life, and a third part after his death.

Cheney, Mrs. Ednah Dow (Littlehale). An American lecturer and miscellaneous writer; born in Boston, 1824. She has been president of the New England Woman's Club and the Massachusetts Woman Suffrage Association. She has written: 'Handbook of American History for Colored People' (1866); 'Gleanings in the Field of Art' (1881); 'Life of Louisa M. Alcott' (1889); and several stories, including: 'Nora's Return,' a sequel to Ibsen's 'A Doll's House'; 'Sally Williams, the Mountain Girl' (1872); besides other books. Died in 1904.

Cheney, John Vance. An American writer of prose and verse; born in Groveland, N. Y., Dec. 29, 1848. Is author of 'The Old Doctor' (1885); 'Thistle-Drift,' poems (1887); a volume of essays; 'Lyrics' (1901); 'Poems' (1902).

Cheney, Theseus Apoleon. An American historian; born in Leon, N. Y., March 16, 1830; died in Starkey, N. Y., Aug. 2, 1878. His publications include: 'Historical Sketch of the Chemung Valley' (1866); 'Historical Sketch of Eighteen Counties of Central and Southern New York' (1868); 'Laron'; 'Relations of Government to Science'; and 'Antiquarian Researches.'

Chénier, André Marie de (shā-nyā'). A notable French poet; born at Constantinople, Oct. 30, 1762; died July 25, 1794. Shortly before the Terror he made a vigorous attack on the Jacobins in the Journal de Paris. He wrote Louis XVI.'s appeal to the people after the death sentence. He celebrated in verse Charlotte Corday. He perished under the guillotine. The maturity, breadth, and soundness of his judgment in poetical composition are demonstrated by his poem on 'Invention,' written in his 24th year. Of the same year is his fine idyl 'Liberty.' Similar in spirit to this, and of perfect Pindaric form, is the 'Dithyrambic on the Tennis Play' (1791). In his prison of St. Lazare he composed a beautiful elegy, 'The Girl Captive.'

Chénier, Marie Joseph de. A French poet and dramatist, younger brother of André M. (1764-1811). He was a Jacobin, and member of the Legislative Assembly in the Revolution. His tragedies — 'Charles IX.' (1789) ; 'Henry VIII.' and 'Calas' (both 1791); 'Caius Gracchus' (1793); and others — brought him fame and success by the accordance of their republican and revolutionary sentiments with the public opinion of the time, rather than by their merits as compositions. His national songs were approved by the best test of such productions,— popularity : one of them, 'The Parting Song' (Partant pour la Syrie), is hardly less famous than the 'Marseillaise.' His satires are full of spirit, point, and wit, but often rancorous and unjust.

Cheraskoff, Michaïl Matvéjevich (čher-äs'-kŏf). A Russian poet (1733-1807) ; born in the government of Poltava. By his contemporaries he was called "the Russian Homer"; but he had little original genius. We have from him several epics after Virgil and Voltaire, according to the orthodox rules of Boileau ; among them 'The Rossiad,' celebrating the conquest of Kasan by Ivan the Terrible, and 'Vladimir,' commemorating the Christianization of Russia. He wrote also a number of dramas, romances, fables, and songs. He excels in description of natural scenery.

Cherbuliez, Charles Victor (shär-bü-lyä'). A distinguished French romancist ; born at Geneva, of a noted family of littérateurs, July 19, 1829 ; died at Combs-la-Ville, July 2, 1899. Having studied in the Universities of Geneva, Paris, Bonn, and Berlin, he was for a time an educator at Geneva ; but in 1864 became one of the editors of the Revue des Deux Mondes. He first gained distinction as art critic and observer of public affairs, as also by his romances, under the pseudonym **"G. Valbert."** He wrote a volume of art travels in Greece ; 'A Horse by Phidias' ; 'Political Spain' ; 'Foreign Profiles'; 'Art and Nature'; etc. His romances are characterized by clever treatment of the problems of domestic and social life and a fine psychological analysis, with a marked bias for description of odd characters. Among his most successful novels—and their success has hardly been less abroad than at home—are : 'Romance of a Respectable Woman' (1866) ; 'Ladislas Bolski's Adventure' (1869) ; 'Samuel Brohl & Co.' (1877). The last two were dramatized, but won little favor on the stage.

Cherville, Gaspard Georges, Marquis de (shär-vēl'). A French novelist ; born at Chartres, 1821. He was for several years collaborator with the elder Dumas ; about 40 volumes were the fruit of the partnership. Independently he contributed to the Paris Temps several admirable sketches and stories of rural life and the chase. A few of his studies have been published in sumptuously illustrated editions ; e. g., 'Life in the Country' (1879). Died 1898.

Chesebro, Caroline. An American novelist; born in Canandaigua, N. Y., about 1828 ; died in Piermont, N. Y., Feb. 16, 1873. She was author of 'Dream-Land by Daylight,' a volume of stories and sketches (1851); 'The Beautiful

Gate and Other Tales' (1863). The novels 'Philly and Kit' (1856); 'Peter Carradine' (1863) ; 'The Foe in the Household' (1871); and various others, are well known.

Chesterfield, Philip Dormer Stanhope, Earl of. An English man of affairs and of the world ; born in London, Sept. 22, 1694 ; died there (?), March 24, 1773. His literary fame rests principally upon his 'Letters to his Son.'

Chettle, Henry. An English dramatist ; born in London (?), about 1565 (?); died there (?), 1607 (?). He was contemporary with Shakespeare, and his best play is probably 'Hoffman,' a tragedy. He wrote various pamphlets, popular in his day.

Chézy, Antoine Léonard de (shä-zē'). A distinguished French Orientalist (1773-1832). For him the first chair of ancient Indian languages in France was founded in 1815. Bopp, W. von Humboldt, F. von Schlegel, Burnouf, Langlois, and other renowned scholars and Orientalists, were his pupils. His principal work is an edition, with French translation, of Kâlidâsa's 'Sakuntala' (1830).

Chézy, Helmina Christiane von. A German poet and novelist ; born (von Klencke) in Berlin, Jan. 26, 1783 ; died in Geneva, Feb. 28, 1856. She produced : 'Poems' (1812); 'Heart Notes during a Pilgrimage' (1833); and similar romantic stanzas; besides 'Emma's Ordeals' (1827), a novel of merit.

Chézy, Wilhelm von. A German novelist and historical essayist, son of Helmine C.; born in Paris, March 21, 1806 ; died in Vienna, March 13, 1865. He acquitted himself creditably as a journalist, and wrote many popular tales : 'The Wandering Pupil' (1835), 'The Six Noble Passions' (1842), and 'The Last Janissary' (1853), among them; as well as 'Chivalry in Picture and Word' (1848), a study of much value.

Chiabrera, Gabriello (kē-ä-brä'rä). An Italian lyric poet (1552-1637) ; born at Savona. Impatient of dependence on the great, he again and again abandoned the courts of noble patrons, and at last settled down in his native Savona. Pindar and Anacreon were his delights among the poets, and his countrymen named him "the Italian Pindar." But his Pindaric odes have little of the grace and force of Pindar; the poet labors too patently for effect in strophe and antistrophe, in bold inversions and composite epithets; he is not spontaneous; he is dull. Yet some of his little songs after Anacreon are models of elegance and grace. His epic and dramatic poems hardly rise above mediocrity. He wrote a charming autobiographical sketch, which shows him to have been ever an honorable man, good lover, good hater, and sincere Christian.

Chiarini, Giuseppe (kē-ä-rē'nē). An Italian poet and critic; born at Arezzo, Aug. 17, 1833. He is a student of foreign literatures, especially English and German, and has been editor of literary journals. His verse is mostly lyrical, and has been collected under the titles

Poems (1874); 'In Memoriam' (1875); 'Lacrymæ' (1879); etc. It gives proof of deep poetic sensibility. He has translated some of Heine's poems, and has published critical essays on English and German poets.

Chiavacci, Vincenz (kē-ä'vä-chē). An Austrian humorist; born at Vienna, June 15, 1847. As "Dame Sopherl, a Woman of Standing" — keeping a stand in the fruit market — he began in 1883 to contribute to the Vienna journals a series of humorous remarks, in the Vienna slang, on the occurrences of the preceding week. Dame Sopherl and her whole circle of gossips, male and female, were put upon the stage (1890) and afforded infinite amusement. The author has worked this and similar veins of humor with distinguished success in a series of volumes.

Child, Francis James. An American poet and prose-writer; born in Boston, Mass., Feb. 1, 1825; died at Cambridge, Sept. 11. 1896. He was professor of rhetoric and oratory at Harvard from 1851 till 1876, when he took the chair of English literature. His principal work, 'English and Scottish Ballads,' a subject on which he was the highest authority in this country, he improved and enlarged for publication in 1886. Among his other works are: 'Four Old Plays' (1848); and a collection of 'Poems of Sorrow and Comfort' (1865).

Child, Lydia Maria. An American prose-writer; born in Medford, Mass., Feb. 11, 1802; died in Wayland, Mass., Oct. 20, 1880. Her first novel, 'Hobomok,' was written and published in 1821. She was an ardent abolitionist, and published the first book written on that subject, entitled 'Appeal for that class of Americans called African.' Dr. Channing went over to Roxbury to thank her for it. Among her numerous works are: 'Philothea,' a romance of Greece in the days of Pericles (1835); 'Fact and Fiction' (1846); 'Looking Toward Sunset' (1864); 'Miria: A Romance of the Republic' (1867); and 'Aspirations of the World' (1878). A collection of her letters, with an introduction by John G. Whittier, and an appendix by Wendell Phillips, was published in 1882.

Childs, George William. An American philanthropist, publisher, and memoir writer; born at Baltimore, Md., May 22, 1829; died at Philadelphia, Feb. 3, 1894. He published the Philadelphia Public Ledger, 1864-94. He gave a Shakespeare memorial fountain to Stratford-on-Avon, a memorial window in Westminster Abbey to Cowper and Herbert, and assisted in establishing a home for printers at Colorado Springs. He published: 'Recollections of General Grant' (1885); and 'Personal Recollections' (1889).

Chiles, Mrs. Mary Eliza (Hicks) (Hemdin). An American novelist and writer of verse; born in Kentucky, 1820. She has published: 'Louisa Elton,' a reply to 'Uncle Tom'; 'Oswyn Dudley'; etc.; and 'Select Poems.'

Chillingworth, William. An English divine and theological writer; born at Oxford, 1602; died January, 1643-44. His fame rests upon 'The Religion of Protestants a Safe Way to Salvation' (1637).

Chittenden, Lucius Eugene. An American lawyer and historical writer; born in Vermont, 1824; died at Burlington, Vt., July 22, 1900. His home was in New York. He wrote: 'Recollections of Lincoln and his Administration'; 'Personal Reminiscences, 1840–1890'; etc.

Chivers, Thomas Holley. An American writer of verse; born 1807; died 1858. His home was in Georgia. He wrote: 'Virginalia, or Songs of my Summer Nights' (1853); 'Atlanta' (1855); 'The Lost Pleiad.'

Chmelnizkij, Nikoláj Ivanovich (ċhmel-nits'-skē-ē). A Russian writer of comedy (1789–1846). He contributed largely to the reformation and elevation of the Russian stage, both by his original productions and by his translations of Regnard, Molière, and other great masters. Among his comedies are: 'The Babblers'; 'Air Castles'; 'The Waverer.' He wrote also a historical drama: 'Zenobius Bogdan; or, The Incorporation of Little Russia.'

Chmielovski, Peter (shmēl-ov'skē). A Polish historian of literature, and critic; born 1848. His early studies were made in Leipsic, but the theatre of his journalistic and literary activities has long been Warsaw. His investigations have been mostly in nineteenth-century subjects. 'Adam Mickiewicz' (1886) and 'Studies and Sketches in the History of Polish Literature' (1886) are among the important results of his labors.

Choate, Rufus. A famous American lawyer, orator and statesman; born at Essex, Mass., Oct. 1, 1799; died at Halifax, N. S., July 13, 1859. He succeeded Daniel Webster in the United States Senate (1841-45), and was long the acknowledged leader of the Massachusetts bar. He was one of the most distinguished of American orators. His works were published in 1863 (2 vols.).

Chodzko, Alexander (ċhōds'kō). A Polish poet and scholar; born in Krzywicze, July 11, 1804; died in Juvisy, Dec. 20, 1891. His versions of numerous masterpieces of Oriental literature are esteemed; but he is happiest in the 'Slav Legends of the Middle Ages' (1859) and 'Bulgarian Studies' (1875).

Chodzko, Ignacy. A Polish poet and sketch-writer; born in Zabloczyzna, Jan. 15, 1795; died there, Aug. 1, 1861. He first attempted odes in the classical style; but subsequently produced 'Lithuanian Pictures' (1840-62) and 'Lithuanian Traditions' (1852-58), vivid prose sketches of manners and people, portraying especially the Lithuanian nobility of the 18th century.

Chomjakoff, Alexéj Stepánovich (ċhōm'yä-kōf). A Russian poet, dramatist, and controversialist; born in Moscow, May 13, 1804; died there, Oct. 5, 1860. His writings — particularly 'The Pseudo-Demetrius' (1833: a tragedy), his collected 'Poems' (1844), and 'Letters to the

Slavs in Moscow' (1860)—embody an essentially Russian conservatism.

Chorley, Henry Fothergill. An English critic and miscellaneous writer; born in Blackley Hurst, Lancashire, Dec. 15, 1808; died in London, Feb. 16, 1872. His criticisms appeared mostly in the Athenæum, of London, displaying fine perception and exquisite taste in matters connected with literature and music. His novels, however ('Conti,' 'The Prodigy,' and 'The Lion'), are failures from the popular point of view, although finely written; and his plays, with the exception of 'Old Love and New Fortune,' are weak.

Chortatzis, Georgios (chor-täts'ēs). A modern Greek dramatic poet, who seems to have been a native of Crete and to have flourished about 1620. His tragedy of 'Erophile' (1637; new ed. 1879) is the first play written in the "new" or modern Greek; the work possesses many merits, and was at one time very popular because of its epigrammatic sententiousness, but its imitation of Giraldi's 'Orbecche' is palpable.

Chrétien de Troyes (kret-yen dĕ trwä). The greatest of the early French romancers; 12th century. Though he won high fame as a lyrist, his renown is based on his epic compositions, especially on his stories of King Arthur and the Round Table. His epic of 'King Marcus and the Fair Ysault' is lost; but these remain: 'Irec and Enid'; 'Cligès'; 'The Knight of La Charette'; 'The Knight with the Lion'; 'Perceval the Welshman.' The last is his most considerable work, but it does not come from his hand alone, being continued and completed by Gautier de Denet and Menassier. In this piece are wrought into one story the legend of the Holy Grail and that of Arthur, which thereafter were not divorced. His language and versification were models for troubadours and romancers for a long time; and from him the Arthurian poets to the end of the 13th century borrowed episodes, themes, situations, characters, and all manner of poets' devices. Chrétien was a master of invention, fashioned for himself a competent literary vehicle, and made most effective use of his large knowledge of men and manners.

Christen, Ada (kris'ten), pseudonym of Christiane Breden. An Austrian poet and novelist; born in Vienna, March 6, 1844. Her first success was the volume of poems 'Songs of One Lost' (1868); a collection evincing delicacy of sentiment blended with the vigor of health. Her subsequent verse, in 'Shadows' (1873) and 'From the Deep' (1878), revealed an accession of power. Her novel of 'Ella' (1873) is a fair production, and the drama 'Faustina' (1871) merits praise; but her best prose is in the book of tales and sketches called 'From Life' (1876).

Christiansen, Arne Einar (krist'yen-sen). A Danish poet; born at Copenhagen, July 20, 1861. His first very promising prose comedy, 'Lindow's Bairns' (1881). was followed by the

prose tragedy 'Nero' (1885). The author had meantime traveled extensively in Europe and the East; then, together with a series of prose dramas, he produced three historical and romantic plays in verse. He makes dexterous use of the resources of dramaturgic art, and gives his native genius free play regardless of literary fashions and conventions.

Christopulos, Athanasios (kris-top'ö-los). A Greek poet and scholar; born in Kastoria, Macedonia, 1772 (or 1770); died in Wallachia, Jan. 29, 1847. His best work is 'Love's Self-Vindication' (Paris, 1833), a collection published originally as 'Erotica and Bacchica' (1811), and comprising love lays and drinking songs.

Chrysander, Friedrich (kris-än'der). A German historian of music; born in Lübtheen, Mecklenburg, July 8, 1826; died at Bergersdorf, Sept. 4, 1901. He was an authority on the annals and epochs of music, a biography of Handel (1858–67, vols. i.–iii., first half) being his masterpiece. He also wrote many critical papers on the oratorio and other forms, in addition to editing musical periodicals; but his attempts in musical composition were not happy.

Chrysippus (kris'ip-us). A famed Greek philosopher; about 280–206 B.C.; born probably at Soli in Cilicia. He attended at Athens the lectures of Zeno, at least of Cleanthes; after the death of Cleanthes he became head of the school. His writings were exceedingly numerous, but only fragments remain. The loss is not very much to be regretted, if we may judge of the quality of the whole mass by specimens preserved for us in ancient authors. But there were precious gems of thought scattered through the rubbish of hair-splitting refinements and mere anilities; and it is to be regretted that these were not timely "tried out" and the rest shot into the dust-hole. This service Seneca could have done most acceptably,—a reverent disciple of Chrysippus, but also an outspoken critic of his writings, as we see in his treatise on 'Kindnesses': "I may seem to be setting Chrysippus to rights: he is a great man, but after all a Greek; his all too fine analysis is worked overmuch; even when you think he is getting at the heart of the matter, he punctures only, instead of boring through."

Chrysoloras, Manuel (kris-ō-lō'räs). A Greek scholar; born in Constantinople, about 1355; died at Constance, April 15, 1415. He was the first to attain eminence in Italy as a teacher of the literature and language of Greece: a work by him called 'Queries' (Erotemata) long remained authoritative on Greek grammar.

Chrysostom, St. John. A Greek Church father; born in Antioch, Syria, 350 (?); died at Comana, 407. His works, consisting of homilies, commentaries, liturgies, epistles, etc., are comprised in 13 vols. fol. (1718).

Church, Mrs. Ella Rodman (MacIlvane). An American miscellaneous writer, better known as "Ella Rodman"; born in New

York State, 1831. She has written: 'Flights of Fancy'; 'Grandmother's Recollections' (1851); 'Flyers and Crawlers, or Talks about Insects' (1884); 'How to Furnish a Home'; 'Money-Making for Ladies'; etc.

Church, Francis Pharcellus. An American editor; born in Rochester, N. Y., Feb. 22, 1839. First publisher and editor of the Army and Navy Journal; afterward, with his brother, established and edited the Galaxy magazine. He is also a leading editorial writer of the daily journals of New York. Died 1906.

Church, William Conant. An American journalist; born in Rochester, N. Y., Aug. 11, 1836. He became the publisher of the New York Sun in 1860, and was war correspondent of the Times (1861-62). In conjunction with his brother Francis he established the Army and Navy Journal (1863) and the Galaxy magazine (1866); and has been a contributor to the Century and other periodicals. He has written a notable biography of General Grant.

Churchill, Charles. An English satirical poet; born in Westminster, February 1731; died at Boulogne, Nov. 4, 1764. He won his fame with 'The Rosciad,' a satire upon the actors of the time, in which only Garrick and some few popular actresses are praised. His capacity for ridicule was so great that 'The Ghost'; 'The Farewell'; 'The Conference'; 'The Author'; and 'The Prophecy of Famine,' proved exceedingly popular. He is almost without a peer in his special field.

Chwostoff, Dmitrij Ivanovich, Count (kvos'-tŏf *or* kwos'tŭf). A Russian poet and states man; born in St. Petersburg, July 19, 1757; died there, Nov. 3, 1835. His public career was distinguished. The four volumes of his 'Works' (1817) comprise odes and miscellaneous poems.

Ciampi, Ignazio (chē-äm'pē). An Italian poet and historian (1824-80); born in Rome. He was a jurist, and from 1874 till his death was professor of modern history in the University of Rome. Among his poetical works are some imitations of the Russian Pushkin; an epic, 'Stella'; and two volumes of 'Various Poems.' He wrote several works on the history of literature, also biographies and histories of special periods. His principal work appeared posthumously: 'Modern History,' from 1492 to the Peace of Westphalia.

Ciampoli, Domenico (chē-äm'pō-lē). An Italian novelist; born at Atezza in Abruzzi, Aug. 25, 1855. His stories and romances are to a great extent pictures of life among the peasantry and mountain folk of Southern Italy. He has also written romances of a less local character: 'Diana'; 'The Unknown.' He has devoted special study to Slavic literature, and published several volumes on that subject.

Cibber, Colley. An English dramatist; born in London, Nov. 6, 1671; died there, Dec. 12, 1757. He was one of the most successful stagers of plays in the history of the theatre,

and he saw every effect with the eyes of the audience. Hence his dramatic works—particularly 'Love's Last Shift,' a farce; 'Love Makes a Man'; 'She Would and She Would Not'; and 'The Careless Husband,' comedies—are masterpieces of construction, although their literary qualities are not up to the high level one might expect. He portrayed the fop, however, with an infinite felicity; and not a few of his scenes are unexampled as specimens of effective action unmarred by meaningless detail.

Cicci, Maria Luigia (chē'chē). An Italian poet; born in Pisa, Nov. 14, 1760; died March 8, 1794. She fell early under the influence of Dante's great poem, and applied herself devotedly to letters, philosophy, physics, and history; her collected 'Poems' (1796) showing the results in refinement of imagery, and polished though perhaps pedantic taste.

Cicero, Marcus Tullius (sis'ẹ-rō). The prince of Roman orators, a statesman, and a distinguished writer on philosophy, rhetoric, morals, etc. (106-43 B. C.); born at Arpinum. He wrote several treatises on the art of oratory, the chief of these being: 'The Orator, to Marcus Brutus'; 'Of the Orator'; and 'Brutus, or of Illustrious Orators.' Of his philosophical writings we have: 'The Academics'; 'Tusculan Disputations'; 'Of Definitions of Good and Evil.' Of discussions of moral questions we have the practical treatise 'Of Mutual Offices.' Theological notions are examined in the two treatises 'Of Divinations' and 'Of the Nature of the Gods.' In the shorter treatises 'Of Old Age,' 'Of Friendship,' 'Of Consolation,' he collects such precepts of philosophy as have special application in the decline of life. The letters of Cicero to his friends (and some of theirs to him) are extant to the number of 864, distributed under these titles: 'To Intimate Friends' (16 books), extending over the years 62-43 B.C.; 'To Atticus' (also 16 books), years 68-43; 'To Quintus,' his brother (3 books), years 60-54; and 'Correspondence with M. Brutus' (2 books), belonging to the time immediately after Cæsar's assassination.

Ciconi, Teobaldo (chē-kō'nē). An Italian comic poet (1824-63); born at San Daniele in the district of Friuli. His first collection of lyric poems was published in 1853, and the same year his drama 'Eleonora of Toldo'; neither had much success. But in 1857 his comedy 'The Little Stray Sheep' was received with hearty favor throughout Italy; and not less gratifying was the success of the pieces which succeeded it.

Cieco da Ferrara (chē-ā'kō). An Italian poet of the latter half of the 15th century. The true name of this « Blindman of Ferrara » was Francesco Bello. His romantic epic 'The Man of Mamre' celebrates in 45 cantos the adventures of an Oriental prince. It is planless, and makes a curious jumble of Christian ideas and ancient myths; yet it is not without traits of lively invention and scintillations of wit. It was first printed after the Cieco's death.

Cienfuegos, Nicasio Alvarez de (thē-enfwä'gōs). A Spanish poet (1764-1809); born in Madrid. He was an alumnus of the School of Poets at Salamanca, and passed his life at Madrid wholly in the service of the Muses. His tragedy 'Pitaco' won him membership in the Spanish Academy: it is his masterpiece. He wrote two other tragedies; and a comedy, 'The Magnanimous Sisters.' His tragedies are hampered by the rules of a pseudo-classicism, but betray the inspiration of noble ideas. His genius was lyric; and in songs, odes, and elegies he proved himself a genine poet.

Cinna, C. Helvius (sin'ä). A Roman poet, the companion of Catullus. His poem 'Smyrna' has perished, all but a few fragments. He was killed by a mob on the night of Julius Cæsar's funeral.

Cino da Pistoja (chē'nō dä pēs-tō'yä). An Italian poet (1270-1337); born at Pistoia. By profession he was a jurisconsult, and he wrote a celebrated commentary on the Justinian Code. Thereafter till his death he was professor of jurisprudence in Italian universities. He was an intimate friend of Dante. His love songs ('Rimes') addressed to his mistress Selvaggia are full of tender passion; they entitle him to a place among the lyric precursors of Petrarch.

Cintio or **Cinzio.** See **Giraldi.**

Cladel, Léon (klä-del'). A French romancist (1855-92); born at Montauban. He rose suddenly into prominence with his story 'The Ridiculous Martyrs' (1862), a satirical description of the lower walks of literature in Paris. This first success was repeated with the later novels: 'Eral the Tamer'; 'One Qouael'; the 'My Peasants' series; 'Barefoot'; 'A Woman under Ban' (for this he suffered four weeks' imprisonment); and many others.

Claflin, Mary Bucklin. An American prose-writer; born in Hopkinton, Mass., July 1825; died in Whitinsville, Mass., June 13, 1896. She was the wife of Governor Claflin of Massachusetts. For eighteen years she was a trustee of Boston University; and of Wellesley College from its foundation till her death. Among her publications are: 'Brampton Sketches'; 'Recollections of Whittier'; and 'Under the Elms.'

Clairmonte, Mrs. See **Egerton, George.**

Clairville, Louis François (klär-vēl'). A French writer of light comedy (1811-79); born at Lyons. Author of more than 220 comedies, farces, and comic-opera libretti. Among his most successful operettas are: 'Daphnis and Chloe' (1849); 'Mme. Angot's Daughter' (1873); among his vaudevilles: 'Property Is Robbery' (1848); 'Antoinette's Temptations' (1850); 'Cinderella' (1866).

Clare, John. An English poet; born in Helpstone, near Peterborough, July 13, 1793; died at Northampton, May 20, 1864. He was an agricultural laborer, absolutely uneducated; and wrote 'Poems, Descriptive of Rural Life and Scenery,' in which a talent not far removed from genius attains many fervent and moving effects.

Clarendon, Edward Hyde, Earl of. An English historian and statesman; born at Dinton, Wiltshire, Feb. 18, 1608-9; died in exile at Rouen, France, Dec. 9, 1674. His 'History of the Rebellion and Civil Wars in England' and 'History of the Civil War in Ireland' are among the foremost authorities for the events and the political biography of the time; and their force, acuteness, and dignified elevation of style give them a high place as literature. His 'Essay on an Active and Contemplative Life' also contains many observations good in matter and style.

Claretie, Jules (klär-tē'). A French novelist and dramatist; born at Limoges, Dec. 3, 1840. He has written a long series of very successful novels, the most noteworthy of them being: 'Madeleine Bertin' (1868); 'The Million' (1882); 'Monsieur the Minister,' (1882); 'Noris, Manners of the Time' (1883); 'The American Woman' (1892). He wrote also some striking chapters of contemporary history, as 'The Revolution of 1870-71'; 'Paris Besieged'; 'Five Years After: Alsace and Lorraine since Annexation.' His dramatic compositions relate mostly to the time of the great Revolution. He became administrator of the Comédie Française in 1885, and was chosen member of the Academy in 1888.

Clark, Alexander. A prominent American Methodist divine and miscellaneous writer; born in Jefferson county, O., 1834; died in Georgia, July 6, 1879. He was editor of the Methodist Recorder (1870-79). He wrote: the 'Old Log Schoolhouse' (1864); 'Workaday Christianity' (1870); 'Rambles in Europe' (1877); 'Ripples on the River,' verse; etc.

Clark, Charles Heber. ["Max Adeler."] An American journalist and humorist; born 1841. He is attached to the Philadelphia Evening Bulletin, and editor of the Textile Record He has written: 'Out of the Hurly-Burly' (1874); 'Elbow-Room' (1876); 'Fortunate Island, and Other Stories' (1881); 'The Quakeress' (1905).

Clark, George Hunt. An American poet; born in Northampton, Mass., 1809; died in Hartford, Conn., Aug. 20, 1881. He was a frequent contributor to Putnam's, Knickerbocker, and other journals. His published poems include: 'Now and Then'; 'The News'; and a collection of humorous and sentimental pieces entitled 'Undertow of a Trade-Wind Surf.'

Clark, Henry James. An American naturalist and prose-writer; born in Easton, Mass., June 22, 1826; died in Amherst, Mass., July 1, 1873. He was associated in work with Agassiz for several years; also was professor in many of our leading colleges and universities. Among his many contributions to literature are: 'Mind in Nature, or the Origin of Life, and the Mode of Development of Animals' (1865); 'Claims for Scientific Property' (1863).

Clark, James Gowdy. An American song-writer; born in Constantia, N. Y., June 28, 1830; died September 1897. Known as the composer of the words and music of many popular songs, was himself a noted singer, and author of 'Poetry and Song' (1886).

Clark, Lewis Gaylord. An American journalist and humorous writer; born in Otisco, N. Y., March 5, 1810; died in Piermont, N. Y., Nov. 3, 1873. In 1834 he became editor of the Knickerbocker Magazine; and with Irving, Bryant, Longfellow, Halleck, and Willis, as contributors, made it the foremost literary publication of that time, and an inspiration to a higher standard of periodical literature. The 'Editor's Table,' written by him, overflowed with amusing stories and witty sayings. The 'Knickerbocker Sketch-Book' (1850), and 'Knick-Knacks from an Editor's Table' (1853), are his only publications in book form.

Clark, Willis Gaylord. An American poet, twin brother of Lewis Gaylord; born in Otisco, N. Y., March 5, 1810; died in Philadelphia, Pa., June 12, 1841. He became associate editor of the Columbian Star, a religious weekly paper (1830), but resigned shortly after to take charge of the Philadelphia Gazette. His longest poem is 'The Spirit of Life' (1833). A complete edition of his poems, edited by his brother, appeared in 1847.

Clarke, Charles Cowden. An English prose-writer and versifier; born in Enfield, Middlesex, Dec. 15, 1787; died at Genoa, March 13, 1877. He produced 'Tales from Chaucer' and 'Shakespeare's Characters,' besides lectures and essays innumerable; and 'Carmina Minima,' a volume of verse. See also Mary Cowden.

Clarke, Edward Daniel. An English traveler and descriptive writer; born at Willington, Essex, June 5, 1769; died at London, March 9, 1822. He investigated the topographical and kindred antiquities of Greece and the Hellene lands most thoroughly, his great work being 'Travels in Various Countries of Europe, Asia, and Africa' (1810-23); but a dissertation on 'The Tomb of Alexander' (1805) is particularly scholarly, its subject being the sarcophagus now in the British Museum.

Clarke, Hyde. An English writer of miscellaneous prose; born in London, 1815; died there, March 1, 1895. In diplomacy, civil engineering, and scholarship he was equally at home, his versatility being conspicuous in 'Theory of Railway Investment'; 'Colonization in our Indian Empire' (1857); 'Comparative Philology' (1858); and 'Examination of the Legend of Atlantis' (1886). He compiled a useful abridged English Dictionary.

Clarke, James Freeman. An American Unitarian clergyman and prose-writer; born in Hanover, N. H., April 4, 1810; died in Boston, Mass., June 8, 1888. He was one of the clearest thinkers and most lucid and graceful writers of America. In 1852, together with Emerson and William H. Channing, he prepared the 'Memoirs of Margaret Fuller d'Ossoli.' His chief work was 'Ten Great Religions' (1871-83). Among the others were: 'Self-Culture' (1882); 'Anti-Slavery Days' (1884); 'Every-Day Religion' (1886); and 'Vexed Questions' (1886).

Clarke, Marcus Andrew Hyslop. An Australian novelist; born in London, April 24, 1846; died in Melbourne, Australia, Aug. 2, 1881. He went to the island in his twenty-fourth year, took up journalism, and acquired the experience of bush life and the knowledge of antipodean men and things of which such brilliant use is made in 'His Natural Life,' a striking convict story; 'Holiday Peak'; 'Old Tales of a New Country'; and other vivid fictions.

Clarke, Mary Bayard. An American poet and prose-writer; born in Raleigh, N. C., about 1830; died in 1886. While living in Cuba, she published verses signed « Tenella ». After her return in 1855 she wrote 'Reminiscences of Cuba' for the Southern Literary Messenger. Among her works are war lyrics and translations from Victor Hugo; also prose articles signed « Stuart Leigh.» In 1870 was published her poem 'Clytie and Zenobia, or the Lily and the Palm'; and 'Wood Notes,' a compilation of North Carolina verse.

Clarke, Mary Cowden. An English story-writer, essayist, and Shakespearean scholar; born (Novello) in London, June 22, 1809; died at Genoa, Jan. 12, 1898. She married Charles Cowden Clarke, with whom she wrote the 'Shakespeare Key' and compiled an edition of Shakespeare's plays. Her own 'Complete Concordance' is universally known. Her novels are: 'A Rambling Story' and 'The Iron Cousin,' pleasing and graceful prose idyls. 'World-Noted Women' contains able biographical studies.

Clarke, McDonald. An American poet; born in Bath, Me., June 18, 1878; died in New York, March 5, 1842. He was an eccentric character, familiarly known as «the mad poet»; and was the subject of an amusing poem by Halleck, called 'The Discarded.' The subjects of Clarke's verses were usually the belles of the city and topics of the day. His works include: 'Poetic Sketches' (1826) and 'The Belles of Broadway' (1833). One of his poems was « Now twilight lets her curtain down.»

Clarke, Rebecca Sophia. [« Sophie May.»] An American novelist and popular writer of children's stories; born at Norridgewock, Me., 1833. Died Aug. 16, 1906. She wrote the 'Dotty Dimple' series, 'Flaxie Frizzle' stories, etc.; and of novels: 'Her Friend's Lover'; 'The Asbury Twins'; 'Quinnebasset Girls'; etc.

Clarke, Richard H. An American prose-writer; born in Washington, D. C., July 3, 1827. He was made president of the Society of American Authors in 1891. 'The New Crusade of the Nineteenth Century,' relating to the Church and slavery, was an important article. Other works of his are: 'Socialism in

America'); 'Biography of Commodore John Barry, Founder of the American Navy': 'Father Sebastian Rale'; an answer to Gladstone on 'Maryland Toleration'; and an'Illustrated History of the Catholic Church in the United States'; and 'Life of Pope Leo XIII.'

Clarke, Samuel. An English theologian and philosopher; born in Norwich, Oct. 11, 1675; died May 17, 1729. He took holy orders, and almost immediately commanded recognition as a thinker and disputant. In his three masterpieces, 'Demonstration of the Being and Attributes of God' (1705-6); 'Verity and Certitude of Natural and Revealed Religion' (1705); and 'Discourse Concerning the Inalterable Obligations of Natural Religion' (1708), we get the measure of the man, and they adequately explain his contemporary eminence. His edition of Homer is good; as are, in fact, nearly all his varied literary productions.

Clason, Isaac Starr. An American poet and actor; born in New York in 1789; died in London, 1834. He published 'Don Juan, Cantos 17 and 18' supplementary to Byron's poem (1825). It gave him his reputation; and was followed by 'Horace in New York,' a collection of poems full of the local gossip of the time, and containing some touching lines on the death of Thomas Addis Emmet.

Claudianus, Claudius (klâ-di-ā'nus A Roman poet of the 4th century. He stood high in favor with the emperors Honorius and Arcadius, and was promoted to the highest honors of the State. He was the last of the non-Christian poets of Rome, and stands high above his contemporaries, though his style and matter have the faults and blemishes of that decadent period,—bombastic expression and flattery of the great. His greatest work is an epic, 'The Rape of Proserpine.' His 'Epithalamium on the Marriage of Honorius' has appended to it some 'Fescennine Verses': both, especially the latter, would seem to continue the true Roman poetic tradition for that kind of compositions. Such poems would not be tolerated at a marriage feast in our times. Besides the works named, we have a considerable number of other poems by Claudianus.

Claudius, Matthias (klou'dē-ös). A noted German poet; born at Reinfeld, Holstein, Aug. 15, 1740; died at Altona, Jan. 21, 1815. Though his first literary venture, 'Trifles and Tales,' had little originality, being an imitation of a work by Gerstenberg under a similar title, he is in his later works one of the most original of German authors. His simple ballads, 'Join in with Clear and Full Accord'; 'O Crown the Bowl'; 'Once Lived a Giant Goliath,' became popular favorites.

Clauren, H. (klou'ren), pseudonym of Carl Heun. A German story-writer and dramatist; born in Dobrilugk, March 20, 1771; died at Berlin, Aug. 2, 1854. He held numerous official positions after studying law, but story-telling and farce-writing occupied the greater part of his time. 'The Sombre Room' and 'Mimili'

were two of his early and successful tales. His poem 'The King Called, and All, All Came,' and his farces, are still remembered. He blended sentimentality and realism in a popularly taking but inartistic manner.

Clavijo y Fajardo, José (kläv-ē'HŌ ē fä-Här'dō). A Spanish journalist and prose-writer; born in the Canary Islands, about 1730; died at Madrid, 1806. He came young to the Spanish capital, and demonstrated his ability to such purpose that prosperity and fame were his very early, the Pensador and the Mercurio being distinctively journals made by himself. He also translated Buffon's 'Natural History.' He is the hero of Goethe's 'Clavigo.'

Clay, Cassius Marcellus. A distinguished American statesman; born in Madison County, Ky., Oct. 19, 1810. He was one of the most powerful of the Southern Abolitionists. In 1862-69 he was minister to Russia. He wrote his own 'Life and Memoirs.' Died July 22, 1903.

Clay, Henry. An eminent American orator and statesman; born in Hanover, Va., April 12, 1777; died at Washington, D. C., June 29, 1852. He was United States Senator from Kentucky, 1806-7, 1810-11; Member of Congress from Kentucky, 1811-21, 1823-25; Speaker of the House, 1811-14, 1815-20, 1823-25; Presidential candidate, 1824; Secretary of State, 1825-29; United States Senator, 1831-42, 1849-52; Presidential candidate, 1832 and 1844; one of the formulators of the Missouri Compromise, 1820, and of the Compromise of 1850; author of the tariff of 1833. His 'Complete Works' (1857) are edited by Colton.

Cleanthes (klē-an'thēs). A Greek philosopher; born at Assos, 331 B. C.; died, 232 B. C. He was the founder of Stoicism. His works are lost, with the exception of a 'Hymn to Zeus' and some few fragments.

Clemens, Jeremiah. An American statesman, lawyer, and novelist; born at Huntsville, Ala., Dec. 28, 1814; died there, May 21, 1865. He was U. S. Senator from Alabama (1849-53). He wrote: 'Bernard Lisle' (1856); 'Mustang Grey' (1858); 'Tobias Wilson' (1865); etc.

Clemens, Samuel Langhorne. ("Mark Twain.") A distinguished American humorist; born in Missouri, Nov. 30, 1835. His works include: 'The Jumping Frog' (1867); 'The Innocents Abroad' (1869); 'Roughing It' (1872); 'A Tramp Abroad' (1880); 'The Prince and the Pauper' (1882); 'Life on the Mississippi' (1883); 'The Gilded Age' (1874: with Charles Dudley Warner); 'Old Times on the Mississippi'; 'Tom Sawyer'; 'Huckleberry Finn'; 'A Yankee at King Arthur's Court'; 'Pudd'nhead Wilson'; 'The Personal Recollections of Joan of Arc'; 'Following the Equator' (1897); 'The Man that Corrupted Hadleyburg' (1900); 'Articles on Christian Science' (1903); 'A Dog's Tale' (1903); 'A Horse's Tale' (1906).

Clesse, Antoine (kles'e). A Belgian popular poet (1816-89); born at The Hague. To the day of his death he followed his trade of armorer. His first ballad, 'Godfrey de Bouillon,' won for him a gold medal. His popular songs 'Beer' and 'The Family Name' (meaning Belgian, including Fleming, Walloon, etc.), came into great favor with the people. He wrote also a comedy, 'A Poet.' Two volumes of 'Songs' (1866-88) contain all his popular ballads, with the music.

Cleveland, Aaron. An American writer of prose and verse; born in Haddam, Conn., Feb. 3, 1744; died in New Haven, Conn., Sept. 21, 1815. In 1763 was written his best poem, 'The Philosopher and Boy.' In 1775 he published a poem on 'Slavery'; also a number of fugitive verses. He was the great-grandfather of President Cleveland.

Cleveland, Rose Elizabeth. An American prose-writer, sister of Grover Cleveland; born in Fayetteville, N. Y., 1846. After the inauguration of her brother (1885) she became the " mistress of the White House," remaining there until 1886. Miss Cleveland published a book of essays and lectures entitled 'George Eliot's Poetry, and Other Studies' (1885); and 'The Long Run,' a novel (1886).

Clinch, Charles Powell. An American poet and play-writer; born in New York city, Oct. 20, 1797; died there, Dec. 16, 1880. For many years he was editorial writer, and literary and dramatic critic, for the press; also writer of many poems, theatrical addresses, and dramas. Among the latter are: 'The Spy'; 'The Expelled Collegiates'; and 'The First of May.'

Clinton, De Witt. A famous American lawyer and statesman; born at Little Britain, N. Y., March 2, 1769; died at Albany, N. Y., Feb. 11, 1828. He was United States Senator from New York (1802); mayor of New York city (1803-7, 1809-10, 1811-15); lieutenant-governor (1811-13); candidate for President (1812); governor (1817-23, 1825-28). He was the chief originator of the Erie Canal (1817-25). Besides purely political works, addresses, etc., he wrote: 'Antiquities of Western New York'; 'Natural History and Internal Revenues of New York'; etc.

Clough, Arthur Hugh (kluf). An English poet; born in Liverpool, Jan. 1, 1819; died at Florence, Italy, Nov. 13, 1861. His works comprise: 'The Bothie of Toper-na-Fuosich [afterwards Tober-na-Vuolich], a Long Vacation Pastoral' (1848); 'Ambarvalia: Poems by Thomas Burbidge and A. H. Clough' (1849); 'Plutarch's Lives: the Translation called Dryden's Corrected' (1859-64 and 1876); 'Poems with Memoir' (by F. T. Palgrave) (1862); 'Poems and Prose Remains' (1869); and one or two more.

Clymer, Ella Dietz. An American poet; born in New York, 185-. She began her career as an actress in 1872; in 1881 she abandoned the stage. She has contributed to literature three volumes of poems: 'The Triumph of Love' (1878); 'The Triumph of Time' (1884);

and 'The Triumph of Life' (1885). She was one of the founders of the " Sorosis" Society, and its president in 1889.

Coan, Titus (kō'an). A noted American missionary; born at Killingworth, Conn., Feb. 1, 1801; died at Hilo, Hawaii, Dec. 1, 1882. After spending several months (1833-34) on a dangerous exploring expedition in Patagonia, he went to the Sandwich Islands (1835), occupying the Hilo station forty-seven years, and in that time converting 14,000 natives. He wrote: 'Adventures in Patagonia' (1880); 'Life in Hawaii' (1881).

Coan, Titus Munson. An American man of letters and critic, son of Titus M. the elder; born in the Sandwich Islands, 1836. He now resides in New York. He has written 'An Ounce of Prevention'; Topics of the Time'; 'Hawaian Ethnography.'

Coates, Florence (Earle) [Mrs. Edward H.]. An American poet; born 1850, and now residing in Philadelphia, Pa. She has made many contributions to various magazines. Among her uncollected poems are: 'Conscience'; 'Song'; 'To France — 1894'; 'Combatants'; 'Survival'; 'Mine and Thine' (1904).

Cobb, Joseph Beckham. An American novelist and miscellaneous writer; born in Georgia, 1819; died 1858. He wrote: 'The Creole' (1850), a novel; 'Mississippi Scenes' (1851); 'Leisure Labors' (1858).

Cobb, Sylvanus. An American novelist; born in Waterville, Me., 1823; died in Hyde Park, Mass., July 2, 1887. He was editor and publisher of a periodical called the Rechabite. Besides contributing to other publications, he was a most prolific story-writer. His most popular novels are: 'The King's Talisman' (1851); 'The Patriot Cruiser' (1859); and 'Ben Hamed' (1864).

Cobbe, Frances Power. An Irish writer on religion and morals; born in Dublin, 1822. She has written 'Intuitive Morals' (1855); 'Religious Duty'; 'Hours of Work and Play' (1867); 'Duties of Women'; 'The Hopes of the Human Race, Hereafter and Here'; and other important works. She has been praised for her expositions of the views of Theodore Parker. Died at Hengurt, Wales, April 5, 1904.

Cobbett, William. An English essayist and political writer; born in Farnham, March 9, 1762; died at Normandy Farm, near Farnham, June 1835. The son of a farm hand, he had no early advantages, but a great gift for controversy; and he plunged warmly into the social and economic and political discussions of his day. He visited this country, and wrote here for a time under the name of " Peter Porcupine." He is at his best in his countless pamphlets, and in 'The Political Proteus,' 'Legacy to Laborers,' and 'Advice to Young Men.'

Cobden, Richard. A great English political economist; born in Sussex, June 3, 1804; died

8

at London, April 2, 1865. He was a manufacturer, but opposed his class; led the Corn Law agitation; and entered Parliament in 1841. He visited this country in 1854. His 'Political Writings' (1867) and 'Speeches on Questions of Public Policy' (1870) are very notable in the history of agitation.

Codemo, Luigia (kō-dā'mō). An Italian novelist; born Sept. 5, 1828, died 1898. She made extensive travels (1838–50), and in 1851 became the wife of the Chevalier Karl von Gerstenbrand. Her first work, 'Memoirs of a Peasant' (1856), evinced a true insight into lowly life; and in the numerous sketches and tales that followed it, she showed a profound sympathy with the common people. Her writings passed through several editions. Among her works are: 'Miseries and Splendors of the Poor'; 'The New Rich'; 'A Lady of Heart.'

Codman, John. A noted American sea-captain and miscellaneous writer; born in Dorchester, Mass., Oct. 16, 1814; died in Boston, April 6, 1900. He wrote: 'Sailors' Life and Sailors' Yarns' (1847); 'The Mormon Country' (1876); 'Round Trip by Way of Panama, etc.' (1879); 'Winter Sketches from the Saddle' (1888), etc.

Coffin, Charles Carleton. An American novelist and lecturer; born in Boscawen, N. H., July 26, 1823; died in Brookline, Mass., March 2, 1896. He began life as a civil engineer; afterward gave his attention to telegraphy. In 1851 he began to write for the Boston papers; and during the Civil War and the Austro-Prussian War of 1866 was war correspondent for the Boston Journal, writing over the signature of "Carleton." His books include: 'Days and Nights on the Battle-Field' (1864); 'Our New Way Round the World' (1869); 'Story of Liberty' (1878); 'Life of Garfield' (1883); and 'The Drum-Beat of the Nation' (1887), the first volume of a series.

Coffin, Robert Barry. An American journalist and miscellaneous writer; born in Hudson, N. Y., July 21, 1826; died in Fordham, N. Y., June 10, 1886. He was on the staff of the Home Journal of New York (1858), and was also art critic of the Evening Post. His humorous sketches, which have appeared in many periodicals over the pen-name "Barry Gray," have been extensively read. Among his publications are: 'My Married Life at Hillside' (1865); 'Cakes and Ale at Woodbine' (1868); and 'The Home of Cooper' (1872).

Coffin, Robert Stevenson. An American poet; born in Brunswick, Me., July 14, 1797; died in Rowley, Mass., May 7, 1827. His first contributions in verse to the periodicals were over the signature of "The Boston Bard." He published 'The Oriental Harp: Poems of the Boston Bard' (1826), in which are included his most notable verses.

Coggeshall, William Turner. An American journalist; born in Lewistown, Pa., Sept. 6, 1824; died in Quito, Ecuador, Aug. 2, 1867. From 1841 to 1866 he was editorially connected with a number of newspapers, including the Cincinnati Gazette, the Springfield Republican (1862), and the Ohio State Journal (1865). He was United States minister to Ecuador from June 1866 until his death. His works include: 'Home Hits and Hints' (1859); 'Poets and Poetry of the West' (1860); and 'The Journeys of Lincoln as President-Elect, and as President Martyred' (1865).

Colardeau, Charles Pierre (kō-lär-dō). A French poet; born at Janville, 1732; died 1776. He was elected to the French Academy in 1776, having written 'The Men of Prometheus' and 'Epistle to M. Duhamel.'

Colban, Adolphine Marie (kol'bän). A Norwegian novelist (1814–84). Left a widow without resources at 36, she went to Paris, where a lady of quality sent to the printer some of the widow's letters to her, entitling the collection 'Letters of a Barbarian.' Parisian society was captivated, and the author decided to exercise her newly discovered talent by writing stories in her own language. Between 1869 and 1881 she published seven volumes of tales, charming for their fine spiritual insight and their warm human sympathy; they were nearly all translated into German. Among them 'Jeg Lever' is perhaps the most noteworthy.

Colenso, John William. An English theologian; born 1814; died 1883. He became Bishop of Natal, South Africa, and wrote 'The Pentateuch and Book of Joshua Critically Examined' (1862).

Coleridge, Hartley. An English poet and literary critic (1796–1849), son of Samuel Taylor; born at Cleveden. From Oxford he went to London, and there published some exquisite sonnets in the London Magazine. He inherited defects of character and will, and never realized the promise of his great talents. His writings in prose are 'Biographia Borealis' (1833); 'The Worthies of Yorkshire and Lancashire' (1836); and a volume of 'Essays and Marginalia.' His brother Derwent published a biography and his poems (2 vols., 1850).

Coleridge, Samuel Taylor. An English poet and philosopher; born at Ottery St. Mary, Devonshire, Oct. 21, 1772; died July 25, 1834. The authorities on the works of Coleridge are very numerous and important. Among the many titles under which his works were published, the following are probably most noteworthy: 'Fall of Robespierre' (1794), a play of which he wrote the first act; 'Moral and Political Lecture Delivered at Bristol' (1795); 'Conciones ad Populum' (1795), being addresses to the people; 'The Plot Discovered' (1795), a political pamphlet; 'Poems on Various Subjects' (1796); 'The Destiny of Nations' (1828), first published in Southey's 'Joan of Arc'; 'Ode to the Departing Year' (1796); 'Fears in Solitude' (1798); 'Wallenstein' (1800); 'Remorse, a Tragedy' (1813); 'Christabel,' with 'Kubla Khan' and 'Pains of Sleep' (1816); 'Biographia Literaria' (1817); 'Aids to Reflection'

(1825); 'Table Talk' (1835); 'Confessions of an Inquiring Spirit' (1840), the last two posthumous. The 'Ancient Mariner' was first published in 1798, in a volume of 'Lyrical Ballads' (with Wordsworth).

Coleridge, Sara. An English poet, daughter of Samuel Taylor; born at Greta Hall, near Keswick, Dec. 22, 1802; died in London, May 3, 1852. The genius of her father seemed almost to have inspired her 'Phantasmion,' a ballad of fairyland. Her classical learning and scientific attainments made her an authority on some of the most abstruse subjects.

Coles, Abraham. An American prose-writer and poet; born in Scotch Plains, N. J., Dec. 26, 1813; died in Monterey, Cal., May 3, 1891. In 1835 he graduated from Jefferson Medical College, Philadelphia. He has published thirteen original translations of the celebrated hymn 'Dies Iræ' (1859); 'Old Gems in New Settings' (1866); 'The Microcosm'; and 'The Light of the World' (1884). In 1871 Princeton gave him the degree of LL. D.

Colet, Louise Revoil (ko-lā'). A French poet and novelist (1810–76). Four times between 1839 and 1855, poems of hers were crowned by the French Academy. She was a graceful lyrist, and often struck the chord of deep passion with effect. Of her verses, poured forth with marvelous facility, 'The Woman's Poem' is perhaps her best after the four offered to the Academy. Among her numerous novels, 'Bruised Hearts' (2 vols., 1843) may be mentioned. She also wrote several narratives of travel.

Collé, Charles (kō-lā'). A French dramatist (1709–83). For the Duke of Orleans's theatre he composed several light comedies, 'There's Truth in Wine,' 'The Knave Gallant,' etc., full of lively dialogue and intensely comic situations. Of his continental pieces, 'Henri IV.'s Hunting Party' is best known. As a lyrist he holds a place next after Béranger among French poets. His 'Historic Journal' (3 vols.) is for the most part a mass of calumnies against his contemporaries.

Collet, Jakobine Camilla (kol'let). A Norwegian novelist; born at Christiansand, Jan. 23, 1813. Her works, in many of which she champions the political emancipation of women, have had very wide circulation. Among them are: 'In the Long Nights'; 'A Bright Picture in a Dark Frame'; 'Against the Current'. D. 1895.

Colletet, Guillaume (kol"ẹ-tā"). A French poet; born at Paris in 1598; died in 1659. He wrote a number of poems that are not without merit, possessing as they do liveliness and originality. Some of his epigrams are ingenious and pungent. His best works are: 'Banquet of the Poets' (1646); 'Selected Poems' (1656). He was one of the five poets selected by Richelieu to put his dramatic works in verse, and was also one of the original members of the French Academy.

Collier, Mrs. Ada (Langworthy). An American writer of verse; born in Iowa, 1843. Her home is in Dubuque. Her principal work is 'Lilith, the Legend of the First Woman' (1885).

Collier, John Payne. An English critic and antiquary; born in London, 1789; died Sept. 17, 1883. He is famed for his 'Poetical Decameron' (1820); 'History of English Dramatic Poetry to the Time of Shakespeare, and Annals of the Stage to the Restoration' (1831); and his edition of Shakespeare (1844).

Collier, Robert Laird. An American Unitarian clergyman, religious writer, and essayist; born at Salisbury, Md., 1837; died 1890. Starting in life as an itinerant Methodist preacher, he held prominent Unitarian pulpits in Chicago and Boston, and became noted as a preacher and lecturer. In later life he was London correspondent of the New York Herald. Besides religious writings, he published: 'Henry Irving, a Sketch and a Criticism'; 'English Home Life' (1885).

Collin, Heinrich Joseph von (kol'lin). An Austrian dramatist and lyrist (1771–1811); born at Vienna. He wrote several tragedies, mostly on antique themes; of these, 'Regulus,' the first of the series, is the best. His powerful 'Songs for the Militia' (1809) give him a high rank among the balladists of the war of liberation. Of his historical ballads, 'Kaiser Max on the Walls of St. Martin's' is best known.

Collin d'Harleville, Jean François (kōl-an därl-vēl'). A French dramatist (1755–1806). He worked a genuine vein of comedy, yet never slighted the moral side of conduct. Notable among his works are 'The Old Bachelor,' his masterpiece, and 'Castles in Spain.'

Collins, John. An English poet; born in Bath, 1742; died at Birmingham, May 2, 1808. He was a stay-maker turned actor; and his poetic fame rests upon 'Scripscrapologia,' a collection of poems, among which 'To-Morrow' is especially readable.

Collins, Mortimer. An English novelist and poet; born in Plymouth, June 29, 1827; died at Knowl Hill, Berkshire, July 28, 1876. His 'Idyls and Rhymes,' 'Summer Songs,' and 'The British Birds,' are the efforts of an inspired verse-maker. His novels: 'Who Is the Heir?' (1865); 'Sweet Anne Page' (1868); 'The Ivory Gate' (1869); 'The Vivian Romance' (1870); 'The Marquis and Merchant' (1871); 'Two Plunges for a Pearl' (1872); 'Blacksmith and Scholar' (1875); and others, are much admired.

Collins, William. An English poet; born in Chichester, Dec. 25, 1721; died there, June 12, 1759. His melancholy temperament and poetic musings marked him as a boy, as a youth at Oxford, and even as a madman in the asylum where he died. 'The Passions,' with "its grace and vigor, its vivid and pliant dexterity of touch"; the 'Ode to Evening,' a mosaic of euphonies; the 'Dirge in Cymbeline'; and the

'Ode on the Death of Thomson,' chiefly perpetuate his fame.

Collins, William Wilkie. An English novelist; born in London, Jan. 8, 1824; died there, Sept. 23, 1889. He was a master of constructive art and fascinating plot. His greatest novels are admittedly ' The Moonstone ' (1868) and ' The Woman in White ' (1860); next in merit are ' The New Magdalen ' (1873) and 'No Name' (1862). The others are: ' Antonina' (2d ed. 1850); ' Basil ' (1852); ' The Dead Secret' (1857); ' Armadale ' (1866); ' Man and Wife' (1870); ' Poor Miss Finch' (1872); ' Miss or Mrs.?' (1873); ' The Law and the Lady' (1875); ' The Two Destinies' (1876); ' Heart and Science' (1883); ' I Say No' (1884); ' The Legacy of Cain' (1888); ' Blind Love' (1889 : completed by Walter Besant). He wrote also a biography of his father, William Collins the painter (1848).

Collyer, Robert. An American clergyman and prose-writer; born in Keighley, Yorkshire, England, Dec. 8, 1823. He came to America in 1849, being then a Wesleyan preacher and a blacksmith; but became a Unitarian, and preached some years in Chicago, where he founded Unity Church in 1860. He was made pastor of the Church of the Messiah, New York city, September 1879, and is now pastor emeritus. Included in his publications are : ' Nature and Life' (1866); ' The Life that Now Is' (1871); ' A History of the Town and Parish of Ilkley' (England, 1886, written in connection with Horsefall Turner) and ' Lectures to Young Men and Women ' (1886); ' Things New and Old.'

Colman, George, the Elder. An English dramatist; born in Florence, Italy, April 28, 1733; died in London, Aug. 14, 1794. Taste, humor, and brilliancy are the leading qualities of his work; ' The Deuce Is in Him'; ' New Brooms'; ' The Separate Maintenance'; and several other comedies, proclaiming him a man of wit, a writer, and a playwright of rare merits.

Colman, George, the Younger. An English dramatist and humorous poet; born in London (?), Oct. 21, 1762; died there, Oct. 17, 1836. ' The Iron Chest,' ' John Bull' (for which he received an unprecedentedly large sum), and ' The Heir-at-Law,' are most widely known among his racy and rather noisy but most laughable comedies. ' Broad Grins' and ' Poetic Vagaries' are very amusing rhymes.

Colombi, Marchioness (kō-lum'bē), pseudonym of Maria Torelli-Torriani. An Italian novelist of to-day; born at Novara. Most noteworthy among her stories is ' In Risaia,' a powerful description of the miseries of Italian peasant life.

Colonna, Vittoria (kō-lon'nä). A poet of Italy (1490–1547); born at Marino. Left a widow in 1525 by the death of her husband, the Marquis of Pescara, she lived thereafter in retirement. She was the correspondent and counselor of the foremost men of her time in Italy, especially Michel Angelo. Her ' Verses,' celebrating the virtues of her deceased husband and the beauties and consolations of religion, were very highly esteemed by her contemporaries, and perhaps overpraised. Her ' Correspondence' was published at Turin in 1888.

Colton, Walter. An American miscellaneous writer; born in Rutland, Vt., May 9, 1797; died in Philadelphia, Pa., Jan. 22, 1851. Became professor of moral philosophy and belles-lettres at Middletown Academy, Conn. (1825) ; in 1828–30 was editor of the American Spectator, Washington. In 1845 he went to California, and in Monterey established the first newspaper of the State, called the Californian. He wrote many books of interest, including ' A Visit to Athens and Constantinople' (1836) and 'Three Years in California' (1850). In 1851 Dr. Cheever edited ' The Sea and Sailor, Notes of France and Italy, and Other Literary Remains,' with a biography of the author.

Columella, Lucius Junius Moderatus (kol-u-mel'ä). A Latin author; born at Gades (?) (Cadiz), and flourished in the first century. His treatise ' Concerning Rustic Affairs' is a very important work, showing the condition of agriculture in Roman times.

Colvin, Sidney. An English critic; born in Norwood, Surrey, June 18, 1845. He became professor of fine arts at Cambridge in 1873. His writings include ' Children in Italian and English Design' (1872), and books on Landor, Dürer, and other writers and artists.

Combe, George. A Scotch phrenologist; born in Edinburgh, 1788; died 1858. He wrote ' The Constitution of Man Considered in Relation to External Objects' (1828) and many other works based upon phrenological science, as well as a volume of American notes.

Combe, William. An English ne'er-do-weel and fertile writer in prose and verse; born in Bristol, 1741; died at Lambeth, June 19, 1823, after 43 years within the rules of a debtor's prison, and previous fortunes from officer to cook. His ' Tour of Dr. Syntax in Search of the Picturesque' was once very popular.

Comegys, Benjamin Bartis. An American religious, ethical, and juvenile writer; born in Delaware, 1819; died Philadelphia, where he was a bank president, ——, 1901. He wrote : 'Tour round my Library'; 'How to Get On' (1885); 'Old Stories with New Lessons' (1888); etc.

Comenius, Johann Amos (ko-mē'ni-us). A noted Czech pedagogue and theologian, one of the world's great educators; born at Nivnitz (?), Moravia, March 28, 1592; died at Amsterdam, Nov. 15, 1671. In the ' Gate of Languages Unlocked' (Janua Linguarum Reserata), the ' World of Sense Depicted' (Orbis Pictus Sensualium), and ' Great Didactics, or the Whole Art of Teaching Everything' (Didactica Magna, seu Omnes Omnia Docendi Artificium), he shows the prodigious scope of his learning and his no less prodigious skill in the application of it.

Comines, Philippe de (kō-mēn'). A noted French chronicler; born at Comines, about 1445; died at the château of Argenton, Oct. 17, 1510. He was the trusted counselor of Philip the Good, Duke of Burgundy, of his son and successor Charles the Bold, of Louis XI., King of France, and of his successor Charles VIII. His 'Memoirs' supply the most trustworthy material we have for the history of his age, and the fullest; according to Hallam, they "almost make an epoch in historical literature." He analyzes the motives of kings and statesmen, and notes the manners of the time. He had a conception of a philosophy of history. In the current of events he sees problems working out; and his study is to trace their solution through the tangle of intrigue and personal ambitions. The first six books of the 'Memoirs' were written between 1488 and 1494, and the last two between 1497 and 1501; they were first printed in 1524-25.

Commodianus (kō-mō-di-ā'nus). A Latin Christian poet who lived in the third or fourth century. He wrote 'Instructions against the Gods of the Gentiles,' an acrostic poem.

Comnena, Anna (kom-nē'na). A Byzantine princess; born 1083; died 1148. She wrote 'The Alexiad,' a life of her father Alexis, Byzantine Emperor,— a work of importance.

Comte, Auguste (kônt). A noted French philosopher, founder of the Positive Philosophy; born at Montpellier, Jan. 19, 1798; died at Paris, Sept. 5, 1857. In his view the problem for philosophy is to ascertain the positive and verifiable basis of all knowledge, science, and religion—of the whole intellectual, moral, and religious world of man. In working out this problem, Comte studied the basis of the State or civil society; and set forth his conclusions in 'The Positive Polity.' He bases the law of morals or of conduct on the "social feeling" or Altruism. The central fact of religion and the one object of religious worship is Humanity conceived as a personality. The uttermost conclusions from such an idea of religion were drawn by Comte, and he contemplated the constitution of a priesthood whose authority, though of course not enforceable by pains and penalties, was to have as wide a reach as the authority of the popes in mediæval times. His 'Positive Philosophy,' 'Positivist Catechism,' and 'Positive Polity,' have been translated into English.

Conant, Thomas Jefferson. An American Baptist divine and Biblical scholar; born at Brandon, Vt., Dec. 13, 1802; died at Brooklyn, N. Y., April 30, 1891. He translated Gesenius's Hebrew Grammar (1839), and published annotated versions of 'Job' (1857); 'Matthew' (1860); 'The Book of Proverbs'; 'Isaiah'; 'Historical Books of the Old Testament from Joshua to Second Kings'; etc.

Condillac, Étienne Bonnot de Mably de (kôn-dē-yäk'). A French philosopher; born in Grenoble, Sept. 30, 1715; died at his estate near Beaugency, Aug. 3, 1780. He founded an international reputation upon 'The Essay on the Origin of Human Knowledge (or Sense Perceptions)' (1746); duly succeeded by the celebrated 'Treatise on the Sensations' (1754), the central standpoint of these and other works being what is, philosophically speaking, sensationalism; a belief, that is, that what we know we know only through the senses, and hence our ideas of deity, love, the soul, etc., are largely modified forms of the objects that impress us in our daily material experience. These standpoints were practically those of French philosophy until the advent of Cousin.

Condorcet, Marie Jean Antoine Nicolas Caritat, Marquis de (kon-dor"sä'). An illustrious French mathematician, philosopher, and economist; born at Ribemont, Picardy, Sept. 17, 1743; died at Bourg-la-Reine, March 28, 1794. He was one of the conspicuous figures of the French Revolution, and killed himself in prison. 'Historical Sketch of the Progress of the Human Mind' (1795) is deemed his greatest work.

Cone, Helen Gray. An American poet; born in New York, 1859. She is a teacher in the Normal College, New York. She has written: 'Oberon and Puck' (1885); 'The Ride to the Lady and Other Poems.'

Confucius or **Khoong-Foo-tse** (kon-fu'shē-us). The head of Chinese religious and social philosophy; born about 551 B. C.; died 479 B. C. His 'Analects' is an exposition of his philosophy, and he is said to have written the preface to the 'Book of Historical Documents.' He is also credited with having compiled the 'Ancient Poems,' about 300 pieces. His last work is called the 'Annals of Lee' or 'Spring and Autumn,' a sort of philosophical history and ethical manual. His writings have been translated into English, and form a volume in the series edited by Prof. Max Müller, 'Sacred Books of the East,' published for Oxford University by the Clarendon Press.

Congdon, Charles Taber. An American journalist; born in New Bedford, Mass., April 7, 1821; died in New York city, Jan. 18, 1891. He edited for a time the organ of the People's Party in the Dorr Rebelion in Rhode Island, 1842. From 1857 to 1882 he was on the editorial staff of the New York Tribune, and a frequent contributor of critical and literary articles to the magazines. In 1861 he published a poem; in 1869 'Tribune Essays'; and in 1880 'Reminiscences of a Journalist.'

Congreve, William. A noted English dramatist; born in Bardsley, near Leeds, April 5, 1670; died at London, Jan. 19, 1729. A man of fashion, his comedies show a wit more brilliant than decorous and a taste less moral than critical. 'The Old Bachelor'; 'The Double Dealer'; 'Love for Love'; and a few others, show great wit and facility. He is regarded as the most eminent of the 'Restoration' dramatists.

Connelly, Mrs. Celia (Logan). An American journalist and playwright; born in Pennsylvania, 1837. Her home is in Washington, D.C. 'An American Marriage' is one of her most successful plays. Died New York, June 18, 1904.

Conrad, Georg (kōn'räd), pseudonym of Prince George of Prussia. A German dramatist; born Feb. 12, 1826. He has experimented successfully with various forms of dramatic literature; and among his productions, 'Phædra,' a metrical drama, 'Where Is Happiness?' a comedy, and 'The Marchioness of Brinvilliers,' a tragedy, may be cited as specimens of a trained and true talent. Died 1902.

Conrad, Michael Georg (kōn'räd). A German novelist; born at Gnodstadt, in Franconia, April 5, 1846. He founded at Munich, in 1885, Society, a journal intended to be an organ of the «naturalistic» school. He spent several years in Paris, and many of his sketches relate to phases of life in France. Among his novels are: 'The Wise Virgins'; 'The Fool's Confession.' He is author of a comedy, 'The Emancipated,' and the drama 'The Firm of Goldberg.' On social and political questions he has written: 'The German Reveille'; 'Justice, the State, and the Modern Spirit.'

Conrad, Robert Taylor. An American lawyer and dramatist; born in Philadelphia, June 10, 1810; died there, June 27, 1858. He wrote: 'Aylmere' (1852), a tragedy in which Edwin Forrest played the rôle of Jack Cade; 'Conrad of Naples,' a tragedy; 'Poems' (1852) ; etc.

Conradi, Hermann (kōn-rä'dē). A German literary critic and essayist (1862–90); born at Jetznitz. As lyrist and critic he was a representative of radical realism, a follower of Tolstoy, Ibsen, and Nietzsche. His genius was forceful, but ,undisciplined, and his writings lack repose and polish. With his too radical story of 'Adam Man' (1889) he incurred the penalties of the law against publications that offend morality.

Conscience, Hendrik (kôn-syoṅs'). A great Flemish novelist, one of the re-creators of Flemish literature; born at Antwerp, Dec. 3, 1812; died in Brussels, Sept. 10, 1883. His first story, 'In the Wonder-Year 1566,' was received with unbounded popular favor, and his delineations of lowly Flemish home life soon became familiar throughout Europe. His historical novels 'The Lion of Flanders' (1838), and others, won his widest fame; but his distinctive power and merit were in his peasant studies, of which the masterpieces are: 'Siska van Roosmael' (1844); 'The Conscript' (1850); 'Rikke-tikke-tak' (1851); 'The Poor Nobleman' (1851); 'The Luck to be Rich' (1855); 'The Young Doctor' (1860). He wrote a musical drama, 'The Poet and His Dream' (1872).

Constant de Rebecque, Henri Benjamin (kôn-stoṅ'dĕ rẹ-bek'). A French publicist; born at Lausanne, Switzerland, Oct. 23, 1767; died at Paris, Dec. 8, 1830. Popularly remembered as the lover of Mme. de Staël. A member of the Revolutionary Tribunate, he was banished by Napoleon, and later by the Bourbons for accepting Napoleon. Besides many works on political questions and the history of political constitutions, and two on the history of religion,— viz., 'Religion Considered in its Source, its Forms, and its Developments,' and 'Roman Polytheism,'— he wrote a romance, 'Adolphe' (1816), which profoundly influenced European literature.

Conti, Amélie Gabrielle Stephanie Louise, Princess of (kon'tē). An Italian writer of memoirs. The narrative of her misfortunes, in 2 vols. (1797), attracted the attention of all Europe, and gave to Goethe the material of his 'Natural Daughter.'

Conway, Hugh. See **Fargus.**

Conway, Katharine Eleanor. An American journalist and poet; born at Rochester, N. Y., 1853. She is attached to the Boston Pilot. She has written: 'Songs of the Sunrise Slope' (1881); 'A Dream of Lilies' (1892), both in verse; 'Making Friends and Keeping Them'; 'A Lady and her Letters'; and 'In the Footprints of the Good Shepherd.'

Conway, Moncure Daniel. Born in Stafford County, Va., March 17, 1832. He became a Methodist minister; but changing his opinions on theology, and especially on slavery, settled in Cincinnati, O., as a radical Unitarian preacher. During the Civil War he left this country and preached in London for several years, finally returning and settling in New York. His literary activity has been great, his writings having been published under the following titles: 'The Rejected Stone'; 'Idols and Ideals'; 'Demonology and Devil Lore'; 'The Wandering Jew'; 'Sketch of Carlyle'; 'The Earthward Pilgrimage'; 'Sacred Anthology,' a compilation; 'Emerson at Home and Abroad'; 'George Washington and Mount Vernon'; 'Omitted Chapters in Life and Letters of Edmund Randolph'; 'Life of Thomas Paine'; 'Tracts for To-Day'; 'Natural History of the Devil'; 'The Golden Hour'; Testimonies Concerning Slavery'; 'Human Sacrifices in England'; 'Lessons for the Day'; 'Travels in South Kensington'; 'A Necklace of Stories'; 'Pine and Palm,' a novel; 'Prisms of Air,' a novel. Died Nov. 16, 1907, at Paris.

Conyngham, David Power. An Irish-American journalist and miscellaneous writer; born in Ireland, 1840; died 1883. He was editor of the New York Tablet. He wrote: 'Sherman's March through the South' (1865); 'Lives of the Irish Saints and Martyrs' (1870); and a number of Irish novels, including 'Sarsfield' (1871).

Cook, Clarence Chatham. An American journalist, and distinguished art critic; born in Dorchester, Mass., Sept. 8, 1828; died at Fishkill Landing, N. Y., June 1, 1900. He contributed to the New York Tribune a series of articles on American art, 1863-69; subsequently was its Paris correspondent. He was editor of the Studio until its suspension. He published : 'The Central Park' (1868); 'The House Beautiful' (1878); 'Stools and Candlesticks'; 'Essays on Beds and Tables'; and edited with notes a translation of the 7th German edition of Wilhelm Lübke's 'History of Art' (2 vols., 1878).

Cook, Eliza. An English poet; born in London, 1818; died at Wimbledon, Sept. 23, 1889. 'Melaia and Other Poems' made her name known. She also published Eliza Cook's Journal. Her most familiar poem is 'The Old Arm-Chair.' She wrote also 'The Old Farm Gate'; 'The Home in the Heart'; and 'I Miss Thee, My Mother.' 'New Echoes and Other Poems' is one of her volumes.

Cook, Flavius Josephus. A noted American lecturer on religious and social topics; born at Ticonderoga, N. Y., Jan. 26, 1838; died there June 25, 1901. He carried on the Monday lectureship in Boston (1874-80); was in Europe and Asia in 1880-82, resuming the lectures in Boston in 1883. His published works include : 'Boston Monday Lectures' (10 vols., 1877); 'Current Religious Perils, with Other Addresses.' In 1888 he founded Our Day, a monthly reform magazine.

Cooke, George Willis. An American miscellaneous writer; born in Comstock, Mich., April 23, 1848. His chief works are: 'Ralph Waldo Emerson : his Life and Writings' (1881); 'Life of George Eliot' (1883); 'A Guide Book to the Poetic and Dramatic Works of Robert Browning' (1891); 'Poets and Problems'; 'The Clapboard Trees Parish'; and 'Dedham, a History.'

Cooke, John Esten. An American novelist; born in Winchester, Va., Nov. 3, 1830; died near Boyce, Va., Sept. 27, 1886. He was an extensive contributor of stories, sketches, and verses to various periodicals, and has written many books, in which are included : 'The Virginia Comedians' (1854); 'Hilt to Hilt' (1869); 'Life of Gen. Robert E. Lee' (1871); 'Virginia, a History of the People' (1883); 'The Youth of Jefferson'; 'Surry of Eagle's Nest'; 'Wearing the Grey'; 'Pretty Mrs. Gaston'; 'Virginia Bohemians'; etc.

Cooke, Josiah Parsons. A distinguished American chemist; born at Boston, Oct. 12, 1827; died at Newport, R. I., Sept. 3, 1894. He was professor of chemistry at Harvard University (1850-94), and lectured on scientific subjects in various cities and towns throughout the country. Besides a number of technical works, he wrote : 'Religion and Chemistry' (1864); 'Scientific Culture' (new ed. 1885); 'The Credentials of Science the Warrant of Faith' (1888).

Cooke, Philip Pendleton. An American poet and prose-writer; born in Martinsburg, Va., Oct. 26, 1816; died near Boyce, Va., Jan. 21, 1850. His first poems were published in the Knickerbocker Magazine. His works in book form include: 'Froissart Ballads and Other Poems' (1847); the tales of 'John Carpe' and 'The Crime of Andrew Blair'; and his short lyric poem, 'Florence Vane,' which was set to music.

Cooke, Philip St. George. A United States army officer and military writer; born near Leesburg, Va., June 13, 1809; died at Detroit, Mar. 28, 1895. He also studied law and was admitted to practice. Besides works on tactics, he wrote: 'Scenes and Adventures in the Army' (1856); 'Conquest of New Mexico and California' (1878).

Cooke, Mrs. Rose (Terry). A distinguished American poet and short-story writer; born at West Hartford, Conn., Feb. 17, 1827; died at Pittsfield, Mass., July 18, 1892. Her complete poems were published in 1888: 'The Gentian' and 'The Two Villages' are good representatives. Her best short stories treat of New England rural life. The novel 'Steadfast' appeared in 1889. Her most acceptable work appeared originally in the Atlantic Monthly and other periodicals.

Cooke, Thomas. An English poet and prose-writer, commonly called Hesiod Cooke; born at Braintree, Dec. 16, 1703; died at Lambeth (London), Dec. 20, 1756. 'The Battle of the Poets' is an attack on Pope, Swift, and others, which gained him an unenviable conspicuity in the 'Dunciad.' As a translator from the classics, notably Hesiod, he is very successful.

Coolbrith, Ina Donna. An American poet; born near Springfield, Ill., 18—. She became librarian of the Oakland Public Library, California, in 1874. She has written 'The Perfect Day and Other Poems' (1881); 'Songs of the Golden Gate.'

Cooley, Thomas McIntyre. An American jurist; born at Attica, N. Y., Jan. 6, 1824; died at Ann Arbor, Sept. 12, 1898. He was professor of law in the University of Michigan (1859 and 1881); Chief Justice of that State (1868-69); chairman of the United States Interstate Commerce Commission (1887-91). He wrote: 'A Treatise upon Wrongs and their Remedies' (Vol. i., 1878); 'General Principles of Constitutional Law in the United States' (1880); etc.

Coolidge, Susan. See **Woolsey, Sarah.**

Coombe, William. See **Combe.**

Coombs, Mrs. Annie (Sheldon). An American novelist; born at Albany, N. Y., 1858; died 1890. Her home was in New York. She wrote: 'As Common Mortals' (1886); 'A Game of Chance' (1887); 'The Garden of Armida.'

Cooper, James Fenimore. An American novelist and historian; born in Burlington, N. J., Sept. 15, 1789; died at Cooperstown, N. Y., Sept. 14, 1851. His novels comprise: 'Precaution' (1820); 'The Spy' (1821); 'The Pioneers' (1823); 'The Pilot' (1823); 'Lionel Lincoln' (1825); 'The Last of the Mohicans' (1826); 'The Red Rover' (1827); 'The Prairie' (1827); 'The Traveling Bachelor' (1828); 'Wept of the Wish-ton-Wish' (1829); 'The Water-Witch' (1830); 'The Bravo' (1831); 'The Heidenmauer' (1832); 'The Headsman' (1833); 'The Monikins' (1835); 'Homeward

Bound' (1838); 'Home as Found' (1838); 'The Pathfinder' (1840); 'Mercedes of Castile' (1840); 'The Deerslayer' (1841); 'The Two Admirals' (1842); 'Wing and Wing' (1842); 'Ned Myers' (1843); 'Wyandotte' (1843); 'Afloat and Ashore' (1844); 'Miles Wallingford' (1844); 'The Chainbearer' (1845); 'Satanstoe' (1845); 'The Redskins' (1846); 'The Crater' (1847); 'Jack Tar' (1848); 'Oak Openings' (1848); 'The Sea Lions' (1849); 'The Ways of the Hour' (1850). He also wrote 'Notions of the Americans' (1828) to vindicate his countrymen from the false ideas of foreigners—after which the foreign journals at once ceased praising his novels and became unsparing in censure; a 'History of the Navy of the United States' (1839); 'The Battle of Lake Erie' (1842), in answer to criticisms on the preceding; 'Lives of American Naval Officers' (2 vols.); and others.

Cooper, Peter. A famous American inventor, manufacturer, and philanthropist; born in New York, Feb. 12, 1791; died there, April 4, 1883. A coachmaker by trade, he became a successful inventor and glue manufacturer, and acquired a large fortune. He built, after his own designs, the first locomotive engine constructed on this continent (1830); was one of the original promoters of the electric telegraph, actively interested in the construction of the New York State canals, etc. He was the candidate of the « Greenback » party for President in 1876. He is best known by the institution that was dearest to his own heart, the « Cooper Union » of New York, founded for the instruction of the industrial classes (1854–59). He wrote: 'Political and Financial Opinions, with an Autobiography' (1877); 'Ideas for a Science of Good Government' (1883).

Cooper, Susan Fenimore. An American prose-writer, daughter of Fenimore Cooper; born in Scarsdale, N. Y., 1813; died in Cooperstown, N. Y., Dec. 31, 1894. During the last years of her father's life she was his secretary and amanuensis. She has written: 'Rural Hours' (1850); 'Fields Old and New' (1854); 'The Shield: A Narrative'; 'Mt. Vernon to the Children of America' (1858); 'Rhyme and Reason of Country Life'; and others.

Cooper, Thomas. An English poet and novelist, best remembered as a Chartist politician; born at Leicester, March 28, 1805; died at Lincoln, July 15, 1892. A shoemaker by trade, he engaged in politics, and soon found himself in prison, where he wrote 'The Purgatory of Suicides,' a moving epic of proletarianism. His 'Captain Cobbler,' a story, and his 'Poetical Works,' are favorably known.

Coornhert, Dirck Volckertsen (kōrn'hert). A Dutch poet and scholar (1522–90). By his poetical writings, 'Book of Songs' (1575), 'Right Use and Abuse of Worldly Possessions' (1585), and several dramas, as also by his elegant translations from Boccaccio and the classics, he earned the title of « restorer of the Dutch language. »

Copernicus, Nikolaus (kō-pėr'ni-kus). A famous Polish astronomer; born in Thorn, Poland, Feb. 19, 1473; died at Frauenburg, Prussia, May 24, 1543. He wrote: 'Revolutions of the Celestial Orbs' (De Orbium Cœlestium Revolutionibus), in which is proclaimed the fact that the sun and not the earth is the centre of our planetary system.

Coppée, François (ko-pā'). An eminent French poet, romancer, and dramatist; born in Paris, Jan. 12, 1842. He was trained for what the Parisians call a ministerial career, but wrote 'The Reliquary' and 'Intimacies,' books of verse. In 'Modern Poems,' 'The Benediction,' and 'The Strike of the Smiths,' we have a very modern note. Died May 23, 1908.

Coppée, Henry. An American soldier, educator, and miscellaneous writer; born at Savannah, Ga., Oct. 13, 1821; died March 21, 1895. He served in the Mexican War (1846–48); was instructor at West Point (1848–49, 1850–55); professor of English literature and history at the University of Pennsylvania (1855–56); president of Lehigh University (1866–75); professor of history there (1875–95). Besides various educational and military works, he wrote: 'Grant and his Campaigns' (1866); 'History of the Conquest of Spain by the Arab-Moors' (2 vols., 1881).

Coppi, Antonio (kop'pē). An Italian economist and historian; born in Andezeno, Piedmont, April 12, 1782; died at Rome, Feb. 24, 1870. He wrote a 'Continuation of Muratori's Annals of Italy, from 1750' (1824–68); and a study 'On the Finances of Mediæval Rome' (1855).

Copway, George. Native name, Kah-ge-gagaw-bowh. An Indian journalist, lecturer, and miscellaneous writer; born in Michigan, 1818; died about 1869. He belonged to the Ojibway tribe, and was settled in New York. He wrote: 'Recollections of a Forest Life'; 'The Ojibway Conquest,' a poem; 'Running Sketches of Men and Places in Europe'; etc.

Coquelin, Bénoît Constant (kōk-lan'). A French actor; born at Boulogne-sur-Mer, Jan. 23, 1841. He is at the head of his profession in comedy, and excels in melodrama. He has written: 'Art and the Comedian' (1880); 'Molière and the Misanthrope' (1881); 'Tartuffe.'

Corbet, Richard. An English poet; born in Surrey, 1582; died at Norwich, July 28, 1635. A noted ecclesiastic and disposed to be gay, he wrote a 'Journey to France' and a 'Farewell to the Fairies,' poems in which he is revealed a jolly parson and the maker of some tolerable verse.

Corbière, Edouard (kor-byär'). A French poet and novelist; born at Brest, 1793; died at Morlaix, Oct. 20, 1875. He published 'The Banian' (1835); 'The Slave'; and other sea tales.

Corbin, Mrs. Caroline Elizabeth (Fairfield). An American story-writer; born in

Connecticut, 1835. She was long a resident of Chicago. Her works include: 'Rebecca'; 'His Marriage Vow'; 'Belle and the Boys'; 'A Woman's Philosophy of Love,' a psychological treatise.

Corbin, John. An American man of letters; born in Illinois, 1870. He has published 'The Elizabethan Hamlet' (1895), 'Schoolboy Life in England: an American View' (1897); 'The first Loves of Perilla'; 'The Cave Man.'

Cordeiro, João Ricardo (kōr-dā'ē-rō). A Portuguese dramatist (1836-81); born at Lisbon. He both wrote several plays, as 'Love and Art'; 'A Cure of Souls'; and also translated into Portuguese and adapted to the Portuguese theatre many of the dramatic compositions of Scribe, Hugo, Legouvé, etc.

Corelli, Marie. See **Mackay, Minnie.**

Corinna (kō-rin'ä). A famed Greek poet; born at Tanagra, Bœotia, about 500 B.C. She was a contemporary of Pindar, sometimes his competitor for poetical prizes. She was celebrated for her beauty, and nicknamed « The Fly » to distinguish her from another poet called « The Bee. » Only fragments of her poems have been preserved.

Corneille, Pierre (kor-nay"). A French dramatist; born at Rouen, June 6, 1606; died in Paris, Sept. 30, 1684. His works comprise: 'Mélite'; 'Clitandre' (1632); 'The Widow'; 'The Gallery of the Palace'; 'The Lady's Maid'; 'The Palais Royal'; 'Medea' (1634-35); 'The Dramatic Illusion' (1635?); 'The Cid' (1636); 'Horace' (1640); 'Cinna' (1640-41); 'Polyeuctus' (1643); 'Pompey' (1643-44); 'The Liar' (1644); 'The Sequel to the Liar' (1645); 'Rodogune' (1645); 'Theodore' (1646); 'Heraclius' (1647); 'Don Sancho' (1649); 'Attila' (1667); and many more. 'Cinna' and 'Polyeucte' are considered the greatest, followed by 'The Liar' and the 'Golden Fleece.'

Corneille, Thomas. A French dramatist, brother of Pierre (1625-1709). He made his first success with a comedy, 'Chance Engagements' (1647), after Calderon, and continued for a while to follow Spanish models. Some of his tragedies were much admired; and one, 'Timocrates,' held the boards for six months. In Voltaire's judgment 'Ariana' is the best of his tragedies; both that play and 'The Earl of Essex' are still seen on the French stage. By his 'Dictionary of Arts and Sciences' and other similar works, he was a forerunner of the French Encyclopedists.

Cornelius Nepos. See **Nepos.**

Cornwallis, Kinahan. An English-American journalist, novelist, etc.; born in England, 1839. He came to America about 1860. He has written: 'Yarra Yarra, or the Wandering Aborigine' (5th ed. 1855), in verse; 'Howard Plunkett' (1857); 'My Life and Adventures' (1860); 'Pilgrims of Fashion' (1862); 'The Gold Room and the New York Stock Exchange' (1879); 'The War for the Union' (1899).

Cornwell, Henry Sylvester. An American poet; born in New Hampshire, 1831; died 1886, at New London, Conn., where he was a physician. From many poems published by him he issued but one collection, 'The Land of Dreams and Other Poems' (1878).

Coronado, Carolina (kō-rō-nä'THō). A Spanish poet; born at Almendralejo in the province of Badajoz, in 1823. About 1848 she married Horace Perry, an American. She was precocious, and published a collection of poems in 1843. Her lyrics are distinguished for melody and depth of feeling. Her few dramatic pieces had little success; but her novels and short stories,— especially 'Jarilla' (1850) and 'The Wheel of Misfortune' (1874),— and her little sketch of travel 'From Tagus to Rhine,' won popular favor.

Corrodi, August (kor-rō'dē). A Swiss poet (1826-85); born at Zürich. Till 1881 he was an artist-painter, and for some time was professor of the arts of design at Winterthur. His first volume of 'Songs' (1853) exhibited graceful versification and deep sympathy with nature. His songs and dramatic compositions in the local dialect —'Mr. Professor, an Idyll of Zürich'; 'The Vicar, a Winter Idyll'; etc. — had extraordinary success. He translated several of Burns's songs into the Swiss-German dialect; and published 'Shakspere: Life Wisdom from his Works.' His works are very numerous and possess enduring merit.

Corson, Hiram. An American prose writer; born in Philadelphia, Pa., Nov. 6, 1828. He became professor of rhetoric and English literature at St. John's College, Annapolis (1866). In 1870 he became professor of English language and literature, rhetoric, and oratory in Cornell, and still holds the position. Among his well-known publications are: a 'Hand-Book of Anglo-Saxon and Early English' (1871); 'An Introduction to the Study of Robert Browning' (1886); 'Jottings in the Text of Hamlet'; 'Lectures on the English Language and Literature'; 'The Aims of Literary Study'; 'The Voice and Spiritual Education.'

Cort, Frans de (kort). An eminent Flemish poet (1834-78); born near Brussels. As singer of the quiet joys of home life and conjugal happiness he has few peers in any literature. His original homely lyrics appeared in 'Songs' (2 vols., 1857-59); 'Zing-Zang' (1866); and another volume of 'Songs' (1868). He also translated into Flemish verse 'The Finest Songs of Robert Burns' (1862).

Cosel, Charlotte von. See **Auer.**

Cossa, Pietro (kōs'sä). An Italian dramatist (1830-81); born at Rome. He was for some years professor of Italian literature. At first an unsuccessful dramatist, his 'Nero' (1871) was received with the most enthusiastic approval for its dramatic power, despite certain marked technical defects of composition. His following plays confirmed the popular estimate of his greatness: 'Messalina'; 'Julian the Apostate'; and especially 'Cleopatra.' He wrote also a volume of 'Lyric Poems.'

Costa, Isaak da (kos'tä). A Dutch poet (1798–1860) ; born at Amsterdam. Among his works, which rank among the best specimens of modern Dutch poetry, may be cited : 'Prometheus ' (1820) ; 'Festival Songs' (1828) ; 'Five-and-Twenty Years,' a great poetico-historical work (1840) ; 'Hagar' (1847); and 'The Battle of Nieuwpoort' (1859). He wrote also some theological tractates.

Coster, Samuel (kos'ter). A Dutch dramatist (1579–1662). He was one of the founders of the Dutch Academy. He is best known for his delightful comedies 'The Play of Tiisken van den Schilden' (1613), and 'The Play of the Rich Man' (1615). He also wrote tragedies, including : 'Iphigenia'; 'Polyxena'; 'Isabella.'

Costetti, Giuseppe (kos-tet'tē). An Italian dramatist; born at Bologna, Sept. 13, 1834. He early won fame by his dramas 'The Malibran,' ; 'The Lion's Den,' etc., and heightened it greatly by his comedies ' The Son of the Family' (1864) ; 'The Old Story' (1875); 'Cain's Wife' (1887) ; 'Confessions of a Dramatic Author.'

Cota, Rodrigo (kō'tä). A Spanish poet of the 15th century. He is believed to be the author of 'The Couplets of Mingo Revulgo' and of a 'Dialogue between Love and an Old Knight,' both reckoned among the earliest of Spanish dramatic compositions. His authorship of the famous poem 'Celestina' is contested, it being now attributed to Fernando de Rojas.

Cotin, Charles (kō-tan'). A French versifier (1604–82). He was a prolific writer, but his amorous and religious poems are nearly forgotten. His name survives in Boileau's satires and Molière's 'Femmes Savantes': there he figures as Trissotin.

Cottin, Marie (kō-tan'). A French novelist (1770–1807). Her romances, 'Claire d'Albe' (1799) ; 'Malvina'; 'Elizabeth, or the Exiles of Siberia', her most notable work (1806), are admirable for style and character-drawing.

Cotton, Charles. An English poet; born in Beresford, Saffordshire, April 28, 1630; died at London (?), Feb. 16, 1686–7. The friend of Izaak Walton, his was an angler's Muse ; and he wrote an addition to Walton's book, besides translations and a poor parody of Virgil.

Cotton, John. An American prose-writer and clergyman; born in Derby, England, Dec. 4, 1584; died in Boston, Mass., Dec. 23, 1652. Upon his arrival in America he became "teacher" of the first church of Boston. A religious controversy with Roger Williams called forth his work 'The Bloody Tenet, Washed and Made White in the Blood of the Lamb.' Cotton was an industrious worker, and published nearly fifty books.

Coues, Elliott (kouz). An American naturalist; born at Portsmouth, N. H., Sept. 9, 1842; died at Baltimore, Dec. 25, 1899. He was lat-terly connected with the Smithsonian Institute. He wrote : 'Key to North American Birds' (1872); 'Field Ornithology' (1874); 'Check-List of North American Birds' (1882); 'Biogen'; 'The Dæmon of Darwin'; etc. With J. S. Kingsley, he edited the 'Standard Natural History' (3 vols., 1883). He was actively interested in Theosophy.

Courier (de Méré), Paul Louis (kö-ryā'). A French Hellenist and political pamphleteer; born in Paris, Jan. 4, 1772; assassinated near Veretz, Aug. 18, 1825. In 1813 he made an elegant translation of 'Daphnis and Chloe,' an ancient romance by Longos, discovered by him at Florence; he also translated 'The Luciad, or the Ass of Lucius of Patras,' published with the Greek text (1818). His numerous pamphlets, especially his 'Pamphlet of Pamphlets,' are masterpieces of style, of marvelous conciseness, and noteworthy documents for the history of the ancient political and ecclesiastical contentions.

Courtmans, Joanna Desideria (kört'mäns). A Flemish poet and novelist (1811–90). Besides dramas and poems, she wrote 22 volumes of stories. She excels particularly in her descriptions of the life of the common people. The most notable of her tales are : 'The Hunter's Gift'; 'Dame Daneel'; 'The Cowherd'; 'Aunt Clara's Bonnet.'

Cousin, Victor (kö-zan'). A distinguished French philosopher; born in Paris, Nov. 28, 1792; died at Cannes, Jan. 2, 1867. He founded a school of Eclectic philosophy; combining the doctrines of the Scotch school of Reid and Stewart, based on sensation, with those of Schelling and Hegel, which rest on the opposite principle of idealism or intuition. He was not an original thinker in philosophy, but he possessed in a high degree the faculty of clear exposition; for that reason his lectures and his writings enjoyed a great popularity. He rendered a memorable service both to philosophy and literature by his translation of 'Plato,' praised by Jowett. Besides his 'History of Philosophy' and other works on that theme, he is author of a few biographical sketches, mostly of characters related to the spiritual and intellectual movements of the 17th century : as 'Jacqueline Pascal'; 'Mme. de Longueville'; 'Mme. de Hautefort'; 'French Society in the 17th Century' (2 vols.).

Cowan, Frank. An American lawyer, physician, journalist, and miscellaneous writer; born in Pennsylvania, 1844. Making the tour of the world in 1880–81 and 1884–85, he entered Corea before that country had made treaties with other nations. He wrote: 'Zomara, a Romance of Spain' (1873) ; 'The City of the Royal Palm and Other Poems' (1884); 'Fact and Fancy in New Zealand' (1885). Died 1905.

Cowley, Abraham. A English poet and essayist; born in London in 1618; died at Chertsey, Surrey, July 28, 1667. Well educated and high in royal favor, he was a fashionable and fortunate poet till the Civil War made havoc of royal favorites. His volumes 'The Mistress,' 'Poems,' various Virgilian elegies and anacreontic love songs, and his essays, were set in the first rank by contemporaries; but are mainly curios now, though some poems are familiar. The first collection of his works, in one volume, appeared in 1668.

Cowper, William. An English poet; born in Great Berkhamstead, Hertfordshire, November 1731; died at East Dereham, Norfolk, April 25, 1800. His works include: 'Poems' (1782); 'The Task' (1785); 'Homer's Iliad and Odyssey' (1791); 'Poems' (1798); etc. 'John Gilpin' first appeared in book form with 'The Task.' Some of his hymns are among the best known of English religious pieces.

Cox, Palmer. An American artist and writer for young people; born at Granby, Quebec, 1840. Since 1875 his home has been in New York. His works are both written and illustrated by himself. He is best known by his 'Brownie Books,' a very popular series containing humorous pictures and verse for children. Other productions are: 'Hans Von Petter's Trip to Gotham' (1878); 'How Columbus Found America' (1878); 'The Brownies in the Philippines.'

Cox, Samuel Sullivan. An American statesman and author; born in Zanesville, O., Sept. 30, 1824; died in New York, September 1889. He served some terms in Congress, and became minister to Turkey. His works are: 'Eight Years in Congress'; 'Why We Laugh'; 'Diversions of a Diplomat in Turkey'; 'A Buckeye Abroad'; 'Arctic Sunbeams'; 'Orient Sunbeams'; 'Search for Winter Sunbeams'; 'Free Land and Free Trade'; and others.

Coxe, Arthur Cleveland. An American writer of prose and verse, and second Bishop of the Protestant Episcopal Church in the diocese of Western New York; born in Mendham, N. J., May 10, 1818; died at Clifton Springs, N. Y., July 20, 1896. Among his many publications are: 'Christian Ballads' (1840); 'Athanasion and Other Poems' (1842); 'The Pascal,' a collection of Easter poems (1889); and many valuable contributions to current literature in both English and French.

Cozzens, Frederick Swartwout. An American humorist; born in New York city, March 5, 1818; died in Brooklyn, N. Y., Dec. 23, 1869. A merchant, to whom literature was a recreation. In Yankee Doodle (1847) were published his earliest humorous poems and sketches. In 1853 a volume entitled 'Prismatics' was published under the pen-name of "Richard Haywarde"; and in 1856 the 'Sparrowgrass Papers,' which attained great popularity. Among his other published works are 'Memorial of Col. Peter A. Porter' and a 'Memorial of Fitz-Greene Halleck' (1868).

Crabbe, George. An English poet; born in Aldeburgh, Suffolk, Dec. 24, 1754; died at Trowbridge, Wiltshire, Feb. 3, 1832. His poems have to do with the life and sorrows of the toiling poor, and English poverty is portrayed in 'The Village'; 'The Parish Register'; 'The Borough'; 'Tales in Verse'; etc.

Craddock, Charles Egbert. See Murfree.

Craigie, Pearl Richards. See Hobbes.

Craik, Dinah Maria Mulock. An English novelist; born in Stoke-upon-Trent, April 20, 1826; died at London, October 1887. 'The Ogilvies'; 'John Halifax, Gentleman'; 'Two Marriages'; 'A Brave Lady'; and 'A Noble Life,' are the best known of her works.

Craik, Georgiana. An English novelist; born in London, April 1831. Her fictions are concerned with domestic life. 'Dorcas' contains some exquisite portrayal of character; 'Riverston,' 'Lost and Won' and 'Only a Butterfly' are also good.

Cram, Ralph Adams. An American poet and story-teller; born in New Hampshire, 1868. He is an architect in Boston. He has written: 'The Decadent, Being the Gospel of Inaction'; 'Black Spirits and White,' a book of ghost stories; 'In the Island of Avalon,' a volume of verse. 'The Gothic Quest.'

Cramer, Karl Gottlob (krä'mèr). A German story-teller (1758–1871). He wrote more than 40 novels and tales, which were read with delight in his day. The best of them, and indeed a work of no little force and originality, is 'The Life and Opinions of Erasmus Sneaker, Traveling Mechanic.'

Cranch, Christopher Pearse. An American poet and artist; born in Alexandria, Va., March 8, 1813; died in Cambridge, Mass., Jan. 20, 1892. Included in his publications are: 'Poems' (1844); 'The Last of the Huggermuggers' (1856); a translation of the Æneid of Virgil into English verse (1872); and 'Ariel and Caliban, with Other Poems' (1887).

Crane, Stephen. An American story-writer; born at Newark, N. J., Nov. 1, 1871; died at Baden Weiler, Black Forest, June 5, 1900. He wrote: 'Maggie,' 'The Red Badge of Courage,' and 'George's Mother' (1898), stories; 'The Black Riders and Other Lines' (1895), verse; etc.

Crane, Thomas Frederick. An American scholar; born in New York State 1844. He is professor of Romance languages at Cornell University (1881). Besides many contributions to periodicals, he has written: 'Italian Popular Tales' (1885); 'Pictures of the French Revolution' (6th ed. 1892); 'French Romanticism' (3d ed. 1890); 'Popular Songs of France' (1891); 'French Society in the 17th Century.'

Crashaw, Richard. An English poet; born in London, 1613 (?); died at Rome or Loreto, May or June 1649. A convert to Catholicism, he wrote 'Steps to the Temple' and 'Sacred Poems,' productions of great imaginative power.

Craven, Madame Augustus (Pauline de la Ferronays). A French novelist; born in London, April 12, 1808; died at Paris, April 1, 1891. Her 'Family Memories'; 'The Story of a Sister'; 'The Labor of a Soul'; and other fictions, are well known.

Craven, Elizabeth Berkeley, Lady, subsequently Margravine of Ansbach. An English descriptive prose and verse writer; born in 1750; died at Naples, Jan. 13, 1828. She produced various sentimentalities in verse and in prose fiction; a meritorious record of ,travel, 'Journey through the Crimea to Constantinople' (1789); and very readable 'Memoirs of the Margravine of Ansbach, Formerly Lady Craven, Written by Herself' (1825).

Crawford, Francis Marion. An American novelist; born in Bagni di Lucca, Italy, Aug. 2, 1854. His works include: 'Mr. Isaacs' (1882); 'Dr. Claudius' (1883); 'To Leeward' (1883); 'A Roman Singer' (1884); 'An American Politician' (1884); 'Zoroaster' (1885); 'A Tale of a Lonely Parish' (1886); 'Saracinesca' (1887); 'Marzio's Crucifix' (1887); 'Paul Patoff' (1887); 'With the Immortals' (1888); 'Greifenstein' (1889); 'Sant' Ilario' (1889); 'A Cigarette-Maker's Romance' (1890); 'The Witch of Prague' (1891); 'Khaled' (1891); 'The Three Fates' (1892); 'Love in Idleness' (1894); 'Katharine Lauderdale,' and its sequel 'The Ralstons' (1895); 'Casa Braccio' (1895); Taquisara' (1896); 'A Rose of Yesterday' (1897); 'Corleone' (1897); 'Ave Roma Immortalis' (1898); 'In the Palace of the King' (1900); 'The Rulers of the South' (1901); 'Marietta, a Maid of Rome' (1901); 'The Heart of Rome' (1903); 'Venetian Gleanings' (1905); 'Arethusa' (1907); 'The Little City of Hope' (1907). He died at Sorrento, April 9, 1909.

Crawford, Louise Macartney. An American author; born in London, 1808. Her most famous song is 'Kathleen Mavourneen,' erroneously attributed to Frederick Crouch.

Crawford, Mary Caroline, an American authoress born in 1874. She is a close student of sociology and of New England romance, and an authority on the higher education of women in America. Her writings include 'The Romance of Old New England Churches' (1903); 'The College Girl of America' (1904); 'St. Botolph's Town' (1909).

Crébillon, Claude Prosper Jolyot de (krä-bē-yôn'), the Younger. A French novelist, son of P. J.; born in Paris, Feb. 14, 1707; died there, April 12, 1777. Author of several licentious novels; personally his life was above reproach. For certain strictures on the Papal bull «Unigenitus» in one of these novels, he was immured for a time in the Bastille. To the most objectionable of all his stories he gave the title 'Sopha: A Moral Tale,' after the manner of other impure writers. He possesses a rich invention, and his characters are drawn by a master's hand; his style is elegant and refined almost to unintelligibility.

Crébillon, Prosper Jolyot de. A noted French dramatist; born at Dijon, Jan. 13, 1674; died in Paris, June 14, 1762. His plays include: 'The Death of Brutus's Children'; 'Idomeneus'

(1705); 'Atreus and Thyestes' (1707); 'Electra' (1708); 'Rhadamistus and Zénobia' (1711); 'Xerxes' (1714); 'Semiramis' (1717); 'Pyrrhus' (1726); 'Catalina' (1748); etc.

Cremer, Jacobus Jan (krä'mär). A Dutch novelist (1827-80); born at Arnheim. He was a painter, but quit the pencil for the pen. His series of 'Stories of Betuwe' (a rural district) are specimens of idiomatic expression, faithful portraiture, and unsophisticated humor. The same traits distinguish all his works; but he is at his best amid rural scenes. He published a volume of 'Poems' (1873).

Crespo, Antonio Candido Gonçalves (kres'-pō). A Portuguese poet; born of a slave mother at Rio Janeiro, March 11, 1846; died at Lisbon, June 11, 1883. He graduated in jurisprudence at the Coimbra University, but devoted himself almost exclusively to the Muses at Lisbon. He published only two small volumes: 'Miniatures' (1870); 'Nocturns' (1882). In collaboration with his wife Maria Amalia Vaz de Carvalho, herself a notable writer, he is author of 'Stories for our Children' (1882). His poems show high sensibility and great power of poetic form and expression.

Creuz, Friedrich Karl Kasimir, Baron von (kroits). A German poet and philosopher (1724-70); born at Homburg vor der Höhe. He is author of several works on archæology and philology. He wrote a philosophical poem, 'The Graves,' a work of considerable merit, showing the influence of Young's 'Night Thoughts.' He published several volumes of 'Odes and Lays'; and a tragedy, 'The Dying Seneca.'

Crockett, David. A noted American pioneer, hunter, politician, and humorist; born at Limestone, Tenn., Aug. 17, 1786; killed at Fort Alamo, San Antonio, Texas, March 16, 836. He was member of Congress from Tennessee; served in the Texan war; and was one of the eccentric characters of the Southwest, about whom numerous stories are still told,—notably of the coon who voluntarily agreed to «come down.» He wrote his 'Autobiography' (1834); 'Tour to the North and Down East' (1835); 'Sketches and Eccentricities' (1847); etc.

Crockett, Samuel Rutherford. A Scotch novelist; born in Little Duchrae, Galloway, in 1862. He was a tutor and university pupil-teacher at an early age; but a volume of verse, 'Dulce Cor,' and 'The Stickit Minister,' volume of prose stories, showed literature to be his vocation. 'The Raiders'; 'Mad Sir Ughtred of the Hills'; 'The Lilac Sun-Bonnet'; 'The Men of the Moss Hags'; 'Sweetheart Travelers'; 'Cleg Kelly, Arab of the City'; 'The Grey Man of Auchendrayne,'; 'An adventurer in Spain'; and 'Red Cape Tales,' are among his books

Croffut, William Augustus. An American prose-writer and poet; born in Redding, Conn., Jan. 29, 1835. He is a journalist of wide experience, having been connected with various newspapers. His works include: 'A Helping

Hand' (1861); 'A Midsummer Lark' (1882); 'Bourbon Ballads'; 'The Folks Next Door'; and 'The Vanderbilts.' He has long been connected with the United States Geological Survey.

Croker, John Wilson. An Irish miscellaneous writer; born in Galway, Dec. 20, 1780; died at Old Brompton, Aug. 10, 1857. His capacity for satire revealed itself in 'An Intercepted Letter from Canton,' and his 'Songs of Trafalgar' spread his fame as a poet. Macaulay's review of his edition of Boswell's 'Life of Johnson,' and his counterblast upon Macaulay's 'History of England,' are among the celebrities of literary duels. He was a Tory politician of intense fervor, permanently resigning his seat in Parliament because of the passage of the Reform Bill of 1832.

Croker, Thomas Crofton. An Irish antiquary and folklorist; born in Cork, Jan. 15, 1798; died at Old Brompton, Aug. 8, 1854. 'Researches in the South of Ireland'; 'Fairy Legends'; and 'Legends of the Lakes, or Sayings and Doings at Killarney,' show his talent in its happiest moods. His learning was profound and accurate, and his style brilliant and pleasing.

Croly, David Goodman. An American journalist; born in New York, Nov. 3, 1829; died there, April 29, 1889. He was at different times connected with various prominent New York papers. He wrote: 'Life of Horatio Seymour' (1868); 'History of Reconstruction' (1868); 'Glimpses of the Future' (1888); etc.

Croly, George. An Irish poet, dramatist, and novelist; born in Dublin, Aug. 17, 1780; died in London, Nov. 24, 1860. His works include: 'Paris in 1815' (1817); 'The Angel of the World' (1820); 'May Fair' (1820); 'Salathiel' (1829); 'Marston' (1846); 'The Modern Orlando' (1846); 'Life and Times of George IV.'; and others.

Croly, Jane (Cunningham), ("Jennie June.") An American prose-writer, wife of D. G. Croly; born in Market Harborough, England, Dec. 19, 1831; died in New York city, Dec. 23, 1901. From 1860 for many years she was editor of W. J. Demorest's magazine, and was also editor of others. She was one of the founders of "Sorosis" and its president for fourteen years, and one of the most active promoters of the Federation of Woman's Clubs. She published: 'Talks on Women's Topics' (1863); 'For Better or Worse' (1875); and 'Three Manuals for Work' (1885–89); etc.

Cronegk, Johann Friedrich, Baron von (krō'nek). A German dramatist (1731–58); born at Ansbach. Lessing pronounced his ode 'War' one of the finest produced in that day. His tragedy 'Codrus' won a prize in 1757; it is admirable for its smooth and stately verse, but it lacks the true poet's inspiration. He was also author of some comedies, didactic poems, epigrams, and spiritual songs.

Crosby, Howard. A distinguished American Presbyterian divine and educator; born in New

York, Feb. 27, 1826; died there, March 29, 1891. He was chancellor of the University of New York 1870–81; one of the New Testament Revision Committee; and interested in every reform of his day. He wrote: 'Lands of the Moslem' (1850); 'Life of Jesus' (1871); 'The Christian Preacher' (1880, Yale lectures for 1879–80); etc.

Crosswell, William. An American poet and hymn-writer; born in Hudson, N. Y., Nov. 7, 1804; died in Boston, Mass., Nov. 9, 1851. Many of his religious poems and hymns appeared in the collection of 'Poems, Sacred and Secular,' edited by Arthur Cleveland Coxe (1859).

Crowe, Catherine. An English story-teller; born (Stevens) at Borough Green, Kent, about 1800; died 1876. She made her first essay with a tragedy, 'Aristodemus,' and then turned to prose fiction. 'Lily Dawson' (1847) is regarded as the best of her novels. She became an ardent devotee of spiritualism and animal magnetism, and in 1852 published her most notable work, 'The Night Side of Nature' (2 vols., 1852).

Crowe, Eyre Evans. An English historian and prose-writer; born 1799; died 1868. His 'History of France 1830–44' is well known.

Crowe, Joseph Archer. An English historian of art and miscellaneous writer; born in London, Oct. 20, 1825; died at Gamburg, Sept. 6, 1896. He was long eminent as a journalist, and for a time served in the British diplomatic service. His celebrity rests mainly upon the 'History of Painting in Italy' (1864–71), the most important work on this subject, written in collaboration with G. B. Cavalcaselle. He also published other volumes on art subjects.

Crowe, William. An English poet; born in Midgham, Berkshire, October (?) 1745; died at Bath, Feb. 9, 1829. He was a clergyman and the friend of Samuel Rogers. His work, especially 'Lewesdon Hill,' a descriptive poem, was praised by Wordsworth, Coleridge, and Moore as noble in diction and elevating in imagery.

Crowne, John. An English dramatist; born in Nova Scotia, about 1656; died at London (?), about 1703. He was esteemed at court for 'Sir Courtly Nice,' a comedy.

Cruden, Alexander. A Scotch writer; born in Aberdeen, 1700; died 1770. He was noted for his eccentricity. His 'Concordance to the Old and New Testaments' is the familiar authority on the subject.

Cruger, Mrs. Julia Grinnell (Storrow). "Julien Gordon." A popular American novelist; born in France, 18—. Her home is in New York. She has written : 'A Diplomat's Diary'; 'Mademoiselle Réséda'; 'A Puritan Pagan'; 'Marionettes'; 'A Successful man'; 'Vampires'; 'Poppæa'; 'World's People'; 'Poems.'

Cruger, Mary. An American novelist; born in New York State, 1834. Her home is in Montrose, N. Y. She has written: 'Hyperæsthesia' (1885); 'A Den of Thieves' (1886); 'The

Vanderheyde Manor House' (1887); 'How She Did It, or Comfort on $150 a Year' (1888); Brotherhood' (1891).

Crusenstolpe, Magnus Jakob (krö'zen-stol-pe). A Swedish novelist and publicist (1795–1865). He won considerable distinction with a series of historico-romantic tales, 'Little Stories'; but his fame rests mainly on his work as a public journalist, historian, biographer, and politician. His works of fiction became in a degree political or progressist pamphlets; e. g., 'The Moor, or the House of Holstein-Gottorp in Sweden.'

Cruz, Juana Ines de la (krōth). A Mexican poet (1651–95). Retiring from the vice-regal court at the age of 17, she became a nun of the Hieronymite order, and devoted herself to poetry, music, and mathematics, leading at the same time a life of great austerity. Her writings consist of songs, dramas (all these except two on religious themes), prologues, and dramatic sacred allegories. Her contemporaries styled her « the Tenth Muse » and « the Mexican Phœnix. »

Cruz, Ramon de la. A Spanish dramatic poet (1731–99). He rescued the native Spanish drama from an inundation of French influence. A marvelously prolific writer, he produced some 300 pieces in all departments of dramatic composition. But of them all only some interludes can now command attention; these are alive in every line, reflecting with absolute truth the life of the lowest orders.

Cruz, San Juan de la. (St. John of the Cross.) A Spanish mystic and poet (1542–91). He was a Carmelite friar, canonized in 1674. His prose writings on the inner life won for him the title « The Ecstatic Doctor »; famous among them is 'The Soul's Darksome Night.' In form and spirit his poetry is noble, deep, and inspired by profound feeling. His complete 'Spiritual Works' were first published in 1619, and in a 12th edition 1703.

Crinkle, Nym. See **Wheeler.**

Császár, Ferencz (chä'zär). A Hungarian poet (1807–58). His 'Poems,' mostly sonnets in the Italian style and nautical songs, entitle him to a place among true poets. He translated several works of Alfieri, Beccaria, Silvio Pellico, and other Italian writers, into Hungarian.

Csiky, Gregor (chēk'ē). A Hungarian dramatist (1842–91); born at Buda-Pesth. He wrote several very successful comedies, among them 'The Oracle' and 'Suspicion.' His tragedies also — 'Janus'; 'Spartacus'; 'The Magician' — were received with great popular favor. He wrote several novels, and translated plays of Sophocles, Euripides, Plautus, Molière, and British dramatists.

Csokonay, Vitéz Mihály (chō'kō-noi). A Hungarian poet (1773–1805). He drew from the well of the national poesy, and so contributed to the formation of a native lyricism.

His principal works are: 'The Hungarian Muse' (1797); 'Dorothea,' a comic epos (1804); 'Odes' (1805); 'The Shepherd King' (1806); 'Anacreontics'; 'Battle of Frogs and Mice.'

Cuellar, José T. de (kwāl'är). A Mexican novelist, dramatist, and poet; born at San Luis Potosi, Aug. 15, 1835. His reputation rests mainly on his novel 'The Sin of the Century,' published at San Luis Potosi in 1868. His comedies and dramas include: 'Duties and Sacrifices'; 'Redemption'; and 'A Voyage to the Orient.' Among his novels are: 'Isolina, the Ex-Ballet Girl'; and 'Gabriel the Locksmith.' He has also written several poems.

Cueva, Juan de la (kwā'vä). A Spanish poet (1550–1607); born at Seville. A poet attempting all forms, he excelled most as a dramatist: he is one of the founders of Spanish national drama. In a volume of 'Works' (1582) he published a number of lyric poems, sonnets, songs, and elegies, including the 'Lament of Venus over Adonis'; noteworthy is his 'Phœbean Chorus of Historical Romances' (1587). His greatest epic is 'The Conquest of Betica' (1603). He wrote four tragedies, one of them on 'The Sack of Rome' by the Constable Bourbon; and ten comedies, one of the best being 'The Aged Lover.'

Cumberland, Richard. An English dramatist, novelist, essayist, and poet, grandson of Richard Bentley; born at Cambridge, Feb. 19, 1732; died at Tunbridge Wells, May 7, 1811. Of good family and the highest prospects, he was discredited and impoverished in public service, and made literature a profession. His comedies, 'The West Indian'; 'The Wheel of Fortune'; 'The Jew'; and 'The Fashionable Lover,' are an epitome of the culture of the time; as are his essays, collected under the title of 'The Observer.' He wrote novels, tracts, religious and didactic poems, not now important; 'Anecdotes of Eminent Painters in Spain'; 'Memoirs' (1806).

Cummins, Maria Susanna. An American novelist; born at Salem, Mass., April 9, 1827; died at Dorchester, Mass., Oct. 1, 1866. Her novel 'The Lamplighter' (1853) had enormous success and was translated into foreign languages; it is still remembered for the idyllic charm and tenderness of its first few chapters, but the rest is commonplace. Her other books are 'Mabel Vaughn' (1857); 'El Fureidis' (1860); 'Haunted Hearts' (1863).

Cunningham, Allan. A Scottish poet and miscellaneous writer; born in Keir, Dumfries-shire, Dec. 7, 1784; died in London, Oct. 30 (not 29), 1842. When a youth he served as an apprentice to a stone-mason; but later became a reporter in London, and wrote 'Sir Marmaduke Maxwell,' a dramatic poem, and 'Lord Roldan' and 'Paul Jones,' interesting but rather theatrical romances. His 'Critical History of the Literature of the Last Fifty Years' and other books prompted Sir Walter Scott to call him a genius.

Cupples, George. A Scotch sketch and story writer; born in Legewood, Aug. 2, 1822; died Oct. 7, 1891. In 'The Green Hand' he gives us a stirring tale of the sea; while his papers on outdoor sports and tastes, and his essays on literary topics, denote the scholar and man of true feeling.

Curtin, Jeremiah. An American linguist and antiquarian writer; born in Milwaukee, 1840. He has written: 'Myths and Folk-Lore of Ireland'; 'Tales of the Fairies and the Ghost World'; 'Myths and Folk-Tales of the Russians, Western Slavs, and Magyars'; etc. He is a proficient in the Slavic tongues; has made addresses in Czech, and translated much from Russian and Polish. Died Dec. 14, 1906.

Curtis, Mrs. Caroline Gardiner (Cary). ("Carroll Winchester.") An American novelist; born in New York State, 1827. Her home is in Boston. She has written: 'From Madge to Margaret' (1880); 'The Love of a Lifetime' (1883).

Curtis, George Ticknor. An American lawyer; born in Massachusetts, 1812; died March 28, 1894. In addition to his eminence at the New York bar, he was noted as the author of an authoritative 'History of the Constitution of the United States'; he published likewise: 'Digest of English and American Admiralty Decisions'; 'American Conveyancer'; 'Life of James Buchanan'; 'Life of Daniel Webster'; 'Creation or Evolution'; and 'John Charaxes,' a novel.

Curtis, George William. An American author; born in Providence, R. I., Feb. 24, 1824; died at Staten Island, Aug. 31, 1892. He was an early abolitionist, and a leader in the Republican party from the first; for many years the editor of Harper's Weekly, and the writer of the 'Editor's Easy Chair' in Harper's Monthly, besides the 'Manners upon the Road' series for Harper's Bazar (1867–73). He was also a lecturer of great popularity. His works include: 'Nile Notes of a Howadji' (1851); 'The Howadji in Syria' (1852); 'Lotus Eating' (1852); 'Potiphar Papers' (1853); 'Prue and I' (1856); 'Trumps' (1862); and others.

Curtis, William Eleroy. An American journalist and writer of travels; born in Ohio, 1850. He has written: 'Capitals of Spanish America' (1888); 'The Land of the Nihilist' (1888); 'Japan Sketches'; 'Venezuela'; 'Life of Zachariah Chandler'; 'The Yankees of the East'; 'The True Abraham Lincoln'; 'Modern India.'

Curtius, Ernst (kör'tsē-ös). A distinguished German archæologist and historian; born at Lübeck, Sept. 2, 1814; died at Berlin, July 11, 1896. His studies were devoted to Grecian antiquity, and he visited Greece repeatedly on scientific missions. In 'Peloponnesus' (2 vols., 1851) he gives the history of that peninsula, its traditions, and its works of art. His 'Greek History' is a popularization of the results of scholarly research, and is written in a pleasing and popular style. His works on 'Olympia'

and other ancient cities are addressed rather to scholars than to the general public.

Cushing, Caleb. A famous American jurist, statesman, and diplomatist; born at Salisbury, Mass., Jan. 17, 1800; died at Newburyport, Mass., Jan. 2, 1879. He was United States commissioner to China (1843–44); Attorney-General (1853–57); Counsel before the Geneva arbitration tribunal (1871–72); minister to Spain (1874–77). He published: 'Reminiscences of Spain'; 'Life of William Henry Harrison' (1840); 'History of Newburyport' (1826); etc.

Custer, Elizabeth (Bacon). An American prose writer; born in Monroe, Mich., 18—; wife of Gen. George A. Custer. She is author of 'Boots and Saddles, or Life in Dakota with General Custer' (1885); 'Tenting on the Plains, or General Custer in Kansas and Texas' (1887); and 'Following the Guidon.'

Custine, Astolphe, Marquis de (küs-tēn'). A French novelist and writer of travels (1790–1857); born near Metz. He traveled in the British Isles, Switzerland, and Southern Italy (1811–22), and afterward in Spain and Russia. The results of his observations in Russia were of considerable importance, and were published in 4 vols., 1843. He wrote a tragedy, 'Beatrice Cenci'; and some romances, among them 'Aloysius, or the Monk of St. Bernard'; 'Romuald, or the Vocation.' His 'Letters to Varnhagen von Ense and Rachel Varnhagen von Ense' were published in 1870.

Custis, George Washington Parke. An American writer; born at Mt. Airy, Md., April 30, 1781; died at Arlington House, Fairfax County, Va., Oct. 10, 1857. He was the adopted son of George Washington. He wrote 'Recollections of Washington' (1860), and several plays and orations.

Cutler, Elbridge Jefferson. An American educator and miscellaneous writer; born in Holliston, Mass., Dec. 28, 1831; died in Cambridge, Mass., Dec. 27, 1870. From 1865 until his death he was professor of modern languages at Harvard. His contributions appeared in the Atlantic Monthly and other periodicals. 'War Poems' was published in 1867, and 'Stella' in 1868.

Cutler, Mrs. Lizzie (Petit). An American novelist; born in Virginia, 1836. Her home is in New York. She has written: 'Light and Darkness'; 'Household Mysteries,' a romance of Southern life; 'The Stars of the Crowd.'

Cuvier, Georges Léopold Chrétien Frédéric Dagobert (kü-vyä'). A celebrated French zoölogist; born at Montbéliard, Aug. 23, 1769; died at Paris, May 13, 1832. His first great work, fruit of most laborious researches, was 'Lectures on Comparative Anatomy' (5 vols., 1801), comprising for the most part only such points of molluscan anatomy as he himself had developed. It was the same with all his works: they are records of most painstaking labor and study. His grand generalizations on the facts of nature appear in the 'Discourse on the Revolutions of the Earth's Surface and on the Changes They have Brought About in the Animal Kingdom.' His master work is 'The Animal Kingdom' (4 vols., 1817).

Cuyler, Theodore Ledyard. A noted American Presbyterian divine and miscellaneous writer; born at Aurora, N. Y., Jan. 10, 1822. Besides numerous contributions to newspapers and other periodicals, he has written. 'Heart Life' (1871); 'From the Nile to Norway' (1881); 'Stirring the Eagle's Nest' (1890); Help and Good Cheer' (1902); 'Our Christmastides' (1904).

Cyrano de Bergerac, Savinien (sēr-ä-nō dẹ berzh-räk'). A French writer of literary extravaganzas (1619–55); born at Paris. He was a famous duelist, and fought more than a thousand single combats, most of them provoked by comments on his enormously overgrown nose. In style and composition he is without taste or judgment; but he is always sprightly and fanciful, often witty and ingenious. Boileau noted his «daring burlesque.» He wrote: 'Letters,' amorous or satirical; a 'Comic History of the States and Empire of the Moon,' and another 'Of the Sun,' both full of metaphysical and satirical passages in the vein later made famous by Swift, to whom they are thought to have suggested 'Gulliver.' His one tragedy, 'Agrippina,' evinces great dramatic power; he wrote also a clever comedy, 'The Pedant Laughing-Stock.'

Czajkovski, Michal (chĭ-kov'skē). A Polish novelist (1808–76). He entered the Turkish army in 1851, embraced Mohammedanism and rose to high rank (Pasha Sadyk); later he went back to the Ukraine and conformed to the Russo-Greek religion. He struck a new and original vein in fiction-writing. The force and fire of his characterizations are extraordinary. His greatest work is 'Vernyhora,' a historical novel of the year 1768, which has been translated into nearly all the languages of Europe. Hardly less celebrated is 'The Hetman of the Ukraine.'

Czuczor, Gergely (tsö tsor or chö'chor). A Hungarian poet and philologist (1800–66). His two fine hero-ballads, 'The Battle of Augsburg' (1824) and 'The Diet of Arad' (1828), brought him instant celebrity. He was a Benedictine monk, and the eroticism of the first collection of his 'Poetical Works' (1836) brought on him stern animadversion from his superiors. In 1848 he published 'Reveil,' a passionate appeal to Hungarian national sentiment, and was imprisoned for it.

D

Daae, Ludvig (dä'ĕ). A Norwegian historian; born in Aremark, near Frederikshald, Dec. 7, 1834. He has paid particular attention to the annals of his own country; his best-known works being: 'Norwegian Village Legends' (1870–72); 'Norway's Saints' (1879); 'The Migrations of the Norsemen to Holland and England' (1880); and others in this field.

Dabney, Robert Lewis. An American prose-writer; born in Louisa County, Va., March 5, 1820. He was a Presbyterian clergyman, and since 1883 has filled the chair of moral philosophy in the University of Texas. Dr. Dabney has published: 'Life of General T. J. (Stonewall) Jackson' (1864); 'Sacred Rhetoric' (1866); 'Sensualistic Philosophy' (1878); and 'The Christian Sabbath' (1881). 'Collected Discussions' is one of his late works. D. 1898.

Dabney, Virginius. An American prose-writer; born at Elmington, Va., Feb. 15, 1835. His publication of 'The Story of Don Miff, as Told by his Friend, John Bouche Whacker, a Symphony of Life' (1886), reached its fourth edition in six months. He also published 'Gold that Did not Glitter.'

Daboll, Nathan. An American educator and writer; born about 1750; died in Groton, Conn., March 9, 1818. He wrote the 'Schoolmaster's Assistant' (1799) and the 'Practical Navigator.' He is best known for his share in the universally used 'New England Almanac,' which he began in 1773.

Daboll, Nathan. An American writer; born in Connecticut, 1782; died 1863. He was son of the preceding, and compiled the 'New England Almanac' begun by his father. He is the author of 'Daboll's New Arithmetic,' long a terror to the American schoolboy.

Dach, Simon (däch). A German lyrist (1605–59); born at Memel. His numerous hymns and songs are found in various collections, his hymns especially in the 'Spiritual Arias' of Heinrich Albert. He wrote several occasional poems in honor of the Electoral House of Brandenburg,—'Electoral Brandenburgian Rose, Eagle, Lion, and Sceptre.' He often followed his native poetic bent, disregarding the hard and fast rules of the poetic schools of his time; and then he was spontaneous, natural, and spoke directly to the popular heart. His 'Annie of Tharau,' a Low-German lay for the wedding of his friend Parson Portatius with Anna Neander, became a popular favorite; his 'Praise of Friendship' seems to belong to a better age; and his spiritual songs, 'In Thy Control, O Lord,' 'Be Comforted, my Soul,' etc., are hardly surpassed by any compositions of his day.

Da Costa, Izaak (dä kos'tä). A Dutch poet and theologian; born at Amsterdam, Jan. 14, 1798; died at Leyden, April 28, 1860. Among his works are: 'Prometheus' (1820); 'Poems' (1821–22); 'Gala Songs' (1828); and 'Hagar' (1840).

Dacre, Barbarina Brand, Lady. An English poet and dramatist; born (Ogle) 1768; died in London, May 17, 1854. Her singular gifts and her faculty for poetic imagery are richly shown in 'Gonzalvo of Cordova' (1810); a drama, 'Pedarias' (1811), a tragedy of ancient Peruvian civilization; and the five-act masterpiece 'Ina'; in addition to which a series of 'Translations from the Italian' are both spirited and accurate.

Daems, Servaas Domien (däms). A Flemish poet; born at Noorderwyk, about 1838. His verse is seen at its best in the collection called 'Luit en Fluit' (1884). Died 1903.

Dahl, Konrad Neuman Hjelm (däl). A Norwegian story-teller; born in the parish of Drontheim, June 24, 1843. He is author of a series of stories and novels of Norwegian and Lapp life, with much insight into nature and into the heart of the people. Most notable among them are: 'The Finnish Youth' (1873); 'The Lion' (1874); 'Eda Mansika' (1875); 'The Voyager in the Icy Sea'; 'Lonely People.'

Dahl or Dal, Dalj, Vladimir Ivanovitch (däl). A Russian story-writer and etymologist; born in Lugan, Nov. 22, 1801; died in Moscow, Oct. 4, 1872. He wrote many powerful realistic tales, besides an 'Expository Dictionary of 'The Living Russian Languages' (1861-68) and a dictionary of proverbs.

Dahlgren, Fredrik August (däl'gren). A Swedish poet and dramatist; born at Taberg, Sept. 20, 1816; died at Djursholm, Feb. 16, 1895. He wrote many dialect songs and ballads, collections of which were published in three volumes (1876). These have attained an extraordinary degree of popularity. Of his dramas many were very successful; his 'Vermlandingarne,' a musical drama (1846), had more than 100 consecutive representations. He translated many dramas from foreign languages, and wrote a history of the Swedish stage.

Dahlgren, Karl Fredrik. A Swedish poet and humorist (1791-1844); born at Stensbruk in East Gothland. He excelled in descriptions of nature and in the idyllic burlesque. Many of his songs and ballads have a permanent place in the treasury of Swedish popular song. For years he published a Muses' Almanac, containing his stories and comic sketches. His novel 'Nahum Fredrik Bergström's Chronicle' (1831) is a work of distinguished merit.

Dahlgren, Madeleine Vinton. An American prose-writer and poet, wife of Admiral Dahlgren; born in Gallipolis, O., about 1835; died at Washington, May 28, 1898. Her works include: 'Idealities' (1859); 'South Sea Sketches' (1881); 'Etiquette of Social Life in Washington' (1881); 'Memoirs of John A. Dahlgren' (1882); 'The Lost Name'; and 'Lights and Shadows of a Life' (1886). For her Spanish translation of Donoso Cortes's 'Catholicism, Liberalism, and Socialism,' she received the thanks of Pius IX.

Dahlmann, Friedrich Christoph (däl'män). A German historian and publicist; born in Wismar, May 13, 1785; died in Bonn, Dec. 5, 1860. His attainments and popularity gave him great influence in Hanoverian politics, but he lost his professorship at Göttingen because of his liberal opinions, and after many vicissitudes devoted himself to historical writing. His 'History of the English Revolution' (1844) and 'History of the French Revolution' (1845) are magnificent studies; but it is in the 'History of Denmark (1840-43) that his powers are most brilliantly displayed.

Dahn, Felix (dan). A distinguished German poet, novelist, and historian; born at Hamburg, Feb. 9, 1834. He was professor of jurisprudence successively in the universities of Munich, Würtzburg, Königsberg, and Breslau. Among his historical works is 'The Kings of the Germans,' his masterpiece in this department (6 vols., 1861-71). He is author also of many tractates on the jurisprudence of the ancient Germans, and the civil and criminal law and procedure of modern German States. He has also written epic and lyric poems remarkable for strong thought, wide horizon, and verbal richness. Of the epics may be named 'Harald and Theano' (1856); of the lyrics, 'Ballads and Songs' (1878). He is author also of several historical novels, uniting profound scholarship with poetic fancy, foremost among them 'The Struggle for Rome' (1876), with scene laid in the 6th century. He has written stories of contemporary life as well; and dramas, as 'German Fidelity'; 'King Roderick,' and 'Markgrave Rüdeger of Bechelaren.'

D'Alembert. See Alembert.

Dalin, Olof von (däl'in). A distinguished Swedish poet and historian, "father of modern Swedish literature"; born at Vinberga, in Halland, August 29, 1708; died Aug. 12, 1763. He found Swedish poetry over-austere and melancholy; he infused into it a sense of the joy of existence. He at the same time enriched the Swedish mother tongue with elements of vocabulary and forms of expression from foreign languages and literatures, which to some extent modified the native speech. The influence of the study of the French classical drama is seen in his epic poem 'Sweden's Liberties' (1742), his drama 'Brynhilda' (1738), and his comedy 'The Jealous Man' (1738). But in his numerous songs and ballads he is a Swede, with a rich fund of humor. His 'History of the Kingdom of Sweden' (4 vols.), reaching to the death of Charles IX., holds an honorable place in Swedish historical literature.

Dall, Caroline Wells. An American prose-writer; born in Boston, Mass., June 22, 1822. She has been an industrious literary worker, and is the author of many books, in which are included: 'Essays and Sketches' (1849); 'Woman's Right to Labor' (1860); 'Egypt's Place in History' (1868); 'Patty Gray's Journey to the Cotton Islands'; and 'What We Really Know about Shakespeare' (1885).

Dall, William Healey. An American naturalist and author; born in Boston, Mass., Aug.

21, 1845; is a member of many of the scientific societies at home and abroad. His scientific articles include about two hundred titles. Among his published books are : ' Alaska and its Resources' (1870) ; ' The Currents and Temperatures of Bering Sea and the Adjacent Waters' (1882) ; and ' Report on the Mollusca, Brachiopoda, and Pelecypoda' of the Blake dredging expedition in the West Indies (1886). He has further published ' Pacific Coast Pilot' and 'Coast Pilot of Alaska' ; ' Alaska and its Resources.'

Dallas, Robert Charles. An English poet, novelist, and dramatist; born in Kingston, Jamaica, 1754; died in Normandy, France, 1824. His publications include : ' Poems' ; ' Lucretia,' a tragedy' ; ' Moral Essays' (1797) ; ' Aubrey,' a novel; and ' The Morlands, Tales Illustrative of the Simple and the Surprising' (1805). He was both friend and adviser of Lord Byron, and in the last year of his life published ' Recollections of the Life of Lord Byron from 1808 to the End of 1814.'

Dall' Ongaro, Francesco (dal'ong-gär'ō). An Italian poet (1808–73) ; born at Mansue in Treviso. He was a priest; being also an ardent patriot, he came into disfavor with the ecclesiastical and civil authorities at Padua, and was suspended from priestly functions. In 1848 he took part in the revolutionary movement, and after its suppression was an exile till 1859. His voluminous writings, both prose and verse, are in part literary, in part political, but all inspired by liberalism and patriotic sentiment. His principal works are : ' Poems' (2 vols., 1840) ; several dramas—one of them, ' Bianca Capello,' written for Ristori; some comedies; several novels; besides legendary stories, hymns, and several popular ballads.

Dalrymple, Sir David, Lord Hailes. A Scotch jurist and historian; born in Edinburgh, Oct. 28, 1726; died Nov. 29, 1792. He was on the bench for many years. His writings include 'Annals of Scotland,' a valuable work, embracing the period from Malcolm Canmore to the accession of the house of Stuart.

Dalsème, Achille (däl-sām'). A French journalist, topical writer, and novelist; born in Nice, Sept. 4, 1840. He connected himself with various political sheets in the capital, and wrote : ' Claude's Folly' (1884), ' The Sins of Themis' (1889), and other studies of contemporary manners; ' The Bazaine Affair' (1873); and ' The Art of War' (1883), a collection of light sketches.

Daly, Charles Patrick. An American jurist and author; born in New York city, Oct. 31, 1816 ; died near Sag Harbor, L. I., Sept. 19, 1899. He had a distinguished career, becoming justice of the court of common pleas in 1844, first judge of the court in 1857, and chief justice in 1871, retiring in 1886. He was president of the American Geographical Society. His works include : ' First Settlement of Jews in North America '); ' What We Know of Maps and Map Drawing before Mercator ' ; and similar investigations.

Daly, [John] Augustin. An American dramatist, and proprietor of Daly's Theatre, New York; born in Plymouth, N. C., July 20, 1838 ; died in Paris, June 7, 1899. Among his plays are : ' Divorce ' ; ' Pique ' ; ' Horizon ' ; ' Under the Gaslight ' ; and a story called ' Peg Woffington, a Tribute to the Actress and the Woman.'

Dana, Charles Anderson. An eminent American journalist and man of letters; born at Hinsdale, N. H., Aug. 8, 1819; died at Dosoris, Long Island, Oct. 17, 1897. Studied at Harvard. In 1842 he was a member of the Brook Farm Association. His first journalistic experience was in Boston. From 1847 until 1862 he was managing editor of the New York Tribune; he was Assistant Secretary of War in 1863 and until the close of the war. The New York Sun was reorganized in 1868, from which year until his death he was its editor. With George Ripley he edited ' The American Cyclopædia' (1857–63 ; revised edition was published in 1873–76) ; he also edited ' The Household Book of Poetry' (1857), of which many editions have been printed. His war reminiscences are now (1897) being published.

Dana, James Dwight. An American scientist ; born at Utica, N. Y., Feb. 12, 1813 ; died at New Haven, April 14, 1895. His researches into geology made him famous, and his professorship at Yale proved epoch-making in the history of that seat of learning. He published: 'System of Mineralogy'; 'Manual of Mineralogy'; 'Text-Book of Geology'; 'Corals and Coral Islands'; 'The Geological Story Briefly Told'; etc.

Dana, Mrs. Mary. See **Shindler.**

Dana, Richard Henry, the Elder. An American poet and essayist; born at Cambridge, Mass., Nov. 15, 1787; died Feb. 2, 1879. His lectures on Shakespeare's characters, delivered in the principal cities of the Atlantic coast (1839–40), awakened a deep public interest. His principal poems are: ' The Change of Home' (1824) ; ' The Dying Raven' (1825) ; ' The Buccaneers' (1827), specially noteworthy for its magnificent descriptions of the vicissitudes of ocean scenery. To a periodical publication, The Idle Man (N. Y., 1821–22), of which he was editor, he contributed critical papers and several short stories; among them ' Paul Fenton,' and ' Edward and Mary.'

Dana, Richard Henry, the Younger. A distinguished American publicist, son of R. H. the Elder; born at Cambridge, Mass., Aug. 1, 1815; died Jan. 6, 1882. Obliged to suspend college studies because of an affection of the eyes, he shipped as a seaman on board a whaling vessel. His observations during the two years of his life as a common sailor are contained in his celebrated narrative ' Two Years Before the Mast' (1837). Returning to Boston, he studied law and was admitted to the bar. In 1841 he published ' The Seaman's Friend,' often afterward republished under the title ' The Seaman's Manual.' He details his experiences and observations during a visit to Cuba, in the little volume 'To Cuba and Back' (1859). He edited Wheaton's 'Elements of International Law' (1866), and wrote a series of 'Letters on Italian Unity' (1871).

Danby, Frank; an English novelist; born July 30, 1864. She wrote: 'A Babe in Bohemia' (1882); 'Pigs in Clover.' (1902); 'Sebastian' (1909).

Dancourt (dän-kör), properly Florent Carton. A French playwright and dramatic artist (1661-1725); born at Fontainebleau. His best low comedies or farces are; 'The Fashionable Chevalier'; 'The Winsome Gardener.' He presents village life with perfect truth, and is master of village *patois*. Voltaire ranks him next after Molière for low comedy.

Dändliker, Karl (den'dlik-er). A Swiss historian; born in Rorbas, Zürich, May 6, 1849. Among his works are: 'Manual of the History of the Swiss People' (1875), and 'Smaller History of Switzerland' (1889); 'History of Switzerland' (1900).

Daneo, Giovanni (dän'ä-ō). An Italian dramatist; born at St. Remy in Piedmont, May 16, 1824. He wrote some dramas of very considerable merit: 'Suleika'; 'Elisa di Montalpino'; also novels: 'Memoirs of a Gentleman' and 'The Castle of Bardespina.' His poetical works consist of two volumes of miscellaneous 'Poems' and 'Verses,' with 'Gotama' and 'Rafaello Sanzio.'

Danforth, Samuel. An American clergyman of learning and influence. He was born in Roxbury, Mass., Dec. 18, 1666, and died in Taunton, Mass., Nov. 14, 1727. For a long period he was pastor of the Congregational Church at Taunton, Mass., and during a religious awakening wrote three famous descriptive letters. He published a 'Eulogy on Thomas Leonard' (1713); 'Essay Concerning the Singing of Psalms' (1723); and prepared an Indian dictionary now the property of the Massachusetts Historical Society.

Dangeau, Philippe de Courcillon, Marquis de (dän-gō'). A French writer of memoirs; born in 1638; died in Paris (?) in 1720. He was one of the courtiers about Louis XIV.; his 'Memoirs' and 'Journal,' particularly as regards the period between 1684 and 1720, being a rich mine from which much history has been quarried.

Daniel, Samuel. An English poet, historian, and rhyming chronicler; born near Taunton, Somersetshire, 1562; died near Beckington, Wiltshire, October 1619. He was conspicuous at the courts of Elizabeth and James I., writing a rhymed 'History of the Civil Wars between the Houses of York and Lancaster' (1595), and a prose 'History of England' (to Edward III.: 1613-18). His style as a sonneteer and lyrist appears in the collection named 'Delia' (1592).

Daniels, Mrs. Cora (Linn). An American novelist; born in 1852. She resides at Franklin, Mass., and has written: 'Sardia, a Story of Love'; 'As It Is to Be'; 'Psychical Philosophy.'

Daniels, William Haven. An American prose-writer; born in Franklin, Mass., May 18, 1836. His literary works are: 'That Boy: Who Shall Have Him?' (1878); 'The Temperance Reform and its Great Reformers' (1878); 'Moody, his Words, Work, and Workers' (1879); and 'A Short History of the People Called Methodist' (1882).

Danilevskij, Grigórij Petróvich (dän-ēl-ef'skē). A Russian story-teller (1829-90); born at Danilovka in the government of Charkof. His stories are either descriptive of ethnographical peculiarities, and on that account specially valuable, or they are historical novels. To the former class belong: 'The Refugees'; 'The Refugees' Return'; 'Liberty.' His principal historical novels are: 'Mirowitsh'; 'The Burning of Moscow'; 'The Black Year.'

Dannelly, Mrs. Elizabeth Otis (Marshall). An American Southern verse-writer. She was born in Georgia in 1838. She has written: 'Cactus, or Thorns and Blossoms'; 'Wayside Flowers.'

Dante Alighieri (dän'te äl-ē-gyä'rē). The greatest of Italian poets; born in Florence, 1265; died in Ravenna, Sept. 14, 1321. His chief works are: 'Poems'; 'The New Life'; 'The Banquet'; 'On Monarchy'; 'A Guide to Poetical Literature'; and 'The Divine Comedy.'

Da Ponte, Lorenzo. An Italian dramatist and author; born in Venice, March 10, 1749; died in New York, Aug. 17, 1838. He wrote the libretti for Mozart's operas 'Don Giovanni' and 'Figaro.' He came to America in 1805, and in 1828 was professor of Italian in Columbia College. He wrote many plays, sonnets, and translations, and published several works of instruction in the Italian language; also his own 'Life' (1823); 'History of the Florentine Republic and the Medici' (1833).

D'Arblay, Madame. See **Burney**.

Dargan, Clara Victoria. (Mrs. Maclean.) An American poet and prose-writer; born near Winnsboro, S. C., about 1840. Her writings include the poem 'Forever Thine' (1859), under the pseudonym of "Claudia," and stories signed "Esther Chesney" (1860). She was literary editor of the Edgefield Advertiser (1863); and is author of 'Riverlands,' a story of life on the Ashley River.

Darimon, Alfred (där-ē-môn'). A French journalist and writer; born in Lille, Dec. 17, 1819. An aptitude for politics and political writing occasioned his most telling work with the pen, especially 'The History of Twelve Years, 1857-69, Notes and Recollections' (1883); 'Through a Revolution' (1884); 'The Agony of the Empire' (2d ed. 1891); and others equally popular.

Darley, Felix Octavius Carr. An American artist; born in Philadelphia, June 23, 1822; died in Claymont, Del., March 27, 1888. His illustrations of literary masterpieces gave pleasure to thousands, and made him famous. His best work comprises his drawings to accompany the text of 'Rip Van Winkle'; 'Sleepy Hollow'; 'Courtship of Miles Standish'; 'Scarlet

Letter'; 'Evangeline'; the novels of Cooper, Dickens, and others, besides many special pictures. His book 'Sketches Abroad with Pen and Pencil' (1868) is well known.

Darley, George. An Irish poet and critic; born in Dublin, 1795; died near Rome (?), Nov. 23, 1846. He wrote valuable studies of other men's work, and was a mathematician of profundity; in addition to which claims to attention, he is the author of 'Sylvia, or the May Queen' (1827), a fine dramatic poem; 'Errors of Extasie and Other Poems'; and 'Nepenthe,' a weird self-revelation in morbid verse.

Darling, Mrs. Flora (Adams). An American novelist; born in New Hampshire in 1840. Among her works are: 'Mrs. Darling's Letters' (1884); 'A Wayward Winning Woman'; 'The Bourbon Lily'; 'A Social Diplomat'; 'The Senator's Daughter'; 'Memories of Virginia.'

Darlington, William. An American scientist, well-known botanist, and author. He was born in Birmingham, Pa., April 28, 1782; died in Westchester, Pa., April 23, 1863. He was a soldier in the War of 1812, and a Member of Congress from 1815 to 1817 and 1819 to 1823. He published a descriptive catalogue of plants in Pennsylvania: 'Flora Cestrica' (1837 and 1853); 'Mutual Influence of Habits and Disease' (1804); 'Agricultural Botany' (1847); and in 1853 a genus of pitcher plant found in California was named in his honor, 'Darlingtonia.'

Darmesteter, Agnes Mary Frances (Robinson). An English poet; born in Leamington, 1857. She has attained great proficiency in Greek studies, her verse showing the influence of Hellenic literature. In 1888 she married James Darmesteter, the Orientalist. Her writings include: 'A Handful of Honeysuckle' (1878); 'An Italian Garden' (1886); 'Lyrics' (1891); 'Retrospect' (1893); 'Life of Renan' (1897); 'The Queen of Navarre' (1900); 'The Return to Nature' (1904).

Darmesteter, James (där-me-ste-tär'). A distinguished French Orientalist; born at Château-Salins, March 28, 1849; died Oct. 19, 1894. Besides works of strict scholarship on the Oriental literatures, as 'Ormazd and Ahriman'; 'Iranian Studies'; 'Origins of Persian Poetry,' he wrote many essays on miscellaneous subjects. There is an English translation of some of his 'Selected Essays.' He translated with Mills the 'Zend-Avesta' for the 'Sacred Books of the East' series, published by the University of Oxford and edited by Max Müller.

Daru, Count Pierre Antoine (dä-rü). A French historian and poet; born in Montpellier, Jan. 12, 1767; died on his estate near Meulan, Sept. 5, 1829. A translation of Horace into French verse (1800) was greatly admired; but his masterpiece is a 'History of the Republic of Venice' (1819), although his 'Cléopédie, or Theory of Literary Reputations' (1800) is a poem containing much to recommend it.

D'Arusmont, Madame Frances (dä-rüs-môn). (Maiden name Fanny Wright.) An American philanthropist and author; born in Dundee, Scotland, Sept. 6, 1795; died in Cincinnati, O., Dec. 2, 1852. She visited this country several times, and in 1825 made an unsuccessful attempt to establish a settlement for the elevation of the negro at Memphis, Tenn. In later years she lectured on social, religious, and political questions. Among her works are: 'Views on Society and Manners in America'; 'Altorf,' a tragedy (1819); 'Lectures on Free Inquiry' (1836).

Darwin, Charles Robert. A celebrated English naturalist and philosopher; born at Shrewsbury, Feb. 12, 1809; died April 19, 1882. His life work as a naturalist began in 1831, when he sailed with Captain Fitzroy in the Beagle for a surveying expedition round the globe. From this expedition Darwin returned toward the end of 1836; in 1839 appeared his 'Journal of Researches,' afterward revised and published under the better known title 'A Naturalist's Voyage.' Several monographs followed on various points of land and marine zoölogy; but not until 1859 did the work appear which brought to Darwin world-wide and enduring fame — 'On the Origin of Species by Means of Natural Selection.' 'The Descent of Man and Selection in Relation to Sex' appeared in 1871, and 'The Expression of the Emotions in Men and Animals' in 1872. In 1868 he published 'The Variation of Animals and Plants under Domestication.' He is buried in Westminster Abbey.

Darwin, Erasmus. An English naturalist and poet, grandfather of Charles R.; born in Elston, Nottingham, Dec. 12, 1731; died at Breads Priory, near Derby, April 18, 1802. «The permanent interest in his writings depends upon his exposition of the form of evolutionism afterwards expounded by Lamarck. He caught a glimpse of many observations and principles afterwards turned to account by his grandson, Charles Darwin; but though a great observer and an acute thinker, he missed the characteristic doctrine which made the success of his grandson's scheme.» His literary works are: 'The Botanic Garden' (1781); a descriptive poem, 'The Temple of Nature, or the Origin of Society' (1803), a specimen of highly didactic versification; and 'Zoönomia' (1794-98), a prose work on organic life. As a poet he is lofty and instructive.

Dasent, Sir George Webbe. An English philologist and novelist; born in the island of St. Vincent, May 22, 1817; died at Ascot, June 11, 1896. He was for a while one of the editors of the London Times, and was one of the Civil Service Commissioners. He was eminent as a scholar in the Norse languages, particularly Icelandic, and translated the 'Younger Edda,' besides other ancient stories and legends of Iceland, and wrote 'The Norseman in Iceland' (1858). Among his original stories are: 'Annals of an Eventful Life'; 'Three to One'; 'Half a Life.'

Dash, Countess (däsh), pseudonym of Gabrielle Anne Cisterne de Courtiras, Vicomtesse de Saint-Mars. A French novelist (1804-72); born at Poitiers. She was a very prolific writer, producing often five or six stories in the course of a year. Life in high society is her theme, and especially wayward love in high society, as the very titles of most of her novels indicate: 'Bussy-Rabutin's Amours'; 'Gallantries of the Court of Louis XV.'; 'Last Amours of Mme. du Barry'; 'Adventures of a Young Married Woman.'

Dassoucy or d'Assoucy, Charles Coippeau, called (dä-sö-sē'). A French burlesque poet; born in Paris, Oct. 16, 1605; died there (?), 1679. He acquired notoriety as the writer of 'Ovid in a Good Humor,' and of a burlesque of Claudian's 'Rape of Proserpine'; but he is remembered mainly because of a contemptuous allusion to him by Boileau. He seems to have possessed some talent for musical composition, but called himself "the emperor of burlesque."

Daubenton, Louis Jean Marie (dō-banton'). A French botanist and naturalist; born in Montbar, Burgundy, May 29, 1716; died in Paris, Dec. 31, 1799. He contributed to the first five volumes of Buffon's 'Natural History' anatomical supplements which form, from a scientific point of view, the most important part of that work.

D'Aubigné, Jean Henri Merle (dō-bēn-yā'). A celebrated Swiss Protestant church historian; born near Geneva, Aug. 16, 1794; died at Geneva, Oct. 24, 1872. He was professor of historical theology at Geneva (1831-72). His great work was 'History of the Reformation' (1835-53; new ed. 1877-78), with its continuation 'History of the Reformation in the Time of Calvin' (1863-76).

Daudet, Alphonse (dō-dä). A distinguished French novelist; born at Nîmes, May 13, 1840; died Dec. 16, 1897. He sought fortune in Paris in 1857: two booklets of poems were failures; two plays—'The Last Idol' (1862) and 'The White Daisy' (1865)—had more success; after some years he discovered his true field. His charming little stories, 'The Little Thing: Story of a Child' (1868); 'Letters from my Mill' (1869); 'Monday Tales' (1873), established his reputation; and his next novel—'Fromont Jr. and Risler Sr.' (1874)—was translated into all the European languages. Not less celebrated are: 'The Nabob' (1878); 'Kings in Exile' (1880); 'Numa Roumestan' (1882); 'The Gospeller' (1883); 'Sappho' (1884). He struck a new and a happier vein in the 'Tartarin' series: 'Prodigious Adventures of Tartarin'; 'Tartarin in the Alps'; 'Port Tarascon.' He writes reminiscences of his early years in the French capital in 'Thirty Years of Paris' (1888), and in 'Recollections of a Man of Letters' (1889).

Daudet, Ernest. A French novelist, brother of Alphonse D.; born at Nîmes, May 31, 1837. His most notable novels are: 'The Venus of

Gordes'; 'The Bloom of Sin'; 'Martha.' He is author of an autobiographical sketch, 'My Brother and Myself' (1882); and has written some historical sketches, as a 'History of the Royalist Conspiracies in the South during the Revolution'; 'History of the Emigration.'

Daumer, Georg Friedrich (dou'mer). A German poet and philosophical writer (1800-75); born in Nuremberg. He underwent some remarkable revolutions of thought concerning religion: in his student days he leaned strongly to Pietism; next he was the declared foe of the Christian religion; about 1859 he embraced Catholicism and became one of its foremost champions. He wrote among many other philosophical tractates: 'Hints toward a System of Speculative Philosophy' (1831); to his second period belongs: 'The Fire and Moloch Worship of the Hebrews' (1842); to his third: 'My Conversion' (1859). Of his poetical works, the 'Flowers of Song from Hafiz' may be named,—a very beautiful transcription of the Oriental poet, with free variations in the very spirit of Hafiz himself. He wrote also 'Beautiful Souls: a Little Wreath of Legends and Poems' (1862); 'Legends and Poems of St. Mary.'

Davenant, William. An English poet and playwright; born at Oxford in Feb., 1605-06; died April 7, 1668. A story was current in his lifetime that he was an illegitimate son of Shakespeare, and "he seemed contented enough to be thought his son." He wrote many plays and poems, but none possessing any distinguished merit; he succeeded Ben Jonson as poet laureate of England, however. He attempted epic composition in 'Gondibert,' and an opera, 'The Siege of Rhodes.'

Davenport, John. An American divine; born in Coventry, England, 1597; died in Boston, March 15, 1670. Author of 'The Knowledge of Christ' (1653); 'The Saint's Anchor Hold' (1701). He was one of the founders of New Haven, Conn. In 1660 he hid the regicides Goffe and Whalley from their pursuers.

Davenport, Robert. An English poet and dramatist, who flourished about 1623 and died after 1651, but whom we know only through his 'A Crowne for a Conquerour and Too Late to Call Backe Yesterday. Two Poems, the One Divine, the Other Morall' (1623); 'King John and Matilda' (1655), a tragedy; and two comedies: 'A New Trick to Cheat the Divell' (1639), and 'The City Night Cap' (printed 1661). That he was associated with Shakespeare in producing 'Henry I. and Henry II.' seems established, and it is almost certain that he is the author of a play called 'The Pirate.'

Davids, Thomas William Rhys. An English publicist, lawyer, and scholar; born at Colchester, England, May 12, 1843. He was educated at the University of Breslau; from 1866 on, filled judicial places in Ceylon and acted as Archæological Commissioner. In 1877 he was called to the London bar, and is now professor of Pali and Buddhist literature in University College, London. Among his works are: 'Buddhism' (1877); translation of 'Buddhist Birth Stories' (1880); 'Buddhist Suttas' and 'Vinaya Texts' (1881), published in 'The Sacred Books of the East'; 'Buddhism; Its History and Literature.'

Davidson, John. A Scotch poet, novelist, and miscellaneous writer; born at Barrhead, Renfrewshire, 1857. He was at first a teacher, but in 1890 went to London and adopted the literary career, writing for the Speaker and other journals. He has written: 'Fleet Street Eclogues' (1893); 'A Random Itinerary' (1894); 'Ballads and Songs' (1894); 'Plays' (1894); 'Earl Lavender' (1895); and two novels: 'Perfervid' and 'Baptist Lake' (1894).

Davidson, Lucretia Maria. An American poet; born in Plattsburg, N. Y., Sept. 27, 1808; died there, Aug. 27, 1825. She was remarkably precocious, and at the age of nine years wrote her first poem: 'Epitaph on a Robin.' Her poetical writings include 278 poems of various lengths. In 1829 S. F. B. Morse collected and published her writings under the title 'Amir Khan and Other Poems.'

Davidson, Thomas. A Scottish-American philosopher and writer; born at Deer, Aberdeen, Oct. 25, 1840; died at Montreal, Sept. 14, 1900. He came to the United States in 1867, and was subsequently professor of classics in the St. Louis High School. In 1875 he settled in Cambridge, Mass. Later he traveled in Greece and Italy, where much of his literary work was perfected. Included in his publications are: 'A Short Account of the Niobe Group' (1874); 'The Place of Art in Education' (1886); 'Giordano Bruno, and the Relation of his Philosophy to Free Thought' (1886); a 'Hand-Book to Dante, from the Italian of Scartazzini, with Notes and Additions' (1887); 'Prolegomena to Tennyson's 'In Memoriam''; 'Aristotle and Ancient and Modern Educational Ideals'; 'The Education of the Greek People and its Influence on Civilization.'

Davies, Sir John. An English poet and judge; born in Tisbury, Wiltshire, March (?) 1569; died in London (?), Dec. 7 or 8, 1626. His legal and judicial career was one of great distinction, cut short by sudden death. His rank as a poet is conferred by 'Know Thyself,' 'The Orchestra,' and 'Hymns to Astræa,' and others, in which sustained power and a wealth of moving diction are equally in evidence.

Davies, Thomas Alfred. An American prose writer; born in St. Lawrence County, N. Y., December 1809; graduated from West Point in 1829. A few selections from his published works are: 'Cosmogony, or Mysteries of Creation' (1858); 'Genesis Disclosed' (1860); 'Answer to Hugh Miller and Theoretical Geologists' (1861); and 'How to Make Money, and How to Keep It' (1866). Died ——, 1899.

Davila, Arrigo Caterino (dä-vel'ä). An Italian historian and statesman; born in Pieve di Sacco, near Padua, Oct. 30, 1576; assassin-

ated at San Michele, near Verona, about 1631. His eminence in diplomacy and in statecraft has been adequately supplemented in literature by a 'History of the Civil Wars in France'; one of the richest sources of information on the subject, as far as it extends (1560 to 1597), and very little discredited by the work of subsequent investigators.

Davis, Andrew Jackson. An American spiritualist and author; born in Orange County, N. Y., in 1826. He is a resident of Poughkeepsie, N. Y., and is the author of thirty volumes, chief among which are: 'The Great Harmonia'; 'Harmonial Man'; 'Philosophy of Spiritual Discourse'; 'The Penetralia.'

Davis, Edwin Hamilton. An American archæologist; born in Ross County, O., Jan. 22, 1811; died in New York city, May 15, 1888. He was author of 'Ancient Monuments of the Mississippi Valley' (1848), which was described by A. Morlot, the distinguished Swiss archæologist, as being "as glorious a monument of American science as Bunker Hill is of American bravery."

Davis, Henry Winter. An American statesman and orator; born in Annapolis, Md., Aug. 16, 1817; died in Baltimore, Md., Dec. 30, 1865. He was Member of Congress for three terms (1856-65), and took a leading part in advocating emancipation and loyalty to the Union. His published works are: 'The War of Ormuzd and Ahriman in the 19th Century' (1853); 'Speeches and Addresses in Congress' (1867).

Davis, Jefferson. An American statesman; born in Christian County, Ky., June 3, 1808; died in New Orleans, La., Dec. 6, 1889. Educated at the United States Military Academy. Served in the Black Hawk War; went to Congress in 1845; served in the Mexican War; was United States Senator in 1847-51; Secretary of War in 1853-57; was appointed President of the Confederate States, Feb. 9, 1861; the following November he was elected President for six years. He was confined as a prisoner of State for two years in Fortress Monroe, indicted for high treason, released on bail; never tried, being included in the general amnesty of 1868. He wrote 'The Rise and Fall of the Confederate Government' (1881).

Davis, John Chandler Bancroft. An American lawyer and diplomatist; born in 1822. A Harvard graduate and a lawyer. In 1849 he went to London as secretary of legation. In 1854 he became American correspondent of the London Times. In 1869, and again in 1881, he was Assistant Secretary of State. He represented the United States in the "Alabama" contest, zealously pushing the "indirect" claims. He is the author of: 'The Massachusetts Justice' (1847); 'Mr. Sumner, the Alabama Claims, and their Settlement' (1878); and a work published in French entitled 'Process Tribunals of the United States' (1878).

Davis, Mrs. Mary Evelyn (Moore). An American poet; born in Talladega, Ala., 1852. She has written ('Minding the Gap and Other Poems' (1870); and 'In War Times at La Rose Blanche' (1887); 'The Price of Silence' (1907).

Davis, Rebecca (Harding). An American novelist; born in Washington, Pa., June 24, 1831. She contributed many short stories and sketches to periodicals, and has written several novels, including: 'Life in the Iron Mills' (1861); 'A Story of To-Day' (1861) published later under the title 'Margaret Howth'; and 'A Law Unto Herself' (1878). She was the first writer in this country to introduce the labor question into fiction. Her later works include: 'Waiting for the Verdict'; 'Dallas Galbraith'; 'Natasqua'; 'Frances Walstrup'; and others.

Davis, Richard Harding. An American novelist, short-story writer, and contributor to periodical literature; born in Philadelphia, April 18, 1864. He graduated at Lehigh University, and entered journalism in Philadelphia. His first purely literary success was the story of 'Gallegher,' based upon his newspaper experiences, and published with other stories in a volume (1891). He has since been constantly engaged in story-writing, and descriptive narration of events, places, and people. Among his works are: 'Stories for Boys' (1891); 'The West from a Car Window' (1892); 'Van Bibber and Others' (1892); 'Our English Cousins' (1894); 'The Rulers of the Mediterranean' (1894); 'The Princess Aline' (1895); 'About Paris' (1895); 'Three Gringoes in Venezuela and Central America' (1896); 'Soldiers of Fortune' (1897); 'Real Soldiers of Fortune' (1907).

Davis, Thomas Osborne. An Irish poet; born in Mallow, County Cork, 1814; died in Dublin, 1845. His verse was mainly on patriotic themes, and appears, collected, in Duffy's 'Library of Ireland.'

Davy, Sir Humphry. An eminent English chemist, philosopher, and man of letters; born at Penzance, Cornwall, Dec. 17, 1778; died at Geneva, Switzerland, May 29, 1829. In addition to the revolution he brought about in the domain of chemistry and applied physics, he embodied his discoveries and researches in fascinating literary form in 'Consolations in Travel, or the Last Days of a Philosopher' (1830); 'Chemical and Philosophical Researches' (1800); 'On the Safety Lamp and on Flame' (1828); and numerous equally interesting productions.

Davydoff, Denis Vasiljevich (dä-vē-dôf'). A Russian poet and writer on military affairs (1784–1839); born at Moscow. His compositions in verse were mostly written in camp, and consisted of satires, elegies, dithyrambics, and soldier ballads: the latter especially had a wide circulation. Among his prose writings were: 'Recollections of the Battle of Prussian-Eylau' and 'An Essay toward a Theory of Partisan Warfare.'

Dawes, Anna Laurens. An American writer on political topics, daughter of Henry L. Dawes of Massachusetts. She was born in 1851, and has written much for periodicals; among her essays being: 'How We Are Governed'; 'The Modern Jew: His Present and Future'; 'Biography of Charles Sumner.'

Dawes, Rufus. An American poet; born in Boston, Jan. 26, 1803; died in Washington, D. C., Nov. 30, 1859. He wrote: 'The Valley of the Nashaway, and Other Poems' (1830); 'Geraldine' (1839), resembling Don Juan in form and treatment; the successful romance 'Nix's Mate' (1840). His verses were sung at the laying of the corner-stone of Bunker Hill monument.

Dawson, Sir John William. A Canadian geologist and writer; born in Pictou, Nova Scotia, Oct. 13, 1820; died at Montreal, Nov. 19, 1899; made many important discoveries in the science of geology, and wrote largely on geological subjects. His publications include: 'Archaia, or Studies of Creation in Genesis' (1859); 'Air Breathers of the Coal Period'; 'Chain of Life' (1884); and 'Egypt and Syria' (1885). His scientific papers include: 'The Formation of Gypsum,' and 'The Renewal of Forests Destroyed by Fire.' He also published 'Hand-Book of Geography and National History of Nova Scotia.'

Dawson, William James. An English poet; born in Towcester, Northamptonshire, 1854. He is a clergyman by profession. His works include: 'Arvalon: a First Poem' (1878); 'A Vision of Souls' (1884); and 'Poems and Lyrics' (1893); 'Savonarola'; 'The Quest of Simple Life.'

Day, John. An English dramatist; born perhaps about 1575; flourished about 1606, and died later than 1623. Of the half-dozen of his plays which have outlived the vicissitudes of manuscript, the 'Parliament of Bees' (1607), a comedy, is of surpassing charm; while the 'Isle of Gulls,' a drama impregnated with wit, contains many strong passages.

Day, Richard Edwin. An American poet; born in West Granby, Oswego County, N. Y., April 27, 1852. He has published 'Lyrics and Satires' (1883), and 'Poems' (1888).

Day, Thomas. An English poet and prose-writer; born in London, June 22, 1748; died Sept. 28, 1789. He was an ardent sympathizer with the American patriots. Among his works are: 'The Devoted Legions,' a poem against the war with America (1776); 'The Desolation of America'; 'Letters of Marius' (1784). He is the author of the celebrated 'History of Sanford and Merton.'

D'Azeglio. See Azeglio.

Dean, John Ward. An American antiquarian scholar and writer; born at Wiscasset, Me., March 13, 1815; died in Boston, Jan. 22, 1902. He was editor of the 'New England Historical and Genealogical Register'; and the author of 'Memoir of Rev. Nathaniel Ward' (1868); 'Memoir of Rev. Michael Wigglesworth' (1871); and 'Life of John H. Shephard.'

Deane, Silas. An American diplomatist; born Dec. 24, 1737, in Groton, Conn.; died in

Deal, England, Aug. 23, 1789. With Franklin and Lee he negotiated the treaty between France and the United States in 1778; was afterwards greatly misrepresented, and died abroad in neglect and poverty. He published in his own defense: 'Letters to Hon. Robert Morgan' (1784); 'An Address to the Citizens of the United States' (1784); and 'Paris Papers, or Mr. Silas Deane's Intercepted Letters to his Brother and Other Friends' (1781).

Debraux, Paul Emile (dě-brō'). A French balladist; born at Ancerville, Dept. Meuse, Aug. 30, 1796; died in Paris, Feb. 12, 1831. He was an ardent Republican, and wrote for the common people lively songs of wine and love, which were sung everywhere in tavern and workshop. He was called "the Béranger of the rabble." His best-known songs are: 'Mt. St. John'; 'Belisarius'; 'Say, Do You Remember?'; 'The Soldier's Widow'; 'Marengo.' Béranger published a complete collection of his 'Songs' (3 vols.).

Dechez, Louis. See **Jenneval.**

Decken, Auguste von der. See **Elbe, A. von der.**

Decker, Jeremias de (deck'er). A Dutch poet (1609–66); born at Dort. He translated into Dutch, Buchanan's 'Baptist,' and into Dutch verse 'The Lamentations of Jeremiah.' Of his original works the best are his household poems and his collection of epigrams. His 'Good Friday' recounts scenes of Christ's passion. His satirical poem 'Praise of Avarice' is of little worth.

De Costa, Benjamin Franklin. An American clergyman and writer; born in Charlestown, Mass., July 10, 1831. Included in his many publications are: 'The Pre-Columbian Discovery of America by the Northmen' (1869); 'The Moabite Stone' (1870); and 'The Rector of Roxburgh,' a novel, under the pen-name of "William Hickling" (1873). He became president (1884) of the first branch of the "White Cross Society." Died New York, Nov. 4, 1904.

De Coster, Charles Théodore Henri (dě kos'ter). A Belgian poet (1827–79); born at Munich. His first poetical composition was 'The Owls' Mirror'; then followed 'Flemish Legends' (1856); 'Brabant Stories' (1861), a spirited description of lowly life; 'The Wedding Tour' (1872); and the little comedy 'Jenny' (1865).

Decourcelle, Pierre (dě kör-sel'). A French dramatist; born at Paris, Jan. 25, 1856. His first work was the five-act drama, 'The Ace of Clubs,' written for Sara Bernhardt; it had an extraordinary success. Then followed a succession of comedies, dramas, comic-opera libretti, and dramatizations of popular novels, written by him individually or in collaboration with other authors; among them: 'The Amazon' (1885); 'Madame Cartridge'; 'The Abbé Constantin' (founded on Halévy's story); 'The Man with the Broken Ear' (after About). He wrote also a sensational novel, 'The Gray

Hat' (1887), and 'Fanfan' (1889), both of which were received with great popular favor.

Dedekind, Friedrich (ded'ě-kind). A German poet (1525–98); born at Neustadt on the Leine. His principal work is 'Grobianus' (1549), a satire in Latin distichs against drunkenness and obscenity; it had wide circulation, and was translated into German, Dutch, and English. He wrote two dramas having a religious polemic end in view: 'The Christian Knight' and 'The Converted Papist.'

Deems, Charles Force. An American clergyman and writer; born in Baltimore, Md., Dec. 4, 1820; died in New York city, Nov. 18, 1893. From 1866 to his death he was pastor of the Church of the Strangers of New York city, and was widely noted as editor and author. Included in his publications are: 'Triumph of Peace and Other Poems' (1840); 'The Light of the Nations' (1870); 'Weights and Wings' (1872); 'Chips and Chunks for Every Fireside'; and 'My Septuagint' (1892).

Deffand, Marie de Vichy-Chamrond, Marquise du (def-fän'). A French wit and letter-writer, mistress of a most brilliant salon; born in Burgundy, 1697; died at Paris, Sept. 24, 1780. Her correspondence with Horace Walpole was published in 1780, with d'Alembert and other great Frenchmen in 1809 (2 vols.), with Voltaire in 1810 (4 vols.), with the Duchess de Choiseul and others in 1859 (3 vols.).

Defoe, Daniel. The author of 'Robinson Crusoe'; born in St. Giles Parish, Cripplegate, 1660 or 1661; died near London, 1731. His works comprise political tracts, verse, polemic writings, economic and social pamphlets, romances, histories, and biographies. Among them are: 'The Storm' (1704); 'Apparition of Mrs. Veal' (1706); 'Robinson Crusoe' (1719); 'Further Adventures of Robinson Crusoe' (1719); 'King of Pirates' (1719); 'Duncan Campbell' (1720); 'Mr. Campbell's Pacquet' (1720); 'Memoirs of a Cavalier' (1720); 'Captain Singleton' (1720); 'Moll Flanders' (1722); 'Journal of the Plague Year' (1722); 'Cartouche' (1722); 'Colonel Jacque' (1722); 'The Highland Rogue' (1723); 'The Fortunate Mistress' (1724); 'Narrative of Murders at Calais' (1724); 'John Sheppard' (1724); 'Account of Jonathan Wild' (1725); and other romances. His pamphlets include: 'Essay upon Projects' (1698); 'Shortest Way with Dissenters' (1702); and 'Political History of the Devil' (1726).

De Fontaine, Felix. An American journalist; born in Boston, Mass., 1832; died in Columbus, S. C., Dec. 11, 1896. The first statement given to the North, of the attack on Fort Sumter, was written by him; and he was correspondent of the Charleston Courier from the principal battle-fields during the Civil War. Subsequently he came to New York city, and was connected with the Herald most of the time until his death. He was the author of 'Cyclopædia of the Best Thoughts of Charles Dickens'; 'Gleanings from a Confederate

Army Note-Book'; and 'Birds of a Feather Flock Together.'

De Forest, John William. An American novelist, born in Humphreysville (near Seymour), Conn., March 31, 1826. Without entering college he passed many years in independent study and foreign travel, becoming a proficient in several languages; entered the army as captain at the outbreak of the Civil War, and rose to major; and since 1850 has been a fertile writer of essays, short stories, and novels for the leading magazines, taking prominent rank among American novelists. Among his works are: 'History of the Indians of Connecticut' (1853); 'Oriental Acquaintance' (1856); 'Witching Times' (1856); 'European Acquaintance' (1858); 'Seacliff' (1859); 'Miss Ravenel's Conversion' (1867); 'Overland' (1871); 'Kate Beaumont' (1872); 'The Wetherell Affair' (1873); 'Honest John Vane' (1875); 'Justine Vane' (1875); 'Playing the Mischief' (1876); 'Irene Vane' (1877); 'Irene, the Missionary' (1879); 'The Oddest of Courtships. Died July 18, 1906.

De Gubernatis. See Gubernatis.

De Kay, Charles. An American poet, grandson of Joseph Rodman Drake; born in Washington, D. C., July 25, 1848. His poems are mostly founded on themes from Oriental, classical, and literary history. Among his works are: 'The Bohemian' (1878); 'Hesperus and Other Poems' (1880); 'The Vision of Nimrod' (1881); 'The Vision of Esther' (1882); 'The Love Poems of Louis Barnaval, Edited [and written] by Charles De Kay' (1883); and many occasional poems. His prose includes: 'Life and Works of Antoine Louis Barye, Sculptor' (1889); and 'The Family Life of Heinrich Heine' (1892), a translation.

Dekker, Eduard Douwes (dek'er). A Dutch novelist (1820–87), pseudonym "Multatuli"; born at Amsterdam. He spent several years in government service in the Dutch East Indies. His story 'Max Havelaar' (1860) is a shocking accusation of wrongs and scandals against the Dutch administration of Java. He later published many satirical works on social, political, and philosophical questions, among them a volume of admirable 'Parables'; a novel, 'The Blessed Virgin'; a drama; and 'The School of Princes.'

Dekker, Thomas. An English dramatist; born in London, about 1570; died some time after 1637. He wrote a great number of plays, but only a few of them were published, among them the two comedies 'The Shoemaker's Holiday' and 'Old Fortunatus'; they are both specimens of whatever is best and most genuine in English humor, and the second in particular abounds in passages of consummate poetic beauty. Of other writings of his we have 'The Wonderful Year,' a pamphlet describing graphically the horrors of the plague; an amusing tract, 'The Bachelor's Banquet,' a satire on henpecked husbands; and many other fugitive

pieces lashing the vices and follies of the age. He also collaborated with other dramatists.

De Lancey, Edward Floyd. An American historical writer; born in Mamaroneck, N. Y., Oct. 23, 1821. He is author of 'Documentary History of New York' (1851); 'The Capture of Fort Washington the Result of Treason' (1877); and 'Origin and History of Manors in the Province of New York'. Died 1905.

Deland, Ellen Douglass. An American writer of juvenile works; born in New York in 1860. She has published: 'Oakleigh'; 'In the Old Herrick House'; 'Malvern'; 'Josephine.'

Deland, Margaret Wado (**Campbell**). An American poet and novelist; born in Allegheny, Pa., Feb. 23, 1857. She is now a resident of Boston. Her fame rests mainly upon her theological polemic novel 'John Ward, Preacher' (1888), which has been very widely read. Among her other well-known works are: 'The Story of a Child'; 'Mr. Tommy Dove and Other Stories'; 'Philip and his Wife'; 'Florida Days,' a collection of sketches of travel; and 'Sydney.' Her most popular poems are contained in the volume entitled 'The Old Garden and Other Verses.'

Delaporte, Michel (dĕ-lä-port'). A French playwright (1806–72); born in Paris. He wrote a long series of vaudevilles, many of them in collaboration with others. Of pieces of his own composition may be named 'The Housewife' (1851), 'Toinette and her Carbineer' (1856), as the most successful. In association with Varin he wrote: 'A Hercules and a Pretty Woman' (1861); 'Ah, 'Tis Pleasant to Love'; 'The Gillyflower Woman' (1869).

Delavigne, Jean François Casimir (de-lä-vēn'). A French lyric poet and dramatist (1793–1843); born at Havre. He struck a patriotic and popular chord in his 'Messenian Odes' (1818), satires directed against the monarchy of the Restoration. His historical dramas and tragedies are numerous; among them are: 'Louis XI.'; 'The Sicilian Vespers'; 'Marino Faliero'; 'Don John of Austria.' His plays are no longer seen on the stage.

De Leon, Edwin. An American prose-writer; born in Columbia, S. C., 1828; died in New York city, 1891. From 1854 to 1862 he was engaged in editorial work; from 1862 to 1870 held the office of United States consul-general and diplomatic agent at Cairo, Egypt. His published works include: 'Thirty Years of my Life on Three Continents'; 'The Khédive's Egypt,' a novel; 'Askaros Kassis, the Captain'; and 'Under the Star and Under the Crescent.'

Deléry, François Charles (dĕ-lā'rē). An American prose-writer; born in St. Charles Parish, La., Jan. 28, 1815; died in Bay St. Louis, Miss., June 12, 1880. His works were written in French, and include: 'Essay on Liberty' (1847); 'Studies of the Passions' (1849); 'King Cotton'; and 'Confederates and Federals' (1864).

Delitzsch, Franz. A German theologian; born in Leipzig, Feb. 23, 1813; died there, March 4, 1890. In 1867 he became professor of theology at Leipzig. Among his numerous devotional and theological works may be mentioned: 'History of Jewish Poetry' (1836); 'The House of God' (1848); 'A Day in Capernaum' (1871); and the well-known translation of the New Testament into Hebrew (1st ed. 1877, 2d ed. 1886).

Del Mar, Alexander. An American political economist; born in New York city, Aug. 9, 1836. He established the Social Science Review and was its editor 1864-66. He is the author of 'Gold Money and Paper Money' (1862); 'Essays on Political Economy' (1865); 'Letter on the Finances' (1868); 'History of Money in Ancient Countries' (1884); 'The Science of Money'; 'The National-Banking System'; and 'Statistical Almanac'; 'Sophisms of Money.'

Delmonté, Felix Maria (del-môn'te). A Dominican lawyer and poet; born in Santo Domingo city, Dominican Republic, about 1810. Has been many times a member of the Dominican Congress. He is the author of 'Las Vérgenes de Galindo,' a historical tale in verse; 'El Mendigo,' a drama; 'Ozama,' a drama; and many lyrical poems.

Delmonte y Tejada, Antonio (del-mōn'te ē tē-yä'dä). A Dominican historian; born in Santiago de los Caballeros, Santo Domingo, in 1783; died in 1861. He is the author of 'Historia de Santo Domingo' (3 vols.), a history of the island from its discovery.

Deloney, Thomas. An English ballad writer and pamphleteer; born in London (?), about 1543; died there about 1600. He turned all current topics, from the Armada to a murder, into racy ballads and snatches, some happy, others execrable, all popular; the 'Strange Histories' (1607) comprising most of the good ones, while in 'The Gentle Craft' (1597), a eulogy of shoemakers, we have a specimen of his pamphlets.

De Long, George Washington. An American Arctic explorer, and officer in the United States navy; born in New York city, Aug. 22, 1844; died in Siberia, Oct. 30, 1881. Graduating from the Naval Academy in 1865, he reached the grade of lieutenant-commander, and perished of cold and exposure while in command of the Jeannette Expedition in 1879-81. His journals have been published, entitled 'The Voyage of the Jeannette' (1883); and the story of the search for the survivors is told in Melville's 'In the Lena Delta' (1884).

Delord, Taxile (dė-lôr'). A French historian, journalist, and topical prose-writer; born in Avignon, Nov. 25, 1815; died in Paris, May 16, 1877. He was successful politically, and edited important Parisian journals, his permanent work being contained in 'Physiology of the Parisian Woman' (1841); 'History of the Second Empire' (1868–75); and 'Literary Mornings' (1860).

Delpit, Albert (del-pē') A French novelist and dramatist; born in New Orleans, Jan. 30, 1849; died in Paris, Jan. 4, 1893. When quite young he assisted the elder Dumas in editing the journals Le Mousquetaire and Le D'Artagnan. After the war with Germany, in which he served, he won academic prizes with a volume of poems, 'The Invasion'; and the poem 'Repentence, or the Country Parish Priest's Story.' He had little success till 'Coralie's Son' (1879) gained the highest recognition both from the reading public and theatre-goers. 'Odette's Marriage' obtained him a pronounced success in high society. He wrote also 'Cruel Loves'; 'As in Life'; and other plays.

Delvau, Alfred (del-vō'). A French Revolutionary prose-writer; born in Paris, 1825; died there, May 3, 1867. A 'History of the Revolution of February' (1850), and 'Henri Murger and Bohemianism' (1866), sufficiently denote the range of his partisan, but more than mediocre, capacities.

Delwig, Anton Antónovich, Baron (del'vig). A Russian lyrist (1798–1831); born in Moscow. He was a schoolfellow and lifelong friend of Pushkin. He held government office, but his St. Petersburg house was the rallying-place of the literary world, especially of the younger set,—Pushkin, Glinka, Baratinsky, Vlasemsky. Among his poetical compositions those written in the tone of the popular ballad are the best, and some of them are in great favor.

Demeter, Dimitrija (dem'ė-ter). A Croatian dramatist and poet; born at Agram, July 21, 1811; died there, June 24, 1872. His principal dramas are: 'Love and Duty'; 'Blood-Revenge'; and the tragedy 'Teuta.' He wrote a lyro-epic poem, 'The Battlefield of Grobnik,' and several stories. He translated several foreign dramatic works into Croatian.

De Mille, Henry Churchill. An American playwright; born in North Carolina, about 1853; died at Pompton, N. J., Feb. 10, 1893. He graduated at Columbia College, and was by turns preacher and school-teacher until 1882, when he became examiner of plays at the Madison Square Theatre, and later for a short time an actor. His first successful play was the 'Main Line,' in which he collaborated with Charles Barnard. In 1887, having become associated with David Belasco, he wrote the well-known society dramas: 'The Wife' (1887); 'Lord Chumley' (1888); 'The Charity Ball' (1889); 'Men and Women' (1890). His last work was a melodrama adapted from the German, entitled 'Lost Paradise,' which was successfully produced in 1892 and is still a favorite.

De Mille, James. A Canadian novelist; born in St. John, N. B., August 1837; died in Halifax, N. S., Jan. 28, 1880. Graduated at Brown College (1854). He was professor of classics in Acadia College (1860–65), and of history and rhetoric in Dalhousie College, Halifax, from 1865 until his death. Among his publications are: 'The Dodge Club' (1866);

'Cord and Creese' (1867); 'A Comedy of Terrors' (1872); 'The Living Link' (1874); and many books for boys, including 'Treasures of the Sea.' A treatise of his on rhetoric was published in 1878.

Deming, Philander. An American humorous writer of dialect sketches. He was born in 1829. His work is very original, and has been published in 'Adirondack Stories'; 'Tompkins and Other Folks'; 'The Story of the Pathfinder.'

Demogeot, Jacques Claude (dem-ō-zhō'). A French literary historian and poet; born at Paris, July 5, 1808. He wrote a 'Study on Pliny the Younger'; the prize essay 'Letters and Men of Letters in the 19th Century'; 'French Literature in the 17th Century,' his greatest work. His poetical writings are a drama, 'Romeo and Juliet' (1852); 'New Paris,' consisting of epico-lyric descriptions; and 'Stories and Talks in Verse' (1860). Died 1894.

Demosthenes (dē-mos'thē-nēz). An Athenian orator; born about 384 B. C.; died at Calauria, 322 B. C. Necessity drove him to take up the business of writing pleas and defenses of suitors and defendants in the law courts; afterward he appeared himself in the courts and the assemblies, and became a foremost leader of the party of independence against the designs of Philip of Macedon. The 'Olynthiacs' and the 'Philippics' were part of this warfare; and his greatest speech, 'On the Crown,' was a vindication of his course. Sixty orations ascribed to him are extant, but some of them are spurious.

Dempster, Charlotte Louisa Hawkins. An Scotch novelist; born in Forfarshire, Scotland, in 1835. She has traveled extensively, and is at present a resident of Cannes, France. She has been a frequent contributor to English periodicals. Her first book was: 'The Hôtel du Petit St. Jean: A Gascon Story' (1869); the second, 'Véra' (1872) established her reputation. Her other works include: 'Essays' (1872); 'Iseulte' (1875); 'Blue Roses' (1877); 'Within Sound of the Sea' (1878), a Scotch story; 'Ninette' (1888), an idyl of Provence.

Denham, Sir John. An English poet; born in Dublin in 1615; died in London (?), March 15 (?), 1669. He figured at the court of Charles II., translated the 'Æneid' (1656 ?), produced the tragedy of 'The Sophy' (1642), and in 'Cooper's Hill' (1642) rose above mediocrity.

Denis, Jean Ferdinand (den-ē'). A French explorer and historical writer; born in Paris, France, Aug. 13, 1798; died Aug. 2, 1890. He was an extensive traveler and a voluminous writer. Among his works are: 'History of Brazil' (1821); 'Buenos Ayres and Paraguay' (2 vols., 1823). He is also the author of a series of historical novels: 'Ysmael-ben-Kaisar, or the Discovery of the New World' (3 vols., 1829).

Denison, Charles Wheeler. An American poet and prose-writer; born in New London, Conn., Nov. 11, 1809; died Nov. 14, 1881. He published: 'The American Village and Other Poems' (1845); 'Out at Sea,' poems (1867). His prose works include 'The Child Hunters' (1867) and a series of biographies: 'The Tanner Boy' (Grant); 'Winfield the Lawyer's Son' (Hancock); and others.

Denison, John Ledyard. An American historian; born in Stonington, Conn., Sept. 19, 1826. He published a 'Pictorial History of the Wars of the United States,' and edited an 'Illustrated History of the New World' in English and in German. Died 1906.

Denison, Mary (Andrews). An American novelist, wife of C. W.; born in Cambridge, Mass., May 26, 1826. Assisted in editing the Olive Branch, in which her husband was interested; also contributed to American and English periodicals. Her works include: 'Home Pictures' (1853); 'That Husband of Mine,' of which it is said the sale reached 200,000 copies; and 'What One Boy can Do' (1885); 'Her Secret.'

Denne, Henry. An English Puritan divine, who flourished in the seventeenth century and was noted for his attacks upon the vices of the clergy. He published 'The Man of Sin' (1645); 'The Drag Net of the Kingdom of Heaven' (1646); 'Grace, Mercy, and Truth'; etc. His sermons and other works were published in London, 1642–60.

Denne-Baron, Pierre Jacques René (dän-bär-ôn). A French poet and essayist; born in Paris, Sept. 6, 1780; died there, June 5, 1854. He had much learning and a faultless taste; 'Hero and Leander' (1806) and 'Poetic Flowers' (1825) being delightful though not great, while his 'Dictionary of Conversation' is widely known.

Dennery or **d'Ennery, Adolphe Philippe** (den-er-ē'). A French dramatist; born at Paris, June 17, 1811. He has produced, either alone or in collaboration, about 200 separate compositions. Among his own productions are the dramas 'My Daughter's Honor' (1835); 'The Pearl of Savoy' (1842); 'Mary Jane' (1845), one of the strongest popular plays of our time; 'The Two Orphans' (1873); the comedies and vaudevilles 'The Change of Uniform' (1836), and 'Robber Paris' (1844); and the fairy spectacles 'Aladdin, or the Wonderful Lamp' (1863), and 'The Tribute of Zamora.' Died 1899.

Dennie, Joseph. An American journalist; born in Boston, Aug. 30, 1768; died in Philadelphia, Jan. 7, 1812. Published 'The Farrago' (1795), essays on life and literature. From 1796 to 1798 edited with great success the Farmer's Weekly Museum at Walpole, N. H. In this appeared his essays signed "The Lay Preacher," whose droll and easy style made him popular. In Philadelphia (1801), assisted by Asbury Dickens, he founded the Portfolio, which he edited till his death under the pen-name of "Oliver Old-School." Two collections of his writings have been published: 'The Lay Preacher, or Short Sermons for Idle Readers' (1796); and 'The Lay Preacher' (1817).

Dennis, John. An English dramatist and critic (1657-1734); born in London. Of his dramas none had much success or deserved it. He was a savage critic, but he had some just views of dramatic art and poetry, as is proved by his 'Three Letters on the Genius and Writings of Shakespeare' (1711). His fame is perpetuated not by his own writings, but by the satires and anecdotes of his enemies, Pope's 'Dunciad' in particular. He invented a new species of stage thunder; and the phrase "stealing one's thunder" is due to his angry outburst at some managers who used it in a successful play when one of his had been damned.

Deotyma (dā-ō-tē'mä), pseudonym of Jadviga Luszczevska. A Polish poet and storywriter; born in Warsaw, October 1830. She has long been celebrated for the power and charm of her prose and versification; 'At the Parting Way' (1876) being a story of rare merit, and 'The Pole in Song' (1859) containing many of her finest stanzas.

Depew, Chauncey Mitchell. An American lawyer; born in Peekskill, N. Y., April 23, 1834. He is president of the New York Central and Hudson River R. R. Co. Noted as a political orator and an after-dinner speaker. Published 'Orations and After-Dinner Speeches' (1890).

De Peyster, John Watts (dē-pēs'ter). An American miscellaneous writer; born in New York city, March 9, 1821. He has contributed much to periodicals, and written a vast number of monographs, often polemic,— one being in defense of his Loyalist grandfather, second in command at King's Mountain on the British side. He is author of: 'Life of Field Marshal Torstenson' (1855); 'The Dutch at the North Pole' (1857); 'Life of Baron Cohorn' (1860); and 'Personal and Military History of General Philip Kearney' (1869). D. May 5, 1907.

De Puy, Henry Walter. An American miscellaneous writer; born in Pompey Hill, Onondaga County, N. Y., in 1820; died Feb. 2, 1876. He constantly contributed political articles to the press; he wrote several popular poems, and was the author of 'Kossuth and his Generals,' with a brief history of Hungary (1851); 'Louis Napoleon and his Times,' with a memoir of the Bonaparte family (1853); 'Three Score Years and Beyond' (1873); and 'Ethan Allen and the Green Mountain Boys of 1876.'

De Puy, William Harrison. An American clergyman and writer; born at Penn Yan, N. Y., Oct. 31, 1821; died at Canaan, Ct., Sept. 4, 1901. His works include: 'Statistics of the Methodist Episcopal Church'; 'Home and Health'; etc.

De Quincey, Thomas. A celebrated English author; born in Manchester, Aug. 15, 1785; died Dec. 8, 1859. He was a very prolific writer; but his works are mostly occasional essays, and papers on historical, literary, and miscellaneous topics. Besides collections of these, his published works include: 'Confessions of an English Opium Eater' (1821); 'Letters to a Young Man Whose Education has been Neglected' (1823); 'Logic of Political Economy' (1844); 'Klosterheim' (1839); etc.

Derby, George Horatio. ["John Phœnix."] An American humorist; born in Dedham, Mass., April 3, 1823; died in New York, May 15, 1861. Graduated at West Point (1846), and served in the army during the Mexican War (1846-47). He wrote under the name "John Phœnix" a series of sketches and burlesques, entitled 'Phœnixiana' (1855), and 'The Squibob Papers' (1859).

Derby, James Cephas. An American publisher of New York and San Francisco; born 1818; died 1892. He is the author of 'Fifty Years among Authors, Books, and Publishers.'

Dernburg, Friedrich (dern'bürg). A German journalist and descriptive writer; born in Mainz, Oct. 3, 1833. After a university course, he rapidly acquired eminence in both journalism and politics, being one of the companions of the German Crown Prince (now Emperor) in a trip to Rome, and later a well-known personality at the Columbian Exposition. 'From the White City' (1893), a series of World's Fair sketches; 'In the Bonds of Guilt' (1894); and 'The Over Proud' (1889), afford typical specimens of his fact and fiction.

De Rosny, Leon. A celebrated French Orientalist; born at Loos, France, Aug. 5, 1837. Professor of Japanese at the Special School of Languages, since 1868, and founder of the International Congress of Orientalists. Among his numerous works are: 'Asiatic Studies' (1864); 'The Origin of Language' (1869); 'Japanese Anthology' (1871); 'A Grammar of the Chinese Language' (London, 1874) 'Japanese Religion' (1881); 'The Written Documents of American Antiquity' (1882); 'Introduction into the Study of Japanese Literature.'

Déroulède, Paul (dê-rö-läd'). A French poet; born at Paris, Sept. 2, 1846. His 'Soldier Songs' (1872) and 'Military Refrains' (1888) were immensely popular, and won him the presidency of the Patriotic League; an association intensely hostile to Germans, and whose agitation seemed likely to lead to a collision with Germany, wherefore the poet was prevailed upon to retire from the presidency. He has written a drama of patriotism, 'The Hetman,' and the semi-religious drama 'The Moabitess.'

Derzhávin, Gavriil Románovich (der-shä'-vin). A noted Russian poet; born at Kasan, July 14, 1743; died on his estate in the government of Novgorod, July 21, 1816. He won the favor of Catharine II. by his ode 'Feliza' (1782), and afterward rose to high office. His last thirteen years were passed in retirement. The characteristics of his poetry are originality of conception, splendor of imagery, forcefulness and mastery of language. His admiration for Catharine II. inspired him with the true poetic afflatus, though some of his poems are mere strings of hollow phrases. He was nevertheless a lover of truth, an honest, downright, hot-tempered man. His best poem is the ode 'God,' which has been translated into all European languages and into Japanese.

De Sanctis, Francesco (dĕ sänk'tis). An Italian literary historian and critic (1818-83); born at Morra. His revolutionary critical disquisitions on the great poets gained him distinction. He was general secretary of the department of public education in the revolutionary government of 1848; after restoration of the monarchy he spent three years in prison, where he studied German literature, and translated parts of Goethe and Schiller and Hegel's 'Logic.' Afterward he was minister of education, and professor in the University of Naples. His most important works are a 'History of Italian Literature' and 'Critical Essays,' the latter a work of high authority.

Désaugiers, Marc Antoine Madeleine (dĕ-sō-zhā'). A noted French song-writer and dramatist; born at Fréjus, Nov. 17, 1772; died at Paris, Aug. 9, 1827. His life till 1797 was full of adventure; he was at one time a prisoner of the revolted blacks in San Domingo and in momentary fear of death. Going on the stage in Paris, in 1805, his parody of the opera 'Danaids' ('The Little Danaids') was acted for 300 consecutive nights. His vaudevilles were remarkably successful. As a light song-writer he is second only, if indeed second, to Béranger. Many of his songs will live long; e. g., 'The Consolations of Old'Age'; 'The Picture of New Years.' Many of them are exquisite little gems of art; e. g., 'The Market'; 'Sunday Pleasures'; 'The Palais Royal.'

Desbordes-Valmore, Marceline (dä-bord"-väl-mōr"). A French poet (1785-1859); born at Douai. She made her début at the age of 16 in comic opera, but shortly after quit the stage. She wrote several volumes of poems: 'Elegies and Romances'; 'New Elegies and Poems'; 'Tears'; 'Poor Flowers'; 'Bouquets and Prayers'; and 'Poems of Childhood.' All her poems are distinguished by great sweetness and unaffected pathos. Her most perfect song is perhaps 'If He had Known.' She wrote also several stories.

Descartes, René (dä-kärt'). An illustrious French philosopher; born at La Haye, Touraine, March 31, 1596; died at Stockholm, Feb. 11, 1650. His works comprise: 'Discourse on Method' (1637); 'Meditations in Elementary Philosophy'; 'Philosophical Beginnings'; 'Dioptrique'; 'Meteors'; 'Geometry'; 'Letters to the Princess Elizabeth'); and many controversial amplifications of his doctrines, among them 'Treatise on the Passions' (1649).

Deschamps, Eustache, called Morel. A French poet; born about 1330 at Vertus, Dept. Marne; died after 1415. He composed a multitude of short poems of a political or moral nature. The 'Mirror of Marriage' comprises 13,000 lines. He wrote an 'Art of Poetizing,' the earliest mediæval work of its kind.

Deschamps de Saint Amand, Antony (dä-shon). A French poet (1800-69); born at Paris. After translating from Dante, he published (1831) 'Political Satires,' notable for vigor and poetic form. But his mind already showed signs of organic disorder, and his 'Last Words' (1835) reveal it plainly. He also wrote: 'Resignation' (1839); 'Studies of Italy' (1835); and many short poems.

Deschamps de Saint Amand, Émile. A French poet, elder brother of Antony (1791-1871); born at Bourges. His song 'Peace Won by Arms' (1812) attracted the notice of Napoleon. In 1818, with Latouche, he produced the successful comedy 'The Round of Favor.' To the journal La Muse Française, founded by him and Victor Hugo (1824), he contributed poems, stories, and critical essays, and stood as leader of the romantic school. He published several volumes of miscellaneous poems, essays on Goethe, Schiller, and Shakespeare, and many sprightly but earnest dramas, which were set to music by Bellini, Halévy, Rossini, and Auber; also a volume of 'Philosophical Stories' (1854).

Deshoulières, Antoinette (dä-zö-lyār'). An eminent French poet; born in Paris, Jan. 1, 1638; died there, Feb. 17, 1694. She was educated in the spirit of the "précieuses" of the Hôtel Rambouillet, and so assimilated their spirit and methods as to be called the "tenth Muse" for her tragedies, comedies, and operas. But her verses sound hollow and insincere. Her best work and inspirations are found in her 'Idylls,' especially in 'The Sheep'; 'The Flowers'; 'The Birds.'

Desjardins, Paul (dä-zhär-dan'). A French writer of essays on social and moral questions; born 18—. He is professor of rhetoric in the St. Stanislas College, Paris, and member of the editorial staff of the Journal des Débats. His studies of social phenomena were collected under the general title 'Contemporary Notes.' One of his works led to the formation of the Union for Moral Action.

Deslys, Charles (dä-lē'). A French novelist (1821-85); born at Paris. The most notable of his numerous stories are: 'The Millionairess' (1852); 'The Last Grisette' (1853); 'The King of Yvetot' (1866); 'Stories of La Grève' (1866), which won an Academy prize; 'The Stonebreaker' (1867).

Desmarets de Saint-Sorlin, Jean (dä-mär-ā' dĕ san-sor-lan'). A French poet (1595-1676); born at Paris. He was a favorite of Cardinal Richelieu, and one of the first members of the Academy. He wrote several plays; among them a character comedy, 'The Visionaries' (1637), received with great favor. Some of his comic figures had Molière for their original. He wrote also epics; among them 'Clovis' (1657) and 'Mary Magdalene' (1669). In his early years he led a wild, disordered life; but later became a devotee, and wrote many religious poems and anti-Jansenist polemics.

Desnoiresterres, Gustave (dā-nwär-tār'). A French novelist and literary historian (1817–92); born at Bayeux. Among his novels are (The Black Chamber' (1843); 'Love on a Stage Coach' (1853). He wrote several very valuable essays and monographs on the history of French literature and of French manners. The Academy crowned his greatest work: (Voltaire and French Society in the 18th Century' (8 vols., 1855).

Desnoyers, Louis (dān-wī-ā'). A French journalist and novelist (1805–68); born at Replonges, Dept. Ain. He founded the journal Charivari (1832), and was one of the founders of the Siècle. He wrote some vaudevilles, and several novels, such as 'Adventures of Jean-Paul Choppart' (1836); 'Memoirs of a 20-Sous Piece' (1837).

Despériers, Bonaventure (dā-per-yā'). A French story-teller; born at Arnay-le-Duc, about 1505; died 1544. He was secretary to Margaret of Navarre. He wrote a series of 90 stories : (New Recreations and Merry Conceits,' printed in 1558. In 1537 was published his 'Cymbalum Mundi in French,' a virulent and contemptuous attack on the Christian religion, which was burned by the common hangman, and of which only one copy is in existence. The author probably escaped a like fate by suicide.

Desportes, Philippe (dā-port'). A French poet (1546–1606) ; born at Chartres. His poems are marked by purity of style and well-knit metrical form. Besides his numerous beautiful and musical elegies and sonnets (457 of these), he made a translation of the (Psalms,' and published a volume of 'Christian Prayers and Meditations' in prose.

Destouches, Philippe Néricault (dā-tösh'). A French dramatist (1680–1754) ; born at Tours. His poetical talents won him the patronage of the Duke of Orleans, and he was employed on a diplomatic mission to England. His comedy (The Boaster' (1732) is a masterpiece in matter, in elaboration, and in character delineation ; Lessing classes that work, with its companion piece (The Spendthrift' (1736), as "models of the finer high comedy." Hardly inferior to these is (The Married Philosopher' (1727), largely based on the the author's own life.

Destutt de Tracy, Antoine Louis Claude, Count (de-stüt' dè tra-sē'). A French philosophical and metaphysical writer; born in Paris, July 20, 1754 ; died there, March 10, 1836. Though in repeated peril during the French Revolution, he survived to write 'Elements of Ideology' (1817), a development of Condillac's philosophy, and in part an exposition of what passed then for economics. His 'Delineation of the Politics of the World's Nations' (1820), and prior works, received considerable notice in this country through Jefferson's praise in his letters.

De Tabley, Lord—John Byrne Leicester Warren. An English poet; born at Tabley House, Cheshire, April 26, 1835 ; died, Nov. 22, 1895. The beauty and refinement of his lyrics was much admired.

He published : (Eclogues and Monodramas' (1864) ; 'Rehearsals' (1870). He was also known as an authority on " book-plates."

Detlef, Karl (det'lef), pseudonym of Klara Bauer. A German novelist; born in Swinemünde, June 23, 1836; died in Breslau, June 29, 1876. Her 'Indissoluble Bonds', (1877) and 'Must It Be ?' (1872) are, valuable and engrossing studies of character.

Deus, João de (dā-üsh). A Portuguese lyric poet; born at São Bartolomeu de Messines, in the province of Algarve, March 8, 1830. He is regarded by his countrymen as introducer of a new era of Portuguese poetry. National spirit, originality, sensibility, and rhythmic melody characterize his poems. They are published in (Field-flowers' (1870); 'A Branch of Blooms' (1870) ; and other works. Died 1897.

De Vere, Sir Aubrey. An Irish poet (1788–1846). His works are: 'Julian the Apostate : a Dramatic Poem' (1822); 'The Duke of Mercia : an Historical Drama,' the volume containing also 'The Lamentations of Ireland' (1823) ; 'The Song of Faith, Devout Exercises and Sonnets' (1842) ; and 'Mary Tudor : an Historical Drama,' published posthumously (1847). His sonnets Wordsworth declared to be "the most perfect of our age."

De Vere, Sir Aubrey Thomas. An Irish poet and descriptive and political essayist, son of Sir Aubrey; born at Curragh Chase, Limerick, Jan. 10, 1814 ; died, Jan 2ɔ, 1902. (Poems' (1843) first revealed his inheritance of talent ; and in (Irish Odes' (1869) and 'Alexander the Great' (1874) he vindicated his title to high poetic rank. In prose, his 'Picturesque Sketches of Greece and Turkey' (1850) and 'Constitutional and Unconstitutional Political Action' (1881) show facility of style.

De Vere, Mary Ainge. (" Madeline Bridges.") An American poet; born in Brooklyn, N. Y., 18—. Has contributed much to the periodicals ; is the author of (Love Songs and Other Poems' (1870) and 'Poems' (1890).

De Vere, Maximilian Schele. A noted philologist; born near Wexio, Sweden, Nov. 1, 1820; came to the United States in 1843; in 1844 became professor of modern languages and belle-lettres in the University of Virginia. His contributions to the leading magazines have been both literary and scientific. His works include : (Outlines of Comparative Philology' (1853); 'Stray Leaves from the Book of Nature' (1856); 'Studies in English'; 'Glimpses of Europe in 1848'; 'Romance of American History'; 'Wonders of the Deep'; etc.

De Walden, Thomas Blaides. An English dramatist; born in London, England, 1811; died in New York city, Sept. 26, 1873. He came to America in 1844 and began his career as an actor; but he made his greatest success as a dramatist, writing and adapting more than one hundred plays, including (Sam' for F. S. Chanfrau, and (The Hypochondriac.'

Dewey, Orville. A prominent American clergyman and man of letters; born in Sheffield, Mass., March 28, 1794; died there, March 21, 1882. He entered the Unitarian ministry in 1819, and became prominent as a pastor in New Bedford and New York. For two years he was Dr. Channing's assistant in Boston. In 1862 he retired and devoted himself to study. Among his works are: 'Discourses on Human Nature' (1847); 'Discourses on the Nature of Religion' (1847); 'The Problem of Human Destiny' (1864).

Dexter, Henry Martyn. An American clergyman and religious writer; born at Plympton, Mass., Aug. 13, 1821; died Nov. 13, 1890. Educated at Yale and Andover. He was pastor in Manchester, N. H., 1844–49; and of the Berkeley Street Congregational Church, Boston, Mass., 1849–67, when he became editor of the Congregationalist. His chief work is 'The Congregationalism of the Last Three Hundred Years' (1880).

Diamante, Juan Bautista (dē-ä-män'tĕ). A Spanish playwright; born about 1626; died toward the end of the century. Of his plays, 45 are extant. All are founded on Spanish history; two on legends of the Cid, one—'Who Honors his Father'—being verbatim coincident with Corneille's 'Cid' throughout entire scenes. Which is the original? Recent critics lean strongly to the Spaniard. Diamante wrote some religious or "spiritual" plays, and a few musical dramas; of the last class, 'Alpheus and Arethusa' is held the best.

Diaz, Mrs. Abby (Morton). An American story-writer; born in Massachusetts, 1821; was a member of the famous Brook Farm Association, and has been an earnest worker in social reforms. Her books for children include: 'The Cat's Arabian Knights'; 'The John Spicer Lectures'; 'Polly Cologne'; 'Jimmyjohns'; and 'The William Henry Letters.' Other works are: 'Bybury to Beacon Street, a Discussion of Social Topics'; 'Domestic Problems'; 'Only a Flock of Women.' Died Belmost, April, 1904.

Diaz or Dias, Antonio Gonçalves (dē'äs). A Brazilian poet; born at Caxias, Brazil, 1823; died at sea, 1864 or 1866. His lyric poems are comprised in the volumes entitled 'First,' 'Second,' and 'Last Songs.' His other works are an epic left incomplete and four dramas. His verses give proof of great originality, with tenderness of feeling and a lively wit.

Diaz de Escobar, Narciso (dē'äth dĕ es-kō-bär'). A Spanish poet; born at Malaga, June 25, 1860. He won great popularity with his lyric poems, and several of his dramatic compositions have been very successful: 'A Morisco Episode'; 'The Young Men of the Day'; 'Two Husbands and a Wife.' In collaboration with other writers, he has published a volume of 'Character Sketches from Madrid.'

Diaz del Castillo, Bernal (dē'äth del käs-tēl'yō). A Spanish chronicler of the conquest of Mexico; born about 1498; died in Mexico

about 1593. His 'True History of the Discovery and Conquest of New Spain' was published at Madrid in 1632. He had little literary skill and no scientific knowledge; but he was a keen observer with a good memory, and an effective story-teller with a fine taste for marvelous feats and the supernatural, though trustworthy for ordinary happenings.

Dibdin, Charles. An English lyric and dramatic poet and actor; born at Southampton, 1745; died July 25, 1814. He opened a little playhouse in London, the Sans Souci Theatre, and there brought out his own plays, enlivened with his own songs, set to music of his own composition, and with himself as the leading actor. He wrote probably fifty plays and operettas (best remembered among them 'The Quaker,' an operetta), two novels, a 'History of the Stage,' and over a thousand songs. His 'Sea Songs' are popular favorites still. He wrote an autobiography: 'Professional Life' (4 vols., 1803).

Dibdin, Thomas Frognall. An eminent English bibliographer; born in Calcutta, India, 1775 or 1776; died in Kensington, London, Nov. 18, 1847. Books, not as literature merely, but as things, were the objects of his study and delight, with such results as the 'Bibliographical Decameron' (1817); 'Bibliophobia' (1832); and 'Reminiscences of a Literary Life' (1836),—works in which the collection of books is dealt with from the point of view of a lover of the printing, binding, and illustrating arts.

Dibdin, Thomas John. An English dramatist; born in London, March 21, 1771; died there, Sept. 16, 1841. Prolific in plays of an ephemeral character, 'Blindman's Buff,' 'The Pirates,' and similar things of an hour, he lived well, worked hard, and died poor, leaving interesting 'Reminiscences' (1827) behind him.

Dicey, Edward. An English journalist, traveler, and author; born in Leicestershire, England, in 1832. He graduated with distinction at Trinity College, Cambridge, and entered journalism. He was identified for a short time with the Daily Telegraph and Daily News, and from 1870 to 1889 was editor of the Observer. Among his works are: 'Rome in 1860' (1861); 'The Battlefields of 1866' (1866); 'A Month in Russia during the Marriage of the Czarewich' (1867); 'England and Egypt' (1881).

Dickens, Charles. An English editor, eldest son of Charles Dickens; born in 1837; died July 20, 1896, at West Kensington, England. He was educated at King's College, Eton, and at Leipsic; became assistant to his father as editor of All the Year Round, and subsequently chief partner in a printing firm. He edited a 'Life of Charles Mathews'; 'The Dictionary of London'; 'Paris and the Thames.'

Dickens, Charles. A famous English novelist; born at Landport in Portsea, Feb. 7, 1812; died June 9, 1870. His works include: 'Sketches by Boz' (1835–36); 'Pickwick Papers' (1837); 'Oliver Twist' (1838–39); 'Nicholas

Nickleby' (1839); 'Master Humphrey's Clock' (1840–41), a weekly issue in periodical form, comprising among others the installments of 'Old Curiosity Shop' and 'Barnaby Rudge'; 'American Notes' (1842); 'A Christmas Carol' (1843); 'Martin Chuzzlewit' (1844); 'The Chimes' (1844); 'The Cricket on the Hearth' (1845); 'Pictures from Italy' (1846); 'The Battle of Life' (1846); 'Dombey and Son' (1848); 'The Haunted Man' (1848); 'David Copperfield' (1850); 'Bleak House' (1853); 'A Child's History of England' (1854); 'Hard Times' (1854); 'Little Dorrit' (1857); 'A Tale of Two Cities' (1859); 'Great Expectations' (1861); 'Our Mutual Friend' (1865); 'The Mystery of Edwin Drood' (1870), unfinished; and many short pieces and humorous essays, stories, and sketches.

Dickens, Mary Angela (Evans). An English novelist, daughter of William Evans; born in London, March 6, 1838; died, June 22, 1896. In 1861 she married the eldest son of Charles Dickens. Her best-known novel is 'A Mere Cipher' (1893). She also wrote 'Cross Currents' (1892); 'Valiant Ignorance' (1894); 'Some Women's Ways,' a volume of short stories.

Dickinson, Anna Elizabeth. Orator, novelist, and playwright; born in Philadelphia, Oct. 28, 1842. At the outbreak of the Civil War she became known as a speaker, and under the stimulus of the great events became an orator of great power and persuasiveness, who created by her youth, real pathos, and brilliant rhetoric, the greatest enthusiasm wherever she was heard; no name was better known the country through. She was called the «Joan of Arc» of the war. Some of her books are: 'What Answer' (1868), a novel; 'A Paying Investment' (1876); 'A Ragged Register of People, Places, and Opinions' (1879). She was the author of two plays of excellent dramatic quality, 'Anne Boleyn' and 'Marie Tudor' (1875), in which she played the title rôles.

Dickinson, Emily. An American poet; born in Amherst, Mass., Dec. 10, 1830; died there, May 15, 1886. Living the life of a recluse, she wrote much verse in forms peculiar to herself, but she published almost nothing; although the few pieces that appeared attracted much attention. In 1892 a collection of her poems was issued which received warm praise from competent critics. In all, three volumes of her verse and prose have appeared.

Dickinson, John. An early American political writer and statesman. He was born in Maryland, Nov. 13, 1732, and died at Wilmington, Del., Feb. 14, 1808. He wrote a series of State papers — 'Address to the Inhabitants of Quebec'; 'Petitions to the King'; 'Address to the Armies' — that had great influence in their day. He was the author of 'Letters from a Pennsylvania Farmer to the Inhabitants of the Colonies' (1767), and 'Essay on Constitutional Power of Great Britain over the American Colonies' (1774). Dickinson College at Carlisle, Pa., was named in his honor.

Diderot, Denis (dē-drō'). A distinguished French philosopher, foremost of the «Encyclopedists»; born at Langres, Oct. 5, 1713; died July 31, 1784. 'Philosophic Reflections'—burned by the hangman and therefore widely circulated —and 'A Skeptic's Walk' (1747) were part of a warfare against the Church. In the compilation of the 'Encyclopedia' Diderot bore the main burden. He wrote all the articles on technology and industries, besides many of those on points of philosophy, and even on physics and chemistry. Further proof of his versatility is seen in the admirable reports he wrote (1765–67) of the art expositions at the Paris Academy. He wrote some dramas, but none of them possess any great merit. On the other hand, his novel 'The Nun' and his dramatic dialogue 'Rameau's Nephew' are wonderfully effective pictures of the corrupt society of the time. His little sketches 'Little Papers' are pearls of kindly humor and of witty narrative.

Didier, Charles (dēd-yā'). A French poet and novelist (1805–64); born at Geneva. He wrote some novels designed to awaken patriotic sentiment in Italy, and to make known the struggles of the Carbonari and other revolutionists against Austrian and papal dominion. Among these novels are: 'Underground Rome' (2 vols., 1833); 'The Roman Campagna' (1842); and 'Fifty Years in the Wilderness' (1857): they contain masterly descriptions of the state of Italy. His lyric poems, 'Melodies' (1827), are characterized less by force than by sweetness.

Didier, Eugene Lemoine. An American prose-writer; born in Baltimore, Md., Dec. 22, 1838. Many of his writings have appeared over the signatures «Lemoine» and «Timon.» He published the 'Life of Edgar A. Poe' (1876); 'Life and Letters of Madame Bonaparte' (1879), republished in London and translated into French and Italian; and a 'Primer of Criticism' (1883).

Dieffenbach, Christian (dēf'en-bäch). A German poet and theologian; born in Schlitz, Hesse, Dec. 4, 1822. His talent finds most congenial expression in 'Songs of Childhood' (1852) and 'In the German Springtime' (1871), the latter a volume of inspiring war song. D. 1901.

Dierx, Léon (dērx). A French poet; born in the Isle of Reunion, 1838. He was educated for a civil-service career, but has devoted his highest capacities to verse. His maiden volume, 'Aspirations' (1858), sounds a new note; while 'Closed Lips' (1867) and 'The Lovers' (1879) maintain him in the supremacy he has attained in the so-called «Parnassian» school.

Dietrickson, Lorents Henrik Segelcke (dē-trik-son). A Norwegian poet and historian of art and literature; born at Bergen, Jan. 1, 1834. While an undergraduate in the University of Christiania, he composed many clever student songs which were collected and published in 1859. He published the poem 'Olaf Liljekranz' in 1857, and 'Kivleflåtten' in 1879. His writings on art and literature are numerous and of high authority.

Dieulafoy, Jeanne Rachel (Mayre) (dyè-lä-fwä). A French descriptive writer and novelist; born (Mayre) in Toulouse, June 29, 1851. Her narrative of travel in 'Persia, Chaldæa, and Susa' (1886), and her fiction 'Parysatis' (1890), 'Brother Pelagus' (1894), are evidences of her talent.

Diez, Friedrich Christian (dētc). A German critic and historian of literature, founder of Romance philology; born in Giessen, March 15, 1794; died in Bonn, May 29, 1876. At 27 he achieved celebrity with his philological studies of 'Old Spanish Romances' (1821), etc.; but his masterpieces in this field are 'The Poetry of the Troubadours' (1826) and 'Lives and Works of the Troubadours' (1829). 'An Etymological Dictionary of the Romance Languages' (1853), and editions of Romance poems and other works, sustain his pre-eminence.

Diez, Katharina. A German poet and story-writer; born at Netphen, Westphalia, Dec. 2, 1809; died there, Jan. 22, 1882. Her simple but fresh and pleasing talent is evinced in 'Song Wreath' (1842), and 'Poems' (1857), in part by a sister; and 'A Youthful Friendship' (1861), a story of village life.

Dilke, Charles Wentworth. An English publicist and critic; born Dec. 8, 1789; died at Hants, Aug. 10, 1864. A journalist and book reviewer of celebrity, his best work is in 'The Papers of a Critic' (1875).

Dilke, Sir Charles Wentworth. An English publicist and critical and political writer; born in London, Sept. 4, 1843. A brilliant but checkered political career has been varied by literary work : 'Greater Britain' (1868), a record of travel in the English colonies; 'Problems of Great Britain'(1890); 'The British Army'; 'Imperial Defense'; and various essays on current style.

Dilke, Emilia Frances, Lady. An English art critic and miscellaneous writer; wife of Sir Charles W. She was for many years a writer for the Saturday and Westminster Reviews, and at one time art critic of the Academy. Her chief work is 'The Renaissance in France,' illustrated by herself. Her other publications include: 'The Shrine of Death' (1886); 'Art in the Modern State' (1888); 'The Shrine of Love.'

Dincklage-Campe, Emmy von (dink'läg-è-ƙäm'pè). A German novelist (1825–91); born at Campe, Osnabrück. Her first novel, 'The Loving Old Couple,' was published in 1857. Though she traveled extensively and observantly in Europe and America, her themes for stories were nearly all from her loved countryside; and she is called "the poetess of the Ems valley." Among her novels may be named: 'The School of the Heart'; 'Tales of Home'; 'Pictures of Emsland'; (posthumously) 'Poems,' and a story, 'The Woman Nihilist.'

Dingelstedt, Franz von, Baron (din'gel-stet). A German poet and dramatist; born at Halsdorf in Upper Hesse, June 30, 1814; died at Vienna, May 15, 1881. His 'Songs of a Cosmopolitan Nightwatchman' (1841) shocked all officialdom, but had a great popular success; and his 'Poems' (1845) showed true poetic feeling and great descriptive power, the latter also visible in his travel sketches and stories; one of the most successful of the latter is 'The Amazon,' a society novel. His tragedy 'The House of the Barneveldts' (1851) was a splendid success. He adapted plays from Molière, Shakespeare, and others, to the German stage, and wrote a volume of 'Studies and Copies after Shakespeare.'

Diniz, Julio (dē'nēs), pseudonym of Joaquim Guilherme Gomes Coelho. A Portuguese novelist and poet; born at Oporto, Nov. 14, 1839; died there, Sept. 12, 1871. He introduced the village story into Portuguese literature. His first work, 'The Rector's Wards' (1866), is also his best; it was followed by 'An English Family' (1867), describing middle-class life in Oporto. His poems were published in 1880.

Diniz da Cruz e Silva, Antonio (dē'nēs dä kröth ē sēl'vä). A Portuguese poet (1731–99); born at Lisbon. A lawyer and official, in 1776 he was made counsel to the superior court at Rio Janeiro, and died there. He was one of the founders of the celebrated literary society, the Lisbon Arcadia. His poetry comprises sonnets (over 300), eclogues, elegies, songs, epigrams, epistles, and several volumes of Pindaric odes; a lengthy poem, 'Brazil's Metamorphoses'; and a heroi-comic epic, 'Hyssop,' — modeled on Boileau's 'Lutrin,' but a spirited, original composition, far superior to Boileau's,— which was republished several times in France, translated into French prose.

Dinnies, Anna Peyre (Shackelford). An American poet and prose-writer; born in Georgetown, S. C., 1816. She was a frequent contributor to Southern periodicals. Her best work is 'The Floral Year' (1847); a collection of 100 poems, arranged in twelve groups, typifying bouquets of flowers. Died in 1886.

Diogenes Laertius (dī-oj'e-nēz lā-er'shus). A Greek compiler of anecdotes, flourishing probably around 200–250 B.C.; native of Laerte in Cilicia. He wrote in 10 books a collection of notes and memoranda 'On the Lives, Teachings, and Sayings of Famous Men,' particularly the philosophers. Drawn from divers sources without any judgment or discrimination, the notes are of very unequal value. The fullest memoranda concern Epicurus, for nearly all the fragments of whom that we possess we are indebted to this compiler.

Disraeli, Benjamin. See **Beaconsfield**.

D'Israeli, Isaac. A notable English literary essayist, compiler, and historian, father of Benjamin; born at Enfield in Middlesex, May 1766; died Jan. 9, 1848. He was of Spanish-Jew stock, but left the Jewish communion,

Rejecting a career of trade, he frequented the British Museum and compiled an interesting collection of literary miscellanea or "ana," the 'Curiosities of Literature,' etc., which he published anonymously in 1791. The author expected little sale, and presented the copyright to the publisher, but bought it back a few years later on its remarkable success; it is still continually republished. A series of like collections followed, with the same success: 'Calamities of Authors'; 'Quarrels of Authors'; 'Miscellanies, or Literary Recollections.' He wrote some unsuccessful romances; among them is 'Mejnoun and Leila,' probably the earliest Oriental romance in the language. His 'Commentaries on the Life and Reign of Charles I.' marked a distinct advance in the methods of historical research.

Ditson, George Leighton. An American historical writer and traveler; born in Westford, Mass., Aug. 5, 1812; has published 'Circassia, or a Tour to the Caucasus' (1850); 'The Para Papers on France, Egypt, and Ethiopia' (1858); 'Adventures and Observations on the Northern Coast of Africa' (1859); 'The Federati of Italy' (1871).

Dix, Dorothea Lynde. An American philanthropist and author; born in Maine in 1802; died in Trenton, N. J., July 19, 1887. In early life she kept a school for girls. Later she gave her attention to ameliorating the condition of paupers, criminals, and insane persons. During the Civil War she was superintendent of hospital nurses for the Union army. Among her works — many of which were published anonymously — are : 'The Garland of Flora' (1829); 'Prisons and Prison Discipline' (1845).

Dix, John Adams. An American statesman and general; born at Boscawen, N. H., July 24, 1798; died in New York city, April 21, 1879. He was with his father in the war of 1812, and subsequently held other commissions in the army; but resigned in 1828, settled in Cooperstown, N. Y., and began the practice of law, which he had studied during his military service. Thereafter he was prominent in the politics of his adopted State, and was elected to the United States Senate in 1845. He was Secretary of the Treasury during a brief period in 1861 under Buchanan, during which time he telegraphed to a naval officer the famous phrase : "If any one attempts to haul down the American flag, shoot him on the spot!" During the Civil War he was made major-general of volunteers. From 1867 to 1868 he was Minister to France, and in 1872 was elected Governor of New York. Among his works are : 'Resources of the City of New York' (1827); 'A Winter in Madeira, and a Summer in Spain and France' (1855); 'Speeches and Occasional Addresses' (2 vols., 1864). He translated 'Dies Iræ' (1863), and 'Stabat Mater' (1868), both privately printed.

Dix, Morgan. An American clergyman and writer, son of John A.; born in New York city, Nov. 1, 1827; rector of Trinity parish, New York city, since Nov. 10, 1862. His publications include : 'Essay on Christian Art' (1853); 'Memoirs of John Adams Dix' (1883); 'The Gospel and Philosophy, Six Lectures' (1886); and two vols. of 'Sermons' (1878–86). Died April 29, 1908.

Dixon, James. An American lawyer and statesman; born in Enfield, Conn., Aug. 5, 1814; died in Hartford, Conn., March 27, 1873. He graduated at Williams College; achieved distinction in the practice of the law, in partnership with Judge W. W. Ellsworth; but turning his attention to public affairs, was repeatedly elected to the Connecticut Legislature as a Whig, served two terms in the United States House of Representatives, and was a member of the United States Senate from 1857 to 1869. In 1862 he received the degree of LL.D. from Trinity College. He excelled as a writer of both prose and poetry, and his poems occupy a conspicuous place in Everest's 'Poets of Connecticut.' Several of his sonnets have an honorable place with those of Lowell and Bryant in Leigh Hunt's 'The Book of the Sonnet.'

Dixon, Richard Watson. An English poet and historian; born in London in 1833. He was a minister of the English Church. He was associated with Burne-Jones, Rossetti, and Morris, in founding the Oxford and Cambridge Magazine, the organ of the pre-Raphaelite school. His poetical works are: 'Christ's Company and Other Poems' (1861); an epic 'Mano' (1883); 'Odes and Eclogues' (1884); 'Lyrical Poems' (1887). His principal historical work is a 'History of the Church of England' (4 vols., 1880–91). Died Jan., 1900.

Dixon, William Hepworth. An English critic, biographer, and historian ; born at Great Ancoats, June 30, 1821; died in London, Dec. 27, 1879. He is peculiarly successful in exploiting the altruistic side of human nature, 'John Howard and the Prison World of Europe' (new ed. 1854); 'William Penn' (1851); and 'Robert Blake' (1852); while the 'History of England During the Commonwealth' and the 'Personal History of Lord Bacon' (1861) are contributions of enduring value to historical science. Visits to America inspired the 'White Conquest' (1876), giving much information about the negroes, Indians, and Chinese.

Dmitriyev, Iván Ivánovich (dmē'trē-ef). A Russian poet (1760-1837); born in the government of Simbirsk. After a high official career, he retired to private life in 1802, and devoted himself till his death to literature. His first poem, a song, 'The Dove,' led Karamsin to advise him to keep on working the lyric vein; he took the French poets for his models, and thus attained a grace of form before unknown in Russian poetry. He made an admirable translation of Lafontaine into Russian verse. His greatest original work is an epico-dramatic poem : 'Jermak, Conqueror of Siberia.' Many of his songs are popular favorites. He wrote a highly interesting autobiography: 'A Glance at my Life.'

Doane, George Washington. An American bishop of the Episcopal Church; born in Trenton, N. J., May 27, 1799; died April 27, 1859. His publications consist of public addresses, and a book of poems entitled 'Songs by the Way' (1824). Many of his verses are found in collections; among which are the familiar lines, 'What Is that, Mother?'; 'Softly Now the Light of Day'; and 'Thou Art the Way.'

Doane, William Croswell. An American bishop of the Episcopal Church, son of George W.; born in Boston, March 2, 1832. He has been a prolific writer on current events, contributing to reviews and other periodicals. He has written a number of poems, among which 'The Sculptor Boy' is best known. Included among his published works are: 'Sermons'; 'Mosaics for the Christian Year'; and 'Life and Writings' of his father, George Washington Doane, with a memoir (4 vols., 1860-61).

Dobell, Sydney Thompson. An English poet (1824-74); born at Cranbrook in Kent. A passionate interest in Italian freedom inspired his dramatic poem 'The Roman,' published in a crisis of Italian affairs (1850), and very successful. His services to the cause of free institutions were heartily acknowledged by Kossuth and Mazzini. A later poem, 'Balder,' had less vogue. In 1856 he published a volume of dramatic and descriptive verses relating mostly to the Crimean war, 'England in Time of War,' many of which have found a place in anthologies. After his death a volume of essays was published: 'Thoughts on Art, Philosophy, and Religion.'

Döbrentey, Gabriel (dě-bren'tä-ē). A Hungarian poet (1786-1851); born at Nagyszölös. After study in German universities, he became a schoolmaster in Transylvania, and founded a journal, the Transylvanian Museum, which had a notable influence in developing the Magyar language and literature. He then settled at Pesth, and was one of the founders of the Hungarian Academy. He edited the Academy's 'Monuments of Ancient Hungarian Speech,' and with Andrew Fay was director of the new Hungarian Theatre. His many songs, odes, epigrams, elegies, etc., despite their frequent turgidity, must be ranked with the better specimens of the national literature, and not a few of them were translated into foreign languages; e. g., 'The Alpine Violet' and the 'Hussar Songs.' He rendered valuable service to the Hungarian stage by introducing the plays of Shakespeare and Schiller. His historical writings are of great and permanent value.

Dobrolyúbov, Nicolai Alexandrovitch (dōbrŏl'yu-bov). A Russian critic; born in Nishni-Novgorod, Feb. 5, 1836; died Nov. 29, 1861. The study of Ostroffski's plays, entitled 'The Dark Kingdom,' and the analysis of Gontcharof's romance 'Oblomoff,' among others, show him to have been a profound and gifted literary critic.

Dobrovsky, Joseph (dō-brov'skē). An eminent Bohemian critic, literary historian, and philologist, the rejuvenator of his country's literature; born in Gyermet, Hungary, Aug. 17, 1753; died in Brünn, Jan. 6, 1829. He was without a peer in Bohemian learning, ranking among the greatest philologists and critics with his 'History of the Bohemian Language and Literature' (1792); 'Principles of the Old Slavic Dialect' (1822); 'Grammar of the Bohemian Language'); and a wealth of similar works, all characterized by accuracy and sound judgment, and conferring unparalleled obligations on Bohemian letters.

Dobson, Austin. An English poet and man of letters; born at Plymouth, Jan. 18, 1840. Intended for a civil engineer, and educated abroad, he accepted a place under the Board of Trade. His poems are inimitable in their artistic finish and grace of fancy. They are contained in the volumes: 'Vignettes in Rhyme and Vers de Société' (1873); 'Proverbs in Porcelain' (1877); 'Old-World Idyls' (1883); 'Eighteenth-Century Vignettes' (1892). He has written biographies of Hogarth, Fielding, Steele, Goldsmith, and other literary notables, and contributed many articles to the English 'Dictionary of National Biography.'

Dóczy, Ludwig von (děk'tsē). A Hungaro-German poet and publicist; born at Ödenburg, Nov. 30, 1845. He was correspondent of the Vienna Presse at Buda-Pesth in 1866; soon became a leader among the younger journalistic supporters of the Deak party, and rose to official prominence. He translated the first part of Goethe's 'Faust'; produced a comedy, 'The Kiss' (1871), which was a striking success both at home and (in his translation) in the German theatres, and others. 'Mixed Marriages' was very successful. He wrote also the tragedy 'The Last Prophet,' and some free-flowing lyrics, besides several novels.

Dodd, Anna Bowman (Blake). An American prose-writer; born in Brooklyn, N. Y., 1850. She has written criticisms for the London Art Journal and Harper's Magazine, and published 'Cathedral Days' (1886); 'The Republic of the Future' (1887); and 'Glorinda: a Story' (1888).

Dodd, Mary Ann Hanmer. An American poet; born in Hartford, Conn., March 5, 1813; graduated at Mrs. Kinnear's Seminary (1830); was contributor to the Ladies' Repository and the Rose of Sharon (1835). A volume of her poems was published in 1843, including 'The Lament' and 'The Dreamer.'

Doddridge, Philip. An English nonconformist divine; born in London, June 26, 1702; died in Lisbon, Portugal, Oct. 26, 1751. He was educated for the ministry at an academy in Kibworth, Leicestershire, where he became pastor in 1722. In 1729 he took charge of a theological academy in Northampton, and continued to preach and prepare students for the ministry until near his death. His chief works are: 'The Rise and Progress of Religion in the Soul' (1750), and 'The Family Expositor' (1760-62), which have been translated into several European languages. He also wrote 'Evidences of Christianity' (1742-43), which has long been a text-book in St. John's College, Cambridge; and several popular hymns.

Dodge, Mary Abigail. An American journalist and author; born in Hamilton, Mass., in 1838; died there, Aug. 17, 1896. For several years she was instructor in the High School at Hartford, Conn. From 1865 to 1867 she was one of the editors of Our Young Folks. Besides numerous contributions to current literature, she has written, under the pseudonym of "Gail Hamilton": 'Gala Days' (1863); 'Woman's Wrongs' (1868); 'The Battle of the Books' (1870); 'Woman's Worth and Worthlessness' (1871); 'The Insuppressible Book' (1885); 'A New Atmosphere'; 'Red-Letter Days'; 'Country Living and Country Thinking'; 'A Washington Bible Class'; 'Twelve Miles from a Lemon'; and 'Biography of James G. Blaine.'

Dodge, Mary Barker (Carter). An American poet; born in Bridgewater, Bucks County, Pa., 18—. Is author of 'Belfry Voices' (1870); 'The Gray Masque, and Other Poems' (1885).

Dodge, Mrs. Mary Elizabeth (Mapes). An American editor, author, and poet; born in New York city in 1840 (?). Since 1873 she has been the editor of St. Nicholas (magazine), New York. Her best-known work is 'Hans Brinker, or the Silver Skates' (1876), which has gone through many editions and been translated into five foreign languages. Among her other works, chiefly for young readers, are: 'Irvington Stories' (1864); 'Theophilus, and Others' (1876); 'Along the Way' (1879); 'Donald and Dorothy' 'The Land of Pluck.' Died, 1905.

Dodge, Richard Irving. An American soldier (colonel in the United States army) and prose-writer; born in Huntsville, N. C., May 19, 1827; died in Sackett's Harbor, N. Y., June 16, 1895. Col. Dodge graduated from West Point Military Academy in 1848. He is the author of 'The Black Hills' (1876); 'The Plains of the Great West' (1877), republished in London as 'Hunting Grounds of the Great West'; and 'Our Wild Indians' (1881).

Dodge, Theodore Ayrault. An American soldier and military writer; born in Pittsfield, Mass., May 28, 1842; received his military education abroad. Returning to this country, he enlisted (1861) in the service of the United States as a private, attaining the rank of colonel, Dec. 2, 1865. He published: 'The Campaign of Chancellorsville' (1881); a 'Bird's-Eye View of the Civil War' (1883); 'A Chat in the Saddle' (1885); and a series of studies called 'Great Captains,' comprising volumes on Alexander the Great, Hannibal, Gustavus Adolphus, and others.

Dodgson, Charles Lutwidge. See **Carroll.**

Dodsley, Robert. An English poet and dramatist (1703-64); born at Mansfield, Notts. He was a noted bookseller and publisher in London, and had close relations with the authors of the time: Pope, Johnson, Goldsmith, Burke, etc. His first volume of verses, 'The Muse in Livery,' was received with great favor, as was his satiric drama 'The Toy-Shop,' brought out at Covent Garden through the influence of Pope. Among his other plays which became popular favorites were the comedies 'The King and the Miller of Mansfield'; 'Sir John Cockle at Court'; and the tragedy 'Cleone.'

Doesticks, Q. K. Philander. See **Thompson.**

Dohm, Ernst (dōm). A German humorist (1819-83); born at Breslau. Settling in Berlin, he wrote for various literary journals, helped found the comic journal Kladderadatsch, and after a year became its head director till death. Many of his poems in it possess lasting value. Foremost of his comedies is 'The Trojan War,' cleverly satirizing German political and social leaders. Other comedies and farces are: 'The First Début'; 'Instantaneous Portraits: an Unrhymed Chronicle.' He translated Lafontaine's 'Fables.' His wife, Hedwig D., born at Berlin, Sept. 30, 1833, wrote several volumes on woman's rights, as 'Jesuitry in the Household'; 'Woman in Science'; 'Woman's Nature and Woman's Right': also some little comedies, as 'The Soul-Saver'; 'A Shot into the Bull's-eye'; and the novels 'Mrs. Tannhäuser'; 'Open Air.'

Dolbear, Amos Emerson. An American physicist and inventor; born in Norwich, Conn., Nov. 10, 1837; has been a valuable contributor to science. Among his publications are: 'The Art of Projecting' (1876); 'The Speaking Telephone' (1877); 'Sound and its Phenomena'; and 'Matter, Ether, and Motion.' He patented the magneto-electric telephone and the static telephone in 1879.

Dolce, Lodovico (dōl'chä). An Italian poet and scholar (1508-68); born at Venice. His poems and prose works are of almost incredible number and variety; most memorable is the epic 'First Impressions of the Enamored Orlando,' which, though not to be compared with Ariosto, is one of the best specimens of the romantic epic of the 16th century. His elaborations of the Amadis legend, his romantic versions of the 'Æneid' and the 'Odyssey,' and his tragedies and comedies, are mediocre.

Dole, Charles Fletcher. An American prose-writer; born in Maine, 1845; a Unitarian minister of Boston. Is the author of: 'The Citizen and the Neighbor'; 'Jesus and the Men about Him'; 'A Catechism of Liberal Faith'; 'The American Citizen'; 'The Coming People'; 'The Spirit of Democracy.'

Dole, Nathan Haskell. An American miscellaneous writer; born in Massachusetts, 1852. One of his most notable works is a variorum edition of the Rubáiyát of Omar Khayyám. He is the author of: 'Not Angels Quite'; 'History of the Turko-Russian War of 1877–78'; 'On the Point, a Summer Idyl'; 'Flowers from Foreign Gardens.' He has translated Tolstoi and others from the Russian.

Döllinger, John Joseph Ignatius. A German Catholic priest, politician, and historian; born at Bamberg, Bavaria, in 1799; died in Munich, 1890. He won distinction as a learned writer on Church history. In 1845 he was elected to the Bavarian Parliament, and in 1851 to the Parliament at Frankfort. He was a vigorous advocate for the separation of the Church from the State. In 1870 he refused assent to Papal Infallibility, and was excommunicated, but received honorary degrees and other tokens of esteem from foreign institutions. In 1872 he was appointed president of the Academy of Science at Munich. Among his works are: 'Origins of Christianity' (1833–35); 'The Reformation' (1846–48); 'The Church and the Churches' (1860); 'Prophecies and the Prophetic Spirit in the Christian Era' (1872).

Domett, Alfred. An English poet; born in Surrey, 1811; died in London, 1887. Said to have been the original of Browning's 'Waring.' He was a colonial statesman of eminence. His verse attracted much attention, the best specimens being in the volumes 'Ranolf and Amohia' (1872), and 'Flotsam and Jetsam: Rhymes Old and New' (1877).

Donne, John. An English poet; born in London, 1573; died March 31, 1631. He was a minister of the Established Church, and one of the preachers at Lincoln's Inn: Izaak Walton describes him as a singularly eloquent pulpit orator. His 'Satires' are his most important contributions to literature. A collection of his sermons, with a memoir, has just (1897) been issued by Augustus Jessopp.

Donnelly, Eleanor Cecilia. An American writer of religious verse, sister of Ignatius; born in Philadelphia, Sept. 6, 1838. A few of her poetical publications are: 'Domus Dei' (1874); 'Hymns of the Sacred Heart' (1882); 'Our Birthday Banquet,' in prose and verse (1885); and 'Signori Leaflets' (1887). Her writings have received the special apostolic benediction of Pope Leo XIII.

Donnelly, Ignatius. An American prose-writer; born in Philadelphia, Nov. 3, 1831; died at Minneapolis, Minn., Jan. 1, 1901. He wrote: an 'Essay on the Sonnets of Shakespeare'; 'Atlantis, the Antediluvian World' (1882); and 'Ragnarok' (1883). In 'The Great Cryptogram' he endeavors to prove that Bacon was the author of Shakespeare's plays. His best known novel is 'Cæsar's Column.'

Dora d'Istria (dō'rä dis'trē-ä), pseudonym of Elena Chica, who married the Russian prince Kolzow-Massalsky. A voluminous Roumanian writer of travel sketches, mostly in French (1828–88); born at Bucharest. Most of her writings are polemic; e. g., her first work,

'Monastic Life in the Eastern Church,' alleges monasticism to be the principal obstacle to civilization in Eastern and Southern Europe. Her other works include: 'German Switzerland' (4 vols.); 'Women in the East'; 'Women, by a Woman.' She contributed many literary and historical essays to German, Italian, French, and Greek periodicals. Her studies on Albanian poetry gave rise to a nationalistic and literary movement among the Albanians. The Greek chamber of deputies, in April 1868, named her "high citizeness of Greece."

Doran, John. An English essayist and critic; born in London, Mar. 11, 1807; died there Jan. 25, 1878. He wrote 'The Wandering Jew' when he was fifteen, and the Surrey Theatre staged it. His maturer performances, 'Table Traits and Something on Them' (1854), 'New Pictures and Old Panels' (1859), and a 'History of Court Fools' (1858), have merit.

Dorer-Egloff, Eduard (dōr'er-eg'lof). A Swiss poet and critic; born in Baden, Aargau, Nov. 7, 1807; died March 27, 1864. He was an accomplished student and critic of Goethe, and a versifier and prose-writer of no mean capacity. 'Lenz and his Writings' (1857), and 'Poems,' the latter a posthumous collection, are among his ablest efforts.

Dorgan, John Aylmer. An American lawyer and writer; born at Philadelphia, Jan. 12, 1836; died there, Jan. 1, 1867. He was a lawyer by profession, but wrote for the Atlantic Monthly and other periodicals. He published his first volume of poems, 'Studies,' in 1862; a second edition of same in 1864, and a third in 1866.

Dorr, Mrs. Julia Caroline (Ripley). An American poet and novelist; born in Charleston, S. C., Feb. 13, 1825. Among her volumes of verse are: 'Daybreak, an Easter Poem'; 'Afternoon Songs'; 'Poems'; and others. Her novels include: 'Lanmere'; 'Sibyl Huntington'; 'Expiation'; and 'Farmingdale.' She has also written: 'Bermuda,' a volume of travel; 'Bride and Bridegroom, or Letters to a Young Married Couple'; 'The Flower of England's Face'; and 'A Cathedral Pilgrimage.'

Dorsch, Eduard (dorsh). A German-American journalist and miscellaneous writer; born in Würzburg, Jan. 10, 1822; died in (Monroe?) Michigan, Jan. 10, 1887. He was a physician who came to this country in 1849, practiced with distinction, acquired note as a journalist, and succeeded in Michigan politics. 'Short Letters to the German People on Two Sides of the Ocean' (1851) and 'From the Old and New Worlds' (1883) represent his prose and poetry respectively.

Dorset, Charles Sackville, Earl of. An English poet; born in Witham, 1637; died in Bath, 1706. Elegant and agreeable as a man and as a poet, he will be longest remembered for the effusion, 'To All You Ladies Now at Hand,' a song unequaled for its sea-fighting spirit.

Dorsey, Anna Hanson. An American poet, novelist, and dramatist; born in Georgetown, D. C., Dec. 12, 1815; died in Washington, D. C., Dec. 26, 1896. Many of her works have been reprinted in foreign countries; among them being ‹May Brooke› (1856) and ‹Oriental Pearl,› translated into German (1857). Her novels, ‹Warp and Woof› and ‹Palms,› were published in 1887.

Dorsey, James Owen. An American ethnologist; born in Baltimore, Md., Oct. 31, 1848; died in Washington, D. C., Feb. 4, 1895. He was ordained a deacon in the Protestant Episcopal Church, and was engaged in parish work in Maryland from 1873 to 1878. He was then appointed ethnologist to the United States Geological and Geographical Survey of the Rocky Mountains; and after spending some time at the Omaha Reservation in Nebraska, was transferred to the United States Bureau of Ethnology. His chief works are: ‹On the Comparative Phonology of Four Siouan [Sioux] Languages› (1883); ‹Siouian Folklore and Mythologic Notes› (1884); ‹Kansas Mourning and War Customs› (1884); ‹Indian Personal Names› (1886).

Dorsey, Sarah Anne. An American prose-writer; born in Natchez, Miss., Feb. 16, 1829; died in New Orleans, La., July 4, 1879. She was a linguist and a student of Sanskrit. Her literary work began with the (Episcopal) Churchman. Included in her writings are: ‹Lucia Dare› (1867); ‹Panola, a Tale of Louisiana› (1877); ‹Atalie›; and ‹Agnes Graham.› She was amanuensis to Jefferson Davis in the preparation of his ‹Rise and Fall of the Confederate Government.›

Dostoévsky, Feodor Michailovitch. (dŏs-tō-yev′skē). A notable Russian novelist; born at Moscow, Nov. 11, 1821; died at St. Petersburg, Feb. 8, 1881. His first book, ‹Poor Folk› (1846), an example of his talent for psychological analysis, was followed by the short stories ‹A Black Heart,› ‹The Little Hero,› and others. He was condemned to the Siberian mines in 1849 for a socialist conspiracy, but in 1859 returned to St. Petersburg and resumed literary work. The thrilling ‹Memoirs of a Dead House› describes penal life in Siberia. ‹Raskolnikov› traces with wonderful skill the origin and effects on the soul of a criminal act. ‹Complete Works,› 14 vols. There are translations of several of his works.

Doucet, Charles Camille (dö-sā′). A French dramatist; born at Paris, May 16, 1812; died there April 1, 1895. He became in 1853 a government official in the theatrical department; was elected to the Academy in 1876, and soon after made its standing secretary. The best known of his comedies are: ‹A Young Man› (1841); ‹Lawyer in His Own Cause› (1842); ‹Forbidden Fruit› (1857); ‹Consideration.› His lyric pieces for the stage, ‹Velasquez› (1847) and ‹Antonio's Barque› (1849), were crowned by the Academy.

Doudney, Sarah. An English writer of fiction; born near Portsmouth, England, in 1842; resides in London. She began contributing to magazines at 18, and is very popular, chiefly as a writer of stories for girls. Her poem ‹The Lesson of the Water Mill› is a familiar favorite. Her prose works, over forty in number, include: ‹Under Grey Walls› (1871); ‹The Pilot's Daughters› (1874); ‹Nothing but Leaves› (1882); ‹Under False Colours›; ‹Silent Strings.›

Douglas, Alice May. An American writer of verse and stories; born in Maine, 1865. Her writings are for young readers, and include in verse: ‹Phlox›; ‹May Flowers›; ‹Gems without Polish›; in stories: ‹Jewel Gatherers›; ‹The Peacemaker›; and ‹Self-Exiled from Russia.›

Douglas, Amanda Minnie. An American story-writer; born in New York city, July 14, 1837; was carefully educated in English literature. She has written many stories, which include: ‹Kathie's Stories for Young People› (6 vols., 1870-71); ‹From Hand to Mouth› (1877); and ‹Foes of her Household› (1886).

Douglas, Gavin. A Scotch poet; born in Perth (?), 1474 (?); died in London, September 1522. He lived "a man of peace amid resounding arms"; writing ‹The Palice of Honour› (1553) while a cloistered youth, and ‹King Hart,› an allegory of the state of man, after he had become famed as a churchman, translating also all of the ‹Æneid.› Heroic in figure and in strain, he towers among his country's ancient bards.

Douglas, Robert Kennaway. An English librarian and educator; born at Ottery St. Mary, Devon, 1838. He was consular interpreter in China, and subsequently acting vice-consul at Taku, 1858-64. On his return to England he occupied several important positions, including a librarianship in the British Museum. In 1873 he was appointed professor of Chinese at King's College, London. Among his publications are: ‹Confucianism and Taouism› (1879); ‹China› (1882); ‹Chinese Stories› (1893).

Douglass, Frederick. An American emancipator and orator; born a slave in Tuckahoe, Md., February, 1817; died near Washington, Feb. 20, 1895. He escaped from slavery in 1838; edited the North Star at Rochester from 1847 until the abolition of slavery. He was renowned as a lecturer and an orator. He published: ‹The Life and Times of Frederick Douglass› (1882); ‹My Bondage and My Freedom›; ‹Narrative of my Experience in Slavery›; etc. He held important government posts.

Dovalle, Charles (dō-väl′). A French poet; born at Montreuil-Bellay, June 23, 1807; died Nov. 30, 1829. He was a poor provincial who came to Paris unknown, studied law, and burst on the literary world with ‹The Oratory in the Garden› and other delightful poems of a like nature, besides an ‹Ode on Liberty.› His promising career was closed at 22 in a duel, the challenger being enraged at a literay criticism.

Dovizi or **Dovizio, Bernardo.** See **Bibbiena.**

Dowden, Edward. An Irish poet and historian of literature; born at Cork, May 3, 1843. He is professor of English literature in Trinity College, Dublin. He published a volume of 'Poems' (1876); his other writings are biographical and critical: *e. g.*, 'Shakespeare, his Mind and Art' (1872), a work of high authority, which reached a fifth edition (1887) and has been translated into German; 'Southey' (1879); 'Life of Percy Bysshe Shelley' (1886); 'Studies in Literature' (3d ed 1887); 'Introduction to Shakespeare' (1893); 'Primer of French Literature' (1897); 'Puritan and Anglican' (1900), 'Robert Browning' (1904). He visited this country in 1896, delivering a notable series of lectures at Princeton.

Dowling, Bartholomew. An Irish poet; born in Limerick, 182-. He lived for a time in this country. He is noted for his lyric 'The Brigade at Fontenoy' and for 'The Revel.'

Downes, William Howe. An American journalist; born in Connecticut, 1854. He is on the staff of the Boston Transcript, and is an art critic. His publications are: 'Spanish Ways and By-Ways'; 'The Tin Army of the Potomac, or a Kindergarten of War.'

Downing, Andrew Jackson. An American landscape-gardener; born in Newburg, N. Y., Oct. 20, 1815; drowned near Yonkers, N. Y., July 28, 1852. His 'Landscape Gardening and Rural Architecture' (1841); 'Cottage Residences' (1842); 'Fruits and Fruit Trees of America' (1845), were long considered authorities on the subjects of which they treat.

Downing, Fanny Murdaugh. An American poet and novelist; born in Portsmouth, Va., about 1835; died 1894. Included in her novels are 'Nameless' (1865); 'Perfect through Suffering'; her poems are 'The Legend of Catawba' and 'Dixie' (1867). Her pen-names were "Viola" and "Frank Dashmore."

Doyle, Sir A. Conan. A Scotch story and romance writer; born in Edinburgh, 1859. He was carefully trained for a physician, but went to London at 20 and adopted literature as a profession. His greatest success was won with the series of detective tales known as the Sherlock Holmes stories: 'The Adventures of Sherlock Holmes,' etc. He has also written: 'The Adventures of Brigadier Gerard' (1895), a Napoleonic romance; 'The Stark-Munro Letters' (1895), a series of portraitures: and 'Uncle Bernac' (1897); 'The Great Boer War'; 'Return of Sherlock Holmes.'

Doyle, Sir Francis Hastings. An English poet; born in Yorkshire, 1810; died 1888. He was long professor of poetry at Oxford. He published 'The Return of the Guards, and Other Poems' (1866).

Drachmann, Holger (dräch'män). A Danish poet and novelist; born at Copenhagen, Oct. 9, 1846. He is essentially an improvisatore; and his works show a lively fancy, and excel in descriptions of the life of the common people, especially fishermen and mariners. His

'Poems' appeared in 1872. His novels are 'Condemned' and 'Once upon a Time.' D. 1908.

Drake, Benjamin. An American biographical writer; born in Mason County, Ky., in 1794; died in Cincinnati, O., April 1, 1841. He established and for many years edited the Western Agriculturist. Among his publications are: 'Adventures of Black Hawk' (1838); 'Life of William Henry Harrison' (1840); and 'Life of Tecumseh' (1841). The last work is considered of especial historic value.

Drake, Francis Samuel. An American historical writer; born in Northwood, N. H., Feb. 22, 1828; died in Washington, D. C., Feb. 22, 1885. He prepared a 'Dictionary of American Biography' (1872). He also published: 'Life of Gen. Henry Knox' (1873); 'Tea Leaves' (1884); and 'Indian History for Young Folks' (1885). Before his death he had gathered material for a new edition of his 'Dictionary,' which is to be found in 'Appleton's Cyclopædia of American Biography.'

Drake, Joseph Rodman. An American poet; born at New York, Aug. 7, 1795; died Sept. 21, 1820. The poems for which he is gratefully remembered are 'The Culprit Fay' (1819) and 'The American Flag' (1819). He wrote also some shorter pieces, notably a poem: 'Abelard to Heloïse.' With Fitz-Greene Halleck, under the signature "The Croakers," he published in a New York journal in 1819 a series of short lyrics, mostly of a humorous kind, on the political affairs of the time.

Drake, Samuel Adams. An American journalist and miscellaneous writer; born at Boston, Dec. 20, 1833. He entered journalism in 1858 as correspondent of the Louisville Journal and St. Louis Republican. In 1861 he joined the army and served throughout the war, becoming brigadier-general in 1863. He returned to Boston in 1871 and resumed literary work. His most important publications are: 'Old Landmarks of Boston' (1872); 'Around the Hub' (1881); 'New England Legends.' D. 1905.

Drake, Samuel Gardner. An American antiquarian; born in Pittsfield, N. H., Oct. 11, 1798; died in Boston, Mass., June 14, 1875. Published 'The History and Antiquities of Boston' (1856), and 'History of the French and Indian War' (1870).

Dranmor (drän'mōr), pseudonym of Ferdinand von Schmid. A Swiss poet; born in Muri, Switzerland, July 22, 1823; died in Bern, March 17, 1888. He was in mercantile life and also in the Austrian diplomatic service for years; but his 'Poetic Fragments' (1860) and 'Requiem' (1870) have added his name to the list of true poets.

Draper, John William. An American physiologist, chemist, historical and miscellaneous prose-writer; born near Liverpool, England, May 5, 1811; died at Hastings-on-the-Hudson, N. Y., Jan. 4, 1882. He came to this country in 1833, and took his degree as M. D. at the

University of Pennsylvania in 1836. He became professor of chemistry in the University of New York in 1841, and in 1850 professor of physiology. Among his works are: 'Human Physiology' (1856); 'History of the Intellectual Development of Europe' (1862), a work of great importance and very widely read; 'History of the American Civil War' (1867–70); 'History of the Conflict between Religion and Science' (1875), which ran through many editions and was translated into nearly all the languages of Europe.

Draper, Lyman Copeland. An American antiquarian; born in Hamburg, N. Y., Sept. 4, 1815; died in Madison, Wis., Aug. 26, 1891. He removed to Madison in 1853; became corresponding secretary of the State Historical Society, and it was mainly through his efforts that the State secured its library and its important antiquarian collection. The State University gave him the degree of LL.D. in 1871. He has published 'Collections' of the State Historical Society (10 vols., 1853–87); 'Madison the Capital of Wisconsin' (1857); 'King's Mountain and its Heroes' (1881).

Dräxler-Manfred, Karl Ferdinand (drex'ler män'fred). An Austrian poet and story-writer; born in Lemberg, June 17, 1806; died in Darmstadt, Dec. 31, 1879. His collected 'Poems' (1839), and the verse collection 'Joy and Pain' (1858), have profoundly impressed thousands of earnest men and women, while his tales in prose are original and pleasing.

Drayton, Michael. An English poet; born near Atherstone in Warwickshire in 1563; died in 1631. His first poem, 'Harmonie of the Church,' was condemned. Then followed 'The Shepherd's Garland,' and poems on the wars of England. His most celebrated composition is 'Polyolbion.' He wrote also several dramas, among them 'Sir John Oldcastle'; and 'Poems Lyric and Pastorall' (1605), including the celebrated 'Ballad of Agincourt.'

Dreyfus, Abraham (drä-füs'). A French playwright; born at Paris, June 20, 1847. He has a fine vein of kindly humor, and it pervades both his contributions to the public journals and his theatrical compositions, which are mostly in one act. Among them are: 'A Gentleman in Black'; 'The Victim'; 'The Klepht'; 'A Break.' His four-act play 'The St. Catherine Institution,' a comedy of manners, was brought out at the Odéon (1881).

Drinker, Anne. An American poet; born at Philadelphia, Pa., Dec. 3, 1827. She is best known by her nom de plume "Edith May." She has published: 'Poems by Edith May' (1854); 'Tales and Verses for Children' (1855); and 'Katy's Story.'

Driver, Samuel Rolles. An English educator and eminent Hebraist; born in Southampton in 1846. Fellow of and tutor in New College, Oxford, in 1882, he became professor of Hebrew there. He was a member of the Old Testament Revision Company. His best-

known works are: 'Isaiah' (1888); 'Notes on the Books of Samuel' (1890); 'Introduction to the Literature of the Old Testament' (4th ed. 1893); and a new Hebrew and English Lexicon.

Drobisch, Gustav Theodor (drō'bish). A German humorist and versifier; born in Dresden, Dec. 26, 1811; died there, April 15, 1882. His perception of the droll side of things is keen and irresistible in 'Conceits and Satires' (1843) and many similar collections of prose and rhyme.

Droogenbroeck, Jan van (drö'gen-brěk). A Flemish poet; born in St. Amand-on-Scheldt, Jan. 18, 1835. He has long been an educator of eminence, and issued his first verse collection, 'Ghazels and Makames' (Arabian terms for stanzas and songs) in 1866, under the pseudonym of "Jan Fergunt"; his subsequent volumes, on Camoens and other important subjects, fully sustaining his reputation. Died 1902.

Drossinis, Georg (drōs'in-is). A Greek poet; born at Athens, Dec. 21, 1859. He has published five volumes of lyrics: 'Spiders' Webs' (1880); 'Stalactites' (1881); 'Idylls' (1885); 'Straw Flowers' (1890); 'Amaranths' (1891): also some stories and other minor works in prose. A charming simplicity of language and an unsophisticated sensibility characterize all his works.

Droste-Hülshoff, Annette Elisabeth von, Baroness. A German poet (1797–1848); born at Hülshoff near Münster. Learned in science, she resided for years at Coblentz, Cologne, and Bonn, in intimate friendship with the ablest men there; from 1840 on she lived in studious retirement at Meersburg Castle on Lake Constance. Her poetry is comprised in a volume of 'Poems' (1838), with two posthumous volumes: 'The Church Year, with an Appendix of Religious Poems' (1852), and 'Last Gifts' (1860). It is vigorous, original, unaffected, and perfect in form. Her simple devoutness is specially marked in the fragments 'A Nobleman of Lusatia' and 'A Country Priest's Ways.' She excelled also as a novelist.

Droysen, Johann Gustav (droi'sen). A German historian and biographer; born in Treptow, on the Rega, July 6, 1808; died in Berlin, June 19, 1884. He was noted for ripe scholarship and for versions of Æschylus long before the production of his masterpiece: 'The Life of Field Marshal Count York of Wartenburg' (1851), and 'The History of Prussian Politics' (1855), politics meaning statecraft.

Droz, Gustave (drō). A French story-teller; born at Paris, June 9, 1832; died there Oct. 23, 1895. He was trained for a painter, but in 1864 gave up the pencil for the pen. The extraordinary success of his first volume of stories, 'Monsieur, Madame, and Baby,' justified the change. He excels in little sketches of life and manners, and his lively, playful descriptions of bachelorhood and married life captivate the public. He wrote: 'Sadnesses and Smiles' (1883);

'A Bunch of Letters'; 'At a Spring'; 'The Child'; etc.

Drummond, Henry. A Scotch geologist and writer; born at Stirling, Aug. 17, 1851; died at Tunbridge Wells, England, March 11, 1897. He studied theology at Edinburgh University, but did not adopt the clerical profession. In 1877 he was appointed professor of natural science in the Free Church College, Glasgow. 'Natural Law in the Spiritual World' (1883), and its successor 'The Ascent of Man,' applications of modern scientific methods to the immaterial universe, have made his popular fame. He traveled in Central Africa (1883–84) studying its botany and geology, and later wrote the highly interesting and instructive volume on 'Tropical Africa' (1888). Other semi-religious writings of his are: 'Pax Vobiscum' (1890); 'The Greatest Thing in the World' (1890); 'The Programme of Christianity' (1892).

Drummond, William, of Hawthornden. A Scotch poet; born at Hawthornden near Edinburgh, Dec. 13, 1585; died Dec. 4, 1649. His principal works are: 'Tears on the Death of Mœliades' (1613), Mœliades being Prince Henry, son of James I.; 'Poems Amorous, Funerall, Divine, Pastorall, in Sonnets, Songs, Sextains, Madrigals' (1616); 'Forth Feasting' (1617); 'Flowers of Zion.' After a visit from Ben Jonson, Drummond printed notes of their conversations; a very interesting chapter in literary history.

Drushinin, Alexander Vassilyevitch (drö'-shē-nēn). A Russian critic and story-writer; born in St. Petersburg, Oct. 20, 1824; died there, Jan. 31, 1864. He is best known by his tales, especially that of 'Pauline Sachs' (1847); but his essays on literary topics, notably 'Johnson and Boswell,' and his translations from Shakespeare, are meritorious.

Dryden, John. An eminent English poet; born at Aldwinkle, Northamptonshire, Aug. 9, 1631; died in London, May 1, 1700. His first poems include 'Astræa Returned' (Astræa Redux) and the 'Year of Wonder' (Annus Mirabilis). The best of his plays are: 'The Conquest of Grenada' (1670); 'Marriage à la Mode'; 'Aurungzebe'; 'All for Love' (1677); 'The Spanish Friar' (1681); 'Don Sebastian' (1689). Much more worthy of his talents and his fame are 'Absalom and Achitophel' and 'The Hind and the Panther.' His Pindaric odes are not surpassed by the work of any English poet; and his 'Alexander's Feast' stands supreme in its kind. He made spirited translations of Virgil and Juvenal; and elaborated into 'Fables,' stories culled from foreign authors or earlier English.

Duboc, Charles Edouard. See Waldmüller.

Duboc, Julius (dü'bōk). A German essayist and critic; born in Hamburg, Oct. 10, 1829. In periodical literature his distinction was marked, and as a student of men and things he worked to good purpose in 'The Psychology of Love' and other books. Died at Dresden, June 13, 1903.

Du Boccage, Marie Anne Fiquet (dü-bōk-äzh'). A French poet (1710–1802); born (Le-page) at Rouen. She accompanied her husband in his European travels, and everywhere won great celebrity for wit and beauty: "A Venus for form, a Minerva for art." Her principal works are an imitation of 'Paradise Lost'; a paraphrase of Gessner's 'Death of Abel'; an original epic, 'The Columbiad'; a tragedy, 'The Amazons,' well received. Her 'Letters on England,' etc., give full report of the honors showered upon her.

Du Boisgobey. See Boisgobey.

Du Bois-Reymond, Emil (dü-bwä'rā-mōn'). An eminent German scientist; born in Berlin, Nov. 7, 1818; died there Dec. 26, 1896. His career was a series of services to chemical, electrical, and physiological science, well attested by his 'Extant Conclusions of the Ancients with Reference to Magnetism in Fishes' (1843); 'The Limits of Our Knowledge of Nature (6th ed. 1884); and 'Investigations into Animal Magnetism' (1848–84).

Dubos, Jean Baptiste (dü-bō'). A French critic and essayist; born in Beauvais, 1670; died in Paris, March 23, 1742. He elevated criticism to a place among the arts with his 'Critical Reflections on Poetry, Painting, and Music' (1719), and other works on æsthetic topics.

Du Camp, Maxime (dü-kon'). A French writer of history and travels; born at Paris, Feb. 8, 1822; died at Baden-Baden, Feb. 8, 1894. 'Egypt, Nubia, Palestine, and Syria' (1852) explains itself. He wrote the history of the Paris Commune: 'The Convulsions of Paris' (4 vols., 1878–79), and other historical sketches. His greatest work is 'Paris: Its Organs, its Functions, and its Life' (6 vols., 1869–75). He wrote some lyric poems: 'Modern Chants' (1855); 'Convictions' (1858); and several novels, among them: 'Memoirs of a Suicide' (1853); 'The Six Adventures' (1857); 'The Man with the Gold Bracelet' (1862).

Du Cange, Charles Dufresne, Sieur (dü-känzh'). A celebrated French scholar, lexicographer, and historian; born at Amiens, Dec. 18, 1610; died at Paris, Oct. 23, 1688. A jurisconsult, advocate of the Paris Parliament, he gave up the post to study. His 'Glossary of Middle and Low Latin' (3 vols., 1678; completed and extended to 6 vols. by the Benedictines of St. Maur, 1733–36; latest ed. by La Fayre, 10 vols., 1883-88) is still indispensable in reading mediæval books. He is author of a similar work on Greek: 'Glossary for the Authors of Middle and Low Greek' (2 vols., 1688). Besides these he wrote in French a 'History of the Empire of Constantinople under the Frank Emperors' (1657), and in Latin a 'Byzantine History.' Another important historical work written by him is 'Of the Princedoms Oversea,' first published (1869) under the title 'Families of Oversea.'

Ducange, Victor Henri Joseph Brahain. A French poet and story-teller (1783–1833); born at the Hague. His first stories, 'Agatha' and 'Valentine,' were received with great favor; but for his too realistic description in 'Valentine' of the excesses of the royalist bands, he was sent to jail for six months. Released, he was again imprisoned, ostensibly for vilifying the French Academy. Once more he offended with 'Thelene, or Love and War,' and had to take refuge in Belgium. Other novels are: 'The Confessor-Doctor'; 'The Artist and the Soldier'; etc. Of his numerous plays the best and most famed is 'Thirty Years, or the Life of a Gambler.' His novels are vividly dramatic and descriptive, but he loves the horrible too well.

Du Chaillu, Paul Belloni (dü-shī-yü'). A French-American explorer and writer; born in Paris, July 31, 1835. His travels in Africa, in which he discovered the gorilla and the Pigmies, are detailed charmingly in 'A Journey to Ashango Land' (1867), and 'My Apingi Kingdom' (1870). 'The Land of the Midnight Sun' (1881) deals with Norway. 'The Viking Age' (1887) is a more ambitious work, intended to re-create the old Norse civilization, and is full of interest and picturesque touches. He died at St. Petersburg, April 30, 1903.

"Duchess, The." See **Hungerford.**

Ducis, Jean François (dü-sē'). A French dramatist (1733–1816); born at Versailles. His adaptations of Shakespeare, all conformed to the classic traditions of the French stage, were very successful. His first original play, 'Abufar, or the Arab Family,' met with hearty approbation. A royalist, and secretary to the Count d'Artois, during the Revolution and Consulate he lived abroad; he returned when the Empire was set up, but declined Napoleon's offers of a place in public life.

Duclos, Charles Pinot (dü-klō'). A French historian (1704–72); born at Dinant. He made his literary début as a story-teller, in 'Confessions of Count . . .' (1742), which had great success. Turning to history, he published the 'History of Louis XI.' (4 vols., 1745). This was followed by his greatest work but one, 'Considerations on the Manners of the Present Age' (1749). His 'Secret Memoirs upon the Reign of Louis XIV., the Regency, and the Reign of Louis XV.' (2 vols., 1791) give him a place among the most celebrated memoirists.

Dudevant, Madame. See **Sand, George.**

Duff, Mountstuart Elphinstone Grant, Sir. An English barrister and statesman; born in 1829. Graduated from Oxford. He was a lawyer, and M. P. 1857–81; Under-Secretary of State for India, and later for the colonies, in Mr. Gladstone's cabinets. He was the successful governor of Madras, 1881–86. Of his notable works, the best known are: 'Studies in European Politics' (1866); 'A Political Survey' (1868); 'Elgin Speeches' (1871); 'Notes of an Indian Journey' (1876); 'Notes from a Diary' (1901).

Dufferin, Frederick Temple Hamilton Blackwood, Marquis of. A British statesman; born in Florence, Italy, June 21, 1826; died at Clandeboye, Ire., Feb. 12, 1902. He was governor-general of Canada (1872), viceroy of India, and ambassador at Paris. Harvard gave him the degree of LL. D. His works include: 'Letters from High Latitudes' (1860); 'Irish Emigration and the Tenure of Land in Ireland' (1867); 'Mr. Mill's Plan for the Pacification of Ireland Examined' (1868); 'The Honourable Impulsia Gushington'; 'Speeches and Addresses' (1882); 'Speeches delivered in India, 1884–88' (1880); etc. His wife (born Hamilton) has written 'Our Viceroyal Life in India' (1890) and 'My Canadian Journal' (1892).

Dufferin, Helena Selina (Sheridan), Lady. A British poet; born 1807; died 1867. She was granddaughter of Richard Brinsley Sheridan, and sister of the Hon. Mrs. Norton. Her songs and lyrics are collected into a volume bearing date 1895, her son being the editor.

Duffield, Samuel Willoughby. An American clergyman; born in Brooklyn, N. Y., in 1843; died in Bloomfield, N. J., May 12, 1887. Under the pen-name of «Anselmus» he contributed to the Evangelist. His publications, in part, are: 'The Heavenly Land,' from the 'De Contemptu Mundi' of Bernard de Morlaix (1868); 'Warp and Woof' (1870); 'English Hymns, their Authors and History' (1886); and 'Latin Hymn-Writers' (1887).

Dufresny, Charles de la Rivière (dü-frä-nē). A French poet (1654–1724); born at Paris. He was great-grandson of Henry IV.'s favorite, «la belle jardinière d'Anet,» and was given lucrative offices by Louis XIV. He was a reckless spendthrift, and often reduced to want. His comedies, though weak in construction and character-drawing, are very lively in dialogue, especially 'The Spirit of Contradiction'; 'The Double Widowhood'; 'The Village Flirt'; 'The Match Made and Unmade.' He wrote also a volume of 'Divers Poems'; one of 'Historical Tales'; and 'Serious and Comic Amusements of a Siamese,' which suggested Montesquieu's 'Persian Letters.'

Duganne, Augustine Joseph Hickey. An American poet and prose-writer; born in Boston, 1823; died in New York, Oct. 20, 1884. His poems were patriotic, political, and sentimental. His prose comprised philosophical, historical, and dramatic works. He published: 'Hand Poems' (1844); 'A Comprehensive Summary of General Philosophy' (1845); 'The Iron Harp' (1847); 'The Lydian Queen' (1848); 'MDCCCXLVIII' (1849); 'Parnassus in Pillory' (1851); 'A Class Book of Government and Civil Society' (1859); 'Fighting Quakers' (1866); and others.

Dugdale, William, Sir. A celebrated English antiquarian; born at Shustoke, Warwickshire, Sept. 12, 1605; died there, Feb. 10, 1686. In 1638 he was created pursuivant-at-arms extraordinary. A royalist in the civil war, he was knighted by Charles II. at the Restoration. His monumental work is the

'Monasticon Anglicanum' (1655), reissued with additions 1817-30 and 1846; a mine of information on the history and biography of English cathedrals, and English history in general. Among his other works are: 'The Antiquities of Warwickshire' (1656); 'Short View of the Late Troubles in England' (1681).

Duguay-Trouin, René (dü-gā'trö-an'). A French naval commander of the first distinction; born in St. Malo, June 10, 1673; died in Paris, Sept. 27, 1736. In his 'Memoirs,' published surreptitiously in 1730, but with authority ten years later, he relates, with becoming modesty, the series of events which gave him such heroic proportions as a conqueror on the sea.

Duhring, Julia. An American essayist; born in Philadelphia, Feb. 23, 1836. She has been an extensive traveler in the United States, Europe, Asia, and Africa; and published two volumes of critical essays on social life, the titles to which are: 'Philosophers and Fools' (1874); 'Gentlefolks and Others'; 'Amor in Society'; 'Mental Life and Culture.'

Dulaurens, Henri Joseph (dü-lōr-än'). A French satirical poet and novelist; born at Douai, in 1719; died at Marienbourg, Belgium, in 1797 (1787?). He wrote with his friend Groubenthal the 'Jesuitics' (1761: modeled on Demosthenes's 'Philippics') against the Jesuits; but executed a more enduring task in the 'Jesuit Priest (or Companion) Matthew' (Compère Mathieu: 1776), a novel of genuine literary merit, and of great vogue even within a recent time.

Dulk, Albert Friedrich Benno (dülk). A German dramatist and polemic prose-writer; born in Königsberg, June 17, 1819; died in Stuttgart, Oct. 30, 1884. His 'Arla' (1844); 'Jesus the Christ' (1865); 'Lea' (1874); and other dramas, are rich in subtleties and in powerful appeals to the loftier side of human nature, but lack poetic feeling. He advocates a new religious evolution, as against Christianity, in 'Beast or Man?' (1872); 'What Is to be Expected from the Christian Church?' (1877); and other like argumentative works.

Duller, Eduard (dül'ler). A German poet and historian (1809-53); born at Vienna. His drama 'Master Pilgram' was produced with success at 17, and followed by 'The Swan Song of Revenge,' a tragedy (1834). He was a passionate champion of free thought; this made Vienna under Metternich too warm for him, and he lived at Munich, Trier, and other places. The lyric poem 'Prince of Love' (1842), and the volume of 'Collected Poems' (1845), are his least polemic and literarily best works. His novels are pompous. He wrote a 'History of the German People' and a 'History of the Jesuits.'

Dulles, John Welch. An American clergyman and editor; born in Philadelphia, Nov. 4, 1823; died there, April 13, 1887. Princeton gave him the degree of D. D. in 1871. He was the author of 'Life in India' (1855);

'The Soldier's Friend' (1861); and 'The Ride through Palestine' (1881).

Dumanoir, Philippe (dü-män-wär'). A French playwright (1806-65); born at Pau. He wrote, alone or in collaboration, some 200 vaudevilles. Of his own solely, there may be cited: 'The Marquise de Prétintaille'; 'The Lambs' School'; 'Terrible Women'; 'The Childless House.' The famous actress Déjazet found many of her best rôles in his pieces.

Dumas, Alexandre, the Elder (dü-mä). A celebrated French romancist and dramatist; born at Villers Cotterets, Aisne, July 24, 1802; died near Dieppe, Dec. 5, 1870. He was grandson of a French marquis and a San Domingo negress. A few of the great multitude of his famous romances are: 'The Count of Monte Cristo' (1844); 'The Three Musketeers' (1844); 'Twenty Years After' (1845); 'The Knight of Maison-Rouge' (1846); 'Viscount de Bragelonne' (1847); 'Queen Margot' (1847). Many of his stories were of great length, six to twelve volumes. Besides pure fiction he wrote a number of historical romances, as 'Joan of Arc' (1842); 'Michelangelo and Raffaelle' (1846); 'Louis XIV. and his Age' (1847). His plays, which had extraordinary success, include: 'Henri III. and his Court' (1829); 'Antony' (1831); 'Charles VII. with his Grand Vassals' (1831); 'Napoleon Bonaparte' (1831); 'Mdlle. de Belle-Isle' (1839); 'Marriage under Louis XV.' (1841); 'The Misses St. Cyr' (1843). Nearly all his novels were put on the stage also. He wrote entertaining narratives of his travels in Switzerland, Italy, Germany, Spain, North Africa, Egypt, Syria, etc.

Dumas, Alexandre, the Younger. A great French dramatist and romancist, son of the preceding; born at Paris about 1824; died there Nov. 27, 1895. He published a small volume of poems, 'Sins of Youth,' at 17. Accompanying his father in travels through Spain and Northern Africa, on his return he published his first romance: 'Story of Four Women and a Parrot' (6 vols. 1847), which found little favor. Among his romances are: 'A Woman's Romance'; 'Cesarine'; 'Camille' (La Dame aux Camélias); all in 1848. His dramas include: 'Diana de Lys' (1853) and 'The Demi-Monde' (1855). He also wrote the romance 'The Clémenceau Case' (1864), dramatized under the same name; the pamphlets: 'Women Murderers and Women Voters' (1872); 'The Divorce Question' (1880); and the dramatic pieces: 'The Natural Son' (1858); 'The Friend of Women' (1864); 'Claude's Wife' (1873); 'The Danicheffs' (1876); 'Joseph Balsamo' (1878); 'Francillon' (1887); and others.

Du Maurier, George Louis Palmella Busson (dü-mō-ryā'). The famous delineator of English society in Punch, and in later years a novelist; born in Paris, March 6, 1834; died in London, Oct. 6, 1896. In his childhood his parents settled in London. He began in 1850 to study art in London, Paris, and Antwerp; returning to London he was employed on the illustrated periodicals, and from 1864 to his death was of the regular staff of Punch. He wrote and illustrated three stories : ‹ Peter Ibbetson › (1891) ; ‹ Trilby › (1894) ; ‹ The Martian › (1897).

Dumersan, Théophile Marion (dü-mär-säṅ'). A French playwright (1780-1849) ; born near Issoudun. He was employed in the Paris mint. He wrote many plays, all marked by keen observation and comic spirit. His ‹ Angel and Devil,› a five-act drama, had a « run » of over 100 presentations ; still more successful was his ‹ Mountebanks,› his masterpiece and a classic in its kind. Other very successful plays written by him are : ‹ The Wigmaker, or Heads à la Titus › ; ‹ Ridiculous Englishwomen.› Worthy of mention is his volume of ‹ National and Popular Songs of France.›

Dumont, Julia Louisa. An American prose and verse writer ; born in Waterford, O., October 1794 ; died at Vevay, Ind., Jan. 2, 1857. She has the distinction of being one of the earliest women of the West whose writings have been preserved. She contributed largely to periodicals both in prose and verse. A collection of her writings was published in a volume, ‹ Life Sketches from Common Paths › (1856).

Dunbar, Paul Laurence. American negro poet and novelist. Born, Dayton, O., June 27, 1872, died Feb. 9, 1906. ‹ Lyrics of Lowly Life› (1896); ‹ Folks from Dixie› (1898); ‹The Uncalled› (1898); ‹Poems of Cabin and Field› (1899); ‹The Strength of Gideon › (1900) ; etc. Died 1906.

Dunbar, William. A renowned Scottish poet ; born at Salton in Lothian, about 1465 (?); died about 1530 (?). He was a Franciscan friar, but was often employed by James IV. in affairs of State. Among his works is the panegyric poem ‹ The Thistle and the Rose,› written (1503) on the marriage of James with Margaret of England ; ‹ The Golden Targe › (1508), consisting of allegories in the fashion of the time and of Chaucer, among them a poem on ‹ The Dance of the Seven Deadly Sins through Hell.› He is at his best in burlesque poetry, as witness the autobiographical ‹ Visitation of St. Francis.› He is « as rich in fancy as Spenser ; as homely and shrewd as Chaucer in the ‹ Miller's Tale › ; as pious as Cowper in his hymns ; and as wittily grotesque as Burns in ‹ Death and Dr. Hornbook.› »

Duncker, Dora (dünk'er). A German story-writer and humorist ; born March 28, 1855. The conceits ‹ Incurable › (1893), ‹ The Sphinx,› and other tales and comedies, have succeeded ; while in ‹ Modern Masters › (1883) she has evolved excellent character studies.

Duncker, Max Wolfgang. A German historian ; born in Berlin, Oct. 15, 1811 ; died in Anspach, July 21, 1886. Politics interested him in early years, but his later energies were given to elaborate historical investigations, of which the best fruits are : ‹ The Crisis of the Reformation › (1845); ‹ Feudalism and Aristocracy › (1858) ; and the masterpiece ‹ Ancient History › (1852-57).

Dunlap, William. An American dramatist and painter ; born at Perth Amboy, N. J., Feb. 19, 1766 ; died at New York, Sept. 28, 1839. He painted George Washington's portrait, still authentically existent, and for five years (1784-89) worked under West in London. Returning, he wrote several successful plays, including : ‹ The Father › (1789), a comedy ; ‹ Leicester › (1794), a tragedy ; ‹ André › (1798), a tragedy. He also published : ‹ Life of George Frederick Cooke › (1813); ‹ Life of Charles Brockden Brown › (1815); ‹ History of the American Theatre › (1832) ; ‹ History of the Rise and Progress of the Art of Design in the United States › (1834) ; and similar works. He was one of the founders of the National Academy of Design.

Dunlop, John. A Scottish song-writer ; born in Carmyle, Lanarkshire (?), November 1755 ; died at Port Glasgow, Sept. 4, 1820. Convivial and prosperous, those qualities are reflected in his ‹ Oh Dinna Ask Me Gin I Lo'e Ye › and similar lines, all sung with enthusiasm by Scots.

Dunlop, John Colin. An important Scotch literary historian, son of John ; born near Glasgow, 1786 (?) ; died at Edinburgh in February 1842 (not 1834). His ‹ History of Fiction › (1814) broke much new ground, and remains authoritative despite manifold efforts to impeach it ; besides which his ‹ History of Roman Literature › (1823-28), and like studies, are characterized by discernment and scholarship.

Dunning, Annie (Ketchum). (« Nellie Graham.») An American story-writer ; born in New York, Nov. 2, 1831. Her first story, ‹ Clementina's Mirror,› appeared in 1857. She later wrote ‹ Contradictions › and ‹ Broken Pitchers.›

Dunraven, Wyndham Thomas Wyndham-Quin, Fourth Earl of. An Irish journalist, statesman, and author ; born at Adare Abbey, Ireland, Feb. 12, 1841. After graduating from Oxford he entered the army ; but left it in 1867 for journalism, being war correspondent for the Daily Telegraph in Abyssinia, and afterwards in the Franco-Prussian War. He was under-secretary for the colonies in Lord Salisbury's administrations. Of recent years he has been conspicuous as a yachtsman, having twice been challenger for the American Cup. Besides various magazine articles on hunting, he published : ‹ The Great Divide › ; ‹ Notes on Irish Architecture › ; ‹ The Soudan : Its History, Geography, and Characteristics › ; ‹ The Irish Question.›

Duns Scotus, Joannes (duns skō'tus). A Scotch metaphysician, head of the Schoolmen, called « the subtle doctor » ; born in Scotland (?), 1265 or 1274 ; died at Cologne (?), Nov. 8, 1308 (?). His opposition to the Thomists or adherents of Thomas Aquinas was spirited. He wrote an ‹ Exposition of ‹ Aristotelian Physics › ; ‹ Questions on Aristotle's Work on the Soul › ; and similar works. The word dunce, in its present application, probably comes from his name used ironically.

Dupanloup, Félix Antoine Philippe (dü-poṅ-lö'). An eminent French controversialist and prelate; born in St. Felix, Savoy, Jan. 3, 1802; died near Grenoble, Oct. 11, 1878. He became Bishop of Orleans; wrote on education and faith.— his 'Christian Marriage' (7th ed. 1885); 'History of our Savior Jesus Christ' (1869); 'Intellectual Higher Education' (1866), etc., attracting great attention. He headed the movement to canonize Joan of Arc.

Dupaty, Emmanuel (dü-pä-tē'). A French poet (1775-1851); born at Blanquefort. His light comedies and vaudevilles gave delight on every stage with their sparkle of wit and their lively dialogue. Of his many pieces, 'The Military Prison' is esteemed the best. 'Informers,' a satiric poem, and 'The Art of Poetry,' are works of great merit.

Duperron, Jacques Davy, Cardinal (dü-perrôn'). A French theologian, Pietist, and miscellaneous writer; born at St. Lô, Normandy, or at Bern, Switzerland, 1556; died in Paris, 1618. He was the son of a Protestant minister, but was converted to Catholicism in his youth and had a distinguished ecclesiastical career. 'A Treatise on the Sacrament of the Eucharist' is his most celebrated prose effort; as a poet he is remembered for the verses styled 'The Temple of Inconstancy.'

Dupont, Pierre (dü-pôn'). A French popular poet (1821-70); born at Lyons. He came to Paris in 1839, and wrote Legitimist odes which the newspapers published. His poem 'The Two Angels' won the Academy's prize in 1842, and he got employment on its 'Dictionary.' Then he won wide popularity with six songs for the people. He was above all things the poet of peasant life. After the February Revolution he was converted to socialism, and his 'Song of the Nations,' 'Song of the Workmen' (now known as the 'Workmen's Marseillaise'), etc., are socialist pamphlets in verse. His native city erected a statue to him.

Dupont de Nemours, Pierre Samuel (düpôn dè nā-mör'). A French economist; born in Paris, Dec. 14, 1739; died near Wilmington, Del., Aug. 6, 1817. He was a Physiocrat, or adherent of Quesnay's theory that all value is derived from land; and strove to propagate this system in 'Physiocratie' (1768). Later he became involved in the French Revolution, took refuge in the United States, and founded a great manufacturing house. His writings were neglected till Jevons, the Duke of Argyll, and later Henry George, revived the old Physiocratic idea.

Dupuy, Eliza Ann. An American storywriter; born in Petersburg, Va., about 1814; died in New Orleans, January 1881. 'The Conspirators,' her first novel, has Aaron Burr as the principal character. Most of her stories, about forty in number, were published in the New York Ledger.

Duran, Agustin (dö-rän'). A distinguished Spanish critic (1789-1862), who had a decisive influence on recent Spanish literature. His first work, anonymous, 'On the Decadence of the Spanish Theatre' (1828), led to the reform of the Spanish stage and its liberation from the French yoke. Of still greater service in arousing love for the native poesy was his 'Collection of Romanceros and Balladists' (5 vols., 1828-32). As a poet he won greatest distinction by his poem of chivalry 'The Three Citrons in the Garden of Love' (1856), written in 15th-century Castilian.

Durand, Alice. See **Gréville, Henry.**

Durandi, Jacopo (dü-ran'dē). An Italian dramatic poet and historian; born in Sant' Agata, Vercelli, July 25, 1737; died in Turin, Oct. 28, 1817. 'Armida' (1770) and 'Hannibal in Turin' (1771) are his best-known plays; his other gift displays itself in a 'History of the Ancient Peoples of Italy' (1769).

Durant, Gilles (dü-roñ'). A French poet; born in Clermont, 1554; died at Paris, 1615 (?). He tried his hand at every species of metrical composition,— odes, elegies, sonnets, and imitations of the Psalms; but his important work is contained in a 'Menippean Satire,' written to ridicule the League against Henry IV.,— the sub-title being 'Lamentation for a Leagued Ass, that Died in 1590, when the States Were in Session.'

Duranti, Durante, Count (dö-rän'tē). An Italian poet and orator (1718-80); born at Brescia. Among his poetical writings, all characterized by wit and refined taste, the best is the didactic poem 'Use,' in which he portrays his hero in the three periods of bachelor, husband, and widower. He wrote two tragedies, 'Virginia' (1764) and 'Attilius Regulus' (1771); and a volume, 'Rime,' containing miscellaneous verse.

Duras, Claire Lechat de Kersaint, Duchess of (dü-rä'). A French novelist; born in Brest, 1777; died in Paris, 1828. Well born, accomplished, and brilliantly married, she was seized with the sentimental sickness of the day, and wrote 'Ourika' (1823), the tale of a negress who fell in love with a white man; and 'Edward' (1825), a novel in which it was the gentleman's turn to throw his heart in an indiscreet direction,

Durbin, John Price. An American clergyman and miscellaneous writer; born in Bourbon County, Ky., in 1800; died in New York city, Oct. 17, 1876. He contributed extensively to current literature, and was the author of 'Observations in Europe, Principally in France and Great Britain' (2 vols., 1844); and 'Observations in Egypt, Palestine, Syria, and Asia Minor' (2 vols., 1845).

D'Urfey, Thomas, usually called Tom. An English dramatist and poet; born in Exeter, 1653; died in London (?), Feb. 26, 1723. He was a good-natured, simple-hearted, thoroughly vulgar and unliterary writer. His dramas, comedies, operas, tragedies, and songs, are exactly like what Sancho Panza would have written if he had taken to letters. Many, like 'The Siege of Memphis' (1676), an extravagant tragedy, and 'The Plotting Sisters' (1691), a comedy, are vestured in a regal pomp of verbiage; others, like the 'Songs Complete' (1699), are of virginal simplicity, but not of virginal modesty.

Düringsfeld, Ida von (dör'ings-feld). A German story-teller (1815-76); born at Militsch in Lower Silesia. Her 'Poems' (1835) and the cycle of stories 'The Star of Andalusia' (1838) were issued under the pseudonym "Thekla," and yearly volumes thereafter anonymously or pseudonymously; 'The Women of Byron' appeared in her own name in 1845, when she married Otto von Reinsberg. Extensive travels later bore fruit in numerous stories, collections of national songs, descriptions of national usages, etc.; all were highly prized, including in the latter line: 'Proverbs of German and Roumanian Speech' (2 vols., 1872-75); and 'The Wedding Book : Usages and Beliefs Regarding the Wedding among the Christian Nations of Europe' (1871).

Durivage, Francis Alexander. An American author, nephew of Edward Everett; born in Boston, Mass., 1814; died in 1881. He contributed light literature in prose and verse to magazines; wrote novelettes; and jointly with W. S. Chase translated Lamartine's 'History of the Revolution of 1848.' He was also author of several plays, and of 'Life Scenes from the World around Us' (1853); 'Cyclopædia of History'; and 'The Fatal Casket.'

Duruy, Georges (dü-rüë'). A French writer on history; born in 1853, at Paris, where he became professor of French literature in the Polytechnic School in 1891. He wrote some novels that became popular favorites, as 'The Lifeguard'; 'A Soul's Victory'; 'Dream-End.' His principal historical works are: 'History of Turenne'; 'Short Popular History of France.' His 'Cardinal Carlo Carafa : a Study on the Pontificate of Paul IV.' (1883) was crowned by the Academy.

Duruy, Victor. A distinguished French historian; born at Paris, Sept. 11, 1811; died there Nov 25, 1894. He assisted Napoleon III. in compiling 'The Life of Julius Cæsar'; was made minister of public instruction in 1863. Among his works are: 'History of the Romans' (2 vols., 1843); 'State of the Roman World toward the Time of the Founding of the Empire' (1853); 'General Introduction to the History of France' (1865); 'History of the Greeks' (3 vols., 1886). He also wrote the greater part of a 'Universal History.' His works have been translated in part under Professor Mahaffy's editorship.

Dutra É Mello, Antonio Francisco (dö'trä ä mel'ö). A Brazilian poet; born in Rio Janeiro, Aug. 8, 1823; died Feb. 22, 1843. His verses are considered among the best of South American poetry. Among his choicest works are: 'A'noite Inspiracão Poetica'; 'A'noite de S. Toão'; and 'Historia Critica da Lingua Latina.'

Dutt, Toru (döt). A Hindoo poet (1856-77). She received a good European education, and had the advantage of four years' travel in the West. She translated into English many French poems,—from Béranger, Gautier, Coppée, etc., —and a collection of these was published as 'A Sheaf Gleaned in French Fields' (1876). She also rendered into English some of the 'Ancient Ballads of Hindustan.' She wrote in French a story : 'Miss d'Arvers's Diary.'

Duval, Alexandre (dü-väl'). A French dramatist (1767-1842); born at Rennes. He served in the French fleet during the American Revolutionary War, and on his return to France was an engineer and architect; but finally devoted himself to writing plays which won great favor from their skillful construction, interesting situations, and fine dialogue. The best are: 'Edward in Scotland'; 'The Domestic Tyrant'; 'The Chevalier of Industry.' He wrote the text of the very successful opera 'Joseph in Egypt.'

Duvar, John Hunter. See **Hunter-Duvar.**

Duvergier d'Hauranne, Prosper (dü-verzh-yä' dō-rän'). A French political writer; born in Rouen, Aug. 3, 1798; died in Paris, May 19 or 22, 1881. Prominent in politics, his writings reflect his opinions; particularly his 'Principles of Representative Government' (1838) and 'History of Parliamentary Government in France' (1857-73).

Duveyrier, Charles (dü-vā-ryä'). A French dramatist (1803-66); born at Paris. He was a disciple of Saint-Simon, and passed a year in jail for a newspaper article on 'Woman's Place' under the Saint-Simonian system. From unsuccessful he grew to be a successful playwright, especially in collaboration. Of the 300 or more pieces which bear his name, there may be mentioned: 'Frontin the Husband-Bachelor'; 'Valerie,' in which Mdlle. Mars made a brilliant success; 'The Cat Metamorphosed into a Woman'; 'Figaro's Daughter'; 'The Burgomaster of Saardam.'

Dux, Adolf (döx). A Hungaro-German poet (1822-81); born at Poszony (Presburg). He made admirable versions of Hungarian poems and novels into German, including those of Katona, Arany, Jókai, Gyulai, and Eötvös. He was the first to translate Petöfi's Select Poems. His own works comprise novels and studies in literary history.

Duyckinck, Evert Augustus. An American author; born in New York city, Nov. 23, 1816; died there, Aug. 13, 1878. Graduating from Columbia College, he studied law, was admitted to the bar in 1837, and went to Europe for a year, after which he devoted himself to literature, in which he was fertile and successful. In 1847 he edited the Literary World. In 1854, with his brother George, he prepared the 'Cyclopædia of American Literature' (2 vols., 1855; enlarged eds. 1865 and 1875). He was a voluminous and successful writer, and added much to the literature of his times. His last work was the preparation, with William Cullen Bryant, of an edition of Shakespeare.

Duyckinck, George Long. An American prose-writer; born in New York, Oct. 17, 1823; died there, March 30, 1863. He graduated at the University of New York in 1843, and was admitted to the bar, but did not practice. With his brother Evert he edited the Literary World and prepared the 'Cyclopædia of American Literature'; he also wrote several biographies.

Duyse, Prudens van (doi'ze). A Flemish poet (1804–59); born at Dendermonde. He was a very prolific author, and wrote poems of every kind,—epic, lyric, dramatic. They are all mediocre, but served to reawaken a love of the Flemish tongue. He wrote many valuable works on Flemish history.

Dwight, John Sullivan. An American musical critic; born at Boston, May 13, 1813; died Sept. 5, 1893. After two years in the Unitarian ministry, he became one of the founders of Brook Farm, and was editor of its organ the Harbinger. In 1852 he established Dwight's Journal of Music, in which appeared most of his scholarly musical criticisms. His best-known poem is 'God Save the State.'

Dwight, Theodore. An American journalist, brother of Timothy; born Dec. 15, 1764; died June 12, 1846. He was a well-known Federalist, a Member of Congress, and wrote 'History of the Hartford Convention' (of 1814) and 'Character of Thomas Jefferson.'

Dwight, Theodore. An American miscellaneous prose-writer, son of Theodore; born March 3, 1796; died Oct. 16, 1866. He wrote 'Tour in Italy'; 'Summer Tour in New England'; 'The Northern Traveler'; 'The Kansas War'; Life of Garibaldi'; besides gazetteers, histories, and school-books.

Dwight, Timothy. An American Congregational clergyman of great distinction; born in Northampton, Mass., May 14, 1752; died in New Haven, Conn., Jan. 11, 1817. He was president of Yale College from 1795 to 1817, and was a very conspicuous figure in theology and education. His 'Theology Explained and Defended' consists of a course of 173 sermons which has passed through as many as a hundred editions. In addition to theological works he wrote 'Essay on Light'; 'Observations on Language'; 'Travels in New England and New York,' which is still widely quoted. He also wrote verse: an epic called 'The Conquest of Canaan'; 'Greenfield Hill,' a pastoral; 'The Triumph of Infidelity,' a satire.

Dwight, Timothy. An American Congregational clergyman; born in Norwich, Conn., Nov. 16, 1828; grandson of Timothy Dwight. He has been president of Yale University, to which post he was elected in 1886. He was one of the members of the New Testament Revision Committee. He has published 'The True Ideal of an American University.'

Dyce, Alexander. An English literary critic and historian; born in Edinburgh, June 30, 1798; died in London, May 15, 1869. As editor of definitive editions of the British poets, he has rendered lasting service to the native Parnassus; his capital achievements, 'Works of Shakespeare' (1853–58) and 'A Few Notes on Shakespeare' (1853), leaving little room for improvement, although subsequent discoveries may supplement them.

Dyer, Sir Edward. An English elegiac poet; born at Sharpham Park, Somersetshire; died in London(?), May(?) 1607. An elegant courtier, he advanced himself in royal favor by court verse. 'My Mind to Me a Kingdom Is' is the best of his effusions. His works, 'The Shepherd's Conceit of Prometheus' and other poems, were not collected until 1872.

Dyer, John. An English didactic and descriptive poet; born in Aberglasney, Wales, in 1700 or 1699; died in Lincolnshire (?), July 24, 1758. He presented himself before the Muses with 'Grongar Hill' (1726), an engaging but excessively correct piece of poetry; nor did he unbend until 'The Ruins of Rome' (1740) inspired him. His final effort, 'The Fleece' (1757), was suffused with tender romanticism.

Dyer, Sidney. An American poet and prose writer; born in Cambridge, N. Y., Feb. 11, 1814; died ——, 1898. He published poems entitled 'Voices of Nature' (1850); 'Songs and Ballads' (1857); 'Great Wonders in Little Things' (1871); 'Ocean Gardens and Palaces' (1877); 'Elmdale Lyceum' (1879); etc.; also 'Psalmist for the Use of Baptist Churches.'

Dyer, Thomas Henry. An English historian; born in London, May 4, 1804; died at Bath, Jan. 30, 1888. He traveled and studied for years to prepare a 'History of Modern Europe' (1861); 'History of the City of Rome' (1865); and 'Ancient Athens' (1873); all monuments of learning and critical insight.

Dygasinski, Adolf (dï-gäs-in'skē). A Polish story-writer; born in the Russo-Polish government of Kjebzy in 1839. His stories are remarkable for charming descriptions of scenery; among them: 'On the Manor'; 'From Village, Field, and Forest' (1887); 'From City and Country' (1889). He has translated works by Max Müller, Tyndall, Mill, and others. D. 1902.

Dyherrn, Baron George von (dē'härn). A German poet and novelist; born in Glogau, Jan. 1, 1848; died in Rothenburg, Silesia, Dec. 27, 1878. He wrote many poems and tales of great merit; 'In the Still Hour' (1870) being a collection of his best verse, and 'From Society' (1880) and 'Heights and Depths' (1881), his ablest fictions.

Dzierzkovski, Joseph (tsērts'kōf-skē). A Polish novelist (1807–65); born at Xaverov, Galicia, in 1807; died in Lemberg, Jan. 13, 1865. He loves to contrast the selfish dissipation of the upper classes with the humble virtues of the lowly. 'Salon and Street' (1847); 'The Twins' (1854); 'The Jugglers' (1855); 'The Crown of Thorns' (1856), are noteworthy; 'Polish Chivalry' (1858), a historical novel, is one of his best. He also wrote a drama, 'The Spark of Poesy' (1860).

E

Eadie, John. A Scotch religious writer; born at Alva, Stirlingshire, May 9, 1810; died in Glasgow, June 3, 1876 (not 1870). He wrote on theology with great vogue among the unlearned; his books including 'The Divine Love' (1855), 'Paul the Preacher' (1859), etc., in addition to scholarly treatises and commentaries.

Eadmer or **Edmer.** A British historian and biographer, who lived, a monk, at Canterbury, between 1090 and 1115, and died about 1124. An enduring fame has been the outcome of his 'History of Recent Events' (Historia Novorum); 'Life of St. Anselm'; and other works.

Eagles, John. An English artist, art critic, and poet; born in Bristol, 1783; died at Clifton, Nov. 8, 1855. He contributed essays on art to periodicals, and brought out 'The Sketcher,' a collection of miscellaneous prose and verse. A book of 'Sonnets' appeared posthumously.

Earle, Mrs. Alice Morse. An American writer; born in Massachusetts in 1851. She has written extensively upon the manners and customs of the colonial period in New England and New York. Among her numerous works are: 'Curious Punishments of Bygone Days'; 'Customs and Fashions in Old New England'; 'Colonial Dames and Goodwives'; 'Colonial Days in Old New York'; 'Two Centuries of Costume in America.'

Earle, John. An English clergyman and author; born in York, England, in 1601; died at Oxford, Nov. 17, 1665. He was chaplain and tutor to Charles II., and his companion in exile; later Bishop of Worcester. His literary fame is due to the famous 'Microcosmographie, or a Peece of the World discovered in Essayes and Characters' (1628), a series of sketches full of wit and humor, which throw much light on the social condition of the time.

Early, Jubal Anderson. An American general and lawyer; born in Franklin County, Va., Nov. 3, 1816; died March 2, 1894. He graduated from West Point in 1837; served in the Seminole War (1837-38); resigned in 1838 to study law; and was prominent in the Mexican War (1847-48). He became a Confederate major-general in the Civil War; took part at Bull Run and Gettysburg, and in 1864 invaded Maryland, but was checked by Sheridan. After the war he practiced law at Richmond and Lynchburg, Va., and New Orleans, La. His works include: 'A Memoir of the Last Year of the War for Independence in the Confederate States' (1867); 'Campaigns of General Lee' (1872).

Eastcott, Richard. An English writer on music; born at Exeter, about 1740; died at Livery Dale (?), Devonshire, 1828. A volume of 'Sketches of the Origin, Progress, and Effects of Music, with an Account of the Ancient Bards and Minstrels' (1793), met with very general approval.

Eastlake, Sir Charles Lock. An English artist, and critic and historian of art; born in Plymouth, Nov. 17, 1793; died in Pisa, Italy, Dec. 14, 1865. His paintings were noteworthy; and in such books as 'Materials for a History of Oil Painting' (1847-69) and 'History of the Gothic Revival' (1871), he manifests taste and discrimination.

Eastman, Charles Gamage. An American poet; born in Fryeburg, Me., June 1, 1816; died in Burlington, Vt., 1861. He published (1848) a volume of 'Poems' descriptive of rural life in New England, and marked by a high degree of metrical finish. He edited the Vermont Patriot at Montpelier from 1846 until his death, and was a contributor of poetry to magazines.

Eastman, Julia Arabella. An American story-writer; born in Fulton, N. Y., July 17, 1837. Included in her juvenile story-books are: 'Short Comings and Long Goings' (1869); 'Beulah Romney' (1871); and 'Young Rick' (1875). She also contributed sketches and poems to magazines.

Eastman, Mary (Henderson). An American prose-writer; born in Warrenton, Va., in 1818. She has published: 'Dacotah, or Life and Legends of the Sioux' (1849); 'Romance of Indian Life' (1852); 'Tales of Fashionable Life' (1856); and many stories and sketches.

Eastwick, Edward Backhouse. An English Orientalist and diplomatist; born in Berkshire in 1814; died at Ventnor, Isle of Wight, July 16, 1883. He was a voluminous writer on Oriental (especially East-Indian) subjects, and has rendered very important service to English literature by many translations from Persian and Hindu: e. g., Sadi's 'Gulistan' or 'The Rose Garden' in 1852, and the version of Pilpay's fables called 'Anvār-i-Suhailī' in 1854. He also wrote a 'Journal of a Diplomat's Three-Years' Residence in Persia' (2 vols., 1864), and 'Venezuela,' or 'Sketches of Life in a South-American Republic' (1868). Between 1878 and 1882 he brought out a sumptuous 2-vol. edition of the 'Kaisar-nama-i-hind,' or 'Lay of the Empress.' He was a frequent contributor to literary journals.

Eaton, Arthur Wentworth Hamilton. An American clergyman and author; born at Kentville, N. Y., in 1849. He is a minister of the Episcopal Church in New York city. Among his works are: 'The Heart of the Creeds' (1888);

'Acadian Legends and Lyrics' (1889); 'Tales of a Garrison Town'; 'The Lotus of the Nile.'

Ebeling, Adolf (ā'bel-ing). A German descriptive and historical writer; born in Hamburg, Oct. 10, 1823; died at Cologne, July 23, 1896. 'Living Pictures from Modern Paris' (1863-67); 'Rainbows in the East' (1868), a series of Oriental epics, legends, or ghazels; 'Napoleon III. and his Court' (1891-93); are the fruit of large travel and study. He has written also many biographical studies and travel sketches.

Ebeling, Christoph Daniel. A German scholar and historian; born in Hildesheim, about 1741; died in Hamburg, June 30, 1817. He was for many years professor of history and Greek at Hamburg. His chief work is a 'Geography and History of North America' (5 vols., 1793-99), for which he received a vote of thanks from Congress.

Eborhard, Christian August Gottlob (ā'berhärd). A German poet and descriptive writer; born in Belzig, Jan. 12, 1769; died in Dresden, May 13, 1845. His verse is a reminiscence of the 18th-century style and of the school of Gleim, the idyl 'Little Hans and the Cookie' (1822) and 'Various Poems' (1833) eminently so. His best prose is in 'Italy as It Impressed Me' (1839).

Eberhard, Johann August. A German philosophical writer; born in Halberstadt, Aug. 31, 1739; died in Halle (?), Jan. 6, 1809. He first attracted attention with a 'New Apology [or plea] of Socrates' (1772), an attack upon the narrow theology of the day, to which succeeded 'Universal History of Philosophy' (1788); 'Handbook to Æsthetic' (1803-5); and other works from a Wolfian standpoint, in harmony with Leibnitz and opposition to Kant.

Ebers, Georg Moritz (ā'bers). A German Egyptologist and novelist; born in Berlin, March 1, 1837; died at Munich, Aug. 7, 1898. His historical romances comprise: 'An Egyptian Princess' (1864); 'Uarda' (1877); 'Homo Sum' (1878); 'The Sisters' (1879); 'The Emperor' (1880); 'Serapis' (1885); 'The Bride of the Nile' (1886); 'Joshua' (1889); 'Per Aspera' (1892); 'Cleopatra' (1894); and 'Elifên,' in verse (1888). The first two have been translated into many languages. Between times he has written several other historical novels; including 'The Burgomaster's Wife' (1881), of the Spanish domination in the Low Countries. His contributions to Egyptology are almost numerous. Died Aug. 8, 1898.

Ebert, Johann Arnold (ā'bert). A German translator and poet; born in Hamburg, Feb. 8, 1723; died in Brunswick, March 19, 1795. His friend Klopstock addressed a pleasing ode to him. He is better known through his translations of Young's 'Night Thoughts' and other poems than by his own work, which appears in 'Epistles and Miscellaneous Verse' (1789).

Ebert, Karl Egon. An Austrian poet and dramatist (1801-82); born at Prague. He began with dramas of Bohemian history, many of which were staged but only one printed, 'Wratislav and Jutta' (1835). As a lyric poet and balladist he was more successful; his 'Poems' (1824) contain fine lyrics, and 'Schwerting the Saxon Duke' is still high in popular favor. His longer poems—'Vlasta, a National Hero-Poem of Bohemia,' and 'The Monastery,' are fluent in style, pure and elegant in language. 'A Monument to Karl Egon, Prince of Fürstenberg' consists of a garland of sonnets; 'Devout Meditations of a Man of the World' is a didactic poem.

Ebner-Eschenbach, Baroness Marie von (ab'ner esh'en-bäch). An eminent Austrian novelist and poet; born (Countess Dubsky) at Castle Zdislavic, Moravia, Sept. 13, 1830. Beginning in 1860 as a playwright, 'Mary Stuart in Scotland' (1860) and the tragedy 'Marie Roland,' with the one-act dramas 'Doctor Ritter,' 'Violets,' and 'The Disconsolate One,' were but moderately successful. Turning to fiction, 'The Princess of Banalia' (1872), a satiric tale, made little impression; but 'Two Countesses' (1885), a story of Austrian high society, met with striking favor, and its successors place her among the great writers. They include: 'Tales of Village and Castle'; 'The Child of the Parish'; 'The Rival.' She has epic power, keen psychological insight, and quick sensibility; and is unsurpassed in grace of form and precision of style.

Ebrard, Johannes Heinrich August (ā'brärd). A German Protestant theological writer, dramatist, and literary critic; born in Erlangen, Jan. 18, 1818; died there, July 23, 1888. He led a general reform movement in theology, producing: 'Philosophical Criticism of Evangelical History' (1842); 'The Dogma of the Last Supper and its History' (1845-46); 'Practical Theology' (1856); etc.; while under the pseudonym of "Gottfried Flammberg" he wrote 'Duplessis-Mornay' (1859), and other dramas, and 'A Life in Song' (2d ed. 1872), a collection of verse. His other pseudonym, "Christian Deutsch," has served in connection with 'Stephen Klinger' (1872), a play, and studies of the Ossian creations.

Ebsworth, Joseph. An English dramatist and musician; born in London, Oct. 10, 1788; died in Edinburgh, June 22, 1868. He wrote, adapted, or translated many successful plays; among them 'The Rival Valets' (1825), a comedy drama, and 'The Crusaders' (1850-51), a drama. He was an adapter rather than a creator. His songs, learning, and versatility made him a distinguished figure in Edinburgh circles. He wrote also in collaboration with his wife, Mary Emma (Fairbrother).

Eça de Queiroz, José Maria (ā'sä dē kā-rōz). A Portuguese novelist; born at Póvoa do Varzim, Nov. 25, 1845. At first a journalist, he traveled and was in the consular service in many parts of the world. He introduced the naturalistic school into Portugal. His powers of observation and description are great, and in his novels—'The Crime of Father Amaro'

(1874, rewritten in 1880); 'The First Monk of St. Basil' (1877); 'A Relic' (1886)—he portrays in master strokes the failings of Portuguese society. His strange, half realistic, half fanciful story, 'The Relic,' weaves into a narrative of Oriental travel a dramatic representation of the Passion of Christ in the form of a dream. In collaboration with Ramalho-Ortagão he wrote the spirited tale of adventure, 'The Mystery of Cintra Street.' Died 1900.

Echard or **Eachard, Laurence.** An English historian; born at Barsham, Suffolk, 1670 (?); died at Lincoln, Aug. 16, 1730. A clergyman and a scholar, his 'History of England from the First Entrance of Julius Cæsar and the Romans to the End of the Reign of James the First' (1707) contains a wealth of information, including the particulars of Cromwell's interview with the Devil on the morning of the battle of Worcester. Other historical and scholarly works increased his reputation.

Echegaray, José (ā-chā-gär-ā'). A notable Spanish dramatist; born in Madrid, 1832. He is author of several treatises on mechanics and civil engineering, and was for a time minister of commerce and of public instruction. Since 1874, when the production of 'The Avenger's Wife' opened a new and brilliant life for the Spanish stage, he has given himself wholly to the drama; producing in a few years thirty plays rich in imagination, dramatic force, and lyric talent, though with the true Spaniard's love of the horrible. Of his greatest pieces may be named: 'The Great Galeotto'; 'Madman or Saint'; 'Conflict between Two Duties'; 'A Merry Life and a Sad Death'; 'Mariana.'

Echeverria, Estéban (ā-chā-vā-rē'ä). A notable Argentine poet; born in Buenos Ayres, 1809; died in Montevideo, 1851. He published a book of 'Rhymes' at 19; passed some time in France, became a devotee of Byron and Lamartine, and on his return published another volume whose exuberance explains its failure. But later volumes of short poems— 'Counsels'; 'The Female Captives'; 'Guitar' —prove him a genuine poet.

Eckardt, Ludwig (eck'ärt). An Austrian literary historian, essayist, and dramatist; born in Vienna, May 16, 1827; died at Tetchen, Bohemia, Feb. 1, 1871. His career was one of vicissitudes owing to his political opinions, but he wrote: 'Josephine,' a drama; 'Lectures on Goethe's Torquato Tasso' (1852); 'Dramatic Studies' (1853); and other critical and biographical studies, attaining distinction as a scholar.

Eckermann, Johann Peter (ek'er-män). A German poet (1792–1854); born at Winsen in Hanover. He has permanent place in literature through his deeply affectionate record of 'Conversations with Goethe in the Last Years of his Life' (2 vols., 1823–32); it has been translated into nearly all the languages of Europe, even Turkish. He edited the 40-vol. edition of Goethe's works (1839–40).

Eckstein, Ernst (ek'stin). A German humorist, poet, and novelist; born at Giessen, Feb. 6, 1845; died in Dresden, Nov. 18, 1900. From the university he went to Paris, and there completed his comic epos 'Check to the Queen' (1870), and wrote 'Paris Silhouettes' (1873), the grotesque night-piece 'The Varzin Ghosts' and the 'Mute of Seville.' Later he visited different places, and wrote the stories 'Margherita'; 'At the Tomb of Cestius'; 'The Mosque at Cordova.' He was editor of a literary and critical journal, Hall of Poets, and of a humorous weekly, The Wag, at Leipsic for some years, and in 1885 settled in Dresden. He was a very prolific and inventive writer, a master of technique. Besides many brilliant humorous sketches, he wrote many stories of ancient classic life, as 'The Claudii'; 'Aphrodite, a Story of Ancient Hellas'; 'Decius the Fluteplayer: a Merry Story of a Musician in Ancient Rome.'

Écrevisse, Peter (ā-krā-vēs'). A Flemish novelist (1804–1879); born at Obbicht in Limburg. In 1860 he withdrew from a promising political career and devoted himself to literature. He is noted for his power of description and his simple earnest style. Of his numerous historical novels must be mentioned: 'The Destruction of Maestricht'; 'The De Witt Brothers.' He is author also of some novels of society: 'The Cancer of Cities'; 'The Stepson'; 'The Servingman of Kempen.'

Eddy, Daniel Clark. An American clergyman and writer; born in Salem, Mass., in 1823; died in Martha's Vineyard, Mass., July 26, 1896. Among his numerous works are: 'Burman Apostle' (1850); 'Percy Family' (1852); 'The Young Woman's Friend' (1855); 'The Angel's Whispers'; 'Waiting at the Cross'; 'Europa, or Scenes in the Old World'; and 'The Young Man's Friend.'

Eden, Emily. An English novelist and descriptive writer; born in Westminster, March 3, 1797; died at Richmond, Surrey, Aug. 5, 1869. Her 'Semi-Detached House' (1859) and 'Semi-Attached Couple' (1860) possess realistic charm; while 'Portraits of the People and Princes of India' (1844), and other impressions of travel, do equal honor to her descriptive excellence.

Eden, Sir Frederick Morton. An English writer on sociology and economics; born in Kent(?), 1766; died in London, Nov. 14, 1809. His painstaking study of 'The State of the Poor' (1797) is a sociological classic.

Edersheim, Alfred (ā'der-shīm). A Jewish-Christian Biblical writer; born at Vienna, 1825; died at Mentone, France, March 16, 1889. From the universities of Vienna and Berlin he passed to that of Edinburgh, where he studied theology and became a minister of the Scotch Free Church. He wrote a 'Bible History' (7 vols.); 'Sketches of Jewish Social Life in the Days of Christ'; 'History of the Jewish Nation after the Destruction of Jerusalem by Titus'; 'Life and Times of Jesus the Messiah.'

Edgar, John George. An English biographer and historian; born in 1834; died in 1864. In business at Liverpool, he left it for literature: edited Every Boy's Magazine, contributed to the London press, and wrote biographies and histories, mainly for the young; among them: 'The Boyhood of Great Men' (1853); 'Footprints of Famous Men' (1853); 'Crusades and Crusaders' (1859); 'Sea Kings and Naval Heroes' (1860); 'Cavaliers and Roundheads' (1861).

Edgcumbe, Richard. An English poetaster and wit; born in Lancaster (?), 1716; died in Cornwall, May 10, 1761. He was a gay spirit, and enriched the literature of conviviality with 'The Fable of the Ass, Nightingale, and Kid'; 'Ode to Health'; and other poems which were deemed witty in their day.

Edgeworth, Maria. A distinguished English novelist; born in Black Bourton, Oxfordshire (not in Berkshire), Jan. 1, 1767; died in Edgeworthstown, Ireland, May 1849. She did her first literary work in conjunction with her father, upon whose Irish estate she acquired that knowledge of genial prodigality and hospitable beggary to which many of her tales owe their humor. Her principal works are: 'Castle Rackrent' (1800); 'Early Lessons' (1801); 'Belinda' (1801); 'Moral Tales' (1801); 'The Modern Griselda' (1804); 'Leonora' (1806); 'Tales of Fashionable Life' (1809–12); 'Patronage' (1814); 'Ormond' (1817); and 'Helen' (1834).

Edgren, Anne Charlotte Leffler- (ed'gren). A Swedish novelist, eminent in the realistic school; born at Stockholm, Oct. 16, 1849; died at Naples, Oct. 24, 1892. A volume of short tales, 'By Chance,' and the dramas, 'The Actress,' 'The Curate,' etc., were a great success anonymously; and she then put her own name to three successive volumes of short stories called 'From Life,' followed by 'A Summer Story,' 'Woman and Erotism,' and many others. 'Ideal Women,' 'The Struggle for Happiness,' and 'A Rescuing Angel' (the most successful of her plays) are most notable among her later dramas.

Edgren, August Hjalmar. A Swedish author; born in Wermland, Sweden, October 1840. He came to the United States in 1860, and joined the 99th New York Regiment as 2d lieutenant January 1862; August 1863 entered the engineer corps. He was connected with Yale University from 1874 to 1880, and professor of modern languages and Sanskrit in Nebraska University from 1880 to 1884. His numerous publications include a Swedish work on the 'Literature of America' (1878); 'Swedish Literature in America' (1883); and 'American Antiquities' (1885); besides many valuable papers for students, pertaining to Sanskrit, Romance, and Germanic philology.

Edler, Karl Erdmann (ād'ler). An Austrian novelist; born at Podêbrad in Bohemia, May 8, 1844. His stories have nearly all a historical background, truthfully portrayed. Among them may be named: 'Wilfried, a Story of the Middle Age' (1874); 'Gabor, a Picture of the Steppe' (1874); 'The Last Jew' (1885); 'Baldine' (1881); 'A Bell-Ringer's Journey'; 'Notre Dame des Flots' (Our Lady of the Billows). The last three were translated into English by Lord Lytton.

Edmonstone, Sir Archibald. An English descriptive writer, dramatist, poet, and Pietist; born in London, March 12, 1795; died there, March 13, 1871. He was an extensive traveler, and wrote 'A Journey to Two of the Oases of Upper Egypt' (1822); in addition to which 'Leonora' (1832), a tragedy, 'The Progress of Religion' (1842), a poem, and 'The Christian Gentleman's Daily Walk' (1840), evince fair talent.

Edward VI. King of England; born at Hampton Court, Oct. 12, 1537; died at Greenwich, July 6, 1553. His 'Journal,' a chronicle of his every-day experiences from the time of his accession until the year preceding his death, and various essays and declamations in French, Greek, and Latin, give a favorable impression of his literary capacity.

Edwards, Amelia Blandford. An English Egyptologist and writer of novels; born in London, 1831; died in Weston-super-Mare, Somersetshire, April 15, 1892. Her novels include: 'My Brother's Wife' (1855); 'Hand and Glove' (1859); and 'In the Days of her Youth' (1873). Later, she achieved great celebrity through her writings and lectures on the antiquities of Egypt; her best-known works in this field are 'A Thousand Miles up the Nile' (1877), and 'Pharaohs, Fellahs, and Explorers' (1891).

Edwards, Edward. An English librarian and writer on library lore; born in London (?), 1812; died at Niton, Isle of Wight, Feb. 10, 1886. In the 'Memoirs of Libraries' (1859), 'Lives of the Founders of the British Museum' (1870), and 'Sir Walter Raleigh' (1885), the latter an experiment in biography, his mastery of his subjects is authoritative.

Edwards, George. An English or Scotch writer on sociology and social reform; born in 1752; died in London, Feb. 17, 1823. Possessed of the conviction that he held the precious secret of the relief of man's estate, he wrote some fifty books to disseminate the information, among which is one with the long title: 'The Practical System of Human Economy, or the New Era at Length Fully Ascertained, Whereby We are Able in One Immediate Simple Undertaking to Remove the Distress, Burdens, and Grievances of the Times, and to Bring All our Interests, Public, Private, and Commercial, to their Intended Perfection' (1816).

Edwards, George Wharton. An American artist and author; born in Connecticut in 1859. He is a resident of Plainfield, N. J. Most of his stories have appeared in the Century Magazine. His works include: 'P'tit Matinic', and Other Monotones'; 'Thumb-Nail Sketches'; 'Break o' Day, and Other Stories.'

Edwards, Harry Stillwell. An American journalist and author; born in Macon, Ga., April 23, 1855. He graduated from the law department of Mercer University, and practiced law, but in 1871 entered journalism in his native city. He is well known as a writer of dialect stories. Among his works are: 'Two Runaways, and Other Stories' (1889); 'Sons and Fathers'; 'The Marbeau Cousins.'

Edwards, Henry Sutherland. An English descriptive writer, essayist, biographer, and novelist; born in London, 1828. He traveled and studied in Russia, Turkey, and Central Europe, acting as newspaper correspondent. He produced 'The Polish Captivity' (1863); 'Life of Rossini' (1869); 'The Germans in France' (1874); 'The Slavonian Provinces of Turkey' (1876); 'The Prima Donna: her History and Surroundings from the 17th to the 19th Century' (1888); 'Dutiful Daughters' (1890); 'The Russians at Home and Abroad' (1890); 'The Romanoffs'; 'Old and New Paris' (1893-94.)

Edwards, John. An American poet; born on the banks of the river Twrch in Wales (whence known as Eos-Glan-Twrch or "the nightingale of the Twrch"), April 15, 1806; died near Rome, N. Y., Jan. 20, 1887. He did much to promote the publication in America of Welsh periodicals. His published poems include 'The Crucifixion' (1853), and 'The Omnipresence of God' (1859).

Edwards, John, or **Sion Ceiriog.** A Welsh poet; born in Crogen Wladys, Glyn Ceiriog, 1747; died in London, September 1792. He wrote a St. David's Day ode and other pieces, and seems to have been a popular and accomplished character.

Edwards, John, or **Sion y Potiau.** A Welsh poet; born in Glyn Ceiriog, Denbighshire, about 1700; died in 1776. He translated Bunyan's 'Pilgrim's Progress' and wrote poetry.

Edwards, Jonathan. An American divine and theological writer of world-wide fame; born in East Windsor, Conn., Oct. 5, 1703; died at Princeton, N. J., March 22, 1758. He was the son of Timothy Edwards, a Congregational minister, and was himself minister at Northampton, Mass., 1727-50. From 1751 to 1758 he was an Indian missionary, and at the time of his death he was president of the College of New Jersey (now Princeton University). His works are the recognized exponents of essential Calvinism next to those of its founder, and rank high in the theological metaphysic of all time. They include among others: 'An Inquiry into the Modern Prevailing Notions respecting that Freedom of the Will which is Supposed to be Essential to Moral Agency' (1754); 'The Great Christian Doctrine of Original Sin Defended' (1757?); and 'A Dissertation concerning the End for which God Created the World' (1789).

Edwards, Mathilda Barbara Betham. An English novelist; born in Westerfield, Suffolk, 1836. Her sprightly fancy and the ingenuity of her plots impart exceptional interest to 'The White House by the Sea' (1857); 'Kitty' (1869); 'For One and the World'; 'A Humble Lover.'

Eeden, Frederik van (ā'den). A Dutch poet; born at Haarlem, about 1860. He is unconventionally graphic and original in his figures of speech, and in true poetry has few contemporary equals. The famous 'Little Johnny' (1887) is a seemingly simple nature poem conveying profound thought. 'Don Torrileio' and other plays had successful stage careers.

Eekhoud, Georges (ēk'hout). A notable Belgian novelist; born at Antwerp, May 27, 1854. He first published two volumes of poetry, 'Myrtles and Cypresses' and 'Poetic Zig-Zags'; then became a newspaper literary critic in Brussels, and wrote a few short stories. His first considerable novel, 'The Militia of St. Francis,' is a masterly portrayal of Flemish peasant life, especially its naïve mystic religiousness. His masterpiece, 'New Carthage,' paints Antwerp life in its naked actuality. Notable also is 'The Fusillades at Mechlin,' a story of the peasants' uprising against the French in 1798. In poetry he has developed from romanticism to pronounced realism.

Effen, Justus van (ef'en). A Dutch essayist; born in Utrecht, Feb. 21, 1684; died in Herzogenbusch, Sept. 18, 1735. His masterpiece, long a classic, The Dutch Spectator (1731-35), is an imitation of Addison and Steele.

Egan, Maurice Francis. An American man of letters; born in Philadelphia, May 24, 1852. He early achieved distinction by his writings, and was long professor of English literature at the University of Notre Dame; holding a like post at present at the Catholic University of America, Washington. His works include: 'That Girl of Mine'; 'That Lover of Mine'; 'A Garden of Roses'; 'Stories of Duty'; 'The Life around Us'; 'Lectures on English Literature'; 'A Primer of English Literature'; 'A Gentleman'; 'The Flower of the Flock.' His poetry includes the volumes 'Preludes,' 'Songs and Sonnets,' etc.

Egan, Pierce, the Elder. An English sporting writer; born in London (?), 1772; died there, Aug. 3, 1849. A prolific "historian of the ring" and kindred institutions, he dashed off the wildly popular 'Life in London' (1821), in which we have to do with Jerry Hawthorn, Esq., and his "elegant friend," Corinthian Bob, in addition to Bob Logic the Oxonian, the three enjoying together many "Rambles and Sprees through the Metropolis."

Egan, Pierce, the Younger. An English novelist, son of Pierce the Elder; born in London, 1814; died there, July 6, 1880. At first an artist, he turned to fiction, winning fame with 'Robin Hood' (1840), 'Wat Tyler' (1841), and similarly conceived romances; while his later and more sensational tales, 'Imogen,' 'Fair Lilias,' and others, appeared for the most part as serials only.

Egelhaaf, Gottlob (ā'gel-häf). A German historian; born in Gerabronn, Würtemberg, March 1, 1848. He has distinguished himself with 'A History of Germany during the Reformation' (3d ed. 1893); 'Emperor William' (3d ed. 1888); 'A History of Germany during the Sixteenth Century until the Peace of Augsburg.' (1888–92); 'Outlines of German Literary History' (1900).

Egerton, Francis. See **Ellesmere.**

Egge, Peter (eg-ga). A Norwegian story-writer; born in 1869. He has embodied the experiences of a not too happy youth in such tales as 'People' and 'Skibsgud.'

Eggeling, Julius (āg'el-ing). A German Sanskrit scholar and critic; born in Hecklingen, Anhalt, July 12, 1842. He has held Sanskrit professorships in England and Scotland, and conferred lasting obligations upon philology in his 'The Çatapatha-Brâhmana, Translated According to the Text of the Mâdhyandina School' (1882–86); 'Catalogue of Sanskrit Manuscripts' (1887–89).

Egger, Émile (eg'er or ā-zhā). An eminent French scholar; born in Paris, July 18, 1813; died at the Royal Baths, Aug. 30, 1885. His masterpieces are: 'Essay on the History of Criticism among the Greeks' (1849); 'The Poetic Element in Aristotle' (1874); and 'Greek Literature' (1890).

Eggleston, Edward. An American historian and novelist; born in Vevay, Ind., Dec. 10, 1837. In fiction he has achieved celebrity with stories of life in Southern Indiana in pioneer days, while as a historian he makes a specialty of American subjects. His works include: 'The Hoosier Schoolmaster'; 'The End of the World'; 'The Circuit Rider'; 'Roxy'; 'The Graysons'; 'The Faith Doctor'; 'The Hoosier Schoolboy'; 'Queer Stories for Boys and Girls'; 'Schoolmasters' Stories'; 'Mr. Blake's Walking-Stick'; 'Duffels'; 'School History of the United States'; 'Household History of the United States'; 'First Book in American History'; 'The Beginners of a Nation,' the first volume of a 'History of Life in the United States'; etc, Died at Lake George, Sept. 2, 1902.

Eggleston, George Cary. An American journalist and miscellaneous writer, brother of Edward; born in Vevay, Ind., Nov. 26, 1839. He has long been connected in an editorial capacity with one or another New York newspaper, including the World, the Evening Post, and the Commercial Advertiser. A few of his many books are: 'A Man of Honor'; 'A Rebel's Recollections'; 'The Wreck of the Red Bird'; 'Red Eagle'; 'Juggernaut' (with Dolores Marbourg); and for young people: 'How to Educate Yourself'; 'How to Make a Living'; 'Our First Century'; Long Knives.'

Egill Skallagrimsson (ā'gel skäl''lä-grēm'-sōn). A celebrated Icelandic skald of the 10th century, who did heroic and daring deeds as well as sung of them; he was a brave fighter and a reckless sea-rover. The story of his life, in 'Egillsaga' or 'Eigla,' tells how he was a poet at three and killed his man at seven; and how he roamed in quest of adventure over northern Europe, in the wildest vicissitudes of fortune, and finally died blind at a good old age. It is reputed to belong to the 13th century, but contains several indisputably genuine compositions of Egill; including the song of 'The Life (or Head) Redeemed,' which placated King Ethelstan when resolved to put the rover to death; the lament for 'His Son's Death'; the song in 'Praise of Arinbjörn.'

Egilsson, Svoinbjörn (ā'gēl-sōn). An Icelandic scholar and critic; born in Gullbringasysla, Feb. 24, 1791; died at Reikiavik, Aug. 17, 1852. He investigated ably the native antiquities, edited a series of Icelandic historical works, and completed a 'Poetic Lexicon of the Ancient Tongue of the North' (1855–60), published posthumously.

Eginhard or **Einhard** (āg'in-härt, īn'härt). A German historian; born in Maingau, about 770; died in Seligenstadt, March 14, 840. He was educated by Alcuin, and afterwards became Charlemagne's private secretary and superintendent of public buildings. He married Imma,—a noble lady, legendarily confounded with Emma, Charlemagne's daughter. His chief work, a 'Life of Charlemagne,' is one of the most important of mediæval histories. He also wrote: 'Annals of the Franks,' 741–829; 'Epistles'; and 'An Account of the Transfer of the Relics of St. Marcellinus and St. Peter.'

Eguilaz, Luis (ā-gēl-äth'). A Spanish dramatist (1830–78); born at Xeres de la Frontera; settled at Madrid. His plays 'Bitter Truths' and 'The Life of Soldier John' gave him fame, and he poured forth others in a great stream, strong in character-drawing and very successful. Among them are: 'The Quarrels of the Philosopher King'; 'Matrimony's Cross'; 'Leaden Sibilics.'

Ehlert, Louis (āl'ert). A German composer and writer on music; born in Königsberg, Jan. 13, 1825; died in Wiesbaden, Jan. 4, 1884. 'Letters on Music to a (Female) Friend' (1859), 'Roman Days' (1867), and 'From the World of Harmony' (2d ed. 1882), are his literary successes.

Ehrlich, Alfred Heinrich (ār'liċh). An Austrian musician, novelist, and writer on music; born in Vienna, Oct. 5, 1822. His best literary work is contained in 'Art and Handiwork' (1862), a novel; 'The Development of Musical Æsthetics from Kant's Time to our Own' (1881); and 'The Art of Living and the Art Life' (1884); 'Modern Music Life.' Died 1899.

Eichendorff, Baron Joseph von (ī'ċhen-dôrf). A distinguished German poet; born at the castle of Lubowitz in Silesia, March 10, 1788; died at Neisse, Nov. 26, 1857. He was the most gifted and original romantic lyrist of Germany, and the last great one. He was a high Prussian official till 1845, when he retired. His principal works are: 'Presage and Presence';

'War to the Philistines,' a dramatic story; 'The Life of a Good-for-Nothing,' idealizing vagabondage; the tragedies 'Ezzelin von Romano,' 'The Last Hero of Marienburg,' and other plays. 'When God his Favor would Bestow,' 'In Some Cool Retreat,' and others might be called popular ballads. He is sweet, visionary, dreamily nature-loving, but not of great force.

Eichhorn, Johann Gottfried (ĭch'horn). A German historian and Oriental scholar; born in Dörrenzimmern, Oct. 16, 1752; died in Göttingen, June 25, 1827. 'A Critical and Historical Introduction to the Old Testament' (1780–83); 'General History of Literature and Culture in Modern Europe' (1796–99); and 'History of Literature' (1799); besides other studies, happily embody great research and sympathetically vitalized learning.

Eichrodt, Ludwig (ĭch'rōt). A German humorous poet (1827–92); born near Karlsruhe. His pieces in the comic papers—which began in 1848 with 'The Itch for Travel,' in Fliegende Blätter—were collected as: 'Poems in All Humors'; 'Lyric Caricatures'; 'The Tailor's Pocketbook'; 'Life and Love' (poems). Among his dramatic poems are 'The Counts Palatine, or a Night in the Lanes of Heidelberg,' and 'Alboin.' His 'Collected Poems' (2 vols., 1890) comprise his best pieces. His verse, though witty, is never without serious purpose.

Eichtal, Gustave d' (ĭch'täl *or* esh-täl'). A French historical and ethnological writer; born in Nancy, March 22, 1804; died in Paris, April 9, 1886. He began studying social problems, but subsequently applied himself to such topics as 'The Black Race and the White Race' (partly by J. Urbain: 1839), 'Critical and Comparative Investigation of the First Three Gospels' (1863), and 'Christianity and the Three Great Mediterranean Peoples' (1864), with the most valuable results.

Elbe, A. von der (äl'bĕ), pseudonym of Auguste von der Decken. A German novelist, daughter and wife of important public men. Her novels were very successful: 'An Old Debt' (1890), 'True Love' (1891), and 'The World of Sham' (1892), increase in popularity.

Elder, Susan Blanchard. An American poetic and dramatic writer; born in Fort Jessup, La., April 19, 1835. Educated in St. Michael's Convent of the Sacred Heart, New Orleans. She began to write for the press, under the name "Hermine," when quite young. She has published: 'The Loss of the Papacy'; 'James the Second'; 'Savonarola.' Her contributions to Roman Catholic publications are numerous, and her devotional poems are very popular. Her dramas are meant for representation in Roman Catholic colleges.

Elder, William. An American miscellaneous writer; born in Somerset, Pa., July 23, 1806; died in Washington, D. C., April 5, 1885. Prior to the Civil War he was well known as an abolitionist, a forceful writer, and an eloquent speaker. His publications include: 'Periscopics' (1854); 'The Enchanted Beauty' (1855); 'Life of Dr. E. K. Kane' (1857); 'Questions of the Day' (1871); and 'Conversations on Political Economy' (1882).

Elderton, William. An English balladwriter; died 1592 (?). He wrote much, 'A New Yorkshyre Song' being among his productions, all vastly popular in the sixteenth century.

Eliot, Charles William. Late President of Harvard University; born in Massachusetts, 1834. He has published 'Manuel of Qualitative Chemical Analysis'; 'Manual of Inorganic Chemistry' (with Storer); 'Five American Contributions to Civilization.' He is a constant writer on education and other prominent questions of the day.

Eliot, George, pseudonym of Mary Ann Evans. A great English novelist; born at Arbury Farm, Chilvers Coton, Warwickshire, Nov. 22, 1819; died in London, Dec. 22, 1880. Her publications are: 'Strauss's Life of Jesus' (anon.: 1846); 'Ludwig Feuerbach's Essence of Christianity, by Marian Evans' (1854); 'Scenes of Clerical Life' (1858); 'Adam Bede' (1859); 'The Mill on the Floss' (1860); 'Silas Marner' (1861); 'Romola' (1863; previously in the Cornhill, July 1862 to August 1863; an "edition de luxe," with Sir Frederick Leighton's illustrations, appeared in 1880); 'Felix Holt' (1886); 'The Spanish Gypsy' (1868); 'Agatha,' a poem (1869); 'Middlemarch' (1872; in parts, December 1871 to December 1872); 'Jubal and Other Poems'; 'Daniel Deronda' (1876); 'Impressions of Theophrastus Such' (1879). Two short stories, 'The Lifted Veil' and 'Brother Jacob,' appeared in Blackwood in 1860. In addition to these, she wrote a very large number of papers for the reviews, such as: 'Carlyle's Life of Sterling' (1852); 'Women in France' (1854); 'Prussia and Prussian Policy' (Stahr, 1855; Dryden, 1855); 'Evangelical Teachings' (1855); 'Silly Novels by Lady Novelists' (1856); 'German Wit' (Heine, 1856); 'Natural History of German Life' (1856); 'Three Months at Weimar' (1855); 'Influence of Rationalism' (1865); 'Lecky's History' (1865); 'Address to Workingmen by Felix Holt' (1866); and 'Leaves from a Note Book.' The 'Life of George Eliot' was published by her husband in 1884.

Eliot, John. The "Apostle to the Indians"; born at Widford, Hertfordshire, England, in 1604; died at Roxbury, Mass., May 21, 1690. He was educated at Cambridge University, England; emigrated to Boston in 1631. In 1646 he began his efforts to convert the Indians. His Indian version of the New Testament was printed at Cambridge, Mass., 1661. Two years later the Old Testament appeared. He published: 'The Christian Commonwealth' (1654); 'The Communion of Churches' (1665); and 'The Harmony of the Gospels' (1678).

Eliot, Samuel. An American author and teacher; born at Boston, Mass., Dec. 22, 1821;

died at Beverly, Mass., Sept. 14, 1898. He filled the chair of political science and constitutional law in Trinity College, Hartford, Conn. Columbia gave him the degree of LL. D. in 1863, Harvard in 1880. Among his publications are: 'Passages from the History of Liberty' (1847); 'The Liberty of Rome' (2 vols., 1849); 'Manual of United States History between the Years 1792 and 1850' (1856; revised ed. 1873); and 'Stories from the Arabian Nights' (1879).

Elizabeth, Queen of Roumania. See **Sylva.**

Ellesmere, Francis Egerton, Earl of. An English statesman, man of letters, and poet; born in London, Jan. 1, 1800, died there, Feb. 18, 1857. His 'The Pilgrimage and Other Poems' (1856) constitutes his most valid title to fame, although he wrote much and well on biographical, historical, and literary subjects.

Ellet, Elizabeth Fries. An American prose-writer; born in Sodus Point, N. Y., in 1818; died June 3, 1877. Among her books are a translation of Silvio Pellico's 'Euphemia of Messina' (1834); 'Poems, Original and Selected' (1835); 'Characters of Schiller' (1842); 'Pioneer Women of the West' (1852); 'Queens of American Society' (1867); 'Court Circles of the Republic,' with Mrs. R. E. Mack (1869); 'The Practical Housekeeper'; 'Evenings at Woodlawn'; 'Women Artists in All Ages.'

Ellinwood, Frank Field. An American clergyman and author; born in Oneida County, N. Y., about 1826. He graduated at Hamilton College in 1849; was ordained a minister in the Presbyterian Church in 1853; and became secretary of foreign missions for that denomination in 1871. His chief works are: 'The Great Conquest' (1876); 'Oriental Religions and Christianity' (1892); 'Questions and Phases of Modern Missions.'

Elliot, Sir Gilbert. A Scotch statesman, philosopher, and poet; born in Teviotdale, Minto Parish (?), September 1722; died at Marseilles, Jan. 11, 1777. His song of 'Amynta,' beginning "My sheep I neglected, I broke my sheep hook," is famous; and he wrote occasional philosophical papers.

Elliot, Henry Rutherford. An American journalist and story-writer; born 1849. He has written: 'The Basset Claim, a Story of Life in Washington'; 'The Common Chord, a Story of the Ninth Ward'; and other fictions. D. 1906.

Elliot, Jane. A Scotch poet, sister of Sir Gilbert; born in Teviotdale, 1727; died there, March 29, 1805. She wrote 'The Flowers of the Forest' (1756), a song of Flodden field.

Elliott, Charles Wyllys. An American novelist and historian; born in Guilford, Conn., May 27, 1817; died Aug. 23, 1883. Settling in New York, he was one of the founders and trustees of the Children's Aid Society in 1853, and in 1857 was one of the commissioners for laying out Central Park. He published among other works: 'Cottages and Cottage Life' (1848); 'Mysteries, or Glimpses of the Supernatural' (1852); 'The Book of American Interiors'; 'Pottery and Porcelain'; 'Remarkable Characters and Places in the Holy Land'; 'St. Domingo, its Revolution and its Hero'; 'Wind and Whirlwind,' a novel; and others.

Elliott, Charlotte. An English hymn-writer; born March 17, 1789; died at Brighton, Sept. 22, 1871. Her sacred songs were exceedingly popular; 'Just as I Am' (1834) being universally adopted.

Elliott, Ebenezer. An English popular poet, born in Masborough, near Sheffield, March 17, 1781; died at Great Houghton, near Barnsley, Dec. 1, 1849. At first a foundry hand, his poetic gift was used in denouncing the exploitation of the proletariat by a capitalistic oligarchy; yet the bitterness and exaggerated rhetoric one would expect are wholly absent from 'Corn Law Rhymes' (1831) and 'More Prose and Verse' (1850).

Elliott, Sir Henry Miers. An English historian; born in Westminster, 1808; died at Simon's Town, Cape of Good Hope, Dec. 20, 1853. Long an Indian civil servant, he compiled 'Memoirs of the History, Folk Lore, and Distribution of the Races of the North-western Provinces of India' (1869), and 'The History of India as Told by its Own Historians: The Muhammedan Period' (1867-77), which appeared posthumously.

Elliott, Henry Wood. An American prose-writer; born in Cleveland, O., Nov. 13, 1841. He edited the Cleveland Daily Herald in 1879; was sent by the government to Alaska as special agent of the Treasury Department. Upon his return he published 'Monograph of the Seal Islands' (1881), and 'Our Arctic Province, Alaska, and the Seal Islands' (1886).

Elliott, Maud (Howe). An American novelist, daughter of Julia Ward Howe; born in Boston, Mass., Nov. 9, 1855. Her writings include: 'A Newport Aquarelle' (1883); 'The San Rosario Ranch' (1884), 'Atalanta in the South' (1886); 'Mammon' (1888); 'Honor'; 'Phyllida'; and 'Roma Bêata' (1904).

Elliott, Sarah Barnwell. An American novelist, granddaughter of Stephen Elliott of South Carolina. Her best-known works are: 'The Felmeres' (1879); 'Jerry'; 'John Paget,' a novel of New York and Newport; 'Sam Houston.'

Elliott, William. A miscellaneous writer; born in Beaufort, N. C., April 27, 1788, died there, February 1863. He was educated at Yale; devoted himself mainly to agriculture and rural sports. His contributions to the Southern Review were numerous. His published works include an 'Address before the St. Paul's Agricultural Society' (1850); 'Fiesco,' a tragedy (1850); and 'Carolina Sports by Land and Water' (1856)

Ellis, Edward Sylvester. An American writer of school text-books and juvenile literature; born in Ohio in 1840. For some years he was an instructor at Trenton, N. J. Besides 'The People's Standard History of the United

States' and several school histories, his works include : 'The Boy Pioneer Series' (1883–84); 'The Camp Fires of General Lee' (1887); 'The Hunters of the Ozark' (1887); 'The Great River Series' (1888); 'Storm Mountain.'

Ellis, George. An English versifier; born in Jamaica (?), 1753; died April 10, 1815. He contributed to the Anti-Jacobin and other periodicals; producing also 'Poetical Tales by Sir Gregory Gander' (1778), and other verse.

Ellis, George Edward. An American clergyman, biographer, and historical writer; born in Boston, Mass., Aug. 8, 1814; died there, Dec. 20, 1894. He was pastor of the Harvard (Unitarian) Church, Charlestown, Mass., 1840–69; and held the professorship of systematic theology in the Cambridge Divinity School, 1857–63. As president of the Massachusetts Historical Society he has made valuable contributions to early colonial history. Among his publications may be noticed : 'A Half-Century of the Unitarian Controversy' (1857); 'History of the Battle of Bunker's Hill' (1875); 'The Red Man and the White Man' (1882); 'The Puritan Age and Rule in the Colony of Massachusetts Bay, 1629–85'; various memoirs, and several biographies in Sparks's 'American Biography.'

Ellis, Robert. An English classicist; born 1820 (?); died at Exeter, Dec. 20, 1885. He made a profound study of Latin and Greek subjects and philology, his 'Hannibal's Passage of the Alps' (1853) being generally known.

Ellis, Robert or **Cynddelw.** A Welsh clergyman and poet; born in Ty'n-y-meini, Llanrhaiadr yn Mochnant; died at Gartheryr, Aug. 20, 1875. His works include a highly prized 'Awdl (or Ode) on the Resurrection' (1849), and 'Poems' (1877) of pleasing inspiration.

Ellis, Sarah Stickney, Mrs. An English miscellaneous writer, wife of Rev. William; born in 1812; died in 1872. For many years she was principal of a girls' school in Hertfordshire. Of her numerous works of a moral and instructive character, the best known are : 'The Poetry of Life' (1838); 'Summer and Winter in the Pyrenees' (1841); 'The Wives of England' (1843); 'The Island Queen' (1846), a poem; 'Fireside Tales' (1848); and the stories 'The Brewer's Family' (1863); 'William and Mary' (1865); 'Northern Roses,' descriptive of Yorkshire life.

Ellis, William. An English economic essayist, critic, and text-book writer; born in London (?) of Franco-Italian parentage, January 1800; died there (?), Feb. 18, 1881. An ardent disciple of John Stuart Mill, he wrote : 'Outlines of Social Economy' (1846); 'Thoughts on the Future of the Human Race' (1866); and many other works of consequence.

Ellwanger, George Herman. An American writer; born in New York State in 1848. He is a resident of Rochester, N. Y. Among his works are : 'The Garden's Story'; 'The Story of my House'; 'In Gold and Silver'; 'Idyl-

lists of the Country-Side,' prose; and 'Love's Demesne, a Garland of Contemporary Love Poems.' Died 1906.

Ellwood, Thomas. An English Quaker controversialist; born in Crowell, Oxfordshire, October 1639; died at Amersham, Bucks, March 1, 1713 (or 1714). His many works include a 'Sacred History' (1705; part ii., 1709), and he is noted for his friendship with Milton.

Elmes, James. An English writer on architecture and general art topics; born in London, Oct. 15, 1782; died at Greenwich, April 2, 1862. He wrote : 'Sir Christopher Wren' (1823); 'The Arts and Artists' (1825); and similar works.

Elmham, Thomas. A British historian and monk, born in North Elmham, Norfolk (?), probably about 1390; died about 1440. Little is known of him beyond the fact that he left a 'Life of Henry V.,' in prose and verse, and a 'History of St. Augustine's Canterbury Monastery,' which is, in spite of its name, a sort of general chronicle of the kingdom.

Elmsley, Peter. An English classical scholar; born in 1773; died at Oxford, March 8, 1825. Editions of Euripides and other Greek authors reveal his learning.

Elphinston, James. A Scotch versifier, essayist, and etymologist; born in Edinburgh (?), Dec. 6, 1721; died at Hammersmith, England, Oct. 8, 1809. He produced metrical versions of Martial, Fénelon, and other great writers, an 'English Grammar' (1765), and many other works. He was a zealous spelling-reformer.

Elsholtz, Franz von (els'hölts). A German dramatist (1791–1872); born at Berlin. He won some fame with his first theatrical piece, 'Come Hither,' a travesty; and in 1827 was appointed organizer and director of the Court Theatre at Gotha. 'The Court Lady' was much admired by Goethe. His plays are published in three volumes, but not now acted.

Elson, Louis Charles. An American musical critic, lecturer, and author; born in Boston, Mass., April 17, 1848. He studied music at the Leipsic Conservatory. In 1877 he became assistant editor of the Vox Humana, and in 1879 sole editor. He is at present musical critic of the Boston Advertiser, and lecturer at the New England Conservatory of Music. His works include : 'History of Music'; 'History of German Song'; 'Curiosities of Music'; 'Music Dictionary.'

Elton, Sir Charles Abraham. An English minor poet; born at Bristol, Oct. 31, 1778; died at Bath, June 1, 1853. He was a gallant soldier and no inelegant verse-maker, his 'Poems' (1804) and versions of classics being his best-known work.

Elvenich, Peter Joseph (el'vän-iċh). A German Catholic philosopher; born in Embken, Jan. 29, 1796; died in Breslau, June 16, 1886. He is easily first among the champions of the movement known as Hermesianism, after George Hermes, its founder; and has written :

'Pius IX., the Hermesians, and Archbishop von Geissel' (1848); 'The Infallible Pope' (1875); and other polemics.

Elwyn, Alfred Langdon. An American poet and prose-writer; born in Portsmouth, N. H., July 9, 1804; died in Philadelphia, March 15, 1884. He originated the Pennsylvania Agricultural Society and Farm School, and was greatly interested in institutions for the blind and feeble-minded. He published: 'Bonaparte,' a poem (1848); 'Glossary of Supposed Americanisms' (1860); 'Melancholy and its Musings' (1881).

Ely, Richard Theodore. An American political economist; born in Ripley, N. Y., April 13, 1854. He graduated at Columbia, and afterward studied at Heidelberg. Since 1892 he has been professor of political economy at Wisconsin University. He has published: 'French and German Socialism in Modern Times'; 'The Past and Present of Political Economy'; 'Taxation in American States and Cities'; 'Problems of To-Day'; 'Political Economy'; 'Social Aspects of Christianity'; 'Outlines of Economics'; and others.

Elyot, Sir Thomas. An English diplomatist and moral essayist; born 1490; died March 20, 1546. He wrote: 'The Governour' (1531), a system of training young gentlemen for government places; 'Of the Knowledge which Maketh a Wise Man' (1533); 'The Castel of Helth' (1534), in which he poached on the profession's preserves, and was roundly abused by them: but the book sold.

Elze, Karl (elts'ē). A German historian of literature (1821–89); born at Dessau. His specialty was English literature; he was professor of English philology in the University of Halle (1875–89. One of his first works was compiling a 'Treasury of English Song.' He produced critical editions of Shakespeare and other English dramatists, and wrote biographies of Byron and other English authors. Specially noteworthy is his 'Outline of English Philology.' 'Westward' (1860) contains translations of English and American poems.

Emants, Marcellus (em'änts). A Dutch poet and descriptive writer; born at Voorburg near The Hague, Aug. 12, 1848. His travels gave play to his keen observation and his poetical imagination: Among his best are: 'A Journey through Sweden' (1877); 'Monaco' (1878); 'Along the Nile' (1884); 'From Spain' (1886). He holds a permanent place in the literature of the Low Countries through his charming narrative poems 'Lilith'; 'The Shimmer of the Gods'; and his dramas 'He'; and 'A Crisis.'

Embury, Emma Catherine. An American poet; born in New York city in 1806; died in Brooklyn, N. Y., Feb. 10, 1863. Much of her work for periodicals was over the pen-name "Ianthe." Among her published works are: 'Guido and Other Poems' (1828); Female Education'; 'The Blind Girl, and Tales'; 'Love's Token Flowers' (1846); and 'Poems' (1869).

Emerson, Mrs. Ellen (Russell). An American author; born in Massachusetts in 1837. Her works are: 'Indian Myths' (1884); 'Masks, Heads, and Faces, with Considerations Respecting the Rise and Development of Art.'

Emerson, Ralph Waldo. An eminent American philosopher, poet, essayist, and lecturer; born in Boston, May 25, 1803; died at Concord, Mass., April 27, 1882. At first a Unitarian minister in Boston, he resigned his pulpit in 1832, retiring to Concord, where his home became a centre of intellectual influence. The works of Emerson comprise the following: 'An Historical Discourse delivered before the Citizens of Concord' (1835); 'Nature' (1836); Carlyle's 'Sartor Resartus,' (edited: 1836); an oration, 'The American Scholar' (1837); 'Carlyle's Essays' (edited: 1838); 'Method of Nature,' an oration (1841); 'Essays' (1841); Carlyle's 'Past and Present' (edited: 1843); 'Man the Reformer' (1844), a lecture; 'The Young American' (1844), a lecture; 'Essays' (second series, 1844); 'An Address' (1844); 'Poems' (1847); 'Nature: Addresses and Lectures' (1849); 'Representative Men,' seven lectures (1850); 'English Traits' (1856); 'Miscellanies' (1856); 'The Conduct of Life' (1860); 'May Day and Other Pieces' (1867); 'Society and Solitude' (1870); 'Tribute to Walter Scott' (1871); 'Letters and Social Aims' (1876); 'Selected Poems' (1876); 'The Fortune of the Republic' (1878), a lecture; 'Complete Works' (1883–84); 'Natural History of Intellect, and Other Papers' (1893). He also contributed much to the Dial, and edited the Massachusetts Quarterly Review (1847–50).

Emerton, Ephraim. An American historical writer; born in Salem, Mass., Feb. 18, 1851. Graduating from Harvard in 1871, he studied two years at Berlin and Leipsic, the latter giving him his Ph. D. in 1876. The same year he was appointed instructor at Harvard, and in 1882 professor of ecclesiastical history. His works include: 'An Introduction to the Study of Mediæval History'; 'Synopsis of the History of Continental Europe'; 'The Practical Method in Higher Historical Instruction'; 'Mediæval Europe, 814-1300.'

Emerton, James Henry. An American naturalist; born in Salem, Mass., 1847. He has distinguished himself by his illustrations for many scientific works, and is the author of 'Notes and Additions' to a second edition of Hentz's 'Spiders of the United States' (1875); 'Structures and Habits of Spiders' (1877); and 'Life on the Sea-Shore' (1880).

Emine, Nikita Ossipovich. An Armenian historian and distinguished scholar; born near Ispahan, Persia, about 1815; died in Moscow, Jan. 7, 1891. He was educated at the Lazareff Institute for Oriental Tongues and at the University, Moscow. Russian learning is indebted to him for his translation into Russian of all the Armenian historians. His monumental work, a 'History of Armenia,' is known to the world through a French translation.

Eminescu, Michael (ă-min-es'kö). The great lyric poet of Roumania (1849–89); born at Bucharest. He was for a time editor of The Times, a strong Conservative journal, and the fierceness of political strife would seem to have spoilt his fine poetical genius. He died in a madhouse. His fame is built on his first volume of 'Poems,' notable alike for the depth and elevation of the thought and the melodiousness of the verse; they are mostly elegiosatiric, and touch questions political, social, religious, and moral. Some of his poems have been rendered into German by Carmen Sylva.

Empáran, Diego de (em-pär'än). A distinguished Mexican controversial writer; born in Puebla, April 5, 1718; died in Ravenna, Italy, about 1807. His book 'The Jesuits and the Pope' (1746), published soon after entering the priesthood, gained him five years' imprisonment. The year after his release he issued a bitter criticism of the Church dignitaries, for which he was deposed from the priesthood and imprisoned in the castle of Sant' Angelo, but released later. His work was burned by the executioner; the single copy saved from the flames is now in the National Academy of Mexico. His works include : 'The Tombs of Mohammed and Christ'; 'Voltaire and his School'; 'Science and Superstition'; and 'Religion and Hygiene.'

Empedocles (em-ped'o-klēz). A celebrated Sicilian Greek philosopher; born at Agrigentum about B. C. 500; died probably in the Peloponnesus about B. C. 440. He was physician, philosopher, and seer, and a poet too, for his treatises or speculations were written in verse. We have some considerable fragments of his work on 'Nature' (or 'Natural Things' or 'Natural Philosophy'). Of another of his works, on 'Lustrations' or 'Purifications,' there remain but a few short fragments.

Empis, Adolphe (em-pē'). A French dramatist (1795–1868); born at Paris. His comedies combine true humor, elegance and keen observation, with a wholesome moral tone. Among his works are : 'Lambert Symnel; or, The Political Manikin' (1826); 'Generous Through Vanity' (1827); 'Mother and Daughter' (1830); 'Stockjobbery; or, The Fashionable Trade' (1835); 'Lord Novart' (1836); and 'The Heiress' (1844). His strongest work, 'The Wives of Henry VIII.,' failed of success, but is a happy imitation of Shakespeare.

Enault, Louis (en-ō'). A French story-teller and writer of travels; born at Isigny in 1822; died Mar. 27, 1900. He wrote travel and fiction based on extensive journeys. The travel sketches comprise : 'Constantinople and Turkey'; 'Norway'; 'The Mediterranean'; 'London.' The more notable of his stories are : 'The Virgin of the Libanus'; 'Love in Lapland'; 'The Baptism of Blood'; 'Tragic Loves.'

Encina, Juan del (en-thē'nä). A celebrated Spanish dramatist; born at Salamanca, about 1469; died there about 1534. His first volume of poems, 'The Song-Book,' contained also a dissertation on 'The Art of Castilian Poesy' or 'The Art of Poetic Invention.' His lyrics are full of charm and lively wit. He wrote fourteen dramas : eight are shepherd-plays or eclogues, the rest are pieces for Church holy seasons. He made the Jerusalem pilgrimage, and described it in the poem 'Tribagia; or, The Sacred Way of Jerusalem.'

Encisco, Diego Ximenez de (en-thēs'kö). A Spanish dramatist; born in Andalusia. He flourished in the sixteenth century, and his works are quite noted, although little is known of his life. His best-known play is 'The Medicis of Florence.'

Endicott, Charles Moses. "Junius Americanus." An American historical writer; born in Danvers, Mass., 1793; died in Northampton, Mass., in 1863. He contributed to the New England Historical and Genealogical Register and to the Boston Gazette. He wrote a 'Life of John Endicott'; 'The Persian Poet, a Tragedy'; 'Essays on the Rights and Duties of Nations'; and 'Three Orations.'

Engel, Eduard (eng'el). A German literary critic; born at Stolp in Pomerania, Nov. 12, 1851. He made a German translation of 'Italian Love-Songs' (1875); and wrote 'Lord Byron : An Autobiography from Journals and Letters' (1876); 'Psychology of French Literature' (1884); 'Did Bacon Write Shakespeare's Plays ?' 'History of English Literature : With Appendix, American Literature.' In his two published collections of short stories — 'Wall to Wall' (1890); and 'Exiled and Other Stories' (1891) — he appears as a moderate realist.

Engel, Johann Jakob. A German philosopher (1741–1802); born at Parchim in Mecklenburg. He was professor of philosophy and philology in Berlin, and afterward preceptor to the future Frederic William III. Æsthetic criticism and art theory owe him much. His 'Philosopher for All the World,' often reprinted, consisting of narratives, dialogues, letters, and essays, his 'First Foundations for a Theory of the Different Kinds of Poetry,' and above all his 'Herr Lorenz Stark,' with its fine delineation of everyday life, give him a place among the leading representatives of serious literature in his time.

English, George Bethune. An American controversial writer; born in Cambridge, Mass., March 7, 1787; died in Washington, D. C., Sept. 20, 1828. He graduated at Harvard, studied law, and left it for theology. In 1813 he wrote a book, 'The Grounds of Christianity Examined,' to which Edward Everett wrote a reply. English responded with 'Five Smooth Stones out of the Brook.' Besides these, he published replies to William Ellery Channing's two sermons on 'Infidelity' (1813).

English, Thomas Dunn. An American physician and poet; born in Philadelphia, June 29, 1819; died at Newark, N. J., April 1, 1902. He graduated from the University of Pennsylvania in 1839, and wrote the famous song 'Ben Bolt' in 1843. He published 'Walter Woolfe', 'American Ballads', 'Jacob Schuyler's Millions', etc.

English, William. An Irish poet; born in Newcastle, Limerick (?); died at Cork, Jan. 13, 1778. His themes were those of humble life; the well-known ballad 'Cashel of Munster' is a fine specimen of Gaelic vernacular.

Ennes, Antonio (en'nās). A Portuguese dramatist; born at Lisbon in 1848. He was for some years prominent in journalism, and afterward held high government offices. His first play, 'The Lazarists,' had extraordinary success in Portugal and Brazil, and long held the stage. It was followed by the comedy 'Eugenia Milton' (1874), and the dramas 'The Troubadours'; 'The Mountebank'; 'The Emigration'; 'A Divorce.' The last was translated into Italian and French.

Ennius, Quintus (en'i-us). A Roman poet; born at Rudiæ in Calabria, 239 B.C.; died in 169 B.C. While a centurion in the army, he was induced by Cato the elder to visit Rome, and came into close association with Scipio Africanus and the other great men there. A Calabrian with Greek culture, he was doubtless the most learned Latin of his time. He essayed nearly every kind of poetry,—narrative or epic (in his metrical 'Annals'), dramatic (tragedy and comedy), didactic (on natural philosophy, theology or mythology, and gastronomy). Nothing of his has come down to us complete, but many considerable fragments are preserved in the works of classic writers and anthologists.

Enriquez Gomez, Antonio (en-rē'kĕth). [Properly Enriquez de Paz.] A Spanish poet; born about 1600 at Segovia. His Jewish blood brought him under suspicion and persecution; he fled to Amsterdam, professed Judaism, and was burned in effigy at Seville in 1660. The dramas 'Cardinal de Albornóz' and 'Fernan Mendez Pinto,' written before exile, found great popular favor; his later ones were entered under the name of Calderon, and were mostly very successful.

Ensor, George. An Irish political writer; born in Dublin, 1769; died at Ardress, Armagh, Dec. 3, 1843. His attacks on the English government of Ireland, especially the pamphlets 'On National Government' (1810) and 'The Poor and their Relief' (1823), are very sarcastic and suffused with hatred of the oppressor.

Eötvös, Baron József (ĕt-vĕsh). A Hungarian novelist and statesman; born at Buda, in September 1813; died Feb. 2 or 3, 1871. The comedies 'The Critics' (1830) and 'The Merry Wedding Party' (1833), and the tragedy 'Revenge' (1834), were his first productions. His best-known novel is 'The Village Notary' (1845), scarifying the Hungarian system of county government; 'The Carthusian' is perhaps finer as literature. He wrote also historical novels, as 'Hungary in 1514' and 'The Peasants' War in Hungary'; and books on political and social questions, among them: 'Observations on Prison Reform' (1842); 'Influence of the Dominant Ideas of the Nineteenth Century upon the State' (1851); 'Equal Rights of the Nationalities in Austria' (2d ed. 1851).

Epicharmos (ep-i-kär'mus). An ancient Greek comic poet; born in the island of Cos, 540 B.C., but lived at Syracuse. He is the founder of the Doric-Sicilian comedy, so-called. Only a few fragments of his works survive; they were mostly travesties of myths, with some scenes from life. They were witty dialogues containing homely aphorisms.

Epictetus (ep-ik-tē'tus). A Greek Stoic philosopher; born at Hierapolis in Phrygia, about 50 A.D. A slave and then a freedman at Rome, he taught philosophy there till 94, when all philosophers were banished by Domitian; apparently returned later and lived into Hadrian's reign. The essential tenets of Stoicism are nowhere more clearly or feelingly set forth than by him. No writings of his are known; but his maxims were gathered and published in the 'Encheiridion,' or Handbook, and the 'Commentaries,' in eight books, of which four are lost. The latest English translation of the latter, Col. Higginson's (1891), is entitled 'The Discourses of Epictetus.'

Epicurus (ep-i-kū'rus). A famous Grecian philosopher; lived from about 341 B.C. to 270 B.C. He was a teacher of philosophy rather as a rule of life than as a system of knowledge, and began to teach when he was about 32 years old, first at Mitylene, then at Lampsacus; but his great school was at Athens, where he settled about 305 B.C. His discipleship there led a life of austere abstemiousness in common, after the manner of a conventual establishment, but the membership comprised both men and women. Their common dwelling was a country-house surrounded by a garden, which yielded to the labor of the brethren the simple material of their frugal fare. Of his numerous writings little remains. According to him the supreme good of life is found in pleasure, but not in the momentary gratification of sense, rather in the delight inseparable from the practice of virtue. Rightly interpreted, the doctrine of Epicurus is as adverse to all sensualism as that of La Trappe; but the Epicurean doctrines were in time misinterpreted and misunderstood, and Epicureanism became a synonym of self-indulgent and sensuous pleasure.

Épinay, Madame de la Live d' (ep-ē-nā'). A notable French writer of memoirs; born at Valenciennes, March 11, 1726; died April 17, 1783. Having a worthless husband, she cultivated intellectual society—Grimm, D'Holbach, Diderot, Rousseau; for the latter she erected in her château garden at Montmorency a cottage, "The Hermitage." She published a valued work on education, 'The Conversations of Emilie'; 'Letters to my Son'; and My Happy Moments.' Her posthumously published 'Memoirs' constitute a charming autobiography written with the freedom of an artist.

Erasmus, Desiderius (er-az'mus). [A Latin paraphrase of his Dutch name.] A celebrated Dutch humanist; born at Rotterdam, 1465 or 1467; died July 12, 1536. All his writings are in Latin. He made a collection of ' Adages ' (1500), with applications to the time; wrote a very popular volume of ' Colloquies ' (1521); and a sweeping satire, ' The Praise of Folly.' His editions of works of the ancients — Cicero, Seneca, Aristotle, St. Augustine, St. Jerome, etc. — are innumerable; and he made an elegant translation of the New Testament, which was used by Luther in his German version. In his later years he was caught up in the general polemic current and wrote against the new doctrines; his treatise on ' Free-Will ' calling forth a reply from Luther in a pamphlet entitled ' On Slave Will.' ('Complete Works,' 10 vols. folio, 1703-6.)

Erben, Karl Jaromir (er'ben). A Bohemian poet, dramatist, and scholar; born in Miletin, Nov. 7, 1811; died in Prague, Nov. 21, 1870. A comedy, ' The Brewers ' (1837) ; ' Bohemian Folk Songs and Proverbs ' (1864); ' Melodies ' (1844-47); and many philological studies, speak for nis genius and versatility.

Erceldoune, Thomas of. [Called the Rhymer, and Learmont.] A Scotch poet and seer, who flourished probably between 1220 and 1297, and wrote a poem called ' Sir Tristrem.' He occupies a very conspicuous position in the annals of Anglo-Saxon literature, but not very much is known of his life, and there is even some dispute respecting his authorship of various pieces attributed to him.

Ercilla y Zuñiga, Alonso de (är-thĕl'yä ē тнön-yē'gä). A Spanish poet; born in Bermeo, Aug. 7, 1533; died 1595. He served against the Araucanian natives of Chili, and wrote a historico-epical poem, ' The Araucanian Woman,' in 37 cantos, which apart from a few episodes is a faithful narrative of what he saw. In its portraiture of character it is admirable, and in its literary form it is classical. Cervantes in ' Don Quixote ' ranks it with the finest of the Italian epics.

Erckmann-Chatrian (erk'män-shä-trē-oñ'). Joint name of two French novelists: Émile Erckmann, born at Pfalzburg, May 20, 1822; died at Luneville, Mar. 14, 1899; and Alexandre Chatrian, born near the same town, Dec. 18, 1826, died Sept. 5, 1890. They were schoolfellows, later companion glass-blowers, finally literary copartners. ('The Illustrious Doctor Mathéus' (1859) was their first novel, and highly successful; among the others are : 'Stories from the Banks of the Rhine' (1862); 'Madame Thérèse'(1863); 'Friend Fritz' (1864); 'Story of a Conscript of 1813' (1865), and its sequel 'Waterloo' (1865); 'Brigadier Frederic' (1874); 'Banished' (1882). They portray Alsatian life and the Napoleonic era with great fidelity and sympathy. They also wrote successful plays, as 'The Polish Jew' (1869); 'Friend Fritz' (1877); 'The Rantzaus' (1882).

Erdélyi, János (er'dāl-ye). A Hungarian lyric poet and folklorist; born in Kapos, Ung, April 1, 1814; died in Sárospatak, Jan. 23, 1868. He shows taste and feeling in a volume of miscellaneous ' Poems ' (1844), and great power as a prose stylist in ' Legends and Popular Tales of Hungary ' (1845-48).

Erdmann, Johann Eduard (erd'män). A German philosophical writer; born in Volmar, Livonia, June 13, 1805; died at Halle, June 12, 1892. As a Hegelian he takes high rank with ' An Attempt at a Scientific Exposition of the History of Later Philosophy ' (1834-53); ' Outlines of the History of Philosophy ' (1865); and kindred works.

Erdmannsdörffer, Bernhard (erd'mänsder"fer). A German historian and biographer; born in Altenburg, Jan. 24, 1833. ' On the Commerce between Venice and the German States in the Middle Ages ' (1858), and ' Count George Frederick von Waldeck: a Prussian Statesman of the Seventeenth Century ' (1869), etc., are distinguished for scholarship and style. Died 1901.

Ericeira or **Ericeyra, Francisco Xavier de Menezes, Count of** (är-ē-sā'rä). A Portuguese soldier and poet; born in Lisbon, 1673; died in 1743. He is a prominent figure in the literature of his country as the author of the ' Henriqueida ' (1741), an epic poem, and a translator of Boileau.

Ernouf, Alfred Auguste (är-nöf'). A French historical writer and publicist; born in Paris, Sept. 21, 1817; died there, Feb. 15, 1889. ' New Studies of the French Revolution ' (1852-54), ' The French in Prussia, 1807-8 ' (1872), and other works, show research and impartiality.

Errante, Vincenzo (er-ränt'ė). An Italian poet and statesman; born at Palermo, July 16, 1813; died in Rome, April 29, 1891. He was many years an exile for his share in Sicilian politics. His works are two volumes of ' Tragedies and Lyrics ' (1874); the dramas ' The Feast of St. Felix ' and ' Suleiman the Great '; the poems ' The Ideal ' and ' Liberty.' He wrote also a ' History of the Osmanli Empire from Osman to the Peace of Carlowitz.'

Erskine, Sir David. A Scotch dramatist and antiquary; born 1772; died in Berwickshire, Oct. 22, 1837. His writings include ' King James the First of Scotland ' (1828), a tragedy, and ' Love amongst the Roses ' (1827), a military opera.

Eschenbach, Wolfram von. A celebrated German mediæval poet; born of a noble family at Eschenbach, near Ansbach, Bavaria, in the second half of the twelfth century; died between 1218 and 1225. He was one of the most prominent minstrels at the court of Hermann, landgraf of Thuringia; and his epics rank among the greatest German imaginative works. Besides several love songs, he wrote ' Parcival,' ' Wilhelm von Orange,' and ' Titurel.'

Escherny, François Louis (āsh-är-nē'). A French philosophical and historical essayist and critic; born in Neuchâtel, Nov. 24, 1733; died in Paris, July 15, 1815. He shows friendship to the French Revolution and the ideas of Rousseau, in 'Equality' (1796); 'Philosophy of Politics' (1798); 'Historic Picture of the Revolution' (1815); and other well-written books.

Escosura, Patricio de la (es-kō-sö'rä). A Spanish novelist and poet; born at Madrid, Nov. 5, 1807; died there, Jan. 22, 1878. After political and military ups and downs and being twice exiled, he became Under-Secretary of State, and afterward ambassador variously. He wrote the historical novels 'The Count de Candespina,' 'Neither King nor Pawn,' and 'The Patriarch of the Valley'; the epics 'The Bust in Black Cloak' and 'Hernan Cortés at Cholula'; several dramas, the most successful of which was 'Hernan Cortés's Debaucheries'; and many historical works, among them a 'Constitutional History of England.'

Esling, Charles Henry Augustine. An American prose-writer and poet; born in Philadelphia, 1845. He has written many articles pertaining to the religious thought of the day for the Catholic Record and other periodicals, and has published the 'Life of St. Germaine Cousin, the Shepherdess of Pibrac,' and several poems, one of which is 'The King's Ring, a Legend of Merry England.' He has written many verses that have been widely popular; his best-known poem is 'The Overture.' D. 1907.

Esménard, Joseph Alphonse (ās-mā-när'). A French poet (1770–1811). He spent years in foreign countries and at sea during the Revolution; returning, Napoleon made him theatrical censor. His best work is a didactic poem, 'Navigation' (1805); other noteworthy ones are: an ode, 'The Oracle of the Janiculum,' in honor of Napoleon's marriage; a collection of Bonapartist poems and ballads, 'Napoleon's Poetic Crown'; two operas, 'The Triumph of Trajan' and 'Hernan Cortés.'

Espinasse, Mademoiselle de l'. See **L'Espinasse.**

Espinel, Vicente de (es-pē-nel'). A Spanish poet and musician (1551–1634). He was in great favor in society from his musical talent, and among poets for inventing a new form of stanza. His 'Rhymes' were published in 1591. He wrote a picturesque romance, 'Life of the Esquire Marcos de Obregon,' from which Le Sage was accused of plagiarizing 'Gil Blas.'

Espronceda, José de (es-prōn-thä'dä). A Spanish poet; born at Almendralejo in Estremadura, in 1810; died May 23, 1842. A precocious poet and revolutionist, he wrote the epic fragment 'Palayo' in confinement, and was repeatedly exiled. His Byronic mannerism and theories exaggerate Byron. His most notable poems are: 'The Pirate'; 'The Beggar,' preaching socialism; 'The Headsman'; the gruesome 'Student of Salamanca'; finally his greatest though incomplete piece, 'The Clean Demon' (1841). The volume 'Forgotten Pages' was issued in 1874.

Esquiros, Henri Alphonse (es-kē-rōs'). A French historical writer and radical; born at Paris, May 23, 1814; died May 12, 1876. His best-known writings are: 'Charlotte Corday' (1840); 'The People's Gospel' (1840), portraying Christ as a revolutionist — he spent eight months in jail for this; 'The Foolish Virgins,' 'The Martyr Virgins,' 'The Wise Virgins,' (1841–42), in the interest of socialism. The 'History of the Montagnards' (2 vols., 1847) and the 'History of Liberty's Martyrs' (1851) were very popular. While banished from France he contributed to the Revue des Deux Mondes from London a series of studies on 'England and English Life,' afterward published in 5 vols. (1859–70).

Estrées, François Annibal, Duke d' (es-trä'). A French prelate, soldier, diplomat, and historical writer; born 1573; died May 5, 1670. He wrote 'Memoirs of the Regency of Marie de' Medici' (1666), and similar works of great value in consequence of his participation in the events he narrates.

Ethelred, Æthelred, Ailred, or Ælred. A British historian; born at Hexham, 1109 (?); died Jan. 12, 1166. He wrote 'The Life and Miracles of King Edward the Confessor,' and many other records.

Etherege or **Ethrygg, George.** An English classical poet and scholar; born at Thame, Oxfordshire, 1514 (?) or 1520 (?); died after 1588. He wrote 'Various Poems' and a Latin translation of Justin Martyr, in addition to numerous verses in Greek and Latin.

Etherege, Sir George. An English comedy-writer and poet; born in Oxfordshire (?), 1635 (?); died in Paris, 1691. 'The Comical Revenge, or Love in a Tub' (1664), 'She Would if she Could' (1667), and other comedies are mainly notable for indecency, though his characters have originality; the hurried verse ascribed to him is not very successful.

Étienne, Charles Guillaume (et-yen'). A distinguished French dramatist (1778–1845). Under the first empire he was censor, editor-in-chief of the Journal of the Empire, and a member of the Academy; at the Restoration he was expelled from the Academy, and thereafter as editor of the Constitutionnel was a power on the side of the opposition. His comedies give proof of his brilliant fancy, elegant style, and great constructive skill: 'The Two Sons-in-Law' is the best comedy of the Imperial era, and not unworthy Molière. He composed many farces, vaudevilles, operettas, and spectacular pieces, which had unbounded success; his operas 'Cinderella' and 'Joconde' were the delight of Paris. He wrote a 'History of the French Theatre.'

Etlar, Carit (ät'lär), pseudonym of **Carl Brosöll.** A Danish realistic novelist, also dramatist and poet; born in Fridericia, April 7, 1816; died May, 1900. The historical tale of 'The Queen's Captain of the Guard' and the story 'The People in Need' (1878) are exceedingly popular. 'The Smuggler's Son' (1839) is one of the best of his plays, and his verse has merit.

Ettmüller, Ludwig (et'mül-er). A German philological critic, poet, and historian; born in Gersdorf, Saxony, Oct. 5, 1802; died in Zurich, April 15, 1877. He rescued many mediæval masterpieces from oblivion. He was also author of 'German Dynasty Founders' (1844) and other epic poems, besides the 'Anglo-Saxon Lexicon' (1852).

Eupolis (ū'po-lis). An Athenian comic poet; born at Athens about 445 B.C.; died before 404. After Cratinus and Aristophanes he was the chief representative of the older Attic comedy; he had a comedy acted at 17. From the extant fragments we infer that, like Aristophanes, he idealized the old ways. According to the ancient critics he combined felicitous invention, masterly handling of plot, and rare grace of style.

Euripides (ū-rip'i-dēz). A great Greek tragic poet; born at Athens about 480 B.C.; died about 406. His dramas, according to the ancient Alexandrine grammatists, numbered 92. Of these, 19 have come down to our time: namely, the tragedies 'Alcestis,' 'Andromache,' 'Bacchæ,' 'Hecuba,' 'Helena,' 'Electra,' 'Heraclidæ,' 'The Mad Hercules,' 'The Suppliants,' 'Hippolytus,' 'Iphigenia at Tauris,' 'Iphigenia at Aulis,' 'Ion,' 'Medea,' 'Orestes,' 'Rhesus' (not genuine, however), 'The Trojan Women,' 'The Phœnissæ'; finally the satyr-play 'Cyclops.' Of his other plays we have only short fragments.

Eusden, Laurence. An English poet; born in Spofforth, Yorkshire (?), 1688; died at Coningsby, Lincolnshire, Sept. 27, 1730. He attracted much attention by his 'Original Poems' (1714), 'Ode for the New Year' (1720), and other poems, resulting in his appointment in 1718 as poet laureate.

Eusebius Pamphili. A Greek theologian and historian, the father of ecclesiastical history; born in Palestine, about 260 A.D.; died about 340. He became Bishop of Cæsarea in 315, and was the head of the Semi-Arians or moderate party in the Council of Nice (325). His chief works are: 'Ecclesiastical History from the Christian Era to 324 A.D.'; 'Chronica,' a history of the world down to 327; 'Life of Constantine'; 'On the Demonstration of the Gospel.'

Eutropius, or **Flavius Eutropius.** A Latin historian, who flourished 350–370 A.D. He was secretary to Constantine, and took part in Julian's expedition against the Persians. He wrote an 'Epitome of Roman History,' a brief narrative of Rome from its foundation to the time of Valens. It is written in a simple and forcible style, and has been used as a text-book for centuries.

Evans, Abel. An English poetaster and epigrammatist; born in London (?), 1679; died at Cheam, Surrey, Oct. 18, 1737. His wit was acknowledged even by Pope; and 'The Apparition' (1710) and fugitive stanzas made a hit, one or two of the couplets he penned being still occasionally quoted.

Evans, Augusta Jane (Wilson). A popular American novelist; born in Columbus, Ga., May 8, 1835. Her writings include: 'Inez, a Tale of the Alamo' (1856); 'Beulah,' the most distinguished of her novels (1859); 'St. Elmo' (1866); and 'At the Mercy of Tiberius' (1887).

Evans, Daniel or **Du o Geredigion.** A Welsh poet; born at Maes y Mynach, Llanvihangel-ystrad, 1792; committed suicide, March 28, 1846. He was well educated and talented, but led a disorderly life; his 'Collected Works' (Gwinllan y Bardd; sef prydyddwaith ar amrywiol destunau a gwahanol fesurau: 1831) evincing great but erratic powers.

Evans, Edward. A Welsh poet; born 1716; died June 21, 1798. A clergyman, and said to be directly descended from the Druids, he cherished the rites of Britain's ancient bards, and sang to Glamorgan's chair in many fiery stanzas; his 'Works' (1778) running through frequent editions.

Evans, Edward Payson. An American prose-writer; born in Remsen, N.Y., Dec. 8, 1831. He has made a special study of Oriental languages. Since 1884 he has been connected with the Allgemeine Zeitung of Munich in Europe, to which he has contributed many articles on the literary, artistic, and intellectual life of the United States. He has published 'Abriss der Deutschen Literaturgeschichte' (1869); and a 'Progressive German Reader' (1870).

Evans, Elizabeth Edson Gibson. An American prose-writer; born in Newport, N.H., March 8, 1833. Her essays and short stories contributed to periodicals, and her novel 'Laura' (1884), constitute her best work. Her 'Story of Kasper Hauser' deals with a strongly controverted subject. She also wrote 'The Christ Myth'.

Evans, Evan. A Welsh poet and antiquary; born at Cynhawdref, Lledrod, Cardiganshire, May 20, 1731; died there, August 1789. He translated Welsh masterpieces into English, and wrote in English 'The Love of our Country' (1772), a poem which won general recognition as original and pleasing.

Evans, Frederick William. ["Elder Evans."] An American lecturer and writer; born at Bromyard or Leominster, England, June 9, 1808; removed to the United States in 1820; died in Mt. Lebanon, N.Y., March 6, 1893; joined the United Society of Believers (Shakers) at Mt. Lebanon, N.Y., in 1830. His works deal with the history and doctrines of that sect. The best known are: 'Compendium of the Origin, History, and Doctrines of Shakers' (1859); 'Autobiography of a Shaker' (1869); 'Shaker Communism' (1871).

Evans, John. A Welsh poet. See **Ffraid.**

Evans, John. An English antiquarian; born at Market Bosworth, Leicestershire, in 1823. He is a paper-manufacturer, but has devoted considerable attention to archæology, geology, and numismatics. His first work, 'The Coins of the Ancient Britons' (1864), received a prize from the French Academy; and his 'Ancient Stone Implements, Weapons, and Ornaments of Great Britain' (1872) was translated into French. 'The Ancient Bronze Implements of Great Britain' appeared in 1881.

Evans, Mary Ann. See **Eliot, George.**

Evans, Thomas or **Telynog.** A Welsh poet; born at Cardigan, 1840; died April 29, 1865. He was a coal-miner at twelve, and famous for a poem on 'Humility' at sixteen; but excessive labor with pick and shovel killed him. His 'Poems' (1866) show undeniable genius and a pathos blended with sprightliness.

Evans, Thomas or **Tomos Glyn Cothi.** A Welsh poet; born at Capel St. Lilin, Carmarthenshire, June 20, 1766; died at Aberdare, Jan. 29, 1833. A song, 'Liberty' (1797), a Welsh-English dictionary, and much miscellaneous verse, preserve his memory.

Evelyn, John. A celebrated English diarist; born at Wotton in Surrey, Oct. 31, 1620; died Feb. 27, 1706. His 'Diary' was commenced at 11; it begins to be valuable about 1641, when he left England and spent ten years on the Continent; the last entry is twenty-four days before his death. It thus covers the varied period of English history from the gathering clouds of the Civil War to the accession of Queen Anne. It was written solely for private family reading, and hence contains frank judgments and inside facts obtainable nowhere else. Evelyn wrote many other works : 'Sylva,' an elaborate treatise on arboriculture; 'A Parallel of Ancient and Modern Architecture'; 'Sculptura, or the History and Art of Chalcography and Engraving on Copper'; etc.

Everett, Alexander Hill. An American diplomatist; born in Boston, March 19, 1792; died in China, June or May, 1847. Soon after graduating at Harvard, he entered the United States diplomatic service, serving as secretary at St. Petersburg. Later he was minister to the Netherlands and to Spain, and was sent as commissioner to China in 1845. He published two volumes of 'Critical and Misc llaneous Essays' (1845-46); 'Poems'; 'Europe: A General Survey'; 'America: A General Survey'; etc.

Everett, Charles Carroll. An American clergyman and writer; born in Brunswick, Me., June 1829. In 1878 he was made dean of the theological faculty of Harvard. Included in his published works are: 'The Science of Thought' (1869); 'Religions before Christianity'; and 'Fichte's Science of Knowledge: A Critical Exposition.' Died at Cambridge, in 1900.

Everett, David. An American journalist and miscellaneous writer; born at Princeton, Mass., March 29, 1770; died at Marietta, O., Dec. 21, 1813. He studied law in Boston, and while

there wrote for Russell's Gazette and a literary paper called the Nightingale. He edited the Boston Patriot (1809) and the Pilot (1812). His works include : 'The Rights and Duties of Nations,' an essay; 'Darenzel, or the Persian Patriot,' a tragedy (1800); 'Common Sense in Déshabillé, or the Farmer's Monitor.' He wrote the famous lines beginning—

> "You'd scarce expect one of my age
> To speak in public on the stage."

Everett, Edward. An American statesman; born at Dorchester, Mass., April 11, 1794; died Jan. 15, 1865. Graduating at Harvard College in 1807, he studied theology and became a Unitarian minister; but the Greek professorship at Harvard having been offered to him, he gave up the ministry and went to Germany for further study. Returning, he assumed the duties of his professorship, and by his lectures on Greek literature awakened a wide interest in Hellenic studies. He was at the same time editor of the North American Review. In 1824 he entered political life: was Member of Congress (1825-35), Governor of Massachusetts (1836-40), and minister to England (1841-45). He was president of Harvard College (1846-49). He succeeded Daniel Webster as Secretary of State on Webster's death in 1852, and while still in office was elected to the Senate (1853), but resigned the following year on account of ill health. His oration on Washington, delivered in the leading places of the Union, brought a large sum to the fund for the purchase of the Washington homestead at Mt. Vernon. Among his works should be mentioned 'Defense of Christianity'; 'Orations and Speeches'; and 'Mount Vernon Papers.'

Everett, James. An English religious poet and historian; born at Alnwick, Northumberland, 1784; died at Sunderland, May 10, 1872. A controversial divine, he wrote 'History of Methodism in Sheffield and its Vicinity' (1823), and other local chronicles of the sort; besides 'Edwin, or Northumbria's Royal Fugitive Restored' (1831), a metrical tale of Saxon times.

Everett, William. An American miscellaneous writer, youngest son of Edward; born in Watertown, Mass., Oct. 10, 1839. From 1870 to 1877 he was assistant professor of Latin at Harvard, receiving in 1875 the degree of Ph.D. in classics. In 1887 he was master of Adams Academy at Quincy, Mass.; in 1893 was elected to Congress. Mr. Everett has published 'On the Cam' (1865); 'Changing Base' (1868) and 'Double Play' (1870), two books for boys; a poem, 'Hesione, or Europe Unchained' (1869); 'School Sermons' (1881); together with many pamphlets on political, literary, and religious subjects.

Ewald, Georg Heinrich August (ā'vält). A German Biblical scholar and interpreter of Hebrew literature; born in Göttingen, Nov. 16, 1803; died there, May 4, 1875. He studied profoundly Arabic, Hebrew, and other Oriental languages and literatures. His works include: 'The Metres of Arab Songs' (1825); 'Critical

Grammar of the Hebrew Language' (1827); 'Hebrew Manual for Beginners' (1842); and 'Critical Grammar of the Arabic Tongue' (1831–33). His great fame, however, rests upon his 'History of the People of Israel,' of which a third edition appeared 1864–68, and which was succeeded by many works of importance.

Ewald, Herman Frederik. A Danish novelist; born at Copenhagen, Dec. 13, 1821. The most noteworthy of his novels are: 'Valdemar Krone: Story of his Youth' (1860), a tale of high life; 'The Nordby Family' (1862); 'Johannes Falk' (1865); 'Charles Lyng,' a fine character-study. He also wrote several historical novels popular both in the original and in German translations: 'The Swedes at Kronborg' (1867); 'Anna Hardenberg' (1880); 'Clara Bille' (1892); 'Daniel Rantzow' (1900).

Ewald, Johannes. The foremost of Danish lyric poets; born at Copenhagen, Nov. 18, 1743; died March 17, 1781. When a boy he ran away to the army, and was in several battles of the Seven Years' War; returning, studied for the Lutheran ministry; then gave himself to studying poetry and drama. He produced 'The Temple of Fortune' (1764); the 'Dirge-Cantata on the Death of Frederic V.' (1766); the drama 'Adam and Eve' (1765, remodeled 1769), with fine lyric interludes. His finest plays are 'Balder's Death' (1773) and 'The Fishers' (1778). In the latter occurs the lyric "King Christian stood by the lofty mast," which is now the Danish national song. 'The Brutal Clacqueurs' (1771) and 'Harlequin the Patriot' (1772) were successful farces. He left a notable autobiography, 'J. Ewald's Life and Opinions.'

Ewbank, Thomas. An American scientist and writer; born in Durham County, England, March 11, 1792; died in New York, Sept. 16, 1870. In 1836 he retired from commercial life for literary and scientific work. His publications include: 'The World a Workshop, or the Physical Relation of Man to the Earth' (1855); 'Life in Brazil,' with an appendix on a collection of American antiquities (1857); 'Thoughts on Matter and Force' (1858); 'Reminiscences in the Patent Office' (1859); and 'Inorganic Forces ordained to Supersede Human Slavery,' an essay.

Ewen, John. A Scotch song-writer; born in Montrose, 1741; died near Aberdeen, Oct. 21, 1821. "O weel may the boatie row" is a lay that has given him celebrity.

Ewing, Hugh Boyle. An American prose-writer; born in Lancaster, O., Oct. 31, 1826; received his education at West Point, and served during the Civil War. From 1866 to 1870 he was minister to Holland. He is author of 'The Grand Ladron, a Tale of Early California,' and 'A Castle in the Air' (1887). D. 1905.

Ewing, Juliana Horatia. An English story-writer and poet; born (Gatty) at Ecclesfield,

Yorkshire, 1841; died at Bath, May 13, 1885. Her stories for children long enjoyed a universal popularity. They comprise 'Daddy Darwin's Dovecot'; 'Dandelion Clocks and Other Tales'; 'A Flat-Iron for a Farthing'; 'A Great Emergency and Other Tales'; 'Jackanapes'; 'Jan of the Windmill'; and many more.

Expilly, Jean Charles Marie (ex-pēl-ē'). A French novelist and historian; born in Salon, Bouches-du-Rhône, Sept. 8, 1814; died at Tain, Drôme, Feb. 12, 1886. The years 1852–58 he spent in South America studying the state of the country, writings on which gave him great distinction. Among his many publications are: 'The Truth concerning the Conflict involving Brazil, Buenos Ayres, Montevideo, and Paraguay in Presence of Civilization' (1866); 'The Political and Commercial Consequences of the Opening of the Amazon' (1869); and several novels, including 'The Sword of Damocles' (1843) and 'The Black Pirate' (1838).

Eye, August von (i'é). A German æsthetic historian and critic; born in Fürstenau, Hannöverschen, May 24, 1825. 'The Kingdom of the Beautiful' (1878), 'The Life and Work of Albert Dürer' (1860), together with studies in art developments and tendencies, have been widely read and generally accepted. Died 1896.

Eyma, Louis Xavier (i-mä'). A French writer; born in St. Pierre, Martinique, West Indies, Oct. 16, 1816; died in Paris, March 29, 1876. After a tour through the United States, he returned to France and published several works, of which the best-known are: 'Les Femmes du Nouveau Monde' (1853); 'Les Peaux Rouges' (1854); 'Les Peaux Noires' (1856); 'La Republique Americaine: Ses Institutions; ses Hommes' (2 vols., 1861); 'La Chasse à l'Esclave' (1866); and many novels.

Eyre, Edmund John. An English dramatist; born in Cambridgeshire (?), May 20, 1767; died at London (?), April 11, 1816. He wrote 'The Dreamer Awake' (1791), a farce; 'The Maid of Normandy' (1793), a tragedy; and a few other plays.

Eyster, Nellie. An American story-writer; born in Frederick, Md., 1836. She has published 'Sunny Hours' (1865); 'On the Wing' (1869); 'Robert Brent's Three Christmas Days'; 'Lionel Wintour's Diary' (1882); 'A Chinese Quaker.'

Eyth, Eduard (it). A German poet; born in Heilbronn, Würtemberg, July 2, 1809; died at Neu-Ulm, April 28, 1884. He is the author of a volume of 'Poems' (1843); 'Pictures in Frames' (1856); and a version of the Odyssey.

Eyth, Julie. A German romantic and sentimental impressionist, wife of Eduard; born Capoll. Her 'Pictures without Frames: From the Papers of an Unknown; Communicated —not by Herself' (1852) won considerable popularity at the time of their appearance.

F

Faasen, Pieter Jacobus or **Rosier** (fä'sen). A Dutch playwright; born at The Hague, Sept. 9, 1833. He was one of the most celebrated Netherland actors of his time, and wrote plays remarkable for character-drawing and very successful. Among them are: 'The Old Cashier' (1875); 'Manus' (1878); 'Anne Mie' (1878), which won the first prize in an international competition and was acted in London.

Fabbri, Cora Randall (fäb'rē). An American poet; born in New York, 1871; died 1892. She was of Italian descent. A volume of her 'Lyrics' appeared but a few days before her death.

Fabens, Joseph Warren. An American miscellaneous writer; born in Massachusetts, 1821; died 1875. Among his works are: 'The Camel Hunt,' a narrative of personal adventure; 'Facts about Santo Domingo'; and 'The Last Cigar,' a book of poems.

Faber, Cecilia Böhl de. See **Caballero.**

Faber, Frederick William. An English hymn-writer; born in Calverley, Yorkshire, June 28, 1814; died at the Oratory, Brompton, Sept. 26, 1863. He was long in the Anglican priesthood, and wrote hymns of singular sweetness and spirituality; going over at last to Rome and voicing his new fervor in much sacred song. A collection of the 'Hymns' (1848) has gone through more than one edition.

Fabié, François Joseph (fä-byā'). A French poet; born at Durenque, Aveyron, Nov. 3, 1846. He has filled important chairs in different colleges, attaining distinction as the author of 'The Poesie of the Foolish Ones' (1879), a collection of his verse, succeeded by others of equal merit; and by 'Roupeyrac's Mill,' a rustic drama, and other plays.

Fabre, Amant Joseph (fäbr). An influential French historical and philosophical writer, dramatist, and publicist; born in Rodez, Dec. 10, 1842 (or 1843). A drama, 'Joan of Arc' (1890), has made his name most widely known; his other work being largely represented by such books as 'A Course in Philosophy' (1870) and 'Washington, the Liberator of America' (1882).

Fabre, Ferdinand. A French novelist; born at Bédarieux, Hérault; in 1830; died at Paris, Feb. 11, 1898. He published 'Ivy Leaves', poems (1853); then the novels 'The Courbezons' (1861), and 'Julien Savignac' (1863). But the remarkable novel 'Abbé Tigrane' (1873)—one of the most noteworthy in modern French fiction, especially by its insight into French priestly life—first won him great distinction ; 'Lucifer' (1884), portraying the struggle among the clergy between Gallicanism and Ultramontanism, is doubtless his greatest work. Shorter stories like the 'Abbé Roitelet' (1891), 'Norine' (1890), 'Germany' (1891) are admirable for tenderness and sympathy with nature; 'Ma Vocation' (1889) is a very interesting little volume of leaves from his student diary.

Fabre, Jean Raymond Auguste. A French poet, brother of Ferdinand; born in Jaujac, June 24, 1792; died in Paris, Oct. 23, 1839. He succeeded in journalism; and in 'Caledonia, or the Patriotic War' (1823), 'The Story of the Siege of Missolonghi' (1827), and other books, displayed a felicitous gift for poesy.

Fabre, Victorin. A French rhetorician and versifier; born in Jaujac, Languedoc, July 19, 1785; died in Paris, May 19, 1831. Euphony and elegance are the characteristics of 'Little Works in Prose and Verse' (1806); 'The Death of Henry IV.' (1808), a poem; and the eulogies on Boileau, Montaigne, and La Bruyère, which constitute his most important work.

Fabre d'Eglantine, Philippe François Nazaire (fäbr dā-glon-tēn'). A French poet; born at Carcassonne, Dec. 28, 1755; died April 5, 1794. The "eglantine" denotes the prize he won in the "floral plays" at Toulouse. Going on the stage with little success, he turned to play-writing; and his comedy 'Molière's Philinte,' a biting satire on "the best society," was received with extraordinary favor. 'The Epistolary Intrigue'; 'The Convalescent of Quality'; 'The Preceptors'; and others, followed with great acceptance. They are spirited, and bold in drawing, but literarily faulty. The song "'Tis raining, Shepherdess, 'tis raining," became a popular favorite.

Fabre d'Olivet, Antoine (fäbr dōl-ē-vä). A French fanciful writer; born in Ganges, Hérault, 1768; died 1825. He came as a lad to Paris to learn silk-making, but speedily began to pour forth mystical works based on Oriental word-and-letter symbolism : 'The Fourteenth of July' (1790), and similar dramas; 'Philosophic History of the Human Race' (1824); and a score of other productions.

Fadeyev, Rostislav Andreievitch (fä'de-yev). A Russian military writer; born 1824; died in Odessa, Jan. 12, 1884. He made more than one campaign in the Caucasus; achieving a reputation as a scientific soldier that commands respect for his 'Russian Military Power' (1868); 'My Opinions of the Oriental Problem' (1870); 'Letters on Russia's Present Position' (1881); and many similar writings.

Fagiuoli, Giambattista (fä-jö-ō'lē). An Italian poet (1660–1742). His lyric poems, partly

12

burlesque, appeared in six volumes (1729–34), and a seventh volume in 1743, under the title 'Pacific Rimes.' Later he published his twenty-two 'Comedies' in six volumes. He hits off the manners of the time admirably; his dialogue is fluent and free : but he lacks the true comic vein and has little dramatic power.

Faguet, Émile (fä-gā'). A French historian of literature; born in La Roche-fur-Yon, Dec. 17, 1847. As a writer for periodicals he has attracted a wide circle of readers. Among the volumes upon which his fame rests are included ' French Tragedy of the Sixteenth Century' (1883) and 'Corneille' (1888); but in 'The Great Masters of the Seventeenth Century' (1885) his learning and ability appear at their best.

Fahlcrantz, Christian Erik (fäl'kränts). A Swedish poet and theological writer (1790–1866). He was a bishop in the Swedish State Church. His poem 'Noah's Ark' is the work of a wit and a thinker. His lyrico-epic 'Ansgarius,' in 14 cantos, gives proof of a lively fancy. He wrote several volumes of religious polemic; in particular one against the Roman propaganda, ' Rome Formerly and Rome Now.'

Faidit, Gaucelm (fä-ē-dē). A Provençal troubadour; born in Uzerche, Limousin, and flourished 1180–1216 or 1190–1240. He was evidently both gifted and magnetic, as Richard the Lion-Hearted, various prelates, and the beautiful Guillelma were all fascinated by him. For years he wandered, singing as he went, with Guillelma following him; accompanying Richard on his crusade to the Holy Land, and mourning that monarch's death in a magnificent song. Some sixty of his pieces are preserved, and they are tender and sweet.

Faillon, Michel Étienne (fä-yôn'). A French historical writer; born in Tarascon, France, in 1799; died in Paris, Oct. 25, 1870. He visited Canada in 1854. He wrote lives of the 'Ven. M. Olier' (1853); 'Marguerite Bourgeoys'; 'Mlle. Maure'; 'Madame d'Youville'; 'Mlle. le Ber'; and a comprehensive history of the French in Canada, three volumes of which appeared before his death.

Fairchild, Ashbel Green. An American clergyman and author; born in Hanover, N. J., May 1, 1795; died in Smithfield, Pa., in 1864. He wrote many contributions to the religious press. His most popular work, 'The Great Supper,' was translated into German, and had an immense sale. He also published ' Baptism,' ' Faith and Works,' and 'Confession of Faith.'

Fairchild, James Harris. An American educator and author ; born at Stockbridge, Mass., Nov. 25, 1817; died at Oberlin, O., March 19, 1902. He was elected president of Oberlin College in 1886, after a service of twenty-six years as tutor, professor of languages, professor of mathematics, and professor of moral philosophy. Besides editing the ' Memoirs of Charles G. Finney' (1876) and Finney's 'Systematic Theology' (1878), he was the author of ' Moral

Philosophy' (1869) ; 'Oberlin, the Colony and the College' (1833); and 'Woman's Right to the Ballot' (1870).

Fairfax, Edward. An English poet; died about 1635; the time of his birth is unknown. He made a metrical translation, 'Godfrey of Boulogne' (1600), of Tasso's 'Jerusalem Delivered,' and dedicated it to Queen Elizabeth; it was highly esteemed by James I., is still highly valued; and on this, rather than on his own 'Eclogues,' the fame of Fairfax as a poet rests. He is also author of a 'Discourse on Witchcraft,' first published in 1858.

Fairfield, Genevieve Genevra. An American miscellaneous writer; born in New York, 1832. She has written 'Genevra'; 'The Wife of Two Husbands'; 'Irene'; etc.

Fairfield, Sumner Lincoln. An American poet and prose-writer; born in Warwick, Mass., June 25, 1803; died at New Orleans, La., March 6, 1844. He began the publication of the North American Magazine in 1833; and continued to edit and publish it for five years. His published volumes include 'Lays of Melpomene' (1824) ; 'Cities of the Plain' (1828); 'Poems and Prose Writings' (1840).

Falconer, William. A Scotch poet (1732?–69). All his family but himself were deafmutes. He was orphaned in boyhood, and at 18 was a seaman on board a Mediterranean vessel that foundered in a storm off Cape Colonna, Greece. He with two others was saved, and his poem 'The Shipwreck' (1762) commemorates the event: it was received with great favor. The author was made midshipman and afterward purser in the navy through the influence of the Duke of York; and in gratitude he wrote ' The Demagogue' (1765), a satire against Chatham, Wilkes, and Churchill. He wrote other poems (odes, satires, etc.); and a valuable 'Universal Dictionary of the Marine' (1769).

Falenski, Felicyan (fä-len'skē). A Polish poet; born in Warsaw, 1825. 'Flowers and Thorns,' 'Mountain Echoes,' and other poems of his, display vigor and imagination. He has tried his hand successfully at play-writing, with ' Althea'; and his versions of Horace, Dante, and Béranger are fine.

Falk, Johannes Daniel (fälk). A German humorist, philanthropist, and man of letters; born in Danzig, Oct. 28, 1768; died Feb. 14, 1826. His capacity for satire was considerable: a 'Pocket Book for Friends of Jest and Satire' (1797) proving very popular, as did 'Men and Heroes' (1796), a satire in verse, and 'Prometheus' (1804), a dramatic poem. His volume on Goethe is still valuable.

Falke, Jacob von (fäl'ke). A German connoisseur and historian of taste; born in Ratzeburg, June 21, 1825. His administrative capacity has placed many art galleries and repositories of art treasures in Germany and Austria upon a successful basis. His writings, particularly

'Knightly Society in the Days of Homage to Womanhood' (1862); 'History of Modern Taste' (1866); 'Art and Art Study' (1878); 'Hellas and Rome' (1879); and 'History of Taste in the Middle Ages' (1893), are notable for both learning and judgment. Died 1897.

Fallmerayer, Jacob Philipp (fäl-mer-ī'er). A German historian and voyager; born in the Tyrol, Dec. 10, 1790; died in Munich, April 26, 1861. As a scholar, especially linguist, and as an explorer of the Orient, his fame is international and his work authoritative; witness 'Fragments from the Orient' (1845), 'History of the Peninsula of Morea in the Middle Ages' (1830), and other important writings.

Falloux, Alfred Frédéric Pierre (fä-lö'). A French historical, political, and controversial writer and publicist; born in Angers, May 7, 1811; died there, Jan. 7, 1886. Legitimist and clerical sympathies influenced his career, his typical writings being: 'Madame Swetchine, her Life and Works' (15th ed. 1884); 'Story of Louis XVI.' (6th ed. 1881); and 'Political Speeches and Miscellany' (1882).

Falsen, Enevold de (fäl'sen). A Danish poet (1755–1808). He held several high offices, judicial and political. His dramas long enjoyed public favor. Among them are 'Idda,' a tragedy; and the comedies 'The Droll Cousins,' 'The Art-Deemster,' 'The Child that Brings Luck.' In despair over the ills that had befallen his country in the Napoleonic times, he ended his life by his own hand.

Falster, Christian (fäl'stēr). A Danish poet (1690–1752). His 'Satires' on his age, modeled on Juvenal, give him eminent rank among the native poets. He wrote three volumes of 'Philological Amenities or Various Discourses,' containing a mass of highly interesting observations on the affairs of the time. His translation of Ovid's 'Tristia' also is worthy of mention.

Fambri, Paul (fam'brē). An Italian dramatist, story-writer, military and literary essayist, and scholar; born in Venice, about 1827. His energies have expended themselves in a great variety of ways. 'The Corporal of a Week,' a comedy; 'Agrippa Postumus,' a tragedy; 'Pietro Aretino,' a metrical play; 'The Law of Dueling,' a text-book of the code of honor; 'Giddy Outsets [Pazzi Mezzi] and a Serious End [e Serio Fine],' a novel; and 'Mary Queen of Scots, according to Tennyson and according to Hugo,' a critique, show his versatility.

Fanfani, Pietro (fän-fä'nē). An Italian philologist, humorist, and novelist (1815–79). He founded in 1847 the Philological Record, and afterward edited several other periodicals of a like character. His 'Vocabulary of Tuscan Usage' and other «vocabularies» are works of high authority. The 'Writ at Random,' and the whimsical satire 'The Laughing Democritus: Literary Recreations,' are specimens of his brimming humor. His novels are: 'Cecco

of Ascoli'; 'Paolina'; 'The Coachman and his Family'; etc.

Fanshawe, Anne Harrison, Lady. An English memoirist; born (Harrison) in London, March 25, 1625; died there, Jan. 30, 1679 or 1680. Her admirably written and accurate observations of life and manners in many lands, preserved in 'Memoirs,' from which extracts have been published, are of historical value.

Fanshawe, Catherine Maria. An English poet; born in Chipstead, Surrey, July 6, 1765; died at Putney Heath, April 17, 1834. A lively fancy, brilliant wit, sound sense, and personal charm made this lady and her poetry admired in her own circle; but she rarely consented to publication, and only her riddle on the letter H, sometimes credited to Byron, is generally known, her stanzas not having been collected.

Faraday, Michael. An English physicist and chemist of great authority; born in Newington Butts, near London, Sept. 22, 1791; died in Hampton Court, Aug. 25, 1867. His achievements in the departments of chemistry and electrical induction and magnetism are of permanent importance; and his works, particularly 'Experimental Researches in Electricity' (1832–55); 'Chemical Manipulations' (1843); 'Experimental Researches in Chemistry' (new ed. 1882); and 'Lectures on the Chemical History of a Candle' (3d ed. 1874), are repositories of valuable knowledge.

Fargus, Frederick John. ("Hugh Conway.") An English novelist (1847–85). His death cut short what seemed a promising career. He is best known by his novel 'Called Back,' but he wrote 'Dark Days' and other stories.

Faria, Manoel Severim de (fä-rē'ä). A Portuguese biographer, essayist, and scholar; born in Lisbon, 1583; died at Evora, Sept. 25, 1655. He devoted many years to the study of his country's literature, giving his researches and thought a lasting form in 'Various Essays' (1624), containing appreciations and biographies of Camoens and other great writers. He also wrote 'Jottings of Portugal' (1655).

Faria y Sousa, Manoel de (fä-rē'ä ē sō'zä). A Portuguese poet and historical writer (1590–1649). His four volumes ("Fount of Aganippe") of sonnets, eclogues, songs, and madrigals, are eccentric but original. He wrote a 'History of the Kingdom of Portugal,' a history of 'Portuguese Asia,' 'Portuguese Africa,' etc., besides many essays in literary criticism. Most of his works are in Spanish.

Farina, Salvatore (fä-rē'nä). A distinguished Italian novelist; born at Sorso in Sardinia, Jan. 10, 1846. His tales were successful from the first, which was 'Two Amours' (1869). Among the others are 'A Secret' (1870); 'Forbidden Fruit'; 'Romance of a Widower'; 'Dounina's Treasure'; 'Courage and Onward'; 'Little Don Quixote' (1890); 'Living for Love' (1890); 'For Life and for Death' (1891). The sympathy with lowly life and the rich humor of his stories have gained him the title of 'The Italian Dickens.' He is the best known abroad of all Italian novelists.

Farini, Carlo Luigi. An Italian statesman and historian; born at Russi, Oct. 22, 1812; died Aug. 1, 1866. He studied medicine at Bologna, but early entered upon a political career, becoming Minister of Public Instruction in 1850, of Commerce in 1861, and President of the Council in 1862 during Cavour's administration. His influence contributed much to the union of Central Italy with the kingdom of Victor Emmanuel II. His 'History of the Roman State from 1815 to 1850' (1850) was translated into English; and his 'History of Italy,' a continuation of Botta's celebrated work, is a performance of standard merit.

Farjeon, Benjamin Leopold. An English journalist and novelist; born in London in 1833. He went to Australia in early life, and after some experience in the gold diggings of Victoria, migrated to New Zealand, where he became business manager of the Otago Daily Times at Dunedin. He returned to London in 1869 and devoted himself to literature. His first novel, 'Grif' (1870), a story of Australian life, made his reputation; and has been followed by 'Joshua Marvel' (1871); 'Christmas Stories' (1874); 'Jessie Trim' (1874); 'Duchess of Rosemary Lane' (1876); 'The Sacred Nugget' (1885); 'Toilers of Babylon' (1888); 'A Fair Jewess' (1894); 'The King of No Land'; and others. Died at London, July 23, 1903.

Farley, Harriet. An American editor and writer; born in New Hampshire, 1817. She was employed in a mill at Lowell, Mass., and became editor of the Lowell Offering, a periodical supported by the factory operatives, who were also contributors to it. Her works include 'Mind among the Spindles,' a collection of her miscellany, and 'Fancy's Frolics.'

Farley, James Lewis. An Irish journalist, topical and descriptive writer; born in Dublin, Sept. 9, 1823; died in London, Nov. 12, 1885. Established in Turkey as a bank official, he became correspondent of two or three great London dailies and speedily made himself an authority on Turkish questions. His books include: 'The Resources of Turkey' (1862); 'Turkey: Its Rise, Progress, and Present Condition' (1866); and 'Modern Turkey' (1872).

Farlow, William Gilson. An American botanist; born in Boston, Mass., Dec. 17, 1844. After graduating at Harvard, he spent several years in Europe pursuing his favorite study. His publications treat mainly of marine algæ, fungi, and diseases of plants. Upon these subjects, and particularly upon cryptogamic botany, he is considered an authority. He also published 'The Potato Rot' (1875); 'Diseases of Olive and Orange Trees' (1876); 'The Marine Algæ of New England' (1881).

Farman, Ella. See **Pratt.**

Farmer, Henry Tudor. An American poet, born in England in 1782; died in Charleston, S. C., January 1828. While very young he emigrated to Charleston, S. C., where he continued to reside until his death. He published a small volume of poems entitled 'Imagination, the Maniac's Dream, and Other Poems' (1819). He also published an 'Essay on Taste.'

Farmer, Mrs. Lydia Hoyt. An American miscellaneous writer; born in Ohio, 1842. Her books include 'Aunt Belindy's Points of View' and 'The Doom of the Holy City.' Died, Cleveland, Ohio, Dec. 27, 1903.

Farnham, Eliza Woodson. An American prose-writer; born in Rensselaerville, N. Y., Nov. 17, 1815; died in New York city, Dec. 15, 1864. A philanthropist, and the author of 'California, Indoors and Out'; 'My Early Days' (1859); and 'Woman and her Era' (1864).

Farquhar, George. An Irish playwright (1678–1707). On leaving Dublin University he joined a troop of players, but quitted the stage before long, having accidentally stabbed to death one of his fellows. He wrote eight comedies which are ranked among the best of the Restoration drama. Among them are: 'Love and a Bottle' (1698); 'The Constant Couple' (1699), and its sequel 'Sir Harry Wildair' (1701); 'The Recruiting Officer' (1706); 'The Beaux' Stratagem' (1707).

Farrar, Charles A. J. An American miscellaneous writer, born 18—; died 1893. He published 'Moosehead Lake and the North Maine Wilderness'; 'Camp Life in the Wilderness'; 'From Lake to Lake'; etc.

Farrar, Eliza Ware. An American story-writer; born in Flanders (Belgium), in 1791; died in Springfield, Mass., April 22, 1870. Her works include: 'The Children's Robinson Crusoe'; 'The Story of Lafayette'; 'The Youth's Love-Letters'; 'Congo in Search of his Master' (1854); and 'Recollections of Seventy Years' (1865).

Farrar, Frederick William. An English clergyman, dean of Canterbury; born at Bombay, India, Aug. 7, 1831. Of his religious and theological writings the most notable are: 'The Witness of History to Christ' (1871); 'The Life of Christ' (2 vols., 1874), a work written for the people and which has had a large circulation; 'Life and Works of St. Paul' (2 vols., 1879); 'The Early Days of Christianity' (2 vols., 1882); 'Eternal Hope,' a work which has been severely criticized by the strait orthodox school on account of its lax doctrine regarding the question of everlasting punishment. He is author also of works on language, as 'The Origin of Language' (1860); 'Chapters on Language' (1865); 'Families of Speech' (1870); 'Language and Languages' (1878); He died in London, March 22, 1903.

Fastenrath, Johannes (fäs'ten-rät). A German poet and story-teller; born at Remscheid, May 3, 1839. A brief sojourn in Spain (1864) filled him with a permanent enthusiasm for the land and literature which has inspired nearly all his life-work. He translated Juan Diana's comedy 'Receipt against Mothers-in-Law'; and compiled a series of volumes which are less translations than transcriptions in the spirit of the originals,—'A Wreath of Spanish Romances'; 'Hesperian Blooms'; 'The Book of my Spanish Friends'; 'Voices of Christmas.' He also wrote many works on the history of Spanish literature; and in Spanish, 'Passion-Books of a German-Spaniard,' a description of the Oberammergau Passion Play; and 'Walhalla and the Glories of Germany' A volume of war songs dedicated 'To the German Heroes of 1870' is also his.

Fauriel, Claude (fō-rē-el'). A French historian; born in St. Étienne, Oct. 21, 1772; died in Paris, July 15, 1844. He shone in the most brilliant literary society of his time and studied diligently before producing his great 'History of Southern Gaul under its German Conquerors' (1836). Other noteworthy books by him are: 'The Origin of the Epic of the Middle Ages' (1833); 'History of Provençal Poetry' (1846); and 'Dante and the Origin of the Italian Language and Literature' (1854); all charmingly written.

Fava, Onorato (fä'vä). An Italian story-writer, versifier, and essayist; born in Collobiano, Piedmont, July 7, 1859. He is versatile and sprightly in 'Against the Majority' (1888); a novel, 'In the Country of the Stars' (1889); a juvenile, 'Our Life' (1885); and many other capitally written and original things.

Favart, Charles Simon (fä-vär'). A French dramatist; born at Paris, Nov. 13, 1710; died May 18, 1792. His very youthful poem 'France Freed by the Maid of Orleans' won the prize of the Floral Plays; and at 24 he was writing successful comedies. These and his operettas number about 150 (his wife, Marie Justine Bénédicte Duronceray, 1727–72, being his constant collaborator), and are for the most part pretty and realistic scenes of love in the country; but some of them are amusing drolleries like the mediæval fabliaux. His most celebrated compositions are 'Annette and Lubin'; 'The Village Astrologer'; 'Ninette at Court'; 'The Three Sultanas'; 'The Englishman at Bordeaux.' His 'Memoirs and Correspondence' (3 vols., 1808) is of great value for the history of literature.

Fawcett, Edgar. An American novelist, poet, and dramatist; born in New York city, May 26, 1847. Among his novels are: 'Purple and Fine Linen' (1873); 'A Hopeless Case' (1880); 'A Gentleman of Leisure' (1881); 'An Ambitious Woman' (1883); 'Rutherford' (1884); 'The Adventures of a Widow' (1884); 'The Confessions of Claude' (1886); 'The House at High Bridge' (1887); 'Miriam Balestier' (1888); 'A Man's Will' (1888); 'Olivia Delaplaine' (1888); 'A Demoralizing Marriage' (1889); 'Fabian Dimitry' (1890); 'A New York Family' (1891); 'An Heir to Millions' (1892); 'Women Must Weep' (1892); 'A Mild Barbarian' (1894); 'Outrageous Fortune' (1894). His poetical works include: 'Short Poems for Short People' (1872); 'Fantasy and Passion' (1877); 'Song and Story' (1884); 'Romance and Revery' (1886). Died London, May 2, 1904.

Fawcett, Henry. An English political economist and publicist; born in Salisbury, Aug. 26, 1833; died in Cambridge, Nov. 6, 1884. An accident which deprived him of sight early in life did not prevent his attainment of distinction as postmaster-general under Gladstone, and as a writer of force in 'Manual of Political Economy' (6th ed. 1883); 'The Economic Position of the British Labourer' (1865); 'Pauperism: Its Causes and Remedies' (1871); and 'Protection and Reciprocity' (6th ed. 1885), in which the liberal theory of the younger Mill is carried to its logical extreme.

Fawcett, Millicent (Garrett) Mrs. An English writer, widow of Henry; born at Aldburgh, Suffolk, June 11, 1847. She is a leader in the movement for university education for women. Her published works comprise: 'Political Economy for Beginners' (1870); 'Tales in Political Economy' (1874); 'Janet Doncaster' (1875), a novel; 'Some Eminent Women of Our Time' (1889); 'Life of Sir Wm. Mollesworth.'

Fawkes, Francis. An English poet and translator; born in Doncaster (?), March (?), 1720 (?); died at Hayes, Kent (?), Aug. 26, 1777. He is happiest in depicting emotional states and sentiments, notably in 'Original Poems and Translations' (1761); his versions of Anacreon, Sappho, Bion, and Moschus earned him a reputation as the ablest worker in this field since Pope,—a reputation which later changes in taste have much diminished.

Fáy, Andreas (fī *or* fäy). A Hungarian poet and novelist; born at Koháný (Zemplin), May 30, 1786; died July 26, 1864. Till the appearance of Kossuth on the scene (1840) he was the foremost leader at Pesth of the Opposition party; thereafter he took no considerable part in politics, but promoted many important national enterprises. His volume of poems 'New Garland' (1818) established his fame as a poet, but his admirable prose 'Fables' (1820) attained a far wider popularity. Among his dramatic works are the tragedy 'The Two Báthorys' (1827); and several comedies, the most notable being 'The Old Coins; or the Transylvanians in Hungary' (1824), and 'The Hunt in the Matra' (1860). His social novel, 'The House of the Béltekys' (2 vols., 1832), and a number of short stories, entitle him to a place among the great masters of Hungarian prose.

Fay, Theodore Sedgwick or **Sedgewick.** An American poet, story-writer, and essayist; born in New York, Feb. 10, 1807; died in Berlin, Nov. 17, 1898. Eminent in periodical journalism. To this period belongs his book, 'Dreams and Reveries of a Quiet Man' (1832). He served with ability in the United States diplomatic service, and wrote 'The Countess Ida' (1841), a tale; 'Ulric' (1851), a poem; 'The Three

Germanys' (1889); 'Great Outlines of Geography'; 'History of Switzerland'; various volumes of verse, travel, description, etc.

Fazio degli Uberti (fät'se-ō dāl'yē ö-bār'tē). An Italian poet; born in Pisa (?) or in Florence about 1300; died at Verona, about 1367. He seems to have led a life of political turmoil. He very early yearned to place his name beside Dante's; the result being a curious poem, 'The World Described,' a servile but not entirely contemptible imitation of the 'Divine Comedy.' He wrote also inferior stanzas and sonnets.

Fearing, Lillien Blanche. An American writer of verse; born in Davenport, Iowa, 1863. She was a member of the Chicago bar. Her works are: 'The Sleeping World and Other Poems' (1887); 'In the City by the Lake,' poems; 'Roberta.' Died in Chicago, ———, 1901.

Fechner, Gustav Theodor (fech'ner). A German humorist and writer on physics and psychiatry; born in Great Särchen in the Niederlausitz, April 19, 1801; died in Leipsic, Nov. 18, 1887. His works on purely scientific topics, 'Elements of Psychophysics' (1860) and 'Text Book of Experimental Physics' (1828) among them, and his 'Three Motives and Grounds of Faith' (1863), have made him eminent; while under the name of "Doctor Mises" he has written various popular humorous tales and fancies, notably 'A Proof that the Moon is Made of Iodine' (1821), 'Comparative Anatomy of the Angels' (1825), and 'The Little Book of Life after Death' (1836).

Federici, Camillo (fā-dā-rē'chē). [Properly Giovanni Battista Viassolo, or (according to others) Ogeri.] An Italian comedy-writer; born at Poggiolo di Garessio, Mondovì, April 9, 1749; died in Turin, Dec. 23, 1802. He set up as a lawyer, but turned to the stage and wrote several comedies, including 'A Word of Advice to Husbands'; 'The Sculptor and the Blind Man'; and 'Falsehood is Short-lived.'

Fedkovic, Joseph Horodencuk (fed-kō'vich). A Ruthenian (Austria) poet and story-writer; born in Bukovina, 1834; died at Czernowitz, Jan. 11, 1888. He was early a journalist of repute, and took to the writing of German verse; producing subsequently poems in his native Ruthenian. 'Poems' (1862) and 'Stories' (1876) show an engaging realism in local color.

Feis, Jakob (fīs *or* fvīs). A German dramatist, essayist, and translator; born in Deidesheim, July 10, 1842. Long a resident of London, he has studied the literature of England thoroughly; translating Tennyson's 'Locksley Hall Sixty Years Later' (1888), and producing the series of studies on 'Shakespeare and Montaigne' (1884) to which his chief celebrity is due. 'Johanna Grey' (1881) and 'The New Master' (1891) are well-written dramas on contemporary social questions.

Feisi, Abul-Feis ibn Mubárak (fā-ē-sē'). A celebrated Indo-Persian poet and scholar; born at Agra, 1547; died 1595. He surpassed all his contemporaries in philological, philosophical, historical, and medical knowledge, and about 1572 was crowned "king of poesy" in the court of the Emperor Akbar. Of his poems the most noteworthy are his lyrics,—odes, encomia, elegies, and specially his four-line pieces or apothegms. Their exalted pantheism brought on him the enmity of the orthodox Muslim clergy. He wrote also many double-rhymed poems; and a Persian imitation of the famous Indian epic 'Nala and Damajanti,' designed to form the third member of an epic cycle, of which the first was to be 'The Centre of the Circle,' the second 'Solomon and Balkis' (the Queen of Sheba), the fourth 'The Seven Zones of the Earth,' and the fifth 'The History of Akbar': only the first and third were completed. His scientific treatises were numerous·

Feitama, Sybrand (fī'tä-mä). A Dutch minor poet and critic; born in Amsterdam, Dec. 10, 1694; died there, June 13, 1758. Quite destitute of originality, but of faultless taste, he made his literary verdicts respected; and translated Voltaire's 'Henriade,' Fénelon's 'Telemachus,' and other French plays into correct if somewhat insipid Dutch verse of marked Gallic flavor.

Feith, Rhijnvis (fīt). A Dutch poet and story-teller; born at Zwolle in Oberyssel, Feb. 7, 1753; died Feb. 8, 1824. Among his 'Odes and Poems' (5 vols., 1796–1810) are several that show true poetic inspiration. His tragedies are: 'Thirza' (1784); 'Lady Jane Grey' (1791); 'Inez de Castro' (1793); 'Mucius Cordus' (1795); and 'The Resuscitation of Lazarus' (1811). He wrote also some stories— 'Julia' (1783); 'Ferdinand and Constance' (1785)—which, like his odes and his didactic poem 'The Count,' show plainly the influence of German poetry in the "Werther" period.

Felder, Franz Michael (fel'der). An Austrian story-writer; born at Schoppernau, in the Bregenzer Wald, May 13, 1839; died at Bregenz, April 26, 1869. Though condemned to the labor of the field and "by poverty oppressed," his 'Out of the Ordinary: Life and Character Pictures of the Bregenzer Wald' (1867), and 'Rich and Poor' (1868), markedly original in style and view, gave him an acknowledged literary standing.

Feldmann, Leopold (feld'män). A German dramatist and journalist; born at Munich, May 22, 1802; died March 26, 1882. In 1835 appeared his 'Lays of Hell,' on the theme of unrequited love; next the comedy 'The Son on his Travels,' which made a brilliant success at Munich. After five years in travel, chiefly in Greece, as correspondent of the Allgemeine Zeitung, in 1850 he settled in Vienna for life. His comedies were very popular in their day; the most worthy of mention are: 'Free Choice'; 'Sweetheart's Portrait'; 'The Late Countess'; 'The Comptroller and his Daughter.'

Feletz, Charles Marie Dorimond de (fä-lets'). A French critic and essayist; born at Grimont,

Limousin (?), about 1767; died in Paris (?), Feb. 11, 1850. After some thrilling experiences in the Revolutionary period, he settled down to journalism in Paris, writing many celebrated essays and reviews, and entering the French Academy. The volumes of 'Philosophical, Historical, and Literary Miscellany' (1828), and 'Historical and Literary Estimates' (1840), contain his finest studies.

Fellows, Sir Charles. An English archæologist and writer on classical antiquities; born in Nottingham, Aug. 1799; died in London, Nov. 8, 1860. Learning and accuracy are manifest in 'An Account of Discoveries in Lycia' (1841), 'The Xanthian Marbles' (1843), and many like investigations.

Fellows, John. An American prose-writer; born in Sheffield, Mass., in 1760; died in New York city, Jan. 3, 1844. His publications include 'The Veil Removed' (1843); 'Exposition of the Mysteries or Religious Dogmas and Customs of the Ancient Egyptians, Pythagoreans, and Druids'; 'Mysteries of Free-Masonry'; and a work on the authorship of the Junius Letters.

Felt, Joseph Barlow. An American historical writer; born in Salem, Mass., Dec. 22, 1789; died there, Sept. 8, 1869. He was well known for his extensive and accurate knowledge of New England history. Among his publications are: 'Annals of Salem,' said by Bancroft to be "an accurate and useful work" (1827; 2d ed., 2 vols., 1845-49); 'The Customs of New England' (1853); and 'Ecclesiastical History of New England' (2 vols., 1855-62).

Felton, Cornelius Conway. An American scholar and writer; born in Newbury, Mass., Nov. 6, 1807; died in Chester, Pa., Feb. 26, 1862. In 1834 he became professor of Greek literature at Harvard; in 1860 its president. His publications include many translations from German, French, and Greek, of which 'The Clouds' and 'The Birds' of Aristophanes are the most distinguished; also 'Familiar Letters from Europe' (1864); 'Greece, Ancient and Modern' (1867); 'Selections from Modern Greek Writers'; etc.

Fénelon, François de Salignac de la Mothe (fān-lôn'). A French theologian and writer; born in the Château Fénelon in Périgord, Dordogne, Aug. 6, 1651; died Jan. 7, 1715. He is especially famous for his story 'Telemachus.' His other writings include: 'Treatise on the Education of Young Girls'; 'Fables'; 'Dialogues of the Dead'; 'Life of Charlemagne'; 'Exposition of the Maxims of the Saints Regarding the Inner Life'; and many others.

Fenn, George Manville. An English story-writer; born in London, Jan. 3, 1831. He graduated from journalism into fiction, gaining prominence by 'Eli's Children' (1882), a tale of clerical life; 'The Golden Magnet' (1884), a story for boys; 'The Master of the Cere-

monies' (1886), a novel of old-fashioned England; 'Uncle Bart' (1900); 'Old Gold' (1901).

Fenton, Elijah. An English poet, dramatist, and biographer; born at Shelton, Staffordshire, May 20, 1683; died in Berkshire, August (not July) 1730. He worked with Pope at the translation of the Odyssey, wrote 'Mariamne,' a tragedy, and produced a 'Hymn to the Sun,' with other verse displaying taste and talent.

Ferguson, Adam. A Scotch historian and ethical writer; born June 20, 1723; died at St. Andrews, Feb. 22, 1816. As a professor, and later as traveling companion to the young Lord Chesterfield, he exhibited the taste, refinement, and charm which characterize no less his writings than his personality as revealed by his contemporaries. 'Institutes of Moral Philosophy' (1769), 'Observations on Civil and Political Liberty' (1776), and 'History of the Progress and Termination of the Roman Republic' (1805), are a few of his interesting books.

Ferguson, Sir Samuel. An Irish lawyer, antiquarian, and poet; born in Belfast, Ireland, in 1810; died in 1886. In early life he was a prominent member of the Irish bar; in 1867 was appointed Deputy Keeper of the Public Records of Ireland; and in 1878 was knighted in recognition of his antiquarian and literary accomplishments. He will best be remembered as the author of the stirring poem, 'The Forging of the Anchor,' which first appeared in Blackwood's Magazine. Chief among his other publications are: 'Lays of the Western Gael' (1864); 'Congal' (1872), a poem in five books; 'Poems' (1880); 'Shakespearean Brevities' (1882).

Fergusson, James. A celebrated Scotch writer on architecture; born at Ayr, Scotland, Jan. 22, 1808; died in London, Jan. 9, 1886. His early travels in the Orient resulted in the 'Historical Inquiry into the True Principles of Art' (1849). His monumental achievement, which constitutes him perhaps the greatest of writers on the subject, is 'History of Architecture in All Countries' (3d ed. 1894). Among his titles, which include volumes incorporated into his great history, are 'Illustrated Handbook of Architecture' (1855); 'History of the Modern Styles of Architecture'; 'The History of Indian and Eastern Architecture'; 'Fire and Serpent Worship'; and innumerable pamphlets on the scientific and æsthetic aspects of architecture and kindred themes.

Fergusson, Robert. A Scotch poet; born in Edinburgh, Sept. 5, 1750; died there, Oct. 16, 1774. He had a precocious and versatile poetical genius, but of the kind nearly allied to madness; and after publishing 'Poems' (1773), a collection of many gems, he was carried to an insane asylum.

Fern, Fanny. See **Parton.**

Fernald, Chester Bailey. An American writer; born in 1869. He is a resident of San Francisco, Cal. He is a contributor to magazines, and the author of 'The Cat and the Cherub, and Other Stories'; 'John Kendrys' Idea.'

Fernández, Diego (fer-nän'deth). A Spanish-American historian; born in Palencia, Spain, 1530 (?); died in Seville, Spain, 1581. He was apparently a soldier of fortune, lured to the scene of Pizarro's great conquest in the hope of fabulous wealth; the upshot being some fighting experiences, and 'The First and Second Parts of the History of Peru' (1571), a warm and interesting, although perhaps partisan, narrative of the subjugation of the Incas.

Fernandez, Lucas. A Spanish dramatist of the sixteenth and seventeenth centuries. His works, published under the general title 'Farces and Eclogues in the Pastoral Style and Manner' (1514), consist of six pastoral dramas in his native Castilian dialect : three religious, the others pictures of actual pastoral life, with shepherds acting simply and discoursing in their naïve way.

Fernandez de los Rios, Angel (fer-nän'deth dä lōs rē'ōs). A Spanish publicist, topical and descriptive writer, and journalist; born in Madrid, July 27, 1821; died near Paris (?), 1879. Active in politics and political journalism at home, he was banished at last, and became a man of letters in Paris. To his credit are placed 'All or Nothing' (1876), an anti-Bourbon prose study of social conditions; 'A Week in Lisbon' (1876); and many essays of value on the politics and resources of the Peninsula.

Fernandez de Piedrahita, Lucas (fer-nän'deth dä pyā-drä-ē'tä). A South-American historian and prelate; born in Bogota, Colombia, 1624; died in Panama, 1688. Educated by the Jesuits, he was soon noted as far as Rome for his learning, piety, and capacity; his promotion to episcopal rank coming early. A 'History of the Kingdom of New Granada' (1688), the result of many years' researches, is an inestimable storehouse, from which every subsequent worker has drawn treasures; the performance remaining incomplete, however, in consequence of the disappearance of the author's manuscript after his death.

Fernandez-Guerra y Orbe, Aureliano (fer-nän'deth ger'ä ē or'bè). A Spanish poet, dramatist, and critic; born in Granada, June 16, 1816 (not 1817). A long life devoted to literary studies has resulted in 'The Lovers' Punishment' (1838), a comedy; 'Odes and Romances' (1842), a collection of verse; a critical edition of the works of Francisco de Quevedo; and many other performances as brilliant. D. 1894.

Fernandez-Guerra y Orbe, Luis. A Spanish dramatist and verse-writer, brother of Aureliano; born in Granada, April 11, 1818. The law was his first calling, but he wrote 'A Vow,' 'Her Highness's Hair-Dresser,' and other stage skits, and established himself in literature; producing much verse, and a highly prized critical work on the eminent dramatist Alarcon y Mendoza. He died Sept. 7, 1894.

Fernandez-Lizardi, José Joaquin (fer-nän'-deth lē-thär'dē). A distinguished Mexican novelist; born in the City of Mexico in 1771; died there, June 1827. His most famous work is 'Periquillo Sarniento' (1816; new ed., illustrated, 2 vols., 1884). He also published two novels, 'Sad Nights and Gala Days' (1823) and 'Life and Exploits of the Famous Knight Don Catrin de la Facheuda' (1832).

Fernández-Madrid, José. A South-American poet; born in Cartagena, Colombia, Feb. 9, 1789; died near London, England, June 28, 1829. He published a volume of poems, 'Las Rosas' (1822); also two tragedies, 'Atala' (1822) and 'Guatimozin' (1827).

Fernandez y Gonzalez, Manuel (fer-nän'-deth ē gōn-thä'leth). A Spanish poet and novelist; born at Seville, 1826; died Jan. 16, 1888. A boyhood in Granada and seven years' army service gave him varied experience of life and men. From 1846 he gave himself to literature; and the plays 'Struggling Against Fate' (1848); 'The Cid' (1858); 'A Duel on Time' (1859); 'Imperial Adventures' (1864), well constructed and full of humor, won great popularity. Among his more notable novels, which circulated widely, are: 'The Seven Children of Lara' (1862); 'The Bloody Queen' (1883); 'The Plantagenet Brothers' (1889).

Ferrand, Eduard (fe-roñ'), pseudonym of Eduard Schulz. A German poet and story-writer; born in Landsberg-on-the-Warta, Jan. 23, 1813; died in Berlin, Oct. 23, 1842. In various 'Poems' (1834), and collected 'Tales' (1835), and in 'Experiences of the Heart' (1839), he shows imaginativeness, and great susceptibility to love in all its exquisite emancipation from the practical.

Ferrari, Giuseppe (fer-rä'rē). An Italian historian and philosophical writer; born in Milan, 1812; died in Rome, July 1, 1876. Early trained to an unsparingly material and realistic standpoint, he became noted for the vigor and democratic impartiality of his 'On Error' (1840); 'Campanella's Religious Opinions' (1840); 'Machiavelli as Judge of the Revolutions of our Time' (1849); 'Philosophy of Revolutions' (1851); 'History of Italian Revolutions, or Guelphs and Ghibellines' (1856–58); etc.,—mostly happy in style, and profoundly influential in molding contemporary thought.

Ferrari, Paolo. An Italian dramatist; born at Modena, April 5, 1822; died March 9, 1889. His early comedies had little success; and his masterpiece, 'Goldoni and his Sixteen Comedies' (1852) was refused production for two years, but when acted won both a popular and a critical ovation. Its successor, 'Parini and Satire' (1857), gained equal favor. Among his others are : 'The Modern Tartuffe' (1862); 'Suicide' (1875); 'The Rival Friends' (1878); 'Antonietta' (1880); 'Fulvio Testi' (1889).

Ferrari, Severino. An Italian poet and scholar; born in Alberino, near Bologna, 1856. Much study and cunning workmanship are manifest in the verse collections 'For Him and His' (1876); 'New Stanzas' (1888); and in longer experiments.

Ferrazzi, Giuseppe Jacopo (fer-äts'ē). An Italian critic, essayist, and Dante scholar; born in Cartigliano, near Bassano, March 20, 1813; died at Bassano, 1887 (not 1881). He is best known for his invaluable 'Handbooks to Dante' (1865-77); but 'Torquato Tasso: a Biographical, Critical, and Bibliographical Study' (1880), and studies of Ariosto, besides an 'Italian Anthology' (1858-59), would in themselves make him a conspicuous literary figure.

Ferreira, Antonio. A celebrated Portuguese poet and dramatist; born at Lisbon in 1528; died of the plague in 1569. He held a professorship at the University of Coimbra, subsequently became judge of the supreme court at Lisbon. During his leisure he composed sonnets, odes, and epigrams, which earned for him the title of the "Portuguese Horace." His high literary reputation, however, is due to his 'Epistles' and the tragedy of 'Inez de Castro,' the second regular tragedy produced in Europe. The subject is a popular Portuguese legend; the play is modeled upon the Greek tragic drama.

Ferreira de Vasconcellos, Jorge (fer-rā'ē-rä dä vas''kon-sel'ösh). A Portuguese dramatist; died 1585. His prose comedies, 'Euphrosyne' (1560), 'Usilippo' (1618), 'Aulegraphia' (1619), are strictly national, and are valuable both philologically and for the proverbs in which they abound. He wrote also a romance of chivalry, 'The Triumph of Sagramor' (1567).

Ferreras, Juan de (fer-rā'ras). A Spanish historian and poetaster; born in Labañeza, June 7, 1652; died (probably) near Madrid, June 8, 1735. He was a scholarly and respected priest, whose careful 'History of Spain' (1700-27) is authoritative for the period prior to 1598; his 'Poems' (1726) are less important.

Ferrero Guglielmo, an Italian historian, born at Portici, in 1871; wrote the brilliant works 'The Greatness and Decline of Rome,' and 'Characters and Events of Roman History' (1901). This work, a departure in historical writing, consists of a series of studies of ancient Rome's great men and women, and of critical moments and events in Roman history. He, in 1909, delivered a course of lectures in the United States.

Ferreyra de la Cerda, Bernarda (fer-rī'rä dä lä ther'dä). A Portuguese poet; (1595-1644). She became, when a little more than twenty, a cherished verse and play writer, of pleasing style and great beauty of diction and imagery. 'Liberated Spain,' a sort of poetic history, exemplifies her merits.

Ferrier, Susan Edmonstone. A Scotch novelist (1782-1854). She wrote three tales: 'Marriage' (1818); 'The Inheritance' (1824); 'Destiny' (1831). In them is seen a faithful and spirited delineation of Scotch character; and her pages are illumined by a genial wit and a quick sense of the ludicrous.

Ferrigni, Piero Francesco Leopoldo Coccoluto (fer-ēn'yē). An Italian journalist, and topical and descriptive writer; born in Livorno (Leghorn), Nov. 15, 1836. A genius for throwing literary flash-lights on the subjects of the day has made him a prodigious favorite; among the many stepping-stones to his popularity being 'Among Pictures and Statues' (1872); 'See Naples and . . .'; 'Up and Down in Florence' (1877); 'The King Is Dead' (1878); 'Jousts and Tourneys'. D. 1895.

Ferris, George Titus. An American writer on music and musicians. His works include: 'Great German Composers' (1879); 'Great Italian and French Composers' (1879); 'Great Singers' (1880-81); 'Great Violinists and Pianists' (1881).

Ferry, Gabriel (fe-rē'), the Elder, pseudonym of Eugène Louis Gabriel Ferry de Bellemare. A French story-teller (1809-52). His stories appeared first serially in the Revue des Deux Mondes. He made repeated voyages to America: in his last voyage, to California, he lost his life in the burning at sea of the ship Amazon. Among his tales are: 'The Woodranger'; 'Hunting with Cossacks'; 'Costal the Indian'; 'Scenes of Military Life in Mexico'; 'The Squatters.'

Ferry, Gabriel, the Younger. A French dramatist and novelist, son of Gabriel the Elder and continuing his pseudonym; born in Paris, May 30, 1846. He has produced plays,—'Réginah' (1874), being one of the best; while his miscellaneous prose includes 'The Last Years of Alexandre Dumas, 1864-70' (1883); 'Balzac and his (Feminine) Friends' (1888); and 'The Exploits of Cæsar: A Parisian Novel' (1889); 'The Last Days of King-Sun' (1896).

Fessenden, Thomas Green. An American who wrote partly under the name "Christopher Caustic"; born in Walpole, N. H., April 22 1771; died in Boston, Mass., Nov. 11, 1837. He graduated from Dartmouth. While in college he wrote a ballad, 'Jonathan's Courtship.' He went to London in 1801, and while there published anonymously a satirical poem, 'Terrible Tractoration' (1803). He returned to the United States; did literary work in New York; went to Boston and founded the New England Farmer (1822). Some of his publications were 'The American Clerk's Companion' (1815), 'The Ladies' Monitor' (1818); and 'Laws of Patents for New Inventions' (1822).

Feszler, Ignaz Aurelius (fes'ler). A Hungarian historian and novelist (1756-1839). A Capuchin priest, his secret communication to Joseph II. in 1781 regarding the monasteries brought about a radical reformation of them. Appointed professor of Oriental languages in the Vienna University, he had to leave the post and Austria for his atheistic and seditious tragedy 'Sidney' (1787); similar reasons cost him a professorship in the Alexander Nevsky Academy of St. Petersburg; afterward he became general superintendent of the Lutheran congregations in that city. He wrote the historical novels 'Marcus Aurelius' (1790); 'Aristides and Themistocles' (1792); 'Matthias Corvinus' (1793); 'Attila' (1794). His greatest work is a 'History of Hungary' (10 vols., 1812–25). He wrote voluminously on Freemasonry, and published an interesting autobiography, 'A Review of my Seventy Years' Pilgrimage' (1826).

Fet, A. (fet), pseudonym of Afanasy Afanasievitch Shenshin. A Russian poet; born in Orel, Dec. 5, 1820; died at Moscow, Dec. 4, 1892. A versifier almost from his cradle, he made himself noted in early manhood by his many charming poems: his most enduring fame resting upon the collection called 'Evenings and Nights' (1883), although versions of Horace, Juvenal, Goethe, and even Shakespeare, show his scholarly and literary attainments.

Fétis, François Joseph (fā-tēs'). A Belgian composer and authority on music; born at Mons, March 25, 1784; died in Brussels, March 26, 1871. His music is admired for original harmony and a sympathetic interpretation of emotion; and his writings, especially the 'History of Music' (1868) and 'Biography and Bibliography of Music and Musicians' (1837), are respected by experts.

Feuchtersleben, Baron Ernst von (foïch'-ters-lā"ben). An Austrian poet and physician; born at Vienna, April 29, 1806; died there, Sept. 3, 1849. In medicine he stood in the foremost rank as a practitioner; and his works, especially on psychiatry, were widely read for authority and lucid exposition. Among his 'Poems' (1836) is the lyric—now become a popular melody—"It stands in God's decrees" (Es ist bestimmt in Gottes Rat).

Feuerbach, Anselm (foi'er-bäch). A German archæologist, brother of Ludwig; born Sept. 9, 1798; died Sept. 8, 1851. His 'Vatican Apollo' (1833), and essays and studies in classic art and art history, are of great merit and importance.

Feuerbach, Ludwig Andreas. A noted German philosopher; born in Landshut, July 28, 1804; died in the Reichenberg, near Nuremberg, Sept. 13, 1872. He was a Hegelian and materialist whose opinions hindered a professional career, and who devoted himself to metaphysics in retirement; but in his masterpiece, 'The Essence of Christianity' (4th ed. 1883), he is no longer a Hegelian. In his 'Theogonie' (2d ed. 1866), he deals with worship from the historical standpoint.

Feuerbach, Paul Johann Anselm von. An eminent German criminalist and reformer of the penal laws; born in Hainichen, near Jena, Nov. 14, 1775; died at Frankfort-on-the-Main, May 29, 1833. He is at his best in: 'Review of the Fundamental Principles and Ideals of Penal Law' (1799); 'Exposition of Remarkable Crimes' (1828); 'Kaspar Hauser: An Instance of a Crime against a Soul' (1832).

Feuillet, Octave (fė-yā'). A distinguished French novelist; born at St. Lô, Aug. 11, 1821; died at Paris, Dec. 29, 1890. 'The Great Old Man' (1845) was his first story; but the 'Romance of a Poor Young Man' (1858), which

was dramatized, first made him famous. Among his numerous other novels are: 'The History of Sibylla' (1862), a romance of mysticism; 'Julia de Trécœur' (1872), dramatized as 'The Sphinx'; 'A Marriage in High Life' (1875); 'Story of a Parisienne'; 'La Morte' (1886). He was also a successful playwright: 'Montjoye' (1863) mirrored the moral rottenness of the Second Empire. He was elected to the Academy in 1863. Beginning as a young-girls' novelist of the discreetest sort, he ended in much the usual French fashion.

Feuillet de Conches, Baron Félix Sébastien (fė-yā dė kôñsh). A French writer of biographical and historical miscellany; born in Paris, Dec. 4, 1798; died there, Feb. 6, 1887. Literary criticism is the mother of 'Metaphysical Meditations and Correspondence of Malebranche' (1841) and 'Léopold Robert: His Life, Labors, and Letters' (1849); while a gossipy fluency imparts interest to 'An Old Child's Tales' (1860) and a 'History of the English School of Painting' (1883).

Féval, Paul (fā-väl'). A notable French novelist; born at Rennes, Sept. 27, 1817; died at Paris, March 8, 1887. His first story, 'The Seals' Club' (1841), and others, having given him some note, he was offered a large sum to write, under the pseudonym "Francis Trollope" (as though an Englishman), a sensational story 'The Mysteries of London,' after the manner of Sue's 'Mysteries of Paris.' It was done in 11 vols., was immensely successful, widely translated, and put on the stage. He remained a very fertile, spirited, and popular writer, often dramatized, with long runs. Especially successful were: 'The Son of the Devil' (1847); 'The Hunchback' (1858); 'Mrs. Gil Blas'; 'The Last Man Alive' (1873); 'The Wonders of Mt. St. Michael' (1879).

Feydeau, Ernest (fā-dō'). A French novelist (1821–73). His ill-famed story 'Fanny' (1858) had an unprecedented success. It was followed by 'Daniel' (1859); 'Catherine d'Overmeire' (1860); 'Sylvie' (1861); and 'A Début at the Opera' (1863). Of his later works one only had any marked success, 'The Countess de Chalis, or the Morals of our Day' (1868). He tried, but with little success, to write for the stage. He repeatedly felt the need of rebutting the charge of indecency: 'On the Luxury of Women; on Morals, Literature, and Virtue' (1866) is an elaborate apologia.

Ffraid, I. D., pseudonym of John Evans. A Welsh poet and essayist; born at Ty Mawr, Llansantffraid yn Nghonwy, July 23, 1814; died there (?), March 4, 1876. He wrote brilliant papers for the Baner and other journals; while his 'Mixed Poems' (Difyrwch Bechgyn Glanau Conwy) (1835) aroused general admiration.

Fibiger, Johannes Henrik Tauber (fib'ē-ger). A Danish poet; born at Nykjöbing, Jan. 27, 1821. He wrote dramas founded on Biblical history,—'Jephtha's Daughter' (1849); 'Jeremiah' (1850); 'John the Baptist' (1857); also a few secular tragedies, the most notable among them being 'Cross and Love' (1858) and 'The Everlasting Struggle' (1866); and a narrative poem in 16 cantos, 'The Gray Friars' (1882).

Fichte, Immanuel Hermann von (fich'te). A German philosopher, son of Johann; born in Jena, July 18, 1796; died in Stuttgart, Aug. 8, 1879. He was a mystic theist, but tried to frame a compromise which should not exclude disbelief in a supreme being. 'Speculative Theology' (1847); 'System of Ethics' (1850); and 'The Soul Question: A Philosophic Confession' (1859), are his typical works.

Fichte, Johann Gottlieb. A celebrated German philosopher; born at Rammenau in Upper Lusatia, May 19, 1762; died at Berlin, Jan. 27, 1814. He wrote his treatise 'Essay toward a Critique of All Revelation' (1792) as a "letter of introduction" to Kant. He was appointed professor of philosophy in the University of Jena in 1794; and the following year published his 'Doctrine of Science,' a fundamental departure from Kant. Of his philosophical writings the most important are: 'The Doctrine of Science' (1794); 'Foundations of the Whole Doctrine of Science' (1794); 'Introduction to the Doctrine of Science' (1798); 'System of Moral Doctrine' (1798); 'Man's Destiny' (1800).

Field, Mrs. Caroline Leslie (Whitney). An American writer, daughter of Mrs. A. D. T. Whitney; born at Milton, Mass., Nov. 10, 1853; died there Dec. 1, 1902. Her works are: 'High Lights' (1885), a novel; 'The Unseen King, and Other Verses' (1887).

Field, Eugene. An American poet and humorous journalist; born at St. Louis, Mo., Sept. 2, 1850; died Nov. 4, 1895. His latter years were spent in Chicago. By his poems and tales in the press he won a high reputation in the West, which before his death had become national. His poems for children are admirable in their simplicity and in their sympathetic insight into the child's world of thought and feeling. His complete works comprise: 'Love Songs of Childhood'; 'A Little Book of Western Verse'; 'A Second Book of Verse'; 'The Holy Cross, and Other Tales'; 'The Love Affairs of a Bibliomaniac.' He made, in collaboration with his brother Roswell Martin Field, some good translations from Horace — 'Echoes from the Sabine Farm.'

Field, Henry Martyn. An American clergyman and scholar; born in Stockbridge, Mass., April 3, 1822. He is a graduate of Williams College, and was ordained to the ministry in 1842. In 1854 he became editor and proprietor of the New York Evangelist. He has been a lifelong traveler. Among his works are: 'Summer Pictures from Copenhagen to Venice' (1859); 'History of the Atlantic Telegraph' (1866); 'From the Lakes of Killarney to the Golden Horn' (1876); 'From Egypt to Japan' (1878); 'On the Desert' (1883); 'Among the Holy Hills' (1883); 'The Greek Islands and Turkey after the War' (1885); 'Our West-

ern Archipelago'; 'The Barbary Coast'; 'Old Spain and New Spain'; 'Gibraltar'; 'Bright Skies and Dark Shadows'; 'The Story of the Atlantic Cable.' Died Jan. 26, 1907.

Field, Kate. [Mary Katherine Kemble.] An American author and lecturer; born in St. Louis, Mo., about 1840; died in Honolulu, Hawaii, May 19, 1896. During several years she was European correspondent of the New York Tribune and other journals. She founded Kate Field's Washington (1889), in Washington, D. C. Among her books are: 'Planchette's Diary' (1868); 'Ten Days in Spain' (1875); 'History of Bell's Telephone'; 'Life of Fechter'; etc.

Field, Maunsell Bradhurst. An American prose and verse writer; born in New York city, March 26, 1822; died there, Jan. 24, 1875. Among his published works are a volume of poems (1869). In collaboration with G. P. R. James he wrote 'Adrian; or the Clouds of the Mind' (1852), and 'Memoirs of Many Men and Some Women' (1874).

Fielding, Henry. A celebrated English novelist; born at Sharpham Park, Somersetshire, April 22, 1707, of the blood of the Hapsburgs; died at Lisbon, Oct. 8, 1754. After ill success as playwright and lawyer he wrote 'The Adventures of Joseph Andrews' (1742), to burlesque Richardson's 'Pamela'; it grew in his hands into a strong novel of a new type, and his career and fame were determined. His masterpiece is 'Tom Jones; or the History of a Foundling' (1749). His last novel, 'Amelia' (1752), is characteristic of his sentiments rather than of his genius. 'The History of Jonathan Wild' is a piece of irony directed against the professors of conventional morality.

Fielding, Sarah. An English novelist, sister to Henry; born in East Stour, Dorsetshire, Nov. 8, 1710; died at Bath, 1768. Contemporaries adjudged her to show something like genius in her novels 'The Adventures of David Simple in Search of a Faithful Friend' (1744), and 'The Governess' (1749). She also did a few important biographies and translations.

Fields, Annie (Adams). An American poet and essayist, wife of James T. Fields; born in Boston, 1834. She has been a leader in charity organization and work. She published: 'Under the Olive,' poems (1881); 'Biography of James T. Fields' (1884); 'How to Help the Poor' (1885); 'The Singing Shepherd'; 'Authors and their Friends'; 'A Shelf of Old Books' (1896); 'Life and Letters of Harriet Beecher Stowe' (1897); 'Orpheus' (1900).

Fields, James Thomas. An American publisher and author; born in Portsmouth, N. H., Dec. 31, 1817; died in Boston, Mass., April 24, 1881. The various publishing firms of which he was partner, with Ticknor, Osgood, and others, were of the first rank. He edited the Atlantic Monthly in 1862-70; and was an acceptable lecturer on literary subjects and authors. He published: 'Poems' (1849); 'A Few Verses for a Few Friends' (1858); 'Yesterdays with Authors' (1872); 'Hawthorne' (1875); 'Old Acquaintance: Barry Cornwall and Some of his Friends' (1875); 'In and Out of Doors with Dickens' (1876); 'Underbrush' (1881), essays; 'Ballads and Other Verses' (1881); and (with Edwin P. Whipple) edited 'The Family Library of British Poetry' (1878).

Fiévée, Joseph (fyā-vā'). A French political writer and journalist; born in Paris, April 9, 1767; died there, May 7, 1839. His experiences during the French Revolution were not happy, largely in consequence of his work 'On the Necessity of a Religion' (1795); but the Napoleonic rule proved more favorable to him. He produced 'Suzette's Dowry' and 'Frederick,' two rather colorless fictions, besides a variety of historical works on aspects of the republic, consulate, and empire.

Figueroa, Cristóval Suarez de (fē-gä-rō'ä). A Spanish poet of the first half of the seventeenth century. His most celebrated poems are a translation of the 'Faithful Shepherd' (1602) of Guarini, and 'Constant Amaryllis' (1609). He wrote a history of 'The Deeds of Don Garcia Hurtado de Mendoza' (1613) in the wars with the Araucanians, interesting but written in an inflated style; also an epic, 'Spain Defended' (1612).

Figueroa, Francisco de. A Spanish poet (1540?-1620?). He was called by his contemporaries "the Divine Figueroa," and at Rome he won the poet's crown. He wrote verse with equal facility and elegance in Castilian and Italian. When dying he burned all his verses; but they were published — including the celebrated volume of eclogues in blank verse, the 'Tirsi'— from copies in the hands of his friends.

Figueroa, Francisco. A Mexican annalist, diarist, and theologian; born in Toluca, 1730 (?); died in the City of Mexico, 1800 (?). He was a Franciscan priest, and taught and lectured well; but his great service to literature consisted in the compilation of materials for a history of Mexico, among them a 'History of the Conquest of New Galicia,' by Mota Padilla, besides diaries and letters.

Figueroa, Francisco Acuña de. A Uruguayan poet; born in Montevideo, 1791; died there, Oct. 6, 1862. A civil-service post afforded him leisure to prepare his 'Poetic Mosaic' (1857), a verse collection, and his more notable 'Paraphrases of the Psalms,' and 'The Toráidas,' a series of Paraguayan notes. He has been assigned a high rank by competent European critics; lofty inspiration and sonorous diction being his characteristics, exemplified in the 'National Hymn of Uruguay.'

Figuier, Guillaume Louis. A French scientific writer; born at Montpellier, Feb. 15, 1819; died at Paris, Nov. 9, 1894. He has done much for the popularization of science as editor of the scientific column of the Presse, and as author of 'The Exposition and History of the

Principal Modern Scientific Discoveries' (1851-53); 'Alchemy and Alchemists' (1854); 'Great Ancient and Modern Inventions' (1864, 3d ed.); 'The Earth before the Deluge' (1866, 5th ed.); 'Lives of Illustrious Savants' (1866); 'Marvels of Science' (1867-69).

Fileti - Ramondetta, Concettina (fē-lä'tē-ra-mon-det'tä). An Italian poet; born (Ramondetta) in Palermo, Dec. 31, 1830. Although of a distinguished family, her childhood was passed in comparative poverty, and she had little formal schooling. Her talent was precocious, and at sixteen she wrote verses which captivated the public. Becoming a wife and mother, however,— with ten children at that,— her association with the Muse has been intermittent in recent years; but she has made even this of some literary service, as in her later 'Poems' (1887).

Filicaja, Vincenzo da (fē-lē-kä'yä). A distinguished Italian poet (1642-1707). He lived several years in retirement, devoted to political study and composition, but publishing nothing till 1684, when appeared his grand odes on the rescue of Vienna from the Turks, which won for him the admiration of all Italy, and honorable notice on the part of the Emperor Leopold and King John Sobieski of Poland. Queen Christina of Sweden named him a member of her newly founded Academy. In depth and nobility of thought, in beauty of expression, and in the melodiousness of his verse, Filicaja is one of the foremost lyrists of Italy; nevertheless he trusts perhaps too much to art and less to nature and inspiration.

Filon, Auguste (fē-lôn'). A French historian; born in Paris, June 7, 1800; died there, Dec. 1, 1875. A commanding point of view and an alluring style are conspicuous throughout his 'Comparative History of France and England' (1832); 'The Spiritual Power in its Relations with the State' (1844); 'History of the Roman Senate' (1850); 'History of the Athenian Democracy' (1854); and several other important works.

Finch, Francis Miles. An American poet, and a judge of the U. S. District Court; born in Ithaca, N. Y., June 9, 1827. He graduated at Yale; and is the author of the well-known lyrics 'Nathan Hale' and 'The Blue and the Gray,' and a popular college song beginning "Floating away like the fountain's spray." Died 1907.

Finck, Henry Theophilus. An American musical critic and author; born in Bethel, Mo., Sept. 22, 1854. He graduated at Harvard in 1876; and from 1878 to 1881 studied physiological psychology at Berlin, Heidelberg, and Vienna. He is musical critic of the New York Evening Post, and a contributor to the Nation. His works include: 'Wagner and Other Musicians' (1887); 'Romantic Love and Personal Beauty' (1887); 'The Pacific Coast Scenic Tour' (1890); 'Chopin, and Other Musical Essays'; 'Lotos Time in Japan' (1895); and 'Spain and Morocco'; 'Edward Grieg' (1905).

Finlay, George. An English historian of the first rank; born in Faversham, Kent, of Scotch blood, Dec. 21, 1799; died in Athens, Greece, Jan. 26, 1875. An ardent Philhellene, he joined Byron's company at Missolonghi in 1823 to assist in liberating Greece from the Turks; and ended by residing there permanently,—at first a cultivator, and then a student of and writer upon Greek history. He was for many years the Athens correspondent of the London Times. His 'Greece under the Romans, B. C. 146 to A. D. 717' (1844) raised him at once to a place among the few foremost historians: Edward A. Freeman declared it to be the most truly original historical work of modern times; and for sound broad humanity, acute judgment, and luminous common-sense on both the practical and the philosophic sides of history, it has few equals of any age. It is not in the form of detailed annals except in the last part, most of it being a set of essays on the political and social conditions of Greece as a subject province. Succeeding volumes carried the story more in detail down to modern times, ending with two volumes on the Greek Revolution. The whole, revised and some volumes wholly rewritten by the author, was published posthumously in 7 vols. (1877).

Finley, John. An American poet; born at Brownsburg, Va., Jan. 11, 1797; died in Richmond, Ind., Dec. 23, 1866. He was one of the editors of the Richmond Palladium, 1831–34. His poems were collected in one volume, 'The Hoosier's Nest, and Other Poems' (1865).

Finley, Martha. An American novelist; born in Chillicothe, O., April 26, 1828. She is the author, under the name of "Martha Farquharson," of a number of novels, including 'Elsie Dinsmore' (1868); 'Wanted — A Pedigree' (1872); and 'The Thorn in the Nest' (1886). She has written in all over twenty 'Elsie Books,' as well as 'The Mildred Books,' etc.

Finotti, Joseph Maria. An American clergyman and author; born at Ferrara, Italy, in 1817; died at Denver, Col., in 1879. He studied theology in the Jesuit College, Rome, and in 1845 removed to the United States. He was ordained priest, and stationed at Alexandria, Va. In 1852 he left the Jesuit Society and became literary editor of the Boston Pilot. His health having failed, he removed to Cincinnati, and afterwards to Omaha, and to Central City, Col. His works include: 'A Month of Mary' (1853); 'Italy in the Fifteenth Century'; 'The French Zouave' (1863); 'American Catholic Bibliography' (unfinished).

Firdausi or **Firdusi** (fēr-dou'sē). A celebrated Persian poet who lived from about 935 to about 1020. He is the greatest of Persian epic poets. In 1010, after 35 years of labor, was completed his first heroic epic, the 'Shāh-Nāmah' (King's Book) in about 60,000 distichs: it recounts the ancient Persian traditions of heroism. His other great poem, 'Jussuf and Zulīkha,' a religious-romantic epos, is founded on the Biblical story of Joseph and Potiphar's wife. There are English translations of sundry passages from the 'Shāh-Nāmah,' and a German translation of the whole of the 'Jussuf and Zulīkha.'

Firenzuola, Agnolo (fē-rents-wō'lä). [Properly Girolamo Giovannini.] An Italian poet; born in Florence, Sept. 28, 1493; died at Prato or in Rome, about 1545. His works consist of burlesque poems; two comedies, including 'The Shining Ones'; a translation of Apuleius's 'Golden Ass'; a didactic story, 'Discourses about Animals'; 'Dialogue on the Beauties of Women'; and ten "novels," mostly stories in the vein of Boccaccio. He writes in a style of great elegance, but with unpardonable lubricity.

Firmenich-Richartz, Johannes Matthias (fēr'men-ich-rich'ärts). A German poet, philological literary critic and student, and dramatist; born in Cologne, July 5, 1808; died in Potsdam, May 10, 1889. His play 'Clotilde Montalvi' (1840), a romantic tragedy, and 'After a Hundred Years,' a humorous composition in dialogue, as well as poems in various languages, are highly meritorious; but his monumental achievement is 'Germany's Folk-Voices: A Collection of German Dialect Poems, Songs, Fables, Sagas, etc.' (1843–66, sup. 1868), showing the most profound learning and scholarly acuteness.

Fischart, Johann (fish'ärt). A famous German satirist (about 1545–91). He took the doctor's degree in the University of Basel 1574, and afterward was an official of the Imperial Chamber of Justice at Spires. The period of his literary production lies between 1575 and 1581, while he assisted his brother-in-law Jobin, who had a printing-office in Strasburg. He was a man of deep patriotic feeling, a notable poet, and the greatest Protestant publicist of his time. Among his compositions in verse may be mentioned: 'The Jester in Rhyme,' a satire on the Dominicans and Franciscans (1571); 'Description of the Four-Cornered Hat' (1580), against the Jesuits; the 'Flöhhatz Weibertratz' (1573), in which he describes a contest at law between fleas and women; 'Podagramic Book of Consolation' (1577), showing how the gout (podagra) spares the laboring poor and kindly chastens the rich, while leaving their minds free for wit and humor; 'The Hive of the Holy Roman Swarm' (1579). In imitation of Rabelais's 'Gargantua,' but giving free play to his own native humor and wit, he wrote of 'The Wondrous Deeds, Thoughts, and Words of the Famous Heroes and Lords Grandgusier, Gargantua, and Pantagruel' (1575). Here, in full accord with the spirit of the Reformation, he "contrasts the sound human understanding with the vagaries of idealism, the common people's bluntness and uncouthness with the aristocratic-romantic perversity of the upper class"; all the while glorifying intellectual progress. As a treasury of ingeniously contrived word compounds the work is of great value to the philologist.

Fischer, Johann Georg (fish′er). German poet; born at Gross Süssen, Oct. 25, 1816; died at Stuttgart, May 4, 1897. His lyric poems are in 8 vols. (1854–91). He excels in popular songs and ballads; he has the gift of combining humor with gravity. In his love songs he nobly idealizes nature and passion. He wrote four dramas: 'Saul' (1862); 'Frederic II. of Hohenstaufen' (1863); 'Florian Geyer' (1866); 'Emperor Maximilian of Mexico' (1868). In 'From Bird Life' (1863) he notes the characteristic phenomena of the psychic life of animals with the acuteness of a naturalist and the sympathy of a poet.

Fischer, Kuno. A German historian of philosophy; born at Sandewalde, in Silesia, July 23, 1824. He was interdicted from teaching philosophy at Heidelberg in 1853; but after filling professorships in Berlin and Jena, he had the satisfaction of being called to the chair of philosophy at Heidelberg in 1872. He is of the school of Hegel. His principal writings are: 'Diotima: The Idea of the Beautiful' (1849); 'Logic and Metaphysic, or the Doctrine of Science' (1852); 'History of Modern Philosophy' (8 vols., 1852–93), his greatest work, written in the form of brilliant monographs on Descartes, Kant, Fichte, Schelling, and other great philosophers down to Schopenhauer; 'Francis Bacon and his Successors' (1856); 'Lessing's Nathan the Wise' (1864); 'Spinoza's Life and Character' (1865); 'Origin and Evolution-Forms of Wit' (1871). D. July 4, 1907.

Fisher, George Park. An American divine and writer; born in Wrentham, Mass., Aug. 10, 1827; became professor of divinity at Yale (1854), and professor of ecclesiastical history (1861). Included in his works are: 'Essays on the Supernatural Origin of Christianity'; 'History of the Reformation' (1873); 'Faith and Rationalism' · (1879); 'Outlines of Universal History'; 'History of the Christian Church' (1888); 'Nature and Method of Revelation' (1890); 'Colonial History of the United States.'

Fiske, Daniel Willard, scholar and librarian; born in Ellisburg, Jefferson County, N. Y., Nov. 11, 1831; was educated at Hamilton College, N. Y., and Upsala University, Sweden. He was secretary of the New York Geographical Society, and attached to the American Legation at Vienna under Motley. He is an adept in many modern languages; in 1869 was made professor of North-European languages, and librarian, at Cornell; and has been a voluminous contributor to Swedish, German, Icelandic, Italian, English, and American journals. He has made the largest existing collections of Icelandic and of Petrarch, and the largest in America of Dante. He is now engaged in trying to create a written Egyptian language.

Fiske, John. A famous American historian; born at Hartford Conn., March 30, 1842; died at E. Gloucester, Mass., July 4, 1901. He graduated at Harvard College in 1863, and studied law, but never practiced. He was lecturer on philosophy at Harvard, and in 1872–79 assistant librarian. He wrote 'Myths and Myth-Makers' (1872); 'Outlines of Cosmic Philosophy' (2 vols., 1875), his principal work, in which he gives an exposition of the philosophy of natural evolution; 'The Unseen World' (1876); 'Darwinism' (1879); 'The Idea of God' (1885). On phases of American history, he has written: 'American Political Ideas' (1885); 'The Critical Period of American History, 1783–89' (1888); 'The Beginnings of New England' (1889); 'The American Revolution' (3 vols., 1891); 'Discovery of America' (2 vols., 1892).

Fitch, William Clyde. An American playwright and author; born in 1865. He was educated at Hartford, Conn., and Amherst College, Amherst, Mass. He has written and adapted a number of successful plays, among them 'Beau Brummell' and 'Bohemia.' He is also the author of 'The Knighting of the Twins, and Ten Other Tales' (1891); 'Some Correspondence and Six Conversations'; 'The Truth'; 'The Woman in the Case'; 'The Straight Road'; 'The Girl who has Everything'; 'The Blue Mouse.' He died Sept. 4, 1909.

Fitts, James Franklin. An American journalist and novelist; (1840–1890). Of his novels the most popular were: 'The Parted Veil'; 'A Version'; 'A Modern Miracle'; 'Captain Kidd's Gold.'

Fitzgerald, Edward. A great English poet; born at Bredfield House, near Suffolk, March 31, 1809; died June 14, 1883. (Fitzgerald was his mother's family name, assumed by his father John Purcell.) His writings are mostly remodeled translations of foreign poems; among them are versions of 'Six Dramas from Calderon' (1853), and two more, and far finer ('The Mighty Magician' and 'Such Stuff as Dreams are Made Of') subsequently; 'The Rubáiyát of Omar Khayyám' (1859), which ultimately won him assured immortality, though at first published anonymously and utterly neglected; Æschylus's 'Agamemnon' and Sophocles's 'Œdipus' plays, and part of Attár's 'Bird Parliament.'

Fitzgerald, Percy Hethrington. A pleasing Irish novelist and biographical essayist; born in Fane Valley, Louth, Ireland, 1834. He wrote: 'The Romance of the English Stage' (1874); 'Lives of the Sheridans' (1887); and of novels, 'Never Forgotten,' 'Diana Gay,' 'Bella Donna,' 'Dear Girl,' etc.

Fitzpatrick, William John. An Irish biographer and topical historian; born in Dublin Aug. 31, 1830; died there, Dec. 24, 1895. From his graduation at the Catholic College, Clongowes Wood, he devoted himself to the study of Ireland's rights and wrongs, and of the actors in Irish history. 'Lord Edward Fitzgerald and his Betrayers' (1859); 'The Sham Squire and the Informers of 1798' (1866); and 'Daniel O'Connell, the Liberator' (1888), are a few among his many widely read productions.

Flagg, Edmund. An American novelist and journalist; born in Wiscasset, Me., Nov. 24,

1815. He was the author of a number of novels and other prose writings. His best work is 'Venice, the City of the Sea' (2 vols., 1853). He contributed to the New World Magazine seven historical romances, based on the dramas of Victor Hugo. 'Edmond Dantès,' a sequel to 'Monte Cristo,' was written by him, as also was 'Mary Tudor.' He died in 1890.

Flagg, Wilson. An American naturalist, scientific and political writer; born in Beverly, Mass., Nov. 5, 1805; died in North Cambridge, Mass., May 6, 1884. Some of his books are: 'Studies in the Field and Forest' (1857); 'Halcyon Days'; 'A Year among the Trees' (1881); and 'A Year among the Birds.'

Flammarion, Camille (flä-mä-rē-ôn'). A French astronomer, writer on descriptive astronomy, and "astronomical novelist"; born in Montigny-le-Roi, Feb. 25, 1842. He was designed by his parents for the Church, but went over to science, and by a long course of writings of a more or less popular character has made his name widely known. 'The Plurality of Inhabited Worlds' (1862); 'Celestial Wonders' (1865); 'The Atmosphere' (1872); 'Urania' (1889); and 'The Planet Mars and its Habitability' (1892), are his best-known works, not to mention an experiment or two in "romance" of the "astronomical creation."

Flash, Henry Lynden. An American writer of verse; born in Cincinnati, O., Jan. 20, 1835. He is the author of 'Poems' (1860), and of many popular ballads which appeared during the Civil War.

Flassan, Gaétan Raxis, Count de (fläs-än'). A French diplomatist and historian of diplomacy; born at Bedouin, Venaissin, 1770; died in Paris, March 20, 1845. His career in the diplomatic service was fairly distinguished, enabling him to gather material for a valuable 'History of French Diplomacy from the Foundation of the Monarchy to Aug. 10, 1792' (1808–11), and one or two works of less importance.

Flaubert, Gustav (flō-bär'). A distinguished French novelist; born at Rouen, Dec. 12, 1821; died there, May 8, 1880. His greatest novel was his first, 'Madame Bovary' (1857). He next wrote a historical novel, 'Salammbô,' the scene laid in the most flourishing period of Carthage,—a splendid description of ancient Punic life, but having lively interest as a story; 'The History of a Young Man' (1869), like 'Madame Bovary' a pessimistic picture of social life; 'The Temptation of St. Anthony' (1874), a piece of imaginative writing dealing with philosophical problems; and 'Three Stories' (1877), which had a favorable reception. The posthumous novel 'Bouvard and Pécuchet' (1881) is a satire on humanity in general. His comedy 'The Candidate' (1874) failed on the stage.

Fléchier, Esprit (flā-shyā'). A notable French pulpit orator and writer; born at Pernes, in the Venaissin, June 10, 1632; died at Montpellier, Feb. 16, 1710. His funeral orations, especially those on Montausier and Turenne, are models of elegiac oratory. He wrote a 'History of Theodosius the Great' (1679); 'Panegyrics of Saints' (1690); 'History of Cardinal Ximenes' (1693).

Fleming, George. See **Fletcher, Julia.**

Fleming, Mrs. May Agnes (Early). A Canadian story-writer; born in New Brunswick, 1840; died 1880. She was a prolific author of romances, mostly sensational, among them being: 'Guy Earlscourt's Wife'; 'Lost for a Woman'; 'Pride and Passion'; etc.

Fleming, Paul (flem'ing). A distinguished German poet; born at Hartenstein in Saxony, Oct. 5, 1609; died at Hamburg, April 2, 1640. As an attaché of an embassy to Russia and Persia, he had an opportunity (1635–39) of studying many peoples. His 'German Poems,' which appeared in 1642, were often republished. His poetry is a true reflection of his inmost thought: he is seen to be a man of unsophisticated tastes, of childlike piety, and yet of virile sense and passion.

Fletcher, Giles. An English clergyman and poet, cousin to John; born in London about 1580; died at Alderton in 1623. His only notable composition was a sacred poem entitled 'Christ's Victorie and Triumph in Heaven and Earth over and after Death' (1610), rich in imagery and descriptions of natural scenery. Parts of it were utilized by Milton in his 'Paradise Regained.'

Fletcher, John. An English dramatist; born in Rye, Sussex, in December 1579; died in London during the plague, in August 1625. His partnership with Beaumont is called by Swinburne "the most perfect union in genius and friendship." 'The Woman Hater,' published anonymously in 1607 and usually accorded to Fletcher, Swinburne and Bullen assign to Beaumont. Fletcher survived his friend nine years, during which he produced many plays with and without collaborators; the latter include Massinger, Middleton, Rowley, Shirley, and others. It is certain that he wrote alone 'The Faithful Shepherdess,' 'Bonduca,' 'Valentinian,' 'The Wild Goose Chase,' and 'Monsieur Thomas,' his greatest works; 'Rule a Wife and Have a Wife'; 'The Loyal Subject'; 'Wit Without Money'; 'A Wife for a Month'; 'The Chances'; 'The Mad Lover'; and 'The Humorous Lieutenant.' Bullen, the most authoritative critic of Elizabethan literature, says he had Massinger's aid in 'The Knight of Malta,' 'Thierry and Theodoret,' 'The Little French Lawyer,' 'The Beggar's Bush,' 'The Spanish Curate,' 'The False One,' and 'A Very Woman.' The same authority gives 'The Queen of Corinth' with Massinger, Rowley, and Middleton; 'The Jeweller of Amsterdam' with Massinger and Field; 'The Bloody Brother' with Ben Jonson, revised by Middleton; 'Two Noble Kinsmen' with Massinger, after Shakespeare's death; and considers 'Henry VIII.' the work of Fletcher and Massinger with Shakespearean passages.

Fletcher, Julia Constance. ["George Fleming."] An American novelist; born in Indianapolis, ――――, 1858, daughter of James C. Fletcher, who was a missionary to Brazil and wrote 'Brazil and the Brazilians.' Among her novels are: 'Kismet' (1877); 'The Head of the Medusa' (1880); 'Andromeda' (1885); 'The Truth about Clement Ker' (1889) ; 'For Plain Women Only'; 'The Canary.'

Fleury, Claude (flĕ-rē'). A French Church historian and pedagogue; born in Paris, Dec. 6, 1640; died there (?), July 14, 1723. His learning and unaffected simplicity made him a notable figure at the court of Louis XIV., and later at that of Louis XV., whose confessor he became. An 'Ecclesiastical History' (1691–1720) forms his claim to enduring renown; the work coming down to 1414, at which point a later writer has attempted, although not sympathetically, to round out the master's performance. 'A History of French Law' (1674) and a 'Historical Catechism' (1679) are less important achievements.

Fleury-Husson, Jules. See **Champfleury.**

Flint, Timothy. An American clergyman and miscellaneous writer; born in North Reading, Mass., July 11, 1780; died in Salem, Mass., Aug. 16, 1840. He was a Congregational minister during 1812–14; subsequently he devoted himself to editorial work, descriptive writing, and fiction. In these departments his most important work is included in: 'The Geography and History of the Mississippi Valley'; 'Indian Wars in the West'; and in fiction, 'Francis Berrian'; 'George Mason'; and 'The Shoshone Valley.'

Floquet, Pierre Amable (flō-kā'). A French historian and biographical writer; born in Rouen, July 9, 1797; died in Formentin, Aug. 6, 1881. He made Normandy's annals and personages the objects of his painstaking study in 'Norman Anecdotes'; 'History of the Parliament of Normandy' (1840–43); 'Studies in the Life of Bossuet' (1855); of which the last two were crowned by the Academy. Subsequent volumes show the rich harvest the field has yielded him.

Florez, Henrique (flō'reth). A Spanish historian and antiquarian; born in Valladolid, Feb. 14, 1701; died in Madrid, Aug. 20, 1773. He was an Augustinian ordinary who taught theology and history with brilliant success, and charmed his classes by presenting dogmas and annals from the standpoint of their human interest. 'Sacred Spain' (1747–73), on the history and dominion of the Church in the peninsula, brought down to the present time by a recent writer; 'Memorials of Catholic Queens'; and other works of importance, justify the high opinion entertained of him.

Florian, Jean Pierre Claris de (flō-ryoṅ'). A French poet and romancer (1755–94). At 10 he captivated Voltaire by his quick repartee and sprightliness. He made his début with some pleasing farces (1779), and added greatly to his fame with the two pastoral stories 'Galatea' (1783) and 'Estelle' (1787); but both are sentimental romances in the dominant taste of that time. A like judgment is to be passed on his metrical romances 'Numa Pompilius' (1786) and 'Gonsalvo of Cordova' (1791). He also wrote 'Medleys of Poetry and Literature'; and 'Florian's Youth,' in which he recounts the story of his boyhood.

Flourens, Marie Jean Pierre (flö-roṅ'). An eminent French writer on physiology and anatomy; born in Maurilhan, Hérault, April 15, 1794; died at Montgeron, near Paris, Dec. 5, 1867. His special studies were neurology, osteology, and cellular pathology. The following partial list of his writings indicates his wide scope and massive knowledge: 'Physical Researches into Irritability and Sensibility' (1822); 'General Anatomy of the Skin and of its Mucous Membranes' (1843); 'Life and Intelligence' (1857); 'Natural Ontology' (1864); and works. in which he traces with admirable lucidity the connection between the respective aspects of physical, intellectual, and ethical states.

Flower, Benjamin Orange. An American editor and author; born in Illinois in 1858. He was until recently the publisher and editor of the Arena, Boston, Mass. Among his numerous works are : 'Civilization's Inferno; or Studies in the Social Cellar' (1893) ; 'The New Time' (1894) ; 'Persons, Places, and Ideas'; 'Gerald Massey: Poet, Prophet, and Mystic' (1895); 'How England Averted a Revolution of Force' (1901).

Flower, Frank Abial. An American historical writer; born in Cottage, N. Y., May 11, 1854. Has written several local histories. Among his works are to be found : 'Old Abe, the Wisconsin War Eagle' (1880) ; 'The Life of Matthew H. Carpenter' (1883); and a 'History of the Republican Party' (1884) ; 'International Deep Waterways'; 'Life of E. M. Stanton.'

Flügel, Johann Gottfried (flü'gel). A German lexicographer and compiler of language manuals; born in Barby on the Elbe, Nov. 22, 1788; died in Leipsic, June 24, 1855. He spent many years in this country in business, diplomatic, and official occupations, and compiled (with J. Sporschil) a 'Complete English-German and German-English Dictionary' (1830), besides publishing 'A. Series of Commercial Letters' (9th ed. 1874); 'Practical Handbook of English Business Correspondence' (9th ed. 1873); 'Triglot; or Mercantile Dictionary in Three Tongues—German, English, French' (2d ed. 1854); and other useful manuals, all revised, or brought down to contemporary needs, by his son.

Flygare-Carlén. See **Carlén.**

Fogazzaro, Antonio (fō-gäts-är'ō). An Italian poet and story-teller; born at Vicenza, 1842. He first came into notice with 'Miranda,' a story in verse (1874), and added greatly to his reputation as a poet with 'Valsonda,' a volume of lyrics (1876). He is author of several novels which were received with marked favor, among them 'Master Chicco's Fiasco'; 'Daniel Cortis'; 'The Poet's Mystery'; 'The Little Modern World.'

Foglar, Ludwig (fō'glär). An Austrian poet; born in Vienna, Dec. 24, 1819; died at Kammer, Aug. 15, 1889. Among his poems, mostly lyric, are 'Cypresses' (1842); 'Sunbeams and Shadows' (1846); 'Clara von Vissegrad' an epic (1847); 'Freedom's Breviary' (1848); 'Joyful and Sorrowful' (1867); 'Saint Velocipede' (1869), a satire (under the pseudonym "Leb erecht Flott").

Fokke Simonsz, Arend (fōk'ē). A Dutch essayist; born at Amsterdam, July 2, 1755; died there, Nov. 15, 1812. All his writings, especially his 'Catechism of Arts and Sciences' (11 vols., 1785-1804), give proof of the extraordinary compass of his learning; but he is most celebrated for his popular scientific works, mostly written in a burlesque or a satiric vein. From him we have the delightful literary satires 'The Modern Helicon' (1792) and 'Apollo, Sergeant of the Burghers' Guard'); 'Life of Lucifer' (1799), a history of demonology in form of a comic romance; the psychological disquisition 'The Different Aspects of Human Life' (1786); 'Woman Is Boss' (1807).

Folengo, Teofilo (fō-len'gō). [Pseudonym "Merlino Coccajo."] An Italian poet (1491-1554). He was the first to win fame as a writer of macaronic verses. His 'Macaronic Work of Merlino Coccajo, Mantuan Poet' — first published in 17 cantos (1517), and four years later in 25 — comprises the comico-heroic poems 'Baldus' and 'Moscæa' (War of the Midges). His satire is mostly against monachism. He writes in cynic humor, but under his burlesque lies a vein of serious purpose : to him Rabelais owes not a little. Under the pseudonym "Limerno Pitocco" he wrote in Italian the epic satire 'Orlandino' (1526) in ridicule of the story of Roland; then, partly in macaronic, partly in pure Italian, partly in pure Latin, 'The Chaos of Three by One' (1527), in which he darkly recounts the events of his own life. He wrote them while a vagrant from his monastery; he returned later and composed some religious poems of little value.

Follen, August (fōl'len). A German poet of patriotism, and popular song-writer; born in Giessen, Jan. 21, 1794; died in Bern, Dec. 26, 1855. He was a little of a soldier, a little of a lawyer, and a good deal of an enthusiast, suffering imprisonment for alleged demagogy. He became intensely popular as the author of 'Sons of Fatherland,' a patriotic hymn; 'Malegys and Vivian' (1829), a romance of chivalry; and numerous fine translations and poetic appeals to the instinct for liberty.

Follen, Eliza Lee (Cabot). An American prose-writer and poet; born in Boston, Aug. 15, 1787; died in Brookline, Mass., Jan. 26, 1860. She was the wife of Charles T. C. Follen, whose memoir she wrote (1842). Her other

works are : 'Poems' (1839); 'Twilight Stories' (1858); and 'Home Dramas' (1859).

Folz, Hans (fōlts). A German master-singer; native of Worms; died about 1515, at Nuremberg, where he followed the trade of barber-surgeon. He is best known for his Shrove Tuesday plays; but he wrote also many jests, New-Year's lays, minstrel songs, etc., highly prized by his contemporaries, but all of them marred by indelicacy. In better tone are some of his poems on the events of his time, as 'The Plague' (1482); 'Investiture of the Emperor Maximilian' (1491).

Fontan, Louis Marie (fôn-tän'). A French dramatist, pamphleteer, and journalist; born in Lorient, Nov. 4, 1801; died in Thiais, Seine, Oct. 10, 1839. His newspaper articles and political pamphlets, particularly 'The Rabid Sheep' (1829), got him into prison, from which he was freed by the Revolution of July. His eminence as a writer for the stage rests upon 'The Reckless Girl Jeanne'); 'The Monk'; 'The Count of St. Germain'; and a few others. He produced also a volume of 'Odes and Epistles' (1825).

Fontana, Ferdinand (fôn-tä'nä). An Italian poet; born in Milan, Jan. 30, 1850. He made his mark early in journalism, and wrote some good librettos — e. g., 'Colomba' (1887); but his is essentially a poet's fame, — 'The Song of Hate,' 'Socialism,' and 'The Meeting' being effective and beautiful compositions.

Fontane, Theodore (fon-tä'ne). A German poet and novelist; born at Neu-Ruppin, Dec. 30, 1819; died at Berlin, Sept. 21, 1898. He visited England several times on literary quests, particularly of old ballad poetry. Among his writings are three volumes on England, one 'A Summer in London' (1854); 'The Sleswick-Holstein War of 1864' (1866), and other war histories. His first volume of lyrics, 'Men and Heroes,' was published in 1850; his collected 'Ballads' in 1892. They are full at once of fire and of firmly exact phrasing. He was the author of many masterly stories of North German life, as 'Count Petöfy'; 'Under the Pear-Tree' (1885); 'Mrs. Jenny Treibel' (1892). He was a thorough realist, yet had a kindly, homely humor.

Fontanes, Marquis Louis de (fôn-tän'). A French poet and statesman; born at Niort, March 6, 1757; died March 17, 1821. Proscribed by the Revolution for editing papers opposed to the Terror, he fled to England, where he became intimate with Châteaubriand. Returning when it was safe, he attained high office under Napoleon and the restored Bourbons. He was a brilliant orator and also literary critic; and wrote several most graceful descriptive poems — among them 'The Forest of Navarre' (1778); 'The Carthusian Nun'; and 'All-Souls' (1796), an imitation of Gray's 'Elegy' — and a translation of Pope's 'Essay on Man.'

Fontenelle, Bernard le Bovier de (fônt-nel'). A distinguished French essayist; born at Rouen,

Feb. 11, 1657; died at Paris, Jan. 9, 1757. A gift of luminous popular exposition made his historical, philosophical, moral, and scientific writings highly esteemed. Best known among his prose writings are: 'Dialogues of the Dead, after the Manner of Lucian' (1683); 'Conversations on the Plurality of Worlds' (1686), which was translated into many languages and is still republished; 'History of the Oracles' (1686). He was unsuccessful as a writer for the stage.

Fonvielle, Wilfried de (fôn-vyäl' or fôn-vyä'). A French popular scientific prose-writer; born in Paris, July 21, 1828 He has long aimed to propagate scientific truths by his writings, of which the best known are: 'Fossil Man' (1865); 'Balloons in the Siege of Paris' (1871); 'The Physics of Miracles' (1872); 'The Conquest of the North Pole' (1877); 'The Wonders of the Invisible World' (5th ed. 1880); and 'Thunders and Lightnings' (4th ed. 1885);—besides one or two minor historical works.

Fonvizin (Von Wisin), Denis Ivanovich (fon-vis'in). A Russian dramatist, satirist, and epistolary writer; born in Moscow, April 14, 1745; died in St. Petersburg, Dec. 12, 1792. His fame as the Molière of his country arises from the merit of two comedies, 'The Brigadier' (1766) and 'The Minor' (or 'Mother's Favorite Son': 1782), ridiculing certain peculiarities of Russian character. A burlesque, 'Court Grammar,' and mock "correspondence" of a facetious sort, add to his renown.

Foote, Henry Stewart. An American statesman and author; born in Fauquier County, Va., Sept. 20, 1800; died in Nashville, Tenn., May 20, 1880. In 1847 he was chosen to the United States Senate; resigning in 1852 to serve as governor of his State. Subsequently he was elected to the Confederate Congress. His publications include: 'Texas and the Texans' (2 vols., 1841); 'The War of the Rebellion, or Scylla and Charybdis' (1866); and 'Personal Reminiscences.'

Foote, Mary (Hallock). An American novelist, descriptive writer, and illustrator; born at Milton, N. Y., Nov. 19, 1847; married a mining engineer, and lives mainly in the Rocky Mountain districts. She is the author of several novels and collections of short stories on the life of these regions: 'The Led Horse Claim' (1883); 'John Bodewin's Testimony' (1886) ; 'In Exile'; 'The Chosen Valley'; 'Cœur d'Alène'; 'The Cup of Trembling and Other Stories'; 'The Prodigal'); 'The Desert and the Town.'

Foote, Samuel. An English wag, impersonator, and comic playwright; born at Truro in Cornwall, 1720; died at Dover, Oct. 21, 1777. From Oxford he went to London to study law, but had to go on the stage for a living; tried tragic parts and failed; then began to give entertainments of a sort now familiar but then new, impersonating real and imaginary people and acting little farces by himself. Later he wrote regular farce-plays, 22

in number; the most notable being 'The Minor' (1760), a skit at the Methodists; 'The Liar'; 'The Mayor of Garratt.' His repartees are famous, and have been collected into a volume.

Foran, Joseph K. A Canadian poet and novelist; born in Greenpark, Aylmer, P. Q., 1857. Among his poems the best known are a 'Lament for Longfellow' and 'Indian Translations.' From 1879 till 1883 he published a series of essays on monuments, coins, art; and subsequently 'Irish-Canadian Representatives: Their Past Acts, Present Stand, and Future Prospects'; 'The Spirit of the Age'; also two novels—'Tom Ellis, a Story of the Northwest Rebellion,' and 'Simon, the Abenakis.'

Forbes, Archibald. A British war correspondent and journalist; born in Morayshire, Scotland, 1838; died in London, March 30, 1900. He became famous during the Franco-German war and the Paris communard insurrection by the vivid power of his letters to the London Daily News. He also did distinguished work during the Russo-Turkish war. His books include: 'Drawn from Life' (1870); 'My experiences of the War between France and Germany' (1871); 'Chinese Gordon, a Succinct Record of his Life' (1884), a very able work; 'Soldiering and Scribbling'; 'Glimpses through the Cannon Smoke'; 'Life of Colin Campbell, Lord Clyde' (1895); 'Memories and Studies of War and Peace' (1895); 'Czar and Sultan'; etc.

Forbes, David. An English geologist and traveler; born at Douglas, Isle of Man, Sept. 6, 1828; died in London, Dec. 5, 1876. As a civil engineer he traveled all over the world, studying rock formations and fossils, and writing 'On the Relations of the Silurian and Metamorphic Rocks of the South of Norway' (1855); 'On the Geology of Bolivia and Southern Peru' (1861); and kindred treatises.

Forbes, Edward. An eminent English naturalist; born in Douglas, Isle of Man, Feb. 12, 1815; died in Edinburgh, Nov. 18, 1854. Scarcely any department of botany, palæontology, geology, and the allied sciences, remained without obligation to his energy and research. The 'History of British Starfishes' (1841), 'Description of Fossil Invertebrate from South India' (1846), 'Zoölogy of the European Seas' (posthumous, 1859), and like studies, remain monuments of his scientific attainments.

Forbes, Henry O. A Scotch naturalist; born in Drumblade, Aberdeen, Jan. 30, 1851. His learning, supplemented by pilgrimages to Java, Sumatra, Timor, and New Guinea, has enriched the literature of science with 'A Naturalist's Wanderings in the Eastern Archipelago' (1885); 'Three Months' Exploration in the Tenimbur Islands of Timor Laut' (1884); and 'New Guinea' (1886), which last domain he has most exhaustively explored.

Forbes, James. An English writer of memoirs, and Indian civil servant; born in London, 1749; died at Aix-la-Chapelle, Germany,

Aug. 1, 1819. He lived almost a generation in the vicinity of Calcutta, where he obtained his material for the 'Oriental Memoirs' (1813-15), a narrative of his experiences and impressions.

Forbes, James David. A noted English physicist; born in Edinburgh, April 20, 1809; died in Clifton, Dec. 31, 1868. He investigated glacial formation, recording his deductions in 'Travels through the Alps of Savoy' (1843); 'Illustrations of the Viscous Theory of Glacier Motion' (1845); 'Norway and its Glaciers' (1853); etc.; in addition to which a 'Review of the Progress of Mathematical and Physical Science' (1858), and 'Experiments on the Temperature of the Earth' (1846), must be cited.

Force, Manning Ferguson. An American general in the Civil War; born in Washington, D. C., Dec. 17, 1824. He joined the Federal Army in 1861, and continued in active service until the close of the war. His publications include: 'From Fort Henry to Corinth' (1881); 'Marching Across Carolina' (1883); 'The Mound Builders'; 'Prehistoric Man'; and 'Personal Recollections of the Vicksburg Campaign' (1885). Died 1899.

Force, Peter. An American historical writer and journalist; born near Little Falls, N. J., Nov. 26, 1790; died in Washington, D. C., Jan. 23, 1868. His life work, entitled 'American Archives,' a valuable collection of 22,000 books and 40,000 pamphlets, was bought by the government (1867) and placed in the library of Congress. He has published also 'Grinnell Land: Remarks on the English Maps of Arctic Discoveries in 1850-1' (1852); and 'Notes on Lord Mahon's History of the American Declaration of Independence' (1855).

Forcellini, Egidio (for-chel-ē'nē). A notable Italian lexicographer; born in Feltre, Belluno, Aug. 26, 1688; died in Padua, April 4, 1768. Notwithstanding a humble origin and impoverished circumstances, he acquired scholarly distinction early in life, and consecrated his best years and efforts to a 'Dictionary of all Latinity' (1771), published posthumously; and so thoroughly well done that every subsequent work of the kind has been indebted to it. The success of the volumes was largely due to the guidance and support of Facciolati, his collaborator.

Forchhammer, Peter Wilhelm (forch'häm-mer). A German classical scholar and antiquarian; born in Husum, Oct. 23, 1801; died in Kiel, Jan. 9, 1894. Topography and mythology were his special fields; and in 'Hellenica' (1837); 'The Topography of Athens' (1841); 'Description of the Plain of Troy' (1850); and works on the interpretation of myth, he places scholars under great obligations.

Ford, James Lauren. An American journalist and author; born in Missouri in 1854. He has written several volumes of short stories and essays, among which are: 'Hypnotic Tales' (1891); 'The Literary Shop' (1894); 'Bohemia Invaded'; 'Dolly Dillenback.' He is also the author of two books for young readers; 'Dr. Dodd's School' (1892) and 'The Third Alarm' (1893); 'The Brazen Calf'; 'The Wooing of Folly.'

Ford, John. An English dramatist; born at Islington in Devon, April 1586; died about 1640. He turned from law to devote himself to the drama. His first poem was 'Fame's Memorial,' an elegy on the Earl of Devonshire. Alone and in collaboration he wrote a series of very successful plays. His tragedies sometimes go beyond even the elastic Elizabethan limits of the permissible, and are Greek in repulsiveness of theme; his comedies are sometimes distasteful: but as a poet he ranks among the foremost outside of Shakespeare. Among his best plays are: 'The Lover's Melancholy'; 'The Broken Heart'; 'Love's Sacrifice.'

Ford, Paul Leicester. An American historian and novelist; born in Brooklyn, N. Y., March 23, 1865; died in New York, May 8, 1902. Among his works are: 'The Honorable Peter Stirling' (1894); 'The Great II. & A. Train Robbery' (1897); 'The True George Washington' (1896); 'The Many-Sided Franklin' (1898); 'Franklin Bibliography'; 'Works of Thomas Jefferson' (1897); 'The Story of an Untold Love' (1897); 'Janice Meredith' (1899); 'Wanted—a Matchmaker' (1900); etc.

Ford, Sallie Rochester. An American story-writer; born in Rochester Springs, Boyle County, Ky., in 1828. Together with her husband she edited the Christian Repository and the Home Circle for many years. Among her published works are: 'Grace Truman' (1857); 'Mary Bunyan' (1859); 'Morgan and his Men' (1864); and 'Ernest Quest' (1887).

Fornáris, José (for-nä'rēs). A Cuban poet; born in Bayamo, Cuba, 1826. He wrote the dramas 'The Daughter of the People' and 'Love and Sacrifice'; and is the author of 'The Harp of the Home,' 'Songs of the Tropics,' and other volumes of verse.

Forneron, Henri (for-nē-rôn'). A French historian and biographer; born in Troyes, Nov. 16, 1834; died in Paris, March 26, 1886. He was connected with the ministry of finance, but preferred historical and biographical studies, the results of which were highly profitable and entertaining, particularly his 'Amours of Cardinal Richelieu' (1870); 'History of the Political Debates in the English Parliament since the Revolution of 1688' (1871); 'The Dukes of Guise and their Time' (1877); and 'History of Philip II.' (1880-82).

Forney, John Weiss. An American politician, journalist, and author; born in Lancaster, Pa., Sept. 30, 1817; died in Philadelphia, Pa., Dec. 9, 1881. He was apprenticed in the office of the Lancaster Journal in 1833; was clerk of the House of Representatives from 1851 to 1855; and secretary of the United States Senate from 1861 to 1868. He was connected with several papers in Philadelphia and Washington. Among his works are: 'What I Saw in Texas' (1872); 'Anecdotes of Public Men'

(1873); 'Forty Years of American Journalism' (1877).

Förster, Ernst (fêr'ster). A German artist, art writer, and critic; born in Münchengosserstädt on the Saale, April 8, 1800; died in Munich, April 29, 1885. His capacity with pencil and brush speedily made him known; and in 'The Truth about Jean Paul's Life' (1827-33), 'History of German Art' (1851-60), 'History of Italian Art' (1869-78), and numerous kindred studies, he showed his literary skill. His essays on the works of the old masters are invaluable to tourist and student.

Förster, Friedrich Christoph. A German historian, poet, essayist, and critic; born in Münchengosserstädt on the Saale, Sept. 24, 1791; died in Berlin, Nov. 8, 1868. He fought in the war of liberation, and with a 'Battle-Cry to the Aroused Germans' won fame as a song-writer: but 'The Courts and Cabinets of Europe in the Eighteenth Century' (1836-39); 'Gustavus Adolphus' (1832), a historical drama; 'Prussian Heroes in War and Peace,' a history in detached studies; 'Poems' (1838), a verse collection; and many short fictions, comprise his enduring works.

Forster, Georg (fôrs'tér). A German tourist and writer of travel, son of Johann Reinhold; born 1754; died 1794. He wrote 'Views on the Lower Rhine,' and 'Minor Writings' on philosophy.

Forster, Johann Reinhold. A German naturalist and voyager; born in Dirschau, West Prussia, Oct. 22, 1729; died in Halle, Dec. 9, 1798. An inveterate student and investigator, he was master of seventeen languages, besides his accomplishments in the physical sciences, theology, and metaphysics. His specialties are indicated by the titles of his brilliant and famous works: 'Introduction to Mineralogy' (1768); 'Flora of South America' (1771); 'Description of the Kinds and Qualities of Plants Gathered during a Journey to the Islands of the South Sea, 1772-75' (1776); 'Observations Made during a Voyage Round the World' (1778); and many more.

Forster, John. An English biographer and historical writer; born in Newcastle-on-Tyne, April 2, 1812; died in London, Feb. 2, 1876. He was educated for the law; held one or two public offices, and finally engaged in literature and journalism. He is noted for his 'Life of Charles Dickens' (1871-74). He also wrote: 'Statesmen of the Commonwealth of England' (1831-34); 'Life of Oliver Goldsmith' (1848); 'Biographical and Historical Essays' (1859); etc.

Förster, Karl August (fêrs'ter). A German poet and translator of poetry; born in Naumburg on the Saale, April 3, 1784; died in Dresden, Dec. 18, 1841. His versions of Petrarch, of Tasso's choicer lyric verse, and of Dante's 'New Life' (1841), won admiration. He wrote a work on 'Raphael' (1827), and has published a volume of 'Poems' (1842).

Forsyth, Joseph. A Scotch descriptive writer; born in Elgin, Feb. 18, 1763; died there, Sept. 20, 1815. He was a man of taste and training who gratified a life's ambition by visiting Italy, where he observed and studied much; afterwards writing 'Remarks on Antiquities, Arts, and Letters, during an Excursion in Italy in the Years 1802 and 1803' (1813), a work of such merit that it has run through many editions.

Forsyth, William. A Scotch poet and journalist; born in Turriff, Aberdeenshire, Oct. 24, 1818; died at Aberdeen, June 21, 1879. Soldiering songs and descriptive poems show him favorably as a poet; 'Idylls and Lyrics' (1872), a miscellaneous collection, being probably his best work.

Forteguerri, Giovanni (for-tā-gwä'rē). An Italian story-writer; born 1508; died in Pistoja, 1582. He is remembered for a series of tales cast in the Boccaccian mold, and interesting as revelations of contemporary life and specimens of Italian in the course of its development.

Fortier, Alcée. A distinguished American educator and miscellaneous prose-writer; born in Louisiana, 1856. He won distinction when very young, with stories of life in his native State. He is now professor in Tulane University. His works include: 'Le Château de Chambord'; 'Gabriel d'Ennerich,' a historical tale; 'Bits of Louisiana Folk-Lore'; 'Sept Grands Auteurs du XIXᵉ Siècle'; 'Histoire de la Littérature Française'; 'Louisiana Studies'; 'Louisiana Folk Tales'; 'History of Mexico.'

Fortiguerri, Niccolò (for-tē-gwä'rä). An Italian poet (1674-1735). He wrote a comico-satirical epic 'Ricciardetto' (1737), in which he, a canon of Santa Maria Maggiore and secretary of the Propaganda, lashes the vices of the clergy: it revived the ironic romantic spirit of Ariosto with admirable taste.

Fortis, Giovanni Battista (for'tēs). An Italian descriptive writer, naturalist, versifier, and biographer; born in Padua, Nov. 11, 1741; died in Bologna, Oct. 21, 1803. He is sometimes alluded to as Alberto. He was a priest of attractive personality and great versatility, besides being a noted conversationalist. His best-known work is 'Travels in Dalmatia' (1774).

Fortlage, Karl (fort'läg-è). A German philosopher; born in Osnabrück, June 12, 1806; died in Jena, Nov. 8, 1881. A Hegelian in his student days, he arrived finally at what we might designate «transcendental pantheism»; his chief works being the 'Genetic History of Philosophy since Kant' (1852) and 'A System of Empirical Psychology' (1855). In the latter he emphasizes the importance of introspection.

Fortunatus, Venantius Honorius Clementianus. A Latin poet; born near Treviso, in northern Italy, about 530; died at Poitiers, France, about 609. He was educated at Milan and Ravenna; in 565 went to France, where he was welcomed at the court of Sigebert, king of Austrasia. At Poitiers he became chaplain to Queen Radegonda, and about 592 succeeded to the episcopate of Poitiers. His prose is mechanical, but his poetry has an easy rhythmical flow. Besides the beautiful hymn beginning "Vexilla regis prodeunt" (The banners of the king advance), which has been translated into several modern languages, he wrote lives of St. Martin of Tours, Saint Radegonda, etc.; hymns; epitaphs, poetical epistles, and some other verses.

Fortune, Robert. An English botanist; born at Kelloe, Berwickshire, Sept. 16, 1813; died at South Kensington, April 13, 1880. His 'Three Years' Wanderings in China' (1847) and 'A Residence among the Chinese, Inland, on the Coast, and at Sea' (1857), in addition to the charm of their plant lore, possess literary grace.

Fosbroke, Thomas Dudley. An English antiquary; born in London, May 27, 1770; died at Walford, Herefordshire, Jan. 1, 1842. His devotion to archæology and the older Anglo-Saxon lore inspired 'British Monachism' (1802) and an 'Encyclopædia of Antiquities' (1825), which show learning and patient investigation.

Foscolo, Ugo (fos'kō-lō). A celebrated Italian poet and patriot; born on the island of Zante, Jan. 26, 1778; died Oct. 10, 1827, in London. His tragedy 'Thyeste' was received with great favor at Venice in 1797. ('The True Story of Two Luckless Lovers, or Last Letters of Jacopo Ortis' (1799), afterward rewritten and renamed 'Italy' (1802), voices his disappointment that the French armies did not liberate Italy; as did an outspoken apostrophe to Bonaparte. In 1807 was published his finest poem, 'The Graves.' His second tragedy, 'Ajax,' brought out at Milan in 1809, caused his expulsion from Lombardy; he went to Florence and there produced the tragedy 'Ricciarda' (1813); compelled to flee from Italy, he composed in Switzerland the bitter satire against his one mies, 'The One-Volume Book of the Super-Revelations of the Cleric Didymus, Least of the Prophets.' He wrote many critical and literary essays.

Fosdick, Charles Austin. A popular American writer of juvenile books; born at Randolph, N. Y., in 1842. He served in the Union navy in the Civil War from 1862 to 1865. Besides contributions to periodicals, he has published under the pseudonym "Harry Castlemon" over thirty books for boys, among which are: 'The Gunboat Series' (1864–68); 'Rocky Mountain Series' (1868-71); 'Rod and Gun Series' (1883–84); 'The Buried Treasure', 'The Steel Horse'; 'The White Beaver'; 'Carl the Trailer.'

Fosdick, William Whiteman. An American poet; born in Cincinnati, O., Jan. 28, 1825; died there, March 8, 1862. He gained some distinction as a poet by a drama entitled 'Tecumseh.' He also published 'Malmiztic the Toltec' (1851) and 'Ariel and Other Poems' (1855).

Foster, Hannah (Webster). An American novelist; born 1759; died at Montreal, Canada, April 17, 1840. Her published works are: 'The Coquette, or the History of Eliza Wharton,' one of the earliest of American novels; 'The Boarding School' (1796); and 'Lessons of a Preceptress' (1798).

Foster, John. An English essayist; born (probably) in Halifax, Yorkshire, Sept. 17, 1770; died at Stapleton, near Bristol, Oct. 14 or 15, 1843. A clergyman, self-educated and with an advanced point of view, he wrote regularly and delightfully; but his volume of 'Essays' (1805) constitutes his chief title to recognition. Four in number, these compositions are respectively: 'On a Man's Writing Memoirs of Himself'; 'On Decision of Character'; 'On the Application of the Epithet Romantic'; and 'On Some of the Causes by which Evangelical Religion has been Rendered Less Acceptable to Persons of Cultivated Taste.'

Foster, Stephen Collins. A famous American song-writer and composer; born at Pittsburg, Pa., July 4, 1826; died in New York city, Jan. 13, 1864. He was educated at Athens Academy and Jefferson College, Pennsylvania. He composed the music and wrote the words of over 125 popular songs and melodies, among which are: 'Old Folks at Home'; 'Nelly Bly'; 'Old Dog Tray'; 'Come Where my Love Lies Dreaming'; 'Suwanee River'; etc.

Fothergill, Jessie. An English story-teller; born at Manchester, June 7, 1851; died at London, July 1891. Her stories show a keen faculty of observation; among them are: 'Healey, a Romance' (1875); 'The First Violin' (1878), in which German life is faithfully portrayed; 'Probation' (1879); 'Kith and Kin' (1881); 'The Lasses of Laverhouse' (1888); 'Oriole's Daughter' (1893).

Foucher, Paul (fö-shā'). A French playwright (1810–75). Partly in collaboration with others and partly alone, he composed about 70 romantic dramas of very unequal value for the Boulevard Théâtre of Paris. His 'Notre Dame de Paris,' after Victor Hugo's novel, alone of all his pieces now holds the stage.

Foucher de Careil, Louis Alexandre, Count (fö-shā' dĕ kär-ā'ē). A French diplomatist and philosophical essayist and critic; born in Paris, March 1, 1826; died there, Jan. 10, 1891. He aimed at popularizing, or at least propagating, the philosophy of Leibnitz; for which purpose he wrote 'Letters and Minor Works of Leibnitz' (1854), 'Leibnitz, Descartes, and Spinoza' (1863), and other books; as well as 'Goethe and his Work' (1865), and studies of Hegel and Schopenhauer.

Fouqué, Baron Friedrich de la Motte (fö-kā'). A German romancist in various forms; born at Brandenburg, Feb. 12, 1777; died at Berlin, Jan. 23, 1843. His first contributions to literature were: 'Romances from the Vale of Roncesval' (1805); 'Story of the Noble Knight Galmy and a Fair Duchess of Britany' (1806); 'Alwin' (1808); followed by the hero-drama 'Sigurd the Snake-Killer' (1808): the titles show his thoughts to have been filled with legends of mediæval France and the Scandinavian North. The work by which he is chiefly known to-day is 'Undine' (1811); 'Sintram' is also still familiar. Among his other works are: 'The Voyages of Thiodulf the Icelander' (1815); 'Short Stories' (6 vols., 1814-19); several dramas, as 'Alf and Yngwi,' 'Runes,' 'The Jarl of the Orkneys'; the epics 'Corona,' 'Charlemagne,' 'Bertrand du Guesclin.' Karoline Auguste, his second wife (1773-1831), wrote many novels and tales, including: 'Roderic' (1807); 'The Heroic Maid of La Vendée' (1816); 'Valerie' (1827).

Fouquier, Jacques François Henri (fō-kyä'). A French journalist and topical writer; born in Marseilles, Sept. 1, 1838; died at Neuilly, Dec. 25, 1901. He long enriched the columns of Gil Blas, Figaro, and L'Echo de Paris, both over his own name and such pseudonyms as «Nestor,» «Columbine» and «Columba.» 'Artistic Studies' (1859), 'In the Last Century' (1884), and 'Parisian Goodness' (1885), are happy dashes at men and women and things.

Fourier, François Marie Charles (fō-ryä'). A French social economist, a very original and interesting figure; born in Besançon, April 7, 1772; died in Paris, Oct. 10, 1837. At first in trade, then in the army, the seeing a cargo of rice thrown into the sea to raise its price led him to attempt a reform abolishing the competitive system, by means of associated production and life in «phalansteries.» 'The Theory of the Four Movements' (1808), 'The New Industrial and Social World' (1829), and 'False Industry' (1835), set forth his scheme.

Fourier, Jean Baptiste Joseph, Baron. A celebrated French mathematician and physicist; born in Auxerre, March 21, 1768; died in Paris (?), May 16, 1830. He was an active Jacobin during the French Revolution. His later energies were divorced from politics and given up to science. 'Analytical Theory of Heat' (1822) is his most noted work; but in mathematics his speculations and methods are of high permanent utility.

Fournel, François Victor (för-nel'). A writer on the antiquities and curiosities of Paris; born near Varennes, Feb. 8, 1829. Among his writings are: 'What One Sees in the Streets of Paris' (1854); 'Theatrical Curiosities' (1859); 'Pictures of Old Paris' (1863); 'Paris and its Ruins in 1871' (1874); 'Paris Cries' (1886). He also wrote 'The Contemporaries of Molière' (1863); 'To the Sun Lands,' sketches of travel (1883); 'Contemporary French Artists.' D. 1894.

Fournier, August (för-nyä'). A distinguished Austrian historian; born in Vienna, June 19, 1850. 'Historical Studies and Sketches' (1885) and 'Napoleon I.: a Biography' (1886-89) have confirmed the presage of a high university standing. He has written also many biographies and sketches of special periods.

Fournier, Édouard. A French historical and descriptive writer; born in Orléans, June 15,

1819; died in Paris, May 10, 1880. The annals of the capital and its topographical features have received interesting treatment at his hands; 'The Street Lamps' (1854), 'Riddles of Parisian Streets' (1859), and 'Paris Through the Ages' (1876), being typical themes. In other lines he is instructive and pleasing, as in 'Music among the People' (1847) and 'La Bruyère's Comedy' (1866).

Fournier, Marc Jean Louis. A French dramatist; born in Geneva, 1818; died in St. Mandé, Jan. 5, 1879. He first entered journalism, but afterwards wrote several strong and original plays, 'Nights on the Seine' (1852) among them; besides work done in collaboration, notably 'Paillasse' (1849) and 'Manon Lescaut' (1852).

Fowler, William Worthington. An American prose-writer; born in Middlebury, Vt., June 24, 1833; died in Durham, Conn., Sept. 18, 1881. He was the author of 'Ten Years in Wall Street' (1870); 'Fighting Fire' (1873); 'Woman on the American Frontier' (1877); 'Twenty Years of Inside Life in Wall Street' (1880).

Fox, George. Founder of the sect of Quakers, and an English diarist and epistolary and doctrinal writer; born at Fenny Drayton, Leicestershire, July 1624; died in London, Jan. 13, 1691. His works are his 'Journal' (1694); 'Epistles' (1698); and 'Doctrinal Pieces' (1706): the first especially made a very deep impression.

Fox, John (William). An American writer of dialect stories; born about 1860. He is a contributor to magazines, and has published 'The Cumberland Vendetta, and Other Stories' (1895); 'Hell Fer Sartain, and Other Stories' (1897); 'Knight of the Cumberland' (1906).

Foxe, John. An English divine and martyrologist; born at Boston, Lincolnshire, in 1516; died April 1587. He studied at Oxford, but was expelled in 1545 after becoming a convert to Protestantism. His fame as an author mainly rests upon his 'History of the Acts and Monuments of the Church,' commonly known as 'Foxe's Book of Martyrs.' This celebrated work, upon which he labored for eleven years, was published in 1563.

Fraknói, Wilhelm (fränk-nō'). A Hungarian historian; born in Ürmény, Feb. 7, 1843. His country's annals and vicissitudes are graphically and accurately elaborated in 'Peter Pázmán and his Time' (1868-69); 'History of Hungary' (1873-74); and 'Hungary and the League of Cambray' (1883).

France, Anatole (fräns). [Jacques Anatole Thibault.] A French novelist and poet of great perfection and distinction of style; born at Paris, April 16, 1844. His first volume of 'Poems' was published in 1873, and his dramatic poem 'Corinthian Revels' in 1876. The humorous story 'Jocaste and the Lean Cat' (1879) was received with indifference; but he had brilliant success with 'The Crime of

Sylvester Bonnard' (1881); 'The Yule Log' (1881); and 'The Wishes of Jean Servien' (1881). His other works include: 'Our Children: Scenes in Town and in the Fields' (1886); 'Queen Pédauque's Cook-Shop'; 'Opinions of the Abbé Jérôme Coignard' (1893); 'The Garden of Epicurus'; 'Abeille'; 'My Friend's Book'; 'Our Children'; 'Balthazar'; 'Thaïs'; 'Literary Life'; 'Alfred de Vigny'; etc.

France, Hector. A French novelist; born at Mirecourt, Vosges, 1840. By profession a soldier, he writes ably on military and economic subjects, as 'John Bull's Army' (1887) and several pamphlets evince. His fictions show a loving care of form and effect, also a delight in dwelling on painful and revolting aspects of passion. 'The Pastor's Romance' (1879); 'Love in the Blue Country' (1880); and 'Sister Kuhnegunde's Sins' (1880), exemplify both.

Franchi, Ausonio (frän'kē), pseudonym of Cristoforo Bonavino. An Italian philosopher; born in Pegli, Feb. 24, 1821. He wrote 'The Rationalism of the People' (1856); 'The Religion of the Nineteenth Century' (1853); and other works in which the Kantian standpoint is reconciled as much as possible with deistic mysticism. He died Sept. 11, 1895.

Francillon, Robert Edward. An English novelist; born at Gloucester, 1841. Among his novels are: 'Pearl and Emerald' (1872); 'Queen Cophetua' (1880); 'King or Knave' (1888). He wrote also many Christmas stories, as 'Streaked with Gold'; 'Rare Good Luck'; 'In the Dark'; and the cantatas 'The Rose Maiden' and 'The Corsair.' He delights in realistic descriptions of scenes of adventure.

Francis d'Assisi, St. An Italian preacher, poet, and great spiritual force, founder of the Franciscan order; born at Assisi in Umbria, Italy, 1182; died Oct. 12, 1226. His literary works consist of letters, sermons, ascetic treatises, proverbs, moral apothegms, and hymns. The most celebrated of his hymns is the 'Canticle of the Sun.' His memory is held in great reverence and love on account of his devotion to religion and his love for all living creatures. Many anecdotes on this point are contained in a collection called 'The Little Flowers of St. Francis,' which is still very popular in Italy.

Francis, Philip, Sir. An Irish-English public man and writer, the best accredited of the candidates for authorship of the "Junius" letters; born in Dublin, Oct. 22, 1740; died in London, Dec. 23, 1818. He entered the civil service at 23, and was rapidly advanced, owing partly to his abilities and partly to personal influence curiously accordant with partialities shown in the 'Letters.' Suddenly raised to the lofty position of one of the resident India council appointed by Parliament to control those affairs, he went out to India; spent his time there in a furious contest for supremacy with Warren Hastings; was finally vanquished, but achieved a terrible revenge after his return to England, by inciting Hastings's impeach-ment and coaching Burke; entered Parliament, prepared many pamphlets and made many speeches of much ability and unfailing acrimony. The 'Letters'—savage assaults on the heads of the party in power, up to George III. himself—appeared in the Public Advertiser of London from 1768 to 1772; ceasing with the dispersion of the party faction most liked by Francis, and a year before his great promotion and his departure from England. The case for his authorship is most effectively put in Macaulay's Essay on Warren Hastings.

Franck, Adolphe (fronk). A French philosopher; born in Liocourt, Meurthe, Oct. 9, 1809; died in Paris, April 11, 1893. He has made a specialty of the Jewish side of metaphysical and humanist subjects, being himself of Jewish origin. His works are: 'Sketches of a History of Logic' (1838); 'The Cabbala, or Religious Philosophy of the Hebrews' (1843); 'Oriental Studies' (1861); and many similar productions.

Franck, Johann (frängk). A German hymn-writer; born in Guben, 1618; died in the Niederlausitz, 1677. His hymns are distinguished for a fervent, ecstatic quality, as shown in the collection 'Spiritual Zion' (1674); among the best remembered being 'Adorn Thyself, Loved Soul,' and 'Jesus, My Joy.'

Franck, Sebastian. A German prose Pietist and spiritual and ethical writer; born in Donauwörth, 1499; died in Basle, Switzerland, 1543. He was a priest who enlisted warmly in the cause of the Reformation, and wrote two compilations, 'Proverbs' (1541) and a 'World-Book' (1534), abounding in instructive and edifying miscellany; in addition to which he produced historical and descriptive tracts and monographs.

Francke, Kuno. An American scholar and author; born in Schleswig, Germany, in 1855. He is professor of German literature in Harvard University. His notable book 'Social Forces in German Literature' appeared in 1896.

Franco, Niccolò (frän'kō). An Italian poet (1505–69). He was long the intimate friend of Pietro Aretino, and his rival in licentiousness of verse; at Rome he was punished repeatedly for his offenses against decency, and at last hanged for his satires against Pius V. Among his works are: 'Popular Epistles' (1538); 'Piscatorial Eclogues'; 'Priapea.'

François, Luise von (frän'swä' or fron-swä'). A German novelist (1817–93). Her first considerable story, 'The Last Reckenburgerin' (1871), was very warmly praised by the critics for its power in character delineation: it was followed by 'Frau Erdmuthen's Twin Boys' (1872); 'Climacteric Years of a Lucky Fellow' (1877); 'Judith tne Housekeeper' (1868), a peasant counterpart to 'The Last Reckenburgerin,' and next after that her best story. She wrote a 'Popular History of the Prussian War of Liberation, 1813–15'; and a comedy relating to the Seven Years' War, 'Woman's Station' (1882).

François de Neufchâteau, Nicolas Louis, Count (fron-swä' dĕ nĕ-shä-tō'). A French public man and minor poet; born in Saffais, Meurthe, April 17, 1750; died in Paris (?), Jan. 10, 1828. He was admitted into the Academy as the author of 'Discourse on the Way to Read Verse' (1775); 'New Moral Tales in Verse' (1781); 'Fables and Tales in Verse' (1814); and similar productions.

Francq van Berkhey, Johannes le (frangk fvan berk'hī). A Dutch poet and naturalist; born in Leyden, Jan. 23, 1729; died there (?), March 13, 1812. He was a physician in Amsterdam, whose 'Flora and Fauna of Holland' (1769–79), and 'Natural History of Horned Cattle' (1805–11), received high praise. In his 'Poems' (1776–79), and the 'Song of Gratitude' (1773), he shows talent.

Frankl, Ludwig August, Chevalier von Hochwart (fränkl). An Austrian poet; born at Chrast, Feb. 3, 1810; died at Vienna, March 14, 1894. His début was made with 'A Lay of Hapsburg' (1832), a series of ballads, followed (1836) by the epic 'Christopher Columbus'; the Biblical poem 'Rachel' (1842); a poem 'The University' (1848), the first publication in Austria not subjected to official censorship; 'Don John of Austria,' a heroic poem (1846); 'Lyric Poems,' and 'Epic and Lyric Poetry.'

Franklin, Benjamin. A celebrated American philosopher, statesman, and didactic writer; born in Boston, Jan. 16, 1706; died in Philadelphia, April 17, 1790. Bred a printer from early boyhood, he was a hard student, and a wide and judicious reader. He early contributed political articles to the local press. Removing to Philadelphia, he established a printing business and founded the Pennsylvania Gazette. He was a promoter of every enterprise for the public good. His talent for invention and practical scientific research soon made itself felt. In 1752 he made his memorable discovery of the electrical nature of thunderstorms. He issued the first Poor Richard's Almanac in 1732, to supplant the current almanacs—full of worthless astrological predictions and stupid jests—with maxims of thrift and homely practical philosophy. As Deputy Postmaster-General he organized a paying postal system for the colonies. He was twice agent of Pennsylvania at London to procure redress of grievances; he passed several years abroad in public service before the Revolution, returning to Philadelphia in 1775. Thenceforward, both at home and especially as agent and diplomat in foreign countries, his life was devoted to his country's interests. He wrote his 'Autobiography,' reaching down to the year 1757; it has been edited by John Bigelow, and published in 3 vols. (3d ed. 1893). His 'Works' (10 vols., 1887–89) contain also his fugitive pieces—many of them classics for style and matter, and furnishing some proverbial sayings—and his correspondence.

Franul von Weissenthurn, Johanna (frän'-ŏl fŏn vīs'en-törn). A German dramatist and actress; born at Grünberg in Coblentz, 1773; died in Vienna, May 17, 1845. Her interpretations of stage emotions and characters made her an international celebrity; and her plays, in the edition of 'Newest Dramas' (1821), are works of great power.

Franzén, Frans Michael (fränt-sän'). A Swedish poet; born at Uleåborg in Finland, Feb. 9, 1772; died Aug. 14, 1847. He was professor of literature and ethics in the University of Åbo; but after the annexation of Finland to Russia he settled in Sweden, and in 1831 was made Bishop of Hernösand. As a poet he refused to adopt the didactic manner then regnant in Swedish poetry, and wrote in an unaffected idyllic vein with singular grace of style. His collected works were published in 5 vols. (1824–36).

Franzos, Karl Emil (fränt-sōs'). An Austrian novelist; born in Podolia, Oct. 25, 1848, of Jewish parentage. First studying jurisprudence, he became a newspaper correspondent, traveled extensively in Europe and Asia, edited an illustrated paper in Vienna, and finally studied in Berlin as a man of letters. His first volume—'Semi-Asia: Pictures of Life in Galicia, Bukowina, Southern Russia, and Roumania' (1876)—was a brilliant success all over Europe, being translated everywhere; and he has maintained high rank. Among his lively and graceful novels are: 'A Struggle for the Right' (1881); 'Tragic Stories' (1886); 'Judith Trachtenberg' (1890); 'The Old Doctor's God' (1892); 'The Truth-Seeker' (1894). Died Berlin, Jan. 31, 1904.

Frapan, Ilse (fräp'än), pseudonym of Ilse Levien. A German story-writer; born in Hamburg, Feb. 3, 1852. She is most at home in delineations of the life and traits of the people; as in 'Bitter-Sweet' (1891), 'Familiar Faces' (1893), and other stories in this field.

Fraser, Alexander Campbell. A Scotch philosophical writer; born at Ardchattan, Argyleshire, September 1819. He was a lecturer on mental philosophy in the New College, Edinburgh, 1846; editor of the North British Review 1850–50; professor of logic in Edinburgh University. His principal productions are: 'Essays in Philosophy' (1856); 'Rational Philosophy' (1858); a memoir of Bishop Berkeley, with a collected edition of his works (1871); an annotated edition of 'Locke's Essay on Human Understanding'; and 'Philosophy of Theism.'

Fraser, James Baillie. An English traveler and man of letters; born at Reelick, Invernessshire, June 11, 1783; died January 1856. He went to the West Indies, and thence to India, in 1815 making explorations in the Himalayas. He wrote 'A Historical and Descriptive Account of Persia,' and other works.

Frauenlob (frou'en-lōb), pseudonym of Heinrich von Meissen. A German mastersinger (1250–1318). He was a roving minstrel, practicing his art in the courts of the princes of southern and northern Germany; at last he settled in Mayence, and is believed to have established there the first school of minstrelsy. His pseudonym or nickname, "Panegyric of Woman," he won from contending in a poetical competition for the word "lady" (frau) instead of "woman" (weib). Tradition says that women bore his corpse to the cathedral.

Fréchette, Louis Honoré (frā-shet'). A French-Canadian poet; born at Quebec about 1839. He has written many odes and lyrics exquisite in form and inspired by genuine passion; they are collected in the volumes 'My Leisure Hours'; 'Pell-Mell'; 'The Legend of a People.' He translated for the Théâtre Français of Paris several of Shakespeare's plays. His poem 'Northern Blooms' was crowned by the French Academy. Died May 31, 1908.

Frederic, Harold. An American journalist and novelist; born at Utica, N. Y., Aug. 19, 1856; died at Henley, England, Oct. 19, 1898. He was for years London correspondent for the American press. Among his stories are: 'The Lawton Girl'; 'In the Valley'; 'The Copperhead,' a tale of the Civil War; 'The Damnation of Theron Ware'; 'March Hares,' a study of contemporary social life.

Fredericq, Paul (fred-er-ēk'). A Belgian historian; born in Ghent, Aug. 12, 1850. Accuracy of scholarship, liberality of view, and ease of style are manifest in his 'Essay on the Political and Social Part Played by the Dukes of Burgundy in the Low Countries' (1875), 'The Netherlands under the Emperor Charles V.' (1885), and other studies in Flemish and Netherlandish chronicles.

Fredro, Count Alexander (frād'rō). A notable Polish dramatist, called "the Molière of Poland"; born at Suchorow in Galicia, 1793; died at Lemberg, July 15, 1876. He is the founder of Polish comedy, those who preceded him having worked over French plays. 'Mr. Moneybags' (his first piece, 1821), 'Ladies and Hussars,' 'Man and Wife,' and 'Revenge,' are his titles. The scenes are taken from real life.

Fredro, Johann Alexander. A Polish dramatist, son of Count Alexander (1829-91). He served in the Polish-Hungarian legion in the Hungarian revolt of 1848, and after its suppression lived in exile till 1857. Of his numerous comedies these may be mentioned: 'Before Breakfast' (1864); 'Foreign Elements' (1872); 'The Goloshes' (1879); 'Poor or Rich' (1880).

Freeman, Edward Augustus. A distinguished English historian; born at Harborne in Staffordshire, Aug. 2, 1823; died at Alicante in Spain, May 16, 1892. He was appointed professor of history at Oxford, 1884. The principal of his very numerous works are: 'History and Conquests of the Saracens' (1856); 'History of the Norman Conquest of England' (6 vols., 1867-79); 'General Sketch of European History' (1872); 'Growth of the English Constitution' (1872); 'Reign of William Rufus and Accession of Henry I.' (2 vols., 1882); 'Fifty Years of European History' (1888). At the time of his death he was engaged on a great

'History of Sicily,' of which four volumes have been published. Among his miscellaneous writings are: 'Lectures to American Audiences' (1882) and 'Some Impressions of the United States' (1883). His contributions to the periodicals of his day were frequent and of great weight; and he was a fiery and unvarying champion of national freedom.

Freiligrath, Ferdinand (frī'lig-rät). A notable German poet; born in Detmold, June 17, 1810; died in Cannstatt, March 18, 1876. His first volume of 'Poems' (1838), full of grand Oriental imagery, won universal favor—and a royal pension, which he renounced as discrediting his liberalism, publishing a 'Confession of Faith' in verse (1844). Banished as a sower of sedition, he took refuge in London till the revolution of 1848. Returning, he was tried for high treason for his poem 'The Dead to the Living,' but acquitted; then threatened with prosecution for 'Political and Social Poems'; and once more flying to London, lived there till 1868. His poems are imaginative and passionate, with ringing and spirited diction; many of his songs are widely popular. He was an admirable translator, notably from Scott, Shakespeare, and Longfellow.

Frémont, Mrs. Jessie Benton. An American prose-writer, wife of John Charles; born in Virginia, 1824. Her father was Thomas H. Benton of Missouri. She wrote: 'Story of the Guard: A Chronicle of the War,' with a German translation (1863); a sketch of her father prefixed to her husband's memoirs (1886); 'Souvenirs of my Time' (1887); and 'The Will and the Way Stories.' She died Dec. 27, 1902.

Frémont, John Charles. An American explorer, politician, general, and writer; born in Savannah, Ga., Jan. 21, 1813; died in New York city, July 13, 1890. He was the first Republican nominee for the Presidency, and served as major-general in the United States army during the Civil War. His publications include: 'Report of the Exploring Expedition to the Rocky Mountains in 1842, and to Oregon and Northern California in 1843-44'; 'Frémont's Explorations'; and 'Memoirs of my Life' (1886).

French, Alice. See **Thanet.**

French, Henry Willard. An American lecturer and author; born in Connecticut in 1854. Among his numerous works are: 'Castle Foam' (1880), a Russian story; 'Ego' (1880), a novel; 'Gems of Genius' (1880); 'Nuna, the Brahmin Girl' (1881); 'Our Boys in China' (1883); 'Through Arctics and Tropics'; 'Out of the Night.'

French, L. Virginia (Smith). An American poet; born in Maryland in 1830; died at McMinnville, Tenn., March 31, 1881. She was associate editor of the Southern Lady's Book, a fashion magazine, published in New Orleans (1852). Her collected works are: 'Wind Whispers,' poems (1856); 'Iztalilxo,' a tragedy (1859); and 'Legends of the South' (1867).

Freneau, Philip. An American poet; born in New York city, Jan. 2, 1752; died near Freehold, N. J., Dec. 18, 1832. His connection with Jefferson and other men of the time made him conspicuous. 'The Home of Night,' an imaginative poem, possesses merit and will endure. 'The College Examination,' 'Eutaw Springs,' and 'The Indian Student,' are favorably remembered. A competent critic commends his 'Lines to a Wild Honeysuckle' as sincere and delicate.

Frenzel, Karl Wilhelm (frents'el). A German novelist and essayist; born at Berlin, Dec. 6, 1827. He has published several volumes of historical essays, as 'Poets and Women' (3 vols., 1859–66), 'Busts and Pictures' (1864), 'Renaissance and Rococo' (1878), all marked by fine discernment and just historical perspective; also two volumes of dramatic criticism, 'Berlin Dramaturgy' (1877). Among his numerous historical novels of the eighteenth century are: 'Pope Ganganelli' (1864); 'Charlotte Corday' (1864); 'La Pucelle' (1871); 'Lucifer: A Story of Napoleon's Time' (1873). Outside the field of historical fiction he has written many stories, as 'Mrs. Venus' (1880); 'Chambord' (1883); 'Weary of Life' (1886); 'Woman's Rights' (1892). He is also author of 'German Voyages' (1868).

Frere, John Hookham. An English poet, translator, and diplomatist; born in London (not Norfolk), May 21, 1769; died in Malta, Jan. 7, 1846. He was a Cambridge graduate, and one of the founders of the Anti-Jacobin (see Canning). After a career in the diplomatic service, he produced his original 'Prospectus and Specimen of an Intended National Work . . . Relating to King Arthur and his Round Table' (1817), better known as 'The Monks and the Giants'; a literary burlesque, but full of charming verse and of excellent character-drawing. It naturalized in English the *ottava rima* afterward used by Byron in 'Beppo' and 'Don Juan.' A version of a large part of Aristophanes succeeded this effort.

Frey, Adolf (fri). A German poet, biographer, and essayist; born Feb. 18, 1855. In his 'Poems' (1886), and 'Recollections of Gottfried Keller' (1892), culture and scholarship are conspicuous; and a volume on 'Albrecht von Haller and his Importance in German Literature' (1879) shows great critical acumen.

Frey, Friedrich Hermann. See **Greif.**

Frey, Jakob. A Swiss novelist; born at Gutenschwyl in Aargau, May 13, 1824. His novels are few in number, but they are to be classed with the finest productions of Swiss literary genius. They are: 'Between Jura and Alps' (1858); 'The Orphan Girl of Hollizen' (1863); 'Swiss Portraits' (in three parts, 1864–77).

Freylinghausen, Johann Anastasius (fri'ling-hou''zen). A German theologian and hymnist; born in Gandersheim, Dec. 2, 1670; died in Halle, Feb. 12, 1739. His 'Song-Book' (1704) is one of the most voluminous and meritorious compilations of sacred verse ever made; and his work on the 'Foundation of Theology' is the masterpiece of the Pietist movement of Halle.

Freytag, Gustav (fri'täg). A distinguished German poet and novelist; born at Kreuzburg in Silesia, July 13, 1816; died at Wiesbaden, April 30, 1895. His first dramatic composition was 'The Bridal Tour,' a comedy (1844); it was followed by a little one-act tragedy, 'The Savant' (1844), and by a small volume of poems 'In Breslau' (1845); after which he produced 'The Valentine' (1846), 'Count Valdemar' (1847), and 'The Journalists' (1853). Among his works outside of the drama may be mentioned his great novel of social life 'Debit and Credit' (3 vols., 1855; 40th ed. 1893), followed by another novel of social life, 'The Lost MS.' (1864; 23d ed. 1893). His next work, 'Ancestors,' is a cycle of six stories portraying the German civilization from the beginning of historic times.

Frič, Joseph Václav (frich). A Czech journalist, dramatist, agitator, and poet; born in Prague, Sept. 5, 1829; died there, Oct. 14, 1890. Political activity and journalistic independence resulted in his exile, but he was granted amnesty after wandering through Europe and writing anti-Austrian books and papers. His place in his country's literature is due to 'Laments of the Bohemian Crown' (1868), a political pamphlet; 'The Vampire' (1849), a patriotic poem; 'Ulric von Hutten' and 'Mazeppa,' dramas; and various other productions.

Friedländer, Ludwig (frēd'len-der). A German classical philologist and scholar; born in Königsberg, July 16, 1824. His most representative work is 'Typical Studies in the History of Roman Manners and Morals' (6th ed. 1889), written in popular style. 'The Remains of Nicanor's Emendations of the Punctuation of the Iliad' (1850), and like theses, constitute him an authority in Homeric criticism.

Friedmann, Alfred (frēd'man). A German poet and story-teller; born at Frankfort-on-the-Main, Oct. 26, 1845. His poems have every grace of form, but lack original inspiration. Among them are: 'Merlin. Orpheus' (1874), two ballads; 'Biblical Stars' (1875), comprising three idylls; 'Love's Fire Test. Angioletta'; 'Lays of the Heart' (1888). He is the author of many novels, including: 'Two Marriages'; 'Suddenly Rich' (1891); 'The Wild Rose' (1893). 'The Reliable' (1897).

Friedrich, Friedrich (frēd'rich). A German novelist; born in Gross-Vahlberg, Little Brunswick, May 2, 1828; died in Plauen, near Dresden, April 13, 1890. He was the author of many pleasing romances; the best of them — 'War Scenes' (1860); 'The Minister's Wife' (1871); 'Frank and Free' (1872); and 'The Honor of the House' (1884) — evincing a considerable degree of constructive ingenuity.

Friedrichs, Hermann (frēd'richs). A German poet and story-writer; born in St. Goar on the Rhine, June 14, 1854. He has distinguished himself in periodical journalism, and shown taste as a maker of polite literature in 'The Revenge of the Bayadere' (1880), a lyric; 'Love Ordeals' (1888), a volume of stories; and 'Forms and Passions' (1889), poems, all uniting tropical intensity to rhetorical grace and purity of diction.

Fries, Jakob Friedrich (frēs). A German philosopher; born in Barby, Aug. 23, 1773; died at Wartburg, Aug. 10, 1843. He is a link between Kant's system and the so-called historical school. 'The New or Anthropological Critique of Reason' (1807) is his most important book; although his 'Handbook to Psychical Anthropology' (1820), 'System of Metaphysics' (1824), and two or three besides, must be considered in an estimation of his position in German letters.

Friis, Jens Andreas (frēs). A Norwegian philologist, ethnologist, and sketch-writer; born in Sogndal, May 2, 1821. He has exhaustively investigated the language and literature of the Finns and Laps; a 'Lap Grammar' (1856), 'Lap Mythology' (1871), and like works, giving him pre-eminence in this field. 'Holidays among Crags and Mountains' (1876) — hunting and fishing sketches, with the mountains of his country as a background — give another side of his literary power. Died Feb. 16, 1896.

Friman, Klaus (frē'män). A Danish poet; born in Selloë, Norway, Aug. 4, 1746; died in Dawigen, Norway, Oct. 16, 1829. He was a country clergyman. His descriptive poem 'Hornelen' (1777) had merits; but the graceful pastoral lyrics which followed constitute him a poet of strongly individualized charm.

Friman, Peder Harboe. A Danish poet, brother of Klaus; born in Selloë, Nov. 19, 1752; died in Copenhagen, Sept. 31, 1839. He also exploited Hornelen in a pleasing metrical description (1777). He wrote odes, and a poem, 'St. Sunniva's Cloister,' of much beauty.

Froebel, Friedrich (frē'bel). A notable German educator; born at Oberweissbach, April 21, 1782; died at Marienthal, June 21, 1852. He was for some time associated with Pestalozzi, but evolved a theory of education of his own. To explain it he wrote 'The Education of Man' (Vol. i., 1826), a work of deep and original thought. He opened the first Kindergarten or Children's Garden at Blankenburg, Thuringia, 1840.

Froebel, Julius. A German journalist, political and descriptive writer, and publicist; born in Griesheim, near Stadtilm, July 16, 1805; died in Zürich, Switzerland, Nov. 6, 1893. He was active in the popular movements preceding and during 1848. He wrote: 'The Republicans,' a political drama; 'Theory of Politics' (1861-64); 'America: Experiences, Studies, and Travels' (1857-58), the latter work the fruit of much personal observation and a residence there of nine years; and 'A System of Social Politics' (2d ed. 1847). He was a remarkably keen and accurate observer, and a writer of rare plausibility.

Fröhlich, Abraham Emanuel (frē'liċh). A Swiss poet and fabulist (1796-1865). His first work was a volume of 'Fables' (1825), followed (1827) by a small volume of 'Swiss Lays.' 'The Gospel of St. John in Songs' (1835) explains itself. He also wrote 'Elegies on Cradle and Bier' (1835); three epics on the Reformers Zwingli, Ulrich von Hutten, and Calvin; a volume of 'Rhymed Proverbs' (1850); 'Selected Psalms and Spiritual Songs' (2d ed. 1845).

Fröhlich, Karl Hermann. A German juvenile poet and artist; born in Stralsund, April 8, 1821. His silhouettes and figures, accompanied by verse, have delighted childhood in two continents. 'Fables and Tales' (1853-54), and 'New Silhouettes and Rhymes' (1855), are particular favorites. He died at Berlin, 1898.

Frohschammer, Jakob (frō'shäm-er). A German philosopher; born in Illkosen, Bavaria, Jan. 6, 1821; died at the Kreuth, June 14, 1893. He was a Catholic priest when he began the series of writings which called public attention to him and cost him his pastorate. These include 'Christianity and Modern (Nature) Science' (1868); 'The Imagination [Phantasie] as the Fundamental Factor [Grundprinzip] in Cosmic Evolution [Weltprozess]' (1877); and 'Outline System of Philosophy' (Part 1, 1892): in which, and other works, mysticism, "other-worldliness," and the phenomena of the imagination are incorporated among the more ordinary particles of the philosophic mosaic.

Froissart, Jean (froi'särt *or* frwä-sär'). A celebrated French chronicler and poet; born at Valenciennes in Hainault, 1333; died at Chimay, 1410(?). He began at 20 to write the history of the wars of his time. His 'Chronicle' (as the title is usually abbreviated) covering the years 1326-1400, is of capital importance for its period. To a collection of the verses of Wenceslaus of Brabant, Froissart added some of his own, and gave to the whole the title 'Meliador, or the Knight of the Golden Sun.' All his extant poems were published at Brussels in 3 vols., 1870-72.

Fromentin, Eugène (frō-moṅ-taṅ'). A French artist, critic, and writer of travel sketches; born in La Rochelle, Oct. 24, 1820; died in St. Maurice near La Rochelle, Aug. 27, 1876. A journey undertaken in the interest of art resulted in 'A Year in the Sahel' (5th ed. 1884) and 'A Summer in the Sahara' (9th ed. 1888). He has also entered another department of literature with 'The Masters of a Former Day' (1876), a happy bit of appreciation of old painters.

Frommel, Emil (frōm'el). A German popular story-writer and theologian; born in Karlsruhe, Jan. 5, 1828. He was a brave army chaplain, and turned out good sermons to the general edification; but 'Tales for the People'

(9 vols., 1873-86), and similar collections of humorous and realistic compositions, will form his memorials in the future. Died Nov. 9, 1896.

Frontaura, Carlos (frōn-tou'rä). A Spanish story-writer and dramatist; born in Madrid, Sept. 4, 1834. 'The Philanthropist,' a comedy, and 'Fortunes and Misfortunes of Rosita,' a novel, illustrate his talent at its best. His compositions are characterized in general by a light gayety. He was a very prolific writer.

Frontinus, Sextus Julius. A Roman general, public official, and author; born about 40 A.D.; died probably in 103 A.D. He was urban prætor of Rome in 70, and as governor of Britain (76-78) acquired a great reputation by the conquest of the warlike Silures. He was twice consul, and during the reign of Nerva became superintendent of aqueducts, to which appointment we owe his valuable treatise 'On the Aqueducts of Rome.' Of the other works attributed to him, the only genuine one is the 'Strategematicon,' treating of military tactics.

Fronto, Marcus Cornelius (fron'tō). A Roman rhetorician and epistolary writer; born in Cirta, Numidia, about 100 A.D.; died in Rome(?), 180(?). It is in his letters, first brought to light in 1815, that he is revealed as a writer of ability and importance.

Frothingham, Nathaniel Langdon. An American Unitarian clergyman and religious writer; born in Boston, Mass., July 23, 1793; died there, April 4, 1870. He was author of 'Deism or Christianity'; 'Sermons in the Order of a Twelvemonth' (1852); and 'Metrical Pieces' (1855). His writings are marked by grace and refinement.

Frothingham, Octavius Brooks. An American Unitarian clergyman, son of Nathaniel; born in Boston, Nov. 22, 1822; died there, Nov. 27, 1895. His radical views led to the resignation of his pastorate in the Unitarian Church, Salem, Mass. He preached in Jersey City, 1855-59; then organized the Third Unitarian Church in New York city, where he preached very radical and advanced views until the dissolution of the church in 1879. The remainder of his life was devoted to travel and literary pursuits, his home being in Boston. His works were: 'Stories from the Lips of the Teacher'; 'Stories from the Old Testament'; 'The Religion of Humanity'; 'The Cradle of the Christ'; 'Memoir of W. H. Channing'; 'The Safest Creed'; 'Beliefs of the Unbelievers'; 'Creed and Conduct'; 'The Spirit of the New Faith'; 'The Rising and the Setting Faith'; 'Lives of Gerrit Smith, George Ripley, Theodore Parker'; 'Transcendentalism in New England'; 'Recollections and Impressions'; etc.

Froude, James Anthony (fröd). A notable English historian; born at Dartington in Devonshire, April 23, 1818; died in London. Oct. 20, 1894. In the beginning of the Tractarian controversy he was a close friend of Newman, and was a contributor to the 'Lives of the English Saints.' He took orders in the Anglican Church

(1844). Among his works may be mentioned: 'Luther: A Short Biography' (1833); 'Shadows of a Cloud' (1847); 'Nemesis of Faith' (1848); 'History of England from the Fall of Wolsey to the Death of Elizabeth' (12 vols., 1850-70); 'Influence of the Reformation on the Scottish Character' (1867); 'The English in Ireland in the Eighteenth Century' (3 vols., 1872); 'Cæsar: A Sketch' (1879); 'Thomas Carlyle' (1882); 'Spanish Story of the Armada' (1892). He was the successor of E. A. Freeman in the professorship of modern history at Oxford.

Frugoni, Carlo Innocenzio Maria (frö-gō'nē). An Italian poet (1692-1768). He was a Franciscan friar, and was professor of rhetoric at Brescia, Bologna, Modena, etc.; at the court of Parma he was appointed poet laureate and historiographer. His 'History of the House of Farnese' was published in 1729. His poetical works (15 vols., 1779) show great elegance of style, richness of imagery, and harmony of numbers. He was happy in his poetical 'Epistles' after the manner of Horace.

Frullani, Emilio (frö-län'ē). An Italian poet; born at Florence, 1808; died there, Oct. 24, 1879. He holds honorable rank among contemporary Italian lyrists. He is a master of elegiac verse; many of his threnodies on the death of friends—above all, the one entitled 'The Three Souls'—are admirable. His poems are collected in two volumes: 'Verses' (1863); 'New Verses' (1874).

Fry, James Barnet. An American military officer and author; born in Carrollton, Ill., Feb. 22, 1827; died at Newport, R. I., July 11, 1894. He graduated at West Point in 1847; served in the Mexican War (1847-48); and was instructor and adjutant at West Point (1853-59). He saw active service in the Civil War and was provost-marshal-general (1863-66). After the war he was appointed adjutant-general, and retired in 1881. His works include: 'Historical and Legal Effects of Brevets' (1877); 'Army Sacrifices' (1879); 'Operations Under Buell' (1884).

Fryxell, Anders (früks'el). A Swedish historian, literary critic, and grammarian; born in Edsleskog, Dalsland, Feb. 7, 1795; died in Stockholm, March 21, 1881. He was a clergyman and a scholar. His writings are characterized by purity of idiom and great beauty of style; the strongest of his works, 'Stories from Swedish History' (1832-79), is throughout its many volumes admirable in its combination of accuracy with historical insight and literary grace. 'The Prejudice against Aristocracy among Historians of Sweden' (1845-50); 'Contributions to Swedish Literary History' (1860-62); and 'Manual of the Swedish Tongue,' are among his most important works.

Fuà-Fusinato, Erminia (fwä'fö-sēn-ä'tō). An Italian poetess, wife of the poet Arnaldo Fusinato; born of Jewish parents at Rovigo, Oct. 5, 1834; died in Rome, Sept. 27, 1876. Her spirited appeals to national sentiment in 1848 brought her widely into notice. In 1852 was published her 'Verses and Flowers.' She wrote a series of 'Stornelli,' advocating Florence as the national capital instead of Rome. Her complete poetical works, 'Versi,' were published in 1879; her 'Literary Writings' in 1883.

Fulda, Ludwig (föl'dä). A German dramatist; born at Frankfort-on-the-Main, July 15, 1862. One of his first pieces, a comedy in verse, 'Honest Men,' was repeatedly put upon the stage. His most successful plays are the two comedies 'Under Four Eyes' (1886) and 'The Wild Chase' (1888); and the drama of society 'The Lost Paradise' (1890). His dramatic tale 'The Talisman' (1893) was received with extraordinary favor. His special gifts are an easy mastery of the resources of language and of poetical technique, and a lively wit ever conscious of a serious purpose.

Fuller, Anna. An American novelist; born in Massachusetts in 1853. Her works are : 'Pratt Portraits : Sketched in a New England Suburb' (1892) ; 'A Literary Courtship' (1893) ; 'Peak and Prairie' (1894) ; 'A Venetian June' (1896). 'Katharine Day' (1901) ; 'A Bookful of Girls.'

Fuller, Henry B. An American story-writer and novelist; born in Chicago of New England blood, 1857. He was intended for a mercantile career, but entered literature anonymously with 'The Chevalier of Pensieri-Vani' (new ed. 1892), and 'The Châtelaine of La Trinité (1892). He next wrote 'The Cliff Dwellers' (1893), and 'With the Procession' (1895), novels of Chicago life; 'Under the Skylights.'

Fuller, Hiram. An American journalist; born in Plymouth County, Mass., about 1815; died in 1880. Together with N. P. Willis and George P. Morris he published the New Mirror. The three subsequently established the Daily Mirror, which Mr. Fuller edited for fourteen years. He resided for a number of years in London and Paris, and on his return wrote 'Grand Transformation Scenes in the United States; or, Glimpses of Home after Thirteen Years Abroad' (1875).

Fuller, Margaret. See Ossoli, Sarah Margaret Fuller, Marchioness d'.

Fuller, Thomas. A noted English historian (1608–61). He was a presbyter of the Established Church and a prebendary of Salisbury Cathedral. He was a voluminous writer. His works include: 'David's Heinous Sin' (1631), a poem; 'History of the Holy War' (1639); 'A Pisgah Sight of Palestine' (1650); 'Church History of Britain' (1655). The one work for which he is now esteemed is 'The Worthies of England' (folio, 1662), which is full of biographical anecdote and acute observations on men and manners.

Fullerton, Georgiana, Lady. An English novelist, daughter of the first Earl Granville and wife of Alexander Fullerton ; born at Tixall Hall, Staffordshire, Sept. 23, 1812; died at Bournemouth, Jan. 19, 1885. Her first novel,

'Ellen Middleton' (1844) was followed by 'Grantley Manor' (1847). Her later stories, after her conversion to the Catholic faith in 1846, are in a mild way "stories with a purpose," the purpose being to develop the influence of religious belief on life and character; among them are : 'Lady Bird' (1852); 'Too Strange Not to be True' (1864); 'Mrs. Gerald's Niece' (1871); 'A Will and a Way' (1881). She wrote also 'The Gold-Digger, and Other Verses' (1872).

Funck-Brentano, Théophile (fönk"bren-tä"nō). A French philosophical and critical writer; born in Luxembourg, Aug. 23, 1830. His thorough studies in law and medicine have imparted to his philosophical writings an exactitude of thought and inspired a special stress upon method, as in 'New Thoughts and Maxims' (1858); 'Exact Thought in Philosophy' (1869); 'Greek Sophists and Contemporary English Sophists' (1879); and others. As a critic he is esteemed for the happy presentation and careful elaboration of his thought.

Furness, Horace Howard. An American Shakespearean scholar and editor, son of William H.; born in Philadelphia, Nov. 2, 1833. He graduated from Harvard in 1854; studied law, and was admitted to the bar in 1859. The honorary degree of Ph. D. was conferred upon him by the University of Göttingen in recognition of his services to Shakespearean literature. He is the editor of the exhaustive New Variorum Edition of Shakespeare, eight volumes of which have appeared since 1871.

Furness, William Henry. An American clergyman and author; born in Boston, April 20, 1802; died in Philadelphia, Jan. 30, 1896. He was educated at Harvard; studied theology at Cambridge, Mass., and was pastor of the First Unitarian Church in Philadelphia from 1825 to 1875. Among his numerous works are : 'Remarks on the Four Gospels' (1836); 'Jesus and his Biographers' (1838); 'Verses and Translations from the German Poets' (1886); 'Pastoral Offices' (1893).

Furnivall, Frederick James. An English historian of literature; born in Egham, Surrey, Feb. 4, 1825. A lawyer by profession, he became a socialist and reformer, and a student of debatable literary problems. His labors resulted in the production of 'Shakespeare's England' (1877), and many editions of old masterpieces, such as : 'Saint-Graal, the History of the Holy Graal in English Verse, by Henry Lonelich' (1861–63), and 'Caxton's Book of Curtesye' (1868) ; 'The Succession of Shakespeare Works.'

Fürst, Julius (fürst). A Polish Oriental scholar; born in Zerkovo, Posen, May 12, 1805; died in Leipsic, Feb. 9, 1873. His origin was Jewish. He obtained a marvelous mastery of the rabbinical literature, utilized in his great 'History of Jewish General and Literary Culture in Asia,' and 'History of Biblical Literature and of Hellenico-Judaic Letters' (1867–70), etc. He suffered many attacks from critics.

Fusinato, Arnaldo (fö-sēn-ä'tō). An Italian poet; born at Schio in the district of Vicenza, 1817; died at Verona, Dec. 29, 1888. His high poetical gifts were first exercised in humorous poetry, often with a political aim. At the outbreak of the revolution of 1848 he and his brother raised a battalion of volunteers and took part in several actions. His collected 'Poems' were published in 1853, and have since been many times republished in cheap popular editions. His 'Unpublished Patriotic Poems' appeared in 1871.

Fustel de Coulanges, Numa Denis (füs-tel'-dĕ kö-länzh'). A French historian; born in Paris, March 18, 1830; died there, Sept. 12, 1889. His 'Polybius, or Greece Conquered by the Romans' (1858); 'The Ancient City' (12th ed. 1889); and 'History of Political Institu-tions in Old France' (1875–92), are interesting and exhaustive works.

Fyffe, Charles Alan. An English historian; born at Blackheath, Dec. 3, 1845; died in London, Feb. 19, 1892. He graduated at Balliol College, Oxford, in 1868, and was called to the bar in 1876, but never actively practiced. As correspondent of the Daily News during the Franco-Prussian war he is said to have sent to that journal the first account of the battle of Sedan that appeared in print. On account of a false charge, he became depressed and committed suicide. His historical works are distinguished by accuracy and a pleasing, perspicuous style. They include : 'History of Greece' (1875); 'History Primers'; and the well-known 'History of Modern Europe' (1880, 1886, 1890), covering the period from 1792 to 1878.

G

Gaboriau, Émile (ga-bō-ryō'). A French writer of detective stories; born in Saujon, Nov. 9, 1835; died at Paris, Sept. 28, 1873. His early years were a succession of vicissitudes; the army, the law, and even the church, were in turn the objects of his inconstant attentions, until at last he wrote his way to fame and fortune with 'The Lerouge Affair' in 1866. He had previously tried his luck with a humorous tale or two. His works include : 'File No. 113' (1867); 'The Crime of Orcival' (1867); 'Monsieur Lecoq' (1869); 'The Fall' (1871); 'The Rope about the Neck' (1873); etc.

Gage, William Leonard. An American clergyman and author; born in Loudon, N.H., in 1832; died in 1889. He was the pastor of a Congregational church at Hartford, Conn., from 1868 to 1884. Besides several translations from the German, he has written 'Trinitarian Sermons' (1860); 'Songs of War Time' (1863); 'Life of Carl Ritter' (1887); 'Palestine, Historic and Descriptive' (1887).

Gagneur, Louise (gän-yėr'). A French novelist; born at Domblans, in the Jura, January(?) 1832. At 18 she wrote an essay on trades-unionism which attracted the attention of Vladimir Gagneur, a deputy in the Chamber, who married her. She wrote novels of a socialistic and anti-Catholic tendency, many of which proved popular. 'An Expiation'; 'The Black Crusade'; 'The Story of a Priest'; and 'The Crime of the Abbé Maufrac,' are some of the better known among these works, which are characterized by vividness of narration and intense warmth of partisan feeling. Died 1902.

Gairdner, James. A Scotch compiler and historical writer; born in Edinburgh, Scotland, March 22, 1828. Besides memorials and compilations relating to the mediæval period of English history, he has published 'The Houses of Lancaster and York' (1874), in the 'Epochs of History' Series; 'Life and Reign of Richard III.' (1878); the volume 'England,' in the Christian Knowledge Society's series entitled 'Early Chroniclers of Europe' (1879); 'Henry VII.,' in 'Twelve English Statesmen' (1889).

Galdós, Benito Perez (gäl'dōs). A Span-ish novelist; born in Las Palmas, Canary Islands, May 10, 1845. He went to Madrid when a lad to study law; but instead began writing plays, till their persistent rejection by managers caused him to try novel-writing, in which he established his fame and his fortune. 'The Fountain of Gold' is the first, and 'Electra' is one of the latest, of a long series of novels demonstrating that, as regards life, "few see it more clearly than Galdós."

Galen, Philipp (gäl'en), pseudonym of Ernst Philipp Karl Lange. A German novelist; born in Potsdam, Dec. 21, 1813. He was for years an army physician, retiring with a reputation for medical lore; he had also won fame with 'The Island King,' a widely popular story, and 'The Madman of St. James,' by far his best work. 'Fritz Stilling' is the tale of a practicing physician's adventures, and 'Walther Lund' deals with literary life. 'The Diplomat's Daughters' and 'Free from the Yoke' are meritorious fictions. He is a pleasing realist with no special "tendency." D. 1899.

Gall, Richard. A Scottish song-writer; born at Linkhouse, December 1776; died in Edinburgh, May 10, 1801. At first apprenticed to his uncle, a carpenter, afterwards to a printer in Edinburgh, he subsequently became a traveling clerk. Burns and Thomas Campbell were counted among his friends. Several of his songs were set to music, and were popular.

Two of these, 'The Farewell to Ayrshire' and that beginning "Now bank and brae are clad in green," are often credited to Burns.

Gallagher, William Davis. An American journalist and poet; born at Philadelphia, Aug. 21, 1808; died 1894. 'A Journey through Kentucky and Mississippi,' published in the Cincinnati Chronicle in 1828, first drew public attention to him. He wrote 'The Wreck of the Hornet,' a poem; and edited 'Selections from the Political Literature of the West' (1841). 'Fruit Culture in the Ohio Valley' is among the best of his agricultural writings. 'Miami Woods,' and 'A Golden Wedding and Other Poems,' were published in 1881.

Gallardo, Aurelio Luis (gal-yar'-do). A Mexican poet; born in León, Guanajuato, Nov. 3, 1831; died in Napa, Cal., Nov. 27, 1869. He published three volumes of poems: 'Dreams and Visions' (Mexico, 1856); 'Clouds and Stars' (Guadalajara, 1865); and 'Legends and Romances' (San Francisco, 1868); also a collection of poems, 'Home Stories.' He wrote many comedies. The drama 'Maria Antonieta de Lorena' is regarded as his best work.

Gallatin, Albert. An American statesman, financier, and author; born in Geneva, Switzerland, Jan. 29, 1761; came to this country in 1780; died at Astoria, L. I., Aug. 12, 1849. He was in Congress 1795–1801; Secretary of the Treasury 1801–1813; minister to France 1815–1823, and to England 1826–27. Later he engaged in banking. Among his works are: 'Considerations of the Currency and Banking Systems of the United States' (1831); 'Memoir on Northeastern Boundary' (1843); 'Notes on the Semi-Civilized Nations of Mexico, Yucatan, and Central America' (1845).

Gallaudet, Thomas Hopkins. An American writer and educator; born at Philadelphia, 1787; died at Hartford, Conn., 1851. In 1817 founded at Hartford the first deaf-mute institute in America, but in 1830 he resigned the presidency of it. He was afterwards chaplain of the Connecticut Retreat for the Insane from 1838 until his death. He wrote 'Bible Stories for the Young' (1838) and 'The Child's Book of the Soul' (1850).

Gallego, Juan Nicasio (gäl-yä'gō). A Spanish lyric poet; born in Zamora, Dec. 14, 1777; died at Madrid, Jan. 9, 1853. He studied law, philosophy, and theology, at Salamanca; but began a poetical career upon becoming intimate with Valdés, Quintana, and Cienfuegos. His political activity resulted in his imprisonment in 1814, and banishment for a short time subsequently. His first poetry was light and amorous, but he later took up sterner subjects. His 'The Second of May,' and an elegy upon the death of Queen Isabella (1818), have attained particular celebrity. He served in the Spanish Cortes for some years.

Gallenga, Antonio Carlo Napoleone (gälleng'-gä). An Italian publicist and author; born in Parma, Nov. 4, 1810; died at Llandogo, Wales,

Dec. 17, 1895. He left Italy in 1831 for political reasons. He represented Piedmont at Frankfort in 1848–49, and was a member of Parliament from 1854 to 1864. He was long the London Times's special correspondent in Italy. His works, many of them issued under the name of "Mariotti," include: 'Italy, Past and Present' (1841–49); 'Castellamonte, an Autobiography' (1854); 'Mariotti's Italian Grammar,' which went through twelve editions; 'History of Piedmont' (1855–56); 'The Pearl of the Antilles' (1873); and several books of travel.

Galt, John. A Scottish novelist; born at Irvine, Ayrshire, May 2, 1779; died at Greenock, April 11, 1839. Going abroad, he met Lord Byron at Gibraltar, and sailed with him for Greece. Returning to London, he contributed to Blackwood's. 'The Annals of the Parish' was published in 1821, and met a popular welcome. In rapid succession appeared 'Sir Andrew Wylie,' 'The Entail,' 'The Steamboat,' 'The Provost,' 'Ringan Gilhaize,' 'The Spaewife,' and 'Rothelan.' His 'Literary Miscellanies' was published in 1834. He also wrote a 'Life of Byron.'

Galton, Francis. A distinguished English anthropologist and traveler; born at Duddeston, near Birmingham, 1822. He is grandson of Erasmus Darwin, and thus a kinsman of the celebrated author of 'The Origin of Species.' His principal works are: 'Narrative of an Explorer in Tropical South Africa' (1853); 'The Art of Travel, or Shifts and Contrivances in Wild Countries' (1855); 'Hereditary Genius, its Laws and Consequences' (1869); 'Experiments in Pangenesis' (1871); and in the same line of studies, 'English Men of Science, their Nature and Nurture' (1874); 'Inquiry into Human Faculty' (1883); 'Natural Inheritance' (1889); 'Finger Prints' (1893). He has also written several memoirs on anthropometric subjects and kindred topics. He has held official positions in connection with the Royal Society, the Royal Geographical Society, and other scientific bodies. He invented the system of composite photography.

Gama, José Basilio da (gä'mä). A Brazilian poet; born in the district of Rio-dos-Mortes, Brazil, in 1740; died in Lisbon, Portugal, July 31, 1795. Educated by the Jesuits, he joined their order; but about 1786 renounced his allegiance to it, and published the poem 'Uruguay' to expose the alleged Jesuit design of forming an independent State among the Uruguay Indians. He was elected a member of the Academy of Lisbon. He also published 'Lenitivo da Sandade do Principe D. José' (1788), and 'Quitubia' (1791).

Ganghofer, Ludwig (gäng'hōf-ėr). A German dramatist and novelist; born in Kaufbeuren, July 7, 1855; resides in Vienna. At first engaged in mechanics, he later embarked in literature. His first great triumph in the drama was 'The Sculptor of Oberammergau,' written in collaboration with Hans Neuert.

His other plays have been staged in all the European capitals. His novels steadily grow in repute; the most successful are: 'It Was Once Upon a Time,' and 'Discontent.' His volume of lyric poetry, 'From the Tribe of Asia,' has attracted great attention.

Gannett, William Channing. An American clergyman and author; born in Boston, Mass., March 13, 1840. He graduated from Harvard in 1860. He has held the pastorates of several Unitarian churches throughout the West and East. Among his works are: 'Memoir of E. S. Gannett' (1875); 'A Year of Miracle' (1881); 'The Thought of God' (with F. L. Hosmer); 'Of Making One's Self Beautiful.'

Garay, János (gor'oi). A Hungarian dramatist and poet; born in Szegszard, Oct. 10, 1812; died at Buda-Pesth, Nov. 5, 1853. His work was inspired by the German drama; as shown in 'Arbocz,' his best-known historical composition. The poems 'The Skirmisher,' 'Bosnyák Zsofia,' and 'Arpádok,' and a volume of historical ballads, have received warm praise from the best European critics.

Garborg, Arne. A Norwegian novelist; born in Jæderen, Jan. 25, 1851. He was the son of humble parents, and prepared himself with difficulty for a school-teacher's career. He took up literature as a means of expressing his theories, and produced the novels 'Pleasant Students' and 'Mannfolk,' both of a rebellious and often displeasing realism, which brought him fame,—but also trouble, for the truthful portraiture in one of them cost him his post in the government service.

Garção, Pedro Antonio Correa (gär-säṅ'). A Portuguese poet; born in Lisbon, April 29, 1724; died there, Nov. 10, 1772. As a lyric poet he stands very high; while his satires, odes, and epistles,—upon the models of Horace,—are dainty and spiritual. He also wrote successful dramas. The Portuguese esteem him for the perfection with which he employed their language in his works. The 'Hymn to Dido' is one of his most popular productions. He was arrested for a personal satire, and died in prison after a long captivity.

Garcia de Quevedo, José Heriberto (gär-thē'ä dē kā-vā'dō). A South-American author; born in Coro, Venezuela, March 1819; died in Paris, June 1871. Educated in France and Spain, he settled in Paris, and was killed in the communard insurrection of 1871. Among his poems are: 'To Columbus'; 'To Liberty'; 'To Pius IX.'; 'Frenzy'; 'The Life to Come'; and 'The Proscript.' His dramas were well received. He wrote the novels 'The Love of a Girl' and 'Two Duels Eighteen Years Apart.'

Garcia Gutierrez. See **Gutierrez.**

Garcia y Tassara, Gabriel (gär-thē'ä e täs-är'ä). A Spanish poet and publicist; born in Seville, June 16, 1817; died at Madrid, Feb. 14, 1875. Among his noteworthy poems, 'A

Devil into the Bargain' (Un Diablo Más) is reckoned the best. His lyrics are very effective.

Garcilaso de la Vega (gär-thē-läs'ō dā lä vā'gä). [Properly Garcias Laso.] A Spanish poet of high rank; born in Toledo in 1503; died at Nice, Oct. 14, 1536. He appeared very early at the court of Charles V., where his progress was rapid, not alone in letters but in arms. He became ambassador to France and subsequently traveled in Alva's suite, only to lose the Emperor's favor and languish long in prison. He it was who naturalized the smoother of the Italian metres in Spain, and softened the stern outlines of his country's models into a delicate elegance. Theocritus, Virgil, and Petrarch, he copied gracefully but unblushingly, as in his famed 'First Eclogue.' Sonnets, lyrics, pastorals, and canzone were written by him in great profusion, often on the eve of battle. He was mortally wounded while charging an enemy at the head of his troops.

Garczynski, Stephen (gär-chin'skē). A Polish poet; born in Kosmovo, Oct. 13, 1806; died at Avignon, Sept. 20, 1833. He studied law at Warsaw, and heard Hegel lecture at Berlin; after which he took part in the revolution of 1831, and then fled to France. His epic poem, 'The Fate of Waclaw,' and his minor poetry, display a pronounced tendency to mysticism; but they are an earnest expression of the Polish spirit of independence and its yearning for a national life.

Gardiner, Samuel Rawson. An eminent English historian; born at Ropley, Hants, England, March 4, 1829; died in London, Feb. 23, 1902. He was educated at Winchester and Oxford, and later was professor of modern history at King's College, London. His great unfinished ('History of England from the Accession of James I. to the Restoration') is one of the monuments of English historical work. Among his lesser books, but all of the soundest excellence, are 'The Fall of the Monarchy of Charles I.' and 'The Thirty Years' War,' in the 'Epochs of History' series; a 'Students' History of England'; and a volume (1897) on the Gunpowder Plot.

Gardner, Dorsey. An American editor, compiler, and author; born in Philadelphia, Aug. 1, 1842; died in Short Hills, N. J., Nov. 30, 1894. He was at one time connected with the Christian Union and New York Commercial Advertiser; became one of the secretaries of the United States Centennial Commission; and since 1882 had been engaged editorially in the revision of the Webster 'International Dictionary.' He published: 'Quatre Bras, Ligny, and Waterloo' (1882); 'A Condensed Etymological Dictionary of the English Language' (1884).

Garfield, James Abram. Twentieth President of the United States; born at Orange, O., 1831; died at Elberon, N. J., 1881. His 'Collected Works' (2 vols., 1883) have been edited by B. A. Hinsdale.

Garland, Hamlin. An American story-writer and poet; born in La Crosse, Wis., Sept. 16, 1860. His works include: 'Main Traveled Roads' (1891); 'A Spoil of Office'; 'Prairie Folks'; 'Prairie Songs' (1893); 'Crumbling Idols'; 'Little Norsk' (1893); 'Rose of Dutcher's Coolly' '(1895); 'The Long Trail'; 'Money Magic.'

Garnett, Richard. An English librarian, editor, and poet; born in Lichfield, England, Feb. 27, 1835. Keeper of Printed Books in the British Museum. He has edited the works of Shelley, De Quincey, Peacock, Drayton, and others; and is the author of biographies of Carlyle, Emerson, and Milton, in the 'Great Writers' series. Besides contributions to periodicals and encyclopædias, he has published: 'Io in Egypt, and Other Poems' (1859); 'Poems from the German' (1862); 'The Twilight of the Gods, and Other Tales' (1889); 'Iphigenia in Delphi, a Dramatic Poem,' 'A History of Italian Literature.' Died Apr. 13, 1906.

Garnier, Robert (gär-nē-ā'). A French poet; born in La Ferté-Bernard, Maine, in 1534; died at Le Mans, Aug. 15, 1590. He studied law, and sat in the Parliament of Paris, but his 'Floral Diversions' caused him to be more widely known as a poet than as a lawyer. He wrote eight tragedies that attracted much attention, 'Porcie' and 'Bradamante' being the best; but they are scarcely adapted to the stage. He was the predecessor of Corneille, and marks a distinct epoch in the development of French literature.

Garrison, William Lloyd. The famous American abolitionist and journalist; born in Newburyport, Mass., Dec. 10 or 12, 1804 or 1805 (authorities conflict); died in New York city, May 24, 1879. He began life as a printer. After writing for various papers in New England, he became associate editor of the Genius of Universal Emancipation, published at Baltimore, Md. In 1831 he founded the famous anti-slavery paper, the Liberator, in Boston. He was also the founder of the American Anti-Slavery Society, and its president from 1843 to 1865. Among his works are: 'Thoughts on African Colonization' (1832); 'Sonnets and Poems' (1843).

Gárshin, Vsevolod Michailovich (gär'shin). A Russian novelist; born in Bachmut, Yekaterinoslav, Feb. 14, 1855; died at St. Petersburg, April 5, 1888. He took part in the Russo-Turkish war, and was wounded at Charkow. He soon after finished his great work 'Four Days,' in which the sufferings and hallucinations of a wounded soldier are strikingly set forth. 'A Very Little Story,' 'The Night,' and several more novels, came from his pen during the next few years. He developed a tendency to melancholy (occasionally relapsing into insanity), traces of which are to be found in 'Attalea Princeps' and 'Night,' two weird tales; and in the psychiatrical study of 'The Red Flower.' He had intervals of sheer mental blankness.

Garth, Sir Samuel. An English physician and poet; born in Yorkshire (?), 1661, or at Bolam, Durham, 1660 (?); died in London (?), Jan. 18, 1719. His medical practice made him famous; still more so the 'Dispensary' (1699), a polemic poem, written to sustain the physicians in a contemporary war upon the apothecaries. He also translated Ovid, and made stinging epigrams.

Gascoigne, Caroline Leigh (gas'koin). An English novelist and poet; born (Smith) at Dale Park (?), May ?, 1813; died June 11, 1883. Literature was her earliest taste, and after her marriage to a noted soldier she wrote 'Temptation, or a Wife's Perils' (1839); 'The School for Wives' (1839); 'The Next-Door Neighbors' (1855); and other novels showing keen observation of character and of the subjective life. 'Belgravia' (1851) reveals her pleasingly as a poet.

Gascoigne, George (gas-koin'). An English poet; born perhaps in Westmoreland, 1525 (?); died in Stamford, Lincolnshire, Oct. 7, 1577. 'The Steele Glass' (1576) is probably the first English satire written in blank verse; 'Jocasta' is a tragedy modeled upon a play by Euripides; these, his lyrics, and 'The Glass of Government,' a prose comedy intercalated with poesies, were much esteemed in their day.

Gaskell, Elizabeth Cleghorn (Stevenson). An English novelist; born in Chelsea, Sept. 29, 1810; died Nov. 12, 1865. She had been long a wife and mother before she turned her attention to story-writing, which she did for the sake of forgetting a domestic grief. 'Mary Barton,' a book of the class to which Dickens's 'Hard Times' belongs; 'Sylvia's Lovers,' a revelation of the old press-gang's doings; 'Cousin Phillis,' a story of humor and pathos in tasteful alternation; and 'Cranford,' a series of sketches,—the last-named a seemingly enduring classic,—are her best. Her 'Life of Charlotte Brontë' brought her under criticism, but as a writer she belongs to a rank by no means crowded.

Gasparin, Agénor Étienne, Comte de (gaspä-rań'). A French publicist and author; born in Orange, France, July 12, 1810; died near Geneva, Switzerland, May 14, 1871. Elected to the Chamber in 1846, he attracted attention by his advocacy of religious liberty, prison reform, abolition of slavery, and social purity. At the outbreak of the American Civil War he published two books maintaining the justice of the Federal cause, entitled 'The Uprising of a Great People' (1861) and 'America before Europe' (1862). Other important works were: 'Slavery' (1838); 'Christianity and Paganism' (1850); 'Liberal Christianity' (1869); 'Innocent III.,' published posthumously.

Gaspé, Philip Aubert de. A Canadian author; born in Quebec, Oct. 30, 1786; died there, Jan. 29, 1871. A lawyer, afterwards sheriff, he became involved in debt for which he was imprisoned four years; and when

14

released, secluded himself on his estate of St. Jean Port-Joli. His 'Old-Time Canadians' (1862), and his 'Memoirs' (1866), treat of Canadian traditions and folk-lore, and were written in French. The former was perhaps the most popular book ever published in Canada. An English translation was made by Mrs. Pennie.

Gassendi, Pierre (gäs-san-dē). A French philosopher, scholar, and astronomer; born near Digne, Provence, Jan. 22, 1592; died at Paris, Oct. 24, 1655. A child-prodigy at 4, despite poverty and mean birth he fought his way to becoming the academic miracle of his day. A list of his works would be a catalogue of seventeenth-century science: but above the rest stand 'Exercises in Paradox in Opposition to Aristotle'; 'Objections to the Theories of Descartes'; and 'On the Life, Character, and Doctrine of Epicurus.' Either because he was so miscellaneous, or because his mind was more acquisitive than profound, he failed to contribute materially to the sum of human knowledge; but his writings clearly denote that he was gifted with a most subtle intellect.

Gaszynski, Konstantin (gä-shin'ske *or* gäsh-tsin'ske). A Polish poet and novelist; born in Ieziorno, near Warsaw, March 30, 1809; died at Aix, Provence, Oct. 8, 1866. His early literary career was interfered with by the distracted condition of his country, and he took refuge in France in 1831. Among his productions, 'Songs of a Polish Pilgrim'; 'Recollections of an Officer'; 'Poems'; 'Stories and Scenes from Aristocratic Life'; and two or three others, are prominent. He wrote in both Polish and French, and the literary studies to which he devoted himself in Provence are widely quoted as authorities on its language and people.

Gatty, Margaret. An English juvenile writer; born (Scott) at Burnham, Essex, 1809; died in Ecclesfield, Oct. 3, 1873. Her career in letters was inaugurated with 'The Fairy Godmother and Other Tales' (1851); but 'Parables from Nature' (1855–71) is most popular.

Gaudy, Baron Franz von (goud'tē *or* goud'ē). A German poet and novelist; born in Frankfort-on-the-Oder, April 19, 1800; died at Berlin, Feb. 6, 1840. He began life a soldier, but abandoned arms for literature at the age of 33. His bent was toward humorous poetry and epigram; and 'Erato,' his first book of any importance, is in the Heine vein. His lyric poetry is of unequal merit, while his songs are more or less imitations of French popular authors. 'Desangaño,' 'Extracts from the Diary of a Traveling Tailor,' and 'Venetian Sketches,' are distinguished among his works of fiction. He wrote some very good accounts of his travels in Europe.

Gautier, Judith (gō-tyä'). A French novelist, poet, and miscellaneous writer, daughter of Théophile Gautier and Carlotta Grisi the famous Italian singer; born in Paris, 1850. She married Catulle Mendès, but was divorced. When quite young she learned Chinese from a mandarin, a guest of her father, and has ever since evinced great interest in the Oriental languages and literature. Her first work, under the name "Judith Walther," was 'The Book of Jade' (1867), a collection of prose and verse translated from the Chinese; it was followed by 'The Imperial Dragon' (1869), a Chinese romance, signed "Judith Mendès"; 'The Usurper,' a Japanese romance, crowned by the French Academy in 1875; 'Lucienne' (1877); 'The Cruelties of Love' (1878); 'Isoline' (1881); 'Poems of the Dragon Fly' (1884), adapted from the Japanese; 'Potiphar's Wife' (1884), a Persian romance; 'The Merchant of Smiles' (1888), a drama adapted from the Chinese; 'The Marriage of Fingal' (1888), a lyric poem; 'The Contemporaneous' (1901).

Gautier, Léon. A French scholar and critic; born in Havre, Aug. 8, 1832. He held official positions connected with the schools and libraries of his native place till his growing eminence as a writer brought him to Paris. His works, which are criticized for a tendency to overestimate the Middle Ages, count among their choicest few: 'Chivalry'; 'Benedict XI., a Study of the Papacy'; and 'Contemporary Portraits and Present Questions.' Died. 1897.

Gautier, Théophile. A French poet, critic, and novelist; born in Tarbes, Hautes Pyrénées, 1811; died near Paris, 1872. His works include: 'Poems' (1830); 'Albertus' (1833); 'Young France' (1833); 'Mademoiselle de Maupin' (1835). His best work as a critic is the 'History of Romanticism' (1854). As a result of his travels he wrote: 'A Journey in Spain' (1843); 'Italy' (1852); 'Constantinople' (1854); etc.: also the novels 'Miltona' (1847); 'Arria Marcella' (1852); etc. Other stories are: 'The Golden Fleece'; 'Beautiful Jenny'; 'Mademoiselle Dafne'; 'Omphale'; 'The Little Dog of the Marquise'; 'The Nest of Nightingales' (1833); 'The Loving Dead' (1836); 'The Chain of Gold'; 'A Night of Cleopatra's' (1845); 'Jean and Jeannette' (1846); 'The Tiger Skin' (1864–65); 'Spirite' (1866); etc. For the stage he wrote: 'Posthumus Pierrot' (1845); 'The Jewess of Constantine' (1846); 'Look but Do Not Touch' (1847); etc. His works of pure fantasy are: 'Avatar'; 'A Year of the Devil' (1839); and themes for ballets. Some of his poems have been collected under the title of 'The Comedy of Death.' On art he has written: 'Modern Art' (1852); 'The Arts in Europe' (1852); etc.

Gay, Delphine (gā). A French poet and novelist, daughter of Sophie; born in Aix-la-Chapelle, Jan. 26, 1804; died at Paris, June 29, 1855. Carefully educated by her celebrated mother, Sophie Gay, she won fame with her poetry at the age of fifteen, an academic prize at eighteen, and a royal pension at twenty. After her marriage with the famous Émile de Girardin in 1831, she began to write romances, and they proved prodigiously popular. Her poems include 'Sisters of St. Camille,' 'The Vision of Joan of Arc,' and 'The Widow of Nain.' Her best-known works of fiction are 'Lorgnon,' 'The Marquis de Pontanges,' and 'Balzac's Cane.' Her literary work is characterized by a tendency to mysticism and a somewhat lackadaisical style.

Gay, John. An English poet; born near Barnstaple, Devonshire, in August (?) 1685; died at London, Dec. 4, 1732. His life was a series of vicissitudes: starvation and luxury, neglect and admiration, alternating in kaleidoscopic abruptness throughout his bohemian existence. His 'Rural Sports' gave him his start in literature; and 'Trivia, or the Art of Walking the Streets of London' has become a classic. But 'The Beggar's Opera' (the first English comic opera), the 'Fables,' and 'The Shepherd's Week,' must remain his enduring monuments. He wrote also 'The Wife of Bath,' and many other poems which add to his reputation.

Gay, Sophie. A French novelist; born (Nichault de Lavalette) in Paris, July 1, 1776; died there, March 5, 1852. She married M. Liottier, a finai cier, in 1793; was divorced, and married M. Gay, a high government official. Her literary talent asserted itself early; and her romantic and sentimental but not silly novels — especially 'Laure d'Estell,' 'Léonie de Montbreuse,' and 'Anatole' — made her famous early in the century. Her play 'The Marquis of Pomenars' had quite a run.

Gay, Sydney Howard. An American author; born in Hingham, Mass., May 22, 1814; died in New Brighton, N. Y., June 25, 1888. He left Harvard before graduation on account of ill-health; and studied law, but abandoned it because he could not conscientiously take the required oath of allegiance to the Constitution of the United States. He became a "Garrisonian abolitionist," and in 1844 was editor of the Anti-Slavery Standard. In 1858 he became editorially connected with the New York Tribune, of which he was managing editor 1862-66. He wrote a 'History of the United States' (4 vols., 1876-81), of which W. C. Bryant wrote the preface; a 'Life of James Madison' (1884), in the 'American Statesmen' series; etc.

Gayángos y Arce, Pascual de (gī-äng'gōs ē är'thä). A Spanish scholar and historical writer; born in Seville, Spain, June 21, 1809. From 1843 to 1872 he held the professorship of Oriental languages at the University of Madrid; since 1881 he has resided mostly in London. He has published the 'Calendar of Letters Illustrative of the History of England in Connection with that of Spain, during the Reign of Henry VIII.' (7 vols.). In Spanish he has issued: 'Memoria del Mora Raris' (1845); 'Memorial History of Spain' (19 vols.); and contributions to various societies. Died 1897.

Gayarré, Charles Étienne Arthur (gī-ä-rā'). An American lawyer, politician, and historian; born at New Orleans, La., Jan. 9, 1805; died

there, Feb. 11, 1895. He was admitted to the bar in 1829; was several times a member of the Louisiana Legislature; deputy State Attorney-General (1831); Secretary of State of Louisiana (1846-53). Among his works, which deal largely with the history of his native State, are: 'History of Louisiana,' in French (1830); 'Louisiana, its History as a French Colony' (1851); 'Philip II. of Spain' (1866); 'Fernando de Lemos,' a novel (1872).

Gaylor, Charles. An American journalist and dramatist; born in New York city, April 1, 1820; died in Brooklyn, May 28, 1892. He wrote over 200 plays, and at one time had five produced simultaneously at New York theatres. He also wrote the first drama on the Civil War, entitled 'Bull Run.' Among his dramas are: 'The Gold Hunters'; 'Taking the Chances'; 'Lights and Shadows of New York'; 'Fritz.' Among his novels are: 'Out of the Streets' and 'Romance of a Poor Young Man.'

Gazzoletti, Antonio (gäts-ō-let'te). An Italian lyric poet; born in Nago, March 20, 1813; died at Milan, Aug. 21, 1866. He was a lawyer at Trieste for many years, and became a government pleader upon the union of Lombardy and Piedmont. Ballads and lyrics were his poetical forms. 'What Is the Italian's Country?' is an attempt to write a national hymn. 'Verses'; 'Memories and Fancies'; 'Umberto Biancamano'; and a poem written in honor of the Dante sexcentenary, have given him a prominent position among modern Italian authors.

Gebhart, Émile (geb-är'). A French critic and essayist; born in Nancy, July 19, 1839. His numerous writings have to do mostly with the poetry and art of antiquity. 'History of the Poetic Sentiment in Relation to Nature during the Greek and Roman Classical Period'; 'Essay on Genre Painting in Antiquity'; and 'Praxiteles,' are his typical productions.

Geddes, Patrick. A Scotch botanist and author; born in 1854. He was educated at the Normal School of Science under Professor Huxley, and at several foreign universities; and is now professor of botany at University College, Dundee. He is the founder of University Hall, Edinburgh, which is part of a vast scheme of university reform and social reconstruction. Besides numerous monographs and articles in the 'Encyclopædia Britannica,' he has written: 'Chapters in Modern Botany'; 'The Evolution of Sex' (with J. Arthur Thomson); 'The Classification of Statistics' (1882); 'John Ruskin, Economist' (1884); 'An Analysis of the Principles of Economics'; 'Evolution of Sex.'

Geffroy, Mathieu Auguste (zhef-rwä'). A French historian; born in Paris, April 21, 1820; died there, Aug. 15, 1895. He was called to the chair of history at Bordeaux in 1852. He became professor of ancient history at Paris in 1872; and three years later was appointed director of the French school at Rome. Besides several articles in the Revue des Deux Mondes, he published: 'History of the

Scandinavians' (1851); 'Letters of Charles XII.' (1852); 'Gustavus III. and his Court' (1867); 'Rome and the Barbarians' (1875); 'Madame de Maintenon' (1887).

Geibel, Emanuel (gī'bel). A German poet; born in Lübeck, Oct. 18, 1815; died there, April 6, 1884. His early choice was for the clerical life, but he soon turned to poetry and to the study of Greek history and letters. He was a versatile writer, and many productions of exquisite sentiment and pathos, as well as works in lighter vein,—notably 'Master Andrea,' a comedy,—have proceeded from his pen.

Geijer, Erik Gustaf (yī'er). A Swedish historian; born in the province of Wermland, Jan. 12, 1783; died in Stockholm, April 23, 1847. At 20 he won a prize from the Swedish Academy for a eulogy of the great mediæval regent Sten Sture, and at 27 became professor of history at the University of Upsala. He sat in the national Parliament for some years, and was distinguished for his eloquence. His 'History of the Swedish People,' 'History of the State of Sweden from 1718 to 1772,' and various contributions to the history of philosophy, theology, and æsthetics, are epoch-making in Swedish letters. He had considerable musical talent, and many of his compositions have become favorite songs in Sweden.

Geikie, Archibald. A Scotch geologist and scientific writer; born in Edinburgh, 1835. In the course of a brilliant career of discovery and experiment he has written: 'Elementary Lessons in Physical Geography' (4th ed. 1884); 'Scenery of Scotland Viewed in Connection with its Physical Geology' (2d ed. 1887); 'Outlines of Field Geology' (4th ed. 1891); 'Text-Book of Geology'; and 'The Founders of Geology.'

Geikie, James. A Scotch geologist and scientific writer, brother of Archibald; born in Edinburgh, 1839. 'The Great Ice Age' (2d ed. 1877), 'Prehistoric Europe' (1881), and 'Earth Sculpture' are works of profound learning and distinguished by much brilliancy of style.

Geiregat, Pieter (gī-rä-gädt'). A Flemish novelist and dramatist; born in Ghent, Feb. 25, 1828. He began as a journalist, but soon became known as a writer of sketches and stories, and plays of realistic and spectacular character. His best fictions are: 'The Workman's Life' and 'Folk Voices.' He is happy in delineating the national character, and successful also as a historical novelist. Among the most widely known of his plays are: 'Mother Rosa'; 'Egmont'; and 'The Two Sisters.' Died at Ghent, in 1902.

Gellert, Christian Fürchtegott (gel'lert). A German prose-writer of eminence, and a popular poet; born in Hainichen, July 4, 1715; died in Leipzig, Dec. 13, 1769. His place in German literature is that of a restorer and a reformer. He began his literary career proper in 1743 with his famous series of fables, tales, and proverbial sayings. Abandoning a church career, he took up school-teaching; and his

lectures on literary topics won him a new renown. During the Seven Years' War he was visited by princes, Frederick the Great invited him to his palace, and regiments of soldiers attended his class recitations. Later in life he fell into a profound melancholy. 'Spiritual Odes and Songs'; 'Moral Precepts'; 'The Loving Sisters'; 'Moral and Didactic Poems'; and above all, the 'Fables,' are the works most widely read in his own day.

Gelli, Giambattista (jäl'ē). An Italian literary critic and dramatist; born in Florence, Aug. 12, 1493; died there, July 24, 1563. Originally a stocking-weaver, he devoted his leisure to study, became known for his learning, and held thronged public readings upon Dante. His writings, partly in dialogue form, are excellent specimens of the Italian of the sixteenth century. 'Readings in the Florentine Academy,' 'Readings on Petrarch,' 'Lectures on Dante,' and similar studies, are authoritative upon their respective subjects. His comedies — 'Sport,' founded upon the 'Aulularia' of Plautus, and 'Error,' a broad burlesque — are famous in Italian literature.

Gellius, Aulus (jel'i-us). A Latin diarist and prose-writer; born in Rome (?), about 130 A.D.; died about 180. Like other rich youths, he studied in the best schools at Rome and finished off at Athens; in Rome he held judicial office for some years. The 'Attic Nights,' which he must thank for his fame, is based on his diary; and it owes much of its interest to the fact that every modern writer of historical novels dealing with the period from Augustus to Marcus Aurelius is compelled to study its gossipy pages, owing to the unrivaled verisimilitude of its pictures.

Gemmingen, Baron Otto Heinrich von (gem'ing-en). A German dramatist; born in Heilbronn, Nov. 5, 1755; died at Heidelberg, March 15, 1836. He was in the diplomatic service of Baden for a time, and his first dramatic productions saw the light at Vienna. His best-known works are: 'The German Family Man,' a play in metre, founded upon Diderot's 'Father of a Family'; and a brilliant adaptation of Shakespeare's 'Richard II.' He wrote a number of minor plays, most of them metrical.

Genast, Karl Albert Wilhelm (gä-näst). A German poet and dramatist; born in Leipsic, July 30, 1822; died at Weimar, Jan. 18, 1887. He studied law and then entered politics, becoming one of the leaders of the popular party at Weimar. 'Bernhard of Weimar,' a tragedy, 'Little Thorn-Rose,' a volume of poems, and 'Florian Geyer,' a novel, are his most notable works.

Genée, Rudolf (zhā-nā). A German literary critic, dramatist, and poet; born in Berlin, Dec. 12, 1824. He abandoned wood engraving for journalism, and then became an instructor in literature at Berlin. As a reader and interpreter of Shakespeare he attained distinction; but his plays — 'The Prodigy' (1854), 'A

New Timon,' 'In Front of the Cannon,' 'The [female] Hermit,' and adaptations from Sheridan,— raised him to the front rank. His works in criticism, treating of German poetry, the drama, and kindred themes, are standard. 'Marienburg' is his successful historical novel.

Genlis, Stéphanie Félicité Ducrest de Saint-Aubin, Comtesse de (zhoṅ-lēs'). A French miscellaneous writer; born at Champcéri near Autun, Jan. 25, 1746; died at Paris, Dec. 31, 1830. Among her writings, which amount to about 90 volumes, are several little comedies intended to be acted by her pupils, the children of the Duke of Chartres; some stories, among them the romance 'Mademoiselle de Clermont' (1802); 'Unpublished Memoirs on the Eighteenth Century and the French Revolution' (10 vols., 1825); 'Baron d'Holbach's Dinners.'

Gensichen, Otto Fanz (gen'siċh-en). A German dramatist; born in Driesen, Feb. 4, 1847. He has produced a wide variety of pieces, as 'Caius Gracchus' and 'Danton,' tragedies; 'Euphrosyne,' 'Phryne,' and 'Aspasia,' spectacular plays; and several one-act " curtain-raisers." His most brilliant effects have been obtained with historical love-stories. He has produced a volume of miscellaneous poetry and a historical novel of merit.

Gentil-Bernard, Pierre Joseph Bernard called (zhoṅ-tēl' or zhoṅ-tē'bär-när'). A French poet and dramatist; born in Grenoble, Aug. 26, 1708; died at Choisy-le-Roi (?), Nov. 1, 1775. He was educated by the Jesuits at Lyons, and rose to the chief secretaryship on Marshal de Coigny's staff. He became immensely fashionable in all the salons in 1737, when his 'Castor and Pollux' appeared, with music by Rameau. Voltaire wrote him a letter of appreciation, comparing him with Ovid, and bestowing the title of " Gentil-Bernard " upon him. 'The Art of Love,' another of his works, is, like all his productions, highly erotic and in utterly false taste.

Gentz, Friedrich von (gents). A German publicist and controversial writer; born in Breslau, May 2, 1764; died near Vienna, June 9, 1832. His early predilections were favorable to the French Revolution; later he attacked it in various writings, including translations . from Edmund Burke, Mallet du Pan, and Mounier. His political career was very brilliant. He labored assiduously to form the Holy Alliance. He was a very able and persuasive writer of political pamphlets and of books against Napoleon; the most widely read being 'Origin and Character of the War against the French Revolution,' and 'Fragments of a History of the Balance of Power in Europe.'

Geoffrey of Monmouth (jef'ri). A British chronicler; born in Monmouth (?), 1100 (?); died at Llandaff, 1154. In his 'Chronicle or History of the Britons,' we are afforded a myriorama of Albion's Olympus, with Merlin and King Arthur, Lancelot and Tristan, and several ladies, indulging themselves in the characteristically lax and delightful manner of fanciful personages.

George, Amara, pseudonym of Mathilde Kaufmann. A German poet and story-writer; born (Binder) in Nuremberg, Dec. 5, 1835. Her reputation was achieved with 'Blooms of the Night,' a collection of poems. She has written pleasing tales, among them 'Before Daybreak.'

George, Henry. An American political economist; born in Philadelphia, Sept. 2, 1839; died in New York, Oct. 29, 1897. His 'Progress and Poverty' was published in 1879. Mr. George removed to New York in 1880. The following year 'The Irish Land Question' was given to the world. In 1886 he was candidate of the United Labor party for mayor of New York. He subsequently founded the Standard, a weekly newspaper. 'Social Problems' appeared in 1884, and 'Protection or Free Trade' in 1886. 'The Perplexed Philosopher,' etc., followed. A posthumous work on political economy is announced for publication in 1898. He was candidate for mayor of Greater New York at the time of his death.

Gerard, Dorothea (ji-rärd'). A Scotch novelist; born in Rochsoles, Lanarkshire, Aug. 9, 1855. Her youth was passed on the Continent, and she married an Austrian, Major-Genl. Julius de Lorggarde. She wrote with her sister, 'Reata' (1880) and 'Beggar My Neighbor'; and subsequently, alone, 'Lady Baby' and 'Recha' (1890). The latter was esteemed her best. 'Miss Providence' appeared in 1897.

Gérard de Nerval (zhā-rär' dĕ ner-väl'), pseudonym of Gérard Labrunie. A French poet, dramatist, and novelist; born in Paris, May 21, 1808; committed suicide there, Jan. 25, 1855. His 'National Elegies,' written at college and published at 19, reached two editions. He made a brilliant translation of 'Faust'; and had a comedy, 'Tartuffe at Molière's,' brought out at 22. 'The Queen of Sheba,' a play written in collaboration with the elder Dumas; 'A Voyage to Greece,' a book of travel; 'Lorelei,' a novel; 'Misanthropy and Remorse,' an imaginative tale; 'The Alchemist,' a play; and 'Dream and Reality,' a romance, are among his most important later works. But the splendid career and fortune within his reach were ruined by his improvidence and recklessness, which grew on him with age, till he was reduced to the direst poverty, and ended by hanging himself. He was one of the most imaginative and graceful writers of his country. The use of pseudonyms was habitual with him, "Aloysius," " Fritz," and " Lord Pilgrim " among them.

Gerbert de Montreuil (zher-bär' de môṅtrèy'). A French poet of the thirteenth century. His most noted work is a continuation of a romance of the Grail, or tale of knighthood, written by Chrestien de Troyes and entitled 'The Cavalier.' Another production, of about 1225, is the 'Romance of the Violet,' known also as 'Gérard de Nevers'; it is the model taken by Weber for his 'Euryanthe,' and by Shakespeare for 'Cymbeline.'

Gerhardt, Paul (gär'härdt). A German hymn-writer of great eminence; born in Gräfenhainichen, Saxony, March 12, 1607; died at Lübben, June 7, 1676. He was a stubbornly separatist Lutheran clergyman, involved in the political turmoils of the time. The production of his more than 100 famous hymns — including particularly "O Head all blood and wounds," "Now all the woodlands rest," "Oh, how shall I receive Thee?"—began about 1660. They made an epoch in psalmody.

Gerle, Wolfgang Adolf (gär'lè). A German story-writer and dramatist; born in Prague, July 9, 1781; died there by his own hand, June 29, 1846. He was a prolific author of works of light fiction, employing at times different pseudonyms,·such as "G. Erle," "Konrad Spät," "Hilarius Kurzweil," and others. 'Corals,' 'Schelmufsky's Strange Adventure,' and 'Moonlight Pictures and Shadows,' are popular. His plays, some written in collaboration with other authors, have been staged with success.

Gerok, Karl (gā-rōk'). A German religious poet; born in Vaihingen, Jan. 30, 1815; died at Stuttgart, Jan. 14, 1890. 'Palm Leaves,' his first ambitious effort, brought out in 1857, established his reputation; and in the ensuing years he put forth many collections of verse, mostly of a deeply religious and devotional character. They include: 'In Lonely Ways,' 'Flowers and Stars,' 'Beneath the Evening Star,' and 'The Last Nosegay.' His patriotic songs are widely known.

Gerstäcker, Friedrich (ger'stek-er *or* gär'-stek-er). A German writer of travel and fiction; born in Hamburg, May 10, 1816; died in Brunswick, May 31, 1872. He was the son of an opera singer who left him orphaned at an early age. After a seven-years' self-supporting tour in the United States, begun at 20, he returned to Germany and wrote: 'Sight-Seeing and Hunting Trips through the United States,' 'The Regulators of Arkansas,' 'Mississippi Scenes,' and other most interesting books which gave him speedy fame. He afterwards journeyed through Mexico and Venezuela, putting his impressions into works that sold widely. As a story-writer on his experiences of travel — 'California Sketches,' 'Under the Equator,' 'In Mexico,' etc.— he has been fairly successful.

Gerstenberg, Heinrich Wilhelm von (gär'-sten-bärg). A German dramatist, critic, and poet; born in Tondern, Schleswig, Jan. 3, 1737; died at Altona, Nov. 1, 1823. He studied law at Jena, and then entered the Danish army. He subsequently lived in Copenhagen. His literary career began with 'Trifles,' a collection of verse. 'War Songs of the Danish Grenadiers,' 'Song of a Scandinavian Bard,' 'The Bride,' and 'Ariadne in Naxos,' succeeded,— important and in many respects splendid efforts of poetic genius. His 'Letters on the

Striking Things in Literature' and his tragedy of 'Ugolino' have proved very popular. As a critic he pays special attention to Shakespeare and to the old dramatists of England.

Gervinus, Georg Gottfried (ger-fē'nös). A German historian and critic; born in Darmstadt, May 20, 1805; died at Heidelberg, March 18, 1871. His early work, 'History of the Anglo-Saxons,' procured him a place at Heidelberg in 1830, and after some preparatory travel he settled down to scholarship. 'History of German National Literature' and 'History of German Imaginative Poetry and Prose' mark this period. He next became professor of literature and history at Göttingen, bringing out his 'Essentials of Historic Science.' His political activity, however, caused him to lose his professorship, and he began a rather wandering career as writer, educator, and agitator until 1847, when he helped found and edited the Deutsche Zeitung. 'History of the Nineteenth Century,' 'Händel and Shakespeare,' and many important contributions to criticism and the philosophy of history, made during this period, shed lustre upon his name.

Geszner, Salomon (ges'ner). A Swiss poet and painter; born in Zürich, April 1, 1730; died there, March 2, 1788. Painting and etching were his earliest pursuits, and he distinguished himself in both; but his friendship with Wieland and Kleist turned him towards literature. His first success as a poet was in the 'Song of the Swiss to his Armed Sweetheart,' in 1751. 'Daphnis' and a volume of 'Idylls' spread his fame widely, and the 'Death of Abel' had great vogue in its day. He affected a mock-heroic style that is now distasteful.

Gevaert, François Auguste (gè-vär'). A French composer and writer on music; born at Huysse, near Oudenarde, July 30, 1828. He is the composer of several successful operas, and was inspector of music at the Academy of Music, Paris, from 1867 to 1870. Since that time he has devoted himself to the history of music. His publications include: 'History and Theory of Music in Antiquity' (first part, 1875); 'Treatise on Instrumentation'; 'The Origin of the Liturgic Chant in the Latin Church' (1890).

Geyter, Julius de (chä'tèr). A Flemish poet; born in Lede, May 25, 1830. He was in early life a school-teacher and later a law-court official, but for many years he has been connected with a bank in Antwerp. His best-known work is the epic 'Emperor Charles.' His songs, which deal with national heroic topics, and his cantatas, are exquisitely melodious and metrically perfect, and are favorites with his people.

Gherardi del Testa, Tommaso (gā-rär'dē del tes'tä). An Italian comedy-writer; born in Terriciuola, near Pisa, 1815; died near Pistoja, Oct. 13, 1881. After studying at Pisa, he settled as a lawyer in Florence; but in 1848 he enlisted for the war with Austria and was taken prisoner. He had already written 'The Son of an Illegitimate,' a novel; but he now turned his attention entirely to comedy, and rose rapidly to prominence through the inimitable drollery of his dialogue and the originality of his situations. 'George's System,' 'Men Must Not be Trifled With,' and 'The Reign of Adelaide,' are conspicuous among his many productions. Of a less mirthful but more satirical nature are 'The Fashion and the Family,' 'New Life,' 'The False Letters,' and other efforts of his maturer years.

Ghislanzoni, Antonio (gēs-län-zō'nē). An Italian dramatist, journalist, and humorist; born in Lecco, 1824; died there, July 18, 1893. He first studied medicine, then became an opera-singer, finally entering political journalism. In the upheavals of 1848 he had various adventures, including capture on the battlefield. He lost his voice shortly after the return of peace, and for a time supported himself by writing for the comic papers, founding one or two himself. He tried his hand at many kinds of literary work, and was most successful as a writer of librettos, 'Aïda' being probably the best. He has produced 'Book of Oddities,' 'A Forbidden Book,' 'Fashion in Art,' and numerous similar volumes, all of a rather ephemeral nature.

Giacometti, Paolo (jä-kō-met'ē). An Italian dramatist; born in Novi Ligure, March 19, 1816; died at Rome, August 1882. He achieved distinction in his twentieth year with a drama, 'Rosilda,' written during his law-student days in Genoa. Forced into literary work by his family's poverty, his dramaturgic talent attained him a competence. Sickness and domestic adversity did not interfere with his prolific genius, and his plays show astonishing versatility. 'Queen Elizabeth of England,' 'Torquato Tasso,' and 'Lucrezia Davidson,' tragedies; 'Sophocles,' his masterpiece, also a tragedy; and numerous comedies, including 'The Woman with a Second Husband,' are among the popular examples of his work.

Giacomino da Verona (jä-kō-mē'nō dä vā-rō'nä). An Italian poet of the thirteenth century. He owes his importance in literature chiefly to his anticipation of Dante, and such influence as his work may have had upon the form and spirit of the 'Divine Comedy.' He would appear to have been a Franciscan monk, who composed two crude but striking poems in the Veronese dialect on the subjects respectively of heaven and hell, 'The Celestial Jerusalem' being one and 'The Infernal City of Babylon' the other.

Giacosa, Giuseppe (jä-kō'sa). An Italian dramatist; born in Colleretto-Parella, Piedmont, Oct. 21, 1847. A lawyer for many years, the success of one or two plays in metrical form, the fruit of his leisure, led him to turn playwright solely. His wit and taste have long made him popular. 'The Husband in Love with his Wife' and 'Brothers in Arms' are his best productions, but of great merit are 'The Sons of the Marquis' and 'Arthur.' He is the author of both dramas and comedies,

and his treatment of contemporary Italian social life is irresistibly satirical.

Giannone, Pietro (jän-nō'nä). An Italian poet; born in Campo Santo, near Modena, 1790; died at Florence, Dec. 24, 1873. When a lad he entered the army of the first Napoleon, on whose fall he went to Rome and lived by his pen. His political affiliations caused his imprisonment, and later he lived in exile at Paris; but finally settled in Florence. 'The Exile' and 'The Vision' are his masterpieces; but he wrote much and well, patriotism and Italian political evils affording him his inspiration.

Gibbon, Charles. A British novelist; born 1836; died Aug. 15, 1890. The Scotch masses were studied by him with enthusiasm, affording subjects for 'Robin Gray' and the Jacobite tale 'For the King'; but his 'For Lack of Gold' and 'A Heart's Problem,' and one or two more, indicate exhaustion, although 'The Braes of Yarrow' is a fine work.

Gibbon, Edward. A great English historian; born at Putney, Surrey, April 27, 1737; died at London, Jan. 16, 1794. His writings are: 'Essay on the Study of Literature' (1761), in French; 'Critical Observations' (1770), on one of the arguments of Warburton's 'Divine Legation of Moses'; 'History of the Decline and Fall of the Roman Empire' (6 vols., 1776-88); 'Vindication' of the 15th and 16th chapters of the 'History' (1779); 'Miscellaneous Works, with Memoir Composed by Himself' (1796). It has lately been discovered that this Memoir was not printed as written by Gibbon, but had been changed in important particulars by whoever prepared it for the press.

Gibbons, James (Cardinal). An American prelate of great celebrity; born in Baltimore, July 23, 1834. He was raised to the cardinalate June 30, 1886. His contributions to secular and religious reviews are frequent and valuable. Among his published works are: 'The Faith of Our Fathers'; 'Our Christian Heritage'; 'The Ambassador of Christ'; etc.

Gibson, William Hamilton. An American artist and author; born in Sandy Hook, Conn., Oct. 5, 1850; died at Washington, Conn., July 16, 1896. A specialist in botany, he contributed to the American Agriculturist and Hearth and Home, and supplied many natural-history subjects for the 'American Cyclopædia.' Many of his illustrations appeared in the Art Journal and in Picturesque America; and his illustrations of books were numerous and popular. He was a member of the Art Union and the Authors' Club. The essays 'Birds of Plumage,' 'A Winter Idyl,' and 'Springtime,' appeared in Harper's Magazine. His later works included 'Our Edible Toadstools and Mushrooms.'

Giddings, Joshua Reed. An eminent American lawyer, politician, and author; born at Athens, Pa., Oct. 6, 1795; died at Montreal, May 27, 1864. He was admitted to the Ohio bar in 1820; elected a member of its Legislature in 1826, and of Congress in 1838, where he was prominent as an opponent of slavery. In 1861 he was appointed consul-general to British North America. Among his works are: 'The Exiles of Florida' (1858); 'History of the Rebellion' (1864).

Giesebrecht, Ludwig (gē'ze-brècht). A German poet; born in Mirow, Mecklenburg-Strelitz, July 5, 1792; died at Jasenitz, near Stettin, March 18, 1873. He was a clergyman's son; studied at the University of Berlin, and later at Stettin; fought in the German war of liberation (1813); and subsequently became a professor. 'Epic Poems,' 'Wendish Tales,' and poetry in dialect, comprise his most popular productions.

Giffen, Robert, Sir. An English editor, statistician, and writer on economic and financial subjects; born at Strathaven, Lanarkshire, Scotland, in 1837. At first in trade at Glasgow, in 1862 he came to London, where he was subeditor of the Globe till 1866. He was acting editor of the Economist under Walter Bagehot 1868-76; then founded the Statist, and became chief of the Statistical Department in the Board of Trade—since 1882 its assistant secretary. He was John Morley's assistant on the Fortnightly Review 1873-76; and is the author of a number of reports, papers, and essays, which have given him a high rank. 'American Railways as Investments' appeared in 1873, and was followed by 'Stock Exchange Securities' (1877); 'Essays in Finance' (1879); 'The Progress of the Working Classes in the Last Half 'Century'; 'Economic Inquiries and Studies.'

Gifford, William. An English satirical poet, translator, and critic; born at Ashburton, Devonshire, April 1756; died in London, Dec. 31, 1826. His 'Baviad' (1791), based on Juvenal's first satire, and his 'Mæviad' (1795), founded upon Horace, both aimed at the Della Crusca poetlings, gave him an authoritative position in the literary world. He edited the Anti-Jacobin for a time; but his supreme later position was as editor of the Quarterly Review, the great Tory organ, which made him a power in politics as well as letters. He probably wrote the famous review of Keats's 'Endymion,' inaccurately supposed to have killed that poet.

Gil Polo, Gaspar (Hēl po'lo). A Spanish poet; born in Valencia about 1535; died at Barcelona in 1591. He was a lawyer in his native town, and successful; but his principal fame arises from his poems,— one of them, 'Diana Enamored,' being a gem of Spanish literature. It is a continuation of Montemayor's 'Diana,' but excels that production in beauty of style and metre, and in the number and variety of its episodes, lifting its author high above the lyric level of his time.

Gil Vicente (Hēl vē-then'tä). A Portuguese dramatist and actor, father of the drama of his country; born in Lisbon (?), about 1475; died there (?), about 1536 or 1538. He studied law, and was a goldsmith in early manhood.

His first play was a pastoral in Spanish, written in 1502 in honor of the birth of the Portuguese prince royal (afterward John III.). This made an immense hit at court, and thereafter he wrote every new play that was acted at the royal festivals. Farces, comedies, dramas, and tragedies, of keen wit, originality, and great poetic talent, appear among his works, which rank him beside the very great authors not of Portugal only, but of the whole Iberian peninsula. He originated many of the methods and canons of taste that are now the accepted tenets of the European theatre. In construction and dialogue, his 'Dom Duardos' and 'Amadis de Gaula' are masterpieces. 'Inez Pereira' is the best of his farces.

Gil y Zárate, Don Antonio (Hēl ē thä'rä-tä). A Spanish dramatist; born in the Escorial, Dec. 1, 1793; died at Madrid, Jan. 27, 1861. Mathematics and physics were his university specialties; but he entered upon a political career when a young man, attaining an important post in the Ministry of the Interior in 1820. The revolutions in Spain forced him out of public life, and he became a professor at the Madrid Lyceum. About this time he turned to playwriting; and a tragedy, 'Doña Blanca de Borbon,' made his name widely known in 1832. His next efforts were less conventionally classical and more on the romantic order. 'Carlos II., the Bewitched,' is one of his most celebrated tragedies, but 'Guzman the Good' is by far the best. 'Rosmunda' and 'Don Alvaro de Luna' also stand at the head of the collection of plays that have won for him the premiership of the modern Spanish drama.

Gilbert, John Thomas. An Irish historical writer; born in Dublin, Ireland, Jan. 23, 1829; died there, May 23, 1898. He was the editor of a series of important publications entitled 'Historic Literature of Ireland.' To his enterprise and energy is largely due the revival of interest in Celtic studies. His principal published works include: 'History of the City of Dublin' (1854-59); 'History of Affairs in Ireland, 1641-52' (1879-81); 'History of the Irish Confederation and War in Ireland, 1641-49, (1882-90).

Gilbert, Josiah. An English artist and writer on art; born at the Independent College, Rotherham, Yorkshire, Oct. 7, 1814. He was student at the Royal Academy, and practiced as a portrait-painter for several years; but since 1843 has been engaged in literary pursuits and art criticism. He is the author of: 'Art, its Scope and Purpose' (1858); 'Cadore, or Titian's Country' (1869); 'Art and Religion' (1871); was joint author of 'The Dolomite Mountains' (1864); and published 'Landscape in Art before Claude and Salvator' (1885).

Gilbert, Nicolas Joseph Laurent (zhēl-bär). A French poet; born in Fontenoy-le-Chateau, Lorraine, in 1751; died insane at Paris, Nov. 16, 1780. He went to Paris in his teens to make himself a poet. The "philosophers," who then lorded it over all forms of literature at Paris, conceived a violent hatred of his satirical productions, which handled their pet hobbies without gloves. 'Farewells to Life,' 'My Apology,' and 'The Author's Carnival,' are among his best-known pieces.

Gilbert, William. An English novelist and biographer; born 1804; died 1890. His earlier literary activity resulted in various good realistic fictions, conspicuously that revelation of London dark life, 'De Profundis' (1864), followed by 'The Goldsworthy Family' (1864), 'Clara Levesque' (1872), and others; his most serious achievement, however, being a gallant but not apparently very successful effort at a rehabilitation of Lucrezia Borgia (1869).

Gilbert, William Schwenck. An English librettist and comic poet and prose-writer; born in London, Nov. 18, 1836. He prepared for the bar, and practiced successfully; but the fame of the 'Bab Ballads,' and of his librettos to the scores of 'Pinafore,' 'Patience,' 'The Mikado,' and other comic operas, eclipsed his legal attainments,— which however are not inconsiderable, for he is now a magistrate with a jurisdiction near London, and writes for law journals more or less regularly.

Gilder, Richard Watson. An American poet; born in Bordentown, N. J., Feb. 8, 1844. Since 1881 he has been editor-in-chief of the Century. His works include: 'The New Day' (1875); 'The Celestial Passion' (1887); 'Lyrics'; 'Two Worlds, and Other Poems' (1891); 'The Great Remembrance, and Other Poems' (1893); 'Five Books of Song'; 'A Book of Music' (1906).

Gilder, William Henry. An American journalist, Arctic traveler, and author, brother of Richard W.; born in Pennsylvania, Aug. 16, 1838; died at Morristown, N. J., Feb. 5, 1900. He served in the Civil War, and was brevetted a major at its close. He accompanied Lieutenant Schwatka in 1878 on a polar expedition, and in 1881 was a member of the Rodgers expedition as a correspondent of the New York Herald. His chief works are: 'Schwatka's Search' (1881); 'Ice Pack and Tundra' (1883).

Gildersleeve, Basil Lanneau. An American classical scholar; born in Charleston, S. C., Oct. 23, 1831. He graduated at Princeton in 1843, and studied in Germany for several years. He was professor of Greek and Latin at the University of Virginia from 1856 to 1876, when he was appointed professor of Greek at Johns Hopkins University. He is the founder and editor of the American Journal of Philology. Among his works are: 'Satires of Persius Flaccus' (1875); 'Justin Martyr' (1875); 'Odes of Pindar.' He has published a Latin Grammar and a volume of 'Essays and Studies.'

Gildon, Charles. A miscellaneous English writer; born in 1665 at Gillingham in Dorsetshire; died in 1724. The following works are ascribed to him: 'History of the Athenian Society' (1691); 'The Post-Boy Robbed of his Mail'; 'Miscellany, Poems upon Various Occasions' (1692); 'Life and Adventures of

Defoe.' He also wrote several plays. In 1699 he edited Langbaine's 'Dramatic Poets.'

Giles, Chauncey. An American clergyman and author; born at Charlemont, Mass., in 1813; died in 1893. He entered the Swedenborgian Church in 1853, and held pastorates in Cincinnati, New York, and Philadelphia. Among his numerous works, many of which have been translated into French, German, and Italian, are included: 'The Magic Spectacles' (1868); 'The Gate of Pearl' (1869); 'The New Jerusalem' (1874); 'The Valley of Diamonds, and Other Stories' (1881); 'Perfect Prayer' (1883).

Giles, Henry. An American Unitarian minister; born in Crokford, County Wexford, Ireland, Nov. 1, 1809; came to the United States in 1840; died near Boston, July 10, 1882. His published works are in part: 'Lectures and Essays' (2 vols., 1845); 'Christian Thought on Life' (1850); 'Human Life in Shakespeare' (1868); and 'Lectures and Essays on Irish and Other Subjects' (1869).

Gilfillan, Robert. A Scotch poet; born in Dumfermline, July 7, 1798; died at Leith, Dec. 4, 1850. His verse is very popular wherever hearts "warm to the tartan"; and his 'Original Songs' (1831) ran through three editions, the best pieces in the collection being 'The Exile's Song,' 'Peter McCraw,' and 'In the Days o' Langsyne.'

Gille, Philippe (zhēl). A French dramatist and journalist; born in Paris, Dec. 18, 1834. He was originally a sculptor, and his work attracted attention; but he put it aside for dramatic composition and journalism, succeeding in both. He has been on the staff of the Petit Journal, Figaro, and Écho de Paris. As a librettist he has written to the scores of eminent composers. He has produced likewise a variety of successful plays, of the kind adapted to the somewhat peculiar exigencies of the Parisian stage. 'Gladiator's Thirty Millions,' 'Jean de Nevelle,' and 'My Comrade,' show him probably at his best; although several other pieces, written in collaboration and independently, have had long runs. Died March 19, 1901.

Gillette, William. An American actor and playwright; born in Hartford, Conn., July 24, 1853. He is the author of several successful plays, in many of which he has assumed the leading parts. Among his best-known productions are: 'The Professor' (1881); 'Esmeralda' (1881), with Mrs. F. H. Burnett; 'The Private Secretary' (adapted); 'Held by the Enemy' (1886); 'A Legal Wreck' (1888); 'Too Much Johnson' (1895); and 'Secret Service' (1896).

Gilm zu Rosenegg, Hermann von (gilm tsö röz'en-eg"). A German lyric poet; born in Innsbruck, Nov. 1, 1812; died at Linz, May 31, 1864. He studied jurisprudence at the university in Innsbruck, and then began a career in the government service, rising to positions of responsibility by years of valuable service. Of liberal tendencies in religion and politics, and enthusiastic in the cause of the Tyrolese, he wrote 'Sonnets from Tyrol' and 'Songs of the Natter Maids,' which achieved quick success. Other poems by him did much to maintain among the Tyrolese the spirit that prompted their uprising for independence in 1809.

Gilman, Arthur. An American educator and author; born at Alton, Ill., June 22, 1837. He was engaged in the banking business in New York from 1857 to 1862, when he removed to Lenox, Mass., and devoted himself to literary and educational work until 1871. In 1876 he assisted in the organization of the Harvard Annex, now known as Radcliffe College. Among his works are: 'First Steps in English Literature' (1870); 'First Steps in General History' (1874); 'History of the American People' (1883); 'Early American Explorers' (1885); 'Colonization of America'; 'The Making of the American Nation' (1887).

Gilman, Caroline Howard. An American autnor; born in Boston, Mass., Oct. 8, 1794; died in 1888. Her collected writings include: 'Recollections of a New England Housekeeper' (1835); 'Recollections of a Southern Matron' (1836); 'Poetry of Traveling in the United States' (1838); etc. The 'Recollections' have passed through many editions.

Gilman, Daniel Coit. An American educator; born at Norwich, Conn., July 6, 1831. He graduated from Yale in 1852. He was superintendent of schools in Connecticut for several years; professor of physical geography at Yale, and college librarian, 1856–72; president of the University of California, 1872–75; and since 1875 president of Johns Hopkins University, Baltimore, Md. Besides numerous reports and addresses on scientific and educational subjects, he wrote: 'Our National Schools of Science' (1867); 'James Monroe in his Relations to the Public Service.' Died 1908.

Gilmore, James Roberts. ["Edmund Kirke."] An American miscellaneous prose-writer; born in Boston, Mass., Sept. 10, 1823. He was at first in mercantile life, subsequently entering journalism and literature. He wrote: 'Among the Pines'; 'My Southern Friends'; 'Down in Tennessee'; 'Life of Garfield'; 'Among the Guerrillas'; 'Adrift in Dixie'; 'On the Border'; 'Patriot Boys'; 'The Rear-Guard of the Revolution'; 'John Sevier as a Commonwealth Builder'; 'The Advance-Guard of Western Civilization'; etc. Died Nov. 16, 1903.

Gindely, Anton (gin'del-ē). A Bohemian historian; born in Prague in 1829; died Oct. 24, 1892. He was a graduate of the University of Prague, and subsequently became a professor of history there. His most important work was a 'History of the Thirty Years' War,' projected on a vast scale, but only a condensed 4-vol. form completed, which has been translated into English. His 'History of the Bohemian Brethren' (1856–57) is also notable.

Ginsburg, Christian. An eminent Polish Rabbinical writer; born in Warsaw, Poland, in 1830, and received his education in the Rabbinic college there. He was one of the

original members appointed by the English Convocation for the revision of the English version of the Old Testament Scriptures. He is the author of a number of works of vast erudition, among which are: 'A Historical and Critical Commentary on the Song of Songs' (1857); 'The Kariates' (1862); 'The Moabite Stone' (1871); 'The Massorah' (1880–86).

Gioberti, Vincenzo (jō-ber'tē). An Italian philosopher and statesman; born in Turin, in April 1801; died in Paris, October 1852. In 1831 he became chaplain to King Charles Albert; but being accused of favoring the Liberals, he was imprisoned and exiled. He removed to Brussels, where he wrote: 'The Theory of the Supernatural' (1838); 'Introduction to the Study of Philosophy' (1839); 'Civil and Moral Supremacy of the Italians' (1843), in which he advocated the restoration of the unity of Italy; and 'The Modern Jesuit' (1847). On his return to Turin in 1848 he was received with enthusiasm, and subsequently became prime minister.

Gioja, Melchiore (jo'yä). An eminent Italian political economist; born at Piacenza, Italy, in 1767; died at Milan in 1829. Imprisoned by the Austrian government in his youth on account of his republican tendencies, he welcomed with enthusiasm the advent of Napoleon in Italy and the establishment of the Cisalpine Republic, under which he received the office of historiographer. Among his remarkable works are: 'The New Galateo' (1802); 'The French, Germans, and Russians in Lombardy' (1805); 'New View of the Economic Sciences' (1815–19); 'The Philosophy of Statistics' (1826).

Giordani, Pietro (jôr-dä'nē). An Italian essayist, controversialist, and critic; born in Piacenza, Jan. 1, 1774; died at Parma, Sept. 14, 1848. His productions are mainly essays and criticisms on art and literature, theses on æsthetics, pamphlets, panegyrics, and monographs, all of a fugitive nature, which keep their place in letters by their style. His 'Letters,' 'Select Prose,' and 'Orations and Eulogies,' show his style at its best.

Giozza, Pier Giacinto (jôt'sä). An Italian critic, poet, essayist, and student of Dante; born April 24, 1846, in Turin, where he studied literature and philosophy in the university. At the present time he is a professor in the Lyceum at Alessandria. His writings are noted for their poetic qualities and correct taste. 'Fantasies and Scintillations,' 'Excelsior,' 'Sighs of the Soul,' 'God in Dante's Paradise,' 'Investigation of Curious Facts concerning Dante's Poetry,' and 'The Legend of the Inferno,' are among the best of recent Italian writings.

Giraldi, Giglio Gregorio (jē-räl'dē). An Italian poet and scholar; born in Ferrara, June 13, 1479; died there, February 1552. His most valuable works, 'Historia de Diis Gentium,' a historical manual of classical mythology; 'De Annis et Mensibus,' a treatise on the calendar;

'Historiæ Poetarum Græcorum ac Latinorum,' a study in classical literary biography; and several more, are still quoted as authoritative. He helped greatly to spread the taste for knowledge characteristic of the age, and his Latin verses prove him a consummate poet.

Giraldi, Giovanni Battista. An Italian dramatist, novelist, and poet; born in Ferrara, November 1504; died there, Dec. 30, 1573. In early life he was so brilliant in literature, medicine, and philosophy that he became Secretary of State under two successive dukes of Este; but a contest raised by an impostor who claimed the authorship of one of his works brought him into disfavor, and he lost his office (1560). Becoming a distinguished professor of literature, he ended as rhetorician at the Academy of Pavia, where he was admitted about 1570 under the name of Cinthio, Cintio, or Cinzio, signing his works thus variously from this date. Of his plays the best known is 'Orbecche,' perhaps the most powerful tragedy written since the classical period and till Shakespeare. Shakespeare and Beaumont and Fletcher, in fact, appear to have helped themselves to his productions to some extent in the construction of their own.

Girardin, Émile de (zhē-rär-dań'). A French journalistic agitator and political and economic writer, illegitimate son of Count Alexander de Girardin and Madame Dupuy; born in Paris (not in Switzerland), June 22, 1806 (or 1803?); died there, April 27, 1881. His early years were passed in poverty and neglect, but he contrived to educate himself sufficiently to write at 19 a sentimental novel, 'Émile,' which met with popular favor. It was as a journalist that he first made himself known among the French, he being indeed the originator of the cheap popular press of Paris with its enormous circulations. His first wife was Sophie Gay. He accumulated a fortune, and led an anti-Prussian agitation in the war of 1870. 'Political Studies,' 'The Abolition of Authority through the Simplification of Government,' and 'The Periodical Press in the Nineteenth Century,' are among his more solid writings. He was the author of a few clever comedies.

Girardin, Marie Alfred Jules de. A French littérateur and translator; born Jan. 4, 1832; died at Paris, Oct. 26, 1888. He was attached to the Lyceum of Versailles, and at Loches; contributed stories to the European Review, the Revue des Deux Mondes, Paris Illustré, and other French periodicals. Among his works are: 'Brave Men' (1874), crowned by the Academy; 'Uncle Placide' (1878); 'The Captain's Niece'; 'Grandfather' (1880), crowned by the Academy; 'The Gaudry Family' (1884); 'The Second Violin' (1887); and translations.

Giraud, Count Giovanni (zhē-ro'). An Italian comedy-writer; born in Rome, Oct. 28, 1776; died in Naples, Oct. 1, 1834. He was bred to the profession of arms, but relieved the monotony of the camp by writing comedies. They were produced with immense success in Venice, and admired by Napoleon, who gave him an important theatrical post; but on Napoleon's overthrow he entered mercantile life. As a playwright he makes Molière his model. 'The Embarrassed Governor,' 'The Prophesying Fanatic,' and 'The Discontented Capricious One,' are good examples of his talent as a contriver of ludicrous situations, helped out by witty dialogue.

Girndt, Otto (gērnt). A German dramatist, humorist, and writer of fiction; born in Landsberg on the Warthe, Feb. 6, 1835. His profession was law; but the vogue of his comedy 'Y 1,' acted when he was 30, turned him toward the stage, in which he has won great popularity. 'Cæsar Borgia' and 'Charlotte Corday,' dramas, 'Oriental Entanglements,' a comedy that won a prize, and 'Dankelman,' a tragedy, merit special mention. His stories are graceful and replete with incident, though they do not rank high; the best of them, 'The Rescue of the King' and 'Jolly Company,' are fair specimens of a lively style.

Gisecke, Nikolaus Dietrich (gē'zek-ě). A German poet; born in Csó, Hungary, of German parents, April 2, 1724; died at Sondershausen, Feb. 23, 1765. He settled early in Hamburg, where he formed one of a little literary circle. He was a clergyman, and his sermons contain elegant diction; but his literary position is due wholly to a volume of poems, simple and unaffected in style, and voicing a mild melancholy,

Giseke, Robert. A German dramatist, novelist, and poet, great-grandson of Nikolaus; born in Marienwerder, Jan. 15, 1827; died at Leubus, Dec. 12, 1890. Early an accomplished theologian and an authority on philosophy and history, his prospects were destroyed by his political utterances in 1848, and he was driven to journalism for a livelihood. After some years he began to write novels, of which the best is perhaps 'Otto Ludwig Brook.' But his original and striking plays gave him his greatest renown; notably 'The Two Cagliostros,' 'Lucifer, or the Demagogues,' 'The Elector Maurice of Saxony,' and 'A Burgomaster of Berlin.'

Gissing, George. An English novelist; born in Wakefield, 1857. He had made a remarkable study of the London masses, from the ranks of skilled labor to the most noisome human refuse of the slums, the result being half repulsive and wholly powerful; particularly in 'The Nether World,' 'New Grub Street,' 'Demos,' and 'Sleeping Fires.' Died, 1903.

Giusti, Giuseppe (jös'tē). An Italian poet and political satirist; born in Monsummano, May 1809; died in Florence, March 31, 1850. His maiden masterpiece was the 'Dies Iræ,' on the death of the Emperor Francis I.,—a poem in which a mockery of woe blends tellingly with sarcasm. He worked this vein the next ten years, as 'The Boot,' 'The Crowned,' and 'The Investiture of a Knight' demonstrate.

These and the satires written from 1847 to 1849, as well as 'The Papacy of Little Peter,' evince genius.

Gjellerup, Karl Adolf (gyāl'ĕr-öp). A Danish novelist, dramatist, poet, and critic; born in Roholte, Seeland, July 2, 1857. He prepared for the ministry; but published a novel, 'An Idealist,' under the pseudonym "Epigonos," at 21. 'Rödtjörn,' a book of poems, appeared a few years later; followed by the novels 'Romulus,' 'The Pupil of the Germans,' and several others. 'Brynhild' and 'Saint Just' are tragedies; 'The Book of my Love' is an assortment of erotic poems. As a critic his work is discriminating and accurate; but all his productions show the influence of foreign literatures.

Gjorgjic, Ignaz (jôr'jich). A Dalmatian poet and scholar; born in Ragusa, Feb. 13, 1676; died there, Jan. 21, 1737. He was abbot of the Benedictine monastery on the island of Meleda, but was exiled for his part in a political dispute. The Pope interceded for him and had him restored to his cloisters. Of his poems, 'The Sighs of the Penitent Magdalen' is the most deserving of mention. 'Marunko i Pavica' is the humorous story of two Venetian youths, and 'The Slav Psalter' is a hymnal.

Gladden, Washington. An American clergyman and author; born at Pottsgrove, Pa., Feb. 11, 1836. He has held pastorates in Congregational churches in New York, Massachusetts, and Ohio, and served on the editorial staff of the Independent and Sunday Afternoon. Among his numerous works are : 'Plain Thoughts on the Art of Living' (1868); 'From the Hub to the Hudson' (1869); 'The Young Men and the Church' (1885); 'Cosmopolis City Club'; 'Christianity and Socialism.'

Gladstone, William Ewart. A Great English statesman and writer on theological and philological subjects, essayist, and translator from the classics; born in Liverpool, Dec. 29, 1809; died at Hawarden, May 19, 1898. His place in literature has been made enduring by 'Juventus Mundi,' 'Studies in Homer and the Homeric Age,' and a large number of essays, rich in thought and clear and weighty in style. His works include: 'Church and State'; 'Homeric Synchronism'; 'Gleanings of Past Years'; a version of Horace; etc.

Glaisher, James. An English astronomer; born in London, England, April 7, 1809. From 1836 until his retirement in 1874 he was connected with the Royal Observatory, Greenwich. He is the author of more than a hundred books and papers relating to astronomy, meteorology, and the theory of numbers. Between 1863 and 1866 he made twenty-nine balloon ascents for scientific purposes, in one of which he attained the greatest height till then reached (seven miles). The results of his observations are published in the popular 'Travels in the Air' (1870). He translated and edited 'The Atmosphere' by Flammarion, and 'The World of Comets' by Guillemin. Died Feb. 7, 1903.

Glapthorne, Henry. An English dramatist who is known to have flourished about 1639. He wrote many plays, five of which have been printed: 'Albertus Wallenstein'; 'The Hollander'; 'Argalus and Parthenia'; 'Wit in a Constable'; 'The Lady's Privilege'; etc.

Glascock, William Nugent. A Scottish author; born 1787; died Oct. 8, 1847, at Baltinglass. He was captain in the navy; entering service January 1800, and retiring in 1847. His literary works include: 'The Naval Sketch Book' (2 vols., 1826); 'Sailors and Saints; or, Matrimonial Manœuvres' (3 vols., 1829); 'Tales of a Tar: With Characteristic Anecdotes' (1836); 'Land Sharks and Sea Gulls' (3 vols., 1838); 'Naval Service; or, Officers' Manual' (2 vols., 1836), which has had a great sale and been translated for all the Continental services.

Glaser, Adolf (glä'zĕr). A German novelist, poet, dramatist, and translator; born in Wiesbaden, Dec. 15, 1829. He won success in journalism; and published poems under the pseudonym "Reinald Reimar," as well as two or three plays. His first novel, written in 1857, was 'The Schaller Family,' followed by many popular works of fiction. 'What Is Truth?' 'A Magdalen without a Halo,' 'Savonarola,' 'Cordula,' are absorbing tales, in which imagination, humor, and ingenuity of plot are predominating qualities. 'Galileo Galilei,' a tragedy, and a series of translations from Dutch authors, must be included.

Glassbrenner, Adolf (gläs'brän-er). A German humorist; born in Berlin, March 27, 1810; died there, Sept. 25, 1876. He was editing the satiric paper Don Quixote when it was suppressed in 1833, and then turned to comic sketch-writing. 'Berlin as it Is and — Drinks,' with 'Lively Berlin,' published under the pseudonym "Adolf Brennglas," quickly brought him into popularity, which 'Life and Conduct in the Exclusive World' and 'Berlin Folk Life' increased; while 'The New Reineke Fuchs' and 'Forbidden Songs' displayed his versatility. He produced stories for children, and comedies of exquisite drollery. He was a leader in the popular agitation of 1848.

Glazier, Willard. An American author; born in Fowler, N. Y., Aug. 22, 1841. His works include: 'Capture, Prison Pen, and Escape' (1865), which was very popular; 'Three Years in the Federal Cavalry' (1870); 'Battles for the Union'; 'Heroes of Three Wars'; 'Peculiarities of American Cities'; and 'Down the Great River.' Died April 26, 1905.

Gleig, George Robert. A British historian and miscellaneous prose-writer; born in Stirling, Scotland, April 20, 1796; died near Winchfield, England, July 9, 1888. He was a soldier under Wellington in Spain, and commanded a regiment in the American war of 1812, being wounded during the sack of Washington. He wrote 'The Subaltern' (1825), an admirable account of a soldier's life in war, used by Parton in his life of Jackson; 'Campaigns of the

British Army at Washington and New Orleans' (new ed. 1861); 'Lives of Eminent British Commanders' (1831); and many others.

Gleim, Johann Wilhelm Ludwig (glīm). A German poet and patron of literature; born in Ermsleben, Halberstadt, April 2, 1719; died Feb. 18, 1803. He attained an immense prestige and popularity among his countrymen as a sort of Mæcenas. His passion for letters induced him to resign profitable government posts while still young. 'An Essay in Sportive Rhyme,' an early work, shows French influence. The Seven Years' War afforded him themes for his best work : 'Songs of a Prussian Grenadier' are patriotic outbursts. ('Petrarcan Songs,' 'Horatian Odes,' 'Songs in Imitation of Anacreon,' and 'Epigrammatic Verse,' are pleasing, but less interesting. His fables and tales became extremely popular.

Glen, William. A Scottish song-writer; born in Glasgow, Nov. 14, 1789; died there, December 1826. He was trained to mercantile business, but preferred conviviality and the Muse. His fame rests upon his 'Poems, Chiefly Lyrical' (1815): "Wae's me for Prince Charlie," a Jacobite song, is widely known.

Glinka, Avdotia Pavlovna (glink'kä). A Russian writer of stories and devotional works, wife of Fedor; born in Koutousof in 1795; died in 1863. She translated Schiller's 'Song of the Bell,' and wrote many popular books of devotion.

Glinka, Fedor Nicolaievich. A Russian poet, historian, and essayist; born in Smolensk in 1788; died at Tver, March 6, 1880. He distinguished himself in the campaign of Austerlitz at 18, but upon falling into disfavor at court gave up an army career for literature. 'Letters of a Russian Officer on the Campaigns of 1805-6 and 1812-15,' 'Presents to Russian Soldiers,' and 'The Liberation of Little Russia,' are the best known of his books. He also translated the Psalms and the Book of Job into verse.

Glinka, Gregory Andréevich. A Russian historian, dramatist, and poet, cousin of Fedor N.; born near Smolensk in 1774; died at Moscow in 1818. He was in boyhood a page at the imperial court. He entered upon a distinguished career as an educator, and accompanied Alexander I.'s brothers on their Continental tour in 1811. His works include: 'The Ancient Religion of the Slavs'; 'Miscellanies in Prose and Verse'; and a play, 'The Daughters of Love.'

Glinka, Sergius Nicolaievich. A Russian poet and writer of juvenile literature; brother of Fedor; born in Smolensk in 1774 or 1771; died at Moscow in 1847. He entered the military service and rose to the rank of major, when he retired. His literary work was devoted mainly to the young and their training. 'Readings for Children,' 'History of Russia for the Use of Boys and Girls,' and similar books, are highly esteemed. He also composed a few plays in verse, edited the Russian Messenger, and translated Young's 'Night Thoughts.'

Glover, Richard. An English epic poet and dramatist; born in London, 1712; died there, Nov. 25, 1785. He abandoned trade for poetry, and made himself famous with 'Leonidas' (1737), a heroic poem, fiery but rather exaggerated in rhetoric. 'The Athenaid' (1787) is a continuation of it. 'London' (1739), a poem of commerce, and 'Boadicea' (1735), a tragedy, are among his works.

Glümer, Claire von (glüm'er). A German novelist and translator; born in Blankenburg-am-Harz, Oct. 18, 1825. Her youth was spent in France, but she has lived in Germany since 1848. She first attracted attention by the great merit of her translations from English and French authors,— Swift, Daudet, George Sand, and others. A volume of 'Sketches of the Pyrenees,' and studies in fiction,— 'Frau Domina' and 'Young Hearts' among them,— prove her a capable writer and an attentive observer of life.

Glum Eyjolfsson (glöm ī''yōlf'sōn). An Icelandic bard; born about 940; died about 1003. His youth was spent in Norway. He is specially famed for the brave fight he waged in the southwestern part of his native island, the particulars of which he recounted in a poem or saga, orally transmitted to posterity until it was put in writing in the thirteenth century. Shortly before his death he became a Christian. His legend is variously known as the 'Viga-Glumssaga,' the 'Glumssaga,' etc.

Gnedich, Nicolai Ivanovich (gnä'dich). A Russian poet; born in Pultowa, Feb. 2, 1784; died in St. Petersburg, Feb. 15, 1833. He studied classical philology, and made himself the most accomplished Russian scholar of his day. A translation of Schiller's 'Conspiracy of Fiesco' was an early effort; but his masterpiece is the translation of the Iliad into Russian (1829), not unworthy of the original, at which he worked for twenty years. A translation of Shakespeare's 'King Lear,' of Voltaire's 'Tancrede,' and of notable modern Greek poems, occupied his later years. His own poem, 'The Fishers,' is much admired.

Gneist, Rudolph (nīst). A German jurist and historical writer; born in Berlin, Aug. 13. 1816; died there, July 21, 1895. He was a National Liberal, and was in the Prussian Parliament many years. William I. made him instructor in political science to Prince William (now William II.). Among his numerous works are: 'Nobility and Knighthood in England' (1853); 'The English Constitutional and Administrative Law of the Present Day' (1857-63); 'Self-Government in England' (1863); 'History of the English Parliament' (1886); 'The Imperial Law against the Machinations of the Socialists.'

Gobineau, Joseph Arthur, Comte de. A French diplomatist, ethnologist, and romance-writer; born at Bordeaux in 1816; died at Paris,

October 1882. During a long diplomatic career he held important positions at Athens, Copenhagen, and Rio Janeiro; was a member of the embassy to Persia, 1855; Imperial Commissary to the United States, 1861. During his long stay in the East he studied Oriental religions, and brought out his famous work 'Religions and Philosophies in Central Asia' (1865), a vivid and unprejudiced treatise. Among his other notable publications are: 'On the Inequality of Human ʃRaces' (1853–55), which has been the point of departure for a new ethnological school; 'History of the Persians' (1869). In fiction he has produced: 'Typhaine Abbey' (1867), a romance; 'Souvenirs of Travels' (1872), stories; 'Asiatic Tales' (1876), a masterpiece of pure literature and imaginative realization of character — translated into English as 'Romances of the East;' 'Amadis,' a poem in three books (unfinished), published posthumously in 1887.

Göckingk, Leopold Friedrich Günther von (gĕk'ingk). A German poet; born in Gröningen, Halberstadt, July 13, 1748; died at Wartenburg, Silesia, Feb. 18,·1828. His prime was passed in official employment, and in 1789 he was ennobled. He retired some years later, and devoted himself seriously to literature. His principal works are: 'Epigrams' (1772), some of which are admirable; 'Songs of Two Lovers' (1777), greatly admired by his contemporaries, who read between the lines the story of the writer's life; three volumes of 'Poems' (1779); 'Charades and Riddles' (1817); 'Life and Literary Remains of Nicolai' (1800).

Godefroy, Frédéric (god-frwä'). A French lexicographer and historian of literature; born in Paris, Feb. 13, 1826. His life has been given up to literary studies; the results of which, the celebrated 'Comparative Lexicon of the Language of Corneille and of the Seventeenth Century in General,' and 'History of French Literature from the Sixteenth Century to Our Own Day,' have given him an international reputation. His monumental effort, however, is the voluminous 'Dictionary of the Old French Language and of All its Dialects from the Ninth to the Fifteenth Century.' The 8th vol. published 1895.

Godet, Philippe Ernest (gō-dā'). A Swiss poet and historian of literature; born in Neuchâtel, April 23, 1850. He was bred to the law, but abandoned it for journalism. He became instructor in literature in the Academy at Neuchâtel. As a poet he pleases, without stirring any profound depths, in such volumes as 'A Handful of Rhymes,' 'First Poems,' and 'Realities.' In prose he wrote: 'The Literary History of French Switzerland,' his greatest work, which won the French Academy's Guérin prize; 'Studies and Talks'; and a biography of Pierre Viret.

Godfrey, Thomas. An American poet; born in Philadelphia, Dec. 4, 1736; died near Wilmington, N. C., Aug. 3, 1763. He wrote in 1759 'The Prince of Parthia,' a tragedy, believed to be the first dramatic work written in this country. In 1763 he published 'The Court of Fancy: A Poem.' His poems were collected in 1767 by his friend Nathaniel Evans.

Godkin, Edwin Lawrence. An American journalist and essayist; born in Moyne, Ireland, Oct. 2, 1831; died at Brixham, Eng., May 20, 1902. He graduated from Queen's College, and came to this country in early manhood. From 1865 he was prominent in journalism. In addition to a 'History of Hungary,' and editorial work on the New York Nation, which he founded, and Evening Post, he produced volumes of essays; 'The Problems of Modern Democracy' and 'Impressions and Comments,' etc.

Gödsche, Hermann (gĕd'sha). A German journalist, critic, and romance-writer; born in Trachenberg, Silesia, Feb. 12, 1815; died at Warmbrunn, Nov. 8, 1878. At first in the postal service, he began writing in 1849, over the name of "Armin"; and rose to eminence in journalism. As a novelist, his 'Nena Sahib,' 'Villafranca,' and 'Biarritz,' written under the pseudonym of "Sir John Retcliffe," are representative of his talent.

Godwin, Parke. An American author; born at Paterson, N. J., Feb. 25, 1816. He began the study of law, but abandoned it for literary pursuits. From 1837 until recently he was connected with the New York Evening Post, besides contributing frequently to Putnam's Magazine. In addition to translations from the German, and the well-known compilation, 'Handbook of Universal Biography' (1851), he published: 'Constructive Democracy' (1851); 'Vala: A Mythological Tale' (1851); 'Out of the Past' (1870); Essays; 'Biography of Bryant' (1883). He died, New York, Jan. 7, 1904.

Godwin, William. An English political philosopher; born at Wisbeach, Cambridge, March 3, 1756; died in London, April 7, 1836. His principal works are: 'Political Justice' (1793), one of the strongest political essays in the language; 'Caleb Williams; or, Things as They Are' (1794), a novel enforcing the principles of the greater work; 'St. Leon' (1799), a novel of domestic life; several other novels; 'The Inquirer,' a series of essays (1796); 'Antonio,' a tragedy (1801); 'Life of Chaucer' (1803); 'History of the Commonwealth' (1824); 'Thoughts on Man,' a series of essays (1834). His wife, Mary Wollstonecraft (1759–97). wrote a memorable work on 'The Rights of Woman' (1792), and many others.

Goethe, Johann Wolfgang (gĕ'tä). One of the world's greatest poets; born at Frankfort on the Main, Aug. 28, 1749; died at Weimar, March 22, 1832. Among his early works are the tragedy 'Prometheus' (1773); 'Erwin and Elmira' (1774), a comedy; 'Sorrows of Young Werther' (1774); 'Clavigo,' a tragedy (1774); 'Stella' (1775), a drama suggested by Swift's life. In 1776 he became privy counselor to the reigning Duke of Weimar, and for some years was fully occupied with business of State. His leisure he devoted to composing, in prose, his great tragedy 'Iphigenia,' which was recast in verse in 1786; in writing the novel 'Wilhelm Meister'; and in building up his greatest work, 'Faust.' The succession of his works from 1789 forward was: 'Tasso,' a drama (1789); 'Metamorphosis of Plants' (1790); 'The Grand Cophta,' a dramatization of the affair of the Diamond Necklace; 'Wilhelm Meister's Apprenticeship' (1796); 'Hermann and Dorothea' (1796-97); 'Elective Affinities' (1808); 'Fiction and Truth' (1811); 'West-Eastern Divan' (1814); 'Wilhelm Meister's Years of Travel' (1821); second part of 'Faust' (1831: the first part had appeared as 'A Fragment' in 1790).

Goeverneur, Jan Jacob Antonie (gö-ver-nêr'). A Dutch poet; born in Hoevelaken, Feb. 14, 1809; died at Groningen, March 19, 1889. His poems in serious vein appeared over the pseudonym of "Jan de Rijmer"; but they are not so meritorious as his verses for children, which the little people of the Netherlands now know by heart.

Gogol, Nikolai Vasiljevich (gō'gol). A great Russian novelist and humorist; born at Sorochintzy in the government of Poltava, March 31, 1809; died at Moscow, March 4, 1852. His principal works are: 'Evenings on a Farm,' a collection of stories and sketches of life in Little Russia (1831); a second series of the same (1834), including the prose epic 'Taras Bulba,' 'Old-World Proprictors,' and 'How the Two Ivans Quarreled'; then followed stories of life in St. Petersburg,— 'Nevsky Prospect'; 'Akakia Akakievich's New Cloak.' The five last mentioned have been translated into English; as also 'Dead Souls' (1837), the author's masterpiece.

Goiorani, Ciro (gō-yôr-än'-ē). An Italian poet and prose-writer; born in Pescia, Jan. 21, 1834. He got into trouble with the authorities when a student at college in consequence of his political activities; and has been in the same trouble more or less all his life, banishment resulting on two or three occasions. The volume of 'Poems of a Tuscan Exile' adequately typifies his poetry. His prose has been written mostly for political journals.

Goldoni, Carlo (gol-dō'nē). An Italian comedy-writer; born in Venice, Feb. 25, 1707; died at Paris, Jan. 6, 1793. He was brought up by the Jesuits, and began the study of law; succeeding in his practice after some early vicissitudes, but always manifesting his genius for dramatic authorship. 'The Good Father' and 'The Singer' are among his early attempts; but his enduring renown dates from the appearance of 'The Venetian Gondolier,' 'Belisarius,' and 'Rosamond,' although as a writer of pure comedy he is best represented by works like 'The Coffee House.'

Goldschmidt, Meïr Aaron (gōlt'shmit). A Danish novelist and publicist; born in Vordingborg, Oct. 26, 1819; died at Copenhagen, Aug.

15, 1887. He entered journalism when quite young, with recognized power till the government censorship interfered with him. 'A Jew' and 'Homeless' are among the novels to which his international reputation is due. His later years were spent in an exhaustive investigation into the state of public education throughout Europe.

Goldsmid, Frederic John, Sir. An English general and author; born at Milan, Aug. 19, 1818. He held several military staff appointments, both general and regimental. In 1874 he brought out a volume entitled 'Telegraph and Travel'; edited 'Eastern Persia: An Account of the Journeys of the Persian Boundary Commission' (1876); and published 'The Life of Sir James Outram' (1880).

Goldsmith, Oliver. An English-Irish poet, novelist, dramatist, and miscellaneous prose-writer; born in Pallas, County Longford, Ireland, Nov. 10, 1728; died at London, April 4, 1774. His first literary ventures were 'Enquiry into the Present State of Polite Learning in Europe' and 'The Citizen of the World.' Next appeared 'The Traveller'; 'The Deserted Village'; 'The Vicar of Wakefield'; 'The Good-Natured Man'; and 'She Stoops to Conquer.' His essays and his histories, his biographies and his text-books, are numerous and famed.

Goll, Jaroslav (gōl). A Czech poet and historian; born in Chlumetz, July 11, 1846. His 'Poems,' in one volume, include some very popular 'Songs of the Exiles.' His historical works, among them 'The French Marriage: France and England, 1624 and 1625,' are important and popular. He is professor of history at the Czech University in Prague.

Gomberville, Marin Le Roy de (gôn-ber-vēl'). A French romancer and poet, and one of the original members of the French Academy; born in Paris (?) in 1599 or 1600; died there, June 14, 1674. At 14 he brought out a volume of poems, some of them above the current level of popular verse. At 20 he plunged into the writing of interminable and extravagant romances, which won unmerited admiration. 'Polexandre' is the only one now valued,— to this he wrote a sequel, and projected a sequel to this sequel. A sonnet on the 'Blessed Sacrament' attained celebrity; and his 'Discourse on the Merits and Defects of History and the Method of Writing it Well' was extensively quoted by contemporary authors. His Latin poems and his philosophical works are alike preposterous.

Gomes, João Baptista (gō'mes). A Portuguese dramatist; born in Oporto about 1775; died there (?), Dec. 20, 1803. He was a very poor boy, and entered a mercantile house when a young man; while thus employed, he wrote in his early twenties a tragedy, 'The New Castro,' on the love of Dom Pedro for Inez de Castro, which was staged in Lisbon about 1800 and was highly successful. It is rich in effective situations and stately periods, while its dialogue and action adhere to the standards of an almost perfect taste.

Gomes de Amorim, Francisco (gō'mes de ä-mö-rēn'). A Portuguese poet and romance-writer; born in Avelomar, Minho, Aug. 13, 1827, died at Lisbon (?), Nov. 4, 1891 not 1892. His childhood was one of dire poverty, and when a lad he drifted to Brazil, where he lived in privation for several years. He returned to his native land in 1846, and in the revolutionary movements of the next few years employed his poetic talent in the patriotic cause. He has a European reputation as being in the first rank of modern Portuguese poets. 'Morning Songs' and 'Ephemeros' are the most celebrated of his poems. He has also written plays and romances; among the latter, 'Love of Country' may be mentioned.

Gomes Leal, Antonio Duarte (gō'mes lā'äl). A Portuguese poet; born in Lisbon, June 6, 1848. His poems made their appearance when he was quite young, and all are characterized by radical thought and decided heterodoxy in matters of religion. One or two of his more recent productions brought him into conflict with the authorities, and he was arrested and imprisoned. 'Antichrist,' 'Renegade,' and 'The Defense against England' have been most widely read.

Goncharóv, Ivan Aleksandrovich (gōn-chä'rov'). A Russian novelist; born in Simbirsk, June 18, 1812; died at St. Petersburg, Sept. 27, 1891. Upon completing his university studies at Moscow, he obtained a post under the government and was sent to Japan in its service. He studied languages and translated numerous masterpieces of literature into Russian, but soon began the production of works of his own. These include 'Jean Podzabryn,' a tale of life among the high functionaries of the empire, and 'Oblómof.'

Goncourt, Edmond and Jules de (gôn-kör'). French novelists and miscellaneous prose-writers, brothers. Edmond was born in Nancy, May 26, 1822; died at Paris, July 16, 1896. Jules was born in Paris, Dec. 17, 1830; died near Paris, June 20, 1870. From childhood their personal intimacy was as close as their literary union subsequently became. The detailed account of them presented elsewhere makes it necessary to allude only to a work on 'Art in the Eighteenth Century,' many of the pictures in which are from the brush of Jules, who was a finished artist. Both were scholars of no mean attainments, and possessed equally the facile and strenuous talent that made them co-builders of a single renown.

Gondinet, Edmond (gôn-dē-nā). A French dramatist; born in Laurière, March 7, 1828; died at Paris, Nov. 19, 1888. His early comedies, 'Too Curious' and 'The Victims of Money,' were received with a favor which led to his writing regularly for the stage; and the farce 'Christiane' in 1871 approved him as one of the first members of his profession. He draws best from Parisian social life; 'Panazol,'

'Papa's Convictions,' and 'The Ladies' Professor' afford typical examples. His pieces written in collaboration have yielded enormous royalties, especially 'The Happiest of the Three.'

Gondola, Giovanni (gon-dō'lä). See **Gundulìc.**

Góngora y Argote, Luis de (gon'gō-rä ē är-gō'tä). A Spanish poet; born in Cordova, June 11, 1561; died there, May 24, 1627. Intended for the law, he gave himself to poetry instead. He entered the Church in 1606, gaining in consequence a petty clerical post at the court of Philip III., from which he retired disheartened. Now began that singular stream of verse to which he owes his place in letters; the dominant traits in which are studied artificiality, extreme pedantry and obscurity, and violent metaphors. Thus, he says of the beauty of a young girl that "it would inflame Norway with its two suns [eyes?], and whiten Ethiopia with its hands." Gongorism, as this sort of thing was termed, had a horde of imitators, spread rapidly from Spain to France, and spoiled the style of a whole generation in both countries: 'The Story of Polyphemus and Galatea' and 'The Story of Pyramus and Thisbe' are its choicest expositions by its originator.

Gonzaga, Thomaz Antonio (gon-zä'gä). [Known also as "Dirceu."] A Portuguese poet; born in Oporto in August 1744; died at Mozambique in 1807 or 1809. Graduating from Coimbra, he emigrated to Brazil and became a judge for some years. Here he conceived a violent passion for one Doña Maria Seixas, whose connection with the development of his genius suggests the relation of Lesbia to Catullus, giving birth to his celebrated 'Marilia.' These love poems are the most exquisite lyrics in Portuguese literature, flawless in metre and immaculate in style. The marriage was prevented by his banishment to Mozambique on a seemingly trumped-up charge of treason, and a fever there left him permanently insane.

Gonzalès, Emmanuel (gôn-sál-āz'). A French novelist of Spanish origin; born in Saintes, Oct. 25, 1815; died at Paris, Oct. 15, 1887. On very little capital and no encouragement he founded the Revue de France, and established his fame as a writer of fiction in its columns. Émile de Girardin engaged him for the Presse, where he made the hit of a season. 'An Angel's Memoirs,' 'Buckingham's Seven Kisses,' 'The Russian Princess,' and 'The Gold Seekers,' are among the romances in which he most happily shows his genius for narration, vivid style, and fertility of expedient.

González del Valle, José Z. (gōn thä'läth dēl vä'lä). A Spanish author, born in Havana, Cuba, in 1820; died in Madrid, Spain, October 1851. He was professor of natural philosophy in the University of Havana until failing health compelled him to relinquish this post. He was appointed honorary secretary to the Queen. Among his novels are: 'Luisa,' 'Carmen and

Adela,' and 'Love and Death' (1839); 'Tropicales,' a volume of poems (Havana, 1842); 'European Journeys' (1843); 'A Funeral Wreath' (1844); 'Historical Sketch of Philosophy' (1848); and 'Lectures on Meteorology' (1849).

Gonzalo de Berceo (gōn-thä'lō dä ber-thä'ō). A Spanish poet; born in Berceo about 1196; died at the monastery of San Millan de la Cogolla, about 1270; was parish priest of Berceo, and one of the first rhymesters to write in Castilian. He wrote in rhymed quatrains and we have more than 13,000 of his verses on the lives of obscure Castilian Saints, on the Mass, the Dolors of the Virgin Mary, the Judgment Day, etc. His style is rude and inelegant, but the poet writes out of a full simple heart, and he tells a story well. He arrays with wonderful effectiveness the stage properties of the Last Judgment; and his contemplation of Mary at the Cross strikes the chord of human sympathy.

Goodale, Elaine — Mrs. Eastman. An American poet; born in Mt. Washington, Mass., Oct. 9, 1863. She became a teacher in the Hampton Institute in Virginia, and wrote editorially for the Southern Workman (1883). In 1885 she visited the Great Sioux reservation, reporting her views to New York and Boston journals. She taught school at White River Camp, Lower Brulé Agency, Dakota. Her 'Journal of a Farmer's Daughter' was published in 1881. Together with her sister Dora Read, she produced: 'Apple Blossoms: Verses of Two Children' (1878); 'In Berkshire with the Wild Flowers' (1879); and 'Verses from Sky Farm' (1880).

Goodale, George Lincoln. An American botanist; born at Saco, Me., Aug. 3, 1839. He graduated from Amherst in 1860, and from the Harvard Medical School in 1863. For some time he was a lecturer in medical schools in Maine. In 1871 he was appointed professor of Natural Sciences in Bowdoin College. Since 1872 he has been connected with Harvard University, at first as instructor and later as professor of botany. Among his works are: 'Concerning a Few Common Plants' (1879); 'Physiological Botany' (1885); 'Wild Flowers of America' (1886); 'Useful Plants of the Future.'

Goode, George Brown. An American ichthyologist; born at New Albany, Ind., Feb. 13, 1851; died in Washington, Sept. 6, 1896. He was a member of several commissions and scientific societies, and was identified with expositions both here and abroad. Besides over two hundred papers on ichthyology, he published: 'The Game Fishes of the United States' (1879); 'The Beginnings of Natural History in America' (1886); 'Virginia Cousins' (1888); 'Museums of the Future' (1890).

Goodrich, Charles Augustus. An American clergyman and author, brother of Samuel G.; born at Ridgefield, Conn., in 1790; died at Hartford, Conn., Jan. 4, 1862. He graduated at Yale in 1812. He held the pastorates of Congregational churches in Worcester, Mass., and Berlin and Hartford, Conn. Among his works are: 'Lives of the Signers' (1829); 'History of the United States' (1852–55); 'Universal Traveller.'

Goodrich, Frank Boot. ["Dick Tinto."] An American author; born in Boston, Dec. 14, 1826; graduated at Harvard in 1845. His Paris letters to the New York Times, signed "Dick Tinto," first brought him into notice. He published: 'Court of Napoleon'; or, 'Society under the First Empire' (1857); 'Women of Beauty and Heroism' (1859); 'World-Famous Women, from Semiramis to Eugénie' (1870); and others.

Goodrich, Samuel Griswold. ["Peter Parley."] An American author; born in Ridgefield, Conn., Aug. 19, 1793; died in New York, May 9, 1860. He edited the Token, published in Boston from 1828 till 1842. From 1841 till 1854 he edited Merry's Museum and Parley's Magazine. His "Peter Parley" books won great popularity, evidenced by the fact that the pen-name was attached to more than 70 spurious volumes. Among the 200 volumes published by him are: 'The Poetical Works of John Trumbull' (1820); 'Tales of Peter Parley about America' (1827); similar books on Europe, Asia, Africa, and other countries.

Goodwin, Mrs. Maud (Wilder). An American historical novelist; born in New York State in 1856. She is a resident of New York city. Among her works are: 'The Colonial Cavalier'; 'The Head of a Hundred'; 'White Aprons: An Historical Romance'; 'Dolly Madison,' a biography; 'Four Roads to Paradise.'

Goodyear, William Henry. An American writer on art; born in Connecticut, 1846. He has published: 'Roman and Mediæval Art'; 'Renaissance and Modern Art'; 'History of Art'; 'The Grammar of the Lotus'; etc.

Gookin, Daniel (gö'kin). An American colonist; born in Kent, England, about 1612; died at Cambridge, Mass., March 19, 1687. He came to Virginia in 1621, but removed to Massachusetts in 1644. He was appointed superintendent of the Indians of that colony in 1656, and major-general in 1681. His chief work is 'Historical Collections of the Indians in New England,' which was not published until 1792.

Gordon, Adam Lindsey. An Australian poet; born in Fayal, Azores, in 1833; died June 24, 1870. He was an Oxford man, who emigrated to Australia and became a noted lover of the turf. He won considerable reputation as a writer of verse; his 'Poems' (1868), largely bush ballads and lyrics of the antipodes, reaching a fifth edition.

Gordon, Archibald D. An American dramatic critic and playwright; born in Ceylon, Oct. 11, 1848; died in Port Richmond, Staten Island, N. Y., Jan. 9, 1895. He entered a publishing-house in New York city in 1865, and subsequently became connected with New York and Chicago papers as dramatic critic. His works include: 'Trixie'; 'The Ugly Duckling'; 'Is Marriage a Failure?'; 'That Girl from Mexico.'

Gordon, Armistead Churchill. An American poet; born in Albemarle County, Va., Dec. 20, 1855. After graduating from the University of Virginia he became a lawyer in Staunton, Va. In collaboration with Thomas Nelson Page he wrote a volume of verse entitled ' Befo' de War' ; ' Echoes in Negro Dialect' (1888); ' Congressional Currency ' ; ' The Ivory Gate.'

Gordon, Clarence. [" Vieux Moustache."] An American juvenile-story writer; born in New York, 1835. He has written 'Christmas at Under Tor'; 'Boarding-School Days'; etc.

Gordon, Julien. See Cruger.

Gordon-Cumming, Constance Frederica. An English traveler and writer, sister of the famous sportsman Roualeyn Gordon-Cumming ; born at Altyre, Morayshire, Scotland, May 26, 1837. She traveled extensively in Great Britain in her early years, and recently has passed her time in Oriental countries. Among her works are: 'In the Hebrides'; 'Via Cornwall to Egypt'; 'In the Himalayas'; 'At Home in Fiji'; 'A Lady's Cruise in a French Man-of-War'; 'Two Happy Years in Ceylon'; 'Work for the Blind in China.'

Gore, Catherine Grace. An English novelist; born (Moody) in East Retford, Nottingham, 1799; died at Linwood, Hampshire, Jan. 26, 1861. She married a captain in the army, saw much high life, and wrote of it in many novels. 'Women as They Are' (1830), 'Mothers and Daughters' (1831), and 'Cecil' (1845) are the best known of her works.

Gore, Charles. An English clergyman and author; born in 1853. He is a Fellow of Trinity College, Oxford, and is now the Bishop of Worcester. He is best known as the editor of 'Lux Mundi,' and author of the essay on 'The Holy Spirit and Inspiration' in that volume. He has also written: 'The Church and the Ministry'; the Bampton Lecture for 1891 on ' The Incarnation of the Son of God'; and 'Roman Catholic Claims' (1888).

Görner, Karl August (gẽr'ner). A German playwright; born in Berlin, Jan. 29, 1806; died in Hamburg, April 9, 1884. He ran away from home when a lad in order to become an actor; eventually had a company of his own; and wrote over 100 successful plays, beginning with 'The Gardener and his Wife.' 'Niece and Aunt'; 'Black Peter'; 'A Happy Paterfamilias'; and 'The Ennobled Shopkeeper,' are some of the others.

Gorostiza y Cepeda, Don Manuel Eduardo de (gôr-ôs-tē'thä ē thä-pä'THä). A Mexican comedy-writer and diplomat; born in Vera Cruz, Nov. 13, 1791; died at Tacubaya, Oct. 23, 1851. His father was Spanish governor of Mexico. At 25 he had made theatre-goers of Madrid familiar with his name, but his impli-

cation in schemes of Mexican independence interfered with his literary career. He was made Mexican minister to England when independence was secured, and later had himself transferred to Paris, in which city he achieved his most enduring renown as a writer of plays. Among them, 'Bread and an Onion, with Thee, Love,' merits special notice as the source of Scribe's 'A Cottage and its Heart.' His 'Allowance for All' and 'Such as It Is' are masterpieces in comedy construction.

Görres, Joseph (gẽr'es). A celebrated German publicist and philosopher; born at Coblentz, Jan. 25, 1776; died 1848. His Rheinischer Merkur, in which he combatted French republican ideas was by far the most powerful journal in Germany: it was called by Napoleon " the fifth power" of Europe. He was a man of vast learning and great versatility; a few of his writings are: 'Aphorisms on Art'; 'Faith and Science'; 'History of Asian Myths'; 'The Hero-Book of Iran,' translated from Persian; ' The Holy Alliance'; 'Swedenborg, his Visions and his Relation to the Church '; 'Christian Mysticism,' a work of high authority (latest ed. 5 vols., 1879); 'Athanasius,' a strong polemic against Protestantism and Prussian bureaucracy; the author had shortly before embraced Catholicism.

Goschen, George Joachim. An English statesman; born in London, Aug. 10, 1831, of German parentage. From Oxford he entered mercantile life; became vice-president of the Board of Trade and director of the Bank of England; Liberal M. P. 1863; Privy-Councilor 1865; First Lord of the Admiralty 1871-74. He was sent on important missions to Cairo and Constantinople. In 1887 he seceded from the Liberal party and joined the Liberal-Unionists, and was Chancellor of the Exchequer in Lord Salisbury's administration. Besides speeches and addresses on political, educational, and economical questions, he published : ' The Theory of the Foreign Exchanges' (1864; 14th ed. 1890); 'Probable Result of an Increase in the Purchasing Power of Gold.' Died Feb. 7, 1907.

Goslavski, Maurycy (gôs-läv'skē). A Polish poet; born in Podolia in 1802; died in Stanislavof, Aug. 17, 1834. He was a soldier by profession; but published a volume of poetry in 1828. He took part in the war for Polish independence in 1830, at which time he produced his most famous stanzas, 'The Poems of a Polish Uhlan.' They were very popular among his countrymen during the great agitation.

Gosse, Edmund William. An English poet, essayist, and critic; born in London, Sept. 21, 1849. He attracted attention when very young by the grace and finish of papers contributed to London periodicals, and for many years his literary judgments have been regarded as of considerable weight. As a poet he is known by 'Madrigals, Songs, and Sonnets'; 'On Viol and Flute'; 'The Unknown Lover'; etc. Some of his literary criticisms and biographies are contained in 'Seventeenth-Century Studies' and 'From Shakespeare to Pope.'

Gosse, Philip Henry. An English naturalist and author; born in Worcester, 1810; died 1888. In 1827 he started on a scientific tour through Canada, the Southern United States, and Jamaica, and on his return published : 'The Canadian Naturalist' (1840); 'The Birds of Jamaica' (1845); 'A Naturalist's Sojourn in Jamaica.' In 1856 he was elected a Fellow of the Royal Society. His works, which amount to nearly fifty volumes, also include : 'Rambles of a Naturalist on the Devonshire Coast' (1853); 'Aquarium' (1854).

Gosson, Stephen. An English poet and satirist ; born in Kent (?), 1555 ; died at Bishopsgate, Feb. 13, 1623 or 1624. He was a clergyman. The 'School of Abuse' (1576) contains good prose, and the 'Pleasant Quips' (1595) good rhymes, but the latter are disfigured by coarse language.

Goszczynski, Severin (gōsh-chin'skē). A Polish poet ; born 1803, in Ilinze in the Ukraine ; died in Lemberg, Feb. 25, 1876. The influence of Byron is unmistakable in his youthful 'Castle of Kanioff.' In the struggle for independence in 1830 he achieved brilliant feats of arms, and composed national odes that spread his fame throughout Europe. Polish freedom proving a chimera, he wandered through France and Switzerland, writing poetry and prose as occasion served. 'The Terrible Huntsman,' 'The Three Chords,' and 'Dziela' are powerful poems.

Götter, Friedrich Wilhelm (gōt'ter). An important and even epoch-making German poet ; born in Gotha, Sept. 3, 1746 ; died there, March 18, 1797. He wrote dramas while studying foreign literatures at the University ; entered the diplomatic service, but gave it up to become a private tutor, and fell under the influence of Goethe. 'Media,' a drama, a volume of collected 'Poems,' and numerous comedies and minor pieces, represent his highest efforts. He was the last German poet to use French models largely.

Gottfried von Strassburg (got'frēt fōn sträs'börg). A German poet of the middle ages, and the most brilliant bard of chivalry ; born in the twelfth century, and died between 1210 and 1220. In collaboration with Von Eschenbach, he was author of 'Parsifal,' the popular "minna" song of its time ; but he owes his permanent fame to 'Tristan and Isolde,' apparently written between 1204 and 1215, and left unfinished. In this story-poem Tristan is sent to woo Isolde in his uncle's name ; but he having swallowed a philtre, the two young people fall deeply in love. Straszburg's work is graceful and simple, and he chooses his legendary material with nice critical judgment.

Gotthelf, Jeremias (got'helf), pseudonym of Albert Bitzius. A Swiss novelist and poet ; born in Murton, Canton of Freiburg, Oct. 4, 1797 ; died at Lützelflüh, Bern, Oct. 22, 1854. As a pastor in retired districts, he saw the hard conditions of the poor, and in 1837 wrote 'The Peasant's Mirror,' a vividly realistic presentation of peasant life,—the imaginary autobiography of one Jeremias Gotthelf ; the immense success of the book led him to adopt the name as a pseudonym. He worked this vein with unflagging industry : 'Joys and Sorrows of a Schoolmaster,' 'How Five Maids Came to Grief through Brandy,' 'How Uli, the Servant, was Made Happy,' and numerous others, "tendency" novels, followed swiftly.

Gottschall, Rudolf von (got'shäl). A German novelist, poet, and critic ; born in Breslau, Sept. 30, 1823. As a critic his subtlety and acuteness of treatment give him a growing influence. Among his works in criticism are : 'Pictures of Travel in Italy' ; 'Portraits and Studies' ; 'Studies in the Direction of a New German Literature' ; and 'Literary Silhouettes.' His critical studies are not permitted to interrupt the production of brilliant plays, stories, and poems.

Gough, John Ballantine. An eminent American temperance advocate ; born in England, 1817 ; died 1885. He published an 'Autobiography' ; 'Temperance Lectures' ; 'Sunlight and Shadow' ; 'Platform Echoes' ; etc.

Goulburn, Edward Meyrick. An English clergyman and religious writer ; born in 1818. He became head-master of Rugby in 1850, and dean of Norwich, 1886–89. Besides many single sermons and lectures, he has published over forty works, among which are : 'Introduction to the Devotional Study of the Holy Scripture' (1854); 'Manual of Confirmation' (1855); a collection of 'Family Prayers' (1857); 'The Functions of Our Cathedrals' (1869); 'The Holy Catholic Church' (1873); 'Farewell to Norwich Cathedral' (1891).

Gould, Benjamin Apthorp. A distinguished American astronomer ; born in Boston, Sept. 27, 1824 ; died at Cambridge, Nov. 26, 1896. He graduated at Harvard in 1844 and afterwards studied abroad. In 1849 he received an appointment to the United States Coast Survey, and devised methods for determining the longitudes telegraphically. From 1870 to 1885 he was director of the national observatory at Cordova, Argentine Republic, where he completed three extensive catalogues of stars, and conducted meteorological and climatological investigations. He was the founder and editor of the Astronomical Journal (1849–61). His principal works are : 'On the Transatlantic Longitude, as Determined by the Coast Survey' (1869); 'Uranometria Argentina' (1879), which gives the brightness and the position of every fixed star, to the seventh magnitude inclusive, within 100 degrees of the South Pole.

Gould, Edward Sherman. An American prose-writer ; born in Connecticut, 1808 ; died 1885. He published : 'The Sleep Rider' ; 'The Very Age,' a comedy ; 'John Doe and Richard Roe,' a tale of New York life ; etc.

Gould, Hannah Flagg. An American poet ; born in Vermont, 1789 ; died 1865. Among the collections of her verse are 'Hymns and Poems for Children'); 'The Golden Vase'); 'The Youth's Coronal'; etc. The best-known piece by her is 'The Snow-Flake and the Frost.'

Gould, John. An English ornithologist; born in 1804; died in 1881. In 1827 he was appointed curator to the Zoölogical Society's Museum, and in 1838 proceeded to study the Australian birds in Tasmania, South Australia, and New South Wales. The results of his researches are embodied in his great work on the 'Birds of Australia' (7 vols., 1840–48). His other important works are: 'A Century of Birds from the Himalayan Mountains'); 'The Birds of Europe' (1832–37); 'The Mammals of Australia'); 'The Birds of Great Britain.'

Gould, John W. An American story-writer; born in Connecticut, 1814; died 1838. He wrote 'Forecastle Yarns'); 'Private Journal of Voyage from New York to Rio Janeiro'; etc.

Gould, Robert Freeke. An English barrister and writer on Freemasonry; born at Ilfracombe, Devonshire, England, in 1836. From 1860 to 1862 he participated, under the rank of lieutenant, in military campaigns in southern China, and in different expeditions against the Tai Ping rebels. His works include: 'The Atholl Lodges' (1879); 'The Four Old Lodges' (1879); 'The History of Freemasonry : Its Antiquities, Symbols, Constitutions, Customs, etc.' (6 vols., 1884–87).

Goulding, Francis Robert. An American story-writer; born in Georgia, 1810; died 1881. He was a Presbyterian clergyman. He wrote: 'Young Marooners on the Florida Coast'); 'Marooner's Island'); and other tales for boys.

Govean, Felice (gō'vä''än). An Italian dramatist and publicist; born in Racconigi, Piedmont, 1819. He began as a miscellaneous prose-writer, and founded the democratic Gazzetta del Popolo, which reached an immense circulation. His true success, however, was in the drama. His first plays, 'The Waldenses' and 'Jesus Christ,' attracted wide notice; and the success of 'The Siege of Turin' and 'The Siege of Alessandria' made his reputation international. His plays are essentially popular in theme and character. He has written a variety of meritorious short stories.

Gower, John. An English poet; born in Kent (?) in 1325 (?); died at London in August or September 1408. At one time ranked high among Britain's early singers, his note has been decried by modern critics, and to-day he is falling into neglect. Still his 'Mirror of Meditation' (Speculum Meditantis), 'Voice of One Crying' (Vox Clamantis), and 'Lover's Confession' (Confessio Amantis), contain specimens of genuine poetry. He wrote excellent sonnets in French.

Gozlan, Léon (goz-lɔn'). A French novelist; born in Marseilles, Sept. 1, 1803; died at Paris, Sept. 14, 1866. From clerk in a Paris book-store he became a writer for Figaro, and then produced novels; sometimes socialistic, but well conceived and executed, with a vein of peculiar irony, but an over-elaboration that spoils at times his best effects. 'The Notary of Chantilly,' 'A Millionaire's Most Beautiful Dream,' and 'The Lambert Family,' deserve special mention.

Gozzi, Carlo, Count (got'sē). An Italian comedy-writer; born in Venice, Dec. 13, 1720; died there (?), April 4, 1806. Forced into the army by poverty while a boy, he left it for literature; at first under French influence, but later turning his native folk-lore into delightful comedies, worked up with infinite cleverness. 'The Love of the Three Oranges,' 'Lady Serpent,' and 'The Triumph of Friendship,' may be mentioned.

Gozzi, Gasparo, Count. An Italian poet and essayist, brother of Carlo; born in Venice, Dec. 4, 1713; died at Padua, Dec. 25, 1786. He married at 26 Louise Bergalli, the celebrated painter and poet, who was 36, the alliance bringing him into literary and artistic associations. He founded the Gazzetta Veneta, which was a great popular success; but his 'Osservatore Veneto,' on the model of the Spectator, is of a higher order as literature. His polemic writings on Dante's 'Divine Comedy' are classic authorities on the resources of the Italian language. His Horatian poems are graceful; and his literary essays are as good in thought as in style.

Grabbe, Christian Dietrich (gräb'bē). A German dramatic poet; born in Detmold, Dec. 11, 1801; died there, Sept. 12, 1836. Developing from an unhappy boy to a man of brilliant powers and ripe scholarship, his incurable passion for drink spoiled his married life and his fortunes, though Heine, Tieck, and others, persuaded him to spasmodic reform; he was successively lawyer, actor, and soldier. Yet he won a place in German drama second only to Goethe and Schiller. His plays are striking and original in conception, and commanding in execution. The impression they leave is of an uncontrolled, discordant, and unrestful genius. 'Hannibal,' 'Don Juan,' and 'Faust,' the fragment entitled 'Marius and Sulla,' and 'The Hermann Battle,' exemplify these conditions in a marked degree.

Grabovski, Michael (gräb-ov'skē). A Polish novelist, essayist, and critic; born in Volhynia in 1805; died at Warsaw, Nov. 18, 1863. While still a student at Warsaw, he won a literary reputation in the war of the romantic upon the then dominant classical school. 'Thoughts on Polish Literature' and 'Melodies from the Ukraine' were his first noteworthy volumes; but the revolution of 1830 interrupted his literary career for nearly ten years, when he completed 'Criticism and Literature.' Two historical novels, one based on a tragic episode in the Ukraine, and the other upon a peasant outbreak in the same region, entitled respectively 'The Koliszczysna and the Steppe Dwellers' and 'The Storm in the Steppes,' are fine examples of Polish literature. An epoch-making work is his 'The Old and the New Ukraine.'

Graf, Arturo (gräf). An Italian poet, historian of literature, and critic; born in Athens, of German parentage; in 1848. His youth was spent in Roumania; he studied law at Naples; became a tutor at the University of Rome in 1874, and in 1882 professor of literature at Turin, a post he still holds. 'Poems,' light in spirit and substance, 'Medusa,' a powerful but somewhat heavy tragic outburst, and some occasional effusions, speak well for his poetic talent. In prose he is a master when dealing with 'The Origin of the Modern Drama,' 'Historical Literature and its Methods,' and 'The Legend of the Terrestrial Paradise.'

Graffigny, Françoise d'Issembourg d'Happoncourt, Madame de (gräf-fin'yē). A French epistolary writer; born in Nancy, Feb. 13, 1695; died at Paris, Dec. 12, 1758. Married young, but separating from her husband, she took refuge at Cirey with Madame du Châtelet and Voltaire. Her first appearance in literature was with the 'Peruvian Letters,' a palpable imitation of Montesquieu's 'Persian Letters,' but successful. A volume of her letters appeared posthumously under the title 'The Private Life of Voltaire and Madame du Châtelet,' a gossipy and trifling but very readable work.

Graham, Nellie. See **Dunning.**

Grand, Mme. Sarah. An English novelist; born (Frances Elizabeth Clarke) in Ireland. She married a British naval officer almost immediately upon leaving school, and has traveled widely. 'The Heavenly Twins' made her famous. 'Singularly Deluded' and 'Ideala' are among her other works of fiction.

Grand-Carteret, John (grän-kär-ter-ā). A French journalist and critic; born in Paris, about 1850. He is of Swiss origin, and first distinguished himself in French journalism through the accuracy and acuteness with which he treated German themes. Of late years he has made important studies of life and manners in Europe. 'Character and Caricature in Germany, Austria, and Switzerland,' 'France Judged by a German,' 'Woman and Germany,' and 'J. J. Rousseau, Judged by a Frenchman of To-Day,' are among his many successes.

Grant, Alexander, Sir. An English educator and writer; born in New York city, Sept. 13, 1826; died in Edinburgh, Scotland, Nov. 30, 1884. After graduating at Oxford he went in 1859 to Madras, where he became professor of history and political economy. He was subsequently appointed director of public instruction at Bombay, his administration marking an epoch in the history of education in India. From his return to Scotland in 1868 till his death he was principal of the University of Edinburgh. Besides contributions to periodicals and the 'Encyclopædia Britannica,' he published a translation of the 'Ethics of Aristotle' (1857–58), his best-known work; lives of Xenophon and Aristotle in 'Ancient Classics for English Readers' (1871–77); 'The Story of the University of Edinburgh' (1883).

Grant, Anne. A Scotch memoirist and descriptive prose-writer; born in Glasgow, Feb. 21, 1755; died in Edinburgh, Nov. 7, 1838. She was in this country when a child, and from her observations gathered at that time wrote 'Memoirs of an American Lady' (1808), a highly attractive delineation of our colonial life. She is also the author of 'Essays on the Superstitions of the Highlands of Scotland' (1811), besides miscellaneous prose.

Grant, George Monroe. A Canadian clergyman, educator, and author; born at Stellarton, Pictou County, Nova Scotia, Dec. 22, 1835. He received his education in his native province, and subsequently won academic distinction in the University of Glasgow, Scotland. On his return to Nova Scotia he spent some time as a missionary in the Maritime Provinces; became pastor of St. Matthew's Church, Halifax; and in 1877 accepted the principalship of Queen's University. Besides contributions to periodical literature his works include: 'Ocean to Ocean' (1872), an interesting diary of a tour across the American continent; 'Picturesque Canada' (1884), a valuable work on the scenery, industries, and social life of the Canadian Dominion.

Grant, James. A Scottish novelist and historical writer; born in Edinburgh, Aug. 1, 1822; died in London, May 5, 1887. He was a kinsman of Sir Walter Scott. He entered the army in 1839, but resigned in 1843, and devoted himself to literary pursuits. 'The Romance of War' (1845) became at once popular, as also 'The Adventures of an Aide-de-Camp' (1848). Among his other novels are: 'Walter Fenton, or the Scottish Cavalier' (1850); 'Bothwell' (1851); 'Jane Seton' (1853); 'The Phantom Regiment' (1856); 'The Secret Dispatch' (1869); 'Under the Red Dragon' (1872); 'Playing with Fire' (1887), a story of the war in the Soudan. He also wrote: 'Memoirs of Kirkaldy of Grange' (1849); 'Memorials of the Castle of Edinburgh' (1850); 'Old and New Edinburgh' (1881); 'Scottish Soldiers of Fortune' (1889); and others.

Grant, James Augustus. An English military officer, explorer, and author; born at Nairn, Scotland, April 11, 1827; died Feb. 11, 1892. He served in the Indian Mutiny at Multan and Gujerat; and was wounded at Lucknow, when as lieutenant-colonel he commanded the rear guard. In 1860–63 he undertook with Capt. Speke an expedition to find the sources of the Nile, which resulted in the discovery of Lake Victoria Nyanza. In 1868 he received "The Star of India" for services rendered in the Abyssinian campaign. He published: 'A Walk Across Africa' (1863); 'Botany of the Speke and Grant Expedition' (1872); 'Khartoum as I Saw It in 1863' (1885).

Grant, Robert. An American lawyer and author; born in Boston, Mass., Jan. 24, 1852. He graduated from Harvard in 1873 and the Harvard Law School in 1879. Since 1893 he has been a judge of probate and insolvency for Suffolk County, Mass. Among his most popular works are: 'The Little Tin Gods on Wheels' (1879); 'Confessions of a Frivolous Girl' (1880); 'An Average Man' (1883); 'Face to Face' (1886); 'The Reflections of a Married Man' (1892); 'The Art of Living.' He also wrote the well-known boy's stories, 'Jack Hall' (1887); 'Jack in the Bush'; 'The Law-Breakers' (1906).

Grant, Robert Edmond. A Scotch naturalist; born in Edinburgh, Scotland, 1793; died in 1874. He was educated in his native city and on the Continent. Upon his return to Edinburgh in 1819 he became a Fellow of the Royal College of Physicians, and began the practice of medicine. In 1827 he was elected professor of zoölogy and comparative anatomy in University College, London, a position which he occupied for the rest of his life. His chief work is 'Outlines of Comparative Anatomy,' for many years a favorite text-book, not only in Great Britain, but on the Continent and in America.

Grant, Ulysses Simpson. The greatest of American generals, and eighteenth President of the United States; born at Point Pleasant, O., April 27, 1822; died at Mt. McGregor, near Saratoga Springs, N. Y., July 23, 1885. His 'Personal Memoirs' seem destined to give him enduring literary fame.

Gras, Felix. A Provençal poet and novelist; born at Malemort (Vaucluse), France, May 3, 1844; died at Avignon, March 4, 1901. He was a lawyer and « juge de paix» in the department of Vaucluse, and one of the leading Provençal writers, ranking next to Mistral. His most famous work is 'The Reds of the Midi,' a story of the French Revolution, translated into English by Mrs. T. A. Janvier; next in importance, 'Li Carbouniè' (1876), and 'Toloza' (1882), epic poems; 'Lou Roumancero Prouvençau' (1887), shorter poems; 'Li Papalino' (1891), Avignon stories. He was also editor of the «Armana Prouvençau,» a literary annual, and from 1891 was the «Capouliè,» or official head, of the «Félibrige,» the society of Provençal men of letters.

Grassi, Angela (gräs'sē). A Spanish poet, novelist, and playwright; born in Crema, Italy, April 2, 1826. Her childhood was passed at Barcelona, where at 15 she wrote the successful drama 'Crime and Expiation.' 'Riches of the Soul' and 'The Drop of Water' won a prize from the Spanish Academy. 'The Son-in-Law,' 'The First Year of Marriage,' and 'The Snowball' are her best-known novels.

Grattan, Henry. An Irish orator and statesman; born in Dublin, June (?) or July (?) 3, 1746; died in London, June 4, 1820. His works, with the exception of the political pamphlets, the 'Correspondence,' and 'Letter on the Irish Union,' consist wholly of his speeches as the champion of Catholic emancipation and the inviolability of the Irish Parliament. His language is vivid, warm, and «contagious.»

Grattan, Thomas Colley. An Irish novelist and sketch-writer; born in Dublin, 1792;

died in London, July 4, 1864. He abandoned law for the army, and from a wandering life obtained materials for his 'Highways and Byways' (1823), a collection of tales and studies that proved highly popular. 'The Heiress of Bruges' (1828) is a historical novel. Some less important fictions, plays, and translations of French poetry complete the sum of his literary product.

Gravière, Jean Pierre Edmond Jurien de la (gräv-yär'). A French admiral and author; born in Brest, France, Nov. 19, 1812; died in Paris, March 5, 1892. He served with distinction in Chinese waters (1841), the Black Sea, and the Mediterranean; and as commander of the expedition against Mexico arranged the treaty of Soledad (1861). He was chosen a member of the French Academy in 1868. His numerous works include: 'Sardinia in 1841' (1841); 'Souvenir of an Admiral' (1860); 'The Ancient Navy'; 'The Modern Navy'; 'Maritime Wars of the Revolution and Empire'; 'The Navy of the Ancients and the Campaigns of Alexander' (10 vols.), a great work which places the author in the front rank of military historians.

Gray, Asa. An eminent American botanist; born at Paris, N. Y., Nov. 18, 1810; died at Cambridge, Mass., January 1888. He was professor of botany at Harvard from 1842 to 1873, when he resigned to take charge of the herbarium of Harvard. In 1874 he was chosen a regent of the Smithsonian Institution. He was recognized throughout the world as one of the leading botanists of the age. Besides contributions to scientific journals, his numerous works include: 'Elements of Botany' (1836); 'Manual of the Botany of the Northern United States' (1848); 'Botany of the United States Pacific Exploring Expedition' (1854); 'School and Field Book of Botany' (1869); 'Natural Science and Religion' (1880).

Gray, David. An American journalist and poet; born in Edinburgh, Scotland, Nov. 9, 1836; died in Binghamton, N. Y., March 18, 1888. He was on the editorial staff of the Buffalo Courier from 1856 to 1882. A volume of his letters, poems, and selected prose writings was published posthumously in 1888.

Gray, David. A Scotch poet; born in Merkland, Dumbartonshire, Jan. 29, 1838; died there, Dec. 3, 1861. He was the son of a factory operative, and his education was obtained through many difficulties. 'The Luggie,' a poem of the didactic and descriptive order, published posthumously, displays an exquisite though ill-regulated genius.

Gray, Thomas. A great English poet; born at Cornhill, London, Dec. 26, 1716; died at Cambridge, July 24, 1771. He is known in every household for the 'Elegy in a Country Churchyard,' published 1751, though begun seven years before. The 'Ode on a Distant Prospect of Eton College' (1747); 'Ode to Adversity'; 'Progress of Poetry'; and 'The Bard' (1757), are also famous.

Graziani, Girolamo (gräts"ē-än'ē). An Italian poet; born in Pergola in 1604; died there, Sept. 10, 1675. He received his education at Bologna and Padua, and became prominent in the service of various Italian princes, until the Duke of Modena, Francis I., created him Count of Sarzano (or Saryana), when he retired, to devote himself to literature. 'Cleopatra,' a heroic poem on the model of Tasso, and 'The Conquest of Granada,' are his happiest efforts in metre. A tragedy, 'Cromwell,' was extraordinarily popular for a time.

Grazzini, Antonio Francesco (grät-sē'nē). An Italian humorist and poet; born in Florence, March 22, 1503; died there, Feb. 18, 1584. Of much native humor, he graduated from apothecary to writer of literary burlesques. He was one of the founders of the celebrated Florentine Academy; was expelled in consequence of a disputed question of grammar, and established the renowned Accadèmia della Crusca, whose mission was the purification of the Italian tongue. His literary reputation rests on his 'Suppers,' written on the model of Boccaccio, and vastly popular at one time. In style they are pure and refined, and they contributed much to the literary development of the language. Seven highly amusing comedies, of a not high literary flavor, and a burlesque poem, 'The War of Monsters,' complete the list of his remembered achievements.

Greeley, Horace. A famous American editor and controversial writer; born in Amherst, N. H., Feb. 3, 1811; died in New York, Nov. 29, 1872. In the countless articles, papers, and pamphlets that issued from his pen, as well as in 'The American Conflict' and 'Recollections of a Busy Life,' he is revealed as the consistent and able opponent of social wrongs and ills of every description; and as a writer he is gifted with a nervous, living style that powerfully supports the arguments he advances. In 'Glances at Europe' and like works he is happy in description.

Greely, Adolphus Washington. An American soldier, Arctic explorer, and author; born at Newburyport, Mass., March 27, 1844. Belonging to the regular army, in 1881 he commanded an Arctic expedition to establish circumpolar stations for scientific purposes, in accordance with a plan made by the International Congress at Hamburg in 1879. He reached the highest point north attained up to that time, but endured great suffering and loss of men from cold and starvation. Among his works are: 'Three Years of Arctic Service' (1886); 'American Weather' (1888); 'Hand-book of Arctic Discoveries'; 'American Explorers.'

Green, Anna Katharine — Mrs. Rohlfs. An American author; born in Brooklyn, N. Y., Nov. 11, 1846. She graduated at Ripley (female) College, Poultney, Vt., 1867. Her novels are detective stories, and enjoy great popularity. 'The Leavenworth Case' (1878) is one of her best. Included in her publications are: 'Risifi's Daughter' (1866), a dramatic poem; 'The

Sword of Damocles'; 'A Strange Disappearance'; 'Hand and Ring'; 'The Mill Mystery'; 'Behind Closed Doors'; 'X, Y, Z'; 'That Affair Next Door'; 'The Mayor's Wife.'

Green, John Richard. An English clergyman and historian; born in Oxford, 1837; died at Mentone, France, March 7, 1883. He ruined his health and died early through fiery zeal in work among the London poor; much of his vast research and his writing were done in bed. The 'Short History of the English People' is perhaps the highest combination in historical writing of sound scholarship, immense and perfectly assimilated reading, and a literary style of great charm, lucidity, and swiftness. 'The Making of England' and 'The Conquest of England' are studies of special periods.

Green, Joseph. An American poet,—famed for his loyalty to England; born in Boston, Mass., in 1706; died in London, England, Dec. 11, 1780; graduated at Harvard 1726. He was a ready wit and satirist. His works include: 'The Wonderful Lament of Old Mr. Tenor' (1744); 'Poems and Satires' (1780).

Green, Matthew. A British poet; born in 1696; died in Nag's Head Court, in 1737. 'The Spleen,' most noted of his poems for originality and wit, was published (1737) after his death, by his friend Richard Glover. It is one of the best of its class, and was a favorite with Gray. The familiar quotation "Fling but a stone, the giant dies," is from this poem.

Green, Thomas Hill. An English philosopher and humanist; born in Birkin, Yorkshire, April 7, 1836; died at Oxford, March 26, 1882. His profound learning and attractive personal qualities made him a strong influence in British thought, and the chief exponent of the Neo-Hegelian movement. His works include: 'Introduction to Hume'; 'Treatise on Human Nature'; 'Collected Writings'; and 'Prolegomena to Ethics.'

Greene, Aella. An American journalist and poet; born in Chester, Mass., in 1838. He was connected with the press. His works include: 'Rhymes of Yankee-Land'; 'Into the Sunshine' (1881); 'Stanza and Sequel' (1884); 'Gathered from Life.' Died Jan. 8, 1903.

Greene, Albert Gorton. An American lawyer and poet; born in Providence, R. I., Feb. 10, 1802; died in Cleveland, O., Jan. 4, 1868. He wrote the famous poem "Old Grimes."

Greene, Asa. An American author; born in Ashburnham, Mass., 1788; died in New York city, 1837. He graduated at Williams College, and in 1827 received a degree from the Berkshire Medical School. He was a bookseller of the old-fashioned kind, and noted as a humorist. He served for some time as editor of the New York Evening Transcript. His publications include: 'Adventures of Dr. Dodimus Duckworth, A. N. Q.; to which is added, the History of a Steam Doctor' (1833); and 'Debtor's Prison' (1837).

Greene, Francis Vinton. An American soldier and author; born in Providence, R. I., June 27, 1850. He graduated from West Point in 1870, and served until 1886, when he resigned with the rank of captain. He was assistant astronomer on the Northwest Boundary Survey from 1872 to 1876, and was attached to the headquarters of the Russian army during the Russo-Turkish War of 1877–78. His chief works are: 'The Russian Army and its Campaigns in Turkey' (1879); 'Army Life in Russia' (1880); 'The Mississippi' (1882); 'Life of Nathaniel Greene' (1893).

Greene, George Washington. An American historian, grandson of Gen. Nathanael Greene; born in East Greenwich, R. I., April 8, 1811; died there, Feb. 2, 1883. Among his works are: 'History and Geography of the Middle Ages' (1851); 'Historical View of the American Revolution' (1865); 'Life of Nathaniel Greene' (1867–71).

Greene, Homer. An American story-writer; born at Ariel, Pa., in 1853, and resides at Honesdale, Pa. He is the author of 'The Blind Brother, a Story of the Pennsylvania Coal Mines' (1887); 'Burnham Breaker' (1887); 'Riverpark Rebellion'; 'Pickett's Gap' (1902).

Greene, Louisa Lelias, Hon. An English writer of juveniles; born (third Lord Plunket's daughter) in 1833. Her works, widely popular, include: 'A Winter and Summer at Burton Hill' (1861); 'Cushions and Corners' (1864); 'The Schoolboy Baronet' (1870); 'Gilbert's Shadow' (1875); 'Jubilee Hall' (1881). She wrote with her cousin W. H. Wills the dramatist: 'Drawing-Room Dramas'; 'Prince Crœsus in Search of a Wife' (1873), a translation.

Greene, Robert. An English dramatist; born in Norwich about 1560; died in London, Sept. 3, 1592. His works rank him as the most original and perhaps the ablest British dramatist before Shakespeare: especially the 'History of Orlando Furioso'; 'Comical History of Alphonsus, King of Aragon'; 'Honorable History of Friar Bacon and Friar Bungay'; and 'The Scottish Historie of James IV.' His pamphlets and tracts, which he wrote with great rapidity and ability, are noteworthy; 'Never Too Late' and 'Greene's Groat's Worth of Wit Bought with a Million of Repentance' being most widely known.

Greene, Mrs. Sarah Pratt (McLean). An American novelist; born at Simsbury, Conn., in 1856. She was educated at South Hadley Seminary, and for several years taught school in Plymouth, Mass. Her best-known novel is 'Cape Cod Folks' (1881). Among her other works are: 'Towhead, the Story of a Girl' (1884); 'Lastchance Junction'; 'Power Lot' (1906).

Greenough, Sarah Dana (Loring). An American author; born in Boston, Feb. 19, 1827; died in Franzensbad, Austria, Aug. 9, 1885. Among her works are: 'Treason at Home,' a novel (3 vols., 1865); 'Arabesques' (1871); 'In Extremis, a Story of a Broken Law' (1872); and 'Mary Magdalene,' a poem (1880).

Greenwood, Grace. See Lippincott.

Greey, Edward (grē). An English-American story-writer; born in Sandwich, Kent, England, Dec. 1, 1835; died in New York, Oct. 1, 1888. After spending several years in Japan, he came to the United States in 1868, became a citizen, and engaged in commercial pursuits in New York. Among his plays are 'Vendome' and 'Uncle Abner.' His historical works include 'Young Americans in Japan' (Boston, 1881), and 'The Wonderful City of Tokio.' He wrote a pleasing collection of Japanese short stories, 'The Golden Lotus,' etc. (1883); 'The Captive of Love,' founded on a Japanese romance; translated 'The Loyal Ronins'; etc.

Greg, William Rathbone. A religious and economic essayist; born in Manchester, England, in 1809; died in 1881. In 1856 he became a commissioner of customs, and in 1864 was appointed comptroller of the Stationery Office. His views of life were profoundly serious and even melancholy, and his works exerted a great influence from their earnestness and sincerity. The most important are: 'Sketches in Greece and Turkey' (1833); 'The German Schism and the Irish Priests' (1845); 'The Creed of Christendom' (1851), his chief work; 'Essays in Political and Social Science' (1853); 'Enigmas of Life' (1872); 'Literary and Social Judgments' (1877).

Gregorovius, Ferdinand (greg-ō-rō'vē-ös). A German historian and poet; born in Neidenburg, East Prussia, Jan. 19, 1821; died at Munich, May 1, 1891. He studied severely at Königsberg and at home, and wrote essays of deep scholarship; 'Socialistic Elements in Goethe's Wilhelm Meister'; a tragedy, 'The Death of Tiberius,' of the ripest historical learning; 'Corsica'; and other most authoritative books of travel and description, based on close personal study. He wrote also 'Euphorion,' an epic, and other poems of high repute. But his historical works, of unsurpassed learning and vivid realization of the spirit of their times, are the most commanding monument of his genius. 'The City of Rome in the Middle Ages,' 'Lucretia Borgia,' 'Urban VIII.,' 'The Monuments of the Popes,' and 'Athenais,' need but be named.

Gregory, Robert. An English clergyman and writer; born in 1819. He received his education at Oxford; was curate of St. Mary-the-Less, Lambeth (1853–73); became canon of St. Paul's in 1868, and dean in 1890 in succession to Dean Church. Aside from his clerical duties, he has devoted much attention to charitable and educational work. Among his publications are: 'A Plea in Behalf of Small Parishes' (1849); 'Lectures at St. Paul's' (1871–82); 'Position of the Celebrant Aspect in Convocation' (1875).

Greif, Martin (grīf). [An adopted name.] A German poet and dramatist, son of Max Frey the publicist; born in Speyer, June 18, 1839. Designed for public life, he preferred the literary career. 'Hans Sachs,' a successful drama, was followed by a volume of poems, the tragedies 'Corfiz Ulfeldt, the Count Chancellor of Denmark,' 'Marino Faliero,' the light comedy 'Walter's Return to his Country,' and numerous other works of high literary qualities and scholarship. Strikingly successful plays also are 'Francesca da Rimini,' and 'Agnes Bernauer, the Angel of Augsburg.' He is also a noted lyric poet.

Greifenson. See **Grimmelshausen**

Grein, J. T. An Anglo-Dutch attorney, journalist, playwright, and dramatic critic; born in Amsterdam, Oct. 11, 1862. He was educated in Holland, Germany, and Belgium, and from 1879 to 1885 was engaged in the East India trade and banking. He is at present an attorney in London, besides being dramatic critic of Life and the Westminster Review, London editor of three papers in Holland, and correspondent of several French and German journals. In 1891 he founded the Independent Theatre Society. Besides 'A Man's Love,' produced in 1889 with C. W. Jarvis as coauthor, and other plays, his works include (in Dutch): 'Dramatic Essays' (1884); 'Silhouettes' (short novels), published in 1885; 'London: Wealth and Poverty' (1890); ''Twixt Light and Dark,' short stories.

Grénier, Édouard (grān-yā'). A French poet; born in Baumes-les-Dames, Doubs, in 1819; died in Paris, Dec. 5, 1901. He abandoned diplomacy for poetry, 'Little Poems' was his maiden collection; 'The Death of the Wandering Jew' attained repute for delicacy and suggestiveness, and 'Dramatic Poems' for intense power. His lines on 'The Death of President Lincoln' were crowned by the Academy.

Grenville-Murray, Eustace Clare. An English descriptive and topical writer and diplomatist; born 1824; died Dec. 20, 1881. He experimented unsuccessfully in fiction, and then won reputation with 'French Pictures in English Chalks,' a series of humorous sketches; 'History of the French Press' (1874); 'Round about France' (1878); and 'Side Lights on English Society' (3d ed. 1889). 'The Member for Paris' (1871) had some vogue.

Gresset, Jean Baptiste Louis de (gres-sā). A French poet, dramatist, and satirist; born in Amiens, Aug. 29, 1709; died there, June 16, 1777. Early a Jesuit and teacher, he gained some repute from a pleasing ode 'On the Love of One's Native Land'; and rose to fame by 'Vert-Vert,' a highly original and deliciously humorous verse narrative of a parrot brought up in a nunnery but falling into evil society. His tendency to burlesque and irreverence in his poetry caused his expulsion from the order on the appearance of 'The Improvised Carnival' and 'The Living Reading-Desk.' He cared nothing for this, and shortly after rose to the pinnacle of popularity through 'The Naughty Man.' He entered the Academy in 1748, and wrote much popular prose and poetry; but later in life became alarmed concerning his soul, and abjured all his writings.

Gréville, Henry (grā-vēl'), pseudonym of Madame Alice Durand. A French novelist; born (Fleury) in Paris, Oct. 12, 1842. She was educated in Russia, and began her literary career with contributions to St. Petersburg journals. Upon her marriage to Prof. Émile Durand, she returned to France and continued her literary activity, making use of her Russian experiences in a series of novels which became very popular, notably 'Dosia' and 'The Expiation of Saveli.' Her genius is essentially realistic, with an occasional tendency towards the romantic. 'Cleopatra,' 'A Russian Violin,' 'A Crime,' and 'An Ancient Household,' are types of this class of novel. Died in Paris, May 20, 1902.

Greyson, Émile (grā-zôn'). A Belgian poet, novelist, and essayist; born Aug. 17, 1823, in Brussels, where he is a high educational official. His early reputation was through poems, stories, and essays in Belgian papers; his later fame was European. 'Fiamma Colonna' and 'Tales of a Flemish Subject' are his best fictions. His translations and literary papers in the Belgian Review, etc., make him a representative man of letters at home.

Gribojedov, Alexander Sergeievich (grē-bō-yā'dov). A Russian dramatic poet and statesman; born in Moscow, Jan. 15, 1793; killed at Teheran, Persia, Feb. 11, 1829. A distinguished soldier and diplomat, he was assassinated while minister to Persia, during an anti-Russian tumult in Teheran. As a writer his reputation rests mainly upon 'Knowledge Brings Suffering,' a drama in verse, delineating Russian society with bitter fidelity. 'A Georgian Night' and a rendering of the Prelude to 'Faust' are also creditable productions.

Grieben, Hermann (grē'ben). A German poet and journalist; born in Köslin, Feb. 8, 1822; died at Cologne, Sept. 24, 1890. He studied at Breslau and rose to prominence in journalism, editing the Ostsee Zeitung, the Kölnische Zeitung, and other equally important sheets. He wrote 'Too Late,' a tragedy, under the pseudonym of "Roderick," and a valuable volume on Dante; besides poems in three collected editions, including 'Voices of the Time.'

Griepenkerl, Wolfgang Robert (grēp'benkärl). A German poet, dramatist, and essayist; born in Hofwyl, Bern, Switzerland, May 4, 1810; died at Brunswick, Oct. 16, 1868. He became a tutor and professor of literature soon after the completion of his university course. His 'Pictures from Classic Greece,' a collection of poems, attracted attention, and an epic on 'The Sistine Madonna' made him celebrated. He wrote several excellent works on music. 'Artistic Genius in German Literature during the Last Century' was for years an authority upon the subject. As a playwright, 'Maximilian Robespierre' and 'The Girondins' entitle him to no minor place, and his 'Ideal and World' and 'In the Upper Sphere' have been staged many times. He wrote a volume of stories that possess merit.

Griesinger, Karl Theodor (grē′ziNG-er). A German novelist and sketch-writer; born Dec. 11, 1809, in Kirnbach, in the Black Forest; died at Stuttgart, March 2, 1884. He studied theology at Tübingen and became a clergyman, then drifted into authorship. His first hit was made with 'Silhouettes from Suabia'; and he founded the Suabian Humorist, only to meet ruin by the upheavals of 1848. After another attempt to establish a popular paper, and an ensuing term of imprisonment, he visited the United States. 'Living Pictures from America'; 'Emigrant Stories'; 'The Old Brewery, or New York Mysteries of Crime'; and 'Vatican Mysteries', were written upon his return home.

Griffin, Gerald. An Irish novelist, dramatist, and poet; born at Limerick, Dec. 12, 1803; died at Cork, June 12, 1840. In 1823 he went to London and embarked upon a literary career. His first success in fiction was 'Holland Tide; or Munster Popular Tales' (1827), a series of short stories. 'Tales of the Munster Festivals' (1827) also became speedily popular, and 'The Collegians' (1829), a second series of the former, still further increased his reputation; on it Dion Boucicault founded his well-known play 'The Colleen Bawn.' Among his other works are: 'Tales Illustrative of the Five Senses' (1830); 'The Invasion' (1832), a historical novel; 'Tales of my Neighborhood' (1835); 'Gisippus, or the Forgotten Friend,' a tragedy; and many spirited lyrics.

Griffin, Gilderoy Wells. An American lawyer and author; born in Louisville, Ky., in 1840. He was educated at Louisville University, and admitted to the bar in 1861. He was consul to Copenhagen in 1871; to the Samoan Islands in 1876; to Auckland, New Zealand, in 1879; and to Sydney, Australia, in 1884. He wrote: 'Studies in Literature' (1870); 'My Danish Days' (1875); 'New Zealand: Her Commerce and Resources' (1884); etc.

Griffis, William Elliot. An American author; born in Philadelphia, Pa., Sept. 17, 1843. His published works are, in part: 'New Japan Series' Reading Books (5 vols., Yokohama: 1872); 'The Mikado's Empire' (1876); 'Japanese Fairy World' (1880); 'Asiatic History'; 'The Japanese Nation, in Evolution.'

Grigoróvich, Dimitrij Vasilievich (grēg-ŏr′ō-vich). A Russian novelist and prose-writer; born in Simbirsk, March 31, 1822. He began life as a civil engineer. His first stories, 'The Village' and 'Anton the Unfortunate,' achieved wide popularity. 'A Failure in Life,' 'The Fishers,' and 'The Emigrants,' are realistic stories of village life which rank him among the first of Russian novelists. Died 1900.

Grillparzer, Franz (gril′pärts-er). An Austrian poet and dramatist of high rank; born in Vienna, Jan. 15, 1791; died there, Jan. 21, 1872. 'Blanche of Castile,' a tragedy, written at 17, and 'Spartacus,' a tragedy, showed genius; but 'The Ancestress' first called popular attention to him. 'Sappho,' a tragedy based upon classical tradition, made him eminent in scholarship

also. 'The Golden Fleece,' 'The Argonauts,' and 'Medea' constitute a trilogy. 'The Career and End of King Ottokar,' 'A True Servant of his Master,' and 'Woe to Him who Lies' call for mention; but his poem 'Waves of Ocean: Thrills of Love' is the supreme manifestation of his art. 'In thy Camp is Austria!' a poem of the times, created a sensation. Later works of note are 'The Jewess of Toledo,' 'Fraternal Strife in the House of Hapsburg,' and 'Libussa,' plays published posthumously; and a story, 'The Poor Minstrel.'

Grimm, Hermann Friedrich (grim). A German essayist, critic, and biographer, son of Wilhelm; born in Cassel, Jan. 6, 1828; died at Berlin, June 18, 1901. He studied law, but never practiced it. His most famous work is his 'Life of Michael Angelo.' Among others, 'Ten Essays Selected as an Introduction to the Study of Modern Art,' 'Fifteen Essays' (new series), and 'Life of Raphael,' are entitled to mention.

Grimm, Jacob. A German philologist, archæologist, and folk-lorist; born in Hanau, Jan. 4, 1785; died at Berlin, Sept. 20, 1863. He studied at Cassel and Marburg; and at 20 became Savigny's assistant at Paris. His abilities becoming renowned, he was sent as secretary to the Hessian ambassador at the Vienna Congress, and then to Paris to reclaim the plundered treasures of German libraries. He continued in similar employments with increasing reputation till his liberalism in 1848 forced him out of public life. Thenceforward till his death he busied himself with antiquarian and philological researches. 'The Poetry of the Meistersingers,' a 'German Grammar,' 'German Mythology,' 'Antiquities of German Jurisprudence,' 'History of the German Language,' and many similar works, cover the entire field of their subjects, and are among the chief creators of modern philology and its methods. His popular fame rests upon his collaboration with his brother Wilhelm in the 'Fables for Children' ('Grimm's Fairy Tales'), universally known.

Grimm, Wilhelm. A German philologist and folk-lorist, brother of Jacob; born in Hanau, Feb. 24, 1786; died at Berlin, Dec. 16, 1859. In their early work the brothers were practically one: but to Wilhelm's taste, less severely scientific than his brother's, belongs the chief credit for the undertaking and execution of the Fables and other popular works; and he made a special study of mediæval German poetry, publishing 'Old Danish Hero Songs,' 'The Song of Roland,' 'German Hero Songs,' and 'Mediæval German Topics.'

Grimmelshausen, Hans Jakob Christoffel von (grim′mels-hou-zen). ["Samuel Greifenson v. Hirschfeld."] A German romance-writer; born in Gelnhausen about 1625; died at Renchen, Baden, Aug. 16, 1676. In youth he was a military adventurer. According to some accounts he served the Bishop of Strasburg for a time, and became a Catholic. He became celebrated as the author of 'The Adventures of Simplicius Simplicissimus,' the life story of a vagabond adventurer of the Thirty Years' War, who settles into a peaceful old age in the Black Forest. His other romances — ' The World Inside Out,' ' Joseph in Egypt,' and ' Pluto's Council Chamber,' among them — are unimportant.

Grimod de la Reynière (grē-mō' dè lä rän-yār'). A French wit and authority on gastronomy; born in Paris, Nov. 20, 1758; died at Villiers-sur-Orge, Dec. 25, 1837. He was designed for the law, but chose letters and the pleasures of the table. The biting venom of his wit, added to a grotesque hideousness of aspect, made him renowned. His celebrity was heightened by the eccentricities of his costly and delicious banquets. ' Reflections on Pleasure,' ' The Philosophical Lorgnette,' and ' The Almanac of Gourmands,' are in the number of his literary extravagances.

Grimthorpe, Edmund Beckett Denison, Lord. An English barrister and author; born at Carlton Hall, Nottinghamshire, England, May 12, 1816. He was educated at Cambridge; appointed chancellor and vicar-general of York in 1877; and has for many years been a leader of the Parliamentary bar. He has taken much interest in architecture, and designed many churches and houses. His works include : ' Origin of the Laws of Nature ' (1879); ' A Book on Building ' (2d ed. 1880); ' Should the Revised New Testament be Authorized ? ' (1882); ' Astronomy without Mathematics ' (7th ed. 1883); ' Treatise on Clocks, Watches, and Bells ' (7th ed. 1883).

Gringoire, Pierre (graṅ-gwär'). A French poet; born in Caen, about 1475; died about 1539. He made himself a sort of court poet to Louis XII., celebrating among other things the conquest of Milan and the expedition against Naples. He was the creator of French political or topical drama, his best work in that line being ' The Game of the Prince of Fools,' in which the king is said to have collaborated; it was aimed against Pope Julius II., as was his ' Morality of the Obstinate Man.' His name figures in Victor Hugo's ' Notre Dame.'

Grinnell, George Bird. An American ornithologist, editor, and author; born in New York State in 1849. He is the editor of Forest and Stream. His works deal principally with Indian life and folk-lore. Among the best known are : ' The Story of a Prairie People '; ' The Story of the Indian '; ' Pawnee Hero Stories and Folk Tales '; ' Jack, the Young Trapper. '

Grisebach, Eduard (grē'ze-bäch). A German poet, critic, and historian of literature; born in Göttingen, Oct. 9, 1845. He was a consular agent for many years. ' The New Tannhäuser ' and ' Tannhäuser in Rome ' represent his poems. ' German Literature since 1770' and ' The Goethe Period of German Poetry ' are masterpieces. He utilizes philological studies in ' The Faithless Widow,' in tracing an old Chinese legend through its transformations in all literatures. ' Kin-Ku-Ki-Kuan ' is a similar study. His editing of Schopenhauer has been very important.

Griswold, Hattie Tyng. An American writer of prose and verse; born in Boston, Jan. 26, 1842. She wrote many tales and poems; published ' Apple Blossoms ' (1878), and ' Home Life of Great Authors ' (1886). ' Under the Daisies ' is one of her best-known poems.

Griswold, Rufus Wilmot. An American journalist and prose-writer; born in Benson, Vt., Feb. 15, 1815; died in New York, Aug. 27, 1857. He left the pulpit to enter journalism, and edited Graham's Magazine with signal ability. In 1852 he conducted the International Magazine. His works include ' Poets and Poetry of America,' which reached twenty editions; ' Poets and Poetry of England in the Nineteenth Century '; ' Prose Writers of America '; ' Female Poets of America '; etc.

Grosse, Julius (grōs'ė). A very prolific German poet, story-writer, and dramatist; born in Erfurt, April 25, 1828. He was lawyer, playwright, and journalist. His poems include ' The Maid of Capri,' ' Pesach Pardel,' and ' Against France.' Among his stories are: ' Untrue Through Sympathy'; ' An Old Love'; ' A Revolutionist'; and ' Against the Stream,' — dainty and interesting narratives. A tragedy, ' Tiberius.' Died at Forbola, May 2; 1902.

Grossi, Tommaso (grōs'sē). An Italian poet and romance-writer; born in Bellano, Jan. 24, 1791; died at Milan, Dec. 20, 1853. Satirically pungent political poems, ' The Fugitive,' a narrative in verse, made his reputation; and a play, ' Sforza, Duke of Milan ' (in collaboration), was a literary sensation. His ' Ildegonda ' is a poem on a mediæval legend; ' The Lombards in the First Crusade,' a happy essay in metre; ' Marco Visconti,' a historical romance. Of his lyrics, ' The Swallow ' has found most favor. ' Ulric and Lida ' was his last work.

Grosz, Ferdinand (grōs). An Austrian journalist; born in Vienna, April 8, 1849. He wrote while still a boy; but his first success was ' Literary Music of the Future ' (1877). Since then he has traveled extensively and written for the best papers. ' In Passing,' ' Unbound ' ' Passion-Play Letters,' ' Leaves in the Wind,' and other collections, have been very popular. His poems, notably ' Songs from the Mountain Tops,' and his plays, ' The First Letter ' and ' At Three o'Clock,' are of special merit.

Groszmann, Gustav Friedrich Wilhelm (grōs'man). A German dramatist and actor; born in Berlin, Nov. 30, 1746; died at Hanover, May 20, 1796. While in the diplomatic service, he became intimate in a literary circle which included Lessing; and successively wrote in a few days each ' The Fire of Passion,' a comedy, and ' Wilhelmine von Blondheim,' a tragedy, which were extremely successful. He turned actor, rose to high reputation, and produced much-admired comedies.

Grote, George. An English historian of the first order; born in Clay Hill, Kent, Nov. 17, 1794; died in London, June 18, 1871. He was one of the most massive scholars of the century in the classics and in logic, with a mind of rare power, breadth, and discrimination. His works on Plato and Aristotle, and various essays, are alone sufficient to give him a solid reputation; and he was an able Parliamentary speaker and reformer. But his fame rests on his epoch-making 'History of Greece' (12 vols., 1845–56), the first ever written from a democratic standpoint.

Grotius, Hugo. A famous Dutch jurist and scholar; born at Delft, April 10, 1583; died at Rostock, Aug. 29, 1645. His treatise 'On the Law of War and Peace' made him the founder of the modern science of international law. He was also the author of important historical works and Biblical commentaries. Next to Barneveld he was the Remonstrant leader in Holland, and barely escaped sharing his fate.

Groto, Luigi (grō′tō). An Italian poet, called «the Blind Man of Adria»; born there, Sept. 7, 1541; died at Venice, Dec. 13, 1585. He lost his sight when eight days old, but studied literature and philosophy with precocious ability, delivering a speech before the Queen of Poland at 18, gaining commissions from Italian States to compose addresses for public occasions, and taking the part of the blind seer Tiresias in Sophocles's 'Œdipus.' His orations and letters were collected: he left also a small volume of poems; 'The Treasure,' a comedy; and 'Delilah,' a tragedy. His style is affected, but his thoughts are original.

Grove, George, Sir. An English civil engineer, editor, and compiler; born in London, Aug 13, 1820; died there, May 28, 1900. During his early life he was a civil engineer, and secretary of the Crystal Palace Company (1852–73). Subsequently he became editor of Macmillan's Magazine, and from 1882 to 1894 was director of the Royal College of Music at Kensington. He was knighted in 1885. He was one of the principal contributors to Dr. William Smith's 'Dictionary of the Bible'; and compiled 'A Dictionary of Music and Musicians, A. D. 1450–1878' (1878–89), a work of vast and accurate information.

Grübel, Konrad (grü′bel). A German dialect poet; born in Nuremberg, June 3, 1736; died there, March 8, 1809. He was a saddler and harness-maker, and passed his youth in privation; but he possessed genuine poetic gifts, as shown in the pictures he has given of the lives and manners of his countrymen in the three volumes of 'Poems in the Nuremberg Dialect.'

Grün, Anastasius (grün), pseudonym of Anton Alexander, Count of Auersperg. An Austrian poet and statesman; born in Laibach, April 11, 1806; died at Gratz, Sept. 12, 1876. Although of aristocratic birth and breeding, his political leanings were liberal, and he became immersed in the progressive movement of his day His literary work, for the most part, grew out of and developed his public policy. His first volume, 'Leaves of Love,' did not attract much attention. 'The Last Knight' was more successful; it celebrated the chivalry of the first Maximilian's time. 'Strolls of a Viennese Poet' and a second volume of 'Poems' made him known. 'The Nibelungen in a Dress Coat' is a humorous narrative; 'Robin Hood' is a powerful poem in ballad form; 'The Kalenberg Pastor' is a picture of simple life; and 'Popular Songs of the Krains' (inhabitants of Carinthia, Austria) forms a very important collection of native folk-lore.

Grundtvig, Nikolai Frederik Severin (grönt-vig). A Danish theologian, historian, and poet; born in Udby, Island of Seeland, Sept. 8, 1783; died at Copenhagen, Sept. 3, 1872. He was the son of a clergyman, a very precocious child; educated first by his father thoroughly, then at the University of Copenhagen, later taking up a course of study in history, languages, religions, etc., with enormous industry and power of assimilation. His first writings were 'A Masked Ball in Denmark,' a protest in prose and verse against the intellectual frivolity of the time: 'An Abridgment of Norse Mythology'; and 'The Progressive Decadence of Military Prowess and Science in the North.' In 1814 he took part with distinction in the Holstein war. Later becoming a pastor, he had to resign in 1825 on account of his religious opinions, devoting his time thereafter to study. The powerful religious movement known as Grundtvigism — designed to reconstruct Christianity, institutionally and to some extent doctrinally — now began to shape itself in his mind. 'The Manual of Universal History,' a monumental work of great value, clearly reveals his theological point of view. 'The Mythology of the North, or the Language of Symbols Developed and Explained by Means of History and Poetry' (1832) made a sensation in the intellectual world. As a poet, 'Little Norse Poems,' 'Phœnix,' and others, have made his name a household word in the North. 'Roskilde Riin,' 'Danish War Song,' 'The Deliverance of Jutland,' and 'Legends of the Poets and Heroes of the North,' are among his celebrated works.

Gruppe, Otto Friedrich (gröp′pe). A German poet, philosopher, and critic; born in Dantzig, April 15, 1804; died at Berlin, Jan. 7, 1876. He graduated at Berlin, and after some experiences in journalism and public office, he became a professor at his alma mater. He first won attention with his 'Antæus,' a work on speculative philosophy, written in opposition to Hegelianism. 'The Turning-Point of Nineteenth-Century Philosophy,' 'Ariadne, the Tragic Art of the Greeks,' 'Roman Elegy,' 'The Theogony of Hesiod,' and a variety of similar works, have earned him distinction. His poems include: 'The Winds,' an effort at Aristophanean comedy; 'Queen Bertha,' 'Emperor Charles,' and 'Alboin,' three epics of great beauty; 'Poems of Fatherland,' 'The War of 1866,' and other martial poems; 'Otto von Wittelsbach,' a drama. These have fully sustained the reputation made by his earlier work. His books on the history of literature are authoritative.

Gryphius, Andreas (grē'fē-ös *or* grif'i-us). A German poet, dramatist, and scholar; born in Glogau, Silesia, Oct. 11, 1616; died there, July 16, 1664. An orphan who struggled into an education, he was finally left a comfortable legacy by a nobleman he had been tutor for: he traveled, and published his poems; but his naturally morose temper was further soured by the political conditions of his time, and his poetry is tinctured with a deep bitterness. 'Leo Armenius,' 'Catherine of Georgia,' 'The Murdered Royalty; or Charles Stuart,' are powerful but sombre tragedies. He was deemed one of the most profound scholars of his day, having an acquaintance with eleven languages. Among his performances was 'Peter Squenz,' an adaptation from a garbled transcript of Shakespeare's 'Midsummer Night's Dream.'

Guadagnoli, Antonio (gwad''än-yō'lē). An Italian poet; born in Arezzo, in 1798; died at Cortona, Feb. 21, 1858. He belonged to an aristocratic family, but his means were slender during the greater part of his life. His poems, 'The Nose,' 'Prattle,' 'My Clothes,' and 'A Woman's Tongue Put to the Test,' display a lively wit with no malicious ingredient. In Tuscany he was especially popular. His 'Collection of Light Poetry' is much quoted.

Gualandi (gwäl-än'dē). See **Guerrazzi**.

Gualtieri, Luigi (gwäl''tē-ā'rē). An Italian novelist and dramatist; born in Bologna, in 1826; died at San Remo, Dec. —, 1901. At twenty-two he settled in Milan and married the popular actress Giacinta Pezzana, whom he accompanied on her professional tours. His first novel was 'The Mysteries of Italy,' followed by 'The Anonymous,' 'The Serpent of the Viscount,' 'Recollections of Ugo Bassi,' 'God and Man,' and the 'Last Pope,' together with many others, all of which became popular. For the stage he wrote: 'The Duel'; 'The Love of an Hour'; 'Aspects of Marriage'; 'Heidelberg Students'; and others.

Guarini, Giovanni Battista (gwär-ē'nē). An Italian poet; born in Ferrara, Dec. 10, 1538; died at Venice, Oct. 7, 1612. He was a very precocious child, and extremely early became professor of literature and philosophy at the University of Ferrara. He was in diplomatic posts for various Italian princes, but lost them all from a quarrelsome temper, which kept him in hot water all his life. As a poet, his pastoral 'The Faithful Shepherd' (Il Pastor Fido), in the style of Tasso's 'Aminta,' is the jewel in his crown. The theme is on the yearly sacrifice of a maiden to Diana by the Arcadians, and offers opportunities for passages of offensive sensuality as well as of exquisite beauty. 'Idropica,' a five-act comedy; 'Poems,' a small collection of verse; and some miscellaneous writings, complete his productions.

Gubernatis, Angelo de (gö-bār-nä'tēs). An Italian critic, poet, philologist, and historian; born in Turin, April 7, 1840. His profound scholarship and versatility have won him distinction in widely separated departments of literature. 'The First Twenty Hymns of the Rig-Veda' (text and translation, 1865); 'Death of Cato' (1863), a drama in metre; 'King Nala,' an Indo-Brahmin play; 'Gabriel,' a novel; 'Zoölogical Mythology' (1872); and many other works, evince a complete mastery of style, and exhibit his brilliant attainments. Literature is further indebted to him for his invaluable work of reference entitled 'Writers of the Day.'

Guell y Renté, José (gwely' ē rän-tā'). A Spanish poet, historian, statesman, and miscellaneous writer; born in Havana, Cuba, Sept. 14, 1818; died at Madrid, Dec. 20, 1884. He studied law in Havana and Barcelona. A romantic attachment for Doña Josepha de Bourbon, sister of the King, ended in his marriage to her, in spite of tremendous court opposition, in 1848. He sided with the popular party in the revolution of 1854, and was subsequently elected to the Cortes. 'Tears of the Heart' and 'Heart-Chagrin' brought him into prominence as a poet. 'Meditations, Christian, Philosophical, and Political, for the Use of the People,' 'Thoughts, Literary and Political,' and many essays and political pamphlets, comprise his prose writings.

Güell y Renté, Juan. A Cuban poet; born in Havana, in 1815; died in Madrid, Spain, 1875. His first volume was published in 1843. 'Sentiments of the Soul,' poems (1844); 'Last Poems' (1859); and 'Summer Nights' (1861).

Guérin, Eugénie and Maurice de (ga-rañ'). French diarists and prose-writers; sister and brother. Eugénie was born in Languedoc, Jan. 11 (?), 1805; died there (?), May 31, 1848. Maurice was born Languedoc, Aug. 5, 1810; died there, July 19, 1839. The rare and somewhat hectic genius of the brother, enforcing the sister's active participation, led to their joint literary career. The 'Journals' and 'Letters' comprise the result of this partnership.

Guernsey, Alfred Hudson. An American editor; born at Brandon, Vt., 1818; died in New York city, Jan. 16, 1902. He was for several years editor of Harper's Magazine and associate editor of the 'American Cyclopædia' (1872-76). Together with Henry M. Alden he was author of 'Harper's Pictorial History of the Great Rebellion,' writing the Eastern campaigns (2 vols., 1862-65); and 'The Spanish Armada' (1882).

Guernsey, Lucy Ellen. An American juvenile-story writer; born at Rochester, N. Y., Aug. 12, 1826; died, Nov. 3, 1899. She wrote: 'Old Stanfield House'; 'Through Unknown Ways'; 'Winifred'; etc.

Guéroult, Constant (gā-rö'). A French writer of sensational fiction; born in Elbeuf,

Feb. 11, 1814; died at Paris, Nov. 29, 1882. At first engaged in trade, he wrote novels in his leisure, and soon made his fortune. 'The Stranglers of Paris,' written partly in collaboration, is his representative effort; but 'The Beggar of Toledo,' 'Captain Zamore,' 'The Depths of Paris,' and 'The Marcellange Affair' are powerful tales of the sensational order, and gave rise to a school of imitators.

Guerrazzi, Francesco Domenico (gwer-rät'sē). An Italian statesman, romance-writer, and satirist; born in Livorno (Leghorn), Aug. 12, 1804; died there, Sept. 23, 1873. After a turbulent political career, a dictatorship of some months in 1848, and then a cell and exile, he devoted himself mainly to literature. He had already written at 23 'The Battle of Benevento,' a historical novel and his best work in fiction. Other novels are: 'The Siege of Florence,' a romance, published under the pseudonym « Anselmo Gualandi»; 'Beatrice Cenci,' a highly popular story; 'Veronica Cybò, Duchess of San Giuliano' and 'The Hiding-Place in the Wall,' both fine efforts of the imagination. A drama, 'The Whites and the Blacks'; a biographical study, 'The Life of Andrea Doria'; and a volume of orations, all show power. He founded L'Asino (The Ass), a satirical sheet.

Guerrero, Teodoro (gā-ray'rō). A Cuban poet and dramatist; born in Havana in 1825. He was educated in Spain, returning to Cuba in 1845, in which year his first volume of poems was published. His drama 'La Escala del Poder,' and his comedy 'La Cabeza y el Corazón,' were successful. 'Lecciones de Mundo' reached many editions.

Guevara, Antonio de (gā-vä'rä). A Spanish historical and moral essayist; born in Viscaya, about 1490; died in 1545. After a short career at court ne became a Franciscan. Charles V. made him his companion in some of his voyages, and gave him a rich bishopric. His humility was proverbial. His writings were an influence in the development of Spanish letters, being distinguished by a great purity of diction and a courtly and graceful style. He applies the teachings of history to daily conduct. His 'Marcus Aurelius,' for example, is a sort of 'Cyropædia,' and has been translated into many languages. 'The Prince's Time-Piece' and 'The First Ten Cæsars' are manuals for the ethical guidance of youthful royalty.

Guevara y Dueñas, Luis Velez de (gā-vä'-rä ē dwän'yäz). A Spanish dramatist and romancer; born in Ecija, Andalusia, January 1570; died at Madrid, Nov. 10, 1646. As a young lawyer he won the favor of King Philip, who gave him his first literary encouragement. He wrote four hundred plays, all very long and full of wit. 'Empire after Death' and 'The King is More Important than One's Own Flesh and Blood' are the best known. He also wrote a novel or romance, 'The Lame Devil,' from which Le Sage freely borrowed in writing upon the same theme.

Guicciardini, Francesco (gwē-chär-dē'nē). A distinguished Italian historian; born at Florence, March 6, 1483; died May 23, 1540. He was a prominent figure in the Italian public life of his time. His principal work, 'History of Italy,' recounts without passion or partisanship the political events of 1492-1534; it was published in 1561-64, and republished ten times in the fifty years succeeding. Long after his death, appeared as 'Unpublished Works' (1857-67, 10 vols.) his 'Political Reminiscences,' a series of aphorisms on politics; 'The Government of Florence,' an essay on the forms of government suited for an Italian State; and a 'History of Florence.'

Guidi, Carlo Alessandro (gwē'dē). An Italian poet; born in Pavia, June 14, 1650; died at Frascati, June 12, 1712. He attracted notice at the Roman court by his extreme hideousness of aspect and precocious charm of mind and character. The Queen of Sweden lodged him in her villa on the Rialto, and Pope Clement XI. was his patron. His fame depends principally upon his graceful lyrics. 'Poems,' 'Daphne,' 'Six Homilies of Pope Clement XI. Done into Verse,' and 'Endymion,' are his most admired compositions. He was killed by the shock consequent upon discovering a typographical error in one of his works.

Guidiccioni, Giovanni (gwē-dē-chē-ō'nē). An Italian poet and ecclesiastic; born in Lucca, Feb. 25, 1500; died at Macerata in 1541. He lived at the court of the Cardinal Farnese, afterwards Pope Paul III., who employed him in difficult diplomatic missions and made him a bishop. He wrote a small volume of 'Poems,' distinguished by a correct taste and elegant diction.

Guido y Spano, Carlos (gwē-dō ē spä'nō). An Argentine poet; born in Salta, March 8, 1832. He was graduated at the University of San Carlos, Buenos Ayres; practiced law; was elected deputy to the national congress, and became its president. He gained reputation as a poet, and is held in highest esteem by his countrymen. His poems are gathered in the volume entitled 'Hojas al Viento,' published in 1871.

Guild, Curtis. An American journalist and author; born in Massachusetts in 1827. He was the editor of the Boston Commercial Bulletin, which he founded in 1859, and was the author of several popular books of travel. Among his works are: 'Over the Ocean' (1871); 'Abroad Again' (1877); 'Britons and Muscovites' (1888); 'A Chat about Celebrities.'

Guild, Reuben Aldridge. An American prose-writer; born in West Dedham, Mass., May 4, 1822; died at Providence, May 14, 1899. His published works include: 'History of Brown University with Illustrative Documents' (1867); 'Chaplain Smith and the Baptists' (1885). He edited 'Rhode Island in the Continental Congress, 1765-1790,' by Wm. R. Staples, (1870); 'Letter of John Cotton, and Roger Williams' Reply'

(1866); and 'Queries of Highest Consideration,' by Roger Williams (1867).

Guillaume de Lorris (gē-yōm' dē lō-rēs'). A French poet; born at Lorris, about 1211; died between 1240 and 1260. He appears to have been about 25 when he wrote the first part of the famous 'Roman de la Rose.' This poem has been the subject of extravagant eulogy until well within the present century. It has to do with a knight who arrives at the Palace of Pleasure, and has varied experiences with Venus and her alluring but erratic companions. The rose in the story has no particular meaning, though the hero's task is to pluck it. The poem is in two parts, the last being from the pen of Jean de Meung.

Guillaume de Machaut (gē-yōm' dē mä-chō'). A French poet and musician; born in Machaut, Seine-et-Marne, between 1282 and 1284; died at Rheims about 1377. He first appeared in a menial office at the court of Jeanne of Navarre, wife of Philip the Fair; becoming the latter's valet in time, and subsequently clerk to the King of Bohemia. A lady of prominence at the French court — the wife of the Comte de Foix according to some, Péronne d'Armentières according to others — fell in love with him, and their amours are set forth in his 'Voir Dit' or 'Book of Said and Seen.' 'The Taking of Alexandria' narrates the adventures of King Peter I. of Cyprus. His musical compositions were much esteemed.

Guillemard, Francis Henry Hill (gil'-mard"). An English traveler and scientist of French descent; born in Eltham, Kent, in 1852. He is a graduate of Cambridge, and for some time taught there. He has traveled extensively and explored many unfrequented lands. Besides contributions to scientific, literary, and medical reviews, he has published 'The Cruise of the Marchesa to Kamchatka and New Guinea' (1886; 2d ed. 1887), interesting alike to naturalist, traveler, and general reader.

Guiney, Louise Imogen. An American poet and essayist; born in Boston, Jan. 7, 1861. Among her volumes of verse may be mentioned: 'Verse'; 'Songs at the Start'; 'A Roadside Harp'; etc. She has also published: 'Goose-Quill Papers'; 'Brownies and Bogles'; 'Monsieur Henri'; 'A Little English Gallery'; 'Lovers' Saint Ruths'; 'Patrins'; etc. She has edited an edition of Mangan's poems.

Guinicelli, Guido (gwē-nē-chel'ē). An Italian poet; born in Bologna about 1240; died in exile in 1276. He held a judgeship in Bologna until expelled for political reasons. His importance is due to his great influence upon Dante, who pronounced him a model of grace and style, and apostrophized him in the 'Inferno.' The poems, so far as they have survived, scarcely justify Dante's praise. They comprise seven canzone or songs in the style of the ode, and five sonnets, all dealing with love, and characterized more by feeling and beauty of sentiment than by power.

Guinness, Mrs. Fanny E. An English evangelist and religious writer, wife of Henry G.; born (Fitzgerald) in Dublin, Ireland, April 1831. She was one of the earliest woman preachers of the gospel, and was secretary of the first Christian mission on the Congo. Besides works written in collaboration with her husband, she has published: 'She Spake of Him: Being Recollections of Mrs. H. Denning' (1872); 'Sitwana's Story' (1882); 'The Wide World and Our Work' (1886); 'New World of Central Africa.'

Guinness, Henry Grattan. An Irish evangelist and religious writer; born near Dublin, August 1835. His chief work, 'The Approaching End of the Age,' was issued in 1878, and has passed through ten editions. He has also written: 'Preaching for the Million' (1859); and with his wife, 'Light for the Last Days' (1886); 'Romanism and the Reformation' (1887); 'The Divine Programme of the World's History' (1888).

Guiraud, Alexandre, Baron (gē-rō'). A French poet and dramatist; born in Limoux, Dec. 25, 1788; died at Paris, Feb. 24, 1847. He gave up the management of large inherited business interests and took up literary pursuits in Paris, writing poems, plays, and miscellaneous prose. 'The Maccabees,' a tragedy, was his first unqualified success. His ode addressed to the Greeks had attracted some notice; and he now brought out a volume of 'Songs of a Savoyard,' which attained great popularity, especially 'The Little Savoyard.' He wrote several other dramas, and a romance or two.

Guittone d'Arezzo (gwē-tō'nä där-rets'ō). An Italian poet; born in Santa Firmina, near Arezzo, about 1230; died at Florence, 1294. He received a scholarly training and knew several languages. When young he was a military adventurer. In middle life he founded an order of monks. His poetry is remarkable for elegance of form and matter; to him the present fixed form of the sonnet is largely due. He left much verse, of which thirty-five sonnets and four canzone have been preserved.

Guizot, François Pierre Guillaume (gē-zō' or güē-zō'). A great French historian and statesman; born at Nîmes, Oct. 4, 1787; died at Val Richer, near Lisieux, Sept. 12, 1874. His most important works are: 'The History of Civilization in Europe'; 'The History of Civilization in France'; 'History of the English Revolution'; 'Shakespeare and his Time'; and his own 'Memoirs.' He also wrote: 'Memoirs relating to the History of France to the Thirteenth Century'; 'Corneille and his Time' (1852); 'Meditations on the Present State of the Christian Religion' (1865); 'History of France for my Grandchildren' (1870–75).

Guldberg, Frederick Höegh. See Höegh-Guldberg.

Gummere, Francis Barton (gum'ery). An American teacher and author; born at Burlington, N. J., March 6, 1855. He was instructor in Harvard College from 1881 to 1882; and in 1887 became professor of English at Haverford College, Pa. Besides miscellaneous papers in Germanic philology and English literature, he has written: 'The Anglo-Saxon Metaphor' (1881); 'Handbook of Poetics' (1885); 'Germanic Origins' (1862); 'The Popular Ballad' (1907).

Gumpert, Thekla von (göm'pärt). A German juvenile writer; born in Kalisch, June 28, 1810. She was the daughter of a prominent physician. When comparatively young she undertook the training of the Princess Czartoriski's children, developing then her talent as a story-teller. 'The Little Father and his Grandchild,' 'Aunt's Trip to the Baths,' and 'My First White Hair,' are among her greatest successes. In 1856 she married Franz von Schober, under whose name she is also known. Her later productions, especially 'Heart-leaf Pastime,' and 'Treasury of Books for Germany's Daughters,' have maintained her popularity. She died April 2, 1897.

Günderode, Karoline von (gün'de-rō-dè). A German poet; born in Karlsruhe, Feb. 11, 1780; died at Winkel on the Rhine, July 26, 1806. An unfortunate love affair with the scholar Creuzer confirmed her natural tendency to melancholy and mysticism, by which her poetry is much colored, and she finally committed suicide. She sometimes used the pseudonym "Tian." 'Poems and Fancies' and 'Poetic Fragments' are her best efforts.

Gundulic, Ivan (gön'dö-litch). ['Ciovanni Gondola.'] A Dalmatian poet; born in Ragusa, Jan. 8, 1588; died there, Dec. 8, 1638. His writings show extensive acquaintance with the philosophy, jurisprudence, and ethics of his time, but little is known of this first dramatic poet among the Slavs. His greatest poem is 'Osman,' an epic in twenty books, presenting a stirring panorama of the career of one of the Turkish Sultans, with the Polish-Turkish war of 1621 for a background. His dramas are pleasing and finished productions. 'Proserpina,' 'Cleopatra,' 'Arijadna,' and 'Dubravka' show a rich and fertile imagination. Among his elegies, 'The Tears of a Lost Son' is full of lofty and tender expression.

Gunsaulus, Frank Wakeley. An American clergyman, novelist, and poet; born at Chesterville, O., Jan. 1, 1856. He graduated at the Ohio Wesleyan University in 1875. Since 1887 he has been the pastor of a Congregational church in Chicago, and has been for some years director of the Armour Institute. Among his works are: 'The Transfiguration of Christ' (1886); 'Monk and Knight: An Historical Study in Fiction' (1890); 'Phidias and Other Poems' (1892); 'Songs of Night and Day.'

Gunter, Archibald Clavering. An American civil engineer, stock-broker, playwright, publisher, and novelist; born in Liverpool, England, Oct. 25, 1847. When five years old he was taken to California by his parents. He received his education mostly in California,

taking the degree of Ph. B. at University College, San Francisco. He was a mining and civil engineer in the West from 1867 until 1874, when he became a stock-broker. In 1877 he removed to New York, where he devoted himself to writing plays and novels. The best-known of the former are: 'Courage'; 'Prince Karl'; 'The Deacon's Daughter.' His most popular novels are: 'Mr. Barnes of New York' (1887), translated into several foreign languages, and 'Mr. Potter of Texas' (1888), both successfully dramatized; 'That Frenchman' (1889); 'Miss Nobody of Nowhere' (1890); 'Baron Montez of Panama and Paris' (1893); 'A Florida Enchantment.' He died 1907.

Günther, Albert Karl Ludwig Gotthelf (gün'ter). A German librarian and ichthyologist; born at Esslingen, Würtemberg, Oct. 3, 1830. He is co-editor of the 'Annals and Magazine of Natural History,' and author of 'The Reptiles of British India' (1864); 'The Fishes of the South Seas' (1873-78); 'The Gigantic Land Tortoises, Living and Extinct' (1877); 'An Introduction to the Study of Fishes' (1880); 'Reptiles and Batrachians of Central America.'

Günther, Johann Christian. A German poet; born in Striegau, Lower Silesia, April 8, 1695; died at Jena, March 15, 1723. He is celebrated for his 'Peace of Passarowitz' and numerous lyrics.

Gurowski, Adam de, Count (grof'skē). A Polish scholar and author; born at Kalisz, Sept. 10, 1805; died at Washington, D. C., May 4, 1866. In early life he was a leading Polish patriot, and an instigator of the revolution of 1830. Later he became an advocate of Panslavism, and was employed in Russia. In 1841 he left the latter country and studied in Berlin, and in Bern, Switzerland. In 1849 he came to the United States, and from 1861 to 1863 was a translator in the State Department at Washington. Among his works, several of which were written in French and German, are: 'Civilization and Russia' (1840); 'Panslavism' (1848); 'Russia as It Is' (1854); 'The Turkish Question' (1854); 'My Diary: Notes on the Civil War' (1862 to 1866).

Guseck, Bernd von (gös'ek), pseudonym of Gustave von Berneck, a German novelist and writer on military topics; born in Kirchhain, Niederlausitz, Oct. 28, 1803; died at Berlin, July 8, 1871. His novels have for the most part a historical background, and are meritorious without being great. 'The Hand of the Stranger,' 'The First Robbery in Germany,' and 'Katharina von Schwarzburg,' are noteworthy in a somewhat extended list. He wrote a play or two, translated Dante's 'Divine Comedy,' and completed a history of the art of war.

Gustafson, Zadel Barnes Buddington. An American poet and prose-writer; born in Middletown, Conn., about 1841. Her poem 'Little Martin Craghan' was very popular. Among her well-known works are: 'Can the Old

Love?' (1871); 'Meg, a Pastoral'; and other poems, 1879; 'Zophiel, or the Bride of Seven.'

Gustav vom See (gös'täf vōm sā), pseudonym of Gustav von Struensee. A German novelist; born in Greifenberg, Pomerania, Dec. 13, 1803; died at Breslau, Sept. 29, 1875. He gave up law to write the series of romances and novels — notably 'Rancé,' 'The Siege of Rheinfels,' and 'The Egoists' — which have given him a name.

Guthrie, James Cargill. A Scotch poet; born in Forfarshire, Aug. 27, 1814; a prominent clergyman, but for years a librarian at Dundee. He has written some exceedingly happy studies in verse, — 'Village Scenes' (1851), 'Wedded Love' (1865), and 'Woodland Echoes' (1878); besides a volume on 'Old Scottish Customs' (1885), a pleasing work in prose.

Guthrie, Thomas A. See **Anstey.**

Gutierrez, Antonio Garcia (gö-tē-är'eth). A Spanish dramatist; born in Chiclana, Cadiz, in 1812; died at Madrid, Aug. 26, 1884. He gave up medicine for the profession of letters; living at first in great destitution, until the play 'El Trovador' made him famous and immensely popular. He visited the United States in 1844. Later he became a theatrical manager in Madrid, writing 'The Campaign of Huesca,' 'The Page,' and other noble tragedies.

Guttinguer, Ulric (gü-tang-wā'). A French poet, journalist, and man of letters; born in Rouen in 1785; died at Paris, Sept. 21, 1866. He was an extreme partisan of the romantic school. He won fame with 'Nadir,' a collection of criticisms, and essays on literary and sentimental subjects. His masterpiece, however, is the volume of 'Poetic Miscellany,' originally contributed to the Muse Française. He wrote several novels, a 'Dithyramb on Lord Byron's Death,' impressions of travel, and much fugitive verse.

Gutzkow, Karl Ferdinand (göts'kō). A German poet, journalist, dramatist, and critic; born in Berlin, March 17, 1811; died at Sachsenhausen, near Frankfort on the Main, Dec. 16, 1878. He was an early and thorough student of history and literature. His essay 'On the Fate-Decreeing Deities' (De Diis Fatalibus) won him a prize and reputation; and his next performance, 'The Forum of Literature and the Press,' obtained for him a place as assistant to Wolfgang Menzel, then the greatest editor in Stuttgart. 'The Letters of a Fool of a Man to a Fool of a Woman,' and a fanciful tale, 'Maha Guru, the Story of a God,' were very popular. He incurred the censure of the authorities, and brought about a rupture with Menzel, by injudicious utterances in his journal;

and was thrown into prison, where he wrote his 'Philosophy of History.' He had already brought out his 'Wally, the Skeptic,' a novel which added as much to his troubles as to his fame. His plays are considered his best work: notably 'Queue and Sword,' a comedy; 'Uriel Acosta,' a tragedy; 'The King's Lieutenant,' a drama in which the young Goethe is portrayed; and five or six others. Of his novels, 'Die Ritter vom Geiste' (The Knights of the Mind) and 'The Magician of Rome' have attained a wide popular circulation and influence.

Guyot, Arnold Henry (ge-ō'). A Swiss geographer and author; born near Neuchâtel, Switzerland, Sept. 28, 1807; died at Princeton, N. J., Feb. 8, 1884. He studied at several European universities, and graduated as Ph. D. from Berlin in 1835. After four years of study in Paris he became the colleague of Agassiz at the Academy of Neuchâtel, as professor of physical geography there. He removed to the United States in 1848, and from 1854 till his death was professor of physical geography at Princeton, N. J. Among his numerous works are: 'Earth and Man' (1849); 'Directions for Meteorological Observations' (1850); a series of school geographies (1866-75); 'A Memoir of Louis Agassiz' (1883); 'Biblical Cosmogony' (1884).

Gyllembourg - Ehrensvärd, Thomasine Christine, Countess (gul'em-börg" ā'rens-vėrd"). A Danish writer of fiction; born (Buntzen) in Copenhagen, Nov. 19, 1773; died there (?), July 2, 1856. Her first marriage at 16 being annulled at 25 by her husband's exile for liberalism, she married a Swedish nobleman, who, implicated in Gustavus III.'s assassination, had taken refuge in Denmark. At 53 she wrote her first novel, the 'Polonius Family,' as a contribution to her son's paper; and its success induced the production of 'Dream and Reality,' 'Two Ages,' and many others that made her famous. She signed herself "The Author of Every-Day History," and concealed her identity until death.

Gyp. See **Martel de Janville.**

Gyulai, Pál (jö'lī). A Hungarian poet and critic; born at Klausenburg in 1826. He began as a journalist. Later he was made professor of Hungarian literature at the University of Buda-Pesth. His works include 'The Life of Vörösmarty,' 'Memorial Addresses,' and many literary studies and criticisms. His collected poems appeared in 1867, in a volume entitled 'Sketches and Pictures.' For many years past he has been at work upon a satirical poem scathing the present age and its follies, called 'Romhányi' and modeled upon Byron. He edits the Buda-Pesth Szemle, a monthly magazine.

16

H

Haar, Bernard ter (här). A Dutch poet; born in Amsterdam, June 13, 1806; died at Velp, near Arnheim, Nov. 19, 1880. For a time he held the professorship of church history at the Utrecht University. His work, chiefly on the subject of Christianity and its development, is characterized by elegance of diction and wealth of imagery. His 'Herbert and Clara,' first published in 1844, is now one of the most popular pieces of verse with the people of the Netherlands. His other works include 'Eliza's Flight,' and a collected edition of the various poems.

Habberton, John. An American journalist and novelist; born at Brooklyn, N. Y., Feb. 24, 1842. After service in the Civil War, he became literary editor of the Christian Union (1874), and editorial writer on the New York Herald (1877). His best known novel is 'Helen's Babies' (1876), of which over 150,000 copies were sold. Among the others are: 'The Barton Experiment' (1876); 'The Worst Boy in Town' (1880); 'Mrs. Mayburn's Twins' (1882); 'Who was Paul Grayson?' 'Brueton's Bayou'; 'Grown-Up-Babies'; 'Deacon Crankett.'

Haberstich, Samuel. See **Bitter.**

Habicht, Ludwig (häb'icht). A German novelist; born in Sprottau, July 23, 1830. His first success was the novel 'The Town Clerk of Liegnitz,' which still remains his best-known work; but among his popular fictions, 'Will and World,' 'In the Sunshine,' and 'Before the Storm,' are worthy of special mention.

Hackett, Horatio Balch. A distinguished American Baptist divine; born at Salisbury, Mass., Dec. 27, 1808; died at Rochester, N. Y., Nov. 2, 1875. He was one of the committee of New Testament revision, and with Ezra Abbot edited the American edition of Smith's 'Bible Dictionary' (1868-70). His chief work was a 'Commentary on Acts' (1851); besides which he wrote 'Memorials of Christian Men in the War' (1864); 'Tour in the Holy Land' (new ed. 1882); etc.

Hackett, James Henry. A famous American actor; born at New York, March 15, 1800; died at Jamaica, N. Y., Dec. 28, 1871. He was particularly successful in impersonating Yankees and Westerners, but was best known by his Falstaff, which he played first about 1832. He wrote 'Notes and Comments on Shakespeare' (1863).

Hackländer, Friedrich Wilhelm von (häk'len-der). A German romance-writer and humorist; born 1816; died 1877. He was in both military and mercantile life for a time, and based some of his most popular works on his personal experiences. Among his writings are: 'Scenes of Military Life'; 'The Soldier's Life in Peace'; 'Traffic and Trade' (Handel und Wandel); 'Anonymous Stories'; 'Pilgrimage to Mecca'; 'Pictures of Life': 'Forbidden Fruit.' His position in German literature is one of great distinction.

Hadlaub, Johann (häd'loub). A German writer of pleasing minne or love songs; flourished about 1400; lived mostly in or near Zürich. His poetry is of special historical value as affording our sole insight into some customs of private life and the way they were then viewed. Harvests and autumn scenes also afford him themes for attractive lines.

Hadley, Arthur Twining. An American political economist, president of Yale University since 1899; born at New Haven, Conn., April 23, 1856. He has published: 'Railroad Transportation' (1885); 'Private Property and Public Welfare'; and a manual of 'Economics.'

Haeckel, Ernst (hek'el). A German naturalist of the first rank, born at Potsdam, Feb. 16, 1834. His purely scientific works have been translated into many languages. His popular books include: 'On the Division of Labor in Nature and Human Life' (1869); 'On the Origin and Genealogy of the Human Race' (1870); 'Life in the Great Marine Animals' (1870); 'The Arabian Corals' (1873); 'The System of the Medusa' (1880); and 'A Visit to Ceylon'; 'World Riddles' (1899).

Haffner, Karl (häf'ner). An Austrian playwright; born in Königsberg, Nov. 8, 1804; died at Vienna, Feb. 29, 1876. He went on the stage at 16, and rose rapidly to eminence. He wrote a hundred or so dramatic pieces of various kinds; 'Theresa Krones' alone merits notice, the others being local and ephemeral.

Hāfiz, Khwāja Shams-ad-dīn Muhammad (Pers. pro. hâ-fiz). Persia's famous lyric poet; born at Shiraz, about 1300; died there, 1389. The most complete English edition of his works is that of H. Wilberforce Clarke: 'The Dīvān ī Hāfiz, Translated' (1891). Hāfiz seems to be most characteristic in his many 'Ghazels' or odes, whose themes are his own emotions. Sir William Jones was one of the first English translators. Other English translations include: 'Selections from Hāfiz' (1875), by H. Bicknell; 'Persian Poetry for English Readers' (privately printed, 1883), by S. Robinson; 'Ghazels from the Divan of Hāfiz' (1893), by Justin Huntley McCarthy. There is a complete German translation by V. von Rosenzweig (3 vols., 1856-64).

Hagedorn, Friedrich von (hä'ge-dorn). A German poet; born at Hamburg, April 23, 1708; died there, Oct. 28, 1754. He was successively in diplomacy, law, and trade, giving his leisure to literature. A volume of 'Poetry, Fables, and Narratives,' in 1738, after Lafontaine's style, was well received, and followed by 'Odes and Songs,' and versified tales of a moral tendency. He is noted for good taste and a pleasing style.

Haggard, Henry Rider. An English novelist; born at Bradenham, Norfolk, June 22, 1856. His long residence in South Africa afforded him much of the material for his fictions. 'King Solomon's Mines' (1885) and 'Allan Quatermain' (1887) were not particularly successful; but 'She,' an extravaganza of adventure and supernaturalism, made his name really celebrated. His later works include 'Mr. Meeson's Will,' 'Cleopatra,' 'The World's Desire'; 'Stella Fregelius'; 'The Brethren'; etc.

Hague, Arnold. An American geologist; born in Boston, Dec. 3, 1840; graduated at the Sheffield Scientific School of Yale (1863); after which he studied three years at the universities of Göttingen and Heidelberg. In 1867 he was appointed assistant geologist on the United States geological exploration of the 40th parallel, under Clarence King. In part, his published works are: 'The Volcanoes of California, Oregon, and Washington Territory' (1883); 'The Volcanic Rocks of the Great Basin' (1884); 'The Volcanic Rocks of Salvador'); 'Crystallization in the Igneous Rocks of Washoe'; 'Geology of the Yellowstone National Park.'

Hague, William. An American clergyman and prose-writer; born in Pelham, N. Y., Jan. 4, 1808; died in Boston, Aug. 1, 1887. He held pastorates in Baptist churches in Utica, N. Y., Boston, Providence, and New York; and was professor of homiletics in the Baptist Theological Seminary at Chicago in 1869. Besides his writings on religion, he published 'Ralph Waldo Emerson,' and 'Life Notes, or Fifty Years' Outlook.'

Hahn, Yelena Andreyevna (hän). A Russian novelist; born (Fadeyev) in 1814; died at St Petersburg in 1842. Of her stories, 'Utballa,' 'The World's Judgment,' and 'Theophania,' are the most important.

Hahn, Ludwig Philipp (hän). A German dramatist; born in Trippstedt, Pfalz, March 22, 1746; died at Zweibrücken, 1814. His tragedies 'Count Karl of Adelsberg' and 'Robert von Hohenecken' are his ablest efforts. He belongs to the "storm and stress" period of German literature, and displays its traits. He is sometimes confused with Johann Friedrich Hahn, an occasional poet, born about 1750, died in 1779.

Hahn-Hahn, Ida von, Countess (hän'hän). A German novelist; born at Tressow, Mecklenburg-Schwerin, June 22, 1805; died at Mainz, May 12, 1880. Domestic troubles involving a separation from her husband turned her mind to travel and literature. The scenes familiar to her were reproduced in her novels, which met with popular favor, particularly 'Ulrich' and 'Two Women.' At the height of her

career she became a convert to the Catholic faith. She now produced various books of a proselytizing nature, and in 1852 took the veil. Her death took place in a convent founded by herself.

Hake, Thomas Gordon. An English poet and physician; born in Leeds, in 1809; died in London, Jan. 11, 1895. He took his medical degree at Glasgow University in 1831, and practiced his profession in East Anglia, later becoming the physician and friend of Dante Gabriel Rossetti. His poetry is thoroughly original, but quaint, vague, and subtly philosophical. His works include: 'Poetic Lucubrations' (1828); 'Vates: A Prose Epic' (1839); 'New Symbols,' verse (1875); 'Maiden Ecstasy,' verse (1880); 'A Divine Pastoral' (1883).

Hakluyt, Richard (hak'löt). An eminent English geographer; born in Herefordshire (or London?) in 1552 or 1553; died Nov. 23, 1616. He had a passion for and keen insight into cosmographic questions; and introduced globes into English schools. He took holy orders, and held befitting positions under government. In 1598 appeared his great history of the important voyages of English seamen. The Hakluyt Society, of London, which publishes old and rare books on geography and navigation, was named in his honor.

Halderman, Samuel Stehman. An American naturalist and prose-writer; born in Locust Grove, Pa., Aug. 12, 1812; died in Chickies, Pa., Sept. 10, 1880. He was the first to hold the chair of comparative philology at the University of Pennsylvania; was a member of many scientific societies, and was editor of the Pennsylvania Farmers' Journal. Among his published works are: 'Zoölogical Contributions' (1842-43); 'Rhymes of the Poets,' published under the pen-name of "Felix Ago" (1868); 'Pennsylvania Dutch' (1872); 'Outlines of Etymology' (1877); and 'Word Building' (1881).

Hale, Edward Everett. A distinguished American divine and prose-writer; born April 3, 1822, in Boston, Massachusetts, where he resides. He has strongly impressed his individuality upon his time. He is singularly felicitous as a writer of short stories, among which the most widely read are: 'My Double and How He Undid Me'; 'The Man Without a Country'; 'The Skeleton in the Closet'; 'Ten Times One Is Ten'; 'In His Name.' One well-known collection is entitled 'The Ingham Papers.' Among his longer stories are: 'Philip Nolan's Friends'; 'Mr. Tangier's Vacations'; 'Ups and Downs'; 'Fortunes of Rachel'; 'Ralph Waldo Emerson'; 'We the People'; 'New England Ballads'; 'Prayers in the United States Senate'; Foundation of the Republic.' His influence has been marked, and his name is familiarly known and cherished throughout the United States. He died June 10, 1909, at Roxbury, Mass.

Hale, Horatio. An American ethnologist and lawyer; born in Newport, N. H., May 3, 1817; died in Clinton, Can., Dec. 29, 1896. Shortly after graduating at Harvard he was made philologist to the government exploring expedition under Capt. Wilkes, and studied the languages of the Pacific Islands, North and South America, Australia, and Africa. The results of his observations were published in 'Ethnography and Philology' (1846). From 1855 he practiced law at C'inton. His other works are: 'Indian Migrations as Evidenced by Language' (1883); 'The Iroquois Book of Rites' (1883); 'A Report on Blackfoot Tribes' (1885).

Hale, Lucretia Peabody. An American author, sister of E. E. Hale; born in Boston, Mass., Sept. 2, 1820; died there, June 12, 1900. She published, among other works, 'The Lord's Supper and its Observance' (1866); 'The Service of Sorrow' (1867); 'The Wolf at the Door' in the 'No Name Series' (1877); 'The Peterkin Papers' (1882); 'The Last of the Peterkins' (1886). She also wrote 'The New Harry and Lucy' (with E. E. Hale). Her chief fame is as the creator of the Peterkins, who have become recognized types of humorous character.

Hale, Sarah Josepha (Buell). An American editor and writer; born in Newport, N. H., Oct. 24, 1788; died in Philadelphia, April 30, 1879. From 1828 until 1837 she edited the Ladies' Magazine, which was then merged into Godey's Lady's Book, of which she became editor. Among her publications are: 'Sketches of all Distinguished Women from the Creation to the Present Day' (1853); 'The Genius of Oblivion, and Other Poems'; 'Northwood,' a novel (1827); 'Sketches of American Character'; 'Traits of American Life'; and many others.

Hale, Susan. An American artist, writer of travels, and biographer, sister of E. E. Hale; born at Boston, 1838. She has written 'Life and Letters of Thomas Gold Appleton' (1885). With her brother she wrote the 'Family Flight' series of travels for young people.

Hálek Vitězlav (häl'ek). A Czech poet; born at Dolinek, Bohemia, April 5, 1835; died at Prague, Oct. 8, 1874. His lyric poems have met with wider appreciation than his stories among his countrymen. His plays have been staged with success. His best poetry appears in a volume entitled 'Nature.'

Halévy, Ludovic (ä-lā-vē'). A French novelist and dramatist of Jewish extraction; born at Paris July 1, 1834. At first adopting an official career, the success of his librettos for Offenbach turned him towards the drama, where he won fame and fortune. With Henri Meilhac he collaborated in works unique even on the French stage. His peculiar gift is an irony exquisitely adapted to a French audience: 'La Belle Hélène' and 'The Grand Duchess of Gérolstein' are instances. In 1882 appeared 'L'Abbé Constantin,' a novel which has been enormously successful. He has since written three or four others, besides sketches; and in dramatic trifles he is most prolific. He became a member of the Academy in 1886. D. May 8, 1908.

Haliburton, Thomas Chandler. ["Sam Slick."] A Canadian author; born at Windsor, Nova Scotia, in 1796; died at Isleworth, near London, Aug. 27, 1865. Originally a lawyer, he became a judge in Nova Scotia. In addition to his famous 'Sam Slick' papers (1835) he produced serious historical and sociological books, dealing principally with conditions in Nova Scotia. He removed to England after resigning his colonial judgeship, and was a Member of Parliament in 1859.

Hall, Ann Maria Fielding, Mrs. An Irish writer of fiction, wife of Samuel C.; born at Dublin, Jan. 6, 1800; died Jan. 30, 1881. At one time her novels and short stories of Irish life enjoyed great popularity. Besides the works written in collaboration with her husband (for which see his name) she published: 'Sketches of Irish Character' (1829); 'The Buccaneer' (1832); 'Lights and Shadows of Irish Life' (1838); 'Tales of the Irish Peasantry' (1840). Of her dramas the most successful was 'The French Refugee,' produced in 1837.

Hall, Basil. A British naval officer and traveler; born at Edinburgh, Dec. 31, 1788; died at Portsmouth, England, Sept. 11, 1844. He accompanied Lord Amherst's embassy to China (1815-17), assisting in important explorations of the eastern seas; and visited the United States in 1827. He wrote: 'Voyage of Discovery to the West Coast of Corea, etc.' (1818); 'Travels in North America' (1829); 'Fragments of Voyages and Travels' (1831-33), his best work; and others.

Hall, Christopher Newman. An English clergyman and religious writer; born at Maidstone, May 22, 1816; died in London, Feb. 18, 1902. He was minister of Christ Church in Hull. He was a staunch friend of the Northern cause during the Civil War, and afterwards made two tours in the United States to allay the feeling against Great Britain. Of his religious writings a devotional treatise, 'Come to Jesus,' is the best known, having had a circulation of 3,000,000 in twenty languages. He also wrote: 'Antidote to Fear'; 'Homeward Bound'; 'Land of the Forum and Vatican' (1854); 'Pilgrim Songs in Cloud and Sunshine' (1871); 'Gethsemane.'

Hall, Charles Winslow. An American lawyer, and writer of romance and adventure; born 1843. He has written: 'Arctic Rovings' (1861); 'Twice Taken' (1867); 'A Drift in the Icefields' (1877); 'Drifting Round the World' (1881); 'Regiments and Armories of Massachusetts.'

Hall, Fitzedward. An American philologist; born in Troy, N. Y., March 21, 1825, died at Marlesford, England, Feb. 1, 1901. He graduated from Harvard in 1846. He lived long in India, and made a thorough study of its tongues, producing many translations in prose and verse. He had the D. C. L. from Oxford in 1860. Settling in London in 1862, he accepted the chair of Sanskrit and Indian jurisprudence in King's College. He was the first American to edit a

Sanskrit text. Professor Hall discovered the supposed lost works: 'Bhârata's Nâtyasâstra,' 'Harshaacharita,' and a complete copy of the valuable 'Brihaddevatâ.' His contributions to our knowledge of Hindu and allied literatures are of inestimable value, and his text-books in this field are valuable and authoritative. He is one of the chief collaborators in Dr. Murray's great 'Etymological Dictionary.'

Hall, Gertrude. An American poet and writer of short stories; born 1863. Her home is in Boston. She has written: 'Far from To-day,' a collection of short stories; 'Allegretto,' a book of verse; 'Foam of the Sea, and Other Tales'; 'The Wagnerian Romances.'

Hall, Granville Stanley. An American educator and psychologist; born at Ashfield, Mass., May 6, 1845. From 1872 to 1876 he was professor of psychology in Antioch College, Ohio, and in 1882 became a professor of that subject in Johns Hopkins University at Baltimore. On the establishment of Clark University at Worcester, Mass., he was made its president. He is the editor of the American Journal of Psychology and the Pedagogical Seminary, and the author of 'Aspects of German Culture' (1881); 'Hints toward a Bibliography of Education' (1886), with J. M. Mansfield; 'How to Teach Reading'; 'Adolescence.'

Hall, John. An American clergyman and religious writer born in County Armagh, Ireland, July 31, 1829; died at Bangor, Ireland, Sept. 17, 1898. He became pastor of a Presbyterian church in Armagh in 1852, and in 1858 of St. Mary's Abbey, Dublin. In 1867 he was called to the Fifth Avenue Church, New York city. His works include: 'Family Prayers for Four Weeks' (1868); 'Papers for Home Reading' (1871); 'Questions of the Day' (1873); 'Foundation Stones for Young Builders' (1879).

Hall, Samuel Carter. An English editor and miscellaneous writer; born at Topsham, Devonshire, England, in 1801; died March 16, 1889. For over forty years he was the editor of the Art Journal, which he founded in 1839. In collaboration with his wife (see Ann Maria) he published the well-known work, 'Ireland, its Scenery and Character' (1841-43); 'Book of Royalty' (1838); 'A Woman's Story' (1857); 'The Book of the Thames' (1859); 'A Companion to Killarney' (1878); and others. His separate works were: 'A Book of Memories'; 'Book of British Ballads'; 'Baronial Halls.'

Hallam, Henry. An English historian; born at Windsor, July 9, 1777; died at Pickhurst, Kent, Jan. 21, 1859. He was of astonishing precocity both in reading and in composition; graduated from Oxford at 22, and at once settled down to the bar; but marrying one fortune and inheriting another, retired from legal practice and devoted himself to history. In 1818 the appearance of 'A View of the State of Europe during the Middle Ages' gave him an instant and enduring fame such as no other mere compilation has ever

won for a writer; a result due to the sagacity, judgment, and impartiality it displays. Nine years later came the 'Constitutional History of England,' continuing the last chapter of his 'Middle Ages'; and in 1837-39 the 'Introduction to the Literature of Europe during the Fifteenth, Sixteenth, and Seventeenth Centuries.'

Halleck, Fitz-Greene. An American poet; born in Guilford, Conn., July 8, 1790; died there, Nov. 19, 1867. He was one of the original trustees of the Astor Library, and held other posts of responsibility in connection with it. His best known poems include: 'Marco Bozzaris' (1827), and 'Fanny.' He was joint author with Joseph Rodman Drake of the 'Croaker' papers, which appeared in a New York newspaper in 1819.

Haller, Albrecht von (häl'ler). A Swiss German botanist, physiologist, and poet; was born at Bern, Oct. 16, 1708; and died there, Dec. 12, 1777. His scientific writings form a considerable part of the literature of his several specialties; but the most charming of these is his work as a poet. His celebrated lines on 'The Alps' have been quoted as an example of great strength of imagery. His poem 'On the Origin of Evil' shows no falling off in power. In his later years he wrote some political novels, among them 'Alfred, King of the Anglo-Saxons' (1773).

Hallevi. Jehudah (hä'lä-vē). A Spanish-Jewish poet, physician, astronomer, and mathematician, under the Arabic caliphate; born in Toledo, in 1080 (?); died at Jerusalem, about 1150.

Halliday, Samuel Byram. An American Congregational minister; born in New Jersey, 1812; died there ———, 1897. He was for many years assistant of Henry Ward Beecher at Plymouth Church. He has written 'The Little Street Sweeper'; 'The Lost and Found' (1859); 'Winning Souls' (1873); 'The Church in America and its Baptisms of Fire'; etc.

Halliwell-Phillipps, James Orchard. An eminent English Shakespearian and antiquarian; born in London, June 21, 1820; died near Brighton, Jan. 3, 1889. He devoted his life and large wealth to research among old records for traces of Shakespeare, publishing private editions of Shakespeariana, buying singly or with others Shakespeare buildings at Stratford, etc.; and to editing old English works. A large part of the verified knowledge of Shakespeare's personality we possess is due to him.

Hallock, Charles. An American journalist; born in New York, 1834. He was founder and proprietor (1873-80) of Forest and Stream. He has written 'The Fishing Tourist' (1873), a guide for anglers; 'Camp Life in Florida' (1875); 'Our New Alaska' 1886); 'Hallock Ancestry.'

Hallock, William Allen. An American clergyman, noted as the lifelong secretary of the American Tract Society; born in Plainfield, Mass., June 2, 1794; died in New York, Oct. 2, 1880. He published 'Life of Harlan Page'; 'Life of Moses Hallock'; 'Life of Justin Edwards'; and many tracts.

Hallowell, Richard Price. An American writer and merchant; born in Philadelphia, Dec. 16, 1835. He was a follower of Phillips and Garrison in the abolition movement, and wrote much for the Index. Among his works are 'The Quaker Invasion of Massachusetts' (1883), and 'The Pioneer Quakers.' Died 1905.

Halm, Friedrich (hälm). See **Münch-Bellinghausen.**

Halpine, Charles Graham. ["Miles O'Reilly."] An Irish-American miscellaneous writer; born in Ireland, 1829; came to this country at 23; died 1868. He was a New York journalist. He served through the Civil War, attaining the rank of colonel. His writings include: 'Lyrics'; 'Poems'; 'Miles O'Reilly Papers'; 'Life and Adventures of Private Miles O'Reilly'; 'Baked Meats of the Funeral'; 'Poetical Works'; etc.

Hamerling, Robert (hä'mer-ling). An Austrian poet of high and enduring place; born in Kirchberg-am-Walde, March 24, 1830; died at Gratz, July 13, 1889. Of humble parents, but reared and well educated in Vienna, he gained influential patronage by poems published at 20, and became a lecturer in the University of Trieste; but retiring on account of illness, was pensioned during the next twenty years. He produced poems, plays, and romances, which rank him among the first poets of "the new time" for thought, euphony, and technique. His greatest work is 'Ahasuerus in Rome' (1866), a vivid epic of Nero's time and the dying paganism. The later 'King of Zion,' in hexameters; 'Cupid and Psyche'; and 'Homunculus,' a satire on the unspirituality of the present age, are worthy his genius. 'Aspasia' is a powerful, graphic, and erudite, but sometimes tedious, picture of Hellenic life and manners in Pericles's time. 'The Seven Deadly Sins' is a noteworthy but minor flight of fancy. In his latter years he published an autobiography, 'Stages of my Life Pilgrimage.'

Hamerton, Philip Gilbert. An English artist, art-writer, and writer on many topics; born at Laneside, Lancashire, Sept. 10, 1834; died near Boulogne, France, Nov. 4, 1894. His works include: 'Thoughts about Art'; 'Etching and Etchers'; 'Contemporary French Painters'; 'Painting in France'; 'The Intellectual Life'; 'The Graphic Arts'; 'Human Intercourse'; 'The Quest of Happiness'; 'Autobiography' (incomplete, but supplemented by his widow); and two or three novels. His most characteristic work is 'A Painter's Camp in the Highlands.'

Hamilton, Alexander. An American statesman; born in the island of Nevis, West Indies, Jan. 11, 1757; killed in a duel by Aaron Burr, near New York, July 12, 1804. He became a captain in the Continental Army 1776; member of the Continental Congress 1782-83; of the Constitutional Convention 1787. He was Secretary of the Treasury 1789-95. In 1798, during the trouble with France, he was made inspector-general of the army, with the rank of major-general, and was for a short time in 1799 commander-in-chief. His works include the larger part of 'The Federalist,' and numerous political pamphlets and public documents and reports. His 'Collected Works' in 8 vols., edited by his son, appeared in 1851.

Hamilton, Anthony. An English author; born in Tipperary, Ireland, about 1646; died at St. Germain-en-Laye, France, in 1720. Of a Royalist family, and forced to live in France from childhood till the Restoration, his wit and moral tone are rather French than English. His 'Memoirs of the Count de Grammont' (1713) has been universally read and admired; and his mock-Oriental tales are full of grace and subtle irony.

Hamilton, Elizabeth. An Irish miscellaneous writer; born at Belfast, 1758; died at Harrogate, England, 1816. Her first serious work, 'The Letters of a Hindoo Rajah' (2 vols.), appeared in 1796. 'The Modern Philosophers' (1800) was followed by 'Memoirs of Agrippina' and 'Letters to the Daughters of a Nobleman.' The best of her works, 'The Cottagers of Glenburnie,' was published in 1808.

Hamilton, Gail. See **Dodge, Mary Abigail.**

Hamilton, John Church. An American biographer and historian, son of Alexander Hamilton; born in Philadelphia, 1792; died 1882. Besides editing his father's works (1851), he wrote: 'Memoirs and Life of Alexander Hamilton' (2 vols., 1834-40); 'History of the Republic' (4th ed. 1879); 'The Prairie Province' (1876), sketches of travel.

Hamilton, Thomas. A Scottish novelist; born in 1789; died at Pisa, Italy, Dec. 7, 1842. He was educated at Glasgow University. After showing an incapacity for business, he obtained a commission in the 29th Regiment. Retiring from the service about 1818, he soon became known as contributor to Blackwood's. His novel, 'Cyril Thornton,' published in 1827, reached several editions. 'Annals of the Peninsular Campaign' came out in 1829; 'Men and Manners in America' in 1833.

Hamilton, William. A Scottish poet; born in 1704, at Bangour, Linlithgowshire; died March 25, 1754, at Lyons, France. He wrote 'The Braes of Yarrow,' and other poems.

Hamley, Edward Bruce, Sir. An English general; born at Bodmin, England, April 27, 1824; died in London, Aug. 12, 1893. He served through the Crimean War; was professor of military history at Sandhurst 1858-64, and commandant there 1870-77; and was division commander in the Egyptian war of 1882. His chief work is 'Operations of War' (1866; 4th ed. 1878), the recognized text-book of military examinations. Among his other publications are: 'The Story of the Campaign' (1855), a narrative of the Crimean War; 'Wellington's Career' (1860); 'Voltaire' in 'Foreign Classics' (1877); 'The War in the Crimea' (1890).

Hammer, Julius (häm'mer). A German poet and prose-writer; born in Dresden, June 7, 1810; died at Pillnitz, Aug. 23, 1862. His comedy called 'The Strange Breakfast' (1834) was followed by a volume of charming lyric poetry under the title 'Look About You, Look Within You' (1851); and by 'Learn, Live, Love,' and other successful efforts. His novels show talent; but his reputation must rest upon his verse, which is graceful, unhackneyed, and ingenious.

Hammerich, Peter Frederik Adolf (häm'mer-ich). A Danish poet, theologian, and historian; born in Copenhagen, 1809; died there, Feb. 9, 1877. During the Danish-German War he was an army chaplain; and after it he was elected to Parliament, and began to write history. As a poet his 'Hero Songs' deserve special mention.

Hammond, Mrs. Henrietta (Hardy). ["Henri Dangé."] An American novelist; born in Virginia, 1854; died 1883. She wrote: 'The Georgians'; 'A Fair Philosopher'; 'Her Waiting Heart'; 'Woman's Secrets, or How to be Beautiful'; and other books.

Hammond, William Alexander. A distinguished American physician and medical writer, also a novelist; born at Annapolis, Md., Aug. 28, 1828; died in Washington, Jan. 5, 1900. He was surgeon-general in the Civil War (1862–64). Among his novels are : 'Robert Severne' (1866); 'Dr. Grattan' (1884); 'Lal' (1884); 'On the Susquehanna' (1887).

Hanaford, Mrs. Phebe Ann (Coffin). An American miscellaneous writer and Universalist minister; born in Massachusetts in 1829. She was the first of her sex to become a member of the Universalist clergy. In 1887 she was called to a church in New Haven, Conn., and has retained the charge ever since. Her works are : 'Life of Abraham Lincoln'; 'Life of George Peabody'; 'Lucretia the Quakeress'; 'Leonette, or Truth Sought and Found'; 'The Best of Books and its History'; 'Frank Nelson, the Runaway Boy'; 'The Soldier's Daughter'; 'Field, Gunboat, and Hospital'; 'Women of the Century'; 'From Shore to Shore, and Other Poems'; etc.

Hannay, James. An English novelist and essayist; born at Dumfries, Scotland, Feb. 17, 1827; died near Barcelona, Spain, Jan. 9, 1873. He was a midshipman for some years. His contributions to Edinburgh periodicals, since collected, have been widely read; and his novels 'King Dobbs,' 'Singleton Fontenoy,' and 'Eustace Conyers,' went through more than one edition. His ability is in satire and delicate irony rather than in characterization.

Hansen, Maurits Christopher (hän'sen). A Norwegian poet; born in Modum, July 5, 1794,

died at Kongsberg, March 16, 1842. His models in fiction seem to have been Fouqué and Tieck. As a poet he is best represented by the volume of 'Norse Idylls.' His style is limpid, and shows the influence of German studies. He also wrote school grammars, and manuals of literature, that have been widely used in Norway.

Hanslick, Eduard (häns'lik). A German musical critic and writer on æsthetics; born at Prague, Sept. 11, 1825. He surpassed all contemporary workers in the field of musical criticism, holding the position of professor of musical criticism and history in the Vienna University. He is a recognized authority among European authors in music and æsthetics, owing to his wit, imaginative power, thorough knowledge of his specialties, and perfect command of style. Died at Vienna, Aug. 7, 1904.

Hanssen, Ola (hän'sen). A Swedish-German poet and author; born in Hönsing, Sweden, Nov. 12, 1860. He had a passion for travel; going on foot in his impecunious early years, but his first poems were successful enough to improve his means. His masterpiece was 'Love Longings' (Sensitiva Amorosa), brought out in 1887, and since translated into German and French. He has lived in Berlin since 1889, and written in German with grace and facility. His poems combine vigorous thought with delicate workmanship, and his literary essays are those of an able and learned critic.

Hapgood, Isabella Florence. An American translator and writer, who has paid particular attention to Russian subjects; born in Massachusetts in 1851. She has published 'The Epic Songs of Russia'; 'Russian Rambles'; and is well known as a translator of the works of Gogol, Hugo, and other great European writers.

Hapgood, Norman. An American journalist of New York; born in Chicago, March 28, 1868. He graduated at Harvard, and studied in Europe. He has published 'Literary Statesmen and Others'; 'Daniel Webster'; 'Abraham Lincoln'; 'The Stage in America' (1901).

Happel, Eberhard Werner (häp'el). A German writer of fiction and prose miscellany; born in Kirchhain, Hesse, Aug. 12, 1647; died at Hamburg, May 15, 1690. His 'Academic Romance' is important as a contribution to the records of literary and artistic evolution.

Harby, Isaac. An American dramatist; born in South Carolina, 1788; died 1828. His home was in Charleston, S. C. He wrote : 'Alexander Severus'; 'The Gordian Knot'; 'Alberti'; etc.

Hardenberg, Friedrich von. See **Novalis**.

Hardinge, Mrs. Belle Boyd. An American Southern woman who acted as a Confederate spy in the Civil War. She wrote 'Belle Boyd in Camp and Prison' (London and New York, 1865).

Hardy, Alexandre (är-dē'). A French playwright; born at Paris about 1570; died near

Versailles (?), 1631. He is said to have been one of the first French "playwrights," properly speaking. His plays number some hundreds, and he borrowed his materials from Cervantes, Boccaccio, and any other author he found available. His best effort is probably 'Mariamne,' produced in 1610. Such talent as he possessed was for construction and adaptation, and for felicitous dialogue.

Hardy, Arthur Sherburne. An American novelist, poet, and man of letters; born at Andover, Mass., Aug. 13, 1847. He graduated from West Point, and commanded a military post in the South for two years. His poetry consists mainly of lyrics and sonnets, while his novels are full of interest and charm. He is a skilled musician. In 1897 he was appointed minister to Persia. 'But Yet a Woman' and 'The Wind of Destiny' are among the more important of his novels. 'Passe-Rose' is a French idyl. His poems have been published in numerous magazines, and some of his mathematical studies have taken shape in a volume on 'Quaternions.' His latest work is ' His Daughter First ' (1903).

Hardy, Iza Duffus. An English novelist, daughter of Sir Thomas. She began story-writing very early, and has been a frequent contributor to the magazines. Among her numerous novels are : 'Glencairn' (1877); 'Only a Love Story' (1877); 'A Broken Faith' (1878); 'The Love that He Passed By' (1884), an American novel; 'A Woman's Loyalty' (1893); and two volumes of transatlantic reminiscences, 'Between Two Oceans' (1884) and 'Oranges and Alligators: Sketches of South Florida Life' (1886).

Hardy, Thomas. An English novelist; born in Dorsetshire, June 2, 1840. His works include : 'Desperate Remedies' (1871); 'Under the Greenwood Tree' (1872); 'A Pair of Blue Eyes' (1873); 'Far from the Madding Crowd' (1874); 'The Hand of Ethelberta' (1876); 'The Return of the Native' (1878); 'The Trumpet Major' (1880); 'A Laodicean' (1881); 'Two on a Tower' (1882); 'The Mayor of Casterbridge' (1886); 'The Woodlanders' (1887); 'Wessex Tales' (1888); 'A Group of Noble Dames' (1891); 'Tess of the D'Urbervilles' (1891); 'Life's Little Ironies' (1894); 'Jude the Obscure'; 'Poems of the Past and Present.'

Hare, Augustus John Cuthbert. An English descriptive writer; born in Rome, March 13, 1834. He was a graduate of Oxford. The son of a rich father, he was enabled from his earliest youth to gratify a taste for travel, on descriptions of which his fame chiefly rests. Among his happiest efforts are: 'A Winter at Mentone' (1861); 'Walks in Rome' (1870); 'Wanderings in Spain' (1872); 'Walks in London' (1877); 'Days near Paris' (1887); and a narrative of travel in southern France. A volume of personal recollections (1895). He died at Holmhurst, Eng., Jan. 22, 1903.

Hare, Augustus William. An English clergyman and writer; born 1792; died 1834. With his brother Julius Charles he wrote 'Guesses at Truth.'

Hare, Julius Charles. An English theologian; born 1795; died 1855. His works include : 'Mission of the Comforter' (1846); 'The Contest with Rome' (1852); 'Vindication of Luther' (1854). See also Augustus William.

Haren, Onno Zwier van (här'en). A Dutch poet and statesman; born at Leeuwarden, April 2, 1713; died near Wolvega, Friesland, Sept. 2, 1779. An active public man on the Orange side, he was forced into retirement by an obscure scandal after the death of Anne, wife of William IV., and took to literary work. His best production is an epic, 'The Fatherland,' portraying the Dutch struggle for freedom. His lyric poetry is good; and a tragedy, 'William I.,' is still generally read. His work on William IV. is a masterpiece of Dutch prose.

Haren, Willem van. A Dutch poet and statesman, brother of Onno; born at Leeuwarden, Feb. 21, 1710; committed suicide in North Brabant, July 4, 1768. He held important governmental posts but was ruined by speculation. His celebrated poem 'Leonidas' (1742) was written to inspire the Hollanders with his own enthusiasm for liberty and the war of the Austrian succession. Even more meritorious are his odes on human happiness and the vicissitudes of life ; but his epic poem 'Friso,' despite imperfections, won him his greatest fame.

Harington, Sir John. An English poet and wit; born at Kelston, near Bath, in 1561; died there, Nov. 20, 1612. He was a soldier, courtier, and scholar, in favor with Queen Elizabeth, and a power in public affairs. His translation of Ariosto's 'Orlando Furioso,' undertaken by command of Queen Elizabeth, is meritorious; but his talent displayed itself best in epigram. His witty verses in ridicule of his contemporaries got him into trouble occasionally, but never into serious difficulty. He was the Martial of his day, though of less genius.

Harland, Henry. ["Sidney Luska."] An American novelist; born at St. Petersburg, 1861. A few years ago he removed to London, where he died, December 19, 1905. He is author of : 'As It was Written' (1885), a musician's story; 'Mrs. Peixada' (1886); 'The Land of Love' (1887); 'My Uncle Florimond' (1888); 'The Yoke of the Thorah' (1887); 'Mr. Sonnenschein's Inheritance' (1888); 'A Latin Quarter Courtship'; 'The Cardinal's Snuff Box.'

Harland, Marion. See **Terhune.**

Harraden, Beatrice. An English novelist, daughter of an East India agent in London; born Jan. 24, 1864. After schooling and a season in Germany, she took her degree at London University at 21, showing marked excellence in languages. She was then employed in a publishing-house, but ill-health compelled her to leave. Her first novel, 'Ships that Pass in the Night,' was instantly successful. This was followed by 'In Varying Moods' (1894); 'Things will Take a Turn' (1894); 'Hilda Strafford,' a Californian story; 'Katharine Frensham' (1903).

Harrigan, Edward. A noted American actor and playwright; born in New York, 1845. He formed a partnership with Tony Hart (1871–85), when the two opened in New York their first Theatre Comique (1876), bringing out there the 'Mulligan Guard' series of plays. Among his dramas, which are all of humble New York life, strong in character-drawing though weak in a literary sense, may be named 'Squatter Sovereignty' and 'Cordelia's Aspirations.'

Harris, Amanda Bartlett. An American writer of juveniles; born at Warner, N. H., 1824. Besides numerous contributions to periodicals, she has published many pleasing books, including 'How We Went Bird-Nesting'; 'Wild Flowers, and where They Grow'; 'The Luck of Edenhall'; etc.

Harris, Augustus Henry Glossop, Sir. An English actor, manager, and dramatist; born in Paris in 1852; died in Folkestone, England, June 22, 1896. Appearing on the stage in 1873, in 1879 he became lessee and manager of Drury Lane Theatre, where he produced popular pantomimes and melodramas written in collaboration—among them: 'The World'; 'Youth'; 'Human Nature'; 'Run of Luck'; 'Prodigal Daughter'; 'Life of Pleasure'; 'Derby Winner.' He induced the revival of grand opera at Covent Garden. He was made sheriff of London and knighted in 1891.

Harris, George Washington. An American humorist; born in Allegheny County, Pa., 1814; died 1869. While a Tennessee River steamboat captain he wrote, about 1860, for the New York Spirit of the Times, a series of broadly humorous character sketches called 'Sut Lovengood's Yarns,' published in book form in 1867.

Harris, Joel Chandler. An American journalist and story-writer; born at Eatonton, Georgia, Dec. 8, 1848. He began life as a printer's apprentice, and afterwards studied law, drifting finally into journalism. He had a thorough familiarity with the negro of the post-bellum period, and while editing an Atlanta paper he produced for it the series of 'Uncle Remus' sketches and songs which immediately made him known. 'The Folk-Lore of the Old Plantation' appeared in 1880, followed by 'Nights with Uncle Remus' (1883); 'Mingo and Other Sketches' (1883); 'Daddy Jake, the Runaway' (1889) ; 'Uncle Remus' and 'Br'er Rabbit' (1907). In a more serious vein is his biography of the lamented Henry W. Grady, a work of genuine power. He died July 3, 1908.

Harris, Mrs. Miriam (Coles). A well-known American novelist; born at Dosoris, L. I., 1834. Her home is in New York. She has written: 'Rutledge' (1860); 'The Sutherlands' (1862)— both widely read; 'Frank Warrington'; 'A Perfect Adonis'; 'Missy'; etc. A complete edition of her novels appeared in 1885.

Harris, Thomas Lake. A noted American mystic philosopher and religious and social reformer; born at Fenny Stratford, England, May 15, 1823. He founded the Brotherhood of the New Life, of which Laurence Oliphant was a member. Among his numerous works in prose and verse are: 'The Great Republic, a Poem of the Sun' (1867); 'Arcana of Christianity' (2 vols., 1868); 'God's Breath in Man' (1891).

Harris, William Torrey. A distinguished American educator, and writer on education and philosophy; born at Killingly, Conn., Sept. 10, 1835. He established the Journal of Speculative Philosophy (1867), the first publication of its kind in the English language, and became United States Commissioner of Education (1889). Among his works are: 'Hegel's Logic' (1890), a critical exposition; 'The Spiritual Sense of Dante's Divina Commedia' (1891); 'Introduction to Philosophy'; 'Psychologic Foundation of Education.'

Harrison, Mrs. Burton (Constance Cary). An American novelist and miscellaneous writer ; born at Vaucluse, Va., April 25, 1846 ; resides in New York. She has written: 'Woman's Handiwork in Modern Homes' (1881); 'Old-Fashioned Fairy-Book' (1884); 'Bar Harbor Days' (1887); and the novels 'The Anglomaniacs'; 'An Errant Wooing'; 'A Bachelor Maid'; 'A Son of the Old Dominion' (1897); 'A Princess of the Hills'; 'Latter-Day Sweethearts.'

Harrison, Frederic. An English essayist, thinker, and publicist; born in London, Oct. 18, 1831. Since graduation from Oxford he has served on various scientific and legal commissions; writing in connection therewith, reports, essays, books on sociology, law, and ethics. In the domain of philosophy his expositions of Comte have given him an international reputation. 'The Meaning of History' (1862); 'Order and Progress' (1875); 'Choice of Books' (1886); 'Oliver Cromwell' (1888); 'Annals of an Old Manor House'; 'The Study of History'; 'Moral and Religious Socialism'; 'William the Silent' ; 'George Washington and Other American Addresses.'

Harrison, James Albert. An American educator and miscellaneous writer; born at Pass Christian, Miss., 1848. He is now professor of Teutonic languages at the University of Virginia. He has written: 'A Group of Poets and their Haunts' (1875) ; 'Greek Vignettes' (1878); 'Spain in Profile' (1879); 'History of Spain' (1881); 'Autrefois: Tales of Old New Orleans and Elsewhere' (1888); etc.

Harrison, Jane Ellen. An English lecturer and writer on Greek art and mythology; born in 1850. She began her career as a lecturer in 1882 at the British Museum, and has since extended her work to South Kensington and most of the provincial towns. She has been prominently identified with the university extension movement. Among her publications may be mentioned: 'Myths of the Odyssey' (1881) ; 'Introductory Studies in Greek Art' (1885); 'Mythology and Monuments of Ancient Athens'; 'Phœbe'; 'Rosary for Lent'; 'Dear Feast of Lent'; 'A Corner in Spain.'

Harrisse, Henri (har-ēs'). An American critic, bibliographer, and historian; born in Paris, 1830, of Russian-Hebrew parentage. He became a citizen of the United States, and for several years practiced law in New York. He has written 'Christopher Columbus' (2 vols., 1884-85); 'John and Sebastian Cabot' (1883); 'The Discovery of North America'; etc.

Harsdörfer, George Philip (härs'dèrf-er). A German poet; born in Nürnberg, Nov. 1, 1607; died there, Sept. 22, 1658. After legal studies and extensive travel, he settled down to official employment in his native town. In 1644 he helped to found a fraternal literary and horticultural society, the Pegnitz Order, which did good work in improving literary language. Best remembered of his many works are: 'The Poetical Funnel,' for "pouring in knowledge," a satirical "royal road" to poesy; and a 'Manual of Polite Conversation,' which explains itself.

Harsha, David Addison. An American religious writer and biographer; born at Argyle, N. Y., Sept. 15, 1827. He wrote 'Lives' of Charles Sumner, Doddridge, Baxter, Bunyan, Addison, James Hervey, Watts, Whitefield, Abraham Booth, and 'Eminent Orators and Statesmen.' Died at South Argyle, in 1895.

Hart, Albert Bushnell. An American educator, historian, biographer, and essayist; born at Clarksville, Pa., July 1, 1854. He is professor of history at Harvard University. He has written: 'Coercive Powers of the United States Government' (1885); 'Introduction to the Study of Federal Government' (1890); 'Studies in Education'; 'Life of Salmon P. Chase'; 'Practical Essays on American Government'; etc. He edited a series of works on special periods of our national history which were published from 1897-1907.

Hart, Charles Henry. An American art critic, antiquarian, and biographer; born in Philadelphia, 1847. Among his published works are: 'Remarks on Tabasco, Mexico' (1865); 'Memoirs of William Hickling Prescott' (1868); 'Memoirs of William Willis' (1870); 'George Ticknor' (1871); 'Turner, the Dream Painter' (1879); and 'Samuel S. Haldeman' (1881).

Hart, Heinrich (härt). A German poet and critic; born in Wesel, Dec. 30, 1855. His early studies were historical, philosophical, and philological. He is a journalist, a dramatic and literary critic, and one of the leaders of what is known as the naturalistic movement in literature. In collaboration with his brother Julius, he projected a variety of successful periodical publications. His poetical works include a volume of verse; a tragedy, 'Sedan'; and an elaborate 'Song of Mankind,' of which but the first few parts have yet appeared. He has issued a volume of sketches, 'Children of the Light.'

Hart, Julius. A German poet and prose-writer, brother of Heinrich; born in Münster, April 9, 1859; resides in Berlin. His earliest

efforts were in newspaper dramatic criticisms. His poems include: 'Sansara,' a volume of verse; 'Don Juan Tenorio,' a tragedy in lyric form; and 'Homo Sum.' He is a graceful translator of poetry from the Persian, English, and Spanish. His poetry and prose are characterized by euphony and limpidity of style.

Harte, [Francis] Bret. A famous American short-story writer and poet; born in Albany, N. Y., Aug. 25, 1839; died at Camberley, England, May 5, 1902. He published 'Outcroppings' (1866), a collection of verse by Californians; 'The Lost Galleon, and Other Tales' (1867); 'Condensed Novels' (1867); 'The Luck of Roaring Camp, and Other Sketches' (1870); 'Plain Language from Truthful James' (1870), illustrated edition; 'The Heathen Chinee' (1871), special edition; 'Poems' (1871); 'East and West Poems' (1871); 'Stories of the Sierras' (1872); 'Poetical Works' (1872); 'Mrs. Skaggs's Husbands, and Other Sketches'; 'M'liss' (1873); 'An Episode of Fiddletown, and Other Sketches' (1873); 'Echoes of the Foot-Hills' (1875); 'Tales of the Argonauts, and Other Sketches' (1875); 'Gabriel Conroy' (1876); 'Two Men of Sandy Bar' (1876), a drama; 'Thankful Blossom' (1877); 'The Story of a Mine' (1878); 'The Hoodlum Band, and Other Stories' (1878); 'Drift from Two Shores' (1878); 'An Heiress of Red Dog, and Other Tales' (1879); 'The Twins of Marble Mountain, and Other Stories' (1879); 'Complete Works' (1882); 'Flip and Other Stories' (1882); 'In the Carquinez Woods' (1884); 'On the Frontier' (1884); 'Maruja' (1885); 'By Shore and Sedge' (1885); 'Snow Bound at Eagle's' (1885); 'The Queen of the Pirate Isle' (1886); 'A Millionaire of Rough and Ready' (1887); 'Devil's Ford' (1887); 'The Crusade of the Excelsior' (1887); 'The Argonauts of North Liberty' (1888); 'A Phyllis of the Sierras' (1888); 'Cressy' (1889); 'The Heritage of Dedlow Marsh, and Other Tales' (1889); 'A Waif of the Plains' (1890); 'A Ward of the Golden Gate' (1890); 'A Sappho of Green Springs, and Other Stories' (1891); 'Colonel Starbottle's Client and Other People' (1892); 'A First Family of Tasajera' (1892); 'Susy' (1893); 'Sally Dows, and Other Stories' (1893); 'A Protégée of Jack Hamlin's, and Other Stories' (1894); 'The Bell-Ringer of Angel's, and Other Stories' (1894); 'Clarence' (1895); 'In the Hollow of the Hills' (1895); 'Three Partners'; etc.

Harting, James Edmund. An English naturalist; born in London, April 29, 1841. He matriculated at the University of London in 1859, and followed the profession of a solicitor until 1878, when he retired and devoted himself to zoölogical research. He is editor of the natural-history columns of the Field, and also has charge of the Zoölogist. Among his numerous publications are: 'The Ornithology of Shakespeare' (1871); 'Handbook of British Birds' (1871); 'Rambles in Search of Shells' (1875); 'British Animals Extinct within Historic Times' (1880); 'Essays on Sport and Natural History' (1883).

Hartley, Cecil B. An American biographer and miscellaneous writer; born 18—· died 18—. He wrote 'Lives' of Louis Wetzel, the Virginia ranger; of the Empress Josephine (1860); of Francis Marion; and of Daniel Boone. Also 'Hunting Sports of the West.'

Hartmann, Alfred (härt'män). A Swiss author; born Jan. 1, 1814, near Langenthal, Bern. He studied law at German universities, but after a sojourn in Paris abandoned jurisprudence and devoted himself to literary pursuits at Solothurn, where for many years he published a comic periodical called Postheiri. His chief works are the romance 'Master Putsch and his Companions' (1858); 'Martin Disteli' (1861), a biography; 'Gallery of Famous Swiss' (1863–71); 'Tales from the Swiss' (1863); 'Swiss Tales' (1877); 'Fortunatus.' D. Dec. 10, 1897.

Hartmann, Eduard von. A German philosopher; born at Berlin, Feb. 23, 1842. At 22 he chose for his life vocation "thinking," or philosophy, and on his retirement from the Prussian military service (1865), devoted himself wholly for some years to writing his great work 'The Philosophy of the Unconscious' (1868; 10th ed., 3 vols., 1890); in the later editions of this work are incorporated his 'Physiology of the Nerve-Centres' (1876); 'The Truth and the Error in Darwinism' (1875); and 'The Unconscious from the Standpoint of Physiology and the Doctrine of Descent' (1872). Then followed 'The Ethical Consciousness,' or as it was at first entitled, 'Phenomenology of the Ethical Consciousness' (1879); 'The Philosophy of Religion' (2d ed. 1888), comprising 'The Religious Consciousness of Mankind' and 'The Religion of the Soul'; 'Æsthetics' (2 vols., 1886–87), comprising 'German Æsthetics since Kant' and 'The Philosophy of the Beautiful.' Besides these works, which constitute his exposition of a system of philosophy, he has written: 'On the Dialectic Method' (1868); 'The Thing in Itself and its Nature' (1871); 'Critical Grounds of Transcendental Realism' (3d ed. 1885); 'Elucidations of the Metaphysics of the Unconscious' (1874), afterwards styled 'New-Kantianism, Schopenhauerism, and Hegelianism'; 'Self-Destruction of Christianity, and the Religion of the Future' (3d ed. 1888); 'The Crisis of Christianity in Modern Theology' (1880); 'Judaism in the Present and the Future' (1885); 'Lotze's Philosophy' (1888); 'The Ghost-Theory in Spiritism' (1891); 'The Fundamental Social Questions' (1894); 'Shelling's Philosophical System' (1897); 'History of Metaphysics' (1900); 'The Problem of Life' (1906). Died June 6, 1906.

Hartmann, Moritz. An Austrian poet and agitator; born in Duschnik, Bohemia, Oct. 15, 1821; died in Vienna, May 13, 1872. He was from youth an ardent social reformer, and wrote poems under this inspiration. His 'Chalice and Sword' (1845) was distinctly revolutionary. He became a "poet of the people," participated in the movement of 1848, and was elected to the Frankfurt Parliament.

His 'Poetic Chronicle of Father Mauritius' (1849) attained a wide popularity. He lived in exile for some years, but continued to write poetry and prose in his wanderings, his reputation constantly increasing. Deep feeling and love of freedom permeate all his work.

Hartmann von Aue (härt'män fōn ou'é). A German mediæval poet; born about 1170; died between 1210 and 1220. He took part in the Crusades. He was one of the most eminent poets of his time, and through the study and imitation of the poets of Northern France, brought about a revival of poetry in Germany. His chief work is 'Poor Heinrich,' a sentimental legend, on which Longfellow based his 'Golden Legend.' His romances 'Erek' and 'Iwein,' written about 1190 and 1200 respectively, were derived from Chrestien de Troyes. His love songs, the noted "minne" poems, are light and graceful.

Hartshorne, Henry. ["Corinne L'Estrange."] An American physician, writer and poet; born in Philadelphia, March 16, 1823; died at Tokio, Feb. 10, 1897. He was professor in the University of Pennsylvania, Haverford College, and the Woman's Medical College of Pennsylvania. Besides valuable medical works, he wrote 'Woman's Witchcraft,' a dramatic romance, and 'Summer Songs' (1865), a volume of verse.

Hartzenbusch, Juan Eugenio (härts'enbösh). A Spanish poet and playwright; son of a German father and a Spanish mother; born in Madrid, Sept. 6, 1806; died there, Aug. 2, 1880. His plays adapted from the French were produced with success. 'The Lovers of Teruel,' his first original drama and his masterpiece, achieved speedy popularity. Others of his best plays are: 'Doña Mencia'; 'The Bachelor Mendarias'; and 'The Courtesan and the Coward.' They show liveliness of fancy, ingenuity of plot, and good metrical workmanship. He also edited the Spanish playwrights, and wrote pleasing poems and stories.

Haschka, Laurenz Leopold (häsh'kä). An Austrian poet; born in Vienna, Sept. 1, 1749; died there, Aug. 3, 1827. His fame is mainly due to 'God Save Emperor Francis,' the national hymn of its period, and still an Austrian popular song.

Hasebroek, Johannes Petrus (häs'ê-brök). A Dutch poet, preacher, and prose-writer; born in Leyden, Nov. 6, 1812. His collected 'Poems,' and two volumes entitled 'Vesper' and 'Hesperides' respectively, reveal him a pleasing maker of verse; but his best-known work is a collection of droll poems called 'Jonathan's Truth and Dreams.' His sermons have been widely circulated in book form. Died 1896.

Hassard, John Rose Greene. An American journalist and musical and literary critic; born in New York, Sept. 4, 1836; died there, April 18, 1888. He was for many years on the staff of the New York Tribune as an authoritative musical critic. His most important work is 'The Ring of the Nibelung'; but he also achieved distinction with such books as ‘Life of Archbishop Hughes’; ‘Life of Pope Pius IX.’; ‘A Pickwickian Pilgrimage’; etc.

Hassaurek, Friedrich (häs′sour″ek). An Austrian-American prose and verse-writer; born in Vienna, Oct. 9, 1832; died at Paris, Oct. 3, 1885. As a boy he was a volunteer soldier in the Austrian army in 1848, but came to this country the next year, and was long a journalist in Cincinnati. He was United States minister to Ecuador under Lincoln. ‘Four Years among the South-Americans,’ a volume of sketches; ‘The Secret of the Andes,’ a novel; and a collection of verses written in German, are his remembered works.

Hasselt, André Henri Constant van (häs′-selt). A Belgian poet and historian; born in Maastricht, Holland, Jan. 5, 1806; died in Brussels, Nov. 30, 1874. As a naturalized Belgian he early made that country his own from a literary point of view, and became in 1837 a member of the Belgian Academy. His leading historical works are : ‘History of French Poetry in Belgium’; ‘The Belgians in the Crusades’; ‘History of the Belgian People’; and ‘The Glories of Art in Belgium.’ He also produced a variety of verses, stories, and essays. His poems are highly spoken of, especially the one entitled ‘Four Incarnations of Christ.’

Hathaway, Benjamin. An American writer of verse; born in Cayuga County, N. Y., 1822. He wrote poems with chalk on barrel heads while working as a cooper, and was for thirty years a nurseryman and farmer. He has written: ‘Art Life, and Other Poems’ (1877); ‘League of the Iroquois’ (1881); ‘The Finished Creation.’

Hatifi, Maulânâ Abdallah (Pers. pron. hâ-tif′i). A Persian poet; born in Chargird, province of Herat, in the fifteenth century; died 1520 (?). His fame rests upon a series of five epic poems in couplets, in which he takes Nisâmi and Amir Chusrau, of Delhi, as his models. Three of the series are : ‘Laila and Mejnunnun’; ‘Love of the Sassanid Khosru’; ‘Haft Mansar’ (Seven Beauties). The fourth is in a fragmentary state, while the final one is the ‘Book of the Seven Timurs.’ He was one of the last of Persia’s great epic poets, and his genius is of a high order.

Hatton, Joseph. An English journalist, novelist, and miscellaneous writer; born at Andover, Feb. 3, 1837. Beginning journalism on his father’s paper, the Derbyshire Times, he edited the Gentleman’s Magazine (1868–74); and has since been a newspaper correspondent, (particularly for the New York Times), and magazinist. As a novelist he will be remembered for ‘Clytie’ (1874); ‘Queen of Bohemia’ (1877); ‘John Needham’s Double’ (1885), dramatized for E. S. Willard; ‘By Order of the Czar,’ a novel of Russian life; ‘Princess Mazaroff’; ‘Under the Great Seal’; ‘When Greek Meets Greek,’ a novel of the French Revolution successfully dramatized. Among his mis-

cellaneous publications the best known are : ‘Journalistic London’ (1882); ‘The New Ceylon’ (1882); ‘Henry Irving’s Impressions of America’ (1884); ‘Reminiscences of J. L. Toole, Comedian’ (1888).

Hauch, Johannes Carsten (houċh). A Danish poet and novelist; born in Frederikshald, Norway, May 12, 1790; died at Rome, March 4, 1872. A several-years’ European tour ended by the amputation of his foot in Italy. He lectured on physics at Sorö, and was professor of poetry at Kiel. The revolution of 1848 drew him in, and he took permanent refuge in Scandinavia; was made professor of æsthetics in the Copenhagen University, and held the post till his death. His plays won him his first general recognition, and several have had brilliant success both in Scandinavia and Germany. ‘Contrasterne’ and ‘Rosaura’ were the earliest; and ‘Tiberius,’ ‘Don Juan,’ and ‘Tycho Brahe,’ among the later. ‘Hamadryads’ gave him fame in romantic poetry, and his lyrics rank him as Denmark’s foremost poet of nature and sentiment. His romances, especially ‘William Zabern,’ ‘Guldmageren,’ ‘The Story of Thorwald Vidförle,’ and ‘Robert Fulton,’ have passed through many editions. In him, depth of feeling unites with taste and mysticism in a charming whole.

Hauenschild, Richard Georg Spiller von. See **Waldau.**

Hauff, Wilhelm (houf). A German story-writer; born at Stuttgart, Nov. 29, 1802; died there, Oct. 18, 1827. From the monastery at Blaubeuren, he went to Tübingen to study theology, but became tutor in the family of a high official. His works include : ‘Almanach of Fables for 1826’; ‘Extracts from Satan’s Memoirs’; ‘Lichtenstein’; ‘Othello’; ‘The Beggar of the Pont des Arts’; and a medley of the most fascinating and amusing tales. His most delightful creation is ‘Phantasies of the Bremen Rathskeller,’ in which his fertility of resource and sparkling wit seem unfailing.

Haug, Johann Cristoph Friedrich (houg). [Pseudonym “Hophthalmos” used in one book only.] A German poet and epigrammatist; born in Niederstotzingen, Würtemberg, March 9, 1761; died at Stuttgart, Jan. 30, 1829. His fame dates from the appearance of two books: ‘Epigrams and Miscellaneous Poems,’ and ‘Epigrams.’ A fine example of his ever juvenescent wit is ‘Two Hundred Hyperboles upon Herr Wahl’s Enormous Nose.’ He wrote also fables, ballads, and charades, in smooth and elegant metre.

Haupt, William Ayers. [“William A. Mestayer.”] An American actor and playwright; born in Philadelphia, June 8, 1846; died in New York, Nov. 21, 1896. He made his first appearance in 1862. He was a popular comedian, and has played with Edwin Forrest, Lester Wallack, and other well-known actors. During the Civil War he served in the engineering corps of the Army of the Potomac. Among the plays which he wrote or assisted in writing are: 'The Tourist in a Pullman Car'; 'We, Us & Co.'; 'Tobogganing'; 'The Grab Bag'; 'The Kitty'.

Hauptmann, Gerhart (houpt'män). A German dramatist and poet; born Nov. 15, 1862, in Salzbrunn, Silesia. He was a scholar of solid attainments at Jena and Berlin. His taste for practical sociology comes out strongly in his intense and powerful poems and dramas; he settled on a small Silesian farm solely to study peasant life. He traveled widely, visiting the United States in 1894. His first play, 'Promethidenlos' (1885), was conventional; but under Ibsen's inspiration he soon broke away from the old lines, producing 'Before Sunrise' and 'A Family Catastrophe,' tragedies presenting the genetic conditions of proletarianism. These and subsequent plays have given him world-wide repute. He has lately turned to comedy but 'The Weavers' represent his forte. 'The Apostle'; 'Hannele'; 'Poor Henry' and 'The Railway-Guard' are an attempt at fiction.

Haussonville, Gabriel Paul Othenin de Cléron, Comte d' (dōs'ôn-vēl). A French littérateur, son of Count Joseph; born at Guscy-et-Châtcl, Dept. Seine-et-Marne, Sept. 21, 1843. He is a member of the French Academy, and one of the leading contributors to the Revue des Deux Mondes. His reputation rests on literary monographs, among which are 'Sainte-Beuve, his Life and Works' (1875), 'George Sand,' 'Prescott,' etc. (1879-88); and works like 'Across the United States' (1883), notes and impressions; 'Social Studies'; 'Socialism and Charity.'

Haussonville, Joseph Othenin Bernard de Cléron, Comte d'. A French historian; born in Paris, May 27, 1809; died May 28, 1884. He was once in the diplomatic service, but entered parliamentary life. His 'History of the Reunion of Lorraine to France,' and 'History of the Foreign Policy of the French Government from 1830 to 1848,' are valuable.

Haussonville, Louise d'. A French novelist, wife of Joseph; born (Princess de Broglie) in 1818; died 1882. 'Robert Emmet' is her best novel. She wrote much about Byron.

Haven, Gilbert. A distinguished American prose-writer and bishop of the M. E. Church; born in Malden, Mass., Sept. 19, 1821; died there, Jan. 30, 1880. An able writer, a forceful preacher, and a persistent worker, he refused all honorary collegiate degrees. He published 'The Pilgrim's Wallet, or Sketches of Travel in England, France, and Germany'; 'Life of Father Taylor, the Sailor Preacher' (1871); 'Our Next-Door Neighbor, or a Winter in Mexico' (1875); etc.

Havergal, Frances Ridley. An English religious writer and poet; born at Astley, Worcestershire, Dec. 14, 1836; died at Swansea, Wales, June 3, 1879. She began to write hymns and letters in verse at the age of seven, but did not publish anything until 1860. She was a frequent contributor to Good Words. Among over 30 publications, which once enjoyed

considerable popularity, may be noticed: 'The Four Happy Days' (1873); 'Under the Surface' (1874), poems; 'Royal Graces and Loyal Gifts' (6 vols., 1879); 'Under His Shadow' (1879); and a number of posthumous works by various editors.

Haver-Schmidt, François (häv'er-shmit). ["Piet Paaltjens."] A Dutch prose and verse writer; born at Leeuwarden, Feb. 14, 1835; died at Schiedam, Jan. 19, 1894. He studied theology at Leyden, and was pastor of "Reformed" churches in various parts of the Netherlands for some years. While still a student he produced a series of parodies, love songs, and sketches (called in collected form 'Skits and Jests'), which are now known almost by heart to the whole Dutch collegiate world. Later he wrote realistic novels and tales of a somewhat serious tendency. Among them are: 'My Brother's House'; 'The Pastorate of My Grandfather'; and various others. His pictures of Dutch life are vivid and well drawn.

Havlíček, Karel (häv'li-chek). ["Borovsky."] A Czech prose-writer and agitator; born at Borova, Oct. 31, 1821; died at Prague, July 29, 1856. As a tutor at Moscow, he gathered the material for his 'Pictures from Russia.' Later he became an influential journalist in Bohemia. His Czech agitation resulted in imprisonment for some years, during which he wrote 'Tyrolese Elegies,' satires popular with his countrymen. In 1855 he was released. He was the most picturesque figure in the "new Czech" movement. His fierce sarcasm and unsparing wit were the dread of friend and enemy alike, and not until he had been dead some years were the most effective of his epigrams published at all. His posthumous poem, 'The Baptism of St. Vladimir,' appeared first in 1877; and later his collected works were published at Prague.

Haweis, Hugh Reginald (hois). An English clergyman and author; born at Egham, Surrey, April 3, 1839; died in London, Jan. 29, 1901. He was a Cambridge graduate. His terse and vigorous language and capacity for exposition gave his books a wide circulation; among them may be mentioned: 'Music and Morals' (1871; 13th ed. 1885), in which he expounds the emotional theory of music; 'Thoughts for the Times' (1872); 'Shakespeare and the Stage'; 'Unsectarian Family Prayers' (1874); 'Pet, or Pastimes and Penalties' (1874); 'American Humorists' (1883); 'Life of Queen Victoria' (1887); 'The Broad Church.'

Hawes, Joel. An American Congregational divine, and religious and ethical writer; born in Massachusetts, 1789; died 1867. He was settled at Hartford, Conn., 1818-67. He wrote: 'Religion of the East'; 'Looking-Glass for Ladies'; 'Washington and Jay'; 'Tribute to the Pilgrims'; etc.

Hawker, Morwenna Pauline. An English novelist; born 1865. She has written 'Cecilia de Noel' (1891), and other novels, employing the pen-name of "Lanoe Falconer."

Hawkesworth, John. A noted English miscellaneous writer; born in London about 1715; died Nov. 16, 1773. He is best known as editor of the Adventurer, and as author of about half its contents. He wrote also an account of the voyages of Captain Cook, Byron, Wallis, and Carteret (3 vols., 1773); 'Zimri' (1760), an excellent oratorio; 'Edgar and Emeline' (1761), a drama; 'Almoran and Hamet' (1761), a tale; 'Life of Swift' (1765–66); etc. Allibone speaks of him as occupying "the first rank among English classical essayists."

Hawkins, Anthony Hope. A popular English novelist, writing under the name "Anthony Hope"; born in London, Feb. 9, 1863. He was admitted to the bar in 1887. Among his best-known works are: 'A Man of Mark' (1890); 'Father Stafford'; 'The Prisoner of Zenda'; 'The Indiscretion of the Duchess'; 'Phroso'; 'Heart of the Princess Osra.'

Hawkins, Frederick. An English journalist and author; born in 1849. He assisted in establishing the Theatre, a periodical exclusively devoted to the literature and art of the stage, and was its editor until 1879. He was dramatic critic of the Times for a short period, and has been for some time on its editorial staff. His works are: 'Life of Edmund Kean' (1869); 'Annals of the French Stage, from its Origin to the Death of Racine' (1884); and a continuation of it to the Revolution period inclusive under the title of 'The French Stage in the Eighteenth Century' (1882).

Hawks, Francis Lister. An American Episcopal divine; born at New Berne, N. C., June 10, 1798; died in New York, Sept. 26, 1866. Originally a lawyer, he was the first president of the University of Louisiana. Besides legal and religious works he wrote: 'Contributions to the Ecclesiastical History of the United States' (1836–41); 'Narrative of Commodore Perry's Expedition' (1856); 'History of North Carolina' (1857–68); etc.

Hawthorne, Julian. An American novelist and journalist, son of Nathaniel; born in Boston, June 22, 1846. His boyhood was passed in Europe, his youth in New England. Upon leaving Harvard he studied civil engineering in Dresden, but took to authorship almost in spite of himself. His success was not rapid, but popular favor has been accorded to the novels 'Idolatry,' 'Fortune's Fool,' 'Sinfire,' 'Beatrix Randolph,' and 'Garth.' As a journalist he has traveled widely in prosecution of his work, his latest task being a study on the spot of the horrors of the Indian famine plague of 1896–97.

Hawthorne, Nathaniel. An American novelist and short-story writer; born in Salem, Mass., July 4, 1804; died at Plymouth, N. H., May 19, 1864. He graduated at Bowdoin in 1825; held a customs post at Boston from 1838 to 1841; was a member of the Brook Farm community, 1841; was surveyor of the port at Salem from 1846 to 1849, and consul at Liver-

pool from 1853 to 1857, returning to the United States in 1861. Among his works are: 'Fanshawe' (1826); 'Twice-Told Tales' (1837, a second series appearing some years later); 'Mosses from an Old Manse' (1846); 'The Scarlet Letter' (1850); 'The House of the Seven Gables' (1851); 'The Wonder Book' (1851); 'The Blithedale Romance' (1852); 'The Snow Image and Other Twice-Told Tales' (1852); 'Life of Franklin Pierce' (1852); 'Tanglewood Tales' (1853); 'The Marble Faun' (1860); 'Our Old Home' (1863); 'Pansie,' sometimes called 'The Dolliver Romance' (1864); 'Note Books' (1868–72); 'Septimius Felton' (1872); 'Tales of the White Hills' (1877); and 'Dr. Grimshawe's Secret' (1883), the last-named being left in a fragmentary condition.

Hay, John. An American poet and prose-writer; born in Salem, Ind., Oct. 8, 1838. He graduated from Brown University, and settled in Illinois as a lawyer, but went to Washington in 1861 as one of Lincoln's private secretaries, acting also as his aide-de-camp. He served under Gens. Hunter and Gillmore with the rank of major and assistant adjutant-general. He was subsequently in the United States diplomatic service, stationed at Paris, Vienna, Madrid, and London. In 1905 he was made Secretary of State. His literary reputation rests upon 'Pike County Ballads,' the best known of which are perhaps 'Little Breeches' and 'Jim Bludso'; 'Castilian Days,' a volume of travel; and 'Life of Abraham Lincoln' (with J. G. Nicolay). Died July 1, 1905.

Hay, John Charles Dalrymple, Sir. An English admiral and author; born Feb. 11, 1821. He was actively engaged in Borneo (1845–46), in operations against the Chinese pirates (1849), and in the Crimean War (1854–56), retiring with the rank of rear-admiral in 1870. He has been several times a member of Parliament in the Conservative interest. His works include: 'The Reward of Loyalty' (1862), being suggestions in regard to the American colonies; 'Remarks on the Loss of the "Captain"' (1871); 'Ashanti and the Gold Coast: A Sketch' (1871); 'Piracy in the Chinese Sea.'

Hay, Mary Cecil. A popular English novelist; born at Shrewsbury, 1840 (?); died 1886. Her home in later life was at East Preston, Sussex. Among her best works are: 'Hidden Perils' (1873); 'Old Myddleton's Money' (1874); 'The Arundel Motto' (1877); 'For Her Dear Sake' (1880).

Hayes, Augustus Allen. An American novelist; born in Boston, 1837; died in Paris, April 18, 1892. His home was in Brookline, Mass. He wrote: 'New Colorado and the Santa Fé Trail' (new ed. 1880); 'The Jesuit's Ring' (1887), a romance of Mt. Desert; 'The Denver Express'; etc.

Hayes, Henry. See **Kirk.**

Hayes, Isaac Israel. An American explorer and prose-writer; born in Chester County, Pa., March 5, 1832; died in New York city, Dec. 17, 1881. Graduating in medicine at the University of Pennsylvania (1853), he joined Dr. Kane's expedition in search of Sir John Franklin. In 1860, as commander of the ship United States, he sailed for exploration of the open polar sea. His reputation was gained as explorer, author, lecturer, surgeon, and legislator. Among his writings are: 'The Open Polar Sea' (1867); 'The Land of Desolation' (1871).

Haygood, Atticus Green. An American Methodist divine, and religious and miscellaneous writer, born at Watkinsville, Ga., Nov. 19, 1839; died 1896. He became bishop in 1890. He wrote: 'The Monk and the Prince,' a study of Savonarola and Lorenzo de' Medici; 'Our Brother in Black' (1881); 'Pleas for Progress' (1889); etc.

Hayley, William. An English poet; born at Chichester, Oct. 29, 1745; died at Felpham, Nov. 12, 1820. He was the biographer of Cowper, who received his pension through Hayley's influence with Pitt. 'Essay on History' appeared in 1780; 'The Triumphs of Temper' in 1781; an 'Essay on Epic Poetry' in 1782; an 'Essay on Old Maids' in 1785; 'Essays on Sculpture' in 1800; and 'The Triumph of Music' in 1804. He wrote also a 'Life of Milton' (1796). Cowper and Gibbon commended his 'Essay on Epic Poetry.'

Hayne, Paul Hamilton. An American poet; born in Charleston, S. C., Jan. 1, 1830; died at Augusta, Ga., July 6, 1886. At first a lawyer, he turned to journalism, and in 1855 his maiden volume of verse appeared. 'Sonnets and Other Poems' followed it two years later, and then came 'Avolio, a Legend of the Island of Cos.' He served through the war, retired from the field in poverty, and wrote poetry. 'Legends and Lyrics'; 'The Mountain of Lovers'; 'The Wife of Brittany'; and other productions of this period, mark him easily first among Southern poets.

Haynes, Emory James. An American Methodist divine and novelist; born at Cabot, Vt., 1847. He has written: 'Fairest of Three' (1883), a tale of American life; 'Dollars and Duties' (1887); 'A Farmhouse Cobweb,' a Vermont novel; 'Are These Things So?' 'None Such.'

Hays, William Shakespeare. An American popular ballad and song writer; born in Kentucky, 1837. His home is in Louisville, Ky. One of his best-known songs is 'Norah O'Neill.' He has written 'Poems and Songs.' Died 1907.

Hayter, Henry Heylyn. An English statistician and author; born at Eden Vale, Wiltshire, October 1821. He emigrated to Victoria, Australia, in 1852, in 1857 joined the department of the Registrar-General, and in 1874 was made government statist. He soon after originated the well-known Victorian Year-Book, which he still edits. His publications include: 'Notes of a Tour in New Zealand'; 'Notes on the Colony of Victoria' (1875); 'School History of Victoria'; 'My Christmas Adventure, Carboona, and Other Poems' (1887); besides scientific papers. Died at Melbourne, Australia, Mar. 23, 1895.

Hayward, Abraham. An English essayist; born Nov. 22, 1801; died in London, Feb. 2, 1884. Educated as a lawyer, he became a contributor to the Edinburgh Review; also wrote regularly for the Quarterly Review. He translated Goethe's 'Faust' in 1883, and wrote 'Sketches of Eminent Statesmen and Writers' (1880).

Hazard, Samuel. An American writer of travels; born in Pennsylvania, 1834; died 1876. He was an officer in the United States army. He wrote: 'Cuba with Pen and Pencil' (1870); 'Santo Domingo Past and Present' (1873).

Hazeltine, Mayo Williamson. An American journalist; born at Belfast, Me., 1841. Originally a lawyer, he is now the well-known literary editor of the New York Sun. He has published: 'The American Woman in Europe'; 'British and American Education'; 'Chats about Books'; etc.

Hazlitt, William. An English critic and prose-writer; born in Maidstone, Kent, April 10, 1778; died at London, Sept. 18, 1830. He was at first a painter. His characteristic work is interesting but bizarre, like himself. 'Characters of Shakespeare's Plays'; 'Lectures on English Poets'; 'The Spirit of the Age'; and other collected volumes of his essays, are still widely read.

Hazlitt, William Carew. An English compiler and author, son of William; born Aug. 22, 1834. He was a lawyer, but did not follow his profession, and has either written or edited a large body of literature on archæological and popular subjects. He is the author of 'The History of the Venetian Republic' (4 vols., 1860), and is the editor of the works of Henry Constable, Richard Lovelace, Robert Herrick, William Hazlitt, Charles Lamb, and others; 'Old English Jest-Books' (1864); 'Remains of the Early Popular Poetry of England' (1864–66); 'Bibliographical Collections and Notes' (1876-82). 'Venetian Republic: Rise, Growth, Fall' (1900).

Head, Barclay Vincent. An English numismatist; born at Ipswich, England, in 1844. He entered the British Museum in 1864, became Assistant Keeper of the Coin Department in 1871, and Keeper in 1893. He has made a special study of ancient Greek coinage, and was the first to methodize the science of Greek numismatics by introducing a chronological system of classification. His works include: 'History of the Coinage of Syracuse' (1874); 'Guide to the Principal Gold and Silver Coins of the Ancients' (1881), both crowned by the French Institute; 'Historia Numorum' (1887), a complete illustrated historical manual of the whole science of Greek numismatics.

Headley, Joel Tyler. An American prose-writer; born in Walton, N.Y., Dec. 30, 1813; died at Newburgh, Jan. 16, 1897. Graduating from Union College in 1846, he became assistant editor of the New York Tribune. His writings had great currency in their day, and include: 'Napoleon and his Marshals' (1846); 'Washington and his Generals' (1847); 'Grant and Sherman, their Campaigns and Generals' (1865); and 'The Great Rebellion' (1864).

Headley, Phineas Camp. An American Congregational divine and miscellaneous writer, brother of Joel T.; born at Walton, N. Y., June 24, 1819. He has written: 'Women of the Bible' (1850); 'Lives' of Josephine (1850), Kossuth (1852), Lafayette (1855), Mary Queen of Scots (1856), etc.; a series of 'Heroes of the Rebellion' (Grant, Ericsson, Farragut, Sherman, etc.: (1864–65); 'Court and Camp of David' (1868). Died at Lexington, Mass., Jan. 5, 1903.

Hearn, Lafcadio (hḗrn). An American journalist and miscellaneous writer; born of an English father and a Greek mother, at Santa Maura, Ionian Islands, June 27, 1850. He was educated in England and France, and has since resided in this country and in Japan. He has written: 'Some Chinese Ghosts' (1887), six stories exquisitely told; 'Two Years in the French West Indies' (1890); 'Youma' (1890), the story of a West-Indian slave; 'Glimpses of Unfamiliar Japan,' and several other books on Japan, including 'Kokovo; Hints and Echoes of Japanese Inner Life'; 'Gleanings in Buddha Fields,' etc. Died Tokio, Sept. 26, 1904.

Heath, Francis George. An English botanist; born at Totnes, Devonshire, Jan. 15, 1843. He is a surveyor in the customs department, and has supported movements for the extension of open spaces, chiefly in and around London. His works on agricultural subjects include: 'The Romance of Peasant Life' (1872); 'The English Peasantry' (1874); 'The Fern World' (1877); 'Sylvan Spring' (1880); 'My Garden Wild' (1881); 'More about Ferns' (1903).

Heaton, John Henniker. An English journalist and publicist; born at Rochester, May 18, 1848. At the age of sixteen he emigrated to Australia, became connected with the press, and was prominent in all public and philanthropic works in the Australasian colonies. As M. P. for Canterbury, England, he introduced a proposal for a universal international penny postage system. His chief works are: 'The Australian Dictionary of Dates and Men of the Time,' a standard work of reference on Australia; 'The Manners, Customs, Traditions, and Annihilation of the Aborigines of Australia'; 'A Short Account of a Canonization at Rome.'

Hebbel, Friedrich (heb'vel). A German dramatist of the first rank; born in Wesselburen, Holstein, March 18, 1813; died at Vienna, Dec. 13, 1863. A poor but precocious peasant lad, his youthful poems brought him patrons, and education in philosophy and history at Heidelberg. In 1839 appeared his first tragedy, 'Judith,' and his recognition was instantaneous; a volume of short poems in 1842 widened his reputation; an allowance from the Duke of Holstein enabled him to travel. In 1844 the tragedy 'Mary Magdalen' appeared at Paris. He married a celebrated actress, settled in Vienna, and produced 'Herod and Mariamne'; 'Julia'; and other plays. These display great versatility and exhaustless fertility, but are too terrific to be pleasing. Recognizing this himself, he essayed a gentler mood in 'Michael Angelo,' 'Agnes Bernauer,' and others. In the Nibelungen trilogy and in 'Demetrius' he has produced what many consider his masterpieces.

Hebel, Johann Peter (hā'bel). A German dialect poet; born in Basle, Switzerland, May 11, 1760; died at Schwetzingen, Sept. 22, 1826. Educated for the ministry, he held various pastorates and rectorships; and devoted his leisure to poetry, his subjects drawn from the dialect and folk-lore of his parishioners. His 'Alemannische Gedichte,' "for friends of rural life and manners," published in 1803, has attained wide celebrity. This and other poetry owed its vogue to exquisite appreciation of nature, pleasing revelations of rustic simplicity, and vivid realism.

Heber, Reginald. A British hymn-writer and clergyman; born in Cheshire, April 21, 1783; died at Trichinopoly, India, April 3, 1826. Graduating at Oxford with honors, he became prominent as prebendary of St. Asaph, 1812; preacher of Lincoln's Inn, 1822; and Bishop of Calcutta, 1822. The most popular of his hymns, 'From Greenland's Icy Mountains,' appeared in 1819; and his sermon on 'The Personality and Office of the Christian Comforter' also brought him fame. He wrote 'A Journey through India from Calcutta to Bombay.'

Hecker, Isaac Thomas. A distinguished American Roman Catholic clergyman; born in New York, Dec. 18, 1819; died there, Dec. 22, 1888. In early life he was a member of the Brook Farm community. He founded the order of the Paulists (1858), becoming their superior; and established the Catholic World (1865), editing it till he died. He wrote 'Questions of the Soul' (1855); 'The Church and the Age' (1888); etc.

Hector, Annie. See **Alexander, Mrs.**

Hedberg, Frans Theodor (hed'bèrg). A Swedish dramatic poet; born in Stockholm, March 2, 1828. He began life in a store, then turned to wig-making, and at last drifted to the stage. 'The Wedding at Ulfasa,' published in 1865, a historical piece; and 'When You Have No Money,' a comedy brought out in 1854 and afterwards rewritten, are typical of his talent. He has produced many plays, besides writing a history of the Swedish stage.

Hédelin, François. See **Aubignac.**

Hedenstierna, Karl Joseph Alfred (hed'-en-shèr-nä). A Swedish humorist and prose-writer; born in Wedåsa, March 12, 1852. He writes sketches of native peasant life and humorous skits. 'All Kinds of People' is his most popular work.

Hedge, Frederick Henry. A distinguished American scholar and Unitarian divine; born at Cambridge, Mass., Dec. 12, 1805; died there, Aug. 21, 1890. He edited the Christian Examiner (1857-60), and was professor of German at Harvard University (1872-81). Deeply read in philosophy, ecclesiastical history, and German literature, he was a finished writer and a polished orator. Among his writings are: 'Reason in Religion' (1865); 'The Primeval World of Hebrew Tradition' (1870); 'Martin Luther and Other Essays' (1888); etc. His 'Prose Writers of Germany' (1848) is a standard work. He translated and wrote numerous hymns for the Unitarian Church, and introduced German scholarship and literature into this country.

Heemskerk, Johann van (hēmz'kerk). A Dutch poet and jurist; born 1597; died at The Hague, Feb. 27, 1656. He studied law at Leyden and Paris, under his kinsman Grotius. He held important government posts in Holland for years. His 'Batavian Arcadia' (1637) is his principal poetical work, but his love poems and elegies are much admired. His works on jurisprudence are valuable but superseded.

Heeren, Arnold Hermann Ludwig (hā'ren). A German historian of eminence; born near Bremen, Oct. 25, 1760; died in Göttingen, March 6, 1842. His fame rests upon 'Views on the Politics, Commerce, and Mercantile Conditions of the Ancient World' (4th ed. 1824-26), a work characteristic of his method, style, and province as a historian. Scarcely less noteworthy is 'History of the Study of Classical Literature since the Revival of Learning' (new ed. 1822); 'History of the States [Staat] of Antiquity' (5th ed. 1828); 'History of the European State-System' (5th ed. 1839). His 'Historical Works' (1821-26) comprise 15 volumes.

Hefner-Alteneck, Jacob Heinrich von (hef'-ner-äl'te-nek). A German writer on art; born at Aschaffenburg, May 20, 1811. He went through a complete course of artistic education, and then devoted his attention to the history of art, particularly of the Middle Ages. In 1868 he became Conservator General of the artistic monuments of Bavaria, and director of the Bavarian National Museum. His numerous works include: 'Costumes of the Christian Middle Ages' (1840-54); 'Works of Art and Furniture of the Middle Ages and Renaissance' (1848-55); 'Iron Work of the Middle Ages and Renaissance' (1861-86); 'Costumes, Works of Art, and Furniture' (1879-90). D. 1903.

Hegel, Georg Wilhelm Friedrich (hā'gel). An eminent German philosopher; born at Stuttgart, Aug. 27, 1770; died at Berlin, Nov. 14, 1831. Among his writings are: 'On the Difference between the Fichtean and Schellingian Systems' (1801); 'The Orbits of the Planets' (1801); 'Phenomenology of the Human Mind' (1807), the first part of his 'System of Science'; 'Science of Logic' (3 vols., 1812-16); 'Encyclopædia of the Philosophical Sciences' (1817); 'Principles of the Philosophy of Law, or the

Law of Nature and Political Science' (1821). His 'Complete Works' appeared in 18 volumes, 1832-42.

Hegner, Ulrich (heg'ner). A Swiss story-writer and humorist; born in Winterthur, Feb. 7, 1759; died there, Jan. 3, 1840. His reputation was made by 'The Whey Cure' (Die Molkenkur) and 'Susan's Nuptials.' 'Sally's Revolution Days' is an effective picture of conditions in Switzerland at the end of the last century.

Heiberg, Hermann (hī'berc). A German novelist; born in Schleswig, Nov. 17, 1840. He retired in 1870 from the publishing business left him by his father, to devote himself to letters and journalism. His numerous stories, novels, and essays have been widely read, particularly 'Talks with the Duchess of Seeland.' Other successful books include: 'Shoulder to Shoulder'; 'Blind Love'; 'The Golden Serpent'; 'Home'; 'The Black Marit.'

Heiberg, Johann Ludvig. An eminent Danish poet and critic, son of Peter Andreas; born in Copenhagen, Dec. 14, 1791; died at Bonderup, in the island of Seeland, Aug. 25, 1860. His first literary training was received from his father, whose widow became Baroness Gyllembourg-Ehrensvärd. His early attempts in literature were as an exponent of the philosophical system of Hegel. He then turned to playwriting: 'King Solomon and the Hatter' and 'April Fools' were extremely successful, the latter being still popular with Danish audiences. He is known as a sound critic and a graceful essayist. "He was long the undisputed lawgiver of the Danish Parnassus."

Heiberg, Peter Andreas. A Danish dramatic poet, satirist, and political writer; born in Vordingborg, Nov. 16, 1758; died at Paris April 30, 1841. His early political writings resulted in his banishment. He went to Paris and entered the service of Talleyrand, and obtained lucrative posts under the first French empire. His comedies, especially 'Heckingborn,' have been much admired, and successfully produced on the English, French, Danish, and German stage. He had a rare genius for social satire. His 'Life of a Dollar Bill' is a prose fancy.

Heidenstam, Werner von (hī'den-stäm). A Swedish poet and novelist; born at Olshammer, July 6, 1859. He is the originator of the movement in Sweden against extreme realism. He has made Oriental themes his specialty. His novel 'Endymion,' published in 1889, is very popular. 'Pilgrimages,' a collection of poems appearing in 1888, and 'Modern Barbarism' established his international reputation.

Heigel, Karl von (hī'gel). A German poet; born in Munich, March 25, 1835. His father's influence as an official of the Hoftheater introduced him to dramatic authorship. He attracted the attention of King Ludwig II. of Bavaria, for whom he wrote numerous plays, and by whom he was decorated. He has written, besides the plays, several volumes of verse

17

His dramas include 'Marfa,' which has been widely staged. His best-known poems are 'Walpurg,' a Bavarian legend, and his lyrics, which are technically perfect. 'The Way to Heaven,' 'The Theatrical Devil,' and 'The King's Secret,' are among his successful works of fiction.

Heije, Jan Pieter (hī′e). A Dutch poet and critic; born in Amsterdam, March 1, 1809; died there, Feb. 24, 1876. He was a prominent physician in Amsterdam when, with a friend, he founded in 1834 The Muses, as a national organ of the arts. He composed songs and rectified scores; his 'Songs of Childhood' and 'Book of Songs for the People' being two among many works that largely influenced popular melody. His poetry is strongly national. His prose, comprising essays and criticisms, is terse and vigorous.

Heimburg, Wilhelmine (hīm′börg), pseudonym of Bertha Behrens. A German storywriter; born at Thale, Sept. 7, 1850. Her principal works are: 'From the Life of my Old Friend' (1879); 'Lumpenmüller's Lisbeth' (1879); 'The Wendhusen Cloister' (1880); 'Her Only Brother' (2d ed. 1883); 'Crises of the Heart' (1888); 'Under the Linden' (1888), short stories; 'Forest Flowers' (5th ed. 1891), a collection of short stories; 'An Insignificant Woman' (1891); 'Miss Useless' (1893).

Heine, Heinrich (hī′ne). A German poet of the first rank; born at Düsseldorf, Dec. 13, 1799; died at Paris, Feb. 17, 1856. His chief works are: a volume of 'Poems' (1822); two tragedies, 'Almansor' and 'Radcliff' (1823); 'Pictures of Travel' (vols. 1 and 2, 1826–27; to which were added two volumes more, 1830–31); 'Book of Songs' (1827); 'History of Recent Polite Literature in Germany' (2 vols., 1833); 'The Salon' (4 vols., 1835–40); 'The Romantic School' (1836); 'Shakespeare's Maids and Matrons' (1839); 'New Poems' (1844); 'Germany: A Winter's Tale' (1844); 'The Romancers' (1851); 'Doctor Faust' (1851); 'Miscellaneous Writings' (3 vols., 1854). ('Complete Works,' 22 vols., 1861–66.)

Heinrich Julius (hīn′rich), **Duke of Brunswick.** A German dramatist and jurist; born Oct. 15, 1564; died at Prague, July 20, 1613. Contests with the city of Brunswick resulted in his repairing to the imperial court at Prague, where he officiated for a time in the royal privy council. His dramas, mostly written under the pseudonym "Hibaldeha," are palpably inspired by foreign models, English and Italian mainly. The tragedy of 'The Adulteress' is reminiscent of Shakespeare; his comedy 'The Nobleman' suggested Bürger's 'Emperor and Abbot.' 'Vincentius Ladislaus' is the counterpart of an older Italian play and of Plautus's 'Miles Gloriosus.'

Heinrich von Veldecke (hīn′rich fon vel′-de-ke). A German poet of the twelfth century. He celebrated in verse the jousts and tournaments of his day. His love songs are among the most exquisite that have survived from that period. His epic of 'Eneit' is a classic. It is not modeled after Virgil's 'Æneid,' but after the 'Roman d'Énéas,' attributed to Benoit de St. Maure. He practically originated the "minne" or love-song as it has come down to us. His principal work was completed about 1190.

Heinse, Wilhelm (hīn′ze). A German poet, essayist, and romance-writer; born in Langewiesen, Thuringia, Feb. 15, 1749; died at Aschaffenburg, June 22, 1803. His youth was oppressed with poverty. At Jena, where he finished his education, he met Wieland, whose influence over him was very great. A little book of poems brought out at this time commended him to "Father" Gleim, the poet, through whom he obtained good situations and the means wherewith to travel. In 1783 appeared his masterpiece, 'Ardinghello,' a powerful if somewhat Utopian romance of art and æsthetics. 'Hildegard von Hohenthal,' a romance, besides poetical and prose works based upon his classical and artistic studies, testify to his genius which, although great, was marred by mistaken points of view.

Heliodorus (hē-li-ō-dō′rus). A Greek romance-writer; born in Emesa, Phœnicia, about 346; died about 420 (?). He became bishop of Tricca, Thessaly, after what seems to have been a creditable clerical career, but at precisely what date he wrote his famous romance 'Æthiopica' is unknown. The circumstances surrounding the production and preservation of this book make it a unique work of fiction and its author worth remembering.

Heller, Louise R. An American miscellaneous writer; born in Covington, Ky., 1870. She is the author of 'André Chenier,' a memorial volume, and has translated 'Madame Sans Gêne.'

Heller, Robert (hel′er). A German historical novelist; born in Grossdrebnitz, Saxony, Nov. 24, 1812; died at Hamburg, May 7, 1871. He left the law for journalism, subsequently writing 'Busts from St. Paul's Church,' which established his reputation. 'Alhambra,' 'A New World,' and 'The Earthquake at Caracas' are distinguished by vividness, fluency of style, and historic accuracy.

Helmbold, Ludwig (helm′bōld). A German hymn-writer; born in Mühlhausen, Thuringia, Jan. 21, 1532; died there, April 12, 1598. He wrote sacred songs in Latin and German, the best in the latter tongue. Those beginning "Lord Jesus Christ, Thou prince of peace" and "I will not give God up" are most widely known.

Helmers, Jan Frederik (hel′mers). A Dutch poet and dramatist; born in Amsterdam, March 4, 1767; died there, Feb. 26, 1813. He left a mercantile career for the pursuit of letters. In 1789 he produced a tragedy, 'Dinomache,' founded upon Athenian history, following it with a poem, 'Socrates.' His best work was

Inspired by the reverses of his country growing out of the Napoleonic wars. When a Bonaparte ascended the Dutch throne, the poet's patriotism found expression in the 'Fragment of a Tragedy upon the Fall of Corinth.' His finest composition, 'The Dutch Nation,' is a poetical apotheosis of Holland.

Helper, Hilton Rowen. An American prose-writer; born near Mocksville, N. C., Dec. 27, 1829. In 1857 appeared the notable work 'The Impending Crisis of the South,' which the Republican party used as a campaign document, with great effect. 'The Three American Railway' was published in 1881, and was followed by 'Nojoque'; 'The Negroes in Negroland'; 'The Land of Gold'; 'Oddments of Andean Diplomacy'; etc.

Helps, Sir Arthur. A noted English essayist, historian, and miscellaneous writer; born at Streatham, Surrey, July 10, 1813; died in London, March 7, 1875. He was clerk of the privy council of England in 1860, and enjoyed the queen's special confidence. His works, written in a pure style, evince high moral purpose. Among the best of them are: 'Friends in Council' (a series, 1847-59); a collection of essays, 'Companions of my Solitude' (1851); 'Realmah' (1868); 'Spanish Conquest in America' (1855-61); etc. He wrote also several romances and dramas, one of the best of the former being 'Casimir Maremma' (1870).

Helvétius, Claude Adrien (äl-väs'yös"). A French philosopher; born in Paris, 1715; died there, Dec. 26, 1771. He was trained to finance, but the circle of the Encyclopedists drew him into philosophy. His 'On the Understanding,' and, some years later, 'Man: His Intellectual Faculties and His Training,' were celebrated at the time as strong philosophic works, but they are of importance in political history rather than in that of philosophy. He is, however, in sympathy with the new historical school of economics, and may have some revival of interest.

Hemans, Felicia Dorothea Browne. An English Irish poet; born (Browne) in Liverpool, Sept. 25, 1793; died at Redesdale, near Dublin, May 16, 1835. At the age of fourteen she published creditable poems in newspapers. Her highest note was reached in the collections: 'Domestic Affections'; 'Tales and Historic Scenes in Verse'; and 'Lays of Many Lands.' Other compositions are: 'Forest Sanctuary'; 'Songs of the Cid'; and 'The Siege of Valencia, the Last Constantine.'

Henderson, Isaac. An American journalist and novelist; born in Brooklyn, N. Y., 1850. He was part owner and publisher of the New York Evening Post (1872-81); since then he has resided in Europe. He has written two novels, 'The Prelate' (1886), and 'Agatha Page' (1888), the second of which has been dramatized; 'The Silent Battle,' etc.

Henderson, William James. An American journalist and miscellaneous writer; born in New Jersey, 1855; connected with the New York Times. He has written: 'Story of Music'; 'Preludes and Studies'; 'Sea Yarns for Boys'; 'Afloat with the Flag'; 'The Art of the Singer.'

Henley, William Ernest. An English poet, born Gloucester, Eng., Aug. 23, 1849. He was variously engaged in journalism, play-writing and magazine work, but appeared more prominently as a poet. His 'Book of Verses,' followed by 'The Song of the Sword,' shows his poetic genius; his note is strongly modern, and in sympathy with the younger school of British poets. Died at Woking, Eng., July 12, 1903.

Henne-am-Rhyn, Otto (hen'ne äm-rin"). A Swiss historian; born in St. Gall, Aug. 26, 1828. His 'Book of Mysteries' and 'History of the Swiss People' are widely known. He is a graphic and voluminous exponent of Freemasonry and ancient religious rites and ceremonies.

Hennequin, Alfred (en'kañ). A French dramatist; born in Liège, Jan. 13, 1842; died at Épinay, Aug. 7, 1887. 'The Veauradieux Trial' and 'The Pink Dominoes' are his most popular comedies. 'Papa's Wife' was also successfully staged.

Henningsen, Charles Frederick. A Swedish-American soldier, poet, novelist, and miscellaneous writer; born of Swedish parentage in England, 1815; died 1877. He served in the Carlist army in Spain in 1834; in the Russian army in Circassia; took part in the Hungarian revolution of 1848; was with William Walker in Nicaragua, and became a Confederate brigadier-general in our Civil War. He wrote 'Last of the Sophis' (1831), a poem; 'Campaign with Zumalacarregui' (2 vols., 1836); the two novels 'The White Slave' (1845) and 'Sixty Years Hence' (1847); 'Personal Recollections of Nicaragua'; etc.

Henry, Caleb Sprague. An American clergyman and philosophical and miscellaneous writer; born at Rutland, Mass., Aug. 2, 1804; died at Newburg, N. Y., March 9, 1884. He was professor in the University of New York 1838-52. He translated Guizot's 'History of Civilization,' etc., and wrote 'About Men and Things' (1873); 'Satan as a Moral Philosopher' (1877); 'The Endless Future of the Human Race' (1879); and others.

Henry, Patrick. An eminent American orator and public man; born at Studley, Va., May 29, 1736; died at Red Hill, Va., June 6, 1799. His literary fame rests upon his speeches, even the meagre reports of which show the fire and substance of a great orator. He would be a recreant American schoolboy indeed who has not declaimed "But as for me, give me liberty or give me death;" "If this be treason, make the most of it;" "I repeat it, sir, let it come!" His speeches and correspondence may be seen in the 'Life' by William Wirt Henry (3 vols., 1891), the third volume of which is devoted exclusively to them.

Hensel, Luise (hen'sel). A German religious poet; born in Linum, Brandenburg, March 30, 1798; died at Paderborn, Dec. 18, 1876. "I am weary and go to rest" is not only one of the best of her poems, but one of the best pieces of religious verse in the German language. Her poetry has been collected into a volume of 'Songs.'

Hensler, Karl Friedrich (hens'ler). A Swiss-Austrian dramatist; born in Schaffhausen, 1761; died at Vienna, Nov. 23, 1825. Of his countless plays, 'The Little Danube Woman' is best known.

Henty, George Alfred. A popular English novelist and writer for boys; born at Trumpington, Cambridgeshire, Dec. 8, 1832. He edited Union Jack, a journal for boys, and had been war correspondent of the London Standard in various quarters of the globe. A voluminous writer, among his best works are: 'The Young Franc-Tireurs' (1871); 'Winning his Spurs' (1882); 'Facing Death' (1882); 'The Lion of St. Mark's' (1888); and many others. Died at Weymouth, Nov. 16, 1902.

Hentz, Mrs. Caroline Lee (Whiting). An American writer of popular romances; born at Lancaster, Mass., 1800; died at Marianna, Fla., Feb. 11, 1856. Among her works may be named: 'Aunt Patty's Scrap-Bag' (1846); 'The Mob Cap' (1848); 'The Planter's Northern Bride' (1854); etc.

Henzen, Karl Georg Wilhelm (henz'en). A German dramatist; born in Bremen, Nov. 30, 1850. 'Ossian' and 'Ulrich von Hutten' are typical among his dramas. He has employed the pseudonym "Fritz von Sakken."

Hepworth, George Hughes. A prominent American clergyman and journalist; born at Boston, Feb. 4, 1833; died in New York city, June 7, 1902. He was first a Unitarian, afterward a Presbyterian, minister, and finally took an editorial position on the New York Herald. He published: The Whip, Hoe, and Sword' (1864); 'The Criminal the Crime, the Penalty' (1865); Starboard and Port' (1876); a book entitled '! ! ! !'; 'Rocks and Shoals'; 'Brown Studies'; 'Hiram Golf's Religion'; 'They Met in Heaven'; etc.

Heraclitus (her-a-kli'tus). A Greek philosopher; born in Ephesus, about 535 B. C.; died about 475 B. C. His system has been summed up in his own favorite words: "All things flow." By this he is said, according to modern critics, to convey the idea that the law of being is one of perpetual change.

Heraud, John Abraham (her-o'). An English novelist, dramatist, and poet; born in London, July 5, 1799; died there, April 20, 1887. At nineteen he began writing for English periodicals. His first poem was a versified chronicle, 'The Legend of St. Loy.' His eccentric genius evolved 'The Descent Into Hell' in 1830, followed by 'The Judgement of the Flood.' His dramas are somewhat impressive,

notably 'Videna,' and 'Wife or No Wife.' He wrote some good biographies, including a work on Savonarola, and is the author of 'A Study of Shakespeare.' Two romances, 'Uxinal,' and 'Macée de Leodepart,' the latter historic, have gone to third editions.

Herbert, Edward. Lord Herbert of Cherbury. A famous English philosopher, historian, soldier, and diplomatist; born at Eyton, Shropshire, 1583; died in London, Aug. 20, 1648. His philosophy was somewhat mystical. His chief work was 'De Veritate' (On Truth: 1624).

Herbert, George. An English poet; born in Montgomery Castle, Montgomeryshire, April 3, 1593; died at Bemerton, Wiltshire, in 1633. He was of high birth and breeding and profound learning. His genial saintliness is reflected in his devotional poetry. His poem 'Sweet Day, So Cool, So Calm, So Bright' is probably best known and most often quoted. *

Herbert, Henry William. ["Frank Forester."] An American miscellaneous writer; born in London, England, April 7, 1807; died in New York city, May 17, 1858. He graduated from Oxford, and came to this country in 1830, rising to eminence as a writer and scholar of decided versatility. His works include: 'Cromwell'; 'Marmaduke Nyvil'; 'The Puritans of New England'; 'The Fronde'; 'Sherwood Forest'; and other historical novels. His histories comprise 'Captains of the Old World'; 'Cavaliers of England'; 'Captains of the Great Roman Republic'; etc. Over the pseudonym "Frank Forester" he published: 'Field Sports of the United States and British Provinces'; Frank Forester and his Friends'; 'Manual for Young Sportsmen'; etc.

Herculano de Carvalho e Araujo, Alessandro (er-kö-lä'nö de kär-väl'yö ē ä-rou'zhö). A Portuguese poet and scholar; born in Lisbon, March 28, 1810; died near Santarem, Sept. 12, 1877. He early distinguished himself as a political reformer, editor, and poet of reform. He also wrote valuable histories and historical novels. 'The Prophet's Voice' is the best of his poems. 'Eurico' is a strongly original historical novel. The 'History of Portugal' and 'The Origin and Development of the Inquisition in Portugal' are his best efforts in history.

Herder, Johann Gottfried von (her'der). A German philosopher and historian of literature; born at Mohrungen, Aug. 25, 1744; died at Weimar, Dec. 18, 1803. He wrote: 'Fragments on Recent German Literature' (1767); 'Voices of Nations in Song' (1778), translations and imitations of popular songs from several European languages; 'The Cid'; 'Spirit of Hebrew Poetry' (1872-83); 'Ideas for a Philosophy of the History of Mankind' (4 vols., 1784-91), his greatest work. His 'Complete Works' were published in 45 volumes, 1805-20.

Hérédia, José Maria de (ä-rā'Dē-ä). A French poet; born in Fortuna-Cafayere, near

Santiago de Cuba, Nov. 22, 1842. He went to France in boyhood to study art, but preferred belles-lettres. He early attracted notice by the originality and charm of his essays in Parisian periodicals, and his sonnets ' Trophies ' made him famous. In 1894 he was elected to the French Academy. Died Oct., 1905.

Herloszsohn, Karl (her'lǫs-ōn). A German novelist; born in Prague, Sept. 1, 1804; died at Leipzig, Dec. 10, 1849. He plunged into story-writing at an early age, founding also a periodical, The Comet, that continued from 1830 to 1848. His numerous novels show rich fancy, and sustain the interest well, but are marred by hasty execution. The best among them are: ' The Venetians '; ' Wallenstein's First Love '; and ' Christmas Tales.' Financial reverses overtook him, his paper suspended, and he died at a comparatively early age, in a public hospital, poor and friendless.

Herman, Henry. An English novelist and playwright; born in Alsace in 1832; died in London, Sept. 24, 1894. He was collaborator with Henry Arthur Jones in the popular melodrama ' The Silver King ' (1882), and with W. G. Wills wrote ' Claudian,' a classic drama, both of which were features of Wilson Barrett's repertoire for many seasons. His other plays include: ' Jeanne Dubarry ' (1875), and ' Slight Mistakes ' (1876). As a writer of fiction he will be best remembered for 'A Leading Lady,' ' Hearts of Gold and Hearts of Steel,' and other stories; and ' One Traveler Returns ' and ' He Fell Among Thieves,' written with D. C. Murray.

Hermann, Nikolaus (her'man). A churchsong writer; born about 1480; died at Joachimsthal, Bohemia (?), May 3, 1561. His brief but numerous songs are mainly of a liturgical character.

Herndon, William Henry. An American lawyer and biographer; born at Greensburg, Ky., Dec. 28, 1818; died near Springfield, Ill., March 18, 1891. In 1843 he formed a law partnership with Abraham Lincoln, which continued formally till the latter's death. He wrote the well-known ' Life of Abraham Lincoln ' (1889).

Herodianus (he-rō-di-ā'-nus). A Greek historian, who lived in the last part of the second and the first half of the third century A. D. He wrote a history of Rome from the death of Marcus Aurelius (180 A. D.) to the accession of Gordianus III. (238 A. D.), which is of special value for the reigns of the emperors subsequent to Alexander Severus. Although written in a rather declamatory style, it is distinguished for candor and independence of view.

Herodotus (he-rod'o-tus). « The Father of History »; born at Halicarnassus, in Caria, about 500 B. C.; died at Thurii, in Magna Græcia, between B.C. 428 and B.C. 426. He wrote his ' Exposition of History ' in nine books in the Ionic dialect, naming them after the nine Muses.

Herpin, Luce (är-pan). See **Perey**.

Herrera, Fernando de (er-rā'rä). A Spanish poet; born in Seville about 1534; died in 1597. On his ordination to the priesthood he devoted his leisure to the composition of a series of exquisite lyrics, which have earned for him the title of « the divine.» His grace and sonorousness are marred occasionally by an excessive exactness of statement, leading to meaningless repetition. Among his more serious poems are those on the battle of Lepanto and the fall of the Portuguese King Sebastian. His first volume was published under his immediate supervision, comprising a selection entitled, ' Some Works in Verse,' dated at Seville, 1582. This was followed some years later by another collection of ' Verses.' He wrote a ' History of the Cyprus War and the Battle of Lepanto ' and, as one authority declares, a ' Life and Death of Sir Thomas More.' He was the friend of Garcilaso de la Vega, and the founder of a school of poetry.

Herrick, Mrs. Christine (Terhune). An American writer on domestic economy; born at Newark, N. J., 1859. Her home is in New York. She has written: ' Housekeeping Made Easy ' (1888); ' The Little Dinner '; ' Liberal Living upon Narrow Means '; etc.

Herrick, Robert. An English poet; born in London in August 1591; died at Dean Prior, Devonshire, Oct. 15, 1674. He was a royalist clergyman forced from his living during the Civil War, but reinstated upon the restoration. Moody and merry by turns, the many ' Noble Numbers,' as well as the ' Hesperides,' produce in succession laughter and tears, but are sometimes open to the charge of mischievousness. Every revival of the forms of the lighter Muse brings the poet into remembrance.

Herrick, Robert. An American educator and novelist; born in Massachusetts, 1868. He is assistant professor at the University of Chicago. He has written ' The Man Who Wins,' a novel; ' The Real World '; ' The Common Lot.'

Herrick, Mrs. Sophia McIlvaine (Bledsoe). An American editor and microscopist, daughter of Albert T. Bledsoe; born at Gambier, O., 1837. She became editor of the Southern Review in 1877, and afterward joined the editorial staff of Scribner's Monthly. She has written ' Wonders of Plant Life under the Microscope ', ' The Earth in Past Ages '; ' A Century of Sonnets.'

Herrig, Hans (her'ig). A German poet, dramatist, and editor; born in Brunswick, Dec. 10, 1845; died at Weimar, May 4, 1892. He abandoned law for literature and journalism, joining the staff of the Deutsches Tageblatt when it started. His plays have been numerous and successful, notably ' Alexander the Great '; ' Jerusalem '; ' Nero '; and others serious in subject. His greatest success was with the « church play » arranged and written for the Luther Jubilee of 1883, and widely performed. His poetry includes both the light and serious, ' The Fat King ' among the former and 'The Swine' among the latter. His prose works include essays on Schopenhauer and upon the development of the stage.

Herron, George Davis. A prominent American Congregational clergyman, writer, and lecturer; born in Indiana, 1862. He is professor of Applied Christianity in Iowa College. He has published several works on Christian Socialism, among them : 'The Christian Society'; 'The Message of Jesus to Men of Wealth' ; ' The Christian State'; 'The Day of Judgment.'

Herschel, John Frederick William, Sir (hèr'shel). An English astronomer and author, son of Sir F. W. Herschel; born at Slough, March 7, 1792; died at Collingwood, May 11, 1871. He continued the work of his father on double stars and nebulæ, and in 1833 went to the Cape of Good Hope for astronomical investigations, which occupied four years, and are embodied in his ' Results of Observations at the Cape of Good Hope' (1847). Besides several encyclopædia articles, his works include : ' On the Study of Natural Philosophy' (1830); 'Outlines of Astronomy' (1849); 'A Manual of Scientific Inquiry' (1849); 'Physical Geography' (1871); 'Popular Lectures on Scientific Subjects' (new ed. 1880).

Hertz, Henrik (herts). A Danish poet and dramatist ; born in Copenhagen, Aug. 25, 1798; died there, Feb. 25, 1870. He abandoned law for literature. 'Letters of a Ghost,' a poetical satire purporting to be written by the spirit of Jens Baggesen, made him famous. He followed this with 'Nature and Art'; 'Four Letters of Knut the Seelander,' a good piece of word-painting ; 'Tyrfing,' a poem; and miscellanies. As a playwright he has won a permanent place with 'The Savings Bank,' a comedy; 'Svend Dyring's House,' a tragedy; and 'The Daughter of King René,' his masterpiece.

Hertz, Wilhelm. A German poet; born in Stuttgart, Sept. 24, 1835. Upon leaving college he devoted himself to agricultural pursuits, after which he studied at Tübingen. He was encouraged to write by a Munich literary circle including Geibel, Heyse, Bodenstedt, and others. In 1859 appeared his 'Poems,' remarkable for delicate sentiment, warmth of feeling, and perfect technique. Among his best-known productions are: 'Launcelot and Guinevere'; 'Henry of Suabia'; and especially 'Tristan and Isolde.' He was professor of literature at the Technological school in Munich, and a lecturer and critic of high authority. Died 1902.

Hervilly, Ernest d' (är-vi-yē). A French journalist, humorist, and dramatist; born in Paris, May 26, 1839. From railroad operative he became editorial and sketch writer, contributing to the Rappel in 1872 under the pseudonym "Le Passant." A few years later appeared volumes of verse, 'The Kisses' and 'The Harem,' which won general admiration. Humorous sketches—'Tales for Great Personages,' 'Pastime Stories,' 'The Weapons of Women,' and others—extended his fame throughout France ; and his plays, 'The True

Invalid'; 'Bigondis' and 'Midas' especially, have been very successful in Paris.

Herwegh, Georg (her'veg). An eminent German poet; born in Stuttgart, May 31, 1817; died at Baden-Baden, April 7, 1875. His early theological studies were abandoned for poetry. The 'Lyrics of a Live Man' appeared in 1841. His poems, these particularly, display spontaneity and a deep love of liberty; they speedily became popular, even winning a personal tribute from Frederick William IV. He had to flee from Prussia soon afterwards, owing to his letter of protest to the king against his prohibition of a periodical which the poet contemplated founding. He retired to Switzerland, married a wealthy banker's daughter, and plunged into the movement of 1848. He was often pursued by the authorities, and once nearly lost his life while leading a riot, being saved by his wife's daring. He spent his riper years in retirement. His poems are the finest expression in verse of the movement to which he devoted his energies.

Herzen, Alexander (hert'sen). A Russian journalist, novelist, and political writer; born in Moscow, March 25, 1812; died in Paris, Jan. 21, 1870. For his outspoken liberal ideas he was imprisoned, and subsequently banished to Viatka and Vladimir. In 1851 he settled in London and started the weekly paper Kólokol (The Alarm Bell), exposing countless abuses and State secrets of the Russian Government. Copies of the papers were smuggled into Russia, and had a large circulation there. Among his publications (many of which are written in English, French, and German) are : 'Dilettanteism in Science' (1842); 'The Development of Revolutionary Ideas in Russia' (1851); 'Imprisonment and Exile.' In fiction, under the pseudonym of "Iskandar," he issued : 'Doctor Krupov' (1847); 'Whose Fault Is It?' (1847); 'Interrupted Tales' (1854).

Hesekiel, Georg Ludwig (he-zā'kē-el). A German poet and story-writer; born in Halle, Aug. 12, 1819; died at Berlin, Feb. 26, 1874. He was intended for the church, but preferred literature and political journalism. His early prose and poetry were of a trifling and fleeting character, but his 'Prussian Songs' in 1846 made him famous. Then followed numerous political novels, notably 'Before Jena'; 'The Calm Before the Storm'; and his masterpiece, 'Under the Iron Tooth.' Other poems are 'New Songs,' and several volumes devoted to patriotic themes. His 'Prince Bismarck' is a popular and important biographical study.

Hesekiel, Ludovika. A German novelist, daughter of George Ludwig; born in Altenburg, July 3, 1847; died at Neustadt, April 6, 1889. Her forte was historical-romance composition; and she wrote a sequel to one of her father's books, under the title 'From Brandenburg to Bismarck.' Her most successful productions are 'God with Us,' and a collection of short stories. Her study of 'Elizabeth Louise, Queen of Prussia,' is brilliant and valuable.

Hesiod (hē'si-ǫd). A great Greek poet; born at Ascra in Bœotia; he lived in the eighth century B.C. Among his writings which are still extant are the 'Theogony,' or origin of the gods; 'Works and Days,' in which are contained precepts for the conduct of life, education, etc., with counsels regarding agriculture. Of his other works only fragments remain; among which is a piece on 'The Shield of Hercules,' which is complete in itself, but the authenticity of which is doubted.

Hettner, Hermann Theodor (het'ner). A German historian; born in Leisersdorf, March 2, 1821; died at Dresden, May 29, 1882. He studied at Heidelberg, Berlin, and Halle, and filled professorships at Jena and elsewhere. His masterpiece, published in 1856, 'History of Eighteenth-Century Literature,' gave him high rank as a philosophical historian. Previously he had made valuable studies on the art of the ancients. He traveled extensively, especially in Greece and Italy. His writings are varied, but all relate to the historical aspects of literature, painting, and sculpture, ancient and modern.

Hetzel, Pierre Jules (het'zel). See **Stahl.**

Heuff, Az Johan Adrian (hêf). A Dutch prose-writer; born in Avezath, March 5, 1843. He abandoned civil engineering for humorous sketch-writing. Under the pseudonym of «J. Huf van Buren» he wrote a number of historical romances, among them 'Hertog Adolf'; a Dutch adaptation of the 'Pseudolus' of Plautus; and an original comedy entitled 'Oom Frederik,' and other dramatic pieces. Under the pen-name «Cosinus» he produced a humorous novel, 'Kippeveer,' wherein certain leaders of the clerical party are ridiculed. He is most successful in satire and caricature.

Heun, Karl. See **Clauren.**

Hevesi, Ludwig (hev'esh-i). A German-Hungarian story-writer and humorist; born in Heves, Hungary, Dec. 20, 1843. He studied medicine at Vienna, and afterwards entered a business office; then in 1866 he founded the popular comic sheet Borsszem Jankó, read by all classes in the Magyar country. He writes German and Hungarian with equal facility. His humor has found its happiest expression in 'Rainbows'; 'On the Sunny Side'; and above all 'Andreas Jelky,' a sketch of a journeyman tailor and his amusing adventures in the «four quarters of the world.»

Hewit, Augustus Francis. An American Roman Catholic priest and religious writer; *Pseud.*: Nathaniel Augustus; born at Fairfield, Conn., Nov. 19, 1820; died in New York city, July 3, 1897. He had a varied experience, as law student, as Congregational minister, Episcopal deacon, and Roman Catholic priest; joining, under the name of Augustine Francis, the Paulist order founded by Father Hecker, and becoming professor and superior in the Paulist Seminary, New York. He wrote 'Life of Princess Borghese' (1856);

'Problems of the Age' (1868); 'Light in Darkness' (1871); etc.

Hewitt, John Hill. An American ballad and miscellaneous writer; born in New York 1801; died 1890. Engaging in literary work at Baltimore in 1825, he is said to have been a «rival of Poe.» His best-known work is the ballad 'The Minstrel's Return from the War.' He wrote also: 'The Governess,' a comedy; 'Washington,' a play; 'Shadows on the Wall,' a volume of reminiscences; etc.

Hewitt, Mrs. Mary. See **Stebbins.**

Hey, Wilhelm (hi). A German fable-writer; born in Leina near Gotha, March 26, 1789; died at Ichtershausen, May 19, 1854. He was pastor at Töttelstädt and court chaplain at Gotha. His 'Fables for Children,' published in 1833, had an enormous circulation from their first appearance. He wrote a rhyming 'Life of Jesus.'

Heyden, Friedrich August von (hī'den). A German poet, story-writer, and dramatist; born in Nerfken, East Prussia, Sept. 3, 1789; died at Breslau, Nov. 5, 1851. He gave up law and entered the army. Of distinguished family, he was employed in official posts at court in 1843, but fell into disfavor through reluctance to act as a literary censor. His verse is graceful and pleasing. His reputation was made with 'Reginald,' and 'A Woman's Word.' 'The Intriguers' was a highly successful novel. As a dramatist he is not important.

Heyduk, Adolf (hī'dùk). A Czech poet; born in Richenburg, June 7, 1835. He studied in Prague and traveled through Italy and Germany; is now a professor at Pisek. His earlier poetry, beginning in 1859, was of a light order, but his volume 'Cymbal and Violin' established his reputation. An idyl of life among his countrymen, 'Grandfather's Legacy,' and a powerful study in realism, 'The Wood-Cutter,' are extremely popular. 'Cymbal and Fiddle' is considered his best work.

Heyse, Johann Ludwig Paul (hī'za). A German poet and novelist; born in Berlin, March 15, 1830. At twenty-four he became noted for the purity and elegance of his elegiac verses, and the succeeding fertile years have brought him high and enduring renown. 'Francesca da Rimini,' a tragedy; 'The Sabines,' a play that under severe tests won the prize offered by the King of Bavaria in 1857; 'The Brothers'; 'Ourika,' a tale; 'Rafael,' a legend and metrical study,— all poems,— and 'New Tales of Marianne,' a series of prose idyls, the dramas 'Meleager'; 'Hadrian'; 'Alcibiades'; 'Vamina Vamini'; 'Elizabeth Charlotte'; 'The Right of the Stronger' are among his numerous works.

Heywood, John. An English dramatist. His literary fame rests upon such productions as a 'A Mery Play between the Pardoner and the Frere, the Curate and Neybour

Pratte,' printed in 1533. He remained a Catholic, and upon Elizabeth's accession retired to private life.

Heywood, Thomas. An English dramatic poet; born in Lincolnshire (?) about 1575'; died in London (?), 1650 (?). Although he wrote all sorts of poetry and prose, for any who would pay him, his reputation rests upon his sparkling song and still more sparkling comedy. 'A Woman Killed with Kindness,' a play of contemporary middle-class manners; 'The Wise Woman of Hogsdon,' a comedy of low life; 'Love's Mistress,' a travesty introducing Apuleius and Midas; and the amusing 'Rape of Lucrece,' show his range.

Hibbard, George Abiah. An American short-story writer; born in New York State, 1858. His home is in Buffalo, N. Y. He has written: 'Iduna, and Other Stories,' 'Nowadays,' 'The Governor,' and other collections of short stories.

Hichens, Robert S. An English journalist and novelist; born in 1864. Although at the age of seventeen he wrote a novel which was actually published, he seems to have been most bent on a musical career; but he wearied of music, and turned to journalism. In 1893 he visited Egypt for his health, and while there conceived the idea which materialized in the 'Imaginative Man' (1895). 'The Green Carnation' (1894), however, epigrammatic and keenly satirical in tone, first brought him into public notice, and was followed by 'After To-morrow,' and 'New Love' (1895); 'The Folly of Eustace and Other Stories' (1896); 'Flames' (1897).

Hicks, Elias. A famous American Quaker reformer, founder of the sect known as "Hicksite" Quakers; born at Hempstead, L. I., March 19, 1748; died at Jericho, N. Y., 1830. In 1781 he began visiting the meetings and families both of Friends and of other denominations throughout the country, preaching greater consecration. He was a fearless and impressive exhorter. An early and determined foe of slavery, he secured the emancipation of many slaves. He was bred a carpenter, and paid his traveling expenses by working at his trade. His neighbors esteemed him so highly that they often called on him to act as umpire in settling their disputes. Neither he nor his followers ever recognized the name "Hicksite," given them in reproach. He wrote: 'Observations on Slavery' (1811); 'Doctrinal Epistle' (1824); 'Journal' (1828; 3d ed. 1832); etc.

Hiel, Emmanuel (hel). A Flemish poet; born in St. Gilles dez Termonde, Belgium, May 31, 1834. He is professor of rhetoric and music in the Industrial Institute at Brussels. He has been prominent in political reform movements, those of his poems which are not of a sentimental order relating mainly to such themes. His beautiful poem 'The Wind' won a prize, while 'Lucifer' and 'The Scheldt' rank high in popular esteem. His poems for children and one or two oratorios and dramatic compositions are especially notable. He died Aug. 27, 1899.

Higginson, Mary Thacher. ["Mrs. Potter."] An American author and poet, wife of T. W. Higginson; born in Machias, Me., Nov. 27, 1843. Her works are: 'Seashore and Prairies' (1876); 'Such as They Are' (1893), a volume of poems written in collaboration with her husband; 'The Playmate Hours' (1904).

Higginson, Mrs. Sarah Jane (Hatfield). An American writer of stories and sketches; born in Pennsylvania, 1840. Her home is in New York. She has written: 'A Princess of Java' (1887), a tale of the far east; 'Java, the Pearl of the East,' a book of travel; 'The Bedouin Girl.'

Higginson, Thomas Wentworth. A distinguished American essayist, poet, and novelist; born in Cambridge, Mass., Dec. 22, 1823. His interesting and varied career includes having been an active abolitionist, a Unitarian clergyman, and (most striking of all) colonel of the first negro regiment in the Civil War. Among his publications are: 'Out-Door Papers' (1863); 'Malbone, an Oldport Romance' (1869); 'Army Life in a Black Regiment' (1870); 'Atlantic Essays' (1871); 'Oldport Days' (1873); 'Young Folks' History of the United States' (1884); 'Life of Margaret Fuller' (1884); 'The Afternoon Landscape' (1890), a volume of poems. 'A Reader's History of American Literature' (1903).

Hildreth, Charles Lotin. An American novelist, author, and poet; born in New York city, Aug. 28, 1856; died there, Aug. 19, 1896. He served on the staff of the New York World and later on Belford's Magazine. Among his works are: 'Judith' (1876); 'The New Symphony and Other Stories' (1878); and the 'Masque of Death and Other Poems' (1889).

Hildreth, Richard. An American historian; born in Deerfield, Mass., June 22, 1807; died in Florence, Italy, July 11, 1865. He first became known as a miscellaneous prose-writer and political journalist. The 'History of the United States' is his greatest work, covering the period from the discovery of America to the end of President Monroe's first administration (6 vols., 1849–56). Among his other works are: 'Archy Moore,' an anti-slavery romance; 'History of Banks'; 'Theory of Morals'; 'Theory of Politics'; and 'Atrocious Judges as Tools of Tyrants,' compiled for political purposes from Lord Campbell's 'Lives of the Chief Justices.' He went to Italy in 1861 as United States consul.

Hiles, Henry. An English organist, composer, and author; born at Shrewsbury, Dec. 31, 1826. He is a lecturer on harmony and musical composition at the Owens College, Manchester, and professor of harmony at the Royal Manchester College of Music. He is the author of the standard theoretical works: 'The Harmony of Sounds' (1872); 'The Grammar of Music' (1879); 'Part-Writing, or Modern Counterpoint' (1884).

Hill, Mrs. Agnes Leonard (Scanland). An American novelist, writing under the pseudonym «Mollie Myrtle»; born at Louisville, Ky., 1842. She has written 'Myrtle Blossoms' (1863); 'Vanquished' (1866), a novel; 'Heights and Depths' (1871); 'The Cry of the Soul' (1907).

Hill, David Jayne. An American educator; born at Plainfield, N. J., 1850. He was made president of Rochester University, N. Y., in 1888. He has written biographies of 'Washington Irving' (1879) and 'William Cullen Bryant' (1879); 'Principles and Fallacies of Socialism' (1885); etc., besides text-books.

Hill, George. An American writer of verse; born at Guilford, Conn., 1796; died 1871. He held several government clerkships. He wrote: 'Ruins of Athens, and Other Poems'; 'Titania's Banquet, and Other Poems.'

Hill, George Canning. An American biographer and essayist; born in Connecticut, 1825. He has written 'Lives' of Capt. John Smith, Israel Putnam, Benedict Arnold, and Daniel Boone; 'Homespun, or Five-and-Twenty Years Ago, by Thomas Lackland' (pseudonym: 1867); 'Our Parish, or Pen-Paintings of Village Life' (187-).

Hill, Theophilus Hunter. An American writer of verse; born near Raleigh, N. C., 1836. He is a lawyer in Raleigh, and was once State librarian. He has written 'Hesper and Other Poems' (1861), distinguished as being the first book copyrighted by the Confederate government; 'Poems' (1869); 'Passion Flower and Other Poems' (1883); etc. Died 1901.

Hill, Thomas. A distinguished Unitarian clergyman and educator; born at New Brunswick, N. J., Jan. 7, 1818; died at Waltham, Mass., Nov. 2, 1891. He was president of Harvard College from 1862 to 1868. He wrote 'Geometry and Faith' (1849); 'Curvature' (1850); 'In the Woods and Elsewhere' (1888), a collection of poetry, etc., and several text-books.

Hillard, George Stillman. A distinguished American lawyer and miscellaneous writer; born at Machias, Me., Sept. 22, 1808; died at Boston, Jan. 21, 1879. As a Massachusetts legislator he was commended by Daniel Webster, and he was conspicuous as an orator. He published 'Six Months in Italy' (1853); 'Life of George Ticknor' (with Mrs. Ticknor); 'Life of George B. McClellan' (1864); also a series of school readers, and an edition of Spenser.

Hillebrand, Karl (hil'lĕ-bränt'). A German critic and historian; born at Giessen, Sept. 17, 1829; died in Florence, Oct. 19, 1884. For participation in the insurrection in Baden (1849) he was imprisoned, but escaped to France, where he graduated at the Sorbonne, and in 1863 became professor of foreign languages at Douai. On the outbreak of the Franco-Prussian War, he removed to Italy and passed the remainder of his life there. Among his valuable publications in French, German, Italian, and English, are: 'On Good Comedy' (1863); 'Contemporary Prussia' (1867); 'Italian Studies' (1868); 'Times, Peoples, and Men' (7 vols., 1875-85); two volumes of a 'History of France from the Accession of Louis Philippe to the Fall of Napoleon III.' (1877-79); 'Lectures on German Thought' (1880).

Hillern, Wilhelmine von (hil'ĕrn). A German novelist (daughter of Charlotte Birch-Pfeiffer); born in Munich, March 11, 1836. In early life she was an actress. In 1857 she married Baron von Hillern. Her novels began to appear in 1862, winning rapid fame. Since 1882 she has been a widow. 'Double Life'; 'A Physician to the Soul'; 'The Geyer-Wally'; and numerous other works of fiction have had a wide circulation. Her efforts as a dramatist have not endured, but one or two of her novels have been adapted for the stage.

Hillhouse, James Abraham. An American dramatic poet; born at New Haven, Conn., Sept. 26, 1789; died near there, Jan. 4, 1841. A merchant in New York, he retired from business in 1822. He wrote: 'The Judgment, a Vision' (1812); and the dramas 'Percy's Masque' (1820) and 'Hadad' (1825). His 'Dramas, Discourses, and other Pieces' appeared in 1839.

Hilliard, Henry Washington. An American soldier, diplomat, and lawyer; born at Fayetteville, N. C., Aug. 4, 1808; died at Atlanta, Ga., Dec. 17, 1892. He was brigadier-general in the Confederate army, chargé d'affaires in Belgium, and minister to Brazil. He wrote: 'De Vane, a Story of Plebeians and Patricians' (2d ed. 1886); 'Politics and Pen Pictures' (1892); and a volume of 'Speeches and Addresses.'

Hind, John Russell. An English astronomer; born in Nottingham, May 12, 1823; died in Twickenham, Dec. 23, 1895. He became a Fellow of the Astronomical Society in 1843, and received three medals from the Academy of Sciences at Paris for the discovery of asteroids. His most important works are: 'The Solar System' (1854); 'Astronomical Vocabulary' (1852), 'Comets' (1852); 'Illustrated London Astronomy' (1853).

Hindley, Charles. An English bookseller and journalist; died at Brighton, May 1893. He wrote several books, but is best known as the author of 'Mother Shipton's Prophecy.'

Hinton, James. A famous English surgeon and philosophical essayist; born at Reading, 1822; died 1875. He was noted as an aurist. He visited the United States in 1850. His great work 'The Mystery of Pain: a Book for the Sorrowful' appeared in 1866. Other notable productions were: 'Art of Thinking' (1879); 'Philosophy and Religion' (1881); etc.

Hippeau, Célestin (ē-pō'). A French educator and author; born at Niort, Deux-Sèvres, May 11, 1803; died in Paris, May 31, 1883. He filled different positions as a teacher and professor at Strasburg, Paris, Caen, etc., and was sent to England and the United States by the minister of public instruction to study their educational systems. His publications on educational and literary subjects include: 'Norman Writers of the Seventeenth Century'

(1857); 'History of the Government of Normandy' (9 vols., 1863-73); 'Public Instruction in the United States' (1869); 'Dictionary of the French Language in the Twelfth and Thirteenth Centuries' (1873).

Hippel, Theodor Gottlieb von (hip'pel). A German sociological and ethical writer, romancer, and jurisconsult; born in Gerdauen, East Prussia, Jan. 31, 1741; died at Königsberg, April 23, 1796. His great but singularly contradictory character is revealed in his many writings. His best-known work is on 'Marriage.' Other productions include: 'The Education of Woman'; 'The Civil Emancipation of Woman'; and 'Biographies in the Ascending Line, with Supplements A, B, C,' a peculiar piece of fiction in which a sardonic humor is combined with profound observation and knowledge of life. A powerful political satire, 'Carpenter I. and Frederick II., by John Henry Frederick Quincetree, Wood Carver, of Hanover. Printed at Solitude,' and other similar efforts, are characteristic exhibitions of his strange genius.

Hirst, Henry Beck. An American lawyer and writer of verse; born in Pennsylvania, 1813; died 1874. His home was in Philadelphia. He wrote 'Endymion, a Tale of Greece'; 'The Penance of Roland'; 'The Coming of the Mammoth, and Other Poems.' He also published a 'Poetical Dictionary.'

Hita, Gines Perez de (ē-tä'). A Spanish romantic historian of the sixteenth century, author of the celebrated 'History of the Civil Wars of Granada.' He was of Murcian origin, and fought bravely in the campaigns against the Moors 1568-70. His 'History' is the first historical romance produced by the Spaniards, and relates in picturesque and imaginative style, and with exquisite purity of language, the events leading up to the expulsion of the Moors from Spain. The narrative is interspersed with delightful legends and stories. The first portion appeared in 1588, the last in 1604.

Hitchcock, Edward. American geologist and author; born in Deerfield, Mass., May 24, 1793; died at Amherst, Mass., Feb. 27, 1864. In the beginning of his career he was pastor of a Congregational church in Conway, Mass. He was made president of Amherst College in 1845, but resigned in 1854, continuing his professorship there till his death. Amherst College owes to him the founding of its Museum of Natural History, and his writings were among the earliest to call attention in this country to the study of geology. His 'Religion of Geology and its Connected Sciences' marks a distinct epoch in scientific study in this country. He published also 'Reminiscences of Amherst College' in 1863.

Hitchcock, Ethan Allen. An American soldier and miscellaneous writer, grandson of the famous patriot Ethan Allen; born at Vergennes, Vt., May 18, 1798; died at Hancock, Ga., Aug. 5, 1870. A graduate of West Point,

he served in the Florida war, in the Mexican War, and in the Civil War. He wrote: 'The Doctrines of Swedenborg and Spinoza Identified' (1846); 'On the Sonnets of Shakespeare' (1865); 'On the Vita Nuova of Dante' (1866); etc.

Hitchcock, James Ripley Wellman. An American writer on art, etc.; born at Fitchburg, Mass., July 3, 1857; died in New York, March 7, 1901. He wrote: 'The Western Art Movement' (1885); 'A Study of George Genness' (1885); 'Madonnas by Old Masters' (1888), the text to photogravures; 'The Future of Etching'; 'Some American Painters in Water Colors'; 'Etching in America'; 'Notable Etchings by American Artists'; etc.

Hitchcock, Roswell Dwight. A distinguished American Congregational divine and theologian; born at East Machias, Me., Aug. 15, 1817; died at Somerset, Mass., June 16, 1887. He was long president of Union Theological Seminary. He wrote 'Analysis of the Bible' (1869); 'Socialism' (1879); 'Life of Edward Robinson'; 'Hymns and Songs for Social and Sabbath Worship'; 'Eternal Atonement' (with Francis Brown); etc.

Hittell, John Shertzer. An American journalist and writer; born at Jonestown, Pa., Dec. 25, 1825; died in San Francisco, ——, 1901. He wrote: 'Evidences against Christianity' (2d ed., 2 vols., 1857); 'Resources of California' (6th ed. 1874); 'A Brief History of Culture' (1875); etc.

Hittell, Theodore Henry. An American lawyer and historian, brother of John Shertzer; born in Pennsylvania, 1830. His home is in San Francisco. Besides valuable legal works, including 'General Laws of California 1850-64' (1868), commonly known as 'Hittell's Digest,' he has published a critical review of 'Goethe's Faust' (1872); the important 'History of California' (4 vols., 1885-97; 'Review of Goethe's Faust.'

Hlinka, Vojtech [Adalbert] (lēng'kä). A Czech story-writer; born in Nekrasin, near Neuhaus, Bohemia, April 17, 1817. He was a Catholic chaplain at Hrádek. For the past thirty years he has written stories and novels in profusion under the pseudonym of "Frantisek [Francis] Pravda," all of which deal with life among the Czechs, and are exceedingly popular with that people. The tales are of a moral nature, and while lacking high qualities of genius, merit notice as studies in a pleasing school of realism.

Hoadly, Benjamin. An English dramatist; born in London, Feb. 10, 1706; died at Chelsea, Aug. 10, 1757. He was educated at Cambridge. He settled in London and became a Fellow of the College of Physicians. Among his works are the 'Suspicious Husband' (1747), a comedy which was well received. He also wrote 'The Tatlers,' and assisted Hogarth in his 'Analysis of Beauty.'

Hobbes, John Oliver, pseudonym of Pearl (Richards) Craigie, an English novelist; born

1867. She has published: 'The Sinner's Comedy'; 'Some Emotions and a Moral'; 'A Study in Temptations'; 'A Bundle of Life'; 'The Harvest Moon'; etc. Died Aug. 13, 1906.

Hobbes, Thomas. An English philosopher; born in Malmesbury, April 5, 1588; died at Hardwick Hall, Derbyshire, Dec. 4, 1679. One of the greatest and most discriminating intellects employed on metaphysical and social analyses in any age, his thought has left deep traces on all related speculation since, even when adverse. Of his voluminous works, expository and controversial, carried on in the leisure of aristocratic patronage to extreme old age, the most vigorously living one to be constantly reckoned with is 'Leviathan,' dealing with the origins, functions, and possibilities of human society, conceived as an organism.

Hobhouse, John Cam, Lord Broughton. An English statesman and miscellaneous writer; born at Redland, near Bristol, June 27, 1786; died in London, June 3, 1869. He was Secretary of War in 1831, and Secretary of State for Ireland in 1833. He was one of Lord Byron's most intimate friends. He wrote: 'Historical Illustrations of the Fourth Canto of Childe Harold' (2d ed. 1818); 'Journey into Albania' (1813); 'Letters Written by an Englishman During the Last Reign of Napoleon' (1816); 'Essay on the Origin and Intention of Sacrifices'; 'A Defense of the People'; etc.

Hodell, Frans Oscar Leonard (ho'del). A popular Swedish dramatist; born in Stockholm, Aug. 13, 1840; died May 24, 1890. For ten years he was an actor. His original and adapted plays number nearly a hundred. Among the most popular were: 'Andersson, Petersson, and Lundström' (1866); 'The Factory Girl' (1868); 'The Seamstresses' (1868); 'Three Pairs of Shoes' (1881). From 1870 until his death he was editor of the Sunday Puck, a comic paper.

Hoefer, Edmund (hö'fer). A German novelist; born in Greifswald, Oct. 15, 1819; died at Cannstadt, May 23, 1882. He studied philology and history at Heidelberg. In 1852 he resided in Stuttgart, and was associated with Hackländer in founding the Hausblätter. He began early to write fiction, his first stories appearing in collected form under the title 'From the People,' and proving very popular. They were followed by 'Out of the Old Time and the New'; 'As the People Speak'; and 'Days that Are no More.' In 1858, the success of 'Norien, the Recollections of an Old Woman,' encouraged him to write a long story. The novels that followed, especially 'German Hearts'; 'The Demagogue'; 'The Lost Son'; and 'Lost in the World,' have had a wide circulation, but are marred by hasty execution. He was a truthful delineator of character and of the every-day life of the North-German people.

Höegh-Guldberg, Frederick (hěch-göld'-bārG). A Danish poet and philologist; born in Copenhagen, March 26, 1771; died there, Sept. 21, 1852. Son of the eminent statesman Ove Höegh-Guldberg, he early became noted for his patriotic poems, a collected edition of which, in one volume, has sold extensively. He is an authority on Danish grammar.

Hoey, Mrs. Frances Sarah. An Irish novelist and translator; born at Bushy Park, in Rathfarnham, County Dublin, Feb. 15, 1830. She married, in 1846, the late Adam Murray Stewart, Esq., and in 1858, her present husband, Mr. Cashel Hoey. Since 1860 she has been a contributor to Chambers' Journal, Belgravia, and other periodicals. She is the author of the popular novels: 'A House of Cards' (1863); 'A Golden Sorrow' (1872); 'Out of Court' (1874); 'The Blossoming of an Aloe' (1874; new ed. 1880); 'The Lover's Creed' (1884); 'A Stern Chase' (1886). Among her translations from the French are 'Memoirs of Madame de Rémusat'; 'The King's Secret'; 'The Last Days of the Consulate.'

Hofdyk, Willem Jakobsz (hof'dik). A Dutch historian and poet; born in Alkmaar, June 27, 1816; died in Arnheim, Aug. 29, 1888. As village schoolmaster his leisure was devoted to the study of Dutch philology, history, and the arts. From 1850 to 1856 he was instructor in history and literature at the college in Amsterdam. Among his numerous and valuable historical writings are: 'Historic Eras,' in Dutch annals; 'The Netherlands People'; and 'Historical View of the Monasteries in the Netherlands.' The best of his poems is 'Kennemerland'; but his narrative poems 'Helene,' 'Griffo de Saliër,' and some others would give him a conspicuous place in Dutch literature.

Hoffman, Charles Fenno. An American poet and novelist; born in New York, 1806; died at Harrisburg, Pa., June 7, 1884. He was originally a lawyer. He founded the Knickerbocker Magazine, edited the Literary World, and was owner and editor of the American Magazine. His finest work was his songs, the best known being 'Sparkling and Bright,' and 'The Myrtle and Steel.' He wrote the novel 'Grayslaer' (1840). His complete poetical works appeared in 1874.

Hoffman, David. An American lawyer, and legal and historical writer; born at Baltimore, Md., Dec. 25, 1784; died in New York, Nov. 11, 1854. He was professor of law in the University of Maryland 1817-36. He wrote 'Chronicles Selected from the Originals of Cartaphilus, the Wandering Jew' (2 vols., 1853), being the beginning of what he intended to be a history of the world but never completed; 'Thoughts on Men and Things' (1837); 'Viator, or a Peep into my Note-Book' (1841); etc.

Hoffman, Wickham. An American soldier and diplomatist; born in New York, 1821. He served in the Civil War, was secretary of legation at Paris, London, St. Petersburg, and minister to Denmark. He has written 'Camp, Court, and Siege' (1877), narrating personal adventures and observations during the Civil War, and the siege of Paris and the Commune; 'Leisure Hours in Russia' (1883). Died 1900.

Hoffmann, August Heinrich (hof'män), commonly called **Hoffmann von Fallersleben.** A celebrated German philologist and poet; born at Fallersleben, district of Luneburg, April 2, 1798; died at Castle of Korvei, on the Weser, Prussia, Jan. 19, 1874. He was destined for theology, but having made the acquaintance of the brothers Grimm, he devoted himself to philological studies, and traveled through the Rhine countries and Holland in search of popular poetry. In 1830 he was appointed professor of German literature, but the publication of his 'Unpolitical Songs' (1840-41), in spite of their innocent title, led to his dismissal. For several years afterward he wandered through Europe until restored to favor in 1848. His own 'Poems' (1834); 'German Street Songs' (1843); 'Soldier Songs' (1851-52); etc., are characterized by genuine simplicity and pathos: and his other publications—'Belgian Hours' (1830-52), a collection of Low German folk-songs; 'Foundations for the History of the German Language and Literature' (1830-37); 'History of German Church Hymn' (1832), are of great philological value.

Hoffmann, Ernest Theodor Amadeus (originally **Wilhelm**). One of the most original of German story-tellers; born at Königsberg, Prussia, Jan. 24, 1776; died in Berlin, 1822. He led an irregular, dissipated life; ranging at different times from councilor in the Supreme Court at Posen,—where his cleverness at caricature led to his dismissal,—musical conductor at Warsaw, and scene painter. In 1816, having secured a clerical appointment at Berlin, he settled down to a quiet life, but weakened by the excesses of his early career, died in 1822. The magic and demoniac element pervades the majority of his works, among which may be mentioned: 'The Devil's Elixir' (1816); 'Night Pieces' (1817); 'Fantastic Pieces in Callot's Manner'; 'The Brothers of Serapion.'

Hoffmann, Franz. A German writer of juvenile stories; born in Bernburg, Feb. 21, 1814; died in Dresden, July 11, 1882. He was partner with his brother Karl in the book business, but subsequently traveled about and supported himself by writing stories for children. His many books have attained wide popularity, and not a few have been translated into all civilized tongues. He founded a popular periodical for children, Neuer Deutsche Jugendfreund.

Hoffmann, Hans. A German novelist and poet; born in Stettin, July 27, 1848. He studied philology at Bonn and in Italy, and became a professor at the Stettin Academy after the publication in 1871 of his noteworthy dissertation on the Nibelungen. After a brilliant career as an educator, he began, in 1878, the writing of novels and lyrics which rapidly won him reputation. His first fiction was on an Italian theme, 'Under Blue Skies' (1881). Among others, 'Brigitta von Wisby,' 'Ivan the Terrible and his Dog,' and a humorous romance, 'The Iron Captain of the Horse,' met with favor. 'Landsturm' is a tragic tale. His 'In Life's Path' and other volumes of lyrics and narrative poems won instant appreciation, like 'The Harz'; 'Erring Mother's Love.'

Hoffmann, Heinrich. A German physician and humorist; born in Frankfort-on-the-Main, June 21, 1809; died there, Sept. 20, 1894. He made a practice of drawing comical pictures to amuse children while treating their complaints. These were published in 1845 under the title of 'Struwwelpeter,' which has gone through 140 editions and was reproduced in nearly every country of Europe, with translations of the humorous letterpress. He also published several volumes of drama and verse under the assumed name of « Donner.»

Hofmann von Hofmannswaldau, Christian (hof'män fon hof'mäns-väld'ou). A German poet; born in Breslau, Dec. 25, 1617; died there, April 18, 1679. After traveling through England, France, and Italy, he returned to Breslau, and although not of legal age was chosen to the legislative chamber, of which he afterwards became the presiding officer. He was in the diplomatic service for a time. His literary work comprises odes, epigrams, wedding songs, and the like. His 'Occasional Poems' and 'Hero Letters' are admirable, although betraying English influence. He was the great reformer of what is known as the Silesian school of poetic art, and may be said to have founded a distinct movement in German literature.

Hofmann, Friedrich (hof'män). A German editor and miscellaneous writer; born in Coburg, April 18, 1813; died at Ilmenau, Aug. 14, 1888. After graduating at Jena he formed a connection with the editorial staff of Meyer's 'Konversations-Lexikon' and subsequently with other important educational undertakings. He wrote 'The Battle of Focksan,' a drama; 'Childhood Joys,' poems; 'The Harp in the Storm,' a work of a historical nature; 'The Rat Catcher of Hameln'; and many other productions.

Hogan, James Francis. An Irish journalist, statesman, and author. He was born at Nenagh, Tipperary, in 1855, and while still an infant was taken by his parents to Australia. He was educated at St. Patrick's College, Melbourne, and in 1881 joined the staff of the Melbourne Argus, besides contributing to other journals and colonial periodicals. In 1893 he was elected a Member of Parliament for the Mid Division of Tipperary, and organized the Colonial Party. He is the author of 'An Australian Christmas Collection' (1886); 'History of the Irish in Australia' (1887); 'The Australian in London' (1888); 'The Lost Explorer' (1890); 'The Convict King' (1891), the last two being romantic stories of Australian adventure.

Hogg, James. A Scotch pastoral poet; born in Ettrick, Dec. 1 (or Nov. 1, not Jan. 25, 1772), 1770; died at Eltrive Lake, Nov. 21, 1835. He was an "Ettrick shepherd" from his seventh year, and so remained, notwithstanding various ineffectual efforts to become an Ettrick farmer. In 'Scottish Pastorals,' 'Poems and Songs,' and 'The Mountain Bard' his essentially Caledonian and pastoral quality finds happy expression, but 'The Queen's Wake' is his masterpiece.

Hohenhausen, Baroness Elizabeth Philippine Amalie (ho"en hous'en). A German poet, dramatist, and romancer; born in Waldau, near Cassel, Nov. 4, 1789; died at Frankfort-on-the-Oder, Dec. 2, 1857. Her father was General Adam Ludwig von Ochs, and in 1809 she married Baron Leopold von Hohenhausen, who left her a widow in 1848. Her poetry was published in 1817, under the title 'Flowers of Spring.' 'Nature, Art, and Life' is a volume of her recollections, and 'John and Cornelius de Witt' is a historical play of merit.

Holbach, Paul Heinrich Dietrich, Baron von (G. pron. hol'bäch; F. pron. ōl-bäk'). A French philosopher and writer; born at Heidelsheim, in the Palatinate, in 1723; died June 21, 1789. He inherited great wealth from his father, and entertained in his elegant house a number of eminent writers and thinkers of the day, among them Rousseau, Diderot, and Buffon. He was himself a man of no ordinary talent, and held materialistic and atheistic views characteristic of the period preceding the French Revolution, which are expounded in 'Christianity Unveiled' (1767); 'Spirit of the Clergy' (1767); 'Sacerdotal Imposture' (1767); 'The System of Nature' (1770); 'The Social System' (1773).

Holberg, Ludwig (hol'berg). A Danish poet, and "father of Danish comedy"; born in Bergen, Norway, Dec. 3, 1684; died at Copenhagen, Jan. 28, 1754. He wrote: 'Peder Paars' (1719–20), a mock-epic poem; 'Plutus'; 'Ulysses von Ithacia'; 'Melampe'; 'The Arabian Powder'; 'Without Head or Tail', 'Witchcraft'; 'The Busy Man'; 'The Fickle-Minded Woman'; 'Jean de France,' directed against the aping of French fashions; 'The Proper Ambition'; 'Henrich og Pernille'; 'The Political Pewterer,' a satire on "labor politics"; 'Erasmus Montanus'; 'The Fortunate Shipwreck'; etc. He also published 'History of the Kingdom of Denmark'; 'Hero Stories'; etc.

Holcroft, Thomas. An English dramatic author and adapter; born in London, Dec. 10, 1745; died there, March 23, 1809. By turn stable boy, school usher, journalist, and strolling actor, he began to write for the stage about 1778. 'The Road to Ruin,' the best of his many plays, was staged in 1792. At its last London revival in 1873 it ran nearly four consecutive months. His 'Tale of Mystery' (1802) brought into favor the melodrama, which has kept the stage ever since. He translated the 'Mariage de Figaro' and other French and German plays. He left 'Memoirs' pronounced by Thomas Moore the most interesting in the language.

Holden, Edward Singleton. A prominent American educator, and writer on scientific and Oriental topics; born at St. Louis, Mo., Nov. 5, 1846. He became president of the University of California in 1886. Until 1897 he was astronomer in charge of the Lick Observatory at Mount Hamilton, connected with the University of California. He has published: 'Life of Sir William Herschel'; 'The Mogul Emperors of Hindustan', 'Stories of the Great Astronomers'; 'Things in Nature'; 'The Sciences.'

Holder, Charles Frederick. An American popular writer and lecturer on natural history; born at Lynn, Mass., 1851. He was assistant at the American Museum of Natural History, New York, from 1870 to 1877. He has written: 'Marvels of Animal Life' (1886); 'Wonder Wings' (1887); 'A Frozen Dragon, and Other Tales' (1888), a natural-history story-book for young people; 'Life of Agassiz'; 'Big Game at Sea.'

Hölderlin, Friedrich (hèl'der-lin). A German poet; born in Lauffen-am-Neckar, March 20, 1770; died at Tübingen, June 7, 1843. He was a profound Greek scholar, and an instructor at Jena, afterwards private tutor. He was intimate with Goethe, Herder, and Schiller, the latter of whom influenced him strongly. Later he traveled in Holland, Switzerland, and France, showing upon his return symptoms of mental decay which necessitated his being placed under restraint. 'Hyperion, or the Hermit in Greece' (1797) is a brilliant story in epistolary form; 'Empedocles' an unfinished drama; and 'Emily before her Bridal Day' a prose idyl. His translations of the 'Antigone' and 'Œdipus' are powerful, and faithful to the Hellenic spirit. Other works are: 'German Men and Women,' a series of studies; and several volumes of 'Poems.'

Hole, Samuel Reynolds. An English clergyman, lecturer, and author; born Dec. 5, 1819. He was ordained a curate in his native parish in 1844, became canon of Lincoln 1875, and in 1887 was appointed to the deanery of Rochester. He has done much to promote the influence of the Church of England as the church of the poor, and has advocated the principles of the Free and Open Church Association. As a lecturer he is well known to American audiences. Among his works are: 'A Little Tour in Ireland' (1858), illustrated by John Leech; 'A Book About Roses' (1869; 8th ed. 1884), an authority on the subject and translated into several languages; 'Nice and her Neighbors' (1881); 'Memories of Dean Hole' (1892). Died Aug. 27, 1904.

Holinshed, Raphael (hol'inz-hed). An English chronicler; born at Bosley, Cheshire (?), about 1520 (?); died at Bramcote (?), 1580 (?). Nothing is known of his personality. The famous 'Chronicles'—not wholly his, however —reveal an accomplished historical student, specially versed in Scotch affairs, which knowledge, however, may have been drawn from previous workers. The Elizabethan dramatists, especially Shakespeare, drew largely on this work for material.

Holland, Frederick May. An American Unitarian divine and miscellaneous writer; born at Boston, 1836. He has written: ' The Reign of the Stoics ' (1879), giving their history, religion, maxims, etc.; ' Stories from Browning ' (1882); ' Life of Frederick Douglass '; ' Rise of Intellectual Liberty from Thales to Copernicus '; etc.

Holland, Henry Scott. An English clergyman and religious writer; born at Ledbury, Herefordshire, in 1847. He was a theological tutor at Christ Church, Oxford (1872-85); became canon of Truro in 1882, and in 1884 canon, afterwards precentor, of St. Paul's. His published sermons and addresses include: ' Logic and Life ' (1882); ' Creed and Character ' (1886); ' Christ and Ecclesiastes ' (1887); ' On Behalf of Belief ' (1888); ' Pleas and Claims ' (1893).

Holland, Josiah Gilbert. A noted American poet, novelist, and editor; born at Belchertown, Mass., July 24, 1819; died in New York, Oct. 12, 1881. He left the practice of medicine to become editor of the Springfield Republican, which position he held from 1849 to 1866. He was editor of Scribner's Monthly, later the Century Magazine, 1870-81. Among his prose works are: ' Life of Abraham Lincoln '; ' Letters to the Young '; ' Plain Talks on Familiar Subjects '; ' Gold Foil '; and the novels 'Arthur Bonnicastle,' 'Sevenoaks,' and ' Nicholas Minturn.' His poems are published under the titles: ' Bitter-Sweet '; ' Kathrina '; ' The Mistress of the Manse '; ' Garnered Sheaves '; and ' The Puritan's Guest.' Part of his poems were written under the pseudonym « Timothy Titcomb.»

Holland, Thomas Erskine. An English jurist; born at Brighton, July 17, 1835. He was educated at Oxford; was called to the bar in 1863; and in 1874 was elected Chichele professor of international law, which post he still holds. He is a member of several foreign societies, and the recipient of honorary degrees from Oxford, Bologna, and Dublin. His monumental work is ' The Elements of Jurisprudence ' (1880), now in its sixth edition, which has become a text-book in most English and American universities. Among his other publications the most notable are: 'An Essay on Composition Deeds ' (1864); ' The Institutes of Justinian ' (1873); ' The European Concert in the Eastern Question ' (1885); 'A Manual of Naval Prize Law '; (1888); ' The Laws and Customs of War at Land ' (1904).

Holley, Marietta. An American writer of humorous stories; born in Ellisburg, N. Y., 1844. The most noted of her works are: ' My Opinions and Betsey Bobbet's ' (1872), and 'Josiah Allen's Wife ' (1878), both of which had an extensive sale.

Hollingshead, John. An English journalist, theatrical manager, and author; born at Hoxton, Sept. 8, 1827. He was a constant contributor to Household Words, All the Year Round, etc. In 1868 he became lessee and manager of the Gaiety Theatre, and now controls many theatrical enterprises in London and the provinces. Besides several original and adapted plays, his works include: ' Under Bow Bells ' (1859); ' Rubbing the Gilt Off ' (1860); ' Ragged London ' (1861); ' Miscellanies: Stories and Essays ' (1874); ' Footlights ' (1883) ; Gayeties Chronicles ' (1900).

Hollister, Gideon Hiram. An American lawyer and miscellaneous writer; born at Washington, Conn., 1817; died 1881. His home was in Litchfield, Conn. He was minister to Hayti 1868-69. He wrote: ' Mount Hope ' (1851), a historical romance; ' History of Connecticut ' (2 vols., 1855); ' Thomas à Becket, a Tragedy; and Other Poems ' (1866); and ' Kinley Hollow ' (1882), a novel, published posthumously.

Holloway, Mrs. Laura (Carter). An American editor and miscellaneous writer; born at Nashville, Tenn., 1848. She was for twelve years associate editor of the Brooklyn Daily Eagle. She has written: ' Ladies of the White House ' (new ed. 1880); ' The Mothers of Great Men and Women, and Some Wives of Great Men ' (1883); ' The Home in Poetry ' (1884); ' Chinese Gordon ' (1885); ' An Hour with Charlotte Brontë '; ' The Buddhist Diet Book '; etc.

Holmes, Abiel. An American Congregational divine and historical writer; father of Oliver Wendell Holmes; born at Woodstock, Conn., Dec. 24, 1763; died at Cambridge, Mass., June 4, 1837. He was pastor of the First Church, Cambridge, Mass. He wrote: ' Life of Ezra Stiles ' (1798); ' Annals of America ' (enlarged ed. 1829), a work of enduring value; ' Memoir of the French Protestants '; etc.

Holmes, Mrs. Mary Jane (Hawes). An American novelist; born at Brookfield, Mass., 18—. A voluminous writer, her works are mostly domestic in character, and moral in tendency. Some of them are said to have had a circulation of over 50,000 copies. Among them are: ' Tempest and Sunshine ' (1854); ' Lena Rivers ' (1856); ' Marian Gray ' (1863); ' Milbank ' (1871); ' Queenie Hetherton ' (1883); etc. She was for a number of years a resident of Kentucky; her present home is at Brockport, N. Y. Died Oct. 6, 1907.

Holmes, Oliver Wendell. An American man of letters; born at Cambridge, Mass., Aug. 29, 1809; died at Boston, Oct. 7, 1894. His poetical works include: ' Poems ' (1836); ' Urania ' (1846); ' Astræa: the Balance of Illusions ' (1850); ' Songs in Many Keys ' (1861); ' Songs of Many Seasons ' (1875); ' The Iron Gate ' (1880). In prose he wrote: ' The Autocrat of the Breakfast Table ' (1859); ' The Professor at the Breakfast Table ' (1860); ' The Poet at the Breakfast Table ' (1872); which had all previously appeared serially in the Atlantic Monthly. He wrote, also, the novels 'Elsie Venner' (1861) and 'The Guardian Angel' (1868). His other prose works, exclusive of his numerous writings on medical science, are: 'Soundings from the Atlantic' (1864); 'Mechanism in Thought and Morals' (1871); 'John Lothrop Motley' (1879); 'Ralph Waldo Emerson' (1884); 'A Mortal Antipathy' (1885); 'Our Hundred Days in Europe' (1887); 'Over the Teacups' (1891); numerous prefaces and introductions to special volumes; etc. His works on medicine are likewise important, for Dr. Holmes was by profession a physician, and in 1847 was made professor of anatomy and physiology in the medical school of Harvard.

Holst, Hans Peter (hōlst). A Danish poet and novelist; born in Copenhagen, Oct. 22, 1811; died near that city, June 2, 1893. He was made professor of language and literature at the Copenhagen Academy, 1836, and traveled through Europe later at government expense. His writings are exceedingly varied, elegant, and tasteful. The 'Poem in Memory of Frederic IV.,' 'Recollections of Travel,' 'Poems,' and 'National Legends,' represent his early work. 'Gioacchino,' a drama of merit; 'Sicilian Types and Characters,' a sketch of scenery and manners; and 'Eros,' a collection of lyrics, have also spread his fame.

Holst, Hermann Eduard von. A German-American historian; born at Fellin, Livonia, Russia, June 19, 1841. Coming to the United States in 1866, he engaged in literary work and lecturing; he returned to Europe, becoming professor in the universities of Strasburg (1872) and Freiburg (1874); appointed professor in the University of Chicago (1892), he came to this country again. He has written: 'Constitutional and Political History of the United States' (5 vols., 1876-85); 'Lives' of John C. Calhoun and John Brown; 'Constitutional Law of the United States.' Died Jan. 20, 1904.

Holt, John Saunders. An American novelist; born in Alabama, 1826; died 1886. He was a lawyer at New Orleans. He wrote: 'Life of Abraham Page,' a novel; 'What I Know about Ben Eccles'; 'The Quines'; etc.

Holtei, Karl von (hol'tī). A German dramatist, poet, and novelist; born in Breslau, Jan. 24, 1798; died there, Feb. 12, 1880. After serving in the campaign of 1815, and going through the university, he became an actor at Breslau, and married the noted actress Louise Rogée. He then essayed dramatic authorship, his 'Viennese in Berlin' and 'Berliners in Vienna' meeting with great success. Not long after appeared the dramas: 'The Old Commander'; 'Lenore'; 'The Tragedy at Berlin'; 'Poor Peter'; and plays founded on Shakespeare's life. His wife dying, he married another actress, and continued his work in connection with the stage; and also began reading in public. Two volumes of poems, also 'Silesian Poems,' 'German Songs,' 'Voice of the Forest,' and others, extended his renown. His popular novels include: 'The Vagabonds'; 'Christian Lammfell'; and 'Noblesse Oblige.'

Hölty, Hermann (hel'ty). A German poet; born in Ülzen, Hanover, Nov. 4, 1828; died at Rehburg, Aug. 16, 1887. He became a clergyman, and held various pastorates in Hanover. His 'Songs and Ballads,' 'Alpine Charms,' 'From the German Olympus,' and various other volumes, have given him his place in literature. He is a pleasing minor poet.

Hölty, Ludwig Heinrich Christoph. A German elegiac poet; born in Mariensee, near Hanover, Dec. 21, 1748; died at Hanover, Sept. 1, 1776. He was always physically delicate. 'The Fall of the Leaves' shows his attractive if slightly effeminate Muse to perfection. 'Faith and Candor Ever,' an elegy to a country maiden, is a spiritual expression of love. The consciousness that he was destined to an early death infused into his song a rarely pensive note.

Holyoake, George Jacob. An English social and religious reformer, journalist, and author; born at Birmingham, April 13, 1817. He was educated at the Mechanics' Institute in his native city, and has figured as teacher, journalist, and lecturer. He is chiefly known for his advocacy of secularism. His works include: 'Secularism' (1854); 'Life of Robert Owen' (1859); 'The Limits of Atheism' (1861); 'History of Co-operation' (1875-79); 'Among the Americans' (1881); 'A Hundred Days in New Mexico and Canada.' Died Jan. 22, 1906.

Home, John. A Scotch dramatist; born in Leith, near Edinburgh, Sept. 21, 1722; died at Marchiston, near Edinburgh, Sept. 5, 1808. He took part against Charles Edward in the war of 1745, was taken prisoner at Falkirk, but freed after Culloden. He subsequently became a clergyman. His great tragedy 'Douglas,' produced in Edinburgh in 1756, aroused hostility among the Scotch clergy, and he abandoned the church. 'Douglas' met with great success in London, and was followed by 'Agis,' 'The Fatal Discovery,' and 'Alfred.' He aided Macpherson financially in the production of the Ossian poetry, and also wrote a 'History of the Rebellion in Scotland in 1755-56.'

Homer (hō-mėr). The greatest of epic poets, author of the Iliad and Odyssey. The date of his birth is generally set at the eighth or ninth century B. C., but has been the subject of discussion among scholars, with various results, now inclining to a much earlier period,—as early as 1300 B. C.,—in accordance with the general results of archæological investigations.

Homes, Mrs. Mary Sophie (Shaw) (Rogers). An American novelist and writer of verse (pseudonym "Millie Mayfield"); born at Frederick, Md., about 1830. Her home is in New Orleans. She has written: 'Carrie Harrington, or Scenes in New Orleans' (1857); 'Progression, or the South Defended' (1868), verse; 'A Wreath of Rhymes' (1869); etc.

Hone, William. An English clergyman and author; born at Bath, June 3, 1780; died at Tottenham, London, Nov. 6, 1842. He was for some years a publisher and bookseller. During the latter part of his life he preached to a congregation of Dissenters. Of his works: 'The Everyday Book' (1826); 'The Table Book' (1827–28); 'The Year Book' (1829), containing much curious information, descriptions of old customs, etc., were popular in their day, and were more than once imitated. 'The Political House that Jack Built,' a satire, appeared in 1819, and went through nearly fifty editions.

Hood, Edwin Paxton. An English clergyman and author; born in London, Oct. 24, 1820; died in 1885. For many years pastor of a Congregational church in London, editor of the Eclectic Review, and a popular lecturer, he wrote, compiled, and edited nearly fifty volumes, among which are: 'John Milton' (1851); 'The Uses of Biography' (1852); 'Biography of William Wordsworth' (1856); 'Lamps, Pitchers, and Trumpets' (1867), lectures delivered to theological students; 'The World of Anecdote' (1869); 'The Romance of Biography' (1876); 'Oliver Cromwell, his Life, Times, Battle-Fields, etc.' (1884); 'The Throne of Eloquence' (1885).

Hood, Thomas. An English poet, master of humor and pathos; born in London, May 23, 1799; died there, May 3, 1845. He had few early advantages, his genius first asserting itself in his early twenties in 'Whims and Oddities,' a collection of verse. The most playful and humorous of poets, there is yet a melancholy in all his numbers that now and then dominates his song entirely,—'The Hostler's Lament' and 'The Haunted House' constituting examples. 'The Plea of the Midsummer Fairies' is worthy of the hand that wrote 'The Song of the Shirt.' He has had more imitators than any other modern poet.

Hood, Thomas, the younger. An English poet, humorist, and novelist, son of Thomas; born in Wanstead. Essex, Jan. 19, 1835; died at Peckham Rye, Surrey, Nov. 20, 1874. He studied at Oxford, and began his literary career there with 'Pen and Pencil Pictures.' 'Quips and Cranks' was his best production in verse. His successful novels include: 'A Disputed Inheritance'; 'A Golden Heart'; and 'The Lost Link.' His talent for droll stories and sketches was considerable.

Hooft, Pieter Corneliszoon (höft). A Dutch poet and historian; born in Amsterdam, March 16, 1581; died at The Hague, May 25 (or 21), 1647. He was burgomaster of Minden for nearly forty years. His works give him high rank, especially his volume of collected 'Poems.' In prose, the 'History of Henry IV.'; 'History of the House of Medici'; and 'History of the Low Countries,' display a talent worthy of a great annalist and investigator.

Hook, James. Dean of Worcester; born in London, June 1772; died at Worcester, 1828. Educated at Oxford, he took holy orders, rose rapidly in the church, and in 1825 was appointed dean of Worcester. He wrote political pamphlets, sermons, etc. Two of his novels, 'Pen Owen' (1822) and 'Percy Mallory' (1823) attracted much attention.

Hook, Theodore [Edward]. An English humorist, story-writer, and dramatist; born in London, Sept. 22, 1788; died in Fulham, Aug. 24, 1841. His peculiar wit was well adapted to the fashion of his day, and the 'Sayings and Doings' were once much in vogue. The plots of his dramas are mere pegs to hang witticisms on; but 'Gilbert Gurney' and 'Jack Brag' are good stories.

Hooker, Joseph Dalton, Sir. An English botanist, son of Sir William Jackson; born at Halesworth, Suffolk, June 30, 1817. He took his M. D. at Glasgow University in 1839. He was assistant surgeon and naturalist of the famous expedition of Sir James Clark Ross; visited India in 1847; and in 1871 with John Ball ascended the Great Atlas in Morocco. From 1855 to 1885 he was on the directorate of Kew Gardens. Among his works are: 'Botany of the Antarctic Voyage' (1847–60); 'Himalayan Journals' (1854); 'Student's Flora of the British Islands' (1870); 'Botany' (Science Primers), in 1876; 'Journal of a Tour in Morocco and the Great Atlas' (1878), with John Ball.

Hooker, Richard. A famous English divine and theological writer; born at Heavitree, Exeter, Mar., 1553–4; died at Bishopsbourne, near Canterbury, Nov. 2, 1600. He has been called "the judicious Hooker." His great work, the 'Laws of Ecclesiastical Polity' (1592–1648), supporting the ministry, ritual, and ceremonies of the Church of England, is one of the masterpieces of English eloquence. Hallam compares it to Cicero's 'De Legibus,' and Pope Clement VIII. had part of it translated into Latin, that it might be read to him. The best edition is John Keble's third (3 vols., 1845).

Hooker, Thomas. An English nonconformist clergyman; born at Markfield, Leicestershire, in 1586; died at Hartford, Conn., July 7, 1647. He came to America in 1633; in 1636 removed from Newtown (Cambridge, Mass.) to Hartford, and founded that colony, becoming minister of the First Church there. He won eminence as a theological writer and a preacher, and has a permanent historical importance for his instrumentality in drawing up the first written constitution in America—that of the Hartford Colony. His chief work is 'A Survey of the Summe of Church Discipline,' in collaboration with John Cotton.

Hooker, William Jackson, Sir. An English botanist; born at Norwich, in 1785; died at Kew, Aug. 12, 1865. A zealous botanist, he traveled much in his favorite pursuit. He was Regius professor of botany in Glasgow University in 1820–41, when he became director of the Kew Gardens. He was knighted in 1836 on account of his high scientific attain-

ments. His best-known botanical works are: 'Journal of a Tour in Iceland' (1809); 'Muscologia Britannica' (1818), containing the mosses of Great Britain and Ireland; 'The British Flora' (1830), which has gone through several editions; 'British Ferns' (1862); 'Garden Ferns' (1862).

Hooper, Johnson. An American writer of stories; born in North Carolina in 1815; died 1863. He was a lawyer in Alabama. He wrote: 'Adventures of Captain Simon Suggs', 'Widow Rugby's Husband, and Other Alabama Tales.'

Hooper, Lucy. An American sketch-writer and poet; born in Massachusetts, 1816; died 1841. Her home was in Brooklyn, N. Y. She wrote 'Scenes from Real Life,' a volume of prose sketches. Her complete poems appeared in 1848.

Hooper, Mrs. Lucy Hamilton (Jones). An American poet, novelist, and journalist; born in Philadelphia, Jan. 20, 1835; died in Paris, Aug. 31, 1893. She was for some time assistant editor of Lippincott's Magazine. Her husband being United States vice-consul-general in France, she resided after 1874 in Paris, where she was correspondent for several American newspapers. She wrote: 'Poems' (1864 and 1871); and the novels 'Under the Tricolor' (1880) and 'The Tsar's Window' (1881).

Hope, Anthony. See **Hawkins.**

Hope, James Barron. An American lawyer, journalist, and poet; born at Norfolk, Va., 1827; died 1887. He served in the Confederate army in the Civil War. Among his poems are: 'Leoni di Monti' (1857); 'Under the Empire, or the Story of Madelon' (1878); and 'Arms and the Man' (1882).

Hope, Thomas. An English novelist; born about 1770; died Feb. 3, 1831. He was one of three brothers, wealthy merchants in Amsterdam. Among his works are: 'Household Furniture and Decorations' (1805); 'The Costume of the Ancients' (1809); 'Designs of Modern Costumes' (1812). 'Anastasius' (1819) was his best-known work. Byron told the Countess of Blessington that he wept bitterly on reading 'Anastasius,' for two reasons — one that he had not written it, and the other that Hope had.

Hopfen, Hans von (hop'fen). A German poet and novelist; born in Munich, Jan. 3, 1835, winning note at the university there. His 'Necessity,' and other poems of equal merit, are characterized by originality and picturesqueness, while his novels — notably 'The Old Practitioner' — show him a graceful and graphic delineator of character and customs. He ranks among the best contemporary German writers, his versatility not having impaired his quality.

Hopkins, Alphonso Alvah. An American educator, lecturer, journalist, and miscellaneous writer; born in New York State, 1843. He has written in verse: 'Asleep in the Sanctum'; 'Geraldine,' a metrical romance modeled after

'Lucile'; the novels, 'His Prison Bars' (1874); 'Sinner and Saint' (1881); 'Life of General Clinton Fisk' (1888); 'Wealth and Waste' (1896).

Hopkins, Edward Washburn. An American educator and writer; born in Massachusetts, 1857. He is professor of Sanskrit at Yale, successor of Professor Whitney. He has written: 'Mutual Relations of the Four Castes in Manu'; 'Translation of Laws in Manu'; 'Social and Military Position of the Ruling Caste in Ancient India'; 'The Religions of India'; 'India, Old and New.'

Hopkins, John Henry. An American divine and writer, the first Protestant Episcopal bishop of Vermont (1832); born in Dublin, Ireland, Jan. 30, 1792; died in Rock Point, Vt., Jan. 9, 1868. He was originally an iron manufacturer, afterwards a lawyer, and won eminence by his vigorous and versatile writings. Among his works are: 'History of the Confessional'; 'The End of Controversy Controverted'; 'The Primitive Church'; 'Essay on Gothic Architecture'; 'The Church of Rome in her Primitive Purity'; 'Scriptural View of Slavery,' a defense of the institution; 'Law of Ritualism'; 'History of the Church,' in verse; Twelve Canzonets, words and music.

Hopkins, John Henry. An American clergyman and writer, son of John Henry; born 1820; died 1891. He founded and long edited the Church Journal. He wrote: 'Carols, Hymns, and Songs'; 'Poems by the Wayside'; 'Life of Bishop Hopkins'; 'Faith and Order of the Protestant Church in the United States'; etc. He also translated Goethe's 'Autobiography.'

Hopkins, Mrs. Louisa Parsons (Stone). An American educator and writer of verse; born in Massachusetts, 1834; died 1895. Her home was in Boston. Besides several educational works she wrote in verse: 'Motherhood' (1880); 'Breath of the Field and Shore'; 'Easter Carols'; etc.

Hopkins, Mark. A distinguished American educator and religious and ethical writer; born at Stockbridge, Mass., Feb. 4, 1802; died at Williamstown, Mass., June 17, 1887. He was a Congregational divine, and president of Williams College. Among his works are: 'Evidences of Christianity' (1846); 'The Law of Love, and Love as a Law' (1860); 'An Outline Study of Man' (1873); etc.

Hopkins, Mark. An American-English journalist and novelist, son of Mark; born in Massachusetts, 1851. He resides at present in London. He has written 'The World's Verdict' (1888), a novel.

Hopkins, Samuel. A noted American theologian; born at Waterbury, Conn., Sept. 17, 1721; died at Newport, R. I., Dec. 20, 1803. He was one of the leaders in the New England theology (so called), and was instrumental in the extermination of slavery in Rhode Island. His chief work was 'System of Doctrines' (1793). He is said to be the hero of Mrs. Stowe's novel, 'The Minister's Wooing.'

18

Hopkinson, Francis. An American political writer and lawyer and one of the signers of the Declaration of Independence; born in Philadelphia, Sept. 21, 1737; died May 9, 1791. He wrote: 'The Pretty Story' (1774); 'The Prophecy' (1776); 'The Political Catechism' (1777). He also wrote poems and essays. The 'Miscellaneous Essays, and Occasional Writings' appeared posthumously. His humorous ballad, 'The Battle of the Keg,' was once widely known.

Hopkinson, Joseph. An American jurist, son of Francis; born at Philadelphia, Nov. 12, 1770; died there, Jan. 15, 1842. He was one of the ablest lawyers of his day. He wrote the famous patriotic song, 'Hail Columbia' (1798), for the benefit of an actor, calling it at first the 'President's March.'

Hoppin, Augustus. An American illustrator and novelist; born at Providence, R. I., July 13, 1828 · died at Flushing, April 2, 1896. He was originally a lawyer. Besides illustrating works by many well-known authors, he illustrated his own books: 'On the Nile' (1871); 'Recollections of Anton House, by C. Anton' (1881), a novel; 'Two Compton Boys' (1884); 'Married for Fun' (1885), a romance; etc.

Hoppin, James Mason. An American educator and miscellaneous writer; born at Providence, R. I., Jan. 17, 1820. A Congregational clergyman and professor at Yale. Besides religious writings, he has published: 'Life of Rear-Admiral Foote' (1874); 'Greek Art on Greek Soil'; 'Old England' (8th ed. 1886), a highly praised book of travel; 'The Early Renaissance' (1892); etc. Died in 1906.

Hopps, John Page. An English clergyman and religious writer; born in London, Nov. 6, 1834. At first a Baptist minister, he joined the Unitarians, holding pastorates at Sheffield, Glasgow, and Leicester, where he now resides. He is an active social reformer and advocate of co-operation. Among his numerous works are: 'Seven Lectures for the People' (4th ed. 1861); 'Besides the Still Waters' (1879); 'A Scientific Basis of Belief in Future Life' (1881); 'Future Probation' (1886); 'The Bible for Beginners.'

Horace, or **Quintus Horatius Flaccus.** A great Latin lyric poet; born at Venusia, in southern Italy, Dec. 8, B. C. 65; died at Rome, Nov. 27, B. C. 8. His writings, in the order of their production, are: The 'Satires,' or as the poet himself called them, 'Talks' (Sermones), eighteen in number, and written in hexameter verse; 'Epodes,' a collection of lyric poems in iambic and composite metres; 'Odes,' his most exquisite works, and the delight of scholars ever since they were written; 'Epistles,' in hexameter verse, brilliant in wit, perfect in melody, replete with workaday wisdom,— among them is the 'Epistle to the Pisos,' or 'The Art of Poetry,' as it has been aptly called.

Hörmann, Ludwig von (hĕr'män). A German descriptive writer; born in Feldkirch, Oct. 12, 1837. He is a philologist and librarian by profession, and was at one time professor in the Academy at Innsbruck, and since 1878 has been librarian of the university there. His fame depends upon: 'Tyrolese Types'; 'The Life of the People of the Tyrol'; and numerous studies of conditions and manners among the natives of the Alpine region.

Horn, Franz Christoph (horn). A German novelist, historian of literature, and essayist; born July 30, 1781; died July 19, 1837. His romances and tales, 'Guiscardo, the Poet,' 'Battle and Victory,' and 'The Wandering Jew,' were once widely read, but are now forgotten. More noteworthy are: 'Outlines of the History and Nature of German Polite Literature from 1790 to 1818'; 'German Poetry and Rhetoric from Luther's Time to Our Own'; 'Shakespeare's Plays,' a valuable critical work.

Hornaday, William Temple. An American naturalist and writer of travels; born near Plainfield, Ind., 1854. He was for a number of years chief taxidermist of the United States National Museum, Washington. He has written: 'Two Years in the Jungle' (1885); 'The Buffalo Hunt' (1887); 'Free Rum on the Congo' (1887); 'Taxidermy and Zoölogical Collecting'; 'Canoe and Rifle on the Orinoco'; etc. Since 1896, Director of N. Y. Zoölogical Park.

Horne, Richard Henry L. Hengist. An English miscellaneous writer; born Jan. 1, 1803; died March 13, 1884. His principal works are: 'Cosmo de' Medici' (1837) and 'The Death of Marlowe' (1837), tragedies; 'Orion,' an epic poem (1843); 'A New Spirit of the Age' (1844); 'Judas Iscariot, a Miracle Play' (1848); 'The Dreamer and the Worker' (1851); 'Australian Facts and Prospects' (1859); 'Exposition of the False Medium, and Barriers Excluding Men of Genius from the Public' (1883).

Horváth, Andreas (hŏr'vät). A Hungarian poet; born in Pázmánd, Nov. 25, 1778; died there, March 7, 1839. He became a Catholic priest soon after attaining manhood. He created the classic epic in Hungarian literature. His principal works are: 'Memorial of Zircz'; and the heroic poem 'Arpád,' in twelve cantos, for which he was awarded a prize by the Hungarian Academy. He became a member of this body in 1832.

Hosmer, George Washington. An American miscellaneous writer; born in 184-. He is a physician by profession. Among his writings are: 'The People and Politics'; 'As We Went Marching On,' a story of the War; etc.

Hosmer, James Kendall. An American educator and miscellaneous writer; born at Northfield, Mass., 1834. He was professor in Antioch College 1866-72; the University of Missouri, Columbia, Mo., 1872; Washington University, St. Louis, Mo., 1874-92; and is now librarian of the public library of Minneapolis (1892-97). Among his works are: 'The Color Guard' (1864), a record of experiences in the Civil War; 'The Thinking Bayonet' (1865), a

novel; 'History of German Literature' (1879); 'Life of Samuel Adams' (1885); 'How Thankful was Bewitched'; 'Life of Sir Henry Vane'; 'Story of the Jews,' in 'Story of the Nations' series; 'History of the Louisiana Purchase.'

Hosmer, Mrs. Margaret (Kerr). An American novelist and writer for the young; born in Philadelphia, 1830; died at Philadelphia, Feb. 3, 1897. Her home was in San Francisco, where she taught school, and in Philadelphia She wrote the novels, 'The Morrisons' (1864), 'Rich and Poor' (1870), 'The Sin of the Father' (1872), etc.; the juveniles, 'Blanche Gilroy' (1871), 'A Rough Boy's Story' (1873); and also, 'Ten Years of a Lifetime.'

Hosmer, William Henry Cuyler. An American writer of verse; born in New York State, 1814; died 1877. He was a lawyer in western New York. He wrote: 'Fall of Tecumseh'; 'Legends of the Senecas'; 'Yonnondio'; 'Bird Notes'; 'The Themes of Song'; 'The Months'; 'The Pioneers of Western New York'; etc.

Hostrup, Jens Christian (hos'trup). A Danish poet, dramatist, and humorist; born in Copenhagen, May 20, 1818; died there, Nov. 21, 1892. He was intended for the church, but his talent as a writer of songs and plays, comic, patriotic, and sentimental, decided his career. 'The Neighbors,' a farce, made his reputation while yet a theological student. His best play is 'Master and Pupil.' Later, as a clergyman, he brought out more serious work: 'Eva,' a drama; a volume of 'Popular Discourses'; and various other productions. His is one of the foremost names in later Danish literature.

Houghton, George Washington Wright. (hōton). An American journalist and writer of verse; born at Cambridge, Mass., 1850; died 1891. His home was in New York. He wrote: 'Songs from Over the Sea' (1874); 'The Legend of St. Olaf's Kirk' (1881); 'Niagara' (1882); etc.

Houghton, Richard Monckton Milnes, Lord (houton). An English poet, critic, and statesman; born in London, Eng., June 19, 1809; died at Vichy, France, Aug. 11, 1885. A Conservative in Parliament, he joined the Liberals under Lord John Russell, and in 1863 was raised to the peerage. His best poetry appears in: 'Memorials of a Tour in Greece'; 'Memorials of a Residence on the Continent, and Historical Poems'; 'Poems of Many Years'; 'Palm Leaves'; and a few other small volumes. His prose is remarkable for the purity of its Saxon style. It includes: 'Life, Letters, and Literary Remains of John Keats'; 'Monographs, Personal and Political'; etc.

House, Edward Howard. An American journalist and story-writer; born at Boston, Sept. 5, 1836, died at Tokio, Japan, Dec. 18, 1901. He was a musical and dramatic critic in Boston and New York; afterwards professor of English Language and literature in the University of Tokio, Japan (1871–73), acting as correspondent of the New York Herald. He wrote: 'Japanese Episodes' (1881); 'Yone Santo' (1888), a story of life in Japan; 'The Midnight Warning, and Other Stories'; 'The Kagosima Affair'; etc.

Houssaye, Arsène (ö-sā'). A French novelist, dramatist, and critic; born in Bruyères, near Laon, March 28, 1815; died in Paris, Feb. 26, 1896. He came early to Paris, and had written two novels at the age of twenty-one, 'The Sinner' being still remembered. He wrote 'The Caprices of the Marchioness,' 'The Comedy at the Window,' and other successful light plays, and became a stage manager. His later novels include: 'The Beautiful Raffuëlla'; 'Marion's Repentance'; 'Romance of the Duchess'; 'Women as They Are'; 'Women of the Past'; etc. His art and theatrical criticisms are exceedingly good; the 'History of French Art in the Eighteenth Century,' 'Portrait Gallery of the Eighteenth Century,' and 'Studies of Voltaire and Rousseau,' rank high. His style is clear and graceful.

Houssaye, Henri. A French historian and critic, son of Arsène; born in Paris, Feb. 24, 1848. He studied painting, but transferred his attention to the study of Greek antiquity. During the siege of Paris in 1870 his gallant conduct earned him the Cross of the Legion of Honor. His valuable publications include: 'History of Alcibiades and the Athenian Republic' (1875), crowned by the French Academy in 1874; 'Athens, Rome, and Paris' (1878); 'History of the Conquest of Greece by the Romans' (vol. 1. 1885); '1814,' a history of the campaign in France and the Fall of the Empire, published in 1888; 'Waterloo' (1899).

Houwald, Christoph Ernst (hö'väld). A German dramatic poet and story-writer; born at Straupitz, Nov. 29, 1778; died at Neuhaus, Jan. 28, 1845. He wrote fables and juvenile stories, but his literary reputation depends wholly upon his plays. 'The Picture' and 'Curse and Benison' are among his best works. In construction, vigor of style, and ingenuity of situation, he is remarkable. 'The Prince and the Townsman' and 'The Enemies' are striking examples in point.

Hovey, Richard. An American writer of verse; born at Normal, Ill., May 4, 1864; died in New York city, April 24, 1900. He wrote: 'Launcelot and Guenevere'; 'Gandolfo,' a tragedy; 'Songs from Vagabondia'; 'More Songs from Vagabondia' (with Bliss Carman); 'The Laurel,' an ode; 'Seaward'; etc.

Howard, Blanche Willis. See **Teuffel, von.**

Howard, Bronson. A prominent American playwright; born at Detroit, Mich., Oct. 7, 1842; resides in New York. He was connected with several newspapers in that city, 1867–72. Among his very successful plays are: 'Saratoga' (1870); 'The Banker's Daughter' (1878); 'Young Mrs. Winthrop' (1882); 'The Henrietta' (1887); 'Shenandoah' (1889); 'Aristocracy' (1892); 'Kate'; 'Norroy, Diplomatic Agent'; 'Scars on the Southern Seas.'

Howard, Edward. An English novelist: born 18—; died Dec. 30, 1841. After serving in the navy, he wrote sea stories; and was associated with Marryat in editing the Metropolitan Magazine in 1832. Later he joined the staff of the New Monthly Magazine, then edited by Hood. His greatest work, 'Rattlin the Reefer' (1836), met with much success. Among his other works are: 'The Old Commodore' (1837); 'Outward Bound' (1838); 'Memoirs of Admiral Sir Sidney Smith, K. C. B.' (1839); 'Jack Ashore'; 'The Centiad, a Poem in Four Books' (1841); 'Sir Henry Morgan, the Buccaneer;' (1842).

Howard, Oliver Otis. A distinguished American general; born at Leeds, Me., Nov. 8, 1830. A graduate of West Point, he rose to the rank of brevet major-general United States Army in the Civil War, and was president of Howard University (1869-73). He has written: 'Donald's School-Days' (1879); 'Nez Percé Joseph' (1881), a valuable contribution to Indian literature; Isabella of Castile '; 'Our Wild Indians.'

Howarth, Mrs. Ellen Clementine (Doran). An American writer of verse; born at Cooperstown, N. Y., May 20, 1827. She published two volumes of verse (1864 and 1867). The best known of her poems are ''Tis but a Little Faded Flower,' and 'Thou Wilt Never Grow Old.' Her poems have been edited by Richard Watson Gilder (1868). Died at Trenton, N. J., ——, 1899.

Howe, Edgar Watson. An American journalist and novelist; born in Wabash County, Ind., 1854. He is proprietor, publisher, and editor of the Daily Globe, Atchison, Kan. He has written: 'The Story of a Country Town' (1883), which attracted considerable attention; 'The Mystery of the Locks'; 'A Moonlight Boy'; 'A Man Story'; 'Lay Sermons.'

Howe, Henry. An American historical writer and compiler; born at New Haven, Conn., 1816. He published: 'Memoir of Eminent Mechanics' (1839); 'Travels and Adventures of Celebrated Travelers' (1853); 'Adventures and Achievements of Americans' (1858); 'Over the World' (1883); 'Our Whole Country'; 'The Great West'; etc. Died in Cincinnati, ——, 1893.

Howe, Mrs. Julia Ward. A famous American poet, essayist, biographer, writer of travels, and lecturer, daughter of Samuel Ward; born in New York, May 27, 1819. A philanthropist, interested especially in woman's suffrage, she was the wife of Dr. Samuel G. Howe the philanthropist, and with him edited the anti-slavery journal, the Boston Commonwealth. She is best known as the author of the 'Battle Hymn of the Republic' (1861), written during a visit to the camps near Washington. Among her works, besides several volumes of verse, are: 'The World's Own' (1857), a drama; 'Life of Margaret Fuller' (1883); 'Trip to Cuba' (1860); 'Is Polite Society Polite? and Other Essays'; etc. She also wrote: 'Later Lyrics'; 'From the Oak to the Olive'; and 'Sex and Education'; 'Sketches of Representative Women of New England.'

Howell, James. An English author; born probably in Wales about 1594; died in Hol-

born, 1666. As steward of a glass-ware factory and subsequently on public missions, he traveled for several years on the Continent. He became a clerk of council in 1640, was imprisoned during the civil war, and upon the Restoration received the post of historiographer royal as a reward for his loyalty to Charles I. Of forty works on historical, political, poetical, and philological subjects, only the 'Epistolæ Ho-Elianæ; or, Familiar Letters' (1645-55) have survived.

Howells, William Dean. A famous American novelist and poet; born at Martinsville, O., March 1, 1837. He was consul at Venice 1861-65; editor-in-chief of the Atlantic Monthly 1871-81; editor of The Editor's Study in Harper's Magazine 1886-91; editor of the Cosmopolitan 1892. His very numerous productions include the following: 'Poems of Two Friends' (1860), with J. J. Piatt; 'Life of Abraham Lincoln' (1860); six poems in 'Poets and Poetry of the West' (1860); 'Venetian Life' (1866); 'Italian Journeys' (1867); 'No Love Lost: a Romance of Travel' (1869); 'Suburban Sketches' (1871); 'Their Wedding Journey' (1872); 'A Chance Acquaintance' (1873); 'Poems' (1873); 'A Foregone Conclusion' (1875); 'Sketch of the Life and Character of Rutherford B. Hayes' (1876); 'A Day's Pleasure' (1876); 'The Parlor Car' (1876), a farce; 'Out of the Question' (1877), a comedy; 'A Counterfeit Presentment' (1877), a comedy; 'The Lady of the Aroostook' (1879); 'The Undiscovered Country' (1880); 'A Fearful Responsibility, and Other Stories' (1881); 'Dr. Breen's Practice' (1881); 'Buying a Horse' (1881); 'A Modern Instance' (1882); 'The Sleeping-Car' (1883), a farce; 'A Woman's Reason' (1883); 'A Little Girl among the Old Masters' (1884); 'The Register' (1884), a farce; 'Three Villages' (1884); 'The Rise of Silas Lapham' (1885); 'The Elevator' (1885), a farce; 'Indian Summer' (1885); 'Tuscan Cities' (1886); 'The Garroters' (1886), a farce; 'Poems' (1886)· biographical sketch, 'George Fuller: His Life and Works' (1886); 'Modern Italian Poets' (1887); 'The Minister's Charge' (1887); edited with T. S. Perry 'Library of Universal Adventure by Sea and Land' (1888); 'April Hopes' (1888); 'A Sea-Change, a Lyricated Farce' (1888); 'Annie Kilburn' (1889); 'The Mouse Trap and Other Farces' (1889); 'A Hazard of New Fortunes' (1890); 'The Shadow of a Dream' (1890); 'A Boy's Town' (1890); 'Criticism and Fiction' (1891); edited 'Poems' (1892), by George Pellew; 'An Imperative Duty' (1892); 'The Albany Depot' (1892); 'A Letter of Introduction' (1892), a farce; 'A Little Swiss Sojourn' (1892); 'The Quality of Mercy' (1892); 'The World of Chance' (1893); 'The Coast of Bohemia' (1893); 'The Niagara Book' (1893), with S. L. Clemens and others; 'Christmas Every Day, and Other Stories Told for Children' (1893); 'Evening Dress' (1893), a farce; 'My Year in a Log Cabin' (1893); 'The Unexpected Guests' (1893), a farce; 'A Likely Story' (1894), a farce; 'Five O'clock

Tea' (1894), a farce; 'A Traveler from Altruria' (1894), a romance; 'My Literary Passions' (1895); 'Stops of Various Quills' (1895); 'Landlord at Lion's Head' (1896); 'The Day of their Wedding' (1896); 'A Parting and a Meeting' (1896); 'Impressions and Experiences' (1896), largely autobiographical; 'An Open-Eyed Conspiracy' (1897); 'A Previous Engagement' (1897); 'Between the Dark and the Daylight.'

Howison, Robert Reid. An American historian and biographer, born at Fredericksburg, Va., 1820. He has practiced law at Richmond, Va., since 1845. He has written: 'History of Virginia' (2 vols., 1847–48); 'Lives' of Generals Morgan, Marion, and Gates; 'History of the American Civil War'; 'God and Creation.' Died 1906.

Howitt, Mary. An English poet, story-writer, and essayist; wife of and collaborator with William; born (Botham) of Quaker parentage in Coleford, March 12, 1799; died at Rome, Jan. 30, 1888. 'The Desolation of Eyam,' a poem; 'Colonization and Christianity'; 'Rural Life in England'; and volumes of essays and historical studies, besides articles on Spiritualism,—in which both believed,—represent their joint work. Her own are 'The Seven Temptations,' a striking poem; various children's stories; and translations of Fredrika Bremer's novels.

Howitt, William. An English historian, essayist, and miscellaneous writer; born in Heanor, Derbyshire, Dec. 18, 1792; died at Rome, March 3, 1879. For his joint work with Mary, see her name. His separate productions include: 'Popular History of England,' once really popular; 'The Student Life of Germany'; 'Woodburn Grange,' a novel; and a couple of dozen other bulky volumes, besides countless occasional articles, all in an easy, readable style.

Howorth, Henry Hoyle, Sir. An English politician and author; born in Lisbon, Portugal, July 1, 1842. He was a Conservative Member of Parliament in 1886, and again in 1893. In recognition of his works on Eastern history and other subjects, he was created K. C. I. E. in 1892. In addition to over seventy scientific memoirs, contributions to periodicals, etc., he has published: 'History of the Mongols' (3 vols., 1876–80), a large work marked by profundity of research; 'The Mammoth and the Flood' (1887), which discusses the problems arising out of the destruction of the so-called palæolithic man; 'The Glacial Nightmare and the Flood.'

Hoyt, Charles Hale, an American playwright, born in Concord, N. H., July 26, 1860; died in 1900. He is the author of 'A Bunch of Keys'; 'A Rag Baby'; 'A Brass Monkey'; 'A Texas Steer'; 'A Parlor Match'; 'A Trip to Chinatown'; 'A Day and Night in New York'; 'A Dog in the Manger'; etc.

Hubbard, Elbert. An American novelist; born in Illinois, 1856. His home is in East Aurora, N. Y. He is editor of the Philistine. He has written: 'No Enemy but Himself';

'Little Journeys to the Homes of Good Men and Great'; 'Forbes of Harvard'; 'One Day'; 'Little Journeys to the Homes of Famous Women' (1897); etc.

Hubbard, William. An American clergyman and author; born in Tendring, Essex, England, in 1621; died at Ipswich, Mass., Sept. 14, 1704. He emigrated to Massachusetts in 1635, graduated at Harvard in 1642, and was minister of Ipswich for over forty years. In 1688 he was temporary president of Harvard College. His chief works are: 'The Present State of New England' (1677); 'A Narrative of Troubles with the Indians' (1677), containing the first map of New England known to have been made in America; and 'A General History of New England from the Discovery to 1680' (published by the Massachusetts Historical Society in 1815), for which the colonial authorities paid him £50.

Hubbell, Mrs. Martha (Stone). An American novelist and writer for the young; born at Oxford, Conn., 1814; died at North Stonington, Conn., 1856. Besides a number of Sunday-school books, she wrote: 'The Shady Side, or Life in a Country Parsonage' (1853), one of the most widely sold books of its day.

Hubner, Charles William. An American journalist and miscellaneous writer; born in Maryland, 1835. His home is at Atlanta, Ga. He has written: 'Souvenirs of Luther'; 'Poems and Essays'; 'Modern Communism'; 'Cinderella' and 'Prince and Fairy,' two lyrical dramas; 'Representative Southern Poets.'

Huc, Évariste Régis (ük). A French priest, missionary, and author; born at Toulouse, Aug. 1, 1813; died in Paris, March 26, 1860. Ordained a priest in 1839, he went the same year to China as a missionary, traveling through the heart of the empire to Mongolia and Thibet, where he penetrated even to Lhassa. His experiences are recounted in 'Souvenirs of a Journey to Tartary, Thibet, and China' (1852); 'The Chinese Empire' (1854); 'Christianity in China, Tartary, etc.' (1858), all of which were translated into English.

Hudson, Frederick. An American journalist; born at Quincy, Mass., 1819; died 1875. He was connected with the New York Herald for nearly thirty years, retiring in 1866. He wrote: 'History of Journalism in the United States' (1873).

Hudson, Henry Norman. An American Shakespearean scholar and Episcopal divine; born at Cornwall, Vt., Jan. 28, 1814; died at Cambridge, Mass., Jan. 16, 1886. He served as chaplain in the Civil War, and was professor of Shakespeare at Boston University, and was for a time editor of the Churchman. He wrote: 'Lectures on Shakespeare' (1848); 'Campaign with General Butler' (1865); 'Shakespeare, his Life, Art, and Characters' (4th ed. 1883); 'Essays on Education, Etc.' (1883); etc. He edited the Harvard and the University edition of Shakespeare.

Hudson, Mrs. Mary (Clemmer) (Ames). An American journalist and miscellaneous writer; born at Utica, N. Y., 1839; died at Washington, D. C., 1884. She was at one time Washington correspondent of the New York Independent. She wrote : ' Ten Years in Washington ' (1871); ' Memorials of Alice and Phœbe Cary ' (1872); ' Men, Women, and Things ' (1873); ' Poems ' (1882); and several novels, among them ' His Two Wives ' (1874).

Huerta, Vicente Garcia de la (ö-är'tä). A Spanish dramatist, poet, and critic; born at Zafra, 1730; died at Madrid, March 12, 1787. He was government librarian, etc. He wrote indifferent lyrics, good narrative and descriptive verse, and excellent plays, one of the best being the tragedy ' Raquel,' on the love of Alphonso VIII. for a beautiful Jewess.

Huet, Coenraad Busken (hu-ā'). A Dutch journalist and miscellaneous writer; born in The Hague, Dec. 28, 1826; died at Paris, May 1, 1886. He was pastor of a church until 1862, when he became editor of the Haarlemmer Courant. He has produced some of Holland's best literary criticism. ' Literary Phantasies,' ' Dutch Literature,' ' Stories,' and numerous essays, have given him a high place in the literature of Europe.

Hughes, John. A distinguished American Roman Catholic prelate; born at Annalogham, Tyrone, Ireland, June 24, 1797; died in New York, Jan. 3, 1864. He was archbishop of New York in 1850–; special agent of the United States in Europe, 1861–62. He founded St. John's Asylum in 1829, the Catholic Herald 1833, and St. John's College, Fordham, 1839. He was prominent as a controversialist against Rev. John Breckenridge, a Presbyterian (1833–35), on the New York public-school system (1839–42), and against Erastus Brooks on the tenure of church property (1851). (' Works,' 2 vols., 1865.)

Hughes, Thomas. An English story and essay writer; born at Uffington, Oct. 20, 1822; died at Brighton, March 22, 1896. Apart from ' Tom Brown's School Days,' and ' Tom Brown at Oxford,' which brought him unexampled fame and popularity, he wrote persistently and capably in behalf of the form of socialism to which he was wedded, notably ' Our Old Church: What Shall We Do with It ?' and ' Rugby,' an account of a co-operative colony projected in Tennessee. ' The Manliness of Christ ' is a very original addition to the literature of militant Christianity.

Hugo, Victor Marie (hū'gō). A great French man of letters and publicist; born at Besançon, Feb. 26, 1802; died at Paris, May 22, 1885. His poems include : ' Various Odes and Poems ' (1822); ' New Odes ' (1824); ' Odes and Ballads ' (1826); ' The Orientals ' (1829); ' Autumn Leaves ' (1831); ' Twilight Songs ' (1835); ' Inner Voices '(1837); ' Sunbeams and Shadows ' (1840); ' The Chastisements ' (1853); ' The Contemplations ' (1856–57); ' The Legend of the Ages ' (1859); ' Songs of the Streets and Woods ' (1865); ' The Terrible Year ' (1872); ' The Art of Being a Grandfather ' (1877); ' The Legend of the Ages,' second series (1877); ' The Pope ' (1878); ' The Four Winds of the Spirit ' (1881); and other volumes of poetry. His plays include : ' Cromwell ' (1827); ' Amy Robsart ' (1828), adapted from Scott's ' Kenilworth '; ' Marion Delorme ' (1829); ' Hernani ' (1830); ' Le Roi s'Amuse ' (1832); ' Lucretia Borgia ' (1833); ' Marie Tudor ' (1833); ' Angelo ' (1835); ' Esmeralda ' (1836); ' Ruy Blas ' (1838); ' Les Burgraves ' (1843); ' Torquemada ' (1882); ' The Theatre in Freedom ' (1886); etc. His prose includes : ' Han d'Islande ' (1823); ' Bug-Jargal ' (1826); ' The Last Day of a Condemned Man ' (1829); ' Notre Dame de Paris ' (1831); ' Literature and Philosophy Blended ' (1834); ' Claude Gueux ' (1834); ' The Rhine ' (1842); ' Napoleon the Little ' (1852); ' Les Misérables ' (1862); ' Victor Hugo Revealed by a Witness of his Life ' (1863); ' William Shakespeare ' (1864); ' The Toilers of the Sea ' (1866); ' The Man Who Laughs ' (1869); ' Acts and Words ' (1872–76); ' Ninety-Three ' (1874); ' History of a Crime ' (1877–78): (posthumously) ' Things Seen ' (1887); ' Touring: Alps and Pyrenees ' (1890); etc.

Hull, Edward. An Irish geologist; born at Antrim, 1829. As a member of the Geological Survey of Great Britain for twenty years, he geologically mapped a large portion of the central counties of England. In 1869 he became professor of geology at the Royal College of Science, Dublin; and in 1883 commanded an expedition under the auspices of the Palestine Exploration Society to Arabia Petræa and Palestine. Among his important works are : ' The Coal-Fields of Great Britain ' (1865); ' Building and Ornamental Stones ' (1872); ' A Text-Book of Physiography ' (1888); ' Mount Seir, Sinai, and Southern Palestine ' (1885).

Humboldt, Alexander von (hum'bōlt). A German scientist and writer on science; born in Berlin, Sept. 14, 1769; died there, May 6, 1859. His educational opportunities were worthy of his splendid intellectual gifts. From childhood he delighted in zoölogical, physical, and geographical investigations. At 28, on the death of his mother, he began the series of voyages memorable in the annals of science. No name is likely ever to stand higher on his country's roll than his: the ' Cosmos ' is a sufficient proof. ' Voyages to the Equinoctial Regions of the New Continent '; ' View of the Cordilleras and of the Monuments of the Indigenous Races of America '; ' Observations on Zoölogy and Comparative Anatomy '; and a wealth of similar works, attest alike his Titanic genius and the singular charm of his literary style.

Humboldt, Wilhelm von. A German philologist, critic, and statesman, brother of Alexander; born in Potsdam, June 22, 1767; died at Tegel, near Berlin, April 8, 1835. He was educated at Göttingen, and devoted to philological and literary studies; but he had strong practical gifts and elevated social sympathies. In 1789 he visited Paris to study the French Revolution, with which he sympathized, from 1802 to 1819 he was in active official life,—minister to Vienna, member of the Privy Council, Secretary of State, ambassador to London, etc.; finally quitting it in disgust at the corruption he would not share. Meantime and later he wrote critiques on Goethe and Homer, and scientific and literary monographs, and translated Æschylus and Pindar. His main work in philology is 'On the Kawi Language of the Javanese,' but he made other valuable studies of primitive dialects.

Hume, David. A British historian and philosopher; born in Edinburgh, April 26, 1711; died there, Aug. 25, 1776. His works include: 'A Treatise on Human Nature' (1739-40); 'Essays, Moral and Political' (1741-42); 'Philosophical Essays Concerning Human Understanding' (1748), which subsequently had the title 'An Enquiry Concerning Human Understanding'; 'Political Discourses' (1751); 'An Enquiry Concerning the Principles of Morals' (1751); 'Four Dissertations' (1757), 'History of England' (1754-61); 'Natural History of Religion' (1757); 'Two Essays' (1777); 'Dialogues Concerning Natural Religion' (1779), etc.

Hume, Fergus. A New Zealand novelist. He was educated for the law, and was articled in the office of Sir Robert Stout, the well-known New Zealand statesman. His first long work, 'The Mystery of a Hansom Cab,' was published in Melbourne, and later in London, achieving a phenomenal circulation. Since the success of his first novel the author has devoted himself to literature in London. His most popular publications are. 'The Piccadilly Puzzle' (1889); 'Miss Mephistopheles' (1890); 'A Creature of Night' (1891); 'An Island of Fantasy' (1894); 'The Turnpike House' (1902).

Humphry, George Murray, Sir. An English surgeon and author; born at Sudbury, Suffolk, July 1820; died in 1896. He became professor of anatomy at Cambridge in 1866, and since 1883 has held the professorship of surgery in that institution. The honor of knighthood was conferred upon him in 1891, on account of his services to medical science. Among his valuable publications may be mentioned: 'A Treatise on the Human Skeleton' (1858); 'On Myology' (1872); 'Vivisection: What Good Has It Done?' (1882); 'Guide to Cambridge' (1883); 'Old Age and Changes Incidental to It' (1885), an oration.

Hungerford, Mrs. Margaret (Hamilton Argles). ["The Duchess."] A popular Irish novelist; born at Milleen, about 1855; died at Brandon, Jan. 24, 1897. 'Phyllis' (1877; 'Molly Bawn' (1878); 'Airy Fairy Lillian' (1879); 'Beauty's Daughters' (1880); 'Mrs. Geoffrey' (1881); 'Faith and Unfaith' (1881); 'Portia' (1882); 'Loÿs, Lord Beresford, and Other Tales' (1883); 'Rosmoyne' (1883), 'Doris' (1884); 'O Tender Dolores' (1885); 'A Maiden All

Forlorn, and Other Stories' (1885); 'In Durance Vile' (1885); 'Lady Branksmere' (1886); 'A Mental Struggle' (1886); 'Lady Valworth's Diamonds' (1886); 'Her Week's Amusement' (1886); 'Green Pastures and Gray Grief' (1886); 'A Modern Circe' (1887); 'The Duchess' (1887); 'Undercurrents' (1888); 'Marvel' (1888); 'Hon. Mrs. Vereker' (1888).

Hunnewell, James Frothingham. An American bibliographer, and writer of travels and history; born in Massachusetts, 1832. His home is at Charlestown, Mass He has written: 'Historical Monuments of France' (1884); 'England's Chronicle in Stone' (1886), being a study of English cathedrals, castles, and palaces; 'Triumphs of Early Printing.'

Hunt, Freeman. An American biographer and sketch-writer; born in Massachusetts, 1804; died 1858. A publisher in New York, he was the founder of Hunt's Merchants' Magazine. He wrote: 'Lives of American Merchants'; 'Sketches of Female Character'; etc.

Hunt, Leigh. An English poet, critic, essayist, born in Southgate, Oct. 19, 1784; died at Putney, Aug. 28, 1859. His collected poems, called 'Juvenilia,' appeared when he was fifteen. With his brother he founded the Examiner, a strong political journal, a disrespectful article in which on the Prince Regent gained him two years' imprisonment. After his release he produced a rapid succession of essays, criticisms, studies, and miscellany; among them 'Sir Ralph Esher,' a romance; 'A Legend of Florence,' a drama; 'The Story of Rimini,' his best work; and 'Recollections of Byron,' his most abused one.

Hunter, William Wilson, Sir. An English statistician and author; born at Glasgow, July 15, 1840; died at Oxford, Feb. 6, 1900. He was educated at the University of Glasgow and foreign universities, and was appointed to the Bengal Civil Service in 1862. As Director-General of Statistics he made a statistical survey of India, the results of which are embodied in the well-known 'Imperial Gazetteer of India' (1881; 1885-87). He was the author of 'Annals of Rural Bengal' (1868; 5th ed. 1872), continued in 'Orissa' (2 vols., 1872); 'The Life of the Marquess of Dalhousie'; 'A Dictionary of the Non-Aryan Languages of India and High Asia,' 'Brief History of the Indian Peoples,' which has been translated into five languages; and was the projector and editor of the series of biographies known as 'The Rulers of India.'

Hunter-Duvar, John. A Canadian poet; born in England, 1830. He has published 'Annals of the Court of Oberon' (1895), besides other volumes of poetry.

Huntington, Frederick Dan. An American clergyman and religious writer; born at Hadley, Mass., 1819. In early life as a Unitarian minister he held a pastorate in Boston from 1842 to 1855, when he became Plummer professor of Christian morals in Harvard University. In 1860 he withdrew from the Unitarian denomination, was ordained in the Protestant Episcopal Church, and in 1869 was consecrated bishop of Central New York. His writings include : ' Christian Believing and Living ' (1860); ' Lectures on Human Society ' (1860); ' Steps to a Living Faith ' (1873); ' Personal Christian Life in the Ministry ' (1887); ' Forty Days with the Master.' Died July 11, 1904.

Huntington, Jedediah Vincent. An American poet and novelist; born in New York, January 1815; died in France, 1862. Originally a physician, then an Episcopal clergyman, he became a Roman Catholic in 1849, and edited Roman Catholic magazines. He wrote: ' Poems ' (1843); the striking novels, ' Lady Alice, or the New Una,' (1849), ' Alban, or the History of a Young Puritan ' (new ed. 1853, with its sequel ' The Forest,' 1852), ' Blonde and Brunette ' (1859); etc.

Hurlburt, William Henry. An American journalist; born at Charleston, S. C., July 3, 1827; died at Cadenabbia, Sept. 4, 1895. After long journalistic experience in New York, he became editor-in-chief of New York World (1876–83). After 1883 he resided in Europe. He wrote: ' GanEden ' (1854), travels in Cuba; ' General McClellan and the Conduct of the War (1864), etc.

Hurst, John Fletcher. A prominent American Methodist divine and writer; born near Salem, Md., Aug. 17, 1834. He became bishop in the Methodist Episcopal Church in 1880, and chancellor of the American University of his denomination in 1891. He has written : ' Literature of Theology '; ' History of Rationalism '; ' Martyrs to the Tract Cause '; ' Life and Literature in the Fatherland '; ' Outline of Church History '; ' Our Theological Century '; ' Bibliotheca Theologica '; ' Short Histories of the Church '; ' Short History of the Christian Church '; ' Indika,' a large illustrated work on India, and of great importance; translations of theological works and histories; etc. Died at Washington, D. C., May 4, 1903.

Hurter, Friedrich Emanuel, von (hör'ter). A Swiss theologian and historian; born at Schaffhausen, March 19, 1787; died at Gratz, Styria, Aug. 27, 1865. Appointed to a pastorate in his native town, he resigned in 1841, and became a convert to Catholicism. In 1846 he was selected as historiographer to the Emperor of Austria. Of his numerous works, relating chiefly to mediæval and church history, may be mentioned : ' History of King Theodoric and his Reign ' (1807); ' Pope Innocent III. and his Contemporaries ' (1834–42); ' Birth and New Birth ' (1845), in which he gives his reasons for a change of religion; ' Emperor Ferdinand II.' (10 vols., 1850–62); ' Last Four Years of the Life of Wallenstein ' (1862).

Hutcheson, Francis. A Scotch educator and philosopher; born at Drumalig, Ulster, Ireland, Aug. 8, 1694; died in Glasgow, about 1746. For many years a public teacher in Glasgow, he became in 1729 professor of moral philosophy at the university in that city. He is re-

garded as one of the founders of modern philosophy in Scotland. He was the author of : ' Inquiry into the Original of Our Ideas of Beauty and Virtue ' (1720); ' Nature and Conduct of the Passions and Affections ' (1728); ' System of Moral Philosophy ' (1755).

Hutchinson, Ellen Mackay. [" Mrs. Royal Cortissoz."] An American poet and journalist; born in western New York in 18—. She was long one of the editors of the New York Tribune, and was associated with E. C. Stedman in the compilation of the ' Library of American Literature.' Her numerous poems have been collected under the title of ' Songs and Lyrics ' (1881).

Hutten, Ulrich von (höt'ten). A German poet, theologian, and controversial satirist; born in Steckelburg, near Fulda, 1488; died in the island of Ufenau, Lake Zurich, 1523. Of a noble family and destined for the church, he preferred a life of roving adventure. After many vicissitudes, including shipwreck, military service, and absolute beggary, he rose to fame by brilliant contributions to the current religious and political controversies. His works include : ' The Art of Prosody '; ' Nemo,' a satire upon the pedantic learning of his day; ' Dialogues '; and various others, most of them attacking abuses in the church. His most noteworthy production, however (his in part if not wholly), is the ' Letters of Obscure Men ' (that is, men who think and talk obscurely), mercilessly ridiculing the ignorance of the lower clergy. His position in literature is that of a fearless genius and champion of truth; he aimed to regenerate his country, but his means were somewhat Utopian.

Hutton, Laurence. An American essayist and literary critic; born in New York, Aug. 8, 1843. Devoting his earlier years to mercantile pursuits, he at length became dramatic critic of the New York Evening Mail. He has edited, since 1886, Literary Notes in Harper's Magazine. His publications are well known under the titles ' Plays and Players '; ' Edwin Booth '; ' Literary Landmarks '; and essays on London, Edinburgh, Jerusalem, Venice, Florence, and Rome. Died at Princeton, N. J., June 10, 1904.

Hutton, Richard Holt. An English editor and author; born at Leeds, June 2, 1826; died in London, Sept. 9, 1897. He was editor of the London Spectator, a critic of great repute, and the author of ' Studies in Parliament : a Series of Sketches of Leading Politicians ' (1866); ' Essays, Theological and Literary ' (2 vols, 1871); ' Sir Walter Scott' (1878) in ' English Men of Letters ' series ; ' Essays on Some Modern Guides of English Thought in Matters of Faith ' (1887).

Huxley, Thomas Henry. An eminent English scientist; born in Ealing, May 4, 1825; died June 29, 1895. His works include : ' On the Educational Value of the Natural-History Sciences ' (1854); ' On Tape and Cystic Worms ' (1857), translated from the German of C. T. Von Siebold; ' Evidence as to Man's Place in

Nature' (1863); 'On Our Knowledge of the Causes of the Phenomena of Organic Nature: Being Six Lectures to Workingmen' (1863); 'Lectures on the Elements of Comparative Anatomy' (1864); 'An Elementary Atlas of Comparative Osteology' (1864-66); 'Palæontologia Indica: Vertebrated Fossils' (1866); 'Lessons in Elementary Physiology' (1866); 'An Introduction to the Classification of Animals' (1869); 'Protoplasm: the Physical Basis of Life' (1869), new edition entitled 'On the Physical Basis of Life' in 'Half Hours with Modern Scientists'; 'Lay Sermons, Addresses, and Reviews' (1870); 'Essays: Selected from Lay Sermons, etc.' (1871); 'A Manual of the Anatomy of Vertebrated Animals' (1871); 'Critiques and Addresses' (1873); 'American Addresses' (1877); 'Physiography' (1877); 'Hume' (1879), in 'English Men of Letters'; 'Science Primers: Introductory' (1880); 'The Crayfish: an Introduction to the Study of Zoölogy' (1880); 'Science and Culture, and Other Essays' (1881); 'Inaugural Meeting of the Fishery Congress: Address' (1883); with H. N. Martin, 'A Course of Practical Instruction in Elementary Biology' (1888); 'Evolution and Ethics' (1893).

Huygens, Constantyn (hī'genz). A Dutch poet and prose-writer; born in The Hague, Sept. 4, 1596; died March 28, 1687. He was long private secretary to the Prince of Orange. His first volume of poems, 'Otia' (Relaxations), is in Italian, French, Latin, and Dutch. The last two sections were subsequently enlarged and each published separately: the first as 'Momenta Desultoria'; and the second, the widely read 'Corn Flowers,' which contained epigrams, translations, and one or two excellent comedies. His most notable poems are 'Daghwerck,' in memory of his wife, and 'Batave Tempe,' a series of native legends and scenes. His prose comprises memoirs, essays on music, and State papers. He is the most brilliant figure in Dutch literary history.

Huysmans, Jorris Karl (ēs-mäns). A French novelist; born in Paris, Feb. 5, 1848. He studied law and entered the French civil service, but abandoned it for literature. At first a pronounced realist, he turned to idealism and even mysticism. He first attracted notice by the story 'Pack on Back'; then followed 'Martha,' 'The Vatard Sisters,' 'The Ménage,' and others. The latest expression of his theories is in 'Down There' (Là-bas). His style is dreamy and intensely delicate, but obscure at times. D. 1906.

Hyacinthe, Père. See **Loyson.**

Hylton, John Dunbar. An American writer of verse; born in the island of Jamaica, W. I, 1837. He is a physician at Palmyra, N. J. He has written: 'The Bride of Gettysburg' (1878); 'Above the Grave of John Odenswurge' (2d ed. 1884); 'Artaloise' (1887); etc.

Hymans, Louis (ē-mäns). A Belgian historian, journalist, novelist, and poet; born in Rotterdam, 1829; died at Brussels, 1884. He removed to Belgium in boyhood and rose rapidly to distinction as a Liberal journalist. He edited the Belgian Star and the Parliamentary Echo for some years, and was elected to Parliament in 1859. He wrote: 'History of the Marquisate of Anvers,' 'Popular History of Belgium,' and 'Political and Parliamentary History of Belgium'; two popular novels, 'André Bailly' and 'The Buvard Family'; and some pleasing poems.

Hyndman, Henry Mayers. An English journalist, socialistic leader, and author; born in 1842. He acted as special correspondent for the Pall Mall Gazette during the war between France and Italy in 1866, and was one of the founders of the Social Democratic Federation in 1881. Among his works, which deal chiefly with socialism, may be mentioned: 'The Indian Famine and the Crisis in India' (1877); 'Text-Book of Democracy' (1881); 'The Historical Basis of Socialism in England' (1883); 'Will Socialism Benefit the English People?' (1884); 'The Commercial Crisis of the Nineteenth Century' (1892). He was co-author with William Morris of 'A Summary of the Principles of Socialism' (1884).

I

Iamblichus (jam'bli-kus). A Syrian philosopher; born at Chalcis, Cœle-Syria; died about 330 A. D. He was the author of numerous philosophical works written from the Neo-Platonic point of view, among them an ‘Exhortation to Philosophy.’ He also wrote a ‘Life of Pythagoras.’

Ibn Batuta (ibn bä-tö'tä). An Arabic writer of travel; born at Tangier, Morocco, about 1304; died at Fez, about 1377. He made many voyages and wrote his ‘Travels,’ which were translated into French and English. He is sometimes termed Abu Abdallah Mohammed.

Ibn Doreid, Abubekr Mohammed (ibn dō-rīd'). An Arabic poet and philologist; born at Basra, 838; died in Bagdad, 933. He wrote, among other things, a celebrated elegy on the mutability of fortune, which has been translated and commented upon.

Ibn Esra (ibn ez'rä). [Properly Abraham ben Meir ibn Esra.] A Jewish writer and scholar; born at Toledo, about 1092; died 1167. He traveled extensively, studying poetry, grammar, mathematics, astronomy, and philosophy. He wrote a Hebrew grammar, was one of the earliest critics and commentators on the Bible, and composed hymns largely used in the Jewish liturgy.

Ibn Khaldún, Abderrahman (ibn khäl-dön'). An Arabic historian, descended from a noble family of Seville; born in Tunis, 1322; died at Cairo, 1406. He occupied high official positions at the courts of various Mahometan princes, and is considered the greatest of Arabic historians, his chief work being a history of the Arabs and Berbers in several volumes, with a philosophical introduction to the science of history.

Ibn Khallikan (ibn kâl'li-kän). An Arabic scholar and writer; born at Arbe'a, 1211; died at Damascus, 1281. He was renowned in his own day for his numerous works in every department of literature. His best-known work is the ‘Wafiat-ul-Aiyan,’ or ‘Deaths of Eminent Men.’

Ibn Koteiba, Abdallah ibn Muslim. A noted Arabic philologist and historian; born at Bagdad, 828; died there, 890. He composed, among many other things, a ‘Handbook of History,’ brought out in a German translation in 1850; a work on ‘The Art of Poetry’; and ‘Contributions to the Knowledge of Poetry among the Old Arabs.’

Ibn Sînâ (ibn sen'ä). An Arabic philosopher, known also as Avicenna; born in Afshena, Bokhara, 980; died at Hamaden, Persia, 1037. The titles of his works are so numerous that the reader is referred to his biography in the ‘Library’ for an authoritive enumeration of them as well as for a history of his career.

Ibn Tofail (ibn to-fîl'). An Arabic philosopher and physician, who flourished towards the close of the twelfth century in one of the Spanish dominions of the Moors. His most celebrated work is a philosophical romance bearing the title ‘The Improvement of Human Reason Exhibited in the Life of Hai Ebn Yokdhan,’ which has been translated into Hebrew, Latin, and English.

Ibrahim of Aleppo (ib-rä-hēm'). A famed Ottoman writer on jurisprudence; born about 1490 (?); died 1549. He compiled the great code of laws known as ‘Multeka-al-Abhar’ (Confluence of the Seas).

Ibsen, Henrik (ib'sẹn). A Norwegian dramatist; born in Skien, March 20, 1828. His plays are: ‘Brand,’ a drama; ‘A Doll's House,’ a satiric comedy; ‘Peer Gynt,’ a dramatic poem; ‘Emperor and Galilean,’ a historic drama (in two parts: i., ‘Julian's Apostasy’; ii., ‘Julian the Emperor’); ‘The Pillars of Society,’ a satiric comedy; ‘The Warriors at Helgeland,’ a historical drama; ‘Love's Comedy,’ a satirical play; and the series comprising ‘Ghosts,’ ‘An Enemy of the People,’ ‘The Wild Duck,’ ‘Rosmersholm,’ ‘The Lady from the Sea,’ ‘Hedda Gabler,’ and ‘Architect Solness,’ all of which are alike in that they aim to dissect the conventionalities of the social system under which we live. Died May 23, 1906.

Ibycus (ib'i-kus). A Greek lyric poet; born in Rhegium, about B. C. 560 (?); died there (or near Corinth?), B. C. 525 (?). The fragments of exquisite metre that have come down to us, and the picturesque fate that befell him—a fate that suggested to Dante one of his inimitable images—have won for him a distinct renown. The ancients esteemed him highly, although Cicero complains of the impurity of his Muse as a sign of the degeneracy of the Romans who admired it. The story told of him is that the poet went on a journey to Corinth but was captured by bandits near that city, and murdered after having been despoiled. As he expired he called to a flock of passing cranes to avenge him; and as the bandits sat in the theatre not many days later, a flight of the stately birds took place, whereupon the leader of the guilty men called attention, ironically, to the dead poet's «avengers.» The word attracted notice and led to discovery.

Ide, George Barton. An American writer and clergyman; born in Vermont, 1804; died in 1872. He has published ‘Green Hollow’; ‘Bible Echoes, or Lessons from the War’;

'The Power of Kindness,' a juvenile tale; and 'Bible Pictures.'

Idrisi (id'rē-sē). An Arabian geographer, who flourished between 1100 and 1200, and wrote a 'Book About the World' which is of importance in the annals of geographical science.

Iffland, August Wilhelm (if'fländ). A German dramatist and actor; born in Hanover, April 19, 1759; died at Berlin, Sept. 22, 1814. He fled his home and theological studies when a mere youth, in order to go on the stage, and soon became a great actor. As a playwright he captured the public with 'The Hunters' and 'The Crime of Ambition.' He united in a rare degree a mastery of stage-craft with a knowledge of dramatic construction.

Iglesias, José Maria (ē-glä'sē-äs). A Mexican historian and publicist; born in the City of Mexico, Jan. 5, 1823. He has figured very prominently in his country's politics. He has written 'Contribution to a History of the War between Mexico and the United States' (1852), and a 'Historical Review of the French Intervention' (1870).

Iglesias de la Casa, José (ē-glä'sē-äs dä lä kä'sä). A Spanish poet; born in Salamanca, Oct. 31, 1748; died there, Aug. 26, 1791. He was a priest in his native diocese, and in conjunction with Melendez, organized a devoted band of poetasters, the fame of which spread far and wide, under the name of the School of Salamanca, exercising in time no ordinary authority over Spanish poetry. His volume of 'Light Verse' has, under various titles, passed through numerous editions in Spain, where he will probably always be a classic.

Ilsley, Charles Parker. An American author; born in Maine in 1807; died in 1887. He was a resident of Portland, Me., until 1866. Among his works are: 'The Liberty Pole, a Tale of Machias'; 'Forest and Shore,' later republished as 'The Wrecker's Daughter.'

Imbert, Barthelémi (an-bär'). A French poet; born at Nîmes, 1747; died near Paris (?), Aug. 23, 1790. He attained celebrity with 'The Judgment of Paris,' a specimen of delicately wrought and musical versification. He also wrote a 'Book of Fables.'

Imbert de Saint-Amand, Arthur (an-bär' de sant-ä-män). *Pseud. :* Arthur Leon. A French biographer and historian; born in Paris, Nov. 22, 1834: died there, June —, 1900. His career was a diplomatic and official one until he began a study of the lives of the women of the old French courts, of the First Empire, and of the restoration. His 'Women of Versailles' is a graphic presentation of court manners and morals before the Revolution, while the 'Women of the Tuileries' is a bit of realism in biography that brings the era vividly before the reader. His studies of the Napoleonic royalties sustain the reputation established by the earlier works.

Imbriani, Vittorio (ēm-brē-än'ē). An Italian poet and historian of literature; born in Naples, Oct. 27, 1840; died there, Jan. 1, 1886. His life was involved in political turmoil, but he made himself known as a graceful and elegant poet with 'Popular Songs of the Southern Provinces,' and as an ode-writer of strength and dignity in an 'Address to Italy's Queen.' In prose he ranks high, as 'Purloined [or Usurped] Reputations,' a book of literary essays, demonstrates. His 'Philological Studies in Dante' is a valuable contribution to our knowledge of the great Florentine.

Imlah, John. A Scottish poet and songwriter; born in Aberdeen, 1799; died at St. James, Jamaica, 1846. His songs met the popular fancy, and are to be found in all Scotch collections. He published 'May Flowers' in 1827, followed by 'Poems and Songs' (1841).

Immermann, Karl Leberecht (im'mer-män). A German poet, dramatist, and romancer; born in Magdeburg, April 24, 1796; died at Düsseldorf, Aug. 25, 1840. A university course and the campaign of Waterloo supplied his early experiences. As the result of years of hard labor he produced plays above mediocrity but below greatness. 'The Princes of Syracuse' and 'The Eye of Love' merit notice among his comedies, while as a tragedy, his 'Ghismonda' ranks high. He lives in the brilliant and original 'Epigoni.' 'Münchhausen,' his lightest fancy, is well known. It must not be confused with 'Baron Münchhausen.'

Inchbald, Elizabeth (Simpson). An English actress, dramatist, and novelist; born 1753; died 1821. 'A Simple Story,' 'Nature and Art,' are among her best tales. She also wrote: 'Such Things Are'; 'The Married Man'; 'The Wedding Day'; 'The Midnight Hour'; 'Every One Has his Fault'; 'Lovers' Vows'; etc.

Ingalls, Joshua King. An American financier and writer; born 18—. He has published: 'Social Wealth'; 'Economic Equities'; and 'Reminiscences of an Octogenarian' (1897).

Ingelow, Jean. An English poet and novelist; born in Boston, Eng., March 17, 1820; died in London, July 19, 1897. 'A Rhyming Chronicle of Incidents and Feeling,' her maiden volume, reveals her melancholy disposition. The 'Round of Days' brought her fame, and the circle of her admirers constantly widened as 'Home ,Thoughts and Home Scenes,' 'A Story of Doom, and Other Poems,' 'Mopsa the Fairy,' and 'Little Wonder Horn' made evident the full range of her power. Her novels, 'Fated to be Free,' 'Sarah de Berenger,' 'Don John,' and one or two more, did not attract wide attention.

Ingemann, Bernhard Severin (ing'e-män). A Danish poet and novelist; born 1789; died 1862. His 'Procne,' 'Youthful Poems,' and 'The Renegade' display genius. 'Blanca,' 'The Voice in the Desert,' and 'The Battle for the Possession of Walhalla' are wonderful plays, alive with inspiration. 'Waldemar the Great and his Companions,' a historic poem, is his masterpiece, while as a novelist he stands among the chosen few with 'Conqueror Waldemar,' one of the triumphs of the Danish language.

Ingersoll, Charles Jared. An American poet and miscellaneous writer; born in Philadelphia, 1782; died there, 1862. He was the author of 'Chiomara' (1800), a poem; 'Edwy and Elgira' (1801), a tragedy; 'Inchiquin the Jesuit's Letters on American Literature and Politics' (1810); 'Julian' (1831), a poem; and a 'Historical Sketch of the Second War between the United States and Great Britain' (4 vols., 1845–52).

Ingersoll, Ernest. An American naturalist and prose-writer; born in Michigan, 1852. The summer of 1873 he spent with Louis Agassiz in his seaside school on Penikese. After Agassiz died he was naturalist and collector with the Hayden survey in the West. He contributed scientific articles to various newspapers. His writings include: 'Birds'-Nesting' (1881); 'History and Present Condition of the Oyster Industries of the United States' (1881); 'Knocking Round the Rockies' (1882); 'Country Cousins' (1884); 'The Strange Ventures of a Stowaway' (1886); and 'The Wit of the Wild' (1906).

Ingersoll, Luther Dunham. An American writer; born 18—. He is librarian of the War Department at Washington, and has published 'Iowa and the Rebellion'; a 'Life of Horace Greeley'; and a 'History of the War Department.'

Ingei oll, Robert Green. A distinguished American orator, lecturer, and lawyer; born in Dresden, N. Y., Aug. 11, 1833; died at Dobb's Ferry. N. Y., July 21, 1899. He was well known as a free-thinker. He went west when twelve years old, becoming in time a school-teacher. He began to practice law in 1854. He was colonel of Illinois cavalry during the War. In 1866 he was made attorney-general for Illinois. He has published: 'The Gods'; 'Ghosts'; 'Some Mistakes of Moses'; 'Lectures Complete'; 'Prose Poems and Selections'; and many other pamphlets and miscellaneous articles.

Ingleby, Clement Mansfield. An English Shakespearean critic and miscellaneous writer; born at Edgbaston, near Birmingham, Oct. 29, 1823; died at Ilford, Essex, 1886. He was educated at Cambridge for the law, which he abandoned for a literary career, and became famous as a Shakespearean scholar and critic, aiding in the Stanton edition. He wrote : 'The Principles of Acoustics and the Theory of Sound'; 'The Stereoscope'; 'The Ideality of the Rainbow'; 'The Mutual Relation of Theory and Practice'; 'Law and Religion'; 'A Voice for the Mute Creation'; 'Miracles Versus Nature.'

Inglis, Henry David (ing'lz). An English descriptive prose-writer; born in Edinburgh, 1795; died in London, March 20, 1835. From mercantile life he drifted into literature; traveling widely, and under the pseudonym of "Derwent Conway," writing: 'Tales of the Ardennes'

(1825), a very popular book, duly followed by 'Solitary Walks through Many Lands' (1828), 'Rambles in the Footsteps of Don Quixote' (1837), and various similar studies.

Ingraham, Joseph Holt. An American writer and clergyman; born in Maine, 1809; died 1866. He lived for a time in Holly Springs, Miss., and early in life wrote some very sensational romances, among them: 'Lafitte; the Pirate of the Gulf'; 'Captain Kyd'; and 'The Dancing Feather.' After entering the ministry he wrote three religious romances: 'The Prince of the House of David'; 'The Pillar of Fire'; and 'The Throne of David.'

Innsley, Owen. See **Jennison, Lucy White.**

Intra, Giambattista (ēn'trä). An Italian novelist and essayist; born in Calvenzano, near Bergamo, in 1832. He has contributed ably to periodical literature and produced original and interesting fiction, notably 'Agnese Gonzaga,' and 'The Last of the Bonaccolsi'; 'In Villa.'

Ion of Chios (i'on [or ē'ōn] ki'os). A Greek poet and prose-writer; born in Chios about 484 B.C.; died at Athens about 422. Few losses to literature are so serious as the destruction of his works, fragments only of which have descended to us. Richly endowed, intellectually and physically, and accomplished even for the age of Pericles, he established himself in the intimacy of Æschylus, Sophocles, and the other men who ornament that unexampled era. He distinguished himself by his versatility: tragedies, hymns, elegies, epigrams, and essays issued in a splendid if not very deep stream from the perennial springs of his fancy. Brilliant passages in his memoirs, saved to us by a happy accident, tell of the banquet he gave to Sophocles and the things said and done on that typically Hellenic occasion.

Iron, Ralph. See **Schreiner, Olive.**

Irving, John Treat, Jr. An American writer; born 1812; a nephew of Washington Irving, and a lawyer of New York city. He has written: 'Indian Sketches'; 'Hawk Chief'; 'The Attorney'; 'Henry Harson'; and 'The Van Gelder Papers.' He died in 1906.

Irving, Pierre Munroe. An American writer, nephew of Washington Irving; born 1803; died in 1876. He was the author of a 'Life of Washington Irving.' He also edited various compilations and acted as his uncle's literary assistant.

Irving, Washington. An American historian, biographer, and man of letters; born in New York, April 3, 1783; died at "Sunnyside," near Tarrytown, N. Y., Nov. 28, 1859. His works include: 'A Voyage to the Eastern Part of Terra Firma' (1806), a translation; Salmagundi (1807–8), with J. K. Paulding and William Irving; 'History of New York by Diedrich Knickerbocker' (1809); 'The Sketch Book' (1819–20); 'Bracebridge Hall' (1822); 'Letters of Jonathan Oldstyle, Gent.' (1824); 'Life and Times of Christopher Columbus' (1828);

'Conquest of Granada' (1829); 'Companions of Columbus' (1831); 'The Alhambra' (1832); 'Crayon Miscellany' (1835); 'Astoria' (1836); 'The Rocky Mountains: Journal of Captain B. L. E. Bonneville' (1837); 'Life of Oliver Goldsmith' (1840); 'Mahomet and his Successors' (1849-50); 'Wolfert's Roost' (1855); 'Life of Washington' (1855-59). Among his literary labors he made an edition of 'The Poetical Works of Thomas Campbell' (1810), and 'Miscellaneous Works of Oliver Goldsmith.'

Irving, William. An American prose-writer, and brother of Washington Irving; born in New York city, 1766; died there, 1821. He contributed largely in the production of Salmagundi; the political pieces were mostly his, as also were the letters of Mustapha in Nos. 5 and 14.

Isaaks, Jorge (ē'säks *or* ī'zaks). A South American novelist and poet; born in Cali, Colombia. His extraction is partly English-Jewish and partly Spanish. 'María,' a novel, is his masterpiece, but he has written meritorious verse.

Isla, José Francisco de (ēs'lä). A Spanish satirist; born in Vidane, March 24, 1703; died at Bologna, Nov. 2, 1781. He was a Jesuit and taught successfully in the Jesuit seminaries for years, but the expulsion of his order from Spain reduced him to destitution, and he died in want. He is without a rival among his countrymen, Cervantes always excepted, as a wit and satirist; the prodigious popularity of his 'Life and Adventures of Friar Gerundio de Campazas,' upon its first appearance in 1758 (under the pseudonym of "F. Lobon de Salazar"), being but a well-won tribute to its unhackneyed drolleries and epigrammatic style. As a portrait of Spanish life in the eighteenth century it must ever remain a standard work. He made an infelicitous translation of 'Gil Blas' from the French that led to a still more infelicitous controversy over the authorship of that lengthy masterpiece. His other works are without importance.

Isocrates (ī-sok'ra-tēs). A Greek orator and rhetorician; born in Athens in 436 B. C.; died at Athens (?) 338 B.C. He was apparently carefully educated, Socrates having been of the number of his preceptors; and at an early age he was celebrated for the facility with which he used his native tongue, although the weakness of his voice precluded any hope he may once have entertained of distinction in public life. He therefore opened a school of oratory, the fame of which soon filled all Greece, in consequence of the exceptional attainments of its graduates. The ages have spared to us twenty-one of his compositions, rhetorical and epistolary. He is best represented by the discourses known as the 'Areopagiticus' and the 'Panegyricus.'

J

Jablonsky, Boleslav (yab-lon'skē). ["Karl Eugen Tupy."] A leading Czech poet; born Jan. 14, 1813; died in Cracow, March 1881. His love lyric 'Pisne' and his didactic 'The Father's Wisdom' are universally popular.

Jackson, Edward Payson. An American prose-writer; born in Erzeroum, Turkey, March 15, 1840. He graduated at Amherst in 1870. He published: 'Mathematic Geography' (1873); 'A Demi-God' (1886); and 'The Earth in Space' (1887). He died in 1905.

Jackson, Helen Fiske. ["H. H."] An American poet and miscellaneous writer; born 1831; died 1885. She published: 'Poems'; 'Bits of Talk'; 'Hetty's Strange History'; 'Ramona'; 'A Century of Dishonor'; etc.

Jackson, Henry. An English novelist; born in Boston, Lincolnshire, April 15, 1831; died at Hampstead, May 24, 1879. His novels: 'A Dead Man's Revenge'; 'Gilbert Rugge' (1866); and 'Argus Fairburn' (1874), had much vogue.

Jackson, Sheldon. An American missionary; born at Minaville, N. Y., May 18, 1834. He was superintendent of missions for the Rocky Mountain region from 1870 to 1872. In 1885 he was appointed general agent of education in Alaska. Among his works are: 'Alaska and Missions on the North Pacific Coast' (1880); 'Education in Alaska' (1881).

Jacobi, Friedrich Heinrich (yä kō'bē). A German philosopher and metaphysician; born in Düsseldorf, Jan. 25, 1743; died at Munich, March 10, 1819. He obtained recognition from Wieland, Goethe, and other accomplished Germans as one of the most original thinkers of their common country. 'Letters on Spinoza's Philosophy'; 'Things Divine'; 'Letter to Fichte'; 'An Enterprise in Criticism to Render Reason Reasonable'; and 'Woldemar,' a philosophical fiction, are among his most important additions to literature.

Jacobi, Johann Georg. A German poet, brother of Friedrich; born in Düsseldorf, Sept. 2, 1740; died at Freiburg, Jan. 4, 1814. His association with Wieland, Klopstock, Goethe, Herder, and "Father" Gleim, the poet and patron of poets, quickened his talent, and the verse that gives him such eminence among his country's minor bards was the result. 'The Summer Journey' and 'The Winter Journey' are among the prettiest of this poet's pieces.

Jacobi, Mary Putnam. An American physician; born in London, England, Aug. 31, 1842

She graduated from the Woman's Medical College, Philadelphia; College of Pharmacy, New York; and the School of Medicine, Paris. Since 1871 she has practiced in New York city. Among her works are: 'The Value of Life' (1879); 'Hysteria, and Other Essays' (1888). D. 1906.

Jacobsen, Jens Peter (yä'kub-sen). A Danish novelist; born at Thisted, Jutland, April 7, 1847; died at Copenhagen, April 30, 1885. He was a botanist and Darwinian who turned to story-writing and became eminent as a realistic novelist. 'Mogens,' 'Niels Lyhne,' and 'Marie Grubbe' are tales of great merit in plot, construction, and style.

Jacobson, Eduard (yä'kub-son). A German comic poet; born at Great Strelitz, Upper Silesia, Nov. 10, 1833. He studied medicine, but wrote 'Faust and Gretchen' in his college days, and thus learned what he was fitted for. A host of laughable nothings have followed it. Among his best works '500,000 Devils' and 'The Man in the Moon' may be cited. D. 1897.

Jacopone da Todi (yä''kō-pō'ne dä tō'dē). An Italian Pietist poet and satirist; born at Todi about 1230; died at Collazzone, Dec. 25, 1306. He was a prominent lawyer, who lost his wife, became a monk, and got involved in politics. He wrote dialect poems in support of his party; the stinging sarcasm of his rhymes aimed against Pope Boniface VIII. causing them to be particularly remembered. The hymn 'Stabat Mater' is attributed to him, although the authorship has been disputed.

Jacotot, Jean Joseph (zhä-kō-tō). A French authority on education; born in Dijon, March 4, 1770; died at Paris, July 31, 1840. He founded a system of pedagogics that still bears his name, and is based apparently upon the *iter*, *iterumque* of Virgil,—constant repetition, and learning by heart,—together with a harmony of studies. His system is set forth in the 'Universal Instruction,' an elaborate manual in "mother tongue," and in 'Music, Design, and Painting,' works of great vogue at one time, and still widely accepted.

Jäger, Oskar (yä'ger). A German historian and pedagogue; born at Stuttgart, Oct. 26, 1830. As an educator he has attained prestige and official position; while his 'History of Recent Times, from the Congress of Vienna to our Own Day' (1874-75) is an acknowledged masterpiece. 'The Humanist Gymnasium' (1889) is an example of his achievements in pedagogics; and he has written 'The Punic Wars' (1869-70) and 'John Wycliffe and his Significance for the Reformation' (1854), both profound studies; and a 'World History' (1902).

Jago, Richard. An English poet; born in Beaudesert, Warwickshire, Oct. 1, 1715; died at Snitterfield, May 8, 1781. He was a clergyman poetically endowed, whose elegy 'The Blackbirds' (1753) pleases, and whose other works are tasteful.

Jagodynski, Stanislas (yä-gō-din'skē). A Polish poet and prose-writer, who flourished in the sixteenth century, and was, it would seem, a laureate and epigrammatist at court, distinguishing himself by his wit and eloquence. 'Presents for Saxon Ladies,' a biting and dainty satire, directed against the corruption of the times; 'The Courtesans,' a volume of epigrams; and 'The Escape of Rugiera,' a drama, show him at his best.

Jalal-ud-din Rūmī. See **Rūmī**.

James I., King of Scotland. Born at Dunfermline, Aug. 1 (?), 1394; assassinated near Perth, Feb. 20, 1437. His 'Kingis Quair' (King's Booklet: 1404?) is a poem of spirit; and in 'The Ballade of Guid Counsale,' almost certainly his, are many fine passages.

James I., King of England. Born in Edinburgh Castle, June 19, 1566; died at the palace of Theobalds, March 27, 1625. His literary gifts are revealed in 'Essays of a Prentice in the Divine Art of Poetry' (1584); 'Poetical Exercises' (1591); and 'The True Law of Free Monarchies' (1603).

James, George Payne Rainsford. An English novelist; born in London, Aug. 9, 1801; died in Venice, May 9, 1860. His historical novel 'Richelieu' (1829) won encomiums from Scott. Next came 'Darnley' (1830); 'Delorme' (1831); 'Attila' (1837); and many stirring and readable novels. He attempted the historian's rôle, without encouraging results, in 'Dark Scenes of History' (1849), and other books. He wrote as many as seventy historical novels.

James, Henry. An American scholar; born at Albany, N. Y., June 3, 1811; died at Cambridge, Mass., Dec. 18, 1882. He resided at Cambridge. Among the most noted of his works on morals and religion are: 'What Is the State?' (1845); 'Moralism and Christianity' (1852); 'Lectures and Miscellanies' (1852); 'The Nature of Evil' (1855); 'Christianity the Logic of Creation' (1857); 'Substance and Shadow' (1863); 'The Secret of Swedenborg' (1869).

James, Henry. An American novelist and miscellaneous prose-writer, son of Henry (1st); born in New York, April 15, 1843. His works include: 'Transatlantic Sketches' (1875); 'A Passionate Pilgrim and Other Tales' (1875); 'Roderick Hudson' (1876); 'The American' (1877); 'Watch and Ward' (1878); 'French Poets and Novelists' (1878); 'Daisy Miller: a Study' (1878); 'The Europeans: a Sketch' (1878); 'An International Episode' (1879); 'The Madonna of the Future and Other Tales' (1879); 'Hawthorne' (1879); 'A Bundle of Letters' (1880); 'Confidence' (1880); 'The Diary of a Man of Fifty' (1880); 'Washington Square' (1880); 'The Portrait of a Lady' (1882); 'Daisy Miller: a Comedy' (1883); 'The Siege of London; The Pension Beaurepas; and The Point of View' (1883); 'Portraits of Places' (1883); 'Tales of Three Cities' (1884); 'A Little Tour in France' (1885); 'The Art of Fiction' (1885), with Walter Besant; 'Stories Revived' (2 vols.,

1885); 'The Author of Beltraffio' (1885); 'The Bostonians' (1886); 'The Princess Casamassima' (1886); 'Partial Portraits' (1888); 'The Aspern Papers and Other Stories' (1888); 'The Reverberator' (1888); 'A London Life' (1889); 'The Tragic Muse' (1890); 'Port Tarascon' (1891), a translation; 'The Lesson of the Master' (1892), a volume of stories; 'The Real Thing and Other Tales' (1893); 'Picture and Text' (1893); 'The Private Life' (1893), a volume of stories; 'Essays in London and Elsewhere' (1893); 'The Wheel of Time' (1894); 'Theatricals' (1894); 'Terminations' (1895); 'What Maisie Knew' (1897); 'The Awkward Age' (1899); 'The Sacred Fount' (1901); 'The Wings of the Dove' (1902); 'The Better Sort' (1903); 'The Lesson of Balzac' (1905); 'American Scenes' (1906).

James, William. An American scholar and psychlogist, son of Henry (1st); born Jan. 11, 1842. Graduated at Harvard University, and has been a professor since 1872 of anatomy, physiology, and psychology. His published works are: 'Principles of Psychology' (1890); 'Psychology, Briefer Course' (1892); 'Pragmatism' (1907).

Jameson, Anna Brownell. An Irish miscellaneous writer; born (Murphy) in Dublin, May 17, 1794; died in London, March 17, 1860. She was the daughter of a noted artist, and began her literary work with 'The Diary of an Ennuyée' (1826). Then followed 'Loves of the Poets' (1829); 'Celebrated Female Sovereigns' (1831); 'Characteristics of Women'; 'Companion to the Public Picture Galleries of London' (1842); 'Memoirs of the Early Italian Painters' (1845), edited; 'Sacred and Legendary Art' (1848 52), not quite complete; etc.

Jameson, Robert William. A British journalist, novelist, poet, and miscellaneous writer; born in Leith, 1805; died in London, Dec. 10, 1868. Radical in his politics, he wrote brilliantly during the Anti-Corn-Law agitation; evolving between times, 'Nimrod' (1848), a poem in blank verse; 'The Curse of Gold' (1854), a novel; and a tragedy, 'Timoleon,' which reached a second edition in 1852.

Jami, 'Abd-urrahmán (jâ-mē', abd'ör-oimạn). The last of Persia's classic poets, born in Jam, Khorasan, August (?) 1414; died at Herat (?), in May (?) 1492 or 1493. His best-known poetical works are: 'The Abode of Spring' (Behâristân); 'The Chain of Gold'; and 'The Loves of Joseph and Zuleika and of Mejnun and Leila.' He is known in Europe as the Persian Petrarch, while his countrymen call him "the fiery star to which the gold stars bend," a metaphor illustrative of the glories with which he invested the passion of love.

Jamison, Mrs. Celia V. (Hamilton). An American novelist; born in Yarmouth, Can., 1848. Among her best-known works are : 'Tionette's Philip'; 'Lady Jane'; 'Thistledown.'

Jamyn, Amadis (jä-maṅ'). A French poet; born in Chaource, Champagne, about 1538; died there about 1585. He wrote in imitation of Ronsard, producing neat and dainty but rather insipid sonnets, in which we are assured that love, while a grand thing, has yet its inconveniences. 'The Hunt' and 'Liberality' are among his pieces.

Janda, Bohumil (yän'dä). A Bohemian novelist and poet; born at Patek, May 1, 1831; died at Prague (?), Sept. 29, 1875. His poetry and prose deal mostly with historical themes afforded by the annals of his native land. 'Jan Talafus z Ostrova' is his masterpiece in metre, being an epic of a fifteenth-century knight. His novel 'Anna Městecká Bocek' is based upon somewhat similar material.

Jan de Rijmer (yän dě rēmer). See **Goeverneur.**

Janet, Paul (zhän-ā'). A French philosopher and essayist; born in Paris, April 30, 1823. He has received important professorships in acknowledgment of the services conferred upon education by 'The Family' (1855), 'Studies of Dialectic in Plato and in Hegel' (1860), 'Masters of Modern Thought' (1883), and others which show the influence of Cousin. Died Oct. 4, 1899.

Janin, Jules (zhä-naṅ). A French critic, journalist, and novelist; born in St. Étienne, Feb. 16, 1804; died at Paris, June 19, 1874. He caught the fancy of the Parisians with his literary and theatrical criticisms, displaying an incredible aptitude for detecting the public taste, and guiding himself wholly by it. In 1870 he was elected to the French Academy. Among his stories and novels, 'The Dead Donkey and the Guillotined Woman,' 'Confession,' and 'A Heart for Two Loves,' are conspicuous. His permanent work is probably the collection of papers called 'History of Dramatic Literature.'

Janson, Kristofer Nagel (yän'son). A Norwegian poet; born in Bergen, May 5, 1841. He is a clergyman and educator, and settled in this country in 1881. 'Norse Poems,' a collection of lyrics, and 'Praerien's Saga,' are his most popular works, but he has produced many stories of merit. He writes in both Norse and English. He returned to Norway in 1892.

Janssen, Johannes (yän'sen). A German historian; born in Xanten, Düsseldorf, April 16, 1829; died in Frankfort-on the Main, Dec. 24, 1891. Distinguished for the zeal and learning with which he contends for the Catholic point of view in various valuable historical studies, he has produced in 'The History of the German People since the Close of the Middle Ages' (1877-94), a masterpiece of energetic controversialism softened by a happy style.

Janvier, Francis de Haes. An American poet, kinsman of Thomas A.; born in Pennsylvania in 1817; died in 1885. He published: 'The Skeleton Monk, and Other Poems' (1860); 'The Sleeping Sentinel' (1863); 'Patriotic Poems' (1866).

Janvier, Margaret Thomson. ["Margaret Vandegrift."] An American writer of juvenile literature, sister of Thomas A.; born in New Orleans, La., 1845. She is a resident of Philadelphia. Among her best-known works are :

'Clover Beach' (1880); 'Under the Dog Star' (1881); 'The Dead Doll, and Other Verses' (1888) ; 'Little Helpers' (1888); 'Umbrellas to Mend' (1905).

Janvier, Thomas Allibone. An American novelist and miscellaneous writer; born in Philadelphia, 1849. He has published: 'An Embassy to Provence,' a volume of travel; 'Color Studies'; 'Four Stories'; 'The Mexican Guide'; 'Stories of Old New Spain'; 'The Aztec Treasure House,' a romance; 'The Uncle of an Angel, and Other Stories'; 'In Old New York'; etc.

Jarves, James Jackson. An American prose-writer; born in Boston, Aug. 20, 1820; died in Terasp, Switzerland, June 28, 1888. He published : 'History of the Hawaiian or Sandwich Islands' (1843); 'Art Hints: Architecture, Sculpture, and Painting' (1855); 'Art Studies: The Old Masters of Italy' (1861); 'Glimpses at the Art of Japan' (1876); and 'Italian Rambles' (1884); and 'Santa Fé's Partner' (1907).

Jasmin, Jacques (zhäs-mañ). A Provençal poet; born in Agen, Lot-et-Garonne, March 6, 1798; died there, Oct. 4, 1864. His origin was of the humblest, and he earned his livelihood as a barber. He wrote : 'Curl Papers,' a string of quaint verses; 'Souvenirs,' a series of stanzas, the nature of which is sufficiently indicated by the title they bear; and the narrative poem 'Françonette.' He developed the possibilities of the language of Provence as a medium of modern literary expression.

Jasykov, Nicolai Mikhailovich (yäs-ē'kov). A Russian poet; born in Simbirsk, March 16, 1803; died at Moscow, Jan. 7, 1847. His earliest verse was in a light and amatory vein (hence his sobriquet 'The Russian Anacreon'), but ill health changed the current of his thoughts. His first book is a collection of amorous lyrics, and his last a compilation of religious poetry. The good taste with which he uses the Russian language makes his verse notable.

Jauregui y Aguilar, Juan de (hou'rä-gē ē ä'gē-lär). A Spanish poet; born in Seville, about 1570; died at Madrid, Jan. 10 (?), 1649. His name became universally known in Spain upon the appearance of his charming translation of Tasso's 'Aminta.' He wrote 'Orpheus,' a long mediocre poem, and a 'Poetic Discourse' against the poet Gongora, besides rendering Lucan's 'Pharsalia' into Spanish with respectable fidelity to the original, but without its power.

Jay, Antoine (zhä). A French critic, essayist, and biographer; born in Guîtres, Gironde, Oct. 20, 1770; died at Lagorce, April 9, 1855. His early essays on literature won prizes from the French Academy, the reputation thus obtained being fully borne out by his work as an editor on the Journal de Paris; by the 'History of Cardinal Richelieu's Ministry'; and the 'Biographies of Contemporaries,' to which he contributed numerous articles. His 'Eulogy of Corneille' and 'Hermits in Prison' are much quoted.

Jay, John. An American lawyer; born in New York city, June 23, 1817 ; died there, May 5, 1894. He graduated from Columbia College in 1836, and was admitted to the bar in 1839. He actively opposed slavery, and was counsel for many fugitive slaves. From 1869 to 1875 he was minister to Austria, and in 1883 became a member of the New York Civil Service Commission. Among his works are : 'Caste and Slavery in the American Church' (1843); 'America Free, or America Slave' (1856).

Jayadeva (jī-ä-dā'vä). A Sanskrit poet; born in Kenduli (?), about 1150 (?). He is known only as the author of the 'Gita-Govinda' or 'Song of the Cowherd,' an expressively passionate and realistic outburst of the amorous Muse.

Jeafferson, John Cordy (jĕf'erson). An English essayist, biographer and critic; born in Framlingham, Suffolk, Jan. 14, 1831; died in London, Feb. 2, 1901. He was bred to the bar, but became a novelist, changing his mind when his fiction failed and his 'Novels and Novelists from Elizabeth to Victoria' (1858) succeeded; after which time, 'A Book about Doctors' (1860), 'A Book about Lawyers' (1866), and 'A Book about the Clergy' (1870) spread his fame. In biography 'The Real Lord Byron ' (1883) and 'The Real Shelley' (1885) are studies in which the critic and the essayist show knowledge and skill.

Jean Paul. See **Richter.**

Jefferies, Richard. An English essayist and novelist; born in Swindon, Wiltshire, Nov. 6, 1848 ; died at Goring, Sussex, Aug. 14, 1887. His published works include : 'The Goddards of North Wilts' (1873), a local family history; 'The Scarlet Shawl' (1874), a novel; 'Restless Human Hearts' (1875), a novel; 'The World's End' (1877), a novel; 'The Dewy Morn,' a novel; 'Wild Life in a Southern County' (1879), a volume of descriptive sketches: this was followed by similar books, notably, 'Round about a Great Estate'; 'The Life of the Fields'; 'The Open Air'; 'The Amateur Poacher' (1879); 'Hodge and his Masters'; 'The Game Keeper at Home'; etc. His later works were the novel 'Green Ferne Farm' (1880); 'Wood Magic' (1881), a fanciful animal story ; 'Bevis' (1882), a tale of childhood; 'The Story of My Heart' (1883), by many pronounced his masterpiece ; 'Red Deer' (1884), a description of Exmoor; 'After London' (1885), an imaginative tale; 'Amaryllis at the Fair' (1887), a novel of country life ; and some fugitive essays and sketches. 'Field and Hedgerow' was published posthumously.

Jefferson, Joseph. An American actor of great repute and charm; born in Philadelphia, Feb. 20, 1829. He came of a long line of dramatists, and was associated with the most famous actors of his time. His play 'Rip Van Winkle' delighted untold thousands of playgoers. No other American actor ever won so warm a place in the American heart. His 'Autobiography' was published in 1890. He gave frequent lectures and addresses on the art of the actor. He died at Palm Beach, Florida, April 23, 1905.

Jefferson, Thomas. A statesman of the first rank and fame; born at Shadwell, Va., April 2, 1743; died at Monticello, Va., July 4, 1826. The Declaration of Independence is the production of his pen; and he was author of 'Notes on Virginia,' 'Autobiography,' and 'Correspondence.' ('Complete Works,' 10 vols., 1892.

Jeffrey, Francis. A famous Scottish critic; born at Edinburgh, Oct. 23, 1773; died there, Jan. 26, 1850. He was educated for the law, but chose letters, beginning his noted literary career by co-operating in the founding of the Edinburgh Review. He was one of the most conspicuous figures of his day in criticism. His multifarious writings are only partially represented in 'Contributions to the Edinburgh Review' (1843), 'Essay on Beauty,' and 'Nature and Principles of Taste' (1879).

Jeffrey, Rosa Vertner Griffith. An American novelist and poet; born in Natchez, Miss., 1826; died 1894. She contributed to the Louisville Journal under the name "Rosa" in 1850. Her published works are in part: 'Poems, by Rosa' (1857); 'Woodburn,' a novel (1864); 'Daisy Dare and Baby Power,' poems (1871); 'The Crimson Hand and Other Poems' (1881); and 'Marsh,' a novel (1884).

Jenkin, Henrietta Camilla. An English novelist; born in Jamaica about 1807; died in Edinburgh, Feb. 8, 1885. Well educated and clever, she wrote fiction as a means of livelihood. Her 'Cousin Stella' (1859), a portrayal of West-Indian life and manners, made a hit; as did 'Who Breaks, Pays' (1861), in which the flirt is admirably pictured. Her other novels are only mediocre.

Jenkins, Edward. An English political pamphleteer; born in Bangalore, India, 1838, and educated at McGill University, Canada, and the University of Pennsylvania. A Member of Parliament, he has written on social and political questions in the satirical vein; his 'Ginx's Baby' (1870), 'Lord Bantam,' 'Little Hodge,' and other efforts, have had great currency.

Jenkins, John Stilwell. An American prose-writer; born in Albany, N. Y., Feb. 15, 1818; died in Weedsport, N. Y., Sept. 20, 1852. He was a lawyer by profession, but edited the Cayuga Times. Among his works are: 'Generals of the Last War with Great Britain' (1841); an abridgment of Hammond's 'Political History of New York' (1846); 'Alice Howard' (1846); 'Life of Silas Wright' (1847); 'History of the Mexican War' (1848); 'Heroines of History' (1853); etc.

Jenneval (zhen-väl), pseudonym of Louis Dechez. A French-Belgian patriotic song-writer; born in Lyons, 1808; killed in the campaign of Lierre, Oct. 19, 1830. His fame rests upon that most renowned of Belgian patri-

otic songs, 'Brabançonne,' which won its way rapidly to official recognition as the national hymn; and his collected 'Poems' give evidence of a genuine inspiration.

Jennison, Lucy White. ["Owen Innsley."] An American poet; born in Massachusetts in 1850. She has lived mainly in Europe. She published 'Love Poems and Sonnets' (1881).

Jensen, Wilhelm (yen'sen). A prolific German poet, novelist, and miscellaneous writer; born in Heiligenhafen, Holstein, Feb. 15, 1837. He is antithetic and realistic in method. Of his poetry the 'Songs from France' and 'A Dream in a Glade' must win a permanent place. The tragedy 'Dido' is meritorious. Of the novels, 'Eddystone,' 'Under Warmer Skies,' 'Nameless,' and 'After Sunset,' have achieved wide popularity. Impatience and rapidity of production tend to mar his style.

Jerábek, Frantisek (yer'shä-bek). A Czech poet of great eminence; born in Sabotka, Jan. 25, 1836; died at Prague, March 30 (?), 1893. 'Hána' was his first dramatic effort; but 'The Way of Public Opinion' and 'A Servant of his Lord' are deemed the triumphs of his genius. In the historic tragedies of 'The Son of Man' and 'Závist' he obtains the most vivid dramatic effects. Few play-writers of recent times have equaled him in sensational climax and in dignity of diction and movement.

Jerome, Jerome Klapka. An English humorist and story-writer; born in Walsall, May 2, 1859. He wrote: 'On the Stage—and Off' (1885), largely autobiographical; 'Idle Thoughts of an Idle Fellow'; and a comedy, 'Barbara.' 'Three Men in a Boat' (1889) was the success of its year; since which time his labors as dramatist, journalist, and story-teller, have been many.

Jerrold, Douglas William. An English humorist; born in London, Jan. 3, 1803; died there, June 8, 1857. His wit was caustic and keen, and his long-continued contributions to Punch are widely known. He wrote: 'Mrs. Caudle's Curtain Lectures'; 'Story of a Feather'; 'The Rent Day'; 'Time Works Wonders'; and 'Retired from Business'; all jolly good things.

Jerrold, William Blanchard. An English journalist and topical writer, son of Douglas; born in London, Dec. 23, 1826; died there (Westminster), March 10, 1884. He edited Lloyd's newspaper brilliantly, and became half a Frenchman in residence, speech, and manner, his best writings being contained in: 'Paris for the English' (3d ed. 1868); 'The Cockaynes in Paris' (1871); and 'The Best of all Good Company' (1871), a series of recollections of Dickens, Bulwer, and others: but he wrote a good comedy occasionally, and some readable stories, and also a 'Life of Napoleon III.' (1875-77).

Jervey, Mrs. Caroline H. ["Gilman Glover."] An American novelist; born in South

Carolina in 1823; died in 1877. Her works include 'Vernon Grove' and 'Helen Courtenay's Promise.'

Jesse, John Heneage. An English historical writer; born near London, 1815; died there, July 7, 1874. His early verse, 'Mary Queen of Scots' and 'Tales of the Dead,' is of no moment. He is remembered for a series of compilations of historical gossip, generally known as 'Courts and Cabinets' of the Stuarts, George II. and III., etc.; they show neither independent research nor critical judgment, but are convenient as bringing together many scattered bits from the original memoirists. He wrote also 'George Selwyn and his Contemporaries' (1843), and 'London and Its Celebrities' (1850).

Jessup, Henry Harris. An American missionary; born at Montrose, Pa., 1832. He was a missionary to Tripoli and Syria from 1856 to 1860, and is at present stationed at Beyrout. His works include 'The Women of the Arabs' (1873), and 'The Mohammedan Missionary Problem' (1879); 'Syrian Home Life'; 'Kamil.'

Jewett, Sarah Orne. An American short-story writer; born in Maine, 1849. Her works include : 'Old Friends and New'; 'Play Days'; 'Country By-Ways'; 'Deephaven'; 'The Mate of the Daylight, and Friends Ashore'; 'A Country Doctor'; 'A Marsh Island'; 'A White Heron and Other Stories'; 'The Story of the Normans,' a historical work; 'The King of Folly Island, and Other People'; 'Betty Leicester'; 'Strangers and Wayfarers'; 'A Native of Winby, and Other Tales'; 'The Life of Nancy'; 'The Country of the Pointed Firs'; 'The Queen'sTwin'; 'The Tory Lover.'

Jewsbury, Geraldine Endsor. An English novelist; born at Measham, Derbyshire, 1812; died in London, Sept. 23, 1880. Her novels, 'Zoë, the History of Two Lives' (1845), 'The Half-Sisters' (1848), 'Right or Wrong' (1859), and others of like charm and interest, met with success.

Jewsbury, Maria Jane. An English poet and prose-writer, sister of Geraldine; born in Measham, Derbyshire, Oct. 25, 1800; died of cholera at Poonah, India, Oct. 4, 1833. She wrote 'Phantasmagoria, or Sketches of Life and Character,' (1824 ?) and the fascinating 'Letters to the Young' (1828) during a severe illness. Her 'Lays of Leisure Hours' (1829) attracted general admiration, and her 'Three Histories: the History of an Enthusiast, the History of a Nonchalant, the History of a Realist' (1830) ran through four editions. She married Rev. W. K. Fletcher, an Indian missionary.

Jirásek, Aloys (yĕ-räs'ek). A Czech novelist; born in Hronov, Bohemia, 1851. His talent is for the production of faithful and effective word-paintings of Czech life and character; 'Between the Streams,' 'Against All,' and 'In Foreign Service,' being typical examples.

Joachim, Joseph (yō-ä'kĕm). A Swiss story-writer; born at Kestenholz, near Solothurn,

April 4, 1835. The son of a peasant, and without early advantages, he did not take to the pen until mature life; but 'Lonny, the Homeless' (1889), 'The Brothers' (1891), 'Mother Lenen's Revenge' (1892), and other tales of village peasant life, have given him an enviable renown.

Jobez, Alphonse (zhō-bez'). A French historian and writer on social science; born in Lons-le-Saulnier, Aug. 1, 1813. His literary reputation dates from the appearance of 'A Preface to Socialism,' 'Democracy Is the Unknown,' and 'Woman and the Child, or Poverty Entails Oppression.' His history of 'France under Louis XV.' is an authority.

Jodelle, Étienne (zhō-del). A French dramatic poet; born in Paris about 1532; died there (?), 1573. At twenty his tragedy of 'Captive Cleopatra' met with almost unparalleled success. It was an imitation of the later classical models, confused with some of the methods of Seneca. His later plays, 'Dido' and 'The Meeting,' were comparative failures.

Jodrell, Richard Paul. An English dramatist and scholar; born in Derbyshire (?), Nov. 13, 1745; died in London, Jan. 26, 1831. He wrote: 'Seeing Is Believing' (1786), a good comedy; 'The Persian Heroine' (1786), a good tragedy; and 'Philology of the English Language' (1820), a good manual.

John, Eugènie (yōn). See **Marlitt.**

Johnson, Charles Frederick. An American scholar and author; born in New York city in 1836. He graduated from Yale in 1855; and is at present a professor of English literature at Trinity College, Hartford, Conn. His works include 'Three Americans and Three Englishmen' (1886), and 'Forms of English Poetry.'

Johnson, Emily Pauline [Tekahionwake]. A Canadian poet; born in the Six Nations Reserve, Canada. She is of Indian descent. Her first volume of verse was 'The White Wampum' (1894). Her first sketch, 'A Red Girl's Reasoning,' took a prize in the Canadian Magazine.

Johnson, Helen Kendrick. An American author; born 1843; is the author of 'The Roddy Books' (3 vols., 1874-76), and 'Raleigh Westgate' (1889). She edited 'Tears for the Little Ones : Poems and Passages Inspired by the Loss of Children' (1878); 'Poems and Songs for Young People' (1884); and 'The Nutshell Series' (6 vols., 1885).

Johnson, Oliver. An American editor and author; born in Peacham, Vt., Dec. 27, 1809; died in Brooklyn, N. Y., Dec. 10, 1889. He was editor of the Independent from 1865 to 1870; became editor of the Christian Union in 1872; was one of the founders of the New England Anti-Slavery Society in 1832; and published 'William Lloyd Garrison and his Times' (1880).

Johnson, Robert Underwood. An American poet and editor; born in Washington, D. C.,

Jan. 12, 1853. He is associate editor of the Century Magazine. His efforts in behalf of the establishment of international copyright were recognized by the degree of M. A., conferred by Yale University in 1891. He edited, with C. C. Buel, the notable 'Battles and Leaders of the Civil War' (1887-88), and has published two volumes of poems: 'The Winter Hour and Other Poems' (1892); and 'Songs of Liberty' (1897) ; 'Poems' (1902).

Johnson, Rossiter. An American author and editor; born, Rochester, N. Y., Jan. 27, 1840. Editor Rochester Democrat, and later Concord, (N. H.) Statesman, 1869-72. Author of 'Phaeton Rogers'; 'A History of the War Between the United States and Great Britain'; 'Idler and Poet' (poems); 'A History of the War of Secession'; 'The End of a Rainbow'; 'Three Decades' (poems); 'A short History of the War Between the United States and Spain'; 'The Hero of Manila'; 'Morning Lights and Evening Shadows' (poems); 'The Alphabet of Rhetoric,' etc. Editor 'Little Classics'; 'Works of the British Poets'; 'The Annual Cyclopaedia,' etc. Associate editor 'The American Cyclopaedia'; 'The Standard Dictionary'; 'Cyclopaedia of American Biography; 'The Story of the Constitution of the U. S.'

Johnson, Samuel. An English critic, essayist, poet, and lexicographer, the most picturesque figure in British literature; born in Lichfield, Sept. 18, 1709; died in London, Dec. 13, 1784. His works include: 'Voyage to Abyssinia' (1735), a translation; 'London' (1738); 'Marmor Norfolciense' (1739), an essay; 'Life of Richard Savage' (1744); 'Macbeth' (1745), an essay; 'Plan for a Dictionary' (1747); 'Vanity of Human Wishes' (1749); 'Irene' (1749); The Rambler (1750-52); The Adventurer papers (1753); the English Dictionary (1755); The Idler (1758-60); 'Rasselas' (1759); 'Shakespeare with Notes' (1765); 'The False Alarm' (1770); 'A Journey to the Western Isles of Scotland' (1775); 'Taxation No Tyranny' (1775); 'English Poets' (1779-81). ('Collected Works,' 11 vols., 1787.)

Johnson, Virginia Wales. An American prose-writer; born in Brooklyn, N. Y., Dec. 28, 1849. Her publications include: 'Kettle Club Series' (1870); 'Travels of an American Owl' (1870); 'Joseph the Jew' (1873); 'A Sack of Gold' (1874); 'The Catskill Fairies' (1875); 'The Calderwood Secret' (1875); 'A Foreign Marriage' (1880); 'Tulip Place' (1886); 'Miss Nancy's Pilgrimage' (1887); 'The House of the Musician' (1887); 'The World's Shrine' (1902).

Johnston, Richard Malcolm. An American story-writer and essayist; born in Hancock County, Ga., March 8, 1822. He studied for the bar and practiced with distinction, but it was as an educator that he first attracted attention. His studies of character and manners in Georgia began to appear shortly after the war. Noted for humor and realism are his 'Dukesborough Tales,' 'Old Mark Langston,' and 'Ogeechee Cross-Firings.' Died 1898.

Johnston, William Preston. An American educator and author; born in Louisville, Ky., Jan. 5, 1831. He was a colonel in the Confederate army; became a professor in Washington and Lee University (1867-77); president of Louisiana State University (1880-83); and president of Tulane University (1884). His works include 'Life of General Albert Sidney Johnston' (1878), and 'The Prototype of Hamlet' (1890). He died 1899.

Johnstone, Charles. An Irish novelist; born at Carrigogunnel, Limerick, about 1719; died at Calcutta, India, about 1800. He had wit and imagination, which he exploited in 'Chrysal, or the Adventures of a Guinea' (1760-65), "the best scandalous chronicle" of its day; and in 'History of John Juniper, Esq., alias Juniper Jack' (1781). He emigrated to India, where he succeeded in journalism.

Johnstone, Christian Isobel. ["Margaret Dods."] A Scottish novelist; born in Fifeshire, 1781; died in Edinburgh, Aug. 26, 1857. She edited, in association with her husband as publisher, many periodicals and papers, and wrote popular tales, notably: 'Clan Albin: a National Tale' (1815), 'Elizabeth de Bruce' (1827), 'The Edinburgh Tales' (1845-46), and others, described as forceful, brilliant, and entertaining. She also compiled 'The Cook and Housewife's Manual' (1826).

Joinville, Jean, Sieur de (zhwaṅ-vēl'). A noted French chronicler; born in Champagne in 1224; died there (?) in 1317 or 1318. He took part in Louis IX.'s crusade, and on his return spent his leisure composing his invaluable 'Memoirs,' which embody the important 'History of Saint Louis,' sometimes treated as a separate work.

Jókai, Maurice (yō'ko-i). A Hungarian novelist, journalist, and publicist; born in Komorn, Feb. 19, 1825. Few lives have been so busy, and few have been enriched with the accomplishment of so much that is good in the domain of letters. 'The White Rose,' 'The Gold Man,' 'The Man with the Iron Heart,' 'Mine, Thine, His,' 'Pater Pater,' 'The Poor Rich,' and 'Peter the Priest' (1897), must be named among his works. Died May 5, 1904.

Joliet, Charles (zhō-lyā'). A French journalist, essayist, and miscellaneous writer; born in St. Hippolyte-on-the-Doubs, Aug. 8, 1832. He has contributed to every periodical of note in Paris, producing likewise countless volumes, such as: 'The Athenians,' poems; 'The Ladies' Doctor,' a humorous narrative; 'The Viper,' a study of woman; 'The Story of Two Young Wives,' a novel; and others, all evincing the happiest versatility and felicity of style.

Jolin, Johan Kristofer (yō'lin). A Swedish dramatist, novelist, and poet; born in Stockholm, Dec. 28, 1818; died there, Nov. 13, 1884. His work, which is popular and original, includes 'Master Smith,' a drama, and 'Vinglaren,' a novel, besides pleasing verse.

Joly, Guy (zhŏ-lē'). A seventeenth-century French writer of memoirs, who came into some prominence during the Fronde, and compiled 'Memoirs to explain and continue those of the Cardinal de Retz' (1718),—a curious, readable, and accurate, yet partisan work.

Jonckbloet, Willem Jozef Andreas (yonk'-blĕt"). A Dutch historian of literature, also essayist and critic; born at The Hague, July 6, 1817; died in Wiesbaden, Oct. 19, 1885. He is a conceded authority on Dutch letters, his masterpieces on 'The Middle Dutch Epic' (1849), 'The History of Middle Dutch Literature' (1851–54), and 'Study of the Romance of Renard' (1863), exhausting those subjects; and his editions of Dutch classics are the standard.

Jones, Amanda Theodosia. An American poet; born in East Bloomfield, Ontario County, N. Y., Oct. 19, 1835. Some of her war songs were very popular. She published: 'Ulah and Other Poems' (1860); 'Atlantis and Other Poems' (1866); and 'A Prairie Idyl, and Other Poems' (1882); 'Rubayat of Solomon' (1905).

Jones, Charles Colcock, Jr. An American lawyer and author; born in Savannah, Ga., Oct. 28, 1831; died July 19, 1893. He was lieutenant-colonel in the Confederate service during the War, afterward removing to New York, where he practiced law. Among his works are: 'Antiquities of the Southern Indians' (1873); 'Siege of Savannah in 1779' (1874); 'History of Georgia' (1883).

Jones, Ebenezer. An English poet; born in Islington, Jan. 20, 1820; died in London, Sept. 14, 1860. His genius was of the erratic sort, as 'Studies of Sensation and Event' (1843), a collection of miscellaneous poems, showed. 'Winter Hymn to the Snow,' 'When the World Is Burning,' and 'To Death,' are his best-known pieces. Since his death there has been a revival of interest in his poetry.

Jones, Ernest Charles. An English poet, novelist, and agitator; born in Berlin, Jan. 25, 1819; died at Manchester, Jan. 26, 1868. He became a leader in the Chartist agitation, to which he sacrificed a large fortune. His prose and poetry were inspired by his political opinions; 'The Lass and the Lady' (1854) and 'Lord Lindsay' being his best fictions, and 'The Battle Day and Other Poems' (1855) containing his most popular songs.

Jones, Evan. A Welsh poet; born at Bryntynoriad, Sept. 5, 1820; died near Cardiff, Feb. 23, 1852. He was a clergyman, and best known as Ieuan Gwynedd, over which name he produced in his native tongue poems on 'The Huts of Wales,' 'Moses on Mount Pisgah,' 'Peace,' and other themes; in addition to which he edited many periodicals, including Yr Adolygydd, or National Review.

Jones, John B. An American journalist and novelist; born in Baltimore, Md., in 1810; died 1866. He spent many years in journalism, and is author of 'Books of Visions' (1847); 'Rural Sports: a Poem' (1848); 'The Western Mer-chant' (1848); 'Wild Western Scenes' (1849); 'The Rival Belles' (1852); 'Freaks of Fortune' (1854); 'A Rebel War Clerk's Diary at the Confederate States Capital' (1866).

Jones, Joseph Stevens. An American playwriter; born in 1811; died in Boston, 1877. He wrote many plays, some of the best known being 'Solon Shingle'; 'Eugene Aram'; 'The Liberty Tree'; 'Moll Pitcher'; 'The Silver Spoon.'

Jones, Justin. An American novelist, writing under the pseudonym "Harry Hazel." Among his works are: 'The Flying Artillerist' (1853); 'The Yankee Middy' (1865); 'Virginia Graham, the Spy of the Grand Army' (1869); etc.

Jonge, Johan Karel Jacob de (yông'ĕ). A Dutch historian, son of Johannes; born at The Hague, June 17, 1827; died there, March 15, 1880. He has studied the colonial history of his country with effect, as 'The Rise of Netherland Dominion in the East Indies' (1862–78), and other works, demonstrate.

Jonge, Johannes Cornelis de. A Dutch historian; born in Zierikzee, May 9, 1793; died near Ryswick, June 12, 1853. He has quarried indefatigably and with rich results in the Netherland vein; 'Studies in the History of the Low Countries' (1825–27) and 'The History of the Dutch Navy' (1833–48) being the best specimens.

Jonson, Ben. A celebrated English dramatist; born in London in 1572 or 1573; died there August 6, 1637. He was about twenty-three when he tried dramatic authorship, and seems to have been only moderately successful until 'Every Man in his Humour' was written, followed by 'Every Man Out of his Humour,' both comedies being the fruit of a wit so clear and fine that his epitaph "O Rare Ben Jonson" fits him well. His poetry is "excellently bright," and impregnated with the Elizabethan atmosphere and spirit.

Jordan, Cornelia Jane Matthews. An American poet; born in Lynchburg, Va., 1830. She wrote her poem 'Corinth' in 1863; it was published in 1865; by order of Gen. Alfred H. Terry, it was seized and burned in the courthouse yard at Lynchburg as objectionable and incendiary. Her publications include: 'Flowers of Hope and Memory' (1861); 'Corinth and Other Poems of the War' (1865); 'A Christmas Poem for Children' (1865); 'Richmond: Her Glory and Her Graves' (1867); 'Useful Maxims for a Noble Life' (1884).

Jordan, David Starr. An eminent American naturalist; born in Gainesville, N. Y., Jan. 19, 1851. He graduated from Cornell University in 1872, and has held professorships in several universities in the West; was president of Indiana University from 1885 to 1891; was elected the first president of Leland Stanford University (California) in 1891, and is still at its head. He wrote voluminously on ichthyology. Among his works are: 'A Manual of the Vertebrates of the Northern United States' (1876); 'A Synopsis of the Fishes of North America' (1883); 'Evolution and Animal Life' (1907).

Jordan, Wilhelm (yor'dän). A German poet and story-writer, and an eminent publicist; born in Insterburg, Feb. 8, 1819. His early poems and sketches brought him into trouble with the authorities; but he managed, notwithstanding, to rise to a position of power in public life, while as a literary man his eminence has long been unquestioned. As a poet he voices his liberal political aspirations through the medium of a chaste but not severe Muse, 'Bells and Cannon' and 'Earthly Fantasies' being characteristic. In fiction he strives to make propaganda and to demonstrate the necessity of a higher social state by exposing the evils of the existing one, and yet he is neither a revolutionist nor a socialist, as 'The Sebalds' and 'Two Cradles' amply prove. 'Demiurgos,' a philosophical poem, 'The False Prince,' a comedy, and 'The Widow of Agis,' a tragedy, are also his. Died June 25, 1904.

Josephus, Flavius (jō-sē'fus). A Jewish historian; born in Jerusalem, 37 A.D.; died at Rome about 100 A.D. He was of noble birth, and bore a conspicuous part in the contests of his people with the Romans and the imperial government of Rome, rising finally to great favor with the Emperor Vespasian and his two immediate successors. He passed the years of his literary activity at Rome, living in dignified ease upon a royal pension and in a luxurious residence, enjoying also the rights of citizenship. The products of these favoring circumstances are the 'History of the War of the Jews against the Romans, and of the Fall of Jerusalem,' the 'Judaic Antiquities,' and an 'Autobiography.' As an eye-witness of much that he records, his work merits attention; but it is the subject of much controversy and doubt.

Jósika, Baron Nikolaus (yō'shē-ko). A Hungarian novelist; born in Torda, Transylvania, April 28, 1794; died at Dresden, Feb. 27, 1865. The scion of a rich and noble family, he received a finished education, entered the army, and at last became a man of letters. His first efforts were collected into a volume of 'Sketches,' and were greatly admired. As a writer of realistic and historic fiction he achieved fame with 'The Poet Zrinyi,' 'The Last of the Bathory,' 'Abafi,' and 'A Hungarian Family during the Period of the Revolution.' A profound student of the life, manners, legends, and antiquities of his countrymen, gifted with a bewitching style, rich in invention and perennially enticing in his plots, he well merits the praises he has won as "the Sir Walter Scott" of the land that gave him birth.

Joubert, Joseph (zhö-bär'). A French moralist and writer of aphorisms; born in Montignac, Périgord, 1754; died at Paris, 1824. The bulk of his epigrammatic work was published posthumously under the critical supervision of Châteaubriand and Raynal, the titles of the volumes being 'Thoughts' and 'Thoughts, Essays, Maxims, and Correspondence.'

Joubert, Léo. A French biographer and historical writer; born in Bourdeilles, Dordogne, Dec. 13, 1826. He is skillful, accurate, and readable, as a miscellaneous biographical writer; and his best studies, 'Washington and the Formation of the Republic of the United States of America' (1888), 'Alexander the Great' (1889), and 'The Battle of Sedan' (1873), are popular.

Jouy, Victor Joseph Étienne, called de (zhö-ē'). A French librettist, dramatist, and descriptive writer; born in Jouy, near Versailles, 1764; died at Paris, Sept. 4, 1846. He entered upon a military career in connection with the Revolution and the restoration, and wrote an opera libretto, 'The Vestal,' which won him a reputation. 'Ferdinand Cortez' and 'William Tell' came next, followed by 'Sylla,' a tragedy. 'The Hermit of the Chaussée d'Antin' is his best thing in prose. This, and other writings in similar vein, had once a tremendous vogue as witty and faithful portraiture of contemporary folly.

Jovanovic, Jovan (yō-vän'-ō-vitch), surnamed **Zmaj.** A Servian poet, journalist, humorist, and dramatist; born in Neusatz, Nov. 24, 1833. He qualified as a lawyer, but went into journalism, winning fame throughout Austria and Hungary as editor and founder of influential political and satirical sheets. He is called "Zmaj" or the "Dragon," from the name of his most successful paper. The volume 'Withered Roses' contains the finest verse, and his farce 'Saran' is perennially popular on the Servian stage. Died at Belgrade, Servia, June 14, 1904.

Jovellanos (Jove-Llanos), Gaspar Melchor de (Hō-vel-yä'nōs). A Spanish dramatist, prose-writer, and statesman; born in Gijon, Asturia, Jan. 5, 1744; died at Vega, Nov. 27, 1811. His political and official career was not fortunate, although he filled high posts with distinction. As a writer he was happy; applause greeting his tragedy of 'Pelagius,' founded upon the fortunes of the famed Asturian king. His 'Orations and Discourses' are the productions of a finished and talented rhetorician.

Joyce, Robert Dwyer. An Irish poet; born in County Limerick, 1836; died in Dublin, Oct. 23, 1883. In 1866 he came to the United States. He was a versatile writer of ballads, songs, and sketches; and contributed to the Pilot and other Irish journals. His best-known published works are: 'Ballads, Romances, and Songs' (1872); 'Deirdré,' an epic poem, which appeared anonymously as one of the 'No Name Series' (1876); 'Legends of the Wars in Ireland' (1868); 'Fireside Stories of Ireland' (1871); 'Blanid,' a poem (1879); 'The Squire of Castleton.'

Juana Inez de la Cruz (kröth). (See **Mexican Nun.**)

Juan Manuel, Don (Hō-än'), **Infant of Castile.** A Spanish romancer and poet; born in

Escalona, 1282; died 1347. He was a gallant knight who lived for love and fought against the Moors, varying these activities by the gratification of his literary tastes. His best work, 'Count Lucanor,' is a collection of anecdotes, apologues, and apostrophes to the gods of love and war, all set down in flowery style, the Oriental influence being readily discernible.

Judd, Sylvester. An American novelist, poet, and theologian; born in Westhampton, Mass., July 23, 1813; died at Augusta, Me., Jan. 20, 1853. His remarkable romance 'Margaret' will always be remembered. 'Richard Edney' is another romance; 'Philo' is a striking poem; and his discourses on 'The Church' were esteemed.

Judson, Emily Chubbuck. ["Fanny Forrester."] An American missionary and writer of prose and verse; born in Eaton, Madison County, N. Y., Aug. 22, 1817; died in Hamilton, N. Y., June 1, 1854. She wrote: 'Charles Linn' (1841); 'The Great Secret' (1842); 'Allen Lucas' (1843); 'Alderbrook' (2 vols., 1846); 'The Kathayan Slave' (1853). Her poems appeared as 'An Olio of Domestic Verses' (1852). Among her other works are: 'Trippings in Author Land' (1846); 'My Two Sisters' (1854); and a memoir of 'Mrs. Sarah B. Judson' (1850). She married Adoniram Judson, the missionary, in 1846.

Judson, Harry Pratt. An American scholar and author; born in New York State in 1849. He is, since 1907, president of the University of Chicago. His works include: 'Cæsar's Army, a Study of the Military Art of the Romans' (1888); 'Europe in the Nineteenth Century'; 'The Growth of the American Nation'; 'The Essentials of a Written Constitution.'

June, Jennie. See **Croly.**

Junghans, Sophie (yŏng'häns). A German novelist; born in Cassel, Dec. 3, 1845. Her literary career began with the production of short stories and verses; with the appearance of 'Käthe, the Story of a Modern Maid,' and 'The House of Eckberg,' a study of life during the Thirty Years' War, she attracted attention. Her novels, while analytical, and perspicuous where plot is concerned, are strong in style and interesting in incident; 'The American [Woman],' 'A Riddle,' 'An Heiress Against her Will,' and others, exemplifying these qualities pre-eminently.

Jung-Stilling (yŏng-stil'ing), called **Johann Heinrich Jung.** A German writer of fiction and autobiography; born in Grund, Westphalia, Sept. 12, 1740; died at Karlsruhe, April 2, 1817. He was of very humble origin, reared in a narrow and simply pious environment, and sent out into the world for a livelihood; but his eager mind turned thirstily to study, and he worked his way to learning. The novels with which he began his literary career, 'The Story of Florentin von Fahlendorn,' 'The Story of the Lord of Morgenthau,' and others, are chronicles of his career at various stages; but he worked the field at its richest in the series of "Stilling" autobiographies, 'Heinrich Stilling's Youth,' 'Heinrich Stilling's Wanderings,' and the prolific cycle of their successors. The author recounts the incidents and the experiences of his life in these nominal fictions with a realistic power that has seldom been surpassed.

Junius. See **Francis.**

Junot, Madame (zhö-nō'), pseudonym of Laurette de St. Martin-Permon, Duchess of Abrantes; born in Montpellier, 1784; died at Paris, June 6(?), 1838. She married one of Napoleon's generals, and after his death was compelled, by financial embarrassments, to take up literature. 'Recollections of Napoleon, the Revolution, the Directory, the Consulate, the Empire, and the Restoration,' is her most permanent work.

Junqueira Freire, Luiz José (Hŏn-kāy'rä frāy'rä). A Brazilian poet; born in Bahia, Dec. 31, 1832; died there (?), June 24, 1855. He manifested a spiritual purity of mind and heart that drew the attention of his religious instructors while he was yet a boy; and at nineteen years of age he took religious vows, but almost immediately learned that he had mistaken his vocation. He obtained a release from his vows in three years' time, after a period of such agony of soul that we owe to it the most profoundly moving verses in which the breaking of a human heart is recorded,— his 'Inspirations of the Cloister.' He died at twenty-three, the regret and the delight of his country.

Jusserand, Jean Jules (zhüs-rän). A French historian of literature, and diplomat; born in Lyons, Feb. 18, 1855. He has made a specialty of the Elizabethan age, and of the literature of England in the Middle Ages; his most brilliant studies being 'The English Theatre, from the Conquest to the Immediate Predecessors of Shakespeare,' 'The Novel in the Time of Shakespeare,' and 'The English Novel.'

Juvenal (jö'ven-ạl). (**Decimus Junius Juvenalis.**) A Latin poet; born at Aquinum about 60 A. D.; died about 140 A. D. Sixteen of his satires, in fi e books, are extant.

Juvenal des Ursins, Jean. See **Ursins.**

K

Kaalund, Hans Vilhelm (kä'lönd). A Danish poet; born at Copenhagen, 1818; died 1885. After making futile attempts at sculpture and painting, a fortunate poem in honor of Thorwaldsen (1838) turned him to literature. Though he had published before, 'Et Foraar' (A Springtide), a collection of his best poems old and new, which, while not of great scope, were graceful and musical, brought him his first success. 'Fulvia' (1875), a fine drama depicting the struggles of the early Christians, contained many lyrics,— a fault in a play intended for the stage; though, altered, it was successfully acted in 1880. 'En Eftervaar' (Return of Spring: 1877) deserves mention. He excelled in satirical fables, his being the best Denmark has produced.

Ka'b ibn Zahir (käb ibn zä'hēr). A noted Arabic poet; contemporaneous with Mahomet. His father was author of one of the famous seven 'Mu 'allakát' (prize poems). After lampooning his own brother and Mahomet, and being outlawed by the latter, Ka'b composed a eulogy on him, 'The Poem of the Mantle,' his best-known work. It was translated into English by Redhouse in 1880.

Kacic-Miosic, Andrija (kä-chich-mē-ō-shich). A Croatian poet; born at Brist, Dalmatia, 1690; died at Zaostrog, 1760. He performed for his country a service similar to that of Percy in his 'Reliques' to England, or of Allan Ramsay in his 'Evergreen' or 'Tea-Table Miscellany' to Scotland, in publishing 'Recreations of the Slavonic People' (1756). This was an anthology of popular songs which he collected or adapted, celebrating the exploits of South-Slavic heroes from the earliest times. Many editions have appeared, and it is popular to-day with the Southern Slavs.

Kaden, Woldemar (kä'den). A German author and translator; born at Dresden, Feb. 9, 1838. He filled the chair of German language and literature in the University of Naples, but resigned in 1882. He has traveled extensively in Italy, and his writings treat almost exclusively of that country. Prominent among them are: 'Wanderings in Italy' (1874); 'Under the Olives' (1880); 'Pompeiian Tales' (1882); 'Italian Sketches and Pictures of Civilization' (1889); 'Italian Plaster Casts' (1891).

Kaempfen, Albert (kem'pfen). A French novelist and journalist; born at Versailles, April 15, 1826. He wrote under the pseudonyms "Feyrnet," "Henrys," "Henri Este." His romance 'The Cup of Tea' (1866), and the humorous work 'Paris, the Capital of the World' (1877), may be mentioned.

Kaempfer, Engelbert. A German physician and historian; born at Lemgo, Westphalia, in 1651; died there, Nov. 2, 1716. As secretary of legation in the Swedish diplomatic service he visited Russia and Tartary; and later, having joined the Dutch East India Company, visited Arabia, Siam, and Japan. In the latter country he remained two years exploring it. The results of his investigations are given in his accurate and reliable 'History of Japan and Siam,' published in English (1727), and afterwards in Latin, Dutch, French, and German.

Kaiser, Friedrich (kī'zer). A German humorous writer; born at Biberach, April 3, 1814; died at Vienna, Nov. 7, 1874. He is best known by his comedies, which were successfully performed, and of which 'Hans Hasenkopf' (1834) is a good example.

Kajaani, Johan Fredrik (ka-yä'nē). A Finnish writer; born at Sotkamo, 1815; died in 1887. He was the author of the first history of Finland written in Finnish.

Kalb, Charlotte von (kälb). A German memoir-writer; born at Waltershausen, in Grabfeld, July 25, 1761; died at Berlin, May 12, 1843. Best known as the friend of Schiller, Goethe, and Richter. She was a lovely and devoted woman. Schiller's poems 'The Conflict' and 'Resignation' refer to her. The character of Linda in Richter's 'Titan' was drawn from her. Her romance 'Cornelia' is in places incomprehensible, which may be said also of 'Charlotte' (memoirs, 1879). 'Letters to Richter and his Wife' appeared in 1882. She wrote a 'History of the American War of Independence.'

Kalbeck, Max (käl'bek). A German author, playwright, and journalist; born at Breslau, Jan. 4, 1850. He has paid considerable attention to the stage, among other work altering Mozart's 'Don Juan' (1887) and writing for Gluck's music a pastoral libretto, 'The May Queen' (1888). His discussions of Richard Wagner's 'Nibelungen' and 'Parsifal' appeared in 1883; 'Rhymed and Unrhymed,' satirical papers, in 1885; 'Old and New,' collected poems, in 1890. In some respects his intellectual attitude is Greek.

Kaler, James Otis. An American journalist; born in Winterport, Me., March 19, 1848. Under the pen-name of "James Otis" he published tales for the young, including: 'Toby Tyler' (1880); 'Left Behind' (1882); 'Mr. Stubbs's Brother' (1883); a sequel to Toby Tyler; 'Silent Pete' (1885); 'The Wreck of the Ocean Queen' (1907).

Kālidāsa (kä-li-dä'sä). A celebrated Hindu poet; his date is variously placed, but most probably he lived about the sixth century A. D. He was called one of the "nine pearls," i. e., one of the nine poets adorning the court of

King Vikramaditya. His most famous work, and the one most attractive to modern readers, and greatly admired by Goethe, is the drama 'Çakuntalā.' It portrays a love affair that, after surmounting manifold impediments, ends at last happily, and brings home to us in a wonderful way the essential unity of human nature in all ages. It was translated into English by Sir William Jones in 1789, and by Monier-Williams in 1885, and has been adapted to the German stage. Kālidāsa wrote dramatic, epic, and lyric poetry.

Kalina, Jaroslav (ka-lē'nä). A Czech poet; born at Hajda, in 1816; died at Prague, 1847. His ballads are his best works. Ten thousand copies of his poem 'Ksaft' (Last Will and Testament) were sold. The latest complete edition of his verse appeared in 1874.

Kalinka, Valerian (ka-lin'kä). A Polish historian, political writer, and journalist; born in 1826; died in 1886. His masterwork, 'The Great Diet,' was intended to be a thorough study of the political history of Poland; only the first volume appeared (1880).

Kalir or **Kaliri, Eleazar ben** (kä'lèr or ka-lē'rē). A Hebrew poet; born at Kiriat-Sefer, in the eighth century. He wrote 150 liturgical chants, of but slight literary value, for use in the synagogue. His religious fame and influence in Italy, Germany, and France were great. He is known as the creator of the Neo-Hebraic poetry, so called; it imitated the Arabic in having, for instance, verses of fixed length, rhyme, and the acrostic.

Kalisch, David (kä'lish). A German comic poet; born at Breslau, Feb. 23, 1820; died at Berlin, Aug. 21, 1872. Of Jewish birth, and intended originally for business, he devoted himself to journalism, beginning as Paris correspondent for German newspapers. Returning to Germany in 1846, he settled eventually in Berlin, where he founded (1848) the Prussian Punch, Kladderadatsch, with which he was successful for many years. He wrote a series of successful farces, like 'The Gold Uncle.'

Kalisch, Ludwig. A German miscellaneous writer; born at Polnisch-Lissa, Sept. 7, 1814; died at Paris, March 3, 1882. Among his earlier works were: 'The Book of Folly' (1845); 'Shadows' (1845); 'Tales in Verse' (1845), which to fit diction united vividness of portrayal; 'Shrapnels' (1849). Exiled by the revolution of 1848, he described his new places of residence in 'Paris and London' (2 vols., 1851). His later works were: 'Bright Hours' (2 vols., 1872); 'Pictures from my Boyhood' (1872); 'Bound and Unbound' (1876); 'Paris Life' (2d ed. 1882); etc. He was the author also of humorous writings and romances.

Kall, Abraham (käl). A popular Danish historian; born at Copenhagen, 1743; died there, 1821. He became university librarian in 1765, professor of history 1780, councilor of State 1811. His chief work was a 'Universal History' (1776).

Kalousek, Josef (kä-lö'sek). A Bohemian historian; born at Vamberk, April 2, 1838. He is professor of history at the University of Prague, and an authority on Czech history and literature. His publications include: 'Bohemian Constitutional Law' (1871); 'Review of the Ethnographic Literature of the Czechs'; 'Defense of Wenceslas'; 'Biography of Emperor Charles IV. of Bohemia' (1878).

Kaltenbrunner, Karl Adam (käl'ten-brön-er). A popular German poet and prose-writer; born at Enns, Dec. 30, 1804; died at Vienna, Jan. 6, 1867. He was author of a number of volumes of poetry in Austrian dialects, his handling of which was masterly. Duke Maximilian of Bavaria set a number of his songs to music. His drama 'The Three Firs' (1862) had a stage success. He was for a large part of his lifetime an official in the Vienna government printing-house.

Kamaryt, Joseph Klastimil (kä'mä-rit). A Czech poet; born at Velesin, near Budejovice, 1797; died at Tabor, 1833. He entered the church. His 'Parables in Verse' reached a second edition in 1845.

Kames, Henry Home, lord. A famous Scottish author and jurist; born at Kames, Berwickshire, in 1696; died at Edinburgh, Dec. 27, 1782. Educated at the University of Edinburgh, after nearly thirty years' practice as a lawyer he became judge in 1752. Besides important legal works, he wrote on antiquities, metaphysics, ethics, religion, æsthetics, education, agriculture, etc. His chief literary production, 'Elements of Criticism' (3 vols., 1762), forestalled, as regards works of the imagination, the modern psychological school. Of this book, Goldsmith said it was "easier to write than to read." Like his contemporary Lord Chesterfield, he was a great social favorite.

Kampen, Nikolaas Godfried van (käm'-pen). A distinguished Dutch historian; born at Haarlem, May 15, 1776; died at Leyden, March 15, 1839. The son of a gardener, having laid the foundation of vast learning while clerk in a book-store, he became editor and finally professor of English and German in the University of Leyden (1815). Many of his historical and literary works were translated into German, their reputation becoming European. 'History of the Literature of the Netherlands' (1812); 'History of French Domination in Europe' (8 vols., 1815-23); 'History of the Influence of the Netherlands Outside of Europe' (3 vols., 1831-33), are among his finest works.

Kane, Elisha Kent. A celebrated American Arctic explorer; born at Philadelphia, Feb. 3, 1820; died at Havana, Feb. 16, 1857. Was a surgeon in the United States navy. Having previously visited practically every other quarter of the globe, he accompanied the Grinnell expedition in search of Sir John Franklin (1850-52). On his return, by contributing the proceeds of a series of lectures and his pay, he shared in equipping a second expedition, under his own command (1853-55). These adventures were in spite of feeble health and frail constitution. He died young. His two works, 'The United States Grinnell Expedition in Search of Sir John Franklin' (1854) and 'Second Grinnell Expedition' (1856), are very interesting. He started northward the second time so quickly that the first work went through the press without his revision.

Kanitz, Phillpp Felix (kä'nits). A Hungarian explorer and writer on ethnography and archæology; born at Buda-Pesth, Aug. 2, 1829. His series of works on Servia, Bulgaria, Herzegovina, Montenegro, etc., beginning in 1862, gave him a brilliant reputation, and have spread greatly the knowledge of Slavic countries. He was the first to draw correct maps of Bulgaria and the Balkans. Died Jan. 5, 1904.

Kannegiesser, Karl Ludwig (kän'ne-gē-ser). A German writer; born at Wendemark, in Altmark, May 9, 1781; died at Berlin, Sept. 14, 1861. He is best known as the translator into German of Chaucer, Beaumont and Fletcher, Byron, Scott, Dante, Madame de Staël, etc.

Kant, Immanuel (känt). An eminent German philosopher; born at Königsberg, April 22, 1724; died there, Feb. 12, 1804. His three great works were: 'Kritik der Reinen Vernunft' (Critique of Pure Reason: 1781), which attempts to define the nature of those of our ideas which lie outside of experience, and to establish the basis of valid knowledge; 'Kritik der Praktischen Vernunft' (Critique of the Practical Reason: 1788), which bases the ideas of God, freedom, and immortality on the ethical consciousness alone, denying that we have any right to hold them otherwise; 'Kritik der Urteilskraft' (Critique of the Power of Judgment: 1790). He wrote also on cosmic physics, æsthetics, pedagogy, ethics, the metaphysical basis of law, etc. He was professor of logic and metaphysics at the University of Königsberg.

Kantemir, Antiochus Dmitrievitch, Prince (kän'te-mēr). A noted Russian author; born at Constantinople, Sept. 21, 1709; died at Paris, April 11, 1744. His 'Satires,' in the antique form, written in rhyme and syllabic metre, were his most important work, and are valuable as describing Russian life and manners. Many of their verses became proverbs with the Russian peasantry. They were the first fruits of modern Russian literature. He may ,be called the father of secular writing in Russia. ('Works,' 2 vols., St. Petersburg, 1867.)

Kapnist, Vasili Vasilievitch (käp'nist). A celebrated Russian poet and dramatist; born at Oboukhovka, in 1757; died there, Nov. 9, 1824. His chief work, 'Chicancry' (1798), a comedy in verse, forbidden by the censor, was performed by express permission of the emperor. It has been more than once reprinted (last in 1888), was translated into French, and has furnished several proverbs. It is an Aristophanic satire on the old justice in Russia —

showing, as has been wittily said, "the Russian Themis stark-naked." He wrote also many exquisite lyrics. ('Works,' St. Petersburg, 1849.)

Kapp, Friedrich (käp). A German biographer and historian; born at Hamm, Westphalia, April 13, 1824; died at Berlin, Oct. 27, 1884. He left Germany at the outbreak of the revolution of 1848, finally wandering as far as New York (1850). He took active part in American politics. Returning to Germany in 1870, he entered the Reichstag in 1872. Nearly all his works refer to the United States, as 'American Soldier Traffic by German Princes' (1864), 'German Emigration to America' (1868), and his 'Lives' of Kalb and Steuben. A citizen of two hemispheres, he was a pioneer in a style of literature that may be called international.

Karadzic, Vuk Stefanovotch (kä-rä'jitsh) A famous Servian author; born at Trshitch, Nov. 7, 1787; died at Vienna, Feb. 7, 1864. The two great works of his life were the reformation of the Servian literary language (which, up to his time had been a very debased medium, being either rude Slavonian or a hybrid jumble of Serb and Slavonian), and the publication of the 'Popular Serb Songs' (4 vols., 1814-33; 3d ed. 1841-46). His epoch-making 'Dictionary' appeared in 1818. The songs attracted wide-spread attention, and were translated into every European tongue. He was the founder of modern Servian literature.

Karamzin, Nikolai Mikhailovitch (kä-rämzin'). A celebrated Russian historian; born at Mikhailovka, near Simbirsk, Dec. 12, 1765; died near St. Petersburg, June 3, 1826. He left the army to devote himself to literature. His great work, 'History of Russia' (11 vols., 1816-29), created a tremendous sensation, being read even by the court and fashionable ladies. "He appeared," in Pushkin's words, "to have discovered old Russia, as Columbus discovered America." The tone of the work was ultraconservative. Its style has been pronounced perfect, though to-day it seems over-rhetorical. It was translated into French and German. 'Letters of a Russian Traveler' (1797-1801), in the style of Sterne, met with great favor. Of several novels, 'Poor 'Lisa' was much imitated, and with others of his writings, translated into German by Richter. Karamzin was also a translator and journalist. With Lomonosov, he was the creator of Russian prose. ('Works,' St. Petersburg, 1848.)

Karasoutzas, John (kä-rä-sö'tzas). A modern Greek poet; born at Smyrna, July 9, 1824; died April 3, 1873. His verse was not only patriotic, but strong and graceful. It appears in the collections 'Lyrics' (1839); 'Breath of the Morn' (1846); 'Kleonike' (1868), a narrative poem; etc.

Karavelov, Liuben (kä-rä-vä'lof). A Bulgarian author; born at Koprivchtitsa, 1834; died at Rustchuk, Feb. 11, 1879. Was one of the creators of Bulgarian prose. His works consisted of novels, tales, and poems (8 vols., 1887).

Karnovitch, Evgenij Petrovitch (kär-nō'-vich). A Russian historian and novelist; born near Jaroslav, Oct. 22, 1823. His historical work, 'Russia's Part in the Deliverance of the Christians from Turkey's Yoke,' 'Konstantin Pavlovitch,' etc., was important. 'Great Fortunes in Russia' (1885) contained interesting facts. His best-known novel is 'Love and Crown'; it has been translated into several European languages.

Karpinski, Franciszek (kär-pin'skē). A celebrated Polish poet; born at Hotoscow, Galicia, in 1741; died in Lithuania, Sept. 4, 1825. He was one of the illustrious figures at the court of Stanislaus Augustus for a time, but withdrew to his estates in 1793 and engaged in philanthropic work. His poems (1804) are remarkable for energy, simplicity, and patriotism, and still retain a hold upon the people.

Karr, Alphonse (kär). A celebrated French writer; born at Paris, Nov. 24, 1808; died at St. Raphael, Var, Sept. 29, 1890. Among his numerous striking novels were 'The Shortest Way' (1836); 'Genevieve' (1838); 'Clotilde' (1839). 'A Journey around my Garden' (1845), talks on botany and natural history, was in another vein. 'Woman' (1853) was a study of morals. Two dramas, 'The Norman Penelope' (1860) and 'Yellow Roses' (1866), were not very successful. One of his most characteristic efforts was the series of papers called 'Les Guêpes.' They were confidential, anecdotic, critical, witty, satirical, caustic, in fact well-nigh unique; and were the cause of an attempt being made on his life (1844) by an offended woman author whom they had harshly criticized.

Karsh or **Karshin, Anna Luise** (kärsh or kärsh'in). A German poet; born near Schwiebus, Dec. 1, 1722; died at Berlin, Oct. 12, 1791. Self-taught, of low birth and free life, her poetic merit was but slight, though she has been extravagantly called «the German Sappho.»

Kästner, Abraham Gotthelf (kest'ner). A German poet; born at Leipsic, Sept. 27, 1719; died at Göttingen, June 20, 1800. Though a learned mathematician, he is best known by his witty and caustic 'Epigrams' (1781; 2 vols., 1800). As an example of these, on a poor tragedy-writer he wrote:—

«This poet's just the man to reach a tragedy's aim:
We've sympathy with his piece, wild dread of more of
    the same.»

(Poetical and prose works, 4 vols., 1841.)

Kate, Jan Jakob Lodewijk ten (kä'te). A Dutch poet; born at The Hague, Dec. 23, 1819; died at Amsterdam, Dec. 25, 1889. 'De Schepping' (The Creation, 1866) ranks as his best poem. In the form of a vision of Moses from Mt. Sinai, it describes the creation of heaven and earth in seven songs, each beginning with the words of the Bible, then narrating the day's creation just finished, and ending with a hymn. His two next best poems

are 'The Planets' and 'The New Church in Amsterdam.' ('Works,' 12 vols., 1889–93.)

Katona, Joseph (kä'tō-nä). A Hungarian poet; born at Kecskemet, Nov. 11, 1792; died there, Nov. 2, 1830. He wrote 'Bánk-Bán' (1821), the grandest tragedy Hungary has produced. Long unnoticed, it appeared on the stage only in 1834, when it met with success, but did not become generally famous till 1845. Meanwhile its author, embittered by its failure, had renounced poetry, and died, beloved by the people, especially the poor. ('Works,' 3 vols., 1880.)

Kaufmann, Alexander (kouf'män). A favorite German poet; born at Bonn, May 14, 1817; died at Wertheim, May 1, 1893. Popular among his lyrics have been 'The Bride,' 'About Midnight,' 'Morning'; of his ballads, 'King Wenzel,' 'The Stolen Steed,' 'Lifthilde.' His songs were simple, hearty, and fervent,—droll and dreamy, humorous and playful. Of several volumes of verse, the best was 'Under the Vines' (1815).

Kaufmann, Mathilde. See **George.**

Kavanagh, Julia. A popular English writer; born at Thurles, Ireland, Jan. 7, 1824; died at Nice, Oct. 28, 1877. She wrote a large number of novels, the scenes of which were almost invariably laid in France, where she had resided: among them 'Daisy Burns' (3 vols., 1853); also 'Woman in France during the 18th Century' (2 vols., 1850), 'A Summer and Winter in the Two Sicilies' (2 vols., 1858), 'French Women of Letters' (1862). She was best known by the novels she published in magazines. One of the best of recent English authors.

Kaye, John William, Sir (kā). An English administrator and military historian; born in 1814; died in 1876. He was for a number of years an officer in the Bengal artillery, but resigned in 1841, and in 1856 entered the East India Company. Upon the transfer of the government of India to the crown, he succeeded John Stuart Mill in the political department of the India office. His works consist of histories and biographies relating to the East, among them being 'A History of Afghanistan' (1851–53); 'History of the Administration of the East India Company' (1853); 'A History of the Sepoy War in India' (1857–58; London, 1864–75), a comprehensive narrative of the celebrated mutiny down to the fall of Delhi; 'Lives of Indian Officers' (1867).

Keary, Annie. An English novelist; born near Wetherby, Yorkshire, March 3, 1825; died at Eastbourne, March 3, 1879. Beginning with books for children, she made her reputation with stories of Irish life. She was a prolific writer and very popular in her day, 'Castle Daly' (1875) being her best work. Her letters were published in 1883.

Keats, John. An eminent English poet; born in London, 1795; died in Rome, 1821. 'Endymion, a Poetic Romance' (1818), his first important effort, though immature, gave great promise, which was fulfilled in 'Lamia, Isabella, the Eve of St. Agnes, and Other Poems' (1820), containing also the fine unfinished epic 'Hyperion.' 'The Letters of John Keats to Fanny Brawne,' whom he loved, appeared in 1878; 'Letters to his Family and Friends' in 1891. Dying at 25, he succeeded in leaving a name immortal in literature. Shelley wrote the exquisite elegy 'Adonais' in commemoration of his death. ('Works,' 3d ed. 1859.)

Kebbel, Thomas Edward. An English journalist and author; born in Leicestershire, Nov. 23, 1828. Educated at Oxford, he became a lawyer and afterwards engaged in journalism, being connected with the Press (1855) and the Day (1867) as political writer. He has written on political topics: 'Essays upon History and Politics' (1864); 'English Statesmen since the Peace of 1815' (1868); 'A History of Toryism' (1885); and biographies of Lord Beaconsfield and Lord Derby in the 'English Statesmen' series. His more recent works are: 'The Old and the New English Country Life' (1891); 'Sport and Nature' (1893).

Keble, John. A famous English religious poet; born at Fairford, Gloucestershire, 1792; died at Bournemouth, Hampshire, 1866. He was remarkable for great beauty of character. A clergyman of the English Church, he repeatedly refused rich livings from a sense of duty. Of his great work 'The Christian Year' (2 vols., 1827), which he published anonymously, in 1872 appeared the 158th edition; over 500,000 copies in all have been sold. It has been illustrated and illuminated, books have been made from and written on it, including a concordance, and from its profits the author built one of the most beautiful parish churches in England.

Keddie, Henrietta. ["Sarah Tytler."] An English novelist and, miscellaneous writer; born in 1827. She is the author of several graceful and readable stories, the best known being: 'Days of Yore' (1864); 'Citoyenne Jacqueline' (1865); 'Noblesse Oblige' (1869); 'French Janet'; 'Blachall Ghosts.' Of her miscellaneous works, designed chiefly for juvenile readers, may be noticed: 'Modern Painters' (1873); 'Children of a Hundred Years Ago' (1876); 'Jane Austen and her Works' (1880); 'Marie Antoinette: the Woman and the Queen' (1883); 'Three Men of Mark'; 'The Machinations of Janet.'

Keenan, Henry Francis. An American novelist; born at Rochester, N. Y., May 4, 1850. A successful journalist, a New York and a Paris correspondent of note, he deserted journalism for literature in 1883. He published: 'Trajan' (1884); 'The Aliens' (1886); 'One of a Thousand' (1887); 'Conflict with Spain' (1898).

Keightley, Thomas (kīt'ly). An English writer; born at Newton, Ire., 1784; died near Erith, Kent, Nov. 4, 1872. He is best known by his 'Fairy Mythology' (2 vols., 1828), and 'Tales and Popular Fictions' (1834).

Keim, Karl Theodor (kīm). A noted German theologian; born at Stuttgart, Dec. 17, 1825; died at Giessen, Nov. 17, 1878. While a disciple of the modern critical school of theology (of Strauss, Baur, and Renan) he strove to reconcile it with the old faith. He wrote: 'The Historical Christ' (3d ed. 1866), and the great work 'History of Jesus of Nazareth' (3 vols., 1867-72).

Keller, Gerard (kel'er). A Dutch miscellaneous writer; born at Gouda, Feb. 13, 1829. His best works are his books of travel: 'A Summer in the North' (1861); 'A Summer in the South' (1864); 'Paris Besieged' (1871); 'Murdered Paris' (1872); 'Europe Sketched in All her Glory' (1877-80); 'America in Image and in Writing' (1887). Of his numerous novels may be named: 'The Teacher's Household' (1858); 'Within and Without' (1860); 'The Mortgage on Wasenstein' (1865); 'From Home' (2 vols., 1867); 'Over-Perfect' (1871); 'Three Tales' ('The Privy Councilor,' 'How They are Enjoyed,' 'In Our Days,' 1880); 'Our Minister' (1883); 'Flickering Flames' (1884); 'Nemesis' (1885). He is the author also of books for the young, and the dramas 'The Barber's Daughter' (1878), 'The Blue Ribbon' (1881), 'The Dangerous Cousin' (1884). D. 1899.

Keller, Gottfried. A powerful German poet and one of the foremost of German novelists; born at Zürich, July 19, 1819; died there, July 16, 1890. Original in execution, he was a keen observer, genuinely artistic, and with a strong sense of humor, sometimes extravagantly indulged. In his best vein he goes straight to the heart. To romanticism in motifs, processes, and characters, he joined realism in execution. His writings disclose the fact that he was a painter before being an author. An impression of his poetical genius may be obtained from 'Complete Poems' (3d ed. 1888). Of his novels, 'Seldwyla Folk' (1856) is one of the best. ('Works,' 11 vols., 1889-93.)

Kelley, James Douglas Jerrold. An American naval officer and story-writer; born 1847. Besides works relating to the navy, he has written the story 'A Desperate Chance'; 'American Man of War.'

Kelly, William Darrah. An American politician; born at Philadelphia, April 12, 1814; died at Washington, D. C., Jan. 9, 1890. He was a lawyer; was Member of Congress from Pennsylvania 1861-90, and prominent as an abolitionist and a protectionist. Besides addresses and political writings, he published 'Letters from Europe' (1880), 'The New South' (1887), etc.

Kellgren, Johan Henrik (kel'gren). One of the greatest of Swedish poets; born at Floby, West Gothland, Dec. 1, 1751; died April 20, 1795. He excelled especially in lyrics, of which one of his finest is 'Nya Skapelsen' (The New Creation). Gustavus III., whose private librarian and secretary he was, furnished the plots of most of his dramas and operas, he himself contributing merely the versification. ('Works,' 2 vols., 1884.)

Kellogg, Elijah. An American Congregational minister and writer for the young; born at Portland, Me., 1813; died at Harpswell, Me., March 17, 1901. He was author of several series of juvenile books,—'Elm Island' series, 'Good Old Times' series, etc.,—but is probably best known by the 'Address of Spartacus to the Gladiators.'

Kelly, Jonathan Falconbridge. An American prose-writer; born in Philadelphia, in 1818; died in Cincinnati, O., 1854. He was the author of 'The Humors of Falconbridge' (1856).

Kelvin, Lord. See **Thomson.**

Kemble, Frances Anne (Mrs. Pierce Butler). A famous English actress, daughter of Charles Kemble and niece of Mrs. Siddons; born in London, Nov. 27, 1809; died there, Jan. 15, 1893. Among other works, she published her 'Journal' (1834); 'Journal of a Residence on a Georgia Plantation' (1863); 'Recollections of a Girlhood' (3 vols., 1878); 'Recollections of Later Life' (3 vols., 1882); and in the Atlantic Monthly, reminiscences of her theatrical career (1876-77).

Kemény, Zsigmond, Baron (kem'ă-nē). An eminent Hungarian novelist and publicist; born at Magyar-Kapud, 1816; died at Puszta-Kamarás, Dec. 22, 1875. His romances and political writings are classics in Hungarian literature. Of the former, 'Man and Wife' (1852) and 'The Abysses of the Heart' (1854), both psychological studies, are among the best. 'Studies' (2 vols., 1870) is an admirable work. The style of his writings and the tax they impose on thought make them not always easy to read, but what they demand they amply repay in pleasure and profit. He was called "prince of the Magyar journalists."

Kempis, Thomas à (kem'pis). A celebrated German mystic; born at Kempen (whence his name, "Thomas from Kempen"), near Cologne, 1380; died 1471. His true name was Hamerken (Latin, Malleolus). Sub-prior of the monastery of Mount St. Agnes, near Zwolle, he was distinguished for piety and success as an instructor of youth. He was author of the 'Imitation of Christ,' one of the most famous of books, which has been universally read and has moved the hearts of men of all nations, conditions and kinds, for four centuries. Its title describes its contents; it abounds in maxims of humility and resignation, and is such a book as only a man living the most uneventful of lives, withdrawn from the world and spent in contemplation, could have written. It is said that it has been translated into more languages than any other book except the Bible.

Kendall, Amos. A distinguished American politician; born at Dunstable, Mass., Aug. 16, 1789; died at Washington, D. C., Nov. 11, 1869. He was Postmaster-General of the United States 1835-40. He wrote 'Life of Andrew Jackson'; 'Autobiography' (1872).

Kendall, George Wilkins. An American writer; born at Mount Vernon, N. H., about 1809; died at Oak Springs, Tex., Oct. 22, 1867. He was founder of the New Orleans Picayune, which became under his direction one of the leading journals of the South. He wrote 'The War Between the United States and Mexico' (1851).

Kendall, Henry Clarence. An Australian poet; born in Ulladalla district, New South Wales, 1841; died near Sydney, 1882. While a lawyer's clerk in Sydney, three poems were accepted by the London Athenæum in 1862; he then devoted himself to literature, publishing 'Leaves from an Australian Forest' (1869) and 'Songs from the Mountains' (1880), his chief works. Especially happy in description of Australian scenery, he is known as "the poet of the bush." A collection of his poetry appeared in 1886.

Kendrick, Ashael Clark. An American scholar, editor, and miscellaneous writer; born at Poultney, Vt., Dec. 7, 1809; died at Rochester, N. Y., Oct. 21, 1895. Besides bringing out translations and several text-books, and revising and editing Olshausen's 'New Testament Commentary' and Meyer's 'Commentary on John,' he published 'Our Poetical Favorites' (3 vols., 3d ed. 1880); 'Life and Letters of Emily C. Judson' (1862). He was one of the American committee of New Testament revisers.

Kennan, George. A noted traveler and writer on Russian topics; born at Norwalk, Huron County, O., Feb. 16, 1845. In early life, and before the completion of the Atlantic cable, he was a member of the Western Union telegraph expedition to survey a route for a Behring Strait and Siberian telegraph line to Europe. The result of this expedition was the book called 'Tent Life in Siberia' (1870). His journeys through Northern Russia and Siberia in the years 1885-86 for the purpose of investigating the condition of the Siberian exiles, resulted in the publication of a series of papers in the Century Magazine (1890-91), afterwards issued in book form under the title 'Siberia and the Exile System'; 'The Tragedy of Pelée.'

Kennedy, Crammond. An American lawyer and miscellaneous writer; born at North Berwick, Scotland, 1842. He came to New York (1856), became known as the boy preacher, served as chaplain in the Civil War, was managing editor of the Christian Union (1870), and since 1878 has practiced law at Washington, D. C. He has written: 'Corn in the Blade' (1860), verse; 'Liberty of the Press' (1876), a prize essay; 'The Capture of Aguinaldo.'

Kennedy, Grace. An English novelist; born at Pinmore, Ayrshire, 1782; died at Edinburgh, 1825. Her best-known work was 'Father Clement' (1823), which reached a twelfth edition and was translated into nearly every European language. Her works were moral and religious in character.

Kennedy, John Pendleton. An American writer; born at Baltimore, Oct. 25, 1795; died at Newport, Aug. 18, 1870. Best known by his very popular 'Horse-shoe Robinson' (1835). Among his other works was a 'Life of William Wirt, Attorney-General of the United States' (1849). Active in politics and several times Member of Congress, he was Secretary of the Navy under President Fillmore.

Kennedy, Patrick. An Irish antiquarian writer; born in County Wexford, 1801; died at Dublin, March 28, 1873. His studies were given to the archæology and popular traditions of Ireland. His chief work was 'Legendary Fictions of the Irish Celts' (new ed. 1892).

Kennedy, William. A Scottish writer of prose and verse; born at Dublin, 1799; died in Paris, ———, 1871. He resided many years in Galveston, Tex., serving there as British consul. He published: 'My Early Days' (1826); 'The Arrow and the Rose; with Other Poems' (1830); 'The Rise, Progress, and Prospects of the Republic of Texas' (2 vols., 1841).

Kennedy, William Sloane. A well-known American biographer, story-writer, and poet; born at Breckville, O., 1850. His home is at Belmont, Mass. He has written lives of Longfellow, Whittier, and Holmes; 'Wonders and Curiosities of the Railway: Locomotive Stories' (1884); 'In Portia's Garden,' verse; etc.

Kennett, White. An English clergyman and historian; born at Dover, in 1660; died in 1728. From 1718 until his death he occupied the episcopal see of Peterborough. In 1706 he brought out a complete 'History of England,' from the earliest times to the death of William III., a work of great accuracy and interest; and in 1713 'Bibliothecæ Americanæ Primordia,' an attempt towards laying the foundation of an American library.

Kenney, Charles Lamb. An English miscellaneous writer, son of James; born at Bellevue, France, April 29, 1821; died at Kensington, Aug. 25, 1881. Was a friend of Thackeray and Dickens. Secretary of M. Lesseps, his book 'The Gates of the East' (1857) turned English public opinion in favor of the Suez Canal, against Lord Palmerston's opposition. He introduced opera-bouffe in London, writing librettos for 'The Grand Duchess of Gérolstein,' 'La Belle Hélène,' etc. He wrote also several popular songs, among them 'Ever my Queen.'

Kenney, James. An English dramatist; born in Ireland, 1780; died July 25, 1849. He was a bank clerk in London, with a taste for the theatre, and wrote a number of pieces that still hold the stage. Among them were the farces 'Raising the Wind' (1803); 'Turn Him Out' (1812); 'Love, Law, and Physic' (1812); the stock favorite 'Sweethearts and Wives' (1823); and the famous tragedy 'The Sicilian Vespers' (1840).

Kenrick, Francis Patrick. A distinguished American Roman Catholic prelate and theological writer; born at Dublin, Ireland, Dec. 3, 1797; died at Baltimore, Md., July 6, 1863. He founded the seminary of St. Charles Borromeo in Philadelphia in 1832: became archbishop of Baltimore, 1851; honorary primate of the United States, 1859. He was prominent as a controversialist and a Biblical scholar. Among his works were: 'Dogmatic Theology' (4 vols., 1839–40); 'Moral Theology' (3 vols., 1841–43). He also published a revision of the Douai English Bible, with notes.

Kenrick, Peter Richard. An American prelate and writer, brother of Francis Patrick; born in Dublin, 1806; died in St. Louis, 1896, of which city he was the first Roman Catholic archbishop. He published: 'The Holy House of Loretto'; 'Anglican Ordinations'; 'Concio in Concilio Vaticana'; etc.

Kent, James. An eminent American jurist; born at Philippi, N. Y., July 31, 1763; died at New York, Dec. 12, 1847. Author of the famous 'Commentaries on American Law' (4 vols., 1826–30), which holds in this country a position similar to that occupied by Blackstone's commentaries in Great Britain. It contains not only federal jurisprudence, but the municipal law, written and unwritten, of the several States; has proved its general interest and special value by years of use; passed through many editions, and is one of the intellectual monuments of our country. He was chief justice and chancellor of the State of New York.

Kent, William Charles Mark. An English miscellaneous writer; born in London, 1823. He has produced a number of works in prose and verse, besides contributing to the 'Encyclopædia Britannica' and several of the best English reviews, and being active as a journalist. His poem 'Aletheia, or the Condemnation of Mythology' (1850) was praised by Lamartine. Among his prose works may be mentioned 'The Vision of Cagliostro' (1863). 'The Derby Ministry,' under the pseudonym "Mark Rochester," and 'The Gladstone Government,' under that of "A Templar," consisted of sketches of prominent political personages.

Kenyon, James Benjamin. An American poet; born in Frankfort, Herkimer County, N. Y., April 26, 1858. He has contributed to periodicals, and is the author of 'The Fallen, and Other Poems' (1876); 'Out of the Shadows' (1880); 'Songs in All Seasons' (1885); and 'In Realms of Gold'; 'Reed Voices' (1905).

Kepler, Johannes (kep'ler). An eminent German astronomer; born at Weil, Würtemberg, Dec. 27, 1571; died at Ratisbon, Nov. 15, 1630. He was the discoverer of the laws of planetary motion, famous as "Kepler's laws," which revolutionized previous theories of the position of humanity, and formed the foundation for Newton's subsequent labors and modern astronomy. His great work was the 'New Astronomy, with Commentaries on the Motions of Mars' (1609). He also completed (1627) the famous "Rudolphine Tables" of Tycho Brahe, the basis of astronomy for the next hundred yea.s; while his contribution to optics was of first, to mathematics of striking, importance. One of the great epoch-makers of human thought. ('Works,' 8 vols., 1858–71.)

Ker, David. An American journalist and writer of travels, stories, and books for the young; born in England, 18—. Formerly a correspondent of the London Daily Telegraph, he has of late years resided in New York. He has written: 'The Broken Image, and Other Tales' (1870), published anonymously; 'On the Road to Khiva' (1874); 'Into Unknown Seas' (1886), describing the cruise of two sailor boys; etc.

Kératry, Auguste Hilarion de (kā-rä-trē). A French politician; born at Rennes, Oct. 28, 1769; died at Port Marly, Nov. 7, 1859. He wrote on a great variety of subjects, his chief works being 'Moral and Philosophical Inductions' (1817), and 'The Beautiful in the Imitative Arts' (3 vols., 1822).

Kerkhoven, Petrus Frans van (kerk-hō'ven). A Flemish miscellaneous writer; born at Antwerp, 1818; died there, 1857. He was editor of several journals; wrote numerous poems, tragedies, comedies, romances, and novels, among them 'Daniel' (1845); 'Ferdinand the Corsair' (1845). His works appeared in 1869–73 in thirteen volumes.

Kernahan, Coulson. An English poet, novelist, and essayist; born at Ilfracombe, Aug. 1, 1858. His poetry is strong in matter and finished in form. Some of his novels are marked by a play of gloomy fancy not unlike Hawthorne's. The striking story 'A Dead Man's Diary,' published anonymously, soon reached a fourth edition. Two others, 'Stranger than Fiction' (1893) and 'Dead Faces' (1894), are notable. He has shown himself to be also an excellent critic. Some of his best works are 'The Child, the Wise Man, and the Devil'; 'Wise Men and a Fool.'

Kerner, Justinus (kär'ner). A famous German poet and novelist; born at Ludwigsburg, Würtemberg, 1786; died at Weinsberg, 1862. Several of his lyrics—for instance, 'Song of Wandering,' 'The Wanderer in the Saw Mill,'—are popular with the masses, and a number were set to music by Schumann. His poetry can be read in 'The Last Bunch of Blossoms' (1852) and 'Winter Blossoms' (1859). Of his prose works (which included medical writings, he being a physician), 'The Seeress of Prevorst' (5th ed. 1877), a result of his studies in animal magnetism and somnambulism, attracted great attention. Noteworthy too was his 'Picture Book from my Childhood' (2d ed. 1886). His work was marked by keen observation, fancy, satirical power, humor blended with pathos, and thought always busy with the other world. He may be called the romanticist of the Swabian school of poets.

Kerner, Theobald. A German poet and novelist, son of Justinus; born at Gaildorf, June 14, 1817. A physician like his father, like him he has published both medical and literary works. Among the latter, his 'Poems' appeared in 1851; 'Princess Klatschrose' the same year (2d ed. 1894); 'The Flying Tailor,' an opera, in 1862; 'Parson Staber, or the New Ahasuerus,' a comedy, in 1888. 'The Kerner House and its Guests' (1893) consisted of bright and interesting sketches of the inmates and visitors of his famous father's domicile, his own since the latter's death.

Kerr, Orpheus C. See **Newell**.

Kervyn de Lettenhove, Josef Marie Bruno Konstantin (ker-van' de let'en-hō-ve). A Belgian historian; born at St. Michel, West Flanders, Aug. 17, 1817; died at Brussels, April 3, 1891. His principal work was 'History of Flanders' (3d ed., 4 vols., 1874). Among his other works may be mentioned 'The Huguenots' (6 vols., 1883–85), 'Marie Stuart' (2 vols., 1890).

Ketchum, Mrs. Annie (Chambers). An American educator, lecturer, and miscellaneous writer; born in Scott County, Ky., 1824. She was principal of the high school for girls at Memphis, Tenn., 1855–58. She has written: 'Christmas Carillons and Other Poems' (1888); 'Nellie Braden,' a novel; 'Rilla Motto,' a romance; etc. Died Jan 27, 1904.

Ketteler, Wilhelm Emanuel von (ket'e-ler). A distinguished German prelate; born at Münster, Dec. 25, 1811; died at Burghausen, Bavaria, July 13, 1877. One of the ablest of German ultramontanists; bishop of Mentz (1850), for which diocese he obtained special privileges; and member of the first Reichstag (1871). He wrote on the questions of the day. Among his works may be mentioned: 'Freedom, Authority, and Church' (7th ed. 1862); 'The Labor Question and Christianity' (3d ed. 1864), which even Lassalle praised; 'Germany after the War of 1866' (6th ed. 1867).

Kettell, Samuel. An American prose-writer; born in Newburyport, Mass., Aug. 5, 1800; died in Malden, Mass., Dec. 3, 1855. He assisted Samuel G. Goodrich in the preparation of some of his 'Peter Parley' books. Under the pen-names of «Peeping Tom» and «Timothy Titterwell» he contributed many humorous articles to the Boston Courier, afterward becoming its editor. His principal works are: 'Records of the Spanish Inquisition' (1828); and 'Specimens of American Poetry, with Critical and Biographical Notices' (3 vols., 1829).

Kettle, Mary Rosa Stuart (Mackenzie), best known as «Rosa Mackenzie Kettle.» An English novelist; born at Overseale, Leicestershire; died at Callander, Scotland, March 14, 1895. Her stories treat of Cornwall and the South Coast. Her earliest success was 'Fabian's Tower' (1852). She also published: 'La Belle Marie: A Romance of the Cornish Coast' (1862); 'Hillsden on the Moors' (1873); 'My Home in the Shires' (1877); 'The Sea and the Moor' (1877); 'The Sisters of Ombersleigh; or, Under the South Downs' (1888).

Kexel, Olof (chaiks'el). A Swedish miscellaneous writer; born at Kalmar, 1748; died at Stockholm, 1796. He wrote numerous satires, songs, poems, plays, and a historical romance, 'Zalameski.'

Key, Francis Scott. An American poet; born in Frederick County, Md., Aug. 9, 1780; died at Baltimore, Jan. 11, 1843. Author of 'The Star Spangled Banner,' which was suggested and partially written while he was viewing the bombardment of Fort McHenry, near Baltimore, by the British fleet, on which he was a prisoner. It was set to music by J. S. Smith.

Keyes, Erasmus Darwin. A distinguished American soldier; born at Brimfield, Mass., May 29, 1810; died 1895. A graduate of West Point (1832), he rose to the rank of major-general in the Civil War. He wrote 'Fifty Years' Observation of Men and Events' (1884).

Keyser, Jakob Rudolph (ki'zer). One of the foremost Norwegian historians; born at Christiania, Jan. 1, 1803; died there, Oct. 8, 1864. Among his many important works were a 'History of Norway' (2 vols., 1865–70); 'History of the Norwegian Church under Catholicism' (2 vols., 1856–58).

Khayyám, Omar (ki-yäm'). A noted Persian poet, mathematician, and astronomer; born at Nishápúr, 1050 (?); died there, 1123 (?). He is best known for his famous 'Rubáiyát,' or 'Quatrains,'—four-line stanzas with the third unrhymed,—of which about 500 are considered genuine; Fitzgerald gives 101. Though some of these had been already translated into English by Hyde, Ouseley, and Cowell (in prose), the first English translation to make them widely known was Fitzgerald's, editions of which appeared in 1859, 1868, 1872, 1879, 1889. Other English translations have been by Whinfield (London, 1881), McCarthy (ib., 1889), Leslie Garner (Milwaukee, 1888), Le Gallienne (1897). An American edition in 1884 contained the celebrated illustrations by Elihu Vedder. There are also German, French, Norwegian, and Hungarian versions. A valuable work is that of N. H. Dole, containing English, French, and German translations, comparatively arranged, with further selections, notes, biographies, bibliography, etc., and an Introduction (2 vols., 1896). A new translation by John Payne, the famous translator of Villon and the 'Arabian Nights,' is announced, containing some 400 additional quatrains.

Kheraskov, Mikhail (che-räs-kof'). A Russian epic poet; born Oct. 25, 1733; died at Moscow, Oct. 9, 1806. His principal works were the 'Rossiad' (1785), in 12 cantos, on the conquest of Kazan, and 'Vladimir' (1786), in 18 cantos, on the conversion of St. Vladimir.

Khvostchinskáia, Nadezhda Dmitrievna (chvo-schin'skä-ē-ä). A Russian novelist; born at Riazan, 1825; died at Peterhof, July 2, 1889. A prolific writer, her best works were: 'Anna Mikhaïlovna' (1850); 'Waiting for Something Better'; the romance 'The Country Teacher';

'The Great Bear,' the last particularly having a pronounced success. She wrote also good short stories and published poetry. ('Works,' 6 vols., 1859.)

Kidder, Daniel Parish. An American descriptive writer; born at Darien, N. Y., 1815; died at Evanston, Ill., 1891. He was a missionary to Brazil, and very active in the Methodist Episcopal Church; was editor of the Sunday School Advocate. He wrote: 'Mormonism, and the Mormons' (1844); 'Sketches of a Residence and Travels in Brazil' (2 vols., 1845).

Kidder, Frederic. An American prose-writer; born in New Ipswich, N. H., 1804; died in Melrose, Mass., 1885. An antiquarian who gave much attention to the language and religion of the New England Indians. He was author of 'The Expeditions of Capt. John Lovewell' (1865); 'History of the First New Hampshire Regiment in the War of the Revolution' (1868); 'History of the Boston Massacre, March 5, 1770' (1870).

Kielland or **Kjelland, Alexander Lange** (chel'and). One of the most prominent of Norwegian novelists and dramatists; born at Stavanger, 1849. A strong representative of the realistic school, he seeks to introduce European culture into Norway, and is a foe to all forms of ecclesiastical tyranny. His writings have been supposed to show the influence of Balzac and Zola, also of Ibsen and Heine. Notable among his novels are: 'Garman and Worse' (1880), his first; 'Laboring People' (1881); 'Skipper Worse' (1882). The Christmas story 'Else' (1881), one of his best productions, should be read by all who desire to form an opinion of his work. Of his dramas, which differ from his novels only in having the dialogue form, among the best are: 'Betty's Formynder' (Betty's Guardian: 1887), 'Professoren' (1888).

Killigrew, Thomas. An English dramatist, brother of William; born at Handworth, Middlesex, 1611; died in London, 1682. Held several offices under Charles I. and Charles II., among them that of English resident at Venice (1651), and court jester. He succeeded his rival theatre manager, Sir Henry Herbert, as master of the revels (1673). He wrote eleven plays, not all of which were intended for the stage. As was to be expected from his character, his comic dramas surpass the serious ones. A complete edition appeared in 1664.

Killigrew, Sir William. An English dramatist; born at Handworth, 1606; died in London, 1695. His dramas were praised by Waller. 'Selindra' (1665) and 'Ormasdes' (1665), two tragi-comedies,—so called because, though they end happily, they contain violent deaths,—are good specimens of his work. He was a Member of Parliament and a courtier.

Kimball, Hannah Parker. An American poet; born 1861. She has contributed much to magazines, her best collection of verse appearine in the volume 'Victory and Other Verses' (1897).

Kimball, Harriet McEwen. An American writer of religious lyrics; born in Portsmouth, N. H., 1834. Her published works include : 'Hymns' (1867); 'Swallow Flights of Song' (1874); and 'The Blessed Company of All Faithful People' (1879) ; 'Poems' (Compl. Ed. 1889).

Kimball, Richard Burleigh. An American writer; born at Plainfield N. H., Oct. 11, 1816; died at New York, Dec. 28, 1892. He was a lawyer. Among his literary works were: 'Cuba and the Cubans' (1850); 'Romance of Student Life Abroad' (1853); 'Under-Currents of Wall Street' (1862); 'Henry Powers, Banker' (1868).

Kind, Johann Friedrich (kint). A German miscellaneous writer; born at Leipzig, March 4, 1768; died at Dresden, June 25, 1843. His works consisted of poems, novels, and dramas, among the latter being the librettos of Kreutzer's opera 'The Night Camp of Granada' and Weber's 'Der Freischütz' (1821).

King, Alice. An English novelist; born at Cutcombe, March 28, 1839; died there, May, 1894. Though she became blind at the age of seven, she learned seven languages, and was a prolific writer for magazines and author of novels, composing her manuscript by the aid of a typewriter. Among the most popular of her works were: 'Sir Tristram's Will' (1867); 'Hearts or Coronets' (1876); 'Fettered Yet Free' (1883); 'A Strange Tangle' (1885).

King, Mrs. Anna Eichberg. An American short-story writer ; born in Switzerland, 1856. Daughter of Julius Eichberg the musician. She is now Mrs. John Lane of London. Author of 'Brown's Retreat and Other Stories' (1893), and 'Kitwyk Stories' (1895), genuinely Dutch in tone.

King, Captain Charles. An American novelist and descriptive writer; born at Albany, N. Y., 1844. He resigned from the United States army in 1879, becoming professor of military science and tactics at the University of Wisconsin (1881) and devoting his time largely to literature. He wrote a long series of novels treating of army and frontier life and people, among the best of which are: 'The Colonel's Daughter' (1883), describing life in a frontier fort; 'Kitty's Conquest' (1884), very popular; 'Famous and Decisive Battles of the World' (1884); 'The Colonel's Christmas Dinner and Other Stories' (1892); 'Captain Close and Sergeant Crœsus' (1895): also 'Campaigning with Crook' (1890); 'The Iron Brigade' (1902).

King, Clarence. A representative American writer on geology and allied topics; born at Newport, R. I., Jan. 6, 1842; died at Phœnix, Ariz., Dec. 24, 1901. In 1863 he joined the State geological survey of California, making the first detailed surveys of the Yosemite Valley. In 1867 he was in charge of the United States geological survey of the 40th Parallel, and for the next five years did valuable work from the California Sierras to Eastern Wyoming, the results of which were registered in two atlases and the seven quarto volumes entitled 'Professional Papers of the Engineer Department of the United States Survey' (1870–78). The first volume was written entirely by Mr. King. When in 1879 the different geological surveys were united in one bureau of the Department of the Interior, Mr. King was made first director of the Survey, holding the position until 1881, when he resigned. He later carried on independent investigation, and contributed many important papers to scientific periodicals in this country and Europe. He was elected in 1876 a member of the National Academy of Science. His best-known book, 'Mountaineering in the Sierras' (1871), is not merely a contribution to technical knowledge in this field, but a brilliant literary performance; being written in a graphic way, and narrating picturesque and thrilling incidents of Western wild life.

King, Edward. An American miscellaneous writer; born at Middlefield, Mass, July 31, 1848; died at Brooklyn, N. Y., March 27, 1896. He was both a journalist—being well known as a Paris and a war correspondent—and an author. His specialties were our own Southern States and French themes. Among his works were 'My Paris, or French Character Sketches' (1868); 'Kentucky's Love, or Roughing It around Paris' (1872); 'The Great South' (1875); 'A Venetian Lover' (1887), a poem; 'The Gentle Savage' (1888), a popular novel.

King, Grace Elizabeth. An American novelist, short-story writer, and historian; born in Louisiana, 1852. She is one of the most prominent of Southern writers, and her books largely deal with Southern subjects. Her novel 'Monsieur Motte,' which appeared first in the New Princeton Review, was republished in book form in 1888. 'Balcony Stories' was one of her best works; others can be seen in 'Tales of a Time and Place.' Her historical writings embrace 'New Orleans, the Place and the People,' and a 'Life' of Bienville, the founder of New Orleans ; 'De Soto and his Men in Florida.'

King, Horatio. An American statesman, publicist, and writer of travels; born at Paris, Me., June 21, 1811; died at Washington, May 20, 1897. He was Postmaster-General of the United States in 1861. He wrote 'Sketches of Travel' (1878); and 'Turning on the Light : A Survey of the Administration of Buchanan.'

King, Thomas Starr. An American essayist; born in New York, Dec. 17, 1824; died in San Francisco, March 4, 1863. He was a Unitarian clergyman and a popular lecturer, and wrote 'The White Hills : their Legends, Landscape, and Poetry' (1859); 'Patriotism and Other Papers' (1864).

Kinglake, Alexander William. A noted English historian; born at Taunton, Devonshire, Aug. 5, 1809; died in London, Jan. 2, 1891. Having accompanied the English army to the Crimea in 1854, he wrote his masterpiece, 'The

Invasion of the Crimea, its Origin and an Account of its Progress' (8 vols., 1863–87). It is the standard work on the subject, written in an almost perfect style, though perhaps it is slightly diffuse, and partial to his friend Lord Raglan. Before the Crimean War he had written 'Eöthen; or Traces of Travel Brought Home from the East' (5th ed. 1846), a delightful record of personal experiences and a brilliant book of travel, with a light touch yet often penetrating to the springs of Oriental feeling.

Kingo, Thomas (kin'gō). A Danish religious poet; born at Slangerulı, Seeland, 1634; died 1703. His secular poetry was commonplace; but his hymns, of which he wrote 41, elevated in thought and beautiful in style, may be said to have made him the John Keble of Denmark. More than two centuries old, they are sung to-day in the Danish churches, and will continue in use while the Danish tongue endures. They appeal both to the cultivated and the rude. The best of them may be seen in his 'Hymn Book' (1689).

Kingsley, Charles. An English novelist, poet, and philanthropist; born at Holne, near Dartmoor, Devonshire, June 12, 1819; died at Eversley, Hampshire, Jan. 23, 1875. He became curate (1842) and vicar (1844) of Eversley, where he spent a large part of his life. His literary career began with the publication of 'The Saint's Tragedy' (1848), a drama in verse on the story of St. Elizabeth of Hungary. This was followed by a series of novels that caught the attention of the best readers: the first being 'Alton Locke, Tailor and Poet' (1849), which led to the establishment of co-operative associations in England, and contained the author's views as a Christian socialist, as did also 'Yeast' (1851). 'Hypatia' (1853) described pagan and Christian life in Alexandria early in the fifth century. 'Westward Ho!' (1855) narrated the adventures in the New World of Sir Amyas Leigh, with Sir Walter Raleigh, Drake, Hawkins, etc., as fellow characters. 'The Water Babies' (1853) was a fairy tale enjoyed by readers of all ages. Of his verse, 'Poems,' chiefly lyric, appeared in 1856, again in 1875, and 'Andromeda and Other Poems' in 1858. 'Lectures delivered in America' (1875) contained addresses given during his visit to the United States in 1874. His controversy with John Henry (afterward Cardinal) Newman, in 1864, led to the latter publishing his celebrated 'Apologia pro Vita Sua.' Mr. Kingsley became professor of modern history at Cambridge in 1859, chaplain to the Queen in 1860, canon of Westminster in 1873. ('Works,' 28 vols., 1878–81.)

Kingsley, Henry. An English novelist, brother of Charles; born at Barnack, Northamptonshire, Jan. 2, 1830; died at Cuckfield, Sussex, May 24, 1876. An unsuccessful experiment at gold-mining in Australia gave him the material for his first novel, 'The Recollections of Geoffrey Hamlyn' (3 vols., 1859), which was well received. He followed it with a long list of popular novels, among them 'Ravenshoe' (1861), generally considered his best work; 'Austin Elliot' (2 vols., 1863); 'The Hillyars and the Burtons' (3 vols., 1865); 'Leighton Court' (2 vols., 1866). A humorous strain in his writings contrasts forcibly with his brother's work. He was also a worker for reviews and newspapers, being a special correspondent in the Franco-Prussian War. The battle of Sedan, at which he was present, formed the subject of 'Valentin: A French Boy's Story of Sedan' (1872).

Kingston, William Beatty. An English journalist and author; born in London, in 1837. For some years in the Austrian consular service at London and Cardiff, he became a special correspondent of the Daily Telegraph in the principal Continental cities, and subsequently war correspondent for the same journal in the Austro-Prussian, Franco-Prussian, and Russo-Turkish wars. His publications include: 'The Battle of Berlin' (1871); 'William I., German Emperor' (1883); 'Music and Manners' (1887), a volume of personal reminiscences; 'Monarchs I Have Met' (1887).

Kingston, William Henry Giles. An English novelist; born in London, Feb. 28, 1814; died near there, August 5, 1880. He wrote almost though not quite exclusively for boys, producing 130 stories in 30 years; mostly of sea voyage and adventure, instructive as well as pleasing, and very popular. 'Peter the Whaler' (1851), 'The Cruise of the Frolic' (1860), the series beginning with 'The Three Midshipmen' (1873), 'Joviman' (1877), etc., won swarms of readers, both young and old. His articles on Portugal, where his father was a merchant at Oporto, led to the commercial treaty between Portugal and England in 1842.

Kinkel, Johann Gottfried (kink'el). A distinguished German poet and historian of art; born at Obercassel, near Bonn, Aug. 11, 1815; died at Zürich, Nov. 12, 1882. His patriotic and stormy life and political martyrdom contrasted oddly with his peaceful writings. His first volume of verse (1843; 7th ed. 1872), rich in feeling and charming in simplicity, contained the fine narrative poem 'Otto the Archer,' which had afterward enormous success printed alone (56th ed. 1881), also serving repeatedly as an opera libretto; his second (1868), more political and much inferior, contained however the exquisite narrative poem 'The Blacksmith of Antwerp,' one of his best productions. The tragedy 'Nimrod' (1857) aimed to depict the rise of despotism. The village tale 'Margret' became at once a classic. Of a great prose work he projected, 'History of Christian Plastic Art,' only the first part, on 'Ancient Christian Art,' ever appeared (1845).

Kinney, Coates. An American journalist and writer of verse; born in Yates County, N. Y., 1826. He was originally a lawyer, afterwards editor of the Cincinnati Times and the Ohio State Journal. He has written: 'Ke-u-ka,' etc.' (1855); 'Lyrics of the Ideal and the

20

Real' (1888). His best-known poem is probably 'The Rain upon the Roof.' He died in 1904.

Kinney, Elizabeth Clementine (Dodge). An American prose and verse writer; born in New York city, 1810; died at Summit, N. J., 1889. She wrote 'Felicita, a Metrical Romance' (1855); 'Poems' (1867); and 'Bianca Cappello, a Tragedy' (1873).

Kip, Leonard. An American miscellaneous prose-writer, brother of William I. Kip; born in New York city, 1826; died in San Francisco, Cal., 1893. Among his published works are: 'California Sketches' (1850); 'Œnone, a Roman Tale' (1866); 'Under the Bells' (1879); and 'Nestlenook' (1880).

Kip, William Ingraham. An American Episcopal divine, one of the notable men of his denomination; born in New York city, Oct. 3, 1811; died in San Francisco, April 7, 1893. He achieved distinction as missionary bishop of California in 1853, and was made bishop in 1857. He published: 'The Double Witness of the Church' (1844); 'The Catacombs of Rome' (1854); 'The Unnoticed Things of Scripture' (1868); and 'The Church of the Apostles' (1877).

Kipling, Rudyard. An English short-story writer, novelist, and poet; born at Bombay, India, Dec. 30, 1865. Starting with prose, his short stories are: 'Plain Tales from the Hills' (1888), introducing among others the famous creations Mulvaney and Ortheris, who appeared again with Learoyd, the third of the great trio, in 'Soldiers Three' (1889) and others of his works; 'The Phantom Rickshaw' (1889); 'Mine Own People' (1891); 'Life's Handicap' (1891); 'Many Inventions' (1893); 'The Jungle Books' (1894-95). His novels are: 'The Story of the Gadsbys' (1890), in dialogue form; 'The Light that Failed' (1891); 'The Naulahka' (1892), with Wolcott Balestier; 'Captains Courageous' (1897), a story with American characters. His verse can be seen in 'Departmental and Other Ditties' (1890); 'Barrack Room Ballads' (1892); 'The Seven Seas' (1896); 'Traffics and Discoveries' (1904).

Kirby, William. A Canadian novelist, poet, and dramatist; born in Kingston-upon-Hull, England, Oct. 13, 1817. He came to Canada in 1832. From 1841 till 1861 he edited and published the Niagara Mail. Among his published works are: 'U. E.: A Tale of Upper Canada'; 'Niagara,' a poem (1869); 'Chien d'Or,' a Canadian historical romance (1877); 'Joseph in Egypt'; dramas; and many poems.

Kirchbach, Wolfgang (kirch'bäch). A German poet and novelist; born in London, Sept. 18, 1857. Of his numerous works, especially noticeable were: 'Salvator Rosa' (1880), a novel; 'Children of the Kingdom' (1883), "a novel cycle"; 'Selected Poems' (1883); 'Waiblinger' (1886), a modern tragedy; 'The Judge of Men' (1888), a comedy; the dramas 'Gordon Pasha' and 'Eginhard and Emma'; and 'What did Jesus Teach?'

Kirchhoff, Theodor (kirch'hof). A German-American poet; born at Ütersen, Jan. 8, 1828. Residing in the United States, he writes in German and publishes in Germany. With his brother Christian, he published 'Songs of War and Love' (1864), and another volume of poems, 'Adelpha' (1869). Alone, he has written: 'Pictures of Travel and Sketches from America' (2 vols., 1875-76); 'Ballads and Recent Poems' (1883); 'Pictures of Californian Civilization' (1886); 'A Trip to Hawaii' (1890).

Kirk, Ellen Warner (Olney). An American novelist, wife of John Foster Kirk; born at Southington, Conn., 1842. She has been a frequent and welcome contributor to periodicals. Of her books, 'A Midsummer Madness' (1885), and 'A Daughter of Eve' (1889), created a marked impression. 'The Story of Margaret Kent' (1885), published under the pseudonym "Henry Hayes," passed rapidly through many editions. Her latest work is 'Marcia' (1907).

Kirk, John Foster. An American historian; born at Fredericton, N. B., 1824. He moved to the United States about 1842. He is author of 'History of Charles the Bold' (3 vols., 1863-68), and of various historical essays and reviews. He was editor of Lippincott's Magazine for many years. Died Sept. 21, 1904.

Kirkland, Caroline Matilda (Stansbury). An American prose-writer; born in New York city, 1801; died there, 1864. Her works, in part, are: 'Forest Life' (1842); 'Garden Walks with the Poets' (1854); 'Memoirs of Washington' (1857); 'The Destiny of Our Country' (1864).

Kirkland, John Thornton. A distinguished American Unitarian divine, educator, and biographer; born in New York State, 1770; died 1840. He was president of Harvard University (1810-27). He wrote: 'Life of Fisher Ames'; 'Eulogy of General Washington.'

Kirkland, Joseph. An American novelist; born at Geneva, N. Y., Jan. 7, 1830; died at Chicago, April 29, 1894. 'Zury, the Meanest Man in Spring County' (1887) gives a picture of pioneer life in Illinois. In 'The McVeys' (1888) reappear several of the characters of 'Zury.' 'The Captain of Company K' appeared in 1891; 'The Chicago Massacre of 1812' in 1893 (in collaboration with Caroline Kirkland); 'The Story of Chicago' (2 vols.) in 1892-94.

Kirwan. See **Murray, Nicholas.**

Kisfaludy, Károly (kish'fa-lö'dē). A noted Hungarian poet and novelist, brother of Sandor; born at Tét (Raab), Feb. 5, 1788; died Nov. 11, 1830. He was the father of modern Hungarian drama. His noblest tragedy, 'Irene' (1820), has scarcely a peer in Hungarian literature. Next comes the fragment 'Matthew Csák'; overwork on which, injuring his health, compelled him to leave it unfinished. His comedies excelled his tragedies; among the best of them were: 'The Rebels,' 'The Murderer,' 'Illusions,' all bright pictures of modern Hungarian life. He was successful as a lyric poet also; and as a novelist, particularly a humorous one. Soon after his death a Kisfaludy Society was formed in Hungary in support of the national Muse. ('Works,' 6 vols., 1893.)

Kisfaludy, Sándor. A celebrated Hungarian poet; born at Sümeg (Zala), Sept. 27, 1772; died Oct. 28, 1844. He was the first great poet of modern Hungary. His masterpiece was 'Himfy's Love Songs' (1801-7), in two parts, 'Love Unrequited' and 'Love Returned,'—the former being the better, and both showing the influence of Petrarch. His other important work was the epic 'Legends from the Magyar Past' (1807-38), which also contained many love songs. He was the poet of the aristocracy, as Csokonai was of the people. A memorial to him was erected at Lake Platten in 1860. ('Works,' 8 vols., 1892.)

Kiss, Josef (kish). A celebrated Hungarian poet; born at Temesvár, 1843. He is exclusively modern in subjects and treatment, but with a strain of melancholy. His 'Song of the Sewing-Machine' (1884), a glorification of work and a noble eulogy on woman, and 'A Grave' (his mother's), are noted. A fourth edition of his 'Poetical Works' appeared in 1890; 'New Poems' in 1891. Since 1890 he has been editor of The Week, a literary journal.

Kjerkegaard, Sören Aaby (kyer'ke-gōr). An eminent Danish religious writer; born at Copenhagen, May 5, 1813; died there, Nov. 11, 1835. He placed the philosophical basis of Christianity in personal faith; and decried "official" Christianity, making religion a personal matter between each soul and the Supreme Being. His principal work was 'Enten — Eller' (Either — Or: 4th ed. 1878).

Klaczko, Julian (kläch'kō). A Polish statesman, poet, and historical writer; born Nov. 6, 1828, of Hebrew parents. He was at one time a prominent member of the Austrian Landtag, and is a voluminous writer on historical and political subjects in Polish, French, and German. Chief among his publications are: 'The Polish School' (1854); 'The Unitarian Agitation in Germany' (1862); 'Studies in Contemporary Diplomacy' (1866); 'The Preliminaries of Sadowa' (1869); 'The Two Chancellors' (1876), a study of Bismarck and Gortchakoff; 'Florentine Causeries'; 'Dante and Michel Angelo'; 'Rome and the Renaissance.'

Klapp, Michael (kläpp). A German dramatist and novelist; born at Prague, 1834; died at Vienna, Feb. 25, 1888. He was a successful writer of comedies, of which one of the best known was 'Rosenkrantz and Guildenstern' (1878). Others were: 'The Blank Lottery'; 'Miss Councillor of Commerce.' 'The Bank Barons' (2 vols., 1877) deserves mention.

Klaproth, Heinrich Julius von (kläp'rōt). A celebrated German Orientalist; born in Berlin, Oct. 11, 1783; died in Paris, Aug. 20, 1835. He was sent by the Russian government on a mission to Central Asia, and acquired valuable information concerning Oriental languages and customs. In 1815 he took up his residence at Paris, at the same time holding a nominal professorship at the University of Berlin. Among his numerous works may be noticed:

'Travels in Caucasus and Georgia' (1812-14); 'Geographico-Historical Description of Eastern Caucasus' (1814); 'Asia Polyglotto' (1823-29); 'Historical View of Asia' (1824).

Klein, Julius Leopold (klīn). A German dramatist and dramatic historian; born at Miskolcz, Hungary, 1810; died at Berlin, Aug. 2, 1876. Prominent among his dramas were the historical tragedies 'Marie de Médicis' (1841; second part, 'Luines,' 1842); 'Zenobia' (1847); 'Strafford' (1862): among his comedies, 'The Duchess' (1848); 'A Protégé' (1850); 'Voltaire' (1862). Of his dramatic work, it has been said that it chows him to be a man of talent working by a mistaken method. His celebrated 'History of the Drama' (13 vols., 1865-76; index 1886) — a production of vast scope, research, and industry — aimed to give the dramatic history of all peoples, but was unfinished at death.

Kleinpaul, Rudolph (klīn'poul). A German miscellaneous writer; born at Grossgrabe, near Kamentz, March 9, 1845. He wrote several interesting volumes of travel in Egypt, Italy, and along the shores of the Mediterranean, of which 'Crucify Him! Adventures of Italian Travel' reached a second edition in 1882. The drama 'The Abduction of the Princes' appeared in 1884.

Kleist, Ewald Christian von (klīst). A German poet; born at Zeblin, Pomerania, March 7, 1715; died at Frankfort on the Oder, Aug. 24, 1759. His fame rests upon the poem 'Spring' (1749), which contains description eminently true to nature, together with an element of melancholy; this trait marks also his odes, elegies, songs, etc. His second-best poem was the little martial epic 'Cissides and Paches,' breathing patriotism from every line. A lover of nature, he was an ardent admirer of the English poet Thomson. His idyls belong to his best work.

Kleist, Heinrich von. A German poet; born at Frankfort on the Oder, Oct. 18, 1777; died at Wannsee, near Potsdam, Nov. 21, 1811. His dramas rival those of Goethe and Schiller. The best are: 'Penthesilea' (1808), a tragedy; 'Kitty of Heilbronn' (1810); 'The Prince of Homburg' (1821); 'Hermann's Battle' (1821),— the last two being his masterpieces; the comedy 'The Broken Jug' (1812). Though known chiefly as a dramatic poet, he wrote also lyrical verse that made a deep and lasting impression. His fine prose story 'Michael Kohlhaas,' together with others, all showing marked ability, appeared in 'Tales' (2 vols., 1810-11). His fame did not come till after his death. ('Works,' Stuttgart, 1885.)

Klemm, Friedrich Gustav (klem). A German librarian and historian; born at Chemnitz, Nov. 12, 1802; died at Dresden, Aug. 26, 1867. Having studied in Leipsic, he settled in 1825 in Dresden, where he became royal librarian (1852), retaining that post until 1864. Of special value are his historical works, such as: 'Attila according to History, Sagas, and Legends'

(1825); 'History of Bavaria' (1828); 'Handbook of German Archæology' (1835); 'Italica' (1839), Italian travels; 'General History of Civilization' (10 vols., 1843–52); 'Science of Civilization' (1854–55); 'Women' (6 vols., 1854–59).

Klicpera, Václav Kliment (klich'pe-rä). A Czech poet and novelist; born at Chlumec, Bohemia, 1792; died at Prague, 1859. He wrote in a style that was picturesque, but occasionally somewhat coarse. Of a large number of dramas, the tragedy 'Sobeslav'; and the comedies 'The Magic Hat,' 'Ziska's Sword,' 'The Liar,' 'The Comedy on the Bridge,' were successful. Among his novels may be named 'Tocnik' and 'Vilkovic.' He wrote also patriotic verse, etc. ('Works,' 1864.)

Klingemann, Ernst August Friedrich (kling'e-män). A German dramatist; born at Brunswick, Aug. 31, 1777; died there, Jan. 25, 1831. His model was Schiller, and so successful in their day were his dramas, that for years his name and Schiller's were coupled in popular speech. Among his works were: 'Martin Luther'; 'Cromwell'; 'German Faith'; 'Faust.' When belonging to the management of the Brunswick Court Theatre, he was the first to produce, though sorely against his will, Goethe's 'Faust' (1829). ('Works,' 2 vols., 1817–18.)

Klinger, Friedrich Maximilian von (kling'-er). A German poet and novelist; born at Frankfort on the Main, Feb. 17, 1752; died at Dorpat, Feb. 25, 1831. Among his earlier dramas, including 'The Twins' (1776), 'Otto' (1781), 'The Suffering Wife,' etc., was 'Sturm und Drang' (Storm and Stress: 1776), which gave its celebrated name to that period of German literature. He was called at the time he wrote it a «Shakespeare gone mad,» and he himself referred in later life to his early productions as «explosions of youthful brains and ill-humor.» From them his evolution was toward moderation and restraint. Of his novels, best known was the gloomy 'Faust's Life, Deeds, and Journey to Hell' (1791); unless indeed 'The Worldling and the Poet' (1798), consisting of psychological dialogues on the contrast between the actual and the ideal world, were its successful competitor. 'Reflections and Thoughts on Various Subjects of the World and Literature' (3 vols., 1802–5) may also be mentioned. Early left an orphan in wretched circumstances, after various vicissitudes he entered the service of Russia, where he rose to high position. (Latest edition of his works, 1841.)

Klonowicz, Sebastián Fabián (klo-nŏ'vich). A Neo-Latin and Polish poet; born at Sulmierzyce, about 1545; died at Lublin, Aug. 29, 1602. His chief work, 'Roxolania' (1584), was a description in verse of the country and people of Red Russia (eastern Galicia). The didactic poem 'The Victory of the Gods' (1595), also in Latin, and directed against the privileges of birth and other wrongs, contained fine passages, but was too long. 'Flis' (The Waterman: 1595), a Polish poem, described

transportation down the Vistula from Warsaw to Dantzic. 'Judas's Purse' (1600) was a sharp, satirical poem, directed against theft, hypocrisy, etc.

Klopp, Onno (klōp). A German historian; born in Leer, 1822. For a number of years he was a teacher in the gymnasium at Osnabrück, and later became a close friend of George V. of Hanover. A strong anti-Prussian tendency is the only blemish in a series of remarkable historical productions, such as a 'History of East Friesland' (1854–58); 'King Frederick of Prussia and the German Nation' (2d ed. 1867); 'Tilly in the Thirty Years' War' (1861); 'The Fall of the House of Stuart' (14 vols., 1875–87); 'The Thirty Years' War to the Death of Gustavus Adolphus' (1891). D. 1903.

Klopstock, Friedrich Gottlieb (klop'stok). A celebrated German poet; born at Quedlinburg, 1724; died at Hamburg, 1803. In freeing German poetry from the exclusive reign of the Alexandrine verse, he was the founder of a new era in German literature. His great epic 'Messiah' (1748–73), at first partly written in prose and changed afterward to hexameters, made him famous; its effect on German thought was great, and its influence can be traced down succeeding German literature. His most finished work, however, was doubtless his 'Odes,' which represent intellectual originality and truth. Even Schiller and Goethe were artistically indebted to him. His dramas were of less worth. ('Works,' 1879.)

Knapp, Albert (knäp). A German religious poet; born July 25, 1798; died June 18, 1864. Many of his hymns can be found in the manual 'Christoterpe' (1833–53), a collection which had previously appeared in small volumes, one issued each year. His 'Evangelical Treasury of Songs for Church and Home' (1837; 3d ed. 1865) was taken from the liturgies and hymns of all Christian countries. He gave great impetus to the poetry of devotion in Germany.

Knapp, Arthur May. An American Unitarian divine and writer of travels; born in Massachusetts, 1841. His home is at Fall River, Mass. He has written 'Feudal and Modern Japan.'

Knapp, Samuel Lorenzo. An American miscellaneous writer; born in Newburyport, Mass., 1783; died in Hopkinton, Mass., 1838. He attained to eminence in law; was editor of the Boston Gazette and the Boston Monthly Magazine. His works, chiefly biographical, include 'Travels in North America by Ali Béy' (1818); 'Memoirs of General Lafayette' (1824); 'Lectures on American Literature' (1829); 'Lives' of Daniel Webster, Aaron Burr, and Andrew Jackson. He edited 'The Library of American History' (1837).

Kneeland, Samuel. An American miscellaneous writer and naturalist; born in Boston, Mass., 1821; died 1888. He was a member of numerous scientific societies, and has contributed many articles to medical literature. In addition to editing 'The Annual of Scientific Discovery' (1886–89), a translation of 'Andry's Diseases of the Heart' (1847), and Smith's 'History of the Human Species,' he wrote 'Science and Mechanism' (1854); 'The Wonders of the Yosemite Valley and of California' (1871); and 'An American in Iceland' (1876).

Kniashnin, Jakov Borissovitch (knē-äzh'-nen). A Russian poet; born at Pskov, 1742; died at St. Petersburg, 1791. In his tragedies, 'Dido,' 'Roslav,' etc., he tried to imitate Corneille. 'Vladimir' (1793), another tragedy, was destroyed by order of Catherine II. as imperiling public safety. Of his comedies, two, 'The Queer Fellows' and 'The Boaster,' are excellent pieces of work. He wrote also odes, satires, songs, fables, and other minor poems. ('Works,' 2 vols., 1842.)

Kniaznin, Franciszek Dionizy (knē-äzh'-nen). A Polish poet; born at Witebsk, 1750; died at Konskawola, 1807. He may be styled the herald of romanticism in Poland. His works consisted of lyrics, dramas, and numerous occasional pieces. Among them were the drama 'Spartan Mother,' and the tragedy 'Themistocles,' also the opera 'The Gipsies.' He translated into Polish some of La Fontaine's fables. ('Works,' 7 vols., 1828.)

Knigge, Adolf Franz Heinrich von, Baron (knig'ė). A German miscellaneous writer; born at Bredenbeck, near Hanover, Oct. 16, 1752; died at Bremen, May 6, 1796. The most important of his works, 'On Converse with Men' (2 vols., 1788), gave maxims and rules for the conduct of life, of which it showed profound knowledge. 'The Journey to Brunswick' (1839, illustrated) was a humorous novel, and has frequently been reprinted. 'The Romance of My Life' (4 vols., 1781; new ed. 1805) has been a great favorite. He was one of the "Illuminati"; and published a defense of Illuminism in his adept's-name "Philo." ('Works,' 12 vols., 1804–06.)

Knight, Charles. An English miscellaneous writer and publisher; born at Windsor, 1791; died at Addlestone, Surrey, 1873. His life was one of wide activity and increasingly great usefulness to his country, from the time when he became publisher of The Etonian for Praed, Macaulay, Nelson Coleridge, etc., while they were students at Eton. He was editor of Knight's Quarterly Magazine; superintendent of publications to the famous Society for the Diffusion of Useful Knowledge; publisher of the 'Library of Entertaining Knowledge,' in which he wrote several volumes; publisher of the Penny Magazine (1832) and of the 'Penny Cyclopædia' (1833). His great work was the 'Popular History of England' (8 vols., 1854–61), a monument of research, breadth of view, and devotion to the people. His autobiography, 'Passages from a Working Life' (3 vols., 1864–65), is one of the most interesting of books. His 'Pictorial Shakespeare' (8 vols., 1839–41), which he himself probably considered the

work of his life, served a good end; and 'The Shadows of the Old Booksellers' (1865) is a gem of its kind. He wrote also a historical novel entitled 'Begg'd at Court' (1868).

Knight, Francis Arnold. An English writer on country life; born at Gloucester, 1852. A regular contributor, mainly on natural-history subjects, to the Daily News, Speaker, Spectator, and other periodicals, he has published four volumes of essays, entitled 'By Leafy Ways'; 'Idylls of the Field'; 'Rambles of a Dominie'; 'By Moorland and Sea.'

Knight, William Angus. A Scotch philosophical writer and littérateur; born at Mordington, Berwickshire, Feb. 22, 1836. He has been professor of philosophy at the University of St. Andrews since 1876, and made valuable additions to philosophical and general literature. Among numerous publications may be noticed: 'Poems from the Dawn of English Literature to the Year 1699' (1863); 'Colloquia Peripatetica' (1870); 'Studies in Philosophy and Literature' (1879); 'Memorials of Colenton' (1887); 'Wordsworth's Prose' (1893); 'Aspects of Theism' (1894). He has also been the editor of 'Philosophical Classics for English Readers' (15 vols., 1880–90), and 'University Extension Manuals' (18 vols., 1891–94).

Knorring, Sofia Margarete von (knor'ing). A Swedish novelist; born Sept. 29, 1797; died Feb. 13, 1848. Unlike Fredrika Bremer, who described middle-class life, she was the novelist of Swedish society; seeing its follies and frivolities indeed, but lacking that power of satire which makes, for instance, Thackeray's handling of similar material so effective. Vivid and graceful, she wanted simplicity and outspokenness. Her best works were: 'Kusinerna'; 'Axel'; 'Class Parallels'; 'A Peasant and his Surroundings,' the only novel in which she treats of middle or lower class life.

Knortz, Karl (knorts). A German-American miscellaneous writer; born at Garbenheim, near Wetzlar, Aug. 28, 1841. Has resided since 1863 in the United States, where he bends his efforts to upholding German interests. Notable among his works are: 'Tales and Legends of the North-American Indians' (1871); 'American Sketches' (1876); 'Longfellow' (1879); 'From the Wigwam' (1880); 'Indian Legends'; 'Pictures of American Life' (1884). With Dickman (1880) he collaborated on 'Modern American Lyrics'; 'Vestiges of Teutonic Belief and Custom in America' (1903).

Knowles, Herbert. An English poet; born at Gomersal, near Leeds, 1798; died there, Feb. 17, 1817. His reputation rests wholly on the poem 'The Three Tabernacles,' known otherwise as 'Stanzas in Richmond Churchyard,' written Oct. 7, 1816, when he was only eighteen years old. It is a remarkable if not unique production, since, while being so precocious, it is mature in thought and feeling, and apart from one or two blemishes, perfect in form. Its solemnity and pathos have seldom been equaled.

Knowles, James Sheridan. An Irish actor, lecturer, and dramatist; born at Cork, May 12, 1784; died at Torquay, England, Nov. 30, 1862. He made his first appearance as an actor in 1806, but never attained much eminence in that profession. Subsequently he taught elocution for several years at Belfast and Glasgow, and wrote for the stage. He abandoned dramatic work in 1845 from religious scruples, devoted himself to literature, and later became well known as a Baptist preacher. Of his works only the tragedy of ‘Virginius,’ produced 1820, and the comedies ‘The Hunchback’ (1832) and ‘The Love Chase’ (1837), have survived. They are good “acting plays,” and always popular, but possess little literary value. Among his other dramas may be mentioned: ‘Caius Gracchus’ (1815); ‘William Tell’ (1825); ‘Alfred the Great’ (1831); ‘The Wife: A Tale of Mantua’ (1833); ‘The Rose of Aragon’ (1842).

Knox, Mrs. Adeline (Trafton). An American novelist, daughter of Mark Trafton; born at Saccarappa, Me., about 1845. Her home is at St. Louis, Mo. She has written: ‘Katharine Earle’ (1874); ‘His Inheritance’ (1878); ‘An American Girl Abroad’; ‘Dorothy’s Experience.’

Knox, John. The great Scottish religious reformer; born at Giffordsgate, near Haddington, 1505; died at Edinburgh, Nov. 24, 1572. A pioneer of Puritanism; prisoner of war, for nineteen months confined in the French galleys; friend of Calvin and Beza; a preacher of sermons that moved their hearers to demolish convents; with a price on his head, yet never faltering; arrested for treason, an armed “congregation” at his heels; burned in effigy, for years a dictator,—he spent his life forwarding the Reformation in Scotland. His great work, distinguished in Scottish prose, was his ‘History of the Reformation of Religion within the Realm of Scotland’ (1584; new ed. 1831). His famous ‘Letter to the Queen Dowager’ appeared in 1556; the ‘First Trumpet Blast against the Monstrous Regiment of Women’ — inveighing against women taking part in the government, and which offended Queen Elizabeth — in 1558. (‘Works,’ 6 vols., 1864.)

Knox, Thomas Wallace. An American prose-writer and traveler; born in Pembroke, N. H., June 25, 1835; died in New York city, Jan. 6, 1896. He made a journey around the world as a newspaper correspondent in 1886. His published works include: ‘Underground Life’ (1873); ‘How to Travel’ (1880); ‘Lives of Blaine and Logan’ (1884); ‘Decisive Battles since Waterloo’ (1887).

Knox, William. A Scotch poet; born at Roxburgh, in 1789; died in 1825. Except for the well-known poem beginning “Oh, why should the spirit of mortal be proud?” he is almost forgotten, although Sir Walter Scott and his contemporaries had considerable regard for his talents. ‘Mariamne’ and ‘The Lonely Hearth’ also enjoyed a good deal of popularity.

Kobbé, Gustav (kob′ĕ). An American musical and miscellaneous writer; born in New York, 1857. His home is in New York. He has written: ‘Jersey Coast and Pines’; ‘Wagner’s Ring of the Nibelung’; ‘New York City and its Environs’; ‘Wagner’s Dramas Analysed.’ ‘Opera Singers’; ‘Famous American Songs’; ‘Signora.’

Kobbe, Theodor Christoph August von. A German poet and novelist. Of his works we name: ‘TheStudent’s Mortal Pilgrimage’ (1820); ‘The Swedes in the Convent at Ütersen’ (1830) a Romance; ‘Humorous Sketches and Pictures’ (1831); ‘Recent Tales’ (2 vols., 1833); ‘Humorous Reminiscences of my College Days’ (2 vols., 1840); ‘Comicalities from Philistine Life’ (2 vols. 1841). He lived from 1798–1845.

Kobell, Franz von (kō′bel). A German poet; born at Munich, July 19, 1803; died there, Nov. 11, 1882. A mineralogist, he made important contributions to his science. His verse, which belongs to the best German dialect poetry, was marked by humor, freshness, and heartiness. The Upper Bavarian and Palatine dialect poems, ‘Schnadahüpfeln und Sprücheln’ (2d ed. 1852); ‘Palatine Tales’ (1863); ‘Schnadahüpfeln und Geschichteln’ (1872); ‘Hansl o’ Finsterwald,’ etc. (2d ed. 1876), were among his best. A devoted hunter, he was able to depict attractively the mountain life of the Bavarian Alps; ‘Wildanger: Sketches from the Chase and its History’ (1859) pleased sportsmen especially.

Kochanovski, Jan (koch-ä-nof′skē). A Polish poet; born at Sycyna, 1530; died at Lublin, Aug. 22, 1584. He was the most important Polish poet of the 16th century; and has been called the Polish Pindar. The influence he exerted on Polish literature by his endeavor to introduce into it classic models can scarcely be overestimated. Writing at first in both Latin and Polish, he gradually abandoned the former. He wrote epics, panegyrics, political satires, ethical discussions, and a drama, ‘The Dismissal of the Greek Ambassadors’ (1578), which took high rank. His best poem was ‘Lamentations,’ written at the death of his daughter,—whom he called the Slavonic Sappho, and to whom he hoped his genius would be transmitted,—and breathing bereavement and prayer. (‘Works,’ last and best edition, 4 vols., 1884.)

Kochovski, Hieronymus Vespasian (kochof′skē). A Polish poet; born at Gaje, Sandomir, 1633; died 1699. His songs written for the enlivenment of camp life, if occasionally somewhat wild, are always fresh and gay. A collection of his satires, odes, and epigrams appeared in 1674. Among his religious poems was an epic, ‘The Suffering Christ’ (1681), consisting of 5,000 verses. ‘Polish Psalmody’ appeared in 1695. He is the best representative of the Polish poetry of the 17th century. He wrote also several historical works.

Kock, Charles Paul de (kōk). A French novelist and playwright; born at Passy, May 21,

1794; died at Paris, Aug. 29, 1871. A remarkably prolific writer, his long series of novels, nearly all of which he worked over for the theatre, became the fashion with a certain "emancipated" circle of readers on both sides of the ocean. They showed observation and knowledge of their subject, the Parisian lower-class life of his time, and were emphatically realistic. Among the most popular were: 'Georgette' (1820); 'Gustave' (1821); 'Monsieur Dupont' (1824); 'Wife, Husband, and Lover' (1829); 'The Man with Three Pairs of Trousers' (1840); 'A Woman with Three Faces' (1859); 'The Millionaire'(1887). He wrote also popular songs.

Kock, Paul Henri de. A French novelist and playwright, son of Paul; born at Paris, April 21, 1819; died at Limeil, April 18, 1892. He followed closely in his father's footsteps, producing numerous novels and plays, which, however, never enjoyed the same popularity. Titles of some of his novels are: 'The King of the Students and the Queen of the Grisettes' (1844); 'Kisses Accursed' (1860); 'Absinthe Drinkers' (1863); 'The New Manon' (1864); 'Mademoiselle Croquemitaine' (1871).

Koehler, Sylvester Rosa. An American prose-writer and art critic; born in Leipsic, Germany, Feb. 11, 1837; died at Littleton, N. H., Sept. 15, 1900. He came to this country in 1849. He was the editor of the American Art Review and author of 'Art Education and Art Patronage in the United States' (1882). He became afterwards Curator of Prints and Engravings at the Museum of Fine Arts, Boston. He wrote a history of color painting.

Kohl, Johann Georg (kōl). A German traveler and historian; born at Bremen, April 28, 1808; died there, Oct. 28, 1878. Nearly his entire life was devoted to travel and historical investigation in Europe and North America, where he spent four years and published as the fruits of researches: 'Travels in Canada' (1855); 'Travels in the Northwestern Parts of the United States' (1857); 'History of the Discovery of America' (1861); and several essays on American cartography. Other works are: 'Travels in the Interior of Russia and Poland' (1841); 'The British Isles and Their Inhabitants' (1844); 'The Rhine' (1851); etc.

Kohn, Salomon (kōn). A German novelist; born at Prague, March 8, 1825. His first novel, 'Gabriel' (1852; 2d ed. 1875), published anonymously, met with considerable success. His other more important works have been: 'Mirror of the Present' (3 vols., 1875); 'Prague Ghetto Pictures' (1886), containing three short stories; 'The Old Grenadier,' 'The Faithful Old,' 'The Life Saver and Other Tales'; 'Judith Lörach.'

Kohut, Alexander (kō'hŏt). A distinguished Jewish-American theologian, scholar, and preacher; born at Félegyházza, Hungary, May 19, 1842; died in New York, May 25, 1894. He was one of the greatest Orientalists and Semitic scholars of his age. He was member of the Hungarian Parliament; founded the Jewish theological seminary in New York (1886),

in which he was professor (1886–94). His chief work was 'Complete Dictionary of the Talmud' (9 vols., 1878–92). In later years he devoted himself to Arabic-Hebrew literature as recently discovered in the MS. fragments from Yemen. A noble monument has just been raised to him in 'Semitic Studies in Memory of Rev. Dr. A. Kohut,' Berlin, 1897; it is composed of contributions by Max Müller, Canon Cheyne, C. A. Briggs, M. Steinschneider, M. Heimthal, etc.

Kolár, Josef Jiri (kō'lär). A Czech novelist and dramatist; born at Prague, Feb. 9, 1812. Several of his dramas have been successful: for instance, 'Monika' (1847); 'Ziska's Death' (1850); 'Smirick' (1881); 'Primator' (1883). He has also made excellent translations from the dramatic works of Shakespeare, Goethe, Schiller, etc., and written novels. He was an actor, very successful in tragic rôles, especially Shakespearean.

Kölcsey, Ferencz (kėl'chä-i). A Hungarian poet; born in the county of Middle Szolnok, Aug. 8, 1790; died at Pesth, Aug. 24, 1838. In character, life, and writings, he was one of the noblest of Hungarians. He wrote ballads, songs, satires, short novels, critical treatises, and orations, but is best known in literature by his verse. Its first characteristic was, not so much strength of thought or warmth of feeling as a certain melancholy longing for something better. Of his short poems, two of the best are his famous national hymn and the ballad 'Beautiful Lena.'

Kollár, Jan (kōl'lär). A noted Czech poet; born at Mossocz, Thurocz (Hungary), July 29, 1793; died at Vienna, Jan. 29, 1852. A most ardent if not the first Panslavist, he used his pen to inculcate and spread the doctrine. His 'Daughter of Glory' (1821), his most popular work, a collection of 645 original sonnets inspired by love, joy, sorrow, patriotism, etc., produced on the nation an enormous effect and made him famous; it has been pronounced one of the most remarkable productions of the nineteenth century. Dedicated to the same end were a collection of 'Popular Songs' (2 vols., 1827), and 'On the Literary Reciprocity of the Slavic Races and Dialects' (2d ed. 1844). He was the first to give the Panslavic idea literary expression. ('Works,' incomplete, 4 vols., 1862–63.)

Koltsov, or **Kolzov, Alekseï Vasilievitch** (kōlt'-sof). A Russian lyric poet; born at Voronesch, Oct. 14, 1809; died there, Oct. 31, 1842. A dealer in cattle and wood, devouring books in a friendly bookseller's store, he became "the Burns of Russia." His poems, few in number (124), the best of them treating of peasant life, short and even almost uncouth, introduced a new form of art. Their diction was inimitably original and natural, their feeling deep and true; they won their author consideration in the highest Russian literary circles. Good specimens of them are: 'The Harvest'; 'The Young Reaper'; 'The Forest.' ('Poetical Works,' 7th ed. 1880.)

Kondratóvicz, Vladislav (kon-drä-tŏ'vich). ["Ladislas Syrokomla."] A popular Polish poet; born at Smalkov, Sept. 17, 1823; died at Vilna, Oct. 15, 1862. His verse (some of it founded on Polish proverbs), dealing with patriotism, the love, the joy, the sorrow of the every-day characters, went to the heart of the nation. He was full of compassion for the poor and the weak, hard toward worldly success, pitiless to arrogance and selfishness, as can be seen in 'Chit-Chat and Fugitive Rhymes' (1853); 'John the Gravedigger'; etc. His 'Philip of Konopi,' a sort of Polish 'Don Quixote,' was an original creation. Though he himself considered 'Margier' (1855), a dignified epic founded on early Lithuanian history, his best work, beside or even above it must be placed the epic 'John Demborog' (1854), based on a family legend. He wrote also in prose, including a 'History of Polish Literature' and several dramas; and made some translations. He called his pen his "plow." ('Poetical Works,' 10 vols., 1872.)

König, Ewald August (kė'niG). A German novelist; born at Barmen, Aug. 22, 1833; died at Cologne, March 9, 1888. He wrote a long list of works, most of them dealing with crime. Some of the best are: 'Through Conflict to Peace' (1869); 'Guilty?' (4 vols., 1878); 'A Lost Life' (2 vols., 1882); 'The Golden Cross' (2 vols., 1883); 'A Modern Vampire' (3 vols., 1883); 'The Daughter of the Councillor of Commerce' (1886); 'Shadows of Life' (2 vols., 1885); 'On Dishonor's Path' (1885).

König, Heinrich Joseph. A German novelist; born at Fulda, March 19, 1790; died at Wiesbaden, Sept. 23, 1869. He wrote a series of excellent historical novels, of which the best were: 'The Noble Bride' (2 vols., 1833) and especially the artistic and admirable 'Club Members of Mayence' (3 vols., 1847). The latter is his best work, and describes the political and religious influence of the French Revolution in Germany toward the end of the eighteenth century. 'William Shakespeare' (1850) was a successful attempt to depict in a novel the great English dramatist and his time.

Konrad von Würzburg (kon'räd fon vürts'-börG). One of the most celebrated German poets of the Middle Ages; born at Würzburg; died at Basel in 1287. He was of burgher descent, and lived at first at Strasburg and later at Basle. Fertile in imagination, learned, and a perfect master of German versification, he was equally at home in lyric, epic, and didactic poetry. His largest work, 'The Trojan War,' consisting of 40,000 verses, remained unfinished. His fame, however, is due to several shorter legendary poems, such as: 'Otto with the Beard'; 'The Reward of the World'; 'The Golden Smithy,' a glorification of the Virgin Mary; 'The Legends of Sylvester'; 'Alexius'; 'Engehart and Engeltrut'; 'The Golden Smithy.'

Koopman, Harry Lyman. An American writer of verse; born in Maine, 1860. He is librarian of Brown University. He has written: 'The Great Admiral'); 'Orestes,' etc.; 'Woman's Will,' etc.; and others.

Kopisch, August (kop'ish). A German poet; born at Breslau, May 26, 1799; died at Berlin, Feb. 3, 1853. Also an artist, he was an artist in his verse, which was precise in form and largely descriptive; it can be best seen in 'Poems' (1836) and 'All Sorts' (1848). His ballads particularly were exquisitely humorous and brisk. Two extremely popular productions of his were the 'Story of Noah' and the droll 'Heinzelmännchen' (The Brownies).

Kopp, Josef Eutychius (kop). A Swiss historian and poet; born at Beromünster, Luzern, April 25, 1793; died at Luzern, Oct. 25, 1866. The first to apply the scientific method of studying history in Switzerland, to him we owe our modern views of old Swiss legends, especially of that of William Tell. His chief work was 'History of the Allied Leagues' (1882). He has been called the "Niebuhr of Switzerland." He wrote also four volumes of dramatic poems (1855-56).

Koppel, Franz (kop'el). A German miscellaneous writer; born at Eltville, Nassau, Dec. 7, 1840. Among his works are the heroi-comic poem, 'Cervantes on his Travels' (1865); 'Two Brothers in Christ' (1867), a romance; several comedies, including 'Which Meyer?' 'Useless to Worry,' 'On Thorns'; 'Spartacus,' a tragedy; the dramas 'Hans in Luck' (1885) and 'Albert the Brave' (1889). He wrote also opera librettos and celebration poems.

Körner, Karl Theodor (kėr'ner). A noted German lyric poet; born at Dresden, Sept. 23, 1791; died near Gadebusch, in the vicinity of Schwerin, Mecklenburg, Aug. 26, 1813. When Prussia armed against Napoleon I. in 1813, he took the field; where, shortly after a return to his corps from an absence caused by a wound, he fell in battle. His spirited war-songs, which have been the inspiration of Germany since, many of them written in the field, can be found in 'Lyre and Sword' (1814). Among the best of them are the 'Battle Prayer' and 'The Sword Song.' His earlier verse — dramas, opera texts, etc.—although well received at the time, is of minor importance. A Körner museum was founded at Dresden in 1873. ('Works,' 1838).

Korolenko, Vladimir Galaktionovitch (kō"-rō-len'kŏ). A Russian novelist; born at Zhitomir, Volhynia, July 27, 1853. Exiled in 1879, while still a student, to Siberia, he was pardoned in 1885. His pictures of contemporary Russian life are among the best we have. 'Makar's Dream' (1885), his first work, was one of the most successful (see Cosmopolitan Magazine, Vol. vi., p. 147); 'The Vagrant,' etc., a volume of sketches translated into English, appeared in New York in 1888; 'The Blind Musician' and 'In Two Moods' (1890-91), also exist in English; 'In Bad Society' and 'The Forest Murmurs' deserve their popularity.

Körting, Gustav (kĕr'ting). A German philologist; born at Dresden, June 25, 1845. Professor at Münster (1876) and Kiel (1893), he has written many and valuable works in the line of his specialty; and, of particular interest to readers of English, an excellent 'History of English Literature' (2d ed. 1893).

Kortum, Karl Arnold (kor'töm). A German comic poet; born at Mülheim, July 5, 1745; died there, Aug. 15, 1824. His immortal masterpiece, 'The Jobsiad; or the Life, Opinions, and Deeds of Hieronymus Jobs, the Candidate' (1784; 14th ed. 1888), a heroi-comic poem, has been popular in Germany for over a century. Its doggerel verse, somewhat in the style of our 'Mother Goose,' its riotous thought and rhyme, and wild drollery, almost place it in a genus by itself. Describing the college life, as well as the previous and subsequent career of its subject, as it does, it is a great favorite with university students. It was translated into English by Rev. Charles T. Brooks (1863).

Kosegarten, Ludwig Theobul (kō'sĕ-gär-ten). A German poet; born at Grevesmühlen, Feb. 1, 1758; died at Greifswald, Oct. 26, 1818. His novels and dramas were commonplace, but his poetry was of a higher order. Among his most successful volumes of verse were: 'Romantic Poems' (6 vols., 1800); 'Rhapsodies' (3 vols., (1804); 'The Island Journey' (1804); 'Legends' (2 vols., 1816). His best work was his lyrics; though they were more poetic in feeling than in its expression. (Complete lyrical works, 12 vols., 5th ed. 1824-27.)

Kossack, Karl Ludwig Ernst (kos'säk). A German feuilletonist; born at Marienwerder, Aug. 4, 1814; died at Berlin, Jan. 3, 1880. He introduced into Germany, through the medium of the Berlin Monday Post founded by himself in 1854, the French feuilleton. These piquant and very popular productions, by which he was best known, were afterward issued in book form. Among the volumes are: 'Berlin and the Berliners' (1851); 'From a Journalist's Waste-paper Basket' (2d ed. 1859); 'Berlin Silhouettes' (1859); 'Comicalities' (1852); 'Paris Stereoscopic Views' (1855); 'Watering-Place Pictures' (1858); 'Comicalities of Travel' (2 vols., 1862); etc. A collection of his novels, 'Genre Pictures,' appeared in 1839.

Köster, Hans (kĕs'ter). A German dramatist; born near Wismar, Aug. 16, 1818. His earlier works having been coldly received, he abandoned writing for several years, but eventually embraced it again. Best of his dramas have been: 'Alcibiades' (1839), his first play, showing in places the influence of Shakespeare, though it has been said the hero talks too much and acts too little; 'Marie Stuart' (1842), in which Mary is depicted not in adversity but on the throne, and considerable skill is shown in individualizing the characters; 'Paolo and Francesca' (1842); 'Henry IV.: A Trilogy' (1844), containing many strong scenes and several well-developed characters; 'Luther' (1847),

a fine tragedy; 'Ulrich von Hutten' (1846), a tragedy; 'Love in May' (1866), a comedy; 'Emperor and Empire' (1872); etc.

Koster, Samuel. See **Coster**.

Köstlin, Christian Reinhold (kĕst'lēn). ["C. Reinhold."] A German novelist and poet; born at Tübingen, Jan. 29, 1813; died Sept. 14, 1856. Besides important legal works (he being by profession a lawyer), he was a prolific writer of lyric and dramatic poetry, novels, etc. One of his best novels was 'Matilda's Grotto' (1838). His drama 'The Doges' Sons' was performed at Stuttgart in 1838. A 3-vol. collection of his novels appeared in 1847-48, under the title 'Collected Tales and Novels.'

Kostomarov, Nikolai Ivanovich (kos-tō'mä-rōv). A Russian historian, novelist, and poet; born at Ostrogosz, in 1817; died April 19, 1885. His efforts while instructor at the University of Kharkov to promote the development of Little Russian as a separate tongue led to his arrest and temporary banishment. In 1859 he was restored to favor, and appointed to a professorship in the University of St. Petersburg, but resigned in 1861. A brilliant poetical style characterizes his numerous literary and historical works, the best-known being: 'The Cossack War with Poland' (1856); 'The Commerce of Moscow in the Sixteenth and Seventeenth Centuries' (1858); 'Ancient Memorials of Russian Literature' (1861-62); 'History of the Polish Republic' (1870); 'Russian History in Biographies' (1873-76); 'Mazeppa' (1882), a tragedy. Under the pseudonym "Jeremija Halka" he wrote several historical novels, besides dramas and ballads.

Kotliarevsky, Ivan Petrovitch (kot-lē-ä-ref'-skē). A Russian poet; born at Poltava, Sept. 9, 1769; died there, Nov. 10, 1838. He was the founder of modern Little Russian literature, his works being written in that language. They were and are very popular in Russia; his operettas 'Natalka Poltavka' (1819) and 'The Soldier Wizard' still holding the stage there. In his chief work, a satire on the state of Russian society, in the form of a burlesque on Virgil's 'Æneid' (3 vols., 1798), was made the first literary use of genuine Little Russian.

Kotzebue, August Friedrich Ferdinand von (kot'ze-bö). A celebrated German dramatist; born at Weimar, May 3, 1761; died at Mannheim, March 23, 1819. Weak in character-drawing, he had a strong sense for situations, and his works have been a mine for dramatists since. Of about 200 tragedies, comedies, dramas, and farces, many of them very popular at the time of their production, the best known now are: 'Misanthropy and Repentance' (1789), reproduced in Paris as lately as 1862, and famous in the United States and England in Sheridan's adaptation entitled 'The Stranger'; and 'The Spaniards in Peru' (1796), adapted by Sheridan as 'Pizarro.' 'The Indians in England' (1790) won great applause. 'German Provincials' was one of his best comedies.

These excelled his tragedies, but were not delicate in expedients for raising a laugh at any cost. His most celebrated novel was 'Sorrows of the Ortenberg Family' (1785). The famous 'Doctor Bahrdt with the Iron Brow' (1790), published under another's name, contained an attack on Goethe, Schiller, etc., who declined to admit him to their society. He was very fond of publishing his autobiography. During much of his life he was in Russian service; and was once banished to Siberia by the Emperor Paul, who however recalled him a year later through being moved by something in one of his plays, gave him a rich estate, and made him aulic councilor and director of the court theatre at St. Petersburg. He was assassinated in Germany as a Russian spy, by a student. ('Complete Dramatic Works,' 40 vols., 1840–41.)

Kotzebue, Wilhelm von. A German miscellaneous writer, brother of August; born at Neval, March 19, 1813; died there, Nov. 5, 1887. Of his works, may be named: 'A Hard-Hearted Friend,' which scored a success, and 'Two Sinners,' — both dramas under the pseudonym "W. Augustsohn"; 'Moldavian Pictures and Sketches' (1860), 'Small Stories from the Great World' (1862), 'Lascar Viorescu' (1863), 'Artificial and Natural Life' (1869), all anonymous; 'August von Kotzebue' (1884), the romance 'Baron Fritz Reckensteg' (2 vols., 1885), 'Roumanian Folk Songs' (1859), all under his own name.

Kouns, Nathan Chapman (könz). An American novelist; born in Missouri, 1833; died 1890. A lawyer by profession, he was State librarian of Missouri (1886–90). He wrote two historical romances: 'Arius the Libyan,' and 'Dorcas, the Daughter of Faustina.'

Kovalevsky, Sonya (kō-vä-lev'skē). An eminent Russian mathematician, said to be the greatest woman mathematician of any age; born in Moscow, 1850; died at Stockholm, 1891, where she was professor of mathematics at the University. See her 'Recollections of Childhood,' with a biography by the Duchess of Cajanello (Anne Charlotte Leffler-Edgren). Her works include theses on 'Rotation'; 'The Laplace Hypothesis'; 'Light'; etc. She also wrote some popular novels under the pseudonym "Tanya Rerevski"; among them 'The Private Tutor' 'The Rajevski Sisters,' etc.

Krantz, Albert (kränts). A German historian; born in Hamburg, about 1450; died there, Dec. 7, 1517. He became rector of the University of Rostock in 1482, represented the Hanseatic towns in several important diplomatic missions, and was chosen arbitrator by the King of Denmark and the Duke of Holstein, in their dispute over the province of Ditmarsch. His historical works are distinguished by great erudition, and a critical spirit rarely found in his day. He published: 'Vandalia, or the History of the Vandals' (1519); 'Saxonia' (1520); 'Chronicles of the Kingdoms of Sweden, Denmark, and Norway' (1545);

'Metropolis, or History of the Church in Saxony' (1548).

Krapotkin, Peter Alexievich, Prince. A Russian scientist, revolutionist, editor, lecturer, and author; born at Moscow, Dec. 9, 1842. He was in the Russian army for a time, and made extensive journeys in Siberia and Mantchuria. Charged with anarchist affiliations, he was imprisoned two years in Russia, escaped, founded the anarchist paper La Révolte in Geneva (1879), and after being expelled from Switzerland in 1881, commenced a crusade against the Russian government in the English and French press. He was imprisoned in France from 1883 to 1886, under a law directed against the International Workingmen's Association, of which he was a member. He has lectured in various parts of the world; is the author of 'To Young People' (1881); 'Words of a Revolutionist' (1885); 'In Russian and French Prisons' (1887); 'In Search of Bread' (1892); and pamphlets on nihilistic subjects ; 'Prosperity for All' (1896); 'Memoirs of a Revolutionist' (1899); 'Mutual Aid' (1902).

Krasicki, Ignacy (krä-sitz'kē). A Polish ecclesiastic and author; born at Dubiecko, Galicia, in 1734; died at Berlin, Germany, March 14, 1801. He became bishop of Ermeland in 1767, archbishop of Gnesen in 1795, and for many years was one of the most brilliant figures at the court of Frederick II. The characteristics of his productions are caustic wit and a facile and agreeable style, which procured for him the title of "the Polish Voltaire." 'Monachomachia, or the Battle of Monks' is considered his best work, but his 'Satires' (1778) and 'Fables' (1780) also take a high rank.

Krasinski, Sigismund, Count (krä-sin'skē). A noted Polish poet; born in Paris, Feb. 19, 1812; died there, Feb. 23, 1859. On account of his health he lived in various European capitals outside Poland. He became one of Poland's three greatest poets, exerting a wide influence on her literature. The drama 'Iridion,' depicting the contrast between Christianity and paganism in Rome under the Cæsars, appeared in 1836, and is generally thought his finest work. Next best are the symbolic drama 'Nieboska Comedya' (The Undivine Comedy: 1837–48), 'Przedswit' (The Dawn: 1843); and 'Psalmy Przyszlósci' (Psalms of the Future: 1845–48), collections of lyric poems full of religion and patriotism. His writings were all published anonymously or under fictitious names. ('Works,' 4 vols., 1880–88.)

Kraszevsky, Jósef Ignacy (krä shev'skē). A noted Polish novelist; born at Warsaw, July 28, 1812; died at Geneva, March 19, 1887. He was the author of over 500 works, consisting, besides valuable historical writings, of romances, novels, critiques, travels, political treatises, epic poems, etc. Of poetry, among his chief works was the epic 'Anafielas' (1840–43), founded on Lithuanian history. 'The Devil and the Woman' (1841) was an imaginative drama. But his best work was in his romances and novels, over 240 in number. Among them were: 'The Poet and the World' (1839); 'Ulana' (1841), containing pictures of Polish society; 'The Hut beyond the Village' (1855), which became very popular in his country; 'About to Die' (1871). His celebrated series of novels depicting Polish history from the earliest times made him the Walter Scott of Poland. It has been said of him that he taught his countrymen to "know better both their past and themselves."

Krause, Karl Christian Friedrich (krous'e). A German philosopher; born at Eisenberg, Saxe-Altenburg, May 6, 1781; died at Munich, Sept. 27, 1832. For two years he was tutor at the University of Jena, and then traveled about Germany, France, and Italy. Besides treatises on music, language, and philosophy, he published several works on Freemasonry, which best represent his peculiar philosophic ideas. Chief among them are: 'Observations on the History of Freemasonry' (1810); 'The Three Oldest Monuments of Freemasonry' (1810); 'Prototype of Mankind' (1811).

Krehbiel, Henry Edward. An American musical critic; born in Ann Arbor, Mich., 1854. He was musical critic successively on the Cincinnati Gazette and the New York Tribune. His published works include : 'The Technics of Violin Playing' (1880); 'Review of the New York Musical Season' (1885-86): and the same for the season of 1886-87; 'How to Listen to Music' (1896).

Kremer, Alfred von (krä'mer). An Austrian diplomatist and Orientalist; born in Vienna, May 13, 1828. Upon his return from a visit to Syria and Egypt he was made professor of modern Arabic in the Polytechnic School, Vienna; and since 1858 has held important positions in the consular service at Cairo, Galatz, and Beyrout. He published (1875-77) 'A History of Oriental Civilization under the Khalifs,' which has firmly established his reputation as an Orientalist. Other important works are: 'Egypt' (1863); 'Legends of Southern Arabia' (1866); 'History of the Dominant Ideas of Islam' (1868); 'The Idea of Nationality and the State' (1885). Died 1889.

Kremnitz, Mite (Marie) (krem'nits). A prolific German miscellaneous writer; born at Greifswald, Jan. 4, 1852. Of her works on Roumania, may be named : 'Roumanian Sketches' (1877); 'New Roumanian Sketches' (1881); 'Roumanian Tales' (1882). Prominent among her other books are: 'Exiles' (1890), a romance; 'Love's Curse' (1881), written under the pseudonym "George Allan"; 'A Prince's Child' (1882). In collaboration with "Carmen Sylva," she has written : 'Anne Boleyn' (1886); 'From Two Worlds' (3d ed. 1887); 'Astra' (3d ed. 1887); 'Revenge' (2d ed. 1889); 'Astray' (1890); 'Man and Woman' (1902); 'Fatum' (1903).

Krestovskii, Vsevolod Vladimirovich (krestof'ske). A Russian military officer and historian; born at Kiev, Feb. 11, 1840. After a short course of study at the University of St. Peters-

burg, he entered a regiment of uhlans and subsequently was transferred to the Imperial Guard, which he accompanied during the war with Turkey (1877) as official historian attached to the general staff. On his return he published an account of his experiences, in 'Twenty Months in the Active Army' (1879). He is best known, however, as a novelist : his 'Not the First nor the Last' (1859); 'The Sphinx' (1860); 'Slums of St. Petersburg' (1867); 'Egyptian Darkness'; etc., enjoying great popularity in Russia and Germany.

Krestovsky, V., later **Krestovskii** (pseudonym) (kres-tof'ske). See **Khvostchinskáia.**

Kretzer, Max (kretz'er). A German novelist; born at Posen, May 7, 1854. He is a prolific and powerful realist. Several of his works have been on socialism. Among the best of his writings are : 'Berlin Tales and Pictures of Manners' (2d ed. 1887); 'Civil Death' (1888), a drama; 'The Deceived' (2d ed. 1891); 'The Sermon on the Mount' (2d ed. 1891), dealing with social questions; 'The Creator of Millions' (1891); 'Uncle Fifi' (2d ed. 1892); 'The Two Confederates' (3d ed. 1893), dealing with social questions; 'Strange Enthusiasts' (1893); 'The Son of the Woman'; 'The Wandering Dollar.'

Kroeger, Adolph Ernst. An American prose-writer; born in Schwabstedt, Schleswig, 1837; died in St. Louis, Mo., 1882. During the Civil War he served on Frémont's staff. By translations of the works of Fichte, Kant, and Leibnitz, he largely contributed to a better understanding of German literature in this country. He wrote for the St. Louis Journal of Speculative Philosophy. He published Fichte's 'Science of Knowledge' (1868); the same author's 'Science of Rights' (1869). He also issued 'Our Forms of Government, and the Problems of the Future' (1862).

Krüdener, Barbara Juliane von, Baroness (krü'de-ner). A Russian novelist and mystic; born at Riga, Nov. 21, 1764; died at Karassu-Bazar, Dec. 24, 1824. Her checkered and romantic career touched the extremes of life — worldliness and sainthood. After having left her husband, with whom her union had been unhappy and whom she had deceived, and tasted Parisian dissipation, she became a Swedenborgian, and devoted herself to helping the poor and afflicted. Surrounded by a retinue of clergy, she traversed Europe, preaching eloquently to the people a return to primitive Christianity, and being persecuted and expelled by the different governments. She was the friend of Queen Louise of Prussia and of Alexander I. of Russia, and is said to have been very influential in the formation of the Holy Alliance. She foretold Napoleon's triumphant return from Elba. Her death was the result of ascetic practices. Her literary reputation rests upon the famous romance 'Valéria, or Letters of Gustave de Linar to Ernest de G——.' (last ed. 1878), containing the history of her marital relations.

Krüger, Johann Christian (krüg'er). A German dramatist; born at Berlin, 1722; died at Hamburg, Aug. 23, 1750. He studied philology, but became an actor and a playwright. Among his comedies were: ‹The Clergy in the Country›; ‹The Blind Husband›; ‹The Candidates, or the Way to Get in Office›; ‹The Wedded Philosopher›; ‹The Devil's a Coward›; and the universally popular ‹Duke Michael.› (Poetical and dramatic works, 1763.)

Krummacher, Friedrich Adolf (krö'mäch-er). A German writer of parables; born at Tecklenburg, July 1767; died at Bremen, April 4, 1845. A minister in the German Reformed Church and a professor of theology, he became widely known by his ‹Parables› (1805), which ran through many editions and are familiar in an English translation. They were as a rule short, written in simple prose, on such subjects as ‹The Blind Man,› ‹Life and Death,› ‹The Hero,› etc., and became a sort of international property, being even printed in schoolbooks. None of his other writings won popularity.

Kruse, Heinrich (krö'zé). A German poet; born at Stralsund, Dec. 15, 1815. His very successful works consist of dramas, idyls, and lyrics. Of tragedies, the best known are ‹The Countess› (1868, his first attempt); ‹King Eric› (2d ed. 1873); ‹Wullenwever› (3d ed. 1878); ‹The Outlaw› (2d ed. 1881); ‹Brutus› (2d ed. 1882); ‹The Byzantine Maiden› (2d ed. 1885); ‹Arabella Stuart› (1888). Three farces, ‹The Devil at Lubeck,› ‹The Jealous Miller,› and ‹Steadfast Love,› appeared in one volume in 1887; ‹Seven Little Dramas› was published in 1893. In his dramatic work the dialogue is pithy and the characters are sharply defined, while the keen humor that fills the comedies and farces breaks out intermittently in the tragedies also. His idyls can be best seen in ‹Sea Tales› (first collection 1880, 2d ed. 1889; second collection 1889). His lyrics appeared in ‹ Poems › (1891). Died Jan. 13, 1902.

Krylov, Ivan Andréevitch (krē-lof'). A Russian writer of fables; born at Moscow, Feb. 13, 1768; died at St. Petersburg, Nov. 21, 1844. He is the most popular author in Russia; the children learn to read from his books, and many of his verses have become national proverbs. His statue stands in the summer garden at St. Petersburg. He produced 142 fables original in substance and form, and 56 translations or imitations. Without ill-nature, their satire on existing conditions is keen. They are written in verse, simple and attractive in style; — any child or peasant readily understands them. They have been translated into every European language. The first collection appeared in 1890. (‹Works,› 1859.)

Kugler, Franz Theodor (kög'ler). A German writer on art and its history; born at Stettin, Jan. 19, 1808; died at Berlin, March 18, 1858. He was appointed a professor of fine arts in the University of Berlin in 1833, and subsequently became a member of the Academy of Berlin. His works have undoubtedly had great influence on German art and culture: notably a ‹History of Painting from Constantine

the Great to the Present Times› (1837); ‹Handbook of the History of Art› (1841–42); ‹History of Architecture› (1856). He is also the author of a ‹History of Frederick the Great› (1840), which is popular in Germany.

Kühne, Gustav (kü'né). A prolific German novelist and poet; born at Magdeburg, Dec. 27, 1806; died at Dresden, April 22, 1888. Among his novels, the later ones of which show a tendency toward too many reflections and a lack of form, were: ‹A Quarantine in the Madhouse› (1835); ‹Feminine and Masculine Characters› (2 vols., 1838); ‹Portraits and Silhouettes› (2 vols., 1843); ‹Convent Tales› (2d ed. 1862); ‹The Rebels of Ireland› (2d ed. 1863); ‹German Men and Women› (2d ed. 1863); ‹The Freemasons› (2d ed. 1867). Of poems, in addition to those contained in his collected works, he published: ‹ Roman Sonnets › (1869); ‹Christ on his Travels› (1870); ‹Wittenberg and Rome› (3 vols., 1877); ‹Romances, Legends, and Fables› (1880). He wrote also the following dramas: ‹Isaura of Castile›; ‹The Emperor Friedrich III.›; ‹Demetrius›; etc. For several years he edited the celebrated periodicals Journal for the Elegant World, and Europa. He belonged to the « Young Germany» school of literature. (‹Works,› 10 vols., 1862–67.)

Kulmann, Elisabeth Borisovna (köl'män). A Russian poet; born at St. Petersburg, 1808; died 1825, at 17. She was very precocious in language-study and literary aptitude, and wrote in Russian, German, and Italian. Her Russian poems, edited by the Russian Academy, appeared in 1833; the best edition of her German verse is that of 1857; the Italian poems were published at Milan in 1847. Her poetry, written in a simple and clear style, showed keen observation, considerable descriptive power, and a lively imagination: Goethe prophesied for her an honorable place in literature. A monument was erected to her memory by the Russian empress.

Kunstmann, Friedrich (könst'män). A German historical and geographical writer; born at Nuremberg, Jan. 4, 1811; died at Munich, Aug. 15, 1867. He was private tutor to the Princess Donna Amalia of Brazil in Lisbon (1841–46), and on his return to Munich was appointed to a professorship in the university. He contributed papers to the transactions of the Munich Academy, and published: ‹The Latin Penitential Books of the Anglo-Saxons› (1844); ‹Africa before the Discoveries of the Portuguese› (1853); ‹The Discovery of America from the Most Ancient Sources› (1859), with an atlas giving fac-simile copies of early maps.

Kürnberger, Ferdinand (kürn'bärg-er). A German novelist· born at Vienna, July 3, 1821; died at Munich, Oct. 14, 1879. His works are witty, highly poetical, and written in a pithy style. His first novel, ‹Tired of America› (1856), was his most popular one; it described the American civilization of that period as merely material. Of several volumes of tales, 'Selected Tales' (1857) contained his best work. Others of his writings were: the drama 'Cataline' (1855); the volume of essays 'Seal Rings' (1874); the romance 'The Despot of the House' (1876); 'Literary Affairs of the Heart' (1877).

Kurz, Heinrich (körts). A German historian of literature; born at Paris, April 28, 1805; died at Aarau, Switzerland, Feb. 24, 1873. Having suffered two years' imprisonment for articles published in his paper, the Augsburg Times, he removed to Switzerland, where he held several professorships and made a special study of German literature. The results of his investigations are embodied in the well-known 'History of German Literature' (4 vols., 1851; 1868–72). Equally important are: 'Handbook of the National Poetic Literature of the Germans' (1840–43); 'Handbook of German Prose' (1845–52.) 'Manual of Sacred History.'

Kurz, Hermann. A German novelist; born at Reutlingen, Würtemberg, Nov. 30, 1813; died at Tübingen, Oct. 10, 1873. He is best known by his two fine romances, 'Schiller's Life in his Native Place' (2d ed. 1856–57), describing Würtemberg at the time Schiller grew up there; and 'Mine Host of the Sun' (2d ed., 2 vols., 1862), a Swabian popular tale of psychological power. 'From the Days of Dishonor' (1871), another strong work, was historical in tone; 'On Shakespeare's Life and Work' (1868) and the text for Konewka's 'Falstaff and his

Companions' (1872) were critical. He translated from the Italian, Spanish, French, and English masters, and wrote also two volumes of poems. ('Works,' 10 vols., 1874–75.)

Kvitka, Grigorii Fedorovitch (kvit'kä). A Russian novelist; born at Osnova (whence his appellation "Osnovianenko"), near Karkov, Nov. 29, 1778; died at Karkov, Aug. 20, 1843. He wrote both in Great and Little Russian, being one of the chief writers in the latter, his works in which (new ed, 2 vols., 1858) were especially dear to his countrymen for presenting pictures of the familiar national life idealized; the most popular was the novel 'Maroussia.' In Great Russian he published two novels of manners and a number of dramas, the most popular of the latter being 'Selmenko.'

Kyd, Thomas. An English dramatist; flourished in the sixteenth century. He was the most popular English writer of tragedies before Shakespeare, and helped prepare the way for him. His most successful two plays, his first and second works respectively, were 'The Spanish Tragedy, or Hieronimo,' and 'Oratio.' They were very popular and were frequently acted, not only in England, but in Germany and in Holland: but the former was much ridiculed by Shakespeare and his contemporaries, for its bombastic rant; and "Go by, Jeronimy" (i. e., "Get out, you lunatic"), from the ravings of the distracted hero, became a common phrase.

L

Laas, Ernst (lä'äs). A well-known German philosopher and educator; born at Fürstenwald on the Spree, June 16, 1837; died at Strasburg, July 25, 1885. He was one of the chief representatives of positivism in Germany, though his strength lay more in criticism than in construction. His principal work, 'Idealism and Positivism' (3 vols., 1879–84), opposed the views of Plato and Kant. Of his pedagogical writings, the most important are 'German Composition in the Upper Gymnasium Classes' (2d ed. 1877–78), an epoch-making work, and 'German Education in the Higher Institutions of Instruction' (2d ed. 1886).

Labanca, Baldassare (lä-bänk'ä). An Italian philosopher; born at Agnone (Molise), 1829. He has attained great eminence with such works as 'Readings in Natural Philosophy' (1864); 'Concerning the True and the False Spirit in Philosophy' (1857); and many similar ones.

Labarre, called **Louis Labar** (lä-bär'). A Belgian journalist and man of letters; born at Dinan, Namur, May 1, 1810; died at Ixelles, Jan. 17, 1892. His first success was a volume of 'Satires and Elegies' (1836), in which his republican sentiments are strongly expressed.

He has edited Charivari Belge and other journals. His best works include: 'A Revolution to Laugh At,' a comedy; 'Antoine Wiertz' (1867), a biography; 'Waterloo' (1868), a historical study; and other miscellany.

Labé, Louise (lä-bā). A French poet; true name Charlieu; called "the fair rope-maker" from her husband's business (about 1526–66). She was early noted for beauty, linguistic talent, and intrepidity. At 16, disguised as a cavalier, she took part in the siege of Perpignan. After marriage at Lyons, her house became the rendezvous of poets, scholars, artists, and musicians. Her poems are true lyrics, singularly graceful and original, though showing Petrarch's influence. She also wrote in prose a charming allegory, 'Dispute between Folly and Love.'

La Bédollière, Émile Gigault de (lä bād-ōl-yär'). A French historian, and social analyst; born at Amiens, 1812; died in Paris, 1883. He wrote much, his best works being: 'History of Paris' (1864); 'History of the Morals and Private Life of the French' (1847); 'History of Mother Michel and of her Cat' (1851), a delightful mock-serious tale, translated into English by T. B. Aldrich for St. Nicholas.

Labeo, Marcus Antistius (lab'ē-ō). A celebrated Roman jurist of the Augustan age. He wrote some 400 works on jurisprudence; but of them one only has come down to our time, being embodied in the Pandects of the Justinian 'Corpus Juris.'

Laberius, Decimus (la-bē'ri-us). A Roman knight and miscellaneous writer; born about 105 B. C.; died at Puteoli, January 43 B. C. His writings consisted of farces, comic and satirical poems, an epic poem on Cæsar's Gallic war, and a prose work containing anecdotes, etc. He was compelled by Cæsar to appear on the stage in one of his own farces, thereby forfeiting his knighthood, which was restored to him by the dictator.

Labesse, Antoine Édouard Decaudin (läbes'). A French miscellaneous writer; born in Angoulême, April 11, 1848. He is a prolific writer on a variety of subjects, his works including: 'The Terrestrial World,' a popular scientific study; 'Monsieur, Madame, and Baby'; 'My First Case'; 'The King of the Fjords'; and many more.

Labiche, Eugène (lä-bēsh'). An important French comedy-writer; born in Paris, May 5, 1815; died there, Jan. 23, 1888. Of over 100 comedies, vaudevilles, farces, etc., of his writing, almost all possessed strong qualities, including striking dialogue, caustic yet never cruel humor, and stage technique, while several were models of their kind. Among the best are: 'The Italian Straw Hat' (1851); 'The Misanthrope and the Auvergnat' (1853); 'Eye Powder' (with Martin, 1862); 'Célimare the Well-Beloved' (1863); 'Cagnotte' (1864); 'One Foot in Crime' (with Choler, 1866); etc. ('Dramatic Works,' 10 vols., 1878–79.) He wrote a number of pieces in collaboration.

La Boëtie, Étienne de (lä bo-e-tē'). A French anti-monarchical poet; born at Sarlat, Nov. 1, 1530; died at Germignan, Aug. 18, 1563. He was a friend of Montaigne, who brought out an edition of his writings (1570–71). Of these the best known is the 'Discourse on Voluntary Slavery,' a rather flat philippic against monarchy. ('Works,' Paris, 1892.)

Laborde, Alexandre Louis Joseph, Count de (lä-bord'). A French writer of travels; born in Paris, Sept. 17, 1773; died there, Oct. 24, 1842. He wrote: 'Picturesque and Historic Journey in Spain' (4 vols., 1807–18; new ed. 1823); 'Description of the New Gardens and Ancient Castles of France' (1808–15); 'The Monuments of France' (2 vols., 1816–36); 'Picturesque Journey in Austria' (3 vols., 1821–23); 'Descriptive Itinerary of Spain' (3d ed., 6 vols., 1827–31); 'Versailles, Ancient and Modern' (1840). He was a soldier, accompanying Napoleon to Spain and Austria, and a politician.

Laborde, Léon, Marquis de. A French miscellaneous writer, son of Alexandre; born in Paris, June 15, 1807; died there, March 25, 1869. Having accompanied his father on a trip to the East, he wrote: 'Journey in Arabia Petræa' (1830–33); 'Journey in the East' (2 vols., 1837–62); 'History of Engraving' (1839); 'The Dukes of Burgundy' (1849–51); 'Account of the Enamels, Jewelry, and Various Objects on Exhibition in the Galleries of the Louvre' (2 vols., 1853); 'The Renaissance of the Arts at the Court of France. Vol. I.: Painting' (1855). In the revolution of 1830 he was General Lafayette's adjutant, was afterwards in the diplomatic service at London, The Hague, and Cassel, and succeeded to his father's office.

Labouchere, Henry (lä-bö-shär'). An English journalist and politician; born in London, 1831. He was in the diplomatic service, part of the time at Washington, and a member of Parliament. An advanced republican, he used Truth, the journal established by him in 1876 as a society and political organ, for the promulgation of his ideas, often thereby getting into serious difficulties. He wrote 'Diary of a Besieged Resident in Paris' (1871).

Laboulaye, Édouard René Lefebvre de (lä-bö-lä'). A distinguished French jurist, historian, and writer of tales; born at Paris, Jan. 18, 1811; died there, May 25, 1883. He was appointed professor of comparative jurisprudence in the Collège de France in 1849, having already won distinction by several treatises on Roman and French law. His greatest work outside of the field of jurisprudence is a 'Political History of the United States, 1620–1789' (3 vols., 1855–66). He wrote also 'The United States and France' (1862) and the humorous satiric novel 'Paris in America' (1863), which had a very large circulation (27th ed. 1872). His novel of 'Prince Caniche' (1868) reached a 20th edition. But by far his best-known works of fiction are the three series of 'Blue Stories,' —tales of fairies, elves, enchanters, etc., original and retold. Some of his essays on contemporary political and social questions have been collected and published under the titles 'Contemporary Studies of Germany and the Slavic States' (1856); 'Religious Liberty' (1858).

Labrunie. See **Gérard de Nerval.**

La Bruyère, Jean de (lä brü-yär'). A famous French moralist and satirist; born in Paris, August 1645; died at Versailles, May 10, 1696. Appointed tutor of the dauphin, he spent a large part of his life at the court of Louis XIV. His great work, on which his reputation rests, 'The Characters of Theophrastus, Translated from the Greek, with the Characters or Manners of this Century' (1688), was a cloak for the keenest and most sagacious observations on the characters and manners of the court. It abounds in wit, shows him to have been an excellent judge of men, and is written in an admirable style. The number of « characters » was greatly increased as the various editions came out. Numerous keys appeared, the first in 1720. It has been translated into well-nigh every modern language. A true philosopher, desiring but to lead a quiet life with his books and friends, only his worth and tact enabled him always to preserve his dignity among the ignorant and arrogant courtiers.

Lacaille, Nicolas Louis de (lä-käy'). A noted French astronomer (1713-62). In 1750 he proposed to the Paris Academy an astronomical expedition to the Cape of Good Hope; the project being officially sanctioned, he made the voyage to the Cape 1751, and spent three years in the southern hemisphere. He made more observations and calculations than all the other astronomers of his time put together, and his exactitude was not inferior to his diligence. His principal writings are: 'The Foundations of Astronomy' (1757); 'Solar Tables'; 'The Southern Starry Heavens' (1763), a catalogue of 10,000 southern stars; elementary treatises on 'Mathematics' (1741), 'Mechanics' (1743), 'Astronomy' (1746), 'Optics' (1750).

La Calprenède, Gauthier de Coste, Seigneur de (lä käl-pre-näd'). A French romancer (1610-63). He first entered the field of literature with tragedies and tragi-comedies, but had little success. He then wrote a romance of chivalry, 'Cleopatra' (12 vols., 1647-58), in which contemporary personages and manners are portrayed under names and amid surroundings of the age of Augustus. The episodes of intrigue and gallantry are to the last degree prolix and wearisome; but the characters are for the most part well defined, some of the scenes skillfully contrived, and the style always elegant and perspicuous. Among his other romances, in a like vein, are 'Cassandra' (10 vols., 1642-50); 'Pharamond' (7 vols., 1661-70); 'Diversions of the Princess Alcidiana' (1661).

Lacaussade, Auguste (lä-kō-säd'). A French poet; born in the Isle of Bourbon, 1817. His most notable volumes of verse include: 'National Poems' (1871); 'Anacreontics'; etc.

Lacépède, Bernard Germain Étienne de Laville, Count de (lä-sä-ped'). A distinguished French naturalist; born at Agen, Dec. 26, 1756; died at Épinay, Oct. 6, 1825. The perusal of Buffon's 'Natural History' in early life decided his after career. Most noteworthy among his works are: 'History of Oviparous Quadrupeds' (1788); 'Natural History of Reptilia' (1788); 'Natural History of Fishes,' a work of the highest authority (6 vols., 1798-1805); 'Natural History of Man' (posthumous).

Lachambeaudie, Pierre (lä-shon-bō-dē'). A French fabulist; born at Sarlat, Dec. 16, 1807; died at Brunoy, near Paris, July 7, 1872. His principal work was 'Popular Fables' (7th ed. 1849), a number of which have been translated into German.

Lachaud, Georges (lä-shō'). A French story and political writer; born in Paris, 1846. 'The Bonapartists and the Republic' (1877) is a typical specimen of his political writings, and 'Pitiless Love' (1884) of his fiction.

La Chaussée, Pierre Claude Nivelle de (lä shō-sä'). A French dramatist, founder of the so-called "mixed" or "weeping" comedy; born in Paris, 1692; died there, March 14, 1754. His comedy 'The False Antipathy' (1734) was the first French pathetic comedy. Of eighteen dramas written by him, among the best are: 'Fashionable Prejudice' (1735), directed against the idea, then wide-spread, that a man of rank can have no love for his wife; 'School of Friendship' (1737); 'Mélanide' (1741); 'Love for Love' (1742); 'Pamela' (1743); 'School of Mothers' (1745); 'The Governess' (1747). His plays were all written in verse and followed strictly the rules of the classic drama, but inclined to be somewhat tedious in their moralizing. ('Works,' 5 vols., 1762.)

Lachmann, Karl (lach'män). A noted German philologist and critic; born at Brunswick, March 4, 1793; died at Berlin, March 13, 1851. With Jakob Grimm he was the founder of the Old-German philology, and was distinguished for the keenness of his critical method. Among the most important of his works were his treatment of the Nibelungen (1836), arguing that it is composed of twenty old folk songs; 'Views on Homer's Iliad' (1847), aiming to show it to be made up of single songs; and his editions of the Nibelungenlied (1826); Walther von der Vogelweide, Wolfram von Eschenbach, Propertius, Catullus, Tibullus, Lucretius, etc. He was professor at Königsberg (1818) and Berlin (1825).

Laclos, Pierre Ambroise François Choderlos de (lä-klō'). A French novelist; born at Amiens, 1741; died at Taranto, Italy, 1803. He is best known by his 'Dangerous Connections' (4 vols., 1782). He wrote also a satire against Madame Dubarry, 'A Letter to Marget.' His life was spared by Robespierre, for the reason, so it was said, that he composed R.'s speeches for him.

La Condamine, Charles Marie de (lä kon''-dä-men'). A French scientist; born in Paris, Jan. 28, 1701; died there, Feb. 4, 1774. He is best known as having with Bouger and Godin measured an arc of the meridian on the plain of Quito, South America. The expedition lasted nine years (1735-44). On his way home he descended the Amazon, being the first scientist to do so, and the first man to publish accurate maps of the river. He is said to have introduced the knowledge of india-rubber into Europe. He wrote: 'Journal of an Expedition to the Equator by Order of the King' (1751); 'Abridged Account of a Journey Made in the Interior of South America' (1745); 'History of Small-Pox Inoculation' (1773); etc.

Lacordaire, Jean Baptiste Henri Dominique (lä-kor-där'). A noted French pulpit orator and journalist; born at Recey-sur-Ource, May 12, 1802; died at Sorèze, Nov. 22, 1861. He became famous as a preacher at Notre Dame, speaking from the pulpit on the questions of the day, and was a member of the National Assembly. With Lamennais, he founded the democratic journal L'Avenir (The Future: 1830), which was condemned by the Pope. Among his works were: 'Philosophical Considerations on the System of Lamennais' (1834); 'Life of St. Dominic' (1840); 'Detached Sermons and Funeral Orations' (1844-47), the most impressive of which was the oration preached over the remains of Gen. Drouot; and a voluminous correspondence.

Lacretelle, Henri de (lä-kret-el'). A French poet and prose-writer, son of Jean; born Aug. 21, 1815. He was a member of the national legislature. He wrote 'Lamartine and his Friends' (1878).

Lacretelle, Jean Charles Dominique de, the Younger. A noted French historian and journalist, brother of Pierre Louis; born at Metz, Sept. 3, 1766; died at Bel-Air, near Macon, March 26, 1855. He was editor of the Journal des Débats, censor of the press, president of the French Academy, and professor of history at the University of Paris. He wrote a number of histories of France at different periods, among which may be named: 'Compendium of the History of the French Revolution' (6 vols., 1801-6); 'History of France during the Eighteenth Century' (6 vols., 1808). He wrote also interesting memoirs of his own time: 'Ten Years of Trials during the Revolution' (1842); 'Philosophic and Literary Last Will and Testament' (2 vols., 1840).

Lacretelle, Pierre Louis. A French legal and miscellaneous writer; born at Metz, 1751; died Sept. 5, 1824. Besides several legal works, etc., he wrote 'Portraits and Pictures' (2 vols., 1817), containing masterly descriptions of Napoleon I., Mirabeau, and Lafayette. He edited the Mercure de France and the Minerve Française. ('Works,' 6 vols., 1823-24.)

Lacroix, Jules (lä-krwä'). A French poet, dramatist, and novelist, brother of Paul; born in Paris, May 7, 1809; died Nov. 10, 1887. He wrote numerous romances; a volume of poetry, 'Les Pervenches' (The Periwinkles: 1838); several dramas; and 'The Year of Infamy' (1872), a collection of patriotic poems.

Lacroix, Paul. A French novelist and historian; born at Paris, Feb. 27, 1806; died there, Oct. 16, 1884. Under the pseudonym "P. L. Jacob, Bibliophile," he edited with valuable commentaries the works of Rabelais and other great 16th-century authors. Among his works are: 'Dissertations on Some Curious Points of the History of France' (3 vols., 1838); 'The 16th Century in France' (2 vols., 1838); 'History . . . of Napoleon III.' (4 vols., 1853); several historical novels; numerous works of great value on such subjects as 'Historic Costumes of France' (10 vols., 1852); 'Manners, Costumes, etc., of the Middle Ages' (1870); 'The 18th Century: Institutions, Usages, and Costumes' (1879); 'The Directorate and the Empire,' etc. (1883); these works on costumes, usages, etc., are illustrated with most elaborate and accurate designs executed by the foremost artists.

Lactantius Firmianus (lak-tan'shi-us fèr-mi-ā-nus), **Lucius Cælius** or **Cæcilius.** An eminent Christian author of the fourth century,

A. D. A pupil of the rhetorician Arnobius, he became a teacher of rhetoric in Nicomedia, and afterwards tutor to Crispus, son of Constantine the Great. His principal work, 'The Divine Institutes,' a production of a polemical character, earned for him the title of the "Christian Cicero."

Lacy, John. An English dramatist and comedian; born near Doncaster, before 1620; died in London, Sept. 17, 1681. His best play is 'The Old Troop,' of which Scott makes use in 'Woodstock.'

Ladd, George Trumbull. An American educator and philosophical writer; born at Painesville, O., 1842. He was educated at Western Reserve College and Andover Theological Seminary. He was pastor of Spring Street Congregational Church, Milwaukee, Wis., from 1871 to 1879; and professor of philosophy at Bowdoin College from 1879 to 1881, when he assumed the chair of philosophy at Yale. His works include: 'Principles of Church Polity' (1881); 'Doctrine of Sacred Scripture' (1883); 'Elements of Physiological Psychology' (1887); 'Philosophy of Conduct' (1902).

La Dixmerie, Nicolas Bricaire de (lä dēz-mär-ē'). A French man of letters; born 1730; died 1791. His works are able and powerful, but not agreeable. They include: 'Philosophical and Moral Tales' (1765), and 'Eulogy of Voltaire' (1779).

Laet, Jan Jakob de (lät). ["Johan Alfried."] A Flemish poet, novelist, and journalist; born at Antwerp, Dec. 13, 1815; died there, April 22, 1891. He was a physician. After championing Flemish rights and language in several journals, some of them founded for the purpose by himself, he deserted journalism for business, but engaged afterward in politics. Among his best-known works were the romance 'The House of Wesenbeke' (1842); the village tale 'The Player' (1846); 'Poems' (1848; 2d ed. 1883).

La Fare, Charles Auguste, Marquis de (lä fär). A French poet; born at Castle Valgorge, Vivarais, 1644; died in Paris, 1712. A friend of Marshal Turenne, he distinguished himself in the campaigns of 1667 and 1674; but left the army afterward and devoted himself to a life of pleasure, the delights of which he celebrated in verse. The Duke of Orleans wrote the music for his opera of 'Panthée.'

La Farge, John (lä färj). An American artist of the first rank; born in New York city, 1835. He studied under Couture in Paris; became a National Academician in 1869; and a member of the Society of American Artists in 1877. He has executed remarkable paintings, altar pieces, and decorations of interiors—notably of Trinity Church, Boston; and designed stained-glass windows for churches and many other buildings, in the new American manner, which is a revival of the art of making colored glass (instead of painting glass), of which he was the originator, in association with Louis Tiffany. He has published a volume of 'Lectures on Art,' and 'An Artist's Letters from Japan'; 'Artist and Writer.'

La Farina, Giuseppe (lä fä-rē'na). An Italian statesman and historian; born at Messina, July 20, 1815; died at Florence, Sept. 5, 1863. A democratic leader, favoring Italian unity and independence, he lived part of his life as a political refugee; but played an important part in the movements of his time. His principal work was 'History of Italy Narrated to the Italian People' (10 vols., 1846).

La Fayette, Marie Madeleine Pioche de la Vergne, Comtesse de (lä-fī-et' or laf-ā-et'). A distinguished French novelist; born at Paris, 1634; died there, May 25, 1693. All her life she was in the foremost literary circles, after marriage her house being a noted rendezvous of wits and scholars, including Mme. de Sévigné, Lafontaine, and La Rochefoucauld. Her first novel was 'The Princess de Montpensier' (1660); ten years later appeared her second, 'Zaïde,' which among her works ranks next after 'The Princess of Cleves' (4 vols., 1678), her most celebrated work, and one of the classics of French literature. She wrote also a 'History of Henrietta of England' (1720), and 'Memoirs of the Court of France for the Years 1688 and 1689' (1731).

Lafontaine, August Heinrich Julius (lä-fontän'). A German novelist; born at Brunswick, Oct. 5, 1758; died at Halle, April 20, 1831. He wrote more than 150 novels, and founded a school which in its day was regarded with high favor at the court of Prussia for its tone of illiberal moralizing sentimentality. Among his novels may be named: 'Picture of the Human Heart' (1792); 'Descriptions of the Life of Man' (1811); 'The Parsonage on the Lake Side' (1816).

La Fontaine, Jean de. A celebrated French fabulist and poet; born at Château-Thierry, in Champagne, July 8, 1621; died in Paris, April 13, 1695. His first work was an adaptation of Terence's 'Eunuch' (1654). His poem 'Adonis' was published in 1658. His principal works are 'Stories and Novels' (5 books, 1665-95), and the 'Fables' (12 books, 1668-95),—both in verse. The 'Stories' are mostly versions of stories like Boccaccio's and Margaret of Navarre's, and almost unrivaled in variety and vividness; but their licentiousness caused the suppression of one book in 1675 by the public censor. In this respect the 'Fables' are without blemish, while as works of literary art they stand in the foremost rank. He wrote some dramas, of little worth; also a version in prose and verse of 'The Loves of Psyche' (1669).

Lafuente, Modesto (lä-fwen'tä). A Spanish historian; born at Rabanel de los Caballeros, 1806; died there, Oct. 25, 1866. Under the pseudonym "Fray Gerundio" he published a series of satirical sketches which had wide circulation; but his principal work is a 'General History of Spain' (30 vols., 1850-66). It is written without partisanship, and is the fruit of laborious research; the style is excellent.

Lagarde, Paul Anton de (lä-gärd'). A distinguished German Orientalist; born at Berlin, Nov. 2, 1827; died at Göttingen, Dec. 22, 1891. He became professor of Oriental languages at Göttingen, 1869. Of his very numerous writings the majority relate to the books of the Hebrew Scriptures; but he edited and commented on versions of those books and of the books of the New Testament in Greek, Armenian, Arabic, Syriac, Coptic, etc.

Lagrange, Joseph Louis (lä-gränzh'). A great French mathematician; born at Turin, Jan. 25, 1736; died at Paris, April 10, 1813. While still a youth he solved for Euler the "isoperimetrical problem"; when Euler died, he succeeded him as director of the Berlin Academy (1766), and held that office till 1787. In the mean time he contributed to the Proceedings of the Academy a long series of memoirs, and wrote his greatest work, 'Analytical Mechanics.' After the death of Frederick the Great he removed to Paris; there he was lodged in the Louvre, and a pension was settled on him equal to that granted by Frederick. He remained in France during the Revolution, safeguarded by the respect felt for his learning and his virtues even by the judges of the revolutionary tribunals.

La Guéronnière, Louis Étienne Arthur Dubreuil Hélion, Vicomte de (lä gär-ōn-yär'). A French publicist; born at Limoges, 1816; died at Paris, Dec. 23, 1875. He became a zealous partisan of Louis Napoleon after the Coup d'État of 1851, being then chief editor of the Pays. In a celebrated pamphlet, 'Napoleon III. and Italy,' he first heralded the approaching war against Austria in Lombardy (1859). In another pamphlet, 'France, Rome, and Italy' (1861), he brought again to the front the question of the Pope's temporal power. Hardly less celebrated than these were his pamphlets 'Napoleon III. and England' (1858); 'The Pope and the Congress' (1859).

La Harpe, Jean François de (lä ärp). A French literary critic and poet; born at Paris, Nov. 20, 1739; died there, Feb. 11, 1803. After publishing several volumes of mediocre verse, he first came into public notice through his tragedy 'Warwick' (1763), and then added largely to his fame by a number of elegant and spirited 'Éloges' on great French worthies. He was professor of literature in the Lycée, 1786-98, and his lectures were attended by all the fashionables of Paris; the lectures were collected and published in a series of volumes, —'Lycée, or Course of Literature' (1799-1805). Among his numerous works Sainte-Beuve assigns the first rank to 'Cazotte's Prophecy.'

Laing, Malcolm (läng). A Scotch lawyer and historian; born on the Island of Mainland, Orkneys, in 1762; died in the Orkneys, November 1818. He was a lawyer by profession, and later a member of Parliament, but devoted himself principally to historical investigation. He wrote a continuation of Henry's 'A History of Great Britain' (1785), and 'History of Scotland' (2 vols., 1800), which may be regarded as supplementary to Dr. Robertson's History. In the preliminary dissertation he presents an elaborate argument to prove Queen Mary's participation in the murder of Darnley.

Laing, Samuel. An English statesman and philosophical writer; born at Edinburgh in 1810. He has been prominently identified with railway legislation in England, was for many years prominent in Parliament, and from 1861 to 1863 held the office of finance minister to India. Of his works, 'Modern Science and Modern Thought' (1886), and 'A Modern Zoroastrian' (1887), have occasioned some discussion. His other publications of a miscellaneous character include: 'India and China' (1863); 'A Sporting Quixote; or the Life and Adventures of the Hon. Augustus Fitzmuddle' (1886); 'The Antiquity of Man' (1890); 'Human Origins.' He died at Sydenham, Aug. 6, 1897.

Laistner, Ludwig (līst'ner). A German poet; born at Esslingen, Nov. 3, 1845. Among his works are: 'Barbarossa's Marriage-Broker' (1875), an epic poem; 'Cloud-Myths' (1879), relating to German mythology; 'The Sphinx's Riddle: Elements of a History of Mythology' (2 vols., 1889); 'Germanic Names of Peoples' (1892). He died March 22, 1896.

Lalande, Joseph .`‘.me Lefrançais de (lä-länd'). An eminent French astronomer; born at Bourg-en-Bresse, July 11, 1732; died at Paris, April 4, 1807. Among his voluminous works are: 'A Treatise on Astronomy' (1764); 'French History of the Heavens' (1801), in which are determined the places of 50,000 stars; 'Astronomy for Ladies' (1785).

La Mara (lä mär'ä), pseudonym of Marie Lipsius. A noted German writer on music; born at Leipsic, Dec. 30, 1837. Her interesting work, 'Studies of Musicians' Heads' (5 vols., 1868–82), has had a wide circulation. She is author also of 'Musical Thoughts' (1873), a collection of sayings of eminent musicians; 'Letters of Musicians' (1886); 'Classicism and Romanticism in the World of Music' (1892).

Lamarck, Jean Baptiste Pierre Antoine de Monet, Chevalier de (lä-märk'). A celebrated French naturalist; born at Barentin, Aug. 1, 1744; died at Paris, Dec. 18, 1829. He directed his studies first to meteorology, but soon turned mainly to botany: his 'French Flora' (3 vols., 1778) became the basis of De Candolle's more celebrated work. He wrote also an 'Encyclopædic Tableau of Botany' (3 vols., 1791–1823) and a 'Natural History of Plants' (15 vols., 1802). His most celebrated work, 'History of the Invertebrates,' appeared in 1815–22 in seven volumes. His theoretical views are expounded in his 'Zoölogical Philosophy' (2 vols., 1809): there he attacks the doctrine of the immutability of species, and lays the scientific foundations of what later was called the development theory of the origin of species.

Lamartine, Alphonse Marie Louis de (lä-mär-tēn'). A celebrated French poet; born at

Milly, near Macon, Oct. 21, 1790; died at Passy, March 1, 1869. His first volume of poems, 'Poetical Meditations' (1820), was in effect a new departure in French lyrism, expressing sympathy with nature and with religious sentiment which accorded with the then new reaction against materialism. Then followed: 'New Poetical Meditations' (1823); 'Poetic and Religious Harmonies' (1830); 'Recollections, Impressions, and Reflections' (4 vols., 1835); 'Jocelyn' (1836), an idyllic epos in which he reaches the summit of his poetic inspiration; 'The Fall of an Angel' (1838), an imitation of Byron; 'History of the Girondins' (8 vols., 1847); 'Confidences' (1849); 'New Confidences' (1851); 'History of the Restoration' (8 vols., 1852); 'Lettres à L.' (1818–65).

Lamb, Charles. A celebrated English essayist; born in London, Feb. 10, 1775; died at Edmonton, Dec. 27, 1834. His 'Essays of Elia' were originally contributed to the London Magazine, beginning 1820; they were collected and published in a volume in 1823, received with universal public favor, and have a high place among English classics. 'Last Essays of Elia' were published in 1833. Lamb's cheerful philosophy of life, his genuine and spontaneous humor, and the easy grace of his style, are as grateful to readers of to-day as to those of two generations ago. He twice attempted dramatic composition, but without success. With his sister Mary Lamb (1765–1847) he wrote 'Tales from the Plays of Shakespeare' (1807), intended for youthful readers, with whom it has ever since been a favorite work.

Lamb, Martha Joanna Reade (Nash). An American historian; born in Plainfield, Mass., Aug. 13, 1829; died in New York city, Jan. 2, 1893. The best known of her works is the 'History of the City of New York' (2 vols., 1877–81). She also wrote 'The Homes of America' (1879); 'Wall Street in History' (1883). For years she was editor of the Magazine of American History. Mrs. Lamb was a member of many learned societies in this country and Europe.

Lambecius, called Peter Lambeck (läm-bē'shŏs). A German scholar (1628–80). He was teacher of history in the high-school of his native city, Hamburg, from 1652 to 1660, when he became its rector. He then became superintendent of the Imperial Library, Vienna. His principal writings are: 'Introduction to Literary History' (1659), the first methodical work of the kind; 'Notes on the Imperial Library' (8 vols., 1665–79), a work of great value for early German language and literature.

Lamber, Juliette (län-bä') —**Madame Adam** (ä-doñ). A French miscellaneous writer; born at Verberie, 1836. Her writings are mainly on political, social, and literary topics. She founded the Nouvelle Revue. Her works include: 'The Siege of Paris'; 'Garibaldi'; 'A Peasant Woman's Narratives'; 'In the Alps'; 'Laïde'; 'The Hungarian Country'; etc.

Lambert, Johann Heinrich (läm'bert). A distinguished German philosopher and scientist;

born at Mühlhausen, Alsace, Aug. 26, 1728; died at Berlin, Sept. 25, 1777. He was entirely self-educated. At 16 he calculated the period of the comet of 1744, according to the "Lambertine theorem." He became tutor in the household of a nobleman in 1748, and in 1759 was appointed professor in the Munich Academy. He was called to Berlin (1764) by Frederick the Great. His masterpiece in philosophy is the 'New Organon, or Thoughts upon the Research of Truth' (2 vols., 1764); in physics he laid the foundations of photometry, pyrometry, and hygrometry; in his 'Cosmological Letters' (1761), he sets forth the views still held by astronomers regarding the nature of the fixed stars; not less important are his researches in pure mathematics.

Lamennais, Hugues Félicité Robert de (lä-men-ā'). A French ecclesiastic, polemical, and political writer; born at St. Malo, June 19, 1782; died at Paris, Feb. 27, 1854. He was ordained priest in 1817. The same year appeared the first volume of his 'Essay upon Indifference in the Matter of Religion' (4 vols., 1807-20), a work of profound learning and of strict orthodoxy. He developed his views further in 'Religion Considered in its Relation to the Civil and Political Order' (1825), and 'Progress of the Revolution and of the War against the Church' (1829). By degrees he became the critic of Church policy, and his journal L'Avenir (The Future) was condemned by the Pope. Lamennais bowed to Rome's decree; but after a year was published his 'Words of a Believer' (1834), in which he repudiates all authority of popes and bishops. The little volume is written in archaic style, imitating the language of the Hebrew sacred books; it had an enormous circulation among the masses of the people in every country of Europe. It was followed by 'The Book of the People' (1837), and 'The Past and the Future of the People' (1842), in the same tone. He wrote also: 'Sketch of a Philosophy' (3 vols., 1841); 'Religion'; and translated the Gospels, accompanying the text with notes.

La Mettrie, Julien Offray de (lä-met-rē'). A French philosopher; born at St. Malo, Dec. 25, 1709; died at Berlin, Nov. 11, 1751. A fever while he was army surgeon led him to study the question of the parallel decline of mental force and bodily strength: his conclusions, those of materialism and atheism, he states in 'The Natural History of the Soul' (1745). Next he attacked the medical profession in 'The Politics of Dr. Machiavel' (1746). Both works were burnt by the common hangman. In numerous other works, as 'Charlatans Unmasked' (1747), 'The Machine-Man' (1748), 'The Plant-Man' (1748), 'The Metaphysic Venus, or Essay on the Origin of the Soul' (1752), he provoked the enmity of the clergy and of medical men. Frederick the Great had an edition of La Mettrie's 'Philosophical Works' published (1751) at the cost of the royal privy purse.

Lami'i (lä-me-e'). A notable Turkish poet and prose-writer; died about 1530. His prose works are chiefly translations from Jami. Among his poetical works are four epics founded on Persian legend: 'Vamik and Afra'; 'Vis and Ramin'; 'Absál and Selman'; and the 'Ferhádnâmeh.' There is a translation in German, by Pfizmaier, of one of the minor poems,— 'The Glorification of the City of Bursa.'

Lamington, Alexander Dundas Ross Wishard Baillie Cochrane, Baron. An English author and politician; born in November 1816; died in London, Feb. 15, 1890. He was the eldest son of Admiral Sir Thomas J. Cochrane, and one of the leaders of the Young England Party in Parliament. 'Exeter Hall or Church Polemics' (1841); 'Morea,' a poem; 'The State of Greece' (1847); 'Ernest Vane,' a novel; 'Florence the Beautiful' (1854); 'Francis the First, and Other Historic Studies' (1870); 'The Théâtre Français in the Reign of Louis XV.' (1879), constitute his chief works.

Lamon, Ward Hill. An American lawyer and biographer; born, ——, 1828; died at Martinsburg, W. Va., May 8, 1893. He was a law partner of Abraham Lincoln. His works are: 'Life of Abraham Lincoln, from his Birth to his Inauguration as President' (1872); 'Recollections of Abraham Lincoln.'

La Motte, Antoine Houdart de (lä-môt'). A French poet; born at Paris, Jan. 17, 1672; died there, Dec. 26, 1731. His first dramatic composition 'Originals,' was a failure; but some of his operas, his tragedy 'Inès del Castro' (1723), and his comedy 'The Swell,' had great success. The 'Odes' and 'Fables,' like all his lyric compositions, though they show considerable invention, are artificial and lack spontaneity.

La Motté-Fouque. See **Fouqué.**

Lampman, Archibald. A Canadian poet; born at Morpeth, Canada, Nov. 17, 1861; died at Ottawa, Feb. 10, 1899. He was a graduate of Trinity College, Toronto (1882), and after 1883 held an appointment in the Post Office Department at Ottawa. A constant contributor of verse to the papers and magazines of the Dominion and the United States, he published two collections of poems, 'Among the Millet' (1888), and 'Lyrics of Earth' (1895), which reveal a deep love of nature and outdoor life. Mr. Howells ranks him with the strongest of American singers.

Lamprecht the Priest (läm'precht). A German poet of the first half of the twelfth century. He wrote the 'Song of Alexander,' one of the best poems of mediæval Germany: it is an adaptation of a French poem by Alberic of Besançon, of which only a fragment remains.

Lancaster, William Joseph Cosens. An English civil engineer and author; born at Weymouth in 1851. He entered the British navy as a midshipman, but on account of defective eyesight resigned and became a civil engineer, in that capacity visiting different parts of the world. Under the pseudonym of

"Harry Collingwood," he is known to juvenile readers in England and America as the author of the popular nautical romances: 'The Secret of the Sands' (1878); 'Under the Meteor Flag' (1884); 'The Pirate Island' (1884); 'The Congo Rovers' (1885), a story of the Slave Squadron; 'The Missing Merchantman' (1888); 'The Cruise of the Esmeralda'; 'The Castaways.'

Lanciani, Rodolfo Amedeo (län-chē-ä'nē). An Italian archæologist; born in Rome, Jan. 1, 1847. He has attained celebrity by investigating the ruins of classical Rome. Among his works are: 'Ancient Rome in the Light of Recent Discoveries' (Boston: 1888); 'Pagan and Christian Rome' (Boston: 1892); and 'The Ruins and Excavations of Ancient Rome' (Boston: 1897).

Land, Jan Pieter Nicolaas (länt). A Dutch Orientalist and philosopher; born at Delft, April 23, 1834; died at Leyden, April 30, 1897. Among his works are: '(John, Bishop of Ephesus, the First Syrian Church Historian' (1856); '(Syriac Anecdotes' (4 vols., 1862); '(In Memory of Spinoza' (1877); '(Javanese Music' (1891); '(Arnold Geulinex and his Philosophy' (1895).

Lander, Richard and John. African explorers, natives of Cornwall. Richard was born 1804; died 1834. John was born 1807; died 1839. The elder brother accompanied Clapperton on his expedition to the Niger, and after Clapperton's death returned to England, where he published his own and his master's 'Journals.' He was then commissioned by the British government to determine the course of the lower Niger, and on that expedition was accompanied by his brother (1830-31). A detailed narrative of their explorations is given in their 'Journal of an Expedition to Explore the Course and Termination of the Niger' (3 vols., 1832).

Landesmann, Heinrich. See Lorm.

Landois, Hermann (länd-wä' or länt'ois). A German zoölogist; born at Münster, April 19, 1835. He is author of 'Sound and Voice Apparatus of Insects' (1867); 'Text-Book of Zoölogy' (1870); 'Text-Book of Botany' (1872); 'Voices of Animals' (1875); 'Text-Book of Instruction in the Description of Nature'; and other works of a like character, which have been frequently republished.

Landon, Charles Paul (län-dôn'). A French painter and art critic; born at Monant, 1760; died at Paris, March 5, 1826. His more notable writings are: 'Annals of the Musée and of the Modern School of Fine Arts' (29 vols., 1801-17); 'Landscapes and Genre Paintings in the Musée Napoléon' (4 vols., 1805-8); 'The Salons of 1808-24', (13 vols.); 'Selections of Paintings and Statues in the most Celebrated Foreign Museums and Cabinets' (12 vols., 1821 sq.).

Landon, Letitia Elizabeth (later **Mrs. Maclean**). An English poet and novelist; born in Chelsea, London, Aug. 14, 1802; died at Cape Coast Castle, Africa, Oct. 15, 1838. She was a poet of genuine feeling and descriptive power, was at one time connected with the London Literary Gazette, and published under the pseudonym of "L. E. L.": 'The Improvisatrice, and Other Poems' (1824); 'The Golden Violet, etc.,' all collected in 1841; and several novels. In June 1838, she married Mr. George Maclean, governor of Cape Coast Castle, and a few months later died from an accidental overdose of prussic acid, which she had been in the habit of taking for the alleviation of spasms. The theory of suicide is now generally discredited.

Landon, Melville De Lancey. ["Eli Perkins."] An American humorist; born in New York State in 1839. Among his works are: 'The Franco-Prussian War in a Nutshell' (1871); 'Saratoga in 1901' (1872); 'Eli Perkins's Wit, Humor, and Pathos' (1883); 'Fun and Fact'; 'Money'; 'Thirty Years of Wit.'

Landor, Walter Savage. A distinguished English poet and prose-writer; born at Ipsley Court, Warwickshire, Jan. 30, 1775; died at Florence, Sept. 17, 1864. He inherited a very large fortune; entered the military service of Spain 1808, with a body of troops maintained at his own expense; in 1815 he fixed his residence at Florence. His most celebrated work is 'Imaginary Conversations of Literary Men and Statesmen' (1st series, 3 vols., 1824-28; 2d series, 3 vols., 1829). Among his other works are: 'Poems' (1795); 'Gebir' (1798); 'Count Julian; a Tragedy' (1812); 'Heroic Idylls' (1814 and 1820), two volumes of Latin verse; 'Sati e upon Satirists and Admonition to Detractors' (1836), an attack upon Wordsworth; 'The Pentameron,' conversations of Petrarch and Boccaccio (1837); 'Andrea of Hungary and Giovanni of Naples' (1839); 'Fra Rupert, the Last Part of a Triology' (1840); 'The Hellenics' (1847); 'Italics,' verses (1848); 'Popery, British and Foreign' (1851); 'Letters of an American, mainly on Russia and Revolution' (1854); 'Letter to R. W. Emerson' (1856), on Emerson's 'English Traits'; 'Antony and Octavius: Scenes for the Study' (1856); 'Dry Sticks Fagoted by W. S. Landor' (1858); 'Savonarola and the Prior of St. Mark' (1860); 'Heroic Idylls, with Additional Poems' (1863).

Lane, Edward William. An English Orientalist, one of the most accomplished men of his time; born at Hereford, Sept. 17, 1801; died at Worthing, Aug. 10, 1876. He published 'Manners and Customs of the Modern Egyptians' (1836), and made one of the most famous translations of the 'Arabian Nights' (1838-40). This work was the first translation of consequence into English which was made directly from the Arabic, all previous translations having been made through the French. It contained valuable illustrations and numerous scholarly and indispensable notes. The translations of Burton and Payne were subsequent to it. The world is indebted to him for many valuable works on Egypt, and especially for his 'Arabic-English Lexicon' (1863-74), which cost him twenty years of unremitting labor. The succeeding parts came out from 1877 to 1882 under the editorship of S. Lane-Poole, the whole forming a dictionary indispensable to the student of Arabic. He also published 'Selections from the Ku-rân.'

Lane-Poole, Stanley. An English historical and archæological writer, nephew of Edward William Lane and editor of many of his works; born in London, Dec. 18, 1854. He is famed for his knowledge of the civilizations and peoples of antiquity and of the mediæval period. Among his works are: 'Arabian Society in the Middle Ages' (1883); 'Social Life in Egypt' (1883); 'The Moors in Spain' (1886); 'The Mogul Emperors' (1892); 'Mediæval India.'

Lanfrey, Pierre (loñ-frā'). A French historian; born at Chambéry, Savoy, Oct. 26, 1828; died at Pau, Nov. 15, 1877. He wrote 'The Church and the Philosophers of the 18th Century' (1855) and an 'Essay on the French Revolution' (1858); both works show profound research and impartial judgment. Besides a number of minor historical studies he wrote a 'History of Napoleon I.' (5 vols., 1867-75), which is his principal work: it is a severe criticism of Napoleon, based on all the accessible historic material. It only comes down to just before the Russian campaign, his death supervening.

Lang, Andrew. An English poet, story-teller, and literary critic; born at Selkirk, Scotland, March 31, 1844. He has written many volumes of verse, characterized by grace of style, harmony of numbers, and a lively, playful fancy. Among his poems are: 'Ballads and Lyrics of Old France' (1872), some of the pieces translated or adapted from the old French, others written new in the tone and spirit of the ancient singers; 'Ballads in Blue China' (1881); 'Helen of Troy' (1883). His 'Letters to Dead Authors' (1886) is worthy of a place on the same shelf with Lucian's 'Dialogues of the Dead' and Landor's 'Imaginary Conversations.' His 'Custom and Myth' (1884) and his 'Myth, Ritual, and Religion' (1887) belong to the popular literature of archæological and prehistoric research. Among his very numerous volumes are translations of Theocritus, Bion, and Moschus; and, in collaboration with Prof. Butcher and Messrs. Walter Leaf and Ernest Myers, a prose translation of the Iliad and Odyssey.

Lang, John Dunmore. A Scotch clergyman, Australian pioneer, and author; born at Greenock, Aug. 25, 1799; died in Sydney, N.S.W., Aug. 8, 1878. He emigrated to Australia in 1822, was ordained to the Scots Church, in Sydney (1823), and contributed much to the advancement of the colony by his advocacy of immigration, the introduction of a school system, and other public measures. He was a prolific writer, among his important works being: 'A History of New South Wales' (1834); 'Origin and Migration of the Polynesian Natives' (1834); 'New Zealand in 1839'; 'Cook's Land, Australia' (1847); numerous pamphlets;

and a series of poems, 'Aurora Australis' (1826).

Lang, Karl Heinrich Ritter von (läng). A German historian; born at Balgheim, July 7, 1764; died near Ansbach, March 26, 1835. His principal works are: 'Historic Development of the German Tax System' (1793); 'Modern History of the Principality of Bayreuth' (3 vols., 1798-1811); 'History of the Jesuits in Bavaria' (1819). His posthumous 'Memoirs of the Ritter von Lang' (2 vols., 1841) made a great noise when first published; but they are to be used with discretion.

Lang, Wilhelm. A German journalist and essayist; born at Tuttlingen, July 16, 1832. Among his works are: 'Michelangelo Buonarotti as a Poet' (1861); 'David Friedrich Strauss' (1874); 'Wanderings in Peloponnesus' (1878); 'From Suabia: History, Biography, Literature' (in 7 parts, 1885-90), a collection of delightful essays.

Langbein, August Friedrich Ernst (läng'-bïn). A German humoristic poet; born near Dresden, Sept. 6, 1757; died Jan. 2, 1835, at Berlin. His 'Poems' (1788); 'Drolleries' (1792); and 'Later Poems' (1812, 1823), circulated everywhere: they were inspired by the Muse of broad comedy, and at times showed little regard for the proprieties. He wrote also several humorous stories which were received with great popular favor, among them 'Master Zimpfel's Wedding Tour' and 'Thomas Kellerwurm.'

Lange, Friedrich Albert (läng'ě). A German philosopher and political economist; born near Solingen, Sept. 28, 1828; died at Marburg, Nov. 21, 1875. He wrote a valuable 'History of Materialism and Critique of its Importance for the Present Time' (1866; supplementary volume, 1867). His principal writings on political economy are: 'The Labor Question Now and in the Future' (1865; 5th ed. 1894); 'J. S. Mill's Views of the Social Question' (1866).

Lange, Julius Henrik. A Danish art critic; born at Vordingborg, June 19, 1838; died at Copenhagen, Aug. 20, 1896. After leaving the University of Copenhagen he thereafter devoted himself to study of the history of art. Among his works are: 'On Art Values' (1876); 'Danish and Foreign Art' (1879); 'Gods and Men in Homer' (1881); 'Art and Politics' (1885); 'Thorwaldsen's Representation of the Human Figure' (1893).

Lange, Samuel Gotthold. A German poet; born at Halle, 1711; died at Laublingen, June 25, 1781. He wrote a series of 'Horatian Odes' (1747) in praise of Frederick the Great, and a metrical translation of 'The Odes of Horace' (1752), which found a severe critic in Lessing; and published a 'Collection of Letters from Scholars and Friends' (2 vols., 1769-70) which is of considerable value for the literary history of the time.

Langendijk, Pieter (läng'en-dĭk). A Dutch poet and playwright; born at Haarlem, July 25, 1683; died in 1756. Left to the care of an extravagant mother by the early death of his father, he was obliged to abandon his

course of education, and support himself as a
designer in a damask factory. His comedies,
which are the redeeming features of a barren
period of Dutch literature, include: 'Don
Quixote' (1711); 'The Braggart'; 'The Mutual
Marriage Deception'; 'Xantippe'; 'Papirius';
'A Mirror of Our Merchants,' the last three
being comedies of manners.

Langford, John Alfred. An English mis-
cellaneous writer; born in Birmingham, Sept.
12, 1823. He was a prominent educator and pub-
licist in his native city. Among his works are:
'Religious Skepticism and Infidelity' (1850);
'English Democracy' (1855); 'Poems of the
Fields and Town' (1859); and 'Heroes and
Martyrs, and Other Poems' (1890).

Langland, William. An English poet; born
in Shropshire (?), about 1330; died about 1400.
His 'Vision of Piers Plowman' (1362?) is the
poem by which he is known.

Lanier, Sidney. An American poet; born
at Macon, Ga., Feb. 3, 1842; died at Lynn,
N. C., Sept. 7, 1881. He served in the Confederate Army as a private soldier; after the
war studied law, and for a while practiced it
at Macon; but abandoned that profession and
devoted himself to music and poetry. From
1879 till his death he was lecturer on English
literature in Johns Hopkins University. The
poem 'Corn,' one of his earliest pieces (1874),
and 'Clover,' 'The Bee,' 'The Dove,' etc.,
show insight into nature. His poetic works
were collected and published (1884) after his
death. He wrote also several works in prose,
mostly pertaining to literary criticism and to
mediæval history: among the former are 'The
Science of English Verse' (1880); 'The English Novel and the Principles of its Development' (1883). He edited or compiled 'The
Boy's Froissart' (1878); 'The Boy's King Arthur' (1880); 'The Boy's Percy' (1882).

Lanigan, George Thomas. An American
journalist and poet; born in Canada, Dec. 10,
1845; died in Philadelphia, Feb. 5, 1886. In
Montreal, with Robert Graham, he founded
the Free Lance, a journal of satire and humor;
now published under the name Evening Star.
In the United States he was connected with
various journals. His writings include: 'Canadian Ballads' (1864); 'Fables Out of the World'
(1878), by "George Washington Æsop." 'The
Amateur Orlando' and 'A Threnody' (for the
Ahkoond of Swat) are among his most successful humorous poems.

Lankester, Edwin Ray. An English scientist; born in London, May 15, 1847. A graduate of Christ Church, Oxford, he is Linacre
professor of human and comparative anatomy
at that university, and curator of the museum;
and is among the first of living authorities in
biology and physiology. He has been active
and effective in his field of science since 1865;
was made professor of zoölogy in London
University in 1874; he is LL. D. and F. R. S.;
and has published over a hundred scientific
memoirs. He has served as secretary of the

British Association, and president of its biological section; was founder and president of the
Marine Biological University at Plymouth. He
is editor of the Quarterly Journal of Microscopical Science, and a frequent contributor
to Nature and other periodicals. Among his
books are: 'On Fossil Fishes of the Red Sandstone of Great Britain' (1870); 'Comparative
Longevity' (1871); 'On Earth-Worms'; 'Degeneration, a Chapter in Darwinism' (1880);
'The Advancement of Science' (1890); 'Zoölogical Papers,' a collection of his articles in the 'Encyclopædia Britannica' (1891); 'Okapia' (1902).

Lanman, Charles. An American prose-
writer and journalist; born in Monroe, Mich.,
June 14, 1819; died in Washington, D. C.,
March 4, 1895. In 1847 he was connected with
the New York Express; in 1850 was private
secretary of Daniel Webster; and 1871–82 secretary to the Japanese legation. He has written for English and American journals; for
his description of scenery of the Saguenay, and
the mountains of North Carolina, he was called
by Washington Irving "the picturesque explorer of the United States." Among his numerous publications are: 'A Tour to the River
Saguenay' (1848); 'Private Life of Daniel Webster' (1852); 'The Japanese in America' (New
York and London: 1872); 'Curious Characters
and Pleasant Places' (Edinburgh: 1881); 'Hap-
hazard Personalities' (Boston: 1886).

Lanman, Charles Rockwell. An eminent
American Sanskrit scholar; born at Norwich,
Conn., July 8, 1850. He studied Sanskrit under
Prof. Whitney at Yale College, afterwards continuing his work at Berlin, Tübingen, and
Leipsic. Upon his return to the United States
he was appointed to an instructorship at Johns
Hopkins University, Baltimore, and in 1880
became professor of Sanskrit at Harvard University, a post which he still retains. An authority on Oriental languages and literature,
he has published: 'A Sanskrit Reader' (1884),
the chief text-book on the subject; and is the
projector of the 'Harvard Oriental Series.'

La Noue, François de, called **Bras de Fer.**
See **Noue.**

Lansdell, Henry. An English clergyman,
traveler, and author; born at Tenterden, Kent,
in 1841. As secretary to the Irish Church Mission, he has been prominent in philanthropic
movements, traveling extensively about the
world. In Siberia he investigated the prisons,
publishing the results of his observations in
'Through Siberia' (1882); 'Russian Central
Asia' (1885). 'Chinese Central Asia' appeared in 1893.

Lanza, Marchioness Clara (Hammond).
An American novelist; born in Kansas in 1858.
She is a resident of New York city. Among
her works are: 'Tit for Tat' (1880); 'Mr. Perkins's Daughter' (1881); 'A Righteous Apostate'
(1883); 'A Modern Marriage'; 'Horace Everett.'

Lanzi, Luigi (länts'ē). An Italian antiquarian; born at Monte dell' Ormo, 1732; died at

Florence, March 31, 1810. Chief among his works are an 'Essay on the Etruscan Language' (3 vols., 1789) and 'Pictorial History of Italy' (1789). He wrote also 'Notices on the Sculpture of the Ancients' (1789).

Lao-tsze (lä'ō-tsä'). A Chinese philosopher of the sixth century B. C. His 'Taoteh-King,' or 'Doctrine of Reason and Virtue,' has been translated into English, French, and German. He rates as being high above our obligations to country, society, and family those which are founded in our common humanity; and teaches that we ought to repay injuries with benefits. See 'Literature of China.'

Laplace, Pierre Simon, Marquis de (lä-pläs'). A renowned French mathematician and physical astronomer; born at Beaumont-en-Auge, March 28, 1749; died at Paris, March 5, 1827. In his great work 'Mechanism of the Heavens' (5 vols., 1799-1825), he attacks nearly every problem arising out of the movements of the heavenly bodies, and in great part offers the solution. His 'Exposition of the System of the Universe' (2 vols., 1796), may be regarded as a less abstruse presentation of the arguments advanced in the 'Mechanism'; in the former he hits on the same hypothesis to account for the origin of the planets which had been a little before offered by Kant. His famous researches into the laws of probability are summed up in the two works, 'Analytic Theory of Probabilities' (1812), and 'Philosophical Essay on Probabilities' (1814).

Lappenberg, Johann Martin (läp'en-berG). A German historical writer; born at Hamburg, July 30, 1794; died Nov. 28, 1865. His task was research into the sources of history rather than historical narrative; as material for the authentic writing of sundry phases of German history his works are of very great and permanent value. Among them are: 'Rise of the Civic Constitution of Hamburg' (1828); 'Early Hamburg Archives' (1842); 'Documentary History of the Hanse Steelyard in London' (1851); 'Hamburg Chronicles' (1852-61).

Laprade, Victor de (lä-präd'). A French poet; born at Montbrison, Jan. 13, 1812; died at Lyons, Dec. 13, 1883. His earliest poems, as 'Magdalen's Precious Ointment' (1839), 'Jesus's Wrath' (1840), showed very plainly the influence of Lamartine; and to the end Lamartine was his model. Besides several volumes of lyric poems,—'Psyche' (1841); 'Odes and Poems' (1844); 'Evangelic Poems' (1852); 'Heroic Idylls' (1858),—he wrote the tragedy 'Harmodius' (1870), and several works in prose; e. g., 'Questions of Art and Morals' (1861); 'Liberal Education' (1873); 'Essays in Idealist Criticism' (1882).

La Ramée, Louise de. See **Ouida.**

Larcom, Lucy. An American poet; born in Beverly, Mass., 1826; died in Boston, 1893. Through her early contributions to the Lowell Offering, she attracted the attention of Whittier, who assisted her in literary work, and was a faithful friend to the close of his life. She edited Our Young Folks, a Boston magazine, from 1866 to its absorption by St. Nicholas in 1874. Her published works include: 'Poems' (1868); 'An Idyl of Work, a Story in Verse' (1875); 'As It Is in Heaven' (1891); and 'The Unseen Friend' (1892).

Lardner, Dionysius. An Irish physicist; born in Dublin, April 3, 1793; died at Naples, April 29, 1859. He wrote several notable mathematical treatises; and edited, himself being one of the chief contributors, an 'Encyclopedia' (132 vols., 1829-46). Among his other writings are: 'Manual of Electricity,' etc. (2 vols., 1841); 'Treatise on Heat' (1844); 'The Steam Engine' (1852); 'Natural Philosophy and Astronomy' (3 vols., 1851-52)

Larivey, Pierre (lä-rē-vä'). A French dramatist (1540-1611). His prose comedies, founded on Italian originals, are full of life and spirit, and had an influence on Molière. Larivey's best comedy, 'Les Esprits,' is an adaptation of Lorenzo de' Medici's 'Aridosio.'

La Roche, Maria Sophie (lä-rōsh'). A German story-teller; born at Kaufbeuren, Dec. 6, 1731; died at Offenbach, Feb. 18, 1807. Her stories show intimate knowledge of the human heart. She was a correspondent of Wieland and of Goethe. She wrote: 'The History of Fräulein von Sternheim' (1771); 'Moral Tales' (1782); 'History of Miss Long' (1789); 'Melusine's Summer Evenings' (1806).

La Rochefoucauld, François, Duc de. See **Rochefoucauld.**

Larousse, Pierre (lä-rös'). A French lexicographer; born at Toucy, Oct. 23, 1817; died Jan. 3, 1875. For several years he compiled valuable educational text-books. In 1864 appeared the first volume of his 'Great Universal Dictionary of the Nineteenth Century' (completed 1876, 15 vols., with supplementary volumes 1878 and 1887). He also published two smaller works of the same class, the 'New Illustrated Dictionary,' and 'Complete Illustrated Dictionary.'

Larra, Mariano José de (lär'ä). A Spanish playwright and journalist; born at Madrid, 1809, committed suicide Feb. 13, 1837. He adapted to the Spanish stage several French comedies, and wrote a tragedy, 'Macias' (1834), on the tragic ending of a famous Galician troubadour. Five volumes of his contributions to the Revista Española were published in 1837; his principal work is 'From 1830 to 1835, or Spain from Fernando VII. to Mendizabal' (1836).

Larrazabal, Felipe (lär-rä-thä'bäl). A Venezuelan biographer and historian; born about 1822; drowned 1873. He wrote a valuable 'Life of the Liberator Simon Bolivar' (2 vols., 1863), collected a large amount of manuscript material on the history of America, and was on his way to Europe to arrange for the publication of several of his works when he was drowned in the wreck of the steamship City of Havre.

La Salle, Antoine de (lä-säl'). A French mediæval romancer (1398–1470). Among his works may be mentioned the 'Chronicle of Little John of Saintré,' a historical romance exemplifying the ideal knightly education of the time. His 'Fifteen Joys of Wedlock' is a witty satire on marriage. He wrote also 'A Hundred New Novels,' stories purporting to be recounted by personages attached to the court of his patron, Philip the Good, of Flanders.

Las Casas. See **Casas.**

Las Cases, Emmanuel Augustin Dieudonné, Marquis de (läs-käz). A French writer; born near Revel, 1766; died May 15, 1842. He was one of the emigrant nobles of 1791, but returned to France in 1799, and set up in Paris as a bookseller. Under the pseudonym « Le Sage » he compiled an 'Atlas, Historical, Geographical, Chronological, and Genealogical' (1803–4) which gained him high office from Napoleon. He accompanied the latter to St. Helena, and began to take down his 'Memoirs' from dictation; but before they were completed, Las Cases's secret correspondence with Napoleon's friends outside was discovered, and he had to quit his master's service. The remainder of the 'Memoirs' is contained in O'Meara's 'Napoleon in Exile.' After Napoleon's death, Las Cases published 'Memorial of St. Helena' (8 vols., 1821–23).

Laskaratos, Andreas (läs-kär'ä-tōs). A modern Greek poet; born in Kephalenia, May 1, 1811. His most notable work is the satire 'The Mysteries of Cephalonia' (1856), which gave great offense to the clergy, and provoked a long and bitter controversy. In defense the poet wrote a 'Reply to the Decision of the Clergy of Cephalonia' (1867), and 'Behold the Man' (1886). He wrote in Italian an account of his sufferings in prison, 'My Sufferings.'

Lasker, Eduard (läs'ker). A German political leader; born at Jarotschin in Posen, Oct. 14, 1829; died at New York, Jan. 5, 1884. His principal works are: 'Constitutional History of Prussia' (1874); 'Future of the German Empire' (1877), 'Ways and Means of Cultural Development' (1881).

Lassalle, Ferdinand (lä-säl'). A German agitator, founder of the German Social Democracy; born of Jewish parents named Lassal, at Breslau, April 11, 1825; died Aug. 31, 1864. Before entering politics he had earned high distinction in philosophical thought, which had brought him to the notice of Humboldt, Böckh, and others. Among his writings of this period are 'Franz von Sickingen,' a historical drama (1859); 'The Philosophy of Heraclitus the Obscure' (2 vols., 1858); 'The System of Acquired Rights' (2 vols., 1860); 'Fichte's Philosophy and the Popular Mind of Germany' (1862). He first came into the political arena as the spokesman of the German workingman in 1862, when he published the 'Workingmen's Programme.' For this he was arrested and imprisoned. Other pamphlets followed: 'Science

and the Workingmen' (1863); 'The Criminal Trial of Lassalle' (1863); 'Indirect Taxation and the Condition of the Laboring Classes' (1863). He further developed the Socialist programme in an 'Open Reply to the Central Committee' (1863). His last work was a spirited attack on one of the foremost opponents of the Social Democracy, 'Herr Bastiat-Schulze von Delitzsch, the Julian of Economics; or Capital and Labor' (1864). His talents won him the admiration even of his enemies.

Lassen, Christian (läs'sen). An eminent German Orientalist; born at Bergen, Norway, Oct. 22, 1800; died at Bonn, May 8, 1876. He has been since 1827 first tutor and then professor of ancient Indian languages and literature at the University of Bonn, where he learned Sanskrit and Arabic; he spent three years in Paris and London. His editions of ancient texts in the languages of India, with translations and commentaries, give ample proof of his accurate and comprehensive scholarship. His greatest work is 'The Science of Indian Antiquity' (4 vols., 1844–61; 2d ed. enlarged, 1867 and 1874); in this he co-ordinates the total results of antiquarian research in India.

Lasson, Adolf (läs-son). A German writer on philosophy; born at Altstrelitz, March 12, 1832. He is author of 'J. H. Fichte in his Relation to Church and State' (1863); 'Civilization and War' (1868); 'Master Eckhart the Mystic' (1878); 'Philosophy of Law' (1881).

Latham, Robert Gordon. A distinguished English ethnologist and philologist; born at Billingborough, 1812; died at Putney, March 9, 1888. He is author of numerous works on the English tongue, among them a 'Treatise on the English Language' (1841; frequently republished); 'History and Etymology of the English Language' (1849); 'Handbook of the English Language' (1851); 'Elements of Comparative Philology' (1862). His principal works on ethnology are: 'Natural History of the Varieties of Man' (1850); 'Man and his Migrations' (1851); 'Ethnology of the British Islands' (1852); 'Ethnology of Europe' (1852); 'Descriptive Ethnology' (2 vols., 1859); 'Russian and Turk' (1878); 'Outlines of General Philology.'

Lathrop, George Parsons. An American poet and prose-writer; born in the Hawaiian Islands, Aug. 25, 1851; died in New York city, April 19, 1898. He was for some years employed editorially on the Atlantic Monthly and the Boston Courier. He wrote: 'Rose and Roof-Tree,' verses (1875); 'A Study of Hawthorne' (1876); 'Afterglow' (1876); 'An Echo of Passion' (1882); 'Spanish Vistas' (1883); 'Gettysburg, a Battle Ode' (1888); 'Would You Kill Him?' (1889); 'Dreams and Days,' verses (1892); 'Gold of Pleasure' (1892), a novel; 'Story of Courage,' with Rose Hawthorne.

Lathrop, Mrs. Rose (H a w t h o r n e). An American poet, daughter of Nathaniel Hawthorne; born in Lenox, Mass., May 20, 1851. She passed her childhood in Europe. In 1871 she married George Parsons Lathrop. She has been prominent in literary circles, has written for the periodicals, and has published 'Along the Shore' (1888) and 'Some Memories of Hawthorne.'

Latimer, Hugh. An English bishop and sermonist; born at Thurcaston, Leicestershire, 1485 (?); died at the stake, Oct. 16, 1555. His 'Sermons' are famous.

Latour, Antoino Tenant de (lä-tör'). A French writer; born at St. Yriein, 1808; died at Sceaux, Aug. 27, 1881. He wrote an 'Essay on the Study of French History in the Nineteenth Century' (1835); a noteworthy study of Luther (1835); an 'Account of a Voyage to the East' (1847); and a series of studies of Spain, the land and the people: the series comprises ten volumes, devoted to separate towns and provinces, as, 'Seville and Andalusia'; 'Toledo and the Banks of the Tagus'; or to general views, as 'Spain, Religious and Literary'; 'Spain: Traditions, Manners, and Literature.'

Latreille, Pierre André (lä-trä'ē). A French zoölogist; born at Brives, Nov. 29, 1762; died at Paris, Feb. 6, 1833. He has contributed materially to the classification of the animal kingdom, as in a 'History of the Salamanders' (1800); 'Natural History of Reptilia' (4 vols., 1802); 'Genera of Crustacea and Insecta'; 'Course in Entomology' (2 vols., 1831–33).

Laube, Heinrich (loub'ě). A German dramatist and novelist; born at Sprottau, Sept. 18, 1806; died at Vienna, Aug. 1, 1884. He was director of theatres in several cities of Germany and Austria between 1849 and 1880. Among his dramatic works are: 'Gustavus Adolphus' (1829); 'Zaganini,' a farce (1829); the tragedy 'Monaldeschi' (1839); 'The Amber Witch' (1842); 'Struensee,' a tragedy (1847); 'The Schoolboys' (1847), a very clever dramatization of an incident in the life of Schiller; 'Lord Essex' (1856), his finest tragedy. Among his stories and works of fiction are: 'Young Europe' (1833); 'Love-Letters'; 'The Actress' (1836); 'The Pretender' (1842); 'Countess Châteaubriand' (1843); 'The Belgian Count' (1845); 'The German War' (9 vols., 1865); 'Life History of Franz Grillparzer' (1884); 'Ruben' (1885).

Laud, William, Archbishop of Canterbury. An English theologian; born at Reading, Oct. 7, 1573; died at London, Jan. 10, 1645. He was an uncompromising upholder of High-Church principles, and exerted all the powers of his high office for the repression of Puritanism. He was brought to trial in the House of Lords on the charge of high treason, Nov. 13, 1643, and was beheaded Jan. 10 following. His writings are but few; his 'Diary' (1695), and his letters, are of value for the history of his time.

Laughlin, James Lawrence. An eminent American political economist; born in Deerfield, O., April 2, 1850. In 1892 he became a professor in Chicago University. His chief

works are: 'The Study of Political Economy' (1885); 'The History of Bimetallism in the United States' (1885); 'The Elements of Political Economy' (1887); 'Industrial America' (1906).

Lauremberg, Johann Wilhelm (lou'remberG). A Low-German satirist; born at Rostock, Feb. 26, 1590; died at Lorö, Feb. 28, 1658. In 'Four Famous Old Comic Poems' (1652), written in the Low-German dialect, he ridicules the fashion of the time in costume, manners, speech, etc. He wrote also some Latin poems; and a few dramatic pieces of little value in High German, with interludes in Low-German.

Laurent, François (lō-roñ'). A Belgian jurist and historical writer; born at Luxemburg, July 8, 1810; died at Ghent, Feb. 11, 1887. His works on law, municipal and international, are written with great breadth of view. He wrote several works in defense of Liberal principles against the Clericals, among them one 'On the Passion of Catholics for Liberty' (1850); and 'Letters on the Jesuits' (1865).

Laurentie, Pierre Sébastien (lō-roñ-tē'). A French journalist and historian; born at Houga, Gers, Jan. 21, 1793; died at Paris, Feb. 9, 1876. An ardent advocate of the royalist cause, he held several important offices until the revolution of 1830, after which he joined the Legitimist journal La Quotidienne, with which he had previously been connected. His extreme royalist sentiments detract from the value of most of his works, among which are: 'History of the Dukes of Orléans' (4 vols., 1832–34); 'History of France' (8 vols., 1841–43); 'Rome and the Pope' (1860); 'History of the Roman Empire' (4 vols., 1861–62), 'The Pope and the Czar' (1862); and numerous brochures, etc.

Lauser, Wilhelm (lou'ser). A German publicist; born at Stuttgart, June 15, 1836. He spent several years in France and Spain, and in foreign travel, and wrote: 'Contemporary Spain' (1872); 'History of Spain from the Fall of Isabella to the Accession of Alfonso XII.' (1877); 'In all Directions: Stories of my Travels' (1889); 'The First Picaresque Romance: Lazarillo de Tormes' (1889). He died Nov. 11, 1902.

Lavater, Johann Kaspar (läv'ä-ter). A Swiss physiognomist and theological writer; born at Zürich, Nov. 15, 1741; died there, Jan. 2, 1801. He was pastor of a church in his native town, and his semi-mystical religious writings won him great fame throughout Germany. In his 'Christian Songs' (first 100, 1776; second 100, 1780), he seeks to counteract the principles of Illuminism and Rationalism; and he has the same aim in the drama 'Abraham and Isaac' (1776), in the epics 'Jesus the Messiah, or the Coming of the Lord' (1780), 'Joseph of Arimathea' (1794), etc. His views of the inner life of the soul find expression in his 'Private Diary of a Self-Observer' (1772–73). But his most celebrated work is 'Physiognomic Fragments' (1775–78), which was received with extraordinary favor by the leading minds of Germany, among them Goethe, Stolberg, Jakobi,

Lavedan, Henri (läv-doń'). A French journalist, critic, novelist, and playwright; born at Orléans, in 1860. He contributed under the pseudonym of «Manchecourt» a series of brilliant articles to Vie Parisienne, Gil Blas, etc., and in the department of fiction has produced: ʻMam'zelle Virtueʼ (1885); ʻQueen Janvierʼ (1886); ʻLydieʼ (1887); ʻInconsolableʼ (1888); ʻHigh Lifeʼ (1891); ʻA New Gameʼ (1892). Of his plays the most notable are: ʻA Family,ʼ a comedy produced at the Comédie Française (1890), and awarded a prize of 4,000 francs by the French Academy; and ʻPrince d'Aurecʼ (acted in 1892).

Laveleye, Émile Louis Victor de (läv-lä'). A Belgian economist; born at Bruges, April 5, 1822; died at Doyon, near Liège, Jan. 3, 1892. Among his numerous writings are: ʻHistory of the Provençal Language and Literatureʼ (1846); ʻThe Question of Goldʼ (1860); ʻProperty and its Principal Formsʼ (1874); ʻContemporary Socialismʼ (1881); ʻElements of Political Economyʼ (1882); ʻMoney and International Bimetallismʼ (1891); ʻGovernment in Democraciesʼ (1891); ʻEssays and Etudesʼ (1894-95).

La Vigne, Andrieu de (lä-vēn'). A French poet (1457-1527). He accompanied Charles VIII. to Naples, and told the story of the march in verse. He also wrote a ʻMystery-Play of Saint Martin,ʼ and several minor poems; among them a sonnet in the Lombard dialect, the first sonnet written by a Frenchman.

La Villemarqué, Théodore Hersart, Vicomte de. See **Villemarqué**.

Lavisse, Ernest (lä-vēs'). A French historian; born at Nouvion-en-Thiérache, Dec. 17, 1842. His historical researches have chiefly to do with Prussia and the German Empire, as in ʻThe Mark of Brandenburg under the Ascanian Dynastyʼ (1875); ʻStudies of the History of Prussiaʼ (1879); ʻFrederick the Great before his Accessionʼ (1893); ʻThree Emperors of Germany: William I., Frederick III., William II.ʼ (1888); ʻOutlines of Europe's Political History.ʼ

Lavoisier, Antoine Laurent (lä-vwä-zyä'). A celebrated French chemist, one of the founders of modern chemistry; born at Paris, Aug. 16, 1743; died there, May 8, 1794. Starting from the discoveries which the phlogistonists had added to the work of the much-libeled alchemists, he demonstrated experimentally the acidifying action of «dephlogisticated air,» or as he renamed it, «oxygen gas.» He was the first to analyze water, and to obtain by synthesis «fixed air,» or as he called it, «carbonic acid.» He first gave system to chemistry; and not least of his services to science was his part in devising — with Guyton de Morveau — a consistent scheme of chemical nomenclature. Besides papers contributed to the proceedings of learned societies, he wrote an ʻElementary Treatise on Chemistryʼ (1789). He was a farmer-general of taxes, and was guillotined for it in the Terror.

Lawless, Emily, Hon. An Irish novelist, daughter of the third Baron Cloncurry; born in 1845. She is the author of several popular romances of Irish life, full of pathos and picturesqueness, among which may be noticed: ʻA Millionaire's Cousinʼ (1885); ʻHurrishʼ (1886), a study; ʻGraniaʼ (1892), her most powerful work; ʻMaelchoʼ (1894), a story of the rebellion of Sir James Fitzmaurice in the 16th century. She is also author of ʻIrelandʼ (1887) in the ʻStory of the Nationsʼ series.

Lawton, William Cranston. An American classical teacher and writer; born at New Bedford, Mass., May 22, 1853. He graduated at Harvard in 1873; studied in Europe from 1880 to 1883; was a classical teacher in New Bedford and Boston for several years; was professor at Bryn Mawr; and is now in Adelphi College, Brooklyn. Besides contributions to the periodicals, he has published: ʻThree Dramas of Euripidesʼ (1889); ʻFolia Dispersa,ʼ a volume of verse; ʻArt and Humanity in Homer.ʼ

Layamon or **Lawemon.** The name of the author of a chronicle of Britain. This chronicle is described as «a poetical semi-Saxon paraphrase,» and it is entitled ʻBrut.ʼ Layamon seems to have modeled his work upon the ʻRoman de Brutʼ of Wace, for there are marked resemblances and not many differences between the two. Nothing is known of the personal history of Layamon, but his ʻBrutʼ is supposed to have been completed about the beginning of the thirteenth century. See the volume ʻNoted Booksʼ in the ʻLibrary.ʼ

Layard, Sir Austen Henry. An English traveler; born at Paris, March 5, 1817; died July 5, 1894. He first became interested in archæological research in 1840, while traveling in Asiatic Turkey, on discovering at Nimrud, a village near the junction of the Tigris with the Zab, the ruins of an ancient city: this was the site of Nineveh. He made excavations on the site, and soon uncovered remains of several palatial edifices. The results of his explorations he published in ʻNineveh and its Remainsʼ (2 vols., 1848), and ʻNineveh and Babylonʼ (1853). He wrote also ʻEarly Adventures in Persia, Susiana, and Babyloniaʼ (2 vols., 1887).

Lazarus, Emma (laz'a-rus). A Hebrew-American poet; born in New York city, July 22, 1849; died there, Nov. 19, 1887. She labored diligently in behalf of her race and devoted her pen largely to Hebrew subjects, publishing a much-discussed article in the Century on ʻRussian Christianity versus Modern Judaism.ʼ Her first volume was composed of ʻPoems and Translationsʼ (1866), written between the ages of fourteen and seventeen. This was followed by ʻAdmetusʼ (1871); ʻAlide; an Episode of Goethe's Lifeʼ (1874); ʻSongs of a Semiteʼ (1882), all of which are marked by naturalness of sentiment, vivid effect, and artistic reserve of expression.

Lazarus, Moritz (lät'sä-rös). A German philosophical writer; born at Filehne (Posen),

Sept. 15, 1824. Among his writings are: 'The Soul's Life in Monographs' (1856); 'Origin of Customs'; 'Ideal Questions' (1878); 'The Allurements of Gaming' (1883); 'The Prophet Jeremiah' (1894). With Steinthal he founded (1859) the Journal of Ethnopsychology and Philology, since 1890 known as the Journal of the Ethnological Society. Died April 13, 1903.

Lea, Henry Charles. An American publisher and historian; born in Philadelphia, Sept. 19, 1825. He entered his father's publishing house in 1843; became the principal in 1865; and retired from business in 1880. Between 1840 and 1860 he wrote many papers on chemistry and conchology. Since 1857 he has devoted his attention to European mediæval history, his chief works being: 'Superstition and Force' (1866); 'An Historical Sketch of Sacerdotal Celibacy' (1867); 'History of the Inquisition of the Middle Ages' (1888); 'History of the Inquisition of Spain' (1906-07).

Leaf, Walter. An English banker, scholar, and translator; born in 1852. After a brilliant career at Cambridge University, where he was Senior Classic, Chancellor's Medalist, and Fellow of Trinity, he entered mercantile life in 1877, retiring in 1892. In addition to his duties as vice-president of the Chamber of Commerce and director of charitable and educational organizations, he is editor of the Journal of Hellenic Studies, and has published: 'The Story of Achilles' (1880), with J. H. Pratt; 'The Iliad of Homer Translated into English Prose' (1882), with A. Lang and E. Myers; 'The Iliad' (1886-88); 'Companion to the Iliad' (1892); 'A Modern Priestess of Isis' (1894), from the Russian; 'Versions from Hafiz.'

Leake, William Martin. An English antiquarian and classical topographer; born at London, Jan. 14, 1777; died at Brighton, Jan. 6, 1860. An officer in the West-Indian service (1794-98), and artillery instructor at Constantinople in early life, he later traveled in the East, and was engaged in surveys and diplomatic business for the British government in Greece (1805-9). Among his publications are: 'Researches in Greece' (1814); 'Topography of Athens' (2d cd. 1841), a learned and still valuable work; 'Historical Outline of the Greek Revolution' (1826); 'Travels in Northern Greece' (4 vols., 1835); 'Peloponnesia' (1846).

Lear, Edward. An English writer and draughtsman of nonsense verses and pictures; born at London, May 12, 1812; died at San Remo, 1888. In early life he was a designer, drawing birds and animals in the way of illustration; his later years were passed in Southern Italy. He wrote a 'Book of Nonsense' (1846); and thereafter 'Nonsense Songs and Stories'; 'Nonsense Songs, Pictures, etc.'; 'Laughable Lyrics'; 'Nonsense Botany'; 'Nonsense Alphabets.' He wrote also: 'Journal of a Landscape Painter in Greece and Albania' (1851); 'Journal of a Landscape Painter in Southern Calabria' (1852); 'Journal of a Landscape Painter in Corsica' (1870).

Learned, Walter. An American poet and translator; born in New London, Conn., June 22, 1847. He is a resident of New London. Besides contributions to current literature, he has written 'Between Times' (1889), a volume of poems; and translated 'Ten Tales' and 'The Rivals' from Coppée.

Lebîd ibn Rabî'a (leb'ed ibn rab'yä). A celebrated Arabian poet (about 575-662). He was at first an opponent of Mohammed, afterward an adherent. His 'Mu'allakat' has been published both in the original language and in French translation by M. de Sacy (1816); and his 'Divan' in the original Arabic, and in German translation by Huber (1887-91).

Lebrun, Pierre Antoine (lē-bruń'). A French poet; born at Paris, Nov. 29, 1785; died there, May 27, 1873. For his 'Ode to the Grand Army' (1805), Napoleon conferred on him a pension of 6000 francs a year; and his 'Ode on the Campaign of 1807' won for him the place of chief collector of indirect taxes. He was elected to the Academy on the publication of his 'Travels in Greece' (1828). He wrote several mediocre tragedies; his 'Mary Stuart' (1820), which still holds a place in the French theatrical repertoire, is half imitation, half translation, of Schiller's play.

Lebrun, Ponce Denis Écouchard, surnamed **Lebrun-Pindare.** A French poet; born at Paris, Aug. 11, 1729; died there, Sept. 2, 1807. His title "Pindar" is due to the form and the mythological allusions of his odes, not to any large poetical merit, either in them or the lyrics; and as a satirist, he alternately groveled before and libeled the same men. His best odes are addressed to Buffon. He excelled in the composition of madrigals and epigrams; the latter relate for the most part to his quarrels with other authors.

Le Chevalier, Jean Baptiste (lē-shev-ä-lyā'). A French archæologist; born at Trelly, July 1, 1752; died at Paris, July 2, 1836. Before the Revolution he made an archæological exploration of the Troad, and published (1794) 'A Visit to the Troad, or the Plain of Troy as It Now Is.' He wrote also 'The Propontis and the Euxine' (2 vols., 1800).

Lecky, William Edward Hartpole. An English historian; born in Dublin, Ireland, March 26, 1838. His first work, 'The Leaders of Public Opinion in Ireland' (1861), is a study, from a Liberal and Union standpoint, of Swift, Flood, Grattan, and O'Connell. His next work was a 'History of the Rise and Influence of the Spirit of Rationalism in Europe' (2 vols., 1865); a semi-controversial essay to prove that the advance of the masses in religious common-sense has been due to the general progress of civilization and not to the arguments of enlightened leaders. Then followed 'A History of European Morals from Augustus to Charlemagne' (2 vols., 1869); 'A History of England in the 18th Century' (8 vols., 1878-90); 'A History of Ireland in the 18th Century' (5 vols., 1892), enlarged from the chapters on this subject in the English History; 'Democracy and Liberty' (1896). Died at Dublin, Oct. 23, 1903.

Leclercq, Michel Théodore (lè-klerk'). A French dramatic poet; born at Paris, April 1, 1777; died there, Feb. 15, 1851. He wrote after the manner of Carmontel a series of 'Dramatic Proverbs,' little pieces for the drawing-room, which, by their pointed, witty dialogue, their fine character-drawing, and their elegant style, won universal favor. The latest edition was in six volumes (1828), and comprised about 80 pieces.

Leconte de Lisle, Charles Marie René (lè-kôṅt' dĕ lēl'). A French poet; born in the Isle of Bourbon (Réunion), Oct. 23, 1818; died at Louveciennes, near Paris, July 17, 1894. Settling in Paris (1846), he was at first an enthusiastic socialist and disciple of Fourier; afterward he became an impassioned admirer of the ancient religions of Greece and India, and a pantheistic conception of the universe dominated all his thoughts. In his 'Antique Poems' (1853), he sings in verse exquisite in form the praises of the ancient gods and heroes; in his 'Barbarian Poems' (1862), with a poet's insight he seeks to interpret the mythological ideas of the Hebrews, Irish, Bretons, Scandinavians, Indians, and Polynesians. His 'Tragic Poems' (1882) were crowned by the French Academy. He made admirable translations of ancient Grecian poets,—Homer, Hesiod, Theocritus, Anacreon, and the dramatists.

Le Conte, Joseph (lè-kont'). An American scientist; born in Liberty County, Ga., Feb. 26, 1823; died in Yosemite Valley, July 6, 1901. He practiced medicine at Macon, Ga., but in 1850 went to Cambridge, Mass., where he studied natural history under Agassiz. He subsequently held several professorships, and after 1869 occupied the chair of geology and natural history in the University of California. 'The Mutual Relations of Religion and Science' appeared in 1874, and was followed by 'Elements of Geology' (1878); 'Light' (1881); 'A Compend of Geology (1884); 'Evolution and its Relation to Religious Thought' (1888).

Ledeganck, Karel Lodewyk (led-è-gänk'). A Flemish poet; born at Eecloo, Nov. 9, 1805; died March 19, 1847. He is one of the most popular of Flemish writers. His first collection of poems was 'Flowers of my Springtide' (1839). His poem on 'The Three Sister Cities'—i. e., Ghent, Bruges, Antwerp—is considered his finest production.

Ledesma Bultrago, Alonso de (lä-dēs'mä bwĕ-trä'gō). A Spanish poet; born in Segovia, 1552; died 1623. He was very mystical and allegorical in his verse, carrying imaginativeness to the point of unintelligibility. 'Spiritual Conceptions' (1600–12) is his best work.

Lee, Eliza Buckminster. An American prose-writer; born in Portsmouth, N. H., in 1794; died in Brookline, Mass., June 22, 1864. Her 'Sketches of New England Life' ap-

peared in 1837, and was followed by 'Delusion' (1839); a translation from the German of the 'Life of Jean Paul Richter' (1842); 'Naomi; or, Boston Two Hundred Years Ago' (1848); 'Parthenia; or, The Last Days of Paganism' (1858); and a translation of Berthold Auerbach's 'Barefoot Maiden' (1860).

Lee, Frederick George. An English clergyman and miscellaneous writer; born at Thame Vicarage, Oxfordshire, Jan. 6, 1832. At Oxford he was both University and College prizeman. He was ordained in 1854, and is at present vicar of All Saints', Lambeth. He is author of nearly fifty poems, essays, lectures, sermons, religious and historical studies, among which are: 'Poems' (2d ed. 1855); 'The Beauty of Holiness' (1859), lectures; 'The Martyrs of Vienne and Lyons' (3d ed. 1866), an Oxford prize poem; 'Glimpses of the Supernatural' (1875); 'A Glossary of Liturgical and Ecclesiastical Terms' (1877); 'Historical Sketches of the Reformation' (1878); 'The Church under Queen Elizabeth' (1880); 'King Edward the Sixth, Supreme Head' (1886); 'Cardinal Reginald Pole' (1887); 'A Manual of Politics' (1889).

Lee, Mrs. Hannah Farnham Sawyer. An American essayist and miscellaneous writer, wife of George Gardiner Lee of Boston; born in Newburyport, Mass., 1780; died in Boston, 1865. Her works, which exerted considerable influence during the first quarter of the nineteenth century, are: 'Grace Seymour' (1835); 'Three Experiments in Living' (1838); 'The Huguenots in France and America' (1842); 'Memoir of Pierre Toussaint' (1853).

Lee, Nathaniel. An English dramatist; born about 1650; died 1692. He wrote several tragedies, including 'The Rival Queens' (1677) and 'Theodosius' (1680).

Lee, Sophia and Harriet. English novelists; born in London—Sophia 1750, Harriet 1757; died—Sophia March 13, 1824, Harriet Aug. 1, 1851. They were daughters of John Lee, actor. Sophia at 29 wrote a very successful comedy, 'The Chapter of Accidents.' In 'The Recess: A Tale of Other Days' (1784) and in 'Canterbury Tales' (5 vols., 1797–1805), which she wrote in conjunction with Harriet, and which soon became a general favorite, is seen the beginning of the historical school in novel-writing. One of the 'Canterbury Tales'— 'Kruitzner; or, The German's Tale'—written by Harriet, suggested to Byron the subject of 'Werner.' She also wrote the stories 'The Errors of Innocence' (5 vols., 1786), and 'Clara Lennox' (1797).

Lee, Vernon, pseudonym of Violet Paget. An English essayist and miscellaneous writer; born in 1856. Her writings include: 'Studies of the Eighteenth Century in Italy' (1880); 'Belcaro' (1882), a volume of essays; 'The Prince of a Hundred Soups' (1883), a fairy tale; 'Miss Brown' (1884), a novel; and many others. She has lived in Italy for years.

Le Fanu, Joseph Sheridan (lĕ-fä'nü or lef'-a-nü). A popular Irish journalist and novelist; born in Dublin, Aug. 28, 1814; died there, Feb. 7, 1873. Having graduated from Trinity College, Dublin, he joined (1837) the staff of the Dublin University Magazine, at first as contributor, and afterwards as editor and proprietor, besides having an interest in the Evening Mail. He made his literary début while in college, but did not attract attention until the publication of two stirring Irish ballads, 'Phaudrig Crookore' and 'Shamus O'Brien.' Among modern Irish novelists he stands next in popularity to Charles Lever. 'The House by the Churchyard' appeared in 1863, and was succeeded by 'Uncle Silas' (1864), his most powerful work; 'Guy Deverell' (1865); 'The Tenants of Malory' (1867); 'The Wyvern Mystery' (1869); 'In a Glass Darkly' (1872).

Leffler, Charlotte. See Edgren.

Le Gallienne, Richard. An English poet and journalist; born in Liverpool, 1866. His first volume of poems, 'My Lady's Sonnets' (1887), was printed privately; among his other works in verse and prose are: 'Volumes in Folio'; 'The Book Bills of Narcissus'; 'English Poems' (1892); 'The Religion of a Literary Man' (1893); 'Prose Fancies' (1894). He has recently put out some translations of Omar Khayyám. He also wrote 'If I were God.'

Legendre, Adrien Marie (lĕ-zhoñdr'). An eminent French mathematician; born in Paris, Sept. 18, 1752; died Jan. 10, 1833. At 22 he was professor of mathematics in the Military School at Paris, and in 1783 was elected member of the Academy. He was one of a commission of three in 1787 to measure a degree of latitude between Dunkirk and Boulogne,—the basis of the metric system; afterward he held high and honorable posts under the government; and in 1824 was Inspector of the Higher Education. From this office he was dismissed in disgrace because he refused, as member of the Academy, to vote for the admission of government nominees. He died in great poverty. His principal works are: 'Elements of Geometry' (1794); 'Theory of Numbers' (1798); 'Treatise on Euler's Elliptical and Integral Functions' (3 vols., 1826–29).

Leger, Paul Louis (le-zhā'). A French scholar and author; born in Toulouse, Jan. 13, 1843. He is professor of the Slav languages at the Collège de France, and has done much to awaken an interest in the history and philology of the Slav peoples by such works as: 'Slav Studies' (1875); 'History of Austria-Hungary' (1878), translated into English; 'Slav Tales' (1882); 'The Save, Danube, and Balkan' (1884); 'Bulgaria' (1885); 'Russians and Slavs' (1890); 'Russian Literature'; 'The Slavic World.'

Leggett, William. An American story-writer and journalist; born in New York city, 1802; died in New Rochelle, N. Y., May 29, 1839. He was on the editorial staff of the New York Evening Post (1829–1836); and wrote: 'Leisure Hours at Sea' (1825); 'Naval Stories' (1834).

Legouvé, Ernest Wilfried (lĕ-gö-vā'). A French dramatist and story-teller; born at Paris, Feb. 15, 1807. In 1827 he won a prize of the Academy with a poem on the art of printing. As instructor in the Collège de France, 1847, lectured on the history of woman's development; and later published 'Moral History of Women' (7th ed. 1882), and 'Woman in France in the Nineteenth Century' (1864). These works, addressed to a feminine public, were received with great favor, and were followed by 'Science of the Family' (1867), and 'Messieurs the Young Folk' (1868). Meanwhile Legouvé was winning high distinction as a playwright with 'Louise de Lignerolles'; 'Adrienne Lecouvreur'; 'Medea'; 'By Right of Conquest'; 'Miss Susanna'; 'Anne de Kerwiler'; 'Consideration'; etc. In 1882 he published 'Recollections of Sixty Years,' and in 1890 'Winter Flowers, Winter Fruits: Story of my Household.' He died in Paris, March 14, 1903.

Lehrs, Karl (lärs). A German philologist; born at Königsberg, Prussia, Jan. 14, 1802; died there, June 9, 1878. He was appointed instructor in philology in the Königsberg University in 1831, and in 1845 became professor. His works deal for the most part with recondite questions, as 'Aristarchus's Studies on Homer' (1833); 'Three Writings of Herodianus' (1848); 'The Scholia to Pindar' (1873); but he wrote also 'Popular Essays on Antiquity, Especially on the Ethics and Religion of the Greeks' (1856; enlarged ed. 1875).

Leibnitz or Leibniz, Gottfried Wilhelm von, Baron. A renowned German philosopher and scholar; born at Leipsic, July 6, 1646; died at Hanover, Nov. 14, 1716. His learning was universal, and in every branch he was master. At 15 he entered Leipsic University for the study of law and philosophy. He then passed to Jena, devoting himself there chiefly to mathematics. In the mean time he composed two disquisitions, with which he proposed to qualify himself for a degree at Leipsic: the degree was refused because of his youth, but in 1666 he took the doctor's degree in law at Altdorf. His scholarship is almost unparalleled in the vastness of its range: he reached the highest eminence among the scholars of his time in languages, history, divinity, philosophy, jurisprudence, political science, physical science, mathematics, even in polite letters. His essays and disquisitions in the field of mere erudition are numerous in the transactions of the learned societies of his time, such as the 'Acta Eruditorum,' 'Miscellanea Berolinensia,' 'Journal des Savants,' and in his voluminous 'Correspondence.' Among his theological and philosophical writings are: 'Essays on God's Goodness, Man's Freedom, and the Origin of Evil' (1710); 'Principles of Nature and Grace' (1717); 'New Essays on the Human Understanding'; 'Refutation of Spinoza,' first printed in 1854. An incomplete edition of his 'Mathematical Works' was published in eleven volumes (1884).

Leichhardt, Ludwig (lich'härdt). A German traveler; born at Trebatsch, Oct. 23, 1813. He visited Australia in 1841, and made several tentative explorations preparatory to his great expedition of 1844-46, which traversed Queensland from Moreton Bay to the Gulf of Carpentaria, and crossing the peninsula of Arnhem Land reached Port Essington (or Victoria) on the west coast of the peninsula. For this he received a reward of $7,000, with which he equipped a second expedition to traverse the continent from west to east: he failed in this attempt, and perished in the wilderness. He published his 'Journal of an Overland Expedition,' etc. (1847).

Leighton, William. An American poet; born in Cambridge, Mass., 1833. Educated at Harvard. He wrote: 'The Sons of Godwin' (1876), a tragedy; 'Change: the Whisper of the Sphinx' (1878), a philosophical poem; 'A Sketch of Shakespeare' (1879); 'The Subjection of Hamlet' (1882).

Leisewitz, Johann Anton (lī'zĕ-vits). A German poet; born at Hanover, May 9, 1752; died at Brunswick, Sept. 10, 1806. His one tragedy, 'Julius of Tarentum' (1776), is one of the characteristic dramas of the period of "storm and stress," and was highly admired by the young Schiller. Several other dramatic pieces he left in an unfinished state; after his death they were destroyed; and all that remains is one scene of a comedy.

Leitner, Gottlieb William (lit'nᵓr). A German Orientalist and traveler; born at Buda-Pesth, Oct. 14, 1840; died at Bonn, March 24, 1899. He was educated at King's College, London, and afterward was professor of modern Greek, Arabic, and Turkish in that Institution. In 1864 he became a member of the Punjab University College faculty, and took a lively interest in the cause of education in the Punjab. He is author of 'The Races and Languages of Dardistan' (1867); 'Theory and Practice of Education'; 'Races of Turkey'; 'History of Indigenous Education in the Punjab' (1883).

Leitner, Karl Gottfried, Ritter von. An Austrian poet; born at Gratz, Nov. 18, 1800; died there, June 20, 1890. By his popular ballads he earned the title of "The Uhland of Styria." He published three volumes of his collected verses: 'Poems' (1825); 'Autumn Flowers' (1870); 'Stories and Poems' (1880).

Leixner, Otto von (līx'ner). A German poet and miscellaneous writer; born at Saar in Moravia, April 24, 1847. Among his poetical works are: a volume of 'Poems' (1868); the drama 'Resurrection of Germany' (1870); 'Twilight' (1886); 'Proverbs and Satiric Rhymes.' He has also written short stories: 'The Two Marys'; 'Memento Vivere'; 'Princess Sunshine' (1882). Among his other works are: 'Marginal Notes by a Hermit'; 'Gossamer' (1886); 'Gossipy Letters to a Young Matron' (1890); 'Lay Sermons' (1894). His 'History of German Literature' is a notable work.

Leland, Charles Godfrey. An American poet and prose-writer; born in Philadelphia, Aug. 15, 1824. He was most widely known for his 'Hans Breitmann's Party, and Other Ballads' (1868); burlesque poems in Pennsylvania Dutch, of which there have been four series. He spent much time abroad, studying gypsy life. His works include: 'Poetry and Mystery of Dreams'; 'English Gypsies'; 'Minor Arts'; 'The Gypsies.' He died March 20, 1903.

Lelewel, Joachim (le'-le-vel). A Polish patriot and historian; born at Warsaw, March 21, 1786; died at Paris, May 29, 1861. While a professor at Wilna he delivered a series of popular lectures on Polish history, which provoked interference by the Russian government; and later for his active participation in the revolution of 1830, he was compelled to leave his native country and locate in France and Belgium. Among his various works on Polish history and antiquities are: 'Ancient Polish Bibliography' (1823-26); 'History of Poland' (1829); 'History of Lithuania and Little Russia' (1830); 'Geography of the Arabs' (1851); 'Geography of the Middle Ages' (1852-57).

Lemaître, François Élie Jules (lĕ-mätr'). A French literary critic and dramatist; born at Vennecy, (Loiret), April 27, 1853. He is the author of five volumes of literary biographies, 'Contemporaries: Being Literary Studies and Portraits' (1885-95). He was for many years dramatic critic of the Journal des Débats. His début as a dramatist was made at the Odéon with 'La Revoltée' (1889), followed by 'Deputy Leveau' (1890), an exceedingly clever political satire. Of his other dramatic compositions may be mentioned: 'The Kings' (1893), and 'The Pardon' (1895). He is the author of two volumes of poems, 'Medallions' (1880) and 'Petites Orientales' (1882); 'Corneille and Aristotle's Poetics' ('1888); 'Myrrha: Stories' (1894) ; 'Lonely Stories' (1900).

Lemay, Léon Pamphile. A Canadian writer of prose and verse; born in Lotbinière, Quebec, Jan. 5, 1837. He published 'Essais Poétiques' (1865). 'The Discovery of Canada' won him the gold medal of Laval University. He translated Longfellow's 'Evangeline' (1879). His best work is said to be found in 'L'Affaire Sougraine' (1884).

Lembcke, Christian Ludwig Eduard (lemb'ke). A Danish poet; born at Copenhagen, June 15, 1815; died at Hadersler, March 20, 1897. He made translations of Shakespeare, Byron, Moore, and other English poets. Published in 1870 a volume of 'Poems and Songs,' in which he laments the defeat of Denmark, in the Schleswig-Holstein war; his ballad 'Our Mother Tongue' is one of the favorite national songs of Denmark.

Lemcke, Karl (lem'ke). A German writer on æsthetics; born at Schwerin, Aug. 26, 1831. His 'Popular Æsthetics' (1865), a work of rare merit, has been often republished, and has been translated into several foreign languages. He is author also of 'Songs and Poems' (1861);

'History of Recent German Poetry'; and of biographies of distinguished painters. Under the pseudonym "Karl Manno" he wrote the novels 'Beowulf' (1882); 'A Lovely Boy' (1885); 'Countess Gerhild' (1892) ; 'Companions of Youth.'

Lemercier, Nepomucène (lĕ-mer-syā'). A French poet; born at Paris, April 21, 1771; died there, June 7, 1840. After many failures he made a brilliant success with his classical tragedy 'Agamemnon' (1795). Elegance of versification, grace of style, and richness of fancy, characterize his 'Four Metamorphoses' (1799), and 'Pinto' (1800), a mixture of tragedy and comedy, in which he attempts to outdo 'Figaro's Wedding.' The most notable of his poems is the philosophical satire 'The Panhypocrisiad, or Infernal Spectacle of the Sixteenth Century' (in 16 cantos; 4 more added in 1832).

Le Moine, James MacPherson. A Canadian historian; born in Quebec, Jan. 24, 1825. His historical works are so fair in spirit and accurate in statement as to disarm adverse criticism. Among his works are : 'L'Ornithologie du Canada' (1860); 'Étude sur les Navigateurs Arctiques Franklin, McClure, Kane, McClintock' (1862); 'The Tourist's Note-Book' (1870); 'Quebec: Past and Present' (1876); and 'The Scot in New France' (1880).

Lemoinne, John Émile (lĕ-mwän'). A French publicist; born in London, Oct. 17, 1815; died at Paris, Dec. 14, 1892. He was political editor of the Journal des Débats. He was elected to the Academy in succession to Jules Janin in 1876, and in 1880 became a senator for life. Some of his political writings were collected and published under the titles 'Critical and Biographical Studies' (1852), and 'New Studies' (1862).

Lemon, Mark. An English humorous writer and playwright; born at London, Nov. 30, 1809; died at Crawley in Sussex, May 23, 1870. Among his comedies and dramas are : 'Domestic Economy'; 'Arnold of Winkelried' (1835); 'Hearts Are Trumps' (1849); 'The Railway Belle' (1854); 'Lost and Won'; 'The Gentleman in Black'; 'Medea, or the Libel on the Lady of Colchis' (1856). He was the first editor of Punch, and for 29 years controlled it. He wrote many fairy tales, among them: 'The Enchanted Doll' (1850); 'Tinykin's Transformations' (1869); and 'A Christmas Hamper.' Memorable among his humorous writings is 'Mark Lemon's Jest-Book.'

Lemonnier, Camille (lĕ-mo-nyä'). A Belgian novelist; born at Brussels, March 24, 1835. He is a pronounced realist. Among his stories are : 'Our Flemings' (1869); 'Flemish and Walloon Stories' (1873); 'Neither Fish nor Flesh' (1884); 'Flemish Christmas Carols' (1887); 'Madame Lupar' (1888); 'The Two Consciences' (1902).

Lemoyne, Camille André (lĕ-mwän). A French poet; born at Saint-Jean-d'Angély (dept. Charente-Inférieure), in 1822. Having suffered financial reverses while studying for the bar, he became a compositor and proof-

reader in the publishing house of Firmin Didot, and subsequently archivist librarian of the School of Decorative Arts. He belongs to the Parnassian school of French poets, and is the author of: 'Last Year's Roses' (1865-69); 'The Charmers' (1867); 'Flowers of the Meadows' (1876); 'Flowers of the Ruins' (1888); 'Flowers of the Evening' (1893), several of which have been crowned by the French Academy. He was decorated with the Legion of Honor in 1870.

Lenartovicz, Teofil (len-art'ō-vĕch). A Polish poet; born at Warsaw, Feb. 27, 1822; died at Florence, Feb. 3, 1893. His popular ballads and songs, 'Lirenka' (1855), are reckoned among the choicest pearls of the national poetry. The most noteworthy of his longer poems are : 'The Polish Land' (1848); 'The Gladiators' (1857); and the 'Italian Album' (1870). He wrote in Italian 'On the Character of Polono-Slavic Poetry' (1886).

Lenau, Nikolaus (lā-nou'), pseudonym of Nikolaus Franz Niembsch von Strehlenau. A celebrated German lyric poet; born at Csatad, Hungary, Aug. 13, 1802; died at Oberdöbling, near Vienna, Aug. 22, 1850. An unhappy love affair made him insane, and he died in a madhouse. He is widely known for his elegies. His works include 'Savonarola' (1837), 'The Albigenses' (1842), and others; all of gloomy tendency.

Leng, John, Sir. An English journalist; born in Hull, in 1828. He began his successful journalistic career in 1847 as sub-editor of the Hull Advertiser; in 1851 became editor and general manager of the Dundee Advertiser, which has since been one of the most influential papers in Great Britain; and he was the founder of the People's Journal, Evening Telegraph, and People's Friend. He was knighted in 1893. Among a number of his books and pamphlets are : 'Impressions of America' (1876); 'Scottish Banking Reform' (1881); 'Practical Politics' (1885); 'Trip to Norway' (1886); 'Home Rule All Round'; 'Glimpses of Egypt and Sicily.'

Lenient, Charles Félix (len-yen'). A French historian of literature; born at Provins, 1826. In 1865 he became professor of poetry in the Sorbonne. His principal works are: 'France in the Middle Ages' (1859); 'Satire in France, or the Militant Literature of the Sixteenth Century' (1866); 'Comedy in France in the Eighteenth Century' (2 vols., 1888); 'Patriotic Poetry in France in the Middle Ages' (1892); and 'Patriotic Poetry in France in Modern Times' (2 vols., 1894).

Lennep, Jacob van (len'nep). A celebrated Dutch poet; born at Amsterdam, March 24, 1802; died at Oosterbeek, Aug. 25, 1868. He translated some of Byron's poems. His first volume of original verse, 'Academic Idylls' (1826), won little attention; but his 'Legends of the Netherlands' were received with universal applause. The 'Legends' comprise among others : 'Adegild' (1828); 'Jacoba and Bertha'

(1829); 'The Struggle with Flanders' (1831); 'Edward van Gelre' (1847).

Lenngrén, Anna Maria (len'gren). A Swedish poetess; born at Stockholm, June 18, 1754; died there, March 8, 1817. She received from her father, Prof. Malmstedt, a very thorough education. Her poems were originally contributed to the Stockholmsposten, of which her husband was editor: they were collected after her death and published under the title of 'Essays in Poesy' (1819; 12th ed. 1890). They consist of humorous satires or epigrams, amusing travesties and idyllic sketches, all distinguished by perfection of form and true poetic sensibility.

Lennox, Charlotte Ramsay. An American novelist; born in New York city in 1720; died in London, Jan. 4, 1804. Educated in England, she received encouragement in her literary work from Samuel Johnson. Her best achievement is 'Shakespeare Illustrated' (2 vols., 1753), and a supplementary volume (1754). She also wrote 'Memoirs of Harriet Stewart' (1751); 'The Female Quixote' (1752); 'Sophia,' a novel (1763); 'The Sisters,' a comedy (1769).

Lennox, William Pitt, Lord. An English writer of biographical memoirs; born 1799; died in London, Feb. 18, 1881. He was son of the fourth Duke of Richmond. He wrote 'Fifty Years' Biographical Reminiscences' (2 vols., 1863); 'My Recollections from 1806 to 1873' (2 vols.); 'Three Years with the Duke of Wellington'; 'Life of the Duke of Richmond'; 'Recreations of a Sportsman' (1862). He wrote several novels, among them 'The Tuft-Hunter' (1843).

Lenormant, Charles (lĕ-nor-män'). A French archæologist and art historian; born at Paris, June 1, 1802; died at Athens, Nov. 24, 1859. He was professor of Egyptian archæology in the Collège de France from 1848 till his death. Among his writings are: 'Thesaurus of Numismatics and Glyptics' (20 vols., 1834–50); 'Introduction to Oriental History' (1838); 'Museum of Egyptian Antiquities' (1835–42); 'Selection of Keramographic Monuments' (4 vols., 1837–61).

Lenormant, François. A French historian and archæologist, son of Charles; born at Paris, Jan. 17, 1837; died there, Dec. 10, 1883. He is one of the foremost of French Assyriologists. His works are very numerous. Among them are: 'Archæological Researches at Eleusis' (1862); 'Political and Economic Organization of Coinage in Antiquity' (1863); 'Ancient History in the East' (3 vols., 1868–69); 'Letters on Assyriology' (5 vols., 1871–79); 'Akkadian Studies' (3 vols., 1873–79); 'The Primitive Language of Chaldea' (1875); 'The Beginnings of History according to the Bible' (3 vols., 1880–84).

Lenz, Jakob Michael Reinhold (lents). A German poet; born at Sesswegen, in Livonia, Jan. 12, 1751; died at Moscow, May 24, 1792. He was an enthusiastic admirer of Shakespeare, and in 1774 published 'Remarks on the Stage, with Translation of Parts of Shakes-

peare's 'Love's Labour's Lost''; and the influence of Shakespeare is seen in his odd comedies, 'The Tutor' (1774); 'The New Menoza' (1774); 'The Soldiers' (1776). He adapted several 'Plays of Plautus for the German Stage' (1774). His finest poem is 'Love in the Country.' His minor songs and ballads are sometimes admirable for their simple and unaffected poetic feeling.

Lenz, Oskar. A German traveler; born at Leipsic, April 13, 1848. He visited the west coast of Africa in the service of the German African Society (1874), and spent three years in exploring the course of the Ogowé; he recounted his observations and experiences in 'Sketches from West Africa' (1878). He next visited Marocco and Timbuctu, and wrote 'Timbuctu: Journey through Marocco, the Sahara, and Soudan' (1884). He wrote also 'Wanderings in Africa' (1895).

Leo I., the Great, Pope. One of the Fathers of the Latin Church; fifth century; Pope 440–61. He was a vigorous asserter in words and in acts of the primacy of the bishop of Rome. He heard the appeal of Celidonius, bishop of Vesontio (Besançon) from the sentence of the synod of Arles deposing him, and pronounced an ecclesiastical censure on Hilarius, the bishop who had presided over the synod. His 'Dogmatic Epistle to Flavianus' set forth the Catholic doctrine in opposition to the heretical teaching of Eutyches, in the form and terms ever since recognized as orthodox in the creeds. His writings consist of 96 'Sermons' or discourses, and 173 'Epistles.' A treatise on 'The Sacraments' and one on 'The Calling of all the Nations' are appended to his undoubtedly genuine works, and attributed to him.

Leo XIII., Pope (Count Gioachino Pecci). He was born at Carpineto, near Anagni, March 2, 1810. He was nuncio to Belgium 1843–45; was made archbishop of Perugia 1845; cardinal 1853; supreme pontiff March 3, 1878. He opened the Vatican archives to scholars desiring to examine them for purposes of historical research. Two of his 'Encyclical Letters' are worthy of special mention; viz., that to «All Patriarchs, Primates, Archbishops,» etc., on 'The Condition of Labor' (1891), and that to «The English People» on 'Church Unity' (1895). He is author of a small volume of lyrics in Latin: 'Lyric Poems [Carmina] of Leo XIII., Supreme Pontiff' (1883). Died July 20, 1903.

Leo, Heinrich. A German historian; born at Rudolstadt, March 19, 1799; died at Halle, April 24, 1878. He was appointed professor of history in the University of Halle, 1830. In early life he was in religion a rationalist, and in political faith a radical; but later he became a conservative and an «obscurantist.» His principal works are: 'History of the Italian States' (5 vols., 1829); 'History of the Netherlands' (2 vols., 1832); 'Natural History of the State' (1833); 'Text-Book of Universal History' (6 vols., 1835–44); 'Anglo-Saxon Glossary' (2 vols., 1872).

Leo Africanus (lē'ō af"rē-kā'nus), properly Alhassan ibn Mohammed Alwazzan. A Moorish traveler and geographer. About 1517 he was captured by pirates while returning from Egypt after extended travels in northern and central Africa, Arabia, Syria, etc. Ultimately he was presented as a slave to Leo X., who assigned him a pension. He wrote a 'Description of Africa' which for a long time was almost the only authority, especially on the Soudan. He also wrote a 'Tractate on the Lives of Arab Philosophers.'

Leon, Luis de. See **Ponce de Leon**.

Leonowens, Anna Harriette Crawford. A noted educator and prose-writer; born in Caernarvon, Wales, Nov. 5, 1834. In 1863 she was appointed governess in the family of the King of Siam. She was four years in the King's household at Bangkok, acting as secretary to the King and instructor to the royal family. The present King of Siam was educated by her. She came to the United States in 1867; opened a school in New York to prepare teachers in the kindergarten system. She has published: 'The English Governess at the Court of Siam' (1870); 'The Romance of the Harem' (1872); and 'Life and Travels in India' (1884).

Leopardi, Giacomo, Count (lā-ō-par'dē). A celebrated Italian poet; born at Recanati in Tuscany, June 29, 1798; died at Naples, June 14, 1837. His family, though noble, was poor, and he acquired a knowledge of the classics and of literature almost unaided in his father's library. Before he was 18 he had produced a Latin translation (with commentary) of Porphyrius's 'Life of Plotinus'; a treatise on 'Some Roman Rhetoricians' of the second century, and a 'History of Astronomy,' both in Latin; and an 'Essay on the Popular Errors of the Ancients,' in Italian, citing over 400 authors. His subsequent works were: 'Ode to Italy' (1818); 'Ode on the Monument to Dante' (1819); 'Ode to Cardinal Mai on the Discovery of Cicero's Tractate on The State' (1820); 'Brutus the Younger' (1823), an ode, and 'Comparison of the Sentiments of Brutus the Younger, and of Theophrastus, when in the Face of Death,' in which two works his pessimistic views first had formal expression; 'Verses,' a collection of his miscellaneous poems (1826); 'Moral Opuscules' (1827), mostly observations, in dialogue form, on ethical questions. 'The Broom-Flower,' 'Sylvia,' and 'The Night Song,' are his most celebrated poems. He left unpublished at his death a volume of 'Thoughts.'

Leopold, Karl Gustaf af (lē'ō-pōld). A Swedish poet; born at Stockholm, Nov. 23, 1756; died there, Nov. 9, 1829. He was for a long time a kind of literary dictator, and was the chief representative in Sweden of the French school of classicism. He attempted all forms of poetry save the epic. Of his tragedies the best-known are 'Odin' (1790), for which Gustavus III. presented him a crown of laurel from Virgil's tomb; and 'Virginia' (1802).

Lepsius, Karl Richard (lep'sē-ös). A distinguished German Egyptologist; born at Naumburg, Dec. 23, 1810; died at Berlin, July 10, 1884. While pursuing his studies in Paris he wrote three disquisitions, which won prizes of the Academy: 'Palæography as a Means of Linguistic Research' (1834); 'Kinship of the Semitic, Indian, Ethiopian, Old Persian, and Old Egyptian Alphabets'; 'Origin and Relationship of Numerical Terms in the Indo-Germanic, Semitic, and Coptic Languages.' In his celebrated 'Letter to Mr. Rossellini on the Hieroglyphic Alphabet' (1837), he propounded a scientific theory of hieroglyphic writing. His translation of the 'Book of the Dead' was published in 1842. That year he visited Egypt, and for four years studied its monuments; the results of his researches and those of his associates are contained in the magnificent 'Monuments of Egypt and Ethiopia' (12 vols., 1849-60). Besides numerous memoirs addressed to the Academy of Berlin and other learned societies, he wrote for the general public 'Letters from Egypt, Ethiopia, and the Sinaitic Peninsula' (1852).

Le Queux, William (lē-kē). An English novelist; born in London, 1864. He has written: 'The Great War in England in 1897' (9th ed. 1895); 'Zoraida'; 'Stolen Souls'; 'Guilty Bonds'; 'Strange Tales of a Nihilist'; and 'The Eye of Istar' (1897); 'The Court of Honor.'

Lermontov, Michail Yuryevitch (ler'montov). A celebrated Russian poet; born at Moscow, Oct. 15, 1814; died July 27, 1841. He was an officer in the Imperial Guards in 1837, when, in a passionate poem, he gave vent to his indignation over the death of Pushkin. The poem, 'The Poet's Death,' gave offense at court, and Lermontov was relegated to the Caucasus, there to serve as ensign in a dragoon regiment. He is at his best in lyric and narrative poetry. The most noteworthy of his rather Byronesque epics are 'The Novice'; 'Ismail Bey'; 'Valerik'; 'The Dæmon.' His fine novel, 'A Hero of Our Time' led to a duel in which he fell.

Leroux, Pierre (lē-rö'). A French socialist philosopher; born at Paris, 1797; died there, April 12, 1871. He was for a while an adherent of Saint-Simon, but afterward developed a humanitarian or socialistic system of his own. Its principles are expounded in 'Equality' (1838); 'Refutation of Eclecticism'; 'Humanity' (2 vols., 1840). After the Coup d'État he was proscribed, and took up his residence in the island of Jersey: there he pursued agricultural experiments, and wrote a philosophical poem, 'The Beach of Samarez' (1864).

Le Roux (R. C. Henri), known as **Hugues.** A French journalist and novelist; born in Havre, in 1860. In early life he was connected with the Political and Literary Review, and subsequently succeeded Jules Claretie as writer of the Paris chronique in the Temps. He is author of a series of popular romances, including 'Médéric and Lisée' and 'One of

22

Us' (1886); 'Souls in Agony' (1888); 'The Parisian Inferno' (1888); 'All for Honor' (1892). His miscellaneous works are : 'In the Sahara' (1891); 'On Board a Yacht: Portugal, Spain, etc.' (1891); two translations from the Russian; etc.

Leroy-Beaulieu, Anatole (lė-rwä' bō-lyė). A French historian; born at Lisieux, 1842. He became professor of modern history in the Free School of Political Sciences, 1881. His principal work, written after extensive travels in Russia, is 'The Empire of the Tsars and the Russians' (3 vols., 1881–89). Among his other writings are : 'A Russian Statesman: Nikolas Milutin' (1884); 'France, Russia, and Europe' (1888); 'Revolution and Liberalism' (1890); 'The Papacy, Socialism, and Democracy' (1893).

Leroy-Beaulieu, Pierre Paul. A French economist; born at Saumur, Maine-et-Loire, Dec. 9, 1843. He is opposed to socialism, and is very conservative in his views. His works include 'The Labor Question in the Nineteenth Century' (1871), 'The Modern State and its Functions' (2d ed. 1891), and others. He is the founder and editor of L'Economiste Français.

Le Sage, Alain René (lė-säzh'). A celebrated French novelist and dramatist; born at Sarzeau, near Vannes, May 8, 1668; died at Boulogne-sur-Mer, Nov. 17, 1747. He abandoned law for literature, with scant success till 1707, when the comedy 'Crispin his Master's Rival' was received with high public favor; as was 'Turcaret' the following year. The latter—a satire on the financiers, trading classes, and nobility—is one of the best comedies in French literature ; every character is drawn with sharp individuality. His novels 'The Devil on Two Sticks' (1707) and 'Gil Blas' (1717), were suggested by Spanish originals; but he owes them nothing beyond suggestion. As author of 'Gil Blas' he is the parent and pattern of Fielding and Smollett. Of his other romances in the same general vein may be mentioned 'The Bachelor of Salamanca' and 'The Life and Adventures of M. de Beauchêne.'

Lescure, Mathurin François Adolphe de (lä-kür'). A French littérateur and historian; born at Bretenoux (Lot), in 1833; died at Clamart (Seine), May 6, 1892. Successively attached to the Ministry of State and the Senate, he acquired a unique reputation by a series of essays and monographs on the Revolutionary and other periods in French history. Among more than forty publications are : 'Confessions of the Abbess de Chelles' (1863); 'Marie Antoinette and her Family' (1865); 'Mary Stuart' (1871); 'Illustrious Mothers' (1881); 'Love under the Terror' (1882); 'Rivarol and French Society during the Revolution and Emigration' (1883), his best work, crowned by the Academy; 'Châteaubriand' (1892); and numerous memoirs.

Leskov, Nikolai Semyonovitch (les'kŏv). A Russian novelist; born in the government of Orel, Feb. 16, 1831; died in St. Petersburg, March 5, 1895. His first story, 'No Way Out' (1865), is a powerful delineation of Russian society, and is tinged with radicalism and nihilism. In the novel 'The Clergy' he portrays the life of the priesthood; in 'To the Knife' he describes in detail the schisms and factions of the intellectual world of Russia. He has also written many tales based on ancient legends.

Lesley, John. A Scotch historian; born Sept. 29, 1527; died in Brussels, Belgium, May 31, 1596. A stanch friend of Mary Queen of Scots, he was implicated in the project for her marriage to the Duke of Norfolk, and in the consequent rebellion in the north of England, and was imprisoned in the Tower. On his release he crossed to the Continent, and subsequently became bishop of Coutances in Normandy. His chief production is a history of Scotland (published at Rome, 1578), in ten books, seven in Latin and the last three in Scotch dialect.

Leslie, Charles Robert. An English painter and writer on art; born in London, Oct. 19, 1794; died there, May 5, 1859. He was brought to America by his parents in 1799, but returning to England (1811), studied art under Allston and West. For a brief period he was instructor in art at West Point, N. Y., and later professor of painting at the Royal Academy (1848–52). His published works include : 'Memoirs of John Constable' (1845); 'Handbook for Young Painters' (1855), an enlarged edition of his Royal Academy lectures; and a 'Life of Reynolds' (completed by Taylor, 1865).

Leslie, Eliza. An American prose-writer; born in Philadelphia, Nov. 16, 1787; died in Gloucester, N. J., Jan. 2, 1858. Her father was a personal friend of Franklin, Jefferson, and other eminent men of his time. Her first successful work was a cookery book; she afterward adopted literature as a profession, and edited The Gift, which attained great popularity. Her published works include : 'Pencil Sketches' (1833–37); 'House Book' (1840); 'Ladies' Receipt Book' (1848); and 'Behaviour Book' (1853).

Lespès, Léo (les-päs'). A French story-teller; born at Bouchain, June 18, 1815; died at Paris, April 29, 1875. He wrote for the minor Paris newspapers, under the signature "Timothy Trimm," a number of short stories, which were received with extraordinary popular favor. He founded the Petit Journal (1862), which immediately reached the then unexampled circulation of 200,000 copies. Among his stories, which were frequently republished, are : 'Stories in Pink and Black' (1842); 'Mysteries of the Grand Opera' (1843); 'A Story to Make You Shudder' (1866); 'Physiology of Champagne' (1866); 'Walks about Paris' (1867).

L'Espinasse, Julie de (les-pē-näs'). A French letter-writer; born at Lyons, about 1732; died at Paris, May 23, 1776. Her drawing-room was a place of assembly for the fashion and wit of Paris. Her 'Letters' (2 vols., 1809), and 'Unpublished Letters' (2 vols., 1877), are of interest more as reflecting the writer's passionate sensibility and enthusiasm than for their literary excellence.

Lesseps, Ferdinand, Vicomte de (les-eps). A French diplomat and engineer; born at Versailles, Nov. 19, 1805; died Dec. 7, 1894. He was employed several years in the French consular and diplomatic service. In 1854, on the invitation of Saïd Pasha, he visited Egypt to study the problem of canalizing the Isthmus of Suez: the results of his studies were stated in a memoir, 'Piercing the Isthmus of Suez.' He was made chief director of the works in 1856. The canal was opened to traffic Aug. 15, 1869. He published (1875-81) five volumes of 'Letters, Journals, and Documents Relating to the Suez Canal'; and in 1887, 'Recollections of 40 Years.' His attempt to pierce the Isthmus of Panama resulted in failure, and in numberless discussions and papers, none of which have been embodied in a book.

Lessing, Gotthold Ephraim (les'ing). A great German poet, and the foremost critic of German literature; born at Kamenz in Upper Lusatia, Jan. 22, 1729; died at Brunswick, Feb. 15, 1781. Among his writings are: 'The Young Savant,' a comedy (1750); 'Trifles,' a collection of his lyric poems (1751); 'Rehabilitations' (1751) — redeeming from obloquy the name and fame of sundry historical personages; 'Miss Sara Sampson' (1755), a tragedy; 'The Free-Thinker,' 'The Jews,' 'The Woman-Hater' (1755), comedies; 'Pope a Metaphysician!' (1755); 'Letters on Literature' (1758); 'Philotas,' a prose tragedy (1759); 'Laocoön: on the Boundaries of Painting and Poetry,' Part i. (1766),—the second part was never written; 'Minna von Barnhelm,' a comedy (1767); 'Antiquarian Letters' (1768); 'Emilia Galotti,' a tragedy (1772); 'Nathan the Wise' (1779); 'Education of the Human Race' (1780); 'Ernst and Falk' (1780).

Lester, Charles Edwards. An American prose-writer; born in Griswold, Conn., 1815; died in Detroit, Mich., 1890. Among his works are: 'The Glory and Shame of England' (2 vols., 1841); 'Artists in America' (1846); 'Life and Public Services of Charles Sumner' (1874); 'History of the United States, Considered in Five Great Periods' (2 vols., 1883).

Lesueur, Daniel. See **Loiseau.**

Lethbridge, Roper, Sir. An English statesman, scholar, and author; born in 1840. He was for many years prominent in educational and political movements in India, as professor in the Bengal Educational Department, and subsequently as Political Agent and Press Commissioner under Lord Lytton's viceroyalty. Among his works are: 'A Short Manual of the History of India' (1881); 'High Education in India'; 'A History of Bengal'; and the

articles on 'Feudatory States' in the Imperial Gazetteer of India. In 1890 he was created Knight Commander of the Indian Empire.

Letronne, Jean Antoine (le-trōn'). A French archæologist; born at Paris, Jan. 2, 1787; died there, Dec. 14, 1848. He is distinguished chiefly for his studies in numismatics and inscriptions. Among his writings are: 'Topography of Syracuse' (1813); 'Fragments of Hero of Alexandria' (1816); 'Valuings of Greek and Roman Coins' (1817); 'Materials to Serve for a History of the Christian Religion' (1833); 'The Vocal Statue of Memnon' (1833); 'Collection of Greek and Latin Inscriptions from Egypt' (1842-48).

Leuckart, Rudolf (loik'ärt). A German zoölogist; born at Helmstedt, Oct. 7, 1822; died at Leipsic, Feb. 6, 1898. He became professor of zoölogy at Giessen in 1855, and of zoölogy and zoötomy at Leipsic in 1869. His studies were chiefly made in the field of lower and lowest forms of animal life,—zoöphytes, sponges, insects, parasites. Among his writings are treatises on 'Trichina Spiralis' (1860); 'Tapeworms'; 'Parthenogenesis of Insects'; 'Anatomy of Bees.'

Leuthold, Heinrich (loit'ōld). A German-Swiss poet; born at Wetzikon, Switzerland, Aug. 9, 1827; died near Zürich, July 1, 1879. With Geibel he made translations of French poetry: 'Five Books of French Lyrism' (1862). A volume of original verse, 'Poems' (1879), showed him to be a gifted poet, possessing perfect mastery of artistic form. The author died insane while his volume was going through the press.

Leva, Giuseppe de (lā'vä). An Italian writer of history; born at Zara in Dalmatia, 1821. Among his works are: 'Life of Cardinal G. Contarini'; 'Giulio della Rovere'; 'Giovanni Grimani'; 'Documentary History of Charles V. in his Relation to Italy' (4 vols., 1863-81).

Levasseur, Pierre Émile (lĕ-vas-ẽr'). A French political economist; born at Paris, Dec. 8, 1828. He is author of 'Public Moneys among the Romans' (1854); 'The Gold Question' (1858); 'The Laboring Classes of France from Cæsar's Time to the Revolution' (2 vols., 1859); the same continued to 1867 (2 vols.); 'The French Population' (1889-91, 3 vols.), an important work; 'France and her Colonies' (1893).

Levay, Joseph (lev'ā). A Hungarian poet; born at Sajo Szent-Peter, Nov. 18, 1825. Besides poems in eulogy of Kazinczy, Paloczy, Deák, etc., and translations of parts of Shakespeare's plays and of Burns's songs, he wrote: 'Songs of Memory' (1850); 'Poems' (1850); 'New Poems' (1856). In his songs he always strikes the chord of national and popular sentiment.

Lever, Charles [James]. An Irish novelist; born at Dublin, Aug. 31, 1806; died at Trieste, June 1, 1872. He wrote: 'Confessions of Harry Lorrequer' (1841); 'Charles O'Malley' (1841); 'Arthur O'Leary' (1844); 'Jack Hinton the

Guardsman' (1844); 'Tom Burke of Ours' (1844); 'The O'Donoghue' (1845); 'Con Cregan' (1849); 'Roland Cashel' (1850); 'The Daltons, or Three Roads in Life' (1852); 'The Dodd Family Abroad' (1854); 'The Fortunes of Glencore' (1857); 'Davenport Dunn' (1859); 'Barrington' (1863); 'Luttrell of Arran' (1865); 'Sir Brooke Fosbrooke' (1866); 'The Bramleighs of Bishop's Folly' (1868); 'Lord Kilgobbin' (1872).

Leverrier, Urbain Jean Joseph (lê-vä-ryä'). A celebrated French astronomer; born at St. Lô, March 11, 1811; died at Paris, Sept. 23, 1877. Till 1837 his studies were wholly in the department of chemistry; in that year he was appointed teacher of astronomy in the Polytechnic School. In 1839 he attained rank among the foremost astronomers by two memoirs presented to the Academy on 'Secular Perturbations of the Planetary System.' He then studied the movements of Mercury and Uranus, and was led to infer the existence of a planet beyond Uranus: the inference was proved true by the finding of the hypothetical planet (Neptune) by Galle. His theories and tables of the several planets are given in the 'Annals of the Paris Observatory.'

Levertin, Oscar. A Swedish poet; born at Stockholm, 1862. He first wrote some stories after the manner of the "realists," but they had little success. Breaking then with realism, he indulged his bent toward romance and mysticism in his poems 'Legends and Tales' (1891), and 'New Poems' (1894). He is at the head of the younger lyric poets of Sweden. In his work 'Gustavus III. as a Dramatist' (1894), he proves himself an acute critic of 18th-century literature.

Levien, Ilse. See **Frapan**.

Lewald, August (le-väld'). A German storyteller; born at Königsberg, Prussia, Oct. 14, 1792; died at Munich, March 10, 1871. He wrote: 'Aquarelles from Life' (1836); 'Story of the Theatre' (5 vols., 1841), autobiographical; 'Clarinette' (3 vols., 1863); 'The Insurgent' (2 vols., 1865); 'Last Travels' (1870).

Lewald, Fanny. A German novelist; born at Königsberg, March 24, 1811; died at Dresden, Aug. 5, 1889. Her principal writings are: 'The Representative' (1841); 'Clementine' (1842); 'Diogena: Story of Iduna, Countess H-H' (1847), a mild satire on Ida, Countess Hahn-Hahn; 'Dunes and Mountain Strata' (1851); 'Pictures of German Life' (1856); 'From Generation to Generation' (1863); 'Woman: Pro and Contra' (1870); 'The Darner Family' (1887); 'Twelve Pictures from the Life' (1888).

Lewes, George Henry. An English historical and miscellaneous writer; born at London, April 18, 1817; died there, Nov. 28, 1878. Among his writings are: 'Biographical History of Philosophy' (1845–46), afterward entitled 'History of Philosophy from Thales to Comte' (1866); 'Life of Robespierre' (1849); 'The Life and Works of Goethe' (1855); 'Seaside Studies' (1858); 'The Physiology of Common Life' (1859); 'Studies in Animal Life' (1862); 'Aristotle: a Chapter from the History of Science' (1864); 'Problems of Life and Mind' (3 vols., 1872–79); 'The Physical Basis of Mind' (1877). He wrote two novels, 'Ranthorpe' (1847), and 'Rose, Blanche, and Violet' (1848); and the dramatic poems 'Lope de Vega and Calderon' and 'The Noble Heart.'

Lewis, Alonzo. An American poet, known as the "Lynn bard"; born in Lynn, Mass., Aug. 28, 1794; died there, Jan. 21, 1861. He was the author of 'Forest Flowers and Sea Shells,' which reached ten editions, and 'History of Lynn' (1829; 2d ed. 1844). N. P. Willis spoke highly of his poems.

Lewis, Charles Bertrand. ["M. Quad."] An American journalist and humorist; born in Liverpool, O., 1842. He received his education at the Michigan Agricultural College. During the Civil War he served in the Union army. For many years he was on the staff of the Detroit Free Press, and since 1891 has been connected with the New York World. He has published: 'Quad's Odds' (1875); 'Goaks and Tears' (1875); 'The Lime Kiln Club.'

Lewis, Charlton Thomas. An American scholar, journalist, and lawyer; born at West Chester, Pa., in 1834. He was professor of mathematics and subsequently of Greek at Troy University (1859–62), revenue commissioner at Washington, D. C., and latterly has practiced law in New York. He wrote a 'History of Germany,' founded on D. Müller's work, and collaborated with Charles Short in the preparation of 'Harper's Latin Dictionary' (1879), etc. Died Morristown, N. J., May 26, 1904.

Lewis, Estelle Anna Blanche Robinson. An American dramatist; born near Baltimore, Md., April 1824; died in London, Nov. 24, 1880. While a schoolgirl she translated the 'Æneid' into English verse; wrote 'Forsaken'; and published 'Records of the Heart' (1844), and 'Hebémah, or the Fall of Montezuma' (1864). Her best dramatic work, 'Sappho of Lesbos,' a tragedy, ran through seven editions, and was translated into modern Greek and played at Athens. Edgar A. Poe spoke of her as the rival of Sappho; Lamartine called her the "female Petrarch."

Lewis, George Cornewall, Sir. An English statesman, scholar, and critic; born at London, April 21, 1806; died at Harpton Court, Radnorshire, April 13, 1863. A graduate of Christ Church, Oxford, with high honors, he became a lawyer, and rose almost to the top in politics, filling three Cabinet places in rapid succession, ending with Chancellor of the Exchequer in 1855. His immense knowledge, sagacious judgment, and cool temper (he said to an excitable colleague, "I am a vegetable and you are an animal"), made him very influential both in public life and in the world of critical scholarship. His most enduring work is the 'Enquiry into the Credibility of Early Roman History'

(2 vols., 1855); mainly a criticism of Niebuhr's assumption that there can be reliable intuitive perceptions of historic fact without a sufficiently tangible basis of evidence to support the test of argument. It is also an excellent analysis of early Roman records and legends. His books on Grecian subjects, on the Romance languages, on early astronomy, etc., are mines of research and good criticism; on Egyptian subjects his over-skepticism led him to the absurd contention that the hieroglyphics could not be deciphered at all. His political writings, as 'On the Use and Abuse of Political Terms' (1835), 'On the Influence of Authority in Matters of Opinion' (1849), 'On the Methods of Observation and Reasoning in Politics' (2 vols., 1852), are clarifying but too prolix.

Lewis, Maria Theresa, Lady. An English biographer, a descendant of the great historian Lord Clarendon and wife of Sir George C. Lewis; born March 8, 1803; died Nov. 9, 1865. She wrote 'Lives of the Friends and Contemporaries of Lord Chancellor Clarendon' (3 vols., 1852).

Lewis, Matthew Gregory. ["Monk" Lewis.] An English poet; born at London, July 9, 1775; died May 14, 1818. His first poem, 'Ambrosio, or the Monk' (1795), became instantly very popular; a court decree stopped its sale for a time; when its sale was resumed many objectionable passages had been expunged. He next wrote a musical drama, 'The Castle Spectre' (1796), long a favorite piece on the stage. He wrote also 'Journal of a West-Indian Proprietor,' published after his death.

Lewis, Tayler. An American scholar and author; born in Northumberland, N. Y., in 1802; died in Schenectady, N. Y., May 11, 1877. Was professor of Greek in the University of New York in 1838, and later of Oriental literature in Union College. He published many volumes. Among these are: 'The Six Days of Creation' (1855); 'Heroic Periods in a Nation's History' (1866); 'The Light by which We See Light' (1875); and many addresses and reviews.

Lewis, Thomas Hayter. An English architect and author; born in London, July 9, 1818. He was professor of architecture at University College (1865–81), and is the author of 'The Holy Places of Jerusalem' (1888), the most important work on the subject issued in recent years. Besides papers relating to architecture and antiquities in the transactions of various societies, he has written also the articles on architecture in the 'Encyclopædia Britannica.'

Leybourn, William. An English mathematician, a pioneer in popularizing arithmetic and astronomy; born 1626; died about 1700. His 'Urania Practica' (1648) was the first English treatise on astronomy; his 'Panarithmologia' (1693) the first English ready-reckoner.

Leyden John (lī'den). A Scotch Orientalist, poet, and author; born in Denholm, Sept. 8, 1775; died at Batavia, Java, Aug. 28, 1811. Soon after obtaining his medical degree he went to India, where his proficiency in Oriental and especially Indo-Chinese languages led to an appointment as professor of Hindustani at Fort William College, Calcutta. He is the author of 'An Historical Account of Discoveries in Northern and Western Africa' (1789), an accurate and useful work for that time; an essay on Indo-Chinese literature in 'Asiatic Researches'; 'Scenes of Infancy,' a poem; and a number of Scotch ballads, much admired by Sir Walter Scott and others.

L'Hôpital, Michel de (lō-pē-tāl'). A French statesman; born at Aigueperse, 1505; died March 13, 1573. He left some elegant Latin poems, also memoirs, discourses, and papers on jurisprudence and political affairs; they were published in five volumes under the title 'Works of Michel de l'Hôpital' (1824).

Libanius (li-bā'ni-us). A Greek sophist of the fourth century; native of Antioch in Syria. Though a heathen, he was beloved by St. Basil and St. John Chrysostom, once his pupils. He was a voluminous writer, and very successfully imitated in his orations the style of Demosthenes; he got the nickname of "the little Demosthenes." Of his orations 68 are extant: they are of value for the history of his time; the same is to be said of his 'Epistles,' of which 1,607 remain.

Libelt, Karol (lē'belt). A Polish miscellaneous writer; born at Posen, April 8, 1807; died near Gollancz, June 9, 1875. His principal work is 'Philosophy and Criticism' (5 vols., 1845–50). He wrote also: 'Mathematical Handbook' (2 vols., 1844); a drama, 'The Maid of Orleans' (1847); 'Humor and Truth' (1848), a volume of brief essays.

Lichtenberg, Georg Christoph (liċht'en-berG). A distinguished German satirical writer and physicist; born near Darmstadt, July 1, 1742; died at Göttingen, Feb. 24, 1799. He gained great celebrity as a lecturer on physical science, chiefly through the ingenious apparatus, contrived by himself, with which he illustrated his lectures. His being a hunchback probably embittered his satiric disposition. The best of his satires are those on the notorious literary pirate Tobias Göbhard; the essay on 'The German Novel'; 'Timorus,' ridiculing Lavater's zeal for proselytizing; and 'Pronunciation of the Wethers of Ancient Greece,' aimed at Voss's system of pronouncing Greek. His brilliant sayings have been collected and published in a separate volume, 'Lichtenberg's Thoughts and Maxims: Light Rays from his Works' (1871).

Lichtenstein, Ulrich von. See **Ulrich von L.**

Lichtwer, Magnus Gottfried (liċht'vär). A German poet; born at Wurzen, Jan. 30, 1719; died at Halberstadt, July 6, 1783. His principal work is 'Four Books of Æsopic Fables' (1748). His didactic poem 'The Right of Reason' (1758), founded on the philosophy of Wolf, is of little value.

Lidner, Bengt (lid'ner). A Swedish poet; born at Göteborg (Gothenburg), March 16,

1757; died at Stockholm, Jan. 4, 1793. He published a volume of 'Fables' after the manner of Lafontaine (1799). In 1781 he was secretary to the Swedish envoy at Paris, and there wrote the tragedy 'Erik the Fjortonde.' He lost his secretaryship through his dissipations. He was a highly gifted poet; but his poems were, like his life, irregular, lacking sobriety and dignity. The best of them are: 'Spastaras Dod' (1783); 'Aret,' (1783); 'Ythersta Domen'; and the opera 'Medea.'

Lie, Jonas Laurits Idemil (lē). A Norwegian poet; born at Eker, near Drammen, June 11, 1833. He published a collection of his 'Poems' (1866); 'The Ghost-Seer,' a novel (1870); 'Pictures from Norway' (3d ed. 1880); 'Lotse and his Wife' (1874); 'Fanfulla,' an italian tale (1875); 'Faustina Strozzi,' a lyrico-dramatic poem (1875). Thereafter he wrote a series of novels; among which were: 'Thomas Ross' (1878); 'Adam Schrader' (1879); 'The Commander's Daughter' (1886); 'Evil Powers' (1890). He also issued the comedies, 'Garbow's Cat' (1880); and 'Merry Wives' (1894).

Lieber, Franz (lē'ber). An eminent American publicist; born at Berlin, Germany, March 18, 1800; died in New York, Oct. 2, 1872. He volunteered as a soldier at 15, and was in the battles of Ligny, Waterloo, and Namur. He served also in the Greek war of independence, recording his experiences in 'Journal in Greece' (1823). He settled in the United States in 1827, and during the next five years was occupied with the compilation of the 'Encyclopædia Americana' (13 vols.). While professor of history and political economy in South Carolina College, he wrote the three great works on which his fame mainly rests: 'Manual of Political Ethics' (1838); 'Legal and Political Hermeneutics' (1839); 'Civil Liberty and Self-Government' (1853). In the beginning of the Civil War he drew up by order of President Lincoln the 'Code of War for the Government of the Armies of the United States in the Field.'

Liebig, Justus, Baron von (lē'biG). A German chemist; born at Darmstadt, May 12, 1803; died at Munich, April 18, 1873. In 1826 he was appointed professor of chemistry in the University of Giessen, and there set up the first chemical laboratory for experimental instruction. He was a very successful lecturer, and attracted students from all over the world. His treatises and memoirs on theoretical and practical chemistry are very numerous, and are of exceptional value; and the term "Liebig's Extract" is certainly a "household word." No other chemist of great rank has so sedulously striven to make the science a tender to practical utilities. Among his writings on the chemistry of agriculture are: 'Principles of Agricultural Chemistry' (1855); 'Theory and Practice of Farming' (1856); 'Scientific Letters on Modern Farming' (1859).

Liebknecht, Wilhelm (lēb'nećht). A German socialist agitator; born at Giessen, March 29, 1826. He is editor-in-chief of the organ of the Social Democratic party, Vorwärts; author of 'The Fundamental Question' (1876); 'A Glance at the New World' (1887), recounting his observations during a visit to the United States; 'Robert Blum' (1890); 'History of the French Revolution' (1890); 'Robert Owen' (1892). His work on 'Woman' is widely known. He died Aug. 7, 1900.

Lieblein, Jens Daniel Carolus (lēb'līn). A Norwegian Egyptologist; born at Christiania, Dec. 23, 1827. He has written works on Egyptology in French, German, Swedish, and Norwegian; among them: 'Egyptian Chronology' (1863); 'Dictionary of Hieroglyphic Names' (1871–92); 'Trade and Shipping in the Red Sea in Ancient Times' (1887).

Liebrecht, Felix (lēb'rećht). A noted German mythologist; born at Namslau, Silesia, March 13, 1812; died at St. Hubert, France, Aug. 3, 1890. He made a study of the sagas and legends of various countries. Among his writings are: translations, with critical annotations, of Giambattista Basile's 'Pentamerone, or the Story of Stories' (1846); of the 'Baarlam and Josaphat' of John of Damascus (1847); and of Dunlop's 'History of Prose Poems.'

Ligne, Charles Joseph, Prince de (lēn). A Belgian soldier and miscellaneous writer; born at Brussels, May 12, 1735; died Dec. 13, 1814. He wrote: 'Military, Literary, and Sentimental Miscellanies' (3 vols., 1795–1811); 'Life of Prince Eugene of Savoy' (2 vols., 1809). From his correspondence, journals, etc., Mme. de Staël compiled two volumes of 'Letters and Thoughts' (1809).

Liguori, Alfonso Maria de (lē-gwō'rē). An Italian theologian and Doctor of the Church; born at Naples, 1696; died Aug. 1, 1787. While bishop of Sant' Agata de' Goti, he founded the religious congregation of Redemptorists. He was "beatified" in 1816; canonized in 1839; proclaimed "Doctor of the Universal Church" in 1871. He wrote 'Moral Theology' (ed. of 1881, 8 vols.), and many books of devotion.

Liliencron, Detlev, Baron von (lēl'yen-krōn''). A German novelist and poet; born at Kiel, June 3, 1844. He wrote: 'The Adjutant's Rides, and Other Poems' (1883); 'A Summer Battle' (1886), a collection of stories; 'Work Ennobles' (1886); 'The Merovingians, a Tragedy' (1888); the novels 'Under Fluttering Banners' (1888), and 'Mæcenas' (1889); and several volumes of collected poems. Died 1909.

Liliencron, Rochus, Baron von. A German philologist; born at Plön in Holstein, Dec. 8, 1820. He is author of 'Runic Writing' (1852); 'Songs and Sayings from the Latest Period of the Minnesingers' (1855); 'Historic Popular Ballads of Germany from the 13th to the 16th Century' (4 vols., 1864–69); 'German Life in the Folk-Song of the 16th Century.'

Lillie, Mrs. Lucy Cecil (White). An American writer of juvenile literature; born in New York State in 1855. Among her most popular works are: 'Prudence' (1882); 'Rolf House'

.(1886); 'The Colonel's Money' (1888); 'The Squire's Daughter' (1891); 'Alison's Adventures' (1895).

Lillo, George. An eminent English dramatist; born at Moorfields, Feb. 4, 1693; died in London, Sept. 3, 1739. The son of a Dutch jeweler, he was brought up to his father's trade, and was for several years in partnership with him. 'Silvia, or the Country Burial' (1730), a ballad opera, was his first piece; and was followed (1731) by the famous 'London Merchant, or the History of George Barnwell,' nowadays better known by its sub-title, which made its author famous, and held the stage for nearly a century. It had a marked influence in its day, and may be regarded as a precursor of the «domestic drama.» His other dramatic productions include: 'Britannia, or the Royal Lovers' (1734); 'Fatal Curiosity' (1736); 'Arden of Feversham,' an adaptation of an Elizabethan play, revised or completed by John Hoadly after Lillo's death.

Lilly, William Samuel. An English controversial writer; born at Fifehead, Dorsetshire, 1840. He is a champion of the Catholic point of view in such works as 'Ancient Religion and Modern Thought' (1884); 'The Claims of Christianity'; 'Christianity and Modern Civilization.'

Limburg-Brouwer, Petrus van (lĕm'börg-brou'er). A Dutch scholar; born at Dordrecht, Sept. 30, 1795; died at Groningen, June 21, 1847. He wrote 'History of the Moral and Religious Civilization of the Greeks' (3 vols., 1833–42), still highly valued; two fine historical novels with the scene laid in ancient Greece,—'Charicles and Euphorion' (1831), and 'Diophanes' (1838); and a novel relating to his own time, 'The Reading Society' (1847).

Limburg-Brouwer, Petrus Abraham Samuel van. A Dutch novelist, son of Petrus; born at Liège, Nov. 15, 1829; died at The Hague, Feb. 13, 1873. He wrote the Oriental romance 'Akbar' (1872), the work of a man of poetic sensibility and most intimate knowledge of Indian literature.

Lincoln, Abraham. Sixteenth President of the United States, the great «War President»; born in Hardin County, Ky., Feb. 12, 1809; died at Washington, April 15, 1865. His 'Address' on the occasion of the dedication of the National Cemetery at Gettysburg, Pa., Nov. 19, 1863, is justly esteemed one of the most memorable utterances of human eloquence; classic also is his 'Second Inaugural Address' of March 4, 1865.

Lindau, Paul (lin'dou). A German novelist and literary critic; born at Magdeburg, June 3, 1839. He has written books of travel, including 'From Venice' (1864); 'From Paris'; works of literary criticism, as 'Harmless Letters of a Provincial German' (2 vols., 1870); 'Literary Trivialities' (1871) 'Molière' (1872); 'Afred de Musset' (1877); 'From Literary France' (1880); and novels, — 'Mr. and Mrs. Brewer' (1882); 'Berlin,' and the drama 'Maria and Magdalena.'

Lindau, Rudolf. A German diplomat and novelist; born at Gardelegen, Oct. 10, 1830. He was for many years engaged in the consular and diplomatic service of Switzerland and Germany. His principal novels are: 'Robert Ashton' (1877); 'Liquidated' (1877); 'Good Company' (1880); 'The Flirt' (1894); 'Silence' (1895). Some of his stories are perfect works of art; all of them mirror with rare fidelity life in the four quarters of the globe, as seen and studied by a man of very extensive travel.

Lindner, Albert (lind'ner). A German dramatist; born at Sulza in Saxe-Weimar, April 24, 1831; died at Berlin, Feb. 4, 1888. His tragedy 'Brutus and Collatinus' won him the Schiller prize. 'The Bloody Nuptials, or St. Bartholomew's Eve' (1871) had extraordinary success upon the stage. He wrote several other tragedies: 'Marino Faliero' (1875); 'Don John of Austria' (1875)); 'The Reformer' (1883). He wrote also 'The Swan of Avon' (1881), and 'The Riddle of Woman's Soul' (1881).

Lindner, Theodor. An Austrian historian; born May 29, 1843. Among his numerous works are: 'The Vehm' (1887); 'German History under the Hapsburgs and Luxemburgs' (1889–93); and 'History of the German People' (1894).

Lindsay, Sir David of the Mount. A Scotch poet; born about 1490; died before May 1555. His satires in rhyme were noted for their ridicule of the clergy. His works include : 'The Dreme' (1528); 'Satyre of the Thrie Estaitis' (1539); and 'Historie of Squier Meldrun' (1548).

Lindsey, William. An American poet and prose-writer; born in Massachusetts in 1858. His works are: 'Apples of Istakhar' (1895), a volume of poems; and 'Cinder-Path Tales' (1896), stories of athletic sports.

Linen, James. A Scottish poet; born 1808; died in New York city, 1873. His dialect poems appeared in the Knickerbocker Magazine and the Scottish-American Journal; a collection, 'Songs of the Seasons, and Other Poems,' was published in 1852; 'The Golden Gate' appeared in 1869.

Ling, Peter Henrik. A Swedish poet; born at Ljunga, Nov. 15, 1776; died at Stockholm, May 3, 1839. He founded Swedish gymnastics, and wrote 'The General Principles of Gymnastics' (1840). He also produced several spirited lyric poems, tragedies, and epics, to inspire his countrymen to emulate the exploits of the ancient heroes of Scandinavia.

Lingg, Hermann (ling). A German poet; born at Lindau, Jan. 22, 1820. He published (1853) a volume of 'Poems' of great originality, and remarkable for wealth of imagery and deep elegiac tone. 'The Migration of Peoples' (3 books, 1866–68) showed grandeur and epic power. His dramas are less admirable; among them are: 'The Doge Candiano' (1873); 'The Sicilian Vespers'; and 'Catiline.' Besides 'Patriotic Ballads' (1868), 'Dark Powers,' and several volumes of collected poems, he has written 'Byzantine Tales' (1881); 'From Forest and Lake,' five stories (1883); 'Clytia, a Scene from Pompeii' (1883).

Linguet, Simon Nicolas Henri (lan-gā'). A French writer of history; born at Rheims, July 14, 1736; died June 27, 1794. He won great fame by his 'History of the Age of Alexander' (1762), and his 'Judiciary Memoirs' (7 vols.). Of his numerous works on laws, politics, science, etc., these may be mentioned: 'History of the Revolutions of the Roman Empire' (2 vols.); 'Theory of the Civil Law' (1767); 'Impartial History of the Jesuits' (1768); 'Memoirs on the Bastille' (1783).

Linnæus, Carolus (lin-nē'us) — **(Karl von Linné)**. A celebrated Swedish naturalist; born at Råshult in Småland, May 13, 1707; died at Upsala, Jan. 10, 1778. Among his writings are: 'The System of Nature, or the Three Kingdoms of Nature Systematically Arranged' (7 vols., 1735); 'Foundations of Botany' (1736); 'Library of Botany' (1736); 'Genera of Plants' (1737); 'Classes of Plants' (1738); 'Philosophy of Botany' (1751); 'System of Plants' (1779).

Linton, Eliza (Lynn). An English novelist, wife of William J.; born in Keswick, Feb. 10, 1822; died in London, July 14, 1898. Her first novel, 'Azeth the Egyptian,' appeared 1846; she also published: 'Witch Stories' (1861); 'The Lake Country' (1864); 'Patricia Kemble' (1874); 'The World Well Lost' (1877); 'My Love' (1881); 'The One Too Many' (1894); etc.

Linton, William James. An English wood-engraver, poet, and miscellaneous writer; born in London, 1812; died Jan. 1, 1898. A draughtsman of repute, and for a period an illustrator on the Illustrated London News, he removed to the United States in 1867 and opened an engraving establishment at New Haven, Conn. Besides works on engraving he wrote a 'Life of Thomas Watson' (the Chartist leader), giving a history of the Chartist movement, in which he shared ardently; a 'Life of Thomas Paine'; 'Claribel and Other Poems' (1865); 'The Flower and the Star' (1869); stories for children; edited 'Rare Poems of the 16th and 17th Centuries' (1883); and was co-editor with R. H. Stoddard of 'English Verse' (1883).

Lippard, George. An American story-writer; born at Yellow Springs, Pa., April 10, 1822; died at Philadelphia, Feb. 9, 1854. His most notorious work was 'The Quaker City' (1845), modeled on Sue's 'Mysteries of Paris,' and implying that Philadelphia was a modern Sodom, though he disclaimed the inference when threatened with legal consequences. 'Mysteries and Miseries of Philadelphia' and 'The Empire City: New York — Its Upper Ten and Lower Million' were companion pieces. He wrote also 'Paul Ardenheim,' a Rosicrucian romance; 'Legends of Mexico' and 'Legends of the Revolution' (1847); 'Washington and his Generals'; and others.

Lippert, Julius (lip'ert). A German historian; born at Braunau in Bohemia, April 12,

1839. He wrote: 'Animism in its Relations to the Ancient Hebrew Religion' (1880); 'Religions of the European Culture-Peoples' (1881); 'Christianism, Popular Beliefs, and Popular Usages' (1882); 'History of the Family' (1885); 'History of Civilization in its Leading Features' (1886); 'History of German Manners and Morals' (1889).

Lippincott, Sarah Jane (Clarke). ["Grace Greenwood."] An American writer of prose and verse; born in Pompey, N. Y., Sept. 23, 1823. She was favorably known as an editor and contributor. 'Ariadne' is one of her best poems. She published: 'Greenwood Leaves' (1850); 'Poems' (1851); 'Merrie England' (1855); 'Records of Five Years' (1868); and 'New Life in New Lands' (1873). Died April 20, 1904.

Lippmann, Julie Mathilde. An American writer of verse and juvenile literature; born in Brooklyn, N. Y., in 1864. She is the author of 'Through Slumbertown and Wakeland'; 'Jock o' Dreams,' a collection of short stories; and 'Miss Wildfire'; 'The Facts in the Case.'

Lipsius, Justus (lip'sē-us). [Properly Joest Lips.] A celebrated Dutch humanist; born at Overyssche, Belgium, Oct. 18, 1547; died at Louvain, March 23, 1606. His strength lay chiefly in the Latin historians and in Roman antiquities; his editions of Tacitus and of Seneca, with commentaries, were prepared with extreme care, and (especially Tacitus) finally determined the genuine text in all essential particulars. In addition he wrote 48 separate treatises and essays, among them: 'The Amphitheatre' (1584); 'On Politics' (1589); 'The Cross' (1593); 'The Military System of the Romans' (1595); 'Vesta and the Vestal Virgins' (1603); 'Introduction to the Stoic Philosophy' (1604); 'Natural Philosophy of the Stoics' (1604).

Lipsius, Marie. See **La Mara**.

Lipsius, Richard Adelbert. A German theologian; born at Gera, Feb. 14, 1830; died at Jena, Aug. 19, 1892. Among his writings are: 'The Pauline Doctrine of Justification' (1853); 'Gnosticism' (1860); 'Chronology of the Bishops of Rome' (1869); 'Sources of the Roman Fable of Peter' (1872); 'Text-Book of Protestant Dogmatic Theology' (1876); 'Philosophy and Religion' (1885); 'Chief Heads of Christian Doctrine' (1889); 'Brief Commentary on the New Testament' (2 vols., 1891); 'Luther's Doctrine of Penance' (1892).

List, Friedrich (list). A German political economist; born at Reutlingen, Aug. 6, 1789; died at Kufstein, Nov. 30, 1846. He emigrated to the United States in 1825, and settled at Harrisburg, Pa. There he wrote 'Outlines of a New System of Political Economy' (1827). He went to Leipsic (1833) as American consul, and did not return to America. He published (1841) Vol. i. of 'The National System of Political Economy' (7th ed. 1884).

Lista y Aragon, Alberto (lēs'tä ē ä-rä-gōn'). A distinguished Spanish poet; born at Triana, near Seville, Oct. 15, 1775; died there, Oct. 5,

1845 He was one of the best lyric poets of his time in Spain, with a rich fancy, deep sensibility, and a philosophic mind. His 'Poems' were published in 2 vols. (2d ed. 1837). He wrote a 'Course of Universal History,' an adaptation of Ségur's work; and 'Literary and Critical Essays' (2 vols., 1884).

Lister, Sir Joseph. An eminent English surgeon; born April 5, 1827. He first suggested the antiseptic mode of treating surgical cases. Among his writings are: 'Early Stages of Inflammation' (1859); 'Ligature of Arteries and the Antiseptic System' (1869); 'The Germ Theory of Fermentative Changes' (1875); 'Lactic Fermentation and its Bearings on Pathology' (1878).

Liszt, Franz (list). A great Hungarian pianist and composer; born at Raiding, near Ödenburg, Oct. 22, 1811; died at Bayreuth, July 31, 1886. At 13 he composed the operetta 'Don Sancho,' which was successfully produced at the Paris Grand Opera in 1825. His chief contributions to the literature of music are: 'Wagner's 'Lohengrin' and 'Tannhäuser'' (1851); 'The Gipsies and their Music in Hungary' (1859); 'Robert Franz' (1872). There is a collection of his 'Letters' (3 vols., 1892–93); also of his correspondence with Richard Wagner (2 vols., 1887).

Litchfield, Grace Denio. An American novelist; born in New York city, 1849. She has lived in Europe for a number of years, and now resides in Washington, D. C. Among her works are: 'Only an Incident' (1883); 'The Knight of the Black Forest' (1885); 'Criss Cross' (1885); 'A Hard-Won Victory' (1888); 'In the 'Crucible'; 'Vita'; 'The Letter.'

Litta, Pompeo, Count (lēt'ä). An Italian writer of history; born at Milan, Sept. 27, 1781; died Aug. 17, 1852. After his death, was published in 183 parts his great work 'Celebrated Italian Families' (1819–82), containing memoirs of 75 noble families.

Littledale, Richard Frederick. An English clergyman and religious writer; born in Dublin in 1833; died in 1890. He was curate of St. Mary Virgin, London, from 1857 to 1861, when he resigned on account of ill-health and devoted himself to the study of religious subjects, particularly the Anglican ritual. Among a number of polemical, historical, exegetic, and other publications, are: 'The Catholic Ritual in the Church of England' (1865); 'Pharisaic Proselytism' (1870); 'Plain Reasons against Joining the Church of Rome' (1880); 'A Short History of the Council of Trent' (1888).

Littleton, Sir Thomas. An English jurist; born in Frankley, Worcestershire, 1402; died there, Aug. 23, 1481. He wrote a treatise on tenures, known through Coke's Commentaries. 'Coke on Littleton' is a secondary course in the bringing up of young lawyers.

Littré, Maximilien Paul Émile (lē-trā'). A celebrated French philologist, philosopher, lexicographer, and author; born at Paris, Feb. 1,

1801; died there, June 2, 1881. He was one of the greatest linguists and scientists of the century, best known for his celebrated 'Dictionary of the French Language' (1863–72). In addition to his labors as a philologist he contributed to various scientific and philosophical journals, was active in politics, translated the works of Hippocrates (10 vols., 1839–61), which admitted him to the Academy of Inscriptions, and Pliny's 'Natural History' (1848), and wrote a 'History of the French Language' (1862); 'Studies of the Barbarians and the Middle Ages' (1867); 'Medicine and Physicians' (1872), 'Literature and History' (1875); 'The Establishment of the Third Republic' (1880); and several treatises on Auguste Comte's positive philosophy, of which he was an ardent advocate. In 1871 he was elected to the French Academy.

Littrow, Heinrich von (lit'trou). An Austrian naval officer and writer on maritime affairs; born at Vienna, Jan. 26, 1820; died April 25, 1895. He is author of a 'Maritime Dictionary' (1851); 'Manual of Seamanship' (1859); 'From the Sea,' a volume of verse (4th ed. 1876); 'Karl Weyprecht, Austrian Polar Explorer' (1881); 'Pictures of Travel' (4th ed. 1883).

Littrow, Josef Johann von. An Austrian astronomer; born at Bischofsteinitz in Bohemia, March 13, 1781; died Nov. 30, 1840. By his writings and public lectures he contributed largely to the diffusion of astronomical knowledge in Austria. His chief works are: 'Theoretic and Practical Astronomy' (2 vols., 1821); 'Wonders of the Heavens' (1834; 8th ed. 1894); 'Atlas of the Starry Heavens' (1838; 3d ed. 1870).

Livermore, Mary Ashton (Rice). An American reformer and lecturer; born in Boston, Dec. 19, 1820. In 1862 she was appointed agent of the Northwestern branch of the United States Sanitary Commission. Since the War she has been conspicuous in her efforts to promote the woman-suffrage and temperance movements. Among her popular lectures are: 'What Shall We Do with Our Daughters?' 'Women of the War'; 'The Moral Heroism of the Temperance Reform.' She is the author of 'Pen Pictures' (1865), 'Thirty Years Too Late' (1878), and a work setting forth her experiences during the War. Died May 23, 1905.

Livingstone, David. A celebrated Scotch traveler; born at Blantyre, March 19, 1813; died in Central Africa, May 1, 1873. He first went out to Africa in the service of the London Missionary Society, 1840. He discovered the Victoria Falls of the Zambezi in 1855, and soon afterward returned to England. He went back to Africa in 1858, and continued his labors as missionary and explorer till 1864; but after a few months he was in the field again, and there remained, without any communication with Europe, till he was found by Stanley. He continued his work in Africa till his death. His works are: 'Missionary Travels and Re-

searches in South Africa' (2 vols., 1857); 'Narrative of an Expedition to the Zambezi and its Tributaries' (1865); 'Last Journals of David Livingstone in Central Africa, from 1865 to his Death' (1874).

Livius Andronicus. See **Andronicus.**

Livy — Titus Livius. A great Roman historian; born at Patavium (Padua), 59 B. C.; died there, 17 A. D. He wrote the 'History of Rome from the Founding of the City' in 142 «books,» of which only 35 have come down to us, — books 1-10, reaching to the year 293 B. C., and books 21-45, covering the years 218-167 B. C.; of the lost books some fragments remain.

Ljunggren, Gustaf Hakon Jordan (lyöng'-gren). A Swedish writer on æsthetics; born at Lund, March 6, 1823. He wrote: 'Winckelmann and Ehrensvärd Compared as Philosophers of Art' (1856); 'The Leading Systems of Æsthetics' (2 vols., 1856); 'The Swedish Drama' (1864); 'Swedish Literature since Gustavus III.' (5 vols., 1873-95); 'History of the Swedish Academy' (2 vols., 1886).

Llorente, Juan Antonio Don (lyō-rän'tā). A Spanish writer of history; born at Rincon de Soto in Andalusia, March 30, 1756; died at Madrid, Feb. 5, 1823. He was ordained priest in 1770; was commissary of the Inquisition at Logroño in 1785, and general secretary of the Inquisition at Madrid in 1789. He was commissioned in 1793 to draw up plans for a general reform of the procedure of the court. His greatest work is the celebrated 'Critical History of the Spanish Inquisition' (4 vols., 1815-17). He wrote also 'Political Portraits of the Popes'; 'Memoirs Relating to the History of the Spanish Revolution' (3 vols., 1815-19).

Lloyd, David Demarest. An American journalist and playwright; born in New York city, 1851; died at Weehawken, N. J., 1889. He graduated at the College of New York, and soon after was attached to the staff of the New York Tribune. As a correspondent at Albany in 1875 he was prominent in exposing the canal ring. Besides contributions to magazines, he wrote four plays: 'For Congress' (1883); 'The Woman Hater' (1885); 'The Dominie's Daughter' (1887); 'The Senator' (1889).

Lloyd, Henry Demarest. An American writer on economics, brother of David; born in New York State in 1847. He received his education at Columbia College, and shortly after graduating joined the editorial staff of the Chicago Tribune. At present he resides in Winnetka, Ill. His chief work is the notable book 'Wealth Against Commonwealth.' He has also written 'A Strike of Millionaires against Miners.' Died Sept. 28, 1903.

Lobo, Francisco Rodrigues (lō'bō). A Portuguese poet; died about 1623. Practically nothing is known of his life. He is one of the most admired of Portuguese poets, among his popular works being: 'Romances' (1596); 'Eclogues' (1605); 'Court in the Country'

(1610), long deemed his masterpiece; and various others.

Locke, David Ross. ["Petroleum V. Nasby."] An American satirist; born in Vestal, N. Y., Sept. 20, 1833; died in Toledo, O., Feb. 15, 1888. He gained celebrity as the author of the widely known 'Nasby Letters' on politics, and produced many pamphlets on literary, political, and social topics. Among his publications are: 'The Moral History of America's Life Struggle'; 'The Morals of Abou ben Adhem, or Eastern Fruit in Western Dishes.'

Locke, Jane Ermina. An American writer of prose and verse; born in Worthington, Mass., April 25, 1805; died in Ashburnham, Mass., March 8, 1859. Her contributions appeared in the Ladies' American Magazine. 'Poems' was published in 1842; 'The Recalled, or Voices of the Past,' 1855; a 'Eulogy on the Death of Webster,' in rhyme, 1855.

Locke, John. A celebrated English philosopher; born at Wrington, near Bristol, Aug. 29, 1632; died at Oates (Essex), Oct. 28, 1704. Among his philosophical writings the first place is held by the 'Essay concerning Human Understanding' (1690). In the field of political science he wrote: 'An Epistle on Tolerance' (1689); a second letter (1690); a third (1692); and 'Two Treatises on Government' (1690). On the subject of religious beliefs he wrote: 'The Reasonableness of Christianity as delivered in the Scriptures' (1695), and a first and second 'Vindication' of the same (1695-97). On education he wrote 'Some Thoughts on Education' (1693), and 'Some Thoughts concerning Reading and Study' (1706). Among his miscellaneous writings were 'The Fundamental Constitutions of Carolina' (1706), and 'Elements of Natural Philosophy' (1706).

Locke, John Staples. An American writer; born in 1836. He is a resident of Saco, Me. Among his works are: 'Picture Rhymes for Happy Times' (1886); 'A Brave Struggle,' a novel (1887); 'Shores of Saco Bay'; 'Historical Sketches of Old Orchard.' He died 190-.

Locker-Lampson, Frederick. An English poet; born at Greenwich, May 29, 1821; died at Rowfant, May 30, 1895. He wrote «society verses», among them: 'London Lyrics' (1857); 'Lyra Elegantiarum' (1867); 'Patchwork' (1879).

Lockhart, John Gibson. A Scotch biographer and poet, son-in-law of Sir Walter Scott; born at Cambusnethan, Lanark, 1794; died at Abbotsford, Nov. 25, 1854. His writings are: 'Peter's Letters to his Kinsfolk' (1819); the novels 'Valerius' (1821), 'Adam Blair' (1822), 'Reginald Dalton' (1823), 'Matthew Wald' (1824); a volume of translations of 'Ancient Spanish Ballads' (1823); 'Life of Robert Burns' (1828); 'Life of Sir Walter Scott' (7 vols., 1839-41), his most celebrated work.

Lockhart, Laurence William Maxwell. A British novelist, nephew of J. G.; born in Lanarkshire, 1831; died at Mentone, March 23,

1882. Among his novels are: 'Double and Quits'; 'Fair to See'; and 'Mine Is Thine.'

Lockroy, Édouard Étienne Antoine Simon (lok-rwä'). A French journalist and statesman; born in Paris, July 18, 1838. He was prominent as a journalist before and after the war with Germany, and suffered several months' imprisonment for his radical articles published in Figaro, The Recall, and The Sovereign People,—a popular political journal, of which he was editor. In recent years he has figured conspicuously in political life, having been Minister of Commerce in 1886, and of Public Instruction in 1888. His published volumes are composed mainly of articles contributed to various journals, and include: 'The Eagles of the Capitol' (1869); 'Down with Progress' (1870); 'The Commune and the Assembly' (1871); 'The Rebel Island' (1877); 'Von Moltke' (1891), memoires; 'A Mission in the Vendée, 1793' (1893); 'From the Weser to the Vistula' (1901).

Lockyer, Joseph Norman. An English astronomer and physicist; born at Rugby, May 17, 1836. He is editor of Nature, the leading scientific weekly publication in England. Among his works are · 'Elementary Lessons in Astronomy' (1868; 44th thousand 1894); 'Contributions to Solar Physics' (1873); 'The Spectroscope and its Applications' (1873); 'Stargazing, Past and Present' (1877); 'The Dawn of Astronomy'; (1894); 'Inorganic Evolution' (1900).

Lodge, Henry Cabot. An American writer of history and biography; born at Boston, May 12, 1850. He was lecturer on history at Harvard 1876-79, and editor of the North American Review 1873-76. He then entered political life, and in 1893 was elected United States Senator from Massachusetts. He is the author of a 'Life of Daniel Webster,' and of lives of Alexander Hamilton and George Washington; also of 'Boston' in the series of 'Historic Towns'; of a 'Short History of the English Colonies in America'; 'Studies in History' (1884); 'Historical and Political Essays'; 'Hero Tales from American History'; 'Certain Accepted Heroes, and Other Essays'; etc.

Lodge, Thomas. An English poet, dramatist, and story-writer; born at London, about 1558; died there, 1625. He wrote: 'A Defense of Poetry, Music, and Stage-Plays' (1579); 'Alarum Against Usurers' (1584); the story of 'Rosalynde, Euphues' Golden Legacie' (1590), the basis of Shakespeare's 'As You Like It'; the play 'Looking-Glasse for London and England'; 'History of Robin the Divell' (1591); 'Life and Death of William Longbeard' (1593); 'Phillis' (1593), a collection of lyrical pieces.

Loftie, William John. An Irish clergyman, editor, and writer on antiquities; born at Tandragee, County Armagh, in 1839. After holding temporary Church appointments, he became assistant minister of the Chapel Royal, Savoy, in 1871; and in 1874 joined the staff of the Saturday Review, besides contributing to the Portfolio and the Magazine of Art. As a writer on antiquarian subjects he successfully combines the qualities of learning and picturesqueness, particularly in 'Round About London' (1877; 4th ed. 1880); 'Memorials of the Savoy' (1879); 'A History of London' (1883); 'Authorized Guide to the Tower of London' (1886); 'The Cathedral Churches of England' (1892); 'Inns of Court and Chancery' (1894) 'London Afternoons.'

Logan, Cornelius Ambrosius. An American dramatist; born in Baltimore, Md., 1806; died near Wheeling, Va., 1853. He made a vigorous reply to Lyman Beecher's attack upon the stage from the pulpit. He wrote successful plays: 'Yankee Land' (1834); 'A Hundred Years Hence,' a burlesque. He also wrote tales and poems.

Logan, John Alexander. An American general and statesman; born in Jackson County, Ill., 1826; died in Washington, D. C., 1886. He distinguished himself both in the field and the forum. He published: 'The Great Conspiracy' (1866); 'The Volunteer Soldier of America' (1887).

Logan, Olive. An American miscellaneous writer; born in Elmira, N. Y., 1839. She began her career as an actress in Philadelphia 1854; retired from the stage in 1868; since then has been a lecturer on social topics, and a contributor to newspapers and magazines. She married W. W. Sikes, a journalist. She is the author of lectures, plays, and books. Among the latter are: 'Château Frissac' (1860); 'Photographs of Paris' (1860); 'Women and Theatres' (1869); and 'Before the Footlights and Behind the Scenes: a Book about the Show Business' (1870).

Logau, Friedrich von (lō-gou'). A German epigrammatist; born at Brockut, Silesia, June 1604; died at Liegnitz, July 24, 1655. He wrote under the pseudonym "Salomon von Golau," anagram of his true name. His works are: 'First Century of German Rhymed Adages' (1638); 'Three Thousand German Epigrams' (1654). He was an original thinker and a forceful writer, but soured by adversity and by contemplation of the evils of his time.

Lohenstein, Daniel Casper von (lō'en-stīn). A Silesian poet; born at Nimpsch in Silesia, Jan. 25, 1635; died at Breslau, April 28, 1683. He wrote a volume of lyric verse, 'Flowers'; six tragedies; and a long hero-romance, 'The Magnanimous General Arminius or Hermann, with his Most Illustrious Thusnelda,' etc. (new ed. 1889-90). This mammoth work, of 3076 double-column pages, and unfinished at that, was in its day regarded as the consummate model of the heroic-gallant romance. His lyrics are tasteless; his tragedies insufferably bombastic.

Löher, Franz von (lè'er). A German miscellaneous writer; born at Paderborn, Oct. 15, 1818; died at Munich, March 1, 1892. He visited the United States and Canada in 1846, to gather material for a history of the Germans in America, and wrote 'Significance of the German Race in the World's History' (1847); 'History of the Germans in America' (1848). He wrote also : ' Land and People in the Old and New Worlds' (1854); 'The Magyars and Other Hungarians' (1874); 'Cyprus' (1878); and many other sketches of history and notes of travel.

Loiseau, Jeanne (lwä-zō'). ["Daniel Lesueur."] A celebrated French poet and romantic writer. She ranks among the best of French contemporary poets, being compared to Meurne, Ackermann, and Sully-Prudhomme. Her 'Flowers of April,' 'Dreams and Visions,' and a translation of the 'Works of Lord Byron' (of which two volumes have appeared), were crowned by the French Academy. Among her successful romances are : 'The Neurotic'; 'Passion's Slave'; 'Woman's Justice'; 'The Hatred of Love.'

Lokmân (lok-män'). An Arabian sage anterior to Mohammed. In legendary story he figures now as King of Yemen, then as a prophet, again as an Abyssinian slave. Under his name we have, besides certain sayings contained in the Koran or current in the common speech, a small collection of 'Fables,' which in no wise merit the praises bestowed upon them. They are an awkward adaptation of Æsop's fables, and are not of earlier date than the sixteenth or the fifteenth century.

Lolli, Giambattista (lōl'lē). A celebrated Italian chess-player. He was a native of Modena. His classical work 'The Game of Chess' appeared in 1763.

Loman, Abraham Dirk (lō'män). A Dutch theologian ; born at the Hague, Sept. 16, 1823. He became professor of theology in the University of Amsterdam in 1877. He is one of the foremost of the Dutch Radical critics of the Scriptures. He wrote : 'The Testimony of the Muratorian Canon' (1865); 'Protestantism and the Authority of the Church' (1868); 'The Gospel of John' (1873); 'Symbol and Fact in the Gospel History'; (1884). Died April 18, 1897.

Lombardi, Eliodoro (lom-bär'dē). An Italian poet and man of letters; born at Marsala, 18—. His 'Songs' (1884), and 'Evolutionary Process in Literature' (1888), are well known.

Lombroso, Cesare (lom-brō'sō). An Italian scientist; born in Venice, November 1836. He has attained world-wide celebrity as an investigator of pathology, psychiatry, nervous diseases, and allied departments of science. His principal works are : 'Researches on Cretinism in Lombardy' (1859); 'Genius and Insanity' (1864); 'Clinical Studies on Mental Diseases' (1865); 'Microcephaly and Cretinism' (1873); 'Love in Suicide and in Crime' (1881); 'The Criminal as related to Anthropology, Jurisprudence, and Prison Discipline' (4th ed. 1889); 'The Man of Genius as Related to Psychiatry' (1889); 'Female Criminals' (1893); 'Anti-Semitism and the Modern Sciences' (1894); 'The Anarchists' (1894); 'Crime ; its Causes and Remedies.' Died 1909.

Loménie, Louis Léonard de (lō-mä-nē'). A French man of letters ; born at St. Yrieix, Haute

Vienne, 1815; died 1878. He had an intimate acquaintance with contemporary European literature. His writings were 'Gallery of Contemporaries' (1840–47); 'Beaumarchais and his Time' (1855); and many more.

Lomonossov, Michail Vasilyévich (lō-mō-nos'ov). A Russian poet and man of science ; born at Dennisowka, Archangel, 1711 or 1712; died at St. Petersburg, April 15, 1765. He is "father of Russian grammar and literature." He was made instructor in chemistry and physics in the Academy in 1742, and professor of chemistry in 1745. He was the first to write polished lyric verse in Russian : his models were the classic poets of France. Among his odes is the celebrated one 'On the Taking of Chotin.' He wrote also songs, didactic poems, and poetical epistles. He failed in tragedy. His principal scientific works are : 'Atmospheric Phenomena Produced by Electricity'; 'Elements of Metallurgy'; 'Causes of Heat and Cold'; etc. Of very great importance are his philological writings; among them are 'On the Utility of Church Slavic for Study of the Russian Language'; 'Russian Grammar,' the publication of which marked an epoch.

Long, Charles Chaillé. An American soldier and author; born at Princess Anne, Somerset County, Md., 1842. He enlisted in the Union army in the Civil War, and attained the rank of captain. In 1869 he was appointed lieutenant-colonel in the Egyptian army; in 1874 he was made chief of staff to General Gordon, and employed on a diplomatic and geographical mission to the interior of Africa. In 1877 he returned to the United States, studied at the Columbia Law School, and was admitted to the bar. He was appointed consul-general in Corea in 1887. His works are : 'Central Africa' (1876); 'The Three Prophets—Chinese Gordon, the Mahdi, and Arabi Pasha'; 'The Sources of the Nile.'

Long, George. An English classical scholar; born at Poulton, Lancashire, 1800; died 1879. He was distinguished for his knowledge of Latin and Greek literature. He published an admirable translation of 'Thoughts of the Emperor M. Aurelius Antoninus' (1862–79) and 'Discourses of Epictetus' (1877).

Longfellow, Henry Wadsworth. An eminent American poet; born at Portland, Me., Feb. 27, 1807; died at Cambridge, Mass., March 24, 1882. He was a graduate of Bowdoin College in 1825. His early years were occupied in travel, and in studies in Spanish, French, and Italian literatures, and translations from each of them. 'Outre Mer, a Pilgrimage Beyond the Sea' was published in serial form in 1833–34 anonymously, but under his own name in 1835; 'Hyperion' followed (1839); 'Voices of the Night' (1839); 'Ballads and Other Poems' (1842); 'Poems on Slavery' (1842); 'The Spanish Student' (1843). His important collection 'Poets and Poetry of Europe,' still a favorite anthology, was published in 1845. Then came 'The Belfry of Bruges and Other Poems' (1846); 'Evangeline, a

Tale of Acadie' (1847); 'Kavanagh, a Tale' (1849); 'The Seaside and the Fireside' (1850); 'A Volume of Poems' (1850); 'The Golden Legend' (1851); 'Song of Hiawatha' (1855); 'Prose Works,' a series of essays, collected (1857); 'Poems,' complete edition (1857); 'Courtship of Miles Standish' (1858); 'Tales of a Wayside Inn' (1863); 'Household Poems' (1865). He translated and published Dante's 'Divine Comedy' in 1867; 'A New England Tragedy' came next (1868); 'The Building of a Ship' (1870); 'Excelsior' (1872); 'Christus: a Mystery,' in a volume comprising several of the foregoing (1872); 'Aftermath' (1873); 'The Hanging of the Crane' (1875); 'The Masque of Pandora and Other Poems' (1875). He edited his 'Poems of Places' in 31 vols. (1876–79); 'Poems of the Old South Church' (1877); 'The Skeleton in Armor' (1878); 'Kéramos and Other Poems' (1879). 'From my Arm-Chair' was printed in 1879; the volume 'Ultima Thule' in 1880; 'Michael Angelo' in 1884; 'Complete Poetical and Prose Works with Later Poems,' with a biographical sketch by Octavius B. Frothingham, in 1880–83.

Longfellow, Samuel. An American clergyman, poet, and author, brother of Henry W.; born in Portland, Me., June 18, 1819; died there, Oct. 3, 1892. He graduated from Harvard in 1839, and from the Divinity School in 1846. He held pastorates in Unitarian churches in Fall River, Mass., Brooklyn, N. Y., and Germantown, Pa. Later he settled in Cambridge, Mass. As a hymn-writer he had few equals. Among his works are: 'Hymns of the Spirit' (with the Rev. Samuel Johnson), published in 1848; 'Life of H. W. Longfellow' (1886); 'A Few Verses of Many Years' (1887).

Longinus, Cassius (lon-ji'nus). A celebrated Greek philosopher and rhetorician; lived about 210–273 A. D.; born at Athens. He taught at Athens till called to Palmyra by Queen Zenobia to be her counselor; he confirmed the Queen in her resolve to resist Roman domination, and on that account was beheaded by order of the Emperor Aurelian. He was a man of vast learning: his biographer calls him a "living library," a "walking museum." Of his voluminous writings, all that have come down to us are the prolegomena to Hephæstion's 'Metrics,' and a fragment of a treatise on rhetoric. The valuable little essay on 'The Sublime,' commonly attributed to him, is the work of some unknown writer of the first century of our era.

Longnon, Auguste Honoré (lôn-yôn'). A French historian and philologist; born at Paris, Oct. 18, 1844. He was a shoemaker, but by diligent cultivation of his rare natural gifts rose to eminence among French scholars. He became professor of history in the Collège de France, 1892. His principal works are: 'Geography of Gaul in the 6th Century' (1878); 'Historical Atlas of France' (1884–89).

Longstreet, Augustus Baldwin. An American lawyer, clergyman, educator, and author; born in Augusta, Ga., Sept. 22, 1790; died at Oxford, Miss., Sept. 9, 1870. He graduated at Yale in 1813, studied law at Litchfield, Conn., and was admitted to the bar in Richmond County, Ga., in 1815. In 1822 he removed to Augusta, Ga., and founded the Sentinel. In 1838 he entered the Methodist Episcopal ministry, and later was president of several Southern universities, chief among them being the University of Mississippi. His works include: 'Georgia Scenes' (1840); 'Letters from Georgia to Massachusetts.'

Longus (long'gus). A Greek romancer; belongs probably to the fifth century of our era. The pastoral romance 'Daphnis and Chloe,' the prototype of 'Paul and Virginia' and similar sentimental tales, is ascribed to him.

Lönnrot, Elias (lèn'rōt). A Finnish philologist; born at Sammatti, in Nyland, April 9, 1802; died there, March 19, 1884. Recognizing the value of the people's songs and ballads for Finnish language-study, he spent years in collecting such material in Finland, Lapland, and adjoining provinces, and published the fruits of his researches in a series of volumes. Among his "finds" is to be numbered the great popular epic 'Kalevala,' of which only a few cantos were previously known to the learned world. He wrote a 'Finnish-Swedish Dictionary' (2 vols., 1866–80). (See 'Kalevala.')

Loosjes, Adriaan (lōs'yes). A Dutch poet and novelist; born on the island of Texel in 1761; died at Haarlem in 1818. He was intended for the Church, but abandoned theology for the trade of bookseller, devoting his leisure to the composition of poems and especially historical romances which made him a favorite in Holland. Among the most popular were: 'Charlotte of Bourbon' (1792); 'Louise de Coligny' (1803); 'Johann de Witt' (1805); 'Maurice Lynslager' (1808). 'Love Songs' (1783); 'De Ruyter' (1784), an epic; and several dramas, constitute his other important works.

Lope de Vega. See Vega

Lopes or **Lopez, Fernão** (lō'päth). The oldest of the Portuguese chroniclers; born about 1380; died after 1459. Appointed chief archivist of the kingdom by Dom João I. in 1434, he devoted his life to historical research and to the composition of chronicles, which for literary and critical value were unsurpassed in his century. His 'Chronicle of Señor Don John I.,' describing the great struggle between Portugal and Castile, has invited comparison with Froissart's writings on account of its picturesqueness and dramatic reality. Equally vigorous are his chronicles of Dom Pedro I. and Don Fernando.

Lopes, Caetano (lo-pes). A Brazilian historian; born in Bahia, October 1780; died in Paris, Dec. 22, 1860. He was a mulatto, educated in Bahia and Paris; he settled in the latter in 1822 and became corresponding member of the Academy of Inscriptions and Belles-lettres. The emperor Pedro held him in high esteem.

The Historical Institute of Rio Janeiro bestowed a gold medal upon him. He was noted for brightness of style and purity of language. His works were numerous, treating of history, biography, and surgery.

Lopez y Planes, Vicente (lō'păth ē plä'nes). An Argentine poet; born in Buenos Ayres in 1784; died there in 1856. He was lawyer, soldier, politician, and author; founded the classic and topographical departments when the university was established. He was Member of Congress, 1819-25; provisional President of the republic, July 5 to Aug. 13, 1827; President of the supreme court of justice; and governor of the province of Buenos Ayres. He wrote the 'Argentine National Hymn' and other poetical works.

Lord, John. An American historian and lecturer; born in Berwick, Me., Sept. 10, 1809; died at Stamford, Conn., Dec. 15, 1894. He spent most of his life in historical study and lecturing; three years. (1843-46) were passed in England, where he spoke on 'The Middle Ages.' His lectures have been delivered in the principal towns and cities of the United States. The degree of LL.D. was given him by the University of New York in 1864. He published 'Modern History for Schools' (1850); 'The Old Roman World' (1867); 'Ancient States and Empires' (1869); and 'Beacon Lights' (1883).

Lord, William Wilberforce. An American verse-writer; born in Madison County, N.Y., 1819. He published a volume of 'Poems' (1845), that were ridiculed by Edgar A. Poe and praised by Wordsworth; 'Christ in Hades' (1851); and 'André, a Tragedy' (1856). He died 1907.

Lorente, Sebastian (lō-ren'tä). A Peruvian historian; born about 1820; died at Lima, November 1884. A professor of history at the University of San Marcos, he made valuable contributions to the historical literature of his country in his 'History of Peru' (5 vols., 1860); 'History of the Conquest of Peru' (1861); and articles in the Peruvian Review.

Lorenz, Ottokar (lō'rentz). A German historian; born at Iglau, Sept. 17, 1832. His first work was 'The Consular Tribunal' (1855). He was appointed professor of history in the University of Vienna, 1862; in 1885 accepted a call to the University of Jena. Among his writings are: 'German History in the 13th and 14th Centuries' (2 vols., 1863); 'Sources of Mediæval German History' (1870); 'History of Alsace' (1871); 'History and Politics' (1876); 'Genealogical Manual of the History of European States' (1895). Died at Jena, May 13, 1904.

Lorenzo de' Medici. See **Medici**.

Lorimer, George Claud. A noted American pulpit orator; born in Edinburgh, Scotland, in 1837; educated at Georgetown College, Ky. He has preached very acceptably in several cities. He was editor of the Watchman in 1876. Among his published works are: 'Under the Evergreens' (1872); 'The Great Conflict' (1876); 'Isms' (1882), etc. Died, Aix-les-Bains, 1904.

Lorm, Hieronymus, pseudonym of Heinrich Landesmann. A German poet and prose-writer; born Aug. 9, 1821, at Nikolsburg, Moravia. Though blind and deaf, he has performed much literary work. His works include 'Poems' (7th ed. 1894); and 'A Child of the Sea' (1882), a novel. He died Dec. 2, 1902.

Lorne, John Douglas Sutherland Campbell, Marquis of, (son-in-law of Queen Victoria). A Scotch miscellaneous writer; born in London, 1845. He has written: 'A Trip to the Tropics' (1867); 'Guido and Lita' (1875), a poem; 'Life of Lord Palmerston' (1890); and 'Life and Times of Queen Victoria' (1901).

Lorris. See **Guillaume de Lorris**.

Lossing, Benson John. An American historian; born in Beekman, Dutchess County, N.Y., 1813; died near Dover Plains, N.Y., June 3, 1891. He was a voluminous writer, and equally at home in historical, biographical, and critical composition; but his most useful and enduring works were his great 'Pictorial Field-Books' of the Revolution, the War of 1812, and the Civil War,—the first published in illustrated numbers 1850-52 (2 vols.), the second in 1868, the third 1866-69 (3 vols.). He was a wood engraver, and himself made the engravings for the works, the scenic ones largely from sketches on the spots. He wrote also 'Outline History of the Fine Arts' (1841); 'Lives of the Presidents of the United States' (1847); 'Biographies of Eminent Americans' (1855); 'A History of England' for schools (1871); etc.

Lotheissen, Ferdinand (lō'tīs-en). A German historian of literature; born at Darmstadt, May 20, 1833; died at Vienna, Dec. 19, 1887. His studies were mainly in the field of French literature; he wrote: 'Literature and Society in France, 1789-94' (1872); 'History of French Literature in the Seventeenth Century' (4 vols., 1878-84); 'Molière, his Life and Works' (1880); 'Margaret, Queen of Navarre' (1885). Among his literary remains was a contribution to the 'History of French Civilization in the Seventeenth and Eighteenth Centuries' (1889).

Lothrop, Harriet Mulford. ["Margaret Sidney."] An American novelist, wife of the publisher D. Lothrop; born in New Haven, Conn., 1844. Among her published works are: 'So as by Fire' (1881); 'The Pettibone Name,' a novel of New England life (1883); 'The Golden West' (1885); 'The Minute-Man' (1886); and 'Dilly and the Captain' (1887).

Loti, Pierre (lō-tē'). A French poet and novelist, whose real name is Louis Marie Julien Viaud; born at Rochefort, Jan. 15, 1850. His works include: 'Aziyadé' (1876); 'Rarahu' (1880), afterwards called 'The Marriage of Loti,' a romance of Tahiti; 'An Iceland Fisherman' (1886); 'Madame Chrysanthème' (1887); 'In Morocco' (1890); 'The Romance of a Child' (1890); 'The Last Days of Peking' 1902.

Lotze, Rudolf Hermann (lōt'sě). A German philosopher; born at Bautzen, Saxony, May 21, 1817; died in Berlin, July 1, 1881. Having graduated in medical science and philosophy at Leipsic, he was appointed professor of mental philosophy there (1843), and in 1844 accepted a call to Göttingen. He ranks among the first of metaphysicians, and has given impulse to the recent development of physiological psychology. Among his numerous works the most important are: 'Metaphysics' (1841); 'Logic' (1843); 'Microcosmos of Philosophie' (3 vols., 1856–64); 'History of Æsthetics in Germany' (1868), several of which have been translated into English.

Lounsbury, Thomas Raynesford. An American scholar; born at Ovid, N. Y., Jan. 1, 1838. He graduated at Yale in 1859, and led the life of a student in Anglo-Saxon and early English, and a writer in critical and biographical works, till 1862, when he enlisted as a volunteer in the Union Army, served as first lieutenant of the 126th New York Volunteers, and was mustered out at the close of the War; since 1871 has occupied the chair of professor of English in the Sheffield Scientific School of Yale University. Among his published works are Chaucer's 'House of Fame' and 'Parlement of Foules'; 'History of the English Language' (1879); biography of James Fenimore Cooper in 'American Men of Letters' series (1883); and his crowning work, which has brought him great celebrity, 'Studies in Chaucer, his Life and Writings' (3 vols., 1892).

Louvet de Couvray, Jean Baptiste (lö-vä′ dè kö-vrä′). A French writer of memoirs; born at Paris, June 11, 1760; died there, Aug. 25, 1797. He wrote a licentious novel, 'Adventures of Chevalier Faublas' (2 vols., 1787–90); 'Some Notes for Use in History' (1795); 'Memoirs upon the French Revolution' (1795).

Lovelace, Richard. An English dramatist and poet; born in Kent, 1618; died in London, 1658. He shone at the court of Charles I., and sacrificed liberty and fortune for that unhappy prince. His 'Lucasta' is a collection of charming verse, 'The Scholar' is a comedy of merit, and 'The Soldier' is a tragedy.

Lover, Samuel. An Irish novelist and songwriter; born at Dublin, 1797; died July 6, 1868. He wrote: 'Legends and Stories of Ireland' (1832); song — 'Rory O'More, a National Romance' (1837); 'Songs and Ballads' (1839), including 'The Low-Backed Car,' 'Widow Machree,' 'The Angel's Whisper' and 'The Four-Leaved Shamrock'; 'Handy Andy, an Irish Tale' (1842); 'Treasure Trove' (1844); 'Metrical Tales and Other Poems' (1860). He edited a collection of 'The Lyrics of Ireland' (1858).

Lowe, Martha Ann. An American verse-writer; born at Keene, N. H., 1829. She published 'The Olive and the Pine' (1859); 'Love in Spain, and Other Poems' (1867); 'The Story of Chief Joseph' (1881); and 'Memoir of Charles Lowe' (1883). She died 1902.

Lowell, Anna Cabot (Jackson). An American prose and verse-writer; born in Boston 1819; died in Cambridge, Mass., Jan. 7, 1874. Among her publications are 'Theory of Teaching' (1841); 'Gleanings from the Poets, for Home and School' (1843); 'Outlines of Astronomy, or the World as It Appears' (1850); and 'Posies for Children: a Book of Verses' (1870).

Lowell, Edward Jackson. An American historical writer; born in Boston, 1845; died there May 11, 1894. He was educated as a lawyer, but later gave himself entirely to literary pursuits. He is the author of 'The Hessians and Other German Auxiliaries of Great Britain in the Revolutionary War' (1884); this work is deemed exhaustive in its scope. He was a frequent contributor to the magazines.

Lowell, James Russell. An eminent American poet and critic; born at Cambridge, Mass., Feb. 22, 1819; died there, Aug. 12, 1891. His principal poetical works are: 'A Year's Life,' a volume of poems (1841); 'Poems' (1848); 'The Biglow Papers' (2 vols., 1849 and 1864); 'Under the Willows and Other Poems' (1868). Among his essays in literary criticism are: 'Among my Books' (two series, 1870 and 1875); 'My Study Windows' (1871); 'Latest Literary Essays and Addresses' (1892). He published also 'Democracy, and Other Addresses' (1887); 'Political Essays' (1888); 'Heartsease and Rue' (1888).

Lowell, Maria (White). An American writer of prose and verse, wife of James Russell Lowell; born in Watertown, Mass., July 8, 1821; died in Cambridge, Mass., Oct. 27, 1853. The best-known of her poems are 'The Alpine Shepherd' and 'The Morning Glory.' The death of Mrs. Lowell, occurring the same night that a child was born to Mr. Longfellow, called forth his poem beginning

"Two angels, one of life and one of death,
Passed o'er our village as the morning broke."

Lowell, Percival. An American traveler, astronomical investigator, and author; born in Massachusetts in 1855. He graduated from Harvard in 1876, and spent some time in Japan and Corea. Among his works are: 'Chosön, a Sketch of Corea' (1886); 'The Soul of the Far East' (1888); 'Noto, an Unexplored Corner of Japan'; 'Occult Japan'; 'Mars and Its Canals' (1906).

Lowell, Robert Traill Spence. An American clergyman, educator, and author, brother of James Russell; born in Boston, Oct. 8, 1816; died Sept. 18, 1891. He graduated from Harvard in 1833; was ordained a Protestant Episcopal minister in Bermuda in 1842; and held pastorates in Newfoundland, New Jersey, and New York. He became principal of St. Mark's School, Southborough, Mass., in 1869; and in 1873 professor of Latin in Union College, Schenectady, N. Y. His best-known work is the novel 'The New Priest in Concepcion Bay' (1864). He also wrote 'Fresh Hearts, and Other Poems' (1860); 'Antony Brade' (1874), a story of school life; 'A Story or Two from an Old Dutch Town' (1878).

Lowry, Robert. An American composer and hymn-writer; born in Philadelphia, March 12, 1826; died at Plainfield, N. J., Nov. 23, 1899. His music and hymns met popular approval. He edited: 'Chapel Melodies' (1868); 'Bright Jewels' (1869); 'Pure Gold' and 'Hymn Service' (1871); 'Brightest and Best' (1875); 'Glad Refrains' (1886); and other sacred collections.

Loyson, Charles (lwä-zôñ'), widely known as « Père Hyacinthe.» A French pulpit orator and writer; born at Orléans, March 10, 1827. His writings include : 'Liturgy of the Gallic-Catholic Church' (4th ed. 1883); 'Neither Clericals nor Atheists' (1890); and 'My Testament' (1893).

Lubbock, Sir John. An English naturalist and palæontologist; born in London, April 30, 1834. His chief writings are : 'Prehistoric Times as Illustrated by Ancient Remains,' etc. (1865); 'The Origin of Civilization and the Primitive Condition of Man' (1870); 'Origin and Metamorphoses of Insects' (1874); 'Ants, Bees, and Wasps' (1882); 'On the Senses, Instincts, and Intelligence of Animals' (1888); 'The Beauties of Nature and the Wonders of the World' (1892); 'The Use of Life' (1894); 'Scenery of Switzerland' (1896); 'Buds and Stipules' (1898); 'Fifty Years of Science' (1882). Died 1901.

Lübke, Wilhelm (lüb'kè). A German historian of art; born at Dortmund, Jan. 17, 1826; died at Karlsruhe, April 5, 1893. Chief among his works are : 'Mediæval Art in Westphalia' (1853); 'Outline of the History of Art' (1860; 11th ed. 1891); 'History of Architecture' (2 vols., 1855); 'History of the Renaissance in France' (1868); 'History of the Renaissance in Germany' (1873); 'History of German Art' (1888); 'Recollections' (1891).

Lubliner, Hugo (löb'lin-er). A German dramatist; born at Breslau, April 22, 1846. His three-act comedy 'The Women's Advocate' (1873) was produced on every stage in Germany. Of inferior merit are his 'The Florentines,' a tragedy; the comedies 'The Woman Without a Mind,' 'On the Wedding Journey,' 'The Poor Rich.' He wrote two novels, 'Creditors of Luck' and 'The Matron of Nineteen Years,' (1887); and the dramas, 'The Fifth Wheel' and 'Dear Enemies.'

Lubovitch, Nikolas löb'ō-vich). A Russian writer of history; born in Podolia, March 16, 1855. He wrote : 'Marnix de Saint Aldegonde as a Political Writer' (1877); 'History of the Reformation in Poland' (1883); 'Duke Albert of Prussia and the Reformation in Poland' (1885); 'Origin of the Catholic Reaction and of the Lapse of the Reformation in Poland' (1890).

Lubovski, Edward (löb-ov'skē). A Polish dramatist; born at Cracow, 1838. His first successful dramatic venture was made with 'Bats.' His dramas, 'The Court of Honor' (1880), and 'Jacus' (1883), are favorite pieces in the theatrical repertoire of Poland. He is the author of two books of fiction : 'A Step Farther' (1885); 'Stories Without a Moral' (1886).

Lucan—Marcus Annæus Lucanus (lö'kän). A Latin poet, nephew of Seneca; born at Cordova, Spain, 39 A. D.; died at Rome, 65 A. D. His uncle introduced him to the court of Nero, and for a time he was a favorite; but Nero envied his poetic talents and banished him from court. His epic poem 'Pharsalia' has for its subject the great battle between Cæsar and Pompey at Pharsalus: in style it is stilted, labored, and rhetorical, yet it shows undoubted poetic talent and nobility of thought.

Luce, Siméon (lüs). A French writer of history; born at Bretteville-sur-Ay, Dec. 29, 1833; died Dec. 14, 1892. He is author of 'History of the Jacquerie' (1859; 2d ed. 1894); 'Chronicle of the First Four Valois' (1862); 'History of Bertrand Duguesclin and his Time' (1876): 'Joan of Arc at Domrémy' (1886); 'France during the 100 Years' War' (1890). He edited Froissart's 'Chronicle' (7 vols., 1869–77).

Luchaire, Achille (lö-chär'). A French historian; born at Paris, Oct. 24, 1846. He has held professorships at Pau, Bordeaux, and Paris, where he now occupies the chair of mediæval history in the Faculty of Letters. An authority on the institutions of France in the Feudal Period, he has published : 'Monarchical Institutions of France under the First Capetians' (1884), 'Studies of the Acts of Louis VII.' (1885), both of which received the Gobert Prize offered by the Academy of Inscriptions. Among his recent works are : 'The French Communes'(1890); 'Louis VI.' (1890); and several monographs written in collaboration with M. B. Zeller. In 1891 he was decorated with the Legion of Honor.

Lucian—Lucianus (lö'shun). A celebrated Greek satirist; born at Samosata, in northern Syria, about 120 A. D.; died about 200 A. D. Very many of his writings are extant, among them : 'Praise of Demosthenes'; 'Dialogues of the Gods'; 'Dialogues of the Sea Gods'; 'Dialogues of the Dead'; 'The True History'; 'Lucius'; or The Ass'; 'On the Syrian Goddess'; 'Death of Peregrinus'; 'The Lover of Lying'; 'The Sea Voyage; or Votive Offerings'; 'The Banquet; or The Lapithæ'; 'The Fisherman'; 'The Sale of Lives'; 'Hermotimus'; 'Alexander, or The False Prophet'; 'Anacharsis.' The genuine writings of Lucian that are extant number 124, not including some fifty epigrams.

Lucilius, Gaius (lö-sil'yus). A Latin poet; born about 180 B. C., at Suessa Aurunca, in Campania; died at Naples, 103 B. C. He first gave form to Roman satiric poetry. Only fragments remain of his thirty books of satires. These show that he wrote in various metres, though mainly in hexameters. In his verses he lashed the vices and follies of his time with perfect freedom and impartiality.

Lucretius Carus, Titus (lö-kre'shus kā'rus). A Roman poet; born about 98 B. C.; died 55 B. C. His one work, 'On Nature,' in six books, was left incomplete; but it is one of the greatest of Latin didactic poems.

Lucy, Henry W. An English journalist and author; born at Crosby, near Liverpool,

Dec. 5, 1845. After some provincial experience as a journalist, he came to London in 1868 and joined the Daily News as special correspondent, chief of the Gallery staff, and writer of the Parliamentary summary. On the death of Tom Taylor, who had written the 'Essence of Parliament' for London Punch, he continued the work as 'The Diary of Toby, M. P.' He is the author of 'Men and Manners in Parliament' (1874); 'A Handbook of Parliamentary Procedure' (1880); 'Gideon Fleyce' (1882), a novel, 'East by West' (1885), an account of a journey round the world; 'A Diary of Two Parliaments' (1885-86).

Luden, Heinrich (lö'den). A German historian; born at Loxstedt, April 10, 1778; died at Jena, May 23, 1847. He was appointed professor of history in the University of Jena, 1810. He rendered a notable service to German historical literature by the example he set of histories written in elegant, spirited style. Among his writings are: 'Manual of Universal History of the Mediæval Nations' (2 vols., 1821); 'History of the German People' (12 vols., 1825-37), his greatest work, but reaching only to the year 1237.

Lüders, Charles Henry. An American poet; born in Philadelphia, 1858; died there, July 12, 1891. Upon the completion of his university studies he visited Europe, subsequently settling in his native city, where he was a prominent member of "The Pegasus," a club of poets. He attained distinction by his contributions of verse to leading magazines, one of his best poems being 'The Dead Nymph.' With S. Decatur Smith, Jr., he published a volume entitled 'Hallo! My Fancy' (188-); and a posthumous volume of his, 'The Dead Nymph' appeared in 189-.

Ludlow, Fitzhugh. An American journalist and author; born in Poughkeepsie, N. Y., Sept. 11, 1836; died in Geneva, Switzerland, Sept. 12, 1870. He received his education at Union College. He was editor of Vanity Fair from 1858 to 1860, and also wrote for the World and Evening Post, besides contributing frequently to Harper's Monthly. His most famous work is 'The Hasheesh Eater' (1857), a glowing portrayal of the early delights and later horrors of addiction to the drug. In 1868 he published 'The Opium Habit,' a warning against that habit, to which he himself later became a victim. He wrote also 'The Heart of the Continent' (1870). His poem 'Too Late' is familiar in anthologies.

Ludlow, James Meeker. An American clergyman and author; born in Elizabeth, N. J., 1841. He is a minister in the Presbyterian Church, and at present is a resident of East Orange, N. J. His best-known works are : 'The Captain of the Janizaries, a Story of the Times of Scanderbeg' (1886) ; 'A King of Tyre' (1891); 'The Angelic Woman'; 'Jesse Ben David' (1906).

Ludolf, Hiob (löd'olf). An eminent German Orientalist; born at Erfurt, Jan. 15, 1624;

died at Frankfort on the Main, April 8, 1704. He traveled extensively through Europe; and while visiting Rome made the acquaintance of the Abyssinian patriarch Gregorius, and from him acquired a knowledge of the Ethiopian language. He is said to have understood 25 languages. He wrote: 'Sketch of the History of Ethiopia' (1681); 'Grammar of the Amharic Language' (1698); 'Ethiopic-Latin Dictionary'; 'Ethiopic Grammar.'

Ludwig, Karl F. W. (löd'-vig). A great German physiologist; born at Witzenhausen, Dec. 29, 1816; died at Leipsic, April 23, 1895. He became professor of physiology at Leipsic University, 1865. There is hardly any department of physiology with which his name is not honorably associated; some of his works were of fundamental importance for medical science and natural history. His principal work is 'Text-Book of Human Physiology' (2 vols., 1852-56).

Ludwig, Otto. An eminent German dramatist and story-writer; born at Eisfeld, Feb. 11, 1813; died at Dresden, Feb. 25, 1865. His first ambition was for music; and, at first self-taught, a melodrama he wrote gained him the means of becoming a pupil of Mendelssohn at Leipsic. But he soon abandoned this, and went into retirement to write novels and dramas; many of the latter he never published, but in 1850 he brought out his tragedy 'The Hereditary Forester,' very faulty in construction though with manifold great excellences. He essayed a higher flight in the tragedy 'The Maccabees' (1855), but again failed in construction. He turned now to story-telling, and began a series of tales of Thuringian life. To this series belongs 'Between Heaven and Earth' (1857), his masterpiece.

Ludwig Salvator, Archduke of Austria. A noted explorer and traveler; born at Florence, Aug. 4, 1847. His principal writings, all illustrated by himself and most of them published anonymously, are: 'Levkosia, Capital of Cyprus' (1873); 'Yacht Voyage to the Syrtes' (1874); 'Los Angeles in Southern California' (2d ed. 1885); 'The Caravan Route from Egypt to Syria' (1878); 'The Balearic Islands,' superbly illustrated (7 vols., 1869-91); 'Around the World without Intending It' (4th ed. 1886); 'The Lipari Islands' (1893).

Luis de Granada, Fray (lö'ēs de grä-nä'dä). A Spanish mystic and preacher; born at Granada, 1504; died at Lisbon, 1588. He entered the order of Preaching Friars or Dominicans in 1523. Though high church dignities were repeatedly offered to him, he remained a simple friar all his life. Of his discourses or sermons, thirteen were committed to writing and have been preserved. He wrote many works of devotion; among them : 'Sinners' Guide' (1556); 'Meditations' (1556).

Luis de Leon. See **Ponce de Leon.**

Lukens, Henry Clay. An American journalist; born in Philadelphia, Aug. 18, 1838. In

23

1884 he was associate editor of the New York Daily News, and subsequently editor of the Journalist, New York. His pen-name is "Erratic Enrique." He has published: 'The Marine Circus at Cherbourg' (1865); 'Lean Nora,' a travesty of Bürger's 'Lenore' (1870); 'Story of the Types' (1881); and 'Jets and Flashes' (1883).

Lumby, Joseph Rawson. An English clergyman, editor, and author; born at Stanningley, Leeds, July 18, 1831; died at Grant, Chester, Nov. 21, 1895. Norris professor of divinity at Cambridge, 1879–92. For the Early English Text Society edited 'King Horn,' 'Ratio Raving, etc.'; for the Pitt Press, Sir Thomas More's 'Life of Richard III.' and 'Utopia.' He wrote: 'A History of the Creed' (1873); 'A Popular Introduction to the New Testament' (1883); and a work on 'Greek Learning in the Western Church during the Seventh and Eighth Centuries.'

Lummis, Charles Fletcher. An American author; born in Massachusetts in 1859. He is a resident of Los Angeles, Cal. He is devoted to the archæology and history of the ~boriginal tribes of the Southwest. Among his works are: 'The Land of Poco Tiempo'; 'The Spanish Pioneers'; 'The Man who Married the Moon'; 'The Gold Fish of the Grand Chimú'; 'A New Mexico David and Other Stories'; 'The Awakening of a Nation'; 'Mexico To-day.'

Lundy, Benjamin. An American anti-slavery agitator; born at Hardwich, N. J., Jan. 4, 1789; died at Lowell, Ill., Aug. 22, 1839. He advocated emancipation in frequent contributions to periodicals, till 1821, when he founded the monthly Genius of Universal Emancipation, which was published under difficulties for some years. He started in Philadelphia a weekly anti-slavery journal, The National Enquirer (1836); and in 1839 was about to revive the Genius of Universal Emancipation at Lowell, when he died. 'The Life, Travels, and Opinions of Benjamin Lundy' was published in 1847.

Lunt, George. An American poet and prose-writer; born in Newburyport, Mass., Dec. 31, 1803; died in Boston, May 17, 1885. During the Civil War he was associate editor, with George S. Hillard, of the Boston Courier. He was a forceful, graceful writer. He published 'Poems' (1839); 'The Age of Gold' (1843); 'The Dove and the Eagle' (1851); 'Lyric Poems' (1854); 'The Union,' a poem (1860); 'Origin of the Late War' (1866); 'Old New England Traits' (1873).

Lunt, William Parsons. An American clergyman; born in Newburyport, Mass., April 21, 1805; died in Akabah, Arabia Petræa, March 20, 1857. His writings are singularly felicitous in purity of taste, and have been much admired. Among his published works are: 'Gleanings'; 'Discourse at the Interment of John Quincy Adams'; 'Union of the Human Race'; 'Sermon on Daniel Webster.' He also compiled The Christian Psalter.'

Luschka, Hubert von (lösh'kä). A German anatomist and physiologist; born at Constance,

July 27, 1820; died at Tübingen, March 1, 1875. He became professor of anatomy in the University of Tübingen in 1855. His principal work is 'Human Anatomy as related to Practical Medicine' (3 vols., 1862–69).

Luska, Sidney. See **Harland, Henry.**

Luther, Martin. The renowned church reformer; born at Eisleben, in Saxony, Nov. 10. 1483; died there, Feb. 18, 1546. Noteworthy among his numerous writings are: 'The Babylonian Captivity of the Church' (1520); the treatise 'Against Henry, King of England' (1522); 'The Slave Will,' Luther's reply to Erasmus's tractate 'On Free Will'; 'Letters' (6 vols., 1825–56); 'Table Talk' (1566). His greatest service to the literature of Germany was his translation of the Bible, the New Testament version being completed in 1522 and the Old Testament in 1534.

Lützow, Karl von (lüts'ou). A German historian of art; born at Göttingen, Dec. 25, 1832. He wrote: 'Munich Antiques' (7 vols., 1861–69); 'Masterpieces of Ecclesiastical Architecture' (1862), fruit of his studies in France and England; 'Monuments of Art,' in association with Lübke (6th ed. 1892); 'History of German Copperplate and Wood Engraving. Died 1897.

Luzan, Ignacio de (lö'thän). A Spanish poet and scholar; born at Saragossa, 1702; died at Madrid, 1754. His work on 'The Poetic Art' (1737) is greatly admired.

Luzzatti, Luigi (löts-ä'tē). An Italian statesman; born at Venice, 1841. He is author of a series of works on political law, among them 'State and Church in Belgium' and 'Embryology and Development of Political Constitutions'; 'The Social Peace at the Paris Exposition.'

Lyall, Alfred Comyns, Sir. An English administrator and author; born at Coulston, Surrey, in 1835. In the course of a long and useful career in India he was Home Secretary, Foreign Secretary, and in 1882 Lieutenant-Governor of the North-West Provinces, having in the previous year been created K. C. B. As an author his reputation is due chiefly to his 'Asiatic Studies, Religious and Social' (1882); a biography of Warren Hastings (1889) in the 'English Men of Action' series; and 'The Rise of the British Dominion in India' (3d ed. 1893); 'Asiatic Studies' (1902).

Lyall, Edna, pseudonym of Ada Ellen Bayly. An English novelist; born at Brighton about 1860; died at Eastbourne, Feb. 9, 1903. Among her works are: 'Won by Waiting'; 'Donovan'; 'Autobiography of a Slander'; 'Knight Errant'; 'A Hardy Norseman'; 'In the Golden Days'; 'We Two'; 'Derrick Vaughan, Novelist'; 'Doreen'; etc.

Lycophron (lī'kof-ron). A Greek poet and grammarian, native of Chalcis in Eubœa; lived in the third century B. C. He had a part in organizing the Alexandrine Library. He was classed as a tragic poet with the "Pleiad," so called. One poem alone of his numerous compositions remains: 'Alexandra,' which contains, in 1474 iambic verses, a prophecy of Cassandra relating to the fall of Troy and the fortunes of the heroes therein concerned.

Lycurgus (lī-kėr'gus). An Attic orator of the fourth century B.C. He was a disciple of Plato and Isocrates, and a zealous adherent of the patriotic party. His 'Orations' against Leocrates are extant: they are notable less for their form than for their noble and dignified exposition.

Lydekker, Richard. An English naturalist; born in 1849, in England; graduated at Trinity College, Cambridge, in 1871; served from 1874 82 in the Geological Survey of India, covering nearly the whole territory of Kashmir. He catalogued the British Museum collections of fossils, mammalia, birds, reptiles and amphibia in 10 volumes. He became chief editor and part owner of Frederick Warne and Company's 'Royal Natural History,' the publication of which began in 1895. His other works include: 'The Deer of All Lands'; 'Fossil Animals of La Plata'; 'Wild Oxen, Sheep, and Goats, of All Lands'; 'Horns and Hoofs.'

Lyell, Sir Charles. A distinguished English geologist; born at Kinnordy, Scotland, Nov. 14, 1797; died at London, Feb. 22, 1875. In his 'Principles of Geology' (3 vols., 1830) he assailed the doctrine of "catastrophism" in geology. He published: 'Elements of Geology' (1837); 'Travels in North America, with Geological Observations' (2 vols., 1845); 'A Second Visit to the United States' (2 vols., 1846): these voyages were made for the purpose of testing his principle of continuous geologic evolution. His last work was 'Geological Evidences of the Antiquity of Man' (1863).

Lyle, William. A Scottish poet; born in Edinburgh, Nov. 17, 1822. Since coming to the United States he has resided in Rochester, N.Y. His poems are widely read in this country and Canada. Among his most popular Scottish dialect poems is 'The Grave of Three Hundred.' He has also written several English poems, including 'Diotima.' 'The Martyr Queen' was published in 1888.

Lyly, John. An English dramatist; born 1554; died in London, 1606. Between 1578 and 1600 he composed several plays, chiefly mythological, which were acted by the boys of St. Paul's School in presence of Queen Elizabeth. But he is noteworthy principally on account of his two books 'Euphues, or the Anatomy of Wit' (1579), and 'Euphues and his England' (1580), which were the first serious attempts in English to use words as mere musical notes, quite subordinating the matter to the sound. Fantastic as the form was, the recognition of new possibilities in the language intoxicated the cultured classes, and set the literary fashion for many years: story-writers who wished to assure themselves an audience entitled their books 'Euphues his ——,' and the influence is clear and strong on Sidney and Spenser.

Lyman, Joseph Bardwell. An American agriculturist; born in Chester, Mass., Oct. 6,

1829; died in Richmond Hill, L. I., Jan. 28, 1872. In 1867 he became agricultural editor of the New York World. The following year he was editor of Hearth and Home, and shortly after joined the staff of the Tribune. He wrote, with his wife, 'The Philosophy of Housekeeping' (1867). He published: 'Resources of the Pacific States' (1865); 'Women of the War' (1866); and 'Cotton Culture' (1867).

Lyman, Laura Elizabeth Baker. An American journalist; born in Kent's Hill, Me., April 2, 1831. Under her pen-name of "Kate Hunnibee," she became widely known from a series of articles which appeared in Hearth and Home. She edited the Home Interest department in the New York Tribune (1869-70), and the Dining-Room Magazine (1876-77).

Lyman, Theodore. An American philanthropist; born in Boston, Feb. 20, 1792; died in Brookline, Mass., July 18, 1849. Graduated at Harvard in 1810. He founded the State Reform School, to which he gave $72,500. Among his works are: 'Three Weeks in Paris' (1814); 'The Political State of Italy' (1820); 'Account of the Hartford Convention' (1823); and 'The Diplomacy of the United States with Foreign Nations' (2 vols., 1828).

Lynch, James Daniel. An American poet and miscellaneous writer; born in Mecklenburg County, Va., Jan. 6, 1836. His best-known poems are: 'The Clock of Destiny,' 'The Star of Texas,' and 'The Siege of the Alamo.' He also published: 'Kemper County Vindicated' (1878); 'Bench and Bar of Mississippi' (1881); and 'Bench and Bar of Texas' (1885).

Lyne, Joseph Loycester. An English divine and religious writer, called "Father Ignatius" and "Ignatius of Jesus"; born in London, Nov. 23, 1837. He was a mission curate in London, but withdrew to begin the attempt of restoring monasticism in the Church of England. He built Llanthony Abbey in Wales, and established there a community of monks on the pattern of the Benedictine order. He is the author of many published sermons, poems, tales, etc., among which are: 'The Catholic Church of England' (1864); 'Brother Placidus' (1870); 'Leonard Morris, or the Benedictine Monk' (1871); 'Mission Sermons and Orations' (1886); 'Tales of the Monastery'; 'Life of Father Ignatius' (1904).

Lysias (liz'i-as). An Attic orator; about 450–380 B.C. Of his anciently accredited 425 orations only 233 were authentic; 31 are still extant, but some even of these, and considerable fractions of others, are suspected to be spurious. All but one of these were written for other persons to deliver in courts or public assemblies; the exception is a speech made by him in court for the conviction of his brother's murderer. They are all written in the purest Attic, and the narration and arguments are managed with extraordinary skill.

Lytle, William Haines (lī-tl). An American general and poet; born in Cincinnati, O.,

Nov. 2, 1826; killed at the battle of Chickamauga, Tenn., Sept. 20, 1863. He graduated at Cincinnati College, and studied law. He was a captain in the Mexican War; and in the Civil War served as colonel in 1861, and later as brigadier-general of volunteers, having been promoted to that rank for gallant conduct. His best-known poems are 'Antony to Cleopatra' and 'Jacqueline.' No complete collection of his works was published.

Lytton, Edward Bulwer, Lord. See Bulwer.

Lytton, Edward Robert Bulwer, Earl of ["Owen Meredith"], the only son of Edward Bulwer-Lytton; born in London, Nov. 8, 1831; died in Paris, Nov. 24, 1891. He was educated at Harrow and Bonn; went to Washington in 1849 as private secretary to his uncle, Lord Dalling (William Henry Lytton Earle); and subsequently had an important diplomatic career in Vienna, Athens, Copenhagen, and Lisbon. He was made viceroy of India in 1876; created Earl of Lytton in 1880; and ambassador to France in 1887. His works include: 'Clytemnestra, The Earl's Return, and Other Poems' (1855); 'The Wanderer' (1859); 'Lucile,' a novel in verse (1860); 'Fables in Song' (1874); 'Glenaveril' (1885); 'King Poppy' (1892); 'The Ring of Amasis,' a novel (1863; new ed. 1890); and 'Marah,' poems, published posthumously (1892).

M

Maartens, Maarten (mär'tenz), pseudonym of J. M. W. Van der Poorten-Schwartz. The most noted Dutch novelist of the day; born in Amsterdam, 1858. He writes his books in English. Among them are: 'The Sin of Joost Avelingh' (1890); 'A Question of Taste' (1891); 'God's Fool' (1892); 'The Greater Glory' (1894); etc.

Mabie, Hamilton Wright. A distinguished American essayist, critic, and editor; born at Cold Spring, N. Y., Dec. 13, 1846. He graduated from Williams College, practiced law for a time in New York city, and then entered journalism, becoming in 1879 associate editor of the Christian Union, now the Outlook. His thoughtful, happily turned, and sound essays, many of which have appeared originally in his paper, have won him the position of a critic of recognized authority and influence. He has insisted on the value of the past and the necessity of a broad culture for the true appreciation of literature, while sympathetic towards the new. The wide sale of his books has done much to stimulate and direct the American taste for letters. He has supplemented the written word by much work on the lecture platform. He is one of the most acceptable lecturers on literary subjects in the country. His books are: 'Norse Stories Retold from the Eddas'; 'My Study Fire'; 'Under the Trees and Elsewhere'; 'Short Studies in Literature'; 'Essays in Literary Interpretation'; 'Essays on Nature and Culture'; 'Essays on Books and Culture.'

Mabillon, Jean (mä-bē-yôn'). A noted French scholar and historian; born at St. Pierremont, Ardennes, Nov. 23, 1632; died at Paris, Dec. 27, 1707. He belonged to the Benedictine order, and lived in the famous Abbey of St. Germain-des-Prés, Paris, after 1664. His critical 'Ancient Analects' (4 vols., 1675–85), and 'Italian Museum' (2 vols., 1687–89), collected in Germany and Italy, possess great value. In 'On Diplomacy' (1681), his chief work, in which are stated the principles of historic inquiry, and which became a classic, he defended his method, which had been attacked by the Jesuits. He wrote also works relating to the Benedictine saints and history.

Mably, Gabriel Bonnot de (mä-blē'). A French publicist, brother of Condillac; born at Grenoble, March 14, 1709; died in Paris, April 23, 1785. The admiration of antiquity prevalent during the French Revolution was largely due to his 'Parallel between the Romans and the French' (1740), 'Observations on the Romans' (1751), and 'Observations on the History of Greece' (1766). His 'Conversations of Phocion' (1763) has been said to contain the germ of modern communism. (Collected Works, 1879.)

MacAfee, Mrs. Nelly Nichol (Marshall). An American novelist, daughter of Gen. Humphrey Marshall of the Confederate army; born at Louisville, Ky., 1845. Among her works are: 'Sodom Apples' (1866); 'Wearing the Cross' (1868); 'A Criminal through Love' (1882); etc.

McAfee, Robert Breckinridge. An American lawyer and historian; born in Mercer County, Ky., February 1784; died there, March 12, 1849. He was United States chargé d'affaires at Bogota, Colombia, from 1833 till 1837; and was a member of the Royal Antiquarian Society of Denmark. He wrote a 'History of the War of 1812' (1816). Much valuable information has been obtained from his private journal, relating to the early history of Kentucky.

McAnally, David Rice. An American educator and prose-writer; born in Tennessee, Feb. 17, 1810. He was long associated with Horace Mann in efforts to improve methods in education. He is the author of 'Life of Martha Laurens Ramsay' (1852); 'Life and Labors of Bishop Marvine' (1878); and 'History of Methodism in Missouri' (1881).

MacArthur, Robert Stuart. An American Baptist divine; born at Dalesville, P. Q., 1841. He has been pastor of Calvary Baptist Church, New York, since 1870, and is editor of the

Christian Inquirer and the Baptist Quarterly Review. He has published 'Quick Truths in Quaint Texts'; 'Calvary Pulpit, or Christ and Him Crucified'; 'The Preeminence of Christ, and Other Sermons' (1905).

Macaulay, Catharine, Mrs. (Sawbridge). An English historian; born in Kent, 1731; died June 22, 1791. She is best known by her 'History of England' (8 vols., 1763–83). Her 'History of England from the Revolution' (1778) was called "the republican history of England," and was severely criticized. Only one volume appeared.

Macaulay, James. A Scottish novelist and writer for the young; born at Edinburgh, 1817. He has been editor of several periodicals, for thirty-five years editor-in-chief of the Religious Tract Society; founded the Boy's Own Paper, and the Girl's Own Paper. He has published 'Across the Ferry' (1871); 'All True' (new ed. 1880); 'From Middy to Admiral of the Fleet'; 'Sea Pictures' (new ed. 1884); 'Victoria, her Life and Reign' (1887); etc.

Macaulay, Thomas Babington, Lord. A famous English historian, essayist, poet, and statesman; born at Rothley Temple, Leicestershire, Oct. 25, 1800; died at Kensington, Dec. 28, 1859. Called to the bar in 1826, he was Member of Parliament 1830–34, 1839–47, 1852–57; member of the Supreme Council in India (residing at Calcutta) 1834–38; Secretary of War 1839–41; Paymaster-General 1846–47. The 'History of England' is his one large work. Vols. i. and ii. appeared in 1849; iii. and iv. in 1855; v., edited by his sister Lady Trevelyan, in 1866. His 'Lays of Ancient Rome' appeared in 1842. His works have been published in innumerable forms in many countries; a complete edition, edited by Lady Trevelyan, appeared in 1866. He was a keen critic, an eloquent and convincing orator, and one of the most delightful of English letter-writers. He has contributed to English literature a vast number of brilliant essays, the enumeration of which will be found in the biographical notice in the 'Library.'

MacCarthy, Denis Florence. An Irish poet; born at Dublin, 1817 (?); died 1882. He was a lawyer by profession, but never practiced. He won the love of his countrymen by his lyrics on Irish history and legend. Among his works are: 'Ballads, Poems, and Lyrics' (1850); 'The Bell-Founder,' etc. (new ed. 1857); 'Underglimpses,' etc. (1857). He wrote also 'Early Life of Shelley' (1872).

McCarthy, Justin. A noted Irish journalist, politician, historian, novelist, and miscellaneous writer; born at Cork, Nov. 22, 1830. He has been a Home Rule Member of Parliament since 1879, and since the fall of Parnell, chairman of the Irish Parliamentary party. He spent three years (1868–70) in the United States, traveling, lecturing, and engaged in literary work, being (amongst other things) connected editorially with the New York Independent. He revisited this country in 1886. Among his

chief works are: 'A History of Our Own Times' (4 vols., 1879–80); 'History of the Four Georges' (4 vols., 1889); the novels 'Lady Judith' (1871); 'A Fair Saxon' (1873); 'Dear Lady Disdain' (1875); 'The Right Honorable' (1886, with Mrs. Campbell-Praed); etc. 'Modern Leaders,' a collection of biographical sketches, appeared in 1872. His latest works are 'The Story of Gladstone's Life'; 'Ireland and her Story.'

McCarthy, Justin Huntley. An Irish journalist, politician, historian, poet, and novelist, son of Justin; born 1860. He has been a Member of Parliament since 1884. He has written: 'Outline of Irish History' (1883); 'Serapion, and Other Poems' (1883); 'England under Gladstone' (2d ed. 1885); 'Camiola, a Girl with a Fortune' (1885). He completed a 'History of the French Revolution' in 1897.

McCaul, John. A Canadian educator and writer; born in Dublin, Ireland, 1807. In 1849 and 1853 he was elected president of Toronto University. He published several volumes of articles and treatises on classical subjects, besides editing portions of Horace, Longinus, Lucian, and Thucydides, as college text-books. He also wrote: 'Britanno-Roman Inscriptions' (1863); and 'Christian Epitaphs of the First Six Centuries.'

Macchetta Blanche (Tucker), Marquise d' Alligre, « Blanche Roosevelt » (mă-ket'a). An American novelist and biographer, daughter of John Randolph Tucker, U. S. Senator from Virginia; born at Sandusky, O., 1856; died in London, Sept. 10, 1898. She wrote: 'Home Life of Henry W. Longfellow' (1882); 'Stage-Struck' (1884); 'Life of Gustave Doré' (1885); etc.

McClellan, George Brinton. A distinguished American general; born in Philadelphia, Dec. 3, 1826; died in Orange, N. J., Oct. 29, 1885. He was commander of the Army of the Potomac, 1861–62. The most important of his works are: 'Report on the Organization and Campaigns of the Army of the Potomac' (1864); 'The Armies of Europe'; 'European Cavalry'; and 'McClellan's Own Story' (1887).

McClelland, Margaret Greenway. An American novelist; born in Norwood, Va., 18—; died Aug. 2, 1895. Besides many stories and poems contributed to magazines, she wrote: 'Oblivion' (1885); 'Princess' (1886); 'Jean Monteith' (1887); 'Madame Silva' (1888); 'Burkett's Lock' (1889); 'Mammy Mystic'; and other novels and tales.

McClintock, John. An American educator and author; born in Philadelphia, Oct. 27, 1814; died in Madison, N. J., March 4, 1870. He was made president of Drew Theological Seminary in 1867. He was the author with James Strong of a large and valuable 'Cyclopædia of Biblical, Theological, and Ecclesiastical Literature' (12 vols.); a work of many years' labor, and intended to cover the whole field embraced in the title. The last volume was published in 1895. He wrote also 'An Analysis of Watson's Theological Institutes' (1850); 'Temporal

Power of the Pope' (1853); and 'Living Words,' a volume of sermons published since his death.

MacColl, Evan. A Canadian poet; born in Kenmore, Argyleshire, Scotland, Sept. 21, 1808. Since emigrating to Canada (1850), he has written many poems, and is called the bard of St. Andrew's Society of Kingston. Among his publications are: 'My Rowan Tree,' best known of his lyrical verses; 'Clarsach Nan Beann, or Poems and Songs in Gaelic' (1837); and 'The Mountain Minstrel, or Poems and Songs in English' (1887).

MacColl, Malcolm. A distinguished English clergyman and religious and political writer; born in Inverness-shire, March 27, 1838. He became canon of Ripon 1884, and Savoy chaplain 1894. He has published: 'Mr. Gladstone and Oxford, by Scrutator' (2d ed. 1865); 'Science and Prayer' (4th ed. 1866); 'The Reformation in England' (2d ed. 1869); 'The Ober-Ammergau Passion Play' (7th ed. 1870); 'Lawlessness, Sacerdotalism, and Ritualism' (3d ed. 1875); 'Christianity in Relation to Science and Morals' (4th ed. 1889); etc.

McConnell, John Ludlum. An American prose-writer; born in Jacksonville, Ill., Nov. 11, 1826; died there, Jan. 17, 1862. His books, descriptive of Western individuality and growth, include: 'Talbot and Vernon' (1850); 'Graham, or Youth and Manhood' (1850); 'The Glens' (1851); and 'Western Characters, or Types of Border Life' (1853).

McCook, Henry Christopher. An American clergyman, naturalist, and miscellaneous writer; born in New Lisbon, O., July 3, 1837. He is vice-president of the American Entomological Society, and of the Academy of Natural Sciences of Philadelphia; and author of 'The Mound-Making Ants of the Alleghanies' (1877); 'The Natural History of the Agricultural Ant of Texas' (1880); 'Tenants of an Old Farm' (1884); 'The Gospel in Nature' (1887); and 'American Spiders and their Spinning-Work' (1888); 'Nature's Craftsmen' (1907).

McCosh, James. A prominent Scottish-American theologian; born in Carskeoch, Ayrshire, Scotland, April 1, 1811; died in Princeton, N. J., Nov. 6, 1894. He came to America in 1868; was president of Princeton College (1868–88), and was one of the foremost men of his day in university life. His principal works include: 'Christianity and Positivism' (1871); 'A Reply to Prof. Tyndall's Belfast Address' (1875); 'The Development Hypothesis' (1876); 'The Emotions' (1880); 'Herbert Spencer's Philosophy as Culminating in his Ethics' (1885).

McCrackan, William Denison. An American political and miscellaneous writer and lecturer; born in Munich, Bavaria, 1864. His home is in New York. He has written: 'Rise of the Swiss Republic'; 'Swiss Solutions of American Problems'; 'Little Idyls of the Big World'; 'The Fair Land Tyrol'; 'Italian Lakes.'

McCrae, George Gordon. An Australian poet; born in Scotland. He has a position in the civil service in Victoria. A number of his poems are based on native Australian legends, the best known being 'Māmba, the Bright-Eyed' (1867), and 'Story of Balladeādro' (1867), both published in Australian periodicals. No collection of his verse has appeared.

MacCrie, Thomas. A Scottish Presbyterian divine and historical writer; born at Duns, November 1772; died at Edinburgh, Aug. 5, 1835. He was professor of divinity at Whitburn, 1817–27. He wrote: 'Life of John Knox' (1812, several editions); 'Life of Andrew Melville' (2 vols., 1819); 'History of the Reformation in Italy' (1827); 'History of the Reformation in Spain' (1829); the two last becoming standard works.

McCulloch, John Ramsay. A famous Scottish statistician and political economist; born at Whithorn, Wigtownshire, March 1, 1789; died in London, Nov. 11, 1864. He was professor of political economy at London University (now University College) 1828–32; editor of the Scotsman 1818–20; comptroller of the stationery office 1838–64; and a regular contributor to the Edinburgh Review. Among the very large number of works he wrote or compiled may be mentioned: 'Principles of Political Economy' (1825), his chief work; 'Dictionary of Commerce' (1832); 'Statistical Account of the British Empire' (1837); etc. He was a disciple of Adam Smith and Ricardo, and edited the works of both, adding a life of the former to his edition of the 'Wealth of Nations.'

McCurdy, James Frederick. A Canadian Oriental scholar; born in Chatham, N. B., Feb. 18, 1847. He has published: 'Aryo-Semitic Speech' (1881); 'The Semitic Perfect in Assyrian' in the 'Transactions of the Congress of Orientalists' (1883); and various essays on subjects connected with Oriental learning.

Macdonald, George. A noted Scottish novelist and poet; born at Huntley, 1824. He was originally an Independent minister, but became a lay member of the Church of England. He has lectured in this country (1872–73). Among his best-known novels are: 'David Elginbrod' (1862); 'Annals of a Quiet Neighborhood' (1866); 'Robert Falconer' (1868). He published poems in 1855, 1857, 1864, 1868, and 1882.

McDowell, Katharine Sherwood. An American poet; born in Holly Springs, Miss., Feb. 26, 1849; died there, July 22, 1884. In 1872 she became private secretary to Longfellow. She wrote: 'The Radical Club,' a poem; 'Suwanee River Tales'; 'Like Unto Like' (1881); and 'Dialect Tales' (1884).

Mace, Frances Parker Laughton. An American poet; born in Orono, Me., Jan. 15, 1836. She published 'Legends, Lyrics, and Sonnets' (1883); 'Under Pine and Palm'; her contributions to magazines include: 'Israfil,' 'Easter Morning,' and 'The Kingdom of a Child.' 'Only Waiting,' a poem, attained great popularity. Died in California, 1899.

Macé, Jean (mä-sä'). A French educator and popular writer for the young; born in Paris, 1815. He served in the French army 1842–45. In 1866 he founded a league of instruction in the Belgian manner. His best-known work is 'Contes du Petit-Château' (1862), called in the English translation 'Home Fairy Tales.' He has also written: 'History of a Mouthful of Bread' (1861); 'Servants of the Stomach' (1866); 'France before the Franks' (1881); etc.

Macedo, Joaquim Manoel de (mä-shā'do). A Brazilian poet; born in San João d'Itaborahi, June 24, 1820; professor of national history in the collège of Rio Janeiro. He has written very successful novels, dramas, and comedies. As a lyric poet he is greatly esteemed. His works include: 'Moreninha,' a novel (1844; 5th ed., revised, 1877); 'O Moço Loura,' a novel of the early stages of the Portuguese conquest (1845); 'A Nebulosa,' a poem (1857); 'Cotie,' a drama; 'Fantasma Branco,' a comedy (1856); and 'Corógraphia do Brasil' (1873). Died 1882.

Macedo, José Agostinho de. A noted Portuguese miscellaneous writer; born at Beja, Sept. 11, 1761; died at Pedrouços, 1831. Among his works are: 'Gama' (1811), an epic; 'A Meditação' (Meditation: 1813), a poem, his chief work; 'Man, or the Limits of Reason' (1815), a philosophical treatise; a number of sarcastic critiques; etc.

Macfarlane, Charles. A Scottish historian; born 18—; died 1858. He traveled extensively in the East, and for many years resided in Italy. He wrote: 'Our Indian Empire' (1844); 'Pictorial History of Scotland' (8 vols., 1849, with G. L. Craik); 'Turkey and Its Destiny' (1850); 'History of British India' (1852); etc.

McGaffey, Ernest. An American writer of verse; born in Ohio, 1861. He is a lawyer in Chicago. He has published 'Poems of Gun and Rod' and 'Poems'; 'Cosmos'; 'Outdoors.'

MacGahan, Barbara. A Russo-American novelist, wife of J. A.; born (Elagina) on her father's estate near Tula, Russia, April, 1850. She graduated from the Tula Female Seminary in 1866. Her first novel was written in Russian under the pseudonym "Pavel Kashirin"; she has written in English one called 'Xenia Repnina.' Her articles in American and European periodicals made her widely known. Died 1904.

MacGahan, Januarius Aloysius. A noted American journalist and war correspondent; born near New Lexington, O., June 12, 1844; died at Constantinople, June 9, 1878. He was war correspondent of the New York Herald during the Franco-Prussian war (1870–71); accompanied the Russian expedition against Khiva in 1873, and the Arctic expedition on the Pandora in 1875. He wrote: 'Campaigning on the Oxus, and the Fall of Khiva' (1874); 'Under the Northern Lights' (1876); 'Turkish Atrocities in Bulgaria' (1876), which appeared originally during the same year as a famous series of war letters in the London Daily News. He is regarded by the Bulgarians as the author of their independence.

MacGillivray, William. A Scottish naturalist; born at Old Aberdeen, 1796; died at Aberdeen, 1852. He was professor of natural history in Marischal College, Aberdeen, 1841–52. His principal work was a 'History of British Birds' (5 vols., 1837–52). He wrote also 'Lives of Eminent Zoölogists' (1834); etc.

MacGregor, John. An English traveler; born at Gravesend, Jan. 24, 1825; died at Boscombe, near Bournemouth, July 16, 1892. He was called to the bar in 1851; was captain of the Royal Canoe Club 1866. He wrote: 'The Rob Roy on the Baltic' (new ed. 1872–79); 'The Voyage Alone in the Rob Roy' (4th ed. 1880); 'The Rob Roy on the Jordan' (new ed. 1880); 'A Thousand Miles in the Rob Roy' (13th ed. 1884); etc.

Mácha, Karel Hynek (mä'kä). A Bohemian poet; born at Prague, Nov. 15, 1810; died at Litomerice, Nov. 7, 1836. His chief work was a lyrico-epic poem, 'Máj' (May: 1836), containing a strain of Byronic pessimism. He wrote also short lyrics and stories, including 'Cikáni' (The Gipsies: 1857). His merit was recognized only after his death. His complete works were published in 1862, a German translation appearing in the same year.

McHenry, James. An American physician, novelist, and poet; born in Larne, County Antrim, Ireland, Dec. 20, 1785; died there, July 21, 1845. He emigrated to the United States in 1817, and settled in Philadelphia in 1824. Included in his many publications are: 'The Pleasures of Friendship,' a poem (1822); 'The Usurper: An Historical Tragedy' (a poetical work); also 'O'Halloran; or, the Insurgent: A Romance of the Irish Rebellion,' reprinted at Glasgow; 'The Wilderness of Braddock's Times: A Tale of the West' (2 vols., 1823); and 'The Betrothed of Wyoming' (2d ed. 1830).

Machiavelli, Niccolo (mak-i-a-vel'li). A famous Italian statesman, and political and historical writer; born at Florence, May 3, 1469; died there, June 22, 1527. Among his works were: 'The Prince' (1513), the famous book on the art of government which has made "Machiavelism" a synonym for perfidy and mercilessness in politics and diplomacy; 'Mandragola' (1513?), a comedy; 'Art of War' (1520); 'Discourses,' etc. (1531), a treatise on republican government; 'Florentine History' (1532). An edition of his works in eight volumes appeared in 1813.

Mackarness, Mrs. Matilda Anne (Planché). An English novelist; born 1826; died 1881. Her numerous works include: 'Trap to Catch a Sunbeam' (1849; 35th ed. 1860); 'Old Joliffe' (7th ed. 1851); 'Cloud with the Silver Lining' (1852); 'False Appearances' (1858); 'Sibert's Wold' (3d ed. 1864); 'Clifford Castle' (new ed. 1885).

Mackay, Charles. A Scottish poet, journalist, and miscellaneous writer; born at Perth,

March 27, 1814; died in London, Dec. 24, 1889, He was editor of the Illustrated London News, 1852–59. He lectured in the United States in 1857–58. While special correspondent of the London Times in New York during the Civil War (strongly favoring the Southern cause), he unearthed the Fenian conspiracy (1862). He wrote: 'The Salamandrine, or Love and Immortality' (1842); 'Voices from the Crowd' (1846); 'Voices from the Mountains' (1847); 'History of the Mormons' (1851); etc.

Mackay, George Eric. A Scotch poet, son of Charles; born in London, Jan, 25, 1851; died there, June 2, 1898. "George Eric Lancaster". Among his works are: 'Songs of Love and Death' (1865); 'Ad Reginam' (To the Queen; 1881, 3 eds.); the popular 'Love Letters of a Violinist' (1886); 'A Lover's Litanies' (1888); 'Nero and Actæa,' a tragedy; etc.

Mackay, Minnie. ["Marie Corelli."] A popular English novelist, daughter of Charles; born 1864. Among her works are: 'A Romance of Two Worlds' (1886); 'History of a Vendetta' (1886); 'Thelma' (1887), a society novel; 'Ardath,' the story of a dead self; etc.

McKenney, Thomas Lorraine. An American prose-writer; born in Hopewell, Md., March 21, 1785; died in New York city, Feb. 19, 1859. He published 'Sketches of a Tour to the Lakes,' etc. (1827). With James Hall he wrote 'A History of Indian Tribes,' illustrated with 120 colored Indian portraits (3 vols., 1838–44); and 'Memoirs, Official and Personal, with Sketches of Travels among the Northern and Southern Indians,' etc. (2d ed. 1846).

Mackenzie, Alexander Slidell. An American naval officer and author, brother of John Slidell the famous Confederate commissioner, — "Mackenzie" being assumed later; born in New York, April 6, 1803; died in Tarrytown, N. Y., Sept. 13, 1848. He published 'A Year in Spain, by a Young American' (2 vols., 1829–31; enlarged ed., 3 vols., 1836), which attained great popularity in England and the United States. Washington Irving commended it highly. He also wrote: 'Popular Essays on Naval Subjects' (2 vols., 1833); 'The American in England' (2 vols., 1835).

Mackenzie, George, Sir. A noted Scottish lawyer and statesman; born at Dundee, 1636; died in London, 1691. As king's counsel in 1677, his ardor in prosecuting witches and the Covenanters earned him the name "Bloody Mackenzie." He wrote: 'A Stoic's Religion' (1663); 'Moral Essay upon Solitude' (1665); 'Moral Gallantry' (1667); etc., besides legal writings. ('Works,' 1716–22.)

Mackenzie, Henry. A Scotch novelist, essayist, and miscellaneous writer; born at Edinburgh, August 1745; died there, Jan. 14, 1831. He was a lawyer at Edinburgh; was appointed comptroller of taxes in 1804. His novels are: 'The Man of Feeling' (1771), — by far his most famous work, and still remembered in the class with Sterne; 'The Man of the World'

(1773); 'Julia de Roubigné' (1777). ('Works,' 8 vols., 1808.)

Mackenzie, Robert Shelton. An American miscellaneous writer; born at Drews Court, County Limerick, Ireland, June 22, 1809; died in Philadelphia, Nov. 30, 1880. He came to the United States in 1852. He wrote: 'Lays of Palestine' (1828); 'Titian: A Venetian Art-Novel'; 'Life of Guizot' (1846); 'Life of Charles Dickens' (1870); and 'Sir Walter Scott: The Story of his Life' (1871). He also edited the 'Noctes Ambrosianæ' (5 vols., 1854).

Mackey, Albert Gallatin. An American writer on Freemasonry; born at Charleston, S. C., March 12, 1807; died at Fortress Monroe, Va., June 20, 1881. His works are authorities. They include: 'A Lexicon of Freemasonry' (1845); 'The Mystic Tie' (1849); 'Book of the Chapter' (1858); 'A Manual of the Lodge' (1862); 'A Text-Book of Masonic Jurisprudence' (1869); and an 'Encyclopædia of Freemasonry' (1874).

Mackintosh, Sir James. A famous Scottish philosopher, lawyer, and politician; born at Aldourie, Inverness-shire, Oct. 24, 1765; died in London, May 30, 1832. He was recorder of Bombay, India, 1804–6; judge of admiralty 1806–11; Member of Parliament, 1813; professor of law and politics at Haileybury College 1818–24; Commissioner of Indian Affairs, 1830. He wrote: 'Dissertation on the Progress of Ethical Philosophy' (1830), in the 'Encyclopædia Britannica'; 'History of England' (1830); 'Life of Sir Thomas More'; etc. Much of his philosophical writing is to be found in 'Modern British Essayists.' ('Works,' 3 vols., 1836.)

McLachlan, Alexander. A Scottish poet; born in Johnstone, Renfrewshire, Aug. 12, 1818; died there, Mar. 20, 1896. In 1841 he went to Canada. His works are: 'Poems,' chiefly in Scotch dialect (1855); 'Poems and Songs' (1874); and 'The Poets and Poetry of Scotland' (1876).

Maclaren, Ian. See **Watson.**

McLean, Sarah Pratt. See **Greene.**

McLellan, Isaac. An American poet; born in Portland, Me., May 21, 1806; died at Greenport, L. I., Aug. 20, 1899. His love for outdoor sports was so intense, and his poems on these themes so numerous, that they won him the title of "the poet-sportsman." His early poems, 'The Death of Napoleon' and 'New England's Dead' are well-known. He is also the author of 'The Fall of the Indian' (1830); 'Mount Auburn' (1843); and 'Poems of the Rod and Gun' (1886).

Macleod, Fiona (mak-loud'). A nom-de-plume of William Sharp the English critic, supposed to be a picturesque Irish poet and novelist whose work was prominent in the Celtic renaissance. Mr. Sharp's death in 1905 revealed the fact that Fiona Macleod was the creation of that critic's fancy. He wrote under her name: 'Pharais' (1895), a romance; 'The Mountain Lovers' (1895); 'The Sin-Eater and Other Tales' (1895); 'The Washer of the Ford' (1896); 'Green Fire' (1896); and a modern version of the old Celtic romance 'The Laughter of Peter-kin.'

Macleod, Norman. A distinguished Scottish divine, and miscellaneous writer; born at Campbeltown, June 3, 1812; died at Glasgow, June 16, 1872. He founded the Evangelical Alliance in 1847; became chaplain to the Queen for Scotland in 1857; edited Good Words 1860-72, making it an educational and literary power. Among his works are: 'The Earnest Student' (1854), a biography; 'Parish Papers' (1862); 'Wee Davie' (new ed. 1865); 'The Starling' (1867, new eds. 1870-77-80), a Scotch story; 'Peeps at the Far East' (1871); 'Character Sketches' (1872); etc.

McLeod, Xavier Donald. An American poet and miscellaneous writer; born in New York, Nov. 17, 1821; killed near Cincinnati, July 20, 1865. An Episcopal clergyman, he became a Roman Catholic in 1852, and later a priest. He wrote: 'Pynnshurst' (1852); 'Life of Sir Walter Scott' (1852); 'The Blood-Stone' (1853); 'Lescure'; 'Life of Mary Queen of Scots' (1857).

McMaster, Guy Humphrey. An American poet; born in Clyde, N. Y., Jan. 31, 1829; died in Bath, Steuben County, N. Y., Sept. 13, 1887. At 19 he wrote 'Carmen Bellicosum,' better known as 'The Old Continentals,' published in the Knickerbocker Magazine, and very popular. Aside from the above, his best-known poems are: 'A Dream of Thanksgiving Eve' (1864); 'The Professor's Guest Chamber' (1880); 'The Commanders' (1887).

McMaster, John Bach. An American historian of celebrity; born at Brooklyn, N. Y., June 29, 1852. He has been professor of American history in the University of Pennsylvania since 1883. He has written 'Benjamin Franklin as a Man of Letters' (1887), etc. His principal work is 'History of the People of the United States'; 'Cambridge Modern History' (1903); 'The Struggle of the Social, Political and Industrial Rights of Man' (1903).

Macneil, Hector. A Scottish poet; born at Rosebank, near Roslin, 1746; died 1818. He wrote: 'Scotland's Skaith' (1795); 'The Waes of War' (1796),—both immensely popular,— and others. His poetical works, 2 vols., appeared in 1801 (3d ed. 1812). He published also 'Scottish Adventurers' (1812), a historical tale; 'Memoirs of Charles Macpherson' (1801), an autobiography; etc.

Macnish, Robert. A noted Scottish medical and miscellaneous writer; born at Glasgow, Feb. 15, 1802; died there, Jan. 16, 1837. He was a contributor to Blackwood's and Fraser's, over the signature "The Modern Pythagorean." His best-known works are: 'Anatomy of Drunkenness' (10th ed. 1854), and 'Philosophy of Sleep' (new ed. 1854). A second edition of his 'Book of Aphorisms' appeared in 1840; 'The Modern Pythagorean' (containing tales, essays, and sketches, with life) in 1844.

McPherson, Edward. An American journalist and political writer; born in Gettysburg, Pa.,

July 31, 1830; died there, Dec. 14, 1895. Among his publications are: 'Political History of the United States during the Great Rebellion' (1865); 'The Political History of the United States during Reconstruction' (1870); and a 'Hand-Book of Politics' (1872).

Macpherson, James. The Scottish author of the "Ossian" poems; born at Ruthven, Inverness-shire, Oct. 27, 1736; died Feb. 17, 1796. Some fragments of Gaelic verse with translations, published by him in 1760, attracted so much attention that funds were raised for sending him to the Highlands to discover more. On his return he published the 'Poems of Ossian,' consisting of 'Fingal, an Epic Poem in Six Books' (1762), and 'Temora, an Epic Poem in Eight Books' (1763). They became at once famous, and were translated into nearly every European language. A fierce controversy has been waged as to their being genuine Gaelic remains. He was secretary to the governor of Florida 1764-66; agent to the Nabob of Arcot 1779; Member of Parliament 1780-90. He wrote also 'History of Great Britain' (1775).

Macquoid, Mrs. Katharine S. A popular English novelist; born in London. Among her numerous works are: 'A Bad Beginning' (last ed. 1884); 'Hester Kirton' (new ed. 1870); 'Patty' (new ed. 1873); 'At the Red Glove' (1885); 'Puff' (1888); etc. Among several books of travel are: 'Through Normandy' (1877), and 'Through Brittany' (1877).

Madách, Emerich (mä'-dätsh). A popular Hungarian poet; born at Alsó-Sztregova, Jan. 21, 1823; died at Balassa-Gyarmath, Oct. 5, 1864. He studied law, and was a notary in his native county. His principal works are: 'Moses' (1861); and 'The Tragedy of Man' (1861), a philosophical dramatic poem treating of the development of mankind since the Fall, produced on the stage in 1883. He wrote also lyrics and dramatic fragments.

Madden, Richard Robert. An English physician and miscellaneous writer; born in Ireland, 1798; died 1886. He was prominent in the English anti-slavery cause. He wrote: 'Travels in Turkey' (2d ed. 1833); 'The Mussulman,' a tale; 'The Infirmities of Genius' (1833); 'Life of Savonarola' (2d ed. 1854); 'Life and Correspondence of the Countess of Blessington' (2d ed. 1855); 'The United Irishmen, their Lives and Times' (4 vols., 1857-60), his great work.

Madison, James. The fourth President of the United States; born at Port Conway, Va., March 16, 1751; died at Montpelier, Va., June 28, 1836. He served two terms as President (1809-17). He was associated with Jay and Hamilton in the composition of the 'Federalist.' 'Madison Papers,' 3 vols., appeared in 1840; 'Letters and Other Writings,' 4 vols., in 1865. His complete works have been published in 6 vols.

Maerlant, Jakob van (mär'-länt). A Flemish poet; born probably at Maerlant, on the island of Voorne, about 1235; died at Damme, near Bruges, 1291. He founded the didactic school of poetry in the Netherlands, and has been called «the father of Dutch poets.» His chief work was 'Mirror of History,' begun in 1283 but left unfinished. A statue has been erected to him at Damme.

Maeterlinck, Maurice (met'èr-lingk). A noted Belgian poet; born in Flanders, 1864. He is the foremost representative of the school calling itself «Young Belgium.» Among his works are the dramas 'The Blind'; 'The Intruder'; 'Princess Maleine' (5th ed. 1891); 'The Seven Princesses' (1891); 'Aglavaine' and 'Sélysette'; 'Monna Vanna'; also the volume of verse 'Hot-House Blooms,' and the essays 'The Treasure of the Humble.'

Maffei, Andrea, Cavaliere (mạ-fä'ē). An Italian poet; born at Riva di Trento, 1802; died at Milan, Nov. 27, 1885. He wrote 'Dal Benaco' (1854); 'Verses Published and Unpublished' (1858); 'Art, Ardors, and Fancies' (2d ed. 1864), containing many rare lyrics. He made numerous translations from the German, English, and Greek. He was also in public life, and became senator.

Magalhaens, Domingo José Gonçalves de (mä-gäl-yä'ens). A Brazilian poet; born in Rio Janeiro in 1811. From 1845 to 1867 he was Brazilian minister to Dresden, Naples, Turin, and Vienna. As a lyric poet he ranks high among his countrymen. His works include: 'Poesias' (1832); and 'Antonio José' and 'Olgiato,' two dramas which had great popularity in Spanish, French, and English translations. He died at Rome, in 1882.

Magariños Cervantes, Alejandro (mä-gä-rēn'yōs ther-vän'tes). A Uruguayan miscellaneous writer; born in Montevideo, 1826. He has written: 'Historical Studies on the River La Plata'; 'Church and State'; several volumes of poems; etc.

Maggi, Carlo Maria (mä'jē). Latin, **Maddius** (mad'i-us). An Italian poet; born at Milan, 1630; died 1699. He was member of the famous Accademia Della Crusca, and professor of Greek at Milan. He wrote poems in Greek, Latin, and Italian; letters; etc. He was one of the restorers of Italian poetry.

Magill, Mary Tucker. An American miscellaneous writer; born in Jefferson County, Va., Aug. 21,1832. She wrote: 'The Holcombes' (1868); 'Women; or, Chronicles of the Late War' (1870); and 'Pantomimes; or, Wordless Poems' (1882). Died at Winchester, Va., ——, 1899.

Maginn, William. An Irish scholar, poet, and journalist, a noted man in his day; born at Cork, Nov. 11, 1793; died at Walton on Thames, Aug. 2, 1842. He was a contributor to the early volumes of Punch, and with Hugh Fraser founded Fraser's Magazine in 1830. The only collection of his writings (and that partial) is the 'Miscellanies' (1855–57), edited by R. Shelton Mackenzie. His best stories are 'The City of Demons' and 'Bob Burke's Duel with Ensign Brady.'

Magnin, Charles (mä-nyan'). A French critic and poet; born in Paris, Nov. 4, 1793; died there, Oct. 8, 1862. He was one of the directors of the National Library in 1832. Besides poetry, he wrote: 'Racine' (1826), a successful comedy; 'The Origins of the Modern Stage' (1838); 'Historical and Literary Talks and Meditations' (1843); 'History of Puppet Shows' (1852); etc.

Magoon, Elias Lyman. An American pulpit orator and author; born in Lebanon, N. H., Oct. 20, 1810; died in Philadelphia, Nov. 25, 1886. Among his published works are: 'Eloquence of the Colonial Times' (1847); 'Proverbs for the People' (1848); 'Republican Christianity' (1849); and 'Westward Empire' (1856).

Magruder, Julia. An American prose-writer; born in Charlottesville, Va., Sept. 14, 1854. She has published 'Across the Chasm,' anonymous (1885); 'At Anchor' (1887); 'A Magnificent Plebeian'; 'Princess Sonya'; 'Violet.' D. 1907.

Mahaffy, John Pentland. An Irish classical scholar and historian; born at Chapponnaire, Switzerland, Feb. 26, 1839. He is professor of ancient history at Trinity College, Dublin. He has published: 'Social Life in Greece' (3d ed. 1877); 'Rambles and Studies in Greece' (2d ed. 1878); 'Greek Life and Thought' (1888); 'Greece under Roman Sway' (1890); 'History of Greek Classical Literature' (3 vols., 2d ed. 1892); 'The Empire of the Ptolemies' (1896); etc.

Mahan, Alfred Thayer. A distinguished American naval officer and writer on naval history; born at West Point, N. Y., Sept. 27, 1840. He served in the Civil War; and was president of the Naval War College, Newport, in 1886–89 and 1890–93. Visiting Europe in command of the Chicago in 1893, he received many honors, among them degrees from both Oxford and Cambridge. His chief work, 'Influence of Sea Power upon History' (1890), with its continuation, 'Influence of Sea Power upon the French Revolution and Empire' (1892), gave him a world-wide reputation. He has published also: 'The Gulf and Inland Waters' (1883); 'Life of Admiral Farragut' (1892); 'The Interest of America in Sea Power, Present and Future' (1897), a compilation of his magazine articles; 'Life of Nelson ' (1897); 'From Sail to Steam' (1907).

Mahan, Asa. A distinguished American Congregational divine and educator; born at Vernon, N. Y., Nov. 9, 1800; died at Eastbourne, England, April 4, 1889. He was president of Oberlin College, 1838–50; of Cleveland University, 1850–56; of Adrian College, Mich., 1860–71. Among his works were: 'System of Intellectual Philosophy' (1845); 'Science of Logic' (1857); 'History of Philosophy' (1883). He published 'Scripture Doctrine of Christian Perfection' (1839) in support of perfectionist views.

Mähly, Jakob (mä'lē). A Swiss poet, miscellaneous writer, and classical scholar; born at Basle, Dec. 24, 1828. He was professor of philology at Basle in 1863. Besides learned works, including 'Richard Bentley' (1868), 'History of Ancient Literature' (2 vols., 1880), etc., he has written 'Rhigmurmel' (1856), a volume of poems in the Basle dialect; the epic poems 'Matilda' (2d ed. 1862) and 'The Earthquake at Basle' (1856); the idyl 'Peace' (1862); stories, comedies, juveniles, etc. He died June 18, 1902.

Maïkov, Apollon Nikolaevich (mä-ē'kof). A distinguished Russian poet; born at Moscow, 1821; died at St. Petersburg, Mar. 20, 1897. He is probably the first of recent Russian poets. The tone of his writings is idealistic, and marked by great finish of form. During the Crimean War he published patriotic poems. His two plays are entitled 'Tri Smerti' (Three Deaths) and 'Dva Mira' (Two Worlds). The fourth edition of his works, in 3 vols., appeared in 1884.

Mailáth, János, Count (mī'lät). A Hungarian historian and poet; born at Buda-Pesth, Oct. 3, 1786; died Jan. 3, 1855. His most important historical works were: 'History of the Austrian Empire' (5 vols., 1834–50), his masterpiece; 'History of the Magyars' (5 vols., 1828–31). His chief poetical writings were: 'Poems' (1824) and 'Magyar Legends, Narratives, and Tales' (1826), together with translations from the German. He and his daughter committed suicide together.

Maimonides, Moses (mī-mon'i-dēz). A famous Jewish philosopher and scholar; born at Cordova, Spain, March 30, 1135; died at Cairo, Egypt, Dec. 13, 1204. He harmonized Judaism and philosophy. Driven with his family from Spain, he resided in Fez; then traveled by way of Palestine to Cairo, becoming there chief rabbi and the caliph's physician. His chief work, written in Hebrew, is 'Mishneh Torah' (Repetition of the Law: 1170–80), a masterly exposition of the whole of the Jewish law as contained in the Pentateuch and the voluminous Talmudic literature. His principal philosophical work, written in Arabic, was 'Dalalt al Ḥaïrïn' (Guide of the Perplexed: 1190). The estimation in which he is held by the Jews can be seen in their saying, "From Moses [the lawgiver] to Moses [Maimonides] there is none like unto Moses."

Maine, Sir Henry James Sumner. A distinguished English jurist; born near Leighton, Aug. 15, 1822; died at Cannes, Feb. 3, 1888. He was professor of civil law at Cambridge 1847–54; reader on Roman law at the Inns of Court, London, 1852; legal member of the council in India 1862–69; professor of jurisprudence at Oxford 1869–78; master of Trinity Hall, Cambridge, 1877; professor of international law at Cambridge 1887. Among his more noted works were: 'Ancient Law' (1861), an epoch-making book; 'Village Communities' (1871); 'Popular Government' (1885); etc.

Maine de Biran, Marie François Pierre Gonthier (mān dē bē-roñ'). A noted French philosopher; born at Bergerac, Nov. 29, 1766; died July 16, 1824. He served in Louis XVI.'s army, and was member of the Council of Five

Hundred in 1797. He was the founder of modern French spiritualism in philosophy. He wrote: 'Influence of Habit upon the Thinking Faculty' (1803); 'Decomposition of Thought' (1805); 'Foundations of Psychology' (1859); etc. ('Works,' 3 vols., edited by Cousin, 1841; 3 vols. additional, by Naville, 1846–59.)

Mair, Charles. A Canadian poet; born in Lanark, Sept. 21 1840. He is the author of 'Dreamland and Other Poems' (1868). and a drama entitled 'Tecumseh' (1886).

Mairet, Jean de (mä-rä'). A French dramatist; born at Besançon, Jan. 4, 1604; died there, Jan. 31, 1686. The precursor of Corneille, like him he furthered the purification of the French stage. He wrote pastorals, tragedies, and tragi-comedies. Among his most original works were the pastoral 'Silvanire' (1625), and the first regular French tragedy, 'Sophonisbe' (1629), his best production.

Maistre, Joseph Marie de, Count (mästr or mätr). A famous French statesman and philosophical and miscellaneous writer; born at Chambéry, April 1, 1754; died at Turin, Feb. 26, 1821. He was senator of Savoy in 1788; chancellor of Sardinia 1799; Sardinian minister at St. Petersburg 1802; minister at Turin 1817. He wrote: 'Thoughts on the French Revolution' (1796); 'Generative Principle of Human Institutions' (1810); 'Examination of Bacon's Philosophy' (1835; new ed. 1864); etc. 'St. Petersburg Evenings' was published in 1821; and his interesting correspondence in 1851 and 1858. ('Works,' 8 vols., 1864.)

Maistre, Xavier de, Count. A noted French soldier, essayist, and novelist; brother of Joseph Marie; born at Chambéry, October 1763; died at St. Petersburg, June 12, 1852. After serving in Piedmont and Italy (1798–99), going to Russia he rose to the rank of major-general. His masterpiece was the much-admired 'Journey Round my Room' (1794) in Sterne's style, written while under arrest for fighting a duel. He wrote besides: 'The Siberian Girl' (1815); 'Prisoners of the Caucasus' (1815); etc. The charm of his work is its dainty style, its power of narration, and its revelations of the author's personality.

Maitin, José Antonio (mä-ē'tēn). A Venezuelan poet; born in Porto Cabello, 1798; died in Choroni, 1874. In 1824 he returned from Havana to his own country from which he had fled on account of persecution, and subsequently lived in the valley of Choroni. In 1844 he made a collection of his best poems and published them under the title 'Echoes from Choroni,' and in 1851 a collected edition of all his works.

Major, Richard Henry. An English historian and geographer; born in London, 1818; died there 1891. He was connected with the British Museum Library 1844–80; honorary secretary of the Hakluyt Society 1849–58; and vice-president of the Royal Geographical Society. He wrote 'Life of Prince Henry of Portugal'

(1868), 'The Discoveries of Prince Henry and their Results' (1877); edited 'Select Letters of Christopher Columbus' (1847); etc.

Malabari, Behramji Merwanji (mä-lä-bä'rē). An eminent social reformer of India, and a poet; born (Mehta) at Baroda, 1853. He has given his fortune and his life to bettering the condition of women in India by the abolition of infant marriage and enforced widowhood. He is editor and proprietor of the Indian Spectator and the Voice of India. Among his works are the fine 'Niti Vinod,' etc., in verse; 'Gujarat and Gujaratis,' liked for its picturesque and humorous style; various political and ethical productions; etc.

Malcolm, Sir John. A distinguished British soldier, statesman, and historian; born at Burnfoot, Dumfriesshire, Scotland, May 2, 1769; died in London, May 30, 1833. Employed by the East India Company, he distinguished himself as a fighter, diplomatist, and ruler; was president of Mysore 1803; won the important battle of Mehidpur over the Mahrattas in 1817; was governor of Malwa 1818–22; of Bombay 1827–30; Member of Parliament 1831–32. He wrote among others: 'Political History of India' (1811); 'History of Persia' (2 vols., 1815), which is still an authority; 'Memoir of Central India' (1823); and above all, 'Sketches of Persia' (1827), still read, and a mine of good stories, legends, travel sketches, descriptions of Oriental life and ceremonial, and manly sense and thought.

Malczewski, Antoni (mäl-chev'skē). A noted Polish poet; born at Warsaw, about 1793; died there, May 2, 1826. The merit of his works, which were marked by a deeply religious spirit, was not recognized till after his death. His masterpiece, the famous epic 'Marya' (Maria: 1825), has been several times edited and translated into English (London, 1836), French, German, and Bohemian. The tomb erected to him at Varsovia bears the inscription: "To the author of Maria." He died in abject poverty.

Malebranche, Nicolas (mäl-broñsh'). A famous French philosopher; born in Paris, Aug. 6, 1638; died there, Oct. 13, 1715. The keynote of his philosophy is to be found in his celebrated principle, "We see all things in God." His chief work, containing the substance of his whole philosophy, was 'Search for Truth' (1674). Other works were: 'Of Nature and Grace' (1680); 'Christian and Metaphysical Meditations' (1683); 'Treatise on Ethics' (1684); etc. Imbued with a deep piety, he felt it to be of the utmost importance to effect a reconciliation between philosophy and religion. ('Works,' 11 vols., 1712; last ed. 1859–71.)

Malesherbes, Chrétien Guillaume de Lamoignon de (mäl-zärb'). A famous French statesman and miscellaneous writer; born in Paris, Dec. 6, 1721; was guillotined there, April 22, 1794. He was censor of the press and president of the excise court 1750–71; Minister of the Interior 1774–76; Louis XVI.'s counsel

before the Convention 1792–93. He wrote 'Public Law of France' (1779); 'Thoughts and Maxims' (1802); 'Book Selling and the Liberty of the Press' (2d ed. 1827); etc. The second edition of his 'Unpublished Works' appeared in 1822.

Malet, Lucas. Pseudonym of Mary St. Leger Harrison, an English novelist, youngest daughter of Charles Kingsley; born 1852, and now wife of Rev. W. Harrison, rector of Clovelly, England. Her novels include: 'Colonel Enderby's Wife'; 'A Counsel of Perfection'; 'Little Peter'; 'Mrs. Lorimer'; 'The Wages of Sin'; 'Carissima'; 'The Gateless Barrier.'

Malherbe, François de (mä-lärb). A famous French poet; born at Caen, 1555; died in Paris, Oct. 16, 1628. He became court poet in 1605. He was the inaugurator of French classicism, and made Parisian French the standard for the kingdom. His poems were marked by purity of diction and harmony of versification, rather than by great poetic feeling. Besides translations from Latin, he wrote but one volume of poetry, containing 'Stanzas,' 'Odes,' 'Sonnets,' 'Epigrams,' and 'Songs.' The best edition of his works is in Lalanne's 'Great Writers' (Paris, 5 vols., 1860–65).

Mallery, Garrick. An American ethnologist; born in Wilkesbarre, Pa., April 23, 1831; died in Washington, Oct. 24, 1894. His works in part are: 'A Calendar of the Dakota Nation' (1877); 'Sign Language among the North American Indians compared with That among Other Peoples and Deaf Mutes' (1881). He, besides, contributed much to periodicals.

Mallet, originally **Malloch, David** (mal'et or mal'lọch). A Scottish poet and dramatist; born at Crieff, Perthshire, about 1705; died in England, April 21, 1765. He was under-secretary to the Prince of Wales, and a friend of Pope, Bolingbroke, and other celebrities of the time. He wrote in verse 'The Excursion' (1728); 'The Hermit' (1747); 'Edwin and Emma' (1760); the tragedies 'Eurydice' (1731), 'Mustapha' (1739); etc. The famous English patriotic song 'Rule Britannia' appeared in 'Alfred: a Masque' (1740), written with James Thomson; its authorship has been claimed for each.

Mallian, Julien de (mä-yän'). A West-Indian dramatist; born in Le Moule, Guadeloupe, 1805; died in Paris, 1851. He gained wide reputation as a writer of comedies and dramas, many of which have been presented on the metropolitan stage. The most popular are: 'Two Roses' (1831), a historical drama of the civil wars in England; 'The Carpenter' (1831), a comedy; and 'The Wandering Jew' (1834).

Mallock, William Hurrell. A distinguished English essayist, novelist, and poet; born in Devonshire, 1849. He is a nephew of Froude the historian. Among his best-known works are: 'The New Republic' (1877), and 'Is Life Worth Living?' (1879). His novels are 'A Romance of the Nineteenth Century'; 'The

Old Order Changeth'); 'A Human Document'); and 'The Heart of Life.' He has published two volumes of poems; and a great number of magazine-articles, some of which have been collected under the titles 'Social Equality' (1882), 'Property, Progress, and Poverty' (1884) and 'Classes and Masses; or Wealth and Wages in the United Kingdom' (1896); 'Religion as a Credible Doctrine' (1902). He credits industrial progress to intellect, not labor.

Malmesbury, William of. A noted English historian; born in Somersetshire, about 1095; died at Malmesbury, about 1143. He was a monk, and librarian of the monastery of Malmesbury. Of his great work, 'History of the Kings of England,' which next to the 'Saxon Chronicle' is the highest authority for Anglo-Saxon times, and its continuation 'Modern History,' both in Latin, the latest and best edition is Hardy's (1840). The latest English translation of the former is in Bohn's Library (1847).

Malmström, Bernhard Elis (mälm'strèm). A Swedish poet and historian of literature; born at Nerike, March 14, 1816; died at Upsala, June 21, 1865. He was professor of æsthetics and literature at Upsala in 1858. He published: 'Poems' (1845-47; latest ed. 1889); 'Ariadne' (1889), of which many editions have appeared; the prose work 'History of Swedish Literature' (5 vols., 1866-68); etc. Much of his poetry has great perfection of form. ('Works,' 8 vols., 1866-69).

Malone, Edmund. A noted Irish Shakespearean scholar and editor; born at Dublin, Oct. 4, 1741; died in London, April 25, 1812. He was originally a lawyer. He edited the works of Sir Joshua Reynolds (1797), Dryden (1800), W. G. Hamilton (1808), with memoirs; he wrote also a 'History of the English Stage' (1790). He is chiefly known for his edition of Shakespeare (11 vols., 1790); and for having collected the material of the Variorum Shakespeare, edited by James Boswell (21 vols., 1821).

Malory, Sir Thomas. The British author of the famous 'Morte d'Arthur'; born probably about 1430; died after 1470. He was probably a priest. The 'Morte d'Arthur' (1469 or 1470) is a prose collection of the romantic traditions concerning King Arthur and the Knights of the Round Table. It was the main source upon which Tennyson drew in writing his 'Idylls of the King.' The latest editions are Sommer's 1890-91 (the standard), and Dent's, with a preface by Professor Rhys (1893).

Malot, Hector (mä-lō'). A French novelist; born near Rouen, May 20, 1830. He has been a prolific writer. Of his numerous works the best known are: 'The Victims of Love,' in three parts; 'The Lovers' (1859); 'Husband and Wife' (1865); 'The Children' (1866); 'Doctor Claude' (1879); 'Accomplices' (1892); 'In the Bosom of the Family' (1893); 'Blue Blood'; 'The Novel of my Novels,' etc. Most of his books treat of French life under the Second Empire.

Malte-Brun, Conrad (mält-brun'), originally Malte Conrad Brunn. A famous French geographer and publicist; born at Thisted, Denmark, Aug. 12, 1775; died in Paris, Dec. 14, 1826. Banished from his native country in 1800, he resided in Paris. His great work was 'Epitome of Universal Geography' (1810-29; latest ed., 6 vols., 1872). He also founded the 'Annals of Travels, Geography, and History' (1808-14); collaborated in 'Mathematical, Physical, and Political Geography' (16 vols., 1804-7) and 'Dictionary of Universal Geography' (8 vols., 1821); wrote 'Scientific and Literary Miscellanies' (3 vols., 1828); etc.

Malthus, Thomas Robert. A famous English political economist; born near Guildford, Surrey, Feb. 17, 1766; died at St. Catherine's, near Bath, Dec. 23, 1834. He was professor of history and political economy at Haileybury College (1805). His celebrated "Malthusian doctrine," as it is called, was announced in 'Principle of Population' (1798; revised ed. 1803). His theory is that population increases faster than the means of subsistence; so that the increase in population must in some way be checked. A ninth edition appeared in 1888.

Mamiani della Rovere, Terenzio, Count (mä-mē-ä'nē del'lä rō'vä-rä). A distinguished Italian statesman, educator, and philosophical writer; born at Pesaro, about 1800; died at Rome, May 21, 1885. He was imprisoned and exiled for taking part in the revolution at Bologna in 1831; made Minister of the Interior in 1848; Minister of Public Instruction in 1860; Minister to Athens. He wrote numerous and important books, among which are: 'Confessions of a Metaphysician' (2d ed. 1865); 'The Religion of the Future' (1879); 'Social Questions' (1882); etc.

Mandeville, Bernard. A Dutch-English medical and miscellaneous writer; born at Dordrecht about 1670; died in London, Jan. 21, 1733. He was a physician in London. He wrote: 'Esop Dressed' (1704), being fables in verse; 'Treatise of the Hypochondriac and Hysteric Passions' (1711); 'Free Thoughts on Religion' (1720); etc. His 'Fable of the Bees; or, Private Vices Public Benefits' (2d ed. 1723) was presented as a nuisance by the grand jury of Middlesex in 1723.

Mandeville, Sir John. A noted (and probably imaginary) English traveler, who or whose inventor flourished in the fourteenth century. He was the reputed author of a popular book of travels of that century, the writer of which claimed to have visited Turkey, Armenia, Tartary, Persia, Syria, Arabia, Egypt, Libya, Ethiopia, Chaldea, Amazonia, and India; to have been in the service of the Sultan of Egypt; etc. It is in fact a most entertaining and curious compilation of legends, miracles, and wonder-stories from many sources, pressed into the service of Christianity and its miracle-working powers.

Manetho (man'e-thō). An Egyptian priest and annalist; born at Sebennytus, in Lower Egypt; lived about 250 B. C. He composed three books in Greek, which purported to give the history of Egypt from the mythical period downward; but only fragments remain, imbedded in the works of Josephus and other writers. His writings, coming down through translations and transliterations of Syncellus, Eusebius, Jerome, and Africanus, have been the chief source of information as to the successive dynasties of Egypt; and with the inscriptions coming to light, assist archæologists in framing its chronology.

Mangan, James Clarence. An Irish poet; born at Dublin, May 1, 1803; died in Meath Hospital, June 20, 1849. His work shows great command of language and skill in versification. He published volumes entitled : ' Romances and Ballads of Ireland ' (1850); ' German Anthology ' (1849); ' Poets and Poetry of Munster ' (1849); etc. A selection of his poems, edited by Louise Imogen Guiney, appeared 1897.

Manley, Mrs. Mary de la Rivière. An English novelist; born in the island of Guernsey, 1672; died at Lambeth Hill, July 11, 1724. She was daughter of Sir Roger Manley. She published ' The New Atlantis ' (1709), a scandalous satire on distinguished public characters, for which she was arrested for libel, but discharged. She published a key to it entitled ' Memoirs of Europe ' (1710). She wrote also ' The Power of Love, in Seven Novels ' (1720), etc.

Mann, Horace. A noted American educator and educational writer; born in Franklin, Mass., May 4, 1796; died in Yellow Springs, O., Aug. 2, 1859. He was Member of Congress from Massachusetts, 1848–53; president of Antioch College, 1852–59. He was one of the foremost men in educational reform; and published, besides his educational lectures and voluminous controversial writings, 'A Few Thoughts for a Young Man ' (1850); ' Slavery : Letters and Speeches ' (1851); and ' Powers and Duties of Woman ' (1853).

Mann, Mary Tyler (Peabody). An American writer, wife of Horace Mann; born in Cambridgeport, Mass., Nov. 16, 1806; died in Jamaica Plain, Mass., Feb. 11, 1887. Her published works are : ' Flower People ' (1838); ' Culture in Infancy ' (1863); ' Life of Horace Mann ' (1865); ' Juanita, a Romance of Real Life in Cuba,' published after her death.

Manning, Henry Edward, Cardinal. A distinguished English Roman Catholic prelate and religious writer; born at Totteridge, Hertfordshire, July 15, 1808; died Jan. 14, 1892. Originally a clergyman of the Church of England, in which he rose to be archdeacon of Chichester (1840), he became a Roman Catholic priest in 1851; archbishop of Westminster in 1865; cardinal in 1875. He founded the Roman Catholic University of Kensington in 1874. He was a friend of the laboring classes. He wrote : ' Unity of the Church ' (1842); ' Temporal Mission of the Holy Ghost ' (3d ed. 1877); ' The Catholic Church and Modern Society ' (1880); ' The Eternal Priesthood ' (1883); ' Religio Viatoris ' (A Traveler's Religion : 3d ed. 1888); etc.

Manrique, Jorge (män-rē′kä). A famous Spanish poet; died 1479. He belonged to one of the oldest and most distinguished families in Spain. His chief work was an ode on his father's death (1492), now known as ' Coplas de Manrique ' (Manrique's Stanzas), one of the most touching poems in the Spanish language. It has often been reprinted, and was translated into English by Longfellow. Several of his love poems also have come down to us.

Mansel, Henry Longueville. A distinguished English metaphysician; born at Cosgrove, Northamptonshire, Oct. 6, 1820; died there, July 30, 1871. He was dean of St. Paul's, London, in 1868. A follower of Sir William Hamilton, he developed his philosophy still further. His chief works were : ' Prolegomena Logica ' (Introduction to Logic : 1851); the article on ' Metaphysics ' in the ' Encyclopædia Britannica ' (1857); ' Bampton Lectures ' (1858); ' Philosophy of the Conditioned ' (1866); etc.

Mansfield, Edward Deering. An American journalist and miscellaneous writer; born at New Haven, Conn., Aug. 17, 1801; died at Morrow, O., Oct. 27, 1880. He wrote : ' Political Grammar ' (1834); ' Life of General Scott ' (1846); ' Legal Rights of Women ' (1847); ' History of the Mexican War ' (1848); ' American Education ' (1850); ' Personal Memoirs ' (1879); ' Utility of Mathematics '; etc. He was for many years a contributor to the New York press over the signature " Veteran Observer."

Mansilla de Garcia, Eduarda (män-sēl′yä dä gär-thē′ä). An Argentine novelist; born (Mansilla) at Buenos Ayres, 1838. She married Manuel Garcia, a diplomatist, in 1855. She has written : ' The Physician of St. Louis '; ' Lucia Miranda '; ' Paul ; or, Life on the Pampas ' (translated into French); etc., all descriptive of Argentine customs or historical episodes.

Mant, Richard. A distinguished English clergyman and religious writer; born at Southampton, Feb. 12, 1776; died at Ballymoney, Ireland, Nov. 2, 1848. He was bishop in the Irish church. He is best known as one of the authors of the ' Annotated Bible ' (3 vols., 1814), known as D'Oyly and Mant's, which had an immense circulation. He wrote also : ' Ancient Hymns ' (1837); ' History of the Church of Ireland ' (1840); etc.

Manuel, Don Juan (mä-nö-el′). A Spanish prince and famous miscellaneous writer; born at Escalona, 1282; died 1347 or 1349. Holding the highest offices in the State,—being joint regent of Spain in 1320,—and twice in arms against his king, as well as commander-in-chief against the Moors, his life was a stormy one. He was one of the first and best of Spanish prose-writers. He is best known by ' El Conde Lucanor ' (Count Lucanor : 1575), a collection of fifty tales in the Eastern style. It was translated into English by James York (new ed. 1888).

Manzano, Juan Francisco (man-thah′no). A Cuban poet; born in Havana, in 1797; died in 1854. A negro, born in slavery, and remaining in servitude for forty years, he obtained his education with great difficulty. While still a slave he succeeded in publishing a small volume of poems entitled 'Passing Flowers.' His drama 'Zafira' was published in 1842. Some of his poems have been translated into French and German.

Manzoni, Alessandro, Count (män-tsō'nē). A famous Italian novelist and poet; born at Milan, March 7, 1785; died there, May 22, 1873. He became senator in 1860. He was the leader of the Italian romantic school. His most celebrated work was the romance 'I Promessi Sposi' (The Betrothed: 1827; English translation in Bohn's Library, 1883). He wrote also the allegorical poem 'Urania' (1807), in honor of poetry; 'Sacred Hymns' (1815); the great tragedies 'The Count of Carmagnola' (1820) and 'Adelchi' (1822); the famous ode on Napoleon's death, 'The Fifth of May'; etc. (Latest edition of his works, 2 vols., 1875–81.)

Map or **Mapes, Walter.** A British theologian, satirist, and poet; born in Gloucestershire or Herefordshire, about 1140; died about 1210. He was archdeacon of Oxford in 1197. He wrote: 'De Nugis Curialium' (Courtiers' Triflings: 1182–92). Probably the Lancelot story in the Arthurian legends is based on an Anglo-French poem by him; and the legends generally have been thought to be largely his work.

Maquet, Auguste (mä-kä'). A French novelist and playwright; born in Paris, Sept. 13, 1813; died at Ste. Mesme, Jan. 8, 1888. He was professor at the Collège Charlemagne in 1831. He collaborated with the elder Dumas in some of his novels. He wrote alone (most of them in both novel and play form): 'Beautiful Gabrielle' (1853), with its sequel 'The Bather's House' (1856); 'The White Rose' (1859); 'Journey to the Country of the Blue' (1859); the play 'The Bercheny Hussar' (1865), which was very successful; etc.

March, Ausias or **Augustin** (märch). A celebrated Spanish poet; born 1390 (?); died about 1460. He is the best of all the Catalan poets. Of his works now extant are ninety-three 'Love Songs'; eight 'Laments'; fourteen 'Moral Poems'; a fine 'Song of Devotion'; etc. He has been called "the Petrarch of Catalonia." (Latest edition of his works, Barcelona, 1884.)

Marchand, Félix Gabriel. A Canadian journalist and dramatist; born at St. John's, P. Q., Jan. 9, 1832. Among his works are the prose comedies 'Fatenville' and 'Mistakes Don't Count'; the comedies in verse 'One Good Fortune Brings Another' and 'The Paste Diamonds'; also a comic opera, 'The University Laureate.'

Marco Polo. See **Polo, Marco.**

Marcus Aurelius Antoninus. See **Aurelius, Marcus.**

Marden, Orison Swett. An American biographer; born in New Hampshire, 1848. His home is in Boston. He has written 'Pushing to the Front' and 'Architects of Fate,' collections of short biographies; 'The Optimistic Life.'

Maréchal, Pierre Sylvain (mä-rā-shäl'). A French atheistical writer; born in Paris, Aug. 15, 1750; died at Montrouge, near Paris, Jan. 18, 1803. He was originally a lawyer. He published 'Fragments of a Moral Poem on God' (1781), modeled upon Lucretius. A parody on the Psalms (1784) cost him his position as sublibrarian of the Collège Mazarin. He wrote an 'Almanac of Honest People' (1788), substituting a list of names of his own invention for the usual calendar of saints; with the astronomer Lalande a 'Dictionary of Atheists' (1800); etc

Marek, Jan Jindrich (mä'rek). A Bohemian novelist and poet; born at Liblin, Nov. 4, 1801; died at Kralovice, Nov. 3, 1853. He became a priest in 1826. He wrote 'Poems' (1823); 'Lilies of the Valley' (2 vols., 1824 and 1826), novels. His works were published in 10 vols. at Prague 1843-47. The first two volumes contain ballads, legends, and short poems; the other eight are novels, including 'The Harper,' 'The Bohemians in Prussia,' 'A Night at Kacerov,' 'The Quack,' etc.

Marenco, Carlo (mä-ren'kō). An Italian tragic poet; born at Cassolnuovo, May 1, 1800; died at Savona, Sept. 20, 1843. He was originally a law student. Among his best-known works are 'La Pia de' Tolomei,' his best production (translated into English by Williams, London, 1856); 'Corso Donati'; 'Arnold of Brescia'; etc. ('Works,' 4 vols., Turin, 1835-40.)

Marenco, Leopoldo, Count. An Italian dramatist, son of Carlo; born at Ceva, Nov. 8, 1831. He was for a time employed in the ministry of finance (1851); and as professor of Italian literature at Bologna 1860-64, and Milan 1864-71. He has written the tragedies 'Piccarda Donati' (1869), 'Sappho' (1880), 'Rosalinda' (1884), etc.; the comedies 'George Gandi' (4th ed. 1882), 'A Bad Example in the Family'; etc. ('Dramatic Works,' 20 vols., Turin, 1883.) He died at Milan, April 30, 1899.

Margry, Pierre (mär-grē'). A French historian; born at Paris, Dec. 8, 1818. He is adjunct curator of the archives of the ministry of marine and the colonies. He has written 'Democracy in France' (1849); 'Navigation of the Mississippi' (1859); 'French Navigation from the 14th to the 15th Century' (1867); 'Conquest of the Canary Isles' (1880); etc.

Marguerite d'Angoulême, or **d'Alençon,** or **de Valois,** or **de Navarre** (mär'gē-rēt dän-gö-läm'). Queen of Navarre, and famous for her stories, poems, and letters; born at Angoulême, April 1492; died in Bigorre, 1549. She was a great patroness of literature. She is best known in literature by the celebrated 'Heptameron,' a collection of tales. A book of her poems, 'Pearls of the Pearl of Princesses,' appeared in 1547 'Letters,' 1841-42.

Marguérittes, Julie de (mär-ger-ēt'). An English dramatic critic; born in London in 1814; died in Philadelphia, June 21, 1866. After successfully appearing in the opera of 'La Gazza Ladra' both in New York and Philadelphia, she retired from the stage and became the dramatic critic of the Philadelphia Sunday Transcript. She was a voluminous writer for the press. Among her books are 'The Ins and Outs of Paris' (1855); 'Italy and the War of 1859' (1859); and 'Parisian Pickings.'

Mariager, P. (mä-rē-ä'ger). A Danish novelist; born 1827. Besides translating a number of works from the French and German, he wrote 'From Hellas' (1881), five stories that were a new departure in Danish literature,— being attempts to reproduce Greek culture as Ebers did Egyptian,—and were translated into several languages; 'The Last Lamia' (1884); 'The Potentate of Rhodes' (1885); 'Sybaris,' a drama; 'A Marriage in the Catacombs' (1893); etc.

Marie. See **Meyn, Antoinette.**

Marie de France (mä-rē' dė froñs). The earliest French poetess; lived probably in the latter half of the 12th century. She spent her life in England. She wrote 'Lais' (Lays), a collection of narrative poems, descriptive especially of love, and belonging to the finest specimens of the Old-French ballad; 'Ysopet,' fables; and a poem on the purgatory of St. Patrick. ('Works,' edited by Roquefort, 2 vols., 1820; 'Lays,' 1885.)

Mariette, Auguste Édouard (mä-ryet'). A distinguished French Egyptologist; born at Boulogne, Feb. 11, 1821; died at Cairo, Egypt, Jan. 18, 1881. He was the principal promoter of the Egyptian museum at Boulak (afterwards at Gizeh), the French School of Egyptology, and the Egyptian Institute; and was inspector-general and guardian of the Egyptian national monuments. He wrote: 'Karnak' (1875); 'Denderah' (4 vols., 1869–80); 'Monuments of Upper Egypt' (Boston, 1890); etc.

Marini, Giovanni Battista (mä-rē'nē). A celebrated Italian poet; born at Naples, Oct. 18, 1569; died there, March 25, 1625. He lived a dissipated and licentious life. The influence of the style he introduced, known as "marinism," was great both in Italy and France, which he visited. He wrote 'Adonis' (1623), his principal work; 'The Massacre of the Innocents' (1633); sonnets; etc.

Marivaux, Pierre Carlet de Chamberlain de (mä-ri-vō'). A distinguished French dramatist and novelist; born in Paris, Feb. 4, 1688; died Feb. 12, 1763. His peculiar style gave rise to the term "marivaudage." His principal plays were: 'Game of Love and Chance' (1730); 'School of Manners' (1732); 'The Legacy' (1736); etc.: his chief novels 'Marianne' (1731–41), his masterpiece, said to have been the model of Richardson's 'Pamela'; 'The Upstart Peasant' (new ed. 1865); etc. ('Works,' 10 vols., 1827–30.)

Markham, Charles Edwin. An American poet; born in Oregon, in 1852. He is professor in Christian College, Santa Rosa. He has written 'In Earth's Shadow' (1890); 'Songs of a Dream-Builder' (1890); 'The Hoe-Man in the Making.'

Markham, Clements Robert. An English traveler, geographer, and historian; born at Stillingfleet, near York, July 20, 1830. He accompanied an Arctic expedition in 1851; visited Peru 1852–54; visited Peru and India as commissioner to introduce cinchona plants into the latter country, 1860; was secretary of the Royal Geographical Society 1863–88; accompanied the Abyssinian expedition 1867–68. He has written: 'Travels in Peru and India' (1862); 'History of the Abyssinian Expedition' (1869); 'History of Peru' (1892); etc. He has edited a number of reprints of works on South America for the Hakluyt Society.

Markoe, Peter. ["A Native of Algiers."] An American poet; born in Santa Cruz, W. I., about 1753; died in Philadelphia about 1792. He published a tragedy, 'The Patriot Chief' (1783); 'Miscellaneous Poems' (1787); a poem called 'The Times' (1788); and 'Reconciliation,' a comic opera (1790).

Mark Twain. See **Clemens.**

Marlitt, E. (mär'lit). Pseudonym of Eugenie John, a popular German novelist; born in Arnstadt on the Gera, Dec. 5, 1825; died there, June 22, 1887. Her novels deal largely with domestic scenes and incidents, and include: 'Gold Else' (1866); 'Blue Beard' (1866); 'The Little Moorland Princess' (1871); 'The Old Mamsell's Secret' (1877); 'In the Schillingscourt' (1880); 'The Eulen House'; etc.

Marlowe, Christopher. A noted English poet and dramatist; born at Canterbury about 1564; killed at Deptford, June 1, 1593. Soon after graduating at Cambridge (1583), he became dramatist to the "Lord Admiral's Company," London, which produced most of his plays. Among them were the tragedies 'Life and Death of Dr. Faustus' (1601); 'The Jew of Malta'; and 'Edward II.' (1593), his best work. Many believe him to have been the author of the second and third parts of Shakespeare's 'Henry VI.' He wrote also the first part of a narrative poem, 'Hero and Leander,' completed afterward by George Chapman. ('Works,' best edition by Dyce, 3 vols., 1850.)

Marmette, Joseph. A Canadian prose-writer; born in Montmagny, P. Q., Oct. 25, 1844. His published works include: 'Charles and Eva' (1868); 'Chevalier de Momac' (1873); and 'The Maccabees of New France' (1878).

Marmier, Xavier (mar-myä'). A French miscellaneous writer; born at Pontarlier, June 24, 1809; died in Paris, Oct. 11, 1892. He was librarian of the library of St. Geneviève, Paris (1846). He was a great traveler. His works include: 'History of Iceland' (1838); 'Letters on Russia,' etc. (2 vols., 1843); 'From the

Rhine to the Nile' (1846); 'The United States and Canada' (1874); the novels 'The Spitzbergen Lovers' (1858), 'The Dramas of the Heart' (1868), 'A Russian Great Lady' (1876); in verse, 'Poetical Sketches' (1830); 'Poems of a Traveler' (1841); etc.

Marmol, José (mar'mōl). An Argentine poet; born in Buenos Ayres, Dec. 5, 1818; died there, Aug. 12, 1871. His principal works are: 'The Pilgrim' and 'Harmonies,' descriptive poems of travels (1856); the dramas 'El Cruzado' (1860) and 'El Poeta' (1862); and 'La Amalia,' a historical romance based upon the War of the Roses in England (1866), — considered his best work, and which has been translated into French and German.

Marmontel, Jean François (mär-môn-tel'). A famous French miscellaneous writer; born at Bort, July 11, 1723; died at Abbeville, Dec. 31, 1799. He was brought up by the Jesuits, and intended for the Church. Among his works were: the popular tragedies 'Dionysius the Tyrant' (1748), 'Aristomenes' (1749), etc.; 'Moral Tales' (1761); the novels 'Belisarius' (1767) and 'The Incas' (1778); etc. Of more lasting value, however, were 'French Poetics' (1763); his contributions to the 'Encyclopédie,' collected as 'Elements of Literature' (1787); and his 'Memoirs' (1804). ('Works,' 17 vols., 1786-87.)

Marnix, Philipp van (mar'niks), **Baron of Saint-Aldegonde**. A Dutch statesman, satirist, and miscellaneous writer; born at Brussels, 1538; died at Leyden, Dec. 15, 1598. He was prominent in the liberation of the Netherlands; formulated the treaty of Breda (1566); was governor of Delft and Rotterdam; defended Antwerp (1584-85). His chief work was 'De Byencorf der h. Roomscher Kercke' (Beehive of the Holy Church of Rome: 1569), a satire on Catholicism (published under the pseudonym "Isaac Rabbotenus") which has become a Dutch prose classic. He wrote the ballad 'William of Nassau,' officially recognized as one of the two national songs of Holland; and a fine poetical version of the Psalms.

Marot, Adolphe Gaston (mä-rō'). A French dramatist; born at Rochefort, Aug. 13, 1837. He was director of the Cluny Theatre (1875). He has written: 'Aristophanes in Paris' (1873, with Clairville); 'The Loves of the Boulevard' (1877); 'Clairon'; 'The French in Tonkin' (1855, with Péricaud); 'Weeping Paris' (1886); 'My Wife's Husband' (1889); the romance 'Mother and Daughter' (1889); etc.

Marot, Clément. A famous French poet; born at Cahors, 1495; died at Turin, 1544. He was easily the first French poet of his age, noted for literary vivacity, facility, and grace. He excelled in elegies, eclogues, and epistles. His metrical version of the Psalms, however, is heavy and prosy. Among his works were 'The Temple of Cupid' (1515), and 'Hell' (1526).

Marquez, José Arnaldo (mär'keth). The best of modern Peruvian — especially lyric —

poets; born about 1825; died Jan. 15, 1881. He published 'Lost Notes' (1862), 'Flor de Abel,' etc.; and a book of travels in the United States. He was editor of several journals. He lost his life in the defense of Lima against the Chilians.

Marradi, Giovanni (mär-rä'dē). An Italian poet; born at Leghorn, 1852. He has written: 'Modern Hymns, by G. M. Labronio' (1878); 'Fancies of the Sea' (1881); 'Lyric Memories' (1884); 'Poems' (1887); 'New Songs' (1891); etc.

Marryat, Florence. A popular English novelist, daughter of Capt. Frederick Marryat; born at Brighton, July 9, 1838; died in London, Oct. 27, 1899. She married first Col. Ross Church, and then Col. Francis Lean. She was a dramatic reader and singer; was editor of London Society (1872-76); and acted in London in her own play 'Her World' (1881). She wrote: 'Too Good for Him' (new ed. 1868); 'Woman Against Woman' (1865); 'Confessions of Gerald Estcourt' (1865); 'Veronique' (1869); 'Fighting he Air' (new ed. 1878); 'A Daughter of the Tropics' (1887). She published 'Life and Letters of Captain Marryat,' 2 vols. (1872).

Marryat, Frederick. ["Captain Marryat."] A famous English novelist; born in London, July 10, 1792; died at Langham, Norfolk, Aug. 9, 1848. Entering the British navy in 1806, he became commander in 1815; and was serving on the St. Helena station at the time of Napoleon's death. Among his best-known works were: 'Frank Mildmay' (1829); 'The King's Own' (1830); 'Peter Simple' (1834); 'Mr. Midshipman Easy' (1836); 'Japhet in Search of a Father' (1836); 'Masterman Ready' (1841).

Marsh, Mrs. Anne (**Caldwell**). A popular English novelist; born in Staffordshire, 1796; died there, October 1874. She published most of her works anonymously. Among them were: 'Two Old Men's Tales' (1834; latest ed. 1849); 'Mount Sorel' (1845); 'Emilia Wyndham' (latest ed. 1849); 'Norman's Bridge' (latest ed. 1849). She wrote also the historical work 'The Protestant Reformation in France' (1847).

Marsh, George Perkins. An American philologist; born in Woodstock, Vt., March 15, 1801; died in Vallombrosa, Italy, July 23, 1882. A graduate of Dartmouth in 1820, he practiced law in Burlington, Vt.; became Member of Congress 1842-49, minister to Turkey 1849-53, and first minister to the new kingdom of Italy 1861, holding the post until his death, a period of over 20 years. As a diplomatist he had great ability. His services to the study of language, especially the history of his own tongue, give him a distinguished place among American scholars. The 'Origin and History of the English Language' remains a standard work. He translated Rask's 'Icelandic Grammar' (1838); and also published 'Lectures on the English Language' (1861); an edition of Wedgwood's 'Etymology'; and 'The Earth as Modified by Human Action' (1874). A revised

24

edition of his complete works appeared in 1885; his ‹ Life and Letters › compiled by his widow in 1888. A part of his fine library of Scandinavian literature was acquired by the University of Vermont.

Marsh, Othniel Charles. A distinguished American palæontologist; born at Lockport, N.Y., Oct. 29, 1831; died at New Haven, Conn., Mar. 18, 1899. A Yale graduate, he studied at Berlin, Heidelberg, and Breslau; and was professor of palæontology at Yale from 1866 to his death. He was authority on the extinct vertebrates of the Rocky Mountains, having conducted many scientific expeditions thither, and discovered more than 1,000 new specimens, many of which he described in the American Journal of Science, and which he presented to Yale University. For twenty years he labored upon a series of government reports containing an illustrated account of his discoveries. Three of these—on the ‹Odontornithes,› the ‹Dinocerata,› and ‹Lauropoda›—have appeared. He was president of the American Association for the Advancement of Science, vertebrate palæontologist of the U. S. Geological Survey, president of the National Academy of Sciences, and fellow of the Geological Society of London. His work has been recognized by honorary degrees from great universities, and in many other ways, bringing him international reputation.

Marshall, John. An eminent American jurist; born at Germantown, Fauquier County, Va., Sept. 24, 1755; died at Philadelphia, July 6, 1835. He served in the Revolutionary War; was United States envoy to France 1797-98; Member of Congress from Virginia 1799-1800; Secretary of State 1800-1; Chief Justice of the United States Supreme Court 1801-35. Among his published works were: ‹ Life of Washington › (5 vols., 1804-7; abridged and improved, 1 vol., 1832); ‹ Writings upon the Federal Constitution.› The greatest American jurist, he was one of the greatest jurists of any age.

Marshall, Nelly Nichol. See **MacAfee.**

Marsham, John, Sir. An English Egyptologist; born 1602; died 1685. His ‹ Diatriba Chronologica › (1649), enlarged into ‹ Chronicus Canon Egyptiacus,› etc. (1672), was a pioneer work in fixing the sequence of ancient history by means of the Egyptian annals.

Marston, John. An English dramatist and poet; born about 1575; died in London, June 25, 1634. He graduated at Oxford in 1594, and became lecturer at the Middle Temple, London, 1593. His chief work was ‹ The Malcontent › (1604), a tragicomedy which he recast from its original form as written by John Webster. The comedy ‹ Eastward Ho!› (1605), written with Ben Jonson and George Chapman, caused the imprisonment of all three on account of its satire on the Scotch. (‹Dramatic Works,› latest edition, 3 vols., 1887. ‹Poems,› 3 vols., 1856.)

Marston, John Westland. An English dramatist, born at Boston, Lincolnshire, Jan. 30, 1819; died in London, Jan. 5, 1890. He was one of

a group of English mystics. Among his dramas were: ‹ The Patrician's Daughter › (1842); ‹ Donna Diana › (1863), his best play; ‹ The Favorite of Fortune › (1866); etc. He wrote also ‹ Our Recent Actors › (1888), a valuable work; a novel; two collections of short stories; and a number of poems,—among the latter ‹ The Death-Ride at Balaklava › (1854), which became very popular.

Marston, Philip Bourke. An English poet, son of John W.; born in London, Aug. 13, 1850; died Feb. 13, 1887. From youth he was almost wholly blind. He was the subject of Hake's poem ‹ The Blind Boy,› and of Mrs. Craik's ‹ Philip, My King.› He wrote: ‹ Song-Tide,› etc. (1871); ‹ A Last Harvest › (1881); ‹ Wind Voices › (1883); etc. His ‹ Collected Poems,› edited by Louise Chandler Moulton, appeared in 1892.

Martel de Janville, Gabrielle de, Countess (mär-tel′ de zhoṅ-vēl′). [" Gyp."] A popular French novelist; born at the Château de Koëtsal, Morbihan, about 1850. She is the creator of several new types, among them Paulette, Loulou, Bob, etc.; and has been a prolific writer. Among her numerous works are: ‹About Marriage › (1883), dramatized the same year; ‹About Divorce › (1886); ‹ Conjugal Joys › (1887); ‹ Miss Eve › (1889); ‹ The Duke › (1892); ‹ The Duchess › (1893); ‹ Baron Sinaï › (1897); ‹ A Household ›; ‹ The Last Cry › (1903).

Martial—Marcus Valerius Martialis (mär′shal). A famous Latin poet; born at Bilbilis, Spain, 40 (?) A. D.; died in Spain about 102 (?) He spent most of his life at Rome, where he enjoyed the favor of the emperors Titus and Domitian. His fame rests upon his ‹ Epigrams,› in fifteen books; they are witty and marked by great felicity of form and expression, but are often sensual and marred by flattery of the great. A late edition, with notes and indices by Friedländer (2 vols.), appeared at Leipzig in 1886.

Martin, Arthur Patchett. An Australian poet and journalist; born at Woolwich, England, 1851. He was one of the founders of the Melbourne Review, and its editor for six years. He has written in verse: ‹ A Sweet Girl Graduate ›; ‹ An Easter Omelette › (1878); in both verse and prose ‹ Fernshawe › (1881; 2d ed. London, 1885); etc.

Martin, Bon Louis Henri (mär-taṅ′). One of the most eminent of French historians; born at St. Quentin, Aisne, Feb. 20, 1810; died in Paris, Dec. 14, 1883. He studied law originally; became a senator in 1876, and member of the Academy in 1878. His great work, the ‹ History of France,› in 16 volumes, appeared in 1855-60; the ‹ Popular History of France › in 1867-75; and the continuation bringing the account down to the present day, ‹ History of Modern France from 1789 › 1878-85. He wrote besides: ‹ France, her Genius and her Destinies › (1847); ‹ Italian Unity › (1865); the heroic drama ‹ Vercingetorix › (1865); ‹ Russia in Europe › (1866); and the Monograph ‹ Jeanne d' Arc › (1872).

Martin, Edward Sanford. An American journalist of New York city; born at "Willowbrook," Owasco Lake, N. Y., in 1856. He is author of 'Slv Ballades in Harvard China'; 'A Little Brother of the Rich, and Other Poems'; 'Windfalls of Observation'; 'Courtship of a Careful Man.'

Martin, Theodore, Sir. An English poet, translator, and biographer; born at Edinburgh, 1816. He became a solicitor in London in 1846; married the actress Helen Faucit in 1851; was elected rector of the University of St. Andrews in 1880. He first became known as an author in London under the pen-name "Bon Gaultier"; and jointly with W. E. Aytoun published the famous 'Book of Ballads' about 1858, also under that pseudonym. He has made many excellent translations from Horace and Catullus, from Dante, from Goethe, Schiller, and Heine, and from mediæval ballads, epigrams, etc. Upon the completion of the 'Life of the Prince Consort' (5 vols., 1874–80), he was knighted. He also wrote 'Life ot the Princess Alice' (1883); and other biographies.

Martin, William Alexander Parsons. A distinguished American Presbyterian missionary and educator; born at Livonia, Ind., April 10, 1827. A missionary originally at Ningpo, China (1850–60), he founded and directed the Presbyterian mission at Pekin, 1863–68; became professor of international law at Tungwên College, Pekin, in 1868; president in 1869; was sent by China to the United States and Europe to report on methods of education in 1880–81; made mandarin of the third rank in 1885. He has published in Chinese, 'Evidences of Christianity' (1855), 'The Three Principles' (1856), etc.; in English, 'The Chinese, their Education, Philosophy, and Letters' (1881); 'Awakening of China' (1907).

Martineau, Harriet (mär'ti-nō). An English reformer and miscellaneous writer, sister of James; born at Norwich, June 12, 1802; died at Ambleside, June 27, 1876. She visited this country in 1834, aiding the abolitionists, and traveled in Palestine and the East in 1846. She wrote a series of stories based on political economy (1832). Among her more important works are: 'Society in America' (1836); 'Deerbrook' (1839), a novel; 'History of England during the Thirty Years' Peace' (1848); 'Philosophy of Comte' (1853); 'British Rule in India' (1857); 'Biographical Sketches' (1869); etc. She labored under the remarkable disability of being all her life without the senses of taste and smell, and at 16 became very deaf.

Martineau, James. An English Unitarian theologian; born at Norwich, April 21, 1805; died in London, Jan. 11, 1900. He was the most profound and brilliant theological and religious writer on the liberal side in England. He was professor of philosophy at Manchester New College, London (1853). He published 'Endeavors after the Christian Life' (1843–47); 'Miscellanies' (1852), edited by T. Starr King; 'Studies of Christianity' (1858). 'Essays, Theological and Philosophical' (2 vols., 1866–68);

'Religion and Modern Materialism' (1874); 'A Study of Spinoza' (1882); 'The Seat of Authority in Religion' (1890); 'Essays, Reviews, and Addresses' (4 vols., 1890–91); etc.

Martinez de la Rosa, Francisco (mär-tē'neth dä lä rō'sä). A distinguished Spanish statesman, poet, dramatist, and miscellaneous writer; born at Granada, March 10, 1789; died at Madrid, Feb. 7, 1862. His best works were the tragedy 'Œdipus,' the drama 'The Venetian Conspiracy,' and the comedy 'The Daughter at Home and the Mother at the Ball.' His novels 'Hernan Perez' and 'Isabel de Solis,' and his 'Spirit of the Age,' are slight.

Martyn, Sarah Towne. An American writer of semi-historical fiction; born in Hopkinton, N. H., Aug. 15, 1805; died in New York, Nov. 22, 1879. Some of her books are: 'Huguenots of France' (1865); 'Sibyl Grey' (1866); 'Women of the Bible' (1868); 'The Crescent and the Cross' (1869); 'Dora's Mistake' (1870); and 'Hillside Cottage' (1872).

Martyn, William Carlos. An American biographical and historical writer; born in New York city, Dec. 15, 1841. He is a Presbyterian divine in that city. In his works are included 'Life of John Milton'; 'Life of Martin Luther'; 'History of the Huguenots' (1866); 'History of the Pilgrim Fathers of New England' (1867); and 'The Dutch Reformation'; 'Christian Citizenship.'

Marvel, Ike. See **Mitchell.**

Marvell, Andrew. An English poet and satirist; born at Winestead, Yorkshire, March 31, 1621; died in London, Aug. 18, 1678. He was Milton's friend, and his assistant in the Latin secretaryship to the Commonwealth (1657). He was called "the British Aristides." He is best known by his 'Poems on Affairs of State' (1689), a collection of satires on Charles II. and the Stuarts; though often coarse, they abound in lofty and generous sentiments. Of his other writings, the best are the 'Horatian Ode on Cromwell's Return from Ireland' (1776); 'The Rehearsal Transposed' (1672–73); the single poem 'The Nymph Complaining'; etc.

Marx, Karl (märks). A famous German socialist; born at Treves, May 5, 1818; died in London, March 14, 1883. He studied jurisprudence, philosophy, and history, at Bonn and Berlin; edited the Journal of the Rhine, 1842–43; on its suppression went to Paris, but was expelled from there (1845), and took refuge at Brussels; founded the New Journal of the Rhine at Cologne (1848); expelled again from Prussia (1849), settled in London. He was the controlling spirit of the International, 1864–72. His great work was 'Das Kapital' (Capital: 1867; new ed. 1885). Vol. i., containing all the essential points of his theory, was translated into English (London, 1887). The entire work, issued under the editorship of Friedrich Engels, appeared in an English translation in 1893.

Marzials, Théophile. An English poet, of French parentage; born at Brussels, 1850. He was educated in Belgium, Switzerland, and England, and has been employed in the British Museum since 1870. He has published 'Gallery of Pigeons and Other Poems' (1873), which has been highly praised. His best-known piece is the song 'Twickenham Ferry.'

Masalskiï, Konstantin Petrovich (mä-säl'-ski-ē). A Russian novelist and poet; born at Jaroslav, 1802; died 1861. He was in the government service till 1842. His principal novels were: 'Terpi Kazak,' etc. (Have Patience, Cossack, You will be Hetman: 1829); 'The Black Trunk'; 'Siege of Uglich'; 'The Russian Icarus'; 'The First Love of the Last of a Race'; etc. ('Works,' 1843–45.)

Mason, Caroline Atherton (Briggs). An American verse-writer; born in Marblehead, Mass., July 27, 1823; died in 1890. She published 'Utterance, a Collection of Home Poems' (1852); and 'Rose Hamilton,' a story (1859). Her poems 'Do They Miss Me at Home?' and 'The King's Quest,' are widely popular.

Mason, William. An English divine and poet; born at Hull, Feb. 12, 1724; died at York, April 7, 1797. He was the friend, executor, and biographer of the poet Gray, and precentor and canon of York. He wrote: 'Elfrida' (1752), and 'Caractacus' (1759), two dramas; 'The English Garden' (1772–82), a poem; 'Memoirs of Gray' (1775); etc. ('Works,' 1811.)

Maspero, Gaston (mäs-pe-rō'). A distinguished French Egyptologist; born in Paris, June 24, 1846. He became professor of Egyptian archæology and philosophy at the Collège de France in 1874; founded a school of Egyptian archæology at Cairo, 1881. Among his works are: 'Popular Tales of Ancient Egypt' (1881); 'Ancient History of the Peoples of the Orient' (4th ed. 1886); 'Egyptian Archæology' (1887); 'Ancient History of the Peoples of the Classical Orient'; 'The Passing of the Empires.'

Massarani, Tullo (mäs-sä-rä'nē). An Italian miscellaneous writer; born at Mantua, 1826. A student of law originally, he was Member of Parliament in 1860–67; then magistrate in Milan. He has written political works, including 'The Italian Idea through the Ages' (1850); the volumes of essays 'Studies in Literature and Art' (1873), 'Studies in Politics and History' (1873), 'Critical Essays' (2d ed. 1883); 'Legnano' (1876), a volume of long and short stories; 'Talks and Rhymes' (2d ed. 1884); etc. He is known also as a painter.

Massey, Gerald. An English poet; born at Tring, May 29, 1828. In youth he worked in a silk-mill and as a straw-braider. He founded and edited the Spirit of Freedom in 1849, and was secretary of the Christian Socialists. He lectured in this country in 1873. He is a firm believer in spiritualism. The titles of his works are: 'Ballad of Babe Christabel,' etc. (5th ed. 1855); 'War Waits' (1855); 'Havelock's March,' etc. (1861); 'My Lyrical Life' (1889); etc.

Massillon, Jean Baptiste (mä-sē-yôn'). A famous French preacher; born at Hyères, June 24, 1663; died at Clermont, Sept. 18, 1742. He was director of the Seminary of St. Magloire, Paris, in 1699; court preacher in 1699, 1701, and 1704; preached the funeral orations on Conti in 1709, the Dauphin in 1711, and Louis XIV. in 1715; became bishop of Clermont in 1717. His sermons are finished in form, and deal with conduct more than dogma. The funeral oration on Louis XIV. was translated into English (London, 1872); also selected sermons (2 vols., 1889–90). ('Works,' 4 vols., Paris, 1886.)

Massinger, Philip. A noted English dramatist; born at Salisbury, 1583; died at the Bankside, Southwark, March, 1639–40. Of 38 plays written wholly or in part by him, he was the sole author of 15. Among the best are: 'The Duke of Milan' (1623); 'The Fatal Dowry' (1632); 'A New Way to Pay Old Debts' (1633), which still keeps the stage, the character of Sir Giles Overreach being almost as familiar as one of Shakespeare's; 'A Very Woman' (1655); 'A City Madam' (1659); etc. He excelled in depicting tragic character and in lofty sentiment without escaping from the limits of possible life; but his verse is prosaic, and often halting and unmelodious.

Masson, Auguste Michel Benoît Gaudichot (mä-sôn'). A French novelist and dramatist; born in Paris, 1800; died 1883. He wrote much in collaboration. Among his works in fiction are: 'Tales of the Workshop' (1832–33); 'A Young Girl's Heart' (1834); 'The Bundle of Straw' (1861); 'The Stubborn Wife' (1865). He also wrote: 'Reminiscences of a Child of the People' (1838–41), autobiographic; 'History of Celebrities' (1838, many editions); the dramas 'The Devil in Love' (1836), 'Madame Favart' (1837), 'A Fixed Idea' (1850), 'The Orphans of Notre Dame Bridge' (1849); etc.

Masson, David. A Scottish biographer, essayist, and critic; born at Aberdeen, Dec. 2, 1822. He was professor of English at University College, London, 1852; later, for a number of years editor of Macmillan's Magazine; professor of rhetoric and English literature at the University of Edinburgh, 1865. His chief work is 'Life of Milton' (6 vols., 1858–79). He wrote besides: 'Essays, Biographical and Critical' (1856); 'British Novelists' (1859); 'The Three Devils' (1874); etc. He died Oct. 7, 1907.

Masudi or **Al-Masudi** (mä-sö'dē). An Arabic historian; born at Bagdad about the close of the ninth century; died in Egypt, 957. He has been called "the Arabian Herodotus." His best work was 'Meadows of Gold and Mines of Gems' (many editions; the latest, text with French translation, 9 vols., Paris, 1861–77). It abounds in information regarding his time, the result of extensive travel, and is the most celebrated of its kind in the language. One volume was translated into English by A. Sprenger (1841).

Mather, Cotton. A famous American clergyman, son of Increase; born in Boston, Feb. 12, 1663; died there, Feb. 13, 1728. A prolific writer of books, his 'Magnalia' is probably better known than any other of the nearly four hundred volumes that he published. 'Memorable Providences relating to Witchcraft and Possessions' appeared in 1685.

Mather, Increase. A noted American Congregational divine, educator, and scholar; born at Dorchester, Mass., June 21, 1639; died at Boston, Aug. 23, 1723. Graduating from Harvard at 17, he went to England; graduated from Trinity College, Dublin, at 19; settled in England as a pastor, but at the Restoration refused to conform and returned to Boston; was president of Harvard 1685-1701; visited England again to convey a vote of thanks to James II. (1688). Of his ninety-two publications, one of the most curious was 'An Essay for the Recording of Illustrious Providences' (1684; London, 1856). It is a collection of remarkable happenings,—sea-deliverances, accidents, witchcraft, apparitions, etc.

Mathers, Helen Buckingham. See **Reeves.**

Mathews, Cornelius. An American novelist, verse-writer, and dramatist; born in Port Chester, N. Y., Oct. 28, 1817; died in New York city, March 25, 1889. His 'Poems on Man in the Republic,' and 'Witchcraft,' were commended by Margaret Fuller in her essay on 'American Literature'; Poe criticized him sharply. Other works of his are: 'Behemoth: a Legend of the Mound-Builders' (1839); 'Pen-and-Ink Panorama of New York City' (1853); 'False Pretences,' a comedy; and 'Indian Fairy Tales' (1868). In 1840, with Evert A. Duyckinck, he edited Arcturus, a monthly magazine.

Mathews, William. An American essayist; born in Waterville, Me., July 28, 1818; resigned the professorship of rhetoric and English literature in the University of Chicago (1875) to devote his time entirely to literary work. His publications include: 'Getting on in the World' (1872); 'The Great Conversers, and Other Essays' (1873); 'Literary Style, and Other Essays' (1881); 'Wit and Humor, their Use and Abuse'; and 'Nugæ Litterariæ; 'Conquering Success' (1903).

Mathieu, Adolphe Charles Ghislain (mä-tyé'). A Belgian poet and journalist; born at Mons, June 22, 1804; died near Brussels, June 13, 1876. He was curator of the public library at Mons, 1840-45; assistant professor at the University of Liège, 1849; chief librarian of the Royal Library, 1864. He wrote: 'Poems of the Belfry' (2d ed. 1846); 'Roland de Lattre' (2d ed. 1840); 'Mons and Brussels' (1852); 'Olla Podrida' (1828-29); 'Memories' (1866); 'Clippings' (1863-71); the dramas 'Two Weddings for One' (1836), 'D'Aubigné' (1854), etc.; 'Mons Biographies' (1848); the political works 'The Reveille of Liberty' and 'France and Belgium.'

Matta, Guillermo (mä'tä). A Chilian politician and poet, born at Copiapó, Chili, 1829.

He was banished in 1859; was deputy 1870 and 1873; governor of Atacama 1875-81. He published in 1853 some short stories that were severely criticized for their freedom of style. His verses, chiefly lyric, are very popular. ('Poems,' 2 vols., Leipzig, about 1880.)

Matthew Paris. See **Paris.**

Matthew, Sir Tobie. An English courtier, diplomat, and writer; born at Salisbury, 1577; died 1655. He was famed for amiability, and for a series of letters published posthumously under the title 'A Collection of Letters made by Sr. Tobie Mat[t]hew, Kt., with a Character of the Most Excellent Lady Lucy' (1660).

Matthews, (James) Brander. An American critic and essayist; born in New Orleans, La., Feb. 21, 1852. He graduated from Columbia College in 1871, and from Columbia Law School in 1873, being admitted to the bar the same year. He soon turned to literature, taking especial interest in the drama, and made himself an authority upon French dramatic literature; has also written several clever comedies. In fiction he has steadily gained in art and reputation, his short studies of New York city life in the realistic vein being among the very best of their kind. He has also written a strong novel of New York life, 'His Father's Son.' He is one of the founders of the Authors' Club of New York, and did valuable work in organizing the American Copyright League. Mr. Matthews is a frequent and acceptable contributor of essays and fiction to periodicals. Of his many writings the following books are the more important: 'The Theatres of France'; 'French Dramatists of the Nineteenth Century'; 'Margery's Lovers, a Comedy'; 'The Last Meeting, a Story'; 'The Secret of the Sea, and Other Stories'; 'A Family Tree, and Other Stories'; 'The Story of a Story'; 'Tom Paulding'; 'Studies of the Stage'; 'Americanisms and Briticisms'; 'Vignettes of Manhattan'; 'Introduction to the Study of American Literature'; 'The Royal Marine'; 'Tales of Fantasy and Fact'; and 'Development of the Drama.'

Maturin, Charles Robert (mat'ū-rin). An Irish novelist; born at Dublin, 1782; died there, Oct. 30, 1824. A clergyman of the Church of England, he was noted for eloquence in the pulpit and hostility to Roman Catholicism. His best novel was 'Melmoth the Wanderer' (1820); others being 'The Wild Irish Boy' (1808), 'The Milesian Chief' (1812), etc. His tragedy 'Bertram,' thought by many to be his best work, was produced by Edmund Kean at Drury Lane in 1816.

Maturin, Edward. An American novelist; born in Dublin, Ireland, in 1812; died in New York city, May 25, 1881. In 1832 he came to America with letters of introduction from Thomas Moore and other literati. He wrote 'Montezuma, the Last of the Aztecs: A Romance' (2 vols., 1845); 'Benjamin, the Jew of Grenada: A Romance' (1848); 'Lyrics of

Spain and Erin' (1850); and 'Bianca, a Tale of Erin and Italy' (1852).

Maudsley, Henry. An English alienist; born at Giggleswick, Yorkshire, Feb. 5, 1835. He was professor of medical jurisprudence in University College, London, 1869-79; and editor of the Journal of Mental Science, 1863-78. He has published: 'Physiology and Pathology of the Mind' (1867); 'Responsibility in Mental Disease' (1874); 'Body and Will' (1883); etc.

Maupassant, Guy de (mō-pä-sôn'). A French novelist; born at the Château de Miromesnil (Seine-Inférieure), Aug. 5, 1850; died at Passy, July 6, 1893. He was for some time clerk at the navy department, Paris. He published over twenty volumes, among them the collections of short stories 'The Sisters Rondoli' (1884), 'Tales of Day and Night' (1885), 'The Left Hand' (1889); the novels 'Peter and John' (1888), 'Strong as Death' (1889), 'Our Heart' (1893); the books of travel 'In the Sunshine' (1884), 'On the Water' (1888), 'A Wandering Life' (1890); 'The Book Agent' (1900). Unsettled by the insanity and death of a brother, he himself died in an asylum.

Maurice, Frederick Denison. A celebrated English divine, and theological and philosophical writer; born near Lowestoft, Suffolk, Aug. 29, 1805; died in London, April 1, 1872. He was professor at King's College, London, in 1840; assisted in founding Queen's College for women, 1848; was principal of St. Martin's Hall, a workingmen's college, 1854; professor of moral philosophy at Cambridge University, 1866. Among his works are: 'Theological Essays' (1853); 'Ancient Philosophy' (1850); 'Mediæval Philosophy' (1857); 'Modern Philosophy' (1862); the novel 'Eustace Conway' (1834). He was known as a leader in the "Broad Church" and in the Christian Socialist movement of his time.

Maury, Matthew Fontaine. An American naval officer, famous in science; born in Spottsylvania County, Va., Jan. 14, 1806; died in Lexington, Va., Feb. 1, 1873. His most distinguished work is 'Physical Geography of the Sea' (1855; revised ed. 1860); he was also author of treatises on navigation, astronomy, and meteorology.

Mauthner, Fritz (mout'nėr). A German novelist; born at Horitz, Bohemia, Nov. 22, 1849. His home since 1876 has been in Berlin. Among his works may be named: 'After Famous Models' (27th ed. 1894; new series, 16th ed. 1883), a collection of witty parodies; 'The Baroness's Sundays' (3d ed. 1884); 'The New Ahasuerus' (1882); 'The Last German of Blatna' (5th ed. 1890); 'Hypatia' (2d ed. 1892); 'The Ghost-Seer' (1894); 'The Bohemian Manuscript' (1897).

Mautner, Eduard. A German poet; born at Pesth, Nov. 13, 1824; died at Baden, near Vienna, July 2, 1889. He wrote: 'The Prize Comedy,' which took the prize offered by the Hofburg Theatre in Vienna (1851), 'Countess Aurora' (1852), 'A Stratagem' (1878), comedies;

the plays 'Eglantine' (1863) and 'The Hour-Glass' (1871); 'Short Stories' (1858); 'Poems' (1847 and 1858); etc. 'Select Poems' appeared in 1889.

Max O'Rell. See **Blouët, Paul.**

Maxwell, Herbert Eustace, Sir. An English politician and miscellaneous writer; born Jan. 8, 1845. He has been a Member of Parliament since 1880; was a lord of the treasury 1886-92, member of the Royal Commission on the Aged Poor in 1893. He has written: 'Passages in Life of Sir Lucian Elphin' (1889), 'The Art of Love' (1890), 'The Letter of the Law' (1891), all novels; 'Meridiana : Noontide Essays' (1892); 'British Fresh Water Fishes.'

Maxwell, Mary Elizabeth (Braddon). See **Braddon.**

Maxwell, William Hamilton. An Irish novelist; born at Newry, County Down, 1792; died at Musselburgh, near Edinburgh, Scotland, Dec. 29, 1850. He may be called the father of the military novel. After serving as an infantry captain in the Peninsular War and at Waterloo, he became rector of Ballagh. There not being a single Protestant in his parish, he devoted his ample leisure to field sports and literature. Among his best works are: 'O'Hara, or 1798' (1825), a novel; 'Sports of the West' (1832), 'Stories of Waterloo' (1834); 'Life of the Duke of Wellington' (1839-41). He was editor of the Military and Naval Almanac for 1840.

Maxwell, William Stirling, Sir. See **Stirling-Maxwell.**

Maxwell Gray. See **Tuttiett, Mary G.**

May, Caroline. An American poet; born in England about 1820; came to New York, 1834. She was author of 'American Female Poets' (1848); 'Treasured Thoughts from Favorite Authors' (1850); 'Poems' (1864); and 'Lays of Memory and Affection.'

May, Lyoff Aleksandrovich (mā). See **Meï.**

May, Samuel Joseph. A noted American reformer; born at Boston, Sept. 12, 1797; died at Syracuse, N. Y., July 1, 1871. He was a Unitarian minister, his longest settlement being at Syracuse (1845-68). One of the first and stanchest abolitionists, his best-known publication was 'Recollections of the Anti-Slavery Conflict' (1869).

May, Sophie. See **Clarke.**

May, Thomas. An English poet, dramatist, and historian; born at Mayfield, Sussex, 1595; died in London, Nov. 13, 1650. He was secretary and historiographer to the Long Parliament. His chief work was 'History of the Long Parliament' (1647). He wrote also two historical poems and five dramas, among the latter the comedy 'The Heir' (1620), and a tragedy entitled 'Julius Cæsar.'

May, Thomas Erskine, Sir—Lord Farnborough. An English writer on the constitution and history of England, etc.; born in

London, Feb. 8, 1815; died in Westminster Palace, May 17, 1886. He was called to the bar in 1838, but the principal part of his life was spent in the service of the House of Commons as librarian and clerk. His principal works are: 'Constitutional History of England' (3d ed. 1871), reprinted in this country, and translated into French and German; and 'History of Democracy in Europe' (2 vols., 1877). Besides these he reduced to order for the first time the 'Rules, Orders, and Forms of the House of Commons' (1854); published a 'Treatise on the Law, Privileges, Proceedings, and Usage of Parliament' (1844), which became a parliamentary text-book; etc.

Mayer, Alfred Marshall. An American scientific writer; born in Baltimore, Md., Nov. 13, 1836. Besides his editorial work on the American Journal of Science, and numerous contributions to other journals, he has published 'The Earth a Great Magnet' (1872); 'Light' (1877); 'Sound' (1878); and 'Sport with Gun and Rod in American Woods and Waters' (1883). He died in 1897.

Mayer, Brantz. An American journalist, descriptive writer, and novelist; born at Baltimore, Md., Sept. 27, 1809; died there, Feb. 23, 1879. He was a lawyer by profession; became editor of the Baltimore American; was attached to the American legation in Mexico, 1841–42; served in the Civil War. He wrote several works on Mexico, including 'Mexico: Aztec, Spanish, and Republican' (2 vols., 1853), his best work; 'Captain Canot' (1854), a novel; etc.

Mayer, Karl (mī'ēr). A German poet and biographer; born at Neckarbischofsheim, Würtemberg, March 22, 1786; died at Tübingen, Feb. 25, 1870. A student of jurisprudence originally, he held several important legal and political positions in his native country. He belonged to the «Suabian School» of poets. He wrote: 'Lenau's Letters to a Friend' (2d ed. 1853); 'Songs' (3d ed. 1864); 'Uhland, his Friends and Contemporaries' (2 vols., 1867); etc.

Mayhew, Henry. An English humorist; born in London, Nov. 5, 1812; died July 25, 1887. He founded the comic paper Figaro, in London; assisted in founding Punch (1841), of which he was for several years chief editor. He was a frequent contributor to the magazines; wrote several juveniles; and with his brothers Horace and Augustus, wrote many popular humorous novels, fairy-tales, and farces. His main work was 'London Labor and the London Poor' (new ed. 1868).

Maynard, François (mä-när'). A French poet; born at Toulouse, 1582; died at Aurillac, 1646. He was for several years secretary of Queen Margaret of Navarre; later a magistrate of Aurillac; toward the end of his life a Councilor of State. One of the most correct and elegant poets of his day, his talent lay in elaboration of form rather than force of matter. Malherbe used to say that of him and Racan

(whose merit was of matter rather than style) together, a great poet might be made. His specialty was epigrams. ('Poetical Works,' 1646. 'Letters,' 1653.)

Mayne, Jasper. An English divine, poet, and dramatist; born in Devonshire, 1604; died 1672. He was archdeacon of Chichester, and chaplain in ordinary to Charles II. Besides sermons and poems, he wrote 'The City Match' (new ed. 1659), one of the best of early English comedies; 'The Amorous Warre' (new ed. 1659), a tragicomedy; etc.

Mayne, John. A Scottish poet; born at Dumfries, 1759; died 1836. He was editor of the London Star. Among his publications are: 'The Siller Gun' (new ed. Edinburgh, 1836); and 'Glasgow' (1803), a descriptive poem.

Mayo, Mrs. Isabella (Fyvie). ["Edward Garrett."] A Scottish novelist; born in London, 1843. She has resided in Aberdeen since 1877. Among her works are: 'Occupations of a Retired Life' (1868); 'Friends and Acquaintances' (2d ed. 1872); 'By Still Waters' (new ed. 1886); 'The Capel Girls' (new ed. 1877); 'The House by the Works' (new ed. 1881); 'Equal to the Occasion' (1887); 'Chrystal Joyce.'

Mayo, Robert. An American historical writer; born in Powhatan County, Va., April 25, 1784; died in Washington, D. C., Oct. 31, 1864. Among his publications are: 'View of Ancient Geography and History' (1813); 'New System of Mythology' (4 vols., 1815–19); and 'The Treasury Department: its Origin, Organization, and Operations' (1847).

Mazade, Charles de (mä-zäd'). A French publicist and critic; born at Tarn et Garonne, March 19, 1820; died in Paris, April 27, 1893. He was one of the most tasteful of French prose-writers. He wrote: 'Contemporary Spain' (1855); 'Modern Italy' (1860); 'Two Women of the Revolution' (Marie Antoinette and Madame Roland: 1866); 'Lamartine's Literary and Political Life' (1872); 'The War of France' (2 vols., 1875); 'Character Studies in the Moral and Political History of the Time' (1875); 'The Royalist Opposition' (1894); etc. He also edited 'Marshal Davoust's Correspondence' (4 vols., 1885).

Maze, Hippolyte (mäz). A French statesman and historian; born at Arras, Nov. 5, 1839; died in Paris, Oct. 25, 1891. He was twice elected deputy for Versailles (1879 and 1881), and twice senator (1886 and 1891). He wrote: 'The Governments of France from the 17th to the 19th Century' (1864); 'The Republic of the United States' (1869); 'The Struggle against Want' (1883); 'The Generals of the Republic' (1889); etc.

Mazères, Édouard (mä-zär'). A French dramatic writer; born in Paris, 1796; died there, 1866. When a young man he was in the army; was prefect of the department at Le Cher. He wrote the comedies 'The Young Husband' (1826); 'Each for Himself' (1828); 'The Friendship of Women' (1849); 'The Pearl Necklace' (1851); etc. His greatest successes came from plays written in collaboration : as 'The Foundling' (1824); 'Three Quarters' (1827), which was very popular, with Picard; 'The Uncle from America' (1826), 'Quackery' (1828), etc., with Scribe; 'Mother and Daughter' (1830), etc., with Empis.

Mazuranic, Ivan (mä-zhö-rän'yich). The greatest of Croatian poets; born at Novi, about 1813. He was procurator-general in 1850; president of the Croat-Slavonian high court of justice, 1861; governor, 1873-80. His chief work is the epic 'Death of Smail-aga Cengic' [Jenghiz Khan] (1846; several editions), translated into Bohemian, Polish, Russian, Slovenic, and German. He wrote the notable political pamphlet 'The Croats to the Magyars.' Died 1890.

Mazzini, Joseph (mät-sē'nē). An Italian patriot ; born at Genoa, June 22, 1805 ; died at Pisa, March 10, 1872. Upon the fall of the Revolutionary government of 1848, in Rome, Mazzini fled to Switzerland, and from there was driven to England. He was concerned in the revolutionary movements of 1852, 1853, and 1857, and so on down to the occupation of Rome in 1870. He wrote much in English and French. His commentaries on Dante's works are very important, and his essays on affairs in Europe and criticisms on the great writers of Europe are most eloquent and discerning. His 'Memoirs' were printed in 1875. ('Complete Works,' 18 vols., 1861-91.)

Mazzoni, Guido (mat-sō'nē). An Italian poet and scholar; born at Florence, June 12, 1859. He became professor of Italian literature in the University of Padua, 1887. He has written : 'Epigrams' (1880); 'Experiments in Metre' (1882); 'Poems' (1883); 'New Poems' (1886); 'Literary Reviews' (1887); 'Among Books and Papers' (1887); etc.

Mead, Edwin Doak. An American historical writer and lecturer; born in Chesterfield, N. H., Sept. 29, 1849. He is the author of 'The Philosophy of Carlyle' (1881), and 'Martin Luther : a Study of the Reformation' (1884); 'The Roman Church and Public Schools.' He is editor of the New England Magazine (1897).

Meason, Malcolm Ronald Laing (mē'zọn). A Scottish soldier, editor, journalist, and storywriter; born at Edinburgh, 1824. Entering the army (1839), he served with distinction in India; edited the Bombay Telegraph 1851-54; has been special correspondent for the London Daily News and Daily Telegraph, the New York Herald, etc. He has written : 'The Bubbles of Finance' (1865); 'The Profits of Panics' (1866); 'Turf Frauds' (1875); 'Three Months after Date, and Other Tales'; 'Sir William's Speculations' (1886); etc.

Medici, Lorenzo de' (med'ē-chē), called the Magnificent. A celebrated Florentine statesman and patron of letters (1449-1492). He wrote many fine poems in Italian and Latin, and contributed much of his wealth to literary undertakings.

Meding, Oskar (mā'ding). ["Gregor Samarow."] A German statesman and historical novelist; born at Königsberg, Prussia, April 11, 1829. After holding office in Prussia, he entered the public service of Hanover (1859), and became councilor of State. He has resided since 1873 in Berlin. Among his works are : 'For Sceptres and Crowns' (1872-76); 'Heights and Depths' (1879-80); 'Summit and Abyss' (1888); 'Memoranda for Contemporary History' (1881-84); a short biography of the Emperor William I., entitled 'Eighty-nine Years in Faith, Struggle, and Victory.' Died 1903.

Meek, Alexander Beaufort (mēk). An American jurist, journalist, and miscellaneous writer; born at Columbia, S. C., July 17, 1814; died at Columbus, Miss., Nov. 30, 1865. He served in the Seminole war, 1836; was attorney-general of Alabama, 1836; judge of Tuscaloosa County, 1842-44; member of the Legislature in 1853, where and when he established the free-school system of Alabama; Speaker of the Alabama House, 1859. Besides a legal digest (1842), he wrote : 'The Red Eagle' (1855); 'Songs and Poems of the South' (1857); 'Romantic Passages in Southwestern History' (1857); 'History of Alabama' (unpublished); etc. His best-known poem is 'The Charge at Balaklava.'

Meï, Lev Aleksandrovich (mā'ē). A Russian poet; born at Moscow, Feb. 13, 1822; died at St. Petersburg, May 16, 1862. He was long in the government employ at St. Petersburg. He wrote a modern rendering of 'The Tale of the Troop of Igor'; the historical dramas 'The Tsar's Bride' (1849), 'Servilia' (1854), 'The Women of Pskov' (1860); numerous short poems, etc. ('Works,' 3 vols., 1863-65.)

Meilhac, Henri (mā-yäc'). A noted French dramatist; born in Paris, Feb. 23, 1831; died there July 6, 1897. He wrote (mostly in collaboration with Ludovic Halévy): 'What Pleases the Men' (1860); 'La Belle Hélène' (1865); 'Bluebeard' (1866); 'The Grand Duchess of Gérolstein' (1867); 'La Périchole'(1869); 'Froufrou'(1869); etc. Several of his pieces have been used by Offenbach as opera-bouffe librettos.

Meinhold, Johann Wilhelm (mīn'hōlt). A German clergyman; born at Netzelkow, Usedom Island, Feb. 27, 1797; died at Charlottenburg, Nov. 30, 1851. He was settled at Usedom and Coserow. His books are 'Maria Schweidler' (1843) and 'Sidonia von Bork,' both purporting to be mediæval manuscripts discovered by Meinhold; his object being to show the Biblical critics, through the deception, that internal evidence as to the antiquity of works is not reliable. Both the works were successful and popular.

Meissner, Alfred (mīs'nẽr). A German poet and novelist; born at Teplitz, Oct. 15, 1822; died at Bregenz, May 29, 1885. He lived at Prague (1850-69) and Bregenz (1869-85). His principal works are : the revolutionary 'Poems' (1845); the epic 'Ziska' (1846); the romances

'Sansara' (3d ed. 1861), 'Dark Yellow' (1862–64), 'Norbert Norson' (1883). ('Works,' 18 vols., 1871–73.)

Melanchthon, Philipp (me-langk'thọn). [A Greek translation of his real name Schwarzerd, «black earth.»] A famous German theologian and religious reformer; born at Bretten, Baden, Feb. 16, 1497; died at Wittenberg, April 19, 1560. He was professor of Greek at Wittenberg (1518), and Luther's chief literary helper in the German Reformation; revised the Augsburg Confession (1530); wrote the 'Apology' (1530); etc. His influence extended even to England. His principal theological work was 'Loci Communes' (Places in Common: 1521), of which over sixty editions were issued during his lifetime. The best edition of his works is in 24 vols., in the 'Corpus Reformatorum' (Body of Reformers: 1834–60).

Meleager (mel-e-ā'jėr). A Greek poet; born at Gadara, Palestine; flourished about the middle of the first century B. C. He is best known as a writer of epigrams on love; and by his 'Stephanos' (Garland), a compilation made up of short poems taken from the writings of some forty poets, alphabetically arranged, with an introduction in verse by himself. The best edition of his own poems, edited by Gräfe, was published at Leipzig, 1811.

Melendez Valdes, Juan, Don (mā-len'deth väl-dās'). A Spanish poet; born at Ribera del Fresno, March 11, 1754; died at Montpellier, France, May 24, 1817. He was professor of the humanities at Salamanca (1781); afterward entered public life; the lasting unpopularity incurred by siding with the French on their invasion of Spain forced him in 1811 into exile, where he died. He was one of the most prominent figures in Spanish literary life during the 18th century. (Poetical works, best edition, Paris, 1820.)

Melgar, Mariano (māl-gar'). A Peruvian poet; born at Arequipa, Peru, 1791; shot at Cuzco, March 10, 1815, having been taken prisoner in Pumacagua's rebellion. Affected by a disappointment in love, nearly all his verse was sad. Many of his lyrics were set to music, and are among the most popular songs of the Spanish-American country-folk.

Meli, Giovanni (mā'lē). The greatest of Sicilian poets; born at Palermo, March 4, 1740; died there, Dec. 20, 1815. He was professor of pharmaceutical chemistry in the University of Palermo (1787). His best work was his songs, some of which recall Anacreon and Theocritus; next, his witty satires and fables. He wrote also two epics, and the heroi-comic poem 'Don Chisciotte,' an elaboration and continuation of Cervantes's 'Don Quixote.' ('Works,' poetical and scientific, 8 vols., Palermo, 1830.)

Meline, James Florant. An American historical writer; born at Sackett's Harbor, N. Y., 1811; died in Brooklyn, N. Y., Aug. 14, 1873. His later years were devoted to literary work.

Three of a series of articles on Savonarola have been published. Most noted of his works are: 'Two Thousand Miles on Horseback' (1867); 'Mary Queen of Scots, and her Latest English Historian,' an attack upon Froude's view of the subject; and 'Life of Sixtus the Fifth' (1871).

Mellin, Gustaf Henrik (mel-lēn'). A Swedish novelist; born at Revolax, Finland, April 23, 1803; died Aug. 2, 1876. He was a pastor at Norra Wram (1851). Most of his novels deal with Swedish history. Among them are: 'The Flower of Kinnekulle' (3d ed. 1831); 'Sivard Kruse's Wedding' (2d ed. 1832); 'Anna Reibnitz' (2d ed. 1833). He produced also historical, biographical, and poetical writings. ('Works,' Stockholm, 1852.)

Melo or **Mello, Francisco Manuel de** (mā'lo or mel'lō). A Portuguese historian and poet; born at Lisbon, Nov. 23, 1611; died there, Oct. 13, 1665. He served with distinction in the Spanish army in Flanders; was imprisoned for nine years, and banished to Brazil, on a false charge of murder. He wrote sometimes in Spanish, sometimes in Portuguese. Among his voluminous works are: 'History of the Disturbances, Separation, and War of Catalonia, in the Time of Philip IV.' (1645; best ed. Paris, 2 vols., 1826–32); 'The Three Muses of Melodino' (1649), containing his poems, mostly satirical and comic.

Melville, George John Whyte. See **Whyte-Melville.**

Melville, Herman. A noted American writer of travel and adventure; born at New York, Aug. 1, 1819; died there, Sept. 28, 1891. Going to sea as a cabin-boy, he spent a number of years in travel. His most famous books were 'Typee' (1846), and 'Omoo' (1847), narrating his adventures in the Marquesas Islands; others were 'White Jacket' (1850), 'Moby Dick' (1851), and a number of other stories, and three volumes of poems. He lectured in the United States in 1857.

Menander (me-nan'dėr). A famous Greek comic poet; born at Athens, 342 B.C.; died about 291 B.C. See Kock's 'Fragments of the Attic Comedians' (vol. 3, Leipzig, 1888), and article 'Philemon, Menander, and the Lost Attic Comedy,' in the 'Library.'

Mencius (men'shi-us). Latinized from **Mengtse** (meng-tse'). A famous Chinese philosopher; born at Tsow-hien, 372 B.C.; died about 289 B.C. He was a follower of Confucius, whose influence he revived. Twenty-nine years he spent in traveling about China preaching, but with small success; his last fifteen years were passed with his disciples in retirement. His sayings are laid down in seven books bearing his name as signature and are contained in the last of the so-called Chinese 'Four Books.'

Mendelssohn, Moses (men'del-sōn). A famous Jewish philosopher; born at Dessau,

Anhalt, Germany, Sept. 6, 1729; died at Berlin, Jan. 4, 1786. He has been called "the German Socrates." He wrote on religious, moral, æsthetic, and practical questions, in a semi-philosophical, common-sense way, popularizing the philosophy of Leibnitz and Wolf, and bringing into notice that of Spinoza. Among his friends were Lessing, Nicolai, Herder, Wieland, etc. He wrote: 'Phædon' (1767), a dialogue on the immortality of the soul, which won a European reputation; 'Jerusalem' (1783); 'Morning Hours' (1785); etc. ('Works,' Leipzig, 1843-45.)

Mendelssohn-Bartholdy, Felix (men'del-sōn-bär-tōl'dē). An eminent German composer and musician, grandson of Moses; born at Hamburg, Feb. 3, 1809; died at Leipzig, Nov. 4, 1847. Apart from his musical works, between one and two hundred in number, he was a voluminous correspondent. His 'Letters' were published in 1861 and 1863 (English translation, 1862-63); 'Letters to the Moscheles' (1888); 'Selected Letters' (London, 1894).

Mendès, Catulle (moñ-des'). A French poet and novelist; born at Bordeaux, May 22, 1843. His verse is marked by extreme devotion to form; his style has been called the cameo-art in literature. The collection entitled 'Poesies' appeared in 1878. In prose he has written 'Love's Follies' (1877), ('Parisian Monsters' (1882), 'To Read at the Bath' (1884), etc.; the dramas 'Captain Fracasse' (1872), 'Fiamette' (1889), etc. His best novels are 'Grande-Maguet' (1888); and 'Rainbow' (1897). Died Feb. 8, 1908.

Mendes Leal da Silva, José (men'däs lä-äl'dä sēl'vä). A distinguished Portuguese statesman and poet; born at Lisbon, Oct. 18, 1818; died at Cintra, Aug. 22, 1886. He was minister of the navy and of foreign affairs; ambassador to France 1874-83; to Spain 1883-86. His 'Songs' were published in 1858. He wrote also a large number of plays, some of them very popular on the Portuguese stage, as 'Uncle Andrew from Brazil' and 'The Sportsman'; and several romances.

Mendez-Pinto, Ferñao or **Fernam** (men'-deth-peñ-to). A Portuguese traveler; born near Coimbra about 1510; died near Lisbon, 1583. He spent many romantic years as a traveler in the East, being repeatedly captured, often sold as a slave, acquiring a large fortune, becoming for a time a Jesuit, founding a Roman Catholic seminary in Japan, etc. He wrote 'Mendez-Pinto's Pilgrimage' (1614), which was translated into the principal European languages, and has become a Portuguese classic.

Mendive, Rafael Maria de (män-dē'vä). A Cuban poet; born in Havana, 1821; died in 1886. His first collection of poems (1847), entitled 'Passion-Flowers,' is widely popular. Banished in 1869, he lived alternately in New York and Nassau, writing legends and stories in verse. He was one of the best of Spanish-American poets; many of his verses received English, French, and Italian translations. A

new edition appeared in 1860, published by the Spanish critic Don Manuel Cañete.

Mendoza, Antonio Hurtado de (men-dō'thä). A Spanish dramatist and poet; born about 1590; died 1644. He was private secretary of Philip IV., and a member of the Inquisition. Among his best plays are 'The Obligations of Lying,' and 'The Husband Makes the Wife.' He wrote also many ballads and lyrics, and a 'Life of Our Lady' in about 800 roundelays.

Mendoza, Diego Hurtado. A distinguished Spanish statesman, satirist, and historian; born in the palace of the Alhambra at Granada, 1503; died at Valladolid, 1575. Intended originally for the Church, he entered the army instead, and rose high in public life. His chief works are, first, the famous satiric romance 'Little Lazarus of Tormes' (1553, and afterward many editions), which was translated into a number of languages (English by Blakeston, 1670), provoked many imitations, and created that new department in Spanish literature which finally produced 'Gil Blas'; and second, the 'War of Granada' (first complete edition, 1776). ('Works,' Vols. iii., xxi., xxxii., xxxvi., of Rivadeneyra's 'Library of Spanish Authors.')

Mendoza, Iñigo Lopez de. See **Santillana.**

Menendez y Pelayo, Marcelino (mä-nen'-deth ē pä-lä'yo). A Spanish scholar, historian, and poet; born at Santander, 1856. He is professor of Spanish literature at the University of Madrid, and one of the most brilliant writers of modern Spain. His 'History of Spanish Heterodoxy' (3 vols., 1880-82), in which he defended the Inquisition, and declared against modern liberalism and science, has excited much discussion. Other prose works are: 'History of Æsthetic Ideas in Spain' (1884-91); 'Calderon and his Plays' (3d ed. 1885); 'Spanish Science' (3d ed. 1887-89). His best poetry is contained in 'Odes, Epistles, and Tragedies' (1883). His last work is 'Origin of the Novel' (1905).

Menken, Adah Isaacs. An American-Jewish poet and actress; born near New Orleans, 1835; died 1868. Her maiden name was Dolores Adios Fuertes. Married four times (once to the pugilist John C. Heenan), she was generally known by the name of her first husband, Alexander Isaacs Menken. Her verses show poetic ability uncultivated. She published: 'Memories'; 'Infelicia' (1868).

Menzel, Wolfgang. A German critic and miscellaneous writer; born at Waldenburg, Silesia, June 21, 1798; died at Stuttgart, April 23, 1873. He was member of the Würtemberg Assembly (1830-38) and Chamber (1848-49); editor for many years of the Literaturblatt (Journal of Literature). His writings were very varied. The best known were: 'German Literature' (1828; English translation in Ripley's 'Specimens of Foreign Literature,' Boston, 1840); a collection of critiques, 'History of the Germans' (6th ed. 1872-73; English translation by Horrocks, London, 1849); 'History of German Poetry' (2d ed. 1875); 'Rübezahl' (1829);

'Narcissus' (1830), two tales; 'Furore' (1851), a romance; etc.

Mercator (Latinized from his real name, **Krémer**), **Gerhard** (mèr-kā'tọr). A celebrated Flemish geographer; born at Rupelmonde, Belgium, March 5, 1512; died at Duisburg, Prussia, Dec. 2, 1594. He invented the "Mercator system" of projection of the earth's surface, made familiar in our atlases. His chief works were 'Geographical Maps according to Ptolemy' (1578–84), and 'Atlas' (1595), which made an epoch in cartography.

Mercier, [Louis] Sébastien (mär-sē-yä'). A French dramatist and essayist; born at Paris, June 6, 1740; died there, April 25, 1814. He was a member of the Five Hundred; professor of history at the Central School, Paris; member of the National Institute. His dramatic works appeared in four volumes at Amsterdam, 1778–84. His most important writings were: 'Picture of Paris' (12 vols., 1781–90), a description of Parisian life; 'New Paris' (6 vols., 1800), a description of Parisian life during the Revolution. 'My Night-Cap' (4 vols., 1784) was an attack on classicism. He was a very prolific writer, and made the first French translation of Schiller's 'Maid of Orleans.'

Meredith, George. A great English novelist and poet; born in Hampshire, 1828. He has published: 'Poems' (1851); 'The Shaving of Shagpat' (1855); 'Farina: a Legend of Cologne' (1857); 'The Ordeal of Richard Feverel' (1859); 'Mary Bertrand' (1860); 'Evan Harrington' (1861); 'Modern Love' (1862), poems; 'Emilia in England' (1864), subsequently republished under the title 'Sandra Belloni'; 'Rhoda Fleming' (1865); 'Vittoria' (1866); 'The Adventures of Harry Richmond' (1871); 'Beauchamp's Career' (1875); 'The Egoist' (1879); 'The Tragic Comedians' (1881); 'Poems and Lyrics of the Joy of Earth' (1883); 'Diana of the Crossways' (1885); 'Ballads and Poems of Tragic Life' (1887); 'A Reading of Earth' (1888); 'One of our Conquerors' (1890); 'The Empty Purse' (1892), poems; 'Lord Ormont and his Aminta' (1894); 'The Amazing Marriage' (1895). His shorter prose tales include: 'The Tale of Chloe'; 'The House on the Beach'; 'The Case of General Ople and Lady Camper.' He died May 17, 1909.

Meredith, Owen. See **Lytton**.

Mérimée, Prosper (mā-rē-mā'). A celebrated French essayist and littérateur; born at Paris, Sept. 28, 1803; died at Cannes, Sept. 23, 1870. He studied law, but never practiced; was senator in 1853. His best-known works were the two novels 'Colomba' (1830), treating of the Corsican vendetta; and 'Carmen' (1840), which furnished the plot of Bizet's opera of the same name. He wrote besides: 'Plays of Clara Gazul' (1825); 'Historic Monuments' (1843); 'Historic and Literary Medleys' (1855), a collection of comedies in the style of the Spanish "intermezzo"; 'Guzla' (1827), a collection of Illyrian lyrics; 'Mateo Falcone,' a

novel; 'Letters to an Unknown' ('Lettres à Une Inconnue': 1873); etc.

Merivale, Charles. An English historian and divine; born at Barton Place, Devonshire, March 8, 1808; died at Ely, Dec. 27, 1893. He was dean of Ely from 1869. He wrote: 'History of the Romans under the Empire' (latest ed. 1890), his principal work, extending from Cæsar's Gallic campaigns to Commodus, where Gibbon begins; 'General History of Rome' (1875); 'Lectures on Early Church History' (1879); etc.

Merivale, Herman. An English statesman, political economist, and historical writer, brother of Charles; born at Dawlish, Devonshire, Nov. 8, 1806; died in London, Feb. 9, 1874. He was professor of political economy at Oxford, 1837–42; under-secretary for the colonies, 1848–60; perpetual under-secretary for India. He wrote: 'Colonization and Colonies' (2 vols., 1841), the best work on the subject; 'Historical Studies' (1865); etc.

Merivale, Herman Charles. An English dramatist, novelist, and poet, son of Herman; born in London, 1839. A lawyer for fifteen years, he withdrew from practice in 1879. He has written the plays 'All for Her' (1874), 'Forget Me Not' (1879), etc.; the stories 'Faucit of Balliol' (1882) and 'Binko's Blues' (1884); the volume of poems 'The White Pilgrim' (1883); 'Florien' (1884). Died Jan. 15, 1906.

Meriwether, Mrs. Elizabeth (Avery). An American novelist; born in Tennessee, 1832. Her home is at Memphis, Tenn. She has written: 'The Master of Red Leaf' (1879); 'Ku-Klux-Klan' (1880), a drama; 'My First and Last Love'; etc.

Meriwether, Lee. An American writer; born in Columbus, Miss., Dec. 25, 1862. He is the author of: 'A Tramp Trip: How to See Europe on Fifty Cents a Day' (1887); 'The Tramp at Home'; and 'Afloat and Ashore on the Mediterranean; 'A Lord's Courtship.'

Merle, Jean Toussaint (märl). A French dramatist, publicist, and critic; born at Montpellier, 1785; died in Paris, 1852. A prolific writer, he collaborated with Ourry, Brazier, Carmouche, etc., on the dramas 'The Old Young-Man' (1812); 'The New-Market Races' (1818); 'The Monster and the Magician' (1826); etc.: and wrote 'Memoirs, Historic, Literary, and Critical, of Bachaumont' (3 vols., 1808–9); 'The English Spy' (1809); 'Of the Opera' (1827); 'Anecdotes, Historical and Political, for a History of the Conquest of Algiers' (1831–32); 'Chambord' (1832); etc.

Merle d'Aubigné. See **D'Aubigné**.

Merlin (mer'lin). Putative author of 'The Prophecy of Merlin'; a British bard and magician supposed to have lived in the 5th century. In the 12th century Geoffrey of Monmouth gave a Latin translation of the 'Prophecy,' which till then had been preserved in Welsh tradition. By natural accretion the 'Prophecy' grew in volume from age to age, and to « Merlin » are ascribed poems which had their rise in the time of King Arthur, as the 'Avallenau' (Apple-Garth), and the 'Hoianau' (Listeners).

Merriam, George Spring. An American essayist and biographer; born in Massachusetts, 1843. He lives at Springfield, Mass. He has written: 'A Living Faith'; 'Life of Samuel Bowles'; 'A Symphony of the Spirit'; 'The Negro and the Nation'; and is a frequent contributor to periodicals.

Merrill, Selah. A well-known American explorer and archæologist; born at Canton Centre, Conn., May 2, 1837. He was chaplain in the Civil War (1864-65); since then has been engaged in explorations in Palestine. He was consul at Jerusalem 1884-86 and 1890-93. Among his works are : 'East of the Jordan' (2d ed. 1883); 'Galilee in the Time of Christ' (1881); 'The Site of Calvary'; 'Ancient Jerusalem.'

Merry, Robert. An English dilettante; born in London, April 1755; died at Baltimore, Md., Dec. 14, 1798. He resigned from the army (1775); became a member of the famous Della Crusca Academy at Florence, Italy (1784-87); on returning to London, wrote plays and poems under the pseudonym "Della Crusca." His affected style found many imitators, and the school that arose was satirized by Gifford in his 'Baviad' and 'Mæviad.' He married an actress, and came to this country in 1796.

Mersliakov, Alexis Theodorovich (mär-zlē-ä-kof'). A noted Russian poet and miscellaneous writer; born at Dolmatov, government of Perm, 1778; died near Moscow, 1830. He was an ardent classicist; professor of rhetoric and literature at the University of Moscow in 1810. He wrote a number of poems which were set to music and became popular songs. His principal literary works were : 'Ancient Poetry and its Influence on Modern Civilization' (1810); and 'Imitation and Translation of Greek and Latin Authors' (1825).

Méry, Joseph (mā-rē'). A French miscellaneous writer; born near Marseilles, Jan. 21, 1798; died in Paris, June 17, 1866. Some of his works became very popular. Among them were the volumes of verse 'Poetic Melodies' (1853), 'Napoleon in Italy' (1859); the romances 'London Nights' (1840), 'Héva' (1843), 'Novel Novels' (1853); the dramas 'The Two Frontins' (1858), 'The Fiancée Worth Millions' (1864). With Barthélemy he wrote satirical verses, and by himself librettos for several operas.

Mesihi (mes'i-hē). A renowned Turkish poet; flourished in the 14th century. He is one of the seven poets called by the Turks « the Pleiades,» and whose names, written in gold, are suspended in the temple of Mecca. Sir William Jones, in his 'Commentaries on Asiatic Poetry,' translated one of his idyls.

Mesonero y Romanos, Ramon de (mā-sō-nä'rō rō-mä'nōs). A Spanish descriptive writer and historian, employing sometimes the pseudonym « El Curioso Parlante » (The Inquisitive Chatterer); born at Madrid, July 10, 1803; died

there, April 1882. He was connected with the national library, Madrid (1845). He wrote: 'Manual of Madrid' (3d ed. 1844), containing apt pictures of life there; 'Madrid Panorama' (2 vols., 1832-35); 'Types and Characters' (1843-62); 'Mementos of Travel in France and Belgium' (1842); 'Ancient Madrid' (1861), a scholarly history; etc. He founded and edited the Spanish Pictorial Weekly (8 vols., 1836).

Mesquita, Salvador de (mäs-kē'tä). A Brazilian poet; born in Rio Janeiro in 1646; died in Rome, beginning of 18th century. His reputation as a poet was assured when he wrote his sacred drama 'Sacrificium Jephtæ' (1680). His best tragedies are 'Demetrius,' 'Perseus,' and 'Prusias of Bithynia' (1690 to 1700).

Metastasio, Pietro (mā"täs-tä'zē-ō). A celebrated Italian poet; born at Rome, Jan. 13, 1698; died at Vienna, April 12, 1782. His real name was Trapassi. He was court poet at Vienna, honored, surrounded by friends, and probably the most famous Continental poet of his time. His fame rests chiefly on his lyrical dramas 'The Gardens of the Hesperides' (1720); 'Demetrius' (1732); 'The Clemency of Titus' (1734); 'Atilius Regulus' (1740-50); and 'Themistocles.' He was a master of the canzonet, and wrote also sonnets, idyls, elegies, criticisms, and letters. Monuments were erected to him at Rome and Vienna. ('Works,' best edition, Paris, 1780-82.)

Metcalfe, Frederick. An English Scandinavian scholar; born 1815; died Aug. 24, 1885. He was a clergyman of the Church of England. He wrote: 'The Oxonian in Norway' (1856); 'The Oxonian in Thelemarken' (1858); 'A History of German Literature' (1858); 'The Oxonian in Iceland' (new ed. 1867); 'The Englishman and the Scandinavian' (1880); etc.

Metternich, Clemens Wenzel Nepomuk Lothar, Prince (met'ter-nich). A celebrated Austrian statesman; born at Coblentz, May 15, 1773; died at Vienna, July 11, 1859. Managing Austria's affairs with consummate skill through the Napoleonic era, he secured for her at the Congress of Vienna (1814) more than a restoration of the territory Napoleon had stripped her of, and a more prominent position than ever, was chancellor of the Austrian empire (1821-48); and dominated for thirty years the Continental politics of Europe (1814-44). (Writings, with autobiography, 8 vols., Vienna, 1880-84).

Mexican Nun, The — Juana Yñez de la Cruz. A Mexican poet (1651-95), nun of the convent of San Gerónimo. She is famous for the beauty of her stanzas 'Learning and Riches'; 'Death in Youth'; etc.

Meyer-Zeigler, Conrad Ferdinand. A Swiss poet and novelist; born at Zürich, Oct. 12, 1825; died, Nov. 28, 1898. His home after 1875 was at Kilchberg, near Zürich. Among his works are in verse, 'Ballads' (1867); 'Romances and Pictures' (1870), 'Hutten's Last Days' (8th ed. 1891), 'Engelberg' (3d ed. 1889); the novels 'The Saint' (12th ed. 1894), 'A Boy'

Suffering> (3d ed. 1889), 'The Monk's Wedding> (5th ed. 1893), 'The Temptation of Pescara> (4th ed. 1889), 'Angela Borgia> (5th ed. 1892); etc. Most of the novels are contained in a collection, the fifth edition of which appeared in 1892.

Meyn, Antoinette (mīn). A Norwegian miscellaneous writer, employing the pseudonyms « Marie » and « Holger Birch.» Most of her works have been translated into Swedish and German. Among them are: 'In the Twilight> (3d ed. 1881); 'Through Struggles> (1876); 'In the Home Circle> (1878); 'The House of Dyocke> (1885); 'Dream and Real Life> (1891); 'From Times Gone By> (1893); etc.

Meynell, Alice (Thompson) (mā'nel). An English poet and essayist; born in London. She spent much of her childhood in Italy, and married (1877) Wilfrid Meynell, editor of Merry England. She has written in verse 'Preludes> (1875; 2d ed. 1893), illustrated by her sister Lady (Elizabeth) Butler; in prose 'Rhythm of Life> (1893); 'John Ruskin> (1900).

Meyr, Melchior (mīr). A German novelist, poet, and philosophical writer; born at Ehringen, near Nördlingen, Bavaria, June 28, 1810; died at Munich, April 22, 1871. He resided in Berlin (1841-52) and Munich (1852-71). His best-known works were: 'Stories from the Ries> (4th ed. 1892), containing delightful descriptions of peasant life in his native district; they are among the very best German village tales. Among the best of his other productions were 'Duke Albert> (1852) and 'Charles the Bold> (1862). He published also 'Poems> (1857), religious-philosophical writings, tragedies, and romances.

Mezeray, François Eudes de (māz-rā'). A French historian; born at Ruy, near Falaise, Normandy, 1610; died in Paris, July 10, 1683. Richelieu made him historiographer, and gave him a pension. His principal work was a 'History of France> (1638-51), published afterward in improved form as 'Chronological Abstract of the History of France> (1668). His method was a radical departure in historical writing, and the forerunner of modern histories, being of the people as well as sovereigns.

Michaud, Joseph François (mē-shō'). A French journalist, poet, and historian; born at Albens, Savoy, June 19, 1767; died at Passy, Sept. 30, 1839. Through the Revolution and the Napoleonic era he remained a stanch Bourbonist. His most popular poem was 'An Exile's Spring> (2d ed. 1827). His chief historical works were: 'History of the Empire of Mysore> (2 vols., 1801); 'History of the Crusades> (3 vols., 1812-22). With his brother he edited the 'Biographie Universelle> (1811-28).

Michel Angelo (mē-kel än'je-lō)—**Michelagnolo Buonarroti.** The eminent Italian sculptor, painter, architect, and poet; born at Caprese, March 6, 1475; died at Rome, Feb. 18, 1564. Of world-wide and lasting renown as an artist and architect, his claim to literary fame

rests upon his sonnets and letters. The best edition of his 'Poems> was published at Florence, 1863; an English translation of the sonnets by Symonds, London, 1892. A volume of 'Letters> was published at Florence, 1865.

Michelet, Jules (mēsh-lā'). A famous French historian; born in Paris, Aug. 21, 1798; died at Hyères, Feb. 9, 1874. He was professor of history at the Collège Rollin, 1821-26; lecturer at the Normal School, 1827; chief of the historical department of the royal archives, 1830; professor of history and morals at the Collège de France, 1838-51. His principal historical works were: 'History of France> (16 vols., 1833-67); 'History of the Revolution> (7 vols., 1847-53); 'Abridgment of Modern History> (1827); etc. Among his polemical writings were: 'Of the Jesuits> (1843); 'Of the Priest, the Wife, and the Family> (1844); 'Of the People> (1845); 'Poland and Russia> (1851); etc. He wrote also, assisted by his wife, the delightful works 'The Bird> (1856); 'The Insect> (1857); 'Love> (1858); 'Woman> (1859); 'The Sea> (1861); 'The Sorceress> (1862).

Michiels, Alfred Joseph Xavier (mē-shi-āl'). A French historian, critic, and miscellaneous writer; born in Rome, Dec. 25, 1813; died in Paris, Oct. 28, 1892. He studied law originally. He wrote 'Studies of Germany> (2d ed. 1850); 'History of Literary Ideas in France in the 19th Century> (3d ed. 1862); 'Journey of a Virtuoso in England> (4th ed. 1872); 'History of Flemish and Dutch Painting> (new ed. 10 vols., 1865-76); 'Architecture and Painting in Europe> (3d ed. 1873); 'Secret History of the Austrian Government> (4th ed. 1879); 'Count Bismarck> (1871); the popular 'Tales of the Mountains> (1857); and 'Political Dramas> (1865); etc.

Mickiewicz, Adam (mits-kē'ā-vich). A celebrated Polish poet; born near Novogródek, Lithuania, Dec. 24, 1798; died at Constantinople, Nov. 26, 1855. He was the greatest of Slavic poets. Banished from Poland for political reasons, he resided principally at Paris after 1828; was professor of the Slavic languages and literature at the Collège de France (1840-44). His great work was the epic 'Pan Tadeusz> (Lord Thaddeus [of Warsaw]: 1834), a picture of Lithuanian life in 1812; though another epic, 'Conrad Wallenrod> (1828), written while an exile in Russia, is hardly less renowned. Other important works were: a third epic, 'Grazyna> (1822); the ballad 'Dziady> (1823); 'Crimean Sonnets> (1826); 'The Books of the Polish People and of the Polish Pilgrimage> (1832); 'Lectures on Slavic Literature,' etc. ('Works,' latest edition, 4 vols., Lemberg, 1893.)

Mickle, William Julius. A Scottish poet; born at Langholm, Dumfriesshire, Sept. 28, 1735; died at Forest Hill, Oct. 28, 1788. He translated into English the 'Lusiad> (new ed. 1798), the national epic of Portugal; and wrote 'Syr Martyn> (1778), 'Almada Hill> (1781), etc. He is said to have been the author of the song 'There's Nae Luck aboot the Hoose.' ('Poetical Works,' with life, 1806.)

Middleton, Conyers. An eminent English theological and classical writer; born at Richmond, Yorkshire, Dec. 27, 1683; died at Hildersham, July 28, 1750. His life was one of embittered controversy, in which he gained immediate opprobrium and material harm, but enduring intellectual consideration. His principal writings were: 'Life of Cicero' (1741), an acute defense of Cicero as statesman; 'Introductory Discourse' (1747); most famous of all, the 'Free Inquiry' (1748),—an argument to prove that the mediæval miracles were false because they grew more plentiful as the need of them grew less.

Middleton, Thomas. An English dramatist; born in London (?) about 1570; died at Newington Butts, 1627. He collaborated with Rowley, Massinger, Fletcher, and Ben Jonson. He wrote: 'A Mad World, My Masters' (1608); 'The Game of Chess' (1623); 'The Spanish Gipsy' (1653); 'Women Beware Women' (1657); a satire on Prince Charles's unsuccessful wooing of the Spanish Infanta; etc. ('Dramatic Works,' 8 vols., London, 1886.)

Mignet, François Auguste Marie (mēn-yā'). A French historian; born at Aix, Provence, May 8, 1796; died in Paris, March 24, 1884. He studied law; was director of the archives of the foreign ministry, Paris, 1830–48. Among his works were: 'Life of Franklin' (1848); 'History of the French Revolution' (13th ed. 1880); 'Charles V.' (10th ed. 1882); 'History of Marie Stuart' (6th ed. 1884); etc. He wrote also a drama entitled 'Antonio Perez and Philip II.' (5th ed. 1881.)

Mikhaïlov, Mikhail Larionovich (mē-kä'ē-lof). A Russian journalist and novelist; born in the Ural Mountains, 1826; died in Siberia, 1865. He was son of a Russian official and a Khirgiz princess. On his return from traveling in Europe (1858–61), political considerations caused his exile. His best novel was: 'Adam Adamovich' (1851). ('Works,' St. Petersburg, 1859.)

Miklosich, Franz von (mik'lō-zich). The founder of Slavic philology; born near Luttenberg, Styria, Nov. 20, 1813; died at Vienna, March 7, 1891. He was member of the Reichstag (1848); professor of Slavic philology at Vienna (1850–86); life member of the Reichstag (1862). He published: 'Comparative Grammar of the Slavic Languages' (1852–74); 'Dialects and Wanderings of the Gipsies of Europe' (1872–77); 'Etymological Dictionary of the Slavic Languages' (1886); etc.

Mikovec, Ferdinand Bretislav (mik'ō-vets). A Bohemian dramatist and archæologist; born at Sloup (Pirkstein), Dec. 24, 1826; died at Prague, Sept. 22, 1862. He took part in the Bohemian and Servian commotions of 1848; founded at Prague the Lumir, the only magazine in Bohemia then devoted exclusively to belles-lettres (1851); also wrote 'Bohemian

Antiquities' (1858). He published 'The Extinction of the Premyslides' (1851), and 'Dimitri Ivanovic' (1856), two successful tragedies; and left two other dramas in MS.

Milá y Fontanals. Manuel (mē-lä' ē fōn-tạ-näls'). A Spanish scholar; born near Barcelona, May 4, 1818; died at Barcelona, July 16, 1884. He was professor of literature at Barcelonia (1845). He devoted himself to history, especially that of Catalonia and Spain, and was an authority on the Romance languages and literatures. Among his works were: 'Catalonian Legends' (2d ed. 1882); 'The Troubadours in Spain' (1861); 'The Popular Heroic Poetry of Spain' (1873); 'Principles of Spanish Literature' (1874); etc.

Milanés, José Jacinto (mē-lä-näs'). A Cuban poet; born in Matanzas, August 1814; died November 1863. His drama 'El Conde de Alarcos' at once gave its author fame, as it contains passages of very passionate poetry. The drama 'A Poet at Court' also met great success. He published 'A Cuban Looker-on,' a series of social sketches (1842). Many of his poems have been translated into English, French, and Italian, and nearly all his works into German.

Milburn, William Henry. A noted American Methodist preacher and lecturer; born in Philadelphia, Sept. 26, 1823. He has been widely known as "the blind preacher," and six times chaplain of the national House of Representatives, once of the national Senate (1893). He has written: 'Rifle, Axe, and Saddle-Bags' (1857); 'Ten Years of Preacher Life' (1859); 'Pioneers and People of the Mississippi Valley' (1860). He died in 1903.

Milelli, Domenico (mē-lel'lē). An Italian poet; born at Catanzaro, Calabria, 1841. Intended for the priesthood, he adopted instead literature of the most realistic sort. A prolific writer, among his works are: 'In Youth' (1873); 'Gioconda' (1874); 'Hiemalia' (1874); 'Pagan Odes' (1879); 'Song Book' (1884); etc. His 'Rime' (Verses), published under the pseudonym "Count of Lara," has been very popular.

Miles, George Henry. An American dramatist and story-writer; born in Baltimore, Md., July 31, 1824; died in Thornbrook, Md., July 23, 1871. His short story 'Loretto, or the Choice,' won the $50 prize offered by the Baltimore Catholic Mirror for the best short story. In 1850 his 'Mohammed' won the $1,000 prize offered by Edwin Forrest for the best play by an American author. He wrote many poems, plays, and sketches; among them 'Christine, a Troubadour's Song; and Other Poems' (1866); and 'Abou Hassan the Wag, or the Sleeper Awakened' (1868).

Milicevic, Milan (mil-i-chev'ich). A Servian geographical, ethnological, and historical writer, and novelist; born near Belgrade, May 7, 1831. He studied theology; was a teacher (1850); and secretary of the Servian minister of education (1861). He has written: 'The

Principality of Servia' (1876); 'Servian Peasant Life' (in the Glasnik: 1867 and 1873); 'Kingdom of Servia' (1884); the stories of Servian life 'Jurmutsa and Fatima,' and 'Winter Evenings' (1879); 'Summer Evenings' (1880).

Mill, James. A noted English philosopher, historian, and political economist; born in Forfarshire, Scotland, April 6, 1773; died at Kensington, June 23, 1836. He studied originally for the church. His great work was 'An Analysis of the Phenomena of the Human Mind' (2 vols., 1829), which laid the foundation of the "association" psychology, since ably developed by Spencer and Bain. He published besides a 'History of British India' (3 vols., 1817-18; new ed. 1872), which got him a position with the East India Company; 'Political Economy' (1821-22); numerous contributions to the Westminster Review; articles in the 'Encyclopædia Britannica'; etc.

Mill, John Stuart. A celebrated English philosophical writer, logician, and political economist, son of James; born in London, May 20, 1806; died at Avignon, France, May 8, 1873. In early childhood he was educated by his father after a unique and rigid system. He became superintendent and proprietor of the Westminster Review (1836-40); chief examiner of the India House (1856); Member of Parliament (1865). Among his most important works were: 'Logic' (1843); 'Political Economy' (1848); 'Essay on Liberty' (1859); 'Utilitarianism' (1862); 'Examination of Sir William Hamilton's Philosophy' (1865); 'Auguste Comte and Positivism' (1865); 'On the Subjection of Women' (1869); etc. His 'Autobiography' appeared in 1873. He was one of the most lucid expositors of abstract ideas who ever wrote in English.

Miller, Cincinnatus Heine, better known as **Joaquin Miller.** An American poet; born in Wabash district, Ind., Nov 10, 1841. His checkered life has included the extremes of being a California gold-miner, editor of an Oregon newspaper, an Oregon lawyer and judge, a social lion in London, journalist at Washington, D.C., etc. The name of "Joaquin" he took from Joaquin Murietta, a Mexican brigand, whom he had once legally defended. His 'Collected Poems' appeared in 1882. Since then he has published 'Songs of Mexican Seas' (1887); and 'Songs of the Soul' (1896). He has written also in prose 'The Baroness of New York' (1877); ''49, or The Gold Seekers of the Sierras' (1884); etc. His novel 'The Danites' (1881) was successfully staged.

Miller, Mrs. Emily (Huntington). An American educator and popular writer for the young; born in Connecticut, 1833. She is president of the Woman's College of the Northwestern University, Ill. Among her works are: 'From Avalon and Other Poems'; 'The Royal Road to Fortune' (1875); the 'Kirkwood' series; etc.

Miller, Harriet (Mann). ["Olive Thorne Miller."] An American writer of children's stories; born in Auburn, N. Y., 1831; particularly distinguished for her descriptive books of birds and their habits. Included in her publications are: 'A Bird-Lover in the West'; 'In Nesting Time'; 'Little Folks in Feathers and Fur'; 'Our Home Pets'; and 'Little People of Asia.'

Miller, Hugh. A noted Scottish geologist, whose writings first made geology popularly known; born at Cromarty, Oct. 10, 1802; died near Edinburgh, Dec. 2, 1856. Beginning life as a stone-mason (1819-36), he became bank accountant at Cromarty (1834), and editor of an Edinburgh newspaper (1840). His chief works were: 'The Old Red Sandstone' (1841); 'Footprints of the Creator' (1847); 'My Schools and Schoolmasters' (1852); 'Testimony of the Rocks' (1857). He published besides 'Poems' (1829); 'Scenes and Legends of the North of Scotland' (1835); etc.

Miller, Joaquin. See **Miller, C. H.**

Miller, Johann Martin. A German novelist and poet; born at Ulm, Dec. 3, 1750; died there, June 21, 1814. He was professor at Ulm (1781); dean and clerical councilor (1810). He was best known by 'Siegwart, a Convent Tale' (1776). He wrote also in prose: 'Contribution to the History of the Tender Passion' (1776); 'Correspondence between Three College Friends' (1776); 'Story of Charles of Burgheim and Emilia of Rosenau' (1778); etc.: while several of his 'Poems' (1783) became popular songs.

Miller, Olive Thorne. See **Miller, Harriet M.**

Miller, Orest Fedorovich (mil'er). A Russian political, archæological, and critical writer; born in Reval, 1833. He is one of the leading Slavophils; teacher of Russian literature in the University of St. Petersburg (1861). He has written: 'The Slav Question in Life and Knowledge' (1865); 'Lomonosov and the Reforms of Peter the Great' (1866); 'Ilja Murovetz and the Heroes of Kiev' (1869), a study of Russian popular myths; 'The Slav World and Europe' (1877), his most successful work; 'Lectures on Russian Literature after Gog l' (3d ed. 1887); etc.

Miller, Stephen Franks. An American lawyer and biographical writer; born in North Carolina about 1810; died 1867. He wrote: 'Bench and Bar of Georgia' (2 vols., 1858), a valuable collection of biographies and historical matter; 'Memoir of General Blackshear and the War in Georgia, 1813-14' (1858); 'Wilkins Wylder' (1860).

Miller, Thomas. An English poet, novelist, and writer on rural life; born at Gainsborough, 1807; died in London, Oct. 24, 1874. He supported himself as a basket-maker, till Rogers the poet enabled him to open a book-store in London. He wrote: 'Royston Gower' (1838), a novel; 'Rural Sketches' (1839), in verse; 'Gideon Giles, the Roper' (1840) and 'Godfrey Malvern' (1843), novels; 'History of the

Anglo-Saxons' (1848; four editions since); etc. With G. W. M. Reynolds, he wrote Vol. v. of the 'Mysteries of London.'

Miller, William. A Scottish poet; born in Bridgegate, Glasgow, August 1810; died at Glasgow, Aug. 20, 1872. Uncertain health preventing his becoming a physician, he adopted the trade of wood-turning. He has been called "the laureate of the nursery." He wrote: 'Scottish Nursery Songs and Other Poems' (1863). One of his most popular single poems was 'Wee Willie Winkie.'

Millet, Francis Davis. An American artist, story-writer, and noted war correspondent; born at Mattapoisett, Mass., Nov. 3, 1846. He was very successful as correspondent of the London Daily News in the Turco-Russian war, and has been a frequent contributor to periodicals. He has published in book form 'A Capillary Crime, and Other Stories'; and 'The Danube from the Black Forest to the Black Sea.'

Mills, Abraham. An American prose-writer; born in Dutchess County, N. Y., in 1796; died in New York city, July 8, 1867. He published 'Literature and Literary Men of Great Britain and Ireland' (2 vols., 1851); 'Outlines of Rhetoric and Belles-Lettres' (1854); 'Poets and Poetry of the Ancient Greeks' (1854); 'Compendium of the History of the Ancient Hebrews' (1856).

Milman, Henry Hart. A distinguished English clergyman, historian, and poet; born in London, Feb. 10, 1791; died near Ascot, Sept. 24, 1868. He was professor of poetry at Oxford, 1821–31; Bampton lecturer 1827; canon of Westminster 1835; dean of St. Paul's 1849. His 'History of the Jews' (1830) excited intense antagonism, being the first attempt to apply secular historical methods to the sacred history, though not irreverently. In 1838 he edited Gibbon's 'Decline and Fall of the Roman Empire,' and in 1839 published a 'Life of Gibbon.' He wrote 'History of Christianity under the Empire' (1840), and published in 1855 his most important work, 'The History of Latin Christianity down to the Death of Pope Nicholas V.' In verse he produced 'Samor' (1818), an epic; 'Fall of Jerusalem' (1820); etc. The drama 'Fazio' (1815), written while he was at Oxford, was performed in 1818 by Charles Kemble and Miss O'Neill, and by Madame Ristori in 1856. He also wrote a history of St. Paul's Cathedral. His 'Essays and Memoirs' were collected by his son in 1870.

Milnes, Richard Monckton (milz). See **Houghton.**

Milton, John. One of the greatest of English poets; born in London, Dec. 9, 1608; died there, Nov. 8, 1674. He graduated at Cambridge in 1629; traveled in Italy, 1638; was Latin secretary of the Commonwealth, 1649; became totally blind in 1652. His greatest works were the famous epics 'Paradise Lost' (1666) and 'Paradise Regained' (1671); the tragedy 'Samson Agonistes' (1671); the poems 'Comus' (1634),

'Lycidas' (1637), 'L'Allegro' (1645), 'Il Penseroso' (1645); and his various sonnets. Of his prose writings the most renowned were 'Areopagitica' (1644), advocating freedom of the press; 'The Tenure of Kings and Magistrates' (1649), justifying the execution of Charles I.; and the 'Defence of the English People' (1654).

Mines, John Flavel. ["Felix Oldboy."] An American journalist, descriptive writer, and writer of verse; born in Paris, 1835; died 1891. Originally a student of theology, he entered the army as chaplain in 1861; but afterward abandoned the ministry, received a commission, and was mustered out as lieutenant-colonel in 1865. He published: 'Heroes of the Last Lustre' (1858), verse; 'Tour around New York, by Mr. Felix Oldboy' (1888).

Minghetti, Marco (min-get'tē). An Italian statesman, journalist, and miscellaneous writer; born at Bologna, Nov. 8, 1818; died at Rome, Dec. 10, 1886. A conspicuous political figure in his day, he occupied for a number of years the highest positions, and was very influential in the government. He wrote: 'Relation of Public Economy to Morality and Right' (2d ed. 1868), his most remarkable work; 'Literary and Economic Pamphlets' (1872); 'Italian Ladies in the Fine Arts' (1877); 'Church and State' (1878); 'Raphael' (1885); a biography; 'My Recollections' (1888–91); 'Parliamentary Speeches.'

Minot, Laurence. An English lyric poet; born 1300 (?); died 1352 (?). Scarcely anything is known of his life. His poetry expressed the militant England of his time, being devoted to the triumph of England over the French and Scots. First printed in 1795; latest edition, edited by Joseph Hall, Clarendon Press, 1887.

Minto, William. A Scottish scholar and miscellaneous writer; born in Alford, Aberdeenshire, Oct. 10, 1845; died at Aberdeen, March 1, 1893. He was editor of the London Examiner, 1874–78; professor of logic and English literature at the University of Aberdeen, 1880. Besides several novels, articles in the 'Encyclopædia Britannica,' contributions to reviews, etc., he published 'English Prose Writers' (1872); and 'English Poets' (1874).

Mira de Mescua or **Amescua, Antonio** (mē'-rä dä mä'-skwä). A Spanish poet and dramatist; born at Guadix, about 1570; died at Madrid, 1635. He was court chaplain at Granada, and afterward chaplain of honor to Philip IV. at Madrid. Calderon and Corneille borrowed from his works. A few of his lyrics can be seen in Vol. xiii., five of his plays in Vol. xiv., of Rivadeneyra's 'Library of Spanish Authors.'

Mirabeau, Gabriel Honoré de Riquetti, Count of (mē-rä-bō'). A famous French orator and revolutionist; born at Bignon, March 9, 1749; died in Paris, April 2, 1791. He rose to the rank of captain in the army; in 1789 was delegate of the Third Estate to the convention of the States-General, where his eloquence made him a power; president of the Jacobin

Club in 1790, of the National Assembly in 1791. Among his writings were : 'The Friend of Men' (1755); 'Rural Philosophy' (1763); 'The Prussian Monarchy' (1788), his chief work; 'Secret History of the Court of Berlin' (1789); etc. He was the one large statesman of the French Revolution. ('Works,' best edition,—though lacking the 'Prussian Monarchy,' — by Blanchard, 10 vols., 1822.)

Mirandola (mē-rän'dō-lä). See **Pico**.

Mirecourt, Eugène de (mēr-kör'). A French novelist and miscellaneous writer; born at Mirecourt, Nov. 19, 1812, died in Tahiti, Feb. 13, 1880. Among his novels were · 'Confessions of Marion Delorme' (1848)· 'Memoirs of Ninon de Lenclos' (1852); 'The Marchioness de Courcelles' (1859). His name was originally Jacquot Mirecourt.

Mistral, Frederi (mēs-träl'). A celebrated Provençal poet; born at Maillane, Bouches-du-Rhône, Sept. 8, 1830. After studying law, he devoted himself to establishing the Provençal dialect as a literary tongue, and became one of the originators of the renowned society of Félibrige (1854), founded for that purpose. His most famous works are the poems 'Mirèio' (1858; several editions, and translated into a number of languages); 'Calendau' (1867); and 'Nerto' (1883). He has published also 'Lis Isclo d'Oro' (1875), a collection of fugitive poems; 'The Poem of the Rhône' (1897); two volumes of 'Lou Tresor dou Felibrige' (1878-86); a Provençal-French dictionary ; etc.

Mitchel, Frederick Augustus. An American novelist and biographer; born 1839. He has written: 'Chattanooga' and 'Chickamauga,' two romances of the Civil War; and 'Ormsby Macknight Mitchel, Astronomer and General' (1887), a biography of his father.

Mitchel, Ormsby Macknight. An American astronomer and soldier; born in Union County, Ky., in 1809 or 1810, died in Beaufort, S. C., of yellow fever, Oct. 30, 1862. He graduated at West Point in 1829; became professor of mathematics and astronomy at Cincinnati College, O., 1834, and was largely instrumental in building and equipping the observatory there, and was director of the Dudley Observatory, Albany, N. Y., 1859. He was made brigadier-general in the Federal service, 1861 ; won the battle of Huntsville, Ala., April 1862; was promoted to major-general and commander of the Department of the South. He delivered many popular lectures on astronomy, and published 'Planetary and Stellar Worlds'; 'The Orbs of Heaven'; 'Elementary Treatise on the Sun'; and 'Astronomy of the Bible.'

Mitchell, Donald Grant. ["Ik Marvel."] A noted American essayist and novelist; born at Norwich, Conn., April 1822. Originally a lawyer, he was consul at Venice 1853-55; he has since lived on his estate Edgewood, near New Haven, Conn. His best-known works are: 'Reveries of a Bachelor' (1850); 'Dream Life' (1851); 'My Farm of Edgewood' (1863);

'Wet Days at Edgewood' (1864). He has written also: 'Doctor Johns' (1866), a novel; 'Bound Together' (1884) ; 'English Lands, Letters and Kings' (1889-90); 'American Lands and Letters' (1897).

Mitchell, John Ames. An American journalist and novelist ; born in New York, Jan. 17, 1845. He is the editor of Life. He has published 'The Summer School of Philosophy at Mount Desert' (1881); 'Romance of the Moon' (1886); 'That First Affair, and Other Stories'; 'The Silent War.'

Mitchell, Langdon Elwyn. ["John Philip Varley".] An American writer, son of S. Weir; born in Philadelphia, 1862. He is author of 'Love in the Backwoods' and 'Becky Sharp.'

Mitchell, Silas Weir. A distinguished American physician, poet, and novelist; born in Philadelphia, Feb. 15, 1829. He is noted as a specialist in toxicology, nervous disorders, etc., the results of his researches being embodied in a number of valuable medical works. He has achieved a high reputation by his purely literary books: 'Hephzibah Guinness, and Other Stories' (1880); 'In War Time' (1885), a novel; 'Poems' (1882-87); 'Characteristics' (1893); 'Hugh Wynne' (1897) ; 'Youth of Washington.'

Mitchell, Walter. An American prose and verse writer ; born in Massachusetts in 1826. He is an Episcopalian clergyman of New York city, and writer of 'Two Strings to his Bow'; 'Bryan Maurice,' a novel ; and 'Tacking Off Shore,' and 'The Mocking Bird,' notable poems.

Mitford, Mary Russell. A distinguished English miscellaneous writer; born at Alresford, Hampshire, Dec. 16, 1787 ; died at Swallowfield, Jan. 10, 1855. Her father (a physician) having dissipated several fortunes, she adopted literature as a means of family support. Her most famous works were : 'Our Village' (5 vols., 1824-32); and 'Recollections of a Literary Life' (1852-54). Other works were the tragedies 'Julian' (1823), 'The Foscari' (1826), and 'Rienzi' (1828), all produced by Macready (of Charles Kemble, the last being the best; 'Belford Regis' (1835), a novel; poems, short stories, juvenile stories, etc.; besides which she was a contributor to periodicals and all sorts of occasional publications.

Mitford, William. An English historian; born in London, Feb. 10, 1744; died at Exbury, Feb. 10, 1827. He was admitted to the bar, but never practiced; was Member of Parliament for over twenty years, and professor of history at the Royal Academy. His most notable work was the 'History of Greece': Vol. i., 1784; Vol. v., 1818. (Best edition, 8 vols., 1838.)

Mivart, St. George Jackson (miv'ärt). An English naturalist; born in London, Nov. 30, 1827; died there, April 1, 1900. He was professor of biology in University College, 1874-77; was professor of the philosophy of natural history at the University of Louvain, Belgium, after 1890. Among his chief works are: 'Genesis of Species' (1870-71); 'Man and Apes' (1873); 'Contemporary Evolution' (1876); 'Origin of Human Reason' (1889); 'Types of Animal

25

Life' (1893). Though an evolutionist, he is well known as denying that evolution accounts for the human intellect.

Moe, Jörgen Ingebrektsen (mō'e). A distinguished Norwegian poet and folk-lorist: born in the district of Ringerike. about 1813; died at Christiansand, 1880 (?). He became bishop of Christiansand in 1875. The influence on Norwegian language, literature, and art, of the popular fairy tales collected at great pains by him, can hardly be exaggerated. He wrote : ' Digte ' (Poems : 2d ed. 1856); ' In the Well and in the Tarn ' (1851), stories for children; ' Norwegian Folk-Tales ' (5th ed. 1874 ; English translation as ' Popular Tales from the Norse ' by Dasent, 3d ed. 1888), with P. C. Asbjörnsen; etc. (' Works,' 1877.)

Moffat, James Clement. An American miscellaneous writer; born in Glencree, Galloway, Scotland, May 30, 1811; died in Princeton, N. J., June 7, 1890. He contributed numerous articles to periodicals, and published 'A Rhyme of the North Countrie' (1847); 'Life of Dr. Thomas Chalmers' (1853); 'Song and Scenery; or, A Summer Ramble in Scotland' (1874); 'Church History in Brief' (1885); 'The Story of a Dedicated Life' (1887).

Moffat, Robert. A noted Scottish missionary; born at Ormiston, Dec. 21, 1795; died at Leigh, Kent, Aug. 8, 1883. Originally a gardener, he went to South Africa as a missionary in 1816, remaining till 1870; he translated parts of the Bible, hymn-books, etc., into the Bechuana and other barbaric languages, and was very successful. He wrote ' Labors and Scenes in South Africa ' (1842). One of his daughters married Dr. Livingstone, the African explorer.

Mohl, Julius von (mōl). A German-French Orientalist; born at Stuttgart, Würtemberg, Oct. 25, 1800; died at Paris, Jan. 4, 1876. He was professor of Oriental literature at Tübingen in 1826; professor of Persian literature in the Collège de France, 1845. His principal work was his edition of Firdausi's ' Shah Namah ' (The Book of the Kings: 6 vols., Paris, 1836–68, text and translation).

Mokry, Otokar (mok'rē). A Bohemian poet and novelist; born at Budweis, 1854. He is State notary at Vodnany, and editor of the ' People's Cheap Library.' He is a romanticist. He has written: in verse, ' Melodies from Southern Bohemia ' (1880), ' Poems ' (1883), ' On the Maiden's Rock ' (1885), ' Reflections and Legends ' (1888); and in prose, ' Short Stories and Arabesques ' (1883), ' Short Stories and Sketches ' (1886); etc.

Molbech, Christian Knud Frederik (mol'-beĉh). A Danish poet and dramatist; born at Copenhagen, July 20, 1821; died at Kiel, May 20, 1888. He was professor of Danish language and literature at Kiel, 1853–64; then a journalist at Copenhagen; censor at the royal theatre, Copenhagen. Among his works were : ' Pictures from the Life of Jesus ' (1840), a volume

of poems; ' The Bride of the Mountain King ' (1845), and ' The Venusberg ' (1845), dramas; ' Twilight ' (1851), poems; ' Poems, Lyric and Dramatic ' (1863); ' The Financier,' a comedy. (' Poetical Works,' new ed. 1879.)

Molesworth, Mrs. Mary Louisa (Stewart). [" Ennis Graham."] An English novelist and writer for children; born of Scotch parentage at Rotterdam, Holland, 1842. She has lived several years in France and Germany. Among her works are the novels ' Lover and Husband ' (new ed. 1873), ' She was Young and He was Old ' (1872), ' Cicely ' (1874), ' Miss Bouverie ' (1880); and the juveniles ' Tell Me a Story ' (1875), ' Carrots ' (1876), ' Children of the Castle ' (1890), ' Hollow Tree House,' etc. (1894); 'The Laurel Walk'; 'Peterkin.'

Molière (mō-lyär'), the stage name of **Jean Baptiste Poquelin**. The greatest of French dramatists; born in Paris, Jan. 15(?), 1622; died there, Feb. 17, 1673. His greatest works were his comedies of character, ' The School for Wives ' (1662); ' Tartuffe ' (1664), thought by many to be his masterpiece; ' Don Juan ' (1665); ' The Misanthrope ' (1666); ' The Miser ' (1668); ' The Tradesman Turned Gentleman ' (1670); ' The Learned Ladies ' (1672); ' The Imaginary Invalid ' (1673). Other renowned dramas were : ' The Affected Ladies ' (1659); ' Sganarelle ' (1660); ' The School for Husbands ' (1661); ' The Physician in Spite of Himself' (1666); ' Georges Dandin ' (1668).

Molina, Juan Ignacio (mō-lē'nä). A Jesuit historian; born in the province of Talca, Chili, June 24, 1737; died at Bologna, Italy, Sept. 12, 1829. After 1774 he resided at Bologna, teaching and devoting his leisure to the composition of valuable historical works on Chili. These were: ' Compendium of Chilian History'; ' Essay on Chilian Natural History ' (1782); ' Essay on Chilian Civil History' (1787), the last-named being translated into several languages, including English; etc.

Molinos, Miguel (mō-lē'nōs). A Spanish mystic, founder of the Quietists; born near Saragossa, Dec. 21, 1640; died at Rome, Dec. 29, 1696 or 1697. He was a priest at Rome. His principal work, ' A Spiritual Guide' (1675), maintained that godliness consists in uninterrupted communion with God through contemplation — the doctrine called " Quietism." This being thought to imperil the doctrine of good actions, the book was condemned (1687); and in spite of recanting, he was imprisoned for life, dying in confinement.

Möller, Peter Ludwig (měl'lěr). A Danish poet and art critic; born at Aalborg, April 18, 1814; died at Rouen, Dec. 7, 1865. He spent the last fifteen years of his life in Paris. He published ' Lyrical Poems ' (1840); ' Critical Sketches ' (1847); ' Pictures and Songs' (1847); ' Falling of the Leaves ' (1855, under the pseudonym of " Otto Sommer"); and the interesting work ' Modern Comedy in France and Denmark ' (1858).

Möller, Poul Martin. A Danish poet, novelist, and philosophical writer; born at Veile, March 21, 1794; died at Copenhagen, March 13, 1838. He was professor of philosophy at Christiania, Norway, 1828-31, and at Copenhagen in 1831. Of a number of fine lyrics, the best-known was his 'Joy over Denmark.' In fiction he wrote 'Eyvind the Skald,' 'A Danish Student's Adventure,' etc. His philosophical writings are contained in his 'Posthumous Works' (3d ed. 1856). He wrote also 'Notes Taken on a Journey to China,' 'Poetry and Prose,' selections, appeared in 1891.

Moltke, Count Hellmuth Karl Bernhard von (molt′kè). The famous Prussian field-marshal; born at Parchim, Mecklenburg-Schwerin, Oct. 26, 1800; died at Berlin, April 24, 1891. Having reorganized the Prussian army (1858-63), he won the Franco-Prussian war, 1870-71; became field-marshal, 1871; life member of the Prussian Upper House, 1872. He published: 'The Russo-Turkish Campaign, 1828-29' (2d ed. 1877); 'History of the Franco-Prussian War' (1891); 'Letters' (1892); 'Letters on Conditions in Turkey' (6th ed. 1893); etc. ('Works,' 1891-93. 'Military Works,' 1892-93).

Mommsen, Theodor (mom′zen). A famous German historian; born at Garding, Schleswig, Nov. 30, 1817. He was professor of law at Leipzig, 1848-50; of Roman law, at Zürich 1852-54, at Breslau 1854-58; of ancient history at Berlin, 1858; member of the Prussian House of Delegates. His great work is 'Roman History' (1854-56; 8th ed. 1888-89; vol. 5, 3d ed. 1886). He has written besides, 'Roman Chronology down to Cæsar' (2d ed. 1859); 'History of Roman Coinage' (1860); 'Roman Investigations' (1864-79); 'History of Roman Political Law' (3d ed. 1888). He was editor-in-chief of the great 'Body of Latin Inscriptions' (15 vols. and supplement, 1863-93). His historical work incorporates the results of vast learning in many fields. Died at Berlin, Nov. 1, 1903.

Monboddo, James Burnet, Lord (mon-bod′-do). A distinguished Scottish judge and philosophical writer; born at Monboddo, 1714; died at Edinburgh, May 26, 1799. He wrote: 'Dissertation on Language' (6 vols., 1773-92), and 'Ancient Metaphysics' (6 vols., 1779-99); both works upholding the theory that the human race was developed from simian stock.

Monier-Williams, Sir Monier. An English Orientalist; born at Bombay, India, 1819; died at Cannes, April 11, 1899. He was professor of Sanskrit at Haileybury College 1844-58, Cheltenham College 1858-60, Oxford 1860. His books include: Sanskrit grammars (1846 and 1860); English-Sanskrit (1851) and Sanskrit-English (1872) dictionaries; editions of Kālidāsa's Çakuntalā (1853) and other Sanskrit texts; 'Rudiments of Hindustani' (1858); 'Indian Epic Poetry' (1863); 'Indian Wisdom' (1875); Hinduism' (1877); 'Modern India and the Indians' (1878); Religious Thought and Life in India' (1883); 'The Holy Bible and the Sacred Books of the East' (1887); and 'Buddhism in its Connection with Brahminism and Hinduism, and in its Contrast with Christianity' —the Duff Lectures (1889).

Monkhouse, William Cosmo. An English art critic, born March 18, 1840; died, July 20, 1901. Among his works are: 'A Dream of Idleness' (1865), verse; 'A question of Honor' (1868), a novel; 'Masterpieces of English Art' (1868); 'Turner' (1879, in the 'Great Artists' series); 'Italian Pre-Raphaelites' (1887); etc.

Monnier, Marc (mo-nyä′). A French scholar and miscellaneous writer; born at Florence, Italy, Dec. 7, 1827; died at Geneva, April 18, 1885. He was professor of comparative literature at Geneva. Among his works were: 'Is Italy the Land of the Dead?' (1830), which made a sensation; 'Permitted Loves' (1861), a novel; 'Figaro's Ancestors' (1868), an essay in dramatic history; 'Plays for Marionettes' (1871); 'Geneva and its Poets' (1874); 'Popular Tales in Italy' (1880); 'History of Modern Literature' (2 vols., 1884-85); and in verse 'Lucioles' (1863), 'Poems' (1872).

Monod, Gabriel Jacques Jean (mo-nō′). A distinguished French historian; born at Ingouville, near Havre, May 7, 1844. Since 1880 he has been a lecturer at the Normal School, Paris. Chiefly noted for his researches in mediæval history, he has published: 'Germans and French' (1872); 'Jules Michelet' (1875); 'Critical Studies on the Sources of Merovingian History' (1872-85); the school text-books, 'Short Universal History' (1883), with M. G. Dhombre, and 'History of France to Louis XI.' (1884), with P. Boudois; 'Bibliography of the History of France' (1888), indispensable to the student; a translation of J. R. Green's 'History of the English People' (with his brother, A. M. Monod); articles in French and English reviews; 'Portraits and Souvenirs' (1897).

Monroe, Harriet. An American poet and biographer; born 1860. She has written 'Columbian Ode' (1893), composed for the opening celebration of the World's Columbian Exposition; 'John Wellborn Root' (1896), a study of his life and work; 'Historical Lutheranism.'

Monroe, James. The fifth President of the United States; born in Westmoreland County, Va., April 28, 1758; died in New York, July 4, 1831. He served in the Revolutionary War, was useful to his State and country in many conspicuous positions, and was President of the United States for two terms, 1817-25. The time of his administration is known as the "era of good feeling," from the lack of party divisions, the Federalist party having been absorbed in the Democratic. Among its chief events were the acquisition of Florida, 1819; the Missouri Compromise, 1820; and the statement of the "Monroe Doctrine," 1823. He published: 'Conduct of the Executive in the Foreign Affairs of the United States' (1798); 'Tour of Observation through the North-Eastern and North-Western States' (1818); 'The People the Sovereigns'; etc.

Monsell, John Samuel Bewley. An English divine and hymn-writer; born at St. Columb's, Derry, Ireland, March 2, 1811; died April 9, 1875, at Guildford, England, his final church living. Among his popular publications of devotional poetry were: 'Parish Musings' (7th ed. 1863); 'Hymns of Love and Praise' (2d ed. 1866); 'The Passing Bell, and Other Poems' (2d ed. 1869); 'Simon the Cyrenian, and Other Poems' (new ed. 1876); 'Spiritual Songs' (6th ed. 1887).

Montagu, Mrs. (Elizabeth Robinson). An English social leader and letter-writer; born at York, Oct. 2, 1720; died in London, Aug. 25, 1800. She married Edward Montagu, grandson of the fifth Earl of Sandwich. She gave every year a famous dinner to the London chimney-sweeps. Her residence in Portman Square was the meeting-place of the celebrated « Blue-Stocking Club » (origin of this famous term). Among her visitors and associates were Lord Lyttelton, Burke, Garrick, Sir Joshua Reynolds, Hannah More, Fanny Burney, etc. She wrote three of the dialogues in Lord Lyttelton's 'Dialogues of the Dead' (4th ed. 1765); 'The Genius of Shakespeare' (1769), an essay; 'Letters' (4 vols., 1809), her best-known work.

Montagu, Mary Wortley, Lady. A famous English letter-writer; born at Thoresby, Notts, May 26, 1689; died in England, Aug. 21, 1762. Her high birth (eldest daughter of an earl afterwards duke) gave her brilliant wit and literary gifts national fame. Accompanying her husband (grandson of the first Earl of Sandwich, and the richest commoner in England) to Constantinople, where he was minister to the Porte (1716–17), she assisted in introducing from the East into England the practice of inoculation. At one time the friend of Pope, she quarreled with him afterward. From 1739 to 1762, having left her husband, she was again abroad, settling in 1758 at Venice. Her 'Letters,' with a life, appear in her works (3d ed. 1887).

Montague, Charles Howard. An American journalist and novelist; born in Massachusetts, 1858; died 1889. He was one of the editors of the Boston Globe. He wrote: 'Romance of the Lilies' (1886); 'The Face of Rosenfel' (1888); 'Countess Muta'; etc.

Montaigne, Michel Eyquem de (môn-tän'). The famous French moral philosopher; born at Château Montaigne, Périgord, Feb. 28, 1533; died Sept. 13, 1592. Having originally studied law, he became a courtier in 1559; was attached to the person of Henry III., 1571; traveled in Germany, Switzerland, and Italy, 1580; was mayor of Bordeaux 1581–85. His masterpiece was his 'Essays' (1580; 5th ed. during his lifetime, with an added book, 1588; many editions since, the best being Le Cleve's, 4 vols., Paris, 1865; the best English translation, Hazlitt's). They are marked by a doubting or inquiring spirit, a tolerant and anti-persecuting temper, and a classic perfection of style.

Montalembert, Charles Forbes de Tryon, Comte de (môn-tä-loñ-bär'). A noted French statesman, historian, and orator; born in London, May 29, 1810; died in Paris, March 13, 1870. He championed the Catholic and clerical interests. He was a member of the Chamber of Peers in 1835; the National Assembly 1848; the Chamber of Deputies 1848–57. His principal writings were: 'Life of St. Elizabeth of Hungary' (1836); 'The Political Future of England' (1855); 'The Monks of the West' (1860–67; 5th ed. 1874–77), his main work; 'Letters to a College Friend' (1874); etc. ('Works,' 1861–68.)

Montalván, Juan Pérez de (mōn-täl-vän'). A Spanish dramatist and story-writer; born at Madrid, 1602; died June 25, 1638. He was a priest at Madrid, and notary of the Inquisition. His best play, 'Teruel's Lovers,' one of the most popular of Spanish dramas, holds the stage at the present day. Among his works were: 'Model Novels' (1624); 'Life and Purgatory of St. Patrick' (1627); 'El Para-Todos' (1632), a collection of diverting stories, anecdotes, and plays; etc. The best of his dramas can be seen in Vol. xiv. of Rivadeneyra's 'Library of Spanish Authors' (Madrid, 1881).

Montalvo, Garcia Ordoñez de (mōn-täl'vō). A Spanish romancer; lived at the end of the 15th century. He was governor of the city of Medina del Campo. He was the author of the earliest Spanish version of the famous 'Amadis of Gaul.'

Montchrestien, Antoine de (môn-krä-tyañ'). A French poet, dramatist, and political economist; born at Falaise, Normandy, about 1570; died near Domfront, October 1621. His life was adventurous and romantic. He wrote a work on political economy (he is said to have been the first to introduce the term into French); several poems, and seven tragedies possessing merit. ('Dramatic Works,' Rouen, last ed. 1607.)

Montégut, Émile (môn-tä-gü'). A French journalist and miscellaneous writer; born at Limoges, June 24, 1825. He became a chevalier of the Legion of Honor in 1865. He has published in book form 'The Netherlands: Impressions of Travel and Art' (1869); 'Poets and Artists of Italy' (1881); 'Literary Types and Æsthetic Fancies' (1882); 'Books and People of the Orient' (1885); 'Critical Miscellanies' (1887); 'A Critic's Reading Hours' (1891); etc.

Montemayor, Jorge de (mōn-tä-mä-yōr'). A celebrated Spanish romance-writer and poet; born at Montemayor, Portugal, about 1520; died at Turin, Feb. 26, 1561. When a young man he was in the army; afterward, being a skillful musician, was attached to the traveling chapel of the prince of Spain (later Philip II.), visiting several countries, particularly Italy and Flanders. His principal work was the famous 'Diana Enamorada' ('Diana in Love,' 1542; latest ed. Madrid, 1795), the most popular

Spanish pastoral romance since 'Amadis of Gaul.' It furnished the model for Sir Philip Sidney's 'Arcadia.' ('Works,' Antwerp, 1554; several editions since.)

Montépin, Xavier Aymon de (môn-tä-pan'). A French novelist and dramatist; born at Apremont, Haute-Saône, March 18, 1824; died at Paris, May 1, 1902. His works abound in sensational incidents and situations. He wrote nearly 100 novels, which have been translated into almost every language, the first being 'The Knights of Lansquenet' (1847); and, alone or with collaborators, about 30 plays.

Montesquieu, Charles de Secondat, Baron de (môn-tes-kyê'). A famous French historian and political philosopher; born near Bordeaux, Jan. 18, 1689; died in Paris, Feb. 10, 1755. He gave up high magistracies to travel widely in order to collect material for the renowned 'Spirit of Laws' (1748); his masterpiece, and one of the most influential works of modern times, establishing the historical method in political science. He wrote besides: 'Persian Letters' (1721), a satire on French society; 'The Temple of Cnidus' (1725), an allegory; 'Causes of Roman Greatness and Decline' (1734), a powerful work; 'Dialogue of Sylla Eucrates and Lysimachus' (1745); etc. ('Works,' best edition, Paris, 1879.)

Montgomery, Florence. An English novelist, daughter of Sir Alexander Montgomery; born 1843. She has written: 'A Very Simple Story' (1867); 'Thrown Together' (1872); 'Thwarted' (1874); 'Wild Mike and his Victim' (new ed. 1878); 'Seaforth' (1878); 'Transformed' (1886); 'The Fisherman's Daughter' (1888); 'Prejudged'; 'An Unshared Secret.'

Montgomery, James. An English poet, best known by his hymns and devotional poetry; born at Irvine, Ayrshire, Scotland, Nov. 4, 1771; died at Sheffield, England, April 30, 1854. He founded and edited the Sheffield Iris, 1794-1825. He published: 'The West Indies' (1809), an anti-slavery poem; 'The World before the Flood' (1813); 'Greenland' (1819); 'Prose by a Poet' (1830-31), lectures on poetry and English literature; 'Original Hymns' (1853), his chief work; etc.

Monti, Luigi (mon'tē). An American miscellaneous writer; born in Palermo, Sicily, in 1830. Being exiled, he came to Boston in 1850. Besides contributions to magazines, he has published 'The Adventures of an American Consul Abroad' (1878); and 'Leone,' a novel in the 'Round Robin' series. Longfellow introduced him in his 'Tales of a Wayside Inn' as the young Sicilian.

Monti, Vincenzo. A celebrated Italian poet; born near Ravenna, Feb. 19, 1754; died at Milan, Oct. 13, 1828. He was secretary of the Cisalpine Republic; professor of rhetoric at Pavia; Napoleon's Italian court historiographer; a member of the Italian Institute. Among his works were the tragedies 'Aristodemus' (1787), 'Caius Gracchus,' etc.; 'Basvilliana' (1793),

a grand poem in four cantos on the death of Hugo Basville; 'Mascheroniana,' a poem on the death of the mathematician Mascheroni; 'Italian Dictionary' (1817-26); etc.

Montiano y Luyando, Agustin de (mōn-ti-ä'nō ē lö-i-än'dō). A Spanish poet and dramatist; born at Valladolid, March 1, 1697; died at Madrid, Nov. 1, 1764. He was director of the Academy of History, Madrid. He wrote 'The Rape of Diana' and 'The Lyre of Orpheus,' poems; 'Virginia' (1750) and 'Athaulpho' (1753), tragedies aiming at a reform of the Spanish drama by bringing it into conformity with the rules of the French stage; and other works.

Montrésor, Frances Frederica. An English novelist, daughter of the late Admiral F. B. Montrésor, R. N. She resides in London. She is the author of several powerful stories of lowly life: the first, 'Into the Highways and Hedges' (1895), met with instant success; and 'False Coin or True' (1896), the story of a workhouse girl, and 'Worth While' (1896), have been favorably received.

Moodie, Susanna. A Canadian poet and prose-writer, sister of Agnes Strickland; born in Reydon Hall, Suffolk, England, Dec. 6, 1803; died in Toronto, Canada, April 8, 1885. She wrote: 'Enthusiasm and Other Poems' (1829), 'Roughing it in the Bush, or Life in Canada' (2 vols., 1852); 'Matrimonial Speculations' (1854); and 'The Monctons' (2 vols., 1856).

Moody, Dwight Lyman. A noted American evangelist; born at Northfield, Mass., Feb. 5, 1837; died there, Dec. 22, 1899. With Ira D. Sankey he held revival meetings in the United States and Great Britain. He founded a School for Christian Workers in Northfield, and a Bible Institute in Chicago. Among his works are: 'Arrows and Anecdotes' (1877); 'Secret Power' (1881); 'Bible Characters' (1888); etc.

Mooney, James. An American ethnologist; born at Richmond, Ind., 1861. From a boy of 12 his specialty has been Indian ethnology. He has written: 'Medical Mythology of Ireland' (1887); 'Funeral Customs of Ireland' (1888); 'Holiday Customs of Ireland' (1890); 'Myths of the Cherokees'; 'Siouan Tribes of the East'; 'The Messiah Religion and the Ghost-Dance'; 'Myths of the Kero Kee.'

Moore, Mrs. Bloomfield. See **Bloomfield-Moore.**

Moore, Charles Leonard. An American writer of verse; born at Philadelphia in 1854. A lawyer there, he was consul at San Antonio, Brazil, 1878-79. He has written: 'Poems, Antique and Modern' (1883); 'A Book of Day-Dreams' in verse; and 'Banquet of Palacios,' a comedy; 'The Red Branch Crests' (1904).

Moore, Clement Clarke. An American educational writer and poet; born in New York city, July 15, 1779; died in Newport, R. I., July 10, 1863. He was the compiler of the first

Hebrew and Greek lexicon published in America, and the author of a book of ‘ Poems’ (1844), in which is included his best-known poem, ‘A Visit from St. Nicholas’ (“ ’Twas the night before Christmas ”). He was the donor of the extensive grounds on which the General Theological Seminary, New York city, stands.

Moore, Edward. An English dramatist and fabulist; born at Abingdon, March 22, 1711–12, died in London, March 1, 1757. He was editor of The World (1753), to which Lyttelton, Pulteney, Chesterfield, Soame Jenyns, Horace Walpole, and others of distinction were contributors. He wrote ‘ Fables for the Female Sex’ (1744); ‘The Foundling’ (1748) and ‘ Gil Blas’ (1751), comedies; ‘The Gamester’ (1753, with Garrick, often reprinted), a highly successful tragedy; ‘Poems, Fables, and Plays’ (1756). (‘Dramatic Works,’ 1788.)

Moore, Frank Frankfort. An English novelist. Among his principal works may be mentioned ‘ Flying from a Shadow’ (1872); ‘The Mate of the Jessica’ (new ed. 1882); ‘Tre, Pol, and Pen’ (1887); ‘ Under Hatches’ (1888); The Opertas : ‘The Queen’s Room’; ‘ The Mayflower.’

Moore, George. An English novelist, poet, and essayist; born 1859. Among his novels are : ‘A Modern Lover’ (1883); ‘A Mummer’s Wife’ (6th ed. 1885); ‘A Drama in Muslin’ (1886); ‘ Confessions of a Young Man’ (1888); ‘Esther Waters’ (1894); etc. He has written also: in verse, ‘Flowers of Passion’ (1877), ‘Pagan Poems’ (1881); and the volumes of essays ‘ Impressions and Opinions’ (1891), ‘Modern Painting’ (1893).

Moore, George Henry. An American historical writer; born in Concord, N. H., April 20, 1823; died in New York city, May 5, 1892. He published: ‘The Treason of Charles Lee’ (1858) ; ‘ Employment of Negroes in the Revolutionary Army’ (1862); ‘ Notes on the History of Slavery in Massachusetts’ (1866); and ‘ Washington as an Angler’ ; ‘The Untilled Field’ (1903).

Moore, Horatio Newton. An American dramatist and novelist; born in New Jersey in 1814; died in Philadelphia, Aug. 26, 1859. His first work of importance, ‘ Orlando, or Woman’s Virtue,’ a tragedy, was published at 19; ‘ The Regicide,’ a five-act drama, at 20. His short novel ‘ Mary Morris’ (1840) was very popular. The ‘ Lives of Marion and Wayne’ was issued in 1854.

Moore, Thomas. A famous Irish poet and song-writer ; born at Dublin, May 28, 1779 ; died near Devizes, Feb. 25, 1852. He was the pet of London society; received an appointment in the civil service in the Bermudas, 1803–4; traveled in the United States, 1803–4; married an actress, 1811. His principal works were a translation of the ‘ Odes of Anacreon’ (1800); ‘ Odes and Epistles’ (1806); ‘ Irish Melodies’ (10 parts, 1807–34); ‘ The Twopenny Post Bag’ (1813); ‘ Lalla Rookh’ (1817); ‘ Loves of the Angels’ (1823); etc. He wrote also : ‘ The Epicurean’ (1827), a romance ; ‘ Lives’ of Sheridan

(1825) and Byron (1830); ‘ History of Ireland’ (1827–35); etc.

Moratin, Leandro Fernandez de (mō-rä-tēn′). A noted Spanish dramatist and poet, son of Nicolas F.; born at Madrid, March 10, 1760; died at Paris, June 21, 1828. He has been called “ the Spanish Molière.” Among his plays were : ‘ The Old Man and the Young Girl’ (1790), his best drama; ‘ The New Comedy’ (1792); ‘ The Baron’ (1803); ‘ The Female Hypocrite’ (1804); ‘ The Girl’s Yes’ (1806); etc. He wrote also ‘ Origins of the Spanish Stage’; lyrical poems; etc. His works can be seen in Vol. ii. of ‘ Library of Spanish Authors.’

Moratin, Nicolas Fernandez de. A Spanish poet; born at Madrid, July 20, 1737; died there, May 11, 1780. He was professor of poetry in the Imperial College, Madrid. His best work, and one of the best epics in the language, was ‘ The Ships of Cortés Destroyed’ (1785). He wrote besides ‘ Diana’ (1763), a fine didactic poem; and many of his short poems were excellent. In the attempt to substitute for the usual religious dramas others more agreeable to the taste of the times, he produced the comedy ‘ The Belle’ (1762), and the tragedies ‘ Lucrecia,’ ‘ Hormesinda’ (1770), ‘ Guzman the Good’ (1777), etc. His works can be seen in Vol. ii. of Rivadeneyra’s ‘ Library of Spanish Authors.’

More, Hannah. An English religious writer; born at Stapleton, Gloucestershire, Feb. 2, 1745; died at Clifton, Sept. 7, 1833. She abandoned a successful worldly literary career at its height to devote her pen to the furtherance of education and religion. Her best-known works were the celebrated tract ‘ The Shepherd of Salisbury Plain’ and the novel ‘Cœlebs in Search of ‘a Wife’ (1809). She wrote also : ‘ Sacred Dramas’ (1782); ‘ Religion of the Fashionable World’ (1791); ‘ Practical Piety’ (1811); etc. Garrick produced her tragedies ‘ Percy’ (1778) and ‘ The Fatal Falsehood’ (1779). (‘Works,’ 11 vols., 1830.)

More, Paul Elmer. An American essayist; born in Missouri, 1864. He is instructor in Sanskrit and Greek at Bryn Mawr College. He has written : ‘ The Great Refusal: Being Letters of a Dreamer in Gotham’; ‘Shelburne Essays.’

More, Thomas, Sir. An eminent English statesman and miscellaneous writer; born in London, Feb. 7, 1478; executed on Tower Hill, July 6, 1535. A great lawyer, he became Lord Chancellor, and was put to death by Henry VIII. for refusing to take the oath renouncing the Pope and abjuring Catherine’s rights. His greatest literary work was the famous ‘ Utopia’ (1516), an account of an imaginary ideal commonwealth supposed to exist on a distant island of the Atlantic. He wrote besides : ‘ Life of John Picus, Earl of Mirandola’ (1510); ‘ History of Richard III.’ (1513); etc. (‘Works,’ Latin and English, Louvain, 1556–57.)

Moréas, Jean (mō-rä-ä′). A French poet, novelist, and romance-writer; born at Athens,

April 15, 1856. He is one of the leaders of the school called the « Decadents.» He has written in verse ' The Quicksands ' (1884), ' Cantilenas ' (1886), ' Iconostasis '; the novel ' The Young Ladies ' (1887); the romances ' The Thin Woman,' ' Tea at Miranda's ' (1887), etc.

Morelli, Giovanni (mō-rel'ē). A distinguished Italian art critic; born in Verona, Feb. 25, 1816; died in Milan, Feb. 28, 1891. He traveled widely throughout Europe, studying the great collections of paintings. His fame rests principally upon the ' Critical Art Studies in Italian Painting ' (1890-93), devoted to the Borghese and Doria Pamfili galleries in Rome, the Munich and Dresden galleries, and that of Berlin. He bequeathed his valuable collection of paintings to his native city. In 1895 a monument was erected to his memory in Milan.

Moreto y Cabaña, Agustin (mō-rā'tō ē kä-bä'nyä). A noted Spanish dramatist; born at Madrid about 1618; died at Toledo, Oct. 28, 1669. He introduced into Spain the comedy of character and manners. ' Disdain for Disdain,' his chief work, was one of the four classical masterpieces of the old Spanish stage; ' The Handsome Don Diego ' contained excellent character-drawing; ' Snares Ahead ' (Trampa Adelante) won high success; and ' The Valiant Justiciary ' and ' The Power of Blood ' were good specimens of his more earnest writing.

Morford, Henry. An American novelist and dramatist; born in New Monmouth, N. J., 1823; died in New York city, 1881. Among his plays are ' The Merchant's Honor ' and ' The Bells of Shandon.' Two volumes of poems were published by him : ' Rhymes of Twenty Years ' (1859); and ' Rhymes of an Editor ' (1873). Among his novels are ' Shoulder Straps ' (1863), ' The Coward ' (1864), ' Utterly Wrecked ' (1866), and ' Only a Commoner ' (1871).

Morgan, Lady (Sydney Owenson). An Irish novelist and miscellaneous writer; born in Dublin, about 1783; died in London, April 14, 1859. The daughter of an Irish actor, she became a leader in London Society. Among her works were the novels ' The Wild Irish Girl ' (1806), her most successful book; ' O'Donnel ' (1814) ; ' Florence Macarthy ' (1816) ; ' The O'Briens and the O'Flahertys ' (1827) ; etc. She wrote also : ' France under the Bourbons ' (1817), and its companion, ' Italy ' (1821), two books which excited furious opposition ; ' Woman and her Master ' (1840) ; ' Autobiography ' (1858) ; songs, comic operas, biographies, travels, etc. See her ' Memoirs,' edited by Hepworth Dixon (2 vols., 1862).

Morgan, Lewis Henry. An American ethnologist and archæologist of great repute; born near Aurora, N. Y., Nov. 21, 1818; died at Rochester, N. Y. (where he was a lawyer), Dec. 17, 1881. Among his important contributions to the science of ethnology is ' Systems of Consanguinity and Affinity of the Human Family,' published by the Smithsonian Institution in 1869, and which remains the standard work on the subject. His ' League of the Iroquois,' published in 1851, is the highest authority on the tribal organization of the Six Nations. His other works include : ' The American Beaver and his Works '; ' Ancient Society ' (1887); ' Horses and Horse Life of the American Aborigines '; etc.

Morier, James Justinian (mō'ri-ėr). An English novelist and writer of travels; born 1780; died at Brighton, March 19, 1849. He was Lord Elgin's secretary during his embassy to Constantinople, and secretary of legation at the court of Persia (1811-15). He wrote two successful books describing travels in Brazil, Asia, Asia Minor, and Turkey. He was best known, however, by his novels depicting Persian life : ' Adventures of Hajji-Baba ' (1824-28; latest ed. 1895); ' Zohrab the Hostage ' (1832); ' Ayesha, the Maid of Kars ' (1834); ' Mirza ' (1841).

Mörike, Eduard (mė'rē-ke). A noted German poet (the last and best of the « Suabian school ») and novelist; born at Ludwigsburg, Würtemberg, Sept. 8, 1804; died at Stuttgart, June 4, 1875. He was a clergyman and teacher, and the greatest German lyrist after Goethe. His best verse can be seen in ' Poems ' (11th ed. 1895), and ' Idylls from the Lake of Constance ' (1846). Of his prose writings, famous are : ' Nolten the Painter ' (3d ed. 1892) and ' Mozart on the Way to Prague ' (5th ed. 1892). He also made fine translations of Anacreon and Theocritus. (' Works,' Stuttgart, 1890.)

Morison, James Augustus Cotter. An English biographer and essayist; born in London, 1832; died Feb. 26, 1888. He was a Positivist in philosophy, and one of the founders of the Fortnightly Review. He wrote ' Life and Times of St. Bernard ' (3d ed. 1877); lives of Gibbon, Macaulay, and Madame de Maintenon ; ' The Service of Man : An Essay toward the Religion of the Future ' (2d ed. 1887); etc.

Morley, Henry. An English scholar and physician; born in London, Sept. 15, 1822; died May 14, 1894. He practiced medicine 1844-48; edited the Examiner; was professor of English language and literature at University College 1865-89, and Queen's College 1878-89, London; principal of University Hall 1882-89. He wrote : ' A Defense of Ignorance ' (1851); several biographies; ' Memoirs of Bartholomew Fair ' (1857); ' First Sketch of English Literature ' (1873); ' English Literature in the Reign of Victoria ' (1881); ' English Writers ' (8 vols., 1887-93); etc.; besides editing many important works, as Boswell's ' Life of Johnson ' (5 vols., 1886); Cassell's ' National Library,' ' Carisbrook Library,' etc.

Morley, John. A distinguished English statesman, editor, biographer, essayist, and critic; born at Blackburn, Lancashire, Dec. 24, 1838. He was admitted to the bar in 1873; edited successively the Literary Gazette, the Fortnightly Review, the Pall Mall Gazette, and Macmillan's Magazine ; became Member of

Parliament 1883 ; chief secretary for Ireland 1886, 1892. He has written lives of Voltaire (1872), Rousseau (1874), Burke (1879), Cobden (1881), Emerson (1884), Sir Robert Walpole (1889); and edited the valuable series known as ' English Men of Letters ' ; ' Life of Gladstone ' (1903).

Morley, Margaret Warner. An American writer of popular scientific, biological, and botanical works. She has written : ' The Song of Life ' (1891); ' Life and Love ' (1895); ' A Few Familiar Flowers ' (1897); ' Flowers and their Friends ' (1897); ' The Renewal of Life '; ' Grasshopper Land.'

Morris, George Pope. An American journalist and song-writer; born in Philadelphia, Oct. 10, 1802; died in New York city, July 6, 1864. In 1846, with N. P. Willis, he founded the Home Journal. He became famous as a writer of songs, among which is included ' Woodman, Spare that Tree.' His books are : ' Briercliff,' a drama ; ' The Little Frenchman '; and ' Poems.'

Morris, George Sylvester. An American prose-writer; born in Norwich, Vt., 1840; died 1889. He has published : ' British Thought and Thinkers ' (1880); ' Kant's Critique of Pure Reason : A Critical Exposition ' (1882); and ' Hegel's Philosophy of the State and of History : An Exposition ' (1887).

Morris, Gouverneur. A famous American statesman; born at Morrisania, N. Y., Jan. 31, 1752; died there, Nov. 6, 1816. He was member of the Continental Congress, 1777–80 ; of the committee that drafted the Constitution, 1787; minister to France, 1792–94; United States Senator from New York, 1800–3. He was noted for ability both in political thought and political action. Specimens of his writing can be seen in Jared Sparks's ' Memoirs of Gouverneur Morris ' (3 vols., 1832), Annie Cary Morris's ' Diary and Letters of Gouverneur Morris ' (2 vols., 1889), etc.

Morris, Harrison Smith. An American poet; born in Philadelphia, Oct. 4, 1856. With John A. Henry he wrote ' A Duet in Lyrics ' (1883). He is author of ' Madonna and Other Poems,' and has edited many editions of standard works.

Morris, Lewis, Sir. An English poet; born at Carmarthen, 1833. He practiced law till 1881 ; became secretary of University College, Wales, in 1877; is now justice of the peace for Carmarthenshire. He has written : ' Songs of Two Worlds ' (three series, respectively in 1871, 1874, and 1875); ' The Epic of Hades ' (1876), his best-known work ; ' Gwen ' (1879), a dramatic monologue ; ' The Ode of Life ' (1880): ' A Vision of Saints ' (1890). Died Nov. 12, 1907.

Morris, William. A celebrated English poet, and writer on socialism; born near London, 1834; died at Hammersmith, Oct. 3, 1896. Having studied painting, he became a designer and manufacturer of artistic household furniture, wall paper, stained glass, etc. (1863). In later life he took great interest in social questions, was a leader in the Socialist League,

and contributed to the Commonweal. His chief poetical work was ' The Story of Sigurd ' (1876). He wrote besides in verse : ' Defence of Guenevere, and Other Poems ' (1858); ' Life and Death of Jason ' (1867); ' The Earthly Paradise ' (1868–70); ' Love Is Enough ' (1872); ' Poems by the Way ' (1892); etc. Translations of the Æneid (1876), the Odyssey (1887), and ' Beowulf ' (1895); and ' The House of the Wolfings ' (1889), ' The Roots of the Mountains ' (1890), etc., represent his prose work. He also published ' Hopes and Fears for Art ' (1882), five lectures; ' Signs of Change ' (1888), a socialistic book ; and others. ✱

Morrison, Arthur. An English writer of fiction; born 1863. During his employment and residence for some years as secretary of a Charity Trust in the East End of London, he made a study of life in the slums, which he has reproduced in his powerful ' Tales of Mean Streets ' (1895), and ' The Child of the Jago ' (1896). A volume of detective stories, entitled ' Martin Hewitt, Investigator,' appeared in 1896.

Morse, Mrs. Charlotte Dunning (Wood). An American novelist, writing under the name " Charlotte Dunning "; born in New York State, 1858. She has written : ' Upon a Cast,' a society novel; ' A Step Aside '; ' Cabin and Gondola.'

Morse, Edward Sylvester. A distinguished American biologist; born at Portland, Me., 1838. He founded the Peabody Academy of Sciences, Salem, Mass., being its curator and president since 1881; was professor at Bowdoin College, 1871–74; professor at the Imperial University, Tokio, Japan, 1877; president of the American Association for the Advancement of Science, 1885–87. Besides numerous scientific and popular papers, he has published : ' First Book in Zoölogy ' (new ed. 1880); ' Japanese Homes ' (1885); ' Mars and Its Mystery ' (1906).

Morse, John Torrey. An American writer of biography; born in Boston, Jan. 9, 1840, and resides in that city as a lawyer. He is editor of the ' American Statesmen Series,' and has published biographies of Alexander Hamilton (2 vols., his strongest work), John and J. Q. Adams, Jefferson, Lincoln, Franklin, and Dr. Holmes; also ' Banks and Banking '; ' Arbitration and Award '; and ' Famous Trials.' His literary work is marked by virile energy, strong grasp, and luminous common-sense.

Morse, Mrs. Lucy (Gibbons). An American novelist; born in New York State, 1839. Her home is in New York. She has written ' Rachel Stanwood '; ' The Chezzles : A Story of Young People ' (1888).

Morse, Samuel Finley Breese. The famous inventor of the electro-magnetic telegraph, also an artist and a publicist; born at Charlestown, Mass., April 27, 1791; died at New York, April 2, 1872. He was professor of natural history at Yale College; the first president of the National Academy of Design, New York (1826–42); and one of the first professors of the University of the City of New York (professor of the fine arts). He wrote 'Foreign Conspiracies against the Liberties of the United States' (1835); 'Our Liberties Defended,' a memoir of Lucretia Maria Davidson (1829); etc.

Morton, John Maddison. An English playwright; born at Pangbourne, Jan. 3, 1811; died Dec. 19, 1891. He wrote over 100 farces, many of great popularity; including the well-known 'Box and Cox,' adapted from the French.

Morton, Sarah Wentworth (Apthorp). An American verse-writer; born in Braintree, Mass., Aug. 29, 1759; died in Quincy, Mass., May 14, 1846. She was the writer of 'Ouabi,' an Indian tale in four cantos (1790), and 'My Mind and its Thoughts' (1823).

Morton, Thomas. An English dramatist; born in the county of Durham, 1764; died in London, March 28, 1838. He abandoned the law for play-writing. Among his dramas, some of which are still favorites, were: 'Children in the Wood' (1793); 'The Way to Get Married' (1796); 'Cure for the Heart Ache' (1797); 'Speed the Plough' (1798), introducing the original Mrs. Grundy, who is heard of but never seen; 'The Blind Girl' (1801); 'Town and Country' (1807); 'School for Grown Children' (1827); etc.

Mosby, John Singleton. A famous Confederate cavalry leader; born in Powhatan County, Va., 1833. After the Civil War he practiced law at Warrenton, Va.; was United States consul at Hong-Kong, 1875–85; afterward practiced law at San Francisco. He wrote 'War Reminiscences' (1887).

Moschus (mos'kus). A celebrated Greek bucolic poet; born at Syracuse; lived about 200 B.C. His extant works are generally published with those of Theocritus and Bion, the latter being his friend and very likely his teacher. They consist of four complete idyls, three small fragments, and an epigram; and are mostly joyous and sportive in character. They can be found in Ahrens's 'Remains of the Bucolic Greek Poets' (1861); English translations by Fawkes, in Chalmers's 'English Poets.'

Mosen, Julius (mō'zen). A German poet, dramatist, and novelist; born at Marieney, Saxony, July 8, 1803; died at Oldenburg, Oct. 10, 1867. He gave up the practice of law at Dresden to become official dramatist of the court theatre at Oldenburg. His chief work was the epic 'Ahasuerus' (1838), based on the legend of the Wandering Jew. He published 'Poems' (1836), some of which became popular songs; the historical dramas 'The Brides of Florence' (1842), 'The Prince's Son' (1858), 'Emperor Otto III.' (1842), 'Henry the Fowler' (1836), etc.; and the novels 'The Blue Flower' (1837), 'Homesickness' (1837), etc. ('Works,' new ed., 6 vols., Leipzig, 1880.)

Mosenthal, Salomon Hermann von (mō'-zen-täl). A German dramatist; born at Cassel, Jan. 14, 1821; died at Vienna, Feb. 17, 1877. He obtained a position in the Austrian government in 1850. His best-known works were

'Deborah' (1850: the original of 'Leah the Forsaken'), and 'Heliotrope Manor' (1857). He wrote also 'The German Actors' (1863); 'The Mayor of Altenbüren' (1868); 'Maryna' (1871); the tragedies 'Düweke' (1860), 'Pietra' (1865); etc. ('Works,' 6 vols., Stuttgart, 1878.)

Möser, Albert (mē'zer). A German poet; born at Göttingen, May 7, 1835. His life has been that of a teacher. He has written 'Poems' (1865; new ed. 1890); 'Night and Stars' (1872); 'Idylls' (1875); 'From the Attic' (1893); 'Pol de Mont' (1893). Died Feb. 27, 1900.

Moser, Gustav von (mō'zer). A prolific German comedy writer; born at Spandau, May 11, 1825. He resigned from the army in 1856 to devote himself to literature. Among his pieces are: 'What do You Think about Russia?'; 'A Modern Barbarian'; 'Ultimo'; 'The Hypochrondriac'; 'The Temptress'; 'The New Governess.' ('Works,' 18 vols., Berlin, 1873–88). D. 1903.

Möser, Justus (mē'zär). A noted German publicist and historian; born at Osnabrück, Dec. 14, 1720; died there, Jan. 8, 1794. He held very important government posts. Modern German historiography may be said to date from him; his theory being that history should describe the development of peoples, laws, customs, and habits, instead of being a mere chronicle of dynasties and wars. His most celebrated works were 'History of Osnabrück' (3d ed. 1819); and 'Patriotic Reveries' (latest ed. 1871), a work of national importance. ('Works,' 10 vols., Berlin, 1842–44.)

Mosheim, Johann Lorenz von (mōs'hīm). A distinguished German church historian and theologian; born at Lubeck, Oct. 9, 1694; died at Göttingen, Sept. 9, 1755. He was the first to treat ecclesiastical history as a sequence of secular causes and effects. He became professor of history and chancellor of the university at Göttingen in 1747. His great work was his 'Institutes of Ecclesiastical History' (new ed. 1755). He published also other historical writings, and was a noted pulpit orator. His published sermons are contained in 'Sacred Discourses' (4th ed., 3 vols., Hamburg, 1765).

Mota-Padilla, Matias de la (mō'tä-pä-dēl'-yä). A Mexican historian; born at Guadalajara, Oct. 6, 1688; died 1766. He was a lawyer, and during the latter part of his life a priest. He wrote among other things 'History of the Conquest of New Galicia' (1870–71), a work of much importance.

Motherwell, William. A Scottish poet and antiquary; born at Glasgow, Oct. 13, 1797; died there, Nov. 1, 1835. He was a journalist and under-secretary of the sheriff of Paisley. His principal works were: 'Minstrelsy, Ancient and Modern' (1827), and 'Poems, Narrative and Lyrical' (1832; latest ed. 1881).

Motley, John Lothrop. A distinguished American historian and diplomatist; born at Dorchester, Mass., April 15, 1814; died in Dorsetshire, England, May 29, 1877. Originally a lawyer, he wrote two novels, became interested in historical research, chose Dutch history for his field, and spent years in Holland working up the original sources. The chief fruits were: 'Rise of the Dutch Republic' (3 vols., 1856); 'History of the United Netherlands' (4 vols., 1860–68); 'Life of John of Barneveld' (1874). He was United States minister to Austria 1861–67, and to Great Britain 1869–70. After 1868 he resided in England.

Moulton, Louise (Chandler). An American poet and prose-writer; born in Pomfret, Conn., April 10, 1835. She is one of the prominent literary women of Boston, and the author of many books, in which are included: 'This, That, and the Other' (1854), stories, essays, and poems; 'Bedtime Stories for Children' (1873); 'Swallow-Flights, and Other Poems' (1878); 'Ourselves and Our Neighbors' (1887); 'Some Women's Hearts' (1888); and 'In the Garden of Dreams, Lyrics, and Sonnets'. D. 1908.

Moultrie, John. An English poet; born in London, Dec. 30, 1799; died at Rugby, Dec. 26, 1874. He was rector of Rugby in 1828. He published: 'My Brother's Grave and Other Poems' (4th ed. 1854); 'The Dream of Life and Other Poems' (last ed. 1854); a volume of 'Sermons' (1852); etc.

Mountcastle, Clara H. ["Caris Sima."] A Canadian poet and story-writer; born at Clinton, Ont. Nov. 26, 1837. She taught drawing and painting 1871–84. She has written: 'The Mission of Love, and Other Poems' (1882); 'Lost, and Other Poems' (1882), 'A Mystery' (1886), verse; and the novel 'Crow's Hollow.'

Mountford, William. An American miscellaneous prose-writer; born in Kidderminster, England, May 31, 1816; came to the United States in 1849; died in Boston, April 20, 1885. Among his publications are: 'Martyria, a Legend' (1846); 'Euthanasy; or Happy Talks toward the End of Life' (1850); 'Beauties of Channing'; 'Miracles, Past and Present' (1870).

Mowatt, Mrs. See **Ritchie.**

Mudford, William. An English journalist and miscellaneous writer; born in London, Jan. 8, 1782; died there, March 10, 1848. He was for many years editor of the London Courier, afterward of the Kentish Observer. Among his works were 'Nubilia in Search of a Husband' (4th ed. 1809); 'The Contemplatist' (1811), essays on morals and literature; 'Life and Adventures of Paul Plaintive' (1811), a novel; 'The Premier' (1831), a novel; 'Tales and Trifles from Blackwood's' (1849), containing the well-known story 'The Iron Shroud,' his best work; etc.

Mügge, Theodor (müg'gĕ). A German novelist and writer of travels; born at Berlin, Nov. 8, 1806; died there, Feb. 18, 1861. For some years he was a journalist. Among his best-known works were the novels 'The Cavalier' (1835), 'Toussaint' (1840), 'Life and Love in Norway' (1858), 'The Prophet' (1860),

etc.; and the volumes of travel 'Sketches from the North' (1844), 'Northern Picture-Book' (3d ed. 1862), etc. (Complete novels, 33 vols., Berlin, 1862–67).

Mühlbach, Luise (mül'bäch), pseudonym of Madame Klara Müller Mundt. A German novelist, wife of Theodor Mundt; born at Neubrandenburg, Jan. 2, 1814; died at Berlin, Sept. 26, 1873. She wrote a number of popular historical novels, including 'Queen Hortense' (5th ed. 1861); 'Emperor Joseph II. and his Court' (9th ed. 1866); 'Marie Antoinette and her Son' (1867); 'Emperor Alexander and his Court' (1868); 'Mohammed Ali and his House' (1871); 'Frederick the Great and his Court' (8th ed. 1882). She was a prolific writer.

Muhlenberg, William Augustus. An American Episcopal clergyman and miscellaneous writer; born in Philadelphia, Sept. 16, 1796; died in New York, April 8, 1877. From 1846 to 1877 he was rector of the Church of the Holy Communion, New York. His time was largely given to educational work and the amelioration of the condition of the poor. Among his writings are: 'St. Johnland: Ideal and Actual' (1867); 'Christ and the Bible' (1869); and 'I Would Not Live Alway,' the story of the hymn (1871).

Muir, John. An American naturalist and explorer; born at Dunbar, Scotland, 1838. He discovered Glacier Bay and the Muir Glacier in Alaska in 1879. Besides contributing a number of illustrated papers to magazines, and editing Picturesque California, he has published 'The Mountains of California' (1894), a valuable and charming work; 'Our National Parks.'

Muir, Sir William. A Scottish Orientalist, brother of John; born at Glasgow, 1819. Entering the Bengal civil service at 18, he was lieutenant-governor of the Northwest Provinces, 1868–74; minister of finance for India, 1874–76; principal of the University of Edinburgh, 1885. He has written: 'Life of Mahomet and History of Islam' (1883); 'The Caliphate: Its Rise, Decline, and Fall' (2d ed. 1892); 'The Mohammedan Controversy' (1897).

Mulford, Elisha. An American Episcopal clergyman and philosophical writer; born at Montrose, Pa., Nov. 19, 1833; died at Cambridge, Mass., Dec. 9, 1885. He wrote 'The Nation' (new ed. 1876) and 'The Republic of God' (1881), two works of great elevation of thought and expression.

Mulford, Prentice. An American journalist and miscellaneous writer; born on Long Island in 1834; died in 1891. He was settled in New York, and afterwards in San Francisco. He wrote: 'The Swamp Angel'; 'Life by Land and Sea'; 'Your Forces, and How to Use Them' (2 vols., 1888).

Mulhall, Michael G. A British statistician; born at Dublin, Sept. 29, 1836; died in London, Dec. 13, 1900. Having removed to South America, he founded the Buenos Ayres Standard (1861), the first English daily paper printed in

South America. He published: 'Handbook of the River Plata' (5th ed. 1885), translated into Spanish; 'Progress of the World' (1880); 'Dictionary of Statistics' (new ed. 1892); etc. His wife, Mrs. Marion Mulhall, has published 'Between the Amazon and the Andes' (1883).

Mullany, Patrick Francis. ["Brother Azarias."] An Irish-American priest, educator, and literary critic; born in Killemain, Ireland, June 29, 1847; emigrated to the United States in childhood; died at Plattsburg, N. Y., Aug. 20, 1893. He joined the order of the Brothers of the Christian Schools. He became in 1866 professor of mathematics and English literature at Rock Hill College, Ellicott City, Md., and in 1878 president, remaining such until 1889, after which he lived in New York and its neighborhood until his death. As a lecturer on literary, philosophic, and pedagogic themes, he was eloquent and influential; his papers on Dante and Aristotle were read at the Concord School of Philosophy, and he was a frequent speaker in different parts of the country. He was also a steady contributor to the periodicals; his essays, afterwards gathered into book form, embodying the results of wise thought and ripe culture, and possessing a fine literary quality. His critical attitude was that of the Christian scholar making a constant appeal to the ideals of the great past, and judging the present thereby. His printed works are: 'The Development of English Literature'; 'Old English Period'; 'Philosophy of Literature'; 'Psychological Aspects of Education'; 'Address on Thinking'; 'Aristotle and the Christian Church'; 'Culture of the Spiritual Sense'; 'Phases of Thought and Criticism.'

Müller, Friedrich (mül'ler). [Called Painter Müller.] A German painter, engraver, poet, and dramatist; born at Kreuznach, Jan. 13, 1749; died at Rome, April 23, 1825. As a poet he belonged to the "storm and stress" school. Among his works may be mentioned: 'Bacchido and Milo' (1775); 'The Satyr Mopsus' (1775); 'Adam's First Awaking and First Happy Nights' (1778); the dramas 'Genoveva' (1808); 'Life of Faust' (latest ed. 1881); the opera 'Niobe' (1778); etc. ('Works,' new ed., Heidelberg, 1825.)

Müller, Friedrich Maximilian. [Universally known in England and America as "Max Müller."] A celebrated German-English Sanskrit scholar and comparative philologist, son of Wilhelm Müller the poet; born at Dessau, Dec. 6, 1823; died at Oxford, Oct. 28, 1900. Removing to England (1846), he became professor of modern languages and literature (1854), and professor of comparative philology (1868-75), at Oxford. He has edited and translated the 'Hitopadeça' (1844), and edited the 'Rig-Veda' (6 vols., 1849-74), etc. He has written: 'History of Ancient Sanskrit Literature' (2d ed. 1860); 'Science of Language' (latest ed. 1891) ; 'Chips from a German Workshop' (latest ed. 1895); 'Science of Religion' (1870) ; 'Essays on Language, Mythology, and Religion' (1881); 'Science

of Thought' (1887) ; the novel 'German Love': and was the editor of the series 'Sacred Books of the East,' now being issued by the Clarendon Press at Oxford, of which some sixty volumes are now ready, and which constitutes the most important translated collection of Oriental literature.

Müller, Johannes von. A celebrated Swiss historian; born at Schaffhausen, Jan. 3, 1752 ; died at Cassel, Prussia, May 29, 1809. He held a number of positions in the service of Mainz, Austria, and Prussia, and when he died was director-general of education in the kingdom of Westphalia. His principal works were : 'History of the Swiss' (new ed., 5 vols., 1786-1808), and '24 Books of Universal History' (3 vols., 1811; new ed. 1852).

Müller, Karl. A German romance-writer; born at Stuttgart, Feb. 8, 1819 ; died there, Nov. 28, 1889. He was editor of several periodicals. He wrote: 'Life's Changes, by Franz von Elling' (1854); 'New Mysteries of Paris' (1863); 'New Mysteries of London' (1865-67); 'The White Woman' (1868-73); 'The Turks before Vienna' (1870); 'At the Court of the Northern Semiramis' (1873); etc. Among his pseudonyms were "Otfried Mylius," "Rod. Nellenburg," etc.

Müller, Karl Otfried. A distinguished German Hellenist and archæologist ; born at Brieg, Aug. 28, 1797 ; died at Athens, Aug. 1, 1840. He was professor of archæology at Göttingen in 1819. His principal works were: 'History of Hellenic Races and States' (2d ed. 1844); 'The Etruscans' (2d ed. 1877-78); 'Introduction to a Scientific Mythology' (1825); 'Handbook of the Archæology of Art' (latest ed. 1878); 'Monuments of Ancient Art' (3d ed. 1876-81); 'History of Greek Literature' (4th ed. 1882-84); maps of ancient Greece; etc.

Müller, Otto. A German novelist; born at Schotten, Hesse, June 1, 1816; died at Stuttgart, Aug. 7, 1894. He edited several periodicals. Among his works were the popular 'Burgher' (3d ed. 1870); 'Charlotte Ackermann' (1854), which he dramatized; 'The Mayor of Frankfort' (3d ed. 1878); 'The Convent Court' (2d ed. 1862); 'Roderich' (2d ed. 1862); 'Tales' (2d ed. 1870); etc.

Müller, Wilhelm. A German lyric poet; born at Dessau, Oct. 7, 1794; died there, Sept. 30, 1827. His life was that of a teacher and a librarian. He wrote in verse 'Poems from the Posthumous Papers of a Traveling Bugler' (1821-24; 2d ed. 1826), 'Songs of the Greeks' (new ed. 1844), 'Romaic National Songs' (1825), 'Lyrical Journeys and Epigrammatic Walks' (1827), etc.; the novel 'The Thirteenth' (1827); the critical essay 'Introduction to Homer' (2d ed. 1836); the book of travel 'Rome, and Rome's Men and Women' (1820); etc. A number of his songs became very popular; some were set to music by Schubert and others. (Miscellaneous writings, with biography, 5 vols., Leipzig, 1830. Poetical works, new ed. Berlin, 1874.)

Müller, Wilhelm. A German historian; born at Giengen, Würtemberg, Dec. 2, 1820; died near Ravensburg, Feb. 7, 1892. He was professor in the gymnasium at Tübingen in 1863. He wrote: 'Guide for Instruction in History' (14th ed. 1890); 'Political History of the Present' (annual, 1867–92); 'Illustrated History of the Franco-Prussian War' (1873); 'Historical Women' (2d ed. 1882); 'Emperor William' (4th ed. 1880); 'Count Moltke' (3d ed. 1889); 'Prince Bismarck' (3d ed. 1890); 'Emperor Frederick' (1888); 'Political History of the Most Recent Times, 1876–90' (4th ed. 1890); etc.

Müller, Wolfgang, called **von Königswinter** (fon ke'nigs-vin-ter). A German lyric and epic poet and novelist; born at Königswinter, Prussia, March 15, 1816; died at Neuenahr, Prussia, June 29, 1873. Originally a physician (1842), he was Member of the Frankfort Parliament in 1848, but abandoned both medicine and politics for literature. Among his works were: 'Poems' (3d ed. 1868); 'Legends of the Rhine in Ballad Form' (4th ed. 1873); 'The May Queen' (1852), a charming village tale in verse; 'Prince Minnewin' (2d ed. 1856); 'Heinrich Heine's Journey to Hell' (1856), published anonymously; 'Aschenbrödel' (Cinderella : 1863), an epic poem; the comedy 'She has Uncovered her Heart'; and in the department of art history 'Düsseldorf Artists' (1854) and 'Munich Sketch Book' (1856). A selection of many of his best poems, entitled 'Verses of a Rhine Poet,' appeared in 6 vols., Leipzig, 1871–76.

Mulock, Dinah Maria. See **Craik, Mrs.**

Munby, Arthur Joseph. An English poet; born in the wapentake of Bulmer, Yorkshire, 1828. His themes are largely pastoral idylls. He has written: 'Verses Old and New' (1865); 'Dorothy' (1880), which was well received; 'Vestigia Retrorsum' (Steps Backward: 1891); 'Vulgar Verses, by Jones Brown' (1891), mostly in dialect; 'Susan' (1893).

Munch, Andreas (mönch). A Norwegian poet and dramatist; born at Christiania, Oct. 19, 1811; died near Copenhagen, June 27, 1884. Originally a student of law, he was an editor (1841–46) and professor in the university (1866) at Christiania. His chief works were 'Ephemera' (1836), his first effort; 'King Sverre's Youth' (1837), a drama; 'The Singer' (1838); 'Poems Old and New' (1848); 'Pictures from North and South' (1848), in prose; 'New Poems' (1850); 'Grief and Consolation' (1852), his most successful production; 'Lord William Russell' (3d ed. 1888), a tragedy; 'An Evening at Giske' (1855), a historical drama. ('Works,' Copenhagen, 5 vols., 1887–90.)

Munch, Peder Andreas. A distinguished Norwegian historian, antiquary, and philologist; born at Christiania, Dec. 15, 1810; died at Rome, May 23, 1863. He was professor of history in the university at Christiania in 1841. His masterpiece was 'History of the Norwegian People' (1851–64). ('Works,' published by the State, 2d ed. Christiania, 1894.)

Münch-Bellinghausen, Eligius Franz Joseph von, Baron (münch' bel'ling-hou"zen), better known as "Friedrich Halm" (hälm). An Austrian dramatist; born at Cracow, April 2, 1806; died at Vienna, May 22, 1871. He studied law, and held various official positions at Vienna. He wrote: 'Griseldis' (10th ed. 1893), which had great success; 'The Adept' (1836); 'Camoens' (1837); 'Imelda Lambertazzi' (1838); 'The Son of the Wilderness' (9th ed. 1894), well known in England and America under the title 'Ingomar'; 'The Fencer of Ravenna' (5th ed. 1893), perhaps his best work; 'Wild Fire' (6th ed. 1894), a romantic comedy; etc. ('Works,' 8 vols., Vienna, 1856-64.)

Munchausen, Baron. See **Münchhausen** and **Raspe.**

Münchhausen, Hieronymus Karl Friedrich von, Baron (münch-hou'zen). A notorious German braggart; born at Bodenwerder, Hanover, 1720; died there, 1797. Having served in the Russian cavalry against the Turks (1737–39), the tales he told of his exploits gave him the reputation of being "the greatest liar in Germany." Ostensibly written out in English by Rudolph Eric Raspe, a German exile, 'Baron Munchausen's Narrative of his Marvelous Travels and Campaigns in Russia' appeared at (Oxford, 1785), and was translated into German by Gottfried A. Bürger the poet (1786). Since then it has often been reprinted. In reality the stories are old "yarns" of various ages collected from other books. See also **Raspe.**

Munday, Anthony. An English miscellaneous writer of great versatility and note; born in London, 1553; died there, August 1633. He wrote a large number of plays, generally in collaboration with Chettle, Drayton, Wilson, Dekker, Webster, and others: among them being 'Richard Cœur de Lion's Funeral' (1589); 'A Chance Medley' (1598); 'The Rising of Cardinal Wolsey' (1601); 'Death of Robert, Earl of Huntington' (1601); and 'The Two Harpes' (1602). He was also a writer of ballads of much note, which were licensed to be sung in London. He wrote, translated, or adapted numerous romances, including 'Palladino of England' (1588) and the two first books of 'Amadis de Gaule' (between 1589 and 1595). His work 'The English Romayne Lyfe' (about 1582) excited the most comment: it was ostensibly an account of his adventures among English Catholic refugees in France and Italy, and was anti-Catholic in tone. His prodigious activity in literature and affairs makes him one of the most notable characters of his time.

Munday, John William. ["Charles Sumner Seeley."] An American writer for boys; born in Indiana, 1844. He is a lawyer at Chicago. He has published 'The Spanish Galleon'; 'The Lost Canyon of the Toltecs.'

Mundt, Klara. See **Mühlbach.**

Mundt, Theodor. A German biographer, writer of travels, critic, and novelist; born at

Potsdam, Sept. 19, 1808; died at Berlin, May 30, 1861. He belonged to the "Young Germany" school. He was professor of the history of literature at Breslau in 1848; professor and librarian at the University of Berlin, 1850. Among his biographical writings and travels, which were his best, were monographs on Prince Pückler, George Sand, Lamennais, and others; 'Walks and World Journeys' (1838–39); 'Italian Conditions' (1859–60). His critical works include : 'Art of German Prose' (2d ed. 1843); 'Universal History of Literature' (2d ed. 1848); 'History of Contemporary Literature' (2d ed. 1853); 'The Pantheon of the Ancient Peoples' (2d ed. 1854); 'History of Society' (2d ed. 1856). He wrote the novels 'Thomas Müntzer' (3d ed. 1860); 'Mendoza, the Father of Rogues' (1847); etc.

Munger, Theodore Thornton. An American Congregational clergyman; born in Bainbridge, N. Y., March 5, 1830. He graduated from Yale in 1851, and Yale Theological School in 1855. Since 1885 he has been pastor of the United Church, New Haven, Conn. He is a Congregational leader in his State; has been active in municipal reform, and is well known as a writer of ability and attractiveness on ethical subjects, and an exponent of broad, progressive theology. He has published : 'On the Threshold'; 'The Freedom of Faith'; 'Lamps and Paths'; and 'The Appeal to Life.'

Munkittrick, Richard Kendall. An American poet and humorous writer; born in England, 1853. He is on the editorial staff of Puck, New York. He has published : 'The Moon Prince,' for children; 'The Acrobatic Muse,' a volume of humorous verse. He has also written serious verse of fine fancy and delicate workmanship.

Munroe, [Charles] Kirk. An American writer for the young; born in Wisconsin, 1856. His present home is in Florida. He has written : 'The Flamingo Feather' (1887); 'Wakulla' (1888); 'Campmates'; 'Canoemates'; 'Raftmates'; 'Rick Dale'; 'Dorymates'; 'The White Conquerors'; 'Big Cypress'; 'At War with Pontiac'; etc.: also a 'Life of Mrs. Stowe' (with her son); 'The Outcast Warrior.'

Murat, Napoléon Achille (mü-rä'). A French-American essayist and political writer; born in France, 1801; died 1847. He was son of Joachim Murat, king of Naples, and hence prince of the Two Sicilies. Coming to this country in 1821, he settled at Tallahassee, Fla., where he was mayor 1824, and postmaster 1826–28. He wrote in French 'Essays Moral and Political on the United States of America'; 'Exposition of the Principles of Republican Government as Perfected in America,' the latter running through over fifty editions.

Muratori, Ludovico Antonio (mö-rä-tō'ri). An Italian historian; born at Vignola, Oct. 21, 1672; died Jan. 23, 1750. He was keeper of the Ambrosian library at Milan (1694), and of the Este library and ducal archives at Modena

(1700). He wrote : 'Writers of Italian Affairs' (25 vols., 1723–51); 'Italian Antiquities of the Middle Ages' (6 vols., 1738–42); 'Annals of Italy' (12 vols., 1744–49); all of great value.

Muravieff, Andreï (mö-rä've-eff). A Russian traveler and miscellaneous writer; born 1798; died 1874. His works enjoyed considerable popularity in Russia. They contained : 'Dante' (1841), a drama; 'History of the Russian Church' (1845); 'Souvenirs of Rome' (1846); 'Souvenirs of the East' (1851); 'Impressions of the Ukraine and Sebastopol' (1859); etc.

Murchison, Roderick Impey, Sir. A Scottish geologist; born at Tarradale (Ross), Feb. 19, 1792; died in London, Oct. 22, 1871. He was one of the founders and often president of the Royal Geographical Society; director-general of the British Geological Survey (1855). He published: 'Geology of Russia and the Ural' (1845); 'Siluria' (1854); 'Geological Atlas of Europe' (1856); etc.

Murdoch, William. A Canadian poet; born in Paisley, Scotland, Feb. 24, 1823; died in St. John, N. B., May 4, 1887. His publications include 'Poems and Songs' (2d ed. 1872); and 'Discursory Ruminations: a Fireside Drama,' with other pieces (1876).

Mure, William. A Scottish historian; born near Caldwell, Ayrshire, July 9, 1799; died in London, April 1, 1860. He was Member of Parliament for Renfrew, 1846–55; and rector of Glasgow University, 1847–48. He wrote 'History of the Language and Literature of Ancient Greece' (5 vols., 1850–57), his main work, but left unfinished; 'Journal of a Tour in Greece and the Ionian Islands' (1842); etc.

Murfree, Fanny Noailles Dickinson. An American novelist, sister of Mary; born in Tennessee, 1845. She has written the novel 'Felicia.'

Murfree, Mary Noailles, better known as "Charles Egbert Craddock." A noted American novelist; born at Murfreesboro, Tenn., Jan. 24, 1850. She was a contributor to the Atlantic Monthly before 1880. Among her best-known books are: 'In the Tennessee Mountains' (1884); 'The Prophet of the Great Smoky Mountains' (1885); 'In the Clouds' (1886); 'The Story of Keedon Bluffs'; 'The Windfall.'

Murger, Henri (mür-zhä'). A noted French littérateur; born in Paris, March 24, 1822; died near there, Jan. 28, 1861. He was at one time secretary of Count Leo Tolstoy. He wrote : 'Scenes of Bohemian Life' (1848), his best-known work, depicting existence in the Latin Quarter of Paris; 'Claude and Marianne' (1851); 'Scenes of Youthful Life' (1851); 'The Last Appointment' (1852); 'The Latin Country' (1852); 'Adeline Protat' (1853); 'The Water Drinkers' (1854); etc. His verse was collected in a volume entitled 'Winter Nights.'

Murner, Thomas (mör'ner). An Alsatian clergyman, and a leading satirist of the 16th century; born at Strasburg, Dec. 24, 1475; died at Oberehnheim, Alsace, about 1536. He was made poet laureate by the emperor Maximilian (1506), and taught for a while logic at Cracow; but in the main led a roaming and unsettled life, drawing large crowds by his witty sermons whenever he preached. He wrote: 'The Rogues' Guild' (1512); 'The Exorcism of Fools' (1512); 'On the Great Lutheran Fool' (1522), a stinging satire on the Reformation; etc.

Murphy, Henry Cruse. An American journalist and historical writer; born at Brooklyn, N. Y., 1810; died 1882. He was a lawyer by profession; was minister to The Hague 1857–61. He wrote: 'Henry Hudson in Holland' (1859); 'Anthology of the New Netherlands' (1865), consisting of translations and memoirs; 'The Voyage of Verrazzano' (1875); etc.

Murray, David Christie. An English novelist; born at West Bromwich, Staffordshire, April 13, 1847. He has been a journalist in London. He has written numerous works, among which are: 'A Life's Atonement' (1879); 'Coals of Fire' (1881); 'The Way of the World' (new ed. 1886); 'The Weaker Vessel' (1888); etc. He died Aug. 2, 1907.

Murray, Grenville. An English miscellaneous writer; born Oct. 2, 1824; died at Passy, France, Dec. 20, 1881. He was in the diplomatic service 1845–68. A voluminous writer, among his works were: 'Dudley Cranbourne' (1845), a novel; 'The Roving Englishman' (1854); 'Embassies and Foreign Courts' (1856); 'The Member for Paris' (1871); 'Young Brown' (1874), both novels; 'Turkey' (1877); 'The Russians of To-day' (1878); 'Under the Lens, Social Photographs' (2d ed. 1885); etc.

Murray, Hugh. A Scottish geographer; born at North Berwick, 1779; died in London, March 4, 1846. He was a clerk in the excise office at Edinburgh, devoting his leisure to literature, especially geography; edited the Scots' Magazine. He wrote: 'Histories of Discoveries and Travels,' consisting of 'Africa' (2 vols., 1817), 'Asia' (3 vols., 1820), and 'North America' (2 vols., 1829); 'Descriptive Geography of British India' (3 vols.); 'China' (3 vols.); 'United States' (3 vols.); 'Marco Polo's Travels' (1 vol., 1839); and 'Encyclopædia of Geography' (1834), his chief work.

Murray, James Augustin Henry. A distinguished British lexicographer; born in Denholm, Roxburghshire, Scotland, 1837. He has long been compiling 'A New English Dictionary on Historical Principles' (first number 1888), founded mainly on materials collected by the Philological Society. The letters A and B, and the greater part of C and E, had appeared by 1893, and G by 1897; and the work is now in continuous publication. The aim of this dictionary "is to furnish an adequate account of the meaning, origin, and history of English words now in general use, or known to have been in use at any time during the past 700 years." Its purpose is "not to dictate to usage, but to record usage." Dr. Murray has also published 'Dialect of the Southern Counties of Scotland,' and similar philological studies.

Murray, John Clark. A Canadian educator and miscellaneous writer; born in Paisley, Scotland, March 19, 1836. In 1872 he became professor of mental and moral philosophy in McGill University, Montreal. He is the author of 'The Ballads and Songs of Scotland' (1874); 'Handbook of Psychology' (1885); and 'Solomon Maimon: an Autobiography,' translated from the German, with notes and additions (1888).

Murray, John O'Kane. An American physician and historian; born in Glenariffe, County Antrim, Ireland, Dec. 12, 1847; died in Chicago, July 30, 1885. He was a man of unusual culture. His most notable work was a 'Popular History of the Catholic Church in the United States' (1876). This was succeeded by 'The Prose and Poetry of Ireland' (1877); 'The Catholic Heroes and Heroines of America' (1878); 'The Catholic Pioneers of America' (1881); and 'Lessons in English Literature' (1883).

Murray, Lindley. whose name was long a synonym for grammar in America, was born in Swatara, Pa., April 22, 1745; died near York, England, Jan. 16, 1826. From 1784 until his death he was devoted to literary work. His publications include: 'Grammar of the English Language' (1795, first ed.), 'The Power of Religion on the Mind' (1787); 'Compendium of Religious Faith and Practice.' 'Memoirs of the Life and Writings of Lindley Murray' was issued in 1826.

Murray, Nicholas. ["Kirwan."] An American Presbyterian clergyman, and controversial and didactic writer; born in Ireland, Dec. 25, 1802; died 1861. He was settled at Elizabethtown, N. J. Among his works were: 'Letters to Bishop Hughes' (collective ed. revised and enlarged, 1855), translated into several languages; 'Romanism at Home' (1852); 'Men and Things as I Saw Them in Europe' (1853); 'Preachers and Preaching' (1860); etc.

Murray, William Henry Harrison. An American preacher, lecturer, and miscellaneous writer; born in Guilford, Conn., April 26, 1840. His publications include: 'The Perfect Horse'; 'Adirondack Tales'; 'How Deacon Tubner Kept New-Year's'; 'Daylight Land'; 'Adventures in the Wilderness'; 'Deacons'; 'Music Hall Sermons'; 'Sermons from Park Street Pulpit'; 'The Doom of Mamelons'; 'Words Fitly Spoken'; etc. Died March 3, 1904.

Musäus, Johann Karl August (mö-zä'ös). A German satirical writer; born at Jena, March 29, 1735; died at Weimar, Oct. 28, 1787. He was professor at the Weimar gymnasium in 1770. Among his works were: 'The German Grandison' (1781–82), satirizing Richardson's novel 'Sir Charles Grandison'; 'Physiognomical Journeys' (1778–79), satirizing Lavater; 'Folk-Tales of the Germans' (latest ed. Hamburg, 1870);

'Ostrich Feathers' (1787), his chief production, and for a long time very popular; etc.

Musick, John Roy. An American novelist and historian; born at St. Louis, Mo., Feb. 28, 1849; died at Omaha, Neb., April 14, 1901. Among his works may be named: 'Calamity Row' (1887); 'Brother Against Brother' (1887); 'Mysterious Mr. Howard'; etc. He wrote a series of twelve American historical novels.

Musset, Louis Charles Alfred de (mü-sā'). One of the greatest three French poets of the nineteenth century; born in Paris, Nov. 11, 1810; died there, May 1, 1857. He studied law and medicine, and tried business, each for a short time; was librarian of the department of the Interior (1838), and the department of Public Instruction (1855). He wrote: 'Tales of Spain and Italy' (1830); 'A Play in an Arm-Chair' (1832); 'A Night of May' (1835); 'A Night of December' (1835); 'A Night of August' (1836); 'A Night of October' (1837),— the last four being his masterpieces; 'Letter to Lamartine' (1836); 'Hope in God' (1838); etc. The 'Nights,' as well as the latter part of the prose story 'Confession of a Child of the Century' (1836), related to his connection with George Sand. Other notable stories were: 'Emmeline' (1837); 'The Two Mistresses' (1837); 'Frederick and Bernerette' (1838); 'Titian's Son' (1838); etc. He produced also a series of graceful and original 'Comedies and Proverbs,' some of which hold the stage to-day; 'One Must Not Play with Love' (1834); 'We Must Swear to Nothing' (1836); 'A Door Must be either Open or Shut' (1845); etc. His life was dissipated. ('Works,' best ed. 10 vols., 1886.)

Muzzey, Artemas Bowers. An American clergyman and miscellaneous writer; born in Lexington, Mass., Sept. 21, 1802; died at Cambridge, April 21, 1892. In 1865 he retired from ministerial work. Included in his numerous publications are: 'The Young Man's Friend' (1836); 'Man, a Soul' (1842); 'The Higher Education' (1871); Personal Recollections of Rev. Dr. Channing' (1874–75); 'Immortality in the Light of Scripture and Science' (1876); and 'Education of Old Age' (1884).

Myers, Ernest James. An English poet, brother of Frederic W. H.; born at Keswick in 1844. He was called to the bar (1874), but never practiced. He has published: 'The Puritans' (1869); 'Poems' (1877); 'Defence of Rome and Other Poems' (1880); 'Judgment of Prometheus and Other Poems' (1886); etc.; besides translating the odes of Pindar (2d ed. 1884).

Myers, Frederic William Henry. An English poet and critic; born at Keswick, Feb. 6, 1843; died in Rome, Jan. 17, 1901. He was classical lecturer at Trinity College, Cambridge, 1865–68. He wrote 'St. Paul' (new ed. 1879), verse; 'Wordsworth' (1880), in 'English Men of Letters'; 'Renewal of Youth, and Other Poems' (1882); 'Essays, Modern and Classical' (1883); 'Science and a Future Life' (1893), a volume of essays; etc. He was one of the foremost writers in English reviews.

Myers, Peter Hamilton. An American story-writer and lawyer; born in Herkimer, N. Y., Aug. 4, 1812; died in Brooklyn, N. Y., Oct. 30, 1878. Among his published works are: 'The First of the Knickerbockers: A Tale of 1673' (1848); 'The Young Patroon, or Christmas in 1690' (1849); 'The King of the Hurons,' republished in England as 'Blanche Montaigne' (1856); and 'The Prisoner of the Border: A Tale of 1838' (1857).

Myers, Philip Van Ness. An American educator and historian; born in New York State, 1846. He was president of Belmont College, Ohio, and has been dean of the University of Cincinnati since 1895. He has written: 'Remains of Lost Empires' (1875); 'Outlines of Ancient History' (1882); 'Outlines of Mediæval and Modern History' (1886); 'General History'; 'The Middle Ages'; 'The Modern Age.'

Myrddin (mēr'din), **Wyllt,**—*i. e.*, the Mad. [Called also **Merlin.**] A Welsh poet; flourished 580 (?). Hardly anything is known of his life. In mediæval Welsh literature he is credited with being the author of six poems, which can be found in the 'Myryrian Archæology' (2d ed., pages 104–18, 348).

N

Nabuco de Araujo, José Tito (nä-bö'kō dä är-ä-ö'zhō). A Brazilian historical and dramatic writer; born in Rio Janeiro, Jan. 4, 1836. He has written 'The Son of Chance,' a drama which has been successfully represented in several of the South-American cities; 'Maxims and Thoughts' (1876); 'Life of Lamartine' (1877); 'Life of General Gurjao' (1878); and 'Poems' (1879).

Nack, James. An American verse-writer; born in New York city, Jan. 4, 1809; died there, Sept. 23, 1879. He labored under the disability of being deaf and dumb. His popular verses include 'Spring Is Coming,' 'Here She Goes and There She Goes,' and the volumes 'The Legend of the Rocks' (1827); 'The Immortal, and Other Poems' (1850); 'Poems' (1852); and 'The Romance of the Ring, and Other Poems' (1859).

Nadal, Ehrman Syme. An American journalist, lecturer, and author; born at Lewisburg, W. Va., Feb. 13, 1843. He was secretary of the United States legation at London, 1870–71 and 1877–84. He is a frequent contributor to magazines. His chief works are: 'Impressions of London Social Life' (1875); 'Essays at Home and Elsewhere' (1882); 'Zwieback, or Notes of a Professional Exile' (1887).

Nadaud, Gustave (nä-dō'). A French song-writer and composer; born in Roubaix, Feb. 20, 1820; died in Paris, April 28, 1893. He published: 'Songs' (1849); 'More Songs' (1873); 'Unpublished Songs' (1876); and 'New Songs' (2d ed. 1892). He composed the music for many of them. He also wrote a novel called 'An Idyll' (2d ed. 1886).

Naden, Constance C. W. An English poet; born in Birmingham, 1858; died in London (?), 1889. She studied sociological problems, and lectured with effect; but is chiefly remembered for her volumes of 'Songs and Sonnets of Springtime' (1881), and 'A Modern Apostle,' etc. (1887).

Nævius, Cneius (nē'vē-us). A Roman poet; born in Campania, B. C. 272 (?); died B. C. 204 (?). He wrote dramas and an epic on the Punic wars, but only fragments of his works are extant. The ancients, Cicero in particular, considered him a great genius.

Naharro, Bartolomé de Torres (nä-är'ō). A Spanish dramatist who flourished in the sixteenth century. He entered the clerical body, but his career otherwise is little known. His pieces are among the earliest specimens of Spanish drama. The best are probably 'Soldadesca' (Soldiery), and the 'Tinelaria.' The 'Propaladia' was condemned by the Inquisition.

Nairne, Lady (Carolina Oliphant). A Scotch poet; born at Gask, Perthshire, 1766; died there, 1845. She attained universal celebrity in Scotland through her poetry, the most popular among her productions being: 'The Land of the Leal' (1798); 'Caller Herrin'; and 'The Laird o' Cockpen.'

Najac, Émile, Count de (nä-zhäk'). A French dramatist; born in Lorient, Morbihan, 1828; died in Paris, 1869. He produced: 'Caged Birds' (1863); 'The Last Doll' (1875); 'Madam Is Served' (1874); and 'Let Us Divorce!' (1880). He has also collaborated with Meilhac, Sardou, and Hennequin.

Nannarelli, Fabio (nä-nä-rel'le). An Italian poet; born in Rome, Oct. 25, 1825; died in Corneto Tarquinia, May 1894. His early studies were elaborate, and he held a professorship of literature at the University of Rome for years. His poetry shows the influence of classic models, particularly the collections entitled 'Poems' (1853), and 'New Poems' (1856). His essays and studies appear in various volumes, and his later poems include 'New Lyrics' (1881).

Nansen, Fridtjof (nän'sen). A Norwegian Arctic explorer; born near Christiania, Oct. 10, 1861. For many years he has devoted himself to Arctic exploration, aiming especially to reach the North Pole, which he has approached much more nearly than any other explorer. His observations, experiences, and discoveries have been carefully noted by him, and published in 'Farthest North'; 'Oceanography of the North Polar Basin.'

Naphegi, Gabor. An American-Hungarian miscellaneous writer; born in Buda-Pesth in 1824; died in 1884. He became a naturalized American citizen in 1868. Among his works are: 'Among the Arabs' (1868); 'An Album of Language' (1869); 'Ghardia; or, Ninety Days in the Desert' (1871); 'The Grand Review of the Dead,' poems.

Napier, Charles James, Sir. An English soldier and military writer; born in London, Aug. 10, 1782; died Aug. 29, 1853. He had a very distinguished military career, and wrote important books based on his experiences; including 'Lights and Shades of Military Life' (2d ed. 1853), and 'Letter on the Defense of England by Corps of Volunteers and Militia' (1852).

Napier, Charles John, Sir. A British vice-admiral and military and naval historian; born in Scotland, March 6, 1786; died Nov. 6, 1860. He held high command, and was a great naval tactician. His writings include: 'The War in Portugal between Pedro and Miguel' (1836); 'The War in Syria' (1842); 'The Navy'

(1850); and 'History of the Baltic Campaign' (1857).

Napier, Henry Edward. An English naval commander and historian, brother of Sir Charles James; born in 1789; died in 1853. His best-known work is 'Florentine History from the Earliest Authentic Records' (6 vols., 1847).

Napier, William Francis Patrick, Sir. A British soldier and historian; born in Ireland, Dec. 17, 1785; died Feb. 10, 1860. He saw much active service, his earliest experiences being in the wars against Napoleon. In literature he ranks among the greatest of military historians through his 'History of the War in the Peninsula' (1828-40), a masterpiece and a classic.

Napoleon III. (Charles Louis Napoleon Bonaparte). Emperor of the French (1852-70); born at Paris, April 20, 1808; died at Chiselhurst, England, Jan. 9, 1873. He was the ostensible author of 'History of Julius Cæsar' (1865-66), an important and valuable work; Victor Duruy was his collaborator.

Nares, Edward. An English story-writer and biographer; born in London, 1762; died 1841. He was a clergyman, who held the professorship of modern history at Oxford for a time. His writings include 'Thinks I to Myself' (1811), a novel; and 'Life and Administration of Lord Burghley' (1828-31).

Naruszewicz, Adam Stanislas (nä-rös'ĕ-vich). A Polish historian and poet; born in Lithuania, 1733; died 1796. He entered the Jesuit order and became a bishop, devoting his leisure to literature. His masterpiece is a 'History of the Polish People' (new ed. 10 vols., 1836). His idyls and satires are the best of his poetic pieces. He made a good Polish version of Tacitus.

Nasby, Petroleum V. See **Locke.**

Nascimento, Francisco Manoël do (näs-chē-men'tō). ["Filinto Elysio."] A Portuguese poet; born in Lisbon, 1734; died 1819. He won a prominent place in his country's literature with a version of La Fontaine's fables, but it is to his 'Odes' and other poems that he owes his greatest eminence.

Nash, Thomas. An English satirical poet, dramatist, and novelist; born in Lowestoft, Suffolk, 1567 (?); died in London, 1601. His 'Anatomy of Absurdities' (1589), a satire, was very successful; as were his 'Return of Pasquil' (1589), and 'Pasquil's Apology' (1590). His best work was the romance called 'The Unfortunate Traveler; or, The Life of Jack Wilton' (1594). 'Summer's Last Will and Testament' (1600), a comedy, is known to students of literature.

Nason, Elias. An American clergyman, biographer, and religious writer; born in Wrentham, Mass., April 21, 1811; died in North Billerica, Mass., June 17, 1887. Among his works are: 'Life of Governor Andrew' (1868); 'Life of Charles Sumner' (1874); 'Lives of Moody and Sankey' (1877); 'Originality' (1882).

Nason, Mrs. Emma (Huntington). An American poet; born in Maine in 1845. She is a resident of Augusta, Me. Her works are 'White Sails' (1888), and 'The Tower, with Legends and Lyrics.'

Navarrete, Manuel Maria de (nä-vä-rā'tä). A Mexican poet; born in Zamora, Mechoacan, June 18, 1768; died in Tlalpujahua, July 17, 1809. His principal work is 'Poem on the Divine Providence' (1808). Before his death he burned his manuscripts. The few which escaped destruction were published under the title of 'Poetical Entertainments' (Mexico, 1823; Paris, 1825).

Navarrete, Martin Fernandez de. A Spanish historian and scholar; born in Abalos, Nov. 9, 1765; died Oct. 8, 1844. He paid particular attention to geographical science and to the historical side of discovery, his best work being 'Collection of Voyages and Discoveries Made by the Spaniards since the End of the Fifteenth Century' (1825-37).

Navarro, Madame de — Mary [Antoinette] (Anderson). An American actress; born in Sacramento, Cal., 1859. She won fame both in the United States and England. In 1890 she retired from the stage and married Antonio F. de Navarro. Her autobiography, 'A Few Memories' (1896), is an interesting work.

Neal, Daniel. An English historian; born in London, 1678; died 1743. He was a widely known Dissenting clergyman. His principal writings are: 'History of the Puritans' (1732-38); and 'History of New England' (1720).

Neal, John. An American poet and author; born in Falmouth, Mass., now Portland, Me., Aug. 25, 1793; died there, June 21, 1876. He was a member of the Society of Friends, but left it at 25. Later in life he figured as editor, lecturer, lawyer, poet, novelist, and teacher of gymnastics. Among his numerous works are: 'Keep Cool' (1817), a novel; 'The Battle of Niagara' (1818), a poem; 'Brother Jonathan' (1825); 'Rachel Dyer' (1828), a novel; 'Downeasters' (1833), a novel; 'Wandering Recollections of a Somewhat Busy Life' (1870).

Neal, Joseph Clay. An American journalist and humorist; born at Greenland, N. H., Feb. 3, 1807; died at Philadelphia, July 18, 1847. He was editor of the Pennsylvanian from 1831 to 1844, when he founded the Saturday Gazette. His works are: 'Charcoal Sketches' (1837); 'Peter Ploddy and Other Oddities' (1844).

Neale, John Mason. A notable English church historian and poet; born in London, Jan. 24, 1818; died at East Grinstead, Aug. 6, 1866. He was an extreme High-Churchman; founded a sisterhood, was inhibited from church ministrations for 14 years, and once burned in effigy. His translations of Latin and Greek hymns are among the finest religious lyrics in the language: the most famous are 'Art Thou Weary' and 'Jerusalem the Golden.' His best-known books are: History of the Holy Eastern Church'; 'Mediæval Hymns'; 'Hymns of the

26

Eastern Church'; and 'History of the So-called Jansenist Church of Holland.'

Neander, Johann August Wilhelm (nā-än'-der). A German church historian; born in Göttingen, Jan. 17, 1789; died at Berlin, July 14, 1850. He was of Jewish extraction, but earnest in the advancement of Christianity. His principal works include: 'The Emperor Julian and his Times' (1812); 'Memorable Occurrences from the History of Christianity and Christian Life' (1822); 'History of the Planting of the Apostolic Church' (1832); 'Universal History of the Christian Religion and Church' (1843); and many others.

Neele, Henry. An English poet; born in London, 1798; died 1828. He was a lawyer, but devoted his leisure to literature, writing 'Dramatic Scenes'; 'Odes and Other Poems' (1817); and editing an edition of Shakespeare.

Negri, Ada (nā'grē) — **Mme. Garlanda.** An Italian poet; born in Lodi, Feb. 3, 1870. She has written in mournful numbers of the sufferings of the poor, the best collection of her verse being in the volume 'Fatality' (or 'Fate': 1892); but excellent poems are contained in 'Storms' (1895).

Negruzzi, Jakob (nā-gröts'ē). A Roumanian poet, son of Konstantin; born in Jassy, Jan. 11, 1843. He is a member of the Roumanian Academy, and founder of the periodical Convorbiri Literare. His volumes of 'Poems,' and 'Copies from Nature,' the latter made up of sketches and tales, have been widely read.

Negruzzi, Konstantin. A Roumanian poet and prose-writer; born in Jassy, 1808; died there, 1868. He wrote many verses and plays, the historical poem 'Aprode Purice,' and the historical sketch 'Alexander Lepusneanu.' His best verse is in the volume entitled 'Youthful Sins.'

Nekrassov, Nikolai Alexejevich (nā-kräs'ov). A Russian poet; born in Podolia, Dec. 4, 1821; died in St. Petersburg, Jan. 8, 1888. He is one of the most important figures in the literature of his country; and his 'Poems' (1845), and 'Last Poems' (1877), gave him great celebrity. He contributed to periodical literature, and edited Sovremmenik (Contemporaries).

Nelson, Henry Loomis. An American journalist and author; born in New York city, Jan. 5, 1846. Edited Harper's Weekly; became professor at Williams College. He wrote: 'Our Unjust Tariff Law' (1884); 'John Rantoul' (1885), a novel; 'The Money We Need' (1896).

Nemcová, Bozena (nyem'tsō-vä). A Czech poet and story-writer; born (Pankl) in Vienna, Feb. 4, 1820; died in Prague, Jan. 21, 1862. She studied the folk-lore of the Czechs, and embodied it in poetic narratives, notably 'Little Grandmother,' and the 'Little Mountain Village.'

Nepos, Cornelius (nē'pos). A Roman biographer and historian; born in Ticinum (?), 99 (?) B. C.; died 24 (?) B. C. His 'Lives'

of eminent men are preserved, and much used as school text-books from their simplicity of style.

Néruda, Jan (nyer-ö'dä). A Czech poet; born in Prague, July 10, 1834; died there, Aug. 22, 1891. He was noted in periodical journalism; while as a poet he is distinguished for his 'Book of Verse' (1867), 'Cosmic Songs' (2d ed. 1878), and various plays, including 'Francesca da Rimini.' His 'Humble Histories' (1878), a series of sketches of Czech life, attained great popularity.

Nerval, Gerard de. See **Gerard de Nerval.**

Nettement, Alfred François (net-män'). A French journalist; born in Paris, 1805; died 1869. He acquired note with his 'History of the Revolution of July 1830' (1833), and 'History of French Literature under the Reign of Louis Philippe.'

Nevay, John. A Scotch poet; born at Forfar, Jan. 28, 1792; died May 1870. His lyrics are contained in 'A Pamphlet of Rhymes' (1818); 'The Child of Nature' (1835), a verse collection; and other volumes.

Nevin, William Channing. An American lawyer and journalist; born in New Athens, O., in 1844. He was admitted to the bar in 1871; and has written for Philadelphia journals. His works include: 'History of All Religions' (1871); 'Ghouls and Gold' (1885); 'In the Nick of Time' (1886); 'A Summer School Adventure' (1887); 'Our New Possessions'; 'A New Start in Life.'

Nevinson, Henry W. An English story-writer; born 18—. He has been a contributor of fiction to London periodicals for some time; a collection of his tales, called 'Slum Stories of London' (1895), being very popular.

Newcastle, Duchess of. See **Cavendish.**

Newcomb, Simon. An American astronomer of distinction, scientist, and author; born of United States parents in Wallace, N. S., March 12, 1835. Among his most important works are: 'Popular Astronomy'; 'School Astronomy,' with E. S. Holden; a series of text-books on 'Algebra,' 'Geometry,' 'Trigonometry,' and 'Calculus'; 'Spherical Astronomy'; 'Lights on Astronomy'; 'The Moon.' Died July 11, 1909.

Newell, Robert Henry. ["Orpheus C. Kerr."] An American journalist and humorist; born in New York city, Dec. 13, 1836; died in Brooklyn, July 11, 1901. He was connected with the New York Mercury and World, and editor of Hearth and Home from 1874 to 1876. He wrote: 'The Orpheus C. Kerr Papers' (1862–68); 'The Palace Beautiful, and Other Poems' (1864); 'The Cloven Foot,' a travesty of Dickens's 'Edwin Drood' (1870); 'Versatilities' (1871); 'There Was Once a Man' (1884); etc.

Newhall, Charles Stedman. An American educator and author; born in Massachusetts in 1842. He is a resident of Asbury Park, N. J. Besides a series of books on the trees, shrubs, and vines of northeastern America, he has written several books for young people. The most popular are: 'Joe and the Howards'; 'Harry's Trip to the Orient' (1885); 'Ruthie's Story' (1888); 'Handbook and Herbarium.'

Newman, Francis William. An English historian and theological writer, brother of John Henry; born in London, June 27, 1805; died at Weston-Super Mare, Oct. 4, 1897. He wrote many important works, including: 'History of the Hebrew Monarchy' (1847); 'The Soul: Its Sorrows and Aspirations' (1849); 'Phases of Faith' (1850); 'Lectures on Ancient and Modern History' (1851); 'Crimes of the House of Hapsburg' (1853); etc.

Newman, John Henry. An English theologian; born in London, Feb. 21, 1801; died in Birmingham, Aug. 11, 1890. His writings include: 'St. Bartholomew's Eve' (1821), a poetic tale; 'Suggestions on Behalf of the Church Missionary Society' (1830); 'The Arians of the Fourth Century' (1833); 'Five Letters on Church Reform' (1833); 'Tracts for the Times' (1834–41); 'Lyra Apostolica' (Verses on Various Occasions: 1834); 'Lectures on the Prophetical Office' (1837); 'Plain and Parochial Sermons' (1837–42); 'Lectures on Justification' (1838); 'Sermons before the University of Oxford' (1843); 'Select Treatise of St. Athanasius' (1842–44); 'Loss and Gain' (1848), a novel; 'Verses on Religious Subjects' (1853); 'Hymns for the Use of the Birmingham Oratory' (1854); 'Callista' (1856), a novel; 'Apologia pro Vita Sua' (1864); 'Essay in Aid of a Grammar of Assent' (1870); 'The Via Media of the Anglican Church' (1877). A new and uniform edition of the 'Works' appeared in 36 vols., 1868–81.

Newman, John Philip. An American clergyman and writer; born in New York city, Sept. 1, 1826; died at Saratoga, July 5, 1899. He was ordained a minister in the Methodist Episcopal Church in 1860, and elected bishop in 1888. He was a preacher of note in Washington, and long chaplain to the Senate. In 1873 he was sent to Asia as inspector of consulates. Among his works are: 'From Dan to Beersheba' (1864); 'Thrones and Palaces of Babylon and Nineveh' (1875); 'America for Americans' (1887).

Newton, Isaac, Sir. The celebrated English philosopher and mathematician; born at Woolsthorpe, Lincolnshire, Dec. 25, 1642 (O.S.), died at Kensington, March 20, 1727. He wrote: 'Theory of Light and Colors' (1675); 'On Motion' (1685); 'Principia' (1687); 'Opticks' (1704); 'Optical Readings' (1728); 'The Chronology of Ancient Kingdoms Amended' (1728); 'Observations upon the Prophecies of Daniel and the Apocalypse of St. John' (1733); and various essays.

Newton, John. An English religious and historical writer, best remembered as Cowper's friend; born in London, 1725; died 1807. He published 'Review of Ecclesiastical History' (1770), 'Cardiphonia,' and various hymns.

Newton, Richard Heber. An American clergyman and religious writer; born in Philadelphia, Oct. 31, 1840. Since 1869 he has been rector of All Souls Church, New York city. He is a Churchman of advanced views. His published works include: 'The Morals of Trade' (1876); 'Philistinism' (1885); 'Social Studies' (1886); 'Church and Creed' (1891); 'Parcifal' (1904).

Newton, William Wilberforce. An American clergyman and miscellaneous writer, brother of Richard H.; born in Philadelphia, Nov. 4, 1843. He is rector of a Protestant Episcopal church at Pittsfield, Mass. His works include: 'Essays of To-Day' (1879); 'The Priest and the Man' (1883), a historical novel, 'Ragnar, the Sea-King' (1888); and a series of sermons for children.

Nicander, Karl August (nē-kän'der). A Swedish poet; born at Strengnäs, 1799; died 1839. His 'Death of Tasso' (1826) is very well known; other noted works by him are: 'The Runic Sword,' a tragedy in verse (1821); 'King Enzio' (1825); and 'Recollections of the South' (1828).

Niccolini, Giovanni Battista (nē-kō-lē'ne). An Italian poet and dramatist; born near Pisa, 1782; died 1861. His tragedies 'Antonio Foscarini' (1827), 'Polissena,' 'Giovanni da Procida' (1830), and 'Filippo Strozzi' (1847), are well known.

Nicephorus (nī-sef'o-rus), known as the "Confessor." A Byzantine historian; born at Constantinople in 758; died in 828. He was appointed patriarch of Constantinople in 806, but on account of his defense of image-worship was persecuted and finally deposed by the Iconoclast Leo V., the Armenian. Retiring to a monastery he wrote a 'Breviarium,' a brief history of Constantinople (602 to 770), distinguished for accuracy and erudition; a 'Chronology' from the beginning of the world; and controversial writings.

Nichol, John. A Scottish littérateur and historical writer; born in Montrose, Forfarshire, Sept. 8, 1833; died in London, Oct. 11, 1894. He was a professor of English literature at the University of Glasgow (1861–89), who did much to make American books popular in England. His numerous publications include: 'Leaves' (1854), verse; 'Tables of European History, 200–1876 A. D.' (1876; 4th ed. 1888); 'Byron' in 'English Men of Letters' series; 'American Literature, 1620–1880' (1882). He was an ardent advocate of the Northern cause during the Civil War, and visited the United States at the close of the conflict.

Nichols, George Ward. An American writer on art and music; born in Mt. Desert, Me., June 21, 1837; died in Cincinnati, O., Sept. 15, 1885. He was on the staff of General Sherman in the Civil War. He was for some years president of the Cincinnati College of Music. Among his works are: 'The Story of the Great March' (1865); 'Sanctuary' (1866), a story of the Civil War; 'Art Education Applied to Industry' (1877); 'Pottery' (1878).

Nichols, John. An English essayist and miscellaneous prose-writer; born in London, 1745; died, 1826. He was one of the publishers of the Gentleman's Magazine, and wrote 'History and Antiquities of Leicestershire' (1795–1811), and 'Literary Anecdotes of the Eighteenth Century' (1812–15).

Nicolardot, Louis (nik-ō-lär-dō). A French essayist and man of letters; born at Dijon, Nov. 28, 1822; died at Paris, Nov. 21, 1888. The most characteristic of his works are: 'Journal of Louis XVI.' (1873); 'The Impeccable Théophile Gautier' (1883); and 'La Fontaine and the Human Comedy' (1885).

Nicolay, John George. An American journalist and historical writer; born at Essingen, Bavaria, Feb. 26, 1832; died in Washington, Sept. 26, 1901. He came to the United States in 1838. He was engaged in journalism in the West; was private secretary of President Lincoln, 1861–5; United States consul at Paris, 1865–69; and marshal of the United States Supreme Court, 1872–87. His chief work is 'Abraham Lincoln: A History' (1891), written in collaboration with John Hay. He also wrote 'The Outbreak of the Rebellion' (1881).

Nicole, François Léon Étienne (nē-kōl). A Haytian poet; born near Grande Rivère in 1731; died at Cap Français in 1773. He was a mulatto. Educated in a Jesuit college, he went to Paris in 1750, where Voltaire introduced him to literary circles. Louis XV. granted him a pension in recognition of his talents. He published: 'The Romance of the Slave' (1766); 'Tropical Flowers' (1770); and 'New Poems' (1772).

Nicole, Pierre. A French theological and philosophical writer; born at Chartres, 1625; died 1695. He is best known for his 'Moral Essays and Theological Instructions' (25 vols., 1671–), a collection of treatises, of which the one entitled 'On the Means of Preserving Peace' is very famous. He also wrote 'Treatise on Human Faith' (1664), and 'The Imaginative and the Visionary' (1667).

Nicoll, Robert. A Scotch poet; born in Perthshire, 1814; died 1837. His 'Poems' (1835) were very popular, but he died at so early an age that the promise of his first book remained unfulfilled.

Nicoll, William Robertson. A Scotch clergyman and editor; born in Lumsden, Aberdeenshire, Oct. 10, 1851. He took an M. A. at Aberdeen University; was minister of the Free Church at Kelso for eight years; on account of ill-health he resigned, in 1887 started the British Weekly, one of the most successful religious papers in England, and within recent years has been English editor of the Bookman. Among his publications are: 'Calls to Christ' (1877); 'The Incarnate Saviour: A Life of Jesus Christ' (1881); 'John Bunyan' (1884) in the 'Evangelical Succession' series; 'Ten-Minute Sermons' (1895); 'The Key of the Grave'; 'Letters on Life.'

Niebuhr, Barthold Georg (nē'bör). A great German historian; born at Copenhagen, Aug. 27, 1776; died at Bonn, Jan. 2, 1831. His 'Roman History' (3 vols., 1811–32) marked a great advance in critical history-writing. Other works by Niebuhr are: 'Lectures on the History of Rome' (2d English ed. 1850); 'Lectures on Ancient History' (3 vols., 1852); 'Grecian Heroic History' (1842); 'Minor Historical and Philological Writings' (2 vols., 1828–43).

Niembsch von Strehlenau, Nikolaus Franz. See Lenau.

Niemcewicz, Julian Ursin (nyem-sē'vitch). A Polish poet, historian, and publicist; born in Lithuania, 1758; died at Paris, 1841. His public career was quite distinguished; and he accompanied Kosciuszko to this country. He married Mrs. Livingston Kean of New York. His principal works are: 'Historical Songs of Poland'; 'History of the Reign of Sigismund III.'; 'Contributions to the Ancient History of Poland'; and a romance called 'John of Tenczyn.'

Nieriker, Mrs. May (Alcott) (nē'rik-ėr). An American artist and author, daughter of A. B. Alcott; born in Massachusetts in 1840; died in 1879. Her works are: 'Concord Sketches' (1869), and 'Studying Art Abroad' (1879).

Nietzsche, Friedrich Wilhelm (nētsh'ĕ). A German writer; born in Röcken, Oct. 15, 1844; died at Weimar, Aug. 25, 1900. His writings have attracted a great deal of attention owing to there extreme character. His principal works include: 'The Birth of Tragedy from the Spirit of Music' (4th ed. 1895); 'Thus Spake Zarathustra' (4th ed. 1895); 'Beyond Good and Evil' (5th ed. 1895); 'The Genealogy of Ethics' (4th ed. 1895); 'The Inversion [Umwertung] of all Values [Werte],' the last remaining incomplete, although deemed his masterpiece.

Nievo, Ippolito (nyä'vō). An Italian poet and story-writer; born in Padua, Nov. 30, 1832; died at sea, March 4, 1861. His best-known work is 'The Confessions of an Octogenarian' (new ed. 1887), a historical novel. His 'Poems' (1883) are admired.

Nikitin, Ivan Savich (nē-kit'in). A Russian poet; born in Varonesh, Oct. 3, 1824; died Oct. 28, 1861. His 'Peasant Hangman' (1858), and 'Poems' (1856), 'Taras,' and other verse, have given him a conspicuous place.

Niles, John Milton. An American lawyer, journalist, and statesman; born in Windsor, Conn., Aug. 20, 1787; died in Hartford, Conn., May 31, 1856. In 1817 he founded the Hartford Times; was twice United States Senator; and in 1840 became Postmaster-General. Besides addresses and speeches he published: 'Lives of Perry, Lawrence, Pike, and Harrison' (1820); 'History of the Revolution in Mexico and South America' (1839).

Nisard, Jean Marie Napoléon Désiré (nē-sär'). A French man of letters; born at Châtillon-sur-Seine, March 20, 1806; died at San Remo, Italy, March 15, 1888. He was noted

as a critic, and also for his 'Studies of Morals and Criticism on the Latin Poets during the Decline of Learning' (1834), and 'History of French Literature' (1844-61).

Nizāmī or Nizamee (nē-shä'mē). A Persian poet; born 1141; died 1202. His works are: the 'Storehouse of Mysteries,' a religious poem; 'Khusrau and Shīrīn,' a metrical tale; 'Lailā and Majnūn,' a romantic epic; 'Seven Portraits,' love stories; and the 'Alexander Book.'

Noah, Mordecai Manuel. An American lawyer, editor, and author; born in Philadelphia, July 14, 1785; died in New York, May 22, 1851. During his journalistic career in New York he was connected with seven newspapers. He made an unsuccessful attempt to found a Jewish colony on Grand Island, in the Niagara River. His chief works are: 'The Siege of Tripoli' and 'The Fortress of Sorrente,' dramas; 'Travels in England, France, and Spain' (1819); 'Gleanings from a Gathered Harvest' (1845).

Noble, Annette Lucile. An American writer of fiction; born in Albion, Orleans County, N. Y., July 12, 1844. She is a frequent contributor to magazines. Among her works are: 'Uncle Jack's Executors' (1880); 'Tarryport Schoolhouse' (1882); 'After the Failure' (1887); 'Rachel's Farm' (1894); 'The Silent Man's Legacy'; 'The Crazy Angel.'

Noble, Louis Legrand. An American poet; born in Lisbon, N. Y., Sept. 26, 1813; died in Ionia, Mich., Feb. 6, 1882. He published: 'Ne-Ma-Min: An Indian Story,' in three cantos (1852); 'The Course of Empire, Voyage of Life, and Other Pictures of Thomas Cole, with Selections from his Letters and Miscellaneous Writings Illustrative of his Life, Character, and Genius' (1853); 'The Lady Angeline, A Lay of the Appalachians; The Hours; and Other Poems' (1857).

Noble, Lucretia Gray. An American novelist; a native of Lowell, Mass.; born 18—. At an early age she removed to Wilbraham, Mass., where she now resides. Besides contributions to magazines, she wrote the popular novel 'A Reverend Idol' (1882).

Nodier, Charles (nōd-yā'). A French romance-writer and poet; born at Besançon, April 1780; died 1844. His works include: 'Entomological Bibliography' (1801); 'Napoleone' (1802), a satiric ode; 'The Painter of Salzburg' (1803), 'The Exiles,' 'Jean Sbogar' (1818), 'Thérèse Aubert' (1819), romances; 'Dictionary of French Onomatopœia' (1808); 'Picturesque and Romantic Travels in Ancient France' (1820); and others.

Noel, Roden Berkeley Wriothesley. An English poet; born Aug. 27, 1834; died at Mainz, May 26, 1894. He published: 'Behind the Veil and Other Poems' (1863); Beatrice and Other Poems, (1868); and various other volumes.

Noel, Thomas. An English poet; born, 1799; died, 1861. He published several volumes of verse, among them 'Rhymes and Roundelayes'

(1841), in which is the poem 'The Pauper's Drive,' often erroneously attributed to Hood.

Nogaret, François Felix (nō-gä-rā'). A French poet and man of letters; born at Versailles, 1740; died 1831. He wrote: 'The Apology for my Taste' (1771), a work on natural history; 'Tales in Verse' (5th ed. 1810); and several plays.

Nomsz, Jan (nomz). A Dutch playwright and poet; born at Amsterdam, 1738; died 1803. His most popular work is 'Maria van Lalain,' a tragedy; 'Zoroaster'; and a poem (1779) of which William I. of Orange is the hero.

Nonius Marcellus (nō'nē-us). A Roman writer on syntax, who flourished in the fourth century. His 'Correctness in [the use of] Words' is important because of its citations from classic works now lost.

Nordau, Max Simon (nôr'dou). A German prose-writer and critic; born at Pesth, Hungary, July 29, 1849. His most celebrated work is 'Degeneration' (1893), but he has written: 'Paris under the Third Republic' (1881); 'The Conventional Lies of our Civilization' (1883); 'Paradoxes' (1886); 'The Sickness of the Century' (1889), a novel; and the drama 'Doctor Kohn' (1898).

Nordhoff, Charles (nôrd'hof). An American journalist and author; born at Erwittee, Westphalia, Aug. 31, 1830; died at Coronado, Cal., July 14, 1901. He came to the United States in 1835, and was a sailor for nine years. He was on the staff of the New York Evening Post from 1861 to 1871, and later correspondent of the New York Herald at Washington, D. C. Among his works are: 'Man-of-War Life' (1855); 'Merchant Vessel' (1855); 'Cape Cod and All Along Shore' (1868); 'Northern California' (1873); 'Politics for Young Americans' (1875); 'Peninsular California' (1888).

Nordmann, Johannes Rumpelmaier (nord'-män). An Austrian poet and descriptive writer; born near Krems, March 13, 1820; died in Vienna, Aug. 20, 1887. He was connected with several prominent periodicals, and also wrote: 'Poems' (1847); 'A Marshal of France' (1857), a tragedy; 'Springtime Evenings in Salamanca' (3d ed. 1880); several novels; and a record of travel called 'My Sundays' (2d ed. 1880).

Noriac, Claude Antoine Jules Cairon (nōr-yäk'). A French novelist and publicist; born at Limoges, 1827; died at Paris, Oct. 1, 1882. His novels include: 'The Countess of Bruges' (1878); 'The Chevalier de Cerny' (1879); and 'Paris as It Is' (1884).

Norman, Henry. An Anglo-American journalist and author; born at Leicester, Eng., Sept. 19, 1858. Educated at Harvard University; has been a member of Parliament since 1900. Besides contributions to magazines he has written: 'The Broken Shaft' (1886); 'The Witching Time' (1887); 'The Real Japan' (1892); 'Peoples and Politics of the Far East' (1895).

Norris, William E. An English novelist; born in London, 1847. His very numerous works include: 'Heaps of Money' (1877); 'Mademoiselle de Mersac' (1880); 'Matrimony' (1881); 'No New Thing'; 'His Grace'; 'A Deplorable Affair'; 'The Countess Radna' (1893); 'My Friend Jim'; 'The Rogue'; 'Nature's Comedian.'

North, Christopher. See **Wilson, John.**

North, Simeon. An American educator and author; born in Berlin, Conn., Sept. 7, 1802; died in Clinton, N. Y., Feb. 12, 1884. He is widely known as president of Hamilton College, 1839–57. His works include: 'The American System of Collegiate Education' (1839); 'Faith in tne World's Conversion' (1842); 'The Weapons in Christian Warfare' (1849); 'Obedience in Death' (1849); 'Half-Century Letter of Reminiscences' (1879).

Norton, Caroline Elizabeth Sarah. An English poet and miscellaneous prose-writer; born in 1808; died 1877. She was a granddaughter of Richard Brinsley Sheridan. Her first book of poetry, 'The Sorrows of Rosalie' (1829), was published when she was seventeen. Her 'The Undying One' (1830), a poem; 'A Voice from the Factories' (1836); 'The Dream, and Other Poems' (1840); and 'Aunt Carry's Ballads' (1847), contain much admired verse. She also wrote 'Stuart of Dunleith' (1847), a novel, and 'Lives of the Sheridans.'

Norton, Charles Eliot. An American scholar and author; born at Cambridge, Mass., Nov. 16, 1827. He was one of the editors of the North American Review 1863–68, and is professor in Harvard University. Among his writings are: 'Notes of Travel and Study in Italy' (1860); 'The New Life of Dante Alighieri, translated, with Essays and Notes' (1867); 'Historical Studies of Church-Building in the Middle Ages.'

Norton, Charles Ledyard. An American journalist and author; born at Farmington, Conn., in 1837. He graduated at Yale in 1859. He was editor of the Christian Union 1869–79, and in 1893 became editor of Outing. His chief works are: 'Canoeing in Kanuckia' (1878), with J. Habberton; 'Handbook of Florida' (1890); 'A Medal of Honor Man; or, Cruising among Blockade-Runners'; 'The Queen's Rangers.'

Norton, Thomas. An English dramatist; born in London, 1532; died, 1583–4. He owes his place in literature to the fact that he was joint author with Sackville of the earliest English blank-verse tragedy, called 'The Tragedie of Gorboduc' (1560–61), based on the legendary history of a British king.

Nott, Eliphalet. An American clergyman and educator; born at Ashford, Conn., June 25, 1773; died at Schenectady, N. Y., Jan. 29, 1866. He was ordained a Presbyterian minister in 1795. After holding pastorates in Cherry Valley and Albany, N. Y., he became president of Union College in 1804, where he remained until his death. His chief works are: 'Counsels to Young Men' (1810), and 'Lectures on Temperance' (1847). His funeral

sermon on the death of Alexander Hamilton was famous, and in the school readers for many years.

Noue, François de la (nö), called **Bras de Fer** (Iron Arm). A French Huguenot commander; born near Nantes, 1531; killed at Lamballe, 1591. His 'Political and Military Discourses' (1587) are deemed masterpieces.

Novalis (nō-väl′ēs), pseudonym of Friedrich von Hardenberg. A German philosopher and mystic; born in Saxony, 1772; died 1801. His works include: 'Hymns to the Night' (1797); 'Disciples at Sais'; and 'Heinrich von Ofterdingen,' his most considerable work.

Noyes, John Humphrey. An American communist; born in Brattleboro, Vt., Sept. 6, 1811; died at Niagara Falls, Canada, April 13, 1886. He is best known as the founder of the Oneida Community. He published: 'The Second Coming of Christ' (1859); 'Salvation from Sin the End of Christian Faith' (1869); 'History of American Socialism' (1870).

Numatianus, Rutilius Claudius (nö-mä-tē-ä′nös). A Roman poet of Gallic birth. He wrote 'Of His Return,' a metrical narrative of a visit to his native country, which had been devastated by the Gothic invader. This poem is supposed to date from 416 A.D., and it has not come down to us complete.

Nuñez, Rafael (nön′yäth). President of Colombia; born in Carthagena, Sept. 28, 1825. He is a brilliant writer, and his poems rank high in Spanish literature. The most widely known are: 'Que Sais-je?'; 'Dulce Ignorancia'; 'Todavía and Möises.' His publications include: 'Ensayos de Critica Social' (1876); 'La Reforma Politica en Colombia' (1885).

Nuñez de Arce, Gaspar (nön′yäth dä är′thä). A Spanish dramatist and poet, known as the "Spanish Tennyson"; born at Valladolid, Aug. 6, 1834. Of his plays the most notable are the comedies 'Who Is the Author?' (1859); 'Neither So Much nor So Little' (1865); 'El Haz de Leña,' a drama in five acts on the subject of Don Carlos. Among his remarkably popular lyric and patriotic poems are: 'The Last Lament of Lord Byron' (23d ed. 1884); 'Battle Cries' (5th ed. 1885); 'Vertigo' (25th ed. 1886); 'An Idyl and an Elegy' (18th ed. 1886); 'The Vision of Friar Luther' (1880).

Nye, Edgar Wilson. An American journalist, lecturer, and humorist; born at Shirley, Me., Aug. 25, 1850; died near Asheville, N. C., Feb. 22, 1896. He settled in Wyoming Territory as a young man, studied law, and was admitted to the bar in 1876. Afterwards he removed to New York city, and became famous as a humorous lecturer and writer under the pseudonym of "Bill Nye." Among his works are: 'Bill Nye and the Boomerang' (1881); 'Forty Liars' (1883); 'Remarks' (1886); 'Fun, Wit, and Humor' (1889), with J. W. Riley; 'Comic History of the United States' (1894); 'Comic History of England' (1896).

O

Ober, Frederick Albion. An American ornithologist, traveler, and author; born in Beverly, Mass., Feb. 13, 1849. He has traveled extensively in Florida, the West Indies, and Mexico; and is the author of a large number of books of travel and descriptive works, principally for young readers. Among the best known are: 'Camps in the Caribbees' (1880); 'The Silver City' (1883); 'Young Folks' History of Mexico' (1883); 'Montezuma's Gold Mines' (1887); 'In the Wake of Columbus' (1893); 'The Heroes of American History' (12 vols., 1907).

Oberholtzer, Mrs. Sara Louisa (Vickers). An American poet; born in Chester County, Pa., May 20, 1841. Her works include: 'Violet Lee and Other Poems' (1872); 'Come for Arbutus' (1882); 'Hope's Heart Bells,' a story of Quaker life (1884); 'Daisies of Verse' (1886); and 'Souvenirs of Occasions.'

O'Brien, Fitz-James. An Irish-American poet and story-writer; born in Limerick, 1828; died April 6, 1862. His writings comprise 'The Diamond Lens and Other Stories,' and many poems. His collected works appeared in 1881.

Occam or Ockham, William. A scholastic philosopher; born at Occam, Surrey, England; died in Munich, Bavaria, in 1347, at an advanced age. Throughout his life he strenuously contested the right of the pope to political power and secular possessions. His skill in logic gave him the name "Doctor Invincibilis." His chief works are: 'Tractatus Logices'; 'Quodlibeta Septem'; 'Super Quatuor Libros Sententiarum'; 'Expositio Aurea super Totam Artem Veterum.' Besides these there are commentaries and polemics.

Occleve or Hoccleve, Thomas. An early English poet and lawyer; supposed to have been born about 1370. He wrote 'The Story of Jonathan' and other poems. His poetry, according to Hallam, "abounds with pedantry, and is destitute of all grace and spirit."

Ochoa y Acuna, Antonio (ō-chō'a ē ä-kö'nä). A Mexican poet; born in Huichapam, April 27, 1783; died in Queretaro, Aug. 4, 1833. His first satirical work appeared in 1806. In 1811 he was admitted to the Arcadia Mexicana, a society of poets; the same year he wrote 'Don Alphonso,' a tragedy. 'Love by Proxy,' a comedy, was presented in 1831. His works, under the name of 'Poems of a Mexican,' have been issued in this country (1820). He was a priest, and wrote under the name of "Pastor Antimio." He is greatly admired by his countrymen.

O'Connell, Daniel. The great Irish orator and statesman; was born at Carhen House, Cahirciveen, County Kerry, Aug. 6, 1775; died in Genoa, Italy, May 15, 1847. His 'Life and Speeches' (1846) appeared under the editorial supervision of his son; and there is also an edition of the 'Correspondence of Daniel O'Connell' by Fitzpatrick. His 'Life' has been written by W. Fagan (1847); M. F. Cusack (1872); J. O'Rourke and O'Keefe (1875); J. A. Hamilton (1888). He wrote 'A Memoir of Ireland, Native and Saxon' (1843).

O'Connor, William Douglas. An American author; born in Boston, Jan. 2, 1833; died in 1889. He was on the editorial staff of the Saturday Evening Post, Philadelphia, from 1854 to 1860, and afterwards held several government positions at Washington, D. C. His chief works are: 'The Ghost' (1856); 'Harrington' (1860), a novel; 'Hamlet's Note-Book' (1886).

O'Conor, John Francis Xavier. An American Catholic clergyman and author; born in New York in 1852. He is a member of the Society of Jesus, and a professor in Boston College. His works include: 'Something Real'; 'Lyric and Dramatic Poetry'; 'Reading and the Mind'; 'Christ, the Man God.'

Oehlenschläger or Öhlenschläger, Adam Gottlob (ĕl'en-shlāg"er). A leading Danish poet; born near Copenhagen, Nov. 14, 1779; died Jan. 20, 1850. His works comprise: 'Poems' (1803); 'First Song of the Edda'; 'A Journey to Langeland'; 'The Life of Christ Annually Repeated in Nature'; 'Earl Hakon'; 'Thor's Journey to Jötunheim'; 'Palnatoke'; 'Axel and Valborg'; 'The Little Shepherd Boy'; and several tragedies, including 'Socrates' and 'Hamlet.'

Oettinger or Öttinger, Eduard Marie (ĕt'-ing-er). A German journalist and novelist; born in Breslau in 1808; died 1872. He edited several satirical journals; and published a number of novels, among which is 'Onkel Zebra' (7 vols., 1843). He also wrote a work entitled 'Rossini' (1847), which is said to be a romance rather than a biography; and 'Bibliographie Biographique Universelle' (2 vols., 1850–54), the most complete work on that subject.

Ohnet, Georges (ō-nä'). A French novelist and dramatist; born in Paris, April 3, 1848. Among his dramatic works are 'Regina Sarpi' (1875) and 'Martha' (1877). His novels have appeared as serials in Figaro, L'Illustration, and the Revue des Deux Mondes, before being published in book form; some of them have been adapted to the stage, notably 'The Forge Master.' Among his stories are: 'Black and Red'; 'Doctor Rameau' (1888); 'Pierre's Soul' (1890); 'Les Dames de Croix-Mort' (1886); 'La Comtesse Sarah'; 'The March to Love' (1902).

O'Keeffe, John. An Irish dramatist; born in Dublin, June 24, 1747; died at Southampton, Feb. 4, 1833. He was designed for an artist; but becoming stage-struck, left Dublin for London, where, failing to procure a theatrical engagement, he devoted himself entirely to dramatic composition. He produced nearly fifty comedies, comic operas, and farces, which were extremely popular. Among the principal ones were: 'The Castle of Andalusia'; Wild Oats'; 'The Poor Soldier'; 'The Young Quaker'; and 'Peeping Tom.'

Oldham, John. An English poet and satirist; born in Shipton, Gloucestershire, in August 1653; died 1683. He was educated at the school of Tedbury, and then at Oxford. He had many patrons, the last being the Earl of Kingston, in whose house he died. His works have been published in three volumes.

Oldmixon, John. An English political writer; born in Bridgewater, Somersetshire, 1673; died 1742. His principal works were: 'A History of England' (2 vols.); 'Life of Arthur Maynwaring'; and 'Life of Queen Anne.' He was distinguished for his hatred of the Stuart family.

Oldys, William. An English biographer and antiquary; born July 14, 1696; died April 15, 1761. In 1737 he succeeded to the care of Lord Oxford's (the Harleian) library, the catalogue of which was partly drawn up by him. He wrote: 'Life of Sir Walter Raleigh'; 'The British Librarian'; 'The Universal Spectator'; 22 lives in the 'Biographia Britannica.' His most valuable and curious work is an annotated copy, now in the British Museum, of Langbaine's 'Account of the Early Dramatick Poets.' Mr. James Yeowell published in 1862 'A Memoir of Oldys, together with his Diary, Choice Notes from his Adversaria, and an Account of the London Libraries.'

Oliphant, Laurence. An English writer and traveler, who was more remarkable than his books. He was born in Cape Town, South Africa, in 1829; died at Twickenham, England, Dec. 23, 1888. Of good family and position, he roamed over the earth, deeply interested in the mystic philosophy of the East; and while sometimes holding official positions, was essentially a dreamer who cared most for the things of the spirit, and gave up brilliant prospects and the pleasures dearest to humanity in order to elevate his soul. He published a dozen books, including three novels; several works of a politico-military nature, such as 'A Narrative of the Earl of Elgin's Mission to China and Japan' (1860); and journalistic and philosophic books, like 'Episodes in a Life of Adventure' (1887) and 'Scientific Religion (1888).

Oliphant, Margaret Oliphant Wilson. A Scotch novelist; born at Wallyford, Scotland, April 4, 1828; died at Windsor, England, June 29, 1897. Her works include: 'Zaidee' (1856); 'Chronicles of Carlingford'; 'The Story of Valentine and his Brother'; 'Sir Tom'; 'In Trust'; 'A House Divided against Itself'; 'The Cuckoo in the Nest'; 'English Literature at the End of the Eighteenth and Beginning of the Nineteenth Century'; 'Victorian Age of English Literature'; 'Makers of Florence, Venice, and Rome.'

Olivier, Juste Daniel (ō-lēv-yā'). A Swiss poet; born in Eysius, Canton of Vaud, Oct. 18, 1807; died in Geneva, Jan. 7, 1876. In 1830 he published his first volume of poems, 'Poèmes Suisses.' This was followed by 'The Future' (1831); 'Songs from Afar' (1833); and many others. He also wrote many works in prose. He spent most of the last years of his life in Paris.

Ollivier, Émile. A French statesman and political writer; born at Marseilles, July 2, 1825. He was elected to the French Academy (1870) as successor to Lamartine. His main works are: 'Democracy and Liberty' (1867); 'Church and State in the Council of the Vatican' (2 vols., 1879); 'Thiers in the Academy and in History' (1880); '1789 and 1889' (1890).

Olmedo, José Joaquin (ol-mä'dō). A South-American poet; born in Guayaquil in 1781; died there, Jan. 19, 1847. His verses have been highly praised. One of his best poems is a 'Song to Bolivar' (1826). His 'Collected Works' (Valparaiso, 1848; Paris, 1853; and Mexico, 1862) have been widely circulated.

Olmsted, Frederick Law. The renowned American architect and designer of public parks; born in Hartford, Conn., April 26, 1822. He designed Central Park in New York, and the park systems of Boston, Chicago, Buffalo, and other cities. His publications include: 'Walks and Talks of an American Farmer in England' (1852); 'A Journey in the Seaboard Slave States' (1856); 'A Journey in Texas' (1857); 'A Journey in the Back Country' (1861). These books may be regarded as diversions,—though some of them are of permanent interest and instructiveness,—as his engineering work has been constant, and is of the highest value and repute. Died Aug. 28, 1903.

Olney, Jesse. An American geographer; born in Union, Conn., Oct. 12, 1798; died in Stratford, Conn., July 31, 1872. In 1828 he first published 'A Geography and Atlas,' which became a standard work for thirty years, and caused a revolution in the methods of teaching geography. He published a series of text-books (1831–52), including a series of 'Readers,' a 'Common School Arithmetic,' a 'History of the United States'; and a volume of poems, 'Psalms of Life.'

Olsson, Olof (ol'sen). A Swedish Lutheran clergyman and educator; born in Björtorp, March 31, 1841. He came to this country in 1868, and was professor and president of Augustana College, Rock Island, Ill. He edited two Swedish journals, and has published: 'At the Cross'; 'Greetings from Afar,' travels in England and Germany (1880); and 'The Christian Hope' (1887). His books have been translated into Swedish and Norwegian. Died, 1900.

O'Mahony, Francis. ["Father Prout."] A noted Irish journalist and poet; born at Cork, about 1804; died in Paris, 1866. Ordained a Roman Catholic priest, he resigned his calling about 1834, and became an author. He published: 'Reliques of Father Prout' (1836), contributed originally to Fraser's Magazine (a final volume appeared in 1876, edited by Blanchard Jerrold); 'Facts and Figures from Italy' (1847), published originally as letters to the Daily News. He died in a monastery, to which he retired in 1864. ('Works,' 1880.)

Omar Khayyám. See **Khayyám.**

Oña, Pedro de (ōn'yä). A Chilian poet; born in Confines, Araucania, about 1560; died in Lima about 1620. His great work 'Arauco Domado' (Conquered Chili: 1596) consisted of nineteen cantos. It is said to be one of the finest of epic poems. A second edition appeared in 1605, and one in 1849. He also wrote a poem 'The Lima Earthquake of the Year 1609'; several sonnets; and a heroic poem, 'Ignacio de Cantabria' (1639).

Ondegardo, Polo (on-dā-gär'dō). A Spanish historian; born in Spain, about 1500; died in Peru, about 1570. From manuscripts written by him and preserved in the archives of Simancas and the Escorial, Prescott obtained information which he used in his 'History of the Conquest of Peru.'

Opie, Amelia. An English writer, wife of John Opie the painter; born in Norwich, Nov. 12, 1769; died there, Dec. 2, 1853. Among her numerous tales, once highly popular, may be mentioned: 'Father and Daughter'; 'Murder Will Out'; 'The Ruffian Boy'; 'Temper'; 'St. Valentine's Day'; 'Illustrations of Lying.' In 1825 she joined the Society of Friends, and after this only published 'Detractions Displayed' and 'Lays for the Dead.'

Opitz, Martin (ō'pïts). A German poet; born in Bunzlau, Silesia, Dec. 23, 1597; died of the plague in Dantzic, Aug. 20, 1639. For more than a century he was called the "father of German poetry." He attained great influence on the literature of Germany, chiefly by his theoretical and critical writings; of which his 'Aristarchus; or, on Contempt for the German Language' (1617) is the most important.

Oppert, Julius. A celebrated French Assyriologist and Orientalist; born at Hamburg, July 9, 1825, of Jewish parents. An expert on the decipherment of cuneiform inscriptions, he has published: 'Assyrian Studies' (1859–64); 'Sanskrit Grammar' (1859); 'History of the Empires of Chaldea and Assyria from the Monuments' (1866); 'The People and Language of the Medes' (1879); 'Chronology of Genesis' (1895).

Oppian or **Oppianus** (op'ē-an). A Greek poet; born at Anazarbus in Cilicia; flourished under Marcus Aurelius. He composed a didactic poem, 'On Fishing,' in five books. The versification is smooth, the style ornate. His works have been edited by J. G. Schneider (Leipzig, 1813), and F. S. Lehrs (Paris, 1846).

Optic, Oliver, pseudonym of William T. Adams. A popular American writer of stories for boys; born in Massachusetts, 1822; died 1897. He was for many years a teacher in the Boston public schools. He wrote 'Army and Navy' series; 'Young America Abroad' series; 'Lake Shore' series; etc.

O'Reilly, John Boyle. An Irish-American poet and prose-writer, for a long time editor of the Pilot, Boston; born near Drogheda, Ireland, June 28, 1844; died at Hull, Mass., Aug. 10, 1890. His works comprise: 'Songs of the Southern Seas' (1873); 'Moondyne' (1878); and many fugitive poems and stories. He was part author of 'The King's Men' (1884).

O'Reilly, Miles. See **Halpine.**

O'Rell, Max. See **Blouët, Paul.**

Orgaz, Francisco (or-gäth'). A Cuban poet; born in Havana in 1815; died in Madrid in 1873. He published a volume of poems, 'Preludes for the Harp' (1841), which placed him among the best lyric poets of Spanish America. A collection of poems, 'Poems of the Tropics' (1850), preserved the uses and customs of the Cuban aborigines. He also wrote several dramas.

Origen (or'i-jen), surnamed "Adamantinos" from his indefatigable study; one of the most learned and spirited of the Christian fathers; born at Alexandria in 185 (?) A. D.; died in Tyre, in 254 (?). Of his many writings only a few have come down to us. Of his 'De Principiis' (Of the Principles), there exists only a free and even interpolated translation by Rufinus. His celebrated treatise on martyrdom is entire. His works were among the earliest printed of the patristic writings.

Orosius, Paulus (ō-rō'si-us). A Latin historian and theologian; born in Spain, probably at Tarragona, at the beginning of the fifth century A. D. He wrote a 'History directed against Pagans' (in seven books), from the beginning of the world to the author's time, especially to disprove the assertions of pagan historians that the calamities of Rome, such as the invasions of the barbarians, were due to Christianity.

Orozco y Berra, Fernando (ō-roth'kō e bär'ä). A Mexican poet; born in San Felipe del Obraje, June 3, 1822; died in Mexico, in 1851. His novel 'The Thirty Years' War' appeared in 1850. He wrote: 'The Coming Fashion,' 'Three Patriots,' 'Three Aspirants,' three-act comedies in verse; and 'Friendship,' a five-act comedy in prose. After his death a collection of his works was published (1886).

Orozco y Berra, Manuel. A Mexican historian; born in the City of Mexico, June 8, 1816; died there, Jan. 27, 1881. Among his published works are: 'History of Geography in Mexico' (1876 and 1880); and 'Ancient History of Mexico,' his most famous work (1880–81), in four parts,—'Civilization,' 'Primitive Man,' 'Ancient History,' and 'The Conquest.'

Orton, James. An American clergyman, naturalist, and traveler; born at Seneca Falls, N. Y., April 21, 1830; died on Lake Titicaca, Peru, Sept. 25, 1877. In 1867, 1873, and 1876, he conducted exploring expeditions to South America. His works are: 'The Andes and the Amazon' (1870); 'Underground Treasures' (1872); 'Liberal Education of Women' (1873); 'Comparative Zoölogy' (1875).

Orton, Jason Rockwood. An American poet and miscellaneous writer; born in Hamilton, N. Y., in 1806; died in Brooklyn, N. Y., Feb. 13, 1867. He was educated as a physician, but abandoned the practice of medicine in 1850, and devoted himself to literature. Besides contributions to periodicals, he published: 'Poetical Sketches' (1829); 'Arnold, and Other Poems' (1854); 'Camp-Fires of the Red Men' (1855); 'Confidential Experiences of a Spiritualist' (1858).

Osborn, Laughton. An American artist and littérateur; born in New York city in 1809; died there, Dec. 12, 1878. He graduated at Columbia College in 1827. His works include: 'Sixty Years of Life' (1831); 'Vision of Rubeta' (1838); 'Arthur Carryl' (1841); 'Travels by Sea and Land' (1868).

Osborne, (Samuel) Duffield. An American novelist; born on Long Island, N. Y., in 1858. His works are: 'The Spell of Ashtaroth' (1888); 'The Robe of Nessus' (1890), a historical novel; 'Macaulay's Lays of Ancient Rome.'

Oscanyan, Hatchik (os-kan'yan). An Armeno-Turkish author, resident in New York; born in Constantinople, April 23, 1818, of Armenian parents. He was educated in the United States, established an Armenian paper in Constantinople in 1841, and was afterwards in the official employ of the Turkish government. He wrote in Armenian: 'Acaby,' a satirical romance (1849); 'Veronica' (1851); and a child's book, 'Bedig.' He published in New York 'The Sultan and his People' (1857), a remarkably popular work.

Osgood, Mrs. Frances Sargent (Locke). An American poet; born in Boston, June 18, 1811; died at Hingham, Mass., May 12, 1850. Besides contributions to magazines she published: 'Wreath of Wild Flowers' (1839); 'Poetry of Flowers' (1841); 'Poems' (1849).

Osgood, Samuel. An American clergyman and author; born in Charlestown, Mass., Aug. 30, 1812; died in New York city, April 14, 1880. He was the pastor of a Unitarian church in New York city from 1849 to 1869, when he resigned and joined the Episcopal Church. Besides translations from the German, his numerous works include: 'Studies in Christian Biography' (1851); 'Mile-Stones in our Life Journey' (1855); 'Student Life' (1860).

O'Shaughnessy, Arthur William Edgar. A British poet; born in 1844; died in 1881. In 1864 he entered the British Museum, and in 1873 married Eleanor, sister of Philip Bourke Marston. He was a follower of Morris and Swinburne and of the French romantic school. He published between 1870 and 1881: 'An Epic of Women'; 'Lays of France,' a free paraphrase of the *lais* of Marie de France; 'Music and Moonlight'; and 'Songs of a Worker.'

Ossian. See the article 'McPherson, James.'

Ossoli, Marchioness d' (os-sō'lē) — **Sarah Margaret Fuller,** best known as "Margaret Fuller." An American writer on literature, art, and society; born at Cambridgeport, Mass., 1810; died at sea, 1850. For some years she was employed as a teacher in girls' schools; for two years edited the Dial (1840-42). Her collected essays on 'Women in the Nineteenth Century' were published in 1843. She contributed regularly to the New York Tribune papers on literature and art, which were collected in a volume published in 1846. At Rome in the same year she married the Marquis d'Ossoli. The pair were on the way to New York when their ship was wrecked and both were lost. Besides the volumes already named, she published other collections of her essays under the titles: 'Art, Literature, and Drama'; 'At Home and Abroad'; 'Life Without and Life Within.'

Ostrovsky, Alexander Nikolaievich (ostrov'skē). A Russian dramatist; born in Moscow, April 12, 1823; died June 14, 1886. One of his best comedies, 'We Get On with our Own Kind,' published in 1849, established his reputation. His works followed each other in rapid succession. Among the best are: 'The Poor Bride' (1852); 'Poverty is Not a Fault' (1853); 'A Profitable Place' (1857); 'The Storm' (1859); and 'A Warm Heart' (1869). He was the author of several translations, especially a remarkable one of 'The Taming of the Shrew.' His complete works were published in St. Petersburg (1887, 10 vols.).

Oswald, Felix Leopold. An American naturalist and miscellaneous writer; born at Namur, Belgium, in 1845. He graduated at Liège in 1864, and became a physician; but later abandoned the practice of medicine, and devoted himself to the study of natural history. He resides in Tennessee. His works include: 'Summer-Land Sketches' (1880); 'Physical Education' (1882); 'The Secret of the East; or, The Origin of the Christian Religion' (1883); 'Days and Nights in the Tropics' (1887). He died in 1906.

Otero, Rafael (ō-tā'r) A Cuban dramatist; born in Havana in 1827; died there in 1876. Among his comedies are: 'A Betrothed of a Day'; 'The Coburger'; 'My Son the Frenchman'; and 'The Dead Commands It,' which were presented in the theatres of Havana and Matanzas. His novel 'La Perla de la Diaria' was published in 1866, and 'Cantos Sociales' in 1868.

Otfried (ot'frēd). A Frankish poet; born near Weissenburg in Alsace; studied at Fulda under Hrabanus Maurus (822-884), and also under Salomon I., bishop of Constance (839-

871); then went back to the Benedictine Monastery in Weissenburg, where he wrote his famous 'Evangilienbuch,' a paraphrase in verse of the Gospels, dedicated about 865 to (King) Louis the German, and to Archbishop Luitbert of Mentz. It is one of the most valuable documents of the Old High German period.

Otis, Harrison Gray. An eminent American statesman and orator, son of James; born in Boston, Oct. 8, 1765; died there, Oct. 28, 1848. He was Member of Congress 1797-1801, and U. S. Senator 1817-22. He was prominent in the Massachusetts Legislature; took an active part in the Hartford Convention of 1814; and was mayor of Boston in 1829. His published works include: 'Letters in Defense of the Hartford Convention' (1824), and 'Orations and Addresses.'

Otis, James. A celebrated American statesman and orator; born at West Barnstable, Mass., Feb. 5, 1725; died at Andover, Mass., May 23, 1783. At an early age he attracted attention by his eloquence in behalf of the colonists against British oppression, and his determined opposition to the "writs of assistance" in 1761. Through his efforts the Stamp Act Congress was assembled in 1765. He was the author of a number of political essays and orations, among which are: 'Vindication of the Conduct of the House of Representatives' (1762); 'Rights of the British Colonies Asserted' (1765); 'Consideration on Behalf of the Colonists' (1765).

Otis, James. See **Kaler.**

Otway, Thomas. An English dramatist; born at Trotton, Sussex, 1652; died 1685. He was educated at Winchester, and at Christ Church, Oxford; served as cornet in the Low Countries; was an unsuccessful actor, and finally wrote for the stage. Of his many plays, one tragedy, 'Venice Preserved,' is among the best remembered of the Restoration drama, and keeps his name familiar in literary allusion. 'The Orphan' ranks next in critical esteem.

Ouida (wē'dä), pseudonym of Louise de la Ramée; an English novelist of French extraction; born at Bury St. Edmunds, 1840. She has published: 'Held in Bondage' (1863); 'Strathmore' (1865); 'Chandos' (1866); 'Cecil Castlemaine's Gage'; 'Idalia'; 'Under Two Flags' (1867); 'Tricotrin' (1868); 'Puck' (1870); 'Folle Farine' (1871); 'A Dog of Flanders'; 'A Leaf in the Storm' (1872); 'Pascarel' (1873); 'Bebée; or, Two Little Wooden Shoes' (1874); 'Signa' (1875); 'In a Winter City' (1876); 'Ariadne' (1877); 'Friendship' (1878); 'Moths' (1880); 'Pipistrello' (1880); 'A Village Commune' (1881); 'In Maremma'; 'Bimbi' (1882); 'Wanda'; 'Frescoes' (1883); 'Princess Napraxine' (1884); 'Othmar'; 'A House Party'; 'Guilderoy'; 'Syrlin'; 'A Rainy June'; 'Don Gesualdo' (1890); 'Moufflou'; 'The Nürnberg Stove'; 'The Tower of Taddeo'; 'The Silver Christ'; 'The New Priesthood' (1893); 'Views and Opinions' (1895); 'Critical Studies.' Died in 1908.

Overskov, Thomas (ō'ver-skov). A Danish dramatist; born in Copenhagen, Oct. 11, 1798; died in 1873. His first comedy (1826) was a complete failure, but later his dramas were successfully performed; one of them, 'Ostergade og Vestergade,' in the style of Sheridan, being his best work, and another, 'Capriciosa,' still keeping its place in the repertory of the Royal Theatre. His most important contribution to literature is a 'History of the Danish Theatre' (7 vols., Copenhagen, 1854-76).

Ovid (Publius Ovidius Naso) (ov'id). The Roman poet; born at Sulmo, March 20, 43 B. C.; died at Tomi, 17 A. D. He wrote: 'Metamorphoses'; 'Fasti' (The Calendar); 'Episties'; 'Amours'; 'Art of Love'; 'Heroids'; and other works.

Oviedo y Valdez, Gonzalo Fernandez de (ōvyä'dō ē väl'däth). A Spanish historian; born in Madrid in 1478; died in Valladolid in 1557. In 1545 he was appointed historian of the Spanish Indies. The first part of his great work appeared as 'General and Natural History of the West Indies,' in 1535; the revision of the entire work was completed in 1548. It was once deemed one of the profoundest works on the natural history of America.

Owen, Goronwy. A Welsh poet; born in Anglesea, North Wales, Jan. 1, 1722; died in St. Andrews parish, Brunswick County, Va., between 1770 and 1780. He became rector of Uppington, Shropshire, in 1745; and while there wrote his celebrated poem 'The Day of Judgment.' He came to the United States in 1775; accepted a position at William and Mary College, and married for his second wife Mrs. Clayton, a sister of the president of the college. He is described as the last of the great poets of Wales. His bardic title was "Black Goronwy of Anglesea." His poems for a long time circulated in manuscript; but in 1780 his collected works were published, succeeding editions being printed in 1810 and 1860. In 1831 his countrymen erected a tablet to his memory in the cathedral church of Bangor.

Owen, Robert. Social reformer and author; born in Newtown, Montgomeryshire, Wales, May 14, 1771; died there, Nov. 17, 1858. He early turned his attention to social questions, publishing in 1812 'New Views of Society; or, Essays upon the Formation of the Human Character, and Book of the New Moral World.' He attempted to found communist societies in England, also in New Harmony, Ind., and later in Mexico. In his later years he became a believer in Spiritualism. His followers bore the name of Owenites, and were among the founders of the English Chartist movement.

Owen, Robert Dale. An American politician, diplomatist, and miscellaneous writer, son of Robert; born in Glasgow, Scotland, Nov. 6, 1801; died at Lake George, N. Y., June 17, 1877. He was educated in Switzerland; removed to the United States in 1823; was Representative to Congress from Indiana (1843-47);

and minister to Naples (1855-58). During the Civil War he was a prominent advocate of negro emancipation. Among his works are: 'Moral Physiology' (1831); 'Footfalls on the Boundary of Another World' (1860); 'Beyond the Breakers' (1870), a novel; 'Threading My Way' (1874).

Ozanam, Antoine Frédéric (ō-zä-näm'). A French scholar and writer; born in Milan, 1813; died September 1853. In 1844 he succeeded Fauriel as professor of foreign literature at the Sorbonne, Paris. He attained eminence as a lecturer, and published besides other works: 'Dante and the Catholic Philosophy in the Thirteenth Century' (1839); 'Germanic Studies for Use in the History of the Franks' (2 vols., 1847-49).

Ozaneaux, Jean George (ō-zä-nō). A French writer of prose and verse; born in Paris, 1795; died 1852. He wrote a 'History of France' (2 vols., 1846), which gained a prize from the Academy; and 'Poetic Errors' (3 vols., 1849).

P

Paalzov, Henrietta Joanna Wach von (päl'-zof). A German story-writer; born at Berlin, 1788; died there, 1847. Among her stories are: 'Godwin Castle' (3 vols., 1837); 'Saint-Roche' (1839); 'Thomas Tyrnau' (1842); 'Jakob von der Nees' (1842). Her plots are very skillfully contrived and elaborated.

Paban, Adolphe (pä-bäň'). A French poet and story-writer; born at Combs-la-Ville, dept. Seine-et-Oise, Nov. 13, 1839. He published three volumes of 'Poems' (1859-62); 'Inspirations' (1868); 'Fanciful Sonnets' (1871); 'A Drama in a Garden,' a story in prose (1874).

Packard, Alpheus Spring. An American naturalist and author; born at Brunswick, Me., Feb. 19, 1839. Since 1878 he has been professor of geology and zoölogy in Brown University. His works include: 'A Guide to the Study of Insects' (1869); 'Half-Hours with Insects' (1875); 'Life Histories' (1876); 'Zoölogy' (1879). He died in 1905.

Packard, Frederick Adolphus. An American lawyer, editor, and author; born in Massachusetts in 1794; died in 1867. He was editor of the publications of the American Sunday-School Union for nearly forty years. Among his important works are: 'The Union Bible Dictionary' (1837); 'The Teacher Taught' (1839); 'Life of Robert Owen' (1866).

Pacuvius, Marcus (pa-kū'vē-us). A Roman tragic poet; born at Brundisium about 219 B. C.; died about 129 B. C. His plays are nearly all founded on Greek subjects connected with the Trojan war: except fragments preserved in the writings of Cicero and in the 'Attic Nights' of Gellius, they are all lost. Among these fragments is one in which the poet is seen to have been a rather bold free-thinker, considering the age in which he lived: "They who understand the notes of birds" (i. e., augurs, haruspices, etc.), "and derive their wisdom more from examining the livers of other creatures than from their own [wit]. I think should be rather heard than heeded."

Paddock, Mrs. Cornelia. An American writer of fiction. Her works are: 'In the Toils' (1879); 'The Fate of Madame la Tour: A Tale of Great Salt Lake' (1881).

Padilla, Pedro de (pä-dē'lyä). A Spanish poet; born at Linares; died about 1595. He was a friend of Cervantes, and a notable improvisator. He renounced the world in his old age and became a Carmelite friar (1585). His works consist of lyric and bucolic poems, satires, spiritual songs, and metrical romances: some of them, especially the eclogues, are among the best of their time. His poems were published under the titles: 'Treasury of Various Poems' (1575); 'Pastoral Eclogues' (1581); 'Romances' (1583); 'Spiritual Garden' (1585); 'Grandeurs and Excellencies of the Virgin Our Lady' (1587).

Page, Thomas Nelson. An American writer of fiction; born in Oakland, Va., April 23, 1853. He was educated at Washington and Lee University, and practiced law at Richmond, Va. His first story, 'Marse Chan' (1887), attracted immediate attention and was widely read. He has written: 'Two Little Confederates' (1888); 'On New-Found River' (1891); 'Elsket and Other Stories' (1891); 'The Old South' (1892); 'Pastime Stories' (1894); 'Unc' Edinburgh' (1895); 'Social Life in Old Virginia' (1897); 'Two Prisoners' (1897); 'Red Rock' (1898); 'Gordon Keith' (1903); 'The Negro—The Southerner's Problem' (1904); 'Bred in the Bone' (1905); 'Under the Cross' (1907).

Paget, Francis Edward. An English story-writer; born May 24, 1806; died Aug. 4, 1882. His most important work is a compilation of 'Some Records of the Ashstead Estate' (1873). His stories deal with church and social reform; among them are: 'Caleb Kniverton, the Incendiary' (1833); 'Milford Malvoisin; or, Pews and Pewholders' (1842); 'The Curate of Cumberworth and the Vicar of Roost' (1859).

Paget, Violet. ["Vernon Lee."] An English story-teller and miscellaneous writer; born at Château St.-Leonard in Normandy. She is author of several works on the history of art and of culture, among them 'Studies of the 18th

Century in Italy' (1880); 'Belcaro: Essays on Sundry Æsthetical Questions' (1881); 'Euphorion: Studies of the Antique and the Mediæval in the Renaissance' (2 vols. 2d ed. 1885); 'Renaissance Fancies and Studies' (1895). Among her stories are: 'Ottilie' (1883); 'Miss Brown' (1884); 'Limbo, Essays' (1897).

Pailleron, Édouard Jules Henri (pä-yer-oñ'). A French dramatic writer; born at Paris, Sept. 17, 1834; died there April 20, 1899. Author of the comedy 'The Parasite' (1860); 'The Parasites,' a volume of satiric poems; the comedies 'Last Quarters,' the last stage of a wedding tour (1863); 'The Second Movement' (1865); 'The World where One is Amused' (1868); 'The World of Boredom' (1881); 'The Mouse' (1887); 'The Strolling Players.' He wrote three volumes of poems; viz., 'Loves and Hatreds' (1869), 'Prayer for France' (1871), 'The Doll' (1884); and 'Academic Discourses' (1886).

Pain, Marie Joseph (pañ). A French dramatist; born at Paris, 1773; died there, 1830. Beginning with 'Saint-Far, or Love's Daintiness,' in the initial crisis of the Revolution (1792), he followed it with a long series of vaudevilles and comedies, some of which had great success; among them: 'A Flat to Let' (1799); 'The Connoisseur' (1800); 'The Duke's Portrait' (1805); 'Love and Mystery; or, Which Is my Cousin?' (1807); 'The Dreamers Awakened' (1813); 'The Ghost' (1816).

Paine, Robert Treat, Jr. An American poet; born in Taunton, Mass., Dec. 9, 1773; died in Boston, Nov. 13, 1811. During the greater part of his erratic career he was engaged in various literary pursuits, although he was at one time in business, and later practiced law for a brief period. He will be best remembered as the author of two songs, 'Rise, Columbia,' and 'Adams and Liberty.' Among his poems are: 'The Invention of Letters' (1795), and 'The Ruling Passion' (1797).

Paine, Thomas. A celebrated American publicist; born at Thetford in Norfolkshire, England, Jan. 29, 1736-7; died at New Rochelle, N. Y., June 8, 1809. He wrote 'Common Sense' (1776); 'The Rights of Man' (2 vols., 1790); 'The Age of Reason' (1793); 'Decline and Fall of the English System of Finance' (1896: it had 14 editions in that year).

Painter, William. An English writer and compiler of stories after the manner of Boccaccio; born about 1540; died Feb., 1893-4. His most famous book is 'The Palace of Pleasure' (2 vols., 1566-67), consisting of stories taken from the 'Heptameron,' from Bandello, and other Italian story-tellers.

Palacky, Frantisek (pä-lạts-kẽ'). A Czech historian; born at Hodoslavitz in Moravia, June 14, 1798; died at Prague, May 26, 1876. He was appointed State historian of Bohemia in 1839. He wrote a 'History of Bohemia' down to the year 1526 (1836-67); 'Beginnings of Bohemian Poetry' (1818); 'Estimate of the Ancient Bohemian Historians' (1830); 'Literary

Travels in Italy in the Year 1837, in Search of Documents for Bohemian and Moravian History' (1838); 'The Earliest Monuments of the Bohemian Language' (1840); 'History of Hussitism' (1868); 'Documents Illustrating the Life, the Cause, and the Teaching of Master John Huss' (1869).

Palaprat, Jean Sieur de Bigot (pä-lä-prä). A French dramatist; born at Toulouse, 1650; died at Paris, 1721. He is best known for certain lively comedies written by him in collaboration with the Abbé Brueys; chief among these are: 'The Mute'; 'The Grumbler' (1681); 'The Ridiculous Concert' (1689); 'The Secret Revealed' (1690). Independently he wrote: 'Quid pro Quo'; 'Hercules and Omphale', 'The Prude.'

Palearius, Aonius, or **Antonio della Paglia** (pä-le-är'ē-us). An Italian polemic writer; born at Veroli in the Pontifical States; died at Rome, 1570. He wrote several theological dissertations, and a notable 'Disputation against the Roman Pontiffs and their Adherents'; his best work is a poem 'On the Immortality of the Soul' (1531), one of the finest specimens of Latin poetry written in the 16th century.

Paley, Frederick Apthorp. An English scholar and writer on architecture, grandson of William. He graduated in 1838 at Cambridge, became a Roman Catholic in 1846, and professor of classical literature in University College from 1874. He edited many Greek and Latin texts, and published a 'Manual of Gothic Architecture' (1846), and other writings on similar subjects. Born Jan. 14, 1815; died, Dec. 9, 1888.

Paley, William. A distinguished English theological writer; born at Peterborough, 1743; died May 25, 1805. He was appointed archdeacon of Carlisle, 1782; prebendary of St. Paul's, London, 1794; dean of Lincoln, 1795. His principal writings are: 'Principles of Moral and Political Philosophy' (1785); 'Horæ Paulinæ; or, The Truth of the Scripture History of St. Paul Evinced,' etc. (1791); 'View of the Evidences of Christianity' (1794), his most celebrated work; 'Natural Theology; or, Evidences of the Existence and Attributes of the Deity Collected from the Appearances of Nature' (1802), in some respects the most remarkable of all his writings.

Pálffy, Albert (päl'fẽ). A Hungarian novelist and publicist; born at Gyula, 1820. In the year of revolutions, 1848, he started a daily journal, The Fifteenth of March, which had a powerful influence in inciting the Hungarian people to insurrection. He was incarcerated for several months after the suppression of the rebellion, and then resumed his labors as a novelist. His principal stories are: 'The Hungarian Millionaire' (1845); 'The Black Book' (1846); 'Stories Left Behind by a Refugee' (1850); 'Mother and Countess' (1886); 'Last Years of Old Hungary' (1890). D. Dec. 23, 1897.

Palfrey, Francis Winthrop. An American historical writer; born in Boston, April 11, 1831;

died in Cannes, France, Dec. 5, 1889. He was educated as a lawyer; served in the Civil War as colonel of the 20th Massachusetts Infantry. He published 'A Memoir of William F. Bartlett' (1879); 'Antietam and Fredericksburg,' being Vol. v. of 'Campaigns of the Civil War' (1882).

Palfrey, John Gorham. An American clergyman and author; born in Boston, May 2, 1796; died in Cambridge, Mass., April 26, 1881. He graduated at Harvard; was pastor of Brattle Street Unitarian Church, Boston; professor in Harvard, 1830–39; member of the State Legislature, 1842–43; Secretary of State of Massachusetts, 1844–48; and member of the Anti-Slavery Congress at Paris, 1867. He published numerous lectures, addresses, and sermons; and wrote 'The Relation between Judaism and Christianity' (1854). His enduring work, however, is 'The History of New England' (4 vols., 1858–64).

Palfrey, Sarah Hammond. ["E. Foxton."] An American novelist and poet, daughter of John G.; born in Massachusetts in 1823. She resides in Cambridge, Mass. Among her poetical works are: 'Prémices'; 'The Chapel'; 'Agnes Wentworth.' She has also published the stories 'Katherine Morne'; 'Hermann, or Young Knighthood' (1866).

Palgrave, Francis, Sir. An English historian of Jewish parentage, originally named Cohen; born in London, 1788; died July 6, 1861. Besides numerous contributions to the reviews, he wrote: 'History of England' (1831); 'Rise and Progress of the English Commonwealth' (1832); 'Detached Thoughts on the Polity and Ecclesiastical History of the Middle Ages'; 'History of Normandy and England' (4 vols., 1851–64); 'Merchant and Friar' (1837), an imaginary history of Marco Polo and Friar Bacon.

Palgrave, Francis Turner. An English poet and art critic, son of Sir Francis; born at Great Yarmouth, Sept. 28, 1824; died in London, Oct. 24, 1897. From 1885 to 1895 he was a professor at Oxford. His books are: 'Idylls and Songs' (1854); the famous anthology 'The Golden Treasury' of English poetry (1861); 'Essays on Art' (1866); 'Hymns' (1868); 'Lyrical Poems' (1871); 'The Visions of England' (1881); 'The Life of Jesus Christ Illustrated from the Italian Painters of the 14th, 15th, and 16th Centuries' (1885); 'Amenophis and Other Poems' (1892). A second 'Golden Treasury' was published in 1897.

Palgrave, Reginald F. D., Sir. An English writer on history and parliamentary law, son of Sir Francis; born at London, June 28, 1829. He wrote: 'The Chairman's Handbook (11th ed. 1895); 'The House of Commons'; 'Oliver Cromwell, the Protector: an Appreciation Based on Contemporary Evidence' (1890), in which he presents the antidote to Thomas Carlyle's 'Life and Letters of Oliver Cromwell.'

Palgrave, William Gifford. An English traveler, son of Sir Francis; born in London, Jan. 24, 1826; died at Montevideo, Sept. 30, 1888.

His chief writings are: Narrative of a Year's Journey through Central and Eastern Arabia' (2 vols., 1862–63); 'Essays on Eastern Questions' (1872); 'Herrmann Agha,' a story (1872); 'Dutch Guiana' (1876); 'Ulysses: Scenes and Studies in Many Lands' (1887); a posthumous poem, 'A Vision of Life: Semblance and Reality' (1891).

Palissot de Montenoy, Charles (pä-lē-so' dĕ môn̄t-nwä'). A French poet; born at Nancy, Jan. 3, 1730; died at Paris, June 15, 1814. At 14 he took the degree of Bachelor of Theology, but gave up the ecclesiastical career for literature, and was appointed director of the Mazarin Library. With his first tragedies he had little success; otherwise with his comedies 'The Guardians' and 'The Barber of Bagdad.' His satiric piece 'The Coterie' (Le Cercle), attacking Rousseau, brought down upon him the enmity of the encyclopedists, who paid him back with 'Little Letters on Great Philosophers' (1757), and the comedy 'The Philosophers' (1760). He lived on pacific terms with Voltaire, and even dedicated to him his 'Dunciad, or War of the Blockheads' (1764).

Palissy, Bernard (pä-lē-sē). A great artistic potter and glass-painter; born at La Chapelle, Biron, in the province of Périgord, 1510; died about 1590, in the Bastille, where he was imprisoned on the charge of heresy. His writings are: 'Veritable Receipt whereby all Men in France can Learn to Multiply and Enlarge their Treasures,' etc. (1564); 'Admirable Discourses on the Nature of Waters and Fountains' (1580).

Pallavicino, Sforza, Cardinal (pä-lä-vē'chenō). An Italian church historian; born at Rome, Nov. 28, 1607; died June 4, 1667. He became a member of the Company of Jesus in 1638; was raised to the cardinalate in 1659. His principal work, 'History of the Council of Trent,' written in Italian, was first published (2 vols., folio) in 1656–57; the second edition (1666) had many changes. The work was written to counteract Sarpi's history of the same council.

Palleske, Emil (pä-lesk'ĕ). A German elocutionist and author; born at Tempelburg, in Pomerania, Jan. 5, 1823; died at Thal, near Eisenach, Oct. 28, 1880. He gave dramatic readings, especially of Shakespeare's plays, throughout Germany. He wrote 'Life and Work of Schiller' (2 vols., 1858–59); 'Charlotte von Kalb: in Memoriam' (1880).

Palma y Romay, Ramón (päl'mä ē rō'mä). A Cuban dramatist and poet; born in Havana, in January 1812; died there, January 1860. His first poems were published in 1830. The drama 'La Vuelta del Cruzado,' performed in 1837, met great success. Volumes of his poems have appeared with the titles: 'Aves de Paso' (1841); 'Hojas Caidas' (1843); and 'Melodias Poéticas' (1846).

Palmeirim, Luiz Augusto (päl-mī'rēm). A Portuguese poet; born at Lisbon, Aug. 9, 1825;

died there, Dec. 4, 1893. His first collection of lyric verse, 'Poesies' (1851), reached a 5th edition in his lifetime, and won for him the title "the Béranger of Portugal." Among his patriotic poems, 'Exiled' is the one best known. His lyrics have been published as 'Popular Songs.' He wrote also some comedies in verse; a 'Gallery of Portuguese Portraits' (1878); and 'The Eccentrics of my Time' (1891).

Palmer, Edward Henry. An English Orientalist; born at Cambridge, Aug. 7, 1840, died in Egypt, 1882. He wrote Arabic and Persian grammars; made a metrical translation of the 'Poetical Works of Behá-ed-din Zoheir of Egypt' (1876); translated the 'Koran' (1880); wrote a 'Life of Haroun Alraschid' (1881); and a series of papers on 'Arab Humour.'

Palmer, John Williamson. An American physician and miscellaneous writer; born in Baltimore, Md., April 4, 1825; died on February 26, 1906. In 1870 he settled in New York; subsequently was connected with the staff of the Century Dictionary. Among his writings are: 'The Golden Dagon; or, Up and Down the Irrawaddi' (1853); 'The New and the Old; or, California and India in Romantic Aspects' (1859); 'After his Kind, by John Coventry,' a novel (1886); and 'Stonewall Jackson's Way,' which was one of the most popular ballads of the Civil War.

Palmer, Joseph. An English miscellaneous writer; born 1756; died at Eastbourne in Sussex, Sept. 4, 1815. He wrote: 'A Fortnight's Ramble to the Lakes,' etc. (1782); 'Half-Pay,' a narrative poem; 'The Lancashire Collier Girl' (1795); 'Siege of Gibraltar' (1795), a poem; 'Windermere' (1798), a poem.

Palmer, Julius Auboineau. An American author; born in Massachusetts in 1840. Among his works are: 'One Voyage and its Consequences' (1889); 'About Mushrooms' (1894); 'Memories of Hawaii' (1894); 'Again in Hawaii' (1895). He died 1900.

Palmer, Mary. An English writer, niece of Sir Joshua Reynolds; born at Plympton Earl in Devonshire, Feb. 9, 1716; died at Great Torrington, May 27, 1794. She wrote 'A Devonshire Dialogue,' the best piece of literature in the Devon dialect.

Palmer, Ray. An American clergyman and hymn-writer; born at Little Compton, R. I., Nov. 12, 1808; died at Newark, N. J., March 29, 1887. He was pastor of Congregational churches in Bath, Me., and Albany, N. Y., and secretary of the Congregational Union, 1866–78. His best-known hymn is 'My Faith Looks Up to Thee,' which has been translated into twenty languages. He has published: 'Spiritual Improvement' (1839); 'Hymns and Sacred Pieces' (1865); 'Hymns of my Holy Hours' (1866).

Palmer, William. An English theologian and archæologist; born at Mixbury in Oxfordshire, July 12, 1811; died at Rome, April 4, 1879. He was a clergyman of the Established Church, but seceded to Rome in 1855. He was a voluminous writer. Among his works are: 'Short Poems and Hymns' (1843); 'Remarks on the Turkish Question' (1858); 'Introduction to Early Christian Symbolism' (1859); 'Egyptian Chronicles' (1861); 'Commentary on the Book of Daniel' (1874).

Palmer, William Pitt. An American poet; born in Stockbridge, Mass., Feb. 22, 1805; died in Brooklyn, N. Y., May 2, 1884. He wrote many poems, some of which became famous; among them are the 'Ode to Light' and 'Orpheus and Eurydice.'

Palmotta, Giunio (päl-mot'tä). A Dalmatian poet; born at Ragusa, 1606; died 1657. Among his works are: 'The Christiad; or, Life of Jesus Christ,' in 24 cantos (1670); some dramas, as 'Atalanta,' 'Œdipus,' 'The Rape of Helen'; and the poem 'Glorious History of the Slav Kings of Dalmatia.'

Paltock, Robert. An English story-writer; born at London, about 1697; died there, March 20, 1767. He is known to fame only through his story 'Peter Wilkins, a Cornishman' (1750).

Paludan-Müller, Frederik (päl'ö-dän-mel'ler). A Danish poet; born at Kjerteminde in the island of Fuynen, Feb. 7, 1809; died at Copenhagen, Dec. 28, 1876. He wrote: 'Love at Court' (1832), a romantic drama; the spirited Byronesque poem 'The Dancers' (1833); 'Cupid and Psyche' (1834); 'Trochees and Iambics' (1837); 'Poems' (2 vols., 1836–38); the dramatic poems 'Venus' (1841), 'Tithon' (1844); the great satirical poem 'The Man Adam' (3 vols., 1841–49), his masterpiece; 'Aeronauts and Atheists' (1853), a versified defense of Christianity; 'Death of Abel'; 'Ahasuerus'; 'Benedict of Nursia' (1854–62). His chief prose writings are 'The Fountain of Youth' (1865), and 'Story of Ivar Lykke' (3 vols., 1866–73). One of his latest poems is 'Adonis,' in which he returns to mythological themes.

Panaieff, Vladimir Ivanovitch (pä-ni'yef). A Russian story-writer and poet; born in the government of Kazan, 1792; died at St. Petersburg, 1854. He wrote 'Panegyrics' of the poet Derzhavin (1817) and the Emperor Alexander I. (1820); 'Idylls' (1820); 'Miscellaneous Poems'; 'Stories.'

Panard, François (pän-är'). A noted French lyric poet; born at Courville near Chartres, about 1694; died at Paris, June 13, 1765. He wrote a series of admirable songs, besides vaudevilles and comic operas. He lived on the bounty of his friends, repaying them with his verses.

Panini (pä'nē-nē). A celebrated Indian philologist of the fourth century B.C. There is extant a philological work written by him, consisting of eight books of Sanskrit grammatical rules: it was published at Calcutta (2 vols., 1809).

Panormita. See **Beccadelli.**

Pansy. See **Alden.**

Pantenius, Theodor Hermann (pän-tē'nĕ-us). A German novelist; born at Mitau in Courland, Oct. 10, 1843. Under the pseudonym of «Theodor Hermann» he wrote: 'Wilhelm Wolfschild' (2d ed. 1873); 'Alone and Free' (1875); 'Ruddy Gold' (1881); 'Stories from Courland' (1892).

Paparrhigopoulos, Constantine (pä''pä-rē-gop'ŏ-los). A modern Greek historian; born at Constantinople in 1815; died at Athens, April 26, 1891. His father was a rich banker of Constantinople, who was put to death during the Greek Revolution of 1821. The son, having escaped to Russia, was educated at Odessa at the expense of the Czar Alexander, and in 1854 became professor of history at the University of Athens. His principal work, 'A History of the Greek People' (5 vols., 1862–77), was translated into French in an abridged form as a 'History of Hellenic Civilization' (1878).

Papillon, Marc de (pä-pē-yôn'), known as "Captain Lasphrise." A French poet; born at Amboise, 1555; died about 1605. In 1590 he published a volume of stanzas, songs, elegies, epigrams, satires, epitaphs, etc. His verses are graceful and enlivened with wit, but many of them are licentious. Toward the end of his life he composed poems on religious subjects; e. g., a versified rendering of the 'Canticle of the Three Children in the Fiery Furnace,' the 'Magnificat,' the 'Lord's Prayer,' etc.

Pardo-Bazán, Emilia (pär-dō-bä-zän'). A Spanish story-teller; born at Coruña, 1852. Most noteworthy among her writings are: 'Pascual Lopez' (1888); 'Mother Nature' (2 vols., 1888); Morriña, a Love Story' (1889); 'The Palpitating Question' (4th ed. 1891). She commenced the publication of the monthly New Critical Theatre in 1890.

Pardoe, Julia. An English historical and miscellaneous writer; born at Beverly, Yorkshire, 1806; died in London, Nov. 26, 1862. She was a most voluminous writer, among her works being: 'Traditions of Portugal' (1833); 'City of the Sultan,' etc. (1837); 'Louis XIV. and the Court and Reign of France' (1847); 'The Jealous Wife' (1847–58); 'The Court and Reign of Francis I.' (1849); 'Marie de' Medici' (1852); 'Episodes of French History, during the Consulate,' etc. (1859); 'A Life Struggle' (1859).

Pardon, George Frederick. An English miscellaneous writer; born at London, 1824; died 1884. He wrote many handbooks of games, sports, and pastimes; several stories, as 'Faces in the Fire' (1856); 'Tales from the Operas' (1858); 'Boldheart the Warrior' (1859); 'Noble by Heritage' (1877); 'Stories About Animals'; 'Stories About Birds'; 'Illustrious Women who have Distinguished Themselves for Virtue, Piety, and Benevolence' (1868).

Parini, Giuseppe (pä-rē'nē). An Italian lyric and satiric poet; born in the village of Bosisio in the Milanese, May 22, 1729; died at Milan, Aug. 15, 1799. His chief work is a social satire in four parts, called 'Morning,' 'Noon,' 'Evening,' and 'Night,' afterward collected and named 'Day.' ('Works,' 6 vols., 1801–4.)

Paris, Gaston Bruno Paulin (pä-rēs'). A distinguished French Romance philologist; born at Avenay, Aug. 9, 1839. He was professor of the French language and literature at the Collège de France, and did much to arouse interest in the study of Romance philology. 'A Poetical History of Charlemagne' (1866); 'Poetry of the Middle Ages' (1885), and 'French Mediæval Literature' (1888), were his most important publications. He was a member of German, Austrian, and Italian academies. Died at Paris, March 6, 1903.

Paris, Matthew. A celebrated mediæval chronicler; his birthplace and date of birth are unknown; he died about 1259. He became a novice in the Benedictine monastery of St. Albans, England, in 1217; was received into the order, and was employed in many weighty affairs of church and State. His principal work is his 'Greater History,' or 'Larger Chronicles' of events down to 1259. Among his other writings is the 'Lives of Twenty-three Abbots of St. Albans.'

Parisius, Ludolf (pär-ē'sē-us). A German publicist; born at Gardelegen, Oct. 15, 1827. Besides several political pamphlets, he wrote: 'Commentary on the Imperial Law against Associations' (1876); 'German Political Parties, and the Ministry of Bismarck' (1877); the novels 'Duty and Obligation' (1873), 'Weary of Freedom' (1873), 'In the Woods and on the Heath'; 'German Popular Songs'; 'Pictures from Ancient Brandenburg' (2 vols., 1882–84).

Park, Andrew. A Scotch poet; born at Renfrew, March 7, 1807; died at Glasgow, Dec. 27, 1863. After an Oriental tour he published 'Egypt and the East' (1856). His poems are: 'The Vision of Mankind'; 'The Bridegroom and the Bride' (1834); 'Silent Love,' a graceful poem (1843); 'Veritas' (1849), a poem of an autobiographical character.

Park, John. A Scotch poet; born at Greenock, Jan. 14, 1804; died at St. Andrews, April 8, 1865. He wrote many songs which have become popular favorites, among them 'O gin I were where Gadie rins,' and 'The Miller's Daughter.' His songs were not published till after his death; then also was published a volume of his 'Lectures and Sermons' (1865).

Park, Mungo. A celebrated Scottish traveler; born at Fowlshiels, Sept. 10, 1771; died in equatorial Africa in 1806. He was sent to Africa under the auspices of the African Association, and explored the Gambia and upper Niger, publishing on his return the well-known 'Travels in the Interior of Africa' (1799). On his second expedition, which was equipped by the British government, he descended the Niger some 1500 miles; and after losing the majority of his men from fever, was treacherously murdered by natives.

Park, Roswell. An American miscellaneous writer; born in Lebanon, Conn., 1807; died in Chicago, Ill., 1869. He published: 'Selections of Juvenile and Miscellaneous Poems' (1836); 'Sketch of the History of West Point' (1840); 'Pantology, or Systematic Survey of Human Knowledge' (1841); and 'Jerusalem, and Other Poems' (1857).

Parker, Edwin Pond. An American clergyman, hymn-writer, and author; born at Castine, Me., 1836. He has been pastor of the South Congregational Church in Hartford, Conn., since 1860. He is the author of several hymns, and has published among other works 'Book of Praise'; 'The Ministry of Beauty'; 'Sermons on Domestic Duties.'

Parker, Sir Gilbert. A Canadian novelist, now living in London; born in Ontario, 1862; Among his works are: 'Pierre and his People'; 'Tales of the Far North'; 'An Adventurer of the North'; 'A Romany of the Snows'; 'A Lover's Diary' (1894); 'The Trail of the Sword' (1894); 'When Valmond Came to Pontiac'; 'The Seats of the Mighty'; 'The Pomp of the Lavillettes'; 'The Trespasser.'

Parker, John Henry. An English archæologist; born in London in 1806; died in 1884. He superintended many excavations in Rome, and was the author of 'The Archæology of Rome' (3 vols., 1874-84), an important work on the walls, aqueducts, tombs, etc., of the Eternal City. His other publications are: a 'Glossary of Architecture' (1836), an important aid to the revival of Gothic art; 'Introduction to the Study of Gothic Architecture' (1849).

Parker, Martin. A noted English balladist; the dates of his birth and death are unknown, but he died probably in 1656. Among his ballads are: 'When the King Enjoyes his Own Again'; 'The King and a Poore Northerne Man'; 'Sailors for my Money'; 'John and Joan; or, A Mad Couple Well Met.'

Parker, Theodore. A distinguished American preacher and reformer; born at Lexington, Mass., Aug. 24, 1810; died at Florence, May 10, 1860. He was pastor of a Unitarian church in Roxbury (1836-43), meanwhile contributing to the Dial essays and reviews in which he gave expression to theological opinions of extreme heterodoxy. His 'Discourse on Matters Pertaining to Religion' (1842), a volume of lectures delivered by him in Boston, made him famous, and he finally left Roxbury and preached regularly in that city. He also lectured in the chief cities of the Union. He published 'Theism, Atheism, and the Popular Theology' (1853), and a volume of 'Ten Sermons on Religion' (1852).

Parkhurst, Charles Henry. An American clergyman and reformer; born at Framingham, Mass., April 17, 1842. He graduated at Amherst College in 1866, and studied theology in Germany. Since 1880 he has been pastor of the Madison Square Presbyterian Church. In 1891, as president of the Society for the Prevention of Crime, he began his attack on the

police department of New York city, and was prominent in the Lexow investigation which followed. His writings include: 'The Blind Man's Creed' (1883); 'Three Gates on a Side' (1891); 'Our Fight with Tammany' (1895).

Parkman, Francis. An eminent American historian; born at Boston, Sept. 16, 1823; died at Jamaica Plain, Mass., Nov. 8, 1893. He wrote: 'The Oregon Trail: Prairie and Rocky Mountain Life' (1849); 'History of the Conspiracy of Pontiac' (2 vols., 1851); 'The Pioneers of France in the New World' (1865); 'The Jesuits in North America' (1866), 'La Salle and the Discovery of the Great West' (1869); 'The Old Régime in Canada' (1874); 'Count Frontenac and New France under Louis XIV.' (1877); 'Montcalm and Wolfe' (2 vols., 1884); 'A Half-Century of Conflict' (2 vols., 1892).

Parley, Peter. See Goodrich.

Parmenides (pär-men'i-dēz). A celebrated Greek philosopher of the fifth century B. C.; born at Elea in Southern Italy. He wrote but one work on philosophy,—a didactic poem in the epic metre and in the Ionic dialect, entitled 'On Nature': fragments of it, in all about 160 lines, have come down to our times. It was divided into three sections, 'Proem,' 'Truth,' 'Opinion.' The fragments have been rendered into English by Thomas Davidson.

Parnell, Thomas. An Irish poet; born at Dublin, 1679; died 1718. He was a minister of the established Irish Church, and held a cure of souls in Ireland, but spent most of his life in England. His works are: a volume of 'Poems,' in which is 'The Hermit'; a 'Life of Homer' prefixed, and a translation of the 'Battle of the Frogs and Mice' always suffixed, to Pope's version of the Iliad.

Parny, Évariste Désiré Desforges, Viscomte de (pär-nē'). A French poet; born in the Isle of Bourbon, Feb. 6, 1753; died at Paris, Dec. 5, 1814. He won celebrity through his volume of 'Erotic Poems,' which first appeared in incomplete form 1778, completed 1781: Voltaire saluted him, "My dear Tibullus." In 1799 he published 'The War of the Gods,' afterward enlarged and named 'The Christianide': it is a cynical and impious attack upon all religions. He published (1805) 'The Stolen Portfolio,' containing 'Venus's Disguises,' 'Gallantries of the Bible,' 'Paradise Lost.'

Parodi, Dominique Alexandre (pä-rō-dē'). A French poet of Greek origin; born in the island of Crete, Nov. 15, 1840. He spent his early years at Smyrna, then lived for a time at Milan, and afterward settled in Paris as a journalist. He wrote: 'The Last of the Popes,' a novel, in Italian; a volume of French verses, 'Passions and Thoughts' (1865); 'Messenian Tales' (1867); 'The Triumph of Peace' (1878); 'Flesh and Soul Cry Out' (1883). He wrote also the tragedy 'Rome Vanquished' (1876), and the Scriptural poem 'Sephora' (1877).

Parr, Samuel. A famous English scholar and educator; born at Harrow-on-the-Hill, Jan.

27

15, 1747; died at Hatton, March 6, 1825. He was chief assistant at Harrow, 1767-71; afterwards master of schools at Colchester and Norwich; and prebend of St. Paul's, London. He was famous for extent and variety of learning and for conversational powers. His writings (8 vols., 1828) include sermons, memoirs, reviews, dissertations, etc.,—a mass of crude scholarship not focused to any special field, and perishing with itself. 'Aphorisms, Opinions, and Reflections by Dr. Parr' (1826) was an effort to preserve some of the talk which helped to make him a popular colossus in his day.

Parrot, Henry. An English epigrammatist; place and date of birth and death unknown. In the first quarter of the 17th century he published six volumes of licentious epigrams and satires. One of the volumes was entitled 'Springes to Catch Woodcocks' (1613), and contains 216 epigrams; another, 'Cures for the Itch : Characters, Epigrams, Epitaphs' (1626).

Parsons, Mrs. Eliza. An English novelist and dramatist; born at Plymouth; died at Leytonstone in Essex, Feb. 5, 1811. She wrote the farce 'Intrigues of a Morning; or, An Hour at Paris' (1792), an adaptation of Molière's 'Monsieur de Pourceaugnac'; the novels 'History f Miss Meredith' (1790); 'The Castle of Wolfenbach' (1793); 'The Peasant of Ardennes Forest'; 'The Mysterious Visits'; and others.

Parsons, Mrs. Frances Theodora (Smith) (Dana). An American writer of Albany, N.Y.; born in New York State in 1861. Under the name of «William Starr Dana» she has published : 'How to Know the Wild Flowers'; 'According to Season'; 'Plants and their Children.'

Parsons, George Frederic. An American journalist and writer; born in Brighton, England, January 15, 1840; died in New York city, July 19, 1893. In 1863 he began journalistic work at Vancouver Island; subsequently was editor of the Sacramento (Cal.) Record Union. In 1883 he joined the editorial staff of the New York Tribune. His works include : 'Life of James Marshall,' discoverer of gold in California (1871); 'Middle Ground,' a novel (1874).

Parsons, Mrs. Gertrude. An English novelist Dorn, 1812; died at Hextmouth, Feb. 12, 1891. Among her novels are : 'Thornberry Abbey' (1846); 'Emma Cross: A Tale' (1859); 'Ruth Baynard's Story' (1861); 'Major Vandermere' (1876). She wrote also 'Life of St. Ignatius of Loyola' (1860); 'Life of St. Colette' (1879).

Parsons, Philip. An English miscellaneous writer; born at Dedham in Essex, 1729; died at Wye, June 12, 1812. His principal work is 'Monuments and Painted Glass in upwards of 100 Churches' (1794). He wrote also : 'Inefficacy of Satire : a Poem' (1766); 'Dialogues of the Dead with the Living' (1779); 'Simplicity : A Poem' (1784).

Parsons, Thomas William. An American poet ; born at Boston, Aug. 18, 1819; died at Scituate, Sept. 3, 1892. He made a metrical translation of the first ten cantos of Dante's 'Inferno' (1843), and afterwards of the others (1867). He published a volume of poems, 'Ghetto di Roma' (1854); 'The Magnolia' (1867); 'The Old House at Sudbury' (1870); 'The Shadow of the Obelisk' (1872).

Parsons, William. An English poet of the 18th century; died 1807. He wrote 'A Poetical Tour' (1787); 'Ode to a Boy at Eton' (1796); 'Fidelity, or Love at First ,ght, with Other Poems' (1798).

Parthenius (pär-thē'nē-us). A Bithynian poet said to have lived in Rome in the first century B. C. He wrote 'Metamorphoses' and other poems, none of which are preserved except one on 'Amatory Affections,' dedicated to the poet Cornelius Gallus.

Partington, Mrs. See **Shillaber.**

Parton, James. An American writer; born at Canterbury, England, Feb. 9, 1822; died at Newburyport. Mass., Oct. 17, 1891. He wrote many valuable biographies, as : 'Life of Horace Greeley' (1855); 'Life and Times of Aaron Burr' (1857); 'General Butler in New Orleans' (1863); 'Life and Times of Benjamin Franklin' (1864); 'Famous Americans of Recent Times' (1870); 'Life of Thomas Jefferson' (1874); 'Life of Voltaire' (1881). Among his other works are : 'Humorous Poetry of the English Language' (1857); 'Triumphs of Enterprise, Ingenuity, and Public Spirit' (1871); 'Topics of the Time' (1871); 'Caricature in all Times and Lands' (1875).

Parton, Sara Payson Willis. [«Fanny Fern.»] An American essay-writer, sister of N. P. Willis and wife of James Parton; born in Portland, Me., July 9, 1811; died in Brooklyn, N. Y., Oct. 10, 1872. She is said to have contributed an article each week, for sixteen years, to the New York Ledger. She published two novels,—'Ruth Hall' (1854), a slightly veiled autobiography, and 'Rose Clark' (1857); and collections from her contributions to the weekly press.

Partridge, John. An English poet and translator; he flourished in the latter half of the 16th century. Besides prose work, he wrote : 'The Most Famouse and Worthie Historie of the Worthy Lady Pendavola'; 'The Worthye Historie of the Most Noble and Valiaunt Knight Plasidas'; 'The Notable Hystorie of the Two Famous Princes of the World, Astianax and Polixena'—all published in 1566.

Partridge, William Ordway. An American sculptor and writer on art; born in France in 1861. He is a resident of Milton, Mass., and the author of 'Art for America' (1894); 'The Song Life of a Sculptor' (1894); 'The Technique of Sculpture' (1895); 'The Czar's Gift' (1906).

Parzanese, Pierpaulo (pär-tsän-ā'ze). An Italian poet; born at Ariano in the kingdom of Naples, about 1800; died 1852. He wrote : 'Popular Songs'; 'Songs of the Poor'; 'Miscellaneous Verses'; 'The Man of Viggiano.'

Pascal, Blaise (päs-käl'). A celebrated French philosopher and mathematician; born at Clermont Ferrand in Auvergne, June 19, 1623; died at Paris, Aug. 19, 1662. Among his writings are: 'Letters Written by Louis Montalte to a Friend in the Provinces,' better known as the 'Provincial Letters' (1656); 'Thoughts on Religion' (Pensées), published several years after the author's death.

Pasqué, Ernst (päs-kā'). A German story-writer and musician; born at Cologne, Sept. 3, 1821; died at Alsbach, March 20, 1892. Among his novels are: 'The Grenadier of Pirmasens' (1875); 'The Prima Donna' (1879); 'The Vagabonds' (1886); 'Stories of Musicians' (1887); 'Magdalena: Story of a German Parisian Lioness' (1890).

Pasquier, Étienne (päs-kyä'). A celebrated French jurisconsult; born at Paris, 1529; died there, 1615. His greatest work is 'Researches on France,' in nine books, treating of the magistracies, States-general, Church affairs, famous trials, origin of French poetry, the French language, etc.; very important are 'Pasquier's Letters' (1619).

Passarge, Ludwig (päs-är'ge). A German miscellaneous writer; born at Wollitnick near Heiligenbeil, East Prussia, Aug. 6, 1825. He traveled extensively in Europe, and wrote: 'From the Weichsel Delta' (1857); 'Fragments from Italy' (1860); 'Sweden, Wisby, and Copenhagen' (1867); 'Summer Tours in Norway (2d ed. 1884. He wrote also: 'Henrik Ibsen' (1883); 'Baltic Stories' (1884); 'From Contemporary Spain and Portugal' (1884); and translated several works of Scandinavian poets.

Passerat, Jean (päs-ėr-ä'). A French poet and scholar; born at Troyes, 1534; died at Paris, 1602. Among his works are: 'Verses of Love and the Chase'; 'Metamorphosis of a Man into a Bird'; he wrote a complete commentary on Rabelais's works, but shortly before his death committed it to the flames.

Pater, Walter Horatio. An English literary and art critic; born at London, Aug. 4, 1839; died at Oxford, July 30, 1894. He wrote: 'The Renaissance: Studies in Art and Poetry' (1873); 'Marius the Epicurean' (1885); 'Imaginary Portraits' (1887); 'Appreciations' (1889); 'Plato and Platonism' (1893); 'Greek Studies' and 'Miscellaneous Studies and Essays,' posthumously published (1895).

Paterculus, Gaius Velleius (pa-tėr'kū-lus). A Roman historian; born about 19 B. C.; died after 30 A. D. He was a prefect or legate in the Roman army under Tiberius, and saw active service in Germania, Pannonia, and Dalmatia. His only extant work is the 'Historiæ Romanæ,' in two books; a compendium of universal, but more particularly of Roman, history. It is generally trustworthy, and valuable for confirmatory evidence.

Patmore, Coventry Kearsey Deighton. An English poet; born at Woodford, July 23, 1823; died at Lymington, Nov. 26, 1896. He wrote: 'The Angel in the House' (4 parts, 1854-62);

7th ed. 1877); 'The Unknown Eros' (1877); 'Amelia' (1878); 'Religio Poetæ' (1893); 'The Rod, the Root and the Flower' (1895); also 'Principle in Art, and Other Essays' (1889).

Patmore, Peter George. An English miscellaneous writer; born at London, 1786; died Dec. 19, 1855. He wrote: 'Imitations of Celebrated Authors, or Imaginary Rejected Articles' (1826); 'My Friends and Acquaintances, being Memorials, Mind-Portraits, and Personal Recollections,' etc. (1854); 'Marriage in Mayfair,' a comedy (1854).

Patten, George Washington. An American poet; born in Newport, R. I., Dec. 25, 1808; died in Houlton, Me., April 28, 1882. Educated at West Point, he served in the Mexican and Seminole wars. He acquired some reputation as a writer, and has been called the "poet-laureate of the army." Among his lyrics are: 'The Seminole's Reply,' once declaimed by most American schoolboys; 'Joys that We've Tasted'; and 'An Episode of the Mexican War.' He published in book-form: 'Artillery Drill' (1861); 'Army Manual' (1863); 'Voices of the Border,' a collection of his poems (1867).

Pattison, Mark. An English critic and historian of literature; born at Hornby in Yorkshire, Oct. 10, 1813; died at Harrogate, July 30, 1884. His writings were for the most part contributions to the quarterlies, and notes and commentaries on classic authors ancient and modern. His chief book is 'Isaac Casaubon' (1875), a life of the great scholar giving a vivid picture of literary life in the 16th century. His autobiographical 'Memoirs' (1883) come down only to the year 1860.

Patton, Jacob Harris. An American historical writer; born in Fayette County, Pa., May 20, 1812. Among his publications are: 'A Concise History of the American People' (2 vols., 1860-82); 'Yorktown, 1781-1881' (1881); 'The Democratic Party, its History and Influence' (1884); and 'The Natural Resources of the United States' (1888).

Paul, John. See **Webb, Charles Henry.**

Paulding, James Kirke. An American novelist; born in Dutchess County, N. Y., Aug. 22, 1779; died at Hyde Park, N. Y., April 6, 1860. He founded, with Washington Irving, the satirical journal Salmagundi. He wrote: 'Lay of a Scotch Fiddle' (1813); 'The United States and England' (1814); 'The Diverting History of John Bull and Brother Jonathan' (1816). His chief novels are: 'Koningsmarke' (1823); 'Tales of a Good Woman by a Doubtful Gentleman' (1823); 'John Bull in America' (1824); 'Merry Tales of the Three Wise Men of Gotham' (1826); 'The Dutchman's Fireside' (1831); 'Westward Ho!' (1832); 'The Puritan and his Daughter' (1849). He wrote also 'Letters on Slavery' (1835), and 'Life of George Washington' (2 vols., 1854).

Pauli, Reinhold (pou'lē). A German historian; born at Berlin, May 25, 1823; died at

Bremen, June 3, 1882. Among his writings are: 'King Alfred and his Place in the History of England' (1851); 'History of England,' continuation of Lappenberg's work (Vols. iii., iv., v., 1853-58); 'Pictures of Ancient England' (1860); 'History of England from the Treaties of Peace 1814-15' (3 vols., 1864-75).

Paulus, Heinrich Eberhard Gottlob (pou'lus). A German theologian and Orientalist; born in Leonberg, Würtemberg, Sept. 1, 1761; died at Heidelberg, Aug. 10, 1851. He was professor of Oriental languages at Jena (1789) and Heidelberg (1811). He was the author of a 'Philological, Critical, and Historical Commentary on the New Testament' (4 vols., 1800-4); 'Exegetic Manual on the First Three Gospels' (1830-33 and 1841-42); and similar works.

Paulus Diaconus (pâ'lus dī-ak'o-nus) (Paul the Deacon). An early Langobardian historian in the eighth century. He wrote a 'Roman History,' coming down to the time of Justinian. In the court of Charlemagne he was one of the chiefs of the literary circle. By the order of Charlemagne he compiled a collection of homilies, 'Omiliarius'; 'he wrote also 'History of the Bishops of Metz,' and a 'History of the Langobardi,' which however he did not live to complete.

Pausanias (pâ-sā'nē-as). A Greek traveler of the second century of our era; a native of Lydia. He wrote in ten books 'The Tour of Greece,' commonly called 'Pausanias's Description of Greece.'

Pautet, Jules (pō-tā'). A French publicist and poet; born at Beaune, 1799; died 1870. Among his writings are: 'Evening Songs' (1838); 'Abdul Medjid,' a lyric chant (1840); 'Ernest, or the Savoyard Vicar's Confession of Faith' (1858); 'The Pope, Austria, and Italy' (1859); 'Vercingetorix and Cæsar,' a poem (1865).

Pavlov, Nikolai Philippovitsh (päv'lov). A Russian story-writer and poet; born at Moscow, 1802; died 1854. He wrote: 'Mary Stuart,' a tragedy (1828); 'Lyric Poems' (1831); two series of 'Stories' (1831-35); and a series of 'Dramas' (1850).

Payn, James. An English editor and novelist. He was born at Cheltenham, Feb. 28, 1830; died in London, March 25, 1898. He graduated at Cambridge in 1854, beginning at once a notable literary career. From 1858 he edited Chambers' Journal, for which he wrote exclusively for many years. In 1882 he became editor of the Cornhill Magazine. His works reach upwards of 100 books, the best-known being: 'Lost Sir Massingberd'; 'By Proxy'; 'The Luck of the Darrells'; 'The Talk of the Town'; 'Some Literary Recollections' (1886); and 'Gleams of Memory' (autobiographical), 1894.

Payne, John. An English poet and Oriental scholar; born in London, Aug. 23, 1842. He studied for the bar, and in 1867 became a solicitor. Among his works are: 'The Masque of Shadow' (1870); 'Intaglios' (1871); 'Songs of Life and Death' (1872); 'Lautrec' (1878); a translation of the 'Poems of Francis Villon' (1878); 'New Poems' (1880); 'Francis Villon—a Biographical Study' (1881); a close and scholarly translation of the 'Arabian Nights' Entertainments,' with the addition of those volumes of 'Arabian Tales' not included in the common (1882 et seq.); and a translation of the 'Rubáiyát' of Omar Khayyám, including over 800 quatrains, several hundred more than have been before translated (1897). He has also made a translation of Dante's 'Divina Commedia,' which is unpublished. Mr. Payne is a profound Oriental scholar, and a writer of vigorous vernacular English.

Payne, John Howard. An American dramatist and author; born in New York city, June 9, 1792; died in Tunis, Africa, April 10, 1852. A precocious child, a successful actor and author, his chief fame rests upon the lyric 'Home, Sweet Home,' which occurs in one of his dramas, the 'Maid of Milan.' From 1841 until his death he was consul at Tunis; his remains were removed to Washington in 1883. Of his plays, 'Brutus,' 'Virginius,' and 'Charles II.' still remain popular.

Payne, William Morton. An American literary critic, editor of the Dial Chicago: born in Massachusetts, 1858. He published 'Our New Education'; 'Little Leaders'; 'Björnstjerne Björnson'; 'The American scholar of the Twentieth Century'; 'Richard Wagner—A Cycle of Sonnets'; 'The Greater English Poets of the Nineteenth Century.'

Paz Soldan, Mariano Felipe (päth sōl-dän'). A Peruvian geographer and historian; born at Arequipá, August 1821; died at Lima, Dec. 31, 1886. He was director of public works, once minister of justice, and the author of 'Geographical Atlas of Peru' (1861); 'History of Independent Peru' (1866); 'Dictionary of the Argentine Republic' (1884); 'History of the War of the Pacific' (1884); etc. During the Chilean occupation he was exiled to Buenos Ayres.

Peabody, Elizabeth Palmer. An American writer and educator, of celebrity; born at Billerica, Mass., May 16, 1804; died at Jamaica Plain, Mass., Jan. 3, 1894. She became a teacher in Boston in 1822; and was one of the first to introduce the kindergarten system in the United States. Besides contributions to periodicals she published: 'First Steps to History' (1833); 'Æsthetic Papers' (1849); 'The Polish-American System of Chronology' (1852); 'Chronological History of the United States' (1856); 'Reminiscences of Dr. Channing' (1880); 'Letters to Kindergarteners' (1886); and 'The Last Evening with Allston, and Other Papers' (1887).

Peacock, John Macleay. A Scotch versewriter; born at Kincardine, March 31, 1817; died at Glasgow, May 4, 1877. His works are: 'Poems and Songs' (1864); 'Hours of Reverie'

(1867); and some previously unpublished verses contained in his 'Life and Works' (1880).

Peacock, Thomas Brower. An American verse-writer; born in Ohio, 1852, and living in Topeka, Kan. He has written: 'Rhyme of the Border War,' and 'The Vendetta: Poems of the Plains'; 'Nil Desperandum.'

Peacock, Thomas Love. An English novelist and poet; born at Weymouth, Oct. 18, 1785; died at lower Halliford, near Chertsey, Jan. 23, 1866. He first wrote poems: 'The Monks of St. Mark' (1804); 'Palmyra' (1806); 'The Genius of the Thames' (1810); 'The Philosophy of Melancholy' (1812); and some dramas. His principal novels are: 'Headlong Hall' (1815); 'Melincourt' (1816); 'Maid Marian' (1822); 'The Misfortunes of Elphin' (1829); 'Crotchet Castle' (1831); 'Gryll Grange' (1860).

Peake, Richard Brinsley. An English dramatist; born at London, Feb. 19, 1792; died Oct. 4, 1847. Among his plays are: 'Amateurs and Actors,' a musical farce (1818); 'The Duel, or my Two Nephews' (1823); 'Presumption, or the Fate of Frankenstein' (1824); 'Comfortable Lodgings, or Paris in 1750' (1827); 'Before Breakfast' (1828); 'The Title Deeds,' a three-act comedy in prose (1847).

Peale, Charles Willson. An American artist, inventor, and miscellaneous writer; born in Maryland, April 16, 1741; died in Philadelphia, Feb. 22, 1827. He attained distinction as a portrait painter, and also as a naturalist. He wrote: 'Essay on Building Wooden Bridges' (1797); 'Discourse Introductory to a Course of Lectures on Natural History' (1800); 'Domestic Happiness' (1816).

Peale, Rembrandt. An American artist and writer on art; born in Bucks County, Pa., Feb. 22, 1778; died in Philadelphia, Oct. 3, 1860. He was a renowned portrait painter, and the author of 'Notes on Italy' (1831); 'Portfolio of an Artist' (1839); 'Graphics' (1845).

Peard, Frances Mary. A popular English novelist, daughter of Commander G. S. Peard, R. N.; born at Exminster, Devon, in 1835. Among her numerous novels and historical romances, which have been popular both in England and the United States, are: 'Unawares' (1870); 'The Rose-Garden' (1872); 'Thorpe Regis' (1874); 'Cartouche' (1878); 'Schloss and Town' (1882); 'The Asheldon School-Room' (1883); 'Prentice Hugh' (1887); 'The Blue Dragon'; 'The Interloper'; 'The Abbot's Bridge.'

Peattie, Mrs. Elia (Wilkinson). An American journalist and miscellaneous writer; born in Michigan in 1862. She is connected with the Chicago press. Her works include: 'The Judge,' a novel (1891); 'With Scrip and Staff,' a story of the Children's Crusade (1891); 'A Mountain Woman, and Other Stories' (1896).

Peck, George Wilbur. An American politician and humorist; born in New York State in 1840. He was at one time mayor of Milwaukee, and subsequently governor of Wisconsin.

In 1883 he published 'Peck's Bad Boy and his Pa,' a humorous book which attained immediate popularity and was subsequently successfully dramatized. His other works include: 'A Compendium of Fun' (1883); 'How Private George W. Peck Put Down the Rebellion' (1887); 'Peck's Bad Boy with the Circus.'

Peck, Harry Thurston. An American scholar and literary critic; born at Stamford, Conn., 1856. He is a graduate of Columbia College, and professor of Latin in that institution, now Columbia University. Since 1895 he has been the American editor of the Bookman. Among his works are: 'The Semitic Theory of Creation' (1886); 'Suetonius' (1889); 'Latin Pronunciation' (1890); 'Dictionary of Classical Antiquities and Literature'; 'Twenty Years of the Republic.'

Peck, Samuel Minturn. A popular American poet; born in Tuscaloosa, Ala., 1854. He was educated at the University of Alabama, and later studied medicine in New York. He is a resident of his native place, where he devotes his time to literature and farming. Among his works are: 'Cap and Bells' (1886); 'Rings and Love Knots' (1892); 'Rhymes and Roses'; 'Fair Women of To-Day'; 'Alabama Sketches.'

Peckham, John. An English mediæval theologian; archbishop of Canterbury; died 1292. He was a voluminous writer on theological and scientific subjects. Among his works are: 'Common Perspective'; 'Theory of the Planets.' In verse he wrote: 'The Nightingale, Harbinger of Pleasant Weather'; 'Defense of the Mendicant Friars.'

Pedersen, Christiern (pä'der-sen). A Danish scholar and historical writer; born about 1480, at Svendborg on the island of Fuynen; died 1554. He was an ardent Reformer. By his translation of Luther's Bible — the 'Bible of Christian III.,' so called — he contributed largely to the formation of the literary language of Denmark. He wrote several historical works, and translated the 'Danish History' of Saxo Grammaticus.

Pedouë, François (ped-ö-ā'). A French poet; born at Paris, 1603; died at Chartres, 1667. His works are: 'Essays in Poetry and in Praise of a Lady' (1624); 'Early Works of the Sieur Pedouë'; and 'The Polished Citizen' (1631). Thereafter he renounced poetry and set about compiling a work on mystical theology, 'The Granada Collection.'

Peebles, Mrs. Mary Louise (Parmlee). ["Lynde Palmer."] An American writer of juvenile tales; born in Lansingburg, N. Y., Dec. 10, 1833. Among her books are: 'The Little Captain' (1861); 'Helps over Hard Places' (1862); 'The Good Fight' (1865); 'The Honorable Club' (1867); 'Drifting and Steering' (1867); 'Archie's Shadow' (1869); 'Jeannette's Cisterns'; 'The Spirit's Pathway'; Five Journeys Around the World.'

Peele, George. An English dramatist; born 1553 (?); died 1597 (?). He wrote: 'The Arraignment of Paris,' a comedy (1584); 'The Chronicle History of Edward I.' (1593); 'The

Battle of Alcazar' (1594); 'The Old Wives' Tale' (1595); 'David and Bethsabe' (1599); 'Sir Clyomon and Sir Clamydes' (1599).

Peet, Stephen Denison. An American clergyman and archæologist; born at Euclid, O., Dec. 2, 1830. He is a Congregational minister of Wisconsin, and an authority on the works of the mound-builders and American archæology in general. Among his works are: 'Ancient Architecture in America' (1884); 'Picture Writing' (1885); 'The Effigy Mounds of Wisconsin' (1888); 'Prehistoric America' (1890-95).

Pelabon, Étienne (pä-lä-bôn). A Provençal poet; born at Toulon, 1745; died at Marseilles, 1808. He wrote a two-act comedy in patois verse (1790), which had extraordinary success. He wrote also: 'Patriotic Reunion,' in verse and in one act; 'Matthew and Anne'; 'The Sansculottes.'

Peladan, Josephin (pä-lä-daň'). ["The Sar."] A French mystical writer; born at Lyons, 1859. He gave himself out to be a descendant of the last of the Babylonian kings, and as such took the name or title of "Sar," and assumed a theatrical garb. He reinstituted the Templar Order of the Rosy Cross, of which he was grand master. For the "salon of the Rosy Cross" he prepared dramatic pieces, among them: 'The Son of the Stars,' a sort of Wagnerian-Chaldaic play in three acts (1892); and 'Babylon,' a tragedy in four acts (1893). His masterpiece is a romantic cyclus, 'Latin Decadence,' a mixture of astrology, mysticism, and esotericism. The first romance in the cyclus is 'The Supreme Vice' (1886); others are 'The Man-Woman' (1890); 'The Woman-Man' (1891). He has written also 'Æsthetic Decadence' and 'Ochlocratic Art'; 'Introduction to History of Painting.'

Pellegrin Simon-Joseph (pel-gran'). A French dramatist; born at Marseilles, 1663; died at Paris, 1745. Among his works are: 'Polydorus,' a tragedy (1705); 'Death of Ulysses' (1706); 'The New World,' comedy (1723); 'Divorce of Love and Reason' (1724); 'Pastor Fido' (1726); 'Hymen's School; or, Her Husband's Sweetheart' (1742). He wrote also a great many religious poems.

Pelletan, Pierre Clément Eugène (pel-toň'). A French publicist; born Oct. 29, 1813; died Dec. 13, 1884. Under the signature "An Unknown," he won distinction as a literary and philosophical critic and writer on social questions in the Paris Presse. Noteworthy among his writings are: 'The Extinguished Lamp,' a philosophical novel (1840); 'Dogma: the Clergy and the State' (1848); 'Rights of Man' (1858); 'Some People and Others' (1873), a curious collection of personal reminiscences.

Pellew, [William] George (pel'ö). An American writer; born in England in 1859; died in New York city, Feb. 18-19, 1892. Among his works are: 'In Castle and Cabin, or Talks in Ireland' (1888); 'Woman and the Commonwealth' (1888); 'Life of John Jay' (1888).

Pellico, Silvio (pel'lē-kō). An Italian poet; born at Saluzzo in Piedmont, June 24, 1788; died at Turin, Jan. 31, 1854. His works are the tragedies 'Laodicea,' 'Francesca of Rimini,' and 'Eufemio of Messina' (1820). During his incarceration in the prison of Santa Margherita in Milan, he wrote the tragedies 'Iginia of Asti,' 'Ester of Engaddi,' and 'Leonerio of Dertonia.' He told the story of his prison life in 'My Prisons.' After his liberation he wrote the tragedies 'Gismonda da Mendrisio,' 'Herodias,' and 'Thomas More'; also some poetical narratives and lyric poems.

Pellissier, Charles Marie Athanase (pel-is-yä'). A French theologian; born at Bordeaux, 1810; died 1871. He entered the ministry of the French Protestant Church 1847, and attained high distinction as a pulpit orator and polemist. He wrote an 'Appeal to Catholics, or Essay on the Duty of Examining'; also several poems; and made a versified translation of the Book of Job.

Pelloutier, Simon (pel-öt-yä'). A German historian; born at Leipsic, 1694; died at Berlin, 1757. He wrote a 'History of the Celts' (2 vols., 1740-50), a work of immense research and written in most attractive style.

Pels, Andreas (pels). A Dutch poet of the 17th century; died at Amsterdam in 1681. His principal works are: 'Death of Dido,' a tragedy; 'Iulfus,' comedy; a poem 'On the Use and Abuse of the Theatre' (1671).

Pemberton, Max. An English journalist, editor, and novelist. He has been a contributor to Vanity Fair, and editor of Chums, a boys' paper, and is now in charge of Cassell's Magazine. He has published: 'The Iron Pirate' (1894), 'Sea-Wolves' (1894), and 'The Impregnable City' (1895), stories of adventure; 'The Little Huguenot'; 'A Puritan's Wife' (1896); 'A Gentleman's Gentleman'; 'Christine of the Hills'; 'Red Moon' (1904); 'The Finishing School' (play), (1904).

Pendleton, Louis [Beauregard]. An American novelist and writer of juvenile literature; born in Georgia in 1861. His works deal principally with Southern scenes and characters, the most popular being: 'In the Wire Grass' (1889); 'King Tom and the Runaways' (1890), a juvenile tale; 'The Sons of Ham' (1895); 'In the Okefenokee'; 'A Forest Drama'; 'In Assyrian Tents.'

Penn, Granville. An English theological writer; born at London, Dec. 9, 1761; died 1844. He made a critical revision of the New Testament — 'The Book of the New Covenant of our Lord' (1836); 'Annotations' to the same (1837); 'Remarks on the Eastern Origination of Mankind and of the Arts of Cultivated Life' (1799).

Penn, John. An English miscellaneous writer; born at London, Feb. 22, 1760; died June 21, 1834. He wrote: 'The Battle of Eddington, or British Liberty,' a drama (1792); a volume of 'Poems' (1794); 'Letters on the

Drama' (1796); 'Virgil's Fourth Eclogue, with Notes' (1825).

Penn, William. The founder of Pennsylvania; born at London, Oct. 14, 1644; died July 30, 1718. He wrote: 'Truth Exalted,' a religious tract expounding the doctrines or principles of the Friends (1668); 'A Sandy Foundation Shaken' (1668), an impeachment of the Athanasian Creed; 'No Cross, No Crown' (1669), written in the prison of the Tower of London, to which he had been committed for publication of the Anti-Athanasian tract without license; 'Reasonableness of Toleration' (1689); 'Primitive Christianity Revived in the Faith and Practice of the People Called Quakers' (1696); and many other works.

Pennell, Henry Cholmondeley. An English poet and writer on angling; born in 1837. After serving in various departments of the Admiralty, he was selected to carry out commercial reforms for the Khedive of Egypt. His poetical works are well known, among them being: 'Puck on Pegasus' (1861); 'The Crescent' (1866); 'The Muses of Mayfair' (1874); 'From Grave to Gay' (1885). On angling and ichthyology he has written: 'The Angler-Naturalist' (1864); 'The Modern Practical Angler' (1873); two volumes on fishing in the 'Badminton Library'); articles in the Fisherman's Magazine and Review, of which he was editor 1864-65.

Pennell, Mrs. Elizabeth (Robins) (pen'el). An American writer, wife of Joseph. For many years she has been a resident of London, and has traveled extensively in Europe. Besides contributions to the Atlantic, the Century, and other magazines, she has published numerous books, illustrated by her husband, and in some cases written in collaboration with him, the best known being: 'A Canterbury Pilgrimage' (1885); 'Two Pilgrims' Progress' (1886); 'Our Journey to the Hebrides' (1889); 'Play in Provence' (1891); 'To Gipsyland' (1892); 'Feasts of Autolycus' (1896).

Pennell, Joseph. An American illustrator and author; born in Pennsylvania in 1860. Besides works written in collaboration with his wife, he has published: 'Pen Drawing and Pen Draughtsmen' (1889); 'The Jew at Home'; 'Modern Illustration'; 'Lithography and Lithographers.'

Pennie, John Fitzgerald. An English dramatic writer; born at East Lulworth in Dorsetshire, March 25, 1782; died at Storborough, near Wareham, July 13, 1848. Among his dramas are: 'The Varangian, or Masonic Honor'; 'Ethelred the Usurper' (1817); 'Ethelwolf, or the Danish Pirates' (1821); he wrote also 'The Royal Minstrel,' an epic poem (1817).

Pentecost, George Frederick. An American clergyman and religious writer; born at Albion, Ill., in 1843. He was at one time connected with the Baptist and Congregational Churches, but of late has been more prominent as an evangelist. His best works are: 'The Angel in the Marble' (1877); 'Out of Egypt' (1884); 'The Christian and the Modern Dance' (1884); 'Bible Studies'; 'Precious Truths.'

Pepys, Samuel (peeps *or* peps). A celebrated English diarist; born in London, Feb. 23, 1632-3; died there, May 26, 1703. He wrote the 'Diary' which bears his name, beginning it in January 1660, and making the last entry May 31, 1669.

Peralta-Barnuevo, Pedro de (pā-räl'tä-bär-nō-ā'vō). A Peruvian historian of the first half of the 18th century. Among his works are: 'The Founding of Lima' (1718); 'History of Spain Vindicated' (1730).

Perce, Elbert. An American writer and littérateur of New York city; born in New York in 1831; died in 1869. He published: 'Old Carl the Cooper' (1854); 'The Last of his Name' (1854); 'The Battle Roll' (1857); 'His Three Voyages'; and several translations from the Swedish.

Percival, James Gates. An American poet and scientist; born in Kensington, Conn., Sept. 15, 1795; died at Hazel Green, Wis., May 2, 1856. During his career he was a professor of chemistry at West Point, army surgeon, botanist, and State geologist of Connecticut; but will be best remembered as a poet. His chief works are: 'Prometheus' (1820); 'Clio' (1822), prose and verse; 'Dream of a Day' (1843).

Percy, Thomas. An English poet; born at Bridgenorth in Shropshire, April 13, 1728 or 1729; died at Dromore, Ireland, Sept. 30, 1811. He was a minister of the English Church; was made dean of Carlisle in 1778, and bishop of Dromore in 1782. He made a collection of old popular ballads and songs, published under the title 'Reliques of Ancient English Poetry' (3 vols., 1765), which ultimately transformed English poetic style and matter. He wrote the ballad 'The Hermit of Warkworth,' and the song 'O Nanny, Wilt Thou Gang wi' Me.'

Pereda, José Maria de (per-ā'dä). A Spanish story-writer; born at Polanco, near Santander, Feb. 7, 1834. He wrote many charming descriptions of life in rural Spain and in Madrid. Among his stories are: 'Sotileza' (1888); 'Don Gonzalo Gonzalez de la Gonzalera' (1889); 'La Puchera'; 'La Montalvez.' Died Mar. 2, 1906.

Pereira da Silva, Joaõ Manuel (pe-rā'rä dä sēl'vä). A Brazilian historian; born at Rio de Janeiro, 1818. He wrote: 'History of the Founding of the Empire of Brazil' (3 vols., 1864-68); 'Brazilian Plutarch' (2 vols., 1866); 'Jeronimo Corte-Real'; 'Portuguese Literature: Its Past and Present' (1866); 'Second Period of the Reign of Dom Pedro I. in Brazil' (1875); 'History of Brazil during the Minority of Dom Pedro II., 1831-40' (1882); 'Epic Poetry' (1889).

Perey, Luce (pär-ā), pseudonym of Luce Herpin. A French critic and essayist; born in Carouge, Switzerland, 1845. Her best works are: 'A Woman of the World in the 18th Century: The Youth of Madame d'Épinay'; 'The

Last Years of Madame d'Épinay'; and 'The Private Life of Voltaire at Délices and at Ferney.'

Perez, Antonio (pā'rāth). A Spanish statesman and historian; born 1539; died at Paris, 1611. His principal work is 'Relations of Antonio Perez, Secretary of State of Philip II.' (1589). As revealing the secrets of Philip II.'s life as a king and a man, it had a wide circulation : from this work was made up a volume of 'Aphorisms of Antonio Perez'; also a volume of 'Noteworthy Passages Taken from the Writings of Don Antonio Perez' (1602).

Perez, Pedro Ildefonso. A Mexican poet; born at Merida in Yucatan, Jan. 23, 1826; died there, Feb. 21, 1869. He wrote : 'The Martyrs of Independence'; 'The Prison of Life'; 'The Smuggler,' a tragedy.

Perez de Zambrana, Luisa (pā'rāth dā thäm-brä-nä). A Cuban story-writer and poet; born at El Cobre near Santiago, 1837. She wrote the novels 'Angelica and Stella,' and 'The Executioner's Daughter'; several of her poems were translated into Italian and French.

Perez Galdos, Benito. See **Galdos.**

Perfall, Karl, Baron von (per'fäl). A German story-writer and art critic; born at Landsberg on the Lech, Dec. 11, 1853. Under the pseudonym «Theodor von der Ammer,» he wrote 'Munich Pictures : Humor and Satire from Isar-Athens' (2d ed. 1878); and under his own name the novels 'Ghosts of Quality' (1883); 'Wedding of Herr von Radenau' (1884); 'Viscountess Bossu' (1885); 'The Langsteiners' (1886); 'Natural Love' (1890) 'The Devout Widow' (2d ed. 1890); 'Lost Eden : Holy Grail' (1894); 'At the Table of Life' (1902).

Perfetti, Bernardino (per-fet'tē). An Italian poet; born at Siena, 1681; died 1747. He was an improvvisatore, and accompanied with the lyre his verses as he composed them; he was as ready to versify a thesis of philosophy or of jurisprudence as to compose a lyric poem. A collection of his verses was published in 1748 under the title 'Poetic Essays.'

Pori, Gian Domenico (per'ē), surnamed « The Poet of the Woods.» An Italian poet; born in the district of Siena, about 1570; died 1638. He wrote 'Comedies of the Woods' and 'Shepherds' Dramas.' After reading the Bible and Tasso, he essayed more ambitious themes, and wrote a poem on the creation of the world, entitled 'Chaos'; but it was never published. He wrote some spirited satires on the corrupt manners of his time in the highest and lowest classes of society.

Perkins, Charles Callahan. An American writer and lecturer on art; born in Boston, March 1823; died at Windsor, Vt., Aug. 25, 1886. He was a prominent art critic and lecturer, and president of the Boston Art Club (1869-79). His published works include : 'Italian Sculptors' (1868); 'Raphael and Michel Angelo' (1878); 'Sepulchral Monuments in Italy' (1883). He was also critical editor of the 'Cyclopædia of Paintings and Painters' (1892).

Perkins, Eli. See **Landon, Melville de Lancey.**

Perkins, Frederic Beecher. An American miscellaneous writer; born in Hartford, Conn., Sept. 27, 1828. He received his education at Yale; studied law, and was admitted to the bar in 1851. He was librarian of the San Francisco Library from 1880 to 1887. Among his works are : 'Scrope; or, The Lost Library' (1874), a novel; 'Devil Puzzlers, and Other Studies' (1877); 'Life of Dickens' (1877); 'The Best Reading' (1877). He died 1899.

Perkins, James Breck. An American lawyer and historical writer of Rochester, N. Y.; born at St. Croix Falls, Wis., Nov. 4, 1847. His chief works are : 'France under Mazarin' (1886); 'France under the Regency' (1892); 'France under Louis XV.'; 'Richelieu' (1900).

Perkins, Justin. An American missionary; born at West Springfield, Mass., March 12, 1805; died in Chicopee, Mass., Dec. 31, 1869. He was educated at Amherst and Andover. In 1833 he went to Persia as a missionary, and was active in establishing schools in that country. His works include : 'Residence of Eight Years in Persia' (1843); 'Missionary Life in Persia' (1861).

Perrault, Charles (pā-rō'). A French poet; born at Paris, Jan. 12, 1628; died there, May 16, 1703. He wrote a poem on 'The Age of Louis the Great' (1687); a 'Parallel between the Ancients and the Moderns'; and a series of immortal fairy-tales in prose : 'Stories of my Mother the Goose' (1697), containing 'Puss in Boots,' 'Red Riding Hood,' 'Bluebeard,' 'Cinderella,' 'Tom Thumb,' etc.

Perrens, François Tommy (per-räns'). A French historian; born at Bordeaux, Sept. 20, 1822; died Feb. 4, 1901. Among his works are : 'Jerome Savonarola' (1854); 'Church and State under Henri IV.' (1872); 'Democracy in France in the Middle Ages' (1873); 'General History of Paris'; 'History of Florence from the Beginning to the Domination of the Medicis' (6 vols., 1877-84); continued down to the fall of the republic (3 vols., 1893).

Perret, Paul (per-ā'). A French novelist; born at Paimbœuf (Loire Inférieure), Feb. 12, 1830. He wrote : 'Life's Seven Crosses'; 'Eve's Fair Daughters'; 'Neither Maid nor Widow' (1879); 'What Love Costs' (1881); 'Half-Marriages' (1881); 'King Margot' (1887); 'The Last Dreamers' (1890).

Perrot, Georges (per-rō'). A celebrated French archæologist and historian of art; born at Villeneuve-Saint-Georges (Seine-et-Oise), Nov. 12, 1832. He became professor of archæology in the Faculty of Letters (1877), and director of the Upper Normal School (1883). During his archæological investigations in Asia Minor, he made the first complete copy of the celebrated inscription on the monument to Augustus at Ancyra. He enjoys a world-wide reputation as co-author, with the architect C. Chipiez, of a 'History of Art in Antiquity' (1881–89), in five volumes, treating of art in Egypt, Chaldæa, Asia Minor, etc. He also wrote 'The Forerunners of Demosthenes' and 'Crete—Past and Future.'

Perry, Bliss. An American educator and writer of fiction; born in Massachusetts in 1860. He was professor of oratory and æsthetic criticism at Princeton University. He has published: 'The Broughton House' (1890); 'Salem Kittredge, and Other Stories' (1894); 'The Plated City' (1895); 'The Powers at Play', 'The Amateur Spirit.'

Perry, Charlotte Augusta. An American poet; born in Wisconsin in 1848. In 1888 she published a volume of poems under the name "Carlotta Perry."

Perry, Mary Alice. An American writer of fiction; born in Massachusetts in 1854; died in 1883. Her works include 'Esther Pennefather,' and 'More Ways Than One.'

Perry, Nora. An American poet and writer of fiction; born at Dudley, Mass., in 1832; died there May 13, 1896. For many years she was a correspondent of the Chicago Tribune and the Providence Journal. She early gained a reputation as a poet, but of late was more widely known as a writer of stories for girls. Her works include: 'After the Ball, and Other Poems' (1875); 'For a Woman' (1885), a novel; 'New Songs and Ballads' (1886); 'A Flock of Girls' (1887); 'A Rosebud Garden of Girls' (1892); 'Hope Benham' (1894).

Perry, Thomas Sergeant. An American educator, critic, and author; born at Newport, R. I., 1845. He graduated at Harvard in 1866; was tutor in German there, 1868–72; and instructor in English, 1877–81. He has spent many years abroad, and is a frequent contributor to magazines. One of his best efforts is 'The Evolution of the Snob' (1887). His other works are: 'English Literature in the 18th Century' (1883); 'From Opitz to Lessing' (1884); 'History of Greek Literature' (1890).

Perry, William Stevens. An American clergyman and writer; born in Providence, R. I., Jan. 22, 1832; died at Dubuque, Iowa, May 13, 1898. He became bishop of Iowa in 1876. He wrote: 'Documentary History of the Protestant Episcopal Church' (1863); 'History of the American Episcopal Church' (1885); 'Life Lessons from the Book of Proverbs' (1885).

Persius Flaccus, Aulus (per'zē-us flak'us). A Latin satiric poet; born at Volaterræ in Etruria, 34 A. D.; died 62 A. D. He wrote but six satires, and they are all extant. The meaning is often very obscure because of unintelligible allusions and excessive brevity.

Pesado, José Joaquin (pā-zä'dō). A Mexican poet; born at San Agustin de Palmar, Feb. 9, 1801; died at Mexico, 1861. His works are collected in the volume 'Original and Translated Poems' (3d ed. 1886).

Pestalozzi, Johann Heinrich (pes-tä-lot'sē). A Swiss educationist; born at Zürich, Jan. 12, 1746; died at Brugg in Aargau, Feb. 17, 1827. Inspired by Rousseau's 'Émile,' he decided to work for the reformation of the systems of popular schooling. He wrote a celebrated story of village life, 'Lienhart and Gertrude' (4 vols., 1781–89); its sequel, 'Christopher and Else' (1782); 'Researches on the Course of Nature in the Development of the Human Race' (1797); 'How Gertrude Teaches her Children: An Essay toward Directing Mothers how to Educate their Children' (1801); 'Life and its Fortunes,' autobiographical (1825); 'The Simplest Way to Educate a Child from the Cradle to the Sixth Year' (1825) ; and his 'Swan Song' (1826).

Peter, Karl Ludwig (pā'ter). A German historian; born at Freyburg on the Unstrut, April 6, 1808; died at Jena, Aug. 11, 1893. Among his works are: 'Epochs in the History of the Roman Constitution' (1841); 'Studies in Roman History' (1863); 'Criticism of the Sources of Ancient Roman History' (1879).

Peters, Samuel Andrew. An American clergyman and author; born at Hebron, Conn., 1735; died in New York, 1826. He was ordained a minister in the Church of England at Hartford in 1760. In 1774 he sailed to England to escape persecution on account of his toryism, and in 1781 published the satirical 'General History of Connecticut,' which gave rise to the misconception as to "Blue Laws," which were in the brain of Peters instead of having ever been on the statute-books of Connecticut.

Petersen, Niels Mathias (pā'der-sen). A Danish historian and philologist; born at Sanderum in the island of Fuynen, Oct. 24, 1791; died at Copenhagen, May 11, 1862. He was appointed professor of Norse languages in the University of Copenhagen in 1845. Among his numerous works are: 'History of the Danish, Norwegian, and Swedish Languages' (2 vols., 1829–30); 'History of Denmark in Heathenism' (3 vols., 2d ed. 1854); 'Norse Mythology' (2d ed. 1862); 'History of Danish Literature' (5 vols., 2d ed. 1867–71).

Peterson, Charles Jacobs. An American publisher and novelist; born in Philadelphia, 1818; died there, 1887. He was the founder of Peterson's Magazine, and the author of several popular novels. His works include: 'Military Heroes of the United States' (1847); 'Cruising in the Last War' (1849); 'Grace Dudley' (1849); Kate Aylesford' (1855); 'Mabel' (1857).

Peterson, Frederick. An American physician and poet; born in Minnesota in 1859. He has published 'Poems and Swedish Translations' (1883); and 'In the Shade of Ygdrasil' (1893); 'A Song of the Latter Day' (1904).

Peterson, Henry. An American journalist and poet, cousin of Charles J.; born in Philadelphia, 1818; died in 1891. For twenty years he was on the editorial staff of the Philadelphia

Saturday Evening Post. Among his works are: 'The Modern Job, and Other Poems' (1869); 'Faire-Mount' (1874); 'Cæsar: A Dramatic Study' (1879).

Petis de la Croix, François (pä-tē' dè lä krwä'). A French Orientalist; born in Paris in 1653; died in 1713. He was secretary to the French ambassador in Morocco, and greatly assisted in negotiating the treaties of peace between France, Tunis, and Tripoli. From 1692 he was professor of Arabic in the Royal College of France. He translated from the Persian 'The Thousand and One Days' (5 vols., 1710–12). His great work 'The History of Timur,' from the Arabic of Ali Yazdi, was published nine years after his death (4 vols., 1722), and translated into English in 1723.

Petit de Julleville, Louis (pe-tē' dè zhül-vēl'). A French historian of literature; born at Paris, July 18, 1841; died there Aug. 28, 1900. He became professor of French literature in the Sorbonne. His principal work is 'History of the Theatre in France' (5 vols., 1880–86); it is very full with regard to the old French theatre. He gives in 'The Theatre in France' (1889) an account of the evolution of the French drama down to the present time. In 1896 he commenced the publication of a 'History of the French Language and Literature,' to be comprised in 8 vols.

Petöfi, Alexander (pä-tē'fē). A celebrated Hungarian poet; born at Kis-Körös, near Pesth, Jan. 1, 1823; died July 31, 1849. Among his chief works are: 'The Wine-Bibbers' (1842); 'The Hangman's Rope'; 'Coriolanus,' translated from Shakespeare (1848); 'Arise, Ye Magyars' (1848).

Petrarch, Francesco (pē'trärk). The greatest of Italian lyric poets; born at Arezzo, July 20, 1304; died at Arquà, July 18, 1374. He wrote mostly in Latin; but his fame rests on his lyrics written in the vulgar tongue, and his 'Rime,' containing sonnets (227), ballads, songs, etc. In Latin verse he wrote: 'Africa,' an epic in hexameters, recounting the feats of Scipio Africanus the Elder; a 'Bucolic Poem'; a volume of 68 'Metrical Epistles.' His chief writings in Latin prose are: 'Of Contempt of the World'; 'Of the Solitary Life'; 'Of the Remedies for Either Fortune'; 'Memoranda,' brief historical and legendary anecdotes; 'Of Illustrious Men'; 'Of True Wisdom'; 'Of his Own and Others' Ignorance.'

Petrie, W. M. Flinders (pē'trē). A celebrated English Egyptologist, grandson of Capt. Flinders the Australian explorer; born June 3, 1853. He made measurements of prehistoric monuments in Britain (1875–80); discovered and excavated the Græco-Egyptian city of Naukratis, in the Delta; and examined the interior of the pyramids at Hawara and Illahun. The results of his researches are found in 'Stonehenge: Plans, etc.' (1881); 'Pyramids and Temples of Gizeh' (1883); 'Tanis' (1885–88); 'Ten Years' Diggings in Egypt' (1892), a popular summary of his Egyptian work; 'Royal Tombs' (1900–01).

Petronius Arbiter (pe-trō'nē-us är'bit-er). A Latin writer of satirical fiction. He lived in the first century of our era, but nothing is known with certainty of his life. Of his story or novel, called 'Satires,' which originally consisted of about 20 "books," there is extant a considerable fragment, 'Trimalchio's Banquet.'

Petrucelli della Gattina, Ferdinando (pä-trö-chel'ē del'lä gät-tē'nä). An Italian politician and journalist; born in Naples, 1813. He wrote: 'Preliminaries of the Roman Question' (1860); 'King of Kings,' a study of Hildebrand (2d ed. 1865); 'Diplomatic History of Conclaves' (4 vols., 1864–65).

Peyrebrune, Georges de—Mathilde Georgina Elisabeth de Peyrebrune de Judicis (pär-brün'). A French novelist; born in Dordogne in 1848. She is one of the most popular women novelists in France, and has written: 'Gatienne' (1882); 'Jean Bernard' (1883); 'A Separation' (1884); 'The Brothers Colombe' (1885), one of her best works; 'A Decadent' (1888); 'The Romance of a Bas-Bleu' (1892), showing the dangers of a literary career for women.

Peyrol, or **Peyrot, Antoine** (pä-rōl'). A Provençal poet; born at Avignon in the beginning of the 17th century; died about 1780. His 'Christmas Carols' (Noëls) are published with those of two other Provençal poets, Saboly and Roumanillo (1852).

Peyton, John Lewis. An American lawyer and author; born in Staunton, Va., Sept. 15, 1824. He studied law at the University of Virginia, and subsequently practiced in Chicago. In 1861 he went to Europe as agent of the Confederacy, and remained abroad until 1880. He has published: 'Adventures of My Grandfather' (1867); 'The American Crisis' (1867); 'Over the Alleghanies' (1869); 'Memorials of Nature and Art' (1881). Died 1896.

Pfau, Ludwig (pfou). A German lyric poet and art critic; born at Heilbronn, Aug. 25, 1821; died at Stuttgart, April 12, 1894. He took a prominent part in the Baden revolution, 1848; and was editor of the Owl-Glass, one of the most spirited comic journals of that day. He wrote: 'Voices of the Time' (1848); 'German Sonnets for the Year 1850' (1849); translated into German 'Breton Folk-Songs' (1859). Among his works in art criticism are: 'Art in the State' (3d ed. 1888); 'Contemporary Art in Belgium'; 'Art and Criticism' (1877).

Pfeffel, Gottlieb Konrad (pfä'fel). A German poet; born at Colmar, June 28, 1736; died there, May 1, 1809. He became totally blind in 1758. He is best known as a fabulist. He wrote 'Ibrahim'; 'The Tobacco Pipe'; 'Theatrical Diversions after French Models' (1765); 'Dramatic Plays for Children' (1769). A selection from his 'Fables and Poetical Narratives' was published in 1810.

Pfeiffer, Ida Reyer (pfi'fer). An Austrian traveler; born at Vienna, Oct. 15, 1797; died there, Oct. 28, 1858. Her travels were made in both hemispheres. Among her books are: 'Travels of a Viennese Woman in the Holy Land' (2 vols., 1843); 'Travels in the Scandinavian North and Iceland' (2 vols., 1846); 'A Lady's Voyage Round the World' (1850); 'My Second Voyage Round the World' (4 vols., 1856); 'Voyage to Madagascar' (2 vols., 1861).

Pfizer, Gustav (pfē'tscr). A German poet; born at Stuttgart, July 29, 1807; died there, July 19, 1890. His principal works are: 'Poems' (1831; a second series 1835); 'Life of Martin Luther' (1836); 'Poems Epical and Epico-Lyrical' (1840); the poem 'The Italian and the German : Æneas Silvius Piccolomini and Gregor von Heimburg' (1844); 'History of Alexander the Great' (1847); 'History of the Greeks.'

Phædrus (fē'drus). A Latin fabulist. He was a native of Macedonia, and was taken to Rome as a slave, but was freed by Augustus. Nearly the whole of the 'Æsopian Fables of Phædrus, Freedman of Augustus' are extant in the original poetic form; besides these, we have three different versions in Latin prose, made in the Middle Ages.

Phelps, Austin. An American clergyman and author; born at West Brookfield, Mass., Jan. 7, 1820; died at Bar Harbor, Me., Oct. 13, 1890. He was pastor of the Pine Street Congregational Church, Boston, 1842–48; and professor of sacred rhetoric in Andover Theological Seminary, 1848–79. He was noted as an original writer and an eloquent preacher. His works include: 'The Still Hour' (1859); 'The New Birth' (1867); 'Men and Books' (1882); 'English Style in Public Discourse' (1883).

Phelps, Charles Henry. An American miscellaneous writer; born at Stockton, Cal., Jan. 1, 1853. He wrote 'Californian Verses' (1882).

Phelps, Elizabeth Stuart. See **Ward, Mrs. Elizabeth Stuart** (Phelps).

Pherecrates (fer-ē-krā'tēs). A Greek comic poet of the fourth century B. C., contemporary of Cratinus, Crates, and Aristophanes. Of his works fragments only remain; among them an 'Address to Old Age,' preserved by Stobæus. He is variously stated to have written 18 or 16 plays.

Pherecydes of Syros (fer-e-sī'dēs). An early Greek philosopher, native of the island of Syros; he lived in the sixth century B. C., being contemporary with Thales and Anaximander. He is credited with having written a work on the origin of things, in which the doctrine of metempsychosis is first propounded.

Philemon (fi-lē'mon). A Greek comic poet; born at Soli in Cilicia, about 361 B. C.; died 263 B. C. He wrote 97 plays, nine of which are extant : the Latin poet Plautus's 'Merchant' and 'Trinummus' are founded on Philemon's 'The Merchant' and 'The Treasure.' See article 'Philemon, Menander, etc.'

Philippson, Martin (fil'ip-son). A German historian; born at Magdeburg, June 27, 1846. He was appointed professor of history in the University of Brussels, 1878. Among his works are: 'Henry IV. and Philip III.: Origin of French Preponderance in Europe, 1598–1610' (3 vols., 1871); 'The Age of Louis XIV.' (1879); 'Origins of Modern Catholicism' (1884).

Philips, Ambrose. An English poet; born in Leicestershire, 1675 (?); died 1749. He wrote a series of 'Pastorals' (1709); 'The Distressed Mother' (1712), a drama adapted from the 'Andromache' of Racine, and highly praised by Addison in the Spectator; 'The Briton' and 'Humphry, Duke of Gloucester,' dramas (1722). He wrote also some epigrams, and made translations of odes of Pindar, Anacreon, and Sappho.

Philips or **Phillips, Edward.** An English miscellaneous writer, nephew of Milton; born at London, 1630; died about 1696. He was a voluminous writer. Among his works are: 'New World of English Words' (1658); 'Mysteries of Love and Eloquence; or, The Arts of Wooing,' etc. (1658); 'Compendious Latin Dictionary' (1682); 'Poem on the Coronation of his Most Sacred Majesty King James II. and his Royal Consort' (1685).

Philips, Francis Charles. An English barrister, playwright, and novelist; born in 1849. After long service as officer in the army, he retired from it and became a barrister. From 1874 to 1880 he was lessee of the Globe Theatre, London. His novels include: 'As in a Looking-Glass' (1885), translated into several languages, and dramatized for Mrs. Beere and Sarah Bernhardt; 'A Lucky Young Woman' (1886); 'The Dean and his Daughter' (1887), dramatized; 'Mrs. Bouverie' (1894). He was also collaborator in the acted plays 'Husband and Wife'; 'Godpapa'; etc.

Philips, John. An English dramatist; born at Bampton in Oxfordshire, 1676; died, 1708-9. He was an ardent student of the ancient classics, and also of Chaucer, Spenser, and Milton. He came into the favorable notice of critics and lovers of poetry with 'The Splendid Shilling' (1703), pronounced by the Tatler "the best burlesque poem in the English language." In a like burlesque vein he wrote 'Blenheim' (1705); then the didactic poem 'Cyder' in imitation of Virgil's 'Georgics.'

Philips, Katherine (Fowler). ["The Matchless Orinda."] An English poet; born in London, Jan. 1, 1631; died June 22, 1664. She wrote many poems, and translated Corneille's 'Horace' and 'Pompée.' She signed herself "Orinda" in correspondence with literary friends, and was pronounced "matchless" for her poetry, first collected in 1678. Dryden, Cowley, Jeremy Taylor, and others eulogized it extravagantly; but personal admiration for the woman probably affected their judgment.

Phillips, George Searle. ["January Searle."] An English-American littérateur; born in

England in 1818; died in 1889. He was a well-known writer and lecturer of Yorkshire, England, who removed to this country and became prominent in literary circles. He published: 'Chapters in the History of a Life'; 'Memoirs of Wordsworth'; and 'The Gypsies of Dane's Dyke.'

Phillips, Henry. An American writer and lawyer of Philadelphia; born there Sept. 6, 1838; died there June 6, 1895. He wrote: (History of American Colonial Paper Currency'; 'History of American Continental Paper Money'; 'Pleasures of Numismatic Science'; 'Poems from the Spanish and German.'

Phillips, Wendell. An eminent American social and political reformer and orator; born at Boston, Nov. 29, 1811; died there, Feb. 2, 1884. He wrote: 'The Constitution a Pro-Slavery Compact' (1840); 'Can Abolitionists Vote or Take Office?' (1845); 'Review of Spooner's "Constitutionality of Slavery"' (1847); 'Review of Webster's Speech of March 7th' (1850); 'Review of Kossuth's Course' (1851); 'Defense of the Anti-Slavery Movement' (1853); 'Addresses' (1859); 'Speeches, Lectures, and Letters' (1863).

Philo the Jew (fi'lō), or Philo Judæus. An Alexandrine Jewish philosopher; born at Alexandria about 20 B. C. About the year 40, in his old age, he went to Rome at the head of a Jewish embassy, to persuade the emperor Caligula to exempt the Jews from the obligation of paying the emperor divine honors; a full account of this mission is given in Philo's extant work 'On the Embassy to Caius.' We have still many of his writings, or considerable fragments of them; an edition of them has been published (8 vols., 1851–54).

Philolaus (fil-o-lā'us). A Greek Pythagorean philosopher, native of Magna Græcia; contemporary with Socrates. Only fragments of his writings have come down to us. He was the first to commit to writing the doctrines of Pythagoras. He taught the doctrine of the earth's motion; that the sphere of the fixed stars, the five planets, and the sun, moon, and earth, move round the "central fire," which is the "hearth of the universe."

Philostratus (fi-los'tra-tus). A Greek rhetorician and sophist; born in the island of Lemnos between 170 and 180 A. D.; died about 250. Of his writings five are extant: viz., 'Life of Apollonius of Tyana,' the famous religious impostor and thaumaturge; 'Lives of the Sophists'; 'Heroics'; 'Images'; and 'Epistles.'

Philoxenus (fi-lok'se-nus). A Greek poet; born in the island of Cythera about B. C. 435; died at Ephesus, B. C. 380. He was taken prisoner in war, conveyed as a slave to Athens, and sold to the musician Melanippides, who gave him a liberal education. At the court of Dionysius, tyrant of Syracuse, he brought upon himself condemnation to servitude in the quarries by refusing to praise the autocrat's verses; when brought again before the tyrant

and asked what he thought of the verses now, he answered, "Take me away to the quarries." He took his revenge on Dionysius in his dithyramb 'Cyclops.' He wrote 24 dithyrambs, and a lyric poem on the genealogy of the Æacidæ. Of his writings only scanty fragments remain.

Phœnix, John. See **Derby.**

Phranza (fran'tsa) or **Phranzes, George** (fran'tsēs). The last of the Byzantine historians; born in 1401; died in 1478. He was chamberlain of Manuel II. (Palæologus), and protovestiary, or wardrobe keeper, to Constantine XIII., whose life he saved at the siege of Patras (1429). After the capture of Constantinople by Mohammed II. he escaped to Corfu, and retiring to a monastery, wrote his interesting and reliable 'Chronicon' or Byzantine history, covering the period from 1259 to 1477.

Phrynichus (frin'i-kus). A Greek tragic poet of the fifth century B. C. Departing from the custom of tragic poets, he took for the subject of his greatest tragedy 'The Capture of Miletus' by the Persians, a contemporary event. It moved the Athenians profoundly, but they fined the poet 1,000 drachmas for harrowing their sensibilities by rehearsing the woes of their allies. Next he wrote: 'The Phœnician Women,' commemorating the defeat of Xerxes at Salamis. He wrote also several tragedies on legendary themes, as 'The Danaids'; 'Actæon'; 'Alcestis'; 'Tantalus.' Only fragments of his plays remain.

Piatt, Donn. An American lawyer, journalist, and author; born in Cincinnati, O., 1819; died in 1891. He began his career as a lawyer; was secretary of the Paris legation in Pierce's administration; served as colonel of volunteers during the Civil War; and subsequently became famous as a journalist in Washington. His works include: 'Memories of Men Who Saved the Union' (1887); 'The Lone Grave of the Shenandoah' (1888); 'Life of General George H. Thomas' (1893).

Piatt, John James. An American journalist and poet, nephew of Donn; born at James' Mills, Ind., March 1, 1835. He became clerk of the U. S. Treasury Department and the House of Representatives; and from 1882 to 1894 was consul at Cork, Ireland. He has written poems of considerable merit and originality. His works include: 'Poems by Two Friends' (1860), with W. D. Howells; 'The Nests at Washington' (1863), with Mrs. Piatt; 'Poems in Sunshine and Firelight' (1866); 'Western Windows' (1868); 'Idyls and Lyrics of the Ohio Valley' (1884); 'The Hesperian Tree' (1900).

Piatt, Mrs. Sarah Morgan (Bryan). An American poet, wife of John J.; born at Lexington, Ky., 1836. Her best-known works are: 'A Woman's Poems' (1871); 'A Voyage to the Fortunate Isles' (1874); 'Dramatic Persons and Moods' (1880); 'The Witch in the Glass' (1888); 'An Enchanted Castle' (1893).

Picard, Louis Benoît (pe-kär'). A French writer of comedy; born at Paris, July 29, 1769;

died there, Dec. 31, 1828. At 20 he was a writer for the stage, but in 1797 he first came into prominence with the comedy 'Mediocre and Groveling' (worked over by Schiller in 'The Parasite'). He then went upon the stage, and in 1801 became director of the Louvois Theatre; but renounced the stage in 1807, was elected to the French Academy, and was appointed director of the Imperial Academy of Music. His best comedies are: 'The Little City'; 'Monsieur Musard' (Mr. Trifler); 'The Puppets'; 'The Two Philiberts.'

Pichat, Michel (pē-shä'). A French dramatist; born at Vienne, 1790; died at Paris, 1828. He wrote the tragedies 'Turnus,' 'Leonidas' (1825), which had great success, 'William Tell'; 'Ali Pasha' (1822), a melodrama; 'Devotion of the French Physicians at Barcelona' (1822), a poem.

Pichler, Adolf (pich'ler). An Austrian poet and naturalist; born at Erl in the Tyrol, Sept. 4, 1819. He wrote narratives of the revolutionary troubles of 1848, viz.: 'The Days of March and October in Vienna, 1848' (1850); and 'The Italo-Tyrolean War' (1849), in which he served as a volunteer. He wrote also a volume of 'Poems' (1853); 'Hymns' (2d ed. 1857); 'From the Tyrol Mountains' (1862); 'Epigrams' (1865); 'All Sorts of Stories from the Tyrol' (1867); 'Boundary Stones,' poetical narratives (1874); 'Literature and Art,' a volume of epigrams (1879); 'In My Time,' personal recollections (1892); 'The Solitary' (1896). Died in 1900.

Pichler, Karoline. An Austrian novelist; born at Vienna, Sept. 7, 1769; died there, July 9, 1843. She was a very prolific writer. Among her stories are: 'Agathocles' (3 vols., 1808); 'Woman's Worth' (4 vols., 1808); 'The Siege of Vienna' (3 vols., 1824); 'The Castle among the Mountains'; 'Black Fritz.'

Pichon, Jérôme Frédéric, Baron (pē-shôn'). A French writer on historical subjects; born at Paris, Dec. 3, 1812. Among his works are: 'The Apparition of Jehan de Meun; or, The Dream of the Prior of Salon' (1845); 'The Count d'Hoym, his Library and his Collections' (2 vols., 1880).

Pickering, Charles. An American naturalist and author; born in Pennsylvania, 1805; died in Boston, 1878. He traveled extensively, and published the volumes: 'The Races of Man and their Geographical Distribution' (1848); 'Geographical Distribution of Animals and Man' (1861); 'Chronological History of Plants' (1879).

Pickering, Henry. An American poet; born in Newburg, N. Y., 1781; died in New York, 1831. His poetical writings include: 'Ruins of Pæstum' (1822); 'Athens and Other Poems' (1824); and 'The Buckwheat Cake' (1831).

Pickering, John. A distinguished American philologist and Oriental scholar; born in Salem, Mass., 1777; died in Boston, 1846. He held many important public positions; was president of the American Academy of Arts and Sciences, and a member of various learned associations at home and abroad. He published a paper on the 'Adoption of a Uniform Orthography for the Indian Languages' (1820); a 'Vocabulary of Words and Phrases Peculiar to the United States' (1816); a 'Greek Dictionary' (1826); and wrote many pamphlets on scientific and political questions.

Pico, Giovanni, Count of Mirandola (pē'kō). An Italian philosopher; lived 1463-1494. He wrote 'Heptaplus,' an allegorical explanation of the creation; 'Philosophical, Cabalistic,' and 'Theological Conclusions' (1486).

Picot, Émile, a French scholar; born Sept. 13, 1844; professor of Roumanian at the School of Oriental Languages in Paris. He published 'The Servians of Hungary' (1874); 'Roumanian Folksongs of Servia' (1889); 'The Italians in France in the XVI. Century' (1902-4).

Picot, Georges (pē-kō'). A French historian; born at Paris, Dec. 24, 1838. He succeeded Thiers as member of the Institute in 1878, and on the death of Jules Simon in 1896 became permanent secretary of the Academy of Sciences. He wrote: 'Elections to the States-General in the Provinces from 1302 to 1614' (1874); 'The Parliament of Paris under Charles VIII.' (1877); 'Judiciary Reform in France' (1881); 'A Social Duty and Workmen's Homes' (1885); 'History of the States-General and their Influence on the Government of France from 1355 to 1614' (4 vols., 1872), his principal work, which twice won the Gobert prize of the Academy; 'The Battle against Social Revolution' (1895).

Piedagnel, François, Alexandre (pyä-dän-yel'). A French verse-writer; born at Cherbourg, Dec. 27, 1831. He published three volumes of poems: 'Yesterday' (1882); 'On the Road' (1886); 'April' (1887). He wrote also: 'Jules Janin' (1874); 'J. F. Millet: Recollections of Barbizon' (1878).

Pierce, Henry Niles. An American Episcopal bishop and author; born in Pawtucket, R. I., 1820. He spent many years in the West as a missionary, and was consecrated bishop in 1870. He published essays, sermons, and reviews; and a volume of poems, 'The Agnostic,' etc. (1884). Died, Sept. 5, 1899.

Pierpont, John. A Unitarian clergyman and poet; born in Litchfield, Conn., April 6, 1785; died in Medford, Mass., Aug. 27, 1866. Among his works is 'Airs of Palestine, and Other Poems' (1840). One of his best-known poems is 'Warren's Address at the Battle of Bunker Hill.'

Piers Plowman. Assumed name of William Longland or Langland. An English satirical writer of the 14th century. His work 'The Vision of Piers Plowman'—a religious and moral allegory, in rhyme—is a picture of the disorders in church and State prevailing at his time.

Pietsch, Ludwig (pētsh). A German traveler and designer; born at Dantzic, Dec. 25, 1824. He wrote: 'The World and Art' (2 vols, 1867)·

'Travels in the East' (1870); 'From Berlin to Paris: War Pictures' (1871); 'Morocco' (1878); 'Pilgrimage to Olympia in 1876' (1879); 'How I Became an Author' (2 vols., 1892–94).

Pigault-Lebrun (pē-go''lĕ-brün'), pseudonym of Antoine P. de L'Épinoy. A French novelist and dramatist; born at Calais, April 8, 1753; died at La Celle Saint Cloud, July 24, 1835. He wrote more than 70 volumes of stories, among them 'The Child of the Carnival' (1792), 'The Barons of Felsheim' (1798), 'Spanish Madness' (1801); and several comedies, as 'The Pessimist' (1789), 'Rivals of Themselves' (1798), 'Love and Reason' (1799). He wrote also 'Literary and Critical Miscellanies' (2 vols., 1816).

Pignotti, Lorenzo (pēn-yot'tē). An Italian poet and historian; born at Figlina, Tuscany, 1739; died at Pisa, 1812. Among his writings are poems 'On the Grave of Shakespeare' (1778); 'The Shade of Pope' (1791). He wrote a book of 'Fables' (1779), which were very popular; and a 'History of Tuscany' (9 vols., 1813).

Piis, Pierre Antoine Augustin (pēs). A French dramatist; born at Paris, 1755; died 1832. Among his very numerous dramatic pieces were: 'Aristotle in Love,' vaudeville (1780); 'Summer Loves' (1781); 'Two Sedan-Chairmen' (1781); 'Marriage in Extremis' (1782), a comedy in one act. His miscellaneous writings included: 'Carlo-Robertiad' (1784), a satire on ballooning; 'Easter Eggs for my Critics' (1786).

Pike, Albert. An American lawyer, journalist, and poet; born in Boston, Dec. 29, 1809; died in Washington, D. C., April 2, 1891. Early in life he went West, entered journalism, and later practiced law in Arkansas. He served as captain of cavalry in the Mexican War, and was a brigadier-general in the Confederate army during the Civil War. His chief works are: 'Prose Sketches and Poems' (1834); 'Hymns to the Gods' (1839); 'Nugæ' (1854); 'Morals and Dogma of Freemasonry' (1870).

Pike, Mrs. Mary Hayden (Green). An American novelist; born in Eastport, Me., Nov. 30, 1825. She will be best remembered as the author of 'Ida May' (1854), a novel dealing with slavery and Southern life, which had a large sale. She also published 'Caste' (1856), and 'Bond and Free' (1858).

Pilch, Frederick Henry. An American verse-writer; born at Newark, N. J., March 5, 1842; died at Bloomfield, N. J., Dec. 3, 1889. He contributed verses to the magazines, and published a collection of 'Homespun Verses' (1889).

Pilkington, Mary. An English story-writer; born at Cambridge, 1766; died 1839. Among her very numerous writings were: 'Edward Barnard; or, Merit Exalted' (1797); 'Mentorial Tales for Young Ladies' (1802); 'The Sorrows of Cæsar; or, Adventures of a Foundling Dog' (1813); 'The Shipwreck; or, Misfortune the Inspirer of Virtuous Sentiments' (1819)

Pillet, Fabien (pē-yā'). A French journalist; born at Lyons, 1772; died at Passy, 1855. He published several volumes of dramatic criticism, and a collection of 'Oddities, Stories, Anecdotes, Epigrams,' etc., relating to the stage (1838).

Pilpay or **Pilpai** (pil-pā'). The supposed author of fables in India, which have been so extensively used by other Oriental countries and in Europe.

Pindar (pin'där). The greatest of the Greek lyric poets; born at Cynoscephalæ near Bœotian Thebes, 522 B. C.; died at Argos, about 450 B. C. The Alexandrine scholars divided his poems into 17 books, comprising Hymns, Pæans, Dithyrambs, Encomia, Songs of Victory. There are now extant, apart from mere fragments, only four books, all songs of victory (epinikia) celebrating the victors in the Olympian, Pythian, Nemean, and Isthmian games.

Pindemonte, Ippolito (pēn''dā-mon'täl). An Italian poet; 1753–1828. He achieved a distinguished reputation by his works: 'Poems of the Fields' (1788), among the best of their kind in Italian literature; 'Various Poems' (1798); 'Epistles in Verse' (1805); a translation of Homer's Odyssey (1809–22); 'Discourses' (1819: Sermoni, after the manner of Horace's 'Satires.'

Pinero, Sir Arthur Wing. A distinguished English dramatist; born in London in 1855; knighted in 1909. He studied for the law, then became an actor, and ultimately left the stage for dramatic authorship. His first comedy, 'Two Can Play at That Game,' was produced in 1877, and has been followed by 'Two Hundred a Year' (1877); 'The Money Spinner' (1880); 'The Magistrate' (1885); 'Dandy Dick' (1887); 'Sweet Lavender' (1888); 'The Profligate' (1889); 'Lady Bountiful' (1891); 'The Second Mrs. Tanqueray' (1893), conceded to be his most powerful work; 'The Notorious Mrs. Ebbsmith' (1895); 'The Benefit of the Doubt' (1896); 'The Princess and the Butterfly' (1897); 'Trelawny of the Wells' (1898); 'The Gay Lord Onex' (1890); 'Iris' and 'Letty' (1903); 'A Wife Without a Smile' (1904); 'His House in Order' (1905).

Pinheiro-Chagas, Manuel (pēn-yä'rō-shä'-gäs). A Portuguese poet and miscellaneous writer; born at Lisbon, 1842. Among his works are: 'A Poem of Youth,' 'The Angel of the Hearth'; some novels, as 'The Court of John V.,' 'The Red Mask,' 'Death's Guerrillas' (1872), 'The Viscountess's Secret'; dramas, 'Senhorita de Valflor' (1867), 'Helen,' 'The Jewish Woman,' 'During the Battle' (1870); some volumes of political comment and satire, as 'Ministers of State, Priests, and Kings,' 'Critical Essays,' 'Portuguese Scenes and Fancies,' 'Celebrated Portuguese,' 'Madrid: Impressions of Travel.'

Pinkerton, Allan G. A famous American detective; born at Glasgow, Scotland, 1819, died in Chicago, 1884. He became involved in the Chartist outbreak in Birmingham, and emigrated to the United States in 1842. He founded his detective agency in Chicago in 1850, and was in charge of the United States secret service during the Civil War. His works include: 'The Molly Maguires' (1877); 'The Spy of the Rebellion' (1883); 'Thirty Years a Detective' (1884).

Pinkney, Edward Coate. An American writer of verses; born at London, 1802; died at Baltimore, Md., 1828. He wrote a volume of 'Poems' (1825; republished 1838 and 1844).

Piozzi, Hester Lynch Salisbury (Thrale) (pē-ots'ē). An Englishwoman, chiefly noted from her friendship with Dr. Johnson. She was born in Carnarvonshire, Jan. 16, 1740-1; died May 2, 1821. She received a good education, and married in 1763 Henry Thrale, a brewer much her elder, taciturn and wholly absorbed in business, and who allowed her little liberty. She first became acquainted with Dr. Johnson the next year; he spent much time at their home and traveling with them. After Thrale's death she married Mr. Piozzi, a cultivated Italian musician of considerable note; Johnson resented the change and left her with reproaches, English society considered it a social descent, and most writers since have echoed their sentiments. Although she has written other things, her 'Anecdotes of Dr. Johnson' and her 'Autobiography' are the works now read.

Piron, Alexis (pē-rôn'). A French poet; born at Dijon, July 9, 1689; died at Paris, Jan. 21, 1773. As an epigrammatist he holds the foremost place in French literature. He wrote many tragedies, comedies, and comic operas, but of these none is now valued except the comedy 'Metromania' (The Poetic Craze). His pungent epigrams made him many enemies; and when he was elected to the Academy, Louis XIV. was prevailed upon to nullify the choice. Hence the witty couplet proposed for his epitaph:—

« Ci gît Piron, qui ne fut rien,
    Pas même académicien; »

that is, "Here lies Piron, who was nothing, not even Academician."

Pisan, Christine de (pē-zän'). A French poet; born at Venice, 1364; died about 1431. Among her poems are: 'An Epistle to the God of Loves' (1399); 'Feats of Arms and of Chivalry' (1404); 'Life and Good Ways of the Wise King Charles V.' [of France] (1404); 'Lamentations over the Evils of the Civil War' (1410); 'Moral Sayings.'

Pisemskij, Aleksei Teofilaktovich (pē-zem'-skē). A Russian novelist; born at Ramene in the government of Kostroma, March 20, 1820; died January 1881. His greatest novel is 'A Thousand Souls' (1858); he wrote also 'The Stormy Sea' (1863), 'The Men of 1840' (1868), 'In the Whirlpool' (1871). Some of his short stories are in every way admirable, among them 'The Wood Demon' and 'Pietershik.'

Pithou, Pierre (pē-tö'). A notable French jurisconsult and historical writer; born at Troyes, Nov. 1, 1539; died at Nogent-sur-Seine, Nov. 1, 1596. Among his writings are: 'Memoirs of the Counts of Champagne' (1572); 'Reasons why the Bishops of France were able to give absolution to Henry of Bourbon, King of France' (1593); 'Comparison of Mosaic and Roman Laws' (1673).

Pitre, Luigi (pē-trā'). An Italian collector of folk-lore; born at Palermo, Dec. 23, 1842. He compiled and edited a 'Library of Sicilian Popular Traditions' (19 vols., 1870-95), and was editor of 'Archives for the Study of Popular Traditions,' founded 1882. He is author of a 'Bibliography of Italian Folk-Lore Literature' (1894); 'Patron Festivals in Sicily' (1901).

Pitre Chevalier, name assumed by Pierre Michel François Chevalier. A French journalist and historical writer; born 1812; died 1863. He wrote several volumes of poems; also 'Studies on Brittany' (6 vols. 1839-42); 'Ancient Brittany' (1844); 'Modern Brittany' (1844); 'History of the War of the Cossacks against Poland' (1859).

Pixérécourt, René Charles Guilbert de (pēx-ā-rā-kör'). A French dramatist; born at Nancy, Jan. 22, 1773; died July 27, 1844. He wrote dramas, among them 'Seligo; or, The Generous Negro' (1793), 'The Castle in the Apennines; or, The Mysteries of Udolfo' (1798); several very successful comedies, as 'The Doctor in Love,' 'The Living Manikin; or, The Wooden Husband,' 'Marcellus; or, The Supposititious Heir' (1801); and many melodramas, comic operas, etc.

Placentius, John Leo (plä-sen'shus). A Belgian versifier, writing in Latin; born about 1500, at St. Trond (Liège); died about 1550. Among his writings are: 'Catalogue of all Bishops of Tongres, Liège,' etc., a fabulous history (1529); two comedies, one in prose, the other in verse; an alliterative poem, 'Battle of the Pigs, by P. Porcius, Poet' (Pugna Porcorum, per P. Porcium, Poetam), in which every word in the 253 verses begins with the letter p. It was printed at Basle, 1552, in conjunction with Hugbald's 'Eologue on Baldheads' (De Calvis), in which every word begins with c.

Planard, François Antoine Eugène (plä-när'). A French dramatist; born at Millau, in Aveyron, Feb. 4, 1783; died at Paris, Nov. 13, 1853. Besides the novel 'Almedan' (1825), and some occasional verse, he wrote many comedies, as 'The Marrier of Old Women' (1808); 'The Family Portrait' (1809); 'The Supposititious Niece' (1813); 'The Lucky Meeting' (1821); and several libretti of comic operas, among them 'Last Wills and Love Letters,' music by Auber; 'The Manikin of Bergamo,' music by Fétis; 'Mina,' music by Ambroise Thomas.

Planché, James Robinson (plon-shā'). An English playwright, archaeologist, and herald; born in London, Feb. 27, 1796; died May 30,

1880. He was an expert on the subject of archæology and costumes; one of the founders of the British Archæological Association; and is credited with the authorship of 200 plays and librettos, original and adapted. Among his miscellaneous works are: 'Lays and Legends of the Rhine' (1826-27); 'History of British Costume' (1834); 'Pursuivant of Arms' (1851), a treatise on heraldry which procured for him the appointment of Rouge Croix Pursuivant; 'Popular Fairy Tales'; 'Recollections' (2 vols., 1872), chiefly literary and theatrical.

Platen-Hallermund, August, Count von (plät'en-häl'ler-mönd). An eminent German poet; born at Ansbach, Oct. 24, 1796; died at Syracuse in Sicily, Dec. 5, 1835. His principal works are: 'Sonnets from Venice' (1824); 'The Fateful Fork' (1826), an Aristophanic comedy ridiculing the reigning literary fashions of the time; 'The Romantic Œdipus' (1828), a comedy with the same subject: then followed a number of lyric poems and odes, with the drama 'The League of Cambrai,' and the epic story 'The Abassides,' written in 1830. His 'Songs of Poland' (1830) gave expression to his deep hate for the Czar; though privately circulated they were not published till after the poet's death.

Plato (plā'tō). The renowned Greek philosopher; born at Athens, in 427 B. C.; died there, 347 B. C. His writings seem to have come down to us complete. They consist of 44 separate works in 64 books, and are all written in dialogue form. These dialogues are classed in three series, marking three periods in the philosopher's life. First, those written during the life of Socrates or during the year or two next following his death: in these Plato is thoroughly under the Socratic influence, and the discussion is ever on conduct, the foundations of morality. The dialogues of this period are: the 'Apology,' 'Lysis,' 'Charmides,' 'Laches,' 'Protagoras,' 'Meno,' 'Gorgias,' 'Io,' 'Euthyphro,' 'Crito,' etc. In the second period the object of research is the objective ground of cognition: to this belong 'Theætetus,' 'The Sophist,' 'The Politician,' 'Parmenides.' The dialogues of the third period deal with the problem of reducing to philosophical unity the data of the several sciences,—physics, ethics, politics, etc.: to this class belong 'Phædrus,' 'Symposium,' 'Phædo,' 'Philebus,' 'The Republic,' 'Timæus,' 'The Laws.' No better guide to the full sense and spirit of Plato's dialogues need be wished than Jowett's translation, as revised by Jowett shortly before his death.

Plautus, Titus Maccius (plâ'tus *or* plou'-tus). A celebrated Roman comic poet; born at Sarsina in Umbria, about 254 (?) B. C.; died at Rome in 184 B. C. According to Varro, 130 comedies passed current in his time as written by Plautus; but of these Varro considered only 21 genuine. Twenty of these are extant. In their plots, leading incidents, and characters, and even in the outlines of the

dialogues, they are borrowed from Greek originals; but Plautus fairly makes this borrowed material his own. Lessing declared Plautus's 'Captives' to be "the best constructed drama in existence"; and the greatest of modern dramatists, as Shakespeare and Molière, did not scruple to draw on the Roman poet for motives of their comedies.

Plavistshikoff, Peter Alexiévich (pläv-ist'shē-kof). A Russian dramatist; born at Moscow, 1760; died there, 1812. Besides lyric and didactic poems, he wrote these dramatic pieces: 'Ruric, Founder of the Russian Monarchy'; 'Takmass Kuli Khan, Prince of Siberia'; 'Yermak, Conqueror of Siberia'; 'The Landless Peasant'; 'The American Savages.'

Pliny the Elder, or the Naturalist (**Caius Plinius Secundus**) (plin'ē). A celebrated Roman compiler of encyclopædic knowledge; born at Novum Comum, the modern Como, 23 A. D.; died 79 A. D. He wrote a 'Natural History' in 37 books, compiled, as the author states in the preface, from more than 2,000 volumes. He begins with physics and astronomy, which occupy books 1 and 2; books 3-6 treat of geography; books 7-19 treat of man, the animal kingdom, and plants; in books 20-32 the author notes the medicinal properties of plants; the remaining books are devoted to mineralogy and the medicinal uses of minerals, and to fine art and anecdotes of artists.

Pliny the Younger (Caius Publius Cæcilius Secundus, Minor). A Roman orator, nephew of Pliny the Elder; born at Comum, A. D. 61; died about 113. Of his writings, one oration is extant, 'The Panegyric,' addressed to the emperor Trajan on the occasion of Pliny's investiture with the insignia of the consulship; and his 'Letters,' including the correspondence between him and Trajan while Pliny was proprætor of Bithynia.

Plotinus (plō-tī'nus). An Alexandrine, the most celebrated representative of Neo-Platonism; born at Lycopolis in Egypt, 205 A. D.; died at Minturnæ in Campania, 270. His writings were collected by his disciple Porphyrius, and divided into six parts, each part subdivided into nine books. The doctrine of Plotinus starts from the basis of Plato's doctrine of ideas; but with that he combines many foreign elements of supernaturalism, mysticism, and extravagant idealism.

Plouvier, Édouard (plöv-yā'). A French dramatist and story-writer; born at Paris, Aug. 2, 1821; died there, Nov. 2, 1876. Among his stories are: 'The Christmas Tree' (1854); 'The Beauty with Golden Hair' (1861). He wrote a volume of songs, 'Sunday Refrains' (1856); and the comedies 'The Steeple-Chase' (1851), 'Winter Night's Dream' (1854), 'A Household Crisis' (1858), 'The Dragooness' (1874); also 'The Late Capt. Octave' (1859).

Plumptre, Anna. An English miscellaneous writer, sister of James; born 1760; died at Norwich, 1818. She wrote: 'Antoinette,' a novel;

'Life of Kotzebue' (1801); 'Narrative of a Three Years' Residence in France' (1810); 'Narrative of a Residence in Ireland' (1817); many other narratives of observations in foreign countries, as South Africa (1806), the Ottoman Empire, Brazil, Japan, etc.; and several stories.

Plumptre, James. An English dramatic and miscellaneous writer; born 1770; died Jan. 23, 1832, at Great Gransden in Huntingdonshire, where he was rector of a church. Among his writings are 'The Coventry Act,' comedy (1793); 'Osway,' tragedy (1795); 'The Lakers,' comic opera (1798); 'A Popular Commentary on the Bible' (1827).

Plutarch (plö'tärk). A celebrated Greek moralist, practical philosopher, and biographer; born at Chæronea in Bœotia about 46 A. D., the time of his death cannot be determined, but he appears to have been living at an advanced age at the death of Trajan, 117 A.D. He wrote 'Parallel Lives' of notable men of Greece and Rome: and a great many 'Moral Treatises,' including 'The Education of Children'; 'The Right Way of Hearing'; 'Precepts about Health'; 'Cessation of Oracles'; 'The Pythian Responses'; 'The Retarded Vengeance of the Deity'; 'The Dæmon of Socrates'; 'The Virtues of Women'; 'On the Fortune of the Romans'; 'Political Counsels'; 'On Superstition'; 'On Isis and Osiris'; 'On the Face of the Moon's Disk'; 'On the Opinions Accepted by the Philosophers.'

Pocci, Franz, Count von (pot'chē). A German poet, musician, and designer; born at Munich, March 7, 1807; died there, May 7, 1876. Besides several light musical dramas he wrote an opera, 'The Alchemist,' and a number of songs and sonatas; a volume of 'Poems' (1843); 'Hunting Songs' (1843); 'Student Songs'; several books for children, admirable alike for literary form and artistic illustration, — e. g., 'The Little Rose Garden,' a prayer-book (3d ed. 1868); 'A Little Book of Proverbs.'

Pocock, Edward. An English Orientalist; born at Oxford, 1604; died 1691. He wrote, or rather edited, with a most learned and elaborate commentary, 'Specimen of the History of the Arabians' (1649); and a similar work, 'Moses's Gate' (1655), one of the writings of Maimonides.

Pocock, Isaac. An English playwright; born at Bristol, 1782; died 1835. Among his most successful productions were: 'John of Paris,' comic opera (1814); 'Zembuca; or, The Net-Maker,' holiday piece (1815); 'The Robber's Wife,' romantic drama (1829); 'King Arthur and the Knights of the Round Table,' Christmas spectacle (1834).

Poe, Edgar Allan. An American poet and story-writer; born in Boston, Jan. 19, 1809; died in Baltimore, Md., Oct. 7, 1849. Left an orphan in early childhood, he was adopted by John Allan of Richmond, Va., and at the age

of 19 left this home and published his first volume of verse at Boston. He was a cadet at the United States Military Academy, 1830-31; and subsequently was editor of the Southern Literary Messenger, 1835-37; of the Gentleman's Magazine, 1839-40; of Graham's Magazine, 1841-42; and of the Broadway Journal, 1845. He also contributed to the Evening Mirror, Godey's Lady's Book, the Whig Review, and other periodicals. He projected a magazine to be called Literary America, and to aid it, lectured in New York city and through the South, 1848-49. He died under distressing conditions at Baltimore in 1849. A complete list of his works in book form includes: 'Tamerlane and Other Poems' (Boston, 1827); 'Al Aaraf, Tamerlane, and Minor Poems' (Baltimore, 1829); 'Poems' (2d ed., including many poems now first published, New York, 1831). The 'Narrative of Arthur Gordon Pym, of Nantucket' (New York, 1838); 'The Conchologist's First Book' (Philadelphia, 1839); 'Tales of the Grotesque and Arabesque' (Philadelphia, 1840); 'The Prose Romances of Edgar A. Poe' (Philadelphia, 1843); 'The Raven and Other Poems' (New York, 1845); 'Mesmerism: In Articulo Mortis' (London, 1846); 'Eureka, a Prose Poem' (New York, 1848). After his death there were republished 'The Literati: Some Honest Opinions about Autorial Merits and Demerits, with Occasional Words of Personality,' etc., edited by R. W. Griswold (New York, 1850); 'Tales of Mystery, Imagination, and Humor; and Poems,' edited by Henry Vizetelly (London, 1852). A collected edition was issued in 3 vols., 1850, 4th vol. 1856. The definitive edition is the one edited by E. C. Stedman and G. E. Woodberry (10 vols., Chicago, 1894-95).

Poggio Bracciolini, Gian Francesco (pod'-jē-o brätch-ē-o-lē'ne). An eminent Italian humanist; born at Castel Terranuova, near Florence, Feb. 11, 1380; died at Florence, Oct. 30, 1459. By his untiring research of the monastery libraries of Switzerland and Germany, he brought to light MSS. supposed to have been lost, of works of the ancient classics, as Quintilian, Valerius Flaccus, Asconius, Statius, Ammianus, and many others. He translated into Latin several of the Greek classics. His own writings are: 'Facetiæ,' a work of the same questionable character as others of the same title — the book had 26 editions at the end of the 15th century; 'Of the Variances of Fortune'; a 'History of Florence'; 'The Miseries of Human Life'; 'The Infelicity of Princes'; 'On Marriage in Old Age'; 'Dialogue Against Hypocrites.'

Pogodin, Michail Petrovich (pō-gō'din). A Russian historian; born at Moscow, Nov. 23, 1800; died there, Dec. 20, 1875. He wrote: 'On the Origin of the Russians' (1823); 'Character of Ivan the Terrible' (1828); 'Complicity of Godunov in the Murder of Demetrius' (1829); 'Marfa Posadniza,' a tragedy (1831); 'Stories' (3 vols., 1833); 'History of the Pseudo-

Demetrius' (1835); 'Russian History' (7 vols., 1846–54: the work was left unfinished); 'Researches on the Historic Basis of Serfdom' (1858); 'The First Seventeen Years of the Reign of Peter the Great' (1875).

Poinsinet, Antoine Alexandre Henri (pwañ-sē-nā'). A French dramatic writer; born at Fontainebleau, 1735; died at Cordova, 1769. His first work was a parody of the opera 'Tithonus and Aurora'; then followed 'The False Dervish,' comic opera (1757); 'The Little Philosopher,' comedy (1760); 'Sancho Panza in his Island,' opera-bouffe (1762); 'Tom Jones,' lyric comedy (1764); 'Ermelinda,' lyric tragedy (1767); 'The Sick Ogre,' spectacular piece; 'Lot and his Daughters.'

Poitevin, Prosper (pwät-vañ'). A French lexicographer and writer; born about 1804; died at Paris, Oct. 27, 1884. He wrote: 'Ali Pasha and Vasiliki,' a poem (1833); and some comedies, among them 'A Night at Potiphar's' (1841), 'The Husband in Spite of Himself' (1842). His works on lexicography and linguistics are numerous; among them 'Universal Dictionary of the French Language' (2 vols., 1854–60), and 'General and Historical Grammar of the French Language' (2 vols., 1856).

Pol, Vincenty (pōl). A Polish poet; born at Lublin, April 20, 1807; died at Cracow, Dec. 2, 1872. He wrote the patriotic 'Songs of Janusz' (1833); 'Song of Our Country' (1843), which won for its author unbounded popularity; 'Pictures from Life and from Travel' (1847), probably his finest work; 'The Starost of Kisla' (1873), a narrative poem on the chase.

Polevój, Nikoláj Alexéjevitsh (pō-lev'oi). A Russian novelist, dramatist, and literary critic; born at Irkutsk, July 4, 1796; died at St. Petersburg, March 6, 1846. His dramatic compositions are 'Ugolino,' 'Parasha,' 'Little Grandfather of the Russian Fleet': they have a place in the repertoire of Russian theatres. He wrote also 'History of the Russian People' (6 vols., 1829–33).

Politian (Angelo Ambrogini) (pō-lish'än). A celebrated Italian humanist; born at Montepulciano in Tuscany, July 1454; died at Florence, 1494. At 15 he wrote epigrams in Latin, at 17 in Greek, and at 18 published an edition of Catullus. He was professor of Greek and Roman literature at Florence, 1480. His translations from Greek into Latin, especially that of the Iliad, were much admired by his contemporaries. Among the Greek works translated by him were those of Epictetus, Herodian, Hippocrates, and Galen, Plutarch's 'Eroticus,' and Plato's 'Charmides.' Among his original works are: 'A Brief Account of the Conspiracy of the Pazzi' (1478); 'Miscellanea' (1489), a collection of his essays in philology and criticism; several poems in elegant Latin, among them 'Manto,' in praise of Virgil; 'Ambra,' an idyllic sketch of Tuscan landscape; 'The Countryman,' celebrating the delights of rural life. He wrote in

Italian the stanzas called 'The Joust,' on Giuliano de' Medici's victory in a tournament; and 'Orpheus,' a lyric drama.

Polko, Elise (pōl'kō). A German story-writer; born at Minden, Jan. 31, 1822; died at Munich, May 15, 1899. She wrote an interesting series of 'Musical Tales' (first instalment 1852); also 'A Woman's Life' (1854); 'In the Artist World'; 'Reminiscences of Felix Mendelssohn Bartholdy' (1868); 'Conversations' (1872); 'From the Year 1870'; 'New Story-Book' (1884).

Pollard, Edward Albert. An American journalist and author; born in Virginia, Feb. 27, 1828; died at Lynchburg, Va., Dec. 12, 1872. As editor of the Richmond Examiner during the Civil War, he was an earnest advocate of the Confederate cause, but an active opponent of Jefferson Davis. Among his numerous works are: 'Black Diamonds' (1859); 'Southern History of the War' (1862); 'The Lost Cause' (1866); 'The Life of Jefferson Davis' (1869).

Pollard, Josephine. An American writer of juvenile literature; born in New York city in 1843; died there, Aug. 15, 1892. Her works include: 'The Gypsy Books' (1873–74); 'Elfin Land' (1882), poems; 'Gellivor, a Christmas Legend' (1882); 'The Boston Tea Party' (1882).

Pöllnitz, Karl Ludwig (pĕl'nits). A German adventurer, known as a writer of memoirs; born 1692; died 1775. He was at one time master of ceremonies at the court of Frederick the Great. He wrote 'La Saxe Galante' (1737: the private life of Augustus of Saxony), and 'Memoirs' of his own life and times (1734).

Pollock, Walter Herries. An English editor, poet, and author, son of Sir W. F. Pollock; born in London in 1850. He was admitted to the bar in 1874, has delivered lectures at the Royal Institution, and from 1884 to 1894 acted as editor of the Saturday Review. Among his miscellaneous literary and poetical publications are: 'Lectures on French Poets'; 'The Picture's Secret,' a novel: 'Songs and Rhymes, English and French'; a translation of De Musset's 'Nights'; 'Old and New,' verse; 'Fencing' in the 'Badminton Library'; 'Animals That Have Owned Us.'

Pollok, Robert. A Scotch poet; born at Moorhouse in Renfrewshire, Oct. 19, 1798; died at Shirley-Commor, near Southampton, Sept. 18, 1827. His poem 'The Course of Time' (1827) is noted. He wrote also 'Tales of the Covenanters' (1833).

Polo, Gaspar Gil. See **Gil Polo.**

Polo, Marco. A famous Italian traveler; born at Venice, 1254; died there, 1324. He accompanied his father and his uncle, Venetian traders, 1271, on their second journey to the court of Kublai, the Khan of Tartary. Marco won the favor of Kublai, and was taken into his service: he was employed on various important missions to the remotest parts of the Khan's dominions, and thus collected information regarding the countries and their inhabitants. The three Venetians started on their return home, 1292, by way of Cochin-China, Sumatra, Ceylon, Ormus, Trebizond, and Constantinople, reaching Venice in 1295. Marco commanded a Venetian galley in the war with Genoa, and was taken prisoner, 1298; while in prison he dictated to Rusticiano of Pisa an account of his travels, which Rusticiano wrote out in French, and nine years later revised and amended. The title of the book is simply 'The Book of Marco Polo.' About 80 MS. copies of it are extant, differing each from each considerably.

Polo de Medina, Salvador Jacinto (pō'lō de mä dē'nä). A Spanish poet; born in Murcia about 1607; died about 1660. He wrote a poem in the form of a vision, 'The Incurables' Hospital; Journey out of this Life into the Next,' a moral treatise which was much admired in his time; 'On Moral Supremacy, to Lælius'; also some fables and some satirical verses.

Polyænus (pol-i-ē'nus). A Greek writer of the second century, native of Macedonia. He wrote a historical collection of instances of military ruses employed by Greeks, Romans, and Barbarians. It was entitled 'Strategics,' or 'Stratagems,' and was inscribed to the emperors Marcus Antoninus and Lucius Verus. The work is extant. It was first printed in 1549, and again in 1887.

Polybius (pō-lib'ē-us). A celebrated Greek historian; born at Megalopolis in Arcadia, 210 B.C., while much of Greece was still independent; died 127, after it had long been a province of Rome, and himself an admired companion of its conquerors. His work, 'Histories,' comprised 40 books, of which only the first five have come down to us complete: it was the author's purpose to write the history of "all the known regions of the civilized world which had fallen under the sway of Rome."

Polyides (pol-ē-i'des). A Greek poet and musician of the fourth century B.C.; famous for his dithyrambs. To him is credited by Welcker the tragedy of ' Iphigenia,' some passages from which are quoted by Aristotle in his ' Poetics.'

Pomeroy, Marcus Mills. ["Brick Pomeroy."] An American journalist and humorous writer; born at Elmira, N. Y., Dec. 25, 1833; died at Brooklyn, May 30, 1896. He was a journalist of La Crosse, Wis., and later of New York city, where he founded Brick Pomeroy's Democrat. His chief publications are: 'Gold Dust' (1872); 'Brick Dust' (1872); 'Perpetual Money' (1878).

Pomfret, John. An English poet; born at Luton in Bedfordshire, 1667; died 1702. His best-known work is ' The Choice: A Poem Written by a Person of Quality' (1700), which had four editions within a year. His other principal writings are: 'A Prospect of Death,' an ode (1700), and 'Reason,' a poem (1700).

Pommier, Victor Louis Amédée (pom-yä'). A French poet; born at Lyons, 1804; died in 1877. Among his writings are: 'The Russian Expedition' (1827); 'The Republic; or, The Book of Blood' (1836); 'The Assassins' (1837); 'Hell' (1853), a most realistic portrayal of the infernal regions as conceived by old-time orthodoxy; 'Algeria and Conquering Civilization' (1848); 'Death of the Archbishop of Paris' (1849); 'Monologues of a Solitary' (1870).

Pompery, Édouard de (pōm-per-ē'). A French miscellaneous writer; born at Couvrelles in Aisne, 1812. He was a socialist democrat, and nearly all his writings deal with social questions. He wrote: 'The Doctor from Timbuktu' (1837); 'Despotism or Socialism' (1849), 'Woman in Human Society: Her Nature, her Rôle, her Social Value' (1864); 'Essay on the True Voltaire' (1873).

Pompignan, Jean Jacques Lefranc, Marquis de (pōm-pēn-yän). A French poet; born at Montauban, 1709; died 1784. His tragedy 'Dido' (1734) had an extraordinary success; it was followed by 'Zoraide,' tragedy; 'The Farewell of Mars,' comedy (1735); 'Trip to Languedoc and Provence,' narrative poem (1740). Some of his odes are works of consummate grace and art, e. g., the 'Ode on the Death of Jean Jacques Rousseau.'

Ponce de Leon, Luis (pōn'thä dä lā-ōn'). A great Spanish lyric poet; born at Granada, 1527; died at Madrigal, 1591. He entered the order of Augustin Friars, 1544, and in 1561 became professor of theology in the University of Salamanca. He suffered five years' imprisonment, by sentence of the Court of Inquisition, for his translation of the 'Song of Songs' into Spanish, with commentary. Among his prose writings is a treatise on the 'Names of Christ' (1583) and 'The Perfect Wife' (1583): both books are still in popular use in Spain. His poems, almost exclusively of a religious character, are to be classed with the highest products of the lyric Muse of Spain. His translations in verse of some of the works of Virgil and Horace, of 40 of the Psalms, and of passages from Greek and Italian poets, are characterized by much spirit and grace of style.

Poncy, Louis Charles (pôn-sē'). A French poet; born at Toulon, 1821; died 1891. He was a stone-mason quite without school education. He published a series of volumes of verse: 'Poems' (1840); 'Marine Views' (1842); 'Marguerite's Posy' (1855).

Pond, Frederick Eugene. An American journalist and author; born in Marquette County, Wis., April 8, 1856. He was among the first to urge the establishment of a National Sportsman's Association, and under the pen-name of "Will Wildwood" has published 'Handbook for Young Sportsmen' (1876); 'Memoirs of Eminent Sportsmen' (1878); and 'Gun Trial and Field Records of America' (1885); 'American Game Reserves.'

Pongerville, Jean Baptiste Aimé Sanson de (pôn-zhā-vēl'). A French miscellaneous writer; born at Abbeville in Somme, March 3, 1782; died at Paris, Jan. 24, 1870. His great work is a scholarly metrical translation of the Latin poet Lucretius. He translated also into French verse some of Ovid's works, under the title 'Mythological Amours.'

Poninski, Anton Slodzin (pō-nin'skē). A Polish poet; died 1742. He wrote 'Hymeneal Song of Augustus III.' (1720), and 'Sarmatides or Satires' (1741).

Ponsard, François (pôṅ-sär'). A French dramatist; born at Vienne, 1814; died at Paris, 1867. His first venture in literature was made with a translation of Lord Byron's 'Manfred' (1837). His 'Lucretia' (1843), in the production of which on the stage of the Odéon the celebrated Rachel acted the leading rôle, was a brilliant success: it marked a reaction against romanticism. Among his other dramatic productions are: 'Agnès de Méranie' (1846); 'Charlotte Corday' (1850); 'Ulysses' (1852); 'Honor and Money' (1853), a fine satiric comedy; 'The Bourse' (1856); 'What Pleases Womankind' (1860), a trilogy, which had little success; 'The Lion in Love' (1866); 'Galileo' (1867).

Ponson du Terrail, Pierre Alexis (pôṅ-sôṅ dü ter-īl'). A French romancer; born at Montmaur near Grenoble, July 8, 1829; died at Bordeaux, Jan. 31, 1871. He wrote an incredible number of works of fiction; among his works are: 'Heritage of a Centenarian'; 'Gown and Sword' (1857); 'The Matrimonial Agency'; 'Memoirs of a Man of the World' (1861); 'Nights at the Gilded House'; 'The King of Navarre's Mistress' (1863); 'The Great World's Bohemians' (1867); 'Dr. Rousselle's Secret' (1869); 'Aurora's Amours' (1870).

Pontmartin, Armand Augustin Joseph Marie (pôṅ-mär-taṅ'). A French story-writer and literary critic; born at Avignon, July 16, 1811; died there, 1890. In 1853 he commenced a series of 'Literary Talks' in the Gazette de France, which, collected, fill 30 volumes. Among his works are: 'Recollections of an Old Lover of Music' (1878); 'Medusa's Raft' (1872); 'Recollections of an Old Critic'; 'My Memoirs' (2 vols., 1885–86); 'Sins of Old Age' (1889); 'Literary Episodes' (1890).

Pontoux, Claude de (pôṅ-tö'). A French versifier; born at Chalons-sur-Saône, about 1530; died there, 1579. He wrote: 'Lamentable Harangues on the Death of Divers Animals'; 'Love's Smiles and Tears' (1576); 'The Idea and Other Works' (1579), 'The Idea' being a lady to whom he paid a hopeless suit.

Pool, Maria Louise. An American journalist and novelist; born in Rockland, Mass., Aug. 20, 1845; died there, May 19, 1898. At one time she was connected with the New York Tribune. Her best-known works are: 'In Buncombe County'; 'A Vacation in a Buggy' (1887); 'Tenting at Stony Beach' (1888); 'Rowena in Boston' (1892); 'In a Dike Shanty' (1896).

Poole, William Frederick. An American librarian and bibliographer; born at Salem, Mass., Dec. 24, 1821; died at Evanston, Ill., March 1, 1894. He was a librarian at Boston, Cincinnati,

and Chicago. His chief work is the celebrated 'Index to Periodical Literature,' which he initiated, and of which in its greatly expanded later form he was co-editor with W. I. Fletcher. Among his other works are 'The Battle of the Dictionaries' (1856), and 'Cotton Mather and Salem Witchcraft' (1869).

Poore, Benjamin Perley. An American journalist, compiler, and author; born at Newbury, Mass., Nov. 2, 1820; died at Washington, D. C., May 30, 1887. He spent several years abroad, and devoted much time to research in French history. Upon his return he became active in journalism, and for thirty years was Washington correspondent of the Boston Journal. His works include: 'The Rise and Fall of Louis Philippe' (1848); 'Early Life of Napoleon' (1851); 'Reminiscences of Sixty Years' (1886).

Poorten-Schwartz, J. M. W. van der. See Maartens.

Poot, Huibert Cornelis (pöt). A Dutch poet; born at Abtswoud, South Holland, Jan. 29, 1689; died at Delft, Dec. 31, 1733. His countrymen called him "the Hesiod of Holland." He published 'Miscellaneous Poems' (1716; to which succeeded a second volume, 1728, and a third, 1735).

Pope, Alexander. A great English poet; born at London, May 21, 1688; died at Twickenham on the Thames, May 30, 1744. His principal works are: 'The Iliad of Homer,' translated (1715–20); 'Homer's Odyssey' (1725); 'Essay on Criticism,' in the manner of Horace (1711); 'The Temple of Fame' (1711); 'Epistle from Eloisa to Abelard' (1716); 'The Rape of the Lock' (1712); 'The Dunciad' (1728, 1742); 'Essay on Man' (1733); 'Imitations of Horace' (1740).

Pope, John. An American general; born at Louisville, Ky., March 16, 1822; died at Sandusky, O., Sept. 23, 1892. He graduated from West Point in 1842, and had important commands in the Civil War. Later in life he had charge of various departments of the regular army in the West. He published: 'The Virginia Campaign of July and August 1862,' a defense of his campaign in command of the Army of the Potomac.

Porphyrius (por-fī'rē-us). A celebrated Neo-Platonic philosopher; born at Batanea in Syria, 233 A.D.; died at Rome, 304 A.D. He was a disciple first of Longinus, then of Plotinus, whose works he edited, and whom he succeeded as master of a school of philosophy at Rome. But few of his writings have come down to us. He wrote a 'History of Philosophy,' to which probably belongs the extant 'Life of Pythagoras.' Some fragments of his work against the Christian religion — condemned to the flames by the emperor Theodosius II. in 453 — are preserved in the writings of his adversaries. We have his tractate 'On Abstinence from Animal Food'; also his 'Homeric Questions,' in 32 chapters; his 'Epistle to Marcella' on the right conduct of life; his letter to the

Egyptian priest Anebon in condemnation of magic and theurgy; 'Introduction to Philosophy,' in which the question of realism and nominalism is first mooted; 'On Deriving a Philosophy from Oracles'; and 'On the Cave of the Nymphs.'

Porson, Richard. An eminent English scholar and critic; born in Norfolk, Dec. 25, 1759; died in London, Sept. 25, 1808. He was educated at Eton and Cambridge, and regius professor of Greek at Cambridge from 1792 till his death. He possessed phenomenal powers of memory, great critical acumen, and a knowledge of Greek unequaled in his day. His emendations and critical notes on the Greek writers are accepted as authoritative. He wrote for the literary reviews on many subjects; edited Æschylus (1795); the 'Hecuba,' 'Orestes,' 'Phœnissæ,' and 'Medea' of Euripides (1797–1801): and published 'Adversaria' (1812); 'Tracts and Criticisms' (1815); 'Aristophanica' (1820); 'Photii Lexicon' (1822); 'Notæ in Suidam' (1834). His Letters to Archdeacon Travis on the "Three Witnesses" are monuments of analytic and argumentative power.

Port, Elizabeth-Marie (port). A Dutch poet and novelist; born in the second half of the eighteenth century. Her writings are: 'The Country' (1792), prose and poetry; 'For the Solitary' (1789); 'Reinhart on Nature and Religion' (1793); 'Elegies' (1794); 'True Enjoyment of Life' (1796); 'My Childhood's Tears' (1804), domestic tableaux; 'Frederick Weit and his Children'; 'On Society and Solitude' (1806); and 'New Poems' (1807).

Porter, Anna Maria. An English novelist; born at Durham, 1780; died 1832. Sister of Jane and Sir R. K.; she wrote 'Artless Tales' (1793–95), which was succeeded by a long series of novels, among them: 'Walsh Colville' (1797); 'The Lakes of Killarney' (1804); 'The Hungarian Brothers' (1807); 'The Recluse of Norway' (1814); 'The Knight of St. John' (1817); 'The Fast of St. Magdalen' (1818); 'Roche Blanche' (1822); 'Honor O'Hara' (1826); 'Barony' (1830); also 'Ballads, Romances, and Other Poems' (1811).

Porter, David. An American naval officer and diplomat; born in Boston, Feb. 1, 1780; died near Constantinople, March 3, 1843. He commanded in several naval engagements of the Tripoli war (1801–6) and the War of 1812. From 1831 to 1843 he held important diplomatic positions at Constantinople. His chief work is 'Constantinople and its Environs' (1835).

Porter, David Dixon. An American admiral, son of David; born at Chester, Pa., June 8, 1813; died at Washington, D. C., Feb. 13, 1891. He came into prominence in the Mexican War, and during the Civil War held important naval commands at New Orleans, Vicksburg, and Fort Fisher. As an author he will be best remembered for his nautical romance, 'The Adventures of Harry Marline' (1886). Among his other works are: 'Life of Commodore David Porter' (1875); 'Allan Dare and

Robert le Diable' (1885), a romance; 'History of the Navy in the War of the Rebellion' (1887).

Porter, Horace. An American general and military writer; born at Huntingdon, Pa., April 15, 1837. He graduated from West Point, and during the Civil War was a staff officer of McClellan and Rosecrans, and subsequently Grant's trusted aide and personal friend in Virginia during the last two years of the War. He is the author of 'Campaigning with Grant,' which first appeared serially in the Century Magazine'; and 'West Point Life.'

Porter, Jane. An English novelist; born at Durham, 1776; died at Bristol, May 24, 1850. Among her stories, some of which still enjoy a wide popularity, are: 'Thaddeus of Warsaw' (1803), which has been translated into several languages, and for which she was elected canoness of the Teutonic Order of St. Joachim; 'The Scottish Chiefs' (1810); 'The Pastor's Fireside' (1815); 'Duke Christian of Lüneburg' (1824); 'Coming Out' (1828); 'The Field of Forty Footsteps' (1828). In collaboration with her sister she wrote 'Tales round a Winter Hearth' (1826). She was long credited with the authorship of 'Sir Edward Seward's Diary' (1831); but it was written by her elder brother, Dr. Wm. Ogilvie Porter.

Porter, John Addison. An American journalist; born at New Haven, Conn., April 17, 1856. He is editor of the Hartford Post. His works are: 'The Corporation of Yale College' (1885); 'Administration of the City of Washington' (1885); 'Sketches of Yale Life' (1886). He is now (1897–98) private secretary to President McKinley. Died in 1900.

Porter, Linn Boyd. An American novelist of Cambridge, Mass.; born about 1840. He is the author of numerous sensational novels, published under the pseudonym of "Albert Ross" which have had a large sale. Among the most popular are: 'Thou Shalt Not' (1889); 'Speaking of Ellen' (1890); 'Out of Wedlock' (1894); 'Love Gone Astray'; 'Stranger than Fiction.'

Porter, Noah. An eminent American clergyman, educator, and author; born at Farmington, Conn., Dec. 14, 1811; died in New Haven, Conn., March 4, 1892. In 1846 he was appointed professor of metaphysics at Yale University; and was president of that institution from 1871 to 1885. The most valuable of his numerous works are: 'Human Intellect' (1868); 'Books and Reading' (1870); 'American Colleges and the American Public' (1870); 'Moral Science' (1885).

Porter, Sir Robert Ker. An English traveler, brother of Jane and Anna Maria; born at Durham, 1777; died at St. Petersburg, May 4, 1842. He traveled extensively in Europe, Asia, and South America; and wrote: 'Traveling Sketches in Russia and Sweden' (1808); 'Letters from Portugal and Spain' (1809); 'Narrative of the Late Campaign in Russia' (1813); 'Travels in Georgia, Persia, Armenia,

Ancient Babylonia, etc., during the Years 1817-20 ' (1821-22).

Posidonius (pos-i-dō'ni-us). A Greek Stoic philosopher; born at Apamea in Syria, but styled **" the Rhodian "** by reason of his long residence in the island of Rhodes; lived from 103 to 19 B. C. He was one of the most learned men of antiquity, his knowledge and his writings extending over every branch of science. Only fragments of his works are extant. His greatest work was a universal history in 52 books, held in high esteem by the ancients: it was a continuation of Polybius, and covered the period 145-82 B. C. His lectures on ' Tactics ' would seem to be the basis of the tractate of his disciple Asclepiodotus on the same subject.

Posnett, Mrs. George. An English novelist; born 18—. Her books are: ' The Touch of Fate ' (1884); ' On the Square ' (1884); ' Her Golden Forget-Me-Not ' (1885); and ' Who Am I? ' (1885).

Potier, Charles Joseph Edward (pōt-yā'). A French actor and dramatic author; born at Bordeaux in 1806; died at Paris in 1870. His principal dramatic works are: ' Factor ' (1834), a five-act drama with Charles Desnoyer and Boulé; ' Because ' (1835), ' The Drunkard's Sister ' (1839), one-act vaudevilles; ' Everybody's Master ' (1840), a two-act comedy with Antony Béraud; ' The Clothing Merchant ' (1841), a five-act drama with Desnoyer and Béraud; ' Estelle and Némorin ' (1844), a two-act pastoral bouffe; and ' The National Sickness ' (1846), a three-act vaudeville with Brissebarre.

Potter, Henry Codman. An American clergyman and author, bishop of New York; born at Schenectady, N. Y., May 25, 1835. Educated in theology in Virginia, he became rector of Grace Church, New York city, in 1868; and was consecrated bishop of New York in 1887. His works include: ' Gates of the East: A Winter in Egypt and Syria ' (1876); ' Sermons of the City ' (1881) ; ' Waymarks ' (1892). D. 1908.

Potts, William. An American writer on nature, also on political and social reform ; born in Philadelphia, May 5, 1838. For many years he was secretary and he is now vice-president of the National Civil Service League. He was chief examiner of the Civil Service Commission for New York State in 1887. He has published a volume of nature studies, ' From a New England Hillside,' and a Sunday-school service book, ' Noblesse Oblige ' ; ' Evolution and Local Reform ' ; ' The Monetary Problem.'

Potvin, Charles (pō-van'). A Belgian poet, and historian of literature; born at Mons, Dec. 2, 1818. He wrote several volumes of lyric poetry: ' Poems and Amours ' (1838); ' Poems, Historical and Romantic ' (2 vols., 1840); ' Political and Elegiac Poems ' (1849); ' Satires ' (1852); ' The Beggar-Woman ' (1856). On the drama he wrote: ' The Theatre in Belgium ' (1862); ' Essays on Dramatic Literature ' (2 vols., 1880) ; and some comedies, as ' Choice

of an Occupation ' and ' War.' He also wrote many volumes of literary history and criticism, among them ' Our Early Literary Periods ' (2 vols., 1870), and ' French Literature in Belgium before 1830.' Died at Ixelles, March 1, 1902.

Pougin, François-Auguste Arthur (pö-zhań'). A French musician and author; born at Chateauroux, 1834. Besides pseudonymous contributions to various journals, he published among others the following volumes : ' French Musicians of the 18th Century ' (1863); ' Meyerbeer: A Biographical Sketch ' (1864); ' William Vincent Wallace ' (1865); ' F. Halévy, Writer ' (1865); ' Bellini, his Life and Works ' (1867); ' Rossini ' (1869); ' Musical Literature in France ' (1869); and ' Albert Grisar ' (1870).

Poujol, Adolph (pö-zhol'). A French dramatic author; born at Paris, 1811 (?). He wrote very many plays in collaboration. Among his writings are : ' A Service of Love ' (1840); The Pastry-Cook of Danaustadt ' (1842); ' Results of a Fault ' (1842); ' Jeanne de Naples ' (1842); ' A Daughter of the Legion of Honor ' (1843); ' December 10 ' (1849); ' Marguerite ' (1851); ' A Maiden's Heart ' (1854); ' Doctor Momus ' (1857); and ' The Art of Managing Women ' (1859).

Poujoulat, Jean Joseph François (pö-zhö-lä'). A French historian; born at La Fare, Bouches-du-Rhône, Jan. 26, 1800; died at Paris, Jan. 5, 1880. His principal works are: ' History of Jerusalem ' (2 vols., 1840-42); ' Cardinal Maury ' (1855); ' History of the French Revolution ' (2 vols., 1855); ' History of France from 1814 ' (4 vols., 1865-67); ' Insanities of the Present Time regarding Religion ' (1877); ' The Bedawîn Woman ' (2 vols., 1835), a novel, crowned by the Academy.

Pouvillon, Émile (pö-vē-yôn'). A French novelist; born at Montauban, 1840. His novel ' Césette ' (1880), a tale of village life, won the Academy's Lambert prize. It was followed by ' Jennie's John ' (1886); ' The Blue Horse ' (1888); ' Singing-Weeping ' ; and ' Bernadotte,' a cabinet drama,— an antithesis of Zola's ' Lourdes.'

Powell, John Wesley. An American soldier, geologist, and author; born in Mount Morris, N. Y., March 24, 1834. He was educated at Oberlin College; was a lieutenant-colonel of artillery at the close of the Civil War; professor of geology in the Illinois Wesleyan University, 1865; explored the cañon of the Colorado River in 1867, and again in 1870-74. He succeeded Clarence King as director of the the United States Geological Survey (1879-96). The special volumes of reports written by Major Powell are : ' Exploration of the Colorado River in 1869-72 ' (1875); ' Geology of the Uinta Mountains ' (1876); ' The Arid Regions of the United States ' (1879); ' Introduction to Study of Indian Languages.' Died in 1902.

Powell, Thomas. An American playwright and author; born in London, Sept. 3, 1809; died in Newark, N. J., Jan. 13, 1887. For many years he was connected with the Frank Leslie publications. Besides two acted plays, 'True at Last' and 'The Shepherd's Well,' he published: 'Florentine Tales' (1847); 'Living Authors of England' (1849); 'Living Authors of America' (1850).

Powers, Horatio Nelson. An American clergyman, literary critic, and poet; born at Amenia, N. Y., April 30, 1826; died in 1890. Among his works are: 'Through the Year' (1875); 'Poems, Early and Late' (1876); 'Ten Years of Song' (1887); 'Lyrics of the Hudson.'

Pradon, Nicolas (prä-dôñ'). A French tragic poet; born at Rouen, 1632; died at Paris, 1698. Besides many fugitive poems, he wrote: 'Tamerlane' (1677); 'Phædra and Hippolytus' (1677); 'The Troad' (1679); 'Statira' (1683); 'Regulus' (1688); 'Scipio Africanus' (1697); and his most famous work, 'Pyramus and Thisbe.'

Pradt, Dominique Dufour de (prät). A French statesman and historian; born at Allanches in Auvergne, April 23, 1759; died March 18, 1837. He wrote: 'Historic Narrative of the Restoration of Royalty in France' (1814); 'History of the Embassy to the Grand Duchy of Warsaw in 1812' (1815); 'The Congress of Vienna' (2 vols., 1815-16); 'Historical Memoirs on the Spanish Revolution' (1816); 'The Colonies and the Present Revolution in [Spanish] America' (2 vols., 1817); 'The Congress of Carlsbad' (2 vols., 1819-20); 'The Four Concordats.'

Praed, Mrs. Campbell Mackworth (präd) (**Rosa Caroline Murray-Prior**). An Australian novelist, wife of the nephew of W. M. Praed; born in Bromelton, Queensland, March 27, 1851. In 1876 she came to London and began to write her noted Australian stories. Her most popular works are: 'An Australian Heroine' (1880); 'Moloch' (1883); 'The Head Station' (1885); 'December Roses' (1892); 'Outlaw and Lawmaker' (1893); 'Nulma' (1897). In collaboration with Justin McCarthy she has written 'The Right Honourable' (1886), and 'The Ladies' Gallery' (1889); 'Fugitive Anne' (1903); 'Nyria' (1904).

Praed, Winthrop Mackworth. An English poet (1802-39); born in London. He wrote society verse and occasional poetry. Among his best-known pieces are: 'The Red Fisherman'; 'Every-Day Characters'; 'Private Theatricals'; 'School and Schoolfellows'; 'A Letter of Advice'; 'Our Ball'; 'My Partner'; 'My Little Cousins'; etc.

Pram, Christen Henriksen (präm). A Danish poet; born at Gudbrandsdal in Norway, 1756; died in the island of St. Thomas, W. I., 1821. He was editor of the periodical Minerva, at Copenhagen; wrote the romantic epic 'Staerkodder' (1785), and two tragedies, 'Damon and Pythias' and 'Frode and Fingal.'

Prati, Giovanni (prä'tē). An Italian lyric poet; born at Dascindo near Trent, Jan. 27, 1815; died at Rome, May 9, 1884. He wrote 'Edmenegarda' (1841), a powerful narrative poem

after the Byronic manner, which was received with extraordinary favor. Then followed several volumes of lyric poetry, which still further enhanced the poet's reputation. His satire 'Satan and the Graces' (1855), and his epics 'Count Riga' (1856), 'Rudolf' (1858), 'Aribert' (1860), were equally successful.

Pratt, Anne (Mrs. John Pearless). Born at Strood, Dec. 5, 1806; died in London, July 27, 1893. An English nature-writer, whose books achieved great popularity. Among them are: 'Flowers and their Associations' (new ed. 1840); 'Field, Garden, and Woodland' (for the young, new ed. 1843); 'Chapters on Common Things of the Seaside' (1850); 'Green Fields, their Grasses' (1852); 'Our Native Songsters' (1852); 'Wild Flowers' (1853); 'Flowering Plants, Grasses, and Ferns of Great Britain' (1854); etc.

Pratt, Mrs. Ella (Farman). An American writer of juvenile literature. She has been editor of Wide Awake, and at present has charge of Our Little Men and Women. Among her works are: 'Anna Maylie' (1873); 'A White Hand' (1875); 'Good-for-Nothing Polly' (1877); 'A Girl's Money.' She died 1907.

Pratt, Orson. A Mormon apostle, educator, and professor; born in Hartford, Conn., Sept. 19, 1811; died in Salt Lake City, Oct. 3, 1881. He was one of the twelve apostles of the Mormon Church (1835), and was in charge of European missions from 1840, many successive years. He was professor of mathematics in Deseret University; also church historian and recorder. His writings include: 'Divine Authenticity of the Book of Mormon' (6 parts, 1851); 'Patriarchal Order, or Plurality of Wives' (1853); 'Cubic and Biquadratic Equations' (1866); 'Key to the Universe' (1879); and 'The Great First Cause.' He left in manuscript a 'Treatise on the Differential Calculus.'

Pratt, Samuel Jackson. An English poet and novelist; born at St. Ives, Cornwall, Dec. 25, 1749; died at Birmingham, Oct. 4, 1814. Besides his translation of Goethe's 'Sorrows of Werther' (1813), his books are: 'Sympathy,' a poem; 'Tears of Genius' (1774), a poem on Goldsmith; 'Landscapes in Verse'; 'Liberal Opinion' (1775), a novel; 'Emma Corbett' (1776), a novel; 'Apology for David Hume' (1777); 'Pupils of Pleasure' (1779), a novel; 'Gleanings through Wales, Holland,' etc. (1795); 'Gleanings in England' (1796); 'The Fair Circassian,' a tragedy; 'Family Secrets' (1797), a novel; 'Cabinet of Poetry' (1808).

Prentice, George Denison. An American journalist, author, and poet; born at Preston, Conn., Dec. 18, 1802; died at Louisville, Ky., Jan. 22, 1870. He was on the staff of the Hartford Weekly Review from 1828 to 1830, when he became editor of the Louisville Journal, and held that position until his death, making the paper famous for satiric wit and exuberant fun. His best-known work is a volume of witticisms entitled 'Prenticeana' (1859). His other publications are 'Life of Henry Clay' (1831), and 'Poems' (1876).

Prentiss, Mrs. Elizabeth (Payson). An American writer of fiction; born at Portland, Me., Oct. 26, 1818; died at Dorset, Vt., Aug. 13, 1878. Her most popular work was 'Stepping Heavenward' (1869), which was translated into several languages. She also published: 'Little Susy's Six Birthdays' (1853); 'Fred and Maria and Me' (1867); 'Aunt Jane's Hero' (1871); 'Pemaquid' (1877); 'Gentleman Jim' (1878).

Preradović, Peter (prer-ä-dō'vich). The most eminent of modern Croatian lyric poets; born at Grabonitza, March 19, 1818; died Aug. 18, 1872. He wrote: 'Firstlings,' a collection of short poems (1846); 'New Songs' (1851); 'The First Men' and 'The Slavic Dioscuri,' epics.

Prescott, William Hickling. An eminent American historian; born at Salem, Mass., May 4, 1796; died at New York, Jan. 28, 1859. His works are: 'History of Ferdinand and Isabella' (3 vols., 1838); 'History of the Conquest of Mexico' (3 vols., 1843); 'History of the Conquest of Peru' (3 vols., 1847); 'History of the Reign of Philip II. of Spain' (3 vols., 1855–58); 'Biographical and Critical Miscellanies' (1843); 'Critical Essays' (1852).

Pressensé, Edmond Déhoult de (prä-soñ-sä'). An eminent French theologian and historian; born at Paris, Jan. 7, 1824; died there, April 8, 1891. Among his numerous writings are: 'The Church and the French Revolution' (1864); 'Jesus Christ, his Life and his Work' (1866; 7th ed. 1884), written in opposition to Renan's 'Life of Jesus'; 'History of the First Three Centuries of the Christian Church' (6 vols., 1858–77); 'The Council of the Vatican' (1872); 'Origins: The Problem of Cognition, the Cosmologic Problem,' etc. (1883); 'Moral and Political Miscellanies' (1885); 'Alexander Vinet and his Unpublished Correspondence with H. Lutteroth' (1890).

Preston, Harriet Waters. An American scholar, translator, and writer; born in Danvers, Mass., in 1843; later resided at Leland Stanford University, California. At an early age she became noted as a linguist, and now has achieved a brilliant reputation as a translator from the Latin and Provençal languages, and as an essayist. Besides her translations of Mistral's 'Mirèio' (1873), Virgil's 'Georgics' (1881), and several others, she has published of her own original work: 'Aspendale' (1881); 'Troubadours and Trouvères' (1876); 'A Year in Eden,' with Louise Dodge (1886); 'Private Life of the Romans' (1893); and 'Love in the Nineteenth Century.'

Preston, Mrs. Margaret (Junkin). An American poet and miscellaneous writer; born in Philadelphia in 1825; died at Baltimore, March 28, 1897. She was a resident of Lexington, Va., and later of Baltimore, Md. Her writings deal chiefly with the period of the Civil War, the best known being: 'Silverwood' (1856), a novel; 'Beechenbrook, a Rhyme of the War' (1866); 'Cartoons' (1875); 'Colonial Ballads' (1887); 'Aunt Dorothy' (1890).

Prévost, Eugène Marcel (prä-vō'). A French novelist; born at Paris, May 1, 1862. His first story, 'The Scorpion' (1887), the tragic history of a clerical tutor in a Jesuit school, made a deep impression because of the fine psychological insight and intimate knowledge of the priestly life it displayed. It was followed by 'Our Helpmate: Provincials and Parisiennes' (1885); 'Chonchette' (1888); 'Mlle. Jaufre' (1889), perhaps his best work; 'Cousin Laura: Stage Morality' (1890); 'A Lover's Confession' (1891); 'Women's Letters' (1892); 'A Woman's Autumn' (1893); 'The Mill at Nazareth' (1894); 'The Demi-Virgins' (1894); 'More of the Women's Letters' (1894); 'Abbot Pierre.'

Prévost d'Exiles, Antoine François (prä-vō-deg-zēl'), commonly called Abbé Prévost. A notable French novelist; born at Hesdin in Artois, April 1, 1697; died near Chantilly, Nov. 23, 1763. He gained great celebrity through his remarkable novels: 'Memoirs of a Man of Quality' (1728); 'Cleveland'; 'Manon Lescaut,' his greatest work (1731); 'Story of a Modern Greek Woman' (1741). He also wrote some historical works and moral essays, and translated Richardson's 'Pamela' and 'Clarissa.'

Prévost-Paradol, Lucien Anatole (prä-vō' pä-rä-dol'). A distinguished French journalist; born at Paris, Aug. 8, 1829; died by suicide at Washington, D. C., July 20, 1870, while he was French envoy to the United States. He wrote: 'Essay on Universal History' (2 vols., 1854); 'Rôle of the Family in Education' (1857); 'Essays on Politics and Literature' (3 vols., 1859–63); 'Pages of Contemporary History' (4 vols., 1862–64); 'Studies on the French Moralists' (1865); 'The New France' (1868).

Price, Eleanor C. An English novelist; born 18—. Her books are: 'One Only' (1874); 'Constantia' (1875); 'A French Heiress in her Own Château' (1878); 'Mrs. Lancaster's Rival' (1879); 'Valentina: A Sketch' (1882); 'The Foreigners' (1883); 'High Aims' (1884); 'Gerald' (1885); 'Alexia' (1887); 'Red Towers' (1888).

Price, Richard. A notable English philosopher and man of science; born at Tynton in Glamorganshire, Feb. 23, 1723; died April 19, 1791. He was a Dissenting minister, and was pastor of a congregation at Hackney. He was the friend of Benjamin Franklin, and sympathized warmly with the American colonists. His tables of vital statistics and calculations of expectancy of life were the basis of modern annuities and life insurance; his economic and financial writings were of a high order, and the younger Pitt consulted him on finance. His principal writings are: 'An Appeal to the Public on the Subject of the National Debt' (1771); 'Civil Liberty and the Justice and Policy of the War with America' (1776); 'Review of the Principal Questions in Morals' (3d ed. 1787); 'The American Revolution and the Means of Rendering It a Benefit to the World' (1784).

Prideaux, Humphrey. An English theologian and historical writer; born at Place in

Cornwall, May 3, 1648; died at Norwich, Nov. 1, 1724. He was a minister of the established Church, and became dean of Norwich in 1702. His chief writings are: 'Validity of the Orders of the Church of England' (1688); 'The Case of Clandestine Marriages Stated' (1691); 'Life of Mahomet' (1697); 'The Old and New Testament Connected in the History of the Jews,' a work of great research and learning (1716).

Priest, Josiah. An American writer; born in New York, about 1790; died about 1850. He was an unschooled man, a harness maker by trade; but published several books, some of which became very popular. Among them were: 'Wonders of Nature' (1826); 'View of the Millennium' (1828); 'Stories of the Revolution' (1836); 'American Antiquities' (1838); and 'Slavery in the Light of History and Scripture' (1843).

Priestley, Joseph. A celebrated English philosopher, theologian, physicist, and chemist; born at Birstall near Leeds, March 13, 1733; died near Philadelphia, Feb. 6, 1804. He was a Dissenting minister of Unitarian or Socinian principles, and served as such in various towns, the last being Hackney, a London suburb. Among his writings are: 'Institutes of Natural and Revealed Religion' (1754); 'History of Electricity' (1767); 'Disquisitions on Matter and Spirit,' his most noteworthy philosophical treatise (1777); 'History of the Corruptions of Christianity' (1782); 'Observations on Different Kinds of Air' (3 vols., 1774-77); 'The Doctrine of Phlogiston Established' (1800).

Prime, Samuel Irenæus. An American clergyman, editor, and author; born at Ballston, N. Y., Nov. 4, 1812; died at Manchester, Vt., July 18, 1885. He was first a minister in the Presbyterian Church. About 1840 he became editor of the New York Observer, and remained in charge until his death. He is the author of over forty volumes, the best known being: 'Travels in Europe and the East' (1855); 'Letters from Switzerland' (1860); 'The Alhambra and the Kremlin' (1873); 'Life of Samuel F. B. Morse' (1874).

Prime, William Cowper. An American man of letters; born at Cambridge, N. Y., Oct. 31, 1825. He wrote: 'Owl Creek Letters' (1848); 'The Old House by the River' (1853); 'Later Years' (1854); 'Boat Life in Egypt and Nubia' (1857); 'Tent Life in the Holy Land'; 'Coins, Medals, and Seals' (1861); a work on the hymn 'O Mother Dear, Jerusalem' (1865); 'I Go a-Fishing' (1873); 'The Holy Cross' (1877); 'Pottery and Porcelain of all Times and Nations' (1878). He edited 'McClellan's Own Story,' with biography (1886). Died in 1905.

Prince. Mrs. Helen Choate (Pratt). An American novelist, granddaughter of Rufus Choate; born in Massachusetts in 1857. She is at present residing in France. Her works are: 'The Story of Christine Rochefort' (1895); 'A Transatlantic Châtelaine'; 'The Strongest Master.'

Prince, John Critchley. An English poet-workingman; born in 1808; died in 1866; a Lancashireman. He wrote: 'Hours with the Muses' (1842); 'Dreams and Realities'; 'Poetic Rosary' (1851); and 'Autumn Leaves' (1856).

Prince, Le Baron Bradford. An American historical writer, descendant of William Bradford of the Mayflower; born in Flushing, L. I., July 3, 1840. He was a prominent jurist of New Mexico. His works include: 'E Pluribus Unum; or, American Nationality' (1868); 'A Nation, or a League' (1880); 'History of New Mexico' (1883); and 'The American Church and its Name' (1887).

Principe, Miguel Agustin (prēn'thē-pä'). A Spanish writer; born at Caspa, 1811. He was at one time professor of literature and history at the University of Saragossa, and afterwards connected with the Royal Library of Madrid. He has written a 'History of the War of Independence'; 'Verses, Serious and Gay'; the three dramas 'Count Julian,' 'Count Julian, Judge of Aragon,' and 'Mauregato,' as well as several comedies, among them 'Periquito' and 'The House of Pero Hernandez.'

Prior, Matthew. A distinguished English poet; born at Wimborne in Dorsetshire, July 21, 1664; died at Wimpole in Cambridgeshire, Sept. 18, 1721. With Charles Montagu, afterward Lord Halifax, he wrote 'The City Mouse and the Country Mouse' (1687), in ridicule of Dryden's 'Hind and Panther.' His other works are: 'Alma; or, The Progress of the Mind' (1718); 'Solomon,' his most ambitious poetic flight (1718); 'Poems on Several Occasions' (1718).

Privat d'Anglemont, Alexandre (prē-vä'-däṅgl-môṅ'). A French man of letters; born at St. Rose, W. I., about 1820; died at Paris, 1859. He first became known through a small volume, 'The Prado' (1846); but all his days he led the life of a bohemian, and finally died in a hospital. He published 'Anecdotes of Paris' (1854); and one of his friends has collected and published Privat's fugitive efforts under the title 'Unknown Paris' (1861).

Proclus (prō'klus.) A Greek Neo-Platonic philosopher; born at Constantinople, 412; died there, 485. He wrote hymns and epigrams, some of which have come down to us. He wrote also works on astronomy and mathematics, among them a 'Commentary on Euclid,' which is extant; and a commentary on Plato's 'Dialogues,' of which the commentary on 'The Republic' has come down to our time.

Procopius (prō-kō'pē-us). An eminent Greek historian of the sixth century, the leading authority for Justinian's reign; born at Cæsarea in Palestine. He was private secretary to Belisarius, then chief of his commissariat and his navy, and prefect of Constantinople under Justinian. Of his writings we have the 'Histories,' or as the author styles them, 'Books about the Wars' of his time,— Persian, Vandal, and Gothic; a treatise 'On Buildings';

'Anecdotes' (posthumous), a supplement to the 'Histories,' consisting of political and personal matter he dared not publish in his lifetime.

Procter, Adelaide Anne. An English poet, daughter of Bryan W.; born at London, Oct. 30, 1825; died Feb. 2, 1864. She wrote 'Legends and Lyrics' (1858), which went through nine editions in seven years; and a second series (1860), which had a like success.

Procter, Bryan Waller. ["Barry Cornwall.] An English poet and man of letters; born at Leeds, Nov. 21, 1787; died at London, Oct. 4, 1874. He wrote: 'Dramatic Scenes and Other Poems' (1819); 'A Sicilian Story' (1820); 'Mirandola,' a tragedy (1821); 'The Flood of Thessaly' (1823); 'English Songs' (1832). His chief prose writings are: 'Life of Edmund Kean' (1835); 'Essays and Tales' (1851); 'Charles Lamb: a Memoir' (1866).

Proctor, Edna Dean. An American poet; born at Henniker, N. H., Oct. 10, 1838. She is a resident of South Framingham, Mass., but was formerly of Brooklyn, N. Y. Her works are: 'Poems' (1866); 'A Russian Journey' (1872); 'The Song of the Ancient People' (1892); 'Songs of America' (1906).

Proctor, Richard Anthony. A distinguished English astronomer and writer on scientific subjects; born at Chelsea, March 23, 1837; died at New York, Sept. 12, 1888. He wrote a great many popular expositions of science; his greatest work, 'Old and New Astronomy,' not quite completed at his death, was completed by another hand and published in parts.

Propertius, Sextus (prō-per'shius). The great Roman elegiac poet; born at Assisium, about 50 B. C.; died about 15 B. C. His poems consist of four "books"; the subjects are either amatory, or political and social, or historical and antiquarian.

Prosper of Aquitaine. A Gallic poet of the first half of the fifth century. He wrote a hexameter poem of about a thousand lines against the Pelagian heresy, 'Against the Ungrateful.' He was a correspondent of St. Augustine, and after that Father's death wrote 'Responsions for Augustine.'

Proth, Mario (prōt). A French writer; born at Sin, 1832. After having finished his studies at Metz, he went to Paris, where he always showed himself a stanch Republican and violent opponent of the Empire. After the revolution of 1870, he was selected to put in order and publish the curious 'Papers and Correspondence of the Imperial Family' found in the Tuileries. Among his own works are: 'To Young People: How to do Battle' (1861); 'Love Letters of Mirabeau, Preceded by a Study of Mirabeau' (1863); 'A Silhouette of the Revolution' (1864); 'The Vagabonds' (1864).

Proudfit, David Law. ["Peleg Arkwright."] An American verse-writer; born in Newburg, N.Y., Oct. 27, 1842; died in New York, Feb. 22, 1897.

His writings have received popular favor. In book-form they are: 'Love among the Gamins,' poems (1877); and 'Mask and Domino' (1888).

Proudhon, Pierre Joseph (prö-dôn'). A French social economist; born at Besançon, July 15, 1809; died at Passy, Jan. 19, 1865. In his early years he was a compositor and afterward proof-reader in a printing-office; and in that situation acquired a knowledge of Latin, Greek, and Hebrew, also of Catholic and patristic theology. He wrote: 'An Essay toward a General Grammar' (1837); 'What Is Property?' (1840), answering the question in the words already used by Brissot, "Property is robbery"; 'System of Economic Contradictions, or Philosophy of Misery' (2 vols., 1846), to which Karl Marx replied with 'The Misery of Philosophy'; 'Justice in the Revolution and in the Church,' a violent attack on all existing institutions of Church and State (1858).

Prout, Father. See O'Mahony, Francis.

Provancher, Léon (prō-vän-shā'). A Canadian priest and naturalist; born in Becancour, P. Q., March 10, 1820. In 1869 he retired from the ministry, and devoted himself to literary work and the study of natural history. He established Le Naturalist Canadien in 1868, and received the degree of D. Sc. in 1880. His publications include: 'Elementary Treatise on Botany' (1858); 'Canadian Plant Life' (1865); 'From Quebec to Jerusalem' (1882); and 'Short History of Canada' (1887).

Proyart, Liévain Bonaventure (Abbé) (prwä-yär'). A French religious writer and historian; born at Artois, 1748; died at Arras, 1808. He took orders, and emigrated at the period of the Revolution, against which some of his writings were directed. Among his works are: 'The Virtuous Pupil,' a small book which has become a classic (1772); a 'Life of the Dauphin, Father of Louis XV.' (1778); 'History of Stanislaus I., King of Poland' (1782); 'The Life and Crimes of Robespierre, Surnamed the Tyrant' (1795); and various others on historical themes.

Prudden, Theophile Mitchell. An American physician and bacteriologist; born at Middlebury, Conn., July 7, 1849. He is professor of pathology in the College of Physicians and Surgeons, New York. His works include: 'Handbook of Pathological Anatomy and Histology' (1885), with F. Delafield; 'Story of the Bacteria' (1889); 'Dust and its Dangers' (1891); 'Water and Ice'; 'On the Great American Plateau.'

Prudentius, Aurelius Publius Clemens (prö-den'shi-us). A Christian poet; born in Spain, about 350 A.D.; died about 410. He wrote: 'Hymns for Days and Seasons'; 'Apotheosis,' 1085 hexameter verses on the divinity of Jesus Christ; 'Hamartigenia,' the origin of sin; 'Psychomachia,' virtue and vice contending for man's soul; 'Against Symmachus'; 'The Martyrs' Crowns'; 'Diptychs,' comprising forty-nine hexameter tetrastichs on Scriptural events and personages.

Prudhomme, René François Armand Sully. See **Sully-Prudhomme.**

Pruszakowa, Séverine Zochowska (prö-sä-kō'vä). A Polish woman of letters; born about 1830. She received an excellent education, and has acquired a style of almost classic purity. She has published both historical and poetical works, among them: 'Tales of Our Times' (1853); 'Poetic Tales' (1855); 'Elizabeth Druzbacka,' a poem (1855); a 'History of Hungary' (1863); 'Sebastian Klouswieg,' one of her finest poetical compositions; and a 'View of the Literature of the Peoples of the Middle Ages, Particularly the Slavs and Germans' (1856).

Prutz, Hans (pröts). A German historical writer, son of Robert Eduard; born at Jena, May 20, 1843. He became professor of history in the University of Königsberg in 1870. He wrote: 'Henry the Lion' (1865); 'Kaiser Frederick I.' (3 vols., 1871–74); 'Phœnicia: Geographical Sketches and Historical Studies' (1876); 'The Possessions of the German Order in the Holy Land' (1877); 'Secret Teaching and Secret Laws of the Templars' (1879); 'Culture-History of the Crusades' (1883); 'Development and Fall of the Order of Knights Templar' (1888).

Prutz, Robert Eduard. A German poet and historian of literature; born at Stettin, May 30, 1816; died there, June 21, 1872. His principal works are: 'The Rhine' (1840); 'Poems,' a collection of his lyrics, in great part erotic (1841); a comedy, 'The Political Lying-in Chamber' (1843); several historical dramas, as 'Charles of Bourbon,' 'Maurice of Saxe,' 'Eric, the Peasants' King'; 'Lectures on the History of the German Theatre' (1847); 'Contemporary German Literature' (1847); 'Men and Books: Biographical Contributions to the History of German Literature in the 18th Century' (1862).

Przezdziecki, Alexander (pzhes-jēts'kē). A Polish miscellaneous writer and historian; born in Podolia, 1814; died in Cracow, 1871. He studied in Berlin; and possessing a large fortune, traveled in all parts of Europe for material relating to the history of his country. He wrote French as easily as his mother tongue. Among his works are: 'Halzka d'Ostrog,' a historical drama (1841); 'The Capitalist,' a comedy (1841); 'Hedwig,' a historical drama (1844); 'Sources for the History of Poland' (1843–44); 'Monuments of the Art of the Middle Ages at the Time of the Renaissance of Poland' (1853–62); 'Dom Sebastian of Portugal,' a comedy. ·

Psalmanazar, George (säl-män-ä-tsär). A noted impostor; born probably in Languedoc, about 1679; died at London, May 3, 1763. He pretended to be a native of Formosa, and in that character traveled through Germany and the Low Countries. At Sluys he made the acquaintance of a Scotch parson, who brought him to England and introduced him to the bishop of London. He published a fictitious 'Historical and Geographical Description of Formosa' (1704), inventing an alphabet and a lingo professing to represent the Formosan tongue; 'Dialogue between a Japanese and a Formosan' (1707); 'An Inquiry into the Objections against George Psalmanazar of Formosa, with George Psalmanazar's Answer,' both inquiry and answer doubtless written by the impostor; 'Essays on Scriptural Subjects' (1753).

Psellus, Michael Constantine (sel'lus). A Byzantine writer on miscellaneous subjects; born at Constantinople, 1018; died about 1079. He wore the title "prince of philosophers," conferred on him by the emperors. Among his writings are: 'Paraphrase of Aristotle on Interpretation' (1503); 'A Work Distributed to the Four Mathematical Sciences, Arithmetic, Music, Geometry, and Astronomy' (printed 1532); 'Synopsis of the Laws,' in iambic verse (1544); 'Dialogue about the Action of Demons'; 'Of the Virtues of [precious] Stones.'

Ptolemy, or **Claudius Ptolemæus** of Alexandria. The most celebrated of ancient astronomers, believed to have been a native of Ptolemais in the Thebaid; he lived in the first half of the second century of our era. His great astronomical treatise was entitled 'Mathematical Arrangement,' and by the Arabian philosophers 'Almagest' (al magiste, "the greatest"); it gives an exposition of the system of the universe, the interrelations and revolutions of the heavenly bodies, as understood in Ptolemy's time. He also wrote treatises on 'Geography,' 'Trigonometry,' 'Chronology,' 'Optics,' and other subjects pertaining to mathematical and physical science. The "Ptolemaic System" was the accepted and ruling astronomical authority down to Copernicus's time, and his work on geography was the chief authority up to the time of the great discoveries of the 15th century. His system of map orientation (north at the top and east at the right) is still the universal one.

Publilius Syrus (pub-lil-yus si'rus). A Latin writer of farces; first century B.C. He was a native of Syria ("Syrus," the Syrian), and was brought to Rome a slave. He made tours of the provincial cities of Italy, acting in his own farces, and everywhere received with great popular favor. All that remains of his works is a collection of 'Sentences,' maxims in iambic and trochaic verse: of these verses about 700 have come down to us.

Pucitelli, Virgile (pö-chē-tel'ē). An Italian poet, who died in Warsaw, 1669. He left his country to attach himself to the court of Wadislas IV., King of Poland, who made him his secretary, and sent him on various diplomatic missions. He received the title of Poet for the King, and composed for him several plays, among them: 'Andromeda' (1634); 'St. Cecilia,' a musical drama; 'The Rape of Helen' (1648); etc.

Pückler-Muskau, Hermann Ludwig Heinrich, Fürst von (pük"ler-mös'kou). A German writer of books of travel; born at Muskau, Silesia, Oct. 30, 1785; died near Kottbus, Feb. 4, 1871. He wrote: 'Letters of a Dead Man' (4 vols., 1830–31), containing outspoken judgments on England and other countries visited by him; 'Hints on Landscape Gardening' (1834); 'Tutti Frutti: From the Papers of the Deceased' (5 vols., 1834); 'Semilasso's Penultimate Tour of the World: Europe' (3 vols., 1835); 'Semilasso in Africa' (5 vols., 1836); 'The Precursor' (1838); 'From Mehemed Ali's Realm' (3 vols., 1844); 'The Return Journey' (3 vols., 1846–48).

Pudlowski, Melchior (pöd-lov´ske). A Polish poet, who died about 1588. He studied at the University of Cracow, and afterwards became secretary of King Sigismund Augustus, being noted as a defender of the Catholic religion against the Protestants. His most noted writings are: 'Lamentation and Admonition of the Polish Republic' (1561); 'Dido to Æneas'; 'An Oration for the Republic and for Religion to the Magistrates of Poland' (1562); and 'A Book of Trifles; That Is, Comic Poems' (1586).

Puech, Jean Louis Scipio (püch). A Provençal poet; born at Aix, 1624; died there, 1688. He took orders, and occupied successively various positions in the Church. He cultivated poetry with much success, showing great talent for versification, a jovial spirit, and a leaning towards satire, many of his verses being full of ingenious and sometimes stinging allusions to events of the times. The most remarkable of his Provençal poems is one called 'The Bohemians'; and in French he published: 'The Burning Chamber'; 'Madeline Dying in the Desert'; 'Christ on the Cross'; etc.

Pufendorf, Samuel von (pöf´en-dorf). An illustrious German publicist; born near Chemnitz in Saxony, Jan. 8, 1632; died at Berlin, Oct. 26, 1694. His tractate 'Elements of Universal Jurisprudence' (1660) won him the office of professor of Roman law in Heidelberg University. Among his principal works are: 'On the State of the German Empire' (1667); 'On the Law of Nature and the Law of Nations' (1672); 'The Duty of the Man and the Citizen' (1673); 'Relation of the Christian Religion to Civil Life' (1687); 'History of Charles Gustavus' (1688); 'Divine Fecial Law' (1695),—i. e., the divine basis of the laws of war and peace.

Pugh, Eliza Lofton. ["Arria."] An American novelist; born in Bayou Lafourche, La., 1841. She is the author of 'Not a Hero' (1867), and 'In a Crucible' (1871).

Puisieux, Madeleine d'Arsant (pwē-syė´). A French woman of letters; born at Paris, 1720; died in the same city, 1798. She had an easy and agreeable style, but lacked warmth and imagination. Her chief works are: 'Advice to a Friend' (1749–50); 'Characters' (1750–55); 'Zamor and Almanzine' (1755); 'Alzarac; or, The Necessity of Being Inconstant' (1762); 'The History of Mademoiselle de Terville' (1768); etc.

Pujoulx, Jean Baptiste (pü-zhö´). A French writer; born at St. Macaire, 1762; died at Paris, 1821. He composed many plays for the theatre, but devoted the last years of his life to the study of natural history and other sciences. Among his works are the comedies 'The Caprices of Proserpine' (1784); 'The Family Supper' (1788); 'Amelia; or, the Convent' (1791). He wrote also 'The New-Rich' (1798); 'Paris at the End of the Eighteenth Century' (1800); and several works on mineralogy, botany, etc.

Pulci, Luca (pöl´che). An Italian poet, brother of Luigi; born at Florence, 1431; died 1470. He wrote: 'The Dryad of Love'; 'Ciriffo Calvaneo'; 'Stanzas for Lorenzo de' Medici's Tourney'; and under the title 'Epistles,' an imitation of Ovid's 'Heroides.'

Pulci, Luigi. An Italian poet, friend of Lorenzo de' Medici; born in Florence, Aug. 5, 1432; died 1484. His greatest work is the romantic epic 'Morgante Maggiore' (first printed 1481). He wrote also some stories.

Pulgar, Fernando de (pul´gär). A Spanish prose-writer of the latter part of the 15th century. He wrote a 'Chronicle' of the reign of Ferdinand and Isabella; 'Notable Men of Castile'; a commentary on the ancient 'Couplets of Mingo Revulgo.'

Pullè, Count Giulio. See **Castelvecchio.**

Pullè, Count Leopoldo. See **Castelnovo.**

Pulszky, Franz Aurelius (pul´ske). A Hungarian writer; born at Eperies (Sáros), Sept. 17, 1814; died at Buda Pesth, Sept. 9, 1897. After completing his studies, he traveled in Germany, Italy, France, and England. He wrote: 'Journal of a Hungarian Traveler in Great Britain' (1837); with his wife, 'White, Red, and Black' (3 vols., 1852), an account of Kossuth's tour in the United States; also a historical novel, 'The Jacobins in Hungary' (2 vols., 1851); 'My Time and my Life' (4 vols., 1879–82); 'The Age of Copper in Hungary' (1884).

Pulszky, Therese. A Hungarian prose-writer, wife of Franz Aurel; born at Vienna, 1815. She accompanied her husband on Kossuth's American tour; see his name for their joint work. She wrote independently: 'Memoirs of a Hungarian Lady' (2 vols., 1850); 'Tales and Traditions of Hungary' (2 vols., 1851).

Pumpelly, Raphael (pum-pel´li). An eminent American geologist and author; born at Oswego, N. Y., Sept. 8, 1837. In his early life he conducted explorations for the governments of Japan and China; was professor at Harvard for several years; and from 1879 to 1892 geologist in charge of the Archæan division of the United States Geological Survey. His chief works are: 'Geological Researches in China, Mongolia, and Japan' (1867); 'Across America and Asia' (1870); 'Mining Industries of the United States'; 'Explorations in Central Asia.'

Purchas, Samuel (pėr-chas). An English compiler of books of travel and exploration;

born at Thaxted, in Essex, 1577; died 1626 — in poverty, and, it is believed, in a debtor's prison. His works are : ' Purchas his Pilgrimage, or Relations of the World and the Religions Observed in all Ages ' (1613; much enlarged in the 4th ed. 1626); ' Purchas his Pilgrim or Microcosmus, or the Historie of Man : Relating the Wonders of his Generation, Varieties in his Degeneration, and Necessity of his Regeneration ' (1619); ' Purchas his Pilgrimes : or Relation of the World in Sea Voyages and Land Travels, by Englishmen and Others ' (4 vols., 1625),— a continuation of Hakluyt, and partly founded on papers left by him.

Pusey, Caleb (pū-zy). An American Quaker colonist; born in Berkshire, England, about 1650; died in Chester County, Pa., Feb. 25, 1727. He came with Penn's company to America in 1682, erected the first mills in the province, held many high places in civil affairs, and was a noted controversialist writer of his day. He published a great number of pamphlets and articles in defense of his creed, among them : 'A Serious and Seasonable Warning,' etc. (1675); 'A Modest Account from Pennsylvania of the Principal Differences in Point of Doctrine between George Keith and those of the People called Quakers ' (1696); ' Satan's Harbingers Encountered,' etc. (1700).

Pusey, Edward Bouverie. An English theological writer, a leader of the Anglo-Catholic (Tractarian) party in the Established Church; born near Oxford, 1800; died Sept. 14, 1882. He was associated with Newman and others in the British Critic, ' Tracts for the Times,' etc.; and his conspicuousness from his social position (nephew of one earl and grandson of another, professor and canon of Christ Church), wealth, and munificent charities, caused the Oxford Movement to be known as " Puseyism," though he was not its initiator and did not at first sympathize with it. He published : 'An Historical Enquiry into the Probable Causes of the Rational Character Lately Predominant in the Theology of Germany ' (1825); 'The Holy Eucharist a Comfort to the Penitent ' (1843), a sermon which resulted in his suspension for three years; two sermons on ' The Entire Absolution of the Penitent ' (1846), equally revolutionary; other sermons on ' The Rule of Faith as Maintained by the Fathers,' etc. (1861), and on ' The Presence of Christ in the Holy Eucharist ' (1853). Of his larger works the most important are : ' The Doctrine of the Real Presence ' (1855); ' The Real Presence of the Body and Blood of Christ the Doctrine of the English Church ' (1857); 'An Eirenicon.'

Pushkin, Alexander Sergéevich(push'kin). A great Russian poet and romancer; born at Moscow, 1799; died 1837. Among his principal works are : ' The Prisoner of the Caucasus ' (1821); ' The Fountain of Bakhchisaraj ' (1822); ' The Robber Brothers ' (1822); ' The Gipsies ' (1824); ' Count Nulin,' a comic epos; ' Poltava ' (1829), an epic poem; ' Journey to Erzerum during the Campaign of 1829 ' (1836);

' The Little House in Kolomna,' a poetical narrative ; the dramas ' The Avaricious Knight,' ' Mozart and Salieri,' and ' The Stony Guest'; ' The Banquet during the Plague '; his masterpiece ' Evgeny Onyegin ' (1833), a romance in verse after the manner of Byron's ' Don Juan ' ; and the historical novels ' The Captain's Daughter ' (1831), ' Dubrovsky,' ' History of Pugachev's Revolt ' (1834);' Pique Dame ' (1834).

Putlitz, Gustav Heinrich Gans, Edler Herr von und zu (pöt'lits). A German poet and novelist; born at Retzien, Prussia, March 20, 1821; died there, Sept. 9, 1890. He began his literary career by writing a number of little comedies dealing with high social life, all in a vein of lively humor; among them are : ' The Heart Forgotten ' ; ' Watering-Places '; ' Family Quarrels.' He wrote also some exquisite short tales,— ' What the Forest Tells,' ' Forget-me-not,' ' Arabesques '; ' Don John of Austria,' a tragedy (1863), and numerous other plays; also a series of novels,— ' The Alpine Bride ' (1870), ' Sparks 'Neath the Ashes ' (1871), ' The Nightingale ' (1872); and ' My Home : Recollections of Childhood and Youth ' (1885).

Putnam, Eleanor. See **Bates.**

Putnam, George Haven. An American publisher and author, son of George P.; born in London, April 2, 1844. He entered the publishing business in 1866, and is at the head of the firm of G. P. Putnam's Sons, New York. His works include : ' International Copyright ' (1879); 'Authors and Publishers' (1883); 'Authors and their Public in Ancient Times ' (1893); 'Books and their Makers during the Middle Ages;' ' The Censorship of the Church of Rome and Its Influence upon the Production and Distribution of Literature.'

Putnam, George Palmer. An American publisher and author (1814-1872). In 1848 he established the publishing house now conducted under the name of G. P. Putnam's Sons; and also founded Putnam's Magazine, which was subsequently merged with Scribner's Monthly. His works include: ' The Tourist in Europe ' (1838); ' American Facts ' (1845); ' The World's Progress ' (1850); ' Ten Years of the World's Progress '; etc.

Putnam, Mrs. Mary (Lowell). An American historical and miscellaneous writer, sister of J. R. Lowell; born in Boston, Dec. 3, 1810. In 1832 she married Samuel R. Putnam, a merchant of Boston. Besides a translation from the Swedish, and numerous magazine articles, she published : ' History of the Constitution of Hungary ' (1850); ' Records of an Obscure Man ' (1861); and two dramatic poems on the subject of slavery, entitled 'The Tragedy of Errors' and 'The Tragedy of Success.' Died in 1898.

Putnam, Mrs. Sarah A. Brock. An American novelist and writer; born at Madison Court-House, Va., about 1845. In 1883 she married the Rev. Richard Putnam, of New York. Her works include : ' Richmond during the War ' (1867); ' The Southern Amaranth ' (1869); ' Kenneth, My King ' (1872); ' Myra,' a novel.

Puymaigre, Théodore Joseph Boudet (pwē-māgr). A French poet and miscellaneous writer; born at Metz, 1816. Among his works are: 'Jeanne Darc,' a dramatic poem (1843); 'Dante Alighieri' (1845); 'Lost Hours,' a collection of poems (1866); 'The Prediction,' in verse (1870); 'The Literary Court of Don Juan II. of Castile' (1894); etc.

Puységur, Armand, Marie Jaques (pwē-sė-gür'). A French soldier and writer; born at Paris, 1751; died at Buzancy, 1825. He entered the artillery service and distinguished himself, afterwards also espousing the cause of the Revolution. His chief fame, however, rests upon the fact of his having been a disciple of the famous Mesmer. His chief writings are: 'Memoirs Touching the History and Establishment of Animal Magnetism' (1784); 'Animal Magnetism, Considered in its Relations with Various Branches of General Physics' (1804-7); 'Truths Travel; Sooner or Later They Arrive' (1814). He has also written some plays, among them 'The Day of Dupes' (1789) and 'The Benevolent Judge' (1799).

Puzynin, Gabrielle Gunther (pzhē'nin). A Polish woman of letters; born in Lithuania about 1820. She has written poetry and novels remarkable for moral tendencies and elegant simplicity of style. Among them are: 'In the Name of God' (1843); 'Further in the World' (1845); 'Lithuanian Children' (1847); 'Collection of Poems Old and New' (1859); etc.

Pyat, Félix (pyä). A French dramatist and politician; born at Vierzon, 1810; died 1889. An extreme radical agitator, his activity and personal hazard extending from the revolution of 1848 to the Communard insurrection of 1871, his part in the latter obliged him to fly the country, and in 1873 he was sentenced to death by the Council of War. During his exile he wrote many inflammatory political pamphlets. His plays also are of political and social tendencies; they are vigorous, and while somewhat sensational, show real originality. Among them are: 'A Revolution of Other Times; or, The Romans at Home'; 'The Brigand and the Philosopher'; 'Ango'; 'Arabella,' a drama (1838); 'Cedric the Norwegian'; 'Diogenes' (1846); 'The Rag-Picker of Paris,' a tragedy (1849); 'Tiberius'; etc.

Pyle, Howard. An American illustrator and author; born at Wilmington, Del., March 5, 1853. For many years he has been an illustrator for Harper's periodicals, and recently has become popular as a writer, chiefly of juvenile literature. His works include: 'Within the Capes' (1885), a novel; 'Pepper and Salt' (1887); 'Otto of the Silver Hand' (1888); 'Buccaneers and Marooners of America' (1891); 'Jack Ballister's Fortunes'; 'Stolen Treasure.'

Pynchon, William. A noted American colonist; born in Springfield, England, about 1590; died in Wraysbury, England, Oct. 29, 1662. He emigrated to New England with Winthrop, and founded the town of Springfield, Mass. In 1650 he published 'The Meritorious Price of Our Redemption,' opposing the Calvinistic view of atonement. The book was denounced as heretical, and the author was compelled to return to England to avoid persecution. His other works are: 'The Jewes Synagogue' (1652); 'How the First Sabbath was Ordained' (1654).

Pypers, Peter (pe'pers). A Dutch poet and dramatic writer; born at Amersfoort, 1749; died 1805. To escape entering the Church as his family wished, he fled to Amsterdam and entered the employ of a merchant; but devoted his leisure to writing poetry and plays, most of them translated or imitated from the French. Among them are: 'Lansus and Lydia,' a tragedy (1777); 'Beverly,' a drama (1781); 'The Widow of Malabar,' a tragedy (1786); 'Stephen, the First Christian Martyr' (1790); 'Jephtha,' a tragedy (1794); 'Iphigenia,' a tragedy (1801). He also published various collections of poems.

Pypin, Alexander Nikolajevich (pip'in). A Russian historian of literature; born at Saratov, 1833. He wrote: 'Sketch of the Literary History of the Ancient Russian Tales and Wonder-Stories' (1859); 'History of the Slavic Literatures' (1865); 'Characteristics of Literary Opinion,' 1820-50' (1874); 'History of Russian Ethnography'; 'History of Russian Literature.'

Pyra, Immanuel Jakob (pir'rä). A German poet; born at Kottbus, July 25, 1715; died at Berlin, July 14, 1744. He wrote: 'Temple of True Poesy' (1737); 'Friendship Songs of Thyrsis (Pyra) and Damon (Lange).'

Pyrrho (pir'rō). A Greek philosopher; born at Elis about 360 B.C., and supposed to have lived to the age of 90. In his earlier years he accompanied Alexander the Great on his expedition to India. He is usually looked upon as the founder of the older School of Skeptics, doubting the existence of anything like positive knowledge. He passed much of his life in solitude, showing a stoical firmness of mind in all danger or pain. His countrymen made him high priest. He left nothing in writing, being known only through the works of others.

Pythagoras (pi-thag'ō-ras). A celebrated Greek philosopher; born at Samos, about 582 B.C.; died about 500. His history is involved in obscurity; but he is believed to have visited Egypt and been inducted into the mysteries and sciences of the priests in the temples there. He founded a society and school, or an exoteric and esoteric community of disciples, at Crotona in Magna Græcia. The societaires took control of the political State of Crotona, and governed it more or less in accordance with the principles of the master's philosophy; but the democracy rose against them, and after an existence of 100 years, or probably much less, the organization was broken up and the Pythagoreans dispersed. No authentic writing of Pythagoras exists. He seems to have materially developed mathematical science; he certainly did much to develop the science of government and of conduct.

Q

Quandt, Johann Gottlob von (kwĕnt). A German writer on art; born at Leipsic, April 9, 1787; died June 18, 1859. He wrote: 'History of Copperplate Engraving' (1826); 'Letters from Italy' (1830); 'Observations and Fancies Regarding Man, Nature, and Art, during a Tour in Southern France' (1846); and a similar work on Spain (1853).

Quarles, Francis. An English sacred poet; born in Rumford, Essex, in 1592; died September 1644. He was educated at Cambridge, and studied for a lawyer. He received several appointments from the Crown, and finally held the position of city chronologer. His leading works were: 'Emblems Divine and Moral' (1635); 'Argalus and Parthenia' (1621); and the 'Enchiridion' (1640) in prose Frequent fine expressions redeem much commonplace.

Quatrefages de Breare, Jean Louis Armand de (kätrfäzh'). A French naturalist; born at Berthezème (Gard), Feb. 10, 1810; died in Paris, Jan. 13, 1892. He became professor of anatomy and ethnology in the Paris Museum of Natural History, 1855. Many of his works have been translated into English. Among them are: 'The Human Species' (1877); 'Recollections of a Naturalist' (1854); 'The Prussian Race' (1879); 'Pygmies' (1887).

Quatremère, Étienne Marc (kätr-mär'). A French Orientalist; born at Paris, July 12, 1782; died Sept. 18, 1857. His father was a merchant, while he was himself a lifelong student. He was successively employed in the Imperial Library, in the chair of Greek at Rouen, in the Academy of Inscriptions, in the Collège de France as professor of Hebrew and Aramaic, and in the School of Living Oriental Languages as professor of Persian. He produced many learned works, among which are: 'Investigations into the Language and Literature of Egypt' (1808); 'Memoir upon the Nabateans' [the Nabathites of the Bible] (1835); together with numerous valuable translations. He left also much lexicographic material.

Quatremère de Quincy, Chrysostome (kätr-mär dè kaṅ'sē). A French archæologist and writer on art; born at Paris, Oct. 28, 1755; died there, Dec. 8, 1849. Among his writings are: 'Dictionary of Architecture' (3 vols., 1786–1828); 'Olympian Jupiter; or, the Ancient Art of Sculpture' (1814); 'Life and Works of Raphael' (1824); 'Ancient Monuments and Works of Art Restored' (2 vols., 1826–28) ; 'Lives of the Most Famous Architects' (3 vols., 1830); 'Canova and his Works' (1834) ; 'Biography of Michael Angelo.'

Queiroz, José Maria Eça de (kä-ē-rōs'). A Portuguese novelist; born in Povoa de Varzim, Nov. 25, 1845. He studied jurisprudence in Coimbra, was editor of a paper, traveled to the Orient, and became consul successively to Havana, Bristol, and Paris, where he went in 1889. He is a naturalist of Zola's school, and introduced this style into Portugal. He is the author of 'The Crime of Father Amaro' (1874); 'The Mandarin'; 'The Dragon's Teeth'; etc.

Quenstedt, Friedrich August (kwen'stet). A German mineralogist and geologist; born at Eisleben, July 9, 1809; died Dec. 21, 1889, at Tübingen, where he was professor in the university. Among his works are: 'Epochs of Nature' (1861), 'Then and Now' (1856), popular expositions of geology ; 'Manual of Mineralogy.'

Quental, Anthero de (ken'täl). A distinguished Portuguese lyric poet; born at Ponta-Delgada in the island of San Miguel, one of the Azores, April 18, 1842; died there, Sept. 11, 1891. While yet a student in the University of Coimbra, he wrote a little volume of 'Sonnets' (1861), which showed a rare command of poetical form; it was followed by 'Modern Odes' (1865); 'Romantic Springtides' (1871); and another volume of 'Sonnets' (1881). He wrote also 'Considerations on the Philosophy of Portuguese Literary History' (1872), and 'General Tendencies of Philosophy in the Second Half of the 19th Century' (1892).

Quesnay, François (kä-nä'). A French physician and economist; born near Paris, June 4, 1694; died Dec. 16, 1774. He was the founder of the school of economists called Physiocrats, and very influential on Adam Smith and all modern political economy. His theory was that all value is derived from the products of land, which should therefore bear all taxation, but also receive all State encouragement. He published several medical works, in addition to his more famous ones (chiefly short articles) on political economy. Among the latter the leading one is the 'Tableau Économique.'

Quesnay de Beaurepaire, Jules (kä-nä' dè bō-rè-pär'). ["Jules de Glouvet."] A French novelist and miscellaneous writer; born at Saumur, 1838. He is author of 'Stories of the Olden Time' (1882); the novels 'The Bourgeois Family' (1883), 'The Ideal' (1884), 'Marie Fougère' (1889); and some volumes of poetry, as 'The Mariner' (1881), 'The Shepherd' (1882); 'The Forester' (1880).

Quesné, Jacques Salbigoton (kä-nä'). A French man of letters ; born at Pavilly, Jan. 1, 1778; died June 13, 1859. He studied with a notary, went to sea for a short time, then served in the army, but after 1800 devoted himself to literary pursuits, although for some years he held an inspectorship. He produced many works, the most important of which was 'Confessions of J. S. Quesné' (1828), an intimate autobiography.

Quesnel, Pierre (kä-nel'). A French abbé and historian; born in Dieppe in 1699; died about 1774. Little is definitely known of his life, but he seems to have been in easy circumstances and of high birth. He traveled much, and spent nearly forty years in preparing for his great work, the 'History of the Jesuits,' in four volumes.

Quesnot de la Chesnée, Jean Jacques (kä-nō' dĕ lä shä-nā'). A French writer of the eighteenth century. Little is known concerning him. He was a French Protestant, an exile from his country after the revocation of the Edict of Nantes; and his productions are chiefly attacks against his country. He wrote: 'The Battle of Ramillies,' a historic pastoral; 'The Battle of Hoogstet,' an operatic tragedy; etc.

Quételet, Lambert Adolphe Jacques (kät-lä'). A Belgian statistician and astronomer; born at Ghent, Feb. 22, 1796; died Feb. 17, 1874. He was educated at the lyceum of Ghent; became professor of mathematics in the athenæum of Brussels in 1819; was lecturer at the Museum of Science and Literature from 1828 to 1834, and was at the same time director of the Royal Observatory. In 1834 he was made secretary of the Brussels Academy. His principal works were 'On Man and the Development of his Faculties,' and 'Anthropometry'; but he wrote many others.

Quevedo, Vasco Mauzinho (kä-vä'thō), known also as Mauzinho Quevedo de Castello Branco. A Portuguese poet, born at Setubal in the latter part of the 16th century; died some time after 1627. He was educated at the University of Coimbra. He wrote a history of Santa Isabel, Queen of Portugal; also 'Affonso Africano' (1611), a brilliant piece of work.

Quevedo y Villegas, don Francisco (kä-vä'tho ē vēl-yä'gäs). A Spanish satirist; born at Madrid, Sept. 26, 1580; died Sept. 8, 1645. He was very witty, very brilliant, and ranks as the greatest satiric writer of his country. His leading works are the 'Sueños' (Dreams), and 'Don Pablo of Segovia,' a romantic satire.

Quicherat, Étienne Joseph (kēsh-rä). A French historian; born at Paris, Oct. 13, 1814; died there, April 8, 1882. His principal work is 'The Trial and Condemnation and Rehabilitation of Joan of Arc' (5 vols., 1841–49). He wrote also: 'History of Costume in France' (1874); 'Archæological and Historical Miscellanies' (2 vols., 1885).

Quicherat, Louis. A French philologist; born at Paris, Oct. 12, 1799; died there, Nov. 17, 1884. He wrote: 'Treatise on Latin Versification' (1826; 29th ed. 1882); 'Elementary Treatise on Music' (1833); 'Poetic Thesaurus of the Latin Language' (1836); 'Latin Prosody' (1839; 32d ed. 1893); 'French-Latin Dictionary' (1858).

Quiller-Couch, A. T. An English writer of fiction; born in Cornwall, Nov. 21, 1863. He was educated at Oxford. He belongs to the staff of the weekly Speaker. Among his notable stories are: 'Dead Man's Rock'; 'The Astonishing History of Troy Town'; 'The Splendid Spur'; 'The Blue Pavilions'; 'The Delectable Duchy'; 'Hetty Wesley'; 'Fort Amity.'

Quillet, Claude (kē-yä'), known also as Calvidius Lætus. A French physician and poet; born in Touraine in 1602; died in 1661. He went to Rome, and lived there until after the death of Richelieu. His chief work was 'Callipædia,' written in Latin and satirizing Mazarin; but on account of the latter's kindness, the satire was changed to eulogy in a second edition.

Quinault, Philippe (kē-nō'). A French dramatist; born in Paris, June 3, 1635; died Nov. 26, 1688. His first play was produced at 18, and was successful. He studied law and continued writing at the same time. He obtained a literary pension, and was made a member of the Academy in 1670. He was a prolific writer, producing comedies, tragedies, and finally libretti for Lulli's operas. It was in the latter work that he made his name. Among his chief works are: 'La Mère Coquette,' a comedy; 'Armide' and 'Hys,' operas.

Quincy, Edmund. An American writer, son of Josiah; born in Boston, Feb. 1, 1808; died May 17, 1877. He wrote a 'Biography' of his father (1867), and edited his speeches (1875), together with some works of his own.

Quincy, Josiah, sometimes called Josiah Quincy, Jr. An American lawyer; born in Boston, Jan. 23, 1744; died April 26, 1775. He graduated from Harvard in 1763. Though noted as a patriot, he joined with John Adams in defending the British soldiers in the "Boston Massacre" case. But he took part in the town-meeting ordering the "Boston tea-party"; and in September 1774 went to England to speak in behalf of the colonists. His best-known works are: 'An Address of the Merchants, Traders, and Freeholders of Boston' in favor of a non-importation act (1770), and 'Observations on the Boston Port Bill' (1774).

Quincy, Josiah. Son of Josiah "Jr."; born in Boston, Feb. 4, 1772; died July 1, 1864. He was a historian and statesman; Member of Congress from Massachusetts, 1805–13; mayor of Boston, 1823–28; president of Harvard, 1829–45. He wrote a 'Memoir' of his father (1825); 'History of Harvard University' (1840); 'Municipal History of Boston' (1852); and other works.

Quinet, Edgar (kē-nā'). A French historian and philosopher; born near Bourg, Feb. 17, 1803; died at Versailles, March 27, 1875. His works fill nearly thirty volumes, of which only a small part has any permanent value, as he is vague and undetermined, in spite of his real learning and ability. He went to Greece on a government mission, and was made professor of foreign literatures at Lyons, and afterwards at the Collège de France in Paris. He was on the staff of the Revue des Deux Mondes, and received the cross of the Legion of Honor in 1838. His principles were strongly republican, and brought him into trouble more than once. His leading works are: 'Ahasuerus' (1834); 'Merlin the Enchanter' (1861); 'The Revolution' (1865); and 'The Creation' (1869). He also wrote several long poems, of which perhaps 'The Slaves' (1853) is the best.

Quintana, Manuel José (kēn-tä'nä). A Spanish poet; born in Madrid, April 11, 1772; died March 11, 1857. He was lawyer, journalist, and man of letters, as well as poet. He was governor or preceptor to the young Queen Isabella, was made senator and peer in 1835, and crowned with laurel in 1855. He was a Liberal in politics, and twice driven from office, being imprisoned from 1814 to 1820. His most famous works are the 'Lives of Celebrated Spaniards' (1807-1833), and 'Odes to Free Spain.'

Quintilian (Marcus Fabius Quintilianus) (kwin-til'yun). A Roman rhetorician; born in 35 A. D., at Calagurris (Calahorra), Spain; died about 95 or 96 A. D. His father was a teacher of rhetoric at Rome, where Quintilian probably received his education. He spent some years in Spain previous to 68 A. D., when he came to Rome again with Galba. He was a pleader in the courts and a professional teacher of rhetoric, and also educated two grand-nephews of Domitian. His own teacher in rhetoric was Domitius Afer, but he made Cicero his model. One of his pupils was Pliny the Younger. Quintilian's great work is the 'Institutio Oratoria,' one of the most famous classical works on rhetoric. His knowledge and cultivation were extensive, and his style delightful.

Quintus Curtius Rufus. A Roman historian, probably of the first century A. D., of whose life nothing is known with certainty. He is the author of 'De Rebus Gestis Alexandri Magni' (Deeds of Alexander the Great), in ten books, the first two of which are lost. It is pleasing in style, but not very accurate.

Quita, Domingo dos Reis (kē'tä). A Portuguese poet; born in Lisbon, Jan. 8, 1728; died 1770. He was left at his father's death the oldest of seven children, and was apprenticed to a barber, but pursued by himself the study of Portuguese literature and that of other countries. The money gained by his writings was lost in the Lisbon earthquake. His most famous work is 'Inez de Castro,' besides which he wrote four other dramas and many poems.

R

Raabe, Wilhelm (rä'bė). A German novelist; born at Eschershausen, Brunswick, Sept. 8, 1831. He is distinguished as a humorist among German novelists of the nineteenth century. His principal works are.: 'The Chronicle of the Sperlingsgasse' (1857); 'Woodland Folk' (1863); 'The Hunger Pastor' (1864) ; 'Horacker' (1876); 'Wunnigel' (1879) ; 'The Horn of Wanza' (1881); 'The Lar'; 'Cloister of Lugan.'

Rabelais, François (räb-lä'). The French satirist; born at Chinon, Touraine, about 1495. died 1553. His fame rests upon the two works called 'Gargantua' (1535) and 'Pantagruel' (1533). 'Gargantua,' although a sequel to the other book, was written before it. He was also the author of scientific treatises, which are now almost entirely forgotten. He is deemed not only the greatest of French satirists, but one of the great satirists of all times.

Racan, Honorat de Bueil (rä-käṅ'). A French poet; born in Touraine in 1589; died in 1670. He was a member of the French Academy, and a friend of Malherbe. He published 'Pastorals' (1628), and a number of other poems, during his lifetime. His works were collected and published at Paris in 1724.

Racine, Jean Baptiste (rä-sēn'). The illustrious French dramatist; born at La Ferté-Milon, Dec. 21, 1639; died at Paris, April 26, 1699. His works include: 'Nymphs of the

Seine' (1660), an ode ; 'Amasie,' a comedy, now lost; 'Ovid's Amours,' a comedy, now lost; 'The Thebaid' (1664), his first staged tragedy, although he had previously written 'Theagenes and Chariclea,' a tragedy, which he suppressed ; 'Alexander' (1665), a tragedy ; 'The Chaplain's Wig' (1665?), a parody of 'The Cid,' and written partly in collaboration; 'Andromache' (1667); 'The Pleaders' (1668), a comedy modeled upon Aristophanes; 'Britannicus' (1669); 'Berenice' (1670); 'Bajazet' (1672); 'Mithridates' (1673); 'Iphigenia' (1674), pronounced by Voltaire the masterpiece of the French theatre; 'Phædra' (1677); 'Esther' (1689); 'Athalie' (1691), his last dramatic work; 'Abridgment of the History of Port Royal'; 'Letters'; and some historical memoranda concerning the campaigns of Louis XIV.

Racine, Louis. A French poet and critic, son of J. B.; born at Paris in 1692; died in 1763. He is chiefly noteworthy for his two poems, 'Grace' (1720), and 'Religion' (1742), which passed through sixty editions. He wrote in prose: 'Reflections upon Poetry'; 'Memoirs of the Life of Racine'; and 'Remarks on Racine's Tragedies.' ('Complete Works,' 1808).

Radcliffe, Ann. An English novelist; born in London, July 9, 1764; died 1823. She was once very popular, but is not now read. Her best-known novel, still familiar by name as a type of the pseudo-mediæval, is 'The Mysteries of Udolpho' (1794), which ran through many editions. She also wrote: 'The Castles of Athlin and Dunboyne' (1789); 'A Sicilian Romance' (1790); 'The Romance of the Forest' (1791); and 'The Italian' (1797).

Rae, Edward. An English traveler and descriptive writer; born at Birkenhead in 1847. His publications include: 'The Land of the North Wind'; 'The Country of the Moors'; 'The White Sea Peninsula'; and 'A Limb of the Law,' a novel: all most favorably received.

Rafn, Carl Christian (räfn). A Danish critic and archæologist; born in Brahesborg, Fünen, Jan. 16, 1795; died in Copenhagen, Oct. 20, 1864. He produced numerous works, the most important being a Danish translation of Norse mythic and romantic sagas (1829-30); an edition of Ragnar Lodbrog's death-song, with philologico-critical remarks (1826); and 'American Antiquities' (1837), his most widely read book, in which he undertakes to prove that America was discovered by Norsemen in the tenth century.

Ragozin, Zénaïde Alexëivna (räg'ō-tsin). A Russian-American Oriental writer; born in 1835. She came to the United States in 1874. Her most important books are: 'The Story of Chaldea' (1886); 'The Story of Assyria' (1887); and 'The Story of Media, Babylon, and Persia' (1888),—all in the 'Stories of the Nations' series; 'Siegfried'; 'Boewulf'; 'Frithjof'; 'Roland.'

Rainsford, William Stephen. An American Episcopal clergyman; born in Dublin, Oct. 30, 1850. He was called to the rectorship of St. George's, New York city, and since that time has been associated with many philanthropic and other reforms. Besides many contributions to current literature, he has published 'Sermons Preached in St. George's' (1887), and 'The Church's Opportunity in the City of To-day'; 'A Preacher's Story of His Work.'

Raleigh, Sir Walter. The famous English admiral; born at Hayes in Devonshire, 1552; executed Oct. 29, 1618. Imprisoned by Queen Elizabeth, he produced poetical and literary fragments, and his 'History of the World.' His poems were not published until nearly two hundred years after his death (1814); his 'Miscellaneous Writings' in 1751; and his 'Complete Works' in 1829.

Ralph, James. An English pamphleteer and poetaster; born in Philadelphia, about 1695; died in Chiswick, Jan. 24, 1762. He went to England in 1725 with Benjamin Franklin, and was unsuccessful in his first efforts to win public favor. His poem on 'Night' (1728) was ridiculed by Pope in his 'Dunciad'; but his continuation of Guthrie's 'History of England' (1744-46) won public praise. He also published 'The Other Side of the Question' (1742), a reply to a criticism on the Duchess of Marlborough.

Ralph, Julian. An American journalist; born in New York in 1853. His publications include: 'On Canada's Frontier'; 'Dixie'; 'Our Great West'; 'Chicago and the World's Fair'; 'People We Pass'; and 'Alone in China, and Other Stories.' Died in New York, Jan. 20, 1903.

Ralston, William Ralston Shedden. An English writer on Russian folk-lore; born 1828; died 1889. He devoted himself to Russian studies, and published: 'Kriloff and his Fables' (1869); 'Liza' (1869); 'Songs of the Russian People' (1872); 'Russian Folk-Tales' (1873); and 'Early History of Russia' (1874).

Rambaud, Alfred Nicolas. An eminent French historian; born at Besançon, department of Doubs, July 2, 1842. Of his works the most important is the 'History of French Civilization' (3 vols., 1885), which is used as a text-book in nearly all universities. His other publications include: 'French Domination in Germany, 1792-1804' (1873); 'Germany under Napoleon I.' (1874); 'The French and the Russians,' etc. (1877); 'History of Russia' (1878); 'History of Contemporary Civilization in France' (1887); 'Jules Ferry' (1903).

Ramée, Louisa de la. See **Ouida.**

Ramirez, Ignacio (rä-mē'reth). A Mexican philosopher; born in San Miguel el Grande, June 23, 1818; died in Mexico, June 15, 1879. He was of pure Aztec blood. He published under the pseudonym of «The Necromancer» many satirical poems and philosophical articles; and also founded the paper Don Simplicio, in 1846. His many literary works were never collected; but his 'Manual of Rudimentary Knowledge,' written in 1873, was published in 1884.

Rammohun Roy (räm-mō-hun'roi). A Hindu rajah; born at Rádhánagar, Bengal, May 1772; died at Bristol, England, Sept. 27, 1833. Rejecting the Hindu religion at an early age, he published 'A Gift to Monotheists,' a protest against idolatry and priestcraft. He embraced the moral principles of Christianity, and issued 'The Precepts of Jesus, the Guide to Peace and Happiness' (1820); an English abridgment of the sacred books of the Vedanta (1826); and numerous pamphlets concerning the condition of India.

Ramsay, Allan. A Scottish poet; born in Leadhills, Lanarkshire, Oct. 15, 1686; died in Edinburgh, Jan. 7, 1758. His fame rests largely upon his 'Gentle Shepherd' (1725), a pastoral drama in the Lowland Scotch dialect, to which songs were added (1728). It is regarded as the best pastoral in any language. His principal works are: 'Tartana; or, The Plaid' (1721); 'Fables and Tales' (1722); 'Fair Assembly' (1723); 'Health' (1724); 'The Tea-Table Miscellany' (1724); 'The Evergreen' (1725); and 'Thirty Fables' (1730).

Ramsay, Andrew Michael. A Scotch mathematician and theologian; born at Ayr, Jan. 9, 1686; died at St. Germain-en-Laye, France, May 6, 1743. A visit to Fénelon at

Cambray resulted in his conversion to Roman-Catholicism and the production of his principal work, 'Travels of Cyrus' (1727), in avowed imitation of 'Télémaque.' He also edited 'Télémaque,' with an introduction: and wrote, in French, a 'Political Essay' on the principles of its author; a 'History of the Life and Works of Fénelon'; besides a number of English poems. His French is remarkable for its purity and perfection of style.

Ramsay, David. An American physician and historian; born in Lancaster County, Pa., April 2, 1749; died at Charleston, May 8, 1815. He devoted his leisure to the study of the Revolutionary struggle, and published: 'History of the Revolution in South Carolina' (1785); 'History of the American Revolution' (1789); 'Life of Washington' (1801); and 'History of South Carolina' (1809). His 'History of the United States' was published posthumously in 1816, and his 'Universal History Americanized' in 1819.

Ramus, Pierre (rä'mus). A French logician; born at Cuth, Vermandois, 1515; was assassinated in the massacre of St. Bartholomew, August 1572. He distinguished himself at 21, upon the occasion of taking his degree, by defending the thesis that "all that Aristotle taught is false." He followed this with 'Criticism of Aristotelian Dialectic' (1543), written in Latin; and with his 'Dialectic,' a French version of his system, the first work of the kind published in the French language. His literary activity produced in all fifty-nine works, all but nine of which appeared before his death. They include treatises on arithmetic, geometry, and algebra.

Rand, Edward Augustus. An Episcopal clergyman and writer of juvenile books; born at Portsmouth, N. H., in 1837. He has published: 'Christmas Jack' (1878); 'Pushing Ahead' (1880); 'The Tent in the Notch' (1881); 'After the Freshet' (1882); 'Little Brown Top' (1883); 'Fighting the Sea' (1887); 'Sailor Boy Bob' (1888); 'When the War Broke Out' (1888); and others. Died Oct. 5, 1903.

Randall, James Ryder. An American songwriter; born in Baltimore, Md., Jan. 1, 1839. His 'Maryland, My Maryland' (1861), called "the 'Marseillaise' of the Confederate cause," was set to music and became very popular. He wrote much in support of the South. His poems include: 'The Sole Entry'; 'Arlington'; 'The Cameo Bracelet'; 'There's Life in the Old Land Yet'; and 'The Battle Cry of the South.'

Randolph, John. An American statesman; born at Cawsons, Va., June 2, 1773; died at Philadelphia, June 24, 1833. His response to Patrick Henry is famous. His 'Letters to a Young Relative' were published in 1834.

Randolph, Sarah Nicholas. An American biographical writer, great-granddaughter of Thomas Jefferson; born at Edge Hill, Va., Oct. 12, 1839. She has published: 'The Domestic

Life of Thomas Jefferson' (1871); 'The Lord will Provide' (1872); 'A Paper on Martha Jefferson Randolph' (1876); and 'Life of Stonewall Jackson' (1876). Died in 1900.

Ranke, Leopold (rän'ĕ). A leading German historian; born at Wiehe, Saxony, Dec. 21, 1795; died May 23, 1886. From early youth till his death at 90 he was engaged in fruitful historical research and production; his chief labors being devoted to the Reformation period, 15th and 16th centuries, all through Europe, though his last work was a great 'Universal History' (the first volume published when he was 85), embodying the ripest results of modern scholarship, but of most value in the earliest part dealing with prehistoric origins. His 'History of the Popes, their Church and State' (1834-36),—which really means the mediæval popes, the earlier papacy being only outlined, — is one of the most widely circulated histories of modern times, and has been translated into English, French, and Dutch. His 'History of Germany during the Reformation' (1839-47) is regarded in Germany as his best production. Among his other important works are: 'Critique on Modern Historians' (1824); 'Princes and Nations of South Europe during the 16th and 17th Centuries' (1827); and 'Genesis of the Prussian States' (1847). His exposé of the reign of Louis XIV. has been compared to that of Voltaire.

Rankin, Jeremiah Eames. An American clergyman and religious writer; born at Thornton, N. H., Jan. 2, 1828. He has written several national hymns, including 'For God and Home and Native Land' and 'Keep your Colors Flying.' He is also the author of 'Bridal Ring' (1866); 'Auld Scotch Mither' (1873); 'Subduing Kingdoms' (1881); 'The Hotel of God' (1883); 'Atheism of Heart' (1884); 'Christ his Own Interpreter' (1884); and 'Ingleside Rhaims' (1887). Died in 1904.

Rapin de Thoyras, Paul de (rä-pan' dĕ twä-rä'). A French historian; born at Castres, Languedoc, March 25, 1661; died at Wesel, Holland, May 16, 1725. He is remarkable for the production of a 'History of England' (1724), to which he devoted seventeen years' labor. It undoubtedly shortened his life, and he survived its publication but a year. It is considered one of the most complete and impartial expositions of English political events ever published. He also wrote: 'A Dissertation on the Whigs and Tories' (1717).

Raspe, Rudolph Eric (räs'pĕ). A German archæologist and mineralogist; born at Hanover in 1737; died in 1794. A refugee in England, most of his books were published in English. He is the author of the well-known 'Baron Munchhausen's Narrative of his Marvellous Travels and Campaigns in Russia' (1785); a recital of many extraordinary adventures taken from ancient German books, but believed by many to have been stories actually related by Baron von Münchhausen (1720-97), who was reputed to have entertained his friends with wonderful tales of his exploits in war, and believed to have been "the greatest liar in all Germany." Among his other writings, apart from his works on mineralogy, may be named 'A Descriptive Catalogue of a General Collection of Engraved Stones' (1791), besides works on philosophy, and historical memoirs.

Rattazzi, Marie Studolmine de Solms (rätäts'ē). A French novelist; born in London (or in Waterford, Ireland) in 1830. Among her many novels, 'The Marriages of the Creole' and 'If I Were Queen' are the most popular. She edited several journals, and wrote poems and dramas. She died in Paris, February —, 1902.

Raupach, Ernst Benjamin Salomo (rou'-päch). A German dramatist; born at Straupitz, Silesia, May 21, 1784; died at Berlin, March 18, 1852. He was popular in his day, but has latterly fallen into neglect, though he has many admirers still. His leading plays include: 'The Princess Chawansky' (1818); 'The Enchained' (1821); 'The Magic Ring of Love' (1824); 'The Friends' (1825); 'Isidor and Olga' (1826); 'Raphael' (1828); and 'The Daughter of the Air' (1829). His comedies were very successful, — among others, 'Critic and Anti-Critic,' 'The Smugglers,' and 'The Spirit of the Time.'

Ravenscroft, Edward. An English dramatist who flourished between 1671 and 1697. He was exceedingly popular in his day. His first play was 'Mamamouchi; or, The Citizen Turned Gentleman' (1675), and was taken from Molière's 'Le Bourgeois Gentilhomme.' His numerous comedies, farces, and tragedies, some posthumous, include 'The Wrangling Lovers' (1676); 'Scaramouch, a Philosopher' (1677); 'King Edgar and Alfreda' (1677); 'Ignoramus' (1678); 'The London Cuckolds' (first published in 1783); 'Dame Dobson' (1683); 'The Canterbury Guests' (1695); and 'The Italian Husband' (1698).

Rawlinson, George. A noted English scholar, historian and theological writer; born at Chadlington, 1812. He was canon of Canterbury Cathedral. His chief works are indispensable classics in their fields: notably the set of 'Great Oriental Monarchies,' ('Five,' 1862-67; 'Sixth,' 1873; 'Seventh,' 1876), and (with his brother Henry and Sir J. G. Wilkinson) the 4-vol. edition of Herodotus (1858-60). He also wrote a 'History of Egypt' (1881), 'Phœnicia' (1889). He died in London, Oct. 5, 1902.

Rawlinson, Henry Creswicke, Sir. An English diplomat and Oriental scholar of great repute, brother of George; born at Chadlington, Oxfordshire, April 11, 1810; died March 5, 1895. He is chiefly remarkable for his researches among the cuneiform inscriptions of Persia, and for his translation of the Behistun inscription, written in one of the old Persian languages. He is the author of 'England and Russia in the East' (1875), and the 'Cuneiform Inscriptions of Western Asia' (1861-84).

Raymond, Henry J. An American journalist; born at Lima, N. Y., Jan. 24, 1820; died in New York, June 18, 1869. He first attracted attention by his editorials in the New York Tribune; and on Sept. 18, 1851, founded the New York Times. He was active in organizing the Republican party; and composed the 'Address to the People' delivered at the National Convention in Pittsburg, February 1856. He has published: 'Political Lessons of the Revolution' (1854); 'Letters to Mr. Yancey' (1860); 'History of the Administration of President Lincoln' (1864); and 'Life and Services of Abraham Lincoln' (1865). He did much to make the newspaper "editorial" the power it now is.

Raynouard, François Juste-Marie (rā-nwär'). A French poet and philologist; born at Brignoles, Provence, September 1761; died at Passy, Oct. 27, 1836. His first tragedies, 'Eleonora of Bavaria' and 'The Templars,' were produced in 1805 with great success. He also wrote during the régime of Napoleon: 'Scipio'; 'The States of Blois'; 'Don Carlos'; 'Charles I.'; 'Deborah'; and 'Joan of Arc at Orléans.' Later he produced a number of books concerning the Provençal language and literature, among them a 'Dictionary of the Language of the Troubadours' (1838-44).

Reach, Angus Bethune. An English journalist; born at Inverness, Scotland, Jan. 23, 1821; died in London, Nov. 25, 1856. His first production, 'Labor and the Poor' (1848), was a very noted series of articles published in the London Morning Chronicle. He wrote: 'The Comic Bradshaw; or, Bubbles from the Boiler' (1848); 'Clement Lorimer; or, The Book with the Iron Clasp,' a romance (1849); 'Leonard Lindsay; or, The Story of a Buccaneer' (1850); 'Claret and Olives' (1852); and many amusing miscellanies and farces.

Read, Opie P. An American journalist; born in Tennessee in 1852. He edited the Arkansaw Traveller for many years. His studies of Arkansas life have been widely read, and include: 'Len Gansett' (1888); 'My Young Master'; 'An Arkansaw Planter'; 'Up Terrapin River'; 'A Kentucky Colonel'; 'On the Suwanee River'; 'Miss Polly Lop, and Other Stories'; 'The Captain's Romance,' and 'The Jucklins'; 'Son of the Swordmaker'; 'The Mystery of Margareth.'

Read, Thomas Buchanan. At American portrait-painter and poet; born in Pennsylvania, March 12, 1822; died in 1872. His most important works are: 'Poems' (1847); 'Lays and Ballads' (1848); 'The House by the Sea' (1856); 'The Wagoner of the Alleghanies' (1862); 'A Summer Story' (1865); and 'Poetical Works' (1867). His best-known poems are 'Sheridan's Ride' and 'Drifting.' He also published: 'Female Poets of America' (1848); 'The Pilgrims of the Great St. Bernard,' a romance; 'The New Pastoral' (1854), his most ambitious poem; 'Sylvia; or, The Lost Shepherd' (1857); 'A Voyage to Iceland' (1857); and 'The Good Samaritans' (1867).

Reade, Charles. The well-known English novelist; born at Ipsden, June 8, 1814; died April 11, 1884. His first great success was 'It's Never Too Late to Mend' (1856); although he had previously written 'Peg Woffington' (1852), and 'Christie Johnstone' (1853). His numerous productions include: 'The Course of True Love Never did Run Smooth' (1857); 'Jack of All Trades' (1858); 'The Autobiography of a Thief' (1858); 'Love Me Little, Love Me Long' (1859); 'The Double Marriage; or, White Lies' (1860); 'The Cloister and the Hearth' (1861); 'Hard Cash' (1863); 'Griffith Gaunt' (1866), 'Foul Play' (1869); 'Put Yourself in his Place' (1870); 'A Terrible Temptation' (1871); 'A Simpleton' (1873); 'The Wandering Heir' (1875); 'A Woman-Hater' (1877); and 'A Perilous Secret,' published posthumously. His plays include: 'Gold' (1850); 'Masks and Faces' (1854); 'The Courier of Lyons'; 'Two Loves and a Life'; 'The King's Rivals' (1854); 'Drink' (1879); besides the dramatization of a number of his novels.

Reade, John. An Irish-Canadian clergyman and journalist; born in Ballyshannon, Donegal, Nov. 13, 1837. He came to Canada in 1856, and has contributed to every magazine or review established in Canada since 1860. His writings include: 'The Prophecy and Other Poems' (1870); 'Language and Conquest' (1883); 'The Making of Canada' (1885); 'Literary Faculty of the Native Races of America' (1885); 'The Half-Breed' (1886); 'Vita Sine Liberis' (1886); and 'Aboriginal American Poetry' (1887).

Reade, William Winwood. An English traveler, novelist, and controversialist; born in Oxfordshire, Jan. 30, 1838; died April 24, 1875. On his return from African journeys, he wrote 'Savage Africa' (1863); 'The African Sketch-Book' (1873); 'Story of the Ashantee Campaign' (1875); and several novels. His masterpiece is probably 'The Martyrdom of Man,' which presents the history of all the forms of human slavery (1872; 13th ed. 1890).

Realf, Richard. An English-American poet; born at Framfield, Sussex, June 14, 1834; committed suicide in Oakland, Cal., Oct. 28, 1878. At 18 he published, under the patronage of several literary people, a collection of poems, 'Guesses at the Beautiful.' In 1854 he came to the United States, enlisted in the army in 1862, and wrote some of his best lyrics in the field. His most admired poems are 'My Slain,' 'An Old Man's Idyl,' and 'Indirection.'

Recke, Ernst von der (reck'é). A Danish romantic poet; born at Copenhagen, Aug. 14, 1848. His earliest and most popular poem is the three-act drama 'Bertran de Born' (1872). He has written much on the art of Danish verse, including 'Principles of Danish Versification as Manifested in its Historic and Systematic Development' (1881); and 'The Rules of Danish Versification Concisely Stated' (1885). Among his other publications include: 'Lyric

Poems' (1876); 'King Liuvigild and his Sons,' a tragedy (1878); 'Archilochus' (1878); 'Knud and Magnus,' a tragedy (1881); 'Short Poems' (1883); 'Miscellaneous Poems' (1890); 'Fru Jeanna,' a tragic opera (1891); and 'The Duchess of Burgundy' (1891).

Reclus, Jean Jacques Élisée (rä-klü'). A French geographer and scientist; born in the Gironde, May 15, 1830. After extensive travels in England, Ireland, and North and South America, he devoted himself to writing on the social and political conditions of these countries, many of his articles appearing in the Revue des Deux Mondes and in the Tour du Monde. Among his numerous writings, 'The Earth' (1867-68), 'The Ocean Atmosphere and Life' (1872), and 'Universal Geography' (1875-88), in thirteen volumes, are most elaborate. D. 1904.

Redpath, James. An American journalist; born in Berwick, Scotland, Aug. 24, 1833; died Feb. 10, 1891. He was known as a fiery abolitionist, and an ardent supporter of the Irish in the land-league troubles. He founded the "Redpath Lyceum Bureau," an agency for lecturers and musicians, in 1867, and conducted it until 1875. He became assistant editor of the North American Review in 1886. He published: 'Handbook to Kansas' (1859); 'The Roving Editor' (1859); 'Echoes of Harper's Ferry' (1860); 'Southern Notes' (1860); 'Guide to Hayti' (1860); 'The John Brown Invasion' (1860); 'Life of John Brown' (1860); and 'Talks About Ireland' (1881).

Redwitz (-Schmölz), Oskar von (red'vitz-shmélts). A German poet; born at Lichtenau, Bavaria, June 28, 1823; died July 7, 1891. He gained wide reputation by his first work, 'Amaranth' (1849), an epic poem written in praise of Roman-Catholicism; and his later works did not fall short of his early promise. They include: 'Tales of the Forest Brook and the Pine'; 'Hermann Stark,' a novel (1868); the remarkable 'Lay of the New German Empire' (1871); 'Odilo' (1878); 'The Wartenberg House' (1884); and 'Hymen' (1887).

Reese, Lizette Woodworth. An American verse-writer and educator; born in Maryland in 1856. Her writings include: 'A Branch of May' (1887); 'A Handful of Lavender'; and 'A Quiet Road.'

Reeve, Clara. An English novelist; born at Ipswich in 1729; died Dec. 3, 1807. Her most famous work is 'The Champion of Virtue: A Gothic Story' (1777), afterwards published under the title of 'The Old English Baron.' She had previously written 'The Phœnix' (1772), a translation from the Latin of Barclay's romance 'Argenis.' Among her other and less important works are: 'The Two Mentors' (1783); 'The Progress of Romance' (1785); and 'The Exiles; or, Memoirs of Count de Cronstadt' (1788).

Reeves, Helen Buckingham (née Mathers). An English novelist; born at Crewkerne, Somersetshire, in 1852. Her novels treat of

domestic English life, and are exceedingly popular. They include : 'Comin' through the Rye'
(1875); 'The Token of the Silver Lily,' a poem
(1876); 'Cherry Ripe' (1877); 'As He Comes
up the Stair' (1878); 'The Land of the Leal'
(1878); 'My Lady Green Sleeves' (1879); 'The
Story of a Sin' (1881); 'Sam's Sweetheart'
(1883); 'Eyre's Acquittal' (1884); 'Jock o'
Hazeldean' (1884); 'Found Out' (1885); 'Murder or Manslaughter ?' (1885); 'The Fashion
of this World' (1886); 'A Study of a Woman'
(1893); and 'A Man of the Time' (1894).

Reeves, Marian Calhoun Legaré. An American novelist; born at Charleston, S. C., about
1854. She began to write in 1866 under the
pseudonym of "Fadette." Her publications include : 'Ingemisco' (1867); 'Randolph Honor'
(1868); 'Sea-Drift' (1869); 'Wearithorne'
(1872); 'A Little Maid of Arcadie' (1888); and
in conjunction with Emily Read, 'Old Martin
Boscawen's Jest' (1878), and 'Pilot Fortune'
(1883).

Regaldi, Giuseppe (rä-gäl'dē). An Italian
poet; born at Novara, November 1809; died at
Bologna, February 1883. He heard the improvisatore Giustiniani, and resolved to rival
him. He accordingly improvised in the principal cities of Italy, in France, Switzerland, and
Germany, and with great success. His volumes
of verse include : 'War' (1832); 'Poems : Extemporaneous and Elaborated' (1839); 'Songs'
(1840); 'National Songs' (1841); 'Prose and
Poetry' (1861-65); 'Selected Poems' (1874);
'Water' (1878). He also wrote 'Dora' (1867),
and 'History and Literature' (1879).

Regnard, Jean François (ren-yär'). A French
comic dramatist; born at Paris in 1656; died
Sept. 4, 1709. By common consent his rank in
France is second to Molière only. His finest
productions are: 'The Gambler' (1696), and
'The Sole Legatee' (1708). He also wrote :
'The Absent-Minded' (1697); 'The Unexpected
Return' (1700); 'The Follies of Love' (1704);
'The Menæchmi' (1705), in imitation of Plau-
tus; and a number of satires and poems.

Regnier, Mathurin (ren-yā'). A French
satirist; born at Chartres, Dec. 21, 1573; died
at Rouen, Oct. 22, 1613. He is famed for
his 'Satires' (1608), sixteen in number, in which
he imitated Horace, Juvenal, and Martial. He
also wrote a number of epistles and elegies.
Editions of his works have appeared in 1853,
1862, 1867, and 1875.

Reid, Christian. See **Tiernan, Frances C.**

Reid, Mayne. An Irish novelist of adventure; born in Ballyroney, County Down, April
4, 1818; died near London, Oct. 22, 1883. He
came to the United States in 1838, and traveled
extensively North, East, South, and West. He
became a captain in the Mexican War Later
he went to London, where he published his
many novels of adventure, including : 'The
Rifle-Rangers' (1850); 'The Scalp-Hunters'
(1851); 'The Quadroon' (1855); 'Osceola'
(1858); 'The Maroon' (1862); 'Cliff-Climbers'

(1864); 'Afloat in the Forest' (1866); 'The
Castaways' (1870); and 'Gwen-Wynne' (1877).

Reid, Thomas. A Scotch professor and philosopher; born at Strachan, Kincardineshire,
April 26, 1710; died Oct. 7, 1796. He was professor of moral philosophy at Glasgow University 1764-80, thenceforward devoting himself
to preparing for publication the substance of
his lectures. They appeared as 'Intellectual
Powers' (1785), and 'Active Powers' (1785).
His other works include : 'An Essay on Quan-
tity' (1748); 'An Inquiry into the Human Mind
on the Principles of Common-Sense' (1764),
his most original work; 'A Brief Account
of Aristotle's Logic' (1774); 'Essays on the
Intellectual Powers of Man' (1785); 'Essays
on the Active Powers of Man' (1788). He is
the leading representative of the school of
"common-sense."

Reid, Thomas Wemyss. An English journalist; born at Newcastle on Tyne in 1842.
He contributed largely to English reviews and
magazines, and published : 'Cabinet Portraits:
Sketches of Leading Statesmen of Both Parties' (1872); 'Charlotte Brontë: A Monograph'
(1877); 'Politicians of To-Day' (1879); 'The
Land of the Bey' (1882); 'Gabrielle Stuart'
(1883); 'A Memoir of John Deakin Heaton'
(1883); 'Gladys Fane : A Story of Two Lives'
(1883); 'Mauleverer's Millions' (1885); 'Life
of Willam Edward Forster'; 'Life of Wm. Black.'

Reid, Whitelaw. An American journalist;
born near Xenia, O., Oct. 27, 1837. During the
Civil War he represented the Cincinnati Gazette in the field; and his letters, under the signature of "Agate," attracted much attention.
Shortly afterward he published 'After the War'
(1866), and 'Ohio in the War' (1868), the most
important of all the State histories of the Civil
War. He became an editorial writer on the
New York Tribune; and upon the death of
Horace Greeley he succeeded him as editor and
principal owner. Besides many contributions to
periodicals, he wrote : 'Schools of Journalism'
(1871); 'The Scholar in Politics' (1873); 'Some
Newspaper Tendencies' (1879); and 'Town
Hall Suggestion' (1881). He was candidate
for Vice-President of the United States in 1892.

Reinbold, Adelheid. See **Berthold.**

Reinick, Robert (rīn'ick). A German poet;
born at Dantzig, Prussia, Feb. 22, 1805; died at
Dresden, Feb. 7, 1852. He studied painting under Schadow and Begas, and these studies influenced all of his lyric productions, which rank
among the best in German literature. His
works include : 'Song-Book for Artists' (1833);
'Song-Book of a Painter' (1837-44); 'Songs and
Fables for the Young' (1844); 'Hebel's Alle-
manic Poems Translated into High German'
(1851); 'Collected Songs' (1852); and 'Book
of Poetic Fables and Stories.' His poetry is
remarkable for its childlike humor, simplicity,
and artistic perfection.

Rellstab, Ludwig (räl'stäb). A German
mathematician and critic; born at Berlin in

1799; died there in 1860. He published romances, dramas, and critical essays, among them being: 'Henrietta,t he Beautiful Singer'; 'Algiers and Paris' (1830–46); 'The Year 1812' (1834); and an 'Autobiography' (1860).

Rémusat, Charles de (rā-mü-sä'). A French philosopher and minister of State; born at Paris in 1797; died June 6, 1875. He published: 'Essays on Philosophy' (1842), which was received with favor; 'Treatise on German Philosophy' (1845); 'Abelard' (1845); 'Bacon, his Life and Time' (1858); 'Religious Philosophy' (1864); and 'History of English Philosophy from Bacon to Locke' (1875).

Rémusat, Claire Élisabeth Jeanne de. A French essayist; born at Paris in 1780; died in 1821. She was the mother of Charles de Rémusat, and companion to the Empress Josephine. She wrote an 'Essay on the Education of Women' (1824). Her 'Memoirs' are very celebrated. They form the substance of her diary, destroyed by fire and rewritten by her from memory. They are very unfriendly to Napoleon.

Rémusat, Jean Pierre Abel. A French Orientalist; born at Paris, September 1788; died June 3, 1832. He devoted himself to the study of Asiatic languages, especially Chinese, and published: 'Researches among the Tartar Languages' (1820); 'Elements of the Chinese Grammar' (1822); 'Asiatic Miscellanies' (1825); and 'New Miscellanies' (1828); besides translations and essays.

Renan, Joseph Ernest (rè-non'). The renowned French Semitic-Orientalist, philologist, historian, and essayist; born at Tréguier, Brittany, Feb. 27, 1823; died at Paris, Oct. 2, 1892. His chief subjects of study were the Semitic languages, and the antecedents and beginnings of Christianity. His works include: 'General History of the Semitic Languages' (1856); the translations 'Job' (1859), 'The Song of Songs' (1860), and 'Ecclesiastes' (1881); 'The Life of Jesus' (1863); 'The Apostles' (1866); 'St. Paul' (1867); 'Anti-Christ' (1873); 'The Gospels' (1877); 'The Christian Church' (1879); 'Marcus Aurelius' (1881); 'The History of the People of Israel' (1887–89). Also the collected essays 'Studies in Religious History' (1857), 'Essays in Criticism and Ethics' (1859), 'Questions of the Day' (1868), 'Miscellanies of History and Travel' (1878), 'New Studies in Religious History' (1884), and 'Discourses and Conferences' (1884); the philosophical dramas 'Caliban,' 'The Water of Youth,' 'The Priest of Nemi,' 'Dialogue of the Dead,' 'The Abbess of Jouarre,' and 'New-Year's Day' (1886); and the autobiographical works 'Recollections of Infancy and Youth' (1883) and 'Stray Leaves' (1892).

Repplier, Agnes. An American essayist; born in Philadelphia in 1855. Her published works include: 'Books and Men'; 'Points of View'; 'In the Dozy Hours'; 'Essays in Idleness'; 'Essays in Miniature'; 'Varia'; 'Compromises.'

Restif, Nicolas Edme (called **Restif** or **Rétif de la Bretonne**) (rè-tēf'). A French novelist; born at Sacy near Auxerre, Nov. 22, 1734; died at Paris, Feb. 3, 1806. He published in all more than 200 volumes, full of wit and imagination, but reflecting the licentious habits of their author and his circle. The most noteworthy are: 'The Foot of Fanchette' (1769); 'The Perverted Countryman' (1774); 'The Life of my Father' (1778), a monument of filial piety; 'The Pornograph' (1796), a plan for regulating prostitution; and the remarkable 'Autobiography of Monsieur Nicolas' (1794–97, 16 vols.).

Reuchlin, Johann (roich'lin). A German classical and Hebrew scholar and humanist; born at Pforzheim, Baden, Feb. 22, 1455; died at Liebenzell, June 30, 1522. He did much to restore Hebrew and Greek letters among his countrymen. His Latin Dictionary, published in 1475, ran through many editions. The results of his Hebrew studies were the works entitled: 'On the Wondrous Word' (1494); 'Hebrew Grammar and Lexicon' (1506); and 'Concerning the Cabbalistic Art' (1517). His famous satire, Epistolæ Clarorum Virorum' (1515), aimed at his enemies, had an influence in developing the Reformation.

Reumont, Alfred von (roi'mont). A German archæologist; born at Aix-la-Chapelle in 1808; died April 27, 1887. He resided in many cities of Europe, and collected material for many books, among the most important being: 'Roman Literature' (1840–44); 'Contributions to Italian History' (1853–55); 'The Youth of Catherine de Medici'; 'Italian Diplomacy.'

Reuss, Eduard Wilhelm Eugen (rois). A noted German theologian; born at Strasburg (then a part of France), July 18, 1804; died there, April 15, 1891. He was made professor in the college of his native city, and published: 'A History of the Books of the New Testament' (1842); 'History of the Christian Religion in the Apostolic Age' (1872); 'A History of the Books of the Old Testament' (1881); and others. He was co-editor of Calvin's Works.

Reuter, Franz (roi'ter). A German novelist and poet; born at Stavenhagen, Mecklenburg-Schwerin, Nov. 7, 1810; died at Eisenach, June 12, 1874. He published: 'My Apprenticeship on the Farm'; 'Funny Tales and Nonsense Rhymes'; 'Nuptial Eve Stories'; 'An Account of a Journey to Belgium'; 'Kein Hüsung'; 'Hanne Nüte und de Lüdde Pudel'; 'Schurr-Murr'; 'Old Camomile Flowers'; 'In the Year 13'; 'Trips to Constantinople.'

Revere, Joseph Warren. An American officer, kinsman of Paul Revere; born in Boston in 1812; died in 1880. He was an officer in the Federal army, and published: 'Keel and Saddle: Retrospect of Forty Years' Military and Naval Service' (1872).

Révillon, Antoine (rev-ē-yôn'). ["Tony."] A French novelist and journalist; born at St. Laurent-les-Mâcon (Ain) in 1832. He has contributed to many periodicals, and published;

'The Happy Youth of F. Lapalud' (1866); 'The Separated One' (1875); and others.

Révoil, Benédict Henri (rev-wäy"). A French novelist and dramatist; born in Aix (Bouches-du-Rhône), Dec. 16, 1816. He lived in the United States for nine years, during which time he collected the material for many of his works. They include: 'Hunting and Fishing of the Other World' (1856); 'The Daughter of the Comanches'; and 'Dramas from the New World' (1864-65), a number of plays which he put on the stage in the United States, and afterwards published in France.

Rexford, Eben Eugene. An American poet; born at Johnsburg, Warren County, N. Y., July 1848; lives in Shiocton, Wis. He began to write when a mere child, contributing to periodicals and magazines. He published in book form the poems 'Brother and Lover' and 'Grandmother's Garden' (1887); and a story, 'John Fielding and his Enemy' (1888). He wrote the popular songs 'Silver Threads among the Gold' and 'Only a Pansy-Blossom.'

Reybaud, Marie Roch Louis (rä-bō'). A French writer on social topics; born at Marseilles, Aug. 15, 1799; died at Paris, Oct. 28, 1879. After traveling extensively, he settled in Paris and devoted himself wholly to literature, producing: 'Stories of the Modern Reformers or Socialists,' published in the Revue des Deux Mondes from 1836-40, and which have since passed through several editions in book form; 'Jérôme Paturot in Search of a Social Position' (1843); 'Jérôme Paturot in Search of the Best Republic' (1848); besides many romances, essays, and criticisms.

Reynolds, Frederic. An English dramatist; born in Lime Street, London, Nov. 1, 1764; died April 16, 1841. His first piece, 'Werter,' founded on Goethe's novel, was produced in 1785; and later was reproduced many times, and printed both in London and Dublin. His second drama, 'Eloisa,' was played in 1786, when he abandoned tragedy for comedy. His first attempt, 'The Dramatist' (1786), was very successful. He produced in all nearly one hundred plays, a novel, and two autobiographical volumes.

Reynolds, Sir Joshua. The great English painter; was born at Plympton Earl's, Devonshire, July 16, 1723; died in London, Feb. 23, 1792. Although it is as a portrait-painter that he is famous, it was his custom to deliver each year at the Royal Academy (of which he was president) a carefully prepared address on some topic immediately connected with art; and these addresses constitute the well-known 'Discourses of Sir Joshua Reynolds,' fifteen in number. He contributed also three essays to The Idler; notes to Mason's translation of Du Fresnoy's 'Art of Painting'; a few notes for Dr. Johnson's edition of Shakespeare; and notes of his tour through Flanders in 1781.

Rhodes, Albert. An American descriptive writer; born at Pittsburg, Pa., Feb. 1, 1840. He has spent most of his time abroad in diplomatic employments and contributing to American, French, and English periodicals. His published works include: 'Jerusalem as It Is' (1867); 'The French at Home' (1875); and 'Monsieur at Home' (1886).

Rhodes, James Ford. An American historian; born in Cleveland, O., in 1848. He was educated at the Universities of New York and Chicago; spent some years in study abroad, and engaged in business until 1891. He has published two volumes of 'History of the United States from the Compromise of 1850' (Vol. ii. 1892). The work is a political history of the events growing out of the slavery question, the Civil War, and the reconstruction era, and will summarize the great debates that took place, and bring into relief the men who took part.

Rhodes, William Barnes. An English dramatic writer; born Dec. 25, 1772; died Nov. 1, 1826. He is famous as the author of a long popular burlesque, 'Bombastes Furioso,' produced anonymously at the Haymarket Theatre in 1810, and published first at Dublin in 1813. Since then it has passed through many editions. He also wrote 'The Satires of Juvenal Translated into English Verse' (1801), and 'Epigrams' (1803).

Rhys, John (rīs). A Celtic philologist; born at Abercaero, Cardiganshire, Wales, June 21, 1840. He has been professor of Celtic in Oxford since 1877, and is the author of 'Lectures on Welsh Philology' (1877); 'Celtic Britain' (1882); 'Studies in the Arthurian Legends' (1891); 'The Welch People' (1900); 'Celtic Folk-lore' (1901).

Ribeiro, Bernardim (rē-bā-ē'rō). A Portuguese poet; born at Tarrão, province of Alemtejo, in 1486 (?); died about 1550. He is a noteworthy figure in Portuguese literature, having been one of the men who introduced the Italian pastoral style that has ever since prevailed in Portugal. Of his works there are now extant five idyls, a pastoral romance in prose, 'Menina e Moça' (first edition, 1554), and a number of lyrics in the style of the older poets of Portugal. Editions of his 'Works' have appeared in 1645, 1785, and 1852.

Ribeiro, Thomaz Antonio Fereiro. A Portuguese poet and politician; born at Parada de Gonta (Beira), July 1, 1831. He has taken high rank among the present-day poets of Spain by his patriotic and exquisite poem 'Jaime' (1861). Among his other works may be mentioned two collections of poems: 'Passing Tones' (1854), and 'Even-Songs' (1858); a poetic recital, 'Delfino' (1868); two books of travel, 'From Tejo to Mondovi' (1864), and 'Among the Palms' (1864). Died Feb. 7, 1901.

Ricardo, David. An English political economist; born in London, April 19, 1772; died at Gatcomb Park, Gloucestershire, Sept. 11, 1823. He stands next to Adam Smith (whose ideas he developed and systematized) in the British free-trade school of political science, and his writings have exerted a vast influence upon all theories of political economy. It has been said that Adam Smith was like the first explorer of a new country, who gives a good description of its general appearance, but omits much and mistakes much; while Ricardo was the first to draw an accurate map of it. After making his fortune in the Stock Exchange in London, he retired to devote himself to the study of mathematics, chemistry, etc. The first result of his studies was a tract entitled 'The High Price of Bullion a Proof of the Depreciation of Bank-Notes' (1809). In 1817 appeared his most important work, 'The Principles of Political Economy and Taxation.' Its leading feature was the theory of rent, now universally accepted, — that it represents the surplus earning power of better or more favorably situated land over that just good enough to be worth utilizing. Many of its other novel conceptions are now commonplaces. He published in addition a number of essays on economics. His 'Works' were edited by MacCulloch (1846). His 'Letters to Malthus' were published in 1887.

Riccobini, Antoine François (rik-ō-bē'nē). An Italian dramatic writer and actor, son of Luigi; born at Mantua; died at Paris in 1772. He wrote: 'The Slave Comedians' (1726); 'Amusements in Fashion' (1732); and an ingenious work called 'Theatrical Art' (1750).

Riccobini, Luigi. An Italian dramatist and descriptive writer; born in Modena in 1675; died in Paris in 1733. He published: 'History of the Italian Theatre' (1728–31); 'The Comedies and Genius of Molière' (1736); 'Reflections on the Theatres of Europe' (1738–50); and several others.

Riccobini, Marie Jeanne Laboras de Mézières. A French actress and novelist, wife of Antoine François; born at Paris in 1713; died there, 1792. She did not succeed upon the stage, and turned to the production of the sentimental novel with no little success. Her first work was the remarkable 'Marquis de Cressy' (1758). This was followed by 'The Letters of Julia Catesby' (1759); 'Ernestine' (1770–98), considered by many her masterpiece; 'The Letters of Sophie de Vallière' (1772); and a number of others.

Rice, George Edward. An American verse-writer; born in Boston, July 10, 1822; died at Roxbury, Mass., Aug. 10, 1861 or 1863. His publications include: 'An Old Play in a New Garb' (1852), a fanciful adaptation of 'Hamlet'; 'Ephemera' (1852), poems, written in conjunction with John Howard Wainwright; 'Myrtilla: A Fairy Extravaganza' (1853); 'Blondel; A Historic Fancy' (1854); and 'Nugamenta' (1859), a book of verse.

Rice, Harvey. An American poet; born at Conway, Mass., June 11, 1800; died 1891. He removed to Cleveland, opened a classical school, and purchased a newspaper, which he issued thereafter as the Plaindealer. He has been a frequent contributor to many periodicals, and in addition has published: 'Mount Vernon and Other Poems' (1864); 'Nature and Culture' (1875); 'Pioneers of the Western Reserve' (1882); 'Select Poems' (1885); 'Sketches of Western Life' (1888); and 'The Founder of the City of Cleveland.'

Rice, James. An English novelist; born at Northampton, Sept. 26, 1843; died in London, April 26, 1882. His reputation was well assured by the publication of 'Ready-Money Mortiboy' (1872), the first of the series of clever novels which he issued in conjunction with Walter Besant. It was subsequently dramatized under the title of 'Ready Money.' This remarkable partnership continued with 'The Golden Butterfly' (1876), 'The Chaplain of the Fleet' (1879), 'The Seamy Side' (1881), and several others. Previous to the partnership he had published 'History of the British Turf' (1879).

Richards, Alfred Bate. An English journalist and dramatist; born at Baskerville House, Worcestershire, Feb. 17, 1820; died at London, June 12, 1876. He produced many tragedies, among them being: 'Crœsus, King of Lydia'; several volumes of poems, including 'Death and the Magdalen' (1846); 'The Dream of the Soul' (1848); and one novel, 'So Very Human' (1871), the title being suggested by a chance phrase of Charles Dickens. In his 'Britain Redeemed and Canada Preserved' (1848), he foreshadowed, thirty years before its construction, the inter-oceanic railway between the Atlantic and the Pacific.

Richards, Laura Elizabeth. An American writer of juvenile books, daughter of Julia Ward Howe; born in Massachusetts in 1850. She has published a great number of children's books, among them being: 'Five Mice' (1880); 'Our Baby's Favorite' (1881); 'Tell-Tale from Hill and Dale' (1886); and 'Toto's Merry Winter'; 'The Piccolo'; 'The Greek Revolution.'

Richardson, Mrs. Abby Sage. An American lecturer and writer; born in Mass., October 14, 1837; died in Rome, Dec. 5, 1900. She wrote: 'Stories from Old English Poetry' (1871); 'The History of Our Country to 1876' (1876); 'Familiar Talks on English Literature' (1881); 'Old Love Letters' (1883); 'Abelard and Heloise: A Mediæval Romance' (1884); etc.

Richardson, Albert Deane. An American journalist; born in Franklin, Mass., Oct. 6, 1833; died in New York city, Dec. 2, 1869. He was famous as the war correspondent of the New York Tribune during the Civil War, and was imprisoned with others for eighteen months as a result of their undertaking to run the batteries of Vicksburg on two barges. The result of his experiences was the work: 'The Field, the Dungeon, and the Escape' (1865). He also wrote: 'Beyond the Mississippi' (1866), and 'A Personal History of Ulysses S. Grant' (1868). A collection of his miscellaneous writings was published by his wife, Abby Sage Richardson, under the title of 'Garnered Sheaves' (1871).

Richardson, Samuel. An English novelist; born in Derbyshire in 1689; died July 4, 1761. He is England's first «a novelist.» All of his books are in the form of letters, long and sentimental. His best-known novels are : ‘Clarissa Harlowe’ (1748); ‘Pamela’ (1740); and a continuation (1741). ‘Sir Charles Grandison’ followed in 1754. His ‘Correspondence,’ edited by Anna Lætitia Barbauld, appeared in 1804.

Richardt, Christian Ernst (rish'ärt). A Danish poet; born in Copenhagen, May 25, 1831; died in 1893. His poems are noted for religious depth, delicacy, and patriotic enthusiasm. He is considered first among the later lyrical poets of Denmark. His first book was ‘Deklarationen’ (1851), a comedy, followed by ‘Short Poems’ (1861); ‘Pictures and Songs’ (1874); ‘Fifty Poems’ (1878); ‘Spring and Autumn’ (1884); and ‘Miscellaneous Poems’ (1891). He also wrote a tragic musical drama, ‘King and Constable’ (1878).

Richebourg, Jules Emile (rēsh-börg'). A French novelist; born at Meury, April 23, 1833; died at Paris, Jan. 25, 1898. He produced light verses and comedies before devoting his attention seriously to romance. After 1858 he produced a great number of novels of adventure, intrigue, and passion, which found great favor among the masses in France. Among them may be named : ‘The Man with the Black Spectacles’ (1864); ‘The Veiled Lady’ (1875); ‘The Beautiful Organist’ (1876); ‘Father Raclot's Million’ (1889); ‘Cinderella’ (1892); and ‘Winter Tales’ (1892).

Richelieu, Armand-Jean du Plessis (rēsh-lyė'). The French duke and cardinal, and statesman; born in Paris, Sept. 5, 1585; died there, Dec. 4, 1642. As prime minister of France he exercised a great influence upon its history, externally and internally, and took great interest in literature and art, enlarging the Sorbonne and the royal library, and giving encouragement to scholars, poets, and artists. He dabbled in literature himself to some extent, writing ‘Miriam’ and ‘The Great Pastoral.’ His ‘Letters, Diplomatic Instructions,’ etc., were edited by Avenel (1853-68). Other works credited to him are of doubtful authenticity.

Richepin, Jean (rēsh-pań'). A French poet, dramatist, and novelist; born at Médéah, Algiers, Feb. 4, 1849. He first attracted attention by his volume of poems ‘The Song of the Beggar’ (1876), which sent him to prison, where he wrote ‘Curious Deaths’ (1887). A most prolific and audacious writer, he is faithful to his principles, or the lack of them, in all his works. They include : ‘Caresses’ (1877), ‘Blasphemics’ (1884), and ‘The Sea’ (1886), in verse; ‘Mme. André’ (1874); ‘Brave Men’ (1888); ‘The Cadet’ (1890); the dramas ‘Monsieur Scapin’ (1886); ‘The Filibuster’ (1888); ‘By the Sword’ (1892); ‘The Martyress’ and ‘The Watchdog’ (1898).

Richmond, Legh. An English religious writer; born at Liverpool, Jan. 29, 1772; died at Turvey, Bedfordshire, May 8, 1827. He was

the author of three famous tales of village life, circulated as tracts in many languages. They are entitled : ‘The Dairyman's Daughter,’ ‘The Negro Servant,’ and ‘The Young Cottager,’ and were printed under the title of ‘Annals of the Poor’ (1814). He also edited ‘The Fathers of the English Church’ (1807-11).

Richter, Jean Paul Friedrich (rich'ter). The celebrated German satirist, philosopher, and humorist; born at Wunsiedel, Bavaria, March 21, 1763; died at Bayreuth, Nov. 14, 1825. He is one of the great humorists of modern German literature, but disregards literary form. His first noteworthy production was the novel ‘The Invisible Lodge’ (1793), followed by ‘Hesperus’ (1795); ‘Biographical Recreations under the Cranium of a Giantess’ (1796); ‘The Life of Quintus Fixlein’ (1796); ‘Flower, Fruit, and Thorn Pieces’ (1797); ‘The Jubilating Senior’ (1797); ‘The Country Valley’ (1797); ‘Titan’ (1803); ‘Wild Oats’ (1804); ‘Introduction to Æsthetics’ (1805), his first philosophical attempt, and regarded by many as the culmination of his genius; and ‘Levana, or Pedagogics’ (1807).

Riddell, Charlotte Eliza Lawson (Mrs. J. H.). A popular English novelist; born Sept. 30, 1832. She published her early novels under the name of «F. G. Trafford.» Her many books include : ‘George Geith’ (1864); ‘The Race for Wealth’ (1866); ‘Far Above Rubies’ (1867); ‘Austin Friars’ (1870); ‘The Ruling Passion’ (1876); ‘The Senior Partner’ (1881); ‘The Struggle for Fame’ (1883); ‘Miss Gascoiagne’ (1887); and ‘Idle Tales’ (1888); ‘Footfall of Fate’ (1900); ‘Poor Fellow’ (1902).

Ridderstad, Karl Fredrik (rid'er-städ). A Swedish novelist and poet; born in Södermannland in 1807; died in 1886. He was a member of the Riksdag, and famous for his eloquence and patriotism. He is the author of several historical romances, the best of which are ‘The Halberdier’ and ‘The Prince’; a number of novels in imitation of Eugène Sue, including ‘Mysteries of Stockholm’ and ‘The Black Hand’; and many lyrics, in which line he was most successful.

Rideing, William Henry. An English-American miscellaneous writer; born in Liverpool, Feb. 17, 1853, now a resident of New York. His books include : ‘Pacific Railways Illustrated’ (1878); ‘A Saddle in the Wild West’ (1879); ‘Stray Moments with Thackeray’ (1880); ‘Boys in the Mountains’ (1882); ‘A Little Upstart’ (1885); ‘The Boyhood of Living Authors’ (1887); ‘In the Land of Lorna Doone’; ‘The Captured Cunarder’; ‘How Tyson came Home.’

Ridpath, John Clark. An American historian and educator; born in Putnam County, Ind., April 26, 1841; died in New York city, July 31, 1900. Among his writings are: ‘Academic History of the United States’ (1875); ‘Grammar-School History of the United States’ (1876); ‘Popular History of the United States’ (1877); ‘Inductive Grammar of the English Language’

(1879); 'Life and Works of Garfield' (1881); 'History of the World' (1885); 'Christopher Columbus: The Epoch, the Man, and the Work' (1890); 'Great Races of Mankind' (1892); and 'The Epic of Life,' a poem (1894).

Riehl, Wilhelm Heinrich (rēl). A German historian, novelist, and publicist; born at Biebrich on the Rhine, May 6, 1823; died Nov. 16, 1897. He is the author of a number of excellent historical and ethnological works, and of a number of novels based upon his studies in these directions. The most prominent ot his works are : 'Natural History of the People as the Foundation of the National Policy' (1851–69); 'Die Pfalzer' (1857); 'Studies of the Civilization of Three Centuries' (1859); 'Enigmas of Life' (1888); and 'From the Corner' (1890).

Riemer, Friedrich Wilhelm (rē'mer). A German littérateur; born at Glatz in Silesia, April 19, 1774; died at Weimar, Dec. 19, 1845. The most important of his publications is a 'Greek-German Dictionary-Manual' (1802–4). His close association with Goethe in Weimar, where he was for some time the instructor of Goethe's son, gave him a poetic bent, and he published 'Leaves and Flowers' (1816), under the pseudonym of "Sylvio Romano"; and under his own name, 'Poems' (1826). He also brought out 'Correspondence between Goethe and Zelter' (1833).

Riethmüller, Christopher James (rēt'müller). An English poet and novelist; born in 18—. His published works include : 'Launcelot of the Lake' (1843), a tragedy; 'Teuton: A Poem' (1861); 'Frederic Lucas: A Biography' (1862); 'Alexander Hamilton and his Contemporaries' (1864); 'Three Legends of the Early Church' (1867); 'Adventures of N. Brooke' (1877); 'Julian the Apostate' (1883); and many others.

Riis, Jacob August (rēs). A New York writer on social topics; born in Denmark, 1849. He has written : 'How the Other Half Lives'; 'The Children of the Poor'; and 'Nibsy's Christmas'; 'The Battle with the Slum'; 'Children of the Tenements' ; 'Theodore Roosevelt, the Citizen.' He is very active in charitable movements in New York.

Riley, James Whitcomb. An American poet; born at Greenfield, Ind., about 1853. In 1875 he began to contribute to local papers verses in the Hoosier dialect, and latterly he has published numerous dialect and serious poems in magazines. His collected works include: 'The Old Swimmin' Hole and 'Leven More Poems' (1883); 'The Boss Girl and Other Sketches' (1886); 'Afterwhiles' (1888): 'Pipes o' Pan at Zekesbury' (1889); 'Green Fields and Running Brooks' (1893); 'Poems Here at Home' ; and 'Armazindy : A Child World'; 'A Defective Santa Claus'; 'Raggedy Man.'

Ring, Bernard Jacques Joseph Maximilien de (rang). A French archæologist; born at Bonn, Rhenish Prussia, May 27, 1799; died at Bischleim, Alsace, in 1875. He devoted himself from his sixteenth year to the study of archæology, and published 'Picturesque Views of the Old Castles of Baden' (1829); 'Celtic Settlement in Southern Germany' (1842); 'Roman Settlement of the Rhine to the Danube' (1852–53), crowned by the French Academy; and 'History of the Opiques People: Their Legislation, Customs, and Language' (1859).

Ring, Max (ring). A German novelist; born at Sauditz, Silesia, Aug. 4, 1817. He has produced a great number of novels, notably 'The Children of God' (1851); 'The Great Elector and the Alderman' (1851); 'The Lost Race' (1867); 'The Friends of the Soul' (1871); 'Chains of Gold' (1881), 'Victory of Love' (1886); and 'Seekers and Strivers' (1888). D. 1901.

Rinuccini, Ottavio (rē-nö-chē'nē). An Italian poet and gentleman; born at Florence in 1565; died in 1621. His pastoral 'Daphne' was put to music and rendered with great success; and his second pastoral, 'Eurydice,' was represented at the marriage of Marie de' Medici and Henry IV., and published in 1600. A later lyric drama, 'Ariadne at Naxos,' is superior to his former productions. His poetry was collected and published in 1622.

Rioja, Francisco de (rē-ō'hä). A Spanish poet; born at Seville about 1585; died at Madrid, Aug. 8, 1659. He was a great scholar, librarian of the royal library and Chronicler of Castile. He was regarded as one of the best poets of his time; and although his poetry is not great, it is distinguished by beauty of form, delicacy of style, and deep feeling for nature. His best-known work is 'Epístola Moral á Fabio,' full of sound advice regarding the superiority of a quiet and unassuming life. He wrote many sonnets under the titles of 'To Riches,' 'To Poverty,' 'To the Spring,' 'To the Rose,' and 'Silvas.' His 'Poems,' with extensive biography, were published in 1867, and additions in 1872.

Riordan, Roger. An Irish-American journalist; born in 1848. He now resides in New York city, and has published: 'A Score of Etchings' (1883); and 'Sunrise Stories: A Glance at the Legislature of Japan.' Died 1904.

Ripley, George. An American scholar and editor; born at Greenfield, Mass., Oct. 3, 1802; died in New York city, July 4, 1880. His ventures along literary lines are almost too numerous to mention. He was the founder and editor of the Dial, and contributed to many journals; was one of the projectors of Brook Farm, and a transcendentalist,—writing articles which covered the whole ground of philosophical speculation. He was long the literary critic of the New York Tribune, and one of the most noted reviewers of his time. He left no extended work, and will be remembered rather as a promoter of learning. In 1838 appeared his first two volumes of 'Foreign Standard Literature,' a series of fourteen in all, which exerted great influence upon the educated mind of New England. They were entitled 'Philosophical Miscellanies.'

Rishanger, William. An English monk of St. Alban's, and chronicler; born about 1250; died about 1312. He rekindled the desire among monks for composing chronicles,—a desire which had almost died out in his day. His most important writing is the 'Narratio de Bellis apud Lewes et Evesham' (Account of the Fights at Lewes and Evesham), with an autobiographical sketch forming part of the manuscript. It extends from 1258 to 1267, and gives with vigor, picturesque detail, and political insight, an excellent account of the barons' wars. Several other works are accredited to him; but their authenticity is doubtful, with the exception of the short chronicle 'Quædem Recapitulatio Brevis de Gestis Domini Edwardi' (Short Account of the Acts and Sayings of King Edward).

Ritchie, Mrs. Anna Cora (Mowatt). An American novelist and dramatist; born (Ogden) in Bordeaux, France, in 1822; died in 1870. She came in early life to New York. A once popular actress, she retired from the stage in 1854, and devoted herself to the production of romances and dramas, with no little success. Some of her books have been published under the pseudonyms of « Isabel » and « Helen Berkley. » They include: 'The Fortune-Hunter' (1842); 'The Mute Singer'; 'Fashion,' a comedy (1847), which was very popular; 'Evelyn' (1845); 'The Autobiography of an Actress' (1854), the best-known and most popular of her productions; 'Mimic Life' (1855); 'Fairy Fingers' (1865); 'The Clergyman's Wife' (1867); and others.

Ritchie, Anne Isabelle (Thackeray.) An English miscellaneous writer, daughter of William Makepeace Thackeray; born in London in 1838. Among her writings are: 'Old Kensington' (1873); 'Toilers and Spinsters' (1873); 'Bluebeard's Keys' (1874); 'Miss Angel' (1875); 'Mme. de Sévigné' (1881); 'Records of Tennyson, Ruskin, and Browning' (1892); 'Lord Tennyson and his Friends' (1893); and with R. Evans, 'Lord Amherst and the British Advance Eastward to Burma'); 'Chapters from some Memoirs.'

Ritson, Joseph. An English antiquary and scholar; born at Stockton-on-Tees, Oct. 2, 1752; died at Hoxton, Sept. 2, 1803. He devoted many years to antiquarian researches, and edited a vast number of reprints of old and rare books. His own works include: 'Observations on Warton's History of English Poetry' (1782); 'Ancient Songs from the Time of King Henry III. to the Revolution' (1790); 'A Collection of Scottish Songs' (1794); 'Robin Hood Ballads' (1795); 'Bibliographia Poetica' (1802); 'Ancient English Metrical Romances' (1802); and many others.

Ritter, Frédéric Louis. An American musician; born in Strasburg, Alsace, 1834; died in 1891. He came to the United States in 1856, and soon made a reputation both here and abroad as a writer on musical topics. Besides many articles in English, French, and German periodicals, he published: 'A History of Music in the Form of Lectures' (1870–74); 'Music in England' (1883); 'Music in America' (1883); 'Manual of Musical History' (1886); and 'Musical Dictation' (1888).

Ritter, Heinrich (rit'ter). A German philosopher; born at Zerbst in 1791; died in 1869. He owes his literary fame to his profound works on the history of philosophy. The most important of them are: 'On the Education of the Philosopher through the History of Philosophy' (1817); 'Introductory Lectures to Logic' (1823); 'History of Philosophy' (1829–53); 'On the Relation between Philosophy and Scientific Life in General' (1835); and 'Encyclopædia of Philosophic Science' (1862–63).

Rivarol, Antoine (rē-vä-rōl'). A French satirist and publicist; born at Bagnols, Languedoc, near 1754; died at Berlin, April 13, 1801. He was one of the most brilliant wits of the eighteenth century. His first work of importance, the discourse 'On the Universality of the French Language,' took the prize at the Academy of Berlin in 1784. His 'Little Almanac of our Great Men' (1788), a volume of satires against authors of his day, and a free translation of Dante's 'Inferno,' were both particularly successful. He also wrote a 'Dictionary of the French Language,' and 'Letters to the Duke of Brunswick.' His 'Works' appeared in 1808.

Rives, Amélie. See **Troubetzkoi.**

Rivet, Gustave (rē-vā'). A French littérateur; born at Domène (Isère), Jan. 25, 1848. He has written a number of dramas, some of which have appeared on the French stage. His writings include: 'Lost Voices' (1874), poems; 'Victor Hugo at Home' (1878); 'The Punishment' (1879), a drama; 'Marie Touchet' (1881), a drama; and 'The Quest of Paternity' (1890).

Rivière, Henri-Laurent (riv-yär'). A French marine officer and littérateur; born in Paris, July 12, 1827; killed in Anam, May 20, 1883. He acquired a speedy popularity by two simple tales, 'Pierrot' (1860), and 'Cain' (1870). He afterward produced many stories, comedies, and works of a more serious character, among them being: 'The French Navy under Louis XV.' (1859); 'The Possessed One' (1863); 'The Journal of a Marine' (1866); 'The Upstart' (1869); 'Adventures of Three Friars' (1875); 'M. Margerie' (1875); and 'The New Caledonia' (1880)

Robert of Gloucester. An English chronicler, living at the time of the battle of Evesham (1265). He is remarkable for a metrical chronicle of England, from the time of the fabulous Brutus to his own, based chiefly upon Geoffrey of Monmouth's book. It extends to ten thousand lines, and is one of the earliest epics of the English language. It was printed by Thomas Hearne in 1724.

Roberthin, Robert (rōb-är'tĕn). A German poet; born at Königsberg in 1600; died there.

April 7, 1648. He published his graceful songs, copies of which have become very rare, under the anagram of " Berintho." His principal work was 'Songs and Airs, Religious and Secular' (1638–50). His poems have also been incorporated in volumes on German poets, etc.

Roberts, Anna S. An American poet; born in Philadelphia in 1827; died in 1858. She published a book of poems entitled 'Forest Flowers of the West' (1851), the most notable of which are: 'The Old Mansion,' 'Two Portraits,' 'The Unsealed Fountain,' and 'A Vision.'

Roberts, Charles George Douglas. A Canadian poet; born in Douglas, N. B., Jan. 10, 1860. He is an earnest advocate of Canadian nationalism, and such of his poetical compositions as relate to this and other distinctly Canadian subjects are particularly excellent. He has published: 'Orion, and Other Poems' (1880), and 'In Divers Tones' (1887); and has edited 'Poems of Wild Life' in the series of 'Canterbury Poets' (1888). In 1897 appeared his 'History of Canada,' and 'The Kindred of the Wild.'

Roberts, Emma. An English descriptive and verse writer; born in 1794; died in Poona, India, Sept. 16, 1840. She lived in India much of her life, devoting herself closely to literature and journalism. Among her many books may be named: 'Memoirs of the Rival Houses of York and Lancaster' (1827); 'Oriental Scenes, Sketches, and Tales' (1832), a volume of poetry; 'Scenes and Characteristics of Hindostan' (1835); 'The East India Voyager' (1839); and 'Hindostan, its Landscapes, Palaces, etc.' (1845–47).

Roberts, Margaret. A Welsh novelist and miscellaneous writer; born at Honyngs, North Wales, in 1833. She has lived much in Italy, France, and Germany, and wrote her first book in Italian, with the exception of the last chapter. Most of her books have been published anonymously. They include: 'Mademoiselle Mori' (1860); 'Denise' (1863); 'Madame Fontenoy' (1864); 'On the Edge of the Storm' (1868); 'Margaret Woodward' (1877); 'Grammar of the French Language' (1882); 'In the Olden Time' (1883); 'Hester's Venture' (1886); 'Under a Cloud' (1888); and many others.

Roberts, Samuel. An English author and pamphleteer; born at Sheffield, April 18, 1763; died there, July 24, 1848. He was known as the " Pauper's Advocate," and is the author of an immense number of books, pamphlets, and broadsheets, dealing with all that he considered unjust or tyrannical. His principal works are: 'Tales of the Poor' (1813); 'The Blind Man and his Son' (1816); 'Defence of the Poor Laws' (1819); 'Life of Queen Mary' (1822); 'The Gipsies: Their Origin, Continuance, and Destination' (1836); and 'Milton Unmasked' (1844). His 'Autobiography and Select Remains' were published in 1849.

Robertson, Frederick William. An English clergyman; born in London, Feb. 3, 1816; died at Brighton, Aug. 15, 1853. His fame rests upon the series of sermons which he delivered at Trinity Chapel, Brighton. His writings and biography have been reprinted in the United States, and widely read, and have exerted great influence in liberalizing religious thought. His works were collected and published after his death under the titles 'Sermons Preached at Trinity Chapel, Brighton' (1855–64); 'Lectures and Addresses on Literary and Social Topics' (1858); 'Expository Lectures on St. Paul's Epistles to the Corinthians' (1859); and 'Notes on Genesis' (1877).

Robertson, James Burton. An English historian; born in London, Nov. 15, 1800; died in Dublin, Feb. 14, 1877. He studied literature, philosophy, and the elements of dogmatic theology, in France; and after various preliminary essays, published a translation of Frederick Schlegel's 'Philosophy of History' (1835), which passed through many editions. His second translation, 'Symbolism, or Exposition of Doctrinal Differences between Catholics and Protestants' (1843), was also widely read in both England and America, and created a profound impression. His original writings include: 'Public Lectures on Some Subjects of Ancient and Modern History' (1859); 'Lectures on Some Subjects of Modern History and Biography' (1864); and many others.

Robertson, Thomas William. An English actor and dramatist; born at Newark-on-Trent, Jan. 9, 1829; died in London, Feb. 3, 1871. His first play was 'A Night's Adventure' (1851); and after its production he settled in London, and devoted himself to play-writing. Several of his dramas were very successful: the best known are 'David Garrick' (1864) and 'Caste' (1868). Other successful ones are: 'Society' (1865); 'Ours' (1866); 'School' (1869); 'Dreams' (1869); and 'M. P.' (1870).

Robertson, William. A Scotch historian; born at Borthwick, Midlothian, Sept. 19, 1721; died at Grange House, near Edinburgh, June 11, 1793. Although ranked with Gibbon and Hume while he lived, and enjoying great popularity, his writings are now but little read. He is the author of many books, chief among which are: 'History of Scotland during the Reigns of Mary and James VI.' (1758–59); 'History of the Reign of the Emperor Charles V.' (1769); 'History of America' (1777); and 'Historical Disquisition concerning the Knowledge which the Ancients had of India' (1791).

Robinson, Agnes Mary Frances. See Darmesteter.

Robinson, Charles Seymour. An American clergyman and hymnologist; born at Bennington, Vt., March 31, 1829. He is famed as a collector of hymns and tunes used in the Presbyterian Church. His publications include: 'Songs of the Church' (1862); 'Songs for the Sanctuary' (1865); 'Church Work' (1873); 'Studies in the New Testament' (1880); 'Laudes Domini' (1884); 'The Pharaohs of the

Bondage and the Exodus' (1887); 'Simon Peter, his Life and Times' (1888); 'From Samuel to Solomon' (1889); 'New Laudes Domini' (1892); 'Annotations upon Popular Hymns' (1893); 'Simon Peter: Later Life and Labors' (1894); and others. He died in 1899.

Robinson, Frederick William. An English novelist; born in Spitalfields, London, Dec. 23, 1830; died at Brixton, Dec. 6, 1901. He was a prolific writer, and published, among many others: 'No Church' (1862); 'Beyond the Church' (1866); 'True to Herself' (1870); 'Her Face was her Fortune' (1873); 'As long as She Lived' (1876); 'The Hands of Justice' (1881); 'The Man She Cared For' (1884); 'Dark Street' (1887); and 'The Youngest Miss Green' (1888).

Robinson, Henry Crabb. An English lawyer and diarist; born at Bury St. Edmunds, March 13, 1775; died in London, Feb. 5, 1867. He acquired a thorough knowledge of modern German literature, and enjoyed the intimate friendship of Goethe, Schiller, the Schlegels, and other prominent Germans. He published but little, but left a copious diary and correspondence (102 volumes in all), selections from which were published under the title of 'Diary, Reminiscences, and Correspondence of H. Crabb Robinson' (1869), very valuable for its description of the men and events of his time in England.

Robinson, Jane. The following volumes, signed "by the author of Whitefriars," are ascribed to the above writer in Olphar Hamst's [Ralph Thomas's] Handbook for Fictitious Names : 'Whitehall; or, The Days of Charles I.' (1845); 'The Maid of Orleans' (1849); 'The Gold Worshipers' (1851); 'The City Banker' (1856); 'Maulever's Divorce' (1858); 'Which Wins?' (1863); 'Dorothy Firebrace' (1865); and others.

Robinson, Mary. An English actress and author; born at Bristol, Nov. 27, 1758; died at Surrey, Dec. 26, 1800. Her first collection of poems was published in 1775, under the patronage of the Duchess of Devonshire. After this she published several books, among them being : 'Celadon and Lydia' (1777), a tale; 'Captivity' (1777), a poem; 'Angelina' (1796); 'Lyrical Tales' (1800); and 'Effusions of Love,' purporting to be her correspondence with the Prince of Wales, afterwards George IV., of whom she was the recognized mistress.

Robinson, Philip Stewart. An English descriptive writer; born at Chunar, India, in 1849. His published works include : 'In my Indian Garden' (1878); 'Under the Punkah' (1881); 'Noah's Ark; or, Mornings in the Zoo' (1882); 'Sinners and Saints : A Tour across the States and Round them' (1883); 'The Valley of Teetotum Trees'; 'In Garden, Orchard and Spinney.'

Robinson, Therese Albertine Luise (von Jakob). [Pseudonym "Talvj,"—her initials.] A German historical and miscellaneous writer; born at Halle, Jan. 26, 1797; died at Hamburg, April 13, 1869. Her most important work is

'A Historical View of the Languages and Literature of the Slavic Nations' (1850). Among her other writings are : 'Psyche: Original Tales' (1824); 'Servian Songs' (1825–26); and 'Characteristics of the Popular Songs of the German Nations' (1840).

Roche, Antonin (rōsh). A French littérateur; born at Puy de Dome, Nov. 10, 1813; died in London, July 9, 1899. He founded in London, classes in literature, history, geography, and astronomy, which proved very successful; and published both in London and Paris, in connection with this work, several educational books, among them being: 'History of France' (1866) ; 'The English Writers of the Nineteenth Century' (1868); 'History of England' (1875) ; and 'History of Principal French Writers' (1878).

Roche, James Jeffrey. An American author; born in Queen's County, Ireland, May 31, 1847. He went to Boston in 1866 and has lived there since ; is an editor of the Pilot, and has published : 'Songs and Satires' (1886); 'Ballads of Blue Water'; 'Life of John Boyle O'Reilly'; 'His Majesty the King'; 'By-Ways of War.'

Roche, Regina Maria. An Irish novelist : born about 1764 in the south of Ireland; died at Waterford, May 17, 1845. She sprang into fame on the appearance of the novel 'The Children of the Abbey' (1798), a story abounding in sentimentality, abductions, secret retreats, etc.,—a cross between the 'Mysteries of Udolpho' and domestic novels like 'Clarissa Harlowe.' From that time until her death she produced many books of the same character, including : 'The Nocturnal Visit' (1800); 'The Tradition of the Castle' (1824); 'The Castle Chapel' (1825); 'The Nun's Picture' (1834); and many others.

Rochefort, Victor Henri (rōsh-for'). A French journalist and republican agitator; born at Paris, Jan. 30, 1830. He was removed from the editorship of Figaro because of his satires on the imperial government; and the papers which he himself founded—La Lanterne, La Marseillaise, and Le Mot d'Ordre—were filled with the same violent attacks. He has more than once been exiled from France for long periods. His last venture, L'Intransigeant, is noted for the virulence of its criticisms upon leading politicians of the day. He has written and published much,—farces, vaudevilles, comic romances, and political works. Among them may be mentioned : 'The Depraved Ones' (1875); 'Return from Nova Scotia' (1877); 'Mlle. Bismarck' (1880); 'Bitter Farces' (1886); 'The [political] Lanterns of the Empire' (1884); 'Fantasia' (1888); 'The Adventures of My Life.'

Rochefoucauld, François, Duc de la (rōsh-fō-kō'), Prince de Marcillac. A great French classic; born at Paris, Sept. 15, 1613; died there, March 17, 1680. His celebrity is due to his small volume of 'Reflections, or Moral Sentences and Maxims,' commonly known as the 'Maxims' (first ed. 1665; final edition of the author 1678, comprising 504 maxims). The dominant note of the 'Maxims' is egoism: virtue and vice are in themselves indifferent. This philosophy of life is set forth with consummate wit, and in a style of faultless elegance. His 'Memoirs' (1662) possess literary merit in a degree hardly inferior to the 'Maxims'; and in historical interest they are equal to the most celebrated memoirs of the time.

Rochester, John Wilmot, Earl of. An English satirist and verse-writer; born at Ditchley, Oxfordshire, April 10, 1648; died July 26, 1680. He became a favorite at the court of Charles II., and wrote songs and satires in accordance with prevailing taste. His 'Poems and Familiar Letters' were posthumously published.

Rochon de Chabannes, Marc Antoine Jacques (rō-shôn" dė shä-bän'). A French dramatist; born in Paris, Jan. 25, 1730; died there, May 15, 1800. He wrote a great number of successful comedies, published under the title of 'Theatre' (1786); besides 'Slothful Nobility' (1756), and 'Philosophic and Moral Discourse' (1768).

Rod, Édouard (rod). A French-Swiss novelist and critic; born at Nyon in 1857. He has published many works of criticism and erudition, among them being: 'À propos de 'L'Assommoir'' (1879); 'The Germans at Paris' (1880); and 'Wagner and the German Æsthetic' (1886). But he is better known as a novelist, and has published: 'The Fall of Miss Topsy' (1882); 'The Deathward Career' (1885); 'The Meaning of Life' (1889); 'Stendhal' (1891); 'The Sacrificed One' (1892); 'A Victor' (1904).

Rodbertus, Johann Karl (rod-bärt'ös) (known as Rodbertus-Jagetzow). A German political economist; born at Greifswald, Pomerania, Aug. 12, 1805; died Dec. 6, 1875. He is regarded by many as the founder of scientific socialism. He maintains that "all commodities can only be considered economically as the product of labor, and cost nothing but labor." His most important works are: 'A Contribution to the Knowledge of Municipal Conditions' (1842); 'Social Letters to Von Kirchmann' (1850–51), published later under the title of 'Capital' (1888); Exposition and Defense of the Existing Credit Note Based upon Real Estate' (1868–69); 'The Normal Working-Day' (1871); 'Letters and Politico-Social Theorems of Dr. Rodbertus-Jagetzow' (1884).

Rodd, Sir James Rennell. An English diplomat and verse writer; born in London, Nov. 9, 1858. He has published: 'Poems in Many Lands' (1883); 'Feda and Other Poems' (1886); 'The Unknown Madonna and Other Poems'; 'Frederick, Crown Prince and Emperor' (1888); 'Customs and Lore of Modern Greece.'

Rodenbach, Georges (rō'den-bäch). A Belgian poet and journalist; born at Tournay, July 16, 1855; died at Paris, Dec. 24, 1898. He is noted for delicacy of sentiment and the grace of his lines.

His great piece is 'Belgium' (1880), a historical poem; and he has also written: 'The Fireside and the Fields' (1877); 'Sorrows' (1879); 'The Beautiful Sea' (1881); 'The Winter of Fashion' (1884); 'White Youth' (1886); 'Silence' (1888); 'Art in Exile' (1889); 'The Reign of Silence' (1891); and one romance, 'Bruges la Morte' (1892).

Rodenberg, Julius (rō'den-berG). A German poet and descriptive writer; born at Rodenberg, Hesse-Nassau, June 26, 1831. He substituted for his own name, Levy, that of his birthplace. He has published accounts of his extensive travels in France, England, Italy, and Belgium, and has written poems of diverse kinds, — epic, heroic-comic, lyrical, dramatic, and opera librettos. His works include: 'Journalistic Life in London' (1859); 'Paris by Daylight and Gaslight' (1867); 'An Educational Tour in England' (1873); 'Pictures of Berlin Life' (1885–88); and the romances 'The Singer of London's Streets' (1863); 'The New Deluge' (1865), translated into many languages; 'By the Grace of God' (1870); 'The Grandidiers' (1879).

Rodger, Alexander. A Scotch minor poet; born at Mid-Calder, Midlothian, July 16, 1784; died at Glasgow, Sept. 26, 1846. He began as a humble hand-loom weaver, and wrote some of his best lyrics while inspector of cloths in Glasgow. His style is somewhat rough, but easy and vigorous. His books include: 'Scotch Poetry, Songs, Odes, Authors, and Epigrams' (1821); 'Poems and Songs, Humorous and Satirical' (1838); 'Stray Leaves from the Portfolios of Alisander the Seer, Andrew Whaup, and Humphrey Henkecke' (1842); and others. His best-known poems are: 'Robin Tamson's Smiddy' and 'Behave Yoursell before Folk.'

Roe, Azel Stevens. An American novelist; born in New York city, Aug. 16, 1798; died at East Windsor Hill, Conn., Jan. 1, 1886. He left the wine business for the production of literature, attaining considerable success. He wrote: 'James Mountjoy' (1850); 'To Love and be Loved' (1852); 'Time and Tide; or, Strive and Win' (1852); 'A Long Look Ahead' (1855); 'The Star and the Cloud' (1856); 'True to the Last' (1859); 'How Could He Help It?' (1860); 'Looking Around' (1865); 'Woman Our Angel' (1866); 'The Cloud in the Heart' (1869); 'Resolution' (1871); and 'True Love Rewarded' (1877).

Roe, Edward Payson. An American novelist; born in Orange County, N. Y., March 7, 1838; died at Cornwall, N. Y., July 19, 1888. He has written a great number of very popular novels, which have been republished in England and other countries. His first novel, 'Barriers Burned Away' (1872), met with immediate success, and was followed by 'What Can She Do?' (1873); 'The Opening of a Chestnut Burr' (1874); 'From Jest to Earnest' (1875); 'Near to Nature's Heart' (1876); 'A Knight of the Nineteenth Century' (1877); 'A Face Illumined' (1878); 'A Day of Fate'

(1880); 'Without a Home' (1880); 'His London Rivals' (1883); 'A Young Girl's Wooing' (1884); 'Nature's Serial Story' (1884); 'An Original Belle' (1885); 'Driven Back to Eden' (1885); 'He Fell in Love with his Wife' (1886); 'The Earth Trembled' (1887); 'A Hornet's Nest' (1887); 'Found, Yet Lost' (1888); 'Miss Lou' (1888); and 'Taken Alive, and Other Stories.'

Roger of Hovedon. An English chronicler, known to have been alive in 1174; probably a native of Howden; died in 1201 (?). His chronicle extends from 732 to 1201; and although careless in chronology, is of the highest value as giving much attention to legal and constitutional details.

Rogers, Henry. An English essayist and reviewer; born at St. Albans, Oct. 18, 1806; died in North Wales, Aug. 20, 1877. Although he was neither philosopher nor theologian, his writings hovered between philosophy and theology, and were widely read. They include: 'Life and Character of John Howe' (1836); 'General Introduction to a Course of Lectures on English Grammar and Composition' (1838); 'The Eclipse of Faith' (1853), a piece of clever dialectics which had great vogue with the religious public of his day; 'Reason and Faith' (1866); 'The Superhuman Origin of the Bible' (1873); and two series of 'Essays' (1850–55).

Rogers, James Edwin Thorold. An English economist; born in Hampshire in 1823; died at Oxford, Oct. 12, 1890. He was professor of political economy at Oxford, and will be remembered as a historian of economics. His principal work is 'The History of Agriculture and Prices in England' (1866–88), of which 'Six Centuries of Work and Wages' (1885) is an abridgment. Among his other writings are: 'Cobden and Modern Political Opinion' (1873); 'The First Nine Years of the Bank of England' (1887); 'The Economic Interpretation of History' (1888); and 'The Industrial and Commercial History of England' (1892).

Rogers, Robert. An American soldier and author; born at Dunbarton, N. H., 1727; died in England in 1800. He commanded during the French and Indian War (1755-63) the celebrated corps known as "Rogers's Rangers." Later he published in England: 'A Concise Account of North America' (1765); 'Journal of Major Robert Rogers' (1765); and 'Ponteach [Pontiac]; or, The Savages of America,' a tragedy in blank verse, copies of which are now very rare. He also left in MS. 'A Diary of the Siege of Detroit in the War with Pontiac,' first published in 1860.

Rogers, Samuel. An English poet; born at Newington Green, London, July 30, 1763; died in London, Dec. 18, 1855. His wealth, liberality, and social qualities, gave his productions a great vogue. His best poem is the 'Pleasures of Memory' (1792), which passed through fifteen editions. He wrote also: 'The Voyage of Columbus' (1812); 'Jacqueline' (1813); 'Human Life' (1819); and 'Italy' (1822),— all highly prized for their exquisite illustrations. He was the intimate friend of nearly all the literary men of his time in Great Britain.

Rohan, Henri de (rō-oṅ'). A French general and military writer; born in Brittany, Aug. 25 (or 21), 1579; died April 13, 1638. He is less remarkable for military achievements than for his four books of memoirs: the first three published under the title 'Memoirs on Events in France from the Death of Henry the Great to June 1629' (1644), covering the civil wars; and the fourth as 'Memoirs and Letters on the War of the Valtelline' (1758), whither Richelieu had sent him to keep off the Imperialists and the Spanish. They rank among the finest of the memoirs written by the aristocracy of the 16th and 17th centuries. He also wrote 'The Perfect Captain' (1636), a political tract; and others.

Rohlfs, Anna Katherine (Green). See Green.

Roig, Jaume (rō'ēg). A Spanish (Valencian) poet of the 15th century. Although physician to Queen Maria (wife of Alphonso V.), he wrote a work full of invectives against the fair sex, intermingled with many moral precepts, under the title of 'Book of very Salutary and Profitable Counsels, as much for the Regulation and Order of a Good Life, as for Augmenting the Devotion to the Purity and Conception of the Virgin Mary' (1531). Copies of this work are now very rare. He occupies one of the first places among the Spanish poets who followed and emulated the troubadours.

Rojas y Zorilla, Francisco (rō'häs ē thō-rēl'yä). A Spanish dramatist; born in Toledo, Oct. 4, 1607; died probably after 1680. Twenty-four of his plays are now extant, which were published in two parts (1640 and 1645). The finest is 'None Below the King,' considered one of the classics among Spanish plays. Other notable ones are: 'There is No Friend for a Friend'; 'What Women Are'; 'Persiles and Sigismunda,' taken from Cervantes's romance; 'The Simpleton's Sport'; and 'The Insult Avenged.'

Roland, Madame — Manon Jeanne Phlipon. A French author and republican politician; born in Paris, March 17, 1754; executed Nov. 8, 1793. She imbibed republican ideas from Rousseau and her classical readings, and her salon was the meeting-place of the Girondist party. She is well known for her 'Memoirs,' written in prison, and edited by Dauban (1864); as were her 'Letters' (1869).

Rolfe, William James. An American editor; born in Newburyport, Mass., Dec. 10, 1827. He is a distinguished Shakespearean scholar, and has published many editions of Shakespeare, annotated; among them 'The Friendly Edition,' in 20 vols. (1870–83), and a 'School Edition,' in 40 vols. He has also published:

'Shakespeare, the Boy'; annotated editions of selections from Tennyson, Scott, Browning, Wordsworth, Gray, Goldsmith, and other English poets; several classical text-books; and 'Tales from English History'; Life of Shakespeare.'

Rolland, Amédée (rol-län'). A French littérateur; born at Paris, February 1819; died July 26, 1868. Besides contributions to many journals, he published two books of verse, 'At the Bottom of the Glass' (1854) and 'The Poem of Death' (1866); and several plays, including 'The Merchant in Spite of Himself' (1858); 'An Upstart' (1859); 'Our Ancestors' (1859).

Rollenhagen, Georg (röl'en-hä''gen). A German poet; born at Bernau, April 22, 1542; died at Magdeburg, May 20, 1609. His great work is the remarkable heroic-comic and didactic poem entitled 'Froschmeuseler, the Grand Court of the Frogs and Mice' (1595); where, under the guise of frogs, rats, mice, cats, and foxes, the author describes the poor people of his day,— their customs, domestic life, temporal and spiritual government, and lastly their military state. He also wrote 'The Limping Courier,' and the dramas, 'Abraham'; 'Tobit'; 'Lazarus.'

Rollett, Hermann (rol'let). An Austrian poet; born near Vienna, Aug. 20, 1819. He has published two collections of 'Wreaths of Song' (1842); 'Wanderings of a Vienna Poet' (1846); 'A Sister' (1847); 'War Songs' (1848); 'Oratorical Poems' (1871); 'Narrative Poems' (1872); and others. An American edition of his writings has appeared as 'Poems from the German of Hermann Rollett.' Died June 20, 1904.

Rollin, Ambrose Lucien (rō-lan'). A West-Indian historian; born at Trois Rivières, Guadeloupe, in 1692; died at Pointe à Pitre, in 1749. He devoted his leisure to researches upon the Caribs and other Indian tribes, and published several works which are still considered authorities upon the subjects he covered. They include: 'History of the Indians' (1739); 'The Indians and the Spanish Conquest' (1840); 'History and Description of the Caribs, their Condition after the Conquest' (1843); 'Civilization of the Indians Compared to their Social Condition' (1845); and 'The Incas of Peru and the Spanish Conquest' (1748).

Rollin, Charles. A French historian and humanist; born in Paris, Jan. 30, 1661; died there, Sept. 14, 1741. His best-known work is the 'Ancient History' (1730-38), often reprinted in France, England, and America, and not useless even yet as an entertaining popular work to create an interest in history. He wrote in an uncritical age, but he was a good story-teller and a keen judge of a good story. His other works include 'Roman History' (1738-48), and a 'Treatise on Study' (1726-31).

Rollinat, André (rō-lē-nä'). A French historian; born at Bordeaux in 1741; died at Nantes in 1793. He devoted himself to researches on the early navigators who have been credited with the discovery of America, and published 'Researches on the Forerunners of Christopher Columbus in America' (1785); 'The Norwegian Sagas and the Scandinavian Navigators' (1788); 'Table of the Tithes Paid to the Treasury of St. Peter during the Thirteenth and Fourteenth Centuries by Vinland' (1790); 'History of the Norse Navigators' (1791); and 'Researches on the Discovery of Brazil by a Dieppe Navigator of the Fifteenth Century' (1791).

Rollinat, Maurice. A French poet; born at Châteauroux (Indre), in 1853. In his first book of poems, 'In the Heaths' (1877), he reproduced in verse the most remarkable passages of George Sand's 'La Petite Fadette' and 'La Mare au Diable.' His other works include: 'Les Névroses' (1883), and 'The Abyss' (1886), besides his musical productions of 'Ten Melodies' (1877) and 'Rondels and Rondeaux' (1883). All of his poems have been received most favorably. Died Oct. 26, 1903.

Rollins, Alice Marland (Wellington). An American verse-writer; born in Boston, June 12, 1847; died Dec. 5, 1897. She has written: 'My Welcome Beyond, and Other Poems' (1885); 'All Sorts of Children' (1886); 'The Three Tetons' (1887); 'Uncle Tom's Tenement' (1888); and 'From Palm to Glacier.'

Romey, Louis Charles Réparat Geneviève Octave (rō-mā'). A French historian and miscellaneous writer; born at Paris, Dec. 26, 1804; died there, April 1874. After extensive travels, and a long sojourn in Spain, where he studied its history and literature, he returned to France and began to work upon his 'History of Spain from its Early Days to the Present Time' (1838-51); a history of great merit, but one which he never completed. His other writings include: 'Chateaubriand as Prophet' (1849); 'Ancient and Modern Russia' (1855); 'A Voyage among my Books' (1861); 'Men and Things of Various Times' (1864); many translations, notably that of 'Uncle Tom's Cabin' (1853); and many valuable contributions to periodicals.

Romieu, Auguste (rōm-yě'). A French administrator and littérateur; born at Paris, Oct. 17, 1800; died Nov. 20, 1855. He spent his youth in dissipation, and in the production of vaudevilles and brilliant witticisms; but after the Coup d'État, published two works of merit which attracted attention, 'The Era of the Cæsars' (1850) and 'The Red Spectre' (1851).

Rondelet, Antonin François (rôn-dlä'). A French professor and economist; born at Lyons, Feb. 28, 1823; died Jan. 24, 1893. His professor in philosophy, the Abbé Noirot, exerted upon him a most important religious and philosophic influence,—one so profound as to be felt in all his writings. He has written: 'Critical Exposition of the Ethics of Aristotle' (1847); 'Spiritualism in Political Economy' (1859); 'Memoirs of a Man of the World' (1861); 'The Science of Faith' (1867); 'Reflections upon Literature and Philosophy, Morals and Religion' (1881); 'The Book of Old Age' (1888); 'An Unfortunate Woman' (1890); and many others.

30

Ronsard, Pierre de (roṅ-sär'). A French poet; born at Château de la Poissonnière, Vendômois, Sept. 11, 1524; died Dec. 27, 1585. He was the first representative of the new school of literature, which completely disregarded the traditions and ideals of the native literature, and substituted the classic models of Rome and Greece. He and his followers began the creation of a new French literature, one which has reigned in France and other countries for centuries. He published: 'Odes' (1550); 'Amours' (1552); 'Hymns' (1555); and four books of his ambitious epic, 'La Franciade' (1572), never completed. His popularity waned after the advent of Malherbe, but his influence was never lost.

Ronsin, Charles Philippe (roṅ-saṅ'). A French dramatist; born at Soissons in 1750 or 1752; guillotined at Paris, March 24, 1794. He wrote six tragedies and two comedies: 'The League of Fanatics and Tyrants' (1791) and 'Arétophile' (1793) were played in Paris with most brilliant success.

Roosevelt, Robert Barnwell. An American lawyer and miscellaneous writer; born in New York city, Aug. 7, 1829. He is an enthusiastic sportsman, and has published: 'The Game Fish of North America' (1860); 'The Game Birds of the North' (1866); 'Superior Fishing' (1866); 'Florida and the Game Water Birds' (1868); 'Five Acres Too Much' (1869), a satire provoked by Edmund Morris's 'Ten Acres Enough'; and 'Progressive Petticoats,' a humorous satire on female physicians. Died 1907.

Roosevelt, Theodore. An American politician and author; born in New York city, Oct. 27, 1858. He allied himself with the civil-service reform movement. Became president of the United States 1901 and 1904. He has written: 'The Naval war of 1812' (1882); 'Hunting Trips of a Ranchman' (1885); 'Life of Thomas Hart Benton' (1887); 'Gouverneur Morris' (1888); 'Essays on Practical Politics' (1888); 'Ranch Life and the Hunting Trail' (1888); 'Winning of the West' (1889); 'History of New York City' (1891); and the 'Wilderness Hunter' (1893); 'American Ideals and Other Essays' (1897); 'Life of Oliver Cromwell' and 'The Strenuous Life' (1902). In 1906 he received the Nobel Prize for Promotion of Industrial Peace. In 1909 he undertook a hunting expedition to the heart of Africa in the interest of the Smithsonian Institution; contributing in the meantime articles for the 'Outlook' of New York, of which he is associate editor.

Root, George Frederick. An American musician and song-writer; 1820–1895. Among the the most popular of his songs are : 'Rosalie, the Prairie Flower' (1855); 'Shouting the Battle Cry of Freedom' (1861); 'Just Before the Battle, Mother' (1863); 'Tramp, Tramp, Tramp, the Boys are Marching' (1864); and the well-known quartet, 'There's Music in the Air.' His cantatas include 'The Flower Queen' (1852) and 'The Haymakers' (1857). He has done much to elevate the standard of music in this country, and has also published methods for the piano and organ, handbooks on harmony and teaching, etc.

Ropes, John Codman. A Russian-American lawyer and military historian; born at St. Petersburg, April 28, 1836, died in Boston, October 27, 1899. Besides contributions to the Military Historical Society of Massachusetts and to periodicals, he wrote : 'The Army under Pope' (1881); 'The First Napoleon' (1885); 'The Campaign of Waterloo'; and 'The Story of the Civil War.'

Roqueplan, Louis Victor Nestor (rōk-plän'). A French littérateur; born at Mallemort (dept. Bouches-du-Rhône), in 1804; died in Paris, April 24, 1870. He gained a reputation at the end of the Restoration by his contributions to literary journals, principally Figaro. He has published a number of clever books, among them being : 'News as Hand'; 'Regain of Parisian Life' (1853); and 'The Green-Rooms of the Opera' (1855).

Roquette, Adrien Emmanuel (rō-ket'). An American poet; born at New Orleans, La., Feb. 13, 1813; died there, July 15, 1887. He was chaplain to the Roman Catholic Seminary at New Orleans, and known as the Abbé Roquette. His principal works include : 'Les Savannes : American Poems' (1841), in which the 'Souvenir of Kentucky' is best known; 'Wild Flowers : Sacred Poetry' (1848); 'Deep Solitude in America' (1852); 'L'Antoniade; or, Solitude with God' (1860); 'Patriotic Poems' (1860); and 'Catherine Tehgahkwita' (1873). He wrote with equal ease and grace in English and French.

Roquette, Otto. A German poet; born at Krotoschin, Posen, April 19, 1824; died at Darmstadt, March 16, 1896. An instructor in Dresden and Berlin, he renounced this career and turned to the exclusive study of literature. He soon acquired a great reputation in his native land by his graceful poems, notably 'Waldermeister's Bridal Tour' (1851). He has published: a 'Song Book' (1852); 'History of German Literature' (1862–63); 'Dramatic Poems' (1867–76); 'Waldermeister's Silver Wedding' (1876); and others. Also a number of dramatic poems, including: 'The Enemy at Home'; 'The Serpent'; and 'The Garden of Roses' (1876).

Rosa, Salvator (rō'sä). An Italian painter and poet; born at Renella, near Naples, about 1615; died March 15, 1673. He wrote many lyric poems, which he set to music; and a number of satires, the best known of which are : 'War,' 'Envy,' 'Babylon,' 'The Painter,' 'Poetry,' and 'Music.' His writings display the same energy and life as are conspicuous in his paintings. His 'Satires' were published in 1710, and were incorporated with his 'Odes and Letters' (1860).

Rosa Gonzales, Juan de la (rō'sä gōn-thä'läs). A Spanish dramatist; born at Valladolid in 1820. His articles in criticism have placed him among the first of Spanish contemporary literary critics. He has also written lyric poetry, and a number of successful dramas, notably 'At the Cock's Mass'; 'With and Without

Reason'); 'The Counsels of Thomas'; 'The Son of the People'; 'The Spanish Adventurer'; and 'Jealousy of a Noble Soul.'

Roscoe, Thomas. An English translator and author; born at Toxteth Park, Liverpool, June 23, 1791; died at St. John's Wood, London, Sept. 24, 1871. He followed literature as a profession until within a few years of his death, and produced and translated many books. His original works include: 'Gonzola the Traitor: a Tragedy' (1820); 'The Tourist in Switzerland and Italy' (1830), followed by six volumes of a similar character; 'Legends of Venice' (1841); 'Life of William the Conqueror' (1846); 'The Last of the Abencerages, and Other Poems' (1850); and others. His translations comprise: 'Memoirs of Benvenuto Cellini' (1822); 'Italian Novelists' (1825); 'German Novelists' (1826); 'Spanish Novelists' (1832); and many others.

Roscoe, William. An English historian; born at Mt. Pleasant, Liverpool, March 8, 1753; died at Toxteth Park, Liverpool, June 30, 1831. His most important work, 'The Life of Lorenzo de' Medici' (1795), did much toward stimulating English interest in Italian literature. His 'The Butterfly's Ball and the Grasshopper's Feast' (1807), a nursery classic in verse, attracted the attention of the king and queen, and was set to music for the young princesses. Among his many other works may be named: 'A General View of the African Slave Trade' (1788); 'The Life and Pontificate of Leo the Tenth' (1805); and 'On the Origin and Vicissitudes of Literature, Science, and Art' (1817).

Roscommon, Wentworth Dillon, Earl of. An Irish poet; born in 1633; died in London, Jan. 17, 1684 or 1685. He devoted himself to the production of literature, much of it in conjunction with Dryden; and produced among other works: 'Essays on Translated Verse' (1684); a blank-verse paraphrase of Horace's 'Ars Poetica' (1680); and a translation of 'Dies Iræ.'

Rose, George. See **Sketchley.**

Rosegger, Petri Kettenfeier (rō'seg-cr). An Austrian poet and novelist; born at Alpl, a small village in the Styrian Alps, July 31, 1843. His youth was one of great poverty, and at 17 he was apprenticed to a tailor; but the exceptional merit of his poetry secured him patronage which enabled him to devote himself exclusively to literature. His first book, 'Zither and Cymbals' (1869), a collection of poems in the Styrian dialect, met with immediate success. The best known of his other works, which include stories, sketches, and novels, concerning the peasant life about him, are: 'Tales of the Alps' (1873); 'Out of the Woods' (1874); 'The Seeker after God' (1883); 'The Last Jacob' (1888); 'Hoch vom Dachstein' (1892); and 'Peter Mayr'; 'The Eternal Light'; 'Sunshine,' etc.

Rosell, Gayetano (rō-sel'). A Spanish littérateur; born in Madrid near 1815. He followed the career of a journalist, writing many

successful articles in criticism and history. He has published: 'The Mother of St. Frederick,' a drama well received; 'Before You Marry,' 'The Hypocrite,' and 'For a Watch and a Hat,' all comedies; 'History of the Naval Combat of Lepanto,' regarded as the best description of that battle ever written; and many translations.

Rosen, George, Baron de (rō'zen). A Russian poet; born at St. Petersburg in 1805; died in 1860. A friend and imitator of Pushkin, his 'Three Poems' (1827) met with immediate success; as did the succeeding volumes, including 'The Mystery' (1828); 'The Virgin among the Angels' (1828); and 'The Birth of Ivan the Terrible.' He has also written tragedies, operas, and translations. His poetry is harmonious, elegant, and full of melancholy; but lacks force and originality.

Rosenkranz, Johann Karl Friedrich (rō'zenkränts). A German philosopher; born at Magdeburg, April 23, 1805; died June 14, 1879. He was the best representative of the « centre » of Hegel's school, and spent much time in rearranging and reclassifying the system. His principal works, nearly all of which have received English versions, are: 'Psychology, or the Science of Subjective Mind' (1837); 'Critical Explanations of Hegel's System' (1840); 'Life of Hegel' (1844); 'Modifications of Logic' (1846); 'System of Science' (1850); 'Æsthetics of the Ugly' (1853); 'Autobiography' (1873); 'The History of Literature' (1875).

Rosenthal-Bonin, Hugo (rō'zen-täl-bō'nēn). A German novelist; born in Berlin, October 14, 1840; died at Stuttgart, April 7, 1897. He wrote a great number of novels, including: 'The Obstacle to Marriage' (1876); 'Subterranean Fire' (1879); 'The Diamond Polisher' (1881); 'Black Shadows' (1884); 'The House with Two Entrances' (1885); and 'The Captain's Daughter' (1887).

Rosetti or Roseti, Constantin (rō-zet'te). A Roumanian poet and politician; born at Bucharest, June 14, 1816; died April 19, 1885. He published a volume of poems under the title of 'Hours of Contentment' (1843); and wrote many political treatises, poems, and translations, a new edition of which appeared in Bucharest in 1885.

Rosier, Joseph Bernard (rōz-yä'). A French dramatist; born at Béziers, Hérault, Oct. 18, 1804; died at Marseilles, Oct. 12, 1880. His well-known comedies are bright and full of wit. They include: 'The Husband of my Wife' (1830); 'A Criminal Case' (1836); 'At Thirty Years' (1838); 'The Protégé' (1839); 'Raymond' (1851); 'Every One for Himself' (1856); and many others.

Rosini, Giovanni (rō-sē'ne). An Italian littérateur; born at Lucignano, Tuscany, June 24, 1776; died May 16, 1855. His poem entitled 'The Marriage of Jupiter and Latona' (1810), written upon the occasion of the marriage of Napoleon with Marie Louise, was awarded an imperial prize of 10,000 francs. His many works of prose and poetry include 'Poems' (1819); three historical romances, translated into many languages, — 'The Nun of Monza' (1829), 'Count Ugolin de la Gherardesca,' and 'Luisa Strozzi' (1833); and a historical drama, 'Torquato Tasso' (1835). He excels as a literary and artistic critic, and his 'History of Italian Painting' (1834) is highly valued.

Rosmini-Serbati, Antonio (roz-mē'nē). A noted Italian philosopher; born at Roveredo, Tyrol, March 25, 1797; died at Stresa, July 1, 1855. He produced some thirty volumes on ontology, theosophy, theodicy, pedagogy, supernatural anthropology, ethics, methodology, and other subjects; and he has disciples who consider his name the greatest in modern metaphysics. English translations of his 'Psychology' and 'Pedagogy' have appeared. But his most important work is 'New Treatises on the Origins of Ideas' (1830).

Rosmini, Carlo de. An Italian historian and biographer; born at Roveredo, Oct. 29, 1758; died at Milan, June 9, 1827. After some attempts at poetry and poetic criticism, he wrote his finest work, 'Life of Victorin de Feltre' (1801). Among his many other books may be named: 'Life of Ovid' (1789); 'Memoirs on the Life and Writings of Clement Baroni Cavalcabro' (1798); 'The Exemplary Life and Death of Marie Josephine Repetti, a Young Milanese' (1815); and 'History of Milan' (1820). He was a most conscientious hagiographer, withdrawing from the world and living almost the life of a hermit that he might devote himself more closely to his work.

Rosny, Antoine Joseph Nicolas de (rō-nē'). A French miscellaneous writer; born at Paris in 1771; died at Valenciennes, Oct. 21, 1814. He was one of the most prolific writers of his century. His first book, 'The Unfortunates of La Galetière' (1796), a romance, was followed with almost inconceivable rapidity by more than eighty volumes, among them being: 'Life of Florian' (1797); 'The Oracle of Apollo' (1800); and 'Literary View of France during the Thirteenth Century' (1809), an attempt to finish the work on the literary history of France, material for which had been collected by the Benedictines of St. Maur. Chagrin at the miserable failure of his project hastened his death.

Ross, Albert. See **Porter, Linn Boyd.**

Ross, Alexander. A Scotch poet; born in Aberdeenshire, April 13, 1699; died at Lochlee, Angus, May 20, 1784. He wrote verses from his childhood, but published nothing until 69, when he brought out 'Helenore, or the Unfortunate Shepherdess' (1768), written in the Buchan dialect, which became exceedingly popular in the north of Scotland. He also left in MS. eight volumes of miscellanies.

Ross, Clinton. An American novelist; born in New York in 1861. He has published: 'The Silent Workman' (1886); 'The Gallery of a Random Collector' (1888); 'The Countess Bettina'; 'The Speculators'; 'Adventures of Three

Worthies'; 'Improbable Tales'; 'Two Soldiers and a Politician'; 'The Puppet'; 'The Scarlet Coat'; 'Battle Tales'; 'Bobbie McDuff'; 'The Meddling Hussy'; and 'Zuleika.'

Ross-Church, Mrs. Florence. See **Marryat, Florence.**

Rossetti, Christina Georgina (rō-set'ē). An English poet, sister of Dante Gabriel; born in London, Dec. 5, 1830; died Dec. 29, 1894. 'Goblin Market' (1862) is regarded as her finest production. Her other writings consist chiefly of lyric poems of great beauty, and sonnets mostly of a grave and simple devotional order. They include: 'The Prince's Progress' (1866); 'Commonplace, and Other Short Stories' (in prose: 1870); 'Sing-Song: A Nursery Rhyme Book' (1872); 'Annus Domini: A Prayer for Each Day in the Year' (1873); 'Speaking Likenesses' (1874); 'Seek and Find' (1879); 'A Pageant, and Other Poems' (1881); 'Letter and Spirit' (1883); 'Verses' (1893); and several posthumous works.

Rossetti, Dante Gabriel. The celebrated English painter and poet; born in London, May 12, 1828; died at Birchington, Kent, April 10, 1882. He was foremost among the founders of the Pre-Raphaelite brotherhood. He began writing verse when but a few years old, and his 'Blessed Damozel' was published at 19; four years later he wrote the remarkable poem 'Sister Helen.' His other works include the translations of 'Early Italian Poets' (1861), reissued as 'Dante and his Circle'; the magnificent ballads 'Rose Mary' (1871), 'The White Ship' and 'The King's Tragedy' (1880); the sonnet-sequence 'The House of Life'; and an imaginative work in prose, 'Hand and Soul.'

Rossetti, Gabriele. An Italian poet, father of Dante Gabriele; born at Vasto, Naples, March 1783; died in London, April 26, 1854. In 1820 he composed the hymn 'The Beautiful One with Seven Stars in her Hair,' which became rapidly popular and is still classed among Italian patriotic songs. Compelled to flee Italy for participation in the insurrections of 1820 and 1821, he established himself in England as a teacher of Italian, and published several works dealing with the esoteric anti-papal significance of the 'Divine Comedy.' They include: 'Divina Commedia' (1826); 'Dante's Beatrice' (1842); and 'The Anti-Papal Spirit which Led to the Reformation' (1832), translated into English by Miss C. Ward (1834).

Rossetti, William Michael. An English poet and art critic, brother of Dante Gabriel; born in London, Sept. 25, 1829. He is the author of 'Dante's Comedy — The Hell, Translated into Literal Blank Verse' (1865); 'Poems and Ballads: A Criticism' [of Swinburne] (1866); 'A Life of Percy Bysshe Shelley' (1869); and 'Life of John Keats' (1887). He has edited the works of many poets.

Rossi, Ernesto (rōs'ē). An Italian actor and dramatist; born at Leghorn, 1829. Though known chiefly as an actor, he has written several plays, including 'Adèla,'—a drama for Mme. Ristori, with whom he has appeared,—'The Hyenas,' a social comedy, and 'The Soldier's Prayer'; also a treatise on 'Hamlet'; 'Dramatic Studies' (1882); 'Forty Years of Artistic Life,' a collection of historical essays and personal recollections; and 'Niccolai' (1887-90). He died June 4, 1896.

Rost, John Christopher (rōst). A German poet; born at Leipsic, April 7, 1717; died in 1765. He made a reputation by his lively satires against the Saxon school; particularly the one entitled 'The Prelude' (1742: a sort of epic satire in five songs), and 'The Devil's Epistle' (1754). He also wrote many pastorals, among them being 'Learned Love' (1742), the grace of which equals its licentiousness; a collection of 'Letters' (1766); and 'Various Poems' (1769).

Rostan, Joseph André de (rōs-tän'). A French dramatist; born at Constantinople, Sept. 13, 1819. He has written, either in French or in Spanish, 'Egill the Demon' (1847), a lyric drama; 'The Last Troubadour'; 'The Daughter of Voltaire' (1859); 'In the Kneading Trough' (1866); besides vaudevilles, librettos of operas, verse, romances, and critical articles. He himself undertook the publication of his 'Works: French and Spanish' (1863).

Rostand, Joseph Eugène Hubert (rōs-tän'). A French poet and littérateur; born at Marseilles, June 23, 1843. The following collections of poems have made his reputation: 'Sketches' (1865); 'The Second Page' (1866); 'Simple Poems' (1874); 'The Paths of Righteousness' ('Les Sentiers Unis': 1886); and the poems of Catullus translated into French verse (1880). He has also published: 'Questions of Social Economy in a Great City' (1889); 'A Visit to Some Bureaus of Pension and Insurance in Italy' (1891).

Rota, Vincent (rō'tä). An Italian littérateur; born at Padua in 1703; died there in 1785. He wrote a great number of theatrical pieces, remarkable for their facility of expression and their witty but not unkind satires; including 'The Dead Alive,' 'The Icy Shepherd,' and 'The Fantasm.' He also wrote 'The Conflagration of the Time of St. Anthony of Padua: A Tale' (1749), in imitation of Boccaccio; and many dialogues and epistles in Latin.

Rotalier, Charles Édouard Joseph (rō-täl-yä'). A French historian and publicist; born at Villerspoz near Colombier, in 1804; died July 21, 1849. He began his literary career with two romances, 'The Captive of Barberousse' and 'The Daughter of the Dey,' suggested by his sojourn in Africa in command of a regiment. But he soon abandoned fiction for more serious work, and wrote the 'History of Algiers,' a strong and brilliant production, still considered an authority upon the subject; and 'France and her Relations with Europe,' a work which at once placed him in the highest rank of the publicists of his day.

Rotgans, Lucas (rot'gäns). A Dutch poet; born in Amsterdam, October 1645; died at Kromwyck, Nov. 3, 1710. He wrote an epic poem of great merit, in eight cantos, of which the hero is William of Orange (William III. of England); two tragedies, 'Æneas and Turnus' and 'Scylla,' played with great success for a long time; 'The Parish Feast,' a descriptive poem in two songs; and 'Miscellaneous Poems.'

Rotrou, Jean (rō-trō'). A French dramatist; born at Dreux, Aug. 21, 1609; died June 27 or 28, 1650. He was but 19 when his first piece was played; it was 'The Hypochondriac' (1628), a tragicomedy in five acts. His chef d'œuvre is 'Venceslas,' a tragedy founded on the Spanish play of Francesco de Rojas, 'One Cannot be Both Father and King.' He produced a great number of other plays, the finest of which are 'St. Genest,' 'Don Bertrand de Cabrère,' and 'Cosroës.'

Rotteck, Karl Wenzeslaus Rodecker von (rot'ek). A German historian; born at Freiburg, Baden, July 18, 1775; died there, Nov. 26, 1840. His 'Universal History' (1813-27), and its minor compendium, 'Universal History of the World' (1830), exercised a great and beneficial influence upon the middle classes of Germany. Both books have been often reprinted and translated into several languages.

Roucher, Jean Antoine (rö-shä'). A French poet; born Feb. 17 or 22, 1745, at Montpellier; guillotined at Paris, July 25, 1794. He wrote an epithalamium on the marriage of Louis XVI. and Marie Antoinette, entitled 'France and Austria at Hymen's Temple.' But his principal production is the didactic poem in five songs, 'The Months' (1779), which was ridiculed on its first appearance, but later acknowledged and admired by the literary world. He also translated Adam Smith's 'Wealth of Nations' (1790). His letters to his family while in prison were published under the title of 'The Consolations of my Captivity' (1797).

Rougemont, Michel Nicolas Balisson de (rözh-môn'). A French dramatist, novelist, and journalist; born at La Rochelle in 1781; died in July 1840. His dramatic compositions are almost innumerable. The most remarkable are: 'The Supposed Husband' (1806); 'The Supper of Henry IV.' (1810); 'The Marriage of Charlemagne' (1811); 'The Fête of Henry IV.' (1826). Among his many other poems, romances, and feuilletons are: 'The Return of the Hero' (1805), a poem; 'Song-Book of the Bourbons' (1814); 'Bonhomme; or, Observations upon Parisian Manners and Customs at the Beginning of the Nineteenth Century' (1818); 'The French Rover' (1816-22); and 'Spain Delivered' (1823).

Rouget de Lisle, Claude Joseph (rö-zhä' dě lēl'). A French officer and song-writer; born at Lons-le-Saunier, May 10, 1760; died at Choisy-le-Roi, June 26 or 27, 1836. He composed both words and music of 'La Marseillaise,' when he was an officer of engineers at Strasburg, on the night of April 25, 1792. It first appeared under the title of 'Song of the Army of the Rhine.' He wrote several other fragments of songs, included in his 'Fifty French Songs, Words of Various Authors, Set to Music by Rouget de Lisle' (1825); and other poems, stories, and plays, of but little merit.

Roumanille, Joseph (rö-män-ēl'). A French (Provençal) poet; born at Saint Remy (Bouches-du-Rhône), Aug. 8, 1818; died at Avignon, May 24, 1891. He was one of the most popular authors of the Society of Félibres. Apart from his improvisations, for which he was noted, he produced: 'Li Margarideto' (1847); 'Le Campano Mountado' (1857); 'Lis Oubreto' (1859); 'Li Conte Provençaueli Cascareleto' (1884); and others.

Roumieux, Louis (röm ye'). A French (Provençal) poet; born at Nîmes in 1829. Among his productions may be named: 'Li Bourgadiero' (1852), a collection of satires in the Nîmois dialect; 'Li Griseto' (1853); and 'Quan vou Prendre dos Lèbre à la Fes n'en Pren Ges' (1863), a comedy.

Rousseau, Jean Baptiste (rö-sō'). A French poet; born at Paris, April 1670; died at Brussels, March 17, 1741. He wrote a great number of odes, epistles, plays, allegories, songs, and epigrams; and although esteemed by his contemporaries "the prince of our lyric poets," is now looked upon as a mediocre writer. He brought out an edition of his 'Works' (1712); and many others have subsequently appeared.

Rousseau, Jean Jacques. The renowned French writer; born in Geneva, June 28, 1712; died at Ermenonville near Paris, July 2, 1778. He published: 'Memoir on the Shape of the Earth' (1738); 'Mme. de Warens' (1739); 'Dissertation on Modern Music' (1743); 'Does the Cultivation of the Arts and Sciences Tend to Promote Morality?' (1750); 'The Village Soothsayer' (1753); 'Narcissus' (1753); 'Letter on French Music' (1753); 'On the Origins and Foundations of Inequality among Mankind' (1755); 'On Political Economy' (1758); 'To D'Alembert on the Article 'Geneva' in the Encyclopedia' (1758); 'Letters to Voltaire,' variously dated; 'A Project of Perpetual Peace' (1761); 'The Social Contract' (1762); 'Émile' (1762); 'To the Archbishop of Paris' (1763); 'The Departure of Silvie' (1763); 'Letters from the Mountain' (1764); 'Theatre Mimicry' (1764); 'Dictionary of Music' (1767); 'Letters on his Exile' (1770). Posthumously appeared 'Émile and Sophie' (1780); 'Consolations of my Life' (1781); 'Government of Poland' (1782); 'Confessions' (1782–90).

Rousseau, Pierre. A French dramatist; born at Toulouse, Aug. 19, 1716 or 1725; died at Bouillon, Nov. 10, 1785. He brought ridicule upon himself by assuming the title of "Rousseau of Toulouse" to distinguish himself from "Rousseau of Geneva." In collaboration with Favart, he published 'A Coquette Without Knowing It' (1744), and 'Mistakes' (1744), played with some success. He also

wrote 'The False Step' (1755), a novel; 'History of the Card-Sharpers' (1758); and others.

Rousseau, Pierre Joseph. A French littérateur; born at Paris in 1797; died there in 1849. He wrote a number of vaudevilles in collaboration with others, signed for the most part with the pseudonyms "James Rousseau" and "Maxime James." Among them are: 'The Lady of the Lake' (1825); 'The Fairy of the Neighborhood' (1826); and 'Love and Fear' (1827); also 'Memoirs of my Creditors' (1828), and other miscellanies.

Rousset, Camille Félix Michel (rö-sā'). A French historian; born at Paris, Feb. 15, 1821; died at Saint Gobain (Aisne), Oct. 20, 1892. Among his published works are: 'History of Louvois' (1861–63); 'The Volunteers of 1791–94' (1870); 'History of the Crimean War' (1877); and 'Beginnings of a Conquest: Algiers from 1830 to 1840' (1887).

Roux, Amédée (rö). A French littérateur; born at Billom, May 9, 1828. Besides a number of translations and the editing of the works of Voiture and letters of Count d'Avaux, he has published: 'A Misanthrope at the Court of Louis XIV.: Montausier' (1860); 'History of Italian Literature under the Régime of Unification' (1869–83); and 'Bird's-Eye View of Three Literatures' (1873).

Rowbotham, John Frederick. A Scotch miscellaneous writer; born in 1859. He resided in Germany several years, collecting material for his elaborate 'History of Music' (1885); after which he turned his attention to the study mediæval poetry, and published 'The Death of Roland: An Epic Poem' (1887); 'A Human Epic' (1902).

Rowe, Nicholas. An English dramatist and poet-laureate; born at Little Barford, Bedfordshire, June 30 (?), 1674; died Dec. 6, 1718. He was a successful courtier and politician, but is best known as the translator of Lucan's 'Pharsalia' (1718), and the author of many successful plays, the most popular of which were the tragedies: 'Tamerlane' (1702); 'The Fair Penitent' (1703); 'Jane Shore' (1714); and 'Lady Jane Grey' (1715).

Rowson, Susanna. An English-American actress, playwright, and novelist; born at Portsmouth, England, in 1762; died at Boston, Mass., March 2, 1824. She appeared on the American stage for about a year; after which she settled in Boston, opening a school and turning her attention to literary pursuits. She is famed as the author of 'Charlotte Temple: A Tale of Truth' (1790), which had an immediate and great success, and has long been a popular classic in America; and its sequel, 'Lucy Temple; or, The Three Orphans' (1828). Among her many other novels and farces may be named: 'Victoria' (1786), the characters of which were drawn from life; and 'The Inquisitor, or Invisible Rambler' (1788).

Roy, Just Jean Étienne (rwä). A French littérateur; born at Marnay (Haute-Saône), Oct.

13, 1794; died at Pontleroy, June 22, 1871. He published, under his own name and the pseudonyms of "Étienne Gervais," "Just Girard," and "Théodore Menard," a number of books, including the series entitled 'History of Fénelon' (1838); 'History of Louis XI.' (1842); 'Illustrations of the History of Germany, England, Egypt, Spain, France, Italy, Russia, and Sweden' (1843-45); 'History of Louis XIV.' (1844); 'France of the Twelfth Century' (1850); 'Modern Algiers' (1855); 'The Empire of Brazil' (1858); 'History of England' (1863); and many others, the greater number of which ran through many editions.

Roy, Pierre Charles. A French poet; born at Paris in 1683; died Oct. 23, 1764. His reputation rests largely upon his two plays, 'Callirhoé' (1712), generally conceded to be his best work, and 'Semiramis' (1718), regarded by some as even superior. His ballet 'The Elements' (1725) added to his reputation. His many odes, epilogues, plays, interludes, and ballets, were collected after his death and published as 'Various Works' (1727). His epigrams have made him famous in his own country; his last one involved him in a fatal quarrel.

Royce, Josiah. An American educator and author; born at Grass Valley, Cal., Nov. 20, 1855. He became professor of the history of philosophy in Harvard in 1892, and has published: 'A Primer of Logical Analysis' (1881); 'The Religious Aspect of Philosophy' (1885); 'California' (1886); 'The Feud of Oakfield Creek' (1887), a novel; 'The Spirit of Modern Philosophy' (1892); 'Outlines of Psychology' (1903); 'The Relation of the Principles of Logic to the Foundations of Geometry' (1905).

Royer, Alphonse (rwä-ā'). A French dramatist and littérateur; born at Paris, Sept. 10, 1803; died there, April 11, 1875. After spending a number of years in the Orient, he turned to the production of dramatic literature, meeting with marked and lasting success. Many of his plays were written in collaboration with his friend Gustave Vaëz. They include: 'The Poor Boys' (1830); 'Venice the Beautiful' (1834); and 'Adventures of Travel' (1837). He also published a 'Universal History of the Theatre' (1869-71), and many literary miscellanies.

Rückert, Heinrich (rük'ert). A German historian, son of Friedrich; born at Coburg, Feb. 14, 1825; died at Breslau, Sept. 11, 1875. His works include the monographs: 'Life of St. Louis, Landgrave of Thuringia' (1850), and 'Brother Philip, of the Order of the Chartreux' (1855); also 'Annals of German History' (1850); 'History of the Middle Ages' (1852); and 'History of German Civilization at the Period of Transition from Pagan to Christian Times' (1853-54); and editions of 'King Rother' and 'Heiland.'

Rückert, [Johann Michael] Friedrich. A distinguished German poet and Orientalist; born at Schweinfurt, Bavaria, May 16, 1788; died at Neuses, near Coburg, Jan. 31, 1866. He published his 'German Poems' (1814),

containing the famous 'Panoplied Sonnets,'—directed against Napoleon,— under the penname of "Freimund Raimar"; that is, "the poet of the free mouth." His poetry is much admired for the ingenuity of its workmanship, its strength and imaginative grace, and is full of inspiration drawn from his patriotism and his studies of the legends of the Orient; but is philosophic rather than spontaneous. He published many translations from the Arabic, and wrote many original poems dealing with Oriental subjects; among them being: 'Oriental Roses' (1822); 'Songs and Legends of the Orient' (1837); 'Rostem and Suhrab: A Heroic Tale' (1838); and 'Brahman Tales' (1839). The most elaborate of all his works is 'The Wisdom of the Brahmans' (1836-39).

Rudagi, Farid-Addin Muhammad (rö-dä'jē). A Persian poet of the tenth century; born in the village of Rudag (whence he derived his name), in the region of Bokhara or Samarkand, toward the end of the ninth century; died about 954. Tradition makes him a sort of blind Homer, but regarding his blindness there is doubt. His literary activity was great. Of his very numerous verses only a very few are now extant, but the fragments show great literary merit.

Rudel, Gauffre or **Godefroy, Prince of Blaye** (rü-del'). A French troubadour of the twelfth century, who attached himself to the suite of Geoffrey, Count of Bretagne, son of Henry II. of England. He went to Syria in search of a fair countess of Tripoli, rumors of whose beauty had reached him; and was so overcome when he finally saw her and heard her voice that he fell dead at her feet. She buried him with great pomp, and retired to a convent to mourn him all her days. Petrarch makes mention of Rudel; and several bits of verse by him are extant in the MSS. of Provençal literature, now in the great libraries of Paris, Venice, and Rome. One of them has been published by Raynouard, as the 'Gem of the Original Poems of the Troubadours.'

Rueda, Lope de (rö-ā'dä). A Spanish dramatist of the sixteenth century; born at Seville; died at Cordova. He was leader of a troupe of actors; and in the elementary state of the stage in his day, himself undertook four rôles,— those of the negress, the brigand, the fool, and the Biscayan. He composed for his company a number of short pieces. His 'Works' (1567) comprise four comedies, notably 'Deceptions' and 'Eufemia'; seven "pasos" in prose; two colloquies; and 'The Wages of Love.'

Ruffini, Giovanni Domenico (rö-fē'nē). An Italian littérateur; born at Genoa, September 1807; died at Taggia, Nov. 2, 1881. Obliged to flee his native land for political reasons, he resided in France, Switzerland, and England, and later returned to Italy. He published in London his first romance, 'Lorenzo Benoni,' a sort of autobiography, related in a very engaging style. He also published 'Doctor Antonio' (1858), his best-known book; 'Les Paragreens' (1860); 'Lavinia'; 'Vincenzo'; 'Carlino.' Many of his works have been translated into French.

Ruge, Arnold (rö'gĕ). A German publicist; born at Bergen, Island of Rügen, Sept. 13, 1802 or 1803; died at Brighton, England, Dec. 31, 1880. He embraced with ardor the doctrines of Hegel, and attracted considerable attention by his philosophical criticisms in the Halle Year-Book. He joined Karl Marx in Paris, and published with him the 'German-French Year-Books' (1843-45). After the suppression of the paper which he started in Berlin, called Reform, he went to London and formed, in connection with Ledru-Rollin and Mazzini, the European Democratic Committee. Among his works are: 'Two Years in Paris' (1845); 'Poetic Pictures' (1847); 'Political Pictures' (1848) 'Our System' (1850); 'In Former Times' (1862-67); and 'Manifesto to the German People' (1886); also the Dramas; 'Schill and His People.' and 'The New World.'

Ruiz, Juan (rō-ēth'). A Spanish poet of the fourteenth century, known as Archpriest of Hita; born at Alcala or Guadalajara, in 1300; died about 1351. He is the most original of mediæval Spanish poets, and has left a poem on love and women, which, while purporting to treat of morality and the follies of earthly love, is in reality a text-book for the man who wishes to become a successful lover. He quotes from Ovid's 'Art of Love,' gives translations from the apologues of Latin and French fabulists, and relates his own experience as well. It is mingled rather incongruously with censures of the capital sins, and with philosophic maxims and verses on the Passion, ending with high praise of the Virgin Mary. It is interspersed with songs, the best of which are the 'Song of Scholars' and 'Song of the Blind.'

Rulhière, Claude Carloman de la (rül-yär'). A French historian and poet; born at Bondy near Paris, in 1735; died at Paris, Jan. 30, 1791. While aide-de-camp to Richelieu, he composed his 'Discourse upon Disputes,' a witty poem which Voltaire inserted in his 'Philosophic Dictionary.' In 1771 he was named political writer to the Minister of Foreign Affairs, and visited London and Poland in that capacity. His historical works are noted for their strict honesty and justice, and his poetry for its ease and freedom of expression. He excels in short tales and epigrams. His historical works include: 'Explanations of the Causes of the Revocation of the Edict of Nantes' (1788); 'Anecdotes of the Russian Revolution in 1762' (1797); and 'History of the Anarchy of Poland' (4 vols., 1807; 4th ed. 1862), his finest work. His poetry includes 'Rough Play' (1808), and many small fragments.

Rumford, Count (Benjamin Thompson). An American scientist, statesman, and philosopher; born at Woburn, Mass., March 26, 1753; died in Auteuil near Paris, Aug. 21, 1814. He was one of the many conservatives at the outbreak of the Revolution who were driven into the British ranks outright by the patriotic harrying of impatient neighbors. After serving England for a time, he entered the service of the Elector of Bavaria, rose to the position of Minister of War, and was finally created a count of the Holy Roman Empire. He took the title Rumford from the village of that name (now Concord, N. H.), where he had married. He spent the last years of his life at Auteuil, busily engaged in scientific researches, — particularly on the nature and effects of heat, studies with which his name is generally associated. As an administrator, military or civil, he showed immense practical capacity in improving the conditions of life for the lower ranks. His works include: 'Essays: Political, Economical, and Philosophical' (1797-1806); and studies in domestic economy, particularly of cookery.

Rūmī, Maulana Jalāl-ad-dīn (rö-mē'). A Persian Súfic poet and philosophic teacher; born at Balkh in Khorásán, Sept. 30, 1207; died Sept. 17, 1273. His great work is the 'Masnawí' or 'Mathnawí,'—a collection of precepts and tales, interwoven with comments on the Koran and sayings of the Prophet, comprising between thirty and forty thousand rhymed couplets; composed in honor of the Maulawí sect of dervishes, of which he was the founder. A versified translation of the first book was published by J. W. Redhouse (1881). He wrote also many spiritual and mystic odes, full of inspiration. His teachings and doctrines are still faithfully adhered to by this order, and studied and revered by the whole Eastern world as the guide to eternal bliss.

Rumohr, Karl Friedrich Ludwig Felix von (rö'mōr). A German historian, antiquary, and poet; born on his family estate of Reinhardsgrimme, near Dresden, in 1785; died at Dresden, July 25, 1843. A most industrious worker, he wrote books on almost every conceivable subject. The most interesting of them are: 'Explanations of Some Assertions regarding the Wealth of Greece in Objects of Plastic Art' (1811); 'Magazine of Art and History' (1816); 'Italian Researches' (1826-31), a profound history of art in Italy, and consulted to this day by students of the subject; 'The Spirit of Culinary Art' (1832); 'School of Good Breeding' (1834), where he lays down rules of etiquette for all classes and conditions of men, from the minister to the postilion and waiter; and 'Researches upon Maso di Finiguerra, Inventor of the Art of Printing upon Wet Paper,' etc. (1841).

Rumohr, Theodor Wilhelm. A Danish novelist; born at Copenhagen, Aug. 2, 1807. His many romances deal with the national heroes of Denmark, and include: 'Jacob Danneford' (1840); 'Niels Juel' (1877); and 'Peter Tordenskjold' (1877). His collected works appeared as 'Historical Pictures of the Fatherland' (1863).

Rundell, Elizabeth (now **Mrs. Andrew Charles**). An English painter, musician, poet, and author; born at Tavistock, Devonshire, 1826 or 1828. All her writings, whether poems or romances, have a deep religious tone. Her first and most widely read book is 'The Chronicles of the Schönberg-Cotta Family' (1863), published anonymously; and all that have followed have appeared as the works of "The Authoress of the Chronicles of the Schönberg-Cotta Family." They include; 'Diary of Mrs. Kitty Trevylyan' (1864); 'The Cripple of Antioch' (1864); 'Winifred Bertram' (1865); 'The Draytons and the Davenants' (1866), 'Against the Stream' (1873); 'Joan the Maid: Deliverer of England and France' (1879); 'Three Martyrs of the Nineteenth Century' (1885); and 'By Thy Glorious Resurrection and Ascension' (1888).

Runeberg, Johan Ludvig (rö'nè-berG). A Swedish poet; born in Jakobsstad, Finland, Feb. 5, 1804; died at Borgå, May 6, 1877. Although his whole life was spent in his native country, he wrote in Swedish. The most celebrated of his writings is 'Ensign Stål's Tales' (1848–60), a collection of ballads on the war between Sweden and Russia, and taking the Swedish side. Among his many poems, lyrics, and dramas, all of which are immensely popular in both Sweden and Finland, are the idyls 'Hanna' (1836), and 'Christmas Eve' (1841); 'The Elk-Hunter' (1832), and 'Nadeschda' (1841), two tales in verse; and 'The Kings at Salamis' (1863), a tragedy in antique form. He was happiest in the lyrical epic, and his style is characterized by a delicate and harmonious grace.

Rusden, George William. An English historian (of Australia); born in Surrey in 1819. He removed to New South Wales in 1834, and made elaborate researches on the history and languages of the Island Continent. He has published: 'Moyarra: An Australian Legend' (1851); 'Discovery, Survey, and Settlement of Port Philip' (1872); 'Translations and Fragments' (1874); 'History of New Zealand' (1883); and 'History of Australia' (1883), a most careful and detailed work.

Ruskin, John. The great English critic and essayist; born in Edinburgh, Feb. 8, 1819; died at Brantwood, Jan. 20, 1900. His books on art comprise: 'Modern Painters' (1843); 'The Seven Lamps of Architecture' (1849); 'The Stones of Venice' (1851–53); 'Pre-Raphaelitism' (1851); 'Giotto and his Works in Padua' (1853–60); 'Elements of Drawing' (1857); 'Political Economy of Art' (1857); 'The Two Paths' (1859); 'Elements of Perspective' (1859); 'Lectures on Art' (1870); 'Aratra Pentelici' (1872); 'Relation between Michael Angelo and Tintoret' (1872); 'The Laws of Fésole' (1877–78); 'The Art of England' (1883); Verona, and Other Lectures' (1893), etc. His many miscellaneous works on ethics, social science, political economy, mythology, botany, etc. published under fanciful titles, include among others: 'Munera Pulveris' (1862–63); 'Sesame and Lilies' (1865), one of his most popular books; 'The Ethics of the Dust' (1866); 'The Crown of Wild Olive' (1866); 'The Queen of the Air' (1869); 'The Eagle's Nest' (1872); 'Love's Meinie' (1873); 'Proserpina' (1875–86); 'Deucalion' (1875–83); and 'St. Mark's Rest' (1874–84). He also wrote a popular fairy tale, 'The King of the Golden River' (1851); 'Arrows of the Chace' (1880), letters to newspapers; 'Præterita,' autobiographical (1885–89); 'Fors Clavigera' (1871–84), miscellaneous counsels, moral, religious, economic, literary, etc.

Russell, Addison Peale. An American journalist and essayist; born in Wilmington, O., in 1826. He has published: 'Half-Tints' (1867); 'Library Notes' (1875); 'Thomas Corwin: A Sketch' (1881); 'Characteristics' (1884); 'A Club of One' (1887); 'In a Club Corner'; and 'Sub Cœlum.'

Russell, Dora. An English novelist; born in 18—. Her romances include: 'The Miner's Oath' (1872); 'Footprints in the Snow' (1877); 'Annabel's Rival' (1881); 'The Broken Seal' (1886); 'The Track of the Storm' (1888); and many others.

Russell, Irwin. An American verse-writer; born at Port Gibson, Miss., June 3, 1853; died at New Orleans, La., Dec. 23, 1879. He was among the first to put the negro character to literary account. His dialect and other verse was collected after his death and published as 'Poems' (1888).

Russell, W. Clark. An English-American novelist; born (of English parentage) in New York city, Feb. 24, 1844. He spent much of his early life at sea, and afterwards settled at Ramsgate, England. He has published a great number of sea stories and novels, among which are: 'The Wreck of the Grosvenor' (1878); 'A Sailor's Sweetheart' (1880); 'My Watch Below' (1883); 'A Sea Queen' (1883); 'Jack's Courtship' (1884); 'A Strange Voyage' (1885); 'The Frozen Pirate' (1887); 'The Death Ship' (1888); 'Marooned' (1889); 'The Romance of Jenny Harlowe' (1889); and 'The Good Ship Mohock' (1895); 'Abandoned'; 'Wrong Side Out' (1904).

Russell, William Howard, Sir. An English journalist; born at Lilyvale near Dublin, March 28, 1821. He was special correspondent of the London Times in the Crimea (1854–55); in India during the Sepoy Mutiny (1857–59); in the United States during the Civil War, and known as "Bull Run Russell"; and its war correspondent in the Franco-German War of 1870. He published: 'Extraordinary Men' (1853); 'The Crimean War' (1855–56); 'My Diary in India'; 'My Diary during the Last Great War' (1873); 'The Prince of Wales's Tour' (1877); 'Hesperothen' (1882); and others. He was knighted in 1895, in recognition of his services to journalism. Died 1907.

Ryan, Abram Joseph. An American priest and verse-writer; born at Norfolk, Va., Aug.

15, 1839; died at Louisville, Ky., April 22, 1886. It was while chaplain in the Confederate army that he wrote his well-known poem 'The Conquered Banner,' composed shortly after Lee's surrender. Later he went North for the purposes of lecturing and publishing his works, which have appeared as 'The Conquered Banner, and Other Poems' (1880); 'Poems, Patriotic, Religious, and Miscellaneous' (1880); and 'A Crown for Our Queen.' Other poems of his which are popular are: 'The Lost Cause,' 'The Sword of Lee,' 'The Flag of Erin,' and the epic 'Their Story Runneth Thus.' At the time of his death he was engaged upon a 'Life of Christ.'

Ryan, William Thomas Carroll. A Canadian author; born in Toronto, Ont., Feb. 3, 1839. Upon leaving the army, where he served during the Crimean War, he devoted himself to journalism and literature. He has edited and published a number of Canadian newspapers, has contributed articles and poems to magazines, and has lectured on the Liberal side. His published works, which he signs « Carroll Ryan,» are: 'Oscar, and Other Poems' (1857); 'Songs of a Wanderer' (1867); 'The Canadian Northwest and the Canadian Pacific Railway' (1875); and 'Picture Poems' (1884).

Rydberg, Abraham Viktor (rid'berG). A Swedish man of letters; born at Jönköping,

Dec. 18, 1829; died at Stockholm, Sept. 21, 1895. He was regarded as one of the best littérateurs of Sweden, and the translator seems to use his books more than those of any other modern Swedish writer. He produced several translations, among them Goethe's 'Faust'); a novel, 'The Last of the Athenians' (1859), a picture of the last conflict between Paganism and Christianity—translated into English, German, and Danish; many poems; a number of æsthetic and historical studies; and a series of works on the philosophy of religion, including 'The Doctrines of Christ according to the Bible' (1862), 'Magic of the Middle Ages' (1864), 'Romish Legends of the Apostles Peter and Paul' (1871), and 'The Primitive Patriarchs' Genealogies in Genesis' (1873). His 'Teutonic Mythology' (1886) is a brilliant piece of work, but useless from a scientific standpoint.

Rymer or **Rhymer, Thomas the** (Thomas Lermont of Erceldoune). A Scotch poet and prophet of the thirteenth century, who occupies an important place in the mythical and legendary literature of Scotland. His name is associated with many fragments of rhymed or alliterative verse, many of which have been collected and published as 'The Prophecies' (1691); and 'Sir Tristem: A Metrical Romance Edited by Sir Walter Scott from the Auchinleck MSS.' (1804).

S

Saar, Ferdinand von (sär). An Austrian poet; born at Vienna, Sept. 30, 1833. Among his works are the tragedies 'Hildebrand' (1865) and 'The Death of Henry' (1867)—these being united under the title 'The Emperor Henry IV.' (1872); 'Tales from Austria' (1877); 'Vienna Elegies'; 'Poems' (1882); 'Three New Novels' (1883); 'The Two De Witts'; 'Thassilo' (1886); 'The Castle of Kostenitz' (1893). He excels as a lyric poet and a story-writer. His lyrics are in a tone of melancholy, but the feeling is genuine and the expression unaffected.

Saavedra, Angel de, Duque de Rivas (sä-vä'drä). A Spanish statesman and poet; born in Cordova, March 10, 1791; died in Madrid, June 22, 1865. He was the author of 'Poetical Essays' (2 vols., 1813); 'Florinda' (1824-25), an epic on the Moorish conquest of Spain; 'The Moorish Foundling' (1834), a national epic; many dramas; a life of Masaniello (1860); and a history of the Neapolitan revolution (2 vols., 1848; new ed. 1881).

Saavedra Guzman, Antonio (sä-vä'drä göth'-män). A Mexican poet; born about 1550; died in Spain about 1620. He gave seven years' special study to the poetical and historical literature of his own country; utilizing the facts in his historical poem 'The Indian Pilgrim'

(1598), in 20 cantos, describing the glories of the Aztec court and the conquest of Mexico. Prescott has given him the name of «the poet-chronicler.»

Saavedra y Faxardo, Diego de (sä-vä'drä ē fä-här'dō). A Spanish moralist; born at Algezarez in Murcia, 1584; died at Madrid, Aug. 24, 1648. His most notable work is 'The Type of a Christian Prince' (1640), written for the instruction of the son of Philip IV., who died before attaining his majority. He wrote also the poem 'The Republic of Letters' (1670); a dialogue between Mercury and Lucian on the follies of European statesmen (first printed 1787); and 'The Gothic, Castilian, and Austrian Crown' (reprinted 1887).

Sabin, Joseph. An American publisher and bibliophile; born in Bramston, England, 1821; died in Brooklyn, N. Y., 1881. His store on Nassau Street, New York, was noted for rare books. He was famous for his knowledge of books, and his reprints of old and curious works. He edited the American Bibliographist; and published a 'Dictionary of Books relating to America' and a 'Bibliography of Bibliographies.'

Sacchetti, Franco (sä-ket'ē). An Italian poet; born at Florence about 1330; died about

1400. His most important work is the 'Three Hundred Stories'—of which only 223 remain, and some of these are mutilated : they give a faithful picture of life in those days, with many satiric allusions. Among his poems the best are the ballads and the madrigals.

Sacher-Masoch (säch'er-mäs'ŏch), **Leopold Ritter von.** An Austrian novelist; born at Lemburg, Jan. 27, 1835; died at Lindheim in Hesse, May 6, 1894. His very numerous stories show great powers of realistic description; among them are : 'Love' (1870); 'False Hermelin,' stories of theatrical life (1873); 'Love Stories from Divers Centuries' (1874); 'The Ideals of our Time' (1876); 'Property' (1877); 'The New Job' (1878); 'The Serpent in Paradise' (1890); 'The Solitaries' (1891); 'Merry Tales from the East' (1893); 'The Filled and the Hungry' (1894). His wife, Aurora von Rümelin, born at Gratz, 1846, wrote : 'Romance of a Virtuous Woman' (1873); 'The True Hermelin' (1879); 'Ladies in Furs' (1881).

Sachs, Hans (sächs). The German meistersinger; born at Nurembreg, Nov. 5, 1494; died Jan. 19 or 20, 1576. A complete collection of his works was published at Nuremberg (1558–79). See 'Hans Sachs' (1765); I. L. Hoffman, 'Hans Sachs' (1847); Kawerau, 'Hans Sachs und die Reformation' (1889); and E. Götze, 'Hans Sachs' (1891).

Sachs, Julius von. A celebrated German botanist; born in Breslau, Oct. 2, 1832; died at Würzburg, May 29, 1897. He paid special attention to the effects of light and heat upon plants. His great work 'History of Botany' (1875) covers the period 1500–1860. He also published 'Lectures on Plant Physiology' (1882), and a series of 'Treatises' (1892) on the same subject ; also a 'Manual of Botany' (English eds. 1875 and 1892).

Saco, José Antonio (sä'kō). A Cuban historical writer and publicist; born at Bayamo, 1797; died at Madrid, 1879. He wrote : 'A Parallel between Cuba and Certain English Colonies' (1838); 'Suppression of the Slave Trade in Cuba' (1845); 'Ideas on the Incorporation of Cuba into the United States' (1848); 'The Political Situation in Cuba and Its Remedy' (1851); 'History of Slavery from the Most Remote Times' (several volumes published in 1876 and years following; but the work is not completed).

Sacy, Antoine Isaac, Baron Silvestre de, a French Orientalist; born at Paris, Sept. 21, 1758 ; died Feb. 21, 1838. In 1792 he became member of the Academy of Inscriptions, and in 1808, professor of the Persian Language at the Collège de France. His writings include 'Arabian Grammar' (1810) ; 'Arabian Chrestomathy' (1806); 'Arabian Grammatical Anthology' (1829) ; 'Memoirs of various Persian Antiquities' (1793) ; a Translation of Abdul-Latif's 'Relation of Egypt' (1810); an edition of the Arabian Work 'Calila and Dimna' (1816) ; 'Memoirs and Translation of Oriental History and Literature' (1818) ; an edition of 'Pendnâmeh' (1819) and 'Makâmen' (1822) ; and his last and most important work 'The Exposition of the Religion of the Druses' (1828).

Sa'di (sä'dē). One of the celebrated Persian poets; born at Shiraz, 1184; died 1291 (?). Besides his 'Divan' he wrote 'Bustân' or The Fruit Garden (1257), and 'Gulistân' or The Rose Garden (1258), his two masterpieces. The 'Bustân' is a didactic poem in ten cantos of double rhymed verse, treating of the highest questions of philosophy and religion : it abounds in sound ethical maxims and noble passages of philosophical speculation. The 'Gulistân' is in prose, with verses interspersed.

Sadlier, Anna Teresa. An American writer and translator; born in Montreal, Canada, 1856. She has written much for the Roman Catholic press, has translated poems and tales from the French and Italian, and published : 'Ethel Hamilton, and Other Tales' (1877); 'The King's Page' (1877); 'Seven Years and Mair' (1878); 'Women of Catholicity' (1885); 'The Silent Woman of Alood' (1887); and a compilation, 'Gems of Catholic Thought' (1882).

Sæmund the Learned (sä'mŏnd). An Icelandic scholar of the 12th century. He traveled widely in pursuit of learning, visiting Paris and Rome, and afterward was a priest at Oddi. He was unknown to scholars till about 1643, when the then newly discovered Elder Edda was ascribed to him by Brynjulf Sveinsson, though the poems of that collection date in all probability back to the 8th or to the 9th century. Sæmund had in his day a great reputation for learning, and was regarded, like Friar Bacon, as a magician. He wrote a 'Book of the Kings' from Harold Fairhair to Magnus the Good. He died in 1133.

Sagard, Théodat Gabriel (sä-gär'). A French missionary to the Hurons in the 17th century. He wrote : 'Travels to the Huron Country, situate in America, toward the Freshwater Sea and the Uttermost Limits of New France, called Canada ; wherein is treated of all matters touching the country, the manners and character of the savages, their government and their ways, as well in their own country as when roaming ; of their faith and belief ; with a dictionary of the Huron language' (1632); also a 'History of Canada and the journey made by the Friars; Minor Recollets thither for the conversion of the unbelievers' (1636). A new edition of both works was published at Paris in 4 vols., 1866.

Saint-Aldegonde (saṅ-täl-dĕ-goṅd). See **Marnix.**

Saint-Amand, Imbert de (saṅt-ä-mäṅ'). See **Imbert.**

Saint-Amant, Marc Antoine Gerard, Sieur de (saṅt-ä-mäṅ'). A noted French writer of bacchanalian verses; born at Rouen, 1594; died at Paris, 1660. He wrote 'Moses Saved' (1653), an epic of the school of Tasso; and a number of short miscellaneous poems, among which those on bacchanalian scenes are the best,— 'The Revel' is one of the most remarkable of convivial poems.

Sainte-Beuve, Charles Augustin (sant-bėv'). A great French literary critic; born at Boulogne-sur-Mer, Dec. 23, 1804; died at Paris, Oct. 13, 1869. His first work, 'Picture of French Poetry in the 16th Century' (1828), made him famous. Then followed, anonymously, a volume of 'Poems' and two other volumes of verse, 'Consolations' (1829) and 'Meditations in August' (1837): in these are seen the influence of Goethe's 'Werther' and Châteaubriand's 'René.' His work in the field of the history of literature was resumed in 1837; and in 1840 began to appear his great work, 'History of Port-Royal' (6 vols., 1840–48; 4th ed. 7 vols. 1878). His celebrated 'Monday Talks' on books and authors were commenced in 1849, and were continued with brief intermissions till his death: they were reprinted in two series, 'Mondays' (15 vols., 1862) and 'New Mondays' (13 vols.). He wrote also: 'Literary Critiques and Portraits' (5 vols., 1832–39); 'Literary Portraits' (2 vols., 1844; 3 vols., 1864); 'Contemporary Portraits' (2 vols., 1846; 5 vols., 1871). His autobiography, 'Recollections and Indiscretions,' was published in 1872, and 4 volumes of his 'Correspondence' in 1877–80.

Saint-Évremond, Charles Marguetel de Saint-Denis, Seigneur de (sant-evr-môn'). A French satirist and literary critic; born at St. Denis near Coutances, in Normandy, April 1, 1610; died at London, Sept. 29, 1703. His chief fame is due to his ability as a literary critic; and his judgments were accepted as decisive on both sides of the Channel. His best works in this department are the satirical sketches 'Comedy of the Academicians' (1650) and his 'Judgment on Seneca, Plutarch and Petronius'; 'Reflections on Ancient and Modern Drama'; 'Discourse on French Historians.'

Saint Francis de Sales (säl *or* sāles). A French ecclesiastic and devotional writer; born 1567; died 1622. He founded the Order of the Visitation. He wrote: 'Introduction to the Devout Life'; 'A Treatise on the Love of God'; etc.

Saint-Gelais, Melin or **Merlin de** (san-zhe-lā'). A French lyric poet; born at Angoulême, Nov. 3, 1487; died at Paris, 1558. He affected the Italian forms of poetry,—the terza rima and sonnet,—and was the first French poet to write madrigals.

Saint-Hilaire, Barthélemy. See Barthélemy-Saint-Hilaire.

Saint-Hilaire, Marco de, pseudonym of **Émile Marc Hilaire** (sant-ē-lār'). A French miscellaneous writer; born about 1796; died Nov. 5, 1887. A literary trifler of small success, he later adopted the line of glorifying Napoleon as the hero of democracy, and contributed in no small degree to foster "Napoleonic ideas" and to prepare the way for the second empire. Among his works of this kind are: 'Recollections of the Private Life of Napoleon' (1838); 'The Emperor's Aides-de-Camp' (1841); 'Popular History of Napoleon' (1842); 'History of the Russian Campaign' (1846–48).

Saintine, originally **Joseph Xavier Boniface** (sant-ēn'). A French littérateur and dramatist; born in Paris, July 10, 1798; died there, Jan. 21, 1865. He wrote about 200 plays. His story 'Picciola' ran through forty editions.

St. John, Bayle. An English miscellaneous writer, son of James A.; born at London, Aug. 19, 1822; died Aug. 1, 1859. Among his works are: 'Eccentric Love: A Novel' (1845); 'Adventures in the Libyan Desert' (1849); 'Views of the Oasis of Siwah' (1850); 'Purple Tints of Paris' (1854); 'Travels of an Arab Merchant in Soudan' (1854); 'The Sub-Alpine Kingdom' (1856); 'Martineto: A Story of Adventure' (1856); 'Legends of the Christian East' (1856).

St. John, James Augustus. An English Orientalist and miscellaneous author; born in Caermarthenshire, Wales, Sept. 24, 1801; died Sept. 22, 1875. He was an extensive traveler. Among his numerous works are: 'Egypt and Mohammed Ali' (1834); 'Description of Egypt and Nubia' (1844); 'Isis: An Egyptian Pilgrimage' (1853); 'The Nemesis of Power' (1854); a treatise on 'The Education of the People' (1858).

St. John, Percy Bolingbroke. An English novelist and miscellaneous writer, son of James A.; born at London, March 4, 1821; died March, 1889. He published among others: 'The Young Naturalist's Book of Birds' (1844); 'Three Days of the French Revolution' (1848); 'An Arctic Crusoe' (1854); 'Quadroona' (1861); 'The Creole Bride' (1864); 'The Snow Ship' (1865); 'The North Pole' (1875); and 'A Daughter of the Sea' (1884).

St. John, Spenser, Sir. An English diplomatist, and writer of books embodying the knowledge so gained; son of James A.; born in London, Dec. 22, 1825. He was private secretary to Rajah Brooke (1848), consul-general to Siam (1850), Borneo (1855), etc.; and published 'Life in the Forests of the Far East' (explorations of Borneo, Sarawak, Suluk Islands, etc.: 2 vols., 1862), and 'Life of Sir James Brooke' (2 vols., 1879). Later he was consul-general to Hayti (1861–62), and many years in the West Indies in different positions; and wrote 'Hayti; or, The Black Republic' (1884), an awful picture of the retrogression of the negro State toward savagery. He was also minister to Peru in 1874 and 1881, and to Mexico in 1884.

St. John-Brennon, Edward. An Irish poet; born at Dublin, Feb. 21, 1847. He wrote: 'Bianca, the Flower Girl of Bologna' (1866); 'Ambrosia Amoris' (1869); 'Two Gallian Laments'; 'The Witch of Nemi'; 'The Tribune Reflects.'

Saint-Lambert, Jean François, Marquis de (san-läm-bār'). A French philosopher and poet; born at Nancy, Dec. 26, 1716; died at Paris, Feb. 9, 1803. He won fame by his poem 'The Seasons' (1769), for which the encyclopedists and Voltaire prophesied immortality;

but it has little merit either in style or in substance. Far better are his 'Fugitive Poems' (1759); and his 'Stories,' republished 1883. His 'Universal Catechism,' despite its materialistic principles, was approved by the Institute in 1810, as a text-book on ethics.

Saint-Marc-Girardin, François Auguste (san-mark' zhē-rär-dan'). A French literary critic; born at Paris, Feb. 12, 1801; died April 11, 1873. With Philarète Chasles he wrote 'View of French Literature in the 16th Century' (1828), which won the first prize of the Academy. He wrote also: 'Political and Literary Notes on Germany' (1835); 'Intermediate Education in Germany' (2 vols., 1835–38); 'Essay on Literature and Morals' (2 vols., 1845); 'Course of Dramatic Literature; or, The Use of the Passions in the Drama' (1843; 11th ed. 5 vols., 1875–77); 'Recollections and Political Reflections of a Journalist' (1859); 'Lafontaine and the Fabulists' (2 vols., 1867); 'J. J. Rousseau, his Life and Works' (2 vols., 1875).

Saint-Pierre, Bernardin de (san-piär'). The celebrated author of 'Paul and Virginia'; born in Havre, Jan. 19, 1737; died at Eragny-sur-Oise, Jan. 21, 1814. His works include: 'Voyage to the Isle of France' (1773); 'Studies of Nature' (1784); 'Vows of a Solitary' (1789); 'The Indian Cottage' (1790); 'Harmonies of Nature' (179–); 'On Nature and Morality' (1798); 'Voyage to Silesia' (1807); 'The Death of Socrates' (1808); 'Essay on Newspapers' (1808); 'Essay on J. J. Rousseau' (1809?); 'Stories of Travel' (1809–12); etc.

Saint-Pierre, Charles Irénée Castel, Abbé de. A French philanthropist; born at St. Pierre (Normandy), Feb. 18, 1658; died April 29, 1743. Among his writings are: 'Project of Universal Peace' (3 vols., 1713); 'Polysynody,' a severe stricture on Louis XIV.'s government, and a plan for the administration of the affairs of the kingdom by a system of councils for each department of the government; and a number of projects for the betterment of society in every way.

Saint-Réal, César Richard, Abbé de (san-rä-äl'). A French historian, called "the French Sallust"; born at Chambéry, 1639; died there, 1692. He was official historian of Savoy, and wrote a 'History of the Spanish Conspiracy of 1618 against the Republic of Venice' (1674), his principal work. His historical novel, 'Don Carlos,' is the chief source of Schiller's drama of that name. His works have been often reprinted (8 vols., 1757).

Saintsbury, George Edward Bateman. An eminent English critic and literary historian; born at Southampton, Oct. 23, 1845. He has been a master in Elizabeth College, Guernsey, head-master of the Elgin Educational Institute (1874–76), and a constant contributor to British reviews. He is noted for his profound learning, sound judgment, and lucid style. Among his numerous works are: 'A Primer of French Literature' (1880), in universal use; 'Life of

Dryden' (1881); 'Short History of French Literature' (1882); 'Life of Marlborough' (1885); 'History of Elizabethan Literature' (1887); 'Essays on French Novelists' (1891); 'The Earl of Derby' (1892); 'Corrected Impressions' (1895), essays on Victorian writers; 'History of 19th-Century Literature, 1780–1895' (1896). He has also edited the 'Pocket Library of English Literature' (6 vols.,); 'The Earlier Renaissance.'

Saint-Simon, Claude Henri, Count de (san sē-mōn'). A French socialist reformer; born at Paris, Oct. 17, 1760; died May 19, 1825. His first work, 'Letters of an Inhabitant of Geneva to his Contemporaries' (1802), proposed a scientific reconstruction of society; to the same end he wrote: 'Reorganization of European Society' (1814); 'The Organizer' (1820); 'The Industrial System' (3 vols., 1821–23); 'Literary, Philosophical, and Industrial Opinions' (1825); 'Industrial Catechism' (1825); 'The New Christianity'; 'Literary, Philosophical and Industrial Opinions.'

Saint-Simon, Louis de Rouvroy, Duc de. A celebrated French annalist; born Jan. 16, 1675; died March 2, 1755. His 'Memoirs' are among the principal sources of the personal history of France during his lifetime. The 'Memoirs' were first published in 20 vols. (1756–58), and afterward in "complete and authentic" form in 21 vols. (1829–30); to them succeeded 'Unpublished Writings' (8 vols., 1886–92) and 'Unpublished Papers, Letters, and Dispatches on the Embassy to Spain' (1880).

Saint Victor, Adam de (san vēk-tor'). A French poet who flourished in the twelfth century, and is especially revered for his beautiful and elevated Latin hymns.

Saint-Victor, Jacques Benjamin Maximilien, Count de. A West-Indian author; born in Fort Dauphin, San Domingo, Jan. 14, 1770; died in Paris, Aug. 8, 1858. He was connected with the Journal des Débats under Napoleon, and established several Roman Catholic and Royalist magazines. His writings include: 'Paris from the Time of the Gauls to our Own Day' (3 vols., 1808–12); 'Poetic Works' (1822); 'Letters on the United States, Written in 1832–33' (2 vols., 1835); and 'Journal of Travel' (2 vols., 1836).

Saint-Victor, Paul Binsse, Count de. A French literary and art critic and journalist; born at Paris, July 11, 1825; died there, July 9, 1881. He rose to distinction first through his weekly critiques of the stage and of the annual exhibitions of fine art. His two principal works are: 'Men and Gods' (1867; 4th ed. 1872), a volume of historico-æsthetic studies, among which the essay on 'The Venus of Milo' merits special mention; and 'The Two Masques: A Tragedy-Comedy' (3 vols., 1880–83), an uncompleted work on the ancient and the modern stage. He wrote also: 'The Women of Goethe' (1869); 'Victor Hugo' (1885); 'Ancients and Moderns' (1886); 'The Theatre of To-day: E. Augier and A. Dumas fils' (1889).

Sala, George Augustus Henry. A famous English newspaper correspondent; born in London, Nov. 24, 1828; died at Brighton, Dec. 8, 1895. During the American Civil War he was correspondent (1863–64) of the London Telegraph, for the same paper in Algiers in 1864 and again in 1875, at the Paris Exposition in 1867, and during the Franco-German War, 1870–71. He published the novels 'Quite Alone' and 'Captain Dangerous'; 'America Revisited' (1882); 'London up to Date' (1894); and his own 'Life and Adventures' (1895). His celebrated 'Cook Book,' which sold enormously in London, shows his versatility and knowledge of human "internal affairs."

Sale, George. An English lawyer, and student of Arabic and Mohammedan history; born probably in Kent, about 1697; died in London, Nov. 13, 1736. He is most celebrated as the translator of the Koran, his version of which is still a standard; his introduction is particularly comprehensive, and appreciative of the Mohammedan religion. He contributed the Oriental biographies to the translation of Bayle's 'General Dictionary,' which was published in London in 10 vols. in 1734; and was one of the learned men selected to make the English 'Universal History,' but his part in the work was not published until 1739, after his death.

Sallust (Gaius Sallustius Crispus). A Roman historian; born in 87 B. C.; died at Rome, about 34 B. C. His known remaining works are : 'The Conspiracy of Catiline' and 'The History of the War against Jugurtha.' A lost history of his covered only the period from B. C. 78 to 67.

Salm-Dyck, Constance Marie de Theis, Princess of (säm-dēk'). A French poet and miscellaneous writer; born at Nantes, Nov. 17, 1767; died at Paris, April 13, 1845. She wrote a series of poetical 'Epistles,' one 'To Women,' another 'On the Blindness of this Age.' She also wrote : ' My Threescore Years' (1833); 'The Twenty-Four Hours of a Sensible Woman'; 'Cantata on the Marriage of Napoleon.'

Salomon ben Judah. See Avicebron.

Saltus, Edgar Everston. An American novelist; born in New York, June 8, 1858. He was educated in Europe, and graduated at the Columbia Law School. He is represented in fiction and miscellany by 'Balzac' (1884); 'The Philosophy of Disenchantment' (1885); 'The Anatomy of Negation' (1886); 'After-Dinner Stories' (1886), a translation from Balzac; ' Mr. Incoul's Misadventure' (1887); 'The Truth about Tristrem Varick' (1888); 'Eden' (1888); 'A Transaction in Hearts' (1888); 'The Pace that Kills' (1889); 'A Transient Guest' (1889); 'Love and Lore' (1890); 'Mary Magdalen' (1891); 'Imperial Purple' (1892); 'Madam Sapphira' (1893); 'Enthralled' (1894); 'When Dreams Come True'; 'The Pomps of Satan '; 'The Lords of the Ghostland.'

Saltus, Francis Saltus. An American poet, brother of Edgar; born 1849; died 1889. He is of the modern school of poets. He published

a book of poems, 'Honey and Gall,' in 1873; and another collection, bearing the title 'The Bayadere and Other Sonnets,' appeared in 1894.

Saltykov, Michail Yevgráfovich (säl'tē-kof); pseudonym, "N. Shtshedrin." A noted Russian satirist; born Jan. 27, 1826; died at St. Petersburg, May 12, 1889. The first work to give him celebrity throughout Russia was 'Sketches from the Provinces' (1856): it was followed by 'Satires in Prose' and 'Innocent Stories' (1863); 'Signs of the Times' (1869); 'Male and Female Pompadours' (1876); 'Across the Frontier'; 'An Idyll of To-day' (1884–86); 'Life's Pettinesses' (1887). The Russian press laws compel the author to use an allegorical style, which makes his meaning unintelligible to foreigners.

Sanborn, Katharine Abbott. An American miscellaneous writer and lecturer; born in Hanover, N. H., 1839. She was professor of English literature in Smith College for several years, and resigned in 1886. Her publications under the name of "Kate Sanborn" include : 'Home Pictures of English Poets'; the 'Round Table Series of Literature Lessons'; 'The Vanity and Insanity of Genius'; 'A Year of Sunshine'; 'Adopting an Abandoned Farm'; 'Abandoning an Adopted Farm '; 'Old Time Wall Papers.'

Sand, George (Baronne Dudevant: born **Amantine Lucile Aurore Dupin).** The celebrated French novelist; born in Paris, July 2, 1804; died at Nohant, June 7, 1876. Her works include : 'A Tourist's Letters' (1830–36); 'Indiana' (1831 ?); 'Valentine' (1832); 'L lie' (1833); 'Aldo the Poet' (1833); 'The Private Secretary' (1834); 'André' (1834); 'Leone Leoni' (1834); 'Jacques' (1834); 'Mauprat' (1836); 'Simon' (1836); 'The Masters of Mosaic' (1837); 'The Last Aldini' (1837); 'Uscoque' (1838); 'A Winter at Majorca' (1838); 'Spiridion' (1838); 'Gabriel' (1839); 'The Seven Strings of the Lyre' (1840); 'The Mississippians' (1840); 'Pauline' (1840); 'Horace' (1841); 'The Companion of a French Tour' (1841); 'Consuelo' (1842); 'The Countess of Rudolstadt' (1843); 'Jeanne' (1844); 'Isidora' (1845); 'Teverino' (1845); 'The Miller of Angibault' (1845); 'The Devil's Pool' (1846); ' M. Antoine's Sin ' (1847); 'Lucrezia Floriani' (1847); 'François le Champi' (1847); 'The Little Fadette' (1849); 'The Castle of Solitude' (1849); 'The Master Ringers' (1853); 'Story of My Life' (1854); 'Mont Revêche' (1855); 'The Devil in the Fields' (1856); 'She and He' (1858); 'The Green Ladies' (1859); 'Laura' (1859); 'The Snow Man' (1859); 'Jean de la Roche' (1860); 'Flavia' (1860); 'Valvedra' (1861); 'Tamaris' (1861); 'Antonia' (1861); 'The Germandre Family' (1861); 'The Fine Gentlemen of Bois-Doré' (1862); 'Mlle. de la Quintinie' (1864); 'A Young Girl's Confession' (1865); 'Monsieur Sylvestre' (1866); 'The Last Love' (1867); 'Cadio' (1868); 'Mlle. Merquem' (1868); 'A Rolling Stone' (1869); 'Daniella' (1869); 'The Little Daughter' (1869); 'Narcissus' (1870); 'Village Walks' (1870); 'Loves of the Golden Age' (1870); 'Cesarine Dietrecht' (1871); 'Journal of a Tourist during the War' (1871); 'Mlle. de Cérignan' (1871); etc. Her dramatic works include: 'Cosima' (1840); 'The King Waits' (1848); 'François le Champi' (1849); 'Claudia' (1851); 'Victorine's Marriage' (1851); 'The Demon of the Hearth' (1852); 'Molière' (1853); 'The Crusher' (1853); 'Mauprat' (1853); 'Flaminio' (1854); 'Master Favilla' (1855); 'Lucia' (1855?); 'As You Like It' (1856); 'Françoise' (1856); 'The Fine Gentlemen of Bois-Doré' (1862); 'The Pavement' (1862); 'The Marquis of Villemer' (1863 64); 'Drac' (1864); 'The Village Don Juan' (1866); 'Cadio' (1868); etc. Many of these were founded on her novels.

Sandback, Mrs. Henry Roscoe. An English poet, granddaughter of William Roscoe the historian. Her works are: 'Amidei: A Tragedy'; 'Poems' (1840); 'Giuliano de' Medici,' a drama (1842); 'Aurora and Other Poems' (1850).

Sandeau, Léonard Sylvain Jules (sän-dō'). A celebrated French novelist and man of letters; born in Aubusson, Feb. 19, 1811; died in Paris, April 24, 1883. He wrote: 'Madame de Sommerville' (1834); 'Marianna' (1840); 'Doctor Herbeau' (1841); 'Fernand' (1844); 'Catherine' (1846); 'Valcreuse' (1846); 'Mlle. de la Seiglière' (1848); 'Madeleine' (1848); 'A Legacy' (1849); 'Bags and Parchments' (1851); 'The House of Penarvan' (1858); 'A Beginning in the Magistracy' (1862); 'J. de Thommeray' (1873); etc.

Sanford, Edward. An American poet and journalist; born in Albany, N. Y., July 8, 1805; died in Gowanda, N. Y., Aug. 28, 1876. Included in his best-known works are a poetical address to Black Hawk, and 'The Loves of the Shell-Fishes.' Many of his verses, which are graceful and humorous, have been published in various collections.

Sanfuentes, Salvador (sän-fwen'täs). A Chilian poet; born in Santiago, Feb. 2, 1817; died there, July 17, 1860. Among his works are: 'Caupolican,' a drama in verse (1835); 'El Campanario' (1838); 'Teudo; or, Memories of a Solitary' (1858); and 'Chile, from the Battle of Chacabuco to that of Maipo' (1850).

Sangster, Charles. A Canadian poet and editor; born in Kingston, Ont., July 16, 1822. He was editor of the Amherstburg Courier (1849), and published 'The St. Lawrence and the Saguenay, and Other Poems' (1856), and 'Hesperus: Poems and Lyrics' (1860).

Sangster, Margaret Elizabeth (Munson). An American poet and prose-writer; born in New Rochelle, N. Y., Feb. 22, 1838. She was editorially connected with Hearth and Home (1871-73) and The Christian at Work (1873-79); since 1889 has been editor of Harper's Bazar. Her most noted poems are: 'Our Own'; 'The Sin of Omission'; and 'Are the Children at Home?' Among her books for girls are: 'May Stanhope and her Friend'; 'Maidie's Problem'; 'The Joyful Life.'

Santayana, George. A Spanish-American poet and educator; born in Spain, 1863. He is professor of philosophy at Harvard, and has published: 'Sonnets and Other Poems,' and 'The Sense of Beauty: An Outline of Æsthetic Theory'; 'The Life of Reason.'

Santillana, Iñigo Lopez de Mendoza, Marques de (sän''tēl-yä'na). A Spanish poet; born at Carrion de los Condes, Aug. 19, 1398; died at Guadalajara, March 25, 1458. He was made marquis for his services in the Moorish wars. He had much to do with the reform of Castilian poetry by subjecting it to the laws of the Italian classic school, and of the later Catalan Provençal school of the court poets. In the Italian-classic style are his 'Proverbs' or 'Hundred Adages,' a collection of 100 proverbs in 8-verse strophes; and the 'Dialogue of Bias against Fortune.' His allegorical poem in dialogue form, the 'Comediette of Ponza,' after the manner of Dante, had an influence on the development of the Spanish drama. Besides poems, he wrote for the Constable of Portugal, Dom Pedro, a memoir which is of great value for the history of ancient Spanish poetry.

Saphir, Moritz (säf'ēr). An Austrian humorist; born at Lovas-Berény in Hungary, Feb. 8, 1795; died near Vienna, Sept. 5, 1858. Among his numerous writings are: 'Album for Play and Earnest, Fun and Humor' (2 vols., 1846; 5th ed. 1875); 'Dictionary of Wit and Humor' (2 ed., 5 vols., 1860).

Sappho (saf'ō). A renowned Greek poet; born in the island of Lesbos about 612 B. C. Of her life little is known. Besides some small fragments of her poems, we have in complete form a 'Hymn to Aphrodite' and an 'Ode to a Beautiful Girl.' In antiquity, as Homer was ever "The Poet" *par excellence*, so Sappho was "The Poetess."

Sarcey, Francisque (sär-sä'). A French author and critic; born at Dourdan (Seine-et-Oise), Oct. 8, 1827: died at Paris, May 16, 1899. As a dramatic critic he was highly esteemed for his independence of judgment, and his wide acquaintance with dramatic literature and the history of the stage. He published: 'History of the Siege of Paris,' which in its first year reached the 30th edition; 'The Word and the Thing,' philosophical conversations (1862); 'Étienne Moret,' a semi-autobiographical story (1875); 'Recollections of Youth' (1884); 'Recollections of Mature Age'; 'Forty Years of the Theatre' (1900).

Sardou, Victorien (sär-dö'). A celebrated French dramatist; born in Paris, Sept. 7, 1831. He began play-writing in early life, although intended originally for the medical profession. Among his plays are: 'The Students' Inn' (1854); 'Monsieur Garat' (1857?); 'Saint Gervais' (1860); 'Blockheads' (1861); 'Piccolino' (1861?); 'Our Intimates' (186-); 'The Butterfly' (1862); 'The Black Devils' (1863); 'Don Quixote' (1864); 'The Benoîton Family' (1865); 'The New House' (1866); 'Seraphine' (1868); 'Fernande' (1870); 'Rabagas' (1872); 'Uncle

Sam› (1873); ‹Ferréol› (1875); ‹Dora› (1877); ‹Daniel Rochat› (1880); ‹Divorçons› (1881); ‹Odette› (1882); ‹Fédora› (1883); ‹Theodora› (1884); ‹Crocodile› (1886); ‹La Tosca› (1887); ‹Thermidor› (1891); ‹Gismonda› (1894); ‹Madame Sans-Gêne›; etc. He was elected to the Academy in 1877 and died Nov. 8, 1908.

Sargent, Charles Sprague. An American botanist and arboriculturist; born in Boston, 1841. He has been director of the botanic garden and arboretum, and professor of arboriculture, at Harvard. He has written many authoritative reports and books, among them: ‹Report on the Forests of North America›; ‹The Woods of the United States›; ‹Notes on the Forest Flora of Japan›; ‹The Silva of North America›; complete and authoritative work on the trees of North America; ‹Report on the Forests of North America›; and ‹Manual of the Trees of North America.›

Sargent, Epes. An American journalist, dramatist, verse and prose writer; born in Gloucester, Mass., Sept. 27, 1813; died in Boston, Dec. 31, 1880. His works include: ‹Change Makes Change,› a comedy; ‹The Priestess,› a tragedy; ‹Wealth and Worth› (1840), a novel; ‹Peculiar: A Tale of the Great Transition› (1863); ‹Life of Henry Clay.› ‹Songs of the Sea› and ‹A Life on the Ocean Wave› are the most popular of his verses. His ‹Cyclopædia of English and American Poetry› was published in 1883.

Sargent, Nathan. [" Oliver Oldschool."] An American journalist and publicist; born in Poultney, Vt., May 5, 1794; died in Washington, D. C., Feb. 2, 1875. He held many public positions, was connected with and established several newspapers, and under his pen-name wrote a series of famous letters from Washington to the United States Gazette. He published a ‹Life of Henry Clay› (1844), and ‹Public Men and Events› (2 vols., 1875).

Sargent, Winthrop. An American lawyer and historical writer; born in Philadelphia, Sept. 23, 1825; died in Paris, May 18, 1870. He lived in New York city, and wrote largely for the press on historical subjects. His ‹History of an Expedition against Fort Duquesne in 1755 under Gen. Braddock› (1855) has been highly esteemed. He wrote ‹The Loyalist Poetry of the Revolution› (1857) and the ‹Life and Career of Major John André› (1861).

Sarmiento, Domingo Faustino (särm-yen'tō). President of the Argentine Republic, and educational writer; born in San Juan, A. R., Feb. 15, 1811; died in Asuncion, Paraguay, Sept. 11, 1888. During 1845–47 he visited Europe and the United States to study the system of primary schools. During his travels he made the acquaintance of Cobden, Guizot, Humboldt, and Horace Mann; under the influence of the latter he wrote ‹Popular Education,› published (1848) by the Chilian government. Other important works of his are: ‹Life of Lincoln› (1866), and ‹The Schools the Foundation of Well-Being in the United States› (1868).

Sartoris, Mrs. Adelaide. An English opera singer and miscellaneous writer; born 1814; died 1879. She wrote: ‹A Week in a French Country House› (1867); ‹Medusa, and Other Tales› (1868); ‹Past Hours› (2 vols., 1880), a collection of the author's fugitive pieces; and an unfinished work, ‹Judith.›

Saulcy, Louis Félicien Joseph Caignart de (sō-sē'). A French numismatist and antiquarian; born in Lille, March 19, 1807; died in Paris, Nov. 3, 1880. He first obtained special attention as a numismatist by his ‹Essay on the Classification of Byzantine Coinage› (1836). Among his works are: ‹Tour in the Holy Land› (1865); ‹Last Days of Jerusalem› (1866); ‹Story of Herod› (1867); and ‹Seven Centuries of Jewish History› (1874).

Saunders, Frederick. An American scholar and miscellaneous writer; born at London, Aug. 13, 1807. He was librarian of the Astor Library, New York, 1859–96. He wrote: ‹Memoirs of the Great Metropolis› (London, 1852); ‹New York in a Nut-Shell› (1853); ‹Salad for the Solitary, by an Epicure› (1853); ‹Salad for the Social› (1856); ‹Pearls of Thought, Religious and Philosophical, Gathered from Old Authors› (1858); ‹Mosaics› (1859); ‹Festival of Song› (1866); ‹About Women, Love, and Marriage› (1868); ‹Evenings with the Sacred Poets› (1869; enlarged 1885); ‹Pastime Papers› (1885); ‹Story of Some Famous Books› (1887). He died at Brooklyn, Dec. 12, 1902.

Saunière, Paul (sōn-yär'). A French story-writer; born at Paris, 1827. He wrote: ‹The Fatal Prediction›; ‹The Bluebeard Nobleman›; ‹Father Grabpenny›; ‹King Misery› (1868); ‹Miss Aglaë› (1874); ‹The True Adventures of Jean Barchalou› (1876); ‹A Son-in-Law at Any Cost› (1879); ‹The Nephew from America› (1881); ‹The Little Marquise› (1883); ‹Mother Michel› (1886); ‹A Daughter of the Pharaohs› (1888); ‹Quicksilver› (1889); ‹The Recluse of Montfleury› (1889).

Saussure, Henri de (sō-sür'). A Swiss naturalist; born at Geneva, 1829. He was a member of the scientific expedition to Mexico, and wrote several memoirs on the insects of that country. He wrote also: ‹Memoir to Serve for the Natural History of Mexico, the Antilles, and the United States› (1872); ‹The Genevan Explorers of the Alps› (1879).

Sauvage, Thomas Marie François (sō-väzh'). A French dramatist; born at Paris, 1794; died there, 1877. Among his plays are: ‹The Portfolio; or, the Impromptu Lord› (1820); ‹Margaret of Anjou› (1826); ‹The Drunkard› (1830); ‹A Provincial Conspiracy› (1832); ‹The Sea Wolf› (1840); ‹The Amazon› (1846); ‹The Carnival of Venice› (1860); ‹My Lord's Coat› (1862).

Savage, John. An American journalist and miscellaneous writer; born in Dublin, Ireland, Dec. 13, 1828; died in 1888. He came to New York in 1848, and subsequently in Washington became proprietor of The States, the organ of

Stephen A. Douglas. Included in his popular war-songs are 'The Starry Flag' and 'The Muster of the North.' Among his other works are: 'Our Living Representative Men' (1860); 'Poems: Lyrical, Dramatic, and Romantic' (1870); 'Picturesque Ireland' (1878-83); and 'Waiting for a Wife,' a comedy (1859).

Savage, Minot Judson. A noted Unitarian clergyman; born in Norridgewock, Me., June 10, 1841. He graduated at the Theological Seminary at Bangor, 1864; went to California as a Congregational home missionary, and preached at San Mateo and at Grass Valley. He removed to Framingham, Mass.; thence was called to Indianapolis, and afterwards to Hannibal, Mo. He accepted a call to the Third Unitarian Church in Chicago in 1873, and after a year there was installed pastor of the Church of the Unity, Boston, where he remained for twenty-two years. He is now in the Church of the Messiah, New York, in association with Dr. Robert Collyer. In his very active career he has published over thirty books on religious, social, and moral questions, among which may be mentioned: 'The Religion of Evolution' (1876); 'Social Problems' (1886); 'My Creed' (1887); 'Jesus and Modern Life' (1893); 'A Man' (1895); 'Religion for To-day' (1897). He has also published 'Bluffton: A Story of To-day' (1878) ; 'Poems,' and 'Life's Dark Problems.'

Savage, Richard Henry. An American novelist; born in Utica, N. Y., June 10, 1846. He wrote many notable works of fiction, among them: 'My Official Wife'; 'A Daughter of Judas'; 'The Anarchist'; 'In the Old Château'; 'The Masked Venus'; 'Miss Devereaux of the Mariquita'; and 'After Many Years, and Other Poems.' Died in N. Y. city, Oct. 11, 1903.

Savage-Armstrong, George Francis. An Irish poet; born at Dublin, 1845. Among his poetical works are: 'Poems, Lyrical and Dramatic' (1879); 'Ugone: A Tragedy' (1870); 'The Tragedy of Israel,' a trilogy (1872-76); 'Stories of Wicklow' (1886); 'One in the Infinite' (1891); 'Queen Empress and Empire' (1897).

Savary, Nicolas (sä-vär-ē'). A French traveler and Orientalist; born at Vitré, Brittany, France, in 1750; died Feb. 4, 1788. He published: 'Letters on Egypt' (3 vols., 1781-85); the Koran in French, with a 'Life of Mohammed' (2 vols., 1783).

Savigny, Friedrich Karl von (sä-vēn-yē'). A distinguished jurist and historian of jurisprudence; born in Frankfort on the Main, Feb. 21, 1779; died in Berlin, Oct. 25, 1861. He stood long at the head of what is termed the historical school of jurisprudence. His principal works were: 'The Legal Right of Property' (1803); 'The Present System of Roman Jurisprudence' (1840-49); 'Contract Law'; 'History of the System of Roman Law in the Middle Ages'; etc.

Savioli, Luigi V. (säv-yō'lē). An Italian poet and historian; born 1729; died 1804. He published in his youth a volume of poems,

'Amours'; translated the works of Tacitus; and at the time of his death was engaged on the composition of a historical work, 'The Annals of Bologna.'

Savonarola, Girolamo (sä-von-ä-rō'lä). One of the great figures of Italian history; born at Ferrara, Sept. 21, 1452; hanged and his body burned May 23, 1498, a victim of the struggles of parties and factions during the pontificate of Alexander VI. (Borgia). The following are the titles of some of his works: 'The Triumph of the Cross'; 'Meditations on the Thirty First Psalm', 'Sermons'; 'Poems,' the latter being few in number; 'Essays'; etc.

Sawyer, Leicester Ambrose. An American clergyman, Biblical scholar, and author ; born in Pinckney, N. Y., July 28, 1807; died at Whitesboro, N. Y., Dec. 29, 1898. He was pastor of churches (1842-59), and published: 'Elements of Biblical Interpretation' (1836); 'Mental Philosophy' (1839); 'Moral Philosophy' (1845); 'Organic Christianity' (1854); 'Reconstruction of Bible Theories' (1862); and 'Final Theology; or, Introduction to the New Testament' (Vol. i., 1879). He published a translation of the New Testament, without the division into verses.

Saxe, John Godfrey. An American humorous poet, very popular in his day; born in Highgate, Vt., June 2, 1816; died in Albany, N. Y., March 31, 1887. In 1872 he became editorially connected with the Albany Evening Journal, and subsequently contributed to Harper's Magazine and the Atlantic Monthly. His most popular verses include 'Rhyme of the Rail' and 'The Proud Miss McBride'; and his published works 'The Flying Dutchman; or, The Wrath of Herr von Stoppelnose' (1862), and 'Leisure-Day Rhymes' (1875).

Saxo Grammaticus. A Danish historian; date of birth not known ; died about 1208. His 'Gesta Danorum' or 'Historia Danica' consists of 16 books, and extends to the year 1185. Much valuable historical material is to be found in the last six books. His surname was given him on account of the correctness and elegance of his Latin, which excited the admiration of Erasmus.

Say, Jean Baptiste (sā). A noted French economist; born 1767; died 1832. He popularized the theories of Adam Smith in France. His best-known work is 'Treatise on Political Economy' (1803); but widely read also were 'Catechism of Political Economy' (1815), 'Complete Course in Practical Political Economy' (1829), and 'Views of Men and Society' (1817). His "theory of markets" attracted great attention.

Sayce, Archibald Henry. An eminent English Orientalist and philologist; born Sept. 25, 1846. His works extend over various fields, and are of great importance for comparative philology and history. They include: 'Assyrian Grammar for Comparative Purposes' (1872); 'Elementary Assyrian Grammar' (1875); 'Lectures on the Assyrian Language' (1877);

31

'Babylonian Literature' (1877); 'Fresh Light from the Monuments' (1884); 'Ancient Empires of the East' (1884); 'Assyria: Its Princes, Priests, and People' (1885); 'Introduction to the Books of Ezra, Nehemiah, and Esther' (1885); 'Hibbert Lectures on the Origin and Growth of Religion, as Illustrated by the Religion of the Ancient Babylonians' (1887); 'The Hittites' (1888); 'Records of the Past' (new series, 1889-92); 'Life and Times of Isaiah' (1889); 'The Races of the Old Testament' (1891); 'Social Life among the Assyrians and Babylonians' (1891); 'A Primer of Assyriology' (1894); 'The Higher Criticism and the Verdict of the Monuments' (1894); 'The Egypt of the Hebrews, and Herodotus' (1895). Special mention should be made of his 'Principles of Comparative Philology'; 'Introduction to the Science of Language,' and 'Religions of Ancient Egypt and Babylonia' (1902).

Scaliger, Joseph Justus (skal'-i-jer). A French critic and classical scholar of great celebrity, son of J. C.; born in Agen, 1540; died at Leyden, 1609. He became one of the most learned men of his age, with a prodigious knowledge of classical antiquities and literature. He was involved in controversy on account of his conversion to Protestantism. Besides notes, criticisms, and essays, on Catullus, Propertius, Virgil, Moschus, and other authors, he wrote: 'The Emendation of Time' (1583), a work on chronology and the calendar; 'The Treasure of Time' (1606), in which he rearranged the whole chronology of classical antiquity; etc.

Scaliger, Julius Cæsar, originally **della Scala.** A celebrated classical scholar, Italian by birth, French by adoption; born at the castle of La Rocca in 1484; died at Agen, 1558. According to some scholars, "no one of the ancients could be placed above him, and the age in which he lived could not show his equal" in learning and talent. He published an 'Oration against Erasmus' (1531), in reply to that scholar's 'Ciceronianus'; 'Poems' (1533-74), in Latin and filling several volumes; 'Comic Metres'; and a variety of dissertations and essays on classical subjects.

Scarron, Paul (skär-rôǹ'). A French poet, dramatist, and novelist; born at Paris about 1610; died there, Oct. 14, 1660. At the age of 30, in consequence of a rheumatic attack, in which he was treated by a quack doctor, he became an invalid for life,—deformed and contorted, and suffering continual pain. His best work is the 'Comic Romance' (2 vols., 1651-57, but never-completed), the story of a band of strolling actors: it paints manners and characters with great vividness. In this novel Scarron draws on Spanish sources, as he does also in the comedies 'The Ridiculous Heir'; 'Jodelet'; 'Don Japhet of Armenia'; 'The Scholar of Salamanca.' His travesty of the Æneid (1648-53) was in its day regarded as a masterpiece of genuine burlesque humor; but it is now rated as unworthy of the author's great talent. He married in 1652 Françoise

d'Aubigné, who afterward, as Mme. de Maintenon, became the wife of Louis XIV.

Schack, Adolph Friedrich, Count von (shäk). A distinguished German Oriental scholar and historian of literature; born in Schwerin, Aug. 2, 1815; died in Rome, April 14, 1894. His works embrace many subjects; but his especial distinction is as a student and critic of Arabic, Persian, and Sanskrit literature. He published: 'History of Dramatic Art and Literature in Spain' (1845-46); 'Poetry and Art of the Arabs in Spain and Sicily' (1865); 'History of the Normans in Sicily' (1889); etc. His translations of Oriental classics are celebrated, and include 'Hero Songs [or epics] of Firdusi' (1851), for which he was decorated by the Shah; 'Firdusi' (1853), additional translations; 'Strophes of Omar Khayyám' (1878); 'Voices from the Ganges,' a series of Hindu poems; 'Mejnun and Leila,' the famous story by Jami; etc. He also wrote original poetry, but not until he had attained his sixtieth year; among his verse being 'Lotus Leaves' (1882), 'Memnon' (1885), 'Epistles and Elegies' (1894), etc. He is the author of an interesting work on 'Mazzini and Unified Italy.'

Schafarik or **Safarik, Pavel Josef** (shä'fä-rik). A celebrated Czech philologist, historian, and philosopher; born at Kobelarova, in the county of Gömör in Hungary, May 13, 1795; died at Prague, June 26, 1861. He began at an early age to collect Slavic folk-songs (published 1823-27). He translated into his native tongue the 'Clouds' of Aristophanes, and Schiller's 'Mary Stuart' (1815). His principal work is 'Slavic Antiquities' (1837). His 'Ground Principles of Old-Czechish Grammar' (1845) marked an epoch in the history of the Czech language. He wrote also: 'History of the Slavic Language and Literature' (1826); 'The Most Ancient Monuments of the Bohemian Language' (1840).

Schaff, Philip (shäf). A distinguished American Presbyterian theologian; born at Coire, Switzerland, Jan. 1, 1819; died in New York, Dec. 20, 1893. He came to the United States in 1844, and until 1863 held the professorship of church history at Mercersburg, Pa. In 1873 he was appointed professor of sacred literature in Union Seminary, New York. He published: 'Principles of Protestantism'; 'History of the Christian Church'; 'Creeds of Christendom'; 'Theological Propædeutics'; 'Christ and Christianity'; 'Critical Edition of the Heidelberg Catechism'; 'Bible Revision'; 'Through Bible Lands'; 'Progress of Religious Freedom'; 'Church and State in the United States'; 'The Person of Christ'; 'Literature and Poetry'; 'A Companion to the Greek Testament and the English Version'; etc. He edited the Schaff-Herzog 'Encyclopedia of Religious Knowledge'; 'Lange's Commentary'; etc.

Schandorph, Sophus (shän'dorf). A Danish poet and story-writer; born at Ringsted, May 8, 1837; died at Fredericksberg, January 1, 1901. His early poems were an echo of the old Romance poetiy; and his dramatic poem 'Out in the Forest' (1868) has a like inspiration. But his native talent was awakened in 1872, chiefly by the lectures of Georg Brandes, and thenceforth he was a pronounced realist. The first fruits of the change to realism are seen in 'From the Provinces' (1876), a collection of short tales, which were followed by 'Youthful Days' (1879); 'Little Folk' (1880); 'Story of Thomas Fris' (1881); 'Reminiscences' (1889); 'William Vang's Student Years' (1894).

Schefer, Leopold (shä'fer). A German poet and story-writer; born at Muskau, Silesia, July 30, 1784; died there, Feb. 16, 1862. From 1816 to 1820 he traveled in Austria, Italy, Greece, the Ionian Islands, Turkey, and Asia Minor, and then began to publish his long series of stories. Among them are: 'The Countess Ufeld' (1834); 'Many Men, Many Minds' (1840), a story of witchcraft; 'Divine Comedy at Rome' (2d ed. 1842); 'The Sibyl of Mantua' (1852), a pointed satire on the modern conventicle. His chief poetical works are: 'Vigils' (1842); 'The Layman's Breviary' (1834; 18th ed. 1884); 'The Secular Priest' (1846); in these the tone is moral and religious, leaning toward pantheism; 'Hafiz in Hellas, by a Hadji' (1853).

Scheffel, Joseph Viktor von (shef'el). A prominent German poet and novelist; born at Karlsruhe, Feb. 16, 1826; died April 9, 1886. In 1854 he published his famous epic poem, 'The Trumpeter of Säckingen.' The historical novel 'Ekkehard' came out in 1855. 'Gaudeamus' (1868) is a collection of lyrics, many of which became favorite student songs. 'Mountain Psalms' (1870) is a collection of poems.

Schelling, Friedrich Wilhelm Joseph von (shel'ling). A celebrated German thinker, one of the four chief metaphysical philosophers of Germany; born at Leonberg, Würtemberg, Jan. 27, 1775; died at the Ragaz baths, Switzerland, Aug. 20, 1854. His system was at first one of idealistic pantheism, akin to those of Fichte and Hegel; later his views were interpreted as furnishing a philosophic basis for Christianity. He had high poetic gifts. His works include: 'On the Possibility of a Form of Philosophy' (1794); 'On the Ego as the Principle of Philosophy' (1795); 'Ideas for a Philosophy of Nature' (1797); 'On the Soul of the World' (1798); 'First Sketch of a System of the Philosophy of Nature' (1799); 'System of Transcendental Idealism' (1800); 'Bruno; or, The Divine and Natural Principle of Things' (1802); 'Philosophy and Religion' (1804); 'On the Relation of Art to Nature' (1807); 'Philosophic Researches on the Essence of Human Liberty' (1809). Four posthumous volumes are of great importance: 'Introduction to the Philosophy of Mythology' (1856); 'Philosophy of Mythology' (1857); 'Philosophy of Revelation,' in two divisions, each separately published in 1858.

Schenkendorf, Max von (shenk'en-dorf). A German poet; born at Tilsit, Dec. 11, 1783; died Dec. 11, 1817. He was educated as a lawyer at the University of Königsberg; he practiced his profession until the breaking out of the war in 1813, when he joined the Prussian army, and with his stirring war-songs inspired his comrades. His 'Gedichte' (1815) is a collection of these songs.

Scherenberg, Ernst (shä'ren-berG). A German poet; born at Swinemünde, July 21, 1839. His first volume was a collection of poems, 'From the Heart's Depths' (1860), which was followed by the cycle 'Banished' (1861), 'Storms in Springtide' (1865), etc. He wrote also the character sketches 'Prince Bismarck' (1885), and 'Emperor William' (1888); and the dramatic poem 'Germania' (1886). He published in 1874 an anthology, 'Against Rome: Voices of German Poets.'

Schérer, Edmond (shä-rär'). A French essayist and critic of celebrity; born in Paris, April 8, 1815; died at Versailles, March 16, 1889. He first attracted general attention in 1860 with a volume entitled 'Miscellanies of Religious Criticism,' containing studies of Joseph de Maistre, Lamennais, Le P. Gratry, Veuillot, Taine, Proudhon, Renan, and others. He has also written: 'Criticism and Belief' (1850); 'Letters to my Pastor' (1853); 'Miscellanies of Religious Criticism' (1860); 'Miscellanies of Religious History' (1864); etc.

Scherer, Wilhelm (shä'rer). An Austrian philologist; born at Schönbrunn, Austria, April 26, 1841; died Aug. 6, 1866. Among his works are: 'German Studies' (1870); 'History of Poetry in the Eleventh and Twelfth Centuries' (1875); 'From Goethe's Youth' (1879). His famous 'History of German Literature' (1883) has been translated into English.

Scherr, Johannes (shär). A German historian; born at Hohenrechberg, Würtemberg, Oct. 3, 1817; died Nov. 21, 1886. He studied philosophy and history at Tübingen; became a prolific writer, and was an accepted critic in German literature. Among his principal works are: 'History of German Literature' (2d ed. 1854); 'History of English Literature' (1854; 3d ed. 1883); 'Blücher, his Life and Times' (3 vols., 1862-63; 4th ed. 1887); 'Germania' (1885).

Schiller, Johann Christoph Friedrich von (shil'ler). A great German poet and dramatist; born in Marbach on the Neckar, Nov. 10, 1759; died at Weimar, May 9, 1805. His works include: 'The Robbers' (1780-81); 'Inquiry into the Connection between the Animal and Spiritual Nature of Man' (1780-81); 'Fiesco' (1783); 'Love and Intrigue' (1784); 'Don Carlos' (1785); 'History of the Revolt of the Netherlands from Spanish Rule' (1788); 'The Ghost Seer' (1789); 'History of the Thirty Years' War' (1792); 'Xenien' (1796), with Goethe; 'Votive Tablets' (1796); 'Wallenstein's Camp' (1798); 'The Piccolomini' (1799); 'Wallenstein's Death' (1799); 'Maria Stuart' (1800); 'The Maid of Orleans' (1801); 'The Bride of Messina' (1803); 'William Tell' (1804); 'Demetrius,' a fragment; and various short poems, tales, and essays.

Schlegel, August Wilhelm von (shlā'gel). A celebrated German Orientalist, critic, and poet, son of J. A.; born at Hanover, Sept. 8, 1767; died May 12, 1845, at Bonn, where he was professor of literature in the university. His most notable works in literary and art criticism are: 'Lectures on Dramatic Art and Literature' (3 vols., 1809–11), translated into nearly all the languages of Western Europe; 'On the Theory and History of the Plastic Arts' (1827). In the field of Orientalism he wrote 'Reflections on the Study of the Asiatic Languages' (1832), and prepared editions of several Indian classics. He translated many of the plays of Shakespeare, and made the English dramatist a German classic; his translations of Dante, Calderon, Camoens, and other foreign masters of literature are admirable; his original poems show consummate art and grace of form. He is at his best in his sonnets, and in the elegy 'Rome' (1812).

Schlegel, Friedrich von. A distinguished German critic and philologist, son of J. A.; born at Hanover, March 10, 1772; died at Dresden, Jan. 12, 1829. He first devoted himself to the study of Greek antiquity, and in 1794 published his great essay 'On the Schools of Grecian Poetry'; following it with many others of a like tenor, as 'The Greeks and Romans' (1797), and 'History of Greek and Roman Poetry' (1798). In his 'Fragments' (1798–1800) he essayed to establish the theory of a new romanticism; in the mean time writing the unfinished romance 'Lucinda,' and a volume of 'Poems.' To this period also belongs his tragedy 'Alarcos,' in which he unsuccessfully sought to combine romantic and classic elements. His work 'Language and Wisdom of the Indians' (1808) was a valuable contribution to the science of language. Among his other writings are lectures on 'Modern History' (1811); 'History of Ancient and Modern Literature' (1815); 'Philosophy of Life.'

Schlegel, Johann Adolf. A German poet; born at Meissen, Sept. 18, 1721; died at Hanover, Sept. 16, 1793. Of his poetry only a few religious poems remain. He translated and published, with additions of his own, Batteux's 'Restriction of the Fine Arts to a Single Principle' (1759).

Schlegel, Johann Elias. A German poet; born at Meissen, Jan. 17, 1719; died at Soröe in Denmark, Aug. 13, 1749. He wrote several tragedies, among them 'Hermann' (the ancient Teutonic hero Arminius) and 'Canute'; and two spirited comedies, 'The Triumph of Good Women' and 'Mute Beauty.'

Schleiermacher, Friedrich Ernst Daniel (shlī'er-mäċh"er). A noted German theologian and philosopher; born at Breslau, Nov. 21, 1768; died at Berlin, Feb. 12, 1834. His principles of theological criticism are laid down in 'Christian Belief according to the Fundamental Doctrines of the Evangelical Church' (2 vols., 1821–22); a sequel to this is 'Christian Morals' (1843); to show the consistency of his

principles with the teachings of Christ, he wrote an 'Introduction to the New Testament' and a 'Life of Jesus' (1850). Among his writings on philosophy are: 'Dialectics' (1830); 'A System of Ethics' (1835); 'Psychology' (1835); 'Æsthetics' (1842).

Schliemann, Heinrich (shlē'män). A German archæologist; born at Neubuckow in Mecklenburg-Schwerin, Jan. 6, 1822; died at Naples, Dec. 26, 1890. His celebrated archæological explorations and excavations at the sites of Troy, Mycenæ, Orchomenos, Tiryns, and other ancient Hellenic cities, are recorded in 'Mycenæ' (1877); 'Ilios' (1880); 'Orchomenos' (1881); 'Troja' (1883); 'Tiryns' (1886); 'Report on the Excavations at Troy' (1890); 'Autobiography' (1891).

Schlosser, Friedrich Christoph (shlos'er). A German historian; born at Jever, Nov. 17, 1776; died at Heidelberg, Sept. 23, 1861. He wrote: 'History of the Iconoclast Emperors of the East' (1812); 'History of the World in Connected Narrative' (9 vols., 1815–24); 'General Historic View of the Ancient World and its Civilization' (9 vols., 1826–34); 'A Judgment of Napoleon and his Latest Traducers and Panegyrists' (3 vols., 1832–35).

Schmid, Ferdinand von. See **Dranmor.**

Schmidt, Heinrich Julian (shmit). A Prussian journalist and author; born at Marienwerder, Prussia, March 7, 1818; died in Berlin, March 27, 1886. He is the author of 'History of Romanticism in the Time of the Reformation and Revolution' (2 vols., 1850); 'History of German Literature since Lessing's Death' (1858); 'History of Intellectual Life in Germany from Leibnitz till Lessing's Death' (1870); and 'History of German Literature from Leibnitz to Our Time' (1886).

Schmidt, Maximilian. A German story-writer; born at Eschlkam in Bavaria, Feb. 25, 1832. He is the author of a series of tales of Bavarian life, as: 'Popular Stories from the Bavarian Forest' (4 vols., 1863–68); 'The Tenth Commandment' (1879); 'The Guardian Spirit of Oberammergau' (1881); 'The Good God's Mantle'; 'The Golden Saturday' (1883); 'The Emmet Witch' (1887); 'On the Golden Stair' (1893).

Schneckenburger, Max (shnek'en-bör"ger). A German verse-writer, author of 'The Watch on the Rhine'; born at Thalheim, Feb. 17, 1819; died at Burgdorf near Bern, May 3, 1849. In the Franco-Prussian war 'The Watch on the Rhine' attained the rank of a national song and melody; and when the war was over, an annual pension of 3,000 marks ($750) was settled on his surviving family, and also on the composer of the melody, Karl Wilhelm.

Schneider, Louis (shnī'der). A German actor and author; born at Berlin, April 29, 1805; died at Potsdam, Dec. 16, 1878. For almost 30 years he was one of the foremost actors of comedy on the German stage. Besides a number of novels and tales of life on the stage, he wrote many successful farces; among them 'The Student on his Travels,' 'The Offer of Marriage in Helgoland,' 'The Orchestra Leader of Venice.' He wrote also 'King William: an Account of his Military Life' (1869); and two other works, entitled 'Emperor William, 1867-71' (1875), and 'From the Life of Emperor William, 1849-73' (3 vols., 1888). He accompanied William during the campaign in France.

Schomburgk, Sir Robert Hermann (shom'-bĕrk *or* shom'hŏrk). An English geographical explorer, whose name has been made familiar through the recent Venezuela boundary controversy; born at Freiburg on the Unstrut, June 5, 1804; died at Schöneberg near Berlin, March 11, 1865. He was commissioned by the British government to explore British Guiana in 1835, and after four years spent in that labor returned to England; he revisited the country in 1840, and remained there till 1845. His writings are: 'Description of British Guiana' (1840); 'Twelve Views of the Interior of Guiana' (1841). His brother Richard (1811-91) accompanied him on his second voyage, and wrote 'Travels in Guiana and on the Orinoco' (1841).

Schoolcraft, Henry Rowe. An American ethnologist and miscellaneous writer, noted as an Indian authority; born in Albany County, N. Y., March 28, 1793; died in Washington, D. C., Dec. 10, 1864. Thirty years of his life he spent among the Indians, and through him many laws were enacted for their protection. Among his numerous publications are: 'Travels in the Central Portions of the Mississippi Valley' (1825); 'Indian Melodies,' a poem (1830); 'The Man of Bronze' (1834); 'Algic Researches,' a book of Indian allegories and legends (1839); and 'The Indian and his Wigwam' (1848).

Schopenhauer, Arthur (shō'pen-hou''er). A celebrated German philosopher; born at Dantzic, Feb. 22, 1788; died at Frankfort on the Main, September 1860. The first great work in his system of philosophical doctrine, 'The World as Will and Representation' (1819; 8th ed. 1891), was in great part written while he was still a student at Jena. His other principal writings are: 'The Fourfold Root of the Principle of the Sufficient Cause' (1813; 5th ed. 1891); 'On Vision and Colors' (1816; 3d ed. 1870); 'The Two Fundamental Problems of Ethics' (1841; 4th ed. 1894); 'Parerga and Paralipomena' (1851; 7th ed. 1891), a collection of his minor writings; and (posthumously) his 'MS. Remains' and his 'Correspondence with Johann August Becker' (1883).

Schouler, James (skö'ler). An American historian; born at Arlington, Mass., March 20, 1839. He graduated at Harvard; practiced law, and served in the army during the Civil War. He is author of legal text-books on 'Domestic Relations'; 'Personal Property'; 'Bailments'; 'Wills'; 'Executors and Administrators.' His best-known works are 'History of the United States under the Constitution'

(5 vols., 1880-91), and 'Constitutional Studies' (1896); 'Eighty Years of Union' (1904).

Schreiner, Olive (shrī'ner). A South-African novelist; born in Basutoland, 1863. She is the daughter of a Lutheran minister, and was married in 1894, to Rev. S. C. Cronwright, an Englishman of the colony. She published her first and most noted book, 'The Story of an African Farm,' under the pseudonym " Ralph Iron " at the age of twenty; 'Dreams' (1890); 'Dream Life and Real Life' (1893); and 'Trooper Peter Halket' (1897); 'An English South African's Views.'

Schubart, Christian Friedrich Daniel (shö'bart). A German poet; born at Obersontheim, March 24, 1739; died at Stuttgart, Oct. 10, 1791. Among his lyrics are: 'Witcheries' (1766); 'Death Songs' (1767); 'The Tomb of the Princes'; 'Ode on Frederick the Great.'

Schubert, Gotthilf Heinrich von (shö'bert). A German philosopher; born at Hohenstein, Saxony, April 26, 1780; died at Munich, July 1, 1860. Among his works are: 'Inklings of a General History of Life' (1806); 'Views of the Night Side of Natural Science' (1808); 'Symbolism of Dreams' (1814); 'The Primordial World and the Fixed Stars' (1822); 'History of the Soul' (1830); 'Old and New concerning the Inner Life of the Soul' (5 vols., 1817-44); 'Ailings and Perturbations of the Human Soul' (1845).

Schücking, Christoph Bernhard Levin (shük'ing). A German novelist; born at Clemensworth, Sept. 6, 1814; died at Pyrmont, Aug. 31, 1883. Among his numerous works are: 'A Castle by the Sea' (1843); a volume of 'Poems' (1846); 'A Son of the People' (1849); 'The Peasants' Prince' (1851); 'Luther at Rome' (1870); 'Saints and Knights' (1873); 'Life Recollections' (1886).

Schücking, Luise. A German novelist and dramatist, wife of Levin; born (Von Gall) 1815; died 1855. She wrote the comedy 'A Bad Conscience' (1842); 'Stories for Ladies' (1845); 'Against the Current' (1851); 'The New Crusader Knight' (1853).

Schulz, Eduard. See Ferrand.

Schulz, Johann Abraham Peter (shölts). A German musical composer and song-writer, born at Lüneburg, March 30, 1747; died at Schwedt, June 10, 1800. Among the most popular of his songs are: 'On the Rhine, On the Rhine'; 'Lo, the Heavens, How Clear'; 'Last Hour of the Year.' His oratorios and choruses, his songs from Racine's 'Athalie,' and his operas 'Minona' and 'Aline,' rank among the best productions of his time.

Schulze, Ernst (shölts'ė). A German poet; born at Celle, March 22, 1789; died there, June 29, 1817. He wrote an epic romance, 'Cecilia' (1818); 'The Magic Rose' (1818), a romantic narrative poem, his best work; 'Miscellaneous Poems' (1820).

Schulze-Delitzsch, Hermann (shölts'ė-dāl'ich). A German social economist; born at Delitzsch, Aug. 29, 1808; died at Potsdam, April 29, 1883. He wrote: 'Chapters of a German Workingman's Catechism' (1863), an anti-socialist tract; 'The Laboring Classes and Associationism in Germany' (2d ed. 1863); 'Money-Advance and Credit Associations as People's Banks' (5th ed. 1876).

Schumann, Robert (shö'män). A noted German songwright, composer, and musical critic; born at Zwickau, Saxony, July 8, 1810; died at Endenich near Bonn, July 29, 1856. He was educated at Heidelberg; in 1843 became professor of composition in the conservatory of Leipsic; and in 1850 musical director at Düsseldorf. While engaged in that place he became insane. His works include almost every art form except oratorio. He wrote four symphonies, several cantatas, an opera, a mass, sonatas, concertos, quartets for strings and also for voices, pieces for the piano, the organ, and a number of songs. His 'Collected Writings on Music and Musicians' appeared in 1854.

Schurman, Jacob Gould. President of Cornell University; born in Freetown, Prince Edward's Island, May 22, 1854. He won the Gilchrist Dominion scholarship, 1875; graduated at London University, 1877; was professor of philosophy in Acadia College, 1880–82; in Dalhousie College, Halifax, 1882–86. He became professor of philosophy at Cornell University, and has been president since 1892. He has published: 'Kantian Ethics' (1881), 'The Ethical Import of Darwinism' (1887), and 'Agnosticism and Religion'; and contributed to many reviews, essays on important subjects.

Schurz, Carl (shörts). A German-American journalist and statesman of eminence; born near Cologne, Prussia, March 2, 1829. His most famous speeches published 1865 contain: 'The Irrepressible Conflict' (1858); 'The Doom of Slavery' (1860); 'The Abolition of Slavery as a War Measure' (1862); and 'Eulogy on Charles Sumner' (1874). He wrote a 'Life of Henry Clay' (1887); and an essay, 'Abraham Lincoln.' His 'Autobiography' (published 1908) is very interesting. Died May 14, 1906.

Schuyler, Eugene. An American writer of note; born in Ithaca, N. Y., Feb. 26, 1840; died in Cairo, Egypt, July 18, 1890. He was United States secretary of legation at St. Petersburg (1870–76); secretary of legation and consul-general at Constantinople (1876–78); and minister to Greece (1882–84). His works include: 'Turkestan: Notes of a Journey in Russian Turkestan, Khokand, Bokhara, and Kuldja' (1876); 'Peter the Great, Emperor of Russia' (2 vols., 1884); and 'American Diplomacy and the Furtherance of Commerce' (1886).

Schwab, Gustav (shväb). A German poet and philosophical writer; born in Stuttgart, June 19, 1792; died Nov. 4, 1850. His poems exhibit purity and feeling. Many of his ballads became very popular. His 'Poems' appeared in 2 vols., 1828–29; a second revised edition, 'New Collection,' in 1838. The best of his prose works is the Life of Schiller' (1840).

Schwartz, Marie Sophie (shvärtz). A Swedish novelist; born at Borås, July 4, 1819; died at Stockholm, May 7, 1894. Her stories deal for the most part with the problems of labor; among them are: 'Labor Ennobles' (1859); 'The Nobleman's Daughter' (1860); 'Birth and Breeding' (1861); 'Changing Fortunes' (1871); 'A Child of the Time' (1873).

Schwatka, Frederick (shwät'kä). An American geographical explorer; born at Galena, Ill., Sept. 29, 1849; died at Portland, Or., Nov. 2, 1892. He graduated from West Point in 1871; commanded an expedition in search of relics of Sir John Franklin's party, 1878–80; made two tours of exploration in Alaska (1883 and 1886). Among his writings are: 'Along Alaska's Great River' (1885); 'Nimrod in the North' (1885); 'The Children of the Cold' (1886).

Schwegler, Albert (shveg'ler). A German philosopher and theologian; born at Michelbach, Würtemberg, Feb. 10, 1819; died at Tübingen, Jan. 5, 1857. His best-known work is his 'History of Philosophy' (1848; 11th ed. 1882). It has been translated into most European languages; into English by J. H. Seelye in America (1856), and by J. H. Stirling in England (1867). His 'History of Greek Philosophy' was published in 1859.

Schweinfurth, Georg August (shvīn'fört). A Russian explorer; born at Riga, Dec. 29, 1836. He studied at Heidelberg, Munich, and Berlin. He investigated the flora and fauna of the valley of the Nile (1864–66), and is the author of 'Nile Vegetation' (1862); 'Contribution to the Flora of Ethiopia' (1867); 'Reliquiæ Kotschyaræ' (1868); 'In the Heart of Africa' (2 vols., 1874).

Scollard, Clinton. An American poet; born in Clinton, N. Y., Sept. 18, 1861. In 1888 he was made assistant professor of rhetoric at Hamilton College, and later professor of English literature. Among his publications are: 'Pictures in Song' (1884); 'With Reed and Lyre' (1886); 'Old and New World Lyrics' (1888); 'Giovio and Gilulia' (1891); 'Songs of Sunrise Lands' (1892); 'The Lutes of Morn'; 'The Cloistering of Ursula'; 'Easter Song.'

Scott, Alexander. A Scotch poet; born about 1525; died about 1584; "the Anacreon of old Scotch poetry." Of his writings thirty-six short poems remain; the most important of these are 'A New Yeir Gift to Quene Mary' and 'The Justing at the Drum.'

Scott, Andrew. A Scottish poet; born in Bowden, Roxburghshire, 1757; died there, May 22, 1839. He served in the British army in this country during the Revolution, and was with Cornwallis at the surrender of Yorktown. While he was encamped on Staten Island he wrote his noted verses 'Betsey Roscoe' and 'The Oak-Tree.' After the war he returned to his native land, and published 'Poems, Chiefly in the Scottish Dialect' (1811), and 'Poems on Various Subjects' (1826).

Scott, Clement William. An English dramatist and critic; born at London, 1841. He wrote: 'Lays of a Londoner' (1882); 'Lays and Legends' (1888); the dramas 'The Cape Mail,' 'Odette,' and 'Sister Mary.' Died 1904.

Scott, Duncan Campbell. A Canadian poet; born at Ottawa, Ont., 1862. He is author of 'The Magic House' (1893).

Scott, Frederick George. A Canadian versewriter; born 1861. He wrote: 'The Soul's Quest' (1888); 'My Lattice, and Other Poems' (1894).

Scott, Lydia, Lady. An English miscellaneous writer. Besides stories, as 'Flirtation,' 'Marriage in High Life,' and 'The Henpecked Husband' (1848), she wrote: 'Exposition of the Types and Antitypes of the Old and New Testament' (1856); 'Incentives to Bible Study' (1860); 'The Dream of a Life' (1862).

Scott, Michael. A Scottish philosopher of the 13th century. Of his life little is known. His nationality even is in doubt: the Italians and the Spaniards claimed him as their countryman as well as the Scots. His great learning won for him the reputation of being a magician. His acquaintance with Arabic enabled him to translate into Latin the works of Avicenna and Averroes, and the Arabic versions of Aristotle with the commentaries of Averroes. His own writings treat of astrology, alchemy, and the occult sciences in general; among them are treatises 'On the Sun and Moon,' 'On Palmistry,' 'On Physiognomy and Human Procreation.'

Scott, Patrick. A British poet, author of 'Oriental Musings, and Other Poems' (1840); 'Love in the Moon,' a poem (1852); 'Thomas à Becket, and Other Poems' (1853); 'Footpaths between Two Worlds, and Other Poems' (1859).

Scott, Sir Walter. The celebrated Scotch novelist and poet; born in Edinburgh, Aug. 15, 1771; died at Abbotsford, Sept. 21, 1832. He wrote: 'Disputatio Juridica' (1792), a legal thesis; 'The Chase' (1796), comprising translations from the German; 'Goetz of Berlichingen' (1799), a translation from Goethe; 'Apology for Tales of Terror' (1799); 'The Eve of St. John: A Border Ballad' (1800); 'Ballads' (1801); 'Minstrelsy of the Scottish Border' (1802-3); 'Lay of the Last Minstrel' (1805); 'Ballads and Lyrical Pieces' (1806), reprints of various poems; 'Marmion' (1808); 'Life of Dryden' (no date); 'The Lady of the Lake' (1810); 'Vision of Don Roderick' (1811); 'Rokeby' (1813); 'The Bridal of Triermain' (1813); 'Abstract of Eyrbiggia Saga' (1814); 'Waverley' (1814); 'Life of Swift' (1814), prefixed to Works; 'The Lord of the Isles' (1815); 'Guy Mannering' (1815); 'The Field of Waterloo' (1815); 'Paul's Letters to his Kinsfolk' (1815); 'The Antiquary' (1816); 'Tales of my Landlord, Collected and Arranged by Jedediah Cleishbotham: The Black Dwarf, Old Mortality' (1817, really 1816); 'Harold the

Dauntless' (1817); 'The Search after Happiness' (1817); 'Rob Roy' (1818); 'Tales of my Landlord, 2d series: Heart of Midlothian' (1818); 'Tales of my Landlord, 3d series: The Bride of Lammermoor, A Legend of Montrose' (1819); 'Description of the Regalia of Scotland' (1819); 'Ivanhoe' (1820); 'The Monastery' (1820); 'The Abbot' (1820); 'Kenilworth' (1821); 'Account of George III.'s Coronation' (1821); 'The Pirate' (1822); 'Halidon Hill' (1822); 'The Fortunes of Nigel' (1822); 'Peveril of the Peak' (1822); 'Quentin Durward' (1823); 'St. Ronan's Well' (1824); 'Redgauntlet' (1824); 'Tales of the Crusaders: The Betrothed, The Talisman' (1825); 'Thoughts on the Proposed Change of Currency' (1826); 'Woodstock' (1826); 'Life of Napoleon Buonaparte, Emperor of the French, with a Preliminary View of the French Revolution' (1827); 'Chronicles of the Canongate: The Two Drovers, The Highland Widow, The Surgeon's Daughter' (1827); 'Tales of a Grandfather' (1st series, 1828; 2d series, 1829; 3d series, Scotland, 1830; 4th series, France, 1830); 'Chronicles of the Canongate, 2d series: St. Valentine's Day; or, The Fair Maid of Perth' (1828); 'My Aunt Margaret's Mirror,' 'The Tapestried Chamber,' and 'The Laird's Jock,' in the Keepsake (1828); 'Religious Discourses, by a Layman' (1828); 'Anne of Geierstein' (1829); 'History of Scotland' (1830); 'Demonology and Witchcraft' (1830); 'House of Aspen,' in the Keepsake (1830); 'Doom of Devorgoil: Auchindrane, or the Ayrshire Tragedy' (1830); 'Essays on Ballad Poetry' (1830); 'Tales of my Landlord, 4th series: Count Robert of Paris, Castle Dangerous' (1832); and many articles for the Edinburgh and Quarterly reviews, historical essays, etc.

Scott, William Bell. A Scottish poet; born near Edinburgh, Sept. 12, 1811; died Nov. 22, 1890. He was a distinguished painter and archæologist. He published: 'Hades, and Other Poems' (1839); 'The Year of the World: A Philosophical Poem' (1846); a 'Memoir' of his brother David (1850); antiquarian 'Gleanings in the North of England' (1849-51); 'Chorea Sancti Viti' (1851); 'Poems' (1854); another volume of 'Poems' (1875).

Scotus Erigena, Joannes (skō'tus e-rij'en-ä). A renowned mediæval philosopher of the 9th century. He was an Irishman, as indicated by the surnames Scotus (which in that age meant Irish) and Erigena (of Irish extraction). His life seems to have been passed mostly in France. He was a Platonist rather than an Aristotelian. His greatest work is 'Of the Division of Nature,' in which he holds for the identity of philosophy and religion, and repels the claim of authority in matters of religious belief.

Scribe, Augustin Eugène (skrēb). A French dramatist; born in Paris, Dec. 24, 1791; died Feb. 20, 1861. For nearly forty years he was the most conspicuous playwright living. His works are seldom placed upon the stage now. His collected 'Œuvres' (76 vols., issued 1874-85) contain all his works, which include novels as well as plays.

Scudder, Horace Elisha. An American man of letters and historian ; born in Boston, Oct. 16, 1838 ; died at Cambridge, Jan. 11, 1902. He was for some years editor of the Atlantic Monthly. He published : ' Seven Little People and their Friends ' ; ' Dream Children ' ; ' Stories from my Attic ' ; ' The Dwellers in Five Sisters' Court ' ; ' Boston Town ' ; ' A History of the United States ' ; ' The Book of Fables ' ; 'The Book of Folk Stories' ; ' Fables and Folk Stories' ; ' George Washington : An Historical Biography ' ; ' Men and Letters ' ; ' Childhood in Literature and Art' ; ' The Bodley Books' ; 'James Russell Lowell : A Biography' (1901); etc.

Scudéry, Georges de (skü-der-ē'). A French poet, brother of Madeleine ; born at Havre, 1601 ; died at Paris, May 14, 1667. He wrote many dramas, all now forgotten with the possible exception of ' Tyrannic Love.' His epic of 'Alaric' (1654) was severely scored by Boileau for its bombastic style.

Scudéry, Madeleine. A French novelist; born at Havre, 1607 ; died at Paris, June 2, 1701. Her stories were greatly admired in their day; but they are now found monotonous and bombastic. This "new Sappho's" most celebrated work is ' Artamenes ; or, The Great Cyrus' (10 vols., 1649-58), in which the author's contemporaries figure under ancient names. She also wrote ' Ibrahim' and ' Clélie,' romances. Besides novels she wrote ' Conversations' ; ' Fables' ; ' Light Verses.'

Sealsfield, Charles, alias of **Karl Anton Postl.** An Austrian novelist and miscellaneous writer; born at Poppitz in Moravia, March 3, 1793; died near Soleure, May 26, 1864. He lived in the United States under the name of Charles Sealsfield, 1822-26, and again 1827-30. He wrote : ' Sketches of Transatlantic Travel' (1834); ' Life Pictures from Both Hemispheres' (1835). Among his novels are : ' Tokeah ; or, The White Rose' (1828); ' Virey and the Aristocrats' (1834); ' German-American Elective Affinities' (1839).

Seawell, Molly Elliot. An American novelist and essayist; born in Virginia, 1860. She has published : ' The Sprightly Romance of Marsac' ; ' Hale Weston ' ; ' Twelve Naval Captains' (1897); and others.

Secundus, Johannes (sā-kön'dös). A Dutch poet; born at The Hague, November 1511 ; died at Utrecht, probably 1536. His best-known work is ' Kisses' (1539), consisting of amatory poems. His ' Poetical Works' were published by his brother in 1541.

Secundus, Publius Pomponius. A Roman poet, who lived in the first century of our era. Tacitus speaks of his tragedies in the highest terms, as does also Quintilian. The elder Pliny wrote his ' Life' in two books Only fragments of Secundus's works remain.

Sedaine, Michel Jean (sed-ān'). A French playwright; born at Paris, July 4, 1719; died there, May 17, 1797. He is regarded as the originator of comic opera. Among his works are the comic operas: ' Playing the Deuce' ; ' The King and the Farmer' ; ' Richard Cœur de Lion' ; 'Aline, Queen of Golconda.' His comedies ' The Philosopher without Knowing It' (1765) and ' The Unexpected Wager' (1768) won for him membership of the Academy; they have still a place in the repertoire of French theatres.

Sedgwick, Catharine Maria. An American novelist; born at Stockbridge, Mass., Dec. 28, 1789; died near Roxbury, Mass., July 31, 1867. She wrote: 'A New England Tale' (1822); 'Redwood' (1824); 'The Traveler' (1825); 'Hope Leslie; or, Early Times in Massachusetts' (1827); 'The Linwoods; or, Sixty Years Since in America' (1835); 'The Poor Rich Man and the Rich Poor Man' (1836); 'Letters from Abroad' (1841); 'Historical Sketches of the Old Painters' (1841); 'Morals of Manners' (1846); 'Married or Single' (1857).

Sedley, Charles, Sir. An English dramatist; born at Aylesford in Kent, 1639; died Aug. 20, 1701. He is author of the favorite song 'Phyllis.' He wrote four comedies, among them ' The Mulberry Garden' (1668) and two tragedies.

Sedley, Henry. An American author; born in Boston, April 4, 1835; died in New York city, Jan. 25, 1899. He was a journalist, at one time one of the editors of the New York Evening Post, Times and Commercial Advertiser; founder and for a time editor of the Round Table. He published : ' Dangerfield's Rest : A Romance' (1864), and ' Marion Rooke; or, the Quest for Fortune' (1865).

Seeley, John Robert, Sir. An English historical scholar ; born in London, Sept. 10, 1834; died at Cambridge (where he was professor of Modern History), Jan. 13, 1895. He came into notice through the book ' Ecce Homo' (a life of Christ), in 1865, which made a great sensation and was reviewed by Mr. Gladstone; he published ' Natural Religion' in 1882; and in ' Lectures and Essays' (1870) he wrote on art, ethics, and education. But his really important work was historical: ' Roman Imperialism,' in the last-mentioned volume; his masterpiece, ' Life and Times of Stein' (3 vols., 1878), a history of the regeneration of Prussia in the Napoleonic period; ' The Expansion of England' (1883: a series of lectures), and cognate works; and ' A Short History of Napoleon the First' (1886: reprinted from the ' Encyclopædia Britannica').

Seely, [Edward] Howard. An American writer of fiction; born in 1856; died in 1894. He published many volumes, among them : 'A Lone Star, Bo-Peep, and Other Stories' ; 'Texan Ranch Life' ; 'A Nymph of the West' ; 'The

Jonah of Lucky Valley, and Other Stories'; 'A Border Leander.'

Seelye, Mrs. Elizabeth (Eggleston). An American author, daughter of Edward Eggleston; born in Minnesota, 1858. She has written: 'The Story of Columbus'; 'Montezuma'; 'Brant and Red Jacket'; 'Pocahontas'; 'Tecumseh'; and 'The Story of Washington.'

Seelye, Julius Hawtry. An American educator; born in Bethel, Conn., Sept. 14, 1824; died at Amherst, Mass., May 12, 1895. He was president of Amherst College (1876 90), and inaugurated the "Amherst system" of self-government, which was productive of good results. His publications include: 'The Way, the Truth, and the Life' (1873), translated into Hindustani, Japanese, and German; 'Christian Missions' (1875); and his revised edition of Hickok's 'Moral Science' (1880).

Seemann, Berthold. A German traveler, naturalist, and author; born in Hanover, Feb. 28, 1825; died in Nicaragua, Oct. 10, 1871. He was naturalist to three exploring expeditions (1846-51), and wrote: 'Voyage of the Herald,' and 'Three Cruises to Arctic Regions in Search of Sir John Franklin' (1852); 'Popular History of Palms' (1855); 'Account of Mission to Fiji Islands' (1862); 'Popular Nomenclature of the American Flora'; and 'Dottings on the Roadside in Panama, Nicaragua, and Mosquito.'

Seemuller, Mrs. Annie Moncure (Crane). An American novelist; born in Maryland, 1838; died in 1872. Her works were at one time very popular, and include the novels 'Emily Chester'; 'Reginald Archer'; 'Opportunity.'

Ségur, Louis Philippe, Comte de (sā-gür'). A French historian; born in Paris, Dec. 10, 1753; died there, Aug. 27, 1830. He received a military education; served in America under Rochambeau; later he was appointed ambassador to Russia. During the Reign of Terror he left public life and devoted himself to literary labor. Among his works are: 'Théâtre de l'Hermitage' (1798); 'Tales, Fables, Songs, and Verses' (1801); 'Memoirs, or Souvenirs and Anecdotes' (1825).

Ségur, Philippe Paul, Comte de. A French writer of history, son of L. P.; born at Paris, Nov. 4, 1780; died Feb. 25, 1873. He wrote: 'History of Napoleon and the Grand Army in 1812' (2 vols., 1824); 'History of Russia and Peter the Great' (2 vols., 1829); 'History and Memoirs, 1789-1848' (8 vols., 1873).

Sejour, Victor (sē-zhör'). A French dramatist; born at Paris, 1816; died Sept. 21, 1874. He was a mulatto. His plays are in the high romantic vein, and call for gorgeous scenery; among them are: 'The Fall of Sejanus' (1849); 'Richard III.' (1852); 'The Devil's Money'; 'The Son of Night' (1856); 'Mysteries of the Temple'; 'The Madonna of the Roses' (1869).

Selden, John. A celebrated English jurist; born at Salvington in Surrey, 1584; died at London, Nov. 30, 1654. He wrote many very learned treatises on law — municipal, international, natural, etc. — and on the legislation of the ancient Hebrews; but he is best remembered for his 'Table Talk,' recorded by his secretary, Richard Milward: of it Coleridge declares that it contains "more weighty bullion sense" than he could find in the same number of pages of any uninspired writer.

Selous, Frederick Courteney. A well-known English explorer and sportsman; born in London, Dec. 31, 1851. He made a name as a gold-prospector, explorer, and elephant-hunter in South Africa, where he has spent many years; and during the Matabele campaign, fought with great gallantry on the side of the colonists. His publications, 'A Hunter's Wanderings in Africa' (1881), and 'Travel and Adventure in Southeast Africa' (1893), have been widely read.

Sénancour, Étienne Pivert de (sen-än-kör'). A French writer of the school of Rousseau; born at Paris, 1770; died at St. Cloud, 1846. Under the direct influence of Rousseau he wrote: 'Reveries on the Primitive State of Man' (1799); his most notable work, 'Obermann' (2 vols., 1804), is in the same vein; then followed 'Love according to Primordial Laws, and according to the Conventions of Society' (2 vols., 1805); 'Free Meditations of an Unknown Solitary on Detachment from the World' (1819); 'Sum of the Traditions of Morality and Religion' (2 vols., 1827), which brought on him legal prosecution for impiety; 'Isabella,' a novel (1833).

Seneca, Lucius Annæus (sen'ē-ka). A celebrated Roman philosopher; born at Corduba, in Spain, about the year 4 B.C.; died 65 A.D. He was Nero's preceptor, and his confidant and adviser in the beginning of his reign. Many of his writings have come down to us, among them 124 'Epistles to Lucilius,' containing admirable counsels and exhortations to the practice of virtue: 'On Providence'; 'Anger'; 'Of Benefits'; 'Natural-History Questions'; several tragedies, among them 'Thyestes,' 'Phædra,' and 'Medea.'

Senior, William. An English miscellaneous writer; author of 'Notable Shipwrecks' (1873); 'Waterside Sketches: A Book for Wanderers and Anglers' (1875); 'By Stream and Sea' (1877); 'Travel and Trout in the Antipodes' (1879); 'A Mixed Bag' (1895).

Serao, Matilde (ser-ä'ō). An Italian novelist; born at Patras in Greece, March 7, 1856. Her best stories are those descriptive of Neapolitan life: as 'Faint Heart' (1881); 'Fantasy' (1883); 'Neapolitan Legends' (1886); 'Opal'; 'Little Minds'; 'Fool's Paradise'; 'Ballet-Girl.'

Serres, Olivia (Wilmot). An English story-writer; born 1772; died 1834. She claimed to be a daughter of the Duke of Cumberland, brother of George III., but failed to make the claim good before a Parliamentary committee. She wrote: 'St. Julian,' a novel (1805); 'Flights of Fancy,' poems (1806); 'Olivia's Advice to her

Daughters'; 'The True Messiah; or, St. Athanasius's Creed Explained (1814).

Servetus, Michael (Miguel Serveto y Reves) (ser-vē'tŭs). A Spanish physician and theological writer; born at Tudela in Navarre, 1511; died at the stake in Geneva, Oct. 27, 1553. He accompanied Charles V. to Germany, as physician to the emperor's confessor Quintana. His work 'On the Errors about the Trinity' was published at Hagenau, 1531, and it was soon afterward ordered to be burnt by the authorities at Basel: the reformer Bucer denounced the writer as deserving of the extremest punishment. Servetus defended his views in another work, 'Dialogues on the Trinity' (1532), and then went to France. At Lyons he published 'The Restoration of Christianism' (1553), and to escape punishment fled to Geneva. There, at the instance of Calvin, he was arrested on the charge of denying God and Christ, and burned as a heretic.

Settle, Elkanah. An English playwright and poet; born at Dunstable, 1648; died at London, 1723. His chief plays are: 'The Empress of Morocco' (1673); 'Love and Revenge' (1675); 'Pastor Fido, or the Faithful Shepherd' (1677), after Guarini; 'The Female Prelate; or, The Life and Death of Pope Joan' (1680); 'Distressed Innocence; or, The Princess of Persia' (1682).

Sévigné, Marie de Rabutin-Chantal, Marquise de (sāv-ēn-yā'). A celebrated French letter-writer; born at Paris, February 1626; died at the Castle of Grignan, in Dauphiny, April 18, 1696. Her 'Letters,' mainly to her daughter, are regarded as models of the familiar epistolary style. The best edition is that in 10 vols., 1818-19.

Sewall, Frank. An American writer and Swedenborgian minister; born in Maine, 1837. He has written many denominational and religious works; among them 'Moody Mike; or, The Power of Love'; 'The Hem of his Garment'; 'The Pillow of Stones'; 'The New Ethics'; 'The New Metaphysics'; 'Angelo and Ariel.' He has been remarkably successful in the translation of Italian and French poetry, and has published a translation of the poems of Carducci, and works on him, notably 'Giosue Carducci and the Hellenic Reaction in Italy'; 'Carducci and the Classic Realism' (1892). His translation of Carducci's sonnet 'The Ox' has been noticed throughout Europe.

Sewall, Harriet (Winslow). An American verse-writer; born at Portland, Me., June 30, 1819; died at Wellesley, Mass., February 1889. She wrote the poem 'Why Thus Longing?' Her other poetical compositions were published in a volume of 'Poems, with a Memoir' (1889).

Sewall, Jonathan Mitchell. An American poet; born at Salem, Mass., 1748; died at Portsmouth, N. H., March 29, 1808. During the Revolutionary war he wrote a ballad, 'War and Washington,' which was very popular; in

his epilogue (1780) to Addison's 'Cato' occur the lines "No pent-up Utica contracts your powers"; his 'Miscellaneous Poems' were collected and published in 1801.

Sewall, Samuel. An American jurist; born in Bishopstoke, England, March 28, 1652; died in Boston, Jan. 1, 1730. He came to America very young, graduated at Harvard in 1675, and became a member of the council; and as judge of the probate court (1692) took a prominent part in the trials during the Salem Witchcraft excitement. He is chiefly remarkable in literary annals for his 'Diary' and 'Letters,' which have been published by the Massachusetts Historical Society (1878-82). He wrote a tract on the rights of slaves, 'The Selling of Joseph' (1711); and published: 'The Accomplishment of Prophecies' (1713); 'A Memorial Relating to the Kennebec Indians' (1721); and 'A Description of the New Heaven' (1727).

Sewall, Stephen. An American Hebrew scholar; born in York, Me., April 4, 1734; died in Boston, July 23, 1804. He became librarian and instructor at Harvard College (1762), and professor of Hebrew (1764-85). He published a 'Hebrew Grammar' (1763); A Funeral Oration in Latin on Edward Holyoke (1769); 'The Scripture Account of the Shechinah' (1794); and left a manuscript 'Chaldee and English Dictionary,' now preserved in Harvard College Library.

Seward, Anna. A English poet; born at Eyam, Derbyshire, 1747; died at Lichfield, March 25, 1809. Her celebrity as a poet was obtained chiefly from her elegies upon her friend Major André (1781), and upon Captain Cook. She published: 'Louisa,' a poetical novel (1782), and 'Sonnets' (1789). Sir Walter Scott published her 'Poetical Works and Correspondence' (3 vols., 1810). She was called "The Swan of Lichfield."

Seward, William Henry. An American statesman; born in Florida, N. Y., May 16, 1801; died in Auburn, N. Y., 1872. In 1838 he was elected the first Whig governor of New York; in 1849 United States Senator, re-elected 1855. He was Secretary of State (1861-69) during the Civil War and through Johnson's term. He published many of his speeches and addresses; a volume on the 'Life and Services of John Quincy Adams' (1849); and, with his adopted daughter Olive Risley Seward, 'Travels Around the World' (1873). His 'Works,' edited by Geo. E. Baker, appeared in 3 vols., 1853; 5 vols., 1884.

Sewrin, Charles A. (sā-ē-raṅ'). A French dramatist and story-writer; born at Metz, 1771; died at Paris, 1853. He wrote among others: — Comic operas: 'The Village School'; 'The Opera in a Village'; 'Of Old and Now-a-days'; 'The Blacksmith of Bassora'; 'The Young Mother-in-Law.' Comedies: 'My Uncle Antony'; 'The Country Cits'; 'Gulliver'; 'The Swiss Milkmaid.' Novels: 'The Story of a Dog' (1801); 'Story of a Cat' (1802); 'A

Family of Liars' (1802); 'The Friends of Henri IV.' (1805).

Sextus Empiricus. A Greek philosopher, who flourished near the end of the second century; a physician of the «empirical» school, whence his surname. In his 'Outlines of Pyrrhonism' he revived the skepticism of Pyrrho; and he wrote a work on skepticism, under the title 'Adversus Mathematicos.'

Seymour, Mary Harrison. An American juvenile-story writer; born in Oxford, Conn, Sept. 7, 1835. She has published: 'Mollie's Christmas Stocking' (1865); 'Sunshine and Starlight' (1868); 'Posy Vinton's Picnic' (1869); 'Ned, Nellie, and Amy' (1870); 'Recompense' (1877); 'Every Day' (1877); and 'Through the Darkness' (1884).

Shadwell, Thomas. An English dramatist; born at Stanton Hall, Norfolk, about 1642; died Nov. 19, 1692. His comedy 'The Sullen Lovers,' produced in 1668, brought him reputation. Among many other plays, he was the author of 'The Virtuoso' (1676); 'Lancashire Witches' (1682); 'The Squire of Alsatia' (1688); and 'Volunteers; or, The Stock-Jobbers' (1693). He became poet-laureate and historiographer royal in 1688, succeeding Dryden in both positions. ('Works,' 4 vols., 1720.)

Shaftesbury, Anthony Ashley Cooper, first Earl of. An English statesman; born in Wimborne, St. Giles, Dorsetshire, July 22, 1621; died in Amsterdam, Jan. 22, 1683. He was a conspicuous figure in the history of his times; was the Achitophel of Dryden's satire. Macaulay gives a brilliant sketch of him in the essay on Sir William Temple. Ashley and Cooper rivers, in South Carolina, received their names from him. His 'Characteristics of Men, Manners, Opinions, and Times' is a collection of his various writings.

Shairp, John Campbell. ["Principal Shairp."] A Scotch poet, critic, and essayist; born at Houstoun, in West Lothian, July 30, 1819; died at Ormsary, in Argyll, Sept. 18, 1885. He was principal of the United College, St. Andrews. Among his works are: 'Kilmahoe, a Highland Pastoral, and Other Poems' (1864); 'Studies in Poetry and Philosophy' (1868); 'Culture and Religion' (1870); 'Poetic Interpretation of Nature' (1877); 'Aspects of Poetry' (1881); and, published posthumously, 'Sketches in History and Poetry' (1887); 'Glen Desseray and Other Poems' (1888).

Shakespeare, William. The poet was born at Stratford-on-Avon, April 22 or 23, 1564; died there, April 23, 1616. His plays, in the order of their production, are given as follows: 'Love's Labour's Lost' (written 1591 (?); revised 1597; published 1598); 'Two Gentlemen of Verona' (written 1591 (?); published posthumously 1623); 'Comedy of Errors' (written 159-; published posthumously 1623); 'Romeo and Juliet' (written 159-; pirated 1597; published with author's sanction 1599); 'Henry VI.' (Part i. written and acted 1592, Parts ii. and iii. following quickly; Part ii. published 1594; Part iii. published 1595); 'King Richard III.' (written 1593 (?); published 1597); 'Titus Andronicus' (written in collaboration 1593 or 1594; acted 1594 (?); published 1600 ?); 'A Merchant of Venice' (written and acted 1594 (?); published 1600); 'King John' (written 1594; acted 159-); 'A Midsummer Night's Dream,' written and acted 1594-95; published 1600; 'King Richard II.' (produced 1595); 'All's Well that Ends Well' (written 1595 (?); acted 159-); 'The Taming of the Shrew' (written 1596 (?); acted 159-; published posthumously 1623); 'Henry IV.' (written or adapted 1597; published, Part i. 1598, Part ii. 1600; revised and republished 1600); 'The Merry Wives of Windsor' (written 159-; acted 159-; published 1602); 'Henry V.' (written 1598; acted 1599; published, text imperfect, 1600); 'Much Ado about Nothing' (written 1599 (?); acted 1599; published 1600); 'As You Like It' (produced 1599); 'Twelfth Night' (written 1599; acted 1601 or 1602); 'Julius Cæsar' (written 1601; acted 1601); 'Hamlet' (written 1602; acted 1602 (?); published by another surreptitiously 1602 or 1603; authorized ed. 1604); 'Troilus and Cressida' (written 1603 (?); acted 1603; published 1608 or 1609); 'Othello' (written 1604 (?); acted 1604; published posthumously 1622); 'Measure for Measure' (written 1604 (?); acted 1604; published posthumously); 'Macbeth' (written 1605-6; acted 1606 (?); revived 1611; published posthumously 1623); 'King Lear' (written 1606; acted 1606; published 1608); 'Timon of Athens' (written in collaboration 1607; acted 160-); 'Pericles' (written in collaboration 1607; published 1608 or 1609); 'Antony and Cleopatra' (written 1607-8; published posthumously 1623); 'Coriolanus' (written 1608 (?); published posthumously 1623); 'Cymbeline' (written 16—; acted 1610); 'A Winter's Tale' (written 16—; acted 1611); 'The Tempest' (written before the winter of 1612-13); 'The Two Noble Kinsmen' (written in collaboration (?); published posthumously 1634); 'Henry VIII.' (portions by Shakespeare written 1613 (?); acted 1613; published posthumously 1623). His poems are: 'Venus and Adonis' (1593); 'The Rape of Lucrece' (1594); 'Sonnets' (written 1591-94; published 1609); 'A Lover's Complaint (written 1594-98 (?); published 1609); 'The Passionate Pilgrim' (1st ed. (?) 1594). The first collected edition of the plays, under the title 'Mr. William Shakespeare's comedies, histories, and tragedies. Published according to the true original copies,' appeared in 1623, and is referred to as «the folio of 1623.» One existing copy has two canceled leaves from 'As You Like It.'

Shaler, Nathaniel Southgate. An American geologist; born near Newport, Ky., Feb. 20, 1841. He was professor of geology at Harvard, and a versatile and interesting writer in many important fields. Among his works are the 'Kentucky Geological Reports and Memoirs' (7 vols., 1876-82); 'On the Nature of Intellectual Property and its Importance to the State' (1878); 'Aspects of the Earth' (1889); 'The Story of our Continent' (1892); 'Nature and Man in North America' (1892); 'The Interpretation of Nature' (1893); 'Sea and Land' (1894); 'The United States of America' (2 vols., 1894); and reports of United States Geological Survey on Marine Marshes, Fresh-Water Swamps, Soils, Harbors, etc. Died Apr. 10, 1906.

Shanks, William Franklin-Gore. An American journalist and author; born in Shelbyville, Ky., April 20, 1837. He was war correspondent for the New York Herald (1861–65), subsequently joined the New York Tribune, and was imprisoned for refusing to divulge the name of a writer of an article in the paper. Besides his contributions to periodicals he has published: 'Recollections of Distinguished Generals' (1865); 'Bench and Bar' (1868); and a play, 'A Noble Treason ' (1876). He died 1905.

Sharp, William. A British critic and man of letters; born 1856. He has traveled extensively, and contributed to leading publications throughout the world. His works include 'Humanity and Man,' a poem; 'The Conqueror's Dream, and Other Poems'; 'Dante Gabriel Rossetti,' a biography; 'Shakespeare's Songs, Poems, and Sonnets'; 'Sonnets of this Century'; 'Shelley,' a biography; 'Romantic Ballads'; etc. Died, 1905.

Shaw, Albert. An American editor and writer on municipal government; born at Shandon, O., July 23, 1857. Since 1891 he has been the editor of the Review of Reviews in America. Included in his publications are: 'Icaria: a Chapter in the History of Communism' (1884); 'Co-operation in a Western City' (1886); and 'The National Revenue' (1888). 'Municipal Government in Great Britain'; 'Municipal Government in Continental Europe'; 'Political Problems of American Development.'

Shaw, George Bernard, an English author, born 1856. Besides numerous novels with strongly socialistic tendencies like 'An Unsocial Socialist'; 'The Quintessence of Ibsenism'; 'Fabianism and the Fiscal Question,' he wrote 'Three Plays for Puritans'; 'Man and Super-man'; and (1909) 'Press-Cuttings,' which was suppressed by the censor. All of his works are filled with epigrams and satirical hits at all phases of society.

Shaw, Henry Wheeler. ["Josh Billings."] An American humorist: (1818–1885). His publications include: 'Josh Billings on Ice' (1875); 'Josh Billings's Complete Works' (1877); and 'Josh Billings's Spice Box' (1881).

Shea, John Dawson Gilmary. An American author and historical writer (1824–1892). He edited the Historical Magazine (1859–65); also Frank Leslie's Chimney Corner. He published: 'Discovery and Exploration of the Mississippi Valley' (1853); 'History of Catholic Missions among the Indians' (1854); 'Account of the New Netherlands in 1643–44' (1862); 'The Catholic Church in the United States' (1856); and 'Life of Pius IX.' (1875).

Shedd, Mrs. Julia Ann (Clark). An American writer on art; born in Newport Me.,

Aug. 8, 1834. Besides contributions to art periodicals she published: 'Famous Painters and Paintings' (1874); 'The Ghiberti Gates' (1876); 'Famous Sculptors and Sculpture' (1881); and 'Raphael, his Madonnas and Holy Families.' Died in Providence, R. I., April 7, 1897.

Shedd, William Greenough Thayer. An eminent educator, author, and Presbyterian clergyman; born in Acton, Mass., June 21, 1820; died November 6, 1894. He was professor in the University of Vermont (1845–52); in Auburn Theological Seminary (1852–54); in Andover Theological Seminary (1854–62); and professor of Biblical literature in Union Seminary from 1863. He has published numerous historical and polemic works. Among them are: 'Lectures on the Philosophy of History' (1856); 'History of Christian Doctrine' (2 vols., 1863); 'Sermons to the Natural Man' (1871); 'Doctrine of Endless Punishment' (1885); and 'Dogmatic Theology' (3 vols., 1888–94).

Shelley, Mary (Godwin). An English writer of works of psychological and historical fiction, second wife of the poet Shelley; born at London, Aug. 30, 1797; died there, Feb. 1, 1851. Her first story, 'Frankenstein' (1818), won for her a place among the imaginative writers of England; it was followed by 'Valperga,' a historical romance (1823); 'The Last Man' (1826); 'Lodore' (1835); 'Falkner' (1837).

Shelley, Percy Bysshe. The celebrated English poet; born at Warnham, near Horsham, Sussex, Aug. 4, 1792; drowned off the coast of Italy, July 8, 1822. He wrote: 'Zastrozzi' (1810), a romance; 'St. Irvyne' (1811), a romance; 'The Necessity of Atheism' (1811 ?), a treatise; 'A Poetical Essay on the Existing State of Things' (1811); 'An Address to the Irish People' (1812); 'Proposals for an Association of those Philanthropists who, Convinced of the Inadequacy of the Moral and Political State of Ireland to Produce Benefits which are, nevertheless, Attainable, are Willing to Unite to Accomplish its Regeneration' (1812); 'Queen Mab: A Philosophic Poem' (1813); 'A Vindication of Natural Diet' (1813); 'A Refutation of Deism' (1814); 'Alastor, or the Spirit of Solitude, and Other Poems' (1816); 'A Proposal for Putting Reform to the Vote throughout the Kingdom' (1817); 'A Six-Weeks' Tour' (1817), in collaboration with Mary Godwin; 'Laon and Cynthia' (1818), subsequently altered and reissued as 'The Revolt of Islam: A Poem' (1818, some few copies being erroneously dated 1817); 'Rosalind and Helen: A Modern Eclogue; with Other Poems' (1819); 'The Cenci: A Tragedy' (1819); 'Prometheus Unbound: A Lyrical Drama' (1820); 'Œdipus Tyrannus, or Swellfoot the Tyrant: A Tragedy in Two Acts; Translated from the Original Doric' (1820); 'Epipsychidion: Verses addressed to the Noble and Unfortunate Lady Emilia V——' (1821); 'Adonais: An Elegy on the Death of John Keats' (1821); 'Hellas: A Lyrical Drama' (1822),—the last of Shelley's works issued during his lifetime. After his death there appeared: 'Posthumous

Poems' (1824); 'The Masque of Anarchy: A Poem; Now First Published' (1832); 'The Shelley Papers' (1833); 'Essays, Letters from Abroad, Translations, and Fragments' (1840); 'The Dæmon of the World: the First Part as Published in 1816 with 'Alastor'; the Second Part Deciphered and now First Printed' (1876).

Shelton, Frederick William. An American clergyman, and humorous and satirical writer; born in Jamaica, N. Y., 1814; died at Carthage Landing, N. Y., June 20, 1881. His publications include: 'The Trollopiad, or Traveling Gentleman in America,' a satirical poem (1837); 'Salander and the Dragon,' a romance (1851); 'Up the River,' a series of rural sketches on the Hudson (1853); 'Peeps from a Belfry; or, Parish Sketch-Book' (1855); 'Use and Abuse of Reason'; 'The Gold Mania'; etc.

Shenshin, Afanasy Afanasievich. See **Fet.**

Shenstone, William. An English poet; born at the Leasowes, near Halesowen, Shropshire, November 1714; died there, Feb. 11, 1763. His best-remembered poems are: 'The Schoolmistress' (1742); 'The Pastoral Ballad' (1743); and 'Written in an Inn at Henley.' His 'Works' and 'Letters' were collected in three volumes (1764-69); and his 'Essays on Men and Manners' were republished in 1868.

Sheppard, Elizabeth Sara. An English novelist; born at Blackheath, 1830; died at Brixton, March 13, 1862. She wrote the noted 'Charles Auchester' (1853), a mystical art novel; 'Counterparts, or the Cross of Love' (1854); 'My First Season' (1855); 'The Double Coronet' (1856); 'Rumor,' a musical and artistic novel (1858).

Sheridan, Philip Henry. A famous American soldier; born in Albany, N. Y., March 6, 1831; died in Nonquitt, Mass., Aug. 5, 1888. He graduated at West Point, July 1, 1853, and rose through a distinguished career of army service during which he became successively major-general, lieutenant-general, and general. He wrote 'Personal Memoirs,' published in 2 vols., 1888.

Sheridan, Richard Brinsley. An eminent British dramatist and parliamentary orator; born at Dublin, Oct. 30, 1751; died at London, July 7, 1816. His principal dramatic works are: 'The Rivals,' comedy (1774); 'The Duenna,' comic opera (1775); 'The School for Scandal,' comedy (1777); 'The Critic,' farce (1779). His most memorable speeches are the 'Begum Speech,' so-called, made in the trial of Warren Hastings, and the 'Perfumery Speech.'

Sherman, Frank Dempster. An American poet; born at Peekskill, N. Y., May 6, 1860. Educated at Columbia College and Harvard University, he became an instructor in the Columbia School of Architecture. He has published: 'Madrigals and Catches'; 'Lyrics for a Lute'; and, with John Kendrick Bangs, 'New Waggings of Old Tales'; 'Little Folk Lyrics'; 'Lyrics of Joy.' His poems are a frequent feature of the magazines.

Sherman, John. An eminent American statesman; born in Lancaster, Ohio., May 10, 1823; died in Washington, Oct. 22, 1900. He was first elected to Congress in 1854; Senator, 1861-73; and 1881-87; Secretary of the Treasury, 1877-81; and Secretary of State from 1897. He is the author of 'Selected Speeches and Reports on Finance and Taxation, 1859-1878' (New York 1879); and 'Recollections of Forty Years in the House, Senate, and Cabinet.'

Sherman, William Tecumseh. One of the most distinguished of American generals; born in Lancaster, O., Feb. 8, 1820, died in New York city, Feb. 14, 1891. He graduated at West Point in 1840; resigned from the army as captain in 1853; was commissioned colonel, May 13, 1861, and after a long career of active service, retired from command on Feb. 8, 1884, as general of the army. He has published: 'Memoirs of Gen. William T. Sherman by Himself' (2 vols., New York, 1875 and 1885).

Sherwood, John D. An American writer; born in Fishkill, N. Y., Oct. 15, 1818. He served as a Federal officer through the Civil War. Besides contributing to periodicals, he has published the volumes: 'The Case of Cuba' (1869); 'Comic History of the United States' (1870).

Shevchenko, Taras Grigorievich (shevchen'kō). A Russian poet; born Feb. 25, 1814; died in St. Petersburg, Feb. 26, 1861. His 'Kobzar,' a volume of lyrics in the Little Russian dialect, appeared in 1840 (new ed. 1860), and became at once popular. 'Haidamaki,' one of the greatest of Russian epics, followed in 1841; after which came 'Hamalia,' 'Maiax,' and others.

Shillaber, Benjamin Penhallow. ["Mrs. Partington."] An American journalist and humorist; born in Portsmouth, N. H., July 12, 1814; died in Chelsea, Mass., Nov. 25, 1890. From 1840 to 1866 he was editor of various journals in Boston. His 'Life and Sayings of Mrs. Partington' (1854) gained for him world-wide popularity. This was followed by 'Knitting-Work' (1857); 'Partington Patchwork' (1873); and 'Wide Swath,' a volume of collected verse (1882).

Shindler, Mrs. Mary Stanley Bunce (**Palmer**) (**Dana**). An American poet and author; born in Beaufort, S. C., Feb. 15, 1810; died in 1883. Her poems, once very popular through the South, include: 'The Southern Harp' (1840); 'The Northern Harp' (1841); 'The Parted Family, and Other Poems' (1842); 'The Temperance Lyre' (1842). She has also written 'Charles Morton; or, The Young Patriot' (1843); 'Forecastle Tom' (1844); and 'Letters on the Trinity' (1845).

Shinn, Charles Howard. An American poet, journalist, and historical writer; born in Austin, Tex., April 29, 1852. He was engaged in periodical work until 1885, when he became connected with the Overland Monthly. He is the author of 'Mining Camps: A Study in

American Pioneer Government' (1885), and 'The Story of the Mine.'

Shinn, Millicent Washburn. An American editor; born in Washington Township, Cal., April 15, 1858. In 1882 she was connected with the Overland Monthly. Her writings include poems, sketches, stories, and critiques, for various magazines.

Shipman, Louis Evan. An American writer; born in Brooklyn, N. Y., Aug. 2, 1869. He has published: 'Urban Dialogues'; 'A Group of American Caricatures'; and an acting play founded on the story of 'Henry Esmond;' 'On Parole'; 'The Admiral.'

Shorey, Paul. An American scholar; born 1857. He is now professor of Greek and Latin literature at the University of Chicago. He published 'The Odes and Epodes of Horace'; 'The Unity of Plato's Thought.'

Shorter, Clement King. An English editor and author. Upon the death of John Latey, he was appointed editor of the Illustrated London News by Sir William Ingram, proprietor of that paper. He also has charge of the Sketch, Album, and English Illustrated Magazine, and is generally regarded as one of the ablest and most acute editors in London. His published works comprise: 'Fifty Years of Victorian Literature, 1837-87' (1888); 'Charlotte Brontë and her Circle' (1896); 'Victorian Literature: Sixty Years of Books and Bookmen' (1897).

Shorthouse, John Henry. An English novelist; born at Birmingham, in 1834. His best-known novel is 'John Inglesant' (1881). His other works include: 'The Little Schoolmaster, Mark' (1883-84); 'Sir Percival' (1886); 'A Teacher of the Violin' (1888); and 'Blanche, Lady Falaise.' Died in London, Mar. 4, 1902.

Sidgwick, Henry. A distinguished English philosopher and political economist; born at Skipton, Yorkshire, May 31, 1838; died at Cambridge, Aug. 28, 1900. He was professor of moral philosophy at Cambridge, and did much for the promotion of higher education of women, having assisted in the foundation of Newnham College. His works include: 'The Methods of Ethics' (1874); 'The Principles of Political Economy' (1883), one of the most important works on the subject; 'Outlines of the History of Ethics' (1886); etc.

Sidney or **Sydney, Algernon.** An English republican patriot; born at Penshurst, Kent (?), 1622 (?); died at London on the scaffold, Dec. 7, 1683. He wrote 'Discourses Concerning Government,' his political confession of faith (1698).

Sidney, Philip, Sir. An English courtier and man of letters; born at Penshurst in Kent, Nov. 30, 1554; died at Arnheim, Oct. 17, 1586. He wrote some 'Sonnets' after the manner of Catullus and Petrarch; a celebrated essay, 'Apology for Poetry' (1595); a pastoral tale, 'Arcadia' (1590); and a versified translation of the 'Psalms.'

Sidonius Appollinaris, Caius Sollius (430-482 A. D). A conspicuous man of affairs and of literary effort in the Roman Empire of the fifth century; bishop of Clermont, in Gaul. Of his work we have 'Panegyrics' of several emperors, and some poems, not valuable; and a collection of letters very valuable as a picture of provincial society just as the barbarians were overwhelming it.

Sienkiewicz, Henryk (sĕ″en-kĕ″ā-vich). A very eminent Polish novelist; born at Vola Okrzejska, 1846. His works comprise: 'No Man Is a Prophet in his Own Country' (1872); 'Hania'; 'Charcoal Sketches'; 'Village Tales'; 'Yanko the Musician'; 'With Fire and Sword' (1884), 'The Deluge' (1886), 'Pan Michael' (1888),—a grand trilogy of historical novels: 'Without Dogma' (1890); 'Quo Vadis' (1895), a historical novel of the time of Nero; 'The Crusaders'; 'Hanna'; 'Comedy of Errors.'

Sigerson, Dora. An Irish verse-writer; born at Dublin; wrote a volume of 'Verses' (1893).

Sigourney, Lydia (Huntley). An American writer of prose and verse; born in Norwich, Conn., Sept. 1, 1791; died in Hartford, Conn., June 10, 1865. In her 'Letters of Life,' published (1866) posthumously, she enumerates forty-six distinct works wholly or partially from her pen, besides over 2,000 articles in prose and verse, contributed by her to nearly 300 periodicals. Among her other publications are: 'Pleasant Memories of Pleasant Lands,' a record of her visit in Europe made in 1840 (1842); 'Scenes in my Native Land' (1844); 'Water Drops: A Plea for Temperance' (1847); 'Gleanings,' poems (1860); and 'The Man of Uz, and Other Poems' (1862).

Sikes, Mrs. W. W. See **Logan.**

Silius Italicus (sil′i-us it-al′i-kus). A Roman poet; born in 25 A. D.; died in 101. His epic poem 'Punica,' in 17 books, is still extant; its theme is the second Punic war, as its story is told by Livy and Polybius, and the author imitates the style of Virgil, but he lacks the true poetic inspiration. To him is attributed 'Homer in Latin,' a Latin translation of a part of the Iliad.

Sill, Edward Rowland. An American poet; born in Windsor, Conn., April 29, 1841; died in Cleveland, O., Feb. 27, 1887. In 1874 he became professor of English literature in the University of California, where he remained until 1882, subsequently removing to Cleveland. His poetical works are included in 'The Hermitage, and Other Poems' (1867); 'The Venus of Milo, and Other Poems' (1883); and 'Poems,' posthumously issued (1888).

Simcox, Edith. An English miscellaneous writer; author of 'Natural Law: An Essay in Ethics' (1877); 'Episodes in the Lives of Men, Women, and Lovers,' stories (1882).

Simms, William Gilmore. An American novelist and poet; born in Charleston, S. C., April 17, 1806; died there, June 11, 1870. His publications include: 'Atalantis: A Tale of the Sea' (1832), the longest and most noted of his poems; 'The Yemassee' (1835; revised ed. 1853); 'Castle Dismal' (1845); 'The Wigwam and the Cabin; or, Tales of the South' (1845-46); 'The Maroon, and Other Tales' (1855); and 'War Poetry of the South' (1867).

Simon, Jules François Suisse (sē-môn'). A notable French statesman and writer on philosophical and political subjects; born at Lorient, Dec. 31, 1814; died at Paris, June 8, 1896. He became a member of the Academy, 1875, and the same year was appointed senator for life. Among his works are: 'Studies on the Theodicy of Plato and Aristotle' (1840); 'History of the School of Alexandria' (2 vols., 1844); 'Duty' (1854; 15th ed. 1892); 'Natural Religion' (1856); 'The Workingwoman' (1861; 9th ed. 1891); 'Labor' (1866; 4th ed. 1877), a work which arrested public attention; 'Free Trade' (1870); 'Reform of Secondary Education' (1874); 'The Twentieth-Century Woman' (1891); 'Four Portraits': Lamartine, Lavigerie, Renan, and Emperor William II. (1896).

Simonds, William. ["Walter Aimwell."] An American juvenile writer; born in Massachusetts, 1822; died 1859. Among his best-known works are: 'The Aimwell Stories'; 'The Boys' Own Guide'; and 'The Boys' Book of Morals and Manners.'

Simonides (sē-mon'id-ēz). A celebrated Greek lyric poet; born in the island of Ceos, about 556 B. C.; died about 468. He was at the height of his fame at the time of the Persian war, and celebrated the heroes of that struggle and their feats. Of his famous 'Epigrams,' a good many have come down to us; but of his Elegies, Dirges, Epinikia, Dithyrambs, Hymns, and Pæans, we have but fragments.

Simpson, John Palgrave. An English story-writer and dramatist; born at Norwich, 1807; died at London, Aug. 19, 1887. He wrote: 'Second Love' (1846); 'Gisela' (1847); 'Letters from the Danube' (1847); 'The Lily of Paris; or, The King's Nurse' (1848); 'Pictures from Revolutionary Paris' (1848); 'Life of Karl Maria von Weber.' His dramatic compositions were about forty in number; among them are 'The World and the Stage,' and 'Sibylla; or, Step by Step.'

Sims, George Robert. An English dramatist and journalist; born in London, Sept. 2, 1847. He is the author of 'The Lights o' London' (1882); 'The Romany Rye' (1883). Some of his contributions to the press are: 'Dagonet Ballads' (1879); 'Three Brass Balls' (1880); 'The Theatre of Life' (1881); 'How the Poor Live' (1883); 'Stories in Black and White' (1885); 'Mary Jane's Memoir'; 'Scarlet Sin.'

Sinclair, Catherine. A Scotch novelist; born in Edinburgh, April 17, 1800; died there, Aug. 6, 1864. Among her writings are: 'Charlie Seymour'; 'Holiday House'; 'Modern Accomplishments,' a study of the education of

girls (1836); 'Shetland and the Shetlanders' (1840); 'Modern Flirtations' (1841); 'Scotch Courtiers and the Court' (1842); 'Jane Bouverie; or, Prosperity and Adversity' (1846); 'Popish Legends; or, Bible Truths' (1852); 'Torchester Abbey' (1857); 'Anecdotes of the Cæsars' (1858); 'Sketches and Short Stories of Scotland' (1859).

Sinclair, Thomas. A British poet and story-writer; born near Thurso, Scotland, 1843. He wrote: 'Poems' (1873); 'The Messenger,' verses (1875); 'Love's Trilogy,' a poem (1876); 'The Goddess Fortune,' a novel (1884); 'The Sinclairs of England'; 'Rulers of Orkney'; 'Essays.'

Sinnett, Alfred Percy. An English journalist; born in London, 1840. He was on the staff of the London Globe in 1859; afterwards edited the Daily Press at Hong Kong. In 1871 he was editor of the Pioneer, at Allahabad, India. Returning to England in 1882, he published 'The Occult World' and 'Esoteric Buddhism' (1883), which immediately connected his name with the Theosophical movement, and with its originator Madame Blavatsky.

Sismondi, Jean Charles Léonard Simon de (sis-môn'dē). A celebrated Swiss historian; born at Geneva, May 9, 1773; died there, June 25, 1842. His principal works are: 'History of the Italian Republics in the Middle Ages' (16 vols., 1807-18); 'History of the New Birth of Liberty in Italy' (2 vols., 1832); 'History of the French' (31 vols., 1821-34); 'History of the Fall of the Roman Empire' (2 vols., 1835); 'Julia Severa; or, The Year 492' (3 vols., 1822); 'Literature of the South of Europe' (1813).

Skeat, Walter William. A distinguished English Anglo-Saxon scholar, philologist, and lexicographer; born in London, Nov. 21, 1835. He is professor of Anglo-Saxon at Cambridge (from 1883); one of the founders of the English Dialect Society; and an authority on early English literature. He has edited 'The Vision of William concerning Piers Ploughman' (1867-85); Barbour's 'The Bruce' (1870-89); 'Specimens of English Literature, 1298-1579' (1871 and 1872); numerous poems, metrical romances, etc.; and has compiled 'An Etymological Dictionary of the English Language' (4 vols., 1879-81; new ed. 1884), his chief work. One of his recent publications is an edition of Chaucer (6 vols., 1894); 'Notes on English Etymology.'

Skelton John. An early English satirical poet; born about 1460; died in 1529. He was academical laureate at Cambridge and Oxford, and afterwards was appointed by Henry VII. tutor to Prince Henry, afterward Henry VIII. He wrote many poems of a jocular and satirical nature, among which are 'Philip Sparrow,' the lament of a maiden over the loss of her pet bird; and 'Colin Clout,' a satire on the clergy.

Sketchley, Arthur, pseudonym of George Rose. An English dramatist and writer of humorous sketches; born at London, May 19, 1817; died there, Nov. 11, 1882. He wrote: 'Pauline,' a drama (1851); 'The Dark Cloud,' drama (1863); 'How will They Get out of It,' comedy (1864); and about 35 volumes of humorous pieces selected from his contributions to the comic journals, among them 'Mrs. Brown's Visit to the Paris Exhibition' (1867), followed by a series of observations of the same imaginary personage: 'In the Highlands' (1869); 'On the Grand Tour' (1870); 'On the New Liquor Law' (1872); 'On the Alabama Claims' (1872); 'On Home Rule' (1881); etc.

Skinner, John. A Scotch song-writer; born at Balfour, in Aberdeenshire, Oct. 3, 1721; died June 16, 1807. His songs were very popular: among them were 'Tullochgorum,' reckoned by Burns "the best Scotch song Scotland ever saw"; 'Ewie wi' the Crookit Horn'; 'John o' Badenyon'; 'The Old Man's Song.' He wrote an 'Ecclesiastical History of Scotland' (2 vols., 1788).

Skipsey, Joseph. An English verse-writer; author of 'Poems, Songs, and Ballads' (1862); 'Miscellaneous Lyrics' (1878). A complete edition of his works, entitled 'Carols from the Coal Fields, and Other Songs and Ballads,' was issued in 1886.

Sladen, Douglas Brooke Wheelton. An English poet; born at London, 1856. He is author of 'Frithjog and Ingebjorg, and Other Poems' (1882); 'Australian Lyrics' (1883); 'A Summer Christmas : A Tale of Sport' (1884); 'Edward the Black Prince,' an epic drama (1886); 'Australian Ballads and Rhymes' (1888); 'The Spanish Armada'; 'Queer Things about Japan.'

Sleidan or **Sleidanus, Johannes** (slī'dan). A celebrated German historian; born at Schleiden near Cologne; died at Strasburg, Oct. 31, 1556. His greatest work is 'Memoirs of the State of Religion and the Civil Government under the Emperor Charles V.' (3 vols., 1555), a history written without partisanship, and in graceful literary style; he wrote also a history of 'The Four Great Empires, Babylonian, Persian, Greek, and Roman' (1556).

Sloane, William Milligan. An American historian; born in Richmond, O., Nov. 12, 1850; graduated at Columbia in 1868; studied in Berlin and Leipsic (1872-76), and during part of that time was private secretary of George Bancroft, then minister at Berlin. He was for several years a professor at Princeton, and is now professor of history at Columbia. He has published: 'The French War and the Revolution'; 'Life of James McCosh'; in 1897 brought out a very important 'Life of Napoleon,' in 2 vols.

Slosson, Mrs. Annie (Trumbull). An American story-writer, sister of J. Hammond and Henry Clay Trumbull; born in Hartford, Conn., 184-. She has devoted much time to the study of entomology, and written many excellent short stories. Her books include: 'Seven Dreamers,' a collection of her magazine stories; 'The Heresy of Mehetable Clark'; 'Anna Malann'; 'The China Hunter's Club'; 'White Christopher.'

Slowacki, Julius (slō-vats'kĕ). A celebrated, Polish poet, born at Kremenecz in Volhynia,

Aug. 23, 1809; died at Paris, April 3, 1849. In his earlier poems he was under the influence of Byron; but escapes from it in the 'Ode to Liberty,' 'Hymn to the Mother of God,' and 'Song of the Lithuanian Legion' (1831). The sentiment of Polish nationality finds fullest expression in the dramatic poem 'Kordyan' (1834), and the tragedy 'Mazeppa.' Slowacki reaches the height of his lyric power in the poem 'In Switzerland.' His last great work, left incomplete, was 'King Spirit,' which he designed to be a «Legend of the Ages» of Polish history.

Smalley, George Washburn. An American journalist; born in Franklin, Mass., June 2, 1833. During the American Civil War, the war between Prussia and Russia, and the Franco-German war, he distinguished himself as war correspondent of the New York Tribune; and as representative of the same in London (1867-95) he gained an eminent rank in journalism. His 'London Letters and Some Others' and 'Studies of Men' were widely popular. He has been American correspondent of the London Times since 1895.

Smart, Christopher. An English poet, and one of the interesting figures of literary history; born at Shipbourne, Kent, April 11, 1722; died May 21, 1771. His fame rests upon a 'Song to David' (1763), pronounced by Dante Gabriel Rossetti "the only great accomplished poem of the eighteenth century." It is said to have been written in a madhouse, "partly with charcoal on the walls, or indented with a key on the panels of his cell," the poet having been deprived of his liberty on account of his debts. Noted also is a version of Horace, which had a wide sale. Other works are : 'Poems' (1752); 'Power of the Supreme Being' (1753); 'The Hilliad : An Epic Poem' (1753); 'Poems on Several Occasions' (1763); 'Translation of the Psalms of David' (1765); and many miscellaneous essays, poems, and translations.

Smart, Mrs. Helen Hamilton (Gardener). An American novelist; born in Virginia, 1858. She has published many works of fiction dealing with social reforms. Among these are: 'An Unofficial Patriot'; 'Is This Your Son, My Lord?' 'Facts and Fictions of Life'; 'Pray You, Sir, Whose Daughter?' 'The Fortunes of Margaret Weld.' She has also written magazine articles, part of them collected as 'Men, Women, and Gods.'

Smiles, Samuel. A British miscellaneous writer; born at Haddington, Scotland, 1812. Many of his writings had a very wide circulation. Among them are: 'Self-Help' (1860); 'Life of George Stephenson' (6th ed. 1864); 'Lives of Engineers' (1862; new ed. 1874, 5 vols.); 'The Huguenots in England and Ireland' (4th ed. 1876); 'Thrift' (1875); 'Men of Invention and Industry.' Died Apr. 16, 1904.

Smith, Adam. A renowned Scotch political economist; born at Kirkcaldy, June 5, 1723; died at Edinburgh, July 17, 1790. He wrote a

'Theory of Moral Sentiments' (1759), in which he finds in human sympathy the cohesive force of social life; 'Origin of Languages' (about 1760); and (in 1776) his great work, 'Inquiry into the Nature and Causes of the Wealth of Nations,' unfairly said to make self-interest the chief motor of society: it only makes that passion the chief motor of making money.

Smith, Albert. An English humorist; born at Chertsey in Surrey, May 24, 1816; died at Fulham in Middlesex, May 23, 1860. He was a leading contributor to Punch. He wrote 'The Adventures of Mr. Ledbury'; 'Christopher Tadpole'; 'Pottleton's Legacy'; a series of "natural histories" of 'The Gent,' 'The Ballet Girl,' 'The Idler upon Town,' 'The Flirt'; and 'The Medical Student,' a small volume of amusing skits.

Smith, Alexander. A Scottish poet; born in Kilmarnock, Dec. 31, 1830; died at Wardie near Edinburgh, Jan. 5, 1867. Among his works, 'A Life Drama' (1853) attracted great attention. He wrote: 'Sonnets of the War,' with Sydney Dobell (1855); 'City Poems' (1857); 'Edwin of Deira' (1861); also the prose works 'Dreamthorpe' (1863), 'A Summer in Skye' (1865), 'Alfred Hagart's Household' (1866), and 'Miss Oona McQuarrie' (1866).

Smith, Buckingham. An American historian and philologist; born in Georgia, Oct. 31, 1810; died in New York, Jan. 5, 1871. He was secretary of legation at Mexico (1850–52), and at Madrid (1855–58). He made an exhaustive study of Mexican history and antiquities, and published many monographs and historical papers. Among them are: 'Narrative of Hernando de Soto' (1854); 'Documents relating to the History of Florida' (1857); 'A Grammatical Sketch of the Heve Language' (1861); 'Grammar of the Pina Language' (1862).

Smith, Charles Henry. ["Bill Arp."] An American humorist; born in Lawrenceville, Ga., June 15, 1826. His literary career began (1861) in a series of letters under the pseudonym above. His publications include: 'Bill Arp's Scrap-Book' (1886); 'The Farm and the Fireside'; and 'Georgia as a Colony and State, 1733–1893.' Died at Atlanta, Ga., Aug. 25, 1903.

Smith, Charlotte (Turner). An English novelist; born 1749; died 1806. She wrote: 'Elegiac Sonnets and Other Essays' (1784); 'Emmeline; or, The Orphan of the Castle' (1788); 'Ethelinde; or, the Recluse of the Lake' (1789); 'Celestina: A Novel' (1791); 'Desmond: A Novel' (1792); 'The Old Manor-House' (1793); 'The Emigrants: A Poem' (1793); 'Natural History of Birds' (1807).

Smith, Edmund. An English poet; born 1672; died 1710. His works are: 'Poem on the Death of Mr. John Philips' (1708); 'Phædrus and Hippolitus: A Tragedy' (1719); 'Monody on Dr. Pocock' (1750); 'Odes' (1719).

Smith, Elizabeth Oakes (Prince). An American writer of prose and verse, noted in her time; wife of Seba; born in Cumberland, Me.,

Aug. 12, 1806; died at Hollywood, N. C., Nov. 15, 1893. Among her numerous works are: 'Riches Without Wings' (1838); 'The Newsboy'; 'The Sinless Child, and Other Poems' (1841); 'Woman and her Needs' (1847); and 'Bald Eagle, the Last of the Rampaughs' (1867). Her children changed their name to Oaksmith to identify themselves with her.

Smith, Francis Hopkinson. An American artist and author residing in New York; born in Baltimore, Md., Oct. 23, 1838. His well-known contributions to the current literature of the day have been illustrated by his own hand. Among his works are: 'Well-Worn Roads of Spain'; 'Holland and Italy'; 'Old Lines in New Black and White'; 'A White Umbrella in Mexico'; 'A Book of the Tile Club'; 'A Day at Laguerre'; 'Colonel Carter of Cartersville,' a novel; 'American Illustrators'; 'A Gentleman Vagabond and Some Others'; 'Tom Grogan,' a novel; 'Espero Gorgoni, Gondolier'; 'The Veiled Lady.'

Smith, George. A celebrated English Assyriologist; born in London, March 26, 1840; died at Aleppo, Aug. 19, 1876. The importance of his contributions to our knowledge of Assyrian history and inscriptions is everywhere acknowledged. Part of his published works are: 'The Chaldean Account of Genesis'; 'Assyria from the Earliest Times till the Fall of Nineveh' (1875); 'Assyrian Discoveries' (1875), an account of his own travels and researches; 'The Assyrian Eponym Canon' (1876); 'History of Babylonia,' edited by A. H. Sayce (1877); 'History of Sennacherib,' edited by A. H. Sayce (1878).

Smith, George Barnett. An English journalist, littérateur, and biographer; born at Ovenden, near Halifax, Yorkshire, May 17, 1841. He was for a time on the staff of the London Globe and Echo; and subsequently contributed literary, critical, and biographical articles to British reviews. His chief publications are: 'Poets and Novelists' (1875); 'Lives' of Shelley, Gladstone, Peel, Bright, Victor Hugo, and Queen Victoria; 'Prime Ministers of Queen Victoria' (1886); and the standard 'History of the English Parliament' (2 vols., 1892).

Smith, Gerrit. An American reformer, antislavery advocate, and philanthropist; born in Utica, N. Y., in 1797; died in New York, Dec. 28, 1874. He was active in the cause of temperance, an uncompromising enemy of slavery, made large donations in aid of the poor, and gave land in New York State to many escaped slaves. He wrote numerous tracts and papers; and published: 'Speeches in Congress' (1855); 'Sermons and Speeches' (1861); 'The Religion of Reason' (1864); 'The Theologies' (1866); 'Nature the Basis of a Free Theology' (1867); and 'Correspondence with Albert Barnes' (1868).

Smith, Goldwin. An eminent English liberal, essayist, and educator, now residing in Canada; born in Reading, Aug. 13, 1823. In 1868 he was professor of English history at

32

Cornell University. In 1871 he removed to Toronto. His works include 'The Relations between America and England'; 'The Political Destiny of Canada'; 'Irish History and the Irish Question'; 'Labor and Capital.'

Smith, Hannah. [" Hesba Stretton."] An English novelist; born at Wellington, Shropshire. She has written many novels and stories; including: 'Jessica's First Prayer' (1866); 'The Clives of Burcot' (1867); 'Paul's Courtship' (1867); 'Hester Morely's Promise' (1868); and 'Bede's Charity' (1882).

Smith, James and Horace. Authors of the 'Rejected Addresses,' and other excellent humorous compositions; born in London; James born 1775, died 1839; Horace born 1779, died 1849. The managers of the new Drury Lane Theatre, completed in 1812 to replace the burned one, offered a prize for the most suitable opening address; the result was a deluge of such ludicrous rubbish that all had to be rejected, and Byron was commissioned to write one. The brothers Smith conceived the idea of burlesquing the style of leading poets and other men of letters and public notorieties, in a set of pieces purporting to be among the real addresses sent in to the committee but declined. Hence the volume of 'Rejected Addresses,' which by 1819 had reached its sixteenth edition, and is a livingly familiar classic still. Its travesties are hardly caricatures so much as genuine reproductions of the spirit as well as manner of their subjects. Horace subsequently published many novels and poems, the best-known among them being the 'Ode to an Egyptian Mummy.' James was afterwards a well-known diner-out, entertainer, and contributor to periodical literature of his day; his best-known pieces are 'The Taking of Sebastopol' and 'Surnames Go by Contraries.'

Smith, (Captain) John. The famous English adventurer and colonist; born in Willoughby, Lincolnshire, January 1579; died in London, June 21, 1631. He was one of the founders of Virginia, who in 1607 settled in Jamestown. His writings are: 'A Map of Virginia,' etc. (1612); 'The Generall Historie of Virginia,' etc. (1624); 'Description of New England'; 'An Accidence, or Pathway to Experience'; 'A Sea Grammar'; 'The True Travels of Captain John Smith.'

Smith, Mary Louise (Riley). An American verse-writer; born in Brighton, N. Y., May 27, 1842. She is author of 'A Gift of Gentians, and Other Verses' (1882); 'The Inn of Rest' (1888); and several booklets, in which are included her notably popular poems 'Tired Mothers,' 'If,' 'His Name,' and 'Sometime.'

Smith, Matthew Hale. A Unitarian minister, journalist, and author; born in Portland, Me., in 1810; died in Brooklyn, N. Y., 1879. As a newspaper correspondent under the name "Burleigh," he attained reputation for vivacity and piquancy. He also made successful lecture tours. His writings include: 'Universalism Exposed' (1842); 'Universalism Not of God' (1847); 'Sabbath Evenings' (1849); 'Mount Calvary' (1866); and 'Sunshine and Shadow in New York' (1868-69).

Smith, Richard Penn. An American dramatist and novelist; born in Philadelphia, March 13, 1799; died at Falls of Schuylkill, Pa., Aug. 12, 1854. Among his most distinguished plays are: 'Caius Marius,' a tragedy, presented by Edwin Forrest in 1831; 'The Disowned'; and 'The Venetians.' His other works include: 'The Forsaken,' a novel (2 vols., 1831); 'Life of David Crockett' (1836); and 'Life of Martin Van Buren' (1836). His 'Complete Works, Embodied in his Life and Correspondence' was published by his son, Horace Wemyss Smith (4 vols., 1888).

Smith, Samuel Francis. An American clergyman and religious verse-writer; born in Boston, Oct. 21, 1808; died there Dec. 23, 1895. He was the author of numerous hymns, including 'America,' which was written in 1832; and published for young readers and others: 'Knights and Sea Kings'; 'Mythology and Early Greek History'; and 'Poor Boys who Became Great.)

Smith, Seba. [" Major Jack Downing."] An American journalist and political satirist; born in Buckfield, Me., Sept. 14, 1792; died in Patchogue, L. I., July 29, 1868. His publications include: 'The Life and Writings of Major Jack Downing,' a series of humorous and satirical letters written during the administration of President Jackson (1833); 'Powhatan,' a poetic romance (1841); 'New Elements in Geometry' (1850); and 'Way Down East' (1855).

Smith, Sydney. A celebrated English wit, clergyman, and essayist; born at Woodford, Essex, June 3, 1771; died in London, Feb. 22, 1845. He was one of the founders of the Edinburgh Review. His writings comprise articles contributed to the Edinburgh Review and republished in book form in 1839; 'Peter Plymley's Letters' (1807-8), in favor of Catholic emancipation; 'Three Letters to Archdeacon Singleton on the Ecclesiastical Commission' (1837-39); 'Letters'; 'Papers'; etc.

Smith, Walter Chalmers. A Scotch poet and story-writer; born 1824. Among his writings are: 'Olrig Grange: A Poem' (1872); 'Hilda among the Broken Gods' (1878); 'Raban, or Life Splinters' (1880); 'North-Country Folk Poems' (1883); 'Kildrostan,' a dramatic poem' (1884); 'A Heretic' (1890).

Smith, William. An English poet and novelist. He wrote: 'Guidone: A Dramatic Poem' (2d ed. 1836); 'Athelwold,' a tragedy (1842); 'Discourse on the Ethics of the School of Paley' (1839); 'Thorndale; or, The Conflict of Opinions' (1857); 'Gravenhurst; or, Thoughts on Good and Evil' (1862).

Smith, William. A distinguished English classical scholar and compiler of classical dictionaries; born at Enfield, 1813; died in London, Oct. 7, 1893. He was of great learning, and his works were very influential in the guidance and extension of scholarship. They include: 'Dictionary of Greek and Roman Antiquities' (1840–42); 'Dictionary of Greek and Roman Biography and Mythology' (1843–49); 'Dictionary of Greek and Roman Geography' (1853–57); 'Dictionary of the Bible' (1860–63); 'Dictionary of Christian Antiquities' (1875–80); 'Dictionary of Christian Biography, Literature, Sects, and Doctrines, during the First Eight Centuries' (1877–87), with Dr. Wace. He also published Greek and Latin text-books, dictionaries, and manuals, besides editing editions of Gibbon, Hume, Hallam, and other historians.

Smith, William Robertson. A Scotch theologian and Orientalist; born at Keig, Aberdeenshire, Nov. 8, 1846; died at Cambridge, March 31, 1894. Upon concluding his theological studies at Edinburgh, Göttingen, and Bonn, he was elected to the chair of Hebrew and Old Testament exegesis in the Free Church College, Aberdeen, and almost immediately began to arouse opposition by the advanced tone of his lectures, essays, and addresses. A crisis in his career came upon the appearance of his Biblical contributions to the ninth edition of the 'Encyclopædia Britannica,' when he was tried for heresy, but finally acquitted in 1880. His article on 'Hebrew Language and Literature' in the 'Britannica' led to his removal from the Free Church College professorship. The views which occasioned the controversy are set forth in 'The Old Testament in the Jewish Church' (1881), 'The Prophets of Israel' (1882), and many important pamphlets. Meanwhile he had been very active in Oriental studies, and in 1883 became professor of Arabic at Cambridge. To this period belong 'Kinship and Marriage in Early Arabia' (1885), and 'Religion of the Semites: Fundamental Institutions' (1889). He was for a time sole editor of the 'Encyclopædia Britannica.'

Smollett, Tobias George. A celebrated British novelist; born at Dalquhurn, Dumbartonshire, Scotland, March 1721; died at Monte Nero, near Leghorn, Italy, Oct. 17, 1771. His works include: 'Advice' (1746?), a satire; 'Reproof' (1746?), a satire; 'The Adventures of Roderick Random' (1748); 'The Regicide' (1749), a tragedy; 'The Adventures of Peregrine Pickle' (1751); 'The Adventures of Ferdinand, Count Fathom' (1753); 'Don Quixote' (1755), a translation from the Spanish of Cervantes; 'Compendium of Voyages and Travels' (1757); 'History of England from the Landing of Cæsar to the Treaty of Aix-la-Chapelle' (1757); 'The Reprisals' (1757), a farce; 'The Adventures of Sir Lancelot Greaves' (1760–61); a translation of 'Gil Blas' (1761); 'The Present State of all Nations: containing a Geographical, Natural, Commercial, and Political History of all the Countries of the Known World' (1763); 'Travels' (1766); 'The Adventures of an Atom' (1769), a political satire; and 'The Expedition of Humphrey Clinker' (1771).

Smyth, Charles Piazzi. A Scotch astronomer; born at Naples, Jan. 3, 1819; died at Ripon, Feb. 21, 1900. His studies of the great Egyptian pyramid led him to the conclusion that it was raised under direct inspiration of God, and that therein were deposited revelations of the great truths of physical Nature. He wrote 'Our Inheritance in the Great Pyramid' (3d ed. 1880).

Smyth, [Samuel] Newman [Phillips]. An American clergyman and religious writer; born in Brunswick, Me., June 25, 1843. His publications include: 'Old Faiths in New Light'; 'The Orthodox Theology of To-day'; 'The Morality of the Old Testament'; 'Personal Creeds'; 'Christian Ethics'; 'The Religious Feeling'; and 'The Reality of Faith.'

Snider, Denton Jaques. Born in Mt. Gilead, O., Jan. 9, 1841. His studies of the great poets, Homer, Shakespeare, Dante, Goethe, and his writings on kindred topics, are very numerous, comprising some eighteen volumes. His book 'A Walk in Hellas' is a remarkable study of Greece as it is to-day, illuminated by what it was in its prime.

Snieders, Jan Renier (snē'ders). A Dutch novelist; born at Bladel in North Brabant, Nov. 22, 1812; died at Turnhout, April 9, 1888. His stories are mostly tales of village life. Among them are 'Amanda'; 'Doctor Marcus'; 'Narda.'

Snoilsky, Carl Johan Gustaf, Count (snoil'-skē). A Swedish poet; born in Stockholm, Sept. 8, 1841. His 'Sonnets' (1871), and his translation of Goethe's ballads (1876), are among the best in Swedish literature. His later poems, 'New Stanzas' (1881), show sympathy for the unfortunate and oppressed.

Snorri or **Snorro Sturluson** (snor'ē stėr'lä-son). An Icelandic historian and statesman; born in 1179; slain 1241. He composed the Prose or Younger Edda; and wrote the 'Heimskringla,' a series of biographies of Norwegian kings, and the poem 'Háttatal.'

Socrates (sok'ra-tēs). The renowned Athenian philosopher; born in Athens in 470 B. C.; died 399 B. C. He left no writings, and his philosophical method and his teaching are to be learned from the works of his disciples and contemporaries, especially Plato and Xenophon. In the 'Dialogues' of Plato, or rather in the earlier dialogues, Socrates is believed to figure in word and in action as he lived, a sincere searcher for truth in all things.

Solomon ben Jehuda ibn Gabirol. See Avicebron.

Solon (sō'lon). The Athenian legislator; lived about 638–559 B. C. The constitution which he gave to Athens is very clearly explained in Grote's 'History of Greece.' Solon himself defined its character and aims in six hexameters which have come down to our time.

Somerville, Mary (Fairfax). A Scottish astronomer and scientist; born at Jedburgh, Dec. 26, 1780; died in Naples, Nov. 29, 1872. She was elected a fellow of the Royal Astronomical

Society. She published: 'Mechanism of the Heavens' (1830), a translation of Laplace's 'Mécanique Céleste,' made at the request of Lord Brougham; 'Connection of the Physical Sciences' (1834); 'Physical Geography' (1849); 'Microscopical and Molecular Science' (1869).

Sophocles (sof'ō-klēz). The great Greek tragic poet was born at Colonus, near Athens, about 495 B. C.; died about 405. His seven extant tragedies are conjectured to have been given to the public in the following order: 'Antigone' (440 B. C.); 'Electra'; 'Trachiniæ'; 'Œdipus Tyrannus'; 'Ajax'; 'Philoctetes'; and 'Œdipus at Colonus.'

Sophocles, Evangelinus Apostolides. A Grecian scholar and educational writer; born in Tsangaranda, Thessaly, Greece, March 8, 1807; died in Cambridge, Mass., Dec. 17, 1883. Coming to America in 1829, he became professor of ancient, modern, and Byzantine Greek in Harvard University in 1860. Among his publications are: 'Romaic Grammar' (1842; 2d ed. Boston, 1857; London, 1866); 'Glossary of Later and Byzantine Greek' (1860, forming Vol. vii., new series of 'Memoirs of the American Academy'); and 'Greek Lexicon of the Roman and Byzantine Periods,' his most important work (1870).

Sophron (sō'fron). A Greek mimetic poet of the fifth century B. C., native of Syracuse. His mimes were dialogues in Doric Greek, half in play, half in earnest, in which the characteristics of the lower orders were faithfully rendered. Only inconsiderable fragments of these compositions have come down to us.

Sordello (sor-del'lō). An Italian poet; born at Goito, near Mantua, about 1180; died about 1255. He composed poems in the language of Provence, of which 34 remain. One of the most celebrated passages in Dante is on the subject of this poet, and Browning's 'Sordello' (1840) is founded upon the story of his life.

Sotheby, William. An English poet; born in London, 1757; died Dec. 30, 1833. He is only remembered now as a translator of Homer and Virgil, and a favorite among the «blue-stockings» of Byron's time, but he wrote among many other things: 'The Battle of the Nile' (1799) and 'Saul' (1807), poems, and 'Italy and Other Poems' (1828); 'The Siege of Cuzco' (1800); 'Julian and Agnes' (1801), 'Orestes' (1802), 'Ivan' (1816), tragedies.

Soulié, Melchior Frédéric (sōl-yē'). A French novelist and poet; born at Foix (Ariège), Dec. 24, 1800; died at Bièvre near Paris, Sept. 23, 1847. He commenced his literary career by publishing a volume of poems, 'French Loves' (1824), followed by 'Romeo and Juliet' (1828). 'Christine at Fontainebleau' and 'Clothilde' (1832) were popular dramas. Some of his novels also achieved public favor, such as 'The Count of Toulouse' (1835); 'A Summer at Meudon' (1836).

Soumet, Alexandre (sō-mā'). A French dramatist; born at Castelnaudary, Feb. 8, 1788; died at Compiègne, March 30, 1845. He won fame with his first elegy, 'The Poor Girl' (1814). His principal tragedies are: 'Clytemnestra' and 'Saul' (1822); 'Joan of Arc' (1825); 'Elizabeth of France' (1828).

South, Robert. An English preacher and controversial writer; born at Hackney, Sept. 4, 1634; died in London, July 8, 1716. His sermons are very noted. The published editions of them are numerous (1692, 6 vols.; 4th ed. 1715; new ed., enlarged, 1744, 11 vols., edited by W. G. T. Shedd; 1867, 5 vols.).

Southerne, Thomas. An English playwright; born in Dublin, 1660; died 1746. His more notable plays are: 'The Persian Prince; or, The Loyal Brother'; 'The Fatal Marriage' (1694); 'Sir Anthony Love; or, The Rambling Lady.'

Southesk, Sir James Carnegie, Earl of. A Scotch poet; born 1827. He wrote: 'Herminius, a Romance' (1862); 'Jonas Fisher: A Poem in Brown and White' (1876); 'Meda Maiden' (1877); 'The Burial of Isis, with Other Poems' (1884); 'Suomiria, a Fantasy' (1897).

Southey, Caroline Ann (Bowles) (south'y or suth'y). An English poet, wife of Robert Southey; born at Lymington, Hampshire, Dec. 6, 1786; died there, July 20, 1854. A collection of her poems published in 1820 brought her to the notice of the world of letters. 'The Pauper's Death-Bed' is well known. She is the author of 'Ellen Fitz-Arthur,' a poem (1820); 'The Widow's Tale, and Other Poems' (1822); 'The Birthday' (1836); 'Tales of the Factories,' in verse (1847).

Southey, Robert. A celebrated English poet and prose-writer; born in Bristol, Aug. 12, 1774; died March 21, 1843. His principal poems are: 'Joan of Arc' (1795); 'The Curse of Kehama,' based upon Hindu mythology (1810); 'A Vision of Judgment,' an apotheosis of George III. (1821). Among his prose works are: 'History of Brazil' (1810-19); 'Life of Nelson' (1813); 'Life of John Wesley' (1820); 'Book of the Church' (1824); 'Life of John Bunyan' (1830); and 'The Doctor' (1834-37). He was made poet-laureate in 1813.

Southwell, Robert. An English poet and Jesuit martyr; born about 1562; executed at Tyburn, Feb. 21, 1595. He wrote: 'Consolation for Catholics' (1586?), a prose work; but his literary fame rests upon his poems, the longest of which is 'St. Peter's Complaint,' while the best is generally considered to be 'The Burning Babe.'

Southworth, Emma Dorothy Eliza (Nevitte). One of the most prolific of American novelists; born in Washington, D. C., Dec. 26, 1818; died there June 30, 1899. Among her sixty-odd stories are: 'Retribution'; 'Unknown'; 'The Family Doom'; 'The Mother's Secret'; and 'An Exile's Bride.' Many of them have been translated into French, German and Spanish, and republished in London, Paris, Leipsic, Madrid and Montreal.

Souvestre, Émile (sö-vestr'). A French dramatist and novelist; born 1806; died 1854. He is celebrated as the author of 'An Attic Philosopher' (1850). His other works include: 'The Last Bretons' (1836); 'Travels in Finisterre'; 'The Confessions of a Workman'; 'Pierre and Jean'; 'The Greased Pole'; 'Man and Money'; etc. His plays include 'Henri Hamelin' and 'Uncle Baptiste.'

Spalding, John Lancaster. An American prelate of the Catholic Church, bishop of Peoria, Ill.; born in Lebanon, Ky., June 2, 1840. He has done much to establish educational institutions in this country, and is widely known as an author and poet. Besides 'Essays and Reviews' (1876), he has published a 'Life of Archbishop Spalding' (1872); 'Religious Mission of the Irish People' (1880); 'Lectures and Discourses' (1882); 'America, and Other Poems'; 'The Poet's Praise'; 'Education and the Higher Life'; 'Songs, Chiefly from the German'; 'Socialism and Labor'; and 'Religion and Art.'

Spalding, Martin John. A Catholic prelate, archbishop of Baltimore; born near Lebanon, Ky., May 23, 1810; died in Baltimore, Feb. 7, 1872. He was distinguished as a controversialist and polemical writer, and published many works; among them: 'D'Aubigné's History of the Reformation Reviewed' (1844); 'Lectures on the General Evidences of Christianity' (1847 and 1866); 'Miscellanies and Reviews' (1885); and 'History of the Protestant Reformation in Germany,' etc. (2 vols., 1860). He also edited 'The General History of the Catholic Church,' by Abbé Darras (4 vols., 1860).

Sparhawk, Frances Campbell. An American novelist and story writer; born at Amesbury, Mass., July 28, 1847. She wrote a large number of serial stories for the Christian Union and other papers, of which the most important is 'Elizabeth: A Romance of Colonial Days.' She is also the author of 'A Lazy Man's Work' (1881); 'Little Polly Blatchley' (1887); 'Miss West's Class in Geography' (1887); 'Onoqua,' an Indian story; and 'Senator Intrigue and Inspector Nosely'; 'Life of Lincoln for Boys.'

Sparks, Jared. An American historian; born in Willington, Conn., May 10, 1789; died in Cambridge, Mass., March 14, 1866. From 1849 to 1853 he was president of Harvard College. He is best known as the editor of the library of American Biography (10 vols., 1834-38), containing twenty-six 'Lives' to which a second series of thirty-four was added later (15 vols., 1844-47); and as the author of several of the biographies,—namely, Ethan Allen, Benedict Arnold, Father Marquette, La Salle, Count Pulaski, Jean Ribault, Charles Lee, and John Ledyard.

Sparks, William Henry. An American verse and prose writer; born on St. Simon's Island, Ga., Jan. 16, 1800; died in Marietta, Ga., Jan. 13, 1882. He published: 'The Memories of Fifty Years' (1870; 4th ed. 1882); 'Father

Anselmo's Ward'; 'Chilecah'; and 'The Woman with the Iron-Gray Hair.' He was also the author of the popular verses 'Somebody's Darling' and 'The Old Church Bell.'

Spaulding, Solomon. An American clergyman and writer; born in Ashford, Conn., in 1761; died in Amity, Pa., Oct. 20, 1816. He was a Revolutionary soldier, a Congregational minister, and afterwards a manufacturer of iron. While living at Conneaut, Pa. (1811-12), he wrote a romance, 'The Manuscript Found,' published in 1812, purporting to have been discovered in an ancient mound. This work was said to have furnished the basis for the 'Book of Mormon'; in denial of which the original manuscript of Spaulding's romance was republished by the Mormons in 1885.

Spears, John Randolph. A New York journalist and story-writer; born in Ohio in 1850. He has published: 'The Gold Diggings of Cape Horn'; 'The Port of Missing Ships, and Other Stories'; 'A Short History of the American Navy.'

Spedding, James. An English critic and literary historian; born near Bassenthwaite, in Cumberland, 1808; died in London, March 9, 1881. The labors of his whole life were concerned with the works of Lord Bacon; and his first work, 'Evenings with a Reviewer' (2 vols., privately printed in 1848, published 1881), was an elaborate review of Macaulay's essay on the great philosopher. He published 'The Works of Francis Bacon' (7 vols., 1857-59); 'Life and Letters of Francis Bacon' (7 vols., 1870-76); 'Life and Times of Francis Bacon' (2 vols., 1878); and a volume of miscellaneous 'Reviews and Discussions' (1869).

Speed, John Gilmer. An American journalist; born in Kentucky, 1853. He has been managing editor of the New York World, has contributed to leading periodicals, and has published a 'Life of Keats.'

Speke, John Hanning. An English explorer; born at Jordans, Somersetshire, May 4, 1827; died near Bath, of an accidental gunshot wound, Sept. 18, 1864. He entered the army, and served in India and in the Crimean war; was with Capt. Richard F. Burton in an expedition which discovered the great lakes of Central Africa; and was at the head of another expedition which discovered the connection of the Nile with those lakes. He published: 'A Journal of the Discovery of the Source of the Nile' (1863); and 'What Led to the Discovery of the Source of the Nile' (1864).

Spencer, Herbert. A celebrated English philosopher; born at Derby, April 27, 1820. He has published: 'The Proper Sphere of Government' (1842); 'Social Statics; or, The Conditions Essential to Human Happiness' (1851), later suppressed by the author; 'Prospectus of a System of Synthetic Philosophy' (1860); 'Education' (1861); 'Essays' (1858-63); 'First Principles' (1862); 'Principles of Biology' (1864); 'Classification of the Sciences' (1864); 'Principles of Psychology' (1872); 'The

Study of Sociology' (1873); 'Principles of Sociology' (1876); 'Ceremonial Institutions' (1879); 'Data of Ethics' (1879); 'Political Institutions' (1882); 'The Man versus the State' (1884); 'Ecclesiastical Institutions' (1885); 'Essays' (1891), being a former work revised; 'Social Statics' (1892), being a former work revised; 'Principles of Ethics' (1893). In 1896 appeared the final volume of 'Principles of Sociology,' completing the 'System of Synthetic Philosophy.' Died Dec. 8, 1903.

Spencer, Jesse Ames. An American educator and author; born at Hyde Park, N. Y., June 17, 1816; died in New York city, Sept. 2, 1898. He was appointed professor of Greek in the College of the City of New York in 1869, and was the author of a volume of religious 'Discourses' (1843): 'History of the English Reformation' (1846); 'History of the United States' (4 vols., 1856–69); 'Greek Praxis' (1870), and a 'Course of English Reading' (1873); 'Memorabilia of Sixty-five Years' (1820–86); etc.

Spencer, William (Loring). An American author, second wife of Gen. Geo. E. Spencer; born in St. Augustine, Fla. She has written: 'Salt Lake Fruit' (1883); 'Story of Mary' (1884), republished as 'Dennis Day' (1887); 'A Plucky One' (1887); and 'Calamity Jane' (1887). Because of her masculine name she has been called « The Major.»

Spencer, William Robert. An English poet; born 1769; died 1834. Among his writings are: 'Urania; or, the Illuminé,' a comedy (1802); 'The Year of Sorrow' (1804); a poetical necrology; a posthumous collection of 'Poems' (1835). He translated Bürger's 'Lenore' in 1796. Some of his songs are still popular favorites, as 'Beth Gelert; or, The Grave of the Greyhound'; 'Wife, Children, and Friends'; 'When Midnight o'er the Moonless Skies'; 'Too Late I Stayed: Forgive the Crime'; 'The Emigrant's Grave.'

Spender, Emily. An English story-writer; born at Bath, 1841. She wrote: 'A Son and Heir' (1864); 'Kingsford' (1866); 'Restored' (1871); 'A True Marriage' (1878); 'Until the Day Breaks' (1886).

Spenser, Edmund. A celebrated English poet, born in London about 1552; died at London, Jan. 16, 1598–9. His works, in their order of publication, are: 'The Shepherd's Calendar' (1579); 'The Faery Queen' (1590), first three books; 'Daphnaida' (1591); 'Complaints' (1591), a collection of poems; 'Colin Clout's Come Home Again' (1595); 'Amoretti' (1595), containing sonnets and 'Epithalamion'; 'Faery Queen' (1596), second three books; 'Four Hymns' (1596); 'Prothalamion' (1596); 'Astrophel' (1596). Posthumously appeared 'View of the State of Ireland' (1633).

Spielhagen, Friedrich (spēl'hä-gen). A prolific German novelist; born in Magdeburg, Feb. 24, 1829. He has published: 'Klara Vere' (1857); 'On the Dunes' (1858); 'Enigmatical Natures' (1860); 'Through Night to Light' (1861); 'The Von Hohensteins' (1863); 'Little Rose of the Court' (1864); 'In Rank and File' (1866); 'The Village Coquette' (1868); 'Hammer and Anvil' (1868); 'German Pioneers' (1870); 'Ever Onward' (1872); 'What the Swallow Sang' (1872); 'Ultimo' (1873); 'The Freshet' (1876); 'Flatland' (1878); 'Quisisana' (1879–80); 'Angela' (1881); 'Uhlenhans' (1884); 'At the Health Springs' (1885); 'What Will That Lead To?' (1886); 'Noblesse Oblige' (1888); 'A New Pharaoh' (1889); 'Sunday's Child' (1893); 'Susi' (1895); and many dramatic works and much miscellany.

Spindler, Karl (spin'dler). A German novelist; born at Breslau, Silesia, Oct. 16, 1796; died at Freiersbach, Baden, July 12, 1855. The best of his works are: 'The Bastard' (3 vols., 1826); 'The Jew' (4 vols., 1827); 'The Jesuit' (3 vols., 1829); and 'The Pensioner' (1831). The latter story is an excellent specimen of the early historical novel in Germany. It delineates the French Revolution and Napoleon's subsequent career.

Spinoza, Benedict (spi-nō'zä). A celebrated philosopher; born at Amsterdam, of Portuguese-Jewish parents, Nov. 23, 1632; died at The Hague, Feb. 21, 1677. He is author of a 'Tractate on God and Man and Man's Felicity' (1655); 'Theologico-Political Tractate' (1670); 'Ethics Demonstrated Geometrically.' The latter is his greatest work; it was not published till after his death.

Spofford, Ainsworth Rand. An American bibliographer and librarian; born in Gilmanton, N. H., Sept. 12, 1825. He was a journalist to 1861, when appointed chief assistant librarian of the Congressional Library, and librarian 1864 to 1897, when he became again « chief assistant.» He is famed for a comprehensive and accurate knowledge of books and their contents, and besides many essays and articles on historical, literary, and scientific subjects for the current journals, has published: 'The American Almanac,' etc. (annually since 1878); and has with others edited: 'Library of Choice Literature' (10 vols., Philadelphia, 1881–88); 'Library of Wit and Humor' (5 vols., 1884); and 'A Practical Manual of Parliamentary Rules' (1884). He died Aug. 11, 1908.

Spofford, Harriet Elizabeth (Prescott). An American novelist and poet; born in Calais, Me., April 3, 1835. Her literary success was assured with the publication of the story entitled 'In a Cellar,' in the Atlantic Monthly (1859). Among her seventeen books are: 'Sir Rohan's Ghost' (1859); 'The Amber Gods, and Other Stories' (1863); 'Azarian: An Episode' (1863); 'New England Legends' (1871); 'The Thief in the Night' (1872); 'The Marquis of Carabas' (1882); 'Poems' (1882); 'Ballads about Authors' (1888); 'A Master Spirit'; 'In Titian's Garden'; 'Priscilla's Love Story'; 'Old Washington.'

Sprague, Charles. An American poet; born in Boston, Oct. 26, 1791; died there, Jan. 22, 1875. He was the author of 'The Winged

Worshipers'; 'Curiosity'; and 'The Family Meeting.' A collection of his works entitled 'Poetical and Prose Writings' was published in 1841.

Sprague, Charles Ezra. An American writer and editor; born in Nassau, N. Y., Oct. 9, 1842. He was an officer through the Civil War, and since, the secretary and president of a New York bank. He is the editor of Volaspodel, the organ of the international language called Volapük, and has written: 'Logical Symbolism' (1882), and 'The Handbook of Volapük' (1888). Also a well-known poem, 'The Story of the Flag' (1886); 'The Philosophy of Accounts.'

Sprague, Mary Aplin. An American novelist; born in Ohio, 1849. She has published the story 'An Earnest Trifler.'

Springer, Mrs. Rebecca (Ruter). An American verse and story writer; born in Indianapolis, Ind., Nov. 8, 1832. Besides a volume of poems, 'Songs of the Sea,' she has written the novels 'Beechwood' (1873) and 'Self' (1881).

Spurgeon, Charles Haddon. An English Baptist preacher and author; born at Kelvedon, Essex, June 19, 1834; died at Mentone, France, Jan. 31, 1892. He was one of the most successful preachers of modern times. From his sermons, thirty-seven volumes have been compiled. He published besides: 'The Saint and his Saviour' (1857); a 'Commentary on the Psalms' (7 vols., 1865-80); 'John Ploughman's Talk' (1868); 'Readings for the Closet' (1869); 'Storm Signals' (1886); 'Messages to the Multitude' (1892).

Squier, Ephraim George. An American archæologist and author; born in Bethlehem, Pa., June 17, 1821; died in Brooklyn, N. Y., April 17, 1888. While a journalist at Chillicothe, O., he prepared an account of discoveries in ancient mounds (he being the principal authority on the subject) for the 'Smithsonian Contributions to Knowledge' (1848). He was chargé d'affaires to the Central American States (1849), consul-general to Peru (1863), and to Honduras (1868). Besides many reports and contributions to periodicals and scientific journals, he published: 'Aboriginal Monuments of the State of New York' (1851); 'Serpent Symbols' (1852); 'Nicaragua' (1852); 'Notes on Central America' (1854); 'States of Central America' (1857); 'Tropical Fibres' (1861); 'Peru: Incidents and Explorations' (1877).

Stabili, Francesco. See **Cecco d'Ascoli.**

Staël-Holstein, Anne Louise Germaine (Necker), Baroness de (stä'el-hol'stīn *or* stä'ęl-ol-staṅ'). A celebrated French writer; born in Paris, April 22, 1766; died there, July 14, 1817. She was the only child of Necker the financier, and of Suzanne Curchod whose name is connected with that of the historian Gibbon. She married, Jan. 14, 1786, the Baron de Staël-Holstein, Swedish ambassador at Paris. Her works include: 'Letters on the Character and

Writings of J. J. Rousseau' (1788); 'Delphine' (1802), a novel; 'Corinne' (1807); 'On Germany' (1810), her best-known work; 'Literature in Relation to Social Institutions'; 'Influence of the Passions on the Welfare of Individuals and Nations'; 'The French Revolution,' a posthumous work; etc.

Stahl, P. J. (stäl). The pseudonym of P. J. Hetzel, a French publisher and author; born in Chartres, Jan. 15, 1814; died at Monte Carlo, March 17, 1886. Of Alsatian origin, he studied law in Germany when a youth, basing upon his experiences during this period his first literary successes: 'The Life of a Student'; 'The Story of a Snuffler'; and others. Among his popular works, most of which were published by himself, may be mentioned: 'The Voyages and Discoveries of Mlle. Lili, and of her Cousin Lucien'; 'The Devil at Paris'; 'The Wit of Woman and the Woman of Wit.'

Stanhope, Lady Hester Lucy, niece of William Pitt the younger; born at Chevening, Kent, England, March 12, 1776; died at Mar Elias, Syria, June 23, 1839. She was confidential secretary to Pitt for ten years prior to his death. In 1810 she visited Syria, Jerusalem, Damascus, Baalbec, and Palmyra. In 1814 she established herself in the deserted convent of Mar Elias, near Sidon, on a crag of Lebanon, became a benefactress to the poor, and studied astrology. Her 'Memoirs' (3 vols., 1845) and 'Seven Years' Travels' (3 vols., 1846) were published by her physician.

Stanhope, Philip Dormer. See **Chesterfield.**

Stanhope, Philip Henry. Fifth Earl Stanhope, better known as Lord Mahon. An English statesman and author; born at Walmer, Kent, Jan. 30, 1805; died at Bournemouth, Hampshire, Dec. 24, 1875. He is author of 'History of the War of Succession in Spain' (1832); 'History of England from the Peace of Utrecht to the Peace of Versailles, 1713-83' (7 vols., 1836-53); 'The Life of Louis, Prince of Condé' (1845); 'A History of England, Comprising the Reign of Anne until the Peace of Utrecht' (1870).

Stanley, Arthur Penrhyn. An English clergyman and author, best known as "Dean Stanley"; born at Alderley, Cheshire, Dec. 13, 1815; died in Westminster, July 18, 1881 His principal works are: 'The Life and Correspondence of Thomas Arnold' (1844); 'Historical Memorials of Canterbury Cathedral' (1855); 'Lectures on the History of the Jewish Church' (Vol. i., 1862; Vol. ii., 1865; Vol. iii., 1876); 'Christian Institutions' (1878).

Stanley, Henry Morton. A celebrated explorer and author; born in Denbigh, Wales, in 1841. Died at London, May 10, 1904. Originally named John Rowlands, he was adopted at 15 by a New Orleans merchant, whose name he took. He served in both the Confederate and Union armies in the Civil War; was a newspaper correspondent in Turkey and Abyssinia in 1868; and started on the search for Dr. Livingstone in October 1869, returning in July 1872. He made an exploration of Equatorial Africa 1874–78; founded the Congo Free State 1879–84; and headed a successful expedition for the relief of Emin Pasha in 1887–90. He has been a Member of Parliament since 1896. His works include : ‹Coomassie and Magdala› (1869); ‹How I Found Livingstone› (1872); ‹Through the Dark Continent› (1878); ‹The Congo and the Founding of its Free State› (1885); and ‹In Darkest Africa› the title best known to general readers in America.

Stannard, Mrs. (Henrietta Eliza Vaughan Palmer). An English novelist, writing under the pseudonyms «John Strange Winter» and «Violet Whyte»; born at York, Jan. 13, 1856. She has written among others : ‹Cavalry Life› (1881); ‹Regimental Legends› (1883) ; ‹Bootle's Baby› (1885), very popular ; ‹ Houp-la › (1885) ; ‹ A Siege Baby › (1887); ‹ Heart and Sword.›

Stanton, Mrs. Elizabeth (Cady). An American reformer and advocate of woman's rights; born in Johnstown, N. Y., Nov. 12, 1815. She called the first convention in behalf of woman suffrage, July 18, 1848. Besides numerous addresses and pamphlets, she wrote — jointly with Susan B. Anthony and F. Gage — a ‹History of Woman's Suffrage› (4 vols., 1880–86); and edited, with others, The Revolution (established 1868). Died in New York city, Oct. 26, 1902.

Stanton, Henry Brewster. An American journalist, reformer, and abolitionist; born in Griswold, Conn., June 29, 1805; died in New York, Jan. 14, 1887. He married Elizabeth Cady in 1840. He was active in the anti-slavery movements (1837–41), was admitted to the bar, and gained reputation in patent law (1847); assisted in organizing the Republican party (1858–60); and from 1868 was an editor of the New York Sun. He contributed to the Liberator, wrote much for periodicals, and published : ‹Sketches of Reform and Reformers in Great Britain and Ireland › (1849); and ‹ Random Recollections › (1886).

Stanton, Theodore. An American journalist, son of H. B. and Elizabeth Cady; born in Seneca Falls, N. Y., Feb. 10, 1851. He was a correspondent for the Tribune at Berlin from 1880, and is now engaged as a journalist in Paris. He translated Goff's ‹Life of Thiers› (1879), and wrote ‹The Woman Question in Europe › (1884); ‹Life of Rosa Bonheur.›

Statham, Francis Reginald. An English poet and miscellaneous writer. He wrote : ‹Alice Rushton and Other Poems› (1868); ‹Glaphyra and Other Poems› (1870); ‹Eucharis : A Poem› (1871); ‹The Second Growth of the Nineteenth Century› (1872); ‹The Zulu Inquiry› (1880); ‹Blacks, Boers, and British : A Three-Cornered Problem› (1881); ‹Free Thought and True Thought› (1884).

Statius, Publius Papinius (stā'shi-us). A Roman poet ; born at Naples about 45 A. D.; died there about 96 A. D. His chief work is

‹The Thebaid,› an epic poem in twelve books, dealing with the struggle between the brothers Eteocles and Polynices of Thebes. Of his epic ‹Achilleis› only fragments remain. His ‹Silvæ,› a series of occasional stanzas, are 32 in number, extending to nearly 4,000 lines, and are deemed his most pleasing work.

Stchedrin (tched'rēn), pseudonym of Mikhail Evgrafovich Saltykov. A Russian satirical writer; born in the government of Tver, Jan. 15, 1826; died in St. Petersburg, May 10, 1889. He is classed among the best satirical writers of his country. Among his best-known works are : ‹Satires in Prose› and ‹Innocent Tales,› both published in 1863; ‹Diary of a Provincial›; ‹The People of Tashkend›; etc. Some of his works have been translated into English, French, and German.

Stead, William Thomas. An English journalist; born at Embleton, Northumberland, July 5, 1849. He is widely known as editor of the Pall Mall Gazette and the Review of Reviews, which last he founded in January 1890. He published ‹The Maiden Tribute of Modern Babylon› (1885). In 1893 he established Borderland, a periodical devoted to Spiritualism. ‹If Christ Came to Chicago› is another of his publications.

Stearns, Frank Preston. An American littérateur and art critic, nephew of Lydia Maria Child ; born in Massachusetts, 1846, and living in Boston. He has written : ‹The Real and Ideal in Literature ›; ‹Life of Tintoretto ›; ‹The Midsummer of Italian Art›; ‹Sketches from Concord to Appledore ›; ‹Modern English Prose ›; and ‹Summer Travel in Europe.›

Stebbins, Mrs. Mary Elizabeth (Moore) (Hewett). An American poet; born in Massachusetts, 1818. She has published : ‹Memorial of F. S. Osgood ›; ‹Songs of Our Lord ›; ‹Heroines of History›; and ‹Poems Sacred, Passionate, and Legendary.›

Stedman, Edmund Clarence. A distinguished American man of letters; born in Hartford, Conn., Oct. 8, 1833. Aside from his original works, his services to literature, both foreign and American, have been very great. His ‹Library of American Literature,› eleven volumes, edited with Miss Hutchinson, was published in 1890–92; ‹Victorian Anthology› in 1895; ‹Victorian Poets,› 1875; ‹Poets of America,› 1886; ‹Nature and Elements of Poetry,› 1892; the Complete Edition of Poe, edited with Professor Woodberry, 1895. His poems and other works are very numerous, and have been published in a volume called ‹A Household Edition,› 1884; and in ‹Poems Now First Collected,› 1897. He died Jan. 18, 1908.

Steel, Flora Annie, Mrs. An English novelist; born (Webster) at Harrow-on-the-Hill, Middlesex, April 2, 1847. At 21 she married an Indian civilian and went to Bengal, where she became prominent in educational affairs, and was appointed inspectress of female schools. On the expiration of her husband's term of service, she returned with him to England and devoted herself to literary work. Her published works include: 'From the Five Rivers' (1893); 'Miss Stuart's Legacy' (1893); 'The Potter's Thumb' (1894); 'On the Face of the Waters' (1897), a stirring tale of the Indian Mutiny'; 'The Hosts of the Lord' (1900).

Steele, Sir Richard. A British author and dramatist; born in Dublin, March 1672; died at Carmathen, Wales, Sept. 1, 1729. He published in 1701, 'The Christian Hero'; in the latter part of the same year he brought out his first comedy, 'The Funeral,' which was followed by 'The Lying Lover' (1703), and 'The Tender Husband' (1705). His fame rests upon his connection with the Tatler and the Spectator. The Tatler (1709–11) contained 271 numbers: 188 were by Steele, 42 by Addison, and 36 by both conjointly. Of 555 numbers of the Spectator, 236 were by Steele and 274 by Addison.

Steele, Thomas Sedgwick. An American artist and writer on out-of-door sports and travel; born in Connecticut in 1845. He has published: 'Canoe and Camera: A Tour through the Maine Forests'; 'Paddle and Portage from Moosehead Lake to the Aroostook River'; 'A Voyage to Vikingland.' Died in 1903.

Steendam, Jacob. The first poet of New York; born in Holland, 1616. The date and place of his death are not known. He lived in New Netherlands, 1632–62; and wrote a small volume of verse, 'Jacob Steendam noch vaster,' which was reprinted with memoir of the author (The Hague, 1861). The poems are descriptive of life in the colony, and are entitled: 'Der Distelvink' (The Thistle Finch); 'Klacht van Nieuw Amsterdam' (The Complaint of New Amsterdam); 'Tlofran Nieuw Nederland' (The Praise of New Netherlands); and 'Prichel Vaarsen' (Spurring Verses).

Stendhal. See **Beyle.**

Stephen, Leslie. A distinguished English critic and man of letters; born in London, Nov. 28, 1832. He was educated at Cambridge, and subsequently edited leading London periodicals. His greatest undertaking was the 'Dictionary of National Biography,' in about 60 volumes, of which he edited the first 26. The work is still in course of publication. He has published: 'Hours in a Library' (1871–79); 'Essays on Free Thinking and Plain Speaking' (1873); 'History of English Thought in the Eighteenth Century' (1876); 'Science of Ethics' (1882); 'Life of Henry Fawcett' (1885); 'An Agnostic's Apology' (1893); 'Life of Sir James Fitzjames Stephen' (1896); 'Social Rights and Duties' (1896); etc. Died at London, Feb. 22, 1904.

Stephens, Alexander Hamilton. An American statesman, vice-president of the Southern Confederacy; born at Crawfordsville, Ga., Feb. 11, 1812; died March 4, 1883. He wrote a 'Constitutional View of the War between the States' (1867–70).

Stephens, Ann Sophia (Winterbotham). An American novelist; born in Derby, Conn., 1813; died in Newport, R. I., Aug. 20, 1886. After 1837 she resided in New York, and was at different times engaged in editorial work. Most noted of her poems is 'The Polish Boy,' and of her novels 'Fashion and Famine' (1854). Among her other publications are: 'The Old Homestead' (1855; 2 vols., 1860); 'Sibyl Chase' (1862); and 'Ahmo's Plot' (1863).

Stephens, Charles Asbury. An American story-writer; born in Maine, 1847. He has published: 'Camping Out', 'Off the Geysers'; 'Left on Labrador'; 'Fox-Hunting'; 'On the Amazon'; 'The Young Moose-Hunters'; 'The Knock-About Club in the Woods,' and the same 'Alongshore' and 'In the Tropics.'

Stephens, James Brunton. An Australian poet and story-writer; born at Borrowstounness in Linlithgowshire, Scotland. He is author of 'Convict Once: A Poem' (1871); 'The Black Gin, and Other Poems' (1874); 'A Hundred Pounds: A Novelette' (1876); 'Miscellaneous Poems' (1880).

Stephens, John Lloyd. An American traveler, the first modern explorer in Yucatan; born in Shrewsbury, N. J., Nov. 28, 1805; died in New York city, Oct. 10, 1852. He wrote a series of letters on travel in the East, entitled 'Incidents of Travel in Egypt, Arabia Petræa, and the Holy Land' (2 vols., 1837); followed by 'Incidents of Travel in Greece, Russia, Turkey, and Poland' (1838); 'Incidents of Travel in Central America, Chiapas, and Yucatan' (1841); and supplemental volumes of explorations and 'Travel in Yucatan' (2 vols., 1843).

Stepniak, Sergius Michael Dragomanov (S. Karchevsky) (step'nyäk). A noted Russian nihilist; born at Gadjatch, government of Poltava, 1841; died at Chiswick, Dec. 23, 1895. Having been exiled in 1876, on account of his criticisms on (the system followed by Count Tolstoy), one of the Ministers of Justice, he settled in Geneva, 1887; went from there to London in 1885. Among his works are 'The Turks Within and Without' (1876); 'Underground Russia' (1881); 'Tyrannicide in Russia' (1881); 'The Career of a Nihilist,' a novel (1889).

Sterling, John. A Scottish editor, essayist, and poet; born at Kames Castle, Isle of Bute, July 20, 1806; died at Ventnor, Isle of Wight, Sept. 18, 1844. He was educated at Glasgow and Cambridge. Among his works are: 'Arthur Coningsby,' a novel (1833); 'Minor Poems' (1839); 'The Election,' a poem (1841); 'Strafford,' a drama (1843); and 'The Onyx Ring' (1856). Thomas Carlyle wrote 'The Life of John Sterling' (1851).

Stern, Daniel, pseudonym of Marie Catherine Sophie de Flavigny, Comtesse d'Agoult (dä-gö'). A famous French writer; born at Frankfort on the Main, Dec. 31, 1805; died at Paris, March 5, 1876. One of her three daughters, that by Franz Liszt, married Von Bülow, and subsequently Richard Wagner. Her works include : 'Moral and Political Essays' (1849); 'History of the Revolution of 1848' (1851); and 'Nélida,' an autobiographical romance which attracted much attention.

Sterndale, Robert Armitage. An English naturalist and story-writer. He is the author of 'Seonee; or, Camp-Life on the Satpura Range' (1877); 'The Afghan Knife' (1879); 'A Natural History of the Mammalia of India,' etc. (1884); 'Denizens of the Jungles.'

Sterne, Laurence. A celebrated English novelist; born at Clonmel, Ireland, Nov. 24, 1713; died 'in London, March 18, 1768. Of 'Tristram Shandy,' Vols. i. and ii. were published in 1760; iii. and iv. in December 1760; v. and vi. in 1762; vii. and viii. in 1765; ix. in 1767. 'A Sentimental Journey through France and Italy' was published in 1768; 'The Sermons of Mr. Yorick' in 1760, as a companion to 'Tristram Shandy.' Posthumously appeared 'Letters to his Most Intimate Friends' (1775).

Stesichorus (stē-sik'o-rus). A Greek lyric poet; born at Himera, Sicily, about 630 B. C.; died in Catania, about 556 B. C. Only fragments of his works remain; but he appears to have dealt with epic subjects, among them the sieges of Troy and Thebes, in lyrical measures. He is looked upon as the greatest of the Dorian lyrists, and is often styled "the lyric Homer." The ancients fabled that he was stricken blind for slandering Helen, but upon retracting his calumnies regained his sight.

Stetson, Charlotte Perkins now **Mrs. G. H. Gilman.** An American poet; born in Hartford, Conn., in 1860. She has published a volume of poems, 'In This our World' (1893) ; 'Human Work' (1904).

Stevens, Abel. An American author, editor, and Methodist clergyman; born in Philadelphia, Jan. 19,1815 ; died at San José, Cal., Sept. 13, 1897. He was editor of the Methodist 1865–74 ; subsequently traveled extensively, and settled in Geneva, Switzerland. He wrote many denominational books, among them: 'Essay on Church Polity' (1847); 'Memorials of the Introduction of Methodism into the Eastern States' (1847–52); 'History of the Religious Movement of the Eighteenth Century called Methodism' (3 vols., 1858–61); 'History of the Methodist Episcopal Church in the United States' (4 vols., 1864–67), a standard authority on this subject. He wrote also a German translation (1867); 'The Centenary of American Methodism' (1865); 'The Women of Methodism,' etc. (1866); 'Madame de Staël' (2 vols., 1881); 'Character Sketches' (1882); 'Christian Work'; 'Tales from the Parsonage'; etc.

Stevens, Henry. An American bibliographer; born in Barnet, Vt., Aug. 24, 1819; died in South Hampstead, England, Feb. 28, 1886. He was a prominent collector and authority on 'Americana,' and the agent for many American libraries. He published : 'Catalogue Raisonné of English Bibles' (1854); 'Historical Collections' ; 'Historical and Geographical Notes' ; 'Bibliotheca Americana' (1861); 'Bibles

in the Caxton Exhibition' (1878); 'Indexes to State Papers in London Relating to Virginia, Maryland, Rhode Island, and New Jersey'; edited 'The Dawn of British Trade to the East Indies' (1886); etc.

Stevens, John Austin. An American historical author; born in New York city, Jan. 21, 1827. He was secretary of the Chamber of Commerce, librarian of the New York Historical Society, and has made a special study of American history. He founded and for many years conducted the Magazine of American History. His works include : 'The Valley of the Rio Grande' (1864); 'Colonial Records of the New York Chamber of Commerce' (1867); 'The Expedition of Lafayette against Arnold' (1878); 'Life of Albert Gallatin' (1883); and others.

Stevenson, Edward Irenæus. An American journalist and littérateur of New York city; born in New Jersey, 1858. He is in editorial connection with the New York Independent since 1881, and also with Harper's Weekly and several musical journals. He has published : 'White Cockades'; 'Janus,' reprinted as 'A Matter of Temperament,' a musical novel; 'Left to Themselves,' reprinted as 'Philip and Gerald' ; 'Mrs. Dee's Encore'; 'A Square of Sevens.'

Stevenson, Robert Louis Balfour. A distinguished Scotch novelist, poet, and essayist; born in Edinburgh, Nov. 13, 1850; died at Apia, Samoa, Dec. 4, 1894. He published : 'An Inland Voyage' (1878); 'Edinburgh: Picturesque Notes' (1878); 'Travels with a Donkey in the Cévennes' (1879); 'Virginibus Puerisque, and Other Papers' (1881); 'Familiar Studies of Men and Books' (1882); 'New Arabian Nights' (1882); 'Treasure Island' (1883); 'The Silverado Squatters' (1883); 'The Dynamiter: More New Arabian Nights' (1885), with Mrs. Stevenson; 'A Child's Garden of Verse' (1885); 'Prince Otto' (1885); 'The Strange Case of Dr. Jekyll and Mr. Hyde' (1886); 'Kidnapped' (1886); 'Underwoods' (1887); 'The Merry Men and Other Tales' (1887); 'Memoirs and Portraits' (1887); 'The Black Arrow' (1888); 'The Master of Ballantrae' (1889); 'Ballads' (1891); 'The Wrecker' (1891-92); 'A Foot-Note to History: Eight Years of Trouble in Samoa' (1892); 'David Balfour' (1893); 'Island Nights' Entertainments' (1893); 'The Ebb Tide' (1894); 'Weir of Hermiston' and 'St. Ives' (1895-96), the last two left not quite complete.

Stewart, Balfour. A Scotch physicist, one of the founders of spectrum analysis; born in Edinburgh, Nov. 1, 1828; died near Drogheda, Ireland, Dec. 19, 1887. He established his scientific reputation with a work on 'Radiant Heat' (1858), in which he formulated his discovery of the equality of the emissive and absorptive powers of bodies. Other works include : 'Treatise on Heat' (1866; 5th ed. 1888); 'Elements of Physics' (1870; 4th ed. 1891); 'Conservation of Energy' (1873; 7th ed. 1887). With Professor Tait he published 'The Unseen Universe; or, Physical Speculations on a Future State' (1875; 17th ed. 1890).

Stewart, Dugald. A distinguished Scotch philosopher; born in Edinburgh, Nov. 22, 1753; died June 11, 1828. His philosophy was "a following-up of the reaction commenced by Reid against the skeptical results that Berkeley and Hume drew from the principles of Locke." He published: 'Elements of the Philosophy of the Human Mind' (Vol. i., 1792; Vol. ii., 1814; Vol. iii., 1827); 'Outlines of Moral Philosophy' (1793); 'Philosophical Essays' (1810); 'Dissertation on the History of Ethical Philosophy' (1815-21); 'Philosophy of the Active and Moral Powers' (1828).

Stifter, Adalbert (stif'ter). An Austrian poet and story-writer; born at Oberplan, in the German Böhmerwald, Oct. 23, 1806; died at Linz, Jan. 28, 1868. His first volume of idyls and tales, 'Studies' (1844), was received with extraordinary public favor; it was succeeded by five other volumes under the same title. Of his stories the more noteworthy are 'The Successor' (1857) and 'Witiko,' (1864).

Still, John. An English writer of comedy; born at Grantham in Lincolnshire, about 1543; died bishop of Bath and Wells, Feb. 26, 1607-8. He is reputed to be the author of "A ryght pithy, pleasant, and merrie comedy, intytuled Gammer Gurton's Needle" (1575): it is believed to be the third English comedy. In the first act occurs the familiar old ballad "I cannot eat but little meat," with chorus, "Backe and side go bare, go bare," supposed to be the first drinking-song in the language.

Still, William. An American philanthropist and anti-slavery advocate, of African descent; born in Shamony, in 1821; died 1902. He was chairman and secretary of the Philadelphia branch of the famous "underground railroad" of 1851-61, and wrote out the narratives of escaping slaves, which constitute the only full account of this organization. His works include: 'The Underground Railroad' (1878); 'Voting and Laboring'; and 'Struggle for the Rights of the Colored People of Philadelphia.'

Stillé, Charles Janeway. An American educator and writer; born in Philadelphia, Sept. 23, 1819; died at Atlantic City, N. J., Aug. 11, 1899. He was long provost of the University of Pennsylvania. He wrote: 'Historical Development of American Civilization'; 'Studies in Mediæval Civilization'; 'Beaumarchais and the Lost Million'; 'History of the United States Sanitary Commission'; 'How a Free People Conduct a Long War'; 'Northern Interest and Southern Independence'; 'John Dickinson'; 'Anthony Wayne'; etc.

Stillman, William James. An American essayist; born at Schenectady, N. Y., June 1, 1828; died at Trinity Green, Surrey, Eng., July 6, 1901. He was for many years a correspondent of the London Times and the New York Evening Post, and was especially conversant with the affairs of Greece; he was consul-general to Crete, 1865-69. He wrote: 'The Acropolis of Athens' (1870); 'The Cretan Insurrection' (1874); 'Herzegovina and the Late Uprising' (1877); 'On the Track of Ulysses' (1887).

Stimson, Frederic Jesup. ["J. S. of Dale."] An American novelist and lawyer; born in Dedham, Mass., July 20, 1855. His works of fiction have been widely read, and his legal text-books are authoritative. He has published: 'Labor in its Relations to Law'; and 'Handbook of the Labor Laws of the United States.' His celebrity as a novelist is due to his 'The Crime of Henry Vane'; 'The King's Men'; 'The Residuary Legatee'; 'The Sentimental Calendar'; 'In the Three Zones'; 'First Harvests'; 'Pirate Gold'; 'King Noanett'; 'Guerndale'; 'The Law of the Constitutions.'

Stinde, Julius (stind'e). A German novelist and miscellaneous writer; born at Kirch-Nüchel in Holstein, Aug. 28, 1841. Among his writings are: 'Talks on Natural Science' (1873); several comedies in Plattdeutsch, as 'Aunt Lotta'; 'The Karstens Family'; two Christmas stories, 'Princess Thousandfair' and 'Prince Naughty'; 'Berlin Art Criticism, with Marginal Notes by Quidam' (1883); and an amusing series of stories of 'The Buchholz Family.'

Stirling-Maxwell, William, Sir (ster'ling-maks'wel). A Scottish biographer and art critic; born near Glasgow, 1818; died at Venice, Jan. 15, 1878. He was Member of Parliament, 1852-79; rector of the University of St. Andrews, 1863; of that of Glasgow, 1872; chancellor of the latter, 1875. He wrote the valuable works: 'Annals of the Artists of Spain' (3 vols., 1848); 'Cloister Life of Charles V.' (1852); 'Velasquez and his Works' (1855); and others.

Stockton, Frank Richard. An American journalist and novelist; born in Philadelphia, April 5, 1834; died in Washington, April 20, 1902. Among his works are: 'Rudder Grange'; 'The Lady, or the Tiger?'; 'The Casting Away of Mrs. Lecks and Mrs. Aleshine'; 'The Dusantes'; 'The Bee-Man of Orn, and Other Fanciful Tales'; 'Tales Out of School'; 'The Hundredth Man'; 'The Late Mrs. Null'; 'Adventures of Captain Horn'; 'The Great Stone of Sardis'; etc.

Stoddard, Charles Warren. An American poet and miscellaneous writer; born in Rochester, N. Y., Aug. 7, 1843. He is a lecturer on English literature in the Catholic University of America, Washington, D. C., and is the author of 'Poems'; 'South-Sea Idyls'; 'Mashallah'; 'The Lepers of Molokai'; 'Summer Cruising in the South Seas'; 'The Dream Lady.'

Stoddard, Elizabeth Drew (Barstow). An American novelist and poet; born in Mattapoisett, Mass., May 6, 1823. She was the wife of R. H.; and the author of three distinguished novels; 'The Morgesons' (1862), 'Two Men' (1865), 'Temple House,' illustrative of English character and scenery (1867); and 'Lolly Dink's Doings.' She died in New York city, August 1, 1902.

Stoddard, Richard Henry. An American lyric poet of distinction; born at Hingham, Mass., July 2, 1825. His poems have been published under the titles: 'Songs of Summer' (1856); 'Abraham Lincoln: A Horatian Ode' (1865); collectively, under 'Poems' (1880), and 'The Lion's Cub' (1890). He made his home in New York. For many years he edited the New York Mail and Express, also at times the New York World. Died, N. Y., May 12, 1903.

Stoddard, William Osborn. An American journalist and miscellaneous writer; born in Homer, N. Y., Sept. 24, 1835. He has been connected editorially with various journals, and was private secretary of President Lincoln, 1861–64. His publications include: 'Verses of Many Days' (1875); 'Dab Kinzer' (1881); 'The Volcano under the City' (1887); and 'Lives of the Presidents' (1886–90). He has also written many books popular among boys.

Stokes, Henry Sewell. An English verse-writer; born at Gibraltar, 1808. He wrote: 'Lay of the Desert: A Poem' (1830); 'Song of Albion,' etc.; 'Vale of Lanberne,' etc. (new ed. 1852); 'Echoes of the War,' etc. (1855); 'Scattered Leaves' (1862); 'Rhymes from Cornwall' (1871); 'Memories: A Life's Epilogue' (1872); 'Poems of Later Years' (1873); 'Restormel: A Legend of Piers Gaveston, the Patriot Priest; and Other Verses' (1874); 'Lantrydock: An Elegy' (1883); 'Voyage of Arundel, and Other Rhymes from Cornwall.' He died April 5, 1895.

Stolberg, Christian, Graf von (stol'berG). A German poet; born at Hamburg, Oct. 15, 1748; died at Windebye in Holstein, Jan. 18, 1821. Most of his poems were published with those of his brother Friedrich Leopold in 1779. He wrote two "choral plays," 'Balthasar' and 'Otanes' (1787); 'Poems of Fatherland' (1815); 'Poems from the Greek' (1782); and a translation of Sophocles (2 vols., 1787).

Stolberg, Friedrich Leopold, Graf von. A German poet and general writer, brother of Christian; born at Bramstedt in Holstein, Nov. 7, 1750; died at Sondermühlen near Osnabrück, Dec. 5, 1819. Some of his poems were published with those of his brother; separately he issued 'Iambics' (1784), satires on the manners of the time. He translated the Iliad and some of Plato's 'Dialogues,' four of Æschylus's dramas, and 'Ossian.' In prose he wrote: 'The Island' (1788), a romance; 'Travels' in Germany, Switzerland, etc. (1794); 'Life of Alfred the Great' (1815); 'History of the Religion of Jesus Christ' (15 vols., 1806–18).

Stone, John Augustus. An American actor and dramatist; born in Concord, Mass., in 1801; died in Philadelphia, June 1, 1834. He appeared on the stage in Boston, New York, and Philadelphia, and wrote many plays; among them 'Metamora,' 'The Ancient Briton,' and 'Fauntleroy' for Edwin Forrest. He also published 'The Demoniac,' 'Tancred,' and 'La Roque.'

Stone, Lucy (Blackwell). An American reformer and prominent advocate of women's rights; born in West Brookfield, Mass., Aug. 13, 1818; died at Boston, Mass., Oct. 18, 1893. She graduated at Oberlin College, 1847. In 1855 she married Dr. Henry B. Blackwell, retaining her own name. She published a protest, 'Taxation without Representation.' In 1869 she helped organize the American Woman's Suffrage Association; became connected with the Woman's Journal in 1872, and was editor after 1888. Her lectures on woman suffrage made her known throughout the country.

Storm, Theodor (Woldsen) (storm). A notable German poet and novelist; born in Husum, Schleswig, Sept. 14, 1817; died at Hademarschen, July 4, 1888. He first attracted attention in literature with 'The Song-Book of Three Friends' (1843), the work of Tycho and Theodor Mommsen and himself. Later, he became universally known as the author of 'Immensee' (43d ed. 1896), a short tale, and a volume of 'Poems' (11th ed. 1897). Among his other works are: 'Aquis Submersus' (1877); 'The Senator's Sons' (1881); 'Knight of the White Horse' (1888); 'Renate'; 'Eekenhof.'

Storrs, Richard Salter. An American Congregational minister, and writer on ecclesiastical history and theology; born at Braintree, Mass., Aug. 21, 1821; died at Brooklyn, June 5, 1900. He is author of 'The Graham Lectures on the Wisdom, Power, and Goodness of God' (1856); 'Conditions of Success in Preaching without Notes' (1875); 'The Divine Origin of Christianity' (1884); 'Bernard of Clairvaux' (1892); and 'Forty Years of Pastoral Life.'

Story, Joseph. A great American jurist; born in Marblehead, Mass., Sept. 18, 1779; died in Cambridge, Mass., Sept. 10, 1845. In 1811 he accepted the appointment of associate justice of the United States Supreme Court, and held the office until his death. His works include: 'Commentaries on the Constitution of the United States' (1833); 'Commentaries on the Conflict of Laws,' considered his ablest effort (1834); and 'Miscellaneous Writings' (1835). In 1851 his 'Life and Letters' was edited by his son, W. W. Story.

Story, William Wetmore. An American sculptor, poet, and essayist, son of Joseph; born in Salem, Mass., Feb. 12, 1819; died at Vallombrosa, near Florence, Italy, Oct. 8, 1895. He published: 'Report of Cases Argued and Determined in the Circuit Court of the United States for the First Circuit' (1842–47); 'Address Delivered before the Harvard Medical Association' (1842); 'Nature and Art: A Poem' (1844); 'Treatise on the Law of Contracts not under Seal' (1844); 'Treatise on the Law of Sales of Personal Property' (1847); 'Poems' (1847); 'Life and Letters of Joseph Story' (1851); 'Poems' (1856); 'The American Question' (1862); 'Roba di Roma' (1862); 'Proportions of the Human Figure' (1866); 'Graffiti d'Italia' (1868); 'A Roman Lawyer in Jerusalem' (1870); 'Nero: An Historical Play' (1875); 'Stephania: A Tragedy' (1875); 'Castle St. Angelo and the Evil Eye' (1877); 'Ode on the Anniversary of the Fifth Half-Century of the Landing of John Endicott at Salem, Mass.' (1878); 'Vallombrosa' (1881); 'He and She' (1883); 'Poems' (1885-86); 'Fiammetta' (1886); 'Conversations in a Studio' (1890); 'Excursions in Art and Letters' (1891); 'A Poet's Portfolio' (1894).

Stowe, Calvin Ellis. A Congregational clergyman and educator; born in Natick, Mass., April 6, 1802; died in Hartford, Conn., Aug. 22, 1886. He graduated at Bowdoin College in 1824, at Andover Seminary in 1828; and edited the Boston Recorder, 1829-30. He became professor of Greek at Dartmouth College, 1830-32, and of sacred literature in Lane Theological Seminary, Cincinnati, O., 1833-35. He married Harriet Elizabeth Beecher, January 1836, and went to Europe to examine the public-school systems. He was professor at Bowdoin, 1850; and at Andover, 1852-64. His works include a translation of Jahn's 'Hebrew Commonwealth' (1829); 'Lectures on the Poetry of the Hebrews' (1829); 'Report on Elementary Education in Europe'; 'Introduction to the Criticism and Interpretation of the Bible' (1835); and 'Origin and History of the Books of the Bible' (1867). Also addresses and pamphlets.

Stowe, Harriet Elizabeth (Beecher). An American novelist; born at Litchfield, Conn., June 14, 1811; died at Hartford, Conn., July 1, 1896. She published: 'The Mayflower; or, Sketches of Scenes and Characters among the Descendants of the Pilgrims' (1843); 'Uncle Tom's Cabin; or, Life among the Lowly' (1852); 'The Two Altars' (1852); 'Key to Uncle Tom's Cabin' (1853); 'Uncle Tom's Emancipation' (1853); 'Sunny Memories of Foreign Lands' (1854); 'The Mayflower, and Miscellaneous Writings' (1855); 'The Colored Patriots of the American Revolution' (1855); 'First Geography for Children' (1855); 'Dred: A Tale of the Great Dismal Swamp' (1856); 'Earthly Care a Heavenly Discipline' (1856), formerly published with 'Uncle Tom's Emancipation'; 'Our Charley and What to Do with Him' (1858); 'The Minister's Wooing' (1859); 'The Pearl of Orr's Island' (1862); 'Agnes of Sorrento' (1862); 'Reply to the Address of Thousands of Women of Great Britain and Ireland to their Sisters of the United States' (1863); 'The Ravages of a Carpet' (1864); 'House and Home Papers' (1864); 'Stories about our Boys' (1865); 'Little Foxes' (1866); 'Religious Poems' (1867); 'Queer Little People' (1867); 'Daisy's First Winter, and Other Stories' (1867); 'The Chimney Corner' (1868); 'Men of our Times' (1868); 'Oldtown Folks' (1869); 'The American Woman's Home' (1869), with Catherine E. Beecher; 'Lady Byron Vindicated' (1870); 'Little Pussy Willow' (1870); 'Pink and White Tyranny' (1871); 'Sam Lawson's Fireside Stories' (1871); 'My Wife and I' (1871); 'Six of One, by Half a Dozen of the Other' (1872); 'Lives and Deeds of our Self-Made Men' (1872); 'Palmetto Leaves' (1873);

'Woman in Sacred History' (1873); 'Betty's Bright Idea, and Other Tales' (1875); 'We and our Neighbors' (1875); 'Deacon Pitkin's Farm, and Christ's Christmas Presents' (1875); 'Footsteps of the Master' (1876); 'Captain Kidd's Money, and Other Stories' (1876); 'The Ghost in the Mill, and Other Stories' (1876); 'Poganuc People' (1878); 'A Dog's Mission' (1881); etc.

Strabo (strā'bō). A Greek geographer; born 63 B.C. (?); died 22 A.D. (?). His 'Geographica,' in 17 books, contains first, criticisms of former geographers, and a treatise on physical geography; then accounts of Spain, Gaul, Britain, and Ireland, Italy, north and east Europe as far as the Danube, Greece, Asia, and Africa. Of his historical work, in 47 books, only fragments remain.

Strabo, Walafrid. A mediæval poet; born in Suabia about 809; died Aug. 18, 849. He wrote a running exegetical commentary on the Scripture, 'The Orderly Gloss' ('Glossa Ordinaria'), which for long was a work of high authority in the schools; a history of the development and growth of ecclesiastical institutions and ordinances — 'Of the Beginnings and Growths of Things Ecclesiastical'; 'Life of St. Gall'; 'Life of St. Othmar'; the poem 'Vision of Saint Wettin,' in which is an episode of the poet's journey to Hell, Purgatory, and Heaven; another poem, 'The Little Garden,' treating of the plants in the garden of the poet's monastery.

Strachey, William. An English voyager. He is said to have sailed with Sir Thomas Gates in 1609, on the vessel Sea Venture; was shipwrecked on the Bermudas, but escaped to Virginia (1610) on a boat that had been constructed from the wreck, and became secretary of the colony during three years. He wrote: 'A True Repertory of the Wracke and Redemption of Sir Thomas Gates, upon and from the Islands of the Bermudas,' which was published in Purchas's 'Pilgrims' (Vol. iv.); 'Historie of Travaile into Virginia Britannia,' a quaint and valuable work of historical reference (about 1618), and first published by the Hakluyt Society from original MS. (No. 6, 1849).

Strahan, Lisbeth Gooch Séguin. An English story-writer. She wrote: 'Children's Pastime: Pictures and Stories' (1874); 'Walks in Algiers' (1878); 'A Little Nineteenth-Century Child, and Other Stories' (1878); 'Life in a French Village' (1879); 'The Black Forest: Its People and Legends' (1879); 'The Country of the Passion-Play' (1880); 'Rural England' (1884); 'A Round of Sunday Stories' (1886); 'The Algerine Slave: A Novel' (1888).

Strang, John. A Scotch miscellaneous writer; born at Glasgow, 1795; died there, Dec. 8, 1863. He wrote: 'Glasgow and its Clubs,' containing notes of local history, anecdotes, etc.; 'Life of Theodore Koerner,' the German poet, with translations of some of his lyrics; 'Germany in 1831'; and 'Traveling Notes of an

Invalid in Search of Health.' He translated also from the German, 'Tales of Humor and Romance.'

Straus, Oscar Solomon. A German-American merchant, reformer, and writer; born in Otterberg, Bavaria, Dec. 23, 1850. He graduated at Columbia College, New York, 1871 ; was minister to Turkey 1887–1898 and 1909; Secretary of Commerce and Labor 1906–09 ; and has been a leader in movements for the reform of local politics, and the improvement of the conditions of the poor. He has published : ' Origin of the Republican Form of Government in the United States ' (1886); 'Roger Williams, the Pioneer of Religious Liberty'; and ' U. S. Doctrine of Citizenship.'

Strauss, David Friedrich. A German writer and critic of great celebrity; born at Ludwigsburg, Würtemberg, Jan. 27, 1808; died there, Feb. 8, 1874. His book ' The Life of Jesus,' published in 1834–35, made him famous. He passed a life of great literary productivity, and was engaged all his life in critical and theological controversies.

Street, Alfred Billings. An American poet of nature; born in Poughkeepsie, N. Y., Dec. 18, 1811; died in Albany, N. Y., June 2, 1881. From 1848 until his death he was State librarian of New York at Albany. He published among other works : 'Fugitive Poems' (1846); 'Woods and Waters' (1860); ' Forest Pictures in the Adirondacks,' poems (1865) ; 'Frontenac'; ' Drawings and Tintings.'

Strickland, Agnes. An English historical writer; born in London, Aug. 19, 1796; died at Southwold, July 13, 1874. Her first work, aided by her sister Susannah, was a volume of ' Patriotic Songs,' followed by 'Worcester Field,' a historical poem. She wrote : ' Queen Victoria from her Birth to her Bridal' (1840); ' Historic Scenes and Poetic Fancies ' (1850); ' Lives of the Bachelor Kings of England' (1861); ' Lives of the Seven Bishops ' (1866); ' Lives of the Tudor Princesses' (1868). Her best works are ' Lives of the Queens of England' (12 vols., 1840–48), and ' Lives of the Queens of Scotland' (8 vols., 1850–59).

Strindberg, August (strēnd'berG). A Swedish novelist and dramatist; born in Stockholm, Jan. 22, 1849. He is the leading apostle of naturalism in Sweden. Among his works are : 'Mästar Olof,' a drama; ' The Red Room,' a social satire; ' The Secret of the Club'; ' Mr. Bengt's Wife'; 'Fröken Julie' (1889) ; ' The Keys to the Kingdom of Heaven' (1892); and the novels ' Utopias in Real Life ' (1885); ' In the Offing ' (1891); and the ' Eight Kings,' dramas.

Strong, Latham Cornell. An American journalist and verse-writer; born in Troy, N. Y., June 12, 1845; died in Tarrytown, N. Y., Dec. 17, 1879. He was editorially connected with the Troy Whig, and contributed verses to other journals and periodicals, besides a series of ' Letters from Europe.' His published volumes include : ' Castle Windows' (1876); ' Poke o'

Moonshine' (1878); ' Midsummer **Dreams'** (1879); and ' Pots of Gold.'

Strong, Nathan. An American Congregational clergyman and author; born in Coventry, Conn., Oct. 16, 1748; died in Hartford, Conn., Dec. 25, 1816. He was a chaplain in the Revolutionary army; projected and sustained the Connecticut Evangelical Magazine (1800–15); founded and conducted the Connecticut Missionary Society (1798–1806); and compiled the ' Hartford Collection of Hymns' (1799). His published works include two volumes of ' Sermons' (1798–1800), and a pamphlet, ' The Doctrine of Eternal Misery Consistent with the Infinite Benevolence of God' (1796).

Strother, David Hunter. [" Porte Crayon."] An American writer and illustrator; born in Martinsburg, Va., Sept. 16, 1816; died in Charleston, W. Va., March 8, 1888. He was a colonel of the Union army in the Civil War. His series of sketches contributed to Harper's Magazine in the years before the War under the pen-name " Porte Crayon," illustrated by himself, were great popular favorites; they were republished in book form under the titles ' The Blackwater Chronicle' (1853), and 'Virginia Illustrated' (1857).

Stryker, Melanchthon Woolsey. An American Presbyterian clergyman and educator; born in New York, 1851. He has been president of Hamilton College since 1892. He has published : ' Miriam and Other Verses'; ' Hamilton, Lincoln, and Other Addresses'; ' The Letter of James the Just'; and many hymns.

Strype, John. An English ecclesiastical historian; born at London, Nov. 1, 1643; died at Hackney, Dec. 11, 1737. His works include: ' Annals of the Reformation in England' (4 vols., 1709–31); ' Lives' of Thomas Cranmer, Sir Thomas Smith, John Aylmer, Sir John Cheke, Edmund Grindall, Matthew Parker, and John Whitgift; and ' Ecclesiastical Memorials' (3 vols., 1721).

Stuart, Esmé. An English story-writer: author of ' The Good Old Days' (1875); ' The Belfry of St. Jude: A Story' (1880); 'Whitechapel: A Story' (1881); ' Isabeau's Hero: A Story of the Revolt of the Cevennes' (1882); ' Jessie Dearlove: A Story' (1885); ' Muriel's Marriage' (1886); ' The Goldmakers' (1887); ' Daisy's King' (1888); ' Joan Vellacot' (1888).

Stuart, Mrs. Ruth (McEnery). An American writer of fiction; born in 1856. Her published writings include : ' A Golden Wedding, and Other Tales'; ' Carlotta's Intended, and Other Stories'; ' The Story of Babette'; 'Solomon Crow's Christmas Pockets ' ; ' Pockets and Other Tales ' ; ' The Second Wooing of Salina Sue.'

Stub, Ambrosius (stöb). A Danish lyric poet; born on the Island of Funen, May 1705; died at Ribe, about 1758. His poems were all (except one) published after his death (1771).

He is the original of the hero of C. K. F. Molbeck's romantic drama 'Ambrosius.'

Stubbs, William. An English historical writer; born at Knaresborough, June 21, 1825; died in London, April 22, 1901. He became bishop of Oxford in 1889. His great work is 'The Constitutional History of England' (3 vols., 1874, 1875, and 1878).

Sturgis, Julian Russell. A British storywriter; born 1848. He wrote 'John-a-Dreams' (1878); 'An Accomplished Gentleman' (1879); 'Little Comedies' (1882); 'Dick's Wanderings'; 'My Friends and I,' etc. Died April 13, 1904.

Sturm, Julius Karl Reinholdt ["Julius Stern"] (störm). A German lyric poet; born at Köstritz in Reuss, July 21, 1816; died there May 2, 1896. He wrote: 'Two Roses; or, the Canticle of Love' (1854); 'Devout Songs and Poems' (1858); 'Israelite Songs' (3d ed. 1881); 'Poems of Battle and Victory' (1870); 'Mirror of the Time in Fables' (1872); 'To the Lord my Song' (1884); 'Palm and Crown' (1887); 'In Joy and in Sorrow' (1896).

Suckling, Sir John. An English poet; born at Whitton, Middlesex, in 1608; died in Paris about 1642. A complete edition of his works was published in 1874.

Sudermann, Hermann (sö'der-man). One of the most distinguished German dramatists and novelists of the day; born at Matziken, East Prussia, Sept. 30, 1857. He published: 'In the Twilight' (1885); 'Dame Care' (1886); 'Brothers and Sisters' (1887); 'Honor' (1888); 'The Cat Bridge' (1889); 'The Destruction of Sodom' (1890); 'Home'; 'Battle of the Butterflies'; 'Iolanthe's Wedding' (1892); 'Once on a Time' (1893); 'John the Baptist'; 'The Joy Living'; 'St. John's Fire'; 'Margot'; 'The Last Visit'; 'The Far-away Princess.'

Sue, Eugène (sü). A famous French romancer; born in Paris, Dec. 10, 1804; died at Annecy, July 3, 1857. He published: 'Kernock the Pirate' (1830); 'History of the French Navy' (1835–37); 'History of the War Navies of all Nations' (1841); 'The Mysteries of Paris' (1843); 'The Wandering Jew' (1845); 'Martin the Foundling' (1847); 'The Seven Deadly Sins' (1847–49); 'The Mysteries of the People' (1849); 'The Jouffroy Family' (1854); 'The Secrets of the Confessional' (1858); etc.

Suetonius—Caius Suetonius Tranquillus (swē-tō'nē-us). A Latin chronicler, grammarian, and critic, who flourished in the early part of the second century of our era. He is celebrated for his 'Lives of the Cæsars.' His other works include: 'Illustrious Grammarians'; 'Distinguished Orators'; and 'Lives,' only partly preserved, of Terence, Horace, Lucan, Juvenal, and Pliny.

Suidas (swē'das). The reputed author of an alphabetically arranged work in Greek, giving an account of persons and places and explanations of words, besides much miscellaneous information. The book is referred to as a 'Lexicon,' and bears evidence of having gone through many hands. It is accompanied by a prefatory statement that "the present book is by Suidas, but its arrangement is the work of twelve learned men." Nothing is known of Suidas, although he is usually placed in the tenth or eleventh century. The 'Lexicon' is valued for its extracts from ancient writers whose works have in many cases perished.

Sullivan, James William. An American writer on social questions; born at Carlisle, Pa., March 9, 1848. He is author of: 'Working-People's Rights' (1885); 'A Concept of Political Justice' (1890), 'Direct Legislation through the Initiative and Referendum' (1892),—this book started the Referendum movement in the United States; 'Tenement Tales of New York' (1894); 'So the World Goes,' a series of short stories (1898).

Sullivan, Thomas Russell. An American novelist and dramatist; born in Boston, Nov. 21, 1849. His novels include 'Tom Sylvester,' 'Roses of Shadow,' 'Day and Night Stories'; and his plays, 'The Catspaw' (1881), 'Merely Players' (1886), and a dramatization of Stevenson's 'Dr. Jekyll and Mr. Hyde' (produced 1886). He was joint author with W. W. Chamberlin of 'Hearts Are Trumps,' produced 1878, and 'Midsummer Madness,' produced 1880.

Sully, Maximilien de Béthune, Duke of (sü-lē'); born at Rosny (Seine-et-Oise), Dec. 13, 1560; died at Villebon, Dec. 22, 1641. He was the close friend, supporter, and finance minister of Henry of Navarre. His 'Memoirs' (1634), followed by two posthumous volumes (1662), are very celebrated.

Sully-Prudhomme, René François Armand (sü-lē'prüd-um'). A French poet; born at Paris, May 16, 1839. He has written: 'Stanzas and Poems' (1865); 'The Broken Vase'; 'The Stables of Augeas'; 'The Wildernesses'; 'Impressions of War' (collected 1872); 'Revolt of the Flowers' (1874); 'Reflections on the Art of Versification' (1892). He died Sept. 7, 1907.

Sulzer, Johann Georg (söl'tser). A Swiss art critic; born at Winterthur, Oct. 6, 1720; died at Berlin, Feb. 25, 1779. His principal work is 'Universal Theory of the Fine Arts' (2 vols., 1771–74). His 'Autobiography' was published 1809.

Sumarokov, Aleksander Petrovich (sö-mär'o-kov). A Russian playwright; born in Moscow, Nov. 23, 1718; died Oct. 12, 1777. His tragedy 'Khorev' (1747) first attracted attention; it was followed by 'Sinav and Truvor' and 'Semira,' which added to his fame. He also wrote comedies, odes, sonnets, madrigals, epigrams, and fables.

Sumner, Charles. A distinguished American statesman; born in Boston, Jan. 6, 1811; died in Washington, D. C., March 11, 1874. His collected works, including speeches, orations, etc., have been published in a 15-vol. edition (1870–83).

Sumner, William Graham. An American educator and author; born in Paterson, N. J.,

Oct. 30, 1840. Since 1872 he has been professor of political and social science at Yale. Among his works are : ' History of American Currency' (1874); 'Andrew Jackson as a Public Man' (1882); 'Economic Problems' (1884); 'Protectionism,' collected essays in political and social science (1885); 'The Financier and Finances of the American Revolution' (1891); and 'Robert Morris' (1892); 'Folkways' (1907).

Swedenborg, Emanuel. The great Swedish religious mystic, philosopher, and author; born in Stockholm, Jan. 29, 1688; died there, March 29, 1772. For an adequate account of his literary works, see article in this 'Library.'

Sweet, Alexander Edwin. An American journalist; born in St. John, N. B., March 28, 1841. He served in the Confederate army in the Civil War; was editor of the San Antonio (Texas) Herald, and of Texas Siftings from 1881. He has published 'Three Dozen Good Stories from Texas Siftings'; and with J. Amory Knox, 'On a Mexican Mustang through Texas.' He died in New York city, May 20, 1901.

Swetchine, Anne Sophie (svech-ēn'). A Russian society dame and letter-writer; born at Moscow, 1782; died at Paris, Sept. 10, 1857. At St. Petersburg her drawing-room was frequented by scholars and men of science; after 1815 she resided in Paris. She was the friend and correspondent of many of the Catholic notables of France,— Joseph de Maistre, Lacordaire, De Falloux, etc. Her 'Life and Works' was published in 2 vols.; and her 'Letters' in several volumes.

Swett, Sophia Miriam. An American writer of stories and juvenile tales; born in Maine in 186-, and now living at Arlington, Mass. She has published : 'The Lollipops' Vacation'; 'Captain Polly'; 'Flying Hill Farm'; 'The Mate of the Mary Ann'; 'Cap'n Thistletop'; and 'The Ponkarty Branch Road ; 'Sonny Boy.'

Swift, Jonathan. A great English prose satirist; born in Dublin, Nov. 30, 1667; died there, Oct. 19, 1745. He wrote : 'Tale of a Tub' (1704); 'Battle of the Books' (1704); 'Meditation upon a Broomstick' (1704); 'Argument to Prove the Inconvenience of Abolishing Christianity' (1708); 'Project for the Advancement of Religion' (1708) ; 'Sentiments of a Church of England Man' (1708); 'Conduct of the Allies' (1711) ; 'Advice to the October Club' (1712); 'Remarks on the Barrier Treaty' (1712); 'Public Spirit of the Whigs' (1714); 'Drapier's Letters' (1724); 'Gulliver's Travels' (1726); 'A Modest Proposal' (1729), for utilizing Irish children as articles of food; etc.

Swinburne, Algernon Charles. A celebrated English poet; born in London, April 5, 1837. He has published : 'The Queen Mother and Rosamund' (1861); 'Atalanta in Calydon' (1864); 'Chastelard' (186–); 'Poems and Ballads' (1866); 'A Song of Italy' (1867); 'Ode on the Proclamation of the French Republic' (1871); 'Songs before Sunrise' (1871); 'Under

the Microscope' (1872); 'Bothwell' (1874): 'Erechtheus' (1875); 'Poems and Ballads' (1878), second series; 'Songs of the Springtides'; 'Songs of Two Nations'; 'Studies in Song'; 'A Century of Roundels'; 'Marino Faliero'; 'Lochrine'; 'Tristram of Lyonesse'; 'The Sisters'; etc. He died April 9, 1909.

Swinton, John. An American journalist and writer on social and labor questions; born in Salton, Scotland, Dec. 12, 1829 ; died in Brooklyn, Dec. 15, 1901. In 1857 he came to New York, and later became chief managing editor of the New York Times, and afterwards of the Sun. From 1883 to 1887 he published a weekly journal, John Swinton's Paper, devoted to labor reform. He wrote : ' The New Issue : the Chinese-American Question'; 'A Eulogy on Henry J. Raymond'; 'John Swinton's Travels '; ' Oration on John Brown '; etc.

Swinton, William. An American journalist educator, and historical writer, brother of John; born in Salton, Scotland, April 23, 1833; died in New York, Oct. 25, 1892. During the Civil War he was war correspondent of the New York Times ; and after 1874 he devoted his time to educational works. His writings include: 'Rambles among Words'; 'Twelve Decisive Battles of the War' ; 'Campaigns of the Army of the Potomac'; 'Word Analysis'; and 'Studies in English Literature.'

Swisshelm, Jane Grey. An American journalist, reformer, and writer; born near Pittsburg, Pa., Sept. 6, 1815; died in Swissvale, Pa., July 22, 1884. She was among the earliest advocates of woman's rights; an ardent opponent of slavery, and while editing the St. Cloud (Minn.) Visitor, had her office and press destroyed by a mob for advocating abolitionism. She was among the first to become a nurse in the Northern army. Besides voluminous contributions to current periodicals, she published: 'Letters to Country Girls' (1853), and an autobiography, 'Half of a Century' (1881).

Sybel, Heinrich von (sē'bel). An eminent German historian ; born in Düsseldorf, Dec. 2, 1817 ; died at Marburg, Aug. 1, 1895. The tone of many of his writings involved him in controversy. He wrote: 'History of the First Crusade' (1841); 'The Development of German Sovereignty' (1844); 'History of the Revolutionary Period from 1789 to 1795' (1853-58), which has passed through many editions and was later brought down to the year 1800 ; 'The German Nation and the Empire ' (1862); 'The Foundation of the German Empire through William I.' (1889-94), already in its fifth edition.

Sylva, Carmen (kär'man sil'va), pseudonym of Elizabeth, Queen of Roumania. A German poet and story-writer; born at Castle Monrepos near Neuwied, Dec. 29, 1843. In 1869 she was married to Charles, then Prince, now King, of Roumania. Among her works (all in German) are : 'Roumanic Poems' (1881); 'Tempests'; 'Songs from the Dimbovitza Valley' (1889). Her tragedy 'Master Manole' (1892) had a brilliant success in the Burgh Teatre, Vienna. In collaboration with Mite Kremnitz, she has written some novels: 'Astra'; 'From Two Worlds'; etc. The gem of the fine tragedy 'Master Manole' is the scene in which are portrayed a wife's longings for motherhood.

Symmachus, Quintus Aurelius (sim'a-kus). A Roman author and orator; born about 350 A. D.; died about 405 A. D. Ten books of his 'Letters' are extant, and are of much historical interest. Fragments of his speeches were discovered by Cardinal Mai, and published in 1815. Symmachus was one of the last champions of paganism, and seems to have been a pure and noble character.

Symonds, John Addington. A distinguished English critic and historian of literature; born at Bristol, Oct. 5, 1840; died at Rome, April 19, 1893. He wrote: 'Introduction to the Study of Dante' (1872); 'Studies of the Greek Poets' (1873); 'Sketches in Italy and Greece' (1874); 'The Renaissance in Italy' (7 vols., 1875–86), his greatest work; 'Sketches and Studies in Italy' (1879); 'Shakespeare's Predecessors' (1884); several volumes of verse both original and translated; 'Lives' of Sir Philip Sidney, Michelangelo, Ben Jonson, Shelley, etc.

Symons, Arthur. A British literary critic; born in Wales, 1865; author of 'Days and Nights' (1889); 'Silhouettes' (1892); 'London Nights.'

Synesius (si-nē'shus). A Greek bishop, philosopher, and poet; born in Cyrene, Africa, about 375; died about 415. He studied philosophy in Alexandria under Hypatia. Among his works which have survived are several essays, including one 'On Dreams'; and a number of orations, among them that delivered before the Emperor Arcadius, 'On Kingship.' His hymns have often been translated into modern languages.

Syrus, Publilius. See **Publilius Syrus.**

Szalay, Laszlo (säl'ī). A Hungarian historian; born at Buda, April 18, 1813; died at Salzburg, July 17, 1864. He succeeded Kossuth as editor-in-chief of the Pesti Hirlap, in 1844. Among his works are 'History of Hungary' (6 vols., 1850–63); 'Michael Eszterházy' (2 vols., 1862–66); and 'The Book of Statesmen,' a collection of political biographies.

Sze-ma or **Sŭma Kwang** (sä'ma). One of the most eminent statesmen and writers of China, and as a historian second only to Sze-ma Ts'ien; born in 1009; died 1086. He is renowned as the author of 'The Comprehensive Mirror of History,' in 294 books, the labor of nineteen years. It covers a period from the beginning of the fourth century B. C. to 960 A. D.

Sze-ma or **Sŭ-ma Ts'ien.** Author of the first general history of China; born at Lung-Mun, in what is now the province of Ho-nan, about 163 B. C. He died in disgrace, about 85 B. C. In 110 B. C. he succeeded his father, Sze-ma T'an, as grand recorder and astronomer, and took up the historical work begun by him. It was finished in 91 B. C., and was named 'Shih-ki,' or Historical Records. It covers from 2697 to 104 B. C. He is also noted for reforming the calendar. The chronology settled on by him still prevails in China.

Szigligeti, Eduard (sēg-lē-get'ē); true name Joseph Szatmáry. A Hungarian dramatist; born at Nagy Varad [Grosswardein], March 18, 1814; died at Pesth, Jan. 19, 1878. He wrote about 100 plays between 1834 and 1872. Several of his comedies and tragedies were crowned by the Academy. Among his best dramas are: 'The Deserter'; 'A Brace of Pistols'; 'The Jew'; 'The Foundling.' He wrote also: 'The Drama and its Different Forms' (1874); 'Biographies of Hungarian Actors' (1878).

T

Tabarî, Abu Djasar Mohammed ibn Djerîr (tä-bä're). A celebrated Mohammedan theologian and historian; born at Amul in Taberistan, 839; died at Bagdad, 921. His two principal writings are: 'Tefsîr' (exegesis), by far the most authoritative exposition of the doctrine of the Koran; and his 'Annals,' in which he gives, on a theological basis, the history of the world from the creation to the year 914.

Tabb, John Banister. An American educator and author born in Virginia, 1845. He is professor of English literature at St. Charles College, Ellicott, City, Md., He has written : 'Poems'; 'Lyrics'; 'An Octave to Mary'; 'Quibbs and Quiddits.'

Tacitus, Publius Cornelius (tas'it-us). A great Latin historian; born about 54 A. D. He was an intimate friend of Pliny the Younger.

The dialogue 'De Oratoribus' is his earliest work; the 'Agricola,' a biography of his father-in-law, C. Julius Agricola, is interesting to English speaking readers on account of the fact that Agricola spent so much of his time in Britain; the 'Germania,' or 'On the Manners of the Germans,' is of great value for its description of early Germany. Of his 'History' only the first four and a half books are extant, giving the history of the years 69–96 A. D., of the 'Annals,' beginning at the death of Augustus and ending at the death of Nero (14–68 A. D.), only the first four books, part of the fifth, the sixth, and from the middle of the eleventh to the middle of the sixteenth, are extant. Many editions of his works have been published. The latest English translation is by Church and Brodribb (London, 1876–77). He died about 117.

Taconnet, Toussaint Gaspard (tä-kō-nā').
A French dramatist and actor; born at Paris,
1730; died there, 1774. Among his works are:
'The Labyrinth of Love' (1749); 'All the
World's Friend' (1762); the farce-tragedy 'The
Death of the Fatted Ox' (1767); 'Stanzas on
the Death of Marie, Queen of France' (1768).

Taillandier, Alphonse Honoré (tī-äṅ-dyā').
A French legist; born at Paris, 1797; died there,
1867. His principal works are: 'Collection
of Ancient French Laws from the Year 420
to the Revolution of 1789' (23 vols., 1821-30);
'Reflections on the Penal Laws of France
and England' (1824).

Taillandier, René Gaspard Ernest, usually
styled Saint-René Taillandier. A French historian and biographer; born at Paris, Dec. 16,
1817; died there, Feb. 24, 1879. He was appointed professor of French poetry in the Sorbonne, 1863. Among his works are: 'Scotus
Erigena and the Scholastic Philosophy' (1843);
'Studies on the Revolution in Germany' (1853);
'The Countess of Albany' (1862); 'Maurice
de Saxe' (1865); 'Ten Years of the History of
Germany' (1875); 'King Leopold and Queen
Victoria' (1878); 'Servia in the 19th Century.'

Taillepied, Noël (tī-pyā'). A French historical writer; born in Normandy, 1540; died
at Angers, 1589. His principal works are:
'Abridgment of the Philosophy of Aristotle'
(1583); 'History of the State and Commonwealth of the Druids' (1585); 'Collection of
the Antiquities and Curiosities of the City of
Rouen' (1587); 'Treatise on the Apparition of
Ghosts' (1602).

Tailliar, Eugène François Joseph (tī-är').
A French juristic writer; born at Douai, 1803;
died there, July 8, 1878. Among his writings
are: 'Essay on the History of the Institutions
of Northern France in the Celtic Era' (1852);
'Usages and Ancient Customs of the County
of Guysnes' (1856); 'Essay on the History of
Institutions' (1859).

Taine, Hippolyte Adolphe (tän). A cele-
brated French historian and critic; born at
Vouziers (Ardennes), April 21, 1828; died at
Paris, March 5, 1893. He published: 'Essay
on La Fontaine's Fables' (1853); 'Essay on
Livy' (1854); 'Journey to the Pyrenees' (1855);
'French Philosophers in the Nineteenth Cen-
tury' (1856); 'Essays in Criticism and His-
tory' (1857); 'Notes on England' (1861);
'Contemporary English Writers' (1863); 'History of English Literature' (1864); 'English
Idealism' (1864); 'English Positivism' (1864);
'New Essays in Criticism and History' (1865);
'Philosophy of Art' (1865); 'Philosophy of Art
in Italy' (1866); 'Tour in Italy, Naples, Rome,
Florence, and Venice' (1866); 'Notes on Paris'
(1867); 'The Ideal in Art' (1867); 'Philosophy
of Art in the Low Countries' (1868); 'Philosophy of Art in Greece' (1870); 'On the
Understanding' (1870); 'Universal Suffrage
and the Method of Voting' (1871); 'Beginnings
of Contemporary France,' a series of works

comprising 'The Old Régime' (1875), 'Anarchy' (1878), 'The Revolutionary Governments' (1884), 'The Modern Régime' (1890).
The last-named was left not quite complete;
the sixth volume was posthumously published,
after revision by Sorel, in 1894. 'Last Essays
in Criticism and History' (1894) is a volume
of miscellany.

Tait, Archibald Campbell. An English
Churchman and theological writer; born in
Edinburgh, Dec. 21, 1811; died in London,
Dec. 1, 1882. He was educated at Glasgow
and Oxford Universities; was one of the leading opponents of the Tractarians or Puseyites;
took orders in the Church of England; was
head-master of Rugby School, dean of Carlisle, bishop of London, and Archbishop of
Canterbury from 1868 to his death. He was
author of 'The Dangers and Safeguards of
Modern Theology' (1861), and 'The Word of
God and the Ground of Faith' (1863), besides
addresses and sermons. His life was published
by Davidson and Benham (2 vols., 1891).

Talbot, Charles Remington. An American
Episcopal clergyman and juvenile-story writer;
born 1851; died 1891. His works include:
'Honor Bright'; 'Miltiades Peterkin Paul';
'Royal Louise'; 'Romulus and Remus'; 'A
Midshipman at Large'; 'The Impostor'; 'A
Romance of the Revolution.'

Talfourd, Sir Thomas Noon. An English
statesman and author; born at Reading, Berkshire, May 26, 1795; died at Stafford, March
13, 1854. He published many speeches and
essays, some of which have been collected
under the title 'Critical and Miscellaneous Essays' (1842). Among his other works are:
'Poems on Various Subjects' (1811); 'An
Attempt to Estimate the Poetical Talent of
the Present Age' (1815); 'History of Greek
Literature'; 'History of Greece' and 'History
of the Roman Republic'; 'Memoirs and Correspondence of Charles Lamb' (1837); 'Final
Memorials of Charles Lamb' (1848); four tragedies, the first two of which had a stage success,—'Ion' (1835), 'The Athenian Captive'
(1838), 'Glencoe' (1840), and 'The Castilian'
(1854); 'Recollections of a First Visit to the
Alps' (1842); 'Vacation Rambles' (1844); and
'Supplement to Vacation Rambles' (1846).

Talleyrand-Perigord, Charles Maurice de
(täl-ā-raṅ'-per-ē-gôr'), Prince of Benevento. A
celebrated French diplomat; born at Paris,
Feb. 13, 1754; died at Valençay, May 17,
1838. His 'Memoirs' were first published in
1891-92 (5 vols.); his 'Correspondence with
Louis XVIII,' during the Congress of Vienna,'
was published in 1881; his 'Diplomatic Correspondence' in 1889-91 (3 vols.); and 'Unpublished Letters of Tallyrand to Napoleon, 1800-
1809,' in 1889.

Talma, Joseph François (täl-mä'). A great
French actor and writer; born in Paris, Jan.
15, 1763; died Oct. 19, 1826. He was educated
at Mazarin College, and afterwards went to

London with his father, a dentist; studied in the hospitals there, and on returning to Paris was apprenticed to a dentist. He had been on the stage, however, both in London and Paris, and made his professional début Nov. 21, 1787, at the Comédie Française. He founded, with a few others, the theatre afterwards known as the Théâtre de la République. He won his fame as a tragedian, but made many improvements in the naturalness of stage productions. He wrote: 'Mémoires de Le Kain, et Réflexions sur cet Acteur et sur l'Art Théâtral' (1825), which was republished in 1856 under a slightly different title. His own 'Mémoires' were edited by Alexandre Dumas (1856).

Talmage, Thomas De Witt. An American Presbyterian clergyman, lecturer and educator; born at Bound Brook, N. J., Jan. 7, 1832; died in Washington, April 12, 1902. He became pastor of Brooklyn Tabernacle, 1869, and later of Lincoln Memorial Church, Washington, D. C. He was the author of many essays, addresses, etc., upon moral and religious subjects, besides volumes of sermons. He edited the Christian at Work (New York, 1873-76); the Advance (Chicago, 1877-78). He wrote: 'The Almond Tree in Blossom' (1870); 'Old Wells Dug Out' (1874); 'Every-Day Religion' (1875); 'The Masque Torn Off' (1879); 'The Marriage Ring' (1886); 'The Pathway of Life'; etc.

Tangermann, Wilhelm (täng'er-man), known under the pseudonym "Victor Granella." A German theological writer; born at Essen on the Ruhr, July 6, 1815. He was a priest of the Roman Catholic Church, but on the fulmination of the Vatican decree of infallibility, he seceded from that communion and became pastor of a schismatical church in Cologne. He wrote: 'Truth, Beauty, and Love,' a series of philosophico-æsthetic studies (1867); 'From Two Worlds: Truth and Fiction' (1871); 'Philosophy and Christianity' (1876); 'New Springtime, New Life' (1889); 'Flowers and Stars,' poems (1896).

Tannahill, Robert. A Scottish poet; born at Paisley, June 3, 1774; drowned himself near their May 17, 1810. He was a weaver, working at the loom all his life, and writing occasionally for periodicals. In 1807 he published 'The Soldier's Return, with Other Poems and Songs, Chiefly in the Scottish Dialect,' which rendered him famous. Several of them became popular favorites, and have remained so. A statue of the poet was erected in Paisley in 1883.

Tansillo, Luigi (tän-sil'lō). An Italian poet; born at Venosa, Italy, in 1510; died at Teano, Dec. 1, 1568. His early poems are: 'The Two Pilgrims,' a pastoral; 'The Vintager' (1532), and some amorous rhymes probably addressed to Maria of Aragon. To his later years belong the 'Balia'; the 'Podere' (1560), an idyl on the charm of country life; and 'St. Peter's Tears,' a religious work written by way of atonement for 'The Vintager.'

Tappan, William Bingham. An American poet; born at Beverly, Mass., 1794; died in 1849. He became general agent of the American Sunday-School Union in 1826. He was author of several volumes of religious poetry; also of 'New England, and Other Poems' (1819); 'Songs of Judah' (1820); 'Lyrics' (1822); 'Poems' (1834); 'Memoir of Capt. James Wilson' (1842); 'Poetry of the Heart' (1847); 'Late and Early Poems' (1849).

Tappert, Wilhelm (täp'pert). A German writer on music; born at Ober Thomaswaldau, in Silesia, Feb. 19, 1830. He wrote: 'Music and Musical Education' (1867); 'Musical Studies' (1868); 'The Wagner Lexicon' (1877), a collection of the words and phrases of contempt, disgust, etc., employed by the critics of Richard Wagner; 'Poems' (1878); 'Richard Wagner, his Life and Work' (1883); 'Stray Melodies' (2d ed. 1890).

Tarbé, Prosper (tär-bā'). A French archæologist; born at Paris, 1809. He has written: 'Rheims, its Streets and Monuments' (1844); 'The Church of Notre-Dame at Rheims' (1845); 'History of the Language and the Dialects of Champagne' (2 vols., 1852).

Tarbell, Ida M. An American writer; born 1857. She is the author of 'Madam Roland'; 'Early Life of Abraham Lincoln' (1896); 'History of the Standard Oil Co.' (1904); 'He Knew Lincoln' (1907).

Tardieu, Jules Romain (tär-dye'). A French story-writer; born at Rouen, 1805; died 1868. Among his stories and sketches are: 'The Art of Being Miserable' (1856); 'The Truce of God: Recollections of a Sunday in Summer' (1862); 'Book for Children who Cannot Read' (1863).

Tarnovski, Stanislav, Count (tär-nov'skē). A Polish historian of literature; born at Dzikov in Galicia, Nov. 7, 1837. Among his numerous monographs on the history of literature are: 'History of the Pre-Christian World'; 'The Polish Novel in the Beginning of the 19th Century'; 'Decline of Polish Literature in the 18th Century'; 'Shakespeare in Poland'; 'Studies in the History of Polish Literature' (1886-92),—his greatest work, and a Polish classic.

Tasso, Bernardo (täs'sō). A Venetian poet; born in 1493; died at Ostiglia, Sept. 4, 1569. In 1536 he married Porzia de' Rossi of Pistoja, and in 1554 retired to Sorrento in order to give himself entirely to literature. There he worked on his epic, 'Amadis of Gaul'; besides this he wrote 'Floridante,' a narrative poem finished by his son Torquato; and also shorter poems called 'Amours,' 'Fishing Eclogues,' and 'Odes.' In prose are the 'Discourse on Poetry,' and numerous interesting letters.

Tasso, Torquato. An Italian poet, son of Bernardo Tasso; born at Sorrento, Italy, March 11, 1544; died at Rome, April 25, 1595. In 1562, he published a romantic epic, 'Rinaldo,' in 12 cantos; and in 1573 he wrote for a court festivity his 'Aminta,' a pastoral drama. In 1575 his 'Jerusalem Delivered' was completed. In 1579 he was confined in a lunatic asylum, where he remained seven years, while his great work was read all over Europe, making his name one of the first of the age. On his release, he roved restlessly from place to place. In 1594 Pope Clement VIII. invited him to come to Rome to be crowned on the Capitoline Hill; but he died before the ceremony could take place. Besides the poems mentioned, he wrote 'Torismondo,' a number of lyrical poems, dialogues, and essays, and a second part of 'Jerusalem Delivered' called 'Jerusalem Conquered.' ('Complete Works,' 33 vols., Pisa, 1821–32.) English translations of the 'Jerusalem Delivered' were made by Edward Fairfax (London, 1600), and by J. K. James (2 vols., 1865).

Tassoni, Alessandro (täs-sō'nē). An Italian poet and critic; born at Modena, Sept. 28, 1565; died there, April 25, 1635. His best-known work is a fine mock-heroic poem, 'The Rape of the Bucket' (1615–22).

Taubert, Emil (tou'bert). A German poet; born at Berlin, Jan. 23, 1844; died there, April 10, 1895. He wrote: 'The Paradise of Youth: Poems for Young and Old' (1869); 'The Clash of Arms' (1870); 'Juventus: New Poems' (1875); 'The Goldsmith of Bagdad'; 'The Cicadas' (1880); 'The Torso' (1881): also some stories, as 'The Antiquary' (1882); 'Sphinx Atropos' (1883); 'The Magic Lantern' (1885); 'Samson' (1886); 'Wife and Bride' (1889).

Tauler, Johannes (tou'ler). A German mystic and writer; born at Strasburg about 1300; died there, June 16, 1361. He entered the order of the Dominicans about 1318; studied theology at their college in Cologne, and afterward in Paris. He was banished with them from Strasburg, and went to Basel in 1339. He was reputed the greatest preacher of his time. His sermons were collected in 1498.

Taunay, Alfredo D'Escragnolle (tō-nä'). An author and statesman; born of French parents in Rio de Janeiro, Brazil, Feb. 22, 1843. In 1865–68 he was attached to the engineer corps of the Brazilian army which invaded Paraguay, and described the history of the campaigns in 'Scenes of Travel' (1868), and 'The Retreat from Laguna' (1871). Besides filling many important political positions, he has written essays, poems, comedies, criticisms, and a series of novels considered the best ever produced by a Brazilian novelist; among which is 'Innocencia,' translated into French and English.

Tautphœus, Baroness von (tout'fē-ös). An Irish novelist; born (Jemima Montgomery) at Seaview, Oct. 23, 1807; died at Munich, Nov. 12, 1893. She wrote the popular novels 'Quits'; 'At Odds'; 'The Initials.'

Tavernier, Jean Baptiste (tä-vern-yā'). A celebrated French traveler; born at Paris, 1605; died at Copenhagen, 1689. He traveled in every country of Europe, in Persia, Mongolia, India, Sumatra, Batavia, etc., and amassed an enormous fortune. He wrote: 'Travels in Turkey, Persia, and India' (1679).

Taylor, Bayard. An American poet, novelist, and traveler; born at Kennett Square, Pa., Jan. 11, 1825; died at Berlin, Germany, Dec. 19, 1878. His works include: 'Ximena, and Other Poems' (1844); 'Views Afoot' (1846); 'Rhymes of Travel, and Other Poems' (1849); 'El Dorado; or, Adventures in the Path of Empire' (1850); 'The American Legend,' poem (1850); 'Handbook of Literature' (edited with George Ripley: 1851); 'Book of Romances, Lyrics, and Songs' (1852); 'Poems and Ballads' (1854); 'A Journey to Central Africa' (1854); 'A Visit to India, China, and Japan' (1855); 'The Lands of the Saracen' (1855); 'Poems of the Orient' (1855); 'Poems of Home and Travel' (1855); 'Northern Travel: Sweden, Norway, and Lapland' (1858); 'Travels in Greece and Russia' (1859); 'At Home and Abroad' (1859); 'At Home and Abroad' (2d series: 1862); 'The Poet's Journal' (1863); 'Hannah Thurston,' novel (1863); 'John Godfrey's Fortunes,' novel (1864); 'Poems' (1865); 'The Story of Kennett,' novel (1866); 'The Picture of St. John' (1866); 'Colorado' (1867); 'Frithiof's Saga' (edited: 1867); 'By-Ways of Europe' (1869); 'Joseph and his Friend,' novel (1870); 'Ballad of Abraham Lincoln' (1870); translation of Goethe's 'Faust' (1870–71); 'The Masque of the Gods' (1872); 'Beauty and the Beast' (1872); 'Illustrated Library of Travel,' etc. (edited: 1872–74); 'Lars,' poem (1873); 'School History of Germany' (1874); 'Egypt and Iceland' (1874); 'The Prophet: A Tragedy' (1874); 'Home Pastorals, Ballads, and Lyrics' (1875); 'The Echo Club, and Other Literary Diversions' (1876); 'Boys of Other Countries' (1876); 'National Ode' (July 4, 1876); Fitz-Greene Halleck Memorial Address (1877); 'Prince Deukalion' (1878). Posthumously: 'Picturesque Europe' (edited: 1878–80); 'Studies in German Literature' (1879); 'Critical Essays and Literary Notes' (1880); 'Dramatic Works' (1880).

Taylor, Benjamin Franklin. An American poet, author, and war correspondent; born at Lowville, N. Y., 1819; died at Cleveland, O., 1887. He wrote: 'Pictures of Life in Camp and Field' (1871); 'The World on Wheels' (1874); 'Song of Yesterday' (1877); 'Between the Gates' (1878); 'Summer Savory' (1879); 'Dulce Domum' (1884); 'Theophilus Trent' (1887).

Taylor, Sir Henry. An English poet of celebrity; born at Bishop-Middleham, Durham, Oct. 18, 1800; died March 28, 1886. In 1824 he became editor of the London Magazine, and obtained a position in the Colonial Office, which he retained until 1872. His dramatic works are: 'Isaac Comnenus' (1827); 'Philip van Artevelde' (1834), his best; 'Edwin the Fair' (1842); 'The Virgin Widow' (1850); and 'St. Clement's Eve' (1862). He published several volumes of essays,—'The Statesman'

(1836), 'Notes from Life' (1847), 'Notes from Books' (1849); also 'The Eve of the Conquest, and Other Poems' (1847); and his 'Autobiography' (1885). In 1888 his 'Letters' appeared, edited by Dowden.

Taylor, Isaac (known as Taylor of Ongar). An English minister and author; born in London, in 1759; died at Ongar, Dec. 12, 1829. He was originally an engraver. Besides sermons, he published many volumes, chiefly for the young; among which are: 'Advice to the Teens'; 'Beginnings of British Biography'; 'Beginnings of European Biography'; 'Biography of a Brown Loaf'; 'Book of Martyrs for the Young'; 'Bunyan Explained to a Child'; 'Child's Life of Christ'; 'Mirabilia; or, The Wonders of Nature and Art'; 'Scenes in America, in Asia, in Europe, in Foreign Lands.'

Taylor, Isaac. An English author, son of Isaac Taylor of Ongar; born at Lavenham, Suffolk, Aug. 17, 1787; died at Ongar, June 28, 1865. Besides contributing to the Eclectic Review, he published many books, including: 'Elements of Thought' (1823); 'History of the Transmission of Ancient Books to Modern Times' (1827); 'The Process of Historical Proof Exemplified and Explained' (1828); 'Natural History of Enthusiasm' (1829); 'Physical Theory of Another Life' (1836); 'Loyola and Jesuitism in its Rudiments' (1849). In 1862 a pension of £100 was bestowed upon him from the civil-service fund "in public acknowledgment of his eminent services to literature, especially in the departments of history and philosophy, during more than forty years."

Taylor, Isaac. An English clergyman and writer, grandson of Isaac Taylor of Ongar; born at Stanford Rivers, May 2, 1829; died at Settrington, May 18, 1901. Was a canon of York. He wrote: 'Words and Places,' an explanation of the local names in Great Britain (1864, 3 eds. since); 'The Family Pen: Memorials Biographical and Literary of the Taylor Family of Ongar' (1867); 'The Alphabet: An account of the origin and Development of letters' (1883); 'The Manx Runes' (1886); 'The origin of the Aryans' (1890), summing up the evidence against the Central-Asian theory.

Taylor, Isidore Justin Séverin, Baron (ti'lor or tä'ler). A French dramatist and writer of books of travel; born at Brussels, 1789; died at Paris, Sept. 8, 1879. Among his dramatic compositions are: 'The Informer'; 'Ismaïl and Marie.' He wrote also: 'Picturesque Tour in Spain, Portugal, and the Coast of Africa' (3 vols., 1826-32); 'Syria, Egypt, Palestine, and Judea' (3 vols., 1835-39); 'Pilgrimage to Jerusalem' (1841); 'The Pyrenees' (1843); and 24 vols. of 'Picturesque and Romantic Travels in Ancient France' (1820-63).

Taylor, Jeremy. A celebrated English theological writer; born August 1613, at Cambridge; died at Lisburn, Ireland, Aug. 13, 1667.

During the civil wars he was chaplain to Charles I., who had the degree of D. D. conferred on him for his treatise 'Episcopacy Asserted against the Acephali and Arians New and Old.' In 1658 he became bishop of Down and Connor in Ireland, and labored earnestly for the establishment of the Protestant Church there. Besides his sermons, his principal works are: 'Discourse on the Liberty of Prophesying' (1647); 'The Great Exemplar of Sanctity and Holy Life' (1649); 'The Rule and Exercise of Holy Living' (1650); 'The Rule and Exercise of Holy Dying' (1651); 'Ductor Dubitantium,' a work on casuistry.

Taylor, John. An English poet; born in Gloucestershire, August 1580; died in London, 1654. He followed the occupation of waterman during a part of his life, and hence was termed "the water-poet." His productions, of which about 140 are known to collectors, are interesting, as they show the manners and customs of the times. They are remarkable for the eccentricity of their titles, as, 'Taylor's Revenge; or, The Rimer, William Fennor, Firkt, Ferrited, and Finely Fetched over the Coals' (1615); 'The Pennyles Pilgrimage; or, The Moneylesse Perambulation of John Taylor, alias the King's Majestie's Water-Poet, from London to Edinborough on Foot' (1618).

Taylor, Philip Meadows. An English soldier and author; born in Liverpool, Sept. 25, 1808; died in Mentone, France, May 13, 1876. He spent a great part of his life in India, in the army and other government service, and married an Indian princess. He was the author of: 'Confessions of a Thug' (1839, new ed. 1858); 'Tippoo Sultaun: A Tale of the Mysore War' (1840); 'Notices of Cromlechs, Cairns, and Other Ancient Scytho-Druidical Remains in the Principality of Sorapur' (1853); 'Tara: A Mahratta Tale' (1863); 'The Student's Manual of the History of India, from the Earliest Period to the Present' (1870); and other works.

Taylor, Thomas. An English author styled "the Platonist"; born in London, May 15, 1758; died there, Nov. 1, 1835. His works comprise 63 vols., of which 23 are large quartos. Among them are treatises on arithmetic and geometry; on the Eleusinian and Bacchic mysteries; an essay on the 'Rights of Brutes,' in ridicule of Thomas Paine's 'Rights of Man'; a 'History of the Restoration of the Platonic Theology'; and a volume of 'Miscellanies in Prose and Verse.' His main labor was the translating of great classical Greek and Latin works. His translation of Plato was in 5 vols., and was printed at the expense of the Duke of Norfolk. Of his translation of Aristotle only fifty complete copies were struck off; the expense being defrayed by W. Meredith, a retired tradesman.

Taylor, Tom. A British dramatist; born at Sunderland, Durham, in 1817; died at Wandsworth, July 12, 1880. He edited Punch in 1874-80; was art critic to the London Times and

Graphic, and wrote more than 100 plays. Among them are : 'Still Waters Run Deep'; 'The Unequal Match'; 'The Overland Route'; 'The Contested Election'; 'Our American Cousin'; 'The Ticket-of-Leave Man.' He translated Villemarqué's 'The Ballads and Songs of Brittany'; and published 'Life and Times of Sir Joshua Reynolds' (1865).

Taylor, William. A world-famous missionary bishop of the American Methodist Episcopal Church, and author; born in Rockbridge County, Va., May 18, 1821; died at Palo Alto, Cal., May 18, 1902. He wrote: 'California Life Illustrated'; 'Seven Years Street Preaching in San Francisco' (1856); 'Model Preacher' (1860); 'Four Years' Campaign in India' (1875).

Tchernytchevskiï, Nikolaï Gavrilovich (cher-ně-chev'skě). A Russian miscellaneous writer; born at Saratov, July 1, 1828; died there, Oct. 29, 1889. He translated into Russian J. S. Mill's 'Principles of Political Economy,' making considerable additions to the first volume. While a suspect he wrote the novel 'What's to be Done?' (1863), which won for him deportation to Siberia. It has been translated into English. In 1883 he was allowed to live in Astrakhan, and was pardoned in 1889.

Teellinck, Evald (tā'link). A notable Dutch anti-papal polemist; born at Zierickzee about 1570; died 1629. He wrote some 20 books, most of them attacking the papal system. Among them are: 'The Paw of the Beast'; 'The Plain Mark of Antichrist'; 'Bileam; or, The Blind Papist.'

Tegnér, Esaias (teng-när'). A Swedish poet; born at Kyrkerud, Wermland, Sweden, Nov. 13, 1782; died at Wexiö, Nov. 2, 1846. His most celebrated work is the epic 'Frithiof's Saga' (1825), a collection of ballads which has been translated into every European language. He also wrote a poem, 'Svea' (1811), which was crowned by the Swedish Academy; 'Nattvärdsbarned' (translated by Longfellow, under the title 'The Children of the Lord's Supper'); 'Axel,' a poem of the time of Charles XII. ('Collected Works,' Stockholm, 7 vols., 1847-51; additional 3 vols., 1873-74).

Teleki, Joseph, Count (tel-ek'ě). A Hungarian statesman and historian; born Oct. 24, 1790; died at Pesth, Feb. 16, 1855. His principal work is 'The Period of the Hunyads in Hungary (5 vols., with 3 supplementary vols. of documentary matter, 1852-55).

Téllez, Gabriel, Maestro Fray (tel'yäth). ["Tirso de Molina."] A Spanish dramatist; born in Madrid, some time between 1570 and 1585; died in Soria, about 1648. He is said to have written about 300 plays, but only 59 are extant. The most famous is 'El Burlador de Sevilla.' He wrote several autos or religious pieces; and two collections of stories after the fashion of the 'Decameron,'—the 'Cigarrales de Toledo' (1621 or 1624), and 'Deleitar Aprovechando' (unfinished, 1625).

Telmann, Konrad (tel'män). A German poet and story-writer; born at Stettin, Nov. 26, 1854; died at Rome, Jan. 23, 1897. His principal works are: 'In Solitude' (1876); 'Waves of Ocean' (1884); 'In Pomerania' (2 vols., 1875), a collection of stories; 'Dissonances and Accords' (1888), stories; 'Sicilian Stories' (1889); 'Athwart Life' (1890); 'Dark Depths' (1895); the novels 'In the Flush of Morning' (1880), 'Væ Victis' (1886), 'On the Sirens' Isle, Capri' (1889), 'Of the Lineage of the Icaridæ' (1891), 'Vox Populi' (1897); etc.

Temme, Jodocus Donatus Hubert (tem'e). A German jurist and story-writer; born at Lette in Westphalia, 1798; died at Zürich, Nov. 14, 1881. Among his stories are: 'German Tales of Crime' (in two series, comprising 14 vols.); 'Darksome Ways' (3 vols., 1862-63); 'The Black Village' (3 vols., 1863); 'The Native Land' (3 vols., 1868).

Tempeltey, Eduard (tem-pel'tī). A German poet; born at Berlin, Oct. 13, 1832. His two dramas, 'Clytemnestra' (1857), and 'Here Guelph, Here Ghibellin!' (1859) were received with extraordinary favor. Among his other dramas is 'Cromwell' (1882), which was also remarkably successful. He wrote also a chaplet of songs, 'Mariengarn' (1866), the theme of which is love in all its phases.

Tencin, Claudine-Alexandrine Guérin de (teñ-sañ'). A French writer; born at Grenoble in 1681; died Dec. 4, 1749. She was the friend of Fontenelle, Marmontel, Bolingbroke, and other noted men, and the mother of D'Alembert. Among her writings are: 'The Siege of Calais'; 'The Misfortunes of Love'; 'Anecdotes of the Court and Reign of Edward II.'; and 'The Count of Comminges,' which is probably her best book.

Ten Kate, Jan Jacob Lodewijk (ten kä'tě). A Dutch poet and theologian; born at The Hague, Dec. 23, 1819. In 1836 his first volume of poems, entitled 'Gedichten,' appeared. In 1837, with a friend, he published a translation of the 'Odes' of Anacreon, the first of a long series of translations that have distinguished him among modern Dutch poets. Among these may be mentioned that of Byron's 'Giaour'; Tasso's 'Gerusalemme Liberata' (1856); Tegnér's 'Frithiof's Saga' (1861); Schiller's 'Marie Stuart' (1866); La Fontaine's 'Fables'; Dante's 'Inferno' (1876); Milton's 'Paradise Lost' (1880). Among his original works are various collections of poems, and many treatises of a religious or philosophical character, some in prose; 'Dead and Alive' (1856); 'The Creation' (1860: English translation by Rev. D. Van de Pelt, 1888); 'The Planets' (1869); 'Eunoë' (1874); 'Palm Leaves and Flowers of Poesy' (1884). He died 1889.

Tennant, William. A Scottish Oriental scholar; born at Anstruther, Fifeshire, May 15, 1784; died Oct. 14, 1848. He was professor of Oriental languages at St. Andrews University from 1834. He published;

'The Anster Concert' (1811), and 'Anster Fair,' both poems descriptive of rural Scottish life; several later poems and dramas; a 'Syriac and Chaldee Grammar' (1840); a 'Life of Allan Ramsay' (1808); and numerous contributions to periodicals, including translations from Oriental poets.

Tennemann, Wilhelm Gottlieb (ten'ĕ-män). A German philosopher; born at Brembach near Erfurt, 1761; died 1819. His most important work is a 'History of Philosophy' (11 vols., 1798 1819); he wrote also: 'Doctrines and Opinions of the Disciples of Socrates on the Immortality of the Soul' (1791); 'Plato's System of Philosophy' (4 vols., 1792–94).

Tenney, Mrs. Sarah (Brownson). An American novelist; born in Massachusetts, 1839; died in New Jersey, 1876. She was daughter of Orestes A. Brownson. Her books are: 'Marion Elwood' (1859); 'At Anchor' (1865); and 'Life of Demetrius Gallitzin, Prince and Priest' (1873).

Tennyson, Alfred, Baron Tennyson. The great English poet; born at Somersby, Lincolnshire, Aug. 6, 1809; died at Aldworth, Oct. 6, 1892. He published, with his brother Charles, a volume entitled 'Poems of Two Brothers' (1827). In 1829 he won the chancellor's gold medal for the prize poem 'Timbuctoo'; in 1830 appeared his first book, 'Poems, Chiefly Lyrical'; in 1832 the first volume containing still recognized masterpieces; in 1850 'In Memoriam'; the same year he was appointed poet-laureate to succeed Wordsworth; in 1855 he received the honorary degree of D. C. L. from Oxford. 'The Princess' was published in 1847; 'Maud and Other Poems' in 1855; 'The Idylls of the King' in 1859; 'Enoch Arden' and 'The Holy Grail' in 1869; 'Queen Mary' in 1875; 'Harold' in 1876; 'The Cup' in 1884; 'Tiresias' in 1885; 'Locksley Hall Sixty Years After,' etc., in 1886; 'The Foresters' and the collection 'Death of Œnone' in 1892.

Tennyson, Charles. See Turner.

Tennyson, Frederick. An English poet, brother of Alfred; born at Louth, Lincolnshire, June 5, 1807; died in London, Feb. 26, 1898. He was educated at Trinity College, Cambridge, and in 1828 took the medal for a Greek poem. He published various volumes of verse, including 'Days and Hours' (1854); 'The Isles of Greece' (1890); 'Daphne, and Other Poems' (1891).

Tennyson, Hallam, Lord. An English biographer, son of Alfred; born 1852. He has written 'The Life of Alfred, Lord Tennyson' (2 vols., 1897), containing a complete bibliography of his father's works.

Teramo, Jacopo Palladino de (tä-rä'mō). An Italian bishop and writer; born at Teramo in the Abruzzi, 1349; died in Poland, 1417. He is noted as author of 'The Trial of Belial,' a vision in which Belial appeals to God for justice for the infringement of his rights by Jesus Christ.

Tercy, Fanny Messageot (tär-sē'), wife of François; born 1781. She wrote several tales, among them 'Louise de Sénancour' (1817); 'The Hermit of Mt. St. Valentin' (1821); 'The Wife of Holofernes' (1829); 'Chronicles of Franche-Comté' (1831).

Tercy, François. A French poet; born at Lons-le-Saulnier in Jura, about 1774; died at Le Mans, Oct. 1, 1841. He wrote: 'Epithalamium of Napoleon and Marie Louise' (1810); 'Birth of the King of Rome' (1811); 'Death of Louis XVI.,' an idyl in the ancient style (1816); 'Death and Apotheosis of Marie Antoinette' (1817); 'Death of Louis XVIII.' (1818).

Terence — Publius Terentius Afer (ter'ens). A Latin writer of comedy; born at Carthage about 190 B. C.; died about 159 B. C. He was a slave, but on account of his talent was carefully educated and was manumitted; after the performance of his first comedy, 'Andria,' in 166 B. C., he enjoyed the friendship of such men as the younger Scipio and Lælius. All his comedies are extant; they are: 'Andria,' 'Hecyra,' 'Heauton-timorumenos,' 'Eunuchus,' 'Phormio,' and 'Adelphi.' There are translations into English by Patrick (1745), Colman (1765), and Riley (1853).

Terhune, Albert Payson. An American journalist and author, son of Mary V.; born 1868. He wrote: 'Syria from the Saddle'; 'Columbia Stories'; 'The Great Cedarhurst Mystery; 'Caleb Conover, Railroader.'

Terhune, Mrs. Mary Virginia (Hawes). ["Marion Harland."] An American novelist, editor, and writer on domestic topics; born in Virginia, 1831. She has contributed largely to magazines, edited departments in Wide Awake, St. Nicholas, etc., and conducted other magazines as chief editor. Among her novels are: 'Alone' (1854); 'The Hidden Path' (1855); 'Moss Side' (1857); 'Miriam' (1860); 'Nemesis' (1860); 'Husks' (1863); 'Sunnybank' (1866); etc. Her works on housekeeping include: 'Common-Sense in the Household' (1871); 'Breakfast, Luncheon, and Tea' (1875); 'The Dinner Year-Book' (1878); 'The Housekeeper's Week.'

Terrasson, Jean (tär-äs-oṅ'). A French miscellaneous writer; born at Lyons, 1670; died at Paris, 1750. He wrote 'Sethos,' a sort of philosophical novel, which contains some curious details regarding the customs of ancient Egypt, and the initiations into the religious mysteries (3 vols., 1731); 'Dissertation on Homer's Iliad' (1715); 'Justification of the India Company' (1720).

Tersteegen, Gerhard. A German lyric poet; born at Mörs, Nov. 25, 1697; died at Mühlheim on the Ruhr, April 3, 1769. Among his works are: 'The Spiritual Garden' (1729); 'Crumbs' (1773). Among his religious songs and hymns the more notable are 'Shout, ye Heavens, for Joy'; and 'The Day is Now Ended.'

Tertullian (Quintus Septimius Florens Tertullianus) (tėr-tul'yạn). A Latin Church

Father and ecclesiastical writer; born at Carthage about 160 A. D.; died about 220 He wrote many works, among which are 'Apologeticum'; 'On the Pretexts of the Heretics'; 'Against Marcion,' in five books; and works on Patience, on Chastity, on Monogamy, on Idolatry, on Theatres, etc.

Testi, Fulvio, Count (tes'tē.) An Italian statesman and poet; born at Ferrara, 1593; died there, 1646. He was one of the most notable lyric poets of Italy in his time. Besides songs and ballads, he wrote: 'Arsinda; or, the Line of the Princes d'Este,' a drama; 'The Isle of Alcina,' a tragedy; an uncompleted epic, 'Constantine'; 'Italy,' a poem in 43 stanzas, in which he portrays the situation of Italy under the Spanish yoke.

Tétard, Jean (tē-tä'). A French philosophical and polemical writer; born at Longvic in Burgundy, 1770; died at Paris, 1841. Among his writings are: 'Moral Essay on Man in his Relation to God' (1818); 'Against Obscurantism and Jesuitism' (1826); 'Indelible and Historic Character of Jesuitism and Doctrinism' (1832).

Teuffel, Blanche Willis (Howard), Mrs. Julius Von. An American novelist; born at Bangor, Me., 1847; died at Munich, Oct. 7, 1898; lived last at Stuttgart. Her books are: 'One Summer' (1875); 'One Year Abroad' (1877); 'Aunt Serena' (1881); 'Guenn' (1883); 'Aulnay Tower' (1885); 'Tony the Maid' (1887); 'The Open Door' (1889); 'A Battle and a Boy' (1892); etc.

Teuffel, Wilhelm (toi'fel). A German philologist; born at Ludwigsburg, Sept. 27, 1820; died at Tübingen, where he was professor in the university, March 8, 1878. His greatest work is the 'History of Roman Literature' (1870). He wrote also: 'Exercises in Latin Style' (1887); 'Studies in Greek and Roman, and also in German Literary History' (1871); and edited with notes several Greek and Roman classics.

Teutsch, Georg Daniel (toitsh). A Transylvanian historical writer; born at Schässburg; died at Hermannstadt, July 2, 1893. He was bishop of the Saxons of Transylvania, and wrote: 'History of the Transylvanian Saxons' (2d ed. 1874); 'Compend of the History of Transylvania'; 'Documents for the History of Transylvania' (1857); 'The Reformation in the Transylvanian Saxonland' (6th ed. 1886); 'Documentary History of the Evangelical Church in Transylvania' (2 vols., 1862–63).

Texier, Charles Félix Marie (tex-yä' or tez-yä'). A French archæologist; born at Versailles, 1802; died 1871. He wrote: 'Description of Asia Minor: Fine Arts, Historic Monuments, Plans of Ancient Cities,' etc. (1839); 'Description of Armenia, Persia, Mesopotamia' (1842); 'The Ancient Ports at the Mouth of the Tiber' (1858); 'Byzantine Architecture' (1865).

Thaarup, Thomas (tär'öp). A Danish poet; born at Copenhagen, 1749; died 1821. Some of his dramatic compositions, among them 'The Birthday' and 'Peter's Wedding,' are regarded as equal to the best in Danish literature. His 'Song of Love and Fatherland' ranks as a lyrical classic.

Thacher, John Boyd. An American critical scholar and bibliographer; born in 1847. He was chairman of the Committee of Awards at the World's Columbian Exposition, Chicago, in 1893; mayor of Albany in 1897. He has published: 'Charlecote: A Drama'; 'The Continent of America, its Discovery and its Baptism'; 'Little Speeches'; 'Christopher Columbus.'

Thackeray, William Makepeace. A celebrated English novelist; born in Calcutta, India, July 18, 1811; died Dec. 24, 1863. His works include: 'The Paris Sketch-Book' (1840); 'Comic Tales and Sketches' (1841), which contained 'Yellowplush Papers,' 'Major Gahagan,' and 'The Bedford Row Conspiracy'; 'The Great Hoggarty Diamond' (1841: in book form 1848); 'A Shabby-Genteel Story' (1841); 'The Chronicle of the Drum' (1841); 'Barry Lyndon' (1842); 'Men's Wives' (1842); 'Irish Sketch-Book' (1843); 'Notes of a Journey from Cornhill to Grand Cairo' (1846); 'Vanity Fair' (Jan. 1847–July 1848); 'Our Street' (1847); 'The Book of Snobs' (1848); 'Mrs. Perkins's Ball' (1848); 'Dr. Birch and his Young Friends' (1848); 'The History of Samuel Titmarsh' (1848), a reissue of various articles; 'The History of Pendennis' (Nov. 1848–Oct. 1850); 'English Humorists of the Eighteenth Century' (1851–52), a series of lectures; 'The History of Henry Esmond' (1852); 'The Newcomes' (1853–55); 'The Rose and the Ring' (1854); 'The Four Georges' (1855–56), a series of lectures; 'The Virginians' (1857–59); 'Lovel the Widower' (1860–61); 'The Adventures of Philip' (1861–62); 'Roundabout Papers' (1862), being a volume of previously printed pieces; 'Denis Duval' (1867), left unfinished. His drawings and caricatures were posthumously published in book form under the title 'Thackerayana' (1876).

Thaer, Wilhelm Albrecht (tä'er). A German agriculturist; born at Lüdersdorf, near Wriezen on the Oder, Aug. 6, 1828. He was appointed professor in the University of Giessen, 1871. He is author of a 'System of Agriculture' (1877); 'Ancient Egyptian Husbandry' (1881); 'Weeds in Rural Economy' (1881); 'Researches in Tenant-Farming' (1890).

Thales (thā'lēs). The earliest of the Greek philosophers, called the father of philosophy; born at Miletus, 640 B. C.; died about 550. He was the founder of the Ionic school, one of the chief sources of Grecian philosophy. He visited Egypt for instruction in the sciences professed by the priesthood. Besides abstract philosophy, he studied geometry and astronomy, and tradition credits him with predicting a solar eclipse. His ancient biographers mention among his services to astronomy a calculation of the length of the year, and of the interval between solstices and equinoxes. He left nothing in writing.

Thanet, Octave, pseudonym of Alice French. An American novelist; born in Massachusetts, 1850. She has published: 'Knitters in the Sun'; 'Otto the Knight'; 'Stories of a Western Town'; 'An Adventure in Photography'; 'Expiation'; 'A Slave to Duty'; 'Man of the Hour.'

Thausing, Moritz (tou'sing). An Austrian art critic; born at Leitmeritz in Bohemia, June 3, 1838; died there, Aug. 14, 1884. He became professor of the science of æsthetics in the University of Vienna, 1873. He wrote: 'Dürer: History of his Life and his Art' (1876); 'J. J. Callot's Sketch-Book' (1881); 'Art Letters from Vienna' (1884).

Thaxter, Mrs. Celia (Leighton). An American poet; born at Portsmouth, N. H., June 29, 1836; died Aug. 26, 1894. She spent her childhood and her later life at the Isles of Shoals. Her works are; 'Poems' (1872); 'Among the Isles of Shoals' (1873); 'Poems' (1874); 'Drift-Weed' (1879); 'Poems for Children' (1884); 'The Cruise of the Mystery,' etc. (1886); 'Idyls and Pastorals' (1886); 'The Yule Log' (1889); 'An Island Garden' (1894); 'Letters' (1895); 'Stories and Poems for Children' (1895).

Thayer, Alexander Wheelock. An American writer on music, whose life was mostly spent abroad; born at South Natick, Mass., Oct. 22, 1817; died at Trieste, July 19, 1897. Contributed to the 'Dictionary of Music'; was musical critic of the New York Tribune; was consul at Trieste, 1859–82. He published: 'Signor Masoni,' etc., (1862); 'The Hebrews and the Red Sea' (1883); three volumes of 'Life of Beethoven' (1866–87.)

Thayer, Mrs. Emma (Homan) (Graves). A writer and artist of Colorado; born 1842. She has written: 'Wild Flowers of Colorado'; 'Wild Flowers of the Pacific Coast'; 'An English American'; 'A Legend of Glenwood Springs.'

Thayer, Joseph Henry. An American clergyman, Biblical scholar, and translator; born in Boston, Nov. 7, 1828; died in Cambridge, Nov. 26, 1901. He graduated from Harvard in 1850, from Andover in 1857. He was a military chaplain, 1859–64; secretary of the American Board of Revision for the New Testament, 1877; and professor in Harvard Divinity School after 1884. He wrote: 'Grammar of the Idiom of the New Testament'; 'Books and Their Use'; translations of 'Grammar of the New Testament Greek'; 'Greek-English Lexicon of the New Testament'; and published a volume of 'Critical Essays.'

Thayer, William Makepeace. An American clergyman, retired from the Congregational church and devoted to literature. He was born at Franklin, Mass., Feb. 23, 1820. His books have attained great popularity, several being reprinted abroad in German, French, Italian, Greek, Swedish, etc. Among his works are: 'The Bobbin Boy' (1859); 'The Pioneer Boy' (1863); a Series of Biographies (10 vols.,

1859–63); 'Youth's History of the Rebellion' (1863–65); 'White House Stories' (1880–85); 'Marvels of the New West' (1887); 'Life of Garfield'; 'Men who Win.' Died April 7, 1898.

Theiner, Augustin (tī'ner). A German canonist; born at Breslau, April 11, 1804; died Aug. 10, 1874. He was appointed prefect of the Vatican archives, 1855; but was deprived of that office during the Vatican Council on the charge of giving to certain oppositionist bishops secret documents of the curia. His first notable work was a tractate in opposition to the rule of clerical celibacy, 'The Introduction of Obligatory Celibacy' (2 vols., 1828; new ed. enlarged, 3 vols., 1856–57). His other principal works are: 'History of the Return of the Reigning Houses of Brunswick and Saxony to the Bosom of the Catholic Church' (1843); an edition of Baronius's 'Church Annals,' with a continuation (3 vols., 1856–57); 'Diplomatic Code of the Temporal Dominion of the Holy See' (1863); 'Temporal Sovereignty of the Holy See Judged by the General Councils of Lyons and Constance' (1867).

Theocritus (thē-ok're-tus). The greatest of Greek bucolic poets; commonly reputed to have been a native of Syracuse, but Cos also claims him; he lived in the first half of the third century B. C. He wrote in the Doric dialect, pastorals and idyls of lowly life, which have ever since been regarded as the consummate models of that kind of poetry. Virgil imitated him in his 'Bucolics.' We have 31 of his idyls and pastorals, and a number of his epigrams: there are English translations by Calverley (1869) in verse, by Andrew Lang (1860) in prose, and by others.

Theodoret (thē-od'ō-ret). A celebrated Greek church historian and theological writer; born at Antioch about 390; died about 460. He became bishop of Cyrrhus, a city in Syria, 423, and there passed the remainder of his life. He wrote voluminous commentaries on the Scriptural books, of which many are extant; we have also his 'Church History' in five books, covering the period 324–429, and several of his theological tractates, besides about 200 of his 'Letters.'

Theognis of Megara (thē-og'nis). A Greek elegiac poet who flourished in the latter half of the sixth century B. C. There are 1389 verses preserved under his name, of importance in enabling us to understand the state of parties and the problems of society in the Greece of that time. Translated by Frere (1842).

Theophrastus of Eresus in Lesbos (thē-o-fras'tus). A Greek philosopher; became the head of the Peripatetic school after the death of its founder Aristotle, presiding over it for 35 years (322–287 B. C.). His treatises on 'Practical Botany,' in nine books, and 'Theoretical Botany,' in six books, are still extant; besides fragments of works on mineralogy, on the senses, and on metaphysics. The work by which he is best known is his treatise called 'Characters.'

Theophylactus, surnamed **Simocatta** (thē-ō-fil-ak'tus). A Byzantine historian; born at Locri about 570 A. D.; died about 640. Three of his works are extant: 'History of the Emperor Maurice'; 'Problems of Physics'; 'Letters, Moral, Rural, and Amorous,'—of these there are 85, in which are imitated the letters of Aristænetus.

Theopompus of Chios (thē"o-pom'pus). A Greek historian and rhetorician; born about 378 B. C. His principal historical works were 'The Hellenics,' in 12 books, and 'The Philippics,' in 58 books; the former being a continuation of Thucydides, and the latter a general history of his own times, with the reign of Philip of Macedon as central point: of both only fragments remain.

Theuriet, André (tėr-yā'). A French poet and novelist; born at Marly-le-Roi, Oct. 8, 1833. He began his literary work with the verses 'In Memoriam' (1857). Subsequent poems are: 'The Road through the Woods' (1867); 'The Peasants of L'Argonne, 1792' (1871); 'The Blue and the Black' (1873); 'Our Birds' (1886). His novels are numerous, comprising among others: 'Tales of Familiar Life' (1870); 'Mlle. Guignon' (1874); 'Dangerous Charm' (1891). Among his dramatic productions are: 'Jean-Marie' (1871); 'The House of the Two Barbeaux' (1885); 'Raymonde' (1887). As an art critic he has also written 'Jules Bastien-Lepage, the Man and the Artist' (1885). D. 1907.

Thibaudeau, Antoine Claire, Count (tē-bō-dō'). A French statesman and historian; born at Poitiers, March 23, 1765; died March 8, 1854. Among his writings are: 'Memoirs on the Convention and the Directory' (1824); 'General History of Napoleon Bonaparte' (5 vols., 1827-28); 'Memoirs on the Consulate and the Empire' (10 vols., 1835); 'History of the States-General' (2 vols., 1843). After his death appeared 'My Biography: My Memoirs 1765-92' (1875).

Thibaut, Anton Friedrich Justus (tē-bō'). A distinguished German legist; born at Hameln, Jan. 4, 1772; died March 28, 1840, at Heidelberg, where he was professor in the university. His greatest work is 'System of the Laws in the Pandects' (1803); some of his other writings are: 'Juristic Encyclopedy and Methodology' (1797); 'Essays on Questions of Civil Law' (1814).

Thierry, Amédée (tyär-ē'). A French historian, brother of J. N. A.; born at Blois, Aug. 2, 1797; died March 27, 1873. Among his works are: 'History of the Gauls to the Roman Domination' (3 vols., 1828); 'History of Gaul under the Roman Domination' (3 vols., 1840-47); 'Later Times of the Western Empire' (1860); 'History of Attila and his Successors' (1864); 'St. Jerome: Christian Society at Rome' (1867).

Thierry, Jacques Nicolas Augustin. A French historian of the "picturesque" school, a member of the Academy; born at Blois, May 10, 1795; died in Paris, May 22, 1856. In 1817 he became a contributor to Le Censeur Européen, edited by Comte; afterward to the Courrier Français, in which he published his 'Letters on the History of France.' In 1825 appeared his 'History of the Conquest of England by the Normans.' He also wrote: 'Ten Years of Historic Studies' (1834); 'Tales of Merovingian Times' (1840); 'Formation and Progress of the Third Estate' (1853). ('Complete Works,' 1856-60.)

Thiers, Jean Baptiste (tyär). A French theological writer; born at Chartres, 1636; died at Vibraye in Maine, 1703. His treatises on theological and ecclesiastical subjects are very numerous; but he owes whatever celebrity he has to his 'History of Wigs, wherein is Shown their Origin, their Use, their Form, the Abuse and Irregularity of Ecclesiastics' Wigs' (1690).

Thiers, Louis Adolphe. A French statesman and author of the first rank; born at Marseilles, April 16, 1797; died at St.-Germain, Sept. 3, 1877. In 1822 he moved to Paris, and became contributor to the Constitutionnel; in 1823 he began to publish his 'History of the French Revolution,' which was finished in 1827, in 10 vols.; in 1830 he founded the National, in connection with Mignet and Armand Carrel; in 1832 he became Minister of the Interior; in 1836 he was made prime minister, and again in 1840; in 1852 he was banished by Louis Napoleon, but returned and lived in retirement until 1863, when he was elected member of the Representative Assembly by Paris; he was elected a member of the National Assembly, Feb. 8, 1871, after the collapse of the monarchy; and on Aug. 31 received the title of "President of the Republic." His great literary work is that comprising the 'History of the French Revolution' (1823-27) and 'History of the Consulate and the Empire' (1845-62). Among his other works are: 'History of John Law' (1826; English translation, 1859); 'On Property' (1848); 'Man and Matter' (1875).

Thirlwall, Connop. An eminent English historian; born at Stepney, London, Feb. 11, 1797; died July 27, 1875, at Bath. He was Bishop of St. David's 1840-74. His principal work is a 'History of Greece' (8 vols., 1835-40; enlarged 1845-52). He made, with J. C. Hare, the English translation of Niebuhr's 'History of Rome' (2 vols., 1828).

Tholuck, Friedrich August Gottreu (tō-lök'). A German theologian and author of great repute; born at Breslau, March 30, 1799; died· at Halle, June 10, 1877. His works, most of which have been often reprinted in Germany and translated into English, were published at Gotha in an edition of 11 vols. (1863-72), and treat of Oriental subjects;

'Sufism; or, Pantheistic Theosophy of the Persians' (1821); 'The Epistle to the Romans' (1824); 'The Gospel of John' (1827; translated into English by Kauffman, 1836); 'The Sermon on the Mount' (1833; translated into English by R. L. Brown, Edinburgh, 1860); 'Early History of Rationalism' (4 vols., 1853-62); 'Church Life of the 17th Century' (1861-62).

Thomas, Augustus, the foremost of living American playwrights; born at St. Louis, Jan. 8, 1859. He is the author of the dramas 'Alabama,' 'Missoura' and 'Arizona.' His plays include 'The Burglar'; 'After-Thoughts'; 'Oliver Goldsmith'; 'On the Quiet'; 'The Capitol'; 'The HoosierDoctor'; 'The Earl of Pawtuket'; 'The Other Girl'; 'Jim De Lancey'; 'The Witching Hour'; 'The Harvest Moon.'

Thomas, Cyrus. An American archæologist now in the government service; born 1825. Of special interest are his 'Study of the Manuscript Troano' (1882); 'Notes on Certain Maya and Mexican Manuscripts' (1884); 'Mound Exploration' (1888);

Thomas, Edith Matilda. An American poet; born in Chatham, O., Aug. 12, 1854; resides in New York. She has contributed to many periodicals, and published in book form: 'A New-Year's Masque,' etc. (1885); 'The Round Year' (1886); 'Lyrics and Sonnets' (1887); 'Children of the Seasons' Series (1888); 'Babes of the Year' (1888); 'Babes of the Nations' (1889); 'Heaven and Earth' (1889); 'The Inverted Torch' (1890); 'Fair Shadow Land' (1893); 'In Sunshine Land' (1895); 'In the Young World' (1895); 'Cassia and Other Verse' (1905).

Thomas, Frederick William. An American journalist and author; born in Charleston, S. C., 1811; died in Washington, D. C., Sept. 30, 1866. He was professor of English literature in the University of Alabama. He contributed much in prose and verse to periodicals, and published: 'The Emigrant,' poem (1833); 'Clinton Bradshaw' (1835), 'East and West' (1836), 'Howard Pinckney' (1840), novels; 'The Beechen Tree, and Other Poems' (1844); 'Sketches of Character,' etc. (1849); and 'John Randolph of Roanoke,' etc. (1853).

Thomas, Isaiah. An American editor, publisher, and littérateur; born in Boston, Jan. 17, 1719; died at Worcester, April 4, 1831. He established and printed the Massachusetts Spy, 1770-1801; imported and used the first font of music type; established the Massachusetts Magazine (1789-96); printed noted editions of the Bible and Watts's 'Psalms and Hymns'; founded the Antiquarian Society, Worcester, Mass., and endowed it with a library and funds for its maintenance; and was the author and publisher of the 'History of Printing.'

Thomas, John R. A Welsh-American song-writer and musician; born in Newport, Wales, in 1830; died 18—. He came to America at an early age, taught music, and sang in opera and oratorio. His songs were highly popular.

Among the best-known are: 'Cottage by the Sea'; 'Happy Be thy Dreams'; 'Some One to Love'; ''Tis but a Little Faded Flower'; 'Beautiful Isle of the Sea'; 'The Flag of the Free'; 'The Mother's Prayer'; and 'No Crown without the Cross.'

Thomas, Lewis Foulke. An American poet and dramatist; born in Baltimore, Md., 1815; died in Washington, 1868. He was author of 'India and Other Poems' (St. Louis, 1842), the first book of poetry published west of the Mississippi; and the tragedies 'Osceola,' successfully performed in Cincinnati (1838), and 'Cortez' (Washington, 1857).

Thomas à Kempis. See Kempis.

Thomas Aquinas or **Thomas of Aquin, Saint** (a-kwi'nas). A great mediæval theologian and philosopher; born at Aquino in the kingdom of Naples, about 1225; died at Fossa Nuova, in the diocese of Terracina, March 7, 1274. His writings are very voluminous, being comprised in 28 vols. quarto. His greatest work is the 'Sum of Theology.' Among his other works are: 'Sum of Catholic Belief against the Heathen'; 'Exposition of all the Epistles of St. Paul.'

Thomas of Celano. An Italian hymnist; born at Celano in the Abruzzi; died about 1255. He was one of the first disciples of St. Francis. He is probably the author of the 'Dies Iræ.' He is also believed to have written the biography of St. Francis found in the Bollandists' 'Acta Sanctorum.'

Thomasius, Christian (tō-mäs'yös). A German legist; born at Leipsic, Jan. 1, 1655; died professor of jurisprudence at Halle, Sept. 23, 1728. Among his writings are: 'Serious but Lively and Sensible Remarks on all Sorts of Juristic Works' (1720); 'Reasonable and Christianlike but not Pharisaical Considerations on all Sorts of Philosophical and Juristic Works' (3 vols., 1723); 'History of Wisdom and Folly.'

Thomasius, Gottfried. A German theological writer; born at Egenhausen, in Franconia, July 26, 1802; died professor of dogmatics at Erlangen, Jan. 24, 1875. Among his writings are: 'Origen' (1837); 'Contributions to Christology' (1845); 'The Person and the Work of Christ' (1852); 'Resuscitation of Evangelical Life in the Lutheran Church of Bavaria' (1867); 'History of Christian Dogma' (1874).

Thompson, Benjamin. See Rumford.

Thompson, Charles Miner. An American journalist, writer on the staff of the Youth's Companion; born 1864. He has written: 'The Nimble Dollar'; 'Life of Ethan Allen.'

Thompson, Francis. An English poet; son of a Lancashire physician. He was educated at Ushaw College, near Durham, and studied medicine at Owens College, Manchester. He determined to take up literature, however, and came to London. His first appearance in print was in the columns of Merry England,

Collected volumes have appeared as follows: 'Poems' (1893); 'Sister-Songs' (1896); 'New Poems' (1897).

Thompson, [James] Maurice. An American essayist and novelist; born in Fairfield, Ind., Sept. 9, 1844; died at Crawfordsville, Ind., Feb. 15, 1901. He was a Confederate soldier in the Civil War; afterwards State Geologist of Indiana, 1885–89. He wrote: 'Hoosier Mosaics' (1875); 'The Witchery of Archery' (1878); 'A Tallahassee Girl' (1882); 'His Second Campaign' (1883); 'Songs of Fair Weather' (1883); 'At Love's Extremes' (1885); 'By-ways and Bird Notes' (1885); 'The Boy's Book of Sports' (1886); 'A Banker of Bankersville' (1886); 'Sylvan Secrets' (1887); 'A Fortnight of Folly' (1888); 'Poems' (1892); 'King of Honey Island' (1892); 'The Ocala Boy' (1895); 'Alice of Old Vincennes' (1900).

Thompson, Mortimer M. [" Q. K. Philander Doesticks, P. B."] An American humorous writer and lecturer; born in 1830; died in 1875. He contributed at first to the daily and in later years regularly to the weekly newspapers, and published in book form in 1855–57: 'Doesticks: What He Says'; 'Plu-Ri-Bus-Tah,' a travesty of 'Hiawatha'; 'The Witches of New York'; 'Nothing to Say'; 'The Elephant Club.'

Thomsen, Vilhelm Ludvig Peder (tom'sen). A Danish philologist; born at Copenhagen, Jan. 25, 1842. His principal works are: 'The Magyar Language' (1866); 'Influence of the Germanic Languages on the Finno-Lappish' (1870); 'Relations between Ancient Russia and Scandinavia' (1879); 'Relations between the Finnish and the Baltic Languages' (1890).

Thomson, Charles. An American patriot and publicist; born in Maghera, County Derry, Ireland, Nov. 29, 1729; died in Lower Merion, Pa., Aug. 16, 1824. At first a teacher at New London, Pa., he became the first secretary of the Continental Congress (1774–79), and was said in compliment to be the " soul of that political body." He destroyed his notes of its proceedings for fear of giving pain to descendants of some of the members. He published: 'An Enquiry into the Causes of the Alienation of the Delaware and Shawaneese Indians,' etc. (1759); a translation of the Greek (Septuagint) Bible (4 vols., 1808), which was the first English version of it; a 'Synopsis of the Four Evangelists' (1815); etc.

Thomson, Edward William. An American writer, editor, and civil engineer; born in Ontario, 1849. He has written: 'Old Man Savarin, and Other Stories'; 'Walter Gibbs,' a book for boys; also the metrical portions of M. S. Henry's Version of 'Aucassin and Nicolette.'

Thomson, James. A Scotch poet; born at Ednam, Sept. 11, 1700; died Aug. 27, 1748. He was educated at Jedburgh School and Edinburgh University, and studied for the ministry. In 1725 he went to London and became a tutor. In 1733 he held a position in the Court of Chancery, and on losing this position was given a pension. In 1744 he was appointed surveyor-general of the Leeward Islands. His most famous poem is 'The Seasons' (1726–1730), and next to this 'The Castle of Indolence' (1748). He wrote some plays, among them being 'Sophonisba' (1730) and 'Tancred and Sigismunda' (1745).

Thomson, James. A Scotch poet; born at Port Glasgow, Nov. 23, 1834; died June 3, 1882. He was brought up in an orphan asylum, and became an army tutor. Most of his life was spent in journalism, though he came to America at one time to investigate a silver mine; thence he was sent to Spain as the New York World's special correspondent. He suffered much from insomnia, which he made the subject of a most powerful poem by that name; and died a victim to the drugs he used to relieve it. His best-known work is 'The City of Dreadful Night' (1870–74); others of high quality are 'The Doom of a City' (1857), and 'Our Ladies of Death' (1861).

Thomson, Joseph. A Scotch traveler; born at Penpont in Dumfriesshire, Feb. 14, 1858; died at London, Aug. 2, 1895. He wrote: 'To the Central African Lakes and Back' (3d ed. 1881); 'Through Masai Land' (1885); 'Ulu, an African Romance' (1888); 'Mungo Park and the Niger' (1890); 'Travels in the Atlas and Southern Marocco' (1890).

Thomson, Sir William — Lord Kelvin. A British physicist, mathematician, engineer, and inventor of the highest rank; born in Belfast, Ireland, June 1824. He has been professor of natural philosophy in the University of Glasgow since he was 22. As such he has not only done enduring work of his own, but has guided the careers of several other great scientists. His scientific papers have been published under the titles 'Reprints of Papers on Electrostatics and Magnetism' (1872); 'Mathematical and Physical Papers' (1882–90); 'Popular Lectures and Addresses'; 'On Heat'; 'On Elasticity.' In 1867, in collaboration with Professor Tait of Edinburgh, he issued his first volume of 'A Treatise on Natural Philosophy' (2d ed. in 2 parts, 1879). From 1846 to 1853 he was editor of the Cambridge and Dublin Mathematical Journal; and also connected with the Philosophical Magazine. He has been president of the British Association for the Advancement of Science, and of the Royal Society of London. He died Dec. 17, 1907.

Thomson, William McClure. An American clergyman of the Presbyterian Church; born in Ohio, Dec. 3, 1806; died in 1894. In 1833 he went as missionary to Syria and Palestine, remaining until 1876. His chief work, 'The Land and the Book' (2 vols., 1859–60; 3 vols., 1880–86), is an accepted authority on Palestine and Syria. He has also published: 'The Land of Promise'; 'Travels in Palestine' (1865).

Thonissen, Jean Joseph (tŏn'is-sen). A Belgian jurist and political economist; born at

Hasselt, Jan. 21, 1817; died Aug. 17, 1891, at Louvain, where he was professor of jurisprudence. Among his writings are: 'Socialism and its Promises' (1850); 'Socialism in the Past' (1851); 'Belgium in the Reign of Leopold I.' (4 vols., 1855); 'The Pretended Necessity of the Death Penalty' (1864); 'The Penal Laws of the Athenian Republic' (1876).

Thorbecke, Heinrich (tör-bek′e). A German Orientalist; born at Meiningen, March 14, 1837; died at Mannheim, Jan. 3, 1890. He was appointed professor in the University of Halle, 1887. His studies were directed mainly to the poetry of the Bedawin and the history of Arabic. He is author of 'Life of Antarah, the Pre-Islamite Poet' (1868); 'Al Ashâ's Song of Praise to Mohammed' (1875); 'M. Sabbâg's Grammar of Conversational Arabic in Syria and Egypt' (1886).

Thorburn, Grant. ["Lawrie Todd."] A Scottish-American craftsman, merchant, and author. He was born at Dalkeith, 1773; emigrated to America, 1794; died at New Haven, Conn., Jan. 21, 1863. As the hero of Galt's novel, 'Lawrie Todd,' he was a well-known figure in New York. His publications in book form include: 'Forty Years' Residence in America' (1834); 'Men and Manners in Great Britain' (1834); 'Fifty Years' Reminiscences of New York' (1845); 'Hints to Merchants,' etc. (1847); 'Notes on Virginia' (1848); 'Life and Writings of Grant Thorburn' (1852–53).

Thoreau, Henry David. A distinguished American writer; born in Concord, Mass., July 12, 1817; died there, May 6, 1862. His works include: 'A Week on the Concord and Merrimac Rivers' (1848); 'Walden; or, Life in the Woods' (1854); 'Echoes of Harper's Ferry' (1860); 'Excursions' (1863); 'The Maine Woods' (1864); 'Cape Cod' (1865); 'Letters to Various Persons' (1865); 'A Yankee in Canada' (1866); 'Early Spring in Massachusetts' (1881); 'Summer' (1884); 'Winter' (1888); 'Autumn' (1892); 'Works' (10 vols., 1894); 'Familiar Letters' (1894); 'Poems of Nature' (1895). The posthumous volumes are made up mostly from his daily journal, begun in 1835, which numbered 30 vols. when he died.

Thoresen, Anna Magdalena· (Kragh) (tö′-re-sen). A Danish novelist; born at Fredericia, June 3, 1819. Among the best of her works are: 'Tales' (1863); 'Signa Historiæ' (Signs of History: 1864); 'Pictures from the West Coast of Norway' (1872); 'Herluf Nordal: A Tale from the Last Century' (1879); 'Short Tales' (1891). She is also the author of several dramas.

Thorild, Thomas (tör′ild). A Swedish poet; born at Kongelf in Bohuslän, 1759; died at Greifswald, 1808. His poetry was of less influence on the thought of his day than his polemics. One of these, 'A Critique of the Critics, with a Project of a Code for the Kingdom of Genius' (1791), had much to do with the development of Swedish poetry. He wrote also

'Maximum, or Archimetria' (1799), an attempt at a system of philosophy.

Thornbury, George Walter. An English author; born in London in 1828; died in London, June 11, 1876. Among his works are: 'Shakespeare's England; or, Sketches of our Social History during the Reign of Elizabeth' (2 vols., 1856); 'Songs of the Cavaliers and Roundheads' (1857); 'Life in Spain' (1859); 'Turkish Life and Character' (1860); 'British Artists from Hogarth to Turner' (1860); 'Life of J. M. W. Turner, R A' (1861); 'Haunted London' (1865); 'Two Centuries of Song' (1866); 'Old and New London' (1873–74).

Thrale, Mrs. See Piozzi.

Thucydides (thö-sid′ē-dēs). A Greek historian. The year of his birth is uncertain; not much earlier than 460 nor later than 454 B. C. The time and manner of his death are likewise uncertain. It is probable that he did not long survive the end of the fifth century. His 'History,' which covers 21 years of the Peloponnesian War, has come down to us in eight books.

Thunmann, Johan (tön′män). A Swedish historian and archæologist; born 1746; died 1778. He wrote: 'The Borderland of History and Poetry' (1772); 'Researches on the History of the Nations of Eastern Europe' (1774); 'The Ancient Poetical Literature of the North' (1775); 'The Discovery of America' (1776); 'Researches on the Ancient History of Some Northern Nations' (1777).

Thwaites, Reuben Gold. An American antiquarian writer, and secretary of the Wisconsin State Historical Society. He was born in Boston, May 15, 1853. His books comprise: 'Historic Waterways'; 'The Story of Wisconsin'; 'Our Cycling Tour in England'; 'The Colonies, 1492–1750'; 'Stories of the Badger State' (1900); 'Father Marquette' (1902); 'Daniel Boone' (1903); 'Brief History of Rocky Mountain Exploration' (1904); 'France in America' (1905). Editor of 'Lahontan's New Voyages to North America,' (1907). He is also editor of 'The Jesuit Relations, and Allied Documents.'

Thwing, Charles Burton. An American physicist, born March 2, 1860; professor of Physics at Syracuse University from 1901–05. He wrote 'Exercises in Physical Measurement' (1896), and 'Elementary Physics' (1900).

Thwing, Charles Franklin. An American author and educator; born Nov. 9, 1853. He is the author of 'American Colleges' (1878); 'The College Woman' (1894); 'The Choice of a College' (1901); 'A Liberal Education and a Liberal Faith' (1903); College Training and the Business Man'; 'A History of Higher Education in America' (1906).

Tickell, Thomas. An English poet, Addison's intimate friend; born at Bridekirk in

Cumberland, 1686; died at Bath, April 23, 1740. His principal works are: 'The Prospect of Peace,' a poem; 'The Royal Progress,' verses celebrating the arrival of George I.; translation of the first book of the Iliad (1715); 'Kensington Garden' (1722); 'Elegy on Addison'; and the popular ballad 'Colin and Lucy';

Ticknor, Caroline. An American novelist and editor. Born in Boston. Author of 'A Hypocritical Romance, and other stories' (1896); 'Miss Belladonna' (1897), etc. One of the assistant editors of 'Masterpieces of the World's Literature,' 'The World's Great Orations,' etc.

Ticknor, George. A distinguished American scholar and historian; born in Boston, Aug. 1, 1791; died there, Jan. 26, 1871. He graduated from Dartmouth College, 1807; was admitted to the bar, 1813; afterwards spent five years in foreign study and travel. He was professor of modern languages at Harvard, 1819–35; one of the founders of the Boston Public Library, and president of its board of trustees 1864–66. He published his chief work, 'A History of Spanish Literature' in 1849, revised editions 1854–63. He wrote also: 'Essays on Spanish History,' etc.; and 'Life of W. H. Prescott' (1864).

Tieck, Johann Ludwig (tēk). A celebrated German poet and miscellaneous writer; born in Berlin, May 31, 1773; died there, April 28, 1853. His works include: 'Peter Lebrecht: A Story without Adventures' (1795); 'William Lovell' (1795–96); 'Abdallah' (1796); 'Ostrich Plumes' (1795–98); 'The Legend of Peter Lebrecht' (1797); 'Franz Sternbald's Wanderings' (1798); 'Prince Zerbino' (1799); 'Romantic Fancies' (1799–1800); 'Life and Death of St. Genevieve' (1800?); 'Love Songs of the Suabian Past' (1803), an adaptation; 'Don Quixote' (1804), and 'Old English Dramatists' (1811), translations; 'Phantasus' (1812); 'Fortunatus'; 'The Paintings' (1813?); 'The Tourists' (1814); 'The Old Man of the Mountain' (1815?) 'Society in the Country'; 'The Betrothal' (1816); 'Musical Joys and Sorrows'; 'The Greek Emperor' (1818); 'Dramatic Pages' ('1825); 'Vittoria Accorombono' (1840), not completed; translations from Shakespeare; essays; editions of noted works; etc.

Tiedemann, Diedrich (tē'de-män). A German philosopher; born at Bremerwörde, 1748; died 1786, at Marburg, where he was professor of philosophy in the university. He wrote: 'Researches on the Origin of Languages' (1772); 'System of the Stoic Philosophy' (1777); 'The First Philosophers of Greece' (1780); 'Origin of the Magic Arts' (1787); 'Spirit of Speculative Philosophy from Thales to Berkeley' (6 vols., 1790–97); 'Theætetus; or, Human Knowledge' (1794).

Tiedge, Christoph August (tēd'chĕ). A German poet; born 1752; died 1841. He enjoys distinction as the author of 'Urania,' and 'Mirror for Women.' He also wrote:

'Wanderings through Life's Market,' and 'Elegies.' His admirers are many, and his poetry has been compared with that of Cowper.

Tiedge, Cornelis Petrus. A Dutch historical writer; born at Leyden, Dec. 16, 1830. Among his writings are: 'The Divine Service of Zarathustra' (1864); 'Compendium of the History of Religion' (2d ed. 1887); 'Western Asia in the Light of Recent Discoveries' (1893); 'Babylonio-Assyrian History' (1887).

Tiernan, Frances C. ["Christian Reid."] An American novelist; born at Salisbury, N. C. Her many works include: 'Valerie Aylmer' (1870); 'Mabel Lee' (1871); 'Morton House' (1871); 'Ebb Tide' (1872); 'Nina's Atonement' (1873); 'Carmen's Inheritance' (1873); 'A Daughter of Bohemia' (1873); 'A Gentle Belle' (1875); 'Hearts and Hands' (1875); 'A Question of Honor' (1875); 'The Land of the Sky' (1875); 'After Many Days' (1877); 'Bonny Kate' (1878); 'A Summer Idyl' (1878); 'Hearts of Steel' (1882); 'Armine' (1884); 'Roslyn's Fortune' (1885); 'Miss Churchill' (1887); 'A Child of Mary' (1887); and 'Philip's Restitution' (1888).

Tighe, Mary (tī). An Irish poetess; born in Dublin in 1772; died at Woodstock, County Kilkenny, March 24, 1810. She published in 1805, for private circulation, her poem 'Psyche.' Her works, which appeared in 1811, passed through several editions. She was the subject of a song by Moore, and a poem by Mrs. Hemans.

Tillemont, Sébastien le Nain de (tē-yė-łżôń'). A French historian; born at Paris, 1637; died 1698. He is author of 'History of the Emperors and Other Princes who Reigned in the First Six Centuries of the Church' (6 vols., 1690–1738); and 'Materials for the History of the First Six Centuries' (16 vols., 1693–1712).

Tillier, Antoine de (tē-yā'). A Swiss historian; born at Bern, 1792; died 1854. His works are: 'History of the Middle Ages' (4 vols., 1829); 'History of the Helvetic Republic, 1798–1848' (11 vols.); 'History of the Republic of Bern' (5 vols.).

Tillières, Le Veneur de, Count (tē-yär'). A French diplomat of the first half of the 17th century. He was ambassador to the English court to arrange the marriage of Prince Charles (Charles I.) with Henrietta Maria. His 'Memoirs' are valuable for the history of the English court: they were first published in 1862.

Tillotson, John. An English archbishop and ecclesiastical writer; born at Sowerby, Yorkshire, October 1630; died in London, Nov. 22, 1694. He ranks among the foremost of English preachers, published in his lifetime several volumes of sermons, and left many more in manuscript. ('Complete Works,' 1820.)

Tilton, Theodore. An American journalist, verse-writer, editor, and lecturer; born in New York city, Oct. 2, 1835. He was long known as editor on the New York Independent (1856–72). He established the Golden Age (newspaper), but retired from it after two years. In 1883 he went abroad, where he has remained. Besides numerous essays and fugitive pieces, he has published: 'The Sexton's Tale, and Other Poems' (1867); 'Sanctum Sanctorum; or, An Editor's Proof Sheets' (1869); 'Tempest-Tossed,' a romance (1873); 'Thou and I' (1880); 'Suabian Stories,' (1882). Died 1907.

Timrod, Henry. An American Southern poet and journalist. He was born at Charleston, S. C., Dec. 8, 1829; died at Columbia, S. C., Oct. 6, 1867. His only volume of 'Poems' was published in 1860; reprinted and edited with memoir by Paul H. Hayne, 1873.

Tincker, Mary Agnes. An American novelist; born in Ellsworth, Me., July 18, 1833. Since 1873 she has resided in Italy, and has published many novels. Among them are: 'The House of Yorke' (1872); 'A Winged Word' (1873); 'Grapes and Thorns' (1874); 'Six Sunny Months' (1878): and the remarkable romances 'Signor Monaldini's Niece' (1878); 'By the Tiber' (1881); 'The Jewel in the Lotus' (1884); and 'Aurora' (1885).

Tindal, Matthew. An English deist; born born at Beer Ferris, Devonshire, in 1657; died at Oxford, Aug. 16, 1733. In 1706 he published 'The Rights of the Church Asserted,' and later two 'Defenses'; in 1710, 'The New High Church Turned Old Presbyterian,' which was ordered publicly burned by the House of Commons. In 1730 his most noted work, 'Christianity as Old as the Creation,' was published.

Tiraboschi, Girolamo (tē-rä-bos'kē). An Italian historian of literature; born at Bergamo, Dec. 28, 1731; died at Modena, June 3, 1794. He wrote a celebrated 'History of Italian Literature' (14 vols., 1772–82); a work of wonderful erudition, accuracy, and completeness, extending from the first beginnings of modern culture in Italy down to the 18th century, and dealing with every branch of literature. Among his other writings are: 'Historical Memoirs of Modena' (4 vols., 1793–94).

Tirebuck, William Edwards. An English journalist, novelist, and miscellaneous writer; born in Liverpool, in 1854; died there, Jan. 22, 1900. At first connected with the Liverpool Mail and Yorkshire Post, he later devoted himself to writing novels; the most popular are: 'Saint Margaret' (1888); 'Dorrie' (1891); 'Sweetheart Gwen' (1893); 'Miss Grace of All Souls' (1895). His other writings include 'Dante Gabriel Rosetti' (1882), and 'Great Minds in Art' (1888). He belongs to the "Liverpool Group" of English Authors, including Hall Caine, Wm. Watson, and Richard Le Gallienne.

Tiro (tī'ro). Cicero's servant and amanuensis; he lived about B. C. 95–A. D. 5. He was emancipated by Cicero, and even treated by him as a friend and co-worker: some of Cicero's letters to him are extant. He invented a system of short-hand, called from him "Notæ Tironianæ."

Tirso de Molina. See **Tellez.**

Tischendorf, Lobegott Friedrich Konstantin von (tish'en-dorf). A celebrated German Biblical antiquarian; born at Lengenfeld in Voigtland, Jan. 18, 1815; died Dec. 7, 1874, at Leipsic, where he was professor of theology. In search of ancient MSS. of the Bible, he visited the East repeatedly, and wrote 'Travels in the East' (1845); 'From the Holy Land' (1862). He edited and published several ancient texts of the Scripture, as 'The Codex of Ephrem Syrus' (1843); 'The Unpublished Palatine Gospel' (1847); 'The Amiatine Codex' (1850); 'The Codex of Claremont' (1852); 'Sacred Palimpsest Fragments' (1854); 'The Sinaitic Codex' (1862); 'The Vatican New Testament' (1867); a critical edition of the 'Septuagint' (7th ed. 1887); 'Apocryphal Acts of the Apostles' (1851); 'Apocryphal Gospels' (1853); 'Apocryphal Apocalypses' (1866). He attempted to solve the question 'When were our Gospels Compiled?' (1865, 4th ed. 1866), but the work found little favor with critics.

Tissandier, Gaston (tē-sän-dyā'). A French aeronaut and chemist; born at Paris, Nov. 21, 1843; died there, August 30, 1899. Besides text-books of chemistry he wrote for the 'Library of Wonders,' 'Water,' 'Coal,' 'Fossils,' 'Photography'; in collaboration with Glaisher, Flammarion, and Fonvielle, he wrote 'Aerial Voyages.'

Tissot, Claude Joseph (tē-sō'). A French philosopher; born at Fourgs (Doubs), Nov. 26, 1801; died at Dijon, Oct. 7, 1876. He translated most of Kant's writings into French. Among his original works are: 'Of the Beautiful, Especially in Literature' (1830); 'Short History of Philosophy' (1840); 'The Mania of Suicide and of Revolt' (1840); 'Parceling of the Land and Division of Property' (1842); 'Principles of Morality' (1866); 'Catholicism and Public Instruction' (1874); 'Insanity Considered Especially in its Relations to Normal Psychology' (1876).

Tissot, Pierre François. A French historical and miscellaneous writer; born at Versailles, 1768; died 1854. Among his works are: 'Reminiscences of Prairial 1st to 3d' (1799), an interesting page of French history; 'Virgil's Bucolics,' in French verse (1800); 'The Three Irish Conspirators; or, Emmet's Shade' (1804); 'The Wars of the Revolution to 1815' (1820); 'Virgil Compared with Ancient and Modern Poets' (4 vols., 1825–30); 'Complete History of the French Revolution' (6 vols., 1833–36).

Titcomb, Timothy. See **Holland.**

Tittmann, Friedrich Wilhelm (tit'män). A German historian; born at Wittenberg, 1784; died 1864. His 'Study on the Amphictyonic League' (1812) was crowned by the Berlin Academy. His principal work is a 'History of Henry the Illustrious' (2 vols., 1845–46). Among his other writings are: 'A View of the Civilization of our Times' (1835); 'On Life and

Matter> (1855); 'Aphorisms of Philosophy> (1859); 'Nationality and the State> (1861).

Tobler, Adolf (tō'bler). A Swiss philologist of Romance languages; born at Hirzel, Zürich, May 24, 1835. He became professor in the University of Berlin, 1867. He wrote: 'French Versification in Ancient and Modern Times> (1880); 'Miscellaneous Contributions to French Grammar> (1886).

Tobler, Titus. A Swiss philologist and traveler, born at Stein, Appenzell, June 25, 1806; died at Munich, Jan. 21, 1877. He wrote: 'A Pleasure Trip to the Land of the Morning> (1839); 'Bethlehem in Palestine> (1849); 'Third Journey to Palestine> (1859); 'Nazareth in Palestine> (1868).

Tocqueville, Alexis Charles Henri Clérel de (tōk-vēl'). A distinguished French publicist and writer; born at Vermeuil (Seine-et-Oise), July 29, 1805; died at Cannes, April 16, 1859. He visited the United States in 1831. In 1835 he published 'Democracy in America.> In 1838 he was made a member of the Academy of Moral and Political Sciences, and in 1839 was elected to the Chamber of Deputies; became a member of the French Academy in 1841; was Minister of Foreign Affairs from June 2 to Oct. 31, 1849. He published 'The Old Régime and the Revolution> in 1856. ('Works,> 9 vols., Paris, 1860-65.)

Todd, John. An American Congregational clergyman; born at Rutland, Vt., Oct. 9, 1800; died at Pittsfield, Mass., where he had long resided, Aug. 24, 1873. His lesson-books and other works for Sunday schools were used all over America for many years. Among his other publications were: 'Hints to Young Men>; 'Summer Gleanings>; etc. He invented the 'Index Rerum> for the use of students.

Todd, Lawrie. See **Thorburn, Grant.**

Toland, John. A British free-thinking philosopher; born at Redcastle near Londonderry, Ireland, Nov. 30, 1670; died near London, 1721-22. He studied theology at Glasgow, Edinburgh, and Leyden. Among many argumentative theological works are: 'Christianity Not Mysterious> (1696); 'Letters to Serena> (1704), Serena being Sophia, Queen of Prussia—in these letters he repudiates the doctrines of a God outside this universe, and of personal immortality; 'Adeisidæmon> (1709), a tractate on belief in dæmons; 'Nazarenus; or, Jewish, Gentile, and Mohametan Christianity> (1718); 'Pantheisticon> (1720).

Toldy, Franz (tol'dē). A Hungarian historian of literature; born at Buda-Pesth, Aug. 10, 1805; died there, Dec. 10, 1875, professor of Hungarian literature. He wrote: 'Manual of Hungarian Poetry> (1828); 'History of the Hungarian National Literature> (1851); 'History of Hungarian Poetry> (1857).

Tollens, Hendrik Caroluszoon (tol'lens). A Dutch poet; born at Rotterdam, Sept. 24, 1780; died at Ryswick, Oct. 21, 1856. Among his best

works are: 'Idylls and Love Songs> (1801-5); 'Poems> (1808-15); 'Account of the Winter Spent by the Dutch at Nova Zembla> (1816); 'Romances, Ballads, and Legends> (1818); 'New Poems> (1821); 'Various Poems> (1840); 'Last Poems> (1848-53).

Tolman, Herbert Cushing, an American linguist, born Nov. 4, 1865; professor of Greek at Vanderbilt University since 1894. He published: 'Tolman's Persian Incriptions> (1892); 'Art of Translating> (1900); 'Mycenæan Tory> (1904); 'Via Crucis> (1907); 'Index of Rites to the Grihya Sutras.> He is editor of the Vanderbilt Oriental Series.

Tolstoy, Aleksii Konstantinovich, Count (tol'stoi). A Russian author; born in St. Petersburg, Aug. 24, 1817; died near there, Sept. 28, 1875. He wrote a number of ballads and lyric poems; one novel, 'Kniaz (Prince) Serbrianyi> (translated by Jeremiah Curtin, 1893); a short drama, 'Don Juan>; and a trilogy, 'The Death of Ivan the Terrible> (1865), 'Tsar Feodor Ivanovich> (1868), and 'Tsar Boris> (1870).

Tolstoy, Count Lyof (or **Lev,** English **Leo**) **Alekséevich.** The great Russian novelist; born on the family estate of Yasnaya Polyana in the government of Tula, Russia, Sept. 9, 1828. He served in the Crimean War, and afterward traveled extensively. In 1861 he took up permanent residence on his country estate. Among his earliest works are: 'Detsvo> (Childhood), 'Otrchestvo> (Boyhood), and 'Iunost> (Youth); also 'Cossacks>, 'Sevastopol,> and a number of military sketches. 'War and Peace> was published in 1865-68; 'Anna Karénina> in 1875-78. His peculiar doctrines are promulgated in 'My Confession,> 'In What my Faith Consists,> etc.; many of them are forbidden in Russia. His later works are: 'The Kreutzer Sonata> (1888); 'Death of Ivan Ilyitch> (1884-86); 'Master and Man> (1895); 'On Art>; 'Resurrection.> Nearly all have been translated into English and most other modern languages.

Tomasini, Jacopo Filippo (tō-mä-sē'nē). An Italian miscellaneous writer; born at Padua, 1597; died 1654, at Citta Nuova in Istria, of which see he was bishop. He wrote: 'Lives of Illustrious Men, with Portraits> (1630); 'Petrarch Come to Life Again> (1635), a work of curious interest; 'On Votive Offerings> (1629).

Tomes, Robert. An American physician and author; born in New York city, March 27, 1817; died in Brooklyn, N. Y., Aug. 28, 1882. Besides many contributions to journals and periodicals, he published: 'The Bourbon Prince> (1853); 'Richard the Lion-Hearted> (1853); 'Oliver Cromwell> (1855); 'Panama in 1855> (1855); 'The Americans in Japan> (1857); 'The Battles of America by Sea and Land> (3 vols., 1861); 'The Champagne Country> (1867); and 'The War with the South> (3 vols., 1864-67).

Tommaseo, Niccolò (tō-mä'sē-ō). An Italian miscellaneous writer; born at Sevenico in Dalmatia, Oct. 9, 1802; died at Florence, May 1, 1874. He wrote the novel 'The Duke of Athens> (1837); 'Commentary on Dante> (1837), a work of great merit; the half mystical, half erotic novel 'Faith and Beauty' (1840); 'Critical Studies' (1843); 'The Death Penalty' (1865). He also compiled a valuable collection of 'Popular Songs: Tuscan, Corsican, Illyrian, Greek' (4 vols., 1844), and a 'Dictionary of Italian Synonyms' (7 vols., 1856).

Tompa, Michael (tōm'pä). A Hungarian poet; born at Rimaszombat, in the county of Gömör, Sept. 29, 1819; died July 30, 1868. He wrote: 'Folk Tales and Popular Sayings' (1846); several allegorical poems, among them 'The Stork' (1847), expressing the popular sympathy with the coming revolution; 'Stories of the Flowers' (1854); 'Mathias Szuhay.'

Tomson, Graham R. See **Watson, Rosamund.**

Tonna, Charlotte Elizabeth Browne. ["Charlotte Elizabeth."] An English religious writer; born in Norwich, Oct. 1, 1790 (or 1792); died July 12, 1846. In her childhood she lost her sight, and regained it. She wrote: 'Judah's Lion'; 'Judæa Capta'; 'Principalities and Powers'; 'Personal Recollections' (1841).

Tooke, John Horne. An English political writer and grammarian; born at Westminster, June 25, 1736; died at Wimbledon, March 18, 1812. The chief of his early works was a pamphlet entitled 'The Petition of an Englishman.' He studied law; took orders in the Church of England; was a friend and adherent of Wilkes, but afterward quarreled with him, and was denounced in the famous 'Junius Letters.' He was sentenced to a year's imprisonment for libel, and while in prison wrote 'A Letter to John Dunning, Esq.,' in which he reviewed the legal aspects of his case. His chief work, 'Epea Pteroenta [Winged Words]; or, The Diversions of Purley,' was published in 1805. He was an active member of the Society of Correspondence formed by the admirers of the French Revolution, and committed to the Tower, but acquitted.

Topelius, Zacharie (top-el'ē-us). A Finnish poet and novelist; born at Kuddräs, E. Bothnia, Jan. 14, 1818; died at Helsingfors, Finland, March 13, 1898. He was editor of the Helsingfors Tidningar 1842–60. His earliest productions appeared in his journal; some of them were issued later in book form under the title 'Ljungblommer' (Heather Flowers: 1845–54). He also wrote a number of dramas, 'Efter Femtio Ar' (Fifty Years Later: 1851); 'Regina af Emmertz' (1854). Many of his juvenile stories have been translated into English. His best-known work is 'Fältskärens Berättelser' (The Surgeon's Stories: 6 vols., 1872–74), a collection of tales dealing with the history of Sweden and Finland during the 17th and 18th centuries.

Töpfer, Karl (tĕp'fer). A German writer of comedies; born at Berlin, Dec. 26, 1792; died at Hamburg, Aug. 22, 1871. Among his comedies are: 'The Best Tone'; 'Courting according to Prescription'; 'Rosenmüller and Finke.' He

wrote also 'Narratives and Stories' (2 vols., 1842–44).

Topin, Marius (tō-pan'). A French historical writer; born at Aix, Dec. 25, 1838. He wrote: 'The Cardinal de Retz, his Genius and his Writings' (1864); 'History of Aigues-Mortes' (1865); 'Europe and the Bourbons under Louis XIV.' (1867); 'The Man in the Iron Mask' (1869); 'Contemporary Novelists' (1876).

Toplady, Augustus Montague. An English clergyman and hymn-writer; born at Farnham, Surrey, Nov. 4, 1740; died at Leicester Fields, London, Aug. 14, 1778. He was editor of the Gospel Magazine, and author of many hymns, chief of which is 'Rock of Ages.'

Toppfer (or **Töpffer**), **Rudolphe** (tōp'fär). A Swiss littérateur; born at Geneva, Feb. 17, 1799; died June 8, 1846. His father was a painter, and he wished to be one also, but an affection of the eyes prevented. He wrote: 'Zigzag Tours' (1843); 'The Heritage' (1834); 'Rosa and Gertrude' (1846); 'Travels and Adventures of Dr. Festus' (1840); etc.

Torelli, Achille (tō-rel'ē). An Italian writer of comedy; born at Naples, May 5, 1844. He wrote at 16 his first comedy, 'Who Dieth Lieth.' Of his others, the most successful were: 'A Court in the 17th Century'; 'The Mission of Woman'; 'Husbands' (1867); 'Sad Reality' (1871); 'Truth' (1875); 'The Color of the Times' (1875).

Torfeson, Thormodur, also known as **Torfæus** (tor'fē-son). A Danish historian; born on the isle of Engoe, off the south coast of Iceland, 1640; died 1719. His principal works, all written in Latin, are: 'History of the Faroe Islands' (1695); 'History of the Orkneys' (1697); 'Line of the Dynasties and Kings of Denmark' (1702); 'History of Old Vinland' (1705); 'Ancient Greenland' (1706); 'The Historic Trefoil' (1707); 'History of Norway' (4 vols., 1711), his greatest work.

Torrey, Charles Cutler, an American orientalist; born Dec. 20, 1863; since 1900 professor of Semitic Languages at Yale University. He wrote 'The Commercial–Theological Terms in the Koran,' and translated from the Arabic 'The Mohammedan Conquest of Egypt and North Africa.'

Torrey, Bradford. An American nature essayist; born in Weymouth, Mass., Oct. 9, 1843. He was educated in the public schools, taught two years, then entered business in Boston. In 1886 he became assistant editor of the Youth's Companion. He is a close student of birds, and writes largely on this subject for the magazines. His essays have been collected into the following volumes: 'Birds in the Bush' (1885); 'The Foot-Path Way'; 'A Rambler's Lease'; 'A Florida Sketch-Book' 'Spring Notes from Tennessee'; 'Nature's Invitation'; 'Friends on the Shelf.'

Tosti, Ludovico (tōs'tē). A distinguished Italian church historian; born about 1800; died 1866. He was a Benedictine monk, and wrote: 'History of Monte Cassino'; 'History of Boniface VIII.,' in which that pope is defended against the accusations of Dante; 'Abelard and his Time'; 'The Countess Matilda and the Roman Pontiffs'; 'The Lombard League,' a spirited account of the struggle of the Italian communes with the German emperors; 'History of the Council of Constance'; 'History of the Greek Schism'; 'Prolegomena to a Universal History of the Church' (2 vols.).

Totten, Charles Adelle Lewis. An American army officer, inventor, lecturer, and writer on military subjects; born at New London, Conn., Feb. 3, 1851. He has written; 'Strategos, the American War Game' (1880); 'Important Question in Metrology' (1883); 'Yale Military Lectures'; 'Nativity, its Facts and Fancies' (1887). His writings are now devoted to questions of prophecy. Died April 12, 1908.

Touchard-Lafosse, G. (tö-chär'lä-fos'). A French novelist and miscellaneous writer; born at La Châtre, 1780; died at Paris, 1847. Among his very numerous writings are: 'Political Puppets' (5 vols., 1829); 'Chronicles of the Œil-de-Bœuf' (8 vols., 1829–33), a collection of scandalous anecdotes; 'Jean Angot: A Story of the 16th Century' (2 vols., 1835); 'Chronicles of the Opera' (2 vols., 1854); 'Recollections of Half a Century' (6 vols).

Tourgee, Albion Winegar. An American lawyer, author, and editor; born at Williamsfield, O., May 2, 1838. He served in the Northern army (1861–65), settled in the South, was a judge, and afterwards editor. He has published: 'The North Carolina Form Book' (1874); 'The North Carolina Code' (1878); 'Legal Digest' (1879); 'North Carolina Reports' (1879). His most popular novels are: 'Figs and Thistles' (1879); 'A Fool's Errand, by One of the Fools' (1879); 'Bricks Without Straw' (1880); 'Hot Plowshares' (1883); 'An Appeal to Cæsar' (1884); 'Black Ice' (1887); and 'Button's Inn' (1887). Died, 1905.

Tourneur, Cyril. An Elizabethan dramatist, the dates of whose birth and death are uncertain. He was author of two plays, 'The Revenger's Tragedy' (1607), and 'The Atheist's Tragedy' (1611); and of a poem entitled 'The Transformed Metamorphosis' (1600).

Towle, George Makepeace. An American journalist, author, and littérateur. He was born in Washington, D. C., Aug. 27, 1841; died in Brookline, Mass., Aug. 10, 1893. He was United States consul at Nantes, France, 1866–68; and at Bradford, England, 1868–70. His works include: 'Glimpses of History' (1865); 'Henry the Fifth' (1866); 'American Society' (1870); 'The Eastern Question' (1877); 'Servia and Roumania' (1877); 'Beaconsfield' (1878); 'Young Folks' Heroes of History' (1878–80); 'Modern France' (1879); 'Men of Mark' (1880); 'England and Russia in Asia' (1885); 'England in Egypt' (1885); 'Literature of the English Language.'

Towles, Mrs. Catharine Webb. An American author; born in Charlemont, Mass., Oct. 25, 1823. She was editor of several Southern magazines, and has published: 'Three Golden Links' (1857); 'Tales for the Freemason's Fireside' (1859); 'Poor Claire; or, Life Among the Queer' (1883).

Townsend, Edward Waterman. An American journalist and writer of dialect stories; born in Ohio, 1855. His stories and sketches, first printed in the daily journals, are collected under the titles: 'Chimmie Fadden, Major Max, and Other Stories'; 'Chimmie Fadden Explains, Major Max Expounds'; 'A Daughter of the Tenements'; 'Near a Whole City Full.' He also wrote: 'A Summer in New York'; 'Reuben Larkmead'; 'Our Constitution'; 'Beaver Creek Farm.'

Townsend, George Alfred. ["Gath."] An American journalist and war correspondent; born in Georgetown, Del., Jan. 30, 1841. He became a journalist in 1860. He was special correspondent for the New York Herald and World (1860–64), afterwards public lecturer, and war correspondent in the Austro-Prussian War (1866). His publications in book form are: 'Campaigns of a Non-Combatant' (1865); 'Life of Garibaldi' (1867); 'Life of Abraham Lincoln' (1867); 'The New World and the Old'; 'Poems' (1870); 'Washington Outside and Inside' (1871); 'Bohemian Days' (1881); 'The Entailed Hat' (1884), and 'Katy of Catoctin; or The Chain-Breakers' (1886), novels; 'Life of Levi P. Morton' (1888); 'Columbus in Love' (1892).

Townsend, Mrs. Mary Ashley. ["Xariffa."] An American poet and author; born in Lyons, N. Y., about 1836; died June 14, 1901. She contributed sketches to the N. O. Delta that attracted attention, and afterwards published, 'Xariffa's Poems'; 'The Brother Clerks' (1859); 'Poems' (1870); 'The Captain's Story' (1874); 'Down the Bayou,' etc. (1884).

Townsend, Virginia Frances. An American author and novelist; born in New Haven, Conn., in 1836. She has edited Arthur's Home Magazine, has contributed to many journals and magazines, and written many popular novels. Among these are: 'While It Was Morning' (1859); 'Amy Deane, and Other Tales' (1862); 'The Well in the Rock,' etc. (1863); 'The Battle-Fields of our Fathers' (1864); 'Janet Strong' (1865); 'Darryl Gap' (1866); 'The Hollands' (1869); 'One Woman's Two Lovers' (1872); 'Elizabeth Tudor' (1874); 'Only Girls' (1876); 'Six in All' (1878); and 'Our Presidents' (1888).

Toy, Crawford Howell. An American Unitarian clergyman and scholar; born in Norfolk, Va., March 23, 1836. He has been professor of Hebrew at Harvard University since 1880. He has written: 'History of the Religion of Israel' (1882); 'Quotations in the New Testament' (1884); 'Judaism and Christianity: Progress of Thought from the Old Testament to the New' (1890); 'Commentary on Proverbs' (1889).

Traill, Catherine Parr (Strickland). An English writer, sister of Agnes; born in London, Jan. 9, 1802; died at Lakeville, Can., Aug. 29,

fd

1899. She removed to Canada in 1833, and made her home for many years at Lakeville, Ont. Among her works are: 'The Backwoods of Canada' (London, 1835); 'Canadian Crusoes' (1852); 'Ramblings in the Canadian Forests' (1854); 'Afar in the Forest' (1869); 'Studies of Plant Life' (1884); 'Pearls and Pebbles' (1895).

Traill, Henry Duff. An English journalist and man of letters; born at Blackheath, Aug. 14, 1842; died in London, Feb. 21, 1900. Graduated from St. John's, Oxford, 1864. He was called to the bar in 1868, but soon took to literature. He wrote 'Lives' of Strafford (a very original work with a new view), William III., Sterne, Coleridge, and others; also 'Central Government' (1881); 'Recaptured Rhymes' (1882); 'The New Lucian' (1884); 'Two Proper Prides;' etc. He lately edited 'Social England: A Record of the Progress of the People,' in six large volumes; and became (1897) editor of the weekly review Literature.

Train, Elizabeth Phipps. An American novelist; born in 1856. Among her works are: 'Dr. Lamar'; 'Autobiography of a Professional Beauty'; 'A Social Highwayman'; 'A Marital Liability'; and translations from the French, 'The Shadow of Dr. Laroque'; 'Recollections of the Court of the Tuileries'; 'A Queen of Hearts.'

Train, George Francis. An American lecturer and writer, noted for his eccentricities; born in Boston, March 24, 1829; traveled extensively in early life; lectured in Great Britain and Ireland, returning to this country in 1862. He has written: 'An American Merchant in Europe, Asia, and Australia' (1857); 'Young America Abroad' (1857); 'Young America in Wall Street' (1858); 'Spread-Eagleism' (1859); 'Every Man his own Autocrat' (1859); 'Observations on Street Railways'; 'Union Speeches' (1862); 'Downfall of England' (1865); and 'Championship of Woman.' Died, N. Y., 1904.

Treat, Mrs. Mary Lou Adelia (Davis) (Allen). An American naturalist; born 1835. She has written: 'Chapters on Ants'; 'Home Studies in Nature'; 'Injurious Insects of the Farm and Garden'; 'My Garden Pets.'

Treitschke, Heinrich Gotthard von (trītsh'-kĕ). A German historian; born at Dresden, Sept. 15, 1834; died at Berlin, April 28, 1896. He wrote: 'The Science of Society' (1859). His chief work is 'German History in the 19th Century' (5 vols., 1879–94). He wrote also: 'Historical and Political Disquisitions' (1865); 'Socialism and its Supporters' (1878); 'A Word on our Jewry' (1890); 'Biographical and Historical Discussions' (1897).

Trelawny, Edward John. An English author of celebrity; born in London, Nov. 13, 1792; died at Sompting, Sussex, Aug. 13, 1881. He is remembered as a picturesque and somewhat theatrical adventurer (supposed to be drawn by Byron in 'The Corsair), the friend of Byron, Shelley, etc., and Byron's companion (1823) in the Greek war of liberation. He

wrote a novel called 'Adventures of a Younger Son' (1830); but his best-known work is 'Recollections of the Last Days of Shelley and Byron' (1858), reissued in 1878 as 'Records of Byron, Shelley, and the Author.' His body was cremated, and the ashes interred near Shelley's at Rome. His portrait is preserved in Millais's painting 'The Northwest Passage.'

Trembecki, Stanislav (trem-bets'kĕ). A Polish poet; born near Cracow, about 1723; died at Tulczyn in Podolia, Dec. 12, 1812. His most considerable poem, 'Zofijovka,' is a description of a park laid out by the poet's patron, Count Potocki, for his wife Sophia.

Trench, Richard Chenevix. An eminent British philologist and essayist; born in Dublin, Sept. 5, 1807; died in London, March 28, 1886. He was dean of Westminster 1856–63; archbishop of Dublin from 1864. He was noted in philology, on which he wrote 'Deficiencies in our English Dictionaries.' Among many other works may be mentioned: 'Poems from Eastern Sources' (1842); 'Elegiac Poems' (1846); 'Poems Collected and Arranged Anew' (1865); 'Notes on the Parables of our Lord' (1841; 15th ed. 1884); 'Notes on the Miracles of our Lord' (1846, 13th ed. 1886); 'On the Study of Words' (1851, 15th ed. 1874); 'English Past and Present' (1855–81); 'The Authorized Version of the New Testament, in Connection with some Recent Proposals for Its Revision' (1858); 'Select Glossary of English Words Used Formerly in Senses Different from their Present' (1859); 'Studies on the Gospels' (1867), 'Lectures on Mediæval Church History' (1877). He edited several volumes of poetry, and 'Remains of the Late Mrs. Richard Trench,' his mother (1862).

Trendelenburg, Friedrich Adolf (tren'delen-börG"). A German philosopher; born at Eutin, Nov. 30, 1802; died at Berlin, Jan. 24, 1872. He set forth the ethical aspect of his philosophy in the treatise 'The Ethical Idea of Right and Law,' and the æsthetic aspect in 'Niobe' (1846) and 'The Cathedral of Cologne' (1853). He wrote also 'Natural Justice on the Ground of Ethics' (2d ed. 1860).

Trent, William Peterfield. An American man of letters, dean of the department of arts and sciences and professor of English and of history in the University of the South; born 1862. He has made a special study of Southern men and times, and has published: 'Life of William Gilmore Simms'; 'English Culture in Virginia'; 'Southern Statesmen of the Old Régime' (1897); 'History of American Literature.'

Trescot, William Henry. An American diplomatist; born in Charleston, S. C., Nov. 10, 1822. He was United States counsel at the Halifax Fishery Commission in 1877; special envoy to South America in 1881; and plenipotentiary with General Grant to negotiate a treaty with Mexico in 1882. He is the author of 'Foreign Policy of the United States' (1849); 'Diplomacy of the Revolution' (1852); 'An

American View of the Eastern Question' (1854); 'Diplomatic History of the Administrations of Washington and Adams' (1857); besides various memoirs, addresses, and pamphlets. Died 1898.

Trevelyan, Charles Edward, Sir. An English statesman and writer; born April 2, 1807; died in London, June 19, 1886. He was Assistant Secretary to the Treasury, 1840; finance minister in India, 1862–65. He married Lord Macaulay's sister. He wrote: 'Education of the People of Ireland' (1838); 'The Irish Crisis' (1848); 'The Purchase System in the British Army' (1867); 'The British Army in 1868' (1869); 'Christianity and Hinduism' (1881); etc.

Trevelyan, George Otto, Sir. An English statesman and author, son of Sir Charles Trevelyan and Hannah Macaulay; born at Rothley Temple, Leicestershire, July 20, 1838. He was secretary for Scotland, 1885–86, and again 1892–95. Among his writings are: 'Letters of a Competition Wallah' (1864); 'Cawnpore' (1865); 'The Ladies in Parliament, and Other Pieces' (1869); 'Life of Lord Macaulay' (1876); 'Early History of Charles James Fox'; 'The American Revolution.'

Trochu, Louis Jules (trō-shü'). A distinguished French soldier; born at Palais in Morbihan, May 12, 1815; died at Tours, Oct. 7, 1896. He wrote: 'The Empire and the Defense of Paris' (1872); 'For Truth and Justice' (1873); 'Politics and the Siege of Paris' (1874); 'Society, the State, and the Army' (1896).

Trogus Pompeius, or **Pompeius Trogus** (trō'gus pom-pē'us). A Roman historian of the Augustan age. Drawing principally on Greek sources, he wrote a universal history from Ninus to his own time, which he called 'Philippian Histories,' because the fortunes of Philip of Macedon and his line formed the central point of the narrative: all that remains of its 44 books is the table of contents and some few fragments.

Trollope, Anthony. A distinguished English novelist; born in London, April 24, 1815; died there, Dec. 6, 1882. He published: 'The Macdermots of Ballydoran' (1847); 'The Kellys and the O'Kellys' (1848); 'La Vendée' (1850); 'The Warden' (1855); 'Barchester Towers' (1857); 'The Three Clerks' (1857); 'Doctor Thorne' (1858); 'The Bertrams' (1859); 'The West Indies and the Spanish Main' (1859); 'Castle Richmond' (1860); 'Framley Parsonage' (1861); 'Tales of All Countries' (1861); 'Orley Farm' (1862); 'The Struggles of Brown, Jones, and Robinson' (1862); 'North America' (1862); 'Rachel Ray' (1863); 'The Small House at Allington' (1864); 'The Belton Estate' (1864); 'Hunting Sketches' (1864); 'Can You Forgive Her?' (1865); 'Miss Mackenzie' (1865); 'Clergymen of the Church of England' (1866); 'Traveling Sketches' (1866); 'Lotta Schmidt, and Other Stories' (1867); 'The Claverings' (1867); 'The Last Chronicle of Barset' (1867); 'Nina Balatka' (anonymous: 1867); 'Linda Tressel' (do.: 1868); 'British Sports and Pas-

times' (edited: 1868); 'Phineas Finn, the Irish Member' (1869); 'He Knew He Was Right' (1869); 'Sir Harry Hotspur of Humblethwaite' (1870); 'An Editor's Tales' (1870); 'The Vicar of Bullhampton' (1870); 'Cæsar's Commentaries' (edited: 1870); 'Mary Gresley' (1871); 'Ralph the Heir' (1871); 'The Eustace Diamonds' (1872); 'The Golden Lion of Granpère' (1872); 'Australia and New Zealand' (1873); 'Phineas Redux' (1873); 'Harry Heathcote of Gangoil' (1874); 'South Australia and Western Australia,' 'Victoria and Tasmania,' and 'New South Wales and Queensland' (all 1874); 'Lady Anna' (1874); 'The Way we Live Now' (1875); 'The Prime Minister' (1876); 'The American Senator' (1877); 'South Africa' (1877); 'Is he Popenjoy?' (1878); 'John Caldigate' (1879); 'An Eye for an Eye' (1879); 'Cousin Henry' (1879); 'Thackeray' in 'English Men of Letters' (1879); 'The Duke's Children' (1880); 'Life of Cicero' (1880); 'Ayala's Angel' (1881); 'Dr. Wortle's School' (1881); 'Why Frau Frohmann Raised her Prices, and Other Stories' (1881); 'The Fixed Period' (1882); 'Kept in the Dark' (1882); 'Lord Palmerston' in 'English Political Leaders' (1882); 'Marion Fay' (1882); 'Mr. Scarborough's Family' (1883). Posthumously appeared: his 'Autobiography' (1883); 'The Land Leaguers' (1883, unfinished); and 'An Old Man's Love' (1884).

Trollope, Frances M. An English author, mother of Anthony; born in Hampshire, about 1780; died in Florence, Italy, Oct. 6, 1863. In 1829 she visited America, and afterwards published a volume entitled 'Domestic Manners of the Americans' (1831). She followed this with the novel 'The Refugee in America' (1832). Among her other works are: 'The Abbess' (1833); 'Tremordyn Cliff' (1835); 'The Barnabys in America' (1843); 'Life and Adventures of a Clever Woman' (1854); and 'Fashionable Life; or, Paris and London' (1856).

Trollope, Thomas Adolphus, elder brother of Anthony; born April 29, 1810; died at Clifton, Nov. 11, 1892. He was a constant contributor to English periodicals, and was Italian correspondent of the New York Tribune. Among his many books are: 'A Summer in Brittany' (1840); 'A Summer in Western France' (1841); 'La Beata' (1861); 'Marietta' (1862); 'Beppo the Conscript' (1864); 'Lindisfarn Chase' (1864); 'History of the Commonwealth of Florence' (4 vols., 1865); 'Dream Numbers' (1868); 'A Siren' (1870); 'Life of Pius IX.' (1877); 'Sketches from French History' (1878); 'What I Remember' (1887–89).

Troubetzkoy, Mrs. Amélie (Rives) (Chanler) (trō-bets'koi). An American novelist; born in Virginia, Aug. 23, 1863. She has lived abroad since her second marriage. She has written: 'A Brother to Dragons, and Other Tales' (1888); 'The Quick or the Dead?' (1888); 'Barbara Dering'; 'The Witness of the Sun'; 'Herod and Mariamne: Drama'; 'Virginia of Virginia'; 'Athelwold'; 'Augustine the Man.'

Trowbridge, John Townsend. An American poet, novelist, and general writer; born in Ogden, N. Y., Sept. 18, 1827. His first poems, 'The Vagabonds,' 'At Sea,' 'The Pewee,' etc., appeared in the Atlantic Monthly, also the story 'Coupon Bonds.' Among his numerous novels, tales of adventure, etc., are: 'Father Brighthopes' (1853); 'Hearts and Faces' (1853); 'Martin Merrivale' (1855); 'Neighbor Jackwood' (1857); 'The Old Battle-Ground' (1859); 'The Drummer Boy' (1863); 'Cudjo's Cave' (1864); 'The Three Scouts' (1865), 'Lucy Arlyn' (1866); 'Coupon Bonds' (1866); 'Neighbors' Wives' (1867); 'The Story of Columbus' (1867); 'The Jack Hazard Series' (1871-75); 'The Emigrant's Story, and Other Poems' (1875); 'The Silver Medal Series' (1877-82); 'The Book of Gold, and Other Poems' (1878); 'A Home Idyl,' etc. (1881); 'The Tide-Mill Series' (1882-87); 'The Lost Earl' (1888) ; 'My Own Story' (1903).

True, Charles Kittridge. An American educator and historical writer; born in Portland, Me., Aug. 14, 1809; died in Brooklyn, N. Y., Jan. 20, 1878. He was pastor of various Methodist churches, and subsequently professor of intellectual philosophy at Wesleyan University (1849-60). He was the author of 'Elements of Logic' (1840); 'Shawmut; or, The Settlement of Boston' (1845); 'John Winthrop' (1875); 'Sir Walter Raleigh' (1878); 'Life and Times of John Knox' (1878); 'Memoirs of John Howard' (1878); 'The Thirty Years' War' (1879); 'Heroes of Holland' (1882).

Trueba y Cosío, Telesforo de (trwä'bä ē kōs'yō). A Spanish poet; born at Santander, 1798; died at Paris, Oct. 4, 1835. He wrote several comedies, as 'The Fickle One' and 'Marrying on 60,000 Duros.' He wrote in English several historical novels, among them 'Gomez Arias' (1828), and 'The Castilian' (1829); and also in English, 'Lives of Cortés and Pizarro' (1830) and the historical drama 'The Royal Delinquent.' The most successful of his works was 'Paris and London' (1833), a portraiture of manners and morals.

Trumbull, Gurdon. An American ornithologist, brother of H. C. and J. H.; born in Stonington, Conn., May 5, 1841. He has published 'American Game Birds; or, Names and Portraits of Birds, with Descriptions. Died 1903.

Trumbull, Henry Clay. An American editor, author, and lecturer; born in Stonington, Conn., June 8, 1830. He was army chaplain 1862-65; afterwards secretary of the American Sunday School Union, 1865-72; and after 1875 editor of the Sunday School Times. He published many books, including: 'Army Sermons' (1864); 'The Knightly Soldier' (1865); 'A Useful Life,' etc. (1866); 'The Captured Scout' (1869); 'Children in the Temple' (1869); 'A Model Superintendent' (1880); 'Kadesh-Barnea' (1884); 'Teaching and Teachers' (1884); 'The Blood Covenant' (1885); 'Yale Lectures on the Sunday School' (1888); 'Studies in Oriental Social Life.' Died Dec. 8, 1903.

Trumbull, James Hammond. An American philologist and librarian, brother of H. C.; born in Stonington, Conn., Dec. 20, 1821; died in Hartford, Aug. 5, 1897. He was Secretary of State of Connecticut during the War, 1861-64, and held many honorable posts connected with historical and educational associations. He was president of the American Philological Association 1874-75. He made the Indian languages of North America a special study; is the acknowledged authority on the Algonkin tongues; and published many essays on Indian philology. He was a frequent contributor to proceedings of historical societies. Among his works are: 'The Colonial Records of Connecticut' (1850-59); 'Historical Notes on some Provisions of the Connecticut Statutes' (1860-61); 'The Composition of Indian Geographical Names' (1870); 'Historical Notes on the Constitution of Connecticut' (1872); 'The True Blue-Laws of Connecticut,' etc. (1876). He edited 'The Memorial History of Hartford County' (1886). His knowledge of books was vast; as a shrewd collector and book-buyer he had few superiors; and his name is associated with the sale of the "Brinley Library," and with the Watkinson Library at Hartford.

Trumbull, John. An American poet and lawyer, famous in his day as a satirist; born in Westbury, Conn., April 24, 1750; died at Detroit, Mich., May 10, 1831. He wrote with Timothy Dwight a series of essays in the Spectator style, which first drew attention to his ability. In 'The Progress of Dulness' (1772-73) he satirized contemporary methods of education; but he won his greatest fame with 'McFingal' (1775-82), a satire on the loyalists of the Revolution time, written in Hudibrastic verse. Thirty pirated editions are said to have been sold; and some of its lines are still "familiar quotations" popularly credited to 'Hudibras.' Later he was associated with Joel Barlow and others in the production of 'The Anarchiad' (1786-87). His 'Poetical Works' were published at Hartford, Conn., in 1820.

Trumpp, Ernst (trömp). A German Orientalist; born at Ilsfeld, Würtemberg, March 13, 1828; died at Munich, April 5, 1885. His principal work is 'The Adi Granth; or, The Holy Scriptures of the Sikhs, Translated from the Original Gurmukhi' (1877). He wrote also: 'The Language of the so-called Caffres in the Hindu Caucasus'; 'Sindi Literature: The Divan of Abd-ul-Latif' (1866); 'The Baptism Book of the Ethiopian Church' (1876).

Tschudi, Johann Jakob von (tshö'dē). A Swiss naturalist and traveler; born at Glarus, July 25, 1818; died at Jakobshof in Lower Austria, Oct. 8, 1889. He traveled extensively in South America in 1838-43, and again in 1857-61. He wrote: 'The Kechua Language' (1853); 'Peru: Sketches of Travel' (1846); 'Peruvian Antiquities' (1851); 'Travels in South America' (5 vols., 1866-69).

Tucker, George. An American lawyer, educator, and author; born in Bermuda in 1775;

died in Albemarle County, Va., April 10, 1861. He was a Member of Congress, 1819-25. For twenty years he was professor of moral philosophy in the University of Virginia (1825-45). He wrote for many journals and periodicals: was the author of 'Letters on the Conspiracy of Slaves in Virginia' (1800); 'Essays on Subjects of Taste,' etc. (1822); 'The Valley of the Shenandoah' (1824), a novel; 'Principles of Rent, Wages, and Profits' (1837); 'Life of Thomas Jefferson' (1837); 'History of the United States from their Colonization to 1841' (4 vols., 1856-58); 'Banks or No Banks' (1857); and 'Essays, Moral and Philosophical' (1860).

Tucker, William Jewett. An American educator and clergyman; born at Griswold, Conn., July 13, 1839. He was professor at Andover Seminary until 1893, and since then president of Dartmouth College. He has written 'The New Movement in Humanity'; 'From Liberty to Unity.'

Tuckerman, Bayard. An American writer; born in New York in 1855. His works include 'A History of English Prose Fiction' (1882); 'Life of Lafayette'; 'William Jay and the Abolition of Slavery'; 'Life of Peter Stuyvesant.'

Tuckerman, Henry Theodore. An American author and critic, of much note in his day; born in Boston, April 20, 1813; died in New York, Dec. 17, 1871. His works include: 'The Italian Sketch Book' (1835); 'Isabel; or, Sicily' (1839); 'Rambles and Reveries' (1841); 'Thoughts on the Poets' (1846); 'Artist Life' (1847); 'Characteristics of Literature' (1849-51); 'The Optimist' (1850); 'Poems' (1851); 'Memorial of Horatio Greenough' (1853); 'Bibliographical Essays' (1857); 'Art in America' (1858); 'The Book of the Artists' (1867); 'The Collector: Essays' (1868). He edited with William Smith 'A Smaller History of English and American Literature' (1870).

Tulloch, John. A Scottish educator and ecclesiastical writer; born near Tibbermuir, Perthshire, June 1, 1823; died at Torquay, England, Feb. 13, 1886. He published: 'Leaders of the Reformation' (1859); 'English Puritanism and its Leaders' (1861); 'Beginning Life' (1862); 'The Christ of the Gospels and the Christ of Modern Criticism'; 'Lectures on Renan's Life of Jesus' (1864); 'Theology and Greek Philosophy in England in the 17th Century' (1872); 'Pascal' (1878); 'Movements in Religious Thought in Britain during the 19th Century' (1885); and several volumes of sermons. He gained the second Burnett prize of £600 for an essay 'On the Being and Attributes of God,' which was published under the title 'Theism: The Witness of Reason and Nature to an All-Wise and Beneficent Creator' (1855). He also did much review work, and wrote 'The Wigtown Martyrs Proved to be Myths.'

Tupper, Martin Farquhar. An English poet; born in London, July 17, 1810; died at Albury, Surrey, Nov. 29, 1889. In 1838 he issued the work by which he is best known, 'Proverbial Philosophy,' which had an immense circulation. He wrote other volumes of prose and verse: 'Hactenus: A Budget of Lyrics'; 'Ballads for the Time'; 'Stephen Langton; or, The Days of King John'; 'Probabilities'; 'An Aid to Faith'; 'My Life as an Author.' He twice visited the United States, and in 1875 wrote a drama in honor of the centenary of American independence.

Tupy, Eugen (tö'pē). ["Voleslav Jablonsky."] A Czech poet; born at Kardasch-Rzetschitz, Jan. 14, 1813; died at Cracow, March 1881. He is one of the foremost of Bohemian lyrists, and his 'Love Songs' in particular are held in great popular favor. He also wrote the didactic poem 'The Father's Wisdom.'

Turgeneff, Ivan (tör-gān'yɐf). A celebrated Russian novelist; born in Orel, Nov. 9, 1818; died in Bougival, near Paris, Sept. 3, 1883. His works include: 'Poems' (1841); 'Parascha' (1843); 'Improvidence' (1843); 'Andrei Kolosov' (1844); 'Andrei' (1845), a volume of poems; 'The Conversation' (1845); 'The Landlord' (1846); 'Three Portraits' (1846); 'Khor and Kalinych' (1847); 'The Bully' (1847); 'Dimitri Rudin' (1852); 'Two Friends' (1853); 'Quiet Life' (1854); 'Rudin' (1856); 'Faust' (1856); 'Asja' (1858); 'A Nest of Noblemen' (1859), also translated as 'Lisa'; 'First Love' (1860); 'Hamlet and Don Quixote' (1860); 'On the Eve' (1862); 'Fathers and Sons' (1862); 'Visions' (1863); 'The Dog' (1863?); 'Story of Lieutenant Jergunov' (1864); 'The Brigadier' (1866); 'Smoke' (1867); 'An Unfortunate' (1868); 'A Strange Tale' (1869); 'A King Lear of the Steppe' (1870); 'Knock! Knock! Knock!' (1870); 'Pegasus' (1871); 'Chertopchanov's End' (1872); 'Punin and Baburin' (1874); 'The Living Skeleton' (1875); 'The Watch' (1875); 'Some One Knocks' (1875); 'The Dream' (1876); 'New' (1877), also translated as 'Virgin Soil'; 'Father Alexei's Story' (1877); 'Song of Triumphant Love' (1881); 'The Old Portraits' (1882); 'The Despairing One' (1882); 'Poems in Prose' (1882); 'Klara Milich' (1883); 'The Conflagration at Sea' (1883).

Turgot, Anne Robert Jacques, Baron de l'Aulne (tör-gō'). An eminent French political economist and statesman; born at Paris, May 10, 1727; died there, March 8, 1781. He was minister of finance under Louis XVI. In political economy he was one of the chief representatives of the Physiocrat school (see Quesnay). It was he who said of Franklin (in a Latin hexameter), "he wrested the lightning from the sky and the sceptre from tyrants."

Turnbull, Robert. A Scottish-American Baptist pastor, editor, and author; born in Scotland, Sept. 10, 1809; came to the United States in 1833; died Nov. 20, 1877, in Hartford, Conn., where he was many years a pastor. He was editor of the Christian Review for two years. Among his many books are: 'The Theatre' (1840); 'Olympia Morata' (1842); 'The Genius of Scotland' (1847); 'The Genius of Italy' (1849); 'Theophany' (1851); 'Pulpit Orators of France and Switzerland' (1853); 'The Student Preacher' (1854); 'The World We Live In' (1855); 'Christ in History' (1856); 'Life Pictures; or, Sketches from a Pastor's Note-Book' (1857).

Turner, Charles Tennyson. An English poet, brother of Alfred Tennyson; born at Somersby, Lincolnshire, July 4, 1808; died at Cheltenham, April 25, 1879. He assumed the name of Turner (1835) by royal license, having inherited some property from his great-uncle, Rev. Samuel Turner. Besides 'Poems of Two Brothers,' written in collaboration with Alfred, he wrote: 'Sonnets and Fugitive Pieces' (1830); 'Sonnets' (1864); 'Small Tableaux' (1868); 'Sonnets, Lyrics, and Translations' (1873); 'Collected Sonnets, Old and New' (1880).

Turner, Sharon. An English historian; born at London, Sept. 24, 1768; died there, Feb. 13, 1847. He wrote: 'History of the Anglo-Saxons' (4 vols., 1799–1805; 7th ed., 3 vols., 1852); 'History of England during the Middle Ages' (3 vols., 1814–23; 7th ed., 4 vols., 1853); 'Modern History of England,' comprising 'The Reign of Henry VIII.' (1826) and 'The Reigns of Edward VI., Mary, and Elizabeth' (1829); 'Sacred History of the World' (3 vols., 1832); and a volume of miscellaneous essays, poems, etc.

Tusser, Thomas. An English poet; born at Rivenhall, Essex, about 1515; died in London, about April 1580. He was the author of 'Five Hundred Points of Good Husbandry, United to as many of Good Housewifery,' etc. (1573), in verse, with metrical autobiography; chiefly valuable for its picture of the manners and domestic life of the English farmer.

Tuttiett, Mary G. (tut'i-et). ["Maxwell Gra."] An English novelist; born in the Isle of Wight, 18—, and resides there. She has written: 'The Broken Tryst' (1879); 'The Silence of Dean Maitland' (1886); 'The Reproach of Annesley' (1889); 'Richard Rosny' (1903).

Twain, Mark. See **Clemens.**

Twesten, Karl (tves'ten). A German miscellaneous writer; born at Kiel; died at Berlin, Oct. 14, 1870. He wrote: 'Schiller in his Relation to Science' (1863); 'Machiavelli' (1868); 'The Religious, Political, and Social Ideas of the Civilized Peoples of Asia and Egypt' (2 vols., 1872).

Twichell, Joseph Hopkins. An American Congregational clergyman, and writer of biography; born in Connecticut, 183-. He has published 'Life of John Winthrop'; and edited 'Some Old Puritan Love Letters.'

Twiss, Sir Travers. A celebrated English writer and authority on international law; born in London, March 19, 1809; died there, Jan 14, 189-. He resigned all his important offices in 1872. He published: 'View of the Progress of Political Economy since the 16th Century' (1847); 'Lectures on International Law' (1856); 'The Law of Nations' (1861); 'Law of Nations in Times of War' (1863); 'Monumenta Juridica' (1871–76); 'Belligerent Right on the High Seas' (1884).

Tycho Brahe (tī'kō brä'e). An illustrious Danish astronomer; born at Knudstrup, Dec. 24, 1546; died at Prague, Oct. 24, 1601. In 'On the New Star' (1573) he treats of the star discovered by him in Cassiopeia. His other writings, most of which were published posthumously, include: 'Astronomical Works'; 'Mechanical Astronomy'; 'Astronomical Letters.'

Tychsen, Olaus Gerhard (tich'sen). A German Orientalist; born at Tondern, Dec. 14, 1734; died at Rostock, Dec. 30, 1815. His greatest work is 'Leisure Hours at Bützow' (6 vols., 1766–69), a valuable repertory of Jewish history and erudition. He also wrote: 'Elements of Arabic' (1792); 'Elements of Syriac' (1793); 'Syriac Natural Science' (1795).

Tychsen, Thomas Christian. A German Orientalist; born at Horsbyll, Silesia, May 8, 1758; died Oct. 23, 1834, at Göttingen, where he was professor of theology. He wrote: 'Principles of Hebrew Archæology' (1789); 'Grammar of Literary Arabic' (1823); and several essays on 'Numismatics,' 'Palæography,' 'The Poetry of the Arabs,' etc.

Tyler, Moses Coit. An American educator and author; born in Griswold, Conn., Aug. 2, 1835; died at Ithaca, N.Y., Dec. 25, 1900. He graduated at Yale in 1857; and was pastor of a Congregational church 1860–62. From 1867 to 1881 he was professor in the University of Michigan; and after that was professor of American history in Cornell University. He published: 'Brawnville Papers' (1868); 'History of American Literature' (1878); 'Manual of English Literature' (1879); 'Life of Patrick Henry' (1887); 'Literary History of the American Revolution, 1763–83' (2 vols., 1887); 'Three Men of Letters' (1895).

Tyler, Royall. An American jurist and author; born in Boston, 1757; died in Brattleboro, Vt., Aug. 16, 1826. In 1794 he was judge of the Supreme Court of Vermont, and in 1800 Chief Justice. He wrote the first American play to be acted by regular comedians: 'The Contrast,' produced in 1786 at New York. He also wrote: 'May-Day: A Comedy' (1787); 'The Georgia Spec.; or, Land in the Moon' (1797); 'The Algerine Captive' (1799); 'Moral Tales for American Youths'; 'The Yankee in London'; and contributed many sketches, verses, and essays to various journals and magazines.

Tylor, Edward Burnett. An English writer on the early history of civilization; born at Camberwell, Oct. 2, 1832. He wrote: 'Anahuac; or, Mexico and the Mexicans' (1861); 'Early History of Mankind and of Civilization' (1865; 3d ed. 1878); 'Primitive Culture: Researches into the Development of Mythology, Philosophy, Religion, Art, and Custom' (1871; 3d ed. 1891); 'Anthropology' (1881).

Tyndall, John. A British physicist and writer on science; born at Leighlin Bridge, near Carlow, Ireland, Aug. 2, 1820; died at Haslemere, Surrey, England, Dec. 4, 1893. He studied in Germany; in 1850 he published in the Philosophical Magazine 'Discoveries in Magnetism.' He was elected a Fellow of the Royal Society in 1852; professor of natural philosophy at the Royal Institution in 1853, and in 1867 its superintendent. He was the first to climb the Weisshorn, and subsequently reached the summit of the Matterhorn; and published: 'Philosophical Transactions in Glaciers of the Alps' (1860); 'Mountaineering in 1861' (1862); and 'Hours of Exercise in the Alps' (1871). 'Heat Considered as a Mode of Motion' appeared in 1863; 'Dust and Disease,' 1870. In 1872 he lectured in the United States: the profits he devoted as a fund "in aid of students who devote themselves to original research." Besides the works mentioned, he published: 'Sound: A Course of Eight Lectures' (2d ed. 1875); 'Faraday as a Discoverer' (1868); 'Nine Lectures on Light' (1870); 'Essays on the Use and Limit of the Imagination in Science' (1871); 'The Forms of Water in Clouds and Rivers, Ice and Glaciers' (1872); 'Essays on the Floating Matter of the Air' (1881); and 'New Fragments' (1892); besides many others. He received honorary degrees from the Universities of Cambridge and Edinburgh, and was made D. C. L. by Oxford.

Tyng, Stephen Higginson. A prominent American clergyman, long rector of St. George's Church, New York; born in Newburyport, Mass., March 1, 1800; died in Irvington, N. Y., Sept. 4, 1885. For several years he edited the Episcopal Recorder, the Protestant Churchman, etc., and he published in book form many volumes; among them: 'Lectures on the Law and Gospel' (1832); 'Sermons' (1839–52); 'Recollections of England' (1847); 'The Israel of God' (1854); 'Christ Is All' (1852); 'The Rich Kinsman' (1856); 'Forty Years' Experience in Sunday Schools' (1860); 'The Prayer Book' (1863–67).

Tyrtæus (tir-tē'us). A Greek lyric poet; he flourished at the time of the second Messenian war in the latter half of the seventh century B. C. Fragments only of his poems have been preserved.

Tyrwhitt, Thomas (ter'it). An English classical scholar and writer; born in London,

March 27, 1730; died there, Aug. 15, 1786. Among his works are: 'Observations on Some Passages of Shakespeare' (1766); a celebrated edition of Chaucer (1773); editions of Isæus's 'Orphica' and Aristotle's 'Poetics'; critical dissertations on Babrius, Euripides, Aristophanes, and Strabo. He was the original editor of 'Rowley's Poems,' for which he furnished a preface and glossary, and subsequently added an appendix to prove that they were written by Chatterton.

Tytler, Alexander Fraser, Lord Woodhouselee. A Scottish historical writer; born in Edinburgh, Oct. 15, 1747; died there Jan. 5, 1813. He wrote, besides many other works, 'Essay on the Principles of Translation' (1791–1813); 'The Elements of General History, Ancient and Modern' (1801), which was long an authoritative text-book; 'Life of Lord Kames' (1807); and 'Life of Petrarch' (1810).

Tytler, Patrick Fraser. A Scottish historian and biographer, son of Alexander F.; born in Edinburgh, Aug. 30, 1791; died at Great Malvern, England, Dec. 24, 1849. His principal works were: Lives of James Crichton of Cluny, commonly called "The Admirable Crichton" (1819), Sir Thomas Craig of Riccarton (1823), and John Wicklyff (1826); 'Scottish Worthies' (1832–33); 'Sir Walter Raleigh' (1833); 'An Historical View of the Progress of Discovery on the Northern Coasts of America,' etc. (1832); 'History of Scotland from 1149 to the Union of the Crowns in 1613' (9 vols., 1828–43; 5th ed. 1866).

Tzetzes, Joannes (tzet'zes). A Greek grammarian and poet; born about 1110; died about 1180. Among his works are: 'The Book of Histories,' a philosophico-historical didactic poem; 'Iliacs,' a poem in continuation of Homer's Iliad; and several other poetical compositions.

Tzschirner, Heinrich Gottlieb (chēr'ner). A German theological writer; born at Wittweida in Saxony, Nov. 14, 1778; died February 1828, at Leipsic, where he was professor of theology. He wrote: 'Protestantism and Catholicism from the Standpoint of Politics' (4th ed. 1824); 'The Fall of Gentilism' (1829); and a continuation of Schröckh's 'Church History.'

U

Ubaldini, Petruccio (ö-bäl-dē'nē). An Italian historian; born at Florence, about 1524; died at London, about 1600. He wrote: 'Life of Charlemagne' (1581); 'Description of Scotland and its Isles' (1588); 'Lives of Illustrious Ladies of England and Scotland' (1591); 'Precepts, Moral, Political, and Economic' (1592).

Uberti, Fazio (or **Bonifacio**) **degli** (ö-bār'tē). An Italian poet; born in Florence; died about 1367. He was a grandson of Uberti, one of

the Florentine leaders of the Ghibelline faction, and was driven into exile by the Guelphs. He wrote an unfinished descriptive poem called 'The News of the World,' which was quite celebrated.

Ubicini, Jean Henri Abdolonyme (ü-bē-sē-nē'). A French publicist; born at Issoudun, 1818; died at Vernon-sur-Brenne, Oct. 27, 1884. He wrote: 'Memoirs Justifying the Roumanian Revolution' (1849); 'The Eastern

Question Confronting Europe' (1854); 'The Serbs in Turkey' (1865); 'Eastern Rumelia since the Treaty of Berlin' (1880); 'Sources of Roman History' (1886).

Uchard, Bernardin, Seigneur de Monspey (ü-shär'). A French poet of the first half of the 17th century. He is noted for two poems written in Southern French patois : 'The Groans of the Poor Farm Laborer over the Dread He Has of War' (1615), and 'The Woman of Piedmont' (1619).

Uchard, Mario. A French playwright and story-writer; born at Paris, Dec. 28, 1824; died there, July 31, 1893. Among his dramatic compositions are: 'The Husband's Return' (1858); 'Second Youth' (1859); 'A Burgomaster's Prosperity' (1864); 'The Charmers' (1864). His novels include: 'Raymon' (1862); 'Gertrude's Marriage' (1862); 'Countess Diana' (1864); 'A Last Passion' (1866); 'My Uncle Barbassou' (1876); 'My Cousin Antoinette' (1891).

Uda, Felice (ö'dä). An Italian poet and publicist, brother of Michele; born at Cagliari in Sardinia, Feb. 25, 1832. He wrote: 'Wishes and Hopes' (1852), a volume of verses, and 'Memories and Affections' (1862), both of which were received with great favor; also 'Literary Sketches' (1863); a series of essays on 'Leopardi and Poerio'; 'Dante and Modern Poetry'; the comedies 'The Heart and the Age' and 'Every-Day Saints'; and 'Miguel Cervantes,' a literary study (1873).

Uda, Michele. An Italian dramatist and novelist; born at Cagliari, 1830. At 20 he joined a band of strolling players, and wrote or adapted comedies for them. Among his original compositions are the comedies 'The Widow's Suitors,' played by Ristori with great success, and 'Mask and Face'; and the dramas 'In the Coffin' and 'The Workingman and his Family.' His finest work is the brilliant comedy 'The Renegades' (1858). Among his novels are 'A Poor Devil,' and 'From Herod to Pilate.'

Udall, Nicholas (ū'dạl). An English dramatist; born in Hampshire, in 1505; died in 1556. He was a Fellow of Corpus Christi College, Oxford, and master of Eton. His schoolbooks were very popular; but he is chiefly remembered as the author of 'Ralph Royster Doyster,' the first regular comedy in the English language, which was certainly in existence as early as 1551. The best edition is one prepared for the Shakspere Society, by William Durrant Cooper (1847).

Ueberweg, Friedrich von (ü'ber-veG). A German philosopher; born in Leichlingen, Jan. 22, 1626; died at Königsberg, June 9, 1871. His chief works are: 'Outline of the History of Philosophy,' published in many editions, the first 1863-66; and 'System of Logic and History of Logical Science.'

Uechtritz, Friedrich (üch'trēts). A German dramatist and novelist; born at Görlitz, Sept. 12,

1800; died there, Feb. 15, 1875. Among his tragedies are: 'Rome and Spartacus,' and 'Rome and Otto III.' (1823); 'Alexander and Darius' (1827); 'The Sword of Honor'; 'Rosamund' (1833). His dramatic poem 'The Babylonians in Jerusalem' (1836) is notable for elevation of thought and lyric grandeur. Among his novels are: 'Albrecht Holm' (5 vols., 1851-53); 'The Bride's Brothers' (3 vols., 1860); and 'Eleazar' (3 vols., 1867), a story of the great Jewish war.

Ughelli, Ferdinando (ö-gel'lē). An Italian historian; born at Florence, 1595; died 1670. He was a Cistercian monk and abbot. His principal work is 'Italia Sacra' (9 vols., 1642-48), an account of all the episcopal sees of Italy, with lists of the bishops and a great deal of general information regarding the history of Italy. He wrote also 'Christian Gaul' (1656).

Ugoni, Camillo (ö-gō'nē). An Italian historian of literature; born at Brescia, 1784; died there, 1855. He wrote 'Italian Literature in the Second Half of the 18th Century' (1856).

Uhland, Ludwig. A celebrated German lyric poet; born at Tübingen, April 26, 1787; died Nov. 13, 1862. His ballads and songs are classic; first collected in 1815, the 60th edition (1875), posthumous, gathered the pieces found among his papers. Besides these he wrote two dramas: 'Ernest, Duke of Suabia' (1817), and 'Ludwig the Bavarian' (1819). In prose he wrote: 'The Old French Epos' (1812); 'Walther von der Vogelweide' (1822); 'The Myth of Thor, according to Norse Tradition' (1836). He made a valuable collection of 'Ancient High and Low German Folk Songs' (1844-45).

Uhlhorn, Gerhard (öl'hôrn). A German theological writer; born at Osnabrück, Feb. 17, 1826. Among his works are: 'The Grounds of Tertullian's Chronology' (1852); 'The Basilidian System' (1855); 'Christmas Customs and Usages' (1869); 'The Struggle of Christianity with Heathenism' (1874); 'Catholicism and Protestantism in Face of the Social Problem' (1887); 'The Church's Care of the Poor as related to the Present Time' (1890). Died 1901.

Uhlich, Leberecht (ö'lich). A German church reformer; born at Cöthen, Feb. 27, 1799; died at Magdeburg, March 23, 1872. He founded the independent ecclesiastical organization styled "Free Parishes." Among his writings are: 'Christianity and Church' (2d ed. 1846); 'The Little Book of the Kingdom of God' (1845); 'Thrones in Heaven and on Earth' (1845).

Ujeski, Corneli (ö-yes'kē). A Polish poet; born in Galicia, 1823. After terminating his studies in his native country, he went to Paris, there devoting himself to the study of ancient and modern literature. Most of his own poetry is inspired by love of his country, whose misfortunes he deplores. Among his works are: 'Lamentations of Jeremiah' (1847), considered one of the masterpieces of Polish literature;

'The Song of Solomon' (1840); 'Odorless Flowers' (1848); 'Marathon,' a poem; 'A Fearful Night'; etc.; as well as collections of shorter poems.

Ujfalvy, Karl Eugen von (ö-i-fäl've), **Mezö-Kövesd.** An Austrian philologist and anthropologist; born at Vienna, May 16, 1842. He is author of: 'French Scientific Expedition to Russia, Siberia, and Turkestan' (6 vols., 1878–80); 'Researches in Biblical Ethnography' (1872); 'Anthropological Results of a Visit to Central Asia' (1880); 'Parsees and Brahmins' (1887).

Ujfalvy, Maria, wife of Karl Eugen. She wrote 'From Paris to Samarcand' (1881), and 'Travels of a Parisian in the Western Himalayas.'

Ukert, Friedrich August (ö'kart). A German classical scholar; born at Eutin in Lubeck, 1780; died 1851. Among his writings are: 'How the Ancients Determined Distances' (1813); 'Homer's Geography' (1815); 'Geography of the Greeks and Romans' (3 vols., 1816–46); 'Demons, Heroes, and Genii' (1850).

Ulbach, Louis (ül-bak'). A French poet and political writer; born in Troyes (Aube) in 1822. He became editor of the Revue de Paris in 1853. He published a volume of poems entitled 'Gloriana' (1844); several tales; and political letters distinguished for their verve and causticity.

Ule, Otto (ö'lė). A German writer on natural science; born at Frankfort on the Oder, Jan. 22, 1820; died at Halle, Aug. 6, 1876. His principal works are: 'The Universe' (3 vols., 3d ed. 1859); 'Wonders of the Starry World' (1861); 'Popular Natural Science' (1865–67); 'The Earth according to its Superficial Phenomena' (1873–76).

Ulfilas, or **Wulfila** (ul'fi-las). The Gothic translator of the Bible; born about 310, in the country of the Goths north of the Danube; died about 381, at Constantinople. He was the first bishop of the Arian Visigoths. He translated the whole of the Bible, except the books of Kings, into Gothic. Of this translation there are extant a considerable part of the Gospels, Corinthians complete, fragments of the other epistles and of Ezra and Nehemiah, and a few passages of Genesis, Ezekiel, and Maccabees. The most considerable MS. copy, called Codex Argenteus, is in the library of the University of Upsala.

Ulliac-Trémandeure, Sophie (ü-yäk'-trä-mon-der'). A French story-writer; born at Lorient, 1794; died at Paris, 1862. Among her stories, all intended for youthful readers, are: 'The Fowler' (1825); 'Old Daniel's Sundays' (1833); 'The Little Hunchback' (1833); 'Mother Goose's Stories' (1842): some of her stories were crowned by the Academy. She wrote also 'An Old Woman's Reminiscences' (2 vols., 1861).

Ullmann, Karl (öl'män). A German theological writer; born at Epfenbach in the Palatinate, March 15, 1796; died at Karlsruhe, Jan. 12, 1865. He was appointed professor in the University of Heidelberg in 1826. Among his works are: 'Gregory of Nazianzus' (1825); 'Reformers before the Reformation' (2 vols., 1841); 'Historical or Mythical?' (1838), a critique of Strauss's 'Life of Jesus.'

Ulloa, Alfonso de (öl-yō'ä). A Spanish writer of history who lived in the 16th century; died about 1580. His principal works are: 'Life of the Emperor Charles V.' (1560); 'Life of the Emperor Ferdinand' (1565); 'History of the Capture of Tripoli in Barbary' (1566); 'History of Europe, 1564–66' (1570).

Ulloa, Antonio de. A Spanish statesman and writer of history; born at Seville, Jan. 12, 1716; died near Cadiz, July 5, 1795. He spent many years in North and South America, and was governor of Louisiana in 1766. Among his writings are: 'Account of a Voyage to South America' (1748); 'American Notes: Physico-Historical Talks on South America and Eastern North America' (1772); 'Secret Information concerning America' (1826), confidential reports made to the Spanish ministry.

Ulloa, Martin de. A Spanish philologist and historical writer; born at Seville, 1730; died at Cordova, 1800. He wrote: 'Memoir on the Origin and Genius of the Castilian Language' (1760); 'Dissertation on the Origin of the Goths' (1781); 'Researches on the First Inhabitants of Spain' (1789); 'Dissertation on Duels' (1789).

Ulloa y Pereira, Luis de (öl-yōä' ē pā-rā'ē-rä). A Spanish poet; born at Toro in Leon, about 1590; died 1660. His most notable work is 'Rachel' (1569), a poem on the amours of Alfonso VIII. and a fair Jewess of Toledo.

Ulpian (ul'pi-an) — Lat. **Ulpianus** (ul-pi-ā'nus), **Domitius.** An eminent Roman jurist; born about 170 A. D. (?) in Tyre; killed 228 A.D. Alexander Severus made him his secretary and prætorian prefect; the prætorian soldiers mutinied and murdered him. He was the author of a work entitled 'Ad Edictum,' and other legal treatises greatly valued, all now lost but a few fragments.

Ulrich von Lichtenstein (öl'rich fon lich'-ten-stin). A Middle High German lyric poet; born about 1200; died about 1275. He belonged to a noble family of Styria, and was long incarcerated as the leader of an unruly faction there. His principal works are: 'Court to the Ladies,' describing his amours and adventures from 1222 to 1255; and 'The Ladies' Book,' from 1257: both valuable monuments of the manners and morals of the age.

Ulrici, Hermann (öl-rē'tsē). A German scholar, critic, and philosopher; born at Pförte, Saxony, March 23, 1806; died at Halle, where he was professor, Jan. 11, 1884. He published in 1833 his 'Characteristics of Ancient Historiography.' This was followed by his 'History of Poetic Art in Greece' (2 vols., 1835), and a 'Treatise on Shakespeare's Dramatic

Art' (1839), which was received with great favor. His philosophical works include 'On the Principle and Method of Hegel's Philosophy' (1841), and 'God and Nature' (1862).

Ulstedt, Philipp (öl'stet). A celebrated German alchemist of the first half of the 16th century. He wrote : 'The Philosopher's Heaven; or, The Secrets of Nature, by Philippus Ulstedt, Patrician of Nuremberg' (1528).

Umbreit, Friedrich Wilhelm Karl (öm'brīt A German theological writer; born in Saxony April 11, 1795; died June 11, 1860. He was professor of theology in the University of Heidelberg. Among his writings are : 'Philological, Critical, and Philosophical Commentary on the Proverbs of Solomon' (1826); 'Fundamental Points of the Old Testament' (1843).

Umpfenbach, Karl Friedrich (ömp'fen-bäċh). A German political economist; born at Giessen, June 5, 1832; professor of political economy in the University of Königsberg. His principal works are : 'Text-Book of the Science of Finance' (2 vols., 1859-60); 'Doctrine of National Economy' (1867); 'Capital as related to Civilization' (1879); 'Old-Age Insurance and State Socialism' (1883).

Underwood, Benjamin Franklin. An American editor and author; born in 1839. He was editor of the Index in Boston; and wrote 'Influence of Christianity upon Civilization,' and 'Essays and Lectures.'

Underwood, Francis Henry. An American man of letters; born in Enfield, Mass., Jan. 12, 1825; died at Leith, Scotland, Aug. 7, 1894. He was an active abolitionist; clerk of the Massachusetts Senate in 1852; afterward literary adviser of Phillips, Sampson & Co. He originated, and assisted in the early management of the Atlantic Monthly; was elected clerk of the superior court in Boston, which position he held for eleven years. In 1885 he was appointed United States Consul at Glasgow ; in 1888 the University of Glasgow conferred upon him the degree of LL. D. His works include a 'Hand-Book of American Literature' (1872); 'Cloud Pictures,' a series of imaginative stories musical in theme (1877); 'Lord of Himself,' a novel of old times in Kentucky (1874); 'Man Proposes' (1880); 'The True Story of Exodus,' an abridgment of Brugsch Bey's work (1880); and biographical sketches of Longfellow (1882), Lowell (1882), and Whittier (1883).

Underwood, Lucien Marcus. An American educator and botanist; born in New York, 1853. He is professor of botany at Syracuse University since 1883, and has published : 'Systematic Plant Record' (1881); 'Our Native Ferns, and How to Study Them' (1881); 'North American Hepaticæ' (1884); 'Our Native Ferns and their Allies' (1888). He died in 1907.

Unger, Franz (öng'er). An Austrian botanist and palæontologist; born at Leutschach in Styria, Nov. 30, 1800; died at Gratz, Feb. 13, 1870. Among his works are : 'On the Influence of Soil on the Distribution of Plants' (1836); 'The Primordial World' (1851); 'Anatomy and Physiology of Plants' (1855); 'Scientific Memorabilia of a Tour in Greece and the Ionian Islands' (1862); 'The Island of Cyprus' (1865).

Upham, Charles W. A Unitarian minister and writer; born in St. John, N. B., in 1802. He published 'Lectures on Witchcraft,' etc. (1831); 'Life of Sir Henry Vane' in Sparks's 'American Biography'); and made numerous contributions to the North American Review, Christian Examiner, etc. He died ——, 1875.

Upham, Thomas Cogswell. An American Unitarian clergyman of Salem, Mass; born in Deerfield, N. H., Jan. 30, 1799; died in New York city, April 2, 1872. Among his works are : 'Outlines of Imperfect and Disordered Mental Action' (1840); 'Life of Madame Guyon,' etc. (1847); 'Life of Faith' (1848); 'American Cottage Life,' a series of poems (1850); 'Letters from Europe, Egypt, and Palestine' (1855); 'Life of Catherine Adorna' (1856); and 'Christ in the Soul' (1872).

Upton, George Putnam. An American journalist and musical critic; born in Roxbury, Mass., Oct. 25, 1834; removed to Chicago, 1855, and has since been identified with musical journalism. He has published: 'Letters of Peregrine Pickle' (1869); 'The Great Fire' (1872); 'Memories' (translated from Max Müller, 1879); 'Woman in Music,' an essay (1880); 'Lives' of Hayden, Liszt, and Wagner (1883-84); 'The Standard Operas' (1885); 'The Standard Oratorios' (1886); 'The Standard Cantatas' (1887); 'The Standard Symphonies' (1888) ; 'Life of Theodore Thomas' (1905).

Urbanski, Ladislas (ör-bän'ski). A Polish dramatist and miscellaneous writer; born in Lithuania, 1796; died at Warsaw, 1857. Among his more noteworthy writings are: 'The Sorcerers,' a poem (1831); 'Paradoxes against Liberty' (1833); 'Venice Saved,' a tragedy (1834); 'Poland, Historical, Poetical, and Literary' (1836); 'Sketch of the Manners of Country People' (1841); 'Russia from the Point of View of European Civilization' (1841).

Urfé, Honoré d'. A noted French romance-writer; born in Marseilles, Feb. 11, 1568; died in Villefranche, June 1, 1625. He is celebrated for his immensely popular bucolic and allegorical romance 'Astrée' (first part, 1610). It introduces us to a sort of ideal world, in which elegant ladies and gentlemen appear clad as shepherds and shepherdesses, and make pretty observations on topics of the period. He left it unfinished, and the conclusion was supplied by his secretary.

Urlichs, Ludwig von (ör'liks). A German archæologist and philologist; born at Osnabrück, Nov. 9, 1813; died Nov. 3, 1889, at Würzburg, where he was professor of classical philology and of æsthetics. His chief works are : 'Charlotte von Schiller and her Friends' (3 vols., 1860-65); 'Contributions to a History of Art'

(1885); 'Elements and History of Classical Archæology' (1886).

Urmy, Clarence [Thomas]. An American musician and versifier; born in California, 1858. He has written 'The Rosary of Rhyme,' and 'A Vintage of Verses.'

Ursins, Jean Jouvenel des (ür-sań'). A French historian; born 1388, at Paris; died 1473, at Rheims, of which he was archbishop. His great work is 'History of Charles VI. and of the Memorable Things which Happened during 42 Years of his Reign, from 1380 to 142?'

Usener, Hermann Karl (ö'ze-ner). A German classical philologist; born at Weilburg on the Lahn, Oct. 13, 1834; professor in the University of Bonn. Among his works are: 'Philology and the Science of History' (1882); 'Ancient Greek Versification' (1887); 'Researches in the History of Religion' (1889); 'Names of Gods: An Attempt to Account for Religious Concepts' (1895).

Ussher, James. An Irish divine and church historian, archbishop of Armagh, nephew of the preceding archbishop; born in Dublin, Jan. 4, 1580–1; died March 21, 1656. He was the first student of Trinity College, Dublin; ordained 1601. In 1612 he published 'The Unbroken Succession of Christian Churches, Especially in the West.' In 1615 he was employed to draw up the articles for the Irish Established Church. He corresponded extensively with European scholars, and employed persons to visit the East for the purchase of manuscripts; two of the most valuable obtained were the Samaritan Pentateuch and the Old Testament in Syriac. In 1639 he printed his 'Antiquities of the British Churches.' His principal other works are: 'Tracts on Episcopacy'; 'The Power of the Prince and the Obedience of the Subject'; 'Annals of the Old and New Testament,' containing his famous scheme of Biblical chronology,— followed without authority, by the printers of the Authorized Version of the Bible. The volume entitled 'A Body of Divinity' (1654, folio) was compiled without his consent from his sermons and notes. He was buried in Westminster Abbey. His library was given to Trinity College, Dublin.

Ussieux, Louis d' (ü-syè'). A French dramatist and historian; born at Angoulême, 1747; died at Chartres, 1805. Among his works are: 'History of the Discovery and Conquest of the Indies by the Portuguese' (1770); 'The French Heroes; or, The Siege of St.-Jean-de-Losne,' a prose drama (1770); 'The French Decameron' 2 vols., 1774).

Ussing, Ludvig. A Danish archæologist; born at Copenhagen, April 10, 1820. He wrote: 'Greek Travels and Studies' (1857); 'Education among the Greeks and Romans' (1863); 'Greek and Roman Metre' (1893); 'Remarks on Vitruvius's Work on Architecture' (1896).

Usteri, Johann Martin (ös'ter-ē). A Swiss poet; born at Zürich, 1763; died there, July 29, 1827. He excels in narratives and idyls, written in the dialect of Zürich; among these his 'Vicar' holds the foremost place. In High German he wrote: 'Enjoy Life' (1793), which became a popular song; and a novel, 'Adventures of a Züricher' (1877).

Uz, Johann Peter (öts). A German poet; born at Ansbach, Oct. 3, 1720; died there, May 12, 1796. He wrote several spirited popular songs and ballads; 'Lyric Poems' (1749); a comic poem in Alexandrine verse, 'The Victory of the God of Love'; a didactic poem, 'The Art of being Always Cheerful' (1760); and a number of 'Epistles,' some of them entirely in verse.

Uzanne, Louis Octave (ü-zän'). A French writer on bibliography and miscellaneous subjects; born at Auxerre, Sept. 14, 1852. He was editor successively of three periodicals devoted to bibliography, the last being Le Livre Moderne. Among his works are monographs on 'The Fan,' 'The Umbrella,' etc.; also 'The Caprices of a Book-Lover' (1877); 'Her Highness, Woman' (1884); 'Our Friends, Books: Talks on Curious Literature' (1886); 'Modern Bindings'; 'Physiology of the Quays of Paris' (1890); 'The Bachelor's Prayer-Book' (1890).

V

Vachell, Horace Annesley. A novelist now residing in California; born in England, 1861. He was formerly an officer in the English service. He has written: 'The Romance of Judge Ketchum'; 'The Model of Christian Gay'; 'The Quicksands of Pactolus'; 'An Impending Sword'; 'The Pinch of Prosperity'; 'Brothers.'

Vacherot, Étienne (väsh-rō'). A French philosopher; born at Langres, July 29, 1809. He wrote a 'Critical History of the School of Alexandria' (3 vols., 1846–51); 'Democracy' (1859); 'Metaphysic and Science' (2 vols., 1858);

'Essays in Critical Philosophy' (1864); 'Religion' (1868); 'Science and Conscience' (1870); 'The External Policy of the Republic'(1881); 'The New Spiritualism' (1884). D. July 28, 1897.

Vacquerie, Auguste (väk-rē'). A French dramatist and journalist; born at Villequier in Seine-Inférieure, Nov. 19, 1819; died at Paris, Feb. 19, 1895. Besides two volumes of miscellaneous poems, he wrote the comedies 'Tragaldabas' (1848), 'Man Changes Oft' (1859), and 'Jean Baudry' (1863); 'Jealousy' (1888), a drama in verse; 'Crumbs of History' (1863);

'My Early Years in Paris' (1872); 'To-day and To-morrow' (1875); 'The Future' (1890).

Vaillant, François (vī-yäñ'). A celebrated French traveler and ornithologist; born in Paramaribo, Dutch Guiana, in 1753; died near Sézanne, November 1824. He passed many years in France and Germany, from 1764 on, studying the habits of birds. He spent 1780–84 in South Africa, exploring among the Kaffirs, etc.; and returning to France, published the interesting 'Journey in the Interior of Africa' (2 vols., 1790–96). He barely escaped death in the Terror, 1793. He published a 'Natural History of the Birds of Africa' (6 vols., 1796–1812), and several minor works on birds.

Valdés, Armando Palacio (väl-däs'). A contemporary Spanish novelist and critic, residing at Oviedo, Spain. A representative of the new realistic school of Spanish fiction, he is best known to English readers by the powerful novels 'Maximina' (1888) and 'Sister St. Sulpice' (1890), translated by N. H. Dole. Next in importance are: 'The Marquis of Peñalta' (English translation 1886); 'Idyl of an Invalid'; 'José'; 'Riverita' (of which 'Maximina' is a sequel); 'Froth.' His critical works include: 'The Athenian Orators'; 'Spanish Novelists'; 'New Journey to Parnassus.'

Valdes, Gabriel de la Concepcion (väl'des) (known as **Placido**). A Cuban poet (colored); born in Havana, 1809; died there, June 28, 1844. He spent his early years in poverty. In 1836 he resided in Matanzas, and published many poems in newspapers and reviews; some of them cost him several months' imprisonment. In 1844 he was falsely accused of implication in a conspiracy of blacks against whites, and was shot as a traitor with nineteen others. He is one of the most popular of Spanish-American poets: his poems have passed through numerous editions at home and abroad; the best is his prayer composed on the eve of death and recited on the way to execution, translated into English by Mary Webster Chapman.

Valentini, Philipp Johann Joseph. An American archæologist; born in Pennsylvania, 1828. His studies were confined to Mexican archæology, among his works being: 'The Landa Alphabet: A Spanish Fabrication'; 'Mexican Copper Tools'; 'The Olmecas and the Tultecas.' He died in 1899.

Valentinus (val-en-tī'nus). An Alexandrian gnostic philosopher; died about 160 A.D. Of the systems of gnosis his is the most profound, as judged by the fragments of his works contained in the writings of his orthodox Christian adversaries, and especially in the supposititious work of Origen, 'The Teachings of the Philosophers.'

Valera, Juan. A Spanish poet and novelist; born at Cabra in the province of Cordova, Oct. 18, 1824. He wrote: 'Poems' (1858); 'Critical Studies' (1864–84); 'Pepita Jimenez,' a novel (1874); 'The Illusions of Doctor Faustino' (1876); 'The Commendador Mendoza' (1877);

'Doña Luz' (1878); 'New Studies' (1884); 'Songs, Romances, and Poems' (1885); 'Stories, Dialogues, and Fantasies' (1887); 'A Good Reputation.' Died at Madrid, April 19, 1905.

Valerius Antias (va-lē'ri-us an'ti-as). A Roman annalist who lived in the first century B.C. He wrote 75 books, sometimes called 'Annals,' sometimes 'Histories,' beginning with the founding of the city of Rome; they survive only in fragments.

Valerius Cato, Publius. A Latin poet and grammarian of the first century B.C. He wrote a short epic, 'Diana' or 'Dictynna,' and 'Lydia,' an erotic poem. To him is ascribed the authorship of two poems in hexameters, both styled 'Portents.'

Valerius Maximus. A Roman anecdotist and rhetorician of the first century A.D. He wrote nine books of 'Memorable Doings and Sayings' of historical characters, Roman, Grecian, and barbarian, all still extant.

Valla, Lorenzo or **Laurentius** (väl'lä). An Italian classical scholar and critic; born about 1407; died Aug. 1, 1457. Among his writings are: 'Elegancies of the Latin Language' (1471); 'Of Pleasure'; a tractate 'Against the Donation of Constantine,' alluding to the fabled concession of the district of Rome to the popes.

Valle y Caviedes, Juan del (väl'yä ē kä-vē-ā'THäs). A Peruvian satirical poet; born at Lima, 1652; died there, 1692. He wrote 'Parnassus's Tooth,' a model of biting satire.

Vallentine, Benjamin Bennaton. A New York journalist, dramatist, and critic; born in England in 1843. He has written the play 'A Southern Romance,' and published: 'The Fitznoodle Papers'; 'Fitznoodle in America'; 'The Lost Train.'

Valmiki (väl-mē'kē). Believed to be the author of the 'Râmâyana' (Fortunes of Rama), a celebrated Indian epic.

Valvasoni, Erasmo di (väl-vä-sō'nē). An Italian poet; born in Friuli, 15—; died in 1593. He wrote 'Angeleida,' a poem on the war among the angels (1590); and 'The Chase,' an admired didactic poem on hunting (1591).

Vambéry, Arminius or **Armin** or **Hermann** (väm-bā're). A noted Hungarian traveler, Orientalist, and historian, now professor at Buda-Pesth; born at Szerdahely, March 19, 1832. He lived many years in Constantinople, and traveled largely in Asia. Among his works are: 'Travels in Central Asia' (1865); 'Wanderings and Adventures in Persia' (1867); 'Sketches of Central Asia' (1868); 'History of Bokhara' (1873); 'Central Asia and the Russian Boundary Question'; 'Islam in the Nineteenth Century' (1875); 'Manners in Oriental Countries' (1876); 'Primitive Civilization of the Turko-Tartar People' (1879); 'Origin of the Magyars' (1882); 'The Future Contest for India' (1886); and various linguistic works, including a 'German Turkish Dictionary,' and 'Etymological Dictionary of the Turko-Tartar Languages' (1878).

Van Anderson, Mrs. Helen. ["Van Metre."] An American lecturer, and minister of Boston; born in Iowa, 1859. She has written: 'The Right Knock'; 'It Is Possible'; 'The Story of Teddy'; 'Journal of a Live Woman.'

Vanbrugh, Sir John (van-brö'). An English dramatist; born about 1663-4; died at London, March 26, 1726. Among his dramatic compositions are: 'The Relapse' (1697); 'Æsop' (1697); 'The Provoked Wife' (1697); 'The False Friend' (1702); 'The Confederacy' (1705); 'A Journey to London,' left unfinished at his death, but completed by Colley Cibber (1728).

Van Buren, Martin. An American statesman; eighth President of the United States; born at Kinderhook, N. Y., Dec. 5, 1782; died there, July 24, 1862. He wrote 'An Inquiry into the Origin and Course of Political Parties in the United States' (1867), and many State papers.

Vancouver, George. A British navigator; born about 1758; died at London, May 10, 1798. He wrote: 'A Voyage of Discovery to the North Pacific Ocean and Round the World' (1798).

Vandegrift, Margaret. See Janvier.

Vandenhoff, George. An actor, elocutionist, and writer; born in England, Feb. 18, 1820. He came to America in 1842; and after success on the stage became famous as a teacher of elocution. He was the author of: 'The Art of Elocution' (1846); 'Dramatic Reminiscences' (1859); 'Leaves from an Actor's Note-Book' (1862); 'Clerical Assistant' (1862); 'Rules for Reading Aloud' (1862).

Van Deusen, Mrs. Mary (Westbrook). An American novelist and verse-writer, living at Rondout, N. Y.; born in New York, 1829. She has published: 'Rachel Dumont'; 'Gertrude Willoughby'; 'Colonial Dames of America'; and a volume of verse, 'Voices of my Heart.'

Van Dyke, Henry. An American Presbyterian clergyman, pastor of Brick Church, New York city; born in Pennsylvania, 1852. Among his numerous works are: 'The Story of the Psalms'; 'The Poetry of Tennyson'; 'The Christ Child in Art'; 'Little Rivers'; 'The Builders, and Other Poems.'

Van Dyke, John Charles. An American art critic, scholar, and author; born in New Brunswick, N. J., April 21, 1856. He studied art abroad (1883-88), and has written: 'Books, and How to Use Them' (1883); 'Principles of Art' (1887); 'How to Judge a Picture' (1888); 'Art for Art's Sake'; 'History of Painting'; 'Old Dutch and Flemish Masters'; 'The Open Door.'

Van Dyke, Theodore Strong. An American lawyer and writer on out-door sports; born in New Jersey, 1842. He resides in Southern California, and has written: 'Rifle, Rod, and Gun, in California' (1881); 'The Still Hunter' (1883); 'Game Birds at Home'; 'Southern California, the Italy of America' (1887); 'Studies in Pictures.'

Van Lennep, Henry John. An American missionary in Asia Minor; born in Smyrna, March 8, 1815; died in Great Barrington, Mass., Jan. 11, 1889. He traveled extensively through the East, was familiar with many Oriental dialects, and published: 'Ten Days among Greek Brigands'; 'Travels in Asia Minor' (1870); 'Bible Lands' (1879); 'The Oriental Album.'

Van Loon, Gerard (van lön). A Dutch historian and antiquary; born in Leyden in 1683. He published among other works a 'History of the Netherlands from 1555 to 1716' (4 vols., 1723), which is considered an authoritative work.

Van Ness, Thomas. An American Unitarian clergyman and author; born in Maryland, 1859. He has published: 'The Coming Religion'; 'The Ideal Commonwealth'; 'My Visit to Count Tolstoy'; 'The Coming Age.'

Van Ness, William Peter. An American jurist and author; born in Ghent, N. Y., in 1778; died in New York city, Sept. 6, 1826. He was the friend of Burr, took his challenge to Hamilton, and was one of Burr's seconds. Under the pen-name of "Aristides" he published: 'Examination of Charges against Aaron Burr' (1803); with John Woodworth edited 'Laws of New York' (2 vols., 1813); also wrote 'Concise Narrative of Gen. Jackson's First Invasion of Florida' (1826).

Van Rensselaer, Mrs. Mariana (Griswold). An American author and art critic; born in New York city, Feb. 23, 1851. She has contributed largely to current periodicals on art and architecture, and published the valuable books: 'Art Out of Doors'; 'English Cathedrals'; 'American Etchers' (1886); 'Henry Hobson Richardson and his Works' (1888); 'One Man who was Content, and Other Stories'; 'Niagara.'

Van Zile, Edward Sims. An American journalist and novelist; born in New York, 1863. He has written: 'Wanted — A Sensation'; 'The Last of the Van Slacks'; 'A Magnetic Man'; 'Don Miguel, and Other Stories'; 'The Manhattaners'; and 'A Crown Prince.'

Vapereau, Louis Gustave (väp-rö'). A noted French scholar and compiler; born at Orleans, April 4, 1819. He was professor of philosophy at the College of Tours for ten years; admitted to the bar in 1854, and about the same time made editor of the famous 'Universal Dictionary of Contemporaries' (1858; 6th ed. 1891-93). Among his other important works are: 'Literary and Dramatic Year' (11 vols., 1859-69); 'Universal Dictionary of Literatures' (1876); 'Historical Elements of French Literature' (2 vols., 1883-85). He was Inspector-General of Public Instruction in 1877, and received the Cross of the Legion of Honor in 1878.

Varin, Charles (vär-añ'). A French vaudeville writer; born at Nancy, 1793; died at Paris, 1869. Among his productions are: 'Borrowed Wives' (1832); 'A Ball in High Life' (1836); 'My Sister Mirette' (1861); 'The Ill-Guarded Girls' (1865); 'Madame Ajax' (1866); etc.

Varnhagen, Francisco Adolpho de, Viscount of Porto Seguro (värn-ä'gen). A celebrated Brazilian diplomatist and historian; born at São João de Ypanema (São Paulo), Feb. 17, 1816; died at Vienna, Austria, June 29, 1878. His youth was passed in Portugal; on his return to Brazil in 1841, he was appointed to diplomatic positions in Lisbon, Paraguay, Peru, Vienna, and other places. He is indisputably the first of Brazilian historians, his works being distinguished by profound research and lucid style. Chief among them are: 'General History of Brazil' (2 vols., 1854-57); 'History of the Struggles with the Dutch in Brazil' (2d ed. 1874); 'Anthology of Brazilian Poetry' (1850-53); biographical studies; monographs on Amerigo Vespucci; etc.

Varnhagen von Ense, Karl A. (värn-ä'gen fon en'sė). A distinguished Prussian diplomatist and author, regarded as one of the best of German prose-writers; born in Düsseldorf, Feb. 21, 1785; died in Berlin, Oct. 10, 1858. In 1814 he married Rahel Levin, an accomplished Jewess, and became conspicuous in Berlin society. His numerous works consist mainly of biographical studies,—including two memorials of his wife, who died in 1833),—tales, criticisms, and poems. Of his 'Diaries' several volumes have appeared.

Varro, Marcus Terentius (var'rō). The most universally learned of ancient Roman scholars; born in 116 B. C. at Reate in the Sabine Territory, and hence surnamed Reatinus; died about 27 B. C. His special object of research was Roman antiquity,—language, usages, laws, public institutions, etc. Among his poetical writings were 150 books of joco-serious 'Menippean Satires,' in prose and verse, after the style of Menippus the Cynic. He wrote among others, 76 books of 'Logistorics,' or notes on the education of children; 41 books on 'Roman Antiquities'; 15 books of 'Portraits' of 700 notabilities, with a prose biography and a metrical eulogium of each; 9 books of 'Sciences,' an encyclopædic work; treatises 'On the Latin Language,' and 'On Farming.' Of all his writings there now remain only the treatise 'On Farming'; six books of the 'Latin Language,' in an imperfect state; and numerous other fragments.

Varro, Publius Terentius, surnamed **Atacinus** from Atax in Narbonese Gaul, his birthplace. A Roman poet; born about 82 B. C.; died about 37 B. C. His works, of which but small fragments remain, are: 'The Sequanian War,' an epic celebrating the exploits of Cæsar in Gaul; some 'Satires,' of which Horace speaks slightingly; 'The Argonauts,' an epic in imitation of Apollonius Rhodius, highly praised by Ovid; a number of other imitations of Greek poets, among them 'Chorography,' a didactic poem on geography, and 'Ephemeris,' a poem on weather prognostics.

Vasari, Giorgio Cavaliere (vä-sä'rē). An Italian painter and writer; born in Arezzo,

1512; died in 1574. He studied under Michael Angelo and other masters; he was then patronized by the Medici family at Florence, where Cardinal Farnese employed him to write the lives of artists. He published these in 1550 with the title of 'Lives of the most Eminent Painters, Sculptors, and Architects' in two volumes, frequently reprinted. An English translation by Mrs. Jonathan Foster was published in London, 1850-53.

Vasconcellos, Carolina Wilhelmina Michaelis de. A German-Portuguese littérateur, wife of J. A.; born at Berlin, March 15, 1851. She is a contributor to the leading literary magazines and reviews of Germany and Portugal, and has written: 'Studies on the Meanings of Spanish Words' (1886); 'Romance Studies' (1891); 'History of Portuguese Literature' (1893); 'Etymological Fragments' (1894).

Vasconcellos, Fonseca e, Joaquim Antonio da (väs''kōn-sel'lōs). A Portuguese biographer and historian; born at Oporto, Feb. 10, 1849; professor of German language and literature in the Lyceum there. His principal works are: 'The Musicians of Portugal' (1870); 'Reform in the Teaching of the Fine Arts' (3 vols., 1877-79); 'Albert Dürer and his Influence in the Peninsula' (1877); 'Francis the Hollander' (1879); 'Goësiana,' 4 vols. 1877-81.

Vasey, George. An English botanist and physician; born near Scarborough, Feb. 28, 1822. He is now connected with the Department of Agriculture at Washington. His published works include: 'The Philosophy of Laughing and Smiling'); 'Descriptive Catalogue of the Native Forest Trees of the United States' (1876); 'The Grasses of the United States' (1883); 'Descriptive Catalogue of the Grasses of the United States' (1885); and 'Grasses of the South' (1887).

Vasfi, Kéfévi, Sheik (väs'fē). A contemporary Turkish poet, critic, and littérateur of considerable repute in his own country. Besides numerous translations of philosophical maxims, moral anecdotes, etc., from the Arabic and Persian, he has written two volumes of original poems, 'Djézébaad' and 'Feïzabad,' which are imbued with the Oriental mysticism.

Vasili, Compte Paul. A pseudonym of Madame Edmond Adam. See **Lamber**.

Vassar, John Guy. An American philanthropist, nephew of Matthew Vassar the founder of Vassar College; born in Poughkeepsie, N. Y., June 15, 1811; died there, Oct. 27, 1888. He was one of the trustees of Vassar College; traveled extensively, and wrote: 'Twenty Years around the World' (1861).

Vattel, Emerich (vä-tel'). A celebrated Swiss publicist and jurist; born at Couvet, Neuchâtel, April 25, 1714; died Dec. 28, 1767. His great work is 'The Law of Nations; or, Principles of the Law of Nature applied to the Affairs of Nations and Sovereigns' (2 vols., 1758). He wrote also: 'Philosophical Leisure

Hours' (1747); 'Literary, Moral, and Political Miscellanies' (1757); 'Questions of Natural Right; or, Observations on Wolf's Treatise on the Law of Nature' (1762).

Vauban, Sébastien Le Prestre de (vō-bon'). A great French military engineer; born at St. Leger de Foucher. Burgundy, May 15, 1633; died at Paris, March 30, 1707. He published nothing during his life, but since his death some of his MSS. have been printed at various times; among them: 'Notes for Instruction in the Conduct of Sieges and the Defense of Places' (1740); 'Marshal de Vauban's Hours of Idleness' (3 vols., 1842); 'Military Works' (3 vols., 1793); 'Attack and Siege of Strong Places.'

Vaudoncourt, François Guillaume de, Baron (vō-dôn-kör'). A French general and military writer; born at Vienna, Sept. 24, 1772; died at Passy near Paris, May 2, 1845. His works comprise: 'History of the Campaigns of Hannibal in Italy' (1812); histories of Napoleon's campaigns in Russia, Germany, and Italy; and 'Fifteen Years of Exile' (4 vols., 1835).

Vaughan, Charles John. An English Broad Church clergyman, religious writer, and commentator; born at Leicester in 1816; died at Llandaff. Wales, Oct. 15, 1897. He was head-master of Harrow, 1844–59; Master of the Temple, 1869–94; chaplain in ordinary to the Queen. Among his works are: 'Memorials of Harrow Sundays' (1859); 'Sundays in the Temple' (1871); 'Heroes of Faith' (1876), lectures; 'Temple Sermons' (1881); 'University Sermons' (1888); single sermons, addresses, pamphlets, etc.

Vaughan, Henry. A British poet, known as " The Silurist," from the ancient Silures of his birthplace; born in Newton, Brecknockshire, Wales, in 1622; died in April, 1695. His works are: 'Olor Iscanus: Select Poems'; 'The Bleeding Heart,' sacred poems; 'Ejaculations'; 'The Mount of Olives; or, Solitary Devotions'; and 'Thalia Rediviva.'

Vaughan, Robert. An English clergyman, editor, and historian; born in 1795; died at Torquay, June, 1868. He was a professor of history in London University; president of the Lancashire Independent College, Manchester, 1842–57; and originator and for twenty years editor of the British Quarterly Review. He published several important historical works, among which are: 'Life of John de Wycliffe' (2 vols., 1828); 'The Protectorate of Cromwell' (1838); 'History of England under the House of Stuart' (2 vols., 1840); 'The Age of Great Cities' (1842); 'Revolutions in English History' (1859–60).

Vauvenargues, Luc de Clapier, Marquis de (vōv-närg'). A French moralist; born at Aix, Aug. 6, 1715; died March 9, 1747. He wrote a valuable 'Introduction to a Knowledge of the Human Mind' (1746), to which are appended 'Reflections' and 'Maxims.' His moral philosophy inclines toward the Stoic school.

Vazoff, Ivan (vä'zof). A notable Bulgarian author; born in Sopot, 1850. Besides numerous poems, he has written 'Under the Yoke' and other widely read novels.

Veeder, Mrs. Emily Elizabeth (Ferris). A novelist and verse-writer of St. Louis, Mo.; born in New York, 1841. She has written: 'Her Brother Donnard'; 'Entranced'; 'The Unexpected'; 'In the Garden, and Other Poems.'

Vega, Lope de (Lope Felix de Vega Carpio). A celebrated Spanish dramatist; born in Madrid, Nov. 25, 1562; died Aug. 21, 1635. He is credited with 1,500 comedies, of which over 500 are extant and 340 well known; 'King and Peasant' is most frequently acted. He also wrote two narrative poems, 'Angelica' and 'Jerusalem Conquered'; five mythological poems, 'Circe,' 'Andromeda,' 'Philomela,' 'Orpheus,' and 'Proserpine'; three historical poems, 'San Isidro,' 'The Dragon,' and 'The Maid of Almudena'; and a comic-heroic poem, 'Gatomachy' (War of Cats); besides sonnets, and several novels, including 'Journey through my Country.'

Vega de la Ventura (vā'gä dā lä vän-tö'rä). An Argentine poet; born in Buenos Ayres, July 14, 1807; died in Madrid, Spain, in 1865. After political imprisonment he held places in the Spanish government; was secretary to Queen Maria Christina, and in 1856 was appointed director of the Royal Conservatory. He wrote: 'The Song of Songs' (Madrid, 1826); 'An Epithalamic Cantata' (1827); 'Agitation,' an ode (1834); 'The 18th of June' (1837); 'The Defense of Seville,' an ode (1838); 'The Man of the World,' a comedy (1840); and the tragedies 'The Death of Cæsar' (1842); 'Don Fernando de Antequera' (1845). He is considered one of the best modern Spanish poets.

Vegetius Renatus, Flavius (ve-jē'tē-us renā'tus). A Latin writer on the art of war, fourth and fifth centuries. He compiled in four books an 'Epitome of the Military Art.' There is an ancient treatise, 'On the Veterinary Art,' credited to him.

Vehse, Karl Eduard (vā'zè). A German historian; born at Freiburg, Saxony, Dec. 18, 1802; died at Striesen near Dresden, June 18, 1870. He was archivist in Dresden, 1825; later settled in Berlin; but was imprisoned and banished for his 'History of the German Courts since the Reformation' (48 vols., 1851–58). Besides this monumental work, he wrote: 'History of the Emperor Otho the Great' (1828); 'Tables of Universal History' (1834); 'Course of Universal History' (1842); and 'Shakespeare as Protestant, Politician, Psychologist, and Poet' (2 vols., 1851).

Veitch, John. A Scottish poet, littérateur, and philosophical writer; born in Peebles, 1829; died there, Sept. 3, 1894. A memoir of his friend Sir William Hamilton first brought him into notice; but he will be best remembered for his poetical and literary works: 'Hillside Rhymes' (1872); 'The Tweed and Other Poems'

(1875); 'The History and Poetry of the Scottish Border' (1878; new ed. 1893), a monumental work; 'Merlin, and Other Poems'; 'The Theism of Wordsworth'; 'The Feeling for Nature in Scottish Poetry,' a delightful book.

Velez-Herrera, Ramón (vä'leth-ā-rā'rä). A Cuban author; born in Havana in 1808; died there in 1887. He abandoned law for literature. The first collection of his poems was published at Havana in 1833, a second in 1837, and a third in 1838. He also published: 'Elvira de Oquendo'; 'The Two Bridegrooms,' a comedy (1848); 'Autumn Flowers,' a collection of poems (1849); 'Cuban Romances' (1856); 'Napoleon in Berlin,' a tragedy (1860); and 'Flowers of Winter,' poems (1882).

Velleius Paterculus (vel-ē'yus pā-ter'kū-lus). A Latin historian of the first century. He wrote a 'History of Rome,' a synopsis of Roman history from the fabled migration of Æneas to 30 A. D. The latter half of the work is not without value for the early empire.

Venable, William Henry. An American author; born in Warren County, Ohio, April 29, 1836. He began to teach at 17, and taught until 1886, afterward devoting himself to literature and lecturing. He has published: 'June on the Miami, and Other Poems' (1871); 'A History of the United States' (1872); 'The School Stage,' a collection of juvenile acting plays (1873); 'Melodies of the Heart, and Other Poems' (1884); 'Footprints of the Pioneers in the Ohio Valley' (1888); 'Biography of William D. Gallagher' (1888); several pamphlets, addresses, etc. He edited 'The Dramatic Actor,' a collection of plays (1874); and 'Dramatic Scenes from the Best Authors'; 'Saga of the Oak.'

Venables. Edmund. An English clergyman and archæologist; born in London, July 5, 1819; died in Lincoln, March 5, 1895. He was canon of Lincoln Cathedral from 1867, and wrote much on architecture and archæology, among his works being: 'Walks through the Streets of Lincoln,' widely popular; 'History of the Isle of Wight' (1860); 'The Church of England: Its Planting, Settlement, Reformation, Renewed Life' (1886); 'Bunyan' (1888).

Venedey, Jakob (ven'e-dī). A German miscellaneous writer; born at Cologne, May 24, 1805; died at Badenweiler, Feb. 8, 1871. He wrote: 'Days of Travel and Rest in Normandy' (1838); 'France, Germany, and the Holy Alliance' (1842); 'Germans and Frenchmen according to their Languages and their Proverbs' (1842); 'John Hampden' (1843); 'Ireland' (1844); 'History of the German People' (4 vols., 1854-62); 'Machiavelli, Montesquieu, and Rousseau' (2 vols., 1850); 'Frederick the Great and Voltaire' (1859); 'Biographies' of Washington (1862), Franklin (1863), Stein (1868); 'The German Republicans under the French Republic' (1870).

Vennor, Henry George. A Canadian meteorologist and writer; born in Montreal, Dec. 30, 1840; died there, July 8, 1884. He was attached to the Geological Survey office till 1881. He published 'Vennor's Almanac' from 1876, which attained a large circulation; and wrote 'Our Birds of Prey' (1875) and many reports for the Geological Survey and the Canadian Naturalist.

Ventignano, Cesare Della Valle, Duke of (ven-tēn-yä' nō). An Italian poet and miscellaneous writer; born in Naples, 1777; died about 1860. Among his works are the tragedies 'The Siege of Corinth' and 'Medea'; an 'Essay on the Education of the Aristocracy and the Laboring Classes'; and a 'Philosophic View of the History of the Human Race' (1853).

Verdy du Vernois, Julius von (vär-dē'dü vär-nwä'). A Prussian soldier; born at Freistadt in Silesia, July 19, 1832. He was made general of infantry in 1888, and in 1889 Prussian minister of war. He wrote: 'The Second Army in the Campaign of 1866'; 'Studies in the History of War' (1876); 'Contribution to the Game of War' (1876); 'Studies on War' (1891-92); 'Personal Reminiscences of the War of 1870-71' (1895). His tragedy 'Alaric' was played at Strasburg in 1894.

Vere, Aubrey Thomas de. See De Vere.

Verena, Sophie (ve-rā'nä). Pseudonym of Sophie Alberti, a German miscellaneous writer; born in Potsdam, Aug. 5, 1826; died there, Aug. 15, 1892. She wrote the popular novel 'A Son of the South' (1859), and a collection of tales entitled 'Old and New' (1879).

Verga, Giovanni (vär'gä). A celebrated Italian poet and novelist; born in Sicily, 1840. His works include: 'Story of a Cricket' (1872); 'Eva' (1873); 'Stories' (1874); 'Nedda' (1874); 'Eros' (1875); 'Royal Tiger' (1876); 'Helen's Husband' (1877); 'Life in the Fields' (1880); 'I Malavoglia' (1881), translated as 'The House under the Medlar Tree'; 'Rustic Tales' (1883); 'Rustic Chivalry' (1884), from which the libretto of Mascagni's famous opera 'Cavalleria Rusticana' was derived; 'The How, the When, and the Wherefore'; etc.

Verlaine, Paul (vär-lān'). A French poet and story-writer; born at Metz, March 30, 1844; died at Paris, Jan. 8, 1896. He led a life of vagabondage, vibrating between prison and hospital. He wrote: 'Saturnine Poems' (1866); 'Gay Festivals' (1869); 'Accursed Poets' (1884); 'Of Old and of Late' (1885). Among his stories are: 'Louise Leclercq' (1886); 'Memoirs of a Widower' (1887); 'Stories Without Words' (1887); 'Love' (1888); 'Dedications' (1890); 'Good Luck' (1891); 'My Hospitals' (1891).

Verne, Jules (värn). A French writer; born in Nantes, Feb. 8, 1828. He has written a comedy in verse entitled 'The Falling-Out' followed by 'Eleven Days at Liège,' and 'The Uncle from America,' and several comic operas; but his fame rests chiefly on his more than sixty romances of science and adventure, many of

35

them translated into many other languages, even Japanese and Arabic. The first was 'Five Weeks in a Balloon' (1863). Among the others are: 'A Journey to the Centre of the Earth' (1872); 'Twenty Thousand Leagues under the Sea' (1873); 'Meridiana'; 'Around the World in Eighty Days' (1874); 'The Mysterious Island' (1875); 'Michael Strogoff' (1876); 'The Purchase of the North Pole.' Died, March, 1905.

Verplanck, Gulian C. An American scholar and writer; born in New York in 1786; died March 1870. He published anonymously in 1819 a brilliant satirical work, entitled 'The State Triumvirate.' In 1825 he was elected to Congress, and published, 1827-30, conjointly with William Cullen Bryant and Robert C. Sands, a miscellany entitled The Talisman. Among his other works are his address before the New York Historical Society entitled 'The Early European Friends of America' (1818); 'Essays on the Nature and Uses of the Evidences of Revealed Religion' (1824); and 'Discourses and Addresses on Subjects of American History, Art, and Literature' (1833). In 1846 he brought out his edition of Shakespeare, with notes, esteemed one of the best that had ever appeared.

Vertot d'Aubœuf, René Aubert de (vär-tō' dō-bèf'). A French priest and historian; born at Château Benetot (Eure), Nov. 25, 1655; died in Paris, June 15, 1735. He was historiographer of the Order of Malta. He published a 'History of the Revolutions of Portugal' (1689); 'History of the Revolutions of Sweden' (1696); 'History of the Revolutions of the Roman Republic' (1719); 'History of the Order of Malta' (1726); all more dramatic and fluent than reliable.

Very, Jones. An American poet; born in Salem, Mass., in 1813; died May 8, 1880. He published some essays and poems in 1839, and was a contributor to the Christian Register, a monthly religious magazine, and other journals. A complete edition of his essays and poems, with a biographical note of the author, was published by James Freeman Clarke, Boston, 1886.

Very, Lydia Louisa Anna. An American poet, sister of Jones Very ; born at Salem, Mass., Nov. 2, 1823; died there, Sept. 10, 1901. She wrote many poems, and her writings appeared in book form under the title 'Prose and Verse.'

Vesalius, Andreas (ve-sā'lē-us). A celebrated physician, founder of the modern science of anatomy; born at Brussels, Dec. 31, 1514; lost at sea in shipwreck off the isle of Zante, on the return from a pilgrimage imposed by the Inquisition in lieu of death, Oct. 15, 1564. His great work 'Of the Structure of the Human Body,' in seven books, illustrated with magnificent plates by Calcar, a pupil of Titian, was published at Basle (3d ed. 1568). (Complete works, edited by Boerhaave and Albinus, 2 vols., 1727.)

Vespucci, Amerigo, Latinized **Americus Vespucius** (ves-pö'chē). The celebrated Italian navigator, eponymus of the New World; born at Florence, March 9, 1451; died at Seville, Feb. 22, 1512. His 'Letters' (1502), giving an account of his voyages, especially of the voyage of 1501, were translated into Latin, Italian, French, and German, and were widely circulated. He wrote a diary called 'The Four Journals,' after his fourth voyage. The suggestion to name the newly discovered continent "America" was first offered by Martin Waldseemüller of St. Dié in Lorraine, in his work 'Introduction to Cosmography' (1507).

Veuillot, Louis (vė-yō'). An eminent French journalist; born in Boynes (Loiret), 1813; died in Paris, April 7, 1883. His works include: 'Pilgrimages in Switzerland' (1839); 'Rome and Loretto' (1841); 'The Virtuous Woman' (1844); 'The French in Algeria' (1845); 'Free-Thinkers' (1848); 'Vindex the Slave' (1849); 'The Day after the Victory' (1850); 'The Droit du Seigneur in the Middle Ages' (1854); 'The Perfume of Rome' (1861); 'The Odors of Paris' (1866); 'Paris during the Two Sieges' (1871); 'Molière and Bourdaloue' (1877); 'Poetic Works' (1878); etc.

Viardot, Louis (vyär-dō'). A French historian and art critic; born at Dijon, July 31, 1800; died at Paris, May 5, 1883. He wrote: 'History of the Arabs and Moors of Spain' (2 vols., 1851); 'The Traditional Rise of Modern Painting in Italy' (1840); 'The Museums of France' (1855); 'Spain and the Fine Arts' (1866); 'Wonders of Painting' (2 vols., 1868-69).

Viaud, Louis Marie Julien. See **Loti.**

Viaud, Théophile de (vė-ō'). A French satirical poet; born in 1590; died in 1626. He wrote elegies, tragedies, etc. In 1623 he was accused of atheism and condemned to death, but escaped, and the sentence was afterward annulled.

Vicente, Gil. See **Gil Vicente.**

Victor, Mrs. Frances Auretta (Fuller) (Barrett). An American poet and author, sister of Metta V., with whom she published an early volume of poems. She wrote 'The River of the West' (1865); 'Life and Adventures in the Rocky Mountains and Oregon' (1870); 'The New Penelope and Other Stories.' She has also contributed chapters on the history of Oregon for H. H. Bancroft's 'Pacific Coast Histories.'

Victor, Mrs. Metta Victoria (Fuller). An American poet, novelist, and sketch-writer, wife of O. J.; born near Erie, Pa., March 2, 1831; died in Hoboken, N. J., June 26, 1886. She published a story, 'The Silver Lute,' at 13; with her sister Frances, 'Poems of Sentiment and Imagination' (1851); alone but anonymously, 'Fresh Leaves from Western Woods' (1853); 'The Senator's Son: A Plea for the Maine Law' (1853), which had a great circulation in England

and America; and 'Two Mormon Wives: A Life Story' (1856). She edited the Home Monthly Magazine in 1856. She wrote many dime novels. The comic sketches 'Miss Slimmens's Window' and 'Miss Slimmens's Boarding House' (1859), and the story 'Too True,' were reprinted from periodicals. She wrote also the novels 'Figure Eight' and 'The Dead Letter'; 'Passing the Portal' (1877); 'The Bad Boy's Diary' (1880); 'The Rasher Family' (1884); 'The Naughty Girl's Diary' (1884); 'Blunders of a Bashful Man' (1885).

Victor, Orville James. An American journalist, editor, and author; born in Sandusky, O., Oct. 23, 1827. He edited the Art Journal; the United States Journal; the 'Dime Biographical Library,' for which he wrote many books; Beadle's Magazine (1866–67): and published 'History of the Southern Rebellion' (4 vols., 1862–65); 'Incidents and Anecdotes of the War' (1863); and 'History of American Conspiracies' (1864); 'Biographies.'

Victoria, full name **Alexandrina Victoria.** Queen of Great Britain and Ireland, and Empress of India; born in London, May 24, 1819, the only child of the Duke of Kent, fourth son of George III. She succeeded to the throne June 20, 1837, on the death of her uncle, William IV., third son of George III., and was crowned June 28, 1838; married Albert, prince of Saxe-Coburg-Gotha (who died Dec. 14, 1861), Feb. 10, 1840. She is author in part of 'Leaves from the Journal of Our Life in the Highlands' (1868), and 'More Leaves from the Journal of a Life in the Highlands' (1884). She supervised the preparation of lives of the Prince Consort. She died at Osborne House, Jan. 22, 1901.

Vicuña-Mackenna, Benjamin (vē-kön'yä). A Chilian historian; born in Santiago in 1831; died in Santa Rosa del Colmo, Jan. 25, 1886. He was concerned in many revolutions, traveled extensively, and held many political positions. In 1870 he acted as war correspondent during the Franco-German war; later as correspondent of the Mercurio in Berlin and Paris. At the opening of the war with Peru he became editor of El Nuevo Ferrocarril; and after the conclusion of the war, his description of it became well known for its impartiality. He wrote: 'The Siege of Chillan in 1813' (1849); 'History of Santiago' (2 vols., 1868); 'Francisco Moyén; or, What the Inquisition in America Meant' (1868); several books on the mineral riches of Chili (1883); 'Album of the Glory of Chili' (1883); 'Dolores' (1883); 'The Isles of Juan Fernandez' (1884); 'At a Gallop' (1885); 'The War in Spain' (1887); and many others.

Vida, Marco Girolamo (vē'dä). A modern Latin poet; born at Cremona, about 1489; died at Alba, Sept. 27, 1566. In his early manhood he won a European reputation with his two didactic poems in Latin, 'The Game of Chess' and 'The Silkworm.' Among his other poems are: 'On the Art of Poetry' (1527); 'The Christiad,' an epic (1535). He also wrote a dialogue 'On the Republic,' in which the interlocutors are Vida and several cardinals whose society he enjoyed at the Council of Trent.

Viehoff, Heinrich (vē'hof). A German historian of literature; born at Büttgen near Neuss, April 28, 1804; died at Treves, 1886. He wrote: 'Introduction to the Art of Poetry' (1860); 'Goethe's Poems: with Notes' (2 vols., 3d ed. 1874); 'Manual of German National Literature' (3 vols., 16th ed. 1881); 'Life and Works of Goethe' (2 vols., 5th ed. 1887), 'Schiller's Poems: with Notes' (3 vols., 6th ed. 1887); 'Life of Schiller' (3 vols., 2d ed. 1888); 'Odysseus and Nausicaa,' a tragedy in five acts, an amplification of Goethe's play. He made many metrical translations of all of Racine's plays, three of Molière's, eleven of Shakespeare's, all the plays of Sophocles, Scott's 'Lady of the Lake,' Longfellow's 'Evangeline,' and Ausonius's 'The Moselle.'

Vigny, Alfred Victor, Comte de (vēn-yē'). A French writer, member of the Academy; born in Loches, March 27, 1799; died in Paris, Sept. 18, 1863. He left military service for literature; and his romance 'Cinq-Mars' (1826) went through several editions. He also wrote several plays; his translation of 'Othello' was acted in 1829, and his 'Chatterton' was a complete triumph. In 1843 he published several poems in the Revue des Deux Mondes. His 'Consultations of Dr. Noir' appeared in 1856.

Villani, Giovanni (vē-lä'nē). An Italian historian; born at Florence about 1275; died there of the plague, 1348. He began a history of his native city, but had only brought it down to 1346 at his death. It was continued, first by his brother Matteo (died 1363, also of the plague), and by Matteo's son Filippo, who lived into the early 15th century.

Villari, Pasquale (vē-lä'rē). An Italian historian; born at Naples, 1827. His principal works are: 'History of Girolamo Savonarola and his Times' (2 vols., 1859–61; new and much improved ed. 1887–88); 'Niccolò Machiavelli and his Times' (3 vols., 1877–82; new ed. 3 vols., 1895); 'Ancient Legends and Traditions Illustrating the Divine Comedy' (1865); 'Essays Critical, Historical, and Literary' (1868); 'Teaching History' (1869); 'The School and the Social Question in Italy' (1872); 'A Treatise on the Social Question in Italy' (1902).

Villaverde, Cirilo (vēl-yä-vär'dä). A Cuban author; born in San Diego de Nuñez in 1812. He graduated in law at Havana, but devoted himself to literature and teaching. He was condemned to death for political action in 1849, but escaped to the United States, and contributed to literary periodicals. He published: 'El Espetori de Oro'; 'Los Dos Amores' (1837); 'El Guajiro' (1840); 'La Pimeta Calada'; 'La Tejedora de Sombreros' (1840–45); and 'Cecilia Valdés' (1881), his masterpiece, a genuine Cuban novel, highly praised by the most competent critics of Spain and Spanish America.

Villegas, Estevan Manuel de (vēl-yā'gäs). A celebrated Spanish lyric poet; born in Old Castile in 1596; died in 1669. He published a collection of poems entitled 'Amatorias' (1620); he also translated Horace and Anacreon into Spanish verse, and made a prose translation of Boethius.

Villehardouin, Geoffrey de (vēl-är-dwań'). A French diplomatist and historian; born at Arcis-sur-Aube about 1165; died about 1213. He participated in the Fourth Crusade and the sack of Constantinople, and wrote a most valuable account of it, entitled 'The History of the Capture of Constantinople by the French and Venetians.' It is supposed to be the oldest prose history in the French language.

Villemain, Abel François (vēl-mań'). A French writer; born in Paris, June 11, 1790; died there, May 8, 1870. He filled the chair of rhetoric at the Lycée Charlemagne, 1810–16, and of French eloquence at the Sorbonne, 1816–26. With Cousin and Guizot he formed the famous trio known as "the three professors." He won the prize offered by the Academy in 1812 with his essay 'Eulogy of Montaigne'; again in 1814 with 'Advantages and Drawbacks of Criticism'; and in 1816 with 'Eulogy of Montesquieu.' The French Academy elected him a member in 1821. His three greatest works are: 'Course of French Literature: A View of the 18th Century'; 'A View of Christian Eloquence in the 4th Century'; 'History of Gregory VII.,' a posthumous publication (1873).

Villemarqué, Théodore Hersart, Vicomte de la (vēl-mär-kā'). A French philologist and antiquarian; born at Quimperté, June 17, 1819. He is author of 'Barzaz-Breiz: Popular Songs of Brittany' (1840); 'Popular Tales of the Ancient Bretons' (1856); 'Celtic Legends of Ireland, Wales, and Brittany' (1859) 'Stories of the Round Table'; 'Breton Poems of the Middle Ages' (1879).

Villena, Enrique de Aragon, commonly styled **Marques de** (vēl-yā'nä). A Spanish scholar and poet; born 1384; died at Madrid, Dec. 15, 1434. He wrote: 'The Troubadour's Art'; 'The Art of Carving'; 'The Labors of Hercules' (1483); 'Treatise on Consolation'; 'Fascinology' (on the evil eye); 'On Leprosy.' He also translated the Æneid and the 'Divine Comedy.'

Villers, Charles François Dominique de (vē-lā'). A French writer of history; born at Boulay in Lorraine, Nov. 4, 1765; left France at the Revolution, settled in Germany and died at Göttingen, Feb. 26, 1815. He wrote: 'Kant's Philosophy; or, Fundamental Principles of Transcendental Philosophy' (2 vols., 1802); 'An Essay on the Spirit and Influence of Luther's Reformation' (1804); 'General View of the Universities' (1808).

Villon, François (vēl-loń'), true name probably **François Montcorbier.** A noted French poet; born 1431; died about 146- (?). He wrote: 'The Greater Testament' (1456), and the 'Smaller Testament: Its Codicil' (1461) both in eight-line stanzas, with ballads and rondeaus interposed; a volume of 'Ballades'; and a collection of poems in a jargon to-day unintelligible, 'Jargon.'

Vilmar, August Friedrich Christian (vēl-mär'). A German theological writer and historian of literature; born at Solz in Lower Hesse; died at Marburg, July 30, 1868. He was professor of Lutheran theology at Marburg, and a resolute opponent of rationalism in theology. He wrote: 'The Theology of Facts versus the Theology of Rhetoric' (1856); 'History of German Civilization in Most Recent Times' (3 vols., 1858–67); 'A Little Handbook for the Friends of the German Folk-Song' (1867); 'Exposition of the Augsburg Confession' (1870); 'Moral Theology' (1871); 'Dogmatic Theology' (1874); 'History of German National Literature' (1845; 24th ed. 1894).

Vincent, Arvède (vań-sän') [**Varine**]. A French miscellaneous writer; born at Paris, Nov. 17, 1840. She wrote: 'Essays and Fantasies' (1887); 'Princesses and Great Ladies: Maria Mancini, Christina of Sweden, the Duchess of Maine,' etc. (1890); 'Bernardin de St. Pierre' (1891); 'A. de Musset' (1893).

Vincent of Beauvais, Latinized **Vincentius Bellovacensis.** A great mediæval encyclopedist; born about 1190; died about 1264. He was a Dominican friar. His voluminous works cover the whole field of mediæval science. The chief is 'The Greater Mirror' (Speculum Majus), a vast encyclopædia of fables, science, literature, etc., in three huge volumes of 80 books and 9,885 chapters; it comprises Natural, Doctrinal, Historical; another part, Moral, is by another hand. Part i. (ed. 1473–76) contains 848 folio pages, and treats of the whole visible world, and even of the Creator, angels, etc.; part ii., Doctrinal, is a summary of the scholastic philosophy, liberal and useful arts, government, grammar, arithmetic, theology, etc. The third part gives the Bible account of creation, the world's secular history down to Constantine, and histories of the German, Frank, English, and other nations.

Vincent of Lerins, or **Vincentius Lerinensis.** An ecclesiastical writer of the first half of the fifth century; he was a native of Gaul and a monk of the monastery of Lerinum, an island (now St. Honorat) opposite Cannes. He is author of a 'Warning against the Profane Novelties of all Heretics.' In that work is for the first time laid down formally the test of Catholicity of doctrine, which is that the Catholic doctrine is "what everywhere, what always, what by all hath been believed" (quod ubique, quod semper, and quod ab omnibus creditum est). He is by some critics believed to be also the author of a treatise favoring the heretical opinions of the Semipelagians, which is the subject of Prosper the Aquitanian's 'Replies, on behalf of Augustine's Teaching, to the Heads of the Vincentian Objections.'

Vincent, Frank. An American traveler and writer; born in Brooklyn, N. Y., April 2, 1848. Yale, his alma mater, gave him an A. M. in 1875. He is a member of many geographical, ethnological, and archæological societies, and has received decorations from the kings of Burmah, Cambodia, and Siam. He has published 'The Land of the White Elephant' (1874); 'Through and Through the Tropics' (1876); 'Two Months in Burmah' (1877); 'The Wonderful Ruins of Cambodia' (1878); 'Norsk, Lapp, Finn' (1881); 'Around and About South America' (1888); and 'The Republics of South America' (1889); 'Actual Africa' (1895).

Vincent, John Heyl. An American clergyman, bishop of the Methodist Episcopal Church; and founder of the Chautauqua Assembly. He was born Feb. 23, 1832, at Tuscaloosa, Ala.; educated at the Wesleyan Institute, and began to preach at 18. He was pastor at Galena, Ill., and Chicago, and in 1865 established the Sunday School Quarterly, and in 1866 the Sunday School Teacher, which contained the lesson system since become international. He was general secretary of the Methodist Sunday School Union, and also of the Tract Society. In 1874, with the Hon. Lewis Miller of Akron, O., he established the Chautauqua Assembly, and has been superintendent of instruction and chancellor up to the present time. In 1888 he became bishop, with residence at Topeka, Kan. Among his published works are: 'Little Footprints in Bible Lands' (1861); 'The Chautauqua Movement' (1886); 'The Home Book' (1886); 'The Modern Sunday School' (1887); 'Better Not'; a series of Chautauqua textbooks (1887); 'The Church at-Home.'

Vincent, Marvin Richardson. An American clergyman; born in Poughkeepsie, N. Y., September, 1834. With Charlton T. Lewis, he translated Johann Albrecht Bengel's 'Gnomon of the New Testament' (2 vols., 1860–62). He has since published, besides tracts, sermons, and review articles, 'Amusement a Force in Christian Training' (1867); 'The Two Prodigals' (1876); 'Gates into the Psalm Country,' a series of descriptions (1878); 'Stranger and Guest'; (1879); 'Faith and Character' (1880); 'The Minister's Handbook' (1882); 'Christ as a Teacher' (1886); and 'Word Studies in the New Testament' (3 vols.,); 'The Inferno of Dante.'

Vinci, Leonardo da (vinche'). A great Italian painter, one of the greatest artists of the world; born at the castle of Vinci in Tuscany, 1452; died in France, May 2, 1519, at the court of Francis I. He lived at Florence; but, brought by an invitation from Ludovico il Moro about 1489 to settle in Milan, he there painted his famous 'Last Supper.' His portrait, painted by himself, is in the Royal Library, Turin. A 'Treatise on Painting'; and his various works on the art of perspective and on the laws of architecture and mathematics are well known. A series of over two hundred drawings of his now belonging to the Royal Academy in London, illustrates in detail the anatomy of the human body.

Vincke, Karl Friedrich Gisbert, Freiherr von (vink'e). A German story-writer and poet; born at Hagen, Sept. 6, 1813; died at Freiburg, Baden, Feb. 6, 1892. He wrote 'Legends and Pictures of Westphalia' (1856); 'Poems' (1860); 'Comedies' (2 vols., 1869 and 1881); 'A Little List of Sins' (4th ed. 1889); and adapted some of Shakespeare's plays.

Vinet, Alexandre Rodolphe (ve-nä'). A Swiss Protestant theologian and historian of literature; born at Ouchy, Vaud, June 17, 1797; died at Clarens, May 4, 1847. He wrote: 'A Memoir in Favor of Freedom of Worship' (1826); 'History of Preaching in the Reformed Churches of France in the 17th Century' (1860); 'Studies on Blaise Pascal' (1848); 'Studies on the Literature of France in the 18th Century' (2 vols., 1853); 'Moralists of the 16th and 17th Centuries' (1859); 'Poets of the Age of Louis XIV.' (1861).

Viollet-le-Duc, Eugène Emanuel (ve-o-lä'-le-dük). A French architect and historian of art; born at Paris, Jan. 27, 1814; died Sept. 17, 1879. He made special and profound study of mediæval architecture in Italy and Southern France; and became professor in the École des Beaux Arts, 1863. His great work is 'Dictionary of French Architecture from the 11th to the 16th Century' (10 vols., 1854–69). His other chief works are: 'Essay on the Military Architecture of the Middle Ages' (1854); 'Dictionary of French House Furniture from the Carlovingian Epoch to the Renaissance' (6 vols., 1854–75); 'Discourses on Architecture' (2 vols., 1858–72); 'Chapels of Notre Dame de Paris' (1867–69); 'Memoir on the Defense of Paris' (1872); 'History of a House,' 'History of a Fortress,' 'History of Human Dwelling-Places,' 'History of a City Mansion and of a Cathedral' (4 vols., 1873–78).

Virchow, Rudolf (fer'chō). A distinguished German pathologist; born at Schievelbein, in Prussia, Oct. 13, 1821. Among his numerous writings are: 'Collected Essays on Scientific Medicine' (1856); 'Four Discourses on Life and Disease' (1862); 'On the Education of Woman for her Calling' (1865); 'On Certain Tokens of Lower Human Races in the Cranium' (1875); 'Freedom of Science in the Modern State.' Died Sept. 5, 1902.

Virgil, Polydore. A celebrated writer and ecclesiastic; born in Urbino, Italy, about 1470; died about 1550. He was sent about 1502 to England by Pope Alexander VI. to collect the tax called "Peter's Pence," and continued to reside there for the greater part of his life. He was successively created archdeacon of Wells; prebendary in the Cathedral of Hereford, Lincoln, and St. Paul's. His principal works are his 'History of Inventions'; 'Historia Anglica,' a history of England brought down to the end of the reign of Henry VII.;

and a treatise against divination, entitled 'De Prodigiis.'

Virgil, or more properly **Vergil — Publius Vergilius Maro.** The greatest of Roman epic poets; born at Andes, a little village near Mantua, Oct. 5, 70 B. C.; died at Brundisium, Sept. 21, 19 B. C. He wrote the epic Æneid, in 12 books; several 'Eclogues' or 'Bucolics,' pastoral poems in imitation of the idylls of Theocritus; and the 'Georgics,' a didactic poem on husbandry, in four books, and 'Moretum.'

Visconti, Ennio Quirino (vis-kon'tē). An Italian archæologist; born at Rome, Nov. 1, 1751; died Feb. 7, 1818. In his 14th year he translated into Italian verse the 'Hecuba' of Euripides. His greatest work is 'Grecian Iconography' (3 vols., 1808). He visited London at the invitation of Lord Elgin to inspect the Elgin Marbles, 1817, and wrote 'Memoirs on the Works of Sculpture from the Parthenon' (1818).

Vitet, Ludovic (vē-tā'). A French statesman, poet, and author, member of the Academy; born in Paris, Oct. 18, 1802; died there, June 5, 1873. While a journalist on L'Univers, he wrote three dramatic poems, 'The Day of the Barricades' (1826), 'The States of Blois' (1827), and the 'Death of Henri III.' (1829), which gave him reputation. Subsequently he held official posts until the revolution of 1848. Of his later works the best known are: 'Fragments and Mélanges' (1846), artistic, literary, and archæological criticisms; 'Studies of the History of Art' (1864); 'Letters on the Siege of Paris' (1870-71).

Vitruvius Pollio (vē-trö'vē-us pol'le-ō). A celebrated Roman military engineer and writer on architecture. He lived in the Augustan age, and wrote ten books 'Of Architecture,' treating of the construction of temples and public and private buildings, as also of waterworks, sun-dials, various machines, etc. The work is still extant.

Vivien de St. Martin, Louis (viv-yeń' de sań mär-tań'). A French geographer; born at Caen, May 22, 1802. He was one of the founders of the Paris Geographical Society, and from 1863 to 1876 edited the Geographical Year, an annual review of geographical exploration. He wrote: 'Description of Asia Minor' (2 vols., 1845); 'Study on the Grecian and Roman Geography of India' (3 vols., 1858-60); 'Study on the Geography of the Primitive Peoples of Northwestern India according to the Vedic Hymns' (1860); 'The North of Africa in Grecian and Roman Antiquity' (1863); 'New Dictionary of Universal Geography' (1876-93); 'Universal Atlas of Geography, Modern, Ancient, and Mediæval' (1877). Died Jan. 3, 1897.

Vizetelly, Henry. An English publisher, journalist, and author; born in London, July 30, 1820; died at Tilford near Farnham, Jan. 1, 1894. He was the first publisher to introduce to English readers 'Uncle Tom's Cabin' and the works of Poe, Zola, and Tolstoy; and in 1843 founded the Pictorial Times, one of the

pioneer journals of the British pictorial press. He acted as Paris correspondent of the Illustrated London News (1866-76), and represented the government at foreign expositions. His earliest work, 'The Story of the Diamond Necklace' (1867), a sketch of the Countess de la Motte, was followed by a translation of Topin's 'Man with the Iron Mask' (1879); 'Berlin under the New Empire' (1879); 'Paris in Peril' (1882), a vivid account of the siege of 1870-71; 'A History of Champagne,' a monograph on wines; 'Glances Back through Seventy Years' (1893).

Vlachos, Angelos (vlak'os). A Greek statesman; born at Athens, 1838. Among his writings are: 'The Homeric Question' (1866); 'New-Greek Chrestomathy' (1870); 'Comedies' (1870); 'Modern Greek-French Dictionary' (1871); 'Lyric Poems' (1875); 'Critics on New-Greek Poets.'

Vogel, Hermann Wilhelm (fō'gel) A German photographer and spectrum-analyst; born at Dobrilugk, Prussia, March 26, 1834. He wrote: 'From the New Witches' Caldron: Sketches of Spiritism' (1880); 'Photographs after Nature' (1882); 'Progress of Photography since 1879' (1883); 'Chemical Action of Light and Photography' (2d ed. 1883); 'Photography of Colored Objects' (1885); 'Practical Spectrum Analysis of Terrestrial Objects' (1889); 'Artistic Photography' (1890). He died Dec. 17, 1898.

Vogel, Jakob, styled **Vogel von Glarus.** A Swiss poet; born at Glarus, Dec. 11, 1816. He is a noted connoisseur and collector of the poetry of Switzerland. His works are: 'Beauties and Terrors of the Swiss Alpine World,' prose (1868); 'Pictures from the Alps,' poems (1874); 'Reminiscences of the Klönthal' (1878); 'Poems' (14th ed. 1890); 'My Home: Selected Poems of Nature' (1893). Died Dec. 7, 1896.

Vogel, Otto. A Plattdeutsch dialect poet; born at Greifswald, Jan. 3, 1838. Among his Plattdeutsch lays are: 'Mirror of Pomerania: From Every Age' (1869) and 'Rose-Leaves, en Strämmel Plattdeutsch.' In High German he wrote 'Reproaches: A Garland of Lays' (1887).

Vogelweide, Walther von der. See Walther von der Vogelweide.

Vogl, Johann Nepomuk (fō'gel). An Austrian lyric poet; born in Vienna in 1802. He published: 'Ballads and Romances'; 'Soldier Songs'; 'Lyric Poems'; and other works. D. 1866.

Vogt, Karl (fōkt). A German naturalist; born at Giessen, July 5, 1817; died May 5, 1895. He was associated with Agassiz in the writing of the works on 'Fossil Fishes,' 'Studies on Glaciers,' and 'Natural History of Freshwater Fishes.' Among his independent writings are: 'Text-Book of Geology and Petrifactions' (1846); 'Physiological Letters' (3 parts, 1846); 'The Ocean and the Mediterranean' (1848); 'Researches on Beast-States,' a political satire (1851); 'Old and New from the Life of Animals and Men' (1859); 'Implicit Faith and Science: A Polemic against Rudolf Wagner' (4th ed. 1856); 'Text-Book of Practical Comparative Anatomy' (1888).

Vogüé, Charles Jean Melchior, Marquis de (vō-gü-ā'). A French archæologist; born at Paris, Oct. 18, 1829. His studies are mainly in the departments of the history of religion and Oriental art. He is author of: 'The Churches of the Holy Land' (1859); 'The Temple of Jerusalem' (1864); 'Civil and Religious Architecture in Central Syria, from the First to the Sixth Century' (2 vols., 1865-77); 'Semitic Inscriptions' (1869-77); 'Memoirs of Villars' (1884-93).

Vogüé, Eugène Melchior, Vicomte de. A French diplomatist and writer, cousin of Charles; born Feb. 25. 1849. He was in the diplomatic service, but left it in 1881 to devote his time to literature. He has published: 'Syria, Palestine, Mount Athos' (1876); 'Oriental Histories' (1879); 'The Son of Peter the Great' (1884); 'The Russian Romance' (1886); 'Souvenirs and Visions' (1887); 'Remarks on the Centennial Exposition' (1889); 'Pages of History' (1902). He is a member of the French Academy.

Voigt, Georg (voit). A German historian; born at Königsberg, April 5, 1827; died at Leipsic, where he was professor of history, Aug. 18, 1891. His chief works are: 'The Renaissance of Classic Antiquity; or, The First Century of Humanism' (1859); 'Enea Silvio de' Piccolomini as Pope Pius II., and his Times' (3 vols., 1856-63); 'Memorabilia of Giordano de Giano the Minorite' (1870); 'Historiography of the Expedition of Charles V. against Tunis, 1535' (1872); 'Maurice of Saxony, 1541-47' (1876).

Voigt, Johannes. A German historian, father of Georg; born at Bettenhausen, in Saxe-Meiningen, Aug. 27, 1786; died at Königsberg, Sept. 23, 1863. He is author of 'Hildebrand as Pope Gregory VII., and his Times' (1815), in which he regards the reign of Gregory VII. as one of the most noteworthy phenomena of the Middle Ages, and Gregory himself as a great reformer; 'History of the Lombard League and its Struggle with the Emperor Frederick I.' (1818); 'History of Prussia from the Earliest Times to the Downfall of the Domination of the Teutonic Order' (9 vols., 1827-39), 'The Westphalian Vehmgerichte as related to Prussia' (1836); 'Margrave Albrecht Alcibiades of Brandenburg-Kulmbach' (1852); 'History of the Teutonic Order in its Twelve Circles in Germany' (2 vols., 1857-59).

Voit, Karl von (foit). A German physiologist; born at Amberg, Bavaria, Oct. 31, 1831. He was appointed professor of physiology in the University of Munich in 1863. His first memorable scientific researches (1854) demonstrated the presence of urea in the muscular tissues of cholera patients; since then he has studied almost exclusively the questions of digestion and assimilation. His principal works are: 'Physiologico-Chemical Researches' (Part i., 1857); 'Researches on the Effects of Common Salt, Coffee, and Muscular Action, on Digestion' (1860); 'Laws of Nutrition in Carnivora' (1860); 'Manual of the Physiology of Assimilation and Nutrition' (1884).

Voiture, Vincent (vwä-tür'). A French poet; born in Amiens, 1598; died May 26, 1648. His letters are the chief basis of his literary reputation. He enjoyed the friendship of Cardinal Mazarin, and through his patronage attained the zenith of his reputation, and enjoyed large pensions.

Volkelt, Johannes Immanuel (folk'elt). A German philosopher; born at Lipnik in Galicia, July 21, 1848. He was made professor of philosophy in the University of Basle, 1883, and in that of Leipsic, 1894. In his studies he has sought to reconcile the contradiction between the ancient and the modern schools of philosophy in their respective theories of the universe. His chief writings are: 'The Unknown and Pessimism' (1873); 'Immanuel Kant's Theory of Cognition Analyzed in its Fundamental Principles' (1879); 'Experience and Thought' (1886); 'Æsthetic Questions of the Times' (1895); 'Arthur Schopenhauer' (1900).

Volkmann, Alfred Wilhelm (folk'män). A German physiologist; born at Leipsic, June 1, 1801; died April 21, 1877, at Halle, where he was professor of physiology. He made special studies of the nervous system and the sense of sight. Among his works are: 'Anatomy of Animals, Illustrated with Plates' (1831-33); 'Contributions to the Physiology of the Sense of Sight' (1836); 'The Independence of the Sympathetic System of Nerves' (1842); 'Dynamics of the Blood' (1850); 'Physiological Researches in the Department of Optics' (1863-64); 'Elasticity of Muscles' (1856).

Volkmann, Richard von. ["Richard Leander."] A German surgeon, story-writer, and poet; born at Leipsic, Aug. 17, 1830; died Nov. 28, 1889, at Jena, where he was professor of surgery. Among his professional writings are: 'Diseases of the Motor Organs' (1865); 'Manual of Surgery' (1865); 'Contributions to Surgery' (1875). He wrote also: 'Reveries at French Firesides,' a series of tales (1871; 22d ed. 1894); 'From Student Times' (1876), 'Poems' (3d ed. 1885); 'Short Poems' (2d ed. 1889); 'Old and New Troubadour Songs' (2d ed. 1890).

Volkmar, Gustav (folk'mär). A German theological writer; born at Hersfeld, Hesse, Jan. 11, 1809; died Jan. 10, 1893. He was professor of theology in the University of Zürich. His principal works are: an edition of 'The Gospel of Marcion' (1852); 'Justin Martyr and his Relation to our Gospels' (1853); 'Sources of the History of Heresies down to the Nicene Council,' vol. i., 'Hippolytus and the Philosophumena' (1853); 'Religion of Jesus and its First Development' (1857); 'Origin of our Gospels' (1866); 'Life and Works of Zwingli' (1870); 'Myths of the Popes' (1873); 'The Synoptics and the Historical Facts of the Life of Jesus' (1877); 'Jesus of Nazareth and the Early Christian Times' (1882); 'Paul from Damascus to the Epistle to the Galatians' (1887).

Vollmar, Georg von (fōl'mär). A German socialist, agitator, and author; born at Munich,

March 7, 1850. He wrote: 'The Isolated Socialist State' (1880); 'The Next Task of the Social Democracy' (1891); 'On State Socialism' (1892).

Vollmöller, Karl Gustav (fōl'mĕl-er). A German philologist; born at Ilsfeld in Würtemberg, Oct. 16, 1848. He was appointed professor of Romanic and English philology in the University of Göttingen, 1881. He has written 'Kürenberg and the Nibelungen' (1874); 'Munich's Brutus' (1877); 'Poem of the Cid' (1879); 'Octavianus' (1883); 'Monuments of the English Language and Literature from the 16th to the 18th Century' (1883). He edits the Critical Annual of the Progress of Romanic Philology (commenced 1892).

Volney, Constantin de, Count (vol-nē'); family name **Chassebœuf** (shas-bĕf) A distinguished French philosopher, author, and traveler; born in Craon (Mayenne), February 1757; died in April 1820. He published in 1789 his 'Travels in Egypt and Syria' (2 vols.), the best description of them to that date. In 1789 he was elected a deputy to the States-General. In 1791 he produced a work still remembered, and on which his fame rests,— 'Ruins; or, Meditations on the Revolutions of Empires.' Imprisoned in 1793, on his release he passed two years in the United States, publishing in 1803 his 'Description of the Climate and Soil' of the country. Among his other works are: 'The Natural Law; or, Physical Principles of Morality' (1793); and 'Researches in Ancient History' (3 vols., 1814).

Voltaire, François Marie Arouet de (vol-tär'). The renowned French writer, whose name of Voltaire was assumed; born in Paris, Nov. 21, 1694; died there, May 30, 1778. His works include: 'Œdipus' (1718); 'Artemire' (1721); 'Mariamne' (1722); 'La Henriade' (1723), originally published as 'The League; or, Henry the Great'; 'History of Charles XII.' (1730?); 'Letters on the English' (1731); 'Brutus' (1731); 'Philosophical Letters' (1732?); 'Zaïre' (1732); 'Eriphyle' (1732); 'Adelaide Duguesclin' (1734); 'The Temple of Taste' (1734?); 'The Death of Cæsar' (1735?); 'Elements of Newton's Philosophy' (1735); 'The Maid of Orleans' (1736); 'Alzire' (1736); 'Zulime' (1740); 'Mahomet' (1741); 'The Prodigal Son' (1742?); 'Mérope' (1743); 'Discourse on Man'; 'The Princess of Navarre' (1746); 'Semiramis'; 'Rome Saved' (174–); 'Orestes' (1750); 'Nanine'; 'Century of Louis XIV.' (1751); 'Diatribe of Doctor Akakia' (1752); 'Amélie' (1752); 'Poem on Natural Law' (1756); 'Candide' (1758); 'History of Russia under Peter I.' (1759); 'Republican Ideas' (1762); 'On Toleration' (1763); 'Catechism of the Honest Man' (1763); 'Tales' (1763); 'Commentary on Corneille' (1764?); 'Agathocles' (1764?); 'Julius Cæsar' (1764), "a translation from the English of W. Shakespeare" (1764); 'Irene'; 'Tancrède' (1765); 'Socrates' (1765?); 'The Bible at Last Explained' (1766); 'Pyrrhonism of History'; 'Century of Louis XV.' (1766?). The au-

thor's habit of secret and anonymous publication makes his bibliography difficult of compilation. The dates of 'Zadig'; 'Micromegas'; 'Jeannot and Colin'; 'The Ingenuous One'; and 'The Princess of Babylon,' are in doubt.

Vondel, Joost van den (von'del). A Dutch dramatic poet; born in Cologne, Nov. 17, 1587; died in Amsterdam, 1679. His is the greatest name in Dutch literature, and he has often been called "The Dutch Shakespeare." He began his literary career with the drama 'Het Pascha,' produced in 1612 before the Rhetorical Chamber, of which he was a member. He wrote the tragedy 'Palamedes,' and 'The Amsterdam Hecuba,' a free version of Seneca (1625); many translations from the classics and versions of classical originals. The dramatic poem 'Lucifer,' the greatest of his works, is considered by many Dutch critics to be an allegorical account of the revolt of the Netherlands against Philip of Spain. His collected works, together with a life of the poet, were published at Amsterdam (1850–69) in twelve volumes.

Von-Visin, Denis Ivanovich (fōn-fēs'in). A Russian poet; born at Moscow, April 14, 1744; died at St. Petersburg, 1792. He wrote: 'The Brigadier,' a comedy (1766), which won for him instant celebrity; it was followed by his masterpiece, the comedy 'Mother's Darling Son' (1782), and the same year appeared his 'Questions to Catherine II.' He left an unfinished autobiography, 'Frank Confession of my Thoughts and Doings.'

Vorosmarty or **Voeroesmarty, Mihály** (vö-rösh-mar'ty). A celebrated Hungarian writer and patriot; born in the county of Fejervar in 1800; died in 1855 while engaged on a translation of Shakespeare. He published 'King Solomon,' a drama in 1821, which was followed by a poem, 'The Triumph of Fidelity' (1827); 'King Sigismund,' a drama (1824); 'The Flight of Zalan,' an epic poem; the tragedy 'Kont' (1825). His narrative poems entitled 'Cserhalom,' and 'The Enchanted Valley,' established his reputation as the first Hungarian poet of his time. He was a contributor to Kisfaludy's Aurora, and was for several years editor of a journal called The Repository of Science. In 1830 he published a patriotic lyric entitled 'The Appeal,' for which he received from the Hungarian Academy a ducat a line.

Vosmaer, Carl (vos'mär). A Dutch journalist, novelist, artist, and writer on art; born at The Hague, March 20, 1826; died at Montreux, Switzerland, June 12, 1888. He is best known outside of his own country as the author of 'The Amazon' (1881), a novel, which was translated into English, French, and other languages. Other works are: 'Studies on War and Art' (1856); 'Sketches' (1860), verse; 'Life of Rembrandt' (1869); 'Franz Hals' (1874); 'Our Contemporary Artists' (1881); a translation of the Iliad and Odyssey.

Voss, Gerhard Johann (fōs), usually styled **Vossius.** A celebrated Dutch philologist; born near Heidelberg 1577; died at Amsterdam, March 17, 1649. In certain departments of archæophilology he made valuable original researches; and he was the first to indicate the historical evolution of the Latin language. Among his writings are: 'Essays on Rhetoric; or, The Institutes of Oratory,' his greatest work (1606); 'The Greek Historians' (1624); 'The Latin Historians' (1627); 'Aristarchus; or, On the Art of Grammar' (1635); 'Of Errors of Speech and Latino Barbarous Terms' (1640); 'Heathen Theology' (1642); 'The Times of the Ancient Poets' (1654); 'Etymology of the Latin Language' (1662). The 'Correspondence of Vossius with Eminent Men' was published in 1691.

Vos, Heinrich. A German philologist, son of Johann H.; born at Otterndorf, Oct. 29, 1779; died Oct. 20, 1822, at Heidelberg, where he was professor of philology, in succession to his father. He was a warm friend of Jean Paul Richter, and his literary executor. He completed his father's translation of Æschylus (1826); this work, as also the 'Correspondence between Heinrich Voss and Jean Paul' and 'Communications regarding Goethe and Schiller, in Letters by Heinrich Voss,' appeared after his death.

Vos, Isaak V., son of Gerhard J.; born at Leyden, 1618; died at Windsor, England, where he held a canonry, Feb. 21, 1689. Among his writings are: 'The Seventy Interpreters: Their Translation and Their Chronology' (1661); 'Of the Singing of Poems and the Power of Rhythm' (1653); 'A Book of Various Observations' (1685).

Voss, Johann Heinrich. A German poet; born in Sommersdorf, Mecklenburg, Feb. 20, 1751; died at Heidelberg, March 29, 1826. His principal original work is the idyl 'Luise,' published in complete form in 1795. His fame is based principally, however, upon his translations of the classical writers, particularly of Homer. He translated the Odyssey (1781); the Iliad, together with a revised version of the Odyssey (1793); Virgil (1799); Horace and Hesiod (1806); Theocritus, Bion, and Moschus (1808); Tibullus (1810); Aristophanes (1821). He is also the author of a number of lyrical poems. His complete poetical works were published in Leipsic, 1835.

Voss, Julius von. A German story-writer; born at Brandenburg, Aug. 24, 1768; died at Berlin, Nov. 1, 1832. His rapidity of literary production was almost without a parallel. His best story is 'The Schildburger' (The Fooltownite: 1823). He wrote a great many comedies, farces, and satirical parodies. In 'The Stralhow Haul of Fish' (1822), a popular piece with songs, in the Berlin patois, he gives the first example of the Berlinese farce.

Voss, Richard. A German poet; born at Neugrape in Pomerania, Sept. 2, 1851. Among his dramatic compositions are: 'Savonarola' (1878); 'Magda' (1879); 'The Patrician Dame' (1881); 'Luigia Sanfelice' (1882); 'Father Modestus' (1883); 'The Czar's Moor' (1883), after a fragment by Pushkin; 'Woe to the Besieged' (1889); 'Eve' (1889); 'Betwixt Two Hearts' (1893); 'At Sedan' (1895). In narrative verse he wrote: 'A Hill Asylum' (1882); 'Roman Village Tales' (1884); 'Messalina' (1881). Among his novels are: 'Life Tragedy of an Actress' (1883); 'The New Romans' (1885); 'Children of the South' (1888); 'Villa Falconieri' (1895); 'Roman Fever' (1902); 'The People of Valdaré.' He excels in description of Italian lowly life.

Vraz, Stanko (fräch). A Croatian poet; born at Zerovec in Lower Styria, June 30, 1810; died at Agram, May 24, 1851. Among his works are: a collection of Slovenian folk-songs from Styria, Ukraine, Carinthia, and Western Hungary (1839); and 'Rose-Apples' (1840), a collection of love-songs.

Vulpius, Christian August (völ'pe-us). A German writer; born in Weimar, 1762; died in 1827. He was a brother-in-law of Goethe, under whose direction he became secretary of the court theatre at Weimar. He published: 'Rinaldo Rinaldini' (1799), a robber romance; 'Dramatic Histories of Former Times'; and a number of dramatic works. He was subsequently first librarian and overseer of the cabinet of coins at Weimar.

W

Waagen, Gustav Friedrich (vä'gen). A German historian of art; born at Hamburg, Feb. 11, 1794; died at Copenhagen, July 15, 1868. He wrote: 'Art Works and Artists of England and Paris' (3 vols., 1837–39); 'Art Works and Artists of Germany' (2 vols., 1843–45); 'The Treasures of Art in Great Britain' (3 vols., 1854); 'The Most Notable Art Monuments in Vienna' (2 vols., 1866–67); 'The Collection of Paintings in the Imperial Hermitage at St. Petersburg' (1867).

Wace, Robert. A Norman-French trouvère, calling himself simply Master Wace; born in the island of Jersey about 1100; died about 1180. His celebrated works are two long romances, the 'Roman de Brut' (Brutus), and the 'Roman de Rou' (Rollo), both in Norman French. The 'Roman de Brut' is in octosyllabic couplets, is presumably founded on Geoffrey of Monmouth's chronicle, and is of commanding literary importance as the source, or supposed source, from which many subsequent poets drew their Merlin and King Arthur tales. The 'Roman de Rou,' mostly octosyllabic also, is a chronicle of the Norman dukes up to 1106.

Wachenhusen, Hans (väch'en-hö-sen). A German miscellaneous writer; born at Treves, January, 1, 1823; died at Marburg, March 23, 1898. He wrote: 'The New Paris' (1855); 'Pictures of Travel in Spain' (1857); 'Journal of the Austro-Italian War' (1859); 'Crescent and Double Eagle' (1860); 'Rome and Sahara,' a novel (3d ed. 1867); 'Paris Photographs' (1868); 'The Poor Egyptian Man' (1871). Among his stories are: 'The Heart's Golgotha'; 'Only a Woman'; 'A Woman's Guilt.'

Wachler, Johann Friedrich Ludwig (väch'-ler). A German historian of literature; born at Gotha, April 15, 1767; died at Breslau, April 4, 1838. His principal writings are: 'Manual of the History of Literary Culture' (2 vols., 1804-5); 'Lectures on the History of German Literature' (2 vols., 1818-19); 'History of Historical Research and Art from the Renaissance' (2 vols., 1812-20).

Wachsmuth, Ernst Wilhelm Gottlieb (vächs'möt). A German historian; born at Hildesheim, Dec. 28, 1784; died at Leipsic, Jan. 23, 1866. Among his works are: 'Outline of a Theory of History' (1820); 'Hellenic Antiquity' (4 vols., 1826-30); 'History of European Morals' (5 vols., 1831-39); 'History of the Age of the Revolution' (4 vols., 1846-48); 'History of German Nationality' (3 vols., 1860-62).

Wachsmuth, Kurt. A German antiquarian; born at Naumburg on the Saale, April 27, 1837. He became professor at Marburg in 1864, and at Leipsic in 1886. His principal works are: 'Timon the Phliasian, and Other Greek Satirists' (1859); 'The Doctrine of the Stoics on Divination and Dæmons' (1860); 'Old Greece in the New' (1864); 'The City of Athens in Antiquity' (2 vols., 1874-90); 'Introduction to the Study of Ancient History' (1895).

Wackenroder, Wilhelm Heinrich (väk'en-röder). A German miscellaneous writer; born at Berlin, 1773; died there, Feb. 13, 1798. His works are: 'Heart Outpourings of an Art-Loving Friar' (1797), written in collaboration with Ludwig Tieck, and received with great favor by the German artists at Rome; 'Franz Sternbald's Wanderings' (1798); 'Fantasias on Art' (1799).

Wackernagel, Jakob (väk'er-nä-gel). A Swiss philologist; born at Basle, Dec. 11, 1853. He became professor of Greek language and literature in the University of Göttingen, 1902. He wrote: 'Origin of Brahmanism' (1877); 'The Study of Classical Antiquity in Switzerland' (1891); 'Palæ-Indian Grammar' (1896).

Wackernagel, Wilhelm. A Swiss linguist and antiquarian; born at Berlin, April 23, 1806; died Dec. 21, 1869, at Basle, where he was professor of German language and literature. His principal writings are: 'German Dictionary' (5th ed. 1878); 'History of Ger-

man Literature' (1848-55); 'Land Laws of the Schwabenspiegel' (1840); 'Old German Sermons and Prayers' (1876)· 'The Little Book of Wine' (1845); and other volumes of poems.

Waddington, William Henry (wod'ing-tọn; Fr. pron. vä-dan-tôn'). A French diplomat, statesman, and archæologist; born of English parentage at St. Remi in Eure-et-Loir, Dec. 11, 1826; died at Paris, Jan. 13, 1894. He was ambassador to England, 1883-93. Among his writings are: 'Travels in Asia Minor in the Interest of Numismatics' (1852); 'Archæological Travels in Greece and Asia Minor' (6 vols., 1847-77); 'Greek and Latin Inscriptions from Syria' (1870).

Wade, Thomas. An English poet; born in 1805; died Sept. 19, 1875. He was an advanced Liberal. His chief works are: 'Tasso and the Sisters' (1825); 'Woman's Love' (played at Covent Garden in 1828, and published in 1829); 'The Jew of Arragon' (1830), a tragedy; 'Mundi et Cordis Carmina' (1835), afterwards reprinted under the English title, 'Songs of the Universe and Heart.' The last-named contained his best work.

Waechter, Karl Georg von (vech'ter). A German jurist; born at Marbach on the Neckar, Dec. 24, 1797; died at Connewitz near Leipsic, Jan. 15, 1880. He is author of: 'Disquisitions on Criminal Law' (1835); 'The German Common Law, Especially Criminal Law' (1844); a commentary on the 'Pandects' of the Justinian Code (2 parts, 1880-81).

Waechter, Oskar von. A German jurist and publicist; son of Karl G.; born at Tübingen, April 29, 1825. He wrote: 'Copyright Systematically Laid Down according to the German Common Law' (1875); 'Copyright in Works of Plastic Art, Photographs, etc.' (1877); 'Encyclopædia of the Laws of Exchange' (1879-80); 'Vehmgericht and Witchcraft Trials' (1882); 'Old Gold in German Proverbs' (1883); 'Johann Jakob Moser' (1885).

Wagenaar, Jan (vä'gen-är). A Dutch historian; born at Amsterdam, Oct. 3, 1709; died there, March 1773. His best-known work is 'History of the Fatherland' (21 vols., 1749-60): the work reaches down to the year 1751. He wrote also: 'Description of the United Provinces of the Netherlands' (12 vols., 1739); 'Description of Amsterdam' (3 vols., 1760-67).

Wagener, Hermann (vä'gen-er). A German writer on political subjects; born at Segelitz near Neu-Ruppin, March 8, 1815; died at Berlin, April 22, 1889. He edited a 'Lexicon of the State and Society' (23 vols., 1858-67); and wrote 'The Policy of Frederick William IV.' (1883); 'My Memoirs of the Periods between 1848 and 1866, and from 1873 till Now' (1884).

Wagner, Adolf (väg'ner). A German political economist, son of Rudolf; born at Erlangen, March 25, 1835. The more important of his writings are: 'Contributions to the Study of Banking' (1857); 'Abolition of Private Land-ownership' (1870); 'Law in the Apparently

Arbitrary Doings of Man' (1864); 'Text-Book of Political Economy,' written in collaboration with other economists (Vol. i., 1876; Vol. vii., 'Finance,' 1880), in which he upholds socialistic views, favoring State ownership of railways; 'The Science of Finance and State Socialism' (1887); 'My Conflict with the Baron von Stumm-Halberg' (1895), the last two in defense of socialism; 'Agrarian and Industrial State' (1902).

Wagner, Ernst. A German novelist; born at Rossdorf, Feb. 2, 1769; died at Meiningen, Feb. 25, 1812. Among his more successful novels are: 'Willibald's Views of Life' (1804); 'The Traveling Painters' (1806); 'Isidora' (1814). He wrote also 'Journeys from Abroad Homeward' (1808).

Wagner, Heinrich Leopold. A German poet; born at Strasburg, Feb. 19, 1747; died at Frankfort on the Main, March 4, 1779. He wrote: 'Prometheus and Deucalion' (1775), a farce ridiculing the critics who carped at Goethe's 'Werther'; 'Voltaire on the Eve of his Apotheosis,' a dramatic satire (1778); 'Repentance After the Act,' a drama (1775); 'The Child-Murderess,' a tragedy (1779).

Wagner, Hermann. A German geographer and statistician, son of Rudolf; born at Erlangen, June 23, 1840. Among his works are: 'The Earth's Population'; 'Wall Map of Germany' (1879); 'Text-Book of Geography' (2 vols., 1894-95); 'Methodical School Atlas' (10th ed. 1902).

Wagner, Moritz. A German traveler and naturalist, brother of Rudolf; born at Bayreuth, Oct. 3, 1813; died by his own hand at Munich, May 30, 1887. He traveled in Algeria, the coastlands of the Black Sea, the Caucasus, Armenia, Kurdistan, Persia, North and Central America, and the West Indies. Among his writings are: 'Travels in the Regency of Algiers' (3 vols., 1841); 'The Caucasus and the Land of the Cossacks' (2 vols., 1847); 'Journey to Colchis' (1850); 'Journey to Ararat and the Armenian Highlands' (1848); 'Travels in Persia and in the Land of the Kurds' (2 vols., 1851); 'Scientific Travels in Tropical America' (1870); 'The Darwinian Theory, and the Law of Migration of Organisms' (1868).

Wagner, Paul. A German agricultural chemist; born at Liebenau in Hanover, March 7, 1843. He was named professor of agricultural chemistry in the University of Darmstadt, 1881. He is author of: 'Text-Book of the Manufacture of Manures' (1877); 'Introduction to Rational Manuring with Phosphoric Acid' (1889); 'Nitrate Manuring' (1892).

Wagner, Richard. The German musical composer and poet; born in Leipsic, May 22, 1813; died in Venice, Italy, Feb. 13, 1883. In addition to the musical compositions upon which his fame is founded, he has written: 'The Judaic in Music' (1852); 'Music of the Future' (1860); 'State and Religion' (1864); 'Letters'; 'Reminiscences from My Life.'

Wagner, Rudolf. A distinguished German physiologist and anthropologist; born at Bayreuth, June 30, 1805; died May 13, 1864, at Göttingen, where he had been professor since 1840. Among his writings are: 'Text-Book of Comparative Anatomy' (1834); 'Text-Book of Physiology' (1839); 'Hand-Dictionary of Physiology' (4 vols., 1842-53); 'Creation of Man and Soul Substance' (1854); 'Of Knowledge and Belief, with Special Reference to the Future of the Soul' (1854); 'The Struggle Over the Soul' (1857); 'Zoölogico-Anthropological Researches' (1861); 'Preliminary Studies toward a Scientific Morphology and Physiology of the Human Brain as an Organ of Soul' (two parts, 1860-62).

Wahrmund, Adolf (vär'mönt). A German Orientalist; born at Wiesbaden, June 10, 1827. His principal works are: 'Hand-Dictionary of the Arabic and German Languages' (3 vols., 1874-77); 'Poems' (1880); 'Babylonianism, Judaism, and Christianism' (1882); 'Practical Manual of the Osmanli-Turkish Language' (2d ed. 1885); 'The Christian School and Judaism' (1885); 'Practical Manual of Modern Arabic' (3d ed. 1886); 'The Law of Nomadism' (1887); 'The War of Civilization between Asia and Europe' (1887); 'Monsieur Jourdan, the Paris Botanist, in the Kara-Bagh: A Comedy in Modern Persian' (1889); 'Abhâsa: A Tragedy' (1890).

Waiblinger, Wilhelm Friedrich (vīb'ling-er). A German miscellaneous writer; born at Heilbronn, Nov. 21, 1804; died at Rome, Jan. 17, 1830. His tales, 'Four Stories from Greece' (1821), and 'Three Days in the Nether World' (1826); and his 'Poems,' were received with extraordinary favor. He wrote also: 'Pocket Book of Italy and Greece' (1829); 'The Britons in Rome,' a humorous story (1844); 'Poems from Italy.'

Waitz, Georg (vītz). A great German historian; born at Flensburg, Oct. 9, 1813; died at Berlin, May 24, 1886. He became professor at Göttingen, 1849. Among his very numerous writings are: 'History of the Formation of Germany' (8 vols., 1843-78; revised ed. 1893), his greatest work. 'The Life and Teaching of Ulfilas' (1840); 'Researches in German History' (1862); 'German Emperors from Charlemagne to Maximilian' (1872).

Waitz, Theodor. A distinguished German psychologist and anthropologist; born at Gotha, March 17, 1821; died May 21, 1864, at Marburg. His more notable works are: an edition of Aristotle's 'Organon' (2 vols., 1844-46); 'Principles of Psychology' (1846); 'Text-Book of Psychology' (1849); 'Anthropology of Savage Peoples' (6 vols., 1859-72), his greatest work; 'The North-American Indians' (1865).

Walch, Johann Georg (välch). A German theological writer; born at Meiningen, June 17, 1693; died Jan. 13, 1775. Among his works are: 'Patristic Library' (1770); 'Philosophical Lexicon' (2 vols., 1726); 'Introduction to the

Theological Sciences' (1747); an edition of the 'Works of Luther' (24 vols., 1740-51).

Walcott, Charles Melton. An English actor and dramatic writer; born in London, in 1815; died in Philadelphia, in May 1868. Besides being an excellent comedian, he has written many plays, among which are : 'The Course of True Love' (1839); 'Washington; or, Valley Forge' (1842); 'Edith' (1846); 'The Custom of the Country' (1848); 'The Haunted Man' (1848); 'David Copperfield' (1848); 'Hoboken' (1849); 'One Cast for Two Suits' (1854); 'Hiawatha' (1855); 'A Good Fellow' (1857). He wrote the songs, 'My Love is a Sailor Boy' and 'My Own Little Rose.'

Waldau, Max (väl'dou), pseudonym of Richard Georg Spiller von Hauenschild. A German poet; born in Breslau, March 24, 1822; died at Tscheidt, Upper Silesia, Jan. 20, 1855. He early rose to prominence through his scholarly attainments, but as a poet he has made his name known wherever German poetry is read. 'A Fairy Fable,' 'Leaves in the Wind,' and 'Rahab : Pictures of Bible Women,' are conspicuous among his volumes of verse. 'Cordula' is a poem admired for its rich metrical effects. He also wrote 'After Nature,' a novel that enjoyed quite a run.

Waldis, Burkard (väl'dis). A German rhyming fabulist; born about 1490; died about 1557. He was a Franciscan friar, but on returning from a pilgrimage to Rome, embraced the doctrines of Luther. He wrote a charming drama in Low German, 'The Parable of the Prodigal Son'; translated the Psalter into German verse; and wrote 'Æsopus,' a collection of about 400 rhymed fables and drolleries.

Waldmüller, Robert (väld'mel-ler), pseudonym of Charles Édouard Duboc. A German poet and miscellaneous writer; born in Hamburg, Sept. 17, 1822. His best work is 'Village Idylls' (1860). Other works are : 'Travel Studies' (1860); 'Sorrow and Joy,' a romance (1874); 'Brunhild,' a drama (1874).

Waldo, Samuel Putnam. An American writer and biographer; born in Connecticut in 1780; died in Hartford, Conn., March 1826. He wrote : 'Narrative of a Tour of Observation by President Monroe' (1818); 'Memoirs of Andrew Jackson' (1820); 'Life of Stephen Decatur' (1821); 'Biographical Sketches of Nicholas Biddle, Paul Jones, Edward Preble, and Alexander Murray' (1823). He edited 'Journal of the Brig Commerce upon the Western Coast of Africa.'

Waldstein, Charles. An eminent American archæologist and writer; born in New York in 1856, and graduated at Columbia College. He was for a time director of the Fitzwilliam Museum at Cambridge, England, which position he resigned in order to take the directorship of the American School of Archæology at Athens. While in this office he was a lecturer on Greek anthology at Cambridge. He is now a fellow of King's College, and a doctor and professor at

Cambridge University. He has written : 'Excavations at the Heraion of Argos'; 'The Balance of Emotion and Intellect'; 'Essays on the Art of Phidias'; 'The Work of John Ruskin'; 'Study of Art in Universities'; 'The Argive Haraeum.'

Waldstein, Louis. An American author, elder brother of Charles; born in New York, 1853. He has written a notable book, 'The Subconscious Self' (1897).

Walewski, Alexandre Florian Joseph Colonna, Duke de (vä-lev'skē). A French statesman; born at Walewice in Poland, May 4, 1810; died at Strasburg, Sept. 27, 1868. He wrote : 'A Word on the Question of Algiers' (1837); 'The English Alliance' (1838); a comedy, 'The School of the World; or, The Coquette Without Knowing it' (1849).

Walford, Mrs. Lucy Bethia. A British novelist, essayist, and biographer; born in Scotland, 1845. She has contributed to Blackwood's Magazine and other periodicals. She has written : 'Mr. Smith' (new ed. 1875); 'Pauline' (last ed. 1885); 'Cousins' (new ed. 1885); 'Troublesome Daughters' (new ed. 1885); 'Dick Netherby' (new ed. 1885); 'Four Biographies' (Jane Taylor, Elizabeth Fry, Hannah More, and Mary Somerville : 1888); 'Her Great Idea, and Other Stories' (1888); 'Baby's Grandmother'; etc.

Walker, Alexander Joseph. An American journalist and editor; born in Virginia in 1819; died in 1893. He successively edited the New Orleans Delta, Times, Jeffersonian, Herald, and Picayune, and subsequently the Cincinnati Enquirer. He published 'Jackson and New Orleans' (1856); 'Life of Andrew Jackson'; 'History of the Battle of Shiloh'; 'Butler at New Orleans'; and 'Duelling in Louisiana.'

Walker, Amasa. An American reformer, merchant, statesman, and political economist; born at Woodstock, Conn., May 4, 1799; died at North Brookfield, Mass., Oct. 29, 1875. He was one of the editors of the Transactions of the Agricultural Society of Massachusetts (7 vols., 1848-54); and published his great work on political economy, 'The Science of Wealth,' in 1866.

Walker, Francis Amasa. An American soldier, educator, and political economist; born in Boston, July 2, 1840; died there Jan. 5, 1897. He edited 'Census Reports' (3 quarto vols.); compiled a 'Statistical Atlas of the United States' (1874); and published 'The Indian Question' (1874); 'The Wages Question' (1876); 'Money' (1878); 'Money, Trade, and Industry' (1879); 'Political Economy' (1883); 'Land and its Rent' (1883); 'History of the Second Army Corps' (1886); 'Life of General Winfield S. Hancock' (1894); and 'The Making of the Nation' (1895). He was president of the Institute of Technology at Boston at the time of his death.

Walker, George Leon. An American writer and Congregational clergyman; born at Rutland, Vt., April, 30, 1830; died at Hartford,

Conn., March 14, 1900. He wrote: 'History of the First Church in Hartford' (1633–1883); 'Thomas Hooker, Preacher, Founder [of Connecticut], Democrat'; 'Aspects of the Religious Life of New England.'

Walker, James. A distinguished American Unitarian divine and educator; born at Burlington, Mass., Aug. 16, 1794; died at Cambridge, Mass., Dec. 23, 1874. He was president of Harvard University, 1853–60; and editor of the Christian Examiner 1831–39. Besides sermons and addresses, editing the works of Dugald Stewart, Dr. Thomas Reid, etc., he published a 'Memoir of Josiah Quincy' (1867), and delivered lectures on 'Natural Religion' and 'The Philosophy of Religion.' He was famous as a pulpit orator.

Walker, James Barr. An American clergyman, journalist, and author; born in Philadelphia, July 29, 1805; died at Wheaton, Ill., March 6, 1887. Besides editorial work, he has written the following: 'The Philosophy of the Plan of Salvation' (1855), a book which commanded wide acceptance; 'God Revealed in Nature and in Christ' (1855); 'Philosophy of Scepticism and Ultraism' (1857); 'The Philosophy of the Divine Operation in the Redemption of Man' (1862); and 'The Living Questions of the Age' (1869).

Walker, John. An English actor, teacher, lecturer, and dictionary-maker; born at Colney Hatch near London, March 18, 1732; died in London, Aug. 1, 1807. His books are a 'Rhyming Dictionary' (1775); 'Elements of Elocution' (1781); 'Rhetorical Grammar' (1785); and a 'Critical Pronouncing Dictionary and Expositor of the English Language' (1791), which was long the standard work of its class, running through forty editions.

Walker, Mrs. Katharine Kent (Child). An American story-writer and translator; born in Pittsfield, Vt., about 1840. She wrote a famous article for the Atlantic Monthly on 'The Total Depravity of Inanimate Things' (Sept., 1864); and has published a version of Bunyan entitled 'Pilgrim's Progress for Children' (1869); 'From the Crib to the Cross' (1869); and a 'Life of Christ' (1869).

Walker, William. An American adventurer; born in Nashville, Tenn., May 8, 1824; shot at Trujillo, Honduras, Sept. 12, 1860. He studied law in Nashville, and medicine in Germany. In 1850 he was an editor in California, and in 1853 organized an expedition against Sonora, Mexico, but was defeated. He landed in Nicaragua in 1855 with 62 followers, captured the city of Granada, and established a government; but was driven from power and surrendered to the U. S. government in May, 1857. In June 1860 he invaded Honduras, was captured, tried by court-martial, and shot. He published 'The War in Nicaragua' (1860).

Walker, William Sidney. A British poet; born at Pembroke, Wales, Dec. 4, 1795; died in London, Oct. 15, 1846. He was a fellow of Trinity College, Cambridge (1822–29), becoming blind during that time. Besides translating a 'Corpus Poetarum Latinorum' (Collection of Latin Poets: new ed. 1854), he wrote 'Gustavus Vasa' (1813), an epic poem; 'Shakspeare's Versification' (3d ed. 1859); 'Critical Examination of the Text of Shakspeare' (3 vols., 1859). 'Poetical Remains,' with a memoir, appeared in 1852.

Walker, Williston. An American clergyman and historical writer, son of George L.; born in Maine, 1860. He has been professor of history in Hartford Theological Seminary since 1880. His works include: 'The Creeds and Platforms of Congregationalism'; 'On the Increase of Royal Power under Philip Augustus'; 'History of the Congregational Church in the United States'; 'John Calvin.'

Wallace, Alfred Russel. A celebrated English naturalist; born at Usk in Monmouthshire, Jan. 8, 1823. He traveled in Brazil, exploring the Amazon and its tributaries (1848–52), and on his return to England published 'Travels on the Amazon and Rio Negro' (1853). He then visited the Malay archipelago, where he spent nearly eight years. One of the fruits of his researches there was the paper 'On the Tendencies of Varieties to Depart Indefinitely from the Original Type,' which was published almost simultaneously with Darwin's first announcement of his theory of natural selection. 'The Malay Archipelago,' 2 vols., was published 1869. He wrote also 'On the Geographical Distribution of Animals' (2 vols., 1876); 'Tropical Nature' (1878); 'Darwinism: An Exposition of the Theory of Natural Selection' (1889). He is author also of 'Miracles and Modern Spiritualism' (1875); 'Land Nationalization: Its necessity and Aims' (1882); 'Darwinism.'

Wallace, Horace Binney. An American author and law editor; born in Philadelphia, Feb. 26, 1817; died in Paris, Dec. 16, 1852. In addition to contributing to literary periodicals, he published anonymously a novel, 'Stanley; or, The Recollections of a Man of the World' (1838); and edited, in conjunction with Judge Hare, 'American Leading Cases in Law' (2 vols., 1847; 3d ed. 1852); Smith's 'Leading Cases' (4th American ed. 2 vols., 1852); and White and Tudor's 'Leading Cases in Equity' (2d American ed. 3 vols., 1852), all copiously annotated. He helped Rufus W. Griswold in his 'Napoleon and the Marshals of the Empire' (2 vols., 1847). 'Art and Scenery in Europe, with Other Papers' (1855), and 'Literary Criticisms, and Other Papers' (1856), are posthumous publications.

Wallace, Lewis. An American general, lawyer, and novelist; born at Brookville, Ind., April 10, 1827. He served in the Mexican War as lieutenant, and in the Civil War attained the rank of major-general. He was Minister to Turkey 1881–85. His works include: 'The Fair God' (1873); 'Ben-Hur' (1880); 'The Life of Gen. Benjamin Harrison' (1888); 'Commodus: A Tragedy' (1889); 'The Boyhood of Christ' (1889); 'The Prince of India' (1893). Died, Crawfordsville, Feb. 15, 1905. *

Wallace, Mrs. (Susan Arnold Elston). An American descriptive and story writer, wife of General Lewis Wallace; born at Crawfordsville, Ind., 1830. Besides contributing to periodicals and reviews, she has published: 'The Storied Sea' (1883); 'Ginevra' (1886); 'The Land of the Pueblos' (1888); 'The Repose in Egypt' (1888); etc. She died in 1907.

Wallace, William Ross. An American lawyer and poet; born in Kentucky, 1819; died in 1881. He has written: 'Perdita'; 'Alban'; 'Meditations in America, and Other Poems.' 'The Liberty Bell' is his best-known poem.

Wallack, Lester [John]. An American actor and manager, son of James William Wallack, the actor and manager; born in New York, Jan. 1, 1820; died in Stamford, Conn., Sept. 6, 1888. He conducted Wallack's Theatre, New York city, for twenty-four years. He was identified with the American stage for more than forty years; and on his retirement in May 1888, was the recipient of an unequaled dramatic testimonial. He wrote the plays 'The Veteran' and 'Rosedale.' His autobiography, 'Memoirs of Fifty Years,' was published the year after his death.

Walloth, Wilhelm (väl'löt). A German story-writer; born at Darmstadt, Oct. 6, 1856. He wrote: 'The King's Treasure House' (3 vols., 1883); 'Paris the Mime' (1886); 'The Gladiator' (1888); 'Tiberius' (2 vols., 1889); 'The Demon of Envy' (1889), 'There Came a Hoar Frost' (1893), 'Love's Fools' (1894), three stories of modern life; and some dramas, as 'Countess Pusterla,' 'John of Suabia,' 'Marino Falieri'; 'The Sacrifice'; 'Alboin.'

Waller, Edmund. An English poet and parliamentarian; born at Coleshill, March 3, 1606; died at Beaconsfield, Oct. 21, 1687. He published a volume of poems in 1645, and again in 1664, which ran through many editions. Of the 25 or more editions of his poems, those of the greatest value are the one of 1711, edited by Bishop Atterbury, with two portraits of the poet; and the one of 1729, with a life by Fenton and a portrait by Vertue. The eighteenth century considered him the first correct versifier, using the heroic couplet with masterful smoothness.

Waller, John Francis. An Irish poet and man of letters, descendant of Edmund Waller; born at Limerick in 1810; died Jan. 9, 1894. He graduated from the Dublin University College. He wrote for the Dublin University Magazine 'The Slingsby Papers,' over the signature of « Jonathan Freke Slingsby.» These were collected in a volume in 1852; his 'Poems' were published in 1854; he was at his best as a lyric poet. He edited the works of Goldsmith, Moore, etc., together with the 'Imperial Dictionary of Universal Biography.'

Wallich, Nathanael (val'lik). A Danish botanist; born at Copenhagen, Jan. 28, 1787; died at London, April 28, 1854. From 1815 till 1847 he was director of the botanic garden at Calcutta. He wrote: 'An Essay on the Flora of Nepâl' (1824-26); 'Rare Asiatic Plants' (3 vols., 1830-32).

Wallin, Johan Olof (väl-lēn'). A Swedish poet; born in Dalarna, Oct. 15, 1779; died at Upsala, archbishop of that see, June 30, 1839. His hymns and religious songs are in high repute in Sweden, and he was called « Sweden's Harp of David.» His finest production is 'The Angel of Death.' He was a notable pulpit orator.

Wallon, Alexandre Henri (vä-lôn'). A French historical writer; born at Valenciennes, Dec. 23, 1812. His principal writings are concerned with the life of Christ, and the writings of the apostles and evangelists. He wrote 'The Life of Jesus and its New Historian' (1864); 'Memoirs on the Years of Jesus Christ'; and other works designed to counteract the effects of Renan's writings. He is author also of 'Political Geography of Modern Times' (1839); 'Slavery in Ancient Times' (3 vols., 1847); 'Joan of Arc' (2 vols., 1860); 'Richard II.' (2 vols., 1864); 'The Reign of Terror' (2 vols., 1873); 'St. Louis and his Times' (2 vols., 1875); 'History of the Paris Revolutionary Tribunal, with the Journal of the Actors' (6 vols., 1880-82); 'The Revolution of May 30th.'

Waln, Robert (wâl). An American and satirical writer; born in 1794; died in 1825. He wrote 'The Hermit in America' (1819); 'American Bards: A Satire'; 'Sisyphi Opus,' etc.; 'Life of Lafayette' (1824).

Walpole, Horace, later **Earl of Orford.** An English author, letter-writer, and dilettante; born in London, Sept. 24, 1717; died there, March 2, 1797. On an estate he bought near Twickenham, in a mansion he built, he established a library and museum, and set up a private press (1757), on which, with others, he printed his own works. He compiled 'A Catalogue of the Royal and Noble Authors of England' (1758); 'Anecdotes of Painters in England' (1761-71); 'Historic Doubts on the Life and Reign of Richard III.' (1768); and other works. He wrote: 'The Castle of Otranto,' a romance (1764); 'The Mysterious Mother,' a tragedy (1768); 'Memoirs of the Last Ten Years of the Reign of George II.' (1822); and other works. His many interesting letters are his chief title to literary fame. They were published in 9 vols., 1857-59.

Walpole, Spencer. An English historian; born Feb. 6, 1839. He has held several government positions, and has also devoted himself to history. Among his books are: his greatest work, 'A History of England from the Conclusion of the Great War in 1815' (1878-86); 'The Electorate and the Legislature' (1881); 'Life of Lord John Russell' (1889); and 'The Land of Home Rule' (1893.) D. 1907.

Walsh, Robert. An American lawyer, journalist, and author; born at Baltimore, Md., in

1784; died Feb. 7, 1859, at Paris, where he had been consul, 1845–51. He wrote for Dennie's Portfolio, and edited the American Review of History and Politics, the first American quarterly (22 vols., 1827–37); most of the articles were from his pen. Others of his publications are: 'Correspondence respecting Russia between R. G. Harper and Robert Walsh, Jr.' (1813); 'An Essay on the Future State of Europe' (1813); biographical prefaces to an edition of the English Poets in fifty small volumes; 'An Appeal from the Judgments of Great Britain respecting the United States of America' (1819). He conducted the American Register (1817–18), the National Gazette (1821–37), and the Museum of Foreign Literature and Science (Vol. i., 1822); and edited 'Didactics: Social, Literary, and Political,' a collection of aphorisms (2 vols., 1836).

Walsh, William Shepard. An American journalist and editor; born in Paris, Feb. 1, 1854. He was connected with J. B. Lippincott & Co. from 1876, and in 1886 became editor of Lippincott's Magazine. He has written many essays, also juveniles, and historical and scientific books for the young; and has published a critical commentary, 'Faust: The Legend and the Poem' (1887), and 'Paradoxes of a Philistine' (1888).

Walter, Ferdinand (väl'ter). A German jurist; born at Wetzlar, Nov. 30, 1794; died at Bonn, Dec. 13, 1879. His principal works are: 'Text-Book of Canon Law' (1822); 'Ancient German Law' (3 vols., 1824); 'History of Roman Law down to Justinian' (1840); 'History of German Law' (1853); 'Sources of Ancient and Modern Ecclesiastical Law' (1862); 'Natural Law and Politics in the Light of the Present' (1863).

Walters, William Thompson. An American merchant and art virtuoso; born in Pennsylvania, 1820; died 1891. He was educated as an engineer; became identified with the coal and iron industry; was art commissioner from the United States at the Paris Expositions (1867–78), at Vienna (1873), and trustee of the Corcoran Gallery at Washington, D.C. His private art gallery is the most extensive and valuable (especially in Oriental ceramics) in this country. He has published: 'Barye' (1885); 'The Percheron Horse' (1886); and 'Notes upon Certain Masters of the XIXth Century' (1886).

Walther von der Vogelweide (väl'ter fon der fō'gel-vī-dė). "The greatest lyric poet of Germany before Goethe, and the first supremely great lyric poet that the nations of modern Europe produced," flourished in the early part of the thirteenth century. The best critical edition of his poems is K. Lachmann's (1827).

Walton, Brian. An English bishop and biblical scholar; born at Seymour, Yorkshire, 1600; died in London, Nov. 29, 1661. He was made chaplain to Charles II. and bishop of Chester at the Restoration. His greatest work is 'Biblia Sacra Polyglotta' (6 vols., folio 1657), including the Hebrew original of the Old Testament, the Samaritan Pentateuch, the Chaldee, Syriac, Arabic, Persian, and Latin Vulgate, with various readings, notes, etc.; still thought to be "the most complete Biblical apparatus in any language." He wrote in 1658 his 'Dissertation on the Antiquity and Authority of his Texts,' in later editions called the 'Prolegomena,' under which name it was published in the original Latin (2 vols., 1827–28). 'The Considerator Considered,' etc. (1659), was written in answer to Dr. John Owen's 'Vindication of the Purity and Integrity of the Hebrew and Greek Texts,' etc. which was a criticism upon his great Biblical work.

Walton, Izaak. The celebrated author of 'The Compleat Angler'; born at Stafford, England, Aug. 9, 1593; died at Winchester, Dec. 15, 1683. He wrote the following biographies, known as 'Walton's Lives': of Dr. John Donne (1640), Sir Henry Wotton (1640), Richard Hooker (1662), George Herbert (1670), and Dr. Robert Sanderson (1678). 'The Compleat Angler; or, The Contemplative Man's Recreation' (1653) is one of the great English classics.

Walworth, Clarence Alphonsus. An American clergyman; born in Plattsburg, N. Y., May 30, 1820. At first a lawyer, afterwards an Episcopalian clergyman, he united with the Roman Catholic Church, and was one of the founders of the Congregation of St. Paul; since 1864 rector of St. Mary's Church, Albany, N. Y. He has written: 'The Gentle Sceptic' (1860); 'The Doctrine of Hell' (1874); 'Andiatorocté, and Other Poems.' Died at Albany, Sept. 19, 1900.

Walworth, Jeannette Ritchie (**Hadermann**). An American novelist; born in Philadelphia, Feb. 22, 1837. She has written for periodicals, and published a number of works, among them: 'The Silent Witness' (1871); 'Nobody's Business' (1878); 'The Bar Sinister' (1885); 'Southern Silhouettes' (1888).

Walworth, Mansfield Tracy. An American novelist, son of Chancellor Walworth; born in Albany, N. Y., Dec. 3, 1837; died in New York city, June 3, 1873. Abandoning the law for literature, he became connected with The Home Journal, and subsequently wrote many novels and romances. He was shot by his son, who was acquitted on the ground of insanity. He wrote: 'Mission of Death'; 'Lulu' (1860); 'Hotspur' (1861); 'Warwick' (1868); 'Beverly' (1873); and two posthumous works, 'Married in Mask' (1888) and 'Tahara' (1888). He had completed a 'Life of Chancellor Livingston'; and was writing 'Lives of the Chancellors of New York State.'

Wang-Chi-Fou (wäng-chē-fö'). One of the greatest Chinese dramatic poets; lived in the 13th century. He was the creator of the Chinese opera (called *Thsa-Khi*, lyrical dramas), and is placed by his countrymen among the ten *Thsaï-tseu*, or writers of genius. He composed thirteen plays, of which only two survive: 'Si-siang-ki' (Western Pavilion) like all

Chinese plays a sort of novel in dialogue,— his best work,— which obtained and still holds great popularity with the Chinese; and the comedy 'The State Minister's Feast.' The former was partly translated into French by Stanislas Julien in 'Europe Littéraire' (Literary Europe).

Wangemann, Hermann Theodor (väng'e-män). A German traveler; born at Wilsnack in Brandenburg, March 27, 1818; died there, June 18, 1894. He was for several years a director of Lutheran missions. He wrote: 'Short History of Evangelical Hymnology' (1855); 'A Year's Travel in South Africa' (1869); 'Pictures of Life in South Africa' (1871); 'South Africa and its Inhabitants' (1881); 'History of the Berlin Missionary Society in South Africa' (1886); 'W. Posselt, the Kaffir Missionary' (1888); 'The Present Lutheran Church in its Relation to the Una Sancta' (7 vols., 1883–84); 'The Church Politics of William III.' (1884).

Wangemann, Otto. A German musician; born at Loitz on the Peene, Jan. 9, 1848. Author of 'Sketch of the History of Music' (1882); 'History of the Organ' (3d ed. 1891); 'History of the Oratorio' (1882); 'The Organ and its Construction' (3d ed. 1895); 'Choral Songs for Gymnasiums.' (3d ed. 1892).

Wappæus, Johann Eduard (väp-pä-ös'). A German geographer and statistician; born at Hamburg, May 17, 1812; died at Göttingen, professor in the university there, Dec. 16, 1879. He edited and largely wrote the Stein-Hörschelmann 'Manual of Geography and Statistics' (10 vols., 1871). He also wrote: 'Researches on the Geographical Discoveries of the Portuguese under Henry the Navigator' (1842); 'The Republics of South America' (1843); 'German Emigration and Colonization' (1846).

Warburton, Eliot Bartholomew George. An Irish barrister and author; born at Aughrim, County Galway, 1810; lost in the burning of the steamer Amazon, off Land's End, Jan. 4, 1852. His works are: 'The Crescent and the Cross; or, Romance and Reality of Eastern Travel' (2 vols., 1844); 'Memoirs of Prince Rupert and the Cavaliers' (3 vols., 1849); 'Reginald Hastings' (3 vols., 1850), a novel of the great rebellion; 'Memoirs of Horace Walpole and his Contemporaries' (2 vols., 1851); 'Darien; or, The Merchant Prince: An Historical Romance' (3 vols., 1851); and 'A Memoir of Charles Mordaunt, Earl of Peterborough' (3 vols., 1853).

Warburton, Peter Egerton. An Australian explorer; born at Northwich, England, Aug. 15, 1813; died near Adelaide, Nov. 16, 1889. He wrote: 'Major Warburton's Diary' (1866); 'Journey Across the Western Interior of Australia' (1875).

Warburton, William. An English author; born at Newark-upon-Trent, Dec. 24, 1698; died June 7, 1779. He became bishop of Gloucester. His defense of Pope's 'Essay on Man' against the charge of atheism won the gratitude of the poet, who made the bishop his literary executor. Warburton thereupon brought out an edition of Pope (1751). He published: 'Miscellaneous Translations in Prose and Verse' (1723); 'An Inquiry into the Causes of Prodigies and Miracles' (1727); 'Alliance between Church and State' (1736); 'Divine Legation of Moses Demonstrated, on the Principles of a Religious Deist, from the Omission of the Doctrine of the Future State of Reward and Punishment in the Jewish Dispensation' (1738–41; 10th ed. 3 vols., 1846); an edition of Shakespeare (very poor, 1747); 'Julian; or, A Discourse Concerning the Earthquake and Fiery Eruption which Defeated the Emperor's Attempt to Rebuild the Temple at Jerusalem' (1750); 'View of Bolingbroke's Posthumous Writings' (1754); and 'The Doctrine of Grace' (1762).

Ward, Adolphus William. An English educator, literary historian, and biographer; born at Hampstead, London, Dec. 2, 1837. In addition to being professor of history and principal of Owens College, Manchester, and contributing to the 'Encyclopædia Britannica' and leading English reviews, he is the author of 'The House of Austria in the Thirty Years' War' (1869); 'Dramatic Literature of the Age of Elizabeth' (2 vols., 1875); 'Lives' of Chaucer (1879) and Dickens (1882) in the 'English Men of Letters' series; translator of Curtius's 'History of Greece' (5 vols., 1868–74); and editor of 'Pope's Poems' (Globe edition, 1869), and of 'Byron's Poems' (Chetham Society's edition); 'Great Britain and Hanover' (1899).

Ward, Artemus. See **Browne, Charles Farrar.**

Ward, Elizabeth Stuart (Phelps). An American novelist and poet; born at Andover, Mass., August 1844. In 1888 she married Herbert D. Ward, with whom she sometimes collaborates. Among her books are: 'The Gates Ajar' (1868), one of the most successful of American stories; 'Men, Women, and Ghosts' (1869); 'The Silent Partner' (1870); 'The Trotty Book' (1870); 'The Story of Avis' (1877); 'Old Maid's Paradise' (1879); 'Beyond the Gates' (1883); 'Dr. Zay' (1884); 'The Gates Between' (1887); 'The Master of the Magicians' (1890); and 'Come Forth' (1890). Jointly with her husband she wrote: 'Poetic Studies,' verse (1885); 'Songs of the Silent World' (1885); and 'The Struggle for Immortality' (1889), a volume of essays. Her most recent work is 'The Story of Jesus Christ' (1897); 'Trixy' (1904); 'The Man in the Case' (1906).

Ward, Herbert Dickinson. An American writer of juvenile books; born in Massachusetts in 1861. He has published: 'The Captain of the Kittie Wink'; 'A Dash to the Pole'; 'The New Senior at Andover'; 'The White Crown,' etc.; 'The Burglar who Moved Paradise'; 'The Last Hero'; 'A Dash to the Pole.'

Ward, Mrs. Humphry (Mary Augusta Arnold). An English novelist of great celebrity; born at Hobart Town, Tasmania, in 1851. She is a granddaughter of Dr. Arnold of Rugby, and was married in 1872 to Thomas Humphry Ward. Her books are : ' Milly and Ollie ' (1881); ' Miss Bretherton ' (1884); a translation of ' Amiel's Journal ' (1885); ' Robert Elsmere ' (1888), a story of religious doubt, stirring up a great interest and having an enormous circulation; ' The History of David Grieve ' (1892); ' Marcella ' (1894); and ' The Story of Bessie Costrell ' (1895). She helped to establish, and still takes an active interest in, University Hall, a social settlement among the London poor.

Ward, Nathaniel. An English-American lawyer, clergyman, and author; born at Haverhill, England, about 1578; died at Shenfield, Essex, about October, 1652. While a pastor in Massachusetts he wrote the ' Body of Liberties,' adopted December 1641, the first code of laws established in New England. His other writings are : ' The Simple Cobler of Agawam ' (1647); ' A Religious Retreat Sounded to a Religious Army ' (1647); ' A Sermon Before Parliament ' (1647); and ' Mercurius Anti-Mechanicus; or, The Simple Cobler's Boy, with his Lap-full of Caveats ' (1648).

Ward, Robert Plumer. An English writer of fiction and miscellaneous works; born in London, 1765; died 1846. His novels, ' Tremaine ' (1825), and ' De Vere ' (1827), published anonymously, were exceedingly popular. His other works include treatises on the law of nations and essays on juristic topics.

Ward, Thomas. An American writer and littérateur of New York city; born 1807; died 1873. He was the author of : ' A Month of Freedom '; ' Passaic '; ' A Group of Poems '; ' Flora : A Pastoral Opera '; ' War Lyrics.'

Ward, William Hayes. An American editor, clergyman, and eminent Assyriologist; born in Abington, Mass., Jan. 25, 1835. He was a pastor of the Congregational church and professor at Ripon College, 1860–68, when he became editor of the Independent. In 1884 he went to Babylon in charge of an expedition. He has written much on Oriental archæology for the Bibliotheca Sacra, and other journals, and prepared the report of the exploring expedition of 1884, and published ' Notes on Oriental Antiquities.'

Warden, David Baillie. An Irish-American scholar; born in 1788; died in Paris, Oct. 9, 1845. He graduated at the New York Medical College, was United States secretary of legation at Paris, and subsequently consul from 1804 to his death. He was a member of the French Institute, and published : ' Inquiry concerning the Intellectual and Moral Faculties and Literature of the Negroes ' (1810); ' Origin and Nature of Consular Establishments ' (1816); ' Description of the District of Columbia ' (1816); ' Statistical, Political, and Historical Account of the United States ' (1819); ' L'Art de vérifier les dates : Chronologie Historique de l'Amérique ' (10 vols., Paris, 1826–44); ' Bibliotheca Americana Septentrionalis,' etc. (1820); ' Recherches sur les Antiquités de l'Amérique Septentrionale ' (1827); and ' Bibliotheca Americana ' (1831).

36

Warden, Florence. Pseudonym of Mrs. George E. James. An English novelist; born Florence Alice Price, 1857. She won note with ' The House on the Marsh ' (1882), which had a wide sale. She has since published : ' At the World's Mercy '; ' A Vagrant Wife '; ' A Prince of Darkness '; ' A Dog With a Bad Name '; ' Doris's Fortune '; ' Scheherazade : A London Night's Entertainment '; ' Morals and Millions.'

Ware, Henry, Jr. An American clergyman and religious writer; born at Hingham, Mass., April 21, 1794; died at Framingham, Mass., Sept. 22, 1843. He took an active part in the organization of the Unitarian movement. Among his writings are : ' Hints on Extemporaneous Preaching ' (1824); ' Recollections of Jotham Anderson ' (about 1824); ' On the Formation of the Christian Character ' (1831); ' Life of the Saviour ' (1832; new ed. 1868); ' The Feast of the Tabernacle,' an oratorio poem (1837); ' Memoirs ' of Rev. Dr. Parker (1834), Dr. Noah Webster, Dr. John Priestley, and Oberlin; and ' Scenes and Characters Illustrating Christian Truth ' (2 vols., 1837). Selections from his writings were published in 4 vols., 1846–47.

Ware, Mrs. Katharine Augusta (Rhodes). An American poet; born in Quincy, Mass., in 1797; died in Paris, in 1843. She edited The Bower of Taste, and published a volume of poems, ' Power of the Passions,' etc. (1842).

Ware, William. An American clergyman, editor, and author; born at Hingham, Mass., Aug. 3, 1797; died at Cambridge, Mass., Feb. 19, 1852. In addition to his pastorates, and his editorship of the Christian Examiner, he wrote the following : ' Letters from Palmyra ' (1837), first published in the Knickerbocker Magazine, subsequently republished as ' Zenobia ; or, The Fall of Palmyra ' (new ed. 1868); ' Probus ; or, Rome in the Third Century ' (1838), republished as ' Aurelian ' (new ed. 1868); ' Julian ; or, Scenes in Judea ' (1841); ' Sketches of European Capitals ' (1851); ' Lectures on the Works and Genius of Washington Allston ' (1852); and a ' Life of Nathaniel Bacon,' in Sparks's series. He edited ' American Unitarian Biography ' (1850).

Warfield, Catharine Ann (Ware). An American poet and novelist; born near Natchez, Miss., June 6, 1816; died in Kentucky, May 21, 1877. She published, with her sister Eleanor, ' The Wife of Leon, and Other Poems ' (1844); ' The Indian Chamber,' etc. (1846): and wrote ' The Household of Bouverie ' (1860); ' The Romance of the Green Seal ' (1867); ' Miriam Monfort ' (1873); ' Hester Howard's Temptation ' (1875); ' A Double Wedding ' (1875); ' Sea and Shore ' (1876); ' The Romance of Beauseincourt ' (1876); ' Ferne Fleming ' (1877); ' The Cardinal's Daughter ' (1877).

Waring, George Edwin. An American sanitary engineer, author and lecturer. Born in Poundridge, N. Y., July 4, 1833; died in New York city, Oct. 28, 1898. He was colonel of the 6th Missouri Cavalry in the Civil War. He was

superintendent of the street-cleaning department of New York city, 1895-98. Soon after
the War he published very spirited stories
of army experience, and has since published
many works on drainage and sanitary science;
also 'A Farmer's Vacation,' 'The Bride of the
Rhine,' 'Village Improvement,' etc.

Warneck, Gustav Adolf (vär'nek). A German theological writer; born at Naumburg,
March 6, 1834. He wrote: 'Missions in the
Light of the Bible' (1878); 'The Relations
between Missions and Modern Civilization'
(1879); 'The Mission in Pictures from its History' (1884); 'Sketch of the History of Missions from the Reformation to the Present
Time'; 'The Ultramontane Art of Fence'
(1889); 'The Romanism of To-day in the Light
of its Missions to the Heathen' (1889); 'The
Evangelical Alliance and its Opponents' (1889);
'Position of the Evangelical Mission Toward
the Question of Slavery'; 'Doctrine of Evangelical Missions.'

Warner, Anna Bartlett. ["Amy Lothrop»]
An American author; born in New York in
1820. In conjunction with her sister, Susan
Warner, she published the novels 'Say and
Seal' (1860); 'Wych Hazel' (1876); and 'The
Gold of Chickaree' (1876). Among her sepa-
rate works, published under her pen-name
"Amy Lothrop," are: 'Dollars and Cents'
(1853); 'My Brother's Keeper' (1855); 'Sto-
ries of Vinegar Hill' (1871); 'The Fourth Watch';
'The Blue Flag,' etc. (1879); 'The Other Shore';
'Three Little Spades,' a child's book; and
'Gardening by Myself'; 'Wayfaring Hymns.'

Warner, Charles Dudley. An American
man of letters and novelist; born in Plainfield,
Mass., Sept. 12, 1829; died at Hartford, Conn.,
Oct. 20, 1900. He graduated at Hamilton College in 1851, was admitted to the bar in 1856,
and practiced in Chicago till 1860, when he removed to Hartford, Conn., became editor of the
Press in 1861, and of the Courant in 1867. He
was connected with Harper's Monthly Magazine, as the contributor of an editorial department, from 1884. His literary work began
while in college, in contributions of stories to
the Knickerbocker and Putnam's Magazine.
His first book was a compilation for the use of
students in schools, called 'A Book of Eloquence' (1853). In 1870 he published 'My Summer in a Garden,' which was followed by
'Saunterings' (1872); 'Backlog Studies' (1872);
'The Gilded Age' (with S. L. Clemens, 1873);
'Baddeck, and That Sort of Thing' (1874);
'Mummies and Moslems' (1876—re-issued under
the title 'My Winter on the Nile'); 'In the
Levant' (1877); 'Being a Boy' (1877); 'In the
Wilderness' (1878); 'The American News-
paper' (1879); 'Studies of Irving' (with W. C.
Bryant and George P. Putnam, 1880); 'Life of
Washington Irving' (1881); edited 'American
Men of Letters' (of this series 'Washington
Irving,' 1881, was the initial volume; the thir-
teenth volume, 'George William Curtis,' by Ed-
ward Cary, appeared in 1894); 'Captain John
Smith, Sometime Governor of Virginia, and

Admiral of New England: A Study of his Life
and Writings' (1881); 'A Roundabout Journey'
(1883); 'Papers on Penology' (with others;
Reformatory Press, Elmira, N. Y., 1886); 'Their
Pilgrimage' (1886); 'On Horseback: A Tour
in Virginia, North Carolina, and Tennessee,
Published with Notes of Travel in Mexico and
California' (1888); 'Studies in the South and
West, with Comments on Canada' (1889); 'A
Little Journey in the World: A Novel' (1889);
'Looking Forward: The Dual Government
Realized' (1890); 'Our Italy, Southern Cali-
fornia' (1890); 'As We Were Saying' (1891);
'Washington Irving' (1892); 'The Work of
Washington Irving' (1893); 'As We Go' (1893);
'The Golden House: A Novel' (1894); 'The
Relation of Literature to Life' (1896); 'The
People for Whom Shakespeare Wrote' (1897);
edited 'A Library of the World's Best Litera-
ture' (1896-98).

Warner, Susan. An American novelist;
born in New York, July 11, 1819; died at
Highland Falls, N. Y., March 17, 1885. Her
books are: 'The Wide, Wide World' (1850);
'Queechy' (2 vols., 1852); a theological treatise,
'The Law and the Testimony' (1853); 'The
Hills of the Shatemuc' (1856); 'Lyrics from
the Wide, Wide World'; 'The Golden Ladder'
(1862); 'The Old Helmet' (1863); 'Wych
Hazel' (1876); and an essay, 'American Female Patriotism.' Her pen-name was "Elizabeth Wetherell."

Warner, William. An English lawyer and
poet; born in London, about 1558; died at
Amwell, March 9, 1609. He wrote: 'Pan his
Syrinx' (1584), a pastoral novel; and 'Albion's
England, a Continued History of the Same
Kingdom from the Originals of the First Inhabitants Thereof,' etc. (1586), a poem, in rhymed
fourteen-syllable lines, of history, legend, and
anecdote, very popular in his day, running
through nine editions, the last being that of
1810.

Warren, Gouverneur Kemble. An American general; born in Cold Spring, N. Y., Jan.
8, 1830; died in Newport, R. I., Aug. 8, 1882.
He graduated at West Point in 1850. He was
a member of many scientific associations, and
contributed to their journals. His published
works include: 'Explorations in the Dacota
Country' (1855-56); 'Explorations in Nebraska
and Dakota' (1858); and a pamphlet, 'The
Battle of Five Forks' (1866), in which he had
a notable part.

Warren, John Byrne Leicester. See **De
Tabley.**

Warren, Mercy Otis. An American poet,
historian, and patriot; born at Barnstable, Mass.,
Sept. 25, 1728; died at Plymouth, Mass., Oct.
19, 1814. An ardent patriot, she corresponded
with the leaders of the Revolution, among them
Samuel and John Adams, and Thomas Jefferson. The 'Correspondence of John Adams
and Mercy Warren' was published by the
Massachusetts Historical Society in 1878. She
wrote dramatic and satirical poems against the

royalists (1773–75), which were included in her volume of 'Poems, Dramatic and Miscellaneous' (1790). She published 'A History of the Rise, Progress, and Termination of the American Revolution, Interspersed with Biographical, Political, and Moral Observations' (3 vols., 1805).

Warren, Samuel. A celebrated English novelist; born in Wales, 1807; died in London, 1877. He was by profession a lawyer. He contributed to Blackwood's the story 'Blucher' when he was in his seventeenth year. His later works include : 'Passages from the Diary of a Late Physician' (1830–31); 'Ten Thousand a Year' (1839); 'Now and Then' (1847); 'Miscellanies' (1854). He wrote several legal works, and also an attack on the Catholic Church, entitled 'The Queen and the Pope' (1850).

Warren, William Fairfield. An American clergyman and educator; born at Williamsburg, Mass., March 13, 1833. He wrote : 'True Key to Ancient Cosmology and Mythological Geography' (1882); 'Paradise Found: The Cradle of the Human Race at the North Pole' (1885), a very curious speculation; 'The Quest of the Perfect Religion' (1887); 'In the Footsteps of Arminius' (1888); 'The Story of Gottlieb,' a study of ideals (1891); 'Constitutional Law Questions in the Methodist Episcopal Church'; 'The Religion of the World and the World-Religion.'

Warriner, Edward Augustus. An American clergyman and writer; born in Massachusetts in 1829. He has written : 'Victor La Tourette'; 'Kear: A Poem'; 'I Am That I Am: A Metrical Essay'; 'The Gate Called Beautiful.'

Warton, Joseph. An English clergyman, critic, and editor; born at Dunsford in 1722; died at Wickham, Feb. 23, 1800. He wrote : 'Odes on Various Subjects' (1746); a poetical translation of the 'Eclogues and Georgics of Virgil' (1753); twenty-four critical papers to the Adventurer (1753–56); an 'Essay on the Genius and Writings of Pope' (2 vols., 1856–82). He edited the works of Pope (9 vols., 1797), and the works of Dryden (4 vols., 1811; completed after his death).

Warton, Thomas. An English clergyman, who was poet-laureate (1785); born at Basingstoke in 1728; died at Oxford, May 21, 1790. He wrote : 'Observations on the Faerie Queene of Spenser' (1754); 'The Life of Sir Thomas Pope' (1772); 'History of English Poetry' (3 vols., 1774–81); and several occasional poems, collected in 1777. He edited the 'Greek Anthology' (1766); the works of Theocritus (2 vols., 1770); and the 'Minor Poems of Milton' (1785).

Washburn, Charles Ames. An American editor, historian, and novelist; born at Livermore, Me., March 16, 1822; died in New York, Jan. 26, 1889. He was editor and proprietor of the Alta California, and the San Francisco Daily Times (1858–61); minister to Paraguay (1861–65), residing in that country also from 1866 to 1868. He wrote 'History of Paraguay' (2 vols., 1871); the novels 'Philip Thaxter' (1861), 'Gomery of Montgomery' (1865); etc.

Washburne, Elihu Benjamin. An American statesman; born in Maine, 1816 ; died 1887. He was made minister to France by President Grant, and remained at his post in Paris during the Commune, a fact which imparts special interest to his 'Recollections of a Minister to France — 1869–77' (1887).

Washburn, William Tucker. An American novelist and versifier ; born in Boston, Aug. 15, 1841. He has written : 'Fair Harvard,' a typical college novel of Harvard University; 'The Unknown City: A Story of New York; and 'Spring and Summer,' a volume of verse ; and 'Poems' (1905).

Washington, George. The first President of the United States; born at Pope's Creek, Westmoreland County, Va., Feb. 22, 1732; died at Mt. Vernon, Va., Dec. 14, 1799.

Wasielevski, Wilhelm Joseph von (vä-sē-ä-lev'skē). A German violinist; born at Gross-Leesen near Dantzic, June 17, 1822; died Dec. 13, 1896. He wrote: 'The Violin and its Masters' (1869); 'R. Schumann: A Biography' (1858); 'The Violin in the 17th Century and the Beginnings of Instrumental Composition' (1874); 'History of Instrumental Music in the 16th Century' (1878); 'Schumanniana' (1883); 'Beethoven' (2 vols., 1888); 'The Violoncello and its History' (1889).

Wasilewski, Edmund (vä-sē-lev'skē). A Polish poet; born at Rogozna, 1814; died 1846. The hardships, misfortunes, and sorrows of his life are reflected in the irony, doubt, despair, resignation, and spiritual revolt of his verse. Among his best productions were: 'The Cracovians' (1840); 'Child of Folly' (1845); 'The Cathedral on the Wesel' (1846); etc. ('Various Poems,' Cracow, 1839.)

Wasson, David Atwood. An American clergyman, poet, and essayist; born at Brooksville, Me., May 14, 1823; died Jan. 21, 1887. He wrote chiefly for periodicals, but his works were collected as 'Bugle Notes,' 'Seen and Unseen,' 'Ideals,' etc.

Waters, Mrs. Clara Erskine (Clement). An American miscellaneous writer; born in St. Louis, Mo., Aug. 28, 1834. In 1883–84 she made a tour round the world. The first of her many publications was the 'Simple Story of the Orient' (1869). 'Legendary and Mythological Art' (1871); 'Artists of the Nineteenth Century and their Works,' with Laurence Hutton (1879); 'Eleanor Maitland,' a novel (1881); 'Stories of Art and Artists' (1886); 'Woman in the Fine Arts' (1904); and a translation of 'Dosia's Daughter,' a novel by Henri Gréville, are included in her works.

Watson, Henry Clay. An American journalist and writer of historical stories; born in Baltimore, 1831; died in Sacramento, Cal., July 10, 1869. He was the author of: 'Camp-Fires of the Revolution' (1851); 'Nights in a Block-House' (1852); 'Old Bell of Independence'

(1852); 'The Yankee Teapot' (1853); 'Heroic Women' (1853); 'The Masonic Musical Manual' (1855); 'Camp Fires of Napoleon' (1856); and 'Lives of the Presidents' (1858).

Watson, John. ["Ian Maclaren."] A noted Scottish Presbyterian preacher, and novelist; born in Essex, 1850. Since 1880 he has been settled over the Sefton Park Church, Liverpool. He has published: 'The Days of Auld Lang Syne' (1893), 'Beside the Bonnie Briar Bush' (illustrated ed., 1896), both very popular; 'The Upper Room' (1895); 'Kate Carnegie' (1896); 'The Cure of Souls' (1896); 'Home Making'; 'The Mind of the Master' (1896); 'Ideals of Strength' (1897); 'The Potter's Wheel' (1897); etc. Died May 6, 1907.

Watson, John Whittaker. An American journalist and poet; born in New York city, Oct. 14, 1824; died there, July 18, 1890. He wrote many stories for periodicals, and is one of the many authors of the poem, 'Beautiful Snow,' contained in 'Beautiful Snow and Other Poems' (1869).

Watson, Paul Barron. An American lawyer and historical writer. He was born in Morristown, N. J., March 25, 1861. He has published: 'Bibliography of the Pre-Columbian Discoveries of America' (1881); 'Life of Marcus Aurelius' (1884); and 'The Swedish Revolution under Gustavus Vasa.'

Watson, Richard. An English theologian; born at Barton-upon-Humber, Feb. 22, 1781; died in London, Jan 8, 1833. His principal works are: 'Theological Institutes' (6 parts, 1823-28); 'The Life of Rev. John Wesley' (1831); 'A Biblical and Theological Dictionary' (1831); 'An Exposition of the Gospels of Matthew and Mark' (1833).

Watson, Rosamund Marriott. An English poet, writing sometimes under the pseudonyms « Graham R. Tomson » and « R. Armytage »; born in London, 1863. She has contributed to English and American periodicals, and has edited several anthologies. Her works include: 'The Bird Bride' (1889); 'A Summer Night, and Other Poems' (1891); 'After Sunset' (1903); 'The Heart of a Garden' (1904).

Watson, Thomas. An English poet; born in London about 1557; died in 1592. His poems, pastoral and amatory, equaled in popularity those of his friends Spenser and Sidney. He translated Sophocles's 'Antigone' into Latin (1581); and wrote: 'Ekatompathia; or, Passionate Century of Love' (1582); 'Meliboeus, Thomæ Watsoni; sive, Ecloga in Obitum Domini Francisci Walsinghami Equitis Aurati' (1590); 'The Tears of Fancie; or, Love Disdained' (1593).

Watson, William. An English poet; born at Wharfedale, Aug. 2, 1858. His works include: 'The Prince's Quest' (1880); 'Epigrams of Art' (1884); in the National Review, a series of political sonnets, 'Ver Tenebrosum' (1885); 'Wordsworth's Grave, and Other Poems' (1891);

'Lachrymæ Musarum' (1892), an elegy on Tennyson; 'Poems' (1893); 'Excursions in Criticism' (1893); 'The Eloping Angels' (1893); 'Odes, and Other Poems' (1894); and 'The Purple East' (1896), an attack on the British government for its failure to act against Turkey for the Armenian massacres; 'For England' (1903).

Wattenbach, Wilhelm (vät'ten-bach). A German historian and palæographist; born at Ranzau, Sept. 22, 1819; died at Frankfort, Sept. 20, 1897; became professor of history at Heidelberg, 1862, and 1873 in Berlin University. He was author of 'Contributions to the History of the Christian Church in Bohemia and Moravia' (1849); 'Introduction to Greek Palæography' (1867); 'Introduction to Latin Palæography' (1869); 'Writing in the Middle Ages' (1871); 'Vacation Travels in Spain and Portugal' (1869); 'The Transylvanian Saxons' (1870); 'The Inquisition against the Waldenses in Pomerania and in the Mark of Brandenburg' (1886); 'The Sect of the Brethren of the Free Spirit' (1887); 'History of the Roman Papacy' (1876).

Watterson, Henry. An American journalist; born in Washington, D. C., Feb. 16, 1840. His first work as journalist was with the Democratic Review, and The States, in Washington, D. C. He edited the Republican Banner, Nashville, Tenn., before and after the War, in the interim serving with distinction in the Confederate army. He edited, in Louisville, Ky., the Louisville Journal (1867-68); and has edited the Louisville Courier-Journal since 1868. He has published, 'Oddities of Southern Life and Character,' and 'History of the Spanish-American War.'

Watts, Alaric Alexander. An English educator, poet, and journalist; born in London, March 16, 1799; died at Kensington, April 5, 1864. His journalistic work was done with the Manchester Courier, the London Standard, and the United Service Gazette. He edited a series of annual volumes, 'Literary Souvenir' (1825-35). He published: 'Poetical Sketches' (1822); and 'Lyrics of the Heart' (1851).

Watts, Isaac. An English clergyman and hymn-writer; born at Southampton, July 17, 1674; died at Theobalds, Newington, Nov. 25, 1748. He wrote many religious and educational treatises, among which are: 'Logic; or, The Right Use of Reason in the Inquiry after Truth' (1725); and 'The Improvement of the Mind' (1741). His 'Psalms and Hymns' have given him a place in the hymnals of all English-speaking denominations.

Waugh, Edwin. An English dialect-writer; born at Rochdale, Lancashire, Jan. 29, 1817; died at New Brighton, April 30, 1890. He wrote 'Sketches of Lancashire Life and Localities' (1855; 4th ed. 1869); 'Poems and Lancashire Songs' (1859); 'Rambles in the Lake Country and its Borders' (1862); 'Tufts of Heather from the Lancashire Moors' (1864); 'Irish Sketches'; 'Home Life of the Lancashire Factory-Folk' (1866); 'Sancno's Wallet'; 'The Chimney Corner' (1879); etc. 'Posies from a Country Garden' (2 vols., 1865) is a selection from his poems.

Wayland, Francis. An American clergyman, educator, and author; born in New York city, March 11, 1796; died in Providence, R. I., Sept. 30, 1865. He graduated at Union College, 1813, was pastor in a Baptist church in Boston 1821–26, and president of Brown University 1827–55. His works include: 'Elements of Moral Science' (1835); 'Elements of Political Economy' (1837); 'The Limitations of Human Responsibility' (1838); 'Thoughts on the Present Collegiate System' (1845); 'Domestic Slavery considered as a Scriptural Institution' (1845); 'Memoirs' of Harriet Ware (1850) and Adoniram Judson (1853); 'Elements of Intellectual Philosophy' (1854); 'Sermons to Churches' (1858); 'Memoir of Thomas Chalmers' (1864).

Webb, Charles Henry. ["John Paul."] An American banker, journalist, and humorist; born at Rouse's Point, N. Y., Jan. 24, 1834. His journalistic work was done on the New York Times (1860–63); the Californian, San Francisco (1863–66); and the New York Tribune, for which, mainly, his humorous articles were written. He invented an adding machine. He wrote several burlesque dramas; 'John Paul's Book' (1874); 'Parodies, Prose and Verse' (1876); and 'Vagrom Verse.' Died, 1905.

Webb, James Watson. An American soldier, journalist, and diplomat; born at Claverack, N. Y., Feb. 8, 1802; died in New York city, June 7, 1884. In journalism he was connected with the Morning Courier, New York (1827–29); The Morning Courier and New York Enquirer (1829–59). He is the author of: 'Altowan; or, Incidents of Life and Adventure in the Rocky Mountains' (2 vols., 1846); 'Slavery and its Tendencies' (1856); and a pamphlet on 'National Currency' (1875).

Webb, Sidney. An English socialist, one of the founders of the Fabian Society; born in London, July 13, 1859. He has written: 'Socialism in England' (1889); 'The Eight Hours' Day' (1891), in collaboration with Harold Cox; and 'The London Program' (1892). His wife, Beatrice (Potter), has written 'The Co-operative Movement in Great Britain,' and together they have written the noted 'History of Trades-Unionism in England' and 'Industrial Democracy.' 'History of Liquor Licensing.'

Weber, Georg (vā'ber). A German educator and historian; born in Bavaria, Feb. 10, 1808; died at Heidelberg, Aug. 10, 1888. His works are: 'Text-Book of General History' (2 vols.); 'History of German Literature'; 'General History of the World for the Educated Classes' (15 vols., 1857–80); and with M. H. Holtzmann, a history of the Hebrew people and the origin of Christianity.

Weber, Karl Julius. A German miscellaneous writer; born at Langenburg, April 16, 1767; died at Kupferzell, July 20, 1832. He wrote: 'Monasticism' (3 vols., 1818–20); 'Knighthood' (3 vols., 1822–24); 'Germany; or, Letters of a German Traveling in Germany' (4 vols., 1826–28); 'Democritus; or, The Literary Remains of a Laughing Philosopher' (5 vols., 1832–35): the last two works being satires on German society.

Weber, Max Maria von. A German railway engineer, son of the celebrated music composer, Karl Maria von W.; born at Dresden, April 25, 1822; died at Berlin, April 18, 1881. Besides numerous technological works, he wrote: 'Karl Maria von Weber: A Life Picture' (3 vols., 1864–66); 'From the World of Work' (1868); 'Works and Days' (1869); 'Looking and Doing' (1878).

Webster, Albert Falvey. An American short-story writer; born in Boston, 1848; died at sea, Dec. 27, 1876. His best stories were printed in Scribner's, Appleton's, and the Atlantic Monthly, and include: 'Our Friend Sullivan'; 'Little Majesty'; 'An Operation in Money'; 'My Daughter's Watch'; 'Miss Eunice's Glove.'

Webster, Julia Augusta (Davies). An English poet and dramatist; born at Poole, Dorsetshire, Jan. 30, 1837; died at Kew, Sept. 5, 1894. She was daughter of Vice-Admiral George Davies. She wrote: 'Blanche Lisle and other Poems, by Cecil Home' (1860); 'A Woman Sold,' etc. (1867); 'In a Day' (1882); dramas and translations of Greek tragedies, etc.

Webster, Daniel. The celebrated American statesman and orator; born in Salisbury, N. H., Jan. 18, 1782; died in Marshfield, Mass., Oct. 24, 1852.

Webster, John. An English dramatist; born near the end of the sixteenth century. He helped Dekker, Chettle, Drayton, Marston, Rowley, Middleton, Munday, Heywood, and Wentworth Smith, in writing some of their plays. Some of his own dramas are: 'The White Devil; or, Vittoria Corombona' (1612); 'The Duchess of Malfi' (1623); 'Appius and Virginia' (1624); and 'The Devil's Law Case.'

Webster, Noah. A celebrated American lexicographer; born at Hartford, Conn., Oct. 16, 1758; died in New Haven, Conn., May 28, 1843. He published: 'A Grammatical Institute of the English Language, etc., in Three Parts' (1783–85), which was spelling-book, grammar, and reader combined; 'A Compendious Dictionary of the English Language' (1807); a 'Philosophical and Practical Grammar of the English Language' (1807); and then his great work, 'American Dictionary of the English Language' (2 vols., 4to, 1828). He superintended the publication of the second edition of his dictionary (1840–41).

Weckherlin, Georg Rudolf (vek'här-lēn). A German poet; born at Stuttgart, about 1584; died at London, in 1653. He was essentially a court poet, and wrote only for the nobility. He was the first to introduce into German literature the ode, sonnet, eclogue, and epigram; his finest pieces are the 'Love Songs to Myrta.' He had his complete poetical works published twice at Amsterdam (2 vols., 1641, 1648).

Wedderburn, James. A Scotch psalmodist; born at Dundee, about 1495; died in France, about 1563. With his brother Robert, he edited: 'Ane Compendious Buike of Godly and Spirituall Sangs, Collectit Out of Sundrie Partes of the Scripture, wyth Sundrie of Uther Ballates Changed Out of Prophane Sangs, for Avoyding of Sinne and Harlotrie' (about 1548). This was the principal psalmbook used in Scotland. He is the reputed author of 'The Complaynt of Scotland' (1548), "the only classic work in old Scottish prose."

Wedmore, Frederick. An English journalist, novelist, and art critic; born at Clifton, July 9, 1844. He has written considerably for the magazines. Among his works are: 'A Snapt Gold Ring' (1871), a novel; 'Two Girls' (1874); 'Studies in English Art' (1876); 'Pastorals of France' (1877); 'Four Masters of Etching' (1883); the novel 'The Collapse of the Penitent.'

Weech, Friedrich von (väċh). A German historian; born at Munich, Oct. 16, 1837. He has written: 'The Emperor Ludwig of Bavaria and King John of Bohemia' (1860); 'Baden under the Grand-Dukes Karl Friedrich, Karl, and Ludwig' (1864); 'History of the Baden Constitution' (1868); 'The Germans since the Reformation' (1878); 'History of Baden' (1890); 'Karlsruhe: History of the City' (1893); 'Journeys to Rome' (1896).

Weed, Thurlow. An American journalist and politician; born at Cairo, N. Y., Nov. 15, 1797; died in New York city, Nov. 22, 1882. He founded the Agriculturist at Norwich, N. Y.; the Evening Journal, Albany, N. Y. (1830); and edited the Commercial Advertiser, New York city (1867-68). His books are: 'Letters from Europe and the West Indies' (1866); and an autobiography, edited by his daughter, and published in 1882. He wrote 'Reminiscences' for the Atlantic Monthly.

Weeden, William Babcock. An American soldier and ethical and historical writer; born at Bristol, R. I., Sept. 1, 1834. He served with distinction in the Union army during the Civil War. He has written: 'Morality of Prohibitory Liquor Laws' (1875); 'Social Law of Labor' (1882); 'Economic and Social History of New England' (2 vols., 1890), his chief work.

Weeks, Edwin Lord. An American artist; born in Massachusetts in 1849. He has written a work of travel, 'From the Black Sea through Persia and India.' Died Nov. 17, 1903.

Weeks, Robert Kelley. An American poet; born in New York city, Sept. 21, 1840; died April 13, 1876. He graduated from Yale in 1862, from the Columbia Law School in 1864, and entered the New York bar the same year, but afterwards left it to devote himself to literary pursuits. He published 'Poems' (1866); and 'Episodes and Lyric Pieces' (1870).

Weems, Mason Locke. An American biographical writer and Episcopal clergyman; born in 1759; died in 1825. His chief work is 'A History of the Life and Death, Virtues and Exploits, of General George Washington' (1800), an entertaining but unreliable and inaccurate book. He also wrote: 'Biographies' of General Francis Marion (1816); Franklin (1817); and William Penn (1829).

Wegele, Franz Xaver (vä'ge-lè). A German historian; born at Munich, Oct. 28, 1823; died at Würzburg, Oct. 16, 1897. He was appointed professor of history in the University of Würzburg, 1851. He wrote: 'Karl August of Weimar' (1850); 'Life and Works of Dante Alighieri' (3d ed. 1879); 'Sources of Thuringian History' (1854); 'Frederick the Peaceful, Margrave of Meissen' (1870); 'Goethe as a Historian' (1875); 'History of German Historiography since the Rise of Humanism' (1885).

Wegscheider, Julius August Ludwig (väg-shī-der). A German theological writer; born at Kübbelingen in Brunswick, Sept. 17, 1771; died at Halle, Jan. 27, 1849. His principal work is 'Institutes of Christian Dogmatic Theology' (1815): this work may be regarded as the classical dogmatic treatise of rationalism.

Wehl, Feodor von (väl). A German novelist and poet; born at Kunzendorf, Silesia, Feb. 19, 1821; died at Hamburg, Jan. 22, 1890. He wrote the lyrico-dramatic poem 'Hölderlin's Love' (1852); a volume of verses, 'From Heart to Heart' (1867); 'Fifteen Years in the Directorship of the Stuttgart Court Theatre' (1886). His plays were published in 6 volumes, 1882. He wrote also: 'Hamburg's Literary Life in the 18th Century' (1856); 'In Leisure Hours' (1867); 'At the Roaring Loom of Time' (1869); 'Time and Men' (1889).

Weil, Gustav (vīl). A German Orientalist and historian; born at Sulzburg, Baden, April 25, 1808; died at Freiburg in Breisgau, Aug. 30, 1889. He was appointed professor of Oriental languages in the University of Heidelberg, 1861. He wrote: 'The Poetry of the Arabs' (1837); a learned 'History of Mohammed the Prophet' (1843); 'Historico-critical Introduction to the Koran' (1844); 'Biblical Legends of the Mussulmans' (1845); 'History of the Khalifs' (5 vols., 1846-62); 'History of the Islamitic People from Mohammed to the time of the Sultan Selim' (1866). He made the first German translation of the 'Thousand Nights and a Night' (4 vols., 1837-41).

Weilen, Joseph von (vī'len). A German educator and dramatist; born at Tetin, Bohemia, Dec. 28, 1828; died in Vienna, July 3, 1889. His works are: 'Fantasies and Songs' (1853); 'Men of the Sword' (1855); 'Tristan' (1860); 'Edda' (1865); 'Drahomira' (1867); 'Count Horn' (1871); and 'The New Achilles' (1881).

Weill, Alexandre (vīl or väl). A French journalist and miscellaneous writer; born at Schiroff in Alsace, 1811. He spent his youth in Germany as teacher, editor, and author. He wrote a series of 'Alsatian Tales' that were very popular; 'The Peasants' War' (1847), a historical study; 'Republic and Monarchy'

(1849); 'Village Tales' (1853); 'Mismorismes: Hymns of the Soul' (1860); 'My Youth, My Adolescence, etc.' (1870), an autobiography; 'Parisian Romances' (1874); 'Genius of Universal History' (1876); etc.

Weingarten, Hermann (vīn'gär-ten). A German church historian; born at Berlin, March 12, 1834; died April 25, 1892, near Breslau, where he was professor of church history. Among his works are: 'Pascal as an Apologist of Christianism' (1863); 'The Revolution Churches of England' (1868); 'Chronological Tables and General Views of Church History' (1870); 'Rise of Monachism in the Post-Constantine Age' (1887).

Weinhold, Karl (vīn'hōlt). A German antiquarian; born at Reichenbach, Silesia, Oct. 26, 1823; died at Bad, Manheim, Germany, Aug. 15, 1901. He held the chair of German philology in various universities, — Breslau, Cracow, Grätz, Kiel, and Berlin. He wrote: 'Christmas Plays and Carols of Southern Germany and Silesia' (1853); 'Researches in German Dialects' (1853); 'Ancient Norse Life' (1856); 'The Giants of German Myth' (1858); 'Heathen Burial in Germany' (1859); 'German Womankind in the Middle Ages' (2 vols., 2d ed. 1882).

Weir, Arthur. A Canadian poet; born at Montreal, 1864. He was for several years a journalist, then an analytical chemist, and is now a banker. He has written 'Fleurs de Lys' (1887); 'The Romance of Sir Richard,' etc. (1890); etc.

Weir, Harrison William. An English illustrator and writer for young people; born at Lewes, May 5, 1824. He is noted for his engravings of animals, and was one of the original members of the Society of Painters in Water-Colors. He has written: 'The Poetry of Nature' (1865); 'Funny Dogs with Funny Tales'; 'The Adventures of a Bear'; 'Bird Stories'; 'Our Cats'; etc.: some of which he illustrated himself. Died Jan. 4, 1906.

Weir, James. An American romance-writer; born in Kentucky, 1821. He has published 'Lonz Powers; or, The Regulators'; 'Simon Kenton'; 'Winter Lodge.' Died in 1906.

Weise, Christian (vī'zė). A German educationist and poet; born at Zittau, April 30, 1642; died there, 1708. He wrote admirable text-books for school instruction; 'Curious Thoughts on German Verse' (2 vols., 1691–95); several dramas and romances; a volume of poems; 'Overflowing Thoughts of Early Youth' (1668). His best works are his satirical tales, as 'The Three Chief Arch-Fools'; 'The Bavarian Machiavel'; 'Kathrine the Shrew.'

Weismann, August (vīs'män). A celebrated German zoölogist; born at Frankfort on the Main, Jan. 17, 1834. He became professor at Freiburg (1871). He denies the possibility of the inheritance of acquired characters. He is one of the leading minds engaged in the study of evolution; his writings have provoked much

discussion, and been a great stimulation to research. Among his principal works are: 'Studies in the Theory of Descent' (1880); 'Essays on Heredity' (London, 1888–92); 'Germ Plasm' (London, 1893); etc.

Weiss, Bernhard (vīs). A German theological writer; born at Königsberg, June 20, 1827. He was made professor of theology at Kiel, 1863, and at Berlin, 1877. His principal writings are: 'Text-Book of Biblical Theology' (1868); 'Life of Jesus' (2 vols., 1882); 'Introduction to the New Testament'; 'Religion of the New Testament.'

Weiss, John. An American clergyman, reformer, and author; born in Boston, June 28, 1818; died there, March 9, 1879. He has published: 'Æsthetic Prose' (1845), a translation of Schiller's philosophical and æsthetic essays; 'Life and Correspondence of Theodore Parker' (2 vols., 1864); 'American Religion' (1871); 'Wit, Humor, and Shakespeare' (1880). He was a disciple of the Transcendental philosophy, an earnest abolitionist, an advocate of woman's political enfranchisement, and a defender of reason in religion.

Weisse, Christian Felix (vī'sė). A German poet and writer for the young; born at Annaberg, Jan. 28, 1726; died at Leipsic, Dec. 16, 1804. He wrote: 'Sportive Lays' (1758), in the Anacreontic vein; 'Lays of the Amazons' (1760); and several tragedies and comedies; he was less successful with these than with his comic operas, which for a long time held the boards of the Leipsic theatre. He wrote also 'Songs for Children' (1776).

Weisse, Christian Hermann. A German philosopher, grandson of Christian F.; born at Leipsic, Aug. 10, 1801; died there, Sept. 19, 1866; he was professor of philosophy at Leipsic from 1845. He wrote: 'The Idea, the Treatment, and the Sources of Mythology' (1828); 'System of Æsthetics as a Science' (2 vols., 1830); 'The Idea of Godhead' (1833); 'Theodicy in German Rhymes' (1834); 'Principles of Metaphysic' (1835); 'The Gospel History Treated Critically and Philosophically' (2 vols., 1838); 'Luther's Christology' (1852).

Weizsäcker, Karl Heinrich (vīts'säk-er). A German Protestant theologian; born at Oehringen, Würtemberg, Dec. 11, 1822; died at Tübingen, Aug. 13, 1899. He was court chaplain at Stuttgart, 1851; member of the superior consistory there, 1859; professor of theology at Tübingen, 1861; chancellor of the university, 1890; privy councilor, 1894. Among his chief works are: 'Researches in Evangelical History' (2d ed. 1891); 'The Apostolic Age of the Christian Church' (2d ed. 1892; English translation 1894); etc. His translation into German of the New Testament (7th ed. 1894) has been greatly liked.

Welby, Amelia (Coppuck). ["Amelia."] An American poet; born at St. Michael's, Md., Feb. 3, 1819; died May 3, 1852. Her collected poems were published in Boston (1844), in New York (1850), and a final collection after her death, in 1860.

Welch, Philip Henry. An American humorist; born at Angelica, N. Y., March 1, 1849; died in Brooklyn, N. Y., Feb. 24, 1889. He has the distinction of being the maker of innumerable newspaper jokes, and short dialogues, the writing of which he made a profession. His books are: 'The Taylor-Made Girl' (1888); and 'Said in Fun' (1889).

Welch, Sarah. An Australian poet. Her home is at Adelaide, South Australia. She is a nurse by profession. She has written 'The Dying Chorister, and the Chorister's Funeral' (1879).

Welcker, Friedrich Gottlieb (vel'ker). A celebrated German classical scholar and archæologist; born at Grünberg, Hesse, Nov. 4, 1784; died at Bonn, Dec. 17, 1868. He was professor of archæology at Giessen, 1809; Göttingen, 1816; at Bonn, 1819. Besides editing editions of a number of Greek authors, he wrote: 'The Æschylean Trilogy' (1824; supplement, 1826); 'Greek Tragedy Arranged with Regard to the Epical Cyclus' (3 vols., 1841), an epoch-making work; 'Ancient Monuments' (5 vols., 1849–64); 'Greek Mythology' (3 vols., 1862); 'The Epical Cyclus' (1865–82); etc.

Welhaven, Johan Sebastian Cammermeyer (vel'hä-ven). A Norwegian journalist, patriot, and poet; born at Bergen, Dec. 22, 1807; died in Christiania, Oct. 21, 1873. He founded a weekly paper, Vidar (1833), which was changed into the daily Constitutionelle (1836). He wrote 'Poetic Art and Character of Henrik Wergeland' (1832), which awakened a great controversy; and 'Norges Daemring' (Norway's Twilight: 1834), political sonnets stirring up great strife of thought. Collections of his unpolemical poems appeared in 1851 and in 1863.

Welldon, James Edward Cowell. An English educator; born at Tunbridge, April 25, 1854. He was head-master of Dulwich College, 1883, and Harrow School, 1885. Besides standard translations of Aristotle's 'Politics,' 'Rhetoric,' and 'Nicomachean Ethics,' he has published 'Sermons Preached to Harrow Boys' (1887), and 'The Spiritual Life and Other Sermons' (1888); 'The Revelation of the Holy Spirit.'

Wells, Charles Jeremiah. An English poet; born in 1800; died in France, Feb. 17, 1879. He left England in 1840, afterwards living chiefly in Marseilles, where he practiced law. He was a friend of Keats, Horne, and Hazlitt. His best work is the dramatic poem, 'Joseph and his Brethren,' published in 1824 under the pseudonym of "H. L. Howard," and reprinted in 1876 with an introduction by Swinburne. He also wrote a little volume called 'Stories After Nature' (1822), now out of print. Some of these tales were afterwards reprinted in the Illustrated Family Journal, and in Linton's Illuminated Magazine.

Wells, David Ames. An American political economist; born at Springfield, Mass., June 17, 1828; died at Norwich, Conn., Nov. 5, 1898. He edited the 'Annual of Scientific Discovery' (16 vols., 1850–65). Some of his earlier works are 'Familiar Science' (1856); 'Elements of Natural Philosophy' (1857); and a widely circulated political pamphlet, 'Our Burden and Our Strength' (1864). Among his financial and economic books are: 'The Creed of the Free-Trader' (1875); 'Production and Distribution of Wealth' (1875); 'Robinson Crusoe's Money' (1876); 'The Silver Question' (1878); 'Our Merchant Marine,' etc. (1882); 'A Primer of Tariff Reform' (1884); 'Practical Economics' (1886); 'A Study of Mexico' (1887); 'A Short and Simple Catechism' (1888); and 'Relation of the Tariff to Wages.'

Wells, H. G. An English novelist; born at Bromley, Kent, 1868. Starting as a teacher in London, he is now a journalist there. He has written: 'The Time Machine' (1895); 'Select Conversations with an Uncle' (1895); 'The Wonderful Visit' (1895), a humorous satire; 'The Island of Dr. Moreau' (1896); 'The Wheels of Chance' (1896); 'Thirty Strange Stories' (1897); 'The Invisible Man' (1897); 'The Food of the Gods'; 'A Modern Utopia.'

Wells, Mrs. Kate Gannett. An American essayist and novelist; born (Catherine Boott Gannett) in 1838. She is the daughter of a Unitarian clergyman of Boston. She has written chiefly for periodicals. Her works have been collected in volumes: 'In the Clearings'; 'Miss Curtis'; 'Two Modern Women'; 'About People'; etc.; also some Sunday-school manuals.

Welsh, Herbert. An American philanthropist; born in Philadelphia, Dec. 4, 1851. He is the Indians' friend and founder of the Indian Rights Association. Among his writings are: 'Four Weeks among Some of the Sioux Tribes of Dakotah'; and 'Report of a Visit to the Navajo, Pueblo, and Hualapai Indians of New Mexico and Arizona'; 'The Other Man's Country.'

Wemyss, Francis Courtney (weems). An actor, manager, and theatrical writer; born in London, May 13, 1797; died in New York, Jan. 5, 1859. He acted in London, 1821; at Philadelphia, 1822; was manager of theatres in several American cities, and secretary of the Dramatic Fund Association from 1852. Among his works are: 'Twenty-Six Years as Actor and Manager' (1847); 'Chronology of the American Stage' (1852); and 'Theatrical Biography.' He edited 'The Minor Drama' (7 vols., 1848–52).

Wendell, Barrett. An American author and educator; born in Boston, Aug. 23, 1855. He has published: 'English Composition' (1891); 'Cotton Mather' (1891), in 'Makers of America' series; and the novels 'The Duchess Emilia' (1885), and 'Rankell's Remains' (1886). His 'Stelligeri, and Other Essays concerning America' (1893), and 'William Shakspere: A Study' (1894); 'The France of To-day' (1907), are widely known. He is American editor of Literature.

Wergeland, Henrik Arnold (ver'gĕ-länd). A Norwegian poet; born at Christiansand, June 17, 1808; died Aug. 12, 1845. His works are:

'The Creation, Man, and the Messiah,' a lyric poem (1830); 'The Jew'; 'Jan van Huysum's Flower-Piece'; 'The English Pilot' (1845); and many tragedies, vaudevilles, farces, etc. He has had a great influence on Norwegian literature and civilization.

Werner, Franz von (vär'ner). ["Murad Effendi."] An Austrian poet and diplomatist; born in Vienna, May 30, 1836; died Sept. 12, 1881. In 1877 he became resident minister at The Hague and Stockholm, and in 1880 was named minister plenipotentiary and envoy extraordinary. He wrote: 'Through Thuringia' (1870); 'Marino Falieri' (1871); 'Inez de Castro' (1872); 'Mirabeau' (1875); 'East and West,' poems (1877); 'Ballads and Pictures' (1879). His dramatic works were collected in 1881.

Werner, Friedrich Ludwig Zacharias. A German dramatist and clergyman; born at Königsberg, Nov. 18, 1768; died in Vienna, Jan. 17, 1823. His works are: 'Sons of the Valley' (1800), inspired by Masonic enthusiasm; 'Cruise in the German Ocean' (1804), set to music by Hoffmann; 'Martin Luther'; and 'The 24th of February,' which made a great sensation. Besides the dramas named, he wrote the tragedies 'Attila,' 'Wanda,' 'Kunegunde,' 'The Mother of the Maccabees'; and lyrical poems, hymns, sermons, etc.

Wesley, Charles. An English clergyman and poet; born at Epworth, Lincolnshire, December 1701; died in London, March 29, 1788. He was "the poet of Methodism," and many of his hymns are to be found in the hymn-books of all Protestant denominations.

Wesley, John. The founder of Methodism; an English preacher and writer; born at Epworth, June 1703; died March 2, 1791. He was educated at Oxford. His works were as follows: 'Primitive Physic' (1747); 'Explanatory Notes on the New Testament' (1755); 'Doctrine of Original Sin' (1757); 'Survey of the Wisdom of God in Creation' (1763); 'Notes on the Old and New Testaments' (1764); 'Preservative against Unsettled Notions in Religion' (1770); 'A Calm Address to Our American Colonies' (1775). His journals are among his best works. He also edited, with his brother Charles, several collections of hymns.

Wesley, Samuel, Sr. An English clergyman and sacred poet; born at Winterborn-Whitchurch, Dorset, 1662; died at Epworth, April 22, 1735. He was the father of Charles and John, and of Samuel, Jr. He wrote 'Life of Christ: An Heroic Poem,' 'Eupolis's Hymn to the Creator,' etc. He is best known by the two hymns to be found in Methodist hymn-books, 'Behold the Saviour of Mankind,' and 'O Thou who when I did Complain.'

Wesley, Samuel, Jr. An English educator and sacred poet, son of Samuel; born in London, Feb. 10, 1690-1; died at Tiverton, Nov. 6, 1739. He was head-master of Blundell's free grammar-school at Tiverton, 1732-39. He remained

with the old High Church party, and did not embrace Methodism with his brothers. Editions of his poems have been published in 1736, 1743, and 1862 (with a Life, by William Nichols). He is best known by his hymns in the Methodist hymn-book, and a poem beginning "The morning flowers display their sweets," written on the death of a young lady.

Wesselhoeft, Mrs. Lily F. (Pope) (wes'selhooft). An American writer of juvenile stories; born in Massachusetts, 1840. Among her works are: 'Jerry the Blunderer'; 'Sparrow the Tramp'; 'Flipwing the Spy'; 'Old Rough the Miser'; 'The Winds, the Woods, and the Wanderer'; 'Frowzle the Runaway.'

Westcott, Brooke Foss. A distinguished English clergyman and Biblical scholar; born near Birmingham, Jan. 12, 1825; died July 28, 1901. He was professor of divinity at Cambridge University, 1870; honorary chaplain to the queen, 1875; bishop of Durham, 1890. Among his works are: 'General View of the History of the English Bible' (2d ed. 1879); 'History of the Canon of the New Testament' (5th ed. 1881); 'Introduction to the Study of the Gospels' (6th ed. 1882); 'The Gospel of the Resurrection' (5th ed. 1884); 'The Bible in the Church' (9th ed. 1885); etc. With Dr. Hart he edited the Greek New Testament (2 vols., 1881).

Westenrieder, Lorenz von (vest'en-rē-der). A German historian; born at Munich, Aug. 1, 1748; died there, March 15, 1829. He was professor of poetry at Landshut, 1774; and of rhetoric at Munich, 1776; literary censor, 1776; clerical senator, 1786; raised to the nobility, 1813. He did much for the elevation of the German language. His statue was erected at Munich in 1854. He wrote 'History of Bavaria' (2 vols., 1785); 'Contribution to the National History, Geography, Statistics, and Agriculture' (10 vols., 1785-1817); etc.

Wetherell, Elizabeth. See **Warner, Susan.**

Weyman, Stanley John (wī'man). An English novelist; born at Ludlow, Shropshire, Aug. 7, 1855. He was educated at Christ Church, Oxford; was classical instructor in the King's School, Chester, 1878; was called to the bar in 1881, and practiced until 1890. He contributed to periodicals in 1883, and published in book form the historical romances: 'The House of the Wolf' (1890); 'Francis Cludde' (1891); 'The New Rector' (1891); 'A Gentleman of France' (1893); 'Under the Red Robe' (1894); 'My Lady Rotha' (1894); 'Count Hannibal'; 'The Long Night.' Several of his stories have been dramatized. His books deal with character and incident not previously written upon and are fresh, original, and popular.

Wharton, Anne Hollingsworth. An American story-writer; born in Pennsylvania about 1845. Among her books are: 'The Wharton Family' (1880); 'Virgilia'; 'St. Bartholomew's Eve'; 'Colonial Days and Dames'; 'Through

Colonial Doorways'; 'Martha Washington: A Biography'; 'Italian Days and Ways.'

Wharton, Thomas. An English statesman; born about 1640; died in London, April 12, 1715. His name is associated with literature by his being the reputed author of the famous Irish ballad, 'Lilliburlero.'

Wharton, Thomas. An American journalist, dramatist, and critic; born in Philadelphia, Aug. 1, 1859; died April 6, 1896. He was an editorial writer on Philadelphia journals, and contributed largely to various periodicals. He published the novels 'A Latter-Day Saint' and 'Hannibal of New York'; and wrote the famous and popular short story, 'Bobbo.'

Whately, Richard. An eminent English clergyman and educator, archbishop of Dublin; born in London, Feb. 1, 1787; died in Dublin, Oct. 1, 1863. He was regarded as one of the "Broad Church" party in the Church of England. He was a voluminous writer; among his works are: 'The Use and Abuse of Party Feeling in Matters of Religion' (1822); 'Elements of Logic' (1826); 'View of the Scripture Revelations concerning a Future State' (1829); 'Bacon's Essays, with Annotations' (1856); 'A General View of the Rise, Progress, and Corruptions of Christianity' (1860); and 'Miscellaneous Lectures and Reviews' (1864).

Wheatley, Henry Benjamin. An English philologist and bibliographer; born at Chelsea, May 2, 1838. He has been an official of various London literary and other societies. Besides editing a number of works, he has written: 'Anagrams' (1862); 'Round About Piccadilly and Pall Mall' (1870); 'Samuel Pepys and the World he Lived In' (1880); 'Decorative Art' (1884); 'How to Form a Library' (1886); 'How to Catalogue a Library' (1887); 'Literary Blunders' (1893); 'Historical Portraits.'

Wheaton, Henry. An eminent American jurist, born in Providence, R. I., Nov. 27, 1785; died in Dorchester, Mass., March 11, 1848. He graduated at Brown University, 1802; practiced law at New York, 1812, and edited the National Advocate. He was a reporter of the United States Supreme Court, 1816 to 1827, and then became chargé-d'affaires to Denmark (1827–35), and in 1835–46 minister to Berlin. His chief writings are: 'Digest of Maritime Law' (1815); 'Life of William Pinckney' (1826); 'Reports of Cases in the Supreme Court' (12 vols., 1827); 'History of the Northmen' (1831); 'Elements of International Law' (1836); 'History of the Law of Nations' (1841).

Wheeler, Andrew Carpenter. ["Nym Crinkle."] An American journalist, critic, and dramatic writer; born in New York, June 4, 1835. He wrote for the New York Times and World, Milwaukee Sentinel, and other journals—and was also a war correspondent. He wrote: 'The Chronicles of Milwaukee' (1861); 'The Twins: A Comedy' (1862); and 'The Primrose Path of Dalliance.' He died at Monsey, N. Y., March 10, 1903.

Wheeler, Crosby Howard. An American writer, who was a missionary to Turkey; born in Maine in 1823. His writings comprise: 'Little Children in Eden'; 'Letters from Eden'; 'Ten Years on the Euphrates'; 'Odds and Ends.' He died in 1896.

Wheeler, William Adolphus. An American lexicographer; born at Leicester, Mass., Nov. 14, 1833; died at Roxbury, Mass., Oct. 28, 1874. He was assistant superintendent of the Boston Public Library in 1867. Besides assisting in the composition of 'Worcester's Dictionary' and of the new illustrated edition of 'Webster's Dictionary' (1864), and editing Hole's 'Brief Biographical Dictionary' (1866) and a 'Dickens Dictionary' (1873), he wrote 'Dictionary of the Noted Names of Fiction' (1865); 'Who Wrote It?' an index to anonymous literature, left unfinished by him, but completed by Charles G. Wheeler (1881); and 'Familiar Allusions' (1882), left unfinished.

Wheelwright, John. An English-American clergyman, who was a classmate of Oliver Cromwell at Cambridge University; born in Lincolnshire, about 1592; died at Salisbury, N. H., Nov. 15, 1679. A brother-in-law of Anne Hutchinson, and defender of her religious opinions, he was banished from Massachusetts for seditious preaching, and founded Exeter on the Squamscott. He published, answering Thomas Welde, 'Mercurius Americanus; or, Observations on a Paper entitled 'Of the Rise, Reign, and Ruin of the Familists, Libertines, etc., in New England' (1654); and a 'Vindication' (1654).

Wheelwright, John Tyler. An American novelist and story-writer; born at Boston, 1856. He has written: 'New Chance Acquaintance' (1880); 'Rollo's Journey to Cambridge' (1880, with F. J. Stimson); 'The King's Men' (1882, with F. J. Stimson, John Boyle O'Reilly, and Robert Grant); 'A Child of the Century' (1887); 'A Bad Penny' (1895).

Whewell, William. A celebrated English scientist and philosopher; born at Lancaster, May 24, 1794; died at Cambridge, March 6, 1866. He was professor of mineralogy at Cambridge University, 1828–32, and of moral theology and casuistical divinity, 1838–55; master of Trinity College in 1841. He wrote: 'Astronomy and Physics with Reference to Natural Theology' (1833); 'History of the Inductive Sciences' (1837); 'Philosophy of the Inductive Sciences' (1840); 'Elements of Morality' (1845); 'Lectures on Political Economy' (1861); etc.

Whichcote, Benjamin. A distinguished English clergyman and religious and ethical writer; born in Shropshire, May 4, 1609; died at Cambridge, May 1683. He was provost of King's College (1644); a leader in, if not the founder of, the latitudinarian school of English divines; a famous preacher, and one of the Cambridge Platonists. His works were all published posthumously: 'Observations and Apophthegms' (1688); 'Moral and Religious Aphorisms' (1703; new ed. 1753); 'Sermons,' etc. (1751).

Whipple, Edwin Percy. An American literary critic; born at Gloucester, Mass., March 8, 1819; died in Boston, June 16, 1886. He published: 'Essays and Reviews' (2 vols., 1848–49); 'Lectures on Subjects connected with Literature and Life' (1849); 'Character and Characteristic Men' (1867); 'The Literature of the Age of Elizabeth' (1868); 'Success and its Conditions' (1871); and posthumously published 'Recollections of Eminent Men' (1887); 'American Literature and Other Papers' (1887); and 'Outlooks on Society, Literature, and Politics' (1888).

Whistler, James Abbott McNeill. An American-English artist; born in Lowell, Mass., 1834. He was eminent in figure, landscape, and portrait painting, and in etching. He has been much written about. He wrote 'The Gentle Art of Making Enemies.' Died, London, 1903.

Whitaker, Alexander. An Episcopal clergyman and author; born in England, 1588; died in Virginia after 1613. He baptized Pocahontas, and officiated at her wedding. He wrote 'Good Newes from Virginia,' one of the first books written in the colonies.

Whitaker, Mrs. Mary Scrimgeour (Furman) (Miller). An American verse-writer and author; born in South Carolina in 1820. She has written: 'Poems'; and 'Albert Hastings: A Novel.'

White, Andrew Dickson. An American scholar and diplomat, former minister to Berlin; born at Homer, N. Y., Nov. 7, 1832. He was the first president of Cornell, to which he has given his historical library of about 20,000 volumes and 10,000 pamphlets, and many rare manuscripts. He has written: 'Outlines of Lectures on Mediæval and Modern History' (1861–72); 'The Plan of Organization for Cornell University' (1868); 'The New Education' (1868); 'Report on Co-education of the Sexes' (1871); and his great work, 'The Warfare of Science' (new ed., much enlarged, 2 vols., 1895); and an 'Autobiography' (1905).

White, Eliza Orne. An American writer of juvenile tales; born in New Hampshire, 1856. She has written: 'Miss Brooks'; 'When Molly was Six'; 'Winterborough'; 'A Little Girl of Long Ago'; 'A Borrowed Sister.'

White, Gilbert. An English clergyman and naturalist; born at Selborne, July 18, 1720; died there, June 26, 1793. He wrote: 'The Natural History and Antiquities of Selborne in the County of Southampton' (1789); and a posthumous work edited from his papers, 'The Naturalist's Calendar, with Observations in Various Branches of Natural History' (1795). Many naturalists have published editions of his works with annotations. John Burroughs writes an introductory to the latest edition (1895, 2 vols.). His 'Letters' were published in 1876. *

White, Greenough. An American educator and Episcopal clergyman; born in Massachusetts, 1863. He was professor of literature and of ecclesiastical history at the University of the South, Sewanee, Tenn., 1885–94. He wrote: Sketch of the Philosophy of American Literature'; 'The Rise of Papal Supremacy'; 'Outline of the Rise of the Philosophy of English Literature.' He died July 2, 1901.

White, Henry Alexander, an American historian; born April 15, 1861; since 1902, professor at Columbia, S. C. Theological Seminary. His numerous publications include 'The Pentateuch in the Light of the Ancient Monuments' (1894); 'History of the United States' (1904); 'Beginners of the History of the United States' (1906); 'Life of Stonewall Jackson' (1907).

White, Horace. An American journalist and editor; born in Colebrook, N. H., Aug. 10, 1834. He settled in Chicago, was editor of the Chicago Tribune (1864–74), and subsequently became connected with the New York Evening Post. He has written many pamphlets and essays upon political, social, and financial topics, the best known being: 'The Silver Question'; 'The Tariff Question'; 'Coin's Financial Fool'; 'Money and Banking Illustrated by American History'; 'The Gold Standard'; and has edited Luigi Cossa's 'Scienza delle Finanze' (1888), and Frédéric Bastiat's 'Sophismes Économiques' (1889).

White, John Blake. An American artist, lawyer, and dramatist; born Sept. 2, 1781, near Eutaw Springs, S. C.; died in Charleston, S. C., Aug. 24, 1859. His dramatic writings include: 'Foscan; or, The Venetian Exile' (1805); 'Mysteries of the Castle' (1806); 'Modern Honor' (1812); 'Triumph of Liberty' (1819); 'Intemperance' (1839).

White, Joseph Blanco. An English clergyman and controversialist; born at Seville, Spain, July 11, 1775; died at Liverpool, May 20, 1841. He edited in England, in the interests of Spanish independence, a monthly journal, El Español (1810–14); also Las Variedades (1822–25); and the London Review (1829). He evolved from a Catholic priest through the Church of England into a Unitarian minister. Some of his publications are: 'Letters from Spain, by Leucadio Doblado' (1822); 'Practical and Internal Evidence against Catholicism' (1825); 'The Poor Man's Preservative against Popery' (1825); 'Second Travels of an Irish Gentleman in Search of a Religion' (2 vols., 1833). Coleridge pronounced his 'Night and Death' the finest sonnet in the English language.

White, Richard Grant. An American journalist, critic and Shakespearean scholar; born in New York city, May 22, 1822; died there, April 8, 1885. His journalistic work was in connection with the New York Courier and Enquirer (1851–58), and World (1860–61); and the London Spectator (1863–67), for which he wrote 'Yankee Letters.' Among his published books are: 'Biographical and Critical Hand-Book of Christian Art' (1853); 'Shakespeare's Scholar' (1854); 'National Hymns: A Lyrical and National Study for the Times' (1861); 'Memoirs of the Life of William Shakespeare, with an Essay towards the Expression of his Genius,' etc. (1865); 'Poetry of the Civil War' (1866); 'Words and their Uses' (1870); 'England Without and Within' (1881); 'The Riverside Shakespeare,' with biography, introductions, and notes (1883, 3 vols.); an annotated edition of Shakespeare (1857-65, 12 vols.). He published one novel, 'The Fate of Mansfield Humphreys' (1884).

Whitefield, George. A famous English Methodist preacher; born at Gloucester, Dec. 27, 1714; died at Newburyport, Mass., Sept. 30, 1770. One of the founders of Methodism, he was one of the greatest sacred orators the Anglo-Saxon race has produced, speaking often three and once seven times a day to immense multitudes, and causing many conversions. He visited America seven times.

Whitehead, Charles. An English poet and novelist, a close friend of Dickens; born in London in 1804; died in Melbourne, Australia, July 5, 1862. He became a journalist in Australia, but fell into poverty and died in a hospital. He wrote many poems, plays, and sketches. His first published work was 'The Solitary' (1831). Other well-known ones were: 'The Autobiography of Jack Ketch'; 'Richard Savage' (1842), which D. G. Rossetti called "a remarkable book"; and 'The Cavalier,' a drama produced at the Haymarket Theatre, London.

Whitehead, Charles Edward. An American writer of hunting stories; born in New York in 1829. He has published 'The Campfires of the Everglades; or, Wild Sports in the South.'

Whitehead, William. An English poet and dramatist; born in Cambridge, 1715; died April 14, 1785. He was educated at Winchester and Cambridge, was secretary and registrar of the Order of the Bath, and became poet-laureate in 1757, succeeding Colley Cibber. He wrote 'The Roman Father,' a tragedy; 'The School for Lovers,' a comedy; and other dramas and poems.

Whitelock, L. Clarkson. An American story-writer. She has written 'A Mad Madonna, and Other Stories'; 'Indian Summer.'

Whiting, Charles Goodrich. An American journalist; born in 1842. His published works include: 'The Saunterer'; 'Essays on Nature.'

Whiting, Henry. A U. S. army officer, poet, and author; born in Lancaster, Mass., in 1790; died in St. Louis, Mo., Sept. 16, 1851. He served with credit in many grades, and retired with the rank of brigadier-general by brevet. His published works include: 'Otway: A Poem' (1822); 'Sannillac: A Poem' (1831); 'The Age of Steam'; 'Life of Zebulon Montgomery Pike.' He was co-author of 'Historical and Scientific Sketches of Michigan' (1834), and edited 'Washington's Revolutionary

Orders,' selected from the MSS. of John Whiting, his father (1844).

Whiting, Lilian. A Boston journalist; born in New York about 1855. She has written: 'The World Beautiful,' two series; 'From Dreamland Sent,' poems; and 'After her Death: The Story of a Summer'; 'Italy, the Magic Land.'

Whitman, Sarah Helen Power. An American poet; born in Providence, R. I., in 1803; died June 27, 1878. She married John W. Whitman, a Boston lawyer. She was once engaged to Edgar Allan Poe, afterwards writing a defense of him entitled 'Edgar A. Poe and his Critics' (1860). She was noted for her conversational powers. She published several volumes of poems, among them being the volume 'Hours of Life, and Other Poems' (1853); also 'Fairy Ballads,' written with her sister, Anna M. Power.

Whitman, Walt. A celebrated American poet; born at West Hills, L. I., May 31, 1819; died at Camden, N. J., March 26, 1892. He published: 'Franklin Evans; or, The Inebriate: A Tale of the Times' (1842); 'Voices from the Press: A Collection of Sketches, Essays, and Poems, by Practical Printers' (Walt Whitman, Woodworth, Willis, Bayard Taylor and others) (1850); 'Leaves of Grass,' 12 poems (1855); do., 32 poems (1856); do., 154 poems (1860-61); do., 178 poems (1867); do., 249 poems (1871); do., 288 poems (1876); do., 283 poems (1881); 'Drum Taps' (1865); 'Passage to India' (1871); 'Democratic Vistas' (1871); After All Not to Create Only' (1871); 'As a Strong Bird on Pinions Free, and Other Poems' (1872); 'Memoranda during the War' (1875); 'Two Rivulets' (1876), including poems previously printed; 'Specimen Days and Collect' (1882-83); 'November Boughs' (1888); 'Leaves of Grass, with Sands at Seventy and a Backward Glance o'er Traveled Roads' (1889); 'Good-Bye, My Fancy' (1891). The 'Complete Works' (1897-98) are published under the supervision of Whitman's literary executors.

Whitney, Adeline Dutton (Train). An American poet and novelist; born at Boston, Sept. 15, 1824. Besides writing a great deal for magazines, she has published: 'Footsteps on the Seas: A Poem' (1857); 'Mother Goose for Grown Folks' (1860; revised ed. 1882); 'The Boys at Chequasset' (1862); 'Faith Gartney's Girlhood' (1863); 'The Gayworthies: A Story of Threads and Thrums' (1865); 'A Summer in Leslie Goldthwaite's Life' (1866); 'Patience Strong's Outings' (1868); 'Hitherto: A Story of Yesterday' (1869); 'Real Folks' (1872); 'Pansies' (1872), verse; 'The Other Girls' (1873); 'Sights and Insights' (1876); 'Bonnyborough' (1885); 'Homespun Yarns' (1887); and two volumes of poems, 'Bird Talk' (1887) and 'Daffodils' (1887). Died March 21, 1906.

Whitney, William Dwight. An American professor, eminent as a philologist and editor; born in Northampton, Mass., Feb. 9, 1827; died at New Haven, Conn., June 7, 1894. He graduated at Williams College, 1845; spent some years abroad in study; in 1854 was made professor of Sanskrit at Yale, in 1870 of comparative philology, holding both positions till death. His writings are authority on all philological questions, and his rank as a Sanskrit scholar is of the first order. From 1849 he was a member of the American Oriental Society, and its president from 1884. His contributions to the North American Review, the New Englander, and other periodicals, were numerous and varied. His earliest work was the preparation, in company with Rudolf Roth of Tübingen, of an edition of the Atharva Veda Sanhita (Berlin, 1856). Among his other works are: 'Language and the Study of Language' (1867); 'On Material and Form in Language' (1872); 'Darwinism and Language' (1874); 'Logical Consistency in Views of Language' (1880); 'Mixture in Language' (1881); 'The Study of Hindoo Grammar and the Study of Sanskrit' (1884); 'The Upanishads and their Latest Translation' (1886). He has also written: 'Compendious German Grammar' (1869); 'German Reader in Prose and Verse' (1870); 'Essentials of English Grammar' (1877); 'Sanskrit Grammar' (1877); and 'Practical French Grammar' (1886). Professor Whitney was the superintending editor of the 'Century Dictionary' (1889–91), and assisted in the preparation of 'Webster's Dictionary' (1864).

Whittaker, Frederick. An American story-writer and journalist, formerly an officer in the United States service; born in 1838. He has written: 'A Defense of Dime Novels, by a Writer of Them'; 'Life of General Custer'; 'Cadet Button: A Tale of American Army Life'; 'Bel Rubio: A Novel.'

Whittemore, Thomas. A distinguished Universalist clergyman and religious writer; born at Boston, Jan. 1, 1800; died at Cambridge, March 21, 1861. He was joint editor of the Universalist Magazine, sole editor and proprietor of the Trumpet (1828–57); member repeatedly of the Massachusetts Legislature; president of the Vermont and Massachusetts railroad. He wrote: 'Modern History of Universalism' (enlarged ed. 1860); 'Autobiography' (1859), besides commentaries, hymns, biographies, etc.

Whittier, Elizabeth H. An American poet, sister of John Greenleaf Whittier; died at Amesbury, Mass., Sept. 3, 1864. Several of her poems can be seen in her brother's 'Hazel Blossoms' (1875), or under that title in any collection of his works.

Whittier, John Greenleaf. A famous American poet; born at Haverhill, Mass., Dec. 17, 1807; died at Hampton Falls, N. H., Sept. 7, 1892. A Quaker in religion, he was remarkable for his consistency and the purity of his life; he was one of the earliest and most influential abolitionists, several times mobbed for his opinions. He was at different periods editor of several journals, among them (1838–40)

the Pennsylvania Freeman, an abolition publication, and the leading contributor to the Washington National Era, 1847–59; was member of the Massachusetts Legislature, 1835–36; one of the secretaries of the American Anti-Slavery Society, 1836. He took great interest in politics. His home, after 1840, was at Amesbury, Mass. Among his best-known poems are: 'Skipper Ireson's Ride' (1860); 'My Playmate' (1860); 'Barbara Frietchie' (1863); 'Laus Deo' (1865); 'My Birthday'; 'Snow-Bound' (1866); 'Maud Muller' (1866); 'The Tent on the Beach' (1867). Perhaps no other of our poets, not even Longfellow, has so reached the popular heart.

Whymper, Edward. An English artist, traveler, and descriptive writer; born in London, April 27, 1840. He is famous as a mountain climber,—was the first to ascend the Matterhorn and other great Alpine peaks, and has ascended several of the greatest of the Andes; traveled in Greenland. He has published, and himself illustrated, 'Swiss Pictures' (1866); 'Scrambles among the Alps' (1869); 'Travels amongst the Great Andes of the Equator' (1892).

Whymper, Frederick. An English writer of travels, brother of Edward; born in London, July 20, 1838. He has written 'Travels and Adventures in Alaska' (1869), and 'Heroes of the Arctic and their Adventures' (1875); and compiled 'The Sea: Its Stirring Story of Adventure, Peril, and Heroism' (4 vols., 1878–81).

Whyte, Violet. See **Stannard.**

Whyte-Melville, George John. An English novelist; born near St. Andrews, Scotland, 1821; died Dec. 5, 1878. A captain in the Coldstream Guards, he retired from the army (1849), but served in the Turkish cavalry during the Crimean war. Among his works were: 'Captain Digby Grand' (1853); 'The Gladiators' (1863); 'Sarchedon' (1871); 'Katerfelto' (1875); etc. He wrote also a volume of 'Songs and Verses' and translated Horace's 'Odes.'

Wichert, Ernst Alexander August Georg (viĥ'ert). A German dramatist and novelist; born in Insterburg, March 11, 1831. He wrote: 'Our General York' (1858); 'Light and Shade' (1861); 'The Fool of Luck' (1869), which took the prize at the Vienna Burg Theatre, and turned the public attention to him; several novels, among them being 'Behind the Scenes' (1872), 'The Green Gate' (1875), 'A Strong Heart' (1878); some historical works, as 'Heinrich von Plauen' (1883); and 'The Great Elector in Prussia' (1886). He died Jan. 21, 1902.

Wickede, Julius von (vik'e-de). A German military writer and littérateur; born in Mecklenburg, July 11, 1819. He has written: 'A History of the War between Germany and France in the Years 1870 and 1871' (1873); 'A History of the Wars of France against Germany in the Last Two Centuries' (1874); 'A Prussian Officer' (1873); 'A German Trooper's Life' (1861); etc. He died March 22, 1896.

Wicksteed, Philip Henry. An English clergyman, economic writer, and critic; born at Leeds, Oct. 25, 1844. He was lecturer on sociology at Oxford University. He has published: ' Dante: Six Sermons ' (1880); ' Alphabet of Economic Science ' (1888); ' Henrik Ibsen: Four Lectures ' (1892); besides translations from the Dutch and French.

Widmann, Joseph Viktor (vid'män). A Swiss poet; born in Moravia, Feb. 20, 1842. He studied theology in Heidelberg and Jena, and in 1866 became organist and musical director in Liestal; in 1807 he was made assistant pastor at Thurgau; in 1868 became director of the Girls' School in Bern, but resigned this position in 1880, becoming associate editor of the Bern Bund. He wrote: ' Iphigenia in Delphi ' (1865), a drama; ' Buddha: An Epic Poem ' (1869); ' Œnone ' (1880), a play; ' The Muse of Aretin.'

Wied, Prince Alexander Philipp Maximilian von (vēd). A German naturalist and traveler; born at Neuwied, Sept. 23, 1782; died Feb. 3, 1867. He became major-general in the Prussian Army, but left it for scientific pursuits. He traveled in Brazil, 1815-17, and in 1833 went on a tour through the United States. As a result of these trips he wrote: ' Travels in Brazil ' (1820); ' Descriptions of the Natural History of Brazil ' (1824-33); and ' A Journey through North America ' (1833-43).

Wieland, Christopher Martin (vē'länt). A German poet and prose-writer; born in Oberholzheim, Suabia, Sept. 5, 1733; died Jan. 20, 1813. He established two periodicals, the German Mercury, and the Attic Museum. His most famous work is the poem ' Oberon ' (1780). Other principal works are: ' Agathon ' (1766-67); ' The New Amadis ' (1771); ' The Golden Mirror ' (1772). He also translated the greater part of Shakespeare into German.

Wiffen, Jeremiah Holmes. An English educator, poet, and translator; born at Woburn in 1792; died at Woburn Abbey, May 2, 1836. He made poetical translations of Garcilaso de la Vega (1823), Tasso's ' Jerusalem Delivered ' (2 vols., 1824-25), and from the Welsh ' Triads.' Besides contributing poems to the annuals, he published several volumes of original verse.

Wiggin, Kate Douglas. An American storywriter; born (Smith) in Philadelphia, Sept. 28, 1857. Her youth was spent in Hollis, Me., and she attended Abbott Academy in Andover, Mass. She went to California in 1876, where she studied the kindergarten system in Los Angeles; later, she taught a year in Santa Barbara College; then went to San Francisco, where she organized the first free kindergarten in the West. In 1880 she organized the California Kindergarten Training School, with her sister Nora A. Smith, and Mrs. S. B. Cooper. In 1880 she married S. B. Wiggin, a lawyer, and they moved to New York, where Mr. Wiggin died in 1889. In 1895 Mrs. Wiggin married Geo. C. Riggs. She has written many stories and books on and for the kindergarten

among them being ' The Story of Patsy,' ' The Birds' Christmas Carol,' ' Polly Oliver's Problem,' ' The Story Hour,' and ' Kindergarten Principles and Practice ' ; ' Finding a Home.'

Wigglesworth, Michael. An American Congregational clergyman and poet; born in England, 1631; died at Malden, Mass., June 10, 1705. His best-known work, ' The Day of Doom ' (1662), was a popular poem in New England for a long period. He published: ' God's Controversy with New England ' and ' Meat Out of the Eater,' in verse; and also ' A Discourse on Eternity.'

Wight, Orlando Williams. An American biographer, editor, and translator; born at Centreville, N. Y., Feb. 19, 1824; died at Detroit, Mich., Oct. 19, 1888. A Universalist minister originally, he practiced medicine in Wisconsin, where he was appointed State geologist and surgeon-general in 1874; health commissioner of Milwaukee, 1878-80; later he was health officer of Detroit. He wrote ' Lives and Letters of Abélard and Héloïse ' (new ed. 1861); ' Maxims of Public Health ' (1884) ; ' People and Countries Visited ' (1888), travels; edited ' Philosophy of Sir William Hamilton ' (1853); ' Standard French Classics ' (12 vols., 1859); ' The Household Library ' (18 vols., 1859); and translated Cousin's ' History of Modern Philosophy ' (1852, with F. W. Ricord); ' Lectures on the True, the Beautiful, and the Good ' (1854); Martin's ' History of France ' (1863, with Mary L. Booth).

Wilberforce, Samuel. An English bishop; born at Clapham, Sept. 7, 1805; killed by a fall from his horse, near Dorking, July 19, 1873. He wrote: ' Note-Book of a Country Clergyman ' (1833); ' Eucharistica ' (1839); ' Sermons Preached Before the University of Oxford ' (2 series, 1839-62), and other volumes of sermons; ' The Rocky Island and Other Parables ' (1840); ' A History of the Protestant Episcopal Church of America ' (1844); ' Heroes of Hebrew History ' (1870); ' Speeches on Missions ' (1874); and many miscellaneous publications.

Wilberforce, William. An English statesman and reformer; born at Hull, Aug. 24, 1759; died in London, July 29, 1833, and was buried in Westminster Abbey, as he had wished, " side by side with Canning, at the feet of Pitt, and within two steps of Fox and Grattan." His great work, achieved by almost twenty years of effort, was abolishing the slave trade throughout the British Empire. He published a volume, ' A Practical View of the Prevailing Religious System of Professed Christians in the Higher and Middle Classes of this Country, Contrasted with Real Christianity ' (1797). His sons wrote the ' Life of William Wilberforce ' (5 vols., 1838); and edited his ' Correspondence ' (2 vols., 1840).

Wilbour, Charles Edwin. An American Egyptologist, journalist, and author; born in Rhode Island, March 17, 1833; died in 1896. He was associated with the New York journals up to 1872, when he began the study of Egyptian antiquities; and was afterwards the companion of Brugsch Bey and Maspero in many exploring expeditions in Upper Egypt. He has published translations from the French: 'Rachel in the New World,' from Léon Beauvallet (1856); Victor Hugo's 'Les Misérables' (1862–63); and Renan's 'Life of Jesus' (1863).

Wilbrandt, Adolf (vēl'bränt). A German poet and dramatist; born at Rostock, Aug. 24, 1837. Among his dramas, which have been successfully presented in all the principal theatres of Germany, are: 'Graf Hammerstein' (1870), 'Gracchus' (1872), 'Arria and Messalina' (1874), 'Giordano Bruno' (1874), 'Nero' (1876), 'Kriemhild' (1877), tragedies; 'Youthful Love' (1872), and 'Natalie' (1878), comedies. He has treated the great social and literary questions of his day in the three novels 'Adam's Sons' (1890), 'Hermann Ifinger' (1892), and 'The Thorny Path' (1894); 'Villa Maria' (1902).

Wilcox, Ella Wheeler. An American poet; born at Johnstown Centre, Wis., about 1855. She has contributed much to current periodicals, and her poems are widely copied. Some of her volumes are: 'Maurine' (1882); 'Poems of Passion' (1883); and 'Poems of Pleasure' (1888). She has published a novel, 'Mal Moulée' (1885); and 'A Woman of the World.'

Wilde, Jane Francesca Elgee, Lady. ["Speranza."] An Irish poet and author, mother of Oscar; born in Wexford, 1826; died in Chelsea, England, Feb. 3, 1896. She wrote: 'Ugo Bassi' (1857); 'Poems' (1864); 'Driftwood from Scandinavia' (1884); 'Ancient Legends, etc., of Ireland' (2 vols., 1886); 'The Glacier Land.'

Wilde, Oscar Fingal O'Flahertie Wills. An Irish poet and author; born in Dublin, Oct. 15, 1856; died in Paris, Nov. 30, 1900. He wrote: 'Poems' (1880); 'The Picture of Dorian Gray,' a novel; 'The Happy Prince, and Other Tales' (1888); 'Guido Ferranti' (1890), and 'The Duchess of Padua,' tragedies; 'Intentions,' essays (1891); 'Lord Arthur Savile's Crimes, and Other Stories' (1891); 'Lady Windermere's Fan,' 'A Woman of No Importance,' and 'The Importance of Being Earnest,' etc.

Wilde, Richard Henry. An American lawyer and author; born in Dublin, 1789; died in New Orleans, 1847. He published: 'Conjectures and Researches concerning the Love, Madness, and Imprisonment of Torquato Tasso' (1842); and wrote many popular lyrics, the best-known one being 'My Life Is Like the Summer Rose.'

Wildenbruch, Ernst von (vēld'en-bröch). A German soldier, lawyer, and dramatist; born at Beyrût, Syria, Feb. 3, 1845. His dramas have been played with great success in most German cities. Some of them are: 'Fathers and Sons' (1882); 'Harold' (4th ed. 1884; English translation 1891); 'Christopher Marlowe' (1884); 'The Mennonite' (3d ed. 1886); 'The Carlovingians' (4th ed. 1887); 'The Quitzows' (1888);

'The New Master' (1891). He has also published a number of short stories and novels, the best of which is 'The Master of Taragra' (1880). In his 'Lays and Songs' (1877) and 'Poems and Ballads' (1884), are some great ballads and hymns, the most popular of which is 'The Witches' Song.' He died in 1909.

Wilder, Alexander. An American physician, and medical and archæological writer; born at Verona, N. Y., May 13, 1823. He was president of the Eclectic Medical College, New York (1867); lecturer on physiology and physiological medicine (1873–77); professor of physiology and of psychological science in the United States Medical College. Besides technical works, he has written 'The Worship of the Serpent' (1877); 'Plato and his Doctrines'; 'Evil'; 'History of Medicine.'

Wildermuth, Madame Ottilie (vēl'der-möt). A German writer; born (Ronschütz) at Rottenburg, Würtemberg, Feb. 22, 1817; died July 12, 1877. She wrote many novels of home life and stories for the young, among which are: 'In Daylight' (1861); 'Augusta' (1865); 'From Mountain and Valley' (1867); etc. 'In the Child World' was published after her death.

Wilhelmine, [Friederike Sophie] (vil-hel-mē'nė), **Margravine of Bayreuth.** A distinguished German writer of memoirs; born at Berlin, July 3, 1709; died October 1758. She was the favorite sister of Frederick the Great. She wrote 'Memoirs' (new ed. 1845).

Wilkes, Charles. An American admiral, explorer, and scientist; born in New York, 1801; died at Washington, D. C., Feb. 8, 1877. In command of an exploring expedition, he visited South America, the Fiji, Samoan, Hawaiian, and other islands in the Pacific, the Antarctic regions, the western coast of North America, etc.; captured the Confederate commissioners Mason and Slidell, on the British steamer Trent (1861); became commodore in 1862, and admiral in 1866. He wrote a 'Narrative' of his expedition (6 vols., 1845); 'Western America' (1849); etc.

Wilkes, George. An American journalist, born in New York city in 1820; died there, Sept. 23, 1885. He was editor of the Spirit of the Times from 1850, and well known as a politician and a traveler. He wrote a 'History of California' (1845); and a book of travel, 'Europe in a Hurry' (1852).

Wilkie, William. A Scottish poet; born at Dalmeny, West Lothian, Oct. 5, 1721; died Oct. 10, 1772. He was professor of natural philosophy at the university of St. Andrews, 1759. He wrote: 'The Epigoniad' (2d ed. 1759), an epic on the taking of Thebes, which won for him the title of the Scottish Homer; and 'Fables' (1768).

Wilkins, John. An English clergyman and scientist; born at Fawsley, Northamptonshire, 1614; died in London, Nov. 19, 1672. He was bishop of Chester (1668), and one of the founders of the Royal Society (1645). His works were one of the most effective agents in the spread of the Copernican system in England. He wrote: 'Discovery of a New World' (1638); 'Discourse concerning a New Planet' (1640); 'Mercury; or, The Secret and Swift Messenger, Showing How a Man May Communicate his Thoughts to a Friend at Any Distance' (1641); 'Mathematical Magic' (1648); 'Essay toward a Real Character and a Philosophical Language' (1668); 'Principles and Duties of Natural Religion' (1675); etc.

Wilkins, Mary Eleanor. An American author; born at Randolph, Mass. Her works, studies of New England country life, are: 'The Adventures of Ann' (1886), 'A Humble Romance' (1887), 'A New England Nun' (1891), and 'Young Lucretia' (1892), collections of short stories; 'Giles Corey, Yeoman' (1893), a play; 'Jane Field' (1893), 'Pembroke' (1894), novels; 'The Long Arm' (1895); 'The Givers' (1904); 'Doc Gordon' (1906).

Wilkinson, Sir John Gardner. An English Egyptologist; born at Haxendale, Oct. 5, 1797; died at Llandover, Wales, Oct. 29, 1875. His principal work is 'Manners and Customs of the Ancient Egyptians' (two series, 6 vols., 1837-41), still valuable, and reissued in 1879. Others are; 'Materia Hieroglyphica' (1828); 'The Topography of Thebes, and General View of Egypt' (1835); 'Modern Egypt and Thebes' (2 vols., 1843), republished as 'Murray's Handbook for Travelers in Egypt' (1847); 'Dalmatia and Montenegro' (2 vols., 1848); 'The Architecture of Ancient Egypt' (1850); 'The Fragments of the Hieratic Papyrus at Turin' (1851); and 'The Egyptians in the Time of the Pharaohs' (1857).

Wilkinson, William Cleaver. An American educator and Baptist clergyman; born in Westford, Vt., Oct. 19, 1833. He is dean of the department of literature and art in the Chautauqua University, for which he has prepared many text-books. Among his works are: 'The Dance of Modern Society' (1869); 'A Free Lance,' etc., (1874); 'The Baptist Principle' (1881); 'Webster: An Ode' (1882); 'Poems' (1883); essay on 'Edwin Arnold' (1884); and 'College Greek Course in English.'

Willard, Emma (Hart). An American educator and author; born in Berlin, Conn., Feb. 23, 1787; died at Troy, N. Y., April 15, 1870. She did much for bettering the education of women. Her books, educational and general, include: 'A Plan for Improving Female Education' (1819); 'A History of the United States' (1828); 'Poems' (1830), containing the popular song 'Rocked in the Cradle of the Deep'; 'Journal and Letters from France and Great Britain' (1833); 'Universal History' (1835); 'Respiration and its Effects'; and 'Morals for the Young' (1857).

Willard, Frances Elizabeth. An American educator, editor and reformer; born at Churchville, N. Y., Sept. 28, 1839; died in New York city, Feb. 18, 1898. She was presi-

dent of the Woman's Christian Temperance Union from 1879, and founded the World's Woman's Christian Temperance Union in 1883. She was editor-in-chief of the Union Signal, the official organ of the woman's temperance movement. Besides contributing to leading periodicals, she published: 'Nineteen Beautiful Years' (1864), a life of her deceased sister; 'Glimpses of Fifty Years' (1889); 'A Great Mother' (1894).

William of Malmesbury. A celebrated English monk and historian; born about 1095; died at Malmesbury, about 1142. He was librarian of the monastery at Malmesbury. He wrote: 'History of the English Kings,' and its continuation 'Modern History,' the two being the source from which all subsequent histories of England have drawn; 'History of the Prelates of England'; 'Lives' of St. Patrick, St. Dunstan, St. Wulfstan; several books of miracles; etc.

William of Tyre. A Syrian historian; born about 1137. He was archbishop of Tyre (1175). He wrote 'History of the Sovereigns of the East,' and 'History of Events in the Lands across the Sea,' a fine record of the Crusades from 1127 to 1184, first printed in 1549. There are German and French translations of the latter.

Williams, Alfred Mason. An American journalist, editor, and poet; born at Taunton, Mass., Oct. 23, 1840; died at St. Kitts, W. I., Mar. 9, 1896. Was editor of the Providence Journal. Published: 'The Poets and Poetry of Ireland'; 'Studies in Folk-Song and Popular Poetry'; 'Sam Houston and the War of Independence in Texas'.

Williams, Mrs. Annie (Bowles). An American juvenile-story writer; born in Connecticut, 1840. She has published: 'Birchwood'; 'The Fitch Club'; 'Professor Johnny'; 'Rolf and his Friends'; 'Who Saved the Ship?'; 'The Giant Dwarf'; 'The Riverside Museum.'

Williams, Mrs. Catharine R. (Arnold). An American author; born in Providence, R. I., about 1790; died there, Oct. 11, 1872. She was the author of 'Original Poems' (1828); 'Religion at Home' (1829); 'Tales, National and Revolutionary' (1830-35); 'Aristocracy,' a novel (1832); 'Fall River' (1833); 'Biography of Revolutionary Heroes' (1839); and 'Annals of the Aristocracy of Rhode Island' (2 vols., 1843-45).

Williams, Francis Howard. An American dramatic writer and poet, residing in Philadelphia; born in Pennsylvania, 1844. Among his plays are: 'The Princess Elizabeth: A Lyric Drama'; 'The Higher Education'; 'A Reformer in Ruffles'; 'Master and Man.' He also wrote 'Theodora: A Pastoral'; 'Atman: A Story'; 'The Flute Player, and Other Poems'; 'Pennsylvania Poets of the Provincial Period'; 'At the Rise of the Curtain.'

Williams, George Washington. An American negro writer and soldier; born in Pennsylvania, 1849. He served in the Northern army in the Civil War, and subsequently as an officer in the army of Mexico (1865–67). He was minister to Hayti, 1885–86. He wrote: 'History of the Negro Race in America'; 'The Negro Troops in the War of the Rebellion'; 'History of Reconstruction.'

Williams, Isaac. A British clergyman and religious poet; born at Cwmcynfelin, near Aberystwith, Wales, Dec. 12, 1802; died at Stinchcombe, England, May 1, 1865. With Keble, Newman, and Pusey, he was active in the Tractarian movement. He wrote: 'The Cathedral' (1838), in verse; 'Hymns' (1839); 'Thoughts in Past Years' (1842); 'The Christian Scholar' (1849); 'Autobiography' (1892), besides other purely religious works.

Williams, Jesse Lynch. An American writer of stories for the young; born in Illinois, 1871. He has published: 'Princeton Stories'; 'The Freshman'; 'The Day-Dreamer'; 'The Stolen Story.'

Williams, John. ["Anthony Pasquin."] An English writer, journalist, and dramatist; born in London about 1765; died in Brooklyn, N. Y., Nov. 23, 1818. Because of his scurrilous political writings he was declared in 1797 to be "a common libeler," and soon after came to the United States. He was connected with the press, wrote several plays, also a volume of poems (1789); 'Legislative Biography' (1795); 'Life of Alexander Hamilton' (1804); and the 'Dramatic Censor' (1811).

Williams, John. An English missionary; born at Tottenham, June 29, 1796; killed and eaten by cannibals, at Erromanga, New Hebrides, Nov. 20, 1839. His adventurous and generally successful life as a missionary extended over a period of more than twenty years (1816–39). He wrote that famous classic of missionary literature, 'A Narrative of Missionary Enterprises in the South Sea Islands' (London and New York, 1837; 56th thousand, 1865).

Williams, Martha McCulloch. An American miscellaneous writer. Besides several stories and poems in Harper's Bazar and Monthly, and a book on botany, she has published 'Field-Farings' (1892), a collection of essays; 'Two of a Trade'; 'A Black Settlement'; 'Sarsaparilla.'

Williams, Roger. An English-American clergyman, and founder of the State of Rhode Island; born about 1604; died about 1683. His chief distinction is in his founding the first State in which there is an absolute guarantee of liberty of conscience to every man,— the government having no authority in matters of religion. He published: 'Key into the Language of America; or, An Help to the Language of the Natives in that Part of America Called New England,' etc. (1643; new ed. 1820); 'Mr. Cotton's Letter,' etc. (1644); and 'The Bloudy Tenent of Persecution for Cause of Conscience, Discussed in a Conference between Truth and Peace,' etc. (1644); 'The Bloody Tenent yet More Bloody,' etc. (1652); 'The Hireling Ministry None of Christ's,' etc.

(1652); 'Experiments of Spiritual Life and Health,' etc. (1652); 'George Fox Digg'd Out of his Burrowes,' etc. (1676); and 'A New England Fire-Brand Quenched,' etc. (1679).

Williams, Samuel Wells. An American philologist and distinguished Chinese scholar; born in Utica, N. Y., 1812; died in New Haven, Feb. 17, 1884. He assisted in preparing a Chinese, and afterwards a Japanese, dictionary; was interpreter for Commodore Perry in Japan, 1853–54; was secretary of legation in China, 1855–57, and again 1862–76. He was professor of Chinese at Yale, 1876–84, and was president of the American Oriental Society. He published: 'Easy Lessons in Chinese' (1842), followed by 'Chinese and English Vocabulary' (1843), and 'Tonic Dictionary of the Chinese' (1874). His greatest work is 'The Middle Kingdom' (2 vols., 1883), which has done excellent service in making Chinese history and conditions known to the public.

Williamson, Julia May. An American writer, living at Augusta, Me.; born 1859. She has written the volumes of poetry 'Echoes of Time and Tide,' and 'The Choir of the Year'; 'Star of Hope and Other Songs.'

Willis, Nathaniel Parker. An American poet and journalist; born at Portland, Me., Jan. 20, 1806; died at Idlewild on the Hudson, N. Y., Jan. 20, 1867. His chief journalistic work was with the New York Mirror (1823–42). Among his numerous writings are: 'Inklings of Adventure' (3 vols., 1836); 'Loiterings of Travel' (3 vols., 1840); 'Letters from Under a Bridge' (1840); 'Poems' (1846); 'People I Have Met' (1850); 'Hurrygraphs' (1851); 'A Health Trip to the Tropics' (1854); 'Famous Persons and Places' (1854); and 'The Convalescent, his Rambles and Adventures' (1859).

Willoughby, Eliza Maria, Baroness Middleton. An English poet. She is daughter of Sir A. P. Gordon-Cumming; married D. W. B. Willoughby (1869), who became Baron Middleton in 1877. She has published: 'On the North Wind, Thistledown' (1874), and 'Ballads' (1878).

Wills, W. R. An Australian poet; born 1837. He has published: 'A Bunch of Wild Pansies' (1885); 'Blossoms of Early Life'; 'Songs for the Weary.'

Wills, William Gorman. An Irish painter and dramatist; born in County Kilkenny, 1830; died in London, Dec. 14, 1891. He is the author of 'Notice to Quit' (3 vols., 1861); 'The Life's Evidence' (3 vols., 1863); and the dramas 'Charles the First' (1872), 'Eugene Aram' (1873), 'Marie Stuart' (1874), 'Jane Shore' (1876), 'Olivia Sedgemoore' (1881), 'Claudian' (1885), 'A Royal Divorce' (1891), and, in conjunction with Sidney Grundy, 'Madam Pompadour.'

Wilmer, Lambert A. An American editor and author; born about 1805; died in Brooklyn, N. Y., Dec. 21, 1863. He was editor of several

37

newspapers, and author of : 'A New System of Grammar' (1851); 'The Quacks of Helicon' (1851); 'The Life of De Soto' (1858); 'Our Press Gang; or, An Exposition of the Corruptions of American Newspapers' (1859).

Wilmshurst, Zavarr. A journalist and author; born in England, Nov. 25, 1824; died in Brooklyn, Jan. 27, 1887. He came to the United States and was editorially connected with several journals in New York city. His plays include a drama on Hawthorne's 'Scarlet Letter'; and 'Nitocria,' a tragedy. His other writings are: 'The Viking,' an epic (1849); 'The Winter of the Heart,' etc. (1874); 'The Siren' (1876); and 'Ralph and Rose' (1879).

Wilson, Alexander. A Scotch-American ornithologist; born at Paisley, Scotland, July 6, 1766; died in Philadelphia, Aug. 23, 1813. In early life he was a weaver and teacher. He published a volume of poems in 1790, but being sentenced for a lampoon in 1793, emigrated to America. He was employed as editor of the American edition of Rees's 'Cyclopædia'; but in his wanderings as peddler, he learned to love birds, and set about writing an ornithology. At his death seven volumes of this work had been published; the eighth and ninth volumes were edited by George Ord, and a continuation by Charles Lucien Bonaparte (4 vols., 1825–33). Volumes of his poems were published at Paisley in 1816, and at Belfast in 1857.

Wilson, Mrs. Augusta Jane (Evans). An American novelist; born at Columbus, Ga., May 8, 1835. She lived some years in Texas; afterwards at Mobile, Ala. Her works at one time had great popularity. They include: 'Inez' (1856); 'Beulah' (1859); 'Macaria' (1864); 'St. Elmo' (1866); 'Vashti' (1869); 'Infelice'; 'At the Mercy of Tiberius'; 'Devota.'

Wilson, Sir Daniel. A Canadian educator and archæologist; born at Edinburgh, 1816; died at Toronto, Aug. 6, 1892. He was president of Toronto University from 1881. He wrote: 'Memorials of Edinburgh in the Olden Time' (1846–49); 'Oliver Cromwell and the Protectorate' (1848); 'Prehistoric Man' (1862); 'Archæology and Prehistoric Annals of Scotland' (revised ed. 1863); 'Chatterton' (1869); 'Reminiscences of Old Edinburgh' (1878); 'The Lost Atlantis' (1892), poems; etc.

Wilson, Henry. [Original name Jeremiah Jones Colbath.] A distinguished American statesman; born at Farmington, N. H., Feb. 16, 1812; died at Washington, Nov. 22, 1875. He was elected to the Vice-Presidency of the United States in 1872, and died while holding this office. His works are: 'History of the Rise and Fall of the Slave Power in America' (3 vols., 1872–75); 'History of the Anti-Slavery Measures of the 37th and 38th Congresses' (1864); and 'History of the Reconstruction Measures of the 39th and 40th Congresses' (1868); besides many addresses and speeches.

Wilson, Henry Bristow. An English clergyman and educator; born in London, 1803; died at Lee, Kent, Aug. 10, 1888. He was professor of Anglo-Saxon at Oxford. He was one of the seven authors of the famous volume of 'Essays and Reviews' (1860); his contribution being 'The National Church.' He wrote: 'The Communion of Saints: An Attempt to Illustrate the Principles of Church Union' (1851), the Bampton lecture contributed to 'Oxford Essays'; etc.

Wilson, Horace Hayman. An English Orientalist; born in London, Sept. 26, 1786; died there, May 8, 1860. Going to India in the service of the East India Company (1808), he was employed in the Calcutta mint; was secretary of the Asiatic Society of Bengal, 1811; professor of Sanskrit at Oxford, 1832; librarian at the East India House, 1836; and director of the Royal Asiatic Society. Besides a Sanskrit dictionary and grammar, translations of the 'Meghaduta,' the 'Vishnu Purana,' part of the 'Rig Veda,' etc., he published: 'Select Specimens of the Theatre of the Hindus' (2d ed. 1835); 'Religious Sects of the Hindus' (1828–32); 'History of British India' (1844–48); etc.

Wilson, James Grant. An American author, editor, and soldier, who served with distinction in the Civil War; born in New York, April 28, 1832. Besides numerous addresses, essays, and articles in periodicals, he has published: 'Biographical Sketches of Illinois Officers' (1862–63); 'Love in Letters, Illustrated in the Correspondence of Eminent Persons' (1867); 'Life of General Grant' (1868–85); 'Life of Fitz-Greene Halleck' (1869); 'Sketches of Illustrious Soldiers' (1874); 'Poets and Poetry of Scotland' (1876); 'Centennial History of the Diocese of New York, 1775–1885' (1886); 'Bryant and his Friends' (1886); 'Commodore Isaac Hull and the Frigate Constitution' (1889). He is the editor — with John Fiske — of 'Appleton's Cyclopædia of American Biography' (6 vols., 1886–89).

Wilson, James Harrison. An American author, and soldier of distinction; born near Shawneetown, Ill., Sept. 2, 1837. He is the author of 'China: Travels and Investigations in the Middle Kingdom' (1887). 'Life of Andrew J. Alexander' (1887); and, in conjunction with C. A. Dana, 'Life of General U. S. Grant' (1868).

Wilson, John. ["Christopher North."] A Scotch essayist, poet, novelist, and editor; born at Paisley, May 18, 1785; died in Edinburgh, April 3, 1854. The son of a rich manufacturer, he was educated at Glasgow University and at Magdalen College, Oxford; noted as a scholar and athlete; settled in Cumberland, and became one of the "Lake Group" with Wordsworth, De Quincey, Southey, and Coleridge. Losing most of his inherited fortune, he removed to Edinburgh and studied law. From the starting of Blackwood's Magazine in 1817 he was a chief contributor, and was for many years its generally accredited head. For it he wrote (with Maginn and others, but largely alone) the 'Noctes Ambrosianæ,' by which he is best remembered, — imaginary dialogues at Ambrose's tavern in Edinburgh, between the leading contributors to the magazine; a selection from these was published in 1876. He also wrote, among other things: 'The Isle of Palms' (1812), and 'The City of the Plague' (1816), poems; 'Lights and Shadows of Scottish Life' (1822); 'The Trials of Margaret Lindsay' (1823); 'The Foresters' (1825); and 'Essay on the Genius and Character of Burns' (1841). He was professor of moral philosophy at Edinburgh University from 1820 to near the end of his life.

Wilson, John Mackay. A Scottish story-writer; born at Tweedmouth, 1804; died at Berwick-on-Tweed, Oct. 2, 1835. He edited for several years the Berwick Advertiser. He was the editor and principal author of 'Tales of the Borders' (1835-40; last ed., enlarged and revised, 24 vols., 1869), of which 150,000 copies have been sold.

Wilson, Robert Burns. An American poet and artist; born in Pennsylvania, Oct. 30, 1850. He resides in Frankfort, Ky. He has published a volume called 'Life and Love.'

Wilson, Sir Robert Thomas. An English soldier and military writer; born in London, 1777; died there, May 9, 1849. He served in the Peninsular war; was British military commissioner at the Russian and allied headquarters, 1812-14; Member of Parliament and governor of Gibraltar, 1842-49. He wrote: 'History of the British Expedition to Egypt' (1802); 'Sketch of the Campaigns in Poland' (1810); 'Military and Political Power of Russia' (1817); 'Narrative of Events During the Invasion of Russia, 1812' (1860); 'Diary' (1861); etc.

Wilson, William. A Scotch-American journalist, publisher, and poet; born in Perthshire, Dec. 25, 1801; died in Poughkeepsie, N. Y., Aug. 25, 1860. He edited the 'Scottish Songs, Ballads, and Poems' of Hew Ainslie (1855), and several other volumes. His 'Poems,' edited by Benson J. Lossing, appeared in 1870, revised and enlarged editions in 1875 and 1884.

Wilson, Woodrow. An American educator and author; born at Staunton, Va., 1856. He has written much on political and literary topics for the magazines and reviews. His books are: 'Congressional Government: A Study of American Politics' (1885), a work popular at home and much used by foreign publicists; 'The State: Elements of Historical and Practical Politics' (1889); 'Division and Reunion,' in 'Epochs of American History' (1893); and 'A History of the American People' (1902). He is now president of Princeton University.

Wilton, Richard. An English clergyman; born at Doncaster, Dec. 25, 1827. He was educated at Cambridge, and took orders in 1852. He published: 'Wood-Notes and Church-Bells' (1873); 'Lyrics, Sylvan and Sacred' (1878);

'Lyra Pastoralis.' Many of his verses have been set to Music.

Winchell, Alexander. An American geologist, author, and educator; born in Dutchess County, N. Y., Dec. 31, 1824; died in Ann Arbor, Mich., Feb. 19, 1891. He lectured extensively and contributed to many journals. His writings include: 'Sketches of Creation' (1870); 'Geological Chart' (1870); 'The Doctrine of Evolution' (1874); 'Science and Religion' (1877); 'Preadamites' (1880); 'Sparks from a Geologist's Hammer' (1881); 'World Life' (1883); 'Geological Studies' (1886); and 'Walks and Talks in the Geological Field' (1886).

Winckelmann, Johann Joachim (vink'el-män). A German critic and archæologist, the founder of scientific archæology and of classic art history as a critical science; born in Stendal, Dec. 9, 1717; died at Trieste, June 8, 1768. He was the first to consider the masterpieces of classical antiquity as representative of a stage in the development of taste, and to formulate the theory of evolution in art. He seems to have obtained his first clue from some observations of Velleius Paterculus and Quintilian. His greatest work is a 'History of the Art of Antiquity' (1764), afterwards supplemented by 'Observations on the History of Art' (1767). He also published: 'Thoughts on the Imitation of Greek Works in Painting and Sculpture' (1755); 'Architecture of the Ancients' (1762); 'Unknown Memorials [or Monuments] of Antiquity' (1767); and many essays and pamphlets.

Wines, Enoch Cobb. An American clergyman and philanthropist; born in Hanover, N. J., Feb. 17, 1806; died in Cambridge, Mass., Dec. 10, 1879. He was noted as secretary of the N. Y. State Prison Association in 1862, and afterwards devoted his life to the promotion of reform in the administration of criminal law and treatment of criminals. His writings include: 'Two Years and a Half in the Navy' (1832); 'A Trip to China' (1832); 'Hints on Popular Education' (1838); 'Commentaries on Laws of Ancient Hebrews' (1852); 'Adam and Christ' (1855); 'Prisons and Reformatories in the United States and Canada' (1867); 'State of Prisons and Child-Saving Institutions' (1880.)

Winslow, Mrs. Catherine Mary (Reignolds). An American actress and public reader; born in 183-. She has written 'Yesterdays with Actors'; 'Readings [with notes] from the Old English Dramatists.'

Winslow, Edward. A Mayflower emigrant and governor of Plymouth Colony; born at Droitwich, England, Oct. 18, 1595; died at sea, between San Domingo and Jamaica, May 8, 1655. He was a hostage to Massasoit, his account of which was in George Morton's 'Relation' (1622). He was the author of 'Good Newes from New England,' etc. (1624), printed in full in Young's 'Chronicles of the Pilgrim

Fathers' (1841); 'Brief Narration; or, Hypocrisie Unmasked,' etc. (1646), reissued as ' The Danger of Tolerating Levellers in a Civill State,' etc. (1649, printed in part in Young's 'Chronicles'); 'New England's Salamander,' etc. (1647); 'The Glorious Progress of the Gospel amongst the Indians of New England' (1649); and 'A Platform of Church Discipline in New England' (1653).

Winslow, Miron. An American missionary; born at Williston, Vt., Dec. 11, 1789; died at the Cape of Good Hope, Oct. 22, 1864. He went as a missionary to Ceylon, 1819; founded the Madras mission, 1836; was president of the native college at Madras, 1840; translated the Bible into Tamil, 1835. He wrote: 'Memoir of Mrs. Harriet Winslow' (1835), his wife, republished in England, and translated into French and Turkish; and 'A Tamil and English Dictionary' (1862), his great work, containing over 67,000 Tamil words.

Winslow, William Copley. An American archæologist and journalist; born at Boston, Jan. 13, 1840. He is an Episcopal clergyman; assisted in founding the University Quarterly, 1861; edited the Hamiltonian, 1862; was assistant editor of the New York World 1862-63, and editor of the Christian Times 1863-65; vice-president, secretary, and treasurer for many years of the Egypt exploration fund for the U. S.; lecturer on archæological subjects and colonial history. He has written: 'Israel in Egypt'; 'The Store City of Pithom' (1885); 'A Greek City in Egypt' (1887); 'The Egyptain Collection in Boston' (1890); 'The Pilgrim Fathers in Holland' (1891); 'Papyri in the United States.'

Winsor, Justin. An American historian and librarian; born at Boston, Jan 2, 1831; died at Cambridge, Oct. 22, 1897. He was librarian of the Boston Public Library, 1868-77, and of Harvard University, 1877-97. He published: ' Bibliography of Original Quartos and Folios of Shakespeare' (1875); 'Reader's Handbook of the American Revolution' (1880); 'Memorial History of Boston' (edited: 4 vols., 1880-82); 'Narrative and Critical History of America' (edited: 8 vols., 1884-89); 'Christopher Columbus' (1891); 'From Cartier to Frontenac' (1894); 'The Mississippi Basin'; and 'The Struggle in America between England and France' (1895). He was the highest authority on the early history of North America.

Winter, John Strange. See **Stannard.**

Winter, William. An American journalist and dramatic critic; born at Gloucester, Mass., July 15, 1836. He has done journalistic work on the Saturday Press, Vanity Fair, the Albion, Weekly Review; and has been dramatic critic for the New York Tribune since 1865. He has written 'The Convent, and Other Poems' (1854); 'The Queen's Domain' (1858), and 'My Witness' (1871), poems; 'Life of Edwin Booth' (1872); 'Thistledown' (1878), poems; 'Poems,' complete edition (1881); 'The Jeffersons' (1881); 'English Rambles' (1883); 'Life of Henry Ir-

ving' (1885); 'Shakspere's England' (1886); 'Stage Life of Mary Anderson' (1886), and 'The Wanderers' (1888); 'The Lives of Actors.'

Winther, Rasmus Villads Christian Ferdinand (vin'ter). A Danish poet; born in Fensmark, July 29, 1796; died in Paris, Dec. 30, 1876. While not the greatest Danish poet, he is one of the truest interpreters of the Danish national character. Some of his numerous publications are: 'Song and Legend' (1841); 'Lyrical Poems' (1849); 'New Poems' (1850); 'The Flight of the Hart' (1856), a lyric romance of the Danish Middle Ages, his greatest work.

Winthrop, John, Governor. Born near Groton, Suffolk, England, Jan. 12, 1587-8; died at Boston, March 26, 1649. He was the first colonial governor of Massachusetts, after the government was transferred to America, holding the office, with but slight interruption, from 1629 to 1649. He wrote a 'History of New England from 1630 to 1649' (2d ed. Boston, 1853), the MS. of which was left by him in the form of a journal correspondence to be found in his 'Life and Letters' (2 vols., 1864-67), by Robert C. Winthrop; 'A Modell of Christian Charity'; 'Arbitrary Government Described.'

Winthrop, Theodore. An American soldier, poet, and novelist; born at New Haven, Conn. Sept. 22, 1828; killed at the head of an assaulting column of Northern troops at Big Bethel, Va., June 10, 1861. The 1861 Atlantic Monthly contained sketches from him of early War scenes. He left completed material for five volumes of novels and essays: 'Cecil Dreeme' (1861); 'John Brent' (1862); 'Edwin Brothercroft' (1862); 'The Canoe and the Saddle' (1862); and 'Life in the Open Air, and Other Papers' (1863). His sister published 'Life and Poems of Theodore Winthrop' (1884).

Wirt, William. An American lawyer and author; born at Bladensburg, Md., Nov. 8, 1772; died at Washington, D. C., Feb. 18, 1834. His writings are: 'Letters of a British Spy,' which first appeared in the Virginia Argus (1803); 'The Rainbow' (1804), which was written for the Richmond Enquirer; and his chief work, 'Sketches of the Life and Character of Patrick Henry' (1817).

Wise, Daniel. An editor, Methodist clergyman, and author; born in Portsmouth, England, Jan. 10, 1813; died at Englewood, N. J., Dec. 19, 1898. He was editor of Zion's Herald at Boston, Mass., and various Sunday-school publications, and published many works on varied subjects, mostly under the pen-names of "Francis Forrester" and "Laurence Lancewood." Among these are: 'Personal Effort' (1841); 'Life of Ulric Zwingli' (1850); 'My Uncle Toby's Library' (12 vols., 1853); 'Vanquished Victors' (1876); 'Heroic Methodists' (1882); 'Boy Travelers in Arabia' (1885); 'Men of Renown' (1886); etc.

Wise, Henry Augustus. An American naval officer and author; born at Brooklyn, N. Y.,

May 12, 1819; died at Naples, Italy, April 2, 1869. Under the pseudonym of "Harry Gringo," he wrote 'Los Gringos; or, An Interior View of Mexico and California, with Wanderings in Peru, Chili, and Polynesia' (1849); 'Tales for the Marines' (1855); 'Scampavias, from Gibel-Tasek to Stamboul' (1857); 'The Story of the Gray African Parrot' (1856), a book for children; and 'Captain Brand of the Centipede' (1860).

Wise, Isaac Mayer. A Jewish rabbi and author; born at Steingrab, April 3, 1819; died at Cincinnati, March 26, 1900. He settled in New York city in 1846. Resided in Cincinnati, O., after 1854, and was president of the Hebrew Union College. He was a leader of the reform movement in American Judaism; and besides editing the Israelite, he wrote extensively. Among his works are: 'History of the Israelitish Nation' (1854); 'Essence of Judaism' (1860); 'Judaism: its Doctrines and Duties' (1862); 'The Martyrdom of Jesus of Nazareth' (1874); 'The Cosmic God' (1876); etc.

Wiseman, Nicholas Patrick Stephen. An English cardinal and archbishop; born at Seville, Spain, Aug. 21, 1802; died in London, Feb. 15, 1865. Among his books are: 'Horæ Syriacæ' (1828); 'Lectures on the Connection between Science and Revealed Religion' (2 vols., 1836); 'The Real Presence' (1836); 'Lectures on the Doctrines and Practices of the Catholic Church' (2 vols., 1836); 'Three Lectures on the Catholic Hierarchy' (1850); 'Essays on Various Subjects' (3 vols., 1853); 'Fabiola; or, The Church of the Catacombs' (1855); 'Recollections of the Last Four Popes' (1858); 'Sermons' (2 vols., 1864); 'The Witch of Rosenburg: A Drama in Three Acts' (1866); and 'Daily Meditations' (1868).

Wissmann, Hermann von (vēs'män). A German African explorer; born at Frankfort on the Oder, Sept. 4, 1853. He crossed the African continent, 1880-82; commanded an expedition sent out by Leopold II., 1884-85; as imperial German commissioner, suppressed the Arab revolt under Bushiri; failed in an attempt to take two steamers to Lake Victoria via Nyassa and Tanganyika, 1892; was governor of German East Africa, 1895; president of the Berlin Geographical Society, 1897. He has written: 'In the Interior of Africa' (3d ed. 1891); 'Under the German Flag across Africa' (latest ed. 1891); 'My Second Crossing of Equatorial Africa' (1891); 'Africa: Descriptions and Advice' (1895); 'In the Wilds of Africa and Asia.'

Wister, Annis Lee (Furness). An American translator; born in Pennsylvania in 1830. She has made many translations of note, among them: E. Marlitt's 'The Old Mamselle's Secret' (1868), 'Gold Else' (1868), 'The Countess Gisela' (1869), 'The Little Moorland Princess' (1873), and 'The Second Wife' (1874); Wilhelmine von Hillern's 'Only a Girl' (1870); Hackländer's 'Enchanting and Enchanted' (1871); Volkhausen's 'Why Did He Not Die?'

(1871); Von Auer's 'It Is the Fashion' (1872); and Fanny Lewald's 'Hulda; or, The Deliverer' (1874).

Wister, Owen. An American short-story writer and lawyer of Philadelphia, son of Sarah B.; born in 1860. Besides stories for the periodicals and magazines, he has written: 'The New Swiss Family Robinson'; 'The Dragon of Wantley,' a romance; 'Red Men and White'; 'The Virginian'; 'Mother'; 'The Seven Ages of Washington.'

Wister, Mrs. Sarah (Butler). An American writer and translator, daughter of Fanny Kemble; born in Pennsylvania, 1835. She has published a poem, 'The Boat of Glass'; and translations from the French of Alfred de Musset.

Wither, George. An English soldier and poet; born at Brentworth, June 11, 1588; died in London, May 2, 1667. For a volume of metrical satires on the manners of the time, 'Abuses Stript and Whipt' (1613), he was cast into prison, where he wrote 'The Shepherd's Hunting' (1615), and, perhaps, 'Fidelia.' Some of his volumes are: 'The Motto' (1618); 'Philarète' (1622); 'Hymns and Songs of the Church' (1623); and 'Hallelujah' (1641). His best-known song is 'Shall I, Wasting in Despair.'

Witherspoon, John. An American Presbyterian divine and educator; born at Yester, Haddingtonshire, Scotland, Feb. 5, 1722; died near Princeton, N. J., Sept. 15, 1794. He was president of Princeton College, 1768; delegate for six years from New Jersey to the Continental Congress; a signer of the Declaration of Independence. He wrote: 'Ecclesiastical Characteristics' (1753); 'Nature and Effects of the Stage' (1757); 'Essays on Important Subjects' (1764); 'Considerations on the Nature and Extent of the Legislative Authority of the British Parliament' (1774); etc. ('Works,' 9 vols., Edinburgh, 1804.)

Withrow, William Henry. A Canadian Methodist divine and miscellaneous writer; born at Toronto, Aug. 6, 1839. Since 1874 he has been editor of the Methodist Magazine, Toronto. He has written: 'Catacombs of Rome' (1874); 'History of Canada' (1878); 'Lawrence Temple' (1881), a novel; 'Valeria, the Martyr of the Catacombs' (1884); 'Life in a Parsonage' (1885); 'Men Worth Knowing' (1886); 'Canada: Scenic and Descriptive' (1889); 'China and its People' (1893); etc.

Witwickie, Étienne (vit'vits-ki). A Polish poet, novelist, and dramatist; born at Krzemienietz; died at Rome, 1847. After the revolution of 1831 he resided in France. He was a romanticist. Among his works were: 'Polish Altar' (with Mickiewicz and B. Zalecoski); 'Towianskism,' a famous book in defense of Catholicism; 'Ballads and Romances' (1824); 'Edmund' (1829); 'Idyllic Poems' (1830); 'Soirées of a Pilgrim' (1837-42); the drama 'A Spoilt Revenge' (1835); etc.

Wolcot or Wolcott, John. [" Peter Pindar."] An English clergyman, physician, and satirical poet; born at Dodbrooke, in May 1738; died in London, Jan. 14, 1819. His satires involved him in many quarrels. So effective were his attacks upon the king, that the ministry silenced him with a pension of £300 per annum. He was an art critic of taste and penetration far beyond his time; his yearly reviews in verse of the Academy Exhibitions are much the best of his work, and still instructive. Some of his satires are: 'Lyric Odes'; 'An Epistle to the Reviewers'; 'Peeps at St. James'; 'Royal Visits'; and 'The Lousiad.'

Wolf, Emma. An American novelist. She has written: 'Other Things Being Equal' (1892); 'A Prodigal in Love' (1894); 'The Joy of Life' (1896); 'Heirs of Yesterday' (1900).

Wolf, Friedrich August (vōlf). A German educator and classical scholar; born at Haynrode, Prussia, Feb. 15, 1759; died at Marseilles, France, Aug. 8, 1824. Among his very many books are his edition of Demosthenes's 'Leptinea' (1790); Plato's 'Symposium,' 'Apology,' 'Phædo,' 'Crito'; Hesiod's 'Theogony'; Cicero's 'Tusculan Disputations,' and other works; and Aristophanes's 'Clouds.' What gave him his greatest notoriety is his 'Prolegomena in Homerum' (1795), an attempt to prove that the Iliad and Odyssey are not the work of one Homer, but a compilation from several sources.

Wolf, Theodore Frelinghuysen. An American physician and littérateur; born in New Jersey, 1847. His books: 'A Literary Pilgrimage among the Haunts of Famous British Authors'; and 'Literary Shrines: The Haunts of Famous American Authors,' are among the popular works of the day. His professional writings include works on tetanus and anæsthesia.

Wolfe, Charles. An Irish clergyman and poet; born at Dublin, Dec. 14, 1791; died at Cove of Cork (now Queenstown), Feb. 21, 1823. His title to literary immortality is his 'Burial of Sir John Moore.' ("Not a drum was heard, not a funeral note.") His 'Poetical Remains, with a Brief Memoir of his Life' was published by Archdeacon John A. Russell in 1825 (8th ed. 1846).

Wolff, Albert V. (vōlf). A German-French journalist and miscellaneous writer; born at Cologne, Dec. 31, 1835. He settled in Paris in 1857, becoming secretary to Alexandre Dumas, père; wrote for the Gaulois, Figaro, Charivari, etc. Some of these articles, collected in book form, were afterwards published as 'Memoirs of the Boulevard' (1866); 'The Two Emperors' (1871); 'Victorien Sardou and Uncle Sam' (1873); etc. He wrote also several novels and farces.

Wolff, Julius. A German poet; born in Quedlinburg in the Harz Mountains, Sept. 16, 1834. In 1869 he founded the Harz News. He joined the army at the time of the Franco-German war, and won the Iron Cross. After this he returned to Berlin, later removing to Charlottenburg. His chief works are: 'War Songs' (1871); 'Tyll Eulenspiegel Redivivus'; 'The Ratcatcher of Hameln,' 'Lingul the Ratcatcher's Songs'; 'The Wild Huntsman' (1877); 'Tannhäuser'; 'Lurlei'; 'The Robber Count'; 'The Bachelor's Law' (1887); 'The Flying Dutchman.'

Wolff, Oskar Ludwig Bernhard. A German novelist and satirist; born at Altona, July 26, 1799; died at Jena, Sept. 16, 1851. He was professor of modern languages at Weimar, 1826, and of modern languages and literature at Jena, 1832. He wrote 'Pictures and Songs' (1840), 'Natural History of the German Student' (2d ed. 1842), 'Bubbles and Dreams' (1844), 'The Minor Ills of Human Life' (1846), 'History of the Novel' (2d ed. 1850), etc.; and edited 'Treasury of National Poetry' (4th ed. 1853), 'Treasury of German Prose' (11th ed. 1875), 'The German People's Treasury of Poetry' (28th ed. 1884), etc.

Wolfram von Eschenbach (vōlf'räm fon esh'en-bäch). Next to Walther von der Vogelweide the greatest of Middle High German poets; died about 1220. He was poor and with a family, and could neither read nor write; but knew French and was of noble birth, which enabled him to frequent the court of Hermann of Thuringia. His chief works were three epic poems: 'Parzival' (about 1210), the greatest of German court epics; 'Titurel' (about 1210?), left unfinished; 'Willehalm' (begun before 1216), left unfinished; both afterward completed by other hands. He wrote also lyrics, among which were four 'Day Songs.'

Wollstonecraft, Mary (Mrs. William Godwin). The noted author of the 'Vindication of the Rights of Women'; born in 1759; died 1797. She was the mother of Mary Godwin, the poet Shelley's second wife. She published: 'Thoughts on the Education of Daughters' (1787); 'Original Stories' (1788); 'Vindication of the Rights of Men' (1790); 'Vindication of the Rights of Women' (1792); 'Historical and Moral Views of the French Revolution' (1794); 'Letters Written in Norway' (1796). Her 'Posthumous Works' appeared in 1798.

Wolseley, Garnet Joseph, First Viscount Wolseley. A distinguished British soldier; born at Golden Bridge House, County Dublin, Ireland, June 4, 1833. He entered the army as ensign in 1852; served in the Crimean War, in India at the relief of Lucknow, and elsewhere; held chief command in the Red River expedition of 1870, and the Ashanti war of 1873–74; was administrator of Natal in 1870; commissioner and commander in Cyprus, 1878 governor of Natal and the Transvaal, 1879–80; gained the victory of Tel-el-Kebir, 1882; commanded the expedition for the relief of Gordon, 1884–85; became commander-in-Chief of the British Army, 1895. Besides technical military works, he has written: 'Narrative of the War with China in 1860' (1860); 'Marley Castle' (1877), a novel; 'The System of Field Manœuvres.'

Wolzogen, Ernst von, Baron (võl-tso'gen). A German novelist, dramatist, and critic, somewhat of a realist; born at Breslau, April 23, 1855. He has written the novels 'One o'Clock Christmas Eve' (6th ed. 1896); 'Mr. Thaddeus's Tenant' (1885), 'Basilla' (1887), 'Red Francis' (1888), 'The Photographs' (1890), humorous sketches; 'The Mad Countess' (1890), etc.; the dramas 'The Last Pigtail' (1884), 'An Unwritten Leaf' (1896), etc.; the critical studies, 'George Eliot' (1885), 'Wilkie Collins' (1885); the pamphlet 'An Earnest Warning to the Ruling Classes' (4th ed. 1895); 'Biography of Hans von Schweinichen' (1885).

Wolzogen, Karoline von. A German novelist; born at Rudolstadt, Feb. 3, 1763; died at Jena, Jan. 11, 1847. She was a sister of Schiller's wife, and his intimate friend; and her 'Life of Schiller' is a charming and trustworthy biography. She published two romances, 'Agnes von Lilien' (2 vols., 1798), for a time thought to be Goethe's work by the most eminent critics; and 'Cordelia' (2 vols., 1840).

Wood, Anthony, called Anthony à Wood. An English antiquary; born at Oxford, Dec. 17, 1632; died there, Nov. 28, 1695. He spent most of his life in collecting data relating to the history of Oxford University. He wrote: 'History and Antiquities of the University of Oxford' (translated into Latin, 1674; published afterwards, rewritten in 2 vols., 1786-90 and 1792-96); 'An Exact History of all the Writers and Bishops who have had their Education in the University of Oxford, from 1500 to 1690' (last ed. 1813-20); 'Modus Salium: A Collection of Pieces of Humor' (1751); and 'The Ancient and Present State of the City of Oxford' (1773).

Wood, Charlotte Dunning. ["Charlotte Dunning."] An American novelist; born at Poughkeepsie, N. Y., 1858. Her works include: 'Upon a Cast' (1885); 'Cabin and Gondola' (1886); 'A Step Aside' (1886).

Wood, Ellen (Price) or Mrs. Henry Wood. An English novelist; born at Worcester, Jan. 17, 1814; died Feb. 10. 1887. She edited the Argosy in 1867; and published many novels, among which are: 'East Lynne' (1861); 'The Channings' (1862); 'The Shadow of Ashlydyat' and 'Verner's Pride' (1863); the 'Johnny Ludlow' stories (1874-80); 'Count Netherleigh' (1881); and 'About Ourselves' (1883).

Wood, George. An American writer and chief of a division in the U. S. Treasury Department; born in Newburyport, Mass., in 1799; died at Saratoga, N. Y., Aug. 24, 1870. He published: 'Peter Schlemihl in America' (1848); 'The Modern Pilgrim' (1855); 'Marrying Too Late' (1856); 'Future Life' (1858), reissued as 'The Gates Wide Open' (1869).

Wood, John George. An English writer on natural history; born in London, 1827; died at Coventry, March 3, 1889. He was a clergyman of the Church of England; edited The Boy's Own Magazine, and Every Boy's Magazine. He wrote the 'Illustrated Natural History' (new ed. 1865-66), with 1,500 original illustrations; 'Homes Without Hands' (1864-65); 'A Popular Natural History' (1866); 'Natural History of Man' (2 vols., 1868-70); 'Bible Animals' (1869); 'The Modern Playmate' (1870), a book of games; 'Man and Beasts, Here and Hereafter' (1874); 'Horse and Man' (1886); etc.

Wood, John Seymour. An American lawyer and littérateur of New York city; born in New York, 1853. He is editor of the Bachelor of Arts, and has published: 'Gramercy Park: A Story of New York'; 'College Days: Yale Yarns'; 'A Coign of Vantage'; 'A Daughter of Venice'; 'An Old Beau, and Other Stories.'

Wood, Mrs. Julia Amanda (Sargent). An American writer of religious stories; born in New Hampshire, 1826. She has written: 'Myrrha Lake'; 'Hubert's Wife'; 'Annette'; 'Strayed from the Fold'; 'From Error to Truth'; 'The Brown House at Duffield.'

Wood, Mrs. Sarah Sayward (Barrell) (Keating). An American writer of fiction; born in Maine, 1759; died in 1855. Her works include: 'Duval'; 'Ferdinand and Almira; or, The Influence of Virtue'; 'Tales of the Night'; and 'The Illuminated Baron.'

Woodberry, George Edward. An American poet and miscellaneous writer; born at Beverly, Mass., May 12, 1855. He was professor of English literature in Nebraska State University 1877-78 and 1880-82; in Columbia College, 1892. Besides numerous articles in magazines and reviews, he has written a 'History of Wood Engraving' (1883); 'Life of Edgar Allan Poe' (1885); and 'The North Shore Watch, and Other Poems' (1890). He has published also an edition of Shelley (1894), and one of Poe (1895), with E. C. Stedman, and 'Great Writers.'

Woodrow, James. A distinguished American Presbyterian clergyman and educator; born at Carlisle, England, May 30, 1828. He edited the Southern Presbyterian Review, 1861-65, and since 1865 has been editor of the Southern Presbyterian. After filling several professorships in various Southern colleges, he became president of South Carolina College in 1891. He has published many review articles, including: 'Geology and its Assailants' (1862); 'An Examination of Certain Recent Assaults on Physical Science' (1873); 'A Further Examination' (1874); etc. He died in 1907.

Woods, Mrs. Kate (Tannatt). An American writer of juvenile tales; born in New York, 1838. Among her books are: 'Six Little Rebels'; 'Out and About'; 'Dr. Dick'; 'The Wooing of Grandmother Grey'; 'Grandfather Grey'; 'Children's Stories'; 'Toots and his Friends'; 'The Duncans on Land and Sea.'

Woods, Katharine Pearson. An American writer of fiction; born in West Virginia, 1853. Her published works include: 'The Crowning of Candace'; 'A Tale of King Messiah'; 'From Dusk to Dawn'; 'A Web of Gold'; 'Metzerott Shoemaker: A Protest against Social Injustice' 'The True Story of Captain John Smith.'

Woods, Margaret L. A noted English novelist; born at Rugby, 1859. She is daughter of Dean Bradley of Westminster, and wife of President Woods of Trinity College, Oxford. She has written: 'A Village Tragedy' (1888); 'Esther Vanhomrigh' (1891); 'Vagabonds' (1894); 'Lyrics and Ballads'; 'The Princess of Hanover.'

Woodworth, Samuel. An American journalist and poet; born at Scituate, Mass., Jan. 13, 1785; died in New York city, Dec. 9, 1842. During the war of 1812-15 he edited, in New York city, The War, a weekly journal, and The Halcyon Luminary, a Swedenborgian monthly. He was one of the founders of the New York Mirror (1823-24); edited the Parthenon (1827); wrote a romantic history of the war, called 'The Champions of Freedom' (2 vols., 1816), and several dramatic pieces. His poetical works were published in 2 vols. in 1861. His famous poem is 'The Old Oaken Bucket.'

Woolley, Mrs. Celia (Parker). An American author and Unitarian minister at Geneva, Ill.; born in Ohio, 1848. She has written: 'Roger Hunt'; 'A Girl Graduate'; 'Rachel Armstrong; or, Love and Theology'; 'The Western Slope.'

Woolman, John. A Quaker preacher and anti-slavery writer; born in Northampton, N. J., August, 1720; died in York, England, Oct. 5, 1772. His writings contain the earliest protest published in America against the slave trade. His works include: 'Some Considerations on the Keeping of Negroes' (Philadelphia, 1753 and 1762); 'Considerations on Pure Wisdom,' etc. (1768); 'Considerations on the True Harmony of Mankind,' etc. (1770); 'Epistles to Quarterly Meetings of Friends,' etc. (1772). His 'Journal of Life and Travels' was published in Philadelphia in 1775, and edited by Whittier, 1871.

Woolner, Thomas. An English sculptor and poet; born at Hadleigh, Dec. 17, 1825; died in London, Oct. 7, 1892. He made busts of Carlyle and Tennyson, and a medallion portrait of Tennyson, engraved for a frontispiece to the Moxon edition of Tennyson. He was a Pre-Raphaelite; and his popular poem 'My Beautiful Lady' (1863) first appeared in the Pre-Raphaelite journal The Germ. His other volumes are: 'Pygmalion' (1881); 'Silenus' (1884); and 'Tiresias' (1886).

Woolsey, Sarah Chauncey. An American author; born at Cleveland, O., about 1845. Under the pen-name "Susan Coolidge" she is a popular writer, especially for children. Some of her writings are: 'The New Year's Bargain' (1871); 'What Katy Did' (1872); 'Verses' (1880); 'A Guernsey Lily' (1881); 'A Little Country Girl' (1885); and 'A Short History of the City of Philadelphia' (1887). She edited: 'The Diary and Letters of Mrs. Delaney' (1878); and 'The Diary and Letters of Madame D'Arblay.' Died April 9, 1905.

Woolsey, Theodore Dwight. An American educator; born in New York city, Oct. 31, 1801; died in New Haven, Conn., July 1, 1889. He edited the 'Alcestis' of Euripides (1833); the 'Antigone' (1835), and the 'Electra' of Sophocles (1837); the 'Prometheus' of Æschylus (1837); and the 'Gorgias' of Plato (1842). He published his inaugural address, 'College Education' (1846); 'Historical Discourse upon Yale College' (1850); 'Introduction to the Study of International Law' (1860); 'An Essay on Divorce and Divorce Legislation' (1869); a book of sermons, 'The Religion of the Present and the Future' (1871). He re-edited Prof. Francis Lieber's 'Civil Liberty and Self-Government' (1874), and his 'Manual of Political Ethics' (1874). He also published a work on 'Political Science' (1877), and one on 'Communism and Socialism' (1879).

Woolson, Mrs. Abba Louisa (Goold). An American lecturer and author; born in Windham, Me., April 30, 1838; died at Venice, Jan. 23, 1894. She gave many lectures on literary, social, historical, and dramatic subjects; and besides contributing to periodicals published: 'Women in American Society' (1873); 'Browsing among Books' (1881); 'George Eliot and her Heroines' (1886); and 'Dress as it Affects the Health of Women' (1874), a series of lectures.

Woolson, Constance Fenimore. An American novelist and poet; born at Claremont, N. H., March 5, 1848; died at Venice, January 1894. Her principal books are: 'Castle Nowhere' (1875); 'Rodman the Keeper' (1880); 'Anne' (1882); 'For the Major' (1883); 'East Angels' (1886); 'Jupiter Lights' (1889); and 'Horace Chase' (1894).

Worcester, Joseph Emerson. A famous American lexicographer, author of 'Worcester's Dictionary'; born in Bedford, N. H., Aug. 24, 1784; settled in Cambridge, Mass., 1820, and died there, Oct. 27, 1865. He graduated at Yale in 1811, and very shortly began his life work as a dictionary-maker. His first publication was: 'A Geographical Dictionary, or Universal Gazetteer' (1817, revised 1823); followed by 'Gazetteer of the United States' (1818); 'Elements of Geography' (1819); 'Sketches of the Earth and its Inhabitants' (1823); 'Elements of History' (1826). In 1830 he published the 'Comprehensive Pronouncing and Explanatory English Dictionary' (enlarged editions appeared 1847-49-55). In 1860 he published the great quarto, 'Dictionary of the English Language' (Illustrated), a standard authority wherever the English tongue is spoken.

Wordsworth, William. A great English poet; born at Cockermouth, Cumberland, April 7, 1770; died at Rydal Mount, April 23, 1850. He was poet-laureate, 1843. A resident of the lake district in Westmoreland and Cumberland, he was one of the celebrated "Lake School" or "Lake Poets," which included also Coleridge and Southey. Among his best-known works were: 'An Evening Walk' (1793); 'Lyrical Ballads' (1798); two volumes of 'Poems' (1807); 'The Excursion' (1814); new edition of 'Poems' (1815); 'The White Doe of

Rylstone' (1815); 'Thanksgiving Ode' (1816); 'Peter Bell' and 'The Waggoner' (1819); 'Yarrow Revisited, and Other Poems' (1835); 'Sonnets' (1838); 'The Prelude' (1850); etc.

Work, Henry Clay. A leading American song-writer; born in Middletown, Conn., Oct. 1, 1832; died in Hartford, Conn., June 8, 1884. He was highly popular in three different classes of songs: of the War, as 'Kingdom Comin',' 'Wake Nicodemus,' 'Babylon is Fallen,' 'Marching Through Georgia'; of temperance, as 'Father, Dear Father, Come Home with Me Now'; sentimental, as 'My Grandfather's Clock' and 'Lily Dale.'

Workman, Mrs. Fanny (Bullock). An American writer of travels; born in Massachusetts, 1859. She has written: 'Algerian Memories'; 'A Bicycle Tour over the Atlas to the Sahara'; 'Ice-bound Heights of the Mustagh.'

Wormeley, Katharine Prescott. An American author, and prominent translator from the French; born in Suffolk, England, July 14, 1832. She is most widely known as a translator of Honoré de Balzac's novels; and has written: 'The Cruel Side of War' (1881); 'Life of Balzac'; 'The U. S. Sanitary Commission' (1863).

Wornum, Ralph Nicholson. An English writer on the fine arts; born at Thornton, North Durham, Dec. 29, 1812; died at Hampstead, Dec. 15, 1877. He was keeper and secretary of the National Gallery (1855). He wrote: 'Analysis of Ornament' (1856); 'Sketch of the History of Painting' (4th ed. 1861); 'Epochs of Painting' (1864); 'Life of Holbein' (1867).

Worsaae, Jens Jakob Asmussen (vor'sâ-e). A Danish historian; born at Veile, Jutland, March 14, 1821; died near Holbäk, Aug. 15, 1885. He was director of the Museum of Northern Antiquities, Copenhagen, from 1866; minister of public worship 1874-75. He wrote: 'Primeval Antiquities of Denmark' (1843); 'Account of the Danes in England, Scotland, and Ireland' (1851); 'The Danish Conquest of England and Normandy' (1863); etc.

Wotton, Henry, Sir. An English diplomatist, poet, and miscellaneous writer; born at Boughton, Malherbe, Kent, March 30, 1568; died at Eton, December 1639. After spending twenty years almost continuously in the diplomatic service, he became provost of Eton in 1625. He wrote: 'Poems,' which have been many times reprinted, generally with those of Raleigh; 'Reliquiæ Wottonianæ' (Wotton's Remains: 1651), his best-known work, edited with a life by his friend Izaak Walton; 'Elements of Architecture'; 'State of Christendom'; etc.

Wotton, William. An English clergyman and scholar; born at Wrentham, Suffolk, Aug. 13, 1666; died at Buxted, Essex, Feb. 13, 1726. He was prebendary at Salisbury 1705. He wrote 'Reflections upon Ancient and Modern Learning' (3d ed. 1795), 'History of Rome' (1701),

etc.; and edited the 'Laws of Howel the Good' (1730), in Welsh and Latin, with glossary.

Wraxall, Sir Nathaniel William. An English statesman and historian; born at Bristol, April 8, 1751; died at Dover, Nov. 7, 1831. Going to India in the service of the East India Company in 1769, he remained there till 1772; then spent several years traveling; was Member of Parliament in 1780. He wrote: 'Kings of France of the House of Valois' (1777); 'History of France' (1795); 'Memoirs of the Courts of Berlin, Dresden, Warsaw, and Vienna' (1799); 'Historical Memoirs of my Own Time' (new ed. 5 vols., 1884), etc.

Wright, Carroll Davidson. An American statistician, lecturer, and writer on political economy; born in Dunbarton, N. H., July 25, 1840. After distinguished service in the Civil War, he was a member of the Massachusetts Legislature, 1871-72; afterwards chief of the State Bureau of Statistics, lecturer at Harvard University, and United States Commissioner of Labor from 1885. He is professor of political science in the Catholic University at Washington, D. C. Besides numerous addresses, pamphlets, and articles in reviews, he has published: 'Reports of Massachusetts Bureau of Labor' (15 vols., 1873-88); 'Census of Massachusetts' (1876-77); 'The Factory System of the United States' (1882); Reports of the U. S. Commissioner of Labor, including 'Industrial Depressions' (1886), 'Convict Labor' (1886), 'Strikes and Lockouts' (1887), 'Railroad Labor'; and 'Battles of Labor.' He has written much on social economy and is authority on statistics.

Wright, Elizur. An American reformer, journalist, and author; born in South Canaan, Conn., Feb. 12, 1804; died in Medford, Mass., Nov. 21, 1885. He graduated at Yale, 1826; taught school, and was professor of mathematics in Western Reserve College, 1829-33. He was identified with the Anti-Slavery movement in 1833; was editor of the newspapers The Emancipator, and Human Rights, and the quarterly Anti-Slavery Magazine. He published several works on life insurance, 'Savings Banks Life Insurance' (1872), 'The Politics and Mysteries of Life Insurance' (1873), etc.; and was Insurance Commissioner of Massachusetts. He wrote an introduction to Whittier's poems (1844); and published a translation in verse of 'La Fontaine's Fables' (1859.)

Wright, Fanny. See D'Arusmont.

Wright, George Frederick. An American geologist and author; born in Whitehall, N. Y., Jan. 22, 1838. He was a Congregational clergyman (1862-72), and professor of Harmony of Science and Revelation in Oberlin College. Since 1884 he has been connected with the U. S. Geological Survey. His works include: 'The Logic of Christian Evidence' (1880); 'Studies in Science and Religion' (1882); 'The Relation of Death to Probation' (1882); 'The Glacial Boundary in Ohio, Indiana, and Kentucky' (1884); 'The Divine Authority of the

Bible ' (1884) ; 'The Ice Age in North America'; ' Man and Glacial Period ' ; ' Asiatic Russia.'

Wright, Henrietta Christian. An American writer for the young. Her works include the ' Golden Fairy Series ' (5 vols., 1883; published also as ' The Little Folk in Green,' illustrated, 1883); ' Children's Stories of American Progress' (1886); ' Children's Stories of the Great Scientists ' (1888).

Wright, Mrs. Julia (McNair). An American author and writer of temperance tales; born in Oswego, N. Y., May 1, 1840. Her books are anti-Catholic in tone, and include : ' Priest and Nun ' (1869); ' Jug-or-Not ' (1870); ' Saints and Sinners ' (1873); ' The Early Church in Britain ' (1874); ' Bricks from Babel ' (1876); ' The Complete Home ' (1879); ' A Wife Hard Won ' (1882), etc. Died Sept. 2, 1903.

Wright, Mrs. Mabel (Osgood). An American writer on nature ; born in New York, 1859. She has written : ' The Friendship of Nature,' a series of outdoor studies ; ' Birdcraft,' a book on New England birds : ' Tommy-Anne: A Natural History Story ' ; 'Citizen Bird,' a book for beginners ; ' Gray Lady and the Birds.'

Wright, Thomas. An English antiquary and historian; born near Ludlow, April 23, 1810; died at Chelsea, Dec. 23, 1877. He was one of the founders of the British Archæological Association, and directed the excavation of Uriconium. A prolific worker, he wrote : ' Queen Elizabeth and her Times ' (1838); ' Essays on the Literature, Popular Superstitions, and History of England in the Middle Ages ' (1846); ' Narrative of Sorcery and Magic ' (1851); ' Wanderings of an Antiquary ' (1854); ' Essays on Archæological Subjects ' (1861); ' Manners and Sentiments in England during the Middle Ages ' (1862); ' Caricature History of the Georges ' (new ed. 1868); ' Womankind in Western Europe ' (1869); ' History of Caricature and the Grotesque ' (2d ed. 1875); ' The Celt, the Roman, and the Saxon ' (5th ed. 1890); etc. He edited ' Early English Poetry ' (1836); ' Piers Plowman ' (1842); ' The Chester Plays ' (1843–47); ' The Canterbury Tales ' (1847–51); ' Works of James Gillray ' (1873); etc.

Wright, William Aldis. An English editor, noted as a Shakespearean scholar; born about 1836. He was the principal contributor in Biblical geography and biography to Dr. Smith's ' Dictionary of the Bible ' (3 vols., 1860–63), and made an abridged edition. He edited Bacon's essays (1862), and his 'Advancement of Learning ' (1869); was co-editor with W. Clark, of the 'Cambridge Shakspeare ' (9 vols., 1863–66), and the ' Globe Shakspeare ' (1 vol., 1864); and edited the ' Bible Word-Book ' (1866), Chaucer's ' Clerk's Tale,' the ' Metrical Chronicle ' of Robert of Gloucester, and other works.

Wright, William Burnet. An American Congregational clergyman ; born in Ohio, 1836. Among his books are : ' Ancient Cities from the Dawn to the Daylight ' ; ' The World to Come ' ; 'Master and Men' ; ' The Sermon on the Mountain Practiced on the Plain'; 'Cities of Paul.'

Wulfila. See **Ulfilas.**

Wundt, Wilhelm Max (vönt). A distinguished German physiologist and philosopher ; born at Neckarau, Baden, Aug. 16, 1832. He has been professor of philosophy at Leipsic since 1875. His works include : ' Science of Muscular Motion ' (1858); ' Manual of Human Physiology ' (4th ed. 1878); ' Ethics ' (2d ed. 1892); ' The Human and the Animal Soul ' (2d ed. 1892; in English, 1894); ' Logic ' (2d ed. 1892–95); ' Elements of Physiological Psychology ' (4th ed. 1893); ' System of Philosophy ' (2d ed. 1897); ' Outline of Psychology ' (2d ed. 1897; in English, 1894); etc. As a physiologist he has advanced psychology by his work. As a philosopher he has introduced the inductive method into sciences previously purely speculative (e. g., logic and ethics), and sought to advance psychology by exact measurements (as of the time needed by a nerve stimulation to reach consciousness and become a percept).

Wuttke, Emma (vöt'kè). A German novelist, wife of Heinrich Wuttke; born at Breslau, March 7, 1833. Her home is at Dresden. She became known under her maiden name, E. Biller, as a writer for the young. Since marrying, she has written the successful historical romances : ' Barbara Ittenhausen ' (6th ed. 1896); ' Barbara of Brandenburg ' (2d ed. 1896); ' Under the Governess's Sceptre ' (1888); ' Duty ' (1896); etc.

Wuttke, Heinrich. A German historian and politician; born at Brieg, Silesia, Feb. 12, 1818; died at Leipsic, June 14, 1876. He was professor at Leipsic (1848), and member of the national assembly; in the latter capacity he was a founder and prominent representative of the "Great German" party. He wrote : ' King Frederick the Great ' (1842–43); ' Poles and Germans ' (1847); ' The Battle of Leipsic ' (1863); ' German Periodicals and the Formation of Public Opinion ' (3d ed. 1876); etc.

Wyatt, Sir Thomas. An English poet and diplomatist ; born at Arlington Castle, Kent, 1503; died at Sherborne, Oct. 11, 1542. He wrote many poems, chiefly love sonnets, in the Italian manner. These were published in 1557, and have been often reprinted. The best edition of his complete works is that by Rev. George F. Nott, along with those of his friend, the Earl of Surrey (2 vols., 1815–16).

Wycherley, William. An English dramatist ; born at Clive, about 1640; died in London, Jan. 1, 1716. Some of his plays were : ' Love in a Wood ' (1672); ' The Gentleman Dancing-Master ' (1673); ' The Country Wife ' (1675); and ' The Plain-Dealer ' (1677). A volume of ' Poems ' was published in 1704. His comedies were in prose, and very coarse. His ' Posthumous Works ' were published in 1728; and his collected ' Plays ' in 1712.

Wyclif, Wickliffe or **Wiclif, John.** Born near Richmond, England, probably some years before 1324; died Dec. 31, 1384. His great work was the translation, with the help of his pupils, of the entire Bible into English (1382). Some of his writings, edited by different hands, have been issued from 1840 to 1880; as: 'Last Age of the Church'; 'Apology for Lollard Doctrines'; 'Three Treatises (1) of the Church and her members; (2) of the Apostacy of the Church; (3) of Antichrist and his Maynee'; 'English Tracts and Treatises,' with 'Selections and Translations from his Latin Works'; 'Select English Works,' including many sermons (3 vols.); 'English Works Hitherto Unpublished,' issued in 1880. Many of his Latin writings remain unpublished.

Wynne, Mrs. Madelene (Yale). An American artist and story-writer, daughter of Mrs. Catharine Brooks Yale; born in New York State, 1847. She has written 'The Little Room, and Other Stories.'

Wyss, Johann Rudolf (vis). A Swiss author; born at Berne, March 13, 1781; died there, March 31, 1830. His writings are: 'Lectures on the Supreme Good' (2 vols., 1811); 'Idylls, Folk-Songs, Legends, and Narratives from Switzerland' (3 vols., 1815–22); and 'Travels in the Bernese Alps' (1808). He edited a series called 'Alpenrose' (20 vols., 1811–30). His 'Swiss Family Robinson' has been translated into many languages.

X

Xacca, Erasmus (Hä'kä). A Sicilian writer; born about 1643; died about 1708. He was doctor of theology, medicine, and laws, and took orders, but devoted much time to literature. He left 'An Exposition of the Psalms of David,' and an original poem, 'A Brief Narrative of the Eruption of Mt. Etna in the Year 1669,' published 1671.

Xanthos (zän'thos). A Greek lyric poet, who lived probably about 650 B. C. Nothing of his poetry has been preserved, but he is highly spoken of by other writers.

Xanthos of Lydia. A Greek historian; living about the sixth century B. C., contemporary with Herodotus. He wrote a work called 'Lydiaca,' being a history of Lydia from heroic times down, and giving also a geographical description of the country; only fragments of it have been preserved.

Xariffa. See Mrs. Mary Ashley Townsend.

Xavier, Francisco (zav'ē-er). The Apostle of the Indies; born at Xaviero, his mother's castle in the Basque country, April 7 (?), 1506; died in the island of Sancian near China, Dec. 2 or 22, 1552. His works comprise: 'Letters,' in five volumes, published at Paris in 1631; a 'Catechism'; and some short treatises. He played a prominent part in the foundation of the Jesuit order, and was canonized in 1622.

Xavier, Jerome (zav'ē-er; Span. pron., Hä-vē-är'). A Spanish Jesuit missionary and writer; born in Navarre; died in Goa, 16—. He wrote both in Latin and in Persian. Among his chief works are: 'A Treatise on the Mysteries of Christianity' (1600); a 'Life of the Apostles'; a 'History of Jesus Christ'; and a 'Directory of Kings for the Government of their Subjects.'

Xenarchus (ze-när'kus). An Athenian comic poet of the Middle Comedy; flourished about 350 to 330 B. C. Fragments of his works are extant.

Xenocles (zen'ō-klēz). A Greek tragic poet; born at Athens, about the fourth century B. C., in the time of Philip of Macedon. Little is known of his life, but he obtained a prize for four plays, 'Œdipus,' 'Lycaon,' the 'Bacchantes,' and 'Athamas.'

Xenocrates (zē-nok'ra-tēz). A Greek writer and philosopher; born in Chalcedon, in 396 B. C.; died 314 in Athens, where he had removed in early youth, and where he joined Plato. He was for some years scholarch, or rector, of the Academy. His writings were numerous, chiefly on metaphysics and ethics, laying special stress upon the latter, and working on Platonic lines. He is said to have first divided philosophy into physic, didactic, and ethic.

Xenophanes (ze-nof'a-nēz). A Greek writer and philosopher; born in Colophon about the third or fourth decade of the sixth century B. C., and died at the age of 92, at Elea, in Southern Italy, where, exiled from his Ionian home, he had established himself. He is the reputed founder of the Eleatic philosophy, and his teachings found expression in both elegiac and epic poems, the most important being 'On Nature' and 'Satires.'

Xenophon (zen'ō-fon). The famous author of the 'Anabasis'; born at Athens, about 430 B. C.; died in Corinth, about 355 B. C. He is the author of the 'Hellenics'; 'Anabasis'; 'Encomium of Agesilaus'; 'Horsemanship'; 'Hipparchicus'; 'Cynegeticus'; 'Lacedæmonian Polity'; 'Cyropædeia'; 'Athenian Finance'; 'Memorabilia of Socrates'; 'Symposium'; 'Œconomicus'; 'Hieron'; 'Apology of Socrates.' 'The Polity of Athens' is now regarded as an anonymous work incorporated into the text of Xenophon, but probably not his.

Xenophon of Ephesus, called **Xenophon the Younger.** A Greek writer, who lived in the second century of the Christian era. Only one work of his has been preserved, a story in five books, called ' Ephesiaca; or, The Loves of Abrocomas and Anthia,' the style of which is pure, elegant, and yet simple, and the action rapid.

Xenos, Stefanos Theodoros (zen'os). A modern Greek historical writer. He resided for many years in London. He wrote: 'The Devil in Turkey; or, Scenes in Constantinople' (London, 1850); 'The Heroine of the Greek Revolution' (1861), republished in America as 'Andronike'; 'East and West' (1865).

Xeres, Francisco (Hār'ās). A Spanish historian, who lived in the sixteenth century, accompanying Pizarro, as his secretary, to Peru, about 1530. Of that expedition he wrote a detailed history, entitled 'A True Account of the Conquest of Peru' (1549), still considered of great value as a source of information.

Ximenes, August Louis (ze-ma-nes'). A French poet of Spanish descent; born at Paris, 1726; died 1815. Among his writings are several tragedies, notably one called 'Don Carlos'; also a poem, 'Cæsar in the Senate,' and critical essays of value.

Ximenes, Enrico Emilio (Hē-mä'nes). An Italian miscellaneous writer; born at Palermo, May 14, 1857. He founded, in 1882, the daily journals Vespers and Democracy at Palermo. He has written 'The Sicilian Vespers' (1882), 'Ninna-Nanna' (1884), in verse; 'Critical Study of Garibaldian Literature' (1885); 'Correspondence of Giuseppe Garibaldi' (2 vols., 1886); 'Syracuse in the Past and Present' (1887); 'Anna Bonanno,' a historical romance; 'Two Years of History'; etc.

Ximenes, Jacques (Hē-mä'nes). A Spanish poet, living in the sixteenth century. Little is known of his life, save that he took part in the war in the Netherlands. He wrote a poem, 'The Invincible Knight, the Cid Ruy Diaz of Bivar' (1579); and left a collection of sonnets (1669).

Ximenes, Peter (shē-ma'nes). A Portuguese-Dutch theologian; born at Middelburg, Holland, 1514; died 1595. He wrote in Latin 'Demonstration of the Catholic Truth.'

Ximenes, Rodrigo. A Spanish prelate and historian, who died 1249. He took part in the war against the Moors, and wrote a 'History of Spain'; 'History of the Huns and Vandals'; a 'History of the Arabs'; and a 'History of Rome.'

Ximenes or Jimenes, de Cisneros, Francisco (dä thēs-nā'rōs). A Spanish churchman and statesman; born at Torrelaguna in Castile, 1436 (?); died at Roa about 1517. He became archbishop of Toledo 1495, and at the same time was appointed grand chancellor of Castile; he was raised to the Cardinalate 1507. He founded the University of Alcalá de Henares 1500, and at his own expense procured the printing of the Complutensian Polyglot Bible, containing the original Hebrew and Greek texts, the Septuagint Greek and the Vulgate Latin translations, and the Targum of Onkelos (6 vols., 1514-17).

Ximeno or Jimeno, Vicente (Hē-mä'nō). A Spanish biographer; born at Valencia, about 1700. He was the author of a 'Literary History of the Kingdom of Valencia' (2 vols., 1747-49).

Xuares, Gaspar (Hwä'rās). A South-American botanist, historian, and biographer; born at Santiago del Estero, Paraguay; died at Rome, 1804. Belonging to the order of Jesuits, he devoted himself to teaching philosophy and theology; after the suppression of his order he removed to Italy, where he occupied himself with botany. He wrote: 'History of Buenos Ayres,' and 'Dissertations,' both remaining in MS.; 'Life of St. Francis Xavier'; etc.

Xylander, Joseph Carl August (ksi-län'der). A German officer and military writer; born at Munich, 1794; died 1854. He wrote: 'A Manual of Tactics'; 'Strategy and its Application' (1818); and many other works, among them a 'History of the War in Sweden in 1808-9' (1825).

Y

Yakhontov, Alexander Nikolaiewich (yä-kon-tof'). A Russian politician and poet; born in the district of Pskov, June 28, 1820. He has held a number of important positions in his native district. He has written for Russian journals (1843-89) a mass of lyrical and satirical poems, from which appeared a 'Collection' in 1884. He has published also several popular historical and scientific works and translations, and translations from Goethe and Lessing.

Yalden, Thomas. An English poet; born at Oxford, 1669-70; died, 1736. He wrote an 'Ode

for St. Cecilia's Day' (1693); 'The Temple of Fame,' on the death of the Duke of Gloucester (1700); 'Æsop at Court,' a collection of fables (1702). His 'Hymn to Light' is the most notable of his poetical compositions. He is best remembered as Swift's friend.

Yale, Mrs. Catharine (Brooks). An American writer, living at Deerfield, Mass. She was born in Vermont in 1818, and is the wife of Linus Yale, inventor of the Yale lock. She has written: 'Story of the Old Willard House of Deerfield, Mass.'; 'Nim and Cum, and the Wonderhead Stories.'

Yanguas y Miranda José (yän'gwäs ē mē-rän'dä). A Spanish archæologist; died about 1860. His principal works are: 'Short History of the Kingdom of Navarre' (1833); 'History of the Conquest of the Kingdom of Navarre, by the Duke of Alva' (1843); 'Dictionary of the Antiquities of the Kingdom of Navarre' (4 vols., 1840-43).

Yanoski, Jean (yä-nos-kē'). A French writer on history; born at Lons-le-Saulnier, 1813; died 1851. He wrote: 'Christian Africa, and the Domination of the Vandals in Africa' (1844); 'Abolition of Ancient Slavery'; 'National Military Forces from the Thirteenth Century to the Reign of Charles VII.'

Yardley, Edward, Jr. An English story and verse writer. He has published: 'Fantastic Stories' (1864); 'Melusine, and Other Poems' (1867); 'Supplementary Stories and Poems' (1870); 'The Supernatural in Romantic Fiction' (1880); besides an English translation of four books of Horace's Odes (1669).

Yardley, Mrs. Jane. An American novelist, who has written in the 'No Name' series: 'Little Sister' (1882); 'A Superior Woman' (1885).

Yarrell, William. An English naturalist; born at Westminster, 1784; died at Yarmouth, September 1856. He is author of 'The History of British Fishes' (2 vols., 1836), and 'The History of British Birds' (2 vols., 1843); both written in an elegant and popular style, and illustrated artistically, yet without impairing the scientific accuracy of the exposition.

Yates, Edmund. An English journalist and novelist; born at Edinburgh, 1831; died London, May 20, 1894. He was a contributor to All the Year Round for several years, and from 1874 till his death conducted the London society journal, The World. He wrote: 'My Haunts and their Frequenters' (1854); 'Black Sheep' (1867); 'Wrecked in Port' (1869); 'Dr. Wainwright's Patient' (1871); 'The Yellow Flag' (1873); 'Personal Reminiscences and Experiences' (2 vols., 1884).

Yazikov (yä-zē-kof'). A Russian lyric poet; born at Simbirsk, 1805; died 1846. He was called "the Russian Anacreon." His earlier verse was notable for sweetness and melody; his later work was more serious in character.

Yearsley, Mrs. Ann. An English poetical and dramatic writer, originally a milk-woman; born in Bristol, about 1756; died 1806. She was befriended by Hannah More, and under her auspices published a romance, 'The Royal Captives,' and a collection of poems.

Yeats, S. Levett. An English novelist. He resides in India, where he is a lieutenant in the Punjaub Light Horse. He has written: 'The Honour of Savelli' (1895); 'A Galahad of the Creeks' (1897); 'The Chevalier D'Auriac' (1897).

Yeats, William Butler. An Irish poet and writer of romance; born in Dublin, June 13, 1865. His first book of poems, containing the 'Island of Statues,' and other brief plays and poems, is included in his later volume, 'The Wanderings of Oisin' (1887). Three volumes of 'Irish Folk Lore,' 'Fairy Tales,' and 'Irish Stories,' were published in the Camelot series. He has also written: 'Celtic Twilight' (1893); 'Poems' (1893); and 'John Sherman and Dhoya' (1893); 'The Secret Rose' and 'The Wind among the Reeds'; 'The Shadowy Waters'; 'In the Seven Woods'; 'The King's Threshold'; 'Deirdre'; 'The Hour Glass'; 'The Unicorn from the Stars'; 'Catherine Ni Honlihan'; 'Rosa Alchemica'; 'Mosada'; 'Countess Cathleen'; 'Golden Helmet.' A complete edition of his works in eight volumes appeared in 1909.

Yelverton, Maria Theresa (Longworth). An English writer of autobiography and travels, and novelist. Besides 'Martyrs to Circumstance' (1861), and 'The Yelverton Correspondence' (1863), both relating to her notorious marriage with Major Yelverton, she has written: 'Zanita: A Tale of the Yosemite' (1871); 'Fifty Thousand Miles of Travel Round the World' (1874); 'Teresina in America' (1875).

Yendis or **Yendys.** See **Dobell.**

Yepez, Antonio de (yā'peth). A Spanish historian; born at Yepez; died 1621. He was a Benedictine monk, and wrote a valuable 'General Chronicle of the Order of St. Benedict' (7 vols., 1609-21).

Yepez, Diego de. A Spanish historian; born at Yepez, near Toledo, 1559; died at Tarragona, 1613, of which see he was bishop. His principal works are: 'History of the Persecution in England Since 1570' (1599); 'Memoir on the Death of Philip II.' (1607).

Ymbert, Jean Albert (añ-bär'). A French writer of comedy; born about 1786; died 1846. He wrote: 'A Husband Unknown to Himself'; 'The Art of Getting Office' (1817); 'A Bachelor's Dinner' (1820); 'The Automaton Man' (1820); 'The Obliging Man' (1820); 'The Propertyless Proprietor' (1820); 'The Neutral City; or, The Burgomaster of Neustadt' (1825).

Yonge, Charles Duke (yung). An English historical writer and classical scholar; born 1812; died 1891. He has published: 'An English-Greek Lexicon' (1849); 'A New Gradus ad Parnassum of the Latin Language' (1850); 'Three Centuries of English History' (1872); 'Three Centuries of English Literature' (1872); 'A Life of Marie Antoinette, Queen of France' (1876); etc.

Yonge, Charlotte Mary. An English novelist; born at Otterbourne, Hampshire, Aug 11, 1823; died there March 24, 1901. She published more than 30 novels, usually of "High Church" tendencies, the most popular of which are: 'The Heir of Redclyffe' (1853) and 'Daisy Chain; or, Aspirations' (1856). Among her historical and biographical works are: 'The Kings of England' (1848); 'Landmarks of History, Ancient, Middle Age, and Modern' (1852–57); 'The Victorian Half-Century' (1887); etc.

Youatt, William. An English writer on veterinary subjects; born in 1777; died in London, 1847. He was for many years professor at the Royal Veterinary College, and co-editor of the Veterinarian, established 1828. He published a standard work on 'The Horse' (1831), also a book on 'The Dog' (1842), and others; all considered of high value in their line.

Youmans, Edward Livingston. An American scientist and writer, long the editor of the Popular Science Monthly; born at Coeymans, N. Y., 1821; died in New York city, 1887. His chief works are: 'Alcohol and the Constitution of Man' (1854); 'Hand-Book of Household Science' (1857); 'Correlation and Conservation of Forces' (1864); 'The Culture Demanded by Modern Life' (1867); etc.

Youmans, William Jay. An American writer and chemist; born at Milton, Saratoga County, N. Y., in 1838; died at Mt. Vernon, N. Y., April 10, 1901. He published a book, 'Pioneers of Science in America' (1895); edited Huxley's 'Lessons in Elementary Physiology,' adding a second part, 'Elementary Hygiene' (1867); many years editor of the Popular Science Monthly, succeeding his brother, Edward L.

Young, Andrew White. An American writer on government; born at Carlisle, N. Y., March 2, 1802; died at Warsaw, N. Y., Feb. 17, 1877. He wrote: 'Introduction to the Science of Government' (1835); 'First Lessons in Civil Government' (1843); 'Citizen's Manual of Government and Law' (1851); 'The American Statesman: A Political History of the United States' (1855); 'National Economy: A History of the American Protective System' (1860).

Young, Arthur. A distinguished English writer on agriculture and social economy; born 1741; died 1820. He made a practical study of agricultural economy, and wrote: 'A Course of Experimental Agriculture' (1770); accounts of tours of observation through different quarters of England, among these, 'A Farmer's Letters to the People of England' (1768), 'A Farmer's Tour through the East of England' (1770); 'Travels in France' (2 vols., 1792), a celebrated book which reveals the true state of the peasant population of France on the eve of the Revolution.

Young, Charles Augustus. An American astronomer; born in Hanover, Dec. 15, 1834. He was professor at Western Reserve College, Ohio, 1856; professor of natural philosophy at Dartmouth College, 1865–77, and of astronomy at Princeton College from 1878. Besides many contributions to scientific journals and magazines, he is the author of 'The Sun' in the 'International Scientific Series' (1882), and a 'Text-Book of General Astronomy.' Died 1908.

Young, Edward. An English poet; born at Upham, Hampshire, 1683; died at Welwyn,

April 5, 1765. After graduating at Oxford, he entered the Church. His masterpiece is 'Night Thoughts' (1742–46), a gloomy but fine poem in blank verse. He also wrote tragedies, among them 'Busiris' (1719), and 'The Revenge' (1721); as well as a collection of satires called 'The Love of Fame' (1725–28).

Young, Edward Daniel. An English traveler; born 1831. He explored the Lake Nyassa country in 1875, and wrote 'Nyassa' (1877). Died 1896.

Young, Frederick, Sir. An English philanthropist, publicist, and writer of travels; born 1817. He aided in securing Victoria Park, London, and Epping Forest to the public, and in establishing the People's Palace; has taken great interest in the emigration question; was one of the earliest advocates of imperial federation; etc. He has written: 'Long Ago and Now'; 'New Zealand: Past, Present, and Future'; 'A Winter Tour in South Africa'; etc.; and edited 'Imperial Federation' (1876).

Young, Jesse Bowman. An American Methodist clergyman, author, and editor; born in Pennsylvania, 1844. He has been editor of the Central Christan Advocate from 1892, and has written 'What a Boy Saw in the Army'; 'Days and Nights on the Sea'; 'The Hungry Christ.'

Young, John. A British clergyman, and religious and philosophical writer. He has published: 'The Province of Reason' (1860); 'Evil and Good' (2d ed. London, 1861); 'The Life and Light of Men' (1866); 'The Christ of History' (6th ed. 1870); 'The Creator and the Creation' (1870).

Young, John Russell. An American writer and journalist; born in Downingtown, Pa., Nov. 20, 1841; died in Washington, Jan. 17, 1899. His journalistic career was notable, including service on the staffs of the New York Herald and Tribune. His most famous work is 'Around the World with General Grant' (2 vols. 1879); and he also wrote numerous pamphlets on important subjects. In 1897 he was appointed by President McKinley Librarian of Congress, which office he held at his death.

Young, Mrs. Julia Evelyn (Ditto). An American verse-writer and novelist, of Buffalo; born in New York, in 1857. She has written: 'Adrift: A Story of Niagara'; 'Glynne's Wife: A Story in Verse'; and 'Thistle-Down,' poems.

Young, Mrs. M., formerly **Mrs. Thomas Postans.** She wrote as Mrs. Thomas Postans: 'Cutch' (1838), sketches of Western India; 'Western India in 1838' (2 vols., 1839); 'Facts and Fictions Illustrative of Oriental Character' (3 vols., 1844). As Mrs. Young: 'Our Camp in Turkey' (2d ed. 1855); 'Aldershot, and All About It' (2d ed. 1858); 'The Moslem Noble' (1857).

Young, William, Sir. An English statesman and historical writer; born in the middle of the eighteenth century; died about 1815. Among his writings are: 'Travels in Italy' (1772); 'The Spirit of Athens: Political and

Philosophical Investigations on the History of that Republic' (1777); 'Rights of Englishmen' (1793); 'The Black Caribs of the Island of St. Vincent' (1795); 'The West Indian Common-Place Book.'

Ypey, Amadeus (ē'pī). A Dutch theological writer; born 1760; died in 1831 at Groningen, where he was professor of church history. He wrote a 'Literary History of Dogmatics' (5 vols., 1793–98); 'History of the Dutch Language' (1812); 'History of the Dutch Church' (4 vols., 1820–27).

Yriarte, Charles Émile (1-rĭ-ŭrt'). A journalist and writer of Spanish descent; born at Paris, Dec. 5, 1832; died at Philadelphia, April 8, 1898. Among his works are: 'Spanish Society' (1864); 'Parisian Portraits' (1865); 'The Life of a Venetian Patrician in the Sixteenth Century' (1874); 'Venice: Its History, Art, Industry, the City and its Life' (1879); 'Italian Sculpture in the Fifteenth Century' (1885); 'Francesca da Rimini' (1882); 'Cesar Borgia' (1888).

Yriarte or **Iriarte, Juan de** (ē-rē-är'tā). A Spanish scholar and writer; born at Orotava on the island of Teneriffe, in 1702; died at Madrid, 1771. He was chief librarian of the Royal Library; and his most important work was 'Codices of the Greek MSS.' (1769). He also wrote epigrams and proverbs in Latin and Spanish, and narrative poems in Latin, published in four volumes (1774).

Yriarte or **Iriarte, Tomas de**. A Spanish poet and dramatist; born at Orotava, island of Teneriffe, 1750; died in Madrid, 1791. His chief works are an excellent didactic poem, 'Music' (1780); and 'Literary Fables' (1782), considered the best fables in the Spanish language. He also wrote the first regular comedies in Spanish, the best being 'The Spoiled Child' and 'The Ill-Bred Young Lady'; besides publishing Spanish translations of French plays and some of the Latin poets.

Ysabeau, Victor Frédéric Alexandre (i-zä-bō'). A French physician and writer on agriculture; born at Rouen, 1793; died at Paris, 1873. Among his works are: 'Gardening; or, The Art of Forming and Managing a Garden' (1854); 'Elementary Lessons in Agriculture' (1857); 'The Vine and Fruit Tree' (1858); 'Popular Natural History of France' (1864); 'Hygiene and Domestic Economy' (1870).

Yule, Henry, Sir. An Anglo-Indian writer and scholar; born at Inveresk, Midlothian, Scotland, 1820; died 1889. He entered the East India Company's military school, and later was employed in India on public works; but finally retired and went to Italy. His chief books are: 'Mission to the Court of Ava' (1856); 'Cathay and the Way Thither' (1866); 'The Book of Ser Marco Polo' (edited: 1891); 'The Diary of William Hedges' (1886); etc.

Yusuf or **Yussuf, Abu Amru** (yös'öf). An Arabic historian and commentator; born at Cordova, 976; died at Xativa, 1070. He was profoundly versed in the traditions of the Oriental Mussulman countries. He wrote: 'Behedjet-Almodjalisyn,' a collection of tales about Mahomet, etc.; 'Tamhyd,' a commentary on one of the chief Mussulman works of religious and civil law; 'History of the Opinions and Doctrines of the Principal Mussulman Sects'; 'History of the Wars against the Christians'; etc.

Yvan, Melchior (ē-voṅ'). A French physician and publicist; born at Digne (Basses-Alpes), 1803; died at Nice, 1873. He wrote: 'China and the Malay Peninsula' (1850); 'Travels and Stories' (1852); 'The Insurrection in China' (1853); 'From France to China' (1855).

Yver, Jacques (ē-vär'). A French story and verse writer; born at Niort, 1520; died there, 1572. He wrote: 'The Springtime of Yver' (1572), in the style of Boccaccio. It has been a number of times republished.

Yvert, Eugène (ē-vär'). A French journalist, poet, and miscellaneous writer; born at Marly-le-Roi, 1794; died at Amiens, Feb. 23, 1878. He was editor of the Picardy Gazette, 1831. He wrote: 'Parliamentary Sketches' (1832), in verse; 'Political Customs' (1845); 'A Ghost' (1852), a two-act comedy in verse; 'Poetic Fancies' (1857); 'Poetical Miscellanies' (1860); etc.

Yves d'Évreux, Pierre (ēv dā-vrē'). A French-Brazilian historian; born at Évreux, Normandy, about 1577; died after 1620. He was a Capuchin missionary at Maranhão, Brazil, 1612–14. He wrote: 'History of the Most Memorable Things that Happened at Maranhão in the Years 1613 and 1614' (Paris, 1615; 2d ed. 1864), a continuation of the history of Claude d'Abbeville; it is a work of great historical value.

Yvon, Claude (ē-vôṅ'). A French theologian; born at Mamers, 1714; died at Paris, 1791. He wrote 'Letters to Rousseau' (1763), in answer to Rousseau's letters to the archbishop of Paris; earlier in life he had been associated with Diderot and the encyclopedists, and wrote 'Liberty of Conscience' (1754), in which he held that the State should be indifferent in matters of religion. Other works are 'Agreement of Philosophy and Religion' (1776), and 'Philosophical History of Religion' (1779).

Z

Zabel, Eugen (tsä'bel). A German miscellaneous writer; born at Königsberg in Prussia, Dec. 23, 1851. During his extensive travels he formed the acquaintance of nearly all the literary celebrities of Europe. Among his works are: 'Berthold Auerbach' (1882); 'Ivan Turgenef' (1883); 'Italian Dramatic Art in Germany' (1892); 'Anton Rubinstein: An Artist's Life' (1892); translations of several of Turgenef's novels, and of French and Spanish dramas; some novels, among them 'Parted Hearts' (1888); and several comedies, as 'The Midnight Sun,' 'A Missed Vocation.'

Zabensing, Johann Christoph (tsä'ben-zing). A German dramatic and miscellaneous writer; born at Augsburg, 1747; died near the end of the century. He was by profession a merchant, but published various original writings, among them a book on the life and writings of Voltaire, and 'The Philosophers à la Mode,' a comedy (1779); 'The Death of Abel,' a drama (1779); and 'Elizabeth; or, The Abduction,' a tragedy (1781).

Zablocki, Frantizek (zä-blots'kē). A Polish dramatist; born 1754; died 1821. He is looked upon as the creator of Polish comedy, his plays holding the stage to the present day. His masterpiece is 'Sarmatyzin,' and others are: 'The Fop who Acts the Gallant with the Ladies'; 'An Irreparable Loss.'

Zaborowski (zä-bō-rov-ski') or **Zaborowski-Moindron** (mwaṅ-drôṅ'). A French publicist; born at La Crèche, 1851. He is secretary of the Paris Anthropological Society, and scientific editor of several Paris journals. He has written: 'On the Antiquity of Man' (2 vols., 1874); 'Prehistoric Man' (1878); 'Origin of Language' (1879); 'Scientific News and Curiosities' (1883); etc.

Zaccaria, Francesco Antonio (dzä-kä-rē'ä). An Italian Jesuit, scholar, and historian; born at Venice, 1714; died 1795. He was professor of ecclesiastical history at the college La Sapienza, Rome. He wrote: 'Literary History of England' (14 vols., 1751); 'Literary Annals of Italy' (3 vols., 1762); 'Numismatic Institutes'; etc.

Zaccone, Pierre (zä-koṅ'). A French dramatic and miscellaneous writer; born at Douai, 1817 (?). Early in life he entered the Post-Office service at Brest, but devoted all his leisure to literature, and was befriended by Émile Souvestre. He published: 'Tableaux of Universal Literary History' (1844); 'Memoirs of a King' (1851); etc. Among his efforts for the theatre, mostly written in collaboration with others, are: 'The Twenty-Fourth of February' (1848); 'Cousin Verdure' (1855); and 'The Sundays of Pampette.'

Zachariä, Heinrich Albert (tsä-ċhä-rē'ä). A German publicist; born at Herbsleben, Saxe-Gotha, Nov. 20, 1806; died at Kannstadt, April 29, 1875, being then professor in the University of Göttingen. Among his works are: 'German States' Rights and Federal Rights' (1841); 'Manual of German Criminal Procedure' (1860); 'German Constitutional Laws of the Present Time' (1855); 'The Question of the Competence of the Empire in View of the Dogma of Infallibility' (1871).

Zachariä, Just Friedrich Wilhelm. A German poet and satirist; born at Frankenhausen, May 1, 1726; died at Brunswick, Jan. 30, 1777. He was professor of belles-lettres in the Carolinum, Brunswick (1761). He wrote: 'The Brawler' (1744), the first burlesque heroic poem that had appeared in German; 'Phaeton'; 'The Handkerchief'; 'Murner in Hell' (1757); 'Fables and Tales' (1771); etc.; and translated into German hexameters Milton's 'Paradise Lost' (1760). ('Poetical Works,' 9 vols., 1763-65; posthumous writings, with biography, 1781.)

Zachariä von Lingenthal, Karl Eduard (tsä-ċhä-rē'ä fon ling'en-täl). A German writer on jurisprudence; born at Heidelberg, Dec. 21, 1812; died at Grosskmehlen, near Merseburg, June 3, 1894. He is regarded as the founder of the science of Græco-Roman jurisprudence. He wrote 'Outline of a History of Græco-Roman Jurisprudence' (1839), 'History of Græco-Roman Private Right' (1864); made a collection of 'Græco-Roman Laws' (1856-84); and edited Justinian's 'Novellæ' (1881).

Zachariä von Lingenthal, Karl Salomo. A German jurist; born at Meissen, Saxony, Sept. 14, 1769; died March 27, 1843. He was professor of law at Wittenberg, 1797-1807, and Heidelberg, 1807-43. He wrote: 'The Unity of State and Church' (1797); 'Forty Books on the State' (2d ed. 7 vols., 1839-43); 'Hand-Book of French Civil Law' (8th ed. 1894-95); etc.

Zachariasiewicz, Jan (tsä-ċha-ri-äs'yä-vich). A Polish novelist and miscellaneous writer; born in East Galicia, about 1825. At various times in his life he became involved in political difficulties, and passed several years in prison; and these experiences have colored all his books. His first publication was 'A Passage from the Life of Unknown People' (1853). In 'The Red Cap' and 'The Secret Fund,' he describes the spy system of the police force; and of like nature are 'Covered Cards' (1875), 'A Bad Business' (1876), etc. He has also written a few art novels.

Zacher, Ernst Julius August (tsä'ċher). A German antiquary; born at Obernigk, Feb. 15, 1816; died March 23, 1887, at Halle where he was professor of German philology. His principal works are: 'Ulfilas's Gothic Alphabet and the Runic Alphabet' (1855); 'German Proverbs' (1852); 'History of the Palgravine Genoveva' (1860); 'Pseudo-Callisthenes' (1867), dealing with the Alexander myth.

Zahir (zä'hēr). An Arabian poet, father of the poet Ka'b; contemporary with Mahomet. He was the author of one of the seven poems of the 'Mu'allakát,' published by Sir William Jones, with an English version, in 1782.

Zahn, Johann Karl Wilhelm (tsän). A German painter, architect, and writer on art; born at Rodenberg, Schaumburg, Aug. 21, 1800; died at Berlin, Aug. 22, 1871. He was professor in the Academy of Arts, Berlin, 1829. Among his works were: 'The Most Beautiful Ornaments and the Most Notable Pictures from Pompeii, Herculaneum, and Stabiæ' (1828-30); 'Ornaments of all Classical Periods of Art' (1832-39); etc.

Zahn, Theodor. A German theological writer; born at Mörs, Oct. 10, 1838. He was appointed professor of theology in the University of Erlangen 1878, and is author of 'Marcellus of Ancyra' (1867); 'The Shepherd of Hermas' (1868); 'Ignatius of Antioch' (1873); 'The Acts of St. John' (1880); 'Cyprian of Antioch and the German Story of Faust' (1882); 'Researches into the History of the New Testament Canon' (5 vols., 1881-93); 'The Gospel of Peter' (1893); 'Introduction to the New Testament' (1897).

Zaleski, Bohdan (zä-les'ski). A noted Polish poet; born at Bohaterka in the Ukraine, 1802; died near Paris, 1886. He passed his childhood in immediate intercourse with the Cossacks, but afterwards studied at Warsaw. After the revolution of 1830, he was obliged to leave Poland, and went to France. Many of his poems depict in vivid colors the scenery of his native country. His chief works are: 'The Spirit of the Steppes' (1842); 'The Most Holy Family'; and collections of shorter poems.

Zalewski, Casimir (zä-lev'ski). A Polish dramatist and journalist; born at Plock, 1848. He abandoned law for literature; founded the journal Wiek (1865). Among his successful dramas are: 'Dowerless' (1868), 'As the World Moves' (1873), 'Before the Wedding' (1876), 'Poor Seed' (1877); the tragedies 'Marco Foscarini' (1878), 'Article 264,' etc.

Zalokostas, Georgios (zäl-ō-kōs'tas). A distinguished Greek poet; born at Syrrhako, Epirus, April 17, 1805; died at Athens, Sept. 3, 1858. At the age of sixteen he fought in the insurrection at Missolonghi. The Greek children learn his songs. Among his best-known poems were: 'Missolonghi'; 'Armatoles and Klephts'; 'The Entrance of Prevesa'; 'Hours of Leisure'; 'Marco Bozzaris'; etc. Several of his pieces have been translated into Italian, Spanish, English, German, French, and Russian. ('Poetical Works,' Athens, 1860.)

Zaluski, Andrew Chrysostom (zä-lös'kē). A Polish statesman and pulpit orator; born about 1650; died 1711. He was bishop of Ermeland and grand chancellor of Poland. He wrote: 'Historico-Familiar Epistles,' an interesting and valuable work.

Zambelios, John (zäm-bē'li-os). A Greek poet; born on one of the Ionian isles, 1787; died at Corfu, 1856. He was a judge at Corfu. He wrote lyric poems, and several successful tragedies. ('Works,' Athens, 1856-57.)

Zambelli, Andrea (dzam-bel'le). An Italian historian; born in Lombardy, 1794; died at Paris, 1862. His chief works are books on 'War' and on 'Religion,' in which he attempts to show the profound difference between ancient and modern nations.

Zamora, Antonio de (thä-mō'rä). A Spanish dramatist; born at Madrid, between 1660 and 1664; died about 1722. He was highly esteemed by his contemporaries as a lyric and dramatic poet. Among his best works are: 'Everybody is his Own Pedigree'; and 'The Wag of Seville,' on which is based the libretto of the opera of 'Don Juan.'

Zanella, Giacomo (dzä-nel'lä). An Italian lyrical poet; born at Chiampo, 1820; died at Vicenza, 1888. After studying for the priesthood, he became professor of philosophy and Italian literature at the seminary in Vicenza. His work is noted for beauty of style and mastery of form; his most popular poem being 'The Fossil Shell.' His first volume of poems, 'Verses,' appeared in 1868, and was followed by several others. Among his poetic tales are: 'The Little Calabrese' (1870); 'Robin Redbreast' (1881); etc.

Zanetti, Bernardino (dzä-net'tē). An Italian historian; born near Treviso, 1690; died 1762. He wrote a 'History of the Lombards' (2 vols., 1753).

Zangemeister, Karl (tsäng'e-mis-ter). A German classical philologist; born at Hallungen, in the Duchy of Gotha, Nov. 28, 1837. He edited the fourth volume of the 'Corpus Inscriptionum Latinarum,' comprising the parietal inscriptions at Pompeii, Herculaneum, and Stabiæ (1871); compiled 'Specimens of Latin MSS. Written in Majuscule Letters' (1882), and 'Fragments of the Old Saxon Bible Poem of the Palatine Library' (1894).

Zangwill, Israel. An English-Jewish novelist; born in London, 1864. He began life as a London teacher, and while teaching, graduated at the London University. He has published: 'The Premier and the Painter' (1888, in collaboration), a romance; 'The Bachelors' Club' (1891); 'The Big Bow Mystery' (1891); 'The Old Maids' Club' (1892); 'Children of the Ghetto' (1892), a collection of stories, his best work; 'Merely Mary Ann' (1893); 'Ghetto Tragedies' (1893); 'The King of Schnorrers' (1894); 'The Master' (1895), a novel; 'Six Persons,' a comedietta; 'Without Prejudice' (1896), published originally, under the same

38

title as 'Causerie' in the Pall Mall Magazine; and the drama 'The Melting Pot' (1909).

Zannowich, Stefano (zän'no-vich). An Albanian writer; born 1751; died 1785. He had a wandering and very adventurous life, but wrote several curious books, among them: 'Turkish Letters' (1877); 'Epistles and Love Songs of an Oriental' (1779); and 'Fragment of a Chapter of 'The Lame Devil,' Sent from the Other World by Le Sage' (1782).

Zanotti, Jean Pierre (zä-not'tē). A painter and poet; born of a Polish family at Paris, 1674; died at Bologna, 1767. He left a number of noted pictures; and published 'Dido,' a tragedy (1718); 'Poems' (1741); and various works on the art of painting.

Zapf, Georg Wilhelm (tsäpf). A German antiquary; born at Nördlingen, 1747; died 1810. A prolific writer, among his works were: 'Bibliography of Ancient and Modern History' (1781); 'The Lives of Celebrated Savants and Artists of All Time' (1806); etc.

Zappi, Giovanni Battista (dzäp'pē). An Italian miscellaneous writer; born at Imola, 1540; died at the end of the century. He published a remarkable book, prose mixed with verse, entitled 'Field of Spiritual Philosophy, in which is Contained the Sum of Christian Living' (1577), treating of the life and character of Christ, the virtues and vices, etc.

Zappi, Giovanni Battista Felice. An Italian lyrical poet; born at Imola, about 1667; died at Rome, 1719. He studied law in Rome, but soon became noted for his poetry, which was distinguished by elegance and grace of style. A collection of his poems was first published in 1770, and consists of sonnets, songs, cantatas, and other verse.

Zarate, Agustin de (thä-rä'tä). A Spanish historian; born about 1492; died at Madrid (?) about 1560. He was comptroller of Castile; accompanied Nuñez Vela, viceroy of Peru, to South America in 1543; was afterward treasurer of the Spanish Netherlands. He wrote: 'History of the Discovery and Conquest of the Province of Peru' (1555). There have been many later editions; and it has been translated into French and Italian.

Zarate, Antonio Gil y. A Spanish dramatic poet; born at San Lorenzo de l'Escurial, Spain, 1795; died 1860. His father, an excellent actor, sent him to study in Paris; and on his return to Spain he became professor of physics in Granada. He afterwards wrote dramas noted for striking situations, lively dialogue, and elegant versification. Among them are: 'Blanche of Bourbon' (1835); 'Guzman the Brave'; 'The Czar Demetrius'; etc. He also published a much-esteemed history of Spanish literature.

Zarncke, Friedrich (tsärn'ke). A German antiquary; born near Brüel in Mecklenburg-Schwerin, July 7, 1825; died Oct. 15, 1891; having been since 1852 professor in the University

of Leipsic. Among his works are: 'The German Cato' (1852); 'The Nibelungen Question' (1854); 'Contributions to the Explanation of the Nibelungenlied' (1857); 'The Trojan Legend of the Franks'; 'German Universities in the Middle Ages' (1857); 'Mediæval Proverbial Poetry' (1863.)

Zbylitowski, André (zbē-lē-tov'skē). A Polish writer, philosopher, and poet; born in Galicia, 1732; died 1813. He was doctor of literature and philosophy in Cracow, and afterwards traveled extensively in Europe and South America. He wrote poetry with much success; some of his idyls being noted for beauty of coloring, elegance, and grace. Among his works are: 'Rhythms in Polish Verse' (1763); 'The Marshal' (historical); 'A Beard,' a novel; and various books on philosophical, political, and grammatical themes.

Zbylitowski, Pierre. A Polish poet and miscellaneous writer; born in the palatinate of Lublin, 1684; died in Warsaw, 1757. He studied at the University of Warsaw, and later traveled extensively in Europe and North America, being a keen observer and profound critic. As a poet he was a disciple of the French school, using sarcasm and irony with brilliant effect. Among his writings are a 'Collection of Satires' (1723); 'Porydia: A Poem' (1734); 'Epigrams' (1735); 'Studies on Voltaire's Works' (1737); 'Lucie: An Erotic Poem' (1739); etc.

Zedlitz, Baron Joseph Christian von (tsed'-lits). An Austrian lyrical poet and dramatic writer; born at Johannisburg in Austrian Silesia, 1790; died in Vienna, 1862. He was educated at Breslau, and afterwards took part in the campaign of 1809. Among his best dramatic writings are: the tragedies 'Two Nights in Valladolid' (1825), 'The Star of Seville' (1830); and the drama 'Prison and Crown' (1834), treating of the last days of Tasso's life. Of poems, he has published a collection, 'Wreaths for the Dead'; a celebrated ballad, 'The Nightly Review'; and poetical tales.

Zeise, Heinrich (tsī'zė). A German poet and translator; born at Altona, 1822. He began life as an apothecary, but graduated at the university. He translated a number of scientific and poetical works from the Danish into German, and also published original efforts, noted for poetical coloring and beauty of form, among them a collection of 'Poems' (1847); 'Battle Songs of Schleswig-Holstein' (1848); 'Songs of Battle and Sword'; etc. also, in prose, 'From the Life and Recollections of a North German Poet' (1888).

Zeising, Adolf (tsī'zing). A German writer on art; born at Ballenstedt, Sept. 24, 1810; died at Munich, April 27, 1876. He wrote: 'New Doctrine of the Proportions of the Human Body' (1854); 'Æsthetic Researches' (1855); 'The Metamorphoses in the Ratios of the Human Figure' (1859); 'Religion and Science, State and Church' (1873); and several novels.

Zeissberg, Heinrich, Baron von (zīs'bärG). An Austrian writer of history; born at Vienna, July 8, 1839. He was appointed professor of history in the University of Vienna, 1873. His principal writings are : ‹ Arno, First Archbishop of Salzburg › (1863); ‹ Polish Historiography in the Middle Ages › (1873); ‹ Minor Sources of Polish History in the Middle Ages › (1877); ‹ Belgium under the General Statthaltership of the Archduke Karl › (1893). Died May 27, 1899.

Zeleguy, Zdenko (tsel'eg-wē). A Moravian poet, writing under the pseudonym of « Franz Vonelsen »; born in Usetin, Jan. 22, 1853. His best-known works are ı ‹ World-Pain Voices › (1887); ‹ Nirvana › (1893); and ‹ Words of Love › (1894).

Zeller, Berthold. Son of Jules S.; born at Rennes, 1848. He is author of ‹ Henri IV. and Marie de' Medici › (1877); ‹ Critical Studies on the Reign of Louis XIII.› (2 vols., 1879–80); ‹ Marie de' Medici and Villeroy › (1897).

Zeller, Christian Heinrich (tsel'er). A German educator; born near Tübingen, March 29, 1779; died at Beuggen, May 18, 1860. His writings are : ‹ Teachings of Experience for Christian Teachers of Rural and Poor Schools › (3 vols., 1827); ‹ Soul-Doctrine, Founded on Scripture and Experience › (1846).

Zeller, Eduard. A noted German theologian, philosopher, and historian; born at Kleinbottmar in Würtemberg, 1814. He studied at Tübingen and Berlin; and despite the very free tendencies of his thought, strongly influenced by that of Strauss, he was professor of theology at Bern, and later professor of philosophy at Heidelberg and at Berlin. Among his chief works are : ‹ Platonic Studies › (1839); ‹ The Philosophy of the Greeks › (1844–52); ‹ The Story of the Apostles, Critically Investigated › (1854); ‹ David Friedrich Strauss Depicted in his Life and Writings › (1874); ‹ Frederick the Great as a Philosopher › (1886); etc.

Zeller, Jules Sylvain (zel-lär'). A French historian; born at Paris, April 23, 1820; died there July 25, 1900. He became professor of history in the Polytechnic School in 1863, and inspector of higher education in 1876. Among his works are : ‹The Roman Emperors : Characters and Portraits› (1863); ‹History of Germany› (1872–91); ‹The Tribunes and the Revolutions in Italy› (1873); ‹Pius IX. and Victor Emmanuel : Contemporary History of Italy› (1879); ‹Short History of Italy, from the Fall of the Roman Empire to our Time› (4th ed. 1886).

Zeno, Apostolo (dzä'nō). An Italian dramatist and historian; born at Venice, 1668; died in the same city, 1750. He has been called the father of Italian opera, and acquired great fame by his dramatic works, published in 1744, in many volumes. Among his other works are : ‹ Historical Dissertations › (1752–53); and ‹ Epistles › (1785).

Zeno of Elea. A Greek philosopher; born about the fifth century B. C.; the date of his death unknown. He spent his later years in Athens. Aristotle calls him the father of dialectics; and Pericles was among his pupils. Of his writings in prose and in dialogue, only fragments have been preserved, but many of them are known to have been on the philosophy of motion.

Zeno the Stoic (zē'nō). A Greek philosopher; born at Citium, a Greek colony on the island of Cyprus, about 350 B. C.; died, as is reported, by his own hand, about 264 B. C. He was the son of a merchant, and followed his father's profession, not visiting Athens till his thirtieth year. He then read Xenophon and Plato, and later founded a school of his own. None of his writings have been preserved, but he is known to have combined the ethics of the Cynic school with the physics of Pythagoras and Heraclitus.

Zerbi, Rocco de (dzăr'bē). An Italian politician, journalist, and miscellaneous writer; born at Reggio, Calabria, 1843. He served in the army, 1860–66; founded the influential Giornaletto of Naples, 1868; became member of the chamber of deputies, 1872. He has written : ‹ Aspirations › (1865), in verse; ‹ Poetry and Prose › (1868), ‹ Without Title › (1870), both romances; ‹ Political Writings › (1876); ‹ Vistilia › (1877), a romance; ‹ Modern Art › (1878); ‹ Church and State › (1878); ‹ Faust › (1878), a notable critical work; etc.

Zernitz, Christian Friedrich (tsär'nēts). A German didactic poet; born at· Tangermünde, 1717; died 1744. All his works were posthumous. His ‹ Didactic Essays › are highly esteemed.

Zesen, Philipp von (tsä'zen). A German poet, and critical and satirical writer; born at Priorau near Dessau, 1619; died at Hamburg, 1689. He devoted himself to the study of philology and poetry; giving special attention to perfecting and purifying his mother tongue. Among his numerous writings in prose and verse are the novels ‹ Adriatic Rosemund › (1645) and ‹ Samson ›; and the poem ‹ Priorau ; or, The Praise of the Fatherland,› as well as some excellent short verse.

Zeuss, Johann Kaspar (tsois). A German philologist and writer of history; born at Vogtendorf in Upper Franconia, July 22, 1806; died there, Nov. 10, 1856. Among his works are : ‹ The Germans and the Neighbor Stocks › (1837); ‹ The Descent of the Bavarians from the Marcomanni › (1839); ‹ Witzenburg Traditions and Possessions › (1842); ‹ The Free Imperial City of Spires from its Destruction › (1843); ‹ Celtic Grammar › (two vols., 1853), his greatest work.

Zevecot, Jacob (zā've-kot'). A Dutch poet and dramatist, considered by his contemporaries the greatest Latin poet of his time; born at Gand, 1604; died 1646. Among his works are : ‹ Elegies ›; ‹ Greek Maria › and ‹ Rosimunda,› tragedies; ‹ Esther,› a tragi-comedy; ‹ The Siege of Leyden> (1626), a tragedy written in Flemish; and various collections of shorter poems.

Zeyer, Julius (zā'yer). A Czech novelist and poet; born at Prague, 1842. After traveling extensively on the Continent, he spent several years teaching in Russia. He has written in prose 'Andrew Cernysev,' a notable romance; 'Miss Olympia'; 'Count Xavier'; 'Madrana's Adventure'; 'Tales of Sosana'; 'The True Friendship of Amis and Amil'; etc.: and in verse, 'Vysehrad,' a series of epic poems, based on Bohemian ancient history.

Zezschwitz, Gerhard von (tsäch'vits). A German theological writer; born at Bautzen, July 2, 1825; died July 20, 1886, at Erlangen, where he was a professor in the university. Among his numerous writings are: 'The Catechisms of the Waldensians and the Bohemian Brethren' (1863); 'The Mediæval Drama, from the End of the Roman Empire' (1878); 'System of Practical Theology' (3 vols., 1876–78); 'Manual of the Theological Sciences' (1883); 'Catechetics' (1883).

Zhukovski, or **Joukovski,** sometimes written **Shukows** (zhö-kof'skē), **Vasilii Andréevich.** A famous Russian poet; born near Bielev in the government of Penza, 1783; died 1852. He succeeded Karamzin as editor of the Viestnik Evropui, 1808; was preceptor of the Emperor Alexande II. in his youth, as well as of Alexand°r's mother. A monument was erected to his memory, 1852. He wrote: 'The Minstrel in the Russian Camp,' a collection of spirited war ballads; 'Ziudmiɪa'; 'Svietlana,' his best work; etc.; and a number of prose essays and tales, the best-known of which was 'Mary's Grove.' He made also numerous translations from the German, English, etc.; his translation of Gray's 'Elegy' being one of the finest ever made.

Ziegler, Carl (tsēG'lär). An Austrian poet; born at St. Martin in Upper Austria, 1812; died at Vienna, 1877. He studied philosophy at the Vienna University, but takes high rank among modern Austrian lyrical poets, both as to substance and form. His language is simple, but the treatment of his subjects original, and full of thought and depth of emotion. He published: 'Poems' (1843); 'Heaven and Earth,' poems (1856); 'Odes' (1866); and a collection of hymns, rhapsodies, etc., many of them full of beauty and power.

Ziegler, Friedrich Wilhelm. A German actor and dramatist; born at Brunswick, 1760; died at Vienna, 1827. He played at the Vienna Court Theatre with steady success for nearly forty years. Several of his dramas hold the stage to-day: as 'Party Rage,' and 'The Four Temperaments.' He wrote: 'Dramatic Works' (5 vols., 1791–94); 'The Dramatic Art' (1821); 'Man with Relation to the Fine Arts, Particularly the Art Dramatic' (1825); etc.

Ziegler, Theobald. A German philosophical writer; born at Göppingen in Würtemberg, Feb. 9, 1846. He became professor of philosophy in the University of Strasburg, 1886. He is author of: 'With Regard to Strauss's Book, 'The Old Faith and the New'' (1874); 'Text-Book of Logic' (1876); 'Republic or Monarchy: Switzerland or Germany' (1877); 'History of Ethics' (1881); 'The Social Question a Moral Question' (1891); 'The German Student at the End of the Nineteenth Century' (6th ed. 1896).

Ziegler und Kliphausen, Heinrich Anselm von (tsēG'lär önt klip'hou-zen). A German romance-writer; born at Radmeritz, Jan. 6, 1653; died near Leipsic, Sept. 8, 1697. His principal work 'The Asiatic Banise' (new ed. 1766), in the heroic-gallant style, has exerted great influence on the formation of the taste of several generations of Germans.

Ziel, Ernst (tsēl). A German poet and miscellaneous writer; born at Rostock, May 5, 1841. He is author of 'Literary Rilievos: Poet Portraits' (4th series, 1885–95).

Zielinski, Felix (zē-lin'ski). A Polish lawyer and miscellaneous writer; born in Volhynia, 1732; died at Warsaw, 1805. He was marshal of the nobility for his district. He wrote: 'The Old and the New Style' (1763); 'Criticism of Karamsin' 1764); 'A Critical Glance at Present Society' (1772); 'Happy-go-Lucky Louise' (1771), humorous; 'A Rustic's Mind' (1775); 'Critical History of Polish Literature' (1776); 'Critical Glance at the Works of Voltaire' (1782); etc.

Zimmermann, Johann Georg (tsim'mermän). A German miscellaneous writer; born in the Swiss canton of Bern, 1728; died 1795. He studied and practiced medicine, but devoted himself to literature as well; publishing a book 'On Solitude' (1784–85), and 'On National Pride' (1789). His style is rich and vigorous; and his books, full of deep sentiment as well as eloquence, have been translated into many other languages.

Zimmermann, Karl. A German theological writer; born at Darmstadt, Aug. 23, 1803; died there June 12, 1877. He wrote: 'Life of Luther' (2d ed. 1855); 'Contributions to Comparative Homiletics' (1866); 'The Evangelical Diaspora' (1868); 'The Gustavus Adolphus Society: Its History, its Constitution, and its Works' (1878).

Zimmermann, Wilhelm. A German poet and historian; born at Stuttgart, 1807; died at Mergentheim, 1878. He studied theology at Tübingen, and occupied various positions, both as a professor and as a clergyman, but devoted himself largely to general literature. He published: 'Poems' (1832); a tragedy, 'Masaniello' (1832); 'History of Würtemberg' (1835); 'German Wars of Liberation against Napoleon' (1836); 'History of the Great Peasant War' (1840–44), considered Zimmermann's best work; 'History of the Poetry of All Nations' (1856); 'Germany's Heroic Struggle' (1870–71)); 'Illustrated History of the German Nation' (1873–77).

Zimmern, Helen (tsim'märn). A German-English story-writer; born at Hamburg, March 25, 1846. From childhood she lived in England. She is author of 'Stories in Precious Stones' (1873); 'Told by the Way' (1874); 'Half-Hours with French Novelists' (1881); 'Stories from Foreign Novelists' (2d ed. 1885). She wrote also 'Schopenhauer, his Life and Philosophy' (1876); 'G. E. Lessing, his Life and Works' (1878); 'The Hansa Towns' (1889).

Zimorowicz, Simon (zē-mō'rō-vich). A Polish poet; born at Lemberg, 1604; died 1629. His work shows much originality, as well as variety. Among his writings are: 'Russian Ladies' (1654); a 'Collection of Idyls' (1654); 'Fortune' (1655); 'The Polish Venus' (1665); 'Grief' (1777); etc.

Zincke, Foster Barham. An English religious and miscellaneous writer. He became vicar of Wherstead, near Ipswich, and chaplain-in-ordinary to the Queen. He wrote: 'Last Winter in the United States' (1868); 'The Egypt of the Pharaohs and of the Khedive' (new ed. 1873); 'A Month in Switzerland' (1873); 'The Swiss Germans' (1874); 'A Walk in the Grisons' (1875); 'The Plow and the Dollar.' Died Aug. 23, 1893.

Zingerle, Ignaz Vincenz (tsing'ärl-ė). An Austrian poet and story-writer, nephew of Pius; born at Meran, June 6, 1825; died at Innsbruck, Sept. 17, 1892. He was made professor of the German language and literature in the University of Innsbruck, 1859. Among his poetical works are: 'Primroses' (1848); 'From the Alps'; 'The Miller's Wife' (1853). He wrote also 'Tyrolese Legends' (1850); 'The Tyrol's Place in German Mediæval Literature' (1851); 'Children's Stories from the Tyrol' (1852); 'Alliteration in the Middle-High-German Poets' (1864); 'Oswald von Walkenstein' (1870).

Zingerle, Pius. An Austrian theological writer and Orientalist; born at Meran, March 17, 1801; died Jan. 10, 1881. He became professor of the Arabic and Syriac languages in the Roman University, 1862. Among works, whether written or edited by him, are: 'Select Work of Ephrem Syrus, Translated from the Greek and Syriac' (6 vols., 1830-37); 'Genuine Acts of the Eastern Martyrs,' from the Syriac (1836); 'Roses of Mary from Damascus' (2d. ed. 1865); 'Life and Deeds of St. Simeon Stylites' (1855); 'Syriac Chrestomathy' (1871); 'Syriac Lexicon,' for use with his 'Chrestomathy' (1873); 'Oriental Elements in German Poetry' (1862).

Zinkeisen, Johann Wilhelm (tsink'ī-zen). A German historian; born at Altenburg, April 11, 1803; died at Berlin, Jan. 5, 1863. He edited at Berlin the Official Gazette (Staats-Zeitung: 1840-51). He wrote: 'History of the Ottoman Empire in Europe' (7 vols., 1840-63); 'History of Greece' (1832-40); etc.

Zinkgref or **Zincgref, Julius Wilhelm** (tsink'gref). A German lyric poet; born at Heidelberg, June 3, 1591; died at St. Goar, Nov. 12, 1635. His principal work was 'German Apothegms' (later ed. 1644), a collection of epigrams, anecdotes, etc.; 'The Soldier's Praise' (1632), his best poem, an imitation of Tyrtæus.

Zintgraff, Eugen (tsint'gräf). A German African traveler; born at Düsseldorf, Jan. 16, 1858. He spent some years in the Congo region and in the Cameroons country, and wrote 'North Cameroons: An Account of Travels in 1886-92' (1895).

Zitelmann, Konrad (tsē'tel-män). A German poet and novelist; born at Stettin, 1854. He studied law at Leipsic, but was obliged to settle in Southern Europe on account of ill health. He has published the collections of poems 'In Solitude' (1876), 'Autumn Days in Meran' (1876), and 'From Foreign Lands' (1889); the novels 'At Dawn' (1880), 'Gods and Idols' (1884), 'The Game is Over,' 'Obscure Lives' (1886), and 'Chords and Discords,' a collection of short stories (1888). Died 1897.

Zittel, Emil (tsit'tel). A German theological writer; born at Lorrach in Baden, Aug. 14, 1831. He wrote: 'All around the Jungfrau: A Tourist's Notes' (1874); 'Dr. Martin Luther, 1483-1517' (1883); 'The Origin of the Bible' (1891); 'Bible Knowledge' (11th ed. 1893); 'How Jesus of Nazareth Became the Messiah or Christ' (1893); 'The Writings of the New Testament Translated and Explained for the German People' (1894). Died Jan. 23, 1899.

Zittel, Karl Alfred. A German geologist and palæontologist; born at Bahlingen, Sept. 25, 1839. He became professor in the University of Munich, 1866. He is author of 'Travels in Sweden and Norway' (1860); 'From Primordial Times' (2d ed. 1875); 'Letters from the Libyan Desert' (1875); 'The Sahara' (1885).

Ziver Pasha (zē-vär'-pä-shä'). A Turkish official and poet; born 1793; died 1862. He was director of the Ministry of Marine, member of the Council of Public Instruction, member of the Council of State and Justice, etc.; and became, a year before his death, a functionary of the first rank. He held the title of imperial poet; his poetry is highly esteemed by the Turks. A collection of it was published at Constantinople, under the title of the 'Divan.'

Zmaj. See Jovanovic.

Zöckler, Otto (tsėk'ler). A German theological writer; born at Grünberg in Upper Hesse, May 27, 1833. He was appointed professor of theology in the University of Greifswald, 1866. Among his numerous works are: 'Natural Theology' (1860); 'Critical History of Asceticism' (1863), afterward rewritten and entitled 'Asceticism and Monasticism' (1897); 'The Augsburg Confession as the Fundamental Symbol of the German Church of the Reformation' (1870); 'God's Witnesses in the Kingdom of Nature' (1881); 'The Apocrypha of the Old Testament' (1891).

Zogbaum, Rufus Fairchild. An American artist; born in Charleston, S. C., Aug. 28, 1849. He was educated in New York, studied abroad; has been successful as a painter of military scenes; and has written 'Horse, Foot, and Dragoons; or, Sketches of Army Life.'

Zogoskin (zo-gos'kin), or **Zagoskin**, or **Sagoskin, Mikhail** (zä-gos'kin). A Russian novelist and dramatist; born in the government of Penza, 1789; died at Moscow, 1852. His chief work is 'The Russians in 1812' (1829). His historical novels have earned for him the name of the Russian Walter Scott.

Zola, Émile (zō'lä). A celebrated French novelist; born in Paris, April 2, 1840. He wrote: 'Tales to Ninon' (1864); 'Claude's Confession' (1865); 'A Dead Woman's Vow' (1866); 'My Hatreds' (1866); 'My Salon' (1866); 'The Mysteries of Marseilles' (1867); 'Edouard Manet' (1867); 'Thérèse Raquin' (1867); 'Madeleine Férat' (1868); 'The Fortune of the Rougons' (1871); 'La Curée' (1872); 'The Maw [Ventre] of Paris' (1873); 'The Conquest of Plassans' (1874); 'New Tales to Ninon' (1874); 'The Sin of Abbé Mouret' (1875); 'His Excellency Eugène Rougon' (1876); 'L'Assommoir' (1877); 'A Page of Love' (1878); 'The French Republic and Literature' (1879); 'Nana' (1880); 'The Experimental Novel' (1880); 'Literary Documents, Studies and Portraits' (1881); 'Naturalism on the Stage' (1881); 'Our Dramatic Authors' (1881); 'The Realistic Novelists' (1881); 'A Campaign' (1881); 'Pot Bouille' (1882); 'Good Luck to the Ladies' (1883); 'The Joy of Living' (1884); 'Germinal' (1885); 'Work' ('L'Œuvre': 1886); 'Earth' ('La Terre': 1887); 'The Dream' ('Le Rêve': 1888); 'The Human Brute' ('La Bête Humaine': 1890); 'Money' (1891); 'The Downfall' ('La Débâcle': 1892); 'Doctor Pascal' (1893); 'Lourdes' (1894); 'Rome' (1895). Died in Paris, Sept. 29, 1902.

Zoller, Edmund von (tsōl'ler). A German miscellaneous writer; born at Stuttgart, May 20, 1822. He is author of: 'The Science of Library Management' (1846); 'Leopold Robert,' a biography (1863); 'German and Austrian Orders and Decorations' (2d ed. 1881); 'The Order of Tunis' (1877); 'The Order of the Golden Fleece' (1879); 'The Order of Charles III.' (1888); and has translated several poems from French, English, Spanish, Portuguese, Dutch, and other languages. He died 1902.

Zöller, Hugo (tsèl-ler). A German journalist and traveler; born at Oberhausen, Prussia, Jan. 12, 1852. He was for a number of years traveling correspondent of the Cologne Gazette, and explored and annexed to Germany various tracts of country in West Africa (1884-85). He has written: 'Round the World' (1881); 'The Panama Canal' (1882); 'The Germans in the Brazilian Primeval Forest' (1883); 'Pampas and Andes' (1884); 'The German Possessions on the West African Coast' (1885); 'German New Guinea' (1891). [

Zolling, Théophile (tsō'ling). A miscellaneous writer; born near Naples, Dec. 30, 1849; died in Berlin, March 23, 1901. He was educated in German Switzerland, studied history and philosophy in Vienna, and later lived in Paris and Berlin. He is known as a lyrical poet, but also wrote a satirical epic 'The Virgin of the Chair' (1876); a drama in collaboration with Alphonse Daudet 'New Love' (1877); the novels 'Gossip' (1889) and 'Madame Love' (1889); etc.

Zöllner, Johann Karl Friedrich (tsèl'ner). A German astronomer and physicist; born at Berlin, Nov. 8, 1834; died April 25, 1882, at Leipsic, where he was professor of physical astronomy in the university. He wrote: 'Outlines of a General Photometry of the Heavens' (1861); 'Photometric Researches with special relation to the Physical Constitution of the Heavenly Bodies' (1865); 'The Nature of the Comets' (1871); 'Principles of an Electrodynamic Theory of Matter' (1876). In his latter years he turned to the study of spiritism and hypnotism; after his death appeared his work 'Are There Unconscious and Hereditarily Transmitted Ideas?' (1879).

Zollogub or **Sollogub** (zol'lō-gŏb), written also **Zollohub** (zol'lō-hŏb), **Vladimir Alexandrovich.** A popular Russian miscellaneous writer; born at St. Petersburg, about 1815; died June 16, 1882. Besides poems, essays, and dramas, he wrote a novel, 'Tarantas,' translated into English and German.

Zonaras, Joannes (zon'ạ-ras). A Byzantine theologian and historian; born at Constantinople, in the twelfth century of the Christian era. He was the author of 'Annals,' from the creation down to his own times, containing valuable extracts from Josephus, and from parts of Dion Cassius that are now lost.

Zöpfl, Heinrich Matthias (tsèpfl). A German jurist; born at Bamberg, April 6, 1807; died at Heidelberg, July 4, 1877. He was professor of public law at Heidelberg, 1839. He wrote: 'On High Nobility and Equality of Birth' (1853); 'Antiquities of the German Realm and Law' (3 vols., 1860-61); 'Principles of the Common German Public Law' (2 vols., 1860); 'History of German Law' (3 vols., 1871-72); 'Outline for Lectures on the Philosophy of Law' (1878), published posthumously; etc.

Zoppio, Melchiore (dzop'yō). An Italian dramatist and miscellaneous writer; born at Bologna, about 1544; died 1634. By profession a physician, he devoted his leisure to philosophy and literature, publishing two comedies, 'Diogenes Accused' (1598), and 'Julian'; and four tragedies, 'Admetus,' 'Medea,' 'Creusa,' and 'Meander' (1629); as well as various philosophical writings.

Zöppritz, Karl (tsèp'prits). A German geographer; born at Darmstadt, April 14, 1838; died March 21, 1885. He is author of 'Pruyssenaere's Travels in the Region of the Upper Nile' (1877); 'Hydro-dynamic Problems of the

Theory of the Tides' (1878); 'Guide to Cartography' (1884).

Zorn, Philipp (tsorn). A German legist; born at Bayreuth, Jan. 13, 1850. He became professor in the University of Königsberg, 1877. Among his writings are: 'State and Church in Switzerland,' written in collaboration with Karl Gareis (2 vols., 1877-78); 'State and Church in Norway to the Close of the Thirteenth Century' (1875) ; 'Public Law of the German Empire' (2 vols., 1880-83); 'Text-Book of Ecclesiastical Law' (1888); 'The Modern German Empire.'

Zoroaster (zō'rō-as''ter). Lived 600 years B. C. He is the founder of the Parsee religion and the author of the Avesta.

Zorrilla y Moral, José (thō-rēl'yä ē mō-räl'). A Spanish poet ; born at Valladolid, Feb. 21, 1818; died at Madrid, Jan. 23, 1893. At his father's wish he studied law, but early showed his talent and ambition as a poet. His first collection of verse appeared in 1837 ; and another, 'Songs of the Troubadour : A Collection of Legends and Traditions,' 1840-41. Then followed a drama, 'Don Juan Tenorio' (1844), reminiscences of 'Faust'; 'Legend of the Cid' (1880); and collections of shorter verse.

Zosimus (zōs'i-mus). A Greek historian, who probably lived during the reign of the Emperor Anastasius, at the end of the fifth century of the Christian era. He wrote a 'Roman History,' composed of six books, in which he attributes the fall of the empire to the Christians alone.

Zouch, Thomas. An English writer of prose and verse; born in York, 1737; died 1815. Among his writings are: 'The Crucifixion,' a poem (1765); and 'Memoirs of the Life and Writings of Sir Philip Sidney' (1808).

Zouche, Richard (zōch). An English writer on jurisprudence; born at Anstey in Wiltshire, about 1590; died at London, March 1, 1661. Among his celebrated treatises, written in Latin, are: 'Elements of Jurisprudence' (1629); 'Description of Feudal Law and Procedure according to the Usages of Milan and Normandy, to serve as Introduction to English Jurisprudence' (1634); 'Description of Ecclesiastical Law and Procedure according to the Canons and Constitutions of England' (1636); 'Explication of Fecial Law and Procedure, or of the Law of Nations' (1650); 'The Competent Judge of an Offending Ambassador' (1657).

Zoukovski. See Zhukovski.

Zrinyi, Niklas, Count (zrēn'yē). A Hungarian soldier and poet; born 1616; died 1664. He wrote idyls and songs; an epic poem, the 'Zrinyade' (1651); and essays in prose.

Zschokke, Johann Heinrich Daniel (tshok'-kĕ). A noted German novelist and miscellaneous writer; born at Magdeburg, 1771; died 1848. He settled in Switzerland, active in politics. He produced a successful drama, 'Abällino the Bandit' (1793), followed by another, 'Julius von Sassen' (1796). He has written a 'History of Bavaria' (1813-18); and a 'History of Switzerland for the Swiss People' (1822); but his fame rests upon a semi-religious work, 'Hours of Devotion,' and his novels, some of the most popular of which are: 'Alamontade the Galley-Slave'; 'The Fool of the Nineteenth Century'; 'Master Jacob'; 'The Goldmaker's Village'; etc.

Zumpt, August (tsömpt). A German classical philologist, nephew of Karl; born at Königsberg, Dec. 4, 1815; died at Berlin, April 22, 1877. His studies had to do mainly with Roman epigraphy in its relation to history. His principal works are: 'The Ancyran Monument' (1845); 'Epigraphical Notes' (2 vols., 1850-54); 'Roman Studies' (1859); 'Criminal Law under the Roman Republic' (4 vols., 1865-69); 'The Birth-Year of Christ' (1869); 'Criminal Trials under the Roman Republic.'

Zumpt, Karl. A German classical philologist; born at Berlin, March 20, 1792; died at Karlsbad, June 25, 1849. He was appointed professor of Roman literature in the University of Berlin, 1836. His greatest work, the 'Latin Grammar' (1818; 13th ed. 1874), was translated into English, and is the basis of several of the Latin grammars since compiled for the use of schools. He also prepared annotated editions of several of the Latin classics; and wrote: 'Annals of Ancient Kingdoms, Nations, etc.' (1819), in Latin; 'The Roman Knights and the Equestrian Order' (1840); 'On the Duration of the Philosophic Schools at Athens, and the Succession of the Scholarchs' (1843); 'On the Law and the Proofs of Extortion' (Repetundarum; 1845); 'The Personal Liberty of the Roman Citizen, and its Legal Guarantees' (1846).

Zunz, Leopold (tsönts). A German writer on Jewish religion and history; born at Detmold, Aug. 10, 1794; died March 17, 1886, at Berlin, where he was head master of the Jewish normal school for teachers. He is the founder of the "Science of Judaism," the plan of which was laid down in his 'A Little about Rabbinic Literature' (1818). Very important was his work 'Jewish Teachings Regarding Worship' (1892). Among his other works are: 'The Synagogue Poetry of the Middle Ages'; 'The Names of the Jews' (1836); 'Jewish Requirements as to Oaths' (1859).

Zupitza, Julius (tsö'pit-sä). A German student of English speech; born at Oberglogau in Upper Silesia, Jan. 4, 1844; died July 6, 1895, at Berlin, where he was professor of English language and literature in the university. Among his works are: 'Introduction to the Study of Middle High German' (1868); 'Exercise Book of Old and Middle English' (1874); 'Alfric's Grammar and Glossary' (1850); 'Specimens of All the Accessible Unprinted MSS. of the Canterbury Tales' (1890).

Zurita, Geronimo (thö-rē'tä). A Spanish historian ; born at Saragossa, 1512; died 1580.

His 'Annals of the Crown of Aragon' (6 vols., 1562–79) are of great value.

Zwecker, J. An English writer of adventures. He is the author of 'Lost among the Afghans,' illustrated (new ed. 1864).

Zweers, Philip (zwärs). A Dutch poet; died 1774. He was a notary at Amsterdam. He wrote: 'Semiramis' (1729), a tragedy; other dramas; and poems. ('Poetical Works,' Amsterdam, 1759.)

Zwinger, Theodore, the Elder (tsving'er) (Lat., **Zwingerus**, zwin-jē'rus). A famous Swiss physician and scholar; born at Basle, 1533; died there, 1588. He was professor of Greek at Basle (1565). He wrote 'Theatre of Human Life' (1565), a collection of anecdotes, etc.

Zwingli, Ulrich (tsving'lē). A Swiss church reformer; born at Wildhaus in the canton of St. Gall, Jan. 1, 1484; fell in battle near Kappel, Oct. 11, 1531. Next after Calvin he was the foremost leader of the Reformation in Switzerland. His principal works, written in Latin, are: 'Of True and False Religion' (1525); 'The Grounds of Faith' (1530); 'A Short and Clear Exposition of Christian Faith' (1538). He wrote in German: 'Baptism, Anabaptism, and Pædobaptism' (1525); 'A Clear Explanation of Christ's Last Supper' (1526).

ADDENDA.

Adler, Hermann. Chief Rabbi of the United Hebrew Congregations of the British Empire; born in Hanover, May 30, 1839. Author of 'Jewish Reply to Colenso,' 'A Volume of Sermons on the Old Testament,' 'Sabbath Readings,' 'Solomon ibn Gebirol, the Poet Philosopher,' and other works.

Argyll, John Douglas Sutherland Campbell. Ninth Duke of; born in London, Aug. 6, 1845; married H. R. H. Princess Louise in 1871. He was Governor-General of Canada 1878–83, and M. P. from South Manchester 1895–1900. Author of 'The United States after the War' (1885); 'Memoirs of Canada and Scotland (1884); 'Canadian Pictures' (1885); 'Life of Palmerston,' 'Life and Times of Queen Victoria' (1901). 'A Gift Book for the Home.'

Aston, William George. An English author and linguist; born near Londonderry, Ire., in 1841. He was appointed student interpreter in Japan, 1864; interpreter and translator to legation at Yedo, 1870, and was successively assistant Japanese secretary at Yedo, acting consul at Hiogo, consul-general for Korea and Japanese secretary to Tokio. Retired on pension in 1889. Among his works are: 'A Grammar of the Japanese Spoken Language,' 'A Grammar of the Japanese Written Language,' 'History of Japanese Literature,' besides various papers for learned societies.

Atherton, Mrs. Gertrude Franklin. An American author; born in San Francisco, Cal., in 18—. Among her published works are: 'The Doomswoman'(1892); 'A Whirl Asunder'(1895); 'His Fortunate Grace' (1897); 'American Wives and English Husbands' (1898); 'The Californians' (1898); 'The Valiant Runaways' (1899); 'Senator North' (1900); 'The Conqueror' (1902); 'Rulers of Kings'; 'Rezanov.'

Bacheller, Irving. An American author and journalist; born in Pierpont, N. Y., Sept. 26, 1859. He was actively connected with the press of New York for many years and was one of the editors of the New York World. His published works are 'The Master of Silence' (1891); 'The Still House of O'Darrow' (1894); 'Eben Holden' (1900); 'Dri and I' (1901); 'Vergilins' (1904); 'Silas Strong' (1906).

Bagot, Richard. An English writer; born in 1860. Among his published works are: 'A Roman Mystery'; 'The Just and the Unjust,' 'Casting of Nets,' 'Donna Diana,' 'Anthony Cuthbert.'

Barton, William Eleazar. An American Congregational clergyman and author; born in Sublette, Ill., June 28, 1861. Among his numerous published works are: 'Life in the Hills of Kentucky' (1889); 'A Hero in Homespun' (1897); 'The Psalms and Their Story' (1898); 'When Boston Braved the King' (1899); 'Pine Knot' (1900); 'The Old World in the New Century'; 'History and Religion of the Samaritans.'

Beard, Daniel Carter. An American artist, author and illustrator; born in Ohio in 1850. Among his works are: 'What to Do and How to Do It,' 'The American Boy's Handy Book,' 'Six Feet of Romance'; 'Moonlight'; 'Field and Forest Handy Book.'

Bell, Lilian. [Mrs. Arthur Hoyt Bogue.] An American author; born in Chicago, Ill., in 1867. Among her works are: 'Love Affairs of an Old Maid' (1893); 'The Under Side of Things' (1896); 'From a Girl's Point of View' (1897); 'As Seen by Me' (1900); 'Yessum' (1901); 'Hope Loring' (1902); 'Carolina Lee.'

Benjamin, Judah P. A jurist and politician of Jewish extraction; born in St. Croix, West Indies, Aug. 11, 1811. He was a famous secessionist and was known as " the brains of the Confederacy." He was Secretary of War in 1861 and Secretary of State of the Confederacy in 1862–65. At the close of the Civil War he fled to England, where he won fame and fortune in the practice of law. His works include 'Digest of Decisions of Supreme Court of New Orleans' (1834); 'Changes in the Practical Operation of the Constitution' (1860); 'Defence of National Democracy' (1860). His 'Law of Sale' (1883), is an authority in English courts. He died in Paris, France, May 7, 1884.

Black, F. Charlton. An American writer and educator and professor of English at Boston University; born in Scotland in 1861. Author of: 'Minor Characters in Shakespeare,' 'Recent Literary Developments.'

Blair, Robert. A Scotch poet and clergyman; born in Edinburgh in 1699. He was ordained minister at Athelstaneford in 1731. His famous poem, 'The Grave,' was published in 1743. He died Feb. 4, 1745.

Blanchard, Amy Ella. An American writer of juvenile stories; born in Baltimore, Md., in 18—. Among her numerous works are: 'Wee Babies' (1882); 'My Own Dolly' (1893); 'Two Girls' (1894); 'Betty of Wye' (1896); 'Miss Vanity' (1899); 'Her Very Best' (1900); 'Twenty Little Maidens'; 'Four Corners in California.'

Boece or Boethius, Hector. A famous Scotch historian; born at Dundee about 1465. His

'History of Scotland' ranks among the best historical works of that period. He died in 1536.

Bolton, Charles Knowles. An American librarian and author, son of Sarah K. Bolton; born in Cleveland, O., Nov. 14, 1867. He became librarian of the Boston Athenæum in 1898. Among his works are : 'Saskia, the Wife of Rembrandt,' 'The Love Story of Ursula Wolcott,' 'The Private Soldier under Washington.'

Bonsal, Stephen. An American journalist and author; born in Virginia in 1863. He served as special correspondent for the New York Herald in the Bulgarian-Servian War, also in Macedonia, in Morocco and in Cuba. He was in the diplomatic service of the United States in Peking, Madrid, Tokio and Korea (1890–96). Among his works are : 'Morocco as It is,' 'The Real Condition of Cuba,' 'The Fight for Santiago.'; 'The Golden Horse Shoe.'

Booth-Tucker, Frederick St. George de Lautour. Commander of the Salvation Army in the United States; born in Bengal, India, March 21, 1853. He held positions in the Indian Civil Service until 1881, when he resigned to join the Salvation Army. Among his published works are : 'Life of Gen. William Booth' (1898); 'In Darkest India and the Way Out' (1899).

Boyle, Mrs. Virginia Frazer. An American author; born near Chattanooga, Tenn. In 1896 she wrote the Prize Centennial Ode for Tennessee, and, besides many short stories for magazines, published 'The Other Side' (1893); 'Brokenburne' (1897); 'Devil Tales' (1900); 'Serena.'

Bradstreet, Mrs. Anne. An English poetess; born at Northampton in 1612. She was the daughter of Thomas Dudley, who became Governor of Massachusetts, and the wife of Rev. Simon Bradstreet, a non-conformist clergyman, with whom she came to New England, June 12, 1630. Her book of poems, 'The Tenth Muse,' was published in 1650. She was considered the most celebrated poet of her time in America. Her death occurred at Andover, Mass., Sept. 15, 1672.

Brady, Cyrus Townsend. An American clergyman and author; born in Allegheny, Pa., Dec. 20, 1861. He was ordained to the Episcopal ministry in 1890, and was chaplain of the 1st Pa. vol. infantry during the Spanish-American War. Among his published works are : 'For Love of Country' (1898); '(The Grip of Honor)' (1899); 'Commodore Paul Jones ' (1900); 'An Apostle of the Plains'; 'The Blue Ocean's Daughter.'

Brooks, John Graham. An American writer and lecturer on economics and president of National Consumers' League; born in Acworth, N. H., July 19, 1846. He was instructor and lecturer on economic subjects at Harvard University and at University of Chicago, and was for two years expert in United States Department of Labor at Washington. Author of : 'The Social Unrest' (1903).

Budge, Ernest A. Wallis. An English writer and the keeper of Egyptian and Assyrian antiquities in the British Museum; born in 18—. He has published over 75 books on Egyptian, Assyrian and various historic subjects, as well as numerous translations, text-books and guides. Among his works are : 'Babylonian Life and History' (1884); 'The Dwellers on the Nile' (1885); 'History of Alexander the Great' (1889); 'A Book of the Dead' (1895); 'A History of Egypt' (8 vols.); 'The Gods of Egypt.'

Buel, James William. An American author; born in Golconda, Ill., Oct. 22, 1849. In 1882 he traveled through Siberia and visited the convict camps. His works include : 'Exile Life in Siberia,' 'The Living World,' 'Story of Man,' 'Heroes of the Dark Continent,' 'World's Wonders,' 'Sea and Land,' 'The Great Operas,' 'Library of American History ' ; 'Hero Tales.'

Bullen, Frank Thomas. An English author and lecturer; born in Paddington, Eng., April 5, 1857. He went to sea at an early age and visited all parts of the world, serving in various capacities up to and inclnding that of chief mate. Among his numerous works are : 'The Cruise of the Cachalot'; 'Idylls of the Sea '; 'The Men of the Merchant Service ' ; 'A Whaleman's Wife '; 'Ocean Freeholders ' ; 'Sea Puritans.'

Burgess, Frank Gelett. An American writer and illustrator; born in Boston, Mass., Jan. 30, 1866. Author of 'The Purple Cow' (1897); 'The Lark Almanac' (1898); 'Goops and How to be Them,' 'Journey Round the Year '(1900); 'The Romantic Mood' (1907).

Burton, John Hill. A Scotch historian and advocate; born at Aberdeen, Scotland, Aug. 22, 1809. His works include, besides antiquarian books on Scotch law and history, 'The Life and Correspondence of David Hume' (1846); 'Political and Social Economy' (1849); 'The History of Scotland from Agricola's Invasion to the Revolution of 1688 ' (1867); 'History of Queen Anne's Reign' (1881); 'The Book Hunter' (1882). He died near Edinburgh, Aug. 10, 1881.

Capes, Bernard. An English author; born in 18—. Among his published works are : 'The Lake of Wine ' (1898); 'The Adventures of the Comte de la Muette'(1898); 'Our Lady of Darkness' (1899); 'From Door to Door' (1900); 'Love Like a Gypsy' (1901); 'Plots' (1901).

Carnegie, Andrew. An American manufacturer, philanthropist and author; born in Dunfermline, Scot., Nov. 25, 1837. He came to the United States in 1848 and amassed a large fortune. He expended many millions in the endowment of a great number of free libraries both in America and Scotland. Among his published works are : 'Triumphant Democracy,' 'An American Four-in-Hand in Britain,' 'Round the World '; 'Wealth '; 'Life of Watt.'

Carryl, Guy Wetmore. An American author; born in New York city, March 4, 1873. He wrote 'Fables for the Frivolous' (1898);

· Mother Goose for Grown-Ups ' (1900) ; ' Grim Tales Made Gay ' (1902). Died April 1, 1904.

Castle, Egerton. An English author and journalist; born March 12, 1858. He was publisher and part owner of the Liverpool Mercury, served on the staff of the Saturday Review, 1885-94; was member of the Council and, until 1901, of the managing committee of the Society of Authors. Among his numerous works are : ' Schools and Masters of Fence ' (1884); ' Consequences of a Novel ' (1891); ' La Bella and Others ' (1892); ' The Light of Scarthey ' (1895); ' The Jerningham Letters ' (1896); ' The Pride of Jennico ' (1898); ' The Bath Comedy ' (these last two novels written with his wife, Agnes Castle); ' Desperate Remedies ' (a play written for Richard Mansfield); ' The Secret Orchard ' (1900) (dramatized for Mr. and Mrs. Kendal); ' The House of Romance,' ' The Star Dreamer ' (1903); ' If Youth but Knew.'

Chalmers, Alexander. A Scotch writer; born in Aberdeen, Scotland, March 29, 1759. He is famous as the author of a General Biographical Dictionary, in thirty-two volumes (1812-17). Edited Johnson's ' British Poets ' and a valuable collection of British Essayists, in forty-five volumes. He died in London, Dec. 10, 1834.

Chanler, William Astor. An American traveler and writer; born in Newport, R. I., in 1867. Author of ' Through Jungles and Deserts,' ' Travels in Eastern Africa.'

Chant, Mrs. Laura Ormiston. An English preacher, lecturer, composer and writer; born in Chepstow, 1848. She taught, nursed in hospitals and took up public advocacy of woman's suffrage, temperance, purity and liberal politics; took relief to the Armenian refugees and conveyed nurses to the Greek frontier and Crete. Among her writings are : ' Verona and Other Poems,' ' Short Stories,' various pamphlets on temperance, poor law, politics and purity, besides a number of hymns and songs.

Chestnutt, Charles Waddell. An American lawyer and author, of African descent; born in Cleveland, O., June 20, 1858. Among his published works are : ' The Conjure Woman ' (1899); ' The Wife of His Youth ' (1899); ' Life of Frederick Douglass ' (1899); ' The House Behind the Cedars ' (1900).

Churchill, Winston. An American novelist; born in St. Louis, Mo., Nov. 10, 1871. He graduated from the United States Naval Academy in 1894, and contributed naval and other stories to the magazines. His published works are ' The Celebrity ' (1898); ' Richard Carvel ' (1899); ' The Crisis '; ' Coniston ' ; ' Mr. Crewe's Career.'

Clark, Imogen. An American writer ; born in New York city in 18—. Author of ' The Victory of Ezry Gardner ' (1897); ' Will Shakespeare's Little Lad ' (1897); ' The Heresy of Parson Medlicott ' (1900); ' God's Puppets ' (1901).

Clarke, Helen Archibald. An American editor, author and composer; born in Philadelphia, Pa.,

in 18—. Founder and editor of Poet Lore, with Charlotte Porter, in 1889, and collaborated with her in editing ' Browning's Complete Works,' ' Mrs. Browning's Complete Works,' ' The Ring and the Book ' ; ' Browning's Italy.'

Cleveland, Stephen Grover. The Twenty-second President of the United States; born in Caldwell, N. J., March 18, 1837. He wrote ' The Self-Made Man in American Life.' D. 1908.

Clews, Henry. An American financier and writer; born in Staffordshire, England, 1840. Author of ' Wall Street and the Nation,' ' Twenty-eight Years in Wall Street,' ' The Wall Street Point of View.'

Coe, George Albert. An American author and professor of philosophy at Northwestern University; born in Monroe County, N. Y., March 26, 1862. Besides being a contributor to philosophical and theological magazines he wrote : ' The Spritual Life; Studies in the Science of Religion ' (1900) ; ' The Religion of a Mature Mind ' ; ' Education in Religion and Morals.'

Cohen, Alfred J. [" Alan Dale."] An American dramatic critic and author; born in Birmingham, Eng., May 14, 1861. He came to the United States, engaged in journalism in New York, and was dramatic critic for the New York Evening World and the New York Journal. Among his published works are : ' Jonathan's home,' ' A Marriage Below Zero,' ' My Footlight Husband,' ' Miss Innocence,' ' A Moral Busybody,' ' Conscience on Ice,' ' A Girl Who Wrote.'

Collier, Jeremy. A famous English theologian and non-conforming bishop; born at Stow, Eng., in 1650. He suffered persecution for his zeal in the expression of his opinions. In 1698 he published his celebrated work, ' A Short View of the Profaneness and Immorality of the English Stage,' which created a great sensation in the literary world and resulted in a reform of the English drama. Among his other works are ' Essays ' on moral subjects. He died in 1726.

Colton, Arthur (Willis). An American author; born in Washington, Conn., May 22, 1868. He was instructor of English literature at Yale College 1893-5, and besides being a contributor to leading magazines, wrote ' Bennie Ben Cree.'

Colvin, Sidney. An English writer; keeper of prints and drawings in the British Museum; born in Norwood, Eng., June 18, 1845. He contributed largely to periodical literature, chiefly upon subjects relative to history and the fine arts. Among his works are : ' Life of Walter Savage Landor ' (1881); ' Life of Keats ' (1887) in Moreley's ' English Men of Letters,' ' A Florentine Picture and Chronicle ' (1898); ' Early History of Engraving in England ' (1901). He edited ' Letters of Keats ' (1887), and ' Letters of R. L. Stevenson ' (1899).

Congreve, Richard. An English author and educator ; born at Leamington, England, Sept. 4, 1818. He taught at Rugby and later became a disciple of Comte. He wrote

'The Catechism of Positivist Religion' (1858); 'Elizabeth of England' (1862); 'Essays: Political, Social and Religious' (1874). He died at Hampstead, England, July 5, 1899.

Connery, Thomas Bernard Joseph. An American author and journalist; born in Ireland, Oct. 13, 1838. He served on the editorial staff of the New York Herald from 1856-84, after which he edited successively New York Truth, Once a Week, and Collier's Weekly. Among his works are: 'Black Friday,' 'That Noble Mexican,' 'My Trip to Mars,' 'Violet Bland ';'Essays on Literary Women in England.'

Conrad, Joseph. An English author and master in the merchant service; born in 18—. Among his works are: 'Almayer's Folly' (1895); 'An Outcast of the Island' (1896); 'Tales of Unrest' (1898); 'Lord Jim' (1900); 'Youth and Other Tales' (1902); 'Romance'(1903).

Conway, Sir William Martin. An English author and Slade professor of fine arts at Cambridge; born in Rochester, Eng., in 1856. He traveled extensively and explored and surveyed many mountain ranges, ascending the most difficult peaks in the Alps, Andes and Himalaya mountains. He was awarded the gold medal for mountain surveys, Paris Exposition, 1900. Among his works are: 'Early Flemish Artists' (1887); 'Dawn of Art in the Ancient World' (1891); 'The Alps from End to End' (1895); 'With Ski and Sledge over Arctic Glaciers' (1898); 'The Bolivian Andes' (1901); 'The Domain of Art' (1902); 'The Alps' (1904).

Corbin, John. An American author and journalist; born in Chicago, Ill., May 2, 1870. After graduating from Harvard University he spent a year at Balliol College, Oxford, and later was dramatic critic for Harper's Weekly and served on the editorial staff of Harper's Magazine and the Encyclopædia Britannica. He wrote: 'The Elizabethan Hamlet' (1895); 'Schoolboy Life in England—An American View' (1898); 'An American at Oxford' (1902); 'The Cave Man' (1907).

Cornish, Francis Warre. An English writer, Vice-Provost of Eton College; born in England, May 8, 1839. Besides contributing to various periodicals, he wrote 'Life of Oliver Cromwell,' 'Sunningwell,' 'Chivalry.'

Cotes, Mrs. Everard. ["Sara Jeanette Duncan."] An English author; born in Brantford, Ont., in 1861. Among her published works are: 'A Social Departure,' 'An American Girl in London,' 'The Story of Tommy Sahib,' 'His Honor and a Lady,' 'The Path of a Star' (1897); 'Those Delightful Americans' (1902).

Coverdale, Miles. An English bishop, reformer and celebrated translator of the first complete English Bible ; born in Yorkshire, England, in 1488. He was educated at Cambridge, became an Augustine monk in 1514, and was one of the first Englishmen who adopted the doctrines of the Reformed Church of England. In 1535 he published an English translation of the Bible, which was reissued in 1537 with royal sanction. This was the first entire Bible ever published in English. He translated from the works of Luther, Calvin, Bullinger and others. He died in London and was buried Feb. 19, 1568.

Croker, Mrs. Bertha M. An English novelist; wife of Lieut.-Col. John Croker. Among her works, most of which have been translated into French and German, also into Norwegian, are: 'Proper Pride' (1882); 'Pretty Miss Neville' (1883); 'Married or Single' (1895); 'Beyond the Pale' (1897); 'Miss Balmaine's Past' (1898); 'Peggy of the Bartons' (1898); 'Infatuation' (1899); 'Angel' (1901); 'The Cat's Paw.'

Crowninshield, Mrs. Mary Bradford. An American author; born in Maine in 1854. Among her published works are: 'Latitude 19°,' 'Where the Trade Wind Blows,' 'All Among the Light-Houses,' 'Plucky Smalls,' 'The Archbishop and the Lady ';'Valencia's Garden.'

Cushing, Frank Hamilton. An American ethnologist and author; born in Northeast, Pa., July 22, 1857. He lived among the Zuñi Indians from 1878-81 in order to study their characteristics. He wrote: 'My Adventures in Zuñi,' 'Mental Concepts: or Hand-Made Mind,' 'The Myths of Creation,' 'The Arrow.' He was in the service of the U. S. Government at the time of his death, which occurred at Washington, D. C., April 10, 1900.

Daskam, Josephine Dodge. An American writer of prose and verse; born in Stamford, Conn., Feb. 17, 1876. Besides being a frequent contributor to magazines, she has published 'Smith College Stories' (1900); 'Sister's Vacation and Other Girl's Stories' (1900); 'Whom the God's Destroyed' (1902); 'Madness of Philip and Other Tales of Childhood' (1902); 'Memoirs of a Baby' (1904).

Dawson, A. J. An English novelist, story writer and traveler; born in Wandsworth in 1871. Among his works are: 'Middle Greyness,' 'Mere Sentiment,' 'God's Foundling,' 'The Story of Robert Kestrel,' 'Half-Caste,' 'Hidden Manna ';'Things Seen in Morocco.'

Dixon, Thomas, Jr. An American clergyman, writer and lecturer; born in Shelby, N.C., Jan. 11, 1864. He was admitted to the bar in 1886, but resigned to enter the Baptist ministry and was ordained in 1887. Among his works are: 'Living Problems in Religion and Social Science' (1891); 'What is Religion' (1892); 'Sermons on Ingersoll' (1894); 'The Leopard's Spots' (1902); 'The Traitor' (1906).

Dodge, Walter Phelps. An American author and lawyer; born in Syria in 1869. He made his residence in London and practiced at the English bar. He wrote: 'Three Great Tales';'As the Crow Flies' ; 'A Strong Man Armed' ; 'The Sea of Love' ; 'The Real Sir Richard Barton.'

Dresser, Horatio Willis. An American author and metaphysician; born in Yarmouth, Me.,

Jan. 15, 1866. He was editor and publisher of the 'Journal of Practical Metaphysics' (1896–98), and a lecturer on practical philosophy for many years. Among his numerous works are : 'The Power of Silence' (1895); 'The Perfect Whole' (1896); 'In Search of a Soul' (1897); 'Voices of Hope' (1898); 'Living by the Spirit'; 'Book of Secrets' ; 'Health and the Inner Life.'

Dromgoole, Will Allen. An American writer of fiction; born in Murfreesboro, Tenn., in 1860. Among her published works are 'The Valley Path,' 'A Moonshiner's Son,' 'Rare Old Chums,' 'A Boy's Battle,' 'Harum-Scarum Joe'; 'The Best of Friends.'

Drummond, James. An English clergyman and author; born in Dublin, Ire., May 14, 1835. He was professor of theology at Manchester New College, London, from 1865 until 1885, when he became principal. Among his many published works are : 'Spiritual Religion' (1870); 'Introduction to the Study of Theology,' 'The Jewish Messiah' (1887); 'Philo-Judæus' (1888); 'Life and Letters of Dr. Martineau' (in union with Prof. Upton) (1902).

Drysdale, William. An American author and journalist; born in Lancaster, Pa., July 11, 1852. He was twenty years on the staff of the New York Times as editor and foreign correspondent. Among his works are : 'In Sunny Lands,' 'The Princess of Montserrat,' 'The Young Reporter,' 'The Fast Mail,' 'The Beach Patrol,' 'The Treasury Club.' Died in 1901.

Dunne, Finley Peter. An American journalist and author; born in Chicago, July 10, 1867. He served on the editorial staffs of various Chicago newspapers and was editor of the Chicago Journal from 1897 to 1900. He wrote 'Mr. Dooley in Peace and War' (1898); 'Mr. Dooley in the Hearts of His Countrymen' (1898); 'Mr. Dooley's Philosophy' (1900).

Eddy, Mary Baker Glover. The discoverer and founder of Christian Science; born in Bow, N. H., in 1821. She began teaching Christian Science in 1867, organized the "Church of Christ, Scientist," Boston, in 1879, and was ordained to the ministry in 1881. Founded Massachusetts Metaphysical College, Boston, 1881, and Christian Science Journal, 1883. Author of 'Science and Health, with Key to Scriptures'; 'Truth versus Error'; also other works and text-books on this subject.

Eliot, Max (Anna B.). [Mrs. Granville Alden Ellis.] An American author, critic and journalist; born in Ohio in 18—. She was London correspondent for the Boston Herald, dramatic critic for the New York Dramatic News, and founded and edited the Amusement Gazette (Boston), 1886–87. Besides contributing to leading American and English magazines, she wrote : 'Sketches in Bermuda,' 'A Tale of Lily-Land,' 'Prima Donnas of To-day,' 'A Tragic Marriage,' 'Part of a Summer.'

Elson, Henry William. An American author and lecturer ; born in Muskingum County, O.,

March 29, 1857. He entered the ministry of the Lutheran Church, but resigned from it in 1895 and became writer and lecturer of the University Extension Society of Philadelphia. Author of : 'Side Lights on American History' (1899–1900); biographies for children of 'Andrew Jackson,' 'U. S. Grant,' 'Daniel Boone,' 'Frances Willard' (1899); 'How to Teach History' (1901); 'Elson's History of the United States'; 'Elson's History' (5 vols., 1905).

Emerson, Edwin. An American author, editor and journalist ; born in Dresden, Saxony, in 18—. He served on the editorial staff of various newspapers, went abroad as foreign correspondent of the Boston Post, and was war correspondent for Leslie's Weekly during the Spanish-American war. He joined the Rough Riders in Cuba and served with the regiment at San Juan and Santiago. He wrote the 'College Yell Book'; 'Peppy's Ghost' (1898); 'In War and Peace'; 'Tales Drolatic'; 'Rough Rider Stories'; 'The Monroe Doctrine in Venezuela.'

Ericsson, John. A famous naval inventor; born in Sweden in 1803. He invented monitor vessels and was the first to apply the screw propeller in navigation. Author of 'Movable Torpedoes,' 'Solar Investigations,' 'Contributions to the Centennial Exhibition,' 'Radiant Heat.' Died in 1889.

Fea, Allen. An English historian and antiquarian; born May 26, 1860. Besides contributing various articles to magazines he wrote : 'The Flight of the King,' 'Secret Chambers and Hiding Places,' 'King Monmouth.'

Fernald, Chester Bailey. An American author and dramatist; born in Charlestown, Mass., March 18, 1869. He was at one time actively connected with the building of war vessels at San Francisco, traveled extensively and settled in London. He wrote : 'The Cat and the Cherub' (1896); 'Chinatown Stories' (1899). His plays, 'The Cat and the Cherub' and 'The Moonlight Blossom,' have been successfully produced.

Field, Roswell Martin. An American journalist and writer; born in St. Louis, Mo., Sept. 1, 1851. Author of 'In Sunflower Land'; 'Madeline.' In 'Echoes from a Sabine Farm' he collaborated with his brother, Eugene Field.

Finn, Francis James. An American Roman Catholic clergyman and author; born in Missouri in 1859. He became a member of the Society of Jesus in 1879, and later was made professor of English literature at St. Xavier's College, Cincinnati. His writings are mainly for young people and include : 'Tom Playfair,' 'Claude Lightfoot'; 'Old Faces and New'; 'Ada Merton'; 'My Strange Friend'; 'The Haunt of the Fairies.'

Fisher, Sidney George. An American lawyer and author; born in Philadelphia, Pa., Sept. 11, 1856. His published works include : 'The Making of Pennsylvania' (1896); 'The Evolution of the Constitution' (1887); 'The True Benjamin Franklin' (1899); 'The True William

Penn' (1900); 'The True History of the American Revolution' (1902).

Fiske, Amos Kidder. An American author and journalist; born in Whitefield, N. H., May 12, 1842. He was associated with George Ticknor Curtis in the preparation of the 'Life of Daniel Webster,' and served for many years on the editorial staff of leading New York papers. Among his works are 'Midnight Talks at the Club' (1890); 'Beyond the Bourn' (1891); 'The Myths of Israel' (1897); 'The Story of the Philippines' (1898); 'The West Indies' (1899); 'The Modern Bank' (1904).

Fiske, Stephen. An American journalist, author and dramatist; born in New Brunswick, N. J., Nov. 22, 1840. He wrote: 'English Photographs,' 'Holiday Tales,' 'Offhand Portraits of Prominent New Yorkers,' and among his plays are 'Martin Chuzzlewit,' 'My Noble Son-in-Law,' 'Robert Rabagas.'

Flandreau, Charles Macomb. An American writer; born in Minnesota in 187-. Author of: 'Harvard Episodes,' 'The Diary of a Freshman'; 'Unmarried.'

Florio, John. An English philologist and grammarian; born in London about 1552 of Italian parents. He is best known for his English translation of 'Montaigne's Essays' (1603). Among his other works are: 'A Perfect Induction of the Italian and English Tongues,' and an 'Italian and English Dictionary,' published under the title of 'A World of Words.' He died at Fulham, Eng., in 1623.

Ford, Worthington Chauncey. An American author and statistician; brother of the late Paul Leicester Ford; born in Brooklyn, N.Y., Feb. 16, 1858. He was chief of Bureau of Statistics at Washington 1885–98, and lecturer of statistics University of Chicago 1901. Author of: 'The Standard Silver Dollar' (1884); George Washington' (1899).

Fowler, Ellen Thorneycroft. An English poet and novelist; born in 18—. Among her published works are: 'Verses Grave and Gay' (1891); 'Cupid's Garden' (1897); 'A Double Thread' (1899); 'Concerning Isabel Carnaby' (1898); 'The Farringdons' (1900); 'Fuel of Fire' (1902); 'Place and Power' (1903).

Fraser, Mrs. Hugh. An English novelist and writer of travels; born in Rome, Italy. Sister of Marion Crawford and an extensive traveler. Author of: 'The Brown Ambassador' (1895); 'Palladia' (1896); 'The Looms of Time' (1899); 'The Splendid Porsenna' (1899); 'A Little Gray Sheep'; 'The Slaking of the Sword.'

Gallon, Tom. An English novelist and dramatist; born in London, Dec. 5, 1866. Among his numerous works are: 'Tatterley' (1897); 'The Kingdom of Hate' (1899); 'Kiddy' (1900); 'A Rogue in Love' (1900); 'The Dead Ingleby' (1902). Plays: 'The Man Who Stole the Castle' (1900); 'Memory's Garden' (1902); 'Tatterley' (1902); 'The Prodigal.'

Garrison, Wendell Phillips. An American author and editor of 'The Nation;' son of William Lloyd; born in Cambridge, Mass., June 4, 1840. Among his published works are: 'Life of William Lloyd Garrison' (1885); 'Parables for School and Home' (1897); 'The New Gulliver' (1898). Died 1907.

Gilder, Jeannette Leonard. An American author, journalist and critic, sister of Richard Watson; born in Flushing, N. Y., Oct. 3, 1849. She was on the editorial staff of Scribner's Monthly (now The Century), the New York Herald and The Critic, and wrote for eighteen years under the pen name of "Brunswick," as New York correspondent for London, Philadelphia and Boston papers. She wrote: 'Taken by Siege' (1886–96; 'Autobiography of a Tomboy' (1900), and edited with Joseph B. Gilder 'Essays from the Critic' (1882); 'Authors at Home' (1889); with Helen Gray Cone, 'Pen Portraits of Literary Women' (1887); and also 'Representative Poems of Living Poets' (1886).

Glasgow, Ellen Anderson Gholson. An American novelist; born in Richmond, Va., April 22, 1874. Author of 'The Descendant' (1897); 'The Phases of an Inferior Planet' (1898); 'The Voice of the People' (1900); 'The Battleground' (1902); 'The Wheel of Life' (1906).

Glyn, Mrs. Clayton. ["Elinor Glyn."] An English writer; born in Toronto, Ont., in 18—. Author of 'The Visits of Elizabeth'; 'Reflections of Ambrosine'; 'The Damsel and the Sage.'

Gordon, Charles W. A Canadian clergyman and author; born in Canada in 1860. He was missionary to the miners and lumbermen in the Rocky Mountains, 1890–93, and became minister of St. Stephen's Church, Winnipeg, in 1894. Among his works are: 'Black Rock.' 'The Sky Pilot,' 'Ould Michael,' 'The Man from Glengarry,' 'Glengarry Days,' 'Glengarry School Days' (1902); 'The Prospector' (1904).

Gordon-Stables, William. An English novelist and journalist; born in Banffshire, N. B., May 21, 1840. He served for nine years in the Royal Navy, traveled extensively and made cruises to the Arctic regions. Author of 114 books, among them 'The Cruise of the Snowbird.' 'To Greenland and the Pole,' 'Our Humble Friends and Fellow Mortals,' 'Leaves from the Log of a Gentleman Gipsy' (1898), and many boys' books. Also 'Popular Medicine and Hygiene' (7 vols.).

Goepp, Philip Henry. An American musician and author; born in New York, June 23, 1864. Composer of numerous songs, anthems, etc. Author of 'Annals of Music in Philadelphia' (1896); 'Symphonies and Their Meaning' (1898–1902).

Gorky, Maxime. [Alicksei Maximovitch Pieshkov.] A Russian novelist; born in Nizni Novgorod, March 14, 1868. During his early career he served successively as peddler, scullery-boy, gardener, watchman and baker's apprentice. Among his numerous works are: 'Song of the Falcon,' ' Twenty-six and One,' 'About the Devil,' ' The Reader,' ' The Outcasts ' (1902); ' Three Men ' (1902).

Graham, Kenneth. An English author and secretary of the Bank of England; born in 18—. He wrote : ' The Golden Age ' (1895); ' Pagan Papers ' (1893); ' Dream Days,' ' The Headswoman ' (1898).

Gregg, David. An American Presbyterian clergyman and writer; born in Pittsburg, Pa., March 25, 1846. Among his published works are ' From Solomon to the Captivity ' (1890); ' Our Best Moods ' (1893); ' The Heaven Life ' (1895); ' Makers of the American Republic ' (1896); 'Between the Testaments' (1907).

Griggs, Edward Howard. An American lecturer and author; born in Owatonna, Mich., Jan. 9, 1868. He was professor of English literature at Indiana University, and of ethics and education at the Leland Stanford, Jr., University. He wrote ' The New Humanism ' (1902).

Guerber, Hélène Adeline. An American educator and author ; born in New York in 18—. Among her many published works are ' Myths of Greece and Rome,' ' Legends of the Rhine,' ' Stories of the Wagner Operas,' ' The Story of the Thirteen Colonies'; ' Legends of Switzerland ' ; 'Yourself' ; ' Cupid and Psyche.'

Gulick, John Thomas. An American Presbyterian missionary and writer; born in Kauai, Hawaiian Islands, March 13, 1832. His writings, which are mostly on Darwinian topics, include ' Diversity of Evolution,' ' Inconsistencies of Utilitarianism.'

Guthrie, William Norman. An American Episcopal clergyman, lecturer and author ; born in Dundee, Scotland. March 4, 1868. His published works are ' Love Conquereth,' (1890); ' Modern Poet Prophets ', ' Essays Critical and Interpretive ' (1897-98); ' To Kindle the Yule Log,' (1899); ' Songs of American Destiny, or Vision of New Hellas ' (1900) ; ' The City of St. Francis ' (1907).

Hall, Ruth. An American journalist and writer; born in Scoharie, N. Y., April 10, 1858. Besides being a frequent contributor to the press she wrote : ' In the Brave Days of Old ' (1898); ' The Boys of Schooley ' (1899); ' The Black Gown ' (1900); ' Downrenter's Son ' (1902).

Hall, Thomas Winthrop. [" Tom Hall."] An American writer of prose and verse; born in Ogdensburg, N. Y., Nov. 13, 1862. Among his prose works are : ' An Experimental Wooing,' ' Tales by Tom Hall,' ' The Fun and Fighting of the Rough Riders,' and among his verses ' When Hearts are Trumps,' ' When Love Laughs,' ' When Cupid Calls.' He died in Hannibal, Mo., Aug. 21, 1900.

Halstead, Murat. An American author and journalist ; born in Ross township, Ohio, Sept. 2, 1829. He served on the editorial staff of several newspapers and went to the Philippines as special correspondent during the war with Spain. Among his works are ' The Story of Cuba,' ' Life of William McKinley,' ' Our Country in War,' ' The Great Century,' ' The Boer and the British War.' Died 1908.

Hamblen, Herbert Elliott. [" Frederick Benton Williams."] An American engineer and author ; born in Ossippee, N. H., Dec. 24, 1849. Among his published works are ' On Many Seas' (1896); ' Tom Benton's Luck,' (1898); ' The Story of a Yankee Boy ' (1898); ' We Win ' (1899), ' Yarn of a Bucko Mate ' (1899); ' The Red Shirts ' (1901).

Hamilton, Sir William. One of the most distinguished of modern metaphysicians; born in Glasgow, Scot., March 8, 1788. In 1821 he became professor of civil history at the University of Edinburgh, and in 1836 was elected to the chair of logic and metaphysics. His celebrated criticism on Cousin (Edinburgh Review, 1829) made him world famous, from which time he continued to publish many essays, lectures and other valuable contributions to mental philosophy and literature. He died May 5, 1856.

Harben, William Nathaniel. [" Will N."] An American author; born in Dalton, Ga., July 5, 1858. Besides being a contributor to leading magazines he was at one time assistant editor of the Youth's Companion. Among his numerous works are ' White Marie ' (1889); ' Almost Persuaded ' (1890); ' The Land of the Changing Sun ' (1894); ' The Caruthers Affair ' (1899); ' The Woman Who Trusted,' (1901); ' Westerfelt ' (1901); ' Ann Boyd.'

Harrison, Benjamin. The twenty-third President of the United States; born in North Bend, Ohio, Aug. 20, 1833. Author of ' This Country of Ours ' (1897). He died in Indianapolis, March 13, 1901.

Hazard, Caroline. An American author and president of Wellesley College; born in Peace Dale, R. I., June 10, 1856. She edited ' Works of R. G. Hazard ' (1889); and wrote ' Life of J. L. Diman ' (1886); ' Thomas Hazard ' (1893); ' Narragansett Ballads ' (1894); ' The Narragansett Friends' Meeting ' (1899).

Hazelton, George Cochrane, Jr. An American lawyer, playwright and author; born in Boscobel, Wis., in 18—. He wrote plays which were successfully produced, entitled ' Edgar Allan Poe ' (1895), and ' Mistress Nell ' (1899); also, ' The National Capitol, its Architecture, Art and History' (1897); ' Mistress Nell.'

Heaton, John Langdon. An American journalist and author; born in Canton, N. Y., Jan. 29, 1860. He wrote ' The Story of Vermont ' (1889); ' Stories of Napoleon ' (1895); ' The Book of Lies ' (1896); ' The Quilting Bee ' (1896).

Heinemann, William. An English publisher and dramatist; born May 18, 1863. He founded the publishing house which bears his name in 1890; married in 1899 Magda Stuart Sindici [" Kassandra Vivaria"]. Among

his dramatic productions are : (The First Step)
(1895); (Summer Moths) (1898); (War)
(1901).

Herford, Oliver. An American humorist,
artist and verse writer. He wrote (The Bashful
Earthquake) (1898); (Alphabet of Celebrities)
(1898); (A Child's Primer of Natural History)
(1896); (Wagner for Infants) (1900).

Herne, James A. An American actor and
playwright; born in Troy, N. Y., in 1839; died
in New York City, June 2, 1901. Among his
published plays are : (Hearts of Oak,) (Margaret Fleming,) (Sag Harbor,) (Drifting Apart,)
(Shore Acres.)

Hewlett, Maurice Henry. An English author;
born in Kent, England, Jan. 22, 1861.
Among his published works are: (Earthwork
Out of Tuscany) (1895); (Songs and Medita-
tions) (1897); (The Forest Lovers) (1898);
(Pan and the Young Shepherd) (1898);
(Richard Yea and Nay) (1900); (New Can-
terbury Tales) (1901); (The Road in Tuscany.)

Hinton, Richard Josiah. An American author
and journalist; born in London, Eng., Nov. 25,
1830. He came to the United States in 1851,
served in the Union army and was the first white
man legally commissioned to recruit and command colored troops. After the war edited several papers, and the last fifteen years of his life
was an active socialist. Among his works are :
(Life of Abraham Lincoln,) (Life of William
H. Seward,) (English Radical Leaders,) (John
Brown,) (The Making of the New West.) Died
in 1901.

Hodges, George. Dean of the Episcopal
Theological School, Cambridge, Mass.; born in
Rome, N. Y., Oct. 6, 1856. Among his pub-
lished writings are : (Beside the Cross) (1889);
(Christianity Between Sundays) (1892); (The
Heresy of Cain) (1894); (The Path of Life)
(1899);(The Year of Grace) ; (Holderness.)

Holcombe, Chester. An American author and
diplomat; born in Winfield, N. Y., Oct. 16,
1844. He was interpreter and secretary U. S.
legation, Peking, China, 1871–85, acting minister during six years and was prominent in
negotiating various important treaties. He wrote
(in Chinese) (Mental Arithmetic) (1873);
(Life of Christ) (1875); (Translation of Declaration of Independence.) In English, (The
Practical Effect of Confucianism upon the Chinese
Nation) (1882); (Travels in Western China)
(1875); (The Real Chinaman) (1895); (The
Real Chinese Question) (1899).

Holland, Clive. An English author; born in
Bournemouth, Eng., April 23, 1866. Besides
being a frequent contributor to English and
American magazines, he was also on the staff of
several London papers. Among his numerous
published works are : (The Golden Hawk)
(1888); (My Japanese Wife) (1895); (The
Lure of Fame) (1896); (A Writer of Fiction)
(1897); (The Seed of the Poppy) (1898); (The
Heart of the Geisha) (play) (1901); (Paris) (1904).

Hopkins, Mrs. Margaret Sutton Briscoe. An
American author ; born in Baltimore, Md.,
Dec 7, 1864. Her writings include : (Perchance
to Dream, and Other Stories) (1892); (Links
in a Chain) (1893); (Jimty and Others) (1898);
(The Sixth Sense, and Other Stories) (1899).

Hornung, Ernest William. An English novelist; born in Middlesborough, Eng., June 7,
1866. Among his works are : (A Bride from
the Bush) (1890); (Under Two Skies) (1892);
(Tiny Luttrell) (1893); (The Unbidden Guest)
(1894); (My Lord Duke) (1897); (Dead Men
Tell No Tales) (1899); (The Black Mask)
(1901); (The Shadow of the Rope) (1902).

Horton, Edward Augustus. An American
Unitarian clergyman and author; born in Springfield, Mass., Sept. 28, 1843. Among his published works are (Story of Israel,) (Scenes
in the Life of Jesus,) (Beginning of Christianity,) (Beacon Lights of Christian History.)

Horton, George. An American author and
journalist; born in Fairville, N. Y., in 1859.
He was appointed consul at Athens by President
Cleveland, and later edited the Chicago-Times
Herald and the Chicago American Saturday
Literary Supplement. Among his works are :
(Songs of the Lowly,) (In Unknown Seas.)
(Aphroessa) ; (A Fair Brigand) (1898); (Like An-
other Helen) (1901); (The Edge of Hazard) (1906).

Hough, Emerson. [" E. Hough."]   An
American traveler and writer; born in Newton,
Ia., June 28, 1857. He traveled over the
wildest parts of the West and explored the Yellowstone Park in the winter of 1895. The Act
of Congress protecting the Park buffalo was due
to this latter trip. Author of : (The Singing
Mouse Stories) (1895); (The Story of the Cowboy) (1895); (The Girl at Half-Way House)
(1900); (The Way of Man) (1907).

Hoyle, Edmond. An English writer on
games; born in England, 1672. He was the
first to write scientifically on whist, or on any
card game. Author of (A Short Treatise on
the Game of Whist) (1742), of which innumerable editions have been issued. He wrote
treatises on chess, backgammon, piquet and
many other games. He died in London, Aug.
29, 1769.

Hyatt, Alpheus. An American scientist and
author; born in Washington, D. C., April 5,
1838. He was curator of the Boston Society of
Natural History and professor of zoology in the
Massachusetts Institute of Technology. Among
his works are (Observations on Fresh Water
Polyzoa,) (About Pebbles,) (Common Hy-
droids.) He died in Cambridge, Mass., Jan.
15, 1902.

Ide, Mrs. Frances Otis. [" Ruth Ogden."]
An American writer of juvenile stories; born at
Long Island, N. Y., 1853. Author of (His
Little Royal Highness) (1897); (A Little
Queen of Hearts) (1892); (Courage) (1894);
(Little Homespun) (1896); (Loyal Hearts and
True) (1900); (The Good and Perfect Gift.)

Ireland, Alleyne. An English author and lecturer; born in Manchester, Eng., Jan. 19, 1871. He traveled extensively from 1887–97, delivered lectures on Tropical Colonization, at Cornell University in 1899, and was appointed lecturer on politics at Chicago University, 1900. Among his works are 'Demerariana' (1897); 'Tropical Colonization' (1899); 'The Anglo-Boer Conflict' (1900); 'China and the Powers' (1901); 'The Far Eastern Tropics' (1905).

Ireland, John. Roman Catholic Archbishop of St. Paul, Minn.; born in Ireland, Sept. 11, 1838. He came to the United States in boyhood, was ordained priest, Dec. 21, 1861, and was chaplain of the Fifth Minnesota regiment in the Civil War. He was consecrated Dec. 21, 1875, and became Archbishop of St. Paul in 1888. Author of 'The Church and Modern Society.'

Ireland, Mrs. Mary B. An American author and translator; born in Calvert, Md., Jan. 9, 1834. She wrote: 'What I told Dorcas' (1895); 'Grandma Elliot's Farm House' (1900). Among her numerous translations from the German are: 'Betty's Decision' (1886); 'The Doctor's Family' (1896); 'Stolen for Ransom' (1901); 'Eric's Vacation' (1901).

Jacobs, Joseph. An English author and journalist; born in Sydney, N. S. W., Aug, 28, 1854. He edited the Literary Year Book and the Jewish Year Book; late secretary of the Russo-Jewish Committee, president of the Jewish Historic Society and literary editor of the Jewish Encyclopædia. Author of: 'English Fairy Tales' (1890); 'Jews of Angevin, England' (1893); 'Literary Studies' (1895); 'As Others Saw Him' (a Jewish Life of Christ) (1895); 'Wonder Voyages' (1896); 'A Story of Geographical Discovery' (1898), and many other works.

Jacobs, William Wymark. An English writer; born in London, Sept. 8, 1863. Author of: 'Many Cargoes' (1896); 'The Skipper's Wooing' (1897); 'Sea Urchins' (1898); 'A Master of Craft' (1900); 'Light Freights' (1901); 'The Lady of the Barge' (1902).

Jarvis, Thomas Stinson. An American novelist and dramatic critic; born in Ontario in 1854. Among his published works are: 'Letters from East Longitudes,' 'Geoffrey Hampstead,' 'Doctor Perdue,' 'The Ascent of Life.'

Jenks, Tudor. An American journalist and author; born in Brooklyn, N. Y., May 7, 1857. Editor on the staff of the St. Nicholas Magazine for many years. Among his published works are: 'Imaginations, or Truthless Tales' (1900); 'Boy's Book of Explorations' (1900); 'Gipsy, the Talking Dog' (1902); 'When America was New.'

Johnson, Clifton. An American author and illustrator; born in Hadley, Mass., Jan. 25, 1865. Among his published writings are: 'The New England Country' (1892); 'The Farmer's Boy' (1894); 'Country Clouds and Sunshine' (1896); 'Among English Hedgerows' (1899); 'Along French Byways' (1900); 'The Land of Heather.'

Johnston, Mary. An American novelist; born in Buchanan, Va., Nov. 21, 1870. She wrote 'Prisoners of Hope' (1898); 'To have and to Hold' (1900); 'Audrey'; 'The Goddess of Reason.'

Jones, Henry. ["Cavendish."] An English writer on whist; born in London, Nov. 2, 1831. While a member of the "Cavendish" Club, he began to make notes upon difficult points in whist and to record interesting hands. He produced in 1862 a manual entitled 'Principles of Whist Stated and Explained by Cavendish,' which was later enlarged and appeared in many subsequent editions. 'Cavendish' soon came to be regarded as the standard authority on whist. He edited several manuals on games and was the author of guides to croquet, euchre, tennis, etc. He died in London, Feb. 10, 1899.

Jowett, Benjamin. An English author and educator; born at Camberwell, Eng., in 1817. He became master of Baliol College in 1870. His most famous work, which is considered an English classic, is 'The Dialogues of Plato,' translated into English with analyses and introductions. He published a translation of 'Thucydides' (1881), and the 'Politics of Aristotle' (1885). He died at Oxford, Oct. 1, 1893.

Kaler, James Otis. ["James Otis."] An American writer of juvenile tales; born in Winterport, Me., March 19, 1848. Among his numerous published works are: 'Raising the Pearl,' 'A Boy Captain,' 'Toby Tyler,' 'Mr. Stubbs's Brother,' 'Silent Pete,' 'The Castaways,' 'When Israel Putnam Served the King,' 'Little Joe'; 'The Wreck of the Ocean Queen.'

Keats, Gwendoline. ["Zack."] An English author; born in 18—. She wrote: 'Life is Life' (1898); 'On Trial' (1899); 'The White Cottage,' 'Tales of Dunstable Weir' (1900).

Kidd, Benjamin. An English author and sociologist; born Sept. 9, 1858. His famous work, 'Social Evolution,' which he was ten years in preparing, published in 1894, was translated into seven different languages. He also wrote: 'The Control of the Tropics' (1898); 'Principles of Western Civilization' (1902); 'South Africa' (1902).

King, William Basil. An American Episcopal clergyman and author; born in Charlottetown, Canada, in 1859. He wrote: 'The Daily Song'; 'Thoughts on the Offices for Morning and Evening Prayer'; 'Griselda'; 'The Giant's Strength.'

Kitto, John. An English writer and Bible student; born at Plymouth, England, Dec. 4, 1804. He published 'The Pictorial Bible' (1838); 'Pictorial History of Palestine' (1843); 'The Lost Senses' (1845); 'The Daily Bible Illustrations,' (8 vols., 1849–53). He died at Cannstadt, Germany, Nov. 25, 1854.

Kropotkin. [Prince Peter Alexcivitch.] A Russian geographer, author and socialist; born in Moscow, Dec. 9, 1842. He received the gold medal of the Russian Geographical Society for his journey across Manchuria in 1864, and explored the glacial deposits in Finland and

Sweden, 1871. He joined the International Working Men's Association in 1872 and was arrested and confined in fortress St. Peter and St. Paul in 1874. Escaped and went to England, and later founded at Geneva the anarchist paper Le Revolte. Expelled from Switzerland in 1881, condemned at Lyons to five years imprisonment in 1884, liberated in 1886. Among his many published works are : ' Researches on the Glacial Period ' (1876); ' In Russian and French Prisons ' (1886); ' L'Anarchie, sa Philosophie, son Ideal ' (1896); ' Memoirs of a Revolutionist ' (1900); ' Modern Science and Anarchism ' (1902); ' The Dessication of Asia.'

Lanier, Clifford Anderson. An American author; born in Griffin, Ga., April 24, 1844. Among his works are : ' Thorn Fruit,' ' The Mate's Race with the Banshees,' ' The Doctor's Legend,' ' Apollo and Keats on Browning ' (1902), and ' Dialect Poems,' with Sidney Lanier.

Law, William Arthur. An English dramatic author; born March 22, 1844. He served eight years in the army and then took up the profession of acting. Among his many dramatic works are : ' A Night Surprise ' (1877); ' A Strange Host ' (1882); ' A Mint of Money ' (1884); ' After Long Years ' (1886); ' The Mystery of a Hansom Cab ' (1888); ' All Abroad ' (1890); 'Culprits ' (1890); ' New Year's Morning '; ' A Country Mouse ' ; ' Bride and Bridegroom.'

Lawrence, William. The seventh Protestant Episcopal bishop of Massachusetts; born in Boston, May 30, 1850. He wrote ' Life of Amos A. Lawrence ' (his father); ' Visions and Service,' ' Roger Wolcott ' (1902).

Lee, Gerald Stanley. An American clergyman, author, lecturer and critic; born in Brockton, Mass., Oct. 4, 1861. He wrote ' About an Old New England Church ' (1893); ' Lost Art of Reading ' (1902); ' The Shadow Christ ' (1896); ' The Voice of the Machines ' (1906).

Lee, Mrs. Jennette. An American novelist, wife of Gerald Stanley Lee; born in Bristol, Conn., Nov. 10, 1860. She wrote, besides numerous magazine stories and sketches, ' Kate Wetherell ' (1900); ' A Pillar of Salt ' (1901); ' Son of a Fiddler ' (1902); ' The Ibsen Secret' (1907).

Lemprière, John, D. D. An English author and educator ; born in the Island of Jersey about 1765. Among his works are a world famous ' Classical Dictionary ' (1788); ' Sermons ' (1791); ' Dictionary of Universal Biography ' (1808). He died in London, Feb. 1, 1824.

Lewis, Alfred Henry. [" Dan Quin."] An American journalist and author; born in Ohio in 1842. Editor and founder of The Verdict (a humorous weekly), and author of : ' Wolfville,' 'Episodes of Cowboy Life,' ' Sandburrs' (1900).

Lilly, William Samuel. An English writer; secretary to Catholic Union of Great Britain; born July 10, 1840. Among his works are : ' Ancient Religion and Modern Thought '

(1884); 'Chapters in European History' (1886); ' On Right and Wrong ' (1890); ' The Great Enigma ' (1893); ' Four English Humorists of the Nineteenth Century ' (1895); ' India and Its Problems '; ' Christianity and Modern Civilization.'

Lincoln, Mrs. Jeanie, Gould. An American author; born in Troy, N. Y., in 18—. Among her published works are : ' A Chaplet of Leaves' (verse) (1869); ' Marjorie's Quest ' (1872); ' Her Washington Season ' (1884); 'An Unwilling Maid ' (1897); ' A Pretty Tory ' (1899).

Lloyd, John Uri. An American author, botanist and chemist; born in West Bloomfield, N. Y., April 19, 1849. Among his works are : ' The Chemistry of Medicine,' ' Elixirs: Their History,' ' The Right Side of the Car,' and ' Stringtown on the Pike.'

London, Jack. An American writer; born in San Francisco, Cal., Jan. 12, 1876. He led a life of adventure, which colors his writings. His published works include ' The Son of the Wolf ' (1900); ' Cruise of the Dazzlers ' (1902);' Daughter of the Snows '; ' The Koad.'

Long, John Luther. An American author; born in 1861. He wrote ' Madam Butterfly,' ' Miss Cherry-Blossom of Tokyo,' ' Fox Woman' (1899); ' The Prince of Illusion '; ' Billy Boy.'

Loomis, Charles Battell. An American writer; born in Brooklyn, N. Y., Sept. 16, 1861. Author of ' Just Rhymes ' (1899); ' The Four-masted Cat-boat ' (1899); ' Yankee Enchantments ' (1900); ' Cheer Up ' (1906).

Lorimer, George Horace. An American journalist and author, son of Rev. George C. Lorimer; born in Louisville, Ky., Oct. 6, 1868. Editor of the Philadelphia Saturday Evening Post. He wrote ' Behind the Veil of Isis,' and ' Letters from a Self-made Merchant to his Son.'

Lumholtz, Carl Sophus. A German traveler and writer; born in 18—. He made extensive researches among the primitive peoples of many nations, whom he studied minutely. Author of : ' Among Cannibals ' (1889); ' Unknown Mexico' (1902).

Lush, Charles Keeler. An American journalist and author; born in La Crosse, Wis., Dec. 5, 1861. He wrote : ' The Federal Judge ' (1897).

McManus, Blanche. [Mrs. M. F. Mansfield.] An American author and illustrator; born in Louisiana, 18—. Among her published works are ' The True Mother Goose,' ' Colonial Monologues,' ' Told in the Twilight,' ' Bachelor Ballads'; ' Ramblers in Normandy and Brittany.'

McManus, Seumas. An Irish writer and humorist; born in Mount Charles County, Donegal, Ire., in 18—. Among his published works are: ' The Bend of the Road,' ' Through Turf and Smoke,' ' The Bewitched Fiddle,' ' A Lad o' the O'Friels ' (1903); ' Donegal Fairy Tales.'

MacGrath, Harold. An American journalist and author; born in Syracuse, N. Y., Sept. 4, 1871. Besides being a contributor to leading magazines and periodicals he wrote 'Arms and the Woman'; 'Hearts and Masks'; 'The Best Man.'

Mackie, Mrs. Pauline Bradford, (Hopkins.) An American writer; born in Fairfield, Conn., July 5, 1873. Among her published works are 'Mademoiselle de Berny' (1897); 'Ye Lyttle Salem Maide,' (1898); 'A Georgian Actress' (1900); 'Story of Kate'; 'The Girl and the Kaiser.'

Major Charles. ["Edwin Caskoden."] An American lawyer and author; born in Indianapolis, Ind., July 25, 1856. He wrote 'When Knighthood Was in Flower' (1898); 'Dorothy Vernon of Haddon Hall' (1902); 'Yolanda.'

Malone, Walter. An American writer of prose and verse; born in De Soto County, Miss., Feb. 10, 1866. Among his published works are: 'Claribel and Other Poems' (1882); 'Narcissus and Other Poems' (1892); 'Songs of Dusk and Dawn' (1894); 'The Coming of the King' (1897); 'Songs of North and South' (1900); 'Songs of East and West' (1906).

Marchmont, Arthur Williams. An English novelist and journalist; born at Southgate, England, in 1852. He engaged in journalism in London and afterwards in the provinces, editing successively the North Eastern Gazette and Lancashire Daily Post. He relinquished journalism for fiction in 1894. Author of 'Isa' (1887); 'By Right of Sword' (1897); 'The Greatest Gift' (1899); 'In the Name of a Woman' (1900); 'For Love or Crown' (1901); 'Sarita the Carlist' (1902); 'The Queen's Advocate.'

Mason, Alfred Edward Woodley. An English novelist; born May 7, 1865. Author of 'A Romance of Wastdale' (1895); 'The Courtship of Morrice Buckler' (1896); 'The Philanderers' (1897); 'Lawrence Clavering' (1897); 'Miranda of the Balcony' (1899), 'Clementina' (1901); 'The Four Feathers' (1902).

Mason, Mrs. Caroline Atwater. An American author; born in Providence, R. I., July 10, 1853. Among her works are: 'A Titled Maiden,' 'A Minister of Carthage,' 'The Quiet King,' 'A Wind Flower,' 'A Woman of Yesterday' (1900); 'Wax Wing' (1905).

Mathews, Frances Aymer. An American author and dramatist; born in New York in 18—. Among her published works are: 'One Man in Ten Thousand,' 'A Married Man,' 'The New Yorkers;' plays, 'Joan D'Arc,' 'A Little Tragedy at Tientsin,' 'Peg Woffington,' 'The Brazilian,' 'Aaron Burr.'

McCutcheon, George Barr. An American journalist and author; born in Tippecanoe County, Ind., July 26, 1866. He wrote 'Graustark' (1900); 'Castle Craneycrow' (1902).

McIlvaine, Charles. ["Toby Hodge."] An American author and scientist; born in Chester County, Pa., May 31, 1840. Besides being a frequent contributor of stories and articles on the subjects of natural science to leading magazines, he wrote: 'A Legend of Polecat Hollow' (1884); 'American Fungi' (1900).

Mead, William Leon. An American author and journalist; born in Margaretville, N. Y., April 27, 1861. He served on the editorial staff of Truth, Tom Nast's Weekly and Form Magazine, besides being a frequent contributor to well-known periodicals. Among his works are: 'In Thraldom' (1877); 'Sky Rockets' (1883); 'The Bow-Legged Ghost and Other Stories' (1899); 'Wild Cat Ledge' (1901); 'A Lost Identity' (1901); 'Romance of R. Fulton.'

Medwin, Thomas. An English author, cousin and biographer of Shelley; born at Horsham, Eng., March 20, 1788. He was intimately associated with Byron and upon his death published a 'Journal of the Conversations of Lord Byron' (1824), which was translated into French and German and excited great controversy. He was the author of several dramatic poems, but is best known for 'The Life of Percy Bysshe Shelley' (1847). He died at Horsham, Aug. 2, 1869.

Merriman, Henry Seton. [Nom de plume of "Hugh Stowell Scott."] An English novelist; born in 18—. Among his numerous works are: 'From One Generation to Another' (1892); 'The Slave of the Lamp' (1892); 'With Edged Tools' (1897); 'Flotsam' (1896); 'The Sowers' (1896); 'In Kedar's Tents' (1897); 'The Velvet Glove'; 'The Vultures.' Died Nov. 19, 1903.

Mifflin, Lloyd. An American poet and artist; born in Columbia, Pa., Sept. 15, 1846. His published works include 'The Hills' (1896); 'At the Gates of Song' (1897); 'On the Slopes of Helicon' (1898); 'Echoes of Greek Idyls' (1899); 'My Lady of Dream' (1906).

Miles, Nelson Appleton. Lieutenant-General commanding the United States Army; born in Westminster, Mass., Aug. 8, 1839. He wrote 'Personal Recollections' (1899), besides many military reports and magazine articles. Ret. 1903.

Miller, Joseph. ["Joe Miller."] An English actor and humorist; born in England in 1684. His name has long been a synonym for a jest or witty anecdote of ancient flavor. His chief reputation rests upon a collection of witticisms attributed to him, entitled 'Joe Miller's Jests,' published after his death (1739) by John Mottley, who, however, secured a part of the collection from other sources. He died in 1738.

Miller, James Russell. An American Presbyterian clergyman and author; born in Harshaville, Pa., March 20, 1840. Among his numerous works are: 'Week Day Religion' (1880); 'In His Steps' (1885); 'Glimpses Through Life's Windows' (1893); 'Blessing of Cheerfulness' (1898); 'Loving My Neighbor' (1900.)

Monroe, Harriet. An American writer of verse; born in Chicago, Ill., Dec. 25, 1860. She wrote the 'Columbian Ode,' which was read and sung at the dedicatory ceremonies of the Columbian Exposition, Oct. 21, 1892. Author of 'Valeria and Other Poems' (1892); 'John Wellborn Root, a Memoir'; 'Historical Lutheranism.'

Moody, William Vaughn. An American writer of verse and instructor in English literature at the University of Chicago; born in Spencer, Ind., July 8, 1869. Author of ' The Masque of Judgment,' a lyrical drama (1900); ' Poems ' (1901); ' History of English Literature' (with R. M. Lovett ' (1902); ' The Great Divide ' (1907.'

Moore, John Trotwood. An American author; born in Marion, Ala., Aug. 26, 1858. He wrote ' Songs and Stories from Tennessee ' (1897); ' Ole Mistis ' (1897); ' A Summer Hymnal ' (1901; ' The Bishop of Cottontown.'

Morris, Clara. An American actress and author; born in Toronto, Can., in 1849. Besides being a contributor to the magazines, she wrote : ' A Silent Singer,' ' Little Jim Crow,' ' Autobiography of Clara Morris,' ' A Paste-Board Crown ' ; ' Life of a Star.'

Morris, Charles. An American author and compiler; born in Chester, Pa., Oct. 1, 1833. Besides being editor of the New Science Review, he wrote much on scientific subjects. Among his works are : ' Inverara,' ' The Aryan Race,' ' King Arthur and the Knights of the Round Table,' ' Historical Tales ' (9 vols.), ' Our War with Spain,' ' Our Island Empire,' ' Man and His Ancestor ' ; ' The Old and the New.'

Munn, Charles Clark. An American writer; born in Southington, Conn., in 1848. Author of ' Pocket Island ' (1900); ' Uncle Terry, a Story of the Maine Coast ' (1900); ' Rockhaven ' (1902); ' Boyhood Days on the Farm.'

Munro, Neil. A Scottish author and journalist; born in Inverary, Scotland, June 3, 1864. He wrote ' The Lost Pibroch, a Series of Celtic Tales and Sketches ' (1896); ' John Splendid, a Highland Romance ' (1898); ' Gilian the Dreamer ' (1899); ' Doom Castle ' (1901); ' The Shoes of Fortune ' (1901) ; ' Erchie '(1904).

Münsterberg, Hugo. An educator and author, and professor of psychology at Harvard College; born in Danzig, Germany, June 1, 1863. He wrote ' Psychology and Life ' (1899); ' American Traits ' (1903); ' Science and Idealism ' (1905); ' Psychotherapy ' (1909).

Noble, Edmund. An English author and journalist; born in Glasgow, Scot., Jan. 8, 1853. He served on the editorial staff of various Liverpool and London papers and was editor of the American edition of ' Free Russia,' 1872-4. Besides being a frequent contributor to magazines on ethical and philosophical subjects, he wrote : ' The Russian Revolt ' (1885); ' Russia and the Russians ' (1900); ' Before the Dawn ' (1901).

Norris, Frank. An American novelist and journalist; born in Chicago, Ill., in 1870. He was war correspondent for McClure's Magazine during the Spanish-American war, and for the San Francisco Chronicle, in South Africa, during the Uitlander insurrection, 1895-96. Among his works are ' McTeague ' (1897); ' A Man's Woman ' (1898); ' The Octopus ' (1901); ' The Pit ' (1903). He died in San Francisco, Cal., Oct. 25, 1902.

Norris, Mary Harriott. An American author and educator; born in Boonton, N. J., March 16, 1848. She was founder and principal of a private school in New York, 1870-98, and dean of women, at Northwestern University, 1898-99. Among her numerous published works are : ' Fraulein Mina ' (1872); ' Ben and Bentie Series ' (1873-76); ' Phebe ' (1890); ' Afterward ' (1893); ' John Applegate, Surgeon ' (1894); ' The Gray House of the Quarries' (1898) ; ' The Veil ' (1907).

North, Sir Thomas. An English translator; born in England about 1535. He exerted a powerful influence on Elizabethan writers and has been called " the first great master of English prose." He is most famous for his unrivalled translation of Plutarch's 'Lives,' published in 1579. He died in 1601.

Nuttall, Thomas. An English naturalist and writer; born in Yorkshire, Eng., Jan. 5, 1786. He devoted his life to scientific pursuits, made extensive explorations, especially in the United States, where he visited nearly every State in the Union and made more discoveries than any other explorer of the botany of North America. He was professor of natural history at Harvard University 1822-34. Among his many important works are : ' Genera of North American Plants ' (1817); ' Geological Sketch of the Valley of the Mississippi,' ' Manual of the Ornithology of the United States and Canada.' He died in England, Sept. 10, 1859.

Ollivant, Alfred. An English author; born in 1874. He was commissioned in the Royal Artillery in 1893, but resigned in 1895, owing to disability caused by a fall from a horse, and turned his attention to literature. He wrote: ' Owd Bob, Son of Battle ' (1898); ' Danny ' (1902).

O'Meara, Barry Edwards. Surgeon to Napoleon and historian of St. Helena; born in Ireland in 1786. He accompanied Bonaparte into exile and was his intimate associate until dismissed from his post July, 1818, as a consequence of his intense partisanship for the unfortunate Emperor. His published works include many famous and valuable reminiscences of Napoleon; among them are ' Napoleon in Exile: or a Voice from St. Helena,' ' The Opinions and Reflections of Napoleon ' 2 vols.). He died in London, January 3, 1836.

Overbury, Sir Thomas. An English statesman and author ; born at Warwickshire, England, in 1581. He wrote ' Observations Upon the State of the Seventeen Provinces,' and a popular volume of ' Characters,' which appeared posthumously. His death occurred Sept. 15, 1613, in the Tower of London, where, for political reasons, he had been subjected to imprisonment and cruel treatment.

Owen, Sir Richard. An English naturalist, lecturer and author ; born in Lancaster, England, July 20, 1804. Among his enormous contributions to scientific literature are ' Lectures on the Comparative Anatomy and Physiology of Invertebrate Animals' (1843); 'Odontography' (1845); 'The Archetypes and Homologies of the Vertebrate System' (1848); 'Nature of Limbs' (1849); Paleontology' (1861). He died at Surrey, England, Dec. 18, 1892.

Oxenham, John. An English author; born in 18—. Among his published works are : 'God's Prisoner' (1889); 'Rising Fortunes' (1899); 'A Princess of Vascovy' (1900); 'Our Lady of Deliverance' (1901); 'John of Gerisan' (1902); 'Under the Iron Flail' (1902) ; 'Hearts in Exile.'

Oxley, James Macdonald. A Canadian lawyer and author; born in Halifax, N. S., Oct. 22, 1855. Among his numerous published works are : 'Bert Lloyd's Boyhood' (1887); 'The Wreckers of Sable Island' (1891); 'Diamond Rock' (1893); 'Baffling the Blockade' (1896); 'Making his Way' (1898); 'Trials and Triumphs' (1899); 'North Overland with Franklin' (1900).

Paine, Albert Bigelow. An American author and editor; born in New Bedford, Mass., July 10, 1861. He served on the New York Herald and the St. Nicholas, and was a frequent contributor to magazines. Among his works are : 'The Mystery of Eveline Delorme' (1894); 'Gobolinks' (with Ruth McEmry Stuart) (1896); 'The Arkansaw Bear' (1898); 'The Deep Woods' (1899); 'The Bread Line' (1900); 'A Sailor of Fortune' (1906).

Palmer, Anna Campbell. [" Mrs. George Archibald."] An American author and journalist; born in Elmira, N. Y., Feb. 3, 1854. Among her published works are : 'Verses from a Mother's Corner' (1889); 'The Summerville Prize' (1890); 'Lady Gay and Her Sister' (1891); 'Three Times Three' (1899); 'Joel Dorman Steele, a Biography' (1900).

Paterson, William Romaine. [" Benjamin Swift."] An English novelist; born in Glasgow, Scotland, July 29, 1871. Among his published works are : 'Nancy Noon' (1896); 'The Tormentor' (1897); 'The Destroyer' (1898); 'Nude Souls' (1900); 'Ludus Amoris' (1902); 'In Piccadilly' (1903).

Peabody, Josephine Preston. An American writer of prose and verse ; born in New York in 1874. Author of 'Old Greek Folk Stories' (1897); 'The Wayfarers' (1898); 'Fortune and Men's Eyes,' (1900). 'Marlowe' (1901).

Peary, Robert Edwin. Lieutenant and civil engineer, U. S. N., arctic explorer and author; born in Cresson, Pa., May 6, 1856. Describes his arctic experiences in his book 'Northward Over the Ice,' 'A Narrative of Life and Work in Northern Greenland in 1886 and 1891-97.'

Penfield, Frederick Courtland. An American author and diplomat; born in Connecticut, April 23, 1855. He was appointed United States vice-consul-general at London, 1855, and was diplomatic agent and consulting general to Egypt 1893-97. He was awarded decorations by many foreign governments, among them France and Turkey. He wrote : 'Present Day Egypt' (1899), besides many articles on economic and international subjects.

Phillpotts, Eden. An English novelist; born in Aboo, India, Nov. 4, 1862. Among his numerous works of fiction are : 'The End of Life' (1890); 'A Tiger's Cub' (1892); 'A Deal with the Devil' (1895); 'Children of the Mist' (1898); 'Loup Garon' (1899); 'The Striking Hours' (1901); 'The River' (1902).

Phillips, Stephen. An English poet; born at Somerton, near Oxford, July 28, 1868. He studied for Civil Service, but abandoned it to go on the stage, and later took up literature as a profession. Among his published works are : 'Marpessa' (1890); 'Eremus' (1894); 'Christ in Hades' (1896); 'Herod' (1900); 'Ulysses' (1902).

Pidgin, Charles Felton. An American author, librettist and statistician; born in Roxbury, Mass., Nov. 1, 1844. Besides being a frequent contributor to periodicals, he wrote many librettos for cantatas, operas and musical comedies, and was also an inventor of considerable note. His novels include 'Quincy Adams Sawyer' (1900); 'Blennerhasset' (1901); 'The Climax' (1902); 'Stephen Holton' (1902); 'Theodosia.'

Pier, Arthur Stanwood. An American writer; born in Pittsburg, Pa., April 21, 1874. He served on the editorial staff of the Youths' Companion, and wrote 'The Pedagogues' (1899); 'The Sentimentalists' (1901); 'The Triumph' (1903); 'The Young in Heart' (1907).

Poole, John. An English dramatist and humorist ; born in England in 1792. Among his successful dramas and farces were : 'Paul Pry' (1825); 'Deaf as a Post,' 'Turning the Tables.' He wrote novels, essays and sketches, among these 'Little Pedlington and the Pedlingtonians' (1838), attained great popularity. He died in London, Feb. 5, 1879.

Poor, Agnes Blake. [" Dorothy Prescott."] An American writer of fiction. Author of 'Brothers and Strangers' (1894); 'Boston Neighbors' (1898); 'Under Guiding Stars' (1907).

Porter, Charlotte. An American editor and author; born in Towanda, Pa., in 1859. She edited Shakespeariana, 1886–88, and founded Poet Lore in 1889, with Helen A. Clarke. Author of : 'Dramatic Motive in Browning's Strafford' (1897), and editor of 'Browning's Complete Poetical Works,' 'Mrs. Browning's Complete Works,' and various others in connection with Helen A. Clarke.

Porter, Horace. An American soldier and statesman and United States Ambassador to France; born in Huntingdon, Pa., April 15, 1837. He was orator at the inauguration of the Washington Arch, New York, May 4, 1895, and at the dedication of Grant's Tomb, New York, April 27, 1897. He wrote : 'Campaigning with Grant,' 'West Point Life.'

Potter, Paul M. An American dramatist; born at Brighton, Eng., June 3, 1852. He was foreign correspondent for the New York Herald and afterwards joined the editorial staff of the Chicago Tribune. Among his numerous plays are : ' The American Minister ' (1892); ' The Victoria Cross ' (1894) ; ' The Conquerors ' (1898); ' Under Two Flags' (1901); ' Nancy Stair ' (1905) He dramatized ' Trilby ' (Du Maurier's novel).

Prichard, Sarah Johnson. An American author; born in Waterbury, Conn., Jan. 11, 1830. Among her works are : ' Martha's Hooks and Eyes ' (1859); ' Nat's Shoes ' (1862); 'The Old Stone Chimney ' (1865); ' Rose Marbury ' (1870); ' History of Waterbury ' (1896); ' The Only Woman in the Town ' (1898).

Prowse, Richard Orton. An English novelist; born at Woodbridge, Suffolk, England, July 22, 1862. Author of ' The Poison of Asps ' (1892); ' A Fatal Reservation ' (1893); 'Voysey' (1901).

Prynne, William. A famous English pamphleteer; born in England in 1600. He was a voluminous writer and published about 200 books and pamphlets. He was instrumental in the recall of Charles II., for whom he was appointed Keeper of the Records. The value of his work lies in these Records, which contain much historic matter of great worth. He died Oct. 24, 1669.

Pugh, Edwin William. An English novelist; born in London, Eng., Jan. 27, 1874. Among his published works are : ' A Street in Suburbia ' (1895); ' The Man of Straw ' (1897); ' King Circumstance ' (1898); ' Mother-Sister ' (1900); ' The Heritage' (1901); ' Fruit of the Vine.'

Pullen, Mrs. Elizabeth. [" Elizabeth Carazza."] An American author, journalist and musical critic; born in Portland, Me., 18—. Among her writings are ' Don Finimondone,' ' The Man from Aidone,' ' Rocco and Sidora,' besides translations from the Italian and the French.

Remington, Frederick. An American artist, sculptor and author; born in Canton, N. Y., Oct. 4, 1861. Besides being famous as an illustrator he wrote ' Pony Tracks,' ' Crooked Trails,' ' Frontier Sketches ' ; ' John Ermine.'

Ridge, William Pett. An English writer; born in Chatham, Eng., in 18—. Among his published works are : ' A Clever Wife ' and ' Minor Dialogues ' (1895); ' Second Opportunity of Mr. Staplehurst ' (1896); ' A Son of the State ' (1899); ' London Only ' (1901); ' Lost Property ' (1902); ' Next Door Neighbors ' (1904).

Risley, Richard Voorhees. An American author; born in New York, Nov. 8, 1874. Besides being a contributor to English and American magazines, he wrote : ' The Sentimental Vikings ' (1897); ' Men's Tragedies ' (1899); ' The Sledge' (1900); ' The Anvil ' (1901); ' Life of a Woman ' (1902). Died 1904.

Rives, Hallie Erminie. An American novelist, cousin of Amelie Rives Trouvetzkoy; born in Christian County, Ky., May 2, 1876. Author of : ' Smoking Flax ' (1896); ' As the Heart Panteth ' (1896); ' A Fool in Spots,' ' Singing Wire,' ' A Furnace of Earth ' (1900); ' Hearts Courageous ' (1902).

Robins, Edward. An American author and critic; born in France in 1862. Among his works are : ' Echoes of the Playhouse, a Review of the Old Time English Theatrical Life,' 'The Palmy Days of Nance Oldfield,' ' Benjamin Franklin, Printer, Statesman, Philosopher and Private Citizen ' ; ' Romances of Early America.'

Robinson, Edith. An American author; born in Massachusetts in 1858. Among her published works are : ' Forced Acquaintances ' (1887); ' A Little Puritan Rebel ' (1898); ' The Captain of the School ' (1901); ' A Puritan Knight Errant ' ; ' A Little Puritan Cavalier.'

Roe, Ven. Henry. Archdeacon of Quebec, Canada; born in Henryville, Province of Quebec, Feb. 22, 1829. Among his works are : ' The Place of Religious Giving in the Christian Economy ' (1880); ' The Place of Laymen in the Spiritual Work of the Church ' (1887); ' The First Hundred Years of the Diocese of Quebec ' (1893).

Rogers, Robert Cameron. An American author; born in Buffalo, N. Y., Jan. 7, 1862. Among his works are : ' Wind in the Clearing and Other Poems,' ' Will o' the Wisp,' ' Old Dorset,' 'For the King and Other Poems ' (1899); 'The Rosary.'

Rood, Henry Edward. An American author and educator; born in Philadelphia, Pa., June 26, 1867. He was on the editorial staff of the Philadelphia Press, New York Herald and Harper's Magazine. Author of ' Hardwicke ' (1902); ' In Pastures New ' (1902).

Rosebery, Earl of. [Archibald Philip Primrose.] Prime Minister of England; born in London, May 7, 1847. He occupied many positions of honor and importance before becoming chief executive and was a diplomatist of note. Author of ' Sir Robert Peel ' (1899); ' The Last Phase ' (1900).

Rosenfeld, Morris. An American Jewish writer; born in Poland in 1862. Author of : ' Songs from the Ghetto.'

Rostand, Edmond. A French author and dramatist; born in Marseilles, France, in 1868. Among his published prose works are: ' Les Romanesques ' (1894); ' Far Away Princess ' (1895); ' La Samaritaine ' (1897) ; ' Cyrano de Bergerac ' (1898) ; and among his poems are ' Les Musadises ' and ' L'Aiglon ' (1900) ; ' The Chanticleer ' ; ' The Lady of Dreams.'

Runkle, Bertha. An American novelist; born in Berkeley Heights, N. J., in 18—. Her historical novel, ' The Helmet of Navarre ' was published 1901 ; ' The Truth about Tolna ' (1906).

Santayana, George. An American writer and assistant professor of philosophy at Harvard College; born in Spain in 1863. Among his published works are : ' Sonnets and Other Poems ' (1894); ' The Sense of Beauty ' (1896); ' Lucifer, a Theological Tragedy ' (1899); ' Interpretations of Poetry and Religion ' (1900).

Saunders, Margaret Marshall. ["Marshall Saunders."] An American author; born in Milton, Nova Scotia, in 1861. Among her numerous works are : 'Beautiful Joe' (1894), for which she was awarded the prize of $200 offered by the American Humane Education Society; 'The House of Armour' (1897); 'Her Sailor' (1899); 'For His Country' (1900); 'Tilda Jane' (1901); 'Beautiful Joe's Paradise' (1902); 'Nita' (1904); 'Alpatok' (1906).

Scidmore, Eliza Ruhamah. An American author and corresponding secretary of the National Geographical Society; born in Madison, Wis., Oct. 14, 1856. Among her published works are 'Jinriksha Days in Japan' (1890); 'From East to West' (1890); 'China, the Long-Lived Empire' (1900); 'Jarva, the Garden of the East' (1897); 'Winter India' (1903).

Scribner, Frank Kimball. An American author and journalist; born in New York, Feb. 22, 1867. Among his published works are : 'The Honor of the Princess' (1897); 'The Fifth of November' (1898); 'In the Land of the Loom' (1899); 'A Continental Cavalier' (1900).

Scudder, Vida Dutton. An American author and associate professor of English literature at Wellesley College; born in Southern India, Dec. 15, 1861. She was actively connected with the formation of College Settlements. Among her published works are 'The Witness of Denial' (1896); 'Social Ideals in English Letters' (1898); 'Introduction to the Study of English Literature' (1901); 'The Disciple of a Saint.'

Searing, Laura Catherine Redden. ["Howard Glyndon."] An American author and journalist; born in Somerset, Md., Feb. 9, 1840. She was Washington correspondent for the Missouri Republican during the Civil War, wrote 'German War Gossip' for the New York Tribune during the Franco-Prussian War and was on the staff of the New York Mail, 1868–76. She wrote: 'Idyls of Battle,' 'Sounds from Secret Chambers,' 'Notable Men in the House of Representatives' (1864); 'Of El Dorado' (1897).

Sharpless, Isaac. An American educator and author; president of Haverford College, Pa.; born in Chester County, Pa., Dec. 16, 1848. Among his works, which are on educational and historical subjects, are 'A Quaker Experiment,' 'Quakers in the Revolution,' 'Two Centuries of Pennsylvania History,' 'English Education in Elementary and Secondary Schools.'

Sheldon, Charles Monroe. An American Congregational clergyman and author; born in Wellsville, N. Y., Feb. 26, 1857. Among his numerous published works are 'Richard Bruce' (1891); 'The Crucifixion of Philip Strong' (1893); 'His Brother's Keeper' (1895); 'Lend a Hand' (1897); 'Born to Serve' (1900); 'Who Killed Joe's Baby'; 'The Heart of the World.'

Sherwood, Mrs. Mary Martha. An English author; born in Worcestershire, England, May 6, 1775. She was the writer of ninety books, many of them juvenile. Among them are 'Little Henry and His Bearer,' 'Henry Milner,' 'Ermina,' and 'The Lady of the Manor.' She died in Twickenham, England, 1851.

Sherwood, Mrs. Mary Elizabeth Wilson. ["Mrs. John Sherwood." "M. E. W. S."] An American author ; born in Keene, N. H., in 1830. Among her writings are 'The Sarcasm of Destiny,' 'A Transplanted Rose,' 'Manners and Social Usages,' 'Sweet Briar,' 'Roxobel,' etc. Died, N. Y. city, Sept. 12, 1903.

Smith, Harry Bache. An American author, dramatist and critic; born in Buffalo, N. Y., in 1860. Among his many opera librettos are 'Robin Hood,' 'Rob Roy,' 'The Fortune Teller,' 'Wizard of the Nile,' 'Foxy Quiller' and 'The Casino Girl.' He also wrote 'Will Shakespeare' (a comedy) (1893); 'Lyrics and Sonnets' (1894); 'Stage Lyrics' (1901).

Snow, Lorenzo. President of the Mormon Church; born in Mantua, O., April 13, 1814. He founded and named Brigham City, Utah, was ordained one of the Twelve Apostles in 1849 and president of the Twelve in 1889. Among his published works are : 'The Italian Mission,' 'The Only Way to be Saved,' 'The Voice of Joseph.' He also translated the 'Book of Mormon' into Italian. Died in Salt Lake City, Utah, Oct. 10, 1901.

Soley, James Russell. An American lawyer and author; born in Boston, Mass., Oct. 1, 1850. He was professor and head of the department of history and law United States Naval Academy 1876–90, and assistant secretary of the navy 1890–3. Among his works are : 'Foreign Systems of Naval Education,' 'The Blockade and the Cruisers,' 'Boys of 1812,' 'Sailor Boys of 1861,' 'Rescue of Greeley' (with Winfield S. Schley) ; 'Admiral Porter.'

Stephens, Robert Neilson. An American author, playwright and journalist; born in New Bloomfield, N. J., July 22, 1867. His plays include 'An Enemy to the King,' and 'The Ragged Regiment,' and among his novels are 'An Enemy to the King' (1897); 'The Continental Dragoon' (1898); 'Philip Winwood' (1900); 'Captain Ravenshaw' (1901). Died 1906.

Stevenson, Burton Egbert. An American journalist and author; born in Chillicothe, O., Nov. 9, 1872. Among his published works are : 'At Odds with the Regent : A Story of the Cellamore Conspiracy' (1900); 'A Soldier of Virginia' (1901); 'The Heritage' (1902); 'Tommy Remington's Battle'; 'That Affair at Elizabeth.'

Stow, John. A celebrated English chronicler and antiquary; born in London about 1525. He was the author of a considerable part of 'Holinshed's Chronicles,' and the world of letters owes much to his valuable historic works and minute researches. He was the most accurate and businesslike of English chroniclers of the sixteenth century. Among his works are : 'Summary of the Chronicles of England,' 'Survey of London.' He died in extreme poverty, April 6, 1605.

Strang, Lewis Clinton. An American writer and dramatic critic; born in Westfield, Mass., Dec. 4, 1869. His published works include : 'Famous Actresses of the Day' (1899); 'Celebrated Comedians of Light Opera and Musical Comedy in America' (1900).

Stratemeyer, Edward. [" Capt. Ralph Bonehill," " Arthur M. Winfield ".] An American writer of juvenile stories; born in Elizabeth, N. J., Oct. 4, 1862. Among his numerous works are ' Last Cruise of the Spitfire' (1894); 'Oliver Bright's Search' (1895); ' Young Auctioneers' (1897); 'Under Dewey at Manilla' (1898); ' Between Boer and Briton' (1900); 'On to Pekin' (1900); ' The Fall of Port Arthur.'

Stringer, Arthur J. A Canadian writer; born in London, Ont., Feb. 26, 1874. Author of ' Watchers of the Twilight,' ' Pauline and Other Poems,' ' Epigrams,' ' The Loom of Destiny.'

Sutherland, Evelyn Greenleaf. An American journalist and playwright; born in Cambridge, Mass., in 18—. For many years dramatic critic on various Boston papers, she also contributed widely to magazines and periodicals. Author of : ' Po' White Trash and Other One-Act Dramas' (1899); ' In Office Hours and Other Vaudeville Sketches' (1899); also, ' Fort Frayne' (with Gen. Charles King), and adapter of ' Monsieur Beaucaire,' with the author.

Sutphen, William Gilbert Van Tassell. An American writer; born in Philadelphia, Pa., May 11, 1861. Author of ' The Golficide' (1898); 'The Golfer's Alphabet' (1899); ' The Cardinal's Rose' (1900); ' The Golfer's Calendar'; ' The Nineteenth Hole'; ' The Doomsman.'

Tanner, Benjamin Tucker. An American Methodist Episcopal bishop of African descent; born in Pittsburg, Pa., Dec. 25, 1835. He was for many years editor of the Christian Recorder, and was founder and editor of the A. M. E. Church Review. He was ordained bishop in 1888. Among his works are : ' The Origin of the Negro,' ' Is the Negro Cursed,' ' A Hint to Ministers,' ' The Color of Solomon.'

Tappan, Eva March. An American author and teacher; born in Worcester, Mass., Dec. 26, 1854. Among her published works are ' Charles Lamb, the Man and the Author' (1896); ' In the Days of Alfred the Great' (1900); ' Our Country's Story' (1902) ; ' America's Literature.'

Tarkington, Newton Booth. An American novelist; born in Indiana, July 29, 1869. His writings include ' The Gentleman from Indiana' (1899); ' Monsieur Beaucaire' (1900); ' Two Vanrevels' (1902); 'Foreign Exchange' (1909).

Thompson-Seton, Ernest. A Canadian artist, writer and naturalist; born in South Shields, England, Aug. 14, 1860. Famous as an animal artist and illustrator, and at one time official naturalist of Manitoba; his works include ' Birds of Manitoba,' ' Mammals of Manitoba,' ' Wild Animals I Have Known,' ' The Biography of a Grizzly.'

Thompson, Hugh Miller. Protestant Episcopal bishop of Mississippi; born in Londonderry County, Ire., June 5, 1830. He was ordained priest in 1856 and consecrated to the bishopric in 1883. He was editor of the American Churchman, Chicago, 1860–70, and of the Church Journal, New York, 1870–77. Among his numerous works are : ' Unity and its Restoration' (1859); ' First Principles' (1863); ' The World and the Kingdom' (1888); ' More Copy' (1897). He died in 1902.

Thompson, Vance. An American journalist, author and playwright; born April 7, 1863. He was editor and founder of M'lle New York (fortnightly review), and published a number of books and dramas. Among the former are : ' Berwyn Kennedy,' ' A Flash of Honor,' ' Writers of Young France,' ' Spinners of Life;' and among the latter ' In Old Japan,' ' The Dresden Shepherdess,' ' Florian's Dream.'

Thorpe, Francis Newton. An American author and lawyer; born in Swampscott, Mass., April 16, 1857. He was fellow-professor of American Constitutional history at the University of Pennsylvania for some years, and wrote extensively on the subject. Among his works are : ' The Government of the People of the United States' (1889); ' The Story of the Constitution' (1891); ' The Constitutional History of the United States, 1765–1895'; ' The Spoils of Empire.'

Thorpe, Mrs. Rose Hartwick. An American author; born in Mishawaka, Ind., July 18, 1850. Especially well known for her poem, ' Curfew Must Not Ring To-night,' she also published many books of prose and verse. Among the former are ' Fred's Dark Days' (1881); ' Nina Bruce' (1886); ' The Chester Girls' (1887); and her verses include ' Temperance Poems' (1887); ' Ringing Ballads' (1887); ' Sweet Song Stories'; ' White Lady of La Jolla.'

Todd, Charles Burr. An American author and journalist; born in Redding, Conn., Jan. 19, 1849. Among his published works are : ' Life and Letters of Joel Barlow' (1886); ' Story of the City of New York' (1895); ' True Aaron Burr'; ' The Confessions of a Railroad Man.'

Todd, David P. An American author and astronomer; born in Lake Ridge, N. Y., March 19, 1855. He was professor of astronomy and director of the observatory at Amherst College, and was in charge of various eclipse expeditions, including those to Texas, Japan, West Africa and East Indies. Author of : ' A New Astronomy' (1897); ' Stars and Telescopes' (1899).

Todd, Mrs. Mabel Loomis. An American author; wife of David P. Todd, born in Cambridge, Mass., in 1858. Besides being a frequent contributor to magazines, she edited ' Poems and Letters of Emily Dickinson' (1890–94); ' A Cycle of Sonnets' (1896); ' Steele's Popular Astronomy' (1899); and wrote ' Footprints' (1883); ' Total Eclipses of the Sun' (1894); 'Corona and Coronet' (1898).

Tomlinson, Everett Titsworth. An American Baptist clergyman and writer of juvenile tales; born in Shiloh, N. J., May 23, 1859. Among his numerous publications are 'The Search for Andrew Field' (1894); 'The Boy Soldiers of 1812' (1895); 'Three Colonial Boys' (1895); 'Two Young Patriots' (1898); 'In the Hands of the Redcoats' (1901); 'The Fruit of the Desert.'

Townsend, Edward Waterman. An American journalist, author and dramatist; born in Cleveland, O., Feb. 10, 1855. He engaged in newspaper work on the New York Sun and became prominent for his studies of the life and dialect of the Bowery. His works include : 'Chimmie Fadden,' 'A Daughter of the Tenements,' 'Major Max,' 'Days Like These,' besides the dramatization of the first-named and the plays 'The Marquis of Michigan,' 'The Sergeant,' 'Our Constitution.'

Townsend, Luther Tracy. An American clergyman and author; born in Orono, Me., Sept. 27, 1838. He entered the Methodist Epicopal ministry in 1864, and was professor of various branches of theology at Boston University, 1868–93. Among his works are : 'Credo' (1869); 'Sword and Garment' (1871); 'Art of Speech' (1880–81); 'Bible Theology and Modern Thought' (1883); 'Evolution of Creation' (1899); 'Anastasis' (1900); 'Collapse of Evolution.'

Trask, Mrs. Kate Nichols. ["Katrina Trask."] An American author and contributor to leading magazines. Among her works are 'Under King Constantine' (1891); 'Sonnets and Lyrics' (1894); 'John Laighton, Jr.' (1898); 'Lessons in Love' (1900); 'Night and Morning' (1906).

Trine, Ralph Waldo. ["Mr. Whitman."] An American writer and lecturer upon social science; born in Mt. Morris, Ill., Sept. 9, 1866. Among his published works are 'What all the World's a-Seeking' (1896); 'In Tune with the Infinite' (1898); 'The Greatest Thing Ever Known' (1898); 'Character-Building Thought Power' (1900); 'In the Fire of the Heart.'

True, John Preston. An American author; born in Bethel, Me., Feb. 13, 1859. He wrote: 'Their Club and Ours' (1883); 'The Iron Star' (1899); 'Scouting for Washington' (1900); 'On Guard against Tory and Tarleton' (1902).

Trumbull, Annie Eliot. An American author; born in Hartford, Conn., March 2, 1857. Among her published works are 'An Hour's Promise,' (1889); 'White Birches' (1893); 'A Cape Cod Week' (1898); 'Rod's Salvation' (1898); 'A Masque of Culture' (play), (1893); 'A Wheel of Progress' (play), (1897); 'Life's Common Way' (1903).

Upham, Grace Le Baron. ["Grace Le Baron."] An American writer of juvenile stories; born in Lowell, Mass., June 22, 1845. Among her numerous published works are: 'Little Miss Faith' (1894); 'The Rosebud Club' (1896); 'Queer Janet' (1897); ''Twixt You and Me' (1898); 'Told Under the Cherry Trees'; 'The Children of Bedford Court.'

Vallentine, Benjamin Bennaton. ["Fitznoodle."] An American author, dramatist and journalist; born in London, Eng., Sept. 7, 1843. He studied for the English bar and later came to the United States and entered into editorial work. Was one of the founders of Puck, and dramatic critic for the New York Herald. Among his works are : 'The Fitznoodle Papers,' 'The Last Train,' 'The Last Circle,' and a number of plays.

Van Noppen, Charles Leonard. An American writer; born in Holland in 1868. He made the only English translation of 'The Lucifer,' by the famous Dutch author, Joost Van Vondel, whose work is thought to have greatly influenced John Milton in the production of 'Paradise Lost.'

Van Rensselaer, May King (Mrs. John King). An American writer of historical fiction; born in New York city, May 25, 1848. Among her published works are 'Crochet Lace' (1882); 'The Devil's Picture Books' (1887); 'New Yorkers of the Nineteenth Century' (1899). She has also edited 'A Girl's Life Eighty Years Ago.'

Vivian, Thomas Jondrie. An American author and journalist; born in Cornwall, England, Aug. 3, 1855. Lecturer on languages and literature at the University of California, Teachers' Institute Los Angeles, and Columbia College, New York. Among his published works are 'With Dewey at Manila,' 'The Fall of Santiago,' 'A Life Wasted,' 'Old Dudley's Monument,' 'Luther Strong.'

Ward, Mrs. May Alden. An American author and lecturer; born in Cincinnati, Ohio, in 1853. She wrote : 'Life of Dante' (1887); 'Petrarch, a Sketch of His Life and Works' (1891); 'Old Colony Days' (1896); 'Prophets of the Nineteenth Century' (1900).

Warman, Cy. An American author and journalist; born in Greenup, Ill., June 22, 1855. He was introduced to public notice as "The Poet of the Rockies," in 1892, by the New York Sun. Rode locomotive from New York to Chicago and wrote his first railroad story, 'A Thousand Miles in a Night,' for McClure's Magazine. Author of: 'Tales of an Engineer' (1895); 'The Express Messenger' (1897); 'Frontier Stories' (1898); 'The White Mail' (1899); 'Short Rails' (1900) ; 'The Last Spike' (1906).

Washington, Booker Taliaferro. An American author of African descent, and principal of the Tuskegee Normal Institute; born near Hale's Ford, Va., 1859. Distinguished as a writer and speaker on racial and educational subjects; among his published works are 'Sowing and Reaping' (1900); 'Up from Slavery' (1901); 'Character Building'; 'The Negro in Business.'

Waterloo, Stanley. An American author and journalist; born in St. Clair County, Mich., May 21, 1846. He served on the editorial staff of several western papers, and among his published works are 'A Man and a Woman,' 'The Story of Ab,' 'Honest Money' (1895); 'The Wolf's Long Howl'; 'The Cassowary.'

Watts-Dunton, Theodore. An English poet, novelist and critic. He was educated as a naturalist and afterwards for the law; made a special study of folk-lore of the East Anglican and Welsh gypsies. He was critic on the Examiner and Athenæum. Among his publications are: 'Jubilee Greeting at Spithead to Men of Great Britain and Other Poems' (1897); 'The Coming of Love : Rhoda Boswell's Story' (1897); 'Aylwin' (1898); 'Snowdon' (1901); 'The Christmas Dream: a Dramatic Idyll' (1901); 'The Renascence of Wonder' (1902).

Wells, Carolyn. An American writer; born in Rahway, N. J., 18—. Author of 'At the Sign of the Sphinx' (1896); 'The Jingle Book' (1899); 'The Story of Betty' (1899); 'Idle Idylls' (1900); 'A Folly Anthology' (1907).

Wells, David Dwight. An American littérateur; born in Norwalk, Conn., April 22, 1868, died there June 15, 1900. He wrote 'Her Ladyship's Elephant,' 'His Lordship's Leopard'; 'Parlous Times.' Died 1900.

Westcott, Edward Noyes. An American banker and author; born in Syracuse, N. Y., Sept. 27, 1847; died there March 31, 1898. His only book, 'David Harum,' published after his death, in 1899, achieved a widespread popularity.

Wharton, Mrs. Edith Newbold (Jones). An American writer of fiction; born in New York in 1862. Author of 'The Greater Inclination' (1889); 'The Touchstone' (1900); 'Crucial Instances' (1901); 'Valley of Decision' (1902).

Webster, Henry Kitchell. An American writer, born in Evanston, Ill., Sept. 7, 1855. Author of : 'The Banker and the Bear: The Story of a Corner in Land' (1900); 'Roger Drake, Captain of Industry' (1902), and (with Samuel Merwin) 'The Short Line War' (1899); 'Calumet 'K'' (1901); 'Traitor and Loyalist.'

Whipple, Henry Benjamin. Protestant Episcopal bishop of Minnesota; born in Adams, N. Y., Feb. 15, 1823. He was active in work for the evangelization of the Indians, and was an authority upon the Indian question, on which he wrote extensively. Author of 'Sermons and Addresses,' and 'Lights and Shadows of a Long Episcopate.' He died at Faribault, Minn., Sept. 16, 1901.

White, Percy. An English novelist and journalist; born in London, Eng., in 18—. He was professor of English language and literature at a French college, later took up journalism and was editor of Public Opinion for ten years. Among his works are : 'Mr. Bailey-Martin' (1893); 'A King's Diary' (1894); 'A Passionate Pilgrim' (1897); 'The Heart of the Dancer' (1900); 'The New Christians' (1902).

White, Trumbull. An American author and journalist; born in Winterset, Ia., Aug. 12,

1868. He was engaged in active editorial work on various Chicago papers, was in charge of news service during the Cuban campaign, 1898, and in 1899 was correspondent from Russia, Central Asia, Turkestan and Siberia. Author of : 'Wizard of Wall Street' (biography of Jay Gould) (1892); 'Reuben and Cynthia at the World's Fair' (1893); 'War in the East, with History of China, Japan and Korea' (1895); 'Our War with Spain' (1898); 'Our New Possessions' (1899); 'San Francisco Earthquake.'

Whitely, Mrs. Isabel Nixon. An American author; born in New York in 1859. She wrote : 'The Falcon of Langeac,' 'For the French Lilies' (1899).

Whitman, Sidney. An English journalist and political writer; born in London, Eng., in 18—. He represented the New York Herald at Constantinople during the outbreak of the Armenian conspiracy in 1896, and accompanied the Turkish mission from the Black Sea to the Mediterranean, 1897–98. Among his works are : 'Imperial Germany' (1888); 'Teuton Studies' (1895); 'A Story of Austria' (1898); 'Life of the Emperor Frederick' (1900); 'My Reminiscences of Prince Bismarck' (1902).

Wilcox, Marrion. An American author and journalist; born in Augusta, Ga., April 3, 1858. He studied law and was admitted to the New York bar; took up editorial work and was on the staff of the Philadelphia Press, New Englander and Yale Review. Besides his regular contributions to magazines and periodicals, his works include : 'Real People' (1886); 'Scenes in General Dayton's Garden' (1889); 'A Short History of the War with Spain' (1898); 'Harper's History of the War in the Philippines' (1900).

Wilkinson, Henry Spenser. An English author and journalist; born in Manchester, Eng., May 1, 1853. In 1892 he spent the winter in India, traveling along the North West Frontier, visiting the camps of exercise in the Punjab, as a guest of Lord Roberts. He published many books on military subjects, among which are : 'Citizen Soldiers' (1884); 'Essays on the War Game' (1887); 'The Command of the Sea' (1894); 'Lessons of the War' (1900); 'War and Policy' (1900).

Willard, Ashton Rollins. An American author; born in Montpelier, Vt., April 14, 1858. Besides being a writer on art subjects for magazines, he published: 'Life and Work of Painter Domenico Morelli' (1895); 'History of Modern Italian Art' (1898); 'Land of the Latins.'

Willets, Gibson. An American author, journalist and traveler; born in Hempstead, N. Y., Aug. 10, 1869. He was special correspondent for various magazines and newspaper syndicates during the Spanish-American War, and in 1900 went to India and journeyed about one thousand miles through the famine district, for the Christian Herald and a syndicate of 200 newspapers. His published works include : 'Anita, the

Cuban Spy'; (His Neighbor's Wife); (The Triumph of Yankee Doodle'; (The Rulers of the World at Home'; (Commercial Invasion of Europe.'

Williams, George Forrester. An American author and journalist; born on the Rock of Gibraltar in 1841. He joined the staff of the New York Times in 1860, served actively throughout the Civil War and acted as war correspondent 1864–65, correspondent during the Franco-Mexican War in 1867, managing editor of the New York Times 1871–73, and of the New York Herald 1874. Author of: (Bullet and Shell,' (Lucy's Rebel,' (The Memorial War Book,' (Unfair in Love and War,' (Across the Lines.'

Wilson, Francis. An American actor and author; born in Philadelphia, Pa., Feb. 7, 1854. He wrote (The Eugene Field I Knew,' (Recollections of a Player,' (Going on the Stage.'

Wilson, Marcius. An American author; born at West Stockbridge, Mass., Dec, 8, 1813. Among his published works are : (Architectural Drawing' (1837); (Civil Polity and Political Economy' (1840); (Grecian History and Mosaics of Bible History' (1882–83); (Wonderful Story of Old' (1888).

Winslow, Helen Maria. An American writer and journalist; born in Westfield, Va., in 1851. Editor of (The Club Woman,' and prominently connected with leading woman's clubs of Boston and vicinity. Author of (The Shawsheen Mills' (1882); (A Bohemian Chapter' (1887); (Salome Shepard, Reformer' (1894); (Concerning Cats' (1900); (Literary Boston of To-day' (1902).

Wister, Owen. An American author and lawyer; born in Philadelphia, Pa., July 14, 1860. Besides being a frequent contributor of prose and verse to magazines, he wrote : (The Dragon of Wantley, His Tail' (1892); (Red Men and White' (1896); (Lin McLean'

(1898); (The Jimmy John Boss' (1900); (U. S. Grant, a Biography' (1900); (The Virginian'; (Mother'; (The Seven Ages of Washington.'

Wood, Henry. An American writer upon metaphysical subjects; born in Barre, Vt., Jan. 16, 1834. Among his works are : (Natural Law in the Business World' (1887); (God's Image in Man' (1892); (Ideal Suggestions' (1893); (Studies in the Thought World' (1896); (The Symphony of Life' (1901).

Woods, Verna. An American educator and author; born in Ohio, in 1864. Besides being a well-known contributor to leading magazines and periodicals she wrote : (A Modern Magdalen,' (The Amazon,' (An Elusive Lover,' (Jason Hildreth's Identity.' Died at Sacramento, Cal., March 5, 1903.

Wright, Marie Robinson. An American author and traveler; born in Newnan, Ga., in 1866. She was five years on the staff of the New York World, was commissioned from Georgia to the Paris Exposition in 1889, the first woman to receive such an appointment, and was decorated by the Mexican Government for her history of that country. Author of (Picturesque Mexico' (Chili'; (The New Brazil' (1901); (Bolivia.'

Wright, Mrs. Mary Tappan. An American author; born in Steubenville, Ohio, Dec. 1851. She wrote (A Truce and Other Stories' (1895); (Aliens' (1902); (The Tower' (1906).

Wyckoff, Walter Augustus. An American author and assistant professor of political economy at Princeton University; born in Mainpuri, India, April 12, 1865. In order to ascertain the actual conditions surrounding the American workingman, he spent two years in toil as an unskilled laborer, and worked his way from Connecticut to California to carry out his experiment. His experiences are related in his book, (The Workers—East and West' (1897–98).